BIOGRAPHICAL DICTIONARY
OF
MATHEMATICIANS

BIOGRAPHICAL
DICTIONARY
OF
MATHEMATICIANS

REFERENCE BIOGRAPHIES FROM THE
Dictionary of Scientific Biography

Volume 4

JERZY NEYMAN – NICCOLÓ ZUCCHI

Listing of Mathematicians by Branch
Chronology
Index

Charles Scribner's Sons
NEW YORK

Collier Macmillan Canada
TORONTO

Maxwell Macmillan International
NEW YORK, OXFORD, SINGAPORE, SYDNEY

Copyright © 1970, 1971, 1972, 1973, 1974, 1975, 1976, 1978, 1980, 1990, 1991
American Council of Learned Societies.

Library of Congress Cataloging-in-Publication Data

Biographical Dictionary of Mathematicians: reference biographies from
the Dictionary of scientific biography.
  p.cm.
  "Published under the auspices of the American Council of Learned
Societies."
  Includes bibliographical references and index.
  ISBN 0-684-19282-9. — ISBN 0-684-19291-8 (v. 4)
  1. Mathematicians—Biography—Dictionaries. I. American Council
of Learned Societies. II. Dictionary of scientific biography.
QA28.B534 1991
510'.92'2—dc20
[B]
                                         90-52920
                                          CIP

Charles Scribner's Sons
Macmillan Publishing Company
866 Third Ave.
New York, New York 10022

Collier Macmillan Canada, Inc.
1200 Eglington Ave. East
Suite 200
Don Mills, Ontario M3C 3N1

JAN 7 1992

1 3 5 7 9 11 13 15 17 19   20 18 16 14 12 10 8 6 4 2

Printed in the United States of America.

BIOGRAPHICAL DICTIONARY
OF MATHEMATICIANS

NEYMAN, JERZY (*b*. Bendery, Russia, 16 April 1894; *d*. Berkeley, California, 5 August 1981)

Early Years. Jerzy Neyman was born in Bendery, Russia, to parents of Polish ancestry. His full name with title, Spława-Neyman, the first part of which he dropped at age thirty, reflects membership in the Polish nobility. Neyman's father, Czesław, who died when Jerzy was twelve, was a lawyer and later a judge, and an enthusiastic amateur archaeologist. Since the family had been prohibited by the Russian authorities from living in central Poland, then under Russian domination, Neyman grew up in Russia: in Kherson, Melitopol, Simferopol, and (after his father's death) in Kharkov, where in 1912 he entered the university.

At Kharkov, Neyman was first interested in physics, but because of his clumsiness in the laboratory abandoned it in favor of mathematics. He was greatly struck by Henri Lebesgue's *Leçons sur l'intégration et la recherche des fonctions primitives*, "the most beautiful monograph that I ever read," as he called it many years later. A manuscript on Lebesgue integration (530 pages, handwritten) that he submitted to a prize competition won a gold medal.

One of his mentors at Kharkov was Sergei Bernstein, who lectured on probability theory and statistics (including application of the latter to agriculture), subjects that did not particularly interest Neyman. Nevertheless, he later acknowledged the influence of Bernstein, from whom he "tried to acquire his tendency of concentrating on some 'big problem.'" It was also Bernstein who introduced him to Karl Pearson's *The Grammar of Science*, which made a deep impression.

After World War I, Poland regained its independence but soon became embroiled in a war with Russia over borders. Neyman, still in Kharkov, was jailed as an enemy alien. In 1921, in an exchange of prisoners, he finally went to Poland for the first time, at the age of twenty-seven.

In Warsaw he established contact with Wacław Sierpiński, one of the founders of the journal *Fundamenta Mathematicae*, which published one of

Neyman's gold medal results (5 [1923], 328–330). Although Neyman's heart was in pure mathematics, the statistics he had learned from Bernstein was more marketable and enabled him to obtain a position as (the only) statistician at the agricultural institute in Bydgoszcz (formerly Bromberg). There, during 1921 and 1922, he produced several papers on the application of probabilistic ideas to agricultural experimentation. In the light of Neyman's later development, this work is of interest because of its introduction of probability models for the phenomena being studied, more particularly a randomization model for the case of a completely randomized experiment. (For more details of Neyman's treatment, see Scheffé, *Annals of Mathematical Statistics,* 27 [1956], 269.) He had learned the philosophy of such an approach from Pearson's book, which laid great stress on models as mental constructs whose formulation constitutes the essence of science.

In December 1922 Neyman gave up his job in Bydgoszcz to take up a position at the State Meteorological Institute, a change that enabled him to move to Warsaw. He did not like the work—being in charge of equipment and observations—and soon left this position to become an assistant at the University of Warsaw and special lecturer in mathematics and statistics at the Central College of Agriculture; he also gave regular lectures at the University of Kraków. In 1924 he obtained his doctorate from the University of Warsaw with a thesis based on the papers he had written at Bydgoszcz.

Since no one in Poland was able to gauge the importance of his statistical work (he was "sui generis," as he later described his situation), the Polish authorities provided an opportunity for Neyman to establish his credibility through publication in British journals. For this purpose they gave him a fellowship to work with Karl Pearson in London. He did publish three papers in *Biometrika* (based in part on his earlier work), but scientifically the academic year (1925–1926) spent in Pearson's laboratory was a disappointment. He found the work of the laboratory old-fashioned and Pearson himself surprisingly ignorant of modern mathematics. (The fact that Pearson did not understand the difference between independence and lack of correlation led to a misunderstanding that nearly terminated Neyman's stay at the laboratory.) So when, with the help of Pearson and Sierpiński, he received a Rockefeller fellowship that made it possible for him to stay in the West for another year, he decided to spend it in Paris rather than in London.

In Paris, Neyman attended the lectures of Lebesgue and a seminar of Jacques Hadamard. "I felt that this was real mathematics worth studying," he wrote later, "and, were it not for Egon Pearson [Karl's son], I would have probably drifted to my earlier passion for sets, measure and integration, and returned to Poland as a faithful member of the Warsaw school and a steady contributor to *Fundamenta Mathematicae.*"

The Neyman-Pearson Theory. What pulled Neyman back into statistics was a letter he received in the fall of 1925 from Egon Pearson, with whom he had had little contact in London. Egon had begun to question the rationale underlying some of the current work in statistics, and the letter outlined his concerns. A correspondence developed and, reinforced by occasional joint holidays, continued even after the end of the Rockefeller year, when Neyman returned to a hectic and difficult life in Warsaw. He again took up his lectures at the university (as docent after his habilitation in 1928), at the Central College of Agriculture, and at the University of Kraków. In addition, he founded a small statistical laboratory at the Nencki Institute for Experimental Biology. To supplement his meager academic income, and to provide financial support for the students and young co-workers in his laboratory, Neyman took on a variety of consulting jobs. These involved different areas of application, with the majority coming from agriculture and from the Institute for Social Problems, the latter work being concerned with Polish census data.

Neyman felt harassed, and his financial situation was always precarious. The bright spot in this difficult period was his work with the younger Pearson. Trying to find a unifying, logical basis that would lead systematically to the various statistical tests that had been proposed by William S. Gossett (also "Student") and Ronald A. Fisher was a "big problem" of the kind for which he had hoped since his student days with Bernstein.

In 1933 Karl Pearson retired from his chair at University College, London, and his position was divided between Fisher and Egon Pearson. The latter lost no time and, as soon as it became available in the spring of 1934, offered Neyman a temporary position in his laboratory. Neyman was enthusiastic. This would greatly facilitate their joint work and bring relief to his Warsaw difficulties.

The set of issues addressed in the joint work of Neyman and Pearson between 1926 and 1933 turned out indeed to be a "big problem," and their treatment of it established a new paradigm that changed the statistical landscape. What concerned Pearson when he first approached Neyman in 1926 was the ad hoc nature of the small sample tests being studied by

Fisher and "Student." In his search for a general principle from which such tests could be derived, he had written to "Student." In his reply "Student" had suggested that one would be inclined to reject a hypothesis under which the observed sample is very improbable "if there is an alternative hypothesis which will explain the occurrence of the sample with a more reasonable probability" (E. S. Pearson, in David, ed., 1966). This comment led Pearson to propose to Neyman the likelihood ratio criterion, in which the maximum likelihood of the observed sample under the alternatives under consideration is compared with its value under the hypothesis. During the next year Neyman and Pearson studied this and other approaches, and worked out likelihood ratio tests for some important examples. They published their results in 1928 in a fundamental two-part paper, "On the Use and Interpretation of Certain Test Criteria for Purposes of Statistical Inference." The paper contained many of the basic concepts of what was to become the Neyman-Pearson theory of hypothesis testing, such as the two types of error, the idea of power, and the distinction between simple and composite hypotheses.

Although Pearson felt that the likelihood ratio provided the unified approach for which he had been looking, Neyman was not yet satisfied. It seemed to him that the likelihood principle itself was somewhat ad hoc and had no fully logical basis. However, in February 1930, he was able to write Pearson that he had found "a rigorous argument in favour of the likelihood method." His new approach consisted of maximizing the power of the test, subject to the condition that under the hypothesis (assumed to be simple), the rejection probability has a preassigned value (the level of the test). He reassured Pearson that in all cases he had examined so far, this logically convincing test coincided with the likelihood ratio test. A month later Neyman announced to Pearson that he now had a general solution to the problem of testing a simple hypothesis against a simple alternative. The result in question is the fundamental lemma, which plays such a crucial role in the Neyman-Pearson theory.

The next step was to realize that in the case of more than one alternative, there might exist a uniformly most powerful test that would simultaneously maximize the power for all of them. If such a test exists, Neyman found, it coincides with the likelihood ratio test, but in the contrary case—alas—the likelihood ratio test may be biased. These results, together with many examples and elaborations, were published in 1933 under the title "On the Problem of the Most Efficient Tests of Statistical Hypoth-

eses." While in the 1928 paper the initiative and insights had been those of Pearson, who had had to explain to Neyman what he was doing, the situation was now reversed, with the leadership having passed to Neyman, leaving Pearson a somewhat reluctant follower.

The 1933 work is the fundamental paper in the theory of hypothesis testing. It established a framework for this theory and stated the problem of finding the best test as a clearly formulated, logically convincing mathematical problem that one can then proceed to solve. Its importance transcends the theory of hypothesis testing since it also provided the inspiration for Abraham Wald's later, much more general statistical decision theory.

Survey Sampling and Confidence Estimation. In the following year Neyman published another landmark paper. An elaboration of work on survey sampling he had done earlier for the Warsaw Institute for Social Problems, it was directed toward bringing clarity into a somewhat muddled discussion about the relative merits of two different sampling methods. His treatment, described by Fisher as "luminous," introduced many important concepts and results, and may be said to have initiated the modern theory of survey sampling.

The year 1935 brought two noteworthy events. The first was Neyman's appointment to a permanent position as reader (associate professor) in Pearson's department. Although at the time he was still hoping eventually to return to Poland, he in fact never did, except for brief visits. The second event was the presentation at a meeting of the Royal Statistical Society of an important paper on agricultural experimentation in which he raised some questions concerning Fisher's Latin Square design. This caused a break in their hitherto friendly relationship and was the beginning of lifelong disputes.

Neyman remained in England for four years (1934 to 1938). During this time he continued his collaboration with Egon Pearson on the theory and applications of optimal tests, efforts that also included contributions from graduate and postdoctoral students. To facilitate publication and to emphasize the unified point of view underlying this work, Neyman and Pearson set up a series, Statistical Research Memoirs, published by University College and restricted to work done in the department of statistics. A first volume appeared in 1936, and a second in 1938.

Another central problem occupying Neyman during his London years was the theory of estimation: not point estimation, in which a parameter is estimated by a unique number, but estimation by means of an interval or more general set in which the unknown parameter can be said to lie with specified confidence (probability). Such confidence sets are easily obtained under the Bayesian assumption that the parameter is itself random with a known probability distribution, but Neyman's aim was to dispense with such an assumption, which he considered arbitrary and unwarranted.

Neyman published brief accounts of his solution to this problem in 1934 and 1935, and the theory in full generality in 1937, in "Outline of a Theory of Statistical Estimation Based on the Classical Theory of Probability."

Neyman's approach was based on the idea of obtaining confidence sets $S(X)$ for a parameter Θ from acceptance regions for the hypotheses that $\Theta = \Theta_0$ by taking for $S(X)$ the set of all parameter values Θ_0 that would be accepted at the given level. This formulation established an equivalence between confidence sets and families of tests, and enabled him to transfer in entirety the test theory of the 1933 paper—lock, stock, and barrel—to the theory of estimation. (Unbeknown to Neyman, the idea of obtaining confidence sets by inverting an acceptance rule had already been used in special cases by Pierre-Simon de Laplace—in a large-sample binomial setting—and by Harold Hotelling.)

In his paper on survey sampling, Neyman had referred to the relationship of his confidence intervals to Fisher's fiducial limits, which appeared to give the same results although derived from a somewhat different point of view. In the discussion of the paper, Fisher welcomed Neyman as an ally in the effort to free statistics from unwarranted Bayesian assumptions, but then proceeded to indicate the disadvantages he saw in Neyman's formulation. The debate between the two men over their respective approaches continued for many years, usually in less friendly terms; it is reviewed by Neyman in "Silver Jubilee of My Dispute with Fisher" (*Journal of the Operations Research Society of Japan*, **3** [1961], 145–154).

Statistical Philosophy. During the period of his work with Pearson, Neyman's attitude toward probability and hypothesis testing gradually underwent a radical change. In 1926 he tended to favor a Bayesian approach in the belief that any theory would have to involve statements about the probabilities of various alternative hypotheses, and hence an assumption of prior probabilities. In the face of Pearson's (and perhaps also Fisher's) strongly anti-Bayesian position, he became less certain, and in his papers of the late 1920's (both alone and with

Pearson), he presented Bayesian and non-Bayesian approaches side by side. A decisive influence was Richard von Mises's book *Wahrscheinlichkeit, Statistik und Wahrheit* (1928), about which he later wrote (*A Selection of Early Statistical Papers of J. Neyman*, 1967; author's note) that it "confirmed him as a radical 'frequentist' intent on probability as a mathematical idealization of relative frequency." He remained an avowed frequentist and opposed any subjective approach to science for the rest of his life.

A second basic aspect of Neyman's work from the 1930's on is a point of view that he formulated clearly in the closing pages of his presentation at the 1937 Geneva conference, "L'estimation statistique traitée comme un problème classique de probabilité" (*Actualités scientifiques et industrielles*, no. 739, 25–57). He states that his approach is based on the concept of "comportement inductif," or inductive behavior, instead of on inductive reasoning. That is, statistics is to use experience not to extract "beliefs" but as a guide to appropriate action.

In other writings (for example, in *Review of the International Statistical Institute*, **25** [1957], 7–22), Neyman acknowledges that a very similar point of view was advocated by Carl F. Gauss and Laplace. It is of course also that of Wald's later general statistical decision theory. This view was strongly attacked by Fisher (for example, in *Journal of the Royal Statistical Society*, **B17** [1955], 69–78), who maintained that decision making has no role in scientific inference, and that his fiducial argument provides exactly the mechanism required for scientific inference.

Move to the United States. By 1937 Neyman's work was becoming known not only in England and Poland but also in other parts of Europe and in the United States. He gave an invited talk about the theory of estimation at the International Congress of Probability held in 1937 at Geneva, and in the spring of 1937 he spent six weeks in the United States on a lecture tour organized by S. S. Wilks. The visit included a week at the graduate school of the Department of Agriculture in Washington, arranged by W. E. Deming. There he gave three lectures and six conferences on the relevance of probability theory to statistics, and on his work in hypothesis testing, estimation, sampling, and agricultural experimentation as illustrations of this approach. These *Lectures and Conferences on Mathematical Statistics*, which provided a coherent statement of the new paradigm he had developed and exhibited its successful application to a number of substantive problems, were a tremendous success.

A mimeographed version appeared in 1938 and was soon sold out. Neyman published an augmented second edition in 1952.

After his return from the United States, Neyman debated whether to remain in England, where he had a permanent position but little prospect of promotion and independence, or to return to Poland. Then, in the fall of 1937, he received an unexpected letter from G. C. Evans, chairman of the department of mathematics at Berkeley, offering him a position in his department. Neyman hesitated for some time. California and its university were completely unknown quantities, while the situation in England—although not ideal—was reasonably satisfactory and offered stability. An attractive aspect of the Berkeley offer was the nonexistence there of any systematic program in statistics, so that he would be free to follow his own ideas. What finally tipped the balance in favor of Berkeley was the threat of war in Europe. Thus in April 1938 he decided to accept the Berkeley offer and immigrate to America, with his wife Olga (from whom he later separated) and his two-year-old son, Michael. He had just turned forty-four and he would remain in Berkeley for the rest of his long life.

The Berkeley Department of Statistics. Neyman's top priority after his arrival in Berkeley was the development of a statistics program, that is, a systematic set of courses and a faculty to teach them. He quickly organized a number of core courses and began to train some graduate students and one temporary instructor in his own approach to statistics. Administratively, he set up a statistical laboratory as a semiautonomous unit within the mathematics department. However, America's entry into World War II in 1941 soon put all further academic development on hold. Neyman took on war work, and for the next years this became the laboratory's central and all-consuming activity.

The building of a faculty began in earnest after the war, and by 1956 Neyman had established a permanent staff of twelve members, many his own students but also including three senior appointments from outside (Michel Loève, Miriam Scheffé, and David Blackwell). Development of a substantial faculty, with the attendant problems of space, clerical staff, summer support, and so on, represented a major, sustained administrative effort. A crucial issue in the growth of the program concerned the course offerings in basic statistics by other departments. Although these involved major vested interests, Neyman gradually concentrated the teaching of statistics within his program, at least at the lower division level. This was an important achievement both in establishing the identity of the program and in obtaining the student base, which alone could justify the ongoing expansion of the faculty. In his negotiations with the administration, Neyman was strengthened by the growing international reputation of his laboratory and by the increasing postwar importance of the field of statistics itself.

An important factor in the laboratory's reputation was the series of international symposia on mathematical statistics and probability that Neyman organized at five-year intervals between 1945 and 1970, and the subsequent publication of their proceedings. The first symposium was held in August 1945 to celebrate the end of the war and "the return to theoretical research" after years of war work. The meeting, although rather modest compared with the later symposia, was such a success that Neyman soon began to plan another one for 1950. In later years the symposia grew in size, scope, and importance, and did much to establish Berkeley as a major statistical center.

The spectacular growth Neyman achieved for his group required a constant struggle with various administrative authorities, including those of the mathematics department. To decrease the number of obstacles, and also to provide greater visibility for the statistics program, Neyman soon after his arrival in Berkeley began a long effort to obtain independent status for his group as a department of statistics. A separate department finally became a reality in 1955, with Neyman as its chair. He resigned the chairmanship the following year (but retained the directorship of the laboratory to the end of his life). He felt, he wrote in his letter of resignation, that "the transformation of the old Statistical Laboratory into a Department of Statistics closed a period of development . . . and opened a new phase." In these circumstances, he stated, "it is only natural to have a new and younger man take over."

There was perhaps another reason. Much of Neyman's energy during the nearly twenty years he had been at Berkeley had gone into administration. His efforts had been enormously successful: a first-rate department, the symposia, a large number of grants providing summer support for faculty and students. It was a great accomplishment and his personal creation, but now it was time to get back more fully into research.

Applied Statistics. Neyman's research in Berkeley was largely motivated by his consulting work, one of the purposes for which the university had appointed him and through which he made himself useful to the campus at large. Problems in astronomy, for example, led to the interesting insight (1948, with Scott) that maximum likelihood estimates may cease to be consistent if the number of nuisance parameters tends to infinity with increasing sample size. Also, to simplify maximum likelihood computations, which in applications frequently became very cumbersome, he developed linearized, asymptotically equivalent methods—his BAN (best asymptotically normal) estimates (1949)—that have proved enormously useful.

Neyman's major research efforts at Berkeley were devoted to several large-scale applied projects. These included questions regarding competition of species (with T. Park), accident proneness (with G. Bates), the distribution of galaxies and the expansion of the universe (with C. D. Shane and particularly Elizabeth Scott, who became a steady collaborator and close companion), the effectiveness of cloud seeding, and a model for carcinogenesis. Of these, perhaps the most important was the work in astronomy, where the introduction of the Neyman-Scott clustering model brought new methods into the field.

Neyman's applicational work, although it extends over many different areas, exhibits certain common features, which he made explicit in some of his writings and which combine into a philosophy for applied statistics. The following are some of the principal aspects.

1. The studies are indeterministic. Neyman has pointed out that the distinction between deterministic and indeterministic studies lies not so much in the nature of the phenomena as in the treatment accorded to them ("Indeterminism in Science and New Demands on Statisticians," in *Journal of the American Statistical Association*, **55** [1960], 625–639). In fact, many subjects that traditionally were treated as deterministic are now being viewed stochastically. Neyman himself has contributed to this change in several areas.

2. An indeterministic study of a scientific phenomenon involves the construction of a stochastic model. In this connection Neyman introduced the important distinction between models that are interpolatory devices and those that embody genuine explanatory theories. The latter he describes as "a set of reasonable assumptions regarding the mechanism of the phenomena studied," while the former "by contrast consist of the selection of a relatively ad hoc family of functions, not deduced from underlying assumptions, and indexed by a set of parameters" ("Stochastic Models and Their Application to Social Phenomena," presented at a joint session of the Institute of Mathematical Statistics, the American Statistical Association, and the American Sociological Society, September 1956; written with W. Kruskal). The distinction is discussed earlier, and again later in Neyman's papers (*Annals of Mathematical Statistics*, **10** [1939], 372–373; and *Reliability and Biometry*, [Philadelphia, 1974], 183–201).

Most actual modeling, Neyman points out, is intermediate between these two extremes, often exhibiting features of both kinds. Related is the realization that investigators will tend to use as building blocks models that, "partly through experience and partly through imagination, appear to us familiar and, therefore, simple" ("Stochastic Models of Population Dynamics").

3. To develop a "genuine explanatory Theory" requires substantial knowledge of the scientific background of the problem. When the investigation concerns a branch of science with which the statistician is unfamiliar, this may require a considerable amount of work. For his collaboration with Scott in astronomy, Neyman studied the astrophysical literature, joined the American Astronomical Society, and became a member of the Commission on Galaxies of the International Astronomical Union. When he developed an interest in carcinogenesis, he spent three months at the National Institutes of Health to learn more about the biological background of the problem.

An avenue for learning about the state of the art in a field and bringing together diverse points of view that Neyman enjoyed and repeatedly used was to arrange a conference. Two of these (on weather modification in 1965 and on molecular biology in 1970) became parts of the then-current symposia. In addition, in 1961, jointly with Scott, he arranged a conference on the instability of systems of galaxies, and in July 1981, with Lucien Le Cam and on very short notice, an interdisciplinary cancer conference.

Epilogue. A month after the cancer conference, Neyman died of heart failure at age eighty-seven. He had been in reasonable health until two weeks earlier, and on the day before his death was still working in the hospital, on a book on weather modification.

Neyman is recognized as one of the founders of the modern theory of statistics whose work on hypothesis testing, confidence intervals, and survey sampling has revolutionized both theory and practice. His enormous influence on the development of statistics is further greatly enhanced through the large number of his Ph.D. students.

His achievements were recognized by honorary

degrees from the universities of Chicago, California. Stockholm, and Warsaw, and from the Indian Statistical Institute. He was elected to the United States National Academy of Sciences and to foreign membership in the Royal Society, the Royal Swedish Academy, and the Polish National Academy. In addition he received many awards, including the United States National Medal of Science and the Guy Medal in Gold of the Royal Statistical Society.

Neyman was completely and enthusiastically dedicated to his work, which filled his life; there was not time for hobbies. Work, however, included not only research and teaching but also social aspects, such as traveling to meetings and organizing conferences. Pleasing his guests was an avocation; his hospitality had an international reputation. In his laboratory he created a family atmosphere that included students, colleagues, and visitors, with himself as paterfamilias.

As an administrator Neyman was indomitable. He would not take no for an answer, and was quite capable of resorting to unilateral actions. He firmly believed in the righteousness of his causes and found it difficult to understand how a reasonable person could disagree with him. At the same time, he had great charm that often was hard to resist.

The characteristic that perhaps remains most in mind is his generosity: furthering the careers of his students, giving credit and doing more than his share in collaboration, and extending his help (including financial assistance out of his own pocket) to anyone who needed it.

BIBLIOGRAPHY

I. ORIGINAL WORKS. A complete bibliography of Neyman's work is given at the end of David Kendall's memoir, in *Biographical Memoirs of Fellows of the Royal Society* (see below). Some of the early papers are reprinted in *A Selection of Early Statistical Papers of J. Neyman* and *Joint Statistical Papers of J. Neyman and E. S. Pearson* (Berkeley, 1967). Neyman's letters to E. S. Pearson from 1926 to 1933 (but not Pearson's replies) are preserved in Pearson's estate.

An overall impression of Neyman's ideas and style can be gained from his *Lectures and Conferences on Mathematical Statistics and Probability*, 2nd. ed., rev. and enl. (Washington, D.C., 1952). The following partial list provides a more detailed view of his major paradigmatic papers: "On the Use and Interpretation of Certain Test Criteria for Purposes of Statistical Inference," in *Biometrika*, **20A** (1928), 175–240, 263–294, written with E. S. Pearson; "On the Problem of the Most Efficient Tests of Statistical Hypotheses," in *Philosophical Transactions of the Royal Society of London*, **A 231** (1933), 289–337,

written with E. S. Pearson; "On the Two Different Aspects of the Representative Method," in *Journal of the Royal Statistical Society*, **97** (1934), 558–625 (a Spanish version of this paper appeared in *Estadística*, **17** [1959], 587–651); "Outline of a Theory of Statistical Estimation Based on the Classical Theory of Probability," in *Philosophical Transactions of the Royal Society of London*, **A 236** (1937), 333–380.

Neyman's other theoretical contributions include "'Smooth' Test for Goodness of Fit," in *Skandinavisk aktuarietidskrift*, **20** (1937), 149–199; "On a New Class of 'Contagious' Distributions, Applicable in Entomology and Bacteriology," in *Annals of Mathematical Statistics*, **10** (1939), 35–57; "Consistent Estimates Based on Partially Consistent Observations," in *Econometrica*, **16** (1948), 1–32, written with E. L. Scott; "Contribution to the Theory of the Chi-Square Test," in J. Neyman, ed., *Proceedings of the Berkeley Symposium on Mathematical Statistics and Probability* (Berkeley, 1949); "Optimal Asymptotic Tests of Composite Statistical Hypotheses," in U. Granander, ed., *Probability and Statistics* (Uppsala, Sweden, 1959), 213–234; "Outlier Proneness of Phenomena and of Related Distributions," in J. S. Rustagi, ed., *Optimizing Methods in Statistics* (New York and London, 1971), 413–430, written with E. L. Scott.

Neyman's position regarding the role of statistics in science can be obtained from the following more philosophical and sometimes autobiographical articles: "Foundation of the General Theory of Statistical Estimation, in *Actualités Scientifiques et industrielles*, no. 1146 (1951), 83–95; "The Problem of Inductive Inference," in *Communications in Pure and Applied Mathematics*, **8** (1955), 13–45; "'Inductive Behavior' as a Basic Concept of Philosophy of Science," in *Review of the International Statistical Institute*, **25** (1957), 7–22; "Stochastic Models of Population Dynamics," in *Science* (New York), **130** (1959), 303–308, written with E. L. Scott; "A Glance at Some of My Personal Experiences in the Process of Research," in T. Dalenius, G. Karlsson, and S. Malmquist, eds., *Scientists at Work* (Uppsala, Sweden, 1970), 148–164; and "Frequentist Probability and Frequentist Statistics," in *Synthèse*, **36** (1977), 97–131.

II. SECONDARY LITERATURE. The most important source for Neyman's life and personality is Constance Reid, *Neyman—from Life* (New York, 1982), which is based on Neyman's own recollections (obtained during weekly meetings over a period of more than a year) and those of his colleagues and former students, and on many original documents. A useful account of his collaboration with E. S. Pearson was written by Pearson for the Neyman festschrift, F. N. David, ed., *Research Papers in Statistics* (New York, 1966). Additional accounts of his life and work are provided by the following: D. G. Kendall, M. S. Bartlett, and T. L. Page, "Jerzy Neyman, 1894–1981," in *Biographical Memoirs of Fellows of the Royal Society*, **28** (1982), 379–412; L. Le Cam and E. L. Lehmann, "J. Neyman—on the Occasion of his 80-th Birthday," in *Annals of Statistics*, **2** (1974), vii–xiii; E. L. Lehmann and Constance Reid, "In Memoriam—Jerzy Neyman, 1894–1981," in *American Statistician*, **36** (1982) 161–162;

and E. L. Scott, "Neyman, Jerzy," in *Encyclopedia of Statistical Sciences*, VI (1985) 215–223.

E. L. LEHMANN

NICHOLSON, JOHN WILLIAM (*b.* Darlington, England, 1 November 1881; *d.* Oxford, England, 10 October 1955)

The eldest son of John William Nicholson and Alice Emily Kirton, Nicholson received his early education at Middlesbrough High School. He studied mathematics and physical science at the University of Manchester from 1898 to 1901. He went on to Trinity College, Cambridge, where he took the mathematical tripos in 1904. At Cambridge he was Isaac Newton student in 1906, Smith's prizeman in 1907, and Adam's prizeman in 1913 and again in 1917. He lectured at the Cavendish Laboratory, Cambridge, and later at the Queen's University, Belfast, before being appointed professor of mathematics at King's College, London, in 1912. In 1921 he became fellow and director of studies in mathematics at Balliol College, Oxford, retiring in 1930 because of bad health. In 1922 he married Dorothy Wrinch, fellow of Girton College, Cambridge; they had one daughter. Their marriage was dissolved in 1938.

Nicholson became fellow of the Royal Astronomical Society in 1911 and fellow of the Royal Society in 1917. He was vice-president of the London Physical Society, president of the Röntgen Society, and member of the London Mathematical Society and the Société de Physique. He received the M.A. from the universities of Oxford and Cambridge, the D.Sc. from the University of London, and the M.Sc. from the University of Manchester.

Nicholson's most original work was his atomic theory of coronal and nebular spectra, which he published in a series of papers, beginning in November 1911, in the *Monthly Notices of the Royal Astronomical Society*. The spectra of the solar corona and galactic nebulae contained lines of unknown origin, which Nicholson, following a common astrophysical speculation at the time, supposed were produced by elements that were primary in an evolutionary sense to terrestrial elements. The presumed simplicity of the primary elements opened the possibility of their exact dynamical treatment. Adapting an atomic model of J. J. Thomson, Nicholson viewed an atom of a primary element as a single, planetary ring of electrons rotating about a small, massive, positively charged nucleus. Associating the frequencies of the unidentified spectral lines with those of the transverse modes of oscillation of the electrons about their equilibrium

path, he accounted for most coronal and nebular lines with impressive numerical accuracy, even predicting a new nebular line that was soon observed.

In his first two papers on celestial spectra, Nicholson had no theoretical means for fully specifying his atomic systems, having to fix empirically the radius and angular velocity of the electron rings from observed spectral frequencies. In his third paper (June 1912) he rectified the incompleteness of his theory by introducing the Planck constant, h. He did so by observing that the angular momentum of primary atoms was a multiple of $h/2\pi$. Niels Bohr read Nicholson's papers in the *Monthly Notices* in late 1912, at the time he was working out his own early thoughts on the relation of the Planck constant to the structure of atoms and molecules. Impressed by the unprecedented spectral capability of Nicholson's theory, Bohr sought its relation to his own theory. In so doing Bohr came to a deeper understanding of his own atomic model, in particular of his need to attribute excited states to it. After Bohr published his theory in 1913, Nicholson challenged it and extended his own theory. But it was Bohr's theory and not his that led to a full understanding of spectra and beyond that to a new quantum atomic physics. The significance of Nicholson's theory for the development of twentieth-century atomic physics lies chiefly in the early impetus it gave Bohr for exploring the spectral implications of his very different quantum theory.

BIBLIOGRAPHY

I. ORIGINAL WORKS. Nicholson's active career spanned the years 1905–1925, during which he published roughly seventy-five papers. His most important papers on coronal and nebular spectra are "The Spectrum of Nebulium," in *Monthly Notices of the Royal Astronomical Society*, **72** (1911), 49–64; and "The Constitution of the Solar Corona," *ibid.*, 139–150; *ibid.* (1912), 677–692, 729–739. In addition to his astrophysical papers, Nicholson published on a wide range of topics that included electric and elastic vibrations, electron theory of metals, electron structure, atomic structure and spectra of terrestrial elements, relativity principle, and special mathematical functions.

Although Nicholson wrote no books, he contributed to Arthur Dendy, ed., *Problems of Modern Science. A Series of Lectures Delivered at King's College—University of London* (London, 1922). He collaborated with Arthur Schuster in revising and enlarging the third ed. of the latter's *An Introduction to the Theory of Optics* (London, 1924); and with Joseph Larmor *et al.* he edited the *Scientific Papers of S. B. McLaren* (Cambridge, 1925).

II. SECONDARY LITERATURE. Nicholson's contribution to modern atomic theory has been recently assessed by John L. Heilbron and Thomas S. Kuhn, "The Genesis of the Bohr Atom," in *Historical Studies in the Physical Sciences*,

1 (1969), 211–290; T. Hirosige and S. Nisio, "Formation of Bohr's Theory of Atomic Constitution," in *Japanese Studies in the History of Science*, no. 3 (1964), 6–28; and Russell McCormmach, "The Atomic Theory of John William Nicholson," in *Archives for History of Exact Sciences*, 3 (1966), 160–184.

In his introduction to Niels Bohr, *On the Constitution of Atoms and Molecules* (Copenhagen, 1963), xi–liii, Léon Rosenfeld has, in addition to discussing Nicholson's theory, published and analyzed letters by Bohr in 1912 and 1913 that bear on his reading of the theory. An older historical discussion of Nicholson's theory is Edmund Whittaker, *A History of the Theories of Aether and Electricity. The Modern Theories 1900–1926* (London, 1953), 107. A contemporary scientific account of Nicholson's theory is W. D. Harkens and E. D. Wilson, "Recent Work on the Structure of the Atom," in *Journal of the American Chemical Society*, 37 (1915), 1396–1421.

For biographical information, see William Wilson, "John William Nicholson 1881–1955," in *Biographical Memoirs of Fellows of the Royal Society*, 2 (1956), 209–214.

RUSSELL MCCORMMACH

NICOMACHUS OF GERASA (*fl. ca.* A.D. 100)

That Nicomachus was from Gerasa, probably the city in Palestine, is known from Lucian (*Philopatris*, 12), from scholia to his commentator Philoponus, and from some manuscripts that contain Nicomachus' works. The period of his activity is determined by inference. In his *Manual of Harmonics* Nicomachus mentions Thrasyllus, who died in A.D. 36; Apuleius, born about A.D. 125, is said to have translated the *Introduction to Arithmetic* into Latin; and a character in Lucian's *Philopatris* says, "You calculate like Nicomachus," which shows that Lucian, born about A.D. 120, considered Nicomachus a famous man.[1] Porphyry mentions him, together with Moderatus and others, as a prominent member of the Pythagorean school, and this connection may also be seen in his writings.[2] Only two of his works are extant, *Manual of Harmonics* and *Introduction to Arithmetic*. He also wrote a *Theologumena arithmeticae*, dealing with the mystic properties of numbers, and a larger work on music, some extracts of which have survived.[3] Other works are ascribed to him, but it is not certain that he wrote any of them.[4]

In the *Manual of Harmonics*, after an introductory chapter, Nicomachus deals with the musical note in chapters 2–4 and devotes the next five chapters to the octave. Chapter 10 deals with tuning principles based on the stretched string; chapter 11, with the extension of the octave to the two-octave range of the Greater Perfect System in the diatonic genus; and the work ends with a chapter in which, after restating the definitions of note, interval, and system, Nicomachus gives a survey of the Immutable System in the three genera: diatonic, chromatic, and enharmonic. He deals with notes, intervals, systems, and genera, the first four of the seven subdivisions of harmonics recognized by the ancients, but not with keys, modulation, or melodic composition. The treatise exhibits characteristics of both the Aristoxenian and the Pythagorean schools of music. To the influence of the latter must be ascribed Nicomachus' assignment of number and numerical ratios to notes and intervals, his recognition of the indivisibility of the octave and the whole tone, and his notion that the musical consonances are in either multiple or superparticular ratios. But unlike Euclid, who attempts to prove musical propositions through mathematical theorems, Nicomachus seeks to show their validity by measurement of the lengths of strings. Hence his treatment of consonances and of musical genera, as well as his definition of the note, are Aristoxenian.

The *Introduction to Arithmetic* is in two books. After six preliminary chapters devoted to the philosophical importance of mathematics, Nicomachus deals with number per se, relative number, plane and solid numbers, and proportions. He enunciates several definitions of number and then discusses its division into even and odd. He states the theorem that any integer is equal to half the sum of the two integers on each side of it and proceeds to give the classification of even numbers (even times even, odd times even, and even times odd), followed by that of odd numbers (prime, composite, and relative prime).[5] The fundamental relations of number are equality and inequality, and the latter is divided into the greater and the less. The ratios of the greater are multiples, superparticulars, superpartients, multiple superparticulars, and multiple superpartients; those of the less are the reciprocal ratios of these. Book I concludes with a general principle whereby all forms of inequality of ratio may be generated from a series of three equal terms.[6] At the beginning of the second book the reverse principle is given. It is followed by detailed treatments of squares, cubes, and polygonal numbers. Nicomachus divides proportions into disjunct and continuous, and describes ten types. He presents no abstract proofs (as are found in Euclid's *Elements*, VII–IX), and he limits himself for the most part to the enunciation of principles followed by examples with specific numbers.[7] On one occasion this method leads to a serious mistake,[8] but there are many other mistakes which are independent of the method of exposition—for example, his inclusion of composite numbers, a class which belongs to all numbers, as a species of the odd. Yet despite its notorious shortcomings, the treatise was influential until the sixteenth century and gave its author the undeserved reputation of being a great mathematician.

NOTES

1. For references to modern discussions, see Tarán, *Asclepius on Nicomachus*, p. 5, n. 3. J. M. Dillon, "A Date for the Death of Nicomachus of Gerasa?" in *Classical Review*, n.s. **19** (1969), 274–275, conjectures that Nicomachus died in A.D. 196, because Proclus, who was born in A.D. 412, is said by Marinus, *Vita Procli*, 28, to have believed that he was a reincarnation of Nicomachus, and because some Pythagoreans believed that reincarnations occur at intervals of 216 years. But Dillon fails to cite any passage in which Proclus would attach particular importance to the number 216 and, significantly enough, this number is not mentioned in Proclus' commentary on the creation of the soul in Plato's *Timaeus*, a passage where one would have expected this number to occur had Dillon's conjecture been a probable one.
2. In Eusebius of Caesarea, *Historia ecclesiastica*, VI, xix, 8.
3. Some of the contents of the *Theologumena* can be recovered from the summary of it given by Photius, *Bibliotheca*, codex 187, and from the quotations from it in the extant *Theologumena arithmeticae* ascribed to Iamblichus.

    In his *Manual of Harmonics*, I, 2, Nicomachus promises to write a longer and complete work on the subject; and the extracts in some MSS, published by Jan in *Musici scriptores Graeci*, pp. 266–282, probably are from this work. They can hardly belong to a second book of the *Manual*, because Nicomachus' words at the end of this work indicate that it concluded with chapter 12. Eutocius seems to refer to the first book of the larger work on music; see *Eutocii Commentarii in libros De sphaera et cylindro*, in *Archimedis Opera omnia*, J. L. Heiberg, ed., III (Leipzig, 1915), 120, ll. 20–21.
4. In his *Introduction to Arithmetic*, II, 6, 1, Nicomachus refers to an *Introduction to Geometry*. Some scholars attribute to him a *Life of Pythagoras* on the grounds that Nicomachus is quoted by both Porphyry and Iamblichus in their biographies of Pythagoras. It is also conjectured that he wrote a work on astronomy because Simplicius, *In Aristotelis De caelo*, Heiberg ed., p. 507, ll. 12–14, says that Nicomachus, followed by Iamblichus, attributed the hypothesis of eccentric circles to the Pythagoreans. A work by Nicomachus with the title *On Egyptian Festivals* is cited by Athenaeus and by Lydus, but the identity of this Nicomachus with Nicomachus of Gerasa is not established. Finally, the "Nicomachus the Elder" said by Apollinaris Sidonius to have written a life of Apollonius of Tyana in which he drew from that of Philostratus cannot be the author of the *Manual*, since Philostratus was born *ca.* A.D. 170.
5. Nicomachus considers prime numbers a class of the odd, because for him 1 and 2 are not really numbers. For a criticism of this and of Nicomachus' classifications of even and odd numbers, see Heath, *A History of Greek Mathematics*, I, 70–74. In I, 13, Nicomachus describes Eratosthenes' "sieve," a device for finding prime numbers.
6. This principle is designed to show that equality is the root and mother of all forms of inequality.
7. Euclid represents numbers by lines with letters attached, a system that makes it possible for him to deal with numbers in general, whereas Nicomachus represents numbers by letters having specific values.
8. See *Introduction to Arithmetic*, II, 28, 3, where he infers a characteristic of the subcontrary proportion from what is true only of the particular example (3, 5, 6) that he chose to illustrate this proportion. See Tarán, *Asclepius on Nicomachus*, p. 81 with references.

BIBLIOGRAPHY

I. ORIGINAL WORKS. The best, but not critical, ed. of the *Introduction to Arithmetic* is *Nicomachi Geraseni Pythagorei Introductionis arithmeticae libri II*, R. Hoche, ed. (Leipzig, 1866), also in English with notes and excellent introductory essays as *Nicomachus of Gerasa, Introduction to Arithmetic*, trans. by M. L. D'Ooge, with studies in Greek arithmetic by F. E. Robbins and L. C. Karpinski (New York, 1926); Boethius' Latin trans. and adaptation is *Anicii Manlii Torquati Severini Boetii De institutione arithmeticae libri duo*, G. Friedlein, ed. (Leipzig, 1867). The *Manual of Harmonics* is in Carolus Jan, *Musici scriptores Graeci* (Leipzig, 1895), 235–265; an English trans. and commentary is F. R. Levin, "Nicomachus of Gerasa, Manual of Harmonics: Translation and Commentary" (diss., Columbia University, 1967).

II. SECONDARY LITERATURE. Ancient commentaries are an anonymous "Prolegomena" in P. Tannery, ed., *Diophanti Opera omnia*, II (Leipzig, 1895), 73–76; Iamblichus' commentary, *Iamblichi in Nicomachi Arithmeticam introductionem liber*, H. Pistelli, ed. (Leipzig, 1894); Philoponus' commentary, R. Hoche, ed., 3 fascs. (Wesel, 1864, 1865; Berlin, 1867); another recension of this commentary in Hoche (Wesel, 1865), pp. ii–xiv, for the variants corresponding to the first book, and in A. Delatte, *Anecdota Atheniensia et alia*, II (Paris, 1939), 129–187, for those corresponding to the second book; Asclepius' commentary, "Asclepius of Tralles, Commentary to Nicomachus' Introduction to Arithmetic," edited with an intro. and notes by L. Tarán, *Transactions of the American Philosophical Society*, n.s., **59**, pt. 4 (1969); there is an anonymous commentary, still unpublished, probably by a Byzantine scholar—see Tarán, *op. cit.*, pp. 6, 7–8, 18–20.

For an exposition of the mathematical contents of Nicomachus' treatise and a criticism of it, see T. Heath, *A History of Greek Mathematics*, I (Oxford, 1921), 97–112.

LEONARDO TARÁN

NICOMEDES (*fl. ca.* 250 B.C. [?])

Nothing is known of the life of Nicomedes. His period of activity can be only approximately inferred from the facts that he criticized the solution of Eratosthenes (*fl.* 250 B.C.) to the problem of doubling the cube and that Apollonius (*fl.* 200 B.C.) named a curve "sister of the cochlioid," presumably as a compliment to Nicomedes, who had discovered the curve known as cochlioid, cochloid, or conchoid.[1] The second inference is far from secure, but what we know of Nicomedes' mathematical investigations fits well into the period of Archimedes (*d.* 212 B.C.).

The work for which Nicomedes became famous was called *On Conchoid Lines* (Περὶ κογχοειδῶν γραμμῶν).[2] We know it only through secondhand references. In

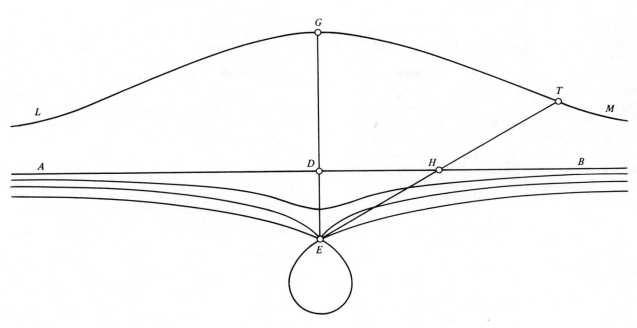

FIGURE 1

it Nicomedes described the generation of a curve, which he called the "first conchoid," as follows (see Figure 1): Given a fixed straight line *AB* (the "canon") and a fixed point *E* (the "pole"), draw *EDG* perpendicular to *AB*, cutting it at *D*, and make *DG* a fixed length (the "interval"); then let *GDE* move about *E* in such a way that *D* is always on *AB* (thus when *D* reaches *H*, *G* will have reached *T*). *G* will then describe a curve, *LGTM*, the first conchoid. The advantages of this curve are that it is very easy to construct (Nicomedes described a mechanical instrument for drawing it)[3] and that it can be used to solve a variety of problems, including the "classical" problems of doubling the cube and trisecting the angle. These are all soluble by means of the auxiliary construction which we may call the "lemma of Nicomedes": Given two straight lines, *X*, *Y*, meeting in a given angle and a point *P* outside the angle, it is possible to draw a line through *P* cutting *X* and *Y* so that a given length, *l*, is intercepted between *X* and *Y*. This is done by constructing a conchoid with "canon" *X*, "pole" *P*, and "interval" *l*; the intersection of this conchoid and *Y* gives the solution.

Nicomedes solved the problem of finding two mean proportionals (to which earlier Greek mathematicians had reduced the problem of doubling the cube) as shown in Figure 2.

Given two straight lines *AB*, *BG*, between which it is required to find two mean proportionals. Complete the rectangle *ABGL*. Bisect *AB*, *BG* in *D* and *E*, respectively. Join *LD* and produce it to meet *GB* produced in *H*. Draw *EZ* perpendicular to *EG*, of

length such that *GZ = AD*. Join *HZ*, and draw *GT* parallel to it. Then draw *ZTK*, meeting *BG* produced in *K*, so that *TK = AD* (this is possible by the "lemma of Nicomedes"). Join *KL* and produce it to meet *BA* produced in *M*. Then

$$\frac{AB}{GK} = \frac{GK}{MA} = \frac{MA}{BG},$$

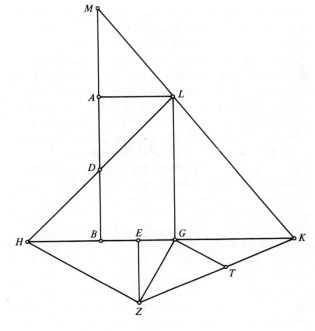

FIGURE 2

and *GK, MA* are the required mean proportionals.[4]

Nicomedes also showed how to trisect the angle by means of his lemma and proved that the "first conchoid" is asymptotic to its "canon."[5] In addition he described what he called the "second, third, and fourth conchoids" and their uses. The ancient sources tell us nothing about them beyond their names, but it has been plausibly conjectured that they are to be identified with the other branch of the curve in its three possible forms. In modern terms the curve is a quartic whose equation is, in polar coordinates,

$$\rho = \frac{a}{\cos \theta} \pm l,$$

or, in Cartesian coordinates,

$$(x - a)^2 (x^2 + y^2) - l^2 x^2 = 0.$$

This curve has two branches, both asymptotic to the line $x = a$. The lower branch (see Figure 1, in the lower part of which the three forms are depicted) has a double point at the pole E, which is either a node, a cusp, or an isolated point according as $l \gtreqless a$ (here l corresponds to the interval, a to the distance from the pole to the canon). This second branch can be constructed in the same way that Nicomedes constructed the first, with the sole difference that the interval is taken on the same side of the canon AB as the pole E.[6]

As far as is known, all applications of the conchoid made in antiquity were developed by Nicomedes himself. It was not until the late sixteenth century, when the works of Pappus and Eutocius describing the curve became generally known, that interest in it revived and new applications and properties were discovered. Viète used the "lemma of Nicomedes" as a postulate in his *Supplementum geometriae* (1593) to solve a number of problems leading to equations of the third and fourth degrees, including the construction of the regular heptagon. Johann Molther, in his little-known but remarkable *Problema deliacum* (1619), used the same lemma for an elegant reworking of the old problem of finding two mean proportionals. The conchoid attracted the attention of some of the best mathematicians of the seventeenth century. Descartes discussed the construction of tangents to it (in his *Géométrie* of 1637); Fermat and Roberval treated the same problem with respect to both branches. Huygens discovered a neat construction of the point of inflection (1653). Newton discussed the curve more than once, and in his *Arithmetica universalis* he recommended its use as an auxiliary in geometry because of the ease of its construction (it is

in fact sufficient to solve any problem involving equations of the third and fourth degrees). In the appendix to the *Arithmetica*, on the linear construction of equations, he makes extensive use of the "lemma of Nicomedes." The seventeenth century also saw the first generalization of the conchoid, produced by taking a circle instead of a straight line for canon: this generates Pascal's limaçon.

NOTES

1. Eutocius, *Commentary on Archimedes' Sphere and Cylinder*, in *Archimedis Opera omnia*, J. L. Heiberg, ed., III, 98; Simplicius, *Commentary on Aristotle's Categories*, Kalbfleisch, ed., p. 192.
2. Eutocius, *loc. cit.* It is uncertain whether Nicomedes called the curve κοχλοειδής, κοχλιοειδής, or κογχοειδής (all three are found in our sources). The first two mean "snail-shaped"; the third, "mussel-shaped."
3. *Ibid.*
4. For a proof see Pappus, *Synagoge*, bk. 4, sec. 43, Hultsch, ed., I, 248–250, repro. in Heath, *History of Greek Mathematics*, I, 260–262. In fact all of the construction after the determination of point K is superfluous, for $ZT = MA$ and therefore GK, ZT are the required mean proportionals. As D. T. Whiteside pointed out to me, this was realized by Molther (*Problema deliacum*, pp. 55–58), and by Newton (*Mathematical Papers*, II, prob. 15, pp. 460–461).
5. On trisection of the angle see Pappus, *Synagoge*, bk. 4, sec. 62, Hultsch, ed., I, 274–276; see also Proclus, *Commentary on Euclid I*, Friedlein, ed., p. 272. On the "first conchoid" being asymptotic to its "canon," see Eutocius, *op. cit.*, in *Archimedis Opera omnia*, J. L. Heiberg, ed., III, 100–102.
6. I do not know who first proposed this identification of Nicomedes' "second, third, and fourth conchoids," but a probable guess is either Fermat or Roberval. In a letter to Roberval of 1636, Fermat (*Oeuvres*, II, 94) mentions the "second conchoid of Nicomedes." Roberval refers to the two branches as "conchoide de dessus" and "conchoide de dessous," respectively ("Composition des mouvemens," in *Ouvrages de mathématique* [1731], p. 28).

BIBLIOGRAPHY

The principal ancient passages concerning Nicomedes are Pappus, *Synagoge*, F. Hultsch, ed., I (Berlin, 1875), bk. 3, sec. 21, p. 56; bk. 4, secs. 39–45, pp. 242–252, and secs. 62–64, pp. 274–276; Eutocius, *Commentary on Archimedes' Sphere and Cylinder*, in *Archimedis Opera omnia*, J. L. Heiberg, ed., 2nd ed., III (Leipzig, 1915), 98–106; Proclus, *Commentary on Euclid I*, G. Friedlein, ed. (Leipzig, 1873), 272; and Simplicius, *Commentary on Aristotle's Categories*, K. Kalbfleisch, ed., which is Commentaria in Aristotelem Graeca, VIII (Berlin, 1907), 192. The best modern account of Nicomedes is Gino Loria, *Le scienze esatte nell'antica Grecia*, 2nd ed. (Milan, 1914), 404–410. See also T. L. Heath, *A History of Greek Mathematics* (Oxford, 1921), I, 238–240, 260–262, and II, 199. There is no adequate account of the treatment of the conchoid in the sixteenth and seventeenth centuries. The best available is Gino Loria, *Spezielle algebraische und transzendente ebene Kurven*, 2nd ed. (Leipzig–Berlin, 1910), I, 136–142, which also gives a good description of the mathematical properties of the curve; see also F. Gomes Teixeira, *Traité des courbes spéciales remarquables*, I, which is vol. IV of his *Obras sobre matematica* (Coimbra, 1908), 259–268.

On generalizations of the conchoid see Loria, *Spezielle . . . Kurven*, pp. 143–152. Viète's *Supplementum geometriae* is printed in his *Opera mathematica*, F. van Schooten, ed. (Leiden, 1646; repr. Hildesheim, 1970), 240–257. Johann Molther's extremely rare opuscule, *Problema deliacum de cubi duplicatione*, was printed at Frankfurt in 1619. For Descartes's treatment of the conchoid see *The Geometry of René Descartes*, trans. by D. E. Smith and M. L. Latham (Chicago–London, 1925), 113–114. The discussions of Fermat and Roberval are printed in Pierre de Fermat, *Oeuvres*, P. Tannery and C. H. Henry, eds., II (Paris, 1894), 72, 82, 86–87. See also Roberval, *Ouvrages de mathématique* (The Hague, 1731), 28–32 (on Pascal's limaçon, see p. 35). Huygens' solution is printed in *Oeuvres complètes de Christiaan Huygens*, XII (The Hague, 1910), 83–86. For Newton's treatment see *The Mathematical Papers of Isaac Newton*, D. T. Whiteside, ed., II (Cambridge, 1968), prob. 15, pp. 460–461, and especially the app. to his "Universal Arithmetick," printed in *The Mathematical Works of Isaac Newton*, D. T. Whiteside, ed., II (New York–London, 1967), 118–134.

G. J. TOOMER

NIELSEN, NIELS (*b.* Ørslev, Denmark, 2 December 1865; *d.* Copenhagen, Denmark, 16 September 1931)

Nielsen's father was a small farmer, and his family lived in modest circumstances. He originally wished to attend the polytechnical institute, but he was early attracted to pure science. In 1885 he began his studies at the University of Copenhagen, where he passed the government examination in 1891 and received his doctorate in 1895. He had been teaching in the secondary schools since 1887, and in 1900 he began to give preparatory courses for the polytechnic institute. From 1903 to 1906 he belonged to the University Inspectorate for secondary schools. In 1905 he became *Dozent* and in 1909 he succeeded Julius Petersen as full professor of mathematics at the University of Copenhagen.

He became a member of the Leopoldina of Halle in 1906 and an honorary member of the Wiskundig Genootschap of Amsterdam in 1907. Nielsen's principal achievements were his many textbooks, which dealt with various classes of special functions. Before he prepared these books he wrote numerous papers. His textbooks on cylindrical functions (1904) and on the gamma function (1906) were widely used.

Nielsen developed no new ideas and did not even present any fundamental theorems, but he possessed great knowledge and the ability to generalize existing formalisms. Moreover, he did make an important contribution to the theory of gamma function and factorial series. The theory originated with W. V. Jensen; Nielsen gave it further impetus, and Nörlund provided its definitive clarification. Nielsen's abilities were thus very restricted. He was a master in the treatment of unmethodical calculations and came up with a multitude of particular points. He playfully conceived new things that were not always in a completed form, and he was a significant influence on his students.

In 1917 Nielsen suffered a breakdown. He never fully recovered but his powers were not perceptibly diminished. He turned his attention to number theory (Bernoulli's numbers, Fermat's equation), which he treated unsystematically. In the history of mathematics he occupied himself primarily with accounts of personalities and the historical development of specific mathematical problems. Two books on Danish mathematicians and two on French mathematicians are the fruits of his work in this area.

BIBLIOGRAPHY

I. ORIGINAL WORKS. Nielsen's works include the following: *Handbuch der Theorie der Zylinderfunktionen* (Leipzig, 1904), which contains sixteen pp. of bibliography; *Theorie der Integrallogarithmus und verwandter Transzendenten* (Leipzig, 1906), which has ten pp. of bibliography, tables, and applications; *Handbuch der Theorie der Gammafunktion* (Leipzig, 1906), which represents twenty years of work and is the first comprehensive treatment of the gamma function since Legendre's *Traité;* and *Lehrbuch der unendlichen Reihen; Vorlesung gehälten an der Universität Kopenhagen* (Leipzig, 1908), an elementary treatment without the use of calculus.

See also *Laeren on Graensvaerdier som indledning til analysen* (Copenhagen, 1910); *Mathematiken i Danmark*, 1528–1800, I; 1801–1908, II (Copenhagen–Oslo, 1910), which contains data on his life and a compilation of his published works; *Elemente der Funktionentheorie Vorlesung gehalten an der Universität Kopenhagen* (Leipzig, 1911); *Géomètres français sous la révolution* (Copenhagen, 1929), treats of seventy-six mathematicians; and *Géomètres français du dix-huitième siècle*, Niels Nörlund, ed. (Copenhagen–Paris, 1929), which is a posthumous work and treats of 153 mathematicians.

II. SECONDARY LITERATURE. Nielsen also published about 100 articles in twenty-one different Danish and foreign periodicals. For further information see Harald Bohr, "Niels Nielsen 2 December 1865–16 September 1931," in *Matematisk Tidsskrift*, 41–45; and Poggendorff, IV, 1073; V, 905; VI, 1855.

H. OETTEL

NIEUWENTIJT, BERNARD (*b*. Westgraftdijk, North Holland, 10 August 1654; *d*. Purmerend, North Holland, 30 May 1718)

Bernard was the son of Emmanuel Nieuwentijt, minister at Westgraftdijk, and Sara d'Imbleville. Although he was expected to enter the ministry, he chose instead to study natural sciences. On 28 February 1675 he was enrolled as a student in medicine at Leiden University; later in the year he was also enrolled at Utrecht University, where he studied law and defended his medical thesis in 1676 [1]. He then settled as a medical practitioner in Purmerend. On 12 November 1684 he married Eva Moens, the widow of Philips Munnik, a naval captain in the service of the Dutch States-General. He was elected a member of the city council and became a burgomaster of Purmerend. As a youth Nieuwentijt was influenced by Cartesianism and he acquired a thorough knowledge of mathematics and natural philosophy. In 1695–1700 he was engaged in a controversy with Leibniz and his school on the foundations of calculus. On 12 March 1699 he married his second wife, Elisabeth Lams, the daughter of Willem Lams, burgomaster of Wormer.

Nieuwentijt became famous in his home country and abroad because of the publication of two lengthy works. One [6] was originally published in Dutch in 1714; according to [12] it was reedited in 1717, 1720, 1725, 1741, and 1759; editions with other dates are incidentally found in various libraries (1715, 1718, 1730; see [13]). The work was translated into English by J. Chamberlayne in 1718 [6a]; a fourth edition (1730) is mentioned. It was also translated into French by P. Noguez [6b]; this translation was published in 1725 (Paris), 1727 (Amsterdam), and 1760 (Amsterdam–Leipzig). A German translation by W. C. Baumann appeared in 1732 and another by J. A. von Segner in 1747 [6c]. The second of his two works [8] was posthumously published in Dutch in 1720; it was published again in 1741 and 1754; and was translated into French (1725) and English (1760). Nieuwentijt's portrait, painted by D. Valkenburg, is in the University of Amsterdam; the portrait in his 1714 publication [6] was engraved by P. van Gunst.

The title of Nieuwentijt's *Analysis infinitorum* [3] reminds the historian of the title of Leibniz' article of 1686, "De geometria recondita et analysi indivisibilium atque infinitorum." Nieuwentijt's [3] was the first comprehensive book on "analysis infinitorum." By L. Euler's *Introductio in analysin infinitorum*, analysis became the name of a mathematical discipline. To this field Nieuwentijt contributed little more than the name. What is surprising, however, is the erudite scholarship of a small-town physician who, except

for limited university study, does not seem to have cultivated many learned colleagues. Nieuwentijt's work reveals his full acquaintance with the mathematics of his period and a remarkable self-reliance.

Nieuwentijt rejected Leibniz' approach to analysis. He did not admit infinitesimals of higher order. Nieuwentijt's method consists, in modern terms, in adjoining to the real field an element e with $e^2 = 0$. Leibniz' answer [9] to Nieuwentijt's objections [2] (see also [4]) was not convincing. Nieuwentijt's objections, however, may have contributed to improving the insight into higher-order differentials. It is disappointing that he did not sufficiently appreciate Leibniz' integral calculus.

His 1714 publication [6], of about 1,000 pages, was intended to demonstrate the existence of God by teleological arguments. Never before had this been tried on such a scale, and none among Nieuwentijt's numerous imitators equaled his completeness. It is not clear, however, whether or to what degree he depended on William Derham, whose *Physico-Theology* [10] (see also [11]) appeared almost simultaneously. Nieuwentijt may have known of Derham's lectures of 1711–1712, which were the nucleus for the work.

It is an old idea that nature, by its purposiveness, betrays the existence of a creator; Nieuwentijt, however, was one of the first who, rather than relying on a few examples, reviewed the whole of natural sciences to show in detail how marvelously things fitted in the world. His work [6] looks like a manual of up-to-date science and as such it may have contributed to the propagation of knowledge. On the other hand, by the abundance of its argumentation, it is tiring reading and full of platitudes. Its fundamental shortcoming is its static world picture and its lack of any trace of the oncoming evolutionary ideas. Its background philosophy, however, is remarkably sound. Nieuwentijt opposed both chance and necessity as explanatory principles of nature. He preferred empiricist above rationalist arguments. Natural laws have, according to Nieuwentijt, factual rather than rational truth, and as such they must have been ordained by a lawgiver.

Nieuwentijt felt that rationalism led to Spinozism and other kinds of atheism. A more methodical struggle against rationalism was fought in his second major work [8]. This is, indeed, a methodology of science which surprises by a seemingly modern view. In fact it is nothing but a philosophy of common sense, and this explains why it fell into oblivion amid more sophisticated philosophies. In this work [8] Nieuwentijt arrived at a clear distinction between what he called ideal and factual mathematics, and at the insight that both avail themselves of the same formal methods, that all ideal statements are conditional, and that the ultimate criterion for factual statements is corroboration by experience. Nieuwentijt distinguished himself from the British empiricists by his closeness to mathematics and exact sciences. Although his influence in philosophy was negligible, his position as a methodologist was unique up to modern times.

BIBLIOGRAPHY

1. *Disputatio medica inauguralis de obstructionibus,* 8 Feb. 1676, Ultraiecti.
2. *Considerationes circa analyseos ad quantitates infinitè parvas applicatae principia, et calculi differentialis usum in resolvendis problematibus geometricis* (Amsterdam, 1694).
3. *Analysis infinitorum, seu curvilineorum proprietates ex polygonorum natura deductae* (Amsterdam, 1695).
4. *Considerationes secundae circa calculi differentialis principia; et responsio ad virum nobilissimum C. G. Leibnitium* (Amsterdam, 1696).
5. "Nouvel usage des tables des sinus au moyen de s'en servir sans qu'il soit nécessaire de multiplier et de diviser," in *Journal littéraire,* **5** (1714), 166–174.
6. *Het regt gebruik der wereltbeschouwingen ter overtuiginge van ongodisten en ongelovigen, aangetoont door . . .* (Amsterdam, 1714).
6a. *The Religious Philosopher, or the Right Use of Contemplating the Works of the Creator*: (I) *In the Wonderful Structure of Animal Bodies,* (II) *In the Formation of the Elements,* (III) *In the Structure of the Heavens, Designed for the Conviction of Atheists,* trans. by J. Chamberlayne, 3 vols. (London, 1718).
6b. *L'existence de Dieu démontrée par les merveilles de la nature, en trois parties, où l'on traite de la structure des corps de l'homme, des élémens, des astres et de leurs divers effets,* trans. by P. Noguez (Paris, 1725).
6c. *Rechter Gebrauch der Weltbetrachtung zur Erkenntnis der Macht, Weisheit und Güte Gottes, auch Überzeugung der Atheisten und Ungläubigen,* trans. by J. A. v. Segner (Jena, 1747).
7. "Brief aen den Heer J. Bernard, zynde een antwoord op de Aenmerkingen van den Heer Bernard, omtrent de werelt-beschouwingen, in de Nouv. de la Repub. 1716, 252," in *Maandelijke Uittreksels, of Boekrael der Geleerde Werelt* (1716), 673–690.
8. *Gronden van zekerheid of de regte betoogwyze der wiskundigen so in het denkbeeldige als in het zakelijke: ter weerlegging van Spinosaas denkbeeldig samenstel; en ter aanleiding van eene sekere sakelyke wysbegeerte, aangetoont door . . .* (Amsterdam, 1720).
9. G. G. L. [Leibniz], "Responsio ad nonnullas difficultates, a Dn. Bernardo Nieuwentijt circa methodum differentialem seu infinitesimalem motas," in *Acta eruditorum* 1695, pp. 310–316.
10. William Derham, *Physico-Theology, or a Demonstra-tion of the Being and Attributes of God From His Works of Creation* (London, 1713).
11. William Derham, *Astro-Theology, or a Demonstration of the Being and Attributes of God From a Survey of the Heavens* (London, 1715).
12. *Nieuw Nederlandsch Biographisch Woordenboek,* **6** (1924), 1062–1063.
13. A. J. J. Van der Velde, "Bijdrage tot de bio-bibliographie van Bernard Nieuwentyt (1654–1718)," in *Bijdragen en Mededelingen Koninklijke Vlaamsche Academie van Taal- en Letterkunde 1926,* 709–718.
14. E. W. Beth, "Nieuwentyt's Significance for the Philosophy of Science," in *Synthese,* **9** (1955), 447–453.
15. H. Freudenthal, "Nieuwentijt und der teleologische Gottesbeweis," in *Synthese,* **9** (1955), 454–464.
16. J. Vercruysse, "La fortune de Bernard Nieuwentyd en France au 18e siècle et les notes marginales de Voltaire," in *Studies on Voltaire and the 18th Century,* **30** (1964), 223–246.
17. J. Vercruysse, "Frans onthaal voor een Nederlandse apologeet: Bernard Nieuwentyd—1654–1718," in *Tijdschrift van de Vrije Universiteit te Brussel,* **11** (1968–1969), 97–120.

HANS FREUDENTHAL

NOETHER, AMALIE EMMY (*b.* Erlangen, Germany, 23 March 1882; *d.* Bryn Mawr, Pennsylvania, 14 April 1935)

Emmy Noether, generally considered the greatest of all female mathematicians up to her time, was the eldest child of Max Noether, research mathematician and professor at the University of Erlangen, and Ida Amalia Kaufmann. Two of Emmy's three brothers were also scientists. Alfred, her junior by a year, earned a doctorate in chemistry at Erlangen. Fritz, two and a half years younger, became a distinguished physicist; and his son, Gottfried, became a mathematician.

At first Emmy Noether had planned to be a teacher of English and French. From 1900 to 1902 she studied mathematics and foreign languages at Erlangen, then in 1903 she started her specialization in mathematics at the University of Göttingen. At both universities she was a nonmatriculated auditor at lectures, since at the turn of the century girls could not be admitted as regular students. In 1904 she was permitted to matriculate at the University of Erlangen, which granted her the Ph.D., *summa cum laude,* in 1907. Her sponsor, the algebraist Gordan, strongly influenced her doctoral dissertation on algebraic invariants. Her divergence from Gordan's viewpoint and her progress in the direction of the "new" algebra first began when she was exposed to the ideas of Ernst Fischer, who came to Erlangen in 1911.

In 1915 Hilbert invited Emmy Noether to Göttingen. There she lectured at courses that were given under his name and applied her profound invariant-theoretic knowledge to the resolution of problems which he and Felix Klein were considering. In this connection she was able to provide an elegant pure mathematical formulation for several concepts of Einstein's general theory of relativity. Hilbert repeatedly tried to obtain her appointment as *Privatdozent*, but the strong prejudice against women prevented her "habilitation" until 1919. In 1922 she was named a *nichtbeamteter ausserordentlicher Professor* ("unofficial associate professor"), a purely honorary position. Subsequently, a modest salary was provided through a *Lehrauftrag* ("teaching appointment") in algebra. Thus she taught at Göttingen (1922–1933), interrupted only by visiting professorships at Moscow (1928–1929) and at Frankfurt (summer of 1930).

In April 1933 she and other Jewish professors at Göttingen were summarily dismissed. In 1934 Nazi political pressures caused her brother Fritz to resign from his position at Breslau and to take up duties at the research institute in Tomsk, Siberia. Through the efforts of Hermann Weyl, Emmy Noether was offered a visiting professorship at Bryn Mawr College; she departed for the United States in October 1933. Thereafter she lectured and did research at Bryn Mawr and at the Institute for Advanced Study, Princeton, but those activities were cut short by her sudden death from complications following surgery.

Emmy Noether's most important contributions to mathematics were in the area of abstract algebra, which is completely different from the early algebra of equation solving in that it studies not so much the results of algebraic operations (addition, multiplication, etc.) but rather their formal properties, such as associativity, commutativity, distributivity; and it investigates the generalized systems that arise if one or more of these properties is not assumed. Thus, in classical algebra it is postulated that the rational, the real, or the complex numbers should constitute a "field" with respect to addition and multiplication, operations assumed to be associative and commutative, the latter being distributive with respect to the former. One of the traditional postulates, namely the commutative law of multiplication, was relinquished in the earliest example of a generalized algebraic structure (William Rowan Hamilton's "quaternion algebra" of 1843) and also in many of the 1844 Grassmann algebras. The entities in such systems and in some of the research of Emmy Noether after 1927 are still termed numbers, albeit hypercomplex numbers. In further generalization the elements of an algebraic system are abstractions that are not necessarily capable of interpretation as numbers, and the binary operations are not literally addition and multiplication, but merely laws of composition that have properties akin to the traditional operations.

If Hamilton and Grassmann inspired Emmy Noether's later work, it was Dedekind who influenced the abstract axiomatic "theory of ideals" which Noether developed from 1920 to 1926. The Dedekind ideals—which are not numbers but sets of numbers—were devised in order to reinstate the Euclidean theorem on unique decomposition into prime factors, a law which breaks down in algebraic number fields. Two of the generalized structures which Noether related to the ideals are the "group" and the "ring."

A group is more general than a field because it involves only a single operation (either an "addition" or a "multiplication") which need not be commutative. It is, then, a system $\{S, \bigcirc\}$ where S is a set of elements, $\bigcirc$ is a closed associative binary operation, and S contains a unit element or identity as well as a unique inverse for every element. A ring is a system $\{S, \oplus, \otimes\}$ which is a commutative group with respect to $\oplus$, an "addition," and which is closed under a "multiplication," that is, a second binary associative operation $\otimes$, which is distributive with respect to the first operation. Finally, a subset of a ring with a commutative multiplication $\otimes$ is called an "ideal" if it is a subgroup of the additive group of the ring—for this it is sufficient that the difference of any two elements of the subset belong to that set—and if it contains all products of subset elements by arbitrary elements of the ring. In a ring with a noncommutative multiplication, there are left ideals and right ideals.

Emmy Noether showed that the ascending chain condition is important for ideal theory. A ring satisfies that condition if every sequence of ideals C_1, C_2, C_3, $\cdots$, in the ring—such that each ideal is a proper part of its successor—has only a finite number of terms. Noether demonstrated that for a commutative ring with a unit element the requirement is equivalent to each of two other requirements: namely, that every ideal in the ring have a finite basis, that is, that the ideal consist of the set of all elements

$$x_1 a_1 + x_2 a_2 + \cdots + x_n a_n,$$

where the a_i are fixed elements of the ring and the x_i are any elements whatsoever in the ring, and that, given any nonempty set of ideals in the ring, there be at least one ideal which is "maximal" in that set.

Having formulated the concept of primary ideals—a generalization of Dedekind's prime ideals—Noether used the ascending chain condition in order to prove that an ideal in a commutative ring can be represented as the intersection of primary ideals. Then she studied the necessary and sufficient conditions for such an ideal to be the product of "prime power ideals." A somewhat different aspect of ideal theory was her use of polynomial ideals to rigorize, generalize, and give modern pure mathematical form to the concepts and methods of algebraic geometry as they had first been developed by her father and subsequently by the Italian school of geometers.

In another area Emmy Noether investigated the noncommutative rings in linear algebras like the Hamilton and Grassmann systems. An "algebra" is a ring in which the two binary operations are supplemented by a unary operation, an external or scalar multiplication, that is, a multiplication by the elements (scalars) of a specified field. From 1927 to 1929 Emmy Noether contributed notably to the theory of representations, the object of which is to provide realizations of noncommutative rings (or algebras) by means of matrices or linear transformations in such a way that all relations which involve the ring addition and/or multiplication are preserved; in other words, to study the homomorphisms of a given ring into a ring of matrices. From 1932 to 1934 she was able to probe profoundly into the structure of noncommutative algebras by means of her concept of the *verschränktes* ("cross") product. In a 1932 paper that was written jointly with Richard Brauer and Helmut Hasse, she proved that every "simple" algebra over an ordinary algebraic number field is cyclic; Weyl called this theorem "a high water mark in the history of algebra."

Emmy Noether wrote some forty-five research papers and was an inspiration to Max Deuring, Hans Fitting, W. Krull, Chiungtze Tsen, and Olga Taussky Todd, among others. The so-called Noether school included such algebraists as Hasse and W. Schmeidler, with whom she exchanged ideas and whom she converted to her own special point of view. She was particularly influential in the work of B. L. van der Waerden, who continued to promote her ideas after her death and to indicate the many concepts for which he was indebted to her.

BIBLIOGRAPHY

I. ORIGINAL WORKS. Among Emmy Noether's many papers are "Invarianten beliebiger Differentialausdrücke," in *Nachrichten von der Gesellschaft der Wissenschaften zu Göttingen* (1918), 37–44; "Moduln in nichtkommutativen Bereichen, insbesondere aus Differential- und Differenzenausdrücken," in *Mathematische Zeitschrift*, **8** (1920), 1–35, written with W. Schmeidler; "Idealtheorie in Ring-bereichen," in *Mathematische Annalen*, **83** (1921), 24–66; "Abstrakter Aufbau der Idealtheorie in algebraischen Zahlund Funktionenkörpern," *ibid.*, **96** (1927), 26–61; "Über minimale Zerfällungskörper irreduzibler Darstellungen," in *Sitzungsberichte der Preussischen Akademie der Wissenschaften zu Berlin* (1927), 221–228, written with R. Brauer; "Hyperkomplexe Grössen und Darstellungstheorie," in *Mathematische Zeitschrift*, **30** (1929), 641–692; "Beweis eines Hauptsatzes in der Theorie der Algebren," in *Journal für die reine und angewandte Mathematik*, **167** (1932), 399–404, written with R. Brauer and H. Hasse; and "Nichtkommutative Algebren," in *Mathematische Zeitschrift*, **37** (1933), 514–541.

II. SECONDARY LITERATURE. For further information about Noether and her work, see A. Dick, "Emmy Noether," in *Revue de mathématiques élémentaires*, supp. 13 (1970); C. H. Kimberling, "Emmy Noether," in *American Mathematical Monthly*, **79** (1972), 136–149; E. E. Kramer, *The Nature and Growth of Modern Mathematics* (New York, 1970), 656–672; B. L. van der Waerden, "Nachruf auf Emmy Noether," in *Mathematische Annalen*, **111** (1935), 469–476; and H. Weyl, "Emmy Noether," in *Scripta mathematica*, **3** (1935), 201–220.

EDNA E. KRAMER

NOETHER, MAX (*b*. Mannheim, Germany, 24 September 1844; *d*. Erlangen, Germany, 13 December 1921)

Max Noether was the third of the five children of Hermann Noether and Amalia Würzburger. Noether's father was a wholesaler in the hardware business—a family tradition until 1937 when it was "Aryanized" by the Nazis. Max attended schools in Mannheim until an attack of polio at age fourteen made him unable to walk for two years and left him with a permanent handicap. Instruction at home enabled him to complete the Gymnasium curriculum; then, unassisted, he studied university-level mathematics.

After a brief period at the Mannheim observatory, he went to Heidelberg University in 1865. There he earned the doctorate in 1868 and served as *Privatdozent* (1870–1874) and as associate professor (*extraordinarius*) from 1874 to 1875. Then he became affiliated with Erlangen as associate professor until 1888, as full professor (*ordinarius*) from 1888 to 1919, and as professor emeritus thereafter. In 1880 he married Ida Amalia Kaufmann of Cologne. She died in 1915. Three of their four children became scientists, including Emmy Noether, the mathematician.

Noether was one of the guiding spirits of nineteenth-century algebraic geometry. That subject was motivated in part by problems that arose in Abel's and Riemann's treatment of algebraic functions and their integrals. The purely geometric origins are to be found in the work of Plücker, Cayley, and Clebsch, all of whom developed the theory of algebraic curves—their multiple points, bitangents, and inflections. Cremona also influenced Noether, who in turn inspired the great Italian geometers who followed him—Segre, Severi, Enriques, and Castelnuovo. In another direction Emmy Noether and her disciple B. L. van der Waerden made algebraic geometry rigorous and more general. Lefschetz, Weil, Zariski, and others later used topological and abstract algebraic concepts to provide further generalization.

In both the old and the new algebraic geometry, the central object of investigation is the algebraic variety, which, in n-dimensional space, is the set of all points $(x_1, x_2, \cdots, x_n)$ satisfying a finite set of polynomial equations,

$$f_i(x_1, x_2, \cdots, x_n) = 0, \quad i = 1, 2, \cdots, r$$

with $r \leqslant n$ and coefficients in the real (or complex) field or, in modern algebraic geometry, an arbitrary field. Thus, in the plane, the possible varieties are curves and finite sets of points; in space there are surfaces, curves, and finite point sets; for $n > 3$ there are hypersurfaces and their intersections.

Following Cremona, Noether studied the invariant properties of an algebraic variety subjected to birational transformations; that is, one-to-one rational transformations with rational inverses, those of lowest degree being the collineations or projective transformations. Next in order of degree come the quadratic transformations, for which Noether obtained a number of important theorems. For example, any irreducible plane algebraic curve with singularities can be transformed by a finite succession of standard quadratic transformations into a curve whose multiple points are all "ordinary" in the sense that the curve has multiple but distinct tangents at such points.

In 1873 Noether proved what came to be his most famous theorem: Given two algebraic curves

$$\Phi(x, y) = 0, \quad \Psi(x, y) = 0$$

which intersect in a finite number of isolated points, then the equation of an algebraic curve which passes through all those points of intersection can be expressed in the form $A\Phi + B\Psi = 0$ (where A and B are polynomials in x and y) if and only if certain conditions (today called "Noetherian conditions") are satisfied. If the intersections are nonsingular points of both curves, the desired form can readily be achieved. The essence of Noether's theorem, however, is that it

provides necessary and sufficient conditions for the case where the curves have common multiple points with contact of any degree of complexity.

Although Noether asserted that his results could be extended to surfaces and hypersurfaces, it was not until 1903 that the Hungarian Julius König actually generalized the Noether theorem to n dimensions by providing necessary and sufficient conditions for the

$$A_1 f_1 + A_2 f_2 + \cdots + A_n f_n = 0$$

form to be possible for the equation of the surface or hypersurface through the finite set of points of intersection of n surfaces ($n = 3$) or n hypersurfaces ($n > 3$),

$$f_1(x_1, x_2, \cdots, x_n) = 0, \cdots, f_n(x_1, x_2, \cdots, x_n) = 0.$$

Noether himself derived a theorem that gives conditions for the equation of a surface passing through the curve of intersection of the surfaces $\Phi(x, y, z) = 0$ and $\Psi(x, y, z) = 0$ to have the form $A\Phi + B\Psi = 0$. Generalization turned out to be complicated and difficult, but Emanuel Lasker, the chess champion, saw that the issue could be simplified by the use of the theory of polynomial ideals which he and Emmy Noether had developed. Thus he was able to derive Noetherian conditions for the

$$A_1 f_1 + \cdots + A_r f_r = 0$$

form to be possible for a hypersurface through the intersection of

$$f_1(x_1, x_2, \cdots, x_n) = 0, \cdots, f_r(x_1, x_2, \cdots, x_n) = 0$$

with $n > 3$, $r < n$, in which case the intersection will, in general, be a curve or a surface or a hypersurface.

The Noether, König, and Lasker theorems all start with a set of polynomial equations that defines a variety the nature of which varies in the different propositions. The objective in every case is the same, namely to see under what conditions a polynomial that vanishes at all points of the given variety can be expressed as a linear combination of the polynomials originally given. Since those polynomials play a basic role, it is especially significant that the representation of a variety as the intersection of other varieties, that is, by a set of polynomial equations, is not unique. Thus a circle in space might be described as the intersection of two spheres, or as the intersection of a cylinder and a plane, or as the intersection of a cone and a plane, and so forth. Hence, in general, the only impartial way to represent a given variety

$$f_i(x_1, x_2, \cdots, x_n) = 0, \quad i = 1, 2, \cdots, r$$

where $r \leqslant n$ and the f_i are polynomials with real or complex coefficients, is not by this one system of equations, but rather in terms of all polynomial equations which points on the variety satisfy. Now if $f(x_1, x_2, \cdots, x_n)$ and $g(x_1, x_2, \cdots, x_n)$ are any two polynomials that vanish at all points of the given variety, then the difference of the polynomials also vanishes at those points, as does the product of either polynomial by an arbitrary polynomial, $A(x_1, x_2, \cdots, x_n)$. By the definition of an ideal, these two facts are sufficient for the set of all polynomials that vanish at every point of the variety to be a polynomial ideal in the ring of polynomials with real (complex) coefficients, and it is that ideal which is considered to represent the variety. The linear combinations $A_1 f_1 + A_2 f_2 + \cdots + A_r f_r$ obviously vanish at all points of the given variety and hence belong to the representative polynomial ideal. These are the linear combinations that were the subject of the special criteria developed in the Noether, König, and Lasker theorems. Other important results related to the representative polynomial ideal are contained in a famous proposition of Hilbert, namely his basis theorem.

BIBLIOGRAPHY

I. ORIGINAL WORKS. Noether's most important papers include "Zur Theorie des eindeutigen Entsprechens algebraischer Gebilde von beliebig vielen Dimensionen," in *Mathematische Annalen*, **2** (1870), 293–316; "Über einen Satz aus der Theorie der algebraischen Functionen," *ibid.*, **6** (1873), 351–359; "Über die algebraische Functionen und ihre Anwendung in der Geometrie," *ibid.*, **7** (1874), 269–310, written with A. W. von Brill; and "Die Entwicklung der Theorie der algebraischen Functionen in älterer und neurer Zeit," in *Jahresbericht der Deutschen Mathematiker-vereinigung*, **3** (1894), 107–566, written with A. W. von Brill.

II. SECONDARY LITERATURE. On Noether and his work, see A. W. von Brill, "Max Noether," in *Jahresbericht der Deutschen Mathematiker-vereinigung*, **32** (1923), 211–233; A. Dick, "Emmy Noether," in *Revue de mathématiques élémentaires*, supp. 13 (1970), 4–8, 19, 53–56, 67–68; W. Fulton, *Algebraic Curves, an Introduction to Algebraic Geometry* (New York–Amsterdam, 1969), 119–129; J. König, *Einleitung in die Allgemeine Theorie der Algebraischen Grössen* (Leipzig, 1903), 385–398; E. Lasker, "Zur Theorie der Moduln und Ideale," in *Mathematische Annalen*, **60** (1905), 44–46, 51–54; F. S. Macaulay, "Max Noether," in *Proceedings of the London Mathematical Society*, 2nd ser., **21** (1920–1923), 37–42; and C. A. Scott, "A Proof of Noether's Fundamental Theorem," in *Mathematische Annalen*, **52** (1899), 593–597.

See also J. G. Semple and L. Roth, *Introduction to Algebraic Geometry* (Oxford, 1949), 94–99, 391; R. J. Walker, *Algebraic Curves* (Princeton, 1950), 120–124; H. Wieleitner, *Algebraische Kurven*, II (Berlin–Leipzig, 1919), 18–20, 45, 88; and the editors of *Mathematische Annalen*, "Max Noether," in *Mathematische Annalen*, **85** (1922), i–iii.

EDNA E. KRAMER

NORWOOD, RICHARD (*b*. Stevenage, Hertfordshire, England, 1590; *d*. Bermuda, 1665)

Norwood's family were gentlefolk who apparently had fallen upon hard times; he attended grammar school, but at the age of fifteen was apprenticed to a London fishmonger. The many seamen he met in London aroused his interest in learning navigation and seeing the world. Eventually he was able to switch his apprenticeship to a coaster plying between London and Newcastle. He tells in his *Journal* how, while forced to lay over for three weeks at Yarmouth, he went through Robert Record's treatise on arithmetic, *The Ground of Arts*. So involved was he in studying mathematics that he almost forgot to eat and caught "a spice of the scurvy." During the following years Norwood made several voyages to the Mediterranean and on his first trip was fortunate to find a fellow passenger with an extensive mathematical library, among which was Leonard Digges's *Pantometria*. On following trips Norwood himself took along mathematical books, including Euclid's *Elements* and Clavius' *Algebra*.

To retrieve a piece of ordnance that had fallen into the harbor at Lymington, Norwood devised a kind of diving bell, descended in it to the bottom, and was able to attach a rope to the lost piece. This exploit brought him to the attention of the Bermuda Adventurers, a company that planned to finance its colonization of Bermuda by exploiting the oyster beds that supposedly surrounded the islands. In 1616 Norwood joined them and sailed for Bermuda. It soon became evident that very few pearls were to be found, and Norwood was then offered the task of surveying the islands. He made several surveys between 1614 and 1617, and upon their completion he returned to London. In 1622 he married Rachel Boughton, and in the same year his map of Bermuda was published by Nathaniel Newbery. No copy of this map is now known to exist, but in 1624–1625 Samuel Purchas reprinted the Newbery version.

Upon his return to London, Norwood taught mathematics and wrote a number of books on mathematics and navigation, which went through many editions. His *Trigonometrie, or, The Doctrine* of Triangles (1631), based on the logarithms of Napier and Briggs as well as on works by Wright and Gunter, was intended essentially as a navigational aid to seamen. In it Norwood explained the common logarithms, the trigonometrical functions, the spherical triangles, and their applications to the problems confronting the navigator. He posed practical problems of increasing complexity; his explanations were clear; and he enabled the navigator to determine his course with the aid of a plane or Mercator chart and the logarithmic and trigonometric formulas. He emphasized great circle navigation by giving the formulas involved and thus facilitated the calculations. In his *The Seaman's Practice* (1637), he set out a great circle course between the Lizard (the southernmost point in Great Britain) and Bermuda.

Norwood was the first to use consistently the trigonometric abbreviations *s* for sine, *t* for tangent, *sc* for sine complement, *tc* for tangent complement, and *sec* for secant.

The Seaman's Practice was especially concerned with the length of a degree and improvements in the log line. In 1635 Norwood measured the length of a degree along the meridian between London and York. His degree was 367,167 English feet, a surprisingly good measurement in view of the crude tools he used. Based on this volume, he reknotted the log line, putting a knot every fifty feet. Running this with a half-minute glass gave sixty sea miles to a degree.

Norwood was a convinced nonconformist, and because of Archbishop Laud's oppressive actions he decided to leave England. He returned to Bermuda in 1638 and established himself as a schoolmaster; planted olive trees and shipped olive oil to London; and made a new survey in 1663. He also corresponded with the newly founded Royal Society.

BIBLIOGRAPHY

I. ORIGINAL WORKS. The British Museum has a copy of Norwood's chart of Bermuda, which, together with his *Description of the Sommer Islands*, was repr. in John Speed, *A Prospect of the Most Famous Parts of the World* (London, 1631). His other works include *Trigonometrie, or, The Doctrine of Triangles* (London, 1631); *The Seaman's Practice; Containing a Fundamental Problem in Navigation, Experimentally Verified* (London, 1637); *Fortification, or Architecture Military* (London, 1639); *Table of the Sun's True Place, Right Ascension, Declination, etc.* (London, 1657); and *A Triangular Canon Logarithmicall* (London, 1665[?]). *The Journal of Richard Norwood, Surveyor of Bermuda; With Introductions by Wesley F. Craven and Walter B. Hayward* (New York, 1945). Norwood wrote this account of his early life when he was 49 years old, but it ends with the year 1620. It is concerned with his religious conversion. The intros. are excellent and the book also contains a biblio. of Norwood's writings (pp. lix–lxiv).

II. SECONDARY LITERATURE. Norwood's contributions to mathematics and navigation are extensively discussed in E. G. R. Taylor, *The Mathematical Practitioners of Tudor and Stuart England* (Cambridge, 1954); and David W. Waters, *The Art of Navigation in England in Elizabethan and Early Stuart Times* (London, 1958).

LETTIE S. MULTHAUF

NOVIKOV, PETR SERGEEVICH (*b*. Moscow, Russia, 15 August 1901; *d*. Moscow, 9 January 1975)

Novikov was the son of Sergei Novikov, a merchant in Moscow, and his wife Alexandra. In September 1919 the young Novikov entered the physics and mathematics department of Moscow University. After serving in the Red Army between March 1920 and July 1922, he returned to the university and was graduated in 1925. During the next four years he was a postgraduate student under Nikolai N. Luzin. Subsequently Novikov taught mathematics at the Moscow Chemical Technological Institute, and in 1934 he was invited to join the newly organized Steklov Mathematical Institute. He worked there in the department of real function theory until 1957, when he organized the department of mathematical logic and became its head. In 1935 Novikov received the doctorate in mathematics, and four years later he became a full professor. In 1953 he was elected a corresponding member, and in 1960 a full member, of the Soviet Academy of Sciences.

In 1935 Novikov married Ludmila Vsevolodovna Keldysh, a well-known mathematician specializing in topology. They had five children. One of their sons, Sergei Petrovich, is president of the Moscow Mathematical Society.

While still a student, Novikov began to work on descriptive set theory. Very soon he became one of the most active members of Luzin's school of descriptive set theory. In his paper "Sur les fonctions implicites mesurables" (1931) Novikov investigated the problem of whether the equations $f_i(\bar{x}, \bar{y}) = 0$ and $(1 \le i \le q)$ with Borel functions f_i can implicitly define a Borel function $\bar{y} = f(\bar{x})$. He discovered a new method that is referred to as the index comparison principle. Using a generalization of this method, he proved, in his 1935 paper, that for the second projective class of sets the following two separability propositions hold: (1) any two CA_2-sets are separable by B_2-sets if they are disjoint; (2) there exist two disjoint A_2-sets that are nonseparable by B_2-sets. These propositions unexpectedly turned out to be dual to the known laws for the first projective class.

In his 1938 paper on mathematical physics, Novikov proved that any two solids having the same constant density must coincide if they both are star-shaped relative to a common point and have the same external gravitational potential. This pioneering result became the basis of many studies by other authors.

In the late 1930's Novikov began to study mathematical logic and the theory of algorithms. In the paper "On the Consistency of Certain Logical Calculus" (1943), he developed a method of providing the consistency based on a notion of "regularity." He also, in the same paper, proved the consistency for the formal arithmetic with recursive definitions using this method. In 1951 Novikov proved the consistency of two propositions in the Gödel system Σ of axiomatic set theory: (1) there exists a CA-set without perfect subsets; and (2) there exists a B_2-set that is not Lebesque-measurable. This proof was based on Gödel's method published in 1940.

The following word problem had been proposed by Max Dehn in 1912: Let a group G be defined by a finite number of generators and defining relations. For an arbitrary word W in the generators of G, decide in a finite number of steps whether or not W defines the identity element of G.

In 1952 Novikov constructed a finitely defined group H with an unsolvable word problem, that is, a group with no algorithm to solve the word problem for H. This result was first announced in his 1952 paper "Ob algoritmicheskoi nerazreshimosti problemy tozhdestva" ("On the Algorithmic Unsolvability of the Word Problem"). The complete proof was published three years later. In 1957 William W. Boone gave another example of a group with an unsolvable word problem, and therefore this result is called the Novikov-Boone theorem. Important corollaries derived from this theorem have suggested that there are many unsolvable algorithmic problems in fundamental branches of classical mathematics. Novikov received the Lenin Prize for this significant achievement in 1957.

Novikov's last important result, proved jointly with S. I. Adian, was a negative solution of the Burnside problem of periodic groups, proposed in 1902. In 1959 Novikov announced the existence of infinite, finitely generated periodic groups of any given exponent $n \geq 72$. The complete proof of the result for odd exponents $n \geq 4,381$ was published in a joint article in 1968. In my book, *The Burnside Problem and Identities in Groups* (1979), there is an exposition of the Novikov-Adian method for any odd exponent $n \geq 665$ and many applications.

The exceptional influence of Novikov on the advancement of mathematics was also due to his lectures at Moscow University and at the Moscow State Teachers Training Institute, where he chaired the department of analysis from 1944 to 1972. He founded a large school in mathematical logic and its applications in the USSR; his book *Elements of Mathematical Logic* (1959) was the first original textbook on the subject in the country. His second book, *Constructive Mathematical Logic from the Point of View of Classical Logic* (1977), has exerted a considerable influence on the development of proof theory.

Novikov retired from the State Teachers Training Institute in 1972 and from the Steklov Mathematical Institute in 1973. He was ill for the last three years of his life.

BIBLIOGRAPHY

I. ORIGINAL WORKS. Novikov's works, up to 1968, are listed in *Uspekhi matematicheskikh nauk*, **26**, no. 5 (1971), 239–241. The most important works are "Sur les fonctions implicites mesurables," in *Fundamenta Mathematicae*, **17** (1931), 8–25; "Sur la separabilité des ensembles projectifs du seconde classe," *ibid.*, **25** (1935), 459–466; "Ob edinstvennosti obratnoi zadachi potentsiala" ("On the Uniqueness of the Inverse Problem of Potential Theory), in *Doklady Akademii nauk*, **18** (1938), 165–168; "On the Consistency of Certain Logical Calculus," in *Matematicheskii sbornik (Recueil mathématique)*, n.s., **12** (1943), 231–261; "O neprotivorechivosti nekotorych polozhenii deskriptivnoi teorii mnozhestv," in *Trudy Matematicheskoro instituta imeni V. A. Steklova*, **38** (1951), 279–316, trans. by Elliott Mendelson as "On the Consistency of Some Propositions of the Descriptive Theory of Sets," in *American Mathematical Society Translations*, ser. 2, **29** (1963), 51–89; "Ob algoritmicheskoi nerazreshimosti problemy tozhdestva" ("On the Algorithmic Unsolvability of the Word Problem"), in *Doklady Akademii nauk*, **85**, no. 4 (1952), 709–712; "Ob algoritmicheskoi nerazreshimosti problemy tozhdestva slov v teorii grupp," in *Trudy Matematicheskogo instituta imeni V. A. Steklova*, **44** (1955), 1–144, trans. by K. A. Hirsch as "On the Algorithmic Unsolvability of the Word Problem in Group Theory," in *American Mathematical Society Translations*, ser. 2, **9** (1958), 1–122; "O periodicheskikh gruppakh," in *Doklady Akademii nauk*, **127**, no. 4 (1959), 749–752, trans. by J. M. Weinstein as "On Periodic Groups," in *American Mathematical Society Translations*, ser. 2, **45** (1965), 19–22; *Elementy matematicheskoi logiki* (Moscow, 1959), trans. by Leo F. Boron as *Elements of Mathematical Logic* (Edinburgh, 1964); "O bezkonechnykh periodicheskikh gruppach" ("On Infinite Periodic Groups"), in *Izvestiia Akademii nauk, seriia matematicheskaia*, **32**, nos. 1–3 (1968), 212–244, 251–254, 709–731, with S. I. Adian; *Constructivnaia matematicheskāia logika s tochki zreniia classicheskoi* ("Constructive Mathematical Logic from the Point of View of Classical Logic"), F. A. Kabakov and B. A. Kushner, eds., preface by S. I. Adian (Moscow, 1977); and *Izbrannye trudy* ("Selected Works"; Moscow, 1979).

II. SECONDARY LITERATURE. S. I. Adian, *The Burnside Problem and Identities in Groups*, John Lennox and James Wiegold, trans. (Berlin and New York, 1979); Kurt Gödel, *The Consistency of the Axiom of Choice and of the Generalized Continuum-Hypothesis with the Axioms of Set Theory*, Annals of Mathematics Studies, no. 3 (1940). See also "Petr Sergeevich Novikov," in *Uspekhi matematidheskikh nauk*, **26**, no. 5 (1971), 231–241; and *Matematicheskaia logika, teoriia algoritmov i teoriia mnozhestv* ("Mathematical Logic, the Theory of Algorithms and Set Theory"), S. I. Adian, ed., in *Trudy Matematicheskogo instituta imeni V. A. Steklova*, **133** (1973), 5–32.

S. I. ADIAN

NUÑEZ SALACIENSE, PEDRO (*b*. Alcácer do Sol, Portugal, 1502; *d*. Coimbra, Portugal, 11 August 1578)

Nuñez's parents are believed to have been Jewish, since he was registered as a "new Christian." He was married at Salamanca in 1523 to Giomar de Arias, daughter of a Spanish Christian, Pedro Fernández de Arias; they had six children. The earliest information on his education places him as an independent student at the University of Salamanca in 1521 and 1522. He moved to Lisbon in 1524 or 1525, at which time he received a bachelor's degree in medicine while simultaneously extending his knowledge of mathematics and studying astrology. This excellent preparation served as a basis for his appointment as royal cosmographer on 16 November 1529. In recognition of his abilities as a practical researcher, he was named on 4 December 1529 to the professorship of moral philosophy at the University of Lisbon, then to the chair of logic (15 January 1530); during 1531 and 1532 he also held the chair of metaphysics. At the same time Nuñez was pursuing his own studies, and on 16 February 1532 he graduated as licentiate in medicine from the University of Lisbon.

The professorship of mathematics at Lisbon was moved to Coimbra in 1537; and on 16 October 1544 Nuñez was named to the post, which he occupied until his retirement on 4 February 1562. On 22 December 1547 he was named chief royal cosmographer and fulfilled the duties of the office until his death.

Nuñez was called to court on 11 September 1572 by his former student Sebastian, grandson of John III.

He remained in Lisbon for two years as adviser for the projected reform of weights and measures, which was promulgated in 1575. He was also appointed professor of mathematics for the instruction of pilots, navigators, and cartographers. After the reform of weights and measures he returned to Coimbra, where he remained until his death.

Considered the greatest of Portuguese mathematicians, Nuñez reveals in his discoveries, theories, and publications that he was a first-rate geographer, physicist, cosmologist, geometer, and algebraist. In addition to works in Portuguese (*Tratado da sphera*), he wrote and published several works in Latin so that his discoveries might be utilized by educated people of other nations. His writings are rigorously scientific and usually contain a profusion of drawings and figures so that they may be understood more easily.

Among Nuñez's students in Lisbon were the brothers of John III, Louis and Henry, the latter the future king and cardinal. While at Coimbra he taught Clavius, known as the sixteenth-century Euclid. Also among his outstanding students were Nicolas Coelho de Amaral, who succeeded Nuñez in his professorship; Manuel de Figueredo, who became chief royal cosmographer; and João de Castro, viceroy of India, and one of the greatest Portuguese navigators.

Nuñez made important contributions in the design of instruments. In astronomical observations the impossibility of precisely measuring small portions of an arc was an impediment, and to overcome this difficulty he conceived the idea of the nonius. In its original form this instrument, consisting of forty-four concentric auxiliary circles, was attached to an astrolabe for measuring fractions of a degree. Upon each circle and upon their quadrants were equal divisions, ranging from eighty-nine on the circle of greatest diameter to forty-six on the circle of least diameter. Each circle had one division less than the one outside it and one division more than the one inside, making it possible to take a reading from the circle that gave the most accurate approximation.

This instrument has not been modified during the four centuries since it was devised, but it has been refined. In 1593 Clavius reduced the auxiliary circles to one divided into sixty-one parts and divided the limb of the astrolabe into sixty; and in 1631 Pierre Vernier let the auxiliary arc move freely by attaching it to the alidade of the astrolabe. (The latter variation is called a vernier in some countries.) With the nonius exceedingly small measures may be read on any scale or system of division, either circular or rectilinear.

As a navigator Nuñez made a significant discovery based on observations reported to him in 1533 by Admiral Martim Afonso de Sousa. They relate to rhumb line sailing and to great circle sailing. The former is the course of the ship while sailing on a single bearing (always oblique to the meridian in the direction of one and the same point of the compass), subsequently (1624) called "loxodrome" by Willebrord Snell. The latter, which is the shortest distance between any two terrestrial points, has been called "orthodrome"; in it the bearing varies. Until that time pilots had considered them equivalent; but Nuñez demonstrated their dissimilarity, an important discovery that exerted great influence on the making of charts for navigation. For this purpose he conceived and drew curved rhumb lines (1534–1537), several years before Mercator made a loxodromic terrestrial globe with rhumb lines for eight sea routes in each quadrant, drawn from various points in different latitudes (1541).

Another of Nuñez's contributions to navigation was his technique for determining latitude by means of two readings of the sun's altitude and the azimuth, with solutions that were quite interesting and ingenious but of little practical use on shipboard; they relate more to the concerns of a scientist in the observatory than to the needs of a practical navigator and therefore have fallen into disuse.

In physics and seamanship Nuñez wrote a commentary on Aristotle's mechanical problem of propulsion by oars. It is a contribution to the geometry of motion —an attempt to determine, at each moment and in every circumstance, the deviation of the boat in relation to the oars.

Nuñez's cosmological theories relating to solar and lunar motions are important, as are his inquiries into the duration of day and night, the transformation of astronomical coordinates, and other problems concerning the motions of celestial bodies. He commented on the planetary theories of Georg Peurbach; worked on the problem of determining the duration of twilight; and solved the problem of afterglow or second twilight.

Nuñez also exhibited mathematical ability in geometry with his original solutions to the problems of spherical triangles. He demonstrated the errors made by Oronce Fine, professor at the Collège de France, in his attempt to solve three problems by means of ruler and compass: trisecting an angle, doubling a cube, and squaring a circle.

Finally, Nuñez was a poet; his highly regarded sonnets were collected and published by Joaquín Ignacio de Fraitas (Coimbra, 1826).

BIBLIOGRAPHY

I. ORIGINAL WORKS. *Tratado da sphera* (Lisbon, 1537) consists of three parts: (1) annotated translations by Nuñez from Sacrobosco's *Tractatus de sphaera*, writings on the theory of the sun and moon by Georg Peurbach, and the first book of Ptolemy's *Geography*; (2) two writings by Nuñez, a treatise on certain difficulties in navigation and a treatise in defense of his navigation chart and tables of the movements of the sun and its declination; (3) an epigram in Latin written to Nuñez by Jorge Coelho. The first part of this work was reprinted at Lisbon in 1911 and 1912, the second part in 1913, and a facs. ed. was published at Munich in 1915. There is an ed. of a French trans. prior to 1562, published in France. The Latin version, *Opera quae complectuntur, primum duos libros . . .* , was published at Basel in 1566 and in subsequent, much improved, eds. in 1573 and 1592. It is in this work that the theory of loxodromic curves is first set forth.

Other works are *De crepusculis liber unus* (Lisbon, 1542; 2nd ed., Coimbra, 1571), which treats the afterglow and the nonius; *Astronomici introductorii De Sphaera epitome* (n.p., n.d. [1543 ?]), with 12 folios thought to be an introduction to *Tratado da sphera*; *De erratis Promtii Orontii Finaei, regii mathematicarum Lutetice professoris* (Coimbra, 1546; 2nd ed. 1571); and *Libro de álgebra en arithmética y geometría* (Antwerp, 1567).

In *De crepusculis*, Nuñez mentions MS treatises, now believed lost, on the geometry of spherical triangles, on the astrolabe, on the geometrical representation of the sphere on a plane surface, on proportions in measurement, and on the method of delineating a globe for the use of navigators. Another MS mentioned is a work on the sea routes to Brazil. In catalog no. 508, item no. 15, of Maggs Bros. bookstore in London, there is a reference to "Codice de circa 1560 de Nunes (Pedro) y Vaz Fraguoso (Pedro)," containing the elements of navigation and routes to the East, which is believed to have been compiled by Vaz Fraguoso.

II. SECONDARY LITERATURE. See the following, listed chronologically: *Diccionario enciclopédico hispano-americano*, XIII (Barcelona, 1813), 1190–1198; Rodolfo Guimaräes, *Sur la vie et l'oeuvre de Pedro Nunes* (Coimbra, 1915); Luciano Pereira da Silva, *As obras de Pedro Nunes, sua cronologia bibliográfica* (Coimbra, 1925); and A. Fontoura da Costa, *Pedro Nunes (1502–1578)* (Lisbon, 1938); and *Quarto centenário da publicaçao de Tratado de sphera de Pedro Nunes* (Lisbon, 1938).

J. M. LÓPEZ DE AZCONA

OCAGNE, PHILBERT MAURICE D' (*b*. Paris, France, 25 March 1862; *d*. Le Havre, France, 23 September 1938)

D'Ocagne was a student and then *répétiteur* at the École Polytechnique. He then became a civil engineer and a professor at the École des Ponts et Chaussées. In 1912 he was appointed professor of geometry at the École Polytechnique. He was elected to the

Académie des Sciences on 30 January 1922.

Active both as researcher and teacher, d'Ocagne published a great many articles, mostly on geometry, in mathematical journals and in the *Comptes rendus . . . de l'Académie des sciences*. His name, however, remains linked especially with graphical calculation procedures and with the systematization he gave to that field under the name of nomography. Graphical calculation consists in the execution of graphs employing straight-line segments representing the numbers to be found. This discipline was reduced to an autonomous body of principles chiefly through the work of Junius Massau (1852–1909). Nomography, on the other hand, consists in the construction of graduated graphic tables, nomograms, or charts, representing formulas or equations to be solved, the solutions of which were provided by inspection of the tables.

The overwhelming majority of formulas and equations encountered in practice can be represented graphically by three systems of converging straight lines. By making a dual transformation on the nomograms d'Ocagne obtained nomograms on which the relationship among the variables consisted in the alignment of numbered points. Hence this type of nomogram is called an aligned-point nomogram.

In a pamphlet published in 1891 d'Ocagne presented the first outline of a rationally ordered discipline embracing all the individual procedures of nomographic calculation then known. Pursuing this subject, he succeeded in defining and classifying the most general modes of representation applicable to equations with an arbitrary number of variables. The results of all these investigations, along with a considerable number of applications, were set forth in *Traité de nomographie* (1899), which was followed by other more or less developed expositions. This material appeared in fifty-nine partial or entire translations in fourteen languages.

D'Ocagne retained a lifelong interest in the history of science and published many articles on the subject, some of which were collected.

BIBLIOGRAPHY

D'Ocagne published many articles in *Comptes rendus . . . de l'Académie des sciences, Revue de mathématiques spéciales, Nouvelles annales de mathématiques, Annales des ponts et chaussées, Bulletin de la Société mathématique de France, Enseignement mathématique, Mathésis,* and other journals. His books include *Nomographie, les calculs usuels effectués au moyen des abaques* (Paris, 1891); *Le calcul simplifié par les procédés mécaniques et graphiques* (Paris, 1893; 2nd ed., 1905; 3rd ed., 1928); *Traité de nomographie. Théorie des abaques, applications pratiques* (Paris, 1899; 2nd ed., 1921); *Calcul graphique et nomographie* (Paris, 1908; 2nd ed., 1914); *Souvenirs et causeries* (Paris, 1928); *Hommes et choses de science,* 3 vols. (Paris, 1930–1932); and *Histoire abrégée des sciences mathématiques,* René Dugas, ed. (Paris, 1955).

JEAN ITARD

OENOPIDES OF CHIOS (*b.* Chios; *fl.* fifth century B.C.)

The notice of Pythagoras in Proclus' summary of the history of geometry is followed by the sentence,[1] "After him Anaxagoras of Clazomenae touched many questions concerning geometry, as also did Oenopides of Chios, being a little younger than Anaxagoras, both of whom Plato mentioned in the *Erastae*[2] as having acquired a reputation for mathematics." This fixes the birthplace of Oenopides as the island of Chios and puts his active life in the second third of the fifth century B.C.[3] Anaxagoras was born about 500 B.C. and died about 428 B.C. There is confirmation from Oenopides' researches into the "great year" (see below), which suggest that he could not have differed greatly in date from Meton, who proposed his own Great Year in 432. Like Anaxagoras, Oenopides almost certainly conducted his researches in Athens.

In the opening words of the *Erastae*, to which Proclus refers, Socrates is represented as going into the school of Dionysius the grammarian, Plato's own teacher,[4] and seeing two youths earnestly discussing some astronomical subject. He could not quite catch what they were saying, but they appeared to be disputing about Anaxagoras or Oenopides, and to be drawing circles and imitating some inclinations with their hands. In the light of other passages in Greek authors, this is a clear reference to the obliquity of the ecliptic in relation to the celestial equator. Eudemus in his history of astronomy, according to Dercyllides as transmitted by Theon of Smyrna, related that Oenopides was the first to discover the obliquity of the zodiac,[5] and there appears to have been a widespread Greek belief to that effect. Macrobius,[6] for example, drawing on Apollodorus, notes that Apollo was given the epithet $\Lambda o \xi i \alpha s$ because the sun moves in an oblique circle from west to east, "as Oenopides says." Aëtius[7] says that Pythagoras was the first to discover the obliquity of the ecliptic, and that Oenopides claimed the discovery as his own, while Diodorus[8] says that it was from the Egyptian priests and astronomers that he learned the path of the sun to be oblique and opposite to the motion of the stars (that is, fixed stars). He is not recorded as having given any value to the obliquity, but it was probably he who settled on the value of 24°, which was accepted in Greece until refined by Eratosthenes.[9] Indeed, if Oenopides did not fix on this or some other figure, it is difficult to know in what his achievement consisted, for the Babylonians no less than the Pythagoreans and Egyptians must have realized from early days that the apparent path of the sun was inclined to the celestial equator.

In the same passage as that already mentioned, Theon of Smyrna[10] attributes to Oenopides the discovery of the period of the Great Year. This came to mean a period in which all the heavenly bodies returned to their original relative positions, but in early days only the motions of the sun and moon were taken into account and the Great Year was the least number of solar years which coincided with an exact number of lunations. Before Oenopides it was calculated that the sun and the moon returned to the same relative positions after a period of eight years, the *octaëteris*, in which three years of thirteen months or 384 days were distributed among five years of twelve months or 354 days, giving the solar year an average of $365\frac{1}{4}$ days and making the lunar month a shade over $29\frac{1}{2}$ days. Oenopides appears to have been the first to give a more exact rendering, possibly in an attempt to take account also of the planetary motions. Aelian records that he set up at Olympia a bronze inscription stating that the Great Year consisted of fifty-nine years, and Aëtius confirms the period,[11] while Censorinus[12] states that he made the year to be $365\frac{22}{59}$ days, which implies a Great Year of 21,557 days. Oenopides no doubt fixed upon a period of fifty-nine years, as P. Tannery[13] first showed, by taking the figures of $29\frac{1}{2}$ days for a lunar month and 365 days for a solar year, and deducing that in fifty-nine years there would on this basis be exactly 730 lunations. Observation would have established, Tannery argued, that in 730 lunar months there were 21,557 days, from which it follows that the year consists of $365\frac{22}{59}$ or 365.37288 days and the month of 29.53013 days. The cycle of nineteen years that Meton and Euctemon proposed in 432 B.C., on which the present ecclesiastical calendar is ultimately based, gives a year of $365\frac{5}{19}$ or 365.26315 days and a month of 29.53191 days. The modern value for the sidereal year is 365.25637 days and for the mean synodic month is 29.53059 days.

Oenopides' figure for the lunar month is, therefore, if Tannery is right, more exact than that of Meton (indeed, very exact, for the error does not exceed a third of a day in the whole fifty-nine years), but his figure for the year is considerably less exact, amounting to seven days for the whole period.

But could Oenopides have calculated at that date so exact a figure for the mean synodic month (which requires a long period of observation) when he had so inaccurate a figure for the solar year (to establish which as about $365\frac{1}{4}$ days would require only a few consecutive observations of the times of the solstices)? In a private communication G. J. Toomer is skeptical. He believes that Oenopides did not assign any specific number of days to the Great Year, and the year-length of $365\frac{22}{59}$ days attributed to him by Censorinus is a later reconstruction. Someone at this later date asked himself what is the length of the year according to Oenopides. He answered the question by taking the standard length of the mean synodic month of his own time, namely (expressed sexagesimally) 29; 31, 50, 8, 20 days. This is found in Geminus as well as the *Almagest* and was a fundamental Babylonian parameter adopted by Hipparchus. The hypothetical investigator multiplied this by the 730 months of Oenopides' period and obtained 21,557 days and a fraction of a day. Dividing 21,557 by the 59 years of the cycle, he declared that Oenopides' year consisted of $365\frac{22}{59}$ days—that is to say, the figure is a later deduction using a completely anachronistic value for the month. This is credible. The critical question is whether Oenopides could have had at his disposal records extending over more than his own adult life showing that in 730 lunations there were 21,557 days; if he did, it would be strange for him not to have known a more exact figure for the year.

Tannery[14] holds that Oenopides' Great Year was intended to cover the revolutions of the planets and of the sun and moon, but he is forced to conclude that Oenopides could not have taken them all into account. The ancient cosmographers gave the time for Saturn to traverse its orbit as thirty years, for Jupiter twelve years, and for Mars two years, which would allow two revolutions for Saturn in the Great Year, five for Jupiter, and thirty or thirty-one for Mars. If the latter figure is taken as the more correct, and the figure of 21,557 days in the Great Year is divided by these numbers, we get values for the revolutions of the three planets which do not differ by more than one percent from the correct values. Tannery considers that the degree of inaccuracy ought rather to be judged by the error in the mean position of the heavenly body at the end of the period; this would be only 2° in the case of Saturn and 9° for the sun, but 107° for Mars. If Oenopides had indicated in which sign of the zodiac the planet would be found at the end of the period, the error would have been obvious when the time came.

According to Achilles Tatius,[15] Oenopides was

among those who believed that the path of the sun was formerly the Milky Way; the sun turned away in horror from the banquet of Thyestes and has ever since moved in the path defined by the zodiac.

Two propositions in geometry were discovered by Oenopides according to Eudemus as preserved by Proclus. Commenting on Euclid I.12 ("to a given infinite straight line from a given point which is not upon it to draw a perpendicular straight line") Proclus[16] says: "Oenopides was the first to investigate this problem, thinking it useful for astronomy. But, in the ancient manner, he calls the perpendicular 'a line drawn gnomon-wise,' because the gnomon is at right angles to the horizon." When he comes to Euclid I.23 ("on a given straight line and at a given point on it, to construct a rectilineal angle equal to a given rectilineal angle") Proclus[17] comments: "This problem is rather the discovery of Oenopides, as Eudemus relates." Heath[18] justly observes that the geometrical reputation of Oenopides can hardly have rested on such simple propositions as these, nor could he have been the first to draw a perpendicular in practice. Possibly he was the first to draw a perpendicular to a straight line by means of a ruler and compass (instead of a set-square), and it may have been he who introduced into Greek geometry the limitation of the use of instruments in all plane constructions—that is, in all problems equivalent to the solution of algebraic equations of the second degree—to the ruler and compasses. He also may have been the first to give a theoretical construction to Euclid I.23.

This question bears on an interesting problem to which Kurt von Fritz[19] has devoted much attention. According to Proclus,[20] "Zenodotus, who stood in the succession of Oenopides but was one of the pupils of Andron, distinguished the theorem from the problem by the fact that the theorem seeks what is the property predicated of its subject-matter, but the problem seeks to find what is the cause of what effect" (as translated by Heath,[21] but Glenn R. Morrow[22] translates τίνος ὄντος τί ἐστιν as "under what conditions something exists"). The meaning was probably no clearer to Proclus than it is to us, but it may be that Oenopides was one of those who helped to create the distinction between theorems and problems. Taken in conjunction with what was said in the previous paragraph, it would appear that he made a special study of the methodology of mathematics.

Oenopides had an original theory to account for the Nile floods. He held that the water beneath the earth is cold in the summer and warm in the winter, a phenomenon proved by the temperature of deep wells. In winter, when there are no rains in Egypt, the heat that is shut up in the earth carries off most of the moisture, but in summer the moisture is not so carried off and overflows the Nile. Diodorus Siculus, who recorded the theory, reasonably objected that other rivers of Libya, similar in position and direction to the Nile, are not so affected.[23]

It is related that Oenopides, seeing an uneducated youth who had amassed many books, observed, "Not in your coffer but in your breast."[24] Sextus Empiricus[25] says that Oenopides laid special emphasis on fire and air as first principles. Aëtius[26] says that Diogenes (of Apollonia), Cleanthes, and Oenopides made the soul of the world to be divine. Cleanthes left a hymn to Zeus in which the universe is considered a living being with God as its soul, and if Aëtius is correct then Oenopides must have anticipated these views by more than a century. Diogenes is known to have revived the doctrine of Anaximenes that the primary substance is air, and presumably Oenopides in part shared this view but gave equal primacy to fire as a first principle.

NOTES

1. Proclus: *Procli Diadochi in primum Euclidis, Elementorum librum commentarii*, G. Friedlein, ed. (Leipzig, 1873, repr. 1967), pp. 65.21–66.4.
2. Plato, *Erastae (Amatores)*, 132 A.B, in J. Burnet, ed., *Platonis opera*, II (Oxford, 1901, repr. 1946). The Platonic authorship of the *Erastae* has been denied, but this does not affect its evidence for Oenopides.
3. The "Vita Ptolemaei e schedis Savilianis descripta" found in a Naples MS (Erwin Rohde, *Kleine Schriften*, I [Tübingen–Leipzig, 1901], p. 123, n. 4) is therefore in error in saying that Oenopides lived "towards the end of the Peloponnesian war" but more accurate in adding "at the same time as Gorgias the orator and Zeno of Elea and, as some say, Herodotus, the historian, of Halicarnassus." Diogenes Laërtius IX.41 (H.S. Long, ed., II [Oxford, 1964], 450. 23–25) says that Democritus "would be a contemporary of Archelaus, the pupil of Anaxagoras, and of the circle of Oenopides"; and he adds that Democritus makes mention of Oenopides—presumably in a work that has not survived.
4. Diogenes Laërtius III. 4 (H. S. Long, ed., I [Oxford, 1964], 122.13).
5. Theon of Smyrna, *Expositio rerum mathematicarum ad legendum Platonem utilium*, E. Hiller, ed. (Leipzig, 1878), 198.14–16. H. Diels's conjecture λόξωσιν ("obliquity") for διάζωσιν ("girdle") is almost certainly correct.
6. Macrobius, *Saturnalia* I.17.31, F. Eyssenhardt, ed., 2nd ed. (Leipzig, 1893), 93.28–94.2.
7. Aëtius, II.12, 2, Ps.-Plutarch, *De placitis philosophorum*, B. N. Bernardakis, ed. (*Plutarchi Chaeronensis Moralia*, Teubner, V [Leipzig, 1893]), 284.8–9.
8. Diodorus Siculus, *Bibliotheca historica*, I.98.3, C. H. Oldfather, ed., I (London–New York, 1933), pp. 334.29, 337.4.
9. Proclus, *In primum Euclidis*, Friedlein, ed., p. 269.11–21, states that Euclid IV.16 (which shows how to construct a regular polygon of fifteen sides in a circle, each side therefore subtending an angle of 24° at the center) was inserted "in view of its use in astronomy." Erastosthenes found the

distance between the tropical circles to be 11/83 of the whole meridian, giving a value for the obliquity of 23°51′20″ as Ptolemy records in *Syntaxis, J. L. Heiberg, ed., I.12 (Leipzig, 1898), p. 68.3–6.

10. Theon of Smyrna, *op. cit.*, p. 198.15.
11. Aelian, *Varia historia*, X.7, C. G. Kuehn ed., II (Leipzig, 1780), 65–67; Aëtius, II.32.2, *op. cit.*, 316.1–7.
12. Censorinus, *De die natali* 19.2, F. Hultsch, ed. (Leipzig, 1867), 40.19–20.
13. Paul Tannery, *Mémoires scientifiques*, II (Toulouse–Paris, 1912), 359.
14. *Ibid.*, 358, 362–363.
15. Achilles Tatius, *Introductio in Aratum* 24, E. Maass ed., *Commentariorum in Aratum reliquiae* (Berlin, 1898), p. 55.18–21. Aristotle, *Meteorologica* I.8, 345A, 13–25, Fobes, ed. (Cambridge, Mass. 1919, repr. Hildesheim, 1967), notes that certain of the so-called Pythagoreans held the same view and pointedly asks why the zodiac circle was not scorched in the same way.
16. Proclus, *In primum Euclidis*, Friedlein, ed., 283.7–10.
17. *Ibid.*, 333.5–6.
18. Thomas Heath, *A History of Greek Mathematics*, I (Oxford, 1921), 175.
19. Kurt von Fritz, "Oinopides" in Pauly-Wissowa, **17** (Stuttgart, 1937), cols. 2267–2271.
20. Proclus, *In primum Euclidis*, Friedlein, ed., p. 80.15–20.
21. Thomas L. Heath, *The Thirteen Books of Euclid's Elements*, 2nd ed., I (Cambridge, 1926; New York, 1956), 126.
22. Glenn R. Morrow, *Proclus: A Commentary on the First Book of Euclid's Elements* (Princeton, 1970), p. 66.
23. Diodorus Siculus I. 41.1–3, *op. cit.*, vol. 1, pp. 144.23–147.17.
24. *Gnomologium Vaticanum* 743, L. Sternbach, ed. (Berlin, 1963), n. 420.
25. Sextus Empiricus, *Pyrrhoniae hypotyposes*, iii. 30.
26. Aëtius, I.7, 17, *op. cit.*, 284.8–9.

BIBLIOGRAPHY

No works by Oenopides have survived, nor are the titles of any known. The ancient references to him are collected in Diels-Kranz, *Die Fragmente der Vorsokratiker*, 6th ed. (Dublin–Zurich, 1969), 41(29), 393–395. The most useful modern studies are Paul Tannery, "La grande année d'Aristarque de Samos," in *Mémoires de la Société des sciences physiques et naturelles de Bordeaux*, 3rd ser., **4** (1888), 79–96, reprinted in *Mémoires scientifiques*, J. L. Heiberg and H. G. Zeuthen, ed., **2** (Paris–Toulouse, 1912), 345–366; Thomas Heath, *Aristarchus of Samos. The Ancient Copernicus* (Oxford, 1913), 130–133; Kurt von Fritz, "Oinopides," in Pauly-Wissowa-Kroll, *Real-Encyclopädie der classischen Altertumswissenschaft*, **17** (Stuttgart, 1937), cols. 2258–2272; D. R. Dicks, *Early Greek Astronomy to Aristotle* (London, 1970), 88–89, 157, 172; Jürgen Mau, "Oinopides," in *Der Kleine Pauly*, IV (Stuttgart, 1972), cols. 263–264.

Ivor Bulmer-Thomas

ORESME, NICOLE (*b.* France, *ca.* 1320; *d.* Lisieux, France, 1382)

Oresme was of Norman origin and perhaps born near Caen. Little is known of his early life and family.

In a document originally drawn in 1348, "Henry Oresme" is named along with Nicole in a list of masters of arts of the Norman nation at Paris. Presumably this is a brother of Nicole, for a contemporary manuscript[1] mentions a nephew of Nicole named Henricus *iunior*. A "Guillaume Oresme" also appears in the records of the College of Navarre at Paris as the holder of a scholarship in grammar in 1352 and in theology in 1353; he is later mentioned as a bachelor of theology and canon of Bayeux in 1376.

Nothing is known of Nicole Oresme's early academic career. Apparently he took his arts training at the University of Paris in the 1340's and studied with the celebrated master Jean Buridan, whose influence on Oresme's writing is evident. This is plausible in that Oresme's name appears on a list of scholarship holders in theology at the College of Navarre at Paris in 1348. Moreover, in the same year he is listed among certain masters of the Norman nation, as was noted above. After teaching arts and pursuing his theological training, he took his theological mastership in 1355 or 1356; he became grand master of the College of Navarre in 1356.

His friendship with the dauphin of France (the future King Charles V) seems to have begun about this time. In 1359 he signed a document as "secretary of the king," whereas King John II had been in England since 1356 with the dauphin acting as regent. In 1360 Oresme was sent to Rouen to negotiate a loan for the dauphin.

Oresme was appointed archdeacon of Bayeux in 1361. He attempted to hold this new position together with his grand-mastership, but his petition to do so was denied and he decided to remain in Navarre. Presumably he left Navarre after being appointed canon at Rouen on 23 November 1362. A few months later (10 February 1363) he was appointed canon at Sainte-Chapelle, Paris, obtaining a semiprebend. A year later (18 March 1364) he was appointed dean of the cathedral of Rouen. He held this dignity until his appointment as bishop of Lisieux in 1377, but he does not appear to have taken up residency at Lisieux until 1380. From the occasional mention of him in university documents it is presumed that from 1364 to 1380 Oresme divided his time between Paris and Rouen, probably residing regularly in Rouen until 1369 and in Paris thereafter. From about 1369 he was busy translating certain Aristotelian Latin texts into French and writing commentaries on them. This was done at the behest of King Charles V, and his appointment as bishop was in part a reward for this service. Little is known of his last years at Lisieux.

Scientific Thought. The writings of Oresme show him at once as a subtle Schoolman disputing the fashionable problems of the day, a vigorous opponent of astrology, a dynamic preacher and theologian, an adviser of princes, a scientific popularizer, and a skillful translator of Latin into French.

One of the novelties of thought associated with Oresme is his use of the metaphor of the heavens as a mechanical clock. It has been suggested that this metaphor—which appears to mechanize the heavenly regions in a modern manner—arises from Oresme's acceptance of the medieval impetus theory, a theory that explained the continuance of projectile motion on the basis of impressed force or impetus. Buridan, Oresme's apparent master, had suggested the possibility that God could have impressed impetuses in the heavenly bodies, and that these, acting without resistance or contrary inclination, could continue their motion indefinitely, thus dispensing with the Aristotelian intelligences as the continuing movers. A reading of several different works of Oresme, ranging from the 1340's to 1377, all of which discuss celestial movers, however, shows that Oresme never abandoned the concept of the intelligences as movers, while he specifically rejected impetuses as heavenly movers in his *Questiones de celo*.[2] In these discussions he stressed the essential differences between the mechanics governing terrestrial motion and that involved in celestial motions. In two passages of his last work, *Livre du ciel et du monde d'Aristote*,[3] he suggests (1) the possibility that God implanted in the heavens at the time of their creation special forces and resistances by which the heavens move continually like a mechanical clock, but without violence, the forces and resistances differing from those on earth; and (2) that "it is not impossible that the heavens are moved by a power or corporeal quality in it, without violence and without work, because the resistance in the heavens does not incline them to any other movement nor to rest but only [effects] that they are not moved more quickly." The latter statement sounds inertial, yet it stresses the difference between celestial resistance and resistance on the earth, even while introducing analogues to natural force and resistance. In other treatments of celestial motions Oresme stated that "voluntary" forces rather than "natural" forces are involved, but that the "voluntary" forces differ from "natural" ones in not being quantifiable in terms of the numerical proportionality theorems applicable to natural forces and resistances.[4] In addition to his retention of intelligences as movers, a further factor prevents the identification of any of Oresme's treatments of celestial movers with the proposal of Buridan. For Buridan, *impetus* was a thing of permanent nature (*res natura permanens*) which was corruptible by resistance and contrary inclination. But Oresme seems

to hold in his *Questiones de celo*[5] that impetus is not permanent, but is self-expending by the very fact that it produces motion. If this is truly what Oresme meant, it would be obviously of no advantage to use such impetuses in the explanation of celestial motions, for unless such impetuses were of infinite power (and he would reject this hypothesis for all such powers) they would have to be renewed continually by God. One might just as well keep the intelligences as movers. An even more crucial argument against the idea that Oresme used the impetus theory to explain heavenly motion is that he seems to have associated impetus with accelerated motion, and yet insisted on the uniform motion of the heavens. Returning to the clock metaphor, it should be noted that in the two places in which the metaphor is employed, Oresme did not apply it to the whole universe but only to celestial motions.

One of these passages in which the clock metaphor is cited leads into one of Oresme's most intriguing ideas—the probable irrationality of the movements of the celestial motions. The idea itself was not original with Oresme, but the mathematical argument by which he attempted to develop it was certainly novel. This argument occurs in his treatise *Proportiones proportionum* ("*The Ratios of Ratios*"). His point of departure in this tract is Thomas Bradwardine's fundamental exponential relationship, suggested in 1328 to represent the relationships between forces, resistances, and velocities in motions:

$$\frac{F_2}{R_2} = \left(\frac{F_1}{R_1}\right)^{\frac{V_2}{V_1}}$$

Oresme went on to give an extraordinary elaboration of the whole problem of relating ratios exponentially. It is essentially a treatment of fractional exponents conceived as "ratios of ratios."

In this treatment Oresme made a new and apparently original distinction between irrational ratios of which the fractional exponents are rational, for example, $(\frac{2}{1})^{\frac{1}{2}}$, and those of which the exponents are themselves irrational, apparently of the form $(\frac{2}{1})^{\sqrt{1/2}}$. In making this distinction Oresme introduced new significations for the terms *pars*, *partes*, *commensurabilis*, and *incommensurabilis*. Thus *pars* was used to stand for the exponential part that one ratio is of another. For example, starting with the ratio $(\frac{2}{1})^{\frac{1}{2}}$, Oresme would say, in terms of his exponential calculus, that this irrational ratio is "one half part" of the ratio $\frac{2}{1}$—meaning, of course, that if one took the original ratio twice and composed a ratio therefrom, $\frac{2}{1}$ would result. Or one would say that the ratio $\frac{2}{1}$ can be divided into two "parts" exponentially, each part being $(\frac{2}{1})^{\frac{1}{2}}$, or more succinctly in modern representation:

$$\frac{2}{1} = \left[\left(\frac{2}{1}\right)^{\frac{1}{2}}\right]^2.$$

Furthermore, Oresme would say that such a ratio as $\left(\frac{3}{1}\right)^{\frac{2}{3}}$ is "two third parts" of $\frac{3}{1}$, meaning that if we exponentially divided $\frac{3}{1}$ into

$$\left(\frac{3}{1}\right)^{\frac{1}{3}} \cdot \left(\frac{3}{1}\right)^{\frac{1}{3}} \cdot \left(\frac{3}{1}\right)^{\frac{1}{3}},$$

then $\left(\frac{3}{1}\right)^{\frac{2}{3}}$ is two of the three "parts" by which we compose the ratio $\frac{3}{1}$, again representable in modern symbols as

$$\left(\frac{3}{1}\right) = \left(\frac{3}{1}\right)^{\frac{2}{3}} \cdot \left(\frac{3}{1}\right)^{\frac{1}{3}}.$$

This new signification of *pars* and *partes* also led to a new exponential treatment of commensurability. After this detailed mathematical treatment, Oresme claimed (without any real proof) that as we take a larger and larger number of the possible whole number ratios greater than one and attempt to relate them exponentially two at a time, the number of irrational ratios of ratios (that is, of irrational fractional exponents relating the pairs of whole number ratios) rises in relation to the number of rational ratios of ratios. From such an unproved mathematical conclusion, Oresme then jumps to his central theme, the implications of which reappear in a number of his works: it is probable that the ratio of any two unknown ratios, each of which represents a celestial motion, time, or distance, will be an irrational ratio. This then renders astrology—the predictions of which, he seems to believe, are based on the precise determinations of successively repeating conjunctions, oppositions, and other aspects—fallacious at the very beginning of its operations. A kind of basic numerical indeterminateness exists, which even the best astronomical data cannot overcome. It should also be noted that Oresme composed an independent tract, the *Algorism of Ratios*, in which he elucidated in an original way the rules for manipulating ratios.

Oresme's consideration of a very old cosmological problem, the possible existence of a plurality of worlds, was also novel. Like the great majority of his contemporaries, he ultimately rejected such a plurality in favor of a single Aristotelian cosmos, but before doing so he stressed in a cogent paragraph the possibility that God by His omnipotence could so create such a plurality.[6]

All heavy things of this world tend to be conjoined in one mass [*masse*] such that the center of gravity [*centre de pesanteur*] of this mass is in the center of this world, and the whole constitutes a single body in number. And consequently they all have one [natural] place according to number. And if a part of the [element] earth of another world was in this world, it would tend towards the center of this world and be conjoined to its mass. . . . But it does not accordingly follow that the parts of the [element] earth or heavy things of the other world (if it exists) tend to the center of this world, for in their world they would make a mass which would be a single body according to number, and which would have a single place according to number, and which would be ordered according to high and low [in respect to its own center] just as is the mass of heavy things in this world. . . . I conclude then that God can and would be able by His omnipotence [*par toute sa puissance*] to make another world other than this one, or several of them whether similar or dissimilar, and Aristotle offers no sufficient proof to the contrary. But as it was said before, in fact [*de fait*] there never was, nor will there be, any but a single corporeal world. . . .

This passage is also of interest in that it reveals Oresme's willingness to consider the possible treatment of all parts of the universe by ideas of center of gravity developed in connection with terrestrial physics.

The passage also illustrates the technique of expression used by Oresme and his Parisian contemporaries, which permitted them to suggest the most unorthodox and radical philosophical ideas while disclaiming any commitment to them.

The picture of Oresme's view of celestial physics and its relationship to terrestrial phenomena would not be complete without further mention of his well-developed opposition to astrology. In his *Questio contra divinatores* with *Quodlibeta annexa* we are told again and again that the diverse and apparently marvelous phenomena of this lower world arise from natural and immediate causes rather than from celestial, incorporeal influences. Ignorance, he claims, causes men to attribute these phenomena to the heavens, to God, or to demons, and recourse to such explanations is the "destruction of philosophy." He excepted, of course, the obvious influences of the light of the sun on living things or of the motions of celestial bodies on the tides and like phenomena in which the connections appear evident to observers. In the same work he presented a lucid discussion of the existence of demons. "Moreover, if the Faith did not pose their existence," he wrote, "I would say that from no natural effect can they be proved to exist, for all things [supposedly arising from them] can be saved naturally."[7]

In examining his views on terrestrial physics, we should note first that Oresme, along with many fourteenth-century Schoolmen, accepted the conclusion that the earth could move in a small motion of translation.[8] Such a motion would be brought about by the fact that the center of gravity of the earth is constantly being altered by climatic and geologic changes. He held that the center of gravity of the earth strives always for the center of the world; whence arises the translatory motion of the earth. The whole discussion is of interest mainly because of its application of the doctrine of center of gravity to large bodies. Still another question of the motion of the earth fascinated Oresme, that is, its possible rotation, which he discussed in some detail in at least three different works. His treatment in the *Du ciel*[9] is well known, but many of its essential arguments for the possibility of the diurnal rotation of the earth already appear in his *Questiones de celo*[10] and his *Questiones de spera*.[11] These include, for example, the argument on the complete relativity of the detection of motion, the argument that the phenomena of astronomy as given in astronomical tables would be just as well saved by the diurnal rotation of the earth as by the rotation of the heavens, and so on. At the conclusion of the argument, Oresme says in the *Questiones de spera* (as he did in the later work): "The truth is, that the earth is not so moved but rather the heavens." He goes on to add, "However I say that the conclusion [concerning the rotation of the heavens] cannot be demonstrated but only argued by persuasion." This gives a rather probabilistic tone to his acceptance of the common opinion, a tone we often find in Oresme's treatment of physical theory. The more one examines the works of Oresme, the more certain one becomes that a strongly skeptical temper was coupled with his rationalism and naturalism (of course restrained by rather orthodox religious views) and that Oresme was influenced deeply by the probabilistic and skeptical currents that swept through various phases of philosophy in the fourteenth century. He twice tells us in the *Quodlibeta* that, except for the true knowledge of faith, "I indeed know nothing except that I know that I know nothing."[12]

In discussing the motion of individual objects on the surface of the earth, Oresme seems to suggest (against the prevailing opinion) that the speed of the fall of bodies is directly proportional to the time of fall, rather than to the distance of fall, implying as he does that the acceleration of falling bodies is of the type in which equal increments of velocity are acquired in equal periods of time.[13] He did not, however, apply the Merton rule of the measure of uniform acceleration of velocity by its mean speed, discovered at Oxford in the 1330's, to the problem of free fall, as did Galileo almost three hundred years later. Oresme knew the Merton theorem, to be sure, and in fact gave the first geometric proof of it in another work, but as applied to uniform acceleration in the abstract rather than directly to the natural acceleration of falling bodies. In his treatment of falling bodies, despite his different interpretation of *impetus*, he did follow Buridan in explaining the acceleration of falling bodies by continually accumulating impetus. Furthermore, he presented (as Plutarch had done in a more primitive form) an *imaginatio*—the device of a hypothetical, but often impossible, case to illustrate a theory—of a body that falls through a channel in the earth until it reaches the center. Its impetus then carries it beyond the center until the acquired impetus is destroyed, whence it falls once more to the center, thus oscillating about the center.[14]

The mention of Oresme's geometrical proof of the Merton mean speed theorem brings us to a work of unusual scope and inventiveness, the *Tractatus de configurationibus qualitatum et motuum*, composed in the 1350's while Oresme was at the College of Navarre. This work applies two-dimensional figures to hypothetical uniform and nonuniform distributions of the intensity of qualities in a subject and to equally hypothetical uniform and nonuniform velocities in time.

There are two keys to our proper understanding of the *De configurationibus*. To begin with, Oresme used the term *configuratio* in two distinguishable but related meanings, that is, a primitive meaning and a derived meaning. In its initial, primitive meaning it refers to the fictional and imaginative use of geometrical figures to represent or graph intensities in qualities and velocities in motions. Thus the base line of such figures is the subject when discussing linear qualities or the time when discussing velocities, and the perpendiculars raised on the base line represent the intensities of the quality from point to point in the subject, or they represent the velocity from instant to instant in the motion (Figs. 1–4). The whole figure, consisting of all the perpendiculars, represents the whole distribution of intensities in the quality, that is, the quantity of the quality, or in case of motion the so-called total velocity, dimensionally equivalent to the total space traversed in the given time. A quality of uniform intensity (Fig. 1) is thus represented by a rectangle, which is its *configuratio*; a quality of uniformly nonuniform intensity starting from zero intensity is represented as to its configuration by a right triangle (Fig. 3), that is, a figure where the slope is constant ($GK/EH = CK/GH$). Similarly, motions of uniform velocity and uniform acceleration are represented, respectively, by a rectangle and a right triangle. There is a considerable discussion of other possible configurations.

Differences in configuration—taken in its primitive

meaning—reflect for Oresme in a useful and suitable fashion internal differences in the subject. Thus we can say by shorthand that the external configuration represents some kind of internal arrangement of intensities, which we can call its essential internal *configuratio*. So we arrive at the second usage of the term configuration, in which the purely spatial or geometrical meaning is abandoned, since one of the variables involved (namely intensity) is not essentially spatial, although, as Oresme tells us, variations in intensity can be represented by variations in the length of straight lines. He suggests at great length how differences in internal configuration may explain many physical and even psychological phenomena, which are not simply explicable on the basis of the primary elements that make up a body. Thus two bodies might have the same amounts of primary elements in them and even in the same intensity, but the configuration of their intensities may well differ, and so produce different effects in natural actions.

The second key to the understanding of the configuration doctrine of Oresme is what we may call the suitability doctrine. It pertains to the nature of configurations in their primitive meaning of external figures and, briefly, holds that any figure or configuration is suitable or fitting for description of a quality, when its altitudes (ordinates, we would say in modern parlance) on any two points of its base or subject line are in the same ratio as the intensities of the quality at those points in the subject. The phrase used by Oresme to describe the key relationship of intensities and altitudes occurs at the beginning of Chapter 7 of the first part, where he tells us that:

> Any linear quality can be designated by every plane figure which is imagined as standing perpendicularly on the linear extension of the quality and which is proportional in altitude to the quality in intensity. Moreover a figure erected on a line informed with a quality is said to be "proportional in altitude to the quality in intensity" when any two lines perpendicularly erected on the quality line as a base and rising to the summit of the surface or figure have the same ratio to each other as do the intensities at the points on which they stand.

Thus, if you have a uniform linear quality, it can be suitably represented by *every* rectangle erected on the given base line designating the extension of the subject (for example, either $ADCB$ or $AFEB$, or any other rectangle on AB in Fig. 1), because any rectangle on that base line will be "proportional in altitude to the quality in intensity," the ratio of any two intensities always being equal to one (that is, $MK/IG = LK/HG = 1$). Similarly, a uniformly difform quality will be represented by *every* right triangle on the given base

$$\frac{MK}{IG} = \frac{LK}{HG} = 1$$

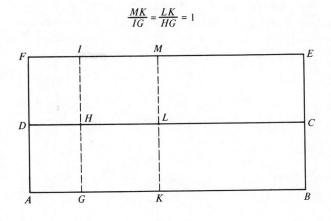

FIGURE 1

line, since two altitudes on any one right triangle will have the same ratio to each other as the corresponding two altitudes over the same points of the base line of any other triangle (that is, in Fig. 2, $DB/FE = CB/GE$).

$$\frac{DB}{FE} = \frac{CB}{GE}$$

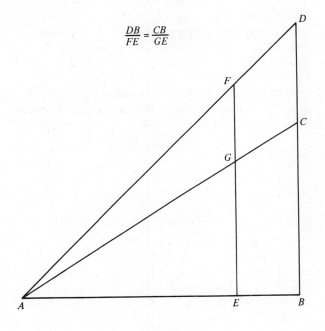

FIGURE 2

The only proviso is, of course, that when we compare figures—say, one uniform quality with another—we must retain some specific figure (say rectangle) as the point of departure for the comparison. Thus, in representing some uniform quality that is twice as intense as the first one, we would have a rectangle whose altitude is everywhere twice as high as that of the rectangle specifying the first uniform quality.

The essential nature of this suitability doctrine was

not present in the *Questiones super geometriam Euclidis*, and in fact it is specifically stated there that some specific quality must be represented by a specific

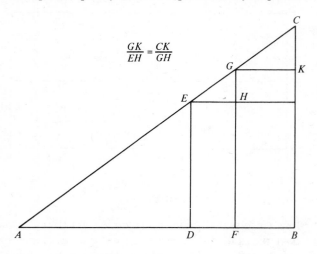

$$\frac{GK}{EH} = \frac{CK}{GH}$$

FIGURE 3

figure rather than a specific kind of figure; that is, a quality represented by a semicircle (Fig. 4) is representable only by that single semicircle on the given base line. But in the *De configurationibus* (pt. 1, ch. 14) Oresme decided in accordance with his fully developed suitability doctrine that such a quality that is representable by a semicircle can be represented by any curved

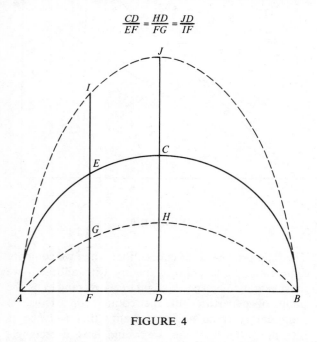

$$\frac{CD}{EF} = \frac{HD}{FG} = \frac{JD}{IF}$$

FIGURE 4

figure on the same base whose altitudes (ordinates) would have any greater or lesser constant ratio with the corresponding altitudes (ordinates) of the semicircle

(for example, in Fig. 4, $CD/EF = HD/FG = JD/IF$). He was puzzled as to what these higher or lower figures would be. For the figures of higher altitudes, he definitely rejected their identification with segments of circles, and he said he would not treat the figures of lower altitudes. Unfortunately, Oresme had little or no knowledge of conic sections. In fact the conditions he specified for these curves comprise one of the basic ways of defining ellipses: if the ordinates of a circle $x^2 + y^2 = a^2$ are all shrunk (or stretched) in the same ratio b/a, the resulting curve is an ellipse whose equation is $x^2/a^2 + y^2/b^2 = 1$. Oresme, without realizing it, has given conditions that show that the circle is merely one form of a class of curves that are elliptical. It is quite evident that Oresme arrived at the conclusion of this chapter by systematically applying the basic and sole criterion of suitability of representation, which he has already applied to uniform and uniformly difform qualities; namely, "that the figure be proportional in altitude to the quality in intensity," which is to say that any two altitudes on the base line have the same ratios as the intensities at the corresponding points in the subject. He had not adequately framed this doctrine in the *Questiones super geometriam Euclidis*, and in fact he denied it there, at least in the case of a quality represented by a semicircle or of a uniform or uniformly difform quality formed from such a difform quality. In this denial he confused the question of sufficiently representing a quality and that of comparing one quality to another.

While the idea of internal configuration outlined in the first two parts of the book had little effect on later writers and is scarcely ever referred to, the third part of the treatise—wherein Oresme compared motions by the external figures representing them, and particularly where he showed (Fig. 5) the equality of a right triangle representing uniform acceleration with a rectangle

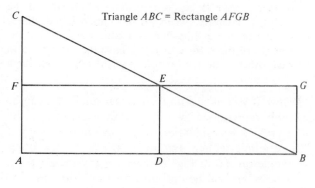

Triangle ABC = Rectangle $AFGB$

FIGURE 5

representing a uniform motion at the velocity of the middle instant of acceleration—was of profound historical importance. The use of this equation of figures can be traced successively to the time of its use by Galileo in the third day of his famous *Discorsi* (Theorem I). And indeed the other two forms of the acceleration law in Galileo's work (Theorem II and its first corollary) are anticipated to a remarkable extent in Oresme's *Questiones super geometriam Euclidis.*[15]

The third part of the *De configurationibus* is also noteworthy for Oresme's geometric illustrations of certain converging series, as for example his proof in chap. 8 of the series

$$1 + \frac{1}{2} \cdot 2 + \frac{1}{4} \cdot 3 \cdots + \frac{1}{2^{n-1}} \cdot n \cdots = 4.$$

He had showed similar interest in such a series in his *Questions on the Physics* and particularly in his *Questiones super geometriam Euclidis.* In the latter work he clearly distinguished some convergent from divergent series. He stated that when the infinite series is of the nature that to a given magnitude there are added "proportional parts to infinity" and the ratio a/b determining the proportional parts is less than one, the series has a finite sum. But when $a > b$, "the total would be infinite," that is, the series would be divergent. In the same work he gave the procedure for finding the following summation:

$$1 + \frac{1}{3} + \frac{1}{9} + \frac{1}{27} + \cdots + \frac{1}{3^n} + \frac{1}{3^{n+1}} + \cdots = \frac{3}{2}.$$

In doing so, he seems to imply a general procedure for the summation of all series of the form:

$$1 + \frac{1}{m} + \frac{1}{m^2} + \frac{1}{m^3} + \cdots + \frac{1}{m^n} + \frac{1}{m^{n+1}} + \cdots.$$

His general rule seems to be that the series is equal to y/x when, $(1/m^i - 1/m^{i+1})$ being the difference of any two successive terms,

$$m^i \left(\frac{1}{m^i} - \frac{1}{m^{i+1}} \right) = \frac{x}{y}.$$

As we survey Oresme's impressive accomplishments, it is clear that his natural philosophy lay within the broad limits of an Aristotelian framework, yet again and again he suggests subtle emendations or even radical speculations.

NOTES

1. MS Paris, BN lat. 7380, 83v: cf. MS Avranches, Bibl. Munic. 223, 348v.
2. Bk. II, quest. 2.
3. Menut text, 70d–71a; 73d.
4. *Questiones de spera*, quest. 9; *Questiones de celo*, bk. II, quest. 2.
5. Bk. II, quest. 13.
6. *Du ciel*, 38b, 39b–c.
7. MS Paris, BN lat. 15126, 127v.
8. *Questiones de spera*, quest. 3.
9. 138b–144c; see also Clagett, *Science of Mechanics*, 600–608.
10. Bk. II, quest. 13.
11. Quest. 6[8]; see also Clagett, *Science of Mechanics*, 608, n. 23.
12. BN lat. 15126, 98v, 118v.
13. *Questiones de celo*, bk. II, quest. 7.
14. *Questiones de celo*, ibid.; *Du ciel*, 30a–b; Clagett, *Science of Mechanics*, 570.
15. Clagett, *Nicole Oresme and the Medieval Geometry of Qualities, etc.*, ch. 2, pt. A.

BIBLIOGRAPHY

I. ORIGINAL WORKS. Oresme's scholarly writings reflect a wide range of interests and considerable originality. He was the author of more than thirty different writings, the majority of which are unpublished and remain in manuscript. They can be conveniently grouped into five categories:

1. Collections of, or individual, *questiones.* These include questions on various works of Aristotle: *Meteorologica* (perhaps in two versions, with MS St. Gall 839, 1–175v being the most complete MS of the vest version); *De sensu et sensato* (MS Erfurt, Amplon. Q. 299, 128–157v); *De anima* (MSS Bruges 514, 71–111v; Munich, Staatsbibl. Clm 761, 1–40v; a different version with an *expositio* in Bruges 477, 238v–264r, may also be by Oresme); *De generatione et corruptione* (MS Florence, Bibl. Naz. Centr., Conv. Soppr. H. ix. 1628, 1–77v; a different version in MS Vatican lat. 3097, 103–146; and Vat. lat. 2185, 40v–61v, may be by him); *Physica* (MS Seville, Bibl. Colomb. 7-6-30, 2–79v); and *De celo* (MSS Erfurt, Amplon. Q. 299, 1–50; Q. 325, 57–90). These also include questions on the *Elementa* of Euclid (edit. of H. L. L. Busard [Leiden, 1961]; additional MS Seville, Bibl. Colomb. 7-7-13, 102v–112) and on the *Sphere* of Sacrobosco (MSS Florence, Bibl. Riccard. 117, 125r–135r; Vat. lat. 2185, 71–77v; Venice Bibl. Naz. Marc. Lat. VIII, 74, 1–8; Seville, Bibl. Colomb. 7-7-13; a different version is attributed to him in Erfurt, Amplon. Q. 299, 113–126). There are other individual questions that are perhaps by him: *Utrum omnes impressiones* (MS Vat. lat. 4082, 82v–85v; edit. of R. Mathieu, 1959), *Utrum aliqua res videatur* (MS Erfurt, Amplon. Q. 231, 146–150), *Utrum dyameter alicuius quadrati sit commensurabilis coste eiusdem* (MS Bern A. 50, 172–176; H. Suter, ed., 1887; see *Isis*, 50 [1959], 130–133), and *Questiones de perfectione specierum* (MS Vat. lat. 986, 125–133v). This whole group of writings seems to date from the late 1340's and early 1350's, that is, from the period when Oresme was teaching arts.

2. A group of mathematico-physical works. This includes a tract beginning *Ad pauca respicientes* (E. Grant, ed., 1966), which is sometimes assigned the title *De motibus sperarum* (MS Brit. Mus. 2542, 59r); a *De proportionibus proportionum* (E. Grant, ed. [Madison, Wisc.,

1966]); *De commensurabilitate sive incommensurabilitate motuum celi* (E. Grant, ed. [Madison, Wisc., 1971]); *Algorimus proportionum* (M. Curtze, ed. [Thorn, 1868], and a partial ed. by E. Grant, thesis [Wisconsin, 1957]); and *De configurationibus qualitatum et motuum* (M. Clagett, ed. [Madison, Wisc., 1968]). These works also probably date from the period of teaching arts, although some may date as late as 1360.

3. A small group of works vehemently opposing astrology and the magical arts. Here we find a *Tractatus contra iudiciarios astronomos* (H. Pruckner, ed., 1933; G. W. Coopland, ed., 1952); a somewhat similar but longer exposition in French, *Le livre de divinacions* (G. W. Coopland, ed., 1952); and a complex collection commonly known as *Questio contra divinatores* with *Quodlibeta annexa* (MS Paris, BN lat. 15126, 1–158; Florence, Bibl. Laurent. Ashb. 210, 3–70v; the *Quodlibeta* has been edited by B. Hansen in a Princeton University diss. of 1973). The first two works almost certainly date before 1364; the last is dated 1370 in the manuscripts but in all likelihood is earlier.

4. A collection of theological and nonscientific works. This includes an economic tract *De mutationibus monetarum* (many early editions; cf. C. Johnson, ed. [London, 1956]; this work was soon translated into French, cf. E. Bridrey's study), a *Commentary on the Sentences of Peter Lombard* (now lost but referred to by Oresme); a short theological tract *De communicatione ydiomatum* (E. Borchert, ed., 1940); *Ars sermonicinandi, i.e.,* on the preaching art (MSS Paris, BN lat. 7371, 279–282; Munich, Clm 18225); a short legal tract, *Expositio cuiusdam legis* (Paris, BN lat. 14580, 220–222v); a *Determinatio facta in resumpta in domo Navarre* (MS Paris, BN lat. 16535, 111–114v); a tract predicting bad times for the Church, *De malis venturis super Ecclesiam* (Paris, BN 14533, 77–83v); a popular and oft-published *Sermo coram Urbano V* (delivered in 1363; Flaccus Illyricus, ed. [Basel, 1556; Lyons, 1597]), a *Decisio an in omni casu* (possibly identical with a *determinatio* in MS Brussels, Bibl. Royale 18977–81, 51v–54v); a *Contra mendicacionem* (MSS Munich, Clm 14265; Kiel, Univ. Bibl. 127; Vienna, Nat.-bibl. 11799); and finally some 115 short sermons for Sundays and Feast Days, *Sacre conciones* (Paris, BN lat. 16893, 1–128v). The dating of this group is no doubt varied, but presumably all of them except the *Commentary on the Sentences* postdate his assumption of the grand-mastership at Navarre.

5. A group of French texts and translations. This embraces a popular tract on cosmology, *Traité de l'espere* (L. M. McCarthy, ed., thesis [Toronto, 1943]), which dates from about 1365; a translation and commentary, *Le livre de ethiques d'Aristote* (A. D. Menut, ed., [New York, 1940]), completed in 1372; a similar translation and commentary of the *Politics—Le livre de politique d'Aristote* (Vérard, ed. [Paris, 1489; cf. Menut's ed., in *Transactions of the American Philosophical Society*, n.s. **60**, pt. 6 (1970)]), completed by 1374; the *Livre de yconomique d'Aristote* (Vérard, ed. [Paris, 1489]; A. D. Menut, ed. [Philadelphia, 1957]), completed about the same time;

and finally, *Livre du ciel et du monde d'Aristote* (A. D. Menut and A. J. Denomy, eds. [Toronto, 1943], new ed., Madison, Wisc., 1968), completed in 1377. To these perhaps can be added a translation of *Le Quadripartit de Ptholomee* (J. F. Gossner, ed., thesis [Syracuse, 1951]), although it is attributed to G. Oresme.

6. Modern editions. These comprise "De configurationibus qualitatum et motuum," in M. Clagett, ed., *Nicole Oresme and the Medieval Geometry of Qualities* (Madison, Wisc., 1968); E. Grant, ed., "*De proportionibus proportionum*" and "*Ad pauca respicientes*" (Madison, Wisc., 1966); *Nicole Oresme and the Kinematics of Circular Motion* (Madison, Wisc., 1971); A. D. Menut, ed., *Le livre de ethiques d'Aristote* (New York, 1940); A. D. Menut and M. J. Denomy, eds., *Le livre de ciel et du monde d'Aristote*, in *Mediaeval Studies*, 3–5 (1941–1943), rev. with English trans. by Menut (Madison, Wisc., 1968).

II. SECONDARY LITERATURE. Only a brief bibliography is given here because the extensive literature on Oresme appears in full in the editions of Grant, Clagett, and Menut listed above. These editions include full bibliographical references to the other editions mentioned in the list of Oresme's works.

Works on Oresme include E. Borchert, "Die Lehre von der Bewegung bei Nicolaus Oresme," in *Beiträge zur Geschichte der Philosophie und Theologie des Mittelalters*, **31**, no. 3 (1934); M. Clagett, *The Science of Mechanics in the Middle Ages* (Madison, Wisc., 1959, 1961); M. Curtze, *Die mathematischen Schriften des Nicole Oresme (ca. 1320–1382)* (Berlin, 1870); P. Duhem, *Études sur Léonard de Vinci*, 3 vols., (Paris, 1906–1913); *Le système du monde*, VI–X (Paris, 1954–1959). See also the following works by A. Maier, *An der Grenze von Scholastik und Naturwissenschaft*, 2nd ed. (Rome, 1952); *Die Vorläufer Galileis im 14. Jahrhundert* (Rome, 1949); *Zwei Grundproblem der scholastischen Naturphilosophie*, 2nd ed. (Rome, 1952); and O. Pederson, *Nicole Oresme, og hans Naturfilosofiske System. En undersøgelse af hans skrift "Le livre du ciel et du monde"* (Copenhagen, 1956).

MARSHALL CLAGETT

ORTEGA, JUAN DE (*b.* Palencia, Spain, *ca.* 1480; *d. ca.* 1568)

Ortega was a member of the Order of Preachers and was assigned to the province of Aragon. He taught arithmetic and geometry in Spain and Italy.

Ortega followed the classical tradition and drew inspiration, like his Spanish contemporaries, from the arithmetic of Boethius. His work reveals the influence of the more important mathematicians of the thirteenth and fourteenth centuries, but he was apparently unfamiliar with fifteenth-century works.

Ortega wrote *Cursus quattuor mathematicarum artium liberalium* (Paris, 1516) and *Tractado subtilisimo d'aritmética y de geometria* (Barcelona, 1512). The first part of the latter was devoted to commercial arithmetic and contains many examples, practical rules, and conversion tables for the various currencies then in use in the different regions of Spain. The second part gives instruction in practical rules of geometry "whereby anybody can measure any figure."

This work is of historical interest mainly for the numerical values that he obtained in extracting square roots, which appear in some of the geometric applications in the second part of the book. Almost identical editions were published in Seville in 1534, 1537, and 1542 (each published by Ortega himself), in which he modified the roots extracted in the first edition. He replaced them with values satisfying the Pell equation $(x^2 - Ay^2 = 1)$; these values thereby gave the best approximation of square roots. Mathematicians have wondered how Ortega managed to evolve a method enabling him to find such closely approximate values, when a general solution of the Pell equation was presumably not achieved before Fermat (1601–1665).

Ortega's *Aritmética* became famous throughout Europe; the work was published in Lyons (1515), Rome (1515), Messina (1522), and Cambray (1612). It was also published in Seville (1552), probably posthumously, as it contained inadmissible changes. (This publication was later corrected.) The Lyons edition was the first book on commercial arithmetic to be published in French.

BIBLIOGRAPHY

Works that discuss Ortega and his work are Cantor, *Vorlesungen über die Geschichte der Mathematik*, II (Leipzig, 1908), 388; J. E. Hofmann, *Geschichte der Mathematik*, trans. into Spanish as *Historia de la Matemática* (Mexico City, 1960), I, 109–110; J. Rey Pastor, "Los matemáticos españoles del siglo XVI," in *Biblioteca scientia*, no. 2 (1926), 67, and "Las aproximaciones de Fr. Juan de Ortega," in *Revista matemática hispano-americana*, **7** (1925), 158.

María Asunción Catalá

OSGOOD, WILLIAM FOGG (*b*. Boston, Massachusetts, 10 March 1864; *d*. Belmont, Massachusetts, 22 July 1943)

Osgood was the son of William Osgood and Mary Rogers Gannett. After preparing for college at the Boston Latin School, he entered Harvard College in 1882 and was graduated second in his class in 1886. He remained at Harvard for a year of graduate work in mathematics and was awarded the A.M. in 1887. Osgood spent much of his first two years at Harvard

studying the classics but was largely influenced by the mathematical physicist Benjamin Osgood Peirce, one of his favorite teachers, and by Frank Nelson Cole. Cole had attended Felix Klein's lectures on function theory and lectured on the subject, following Klein's ideas, at Harvard during 1885–1887. Osgood went to the great German center of mathematics at Göttingen in 1887, largely because of Klein's presence there.

In 1887 there was great mathematical activity in Europe, brought about especially by the introduction of rigor into current research. Under the influence of Klein, Osgood embraced this tendency, which remained a commitment throughout his life. Osgood went to Erlangen in 1889 to continue his graduate work. His dissertation, a study of Abelian integrals of the first, second, and third kinds, was based on previous work by Klein and Max Noether. The topic was part of the theory of functions, to which Osgood devoted much of his later life. After receiving his Ph.D. at Erlangen in 1890, Osgood married Anna Terese Ruprecht of Göttingen and returned to the United States. He then joined the Harvard department of mathematics, where he remained for forty-three years. He brought with him the spirit of research, then new in the United States, as well as that of rigor. A year later Maxime Bôcher returned to Harvard, and the two were influential in fostering the new attitude there.

Osgood's main research papers concerned convergence of sequences of continuous functions, solutions of differential equations, Riemann's theorem on the mapping of a simply connected region, the calculus of variations, and space-filling curves. These topics are classical, and Osgood's results are important and deep. Klein invited Osgood to write an article for the *Encyklopädie* on the theory of functions; the writing of it (1901) gave Osgood an unparalleled knowledge of the field and its history. His *Lehrbuch der Funktionentheorie* (1907) subsequently became the standard treatise. Osgood was one of the world's outstanding mathematics teachers through that work and through others on analytic geometry, calculus, and advanced calculus. Over the years he instilled ideals and habits of careful and accurate thought in hundreds of elementary as well as advanced students. After his retirement from Harvard in 1933, he lectured for two years at the National University of Peking.

Osgood's favorite recreations were travel by car, smoking cigars, and occasional games of tennis and golf. He was kindly although somewhat reserved, but warm to those who knew him. He and his first wife had two sons and a daughter. He married Celeste Phelps Morse in 1932.

BIBLIOGRAPHY

Personal recollections; Harvard Class of 1886 *Reports* for 1886, 1889, 1894, 1898, 1901, 1906, 1911, 1926, 1936; and clippings in Harvard University Archives. See also *Dictionary of American Biography*, supp. 3, 574–575.

J. L. WALSH

OSTROGRADSKY, MIKHAIL VASILIEVICH (*b.* Pashennaya [now in Poltava oblast], Russia, 24 September 1801; *d.* Poltava [now Ukrainian S.S.R.], 1 January 1862)

Ostrogradsky was born on the estate of his father, Vasily Ivanovich Ostrogradsky, a landowner of modest means; his mother was Irina Andreevna Sakhno-Ustimovich. After he had spent several years at the Poltava Gymnasium, the question of his future arose. Ostrogradsky hoped to become a soldier; but the life of an officer was expensive, the salary alone would not support him, and the family had little money to spare. It was decided to prepare him for the civil service and to give him a university education, without which his career would be limited. In 1816 Ostrogradsky enrolled in the physics and mathematics department of Kharkov University, where he received a good mathematical education under A. F. Pavlovsky and T. F. Osipovsky. He was especially influenced by the latter, an outstanding teacher and author of the three-volume *Kurs matematiki* (1801–1823), which was well known in its time, and also of philosophical papers in which he criticized Kant's apriorism from the materialistic point of view. In 1820 Ostrogradsky passed the examinations for the candidate's degree, and the university council voted to award it to him. But the minister of religious affairs and national education refused to confirm the council's decision and proposed that Ostrogradsky take the examinations again if he wished to receive his degree. Ostrogradsky rejected this proposal, and therefore did not obtain a university diploma.

The true reason for the arbitrary reversal of the council's decision was the government's struggle with the nonconformist and revolutionary attitudes prevalent among the Russian intelligentsia. The national educational system was headed by conservative bureaucrats who encouraged a combination of piety and mysticism at the universities. In the autumn of 1820 Osipovsky was suspended after having been rector of Kharkov University for a number of years. The animosity felt toward him was extended to Ostrogradsky, his best and favorite pupil, who, according to his own account later, was at that time a complete materialist and atheist. The ground for the

refusal to grant him a diploma was that, under the influence of Osipovsky, he and the other students of mathematics did not attend lectures on philosophy and theology.

Ostrogradsky continued his mathematical studies in Paris, where Laplace and Fourier, Legendre and Poisson, Binet and Cauchy worked, and where outstanding courses were offered at the École Polytechnique and other educational institutions. Ostrogradsky's rapid progress gained him the friendship and respect of the senior French mathematicians and of his contemporaries, including Sturm. The Paris period of his life (1822–1827) was for Ostrogradsky not only "years of traveling and apprenticeship" but also a period of intense creative work. Between 1824 and 1827 he presented to the Paris Academy several papers containing important new discoveries in mathematical physics and integral calculus. Most of these discoveries were incorporated in his later papers; a memoir on hydrodynamics was published by the Paris Academy in 1832, and individual results in residue theory appeared, with his approval, in the works of Cauchy.

In the spring of 1828 Ostrogradsky arrived in St. Petersburg. There, over a period of several months, he presented three papers to the Academy of Sciences. In the first, on potential theory, he gave a new, more exact derivation of Poisson's equation for the case of a point lying within or on the surface of an attracting mass. The second was on heat theory, and the third on the theory of double integrals. All three appeared in *Mémoires de l'Académie impériale des sciences de St.-Péterbourg*, 6th ser., **1** (1831). On 29 December 1828 Ostrogradsky was elected a junior academician in the section of applied mathematics. In 1830 he was elected an associate and in 1832 a full academician. His work at the Academy of Sciences restored to it the brilliance in mathematics that it had won in the eighteenth century but had lost in the first quarter of the nineteenth.

Ostrogradsky's activity at the Academy was manifold. He contributed some eighty-odd reports in mathematics and mechanics, delivered public lectures, wrote detailed reviews of papers submitted to the Academy, and participated in the work of commissions on the introduction of the Gregorian calendar and the decimal system of measurement. At the behest of the government he also investigated exterior ballistics problems. Ostrogradsky also devoted a great deal of time to teaching and did much to improve mathematical instruction in Russia. From 1828 he lectured at the Naval Corps (later the Naval Academy); from 1830, at the Institute of Means of Communication; and from 1832, at the General Pedagogical Institute.

Later he also lectured at the General Engineering College and at the General Artillery College.

From 1847 Ostrogradsky accomplished a great deal as chief inspector for the teaching of the mathematical sciences in military schools. His textbooks on elementary and higher mathematics include a very interesting course on algebra and an exposition of the theory of numbers. Ostrogradsky's educational views were ahead of their time in many respects, particularly his program for the education of children between the ages of seven and twelve, which is expounded in *Considérations sur l'enseignement* (St. Petersburg–Paris, 1860), written with I. A. Blum.

It was mainly Ostrogradsky who established the conditions for the rise of the St. Petersburg mathematical school organized by Chebyshev, and who was the founder of the Russian school of theoretical mechanics. His direct disciples included I. A. Vyshnegradsky, the creator of the theory of automatic regulation, and N. P. Petrov, the author of the hydrodynamic theory of lubricants. Ostrogradsky's services were greatly appreciated by his contemporaries. He was elected a member of the American Academy of Arts and Sciences in 1834, the Turin Academy of Sciences in 1841, and the Rome Academy of Sciences in 1853; in 1856 he was elected a corresponding member of the Paris Academy of Sciences.

Ostrogradsky's scientific work closely bordered upon the developments originating in the École Polytechnique in applied mathematics and in directly related areas of analysis. In mathematical physics he sought a grandiose synthesis that would embrace hydromechanics, the theory of elasticity, the theory of heat, and the theory of electricity by means of a unique homogeneous method. The realization of this plan was beyond the capacity of one man and beyond the resources of the nineteenth century; it remains uncompleted to date.

Ostrogradsky contributed significantly to the development of the method of separating variables that was so successfully applied by Fourier in his work on the conduction of heat (1822). In "Note sur la théorie de la chaleur," presented in 1828 and published in 1831 (see his *Polnoe sobranie trudov,* I, 62–69), Ostrogradsky was the first to formulate a general schema of the method of solving boundary-value problems, which Fourier and Poisson had applied to the solution of individual problems.

For linear partial differential equations with constant coefficients Ostrogradsky established the orthogonality of the corresponding system of proper functions (eigenfunctions). Auxiliary means of calculation in this determination were Ostrogradsky's

theorem for the reduction of certain volume integrals to surface integrals and the general formula for arbitrary conjugate linear differential operators with constant coefficients for a three-dimensional space, generally called Green's theorem. In terms of modern vector analysis Ostrogradsky's theorem states that the volume integral of the divergence of a vector field A taken over any volume v is equal to the surface integral of A taken over the closed surface s surrounding the volume v:

$$\iiint (\nabla \cdot A)\, dv = \iint A d\bar{s}.$$

(Ostrogradsky himself expressed this proposition in terms of ordinary integral calculus.) This theorem is also called Gauss's theorem, Green's theorem, or Riemann's theorem.

Ostrogradsky next applied his general results to the theory of heat, deriving formulas for the coefficients a_k in the expansion of an arbitrary function $f(x, y, z)$ into a series $\sum\limits_{k=0}^{\infty} a_k u_k$ of eigenfunctions $u_k(x, y, z, \theta_k)$ of the corresponding boundary-value problem—a generalized Fourier series. He noted the difficulty connected with investigating the convergence of this type of series expansion and only touched on the problem of the existence of eigenvalues of θ_k; satisfactory solutions to these questions were not found until the turn of the twentieth century, by Poincaré and V. A. Steklov, among others.

A large part of these discoveries was contained in two memoirs presented by Ostrogradsky to the Paris Academy of Sciences in 1826–1827. In the second of these he solved the problem of the conduction of heat in a right prism with an isosceles right triangle as a base; Fourier and Poisson had previously examined the cases of a sphere, a cylinder, and a right rectangular parallelepiped. Lamé mentioned this solution, which was not published during Ostrogradsky's lifetime, in an 1833 paper. General results in the theory of heat analogous to Ostrogradsky's (but without his integral theorem) were also obtained by Lamé and Duhamel, who presented their papers to the Paris Academy of Sciences in 1829 (published in 1833).

At first Ostrogradsky investigated heat conduction in a solid body surrounded by a medium having a constant temperature. In "Deuxième note sur la théorie de la chaleur," presented in 1829 and published in 1831 (see *Polnoe sobranie trudov,* I, 70–72), he reduced this problem to the case when the temperature of the surrounding medium is a given function of the coordinates of space and time. Finally, in "Sur l'équation relative à la propagation de la chaleur dans l'intérieur des liquides," presented in 1836 and published in 1838 (*ibid.*, pp. 75–79), he derived the corresponding differential equation for an uncompressed moving liquid free of internal friction, thereby confirming Fourier's results by more thorough analysis.

At the same time Ostrogradsky studied the theory of elasticity; in this field his work meshed with Poisson's parallel investigations. Starting from the work of Poisson, who was the first to establish precisely the necessary condition of the extremum of a double integral with variable limits (1833), Ostrogradsky obtained important results in the calculus of variations. In "Mémoire sur le calcul des variations des intégrales multiples," presented in 1834 and published in 1838 (*ibid.*, III, 45–64), he derived equations containing the necessary conditions of the extremum of an integral of any multiplicity. To accomplish this he had to develop substantially the theory of multiple integrals. He generalized the integral theorem which he had found earlier, that is, reduced an n-tuple integral from an expression of the divergent type taken over any hypervolume to an $(n - 1)$-tuple integral taken over the corresponding boundary hypersurface; derived a formula for the substitution of new variables in an n-tuple integral (independently of Jacobi, who published it in 1834); and described in detail the general method for computing an n-tuple integral by means of n consecutive integrations with respect to each variable.

In "Sur la transformation des variables dans les intégrales multiples," presented in 1836 and published in 1838 (*ibid.*, pp. 109–114), Ostrogradsky was the first to derive in a very modern manner (with a geometrical interpretation) the rule of the substitution of new variables in a double integral; he later extended this method to triple integrals. His work in the calculus of variations was directly related to his work in mechanics.

Ostrogradsky made two important discoveries in the theory of ordinary differential equations. In "Note sur la méthode des approximations successives," presented in 1835 and published in 1838 (*ibid.*, pp. 71–75), he proposed a method of solving nonlinear equations by expanding the unknown quantity into a power series in α, where α is a small parameter, in order to avoid "secular terms" containing the independent variable outside the sign of trigonometric functions. This important idea received further development in the investigations of H. Gylden (1881), Anders Lindstedt (1883), Poincaré, and Lyapunov. In "Note sur les équations différentielles linéaires," presented in 1838 and published in 1839 (*ibid.*, pp. 124–126), Ostrogradsky derived,

simultaneously with Liouville, a well-known expression for Wronski's determinant, one of the basic formulas in the theory of differential linear equations.

Ostrogradsky also wrote several papers on the theory of algebraic functions and their integrals (*ibid.*, pp. 13–44, 175–179). The foundation of this theory was laid in 1826 by Abel, whom Ostrogradsky may have met in Paris. From Ostrogradsky's general results there follows the transcendency of a logarithmic function and of the arc tangent. His investigations were parallel to Liouville's work in the same area; they were continued in Russia by Chebyshev and his pupils. In "De l'intégration des fractions rationnelles," presented in 1844 and published in 1845 (*ibid.*, pp. 180–214), Ostrogradsky proposed a method for finding the algebraic part of an integral of a rational function without preliminary expansion of the integrand into the sum of partial fractions. This algebraic (and rational) part is calculated with the aid of rational operations and differentiations. Hermite rediscovered this method in 1872 and included it in his textbook on analysis (1873). It is sometimes called Hermite's method.

In "Mémoire sur les quadratures définies," written in 1839 and published in 1841 (*ibid.*, pp. 127–153), which grew out of his work in ballistics, Ostrogradsky gave a new derivation of the Euler-Maclaurin summation formula with a remainder term in the form in which it is now often presented (Jacobi published an equivalent result in 1834) and applied the general formulas to the approximation calculus of definite integrals. Several articles are devoted to probability theory—for example, one on the sample control of production, presented in 1846 and published in 1848 (*ibid.*, pp. 215–237), and to algebra. In general, however, as a mathematician Ostrogradsky was always an analyst.

Ostrogradsky's memoirs in mechanics can be divided into three areas: the principle of virtual displacements; dynamic differential equations; and the solution of specific problems.

Ostrogradsky's most important investigations in mechanics deal with generalizations of its basic principles and methods. He made a substantial contribution to the development of variational principles. The fundamental "Mémoire sur les équations différentielles relatives au problème des isopérimètres," presented in 1848 and published in 1850 (*ibid.*, II, 139–233), belongs in equal measure to mechanics and the calculus of variations. Because of his mathematical approach Ostrogradsky's investigations significantly deepened the understanding of variational principles.

In the paper just cited Ostrogradsky examined the

variational problem in which the integrand depends on an arbitrary number of unknown functions of one independent variable and their derivatives of an arbitrary order and proved that the problem can be reduced to the integration of canonical Hamiltonian equations, which can be viewed as the form into which any equations arising in a variational problem can be transformed. This transformation requires no operation other than differentiation and algebraic operations. The credit for this interpretation of the dynamics problem belongs to Ostrogradsky. He also eased the restrictions on constraints, which had always been considered stationary, and thus significantly generalized the problem. Therefore the variational principle formulated by Hamilton in 1834–1835 might more accurately be called the Hamilton-Ostrogradsky principle. Jacobi also worked in the same direction, but his results were published later (1866).

At the same time Ostrogradsky prepared the important paper "Sur les intégrales des équations générales de la dynamique," also presented in 1848 and published in 1850 (*ibid.*, III, 129–138). In it he showed that even in the more general case, when the constraints and the force function depend on time (this case was not considered by Hamilton and Jacobi), the equations of motion can be transformed into Hamiltonian form. Generally, the development of the classical theory of the integration of canonical equations was carried out by Hamilton, Jacobi, and Ostrogradsky.

Ostrogradsky's results related to the development of the principle of virtual displacements are stated in "Considérations générales sur les moments des forces," presented in 1834 and published in 1838 (*ibid.*, II, 13–28). This paper significantly broadened the sphere of application of the principle of virtual displacements, extending it to the relieving constraints.

In "Mémoire sur les déplacements instantanés des systèmes assujettis à des conditions variables," presented and published in 1838 (*ibid.*, pp. 32–59), and "Sur le principe des vitesses virtuelles et sur la force d'inertie," presented in 1841 and published in 1842 (*ibid.*, pp. 104–109), Ostrogradsky gave a rigorous proof of the formula expressing the principle of virtual displacements for the case of nonstationary constraints.

"Mémoire sur la théorie générale de la percussion," presented in 1854 and published in 1857 (*ibid.*, pp. 234–266), presents Ostrogradsky's investigations of the impact of systems, in which he assumed that the constraints arising at the moment of impact are preserved after the impact. The principle of virtual displacements is extended here to the phenomenon of inelastic impact, and the basic formula of the analytical theory of impact is derived.

Ostrogradsky also wrote papers containing solutions to particular problems of mechanics that had arisen in the technology of his time. A series of his papers on ballistics deserves special mention: "Note sur le mouvement des projectiles sphériques dans un milieu résistant" and "Mémoire sur le mouvement des projectiles sphériques dans l'air," both presented in 1840 and published in 1841; and "Tables pour faciliter le calcul de la trajectoire que décrit un mobile dans un milieu résistant," presented in 1839 and published in 1841 (*ibid.*, pp. 70–94). In the first two papers Ostrogradsky investigated the motion of the center of gravity and the rotation of a spherical projectile the geometrical center of which does not coincide with the center of gravity; both topics were important for artillery at that time. The third paper contains tables, computed by Ostrogradsky, of the function $\Phi(\theta) = 2 \int d\theta / \sin^3 \theta$, used in ballistics. These papers stimulated the creation of the Russian school of ballistics in the second half of the nineteenth century.

BIBLIOGRAPHY

I. ORIGINAL WORKS. Most of Ostrogradsky's papers appeared in French in publications of the St. Petersburg Academy of Sciences. The most complete bibliography of his works and of writings concerning him is by M. G. Novlyanskaya in Ostrogradsky's *Izbrannye trudy* ("Selected Works"), V. I. Smirnov, ed. (Moscow, 1958), 540–581. Other collections of Ostrogradsky's writings are *Polnoe sobranie sochineny* ("Complete Collected Works"), I, pt. 2, *Lektsii po analiticheskoy mekhanike, 1834* ("Lectures on Analytic Mechanics"), and II, *Lektsii algebraicheskogo i transtsendentnogo analiza, 1837* ("Lectures on Algebraic and Transcendental Analysis"; Moscow-Leningrad, 1940–1946), never completed; and *Polnoe sobranie trudov* ("Complete Collected Works"), I. Z. Shtokalo, ed., 3 vols. (Kiev, 1959–1961), which contains commentaries and articles by I. Z. Shtokalo, I. B. Pogrebyssky, E. Y. Remez, Y. D. Sokolov, S. M. Targ, and others but does not include the 1834 and 1837 works above or the two articles that follow; and "Dokazatelstvo odnoy teoremy integralnogo ischislenia" ("Proof of One Theorem in the Integral Calcuius") and "Memuar o rasprostranenii tepla vnutri tverdykh tel" ("Memoir on the Conduction of Heat Within Solid Bodies"), in *Istoriko-matematicheskie issledovaniya*, **16** (1965), 49–96, Russian translations of two previously unpublished articles presented to the Paris Academy in 1826–1827, with an introduction by A. P. Youschkevitch.

II. SECONDARY LITERATURE. See Y. L. Geronimus, *Ocherki o rabotakh korifeev russkoy mekhaniki* ("Essays on the Work of the Leading Figures in Russian Mechanics"; Moscow, 1952), 13–57; B. V. Gnedenko and I. B. Pogrebyssky, *Mikhail Vasilievich Ostrogradsky (1801–1862). Zhizn i rabota. Nauchnoe i pedagogicheskoe nasledie* (". . . Life and Work. Scientific and Pedagogical Heritage"; Moscow, 1963), the most complete work on his life and accomplishments; A. T. Grigorian, *Mikhail Vasilievich Ostrogradsky (1801–1862)* (Moscow, 1961); and *Ocherki istorii mekhaniki v Rossii* ("Essays on the History of Mechanics in Russia"; Moscow, 1961), see index; *Istoria otechestvennoy matematiki* ("History of Russian Mathematics"), I. Z. Shtokalo, ed.-in-chief, II (Kiev, 1967), see index; A. I. Kropotov and I. A. Maron, *M. V. Ostrogradsky i ego pedagogicheskoe nasledie* ("Ostrogradsky and His Pedagogical Heritage"; Moscow, 1961); *Mikhail Vasilievich Ostrogradsky. 1862–1962. Pedagogicheskoe nasledie. Dokumenty o zhizni i deyatelnosti* (". . . Pedagogical Heritage. Documents on His Life and Activity"), I. B. Pogrebyssky and A. P. Youschkevitch, eds. (Moscow, 1961), a supp. to *Polnoe sobranie trudov* containing a Russian trans. of Ostrogradsky and Blum's *Considérations sur l'enseignement* (St. Petersburg–Paris, 1860), and Ostrogradsky's "Zapiski integralnogo ischislenia" ("Lectures on Integral Calculus"); E. Y. Remez, "O matematicheskikh rukopisyakh akademika M. V. Ostrogradskogo" ("On the Mathematical Manuscripts of Academician M. V. Ostrogradsky"), in *Istoriko-matematicheskie issledovaniya*, **4** (1951), 9–98; S. P. Timoshenko, *History of Strength of Materials* (New York–Toronto–London, 1953); I. Todhunter, *A History of the Progress of the Calculus of Variations During the Nineteenth Century* (Cambridge, 1861); P. I. Tripolsky, ed., *Mikhail Vasilievich Ostrogradsky. Prazdnovanie stoletia dnya ego rozhdenia* (". . . Celebration of the Centenary of His Birth"; Poltava, 1902), which contains short sketches on his life and scientific and educational activities—of special interest are an article by Lyapunov on his work in mechanics (pp. 115–118) and one by Steklov on Ostrogradsky's paper in mathematical physics (pp. 118–131); A. Youschkevitch, *Michel Ostrogradski et le progrès de la science au XIXe siècle* (Paris, 1967); and *Istoria matematiki v Rossii do 1917 goda* ("History of Mathematics in Russia to 1917"; Moscow, 1968), see index; and N. E. Zhukovsky, "Uchenye trudy M. V. Ostrogradskogo po mekhanike" ("Ostrogradsky's Scientific Works in Mechanics"), in Zhukovsky's *Polnoe sobranie sochineny* ("Complete Collected Works"), VII (Moscow–Leningrad, 1950), 229–246.

A. P. YOUSCHKEVITCH

OUGHTRED, WILLIAM (*b.* Eton, Buckinghamshire, England, 5 March 1575; *d.* Albury, near Guildford, Surrey, England, 30 June 1660)

Oughtred's father was a scrivener who taught writing at Eton and instructed his young son in arithmetic. Oughtred was educated as a king's scholar at Eton, from which he proceeded to King's College, Cambridge, at the age of fifteen. He became a fellow of his college in 1595, graduated B.A. in 1596, and was awarded the M.A. in 1600.

Ordained a priest in 1603, Oughtred at once began his ecclesiastical duties, being presented with the living of Shalford, Surrey. Five years later he became rector of Albury and retained this post until his death. Despite his parochial duties he continued to devote considerable time to mathematics, and in 1628 he was called upon to instruct Lord William Howard, the young son of the earl of Arundel. In carrying out this task he prepared a treatise on arithmetic and algebra. This slight volume, of barely 100 pages, contained almost all that was then known of these two branches of mathematics; it was published in 1631 as *Clavis mathematicae*.

Oughtred's best-remembered work, the *Clavis* exerted considerable influence in England and on the Continent and immediately established him as a capable mathematician. Both Boyle and Newton held a very high opinion of the work. In a letter to Nathaniel Hawes, treasurer of Christ's Hospital, dated 25 May 1694 and entitled "A New Scheme of Learning for the Mathematical Boys at Christ's Hospital," Newton referred to Oughtred as "a man whose judgment (if any man's) may be relied on." In Lord King's *Life of Locke* we read: "The best Algebra yet extant is Oughtred's" (I, 227). John Aubrey, in *Brief Lives*, maintained that Oughtred was more famous abroad for his learning than at home and that several great men came to England for the purpose of meeting him (II, 471).

John Wallis dedicated his *Arithmetica infinitorum* (1655) to Oughtred. A pupil of Oughtred, Wallis never wearied of sounding his praises. In his *Algebra* (1695) he wrote: "The *Clavis* doth in as little room deliver as much of the fundamental and useful parts of geometry (as well as of arithmetic and algebra) as any book I know," and in its preface he classed Oughtred with the English mathematician Thomas Harriot.

The *Clavis* is not easy reading. The style is very obscure, and rules are so involved as to make them difficult to follow. Oughtred carried symbolism to excess, using signs to denote quantities, their powers, and the fundamental operations in arithmetic and algebra. Chief among these were X for multiplication, ⊐ for "greater than"; ⊏ for "less than"; and ∼ for "difference between." Ratio was denoted by a dot; proportion, by ::. Thus the proportion $A : B = \alpha : \beta$ was written $A \cdot B :: \alpha \cdot \beta$. Continued proportion was written $\div$. Of the maze of symbols employed by Oughtred, only those for multiplication and proportion are still used. Yet, surprisingly, there is a complete absence of indices or exponents from his work. Even in later editions of the *Clavis*, Oughtred used *Aq, Ac, Aqq, Aqc, Acc, Aqqc, Aqcc, Accc, Aqqcc*, to denote successive powers of *A* up to the tenth. In his *Géométrie* (1637) Descartes had introduced the notation x^n but restricted its use to cases in which *n* was a positive whole number. Newton extended this notation to include fractional and negative indices. These first appeared in a letter to Oldenburg for transmission to Leibniz—the famous *Epistola prior* of June 1676—in which Newton illustrated the newly discovered binomial theorem.

In *La disme*, a short tract published in 1585, Simon Stevin had outlined the principles of decimal fractions. Although a warm admirer of Stevin's work, Oughtred avoided his clumsy notation and substituted his own, which, although an improvement, was far from satisfactory. He did not use the dot to separate the decimal from the whole number, undoubtedly because he already used it to denote ratio; instead, he wrote a decimal such as 0.56 as 0/56.

Oughtred is generally regarded as the inventor of the circular and rectilinear slide rules. Although the former is described in his *Circles of Proportion and the Horizontal Instrument* (1632), a description of the instrument had been published two years earlier by one of his pupils, Richard Delamain, in *Grammelogie, or the Mathematical Ring*. A bitter quarrel ensued between the two, each claiming priority in the invention. There seems to be no very good reason why each should not be credited as an independent inventor. Oughtred's claim to priority in the invention of the rectilinear slide rule, however, is beyond dispute, since it is known that he had designed the instrument as early as 1621.

In 1657 Oughtred published *Trigonometria*, a work of thirty-six pages dealing with both plane and spherical triangles. Oughtred made free use of the abbreviations *s* for sine, *t* for tangent, *se* for secant, *sco* for sine of the complement (or cosine), *tco* for cotangent, and *seco* for cosecant. The work also contains tables of sines, tangents, and secants to seven decimal places as well as tables of logarithms, also to seven places.

It is said that Oughtred, a staunch royalist, died in a transport of joy on hearing the news of the restoration of Charles II.

BIBLIOGRAPHY

I. ORIGINAL WORKS. Oughtred's chief writing is *Arithmeticae in numeris et speciebus institutio . . . quasi clavis mathematicae est* (London, 1631); 2nd ed., *Clavis*

mathematicae (London, 1648). English translations were made by Robert Wood (1647) and Edmond Halley (1694). Subsequent Latin eds. appeared at Oxford in 1652, 1667, and 1693.

His other works are *The Circles of Proportion and the Horizontal Instrument*, W. Forster, trans. (London, 1632), a treatise on navigation; *The Description and Use of the Double Horizontal Dial* (London, 1636); *A Most Easy Way for the Delineation of Plain Sundials, Only by Geometry* (1647); *The Solution of All Spherical Triangles* (Oxford, 1651); *Description and Use of the General Horological Ring and the Double Horizontal Dial* (London, 1653); *Trigonometria* (London, 1657), trans. by R. Stokes as *Trigonometrie* (London, 1657); and *Canones sinuum, tangentium, secantium et logarithmorum* (London, 1657).

A collection of Oughtred's papers, mainly on mathematical subjects, was published posthumously under the direction of Charles Scarborough as *Opuscula mathematica hactenus inedita* (Oxford, 1677).

II. SECONDARY LITERATURE. On Oughtred or his work, see John Aubrey, *Brief Lives*, Andrew Clark, ed. (Oxford, 1898), II, 106, 113–114, 471. W. W. R. Ball, *A History of the Study of Mathematics at Cambridge* (Cambridge, 1889); Florian Cajori, *William Oughtred, a Great Seventeenth-Century Teacher of Mathematics* (Chicago–London, 1916); Moritz Cantor, *Vorlesungen über Geschichte der Mathematik*, 2nd ed., II (Leipzig, 1913), 720–721; Charles Hutton, *Philosophical and Mathematical Dictionary*, new ed. (London, 1815), II, 141–142; and S. J. Rigaud, ed., *Correspondence of Scientific Men of the Seventeenth Century*, I (Oxford, 1841), 11, 16, 66.

J. F. SCOTT

OZANAM, JACQUES (*b.* Bouligneux, Bresse, France, 1640; *d.* Paris, France, 3 April 1717 [?])

Ozanam came from a Jewish family that had converted to Catholicism. As the younger of two sons he was educated for the clergy, but chemistry and mechanics interested him more than theology. He was said to be generous, witty, and gallant; and probably he was too tolerant to have made a good churchman of his day. Except for a tutor who may have helped him slightly, Ozanam taught himself mathematics.

Four years after Ozanam had begun studying for the church, his father died; he then devoted himself to mastering mathematics, with considerable success. He taught mathematics at Lyons without charge until the state of his finances led him to charge a fee. A lucky circumstance took him to Paris, where his teaching brought him a substantial income. Being young and handsome, his gallantry as well as his penchant for gambling drained his resources; Ozanam sought a way out by marrying a modest, virtuous young woman without means. Although his financial problems remained unsolved, the marriage was happy and fruitful; there were twelve children, most of whom died young. After his marriage Ozanam's conduct was exemplary; always of a mild and cheerful disposition, he became sincerely pious and shunned disputes about theology. He was wont to say that it was the business of the Sorbonne doctors to discuss, of the pope to decide, and of a mathematician to go straight to heaven in a perpendicular line.

Following the death of his wife in 1701, misfortune quickly befell Ozanam. In the same year the War of the Spanish Succession broke out; and many of his students, being foreign, had to leave Paris. From then on, the income from his professional activities became small and uncertain. The last years of his life were melancholy, relieved only by the dubious satisfaction of being admitted as an *élève* of the Academy of Sciences. Ozanam never regained his customary health and spirits, and died of apoplexy, probably on 3 April 1717, although there is some reason to believe that it may have been between 1 April and 6 April 1718.

By almost any criterion Ozanam cannot be regarded as a first-rate mathematician, even of his own time. But he had a flair for writing and during his career wrote a number of books, some of which were very popular, passing through many editions. According to Montucla:

> He promoted mathematics by his treatise on lines of the second order; and had he pursued the same branch of research, he would have acquired a more solid reputation than by the publication of his *Course, Récréations,* or *Dictionnaire mathématique*; but having to look to the support of himself and family, he wisely consulted the taste of his purchasers rather than his own [*Histoire des mathématiques,* II, 168].

In short, his contributions consisted of popular treatises and reference works on "useful and practical mathematics," and an extremely popular work on mathematical recreations; the latter had by far the more lasting impact. Ozanam's *Récréations* may be regarded as the forerunner of modern books on mathematical recreations. He drew heavily on the works of Bachet de Méziriac, Mydorge, Leurechon, and Daniel Schwenter; his own contributions were somewhat less significant, for he was not a particularly creative mathematician. The work was later augmented and revised by Montucla and, still later, was translated into English by Hutton (1803).

Ozanam is not to be confounded with a contemporary geometer, Sébastien Leclerc (1637–1714), who upon occasion used the pseudonym Ozanam.

BIBLIOGRAPHY

I. ORIGINAL WORKS. Ozanam's writings include *Méthode pour tracer les cadrans* (Paris, 1673, 1685, 1730); *La géométrie pratique du sr Boulenger* (Paris, 1684, 1689, 1691, 1736, 1764); *Tables de sinus, tangentes et sécantes; et des logarithmes . . .* (Paris, 1685, 1697, 1720, 1741); *Traité de la construction des équations pour la solution des problèmes indéterminez* (Paris, 1687); *Traité des lieux géométriques, expliquez par une méthode courte et facile* (Paris, 1687); *Traité des lignes du premier genre, expliquées par une méthode nouvelle et facile* (Paris, 1687); *Usage du compas de proportion . . . augmenté d'un traité de la division des champs* (Paris, 1688, 1691, 1700, 1736, 1748, 1794); *Usage de l'instrument universel. . . .* (Paris, 1688, 1700, 1748); and *Méthode de lever les plans et les cartes de terre et de mer, avec toutes sortes d'instrumens, et sans instrumens. . . .* (Paris, 1693, 1700, 1750, 1781).

His major works are *Dictionnaire mathématique, ou, idée générale des mathématiques. . . .* (Amsterdam–Paris, 1691), translated and abridged by Joseph Raphson (London, 1702); *Cours de mathématique, qui comprend toutes les parties les plus utiles et les plus necessaires à un homme de guerre, & à tous ceux qui se veulent perfectionner dans les mathématiques,* 5 vols. (Paris, 1693), also 3 vols. in 1 (Amsterdam, 1697), translated as *Cursus mathematicus: Or a Compleat Course of the Mathematicks. . .,* 5 vols. (London, 1712); and *Récréations mathématiques et physiques . . .,* 4 vols. (Paris, 1694, 1696, 1698, 1720, 1725, 1735, 1778, 1790; Amsterdam, 1698), translated as *Recreations Mathematical and Physical . . .* (London, 1708); as *Recreations in Mathematics and Natural Philosophy . . . First Composed by M. Ozanam . . . Lately Recomposed by M. Montucla, and Now Translated into English . . . by Charles Hutton* (London, 1803, 1814), rev. by Edward Riddle (London, 1840, 1844); and as *Recreations for Gentlemen and Ladies, or, Ingenious Amusements . . .* (Dublin, 1756).

Among his other works are *Traité des fortifications . . .* (Paris, 1694), translated by J. T. Desaguliers as *Treatise of Fortification . . .* (Oxford, 1711, 1727); *Nouveaux élémens d'algèbre . . .,* 2 vols. (Amsterdam, 1702); *Géographie et cosmographie* (Paris, 1711); *La perspective, théorique et pratique* (Paris, 1711, 1720); *La méchanique . . . tirée du cours de mathématique de M. Ozanam* (Paris, 1720); *La gnomonique . . . tirée du cours de mathématique de M. Ozanam* (Paris, 1746); and *Traité de l'arpentage et du toisé, nouvelle édition, mise dans un nouvel ordre par M. Audierne* (Paris, 1779). Ozanam also published several articles in the *Journal des sçavans,* including a proof of the theorem that neither the sum nor the difference of two fourth powers can be a fourth power.

His translations or editions of works by others include a revised and enlarged ed. of Adriaan Vlacq, *La trigonométrie rectiligne et sphérique . . . avec tables* (Paris, 1720, 1741, 1765); and *Les élémens d'Euclide du R. P. Dechalles . . . et de M. Ozanam . . . démontrés d'une manière . . . par M. Audierne* (Paris, 1753).

II. SECONDARY LITERATURE. See Heinrich Zeitlinger,

ed., *Bibliotheca chemico-mathematica* (London, 1921), I, 171, and II, 643; Moritz Cantor, *Vorlesungen über die Geschichte der Mathematik*, 2nd ed. (Leipzig, 1913), II, 770, and III, 102–103, 270, 364; Fontenelle, "Éloge . . .," in *Oeuvres diverses*, III (The Hague, 1729), 260–265; Charles Hutton, *Philosophical and Mathematical Dictionary*, II (London, 1815), 144; J. E. Montucla, *Histoire des mathématiques*, II (Paris, 1799), 168; *The Penny Cyclopaedia of the Society for the Diffusion of Useful Knowledge*, XVII (London, 1840), 111–112; and Edward Riddle, *Dr. Hutton's Philosophical Recreations* (London, 1840), v–vii.

WILLIAM L. SCHAAF

PACIOLI, LUCA (*b.* Sansepolcro, Italy, *ca.* 1445; *d.* Sansepolcro, 1517)

Luca Pacioli (Lucas de Burgo), son of Bartolomeo Pacioli, belonged to a modest family of Sansepolcro, a small commercial town in the Tiber valley about forty miles north of Perugia. All we know of his early life is that he was brought up by the Befolci family of Sansepolcro. It has been suggested that he may have received part of his early education in the atelier of his older compatriot Piero della Francesca (1410–1492). As a young man he entered the service of Antonio Rompiansi, a Venetian merchant who lived in the fashionable Giudecca district. Pacioli lived in Rompiansi's house and helped to educate his three sons. While doing so he studied mathematics under Domenico Bragadino, who held classes in Venice, probably at the school that the republic had established near the Church of San Giovanni di Rialto for those who did not want to go to Padua. The experience Pacioli gained in Rompiansi's business and the knowledge he gathered at Bragadino's school prompted him to write his works on arithmetic, the first of which he dedicated to the Rompiansi brothers in 1470. Their father was dead by then and Pacioli's employment probably had ended. He then stayed for several months in Rome as the guest of the architect Leone Battista Alberti.

Sometime between 1470 and 1477 Pacioli was ordained as a friar in the Franciscan order in fulfillment of a vow. After completing his theological studies he began a life of peregrination, teaching mathematics in various cities of Italy. From 1477 to 1480 he gave lessons in arithmetic at the University of Perugia and wrote a treatise on arithmetic for the benefit of his students (1478). In 1481 he was in Zara (now Zadar, Yugoslavia), then under Venetian rule, where he wrote another work on arithmetic. After teaching mathematics successively at the universities of Perugia, Naples, and Rome in 1487–1489, Pacioli returned to Sansepolcro. In 1494 his major work, *Summa de arithmetica, geometria, proportioni et proportionalita*, was ready for the publisher and he went to Venice to supervise the printing. He dedicated the book to the young duke of Urbino, Guidobaldo da Montefeltro (1472–1508), who, it is believed, was his pupil. The dedicatory letter suggests that Pacioli had been closely associated with the court of Urbino. This is confirmed by the altarpiece painted by Piero della Francesca for the Church of San Bernardino in Urbino (now in Milan), in which the figure of St. Peter the Martyr is portrayed by Pacioli. The painting shows Duke Federigo (Guidobaldo's father) praying before the Virgin and Child surrounded by angels and saints. A painting by Jacopo de' Barbari in the Naples Museum shows Pacioli demonstrating a lesson in geometry to Guidobaldo.

In 1497 Pacioli was invited to the court of Ludovico Sforza, duke of Milan, to teach mathematics. Here he met Leonardo da Vinci, who was already in Sforza's employment. That Leonardo consulted Pacioli on matters relating to mathematics is evident from entries in Leonardo's notebooks. The first part of Pacioli's *Divina proportione* was composed at Milan during 1496–1497, and it was Leonardo who drew the figures of the solid bodies for it. Their stay in Milan ended in 1499 with the entry of the French army and the consequent capture of Sforza. Journeying through Mantua and Venice, they arrived in Florence, where they shared quarters. Leonardo's stay in Florence, which lasted until the middle of 1506, was interrupted by a short period in the service of Cesare Borgia.

In 1500 Pacioli was appointed to teach Euclid's *Elements* at the University of Pisa, which had been transferred to Florence because of the revolt of Pisa in 1494. The appointment was renewed annually until 1506. In 1504 he made a set of geometrical figures for the Signoria of Florence, for which he was paid 52.9 lire. He was elected superior of his order for the province of Romagna and shortly afterward (1505) was accepted as a member of the monastery of Santa Croce in Florence. During his stay in Florence, Pacioli also held an appointment at the University of Bologna as *lector ad mathematicam* (1501–1502). At this time the University of Bologna had several *lectores ad arithmeticam*, one of whom was Scipione dal Ferro, who was to become famous for solving the cubic equation. It has been suggested that Pacioli's presence in Bologna may have encouraged Scipione to seek a solution of the cubic equation, but there is no evidence to support this apart from Pacioli's statement in the *Summa* that the cubic equation could not be solved algebraically.

Since his arrival in Florence, Pacioli had been

preparing a Latin edition of Euclid's *Elements* and an Italian translation. He had also written a book on chess and had prepared a collection of recreational problems. On 11 August 1508 Pacioli was in Venice, where he read to a large gathering in the Church of San Bartolomeo in the Rialto an introduction to book V of Euclid's *Elements*. A few months later, on a supplication made by him to the doge of Venice, he was granted the privilege that no one but he could publish his works within the republic for fifteen years. The works listed were the fifteen books of Euclid, *Divina proportione*, "De viribus quantitatis," "De ludo scachorum," and *Summa de arithmetica*. The Latin edition of Euclid and the *Divina proportione* were published in 1509. Pacioli was called once more to lecture in Perugia in 1510 and in Rome in 1514.

On several occasions Pacioli came into conflict with the brethren of his order in Sansepolcro. In 1491, on a complaint made to the general of the order, he was prohibited from teaching the young men of the town; but this did not prevent his being called to preach the Lenten sermons there in 1493. It is likely that certain minor privileges granted to him by the Pope had aroused enmity or jealousy. Although a petition had been sent to the general of the order in 1509, he was shortly afterward elected commissioner of his convent in Sansepolcro. A few years later Pacioli renounced these privileges and in 1517, shortly before his death, his fellow townsmen petitioned that he be appointed minister of the order for the province of Assisi.

The commercial activity of Italy in the late Middle Ages had led to the composition of a large number of treatises on practical arithmetic to meet the needs of merchant apprentices. Evidence of this is found in the extant works of the *maestri d'abbaco* of central and northern Italy. Some of them even contained chapters devoted to the rules of algebra and their application, no doubt influenced by the *Liber abbaci* of Leonardo Fibonacci. The first printed commercial arithmetic was an anonymous work that appeared at Treviso in 1478. By the end of the sixteenth century about 200 such works had been published in Italy. Pacioli wrote three such treatises: one at Venice (1470), one at Perugia (1478), and one at Zara (1481). None of them was published and only the second has been preserved.

Pacioli's *Summa de arithmetica . . .* (1494) was more comprehensive. Unlike the practical arithmetics, it was not addressed to a particular section of the community. An encyclopedic work (600 pages of close print, in folio) written in Italian, it contains a general treatise on theoretical and practical arithmetic; the elements of algebra; a table of moneys, weights, and measures used in the various Italian states; a treatise on double-entry bookkeeping; and a summary of Euclid's

geometry. He admitted to having borrowed freely from Euclid, Boethius, Sacrobosco, Leonardo Fibonacci, Prosdocimo de' Beldamandi, and others.

Although it lacked originality, the *Summa* was widely circulated and studied by the mathematicians of the sixteenth century. Cardano, while devoting a chapter of his *Practica arithmetice* (1539) to correcting the errors in the *Summa,* acknowledged his debt to Pacioli. Tartaglia's *General trattato de' numeri et misure* (1556–1560) was styled on Pacioli's *Summa*. In the introduction to his *Algebra*, Bombelli says that Pacioli was the first mathematician after Leonardo Fibonacci to have thrown light on the science of algebra—"primo fu che luce diede a quella scientia."[1] This statement, however, does not mean that algebra had been neglected in Italy for 300 years. Another edition of Pacioli's *Summa* was published in 1523.

Pacioli's treatise on bookkeeping, "De computis et scripturis," contained in the *Summa*, was the first printed work setting out the "method of Venice," that is, double-entry bookkeeping. Brown has said, "The history of bookkeeping during the next century consists of little else than registering the progress of the *De computis* through the various countries of Europe."[2]

The *Divina proportione*, written in Italian and published in 1509, was dedicated to Piero Soderini, perpetual gonfalonier of Florence. It comprised three books: "Compendio de divina proportione," "Tractato de l'architectura," and "Libellus in tres partiales tractatus divisus quinque corporum regularium." The first book, completed at Milan in 1497, is dedicated to Ludovico Sforza. Its subject is the golden section or divine proportion, as Pacioli called it, the ratio obtained by dividing a line in extreme and mean ratio. It contains a summary of Euclid's propositions (including those in Campanus' version) relating to the golden section, a study of the properties of regular polyhedrons, and a description of semi-regular polyhedrons obtained by truncation or stellation of regular polyhedrons. Book 2 is a treatise on architecture, based on Vitruvius, dedicated to Pacioli's pupils at Sansepolcro. To this he added a treatise on the right proportions of roman lettering. The third book is an Italian translation, dedicated to Soderini, of Piero della Francesca's *De corporibus regularibus*.

Also in 1509 Pacioli published his Latin translation of Euclid's *Elements*. The first printed edition of Euclid (a Latin translation made in the thirteenth century by Campanus of Novara from an Arabic text) had appeared at Venice in 1482. It was severely criticized by Bartolomeo Zamberti in 1505 when he was publishing a Latin translation from the Greek. Pacioli's edition is based on Campanus but contains his own emendations and annotations. It was published in order to vindicate Campanus, apparently at the expense of Ratdolt, the publisher of Campanus' translation.

Among the works that Pacioli had intended to publish is "De viribus quantitatis," a copy of which, in the hand of an amanuensis, is in the University Library of Bologna.[3] The name of the person to whom the work was dedicated has been left blank. It is an extensive work (309 folios) divided into three parts: the first is a collection of eighty-one mathematical recreational problems, a collection larger than those published a century later by Bachet de Méziriac and others; the second is a collection of geometrical problems and games; the third is a collection of proverbs and verses. No originality attaches to this work, for the problems are found scattered among earlier arithmetics and, in fact, a collection is attributed to Alcuin of York. Pacioli himself called the work a compendium. Some of the problems are found in the notebooks of Leonardo da Vinci, and the work itself contains frequent allusions to him.

Pacioli's Italian translation of Euclid's *Elements* and his work on chess, "De ludo scachorum," dedicated to the marquis of Mantua, Francesco Gonzaga, and his wife, Isabella d'Este, were not published and there is no trace of the manuscripts.

Vasari, in writing the biography of Piero della Francesca, accused Pacioli of having plagiarized the work of his compatriot on perspective, arithmetic, and geometry.[4] The accusations relate to three works by Piero—*De prospectiva pingendi*, "Libellus de quinque corporibus regularibus," and *Trattato d'abaco*, all of which have been published only since the turn of the twentieth century.[5] In 1908 Pittarelli came to the defense of Pacioli, pointing out that any accusation of plagiarism in regard to *De prospectiva* was unjust, since Pacioli had acknowledged Piero's work in both the *Summa* and the *Divina proportione*.[6] As for the *Libellus*, it has been established by Mancini that Pacioli's work is a translation of it that lacks the clarity of the original.[7] In the case of the *Trattato*, although Piero can claim no originality for it, it has been possible to find in it at least 105 problems of the *Summa*.[8]

The writings of Pacioli have provided historians of the Renaissance with important source material for the study of Leonardo da Vinci. The numerous editions and translations of the *De computis et scripturis* are evidence of the worldwide esteem in which Pacioli is held by the accounting profession. Pacioli made no original contribution to mathematics; but his *Summa*, written in the vulgar tongue, provided his countrymen, especially those not schooled in Latin,

with an encyclopedia of the existing knowledge of the subject and enabled them to contribute to the advancement of algebra in the sixteenth century.

NOTES

1. Rafael Bombelli, *Algebra* (Bologna, 1572), d 2v.
2. Brown, *History of Accounting*, p. 119.
3. An ed. of the MS by Paul Lawrence Rose of New York University is in press.
4. Vasari, *Vite*, pp. 360, 361, 365.
5. Codex Palat. Parma, published by C. Winterberg (1899); Codex Vat. Urb. lat. 632, published in 1915 by Mancini; Codex Ash. 280, published in 1971 by Arrighi.
6. Pittarelli, "Luca Pacioli . . . ."
7. Mancini, "L'opera 'De corporibus regularibus' . . . ."
8. Jayawardene, "The *Trattato d'abaco* of Piero della Francesca."

BIBLIOGRAPHY

I. ORIGINAL WORKS. Pacioli's writings include *Summa de arithmetica, geometria, proportioni et proportionalita* (Venice, 1494; 2nd ed. Toscolano, 1523)—there are several eds. of the treatise on bookkeeping, "De computis et scripturis," contained in the *Summa*, fols. 197v–210v, in the original Italian and in trans.; *Divina proportione* (Venice, 1509)—there are two extant MSS containing the "Compendio de divina proportione," one in the University of Geneva Library (Codex 250) and the other in the Biblioteca Ambrosiana, Milan (Codex 170, parte superiore), the second published as no. XXXI of Fontes Ambrosiani, Giuseppina Masotti Biggiogero, ed. (Verona, 1956); *Euclid megarensis opera . . . a Campano . . . tralata. Lucas Paciolus emendavit* (Venice, 1509); "De viribus quantitatis" (University of Bologna Library, Codex 250), described by Amedeo Agostini in "Il 'De viribus quantitatis' di Luca Pacioli," in *Periodico di matematiche*, **4** (1924), 165–192, and by Carlo Pedretti in "Nuovi documenti riguardanti Leonardo da Vinci," in *Sapere* (15 Apr. 1952), 65–70.

An unpublished arithmetic, written in Perugia (1478), is in the Vatican Library (Codex Vat. lat. 3129).

II. SECONDARY LITERATURE. Studies of Pacioli's life and work are listed by G. Masotti Biggiogero in "Luca Pacioli e la sua 'Divina proportione,'" in *Rendiconti dell'Istituto lombardo di scienze e lettere*, ser. A, **94** (1960), 3–30.

The earliest biographical sketch, written by Bernardino Baldi in 1589, was not published. Baldassare Boncompagni made a critical study of it with the help of archival documents: "Intorno alle vite inedite di tre matematici . . . scritte da Bernadino Baldi," in *Bullettino di bibliografia e di storia delle scienze mathematiche e fisiche*, **12** (1879), 352–438, 863–872. Other archival documents were published by D. Ivano Ricci in *Luca Pacioli, l'uomo e lo scienziato* (Sansepolcro, 1940). R. E. Taylor, *No Royal Road: Luca Pacioli and His Times* (Chapel Hill, N. C., 1942), is a lively narrative but unreliable as a biography.

Pacioli's work is discussed by L. Olschki in *Geschichte der neusprachlichen wissenschaftlichen Literatur*, I (Leipzig, 1919), 151–239.

Stanley Morison, *Fra Luca Pacioli of Borgo San Sepolcro* (New York, 1933), contains a study of that part of the *Divina proportione* dealing with roman lettering. The history of bookkeeping is discussed by Richard Brown in *A History of Accounting and Accountants* (London, 1905), 108–131.

On the accusations of plagiarism see Giorgio Vasari's life of Piero della Francesca in *Le vite de' più eccellenti architetti, pittori e scultori italiani* (Florence, 1550); G. Pittarelli, "Luca Pacioli usurpò per se stesso qualche libro di Piero de' Franceschi," in *Atti, IV Congresso internazionale dei matematici, Roma, 6–11 aprile 1908*, III (Rome, 1909), 436–440; G. Mancini, "L'opera 'De corporibus regularibus' di Pietro Franceschi detto Della Francesca usurpata da fra Luca Pacioli," in *Memorie della R. Accademia dei Lincei*, classe di scienze morali, storiche e filologiche, ser. 5, **14** (1915), 446–477, 488–580; and Gino Arrighi's ed. of Piero della Francesca's *Trattato d'abaco* (Pisa, 1971), 24–34. See also S. A. Jayawardene, "The *Trattato d'abaco*" of Piero della Francesca," in *Studies in the Italian Renaissance: A Collection in Honour of P. O. Kristeller* (in press).

S. A. JAYAWARDENE

PADOA, ALESSANDRO (*b.* Venice, Italy, 14 October 1868; *d.* Genoa, Italy, 25 November 1937)

Padoa attended a secondary school in Venice, the engineering school in Padua, and the University in Turin, from which he received a degree in mathematics in 1895. He taught in secondary schools at Pinerolo, Rome, and Cagliari, and (from 1909) at the Technical Institute in Genoa.

Padoa was the first to devise a method for proving that a primitive term of a theory cannot be defined within the system by the remaining primitive terms. This method was presented in his lectures at Rome early in 1900 and was made public at the International Congress of Philosophy held at Paris later that year. He defined a system of undefined symbols as irreducible with respect to the system of unproved propositions when no symbolic definition of any undefined symbol can be deduced from the system of unproved propositions. He also said:

> To prove that the system of undefined symbols is irreducible with respect to the system of unproved propositions, it is necessary and sufficient to find, for each undefined symbol, an interpretation of the system of undefined symbols that verifies the system of unproved propositions and that continues to do so if we

suitably change the meaning of only the symbol considered ["Essai . . .," p. 322].

Although it took the development of model theory to bring out the importance of this method in the theory of definition, Padoa was already convinced of its significance. (A proof of Padoa's method was given by Alfred Tarski in 1926 and, independently, by J. C. C. McKinsey in 1935.)

In lectures at the universities of Brussels, Pavia, Bern, Padua, Cagliari, and Geneva, Padoa was an effective popularizer of the mathematical logic developed by Giuseppe Peano's "school," of which Padoa was a prominent member. He was also active in the organization of secondary school teachers of mathematics and participated in many congresses of philosophy and mathematics. In 1934 he was awarded the ministerial prize in mathematics by the Accademia dei Lincei.

BIBLIOGRAPHY

I. ORIGINAL WORKS. A list of 34 of Padoa's publications in logic and related areas of mathematics (about half of all his scientific publications) is in Antonio Giannattasio, "Due inediti di Alessandro Padoa," in *Physis* (Florence), **10** (1968), 309–336. To this may be added three papers presented to the Congrès International de Philosophie Scientifique at Paris in 1935 and published in *Actualités scientifiques et industrielles* (1936): "Classes et pseudo-classes," no. 390, 26–28; "Les extensions successives de l'ensemble des nombres au point de vue déductif," no. 394, 52–59; and "Ce que la logique doit à Peano," no. 395, 31–37.

Padoa's method was stated in "Essai d'une théorie algébrique des nombres entiers, précédé d'une introduction logique à une théorie déductive quelconque," in *Bibliothèque du Congrès international de philosophie, Paris, 1900*, III (Paris, 1901), 309–365. An English trans. (with references to Padoa's method) is in Jean van Heijenoort, ed., *From Frege to Gödel: A Source Book in Mathematical Logic 1879–1931* (Cambridge, Mass., 1967), 118–123. Padoa's major work is "La logique déductive dans sa dernière phase de développement," in *Revue de métaphysique et de morale*, **19** (1911), 828–832; **20** (1912), 48–67, 207–231, also published separately, with a preface by G. Peano (Paris, 1912).

II. SECONDARY LITERATURE. There is no biography of Padoa. Some information on his life and work may be found in the obituaries in *Bollettino dell'Unione matematica italiana*, **16** (1937), 248; and *Revue de métaphysique et de morale*, **45** (1938), Apr. supp., 32; and in F. G. Tricomi, "Matematici italiani del primo secolo dello stato unitario," in *Memorie della Accademia delle scienze di Torino*, 4th ser., no. 1 (1962), 81.

HUBERT C. KENNEDY

PAINLEVÉ, PAUL (*b*. Paris, France, 5 December 1863; *d*. Paris, France, 29 October 1933)

Painlevé's father, Léon Painlevé, and grandfather, Jean-Baptiste Painlevé, were lithographers. Through his grandmother, Euphrosine Marchand, he was a descendant of Napoleon I's valet. As gifted in literature as in the sciences, Painlevé received excellent marks in secondary school.

After hesitating between a career as a politician, engineer, and researcher Painlevé chose the last, which had been offered him by the École Normale Supérieure. Admitted in 1883, he received his *agrégation* in mathematics in 1886. He worked for a time at Göttingen, where Schwarz and Klein were teaching, and at the same time completed his doctoral dissertation (1887). Painlevé became professor at Lille in 1887. In 1892 he moved to Paris, where he taught at the Faculty of Sciences and the École Polytechnique, the Collège de France (1896), and the École Normale Supérieure (1897).

Painlevé received the Grand Prix des Sciences Mathématiques (1890), the Prix Bordin (1894), and the Prix Poncelet (1896); and was elected a member of the geometry section of the Académie des Sciences in 1900. In 1901 he married Marguerite Petit de Villeneuve, niece of the painter Georges Clairin; she died at the birth of their son Jean (1902), who became one of the creators of scientific cinematography.

Painlevé was interested in the infant field of aviation, and as the passenger with Wilbur Wright and Henri Farman he even shared for a time the record for duration of biplane flights (1908). He was a professor at the École Supérieure d'Aéronautique (1909) and president of several commissions on aerial navigation.

In 1910 Painlevé turned to politics. Elected a deputy from the fifth arrondissement of Paris, the "Quartier Latin," he headed naval and aeronautical commissions established to prepare for the country's defense. In 1914 he created the Service des Inventions pour les Besoins de la Défense Nationale, which became a ministry in 1915. Minister of war in 1917, Painlevé played an important role in the conduct of military operations: he supported the efforts of the Army of the Near East in the hope of detaching Austria-Hungary from the German alliance. He conducted the negotiations with Woodrow Wilson over the sending of American combat troops to France. He also had Foch appointed as head of the allied chiefs of staff.

In 1920 Painlevé was commissioned by the Chinese government to reorganize the country's railroads. From 1925 to 1933 he was several times minister of war and of aviation, president of the Council of Ministers, and an active participant in the League of Nations and in its International Institute of Intellectual Cooperation.

As a mathematician Painlevé always considered questions in their greatest generality. After his first works concerning rational transformations of algebraic curves and surfaces, in which he introduced biuniform transformations, he was remarkably successful in the study of singular points of algebraic differential equations. His goal was to obtain general propositions on the nature of the integral considered as a function of the variable and of the constants, particularly through distinguishing the "perfect integrals," definable throughout their domain of existence by a unique development.

In old problems in which the difficulties seemed insurmountable, Painlevé defined new transcendentals for singular points of differential equations of a higher order than the first. In particular he determined every equation of the second order and first degree whose critical points are fixed. This work was presented in notes published in the *Comptes rendus . . . de l'Académie des sciences* beginning in 1887.

The results of these studies are applicable to the equations of analytical mechanics which admit rational or algebraic first integrals with respect to the velocities. Proving, in the words of Hadamard's *éloge*, that "continuing [the work of] Henri Poincaré was not beyond human capacity," Painlevé extended the known results concerning the *n*-body problem. He also corrected certain accepted results in problems of friction and of the conditions of certain equilibriums when the force function does not pass through a maximum.

BIBLIOGRAPHY

I. ORIGINAL WORKS. Painlevé's mathematical writings are "Sur les lignes singulières des fonctions analytiques," in *Annales de la Faculté des sciences de Toulouse* (1888), his doctoral dissertation; "Sur la transformation des fonctions harmoniques et les systèmes triples de surfaces orthogonales," in *Travaux et mémoires de la Faculté des sciences de Lille*, **1** (Aug. 1889), 1–29; "Sur les équations différentielles du premier ordre," in *Annales scientifiques de l'École normale supérieure*, 3rd ser., **8** (Jan.–Mar. 1891), 9–58, 103–140; (Aug.–Sept. 1891), 201–226, 267–284; **9** (Jan. 1892), 9–30; (Apr.–June 1892), 101–144, 283–308; "Mémoire sur la transformation des équations de la dynamique," in *Journal de mathématiques pures et appliquées*, 4th ser., **10** (Jan. 1894), 5–92; "Sur les mouvements et les trajectoires réels des systèmes," in *Bulletin de la*

Société mathématique de France, **22** (Oct. 1894), 136–184; *Leçons sur l'intégration des équations de la dynamique et applications* (Paris, 1894); *Leçons sur le frottement* (Paris, 1895); *Leçons sur l'intégration des équations différentielles de la mécanique et applications* (Paris, 1895); *Leçons sur la théorie analytique des équations différentielles professées à Stockholm* . . . (Paris, 1897); "Sur les équations différentielles dont l'intégrale générale est uniforme," in *Bulletin de la Société mathématique de France*, **28** (June 1900), 201–261; "Sur les équations différentielles du second ordre et d'ordre supérieur dont l'intégrale générale est uniforme," in *Acta mathematica*, **25** (Sept. 1900), 1–80; and contributions to Émile Borel, *Sur les fonctions de variables réelles et les développements en série de polynomes* (Paris, 1905), 101–147; and Pierre Boutroux, *Leçons sur les fonctions définies par les équations différentielles du premier ordre* (Paris, 1908), 141–187.

Painlevé's other works include *L'aviation* (Paris, 1910; 2nd ed., 1911), written with Émile Borel; *Cours de mécanique de l'École polytechnique*, 2 vols. (Paris, 1920–1921); *Les axiomes de la mécanique. Examen critique et note sur la propagation de la lumière* (Paris, 1922); *Cours de mécanique* (Paris, 1929), written with Charles Platrier; *Leçons sur la résistance des fluides non visqueux*, 2 vols. (Paris, 1930–1931); and *Paroles et écrits* (Paris, 1936).

II. SECONDARY LITERATURE. See the collection made by the Société des Amis de Paul Painlevé, *Paroles et écrits de Paul Painlevé* (Paris, 1936), with prefaces by Paul Langevin and Jean Perrin; and Jean Painlevé, *Textes inédites et analyse des travaux scientifiques jusqu'en 1900*.

LUCIENNE FÉLIX

PAPPUS OF ALEXANDRIA (*b.* Alexandria, *fl.* A.D. 300–350)

In the silver age of Greek mathematics Pappus stands out as an accomplished and versatile geometer. His treatise known as the *Synagoge* or *Collection* is a chief, and sometimes the only, source for our knowledge of his predecessors' achievements.

The *Collection* is in eight books, perhaps originally in twelve, of which the first and part of the second are missing. That Pappus was an Alexandrian is affirmed by the titles of his surviving books and also by an entry in the *Suda Lexicon*.[1] The dedication of the seventh and eighth books to his son Hermodorus[2] provides the sole detail known of his family life. Only one of Pappus' other works has survived in Greek, and that in fragmentary form—his commentary on Ptolemy's *Syntaxis* (the *Almagest*). A commentary on book X of Euclid's *Elements*, which exists in Arabic, is generally thought to be a translation of the commentary that Pappus is known to have written, but some doubts may be allowed. A geographical work, *Description of the World*, has survived in an early Armenian translation.

The dates of Pappus are approximately fixed by his reference in the commentary on Ptolemy to an eclipse of the sun that took place on the seventeenth day of the Egyptian month Tybi in the year 1068 of the era of Nabonasar. This is 18 October 320 in the Christian era, and Pappus writes as though it were an eclipse that he had recently seen.[3] The *Suda Lexicon*, which is followed by Eudocia, would make Pappus a contemporary of Theon of Alexandria and place both in the reign of Theodosius I (A.D. 379–395), but the compiler was clearly not well informed. The entry runs: "Pappus, of Alexandria, philosopher, lived about the time of the Emperor Theodosius the Elder, when Theon the Philosopher, who wrote on the *Canon* of Ptolemy, also flourished. His books are: *Description of the World, Commentary on the Four Books of Ptolemy's Great Syntaxis, Rivers of Libya, Interpretation of Dreams*." The omission of Pappus' chief work and the apparent confusion of the *Syntaxis* with the *Tetrabiblos* of Ptolemy[4] does not inspire confidence. The argument that two scholars could not have written in the same city, on the same subject, at the same time, without referring to each other may not be convincing, for that is precisely what scholars are liable, deliberately or inadvertently, to do. But detailed examination shows that when Theon wrote his commentary on the *Syntaxis* he must have had Pappus' commentary before him.[5] A scholium to a Leiden manuscript of chronological tables, written by Theon, would place Pappus at the turn of the third century, for opposite the name Diocletian (A.D. 284–305) it notes: "In his time Pappus wrote."[6] This statement cannot be reconciled with the eclipse of A.D. 320, but it is more than likely that Pappus' early life was spent under Diocletian, for he would certainly have been older than fifteen when he wrote his commentary on the *Syntaxis*.

The several books of the *Collection* may well have been written as separate treatises at different dates and later brought together, as the name suggests. It is certain that the *Collection*, as it has come down to us, is posterior to the *Commentary on the Syntaxis*, for in book VIII Pappus notes that the rectangle contained by the perimeter of a circle and its radius is double the area of the circle, "as Archimedes showed, and as is proved by us in the commentary on the first book of the *Mathematics* [*sc.*, the *Syntaxis mathematica* of Ptolemy] by a theorem of our own."[7] A. Rome concludes that the *Collection* was put together about A.D. 340, but K. Ziegler states that a long interval is not necessary, and that the *Collection* may have been compiled soon after A.D. 320.[8] It has come down to us from a single twelfth-century manuscript, Codex Vaticanus Graecus 218, from which all the other manuscripts are derived.[9]

T. L. Heath judiciously observes that the *Collection*, while covering practically the whole field of Greek geometry, is a handbook rather than an encyclopedia; and that it was intended to be read with the original works, where extant, rather than take their place. But where the history of a particular topic is given, Pappus reproduces the various solutions, probably because of the difficulty of studying them in many different sources. Even when a text is readily available, he often gives alternative proofs and makes improvements or extensions.[10] The portion of book II that survives, beginning with proposition 14, expounds Apollonius' system of large numbers expressed as powers of 10,000. It is probable that book I was also arithmetical.

Book III is in four parts. The first part deals with the problem of finding two mean proportionals between two given straight lines, the second develops the theory of means, the third sets out some "paradoxes" of an otherwise unknown Erycinus, and the fourth treats of the inscription of the five regular solids in a sphere, but in a manner quite different from that of Euclid in his *Elements*, XIII.13–17.

Book IV is in five sections. The first section is a series of unrelated propositions, of which the opening one is a generalization of Pythagoras' theorem even wider than that found in Euclid VI.31. In the triangle

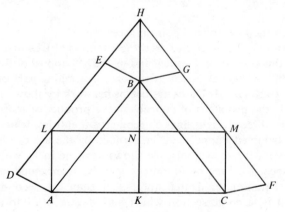

FIGURE 1

ABC let any parallelograms *ABED*, *BCFG* be drawn on *AB*, *AC* and let *DE*, *FG* meet in *H*. Join *HB* and produce it to meet *AC* in *K*. The sum of the parallelograms *ABED*, *BCFG* can then be shown to be equal to the parallelogram contained by *AC*, *HB* in an angle equal to the sum of the angles *BAC*, *DHB*. (It is, in fact, equal to the sum of *ALNK*, *CMNK*; that is, to the figure *ALMC*, which is easily shown to be a parallelogram having the angle *LAC* equal to the sum of the angles *BAC*, *DHB*.)

The second section deals with circles inscribed in the figure known as the ἄρβηλος or "shoemaker's

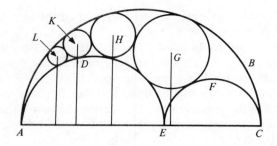

FIGURE 2

knife." It is formed when the diameter *AC* of a semicircle *ABC* is divided in any way at *E* and semicircles *ADE*, *EFC* are erected. The space between these two semicircles and the semicircle *ABC* is the ἄρβηλος. In a series of elegant theorems Pappus shows that if a circle with center *G* is drawn so as to touch all three semicircles, and then a circle with center *H* to touch this circle and the semicircles *ABC*, *ADE*, and so on *ad infinitum*, then the perpendicular from *G* to *AC* is equal to the diameter of the circle with center *G*, the perpendicular from *H* to *AC* is double the diameter of the circle with center *H*, the perpendicular from *K* to *AC* is triple the diameter of the circle with center *K*, and so on indefinitely. Pappus records this as "an ancient proposition" and proceeds to give variants. This section covers as particular cases propositions in the *Book of Lemmas* that Arabian tradition attributes to Archimedes.

In the third section Pappus turns to the squaring of the circle. He professes to give the solutions of Archimedes (by means of a spiral) and of Nicomedes (by means of the conchoid), and the solution by means of the quadratrix, but his proof is different from that of Archimedes. To the traditional method of generating the quadratrix (see the articles on Dinostratus and Hippias of Elis), Pappus adds two further methods "by means of surface loci," that is, curves drawn on surfaces. As a digression he examines the properties of a spiral described on a sphere.

The fourth section is devoted to another famous problem in Greek mathematics, the trisection of an angle. Pappus' first solution is by means of a νεῦσις or verging—the construction of a line that has to pass through a certain point—which involves the use of a hyperbola. He next proceeds to solve the problem directly, by means of a hyperbola, in two ways; on one occasion he uses the diameter-and-ordinate property (as in Apollonius), and on another he uses the focus-directrix property. This property is proved in book VII. Pappus then reproduces the solutions by means of the quadratrix and the spiral of Archimedes; he also gives the solution of a νεῦσις, which he believes

Archimedes to have unnecessarily assumed in *On Spirals*, proposition 8.

In the preface to book V, which deals with isoperimetry, Pappus praises the sagacity of bees who make the cells of the honeycomb hexagonal because of all the figures which can be fitted together the hexagon contains the greatest area. The literary quality of this preface has been warmly praised. Within the limits of his subject, Pappus looks back to the great Attic writers from a world in which Greek had degenerated into Hellenistic. In the first part of the book Pappus appears to be reproducing Zenodorus fairly closely; in the second part he compares the volumes of solids that have equal surfaces. He gives an account of thirteen semiregular solids, discovered and discussed by Archimedes (but not in any surviving works of that mathematician) that are contained by polygons all equilateral and equiangular but not all similar. He then shows, following Zenodorus, that the sphere is greater in volume than any of the regular solids that have surfaces equal to that of the sphere. He also proves, independently, that, of the regular solids with equal surfaces, that solid is greater which has the more faces.

Book VI is astronomical and deals with the books in the so-called *Little Astronomy*—the smaller treatises regarded as an introduction to Ptolemy's *Syntaxis*. In magistral manner he reviews the works of Theodosius, Autolycus, Aristarchus, and Euclid, and he corrects common misrepresentations. In the section on Euclid's *Optics*, Pappus examines the apparent form of a circle when seen from a point outside the plane in which it lies.

Book VII is the most fascinating in the whole *Collection*, not merely by its intrinsic interest and by what it preserves of earlier writers, but by its influence on modern mathematics. It gives an account of the following books in the so-called *Treasury of Analysis* (those marked by an asterisk are lost works): Euclid's *Data* and *Porisms*,* Apollonius' *Cutting Off of a Ratio*, *Cutting Off of an Area*,* *Determinate Section*,* *Tangencies*,* *Inclinations*,* *Plane Loci*,* and *Conics*. In his account of Apollonius' *Conics*, Pappus makes a reference to the "locus with respect to three or four lines" (a conic section); this statement is quoted in the article on Euclid (IV, 427 *ad fin.*). He also adds a remarkable comment of his own. If, he says, there are more than four straight lines given in position, and from a point straight lines are drawn to meet them at given angles, the point will lie on a curve that cannot yet be identified. If there are five lines, and the parallelepiped formed by the product of three of the lines drawn from the point at fixed angles bears a constant ratio to the parallelepiped formed by the product of the

other two lines drawn from the point and a given length, the point will be on a certain curve given in position. If there are six lines, and the solid figure contained by three of the lines bears a constant ratio to the solid figure formed by the other three, then the point will again lie on a curve given in position. If there are more than six lines it is not possible to conceive of solids formed by the product of more than three lines, but Pappus surmounts the difficulty by means of compounded ratios. If from any point straight lines are drawn so as to meet at a given angle any number of straight lines given in position, and the ratio of one of those lines to another is compounded with the ratio of a third to a fourth, and so on (or the ratio of the last to a given length if the number of lines is odd) and the compounded ratio is a constant, then the locus of the point will be one of the higher curves. Pappus had, of course, no symbolism at his disposition, nor did he even use a figure, but his meaning can be made clearer by saying that if $p_1, p_2, \ldots, p_n$ are the lengths of the lines drawn at fixed angles to the lines given in position, and if (*a* having a given length and *k* being a constant)

$$\frac{p_1}{p_2} \cdot \frac{p_3}{p_4} \ldots \frac{p_{n-1}}{p_n} = k \text{ when } n \text{ is even, or}$$

$$\frac{p_1}{p_2} \cdot \frac{p_3}{p_4} \ldots \frac{p_n}{a} = k \text{ when } n \text{ is odd,}$$

then the locus of the point is a certain curve.

In 1631 Jacob Golius drew the attention of Descartes to this passage in Pappus, and in 1637 "Pappus' problem," as Descartes called it, formed a major part of his *Géométrie*.[11] Descartes begins his work by showing how the problems of conceiving the product of more than three straight lines as geometrical entities, which so troubled Pappus, can be avoided by the use of his new algebraic symbols. He shows how the locus with respect to three or four lines may be represented as an equation of degree not higher than the second, that is, a conic section which may degenerate into a circle or straight line. Where there are five, six, seven, or eight lines, the required points lie on the next highest curve of degree after the conic sections, that is, a cubic; if there are nine, ten, eleven, or twelve lines on a curve, one degree still higher, that is, a quartic, and so on to infinity. Pappus' problem thus inspired the new method of analytical geometry that has proved such a powerful tool in subsequent centuries. (See the article on Descartes, IV, 57.)

In his *Principia* (1687) Newton also found inspiration in Pappus; he proved in a purely geometrical manner that the locus with respect to four lines is a conic section, which may degenerate into a circle. It is impossible to avoid seeing in Newton's conclusion to lemma XIX, cor. ii, a criticism of Descartes: "Atque ita Problematis veterum de quatuor lineis ab *Euclide* incaepti et ab *Apollonio* continuati non calculus, sed compositio Geometrica, qualem Veteres quaerebant, in hoc Corollario exhibetur."[12] But in this instance it was Descartes, and not Newton, who had the forward vision. Pappus observes that the study of these curves had not attracted men comparable to the geometers of previous ages. But there were still great discoveries to be made, and in order that he might not appear to have left the subject untouched, Pappus would himself make a contribution. It turns out to be nothing less than an anticipation of what is commonly called "Guldin's theorem."[13] Only the enunciations, however, were given, which state

> Figures generated by complete revolutions of a plane figure about an axis are in a ratio compounded (*a*) of the ratio [of the areas] of the figures, and (*b*) of the ratio of the straight lines similarly drawn to [*sc.* drawn to meet at the same angles] the axes of rotation from the respective centers of gravity. Figures generated by incomplete revolutions are in a ratio compounded (*a*) of the ratio [of the areas] of the figures and (*b*) of the ratio of the arcs described by the respective centers of gravity; it is clear that the ratio of the arcs is itself compounded (1) of the ratio of the straight lines similarly drawn [from the respective centers of gravity to the axis of rotation] and (2) of the ratio of the angles contained about the axes of rotation by the extremities of these straight lines.

Pappus concludes this section by noting that these propositions, which are virtually one, cover many theorems of all kinds about curves, surfaces, and solids, "in particular, those proved in the twelfth book of these elements." This implies that the *Collection* originally ran to at least twelve books.

Pappus proceeds to give a series of lemmas to each of the books he has described, except Euclid's *Data*, presumably with a view to helping students to understand them. (He was half a millennium from Apollonius and elucidation was probably necessary.) It is mainly from these lemmas that we can form any knowledge of the contents of the missing works, and they have enabled mathematicians to attempt reconstructions of Euclid's *Porisms* and Apollonius' *Cutting Off of an Area, Plane Loci, Determinate Section, Tangencies,* and *Inclinations*. It is from Pappus' lemmas that we can form some idea of the eighth book of Apollonius' *Conics.*

The lemmas to the *Cutting Off of a Ratio* and the *Cutting Off of an Area* are elementary, but those to the *Determinate Section* show that this work amounted to a theory of involution. The most interesting lemmas

concern the values of the ratio $AP \cdot PD : BP \cdot PC$, where (A, D), (B, C) are point-pairs on a straight line and P is another point on the straight line. Pappus investigates the "singular and least" values of the ratio and shows what it is for three different positions of P.

The lemmas to the *Inclinations* do not call for comment. The lemmas to the second book of the *Tangencies* are all concerned with the problem of drawing a circle so as to touch three given circles, a problem that Viète and Newton did not consider it beneath their dignity to solve.[14] The most interesting of Pappus' lemmas states: Given a circle and three points in a straight line external to it, inscribe in the circle a triangle, the sides of which shall pass through the three points.

The lemmas to the *Plane Loci* are chiefly propositions in algebraic geometry, one of which is equivalent to the theorem discovered by R. Simson, but generally known as Stewart's theorem:[15] If A, B, C, D are any four points on a straight line, then

$$AD^2 \cdot BC + BD^2 \cdot CA + CD^2 \cdot AB + BC \cdot CA \cdot AB = 0.$$

The remarkable proposition that Pappus gives in his description of Euclid's *Porisms* about any system of straight lines cutting each other two by two has already been set out in modern notation in the article on Euclid (IV, 426–427). The thirty-eight lemmas that he himself provides to facilitate an understanding of the *Porisms* strike an equally modern note. Lemma 3, proposition 129 shows that Pappus had a clear understanding of what Chasles called the anharmonic ratio and is now generally called the cross-ratio of four points. It proves the equality of the cross-ratios that

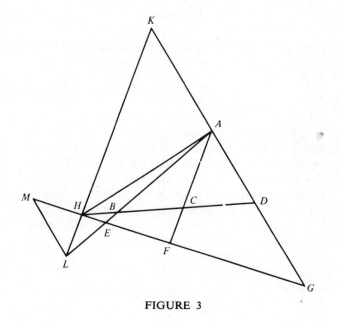

FIGURE 3

are made by any two transversals on a pencil of four lines issuing from the same point. The transversals are, in fact, drawn from the same point on one of the straight lines—in Figure 3 they are *HBCD* and *HEFG*, cutting the lines *AH, AL, AF,* and *AG*—but it is a simple matter to extend the proof, and Pappus proves that

$$\frac{HE \cdot GF}{HG \cdot FE} = \frac{HB \cdot DC}{HD \cdot BC},$$

that is to say, the cross-ratio is thus invariant under projection.

Lemma 4, proposition 130 shows, even more convincingly than the lemmas to the *Determinate Section,* that Pappus had an equally clear grasp of involution. In Figure 4, *GHKL* is a quadrilateral and *ABCDEF* is

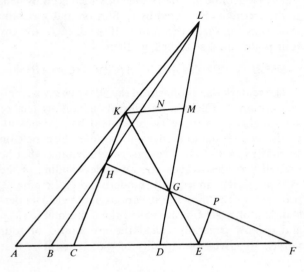

FIGURE 4

any transversal cutting pairs of opposite sides and the diagonals in (*A,F*), (*C,D*), (*B,E*). Pappus shows that

$$\frac{AF \cdot BC}{AB \cdot CF} = \frac{AF \cdot DE}{AD \cdot EF}.$$

(Strictly, what Pappus does is to show that if, in the figure, which he does not set out in detail, this relationship holds, then *F, G, H* lie on a straight line, but this is equivalent to what has been said above.) This equation is one of the ways of expressing the relationship between three pairs of conjugate points in involution. That Pappus gives these propositions as lemmas to Euclid's *Porisms* implies that they must have been assumed by Euclid. The geometers living just before Euclid must therefore have had an understanding of cross-ratios and involution, although these properties were not named for 2,250 years.

Lemma 13, proposition 139 has won its way into text books of modern geometry as "The Theorem of Pappus."[16] It establishes that if, from a point *C,* two transversals *CE, CD* cut the straight lines *AN, AF, AD* (see Figure 5) so that *A, E, B* and *C, F, D* are two sets of collinear points, then the points *G, M, K* are collinear. *GMK* is called the "Pappus line" of the two sets of collinear points.

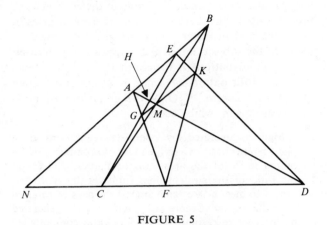

FIGURE 5

In the second of the two lemmas that Pappus gives to the *Surface Loci,* he enunciates and proves the focus-directrix property of a conic, which, as we have seen, he had already once employed. There is only one other place in any surviving Greek text in which this property is used—the fragment of Anthemius' *On Remarkable Mechanical Devices.* G. L. Toomer, however, has recently discovered this property in an Arabic translation of Diocles' treatise *On Burning Mirrors* in Mashhad (Shrine Library, MS 392/5593) and Dublin (Chester Beatty Library, Arabic MS 5255). But Pappus' passage remains the only place in ancient writing in which the property is proved.

Book VIII is devoted mainly to mechanics, but it incidentally gives some propositions of geometrical interest. In a historical preface Pappus justifies the claim that mechanics is a truly mathematical subject as opposed to one of merely utilitarian value. He begins by defining "center of gravity"—the only place in Greek mathematics where it is so defined—gives the theory of the inclined plane; shows how to construct a conic through five given points; solves the problem of constructing six equal hexagons around the circumference of a circle so as to touch each other and a seventh equal hexagon at the center; discourses on toothed wheels; and in a final section (which may be wholly interpolated) gives extracts from Heron's description of the five mechanical powers: the wheel and axle, the lever, the pulley, the wedge, and the screw.

Commentary on the Almagest. A commentary by Pappus on book V (with lacunae) and book VI of Ptolemy's *Syntaxis* exists in the Florentine manuscript designated L (ninth century) and in various other manuscripts. But this commentary is only part of a larger original. In the *Collection* Pappus refers to his commentary (*scholion*) on the first book of the *Almagest*, and in the surviving sixth book he makes the same reference, repeating a proof of his own for Archimedes' theorem about the area of a circle which, he says, he had given in the first book. In the compilation of uncertain authorship known as the *Introduction to the Almagest* there is a reference to a method of division "according to the geometer Pappus," which would seem to hark back to the third book.[17] In the fifth book of the commentary Pappus refers to a theorem in connection with parallax proved in his fourth book.[18] Although there is no direct reference to the second book, there is sufficient evidence that he commented on the first six books, and he may have written on all thirteen. The date of the commentary, as we have seen, must be soon after 320.

At the outset of his fifth book Pappus gives a summary of Ptolemy's fourth book, and at the beginning of his sixth book he summarizes Ptolemy's fifth book, which suggests that his commentary was a course of lectures. This theory is borne out by the painstaking and methodical way in which he explains, apparently for an audience of beginners, the details of Ptolemy's theory.

Ptolemy's fourth book introduces his lunar theory, and he explains the "first or simple anomaly" (irregularity of the movements of the moon) by postulating that the moon moves uniformly round the circumference of a circle (the epicycle), the center of which is carried uniformly round a circle concentric with the ecliptic. Pappus, following Ptolemy closely, explains in his fifth book that this needs correction for a second anomaly, which disappears at the new and full moons but is again noticeable when the moon is at the quadratures—provided that it is not then near its apogee or perigee, an irregularity later called evection. He also explains in detail Ptolemy's hypothesis that the circle on which the epicycle moves (the deferent) is eccentric with the ecliptic, and that the center of the eccentric circle itself moves uniformly round the center of the earth. To account for certain irregularities not explained by these anomalies, Ptolemy postulates a further correction which he calls prosneusis (that is, inclination or verging). In this context prosneusis means that the diameter of the epicycle which determines apogee and perigee is not directed to the center of the ecliptic but to a point on the line joining the center of the eccentric and the center of the ecliptic produced,

and as far distant from the latter as the latter is from the former. After a gap in the manuscript, Pappus begins his comment again in the middle of this subject and proceeds to deal with a further complication. He states that the true position of the moon may not be where it is seen in the heavens on account of parallax, which may be neglected for the sun but not for the moon. He gives details for the construction of a "parallactic instrument" (an alidade) used for finding the zenithal distances of heavenly bodies when crossing the meridian. He had previously given details of "an astrolabe" (really an armillary sphere) described by Ptolemy.[19] He also follows Ptolemy closely in his deduction of the sizes and distances of the sun and moon, the diameter of the shadow of the earth in eclipses, and the size of the earth.

In the sixth book, again following Ptolemy closely, Pappus explains the conditions under which conjunctions and oppositions of the sun and moon occur. This explanation leads to a study of the conditions for eclipses of the sun and moon and to rules for predicting when eclipses will occur. The book closes with a study of the points of first and last contact during eclipses.

Pappus, like Theon after him, not only follows Ptolemy's division into chapters but enumerates theorems as Ptolemy does not. It is clear that Theon had Pappus' commentary before him when he wrote over a century later, and in some cases Theon lifted passages directly from Pappus.

Commentary on Euclid's Elements. Eutocius[20] refers to a commentary by Pappus on the *Elements* of Euclid and it probably extended to all thirteen books. In Proclus' commentary on book I there are three references to Pappus,[21] and it is reasonable to believe that they relate to Pappus' own commentary on the *Elements* as they do not relate to anything in the *Collection*. Pappus is said to have pointed out that while all right angles are equal to one another, it is not true that an angle equal to a right angle is always

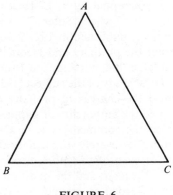

FIGURE 6

a right angle—it may be an angle formed by arcs of circles and thus cannot be called a right angle. He is also alleged to have added a superfluous axiom: If unequals are added to equals, the excess of one sum over the other is equal to the excess of one of the added quantities over the other. He also added a complementary axiom about equals added to unequals, as well as certain axioms that can be deduced from the definitions. He gave a neat alternative proof of Euclid I.5 (the angles at the base of an isosceles triangle are equal) by comparing the triangle ABC with the triangle ACB, that is, the same triangle with the sides taken in reverse order (Figure 6).

Eutocius states that Pappus, in his commentary on the *Elements*, explains how to inscribe in a circle a polygon similar to a polygon inscribed in another circle. This would doubtless be in his commentary on book XII, and Pappus probably solved the problem in the same manner as a scholiast to XII.1, that is, by making the angles at the center of the second circle equal to the angles at the center of the first.[22]

If Pappus wrote on books I and XII it is likely that he also commented on the intermediate books, and the fact that he commented on book X is attested by a scholiast to Euclid's *Data*[23] and by the *Fihrist*, in which it is stated that the commentary was in two parts.[24]

A two-part commentary on the tenth book of Euclid's *Elements* does actually exist in Arabic,[25] and it is usually identified with that of Pappus. It was discovered in a Paris manuscript by F. Woepcke in 1850, but the manuscript lacks diacritical marks and Woepcke himself read the consonantal skeleton of the author's name as Bls, which he interpreted as meaning Valens, probably Vettius Valens, an astronomer of the age of Ptolemy.[26] Heiberg showed this interpretation to be impossible, and was the first scholar to identify the commentary with that which Pappus was known to have written.[27] H. Suter pointed out that the Arabic for Bls could easily be confused with Bbs, and as there is no P in Arabic, Pappus would be the author indicated.[28] This was accepted by T. L. Heath,[29] and indeed generally, but when Suter's translation of Woepcke's text was published in 1922[30] he raised the question whether the prolixity and Neoplatonic character of the treatise did not indicate Proclus as the author. In the latest study of the subject (1930) William Thomson denied the charges of prolixity and mysticism and accepted the authorship of Pappus.[31] It must be admitted that the commentary is in a wholly different style from the severely mathematical nature of the *Collection*, or even of the more elementary commentary on the *Almagest*, and the question of authorship cannot be regarded as entirely free from doubt.

The superscription to the first part of the commentary and the subscription to the second part state that the Arabic translation is the work of Abū 'Uthman al-Dimishqī (*fl. ca.* 908–932), who also translated the tenth book of Euclid's *Elements*. The postscript to the second part adds that the copy of the commentary was written in 969 by Aḥmad ibn Muḥammad ibn 'Abd al-Jalīl, that is, the Persian geometer generally known as al-Sizjī (*ca.* 951–1029).

Some two dozen passages in the commentary have parallels in the scholia to Euclid's book X, sometimes remarkably close parallels. The simplest explanation is that the scholiast made his marginal notes with Pappus' commentary in front of him.

Euclid's book X is a work of immense subtlety, but there is little in the commentary that calls for comment. The opening section has an interest for the historian of mathematics as it distinguishes the parts played by the Pythagoreans, Theaetetus, Euclid, and Apollonius in the study of irrationals. It also credits Theaetetus with a classification of irrationals according to the different means.[32] He is said to have assigned the medial line to geometry ($\sqrt{xy}$ is the geometric mean between x, y), the binomial to arithmetic ($\frac{1}{2}[x + y]$ is the arithmetic mean between x, y), and the apotome to harmony (the harmonic mean $[2xy]/[x + y]$ between x, y is $[(2xy)/(x^2 - y^2)] \cdot [x - y]$, which is the product of a binomial and an apotome.)

Other Mathematical Works. Marinus, in the final sentence of his commentary on Euclid's *Data*,[33] reveals that Pappus also commented on the *Data*. Pappus apparently showed that Euclid's teaching followed the method of analysis rather than synthesis. Pappus also mentions a commentary that he wrote on the *Analemma* of Diodorus, in which he used the conchoid of Nicomedes to trisect an angle.[34]

The *Fihrist* includes among Pappus' works "A commentary on the book of Ptolemy on the *Planisphaerium*, translated by Thābit into Arabic." The entry leaves it uncertain whether Thābit ibn Qurra (*d.* 901) translated Ptolemy's work or Pappus' commentary, but Hājjī Khalīfa states that Ptolemy was the author of a treatise on the *Planisphaerium* translated by Thābit. He also adds that Ptolemy's work was commented on by "Battus al Roûmi [that is, late Greek], an Alexandrian geometer." "Battus" is clearly "Babbus," that is Pappus.[35]

Geography. The *Description of the World* mentioned in the *Suda Lexicon* has not survived in Greek, but the *Geography* bearing the name of the Armenian Moses of Khoren (although some scholars see in it the work of Anania Shirakatsi) appears to be a translation, or so closely based on Pappus' work as to be virtually a translation. The *Geography*, if correctly ascribed to Moses, was written about the beginning of the fifth century. The archetype has not survived, and the manuscripts contain both a long and a short recension. The character of Pappus' work may be deduced from two passages of Moses, or the pseudo-Moses, which may be thus rendered:[36] "We shall begin therefore after the *Geography* of Pappus of Alexandria, who has followed the circle or the special map of Claudius Ptolemy" and "Having spoken of geography in general, we shall now begin to explain each of the countries according to Pappus of Alexandria." From these and other passages J. Fischer[37] deduced that Pappus' work was based on the world map and on the special maps of Ptolemy rather than on the text itself, and as Pappus flourished only a century and a half after Ptolemy it is a fair inference that the world map and the special maps date back to Ptolemy himself. Pappus appears to have written with Ptolemy's maps as his basis, but about the world as he knew it in the fourth century.

Nothing is known of the second geographical work, *Rivers of Libya*, mentioned in the *Suda Lexicon*, or of the *Interpretation of Dreams*. The interpretation of dreams is akin to astrology, and there would be nothing surprising in a work on the subject by an ancient mathematician.

Music. It is possible that the commentary on Ptolemy's *Harmonica*, which was first edited by Wallis as the work of Porphyry, is, from the fifth chapter of the first book on, the work of Pappus. Several manuscripts contain the first four chapters only, and Lucas Holstein found in the Vatican a manuscript containing a definite statement that Porphyry's commentary was confined to the first four chapters of the first book and that Pappus was responsible for the remainder. Montfaucon also noted the same manuscript under the title "Pappi De Musica." Wallis did not accept the attribution because the title of the whole work and the titles of the chapters imply that it is wholly the work of Porphyry and because he could detect no stylistic difference between the parts. But the titles prove nothing, as Porphyry no doubt did comment, or intended to comment, on the whole work, and only missing parts would have been taken from another commentary, and arguments based on differences of style, especially in a technical work, are notoriously difficult. Hultsch and Jan were satisfied that Pappus was the author, but Düring was emphatically of the opinion that the whole is the work of Porphyry, and Ver Eecke agreed.[38] It must be left an open question.

Hydrostatics. An Arabic manuscript discovered in Iran by N. Khanikoff and published in 1860 under the title *Book of the Balance of Wisdom, an Arabic Work on the Water Balance, Written by al-Khazini in the Twelfth Century*[39] attributes to Pappus an instrument for measuring liquids and describes it in detail. The instrument is said by Khanikoff to be nearly identical with the volumeter of Gay-Lussac. If the attribution is correct—and there seems no reason to doubt it—the instrument may have been described in the missing part of the eighth book of the *Collection* or it may have had a place in a separate work on hydrostatics, of which no other trace has survived.

An Alchemical Oath. An oath attributed to "Pappus, philosopher" in a collection of alchemical writings may be genuine—if not *vero*, it is at least *ben trovato*—and if so it may tell us something of Pappus' syncretistic religious views in an age when paganism was retreating before Christianity. It is an oath that could have been taken equally by a pagan or a Christian, and it would fit in with the dates of Pappus. It could be gnostic, it has a Pythagorean element in it, there may be a veiled reference to the Trinity, and there is a Byzantine ring to its closing words. It reads: "I therefore swear to thee, whoever thou art, the great oath, I declare God to be one in form but not in number, the maker of heaven and earth, as well as the tetrad of the elements and things formed from them, who has furthermore harmonized our rational and intellectual souls with our bodies, who is borne upon the chariots of the cherubim and hymned by angelic throngs."[40]

A Vatican manuscript containing Ptolemy's *Handy Tables* has on one folio a short text about the entry of the sun into the signs of the zodiac, which F. Boll has shown must refer to the second half of the third century and which E. Honigmann attributes to Pappus. But this is no more than an unsubstantiated guess, which Boll himself refrained from making.[41]

A Florentine manuscript catalogued by Bandini notices Ἡμεροδρόμιον Πάππου τῶν διεπόντων καὶ πολευόντων, that is, daily tables of governing and presiding stars compiled by Pappus.[42]

NOTES

1. *Suda Lexicon*, Adler, ed., Vol. I, Pars IV (Leipzig, 1935), P 265, p. 26.
2. Pappus, *Collectio*, III.1, F. Hultsch, ed., I, 30.4; VII.1, Hultsch, ed., II, 634.1. Nothing more is known of Hermodorus or of Pandrosion and Megethion, to whom the third and fifth books are dedicated; or of his philosopher-friend Hierius, who pressed him to give a solution to the problem of finding two mean proportionals (Hultsch, ed., III, 3–8). A phrase in Proclus, *In primum Euclidis*, Friedlein, ed. (Leipzig, 1873; repr. Hildesheim, 1967), p. 429.13, οἱ . . . περὶ Πάππον, implies that he had a school.

3. A. Rome, *Commentaires de Pappus et de Théon d'Alexandrie sur l'Almageste*, I (Rome, 1931), 180.8–181.23, *Studi e Testi*, no. 54 (1931). The eclipse is no. 402 in F. K. Ginzel, *Spezialler Kanon der Sonnen und Mond Finsternisse* (Berlin, 1899), p. 87, and no. 3642 in T. von Oppolzer, *Canon der Finsternissen* (Vienna, 1887), repr. translated by Owen Gingerich (New York, 1962), p. 146. Rome, who first perceived the bearing of this eclipse on the date of Pappus, argues that if the total, or nearly total, eclipse of A.D. 346 had taken place, Pappus would certainly have chosen it for his example, and that the better eclipse of A.D. 291 was already too distant to be used (A. Rome, *op. cit.*, pp. x–xiii).

4. So A. Rome, *op. cit.*, I, xvii, note 1, suggests. This is more convincing than the conjecture of F. Hultsch, *op. cit.*, III, viii, note 3, that *Δ* is a copyist's error for *ΙΓ*.

5. A. Rome, *op. cit.*, II, lxxxiii, *Studi e Testi*, no. 72 (1936).

6. Leiden MS, no. 78, of Theon's ed. of the *Handy Tables*, fol. 55. This was first noted by J. van der Hagen, *Observationes in Theonis Fastos Graecos priores* (Amsterdam, 1735), p. 320, and his view was followed by H. Usener, "Vergessenes III," in *Rheinisches Museum*, n.s. **28** (1873), 403–404, and F. Hultsch, *op. cit.*, III, vi–vii, but none of these scholars realized the significance of Pappus' reference to the eclipse of A.D. 320.

7. Pappus, *Collectio* VIII.46, *op. cit.*, III, 1106.13–15. Rome, *op. cit.*, I, 254, note 1, gives reasons for thinking that the third theorem of book V of the *Collectio* is a fragment, all that now survives, of book I of the *Commentary on the Syntaxis*, and that it is an interpolation by an ed.

8. A. Rome, see previous note; K. Ziegler, in Pauly-Wissowa, XVIII (Waldsee, 1949), col. 1094.

9. F. Hultsch, *op. cit.*, I, p. vii–xiv.

10. Thomas Heath, *A History of Greek Mathematics*, II (Oxford, 1921), 357–358. A full and excellent conspectus of the *Collection* is given by Heath, *loc. cit.*, pp. 361–439; Gino Loria, *Le scienze esatte nell'antica Grecia*, 2nd ed. (Milan, 1914), pp. 658–700; and Paul Ver Eecke, *Pappus d'Alexandrie: La Collection mathématique*, I (Paris–Bruges, 1933), xiii–cxiv.

11. René Descartes, *Des matières de la géométrie* (Leiden, 1637), book I, 304–314, book II, 323–350; David Eugene Smith and Marcia C. Latham, *The Geometry of René Descartes With a Facsimile of the First Edition* (New York, 1925; repr. 1954), book I, 17–37, book II, 59–111.

12. Isaac Newton, *Philosophiae naturalis principia mathematica* (London, 1687; repr. London, 1953), "De motu corporum," lib. 1, sect. 5, lemma XIX, pp. 74–75.

13. Pappus, VII.42, *op. cit.*, II, 682.7–15. The whole passage in which this occurs is attributed by Hultsch to an interpolator, but without reasons given, and by Ver Eecke (*op. cit.*, I, xcvi) for unconvincing stylistic reasons and lack of connection with the context. But Heath pertinently observes (*A History of Greek Mathematics*, II, 403) that no Greek after Pappus would have been capable of framing such an advanced proposition. Ver Eecke (*op. cit.*, I, xcv, cxxiii) observes that Paul Guldin (1577–1643) could not have been inspired by the passage in Pappus as Commandino did not include it in his first ed. (Pesaro, 1588) and he could not have seen the second ed. (Bologna, 1660), augmented with this passage by Manolessius. But this conclusion is an error; the passage is in the first no less than the second ed. See also the article on Guldin.

14. F. Vieta, *Apollonius Gallus* (Paris, 1600), problem x, pp. 7–8; Isaac Newton, *Arithmetica universalis* (Cambridge, 1707), problem xli *ad finem*, pp. 181–182, 2nd ed. (London, 1722), problem xlvii *ad finem*, p. 195; *Principia* (London, 1687; repr. London, 1953), lemma XVI, pp. 67–68.

15. Robert Simson, *Apollonii Pergaei locorum planorum libri II restituti* (Glasgow, 1749), pp. 156–221; Matthew Stewart, *Some General Theorems of Considerable Use in the Higher Parts of Mathematics* (Edinburgh, 1746), pp. 1–2. See also

Moritz Cantor, *Vorlesungen über Geschichte der Mathematik*, III (Leipzig, 1898), 523–528.

16. For example, E. A. Maxwell, *Geometry For Advanced Pupils* (Oxford, 1949), p. 97. The term "Pappus' Theorem" is thus used by Renaissance and modern geometers in two different ways.

17. C. Henry, *Opusculum de multiplicatione et divisione sexagesimalibus, Diophanto vel Pappo tribuendum* (Halle, 1879), p. viii; A. Rome, *op. cit.*, **1**, xvi.

18. A. Rome, *op. cit.*, I, 76.19–77.1.

19. For a reconstruction of the astrolabe and parallactic instrument as described by Pappus, with illustrations, see A. Rome, *Annales de la Société scientifique de Bruxelles*, **47** (1927), 77–102, 129–140, and *op. cit.*, **1**, 3–5, 69–77.

20. Eutocius, *Commentarii in libros Archimedis De Sphaera et cylindro*, p. 1.13, *ad init.*, *Archimedis opera omnia*, J. L. Heiberg, ed., 2nd ed., III (Leipzig, 1915), corr. repr. Evangelos S. Stamatis (Stuttgart, 1972), p. 28.19–22: ὅπως μὲν οὖν ἔστιν εἰς τὸν δοθέντα κύκλον πολύγωνον ἐγγράψαι ὅμοιον τῷ ἐν ἑτέρῳ ἐγγεγραμμένῳ, δῆλον, εἴρηται δὲ καὶ Πάππῳ εἰς τὸ ὑπόμνημα τῶν Στοιχείων.

21. Proclus, *In primum Euclidis*, Friedlein, ed., pp. 189.12–191.4, 197.6–198.15, 249.20–250.19.

22. *Euclidis opera omnia*, J. L. Heiberg and H. Menge, eds., V (Leipzig, 1888), scholium 2, 616.6–617.21.

23. *Ibid.*, VI (Leipzig, 1896), scholium 4 *ad definitiones*, 262.4–6: δύναται δὲ καὶ ῥητὸν καὶ ἄλογον δεδομένον εἶναι, ὡς λέγει Πάππος ἐν ἀρχῇ τοῦ εἰς τὸ ι' Εὐκλείδου.

24. H. Suter, "Das Mathematiker Verzeichniss im Fihrist des Ibn abî Ja'kûb an-Nadîm," in *Zeitschrift für Mathematik und Physik*, **37** (1892), suppl. (or *Abhandlungen zur Geschichte der Mathematik*, **6**), p. 22. The whole entry runs, in English: "Pappus the Greek. His writings are: A Commentary on the book of Ptolemy concerning the representation of the sphere in a plane, translated by Thābit into Arabic. A commentary on the tenth book of Euclid, in two parts."

25. Bibliothèque Nationale (Paris), MS no. 2457 (Supplément arabe de la Bibliothèque impériale no. 952.2). The manuscript contains about fifty treatises, of which nos. 5 and 6 constitute the two books of the commentary.

26. Woepcke described the manuscript and translated four passages into French in his "Essai d'une restitution de travaux perdus d'Apollonius sur les quantités irrationelles," in *Mémoires présentés par divers savants à l'Académie des sciences*, **14** (1856), 658–720. He developed his theory about the authorship in *The Commentary on the Tenth Book of Euclid's Elements by Bls*, which he published anonymously and without date or place of publication. Woepcke read the name of the author in the title of the first book of the commentary as B.los (the dot representing a vowel) and in other manuscripts as B.lis, B.n.s, or B.l.s.

27. J. L. Heiberg, *Litterärgeschichtliche Studien über Euklid* (Leipzig, 1882), pp. 169–170. Heiberg points out that one of the manuscripts cited by Woepcke states that "B.n.s le Roumi" (that is, late Greek) was later than Claudius Ptolemy, while the *Fihrist* says that "B.l.s le Roumi" wrote a commentary on Ptolemy's *Planisphaerium*. As Vettius Valens lived under Hadrian, he was therefore older than Ptolemy—an elder contemporary. Moreover the *Fihrist* gives separate entries to B.l.s and Valens. See also Suter, *op. cit.*, p. 54, note 92.

28. H. Suter, "Das Mathematiker Verzeichniss im Fihrist," pp. 22, 54, note 92.

29. T. L. Heath, *The Thirteen Books of Euclid's Elements*, 2nd ed., III (Cambridge, 1905, 1925; repr. New York, 1956), 3; Heath, *A History of Greek Mathematics*, I (Oxford, 1921), 154–155, 209, II, 356.

30. H. Suter, "Der Kommentar des Pappus zum X Buche des Eukleides," in *Abhandlungen zur Geschichte der Naturwissenschaften und der Medizin*, **4** (1922), 9–78; see p. 78 for the question of authorship.

31. William Thomson and Gustav Junge, *The Commentary of Pappus on Book X of Euclid's Elements* (Cambridge, Mass., 1930; repr. New York, 1968), pp. 38–42.

32. There is nothing in the opening section about the rational and irrational being "given," as Pappus is stated by a scholiast (see note 23) to have maintained at the beginning of his commentary. This may be evidence against the ascription of the Arabic treatise to Pappus.

33. *Euclidis opera omnia*, J. L. Heiberg and H. Menge, eds., VI, 256.22–25.

34. F. Hultsch, *op. cit.*, I, 246.1–3. Ἀνάλημμα, as in Ptolemy's work with that title, means the projection of the circles of a celestial sphere on the plane. Neither the work of Diodorus nor the commentary of Pappus has survived. In Ptolemy's work certain segments of a semicircle are required to be divided into six equal parts, and it is easy to see how Pappus would need to trisect an arc or angle.

35. H. Suter, "Das Mathematiker Verzeichniss im Fihrist," p. 22 (see note 24, supra); Ḥājjī Khalīfa, *Lexikon bibliographicum et encyclopaedicum*, G. Fluegel, ed., V (London, 1850), 61–62, no. 9970, *s.v.* Kitab testih el koret. The *Planisphaerium* is a system of stereographic projection by which points on the heavenly sphere are represented on the plane of the equator by projection from a pole.

36. Translated from the French of P. Arsène Soukry, *Géographie de Moïse de Corène d'après Ptolémée* (Venice, 1881), p. 7.

37. J. Fischer, "Pappus und die Ptolemaeus Karten," in *Zeitschrift der Gesellschaft für Erdkunde zu Berlin*, **54** (1919), 336–358.

38. John Wallis, *Claudii Ptolemaei Harmonicorum libri III* (Oxford, 1682), reprinted in *Opera mathematica*, III (Oxford, 1699); the commentary is on pp. 183–355 of the latter work, and the authorship is discussed on p. 187. It has been edited in modern times by Ingemar Düring as *Porphyrios' Kommentar zur Harmonienlehre des Ptolemaios* (Göteborg, 1932). His discussion of the authorship is on pp. xxxvii–xxxix. Lucas Holstenius, *Dissertatio De vita et scriptis Porphyrii* (Rome, 1630), c. vi, p. 55: Neque tamen in universum ἁρμονικῶν opus scripsit Porphyrius, sed in quatuor duntaxat prima capita: cetera dein Pappus pertexuit. Ita enim in alio manuscripto Vaticano titulus indicat: Πορφυρίου ἐξήγησις εἰς δ´ πρῶτα κεφάλαια τοῦ πρώτου τῶν ἁρμονικῶν Πτολεμαίου. Sequitur deinde, Πάππου ὑπόμνημα εἰς τὰ ἀπὸ τοῦ ε´ κεφαλαίου καὶ ἐφεξῆς. Bernard de Montfaucon, *Bibliotheca bibliothecarum manuscriptorum nova*, I (Paris, 1739), 11B. Paul Ver Eecke, *Pappus d'Alexandrie: La Collection mathématique*, I (Paris–Bruges, 1933), cxv–cxvi. F. Hultsch, *op. cit.*, III, xii. C. Jan, *Musici scriptores graeci* (Leipzig, 1895; repr. Hildesheim, 1962), p. 116 and note 1.

39. See *Journal of the American Oriental Society*, **6** (1860), 40–53; and the article on al-Khāzinī, IV, 338–341; and bibliography, 349–351.

40. C. G. Grumer, *Isidis, Christiani et Pappi philosophi Iusjurandum chemicum nunc primum graece et latine editum* (Jena, 1807); M. Berthelot and C. E. Ruelle, *Collection des anciens alchimistes grecs* (Paris, 1888), pp. 27–28, traduction, pp. 29–30; Paul Tannery, "Sur la religion des derniers mathématiciens de l'antiquité," in *Annales de philosophie chrétienne*, **34** (1896), 26–36, repr. in *Mémoires scientifiques*, **2** (1912), 527–539, esp. pp. 533–535. Tannery seems inclined to think that the oath may be correctly attributed to Pappus the mathematician, and he speculates that he may have been a gnostic.

41. Vaticanus Graecus 1291, fol. 9r. F. Boll, "Eine illustrierte Prakthandschrift der astronomischen Tafeln des Ptolemaios," in *Sitzungsberichte der Königliche Bayerische Akademie der Wissenschaften, philosophisch-philologischen und historischen Classe*, **29** (1899), 110–138. E. Honigmann, *Die sieben Klimata und die πόλεις ἐπίσημοι* (Heidelberg, 1929), p. 73.

42. Codex Laurentianus XXXIV plut. XXVIII; A. M. Bandini, *Catalogus Bibliothecae Laurentianae*, II (Florence, 1767), 61.

BIBLIOGRAPHY

I. ORIGINAL WORKS. *Collection.* The only complete ed. of the extant Greek text is F. Hultsch, *Pappi Alexandrini Collectionis quae supersunt e libris manu scriptis edidit latina interpretatione et commentariis instruxit Fridericus Hultsch*, 3 vols. (Berlin, 1876–1878). The Greek text is accompanied by a Latin translation on the opposite page and there are invaluable introductions, notes, and appendixes. Apart from a tendency to invoke interpolators too readily, the work is a model of scholarship.

The only translation of the whole extant text into a modern language is that of Paul Ver Eecke, *Pappus d'Alexandrie, La Collection Mathématique: oeuvre traduite pour la première fois du grec en français avec une introduction et des notes*, 2 vols. (Paris–Bruges, 1933). A German translation of books III and VIII is given by C. J. Gerhardt, *Die Sammlung des Pappus von Alexandrien, griechisch und deutsch herausgegeben*, 2 vols. (Halle, 1871).

The *Collection* first became known to the learned world when Commandino included Latin translations of various extracts in his editions of Apollonius (Bologna, 1566) and Aristarchus (Pesaro, 1572). After Commandino's death, his complete Latin trans. of the extant Greek text, except the unknown fragment of book II, appeared as *Pappi Alexandrini Mathematicae Collectiones a Federico Commandino Urbinate in Latinum conversae et commentariis illustratae* (Pesaro, 1588). Reprints appeared in 1589 (Venice) and 1602 (Pesaro) and a second ed. was published by C. Manolessius in 1660 (Bologna); despite the editor's claims it was inferior to the first ed.

Extracts from the Greek text were published in works by Marc Meiboom (1655), John Wallis (1688; first publication of the missing fragment of book II, which he found in a MS in the Savilian Library at Oxford), David Gregory (1703), Edmond Halley (1706, 1710), Robert Simson (1749), Joseph Torelli (1769), Samuel Horsley (1770), J. G. Camerer (1795), G. G. Bredow (1812), Hermann J. Eisenmann (1824), C. J. Gerhardt (1871).

Commentary on Ptolemy's Syntaxes (Almagest). The only complete ed. of the extant Greek text (part of book V and book VI) is Adolphe Rome, *Commentaires de Pappus et de Théon d'Alexandrie sur l'Almagesie, texte établi et annoté par A. Rome*; vol. I is *Pappus d'Alexandrie: Commentaire sur les livres 5 et 6 de l'Almageste* (Rome, 1931), *Studi e Testi* no. 54. The work lacks only the indexes that would have been published at the end of the commentaries if Rome's design had not been interrupted by the destruction of his papers in the war.

The extant Greek text of book V was printed, with numerous errors and together with Theon's commentary, at the end of the *editio princeps* of the *Almagest*. This ed. was published by Grynaeus and Camerarius (Basel, 1538), but contained no mention of Pappus on the title page. F. Hultsch began, but was not able to complete, an ed. of the commentary by Pappus and Theon; see his "Hipparchos über die Grosse und Entfernung der Sonne," in *Berichte über die Verhandlungen der königlich sachsischen Gesellschaft der Wissenschaften*, Philologisch-Historische

Klasse, **52** (1900), 169–200. This work is vitiated by a fundamental error—what he thought was a working over of Pappus' text by Theon was really the same text—an error he would undoubtedly have recognized had he been able to continue his research.

Commentary on Euclid's Elements. The text of Abū 'Uthman al-Dimishqi's Arabic translation of a Greek commentary on the tenth book of Euclid's *Elements*, generally believed to be part of Pappus' commentary on the *Elements*, is published—with an English trans. and notes—in William Thomson and Gustav Junge, *The Commentary of Pappus on Book X of Euclid's Elements*, VIII in Harvard Semitic Series (Cambridge, Mass., 1930; repr. New York, 1968), 189–260. This supersedes the first printed version of the text by F. Woepcke, *The Commentary on the Tenth Book of Euclid's Elements by Bls* (Paris, 1855)—published without indication of author, place, or date. The Arabic text and trans. are the work of William Thomson. There is a German translation in H. Suter, "Der Kommentar des Pappus zum X Buche des Eukleides," in *Abhandlungen zur Geschichte der Naturwissenschaften und der Medizin* (1922), 9–78.

Commentary on Ptolemy's Harmonics. John Wallis, *Claudii Ptolemaei Harmonicorum libri III (graece et latine), Joh. Wallis recensuit, edidit, versione et notis illustravit, et auctarium adjecit* (Oxford, 1682). The commentary, which follows Ptolemy's text, is the work of Porphyry for the first four chapters, but possibly of Pappus from the fifth chapter on. The work was reprinted in *Johannis Wallis S.T.D. Operum mathematicorum Vol. III* (Oxford, 1699), 183–355, as *Porphyrii in Harmonica Ptolemaei commentarius nunc primum ex Codd. MSS. (Graece et latine) editus,* with (?) Pappus' share of the commentary on pp. 266–355. There is a modern text, with copious notes, by Ingemar Düring, "Porphyrios' Kommentar zur Harmonielehre des Ptolemaios," in *Göteborgs högskolas årskrift,* **38** (1932), i–xliv, 1–217; see also Bengt Alexanderson, *Textual Remarks on Ptolemy's Harmonica and Porphyry's Commentary,* which is *Studia Graeca et latina Gothoburgensia,* XXVII (Göteborg, 1969).

Geography. What is believed to be essentially an early Armenian trans. of Pappus' *Geography* is given, with a French rendering, in P. Arsène Soukry, *Géographie de Moïse de Corène d'après Ptolémée, texte arménien, traduit en français* (Venice, 1881).

II. SECONDARY LITERATURE. *General.* Konrat Ziegler, "Pappos 2," in Pauly-Wissowa, XVIII (1949), cols. 1084–1106; the prefatory matter, notes, and appendices to the works by Hultsch, Rome, and Ver Eecke are cited above; Moritz Cantor, *Vorlesungen über Geschichte der Mathematik,* I, 3rd ed. (Leipzig, 1907), 441–455; Gino Loria, *Le scienze esatte nell'antica Grecia,* 2nd ed. (Milan, 1914), pp. 656–703; T. L. Heath, *A History of Greek Mathematics,* II (Oxford, 1921), 355–439.

Collection. The works cited in the previous paragraph are helpful. See also Robert Simson, *Apollonii Pergaei locorum planorum libri II restituti* (Glasgow, 1749); "De porismatibus tractatus," in *Opera quaedam reliqua*

(Glasgow, 1776), pp. 315–594; Michel Chasles, *Les trois livres de porismes d'Euclide, rétablis pour la première fois, d'après la notice et les lemmes de Pappus* (Paris, 1860); Paul Tannery, "L'arithmetique des Grecs dans Pappus" in *Mémoires de la Société des sciences physiques et naturelles de Bordeaux,* **3** (1880), 351–371, repr. in *Mémoires scientifiques,* **1** (1912), pp. 80–105; "Note sur le problème de Pappus" ("Pappus' problem" in the sense used by Descartes), in *Oeuvres de Descartes,* C. Adam and P. Tannery, eds., VI (Paris, 1902), 721–725, repr. in *Mémoires scientifiques,* **3** (1915), 42–50; J. S. MacKay, "Pappus on the Progressions" (a translation of Pappus on means), in *Proceedings of the Edinburgh Mathematical Society,* **6** (1888), 48–58; J. H. Weaver, "Pappus," in *Bulletin of the American Mathematical Society,* **23** (1916–1917), 127–135; "On Foci of Conics," *ibid.,* 361–365; N. Khanikoff, "Analysis and Extracts of *Book of the Balance of Wisdom,* an Arabic Work on the Water Balance, Written" by al-Khāzinī in the Twelfth Century, in *Journal of the American Oriental Society,* **6** (1860), lecture 1, ch. 7, 40–53; and al-Khāzinī, *Kitāb mīzān al-ḥikma* (Hyderabad, Deccan, A.H. 1359 [A.D. 1940–1941]). For further references see Bibliography to article on al-Khāzinī, in *Dictionary of Scientific Biography,* IV, 349–351. An article by Malcolm Brown, "Pappus, Plato and the Harmonic Mean," is promised for *Phronesis.*

Commentary on Ptolemy's Syntaxis (Almagest). F. Hultsch, *Hipparchos über die Grosse und Entfernung der Sonne* as above; S. Gunther, "Über eine merkwürdige Beziehung zwischen Pappus und Kepler," in *Bibliotheca mathematica,* n.s. **2** (1888), 81–87; A. Rome, "L'astrolabe et le météoroscope, d'après le commentaire de Pappus sur le 5ᵉ livre de l'Almageste," in *Annales de la Société scientifique de Bruxelles,* **47** (1927), 77–102; "L'instrument parallactique d'après le commentaire de Pappus sur le 5ᵉ livre de l'Almageste," *ibid.,* 129–140; *Pappus d'Alexandrie: Commentaire sur les livres 5 et 6 de l'Almageste* as above.

Commentary on Euclid's Elements. F. Woepcke, "Essai d'une restitution de travaux perdus d'Apollonius sur les quantités irrationelles," in *Mémoires présentés par divers savants à l'Académie des sciences de l'Institut de France,* **14** (1856), 658–720; J. L. Heiberg, *Litterärgeschichtliche Studien uber Euklid* (Leipzig, 1882), pp. 169–170; H. Suter, *Der Kommentar des Pappus zum X Buche des Eukleides* as above; William Thomson and Gustav Junge, *The Commentary of Pappus on Book X of Euclid's Elements* as above.

Geography. J. Fischer, "Pappus und die Ptolemaeus Karten," in *Zeitschrift der Gesellschaft für Erdkunde zu Berlin,* **54** (1919), 336–358; *Claudii Ptolemaei Geographiae Codex Urbinas Graecus 82, Tomus prodromus* (Leiden-Leipzig, 1922), 419–436; E. Honigmann, *Die sieben Klimata und die πόλεις ἐπίσημοι* (Heidelberg, 1929), c.x., "Pappus und Theon," pp. 72–81.

Commentary on Ptolemy's Harmonics. Ingemar Düring, "Die Harmonielehre des Klaudios Ptolemaios," in *Göteborgs högskolas årskrift,* **36** (1930); and "Ptolemaios und Porphyrios uber die Musik," *ibid.,* **40** (1934), 1–293.

IVOR BULMER-THOMAS

PARSEVAL DES CHÊNES, MARC-ANTOINE (*b.* Rosières-aux-Salines, France, 27 April 1755; *d.* Paris, France, 16 August 1836)

Little is known of Parseval's life or work. He was a member of a distinguished French family and described himself as a squire; his marriage in 1795 to Ursule Guerillot soon ended in divorce. An ardent royalist, he was imprisoned in 1792 and later fled the country when Napoleon ordered his arrest for publishing poetry against the regime. He was nominated for election to the Paris Academy of Sciences in 1796, 1799, 1802, 1813, and 1828; but the closest he came to being elected was to place third to Lacroix in 1799.

Parseval's only publications seem to have been five memoirs presented to the Academy of Sciences. The second of these (dated 5 April 1799) contains the famous Parseval theorem, given here in his own notation:

If there are two series

$$A + Bf + Cf^2 + Ff^3 + \cdots = T$$
$$a + b\tfrac{1}{f} + c\tfrac{1}{f^2} + f\tfrac{1}{f^3} + \cdots = T'$$

as well as the respective sums T, T', then we obtain the sum of the series

$$Aa + Bb + Cc + Ff + \cdots = V$$

by multiplying T by T' and, in the new function $T \times T'$, substituting

$$\cos u + \sqrt{-1}\,\sin u$$

for the variable f, which will yield the function V'. Then for f substitute

$$\cos u - \sqrt{-1}\,\sin u$$

which will yield the new function V''. We then obtain

$$V = \frac{1}{u} \int \frac{V' + V''}{2}\, du,$$

u being made equal to 180° after integrating.

According to Parseval, the theorem was suggested by a method of summing special cases of series of products, presented by Euler in his *Institutiones calculi differentialis* of 1755. He believed the theorem to be self-evident, suggesting that the reader multiply the two series and recall that $(\cos u + i \sin u)^m = \cos mu + i \sin mu$, and gave a simple example that would "confirm its validity." He noted that it could be used only if the imaginaries in V' and V'' cancel one another, and he hoped to overcome this inconvenience. This hope was realized in a note appended to his next memoir (dated 5 July 1801), in which he gave a simplified version of the theorem. In modern notation the theorem states:

If, in the series $M = A + Bs + Cs^2 + \cdots$ and $m = a + bs + cs^2 + \cdots$, s is replaced by $\cos u + i \sin u$, and the real and imaginary parts are separated so that

$$M = P + Qi$$

and

$$m = p + qi,$$

then

$$\frac{2}{\pi} \int_0^\pi Pp\, du = 2Aa + Bb + Cc + \cdots.$$

(There is an error in Parseval's statement: the 2 in the right-hand side of the last equation is missing.)

In his memoirs, which were not published until 1806, Parseval applied his theorem to the solution of certain differential equations suggested by Lagrange and d'Alembert. The theorem first appeared in print in 1800, in Lacroix's *Traité des différences et des séries* (p. 377). By 1810 Delambre, in his *Rapport historique sur les progrès des sciences mathématiques depuis 1789, et sur leur état actuel*, could report that Prony had given, and published, lectures at the École Polytechnique taking Parseval's procedure into account and that Poisson had used a method dependent on an equation of this type. Since then dozens of equations have been called Parseval equations, although some only remotely resemble the original. Although Parseval's method involves trigonometric series, he never tried to find a general expression for the series coefficients; and hence he did not contribute directly to the theory of Fourier series. It should be noted that although Parseval viewed his theorem as a formula for summing infinite series, it was taken up at the end of the century as defining properties in more abstract treatments of analysis.

BIBLIOGRAPHY

I. Original Works. Parseval's five memoirs appeared in *Mémoires présentés à l'Institut des Sciences, Lettres et Arts, par divers savans, et lus dans ses assemblées. Sciences mathématiques et physiques.* (*Savans étrangers.*), **1** (1806): "Mémoire sur la résolution des équations aux différences partielles linéaires du second ordre" (5 May 1798), 478–492; "Mémoire sur les séries et sur l'intégration complète d'une équation aux différences partielles linéaires du second ordre, à coefficiens constans" (5 Apr. 1799), 638–648; "Intégration générale et complète des équations de la propagation du son, l'air étant considéré avec ses trois dimensions" (5 July 1801), 379–398; "Intégration générale et complète de deux équations importantes dans la mécanique des fluides" (16 Aug. 1803), 524–545; and

"Méthode générale pour sommer, par le moyen des intégrales définies, la suite donnée par le théorème de M. Lagrange, au moyen de laquelle il trouve une valeur qui satisfait à une équation algébrique ou transcendente" (7 May 1804), 567–586.

II. SECONDARY LITERATURE. A brief biography is in *Généalogies et souvenirs de famille; les Parseval et leurs alliances pendant trois siècles, 1594–1900*, I (Bergerac, 1901), 281–282. The memoirs are described in Niels Nielsen, *Géomètres français sous la Révolution* (Copenhagen, 1929), 192–194. The relation of Parseval's theorem to the work of Fourier is discussed in Ivor Grattan-Guinness, *Joseph Fourier, 1768–1830* (Cambridge, Mass., 1972), 238–241, written with J. R. Ravetz.

HUBERT C. KENNEDY

PASCAL, BLAISE (*b.* Clermont-Ferrand, Puy-de-Dôme, France, 19 June 1623; *d.* Paris, France, 19 August 1662), *mathematics, mechanical computation, physics, epistemology.*

Varied, original, and important, although often the subject of controversy, Pascal's scientific work was intimately linked with other aspects of his writings, with his personal life, and with the development of several areas of science. Consequently a proper understanding of his contribution requires a biographical framework offering as precise a chronology as possible.

Pascal's mother, Antoinette Begon, died when he was three; and the boy was brought up by his father, Étienne, who took complete charge of his education. In 1631 the elder Pascal left Clermont and moved to Paris with his son and two daughters, Gilberte (1620–1687), who married Florin Périer in 1641, and Jacqueline (1625–1661), who entered the convent of Port-Royal in 1652.

The young Pascal began his scientific studies about 1635 with the reading of Euclid's *Elements.* His exceptional abilities, immediately and strikingly apparent, aroused general admiration. His sister Gilberte Périer left an account, more doting than objective, of her brother's life and, in particular, of his first contacts with mathematics. According to her, Pascal accompanied his father to the meetings of the "Académie Parisienne" soon after its founding by Mersenne in 1635 and played an important role in it from the first. This assertion, however, is not documented; and it appears more likely that it was at the beginning of 1639 that Pascal, not yet sixteen, began to participate in the activities of Mersenne's academy. In that year Girard Desargues had just published his *Brouillon project d'une atteinte aux événemens des rencontres du cone avec un plan*; but his originality, his highly personal style and vocabulary, and his refusal to use Cartesian algebraic symbols baffled most contemporary mathematicians. As the only one to appreciate the richness of this work, which laid the foundations of projective geometry and of a unified theory of conic sections, Pascal became Desargues's principal disciple in geometry.

Projective Geometry. Grasping the significance of Desargues's new conception of conics, Pascal adopted the basic ideas of the *Brouillon project:* the introduction of elements at infinity; the definition of a conic as any plane section of a cone with a circular base; the study of conics as perspectives of circles; and the involution determined on any straight line by a conic and the opposite sides of an inscribed quadrilateral. As early as June 1639 Pascal made his first great discovery, that of a property equivalent to the theorem now known as Pascal's "mystic hexagram"; according to it, the three points of intersection of the pairs of opposite sides of a hexagon inscribed in a conic are collinear.[1] He also soon saw the possibility of basing a comprehensive projective study of conics on this property. (The property amounts to an elegant formulation, in geometric language, of the condition under which six points of one plane belong to a single conic.) Next he wrote *Essay pour les coniques* (February 1640), a pamphlet, of which only a few copies were published [1].[2] A plan for further research, illustrated with statements of several typical propositions that he had already discovered, the *Essay* constituted the outline of a great treatise on conics that he had just conceived and begun to prepare.

Pascal seems to have made considerable progress by December 1640, having deduced from his theorem most of the propositions contained in the *Conics* of Apollonius.[3] Subsequently, however, he worked only intermittently on completing the treatise. Although Desargues and Mersenne alluded to the work in November 1642 and 1644, respectively, it was apparently not until March 1648 that Pascal obtained a purely geometric definitive general solution to the celebrated problem of Pappus, which had furnished Descartes with the principal example for illustrating the power of his new analytic geometry (1637).[4] Pascal's success marked an important step in the elaboration of his treatise on conics, for it demonstrated that in this domain projective geometry might prove as effective as the Cartesian analytic methods. Pascal therefore reserved the sixth, and final, section of his treatise, "Des lieux solides" (geometric loci composed of conics), for this problem.

In 1654 Pascal indicated that he had nearly completed the treatise [12], conceived "on the basis of a single proposition"—a work for which he had "had the idea before reaching the age of sixteen" and which he then "constructed and put in order." He also mentioned some special geometric problems to which his projective method could usefully be applied: circles or spheres defined by three or four conditions; conics determined by five elements (points or tangents); geometric loci composed of straight lines, circles, or conics; and a general method of perspective.

Pascal made no further mention of this treatise, which was never published. It seems that only Leibniz saw it in manuscript, and the most precise details known about the work were provided by him. In a letter [23] of 30 August 1676 to E. Périer, one of Pascal's heirs, Leibniz stated that the work merited publication and mentioned a number of points concerning its contents, which he divided into six parts: (1) the projective generation of conics; (2) the definition and properties of the "mystic hexagram"—Pascal's theorem and its applications; (3) the projective theory of poles and polars and of centers and diameters; (4) various properties related to the classic definitions of conics on the basis of their axes and foci; (5) *contacts coniques*, the construction of conics defined by five elements (points or tangents); and (6) solid loci (the problem of Pappus). Besides reading notes on a number of passages of Pascal's treatise [15], Leibniz's papers preserve the text of the first part, "Generatio conisectionum" [14].

The content and inspiration of this introductory chapter are readily apparent from the full title: "The Generation of Conics, Tangents, and Secants; or the Projection of the Circumference, Tangents, and Secants of the Circle for Every Position of the Eye and of the Plane of the Figure." The text presents in an exceptionally elegant form the basic ideas of projective geometry already set forth, in a much less explicit fashion, in Desargues's *Brouillon project*.[5] Although these few elements of Pascal's treatise preserved by Leibniz do not provide a complete picture of its contents, they are sufficient to show the richness and clarity of Pascal's conceptions once he had become fully aware of the power of projective methods. It is reasonable to assume that publication of this work would have hastened the development of projective geometry, impeded until then by the obscurity of Desargues's writings and by their limited availability. Despite the efforts of Philippe de la Hire,[6] the ultimate disappearance of the treatise on conics and the temporary eclipse of both *Essay pour les coniques* (which was not republished until 1779) and Desargues's *Brouillon project* (rediscovered in 1864) hindered the progress of projective geometry. It was not truly developed until the nineteenth century, in the work of Poncelet and his successors. Poncelet, in fact, was one of the first to draw attention to the importance of Pascal's contribution in this area.

Pascal was soon obliged to suspend the contact with the "Académie Parisienne" that had encouraged the precocious flowering of his mathematical abilities. In 1640 he and his sisters joined their father, who since the beginning of that year had been living in Rouen as a royal tax official. From the end of 1640 until 1647 Pascal made only brief and occasional visits to Paris, and no information has survived concerning his scientific activity at the beginning of this long provincial interlude. Moreover, in 1641 he began to suffer from problems of health that several times forced him to give up all activity. From 1642 he pursued his geometric research in a more or less regular fashion; but he began to take an interest in a new problem, to the solution of which he made a major contribution.

Mechanical Computation. Anxious to assist his father, whose duties entailed a great deal of accounting, Pascal sought to mechanize the two elementary operations of arithmetic, addition and subtraction. Toward the end of 1642 he began a project of designing a machine that would reduce these operations to the simple movements of gears. Having solved the theoretical problem of mechanizing computation, it remained for him to produce such a machine that would be convenient, rapid, dependable, and easy to operate. The actual construction, however, required relatively complicated wheel arrangements and proved to be extremely difficult with the rudimentary and inaccurate techniques available. In this venture Pascal displayed remarkable practical sense, great concern for efficiency, and undeniable stubbornness. Supervising a team of workers, he constructed the first model within a few months but, judging it unsatisfactory, he decided to modify and improve it. The considerable problems he encountered soon discouraged him and caused him to interrupt his project. At the beginning of 1644 encouragement from several people, including the chancellor of France, Pierre Séguier, induced Pascal to resume the development of his "arithmetic machine." After having constructed, in his words, "more than fifty models, all different," he finally produced the definitive model in 1645. He himself organized the manufacture and sale of the machine.

This activity is the context of Pascal's second publication, an eighteen-page pamphlet [2] consisting of a "Lettre dédicatoire" to Séguier and a report on the calculating machine—its purpose, operating principles, capabilities, and the circumstances of its construction ("Avis nécessaire à ceux qui auront curiosité de voir ladite machine et de s'en servir"). The text concludes with the announcement that the machine can be seen in operation and purchased at the residence of Roberval. Pascal's first work of this scope, the pamphlet is both a valuable source of information on the guiding ideas of his project and an important document on his personality and style.

It is difficult to estimate the success achieved by Pascal's computing machine, the first of its kind to be offered for sale—an earlier one designed by W. Schickard (1623) seems to have reached only the prototype stage. Although its mechanism was quite complicated, Pascal's machine functioned in a relatively simple fashion—at least for the two operations to which it was actually applied.[7] Its high price, however, limited its sale and rendered it more a curiosity than a useful device. It is not known how many machines were built and sold; seven still exist in public and private collections.[8] For a few years Pascal was actively involved in their manufacture and distribution, for which he had obtained a monopoly by royal decree (22 May 1649) [22]. In 1652 he demonstrated his machine during a lecture before fashionable audience and presented one to Queen Christina of Sweden. For some time, however, he had been directing his attention to problems of a very different kind.

Raised in a Christian milieu, Pascal had been a practicing Catholic throughout his youth but had never given any special consideration to problems of faith. Early in 1646, however, he became converted to the austere and demanding doctrine of Saint-Cyran (Jean Duvergier de Hauranne), whose views were close to those of the Jansenists. This event profoundly marked the rest of Pascal's life. The intransigence of his new convictions was underscored at Rouen between February and April 1647, when Pascal and two friends denounced certain bold theological positions defended by Jacques Forton de Saint-Ange. This change in attitude did not, however, prevent Pascal from embarking on a new phase of scientific activity.

Fluid Statics and the Problem of the Vacuum. To understand and evaluate Pascal's work in the statics of gases and liquids, it is necessary to trace the origins of the subject and to establish a precise chronology. In his *Discorsi* (1638) Galileo had noted that a suction pump cannot raise water to more than a certain height, approximately ten meters. This observation, which seemed to contradict the Aristotelian theory that nature abhors a vacuum, was experimentally verified about 1641 by R. Maggiotti and G. Berti. V. Viviani and E. Torricelli modified the experiment by substituting mercury for water, thereby reducing the height of the column to about seventy-six centimeters. Torricelli announced the successful execution of this experiment in two letters to M. Ricci of 11 and 28 June 1644. Describing the experiment in detail, he gave a correct interpretation of it based on the weight of the external column of air and the reality of the existence of the vacuum.[9] Mersenne, informed of the work of the Italian scientists, attempted unsuccessfully to repeat the experiment, which for some time fell into neglect.

In October 1646 Mersenne's friend P. Petit, who was passing through Rouen, repeated the experiment with the assistance of Étienne and Blaise Pascal. At the end of November 1646 Petit described the event in a letter to Pierre Chanut. Meanwhile, Pascal, seeking to arrive at firm conclusions, had repeated the experiment in various forms, asserting that the results contradicted the doctrine of the *horror vacui*. Profiting from the existence at Rouen of an excellent glassworks, Pascal conducted a series of further experiments in January and February 1647. He repeated Torricelli's experiment with water and wine, using tubes of different shapes, some as long as twelve meters, affixed to the masts of ships. These experiments became known in Paris in the spring of 1647. Gassendi wrote the first commentary on them, and Mersenne and Roberval undertook their own experiments. The first printed account of the entire group of Pascal's experiments was *Discours sur le vide* by P. Guiffart, of Rouen, written in April 1647 and published in August of that year. Just as it was published, word reached Paris that a barometric experiment had been conducted at Warsaw in July 1647 by V. Magni, who implicitly claimed priority. Roberval responded on 22 September with a Latin *Narratio* (published at Warsaw in December), in which he established the priority of Torricelli's and Pascal's experiments and revealed new details concerning the latter.

Pascal soon intervened directly in the debate. During the summer of 1647 his health had deteriorated; and he left Rouen with his sister Jacqueline to move to Paris, where their father joined them a year later. Henceforth, Pascal maintained contacts both with the Jansenists of Port-Royal and with the secular intellectuals of Paris, who were greatly interested in the interpretation of the experiments with the vacuum. He had two discussions on this topic with Descartes (23 and 24 September), who may have suggested that he compare barometric observations made at different altitudes.[10] This idea was also proposed by Mersenne in his *Reflexiones physico-mathematicae* (beginning of October 1647).[11] At this time Pascal wrote a report of his experiments at Rouen, a thirty-two-page pamphlet published in October 1647 as *Expériences nouvelles touchant le vide* [3]. In this "abridgment" of a larger work that he planned to write, Pascal admitted that his initial inspiration derived from the Italian barometric experiment and stated that his primary goal was to combat

1916

the idea of the impossibility of the vacuum. From his experiments he had deduced the existence of an apparent vacuum, but he asserted that the existence of an absolute vacuum was still an unconfirmed hypothesis. Consequently his pamphlet makes no reference to the explanation of the barometric experiment by means of the weight of the air, proposed by Torricelli in 1644.[12] According to his sister Jacqueline, however, Pascal had been a firm proponent of this view from 1647.[13] In any case his concern was to convince his readers; he therefore proceeded cautiously, affirming only what had been irrefutably demonstrated by experiment.

Despite his moderate position, Pascal's rejection of the theory of the impossibility of the vacuum involved him in vigorous debate. With the publication of the *Expériences nouvelles*, a friend of Descartes's, the Jesuit Estienne Noël, declared in a letter to Pascal that the upper portion of Torricelli's tube was filled with a purified air that had entered through the pores of the glass.[14] In a dazzling reply (29 October 1647) [4] Pascal clearly set forth the rules of his scientific method and vigorously upheld his position. Several days later Noël reaffirmed the essence of his views but expressed a desire to end the dispute.[15] It was indirectly resumed, however, after Noël published a new and violent critique of the *Expériences nouvelles*.[16] In a letter to his friend F. Le Pailleur [5], Pascal refuted Noël's second letter and criticized his recent publication. In April 1648 Étienne Pascal entered the debate against Noël.[17] The dispute soon ended, however, when Noël published a much more moderate Latin version of his short treatise.[18]

During this controversy scientists in Paris had become interested in the problem of the vacuum, devoting many experiments to it and proposing a number of hypotheses to explain it. Having participated in discussions on the topic, Pascal conceived one of the variants of the famous experiment of the vacuum within the vacuum, designed to verify the hypothesis of the column of air.[19] He seems, however, to have expected a still better confirmation of the hypothesis from a program of simultaneous barometric observations at different altitudes (at Clermont-Ferrand and at the summit of Puy de Dôme), the execution of which he entrusted to his brother-in-law, Périer. One of these observations, now known as the "Puy de Dôme experiment," was carried out on 19 September 1648. Pascal immediately published a detailed, twenty-page account of it, *Récit de la grande expérience de l'équilibre des liqueurs . . .* [6], consisting principally of Périer's letter and report. In a short introduction he presented the experiment as the direct consequence of his *Expériences nouvelles*, and the text of a letter of 15 November 1647 to Périer, in which he explained the goal of the experiment and the principle on which it was based. He concluded by pointing out his analogous experiment at the Tour St. Jacques in Paris and by announcing his conversion to the principles of the existence of the absolute vacuum and of the weight of air.

The *Récit*, which marks an important phase of Pascal's research on the vacuum, gave rise to two heated controversies.[20] The first arose at the end of the seventeenth century, when several authors denied Pascal's priority with regard to the basic principle of the Puy de Dôme experiment. This question, however, is of only secondary importance. While it appears that the principle was formulated simultaneously—on the basis of different presuppositions—by Pascal, Descartes, and Mersenne, only Pascal tested it and integrated it into an exceptionally cogent chain of reasoning.

The second controversy was launched in 1906–1907 by F. Mathieu, who challenged both Pascal's scientific originality and his honesty. He accused Pascal of having fabricated the letter to Périer of 15 November 1647 after completion of the event, in order to take credit for the experiments of the vacuum within the vacuum and of Puy de Dôme. Although the heated debate that ensued did not produce any unanimously accepted conclusions, it did stimulate research that brought to light many unpublished documents. In an assessment of the question J. Mesnard, after examining the arguments and clarifying many points, suggests that Pascal probably did send the contested letter to Périer on 15 November 1647 but may have altered the text slightly for publication. This compromise judgment is probably close to the truth.

At the beginning of 1649 Périer, following Pascal's instructions, began an uninterrupted series of barometric observations designed to ascertain the possible relationship between the height of a column of mercury at a given location and the state of the atmosphere. The *expérience continuelle*, which was a forerunner of the use of the barometer as an instrument in weather forecasting, lasted until March 1651 and was supplemented by parallel observations made at Paris and Stockholm.[21] Pascal continued working on a major treatise on the vacuum; but only a few fragments, dating from 1651, have survived: a draft of a preface [7] on the relationships between reason and authority and between science and religion, and two short passages published by Périer in 1663.[22] In June 1651 a Jesuit accused Pascal of claiming credit for Torricelli's experiment. In two letters [9, 10], of which only the first was printed, Pascal recounted—with several serious errors—the history of that experiment and laid claim to the idea of the Puy de Dôme experiment.

Pascal soon put aside his great treatise on the vacuum in order to write a shorter but more synthetic work. Divided into two closely related parts, this work is devoted to the laws of hydrostatics and to the demonstration and description of the various effects of the weight of air. It was completed about the beginning of 1654 and marked the end of Pascal's active research in physics. It was published posthumously by Périer, along with several appendices, in 1663 as *Traités de l'équilibre des liqueurs et de la pesanteur de la masse de l'air* . . . [13]. The fruit of several years of observations, experiments, and reflection, it is a remarkable synthesis of new knowledge and theories elaborated since the work of Stevin and Galileo. The highly persuasive *Traités*, assembling and coordinating earlier results and recent discoveries, are characterized above all by their rigorous experimental method and by the categorical rejection of Scholasticism. In hydrostatics Pascal continued the investigations of Stevin, Galileo, Torricelli, and Mersenne. He clearly set forth the basic principles of the science, although he did not fully succeed in demonstrating them satisfactorily. In particular he provided a lucid account of the fundamental concept of pressure.

The untoward delay in the publication of the *Traités* obviously reduced its timeliness; for in the meanwhile the study of the weight of air and the existence of the vacuum had been profoundly affected by the work of Otto von Guericke and Robert Boyle.[23] In this area, in fact, the *Traités* essentially systematized, refined, and developed experiments, concepts, and theories that, for the most part, had already been discussed in the *Expériences nouvelles* and the *Récit*. Pascal's influence, therefore, must be measured as much by the effect of these preliminary publications and the contemporary writings of Mersenne and Pecquet, which reflect his thinking, as by the posthumous *Traités*.[24] This influence was certainly considerable, for it partially conditioned all subsequent research on the subject; but it cannot easily be separated from that of, for instance, Roberval and Auzout, who participated in the rapid progress of research on the vacuum at Paris in 1647 and 1648. Nevertheless, for their synthetic treatment of the subject, clarity, and rigor, the *Traités* are indisputably a classic of seventeenth-century science.

Although from October 1646 Pascal had been deeply interested in problems of the vacuum, he was often impeded in his research by poor health and by religious concerns. The death of his father in September 1651 and the entry of his sister Jacqueline into the convent of Port-Royal in January 1652 marked a turning point in his life. In better health and less preoccupied with religious problems, he pursued his scientific work while leading a more worldly existence. Beginning in the summer of 1653 he frequently visited the duke of Roannez. Through the duke he met the Chevalier de Méré, who introduced him to the problems of games of chance. At the beginning of 1654, in an address [12] to the Académie Parisienne de Mathématique, which was directed by F. Le Pailleur, Pascal listed the works on geometry, arithmetic, and physics that he had already completed or begun writing and mentioned, in particular, his recent research on the division of stakes.[25]

Calculus of Probabilities. The Arithmetical Triangle. The year 1654 was exceptionally fruitful for Pascal. He not only did the last refining of his treatises on geometry and physics but also conducted his principal studies on arithmetic, combinatorial analysis, and the calculus of probability. This work can be seen in his correspondence with Fermat [16] and his *Traité du triangle arithmétique* [17].

Pascal's correspondence with Fermat between July and October 1654 marks the beginning of the calculus of probability. Their discussion focused on two main problems. The first concerned the probability that a player will obtain a certain face of the die in a given number of throws. The second, more complex, consisted in determining, for any game involving several players, the portion of the stakes to be returned to each player if the game is interrupted. Fermat succeeded in solving these problems by using only combinatorial analysis. Pascal, on the other hand, seems gradually to have discovered the advantages of the systematic application of reasoning by recursion. This recourse to mathematical induction, however, is not clearly evident until the final section of the *Traité du triangle arithmétique*, of which Fermat received a copy before 29 August 1654.

The *Traité* was printed in 1654 but was not distributed until 1665. Composed partly in French and partly in Latin, it has a complex structure; but the discovery of a preliminary Latin version of the first part makes it easier to trace its genesis.[26] Although the principle of the arithmetical triangle was already known,[27] Pascal was the first to make a comprehensive study of it. He derived from it the greatest number of applications, the most important and original of which are related to combinatorial analysis and especially to the study of the problems of stakes. Yet it is impossible to appreciate Pascal's contribution if it is considered solely from the perspective of combinatorial analysis and the calculus of probability. Several modern authors have shown that Pascal's letters to Fermat and the *Traité du triangle arithmétique* can be fully understood only when they are seen as preliminary steps toward a theory of decision.[28]

As E. Coumet has pointed out, Pascal's concern, beyond the purely mathematical aspect of the problems, was to link decisions and uncertain events. His aim was not to define the mathematical status of the concept of probability—a term that he did not employ—but to solve the problem of dividing stakes. This innovative effort must therefore be viewed in the context of the discussions conducted by jurists, theologians, and moralists in the sixteenth and seventeenth centuries on the implications of chance in the most varied circumstances of individual and community life. Unrecognized until recently, this aspect of Pascal's creative work is revealed in its full significance in the light of recent ideas on game theory and decision theory.

On the other hand, Pascal's research on combinatorial analysis now appears much less original. Considered in the context of the vigorous current of ideas on the subject in the sixteenth and seventeenth centuries, it is noteworthy less for the originality of its results than for the clarity, generality, and rigor with which they are presented.[29] Pascal's contribution to the calculus of probability is much more direct and indisputable: indeed, with Fermat he laid the earliest foundations of this discipline.[30] The *Traité du triangle arithmétique* contains only scattered remarks on the subject; in addition, only a part of the correspondence with Fermat [16] has been preserved, and its late publication (1679 and 1779) certainly reduced its direct influence. Fortunately, through Huygens the original contribution of Pascal and Fermat in this area became quickly known. During a stay in Paris in 1655 Huygens was informed in detail of their work, and he recast their ideas in the light of his own conceptions in his *Tractatus de ratiociniis in aleae ludo*. With its publication in 1657 the essential elements of the new science were revealed.[31] Nevertheless, the calculus of probability did not experience further development until the beginning of the eighteenth century, with Jakob I Bernoulli, P. R. de Montmort, and A. de Moivre.

Unsatisfied by his worldly life and intense scientific activity, Pascal was again drawn to religious concerns. Following a second conversion, during the famous "nuit de feu" of 23 November 1654, he abandoned his scientific work in order to devote himself to meditation and religious activity and to assist the Jansenists in their battle against many enemies, particularly the Jesuits. Working anonymously, between 13 January 1656 and 24 March 1657 Pascal composed the eighteen *Lettres provinciales* with the assistance of his friends from Port-Royal, Antoine Arnauld and Pierre Nicole. A masterpiece of polemic, this eminent contribution to the debate then agitating Christian doctrine was first published as a collection in 1657 under the pseudonym Louis de Montalte. Although Pascal produced other polemical writings, he worked primarily on preparing a defense of Christianity directed to nonbelievers. This unfinished project was the source of several posthumously published writings, the most important being the *Pensées*, published in 1670. The object of numerous commentaries and penetrating critical studies, this basic work fully displays Pascal's outstanding philosophical and literary talents.

Although concerned above all with meditation and religious activities during this period, Pascal was not totally estranged from scientific life thanks to his friends, particularly Carcavi. Around 1657, at the request of Arnauld, Pascal prepared a work entitled *Éléments de géométrie*, of which there remain only a few passages concerning methodology: the brief "Introduction à la géométrie," preserved among Leibniz's papers [18]; and two fragments, "De l'esprit géométrique" and "De l'art de persuader" [19]. Finally, in 1658 Pascal undertook a brilliant, if short-lived, series of scientific studies.

The Calculus of Indivisibles and the Study of Infinitesimal Problems. During 1658 and the first months of 1659 Pascal devoted most of his time to perfecting the "theory of indivisibles," a forerunner of the methods of integral calculus. This new theory enabled him to study problems involving infinitesimals: calculations of areas and volumes, determinations of centers of gravity, and rectifications of curves.

From the end of the sixteenth century many authors, including Stevin (1586), L. Valerio (1604), and Kepler (1609 and 1615), had tried to solve these fundamental problems by using simpler and more intuitive methods than that of Archimedes, which was considered a model of virtually unattainable rigor.[32] The publication in 1635 of Cavalieri's *Geometria* marked the debut of the method of indivisibles;[33] its principles, presentation, and applications were discussed and elaborated in the later writings of Cavalieri (1647 and 1653) and in those of Galileo (1638), Torricelli (1644), Guldin (1635–1641), Gregory of Saint-Vincent (1647), and A. Tacquet (1651). (The research of Fermat and Roberval on this topic remained unpublished.)[34] The method, which assumed various forms, constituted the initial phase of development of the basic procedures of integral calculus, with the exception of the algorithm.

Pascal first referred to the method of indivisibles in a work on arithmetic of 1654, "Potestatum numericarum summa."[35] He observed that the results concerning the summation of numerical powers made possible the solution of certain quadrature problems. As an example he stated a known result concerning the integral of x^n for whole n, $\int_0^a x^n \, dx = a^{n+1}/(n+1)$, in modern notation.[36] This arithmetical interpretation of the theory of indivisibles permitted Pascal to give a sufficiently precise idea of the order of infinitude[37] and to establish the natural relationship between "la mesure d'une grandeur continue" and "la sommation des puissances numériques." In the fragment "De l'esprit géométrique" [19], composed in 1657, he returned to the notion of the indivisible in order to specify its relationship to the notions of the infinitely small and of the infinitely large and to refute the most widespread errors concerning it.

At the beginning of 1658 Pascal believed that he had perfected the calculus of indivisibles by refining his method and broadening its field of application. Persuaded that in this manner he had discovered the solution to several infinitesimal problems relating to the cycloid or *roulette*, he decided to challenge other mathematicians to solve these problems.[38] Although rather complicated, the history of this contest is worth a brief recounting because of its important repercussions during a crucial phase in the birth of infinitesimal calculus. In an unsigned circular distributed in June 1658, Pascal stated the conditions of the contest and set its closing date at 1 October [20a]. In further unsigned circulars and pamphlets [20], issued between July 1658 and January 1659, he modified or specified certain of the conditions and announced the results. He also responded to the criticism of some participants and sought to demonstrate the importance and the originality of his own solutions.

Most of the leading mathematicians of the time followed the contest with interest, either as participants (A. de Lalouvère and J. Wallis) or as spectators working on one or several of the questions proposed by Pascal or on related problems—as did R. F. de Sluse, M. Ricci, Huygens, and Wren.[39] Their solutions having been judged incomplete and marred by errors, Lalouvère and Wallis were eliminated. Their heated reactions to this decision were partially justified by the bias it displayed and the commentaries that accompanied it.[40] This bias, which also appears in certain passages of Pascal's *Histoire de la roulette* [20b, 20d], was the source of intense polemics concerning, in particular, the importance of Torricelli's original contribution.[41] At the end of the contest Pascal published his own solutions to some of the original problems and to certain problems that had been added in the meantime. In December 1658 and January 1659 he brought out, under the pseudonym A. Dettonville, four letters setting forth the principles of his method and its applications to various problems concerning the cycloid, as well as to such questions as the quadrature of surfaces, cubature of volumes, determination of centers of gravity, and rectification of curved lines.

In February 1659 these four pamphlets were collected in *Lettres de A. Dettonville contenant quelques-unes de ses inventions de géométrie . . .* [21].

This publication of some 120 pages has a very complex structure. The first of the *Lettres* consists of five sections with independent paginations, and the three others appear in inverse order of their composition.[42] Thus only by returning to the original order is it possible to understand the logical sequence of the whole, follow the development of Pascal's method, and appreciate the influence on it of the new information he received and of his progress in mastering infinitesimal problems.[43]

When he began the contest, Pascal knew of the methods and the chief results of Stevin, Cavalieri, Torricelli, Gregory of Saint-Vincent, and Tacquet; but he was not familiar with the bulk of the unpublished research of Roberval and Fermat. Apart from this information, and in addition to the arithmetical procedures that he applied, starting in 1654, to the solution of problems of the calculus of indivisibles, Pascal possessed a new method inspired by Archimedes. It was elaborated on a geometric foundation, its point of departure being the principle of the balance and the concepts of static moment and center of gravity. Pascal learned of the importance of the results obtained by Fermat and Roberval—notably in the study of the cycloid—at the time he issued his first circular. This information led him to modify the subject of the contest and to develop his own method further. Similarly, in August 1658, when he was informed of the result of the rectification of the cycloid, Pascal extended rectification to other arcs of curves and then undertook to determine the center of gravity of these arcs, as well as the area and center of gravity of the surfaces of revolution generated by their revolution about an axis. Consequently the *Lettres* present a method that is in continual development, appearing increasingly complex as it becomes more precise and more firmly based. The most notable characteristics of this work, which remained unfinished, are the importance accorded to the determination of centers of gravity, the crucial role of triangular sums and statical considerations, its stylistic rigor and elegance, and the use of a clear and precise geometric language that partially compensates for the absence of algebraic symbolism.[44] Among outstanding contributions of the work are the discovery of the equality of curvature of the generalized cycloid and the ellipse; the deepening of the concept of the indivisible; a first step toward the concept of the definite integral and the determination of its fundamental properties; and the indirect recourse to certain methods of calculation, such as integration by parts.

Assimilated and exploited by Pascal's successors, these innovations contributed to the elaboration of infinitesimal methods. His most productive contribution, however, appears to have been his implicit use of the characteristic triangle.[45] Indeed, Leibniz stated that Pascal's writings on the characteristic triangle were an especially fruitful stimulus for him.[46] This testimony from one of the creators of infinitesimal calculus indicates that Pascal's work marked an important stage in the transition from the calculus of indivisibles to integral calculus. Pascal was unable, however, to transcend the overly specific nature of his conceptions. Neither could he utilize to full effect the power and generality of the underlying methods nor develop the results he obtained. This partial failure can be attributed to two causes. First, his systematic refusal to adopt Cartesian algebraic symbolism prevented him from realizing the necessity of the formalization that permitted Leibniz to create the integral calculus. Second, his preoccupation with mystic concerns led him to interrupt his research only a short time after he had begun it.

Early in 1659 Pascal again fell gravely ill and abandoned almost all his intellectual undertakings in order to devote himself to prayer and to charitable works.[47] In 1661 his desire for solitude increased after the death of his sister Jacqueline and a dispute with his friends from Port-Royal. Paradoxically, it was at this time that Pascal participated in a project to establish a public transportation system in Paris, in the form of carriages charging five *sols* per ride—a scheme that went into effect in 1662.[48] Some writers have asserted that Pascal's doctrinal intransigence had diminished in this period to such a point that at the moment of his death he renounced his Jansenist convictions, but most of the evidence does not support this interpretation.

Pascal was a complex person whose pride constantly contended with a profound desire to submit to a rigorous, Augustinian insistence on self-denial. An exceptionally gifted polemicist, moralist, and writer, he was also a scientist anxious to help solve the major problems of his day. He did not, it is true, produce a body of work distinguished by profound creativity, on the model of such contemporaries as Descartes, Fermat, and Torricelli. Still, he was able to elucidate and systematize several rapidly developing fields of science (projective geometry, the calculus of probability, infinitesimal calculus, fluid statics, and scientific methodology) and to make major original contributions to them. In light of this manifold achievement Pascal, a leading opponent of Descartes, was undoubtedly one of the outstanding scientists of the mid-seventeenth century.

NOTES

1. The first known formulation of this theorem was as lemma 1 of *Essay pour les coniques*. It clearly differs from the modern statement by not referring explicitly to the inscribed hexagon and by apparently being limited to the case of the circle (even though the corresponding figure illustrates the case of the ellipse). According to remarks made by Leibniz, it seems that this theorem, in its hexagonal formulation and under the name "hexagramme mystique," held a central place in Pascal's treatise on conics, now lost. The fact that the *Essay pour les coniques* contains only statements without demonstrations makes it impossible to ascertain the precise role Pascal assigned to this theorem in 1640.

2. The numbers in square brackets refer to the corresponding works listed in sec. 1 of the bibliography. For a more detailed study of the *Essay*, see R. Taton, in *Revue d'histoire des sciences*, 8 (1955), 1–18, and in *L'oeuvre scientifique de Pascal* (Paris, 1964), 21–29; and J. Mesnard, ed., *Blaise Pascal. Oeuvres complètes*, II (1971), 220–225 (cited below as Mesnard).

3. See Mersenne's letter to Theodore Haak of 18 Nov. 1640, in Mesnard, II, 239.

4. On the references by Desargues and Mersenne, see *ibid.*, 279–280, 299. On the problem of Pappus, see Mersenne's letter to Constantijn Huygens of 17 Mar. 1648 in C. Huygens, *Oeuvres complètes de Christiaan Huygens, publiées par la Société Hollandaise des Sciences*, II (1888), 33, and in Mesnard, II, 577–578. On Descartes, see Taton, in *L'oeuvre scientifique de Pascal*, 45–50; and M. S. Mahoney, "Descartes: Mathematics and Physics," in *DSB*, IV, 56.

5. See Taton, in *L'oeuvre scientifique . . .*, 55–59 (for "Generatio conisectionum") and 53–72 (for the treatise as a whole). See also his "Desargues," in *DSB*, IV, 46–51.

6. See Taton, "La Hire, Philippe de," in *DSB*, VII, 576–578.

7. See D. Diderot, "Arithmétique (Machine)," in *Encyclopédie*, I (1751), 680–684.

8. See J. Payen, in *L'oeuvre scientifique de Pascal*, 229–247.

9. See, in particular, C. De Waard, *L'expérience barométrique, ses antécédents et ses explications* (Thouars, 1936), 110–123; M. Gliozzi, "Origine e sviluppi dell'esperienza torricelliana," in *Opere de Evangelista Torricelli*, G. Loria and G. Vassura, eds., IV (Faenza, 1944), 231–294; and W. E. K. Middleton, *The History of the Barometer* (London, 1964).

10. Jacqueline Pascal gave some details of these meetings in a letter to her sister Gilberte of 25 Sept. 1647. (See Mesnard, II, 478–482.) In a letter to Mersenne of 13 Dec. 1647 and in two letters to Carcavi of 11 June and 17 Aug. 1649 (see *ibid.*, 548–550, 655–658, 716–719) Descartes stated that he had suggested this idea, which was the origin of the celebrated Puy de Dôme experiment of 19 Sept. 1648, to Pascal.

11. See *ibid.*, 483–489.

12. Torricelli held that the space above the column of mercury was empty. Considering the horizontal plane determined by the exterior level of the mercury, he asserted that the weight of the column of mercury equaled the weight of a column of air of the same base, which implied simultaneously the existence of the vacuum, the weight of the air, and the finiteness of the terrestrial atmosphere. In 1651 Pascal admitted that he was aware of Torricelli's explanation as early as 1647 (see *ibid.*, 812), but he insisted that at that time the explanation was only a conjecture; it had yet to be verified by experiment, and for this reason he undertook the experiment of Puy de Dôme.

13. Letter to Gilberte Pascal of 25 Sept. 1647 (see *ibid.*, 482).

14. See *ibid.*, 513–518.

15. See *ibid.*, 528–540.

16. It was a brief work with the picturesque title *Le plein du vide* (Paris, 1648); see Mesnard, II, 556–558. This work was reprinted by Bossut in *Oeuvres de Blaise Pascal*, C. Bossut, ed., IV (The Hague, 1779), 108–146.

17. See Mesnard, II, 584–602.

18. E. Noël, *Plenum experimentis novis confirmatum* (Paris, 1648); see Mesnard, II, 585.

19. This experiment is mentioned without details in Pascal's *Récit* . . . (see Mesnard, II, 678). The reality of the experiment is confirmed by the quite precise description of it that Noël gave in his *Gravitas comparata* (Paris, 1648); on this point see Mesnard, II, 635–636, which presents the Latin text, a French translation, and an explanatory diagram derived from an earlier study by P. Thirion. The principle of this experiment consists of conducting Torricelli's experiment in an environment where the pressure can be varied from atmospheric pressure to zero. Other variants were devised at almost the same time by Roberval (Mesnard, II, 637–639) and by Auzout (*ibid.*, 767–771). A fourth variant, easier to carry out in practice, is described in Pascal's *Traités de l'équilibre des liqueurs et de la pesanteur de la masse de l'air* . . . (*ibid.*, 1086–1088).

20. See *ibid.*, 653–676.

21. F. Périer published an account of them in 1663 as an appendix to Pascal's *Traités de l'équilibre* . . . (pp. 195–209); see Mesnard, II, 738–745. The fact that the first observations made at Stockholm were carried out by Descartes appears to indicate that he had become reconciled with Pascal.

22. The preface was not published until 1779, when it appeared under the title "De l'autorité en matière de philosophie" (Bossut, II, 1–12). The passages published by Périer appear at the end of Pascal's *Traités de l'équilibre* . . . (pp. 141–163).

23. See F. Krafft, "Guericke," in *DSB*, V, 574–576; and C. Webster, "The Discovery of Boyle's Law and the Concept of the Elasticity of Air in the Seventeenth Century," in *Archive for History of the Exact Sciences*, **2** (1965), 441–502, esp. 447–458.

24. M. Mersenne, *Reflectiones physico-mathematicae* (Paris, 1647); and J. Pecquet, *Experimenta nova anatomica* (Paris, 1651). To these works should be added publications by Noël, already cited, as well as those of Roberval and of V. Magni (see Webster, *op. cit.*), and, above all, the correspondence of scientists from Italy, France, England, Poland, and other European countries.

25. The word used in French to designate this problem, *parti*, is the past participle (considered as the noun form) of the verb *partir*, understood in the sense of "to share." The problem consists in finding, for a game interrupted before the end, the way of dividing the stakes among the players in proportion to their chances of winning at the time of interruption.

26. See Mesnard, II, which provides an introduction to the texts (pp. 1166–1175) and the texts themselves, both of the first printing, in Latin with French translation (pp. 1176–1286), and of the second, with translation of the Latin passages (pp. 1288–1332).

27. This figure, in more or less elaborated forms that were equivalent to lists of coefficients of the binomial theorem, appeared as early as the Middle Ages in the works of Naṣīr al-Dīn al Ṭūsī (1265) and Chu Shih-chieh (1303). The arithmetical triangle reappeared in the sixteenth and seventeenth centuries in the writings of Apian (1527), Stifel, Scheubel, Tartaglia, Bombelli, Peletier, Trenchant, and Oughtred. But Pascal was the first to devote to it a systematic study linked to many questions of arithmetic and combinatorial analysis.

28. See, for example, E. Coumet, "La théorie du hasard est-elle née par hasard?" in *Annales. Économies, sociétés, civilisations* (1970), 574–598, as well as the studies of G.-T. Guilbaud (1952) and the other works on operational research, cybernetics, game theory, and other fields cited in Coumet's article (p. 575, notes 1 and 2).

29. See E. Coumet, "Mersenne, Frénicle et l'élaboration de l'analyse combinatoire dans la première moitié du XVIIe siècle" (a typescript thesis, Paris, 1968), and "Mersenne: Dénombrements, répertoires, numérotations de permuta-

tions," in *Mathématiques et sciences humaines*, **10** (1972), 5–37.

30. See I. Todhunter, *A History of the Mathematical Theory of Probability From the Time of Pascal to That of Laplace* (Cambridge–London, 1865; repr. New York, 1949), 7–21.

31. See F. Van Schooten, *Exercitationum mathematicarum libri quinque* (Leiden, 1657), 519–534, and H. J. M. Bos's article on Huygens in *DSB*, VI, 600.

32. On Archimedes see the article by M. Clagett in *DSB*, I, 213–231, esp. 215–222, for his infinitesimal methods and 229 for the diffusion of his writings in the sixteenth and seventeenth centuries. It should be noted that at this period mathematicians were aware only of his rigorous method of presentation, which Gregory of Saint-Vincent termed the "method of exhaustion." Archimedes' much more intuitive method of discovery did not become known until the rediscovery of his *Method* in 1906. On the infinitesimal work of Stevin, Valerio, and Kepler, see C. B. Boyer, *The Concept of Calculus* (New York, 1949), 98–111.

33. B. Cavalieri, *Geometria indivisibilibus continuorum nova quadam ratione promota* (Bologna, 1635). On this subject see Boyer, *op. cit.*, pp. 111–123; A. Koyré, in *Études d'histoire de la pensée scientifique* (Paris, 1966), 297–324; and the article on Cavalieri by E. Carruccio in *DSB*, III, 149–153.

34. See Boyer, *op. cit.*, pp. 123–147, 154–165.

35. Reprinted in Mesnard, II, 1259–1272; see esp. 1270–1272. This work is the next to last—but also one of the earliest written—of the brief treatises making up the *Traité du triangle arithmétique* [17].

36. "The sum of all the lines of any degree whatever is to the larger line and to the higher degree as unity is to the exponent of the higher degree" (Mesnard, II, 1271). On Pascal's infinitesimal work see H. Bosmans, in *Archivio di storia della scienza*, **4** (1923), 369–379; Boyer, *op. cit.*, pp. 147–153; F. Russo, in *L'oeuvre scientifique de Pascal* (Paris, 1964), 136–153; and P. Costabel, *ibid.*, 169–206.

37. "In the case of a continuous magnitude (*grandeur continue*), magnitudes of any type (*genre*), when added in any number desired to a magnitude of higher type, do not increase it at all. Thus, points add nothing to lines, [nor] lines to surfaces, [nor] surfaces to solids, or, to use the language of numbers in a treatise devoted to numbers, roots do not count with respect to squares, [nor] squares with respect to cubes . . . . Therefore, lower degrees should be neglected as possessing no value" (Mesnard, II, 1271–1272).

38. The cycloid is the curve generated by a point M of the circumference of a circle (C) that rolls without sliding on a straight line D. AB, the base of the cycloid, is equal to $2\pi r$ (where r is the radius of the circle C). Derived curves are obtained by the displacement of a point M' situated on the interior (curtate cycloid) or M'' on the exterior (prolate cycloid) of the moving circle. Defined by Roberval in 1637,

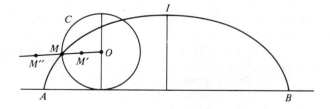

FIGURE 1

these curves had served since that year—under the name of

roulettes, trochoids, or cycloids—as key examples for the solution of various problems pertaining to the infinitesimal calculus. These problems included the construction of tangents to plane curves by the use of the method of indivisibles, the determination of plane areas, the calculation of volumes, and the determination of centers of gravity. The cycloid thus played an important role in the patient efforts that resulted in the transition from the method of indivisibles to the infinitesimal calculus. Between 1637 and 1647 Roberval, then Fermat and Descartes, and finally Torricelli were particularly interested in the solution of infinitesimal problems associated with the cycloid; and bitter priority disputes broke out between Roberval and Descartes and then between Roberval and Torricelli. But in June 1658, when Pascal distributed his first circular, it appears that he had only a very imperfect knowledge of prior work on this subject.

The practice of setting up a contest was very common at the time. A similar contest, initiated by Fermat in January 1657 on questions of number theory, continued to set Fermat against some of the participants, notably Wallis. See O. Becker and J. E. Hofmann, *Geschichte der Mathematik* (Bonn, 1951), 192–194.

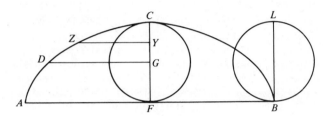

FIGURE 2

The contest problem was the following: Given an arch of the cycloid of base AB and of axis CF, one considers the semicurvilinear surface CZY defined by the curve, the axis, and a semichord ZY parallel to the base. The problem is to find (1) the area of CZY and its center of gravity; (2) the volumes of the solids V_1 and V_2 generated by the revolution of CZY about CY and about ZY, as well as their centers of gravity; and (3) the centers of gravity of the semisolids obtained by cutting V_1 and V_2 by midplanes.

39. In his *Histoire de la roulette* [20b], Pascal mentions the results sent to him by these four authors and notes, in particular, the rectification of the arch of the cycloid communicated to him by Wren. He points out that he has extended this operation to an arbitrary arc AZ originating at the summit of the cycloid and that he has determined the center of gravity of this arc AZ, as well as the areas and centers of gravity of the surfaces of revolution generated by the rotation of AZ about the base or about the axis of the cycloid. Carcavi, the president of the jury, also mentioned the results sent by Fermat, particularly those on the areas of the surfaces of revolution.

40. See A. Lalouvère, *Veterum geometria promota in septem de cycloide libris* (Toulouse, 1660); and J. Wallis, *Tractatus duo, prior de cycloide, posterior de cissoide* (Oxford, 1659). On the latter publication see K. Hara, "Pascal et Wallis au sujet de la cycloïde," in two parts: the first in *Annals of the Japanese Association for the Philosophy of Science*, **3**, no. 4 (1969), 36–57, and the second in *Gallia* (Osaka), nos. 10–11 (1971), 231–249.

41. See, in particular, C. Dati, *Lettera della vera storia della cicloide* (Florence, 1663).

42. This question is raised by K. Hara, in "Quelques additions à l'examen des textes mathématiques de Pascal," in *Gallia* (Osaka), no. 7 (1962); by P. Costabel, in *L'oeuvre scientifique de Pascal*, 169–198; and by J. Mesnard, in Mesnard, I, 31–33.

43. The original order is reproduced in vol. III of Mesnard's ed. of Pascal's works (in preparation).

44. See Bosmans, *op. cit.*; Boyer, *op. cit.*, pp. 147–153; Russo, *op. cit.*, pp. 136–153; and Costabel, *ibid.*, pp. 169–206.

45. See Russo, *op. cit.*, pp. 149–151. It should be noted that the expression "characteristic triangle" was introduced not by Pascal but by Leibniz. See also Boyer, *op. cit.*, pp. 152–153; Boyer points out that this figure had previously been used by Torricelli and Roberval and even by Snell (1624). In modern notation, the characteristic triangle at a point $M(x_0, y_0)$ of a plane curve (C) of equation $y = f(x)$ is a right triangle, the first two sides of which, parallel to the axes Ox and Oy, are of length dx and dy; its diagonal, of length ds, is parallel to the tangent to the curve (C) at M.

46. See a letter from Leibniz to Jakob I Bernoulli of Apr. 1703, in Leibniz, *Mathematische Schriften*, C. I. Gerhardt, ed., III (Halle, 1856), 72–73. This letter is reproduced in part in *Histoire générale des sciences*, 2nd ed., II (Paris, 1969), 245–246. For other statements by Leibniz concerning his knowledge of Pascal's writtings, see P. Costabel, in *L'oeuvre scientifique de Pascal*, 201–205.

47. Pascal wrote again to Fermat (10 Aug. 1660), met Huygens (5 and 13 Dec. 1660), and conversed with the duke of Roannez on the force of rarefied air and on flying. These are the few indications that we have regarding Pascal's scientific activity during the last three years of his life.

48. See M. Duclou, *Les carrosses à cinq sols* (Paris, 1950).

BIBLIOGRAPHY

I. ORIGINAL WORKS. There have been many complete eds. of Pascal's works. The most important from the point of view of scholarship are the following:

a. *Oeuvres de Blaise Pascal*, C. Bossut, ed., 5 vols. (The Hague, 1779), abbrev. as Bossut.

b. *Oeuvres de Blaise Pascal publiées selon l'ordre chronologique*, L. Brunschvicg, P. Boutroux, and F. Gazier, eds., 14 vols. (Paris, 1904–1914), part of the Collection des Grands Écrivains de la France, abbrev. as G.E.

c. *Oeuvres complètes de Blaise Pascal*, J. Chevalier, ed. (Paris, 1954), in Bibliothèque de la Pléiade," abbrev. as PL.

d. *Blaise Pascal. Oeuvres complètes*, J. Mesnard, ed., 2 vols. to date (Paris, 1964–1971); abbrev. as Mesnard. This last ed., which surpasses all previous ones, so far comprises only vol. I (*Introduction générale* and *Documents généraux*) and vol. II (*Oeuvres diverses, 1623–1654*). It has been used in preparing this article.

Each reference to a passage in one of these eds. will consist of the abbreviation, the volume number, year of publication of the volume, and page number. The list below includes most of Pascal's surviving scientific writings, cited in the order in which they were written. For each writing there is the title, its presumed date of composition, and its various eds.: the first (indicated as "orig." if published during Pascal's lifetime and as "1st ed." if posthumous) and the chief subsequent eds. (in separate vols. and in the sets of complete works cited above, as well as any other ed. containing important original material).

1. *Essay pour les coniques* (1639–1640). Orig. (Paris, Feb. 1640); Bossut, IV (1779), 1–7; G.E., I (1908), 243–260 and XI (1914), 347; PL (1954), 57–63, 1380–1382; R. Taton, "L' 'Essay pour les coniques' de Pascal," in *Revue d'histoire des sciences*, **8** (1955), 1–18; Mesnard, II (1971), 220–235.

2. *Lettre dédicatoire à Monseigneur le Chancelier sur le sujet de la machine nouvellement inventée par le sieur B. P. pour faire toutes sortes d'opérations d'arithmétique par un mouvement réglé sans plume ni jetons avec un avis nécessaire à ceux qui auront curiosité de voir ladite machine et de s'en servir* (1645). Orig. (Paris, 1645); Bossut, IV (1779), 7–24; G.E., I (1908), 291–314; PL (1954), 347–358; Mesnard, II (1971), 329–341.

3. *Expériences nouvelles touchant le vide. . . . Avec un discours sur le même sujet . . . dédié à Monsieur Pascal, conseiller du roi . . . par le sieur B. P. son fils. Le tout réduit en abrégé et donné par avance d'un plus grand traité sur le même sujet* (Sept.–early Oct. 1647). Orig. (Paris, Oct. 1647); Bossut, IV (1779), 51–68; G.E., II (1908), 53–76; PL (1954), 359–370; Mesnard, II (1971), 493–508.

4. Pascal's correspondence with Noël (late Oct.–early Nov. 1647). 1st ed., Bossut, IV (1779), 69–108; G.E., II (1908), pp. 77–125; PL (1954), 370–377, 1438–1452; Mesnard, II (1971), 509–540.

5. Pascal's letter to Le Pailleur (Feb. 1648). 1st ed., Bossut, IV (1779), 147–177; G.E., II (1908), 177–211; PL (1954), 377–391; Mesnard, II (1971), 555–576.

6. *Récit de la grande expérience de l'équilibre des liqueurs projetée par le sieur B. P. pour l'accomplissement du traité qu'il a promis dans son abrégé touchant le vide et faite par le sieur F. P. en une des plus hautes montagnes d'Auvergne* (autumn 1648). Orig. (Paris, 1648), repr. in facs. with intro. by G. Hellmann (Berlin, 1893) and in *Traités de l'équilibre des liqueurs et de la pesanteur de la masse de l'air . . .* (Paris, 1663; repr. 1664, 1698); Bossut, IV (1779), 345–369; G.E., II (1908), 147–162, 349–358, and 363–373; PL (1954), 392–401; Mesnard, II (1971), 653–690.

7. Preface to the treatise on the vacuum ("De l'autorité en matière de philosophie") (1651). 1st ed., Bossut, II (1779), 1–12; G.E., II (1908), 127–145, and XI (1914), 348–349; PL (1954), 529–535; Mesnard, II (1971), 772–785.

8. Fragments of "Traité du vide" (1651). 1st ed., in *Traités de l'équilibre des liqueurs et de la pesanteur de la masse de l'air . . .* (Paris, 1663), 141–163; Bossut, IV (1779), 326–344; G.E., II (1908), 513–529; PL (1954), 462–471; Mesnard, II (1971), 786–798.

9. *Lettre de M. Pascal le fils adressante à M. le Premier Président de la Cour des aides de Clermont-Ferrand . . .* (July 1651). Orig. (Clermont-Ferrand, 1651); Bossut, IV (1779), 198–214; G.E., II (1908), 475–495; PL (1954), 402–409; Mesnard, II (1971), 799–813.

10. Continuation of the correspondence with M. de Ribeyre (July–Aug. 1651). 1st ed., Bossut, IV (1779), 214–221; G.E., II (1908), 496–502; PL (1954), 409–411; Mesnard, II (1971), 814–818.

11. Letter from Pascal to Queen Christina of Sweden (June 1652). 1st ed., in F. Granet and P. N. Desmolets, eds., *Recueil de pièces d'histoire et de littérature*, III (Paris, 1738), 117–123; Bossut, IV (1779), 25–29; G.E., III (1908), 23–34; PL (1954), 502–504; Mesnard, II (1971), 920–926.

12. "Celeberrimae matheseos academiae Parisiensis" (Paris, 1654). 1st. ed., Bossut, IV (1779), 408–411; G.E., III (1908), 293–308; PL (1954), 71–74, 1400–1404 (French trans.); Mesnard, II (1971), 1121–1135 (with French trans.).

13. *Traités de l'équilibre des liqueurs et de la pesanteur de la masse de l'air. Contenant l'explication des causes de divers effets de la nature qui n'avaient point été bien connus jusques ici, et particulièrement de ceux que l'on avait attribués à l'horreur du vide* (completed at the latest in 1654). 1st ed. (Paris, Nov. 1663). The text of the *Traités* corresponds to pp. 1–140; pp. 141–163 reproduce the only two fragments known of the great treatise on the vacuum prepared by Pascal in 1651; the rest of the volume contains (pp. 164–194) a repr. of the *Récit de la grande expérience . . .* and (pp. 195–232) texts by F. Périer and others. Important subsequent eds. are those of 1664 and 1698; Bossut, IV (1779), 222–325; G.E., III (1908), 143–292, and IX (1914), 352; PL (1954), 412–471; Mesnard, I (1964), 679–689 (preface by F. Périer), and II (1971), 739–745 (account of Périer's observations), 787–798 (two "Fragments d'un traité du vide"), and 1036–1101 (the actual *Traités*).

14. "Generatio conisectionum" (completed about 1654). 1st ed. in *Sitzungsberichte der K. Preussischen Akademie der Wissenschaften zu Berlin*, **1** (1892), 197–202 (edited by C. I. Gerhardt); G.E., II (1908), 234–243; PL (1954), 66–70, 1382–1387 (French trans.); Mesnard, II (1971), 1108–1119.

15. Leibniz's notes on Pascal's treatise on conics (the notes date from 1676, but the treatise was finished about 1654). 1st ed. (partial) in *Sitzungsberichte der K. Preussischen Akademie der Wissenschaften zu Berlin*, **1** (1892), 195–197, edited by C. I. Gerhardt; G.E., II (1908), 227–233; P. Costabel, in *L'oeuvre scientifique de Pascal* (1964), 85–101 (with French trans.); Mesnard, II (1971), 1120–1131 (with French trans.).

16. Correspondence with Fermat (July–Oct. 1654). 1st ed., P. Fermat, *Varia opera mathematica . . .* (Toulouse, 1679), 179–188 (for the three letters by Pascal; for the other four see Bossut); Bossut, IV (1779), 412–445; Fermat, *Oeuvres*, P. Tannery and C. Henry, eds., II (1894), 288–314, and III (1896), 310–311; PL (1954), 74–90; Mesnard, II (1971), 1132–1158.

17. *Traité du triangle arithmétique, avec quelques petits traités sur la même matière* (1654). 1st ed. (Paris, 1665). Without the first four pages (title page, foreword, and table of contents) and the plate, this work was printed during Pascal's lifetime (1654) but was not distributed. It consists of four parts: the "Traité du triangle arithmétique" itself; two papers devoted to various applications of the triangle; and a fourth paper on numerical orders, powers, combinations, and multiple numbers that is formed of seven sections, the first in French and the rest in Latin. J. Mesnard has identified a preliminary Latin version of the part of this treatise that was published in French.

Subsequent eds.: Bossut, V (1779), 1–134; *Oeuvres complètes de Pascal*, C. Lahure, ed., II (1858), 415–494 (with French trans. of the Latin passages); G.E., III (1908), 311–339, 341–367, 433–598, and XI (1914), 353, 364–390; PL (1954), 91–171, 1404–1432 (translations); Mesnard, II (1971), 1166–1332—repr. with French trans. of the entire preliminary Latin ed., *Triangulus arithmeticus*, followed by the new sections of the *Traité*.

18. "Introduction à la géométrie" (written about the end of 1657). 1st ed. in *Sitzungsberichte der K. Preussischen Akademie der Wissenschaften zu Berlin*, **1** (1892), 202–204 (C. I. Gerhardt, ed.); G. E., IX (1914), 291–294; PL (1954), 602–604, 1476; J. Itard, in *L'oeuvre scientifique de Pascal* (1964), 102–119.

19. "De l'esprit géométrique" and "De l'art de persuader" (written about 1657–1658). 1st ed. (partial), P. N. Desmolets in *Continuation des mémoires de littérature et d'histoire*, V, pt. 2 (Paris, 1728), 271–296; Bossut, II (1779), 12–38, 39–57; G.E., IX (1914), 240–290; PL (1954), 574–602.

20. Various items pertaining to the cycloid competition (June 1658–Jan. 1659).

a. Three circulars addressed to the contestants: the first in Latin (June 1658); the second in Latin (July 1658); the third in French and Latin (dated 7 Oct. in the French text and 9 Oct. in the Latin version).

b. *Histoire de la roulette . . .* (10 Oct. 1658), also in Latin, *Historia trochoidis* (same date).

c. *Récit de l'examen et du jugement des écrits envoyés pour les prix proposés publiquement sur le sujet de la roulette . . .* (25 Nov. 1658).

d. *Suite de l'histoire de la roulette . . .* (12 Dec. 1658, with an addition on 20 Jan. 1659); the Latin version exists only in MS.

A more detailed description of this group of writings is provided by L. Scheler, in *L'oeuvre scientifique de Pascal* (1964), 30–31, and in Mesnard, I (1964), 163–167. Subsequent eds. are Bossut, V (1779), 135–213; G.E., VII (1914), 337–347, and VIII (1914), 15–19, 155–223, 231–246, 289–319; PL (1954), 180–223, 1433–1435 (French trans. of the circulars of June and July 1658).

21. *Lettres de A. Dettonville contenant quelques-unes de ses inventions de géométrie . . .* (Paris, Feb. 1659). This vol. contains a title page (written after the rest of contents), four sheets of plates, and four letters published between Dec. 1658 and Jan. 1659 (in the order 1, 4, 3, 2).

Letter no. 1: *Lettre de A. Dettonville à Monsieur de Carcavy, en lui envoyant: Une méthode générale pour trouver les centres de gravité de toutes sortes de grandeurs. Un traité des trilignes et de leurs onglets. Un traité des sinus du quart de cercle. Un traité des solides circulaires. Et enfin un traité général de la roulette, contenant la solution de tous les problèmes touchant la roulette qu'il avait proposés publiquement au mois de juin 1658*. Orig. (Paris, 1658).

Letter no. 2: *Lettre de A. Dettonville à Monsieur A. D. D. S. en lui envoyant: La démonstration à la manière des anciens de l'égalité des lignes spirale et parabolique*. Orig. (Paris, 1658).

Letter no. 3: *Lettre de A. Dettonville à Monsieur de Sluze, chanoine de la cathédrale de Liège, en lui envoyant: La dimension et le centre de gravité de l'escalier. La dimension et le centre de gravité des triangles cylindriques. La dimension d'un solide formé par le moyen d'une spirale autour d'un cône*. Orig. (Paris, 1658).

Letter no. 4: *Lettre de A. Dettonville à Monsieur Huggyens [sic] de Zulichem, en lui envoyant: La dimension des lignes de toutes sortes de roulettes, lesquelles il montre être égales à des lignes elliptiques*. Orig. (Paris, 1659).

Later eds.: Bossut, V (1779), 229–452; G.E., VIII (1914), 247–288, 325–384, and IX (1914), 1–149, 187–204; PL (1954), 224–340, 1436–1437; a facs. of the original ed. has recently appeared (London, 1966).

Two other important documents relating to Pascal's scientific work are the following:

22. The license for his calculating machine (22 May 1649). 1st ed. in *Recueil de diverses pièces pour servir à l'histoire de Port-Royal* (Utrecht, 1740), 244–248; Bossut, IV (1779), 30–33; G.E., II (1908), 399–404; Mesnard, II (1971), 711–715.

23. Letter from Leibniz to Étienne Périer of 30 Aug. 1676 concerning Pascal's treatise on conics. 1st ed., Bossut, V (1779), 459–462; G.E., II (1908), 193–194; PL (1954), 63–65; J. Mesnard and R. Taton, in *L'oeuvre scientifique de Pascal* (1964), 73–84.

II. SECONDARY LITERATURE. A very complete bibliography of studies on Pascal's scientific work published before 1925 can be found in A. Maire, *Bibliographie générale des oeuvres de Pascal*, 2nd ed., I, *Pascal savant* (Paris, 1925). Most of the more recent works on the subject (except for those dealing with the cycloid) are cited in the bibliographies in Mesnard, II (1971)—geometry, 227–228, 1108; combinatorial theory and the calculus of probability, 1135, 1175; the calculating machine, 327–328; physics, 349, 459, 513, 675–676, 777, 804, 1040; miscellaneous, 1031.

Two general studies in particular should be mentioned: P. Humbert, *L'oeuvre scientifique de Pascal* (Paris, 1947), a survey written for a broad audience; and *L'oeuvre scientifique de Pascal* (Paris, 1964), a joint effort that restates the main aspects of Pascal's career and scientific work (with the exception of the theory of combinations and the calculus of probability). Other recent studies worth consulting are A. Koyré, "Pascal savant," in *Blaise Pascal, l'homme et l'oeuvre* (Paris, 1956), pp. 259–285; K. Hara, "Examen des textes mathématiques dans les oeuvres complètes de Pascal d'après les Grands Écrivains de la France," in *Gallia* (Osaka), no. 6 (1961); "Quelques additions à l'examen des textes mathématiques de Pascal," *ibid.*, no. 7 (1962); and "Pascal et Wallis au sujet de la cycloïde, I," in *Annals of the Japan Association for Philosophy of Science*, 3, no. 4 (1969), 166–187; "Pascal et Wallis . . . , II," in *Gallia*, nos. 10–11 (1971), 231–249; and "Pascal et Wallis . . . , III," in *Japanese Studies in the History of Science*, no. 10 (1971), 95–112; N. Bourbaki, *Éléments d'histoire des mathématiques*, 2nd ed. (Paris, 1969), see index; M. E. Baron, *The Origins of the Infinitesimal Calculus* (London, 1969), esp. 196–205; and E. Coumet, "La théorie du hasard est-elle née par hasard?" in *Annales. Économies, sociétés, civilisations*, **5** (May–June 1970), 574–598.

RENÉ TATON

PASCAL, ÉTIENNE (*b.* Clermont-Ferrand, France, 2 May 1588; *d.* Paris, France, 24 September 1651),

The son of Martin Pascal, treasurer of France, and Marguerite Pascal de Mons, Pascal married Antoinette Begon in 1616. They had three children: Gilberte (1620–1687), who in 1641 married Florin Périer; Blaise (1623–1662), the philosopher and scientist; and Jacqueline (1625–1661), who in 1652 entered the convent of Port-Royal.

Elected counselor for Bas-Auvergne in 1610, Pascal became president of the Cour des Aides in 1625. His wife died in 1626, and in 1631 he left Clermont to settle in Paris with his children. He devoted himself to his son's education while gaining a reputation as a talented mathematician and musician. In 1634 Pascal was one of five commissioners named to examine J. B. Morin's "invention" for the determination of longitudes. As early as 1635 he frequented "Mersenne's academy" and was in contact with Roberval, Desargues, and Mydorge.

In November 1635 Mersenne dedicated to Pascal the "Traité des orgues" of his *Harmonie universelle* (1636). Roberval communicated to Pascal his first discoveries concerning the cycloid and intervened on his side in the debate concerning the nature of gravity (interpreting it in terms of attraction—letter to Fermat of 16 August 1636; Fermat's response of 23 August). At the beginning of 1637 Fermat wrote his "Solution d'un problème proposé par M. Pascal." At about the same time Pascal introduced a special curve, the conchoid of a circle with respect to one of its points, to be applied to the problem of trisecting an angle. Roberval called it the "limaçon de M. Pascal" and determined its tangent by his kinematic method. In February 1638 Roberval joined Pascal in defending Fermat's *De maximis et minimis*, which had been attacked by Descartes.

Having been obliged to return to Auvergne from March 1638 to April 1639, Pascal then moved to Rouen, where he was appointed intendant of the province, a post he held until 1648. He had given his son Blaise a solid foundation in mathematics, and he now fostered the development of his work, mainly through his contacts with many scientists. In October 1646 Pascal participated with his son and P. Petit in the first repetition in France of Torricelli's experiment. In April 1648 he joined in the debate between Blaise and the Père E. Noël concerning the problem of the vacuum. He returned to Paris in August 1648, was in Auvergne from May 1649 to November 1650, then spent his last months in Paris.

BIBLIOGRAPHY

I. ORIGINAL WORKS. The rare documents concerning Pascal's scientific work are reproduced in the major eds. of his son's complete works: *Oeuvres de Blaise Pascal publiées selon l'ordre chronologique*, L. Brunschvicg, P. Boutroux, and F. Gazier, eds., 14 vols. (Paris, 1908–1914), in the collection Grands Écrivains de la France (hereafter cited as G.E.); and *Blaise Pascal. Oeuvres complètes*, J. Mesnard, ed., I, II (Paris, 1964, 1971) (hereafter cited as Mesnard).

They include "Jugement porté par les commissaires Étienne Pascal, Mydorge, Beaugrand, Boulanger, Hérigone sur l'invention du sieur J. B. Morin," in G.E., I, 194–195, and Mesnard, II, 82–99; "Lettre d'Étienne Pascal et Roberval à Fermat, samedi 16 août 1636," in *Oeuvres de Fermat*, P. Tannery, C. Henry, and C. de Waard, eds., 5 vols. (Paris, 1891–1922), II, 35–50 (hereafter cited as Fermat), also in G.E., I, 177–193, and Mesnard, II, 123–140; "Lettre de Fermat à Étienne Pascal et Roberval, 23 août 1636," in Fermat, II, 50–56, and in Mesnard, II, 140–146; "Solutio problematis a Domino de Pascal propositi" (Jan. or Feb. 1637), in Fermat, I, 70–74, also in G.E., I, 196–201, and Mesnard, II, 148–156, also translated into French as "Solution d'un problème proposé par M. de Pascal," in Fermat, III, 67–71, and Mesnard, II, 149–156; "Réponse de Descartes à un écrit des amis de M. de Fermat" (1 Mar. 1638), in *Oeuvres de Descartes*, C. Adam and P. Tannery, eds., II (Paris, 1898), 1–15, also in *Descartes. Correspondance*, C. Adam and G. Milhaud, eds., II (Paris, 1939), 143–153, *Correspondance du P. Marin Mersenne*, C. De Waard and B. Rochot, eds., VII (Paris, 1962), 64–73, and Mesnard, II, 164–174; and "Lettre de M. Pascal le Père au R. P. Noël" (Apr. 1648), in G.E., II, 255–282, and in Mesnard, II, 584–602.

II. SECONDARY LITERATURE. Documents, notices, and details concerning the life and work of Pascal can be found in G.E., I, 5–28, 170–176, and II, 533–562; Mesnard, I, 459–464, 510–515, 571–576, 721–722, 727–729, 754–771, 1077–1079, 1091–1100, and II, 119–123, 157–163, 174–188, 217, 253–254, 841–863; the ed. of Descartes's *Oeuvres* cited above, index, V, 607; the ed. of Descartes's correspondence cited above, II, 379–381 and index; and Mersenne's correspondence cited above, vols. IV–VII, see index.

The catalog of a commemorative exhibition held at the Bibliothèque Nationale in 1962, *Blaise Pascal, 1623–1662* (Paris, 1962), furnishes references to many documents concerning Étienne Pascal: nos. 1, 9, 10, 14, 17, 18, 22–27, 31, 32, 34, 36, 38, 41, 60, 67, 69–72, 76, 77, 168. Other references are in A. Maire, *Pascal savant* (Paris, 1925), 270–275 and index.

Additional details are in M. Cantor, *Vorlesungen über Geschichte der Mathematik*, 2nd ed., II (Leipzig, 1900), 675, 679, 681, 875, 881, 882; J. Mesnard, *Pascal et les Roannez*, 2 vols. (Paris, 1965), see index; and P. Tannery, *Mémoires scientifiques*, X (Paris, 1930), 372, 382–383, and XIII (Paris, 1934), 337–338.

RENÉ TATON

PASCH, MORITZ (*b*. Breslau, Germany [now Wrocław, Poland], 8 November 1843; *d*. Bad Homburg, Germany, 20 September 1930)

Pasch studied chemistry at Breslau but changed to mathematics at the suggestion of Heinrich Schröter, to whom, along with Kambly, his teacher at the Elisabeth Gymnasium, he dedicated his dissertation (1865). Later, at Berlin, he was influenced by Weierstrass and Kronecker. He maintained his mathematical activity with scarcely a break for sixty-five years, for the first seventeen years in algebraic geometry and later in foundations, the work on which his fame rests. His first two papers were written in collaboration with his lifelong friend J. Rosanes. Except for rapid promotion, Pasch's career at the University of Giessen was not unusual: in 1870, *Dozent*; in 1873, extraordinary professor; in 1875, after an offer of an extraordinary professorship from the University of Breslau, ordinary professor. In 1888 he obtained the chair left vacant by the death of Heinrich Baltzer. He was also active in administration, becoming dean in 1883 and rector in 1893–1894. In order to dedicate himself more fully to his scientific work, he retired in 1911. In celebration of his eightieth birthday Pasch received honorary Ph.D.'s from the universities of Frankfurt and Freiburg. He was a member of the Deutsche Mathematiker-Vereinigung. His name is perpetuated in Pasch's axiom, which states that in a plane, if a line meets one side of a triangle, then it meets another. His outward life was simple, although saddened by the early death of his wife and one of two daughters. He died while on a vacation trip away from Giessen.

The axiomatic method as it is understood today was initiated by Pasch in his *Vorlesungen über neuere Geometrie* (Leipzig, 1882; 2nd ed., Berlin, 1926). It consists in isolating from a given study certain notions that are left undefined and are expressly declared to be such (the *Kernbegriffe*, in Pasch's terminology of 1916), and certain theorems that are accepted without proof (the *Kernsätze*, or axioms). From this initial fund of notions and theorems, the other notions are to be defined and the theorems proved using only logical arguments, without appeal to experience or intuition. The resulting theory takes the form of purely logical relations between undefined concepts.

To be sure, there are preliminary explanations, and a definite philosophy is disclosed for choosing the axioms. According to Pasch the initial notions and theorems should be founded on observations. Thus the notion of point is allowed but not that of line, since no one has ever observed a complete (straight) line; rather, the notion of segment is taken as primitive. Similarly, a planar surface, but not a plane, is primitive.

Pasch's analysis relating to the order of points on a line and in the plane is both striking and pertinent to its understanding. Every student can draw diagrams and see that if a point *B* is between point *A* and point *C*, then *C* is not between *A* and *B*, or that every line divides a plane into two parts. But no one before Pasch had laid a basis for dealing logically with such observations. These matters may have been considered too obvious; but the result of such neglect is the need to refer constantly to intuition, so that the logical status of what is being done cannot become clear. According to Pasch, the appeal to intuition formally ceases once the *Kernbegriffe* and *Kernsätze* are stated.

The higher geometry of Pasch's day was projective geometry that used real numbers as coordinates. Pasch therefore considered that the foundation would be laid once the coordinates had been introduced. In doing this he presented notions of congruence, which were nonprojective. This is somewhat disappointing in view of Staudt's 1847 program for founding projective geometry solely on projective terms (though we may emphasize that the congruence axioms are original with Pasch). But F. Klein had uncovered some nonrigorous thinking in Staudt's proof that a one-to-one mapping between two lines that sends harmonic quadruples into harmonic quadruples is uniquely determined by the images of three points—without, however, obtaining notable success in clarifying this matter. Pasch proved this fundamental theorem on the basis of the Archimedean character of the ordering on the line, and not on its completeness, as Klein proposed to do. The congruence notions were introduced, at least in part, in order to state Archimedes' axiom. Once the fundamental theorem was proved, the introduction of coordinates could be easily accomplished—as M. Dehn remarks in a historical appendix to Pasch's *Vorlesungen*—on the basis of the Eudoxian theory of book V of Euclid's *Elements*. But for Pasch this procedure was complicated by his empiricist point of view.

It would be easy to overlook the significance of Pasch's foundational achievements for several reasons. First, it is now a commonplace to present theories in an axiomatic way, so that even logic itself is presented axiomatically. Thus Pasch's innovation achieves the status of being a trifle.

There are also widespread misconceptions as to what is in book I of the *Elements*: it is thought that Euclid had an axiomatic way of presenting geometry. This view is further confounded by a lack of clarity as to what the axiomatic method is and what geometry is. Anyone who looks at book I of the *Elements* with modern hindsight sees that something is wrong, but it would take delicate historical considerations to place the source of the faults in a correct light.

The Greeks of Euclid's time had the axiomatic method; Aristotle's description of it can be considered a close approximation to the modern one. Or, better yet, one may consider Eudoxus' theory of magnitude as presented in book V of the *Elements*. Except for style (which, however, may indicate a difference in point of view), the procedure presented there coincides with Pasch's. It is known, however, that the *Elements* is a compilation of uneven quality, so that even with the definitions, postulates, and common notions of book I, it is unwarranted to assume that book I is written from the same point of view as book V.

In some versions of book I, as it has come down to us, there are five "common notions" and five postulates. T. L. Heath considers it probable that common notions 4 and 5 were interpolations; and P. Tannery maintains that they were none of them authentic. The first three postulates are the "postulates of construction," the fourth states that all right angles are equal, and the fifth is the parallel postulate. It has been argued that the first three postulates were meant to help meet the injunction to limit the means of construction to "straightedge and compass"; that there was no intention to say anything about space. One could eliminate these three, as well as the fourth, without changing the rigor of the book or the points of view disclosed relative to geometry or to the axiomatic method. The fifth does not appear until proposition 29, so that the first twenty-eight propositions (minus the constructions) are, from a modern axiomatic point of view, based on nothing.

Although deduction is a prominent feature of book I of the *Elements*, the contents of the book and the history of the parallel postulate show that geometry was conceived as the study of a definite object, "external space." With the invention of non-Euclidean geometry around 1800, it began to dawn on mathematicians that their concern is with deduction, and not with a supposed external reality. Applications, if any, may be left to the physicist. With G. Fano's miniature projective plane of just seven points and seven lines (1892), the revolution may be considered to have been completed. Hilbert, through his work in geometry and logic, consolidated it.

Pasch initiated the axiomatic method, although the foundational developments of his time were against this point of view. Thus Cantor's striking discoveries were based, from an axiomatic point of view, on nothing. Dedekind rightly contrasted his own treatment of magnitude with Eudoxus'; Dedekind's was constructive, whereas Eudoxus' was axiomatic. As late as 1903 Frege poked fun at the axiomatic method as presented in Hilbert's *Grundlagen der Geometrie*.

The Italian geometers, particularly Peano, continued Pasch's work. In 1889 Peano published both his exposition of geometry, following Pasch, and his treatment of number. It is tempting to see in the former work a source of the latter, although there were many other sources.

Pasch played a crucial role in the innovation of the axiomatic method. This method, with contributions from logic and algebra, is a central feature of twentieth-century mathematics.

BIBLIOGRAPHY

See M. Dehn and F. Engel, "Moritz Pasch," in *Jahresbericht der deutschen Mathematiker-Vereinigung*, **44** (1934), 120–142; P. Tannery, "Sur l'authenticité des axiomes d'Euclide," in *Bulletin des sciences mathématiques et astronomiques* (1884), 162; G. Fano, "Sui postulati fondamentali della geometria proiettiva," in *Giornale di matematiche* (Naples), **30** (1892), 106–132; G. Frege, "Über die Grundlagen der Geometrie," in *Jahresbericht der deutschen Mathematiker-Vereinigung*, **12** (1903), 319–324, 368–375; H. Freudenthal, "Zur Geschichte der Grundlagen der Geometrie," in *Nieuwe Archieff voor Wiskunde*, **5** (1957), 105–142; T. L. Heath, *The Thirteen Books of Euclid's Elements*, 2nd ed. (New York, 1956), esp. 221, 225, 232; and A. Seidenberg, "The Ritual Origin of Geometry," in *Archive for History of Exact Sciences*, **1** (1962), 488–527, esp. 497 f.

A. SEIDENBERG

PATRIZI, FRANCESCO (also **Patrizzi** or **Patricio**; Latin form, **Franciscus Patricius**) (*b*. Cherso, Istria, Italy, 25 April 1529; *d*. Rome, Italy, 7 February 1597)

Patrizi studied at Ingolstadt, at the University of Padua (1547–1554), and at Venice. While in the service of various noblemen in Rome and Venice he made several trips to the East, where he perfected his knowledge of Greek, and to Spain. He lived for a time at Modena and at Ferrara, before being appointed to a personal chair of Platonic philosophy at the University of Ferrara by Duke Alfonso II d'Este in 1578. He remained there until 1592, when Pope Clement VIII summoned him to a similar professorship in Rome, a post he held until his death.

Patrizi had interests in many different intellectual fields; he published works on poetry, history, rhetoric, literary criticism, metaphysics, ethics, natural philosophy, and mathematics, besides translating a number of Greek works into Latin. His thought is a characteristic blend of Platonism (in the widest sense in which the word is used when referring to the Renaissance) and natural philosophy, with a very strong anti-Aristotelian bent. The latter critical tendency is developed in his *Discussiones peripateticae* (Venice, 1571; much enlarged edition, Basel, 1581).

Patrizi's importance in the history of science rests primarily on his highly original views concerning the nature of space, which have striking similarities to those later developed by Henry More and Isaac Newton. His position was first set out in *De rerum natura libri II priores, alter de spacio physico, alter de spacio mathematico* (Ferrara, 1587) and was later revised and incorporated into his *Nova de universis philosophia* (Ferrara, 1591; reprinted Venice, 1593), which is his major systematic work. Rejecting the Aristotelian doctrines of *horror vacui* and of determinate "place," Patrizi argued that the physical existence of a void is possible and that space is a necessary precondition of all that exists in it. Space, for Patrizi, was "merely the simple capacity (*aptitudo*) for receiving bodies, and nothing else." It was no longer a category, as it was for Aristotle, but an indeterminate receptacle of infinite extent. His distinction between "mathematical" and "physical" space points the way toward later philosophical and scientific theories.

The primacy of space (*spazio*) in Patrizi's system is also seen in his *Della nuova geometria* (Ferrara, 1587), the essence of which was later incorporated into the *Nova de universis philosophia*. In it Patrizi attempted to found a system of geometry in which space was a fundamental, undefined concept that entered into the basic definitions (point, line, angle) of the system.

The full impact of Patrizi's works on later thought has yet to be evaluated.

BIBLIOGRAPHY

Lega Nazionale di Trieste, *Onoranze a Francesco Patrizi da Cherso: Catalogo della mostra bibliografica* (Trieste, 1957), presents the most complete listing of primary and secondary works to 1957. Other general works are B. Brickman, *An Introduction to Francesco Patrizi's Nova de universis philosophia* (New York, 1941); P. O. Kristeller, *Eight Philosophers of the Italian Renaissance* (Stanford, 1964), ch. 7; and G. Saitta, *Il pensiero italiano nell'umanesimo e nel Rinascimento*, 2nd ed. (Florence, 1961), II, ch. 9.

Works on Patrizi's concept of space are B. Brickman, "Francesco Patrizi on Physical Space," in *Journal of the History of Ideas*, **4** (1943), 224–245; E. Cassirer, *Das Erkenntnisproblem*, 3rd ed. (Berlin, 1922), I, 260–267; W. Gent, *Die Philosophie des Raumes und der Zeit*, 2nd ed. (Hildesheim, 1962), 81–83; and M. Jammer, *Concepts of Space* (Cambridge, Mass., 1954), 84–85.

CHARLES B. SCHMITT

PEACOCK, GEORGE (*b*. Denton, near Darlington, Durham, England, 9 April 1791; *d*. Ely, England, 8 November 1858)

Peacock is known for his role in the reform of the teaching of mathematics at Cambridge and his writings on algebra. His father, Thomas, was perpetual curate at Denton; and Peacock was educated at home. He entered Trinity College, Cambridge, in 1809 and received the B.A. in 1813, as second wrangler; the M.A. in 1816; and the D.D. in 1839. In 1815 he was named lecturer at Trinity and was a tutor from 1823 to 1839. He was a moderator of the tripos examination in 1817, 1819, and 1821. Peacock was a member of the Analytical Society, founded by Charles Babbage for the purpose of revitalizing mathematical studies at Cambridge. Toward this end Peacock, Babbage, and John Herschel published a translation of an elementary calculus text by Lacroix (1816). In 1820 Peacock published a collection of examples in differential and integral calculus. These works, and his influence as moderator, tutor, and lecturer, were major factors in replacing the fluxional notation and the geometric methods, which had been entrenched at Cambridge since the time of Newton, with the more fruitful analysis and Leibnizian notation.

In 1837 Peacock became Lowndean professor of geometry and astronomy at Cambridge, but in 1839 he was appointed dean of Ely. (He had been ordained in 1822.) Although he moved to Ely and no longer lectured, he remained active in the affairs of Cambridge. In 1841 he published a book on the statutes of the university in which he urged reform, and he served on two government commissions dealing with the question. Peacock was a member of the Cambridge Philosophical Society, the Royal Astronomical Society, the Geological Society of London, and the British Association for the Advancement of Science. He was elected a fellow of the Royal Society in 1818. He married Frances Elizabeth Selwyn in 1847. They had no children.

Peacock's mathematical work, although not extensive, is significant in the evolution of a concept of abstract algebra. In the textbook *A Treatise on Algebra* (1830), revised in 1842–1845, he attempted to put the theory of negative and complex numbers on a firm logical basis by dividing the field of algebra into arithmetical algebra and symbolic algebra. In the former the symbols represented positive integers; in the latter the domain of the symbols was extended by his principle of the permanence of equivalent forms. This principle asserts that rules in arithmetical algebra, which hold only when the values of the variables are restricted, remain valid when the restriction is removed. Although it was a step toward abstraction, Peacock's view was limited because he insisted that if the variables were properly chosen, any formula in symbolic algebra would yield a true formula in arithmetical algebra. Thus a noncommutative algebra would not be possible.

Peacock's other works include a survey on the state of analysis in 1833, prepared for the British Association for the Advancement of Science. It is an invaluable source for a contemporary view of the important problems at that time. Peacock also wrote a biography of Thomas Young and was one of the editors of his miscellaneous works.

BIBLIOGRAPHY

Early works are Sylvestre Lacroix, *An Elementary Treatise on the Differential and Integral Calculus*, translated by Charles Babbage, George Peacock, and John Herschel, with notes by Peacock and Herschel (Cambridge, 1816); and *A Collection of Examples of the Differential and Integral Calculus* (Cambridge, 1820). *A Treatise on Algebra* (Cambridge, 1830) is rare, but there is a rev. ed., 2 vols. (Cambridge, 1842–1845; repr. New York, 1940). Other writings include "Report on the Recent Progress and Present State of Certain Branches of Analysis," in *Report of the British Association for the Advancement of Science* (1834), 185–352; "Arithmetic," in *Encyclopaedia Metropolitana*, I (London, 1845); 369–523; *The Life of Thomas Young* (London, 1855); *Miscellaneous Works of the Late Thomas Young*, vols. I and II, George Peacock, ed., vol. III, John Leitch, ed. (London, 1855); and *Observations on the Statutes of the University of Cambridge* (London, 1841).

A complete bibliography of his writings can be found in Daniel Clock, "A New British Concept of Algebra: 1825–1850" (Ph.D. diss., U. of Wisconsin, 1964), 10–12; this work also contains an extensive discussion of Peacock's life and work.

ELAINE KOPPELMAN

PEANO, GIUSEPPE (*b.* Spinetta, near Cuneo, Italy, 27 August 1858; *d.* Turin, Italy, 20 April 1932)

Giuseppe Peano was the second of the five children of Bartolomeo Peano and Rosa Cavallo. His brother Michele was seven years older. There were two younger brothers, Francesco and Bartolomeo, and a sister, Rosa. Peano's first home was the farm Tetto Galant, near the village of Spinetta, three miles from Cuneo, the capital of Cuneo province, in Piedmont. When Peano entered school, both he and his brother walked the distance to Cuneo each day. The family later moved to Cuneo so that the children would not have so far to walk. The older brother became a successful surveyor and remained in Cuneo. In 1974 Tetto Galant was still in the possession of the Peano family.

Peano's maternal uncle, Michele Cavallo, a priest and lawyer, lived in Turin. On this uncle's invitation Peano moved to Turin when he was twelve or thirteen. There he received private lessons (some from his uncle) and studied on his own, so that in 1873 he was able to pass the lower secondary examination of the Cavour School. He then attended the school as a regular pupil and in 1876 completed the upper secondary program. His performance won him a room-and-board scholarship at the Collegio delle Provincie, which was established to assist students from the provinces to attend the University of Turin.

Peano's professors of mathematics at the University of Turin included Enrico D'Ovidio, Angelo Genocchi, Francesco Siacci, Giuseppe Basso, Francesco Faà di Bruno, and Giuseppe Erba. On 16 July 1880 he completed his final examination "with high honors." For the academic year 1880–1881 he was assistant to D'Ovidio. From the fall of 1881 he was assistant and later substitute for Genocchi until the latter's death in 1889. On 21 July 1887 Peano married Carola Crosio, whose father, Luigi Crosio (1835–1915), was a genre painter.

On 1 December 1890, after regular competition, Peano was named extraordinary professor of infinitesimal calculus at the University of Turin. He was promoted to ordinary professor in 1895. In 1886 he had been named professor at the military academy, which was close to the university. In 1901 he gave up his position at the military academy but retained his professorship at the university until his death in 1932, having transferred in 1931 to the chair of complementary mathematics. He was elected to a number of scientific societies, among them the Academy of Sciences of Turin, in which he played a very active role. He was also a knight of the Order of the Crown of Italy and of the Order of Saint Maurizio and Saint Lazzaro. Although he was not active politically, his views tended toward socialism; and he once invited a group of striking textile workers to a party at his home. During World War I he advocated a closer federation of the allied countries, to better prosecute the war and, after the peace, to form the nucleus of a world federation. Peano was a nonpracticing Roman

Catholic.

Peano's father died in 1888; his mother, in 1910. Although he was rather frail as a child, Peano's health was generally good. His most serious illness was an attack of smallpox in August 1889. After having taught his regular class the previous afternoon, Peano died of a heart attack the morning of 20 April 1932. At his request the funeral was very simple, and he was buried in the Turin General Cemetery. Peano was survived by his wife (who died in Turin on 9 April 1940), his sister, and a brother. He had no children. In 1963 his remains were transferred to the family tomb in Spinetta.

Peano is perhaps most widely known as a pioneer of symbolic logic and a promoter of the axiomatic method, but he considered his work in analysis most important. In 1915 he printed a list of his publications, adding: "My works refer especially to infinitesimal calculus, and they have not been entirely useless, seeing that, in the judgment of competent persons, they contributed to the constitution of this science as we have it today." This "judgment of competent persons" refers in part to the *Encyklopädie der mathematischen Wissenschaften*, in which Alfred Pringsheim lists two of Peano's books among nineteen important calculus texts since the time of Euler and Cauchy. The first of these books was Peano's first major publication and is something of an oddity in the history of mathematics, since the title page gives the author as Angelo Genocchi, not Peano: *Angelo Genocchi, Calcolo differenziale e principii di calcolo integrale, publicato con aggiunte dal D.ʳ Giuseppe Peano*. The origin of the book is that Bocca Brothers wished to publish a calculus text based on Genocchi's lectures. Genocchi did not wish to write such a text but gave Peano permission to do so. After its publication Genocchi, thinking Peano lacked regard for him, publicly disclaimed all credit for the book, for which Peano then assumed full responsibility.

Of the many notable things in this book, the *Encyklopädie der mathematischen Wissenschaften* cites theorems and remarks on limits of indeterminate expressions, pointing out errors in the better texts then in use; a generalization of the mean-value theorem for derivatives; a theorem on uniform continuity of functions of several variables; theorems on the existence and differentiability of implicit functions; an example of a function the partial derivatives of which do not commute; conditions for expressing a function of several variables with Taylor's formula; a counterexample to the current theory of minima; and rules for integrating rational functions when roots of the denominator are not known. The other text of Peano cited in the *Encyklopädie* was the two-volume *Lezioni*

di analisi infinitesimale of 1893. This work contains fewer new results but is notable for its rigor and clarity of exposition.

Peano began publication in 1881 with articles on the theory of connectivity and of algebraic forms. They were along the lines of work done by D'Ovidio and Faà di Bruno. Peano's work in analysis began in 1883 with an article on the integrability of functions. The article of 1890 contains original notions of integrals and areas. Peano was the first to show that the first-order differential equation $y' = f(x, y)$ is solvable on the sole assumption that f is continuous. His first proof dates from 1886, but its rigor leaves something to be desired. In 1890 this result was generalized to systems of differential equations using a different method of proof. This work is also notable for containing the first explicit statement of the axiom of choice. Peano rejected the axiom of choice as being outside the ordinary logic used in mathematical proofs. In the *Calcolo geometrico* of 1884 Peano had already given many counterexamples to commonly accepted notions in mathematics, but his most famous example was the space-filling curve that was published in 1890. This curve is given by continuous parametric functions and goes through every point in a square as the parameter ranges over some interval. Some of Peano's work in analysis was quite original, and he has not always been given credit for his priority; but much of his publication was designed to clarify and to make rigorous the current definitions and theories. In this regard we may mention his clarification of the notion of area of a surface (1882, independently discovered by H. A. Schwarz); his work with Wronskians, Jacobians, and other special determinants, and with Taylor's formula; and his generalizations of quadrature formulas.

Peano's work in logic and in the foundations of mathematics may be considered together, although he never subscribed to Bertrand Russell's reduction of mathematics to logic. Peano's first publication in logic was a twenty-page preliminary section on the operations of deductive logic in *Calcolo geometrico secondo l'Ausdehnungslehre di H. Grassmann* (1888). This section, which has almost no connection with the rest of the text, is a synthesis of, and improvement on, some of the work of Boole, Schröder, Peirce, and McColl. The following year, with the publication of *Arithmetices principia, nova methodo exposita*, Peano not only improved his logical symbolism but also used his new method to achieve important new results in mathematics; this short booklet contains Peano's first statement of his famous postulates for the natural numbers, perhaps the best known of all his creations. His research was done independently of the work of Dedekind, who the previous year had published an analysis of the natural numbers, which was essentially that of Peano but without the clarity of Peano. (This was the only work Peano wrote in Latin.) *Arithmetices principia* made important innovations in logical notation, such as ∈ for set membership and a new notation for universal quantification. Indeed, much of Peano's notation found its way, either directly or in a somewhat modified form, into mid-twentieth-century logic.

In the 1890's he continued his development of logic, and he presented an exposition of his system to the First International Congress of Mathematicians (Zurich, 1897). At the Paris Philosophical Congress of 1900, Peano and his collaborators—Burali-Forti, Padoa, and Pieri—dominated the discussion. Bertrand Russell later wrote, "The Congress was a turning point in my intellectual life, because I there met Peano."

In 1891 Peano founded the journal *Rivista di matematica*, which continued publication until 1906. In the journal were published the results of his research and that of his followers, in logic and the foundations of mathematics. In 1892 he announced in the *Rivista* the *Formulario* project, which was to take much of his mathematical and editorial energies for the next sixteen years. He hoped that the result of this project would be the publication of a collection of all known theorems in the various branches of mathematics. The notations of his mathematical logic were to be used, and proofs of the theorems were to be given. There were five editions of the *Formulario*. The first appeared in 1895; the last was completed in 1908, and contained some 4,200 theorems. But Peano was less interested in logic as a science per se than in logic as used in mathematics. (For this reason he called his system "mathematical logic.") Thus the last two editions of the *Formulario* introduce sections on logic only as it is needed in the proofs of mathematical theorems. The editions through 1901 do contain separate, well-organized sections on logic.

The postulates for the natural numbers received minor modifications after 1889 and assumed their definitive form in 1898. Peano was aware that the postulates do not characterize the natural numbers and, therefore, do not furnish a definition of "number." Nor did he use his mathematical logic for the reduction of mathematical concepts to logical concepts. Indeed, he denied the validity of such a reduction. In a letter to Felix Klein (19 September 1894) he wrote: "The purpose of mathematical logic is to analyze the ideas and reasoning that especially figure in the mathematical sciences." Peano was neither a logicist nor a formalist. He believed rather that mathematical ideas are ultimately derived from our experience of the material world.

In addition to his research in logic and arithmetic, Peano also applied the axiomatic method to other fields, notably geometry, for which he gave several axiom systems. His first axiomatic treatment of elementary geometry appeared in 1889 and was extended in 1894. His work was based on that of Pasch but reduced the number of undefined terms from four to three: point and segment, for the geometry of position (1889), and motion, also necessary for metric geometry (1894). (This number was reduced to two by Pieri in 1899.)

The treatise *Applicazioni geometriche del calcolo infinitesimale* (1887) was based on a course Peano began teaching at the University of Turin in 1885 and contains the beginnings of his "geometrical calculus" (here still influenced by Bellavitis' method of equipollences), new forms of remainders in quadrature formulas, new definitions of length of an arc of a curve and of area of a surface, the notion of a figure tangent to a curve, a determination of the error term in Simpson's formula, and the notion of the limit of a variable figure. There is also a discussion of the measure of a point set, of additive functions of sets, and of integration applied to sets. Peano here generalized the notion of measure that he had introduced in 1883. Peano's popularization of the vectorial methods of H. Grassmann—beginning with the publication in 1888 of the *Calcolo geometrico secondo l'Ausdehnungslehre di H. Grassmann*—was of more importance in geometry. Grassmann's own publications have been criticized for their abstruseness. Nothing could be clearer than Peano's presentation, and he gave great impetus to the Italian school of vector analysis.

Peano's interest in numerical calculation led him to give formulas for the error terms in many commonly used quadrature formulas and to develop a theory of "gradual operations," which gave a new method for the resolution of numerical equations. From 1901 until 1906 he also contributed to actuarial mathematics, when as a member of a state commission he was asked to review a pension fund.

Peano also wrote articles on rational mechanics (1895–1896). Several of these articles dealt with the motion of the earth's axis and had their origin in the famous "falling cat" experiment of the Paris Academy of Sciences in the session of 29 October 1894. This experiment raised the question: "Can the earth change its own orientation in space, using only internal actions as animals do?" Peano took the occasion to apply his geometrical calculus in order to show that, for example, the Gulf Stream alone was able to alter the orientation of the earth's axis. This topic was the occasion of a brief polemic with Volterra over both priority and substance.

By 1900 Peano was already interested in an international auxiliary language, especially for science. On 26 December 1908 he was elected president of the Akademi Internasional de Lingu Universal, a continuation of the Kadem Volapüka, which had been organized in 1887 by the Reverend Johann Martin Schleyer in order to promote Volapük, the artificial language first published by Schleyer in 1879. Under Peano's guidance the Academy was transformed into a free discussion association, symbolized by the change of its name to Academia pro Interlingua in 1910. (The term "interlingua" was understood to represent the emerging language of the future.) Peano remained president of the Academia until his death. During these years Peano's role as interlinguist eclipsed his role as professor of mathematics.

Peano's mathematical logic and his ideography for mathematics were his response to Leibniz' dream of a "universal characteristic," whereas Interlingua was to be the modern substitute for medieval Latin, that is, an international language for scholars, especially scientists. Peano's proposal for an "interlingua" was *latino sine flexione* ("Latin without grammar"), which he published in 1903. He believed that there already existed an international scientific vocabulary, principally of Latin origin; and he tried to select the form of each word which would be most readily recognized by those whose native language was either English or a Romance language. He thought that the best grammar was no grammar, and he demonstrated how easily grammatical structure may be eliminated. His research led him to two areas: one was the algebra of grammar, and the other was philology. The latter preoccupation resulted most notably in *Vocabulario commune ad latino-italiano-français-english-deutsch* (1915), a greatly expanded version of an earlier publication (1909). This second edition contains some 14,000 entries and gives for each the form to be adopted in Interlingua, the classic Latin form, and its version in Italian, French, English, and German (and sometimes in other languages), with indications of synonyms, derivatives, and other items of information.

In his early years Peano was an inspiring teacher; but with the publication of the various editions of the *Formulario*, he adopted it as his text, and his lectures suffered from an excess of formalism. Because of objections to this method of teaching, he resigned from the military academy in 1901 and a few years later stopped lecturing at the Polytechnic. His interest in pedagogy was strong, and his influence was positive. He was active in the Mathesis Society of school teachers of mathematics (founded in 1895); and in 1914 he organized a series of conferences for secondary teachers of mathematics in Turin, which continued through 1919. Peano constantly sought to promote clarity, rigor, and simplicity in the teaching of mathematics. "Mathematical rigor," he wrote, "is very simple. It consists in affirming true statements and in not affirming what we know is not true. It does not consist in affirming every truth possible."

As historian of mathematics Peano contributed many precise indications of origins of mathematical terms and identified the first appearance of certain symbols and theorems. In his teaching of mathematics he recommended the study of original sources, and he always tried to see in his own work a continuation of the ideas of Leibniz, Newton, and others.

The influence of Peano on his contemporaries was great, most notably in the instance of Bertrand Russell. There was also a school of Peano: the collaborators on the *Formulario* project and others who were proud to call themselves his disciples. Pieri, for example, had great success with the axiomatic method, Burali-Forti applied Peano's mathematical logic, and Burali-Forti and Marcolongo developed Peano's geometrical calculus into a form of vector analysis. A largely different group was attracted to Peano after his shift of interest to the promotion of an international auxiliary language. This group was even more devoted; and those such as Ugo Cassina, who shared both the mathematical and philological interests of Peano, felt the closest of all.

It has been said that the apostle in Peano impeded the work of the mathematician. This is no doubt true, especially of his later years; but there can be no question of his very real influence on the development of mathematics. He contributed in great measure to the popularity of the axiomatic method, and his discovery of the space-filling curve must be considered remarkable. While many of his notions, such as area and integral, were "in the air," his originality is undeniable. He was not an imposing person, and his gruff voice with its high degree of lallation could hardly have been attractive; but his gentle personality commanded respect, and his keen intellect inspired disciples. Much of Peano's mathematics is now of historical interest; but his summons to clarity and rigor in mathematics and its teaching continues to be relevant, and few have expressed this call more forcefully.

BIBLIOGRAPHY

I. Original Works. See Ugo Cassina, ed., *Opere scelte*, 3 vols. (Rome, 1957–1959), which contains half of Peano's articles and a bibliography (in vol. I) that lists approximately 80 percent of Peano's publications. A more complete list is in Hubert C. Kennedy, ed., *Selected Works of Giuseppe Peano* (Toronto, 1972). The fifth ed. of the *Formulario mathematico* has been reprinted in facsimile (Rome, 1960).

II. SECONDARY LITERATURE. The most complete biography is Hubert C. Kennedy, *Giuseppe Peano* (Basel, 1974). Ten articles on the work of Peano are in Ugo Cassina, *Critica dei principî della matematica e questioni di logica* (Rome, 1961) and *Dalla geometria egiziana alla matematica moderna* (Rome, 1961). Also see Alessandro Terracini, ed., *In memoria di Giuseppe Peano* (Cuneo, 1955), which contains articles by eight authors. A list of these and other items is in *Selected Works of Giuseppe Peano*.

HUBERT C. KENNEDY

PEARSON, KARL (*b.* London, England, 27 March 1857; *d.* Coldharbour, Surrey, England, 27 April 1936)

Pearson, founder of the twentieth-century science of statistics, was the younger son and the second of three children of William Pearson, a barrister of the Inner Temple, and his wife, Fanny Smith. Educated at home until the age of nine, he was sent to University College School, London, for seven years. He withdrew in 1873 for reasons of health and spent the next year with a private tutor. He obtained a scholarship at King's College, Cambridge, in 1875, placing second on the list. At Cambridge, Pearson studied mathematics under E. J. Routh, G. G. Stokes, J. C. Maxwell, Arthur Cayley, and William Burnside. He received the B.A. with mathematical honors in 1879 and was third wrangler in the mathematical tripos that year.

Pearson went to Germany after receiving his degree. At Heidelberg he studied physics under G. H. Quincke and metaphysics under Kuno Fischer. At Berlin he attended the lectures of Emil du Bois-Reymond on Darwinism. With his father's profession no doubt in mind, Pearson went up to London, took rooms in the Inner Temple in November 1880, read in Chambers in Lincoln's Inn, and was called to the bar in 1881. He received an LL.B. from Cambridge University in 1881 and an M.A. in 1882, but he never practiced.

Pearson was appointed Goldsmid professor of applied mathematics and mechanics at University College, London, in 1884 and was lecturer in geometry at Gresham College, London, from 1891 to 1894. In 1911 he relinquished the Goldsmid chair to become the first Galton professor of eugenics, a chair that had been offered first to Pearson in keeping with Galton's expressed wish. He retired in 1933 but continued to work in a room at University College until a few months before his death.

Elected a fellow of the Royal Society in 1896, Pearson was awarded its Darwin Medal in 1898. He was awarded many honors by British and foreign anthropological and medical organizations, but never joined and was not honored during his lifetime by the Royal Statistical Society.

In 1890 Pearson married Maria Sharpe, who died in 1928. They had one son, Egon, and two daughters, Sigrid and Helga. In 1929 he married a co-worker in his department, Margaret Victoria Child.

At Cambridge, Pearson's coach under the tripos system was Routh, probably the greatest mathematical coach in the history of the university, who aroused in Pearson a special interest in applied mathematics, mechanics, and the theory of elasticity. Pearson took the Smith's Prize examination, which called for the very best in mathematics. He failed to become a prizeman; but his response to a question set by Isaac Todhunter was found, on Todhunter's death in 1884, to have been incorporated in the manuscript of his unfinished *History of the Theory of Elasticity*, with the comment "This proof is better than De St. Venant's."[1] As a result, in the same year Pearson was appointed by the syndics of the Cambridge University Press to finish and edit the work.

Pearson did not confine himself to mathematics at Cambridge. He read Dante, Goethe, and Rousseau in the original, sat among the divinity students listening to the discourse of the university's regius professor of divinity, and discussed the moral sciences tripos with a fellow student. Before leaving Cambridge he wrote reviews of two books on Spinoza for the *Cambridge Review*, and a paper on Maimonides and Spinoza for *Mind*.

Although intensely interested in the basis, doctrine, and history of religion, Pearson rebelled at attending the regular divinity lectures, compulsory since the founding of King's in 1441, and after a hard fight saw compulsory divinity lectures abolished. He next sought and, with the assistance of his father, obtained release from compulsory attendance at chapel; after which, to the astonishment and pique of the authorities, he continued to attend as the spirit moved him.

Pearson's life in Germany, as at Cambridge, involved much more than university lectures and related study. He became interested in German folklore, in medieval and renaissance German literature, in the history of the Reformation, and in the development of ideas on the position of women. He also came into contact with the ideas of Karl Marx and Ferdinand Lassalle, the two leaders of German socialism. His writings and lectures on his return to England indicate that he had become both a convinced evolutionist and a fervent socialist, and that he had begun to merge these two doctrines into his own rather special variety of social Darwinism. His given name was originally Carl; at about this time he began spelling it with a "K." A King's College fellowship, conferred in 1880 and continued until 1886, gave Pearson financial independence and complete freedom from duties of any sort, and during these years he was frequently in Germany, where he found a quiet spot in the Black Forest to which he often returned.

In 1880 Pearson worked for some weeks in the engineering shops at Cambridge and drew up the schedule in Middle and Ancient High German for the medieval languages tripos. In the same year he published his first book, a literary work entitled *The New Werther*, "by Loki," written in the form of letters from a young man wandering in Germany to his fiancée.

During 1880–1881 Pearson found diversion from his legal studies in lecturing on Martin Luther at Hampstead, and on socialism, Marx, and Lassalle at workingmen's clubs in Soho. In 1882–1884 he gave a number of courses of lectures around London on German social life and thought from the earliest times up to the sixteenth century, and on Luther's influence on the material and intellectual welfare of Germany. In addition he published in the *Academy*, *Athenaeum*, and elsewhere a substantial number of letters, articles, and reviews relating to Luther. Many of these were later republished, together with other lectures delivered between 1885–1887, in his *The Ethic of Freethought* (1888).

During 1880–1884 Pearson's mathematical talent was not entirely dormant. He gave University of London extension lectures on "Heat" and served as a temporary substitute for absent professors of mathematics at King's College and University College, London. At the latter Pearson met Alexander B. W. Kennedy, professor of engineering and mechanical technology, who was instrumental in securing Pearson's appointment to the Goldsmid professorship.

During his first six years in the Goldsmid chair, Pearson demonstrated his great capacity for hard work and extraordinary productivity. His professorial duties included lecturing on statics, dynamics, and mechanics, with demonstrations and proofs based on geometrical and graphical methods, and conducting practical instruction in geometrical drawing and projection. Soon after assuming the professorship, he began preparing for publication the incomplete manuscript of *The Common Sense of the Exact Sciences* left by his penultimate predecessor, William Kingdon Clifford; and it was issued in 1885. The preface, the entire chapter "Position," and considerable portions of the chapters "Quantity" and "Motion" were written by

Pearson. A far more difficult and laborious task was the completion and editing of Todhunter's unfinished *History of the Theory of Elasticity*. He wrote about half the final text of the first volume (1886) and was responsible for almost the whole of the second volume, encompassing several hundred memoirs (1893). His editing of these volumes, along with his own papers on related topics published during the same decade, established Pearson's reputation as an applied mathematician.

Somehow Pearson also found the time and energy to plan and deliver the later lectures of *The Ethic of Freethought* series; to complete *Die Fronica* (1887), a historical study that traced the development of the Veronica legend and the history of the Veronica-portraits of Christ, written in German and dedicated to Henry Bradshaw, the Cambridge University Librarian; and to collect the material on the evolution of western Christianity that later formed much of the substance of *The Chances of Death* (1897). In these historical studies Pearson was greatly influenced and guided by Bradshaw, from whom he learned the importance of patience and thoroughness in research. In 1885 Pearson became an active founding member of a small club of men and women dedicated to the discussion of the relationship between the sexes. He gave the opening address on "The Woman's Question," and addressed a later meeting on "Socialism and Sex." Among the members of the group was Maria Sharpe, whom he married in 1890.

In the 1890's the sole duty of the lecturer in geometry at Gresham College seems to have been to give three courses per year of four lectures to an extramural audience on topics of his own choosing. Pearson's aim in applying for the lectureship was apparently to gain an opportunity to present some of his ideas to a fairly general audience. In his first two courses, delivered in March and April 1891 under the general title "The Scope and Concepts of Modern Science," he explored the philosophical foundations of science. These lectures, developed and enlarged, became the first edition of *The Grammar of Science* (1892), a remarkable book that influenced the scientific thought of an entire generation.

Pearson outlined his concept of the nature, scope, function, and method of science in a series of articles in the first chapter of his book. "The material of science," he said, "is coextensive with the whole physical universe, not only . . . as it now exists, but with its past history and the past history of all life therein," while "The function of science" is "the classification of facts, the recognition of their sequence and their relative significance," and "The unity of all science consists alone in its method, not its material . . .

It is not the facts themselves which form science, but the method in which they are dealt with." In a summary of the chapter he wrote that the method of science consists of "(a) careful and accurate classification of facts and observation of their correlation and sequence; (b) the discovery of scientific laws by aid of the creative imagination; (c) self-criticism and the final touchstone of equal validity for all normally constituted minds." He emphasized repeatedly that science can only describe the "how" of phenomena and can never explain the "why," and stressed the necessity of eliminating from science all elements over which theology and metaphysics may claim jurisdiction. The *Grammar of Science* also anticipated in many ways the revolutionary changes in scientific thought brought about by Einstein's special theory of relativity. Pearson insisted on the relativity of all motion, completely restated the Newtonian laws of motion in keeping with this primary principle, and developed a system of mechanics logically from them. Recognizing mass to be simply the ratio of the number of units in two accelerations as "expressed briefly by the statement that mutual accelerations are *inversely* as masses" (ch. 8, sec. 9), he ridiculed the current textbook definition of mass as "quantity of matter." Although recognized as a classic in the philosophy of science, the *Grammar of Science* is little read today by scientists and students of science mainly because its literary style has dated it.

Pearson was thus well on the way to a respectable career as a teacher of applied mathematics and philosopher of science when two events occurred that markedly changed the direction of his professional activity and shaped his future career. The first was the publication of Galton's *Natural Inheritance* in 1889; the second, the appointment of W. F. R. Weldon to the Jodrell professorship of zoology at University College, London, in 1890.

Natural Inheritance summed up Galton's work on correlation and regression, concepts and techniques that he had discovered and developed as tools for measuring the influence of heredity;[2] presented all that he contributed to their theory; and clearly reflected his recognition of their applicability and value in studies of all living forms. In the year of its appearance, Pearson read a paper on *Natural Inheritance* before the aforementioned small discussion club, stressing the light that it threw on the laws of heredity, rather than the mathematics of correlation and regression. Pearson became quite charmed by the concept and implications of Galton's "correlation," which he saw to be a "category broader than causation . . . of which causation was only the limit, and [which] brought psychology, anthropology, medicine and sociology in

large parts into the field of mathematical treatment," which opened up the "possibility . . . of reaching knowledge—as valid as physical knowledge was then thought to be—in the field of living forms and above all in the field of human conduct."[3] Almost immediately his life took a new course: he began to lay the foundations of the new science of statistics that he was to develop almost single-handed during the next decade and a half. But it is doubtful whether much of this would have come to pass had it not been for Weldon, who posed the questions that impelled Pearson to make his most significant contributions to statistical theory and methodology.[4]

Weldon, a Cambridge zoologist, had been deeply impressed by Darwin's theory of natural selection and in the 1880's had sought to devise means for deriving concrete support for it from studies of animal and plant populations. Galton's *Natural Inheritance* convinced him that the most promising route was through statistical studies of variation and correlation in those populations. Taking up his appointment at University College early in 1891, Weldon began to apply, extend, and improve Galton's methods of measuring variation and correlation, in pursuit of concrete evidence to support Darwin's "working hypothesis." These undertakings soon brought him face to face with problems outside the realm of the classical theory of errors: How describe asymmetrical, double-humped, and other non-Gaussian frequency distributions? How derive "best"—or at least "good"—values for the parameters of such distributions? What are the "probable errors" of such estimates? What is the effect of selection on one or more of a number of correlated variables? Finding the solution of these problems to be beyond his mathematical capacity, Weldon turned to Pearson for help.

Pearson, in turn, seeing an opportunity to contribute, through his special skills, to the improvement of the understanding of life, characteristically directed his attention to this new area with astonishing energy. The sudden change in his view of statistics, and the early stages of his rapid development of a new science of statistics are evident in the syllabuses of his lectures at Gresham College in 1891–1894 and in G. Udny Yule's summaries of Pearson's two lecture courses on the theory of statistics at University College during the sessions of 1894–1895 and 1895–1896,[5] undoubtedly the first of their kind ever given. Pearson was an enthusiast for graphic presentation; and his Gresham lectures on "Geometry of Statistics" (November 1891–May 1892) were devoted almost entirely to a comprehensive formal treatment of graphical representation of statistical data from the biological, physical, and social sciences, with only brief mention of numerical descriptive statistics. In "Laws of Chance" (November 1892–February 1893) he discussed probability theory and the concept of "correlation," illustrating both by coin-tossing and card-drawing experiments and by observations of natural phenomena. The term "standard deviation" was introduced in the lecture of 31 January 1893, as a convenient substitute for the cumbersome "root mean square error" and the older expressions "error of mean square" and "mean error"; and in the lecture of 1 February, he discussed whether an observed discrepancy between a theoretical standard deviation and an experimentally determined value for it is "sufficiently great to create suspicion." In "The Geometry of Chance" (November 1893–May 1894) he devoted a lecture to "Normal Curves,"[6] one to "Skew Curves," and one to "Compound Curves."

In 1892 Pearson lectured on variation, and in 1893 on correlation, to research students at University College, the material being published as the first four of his *Philosophical Transactions* memoirs on evolution. At this time he worked out his general theory of normal correlation for three, four, and finally n variables. Syllabuses or summaries of these lectures at University College are not available, but much of the substance of the four memoirs is visible in Yule's summaries. Those of the lectures of November 1895 through March 1896 reveal Pearson's early groping toward a general theory of skew correlation and nonlinear regression that was not published until 1905. His summary of Pearson's lecture of 14 May 1896 shows that considerable progress had already been made on both the experimental and theoretical material on errors of judgment, measurement errors, and the variation over time of the "personal equations" of individual observers that constituted Pearson's 1902 memoir on these matters.

These lectures mark the beginning of a new epoch in statistical theory and practice. Pearson communicated some thirty-five papers on statistical matters to the Royal Society during 1893–1901. By 1906 he had published over seventy additional papers embodying further statistical theory and applications. In retrospect, it is clear that Pearson's contributions during this period firmly established statistics as a discipline in its own right. Yet, at the time, "the main purpose of all this work" was not development of statistical theory and techniques for their own sake but, rather, "development and application of statistical methods for the study of problems of heredity and evolution."[7]

In order to place the whole of Pearson's work in proper perspective, it will be helpful to examine his contributions to distinct areas of theory and practice. Consider, for example, his "method of moments" and

his system of wonderfully diverse frequency curves. Pearson's aim in developing the method of moments was to provide a general method for determining the values of the parameters of a frequency distribution of some particular form selected to describe a given set of observational or experimental data. This is clear from his basic exposition of the subject in the first (1894) of his series of memoirs entitled "Contributions to the Mathematical Theory of Evolution."[8]

The foundations of the system of Pearson curves were laid in the second memoir of this series, "Skew Variation in Homogeneous Material" (1895). Types I–IV were defined and applied in this memoir; Types V and VI, in a "Supplement . . ." (1901); and Types VII–XII in a "Second Supplement . . ." (1916). The system includes symmetrical and asymmetrical curves of both limited and unlimited range (in either or both directions); most are unimodal, but some are U-, J-, or reverse J-shaped. Pearson's purpose in developing them was to provide a collection of frequency curves of diverse forms to be fitted to data as "*graduation curves*, mathematical constructs to describe more or less accurately what we have observed."[9] Their use was facilitated by the central role played by the method of moments: (1) the appropriate curve type is determined by the values of two dimensionless ratios of centroidal moments,

$$\beta_1 = \frac{\mu_3^2}{\mu_2^3} \quad \text{and} \quad \beta_2 = \frac{\mu_4}{\mu_2^2},$$

defined in the basic memoir (1894); and (2) values of the parameters of the selected types of probability (or frequency) curve are determined by the conditions $\mu_0 = 1$ (or $\mu_0 = N$, the total number of observations), $\mu_1 = 0$, and the observed or otherwise indicated values of $\mu_2(= \sigma^2)$, β_1, and β_2. The acceptance and use of curves of Pearson's system for this purpose may also have been aided by the fact that all were derived from a single differential equation, to which Pearson had been led by considering the slopes of segments of frequency polygons determined by the ordinates of symmetric and asymmetric binomial and hypergeometric probability distributions. That derivation may well have provided some support to Pearson curves as probability or frequency curves, rather than as purely arbitrary graduation curves. Be that as it may, the fitting of Pearson curves to observational data was extensively practiced by biologists and social scientists in the decades that followed. The results did much to dispel the almost religious acceptance of the normal distribution as the mathematical model of variation of biological, physical, and social phenomena.

Meanwhile, Pearson's system of frequency curves

acquired a new and unanticipated importance in statistical theory and practice with the discovery that the sampling distributions of many statistical test functions appropriate to analyses of small samples from normal, binomial, and Poisson distributions— such as χ^2, s^2, t, $s_1{}^2 / s_2{}^2$, and r (when $\rho = 0$)—are represented by particular families of Pearson curves, either directly or through simple transformation. This application of Pearson curves, and their use to approximate percentage points of statistical test functions whose sampling distributions are either untabulated or analytically or numerically intractable, but whose moments are readily evaluated, have now transcended their use as graduation curves; they have also done much to ensure the value of Pearson's comprehensive system of frequency curves in statistical theory and practice. The use of Pearson curves for either purpose would, however, have been gravely handicapped had not Pearson and his co-workers prepared detailed and extensive tables of their ordinates, integrals, and other characteristics, which were published principally in *Biometrika* beginning in 1901, and reprinted, with additions, in his *Tables for Statisticians and Biometricians* (1914; Part II, 1931).

As statistical concepts and techniques of correlation and regression originated with Galton, who devised rudimentary arithmetical and graphical procedures (utilizing certain medians and quartiles of the data in hand) to derive sample values for his "regression" coefficient, or "index of co-relation," r. Galton was also the first, though he had assistance from J. D. Hamilton Dickson, to express the bivariate normal distribution in the "Galtonian form" of the frequency distribution of two correlated variables.[10] Weldon and F. Y. Edgeworth devised alternative means of computation, which, however, were somewhat arbitrary and did not fully utilize all the data. It was Pearson who established, by what would now be termed the method of maximum likelihood, that the "best value of the correlation coefficient" (ρ) of a bivariate normal distribution is given by the sample product-moment coefficient of correlation,

$$r = \frac{\Sigma xy}{N s_x s_y} = \frac{\Sigma xy}{\sqrt{\Sigma(x^2) \cdot \Sigma(y^2)}},$$

where x and y denote the deviations of the measured values of the x and y characteristics of an individual sample object from their respective arithmetic means (m_x and m_y) in the sample, Σ denotes summation over all N individuals in the sample, and s_x and s_y are the sample standard deviations of the measured values of x and y, respectively.[11] The expression "coefficient of correlation" apparently was originated by Edgeworth in 1892,[12] but the value of r defined by the above equation is quite properly known as "Pearson's coefficient of correlation." Its derivation may be found in section 4b. of "Regression, Heredity, and Panmixia" (1896), his first fundamental paper on correlation theory and its application to problems of heredity.

In the same memoir Pearson also showed how the "best value" of r could be evaluated conveniently from the sample standard deviations s_x, s_y and either s_{x-y} or s_{x+y}, thereby avoiding computation of the sample product moment ($\Sigma xy/N$); gave a mistaken expression for the standard deviation of the sampling error[13] of r as a measure of ρ in large samples—which he corrected in "Probable Errors of Frequency Constants . . ." (1898); introduced the term "coefficient of variation" for the ratio of a standard deviation to the corresponding mean expressed as a percentage; expressed explicitly, in his discussion of the trivariate case, what are now called coefficients of "multiple" correlation and "partial" regression in terms of the three "zero-order" coefficients of correlation (r_{12}, r_{13}, r_{23}); gave the partial regression equation for predicting the (population) mean value of trait X_1, say, corresponding to given values of traits X_2 and X_3, the coefficients of X_2 and X_3 being expressed explicitly in terms of r_{12}, r_{13}, r_{23} and the three sample standard deviations (s_1, s_2, s_3); gave the formula for the large-sample standard error of the value of X_1 predicted by this equation; restated Edgeworth's formula (1892) for the trivariate normal distribution in improved determinantal notation; and carried through explicitly the extension to the general case of a p-variate normal correlation surface, expressed in a form that brought the computations within the power of those lacking advanced mathematical training.

In this first fundamental memoir on correlation, Pearson carried the development of the theory of multivariate normal correlation as a practical tool almost to completion. When the joint distribution of a number of traits X_1, X_2, . . ., X_p, ($p \geqq 2$) over the individuals of a population is multivariate normal, then the population coefficients of correlation, ρ_{ij}, ($i, j = 1, 2, \ldots, p;\ i \neq j$), completely characterize the degrees of association among these traits in the population—traits X_i and X_j are independent if and only if $\rho_{ij} = 0$ and completely interdependent if and only if ρ_{ij} equals ± 1—and the regression in the population of each one of the traits on any combination of the others is linear. It is clear from footnotes to section 5 of this memoir that Pearson was fully aware that linearity of regressions and this comprehensive feature of population (product-moment) coefficients of correlation do not carry over to multivariate skew frequency distributions, and he recognized "the need of [a] theory of skew correlation" which he proposed to treat "in a memoir on skew correlation."[14] The promised memoir, *On the General Theory of Skew Correlation and Non-Linear Regression*, appeared in 1905.

Pearson there dealt with the properties of the correlation ratio, $\eta(=\eta_{yx})$, a sample measure of correlation that he had introduced in a paper of 1903 to replace the sample correlation coefficient, r, when the observed regression curve of y on x (obtained by plotting the means of the y values, $\bar{y}_{x_i}$, corresponding to the respective x values, $x_1, x_2, \ldots$, as a function of x) exhibits a curvilinear relationship and showed that η is the square root of the fraction of the variability of the N y values about their mean, $\bar{y}$, that is ascribable to the variability of the y means $\bar{y}_{x_i}$ about $\bar{y}$; that $1 - \eta^2$ is the fraction of the total variability of the y values about their mean $\bar{y}$ contributed by the variability of the y values within the respective x arrays about their respective mean values, $\bar{y}_{x_i}$, within these arrays; and that $\eta^2 - r^2$ is the fraction ascribable to the deviations of the points $(\bar{y}_{x_i}, x_i)$ from the straight line of closest fit to these points, indicating the importance of the difference between η and r as an indicator of the departure of regression from linearity.[15] He also gave an expression for the standard deviation of the sampling error of η in large samples that has subsequently been shown to be somewhat inaccurate; classified the different forms of regression curves and the different patterns of within-array variability that may arise when the joint distribution of two traits cannot be represented by the bivariate normal distribution, terming the system "homoscedastic" or "heteroscedastic" according to whether the within-array variability is or is not the same for all arrays, respectively; gave explicit formulas for the coefficients of parabolic, cubic, and quartic regression curves, in terms of $\eta^2 - r^2$ and other moments and product moments of the sample values of x and y; and listed the conditions in terms of $\eta^2 - r^2$ and the other sample moments and product moments that must be satisfied for linear, parabolic, cubic, and quartic regression equations to be adequate representations of the observed regression of y on x.

In a footnote to the section "Cubical Regression," Pearson noted that he had pointed out previously[16] that when a polynomial of any degree, p ($p \leq n$), is fit to all of n distinct observational points by the method of moments, the curve determined by "the method of moments becomes identical with that of least squares"; but, he continued, "the retention of the method of moments . . . enables us, without abrupt change of method, to introduce the need for η, and to grasp at

once the application of the proper SHEPPARD'S corrections [to the sample moments and product moments of x and y when the measurements of either or both are coarsely grouped]."

Pearson clearly favored his method of moments; but the method of least squares has prevailed. However, use of the method of least squares to fit polynomial regression curves in a bivariate correlation situation involves an extension beyond the original formulation and development of the method of least squares by Legendre, Gauss, Laplace, and their followers in the nineteenth century. In this classical development of the method of least squares, one of the variables—x, for example—was a quantity that could be measured with negligible error, and the other, y, a quantity of interest functionally related to x, the observed values of which for particular values of x, Y_x, were, however, subject to nonnegligible measurement errors. The problem was to determine "best" values for the parameters of the functional relation between y and x despite the measurement errors in the observed values of Y_x. The method of least squares as developed by Gauss gave a demonstrably optimal solution when the functional dependence of y upon x was expressible with negligible error in a form in which the unknown parameters entered linearly—for instance, as a polynomial in x. In the Galton-Pearson correlation situation, in contrast, the traits X and Y may both be measurable with negligible error with respect to any single individual but in some population of individuals have a joint frequency or probability distribution. The regression of y on x is not an expression of a mathematical functional dependence of the trait Y on the trait X but, rather, an expression of the mean of values of Y corresponding to values of $X = x$ as a function of x—for example, as a polynomial in x. In the classical least-squares situation, the aim was to obtain the best possible approximation to the correct functional relation between the variables despite variations introduced by unwanted errors of measurement. In the Galton-Pearson correlation situation, on the other hand, the aim of regression analysis is to describe two important characteristics of the joint variation of the traits concerned. Pearson's development of the theory of skew correlation and nonlinear regression was, therefore, not merely an elaboration on the work of Gauss but a major step in a new direction.

Pearson did not pursue the theory of multiple and partial correlation beyond the point to which he had carried it in his basic memoir on correlation (1896). The general theory of multiple and partial correlation and regression was developed by his mathematical assistant, G. Udny Yule, in two papers published in 1897. Yule was the first to give mathematical expressions for what are now called partial correlation coefficients, which he termed "net correlation coefficients." What Pearson had called coefficients of double regression, Yule renamed net regressions; they are now called partial regression coefficients. The expressions "multiple correlation" and "partial correlation" stem from the paper written with Alice Lee and read to the Royal Society in June 1897.[17]

In order to see whether the correlations found in studies of the heredity of continuously varying physical characteristics held also for the less tractable psychological and mental traits, Pearson made a number of efforts to extend correlation methods to bivariate data coarsely classified into two or more ordered categories with respect to each trait. Thus, in "On the Correlation of Characters Not Quantitatively Measurable" (1900), he introduced the "tetrachoric" coefficient of correlation, r_t, derived on the supposition that the traits concerned were distributed continuously in accordance with a bivariate normal distribution in the population of individuals sampled, though not measured on continuous scales for the individuals in the sample but merely classified into the cells of a fourfold table in terms of more or less arbitrary but precise dichotomous divisions of the two trait scales. The derived value of r_t was the value of the correlation coefficient (ρ) of the bivariate normal distribution with frequencies in four quadrants corresponding to a division of the x, y plane by lines parallel to the coordinate axes that agreed exactly with the four cell frequencies of the fourfold table. Hence the value of r_t calculated from the data of a particular fourfold table was considered to be theoretically the best measure of the intensity of the correlation between the traits concerned. Pearson gave a formula for the standard deviation of the sampling error of r_t in large samples. He corrected two misprints in this formula and gave a simplified approximate formula in a paper of 1913.[18]

To cope with the intermediate case, in which one characteristic of the sample individuals is measured on a continuous scale and the other is merely classified dichotomously, Pearson, in a *Biometrika* paper of 1909, introduced (but did not name) the "biserial" coefficient of correlation, say r_b.

The idea involved in the development of the "tetrachoric" correlation coefficient, r_t, for data classified in a fourfold table was extended by Pearson in 1910 to cover cases in which "one variable is given by alternative and the other by multiple categories." The sample measure of correlation introduced but not named in this paper became known as "biserial η" because of its analogy with the biserial correlation coefficient, r_b, and the fact that it is defined by a special

adaptation of the formula for the correlation ratio, η, based on comparatively nonrestrictive assumptions with respect to the joint distribution of the two traits concerned in the population sampled. The numerical evaluation of "biserial η," however, involves the further assumption that the joint variation of the traits is bivariate normal in the population; and its value for a particular sample, say r_η, is taken to be an estimate of the correlation coefficient, ρ, of the assumed bivariate normal distribution of the traits in the population sampled. The sampling variation of r_η as a measure of ρ was unknown until Pearson published an expression for its standard error in large samples from a bivariate normal population in 1917.[19] It is not known how large the sample size N must be for this asymptotic expression to yield a satisfactory approximation.

Meanwhile, Charles Spearman had introduced (1904) his coefficient of rank-order correlation, say r', which, although first defined in terms of the rank differences of the individuals in the sample with respect to the two traits concerned, is equivalent to the product-moment correlation coefficient between the paired ranks themselves. Three years later Pearson, in "On Further Methods of Determining Correlation," gave the now familiar formula, $\hat{\rho} = 2\sin(\pi r'/6)$, for obtaining an estimate, $\hat{\rho}$, of the coefficient of correlation (ρ) of a bivariate normal population from an observed value of the coefficient of rank-order correlation (r') derived from the rankings of the individuals in a sample therefrom with respect to the two traits concerned; he also presented a formula for the standard error of $\hat{\rho}$ in large samples.

The "tetrachoric" and "biserial" coefficients of correlation and "biserial η" played important parts in the biometric, eugenic, and medical investigations of Pearson and the biometric school during the first two decades of the twentieth century. Pearson was fully aware of the crucial dependence of their interpretation upon the validity of the assumed bivariate normality and was circumspect in their application; his discussions of numerical results are full of caution. (A sample product-moment coefficient of correlation, r, always provides a usable determination of the product-moment coefficient of correlation, ρ, in the population sampled, bivariate normal or otherwise. On the other hand, when the joint distribution of the two traits concerned is continuous but not bivariate normal in the population sampled, exactly what interpretations are to be accorded to observed values of r_t, r_b, and r_η is not at all clear; and if assumed continuity with respect to both variables is not valid, their interpretation is even less clear—they may be virtually meaningless.) The crucial dependence of the interpretation of these measures on the uncheckable assumption of bivariate normality of the joint distribution of the traits concerned in the population sampled, together with their uncritical application and incautious interpretation by some scholars, brought severe criticism; and doubt was cast on the meaning and value of "coefficients of correlation" thus obtained. In particular, Pearson and one of his assistants, David Heron, ultimately became embroiled in a long and bitter argument on the matter with Yule, whose paper embodying a theory and a measure of association of attributes free of any assumption of an underlying continuous distribution Pearson had communicated to the Royal Society in 1899. Despite this skepticism, r_t, r_b, and r_n have survived and are used today as standard statistical tools, mainly by psychologists, in situations where the traits concerned can be logically assumed to have a joint continuous distribution in the population sampled and the at least approximate normality of this distribution is not seriously questioned.

Pearson did not attempt to investigate sampling distributions of r or η in small samples from bivariate normal or other population distributions because he saw no need to do so. He and his co-workers in the 1890's and early 1900's saw their mission to be the advancement of knowledge and understanding of "variation, inheritance, and selection in Animals and Plants" through studies "based upon the examination of *statistically large numbers* of specimens," and the development of statistical theory, tables of mathematical functions, and graphical methods needed in the pursuit of such studies.[20] They were not concerned with the analysis of data from small-scale laboratory experiments or with comparisons of yield from small numbers of plots of land in agricultural field trials. It was the need to interpret values of r obtained from small-scale industrial experiments in the brewing industry that led "Student" (W. S. Gosset) to discover in 1908 that r is symmetrically distributed about 0 in accordance with a Pearson Type II curve in random samples of any size from a bivariate normal distribution when $\rho = 0$; and, when $\rho \neq 0$, its distribution is skew, with the longer tail toward 0, and cannot be represented by any of Pearson's curves.[21]

In another paper published earlier in 1908 ("The Probable Error of a Mean"), "Student" had discovered that the sampling distribution of s^2 (the square of a sample standard deviation), in random samples from a normal distribution, can be represented by a Pearson Type III curve. Although these discoveries stemmed from knowledge and experience that "Student" had gained at Pearson's biometric laboratory in London and were published in the journal that

Pearson edited, they seem to have awakened no interest in Pearson or his co-workers in developing statistical theory and techniques appropriate to the analysis of results from small-scale experiments. This indifference may have stemmed from preoccupation with other matters, from recognition that establishment of the small trends or differences for which they were looking required large samples, or from a desire "to discourage the biologist or the medical man from believing that he had been supplied with an easy method of drawing conclusions from scanty data."[22]

In September 1914 Pearson received the manuscript of the paper in which R. A. Fisher derived the general sampling distribution of r in random samples of any size $n \geq 2$ from a bivariate normal population with any degree of correlation, $-1 \leq \rho \leq +1$, and pointed out the extreme skewness of the distribution for large positive or negative values of ρ even for large sample sizes.[23] Pearson responded with enthusiasm, congratulated Fisher "very heartily on getting out the actual distribution form of r," and stated that "if the analysis is correct which seems highly probable, [he] should be delighted to publish the paper in *Biometrika*."[24] A week later he wrote to Fisher: "I have now read your paper fully and think it marks a distinct advance . . . I shall be very glad to publish it . . . [it] shall appear in the next issue [May 1915] . . . I wish you had had the leisure to extend the last pages a little . . . I should like to see some attempt to determine at what value of n and for what values of ρ we may suppose the distribution of r practically normal."[25]

In the "last pages" of the paper, Fisher introduced two transformations of r, $r/\sqrt{1-r^2}$ and $\tanh^{-1} r$, his aim being to find a function of r whose sampling distribution would have greater stability of form as ρ varied from -1 to $+1$, would be more nearly symmetric, or would have an approximately constant standard deviation, for all values of ρ. The first of these two transformations he considered in detail. Denoting the transformed variable by t, and the corresponding transformation of ρ by τ, he showed that the mean value of t was proportional to τ, the constant of proportionality increasing toward unity with increasing sample size. He also gave exact formulas for $\sigma^2(t)$, $\beta_1(t)$, and $\beta_2(t)$, and tables of their numerical values for selected values of τ^2 from .01 to 100 (that is, ρ from .0995 to .995) and sample sizes n from 8 to 53. Although the distribution of t was, by design, much less asymmetric and of more stable form than the distribution of r—this became unmistakably clear when the corresponding values of $\beta_1(r)$ and $\beta_2(r)$ became known in the "Cooperative Study" (see below)—the transformation was not an unqualified success: its distribution was not close to normal except in the vicinity of $\rho = 0$, and $\sigma^2(t)$ was not approximately constant but nearly proportional to $1/(1 - \rho^2)$. In the final paragraph Fisher dismissed the second transformation for the time being with the comment (with respect to the aims mentioned above): "It is not a little attractive, but so far as I have examined it, it does not tend to simplify the analysis . . . ." (He later found it very much to his liking.)

Reasoning about a function of sample values, such as r, in terms of a transform of it, instead of in terms of the function itself, seems to have been foreign to Pearson's way of thinking. He wrote to Fisher:

> I have rather difficulties over this r and t business—not that I have anything to say about it from the theoretical standpoint—but there appear to me difficulties from the everyday applications with which we as statisticians are most familiar. Let me indicate what I mean.
>
> A man finds a correlation coefficient r from a small sample n of a population; often the material is urgent and an answer on the significance has to be given at once. What he wants to know, say, is whether the true value of $r(\rho)$ is likely to exceed or fall short of his observed value by, say, .10. It may be for instance the correlation between height of firing a gun and the rate of consumption of a time fuse, or between a particular form of treatment of a wound and time of recovery. . . . For example, suppose that $\rho = .30$, and I want to find what is the chance that in 40 observations the resulting r will lie between .20 and .40. Now what we need practically are the β_1 and β_2 for $\rho = .30$ and $n = 40$, and if they are not sufficiently Gaussian for us to use the probability integral, we need the frequency curve of r for $\rho = .30$ and $n = 40$ to help us out. . . . Had I the graph of t I could deduce the graph of r, and mechanically integrate to determine the answer to my problem, but you have not got the ordinates of the t-curve and the practical problem remains it seems to me unsolved. It still seems to me essential (i) to determine β_1 and β_2 accurately for r . . . and (ii) determine a table of frequencies or areas (integral curve) of the r distribution curve for values of ρ and n which do not provide approximately Gaussian results. Of course you may be able to dispose of my practical difficulties, which do not touch your beautiful theory.[26]

Pearson then proposed a specific program of tabulation of the ordinates of the frequency curves for r for selected values of ρ and n to be executed by his trained calculators "unless you really want to do them yourself." The letter in which Fisher is said to have "welcomed the suggestion" that the computations of these ordinates be carried out at the Galton laboratory "seems to have been lost through the disturbance of papers during the 1939–45 war."[27] On the other hand,

Fisher seems to have agreed (in this missing, or some other, letter) to undertake the evaluation of the integral of the distribution of r for a selection of values of ρ and n. In a May 1916 letter to Pearson he comments, "I have been very slow about my paper on the probability integral."

When not engaged in war work, Pearson and several members of his staff took on the onerous task of developing reliable formulas for the moments of the distribution of r and calculating tables of its ordinates for ρ from 0.0 to 0.9 and selected values of n. In May 1916, Pearson wrote to Fisher: ". . . the *whole* of the correlation business has come out quite excellently . . . . By [$n =$] 25 my curves [curves of the Pearson system] give the frequency very satisfactorily, but even when $n = 400$, for high values of ρ the normal curve is really not good enough . . . ."[28] It is quite clear from this correspondence between Pearson and Fisher during 1914–1916 that the relationship was entirely friendly, and the implication in some accounts of Fisher's life and work[29] that this venture was carried out without his knowledge is far from correct.

The results of this joint effort of Pearson and his staff were published as ". . . A Cooperative Study" in the May 1917 issue of *Biometrika*. Included were tables of ordinates of the distribution of r for $\rho = 0.0(0.1)0.9$ and $n = 3(1)25, 50, 100, 400$; values of $\beta_1(r)$ and $\beta_2(r)$ for the same ρ when $n = 3, 4, 25, 50, 100, 400$; and of the normal approximation to the ordinates for $n = 100, \rho = 0.9$, and $n = 400, \rho = 0.7(0.1)0.9$. There were also photographs of seven cardboard models showing, for example, the changes in the distribution of r from U-shaped through J-shaped to skew "cocked hat" forms with increasing sample size for $n = 2(1)25$ for $\rho = 0.6, 0.8$, and illustrating the rate of deviation from normality and increasing skewness with increase of ρ from 0.0 to 0.9 in samples of 25 and 50. This publication represented a truly monumental undertaking. Unfortunately, it had little long-range impact on practical correlation analysis, and it contained material in the section "On the Determination of the 'Most Likely' Value of the Correlation in Sampled Population" that contributed to the widening of the rift that was beginning to develop between Pearson and Fisher.

In his 1915 paper Fisher derived (pp. 520–521), from his general expression for the sampling distribution of r in samples of size n from a bivariate normal population, a two-term approximation,

$$\hat{\rho} = r\Big/\Big(1 + \frac{1 - r^2}{2n}\Big),$$

to the "relation between an observed correlation of the sample and the *most probable value* of the correlation of the whole population" [emphasis added]. He referred to his 1912 paper "On an Absolute Criterion for Fitting Frequency Curves" for justification of this procedure.[30] Inasmuch as Pearson had shown in his 1896 memoir that an observed sample from a bivariate normal population is "the most probable" when $\rho = r$ ($\mu_x = m_x$, $\sigma_x = s_x$, $\mu_y = m_y$, and $\sigma_y = s_y$), Fisher's proposed adjustment must have been puzzling to him. The result Fisher obtained is the same as what would be obtained, via the sampling distribution of r, by the method of inverse probability, using Bayes's theorem and an assumed uniform a priori distribution of ρ from -1 to $+1$. This, and Fisher's use of the expression "most probable value," evidently led Pearson, who presumably drafted the text of the "Cooperative Study,"[31] to state mistakenly (pp. 352, 353) that Fisher had assumed such a uniform a priori distribution in deriving his result. Pearson may have been misled also by a "Draft of a Note"[32] that he had received from Fisher in mid-1916, commenting on a paper by Kirstine Smith that had appeared in the May 1916 issue of *Biometrika*, in which Fisher had written: "There is nothing at all 'arbitrary' in the use of the method of moments for the normal curve; as I have shown elsewhere it flows directly from the absolute criterion ($\Sigma \log f$ a maximum) derived from the Principle of Inverse Probability."

Not realizing that Fisher had not only not assumed a uniform a priori distribution of ρ but had also considered his procedure (which he later termed the method of "maximum likelihood") to be completely distinct from "inverse probability" via Bayes's theorem with an assumed a priori distribution, Pearson proceeded to devote over a page of the "Study" to pointing out the absurdity of such an "equal distribution of ignorance" assumption when estimating ρ from an observed r. Several additional pages contain a detailed consideration of alternative forms for the a priori distribution of ρ, showing that with large samples the assumed distribution had little effect on the end result but in small samples could dominate the sample evidence, from which he concluded that "in problems like the present indiscriminate use of Bayes' Theorem is to be deprecated" (p. 359). All of this amounted to flogging a dead horse, so to speak, because Fisher was as fully opposed as Pearson to using Bayes's theorem in such problems. Unfortunately, Fisher probably was totally unaware of this offending section before proofs became available in 1917. Papers such as the "Study" were not readily typed in those days, so that there would have been only a single manuscript of the text and tables prior to typesetting. Had Fisher, who was then teaching mathematics and physics in English public schools,

been in closer touch with Pearson, these misunderstandings might have been resolved before publication of the offending passages.

In August 1920 Fisher sent Pearson a copy of his manuscript "On the 'Probable Error' of a Coefficient of Correlation Deduced From a Small Sample," in which he reexamined in detail the $\tanh^{-1} r$ transformation and, denoting the transformed variable by z and the corresponding transformation of ρ by ζ, showed that z can be taken to be approximately normally distributed about a mean of $\zeta + \dfrac{\rho}{2(n-1)}$ with a standard deviation equal to $1/\sqrt{n-3}$, the normal approximation being extraordinarily good even in very small samples—of the order of $n = 10$. This transformation thus made it possible to answer questions of the types that Pearson had raised without recourse to tables of the integral of the distribution of r, and obviated the immediate need for the preparation of such tables. (It was not until 1931 that Pearson suggested to Florence N. David the computation of tables of the integral. Values of the integral obtained by quadrature of the ordinates given in the "Cooperative Study" were completed in 1934. Additional ordinates and values of the integral were calculated to facilitate interpolation. These improved tables, together with four charts for obtaining confidence limits for ρ given r, were published in 1938.[33])

In his discussion of applications, Fisher took pains to point out that the formula he had given in his 1915 paper for what he then "termed the 'most likely value,' which [he] now, for greater precision, term[ed] the 'optimum' value of ρ, for a given observed r" involved in its derivation "no assumption whatsoever as to the probable distribution of ρ," being merely that value of ρ for which the observed r occurs with greatest frequency." He also noted that one is led to exactly the same expression for the optimum value of ρ in terms of an observed r if one seeks the optimum through the z distribution rather than the r distribution and he commented that the derivation of this optimum cannot, therefore, be inferred to depend upon an assumed uniform prior distribution of ζ and upon an assumed uniform prior distribution of ρ, since these two assumptions are mutually inconsistent. Then, "though . . . reluctant to criticize the distinguished statisticians who put their names to the Cooperative Study," Fisher went on to criticize with a tone of ridicule some of the illustrative examples of the application of Bayes's theorem considered on pp. 357–358 of the "Study," without noting the authors' conclusions from these, and other examples considered, that such "use of Bayes' Theorem is to be deprecated" (p. 359) and when applied to "values observed in a small sample may lead to results very wide from the truth" (p. 360). Fisher concluded his paper with a "Note on the Confusion Between Bayes' Rule and My Method of the Evaluation of the Optimum."

Pearson returned the manuscript to Fisher with the following comment:

> . . . I fear if I could give full attention to your paper, which I cannot at the present time, I should be unlikely to publish it in its present form, or without a reply to your criticisms which would involve also a criticism of your work of 1912—I would prefer you publish elsewhere. Under present printing and financial conditions, I am regretfully compelled to exclude all that I think erroneous on my own judgment, because I cannot afford controversy.[34]

Fisher therefore submitted his paper to *Metron*, a new journal, which published the work in its first volume.[35]

The cross criticism, at cross purposes, conducted by Pearson and Fisher over the use of Bayes's theorem in estimating ρ from r was multiply unfortunate: it was unnecessary and ill-timed; it might have been avoided; and it fostered ill will and fueled the innately contentious temperament of both parties at an early stage of their argument over the relative merits of the method of moments and method of maximum likelihood. This argument was started by Fisher's "Draft of a Note," which Pearson took to be a criticism not only of the minimum chi-square technique that Kirstine Smith had propounded but also of his method of moments, and refused to publish it in both original (1916) and revised (1918) forms on the grounds of its being controversial and liable to provoke a quarrel among contributors.[36] The argument, which grew into a raging controversy, was fed by later developments on various fronts and continued to the end of Pearson's life—and beyond.[37]

In 1922 Fisher found the sampling distribution of η^2 in random samples of any size from a bivariate normal population in which the correlation is zero ($\rho = 0$), and later (1928) derived the distribution of η^2 in samples of any size when the x values are fixed and the y values are normally distributed with a common standard deviation σ about array means $\mu_{y|x}$ which may be different for different values of x, thereby giving rise to a nonzero value of the "population" correlation ratio. In particular, it was found that for any value of the population correlation ratio different from zero, the sampling distribution of η tends in sufficiently large samples to be approximately normal about the population value with standard error given by Pearson's formula; but when the correlation ratio in the population is exactly zero—that is, when sampling from uncorrelated material—the sampling

distribution of η does not tend to normality with increasing sample size for any finite number of arrays. This led to formulation of new procedures, since become standard, for testing the statistical significance of an observed value of η and of $\eta^2 - r^2$ as a test for departure from linearity.

In 1926 Pearson showed that the distribution of sample regression coefficients, that is, of the slopes of the sample regression of y on x and of x on y, respectively, is his Type VII distribution symmetrical about the corresponding population regression coefficient. It tends to normality much more rapidly than the distribution of r with increasing sample size, so that the use of Pearson's expressions for the standard error of regression coefficients is therefore valid for lower values of n than in the case of r. It is, however, not of much use in small samples, since it depends upon the unknown values of the population standard deviations and correlation, σ_y, σ_x, and ρ_{xy}. Four years earlier, however, in response to repeated queries from "Student" in correspondence, Fisher had succeeded in showing that in random samples of any size from a general bivariate normal population, the sampling distribution of the ratio $(b - \beta)/s_{b-\beta}$, where β is the population regression coefficient corresponding to the sample coefficient b, and $s_{b-\beta}$ is a particular sample estimate of the standard error of their difference, does not depend upon any of the population parameters other than β and is given by a special form of Pearson's Type VII curve now known as "Student's" t-distribution for $n - 2$ degrees of freedom. Consequently, it is this latter distribution, free of "nuisance parameters," that is customarily employed today in making inferences about a population regression coefficient from an observed value of the corresponding sample coefficient.

Although the final steps of correlation and regression analyses today differ from those originally advanced by Pearson and his co-workers, there can be no question that today's procedures were built upon those earlier ones; and correlation and regression analysis is still very much indebted to those highly original and very difficult steps into the unknown taken by Pearson at the turn of the century.

Derivation of formulas for standard errors in large samples of functions of sample values used to estimate parameters of the population sampled did not, of course, originate with Pearson. It dates from Gauss's derivation (1816) of the standard errors in large samples of the respective functions of successive sample absolute moments that might be used as estimators of the population standard deviation. Another early contribution was Gauss's derivation (1823) of a formula comparable with that derived by

Pearson in 1903 for the standard error in large samples of the sample standard deviation as estimator of the standard deviation of an arbitrary population having finite centroidal moments of fourth order or higher. Subsequent writers treated these matters somewhat more fully and made a number of minor extensions, but the first general approach to the problem of standard errors and intercorrelations in large samples of sample functions used to estimate values of population parameters is that given in "On the Probable Errors of Frequency Constants . . . ," written by Pearson and his young French mathematical demonstrator, L. N. G. Filon, and read to the Royal Society in November 1897. In section II there is the first derivation of the now familiar expressions for the asymptotic variances and covariances of sample estimators of a group of population parameters in terms of mathematical expectations of second derivatives of the logarithm of what is now called the "likelihood function," but without recognition of their applicability only to maximum likelihood estimators, a limitation first pointed out by Edgeworth (1908).[38] Today these formulas are usually associated with Fisher's paper "On the Mathematical Foundations of Theoretical Statistics" (1922)—and perhaps rightly so, because, although the expressions derived by Pearson and Filon, and by Fisher, are of identical mathematical form, what they meant to Pearson and Filon in 1897 and continued to mean to Pearson may have been quite different from what they meant to Fisher.[39] (This may have been a major obstacle to their conciliation.)

Specific formulas derived by Pearson and Filon included expressions for the standard error of a coefficient of correlation r; the correlation between the sample means m_x and m_y of two correlated traits; the correlation between the sample standard deviations, s_x and s_y; the correlation between a sample coefficient of correlation r and a sample standard deviation s_x or s_y; the standard errors of regression coefficients, and of partial regression coefficients, for the two- and three-variable cases, respectively; and the correlations between pairs of sample correlation coefficients (r_{12}, r_{13}), (r_{12}, r_{34})—all in the case of large samples from a correlated normal distribution. In the process it was noted that in the case of large samples from a correlated normal distribution, the errors of sample means are uncorrelated with the errors of sample standard deviations and sample correlation coefficients; and that through failure to recognize the existence of correlation between the errors of sample standard deviations and a sample correlation coefficient, the formula given previously for the large sample standard error of the sample correlation coefficient r

was in error, because it was appropriate to the case in which the population standard deviations, σ_x and σ_y, are known exactly. Large sample formulas were found also for the standard errors and correlations between the errors of sample estimates of the parameters of Pearson Type I, III, and IV distributions, making this the first comprehensive study of such matters in the case of skew distributions.

Pearson returned to this subject in a series of three editorials in *Biometrika*, "On the Probable Errors of Frequency Constants," prepared in response to a need expressed by queries from readers. The first (1903) deals with the standard errors of, and correlations between, (i) cell frequencies in a histogram and (ii) sample centroidal moments, in terms of the centroidal moments of a univariate distribution of general form. Some of the results given are exact and some are limiting values for large samples. In some instances a "probable error" ($= 0.6745 \times$ standard error) is given, but the practice is deprecated: "The adoption of the 'probable error' . . . as a measure of . . . exactness must not, however, be taken as equivalent to asserting the validity of the normal law of errors or deviations, but merely as a purely conventional reduction of the standard deviation. It would be equally valid provided it were customary to omit this reduction or indeed to multiply the standard deviation by any other conventional factor" (p. 273).

The extension to samples from a general bivariate distribution was made in "Part II" (1913), reproduced from Pearson's lecture notes. Formulas were given for the correlation of errors in sample means; the correlation of errors in sample standard deviations; the standard error of the correlation coefficient r (in terms of the population coefficient of correlation ρ and the β_2's of the two marginal distributions); the correlation between the random sampling deviations of a sample mean and a sample standard deviation for the same variate; correlation between the random sampling deviations of sample mean of one variate and the standard deviation of a correlated variate; the correlation between a mean and a sample coefficient of correlation; the correlation between the sampling deviations of a sample standard deviation and sample coefficient of correlation; and the standard errors of coefficients of linear regression lines and of the means of arrays. In this paper it is also shown that in the case of all symmetric distributions, there is no correlation between the sample mean and sample standard deviation. "Part III" (1920) deals with the standard errors of, and the correlations between, the sampling variations of the sample median, quartiles, deciles, and other quantiles in random samples from a general univariate distribution. The relative efficiency of estimating the standard deviation of a normal population from the difference between two symmetrical quantiles of a large sample therefrom is discussed, and the "optimum" is found to be the difference between the seventh and ninety-third percentiles.

The results given in these three editorials are derived by a procedure considerably more elementary than that employed in the Pearson-Filon paper. Some of the results given are exact; others are limiting values for large samples; and many have become more or less standard in statistical circles.

The July 1900 issue of *Philosophical Magazine* contained Pearson's paper in which he introduced the criterion

$$\chi^2 = \Sigma \frac{(f_i - F_i)^2}{F_i}$$

as a measure of the agreement between observation and hypothesis overall to be used as a basis for determining the probability with which the differences $f_i - F_i$, $(i = 1, 2, \ldots, k)$, collectively might be due solely to the unavoidable fluctuations of random sampling, where f_i denotes the observed frequency (the observed number of observations falling) in the ith of k mutually exclusive categories, and F_i is the corresponding theoretical frequency (the number expected in the ith category in accordance with some particular true or hypothetical frequency distribution), with $\Sigma f_i = \Sigma F_i = N$, the total number of independent observations involved. To this end he derived the sampling distribution of χ^2 in large samples as a function of k, finding it to be a specialized form of the Pearson Type III distribution now known as the "χ^2 distribution for $k - 1$ degrees of freedom," the $k - 1$ being explained by the remark (in our notation) "only $k - 1$ of the k errors are variables; the kth is determined when the first $k - 1$ are known"; he also gave a small table of the integral of the distribution for χ^2 from 1 to 70 and k from 3 to 20. Of Pearson's many contributions to statistical theory and practice, this χ^2 text for goodness of fit is certainly one of his greatest; and in its original and extended forms it has remained one of the most useful of all statistical tests.

Four years later, in *On the Theory of Contingency and Its Relation to Association and Normal Correlation*, Pearson extended the application of his χ^2 criterion to the analysis of the cell frequencies in a "contingency table" of r rows and c columns resulting from the partitioning of a sample of N observations into r distinct classes in terms of some particular characteristic, and into c distinct classes with respect to another characteristic; showed how the χ^2 criterion could be used to test the independence of the two classifications; termed $\phi^2 = \chi^2/N$ the "mean square contingency" and

$$C = \sqrt{\frac{\chi^2}{N + \chi^2}}$$

the coefficient of mean square contingency; showed that, if a large sample from a bivariate normal distribution with correlation coefficient ρ is partitioned into the cells of a contingency table, then C^2 will tend to approximate ρ^2 as the number of categories in the table increases, the correct sign of ρ then being determined from the order of the two classifications and the pattern of the cell frequencies within the $r \times c$ table; and that, when $r = c = 2$, ϕ^2 is equal to the square of the product-moment coefficient of correlation computed from the observed frequencies in the fourfold table with purely arbitrary values (for instance, 0, 1) assigned to the two row categories and to the two column categories.

Pearson made much of the fact that the value of χ^2 and of C is unaffected by reordering either or both of the marginal categories, so that χ^2 provides a means of testing the independence of the two characteristics (such as eye color and occupation) in terms of which the marginal classes are defined without, and independently of, any additional assumptions as to the nature of the association, if any. In view of the above-mentioned relation of C to ρ under the indicated circumstances, C would seem to be a generally useful measure of the degree or intensity of the association when a large value of χ^2 leads to rejection of the hypothesis of independence; and Pearson proposed its use for this purpose. It is, however, not a very satisfactory measure of association—for example, the values of C obtained from an $r \times c$ classification and an $r' \times c'$ classification of the same data will usually be different. Also, some fundamental objections have been raised to the use of C, or any other function of χ^2, as a measure of association. Nonetheless, C played an important role in its day in the analysis of data classified into $r \times c$ tables when the categories for both characteristics can be arranged in meaningful orders— if the categories for either characteristic cannot be put into a meaningful order, then there can be no satisfactory measure of the intensity of *the* association; and a large value of χ^2 may simply be an indication of some fault in the sampling procedure.

In a 1911 *Biometrika* paper, Pearson showed how his χ^2 criterion could be extended to provide a test of the hypothesis that "two independent distributions of frequency [arrayed in a $2 \times c$ table] are really samples from the same population." The theoretical proportions in the respective cells implied by the presumed common population being unknown, they are estimated from the corresponding proportions of the two samples combined. Illustrative examples show that to find P, the probability of a larger value of χ^2, the "Tables for Testing Goodness of Fit" are to be entered with $n' = c$, signifying that there are $c - 1$ "independent variables" ("degrees of freedom") involved, which agrees with present practice. In a *Biometrika* paper, "On the General Theory of Multiple Contingency . . ." (1916), Pearson gave a new derivation of the χ^2 distribution, as the limiting distribution of the class frequencies of a multinomial distribution as the sample size $N \to \infty$; pointed out (pp. 153–155) that if q linear restraints are imposed on the n' cell frequencies in addition to the usual $\Sigma f_i = N$, then to find P one must enter the tables with $n' - q$; and extended the χ^2 technique to testing whether the frequencies arrayed in two ($2 \times c$) contingency tables can be considered random samples from the same bivariate population. In this application of "partial χ^2," Pearson considers the c column totals of each table to be fixed, thereby imposing $2c$ linear restraints on the $4c$ cell frequencies involved. The theoretical proportion, p_{1j}, in the presumed common population, corresponding to the cell in the top row and jth column of either table being unknown, it is taken as equal to the corresponding proportion in this cell of the two tables combined, ($j = 1, 2, \ldots, c$), thereby imposing c additional linear restraints (p_{2j} is, of course, simply $1 - p_{1j}$, [$j = 1, 2, \ldots, c$]). Hence there remain only $4c - 2c - c = c$ "independent variables"; and Pearson notes that the χ^2 tables are to be entered with $n' = c + 1$. These two papers clearly contain the basic elements of a large part of present-day χ^2 technique.

In section 5 of his 1900 paper on χ^2, Pearson pointed out that one must distinguish between a value of χ^2 calculated from theoretical frequencies F_i derived from a theoretical probability distribution completely specified a priori and values of χ_s^2, say, calculated from theoretical frequencies $\tilde{F}_i$ derived from a theoretical probability distribution of specified form but with the values of one or more of its parameters left unspecified so that "best values" for these had to be determined from the data in hand. It was clear that χ_s^2 could never exceed the "true" χ^2. From a brief, cursory analysis Pearson concluded that the difference $\chi^2 - \chi_s^2$ was likely to be negligible. Evidently he did not realize that the difference might depend on the number of constants the values of which were determined from the sample and that, if k constants were fit, χ_s^2 might be zero.

Ultimately Fisher showed in a series of three papers (1922, 1923, 1924) that when the unknown parameters of the population sampled are efficiently estimated from the data in such a manner as to impose c additional linear restraints on t cell frequencies, then, when the total number of observations N is large,

χ_s^2 will be distributed in accordance with a χ^2 distribution for $(t - 1 - c)$ degrees of freedom. Pearson had recognized this in the cases of the particular problems discussed in his 1911 and 1916 papers considered above; but he never accepted Fisher's modification of the value of n' with which the "Tables of Goodness of Fit" were to be entered in the original 1900 problem of testing the agreement of an observed and a theoretical frequency distribution when some parameters of the latter were estimated from the observed data, or in the 1904 problem of testing the independence of the two classifications of an $r \times c$ contingency table.

During Pearson's highly innovative decade and a half, 1891–1906, in addition to laying the foundations of the major contributions to statistical theory and practice reviewed above, he also initiated a number of other topics that later blossomed into important areas of statistics and other disciplines. Brief mention was made above of "On the Mathematical Theory of Errors of Judgment . . ." (1902). This investigation was founded on two series of experiments in which three observers each individually (a) estimated the midpoints of segments of straight lines; and (b), estimated the position on a scale of a bright line moving slowly downward at the moment when a bell sounded. The study revealed that the errors of different observers estimating or measuring the same series of quantities are in general correlated; that the frequency distributions of such errors of estimation or measurement certainly are not always normal; and that the variation over a period of time of the "personal equation" (the pattern of the systematic error or bias of an individual observer) is not explainable solely by the fluctuations of random sampling. The investigation stemmed from Pearson's observation that when three observers individually estimate or measure a series of physical quantities, the actual magnitudes of which may or may not be known or determinable, then, on the assumption of independence of the judgments of the respective observers, it is possible to determine the standard deviations of the distributions of measurement errors of each of the three observers from the observed standard deviations of the differences between their respective measurements of the same quantities. The investigation reported in this memoir is thus the forerunner of the work carried out by Frank E. Grubbs during the 1940's on methods for determining the individual precisions of two, three, four, or more measuring instruments in the presence of product variability.

A second example is provided by Pearson's "Note on Francis Galton's Problem" (August 1902), in which he derived the general expression for the mean value of the difference between the rth and the $(r + 1)$th individuals ranked in order of size in random samples of size n from any continuous distribution. This is one of the earliest general results in the sampling theory of order statistics, a very active subfield of statistics since the 1930's. Pearson later gave general expressions for the variances of, and correlations between, such intervals in random samples from any continuous distribution in a joint paper with his second wife, "On the Mean . . . and Variance of a Ranked Individual, and . . . of the Intervals Between Ranked Individuals, Part I . . ." (1931).

A third example is the theory of "random walk," a term Pearson coined in a brief letter, "The Problem of the Random Walk," published in the 17 July 1905 issue of *Nature*, in which he asked for information on the probability distribution of the walker's distance from the origin after n steps. Lord Rayleigh replied in the issue of 3 August, pointing out that the problem is formally the same as that of "the composition of n isoperiodic vibrations of unit amplitude and of phases distributed at random" (p. 318), which he had considered as early as 1880, and indicated the asymptotic solution as $n \to \infty$. The general solution for finite n was published by J. C. Kluyver in Dutch later the same year and, among other applications, provides the basis for a test of whether a set of orientation or directional data is "random" or tends to exhibit a "preferred direction." With John Blakeman, Pearson published *A Mathematical Theory of Random Migration* (1906), in which various theoretical forms of distribution were derived that would result from random migration from a point of origin under certain ideal conditions and solutions to a number of subsidiary problems were given, results that have found various other applications. Today "random walks" of various kinds, with and without reflecting or absorbing barriers, play important roles not only in the theory of Brownian motion but also in the treatment of random phenomena in astronomy, biology, physics, and communications engineering; in statistics, they are used in the theory of sequential estimation and of sequential tests of statistical hypotheses.

Pearson's involvement in heredity and evolution dates from his first fundamental paper on correlation and regression (1896), in which, to illustrate the value of these new mathematical tools in attacking problems of heredity and evolution, he included evaluations of partial regressions of offspring on each parent for sets of data from Galton's *Record of Family Faculties* (London, 1884) and considerably extended Galton's collateral studies of heredity by considering types of selection, assortative mating, and "panmixia" (suspension of selection and subsequent free interbreeding). Galton's formulation, in *Natural Inheritance* (1889), of

his law of ancestral heredity was somewhat ambiguous and imprecise because of his failure to take into account the additional mathematical complexity involved in the joint consideration of more than two mutually correlated characteristics. Pearson supposed him to mean (p. 303) that the coefficients of correlation between offspring and parent, grandparent, and great-grandparent, . . . were to be taken as $r, r^2, r^3, \ldots$. This led him to the paradoxical conclusion that "a knowledge of the ancestry beyond the parents in no way alters our judgment as to the size of organ or degree of characteristic probable in the offspring, nor its variability" (p. 306), a conclusion that he said in a footnote "seems especially noteworthy" inasmuch as it is quite contrary to what "it would seem natural to suppose."

In "On the Reconstruction of the Stature of Prehistoric Races" (1898), Pearson used multiple regression techniques to predict ("reconstruct") average measurements of extinct races from the sizes of existing bones and known correlations among bone lengths in an extant race, as a means of testing the accuracy of predictions in evolutionary problems in the light of certain evolutionary theories.

Meanwhile, Galton had formulated (1897) his "law" more precisely. After some correspondence Pearson, in "On the Law of Ancestral Heredity" (1898), subtitled "A New Year's Greeting to Francis Galton, January 1, 1898," expressed what he christened "Galton's Law of Ancestral Heredity" in the form of a multiple regression equation of offspring on midparental ancestry

$$x_0 = \frac{1}{2} \frac{\sigma_0}{\sigma_1} x_1 + \frac{1}{4} \frac{\sigma_0}{\sigma_2} x_2 + \frac{1}{8} \frac{\sigma_0}{\sigma_3} x_3 + \cdots,$$

where x_0 is the predicted deviation of an individual offspring from the mean of the offspring generation, x_1 is the deviation of the offspring's "midparent" from the mean of the parental generation, x_2 the deviation of the offspring's "midgrandparent" from the mean of the grandparental generation, and so on, and $\sigma_0\,\sigma_1 \ldots$ are the standard deviations of the distributions of individuals in the respective generations. In order that this formulation of Galton's law be unambiguous, it was necessary to have a precise definition of "sth midparent." The definition that Pearson adopted "with reservations" was "[If] a father is a first parent, a grandfather a second parent, a great-grandfather a third parent, and so on, [then] the mid sth parent or the sth mid-parent is derived from [is the mean of] all 2^s individual sth parents" (footnote, p. 387).

From this formulation Pearson deduced theoretical values for regression and correlation coefficients between various kin, tested Galton's stature data against these expectations, and suggested generalizing Galton's law by substituting $\gamma\beta$, $\gamma\beta^2$, $\gamma\beta^3$, ... for Galton's geometric series coefficients 1/2, 1/4, 1/8, ... to allow "greater scope for variety of inheritance in different species" (p. 403). In the concluding section Pearson claims: "If either [Galton's Law], or its suggested modification be substantially correct, they embrace the whole theory of heredity. They bring into one simple statement an immense range of facts, thus fulfilling the fundamental purpose of a great law of nature" (p. 411). After noting some difficulties that would have to be met and stating, "We must wait at present for further determinations of hereditary influence, before the actual degree of approximation between law and nature can be appreciated," he concluded with the sweeping statement: "At present I would merely state my opinion that, with all due reservations it seems to me that . . . it is highly probable that [the law of ancestral heredity] is the simple descriptive statement which brings into a single focus all the complex lines of hereditary influence. If Darwinian evolution be natural selection combined with *heredity*, then the single statement which embraces the whole field of heredity must prove almost as epoch-making to the biologist as the law of gravitation to the astronomer" (p. 412).

These claims were obviously too sweeping. Neither the less nor the more general form of the law was founded on any clear conception of the mechanism of heredity. Also, most unfortunately, some of the wording employed—for instance, "I shall now proceed to determine . . . the correlation between an individual and any sth parent from a knowledge of the regression between the individual and his mid-sth parent" (p. 391) —tended to give the erroneous idea that the law expressed a relation between a particular individual and his sth parents, and thus to mislead biologists of the period, who had not become fully conscious that regression equations merely expressed relationships that held on the average between the generic types of "individuals" involved, and not between particular individuals of those types.

During the summer vacations of 1899 and 1900 Pearson, with the aid of many willing friends and colleagues, collected material to test a novel theory of "homotyposis, which if correct would imply that the correlation between offspring of the same parents should on the average be equal to the correlation between undifferentiated like organs of an individual." The volume of data collected and reduced was far greater than Pearson had previously attempted. The result was a joint memoir by Pearson and several members of his staff, "On the Principle of Homotyposis and Its Relation to Heredity . . . Part I.

Homotyposis in the Vegetable Kingdom," which was "received" by the Royal Society on 6 October 1900. William Bateson, biologist and pioneer in genetics, who had just become a convert to Mendel's theory, was one of those chosen to referee the memoir, which was "read"—presumably only the five-page abstract[40] and certainly in highly abridged form—at the meeting of 15 November 1900. In the discussion that followed the presentation, Bateson sharply criticized the paper, its thesis being, in his view, mistaken; and other fellows present added criticism of both its length and its content.

The next day (16 November 1900) Weldon wrote to Pearson: "The contention 'that numbers mean nothing and do not exist in Nature' is a very serious thing, which will have to be fought. Most other people have got beyond it, but most biologists have not. Do you think it would be too hopelessly expensive to start a journal of some kind?. . ."[41] Pearson was enthusiastically in favor of the idea—on 13 December 1900 he wrote to Galton that Bateson's adverse criticism "did not apply to this memoir only but to all my work, . . . if the R. S. people send my papers to Bateson, one cannot hope to get them printed. It is a practical notice to quit. This notice applies not only to *my* work, but to most work on similar statistical lines."[42] On 29 November Weldon wrote to him: "Get a better title for this would-be journal than I can think of!"[43] Pearson replied with the suggestion that "the science in future should be called Biometry and its official organ be *Biometrika*."[44]

A circular was sent out during December 1900 to solicit financial support and resulted in a fund sufficient to support the journal for a number of years. Weldon, Pearson, and C. B. Davenport were to be the editors; and Galton agreed to be "consulting editor." The first issue appeared in October 1901, and the editorial "The Scope of *Biometrika*" stated:

> *Biometrika* will include (a) memoirs on variation, inheritance, and selection in Animals and Plants, based upon the examination of statistically large numbers of specimens (this will of course include statistical investigations in anthropometry); (b) those developments of statistical theory which are applicable to biological problems; (c) numerical tables and graphical solutions tending to reduce the labour of statistical arithmetic; (d) abstracts of memoirs, dealing with these subjects, which are published elsewhere; and (e) notes on current biometric work and unsolved problems.

In the years that followed, *Biometrika* became a major medium for the publication of mathematical tables and other aids to statistical analysis and detailed tables of biological data.

The memoir on homotyposis was not published in the *Philosophical Transactions* until 12 November 1901, and only after a direct appeal by Pearson to the president of the Royal Society on grounds of general principle rather than individual unfairness. Meanwhile, Bateson had prepared detailed adverse criticisms. Under pressure from Bateson, the secretary of the Royal Society put aside protocol and permitted the printing of Bateson's comments and their issuance to the fellows at the meeting of 14 February 1901—before the full memoir by Pearson and his colleagues was in their hands, and even before its authors had been notified whether it had been accepted for publication. Then, with the approval of the Zoological Committee, Bateson's full critique was published in the *Proceedings of the Royal Society* before the memoir criticized had appeared.[45] One can thus appreciate the basis for the acerbity of Pearson's rejoinder, which he chose to publish in *Biometrika*[46] because he had been "officially informed that [he had] a right to a rejoinder, but only to such a one as will not confer on [his] opponent a right to a further reply!" (footnote, p. 321).

This fracas over the homotyposis memoir was but one manifestation of the division that had developed in the 1890's between the biometric "school" of Galton, Weldon, and Pearson and certain biologists—notably Bateson—over the nature of evolution. The biometricians held that evolution of new species was the result of gradual accumulation of the effects of small continuous variations. In 1894 Bateson published a book in which he noted that deviations from normal parental characteristics frequently take the form of discontinuous "jumps" of definite measurable magnitude, and held that discontinuous variation of this kind—evidenced by what we today call sports or mutations—is necessary for the evolution of new species.[47] He was deeply hurt when Weldon took issue with this thesis in an otherwise very favorable review published in *Nature* (10 May 1894).

When Gregor Mendel's long-overlooked paper of 1866 was resurrected in 1900 by three Continental botanists, the particulate nature of Mendel's theory of "dominance" and "segregation" was clearly in keeping with Bateson's views; and he became a totally committed Mendelist, taking it upon himself to convert all English biologists into disciples of Mendel. Meanwhile, Weldon and Pearson had become deeply committed adherents to Galton's law of ancestral heredity, to which Bateson was antipathetic. There followed a heated controversy between the "ancestrians," led by Pearson and Weldon, and the "Mendelians," led by Bateson. Pearson and Weldon were not, as some supposed, unreceptive to Mendelian ideas but were concerned with the too ready acceptance of

Mendelism as a complete gospel without regard to certain incompatibilities they had found between Mendel's laws of "dominance" and "segregation" and other work. Weldon, the naturalist, regarded Mendelism as an unimportant but inconvenient exception to the ancestral law. Pearson, the applied mathematician and philosopher of science, saw that Mendelism was not incompatible with the ancestral law but in some circumstances could lead directly to it; and he sought to bring all heredity into a single system embodying both Mendelian and ancestrian principles, with the latter dominant. To Bateson, Mendel's laws were the truth and all else was heresy. The controversy raged on with much mutual incomprehension, and with great bitterness on both sides, until Weldon's death in April 1906 removed the most committed ancestrian and Bateson's main target.[48] Without the help of Weldon's biologically trained mind, Pearson had no inclination, nor the necessary training, to keep in close touch with the growing complexity of the Mendelian hypothesis, which was coming to depend increasingly on purely biological discoveries for its development; he therefore turned his attention to unfinished business in other areas and to eugenics.

During the succeeding decades Mendelian theory became firmly established—but only after much testing on diverse material, clarification of ideas, explanation of "exceptions," and tying in with cytological discoveries. Mendel's laws have been shown to apply to many kinds of characters in almost all organisms, but this has not entirely eliminated "biometrical" methods. Quite the contrary: multiple regression techniques are still needed to cope with the inheritance of quantitative characters that presumably depend upon so many genes that Mendelian theory cannot be brought to bear in practice. For example, coat color of dairy cows depends upon only a few genes and its Mendelian inheritance is readily verified; but the quantitative trait of milk production capacity is so complex genetically that multiple regression methods are used to predict the average milk-production character of offspring of particular matings, given the relevant ancestral information.

In fact, geneticists today ascribe the reconciliation of the "ancestral" and "Mendelian" positions, and definitive synthesis of the two theories, to Fisher's first genetical paper, "The Correlations to be Expected Between Relatives on the Supposition of Mendelian Inheritance" (1918), in which, in response to new data, he improved upon the kinds of models that Pearson, Weldon, and Yule had been considering 10–20 years before, and showed clearly that the correlations observed between human relatives not only could be interpreted on the supposition of Mendelian inheritance, but also that Mendelian inheritance must lead to precisely the kind of correlations observed.

Weldon's death was not only a tremendous blow to Pearson but also removed a close colleague of high caliber, without whom it was not possible to continue work in biometry along some of the lines that they had developed during the preceding fifteen years. Yet Pearson's productivity hardly faltered. During his remaining thirty years his articles, editorials, memoirs, and books on or related to biometry and statistics numbered over 300; he also produced one in astronomy and four in mechanics and about seventy published letters, reviews, and prefatory and other notes in scientific publications, the last of which was a letter (1935) on the aims of the founders of *Biometrika* and the conditions under which the journal had been published.

Following Weldon's death, Pearson gave increasing attention to eugenics. In 1904 Galton had provided funds for the establishment of a eugenics record office, to be concerned with collecting data for the scientific study of eugenics. Galton kept the office under his control until late in 1906, when, at the age of eighty-four, he turned it over to Pearson. With a change of name to eugenics laboratory, it became a companion to Pearson's biometric laboratory. It was transferred in 1907 to University College and with a small staff carried out studies of the relative importance of heredity and environment in alcoholism, tuberculosis, insanity, and infant mortality.[49] The findings were published as Studies in National Deterioration, nos. 1–11 (1906–1924) and in Eugenics Laboratory Memoirs, nos. 1–29 (1907–1935). Thirteen issues of the latter were devoted to "The Treasury of Human Inheritance" (1909–1933), a vast collection of pedigrees forming the basic material for the discussion of the inheritance of abnormalities, disorders, and other traits.

Pearson's major effort during the period 1906–1914, however, was devoted to developing a postgraduate center in order "to make statistics a branch of applied mathematics with a technique and nomenclature of its own, to train statisticians as men of science . . . and in general to convert statistics in this country from being the playing field of *dilettanti* and controversialists into a serious branch of science, which no man could attempt to use effectively without adequate training, any more than he could attempt to use the differential calculus, being ignorant of mathematics."[50] At the beginning of this period Pearson was not only head of the department of applied mathematics, but also in charge of the drawing office for engineering students, giving evening classes in astronomy, directing the biometric and eugenics laboratories, and editing their various publications, and *Biometrika*, a tremendous task for one man. In the summer of 1911, however, he was able to cut back somewhat on these diverse activities by relinquishing the Goldsmid chair of applied mathematics to become the first Galton professor of eugenics and head of a new department of applied statistics in which were incorporated the biometric and eugenics laboratories. But he also assumed a new task about the same time: soon after Galton's death in 1911, his relatives had asked Pearson to write his biography. The first volume of *The Life, Letters and Labors of Francis Galton* was published in 1914, the second volume in 1925, and the third volume (in two parts) in 1930. It is an incomparable source of information on Galton, on Pearson himself, and on the early years of biometry. Although the volume of Pearson's output of purely statistical work was somewhat reduced during these years by the task of writing this biography, it was still immense by ordinary standards.

Pearson was the principal editor of *Biometrika* from its founding to his death (vols. 1–28, 1901–1936), and for many years he was the sole editor. Under his guidance it became the world's leading medium of publication of papers on, and mathematical tables relating to, statistical theory and practice. Soon after World War I, during which Pearson's group was deeply involved in war work, he initiated the series Tracts for Computers, nos. 1–20 (1919–1935), many of which became indispensable to computers of the period. In 1925 he founded *Annals of Eugenics* and served as editor of the first five volumes (1925–1933). Some of the tables in *Tables for Statisticians and Biometricians* (pt. I, 1914; pt. II, 1931) appear to be timeless in value; others are no longer used. *The Tables of the Incomplete Beta-Function* (1934), a compilation prepared under his direction over a period of several decades, remains a monument to him and his co-workers.

In July 1932 Pearson advised the college and university that he would resign from the Galton professorship the following summer. The college decided to divide the department of applied statistics into two independent units, a department of eugenics with which the Galton professorship would be associated, and a new department of statistics. In October 1933 Pearson was established in a room placed at his disposal by the zoology department; his son, Egon, was head of the new department of statistics; and R. A. Fisher was named the second Galton professor of eugenics. Pearson continued to edit *Biometrika* and had almost seen the final proofs of the first half of volume 28 through the press when he died on 27 April 1936.

NOTES

1. Quoted by E. S. Pearson in *Karl Pearson: An Appreciation . . .*, p. 4 (*Biometrika*, **28**, 196).
2. Galton discovered the statistical phenomenon of regression around 1875 in the course of experiments with sweet-pea seeds to determine the law of inheritance of size. Using 100 parental seeds of each of 7 different selected sizes, he constructed a two-way plot of the diameters of parental and offspring seeds from each parental class. Galton then noticed that the median diameters of the offspring seeds for the respective parental classes fell nearly on a straight line. Furthermore, the median diameters of offspring from the larger-size parental classes were less than those of the parents; and for the smaller-size parental classes, they were greater than those of the parents, indicating a tendency of the "mean" offspring size to "revert" toward what might be described as the average ancestral type. Not realizing that this phenomenon is a characteristic of any two-way plot, he first termed it "reversion" and, later, "regression."

    Examining these same data further, Galton noticed that the variation of offspring size within the respective parental arrays (as measured by their respective semi-interquartile ranges) was approximately constant and less than the similarly measured variation of the overall offspring population. From this empirical evidence he then inferred the correct relation, variability of offspring family = $\sqrt{1 - r^2} \times$ variability of overall offspring population, which he announced in symbolic form in an 1877 lecture, calling r the "reversion" coefficient.

    A few years later Galton made a two-way plot of the statures of some human parents of unselected statures and their adult children, noting that the respective marginal distributions were approximately Gaussian or "normal," as Adolphe Quetelet had noticed earlier from examination of each of these variables separately, and that the frequency distributions along lines in the plot parallel to either of the variate axes were "apparently" Gaussian distributions of equal variation, which was less than, and in a constant ratio $\sqrt{1 - r^2}$ to, that of the corresponding marginal distributions. To obtain a numerical value for r, Galton expressed the deviations of the individual values of both variates from their respective medians in terms of their respective semi-interquartile ranges as a unit, so that r became the slope of his regression line.

    In 1888 Galton made one more great and far-reaching discovery. Applying the techniques that he had evolved for the measurement of the influence of heredity to the problem of measuring the degree of association between the sizes of two different organs of the same individual, he reached the conception of an "index of co-relation" as a measure of the degree of relationship between two such characteristics and recognized r, his measure of "reversion" or "regression," to be such a coefficient of co-relation or correlation, suitable for application to all living forms.

    Galton, however, failed to recognize and appreciate the additional mathematical complexity necessarily involved in the joint consideration of more than two mutually correlated characteristics, with the result that his efforts to formulate and implement what became known as his law of ancestral heredity were somewhat confused and imprecise. It remained for Pearson to provide the necessary generalization and precision of formulation in the form of a multiple regression formula.

    For fuller details, see Pearson's "Notes on the History of Correlation" (1920).
3. *Speeches . . . at a Dinner . . . in [His] Honour*, pp. 22–23;

also quoted by E. S. Pearson, *op. cit.*, p. 19 (*Biometrika*, **28**, 211).
4. An examination of *Letters From W. S. Gosset to R. A. Fisher 1915–1936*, 4 vols. (Dublin, 1962), issued for private circulation only, reveals that Gosset (pen name "Student"), played a similar role with respect to R. A. Fisher. When and how they first came into contact is revealed by the two letters of Sept. 1912 from Gosset to Pearson that are reproduced in E. S. Pearson's "Some Early Correspondence . . ." (1968).
5. E. S. Pearson, *op. cit.*, apps. II and III.
6. Pearson was not the first to use this terminology: "Galton used it, as did also Lexis, and the writer has not found any reference which seems to be its first use" (Helen M. Walker, *Studies . . .*, p. 185). But Pearson's consistent and exclusive use of this term in his epoch-making publications led to its adoption throughout the statistical community.
7. E. S. Pearson, *op. cit.*, p. 26 (*Biometrika*, **28**, 218).
8. The title "Contributions to the Mathematical Theory of Evolution" or "Mathematical Contributions . . ." was used as the general title of 17 memoirs, numbered II through XIX, published in the *Philosophical Transactions* or as Drapers' Company Research Memoirs, and of 8 unnumbered papers published in the *Proceedings of the Royal Society.* "Mathematical" became and remained the initial word from III (1896) on. No. XVII was announced before 1912 as a forthcoming Drapers' . . . Memoir but has not been published to date.
9. From Pearson, "Statistical Tests," in *Nature*, **136** (1935), 296–297, see 296.
10. Pearson, "Notes on the History of Correlation," p. 37 (Pearson and Kendall, p. 197).
11. Pearson did not use different symbols for population parameters (such as μ, σ, ρ) and sample measures of them (m, s, r) as has been done in this article, following the example set by "Student" in his first paper on small-sample theory, "The Probable Error of a Mean" (1908). Use of identical symbols for population parameters and sample measures of them makes Pearson's, and other papers of this period, difficult to follow and, in some instances, led to error.
12. Pearson, "Notes on the History of Correlation," p. 42 (Pearson and Kendall, p. 202).
13. In the rest of the article, the term "standard error" will be used instead of "standard deviation of the sampling error." Pearson consistently gave formulas for, and spoke of the corresponding "probable error" (or "p.e.") defined by,

    probable error = $0.674489 \ldots \times$ standard error,

    the numerical factor being the factor appropriate to the normal distribution, and reserved the term "standard deviation" (and the symbol σ) for description of the variation of individuals in a population or sample.
14. Footnote, p. 274 (*Early . . . Papers*, p. 134).
15. There are always two sample η's, η_{yx} and η_{xy}, corresponding to the regression of y on x and the regression of x on y, respectively, in the sample. When these regressions are both exactly linear, $\eta_{yx} = \eta_{xy} = r$; otherwise η_{yx} and η_{xy} are different.

    In this memoir Pearson defines and discusses the correlation ratio, η_{yx}, and its relation to r entirely in terms of a sample of N paired observations, (x_i, y_i), $(i = 1, 2, \ldots, N)$. The implications of various equalities and inequalities between the correlation ratio of a trait X with respect to a trait Y in some general (nonnormal) bivariate population and ρ, the product-moment coefficient of correlation of X and Y in this population, are discussed, for example, in W. H. Kruskal, "Ordinal Measures of Association," in *Journal of American Statistical Association*, **53** (1958), 814–861.
16. In Pearson, "On the Systematic Fitting of Curves to Observations and Measurements," in *Biometrika*, **1**, no. 3

(Apr. 1902), 264–303, see p. 271.

17. Pearson and Alice Lee, "On the Distribution of Frequency (Variation and Correlation) of the Barometric Height at Diverse Stations," in *Philosophical Transactions of the Royal Society*, **190A** (1898), 423–469, see 456 and footnote to 462, respectively.

18. Pearson, "On the Probable Error of a Coefficient of Correlation as Found From a Fourfold Table," in *Biometrika*, **9**, nos. 1–2 (Mar. 1913), 22–27.

19. Pearson, "On the Probable Error of Biserial η," *ibid.*, **11**, no. 4 (May 1917), 292–302.

20. *Ibid.*, **1**, no. 1 (Oct. 1901), 2. Emphasis added.

21. Student, "Probable Error of a Correlation Coefficient," *ibid.*, **6**, nos. 2–3 (Sept. 1908), 302–310. In a 1915 letter to R. A. Fisher (repro. in E. S. Pearson, "Some Early Correspondence . . .," p. 447, and in Pearson and Kendall, p. 470), Gosset tells "how these things came to be of importance [to him]" and, in particular, says that the work of "the Experimental Brewery which concerns such things as the connection between analysis of malt or hops, and the behaviour of the beer, and which takes a day to each unit of the experiment, thus limiting the numbers, demanded an answer to such questions as 'If with a small number of cases I get a value r, what is the probability that there is really a positive correlation of greater than (say) 25 ?' "

22. E. S. Pearson, "Some Reflexions . . .," pp. 351–352 (Pearson and Kendall, pp. 349–350).

23. R. A. Fisher, "Frequency Distribution of the Values of the Correlation Coefficient in Samples From an Indefinitely Large Population," in *Biometrika*, **10**, no. 4 (May 1915), 507–521.

24. Letter from Pearson to Fisher dated 26 Sept. 1914, repro. in E. S. Pearson, "Some Early Correspondence . . .," p. 448 (Pearson and Kendall, p. 408).

25. Letter from Pearson to Fisher dated 3 Oct. 1914, partly repro. *ibid.*, p. 449 (Pearson and Kendall, p. 409).

26. Letter from Pearson to Fisher dated 30 Jan., 1915, partly repro. *ibid.*, pp. 449–450 (Pearson and Kendall, pp. 409–410).

27. *Ibid.*, p. 450 (Pearson and Kendall, p. 410).

28. Letter from Pearson to Fisher dated 13 May 1916, repro. *ibid.*, p. 451 (Pearson and Kendall, p. 411).

29. J. O. Irwin, in *Journal of the Royal Statistical Society*, **126**, pt. 1 (Mar. 1963), 161; F. Yates and K. Mather, in *Biographical Memoirs of Fellows of the Royal Society*, **9** (Nov. 1963), 98–99; P. C. Mahalanobis, in *Biometrics*, **20**, no. 2 (June 1964), 214.

30. R. A. Fisher, "On an Absolute Criterion for Fitting Frequency Curves," in *Messenger of Mathematics*, **41** (1912), 155–160.

This paper marks Fisher's break away from inverse probability reasoning via Bayes's theorem but, although evident in retrospect, the "break" was not clear-cut: not having yet coined the term "likelihood," he spoke (p. 157) of "the probability of any particular set of θ's" (that is, of the parameters involved) being "proportional to the chance of a given set of observations occurring"— which appears to be equivalent to the proposition in the theory of inverse probability that, assuming a uniform a priori probability distribution of the parameters, the ratio of the a posteriori probability that $\theta = \theta_o + \xi$ to the a posteriori probability that $\theta = \theta_o$ is equal to the ratio of the probability of the observed set of observations when $\theta = \theta_o + \xi$ to their probability when $\theta = \theta_o$. He also described (p. 158) graphical representation of "the inverse probability system." On the other hand, he did stress (p. 160) that only the relative (not the absolute) values of these "probabilities" were meaningful and that it would be "illegitimate" to integrate them over a region in the parameter space.

Fisher introduced the term "likelihood" in his paper "On the Mathematical Foundations of Theoretical Statistics," in *Philosophical Transactions of the Royal Society*, **222A** (19 Apr. 1922), 309–368, in which he made clear for the first time the distinction between the mathematical properties of "likelihoods" and "probabilities," and stated:

> I must plead guilty in my original statement of the Method of Maximum Likelihood to having based my argument upon the principle of inverse probability; in the same paper, it is true, I emphasized the fact that such inverse probabilities were relative only . . . . Upon consideration . . . I perceive that the word probability is wrongly used in such a connection: probability is a ratio of frequencies, and about the frequencies of such [parameter] values we can know nothing whatever (p. 326).

31. E. S. Pearson, "Some Early Correspondence . . .," p. 452 (Pearson and Kendall, p. 412).

32. Repro. *ibid.*, pp. 454–455 (Pearson and Kendall, pp. 414–415).

33. F. N. David, *Tables of the Ordinates and Probability Integral of the Distribution of the Correlation Coefficient in Small Samples* (London, 1938).

34. Letter from Pearson to Fisher dated 21 Aug. 1920, repro. in E. S. Pearson, "Some Early Correspondence . . .," p. 453 (Pearson and Kendall, p. 413).

35. R. A. Fisher, "On the 'Probable Error' of a Coefficient of Correlation Deduced From a Small Sample," in *Metron*, **1**, no. 4 (1921), 1–32.

36. Letters from Pearson to Fisher dated 26 June 1916 and 21 Oct. 1918, repro. in E. S. Pearson, "Some Early Correspondence . . .," pp. 455, 456, respectively (Pearson and Kendall, pp. 415, 416).

37. Pearson, "Method of Moments and Method of Maximum Likelihood," in *Biometrika*, **28**, nos. 1–2 (June 1936), 34–59; R. A. Fisher, "Professor Karl Pearson and the Method of Moments," in *Annals of Eugenics*, **7**, pt. 4 (June 1937), 303–318.

38. F. Y. Edgeworth, "On the Probable Error of Frequency Constants," in *Journal of the Royal Statistical Society*, **71** (1908), 381–397, 499–512, 652–678.

39. The identical mathematical form of expressions derived by the method of maximum likelihood and by the method of inverse probability, if a uniform prior distribution is adopted, has been a source of continuing confusion. Thus, the "standard errors" given by Gauss in his 1816 paper were undeniably derived via the method of inverse probability and, strictly speaking, are the standard deviations of the a posteriori probability distributions of parameters concerned, given the observed values of the particular functions of sample values considered. On the other hand, by virtue of the above-mentioned equivalence of form, Gauss's 1816 formulas can be recognized as giving the "standard errors," that is, the standard deviations of the sampling distributions, of the functions of sample values involved for fixed values of the corresponding population parameters. Consequently, speaking loosely, one is inclined today to attribute to Gauss the original ("first") derivation of these "standard error" formulas, even though he may have had (in 1816) no conception of the "sampling distribution," for fixed values of a population parameter, of a sample function used to estimate the value of this parameter. In contrast, the result given in his 1821 paper almost certainly refers to the sampling distribution of s, and not to the a posteriori distribution of σ.

Edgeworth's discussion is quite explicitly in terms of inverse probability. Pearson-Filon asymptotic formulas are derived afresh in this context and are said to be applicable only to "solutions" obtained by "the genuine inverse method," the "fluctuation of the *quaesitum*" so determined "being less than that of any other determination" (pp. 506–507).

The correct interpretation of the formulas derived by Pearson and Filon is somewhat obscured by their use of identical symbols for population parameters and the sample functions used to estimate them, and by the fact that their choice of words is such that their various summary statements can be interpreted either way. On the other hand, their derivation starts (p. 231) with consideration of a ratio of probabilities, introduced without explanation but for which the explanation may be the "proposition in the theory of Inverse Probability" mentioned in note 30 above; and Pearson says, in his letter of June 1916 to Fisher (see note 32), "In the first place you have to demonstrate the logic of the Gaussian rule . . . I frankly confess I approved the Gaussian method in 1897 (see *Phil. Trans.* Vol. 191, A, p. 232), but I think it logically at fault now." These facts suggest that Pearson and Filon may have regarded the "probable errors" and "correlations" they derived as describing properties of the joint a posteriori probability distribution of the population parameters, given the observed values of the sample functions used to estimate them.

40. *Proceedings of the Royal Society*, **68** (1900), 1–5.
41. Quoted by Pearson in his memoir on Weldon, in *Biometrika*, **5**, no. 1 (Oct. 1906), 35 (Pearson and Kendall, p. 302).
42. Letter from Pearson to Galton, quoted in Pearson's *Life . . . of Francis Galton*, IIIA, 241.
43. Quoted by Pearson in his memoir on Weldon, in *Biometrika*, **5**, no. 1 (Oct. 1906), 35 (Pearson and Kendall, p. 302).
44. *Ibid.*
45. W. Bateson, "Heredity, Differentiation, and Other Conceptions of Biology: A Consideration of Professor Karl Pearson's Paper 'On the Principle of Homotyposis,'" in *Proceedings of the Royal Society*, **69**, no. 453, 193–205.
46. Pearson, "On the Fundamental Conceptions of Biology," in *Biometrika*, **1**, no. 3 (Apr. 1902), 320–344.
47. W. Bateson, *Materials for the Study of Variation, Treated With Especial Regard to Discontinuity in the Origin of Species* (London, 1894).
48. For fuller details, see either of the articles by P. Froggatt and N. C. Nevin in the bibliography; the first is the more complete.
49. These studies were not without a price for Pearson: he became deeply involved almost at once in a hot controversy over tuberculosis and a fierce dispute on the question of alcoholism. See E. S. Pearson, *Karl Pearson . . .*, pp. 59–66 (*Biometrika*, **29**, 170–177).
50. From a printed statement entitled *History of the Biometric and Galton Laboratories*, drawn up by Pearson in 1920; quoted in E. S. Pearson, *Karl Pearson . . .*, p. 53 (*Biometrika*, **29**, 164).

BIBLIOGRAPHY

I. ORIGINAL WORKS. A bibliography of Pearson's research memoirs and his articles and letters in scientific journals that are on applied mathematics, including astronomy, but not statistics, biometry, anthropology, eugenics, or mathematical tables, follows the obituary by L. N. G. Filon (see below). A bibliography of his major contributions to the latter five areas is at the end of P. C. Mahalanobis, "A Note on the Statistical and Biometric Writings of Karl Pearson" (see below). The individual mathematical tables and collections of such tables to which Pearson made significant contributions in their computation or compilation, or through preparation of explanatory introductory material, are listed and described in Raymond Clare Archibald, *Mathematical Table Makers* (New York, 1948), 65–67.

Preparation of a complete bibliography of Pearson's publications was begun, with his assistance, three years before his death. The aim was to include all of the publications on which his name appeared as sole or part author and all of his publications that were issued anonymously. The result, *A Bibliography of the Statistical and Other Writings of Karl Pearson* (Cambridge, 1939), compiled by G. M. Morant with the assistance of B. L. Welch, lists 648 numbered entries arranged chronologically under five principal headings, with short summaries of the contents of the more important, followed by a sixth section in which a chronological list, "probably incomplete," is given of the syllabuses of courses of lectures and single lectures delivered by Pearson that were printed contemporaneously as brochures or single sheets. The five major categories and the number of entries in each are the following:

I. Theory of statistics and its application to biological, social, and other problems (406);

II. Pure and applied mathematics and physical science (37);

III. Literary and historical (67);

IV. University matters (27);

V. Letters, reviews, prefatory and other notes in scientific publications (111).

Three omissions have been detected: "The Flying to Pieces of a Whirling Ring," in *Nature*, **43**, no. 1117 (26 Mar. 1891), 488; "Note on Professor J. Arthur Harris' Papers on the Limitation in the Applicability of the Contingency Coefficient," in *Journal of the American Statistical Association*, **25**, no. 171 (Sept. 1930), 320–323; and "Postscript," *ibid.*, 327.

The following annotated list of Pearson's most important publications will suffice to reveal the great diversity of his contributions and their impact on the biological, physical, and social sciences. The papers marked with a single asterisk (*) have been repr. in *Karl Pearson's Early Statistical Papers* (Cambridge, 1948) and those with a double asterisk (**), in E. S. Pearson and M. G. Kendall, eds., *Studies in the History of Probability and Statistics* (London–Darien, Conn., 1970), referred to as Pearson and Kendall.

"On the Motion of Spherical and Ellipsoidal Bodies in Fluid Media" (2 pts.), in *Quarterly Journal of Pure and Applied Mathematics*, **20** (1883), 60–80, 184–211; and "On a Certain Atomic Hypothesis" (2 pts.), in *Transactions of the Cambridge Philosophical Society*, **14**, pt. 2 (1887), 71–120, and *Proceedings of the London Mathematical Society*, **20** (1888), 38–63, respectively. These early papers on the motions of a rigid or pulsating atom in an infinite incompressible fluid did much to increase Pearson's stature in applied mathematics at the time.

William Kingdon Clifford, *The Common Sense of the Exact Sciences* (London, 1885; reiss. 1888), which Pearson edited and completed.

Isaac Todhunter, *A History of the Theory of Elasticity and of the Strength of Materials From Galilei to the Present Time*, 2 vols. (Cambridge, 1886–1893; reiss. New York, 1960), edited and completed by Pearson.

The Ethic of Freethought (London, 1888; 2nd ed., 1901), a collection of essays, lectures, and public addresses on free thought, historical research, and socialism.

"On the Flexure of Heavy Beams Subjected to a Continuous Load. Part I," in *Quarterly Journal of Pure and Applied Mathematics*, **24** (1889), 63–110, in which for the first time a now-much-cited exact solution was given for the bending of a beam of circular cross section under its own weight, and extended to elliptic cross sections in ". . . Part II," *ibid.*, **31** (1899), 66–109, written with L. N. G. Filon.

The Grammar of Science (London, 1892; 3rd ed., 1911; reiss. Gloucester, Mass., 1969; 4th ed., E. S. Pearson, ed., London, 1937), a critical survey of the concepts of modern science and his most influential book.

* "Contributions to the Mathematical Theory of Evolution," in *Philosophical Transactions of the Royal Society*, **185A** (1894), 71–110, deals with the dissection of symmetrical and asymmetrical frequency curves into normal (Gaussian) components and marks Pearson's introduction of the method of moments as a means of fitting a theoretical curve to experimental data and of the term "standard deviation" and σ as the symbol for it.

* "Contributions to the Mathematical Theory of Evolution. II. Skew Variation in Homogeneous Material," *ibid.*, **186A** (1895), 343–414, in which the term "mode" is introduced, the foundations of the Pearson system of frequency curves is laid, and Types I–IV are defined and their application exemplified.

* "Mathematical Contributions to the Theory of Evolution. III. Regression, Heredity, and Panmixia," *ibid.*, **187A** (1896), 253–318, Pearson's first fundamental paper on correlation, with special reference to problems of heredity, in which correlation and regression are defined in far greater generality than previously and the theory of multivariate normal correlation is developed as a practical tool to a stage that left little to be added.

The Chances of Death and Other Studies in Evolution, 2 vols. (London, 1897), essays on social and statistical topics, including the earliest adequate study ("Variation in Man and Woman") of anthropological "populations" using scientific measures of variability.

* "Mathematical . . . IV. On the Probable Errors of Frequency Constants and on the Influence of Random Selection on Variation and Correlation," in *Philosophical Transactions of the Royal Society*, **191A** (1898), 229–311, written with L. N. G. Filon, in which were derived the now-familiar expressions for the asymptotic variances and covariances of sample estimators of a group of population parameters in terms of derivatives of the likelihood function (without recognition of their applicability only to maximum likelihood estimators), and a number of particular results deduced therefrom.

* "Mathematical . . . V. On the Reconstruction of the Stature of Prehistoric Races," *ibid.*, **192A** (1898), 169–244, in which multiple regression techniques were used to reconstruct predicted average measurements of extinct races from the sizes of existing bones, given the correlations among bone lengths in an extant race, not merely as a technical exercise but as a means of testing the accuracy of predictions in evolutionary problems in the light of certain evolutionary theories.

"Mathematical . . . On the Law of Ancestral Heredity," in *Proceedings of the Royal Society*, **62** (1898), 386–412, a statistical formulation of Galton's law in the form of a multiple regression of offspring on "midparental" ancestry, with deductions therefrom of theoretical values for various regression and correlation coefficients between kin, and comparisons of such theoretical values with values derived from observational material.

"Mathematical . . . VII. On the Correlation of Characters not Quantitatively Measurable," in *Philosophical Transactions of the Royal Society*, **195A** (1901), 1–47, in which the "tetrachoric" coefficient of correlation r_t was introduced for estimating the coefficient of correlation, ρ, of a bivariate normal distribution from a sample scored dichotomously in both variables.

* "On the Criterion That a Given System of Deviations From the Probable in the Case of a Correlated System of Variables Is Such That It Can Be Reasonably Supposed to Have Arisen From Random Sampling," in *London, Edinburgh and Dublin Philosophical Magazine and Journal of Science*, 5th ser., **50** (1900), 157–175, in which the "χ^2 test of goodness of fit" was introduced, one of Pearson's greatest single contributions to statistical methodology.

"Mathematical . . . IX. On the Principle of Homotyposis and Its Relation to Heredity, to the Variability of the Individual, and to That of Race. Part I. Homotyposis in the Vegetable Kingdom," in *Philosophical Transactions of the Royal Society*, **197A** (1901), 285–379, written with Alice Lee *et al.*, a theoretical discussion of the relation of fraternal correlation to the correlation of "undifferentiated like organs of the individual" (called "homotyposis"), followed by numerous applications; the paper led to a complete schism between the biometric and Mendelian schools and the founding of *Biometrika*.

* "Mathematical . . . X. Supplement to a Memoir on Skew Variation," *ibid.*, 443–459; Pearson curves Type V and VI are developed and their application exemplified.

* "On the Mathematical Theory of Errors of Judgment With Special Reference to the Personal Equation," *ibid.*, **198A** (1902), 235–299, a memoir still of great interest and importance founded on two series of experiments, each with three observers, from which it was learned, among other things, that the "personal equation" (bias pattern of an individual observer) is subject to fluctuations far exceeding random sampling and that the errors of different observers looking at the same phenomena are in general correlated.

"Note on Francis Galton's Problem," in *Biometrika*, **1**, no. 4 (Aug. 1902), 390–399, in which Pearson found the general expression for the mean value of the difference between the rth and the $(r + 1)$th ranked individuals in random samples from a continuous distribution, one of the earliest results in the sampling theory of order statistics —similar general expressions for the variances of and correlations between such intervals are given in his joint paper of 1931.

"On the Probable Errors of Frequency Constants," in *Biometrika*, **2**, no. 3 (June 1903), 273–281, an editorial that deals with standard errors of, and correlations between, cell frequencies and sample centroidal moments, in terms of the centroidal moments of a univariate distribution of general form. The extension to samples from a general bivariate distribution was made in pt. II, in *Biometrika*, **9**, nos. 1–2 (Mar. 1913), 1–19; and to functions of sample quantiles in pt. III, *ibid.*, **13**, no. 1 (Oct. 1920), 113–132.

Mathematical . . . XIII. On the Theory of Contingency and Its Relation to Association and Normal Correlation, Drapers' Company Research Memoirs, Biometric Series, no. 1 (London, 1904), directed toward measuring the association of two variables when the observational data take the form of frequencies in the cells of an $r \times c$ "contingency table" of qualitative categories not necessarily meaningfully orderable, an adaptation of his χ^2 goodness-of-fit criterion, termed "square contingency," being introduced to provide a test of overall departure from the hypothesis of independence and the basis of a measure of association, the "coefficient of contingency" $c = \sqrt{\chi^2/(\chi^2 + n)}$, which was shown to tend under certain special conditions to the coefficient of correlation of an underlying bivariate normal distribution.

On Some Disregarded Points in the Stability of Masonry Dams, Drapers' Company Research Memoirs, Technical Series, no. 1 (London, 1904), written with L. W. Atcherley, in which it was shown that the assumptions underlying a widely accepted procedure for calculating the stresses in masonry dams are not satisfied at the bottom of the dam, the stresses there being in excess of those so calculated, with consequent risk of rupture near the base—still cited today, this paper and its companion *Experimental Study . . .* (1907) caused great concern at the time, for instance, with reference to the British-built Aswan Dam.

Mathematical . . . XIV. On the General Theory of Skew Correlation and Non-Linear Regression, Drapers' Company Research Memoirs, Biometric Series, no. 2 (London, 1905), dealt with the general conception of skew variation and correlation and the properties of the "correlation ratio" η (introduced in 1903) and showed for the first time the fundamental importance of the expressions $(1 - \eta^2)\sigma_y^2$ and $(\eta^2 - r^2)\sigma_y^2$ and of the difference between η and r as measures of departure from linearity, as well as those conditions that must be satisfied for linear, parabolic, cubic, and other regression equations to be adequate.

"The Problem of the Random Walk," in *Nature*, **72** (17 July 1905), 294, a brief letter containing the first explicit formulation of a "random walk," a term Pearson coined, and asking for information on the probability distribution of the walker's distance from the origin after n steps—Lord Rayleigh indicated the asymptotic solution as $n \rightarrow \infty$ in the issue of 3 Aug., p. 318; and the general

solution for finite n was published by J. C. Kluyver in Dutch later the same year.

Mathematical . . . XV. A Mathematical Theory of Random Migration, Drapers' Company Research Memoirs, Biometric Series, no. 3 (London, 1906), written with John Blakeman. Various theoretical forms of distribution were derived that would result from random migration from an origin under certain ideal conditions, and solutions to a number of subsidiary problems were given—results that, while not outstandingly successful in studies of migration, have found various other applications.

** "Walter Frank Raphael Weldon, 1860–1906," in *Biometrika*, **5**, nos. 1–2 (Oct. 1906), 1–52 (repr. as paper no. 21 in Pearson and Kendall), a tribute to the man who posed the questions that impelled Pearson to some of his most important contributions, with additional details on the early years (1890–1905) of the biometric school and the founding of *Biometrika*.

Mathematical . . . XVI. On Further Methods of Determining Correlation, Drapers' Company Research Memoirs, Biometric Series, no. 4 (London 1907), dealt with calculation of the coefficient of correlation, r, from the individual differences $(x - y)$ in a sample and with estimation of the coefficient of correlation, ρ, of a bivariate normal population from the ranks of the individuals in a sample of that population with respect to each of the two traits concerned.

An Experimental Study of the Stresses in Masonry Dams, Drapers' Company Research Memoirs, Technical Series, no. 5 (London, 1907), written with A. F. C. Pollard, C. W. Wheen, and L. F. Richardson, which lent experimental support to the 1904 theoretical findings.

A First Study of the Statistics of Pulmonary Tuberculosis, Drapers' Company Research Memoirs, Studies in National Deterioration, no. 2 (London, 1907), and *A Second Study . . .: Marital Infection, . . .* Technical Series, no. 3 (London, 1908), written with E. G. Pope, the first two of seven publications by Pearson and his co-workers during 1907–1913 on the then-important and controversial subjects of the inheritance and transmission of pulmonary tuberculosis.

"On a New Method of Determining Correlation Between a Measured Character A, and a Character B, of which Only the Percentage of Cases Wherein B Exceeds (or Falls Short of) a Given Intensity Is Recorded for Each Grade of A," in *Biometrika*, **6**, nos. 1 and 2 (July–Oct. 1909), 96–105, in which the formula for the biserial coefficient of correlation, "biserial r," is derived but not named, and its application exemplified.

"On a New Method of Determining Correlation When One Variable Is Given by Alternative and the Other by Multiple Categories," *ibid.*, **7**, no. 3 (Apr. 1910), 248–257, in which the formula for "biserial η" is derived but not named, and its application exemplified.

A First Study of the Influence of Parental Alcoholism on the Physique and Ability of the Offspring, Eugenics Laboratory Memoirs, no. 10 (London, 1910), written with Ethel M. Elderton, gave correlations between drinking habits of the parents and the intelligence and various physical characteristics of the offspring, and examined the effect of parental alcoholism on the infant death rate.

A Second Study . . . Being a Reply to Certain Medical Critics of the First Memoir and an Examination of the Rebutting Evidence Cited by Them, Eugenics Laboratory Memoirs, no. 13 (London, 1910), written with E. M. Elderton.

A Preliminary Study of Extreme Alcoholism in Adults, Eugenics Laboratory Memoirs, no. 14 (London, 1910), written with Amy Barrington and David Heron. The relations of alcoholism to number of convictions, education, religion, prostitution, mental and physical conditions, and death rates were examined, with comparisons between the extreme alcoholic and the general population.

"On the Probability That Two Independent Distributions of Frequency Are Really Samples From the Same Population," in *Biometrika*, 8, nos. 1–2 (July 1911), 250–254, in which his χ^2 goodness-of-fit criterion is extended to provide a test of the hypothesis that two independent samples arrayed in a $2 \times c$ table are random samples from the same population.

Social Problems: Their Treatment, Past, Present and Future..., Questions of the Day and of the Fray, no. 5 (London, 1912), contains a perceptive, eloquent plea for replacement of literary exposition and folklore by measurement, and presents some results of statistical analyses that illustrate the complexity of social problems.

The Life, Letters and Labours of Francis Galton, 3 vols. in 4 pts. (Cambridge, 1914–1930).

Tables for Statisticians and Biometricians (London, 1914; 2nd ed., issued as "Part I," 1924; 3rd ed., 1930), consists of 55 tables, some new, the majority repr. from *Biometrika*, a few from elsewhere, to which Pearson as editor contributed an intro. on their use.

"On the General Theory of Multiple Contingency With Special Reference to Partial Contingency," in *Biometrika*, 11, no. 3 (May 1916), 145–158, extends the χ^2 method to the comparison of two ($r \times 2$) tables and contains the basic elements of a large part of present-day χ^2 technique.

"Mathematical Contributions . . . XIX. Second Supplement to a Memoir on Skew Variation," in *Philosophical Transactions of the Royal Society*, 216A (1916), 429–457, in which Pearson curves Types VII–XI are defined and their applications illustrated.

"On the Distribution of the Correlation Coefficient in Small Samples. Appendix II to the Papers of 'Student' and R. A. Fisher. A Cooperative Study," in *Biometrika*, 11, no. 4 (May 1917), 328–413, written with H. E. Soper, A. W. Young, B. M. Cave, and A. Lee, an exhaustive study of the moments and shape of the distribution of r in samples of size n from a normal population with correlation coefficient ρ as a function of n and ρ, and of its approach to normality as $n \to \infty$, with special attention to determination, via inverse probability, of the "most likely value" of ρ from an observed value of r—the paper that initiated the rift between Pearson and Fisher.

"De Saint-Venant Solution for the Flexure of Cantilevers of Cross-Sections in the Form of Complete and Curtate Circular Sectors, and the Influence of the Manner of Fixing the Built-in End of the Cantilever on Its Deflection," in *Proceedings of the Royal Society*, 96A (1919), 211–232, written with Mary Seegar, a basic paper giving the solution regularly cited for cantilevers of such cross sections—Pearson's last paper in mechanics.

** "Notes on the History of Correlation. Being a Paper Read to the Society of Biometricians and Mathematical Statisticians, June 14, 1920," in *Biometrika*, 13, no. 1 (Oct. 1920), 25–45 (paper no. 14 in Pearson and Kendall), deals with Gauss's and Bravais's treatment of the bivariate normal distribution, Galton's discovery of correlation and regression, and Pearson's involvement in the matter.

Tables of the Incomplete Γ-Function Computed by the Staff of the Department of Applied Statistics, University of London, University College (London, 1922; reiss. 1934), tables prepared under the direction of Pearson, who, as editor, contributed an intro. on their use.

Francis Galton, 1822–1922. A Centenary Appreciation, Questions of the Day and of the Fray, no. 11 (London, 1922).

Charles Darwin, 1809–1922. An Appreciation. . . ., Questions of the Day and of the Fray, no. 12 (London, 1923).

"Historical Note on the Origin of the Normal Curve of Errors," in *Biometrika*, 16, no. 3 (Dec. 1924), 402–404, announces the discovery of two copies of a long-overlooked pamphlet of De Moivre (1733) which gives to De Moivre priority in utilizing the integral of essentially the normal curve to approximate sums of successive terms of a binomial series, in formulating and using the theorem known as "Stirling's formula," and in enunciating "Bernoulli's theorem" that imprecision of a sample fraction as an estimate of the corresponding population proportion depends on the inverse square root of sample size.

"On the Skull and Portraits of George Buchanan," *ibid.*, 18, nos. 3–4 (Nov. 1926), 233–256, in which it is shown that the portraits fall into two groups corresponding to distinctly different types of face, and only the type exemplified by the portraits in the possession of the Royal Society conforms to the skull.

"On the Skull and Portraits of Henry Stewart, Lord Darnley, and Their Bearing on the Tragedy of Mary, Queen of Scots," *ibid.*, 20B, no. 1 (July 1928), 1–104, in which the circumstances of Lord Darnley's death and the history of his remains are discussed, anthropometric characteristics of his skull and femur are described and shown to compare reasonably well with the portraits, and the pitting of the skull is inferred to be of syphilitic origin.

"Laplace, Being Extracts From Lectures Delivered by Karl Pearson," *ibid.*, 21, nos. 1–4 (Dec. 1929), 202–216, an account of Laplace's ancestry, education, and later life that affords necessary corrections to a number of earlier biographies.

Tables for Statisticians and Biometricians, Part II (London, 1931), tables nearly all repr. from *Biometrika*, with pref. and intro. on use of the tables by Pearson, as editor.

"On the Mean Character and Variance of a Ranked Individual, and on the Mean and Variance of the Intervals Between Ranked Individuals. Part I. Symmetrical Distributions (Normal and Rectangular)," in *Biometrika*, **23**, nos. 3–4 (Dec. 1931), 364–397, and ". . . Part II. Case of Certain Skew Curves," *ibid.*, **24**, nos. 1–2 (May 1932), 203–279, both written with Margaret V. Pearson, in which certain general formulas relating to means, standard deviations, and correlations of ranked individuals in samples of size *n* from a continuous distribution are developed and applied (in pt. I) to samples from the rectangular and normal distributions, and (in pt. II) to special skew curves (Pearson Types VIII, IX, X, and XI) that admit exact solutions.

Tables of the Incomplete Beta-Function (London, 1934), tables prepared under the direction of and edited by Pearson, with an intro. by Pearson on the methods of computation employed and on the uses of the tables.

"The Wilkinson Head of Oliver Cromwell and Its Relationship to Busts, Masks and Painted Portraits," in *Biometrika*, **26**, nos. 3–4 (Dec. 1934), 269–378, written with G. M. Morant, an extensive analysis involving 107 plates from which it is concluded "that it is a 'moral certainty' drawn from circumstantial evidence that the Wilkinson Head is the genuine head of Oliver Cromwell."

"Old Tripos Days at Cambridge, as Seen From Another Viewpoint," in *Mathematical Gazette*, **20** (1936), 27–36.

Pearson edited two scientific journals, to which he also contributed substantially: *Biometrika*, of which he was one of the three founders, always the principal editor (vols. **1–28**, 1901–1936), and for many years the sole editor; and *Annals of Eugenics*, of which he was the founder and the editor of the first 5 vols. (1925–1933). He also edited three series of Drapers' Company Research Memoirs: Biometric Series, nos. 1–4, 6–12 (London, 1904–1922) (no. 5 was never issued), of which he was sole author of 4 and senior author of the remainder; Studies in National Deterioration, nos. 1–11 (London, 1906–1924), 2 by Pearson alone and as joint author of 3 more; and Technical Series, nos. 1–7 (London, 1904–1918), 1 by Pearson alone, the others with coauthors. To these must be added the Eugenics Laboratory Memoirs, nos. 1–29 (London, 1907–1935), of which Pearson was a coauthor of 4. To many others, including the 13 issues (1909–1933) comprising "The Treasury of Human Inheritance," vols. I and II, he contributed prefatory material; the Eugenics Laboratory Lecture Series, nos. 1–14 (London, 1909–1914), 12 by Pearson alone and 1 joint contribution; Questions of the Day and of the Fray, nos. 1–12 (London, 1910–1923), 9 by Pearson alone and 1 joint contribution; and Tracts for Computers, nos. 1–20 (London, 1919–1935), 2 by Pearson himself, plus a foreword, intro., or prefatory note to 5 others.

Pearson has given a brief account of the persons and early experiences that most strongly influenced his development as a scholar and scientist in his contribution to the volume of *Speeches* . . . (1934) cited below; fuller accounts of his Cambridge undergraduate days, his teachers, his reading, and his departures from the norm of a budding mathematician are in "Old Tripos Days" above. His "Notes on the History of Correlation" (1920) contains a brief account of how he became involved in the development of correlation theory; and he gives many details on the great formative period (1890–1906) in the development of biometry and statistics in his memoir on Weldon (1906) and in vol. IIIA of his *Life . . . of Francis Galton.*

A very large number of letters from all stages of Pearson's life, beginning with his childhood, and many of his MSS, lectures, lecture notes and syllabuses, notebooks, biometric specimens, and data collections have been preserved. A large part of his scientific library was merged, after his death, with the joint library of the departments of eugenics and statistics at University College, London; a smaller portion, with the library of the department of applied mathematics.

Some of Pearson's letters to Galton were published by Pearson, with Galton's replies, in vol. III of his *Life . . . of Francis Galton*. A few letters of special interest from and to Pearson were published, in whole or in part, by his son, E. S. Pearson, in his "Some Incidents in the Early History of Biometry and Statistics" and in "Some Early Correspondence Between W. S. Gosset, R. A. Fisher, and Karl Pearson," cited below; and a selection of others, from and to Pearson, together with syllabuses of some of Pearson's lectures and lecture courses, are in E. S. Pearson, *Karl Pearson: An Appreciation . . .*, cited below.

For the most part Pearson's archival materials are not yet generally available for study or examination. Work in progress for many years on sorting, arranging, annotating, cross-referencing, and indexing these materials, and on typing many of his handwritten items, is nearing completion, however. A first typed copy of the handwritten texts of Pearson's lectures on the history of statistics was completed in 1972; and many dates, quotations, and references have to be checked and some ambiguities resolved before the whole is ready for public view. Hence we may expect the great majority to be available to qualified scholars before very long in the Karl Pearson Archives at University College, London.

II. SECONDARY LITERATURE. The best biography of Pearson is still *Karl Pearson: An Appreciation of Some Aspects of His Life and Work* (Cambridge, 1938), by his son, Egon Sharpe Pearson, who stresses in his preface that "this book is in no sense a Life of Karl Pearson." It is a reissue in book form of two articles, bearing the same title, published in *Biometrika*, **28** (1936), 193–257, and **29** (1937), 161–248, with two additional apps. (II and III in the book), making six in all. Included in the text are numerous instructive excerpts from Pearson's publications, helpful selections from his correspondence, and an outline of his lectures on the history of statistics in the seventeenth and eighteenth centuries. App. I gives the syllabuses of the 7 public lectures Pearson gave at Gresham College, London, in 1891, "The Scope and Concepts of Modern Science," from which *The Grammar of Science* (1892) developed; app. II, the syllabuses of 30 lectures on "The Geometry of Statistics," "The Laws of Chance," and 'The Geometry of Chance" that Pearson delivered to general audiences at Gresham College, 1891–1894; app. III, by G. Udny Yule, repr. from *Biometrika*, **30** (1938), 198–203, summarizes the subjects dealt with by Pearson in his lecture courses on "The Theory of Statistics" at University College, London, during the 1894–1895 and 1895–1896 sessions; app. VI provides analogous summaries of his 2 lecture courses on "The Theory of Statistics" for first- and second-year students of statistics at University College during the 1921–1922 session, derived from E. S. Pearson's lecture notes; and apps. IV and V give, respectively, the text of Pearson's report of Nov. 1904 to the Worshipful Company of Drapers on "the great value that the Drapers' Grant [had] been to [his] Department" and an extract from his report to them of Feb. 1918, "War Work of the Biometric Laboratory."

The following publications by E. S. Pearson are useful supps. to this work: "Some Incidents in the Early History of Biometry and Statistics, 1890–94," in *Biometrika*, **52**, pts. 1–2 (June 1965), 3–18 (paper 22 in Pearson and Kendall); "Some Reflexions on Continuity in the Development of Mathematical Statistics, 1885–1920," *ibid.*, **54**, pts. 3–4 (Dec. 1967), 341–355 (paper 23 in Pearson and Kendall); "Some Early Correspondence Between W. S. Gosset, R. A. Fisher, and Karl Pearson, With Notes and Comments," *ibid.*, **55**, no. 3 (Nov. 1968), 445–457 (paper 25 in Pearson and Kendall); *Some Historical Reflections Traced Through the Development of the Use of Frequency Curves*, Southern Methodist University Dept. of Statistics THEMIS Contract Technical Report no. 38 (Dallas, 1969); and "The Department of Statistics, 1971. A Year of Anniversaries . . ." (mimeo., University College, London, 1972).

Of the biographies of Karl Pearson in standard reference works, the most instructive are those by M. Greenwood, in the *Dictionary of National Biography, 1931–1940* (London, 1949), 681–684; and Helen M. Walker, in *International Encyclopedia of the Social Sciences*, XI (New York, 1968), 496–503.

Apart from the above writings of E. S. Pearson, the most complete coverage of Karl Pearson's career from the viewpoint of his contributions to statistics and biometry is provided by the obituaries by G. Udny Yule, in *Obituary Notices of Fellows of the Royal Society of London*, **2**, no. 5 (Dec. 1936), 73–104; and P. C. Mahalanobis, in *Sankhyā*, **2**, pt. 4 (1936), 363–378, and its sequel, "A Note on the Statistical and Biometric Writings of Karl Pearson," *ibid.*, 411–422.

Additional perspective on Pearson's contributions to biometry and statistics, together with personal recollections of Pearson as a man, scientist, teacher, and friend, and other revealing information are in Burton H. Camp, "Karl Pearson and Mathematical Statistics," in *Journal of the American Statistical Association*, **28**, no. 184 (Dec. 1933), 395–401; in the obituaries by Raymond Pearl, *ibid.*, **31**, no. 196 (Dec. 1936), 653–664; and G. M. Morant, in *Man*, **36**, no. 118 (June 1936), 89–92; and in Samuel A. Stouffer, "Karl Pearson—An Appreciation on the 100th Anniversary of His Birth," in *Journal of the American Statistical Association*, **53**, no. 281 (Mar. 1958), 23–27.

S. S. Wilks, "Karl Pearson: Founder of the Science of Statistics," in *Scientific Monthly*, **53**, no. 2 (Sept. 1941), 249–253; and Helen M. Walker, "The Contributions of Karl Pearson," in *Journal of the American Statistical Association*, **53**, no. 281 (Mar. 1958), 11–22, are also informative and useful as somewhat more distant appraisals. L. N. G. Filon, "Karl Pearson as an Applied Mathematician," in *Obituary Notices of Fellows of the Royal Society of London*, **2**, no. 5 (Dec. 1936), 104–110, seems to provide the only review and estimate of Pearson's contributions to applied mathematics, physics, and astronomy. Pearson's impact on sociology is discussed by S. A. Stouffer in his centenary "Appreciation" cited above; and Pearson's "rather special variety of Social-Darwinism" is treated in some detail by Bernard Semmel in "Karl Pearson: Socialist and Darwinist," in *British Journal of Sociology*, **9**, no. 2 (June 1958), 111–125. M. F. Ashley Montagu, in "Karl Pearson and the Historical Method in Ethnology," in *Isis*, **34**, pt. 3 (Winter 1943), 211–214, suggests that the development of ethnology might have taken a different course had Pearson's suggestions been put into practice.

The great clash at the turn of the century between the "Mendelians," led by Bateson, and the "ancestrians," led by Pearson and Weldon, is described with commendable detachment, and its after-effects assessed, by P. Froggatt and N. C. Nevin in "The 'Law of Ancestral Heredity' and the Mendelian-Ancestrian Controversy in England, 1889–1906," in *Journal of Medical Genetics*, **8**, no. 1 (Mar. 1971), 1–36; and "Galton's 'Law of Ancestral Heredity': Its Influence on the Early Development of Human Genetics," in *History of Science*, **10** (1971), 1–27.

Notable personal tributes to Pearson as a teacher, author, and friend, by three of his most distinguished pupils, L. N. G. Filon, M. Greenwood, and G. Udny Yule, and a noted historian of statistics, Harald Westergaard, have been preserved in *Speeches Delivered at a Dinner Held in University College, London, in Honour of Professor Karl Pearson, 23 April 1934* (London, 1934), together with Pearson's reply in the form of a five-page autobiographical sketch. The centenary lecture by J. B. S. Haldane, "Karl Pearson, 1857–1957," published initially in *Biometrika*, **44**, pts. 3–4 (Dec. 1957), 303–313, is also in *Karl Pearson, 1857–1957. The Centenary Celebration at University College, London, 13 May 1957* (London, 1958), along with the introductory remarks of David Heron, Bradford Hill's toast, and E. S. Pearson's reply.

Other publications cited in the text are Allan Ferguson, "Trends in Modern Physics," in British Association for the Advancement of Science, *Report of the Annual Meeting, 1936*, 27–42; Francis Galton, *Natural Inheritance* (London–New York, 1889; reissued, New York, 1972); R. A. Fisher, "The Correlation Between Relatives on the Supposition of Mendelian Inheritance," in *Transactions of the Royal Society of Edinburgh*, **52** (1918), 399–433; H. L. Seal, "The Historical Development of the Gauss Linear Model," in *Biometrika*, **54**, pts. 1–2 (June 1967), 1–24 (paper no. 15 in Pearson and Kendall); and Helen M. Walker, *Studies in the History of Statistical Method* (Baltimore, 1931).

CHURCHILL EISENHART

PECHAM, JOHN (*b.* Sussex, England, *ca.* 1230–1235; *d.* Mortlake, Surrey, England, 8 December 1292)

Pecham was probably born in the vicinity of Lewes in Sussex, possibly in or near the village of Patcham, and received his elementary education at the priory of Lewes.[1] He later matriculated in the arts faculties at Paris and Oxford, probably in that order. He became a Franciscan in the late 1240's or in the 1250's and was sent to Paris to undertake theological studies between 1257 and 1259.[2] In 1269 he received the doctorate in theology and for the next two years served as regent master in theology. Pecham returned to Oxford in 1271 or 1272 as eleventh lecturer in theology to the Franciscan school, a position he held until his appointment as provincial minister of the order in 1275. Two years later he was called to Italy as master in theology to the papal curia, and in 1279 he was elected archbishop of Canterbury. During his thirteen years as archbishop, Pecham maintained a zealous program of reform. He conscientiously endeavored to improve the administration of his province and persistently fought the practices of plurality and nonresidence; he called two reform councils and opposed, at every opportunity, the spread of "dangerous" philosophical novelties.

Of Pecham's intellectual development we know very little, although the major forces shaping his outlook probably came from within his own order. In the thirteenth century the Franciscan Order was a stronghold of Augustinianism and, consequently, of opposition to the new Aristotelian and Averroist ideas penetrating Europe. It is thus no surprise that Pecham became one of the leaders in the resistance against heterodox Aristotelian, and even more moderate Thomist, innovations.[3] But the Franciscan Order could provide more than antagonism toward philosophical and theological novelties. Among the English Franciscans a tradition of mathematical science had been initiated by Robert Grosseteste (who lectured to the Franciscans at Oxford and probably bequeathed his library to them at his death) and advanced by Roger Bacon. There can be little doubt that this tradition influenced Pecham: there is ample evidence that he and Bacon were personally acquainted and, indeed, resided together in the Franciscan friary at Paris during the period when Bacon was writing his principal scientific works. Nevertheless, this should not be taken to mean that Pecham was Bacon's student or protégé (there is no evidence for either) or that the influences on Pecham were limited to the Franciscan Order; Pecham's optical works, for example, reveal the influence not only of Augustine, Grosseteste, and Bacon but also of Aristotle, Euclid, al-Kindī, Ibn al-Haytham, Moses Maimonides, and perhaps Ptolemy and Witelo; and the primary influence in this instance was not Augustine or Grosseteste or Bacon, but Ibn al-Haytham.

Works. Pecham's indisputably genuine works on natural philosophy and mathematical science are *Tractatus de numeris* (or *Arithmetica mystica*); *Tractatus de perspectiva*; *Perspectiva communis*, extant in both an original and a revised version; and *Tractatus de sphera*. In addition to these, a treatise entitled *Theorica planetarum* is attributed to Pecham in several manuscripts and has commonly been regarded as genuine, although the question of its authenticity has in fact never been explored with care. Material of considerable scientific import is also contained in Pecham's treatises on the soul, *Tractatus de anima* and *Questiones de anima*, and his *Questiones de beatitudine corporis et anime*.[4] Two other scientific treatises have also been attributed to Pecham, *Perspectiva particularis* and *Tractatus de animalibus*, but there is no evidence supporting either attribution.

Of Pecham's scientific works only those on optics have been subjected to serious scrutiny; nevertheless, it is possible to make a few remarks about several of the others. The *Tractatus de sphera* was apparently a rival to, rather than a commentary on, Sacrobosco's *De sphaera*.[5] In this work Pecham presents an elementary discussion of the sphericity (or circularity) of the principal bodies of the world (for instance, the heavens, raindrops, and solar radiation passing through noncircular apertures); the rotation of the heavens; the equality and inequality of days; the climatic zones of the terrestrial sphere; the origin of eclipses; and other topics of a cosmologic nature.

The *Tractatus de numeris* begins with the classification of number into abstract and concrete; concrete number is further subdivided into corporeal and spiritual number, spiritual number is divided into five additional categories, and so on. After further discussion of the elementary properties of numbers (odd and even, equality and inequality) and the perceptibility of number by the external senses, Pecham turns to the mystical properties of numbers: he employs number to elucidate the mysteries of the Trinity and concludes with an analysis of the mystical meanings of the numbers 1 to 30, 36, 40, 50, 100, 200, 300, and 1,000.

The earliest of Pecham's optical works was the *Tractatus de perspectiva*, probably written for the Franciscan schools during Pecham's years as a teacher at Paris or Oxford (1269–1275) or possibly during his provincial ministership (1275–1277). It is a rambling piece of continuous prose, not divided into propositions like the later *Perspectiva communis*, that treats the full range of elementary optical matters. Like the *Tractatus de numeris*, and unlike the *Perspectiva com-*

munis, it is filled with quotations from the Bible and patristic sources, especially Augustine, that give it a theological and devotional flavor. With a few exceptions the *Tractatus de perspectiva* and *Perspectiva communis* are identical in theoretical content, although each includes certain topics that the other omits.

The work on which Pecham's fame has chiefly rested is the *Perspectiva communis*, probably written between 1277 and 1279 during Pecham's professorship at the papal curia.[6] In the first book Pecham discussed the propagation of light and color, the anatomy and physiology of the eye, the act of visual perception, physical requirements for vision, the psychology of vision, and the errors of direct vision. In book II he discussed vision by reflected rays and presented a careful and sophisticated analysis of image formation by reflection. Book III was devoted to the phenomena of refraction, the rainbow, and the Milky Way.

The central feature of Pecham's optical system and the dominant theme of book I of the *Perspectiva communis* is the theory of direct vision. Here, as elsewhere, Pecham endeavored to reconcile all the available authorities—Aristotle, Euclid, Augustine, al-Kindī, Ibn al-Haytham, Ibn Rushd, Grosseteste, and Bacon. Following Ibn al-Haytham, Pecham argued that the emission of visual rays from the observer's eye is neither necessary nor sufficient as an explanation of sight; the primary agent of sight is therefore the ray coming to the eye from a point on the visible object. But in an attempt to follow Aristotle, al-Kindī, and Grosseteste as well, Pecham argued that visual rays do nevertheless exist and perform the important, but not always necessary, function of moderating the luminous rays from the visible object and making them "commensurate with the visual power." Thus Pecham, like Bacon, resolved the age-old debate between the emission and intromission theories of vision in favor of a twofold radiation, although, to be sure, priority was given to rays issuing from the visible object.

The rays issuing from points on the visible object fall perpendicularly onto the cornea and penetrate without refraction to the sensitive ocular organ, the glacial humor (or crystalline lens); nonperpendicular rays are weakened by refraction and therefore can be largely ignored. Since only one perpendicular ray issues from each point of the visible object and the collection of such perpendicular rays maintains a fixed order between the object and the eye, a one-to-one correspondence is established between points on the object and points on the glacial humor, and unconfused perception of the visual field is thus achieved. Vision is not "completed," however, in the glacial humor. There is a further propagation of the rays (or species)

through the vitreous humor and optic nerve to the common nerve, where species from the two eyes combine, and eventually to the anterior part of the brain and the "place of interior judgment."

Pecham's optical system included significantly more than a theory of direct vision. He briefly discussed the doctrine of species; treated at length the propagation of rays; and developed a theory to explain how solar radiation, when passing through noncircular apertures, gives rise to circular images. He expressed the full law of reflection and applied it to image formation by plane, spherical, cylindrical, and conical mirrors; in this analysis he revealed an implicit understanding of the nature of the focal point of a concave mirror. Although he did not possess a mathematical law of refraction, he successfully applied the general qualitative principles of refraction to the images that result from refraction at plane and circular interfaces between transparent media of various densities. In his discussion of the rainbow Pecham again attempted to reconcile different theories. He argued that all three kinds of rays (rectilinear, reflected, and refracted) concur in the generation of the rainbow.

Significance and Influence. Pecham saw himself primarily not as a creative scientific thinker but as an expositor of scientific matters in elementary terms. He remarked at the beginning of the *Tractatus de sphera*:

> In the present opusculum, I intend to explain the number, figure, and motion of the principal bodies of the world (as well as related matters) insofar as is sufficient for an understanding of the words of Holy Scripture. And certain of these matters I have found treated in other works, but because of their difficulty, brevity, and in some cases falsity, they are useless for the elementary students that I intend to serve.[7]

In the *Tractatus de perspectiva* he remarked that he had undertaken to discuss light and number "for the sake of my simpler brothers," and in the preface to the *Perspectiva communis* he indicated that his goal was to "compress into concise summaries the teachings of perspective, which [in existing treatises] are presented with great obscurity."[8] Pecham's significance in the history of science is principally the result of his success in achieving this goal. He is most notable not as one who formulated new theories and interpretations, although on many occasions he did, but as one who skillfully presented scientific knowledge to his contemporaries and posterity by writing elementary textbooks.

Pecham's success was greatest in the case of the *Perspectiva communis*. This text is still extant in more than sixty manuscripts and went through twelve printed editions, including a translation into Italian, between 1482 and 1665. It was used and cited by many medieval and Renaissance natural philosophers, including Dominicus de Clavasio, Henry of Langenstein, Blasius of Parma, Lorenzo Ghiberti, Leonardo da Vinci, Albert Brudzewski, Francesco Maurolico, Giambattista della Porta, Girolamo Fabrici, Johannes Kepler, Willebrord Snellius, and G. B. Riccioli. It was lectured upon, in the late Middle Ages, at the universities of Vienna, Prague, Paris, Leipzig, Cracow, Würzburg, Alcalá, and Salamanca.[9] The *Perspectiva communis* was the most widely used of all optical texts from the early fourteenth until the close of the sixteenth century, and it remains today the best index of what was known to the scientific community in general on the subject.

NOTES

1. The evidence for both claims is a letter written by Pecham in 1285, in which he refers to his "nourishment from childhood" in the vicinity of the priory of Lewes and the comforts and honors he has received from its teachers; see *Registrum epistolarum*, III, 902. Several historians have argued that Pecham was born in Kent rather than Sussex.
2. In assigning the latter dates, I am following Douie, *Archbishop Pecham*, p. 8.
3. On Pecham's position vis-à-vis Averroism and Thomism, see Fernand van Steenberghen, *The Philosophical Movement in the Thirteenth Century* (Edinburgh, 1955), 94–104. Van Steenberghen calls Pecham "the true founder of neo-Augustinianism" (p. 103).
4. Scientific content is especially evident in the *Questiones de beatitudine corporis et anime*, in *Johannis Pechami Quaestiones tractantes de anima*, Hieronymus Spettman, ed., which is *Beiträge zur Geschichte der Philosophie des Mittelalters*, XIX, pts. 5–6 (Münster 1918), although Pecham's psychology is apparent in all of them. On Pecham's psychology see Sharp, *Franciscan Philosophy*, 185–203; and *Die Psychologie des Johannes Pecham*, Spettman, ed., which is *Beiträge zur Geschichte der Philosophie des Mittelalters*, XX, pt. 6 (Münster, 1919).
5. According to Thorndike, *Sphere of Sacrobosco*, 24–25.
6. The dating of the *Perspectiva communis* is discussed in Lindberg, *Pecham and the Science of Optics*, 14–18; and in Lindberg, "Lines of Influence in Thirteenth-Century Optics: Bacon, Witelo, and Pecham," in *Speculum*, 46 (1971), 77–83.
7. Latin text in Thorndike, *op. cit.*, 445.
8. See Lindberg's eds. of these two treatises for the texts.
9. For a fuller account of the influence of the *Perspectiva communis*, see Lindberg, *Pecham and the Science of Optics*, 29–32.

BIBLIOGRAPHY

I. ORIGINAL WORKS. The *Perspectiva communis* (in both the original and the revised versions) is available in a recent ed. and English trans. by David C. Lindberg, *John Pecham and the Science of Optics* (Madison, Wis., 1970). The known extant MSS and eleven early printed eds. are listed in the intro. to this ed. Pecham's other optical work, the *Tractatus de perspectiva*, is also available in a modern critical version, David C. Lindberg, ed., in Franciscan Institute Publications, Text Ser. no. 16 (St. Bonaventure, N.Y., 1972).

No other complete scientific work of Pecham has been printed. The first five chapters of the *Tractatus de numeris* have been edited from four MSS and published as an appendix to *Tractatus de anima Ioannis Pecham*, Gaudentius Melani, ed. (Florence, 1948), 138–144. Lynn Thorndike has published the opening paragraphs and incipits of later paragraphs of the *Tractatus de sphera* in *The Sphere of Sacrobosco and Its Commentators* (Chicago, 1949), 445–450; and Pierre Duhem has published the section on pinhole images from this same work in *Le système du monde*, III (Paris, 1915), 524–529. The *Theorica planetarum* is extant only in MS.

For a full listing of Pecham's works, including extant MSS and eds., see Victorinus Doucet, "Notulae bibliographicae de quibusdam operibus Fr. Ioannis Pecham O.F.M.," in *Antonianum*, 8 (1933), 207–228, 425–459; Palémon Glorieux, *Répertoire des maîtres en théologie de Paris au XIIIe siècle*, II (Paris, 1933), 87–98; and *Fratris Johannis Pecham quondam archiepiscopi Cantuariensis Tractatus tres de paupertate*, C. L. Kingsford *et al.*, eds. (Aberdeen, 1910), 1–12.

II. SECONDARY LITERATURE. The best biography of Pecham is Decima L. Douie, *Archbishop Pecham* (Oxford, 1952). Other valuable sources on Pecham's life and thought are David Knowles, "Some Aspects of the Career of Archbishop Pecham," in *English Historical Review*, 57 (1942), 1–18, 178–201; Hieronymus Spettman, "Quellenkritisches zur Biographie des Johannes Pecham," in *Franziskanische Studien*, 2 (1915), 170–207, 266–285; and D. E. Sharp, *Franciscan Philosophy at Oxford in the Thirteenth Century* (Oxford, 1930), 175–207. For a short biographical sketch and additional bibliography, see Lindberg, *Pecham and the Science of Optics*, 3–11.

Pecham's optical work has been most fully analyzed in the following works by David C. Lindberg: *John Pecham and the Science of Optics*; "The *Perspectiva communis* of John Pecham: Its Influence, Sources, and Content," in *Archives internationales d'histoire des sciences*, 18 (1965), 37–53; "Alhazen's Theory of Vision and Its Reception in the West," in *Isis*, 58 (1967), 321–341; and "The Theory of Pinhole Images From Antiquity to the Thirteenth Century," in *Archive for History of Exact Sciences*, 5, no. 2 (1968), 154–176. Brief descriptions of Pecham's other scientific works are found in *Registrum epistolarum fratris Johannis Peckham archiepiscopi Cantuariensis*, Charles T. Martin, ed., III (London, 1885), lvi–cxlv; and Lynn Thorndike, "A John Peckham Manuscript," in *Archivum Franciscanum Historicum*, 45 (1952), 451–461.

DAVID C. LINDBERG

PEIRCE, BENJAMIN (*b.* Salem, Massachusetts, 4 April 1809; *d.* Cambridge, Massachusetts, 6 October 1880)

In an address before the American Mathematical Society during the semicentennial celebration of its founding in 1888 as the New York Mathematical Society, G. D. Birkhoff spoke of Benjamin Peirce as having been "by far the most influential scientific personage in America" and "a kind of father of pure mathematics in our country."

Peirce's background and training were completely American. The family was established in America by John Peirce (Pers), a weaver from Norwich, England, who settled in Watertown, Massachusetts, in 1637. His father, Benjamin Peirce, graduated from Harvard College in 1801, and served for several years as representative from Salem in the Massachusetts legislature; he was Harvard librarian from 1826 until 1831, prepared a printed catalog of the Harvard library (1830–1831), and left a manuscript history of the university from its founding to the period of the American Revolution (published 1833). Peirce's mother, Lydia Ropes Nichols of Salem, was a first cousin of her husband. On 23 July 1833 Peirce married Sarah Hunt Mills, daughter of Harriette Blake and Elijah Hunt Mills of Northampton, Massachusetts. They had a daughter, Helen, and four sons: James Mills Peirce, professor of mathematics and an administrator at Harvard for fifty years; Charles Sanders Peirce, geodesist, mathematician, logician, and philosopher; Benjamin Mills Peirce, a mining engineer who wrote the U.S. government report on mineral resources and conditions in Iceland and Greenland; and Herbert Henry Davis Peirce, a diplomat who served on the staff of the legation in St. Petersburg and who later arranged for the negotiations between Russia and Japan that led to the Treaty of Portsmouth on 5 September 1905.

Peirce attended the Salem Private Grammar School, where Henry Ingersoll Bowditch was a classmate. This relationship influenced the entire course of Peirce's life, since Ingersoll Bowditch's father, Nathaniel Bowditch, discovered Peirce's unusual talent for mathematics. During Peirce's undergraduate career at Harvard College (1825–1829), the elder Bowditch enlisted Peirce's aid in reading the proof-sheets of his translation of Laplace's *Traité de mécanique céleste*. Peirce gave evidence of his own mathematical powers in his revision and correction of Bowditch's translation and commentary on the first four volumes (1829–1839), and also with his proof (in 1832) that there is no odd perfect number that has fewer than four prime factors.

Peirce taught at Bancroft's Round Hill School at Northampton, Massachusetts, from 1829 until 1831, when he was appointed tutor in mathematics at Harvard College; he received his M.A. from that institution in 1833. At Harvard he became University professor of mathematics and natural philosophy (1833–1842), then Perkins professor of astronomy and mathematics (1842–1880). During the early days of his teaching at Harvard, Peirce published a popular series of textbooks on elementary branches of mathematics.

Peirce's continued interest in the theory of astronomy was apparent in his study of comets. Around 1840 he made observations in the old Harvard College observatory; his 1843 Boston lectures on the great comet of that year stimulated the support that led to the installation of the new telescope at the Harvard Observatory in June 1847. Since 1842 Peirce had also supervised the preparation of the mathematics section of the ten-volume *American Almanac and Repository of Useful Knowledge*, and in 1847 he published therein a list of known orbits of comets. In 1849 Charles Henry Davis, a brother-in-law of Peirce's wife, was appointed superintendent of the newly created *American Ephemeris and Nautical Almanac*, and Peirce was appointed consulting astronomer (1849–1867).

Peirce was not only helpful to Davis in planning the general form of the *Ephemeris*, but he also began a revision of the theory of planets. He had become deeply interested in the work of Le Verrier and John Couch Adams that had permitted Galle's discovery of the planet Neptune on 23 September 1846. In cooperation with Sears Walker, Peirce determined the orbit of Neptune and its perturbation of Uranus. Simon Newcomb wrote in his *Popular Astronomy* (1878) that the investigation of the motion of the new planet was left in the hands of Walker and Peirce for several years, and that Peirce was "the first one to compute the perturbations of Neptune produced by the action of the other planets." Peirce was led to believe that Galle's "happily" discovered Neptune and Le Verrier's calculated theoretical planet were not the same body and that the latter did not exist—an opinion that led to considerable controversy.

In conjunction with his work on the solar system, Peirce became interested in the mathematical theory of the rings of Saturn. In 1850 George Phillips Bond, assistant in the Harvard College observatory, discovered Saturn's dusky ring and on 15 April 1851 announced to a meeting of the American Academy of Arts and Sciences his belief that the rings were fluid, multiple, and variable in number. Peirce published several mathematical papers on the constitution of the rings in which he reached the same conclusion concerning their fluidity. His review of the problem at that time led to a most unfortunate priority dispute.

Peirce also enjoyed a distinguished career in the U.S. Coast Survey. In 1852 he accepted a commission —at the request of Alexander Dallas Bache, who was then superintendent—to work on the determination of longitude for the Survey. This project involved Peirce in a thorough investigation of the question of errors of observation; his article "Criterion for the Rejection of Doubtful Observations" appeared in B. A. Gould's *Astronomical Journal* in July 1852. The criterion was designed to determine the most probable hypothesis whereby a set of observations might be divided into normal and abnormal, when "the greater part is to be regarded as normal and subject to the ordinary law of error adopted in the method of least squares, while a smaller unknown portion is abnormal and subject to some obscure source of error." Some authorities regarded "Peirce's criterion"—which gave good discrimination and acceptable practical results—as one of his most important contributions, although it has since been demonstrated to be invalid.

After Bache's death Peirce became superintendent of the Coast Survey (1867–1874), while maintaining his association with Harvard. He arranged to carry forward Bache's plans for a geodetic system that would extend from the Atlantic to the Gulf. This project laid the foundation for a general map of the country independent of detached local surveys. Peirce's principal contribution to the development of the Survey is thought to have been the initiation of a geodetic connection between the surveys of the Atlantic and Pacific coasts. He superintended the measurement of the arc of the thirty-ninth parallel in order to join the Atlantic and Pacific systems of triangulation.

Peirce also took personal charge of the U.S. expedition that went to Sicily to observe the solar eclipse of 22 December 1870, and, as a member of the transit of Venus commission, sent out two Survey parties—one to Nagasaki and the other to Chatham Island—in 1874. Peirce also played a role in the acquisition of Alaska by the United States in 1867, since in that year he sent out a reconnaissance party, whose reports were important aids to proponents of the purchase of that region. In 1869 he sent parties to observe the eclipse of the sun in Alaska and in the central United States.

Peirce's eminence made him influential in the founding of scientific institutions in the United States. In 1847 the American Academy of Arts and Sciences appointed him to a committee of five in order to draw up a program for the organization of the Smithsonian Institution. From 1855 to 1858 he served with Bache and Joseph Henry on a council to organize the Dudley observatory at Albany, New York, under the direction of B. A. Gould. In 1863 he became one of the fifty incorporators of the National Academy of Sciences.

Despite his many administrative obligations, Peirce continued to do mathematics in the 1860's. He read before the National Academy of Sciences a number of papers on algebra, which had resulted from his interest in Hamilton's calculus of quaternions and finally led to Peirce's study of possible systems of multiple algebras. In 1870 his *Linear Associative Algebra* appeared as a memoir for the National Academy and was lithographed in one hundred copies for private circulation. The opening sentence states that "Mathematics is the science which draws necessary conclusions." George Bancroft received the fifty-second copy of the work, and in an accompanying letter (preserved in the manuscript division of the New York Public Library) Peirce explained that

> This work undertakes the investigation of all possible single, double, triple, quadruple, and quintuple Algebras which are subject to certain simple and almost indispensable conditions. The conditions are those well-known to algebraists by the terms of *distributive* and *associative* which are defined on p. 21. It also contains the investigation of all sextuple algebras of a certain class, i.e., of those which contain what is called in this treatise an *idempotent* element.

D. E. Smith and J. Ginsburg, in their *History of Mathematics Before 1900*, speak of Peirce's memoir as "one of the few noteworthy achievements in the field of mathematics in America before the last quarter of the century." It was published posthumously in 1881 under the editorship of his son Charles Sanders Peirce (*American Journal of Mathematics*, **4**, no. 2, 97–229).

In *A System of Analytic Mechanics* (1855) Peirce again set forth the principles and methods of the science as a branch of mathematical theory, a subject he developed from the idea of the "potential." The book has been described as the most important mathematical treatise that had been produced in the United States up to that time. Peirce's treatment of mechanics has also been said, by Victor Lenzen, to be "on the highest level of any work in the field in English until the appearance of Whittaker's *Analytical Dynamics*" in 1904. Peirce was widely honored by both American and foreign scholarly and scientific societies.

BIBLIOGRAPHY

I. ORIGINAL WORKS. Peirce's works include *An Elementary Treatise on Sound* (Boston, 1836); *An Elementary Treatise on Algebra* (Boston, 1837), to which are added exponential equations and logarithms; *An Elementary Treatise on Plane and Solid Geometry* (Boston, 1837); *An Elementary Treatise on Plane and Spherical Trigonometry, . . . Particularly Adapted to Explaining the Construction of Bowditch's Navigator and the Nautical Almanac* (Boston, 1840); *An Elementary Treatise on Curves,*

Functions, and Forces, 2 vols. (Boston, 1841, 1846); and *Tables of the Moon* (Washington, D.C., 1853) for the *American Ephemeris and Nautical Almanac. Tables of the Moon* was used in taking the *Ephemeris* up to the volume for 1883 and was constructed from Plana's theory, with Airy's and Longstreth's corrections, Hansen's two inequalities of long period arising from the action of Venus, and Hansen's values of the secular variations of the mean motion and of the motion of the perigee.

Later works are *A System of Analytic Mechanics* (Boston, 1855); *Linear Associative Algebra* (1870), edited by C. S. Peirce, which appeared in *American Journal of Mathematics,* **4** (1881), 97–229, and in a separate vol. (New York, 1882); and James Mills Peirce, ed., *Ideality in the Physical Sciences,* Lowell Institute Lectures of 1879 (Boston, 1881).

Peirce's unpublished letters are in the National Archives, Washington, D. C., and in the Benjamin Peirce and Charles S. Peirce collections of Harvard University.

II. SECONDARY LITERATURE. On Peirce and his work, see reminiscences by Charles W. Eliot, A. Lawrence Lowell, W. E. Byerly, Arnold B. Chace, and a biographical sketch by R. C. Archibald, in *American Mathematical Monthly,* **32** (1925), repr. as a monograph, with four new portraits and addenda (Oberlin, 1925), which contains in sec. 6 a listing with occasional commentary of Peirce's writings and massive references to writings about him. See also Bessie Zaban Jones and Lyle Gifford Boyd, *The Harvard College Observatory* (Cambridge, Mass., 1971), esp. the chap. entitled "The Two Bonds," which gives a detailed description of the unhappy relationship that developed between Peirce and George and William Bond.

See further R. C. Archibald, in *Dictionary of American Biography* (New York, 1934); A. Hunter Dupree, "The Founding of the National Academy of Sciences—A Reinterpretation," in *Proceedings of the American Philosophical Society,* **101,** no. 5 (1957), 434–441; M. King, ed., *Benjamin Peirce . . . A Memorial Collection* (Cambridge, Mass., 1881); Victor Lenzen, *Benjamin Peirce and the United States Coast Survey* (San Francisco, 1968); Simon Newcomb, *Popular Astronomy* (New York, 1878), esp. pp. 350 (on the rings of Saturn), 363 (on the perturbation of Neptune), and 403 (on comets); H. A. Newton, "Benjamin Peirce," in *Proceedings of the American Academy of Arts and Sciences,* 16, n.s., **8,** pt. 2 (1881), 443–454, repr. in *American Journal of Science,* 3rd ser., **22,** no. 129 (1881), 167–178; James Mills Peirce, in *Lamb's Biographical Dictionary of the United States,* VI (Boston, 1903), 198; and Poggendorff, II (1863), 387–388; and III (1858–1883), 1012–1013. See also F. C. Pierce, *Peirce Genealogy* (Worcester, Mass., 1880).

CAROLYN EISELE

PEIRCE, BENJAMIN OSGOOD, II (*b.* Beverly, Massachusetts, 11 February 1854; *d.* Cambridge, Massachusetts, 14 January 1914)

Peirce's father, who bore the same names, was by 1849 a merchant in the South African trade, having previously been professor of chemistry and natural philosophy at Mercer University, Macon, Georgia. His mother was Mehetable Osgood Seccomb of Salem, Massachusetts. Peirce and his father were close companions, and in 1864 they traveled together to the Cape of Good Hope. They shared a love of music; Peirce's father played the flute and Peirce himself frequently sang in Oratorio and Choral Society performances. Later in his professional career at Harvard, Peirce served as a member of the committee on honors and higher degrees in music.

In 1872, after a two-year apprenticeship as a carpenter (during which he read extensively and perfected the Latin his father had taught him) Peirce was admitted to Harvard College. He became the first research student of John Trowbridge and published, during his junior year, a paper that revealed a "remarkable knowledge of Becquerel, Rowland, Maxwell, and Thomson; a remarkable use of electromagnetic equipment; a remarkable application of mathematics." Under Trowbridge's influence he investigated magnetization; he later developed an interest in problems in heat conduction, and wrote a number of papers on those subjects.

Peirce was graduated in 1876 with highest honors in physics. During the next year, he served as laboratory assistant to Trowbridge and then studied under Wiedemann in Leipzig, where he took the Ph.D. (1879). In 1880 he worked in Helmholtz' laboratory in Berlin, where he met Karl Pearson, who became his lifelong friend. He also met Isabella Turnbull Landreth, a student in the conservatory of music, and they were married in her native Scotland in 1882. They had two daughters.

Peirce's research efforts in Germany were in a sense unrewarding. Edwin Hall wrote of the "unhappy turn of fate" that led Peirce to devote "a year or more of intense labor on gas batteries at a time when physical chemistry was floundering through a bog of experimentation . . . misdirected by the false proposition that the electromotive force of a battery should be calculable from the heat yielded by the chemical operations occurring in it." Peirce exercised the greatest care in testing some 400 batteries, of six different types, and found no data to support this principle, which had been advocated by Wiedemann and by William Thomson. Although he regretfully recorded his findings, he did not openly challenge such authorities, and Wiedemann and Thomson's theorem was only later disproved by J. Willard Gibbs and Helmholtz.

In 1880 Peirce returned to the United States and

taught for one year at the Boston Latin School. He began his teaching career at Harvard University as an instructor in 1881, and in 1888, following Lovering's retirement, was appointed Hollis professor of mathematics and natural philosophy. He soon established himself as an able administrator.

In 1883 Peirce was one of the first scientists to study retinal sensitivity by means of the spectrum instead of revolving discs. But his 1889 work, "Perception of Horizontal and of Vertical Lines," was essentially psychological. The full extent of his mathematical talent was first revealed in 1891, in a paper entitled "On Some Theorems Which Connect Together Certain Line and Surface Integrals." His *Short Table of Integrals*, which eventually became an indispensable reference tool for scientists and mathematicians, was first published as a pamphlet in 1889.

Peirce was a member of various American and foreign societies. In 1913 he served as president of the American Physical Society, which he had helped to organize, and as vice-president of the American Mathematical Society. He also served as an editor of the *Physical Review*. He was a cousin, at several removes, of Charles Sanders Peirce.

BIBLIOGRAPHY

I. ORIGINAL WORKS. Poggendorff, III, col. 1013; IV, cols. 1128–1129; and V, cols. 952–953, gives a detailed bibliography. Peirce's major works are *Elements of the Theory of the Newtonian Potential Function* (Boston, 1888); *A Short Table of Integrals*, issued as a pamphlet in 1889, but subsequently published in Byerly, ed., *Elements of the Integral Calculus* (Boston, 1889) and enlarged in many later eds.; and *Mathematical and Physical Papers, 1903–1913* (Cambridge, Mass., 1926), which contains 56 papers. Peirce's papers and correspondence are preserved in the archives of Harvard College.

II. SECONDARY LITERATURE. For works on Peirce and his work, see *American Men of Science*, 2nd ed. (Lancaster, Pa., 1910), p. 364; R. Archibald, in *Dictionary of American Biography*, XIV, 397–398; *Boston Transcript* (14 Jan. 1914); Edwin Hall, *et al.*, "Harvard University Minute on the Life and Services of Professor Benjamin Osgood Peirce," in the university archives, repr. from *Harvard University Gazette* (21 Feb. 1914); Edwin Hall, "Biographical Memoir of Benjamin Osgood Peirce," in *Biographical Memoirs. National Academy of Sciences*, **8** (1919), 437–466, which also contains a complete bibliography of his mathematical and physical papers; *Lamb's Biographical Dictionary of the United States*, VI (Boston, 1903), 198; J. Trowbridge, "Benjamin Osgood Peirce," in *Harvard Grads's Magazine* (Mar. 1914); A. G. Webster, "Benjamin Osgood Peirce," in *Science* (1914), repr. in

Nation (23 Apr. 1914); and *Who's Who in America, 1912–1913*.

CAROLYN EISELE

PEIRCE, CHARLES SANDERS (*b.* Cambridge, Massachusetts, 10 September 1839; *d.* Milford, Pennsylvania, 19 April 1914)

Peirce frequently asserted that he was reared in a laboratory. His father, Benjamin Peirce, was professor of mathematics and natural philosophy at Harvard University at the time of Charles's birth; he personally supervised his son's early education and inculcated in him an analytic and scientific mode of thought. Peirce attended private schools in Cambridge and Boston; he was then sent to the Cambridge High School, and, for a term, to E. S. Dixwell's School, to prepare for Harvard. While at college (1855–1859), Peirce studied Schiller's *Aesthetische Briefe* and Kant's *Kritik der reinen Vernunft*, both of which left an indelible mark on his thought. He took the M.A. at Harvard (1862) and the Sc.B. in chemistry, *summa cum laude*, in the first class to graduate from the Lawrence Scientific School (1863). Despite his father's persistent efforts to encourage him to make a career of science, Peirce preferred the study of methodology and logic.

Upon graduation from Harvard, Peirce felt that he needed more experience in methods of scientific investigation, and he became a temporary aide in the U.S. Coast Survey (1859). For six months during the early 1860's he also studied, under Louis Agassiz, the techniques of classification, a discipline that served him well in his logic research. Like Comte, Peirce later set up a hierarchy of the sciences in which the methods of one science might be adapted to the investigation of those under it on the ladder. Mathematics occupied the top rung, since its independence of the actualities in nature and its concern with the framing of hypotheses and the study of their consequences made its methodology a model for handling the problems of the real world and also supplied model transforms into which such problems might be cast and by means of which they might be resolved.

Peirce was appointed a regular aide in the U.S. Coast Survey on 1 July 1861 and was thereby exempted from military service. On 1 July 1867 he was appointed assistant in the Survey, a title he carried until his resignation on 31 December 1891. In the early days his assignments were diverse. He observed in the field the solar eclipse of 1869 in the United States and selected the site in Sicily from which an American expedition—headed by his father and including both himself and his wife—observed the solar eclipse of 22 December 1870. He was temporarily in charge of the Coast Survey Office in 1872, and on 30 November of that year his father appointed him to "take charge of the Pendulum Experiments of the Coast Survey." Moreover he was to "investigate the law of deviations of the plumb line and of the azimuth from the spheroidal theory of the earth's figure." He was further directed to continue under Winlock the astronomical work that he had begun in 1869, while an assistant at the Harvard College Observatory; his observations, completed in 1875, were published in 1878 in the still important *Photometric Researches*. He was an assistant computer for the nautical almanac in 1873, and a special assistant in gravity research from 1884 to 1891. During the 1880's, however, Peirce found it increasingly difficult, under the changing administration of the Survey, to conform to the instructions issued him; in 1891 he tendered a forced resignation and left government service. (In 1962 a Coast and Geodetic Survey vessel was named for him, in somewhat belated recognition of his many contributions.)

Peirce's astronomical work, which he began in 1867, was characterized as "pioneer" by Solon I. Bailey, director of the Harvard Observatory in 1920. Peirce attempted to reform existing scales of magnitudes with the aid of instrumental photometry, and he investigated the form of the galactic cluster in which the sun is situated, the determination of which was "the chief end of the observations of the magnitude of the stars."

From April 1875 to August 1876 Peirce was in Europe to learn the use of the new convertible pendulum, "to compare it with those of the European measure of a degree and the Swiss Survey," and to compare his "invariable pendulums in the manner which has been usual by swinging them in London and Paris." In England he met Lockyer, Clifford, Stokes, and Airy; and in Berlin, Johann Jacob Baeyer, the director of the Prussian Geodetic Institute, where Peirce compared the two standards of the German instrument and the American one. He was invited to attend the meetings of the European Geodetic Association held in Paris during the summer of 1875, and there made a name as a research geodesist. His discovery of an error in European measurement, which was due to the flexure of the pendulum stand, led to the important twenty-three-page report that Plantamour read for him at Geneva on 27 October 1877. The first Peirce pendulum was invented in June 1878 and superseded the Repsold model used in the Coast and Geodetic Survey. Although the United States did not become a member of the International Geodetic Association until 1889, Peirce's geodetic work was

widely recognized. His paper on the value of gravity, read to the French Academy on 14 June 1880, was enthusiastically received, and he was invited to attend a conference on the pendulum of the Bureau des Longitudes.

In 1879 Peirce succeeded in determining the length of the meter from a wavelength of light. Benjamin Peirce described this feat, an adumbration of the work of Michelson, as "the only sure determination of the meter, by which it could be recovered if it were to be lost to science." By 1882 Peirce was engaged in a mathematical study of the relation between the variation of gravity and the figure of the earth. He claimed that "divergencies from a spherical form can at once be detected in the earth's figure by this means," and that "this result puts a new face on the relation of pendulum work to geodesy."

Peirce's mathematical inventiveness was fostered by his researches for the Coast Survey. His theory of conformal map projections grew out of his studies of gravity and resulted in his quincuncial map projection of 1876, which has been revived by the Coast Survey in chart no. 3092 to depict international air routes. This invention represented the first application of elliptic functions and Jacobian elliptic integrals to conformal mapping for geographical purposes. Peirce was further concerned with topological mapping and with the "Geographical Problem of the Four Colors" set forth by A. B. Kempe. The existential graphs that he invented as a means of diagrammatic logical analysis (and which he considered his *chef d'oeuvre*) grew out of his experiments with topological graphic elements. These reflect the influence on his thought of Tait's historic work on knots and the linkage problems of Kempe, as well as his own belief in the efficacy of diagrammatic thinking.

Peirce's interest in the linkage problem is first documented in the report of a meeting of the Scientific Association at the Johns Hopkins University, where Peirce was, from 1879 to 1884, a lecturer in logic and was closely associated with members of the mathematics department directed by J. J. Sylvester. (It was Sylvester who arranged for the posthumous republication, with addenda and notes by Charles Peirce, of Benjamin Peirce's *Linear Associative Algebra*.) Peirce had persuaded his father to write that work, and his father's mathematics influenced his own. J. B. Shaw has pointed out that two other lines of linear associative had been followed besides the direct one of Benjamin Peirce, one by use of the continuous group first announced by Poincaré and the other by use of the matrix theory first noted by Charles Peirce. Peirce was the first to recognize the quadrate linear associative algebras identical with matrices in which the units are letter pairs. He did not, however, regard this combination as a product, as did J. W. Gibbs in his "Elements of Vector Analysis" of 1884. Gibbs's double-dot product, according to Percey F. Smith, "is exactly that of C. S. Peirce's vids, and accordingly the algebra of dyadics based upon the double-dot law of multiplication is precisely the matricular algebra" of Peirce. In his *History of Mathematics*, Florian Cajori wrote that "C. S. Peirce showed that of all linear associative algebras there are only three in which division is unambiguous. These are ordinary single algebra, ordinary double algebra, and quaternions, from which the imaginary scalar is excluded. He showed that his father's algebras are operational and matricular." Peirce's work on nonions was to lead to a priority dispute with Sylvester.

By the time Peirce left the Johns Hopkins University, he had taken up the problem of continuity, a pressing one since his logical analysis and philosophical interpretation required that he deal with the infinite. In his 1881 paper "Logic of Number," Peirce claimed to have "distinguished between finite and infinite collections in substantially the same way that Dedekind did six years later." He admired the logical ingenuity of Fermat's method of "infinite descent" and used it consistently, in combination with an application of De Morgan's syllogism of transposed quantity that does not apply to the multitude of positive integers. Peirce deduced the validity of the "Fermatian method" of reasoning about integers from the idea of correspondence; he also respected Bolzano's work on this subject. He was strongly impressed by Georg Cantor's contributions, especially by Cantor's handling of the infinite in the second volume of the *Acta Mathematica*. Peirce explained that Cantor's "class of *Mächtigkeit* aleph-null is distinguished from other infinite classes in that the *Fermatian inference* is applicable to the former and not to the latter; and that generally, *to any smaller class some mode of reasoning is applicable which is not applicable to a greater one.*" In his development of the concept of the orders of infinity and their aleph representations, Peirce used a binary representation (which he called "secundal notation") of numbers. He eventually developed a complete algorithm for handling fundamental operations on numbers so expressed. His ingenuity as an innovator of symbolic notation is apparent throughout this work.

Peirce's analysis of Cantor's *Menge* and *Mächtigkeit* led him to the concept of a supermultitudinous collection beyond all the alephs—a collection in which the elements are no longer discrete but have become "welded" together to represent a true continuum. In his theory of logical criticism, "the temporal succession

of ideas is continuous and not by discrete steps," and the flow of time is similarly continuous in the same sense as the nondiscrete superpostnumeral multitudes. Things that exist form an enumerable collection, while those *in futuro* form a denumerable collection (of multitude aleph-null). The possible different courses of the future have a first abnumeral multitude (two raised to the exponent aleph-null) and the possibilities of such possibilities will be of the second abnumeral multitude (two raised to the exponent "two raised to the exponent aleph-null"). This procedure may be continued to the infinitieth exponential, which is thoroughly potential and retains no relic of the arbitrary existential—the state of true continuity. Peirce's research on continuity led him to make an exhaustive study of topology, especially as it had been developed by Listing.

Peirce's philosophy of mathematics postulated that the study of the substance of hypotheses only reveals other consequences not explicitly stated in the original. Mathematical procedure therefore resolves itself into four parts: (1) the creation of a model that embodies the condition of the premise; (2) the mental modification of the diagram to obtain auxiliary information; (3) mental experimentation on the diagram to bring out a new relation between parts not mentioned in its construction; and (4) repetition of the experiment "to infer inductively, with a degree of probability practically amounting to certainty, that every diagram constructed according to the same precept would present the same relation of parts which has been observed in the diagram experimented upon." The concern of the mathematician is to reach the conclusion, and his interest in the process is merely as a means to reach similar conclusions, whereas the logician desires merely to understand the process by which a result may be obtained. Peirce asserted that mathematics is a study of what is or is not logically possible and that the mathematician need not be concerned with what actually exists. Philosophy, on the other hand, discovers what it can from ordinary everyday experience.

Peirce characterized his work in the following words: "My philosophy may be described as the attempt of a physicist to make such conjecture as to the constitution of the universe as the methods of science may permit. . . . The best that can be done is to supply a hypothesis, not devoid of all likelihood, in the general line of growth of scientific ideas, and capable of being verified or refuted by future observers." Having postulated that every additional improvement of knowledge comes from an exercise of the powers of perception, Peirce held that the observation in a necessary inference is directed to a sort of diagram or image of the facts given in the premises. As in mathematics, it is possible to observe relations between parts of the diagram that were not noticed in its construction. Part of the business of logic is to construct such diagrams. In short, logical truth has the same source as mathematical truth, which is derived from the observation of diagrams. Mathematics uses the language of imagery to trace out results and the language of abstraction to make generalizations. It was Peirce's claim to have opened up the subject of abstraction, where Boole and De Morgan had concentrated on studies of deductive logic.

In 1870 Peirce greatly enlarged Boolean algebra by the introduction of a new kind of abstraction, the dyadic relation called "inclusion"—"the connecting link between the general idea of logical dependence and the idea of sequence of a quantity." The idea of quantity is important in that it is a linear arrangement whereby other linear arrangements (for example, cause and effect and reason and consequent) may be compared. The logic of relatives developed by Peirce treats of "systems" in which objects are brought together by any kind of relations, while ordinary logic deals with "classes" of objects brought together by the relation of similarity. General classes are composed of possibilities that the nominalist calls an abstraction. The influence of Peirce's work in dyadic relations may be seen in Schröder's *Vorlesungen über die Algebra der Logik*, and E. V. Huntington included Peirce's proof of a fundamental theorem in his "Sets of Independent Postulates for the Algebra of Logic" and in *The Continuum* referred to a statement that Peirce had published in the *Monist*. Peirce's contribution to the foundations of lattice theory is widely recognized.

In describing multitudes of systems within successive systems, Peirce reached a multitude so vast that the individuals lose their identity. The zero collection represents germinal possibility; the continuum is concrete-developed possibility; and "The whole universe of true and real possibilities forms a continuum upon which this universe of Actual Existence is a discontinuous mark like a point marked on a line."

The question of nominalism and realism became for Peirce the question of the reality of continua. Nature syllogizes, making inductions and abductions—as, for example, in evolution, which becomes "one vast succession of generalizations by which matter is becoming subjected to ever higher and higher laws." Laws of nature in the present form are products of an evolutionary process and logically require an explanation in such terms. In the light of the logic of relatives, Peirce maintained, the general is seen to be the continuous and coincides with that opinion the medieval Schoolmen called realism. Peirce's Scotistic

stance—in opposition to Berkeley's nominalism—caused him to attack the nominalistic positions of Mach, Pearson, and Poincaré. Peirce accused the positivists of confusing psychology with logic in mistaking sense impressions, which are psychological inferences, for logical data. Joseph Jastrow tells of being introduced by Peirce "to the possibility of an experimental study of a psychological problem," and they published a joint paper, "On Small Differences in Sensation," in the *Memoirs of the National Academy of Sciences* (1884).

William James was responsible for Peirce's world-wide reputation as the father of the philosophical doctrine that he originally called pragmatism, and later pragmaticism. Peirce's famous pragmatic maxim was enunciated in "How to Make Our Ideas Clear," which he wrote (in French) on shipboard before reaching Plymouth on the way to the Stuttgart meetings of the European Geodetic Association in 1877. The paper contains his statement of a laboratory procedure valid in the search for "truth"—"Consider what effects, that might conceivably have practical bearings, we conceive the object of our conception to have. Then, our conception of these effects is the whole of our conception of the object." In a letter to his former student Christine Ladd-Franklin, Peirce emphasized that "the meaning of a *concept* . . . lies in the manner in which it could *conceivably* modify purposive action, and *in this alone*." Moreover "pragmatism is one of the results of my study of the formal laws of signs, a study guided by mathematics and by the familiar facts of everyday experience and by no other science whatever." John Dewey pointed out that reality, in Peirce's system, "means the object of those beliefs which have, after prolonged and cooperative inquiry, become stable, and 'truth,' the quality of these beliefs, is a logical consequence of this position." The maxim underlies Peirce's epistemology, wherein the first procedure is a guess or hypothesis (abductive inference) from which are set up subsidiary conclusions (deductive inference) that can be tested against experimental evidence (inductive inference).

The results of the inductive process are ratios and admit of a probability error, abnormal occurrences corresponding to a ratio of zero. This is valid for infinite classes, but for none larger than the denumeral. Consequently, induction must always admit the possibility of exception to the law, and absolute certainty is unobtainable. Every boundary of a figure that represents a possible experience ought therefore to be blurred, and herein lies the evidence for Peirce's claim to priority in the enunciation of a triadic logic.

Morris Cohen has characterized Peirce's thought as germinal in its initiation of new ideas and in its illumination of his own "groping for a systematic view of reason and nature." Peirce held that chance, law, and continuity are basic to the explanation of the universe. Chance accounts for the origin of fruitful ideas, and if these meet allied ideas in a mind prepared for them, a welding process takes place—a process called the law of association. Peirce considered this to be the one law of intellectual development.

In his educational philosophy Peirce said that the study of mathematics could develop the mind's powers of imagination, abstraction, and generalization. Generalization, "the spilling out of continuous systems of ideas," is the great aim of life. In the early 1890's he was convinced that modern geometry was a rich source of "forms of conception," and for that reason every educated man should have an acquaintance with projective geometry (to aid the power of generalization), topology (to fire the imagination), and the theory of numbers (to develop the power of exact reasoning). He kept these objectives in view in the mathematics textbooks that he wrote after his retirement from the Coast Survey; these works further reflect the influence of Arthur Cayley, A. F. Möbius, and C. F. Klein. Peirce's adoption of Cayley's mathematical "absolute" and his application of it to his metaphysical thought is especially revealing. "The Absolute in metaphysics fulfills the same function as the absolute in geometry. According as we suppose the infinitely distant beginning and end of the universe are *distinct*, *identical*, or *nonexistent*, we have three kinds of philosophy, hyperbolic, parabolic, or elliptic." Again "the first question to be asked about a continuous quantity is whether the two points of its absolute coincide." If not, are they in the real line of the scale? "The answers will have great bearing on philosophical and especially cosmogonical problems." For a time Peirce leaned to a Lobachevskian interpretation of the character of space.

Peirce once wrote to Paul Carus, editor of the *Monist*, "Few philosophers, if any, have gone to their work as well equipped as I, in the study of other systems and in the various branches of science." In 1876, for example, Peirce's thought on the "economy of research" was published in a Coast and Geodetic Survey report. It became a major consideration in his philosophy, for the art of discovery became for him a general problem in economics. It underlay his application of the pragmatic maxim and became an important objective in his approach to problems in political economy, in which his admiration of Ricardo was reflected in his referring to "the peculiar reasoning of political economy" as "Ricardian inference." Peirce's application of the calculus approach of Cournot predated that of Jevons and brought him

recognition (according to W. J. Baumol and S. W. Goldfeld) as a "precursor in mathematical economics."

Peirce also sought systems of logical methodology in the history of logic and of the sciences. He became known for his meticulous research in the scientific and logical writings of the ancients and the medieval Schoolmen, although he failed to complete the book on the history of science that he had contracted to write in 1898. For Peirce the history of science was an instance of how the law of growth applied to the human mind. He used his revised version of the Paris manuscript of Ptolemy's catalogue of stars in his astronomical studies, and he included it for modern usage in *Photometric Researches*. He drew upon Galileo—indeed, his abductive inference is identical twin to Galileo's *il lume naturale*—and found evidence of a "gigantic power of right reasoning" in Kepler's work on Mars.

Peirce spent the latter part of his life in comparative isolation with his second wife, Juliette Froissy, in the house they had built near Milford, Pennsylvania, in 1888. (His second marriage, in 1883, followed his divorce from Harriet Melusina Fay, whom he had married in 1862.) He wrote articles and book reviews for newspapers and journals, including the *Monist*, *Open Court*, and the *Nation*. As an editorial contributor to the new *Century Dictionary*, Peirce was responsible for the terms in logic, metaphysics, mathematics, mechanics, astronomy, and weights and measures; he also contributed to the *Dictionary of Philosophy and Psychology*. He translated foreign scientific papers for the Smithsonian publications, served privately as scientific consultant, and prepared numerous papers for the National Academy of Sciences, to which he was elected in 1877 and of which he was a member of the Standing Committee on Weights and Measures. (Earlier, in 1867, he had been elected to the American Academy of Arts and Sciences.) Peirce also lectured occasionally, notably at Harvard (where he spoke on the logic of science in 1865, on British logicians in 1869–1870, and on pragmatism in 1903) and at the Lowell Institute. None of his diverse activities was sufficient to relieve the abject poverty of his last years, however, and his very existence was made possible only by a fund created by a group of friends and admirers and administered by his lifelong friend William James.

BIBLIOGRAPHY

I. ORIGINAL WORKS. Bibliographies and works by Peirce include Carolyn Eisele, ed., *The New Elements of*

Mathematics by Charles S. Peirce, 4 vols. (The Hague, 1974); Charles Hartshorne and Paul Weiss, eds., *The Collected Papers of Charles Sanders Peirce*, I–VI (Cambridge, Mass., 1931–1935); Arthur W. Burks, ed., VII–VIII (Cambridge, Mass., 1958), with a bibliography in vol. VIII—supp. 1 to this bibliography is by Max Fisch, in Philip Wiener, and Harold Young, eds., *Studies in the Philosophy of Charles Sanders Peirce*, 2nd ser. (1964), 477–485, and supp. 2 is in *Transactions of the Charles S. Peirce Society*, **2**, no. 1 (1966), 51–53. Also see Max Fisch, "A Draft of a Bibliography of Writings About C. S. Peirce," in *Studies*, 2nd ser., 486–514; supp. 1 is in *Transactions of the Charles S. Peirce Society*, **2**, no. 1 (1966), 54–59. Papers in the Houghton Library at Harvard University are listed in Richard S. Robin, *Annotated Catalogue of the Papers of Charles S. Peirce* (Amherst, 1967). In addition, see Richard S. Robin, "The Peirce Papers: A Supplementary Catalogue," in *Transactions of the Charles S. Peirce Society*, **7**, no. 1 (1971), 37–58. Unpublished MSS are in the National Archives, the Library of Congress, the Smithsonian Archives, and in the Houghton Library, Harvard University.

For Peirce's work during 1879–1884, see *Johns Hopkins University Circulars*, esp. "On a Class of Multiple Algebras," **2** (1882), 3–4; "On the Relative Forms of Quaternions," **13** (1882), 179; and "A Communication From Mr. Peirce [On nonions]," **22** (1883), 86–88.

In the period 1870–1885, Peirce published fourteen technical papers as appendices to *Reports of the Superintendent of the United States Coast and Geodetic Survey*. See "Notes on the Theory of Economy of Research," **14** (1876), 197–201, repr. in W. E. Cushen, "C. S. Peirce on Benefit-Cost Analysis of Scientific Activity," in *Operations Research* (July–Aug., 1967), 641–648; and "A Quincuncial Projection of the Sphere," in **15** (1877), published also in *American Journal of Mathematics*, **2** (1879), and in Thomas Craig, *A Treatise on Projections* (1882). See also "Photometric Researches," in *Annals of Harvard College Observatory* (Leipzig, 1878); and preface: "A Theory of Probable Inference"; note A: "Extension of the Aristotelian Syllogistic"; and note B: "The Logic of Relatives," in Peirce, ed., *Studies in Logic. By Members of the Johns Hopkins University* (Boston, 1883).

See also *Charles S. Peirce Über die Klarheit unserer Gedanken* (*How to Make Our Ideas Clear*), ed., trans., and with commentary by Klaus Oehler (Frankfurt am Main, 1968); Edward C. Moore, ed., *Charles S. Peirce: The Essential Writings* (New York, 1972); *Charles S. Peirce Lectures on Pragmatism* (*Vorlesungen über Pragmatismus*), ed., trans., and annotated by Elisabeth Walther (Hamburg, 1973); and Morris R. Cohen, ed., *Chance, Love, and Logic* (New York, 1923).

II. SECONDARY LITERATURE. The *Transactions of the Charles S. Peirce Society* contain a large number of papers on Peirce and his work. There are also interesting biographical notices in a number of standard sources—see esp. those by N. Bosco, in *Enciclopedia filosofica* (Florence, 1967); Murray G. Murphey, in *The Encyclopedia of Philosophy* (New York–London, 1967); Paul Weiss, in

Dictionary of American Biography (New York, 1934); and Philip P. Wiener, in *International Encyclopedia of the Social Sciences* (New York, 1968). See also *Lamb's Biographical Dictionary of the United States* (Boston, 1903); and *American Men of Science* (1906), which contains Peirce's own list of his fields of research.

Recent books, not necessarily listed in the bibliographies cited above, include John F. Boler, *Charles S. Peirce and Scholastic Realism* (Seattle, 1963); Hanna Buczynska-Garewicz, *Peirce* (Warsaw, 1965); Douglas Greenlee, *Peirce's Concept of Sign* (The Hague–Paris, 1973); Edward C. Moore and Richard S. Robin, eds., *Studies in the Philosophy of Charles Sanders Peirce*, 2nd ser. (Amherst, 1964); Murray G. Murphey, *The Development of Peirce's Philosophy* (Cambridge, Mass., 1961); Francis E. Reilly, *Charles S. Peirce's Theory of Scientific Method* (New York, 1970); Don D. Roberts, *The Existential Graphs of Charles S. Peirce* (The Hague–Paris, 1973); Elisabeth Walther, *Die Festigung der Überzeugung und andere Schriften* (Baden-Baden, 1965); Hjamer Wennerberg, *The Pragmatism of C. S. Peirce* (Uppsala, 1962); and Philip P. Wiener and Frederic H. Young, eds., *Studies in the Philosophy of Charles Sanders Peirce* (Cambridge, Mass., 1952).

Especially pertinent to this article are J. C. Abbott, *Trends in Lattice Theory* (New York, 1970); Oscar S. Adams, "Elliptic Functions Applied to Conformal World Maps," in *Department of Commerce Special Publication No. 112* (1925); and "The Rhombic Conformal Projection," in *Bulletin géodésique*, **5** (1925), 1–26; Solon I. Bailey, *History and Work of the Harvard College Observatory* (1931); W. J. Baumol and S. M. Goldfeld, *Precursors in Mathematical Economics* (London, 1968); Max Bense and Elisabeth Walther, *Wörterbuch der Semiotik* (Cologne, 1973); Garrett Birkhoff, *Lattice Theory* (New York, 1948); Rudolf Carnap, *Logical Foundations of Probability* (London, 1950); Clarence I. Lewis, *A Survey of Symbolic Logic* (Berkeley, 1918); James Byrnie Shaw, *Synopsis of Linear Associative Algebra* (Washington, D.C., 1907); Percey F. Smith, "Josiah Willard Gibbs," in *Bulletin of the American Mathematical Society* (Oct. 1903), 34–39; and Albert A. Stanley, "Quincuncial Projection," in *Surveying and Mapping* (Jan.–Mar., 1946).

See also the section "Charles Sanders Peirce," in *Journal of Philosophy, Psychology and Scientific Methods*, **13**, no. 26 (1916), 701–737, which includes Morris R. Cohen, "Charles S. Peirce and a Tentative Bibliography of His Published Writings"; John Dewey, "The Pragmatism of Peirce"; Joseph Jastrow, "Charles Peirce as a Teacher"; Christine Ladd-Franklin, "Charles S. Peirce at the Johns Hopkins"; and Josiah Royce and Fergus Kernan, "Peirce as a Philosopher."

More recently published essays by Carolyn Eisele, not necessarily listed above, include "The *Liber abaci* Through the Eyes of Charles S. Peirce," in *Scripta mathematica*, **17** (1951), 236–259; "Charles S. Peirce and the History of Science," in *Yearbook. American Philosophical Society* (Philadelphia, 1955), 353–358; "Charles S. Peirce, American Historian of Science," in *Actes du*

VIIIe Congrès international d'histoire des sciences (Florence, 1956), 1196–1200; "The Charles S. Peirce-Simon Newcomb Correspondence," in *Proceedings of the American Philosophical Society*, **101**, no. 5 (1957), 410–433; "The Scientist-Philosopher C. S. Peirce at the Smithsonian," in *Journal of the History of Ideas*, **18**, no. 4 (1957), 537–547; "Some Remarks on the Logic of Science of the Seventeenth Century as Interpreted by Charles S. Peirce," in *Actes du 2eme Symposium d'histoire des sciences* (Pisa–Vinci, 1958), 55–64; "Charles S. Peirce, Nineteeth-Century Man of Science," in *Scripta mathematica*, **24** (1959), 305–324; "Poincaré's Positivism in the Light of C. S. Peirce's Realism," in *Actes du IXe Congrès international d'histoire des sciences* (Barcelona–Madrid, 1959), 461–465; "The Quincuncial Map-Projection of Charles S. Peirce," in *Proceedings of the 10th International Congress of History of Science* (Ithaca, 1962), 687; and "Charles S. Peirce and the Problem of Map-Projection," in *Proceedings of the American Philosophical Society*, **107**, no. 4 (1963), 299–307.

Other articles by Carolyn Eisele are "Fermatian Inference and De Morgan's Syllogism of Transposed Quantity in Peirce's Logic of Science," in *Physis. Rivista di storia della scienza*, **5**, fasc. 2 (1963), 120–128; "The Influence of Galileo on the Thought of Charles S. Peirce," in *Atti del Simposio su Galileo Galilei nella storia e nella filosofia della scienza* (Florence–Pisa, 1964), 321–328; "Peirce's Philosophy of Education in His Unpublished Mathematics Textbooks," in Edward C. Moore and Richard S. Robin, eds., *Studies in the Philosophy of Charles Sanders Peirce*, 2nd ser., (1964), 51–75; "The Mathematics of Charles S. Peirce," in *Actes du XIe Congrès international d'histoire des sciences* (Warsaw, 1965), 229–234; "C. S. Peirce and the Scientific Philosophy of Ernst Mach," in *Actes du XIIe Congrès international d'histoire des sciences* (Paris, 1968), 33–40; and "Charles S. Peirce and the Mathematics of Economics," in *Actes du XIIIe Congrès international d'histoire des sciences* (Moscow, 1974).

Essays by Max H. Fisch include "Peirce at the Johns Hopkins University," in Philip P. Wiener and Frederic H. Young, eds., *Studies in the Philosophy of Charles Sanders Peirce* (Cambridge, 1952), 277–312, written with Jackson I. Cope; "Alexander Bain and the Genealogy of Pragmatism," in *Journal of the History of Ideas*, **15** (1954), 413–444; "A Chronicle of Pragmaticism, 1865–1897," in *Monist*, **48** (1964), 441–466; "Was There a Metaphysical Club in Cambridge?," in Edward C. Moore and Richard S. Robin, eds., *Studies in the Philosphy of Charles Sanders Peirce*, 2nd ser. (Amherst, 1964), 3–32; "Peirce's Triadic Logic," in *Transactions of the Charles S. Peirce Society*, **2** (1966), 71–86, written with Atwell Turquette; "Peirce's Progress from Nominalism Toward Realism," in *Monist*, **51** (1967), 159–178; and "Peirce's Ariste: The Greek Influence in His Later Philosophy," in *Transactions of the Charles S. Peirce Society*, **7** (1971), 187–210.

Essays by Victor F. Lenzen include "Charles S. Peirce and *Die Europaische Gradmessung*," in *Proceedings of the XIIth International Congress of the History of Science* (Ithaca, 1962), 781–783; "Charles S. Peirce as Astronomer," in Edward C. Moore and Richard S. Robin, eds., *Studies in the Philosophy of Charles Sanders Peirce*, 2nd ser. (Amherst, 1964), 33–50; "The Contributions of Charles S. Peirce to Metrology," in *Proceedings of the American Philosophical Society*, **109**, no. 1 (1965), 29–46; "Development of Gravity Pendulums in the 19th Century," in United States Museum Bulletin 240: *Contributions From the Museum of History and Technology, Smithsonian Institution*, paper 44 (Washington, 1965), 301–348, written with Robert P. Multhauf; "Reminiscences of a Mission to Milford, Pennsylvania," in *Transactions of the Charles S. Peirce Society*, **1** (1965), 3–11; "The Role of Science in the Philosophy of C. S. Peirce," in *Akten des XIV Internationalen Kongresses für Philosophie* (Vienna, 1968), 371–376; "An Unpublished Scientific Monograph by C. S. Peirce," in *Transactions of the Charles S. Peirce Society*, **5** (1969), 5–24; "Charles S. Peirce as Mathematical Geodesist," *ibid.*, **8** (1972), 90–105; and "The Contributions of C. S. Peirce to Linear Algebra," in Dale Riepe, ed., *Phenomenology and Natural Existence* (*Essays in Honor of Martin Farber*) (New York, 1973), 239–254.

CAROLYN EISELE

PELETIER, JACQUES (*b.* Le Mans, France, 25 July 1517; *d.* Paris, France, July 1582)

Peletier was the ninth of fifteen children born to Pierre Peletier, a barrister in Le Mans, and Jeanne le Royer. His family, educated in theology, philosophy, and law, wanted him to pursue these diciplines. He therefore studied philosophy at the Collège de Navarre (Paris) and read law for five years in Le Mans. But when he became secretary in the late 1530's to René du Bellay, bishop of Le Mans, he decided that his interests were not in philosophy or law.

In 1541 Peletier published *L'art poëtique d'Horace, traduit en vers François*, the preface of which pleaded for a national language, thus anticipating the ideas of the later Pléiade. He also studied Greek, mathematics, and later medicine, always as an autodidact. In 1543 he became rector of the Collège de Bayeux in Paris, a post that soon bored him. He therefore left Paris in 1547 and lived as a vagabond. Among the cities he visited were Bordeaux, Poitiers, Lyons, Paris, and Basel. Working alternately as a teacher in mathematics and as a surgeon, he devoted his life to poetry and science. Peletier shared with the Pléiade, a group of seven poets whose leader was Pierre de Ronsard, a desire to create a French literature. He also stated that French was the perfect instrument for the sciences and planned to publish mathematical books in the vernacular. Temporarily, however, he published only in Latin (1557–*ca.* 1572) because no one would accept his somewhat peculiar French orthography. Peletier's poetry had scientific aspects, especially the second part of *L'amour des amours* (1555), in which he published descriptive-lyric verses on nature, natural phenomena, and astronomy which revealed the influence of Lucretius. He also published two minor works on medicine.

In 1545 Peletier published a short comment on Gemma Frisius' *Arithmeticae practicae methodus facilis*. In 1549 the *Arithmétique* appeared. In this work Peletier tried to satisfy both the theoretical requirements and the practical needs of the businessman. This topic had been previously discussed in Latin by C. Tunstall and Gemma Frisius, but Peletier was the first to combine both in a textbook in the vernacular. Peletier wrote *L'algèbre* (1554) in French in his own orthographic style. In this work he adopted several original and ingenious ideas from Stifel's *Arithmetica integra* (1544) and showed himself to have been strongly influenced by Cardano. Peletier's work presented the achievements already reached in Germany and Italy, and he was the first mathematician to see relations between coefficients and roots of equations.

In the *In Euclidis elementa demonstrationum* (1557) Peletier rejected the method of superposition as non-geometric. His arguments for this opinion, however, were used for the contrary view by Petrus Ramus. A long note on the angle of contact—in Peletier's view not a finite quantity and not an angle at all—was the starting point for various disputes, especially with C. Clavius. This work was vehemently criticized by J. Buteo.

Translations into French or Latin and several reprints, especially of the French editions, indicate that Peletier's works were quite successful. His other mathematical publications were devoted to such topics as the measurement of the circle, contact of straight lines and curves with curves, and duplication of the cube. The basic ideas in these publications often originated in Peletier's discussions with Buteo and Clavius.

BIBLIOGRAPHY

I. ORIGINAL WORKS. An incomplete bibliography of Peletier's works is given by C. Jugé in *Jacques Peletier du Mans* (Paris, 1907). His major works include *Arithmeticae practicae methodus facilis per Gemmam Frisium, huc accesserunt Peletarii annotationes* (Paris, 1545), subsequent eds. between 1549 and 1557; *L'arithmétique departie en quatre livres* (Poitiers, 1549), with later eds. between 1552 and 1969; *L'algebre departie en deus livres* (Lyons, 1545; 3rd ed., 1620), with a Latin trans. as *De occulta parte numerorum* (Paris, 1560); *In Euclidis elementa geometrica*

demonstrationum libri sex (Lyons, 1557; 2nd ed., Geneva, 1610), with a French trans. (Geneva, 1611); *Commentarii tres, primus de dimensione circuli, secundus de contactu linearum, tertius de constitutione horoscopi* (Basel, 1563), an ed. of the second part also appeared (Paris, 1581); *Disquisitiones geometricae* (Lyons, 1567); and *In C. Clavium de contactu linearum apologia* (Paris, 1579).

Peletier's letter *ad Razallium* against Buteo was published at the end of *De occulta parte numerorum*. The *In Euclidis elementa* of 1573, mentioned by Jugé, is not Peletier's work but one of the many eds. "cum praefatione St. Gracilis."

II. SECONDARY LITERATURE. C. Jugé (see above) provides a biography of Peletier. For works on his poetry, see A. Boulanger, *L'art poétique de Jacques Peletier* (Paris, 1830); *Dictionnaire des lettres françaises, le seizième siècle* (Paris, 1951), 561–563; F. Letessier, "Un humaniste Manceau: Jacques Peletier (1517–1582)," in *Lettres d'humanité. Bulletin de l'Association Guillaume Budé*, supp. 9 (1950), 206–263; H. Staub, *Le curieux désir. Scève et Peletier du Mans poètes de la connaissance* (Geneva, 1967); and D. B. Wilson, "The Discovery of Nature in the Work of Jacques Peletier du Mans," in *Bibliothèque d'humanisme et renaissance*, 16 (1954), 298–311. His contacts with the Pléiade are discussed by H. Chamard in *Histoire de la Pléiade* (Paris, 1961–1963), *passim*, and in L. C. Porter's intro. to the repr. of Peletier's *Dialogue de l'ortografe e prononciation françoese* (Poitiers, 1550; repr. Geneva, 1966).

Peletier's mathematics is discussed by H. Bosmans, "L'algèbre de J. Peletier du Mans," in *Revue des questions scientifiques*, 61 (1907), 117–173, which uses the 1556 ed. of *L'algèbre*; N. Z. Davis, "Sixteenth-century French Arithmetics on the Business Life," in *Journal of the History of Ideas*, 21 (1960), 18–48; V. Thebault, "A French Mathematician of the Sixteenth Century: Jacques Peletier (1517–1582)," in *Mathematics Magazine*, 21 (1948), 147–150; M. Thureau, "J. Peletier, mathématicien manceau au XVIᵉ siècle," in *La province du Maine*, 2nd ser., 15 (1935), 149–160, 187–199; and J. J. Verdonk, *Petrus Ramus en de wiskunde* (Assen, 1966), 264–268; on his contacts with P. Nunez, see L. de Matos, *Les Portugais en France au XVIᵉ siècle* (Coimbra, 1952), 123–125.

J. J. VERDONK

PELL, JOHN (*b.* Southwick, Sussex, England, 1 March 1611; *d.* London, England, 12 December 1685)

Pell was the son of John Pell, vicar of Southwick, and Mary Holland, who both died when he was a child. In 1624 he left Steyning School in Sussex for Trinity College, Cambridge. He received the B.A. in 1629 and the M.A. in 1630. By the latter year he was assistant master at Collyer's School in Horsham, and then at Samuel Hartlib's short-lived Chichester academy. On 3 July 1632 he married Ithamaria Reginalds, the second daughter of Henry Reginalds of London. In 1638 the Comenian group, of which Hartlib was a leading member, arranged his move to London; and he soon won a reputation for his knowledge of mathematics and languages. The success of the group was thwarted by political developments; not wanting to take a church living, Pell had to emigrate to secure a mathematical post. In December 1643 he became professor of mathematics at Amsterdam and, in 1646, at the newly opened academy in Breda. From 1654 to 1658 he was a Commonwealth agent in Zurich. After the Restoration, Pell became rector of Fobbing in Essex, vicar of Laindon, and then chaplain to Gilbert Sheldon, bishop of London.[1] For a time he lived with a former pupil at Brereton Hall. He died in London in poverty.[2]

Opinions about Pell's significance as a mathematician have always varied, and a full assessment will be impossible until his writings have been collected and analyzed. Houzeau and Lancaster, and others, have suggested that his "Description and Use of the Quadrant" (1628) and other works were printed. His first publication was undoubtedly *Idea of Mathematics*, which appeared anonymously after circulating in manuscript in an early version before 1630. The work was published in Latin and in English in 1638 and republished as part of John Dury's *The Reformed Librarie-Keeper* in 1650. The *Idea* won Pell "a great deal of repute both at home and abroad" and led to his post at Amsterdam. His arguments are clearly very close to those of Bacon, Comenius, and their followers but also have a large personal element. The tract stressed the importance of mathematics and proposed "the writing of a *Consilarius Mathematicus*, the establishment of a public library of all mathematical books, and the publication of three new treatises." A copy was sent by Pell's patron, Theodore Haak, to P. Mersenne, who circulated the work; Descartes replied approvingly.[3]

At Amsterdam, Pell's fame was enhanced by his *Controversiae de vera circuli mensura* (1647), which attacked C. S. Longomontanus and earned the approbation of Roberval, Hobbes, Cavendish, Cavalieri, Descartes, and others.[4] In 1647 Pell read his *oratio inauguralis* at Breda and was praised by an eyewitness[5] for the excellence of his delivery and his explanation of "the use and dignity" of mathematics.

Most mathematicians know of Pell through his equation[6] $x^2 = 1 + Ay^2$. Some suggest that Euler mistakenly attributed to Pell some work of William Lord Brouncker, but the equivalent equation $x = 12yy - zz$ occurs in Thomas Brancker's 1668 translation, *An Introduction to Algebra*,[7] of J. H.

Rahn's *Teutsche Algebra oder algebraische Rechenkunst* (Zurich, 1659). Pell edited the latter part of the translation. Aubrey, however, stated that "Rhonius was Dr. Pell's scholar at Zurich and came to him every Friday night after he had writt his post-lettres" and claimed that the *Algebra* was essentially Pell's work.[8] If this statement is accepted, Pell should also be credited with innovations in symbolism (particularly $\div$) and with setting out equations in three columns (two for identification and one for explanation), otherwise credited to Rahn. Without further evidence, it is best to assume that there was joint responsibility for these innovations and that Pell's contemporary reputation as a mathematician, and particularly as an algebraist, was not unearned.

NOTES

1. His academic reputation is indicated by his D.D. at Lambeth and election as a fellow of the Royal Society in 1663.
2. Some of his books and manuscripts were acquired by Richard Busby, master of Westminster School, which still has some of his books. The MSS came to the British Museum via Thomas Birch; other manuscripts were left at Brereton.
3. Wallis, "An Early Mathematical Manifesto," *passim*.
4. Dijksterhuis, "John Pell," p. 293.
5. Edward Norgate, quoted by D. Langedijk in " ' De illustre schole ende Collegium Auriacum ' te Brede," p. 131.
6. Whitford, *The Pell Equation*, p. 2. Cajori does not accept or even refer to Whitford's argument.
7. *Loc. cit.*, p. 143, no. 34. The relation between the 1659 and 1668 eds. is discussed in more detail in a forthcoming article by C. J. Scriba.
8. Aubrey's biography was partly checked by Pell himself and later supplemented by Haak.

BIBLIOGRAPHY

I. ORIGINAL WORKS. For a 1967 repr. of the 1638 *Idea* and the 1682 and 1809 versions, see Wallis. Two other anonymous works not cited in the text are *Easter Not Mistimed* (London, 1664) and *Tabula numerorum quadratorum* (London, 1672). See notes for a reference to his many MSS, often mistakenly said to have been published.

II. SECONDARY LITERATURE. Writings on Pell and his work are J. Aubrey's biography of Pell, Bodleian MS 6 f.53, printed in *Brief Lives*, A. Clark, ed., II (Oxford, 1898), 121–131, and in O. L. Dick's 1949–1950 ed.; P. Bayle, in *A General Dictionary, Historical and Critical*, J. P. Bernard et al., eds., VIII (London, 1739), 250–253; T. Birch, *The History of the Royal Society of London*, IV (London, 1757), 444–447; F. Cajori, "Rahn's Algebraic Symbols," in *American Mathematical Monthly*, **31** (1924), 65–71; E. J. Dijksterhuis, "John Pell in zijn strijd over de rectificatie van den cirkel," in *Euclides*, **8** (1932), 286–296; J. C. Houzeau and A. Lancaster, *Bibliographie générale de l'astronomie* (Brussels, 1882–1887, repr., 1964); and D. Langedijk, " 'De illustre schole ende Collegium Auriacum' te Brede," in G. C. A. Juten, ed., *Taxandria: Tijdschrift voor Noordbrabentsche geschiedenis en volks-*

kunde xlii, III (Bergen op Zoom, 1932), 128–132.

For additional information see C. de Waard's biography of Pell in *Nieuw Nederlandsch biografisch woordenboek*, III (1914), cols. 961–965; and "Wiskundige bijdragen tot de pansophie van Comenius," in *Euclides*, **25** (1950), 278–287; P. J. Wallis, "An Early Mathematical Manifesto —John Pell's *Idea of Mathematics*," in *Durham Research Review*, no. 18 (1967), 139–148; E. E. Whitford, *The Pell Equation* (New York, 1912); and A. Wood, in *Fasti Oxonienses*, P. Bliss, ed., I (London, 1815), cols. 461–464, and in 1967 fasc., repr. (New York–London).

P. J. WALLIS

PEMBERTON, HENRY (*b.* London, England, 1694; *d.* London, 9 March 1771)

Little is known of Pemberton's family or youth beyond the significant fact that he was introduced to mathematics at grammar school. He read, independently, Halley's editions of Apollonius and then traveled to Leiden to study medicine with Boerhaave. In Leiden he was further introduced to the work of Newton, the decisive event of his intellectual life. Pemberton interrupted his stay in Leiden to study anatomy in Paris and then returned to London about 1715 to attend Saint Thomas's Hospital. Although he took his degree at Leiden in 1719, he never practiced medicine extensively because of his delicate health. He did, however, serve for several years as professor of physics at Gresham College.

Pemberton's thesis, on the mechanism by which the eye accommodates to objects at different distances (1719), was his most important independent work. Treating the crystalline lens as a muscle, he argued that it accommodates to vision at varying distances by changes in shape. Students of physiological optics in the eighteenth century knew the work, and Pemberton ranks as one of the precursors of Thomas Young.

Pemberton's work on the mechanism of accommodation was nearly his last independent work, for he was determined to join the circle of Newton's epigones. He attempted, unsuccessfully, to approach the master through John Keill. But Richard Mead, Newton's friend and physician, showed Newton a paper in which Pemberton refuted Leibniz' measure of the force of moving bodies—an obsequious essay larded with references to "the great Sir Isaac Newton." Although the measure of the force of moving bodies was not an issue germane to Newtonian mechanics, Newton was apparently pleased with the attack on Leibniz. He made Pemberton's acquaintance; and Pemberton sought to cement the relation by contributing another obsequious essay on muscular motion, which converted itself into a panegyric on Newtonian

method, to Mead's edition of Cowper's *Myotomia reformata*, completed in 1723 and published in 1724. When work on the third edition of Newton's *Principia* began late in 1723, Pemberton was the editor.

Pemberton devoted the major portion of his attention to the edition during the following two and a half years. He was a conscientious editor who carefully attended to the details of style and consistency, but nothing more substantive in the edition bears his stamp. The third edition of the *Principia* (1726) is the primary vehicle by which Pemberton's name has survived. The meagerness of his contribution, in comparison with the promise of his thesis at Leiden, suggests how deadening the role of sycophant can be.

Pemberton had labored assiduously to earn Newton's favor; apparently he intended to make his position near Newton the foundation of a career. Already he was at work on a popularization of Newtonianism for those without mathematics—*A View of Sir Isaac Newton's Philosophy*, which finally appeared in 1728 with prefatory assurances that Newton had read and approved it. He had also announced an English translation of the *Principia* and a commentary on it. In 1728 he received the Gresham position. Other aspiring young men had also courted Newton, however, and they chose to dispute the inheritance. John Machin, secretary of the Royal Society, sponsored and aided Andrew Motte's rival translation, which beat Pemberton's work to the press. Discouraged, he abandoned the commentary and virtually ended his career as a scientist.

Pemberton was thirty-five years old when Motte's translation appeared in 1729. Although he lived more than forty years more, he did almost nothing further to fulfill his earlier promise. During the 1730's, he was drawn into the fringes of the *Analyst* controversy on the foundations of the calculus. In 1739 the College of Physicians engaged him to reedit and translate their pharmacopoeia—*The Dispensatory of the Royal College of Physicians* (1746). He spent the following seven years on the project, attempting, he said, to purge it of the trifles that disgraced it. From the point of view of medical science, the job was undertaken too soon, and it had to be repeated again before the end of the century. At Gresham College he delivered courses of lectures on chemistry and physiology, which his friend James Wilson later published; both were minor works. Toward the end of his life he returned to his early love of mathematics and published four papers in the *Philosophical Transactions of the Royal Society*.

Pemberton was a man of deep friendships and broad learning. His first publication was a mathematical letter addressed to James Wilson, to whom, fifty years later, he left his papers. In his *View of Newton's*

Philosophy he published a poem on Newton by a young friend, Richard Glover, whose continuing poetic efforts evoked pamphlets written by Pemberton praising Glover's work with a show of literary erudition. Glover's political connections led Pemberton to write an essay on political philosophy, which remained unpublished. He also wrote on weights and measures. He was known as a lover of music who never missed a performance of a Handel oratorio.

BIBLIOGRAPHY

I. ORIGINAL WORKS. Pemberton's major works include *Dissertatio physica-medica inauguralis de facultate oculi qua ad diversas rerum conspectarum distantias se accommodat* (Leiden, 1719); *Epistola ad amicum de Cotesii inventis, curvarum ratione, quae cum circulo & hyperbola comparationem admittunt* (London, 1722); "Introduction. Concerning the Muscles and Their Action," in William Cowper, *Myotomia reformata*, Richard Mead, ed. (London, 1724); "A Letter to Dr. Mead . . . Concerning an Experiment, Whereby It Has Been Attempted to Shew the Falsity of the Common Opinion, in Relation to the Force of Bodies in Motion," in *Philosophical Transactions of the Royal Society*, **32** (1722), 57; *A View of Sir Isaac Newton's Philosophy* (London, 1728); *Observations on Poetry, Especially the Epic* (London, 1738); *The Dispensatory of the Royal College of Physicians* (London, 1746); *Some Few Reflections on the Tragedy of Boadicia* (London, 1753); *A Course of Chemistry* (London, 1771); and *A Course of Physiology* (London, 1773).

II. SECONDARY LITERATURE. See I. Bernard Cohen, "Pemberton's Translation of Newton's *Principia*, With Notes on Motte's Translation," *Isis*, **54** (1963), 319–351; and *Introduction to Newton's 'Principia'* (Cambridge, Mass., 1971), 265–286; and the biographical sketch published by James Wilson as the preface to Pemberton's *Course of Chemistry*.

RICHARD S. WESTFALL

PÉRÈS, JOSEPH JEAN CAMILLE (*b.* Clermont-Ferrand, France, 31 October 1890; *d.* Paris, France, 12 February 1962)

The son and son-in-law of distinguished philosophers, Pérès entered the École Normale Supérieure in 1908, became *agrégé* in mathematics in 1911, and was immediately awarded a scholarship to enable him to earn a doctorate. Introduced by Émile Borel to Vito Volterra, he left for Italy to prepare his dissertation under the latter's supervision. He defended the dissertation *Sur les fonctions permutables de Volterra* in 1915, while teaching *mathématiques spéciales* at the *lycée* of Montpellier. After brief stays at the faculties of Toulouse and Strasbourg,

he was from 1921 to 1932 professor of rational and applied mechanics at Marseilles, where in 1930 he founded an institute of fluid mechanics. Called to the Sorbonne in 1932, he devoted his scientific efforts primarily to developing the field of fluid mechanics. But his personal qualities led to his being burdened with ever more numerous and demanding duties. He taught at all the *grandes écoles* and from 1954 to 1961 was dean of the Paris Faculty of Sciences during a difficult time of expansion and profound transformation. Moreover, he fulfilled extensive responsibilities in several major national and international research organizations, notably the Centre National de la Recherche Scientifique and the International Committee of Scientific Unions.

Pérès won prizes from the Académie des Sciences in 1932, 1938, and 1940 and was elected a member in 1942. He was a foreign member of the Accademia Nazionale dei Lincei, Accademia delle Scienze, and the National Academy of Sciences, as well as an active member of the Académie Internationale d'Histoire des Sciences from 1948. Pérès's positions and honors testify to his exceptionally fruitful life, devoted to the combination of teaching and research.

Volterra's initial influence on Pérès and their warm thirty-year friendship account to a large degree for the course of Pérès's research, which was at first oriented toward pure analysis and then toward mechanics. The events of his career simply accentuated a development the outlines of which were determined at the outset.

Pérès's results on integral equations extended those of Volterra, notably regarding composition products of permutable functions with a given function and, later, the composition of functions of arbitrary order. These findings are now considered classical, as is his theory of symbolic calculus, which is more general than Heaviside's. Work of this type in analysis harmonized with the needs of fluid mechanics. In the latter domain, which experienced great progress in France through Pérès's efforts, his work was linked in large part to that of other researchers. Aiming at various applications, especially in aeronautics, Pérès conducted studies on the dynamics of viscous fluids, on the theory of vortices, and on movements with slip streams while refining the method of electrical analogies. In constructing his "wing calculator," as well as analogous devices—for measuring the pressure of lapping waves on jetties, for example—Pérès remained in close contact with those testing the equipment. To his scientific colleagues he remained a circumspect theorist, animator, and promoter.

At the beginning of his career Pérès obtained two results, now bearing his name, that are not connected with the fields mentioned above. One concerned Levi-Civita parallelism (1919); the other, impact with friction (1924). In the second area he achieved one of the last great successes of rational mechanics. The gift for theoretical speculation manifested in these investigations remained the mainspring of his work and of his influence, and the fruitfulness of both is explained by his openness to new ideas.

BIBLIOGRAPHY

I. Original Works. Pérès's books include *Sur les fonctions permutables de Vito Volterra* (Paris, 1915), his diss.; *Leçons sur la composition et les fonctions permutables* (Paris, 1924); *Les sciences exactes* (Paris, 1930); *Cours dé mécanique des fluides* (Paris, 1936); *Tables numériques pour le calcul de la répartition des charges aérodynamiques suivant l'envergure d'une aile* (Paris, 1936), written with L. Malavard and L. Romani; *Théorie générale des fonctionnelles* (Paris, 1936); *Notice sur les titres et travaux scientifiques* (Paris, 1942), submitted with his candidacy to the Academy; and *Mécanique générale* (Paris, 1953).

Among his memoirs published in the *Comptes rendus* of the Academy are "Actions d'un fluide visqueux sur un obstacle," **188** (1929), 310–312, 440–441; "Sur le mouvement limite d'Oseen," **192** (1931), 210–212; "Sur les analogies électriques en hydrodynamique," **194** (1932), 1314–1316, written with L. Malavard; "Sur le calcul analogique des effets de torsion," **211** (1940), 131–133, written with L. Malavard; "Sur le calcul expérimental," *ibid.*, 275–277; and "Calcul symbolique d'Heaviside et calcul de composition de V. Volterra," **217** (1943), 517–520.

His other noteworthy works include the editing of *Leçons sur les fonctions de lignes de Vito Volterra* (Paris, 1913); "Le parallélisme de M. Levi-Civita et la courbure Riemannienne," in *Rendiconti. R. Accademia dei Lincei* (June 1919); "Choc avec frottement," in *Nouvelles annales de mathématiques*, **2** (1924); Pérès edited this journal, with R. Brocard and H. Villat, from 1923 to 1927; "Une application nouvelle des mathématiques à la biologie, la théorie des associations biologiques," in *Revue générale des sciences* (1927); and "Les divers aspects de la mécanique. Quelques notions concernant son enseignement," in *Mécanique*, no. 322 (Feb. 1944), 27-29.

II. Secondary Literature. On Pérès and his work, see the notices by P. Costabel, in *Archives internationales d'histoire des sciences*, **15** (1962), 137–140; H. Villat, in *Comptes rendus . . . de l'Académie des sciences*, **254** (1962); and M. Zamansky, in *Revue de l'enseignement supérieur*, no. 2 (1962), 95–97.

Pierre Costabel

PERSEUS (*fl.* third century B.C. [?])

Perseus is known only from two passages in Proclus. In one passage his name is associated with the investigation of "spiric" curves as that of Apollonius of Perga is with conics, Nicomedes with the conchoids, and Hippias of Elis with the quadratrices.[1] In the second passage, derived from Geminus, Proclus says that Perseus wrote an epigram upon his discovery, "Three lines upon five sections finding, Perseus made offering to the gods therefor."[2]

In another place Proclus says that a spiric surface is thought of as generated by the revolution of a circle standing upright and turning about a fixed point that is not its center; wherefore it comes about that there are three kinds of spiric surface according as the fixed point is on, inside, or outside the circumference.[3] The spiric surface is therefore what is known today as a "tore"; in antiquity Hero of Alexandria gave it the name "spire" or "ring."[4]

These passages throw no light on the provenance of Perseus and leave wide room for conjecture about his dates. He must have lived before Geminus, as Proclus relies on that author; and it is probable that the conic sections were well advanced before the spiric curves were tackled. Perseus therefore probably lived between Euclid and Geminus, say between 300 and 70 B.C., with a preference for the earlier date.

What Perseus actually discovered is also uncertain. In rather more precise language than that of Proclus, a spiric surface may be defined as the surface generated by a circle that revolves about a straight line (the axis of revolution) always remaining in a plane with it. There are three kinds of spiric surfaces, according as the axis of revolution is outside the circle, tangential to it, or inside it (which are called by Proclus the "open," "continuous," and "interlaced"; and by Hero the "open," "continuous," and "self-crossing").

A spiric section on the analogy of a conic section would be a section of a spiric surface by a plane, which it is natural to assume is parallel to the axis in the first place. Proclus says that the sections are three in number corresponding to the three types of surface, but this is difficult to understand or to reconcile with the epigram. G. V. Schiaparelli showed how three different spiric curves could be obtained by a section of an open tore according as the plane of section was more or less distant from the axis of revolution,[5] and Paul Tannery entered upon a closer mathematical analysis that led him to give a novel interpretation to the epigram.[6] If r is the radius of the generating circle, a the distance of its center from the axis, and d the distance of the cutting plane from the axis, in the case of the open tore (for which $a > r$), the following five cases may be distinguished:

$$a + r > d > a \qquad (1)$$
$$d = a \qquad (2)$$

$$a > d > a - r \qquad (3)$$
$$d = a - r \qquad (4)$$
$$a - r > d > 0 \qquad (5)$$

Of these the curve produced by (4) is Proclus' first spiric curve, the "hippopede" or "horse-fetter," which is like a figure eight and had already been used by Eudoxus in his representation of planetary motion; (1) is Proclus' second, broad in the middle; (3) is his third, narrow in the middle; (2) is a transition from (1) to (3); and (5) produces two symmetrical closed curves. If the tore is "continuous" ("closed" in modern terminology), $a = r$, the forms (1), (2), and (3) remain as for the "open" tore, but (4) and (5) disappear and there is no new curve. If the tore is "interlaced" ("reentrant"), $a < r$, and the forms (4) and (5) do not exist; but there are three new curves corresponding to (1), (2), and (3), each with an oval inside it.

Tannery deduced that what the epigram means is that Perseus found three spiric curves in addition to the five sections. In this deduction he has been followed by most subsequent writers, Loria even finding support in Dante.[7] Although the interpretation is not impossible, it puts a strain upon the Greek. It is simpler to suppose that Tannery has correctly identified the five sections, but that Perseus ignored (2) and (5) as not really giving new curves. Thus he found "three curves in five sections." If we suppose that he took one of his curves from the five sections of the "open" tore, one from the five sections of the "continuous," and one from the five sections of the "interlaced," we could reconcile Proclus' statement also, but it is simpler to suppose that Proclus, writing centuries later, made an error.

NOTES

1. Proclus, *In primum Euclidis*, G. Freidlein, ed. (Leipzig, 1873; repr. Hildesheim, 1967), p. 356.6–12.
2. *Ibid.*, pp. 111.23–112.2.
3. *Ibid.*, p. 119.9–13.
4. Heron, *Definitiones* 97, in J. L. Heiberg, ed., *Heronis Alexandrini opera quae supersunt omnia*, IV (Leipzig, 1912), pp. 60.24–62.9.
5. G. V. Schiaparelli, *Le sfere omocentriche di Eudosso, di Calippo e di Aristotele* (Milan, 1875), pp. 32–34.
6. Paul Tannery, *Mémoires scientifiques*, II (Toulouse–Paris, 1912), pp. 26–28.
7. Gino Loria, *Le scienze esatte nell'antica Grecia*, 2nd ed. (Milan, 1914), p. 417, n. 2.

BIBLIOGRAPHY

On Perseus or his works, see T. L. Heath, *The Thirteen Books of Euclid's Elements*, 2nd ed. (Cambridge, 1926; repr. New York, 1956), I, 162–164; *A History of Greek Mathematics*, II (Oxford, 1921), 203–206; G. V. Schiaparelli, *Le sfere omocentriche di Eudosso, di Calippo e di Aristotele* (Milan, 1875), 32–34; and Paul Tannery, "Pour l'histoire des lignes et de surfaces courbes dans l'antiquité," in *Bulletin des sciences mathématiques et astronomiques*, 2nd ser., **8** (Paris, 1884), 19–30; repr. in *Mémoires scientifiques*, **2** (Toulouse–Paris, 1912), 18–32.

IVOR BULMER-THOMAS

PETER PHILOMENA OF DACIA, also known as **Petrus Dacus, Petrus Danus, Peter Nightingale** (*fl.* 1290–1300)

Originally a canon of the cathedral in Roskilde, Denmark, Peter Nightingale first appears as the recipient of a letter from Hermann of Minden (provincial of the German Dominicans, 1286–1290) thanking him for the gift of some astronomical instruments and proposing to him that he leave Italy for Germany.[1] In 1291–1292 he is listed as a member of the University of Bologna,[2] where he taught mathematics and astronomy to pupils who included the astrologer Magister Romanus.[3] During 1292 Peter went to Paris, where in that and the following year he produced many writings. After that the sources are silent about him until 4 July 1303, when a letter from Pope Boniface VIII shows that he had returned to Denmark, in his former position as a canon of Roskilde.[4] The years of Peter's birth and death are unknown; and since he is not mentioned in the necrology of his cathedral, it is probable that he died abroad. Although he was a canon regular, he has often been considered a Dominican[5] and confused with the Swedish Dominican author of the same name. This mistake was corrected by H. Schück in 1895 but nevertheless persists in more recent literature.[6] His identification with another Petrus de Dacia, who in 1327 was rector of the University of Paris, has also been shown to be incorrect.[7]

A recent survey has revealed that there are more than 200 extant manuscripts of Peter's numerous works.[8] These can be divided into two groups, the first of which comprises the following writings:

Commentarius in Algorismum vulgarum (10 MSS). This commentary to Sacrobosco's well-known textbook of arithmetic was completed on 31 July 1291 at Bologna and is the only work of Peter Nightingale that has been edited and printed.[9] It contains some original contributions, notably a new and better method of extracting cube roots.[10]

Tabula multiplicationis (2 MSS). A multiplication table in the sexagesimal system and, accordingly, destined for use by astronomers.

Declaratio super Compotum (2 MSS). A commentary on the twelfth-century *Compotus metricus manualis* of

Gerlandus of Besançon. It has not yet been examined.

Kalendarium with *canones* (56 MSS). This calendar for the period 1292–1369 was computed in Paris as a substitute for the much-used calendar of Robert Grosseteste, which had run out.[11] The appended *canones* give rules for adjusting the calendar for a new seventy-six-year period. Such adjustments were made in 1369 and around 1442. This calendar was intended to give more precise times of the phases of the moon than Grosseteste's work, with which it has often been confused.[12]

Tractatus eclipsorii (2 MSS). This newly found treatise describes the construction and use of a volvelle or equatorium for determining eclipses. It was written in Paris but contains a reference to Roskilde and is presumably the first evidence of Peter's interest in devising astronomical computers. It is followed by:

Tabulae coniunctionum solis et lune, that is, a table of mean conjunctions of the sun and moon;

Tabula temporis diurni, a table giving the length of the day as a function of the declination of the sun, calculated for the middle of the seventh climate (approximately the latitude of Paris);

Tabula diversitatis aspectuum lune ad solem, a table of the lunar parallax in longitude and latitude, for the same latitude as the preceding table, and meant to be used in connection with the *Tractatus eclipsorii*; and

Tabula equacionis dierum, a table of the equation of time as a function of the longitude of the sun.

Tabula lune with *canones* (68 MSS). This was Peter's most popular work. It exists in two versions: a numerical table and a diagram by which the approximate positions of the moon can be rapidly found from its age and the months of the year.

Tabula planetarum with *canones* (8 MSS). A diagram showing the governing planet for each day of the week and each hour of the day.

All the above works are well-authenticated writings by Peter Nightingale, but it is more difficult to ascertain the authorship of the treatises of the second group:

Tractatus de semissis (10 MSS). A long treatise on the construction and use of an equatorium for calculating planetary longitudes, written in Paris in 1293. No specimen of this instrument has survived, but a modern reconstruction based on the text was published in 1967.[13]

Tractatus novi quadrantis (18 MSS). This work was written in 1293 in Paris and describes the "new quadrant" invented some years earlier by Jacob ben Māḥir ibn Tibbon (Profatius Judaeus).[14] Peter's text seems to be a translation from the Hebrew original, provided with a careful introduction explaining the construction of this curious device, in which the

astrolabe is transformed into a quadrant. It is not yet clear whether the other later Latin version dating from 1299 and attributed to Armengoud of Montpellier has anything to do with Peter's treatise.

Tractatus eclipsis solis et lune (1 MS). This is a brief treatise on how the problem of computing eclipses can be solved by geometrical construction.

In many manuscripts the three writings of the second group are attributed to a Petrus de Sancto Audomaro, or Peter of St.-Omer. But two manuscripts of the *Tractatus de semissis* are stated to be by Petrus Danus of St. Audomaro, while another simply calls the author Petrus Danus. Internal evidence and a comparison of astronomical parameters prove the three texts to be works by the same author, who accordingly must have been a very competent astronomer working in Paris at exactly the same time as Peter Nightingale. The latter is a definitely historical person, while it has been impossible to find any other records of the former in contemporary sources. Therefore, there are good reasons to agree with the hypothesis, proposed by E. Zinner in 1932, that the two authors are identical. In that case all the works mentioned above must be attributed to Peter Nightingale, whose possible connection with St.-Omer remains to be explained.

Apart from his works in pure mathematics, Peter Nightingale made two important contributions to medieval science. One was his work on astronomical computing instruments, for which he occupies a very important position in the history of astronomical computing machines. He was not the first Latin writer in this field, which in the later Middle Ages increasingly attracted the attention of astronomers. About 1260 the Paris astronomer Campanus of Novara had constructed a set of six equatoria for calculating longitudes.[15] Peter, however, was the first to invent a computer that solved this problem for all the planets with a single instrument. This device reduced the number of graduated circles and facilitated the construction of the instrument, the main principle of which was later adopted by John of Lignères and Chaucer.[16] The *Tractatus de semissis* also contains Peter's efforts to correct traditional astronomical parameters by new observations.

Peter's second achievement was in the field of astronomical tables, in which his calendar remained in constant use for 150 years. This calendar had the peculiar feature that for each day of the year it listed both the declination of the sun and the length of the day. The same features are found in a contemporary calendar by the Paris astronomer Guillaume de St.-Cloud, who seems to have collaborated with Peter Nightingale during the latter's sojourn in Paris.[17] The prehistory of this calendar was put into perspective by

A. Otto, who in 1933 drew attention to a passage in the partly extant *Liber daticus* of Roskilde cathedral. It appears that in 1274 an unnamed astronomer belonging to the chapter made a series of observations, unique for his time, of the altitude of the sun at noon, from which he calculated the length of the day by a *kardagas sinuum* (a trigonometrical diagram replacing a sine table).[18] Both the altitude and the length of the day were tabulated in the now lost calendar of the cathedral. In this respect the Roskilde calendar may be considered the prototype of the calendar calculated by Peter Nightingale in Paris. This is not to say that he was identical with the unknown Roskilde astronomer of 1274; but there is no doubt that it was he who brought the principle from Denmark to France, thus creating a hitherto unknown link between Scandinavian astronomy and European science in general.

NOTES

1. Published in Paul Lehmann, "Skandinaviens Anteil an der lateinischen Literatur und Wissenschaft des Mittelalters," in *Sitzungsberichte der Bayerischen Akademie der Wissenschaften zu München*, Phil.-hist. Abt. (1936), 53–54.
2. Ellen Jørgensen, "Om nogle middelalderlige forfattere der naevnes som hjemmehørende i Dacia," in *Historisk tidsskrift*, 8th ser., 3 (1910–1912), 253–260.
3. Lynn Thorndike, *History of Magic and Experimental Science*, III (New York, 1934), 647–649.
4. A. Krarup, in *Bullarium danicum*, no. 947 (1932), 834–835.
5. J. Quétif and J. Echard, *Scriptores ordinis Praedicatorum*, II (Paris, 1721).
6. H. Schück, *Illustrerad Svensk literaturhistoria*, I (Stockholm, 1895), 343; G. Sarton, *Introduction to the History of Science*, II (Baltimore, 1931), 996–997.
7. C. E. Bulaeus, *Historia Universitatis Parisiensis*, II (Paris, 1668), 210, 982; cf. H. Denifle and A. Chatelain, *Chartularium Universitatis Parisiensis*, II (Paris, 1891), nos. 863, 955.
8. This survey, by Olaf Pedersen, is not yet completed. It supersedes previous inventories by G. Eneström, "Anteckningar om matematikern Petrus de Dacia och hans skrifter," in *Öfversigt af K. Vetenskapsakademiens förhandlingar* (1885), 15–27, 65–70, and (1886), 57–60; and E. Zinner, *Verzeichnis der astronomischen Handschriften des deutschen Kulturgebietes* (Munich, 1925), nos. 2055–2082.
9. Maximilian Curtze, *Petri Philomeni de Dacia in Algorismum vulgarem Johannis de Sacrobosco commentarius una cum algorismo ipso* (Copenhagen, 1897).
10. G. Eneström, "Über die Geschichte der Kubikwurzelausziehung im Mittelalter," in *Bibliotheca mathematica*, 3rd ser., 14 (1914), 83–84; cf. M. Cantor, *Geschichte der Mathematik*, 2nd ed., II (Leipzig, 1899–1900), 90.
11. E. Zinner, "Petrus de Dacia, en middelalderlig dansk astronom," in *Nordisk astronomisk tidsskrift*, 13 (1932), 136–146; German trans. in *Archeion*, 18 (1936), 318–329.
12. First by J. Langebek, in *Scriptores rerum Danicarum*, IV (Copenhagen, 1786), 260 f., where Grosseteste's calendar was edited and attributed to Petrus de Dacia.
13. O. Pedersen, "The Life and Work of Peter Nightingale," in *Vistas in Astronomy*, 9 (1967), 3–10; cf. O. Pedersen, "Peder Nattergal og hans astronomiske regneinstrument," in *Nordisk astronomisk tidsskrift*, 44 (1963), 37–50.

14. This text has been edited in an unpublished thesis by Lydik Garm, "Profatius Judaeus' traktat om kvadranten" (Aarhus, Institute for the History of Science, 1966).
15. F. J. Benjamin and G. J. Toomer, *Campanus of Novara and Medieval Planetary Theory* (Madison, Wis., 1971).
16. D. J. de Solla Price, *The Equatorie of the Planetis* (Cambridge, 1955), 17 f. (Chaucer) and 188 f. (John of Lignères).
17. P. Duhem, *Le système du monde*, new ed., IV (Paris, 1954), 14 f.; cf. Zinner, *loc. cit.*
18. A. Otto, *Liber daticus Roskildensis* (Copenhagen, 1933), 32–33. The importance of the Roskilde astronomer was first pointed out by A. A. Bjørnbo, "Die mathematischen S. Marco-Handschriften in Florenz," in *Bibliotheca mathematica*, 3rd ser., 12 (1912), 116.

OLAF PEDERSEN

PETERSEN, JULIUS (*b.* Sorø, Denmark, 16 June 1839; *d.* Copenhagen, Denmark, 5 August 1910)

Petersen's interest in mathematics was awakened at school, where his main occupation was solving problems and attempting the trisection of the angle. At the age of seventeen he entered the College of Technology in Copenhagen; but after some years of study he transferred to the University of Copenhagen, from which he graduated in 1866 and received the doctorate in 1871. His dissertation treated equations solvable by square roots with applications to the solution of problems by ruler and compass. During his university years and after graduation Petersen taught in secondary schools. In 1871 he was appointed docent at the College of Technology and, in 1887, professor at the University of Copenhagen, a post he held until the year before his death.

Through his terse, well-written textbooks Petersen has exerted a very strong influence on mathematical education in Denmark. Several of his books were translated into other languages. Worthy of particular mention is his *Methods and Theories for the Solution of Problems of Geometrical Constructions* (Danish, 1866; English, 1879; German, 1879; French, 1880; Italian, 1881; Russian, 1892). His other writings cover a wide range of subjects in algebra, number theory, analysis, geometry, and mechanics. Perhaps his most important contribution is his theory of regular graphs, inspired by a problem in the theory of invariants and published in *Acta mathematica* in 1891.

BIBLIOGRAPHY

Petersen's works are listed in Niels Nielsen, *Matematiken i Danmark 1801–1908* (Copenhagen–Christiania, 1910).

There are obituaries by H. G. Zeuthen, in *Oversigt over det K. Danske Videnskabernes Selskabs Forhandlinger 1910* (1910–1911), I, 73–75; C. Juel and V. Trier, in *Nyt Tidsskrift for Matematik*, A, 21 (1910), 73–77, in

Danish; and C. Juel, "En dansk Matematiker," in *Matematisk Tidsskrift*, A (1923), 85–95.

BØRGE JESSEN

PETERSON, KARL MIKHAILOVICH (*b.* Riga, Russia [now Latvian S.S.R.], 25 May 1828; *d.* Moscow, Russia, 19 April 1881)

Peterson was the son of a Latvian worker, a former serf named Mikhail Peterson, and his wife, Maria Mangelson. In 1847 he graduated from the Riga Gymnasium and enrolled at the University of Dorpat. The lectures of his scientific tutor Ferdinand Minding provided an occasion for Peterson's writing his thesis "Über die Biegung der Flächen" (1853), for which he received the degree of bachelor of mathematics.

Later Peterson moved to Moscow where he worked first as a private teacher then, from 1865 until his death, as a mathematics teacher at the German Peter and Paul School. Becoming intimately acquainted with scientists close to N. D. Brashman and A. Y. Davidov, Peterson took an active part in the organization of the Moscow Mathematical Society and in its work. He published almost all of his writings in *Matematicheskii sbornik*, issued by the society.

In 1879 the Novorossiiskii University of Odessa awarded Peterson an honorary doctorate in pure mathematics for his studies on the theory of characteristics of partial differential equations, in which, by means of a uniform general method, he deduced nearly all the devices known at that time for finding general solutions of different classes of equations. These studies were to a certain extent close to the works of Davidov (1866) and N. Y. Sonin (1874). However, Peterson's principal discoveries are connected with differential geometry.

In the first part of his thesis Peterson established certain new properties of curves on surfaces and in the second part he continued Gauss's and Minding's works on the bending of surfaces. Here he for the first time obtained equations equivalent to three fundamental equations of Mainardi (1856) and Codazzi (1867–1869), which involve six coefficients of the first and the second quadratic differential forms of a surface. Peterson also proved—in different expression—the theorem usually bearing the name of Bonnet (1867): the geometrical form of the surface is wholly determined if the coefficients of both quadratic forms are given. Minding found the thesis excellent, but these results were not published during Peterson's lifetime and found no development in his articles which were printed after 1866. Brief information on Peterson's thesis was first given by P. Stäckel in 1901; a complete Russian translation of the manuscript, written in German and preserved in the archives of the University of Tartu, was published in 1952.

In his works Peterson elaborated new methods in the differential geometry of surfaces. Thus, he introduced the notion of bending on a principal basis, namely, bending under which a certain conjugate congruence of curves on the surface remains conjugate; such congruence is called the principal basis of a surface. Peterson established numerous general properties of conjugate congruences and studied in depth the bending on a principal basis of surfaces of second order, surfaces of revolution, minimal and translation surfaces. All these surfaces and some others constitute a class of surfaces, quite interesting in its properties, named after Peterson.

Although Peterson did not teach at the university, his ideas initiated the studies of B. K. Mlodzeevsky and, later, of his disciples Egorov, S. P. Finikov, and S. S. Bushgens. Peterson's discoveries also found a somewhat belated reputation and extension in other countries, for example, in the works of Darboux and Bianchi. Outside the Soviet Union, however, his remarkable studies on the theory of surfaces are still mentioned but rarely in the literature on the history of mathematics.

BIBLIOGRAPHY

I. ORIGINAL WORKS. Peterson's writings include "Ob otnosheniakh i srodstvakh mezhdu krivymi poverkhnostyami" ("On Relationships and Kinships Between Surfaces"), in *Matematicheskii sbornik*, **1** (1866), 391–438; "O krivykh na poverkhnostiakh" ("On Curves on Surfaces"), *ibid.*, **2** (1867), 17–44; *Über Kurven und Flächen* (Moscow–Leipzig, 1868); "Ob integrirovanii uravnenii s chastnymi proizvodnymi" ("On the Integration of Partial Differential Equations"), in *Matematicheskii sbornik*, **8** (1877), 291–361; **9** (1878), 137–192; **10** (1882), 169–223; and *Ob integrirovanii uravnenii s chastnymi proizvodnymi po dvum nezavisimym peremennym* ("On the Integration of Partial Differential Equations With Two Independent Variables"; Moscow, 1878). For a French trans. of Peterson's works, see *Annales de la Faculté des sciences de l'Université de Toulouse*, 2nd ser., **7** (1905), 5–263. See also "Ob izgibanii poverkhnostei" ("On the Bending of Surfaces"), his dissertation, in *Istoriko-matematicheskie issledovaniya*, **5** (1952), 87–112, with commentary by S. D. Rossinsky, pp. 113–133.

II. SECONDARY LITERATURE. On Peterson and his work, see (listed chronologically) P. Stäckel, "Karl Peterson," in *Bibliotheca mathematica*, 3rd ser., **2** (1901), 122–132;

B. K. Mlodzeevsky, "Karl Mikhailovich Peterson i ego geometricheskie raboty" ("Karl Mikhailovich Peterson and His Geometrical Works"), in *Matematicheskii sbornik*, **24** (1903), 1–21; D. F. Egorov, "Raboty K. M. Petersona po teorii uravnenii s chastnymi proizvodnymi" ("Peterson's Works on Partial Differential Equations"), *ibid.*, 22–29—the last two appear in French trans. in *Annales de la Faculté des sciences de l'Université de Toulouse*, 2nd ser., **5** (1903), 459–479; D. J. Struik, "Outline of a History of Differential Geometry," in *Isis*, **19** (1933), 92–120; **20** (1933), 161–191; S. D. Rossinsky, "Karl Mikhailovich Peterson," in *Uspekhi matematicheskikh nauk*, **4**, no. 5 (1949), 3–13; I. Y. Depman, "Karl Mikhailovich Peterson i ego kandidatskaya dissertatsia" ("Peterson and His Candidature Dissertation"), in *Istoriko-matematicheskie issledovaniya*, **5** (1952), 134–164; I. Z. Shtokalo, ed., *Istoria otechestvennoy matematiki* ("History of Native Mathematics"), II (Kiev, 1967); and A. P. Youschkevitch, *Istoria matematiki v Rossii do 1917 goda* ("A History of Mathematics in Russia to 1917"; Moscow, 1968).

A. P. YOUSCHKEVITCH
A. T. GRIGORIAN

PETROVSKY, IVAN GEORGIEVICH (*b.* Sevsk, Orlov guberniya, Russia, 18 January 1901; *d.* Moscow, U.S.S.R., 15 January 1973)

Petrovsky's major works dealt with the theory of partial differential equations, the topology of algebraic curves and surfaces, and the theory of probability. After graduating from the technical high school in Sevsk in 1917, he worked in various Soviet institutions until 1922, when he entered Moscow University. He graduated from the division of physics and mathematics in 1927 and remained at Moscow until 1930 as a graduate student of D. F. Egorov.

From 1929 to 1933 Petrovsky was assistant professor and *dozent* at Moscow. In 1933 he became professor and, in 1935, doctor of physical-mathematical sciences. From 1951 he was head of the department of differential equations. During World War II he was dean of the faculty of mechanics and mathematics; and from 1951 until his death he was rector of the university.

Petrovsky combined his work at the university with activity at various scientific and teaching institutions. From 1943 he worked at the V. A. Steklov Institute of Mathematics at the Academy of Sciences, of which he was vice-director from 1947 to 1949. For many years he was editor-in-chief of *Matematicheskii sbornik*.

In 1943 Petrovsky was elected corresponding member and, in 1946, full member of the Soviet Academy of Sciences. From 1949 to 1951 he was academician-secretary of the division of physical and mathematical sciences of the Academy, and from 1953 until his death he was a member of the Presidium of the Academy. He was twice awarded the State Prize of the U.S.S.R., and he received the title of Hero of Socialist Labor. He was also a member of the Soviet Committee for the Defense of Peace and vice-president of the Institute of Soviet-American Relations.

Petrovsky's first research dealt with the investigation of the Dirichlet problem for Laplace's equation (1928) and the theory of functions of a real variable (1929). In the early 1930's he began research on the topology of algebraic curves and surfaces in which he achieved fundamental results and methods. In 1933 he proved Hilbert's hypothesis that a curve of the sixth order cannot consist of eleven ovals lying outside each other. The method that Petrovsky devised for this proof was useful in solving the more general problem of embedding components of algebraic curves of any order in a projective plane. In 1949 he generalized certain of his results to include algebraic surfaces in *n*-dimensional space.

The results of Petrovsky's work (1934) on the solvability of the first boundary-value problem for the heat equation were widely applied in the theory of probability, especially in research connected with the Khinchin-Kolmogorov law of the iterated logarithm. Petrovsky's article on the theory of random processes (1934) considerably influenced an investigation of limit laws for the sum of a large number of random variables with the aid of the transition to random processes with continuous time. The work also contains the so-called method of upper and lower sums, which became the basic analytical method of research in the field.

A second work, also published in 1934, examined the behavior, near the origin of the coordinates of integral curves, of a system of equations of the form

$$\frac{dx_i}{dt} = \sum_{k=1}^{n} \alpha_{ik} x_k + \phi_i(x_1, \cdots, x_n).$$

This work was, essentially, the first full investigation of a neighborhood of a singular point in the three-dimensional case.

In 1937–1938 Petrovsky distinguished and studied classes of systems of partial differential equations, which he first identified as either elliptical, hyperbolic, or parabolic. In 1937 he published his proof that the Cauchy problem for nonlinear systems of differential equations, which Petrovsky called hyperbolic, is well-posed. In a work on the Cauchy problem for systems of linear partial differential equations in nonanalytic functions (1938) Petrovsky studied systems for which the Cauchy problem is uniformly well-posed relative to the variation of the surface, for which the original data are given. Petrovsky introduced the concept of parabolic systems and investigated the problem of the analyticity of the solution of such systems in space dimensions. In 1937 he introduced his famous notion of elliptical systems and showed that when the functions are analytic, all sufficiently smooth solutions will be analytic, thereby giving a more complete solution of Hilbert's nineteenth problem. Petrovsky's results were the starting point for numerous investigations, including those of J. Leray and L. Gårding; and they determined the basic direction of the development of the theory of systems of partial differential equations.

In widely known works on the qualitative theory theory of hyperbolic equations (1943–1945) Petrovsky introduced the concept of lacunae and obtained necessary and sufficient conditions for the existence of stable lacunae for uniform hyperbolic equations with constant coefficients. He also solved completely the question of lacunae for linear hyperbolic systems with variable coefficients in the case of two independent variables.

In 1945 Petrovsky investigated the extent of the discontinuitites of the derivatives of the displacements on the surface of a nonuniform elastic body that is free from the influence of external forces; and in 1954 he examined the character of lines and surfaces of a discontinuity of solutions of the wave equations.

Many well-known specialists in the theory of differential equations were students of Petrovsky, whose seminar (the Petrovsky seminar) is a leading center for the study of the theory of partial differential equations. His course texts are widely known.

BIBLIOGRAPHY

I. ORIGINAL WORKS. Petrovsky's major works are "Über das Irrfahrtproblem," in *Mathematische Annalen*, **109** (1934), 425–444; "Ueber das Verhalten der Integralcurven eines Systemes gewöhnlicher Differentialgleichungen in der Nahe lines singularen Punktes," in *Matematicheskii sbornik*, **41** (1934), 107–156; "Zur ersten Randwertaufgabe der Warmeleitungsgleichung," in *Compositia Mathematica*, **1** (1935), 383–419; "Über das Cauchysche Problem für Systeme von partiellen Differentialgleichungen," in *Matematicheskii sbornik*, **2** (1937), 815–870; "On the Topology of Real Plane Algebraic Curves," in *Annals of Mathematics*, **39**, no. 1 (1938), 197–209; "Sur l'analyticité des solutions des systèmes d'équations différentielles," in *Matematicheskii sbornik*, **5** (1939), 3–70; *Lektsii po teorii obyknovennykh differentsialnykh uravneny* ("Lectures on the Theory of Ordinary Differential Equations"; Moscow–Leningrad, 1939); "On

the Diffusion of Waves and the Lacunas for Hyperbolic Equations," in *Matematicheskii sbornik*, **17** (1945), 289–370; *Lektsii po teorii integralnykh uravneny* (Moscow–Leningrad, 1948), trans. into German as *Vorlesungen über die Theorie der Integralgleichungen* (Würzburg, 1953); and *Lektsii ob uravneniakh s chastnymi proizvodnymi* (Moscow–Leningrad, 1948), trans. into English as *Lectures in Partial Differential Equations* (New York, 1954) and into German as *Vorlesungen über partielle Differentialgleichungen* (Leipzig, 1955).

II. SECONDARY LITERATURE. On Petrovsky's work and its influence, see P. S. Aleksandrov *et al.*, "Ivan Georgievich Petrovsky," in *Uspekhi matematicheskikh nauk*, **26**, no. 2 (1971), 3–22, with bibliography, pp. 22–24; *Matematika v SSSR za 40 let* ("Mathematics in the U.S.S.R. for the Last Forty Years"), II (Moscow, 1959), 538–540, for a bibliography of 51 of his publications; and *Matematika v SSSR za 50 let* ("Mathematics in the U. S. S. R. for the Last Fifty Years"), II, pt. 2 (Moscow, 1970), 1035.

S. DEMIDOV

PEURBACH (or **PEUERBACH**), **GEORG** (*b.* Peuerbach, Austria, 30 May 1423; *d.* Vienna, Austria, 8 April 1461)

Georg Peurbach, the son of Ulrich, was born in Upper Austria, about forty kilometers west of Linz. Nothing is known of his early life. He matriculated for the baccalaureate at the University of Vienna in 1446 as Georgius Aunpekh de Pewrbach and received the bachelor's degree in the Arts Faculty on 2 January 1448. Two years later he probably became a licentiate, and on 28 February 1453 he received the master's degree and was enrolled in the Arts Faculty. The last notable astronomer at Vienna, John of Gmunden, had died in 1442, prior to Peurbach's arrival, so it is not clear with whom he studied – if, indeed, he did formally study astronomy at the university. It is possible that he had access to astronomical books and instruments collected by John of Gmunden.

At some time during the period 1448–1453 Peurbach traveled through Germany, France, and Italy. Regiomontanus, in a lecture on the progress and utility of the mathematical sciences delivered at Padua in 1464 (printed with the treatises of al-Farghānī and al-Battānī [Nuremburg, 1537]), says that many in his audience must have heard Peurbach lecture on astronomy in that city. Peurbach also lectured in Ferrara and is said to have been offered positions at Bologna and Padua. It is also said that in Ferrara he made the acquaintance of Giovanni Bianchini, the most noted Italian astronomer of the period, who attempted to persuade him to accept a position at an Italian university. He may have met Nicholas Cusa in Rome at this time and certainly came to know him in later years, since Cusa sent an inscribed copy of his *De quadratura circuli* to Peurbach, who proceeded to point out its errors to Regiomontanus. At any rate, Peurbach seems already to have acquired an international reputation at the time of his Italian sojourn, although, as far as is known, he had written nothing.

After his return to Vienna, Peurbach engaged during the period 1453–1456 in a correspondence (published by Albin Czerny) with Johann Nihil of Bohemia, the court astrologer to Emperor Frederick III in Wiener Neustadt. Ten letters, only two from Peurbach, survive as a result of their inclusion in a collection of specimen letters appended to a treatise on letter writing. On Nihil's advice, Peurbach accepted the position, at a salary of 24 pounds, of court astrologer to King Ladislaus V of Hungary, the young nephew of Frederick. At some later time, perhaps after the death of Ladislaus in 1457, Peurbach became court astrologer to the emperor, since Regiomontanus refers to him as *astronomus caesaris* in the dedication of the *Epitome of the Almagest* and cites his service to Frederick in the lecture given at Padua.

While Peurbach's court appointments were made for his abilities in astronomy and astrology, his responsibilities at the university, to judge by the admittedly scanty evidence, were concerned mostly with humanistic studies. In 1454 and 1460 he lectured on the *Aeneid*, in 1456 on Juvenal, in 1457 possibly on the *Rhetorica ad Herennium*, and in 1458 possibly on Horace. In 1458 he also participated in a disputation, *De arte oratoria sive poetica*, which survives (Munich, Clm 19806, fols. 193–199), as does a treatise from 1458 on letter writing (Clm 18802, fols. 86–97) attributed to Peurbach (written under a pseudonym). A number of undistinguished Latin poems by Peurbach are also known (Vienna, Vin 352, fols. 67a–69b).

Peurbach's student and associate Johannes Müller von Königsberg, known as Regiomontanus, matriculated in the arts faculty at Vienna on 14 April 1450 at the age of thirteen, and received his bachelor's degree on 16 January 1452. His collaboration with Peurbach, to whom he later referred as "my teacher," probably began after Peurbach received his master's degree. Peurbach's own works seem to date from 1454 and later, and a number of them were copied by Regiomontanus in a notebook (Vin 5203) that he kept at Vienna during 1454–1462. The notebook begins with Peurbach's *Theoricae novae planetarum*, completed 30

August 1454, and contains a number of Peurbach's shorter works written during the 1450's. Peurbach says in a letter of 1456 to Nihil (Czerny, 302) that he and Regiomontanus are both calculating ephemerides from Bianchini's tables, checking discrepancies in their calculations by recomputing with the Alphonsine Tables. Both observed Halley's Comet in June 1456; Peurbach mentioned it in a letter to Nihil (Czerny, 298–299) and wrote an astronomical and astrological report on the comet that was not discovered and published until the twentieth century. In June 1457 Peurbach observed another comet; and on 3 September he and Regiomontanus observed a lunar eclipse, finding the observed time of mideclipse to be eight minutes earlier than predicted by the Alphonsine Tables. Evidently Peurbach had not yet completed his own *Eclipse Tables*. In 1460 they observed lunar eclipses on 3 July and 27/28 December, this time comparing the observations with Peurbach's tables, which probably were completed in 1459. These eclipse observations were first published by Johann Schöner (Nuremberg, 1544). Peurbach carried out observations leading to the determination of the latitude 48;22° (correct, 48;13°) for Vienna; and Peurbach and Regiomontanus together found, through some series of observations, an obliquity of the ecliptic of 23;28°.

On 5 May 1460 Johannes Bessarion, archbishop of Nicaea and a cardinal since 1439, arrived in Vienna as legate of Pius II. His mission was to intervene in the continuing dispute between Frederick III and his brother Albert VI of Styria and to seek aid in a planned crusade against the Turks for the recapture of Constantinople. In Vienna he met both Peurbach and Regiomontanus. Bessarion was a figure of considerable importance in the transmission of Greek learning to Italy, and his interests were sufficiently diverse to include the exact sciences. He collected a large number of very fine Greek manuscripts that he later left to the city of Venice, where they form the core of the manuscript collection of the Biblioteca Marciana. One of his plans evidently involved a new translation of the *Almagest* from the Greek to replace Gerard of Cremona's version from the Arabic and to improve upon the inferior translation from the Greek made by George of Trebizond in 1451. He also desired an abridgment of the *Almagest* to use as a textbook. Although Peurbach was unfamiliar with Greek, according to Regiomontanus he knew the *Almagest* almost by heart (*quem ille quasi ad litteram memorie tenebat*) and so took on the task of preparing the abridgment. Further plans were made for Peurbach and Regiomontanus to accompany Bessarion to Italy and there work with him, using Bessarion's Greek manuscripts as the basis of the new translation. Peurbach, however, had completed only the first six books of the abridgment when he died, not yet thirty-eight years old. On his deathbed he made Regiomontanus promise to complete the work, which the latter did in Italy during the next year or two. This account is given by Regiomontanus in his preface to the *Epitome of the Almagest*. The completed work was dedicated to Bessarion by Regiomontanus, probably in 1463, in a very careful and beautifully executed copy (Venice, lat. 328, fols. 1–117).

Peurbach's early death was a serious loss to the progress of astronomy, if for no other reason than that the collaboration with his even more capable and industrious pupil Regiomontanus promised a greater quantity of valuable work than either could accomplish separately. Of their contemporaries, only Bianchini, who was considerably their senior, possessed a comparable proficiency and originality. The equally early death of Regiomontanus in 1476 left the technical development of mathematical astronomy deprived of substantial improvement until the generation of Tycho Brahe.

No systematic effort has been made to collect or enumerate Peurbach's works and the manuscripts containing them, so any catalog is necessarily tentative, in that it probably includes some spurious works and omits some genuine writings that have not yet been located or properly identified. A list was given by Georg Tannstetter Collimitius in the catalog of distinguished mathematicians associated with the University of Vienna that he wrote as an introduction to his 1514 edition of Peurbach's *Tabulae eclipsium* and Regiomontanus' *Tabula primi mobilis*. Tannstetter's list, which was based upon manuscripts collected near the end of the fifteenth century by his teacher Andreas Stiborius Boius (Andreas Stöberl), appears to be generally— and possibly completely—reliable. The works discussed below are listed by Tannstetter, supplemented by some later discoveries. Where manuscripts or printed editions of a given work are known, some, but not all, are listed here. A more extensive list of manuscripts can be found in E. Zinner's *Verzeichnis* (nos. 7691–7761), and some additional manuscripts and printed editions can be found in the text and notes of Zinner's *Regiomontanus*.

Theoricae novae planetarum is an elementary but thorough textbook of planetary theory written by Peurbach to replace the old, and exceedingly careless, so-called *Theorica planetarum Gerardi*, a standard text written probably in the second half of the thirteenth century. The original version of the *Theoricae novae*, completed in 1454 (e.g. Vin 5203, fols. 2a–24a), contained sections on the sun, moon, superior planets, Venus, Mercury, characteristic phenomena and eclipses, theory of latitude, and the motion of the eighth sphere according to the Alphonsine Tables. Peurbach later enlarged the work (e.g. Florence, Magl. XI, 144, fols. 1a–15b) by adding a section on Thābit ibn Qurra's theory of trepidation. Regiomontanus brought out the first printed edition (Nuremberg, *ca.* 1474). Zinner reports no fewer than fifty-six editions through the middle of the seventeenth century; there are also a substantial number of manuscript copies, mostly from the late fifteenth century. A number of printings from the 1480's and 1490's in small quartos (e.g. 1482, 1485, 1488, 1490, 1491), also containing Sacrobosco's *De sphaera* and Regiomontanus' *Disputationes contra Cremonensia in planetarum theoricas deliramenta*, seem to represent the standard school edition and common text, which is generally sound. The colored figures in these editions are copied from Regiomontanus' printing, while contemporary manuscripts contain figures of greater diversity and complexity. The diagrams are of considerable importance, since parts of Peurbach's text would be unintelligible without them.

The *Theoricae novae* contains very careful and detailed descriptions of solid sphere representations of Ptolemaic planetary models that Peurbach based either upon Ibn al-Haytham's description of identical models in his *On the Configuration of the World* (translated into Latin in the late thirteenth century) or upon some later intermediary work. Peurbach's book was of great importance because his models remained the canonical physical description of the structure of the heavens until Tycho disproved the existence of solid spheres. Even Copernicus was to a large extent still under their influence, and the original motivation for his planetary theory was apparently to correct a number of physical impossibilities in Peurbach's models relating to nonuniform rotation of solid spheres.

Since the *Theoricae novae* was intended as an elementary work, much of it is devoted to definitions of technical terms; along with the *Epitome* it helped to establish the technical terminology of astronomy through the early seventeenth century. As the standard textbook of planetary theory, it was the subject of numerous commentaries (see Zinner, *Verzeichnis*, nos. 7700–7714). There were printed commentaries by Albert of Brudzewo (1495), Joannes Baptista [or Franciscus] Capuan (1495, 1499, 1503, 1508, 1513, 1518), Erasmus Reinhold (1542, 1553), Oswald Schreckenfuchs (1556), Pedro Nuñez Salaciense (1566, 1573), and others. The most interesting are those by Reinhold and Nuñez. The *Theoricae novae* was translated into French, Italian, and Hebrew; there are no modern editions or translations.

Possibly related to the *Theoricae novae* is a short work (Vin 5203, fols. 88a–92a) called *Speculum planetarum*, on the making of manuscript equatoria with revolving disks of paper.

Recognized throughout the sixteenth century as a monument of industry, the *Tabulae eclipsium*, completed probably in 1459, is Peurbach's most impressive work and was still used (although critically) by Tycho near the end of the sixteenth century. There are a substantial number of manuscript copies (especially Venice, lat. 342, and Nuremberg, Cent. V 57, fols. 10a–19b and 108a–153b, both copied by Regiomontanus), and the work was printed very beautifully in a version edited by Tannstetter (Vienna, 1514). The tables are based entirely on the Alphonsine Tables, in that the underlying parameters are exclusively Alphonsine; but Peurbach expanded and rearranged the tables needed for every step in eclipse computation, saving the calculator much time and relieving him of a number of tedious procedures. The tables in the printed version run to fully 100 pages; and earlier manuscripts, which tend to squeeze more on a page, have over ninety pages of closely written digits. Most remarkable, and evidently most laborious to compute, are the forty-eight-page double-entry tables (solar and lunar anomaly) of time between mean and true conjunction or opposition and the twelve-page triple-entry tables (solar longitude, lunar anomaly, time from noon) of the difference of lunar and solar parallax in longitude and latitude for the sixth and seventh climates (latitudes about $45°–49°$) that are used to find the time and location of apparent conjunction in solar eclipses.

The tables exist in two forms. Originally they were computed for the meridian of Vienna, and this, with some minor alterations in the instructions, was the version later printed; but a number of manuscripts (such as Vin 5291, fols. 100a–163a) contain a version with the epoch positions shifted 0;30 hours (error for 0;22 hours) to the east to adapt the tables to the meridian of Grosswardein (now Oradea, Hungary). In this version they were dedicated to Johann Vitez, the bishop

of Grosswardein, and were known as the *Tabulae Waradienses*.

The instructions for the use of the tables are very clear and are notable for giving two fully worked examples: the solar eclipse of (civil) 18 July 1460 and the lunar eclipse of (civil) 28 December 1460. The latter was observed by Peurbach and Regiomontanus. Comparison of the observation with computation from Peurbach's tables for (astronomical) 27 December is as follows:

	Observation	Computation
Beginning of eclipse	11;42ʰ	11;32ʰ
Beginning of delay (totality)	12;47ʰ	12;42ʰ
End of delay (totality)	13;55ʰ	13;58ʰ

The agreement is good but, as expected, is no better than the comparison with the Alphonsine Tables made using the lunar eclipse of 3 September 1457.

According to Regiomontanus, Peurbach was responsible for the first six books of *Epitoma Almagesti Ptolemaei* (also known by slight variants of this title), the most important and most advanced Renaissance textbook on astronomy, while books VII–XIII were completed by Regiomontanus after Peurbach's death. But this account of the division of labor and credit probably requires some modification. The introduction and first six propositions of book I, giving the general arrangement of the universe, are in part translated and in part paraphrased from the Greek *Almagest* and must be the work of Regiomontanus, possibly with assistance from Bessarion. Further, this section of the work is not in Venice, lat. 329, a manuscript preserving a version of the text with numerous marginal corrections, largely of Greek forms of proper nouns, that are probably in the hand of Bessarion. Venice, lat. 329, is earlier than any other surviving manuscript and contains a preliminary and incomplete version of the text. With one important exception, all other manuscripts descend from a later, complete version. The exception is Venice, lat. 328, which contains a further revision of the text prepared by Regiomontanus for Bessarion, to whom it is dedicated in a note in Regiomontanus' hand. This is in all likelihood the best manuscript of the *Epitome*, although some comparison with others is still necessary to establish the text correctly. The first printing (Venice, 1496) is very careless; later printings were at Basel (1543) and Nuremberg (1550).

Aside from the introductory section, books I through VI are closely based upon the so-called *Almagesti minoris libri VI*, a doubtless unfinished textbook, apparently of the late thirteenth century, that supplements Ptolemy with information and procedures drawn from al-Battānī, Thābit ibn Qurra, Jābir ibn Aflaḥ, az-Zarqāl, and the Toledan Tables. The *Almagestum minor* divides Ptolemy's sometimes lengthy chapters into individual propositions showing the proof of a geometrical theorem, the derivation of a parameter, or the carrying out of a procedure, and there are occasional digressions adding the work of post-Ptolemaic writers. The *Epitome* adopts exactly this arrangement and sometimes follows the *Almagestum minor* nearly word for word, including all of its supplements to Ptolemy. Evidently Peurbach based the *Epitome* upon the earlier work; and, with all due respect to Regiomontanus' account of his teacher's contribution, one may legitimately ask to what extent the present state of the first six books is really the result of Regiomontanus' revision of what Peurbach may have left as little more than a close paraphrase of the *Almagestum minor*.

With the exception of the introductory propositions in book I, the underlying text of the *Epitome* is that of Gerard of Cremona's translation of the *Almagest*. Although the work contains a number of evidently conjectural emendations by Regiomontanus, they seem to have been made without consultation of the Greek text, except possibly for the correction of proper nouns from their Arabic-Latin forms to their Greek forms entered in Venice, lat. 329. These corrections did not extend through the entire work, and hence in all manuscripts except 328 the corrections are only partial; only in 328 are they complete.

However the credit be divided between Peurbach and Regiomontanus, the *Epitome* served as the fundamental treatise on Ptolemaic astronomy until the time of Kepler and Galileo, and remains the best exposition of the subject next to the *Almagest* itself. Although it runs to about half the length of the *Almagest*, the *Epitome* is nevertheless a model of clarity and includes everything essential to a working understanding of mathematical astronomy and even manages to clarify sections in which Ptolemy omits steps or is somewhat obscure. It has not been superseded even by the excellent modern commentaries on the *Almagest*, and the mathematical astronomy of the sixteenth century is in places unintelligible without it. The *Epitome* is the true discovery of ancient mathematical astronomy in the Renaissance because it gave astronomers an understanding of Ptolemy that they had not previously been able to achieve. Copernicus used it constantly, sometimes in preference to the *Almagest*; and its influence can be seen throughout *De revolutionibus*.

None of Peurbach's other works compares in importance with the three previously described. A provisional list of the remaining works is given below.

Iudicium super cometa qui anno Domini 1456^(to) per totum fere mensem Iunii apparuit (St. Pölten Alumnatsbibliothek XIXa, fols. 143a–149b, published in 1960 by Lhotsky and Ferrari d'Occhieppo) is a report on the appearance of Halley's Comet in 1456. It contains observations of its position, an examination of its physical cause and nature, an estimation of its distance and size, and a judgment of its astrological import. Peurbach concludes that the comet must be at least a thousand German miles above the earth, eighty German miles in length (including the tail), and four German miles in thickness. Its significance includes drought, pestilence, and war, especially for Greece, Dalmatia, Italy, and Spain, where the comet reached the zenith, and certain trouble for individuals whose nativities have Taurus in the ascendant.

Compositio tabulae altitudinis solis ad omnes horas consists of tables of solar altitude for latitude 48° and thus is applicable to Vienna. It is in Vin 5203, fols. 54a–58a, and other manuscripts.

Instrumentum pro veris coniunctionibus solis et lunae is a description of an instrument for the rapid determination of the position of true conjunction. It is in Vin 5203, fols. 67a–69a, and other manuscripts.

Canones astrolabii is probably the work in Vin 4782, fols. 225a–270b, and Vin 5176, fols. 156a–162b.

Compositio quadrantis astrolabii is in Vin 5176, fols. 43b–47a, and other manuscripts.

Canones gnomonis (also known as *Quadratum geometricum*) survives in a manuscript in Vin 5292, fols. 86b–93b; the work was printed at Nuremberg in 1516 and was included in J. Schöner's collection (Nuremberg, 1544). Like the *Eclipse Tables*, it was dedicated to Johann Vitez. It consists of a description of an instrument made up of an open square with two graduated sides and a pointer and sight attached to turn on the vertex opposite the graduated sides. The instrument is used for measuring altitudes of heavenly bodies or objects on the earth and, by taking measurements from different positions, for determining the distance of inaccessible objects on the earth. Instructions and tables were provided for each application. Tannstetter mentions *Plura de quadrantibus*, which could refer to this or to other treatises.

There are a number of writings concerned with sundials and time measurement (Zinner, *Verzeichnis*, nos. 7725–7728a). *Instrumentum universale ad inveniendas horas quocunque climate* is in Vin 5203, fols. 80b–86a, and other manuscripts. Georg Tannstetter lists *Extensio organi Ptolemaei pro usu horarium germanicarum ad omnia climata cum demonstratione* and *Modus describendi horas ab occasu in pariete*. The first could be the work in Vin 5203, and the second seems to concern sundials mounted vertically on walls. Tannstetter also mentions a *Compositio novae virgae visoriae cum lineis et tabula nova* and a *Compositio compasti cum regula ad omnia climata* that could have described portable sundials with attached compasses. Other apparently lost works listed by Tannstetter are *Collectio tabularum primi mobilis et quarundam nova compositio cum singulari usu*, which could have been an extensive collection of tables for spherical astronomy on the order of Regiomontanus' *Tabulae directionum*, and a *Tabula nova proportionis parallelorum ad gradus aequinoctialis cum compositione eiusdem*, probably a table giving the fraction of a degree of the equator for a degree of longitude on parallel circles at intervals of one degree of latitude.

Next to the planetary equation tables in book XI of his copy of the *Almagest* (Nuremberg, Cent. V 25, fol. 80a), Regiomontanus mentions that Peurbach had made more accurate equations. Tannstetter lists *Tabulae aequationum motuum planetarum novae, nondum perfectae et ultimum completae*, which he says Johannes Angelus (Engel) (*d.* 1512) attempted to complete. One may guess that these, like the solar and lunar equation tables in the *Eclipse Tables*, were recomputations of the planetary equations at 0;10° intervals using Alphonsine parameters. Such an expansion simplifies interpolation and thus speeds the computation of positions. Tannstetter mentions a *Tabula nova stellarum fixarum*, which could be the Ptolemaic or Alphonsine star catalog corrected for precession to Peurbach's time. There is an *Almanach perpetuum cum canonibus reduxit ad nostra tempora* that appears to be an almanac at intervals of five or ten days running through an integral number of longitudinal and synodic cycles for each planet, as in the almanacs of az-Zarqāl, Abraham Zacuto, and others. Tannstetter also says that Peurbach calculated ephemerides for many years and made *sphaeras solidas* (celestial globes) and many other instruments. A *Computus* by Peurbach is listed by Zinner (*Verzeichnis*, nos. 7750–7757).

Peurbach wrote a short work on the computation of sines and chords, *Tractatus super propositiones Ptolemaei de sinubus et chordis* (Vin 5203, fols. 124a–128a); the work was twice printed (Nuremberg, 1541; Basel, 1561) along with Regiomontanus' *Compositio tabularum sinuum rectorum* and sine tables. He first explains the computation using *kardagas* (arcs of 15°) according, he says, to the method of az-Zarqāl, and then, at somewhat greater length, sets out Ptolemy's derivation from the first book of the *Almagest*. Tannstetter lists a *Nova tabula sinus de decem minutis in decem per multas millenarias partes cum usu, quae plurimum rerum novarum in astronomia occasio fuit*; and such a table of sines at intervals of 0;10° with a *sinus totus* (unit radius) of 600,000 parts survives in Vin 5291, fols. 165a–173b, and Vin 5277, fols. 288a–289b, but without an explanation of its use. A lesser but evidently popular mathematical work was Peurbach's *Algorismus* or *Elementa arithmetices* or *Introductorium in arithmeticam*, a brief elementary textbook on practical computation with integers and fractions that was printed several times in the late fifteenth and early sixteenth centuries (for instance, Hain*13598-601, 1513, 1534).

BIBLIOGRAPHY

Georg Tannstetter Collimitius's list of Peurbach's works in his *Viri mathematici quos inclytum Viennensis gymnasium ordine celebres habuit* is printed in *Tabulae eclipsium magistri Georgii Peurbachii. Tabula primi mobilis Johannis de Monteregio* (Vienna, 1514). The observations of Peurbach and Regiomontanus were first published in *Scripti clarissimi mathematica M. Ioannis Regiomontani . . . ,* J. Schöner, ed. (Nuremberg, 1544). The fundamental biography of Peurbach is P. Gassendi, "Georgii Peurbachii et Ioannis Mulleri Regiomontani vita," which appears in Gassendi's *Tychonis Brahei, equitis dani, astronomorum Coryphaei vita . . . accessit Nicolai Copernici, Georgii Peurbachi et Ioannis Regiomontani astronomorum celebrium vita,* 2nd ed. (The Hague, 1655), 335–373, repr. in Gassendi's *Opera,* V (Lyons, 1658), 517–534. The next study of value is F. K. F. A. von Khautz, *Versuch einer Geschichte der österreichischen Gelehrten* (Frankfurt–Leipzig, 1755), 33–57. J. B. J. Delambre, *Histoire de l'astronomie du moyen âge* (Paris, 1819), 262–288, considers principally the precession theory of the *Theoricae novae* and other selected topics, using the commentaries of Capuan, Reinhold, and Nuñez Salaciense. G. H. Schubart, *Peuerbach und Regiomontanus* (Erlangen, 1828); J.

Fiedler, *Peuerbach und Regiomontanus* (Leobschütz, Poland, 1870); and J. Aschbach, *Geschichte der Wiener Universität im ersten Jahrhundert ihres Bestehens*, I (Vienna, 1865), 479–493, do not add significantly to earlier sources. Peurbach's correspondence with Nihil is published in A. Czerny, "Aus dem Briefwechsel des grossen Astronomen Georg von Peuerbach," in *Archiv für österreichische Geschichte*, **72** (1888), 281–304.

A distinct advance in research on Peurbach is K. Grossmann, "Die Frühzeit des Humanismus in Wien bis zu Celtis Berufung 1497," in *Jahrbuch für Landeskunde von Niederösterreich*, n.s. **22** (1929), 150–325, esp. 235–254. Grossmann examined numerous MSS, and his study is especially valuable on Peurbach's humanistic activities. The most extensive catalog of MSS containing writings by Peurbach is E. Zinner, *Verzeichnis der astronomischen Handschriften des deutschen Kulturgebietes* (Munich, 1925), 241–243. The most thorough and up-to-date biographical and bibliographical study is E. Zinner, *Leben und Wirken des Joh. Müller von Königsberg genannt Regiomontanus*, 2nd ed. (Osnabrück, 1968). Peurbach is treated separately on 26–49, the notes at the end contain much information on MSS and early printings, and there is a thorough bibliography. Peurbach is considered briefly in most of the standard histories of astronomy and mathematics.

There are no modern eds. or translations of any of Peurbach's major works. The text of the section of the *Theoricae novae* concerning Mercury is given, along with an analysis of the model, in W. Hartner, "The Mercury Horoscope of Marcantonio Michiel of Venice: A Study in the History of Renaissance Astrology and Astronomy," in *Vistas in Astronomy*, **1** (1955), 84–138, repr. in Hartner's *Oriens-Occidens* (Hildesheim, 1968), 440–495, esp. 483–491. Peurbach's report on the comets of 1456 and 1457 is published with extensive analysis in A. Lhotsky and K. Ferrari d'Occhieppo, "Zwei Gutachten von Georgs von Peuerbach über Kometen (1456 and 1457)," in *Mitteilungen des Instituts fur österreichische Geschichtsforschung*, 4th ser., **68** (1960), 266–290; and K. Ferrari d'Occhieppo, "Weitere Dokumente zu Peuerbachs Gutachten über den Kometen von 1456 nebst Bemerkungen über den Chronikbericht zum Sommerkometen 1457," in *Sitzungsberichte der Österreichischen Akademie der Wissenschaften*, Math.-naturw. Kl., Abt. 2, **169** (1961), 149–169.

C. DORIS HELLMAN
NOEL M. SWERDLOW

PFAFF, JOHANN FRIEDRICH (*b.* Stuttgart, Germany, 22 December 1765; *d.* Halle, Germany, 21 April 1825)

Pfaff came from a distinguished family of Württemberg civil servants. His father, Burkhard Pfaff, was chief financial councillor and his mother was the only daughter of a member of the consistory and of the exchequer; Johann Friedrich was the second of their seven sons.

The sixth son, Christoph Heinrich (1773–1852), did work of considerable merit in chemistry, medicine, and pharmacy. He also investigated "animal electricity" with Volta, Humboldt, and others. Pfaff's youngest brother, Johann Wilhelm Andreas (1774–1835), distinguished himself in several areas of science, especially in mathematics, and became professor of mathematics at the universities of Würzburg and Erlangen; but the rapid changes in his scientific interests prevented him from attaining the importance of Johann Friedrich.

As the son of a family serving the government of Württemberg, Pfaff went to the Hohe Karlsschule in Stuttgart at the age of nine. The school, which was well-administered but subject to a harsh military discipline, served chiefly to train Württemberg's government officials and superior officers. Pfaff completed his legal studies there in the fall of 1785.

On the basis of mathematical knowledge that he acquired by himself, Pfaff soon progressed to reading Euler's *Introductio in analysin infinitorum*. In the fall of 1785, at the urging of Karl Eugen, the duke of Württemberg, he began a journey to increase his scientific knowledge. He remained at the University of Göttingen for about two years, studying mathematics with A. G. Kaestner and physics with G. C. Lichtenberg. In the summer of 1787 he traveled to Berlin, in order to improve his skill in practical astronomy with J. E. Bode. While in Berlin, on the recommendation of Lichtenberg, Pfaff was admitted to the circle of followers of the Enlightenment around Friedrich Nicolai. In the spring of 1788 he traveled to Vienna by way of Halle, Jena, Helmstedt, Gotha, Dresden, and Prague.

Through the recommendation of Lichtenberg, Pfaff was appointed full professor of mathematics at the University of Helmstedt as a replacement for Klügel, who had been called to Halle. Pfaff assumed the rather poorly paid post with the approval of the duke of Württemberg.

At first Pfaff directed all his attention to teaching, with evident success: the number of mathematics students grew considerably. Gauss, after completing his studies at Göttingen (1795–1798), attended Pfaff's lectures and, in 1798, lived in Pfaff's house. Pfaff recommended Gauss's doctoral dissertation and, when necessary, greatly assisted him; Gauss always retained a friendly memory of Pfaff both as a teacher and as a man.

While in Helmstedt, Pfaff aided students whose talents he recognized. For example, he was a supporter of Humboldt following his visit to Helmstedt and he recommended him to professors at Göttingen. During this period he also formed an enduring friendship with the historian G. G. Bredow. Their plan to edit all the fragments of Pappus of Alexandria progressed no further than a partial edition (Book 4 of the *Collectio*) done by Bredow alone.

In 1803 Pfaff married Caroline Brand, a maternal cousin. Their first son died young; the second, Carl, who edited a portion of his father's correspondence, became an historian, but his career was abbreviated by illness.

A serious threat to Pfaff's academic career emerged at the end of the eighteenth century, when plans were discussed for closing the University of Helmstedt. This economy measure was postponed—in no small degree as a result of Pfaff's interesting essay "Über die Vorteile, welche eine Universität einem Lande gewährt" (Häberlins *Staatsarchiv* [1796], no. 2)—but in 1810 the university was in the end closed. The faculty members were transferred to Göttingen, Halle, and Breslau. Pfaff went to Halle at his own request, again as professor of mathematics. After Klügel's death in 1812 he also took over the direction of the observatory there.

Pfaff's early work was strongly marked by Euler's influence. In his *Versuch einer neuen Summationsmethode . . .* (1788) he uncritically employed divergent series in his treatment of Fourier expansions. In editing Euler's posthumous writings (1792) and in the inaugural essay traditionally presented by new professors at Helmstedt—"programma inaugurale, in quo peculiaris differentialis investigandi ratio ex theoria functionum deducitur" (1788)—as well as in 1795, Pfaff investigated series of the form

$$\sum_{k=1}^{n} \arctan \frac{f(k+1) - f(k)}{1 + f(k) \cdot f(k+1)}.$$

A friend of K. F. Hindenburg, the leader of the German combinatorial school, Pfaff prepared a series of articles between 1794 and 1800 for *Archiv der reinen und angewandten Mathematik* and *Sammlung combinatorisch-analytischer Abhandlungen*, which were edited by Hindenburg. The articles consistently reflect the long-winded way of thinking and expression of Hindenburg's school, with the single exception of "Analysis einer wichtigen Aufgabe des Herrn La Grange" (1794), which sought to free the Taylor expansion (with the remainder in Lagrange's form) from the tradition that embedded it in the theory of combinations and instead to present it as a primary component of analysis.

In 1797 Pfaff published at Helmstedt the first and only volume of an introductory treatise on analysis written in the spirit of Euler: *Disquisitiones analyticae maxime ad calculum integralem et doctrinam serierum pertinentes*. In 1810 he participated in the solution of a problem originating with Gauss that concerned the ellipse of greatest area that can be inscribed in a given quadrilateral. This led him to investigate conic pencils of rays.

Pfaff presented his most important mathematical achievement, the theory of Pfaffian forms, in "Methodus generalis, aequationes differentiarum partialium, necnon aequationes differentiales vulgares, utrasque primi ordinis, inter quotcunque variabiles, complete integrandi," which he submitted to the Berlin Academy on 11 May 1815. Although it was printed in the *Abhandlungen* of the Berlin Academy (1814–1815) and received an exceedingly favorable review by Gauss, the work did not become widely known. Its importance was not appreciated until 1827, when it appeared with a paper by Jacobi, "Über Pfaff's Methode, eine gewöhnliche lineare Differentialgleichung zwischen 2 *n* Variabeln durch ein System von *n* Gleichungen zu integrieren" (*Journal für die reine und angewandte Mathematik*, **2**, 347 ff.).

Pfaff's "Methodus" constituted the starting point of a basic theory of integration of partial differential equations which, through the work of Jacobi, Lie, and others, has developed into the modern Cartan calculus of extreme differential forms. (On this subject see, for example, C. Carathéodory, *Variationsrechnung und partielle Differentialgleichungen 1. Ordnung*, I [Leipzig, 1956].)

The core of the method that Pfaff made available can be described as follows: In the title of the "Methodus" the expression "aequationes differentialis vulgares" appears; by this Pfaff meant equations of the form

$$\sum_{i=1}^{n} \varphi_i(x_1, x_2, \cdots, x_n) \, dx_i = 0,$$

the left side of which, in modern terminology, is a differential form in *n* variables (Pfaffian form). The equation itself is called a Pfaffian equation. Now, by means of a first-order partial differential equation in $n + 1$ variables,

$$F(x_1, x_2, \cdots, x_n; z; p_1, p_2, \cdots, p_n) = 0,$$

where the partial derivatives

$$p_i = \frac{\partial z}{\partial x_i}, \qquad i = 1, 2, \cdots, n,$$

one can easily transform the equation

$$dz - \sum_{i=1}^{n} p_i \, dx_i = 0$$

into a Pfaffian equation in $2n$ variables by eliminating dz.

The significance of the reduction of a partial differential equation to a Pfaffian equation had previously been recognized by Euler and Lagrange. The reduction could not be exploited, however, for lack of an integration theory of the Pfaffian forms which would be valid for all n; it was this deficiency that Pfaff's "Methodus" in large measure remedied. Gauss justifiably emphasized this aspect of Pfaff's work in his review in *Göttingische gelehrte Anzeigen* (1815).

Pfaff's theory is based on a transformation theorem that in current terminology, and going a little beyond Pfaff, can be stated in the following manner: A Pfaffian form $\sum_{i=1}^{n} \varphi_i \, dx_i$ with an even number of variables can be transformed, by means of a factor $\rho(x_1, x_2, \cdots, x_n)$ into a Pfaffian form of $n-1$ variables. Moreover, for the case $n = 2$, ρ is simply the Euler multiplier or integrating factor of the differential equation $\varphi_1 \, dx_1 + \varphi_2 \, dx_2 = 0$. For $\sum_{i=1}^{4} \varphi_i \, dx_i$, therefore, there is a multiplier ρ, so that $\rho \sum_{i=1}^{4} \varphi_i \, dx_i$ can be written in the form $\sum_{i=1}^{3} \psi_i(y_1, y_2, y_3) \, dy_i$ and the y_i's are independent functions of $x_1, \cdots, x_4$.

For a Pfaffian form with an odd number of variables there is in general no corresponding multiplier that will enable one to reduce the number of variables.

In the 1827 article cited above, Jacobi later provided a suitable method of reduction: a Pfaffian form $\sum_{i=1}^{n} \varphi_i \, dx_i$ with an odd number of variables can, through subtraction of a differential dw, which is always reducible by means of the transformation $x_i = f_i(y_1, y_2, \cdots, y_{n-1}, t)$ $i = 1, 2, \cdots, n$, be brought to the form $\sum_{i=1}^{n-1} \psi_i \, dy_i$, where the ψ_i's are functions of the y_i's.

Through alternately employing transformation (following Pfaff) and reduction (following Jacobi) one can finally bring every Pfaffian form with arbitrary number of variables into a canonical form: for $n = 2p$, into the form $z_1 \, dz_2 + z_3 \, dz_4 + \cdots + dz_{2p-1} \, dz_{2p}$; and for $n = 2p + 1$, into the form $dz_1 + dz_2, dz_3 + \cdots + z_{2p} \, dz_{2p+1}$.

Lie later gave the relationship between partial differential equations and Pfaffian forms a geometrical interpretation that possessed a greater intuitive clarity than the analytic approach.

BIBLIOGRAPHY

I. ORIGINAL WORKS. There is a list of Pfaff's writings in Poggendorff, II, cols. 424–425. They include *Versuch*
einer neuen Summationsmethode nebst anderen damit zusammenhängenden analytischen Bemerkungen (Berlin, 1788); "Analysis einer wichtigen Aufgabe des Herrn La Grange," in Hindenburg's *Archiv der reinen und angewandten Mathematik*, **1** (1794), 81–84; *Disquisitiones analyticae maxime ad calculum integralem et doctrinam serierum pertinentes* (Helmstedt, 1797); "Methodus generalis, aequationes differentiarum partialium, necnon aequationes differentiales vulgares, utrasque primi ordinis, inter quotcunque variabiles complete integrandi," in *Abhandlungen der Preussischen Akademie der Wissenschaften* (1814–1815), 76–135, also translated into German by G. Kowalewski as no. 129 in Ostwald's Klassiker der exakten Wissenschaften (Leipzig, 1902); and *Sammlung von Briefen, gewechselt zwischen Johann Friedrich Pfaff...*, Carl Pfaff, ed. (Leipzig, 1853).

II. SECONDARY LITERATURE. See G. Kowalewski, *Grosse Mathematiker*, 2nd ed. (Munich–Berlin, 1939), 228–247; and Carl Pfaff's biographical introduction to his ed. of his father's correspondence, pp. 1–35. Also see articles on Pfaff in *Neuer Nekrolog der Deutschen*, **3** (1825), 1415–1418; and *Allgemeine deutsche Biographie*, XXV (Leipzig, 1887), 592–593.

H. WUSSING

PICARD, CHARLES ÉMILE (*b.* Paris, France, 24 July 1856; *d.* Paris, 11 December 1941)

Picard's father, the director of a silk factory, was of Burgundian origin; his mother was the daughter of a doctor from northern France. At the death of her husband, during the siege of Paris in 1870, she was obliged to seek employment in order to care for her two sons. Picard was a brilliant student at the Lycée Henri IV and was especially interested in literature, Greek, Latin, and history. An avid reader with a remarkable memory, he acquired a rare erudition. For many years he retained a liking for physical exercise—gymnastics and mountain climbing—and an interest in carefully planned travel. He chose his vocation after reading a book on algebra at the end of his secondary studies. In 1874, after only one year of preparation, he was accepted as first candidate by the École Normale Supérieure and as second candidate by the École Polytechnique. After a famous interview with Pasteur, he chose the former, where he would be permitted to devote himself entirely to research. He placed first in the competition for the *agrégation* in 1877 but had already made several important discoveries and had received the degree of *docteur ès sciences*.

From 1877 to 1878 Picard was retained as an assistant at the École Normale Supérieure. Appointed professor at the University of Toulouse in 1879, he returned to Paris in 1881 as lecturer in physical and experimental mechanics at the Sorbonne and as lecturer in mechanics and astronomy at the École Normale Supérieure. Although he accepted these teaching posts outside his preferred field, Picard continued his work in analysis, and the first of the two famous theorems that bear his name dates from 1879, when he was twenty-three. In 1885 he was unanimously elected to the chair of differential and integral calculus at the Sorbonne, where he served as his own *suppléant* before reaching the prescribed age of thirty for the post. In 1897, at his own request, he exchanged this chair for that of analysis and higher algebra, where he was able to train students for research.

Nominated in 1881 by the section of geometry for election to the Académie des Sciences, he was elected in 1889. In 1886 he received the Prix Poncelet and in 1888 the Grand Prix des Sciences Mathématiques for a memoir that was greatly admired by Poincaré. Picard's mathematical activity during the period 1878–1888 resulted in more than 100 articles and notes. A member of the Académie Française (1924), he received the Grande Croix de la Légion d'Honneur in 1932 and the Mittag-Leffler Gold Medal from the Swedish Academy of Sciences in 1937. He received an honorary doctorate from five foreign universities and was a member of thirty-seven academies and learned societies.

Picard was chairman of numerous commissions, including the Bureau des Longitudes; and his administrative abilities and his sincere and resolute character earned him great prestige. As permanent secretary of the Académie des Sciences from 1917 to his death in 1941, he wrote an annual notice on either a scientist or a subject of current interest. He also wrote many prefaces to mathematical books and participated in the publication of works of C. Hermite and G.-H. Halphen.

An outstanding teacher, Picard was devoted to the young, and from 1894 to 1937 he trained more than 10,000 engineers at the École Centrale des Arts et Manufactures. He was responsible, with extraordinary success, for choosing pupil-teachers at the École Normale Supérieure de Jeunes Filles de Sèvres (1900–1927). He was director of the Société des Amis des Sciences, founded by Pasteur to look after needy scholars and their families.

In 1881 Picard married the daughter of his mentor and friend Charles Hermite. His life of uninterrupted professional success was clouded by the death of his daughter and two sons in World War I. His grandsons were wounded and captured in World War II, and the invasion and occupation of France darkened the last two years of his life. He died in

the Palais de l'Institut, where he lived as *secrétaire perpétuel* of the Academy.

Picard's works were mostly in mathematical analysis and algebraic geometry. As early as 1878 he had studied the integrals of differential equations by making successive substitutions with equations having suitable partial derivatives. The following year he discovered the first of the two well-known theorems that bear his name. The first states: Let $f(z)$ be an entire function. If there exist two values of A for which the equation $f(z) = A$ does not have a finite root, then $f(z)$ is a constant. From this theorem it follows that if $f(z)$ is an entire function that is not a constant, there cannot be more than one value of A for which $f(z) = A$ has no solution.

Picard's second theorem, which extended a result stated by Weierstrass, states: Let $f(z)$ be a function, analytic everywhere except at a, where it has an essential isolated singularity; the equation $f(z) = A$ has in general an infinity of roots in any neighborhood of a. Although the equation can fail for certain exceptional values of the constant A, there cannot be more than two such values (1880). This result led to a classification of regular analytic functions; and it was the origin of important work carried out especially by Émile Borel and Otto von Blumenthal. The latter established generalizations that he called Picard's little theorem and Picard's big theorem. Picard's theorems revealed the fruitfulness of the idea of introducing, in the terms of a problem, a restriction bearing on the case of an exception that can be shown to be unique.

From 1883 to 1888 Picard extended Poincaré's investigations on automorphic functions to functions of two complex variables, which he called hypergeometric and hyperfuchsian (1883, 1885). These functions led Picard to the study of algebraic surfaces (1901). Setting himself the task of studying the analogies between the theory of linear differential equations and the theory of algebraic equations, Picard took up Galois's theory and obtained for a linear differential equation a group of transformations now called the Picard group.

Picard's method for demonstrating the existence of the integrals of differential equations by successive approximations at first appears very simple. The introduction of n functions $u_1, u_2, \ldots, u_n$ reestablishes the system

$$\frac{du_i}{dx} = f_i(x, u_1, u_2, \cdots, u_n), \qquad i = 1, 2, \cdots, n,$$

with the initial conditions $x = x_0$ gives $u_i = a_i$. There is then resolved by n quadratures the system

$$\frac{dv_i}{dx} = f_i(x, a_1, a_2, \cdots, a_n),$$

the v_i satisfying the initial conditions and the same being true of

$$\frac{dw_i}{dx} = f_i(x, v_1, v_2, \cdots, v_n)$$

and so forth. It remains to prove—and this is the essential point—that under certain conditions (identified by Cauchy) the functions that are successively introduced tend toward limits that are precisely the desired integrals in the neighborhood of x_0. Picard himself extended his method to numerous cases, particularly to the equations of complex variables and also to integral equations. He, as well as his successors, thus demonstrated the preeminence of his method. Integral equations became of considerable importance in mathematical physics, with much of the genuine progress due to Fredholm. By completing the earlier works, Picard made more precise the necessary conditions for the existence of the various types of equations.

These works, as well as many dispersed results found in notes, were assembled in Picard's three-volume *Traité d'analyse*, which immediately became a classic and was revised with each subsequent edition. The work was accessible to many students through its range of subjects, clear exposition, and lucid style. Picard examined several specific cases before discussing his general theory.

In theoretical physics Picard applied analysis to theories of elasticity, heat, and electricity. He was particularly successful in achieving an elegant solution to the problem of the propagation of electrical impulses along cables (*équation des télégraphiques*). This research was to have been collected in a fourth volume of his treatise on analysis; but it appeared instead in four fascicles of *Cahiers scientifiques*.

After 1900 Picard published several historical and philosophical reflections, in particular *La science moderne et son état actuel* (1905), and speeches and reports. When he was more than eighty years old he presented considerations on the questions of homogeneity and similarity encountered by physicists and engineers.

Throughout his life Picard supported the innovations of other mathematicians, including the early work of Lebesgue. With Poincaré he was the most distinguished French mathematician of his generation.

BIBLIOGRAPHY

I. ORIGINAL WORKS. Picard's writings include "Sur la

forme des équations différentielles du second ordre dans le voisinage de certains points critiques," in *Comptes rendus hebdomadaires des séances de l'Académie des sciences*, **87** (1878), 430–432, 743–746; "Mémoire sur les fonctions entières," in *Annales scientifiques de l'École normale supérieure*, 2nd ser., **9** (1880), 145-166; "Sur la réduction du nombre des périodes des intégrales abéliennes," in *Bulletin de la Société mathématique de France*, **11** (1883), 25–53; "Sur les fonctions hyperfuchsiennes provenant des séries hypergéométriques de deux variables," in *Annales scientifiques de l'École normale supérieure*, 3rd ser., **2** (1885), 357–384; "Mémoire sur la théorie des fonctions algébriques de deux variables indépendantes," in *Journal de mathématiques pures et appliquées*, 4th ser., **5** (1889), 135–319; *Traité d'analyse*, 3 vols. (Paris, 1891–1896); and *Théorie des fonctions algébriques de deux variables indépendantes*, 2 vols. (Paris, 1897–1906), written with Georges Simart.

Subsequent writings include "Sur la résolution de certaines équations à deux variables," in *Bulletin de la Société mathématique de France*, **25** (1901); *Sur le développement de l'analyse et ses rapports avec diverses sciences* (Paris, 1905); *La science moderne et son état actuel* (Paris, 1905); *L'histoire des sciences et les prétentions de la science allemande* (Paris, 1916); *Les sciences mathématiques en France depuis un demi-siècle* (Paris, 1917); *Discours et mélanges* (Paris, 1922); and *Mélange de mathématiques et de physique* (Paris, 1924).

His later writings are "Leçons sur quelques types simples d'équations aux dérivées partielles avec des applications à la physique mathématique," in *Cahiers scientifiques*, fasc. 1 (1925); "Leçons sur quelques équations fonctionnelles avec des applications à divers problèmes d'analyse et de physique mathématique," *ibid.*, fasc. 3 (1928); "Leçons sur quelques problèmes aux limites de la théorie des équations différentielles," *ibid.*, fasc. 5 (1930); "Leçons sur quelques équations fonctionnelles," *ibid.*, fasc. 6 (1930); *Un coup d'oeil sur l'histoire des sciences et des théories physiques* (Paris, 1930); "Quelques applications analytiques de la théorie des courbes et des surfaces algébriques," in *Cahiers scientifiques*, fasc. 9 (1931); and *Discours et notices* (Paris, 1936).

II. SECONDARY LITERATURE. An early biography of Picard is Ernest Lebon, *Émile Picard, biographie, bibliographie* (Paris, 1910), which has details of 256 of his works. See also René Garnier, ed., *Centenaire de la naissance d'Émile Picard* (Paris, 1957), which has reports of speeches by colleagues and pupils.

His mathematical discoveries are discussed in Émile Borel, *Leçons sur les fonctions méromorphes* (Paris, 1903), ch. 3; and Otto Blumenthal, *Principes de la théorie des fonctions entières d'ordre infini* (Paris, 1910), ch. 7.

LUCIENNE FÉLIX

PIERI, MARIO (*b*. Lucca, Italy, 22 June 1860; *d*. Sant' Andrea di Còmpito (Lucca), Italy, 1 March 1913)

Pieri's father, Pellegrino Pieri, was a lawyer; his mother was Erminia Luporini. He began his university studies in 1880 at Bologna, where Salvatore Pincherle was among the first to recognize his talent; but he obtained a scholarship to the Scuola Normale Superiore of Pisa in November 1881 and completed his university studies there, receiving his degree on 27 June 1884. After teaching briefly at the technical secondary school in Pisa he became professor of projective geometry at the military academy in Turin and also, in 1888, assistant in projective geometry at the University of Turin, holding both posts until 1900. He became *libero docente* at the university in 1891 and for several years taught an elective course in projective geometry there.

On 30 January 1900, following a competition, he was named extraordinary professor of projective and descriptive geometry at the University of Catania. In 1908 he transferred to Parma, where in the winter of 1911 he began to complain of fatigue. His fatal illness, cancer, was diagnosed a few months later.

For ten years following his first publication in 1884, Pieri worked primarily in projective geometry. From 1895 he studied the foundations of mathematics, especially the axiomatic treatment of geometry. Pieri had made a thorough study of Christian von Staudt's geometry of position, but he was also influenced by his colleagues at the military academy and the university, Giuseppe Peano and Cesare Burali-Forti. He learned symbolic logic from the latter, and Peano's axiom systems for arithmetic and ordinary geometry furnished models for Pieri's axiomatic study of projective geometry.

In 1895 Pieri constructed ordinary projective geometry on three undefined terms: point, line, and segment. The same undefined terms were used in 1896 in an axiom system for the projective geometry of hyperspaces, and in 1897 he showed that all of the geometry of position can be based on only two undefined terms: projective point and the join of two projective points. In the memoir "I principii della geometria di posizione composti in un sistema logico-deduttivo" (1898) Pieri combined the results reached thus far into a more organic whole. Here the same two undefined terms were used to construct projective geometry as a logical-deductive system based on nineteen sequentially independent axioms—each independent of the preceding ones—which are introduced one by one as they are needed in the development, thus allowing the reader to determine on which axioms a given theorem depends. Of this paper Bertrand Russell wrote: "This is, in my opinion, the best work on the present subject" (*Principles of Mathematics*, 2nd ed. [New York, 1964], 382), a

judgment that Peano echoed in his report in 1903 to the judging committee for the Lobachevsky Award of the Société Physico-Mathématique de Kasan. (Pieri received honorable mention, the prize going to David Hilbert.)

In their axiom systems for ordinary geometry, Pasch had used four undefined terms, and Peano three. With Pieri's memoir of 1899, "Della geometria elementare come sistema ipotetico-deduttivo," the number was reduced to two—point and motion—the latter understood as the transformation of one point into another. Pieri continued to apply the axiomatic method to the study of geometry, and in several subsequent publications he investigated the possibility of using different sets of undefined terms to construct various geometries. In "Nuovi principii di geometria proiettiva complessa" (1905) he gave the first axiom system for complex projective geometry that is not constructed on real projective geometry.

Two brief notes published in 1906–1907 on the foundations of arithmetic are notable. In "Sur la compatibilité des axiomes de l'arithmétique" he gave an interpretation of the notion of whole number in the context of the logic of classes; and in "Sopra gli assiomi aritmetici" he selected as primitive notions "number" and "successor of a number," and characterized them with a system of axioms that from a logical point of view simplified Peano's theory. In 1911 Pieri may have been on the point of beginning a new phase of his scientific activity. He was then attracted by the vectorial calculus of Burali-Forti and Roberto Marcolongo, but he left only three notes on this subject.

Pieri became one of the strongest admirers of symbolic logic; and although most of his works are published in more ordinary mathematical language, the statements of colleagues and his own statements show that Pieri considered the use of Peano's symbolism of the greatest help not only in obtaining rigor but also in deriving new results.

Pieri was among the first to promote the idea of geometry as a hypothetical-deductive system. His address at the First International Congress of Philosophy in 1900 had the highly significant title "Sur la géométrie envisagée comme un système purement logique." Bertrand Russell wrote in 1903: "The true founder of non-quantitative Geometry is von Staudt. . . . But there remained one further step, before projective Geometry could be considered complete, and this step was taken by Pieri. . . . Thus at last the long process by which projective Geometry has purified itself from every metrical taint is completed" (*Principles of Mathematics*, 2nd ed. [New York, 1964], 421).

BIBLIOGRAPHY

I. ORIGINAL WORKS. A chronological list of Pieri's publications appears in Beppo Levi, "Mario Pieri," in *Bullettino di bibliografia e storia delle scienze matematiche*, **15** (1913), 65–74, with additions and corrections in **16** (1914), 32. The list includes 57 articles, a textbook of projective geometry for students at the military academy, a translation of Christian von Staudt's *Geometrie der Lage*, and four book reviews.

II. SECONDARY LITERATURE. Besides the obituary by Beppo Levi (cited above), see Guido Castelnuovo, "Mario Pieri," in *Bollettino della mathesis*, **5** (1913), 40–41; and [Giuseppe Peano], "Mario Pieri," in *Academia pro Interlingua, Discussiones*, **4** (1913), 31–35. On the centennial of Pieri's birth Fulvia Skof published "Sull'opera scientifica di Mario Pieri," in *Bollettino dell'Unione matematica italiana*, 3rd ser., **15** (1960), 63–68.

HUBERT C. KENNEDY

PINCHERLE, SALVATORE (*b*. Trieste, Austria [now Italy], 11 March 1853; *d*. Bologna, Italy, 10 July 1936)

Born of a Jewish business family, Pincherle completed his preuniversity studies in Marseilles, where his family had migrated. The unusually sophisticated teaching of science there seems to have been a decisive factor in diverting his interest from the humanities to mathematics; and by 1869, when he entered the University of Pisa, the decision to study mathematics had already matured. His teachers at Pisa included Betti and Dini; Pincherle was greatly affected by both of them. After graduating in 1874, Pincherle became a teacher at a *liceo* in Pavia. A scholarship for study abroad enabled him to spend the academic year 1877–1878 in Berlin, where he met Weierstrass, who influenced all his subsequent work. In 1880 Pincherle became professor of infinitesimal analysis at the University of Palermo. He remained there only a few months, having been appointed to a chair at the University of Bologna. He retired in 1928.

Pincherle greatly improved the level of mathematics at the University of Bologna, which had badly deteriorated during the final years of papal domination. The university later acknowledged his contribution by naming the mathematics institute for him during his lifetime. In Bologna, Pincherle also founded (1922) the Italian Mathematical Union, of which he was the first president. At the Third International Congress of Mathematicians, held at Bologna in 1928, of which he was president, Pincherle restored the truly international character of international mathematical congresses by reopening participation to German and other mathematicians who had been excluded since World War I.

Pincherle's contributions to mathematics were mainly in the field of functional analysis, of which he was one of the principal founders, together with Volterra. Remaining faithful to the ideas of Weierstrass, he did not take the topological approach that later proved to be the most successful, but tried to start from a series of powers of the D derivation symbol. Although his efforts did not prove very fruitful, he was able to study in depth the Laplace transformation, iteration problems, and series of generalized factors. He was the author of several textbooks, notably for secondary schools, at which he had had direct practical experience.

Pincherle was a member of the Accademia Nazionale dei Lincei and the Bayerische Akademie der Wissenschaften, which, despite the rise of Nazism, sent him a warm message on his eightieth birthday in 1934. In 1954 the city of Trieste held a solemn celebration of the centenary of his birth.

BIBLIOGRAPHY

There is an accurate bibliography of Pincherle's writings from 1874 to 1936, with 245 references, by Ettore Bortolotti, in *Bollettino dell'Unione matematica italiana*, **16** (1937), 37–60. On his life and work, see the notices by Ugo Amaldi, in *Annali di matematica pura ed applicata*, 4th ser., **17** (1938), 1–21; and Leonida Tonelli, in *Annali della Scuola normale superiore*, 2nd ser., **6** (1937), 1–10; and F. G. Tricomi, *Salvatore Pincherle nel centenario della nascità*, Pubblicazioni della Facoltà di scienze e d'ingegneria, Università di Trieste, ser. A, **60** (1954).

F. G. TRICOMI

PITISCUS, BARTHOLOMEO (*b*. Grünberg, Silesia [now Zielona Góra, Poland], 24 August 1561; *d*. Heidelberg, Germany, 2 July 1613)

Very little is known of Pitiscus' life. He was court chaplain at Breslau, pursued theological studies in Heidelberg, and for more than a score of the last years of his life he was court chaplain and court preacher for Elector Frederick IV of the Palatinate. Although Pitiscus worked much in the theological field, his proper abilities concerned mathematics, and particularly trigonometry. His achievements in this field are important in two respects: he revised the tables of Rheticus to make them more exact, and he wrote an excellent systematic textbook on trigonometry, in which he used all six of the trigonometric functions.

The word "trigonometry" is due to Pitiscus and was

first printed in his *Trigonometria: sive de solutione triangulorum tractatus brevis et perspicuus*, which was published as the final part of A. Scultetus' *Sphaericorum libri tres methodicé conscripti et utilibus scholiis expositi* (Heidelberg, 1595). A revised edition, *Trigonometriae sive de dimensione triangulorum libri quinque*, was published at Augsburg in 1600. It consists of three sections, the first of which comprises five books on plane and spherical trigonometry. The second section, "Canon triangulorum sive tabulae sinuum, tangentium et secantium ad partes radij 100000 et ad scrupula prima quadrantis," contains tables for all six of the trigonometric functions to five or six decimal places for an interval of a minute, and a third section, "Problemata varia," containing ten books, treats of problems in geodesy, measuring of heights, geography, gnomometry, and astronomy. The second enlarged edition of the first and third section was published at Augsburg in 1609. The largely expanded tables in "Canon triangulorum emendatissimus" are separately paged at the end of the volume and have their own title page, dated 1608. The same arrangement as in the first edition occurs in the third edition of Frankfurt (1612). In this edition the "Problemata varia" are enlarged with one book on architecture.

Soon after its appearance on the Continent, the *Trigonometria* of Pitiscus was translated into English by R. Handson (1614); the second edition of this translation was published in 1630; the third edition is undated. Together with these editions were also published English editions of the "Canon" of 1600: "A Canon of Triangles: or the Tables, of Sines, Tangents and Secants, the Radius Assumed to be 100000." There exists also a French translation of the "Canon" of 1600 published by D. Henrion at Paris in 1619. Von Braunmühl remarks in his "Vorlesungen" that in the Dresden library there is a copy of a lecture of M. Jöstel entitled "Lectiones in trigonometriam (Bartholomaei) Pitisci. Wittenbergae 1597," which indicates that the *Trigonometria* was one of the sources for the lectures in trigonometry that were given in the universities of Germany at the close of the sixteenth century.

The first book of the *Trigonometria* considers definitions and theorems from plane and spherical geometry. The names "tangent" and "secant" that Pitiscus used proceeded from the *Geometria rotundi* (Basel, 1583) by T. Finck; instead of "cosinus," Pitiscus wrote "sinus complementi." The second book is concerned with the things that must be known in order to solve triangles by means of the tables of sines, tangents, and secants. This book includes the definitions of the trigonometric functions, a method

for constructing the trigonometric tables, and the fundamental trigonometric identities. From the "sinus primarii," that is, the sines of 45°, 30°, and 18°; Pitiscus derived the remaining sines, the "sinus secundarii." Book III is devoted to plane trigonometry, which he consolidated under six "Axiomata proportionum," the first three of which he combined into one in his editions of 1609 and 1612. What other authors designated propositions or theorems, Pitiscus called axioms. The spherical triangle is considered in Book IV, which he drew together in four axioms, the third of which is the sine law; the fourth is the cosine theorem for which Pitiscus was the first to give a real proof (for the theorem relative to angles). By means of these four axioms Pitiscus solved right and oblique spherical triangles. He did not study the polar triangle in this book on spherical triangles but treated it briefly in Book I in much the same way as P. Van Lansberge did. Book V contains such propositions as: "The difference of the sine of two arcs which differ from sixty degrees by the same amount is equal to the sine of this amount." Pitiscus referred to T. Finck and Van Lansberge as also giving this theorem; his proof is the same as the one given by Clavius. After publication in Leipzig of his "Canon doctrinae triangulorum" in 1551, and for at least a dozen years before his death in 1576, Rheticus and a corps of calculators carried on colossal computations in preparing the manuscript for his *Opus Palatinum de triangulis* (Neustadt, 1596). Shortly after the *Opus Palatinum* was published, it was found that the tangents and secants near the end of the quadrant were very inaccurate. Pitiscus was engaged to correct the tables. Because Rheticus seems to have realized that a sine or cosine table to more than ten decimal places would be necessary for such correction, Pitiscus sought the manuscript and finally after the death of V. Otho, a pupil of Rheticus, he found that it contained (1) the ten-second canon of sines to fifteen decimal places; (2) sines for every second of the first and last degree of the quadrant to fifteen decimal places; (3) the commencement of a canon for every ten seconds of tangents and secants, to fifteen decimal places; and (4) a complete minute canon of sines, tangents, and secants, to fifteen decimal places. With the canon (1) in hand Pitiscus recomputed to eleven decimal places all of the tangents and secants of the *Opus Palatinum* in the defective region from 83° to the end of the quadrant. Then eighty-six pages were reprinted and joined to the remaining pages of the great table. In 1607 the whole was issued with a special title page. After his discovery of the new Rheticus tables, Pitiscus started to prepare a second work, *Thesaurus Mathematicus*, which was finally published in 1613 and contained the following four parts: (1) (Rheticus) canon of sines for every 10″ to fifteen decimal places; (2) (Rheticus) sines for 0 (1″) 1°, 89° (1″) 90°, to fifteen decimal places; (3) (Pitiscus) the fundamental series from which the rest were calculated to twenty-two decimal places; and (4) (Pitiscus) the sines to twenty-two decimal places for every tenth, thirtieth, and fiftieth second in the first thirty-five minutes.

BIBLIOGRAPHY

For the full titles of the Pitiscus editions, see R. C. Archibald, "Bartholomäus Pitiscus (1561–1613)," in *Mathematical Tables and Other Aids to Computation*, **3** (1949), 390–397; and "Pitiscus' Revision of the Opus Palatinum Canon," *ibid.*, 556–561.

Secondary literature includes A. von Braunmühl, *Vorlesungen über Geschichte der Trigonometrie*, I (Leipzig, 1900), 221–226; G. J. Gerhardt, *Geschichte der Mathematik in Deutschland* (Munich, 1877), 93–99; N. L. W. A. Gravelaar, "Pitiscus' Trigonometria," in *Nieuw archief voor wiskunde*, V. 3, S. 2 (Amsterdam, 1898), 253–278; and M. C. Zeller, *The Development of Trigonometrie From Regiomontanus to Pitiscus* (Ann Arbor, Mich., 1944), 102–104.

H. L. L. Busard

PLANA, GIOVANNI (*b.* Voghera, Italy, 6 November 1781; *d.* Turin, Italy, 20 January 1864)

Plana was the son of Antonio Maria Plana and Giovanna Giacoboni. In 1796 his father sent him to complete his studies in Grenoble, where two of his uncles lived. Plana soon became noted for his scientific ability; in 1800 he was admitted to the École Polytechnique at Paris, where he remained for the next three years. This period was decisive in shaping his career, for one of his teachers was Lagrange. In Grenoble, Plana became a close friend of his famous contemporary Stendhal.

In 1803 Plana returned to Italy. Fourier, greatly impressed by Plana, had tried unsuccessfully to procure his nomination as professor of mathematics at the artillery school of Grenoble but managed to obtain a similar post for him at the artillery school in the Piedmont, which was then annexed to France; the school was located partly at Turin and partly at Alessandria. In 1811, on Lagrange's recommendation, Plana was named professor of astronomy at the University of Turin. He remained there until his death, teaching astronomy and infinitesimal analysis, as well as other subjects at the local military academy. For half a century he also directed and stimulated the development of the astronomical observatory of Turin.

Plana is generally considered one of the major Italian scientists of his age because, at a time when the quality of instruction at Italian universities had greatly deteriorated, his teaching was of the highest quality, quite comparable with that of the *grandes écoles* of Paris, at which he had studied.

Plana's scientific contributions cover a wide range: mathematical analysis (Eulerian integrals, elliptical functions), mathematical physics (the cooling of a sphere, electrostatic induction), geodesy (the extension of an arc of latitude from Austria to France), and astronomy (particularly the theory of lunar movement). His study of the moon was inspired by Barnaba Oriani, director of the Brera Observatory in Milan. Oriani had suggested that he and Francesco Carlini, who had done geodetic work with Plana, should attempt to compile reasonably precise lunar tables solely on the basis of the law of universal gravity—that is, using only the observational data essential to determine the arbitrary constants of the problem. Plana soon quarreled with Carlini, who withdrew in disgust; and Plana succeeded alone, after almost twenty years. The results were presented in the three-volume *Théorie du mouvement de la lune* (Turin, 1832). The work was not widely read and received criticism that was not always unfounded; but it is of notable scientific and philosophical value, and as such it was well received.

In 1827 Plana was named astronomer royal; in 1844 he became a hereditary baron; in 1848, a senator; and in 1860, *associé étranger* of the Paris Academy of Sciences.

BIBLIOGRAPHY

A list of about 100 works by Plana is in Poggendorff, II, cols. 460–463. Most of Plana's writings and his portraits are listed in Albert Maquet, "L'astronome royal de Turin, Giovanni Plana (1781–1864); un homme, une carrière, un destin," in *Mémoires de l'Académie royale de Belgique. Classe des sciences*, **36** (1965), fasc. 6.

The following articles were published on the centenary of Plana's death: G. Agostinelli, "Della vita e delle opere di Giovanni Plana," in *Atti dell'Accademia delle scienze*, **99** (1964–1965), 1177–1199; Jacopo Lanzi de Rho, ed., "Ultrapadum," in *Bollettino della Società di storia . . . dell'Oltrepò (pavese)*, **17** (Dec. 1964; pub. Dec. 1966), fasc. 27; and F. G. Tricomi, "Giovanni Plana (1781–1864). Cenni commemorativi," in *Atti dell'Accademia delle scienze*, **99** (1964–1965), 267–279.

F. G. Tricomi

PLANUDES, MAXIMUS (*b*. Nicomedia, Bithynia, *ca*. 1255; *d*. Constantinople, 1305)

Manuel Planudes, as he was named by his well-to-do family, was probably brought to Constantinople shortly after Michael VIII recovered the city from the Latins in 1261. When he became a monk, in or shortly before 1280, he took the name Maximus, by which he is now known. He was a leading intellectual and teacher in Byzantium in the early Palaeologan period, first at the Chora monastery and, after *ca*. 1300, at the Akataleptes monastery.

His knowledge of Latin was sufficient for him to translate many theological and classical works into Greek, including à translation of Macrobius' *Commentum in somnium Scipionis*. It has also been claimed that he is the translator of the Aristotelian *De plantis* from the Latin of Alfred Anglicus. But his primary scholarly interest was the editing of texts and the training of younger scholars, such as Demetrius Triclinius and Manuel Meschopulus, to carry on this work. His school was concerned mainly with editing and commenting on the Greek poets and dramatists, although it did not neglect authors of prose. His editions include Aratus' *Phaenomena*, with scholia; Theodosius' *Sphaerica*; Euclid's *Elements*; Ptolemy's *Geography*; pseudo-Iamblichus' *Theologumena arithmeticae*; and Diophantus' *Arithmetica*, with scholia on the first two books.

Another scholarly activity in which Planudes delighted was the compilation of florilegia. His anthology of Greek poetry, the *Anthologia Planudea*, is well known; and his *Very Useful Collection Gathered From Various Books* preserves much of what we possess of John Lydus' *De mensibus*.

For historians of science his most important original work is *Calculation According to the Indians, Which Is Called Great*, which deals with addition, subtraction, multiplication, division, sexagesimals, and squares and square roots. Although it contains little original material, it is significant for its use of the eastern Arabic form of the Indian numerals. Planudes' source may have been his contemporary, Gregory Chioniades, who had studied astronomy at Tabriz in the early 1290's and was using the same forms of the Indian numerals in Byzantium in 1298–1302. The medical works sometimes attributed to Planudes—that on uroscopy, for example—were probably written by Nicophorus Blemmydes.

BIBLIOGRAPHY

The fundamental articles remain C. Wendel, "Planudea," in *Byzantinische Zeitschrift*, **40** (1940), 406–445; and his article in Pauly-Wissowa, XX, 2202–2253.

DAVID PINGREE

PLATO (*b*. Athens [?], 427 B.C.; *d*. Athens, 348/347 B.C.)

Plato's enthusiasm for mathematics, astronomy, and musical theory appears everywhere in his writings, and he also displays a far from superficial knowledge of the medicine and physiology of his day. In ancient times competent judges held that he had promoted the advance of mathematics, especially geometry, in his lifetime.[1] Theodore of Cyrene and Archytas of Tarentum were his friends, and Eudoxus of Cnidus, Theaetetus, and Menaechmus his colleagues or pupils. His critics assert that his theory of knowledge rules out any empirical science and that, owing to his idealism, he had a radically false idea of the procedure and value of the mathematics that he admired. Even so, it can be said that the Academy, founded by him at Athens at a date not exactly known (380 B.C.?), became a center where specialists—not all of them sympathizers with his philosophy and epistemology—could meet and profit by discussion with him and with one another.

Our object here must be to trace Plato's intellectual development and, incidentally, to submit part of the material upon which an estimate of his services or disservices to science must be based. It must be considered how far he is likely to have carried out in his school the project, sketched in the *Republic*, of a mathematical training preparatory for and subordinate to dialectic, and whether, in the writings believed to belong to the last twenty years of his life, he took note of recent scientific discoveries or was influenced by them in matters belonging to philosophy.

As for sources of information, the account of Plato's life and doctrine by Diogenes Laertius (probably early third century A.D.) is based on previous authorities of unequal value. He reports some evidently reliable statements by men who were in a position to know the facts and who were neither fanatical devotees nor detractors, and he has preserved the text of Plato's will. Aristotle gives us a few details, and Cicero a few more.

The Epistles, ascribed to Plato and printed in the Herrmann and Burnet editions of the Greek text of his works, would, if genuine, furnish us with a personal account of his conduct at important crises in his life; and, what is more, they would tell far more about his ideals of education and the work of the Academy than can be gathered from the dialogues. Unfortunately, opinion regarding authenticity of the *Epistles* is so divided that caution is essential. In the ensuing account, where reference is made to this source, the fact has been indicated.

Plato's writings have been preserved entire. But the double fact that they are dialogues and that the scene is usually laid in the past leads to difficulties of interpretation which are sufficiently obvious. Moreover, nothing definite is known about either the manner of their first publication or their relative order, still less the dates. Some hypothesis about the latter is a presupposition of fruitful discussion of Plato's development.

A statistical study of the style of Plato's works, in which the pioneer was the Reverend Lewis Campbell (1869), has led to results which have met with wide approval: many scholars hold that *Parmenides* and *Theaetetus* were written later than the *Republic*, and that a group of dialogues having close stylistic affinity to one another and to the *Laws* (which is plainly a work of old age) came still later. This is credible from a philosophical point of view, and its correctness is assumed here; but such a method can only yield a probable result.

Several members of Plato's family are mentioned, or appear as characters, in his dialogues. He himself was the son of Ariston[2] and Perictione, and was born either at Athens or Aegina, where his father may have gone as a settler when the Athenians occupied the island. Nothing reliable is known of his father's ancestors, but those on his mother's side were men of distinction. Perictione was descended from Dropides, a close friend (some say brother) of Solon, the famous poet-statesman of the sixth century B.C. She was a cousin of Critias, son of Callaeschrus, an intellectual daring in both speculative thought and action. It was Critias who in 404 B.C. led the extremists among the Thirty Tyrants and put to death the moderate Theramenes. He became guardian of Perictione's brother Charmides and drew him into public affairs. Both perished in the battle which put an end to the Thirty's six months of power.

Plato was one of four children. His brothers Adeimantus and Glaucon take a leading part in the *Republic*, where they are depicted with admiration and a clear impression of their personality is left. They appear once more briefly in the *Parmenides*, and Xenophon presents Socrates proving to Glaucon the folly of his trying to address the Assembly when he is not yet twenty.[3] The brothers were considerably older than Plato, and his sister Potone (mother of Speusippus, who followed him as head of the Academy) was doubtless born in the interval.

Plato's father, Ariston, appears to have died young. Perictione then married Pyrilampes, son of Antiphon, who had been prominent in state affairs as a close associate of Pericles; he was probably her uncle. Another son, called Antiphon after his grandfather, was born; this half brother of Plato's has a part in the *Parmenides*. Most of these persons are mentioned either in *Charmides* (155–158), or in *Timaeus* (20E), or at the opening of *Parmenides*.[4]

Plato's social position was such that he might well have aspired to an active part in public affairs, but it could not have been easy for him to decide what role to assume. Some scholars take it for granted that the example and writings of Critias left a deep impression upon him; others point out that it was only in the concluding phase of the Athenian struggle against the Peloponnesians that Plato's maternal relatives emerged as reactionary extremists, and that in his stepfather's home he would have been imbued with liberal opinions and respect for the memory of Pericles.

No one can say with certainty what the complexion of his views was at the age of twenty-four, except that he was obviously no friend to egalitarianism and full democracy. The story which he tells, or is made to tell, in Epistle VII seems probable. His friends and relatives among the Thirty at once called upon him to join them, but instead he determined to wait and see what they would do. They soon made the former regime seem highly desirable by comparison. Socrates was commanded to help in the arrest of a man who was to be put to death illegally under a general sentence, so that he would either be involved in their impious actions or refuse and thus expose himself to punishment. When the Thirty were overthrown, Plato again thought of public affairs—but with less eagerness than before. The democratic leaders restored to power showed moderation at a time when ruthless acts of revenge might have been expected. Nevertheless Socrates was brought to trial on the pretext of impiety and found guilty. As Plato grew older and the politicians, laws, and customs of the day displeased him more and more, he was thrown back on a theorist's study of ways of reform.[5]

None of this is inconsistent with what is otherwise known. Socrates' disobedience to the illegal command of the Thirty was a fact widely spoken of. Plato would probably have been impressed to an equal degree by Socrates' courageous independence in such matters and by his faith in argument (argument with himself when he could not find a respondent). He became conspicuous among Socrates' habitual companions, as distinct from the occasional listeners to his conversation. With Adeimantus he heard Socrates' provocative defense in court against the charge of impiety;[6] when a majority had found him guilty, Plato was one of those who induced Socrates to offer to pay a substantial fine, for which he would be a guarantor.[7]

Owing to illness, Plato was absent from the last meeting of Socrates with his friends.[8] After the tragedy, he retired, with other Socratics, to Megara, the home of Euclid.[9] The attack on Socrates was personal, and perhaps the prosecutors did not desire his death. His Athenian friends can hardly have been in danger. But there are some hints in the *Phaedo* that he advised those present, among whom were the Megarians Euclid and Terpsion, to pursue the search for truth in common and not lose heart when plausible reasoning led them nowhere; rather, they must make it their business to master the "art of argument," *logōn technē*.[10]

Probably his wish was piously carried out by his followers, and a few years elapsed before the different direction of their interests became clear. As a metaphysician Euclid was a follower of Parmenides, and accepted the Socratic thesis that there is a single human excellence, not a plurality of "virtues." His thought had no religious coloring, nor was he an educational reformer. His younger disciples turned in earnest to the hoped-for *logōn technē*, and not without result; they prepared the way for the propositional logic of the Stoic school.[11] This might be supposed to go together with an interest in the sciences, but this is not recorded of the Megarians. Plato, on the other hand, began to turn in that direction; his first dialogues and the *Apology* must have been written during the years 399–388 B.C. He felt it his duty to defend the memory of Socrates, especially since controversy about his aims had been revived by hostile publications. As the chance of political action remained remote, he gradually developed the idea of a training of the young not in rhetoric but in mathematics—and in Socratic interrogation only after the mathematical foundation had been laid. Part of his diagnosis of the ills of Athens was that young men had bewildered themselves and others by engaging too soon in philosophical controversy; these ideas probably found little sympathy among the Megarians. How long he remained among them is not recorded, but he was liable to Athenian military service, probably as a cavalryman. A statement has indeed come down to us[12] that he went on expeditions to Tanagra (in Boeotia) and Corinth. This is credible in itself, and in the latter case the reference could be to an engagement in 394 B.C. outside Corinth, in which the Spartans and their allies defeated the Athenians and Thebans. But neither does it seem inconsistent with Plato's regarding Megara for a time as his home. About 390 he resolved to visit the West, where Archytas of Tarentum survived as a maintainer of the Pythagorean system of education and was also active in research.

Plato's views at the time of departure on his journey to the West are well seen in the *Gorgias*. It is his first major constructive effort as a moralist, but there is as yet no positive doctrine of knowledge and reality. When Callicles spurns conventional justice, as a means of defrauding the strong and energetic of what naturally belongs to them, and declares that temperance is not a virtue (why should a clear-sighted man choose to curb his own desires?), Socrates confidently develops an answering thesis: the supervision of the soul must be supposed comparable in its operation to the arts, which impose form and design (*eidos, taxis*) and preserve the natural subordination of one part of a subject to another (*kosmos*). Human good does not consist in the ceaseless satisfaction of desires, irrespective of their quality (if it did, man would stand apart from the general world order), and self-discipline is the basis of happiness. But the statesmen of Athens, the dramatists and musicians, the teachers and learners of rhetorical persuasion, have all alike failed to understand this and have flattered rather than guided the public.

In his use of the varied senses of *kosmos* (which, according to the context, means world or world order, moral discipline, or adornment), Socrates is here on Pythagorean ground; and ideas are already present which Plato expanded only in his later writings and his oral instruction.[13] The *Gorgias* passage is also an emphatic answer to the friends who had sought to draw Plato into Athenian politics.[14]

Concerning the journey itself, in Epistle VII Plato says, or is made to say, that he was then forty years old (324A) and that in Italy and Sicily he was appalled by the sensuous indulgence which he found taken for granted there. On crossing to Syracuse he made the acquaintance of Dion, the young brother-in-law of the tyrant Dionysius the Elder, who listened attentively to his discourses and aroused his admiration by his intelligence and preference for a sober life. In the tyrant's entourage this was viewed as an affectation of singularity and led to Dion's becoming unpopular.[15]

If this evidence is set aside as suspect, the next best source is Cicero.[16] He says that Plato visited Egypt before proceeding to Italy; that he spent a considerable time with Archytas and with Timaeus of Locri; and that the object of the voyage was to gain acquaintance with Pythagorean studies and institutions. To this some reservations must be made. First, it can hardly be true—if Cicero means this—that when he boarded the ship Plato was altogether ignorant of mathematics. In his own dialogues there is clear evidence that the sciences were to some extent taught to boys at Athens and that there was an opportunity of learning from specialists in mathematics and astronomy, no less than from those in music, meter, and grammar. About Pythagoreanism also Plato already had some information, judging from the *Gorgias* passage mentioned above; he could have obtained this (as Wilamowitz suggests) from the Thebans Simmias and Cebes, pupils of Socrates who are said to have met Philolaus.[17]

Secondly, it does not seem likely that Timaeus of Locri was still alive at the time of Plato's journey. In *Timaeus* 20A he is described as a man of intellectual distinction who has already held high office, and this is at a time certainly previous to 415 B.C. (It is possible that at this time Plato met Philistion of Locri, and derived from him the interest in the physiology of the Sicilian Empedocles, which is visible in both *Meno* and *Phaedo*.) Cicero's report may be wrong in some of its detail, but it seems true in spirit. Plato's purpose in visiting the West was to see for himself how the Pythagoreans conducted their science-based educational system, and he did at this time establish a connection with Archytas.

Plato returned to Athens, after two years' absence, in 388 B.C. (Ancient biographers related, with some circumstantial detail, that at Syracuse he had exasperated the tyrant Dionysius the Elder by open criticism of his rule and had been handed over as a prisoner to a Spartan envoy. But such insolence is hardly in character for Plato, and probably his voyage home was of a less sensational kind.) He might at this time have visited the Pythagoreans at Phlius, in the Peloponnesus. The setting of the *Phaedo* suggests personal acquaintance with their leader Echecrates, and Cicero confirms this.[18]

Nothing definite is recorded about Plato's personal life during the ensuing twenty-two years. But the Academy was founded, or gradually grew up, during this time, and he composed further dialogues in Socratic style. The *Meno* and *Euthyphro*, *Euthydemus*, *Phaedo*, *Symposium*, and *Republic* must all be assigned to these years. In them he puts forward the distinctive account of knowledge which has taken shape in his mind; explains his purpose and method in education and shows the continuity of his aims with those of Socrates; and differentiates himself, where necessary, from the Italian Pythagoreans. It is natural to place the *Republic* at the end of this series, and to regard it as either a prospectus for a proposed school or as a statement to the Athenian public of what was already being carried out among them.

Aristotle gives a clear analysis of the factors which produced Plato's doctrine of Forms.[19] Plato was acquainted from youth with an Athenian named Cratylus, who declared with Heraclitus that there is no stable substance, or hold for human knowledge, in the sense world. Plato did not deny this then or later but, wishing to take over and continue the Socratic search for universals, in the sphere of morals, which do remain permanent, he necessarily separated the universals from sensible particulars. It was he who termed them Ideas and Forms. In his view particulars (that is, things and states of things, actions and qualities) derive reality from Forms by "participation"; and when we name or speak of these particulars, we in effect name Forms.

In the dialogues Plato often starts from a contrast between knowledge and opinion. To live in a state of opinion is to accept assertions, either of fact or of principle, on authority or from mere habit. The opinion may be true and right; but since it is held without a rational ground, it may be driven from the mind by emotion and is less proof against forgetfulness than knowledge is. The holder of it may also be deceived in an unfamiliar instance. Based as it is on habit, an opinion cannot easily be transmitted to another; or, if the transmission takes place, this is not teaching. In terms of the theory of Forms, the holder of knowledge knows the Forms and can relate particular instances to them (although Plato did not successfully explain how this occurs), whereas the contented holder of opinions moves about among half-real particulars.

In middle life, then, Plato had advanced from his Socratic beginnings toward beliefs, held with assurance, from which many practical consequences flowed. The chief elements were the knowledge-opinion contrast; the belief in a realm of immutable Forms, with which human minds can make intermittent contact and which on such occasions the minds recognize as "their own" or as akin to them;[20] given this, the soul, or its intellectual part, is seen to be likewise eternal; and the belief that the Forms, each of which infuses reality into corresponding particulars, in turn derive their existence, intelligibility, and truth from one supreme Form, the Good.

The advance from the plurality of Forms to their source is in consequence regarded as the ultimate stage in human study, *megiston mathēma*;[21] it is a step which will be taken by only a few, but for the welfare of mankind it is important that a few should take it. Within the dialogue it is described but cannot be accomplished. There are hints of a methodical derivation of the other Forms from the Good; but for the present the image, whereby the Good is shown to have the same relation to other objects of intellection as the sun has to other visible things, takes its place. In reading the *Republic* and later dialogues, one must therefore reckon with the possibility that in the school Plato amplified or corrected the exposition which he chose to commit to writing.

The Athenians thought it suitable that young men should exercise themselves in argument on abstract themes before turning to serious business, and were prepared to tolerate "philosophy" on these terms. But Plato, as has been said, speaks out against this practice and holds that it has brought philosophy into discredit.

Indeed, according to him, the order of procedure should be reversed. Argument, or its theory, is the hardest branch of philosophy and should come later. Men and women to whom legislation and administration are ultimately to be entrusted should undergo discipline in the sciences (including reflection on their interrelation) before they embark, say, at the age of thirty, on dialectical treatment of matters which have to be grasped by the intellect without the help of images. Such a discipline will single out those who have capacity for dialectic. To them will fall the task of making good laws, if these are not found in existence, and of interpreting and applying them if they are. For this purpose knowledge must be reinforced by experience.[22] Lawless government is the common fault of despotism and democracy.

Plato holds that ignorance of mathematical truths which are in no way recondite, for example, the wrong belief that all magnitudes are commensurable, is a disgrace to human nature.[23] It is not, however, this that is emphasized in his educational plan in the *Republic*. He explains that it is characteristic of mathematical studies that they gently disengage the intellect from sensible appearances and turn it toward reality; no other discipline does this. They induce a state of mind (which Plato terms *dianoia*, discursive thought) clearer than "opinion" and naïve trust in the senses but dimmer than knowledge and reason. In geometry, for instance, the learner is enabled or compelled, with the aid of figures, to fix his attention on intelligible objects. Also, mathematicians "lay down as hypotheses the odd and even, various figures, and the three kinds of angles and the like"[24] but leave them unexamined and go on to prove that the problem that gave rise to their investigation has been solved. In this respect mathematical procedure tends to divert the mind from reality and can provide only conditional truth. But such studies, pursued steadily and without continual talk of their practical use, are a good preparation for methodical treatment of such relations among Forms as cannot be visibly depicted.

Arithmetic and plane geometry will be the basis of an education which is to end in knowledge; the geometry of three-dimensional figures must also be studied. When, in the dialogue, Glaucon observes that this hardly yet exists as a science, Socrates says that there are two reasons for this: first, no state at present honors the study and encourages men to devote themselves to it; and second, a director is needed in order to coordinate the research.[25] Such a man will be hard to find; and at present even if he existed the researchers are too self-confident to defer to him. Even without these conditions, and even when the researchers do not succeed in explaining what they are striving to achieve, the intrinsic charm of the study of three-dimensional figures is carrying it forward. This is one of the passages in which speakers in Plato's dialogues refer prophetically, but in veiled terms, to circumstances at the time of writing. It is somewhat enigmatic for us. The intention is perhaps to compliment Theaetetus, who had discovered constructions for inscribing in a sphere the regular octahedron and icosahedron. Either he or Plato himself is cast for the role of a director, and there is a plea for public support of the Academy so that research can continue.

There is a similar personal reference in the treatment of the sciences of astronomy and musical theory.[26] Socrates dissociates himself from the Pythagoreans while approving of their statement that the two sciences are closely akin. Their theory of harmony is restricted to a numerical account of audible concords; and the aim of their astronomy is to discover the proportion between month, year, and the period of revolution of the planets. Instead of this, heard harmonies should be studied as a special case of the harmonies between numbers; and the proportion between month, year, and so forth (which is doubtless not unvarying) as an application of some wider theory dealing with the spatial relations of any given number of bodies of any shape, moving at any regular speeds at any distances. The visible universe will be to the "true astronomer" what a beautifully contrived diagram might be to the geometer, that is, an aid to the science, not the object of contemplation. Here Plato is indicating that he has not simply established on Athenian soil a replica of the Pythagorean schools. Attachment to the sense world must be loosened and the sciences taught with emphasis on their affinity to one another; for it is the power of synopsis, the perception of common features, that is to be strengthened. Those few who excel in this are to be set apart and trained to pursue another method which treats hypotheses as provisional until they have been linked to the unconditionally real and so established.[27]

There is no question here, as some have thought, of a fusion of the existing special sciences. The ideal held out is probably this: The One is an aspect of the Good (this was common ground to Euclid of Megara and Plato); from the concept of unity, the number series can be made to emerge by deduction; and from the Good, by a process which makes more use of Socratic questioning, the system of moral and aesthetic concepts can likewise be evolved.[28]

Boys will have some introduction to all the sciences that have been mentioned. Compulsion is to be avoided in the training of the mind, especially since what is learnt under duress leaves no lasting impression. At the age of twenty when state-enforced physical exercise is to cease, those judged capable of further progress must begin to bring together the knowledge that they have hitherto acquired randomly and to consider in what way the sciences are akin to one another and to reality. Until they are thirty this will be their occupation. After this there can follow five years of that dialectical exercise that Athenian custom regards as a fitting occupation for mere adolescents.[29]

The program here outlined is our safest guide to the actual institutions of the Academy. But it is an ideal that is sketched, and one need not insist that it was carried out in detail. For instance, Plato did not admit women, and it is highly improbable that he gave no philosophical instruction to those under thirty; it would doubtless occur to him that since he could not prevent them from obtaining such instruction, it would be better to make sure that they were well taught.

"Academy" was an area to the northeast of the city which had been laid out as a park, including a public gymnasium. According to Lysias, the Spartans encamped there during the troubled year 403 B.C. Plato may have commenced teaching in the gymnasium itself; but he soon purchased an adjoining garden and erected buildings there, and from this moment he may be said to have instituted a school. Hitherto he could not exclude chance listeners. The buildings may have included lodgings for students or visitors, and Plato himself presumably lived in the neighborhood. Common meals had been a feature of Pythagorean life, and this precedent was followed. Legal recognition was secured by making the Academy a religious fraternity devoted to the Muses.

Plato nominated his nephew Speusippus to be his successor, but later the head seems to have been elected. Presumably the power of admission rested with the head, and those accepted contributed to the maintenance of the school according to their means. The story that the words "Let no man unversed in geometry enter" were inscribed over the door cannot be traced back further than John Philoponus (sixth century). In the first century B.C., "academic" teaching was being given in the gymnasium of Ptolemy near the agora of Athens.[30]

In the teaching, Plato will doubtless have been assisted from an early stage by Theaetetus, who, as the dialogue named after him shows, was a boy of exceptional promise in 399 B.C. He was an Athenian. The dialogue records his death from wounds received in battle at Corinth, complicated by illness, and was obviously written soon afterward (ca. 368–367 B.C.). Hence his collaboration with Plato may have lasted about fifteen years.

Somewhat later, Eudoxus of Cnidus resided occasionally at the Academy. He is known to have died at the age of fifty-three, and the dates for his life now usually accepted are ca. 400–ca. 347 B.C. In mathematics he was a pupil of Archytas, but it is not clear when this instruction was received. During a first visit to Athens at the age of twenty-three, he heard lectures from Plato. Later he established a school at Cyzicus in northwest Asia Minor, one of those Greek cities which had been abandoned to Persian control under the Peace of Antalcidas in 387 B.C.; Eudoxus probably felt insecure there and was glad to maintain a connection with the Platonists.

Eudoxus was at Athens when Aristotle first arrived as a student in 367 B.C., and it is plain from several Aristotelian passages[31] that he deeply influenced his juniors and played an important part in the life of the school. In Plato's *Philebus* there is probably some concealed allusion to him. Mathematics and astronomy were his main business, but he took part as a friendly outsider in philosophical debate arising from Plato's writings. He was not one to pledge himself to accept philosophical dogmas, nor was this expected of him, and his work exhibits the close attention to phenomena which the Socrates of the *Republic* deprecates.

But Eudoxus recognized that philosophy has a legitimate role in criticizing the procedure of specialists. His explanation of the celestial movements in terms of homocentric spheres, rotating about a stationary spherical earth, was put forward in answer to a problem posed by Plato: "What are the uniform and ordered movements by the assumption of which the apparent movements of the planets can be accounted for?" Eudoxus did not abandon his own school and merge it with that of Plato; and Proclus' statement that he "became a companion of Plato's disciples" does not mean this, for we know that Aristotle later carried on the connection with Cyzicene mathematicians which Plato had established. Epistle XIII, ascribed to Plato, mentions Helicon as a pupil of Eudoxus and implies the presence of other Cyzicenes at Athens in the period 365–362 B.C.

If we consider Plato's relation to Theaetetus and Eudoxus and also bring in the evidence of Aristotle, his personal role in the Academy begins to appear. He probably committed all the specialist instruction to them. He took note of their research and sometimes criticized their methods, speaking as a person with authority; he guided the juniors in that reflection about first principles and about the interrelation of sciences that in *Republic* VII is designated as suitable for them;[32] and he confided to some an ethico-mathematical philosophy in which two ultimate principles, from which Form-Numbers were derived, were found by analysis.

The last item is outside the scope of this article, and concerning the other two a few examples must suffice. Theaetetus added to previously known constructions of regular solid figures those for the octahedron and icosahedron, and gave a proof[33] that there can be no more than five regular solids. He also tried to classify incommensurable relations, connecting them with the three kinds of means. Plato's inspiration may be seen in this effort to systematize. Plato is credited by Proclus with beginning the study of conic sections, which his followers developed, and with either discovering or clearly formulating the method of analysis, which proved fruitful in geometry in the hands of Leodamas of Thasos.[34] According to Plutarch, Plato criticized Eudoxus, Archytas, and Menaechmus for trying to effect the duplication of the cube by mechanical means and so losing the benefit of geometry.[35] Aristotle says that Plato (in oral instruction) "used to object vigorously to the point, as a mathematical dogma, and on the other hand often posited his indivisible lines."[36]

The view that the sciences contemplate objects situated halfway between Forms and sensibles and having some of the characteristics of both, which is not found in Plato's dialogues, was probably at home in the same discussion. Observation of the heavens went on, perhaps under the direction of Eudoxus or his companions. Aristotle says that he had seen an occultation of Mars by the moon (then at half-moon); this must have been in April or May 357 B.C., a calculation first made by Kepler.[37]

It was maintained by H. Usener in 1884 that the Academy was the first known institute for scientific research, a statement which initiated a debate not yet closed. It has been opposed from one point of view by those who compare the Academy to a modern school of political science (and perhaps jurisprudence) thoroughly practical in its orientation; and from another especially by Jaeger, who thinks that it was no part of Plato's intention to teach science in encyclopedic fashion and promote its general advance.[38] The Academy was not a place in which *all* science was studied for its own sake but one in which selected sciences were taught and their foundations examined as a mental discipline, the aim being practical wisdom and legislative skill, which in Plato's opinion are inseparable from contemplative philosophy.

Evidently the crux of this matter is whether empirical sciences, which had no place in the curriculum projected for the guardians in the *Republic*, were, in fact, pursued under Plato's auspices. Jaeger seems to be right in his skepticism about the apparent evidence of such activity. It may be added that proofs that Plato was personally interested in (for instance) medicine and physiology, which *Timaeus* affords, are not quite what is wanted. One might argue that he was indeed an empirical scientist manqué, pointing to his interest in the manufacturing arts in the *Statesman*, his marvelous sketch of the geology of Attica in the *Critias*, and his attention to legislative detail in the *Laws*. It was an imperfectly suppressed love of the concrete and visible, rather than any retreat from his avowed opinions, that led him to pose the problem concerning celestial phenomena which Eudoxus later solved. But it is a long step from these admissions to the pronouncement that the Academy became an institute of scientific research.

Plato's activity at Athens was interrupted by two more visits to Sicily. When Dionysius the Elder died in the spring of 367 B.C., two problems in particular demanded solution: what the future form of government Syracuse itself should be; and when and how several Greek cities, whose populations had been transferred elsewhere under Dionysius' policy, should be refounded. Plato's admirer Dion planned to make his nephew, Dionysius the Younger, a constitutional monarch, and appealed for Plato's aid in educating him for his responsibility. His proposal was that Plato should come to Syracuse and take charge of a group of earnest students, which Dionysius might unobtrusively join.

Plato yielded to pressure and arrived in the spring of 366 B.C. But, according to Epistle VII, he found a situation of intrigue. Some Syracusans believed that Dion's aim was to occupy his nephew with interminable study while he himself wielded effective power. From another side there was pressure for the restoration of full democracy. A war with Carthage (or against the Lucanians) was in progress. Three months after Plato's arrival the young ruler charged Dion with attempting to negotiate with the Carthaginians and expelled him. Plato left the following year (365 B.C.), after obtaining what he took to be a promise that Dion would be recalled.

In 362 B.C. he once more left the Academy (appointing, it is said, Heraclides Ponticus as his deputy) and returned to Syracuse. There were reports that Dionysius was now genuinely interested in philosophy; but in consenting to go Plato was more influenced, according to Epistle VII, by a promise that a favorable settlement of Dion's affairs could be reached on condition that he return. Dion had spent his years of exile in Athens and had become a friend of Plato's nephew Speusippus.

Plato's mission ended in failure. Dion's agents were forbidden to send him the revenue from his estates; and Plato made his escape with some difficulty, returning home in 361 B.C. Dion thereupon took steps to effect his return to Syracuse by force, urging Plato to aid him and to punish Dionysius as a violator of hospitality. But Plato answered (still according to the Epistle) that he was too old, that after all Dionysius had spared his life, and that he wished to be available if necessary as a mediator. Other members of the Academy, however, joined the expedition. Dion succeeded in his enterprise but failed to reconcile the warring parties; and after a brief period of power he was murdered by the Athenian Callippus (354 B.C.). Epistles VII and VIII, addressed to Dion's partisans, belong to this time or were fabricated as belonging to it. They contain constructive advice which, in language and spirit, closely resembles *Laws* III. Plato died in 348/347 B.C., at the age of eighty.

Was Plato at all influenced in his later years by progress in the special sciences? It may be replied that later modifications in his general theory of knowledge seem to have been the product of his own reflection rather than of any remarkable discoveries and were not such as to affect his educational ideals. He did, however, absorb new scientific ideas and make use of them for his purposes as a moralist. This is seen in one way in the *Timaeus*, where the world is shown to be a product of beneficent rational design, and in another in the *Laws*, where theological consequences are drawn from the perfect regularity of the planetary movements.

In the *Timaeus*, Plato has not abandoned his theory of Forms, for Timaeus declares that the perpetually changing, visible cosmos can at best be an object of "right opinion." The view earlier attributed to Socrates in *Phaedo*—that the only satisfactory explanation of physical facts is a teleological one—is assumed from the start and carried out in detail. Timaeus opposes mechanistic views with a superior atomism, in which Theaetetus' construction of the mathematical solids plays a part. Sicilian influence is especially strong. From Empedocles' system the doctor Philistion of Locri, with whom Plato was personally acquainted,[39] developed a theory whereby the heart is the center of life and consciousness, and the veins and arteries carry pneuma along with blood. Timaeus adopts this physiology and the explanation of disease which went with it, except that in making the brain the organ of consciousness he follows Alcmaeon. (It appears then to have been the Academy, with its Sicilian connections, which brought the knowledge of Empedoclean medicine to the mainland.) All this leads up to the conclusion that man can learn to regulate his life by study of the cosmos, which is a divine artifact but also an intelligent being.

The Athenian Stranger in the *Laws* says that he was no longer a young man when he became persuaded that each of the planets moves in a single path, and that we malign them when we call them "wanderers." He evidently speaks for Plato, and the remark is a formal withdrawal of what was said in *Republic* VII of the erratic celestial movements; but in favor of what new system? Surely that of Eudoxus. This may not have lasted long, and was open to an objection that was soon seen, but it was the first scientific astronomy. From it Plato could, and did, argue that all movement stems from a soul (matter is inactive); perfectly regular movement stems from a wise and beneficent soul; and the rotation of the stars, sun, and planets is perfectly regular.

In these later developments Plato may appear not as a lover of science but as a biased user of it. But "an intense belief that a knowledge of mathematical relations would prove the key to unlock the mysteries of the relatedness within Nature was ever at the back of Plato's cosmological speculations" (Whitehead, *Adventures of Ideas*, p. 194).[40]

NOTES

1. Proclus in his commentary on Euclid's *Elements* gives a summary account of the development of geometry from the time of Thales. He claims that Plato brought about a great advance, and names some of those who worked with his encouragement in the Academy. Closely similar language is used in a fragmentary papyrus found at Herculaneum, "Academicorum philosophorum index Herculanensis," where Plato's role is said to be that of a supervisor who propounded problems for investigation by mathematicians. Simplicius in his commentary on Aristotle's *De Caelo* informs us that Eudoxus' astronomical system was a solution of a carefully formulated problem set by Plato. The common source of the first two reports is probably the history of mathematics by Eudemus of Rhodes, and Simplicius says that his statement is derived from Book 2 of Eudemus' *History of Astronomy*. Greek texts are in K. Gaiser, "Testimonia Platonica" (Appendix to *Platons Ungeschriebene Lehre*), nos. 15–21, 460–479. An English translation of the latter part of the Proclus passage is in Heath, *A Manual of Greek Mathematics*, 184–185.
2. *Apology* 34A; *Republic* II, 368A.
3. *Memorabilia* III, 6.
4. For a family tree, see John Burnet, *Greek Philosophy From Thales to Plato* (London, 1924), appendix; or C. Ritter, *Platon*, I, 13.
5. *Epistles* VII, 324–326.
6. *Apology* 34A.
7. *Ibid.*, 38B.
8. *Phaedo* 59B, C.
9. Diogenes Laërtius III, 6, and II, 106, quoting Hermodorus, a pupil of Plato.
10. *Phaedo* 78A, 107B.
11. W. and M. Kneale, *The Development of Logic* (Oxford, 1962), ch. 3; B. Mates, *Stoic Logic* (Berkeley–Los Angeles, 1961), intro.
12. Aelian, V, 16; VII, 14; and Diogenes Laërtius, III, 8, where there is confusion between Plato and Socrates.
13. Robin, *Platon*, pp. 101–103.
14. Cornford, *Republic of Plato*, Intro., p. xvii.

15. *Epistles* VII, 326–327.
16. *De Republica* I, 10.
17. *Phaedo* 61D.
18. *De finibus* V, 29.87.
19. *Metaphysics*, 987A32.
20. *Phaedo* 75E, 76E.
21. *Republic* VI, 503–505.
22. *Republic* VI, 484C, D.
23. *Laws* VII, 819–820.
24. *Republic* VI, 510C.
25. *Ibid.*, VII, 528B.
26. *Ibid.*, 528E ff.
27. *Ibid.*, 533.
28. Cornford, who gives this exposition, relies upon *Parmenides* 142D ff. See his trans. of the *Republic*, p. 245, and his "Mathematics and Dialectic in the *Republic* VI–VII."
29. *Republic* VII, 535–540.
30. See Cicero, *De finibus* V, 1, for an eloquent description of a walk to the gymnasium's original site, now deserted.
31. Especially *Nicomachean Ethics* X, ch. 1.
32. *Republic* VII, 535–540.
33. Euclid XIII, 18A.
34. See Cornford, "Mathematics and Dialectic in the *Republic* VI–VII," pp. 68–73.
35. *Quaestiones convivales* 718F.
36. *Metaphysics* A, 992a20; see Ross *ad. loc.*
37. See Stocks's note in Oxford trans. of Aristotle, vol. II; and Guthrie's ed. of Aristotle's *On the Heavens* (Loeb), p. 205.
38. Aristotle, p. 18 and elsewhere.
39. *Epistles* II, 314D.
40. That the system presented through Timaeus is formulated in antithesis to mechanist atomism—whether or not Plato knew of Democritus as its chief author—is clearly shown by Frank, *Platon u. die sogenannten Pythagoreer*, pp. 97–108. On the meaning of *Timaeus* 40B, C, concerning the earth's rotation, see Cornford, *Plato's Cosmology*, pp. 120–134. On Philistion, see Jaeger, *Diokles von Karystos*, pp. 7, 211. For the argument that *Laws* 822A–E can refer only to the system of Eudoxus, and for Plato's astronomy in general, see Burkert, *Weisheit und Wissenschaft*, pp. 302–311.

BIBLIOGRAPHY

I. ORIGINAL WORKS. For present purposes the most important dialogues are *Meno*, *Phaedo*, *Republic*, *Parmenides*, *Theaetetus*, *Timaeus*, and *Laws*. The *Epistles* and *Epinomis*, even if they are not authentic, are informative. There are translations with introductions and notes in many modern languages.

Some useful English versions are *Phaedo*, R. Hackforth, trans. (Cambridge, 1955); *Republic*, F. M. Cornford, trans. (Oxford, 1941); *Theaetetus*, *Parmenides*, and *Timaeus*, F. M. Cornford, trans., in vols. entitled, respectively, *Plato's Theory of Knowledge* (London, 1935), *Plato and Parmenides* (London–New York, 1939), and *Plato's Cosmology* (London, 1937); *Timaeus* and *Critias*, A. E. Taylor, trans. (London, 1929); *Philebus and Epinomis*, A. E. Taylor, trans., R. Klibansky *et al.*, eds. (Edinburgh–London, 1956), with intro. to the latter by A. C. Lloyd; *Epinomis*, J. Harward, trans. (Oxford, 1928); *Epistles*, J. Harward, trans. (Cambridge, 1932); *Epistles*, Glenn R. Morrow, trans. (Urbana, Ill., 1935; repr. New York, 1961); *Laws*, A. E. Taylor, trans. (London, 1934; repr. 1960).

The appropriate vols. in the French trans., *Oeuvres complètes*, 13 vols. in 25 pts. (Paris, 1920–1956), published under the patronage of the Association Guillaume Budé, should also be consulted.

II. SECONDARY LITERATURE. On Plato's life, see H. Leisegang, *Platon*, in Pauly-Wissowa, *Realenzyklopädie*, 1st ser., XX. The following books and articles are important for his views concerning method and for an estimate of his understanding of science.

J. Adam, *The Republic of Plato*, II (Cambridge, 1902); W. Burkert, *Weisheit und Wissenschaft* (Nuremberg, 1962), containing a useful bibliography; F. M. Cornford, "Mathematics and Dialectic in the *Republic* VI–VII," in *Mind*, **41** (1932), 37–52, 173–190, repr. in *Studies in Plato's Metaphysics*, R. E. Allen, ed. (London, 1965), 61–95; and E. Frank, *Platon und die sogenannten Pythagoreer* (Halle, 1923).

See also K. Gaiser, *Platons ungeschriebene Lehre*, 2nd ed. (Stuttgart, 1968), which contains in an app. the *Testimonia Platonica*, ancient evidence relative to the organization of the Academy and to Plato's esoteric teaching; and "Platons *Menon* und die Akademie," in *Archiv für Geschichte der Philosophie*, **46** (1964), 241–292; T. L. Heath, *History of Greek Mathematics* (Oxford, 1921), and *Aristarchus of Samos* (Oxford, 1913), esp. chs. XV and XVI; G. E. R. Lloyd, "Plato as Natural Scientist," in *Journal of Hellenic Studies*, **88** (1968), 78–92; C. Ritter, *Platon*, 2 vols. (Munich, 1910–1922), containing a chapter on Plato's doctrine of nature and his attitude toward the problems of science; L. Robin, *Platon* (Paris, 1935); F. Solmsen, "Platonic Influences in the Formation of Aristotle's Physical System," in I. Düring and G. Owen, eds., *Aristotle and Plato in the Mid-Fourth Century* (Göteborg, 1960); and A. E. Taylor, *Plato, the Man and His Work*, 4th ed. (London, 1937).

There is a review of literature relating to Plato, 1950–1957, by H. Cherniss in *Lustrum*, **4** (1959), 5–308, and **5** (1960), 323–648; sec. II.B deals with the Academy, sec. V.E with mathematics and the sciences.

On the Academy, the comprehensive account in E. Zeller, *Philosophie der Griechen*, 6th ed. (Hildesheim, 1963), has not yet been superseded; and H. Usener, "Organisation der wissenschaftlichen Arbeit," in *Preussische Jahrbücher*, **53** (1884), repr. in *Vorträge und Aufsätze* (1907), 67 ff., has been a starting point for later discussion. See also E. Berti, *La filosofia del primo Aristotele* (Padua, 1962), pp. 138–159; H. Cherniss, *The Riddle of the Academy* (Berkeley, 1945); H. Herter, *Platons Akademie*, 2nd ed. (Bonn, 1952); W. Jaeger, *Aristotle*, 2nd ed. (Oxford, 1948), *Diokles von Karystos* (Berlin, 1938), and *Paideia* (Oxford, 1944), II and III; G. Ryle, *Plato's Progress* (Cambridge, 1966); P. M. Schuhl, "Une école de sciences politiques," in *Revue philosophique de la France et de l'étranger*, **84** (1959), 101–103; J. Stenzel, *Platon der Erzieher* (Leipzig, 1928); and U. von Wilamowitz, *Platon* (Berlin, 1919; 5th ed. 1959).

On Eudoxus, see K. von Fritz, "Die Lebenszeit des Eudoxos v. Knidos," in *Philologus*, **85** (1929–1930), 478–481; H. Karpp, *Die Philosophie des Eudoxos v. Knidos*

(Würzburg, 1933); and E. Frank, "Die Begründung der mathematischen Naturwissenschaft durch Eudoxus?" in L. Edelstein, ed., *Wissen, Wollen, Glauben* (Zurich, 1955), 134–157.

On the mathematical intermediates in Plato's philosophy, see W. D. Ross, *Metaphysics of Aristotle* (Oxford, 1924), I, 166 ff.; J. A. Brentlinger, "The Divided Line and Plato's Theory of Intermediates," in *Phronesis*, **7**, no. 2 (1963) 146–166; S. Mansion, "L'objet des mathématiques et de la dialectique selon Platon," in *Revue philosophique de Louvain*, **67** (1969), 365–388.

On the number in *Republic* VIII, 546, see *The Republic of Plato*, Adam, ed., II, 201–203, 264–312; A. Diès, "Le Nombre de Platon," in *Mémoires de l'Académie des inscriptions*, **14** (1940); Gaiser, *Platons ungeschriebene Lehre*, pp. 271–273, 409–414. On the shape of the earth in the *Phaedo*, see Burkert, *Weisheit und Wissenschaft*, pp. 282–284, and earlier literature there mentioned. On Plato as geographer and as physicist, see P. Friedländer, *Platon*, 2nd ed. (Berlin, 1954), I, chs. 14, 15. On the *Epinomis* and the history of science, see E. des Places, "Notice" to the *Epinomis*, in *Platon, Oeuvres complètes*, Collection Budé, XII, 118–128.

D. J. ALLAN

PLATO OF TIVOLI (*fl.* Barcelona, first half of twelfth century)

Presumably an Italian, Plato is known only through his work, at least part of which was produced at Barcelona between 1132 and 1146. He was one of the first scientist-scholars active in the Iberian Peninsula to provide the Latin West with some of the works of Greek authors as transmitted or elaborated in Arabic and Hebrew and with works originally written in those languages; he was the first to edit Ptolemy in Latin and to help in the translation of the most important Hebrew treatise on geometry. His name appears only as a translator from the Arabic and Hebrew—or, better, as an editor of translations made in collaboration with the Jewish mathematician and polymath Abraham bar Ḥiyya ha-Nasi (Savasorda). It is impossible to determine to what extent the translations ascribed to Plato alone or to both men reflect Plato's linguistic and scientific knowledge; the editor of the most difficult of the translations finds the Latin rendering exact and clear. In the introductions to two translations Plato says that he was prompted by selective interests: he preferred al-Battānī to Ptolemy because al-Battānī was less verbose, and Ibn al-Ṣaffār to many other authors on the astrolabe because he was more reliable and scientific. He was a friend of at least one other translator of Arabic scientific literature, John, son of David, to whom he dedicated his translation of the work on the astrolabe. In the middle of the thirteenth century Plato was mentioned as an eminent Christian mathematician by the author of the *Summa philosophie* wrongly ascribed to Robert Grosseteste. His influence as a translator and editor is shown by the use of his versions by Leonardo Fibonacci and Albertus Magnus, by the relatively large number of manuscripts of his texts still surviving, and by the number of printed editions of some of them produced in the late fifteenth and sixteenth centuries.

The four truly scientific works—two mathematical and two astronomical—that in manuscripts or printed editions carry the name of Plato of Tivoli, with or without the name of Abraham bar Ḥiyya, as a translator are the following:

1. The *Liber Embadorum* ("Book of Areas," or "Practical Geometry") of Savasorda, identified by Steinschneider as the *Ḥibbur ha-meshiḥah we-ha-tishboret* of Abraham bar Ḥiyya, translated from the Hebrew in 1145 [the manuscripts give the right astronomical equivalent of this date but the wrong Hegira year, 510/1116 instead of 540/1145] and preserved in at least five manuscripts.

2. The *Spherica* by Theodosius of Bithynia, translated from the Greco-Arabic version of Ḥunayn ibn Isḥāq or of Qusṭā ibn Lūqā and extant in eleven manuscripts and four early editions.

3. Al-Battānī's *al-Zīj* ("Astronomical Treatise"), or *De motu stellarum*, in ten manuscripts and two editions.

4. The *De usu astrolabii* of Abu'l-Qāsim Maslama (Ibn al-Ṣaffār), in three manuscripts—quite convincing linguistic reasons have been given by M. Clagett to confirm a suggestion (based on the place of this text in the three existing manuscripts) that Plato is the author of the Latin translation from the Arabic of Archimedes' *In quadratum* [for *Quadratura*?] *circuli*, or *De mensura circuli*.

The translations from the Arabic of seven other works (five astrological, one geomantical, and one medical [now lost]) are ascribed to Plato, with or without Abraham bar Ḥiyya, in the manuscripts.

1. Ptolemy's *Quadripartitum*, translated in 1138 and preserved in nine manuscripts and five editions.

2. The *Iudicia Almansoris*, which is the *Centum* (or *Centumquinquaginta*) *propositiones* or *Capitula* (*Stellarum*) by, or dedicated to, one al-Manṣur (or by ar-Rāzī [?]), translated in 1136 and preserved in over forty manuscripts and a dozen printed editions.

3. The *De electionibus horarum* of 'Ali ibn Aḥmad al-Imrani, translated in 1133 or 1134 and extant in eighteen manuscripts.

4. The *De nativitatibus* or *De iudiciis nativitatum* of Abu 'Ali al-Khayaṭ, translated in 1136 and preserved

in nine manuscripts.

5. The *De revolutionibus nativitatum* by Abū Bakr al-Ḥasan (Albubather), preserved in one manuscript.

6. The *Questiones geomantice* or *Liber Arenalis scientie* by "Alfakini, son of Abizarch" or "son of Abraham," probably translated in 1135 and preserved in two printed editions and one manuscript (copied from the earlier edition [?]).

7. A *De pulsibus et urinis* by "Aeneas" (Ḥunayn ibn Isḥāq [?]), now lost.

A translation of an anonymous *Commentary on the Tabula Smaragdica*, extant in one manuscript, has been tentatively attributed to Plato by its recent editors.

The translation of Abraham bar Ḥiyya's *Geometry* (*Liber embadorum*) contributed much to both the structure and the contents of Leonardo Fibonacci's *Practica geometriae*. In particular it was the first work to introduce into the Latin study of mathematics the solution of quadratic equations and, with Theodosius' *Spherica*, it furthered the development of trigonometry. As late as 1819, Plato of Tivoli's translation of al-Battānī's *al-Zij* was the basis for Delambre's detailed study of that work.

BIBLIOGRAPHY

I. ORIGINAL WORKS. Printed eds. of the works cited in text are Abraham bar Ḥiyya, *Liber embadorum*, M. Curtze, ed., in *Urkunden zur Geschichte der Mathematik im Mittelalter und der Renaissance*, I, which is vol. XII of *Abhandlungen zur Geschichte der Mathematischen Wissenschaften* (Leipzig, 1902), 10–182, with German trans. on facing pages; Theodosius of Bithynia, *Spherica* (Venice, 1518; Vienna, 1529; Messina, 1558); al-Battānī, *De motu stellarum* (Nuremberg, 1537; Bologna, 1645), both eds. with additions and notes by Regiomontanus; Archimedes, *In quadratum circuli*, Marshall Clagett, ed., in "The *De mensura circuli*," in *Osiris*, 10 (1952), 599–605, and in Clagett's *Archimedes in the Middle Ages*, I (Madison, Wis., 1964), 20–26, with English trans. on opposite pages— see also 691–708 for a selective index of geometrical terms that includes those used in this trans.; Ptolemy, *Quadripartitum* (Venice, 1484, 1493; Basel, 1551); *Iudicia Almansoris* (Venice, 1484, 1492; Basel, 1533; Ulm, 1641, 1647); al-Imrani, *De electionibus horarum*, partly edited by J. M. Millás-Vallicrosa in *Las traducciones orientales* . . . (see below), 328–339; *Questiones geomantice* (Verona, 1687, 1705); and *Commentary on the Tabula Smaragdica*, R. Steele and D. W. Singer, eds., in *Proceedings of the Royal Society of Medicine*, Hist. sec., 21 (1928), 41–57.

No printed eds. are known to exist of *De usu astrolabii*, *De iudiciis nativitatum*, *De revolutionibus nativitatum*, and *De pulsibus et urinis*.

No complete list of MSS containing the translations ascribed to Plato of Tivoli has been published, but many

are mentioned in L. Thorndike and P. Kibre, *A Catalog of Incipits of Mediaeval Scientific Works in Latin*, rev. ed. (Cambridge, Mass., 1963), see index, col. 1889. See also the works of Boncompagni, Carmody, Haskins, Millás-Vallicrosa, Sarton, and Steinschneider cited below.

II. SECONDARY LITERATURE. The four essential works dealing with Plato of Tivoli are F. J. Carmody, *Arabic Astronomical and Astrological Sciences in Latin Translation: A Critical Bibliography* (Berkeley–Los Angeles, 1956), see index, 192; C. H. Haskins, *Studies in the History of Mediaeval Science* (Cambridge, Mass., 1927), 9–11; G. Sarton, *Introduction to the History of Science*, II, pt. 1 (Baltimore, 1931), 177–179; and M. Steinschneider, *Die Europäischen Übersetzungen aus dem Arabischen bis Mitte des 17ten Jahrhunderts* (1904–1905; repr. Graz, 1956), 62–66.

Further information is in the introductions to the modern eds. of Plato's works and in B. Boncompagni, "Delle versioni fatte da Platone Tiburtino," in *Atti dell' Accademia pontificia dei Nuovi Lincei*, 4 (1851), 249–286; J. A. von Braunmühl, *Vorlesungen über die Geschichte der Trigonometrie*, I (Leipzig, 1900), 48–50; C. H. Haskins, "The Translations of Hugo Sanctallensis," in *Romanic Review*, 2 (1911), 2, a note on the date of the *Liber embadorum*; J. M. Millás-Vallicrosa, *Assaig d'història de les idees fisiques i matemàtiques a la Catalunya medieval*, I (Barcelona, 1931), 29 ff., on the *De usu astrolabii*; *Las traducciones orientales en los manuscritos de la Biblioteca catedral de Toledo* (Madrid, 1942); and *Estudios sobre historia de la ciencia española* (Barcelona, 1949), 219 ff., "La obra enciclopédica de Abraham bar Ḥiyya"; C. A. Nallino's ed. of al-Battānī, *Opus astronomicum* (*De motu stellarum*), Arabic text and new Latin trans., I (Milan, 1903), l–lvi; M. Steinschneider, "Abraham Judaeus: Savasorda und Ibn Esra . . .," in *Zeitschrift für Mathematik*, 12 (1867), 1–44, important for the relationship between Plato and Abraham, for the authorship of the *Iudicia Almansoris*, and for al-Imrani's *De electionibus horarum*; L. Thorndike, *A History of Magic and Experimental Science*, II (London, 1923), esp. 82–83; and P. Ver Eecke's introduction to his French trans. of Theodosius of Bithynia's *Spherica* (Bruges, 1926; repr. Paris, 1959), xxxv–xli, on the Latin printed eds., on the use made of them, and on Regiomontanus.

LORENZO MINIO-PALUELLO

PLAYFAIR, JOHN (*b.* Benvie, near Dundee, Scotland, 10 March 1748; *d.* Edinburgh, Scotland, 20 July 1819)

Playfair was the eldest son of the Reverend James Playfair. At the age of fourteen he went to the University of St. Andrews, primarily to qualify for the ministry, but he also showed remarkable mathematical ability. In 1769 he left St. Andrews for Edinburgh. On the death of his father in 1772, he succeeded him in the living of Benvie, which he resigned in 1782 to become tutor for a private family. From 1785 to 1805 Playfair held a professorship of mathematics at the University of Edinburgh. He edited the *Transactions of the Royal Society of Edinburgh* for many years, and most of his papers appeared in that periodical. They were concerned almost entirely with mathematics, physics, and biographies. His *Elements of Geometry* was published in 1795. Following the death in 1797 of his friend James Hutton, Playfair proceeded to make a careful analysis, clarification, and amplification of Hutton's *Theory of the Earth*, which had originally been presented as a paper read in 1785 to the Royal Society of Edinburgh and was expanded into the two-volume work of 1795. Playfair's efforts resulted in *Illustrations of the Huttonian Theory of the Earth* (1802). In 1805 he became professor of natural philosophy at Edinburgh, where his lectures now embraced physics and astronomy. His *Outlines of Natural Philosophy* was published in 1814.

Playfair's professional work was thus in mathematics and physics. His book on geometry is a full presentation of the first six books of Euclid, with much additional material. The formal treatment of linear parallelism requires axioms. Finding Euclid's axioms on this matter to be unsatisfactory, Playfair proposed "that two straight lines, which intersect one another, cannot be both parallel to the same straight line." This is what became known as "Playfair's axiom," as it is given in his *Elements of Geometry*.

Playfair's fame as a scientist, however, rests almost entirely on his work in geology—hardly a "professional" study at the time—in presenting Hutton's momentous theory in a clear and palatable form (which Hutton himself had failed to do), and in adding materially to the geological knowledge of the time. The precision and elegance of the style of his mathematical exposition is here applied to a descriptive, inductive science. As Archibald Geikie remarked (1905): "How different would geological literature be to-day if men had tried to think and write like Playfair!" The publication of the *Illustrations* is indeed one of the most conspicuous landmarks in the progress of British geology. It ended the early period in the history of that science, a termination that happened to coincide with the end of the eighteenth century. There was a pause in the advance of geology during the early years of the nineteenth century; but powerful forces were gathering an impetus that was released in the second decade with the publication of important works by William Smith, John Farey, and Thomas Webster, which were summarized in the next landmark of the literature, Conybeare and Phillips' *Outlines of the Geology of England and Wales* (1822). Playfair lived well into this second period of activity but did not take

any part in it. A project that was very much in his mind was the preparation of a comprehensive work on geology, which was to have been a greatly amplified edition of his *Illustrations*. The peace of 1815 enabled Playfair to make an extensive tour of France, Switzerland, and Italy, in order to extend his observations for this purpose; but although we have details of the journey, nothing of the projected work was composed.

By the end of the eighteenth century the rocks of Britain had been classified into two main groups, the Primary (at first called "Primitive") and the Secondary. This division was based on observed superposition, particular attention being paid to unconformities and, as the names show, on the consequently inferred relative ages. The grouping is in fact a natural twofold occurrence in many regions, but the stratigraphical (time) gap is not everywhere at the same part of the general succession; for instance, over much of Scotland it is below the Old Red Sandstone, in northwest England below the Carboniferous, and in south Wales and southwest England below the Permo-Triassic or the Lias. This discrepancy was not known at the time; and long after the end of the eighteenth century the Devonian and Carboniferous rocks of Devon and Cornwall were thought to be equivalent in age to rocks below the Old Red Sandstone elsewhere. As for the igneous rocks, the large granite masses were generally believed to be among the most ancient; but since their intrusive nature had been demonstrated, this assumption was found to rest on no very secure basis. They had not, however, yet been discovered as being intrusive into any but Primary rocks. The smaller intrusions, dikes and sills, found among Secondary rocks, were necessarily accepted as being comparatively young. In fact, the logical position had been reached of a preliminary classification of rocks, regardless of age, into the two lithological groups: igneous and sedimentary.

It is not surprising that no classification of the Primary rocks had been attempted. Particular rocks were simply described by such lithological or mining terms as schistus, slate, killas, and clay-slate, which had no very precise meaning. Within the Secondary group a very rough succession from the Coal Measures to the Chalk had been given by John Strachey (1725), and John Michell (1788) had offered a more accurate succession of the same range of strata. In those regions where the Carboniferous succession had been observed—in Scotland (by John Williams, 1789) and, particularly, in Derbyshire (by John Whitehurst, 1778)—the Limestone was found to underlie the Coal Measures, with Millstone Grit (if present) intermediate. It does not seem that the stratigraphic relation of the Old Red Sandstone (the equivalent in age to the marine

Devonian) to the Carboniferous rocks had been observed. The question arises of the extent to which a geological map of Britain could have been constructed from the observations recorded up to 1802. The map would have been very sketchy; and no one made any serious attempt at such a compilation, although William George Maton drew a very inaccurate "mineralogical map" of southwest England in 1797. The geological researches of William Smith had begun about 1790. In 1801 he colored geologically a small map of England and Wales, and in 1815 his great map of England and Wales was published.

Such was the position when Playfair wrote his book, which divided two eras in the history of geological investigation. His own observations, inferences, and expressions were the final contributions to the first era and can be classed under three heads.

First, Playfair realized the importance of unconformity in the manifestation of the geological cycle; and he searched throughout Britain for signs of this kind of structural relation, to add to the instances already recorded by Hutton. (Unconformity implies the operation of the "geological cycle"—deposition, deformation, emergence, erosion, submergence, and deposition. The concept of the geological cycle is the essence of Hutton's theory.) Thus Playfair observed the unconformity between the Permo-Triassic and Devonian to be seen at places on the coasts of both north and south Devonshire, and that between the Old Red Sandstone and Dalradian ("Primary schistus") on the east and west coasts of Scotland. He graphically described the unconformity between the Carboniferous Limestone and pre-Devonian rocks in the Ingleborough district of Yorkshire (the British region that shows this phenomenon most clearly) and gave a glimpse of the structure of the English Lake District with its rim of unconformable Carboniferous rocks.

Second, Playfair made miscellaneous observations, of which the more significant were the fossiliferous nature of the Primary Devonian limestone at Plymouth; the fractures, curiously plane without shattering, in the Old Red Sandstone conglomerate at Oban in Scotland; the general constancy of the east-northeast/west-southwest trend in the structure of the older rocks of Britain; the form of the intrusive sill at Salisbury Craigs and the metamorphism at the volcanic neck of Arthur's Seat, in the neighborhood of Edinburgh; the small-scale folding in the Dalradian schist of Ben Lawers, which he noticed resembled that in the Alpine region; intrusive veins in Ayrshire and Arran and the contact metamorphism produced by them; the flint-gravels of southern England as the residue of dissolved flinty chalk; and the submerged forest of the Lincolnshire coast.

Third, Playfair's book used many more-or-less ordinary words (arenaceous, consolidated, petrifaction) in modern geological senses, most of them probably for the first time, and introduced several highly significant terms into geological literature (geological cycle, igneous origin). His name is attached to a geomorphological "law," "Playfair's law of accordant junctions," which, as given in the *Illustrations*, states that "Every river appears to consist of a main trunk, fed from a variety of branches, each running in a valley proportioned to its size, and all of them together forming a system of vallies, communicating with one another, and having such a nice adjustment of their declivities that none of them join the principal valley on too high or too low a level,—a circumstance which would be infinitely improbable if each of these vallies were not the work of the stream that flows in it."

BIBLIOGRAPHY

I. ORIGINAL WORKS. Playfair's chief writings are *Elements of Geometry* (Edinburgh, 1795); *Illustrations of the Huttonian Theory of the Earth* (Edinburgh, 1802); *Outlines of Natural Philosophy* (Edinburgh, 1814); and *A General View of the Progress of Mathematical and Physical Science Since the Revival of Letters in Europe*, vols. II and IV of *Encyclopaedia Britannica*, supp. (1816). In *The Works of John Playfair*, James G. Playfair, ed., 4 vols. (Edinburgh, 1822), "are contained all the publications to which Mr. Playfair affixed his name, with the exception of the *Elements of Geometry*, and of the *Outlines of Natural Philosophy*, which were intended only for the use of students, and although excellently adapted to their object, would possess but little interest for the general reader." Vol. I contains a biographical memoir (see below) and *Illustrations of the Huttonian Theory*; vol. II, the *Progress of Mathematical and Physical Science*; vol. III, various papers on mathematics and physics, plus a "lithological survey of Schehallien" (in Scotland), all of which had appeared either in *Transactions of the Royal Society* or *Transactions of the Royal Society of Edinburgh*; and vol. IV, various biographical accounts and reviews, a biography of James Hutton being particularly important. His works are listed in the British Museum *General Catalogue of Printed Books*, CXCI, cols. 378–379.

II. SECONDARY LITERATURE. The source for details of the life of Playfair is F. Jeffrey, "Biographical Account of the Late Professor Playfair," prefixed to J. G. Playfair's ed. of the *Works* (see above). See also B. B. Woodward, in *Dictionary of National Biography*, XLV (1896), 413–414. In reviewing Hutton's theory, Playfair's *Illustrations* is nearly always referred to, since it is an essential part of the authoritative exposition of Hutton's principles. See particularly A. Geikie, *The Founders of Geology* (London, 1905), 280–316; and "Lamarck and Playfair," in *Geological*

Magazine, **43** (1906), 145–153, 193–202; C. C. Gillispie, *Genesis and Geology* (New York, 1951; repr. 1959), *passim*; and R. J. Chorley *et al.*, *The History of the Study of Landforms* (London, 1964), 57–68. Playfair's original contributions to geological knowledge are reviewed in J. Challinor, "The Early Progress of British Geology—III," in *Annals of Science*, **10** (1954), 107–148, see 137–143.

JOHN CHALLINOR

PLÜCKER, JULIUS (*b*. Elberfeld, Germany, 16 June 1801; *d*. Bonn, Germany, 22 May 1868)

Plücker was descended from a Rhenish merchant family of Aix-la-Chapelle (Aachen). After graduating from the Gymnasium in Düsseldorf, he studied at the universities of Bonn, Heidelberg, Berlin, and Paris until 1824, when he earned his doctorate *in absentia* from the University of Marburg. In 1825 he became *Privatdozent* at the University of Bonn, where in 1828 he was promoted to extraordinary professor. In 1833 he served in Berlin simultaneously as extraordinary professor at the university and as teacher at the Friedrich Wilhelm Gymnasium. In 1834 he became ordinary professor at the University of Halle. He then served as full professor of mathematics (1836–1847) and physics (1847–1868) at Bonn, where he succeeded Karl von Münchow. In 1837 he married a Miss Altstätten; his wife and one son survived him.

Although Plücker was educated primarily in Germany, throughout his life he drew much on French and English science. He was essentially a geometer but dedicated many years of his life to physical science. When Plücker began his work in mathematics, the only German mathematician of international repute was Gauss. In 1826, however, Crelle founded, in Berlin, his *Journal für die reine und angewandte Mathematik*; and the work of Plücker, Steiner, and others soon became well known. Their field of research was not the differential geometry of Monge and Gauss, but rather the analytic and projective geometry of Poncelet and Gergonne. But differences between the synthetic school in geometry, of which Steiner was the head in Berlin, and Plücker's analytical school—together with a conflict of personality between the two men—resulted in Plücker's being resident at Berlin for only a year.

In 1828 Plücker published his first book, volume I of *Analytisch-geometrische Entwicklungen*, which was followed in 1831 by volume II. In each volume he discussed the plane analytic geometry of the line, circle, and conic sections; and many facts and theorems—either discovered or known by Plücker—were demonstrated in a more elegant manner. The point coordinates used in both volumes are nonhomogeneous affine; in volume II the homogeneous line coordinates in a plane, formerly known as Plücker's coordinates, are used and conic sections are treated as envelopes of lines. The characteristic features of Plücker's analytic geometry were already present in this work, namely, the elegant operations with algebraic symbols occurring in the equations of conic sections and their pencils. His understanding of the so-called reading in the formulas enabled him to achieve geometric results while avoiding processes of elimination, and his algebraic elegance was surpassed in some matters only by Hesse. Plücker's careful treatment, in the first book, of conic sections that osculate with one another in different degrees is still noteworthy.

In 1829 Plücker introduced the so-called triangular coordinates as three values that are proportional to the distances of a point from three given lines. Simultaneously, Möbius introduced his barycentric coordinates, another type of homogeneous point coordinates. In his *Analytisch-geometrische Entwicklungen*, however, Plücker used only nonhomogeneous point coordinates. At the end of volume II he presented a detailed explanation of the principle of reciprocity, now called the principle of duality. Plücker, who stood in the middle of the Poncelet-Gergonne controversy, was inclined to support Poncelet's position: Plücker introduced duality by means of a correlation polarity and not in the more modern sense (as in Gergonne) of a general principle. Thus Plücker's work may be regarded as a transitional stage preceding the pure projective geometry founded by Staudt.

After 1832 Plücker took an interest in a general treatment of plane curves of a higher degree than the second. Although his next book, *System der analytischen Geometrie, insbesondere eine ausführliche Theorie der Kurven 3. Ordnung enthaltend* (1835), discussed general (or projective) point and line coordinates for treating conic sections, the greater part of the book covered plane cubic curves. Plücker's consideration of these curves began with the following theorem by Poncelet. The three finite points where the three asymptotes of a cubic intersect the curve lie on a straight line. Analytically this theorem is equivalent to the possibility of writing the curve equation in the form $pqr + \lambda s^3 = 0$ (p, q, r, s linear forms). A cubic curve is determined by the 4 lines with equations $p = 0$, $q = 0$, $r = 0$, $s = 0$, and one point on the curve. Plücker gave constructions for the cubics thus determined. A real affine classification based upon these constructions leads to 219 different types.

Plücker devoted the greater part of *Theorie der*

algebraischen Kurven (1839) to the properties of algebraic curves in the neighborhood of their infinite points. He considered not only the asymptotic lines, but also asymptotic conic sections and other curves osculating the given cubic in a certain degree. For the asymptotic lines he corrected some false results given by Euler in *Introductio in analysin infinitorum* (1748).

Although the increasing predominance of projective and birational geometry abated interest in these particulars about the behavior of curves at infinity, the second part of *Theorie der algebraischen Kurven* was of more permanent value. It contained a new treatment of singular points in the plane, a subject previously discussed in Cramer's work (1750) on the theory of curves. Plücker's work also resolved several doubts concerning the relation between the order and class of curves in the work of Poncelet and Gergonne.

In his 1839 publication Plücker proved the following celebrated formulas, known as "Plücker's equations":

$$k = n(n - 1) - 2d - 3s, \quad n = k(k - 1) - 2\delta - 3\sigma,$$

connecting the order n and class k of a curve, which contains as singular points d double points and s cuspidal points, and as dual singularities δ double tangents and σ inflexions. The same assumptions validate Plücker's formulas of the second group:

$$\sigma = 3n(n - 2) - 6d - 8s, \; s = 3k(k - 2) - 6\delta - 8\sigma.$$

A cubic without singular points therefore contains nine inflexional points, and Plücker discovered that no more than three inflexional points can be real. He thus prepared the foundation for the results later obtained by Hesse. In the last chapter of *Geometrie der algebraischen Kurven* Plücker dealt with plane quartic curves and developed a full classification of their possible singular points. A nonsingular quartic curve that possesses twenty-eight double tangents is the central fact in his theory of these curves.

Although Plücker's treatment of quartic curves and his theorems on their configuration were all wrong (Hesse later corrected his errors), Plücker had a clear insight, which eluded his predecessors, into the meaning of the so-called Cramer paradox and its generalizations. The crux of the paradox is that $1/2\, n(n + 3) - 1$ common points of two curves of degree $n \geqslant 3$ determine another set of $1/2(n - 1)$ $(n - 2)$ common points. Severi, in his conferences and books on enumerative geometry, underlined the so-called Plücker-Clebsch principle in the following form: If a system of algebraic equations, depending on certain constants, generally has no common solution—except when the constants fill certain conditions—then the system in this latter case has not only one, but also infinitely many solutions.

In 1829, independent of Bobillier, Plücker extended the notion of polars (previously known only for conic sections) to all plane algebraic curves. He also studied the problem of focal points of algebraic curves, the osculation of two surfaces, and wave surface, and thus became concerned with algebraic and analytic space geometry. This field was also discussed in *System der Geometrie des Raumes in neuer analytischer Behandlungsweise* (1846), in which he treated in an elegant manner the known facts of analytic geometry. His own contributions in this work, however, were not as significant as those in his earlier books.

After 1846 Plücker abandoned his mathematical researches and conducted physical experiments until 1864, when he returned to his work in geometry. His mathematical accomplishments during this second period were published in *Neue Geometrie des Raumes, gegründet auf die Betrachtung der Geraden als Raumelement*, which appeared in 1868. Plücker's death prevented him from completing the second part of this work, but Felix Klein, who had served as Plücker's physical assistant from 1866 to 1868, undertook the task. Plücker had indicated his plans to Klein in numerous conversations. These conversations served also as a source for Plücker's ideas in *Neue Geometrie*, in which he attempted to base space geometry upon the self-dual straight line as element, rather than upon the point or in dual manner upon the plane as element. He thus created the field of line geometry, which until the twentieth century was the subject of numerous researches (see Zindler, "Algebraische Liniengeometrie," in *Encyklopädie der mathematischen Wissenschaften*, III, 2 [1921], 973–1228).

Plücker's work in line geometry can be related to several earlier developments: the notion of six line coordinates in space as well as a complex of lines intersecting a rational norm curve had already been discussed by Cayley; the researches of Poinsot and Möbius on systems of forces were closely related to line geometry; and researches on systems of normals to a surface were made by Monge and later generalized by W. R. Hamilton to a differential geometry of ∞^2 rays.

Notwithstanding these developments, Plücker's systematic treatment of line geometry created a new field in geometry. He introduced in a dual manner the six homogeneous line coordinates p_{ij}, now called "Plücker's coordinates," among which a quadratic relation $Q_4(p_{ij}) = 0$ exists. Subsequent work by Klein and Segre interpreted line geometry of R_3 as a geometry of points on a quadric Q_4 of P_5. But this development, as well as further generalizations of an

S_k geometry in S_n to be interpreted as a point geometry on a Grassmannian variety $G_{n,k}$, was not anticipated by Plücker, who restricted his work to the domain of ordinary space and conceived therein a four-dimensional geometry with the line as element.

Plücker's algebraic line geometry was distinct, however, from the differential line geometry created by Hamilton. Plücker introduced the notions (still used today) of complexes; congruences; and ruled surfaces for subsets of lines of three, two, or one dimension. He also classified linear complexes and congruences and initiated the study of quadratic complexes, which were defined by quadratic relations among Plücker's coordinates. (Complex surfaces are surfaces of fourth order and class and are generated by the totality of lines belonging to a quadratic complex that intersects a given line.) These complexes were the subject of numerous researches in later years, beginning with Klein's doctoral thesis in 1868. In *Neue Geometrie* Plücker again adopted a metrical point of view, which effected extended calculations and studies of special cases. His interest in geometric 'shapes and details during this period is evident in the many models he had manufactured.

In assessing Plücker's later geometric work it must be remembered that during the years in which he was conducting physical research he did not keep up with the mathematical literature. He was not aware, for example, of Grassmann's *Die Wissenschaft der extensiven Grösslehre oder die Ausdehnungslehre* (1844), which was unintelligible to almost all contemporary mathematicians.

Plücker was professor of mathematics and physics at the University of Bonn; he is said to have always been willing to remind other physicists that he was competent in both fields. It is particularly noteworthy that Plücker chose to investigate experimental rather than theoretical physics; Clebsch, in his celebrated obituary on Plücker, identified several relations between Plücker's mathematical and his physical preoccupations. In geometry he wished to describe the different shapes of cubic curves and other figures, and in physics he endeavored to describe the various physical phenomena more qualitatively. But in both cases he was far from pursuing science in a modern axiomatic, deductive style.

Plücker's guide in physics was Faraday, with whom he corresponded. His papers of 1839 on wave surface and of 1847 on the reflection of light at quadric surfaces concerned both theoretical physics and mathematics, though often counted among his forty-one mathematical papers. Plücker also wrote fifty-nine papers on pure physics, published primarily in *Annalen der Physik und Chemie* and *Philosophical Transactions of the Royal Society*. He investigated the magnetic properties of gases and crystals and later studied the phenomena of electrical discharge in evacuated gases. He and his collaborators described these phenomena as precisely as the technical means of his time permitted. He also made use of an electromagnetic motor constructed by Fessel and later collaborated with Geissler at Bonn in constructing a standard thermometer. Plücker further drew upon the chemical experience of his pupil J. W. Hittorf in his study of the spectra of gaseous substances, and his examination of the different spectra of these substances indicates that he realized their future significance for chemical analysis.

In 1847 Plücker discovered the magnetic phenomena of tourmaline crystal; and in his studies of electrical discharges in rarefied gases he anticipated Hittorf's discovery of cathodic rays. His discovery of the first three hydrogen lines preceded the celebrated experiments of R. Bunsen and G. Kirchhoff in Heidelberg. Although Plücker's accomplishments were unacknowledged in Germany, English scientists did appreciate his work more than his compatriots did, and in 1868 he was awarded the Copley Medal.

BIBLIOGRAPHY

I. ORIGINAL WORKS. Plücker's major works are *Analytisch-geometrische Entwicklungen*, 2 vols. (Essen, 1828–1831); *System der analytischen Geometrie* (Berlin, 1835); *Theorie der algebraischen Kurven* (Bonn, 1839); *System der Geometrie des Raumes in neuer analytischer Behandlungsweise* (Düsseldorf, 1846); *Neue Geometrie des Raumes, gegründet auf der geraden Linie als Raumelement* (Leipzig, 1868–1869); and *Gesammelte wissenschaftlichen Abhandlungen*, 1 vol. (Leipzig, 1895–1896).

II. SECONDARY LITERATURE. On Plücker and his work, see A. Clebsch, "Zum Gedächtnis an Julius Plücker," in *Abhandlungen der K. Gesellschaft der Wissenschaften zu Göttingen*, **15** (1872), 1–40; Dronke, *Julius Plücker* (Bonn, 1871); and Wilhelm Ernst, *Julius Plücker* (Bonn, 1933).

WERNER BURAU

POINCARÉ, JULES HENRI (*b.* Nancy, France, 29 April 1854; *d.* Paris, France, 17 July 1912)

The development of mathematics in the nineteenth century began under the shadow of a giant, Carl Friedrich Gauss; it ended with the domination by a genius of similar magnitude, Henri Poincaré. Both were universal mathematicians in the supreme sense, and both made important contributions to astronomy and mathematical physics. If Poincaré's discoveries in number theory do not equal those of Gauss, his achievements in the theory of functions are at least on the same level—even when one takes into account the theory of elliptic and modular functions, which must be credited to Gauss and which represents in that field his most important discovery, although it was not published during his lifetime. If Gauss was the initiator in the theory of differentiable manifolds, Poincaré played the same role in algebraic topology. Finally, Poincaré remains the most important figure in the theory of differential equations and the mathematician who after Newton did the most remarkable work in celestial mechanics. Both Gauss and Poincaré had very few students and liked to work alone; but the similarity ends there. Where Gauss was very reluctant to publish his discoveries, Poincaré's list of papers approaches five hundred, which does not include the many books and lecture notes he published as a result of his teaching at the Sorbonne.

Poincaré's parents both belonged to the upper middle class, and both their families had lived in Lorraine for several generations. His paternal grandfather had two sons: Léon, Henri's father, was a physician and a professor of medicine at the University of Nancy; Antoine had studied at the École Polytechnique and rose to high rank in the engineering corps. One of Antoine's sons, Raymond, was several times prime minister and was president of the French Republic during World War I; the other son, Lucien, occupied high administrative functions in the university. Poincaré's mathematical ability became apparent while he was still a student in the *lycée*. He won first prizes in the *concours général* (a competition between students from all French *lycées*) and in 1873 entered the École Polytechnique at the top of his class; his professor at Nancy is said to have referred to him as a "monster of mathematics." After graduation he followed courses in engineering at the École des Mines and worked briefly as an engineer while writing his thesis for the doctorate in mathematics which he obtained in 1879. Shortly afterward he started teaching at the University of Caen, and in 1881 he became a professor at the University of Paris, where he taught until his untimely death in 1912. At the early age of thirty-three he was elected to the Académie des Sciences and in 1908 to the Académie Française. He was also the recipient of innumerable prizes and honors both in France and abroad.

Function Theory. Before he was thirty years of age, Poincaré became world famous with his epoch-making discovery of the "automorphic functions" of one complex variable (or, as he called them, the

"fuchsian" and "kleinean" functions). The study of the modular function and of the solutions of the hypergeometric equation had given examples of analytic functions defined in an open connected subset D of the complex plane, and "invariant" under a group G of transformations of D onto itself, of the form

$$T: z \to (az + b)/(cz + d)$$
$$(a, b, c, d \text{ constants}, ad - bc \neq 0) \qquad (1)$$

G being "properly discontinuous," that is, such that no point z of D is the limit of an infinite sequence of transforms (distinct from z) of a point $z' \in D$ by a sequence of elements $T_n \in G$. For instance, the modular group consists of transformations (1), where a, b, c, d are integers and $ad - bc = 1$; D is the upper half plane $\mathscr{I}z > 0$, and it can be covered, without overlapping, by all transforms of the fundamental domain defined by $|z| \geqslant 1$, $|\mathscr{R}z| \leqslant 1/2$. Using non-Euclidean geometry in a very ingenious way, Poincaré was able to show that for any properly discontinuous group G of transformations of type (1), there exists similarly a fundamental domain, bounded by portions of straight lines or circles, and whose transforms by the elements of G cover D without overlapping. Conversely, given any such "circular polygon" satisfying some explicit conditions concerning its angles and its sides, it is the fundamental domain of a properly discontinuous group of transformations of type (1). The open set D may be the half plane $\mathscr{I}z > 0$, or the interior or the exterior of a circle; when it is not of this type, its boundary may be a perfect non-dense set, or a curve that has either no tangent at any point or no curvature at any point.

Poincaré next showed—by analogy with the Weierstrass series in the theory of elliptic functions—that for a given group G, and a rational function H having no poles on the boundary of D, the series

$$\Theta(z) = \sum_k H(T_k \cdot z)\,(c_k z + d_k)^{-2m} \qquad (2)$$

where the transformations

$$T_k: z \to (a_k z + b_k)/(c_k z + d_k)$$

are an enumeration of the transformations of G, and m is a large enough integer, converges except at the transforms of the poles of H by G; the meromorphic function Θ thus defined in D, obviously satisfies the relation

$$\Theta(T \cdot z) = (cz + d)^{2m}\,\Theta(z)$$

for any transformation (1) of the group G. The quotient of two such functions, which Poincaré called thetafuchsian or thetakleinean, corresponding to the same integer m, gives an automorphic function (meromorphic in D). It is easy to show that any two automorphic functions X, Y (meromorphic in D and corresponding to the same group G) satisfy an "algebraic" relation $P(X, Y) = 0$, where the genus of the curve $P(x, y) = 0$ is equal to the topological genus of the homogeneous space D/G and can be explicitly computed (as Poincaré showed) from the fundamental domain of G. Furthermore, if $v_1 = (dX/dz)^{1/2}$, $v_2 = zv_1$, v_1, and v_2 are solutions of a linear differential equation of order 2:

$$d^2v/dX^2 = \varphi(X, Y)\, v,$$

where φ is rational in X and Y, so that the automorphic function X is obtained by "inverting" the relation $z = v_1(X)/v_2(X)$. This property was the starting point of Poincaré's researches, following a paper by I. L. Fuchs investigating second-order equations $y'' + P(x)\, y' + Q(x)\, y = 0$, with rational coefficients P, Q, in which the inversion of the quotient of two solutions would give a meromorphic function; hence the name he chose for his automorphic functions.

But Poincaré did not stop there. Observing that his construction of fuchsian functions introduced many parameters susceptible of continuous variation, he conceived that by a suitable choice of these parameters, one could obtain for an "arbitrary" algebraic curve $P(x, y) = 0$, a parametric representation by fuchsian functions, and also that for an arbitrary homogeneous linear differential equation of any order

$$y^{(n)} + P_1(x)\, y^{(n-1)} + \cdots + P_n(x)\, y = 0,$$

where the P_j are algebraic functions of x, one could express the solutions of that equation by "zeta-fuchsian" functions (such a function $\mathbf{F}$ takes its value in a space $\mathbf{C}^p$; in other words, it is a system of p scalar meromorphic functions and is such that, for any transformation (1) of the fuchsian group G to which it corresponds, one has $\mathbf{F}(T \cdot z) = \rho(T) \cdot \mathbf{F}(z)$, where ρ is a linear representation of G into $\mathbf{C}^p$). The "continuity method" by which he sought to prove these results could not at that time be made rigorous, due to the lack of proper topological concepts and results in the early 1880's; but after Brouwer's fundamental theorems in topology, correct proofs could be given using somewhat different methods.

Much has been written on the "competition" between C. F. Klein and Poincaré in the discovery of automorphic functions. Actually there never was any real competition, and Klein was miles behind from the start. In 1879 Klein certainly knew everything that had been written on special automorphic functions, a theory to which he had contributed by several

beautiful papers on the transformation of elliptic functions. He could not have failed in particular to notice the connection between the fundamental domains of these functions, and non-Euclidean geometry, since it was he who, after Cayley and Beltrami, had clarified the concept of Euclidean "models" for the various non-Euclidean geometries, of which the "Poincaré half plane" was a special example.

On the other hand, Poincaré's ignorance of the mathematical literature, when he started his researches, is almost unbelievable. He hardly knew anything on the subject beyond Hermite's work on the modular functions; he certainly had never read Riemann, and by his own account had not even heard of the "Dirichlet principle," which he was to use in such imaginative fashion a few years later. Nevertheless, Poincaré's idea of associating a fundamental domain to any fuchsian group does not seem to have occurred to Klein, nor did the idea of "using" non-Euclidean geometry, which is never mentioned in his papers on modular functions up to 1880. One of the questions Klein asked Poincaré in his letters was how he had proved the convergence of the "theta" series. It is only after realizing that Poincaré was looking for a theorem that would give a parametric representation by meromorphic functions of all algebraic curves that Klein set out to prove this by himself and succeeded in sketching a proof independently of Poincaré. He used similar methods (suffering from the same lack of rigor).

The general theory of automorphic functions of one complex variable is one of the few branches of mathematics where Poincaré left little for his successors to do. There is no "natural" generalization of automorphic functions to several complex variables. Present knowledge suggests that the general theory should be linked to the theory of symmetric spaces G/K of E. Cartan (G semisimple real Lie group, K maximal compact subgroup of G), and to the discrete subgroups Γ of G operating on G/K and such that G/Γ has finite measure (C. L. Siegel). But from that point of view, the group $G = \mathbf{SL}(2, \mathbf{R})$, which is at the basis of Poincaré's theory, appears as very exceptional, being the only simple Lie group where the conjugacy classes of discrete subgroups Γ depend on continuous parameters (A. Weil's rigidity theorem). The "continuity" methods dear to Poincaré are therefore ruled out; in fact the known discrete groups $\Gamma \subset G$ for which G/Γ has finite measure are defined by arithmetical considerations, and the automorphic functions of several variables are thus much closer to number theory than for one variable (where Poincaré very early had noticed the particular "fuchsian groups" deriving from the arithmetic theory of ternary quadratic forms, and the special properties of the corresponding automorphic functions).

The theory of automorphic functions is only one of the many contributions of Poincaré to the theory of analytic functions, each of which was the starting point of extensive theories. In a short paper of 1883 he was the first to investigate the links between the genus of an entire function (defined by properties of its Weierstrass decomposition in primary factors) and the coefficients of its Taylor development or the rate of growth of the absolute value of the function; together with the Picard theorem, this was to lead, through the results of Hadamard and E. Borel, to the vast theory of entire and meromorphic functions that is not yet exhausted after eighty years.

Automorphic functions had provided the first examples of analytic functions having singular points that formed a perfect non-dense set, as well as functions having curves of singular points. Poincaré gave another general method to form functions of this type by means of series $\sum_n \frac{A_n}{z - b_n}$ of rational functions, leading to the theory of monogenic functions later developed by E. Borel and A. Denjoy.

It was also a result from the theory of automorphic functions, namely the parametrization theorem of algebraic curves, that in 1883 led Poincaré to the general "uniformization theorem," which is equivalent to the existence of a conformal mapping of an arbitrary simply connected noncompact Riemann surface on the plane or on an open disc. This time he saw that the problem was a generalization of Dirichlet's problem, and Poincaré was the first to introduce the idea of "exhausting" the Riemann surface by an increasing sequence of compact regions and of obtaining the conformal mapping by a limiting process. Here again it was difficult at that time to build a completely satisfactory proof, and Poincaré himself and Koebe had to return to the question in 1907 before it could be considered as settled.

Poincaré was even more an initiator in the theory of analytic functions of several complex variables—which was practically nonexistent before him. His first result was the theorem that a meromorphic function F of two complex variables is a quotient of two entire functions, which in 1883 he proved by a very ingenious use of the Dirichlet principle applied to the function $\log |F|$; in a later paper (1898) he deepened the study of such "pluriharmonic" functions for any number of complex variables and used it in the theory of Abelian functions. Still later (1907), after the publication of F. M. Hartogs' theorems, he

pointed out the completely new problems to which led the extension of the concept of "conformal mapping" for functions of two complex variables. These were the germs of the imposing "analytic geometry" (or theory of analytic manifolds and analytic spaces) which we know today, following the pioneering works of Cousin, Hartogs, and E. E. Levi before 1914; H. Cartan, K. Oka, H. Behnke, and P. Lelong in the 1930's; and the tremendous impulse given to the theory by cohomological ideas after 1945.

Finally, Poincaré was the first to give a satisfactory generalization of the concept of "residue" for multiple integrals of functions of several complex variables, after earlier attempts by other mathematicians had brought to light serious difficulties in this problem. Only quite recently have his ideas come to full fruition in the work of J. Leray, again using the resources of algebraic topology.

Abelian Functions and Algebraic Geometry. As soon as he came into contact with the work of Riemann and Weierstrass on Abelian functions and algebraic geometry, Poincaré was very much attracted by those fields. His papers on these subjects occupy in his complete works as much space as those on automorphic functions, their dates ranging from 1881 to 1911. One of the main ideas in these papers is that of "reduction" of Abelian functions. Generalizing particular cases studied by Jacobi, Weierstrass, and Picard, Poincaré proved the general "complete reducibility" theorem, which is now expressed by saying that if A is an Abelian variety and B an Abelian subvariety of A, then there exists an Abelian subvariety C of A such that $A = B + C$ and $B \cap C$ is a finite group. Abelian varieties can thus be decomposed in sums of "simple" Abelian varieties having finite intersection. Poincaré noted further that Abelian functions corresponding to reducible varieties (and even to products of elliptic curves, that is, Abelian varieties of dimension 1) are "dense" among all Abelian functions—a result that enabled him to extend and generalize many of Riemann's results on theta functions, and to investigate the special properties of the theta functions corresponding to the Jacobian varieties of algebraic curves.

The most remarkable contribution of Poincaré to algebraic geometry is in his papers of 1910–1911 on algebraic curves contained in an algebraic surface $F(x, y, z) = 0$. Following the general method of Picard, Poincaré considers the sections of the surface by planes $y = $ const.; the genus p of such a curve C_y is constant except for isolated values of y.

It is possible to define p Abelian integrals of the first kind on $C_y, u_1, \ldots, u_p$, which are analytic functions on the surface (or rather, on its universal covering). Now, to each algebraic curve Γ on the surface, meeting a generic C_y in m points, Poincaré associates p functions $v_1, \ldots, v_p$ of y, $v_j(y)$ being the sum of the values of the integral u_j at the m points of intersection of C_y and Γ; furthermore, he is able to characterize these "normal functions" by properties where the curve Γ does not appear anymore, and thus he obtains a kind of analytical "substitute" for the algebraic curve. This remarkable method enabled him to obtain simple proofs of deep results of Picard and Severi, as well as the first correct proof of a famous theorem stated by Castelnuovo, Enriques, and Severi, showing that the irregularity $q = p_g - p_a$ of the surface (p_g and p_a being the geometric and the arithmetic genus) is exactly the maximum dimension of the "continuous nonlinear systems" of curves on the surface. The method of proof suggested by the Italian geometers was later found to be defective, and no proof other than Poincaré's was obtained until 1965. His method has also shown its value in other recent questions (Igusa, Griffiths), and it is very likely that its effectiveness is far from exhausted.

Number Theory. Poincaré was a student of Hermite, and some of his early work deals with Hermite's method of "continuous reduction" in the arithmetic theory of forms, and in particular the finiteness theorem for the classes of such forms (with nonvanishing discriminant) that had just been proved by C. Jordan. These papers bring some complements and precisions to the results of Hermite and Jordan, without introducing any new idea. In connection with them Poincaré gave the first general definition of the genus of a form with integral coefficients, generalizing those of Gauss and Eisenstein; Minkowski had arrived independently at that definition at the same time.

Poincaré's last paper on number theory (1901) was most influential and was the first paper on what we now call "algebraic geometry over the field of rationals" (or a field of algebraic numbers). The subject matter of the paper is the Diophantine problem of finding the points with rational coordinates on a curve $f(x, y) = 0$, where the coefficients of f are rational numbers. Poincaré observed immediately that the problem is invariant under birational transformations, provided the latter have rational coefficients. Thus he is naturally led to consider the genus of the curve $f(x, y) = 0$, and his main concern is with the case of genus 1; using the parametric representation of the curve by elliptic functions (or, as we now say, the Jacobian of the curve), he observes that the rational points correspond on the Jacobian to a subgroup, and he defines the "rank" of the curve as the rank of that subgroup. It is likely that Poincaré conjectured that the rank is always finite; this fundamental fact was proved by L. J. Mordell in 1922 and generalized to curves of arbitrary genus by A. Weil in 1929. These authors used a method of "infinite descent" based upon the bisection of elliptic (or Abelian) functions; Poincaré had developed in his paper similar computations related to the trisection of elliptic functions, and it is likely that these ideas were at the origin of Mordell's proof. The Mordell-Weil theorem has become fundamental in the theory of Diophantine equations, but many questions regarding the concept of rank introduced by Poincaré remain unanswered, and it is possible that a deeper study of his paper may lead to new results.

Algebra. It is not certain that Poincaré knew Kronecker's dictum that algebra is only the handmaiden of mathematics, and has no right to independent existence. At any rate Poincaré never studied algebra for its own sake, but only when he needed algebraic results in problems of arithmetic or analysis. For instance, his work on the arithmetic theory of forms led him to the study of forms of degree $\geqslant 3$, which admit continuous groups of automorphisms. It seems that it is in connection with this problem that his attention was drawn to the relation between hypercomplex systems (over **R** or **C**) and the continuous group defined by multiplication of invertible elements of the system; the short note he published on the subject in 1884 inspired later work of Study and E. Cartan on hypercomplex systems. A little-known fact is that Poincaré returned to noncommutative algebra in a 1903 paper on algebraic integrals of linear differential equations. His method led him to introduce the group algebra of the group of the equation (which then is finite), and to split it (according to H. Maschke's theorem, which apparently he did not know but proved by referring to a theorem of Frobenius) into simple algebras over **C** (that is, matrix algebras). He then introduced for the first time the concepts of left and right ideals in an algebra, and proved that any left ideal in a matrix algebra is a direct sum of minimal left ideals (a result usually credited to Wedderburn or Artin).

Poincaré was one of the few mathematicians of his time who understood and admired the work of Lie and his continuators on "continuous groups," and in particular the only mathematician who in the early 1900's realized the depth and scope of E. Cartan's papers. In 1899 Poincaré became interested in a new way to prove Lie's third fundamental theorem and in what is now called the Campbell-Hausdorff formula; in his work Poincaré substantially defined for the first time what we now call the "enveloping algebra" of a Lie algebra (over the complex field) and gave a description of a "natural" basis of that algebra deduced from a given basis of the Lie algebra; this theorem (rediscovered much later by G. Birkhoff and E. Witt, and now called the "Poincaré-Birkhoff-Witt theorem") has become fundamental in the modern theory of Lie algebras.

Differential Equations and Celestial Mechanics. The theory of differential equations and its applications to dynamics was clearly at the center of Poincaré's mathematical thought; from his first (1878) to his last (1912) paper, he attacked the theory from all possible angles and very seldom let a year pass without publishing a paper on the subject. We have seen already that the whole theory of automorphic functions was from the start guided by the idea of integrating linear differential equations with algebraic coefficients. Poincaré simultaneously investigated the local problem of a linear differential equation in the neighborhood of an "irregular" singular point, showing for the first time how asymptotic developments could be obtained for the integrals. A little later (1884) he took up the question, also started by I. L. Fuchs, of the determination of all differential equations of the first order (in the complex domain) algebraic in y and y' and having fixed singular points; his researches were to be extended by Picard for equations of the second order, and to lead to the spectacular results of Painlevé and his school at the beginning of the twentieth century.

The most extraordinary production of Poincaré, also dating from his prodigious period of creativity (1880–1883) (reminding us of Gauss's *Tagebuch* of 1797–1801), is the qualitative theory of differential equations. It is one of the few examples of a mathematical theory that sprang apparently from nowhere and that almost immediately reached perfection in the hands of its creator. Everything was new in the first two of the four big papers that Poincaré published on the subject between 1880 and 1886.

The Problems. Until 1880, outside of the elementary types of differential equations (integrable by "quadratures") and the local "existence theorems," global general studies had been confined to linear equations, and (with the exception of the Sturm-Liouville theory) chiefly in the complex domain. Poincaré started with general equations $dx/X = dy/Y$, where X and Y are "arbitrary" polynomials in x, y, everything being real, and did not hesitate to consider the most general problem possible, namely a qualitative description of all solutions of the equation. In order to handle the infinite branches of the integral curves, he had the happy idea to project the (x, y) plane on a sphere from the center of the sphere (the center not lying in the plane), thus dealing for the first time with the integral curves of a vector field on a compact manifold.

The Methods. The starting point was the consideration of the "critical points" of the equation, satisfying $X = Y = 0$. Poincaré used the classification of these points due to Cauchy and Briot-Bouquet (modified to take care of the restriction to real coordinates) in the well-known categories of "nodes," "saddles," "spiral points," and "centers." In order to investigate the shape of an integral curve, Poincaré introduced the fundamental notion of "transversal" arcs, which are not tangent to the vector field at any of their points. Functions $F(x, y)$ such that $F(x, y) = C$ is a transversal for certain values of C also play an important part (their introduction is a forerunner of the method later used by Liapunov for stability problems).

The Results. The example of the "classical" differential equations had led one to believe that "general" integral curves would be given by an equation $\Phi(x, y) = C$, where Φ is analytic, and the constant C takes arbitrary values. Poincaré showed that on the contrary this kind of situation prevails only in "exceptional" cases, when there are no nodes nor spiral points among the critical points. In general, there are no centers—only a finite number of nodes, saddles, or spiral points; there is a finite number of closed integral curves, and the other curves either join two critical points or are "asymptotic" to these closed curves. Finally, he showed how his methods could be applied in explicit cases to determine a subdivision of the sphere into regions containing no closed integral or exactly one such curve.

In the third paper of that series Poincaré attacked the more general case of equations of the first order $F(x, y, y') = 0$, where F is a polynomial. By the consideration of the surface $F(x, y, z) = 0$, he showed that the problem is a special case of the determination of the integral curves of a vector field on a compact algebraic surface S. This immediately led him to introduce the genus p of S as the fundamental invariant of the problem, and to discover the relation

$$N + F - C = 2 - 2p \qquad (3)$$

where N, F, and C are the numbers of nodes, spiral points, and saddles. He then proceeded to show how his previous results for the sphere partly extend to the general case, and then made a detailed and beautiful study of the case when S is a torus ($p = 1$), so that there may be no critical point; in that case, he is confronted with a new situation—the appearance of the "ergodic hypothesis" for the integral curves. He was not able to prove that the hypothesis holds in general (under the smoothness conditions imposed on the vector field), but later work of Denjoy showed that this is in fact the case.

In the fourth paper Poincaré finally inaugurated the qualitative theory for equations of higher order, or equivalently, the study of integral curves on manifolds of dimension ≥ 3. The number of types of critical points increases with the dimension, but Poincaré saw how his relation (3) for dimension 2 can be generalized, by introducing the "Kronecker index" of a critical point, and showing that the sum of the indices of the critical points contained in a bounded domain limited by a transversal hypersurface $\sum$ depends only on the Betti numbers of $\sum$. It seems hopeless to obtain in general a description of all integral curves as precise as the one obtained for dimension 2. Probably inspired by his first results on the three-body problem (dating from 1883), Poincaré limited himself to the integral curves that are "near" a closed integral curve C_o. He considered a point M on C_o and a small portion $\sum$ of the hypersurface normal to C_o at M. If a point P of $\sum$ is close enough to M, the integral curve passing through P will cut $\sum$ again for the first time at a point $T(P)$, and one thus defines a transformation T of $\sum$ into itself, leaving M invariant, which can be proved to be continuously differentiable (and even analytic if one starts with analytic data). Poincaré then showed how the behavior of integral curves "near C_o" depends on the eigenvalues of the linear transformation tangent to T at M, and the classification of the various types is therefore closely similar to the classification of critical points.

After 1885 most of Poincaré's papers on differential equations were concerned with celestial mechanics, and more particularly the three-body problem. It seems that his interest in the subject was first aroused by his teaching at the Sorbonne; then, in 1885, King Oscar II of Sweden set up a competition among mathematicians of all countries on the n-body problem. Poincaré contributed a long paper, which was awarded first prize, and which ranks with his papers on the qualitative theory of differential equations as one of his masterpieces. Its central theme is the study of the periodic solutions of the three-body problem when the masses of two of the bodies are very small in relation to the mass of the third (which is what happens in the solar system). In 1878 G. W. Hill had given an example of such solutions; in 1883 Poincaré proved—by a beautiful application of the Kronecker index—the existence of a whole continuum of such solutions. Then in his prize memoir he gave another proof for the "restricted" three-body problem, when one of the small masses is neglected, and the other μ is introduced as a parameter in the Hamiltonian of the system. Starting from the trivial existence of periodic solutions for $\mu = 0$, Poincaré

proved the existence of "neighboring" periodic solutions for small enough μ, by an application of Cauchy's method of majorants. He then showed that there exist solutions that are asymptotic to a periodic solution for values of the time tending to $+\infty$ or $-\infty$, or even for both ("doubly asymptotic" solutions). It should be stressed that in order to arrive at these results, Poincaré first had to invent the necessary general tools: the "variational equation" giving the derivative of a vector solution $\mathbf{f}$ of a system of differential equations, with respect to a parameter, as a solution of a linear differential equation; the "characteristic exponents," corresponding to the case in which $\mathbf{f}$ is periodic; and the "integral invariants" of a vector field, generalizing the particular case of an invariant volume used by Liouville and Boltzmann.

Celestial Mechanics. The works of Poincaré on celestial mechanics contrasted sharply with those of his predecessors. Since Lagrange, the mathematical and numerical study of the solar system had been carried out by developing the coordinates of the planets in series of powers of the masses of the planets or satellites (very small compared with that of the sun); the coefficients of these series would then be computed, as functions of the time t, by various processes of approximation, from the equations obtained by identifying in the equations of motion the coefficients of the powers of the masses. At first the functions of t defined in this manner contained not only trigonometric functions such as $\sin(at + b)$ (a, b constants) but also terms such as $t \cdot \cos(at + b)$, and so forth, which for large t were likely to contradict the observed movements, and showed that the approximations made were unsatisfactory. Later in the nineteenth century these earlier approximations were replaced by more sophisticated ones, which were series containing only trigonometric functions of variables of type $a_n t + b_n$; but nobody had ever proved that these series were convergent, although most astronomers believed they were. One of Poincaré's results was that these series cannot be uniformly convergent, but may be used to provide asymptotic developments of the coordinates.

Thus Poincaré inaugurated the rigorous treatment of celestial mechanics, in opposition to the semiempirical computations that had been prevalent before him. However, he was also keenly interested in the "classical" computations and published close to a hundred papers concerning various aspects of the theory of the solar system, in which he suggested innumerable improvements and new techniques. Most of his results were developed in his famous three-volume *Les méthodes nouvelles de la mécanique céleste* and later in his *Leçons de mécanique céleste*.

From the theoretical point of view, one should mention his proof that in the "restricted" three-body problem, where the Hamiltonian depends on four variables (x_1, x_2, y_1, y_2) and the parameter μ, and where it is analytic in these five variables and periodic of period 2π in y_1 and y_2, then there is no "first integral" of the equations of motion, except the Hamiltonian, which has similar properties. Poincaré also started the study of "stability" of dynamical systems, although not in the various more precise senses that have been given to this notion by later writers (starting with Liapunov). The most remarkable result that he proved is now known as "Poincaré's recurrence theorem": for "almost all" orbits (for a dynamical system admitting a "positive" integral invariant), the orbit intersects an arbitrary nonempty open set for a sequence of values of the time tending to $+\infty$. What is particularly interesting in that theorem is the introduction, probably for the first time, of null sets in a question of analysis (Poincaré, of course, did not speak of measure, but of "probability").

Another famous paper of Poincaré in celestial mechanics is the one he wrote in 1885 on the shape of a rotating fluid mass submitted only to the forces of gravitation. Maclaurin had found as possible shapes some ellipsoids of revolution to which Jacobi had added other types of ellipsoids with unequal axes, and P. G. Tait and W. Thomson some annular shapes. By a penetrating analysis of the problem, Poincaré showed that still other "pyriform" shapes existed. One of the features of his interesting argument is that, apparently for the first time, he was confronted with the problem of minimizing a quadratic form in "infinitely" many variables.

Finally, in one of his later papers (1905), Poincaré attacked for the first time the difficult problem of the existence of closed geodesics on a convex smooth surface (which he supposed analytic). The method by which he tried to prove the existence of such geodesics is derived from his ideas on periodic orbits in the three-body problem. Later work showed that this method is not conclusive, but it has inspired the numerous workers who finally succeeded in obtaining a complete proof of the theorem and extensive generalizations.

Partial Differential Equations and Mathematical Physics. For more than twenty years Poincaré lectured at the Sorbonne on mathematical physics; he gave himself to that task with his characteristic thoroughness and energy, with the result that he became an expert in practically all parts of theoretical physics, and published more than seventy papers and books on the most varied subjects, with a predilection for the theories of light and of electromagnetic waves. On two occasions he played an important part in the development of the new ideas and discoveries that revolutionized physics at the end of the nineteenth century. His remark on the possible connection between X rays and the phenomena of phosphorescence was the starting point of H. Becquerel's experiments which led him to the discovery of radioactivity. On the other hand, Poincaré was active in the discussions concerning Lorentz' theory of the electron from 1899 on; Poincaré was the first to observe that the Lorentz transformations form a group, isomorphic to the group leaving invariant the quadratic form $x^2 + y^2 + z^2 - t^2$; and many physicists consider that Poincaré shares with Lorentz and Einstein the credit for the invention of the special theory of relativity.

This persistent interest in physical problems was bound to lead Poincaré into the mathematical problems raised by the partial differential equations of mathematical physics, most of which were still in a very rudimentary state around 1880. It is typical that in all the papers he wrote on this subject, he never lost sight of the possible physical meanings (often drawn from very different physical theories) of the methods he used and the results he obtained. This is particularly apparent in the first big paper (1890) that he wrote on the Dirichlet problem. At that time the existence of a solution inside a bounded domain D limited by a surface S was established (for an arbitrary given continuous function on S) only under rather restrictive conditions on S, by two methods due to C. Neumann and H. A. Schwarz. Poincaré invented a third method, the "sweeping out process": the problem is classically equivalent to the existence of positive masses on S whose potential V is equal to 1 in D and continuous in the whole space. Poincaré started with masses on a large sphere Σ containing D and giving potential 1 inside Σ. He then observed that the classical Poisson formula allows one to replace masses inside a sphere C by masses on the surface of the sphere in such a way that the potential is the same outside C and has decreased inside C. By covering the exterior of D by a sequence (C_n) of spheres and applying repeatedly to each C_n (in a suitable order) the preceding remark, he showed that the limit of the potentials thus obtained is the solution V of the problem, the masses initially on Σ having been ultimately "swept out" on S. Of course he had to prove the continuity of V at the points of S, which he did under the only assumption that at each of these points there is a half-cone (with opening $2\alpha > 0$) having the point as vertex and such that the intersection of that half-cone and of a neighborhood of the vertex does not meet D (later examples of Lebesgue showed that such a restriction cannot be eliminated). This very original method was later to play an important part in the renewal of potential theory that took place in the 1920's and 1930's, before the advent of modern Hilbert space methods.

In the same 1890 paper Poincaré began the long, and only partly successful, struggle with what we now call the problem of the eigenvalues of the Laplacian. In several problems of physics (vibrations of membranes, cooling of a solid, theory of the tides, and so forth), one meets the problem of finding a function u satisfying in a bounded domain D an equation of the form

$$\Delta u + \lambda u = 0 \qquad (4)$$

and on the boundary S of D the condition

$$u + k(du/dn) = 0 \qquad (5)$$

where du/dn is the normal derivative and λ and k are constants. Heuristic variational arguments (generalizing the method of Riemann for the Dirichlet principle) and the analogy with the Sturm-Liouville problem (which is the corresponding problem for functions of a single variable) lead to the conjecture that for a given k there exists an increasing sequence of real numbers ("eigenvalues"),

$$\lambda_1 < \lambda_2 < \cdots < \lambda_n < \cdots$$

such that the problem is only solvable when λ is equal to one of the λ_n, and then has only one solution u_n such that $\int_D u_n^2 \, d\tau = 1$, the "eigenfunctions" u_n forming an orthonormal system. In the case of the vibrating membrane, the u_n corresponds to the experimentally detectable "harmonics." But a rigorous proof of the existence of the λ_n and the u_n had not been found before Poincaré; for the case $k = 0$, Schwarz had proved the existence of λ_1 by the following method: the analogy with the Sturm-Liouville problem suggested that for any smooth function f, the equation

$$\Delta u + \lambda u + f = 0 \qquad (6)$$

would have for λ distinct from the λ_n a unique solution $u(\lambda, \mathbf{x})$ satisfying (5), and which would be a meromorphic function of λ, having the λ_n as simple poles. Schwarz had shown that, as a function of λ, the solution $u(\lambda, \mathbf{x})$ was equal to a power series with a finite radius of convergence. Picard had been able to prove also the existence of λ_2. In 1894 Poincaré (always in the case $k = 0$) succeeded in proving the above property

of $u(\lambda, \mathbf{x})$, by an ingenious adaptation of Schwarz's method, using in addition an inequality of the type

$$\iiint_D V^2 dx \, dy \, dz \leqslant$$

$$C \iiint_D \left[\left(\frac{\partial V}{\partial x} \right)^2 + \left(\frac{\partial V}{\partial y} \right)^2 + \left(\frac{\partial V}{\partial z} \right)^2 \right] dx \, dy \, dz \qquad (7)$$

(C constant depending only on D)

valid for all smooth functions V such that $\iiint_D V \, dx \, dy \, dz = 0$ (the forerunner of numerous similar inequalities that play a fundamental part in the modern theory of partial differential equations). But he could not extend his method for $k \neq 0$ on account of the difficulty of finding a solution of (6) having a normal derivative on S (he could only obtain what we now would call a "weak" derivative, or derivative in the sense of distribution theory).

Two years later he met similar difficulties when he tried to extend Neumann's method for the solution of the Dirichlet problem (which was valid only for convex domains D). Through a penetrating discussion of that method (based on so-called "double layer" potentials), Poincaré linked it to the Schwarz process mentioned above, and was thus led to a new "boundary problem" containing a parameter λ: find a "single layer" potential φ defined by masses on S, such that $(d\varphi/dn)_i = -\lambda(d\varphi/dn)_e$, where the suffixes i and e mean normal derivatives taken toward the interior and toward the exterior of S. Here again, heuristic variational arguments convinced Poincaré that there should be a sequence of "eigenvalues" and corresponding "eigenfunctions" for this problem, but for the same reasons he was not able to prove their existence. A few years later, Fredholm's theory of integral equations enabled him to solve all these problems; it is likely that Poincaré's papers had a decisive influence on the development of Fredholm's method, in particular the idea of introducing a variable complex parameter in the integral equation. It should also be mentioned that Fredholm's determinants were directly inspired by the theory of "infinite determinants" of H. von Koch, which itself was a development of much earlier results of Poincaré in connection with the solution of linear differential equations.

Algebraic Topology. The main leitmotiv of Poincaré's mathematical work is clearly the idea of "continuity": whenever he attacks a problem in analysis, we almost immediately see him investigating what happens when the conditions of the problem are allowed to vary continuously. He was therefore bound to encounter at every turn what we now call topological problems. He himself said in 1901, "Every problem I had attacked led me to *Analysis situs*," particularly the researches on differential equations and on the periods of multiple integrals. Starting in 1894 he inaugurated in a remarkable series of six papers—written during a period of ten years—the modern methods of algebraic topology. Until then the only significant step had been the generalizations of the concept of "order of connection" of a surface, defined independently by Riemann and Betti, and which Poincaré called "Betti numbers" (they are the numbers $1 + h_j$, where the h_j are the present-day "Betti numbers"); but practically nothing had been done beyond this definition. The machinery of what we now call simplicial homology is entirely a creation of Poincaré: concepts of triangulation of a manifold, of a simplicial complex, of barycentric subdivision, and of the dual complex, of the matrix of incidence coefficients of a complex, and the computation of Betti numbers from that matrix. With the help of these tools, Poincaré discovered the generalization of the Euler theorem for polyhedra (now known as the Euler-Poincaré formula) and the famous duality theorem for the homology of a manifold; a little later he introduced the concept of torsion. Furthermore, in his first paper he had defined the fundamental group of a manifold (or first homotopy group) and shown its relations to the first Betti number. In the last paper of the series he was able to give an example of two manifolds having the same homology but different fundamental groups. In the first paper he had also linked the Betti numbers to the periods of integrals of differential forms (with which he was familiar through his work on multiple integrals and on invariant integrals), and stated the theorem which G. de Rham first proved in 1931. It has been rightly said that until the discovery of the higher homotopy groups in 1933, the development of algebraic topology was entirely based on Poincaré's ideas and techniques.

In addition, Poincaré also showed how to apply these new tools to some of the problems for which he had invented them. In two of the papers of the series on analysis situs, he determined the Betti numbers of an algebraic (complex) surface, and the fundamental group of surfaces defined by an equation of type $z^2 = F(x, y)$ (F polynomial), thus paving the way for the later generalizations of Lefschetz and Hodge. In his last paper on differential equations (1912), Poincaré reduced the problem of the existence of periodic solutions of the restricted three-body problem (but with no restriction on the parameter μ) to a theorem on the existence of fixed points for a continuous transformation of the plane subject to certain conditions, which was probably the first example of an existence proof in analysis based on algebraic topology. He did not succeed in proving

that fixed point theorem, which was obtained by G. D. Birkhoff a few months after Poincaré's death.

Foundations of Mathematics. With the growth of his international reputation, Poincaré was more and more called upon to speak or write on various topics of mathematics and science for a wider audience, a chore for which he does not seem to have shown great reluctance. (In 1910 he even was asked to comment on the influence of comets on the weather!) His vivid style and clarity of mind enhanced his reputation in his time as the best expositor of mathematics for the layman. His well-known description of the process of mathematical discovery remains unsurpassed and has been on the whole corroborated by many mathematicians, despite the fact that Poincaré's imagination was completely atypical; and the pages he devoted to the axioms of geometry and their relation to experimental science are classical. Whether this is enough to dub him a "philosopher," as has often been asserted, is a question which is best left for professional philosophers to decide, and we may limit ourselves to the influence of his writings on the problem of the foundations of mathematics.

Whereas Poincaré has been accused of being too conservative in physics, he certainly was very open-minded regarding new mathematical ideas. The quotations in his papers show that he read extensively, if not systematically, and was aware of all the latest developments in practically every branch of mathematics. He was probably the first mathematician to use Cantor's theory of sets in analysis; he had met concepts such as perfect non-dense sets in his work on automorphic functions or on differential equations in the early 1880's. Up to a certain point, he also looked with favor on the axiomatic trend in mathematics, as it was developing toward the end of the nineteenth century, and he praised Hilbert's *Grundlagen der Geometrie*. However, Poincaré's position during the polemics of the early 1900's about the "paradoxes" of set theory and the foundations of mathematics has made him a precursor of the Intuitionist School. He never stated his ideas on these questions very clearly and mostly confined himself to criticizing the schools of Russell, Peano, and Hilbert. Although accepting the "arithmetization" of mathematics, Poincaré did not agree to the reduction of arithmetic to the theory of sets nor to the Peano axiomatic definition of natural numbers. For Poincaré (as later for L. E. J. Brouwer) the natural numbers constituted a fundamental intuitive notion, apparently to be taken for granted without further analysis; he several times explicitly repudiated the concept of an infinite set in favor of the "potential infinite," but he never developed this idea systematically. He obviously had a blind spot regarding the formalization of mathematics, and poked fun repeatedly at the efforts of the disciples of Peano and Russell in that direction; but, somewhat paradoxically, his criticism of the early attempts of Hilbert was probably the starting point of some of the most fruitful of the later developments of metamathematics. Poincaré stressed that Hilbert's point of view of defining objects by a system of axioms was only admissible if one could prove a priori that such a system did not imply contradiction, and it is well known that the proof of noncontradiction was the main goal of the theory which Hilbert founded after 1920. Poincaré seems to have been convinced that such attempts were hopeless, and K. Gödel's theorem proved him right; what Poincaré failed to grasp is that all the work spent on metamathematics would greatly improve our understanding of the nature of mathematical reasoning.

BIBLIOGRAPHY

See *Oeuvres de Henri Poincaré*, 11 vols. (Paris, 1916–1954); *Les méthodes nouvelles de la mécanique céleste*, 3 vols. (Paris, 1892–1899); *La science et l'hypothèse* (Paris, 1906); *Science et méthode* (Paris, 1908); and *La valeur de la science* (Paris, 1913).

On Poincaré and his work, see Gaston Darboux, "Éloge historique d'Henri Poincaré," in *Mémoires de l'Académie des sciences*, **52** (1914), lxxxi–cxlviii; and Poggendorff, III, 1053–1054; IV, 1178–1180; V, 990; and VI, 2038. See also references in G. Sarton, *The Study of the History of Mathematics* (Cambridge, Mass., 1936), 93–94.

JEAN DIEUDONNÉ

POINSOT, LOUIS (*b.* Paris, France, 3 January 1777; *d.* Paris, 5 December 1859)

At the end of October 1794 Poinsot, who was a student in his last year at the Collège Louis-le-Grand in Paris, presented himself as a candidate in the first competitive entrance examination to the future École Polytechnique. Admitted despite an insufficient knowledge of algebra, he left in 1797 in order to enter the École des Ponts et Chaussées, where he remained for three years. Neglecting his technical studies—which held little attraction for him—in favor of mathematics, he eventually gave up the idea of becoming an engineer. From 1804 to 1809 he taught mathematics at the Lycée Bonaparte in Paris; he was then appointed inspector general of the Imperial University.

Despite the frequent travels to the provinces necessitated by this new post, on 1 November 1809 Poinsot was named assistant professor of analysis and mechanics at the École Polytechnique, substituting for Labey. Although he held this position until the school was reorganized in September 1816, he actually taught there for only three years, after which time he arranged for A. A. L. Reynaud and later for Cauchy to substitute for him. He owed his appointment at the Polytechnique to the favorable reception given to his *Éléments de statique* (1803) and to three subsequent memoirs that dealt with the composition of momenta and the composition of areas (1806), the general theory of equilibrium and of movement in systems (1806), and polygons and polyhedra (1809). His reputation also resulted in his election on 31 May 1813 to the mathematics section of the Académie des Sciences, replacing Lagrange.

From 1816 to 1826 Poinsot served as admissions examiner at the École Polytechnique, and on several occasions after 1830 he worked with the school's Conseil de Perfectionnement. Although in 1824 he gave up his duties as inspector general, his nomination in 1840 to the Conseil Royal de l'Instruction Publique kept him informed of university problems. Meanwhile he continued research on number theory and on mechanics, publishing a small number of original and carefully executed memoirs. Named to the Bureau des Longitudes in 1843, he displayed a certain interest in celestial mechanics. Moderately liberal in his political opinions, he protested against the clericalism of the Restoration but later accepted nomination to the Chambre des Pairs (1846) and to the Senate (1852).

Poinsot was determined to publish only fully developed results and to present them with clarity and elegance. Consequently he left a rather limited body of work, which was devoted mainly to mechanics, geometry, and number theory. He showed almost no interest in algebra except for his early investigations concerning the fifth-degree equation and his remarkable analysis of Lagrange's *Traité de la résolution des équations numériques de tous les degrés* (1808). Similarly, the infinitesimal calculus appears in his work only in the form of extracts (published in 1815) from his course in analysis at the École Polytechnique.

Poinsot's contributions to number theory (1818–1849) have been analyzed by L. E. Dickson. They deal primarily with primitive roots, certain Diophantine equations, and the expression of a number as a difference of two squares.

A fervent disciple of Monge, Poinsot was one of the principal leaders of the revival of geometry in France during the first half of the nineteenth century. In particular, he was responsible for the creation in 1846 of a chair of advanced geometry at the Sorbonne, which was intended for Chasles. Poinsot, who had a presentiment of the importance of the geometry of position, established the theory of regular star polygons and discovered several types of regular star polyhedra (1809), a general study of which was carried out by Cauchy shortly afterward.

Yet it was in mechanics that Poinsot most effectively displayed his gift for geometry. Although *Éléments de statique* (1803) was merely a manual designed for candidates to the École Polytechnique, the work possessed the great merit of applying geometric methods to the study of elementary problems of mechanics and of introducing the concept of the couple. The latter notion, moreover, held a central place in two more highly developed memoirs that Poinsot presented to the Académie des Sciences in 1804 and published in the *Journal de l'École polytechnique* in 1806. The second of these memoirs inspired an interesting debate between Poinsot and Lagrange concerning the principles of mechanics.

Among Poinsot's other writings on mechanics, the most important is *Théorie nouvelle de la rotation des corps* (1834). Pursuing the theoretical study undertaken in the eighteenth century by Euler, d'Alembert, and Lagrange, Poinsot established in a purely geometric fashion the existence of the axes of permanent rotation and worked out a very elegant representation of rotary motion by the rolling of the ellipsoid of inertia of a body on a fixed plane (Poinsot motion). This theory was developed by Sylvester and was applied by Foucault to the discovery of the gyroscope. Poinsot's remarkable geometric intuition also enabled him to elaborate a purely geometric theory of the precession of the equinoxes (1858).

In frequent opposition to the French analytic school of the first half of the nineteenth century, Poinsot produced an original body of work by successfully submitting to geometric treatment a certain number of fundamental questions in the mechanics of solids.

BIBLIOGRAPHY

I. ORIGINAL WORKS. Poinsot's best known work, *Éléments de statique* (Paris, 1803), went through many editions: the 9th ed. (1848) was the last to appear in his lifetime; 12th ed. (1877). This work was accompanied, progressively, by some of his most important papers on statics; the 8th through 10th eds. contain four memoirs on the composition of momenta and of areas, on the unchanging plan of the system of the world, on the general theory of equilibrium and of the movement of systems and on a new theory of the rotation of bodies. There is an English trans. of this work by T. Sutton (Cambridge, 1847).

Most of Poinsot's other publications are listed in Royal Society *Catalogue of Scientific Papers*, IV, 960–961, which includes 31 articles and memoirs on mechanics, algebra, number theory, infinitesimal calculus, geometry, infinitesimal geometry, and celestial mechanics, all of which were published in various academic collections or in mathematical or astronomical reviews. Many of these papers were also published as offprints and enjoyed a fairly broad distribution.

An important analysis of the 2nd ed. of Lagrange's *Traité de la résolution des équations numériques de tous les degrés* is in *Magasin encyclopédique*, **4** (1808), 343–375 (repr. in 1826 in the 3rd ed. of this work, pp. v–xx), as well as two pamphlets that do not appear to be offprints: *Recherches sur l'analyse des sections angulaires* (Paris, 1825) and *Théorie nouvelle de la rotation des corps présentée à l'Institut le 19 mai 1834* (Paris, 1834), with English trans. by C. Whitley (Cambridge, 1834).

The bulk of Poinsot's MSS have been preserved in Paris at the Bibliothèque de l'Institut de France (MSS 948–965, 4738); MS 4738, which is an offprint of one of Poinsot's first memoirs, "Théorie générale de l'équilibre et du mouvement des systèmes," in *Journal de l'École polytechnique*, **6** (1806), 206–241, contains in the margin MS criticisms by Lagrange and Poinsot's responses.

II. SECONDARY LITERATURE. Poinsot's life and work have not yet been subjected to the detailed study they merit. His geometric writings have been analyzed in detail by M. Chasles, in *Aperçu historique* . . . (Brussels–Paris, 1837), see index; and in *Rapport sur les progrès de la géométrie* (Paris, 1870), 13–17; those on number theory have been analyzed by L. E. Dickson, in *History of the Theory of Numbers*, 3 vols. (Washington, 1919), see index. Other aspects of his work remain to be examined.

The most complete study of Poinsot's work is J. Bertrand, "Notice sur Louis Poinsot," in *Journal des savants* (July 1872), 405–420; and in Poinsot, *Éléments de statique*, 11th ed. (Paris, 1872), ix–xxviii. See also J. Bertrand, "Éloge historique de Louis Poinsot, lu le 29 décembre 1890," in *Revue générale des sciences pures et appliquées*, **1** (1890), 753–762, repr. in *Mémoires de l'Académie des sciences de Paris*, **45** (1899), lxxiii–xcv, and in J. Bertrand, *Éloges académiques*, n.s. (Paris, 1902), 1–27.

Other articles (listed chronologically) include G. Vapereau, in *Dictionnaire universel des contemporains*, 2nd ed. (Paris, 1861), 1408; E. Merlieux, in F. Hoefer, ed., *Nouvelle biographie générale*, XL (Paris, 1862), 562–563; P. Mansion, in *Résumé du cours d'analyse infinitésimale* (Paris, 1887), 289–291; M. d'Ocagne, in *Histoire abrégée des sciences mathématiques* (Paris, 1955), 200–202; and P. Bailhache, "La théorie générale de l'équilibre et du mouvement des systèmes de Louis Poinsot et sa signification critique" (thesis, Paris, 1974).

RENÉ TATON

POISSON, SIMÉON-DENIS (*b.* Pithiviers, Loiret, France, 21 June 1781; *d.* Paris, France, 25 April 1840)

Poisson was an example of those scientists whose intellectual activity was intimately linked to a great number of educational or administrative duties and to the authority derived from them. This responsibility and authority earned him more misunderstanding than esteem, and his reputation in the French scientific community was challenged during his lifetime as well as after his death. It was only outside France that certain results of his prodigious activity were best understood and considered worthy of perpetuating his memory. His life and work are thus of special interest for the history and philosophy of science. The same institution that gave him his training, the newly founded École Polytechnique, also assured his success. An exemplary product of a certain type of training and of a particular attitude toward scientific research, he devoted his life to both, exhausting in their service his remarkable capacity for hard work. His activities, which continued unabated through a succession of political regimes, exercised a major influence on French science. Although his ambition to continue Laplace's work by giving a true *summa* of mathematical physics was not to be realized, his numerous efforts toward this goal offer a lesson concerning the application of mathematics to natural phenomena that is still worth examining.

Poisson came from a modest family. His health, like that of several older siblings who died in childhood, was weak; and his mother had to entrust him to a nurse. His father, formerly a soldier, had been discriminated against by the noble officers, and after retiring from military service he purchased a low-ranking administrative post. Apparently it was he who first taught Poisson to read and write. The Revolution, which the elder Poisson welcomed with enthusiasm, enabled him to become president of the district of Pithiviers, which post afforded him access to information useful in choosing a career for his son. The latter had been entrusted to an uncle named Lenfant in Fontainebleau in order to learn surgery, but he lacked the prerequisite manual dexterity and showed little interest in the profession. Having failed as an apprentice, he was guided by his father toward those professions to which access had been eased by measures recently adopted by the republican regime. In 1796 he was enrolled at the École Centrale of Fontainebleau, where he soon displayed a great capacity for learning and was fortunate in having a dedicated teacher. He made rapid progress in mathematics and was encouraged to prepare for the competitive entrance examination at the École Polytechnique, to which he was admitted first in his class in 1798.

On his arrival in Paris, fresh from the provinces, Poisson had to adapt himself in several ways to a radically new life for which he had been little prepared. His easy success in his studies left him time to make this adjustment much more quickly than is usual in such cases. Lagrange, who had just begun his courses on analytic functions, found in Poisson an attentive student always capable of contributing pertinent remarks in class; and Laplace was even more impressed by Poisson's ability to assimilate difficult material. The reputation that Poisson enjoyed among his fellow students is mentioned in an article on him by Arago, whom he preceded by five years at Polytechnique. This comment is certainly an echo of direct testimony, and there is no reason to doubt Arago's assertion that during these years Poisson evinced a lively interest in the theater and in other aspects of cultural life. An openness to every new experience and a passion for learning allowed him to circumvent the difficulties that he might otherwise have encountered on account of his limited early education. However, his teachers were apparently unable to correct his innate clumsiness, for he could never learn to draft acceptable diagrams. This deficiency prevented him from advancing in descriptive geometry, which subject Monge had made a central element of the new school's curriculum and which contributed greatly to its reputation. On the other hand, Poisson possessed undoubted ability in mathematical analysis and displayed this gift in 1799–1800 in a paper on the theory of equations and on Bezout's theorem. At a time when it was difficult to recruit suitably qualified teaching personnel, this asset was sufficient to gain him nomination as *répétiteur* at Polytechnique immediately after his graduation in 1800.

Poisson owed this appointment principally to the backing of Laplace, who unwaveringly supported him throughout a career qualified as "easy" by Victor Cousin. The main reason that "easy" is the right word was that Poisson was enabled to stay in Paris in the milieu of Polytechnique. He was named deputy professor in 1802 and four years later replaced Fourier as titular professor. Thereupon, Poisson had to wait only a short time to obtain supplementary posts outside the school. In 1808 he was appointed astronomer at the Bureau des Longitudes and, in 1809, professor of mechanics at the Faculty of Sciences. It would appear that he never disdained worldly connections or the advantages to be gained through the salons, but it would be completely unjust to assume that he systematically cultivated these means of social advancement. As a participant in the Société Philomathique from 1803 and later in the Société d'Arcueil, he had no intellectual reservations about the idealism that animated Polytechnique; and if his friendships were useful, he did not cultivate them out of self-serving motives.

On 23 March 1812 Poisson was elected to the physics section of the Institute (to the place left vacant by Malus' death), and by 14 April his nomination had received the imperial approbation. This rapid confirmation shows that the authorities had not forgotten the acquiescent attitude that he had adopted in 1804. In that year Poisson prevented the students of the École Polytechnique from publishing a petition against the proclamation of the empire. He had taken this step, however, primarily to avoid a crisis at the institution to which he was devoted. He felt no genuine allegiance to the Napoleonic regime and easily accommodated himself to its overthrow. The restoration of Louis XVIII in 1814 caused no hiatus in his career, and he continued to accumulate official responsibilities. To the responsibilities he already exercised, he added that of examiner at the École Militaire in 1815 and of examiner of graduating students at Polytechnique the following year.

Within this pattern of continuity, however, Poisson's life and career entered upon a new phase at about this time. In 1817 he was married to Nancy de Bardi, an orphan born in England to émigré parents. The marriage constrained his life severely, leaving no time for anything but family, research, and professional obligations. His nomination in 1820 to the Conseil Royal de l'Université introduced him into the national educational system at the highest administrative level—at the very moment when the government's conservative general political stance was issuing in a campaign against the scientific programs and policies adopted during the Revolutionary and Napoleonic periods. Enlisting the aid of colleagues, notably Ampère, he managed to resist this pressure. His efforts in defense of science, which continued until the end of his life, constitute a considerable achievement.

While assuming these weighty pedagogical responsibilities, Poisson was becoming steadily more influential within the Academy of Sciences. Following Laplace's death in 1827, he felt it to be his mission to build upon the latter's scientific legacy; and Cauchy's exile in 1830 contributed still further to casting Poisson in the role of France's leading mathematician. It was primarily against him that Evariste Galois directed his celebrated criticism of French mathematics, and historians have been too eager to accept its validity at face value. Circumstances thrust upon Poisson more responsibil-

ity than any one man could have borne. It is all the more remarkable, then, that he published virtually all of his books during the last ten years of his life. To be sure, none of them manifests a profound originality. His many articles and memoirs (of which he himself prepared a list) must therefore be considered in order to arrive at a just assessment of his *oeuvre*. It must also be acknowledged that his books exhibit an uncommon gift for clear exposition and constitute an ambitious project for the instruction of future generations of students. He exhausted himself in the attempt to realize this project and died regretting that he had left it unfinished. Accordingly, any final judgment of his work and influence must give considerable weight to his role as educator.

It was precisely this aspect of Poisson's contribution that was ignored in the unsigned article on him published in Larousse's *Grand dictionnaire universel du XIX siècle* (1874). The author wrote: "The reputation of a mathematician really depends on extraordinary powers of analysis. The experimental scientist, whose physical discoveries the analyst formulates in incomprehensible expressions, is generally incapable of verifying the quality of the help that he is getting. . . . To the layman, what is most striking in the procedures of mathematicians, even though it really has almost no merit, is the art of making transformations. Poisson possessed that skill in a high degree. He amazed people and was taken for a great man. But, in order to be remembered, a scientist needs to have ideas, and Poisson had only those of others. Moreover, when he had to choose, as between two opposing ideas, the one that he would dignify with an application of his analysis, he generally made the wrong choice."

Although this criticism is so hostile as to amount to denigration, it does serve to bring out several of Poisson's characteristic traits. First, it stresses that the tireless manipulation of mathematical equations was his special province. His zeal for extending as far as possible the type of activity for which he had a gift was natural; and the limitations or deficiencies of his results are less interesting than what they reveal about the historical context, which was one of intense scientific activity.

Two authors who were very close to Poisson during the last decade of his life have left accounts that substantially agree as to his position within French science. Their gratitude for his help, moreover, did not lead them to abstain from criticism, and they provide several details that are not available elsewhere.

In 1840 Guillaume Libri, who had not yet become notorious for his bizarre administration of the French national archives, wrote an *éloge* of Poisson in which he affirmed, "Surely no one would dare to say that Poisson lacked inventiveness, but he especially liked unresolved questions that had been treated by others or areas in which there was still work to be done." In a note he added that Poisson, who refused to attend to two matters at once, had a small wallet for papers on which he jotted down information and recorded observations of subjects to be examined later. Libri, who evidently had the document in his possession, stated by way of example that Poisson considered research on algebraic equations and definite integrals to be hopeless. By contrast, he seems to have found it more important to pursue Euler's works on problems of *géométrie dépendant des différences mêlées*, that is, on problems of mathematical physics involving partial differential equations.

Cournot, who owed his university career to Poisson and replaced him in 1839 as chairman of the Jury d'Agrégation in mathematics, recorded in his *Souvenirs* that "the abundance, adaptability, and resourcefulness" that his benefactor displayed to a greater degree than anyone else "in involved calculation" [*dans les hauts calculs*] was combined with an eagerness to examine "all questions and preferably those that are significant for natural philosophy. . . . Despite that, or because of it," Cournot adds with discernment, "he did not enjoy the rare good fortune of developing one of those completely new and striking conceptions that forever establish the fame of their innovator in the history of science. He proceeded steadily along his path, rather than crossing into any new domain."

Although this judgment must be slightly modified, as will be seen below, it epitomizes the essential aspects of Poisson's mathematical work. Poisson was succeeded on the Conseil Royal de l'Université in 1840 by Poinsot, with whose scientific personality Cournot compared Poisson's in a felicitous contrast: "Poinsot took the opposite course to Poisson: he stuck to a few simple, ingenious ideas that were completely his own. He considered them and reconsidered them at his leisure, without worrying about producing a great deal and even (let us speak plainly) without possessing much knowledge." Although Cournot adds only that "it would take too long to explain to someone who is not a member of the profession all the different ways in which mathematics can be cultivated." Cournot obviously preferred Poinsot's originality tempered by laziness. It is also clear that Cournot was more impressed by the "abundance" of Poisson's works

than he was concerned to submit them to a genuine historical critique.

Although Poisson's list of his own publications has greatly impressed posterity by its length, it has not aroused adequate critical interest. Historians of science are aware that in citing his memoirs Poisson also listed the extracts derived from them, which appeared mainly in the *Bulletin de la Société philomathique de Paris* and in the *Annales de chimie et de physique*. Accordingly, they have eliminated from the list those works thought to be duplicate or even triplicate entries and have been content to wonder at the remainder, which consists of nearly 300 original titles. But the classification by chronological order and by subject matter obliges the historian, precisely because of the lack of exact bibliographical data, to undertake laborious research in order to reconstruct the actual conditions under which Poisson produced his work during the Empire and the Restoration. The delay in publication of official periodicals such as the *Journal de l'École polytechnique* and the *Mémoires de l'Académie des sciences* deprived them of much of their importance as disseminators of new knowledge. Other private publications, originating in various scientific circles and learned societies, were more effective from this point of view; but they too experienced difficult periods, during which they substituted for each other. One reason for the abundance of Poisson's titles, therefore, lies in the special circumstances of the scientific life of the age.

Before considering Poisson's scientific work, let us try to complete a portrait of its author. At the end of his article Arago delivered a parting shot to the effect that Poisson had the habit of saying "Life is good for only two things: to study mathematics and to teach it." Since we cannot assume that the permanent secretary of the Academy of Sciences wrote this purely and simply for the pleasure of coining a *bon mot*, it is reasonable to believe that it contains an element of truth. Here again, Cournot furnishes the necessary context.

Cournot was told that Poisson wished to receive a visit from him, but the young *docteur ès sciences* postponed the visit for several years, fearing that he would be recruited as a *lycée* professor. Thus, Cournot's image of Poisson was very much like Arago's sketch—that of a narrow mathematical zealot. Cournot's change of opinion after several years of direct contact may therefore be accepted with confidence.

Cournot was eager to elaborate on his first impression of Poisson. Alluding to both his appearance and his style of a straightforward man of the common people, he reports that "With a formal and even elaborate manner Poisson combined great intellectual subtlety and a large store of common sense and forbearance that disposed him toward conservative ideas. Given the distinguished reputation that he enjoyed in the scientific world [in 1815], the royalist party were quite willing to take his conservative outlook for royalism, and he went along with this! . . . When the Revolution of 1830 occurred, Poisson saw no grounds for withholding his support from a government that aimed at being sensible and moderate; and he resolved to tolerate Cousin's philosophical declaration, as he had tolerated others, provided that he was not obligated to subscribe to its tenets personally and that in public life, as in mathematics, things would run their course." This portrait is very probably close to the truth. When in 1837 Poisson accepted elevation to the nobility (he became a baron), even as Laplace had done, he was displaying not so much a political conformism as the desire to neglect no measures likely to be useful in promoting the interests of science.

Reporting further on his contacts with Poisson, Cournot wrote that "At the very end of his life, when it had become painful for him to speak, I saw him almost weep from the chagrin that he had experienced as chairman of a competitive examination [for the *agrégation*], for he had become convinced that our young teachers were concerned solely with obtaining a post and possessed no love for science at all." Perhaps it was when confronted with such an audience and sensing its debased motivation that the aging teacher adopted the habit of bluntly uttering the aphorism cited by Arago. Poisson undoubtedly had forgotten how fully he himself had been protected in his youth from the cares borne by senior colleagues of the scientific establishment. Still, he had always scrupulously fulfilled all his official duties, without ever taking time from his own exhausting program of research. This conscientiousness is proof that Poisson, an unbeliever in religion, had found an ideal to which he had become increasingly willing to sacrifice even his health. Such conduct can evoke only respect.

The number and variety of the subjects that Poisson treated make it impractical to offer an exhaustive account of his scientific work. Accordingly, we shall attempt only to outline its most important aspects. In Poisson's case, a classification by subject matter would be less helpful than one by chronological order, which reveals the shifts in his interests during his long career.

The early stages of Poisson's research can be studied in the eleventh through fourteenth *cahiers* of the *Journal de l'École polytechnique* and in the second series of the *Bulletin de la Société philomathique de Paris*. In each instance the year 1807 is seen to be the *terminus ad quem* of the period in which he completed his mathematical training and was clearly seeking out subjects that readily offered scope for further development. Libri's remarks, cited above, are quite illuminating for this period. They indicate that he was particularly drawn to the integration of differential and of partial differential equations, and to their possible application in the study of the oscillations of a pendulum in a resisting medium and in the theory of sound. Naturally, coming in the wake of the great works of the preceding century, the choice of these topics did not demonstrate any particular originality. Still, this initial selection was decisive for his career, since it continued to guide all his subsequent research.

From 1808 to 1814 Poisson clearly set out to make an original contribution. At the beginning of this period the Academy of Sciences was emerging from an administrative crisis and was preparing to resume its role and assure the publication of its periodicals. This auspicious situation provided Poisson with a favorable opportunity for advancement. Fourier's first memoir on the theory of heat, read to the Institute in December 1807, was not favored with a report; and it was only through Poisson's efforts that it appeared three months later, in abridged form, in the *Bulletin de la Société philomathique de Paris*, of which journal Poisson soon assumed editorial direction. This fact is especially noteworthy. Poisson himself was not impeded by the obstacles encountered in scientific publishing, at their worst around 1810. He submitted three major papers to the Academy, all of which received flattering reports from committees that included Laplace: "Sur les inégalités des moyens mouvements des planètes" (20 June 1808), "Sur le mouvement de rotation de la terre" (20 March 1809), and "Sur la variation des constantes arbitraires dans les questions de mécanique" (15 October 1809). Poisson's career was thus off to a most promising start, and his election to the Academy came just at the moment when Biot was scheduled to report on his fourth major memoir, "Sur la distribution de l'électricité à la surface des corps conducteurs" (9 March 1812). This report was never delivered, since Poisson himself had become one of the judges. During this period he composed two other works, a new edition of Clairaut's *Théorie de la figure de la terre* (1808) and the two-volume *Traité de mécanique* (1811), a textbook. Yet these, taken together with the four memoirs, do not seem to constitute a body of work of sufficient significance to justify such a rapid rise.

Nevertheless, the memoirs are not without a certain importance. In the first, Poisson simply pursued problems raised and mathematically formulated by Laplace and Lagrange regarding the perturbations of planetary motions with respect to Kepler's solution of the problem of motion for two bodies. Even here, however, he improved the demonstration of the stability of the major axes of the orbits and of the mean motions. In finding approximate solutions by means of various series expansions, he also showed that determination of the possibility of secular inequalities required the inclusion of higher-order terms in the calculation. Finally, he simplified the mathematical treatment of these difficult equations by perceptive suggestions regarding the notation and disposition of the terms representing the perturbing function.

Poisson's remarks so impressed Lagrange that he was led to reconsider the bases of his earlier work on the subject. Specifically, he improved the analytic method of integrating the differential equations of motion subject to perturbing forces which appeared in the supplement to Laplace's *Mécanique céleste*, Book VIII (1808), where it is known as the variation of arbitrary constants. Lagrange presented his results to the Institute, and they gave rise in turn to Poisson's memoir of October 1809. In order to grasp fully what was involved in this affair, a certain amount of technical detail is necessary. The terminology and notation in the following account have been somewhat modernized for ease of comprehension.

Consider a material system described by k coordinates q_i satisfying k second-order differential equations (1) of the Lagrange type. From these equations, obtain a second set (2) by adding to the second members of (1) the partial derivatives $\delta\Omega/\delta q_i$ of a function that yields the perturbing force. It is known that every integral of the first set of equations (1), whether or not it can be completely expressed in an analytic form, depends on $2k$ arbitrary constants a_r. The method called variation of constants consists in asking which functions of time can be substituted for a_r in order that the integrals of (1), corresponding to a_r, can satisfy (2).

Lagrange's contribution was to develop fully the implications of Laplace's observation that, since the number of a_r is twice the number of the equations (1) or (2), these constants can be submitted to k well-chosen conditions. Lagrange's choice results in showing that the derivatives of the sought-for functions a_r with respect to time are the solutions of a linear system in which the coefficients of the unknowns are independent of time.

This result, simple in the formulation just cited, is what seemed to Poisson to call for a more direct derivation, which he arrived at thanks to his ingenious idea of modifying the very nature of the general problem. He introduced, besides the parameters q_i, new variables $u_i = \dfrac{\delta T}{\delta q_i'}$, with T being half the live force, a homogeneous quadratic form with respect to the time derivatives q_i. The systems of equations (1) and (2) then take "the simplest form that can be given to them," namely $\dfrac{du_i}{dt} = \dfrac{\delta R}{\delta q_i}$, which form subsists on introduction of the perturbation function Ω. One obtains a system of $2k$ first-order differential equations with respect to the $2k$ unknowns q_i, u_i as a function of time. Let (1') be those that correspond to (1). The a_r previously considered can be identified with the first integrals of (1'): $a_r = f(t; q_i, u_i)$, and Poisson directly expressed the values of da_r/dt needed to satisfy (2'). These values are obviously nothing other than the result of the linear system proposed by Lagrange, the only difference lying in the form of the calculations and of the result.

Accordingly, there is nothing surprising about Lagrange's reaction, as expressed in the second edition of his *Mécanique analytique* (1811; Part Two, Section 8). Poisson, he writes, "has produced a fine memoir," but "perhaps he never would have thought of writing it . . . had he not been assured in advance" of the nature of the results. Lagrange adds, moreover, that the advantage of the new calculations is only apparent. For he contends that the form of the constant coefficients that he himself had given, $[a_r, a_s] = \dfrac{\delta q_i}{\delta a_r} \cdot \dfrac{\delta u_i}{\delta a_s} = \dfrac{\delta q_i}{\delta a_s} \cdot \dfrac{\delta u_i}{\delta a_r}$, is more practical, since first priority should be given to all the problems in which the integration of (1') yields expressions of q_i and u_i as a function of a_r and of time.

This was perhaps the first occasion on which Lagrange expressed dissatisfaction with Poisson's work, but his criticism was not totally justified. The property that he called singular, namely the constancy of the coefficients $[a_r, a_s]$ is undoubtedly the same in the case of Poisson's coefficients: $(a_r, a_s) = \dfrac{\delta a_r}{\delta q_i} \cdot \dfrac{\delta a_s}{\delta u_i} = \dfrac{\delta a_r}{\delta u_i} \cdot \dfrac{\delta a_s}{\delta q_i}$; although one should not be too hasty in minimizing the importance of the changes in form.

Considering a_r, as first integrals, rather than thus designating the constants of integration, opened a new perspective on the problem. For if it is assumed that there are two first integrals α, β of the system (1'), that is to say, that two functions of the q_i, u_i, and t that remain constant because of (1') can be determined, then the algorithm of Poisson's parenthesis (α, β) also yields a function that remains constant. It may be asked if (α, β) is not a third first integral. As Joseph Bertrand perceptively observed in 1853, (α, β) must not, in being constant, reduce to an identity because of the nature of the functions α, β. This condition limits the scope of "Poisson's theorem"; but to limit is not to destroy, and the theorem retains some interest.

At the end of his memoir Poisson noted that his method of computation immediately clarifies the identity of the mathematical problem involved when passing from the perturbations of the rotation of solids to those of a material point attracted to a center. Lacroix, who was assigned to report on the memoir to the Academy, was much impressed by this fact, but apparently few other members shared his enthusiasm. Hamilton, and then Jacobi, later derived inspiration from Poisson's calculations in creating the mathematical techniques that underlay the great developments in theoretical physics up to the start of the twentieth century. With a bit of patriotic exaggeration Bertrand stated that Jacobi, upon discovering Poisson's "parenthesis" around 1841, found it "prodigious." The truth is more modest. In *Vorlesungen über Dynamik* (1842) Jacobi proclaimed that "Poisson made the most important advance in the transformation of equations of motion since the first version of *Mécanique analytique*." This is a fair judgment. It must simply be added that, in the works preceding his election to the Academy, Poisson displayed something more than skilled calculation. His sense of formalization led him to discover analogies, to unify problems and topics previously considered distinct, and to extend definitively "the domain of the calculus" (*l'emprise du calcul*).

This expression was not peculiar to Poisson, although he used it often. In his efforts to extend the use of mathematics in the treatment of physical problems, he studied many subjects. In some cases he limited himself to brief outlines, one of which, that concerning the potential in the interior of attracting masses (1813), later gave rise to important results in electrostatistics. He was more ambitious in the memoirs on electricity and magnetism and on the theory of elastic surfaces. The second of these, read to the Academy on 1 August 1814, represented his attempt to block the progress of Sophie Germain, who he knew was competing—under the guidance of Legendre—for the prize in physics.

Political events once again interrupted French scientific life, and several years elapsed before the delays in publication of specialized journals were reduced to the point where they no longer hindered the exchange of ideas. The period 1814–1827, from the fall of the Empire to the death of Laplace, constitutes the third period of Poisson's career. He worked closely with Laplace, under whose influence he investigated a number of topics. One of these was the speed of sound in gases; here Laplace in 1816 had simply stated, without demonstration, a correction to Newton's formula. In other studies Poisson considered the propagation of heat, elastic vibration theory, and what was later called potential. He took up ideas that Laplace had proposed and at the same time conducted a vast amount of his own research. It is somewhat difficult to gain a clear view of all this varied activity, but the many debates in which Poisson participated offer considerable insight into his thinking and reveal the beginnings of an ambitious plan.

Poisson's relations with Fourier began to deteriorate in 1815 with Poisson's publication in the *Bulletin de la Société philomathique de Paris* and *Journal de physique* of sketches concerning the theory of heat. Fourier wrote on this occasion: "Poisson has too much talent to apply it to the work of others. To use it to discover what is already known would be to waste it. . . . He adds, it is true, that his method differs from mine and that it is the only valid one. But I do not agree with these two propositions. With regard to the second claim, which is unheard of in mathematics, if Poisson wants others to accept it, he must eliminate from his memoir the part [that I indicated] and take care never to eliminate from below the exponential or trigonometric signs the quantities of which the absolute value is not infinitely small" (manuscript notes written for Laplace, Bibliothèque Nationale, MS Fr. 22525, fol. 91). Fourier's slashing criticism was justified, and Poisson accepted it in three memoirs (1820–1821), which he published in the eighteenth (1820) and nineteenth (1823) *cahiers* of the *Journal de l'École polytechnique* (1820–1821). In a note to one of these papers, moreover, he admitted that he had been to the office of the secretary of the Academy to consult Fourier's prize manuscript of 1812. Nevertheless, in preceding Fourier in publication, he involved himself in an unfortunate enterprise. In dealing with "the manner of expressing functions by series of periodic quantities and the use of this transformation," he proved to be less adroit than in the formalization of mechanics. He scarcely improved either the manner or the use, and his contribution amounted to no more than an emphasis on the necessity of deepening the notion of convergence for the series under consideration.

Furthermore, it was not only with respect to integrals of the differential equations of the propagation of heat that Poisson felt uncomfortable at the kinds of calculation he was encountering. He recurred to a remark that Laplace had made in 1809 to the effect that Fourier's method involved the serious mistake of equating two infinitesimals of different orders. Poisson expended much effort in modifying the infinitesimal derivation of the fundamental equation of the motion of heat, claiming that what he cared about was rigor.

In fact, however, Poisson had misunderstood Fourier's point of view. Where Fourier was considering the flow of heat across a surface, he was thinking—like Laplace before him—of bodies being heated by intercorpuscular action. He held the caloric model of heat to be indispensable to theory. Particles of caloric combine with particles of ponderable matter engendering repulsive forces between the latter at distances too small to be detected. Inasmuch as he substituted this mechanistic model for Fourier's analysis in order to derive the same type of equations as his rival, his reasoning is artificial—not to say byzantine—in its complexity. No more than Fourier did he, at least at this juncture, reckon with the difficulties arising from the nature and physical dimensions of the constants introduced in the course of calculation. Later on, to be sure, he made some headway on that score. We shall come back to that problem.

The physics of heat, which was attracting a growing number of researchers during this period, consists of phenomena other than those that, like radiation, suggest the adoption of a hypothesis concerning events occurring on an infinitesimal, molecular scale. Poisson made worthwhile contributions to the understanding of these other areas, largely through his insistent amassing of theoretical and experimental data.

In "Sur la chaleur des gaz et des vapeurs," published in August 1823 in *Annales de chimie et de physique*, Poisson developed ideas published four months before by Laplace in Book XII of *Mécanique céleste*. Poisson introduced all the precautions needed to render the confused notion of quantity of heat susceptible to mathematical analysis. He called quantity of heat the magnitude that characterizes the transition of a given mass of gas from an arbitrary initial state of temperature and pressure to another state. This definition makes more abstract the quantitative aspect that naturally follows from the concept of heat as a caloric fluid. Poisson could thus deal comfortably with this magnitude, since for him it is simply a function q of p, ρ, and θ (pressure, density, and temperature). The equation of state $p = a\rho(1 + \alpha\theta)$ was already classic, and the growing acceptance of the notions of specific heats, at constant pressure and constant volume, allowed him to write the simple partial differential equation of which q should be the integral. He also showed that independently of any additional hypothesis, and whatever the arbitrary function used in the integration, the adiabatic transformations (the term did not yet exist) correspond to the formulas $p \cdot \rho^\gamma =$ constant and $(\theta + 266.67) \cdot \rho^{1-\gamma} =$ constant, γ being the ratio of the specific heats, assumed constant.

Sadi Carnot, who read this article, unfortunately took no interest in these formulas. He devoted his attention solely to the calculations in which Poisson's choice of the arbitrary function of integration was based on a hypothesis taken from Laplace. These calculations led Poisson to propose formulas for the saturated steam pressure H at temperature θ and for the quantity of heat of a given mass of steam. Although Carnot did not pick out from this memoir the results that could have been of greatest help to him, he did discover an interesting numerical fact in another article by Poisson published in the same volume of *Annales de chimie et de physique*.

In this brief note on the relative velocity of sound, Poisson discussed the formula that Laplace had proposed to correct Newton's treatment. The new formulation took account of variations in temperature produced by vibrations of the air. He reported that a comparison of this formula with observations led him to conclude that atmospheric air subjected to a sudden compression of 1/116 is heated 1°C. This "indirect" manner of investigating the physics of gases agrees "very closely" with the interpretation of the experiments of Clément and Desormes. Carnot was their disciple, and mention of them in the article was probably what attracted his interest to it. Considering the place of this numerical value in *Réflexions sur la puissance motrice du feu* (1824), it is important to explain both the origin and the nature of Carnot's concern with this aspect of the subject—especially as the explanation challenges simplistic notions of scientific progress. We must, however, resist the temptation to study all such examples offered by Poisson's activity. These may clearly be seen in the records of his debates with Fresnel on light and with Sophie Germain and Navier on the vibration of elastic surfaces. Poisson continued to depend on the notion of the corpuscle and the forces to which it is subject as his fundamental conceptual tool in studying all areas of physics. Accordingly, it is not surprising that while he became increasingly interested in vibratory models, he never took the final step of admitting transverse vibrations—or, indeed, any oscillation occurring in a direction different from that of the pressures constituting the corpuscular equilibrium. For this reason he was incapable of providing creative solutions to problems arising in this domain.

Poisson was justly accused by his opponents of having failed to cite contemporary scientists in his writings. But this oversight—which, in any case, was never complete—can readily be repaired by internal criticism. For example, Poisson's work reflects Sophie Germain's critical remarks, which were as cutting as Fourier's, concerning his method for mathematizing the treatment of elasticity. Specifically, he added to his molecular hypotheses a coefficient for determining the macroscopic relationship between lengthening or extension of elastic materials and variation in thickness. Similarly, his dispute with Navier over the general laws of elasticity led Poisson to demonstrate the importance of the notion of the normal state. On the same occasion, he showed that in calculating the deformed state it is illusory to conserve coefficients expressed by definite integrals that have a value of zero in the normal state and that remain approximately zero. In sum, it cannot be denied that Poisson showed real tact in "subjecting" physical phenomena to mathematical calculation.

It is in this context that Poisson's contribution to the mathematical treatment of attractive force must be mentioned. His interest in this subject dates from his analysis in 1812–1813 of James Ivory's work; and here again Laplace was the source for his examination of the integral V of the inverse of the distance function, which function was first called potential by George Green. Late in 1813 Poisson pointed out that in addition to the equation for the attraction exerted by a mass on an external point, namely

$$\Delta V = \frac{\partial^2 V}{\partial x^2} + \frac{\partial^2 V}{\partial y^2} + \frac{\partial^2 V}{\partial z^2} = 0,$$

the equation $\Delta V = -4\pi\rho$ must also be considered, where ρ is the density around the point x, y, z, when this point is inside the attracting mass. The demonstration provoked several objections, and Poisson attempted to prove it, notably in two memoirs of 1824 published in the *Mémoires de l'Académie des sciences* (**5** [1821–1822/1826], 247–338, 488–533). In 1826 he stated the triple equation,

$$\Delta V = 0, \quad = -2\pi\rho, \quad = -4\pi\rho,$$

depending on whether the point x, y, z is internal to, on the surface of, or external to the attracting mass.

"Mathematicians have long known of the first of these cases," he added. "An investigation several years ago led me to the third. To it I now add the second, thus completing this equation. Its importance in a great number of questions is well known ("Sur la théorie du magnétisme en mouvement," *ibid.*, **6** [1823/1827], 463).

Actually, it was Green who saw how to exploit Poisson's formulation. Green seized on the importance of the above memoirs in his *Essay on the Application of Mathematical Analysis to the Theories of Electricity and Magnetism* (1828), although he showed little interest in resolving the analytical difficulties still inherent in them. In 1839 Gauss emphasized the need for an improved demonstration of the intermediate equation $\Delta V = -2\pi\rho$, which was not given until 1876 (Riemann). Poisson apparently never knew that he had inspired Green's work. Indeed, up until 1828 the discussions that we have summarized above were continued mainly in relation to an ambitious project for promulgating a charter for applied mathematics.

In the preface to the long "Mémoire sur l'équilibre et le mouvement des corps élastiques" (14 April 1828), the hints yield to explicit declaration. In applying mathematics to physics, Poisson stated, it was necessary at first to employ abstraction and "in this regard, Lagrange has gone as far as possible in replacing physical ties by equations between coordinates." Now, however, "along with this admirable conception," it is necessary to "construct physical mechanics, the principle of which is to reduce everything to molecular actions." In other words, the death of Laplace the previous year enabled Poisson to move boldly ahead with his longrange plans and to present himself as Laplace's successor.

The last period of Poisson's life was dominated by his feeling of being the chosen leader of French science—at a time when he already felt called upon to guide the future of the French university system. Since it was during this last period that he decided to publish books, this sense of a twofold mission determined the form that they took; and these works are therefore treatises, concerned primarily with pedagogical matters. Although ably written and including clear historical accounts of the topics treated, they did little to advance contemporary research. Poisson was always reticent about the contributions of his contemporaries. He even omitted Poinsot's name at the very place in the second edition of *Traité de mécanique* (1833) where he was expounding the new mechanics of solids. Nevertheless, Poisson did have a genuine talent for summarizing the state of knowledge and the theoretical situation in areas of active research. This skill is evident in the report that he presented to the Academy on Jacobi's *Fundamenta nova theoriae functionum ellipticarum*, which was published in 1831.

It would, however, be unfair to reduce Poisson's work during the last period merely to an intelligent reformulation of data commingling his own results with those from other sources. In *Théorie mathématique de la chaleur* (1835), reprinted in 1837 with an important supplement, he offered evidence of his own originality in his treatment of the integration of the auxiliary differential equation

$$\frac{d^2P}{dx^2} - \frac{m}{x^2}P + \alpha^2 P = 0,$$

which is encountered in the problem of heat distribution inside bodies. He showed that the same integral series that is derived from Bessel's work has the sum

$$P = A\, x^{i+1} \int_0^\pi \cos(\alpha x \cos \omega)\, \sin^{2i+1} \omega\, d\omega,$$

i being such that $m = i(i + 1)$.

Although he was concerned only with those cases in which this equation leads to simple results in finite form, the expression for the Bessel function that it gives rise to is often—and justly—called Poisson's integral.

Similarly, as Gaston Bachelard observed, Poisson scored a point in this work by demonstrating how the conductibility of heat in the interior of bodies, far from being contained in the notion of flux as Fourier had held, must be derived from an absorption coefficient that restores a neglected functional dimension. It was in this area that the contribution mentioned in connection with Poisson's mechanical model for conduction of heat was the most fruitful. That conception enabled Poisson to understand on the molecular scale that the complete and correct equation for radiation of heat is

$$C\frac{\partial u}{\partial t} = K\left(\frac{\partial^2 u}{\partial x^2} + \frac{\partial^2 u}{\partial y^2} + \frac{\partial^2 u}{\partial z^2}\right)$$
$$+ \left(\frac{dK}{du}\right)\left[\left(\frac{\partial u}{\partial x}\right)^2 + \left(\frac{\partial u}{\partial y}\right)^2 + \left(\frac{\partial u}{\partial z}\right)^2\right],$$

where *u* is the temperature at the point *x, y, z*, as a function of time *t*; *C* is the specific heat; and *K* is the coefficient of conductibility. Fourier's method, on the other hand, led to the omission of the factor *dK/du*.

Whatever the value of Poisson's argument in this regard, the admirable program of physical mechanics, as he conceived it, did not provide a model of natural phenomena that could successfully withstand the passage of time.

Poisson believed that he had corrected an error in Laplace's treatment of capillarity by introducing a variation of the liquid density to characterize the action of the container walls, but he was as mistaken in this area as he was in his handling of the radiant heat of the earth and of the atmosphere. Were it not for the titles of these treatises, one would not guess that they were intended as the first draft of a course on mathematical physics.

Toward the end of his life, Poisson turned his attention to other subjects, producing two works of considerable repute. The first, *Recherches sur la probabilité des jugements en matière criminelle et en matière civile* (1837), is significant for the author's participation in an important contemporary debate. The legitimacy of the application of the calculus to areas relating to the moral order, that is to say within the broad area of what is now called the humanistic sciences, was bitterly disputed beginning in 1820 in politically conservative circles as well as by Saint-Simonians and by such philosophers as Auguste Comte. Poisson was bold enough to take pen in hand to defend the universality of the probabilistic thesis and to demonstrate the conformability to the order of nature of the regularities that the calculus of probability, without recourse to hidden causes, reveals when things are subjected to a great number of observations. It is to Poisson that we owe the term "law of large numbers." He improved Laplace's work by relating it explicitly to Jacob Bernoulli's fundamental theorem and by showing that the invariance in the prior probabilities of mutually exclusive events is not a necessary condition for calculating the approximate probabilities. It is also from Poisson that we derive the study of a problem that Laplace had passed over, the case of great asymmetry between opposite events, such that the prior probability of either event is very small. The formula for evaluation that he proposed for this case, which is to be substituted for Laplace's general formula, was not recognized or used until the end of the nineteenth century. The formula states that $P = \sum_1^n \frac{\omega^n}{n!} e^{-\omega}$ expresses the probability that an event will not occur more than n times in a large number, μ, of trials, when the probability that it will occur in any one trial equals the very small fraction ω/μ. In fact, Poisson's work in this area was not accepted or applied by his contemporaries except in Russia under Chebyshev; it seemed, rather, an echo of Laplace's and was barely accorded the attention appropriate to an excellent popularization. It was many years before the importance of the Poisson distribution was recognized.

The second work in this category, *Recherches sur le mouvement des projectiles dans l'air* (1839), was far better known in its day. It is the first work to deal with the subject by taking into account the rotation of the earth and the complementary acceleration resulting from the motion of the system of reference. A decade after its publication it inspired Foucault's famous experiment demonstrating the earth's rotation. Poisson, who had supervised Coriolis' doctoral research, recognized the importance of his invention of a term to correct for the deviations from the law of motion that arise in a rotating reference system. Unfortunately, Poisson did not consider himself obliged to cite the name of the actual inventor of the term.

The very multiplicity of Poisson's undertakings might be considered a reason for his failure to enjoy the good fortune of which Cournot spoke. He constantly exploited the ideas of other scientists, often in an unscrupulous manner. Still, he was frequently the first to show their full significance, and he did much to disseminate them. In the last analysis, however, what was the scientific value of his own contribution? It is tempting to reply that he merely displayed a singular aptitude for the operations of mathematical analysis. And it is no accident that he rejected the view of Lagrange and Laplace that Fermat was the real creator of the integral and differential calculus. To be sure, he waited until he was free to voice his disagreement; for it was not until 1831, in "Mémoire sur le calcul des variations," that, ignoring French chauvinism, he dared to assert "This [integral and differential] calculus consists in a collection of rules . . . rather than in the use of infinitely small quantities . . . and in this regard its creation does not predate Leibniz, the author of the algorithm and of the notation that has generally prevailed." In discussing this question in its historical context, Poisson clearly revealed that aspect to which he was most sensitive and for which he was most gifted.

Is this all that can be said? We do not think so. Having reproached Poisson for being unable or unwilling to understand him, Galois wrote, perhaps thinking of him: "The analysts try in vain to conceal the fact that they do not deduce; they combine, they compose. . . . When they do arrive at the truth, they stumble over it after groping their way along." But—and this is precisely the point—Poisson was not one of those analysts who attempt to obscure the way in which they really work. He did combine a great deal, compose a great deal, and stumble frequently—and often guess right. He had a tremendous zeal for changing the manner of treating problems, for fashioning and refashioning formulas, and for taking from the experiments of others that material to which his mathematical techniques would be applied. This zeal occasioned criticism and ironic comments, but it was nevertheless rooted in genuine ability, one capable of motivating an experimental approach.

Poisson was certainly not a genius. Yet, just as surely, he was one of those without whom progress in French science in the early nineteenth century would not have occurred.

BIBLIOGRAPHY

I. ORIGINAL WORKS. *Catalogue des ouvrages et mémoires scientifiques*, based on Poisson's MS, groups the titles by the periodicals in which they were published and includes summaries; it was reprinted in *Oeuvres complètes de François Arago*, II (Paris, 1854), 672–689. His books include *Traité de mécanique*, 2 vols. (Paris, 1811; 2nd ed., enl., 1833); *Formules relatives aux effets du tir du canon sur les différentes parties de son affût* (Paris, 1826; 2nd ed., 1838); *Nouvelle théorie de l'action capillaire* (Paris, 1831); *Théorie mathématique de la chaleur* (Paris, 1835), 2nd ed. printed with *Mémoire et notes formant supplément . . .* (Paris, 1837); *Recherches sur la probabilité des jugements en matière criminelle et en matière civile* (Paris, 1837); and *Recherches sur le mouvement des projectiles dans l'air en ayant égard à leur figure et leur rotation, et à l'influence du mouvement diurne de la terre* (Paris, 1839).

II. SECONDARY LITERATURE. On Poisson and his work, see François Arago, *Oeuvres complètes*, II (Paris, 1854), 591–698; Gaston Bachelard, *Étude sur l'évolution d'un problème de physique; la propagation thermique dans les solides* (Paris, 1927; 2nd ed., 1973), 73–88; Joseph Bertrand, "Sur un théorème de Poisson," in J. L. Lagrange, *Mécanique analytique*, 4th ed. (Paris, 1867), 484–491; Henri Pierre Bouasse, *Dynamique générale* (Paris–Toulouse, 1923), 316–317; Antoine Augustin Cournot, *Souvenirs* (Paris, 1913), 160–167; Sophie Germain, *Recherches sur la théorie des surfaces élastiques* (Paris, 1821), preface and 1–12; "Examen des principes qui peuvent conduire à la connaissance des lois de l'équilibre et du mouvement des solides élastiques," in *Annales de chimie et de physique*, **38** (1828), 123–131; and *Oeuvres philosophiques* (Paris, 1879), 344–348, 353; C. G. J. Jacobi, *Vorlesungen über Dynamik* (Berlin, 1866), 6, 51, 67; and Guillaume Libri, "Troisième lettre à un américain sur l'état des sciences en France," in *Revue des deux mondes*, 4th ser., **23** (1 Aug. 1840), 410–437.

PIERRE COSTABEL

POLENI, GIOVANNI (*b.* Venice, Italy, 23 August 1683; *d.* Padua, Italy, 15 November 1761)

Poleni was the son of Jacopo Poleni and carried his title of marquis of the Holy Roman Empire, conferred by Emperor Leopold I and confirmed in 1686 by the Republic of Venice. In his early life he followed a variety of studies, and his intellectual endowment was soon known to be extraordinary. After completing his studies, first in philosophy and then in theology, at the school of the Padri Somaschi in Venice, he began, with his parents' encouragement, a judicial career. At the same time his father introduced him to mathematics and physics, and it became clear that the natural sciences were going to be his most prominent field of activity.

At the age of twenty-six he married Orsola Roberti of a noble family of Bassano del Grappa and accepted the chair of astronomy at the University of Padua; six years later he became professor of physics as well. The Venetian Senate invited him to investigate problems of hydraulics pertinent to the irrigation of lower Lombardy, Poleni soon acquired such proficiency in this field that he became the accepted arbiter of all disputes between states bordering on rivers. In 1719 he assumed the chair of mathematics at the University of Padua left vacant by Nikolaus I Bernoulli, upon the latter's return to Basel. His noteworthy opening lecture was published in 1720 as *De mathesis in rebus physicis utilitate*.

In 1738 Poleni established within a few months an up-to-date laboratory of experimental physics and began to lecture on that subject. He simultaneously conducted meteorological observations, corresponded with French, English, German, and Italian savants (particularly Euler, Maupertuis, the Bernoullis, and Cassini III), published memoirs on various subjects, and participated in the study of calendar reform that had been sponsored by Pope Clement XI. In 1733 Poleni received a prize from the Royal Academy of Sciences of Paris for a paper on a method of calculating—independently of astronomical observations

—the distance traveled by a ship; and in 1736 he was awarded a prize for a study of ships' anchors. In 1739 he became a foreign member of the Academy, and in 1741 he received a prize for a study of cranes and windlasses.

Poleni's scientific activities were paralleled by classical researches, which were described in treatises on the temple of Ephesus, on ancient theaters and amphitheaters, on French archaeological findings, on an Augustan obelisk, and on several architectural topics. In 1748 he was called to Rome by Pope Benedict XIV to examine the cupola of St. Peter's basilica and to propose means of preventing its further movement, but he was soon recalled to Padua to assume judicial duties. Excessive work gradually affected his health, although not his enthusiasm, until his death at the age of seventy-eight. His remains were laid in the Church of St. Giacomo in Padua, where his sons placed a monument in his honor. The citizens of Padua subsequently decreed that a statue (one of the earliest works of Antonio Canova) of Poleni be placed among those of illustrious men in the Prato della Valle. A medal in his honor was struck by the Republic of Venice.

BIBLIOGRAPHY

I. ORIGINAL WORKS. Poleni's earliest paper was *Miscellanea: de barometris et thermometris; de machina quadam arithmetica; de sectionibus conicis in horologiis solaribus describendis* (Venice, 1709). A treatise on assorted topics, it includes a dissertation on barometers, which was followed by a second dissertation on this instrument, in *Giornale letterario d'Italia* (1711), and on thermometers, in which several improvements are proposed; also included is the design of an arithmetic machine based on reports that Poleni had received of those of Pascal and of Leibniz. Poleni actually built this machine, which was reportedly very simple and easy to operate; but when he heard of another machine presented to the emperor by the Viennese mechanician Brauer, he destroyed his own and never rebuilt it. A planned 2nd ed. of *Dialogus de vorticibus coelestibus* (Padua, 1712) was unrealized. His lecture, *De physices in rebus mathematicis utilitate oratio* (Padua, 1716), was reprinted in 1720, with some observations by J. Erhard Kapp, in *Clarissimorum virorum orationes selectae* (Leipzig, 1722).

Poleni's works on hydraulics and hydrodynamics include *De motu aquae mixto libri duo* (Padua, 1717), which contains information on estuaries, ports, and rivers; and *De castellis per quae derivantur aquae fluviorum habentibus latera convergentia liber* (Padua, 1718), with reports on experiments on water flow and on the force exerted by an impacting fluid. On the same subject are his corrections on Frontinus' treatise, *L. Julii Frontini de aquaeductibus urbis Romae commentarius restitutus atque explicatus* (Padua, 1722), which were in large part incorporated in

Rondelet's trans. (1820) of Frontinus' commentary. A paper combining astronomical and anatomical subjects followed in 1723: "Ad abbatem Grandum epistolae duae de telluribus forma; observatio exlipsis lunaris Patavii anno 1723; et de causa motus musculorum." The memoir on the solar eclipse of 1724, *Ad Johan. Jacob. Marinonum epistola in quo agitur de solis defectu anno 1724 Patavii observato* (Vienna, 1725), was reprinted in *Acta eruditorum Lipsensium* (Leipzig, 1725). A collection of Poleni's letters is in *Epistolarum mathematicarum fasciculus* (Padua, 1728), to which Poleni appended a now very rare short treatise by Giovanni Buteo, *Misura delle acque*.

Some studies of the ancient world followed: a collection of ancient writings, *Utriusque thesauri antiquitatum Romanarum Graecarumque supplementa* (Venice, 1735); a study of Vitruvius' work, *Exercitationes Vitruvianae, seu commentarius criticus de Vitruvii architectura* (Venice, 1739); and an architectural criticism, *Dissertazione sopra il tempio di Diana in Efeso* (Rome, 1742). A reply to an anonymous critic of the latter work appeared in *Giornale dei Dotti* (July 1748). A description of the means employed by Poleni for the restoration of the cupola of St. Peter's Church is found in *Memorie istoriche della gran cupola del tempio Vaticano* (Padua, 1748). Other papers, too numerous to list, may be found in *Acta Lipsiensia*, in the memoirs of the Imperial Academy of Sciences at St. Petersburg, and in *Transazioni filosofiche*.

II. SECONDARY LITERATURE. Particulars about Poleni's life are in *Memorie per la vita, gli studi e i costumi del signor Giovanni Poleni* (Padua, 1762) and in his eulogy, which was inserted by Grandjean de Fouchy in the collection of Poleni's writing issued by the Academy of Sciences (1763) and by Fabroni in *Vitae Italorum*, XII, no. 2 (1763). A good biography of Poleni is in *Biografia universale antica e moderna*, XLV (1828), and in the 2nd French ed. of the same work (Paris, 1854). A more detailed account of his life appeared in E. de Tipaldo, ed., *Biografia degli Italiani illustri* (Venice, 1834).

BRUNO A. BOLEY

PONCELET, JEAN VICTOR (*b.* Metz, France, 1 July 1788; *d.* Paris, France, 22 December 1867)

Poncelet was the natural son (later legitimated) of Claude Poncelet, a rich landowner and advocate at the Parlement of Metz, and Anne-Marie Perrein. At a very early age Poncelet was entrusted to a family of the little city of Saint-Avold, and they saw to his earliest education. In 1804 he returned to Metz. After brief and highly successful studies at the city's *lycée*, he entered the École Polytechnique in October 1807, but fell behind a year on account of poor health. During his three years at the Polytechnique, his teachers included Monge, S. F. Lacroix, Ampère, Poinsot, and Hachette.

In September 1810 Poncelet was admitted to the corps of military engineers. Upon graduating from the École d'Application of Metz in February 1812, he was assigned to work on fortification on the Dutch island of Walcheren. Beginning in June 1812 he participated in the Russian campaign as a lieutenant attached to the engineering general staff. In the course of the subsequent retreat, on 18 November 1812, he was taken prisoner at the Battle of Krasnoï and brought to a camp on the Volga River at Saratov where he was held until June 1814. He profited from his enforced leisure by resuming his study of mathematics. Since he had no books at his disposal he was obliged to reconstruct the elements of pure and analytic geometry before undertaking the original research on the projective properties of conics and systems of conics that established the basis for his later important work in this domain. The notes from this period, which he later designated by the name "cahiers de Saratov," were published in 1862 in volume I of his *Applications d'analyse et de géométrie.*

Upon his return to France in September 1814, he was appointed captain in the engineering corps at Metz, where until May 1824 he worked on various projects in topography and fortification, and also on the organization of an engineering arsenal. Consequently, he was able to acquire a firm knowledge of the problems of fortification and industrial mechanics. Among the innovations to his credit is the development, in 1820, of a new model of the variable counterweight drawbridge, the description of which he published in 1822. His position as a military engineer left him sufficient time to pursue the research on projective geometry that he had commenced in Saratov.

After several preliminary works, which were not published until 1864 (in *Applications d'analyse et de géométrie* II), Poncelet published several articles in Gergonne's *Annales de mathématiques pures et appliquées* (starting in 1817). On 1 May 1820 he presented to the Académie des Sciences an important "Essai sur les propriétés projectives des sections coniques," which contained the essence of the new ideas he wished to introduce into geometry. The original version of this fundamental memoir also was not published until 1864 (in *Applications d'analyse . . . II*). Poncelet sought to show—taking the example of the conics—that the language and concepts of geometry could be generalized by the systematic employment of elements at infinity and of imaginary elements. This goal was within reach, he contended, thanks to the introduction of the concept of "ideal chord" and the use of the method of central projections and of an extension procedure called the "principle of continuity." Here Poncelet made explicit some of the ideas and methods underlying Monge's work. Thus in this remarkable paper, the fruit of investigations begun in 1813, Poncelet resolutely opened the way to the development of the subject of complex projective geometry. Cauchy, the Academy's referee, was little disposed to accept Poncelet's high estimation of the value of geometric methods. Cauchy criticized one of the paper's fundamental components, the principle of continuity, characterizing it as a "bold induction," "capable of leading to manifest errors" (report of 5 June 1820).

Poncelet was deeply affected by this serious criticism for in effect it made the principle of extension, which he considered to be an axiom, dependent on algebraic identities. Rejecting this recourse to analysis, he intransigently maintained his position against Cauchy, despite the latter's great authority. Next he reworked his 1820 "Essai" in order to make it the first section of a large *Traité des propriétés projectives des figures* (Metz–Paris, 1822). This work (discussed below) contained many extremely important innovations, ideas, methods, and original results, and it played a decisive role in the development of projective geometry in the nineteenth century.

Pursuing his geometric studies along with his professional duties, Poncelet then undertook the preparation of four important memoirs. The first two (on centers of harmonic means and on the theory of reciprocal polars) were presented to the Academy in March 1824, but the other two memoirs remained unfinished for several years following an important change in Poncelet's career.

On 1 May 1824, after long hesitation, Poncelet agreed, at the urging of Arago, to become professor of "mechanics applied to machines" at the École d'Application de l'Artillerie et du Génie at Metz. In preparing the courses he was scheduled to give starting in January 1825, Poncelet soon displayed an increasingly lively interest in the study of the new discipline he was to teach and in various aspects of applied mechanics. As a result he interrupted the elaboration of his geometric work, returning to it only occasionally to defend certain of his ideas or to complete unfinished papers.

In 1828 Poncelet published in Crelle's *Journal für die reine und angewandte Mathematik* his first memoir of 1824, on the centers of harmonic means. A second 1824 memoir, on the theory of reciprocal polars, was not published until the beginning of 1829 in Crelle's *Journal*, because Cauchy had delayed his report on it until February 1828. On account of the long delay in publication, Poncelet had the misfortune of seeing certain of his ideas and a portion of his results attributed to other authors. Thus various articles

appearing in 1826 and 1827 in Gergonne's *Annales de mathématiques* and Férussac's *Bulletin des sciences mathématiques* accorded priority to Gergonne and Plücker concerning the principle of duality and its chief applications, conceding merely vague anticipations to Poncelet. In December 1826 the latter vigorously protested to Gergonne and sent him an analysis of his memoir, which was published in March 1827 in the *Annales* accompanied by Gergonne's critical remarks. A regrettable priority dispute began; it lasted until May 1829 and opposed Poncelet first to Gergonne and then to Plücker. This distressing affair greatly upset Poncelet, who was already very hurt by Cauchy's criticisms and by the unenthusiastic welcome given his work by a group of the mathematicians at the Académie des Sciences.

Accordingly, Poncelet abandoned to his rivals the task of continuing the important work he had accomplished in projective geometry. He confined himself to completing, in the winter of 1830–1831, the two memoirs left unfinished since 1824. Even so, he published only the first memoir in the winter of 1832; in it he took up the application of the theory of transversals to curves and geometric surfaces. The second memoir he withheld until 1866, when it was included in volume II of the second edition of the *Traité des propriétés projectives des figures*.

Beginning in 1824 Poncelet had essentially shifted his attention from geometry to applied mechanics. Although he had previously studied certain machines and ways of improving them, it was during the summer of 1824 that he achieved his first important innovation: the design and realization of an undershot waterwheel with curved paddles, which possessed a much increased efficiency. The paper he wrote on this subject gained him a prize in mechanics from the Académie des Sciences in 1825. After new trials conducted on full-scale models, he presented a revised version of his study in 1827. Yet, most of his activity at this period was devoted to elaborating and continually updating the course in mechanics applied to machines that he gave from 1825 to 1834. In addition, he prepared a parallel course in industrial mechanics on a more elementary level which he gave to artisans and workers of Metz from November 1827 to March 1830.

In preparing these courses Poncelet drew on many earlier works concerning the theory of machines and the various branches of mechanics: theoretical, experimental, and applied. In addition, he kept himself informed about all the innovations in these fields. He also profited from his practical professional experience, which he rounded out during a trip taken in 1825 for the purpose of studying the machines in the principal factories of France, Belgium, and

Germany.

Poncelet's course on mechanics applied to machines was lithographed for the students at Metz. Three main versions of the work were prepared under his personal supervision: the first (partial), in 1826; the second, in 1832, with the assistance of A. T. Morin; the third (definitive), in 1836. But many other editions, both lithographed and printed, were produced without his knowledge, thus giving his work a broad distribution. The first authentic printed edition, brought out by his disciple X. Kretz, reproduced—with some notes added to bring the work up to date—the text of the lithographed version of 1836 (*Cours de mécanique appliquée aux machines* [Paris, 1874–1876]).

As for the course on industrial mechanics, a first draft, written up by F. T. Gosselin, was lithographed in three parts between 1828 and 1830. Poncelet himself wrote up a more complete version of the first part, dealing with fundamental principles and applications; it was printed in 1829 and rapidly sold out. The following year the work was reprinted as the opening section of a general treatise. The printing of the latter, interrupted on four occasions, dragged on until 1841, when it finally appeared as *Introduction à la mécanique industrielle, physique ou expérimentale*, with the peculiar feature of containing successive passages printed at different dates. In addition to numerous pirated editions, this work was brought out in a third edition by Kretz in 1870.

All this writing and correcting obliged Poncelet to rethink the presentation of the principles of mechanics with a view to applying the theoretical results to the various machines employed in industry. His chief goal was to understand and to explain the functioning of real machines in order to attempt to improve them and to increase their efficiency. For him theory was only a tool in the service of practice. Along with this sort of work, Poncelet carried out several series of experiments on the laws of the discharge of water from large orifices (in 1827 and 1828, with J.-A. Lesbros) and on the formation of ripples on the surface of water (1829); the results were published a short time later.

In 1830 Poncelet became a member of the municipal council of Metz and secretary of the Conseil Général of the Moselle. Hence, it appears that he wished to remain permanently in his native city. In 1834 his nomination as scientific *rapporteur* for the Committee of Fortifications and as editor of the *Mémorial de l'officier du génie*, together with his election to the mechanics section of the Académie des Sciences, led him to move to Paris. He seems then to have forgotten his initial vocation for geometry, to which he made no more than brief references, in 1843 and in 1857.

Contrariwise, he drew extensively on his technical knowledge in the memoirs he wrote for the *Mémorial* and in the reports he prepared at the request of the Académie des Sciences and of various official commissions.

Meanwhile he appears to have wanted to do more teaching, and at the end of 1837 he happily agreed to create a course on physical and experimental mechanics at the Faculty of Sciences of Paris. His assignment was of a different kind from what he had at Metz, and he sought to develop for his students a concrete conception of mechanics, midway between abstract theory and industrial application. Although his courses, which he gave until April 1848, were not published, they provided the inspiration, in part, for several books, including the last part of his *Introduction à la mécanique industrielle, physique ou expérimentale* (Metz–Paris, 1841) and H. Résal's *Éléments de mécanique* (Paris, 1851). In this manner a new current was introduced into the teaching of mechanics in France, which until then had an exclusively theoretical orientation.

In 1842 Poncelet married Louise Palmyre Gaudin. By this date he was no longer conducting truly original research. Dividing his time between teaching at the Sorbonne, his duties as an academician and military officer, and technical investigations for *Mémorial de l'officier du génie*, he waited for 1848, when he could retire as a colonel in the engineering corps.

But the Revolution of February 1848 abruptly changed this rather calm existence. Following his successive nominations as member of a commission for curriculum reform and then as professor of mechanics at an ephemeral school of administration created under the control of the Collège de France, he gave up his chair of physical and experimental mechanics at the Faculty of Sciences (16 April). A few days later he was entrusted with new responsibilities that soon monopolized his time. Having been elected to the Constituent Assembly at the end of April as deputy of the Moselle, he regularly participated as a moderate republican in the work of that body during its brief existence. At the same time, Arago, the new minister of war, appointed him brigadier general and then designated him for the post of commandant of the École Polytechnique, which he filled until October 1850. Entrusting the responsibility for current administration to his assistant, Poncelet devoted himself mainly to projects for reforming the school's curriculum. He also had to intervene directly to contain and to direct the activity of the school's students during the riots of May and June 1848.

Having retired at the end of October 1850, Poncelet

gladly accepted the chairmanship of the division of industrial machines and tools at the Universal Expositions of London (1851) and Paris (1855). Profoundly interested in the rapid progress of mechanization, he transformed the simple report he was supposed to make on the London Exposition into a vast inquiry into the advances made since the beginning of the century in the conception and use of the different types of machines and tools employed in industry (textile and others). This work, to which he devoted nearly seven years, was published in 1857 in two large volumes that constitute a precious documentary source.

Several years later Poncelet undertook to regroup and edit the whole of his published and unpublished work. Of this ambitious project he was able to bring out only the four volumes of his writings on geometry, the two volumes of the *Applications d'analyse et de géométrie* (1862–1864), and the two volumes of the second edition of the *Traité des propriétés projectives des figures* (1865–1866). Certainly this was not a disinterested enterprise; the polemical character of the commentaries and introductions is obvious. Nevertheless, the compilation of these texts—to which were added a number of commentaries and notes intended to bring them up to date—does allow us to follow closely the evolution of Poncelet's thought, especially since the presentation is chronological: the unpublished notebooks from Saratov (1813–1814) in volume I of the *Applications;* published and unpublished geometric works of the period from 1815 to 1821 in volume II; republication of the original version of the *Traité des propriétés projectives des figures* (1822) in volume I of the *Traité;* and geometric works of the period 1823 to 1831 (including the writings from the polemic with Gergonne and Plücker) in volume II of the *Traité.*

Poncelet began similar work on his writings on the theory of machines and on industrial, physical, and experimental mechanics; but his death in 1867 interrupted this project. At the request of Mme Poncelet the project was resumed by Kretz, who republished the courses on industrial mechanics and on mechanics applied to machines that Poncelet had given at Metz. Kretz did not publish his course on physical and experimental mechanics given at the Faculty of Sciences, despite the many documents at his disposition. Unfortunately these documents disappeared along with the bulk of Poncelet's manuscripts during World War I.

Poncelet's scientific and technical work was concentrated in two very different areas, corresponding to two successive stages in his career: projective geometry and applied mechanics. In geometry, his work, conceived for the most part between 1813 and 1824, was published between 1817 and 1832, except for some writings that appeared too late to influence the development of this field. The most significant portion of this work is the *Traité des propriétés projectives des figures*, which was the first book wholly devoted to projective geometry, a new discipline that was to experience wide success during the nineteenth century. In this domain Poncelet considered himself the successor to Desargues, Blaise Pascal, and Maclaurin and the continuator of the work of Monge and his disciples. Concerned to endow pure geometry with the generality it lacked and to assure its independence *vis-à-vis* algebraic analysis, Poncelet systematically introduced elements at infinity and imaginary elements, thus constructing the space employed in complex projective geometry. Basing his efforts on the principle of continuity and the notion of ideal chords, he also made extensive use of central projections and profitably utilized other types of transformations (homology and transformation by reciprocal polars in two or three dimensions, birational transformation, and so forth).

The distinction Poncelet made between projective and metric properties prefigured the appearance of the modern concept of structure. Among the many original results presented in the *Traité* are those stating that in complex projective space two nondegenerate conics are of the same nature and have four common points (a finding that led to the discovery of cyclic points, imaginary points at infinity common to all the circles of a plane), and that all quadrics possess (real or imaginary) systems of generatrices. The decisive influence that *Traité des propriétés projectives des figures* exercised on the development of projective geometry—an influence underestimated by Chasles, Poncelet's direct rival—is brought to light by most commentators, particularly by E. Kötter, who made the most complete analysis of it, but also by A. Schoenflies and A. Tresse, J. L. Coolidge, C. B. Boyer, N. Bourbaki, and others (see Bibliography). Of the later memoirs, the most striking is devoted to the theory of reciprocal polars, which in Poncelet's hands became an extremely fruitful instrument of discovery, although he did not perceive the more general character of the principle of duality, which was pointed out shortly afterward by Gergonne, Plücker, Möbius, and Chasles. Although it was prematurely interrupted, Poncelet's geometric work marks the first major step toward the elaboration of the fundamental theories of modern geometry.

The bulk of Poncelet's work in applied mechanics and technology was conceived between 1825 and 1840. With regard to technological innovation, his principal contributions concern hydraulic engines (such as Poncelet's waterwheel), regulators and dynamometers, and various improvements in the techniques of fortification (a new type of drawbridge, resistance of vaults, stability of revetments). In applied mechanics Poncelet made important contributions to three broad, interrelated fields: experimental mechanics, the theory of machines, and industrial mechanics. He achieved remarkable successes by virtue of his training at the École Polytechnique, his experience as a military engineer, and his vast knowledge—all of which allowed him to utilize and combine the resources of mathematics and theoretical science, the results of systematic experiments, and the teaching of industrial and craft practice.

Poncelet, whose goal was always real applications, placed experimental and practical findings above theories and hypotheses. In the theory of machines, for example, he refused to make any theoretical classification such as Monge had, relying instead on the more concrete principles set forth by G. A. Borgnis in 1819. Instead of vast syntheses he preferred precise and limited studies, informed by a profound knowledge of the technical imperatives involved. Consequently his original work is to be found to a much greater degree in the realms of organization and improvements than in that of brilliant innovations. The influence of his thinking—a mixture of the theoretical and the concrete—on the creation of the field of applied mechanics is indicated by the success of his two lecture courses. From the two chief aspects of his work, the mathematical and the technological, it appears that Poncelet wished to contribute to the concurrent development of both pure science and its applications.

BIBLIOGRAPHY

I. ORIGINAL WORKS. Nearly complete—although occasionally imprecise—lists of Poncelet's various publications are in I. Didion, *Mémoires de l'Académie de Metz*, **50** (1870), 149–159; and in H. Tribout, *Un grand savant: Le général Jean-Victor Poncelet* (Paris, 1936), esp. 204–220. Accessible, but much less complete, are the bibliographies in Poggendorff, **2** (1863), cols. 496–497; **3** (1898), 1057–1058; and in Royal Society *Catalogue of Scientific Papers*, IV (London, 1870), 479–481, which cites 41 articles. A partial supp. is in *Catalogue général des livres imprimés de la Bibliothèque nationale*, CXL (Paris, 1936), cols. 490–495.

As none of these bibliographies is fully satisfactory, we shall present here a selective bibliography based on the list of articles in Royal Society *Catalogue of Scientific Papers* and divided into 3 sections: geometry, other mathematical works, and applied mechanics (industrial and experimental).

Geometry. The list of the Royal Society *Catalogue of Scientific Papers*—from which the first entry, by an homonymous author, must be eliminated—contains 16 memoirs on geometry: nos. 2–9, 40 (published between 1817 and 1825), nos. 13–15 (1827–1829), nos. 18–20 (1832), and no. 31 (1843). Several works should be added to this list: "Problèmes de géométrie," in *Correspondance sur l'École polytechnique*, **2**, sec. 3 (1811), 271–274; various nn. on the projective properties of figures, on the principle of continuity, and on an instrument for tracing conics, are in *Mémoires de l'Académie de Metz*, **1–4** (Metz, 1820–1823), details of which can be found in the bibliographies of Didion and Tribout cited above; and certain items stemming from the polemic Poncelet commenced against Gergonne and Plücker: "Analyse d'un mémoire présenté à l'Académie royale des sciences," in *Annales de mathématiques pures et appliquées*, **17**, no. 9 (1827), 265–272, which is a partial text of a letter by Poncelet dated 10 December 1826; it is followed by Gergonne's "Réflexions," *ibid.*, 272–276; "Note sur divers articles . . .," in Férussac, ed., *Bulletin des sciences mathématiques*, **8** (1827), 109–117 (this note is cited as no. 13 in the list of Royal Society *Catalogue of Scientific Papers* in accord with its republication in the *Annales de mathématiques pures et appliquées*, **18**, no. 5 [1827], 125–149, with Gergonne's critical remarks and the corresponding passages from Poncelet's letter of 10 December 1826).

See also "Sur la dualité de situation et sur la théorie des polaires réciproques," *ibid.*, **9** (May 1828), 292–302; "Réponse de M. Poncelet aux réclamations de M. Plücker," *ibid.*, **10** (May 1829), 330–333; and "Sur la transformation des propriétés métriques des figures au moyen de la théorie des polaires réciproques," in *Comptes rendus hebdomadaires des séances de l'Académie des sciences*, **45** (1857), 553–554.

Three of Poncelet's important memoirs on geometry first became known through the critical reports on them that Cauchy presented to the Académie des Sciences. See Cauchy's reports on "Mémoire relatif aux propriétés projectives des coniques," in *Annales de mathématiques pures et appliquées*, **11**, no. 3 (1820), 69–83; on "Mémoire relatif aux propriétés des centres de moyennes harmoniques," *ibid.*, **16**, no. 11 (1826), 349–360; and on "Mémoire relatif à la théorie des polaires réciproques," in *Bulletin des sciences mathématiques*, **9** (1828), 225–229.

Poncelet's geometric *oeuvre* also includes two important books. The famous *Traité des propriétés projectives des figures* (Metz-Paris, 1822), the 2nd ed. of which (2 vols., Paris, 1865–1866) reproduces the text of the 1st ed., with annotations (in vol. I) and Poncelet's geometric articles posterior to 1822 and also the principal items from his polemic with Gergonne and Plücker (1825–1829) (in vol. II).

The 2nd book is *Applications d'analyse et de géométrie . . .*, 2 vols. (Paris, 1862–1864). Its first vol. contains, with some nn. and additions, the text of the 7 notebooks in analytic and pure geometry dating from his imprisonment at Saratov (1813–June 1814); the last notebook is the first, incomplete sketch of his future treatise on projective properties. The 2nd vol. contains the text of various geometric works dating from the period 1815–1817 (notebooks 1 to 3), an unpublished memoir from 1818–1819 on the principle of continuity (no. 4), the "Essai sur les propriétés projectives des figures," presented to the Académie des Sciences on 1 May 1820 (no. 5), the text of the articles published in *Annales* between 1817 and 1822 (no. 6), and a few letters and polemical writings (no. 7).

Other Mathematical Works. This relatively secondary portion of Poncelet's *oeuvre* is virtually limited to the 4 articles and memoirs cited as nos. 21–23 (1835) and no. 37 (1848) in Royal Society *Catalogue of Scientific Papers.*

Applied Mechanics (Industrial and Experimental). The Royal Society *Catalogue of Scientific Papers* mentions 20 articles from 1825 to 1852, dealing with this fundamental aspect of Poncelet's *oeuvre*: nos. 10–12, 16, 17, 24–30, 32–36, 38, 39, and 41.

To this very incomplete list should be added the reports and communications presented to the Académie de Metz between 1820 and 1834 and a portion of the reports presented to the Académie des Sciences between 1834 and 1857 (the bibliographies of Didion and Tribout cited above give references to the corresponding publications).

Eight important technical memoirs published between 1822 and 1844 are in different fascs. of the *Mémorial de l'officier du génie*: "Mémoire sur un nouveau pont-levis à contrepoids variable," no. 5 (1822); "Notice sur un pont-levis à bascule mouvante," no. 10 (1829); "Solution graphique des principales questions sur la stabilité des voûtes," no. 12 (1835); "Mémoire sur la stabilité des revêtements et de leurs fondations," no. 13 (1840); "Note additionnelle sur les relations analytiques qui tiennent entre elles la poussée et la butée des terres," *ibid.*; "Rapport et mémoire sur la construction et le prix des couvertures en zinc," *ibid.*; "Observation sur le mode d'exécution et de restauration du pont-levis à contrepoids variable," *ibid.*; and "Résumé historique de la question du défilement des tranchées," no. 14 (1844). See, in addition, the two short notes, "Extrait d'un mémoire sur les projets d'usines et de machines pour l'Arsenal du génie de Metz," in *Bulletin de la Société d'encouragement pour l'industrie nationale*, **23** (1824), 66–68; and "Réclamation de M. Poncelet," in *Bulletin de Férussac*, **13** (1830), 7–9.

Poncelet was also the author of two lecture courses, one on "mechanics applied to machines" and another on industrial mechanics. In addition, he wrote an important two-volume study on the different types of industrial machines and tools.

The course, *Cours de mécanique appliquée aux machines*, which grew out of lectures Poncelet had given from 1825 to 1834 to students at the École d'Application de l'Artillerie et du Génie de Metz, went through a large number of editions. The only ones among these that Poncelet himself supervised are a lithographed ed. of 1826, "Première partie du cours de mécanique appliquée aux machines . . ."; a lithographed reedition, in 1832, of secs. 1 and 3 and an ed. in the same year, with the assistance of A. T. Morin, of two supplementary sets of notes: "Leçons préparatoires

au lever d'usines," which became secs. 6 and 7 of the course, and "Leçons sur les ponts-levis" (sec. 8); and a lithographed reedition, in 1836, of the whole of the course (the 4th sec. now including the 5th).

These eds.—each containing original or additional material—of the course went through many other printings, certain of which were done for the use of the students at the École de Metz; other printings were done without Poncelet's knowledge. Printed eds. were also brought out without the author's authorization (e.g., *Traité de mécanique appliquée aux machines*, 2 vols. [Liège, 1845]); these contained, in addition to the 6 secs. of the lithographed edition of 1836, a brief 4th sec. on friction in gears. See also definitive posthumous ed., *Cours de mécanique appliquée aux machines*, 3rd. ed. in 2 vols. (Paris, 1874–1876).

The course, *Cours de mécanique industrielle*, stemmed from lectures Poncelet gave between 1827 and 1830 to artisans and workers of Metz. It went through several eds., which are sometimes difficult to identify.

A lithographed version, prepared with Poncelet's permission by his colleague F. T. Gosselin, was published in 3 pts. as *Cours de mécanique industrielle fait aux artistes et ouvriers messins . . .*: Première Partie: "Résumé des leçons du Cours de mécanique industrielle . . ." (Metz, 1828), of which there also exists a more detailed version; Deuxième Partie: "Cours de mécanique industrielle professé de 1828 à 1829" (Metz, 1829; 2nd ed., 1831); and Troisième Partie: "Cours de mécanique industrielle professé du mois de janvier au mois d'avril 1830."

Several other unauthorized lithographed versions of this course were also produced. Poncelet published a partial printed version of the course, *Première partie du Cours de mécanique industrielle, fait aux ouvriers messins* (Metz, 1829). An ed. of the entire course, begun in 1830 and continued in 1835, 1838, and 1839, was completed in 1841: *Introduction à la mécanique industrielle, physique ou expérimentale*, 2nd ed. (Metz–Paris, 1841), which was republished under the same title (Paris, 1870).

Poncelet's report, *Inventaire des machines et outils. Travaux de la Commission française* [at the Universal Exposition of 1851], III: *Rapport fait au jury international . . . sur les machines et les outils employés dans les manufactures* (Paris, 1857), appeared in 2 vols.: I, *Machines et outils des arts divers*; II, *Machines et outils appropriés aux arts textiles.*

II. SECONDARY LITERATURE. Major accounts of Poncelet's life and work are I. Didion, "Notice sur la vie et les ouvrages du général J.-V. Poncelet," in *Mémoires de l'Académie de Metz*, **50** (1870), 101–159; J. Bertrand, "Éloge historique de Jean-Victor Poncelet," in *Mémoires de l'Académie des sciences de l'Institut de France*, **41**, pt. 2 (1879), i–xxv, repr. in J. Bertrand, *Éloges académiques* (Paris, 1890), 105–129; and H. Tribout, *Un grand savant: Le général Jean-Victor Poncelet* (Paris, 1936).

Among the briefer notices, see F. Hoefer, in *Nouvelle biographie générale*, **40** (Paris, 1862), cols. 735–736; J.-B. Dumas, C. Dupin, and M. Rolland, *Discours prononcés aux funérailles de M. le général Poncelet* (Paris,

1867), E. T. Bell, in *Les grands mathématiciens* (Paris, 1939), 226–238; and M. D'Ocagne, in *Histoire abrégée des sciences mathématiques* (Paris, 1955), 205–209.

Poncelet provided an analysis of his own work in geometry and applied mechanics before 1834, in *Notice analytique sur les travaux de M. Poncelet* (Paris, 1834).

Many studies have been devoted to Poncelet's geometric work. The principal studies are M. Chasles, *Aperçu historique sur le développement des méthodes en géométrie . . .* (Brussels, 1837), see index; and *Rapport sur les progrès de la géométrie* (Paris, 1870), 38–45; E. B. Holst, *Om Poncelet's betydning for Geometrien* (Christiania [Oslo], 1878); E. Kötter, "Die Entwicklung der synthetischen Geometrie von Monge bis auf Staudt (1847)," in *Jahresbericht der Deutschen Mathematiker-Vereinigung*, **5**, pt. 2 (Leipzig, 1901), see index; A. Schoenflies and A. Tresse, in *Encyclopédie des sciences mathématiques*, III, vol. 2, fasc. 1 (Leipzig–Paris), esp. pp. 6–15; J. L. Coolidge, *A History of Geometrical Methods* (Oxford, 1940), see index; and *A History of the Conic Sections and Quadric Surfaces* (Oxford, 1945), see index; C. B. Boyer, *A History of Analytic Geometry* (New York, 1956), see index; and N. Bourbaki, *Éléments d'histoire des mathématiques*, (Paris, 1969), 165–168.

No comprehensive study has as yet been devoted to Poncelet's technical work. Its essential aspects are briefly outlined in M. Daumas, ed., *Histoire générale des techniques*, III (Paris, 1968), see index.

On Poncelet's work in applied mechanics, see C. Comberousse, in *Nouvelles annales de mathématiques*, 2nd ser., **13** (1874), 174–185; and an anonymous author, "J. V. Poncelet. Son rôle en mécanique," in *Revue scientifique*, 2nd ser., **11** (1876), 256–258.

RENÉ TATON

PORETSKY, PLATON SERGEEVICH (*b.* Elisavetgrad [now Kirovograd], Russia, 15 October 1846; *d.* Joved, Grodno district, Chernigov guberniya, Russia, 22 August 1907)

The son of a military physician, Poretsky graduated from the Poltava Gymnasium and from the Physical-Mathematical Faculty of Kharkov University; in 1870 he was attached to the chair of astronomy to prepare for a professorship. For several years Poretsky worked as an astronomer-observer at the Kharkov observatory and, from 1876, at Kazan University, where he conducted observations of stars in the Kazan zone according to the program of the International Astronomical Society. In 1886 he defended a thesis for his master's degree, the theoretical portion of which dealt with reducing the number of unknowns and equations for certain systems of cyclic equations that occur in practical astronomy. For this work he was awarded a doctorate in astronomy. In the same year Poretsky became *Privatdozent* at Kazan University

and in 1887-1888, for the first time in Russia, he lectured on mathematical logic, in which he had become interested soon after going to Kazan through the influence of A. V. Vasiliev.

From 1882 to 1888 Poretsky was secretary and treasurer of the Physical-Mathematical Section of the Kazan Society of Natural Science, supervising the publication of its *Proceedings*; for several years he edited a liberal newspaper, *Kazansky telegraf*, sometimes publishing in it his translations of Pierre Béranger's poems. At the beginning of 1889 poor health forced Poretsky to retire, but he continued his research in mathematical logic for the rest of his life.

Poretsky's main achievement was the elaboration of the Boolean algebra of logic; he considerably augmented and generalized the results obtained by Boole, Jevons, and E. Schröder. In papers published from 1880 to 1908, Poretsky systematically studied and solved many problems of the logic of classes and of propositions. He developed an original system of axioms of logical calculus and proposed a very convenient mode of determining all the conclusions that are deducible from a given logical premise, and of determining all possible logical hypotheses from which given conclusions may be deduced. He also applied the logical calculus to the theory of probability. Poretsky was the first eminent Russian scholar in mathematical logic. His research was continued by E. Bunitsky, Couturat, Archie Blake, and N. Styazhkin.

BIBLIOGRAPHY

A nearly complete list of Poretsky's writings is in the work by Styazhkin (see below), 291–292.

Secondary literature includes A. Blake, *Canonical Expressions in Boolean Algebra* (Chicago, 1938); L. Couturat, *L'algèbre de la logique* (Paris, 1905); D. Dubyago, "P. S. Poretsky," in *Izvestiya Fiziko-matematicheskogo obshchestva pri (Imperatorskom) kazanskom universitete*, 2nd ser., **16** (1908), 3–7; and N. I. Styazhkin, *Stanovlenie idei matematicheskoy logiki* (Moscow, 1964), ch. 6, sec. 2, trans. into English as *History of Mathematical Logic From Leibniz to Peano* (Cambridge, Mass., 1969).

A. P. YOUSCHKEVITCH

PORTA, GIAMBATTISTA DELLA (*b.* Vico Equense, Italy, between 3 October and 15 November 1535; *d.* Naples, Italy, 4 February 1615)

The modest fortunes of the Porta family, who belonged to the ancient nobility of Salerno, were improved when Nardo Antonio della Porta, father of

Giambattista, entered the service of Emperor Charles V in 1541. From that year the family residence alternated between a villa in Vico Equense and a house in Naples. Giambattista was the second of three sons. Only two of his teachers are known: Antonio Pisano, a royal physician in Naples, and Domenico Pizzimenti, a translator of Democritus. The nature of his formal education is unknown, but early accounts of his life suggest that he was self-taught. His informal education, however, was clearly the convivial, and sometimes profound, discussion of scientific and pseudoscientific topics.

Porta was examined by the Inquisition some time prior to 1580, and in 1592 all further publication of his works was prohibited. This ban was not lifted until 1598. In the same period his religious activity is first mentioned. By 1585 he had become a lay brother of the Jesuits, and his participation in the charitable works of both the Jesuits and the Theatines in Naples demonstrates his devotion to the ideals of the Catholic Reformation. The relationship of this overt piety to his difficulties with the Inquisition and to his personal relations with Fra Paolo Sarpi in Venice after 1579 and with Campanella in Naples in 1590 cannot easily be determined.

Nothing is known of Porta's marriage except that it produced his only child, a daughter, about 1579. He suffered from various psychosomatic ailments, which by his own account were cured when his anxiety was relieved. His most frequent illness was a persistent fever, which on occasion confined him to bed for several months.

Porta's relationship to the academies of late Renaissance Italy is of great importance. The academies of Naples were closed under suspicion of political intrigue in 1547 and began to reopen only after 1552. In the following decade the Altomare was the outstanding literary academy of Naples, and several of Porta's close friends were members. Porta himself established the Accademia dei Segreti (Academia Secretorum Naturae) some time prior to 1580. It met in Porta's house in Naples; was almost certainly founded on the model of the earlier literary academies; and was devoted to discussion and study of the secrets of nature. It seems to have been closed by order of the Inquisition and may have been the cause for Porta's original process by the Inquisition.

This early academy was but a vague anticipation of the Accademia dei Lincei, founded at Rome in 1603 by Federico Cesi and three friends. The relationship of Porta to the Lincei is difficult to establish. In 1604 Cesi traveled to Naples and often visited Porta. In the same year Porta wrote a compend of the history of the Cesi family. Cesi, who wrote the constitution of the Lincei, known as the *Lynceographum*, acknowledged that the idea of such an academy preceded the fact; and he seems to have known of Porta and his academy. The documented meeting of Cesi and Porta in 1604 was followed by a respectful correspondence which culminated in the enrollment of Porta among the Lincei on 6 July 1610. Porta's reputation among his contemporaries was second only to that of Cesi, but the enrollment of Galileo on 25 April 1611 soon overshadowed Porta and gave a new direction to the academy. It is significant, however, that the choice of the lynx with the motto "Auspicit et Inspicit" for the Lincei was derived from Porta's *Phytognomonica* (Naples, 1588). In 1611 Porta was enrolled among the Oziosi in Naples, then the most renowned literary academy.

Porta's first book, published in 1558 as *Magiae naturalis*, was a treatise on the secrets of nature, which he began collecting when he was fifteen. The secrets are arranged in four books, and the conception implied in the title is that natural magic is the perfection of natural philosophy and the highest science. This small collection of secrets constituted the basis of a twenty-book edition of the *Magiae naturalis* published in 1589, which is Porta's best-known work and the basis of his reputation. It is an extraordinary hodgepodge of material representing that unique combination of curiosity and credulity common in the late Renaissance. But combined with the author's insatiable desire for the marvelous and apparently miraculous is a serious attempt to define and describe natural magic and some refined application of both mathematical and experimental techniques in science. Book XVII, on refraction, is the basis of the attribution of priority to Porta in inventing the telescope and demonstrates his involvement with both theory and practice.

Natural magic is no longer quite so pretentiously conceived as in the first edition. It presumes an orderly and rational universe into which the magician-scientist has insights that are revealed to him because of his virtue and his study. Natural magic entails a survey of the whole of nature, but with a modicum of modesty Porta acknowledges that it may merely be the practical part of natural philosophy. The 1589 edition represents in part the work, discussions, and experiments that took place at Porta's academy— hence the emphasis on experimentation and application in his definition of natural magic.

Behind Porta's conception of natural magic lie the Hermetic and Neoplatonic traditions given new life in Renaissance philosophy, and these traditions present Porta with the possibility of an intellectual synthesis founded on the conviction that rational orderliness exists behind all the marvels and prodigies of nature that he has collected. In this belief he is a philosophical, if not a religious, mystic. But natural magic is the art and practice of such mysticism. Natural magic is not simply philosophy or religion; it is both of these brought into practice and subjected to experiment. And experiment is merely refined experience. The contribution of Porta's conception and practice of natural magic to the emerging idea of science is not merely rational or theoretical or contemplative. Rather, science must represent theory and contemplation coming to practical and experimental expression. Such a conception of natural magic as science is ideally represented in his work on concave and convex lenses. His theoretical and experimental work prepared the way for the invention of the telescope.

The range of Porta's scientific and literary interests is easily demonstrated by his works. The first published after the *Magiae* was a treatise on cryptography, *De furtivis literarum notis*, in 1563. It was followed in 1566 by *Arte del ricordare*, a book on the art of memory and mnemonic devices. Both reveal his fascination with hidden and marvelous things. In the 1570's Porta composed his first plays and wrote a treatise on the physiognomy of hands. The latter, based on his observations in the prisons of Naples, is often cited as a precursor of criminal physiognomy. The plays were not published until much later, and the treatise on the physiognomy of hands did not appear until after his death.

The early biographies of Porta suggest that his writing of drama was occasioned by the Inquisition's scrutiny of the activity of his academy, and Porta himself says that he turned to comedy as a diversion from his more serious studies. In 1584 and in 1585 he published treatises on horticulture and agriculture that were based on careful study and practice. In 1586 he published a treatise on human physiognomy, *De humana physiognomonia*, in which he clearly established the doctrine of the correspondence between the external form of the body and the internal character of the person. The doctrine of signatures— that the external form of a plant indicates its medicinal properties—is worked out in Porta's treatise on the physiognomy of plants, *Phytognomonica* (1588), in which he established the claim that physiognomy of plants is the theoretical part of agriculture. His work on physiognomy attracted the attention of the Inquisition, and a proposed Italian edition of his treatise on human physiognomy was prohibited in 1593.

In the same year, Porta published *De refractione optices*, an expansion of book XVII of the *Magiae* of 1589 on the properties of refracting lenses. In 1601 he brought out a curious treatise on celestial physiognomy, in which, after a prefatory denunciation of astrology, he proceeded to develop a theory of astral signatures that he had confirmed by experience and observation. Also in 1601 he published a small book on the mechanics of water and steam and another on the elements of curved lines in which he addressed, with some finesse, the ancient topic of squaring the circle. In 1605 he issued a translation of book I of Ptolemy's *Almagest* together with the commentary of Theon of Alexandria. In 1608 there appeared his short treatise on military fortification and a longer study on the alchemical technique of distillation (*De distillatione*). The last book published during Porta's lifetime was a treatise on meteorology (1610). Among his many special studies, those on agriculture and refraction have received the highest praise from both his contemporaries and posterity. The others are modest, even though careful study usually reveals that they are not devoid of merit.

Porta's contribution to the theory and practice of Renaissance optics is found in book XVII of the *Magiae* of 1589 and in the *De refractione* of 1593. He did not invent the camera obscura, but he is the first to report adding a concave lens to the aperture. He also juxtaposed concave and convex lenses and reports various experiments with them. But in both the 1589 and 1593 treatises he limits his purposes to clarifying the image and to a geometrical explanation of the refracting properties of such lenses. Despite his claim to priority he did not invent the telescope. His comparison of the lens in the camera obscura to the pupil in the human eye did provide an easily understandable demonstration that the source of visual images lay outside the eye as well as outside the darkened room. He thus ended on a popular level an age-old controversy. Porta's work lies conceptually and chronologically between Risner's *Opticae thesaurus* of 1572 and Kepler's *Ad Vitellionem paralipomena* of 1604. He was thoroughly familiar with the former and did not attain the geometrical certainty of the latter.

Both Porta and his position in the history of late Renaissance science are tragically revealed in two of his unpublished works. The first is a treatise known as "De telescopiis." Among the Lincei, Porta was thought to have priority in the invention of the telescope, but this treatise reveals his secondary position both in theory and in practice. He acknowledges that Galileo brought his early (1589) theory to fruition, but he fails to go beyond Galileo in any way. He returns to the elusive quest for a parabolic mirror that will permit him to see to infinity. The second treatise, known as the "Taumatologia," is an unfinished work that exists only in manuscript; but when trying to get it published, Porta claimed that it would be the consummation of his lifework. His correspondence about it reveals his return to his youthful enthusiasm for the secrets of nature and for the arcane and marvelous. It was to be another expanded version of his *Magiae*. Thus Porta devoted his last years more to discovering the philosophers' stone and the quintessence of nature than to the disciplined mathematical and experimental work of his younger contemporary Galileo. His devotion to experiment and his study of mathematics brought him in the 1580's to the verge of greatness, but he was soon overwhelmed again by the lure of the occult and the marvelous. Perhaps Porta's most compelling virtue and weakness was this youthful enthusiasm for the things of nature. There is a joy in his studies that not even the fatigue of working on the telescope and parabolic mirrors could diminish.

BIBLIOGRAPHY

I. ORIGINAL WORKS. Porta's first published work is *Magiae naturalis libri iiii* (Naples, 1558), repr. several times before publication of the expanded *Magiae naturalis libri xx* (Naples, 1589). There were Italian and other translations of both eds. There is an English trans., *Natural Magick* (London, 1658; repr. New York, 1957). There is a convenient list of the 1st eds. of all of Porta's scientific and literary works in Louise George Clubb, *Giambattista Della Porta, Dramatist* (Princeton, 1965), 316–342. Fuller bibliographical information for all eds. and translations is in Giuseppe Gabrieli, "Bibliografia Lincei I: G. B. della Porta," in *Atti dell'Accademia nazionale dei Lincei. Rendiconti*, Cl. Sc. Mr., 6th ser., **8** (1932), 206 ff.

The most important MSS of Porta are in the Library of the Accademia dei Lincei in Rome. MS Archivio Linceo IX contains an autograph copy of the index of the "Taumatologia." MS Archivio Linceo X is the MS base for Porta's book on distillation. MS Archivio Linceo XIV contains primarily the text for Porta's proposed book on the telescope. This portion of the MS has been edited and published by Vasco Ronchi and Maria Amalia Naldoni as *De telescopio* (Florence, 1962). MS Archivio Linceo XV contains the MS base for Porta's book on meteorology published in 1610. The library of the Faculty of Medicine of the University of Montpellier, MS H 169, contains parts of the "Taumatologia" as well as treatises on the magnet and the physiognomy of the hand. MS portions of the treatise on the physiognomy of the hand are also in Naples, Paris, and Toronto but are of minor importance.

II. SECONDARY LITERATURE. In addition to the book by Louise G. Clubb, three articles by Giocchino Paparelli are important: "La Taumatologia di Giovambattista Della Porta," in *Filologia romanza*, **2** (1955), 418–429; "La data di nascita di G. B. Della Porta," *ibid.*, **3** (1956), 87–89; and "Giambattista Della Porta: Della Taumatologia e liber medicus," in *Rivista di storia delle scienze mediche e naturali*, **47** (1956), 1–47.

M. HOWARD RIENSTRA

POST, EMIL LEON (*b.* Augustów, Poland, 11 February 1897; *d.* northern New York, 21 April 1954)

Post was the son of Arnold J. and Pearl D. Post. In May 1904 he arrived in America, where his father and his uncle, J. L. Post, were in the fur and clothing business in New York. As a child Post's first love was astronomy, but the loss of his left arm when he was about twelve ruled that out as a profession. He early showed mathematical ability, however; and his important paper on generalized differentiation, although not published until 1930, was essentially completed by the time he received the B.S. from the College of the City of New York in 1917. Post was a graduate student, and later lecturer, in mathematics at Columbia University from 1917 to 1920, receiving the A.M. in 1918 and the Ph.D. in 1920.

After receiving the doctorate, Post was a Proctor fellow at Princeton University for a year and then returned to Columbia as instructor, but after a year he suffered the first of the recurrent periods of illness that partially curtailed his scientific work. In the spring of 1924 he taught at Cornell University but again became ill. He resumed his teaching in the New York City high schools in 1927. Appointed to City College in 1932, he stayed there only briefly, returning in 1935 to remain for nineteen years. Post's family was Jewish; while not orthodox in his adult years, he was a religious man and proud of his heritage. He married Gertrude Singer on 25 December 1929 and they had one daughter.

Post was a member of the American Mathematical Society from 1918 and a member of the Association for Symbolic Logic from its founding in 1936. His extrascientific interests included sketching, poetry, and stargazing.

Post was the first to obtain decisive results in finitistic metamathematics when, in his Ph.D. dissertation of 1920 (published in 1921), he proved the consistency as well as the completeness of the propositional calculus as developed in Whitehead and Russell's *Principia mathematica*. This marked the beginning, in important respects, of modern proof theory. In this paper Post systematically applied the truth-table method, which had been introduced into symbolic logic by C. S. Peirce and Ernst Schröder. (Post gave credit for his method to Cassius J. Keyser when he dedicated his *Two-Valued Iterative Systems* to Keyser, "in one of whose pedagogical devices the author belatedly recognizes the true source of his truth-table method.") From this paper came general notions of completeness and consistency: A system is said to be complete in Post's sense if every well-formed formula becomes provable if we add to the axioms any well-formed formula that is not provable. A system is said to be consistent in Post's sense if no well-formed formula consisting of only a propositional variable is provable. In this paper Post also showed how to set up multivalued systems of propositional logic and introduced multivalued truth tables in analyzing them. Jan Łukasiewicz was studying three-valued logic at the same time; but while his interest was philosophical, Post's was mathematical. Post compared these multivalued systems to geometry, noting that they seem "to have the same relation to ordinary logic that geometry in a space of an arbitrary number of dimensions has to the geometry of Euclid."

Post began a scientific diary in 1916 and so was able to show, in a paper written in 1941 (but rejected by a mathematics journal and not published until 1965), that he had attained results in the 1920's similar to those published in the 1930's by Kurt Gödel, Alonzo Church, and A. M. Turing. In particular, he had planned in 1925 to show through a special analysis that *Principia mathematica* was inadequate but later decided in favor of working for a more general result, of which the incompleteness of the logic of *Principia* would be a corollary. This plan, as Post remarked, "did not count on the appearance of a Gödel!"

If Post's interest in 1920 in multivalued logics was mathematical, he also wrote in his diary about that time: "I study Mathematics as a product of the human mind and not as absolute." Indeed, he showed an increasing interest in the creative process and noted in 1941 that "perhaps the greatest service the present account could render would stem from its stressing of its final conclusion that *mathematical thinking is, and must be, essentially creative.*" But this is a creativity with limitations, and he saw symbolic logic as "the indisputable means for revealing and developing these limitations."

On the occasion of Post's death in 1954, W. V. Quine wrote:

> Modern proof theory, and likewise the modern theory of machine computation, hinge on the concept of a recursive function. This important number-theoretic concept, a precise mathematical substitute for the vague idea of "effectiveness" or "computability," was discovered independently and in very disparate but equivalent forms by four mathematicians, and one of these was Post. Subsequent work by Post was instrumental to the further progress of the theory of recursive functions.

If other mathematicians failed to recognize the power of this theory, it was forcefully shown to them in 1947, when Post demonstrated the recursive unsolvability of the word problem for semigroups, thus solving a problem proposed by A. Thue in 1914. (An equivalent result had been obtained by A. A. Markov.) When reminded of his earlier statement, Quine in 1972 confirmed his opinion, adding: "The theory of recursive functions, of which Post was a co-founder, is now nearly twice as old as it was when I wrote that letter. What a fertile field it has proved to be!"

BIBLIOGRAPHY

I. ORIGINAL WORKS. Except for abstracts of papers read at scientific meetings, the following is believed to be a complete list of Post's scientific publications: "The Generalized Gamma Functions," in *Annals of Mathematics*, **20** (1919), 202–217; "Introduction to a General Theory of Elementary Propositions," in *American Journal of Mathematics*, **43** (1921), 163–185, his Ph.D. dissertation, repr. in Jean van Heijenoort, ed., *From Frege to Gödel. A Source Book in Mathematical Logic, 1879–1931* (Cambridge, Mass., 1967), 264–283; "Generalized Differentiation," in *Transactions of the American Mathematical Society*, **32** (1930), 723–781; "Finite Combinatory Processes. Formulation I," in *Journal of Symbolic Logic*, **1** (1936), 103–105, repr. in *The Undecidable* (see below), 289–291; "Polyadic Groups," in *Transactions of the American Mathematical Society*, **48** (1940), 208–350; *The Two-Valued Iterative Systems of Mathematical Logic*, Annals of Mathematics Studies no. 5 (Princeton, 1941); "Formal Reductions of the General Combinatorial Decision Problem," in *American Journal of Mathematics*, **65** (1943), 197–215; "Recursively Enumerable Sets of Positive Integers and Their Decision Problems," in *Bulletin of the American Mathematical Society*, **50** (1944), 284–316, repr. in *The Undecidable* (see below), 305–337, Spanish trans. by J. R. Fuentes in *Revista matemática hispano-americana*, 4th ser., **7** (1947), 187–229; "A Variant of a Recursively Unsolvable Problem," *ibid.*, **52** (1946), 264–268; "Note on a Conjecture of Skolem," in *Journal of Symbolic Logic*, **11** (1946), 73–74; "Recursive Unsolvability of a Problem of Thue," *ibid.*, **12** (1947), 1–11, repr. in *The Undecidable* (see below), 293–303; "The Upper Semi-Lattice of Degrees of Recursive Unsolvability," in *Annals of Mathematics*, 2nd ser., **59** (1954), 379–407, written with S. C. Kleene; and "Absolutely Unsolvable Problems and Relatively Undecidable Propositions—Account of an Anticipation," in Martin Davis, ed., *The Undecidable* (Hewlett, N.Y., 1965), 338–433.

II. SECONDARY LITERATURE. There is an obituary of E. L. Post in *The Campus* (City College), 27 April 1954. Part of Post's work was carried to a conclusion by S. V. Yablonsky and his students. See S. V. Yablonsky, G. P. Gavrilov, V. B. Kudryavtsev, *Funktsii algebry logiki i klassy Posta* (Moscow, 1966); translated into German as

Boolesche Funktionen und Postsche Klassen (Brunswick, 1970).

HUBERT C. KENNEDY

PRATT, JOHN HENRY (*b.* London, England, 4 June 1809; *d.* Ghazipur, India, 28 December 1871)

Pratt was the son of Rev. Josiah Pratt, secretary of the Church Missionary Society. He received the B.A. at Gonville and Caius College, Cambridge, in 1833 and the M.A. at Christ's and Sidney Sussex colleges in 1836. His missionary zeal, coupled with his exceptional scientific aptitude, propelled him into both arenas, sometimes separately, sometimes simultaneously.

Through the influence of Bishop Daniel Wilson, Pratt obtained a chaplaincy appointment with the East India Company in 1838 and, in 1844, became chaplain to the bishop of Calcutta. He was appointed archdeacon of Calcutta in 1850, a post he held until he died. In 1866 he became a fellow of the Royal Society.

Of Pratt's several books only his first, *The Mathematical Principles of Mechanical Philosophy* (Cambridge, 1836; revised 1842; expanded and republished in 1860 as *A Treatise on Attractions, LaPlace's Functions, and the Figure of the Earth*), is exclusively concerned with science. The focal point of this book is the shape of the earth.

The theory of fluids suggests that the earth is essentially spheroidal. Pratt began by calculating the Newtonian attractive force exerted by a homogeneous sphere on a point, then successively relaxed the constraints on composition and shape. He ended the first part of the treatise by considering local gravitational effects, those due to irregularities in the earth's crust.

In the second part Pratt turned his attention to the fact, first demonstrated by Newton, that the earth is not a sphere, showing that the fluid hypothesis leads to an oblate spheroidal shape. He next produced a sequence of arguments intended to show that the lower bound of the thickness of the earth's crust is 1,000 miles (current estimates range from five to eight miles). Pratt concluded by showing that the precession of the equinoxes, the period differential for pendulums as a function of latitude, and geodetic data all support the conclusion that the earth is an oblate spheroid. He gave the difference between the equatorial and polar axes as 26.9 miles, a figure that compares favorably with current measurements.

For most of his professional life Pratt was concerned primarily with the propagation of the faith. He was a not undistinguished member of that informal fraternity committed to the proposition that revelation and science are complementary avenues to the acquisition of knowledge.

BIBLIOGRAPHY

With the exception of *A Treatise on Attractions*, Pratt's works do not appear to have survived in the major collections; nor have his publishers, through a complex of unfortunate circumstances, been able to preserve copies of his works, the more scientifically oriented of which include *Scripture and Science Not at Variance; With Remarks on the Historical Character, Plenary Inspiration, and Surpassing Importance of the Earlier Chapters of Genesis Unaffected by the Discoveries of Science* (London, 1856; 7th ed. 1872); *The Descent of Man, in Connexion With the Hypothesis of Development* (London, 1871); and *Difficulties in Receiving the Bible as a Divine Revelation Arising From the Progress of Human Knowledge* (Calcutta, 1864).

JEROME H. MANHEIM

PRÉVOST, ISAAC-BÉNÉDICT (*b.* Geneva, Switzerland, 7 August 1755; *d.* Montauban, France, 10 June 1819)

Prévost was an astute observer whose knowledge of the sciences was largely self-acquired. His memoir of 1807 on the cause of the smut or bunt of wheat was remarkable in its time and its validity has endured. Although its implications in identifying a plant parasite as the agent of the disease were not fully appreciated then, the work later became influential and contributed to the background against which developed an understanding of contagious disease.

The son of Jean-Jacques Prévost and Marie-Élisabeth Henri, young Isaac-Bénédict was sent to a nearby village boarding school but had neither the disposition nor the opportunity to obtain more than the essentials for his later scholarship. He worked briefly as an engraver's apprentice and then as an apprentice in a grocery house, where he mulled over questions of weight and force, odors, and other subjects that were later to concern him. Deciding against a commercial career, he resolved instead to devote himself to the sciences. He became tutor to the sons of M. Delmas of Montauban; Montauban was his home and the family were his friends until his death. Encouraged by the family, Prévost decided to give his full energies to his studies, and he set out to remedy his education. At first, he was most attracted to mathematics but later turned to physics and natural history, which he was able to study when the family spent part of each year in the country. Although the necessary books were sometimes hard to obtain, he persevered in reading, observing, and experimenting.

A founding member of the Société des Sciences et des Arts du Département du Lot in Montauban, Prévost belonged to a number of learned societies and corresponded with many colleagues, including his cousin Pierre Prevost. He communicated papers on various subjects to the scientific journals and established himself as a savant. Although he had declined in 1784 an offer to succeed Pierre Prevost at the Berlin academy, he later accepted an appointment (1810) as professor of philosophy at the new Protestant academy in Montauban.

La carie or *charbon* (the bunt, smut, or stinking smut of wheat) was vastly destructive of crops when Prévost began a ten-year study to find the direct cause of the disease. Within the affected kernels, forming a dark powder, were the particles Tillet had described but considered a contaminating virus (1755). Prévost examined these brown-black, spherical granules beneath the microscope and estimated that millions were contained in a bunted kernel. He noted their likeness to the globules seen in certain uredos and recognized them specifically as the seeds of a cryptogam. By placing the spores in water, he was able to cultivate microscopic plants; and with the use of controls, he experimented in the fields to observe the destruction of young wheat plants. Although he could not discern the mycelia, he inferred that the penetrating parasite ultimately reached the kernel, there forming its gemmae. Prévost also discovered that copper solutions (particularly copper sulfate) can prevent the disease.

In 1807 Prévost finally identified a fungus parasite as the causative agent. Since at that time the spontaneous generation of lower plants was still an accepted hypothesis, Prévost's discovery was extraordinarily important. His work gained wider recognition in 1847, when the Tulasnes cited his memoir in their own studies.

BIBLIOGRAPHY

I. ORIGINAL WORKS. Prévost's most important work was *Mémoire sur la cause immédiate de la carie où charbon des blés, et de plusieurs autres maladies des plantes, et sur les préservatifs de la carie* (Paris, 1807), trans. by George Wannamaker Keitt as *Memoir on the Immediate Cause of Bunt or Smut of Wheat, and of Several Other Diseases of Plants and on Preventives of Bunt*, Phytopathological Classics, no. 6 (Menasha, Wis., 1939).

II. SECONDARY LITERATURE. The main source on Prévost's life and character is Pierre Prevost, *Notice de la vie et des écrits d'Isaac-Bénédict Prévost* (Geneva–Paris, 1820), which describes published and unpublished works, journals, notes, and correspondence. A shorter biography, P. P. [Pierre Prevost], "Prévost, (Isaac-Bénédict)," is in the *Biographie Universelle, Ancienne et Moderne*, XXXVI (1823), 59–60. Keitt (see above) includes a biography and an evaluation of the *Mémoire*; see also G. W. Keitt, "Isaac-Bénédict Prévost, 1755–1819," in *Phytopathology*, **46** (1956), 2–5; E. C. Large, in *The Advance of the Fungi* (New York, 1940; 2nd ed., 1962), 76–79, also assesses Prévost's work.

GLORIA ROBINSON

PRINGSHEIM, ALFRED (*b.* Ohlau, Silesia, Germany, 2 September 1850; *d.* Zurich, Switzerland, 25 June 1941)

Pringsheim studied at Berlin and Heidelberg in 1868–1869, received the Ph.D. at Heidelberg in 1872, and qualified as *Privatdozent* at Munich in 1877. He was appointed extraordinary professor at Munich in 1886 but did not become full professor until 1901. He retired in 1922. Pringsheim was a member of the Bavarian Academy of Sciences.

Pringsheim, who came from a rich family, was a lover and promoter of music and fine arts. In his youth he had been a friend of Richard Wagner; and with his wife, Hedwig Dohm, he made his home into a center of Munich's social and cultural life. The novelist Thomas Mann, who was his son-in-law, wrote a novel based on the Pringsheim family. Pringsheim's refined wit was famous. His sprightly *Bierrede* was the acme of the yearly meeting of the Deutsche Mathematiker-Vereinigung and was mentioned by mathematicians throughout the year. His puns were famous: Once when he was asked about his son, who at that time worked as a physicist under Nernst, he answered "Peter ist in Berlin und lernt da den Nernst der Lebens kennen."

After 1933 he was subjected to persecution as a "non-Aryan"; Pringsheim was forced to sell his house to the Nazi party, which tore it down to erect a party building. Having been forced to give up his library and to move several times, he was finally allowed to sell his celebrated majolica collection to a London dealer, although he had to surrender the greater part of the proceeds. In 1939 he moved to Zurich, where he died two years later.

In mathematics Pringsheim was the most consequent follower of Weierstrass. His field was pre-Lebesgue real functions and complex functions; his work is characterized by meticulous rigor rather than by great ideas. His best-known discovery concerns power series with positive coefficients: they have a singularity in the intersection of the positive axis and the circle of convergence. His elaboration of the theory of integral transcendental functions was exemplary and influential, and his extremely simple proof of Cauchy's integral theorem has been generally accepted.

Pringsheim was a brilliant lecturer and conversationalist, but his writings do not reflect this brilliance. This is even true of his celebrated *Festrede*, a paragon of stylistic and oratorical splendor only for those who had heard him speak. The voluminous edition of his courses is one of the dreariest specimens of epsilontics.

BIBLIOGRAPHY

Pringsheim's writings include *Die Grundlagen der modernen Wertlehre: Daniel Bernoulli, Versuch einer neuen Theorie der Wertbestimmung von Glücksfällen*, Sammlung Älterer und Neuerer Staatswissenschaftlicher Schriften, no. 9 (Leipzig, 1896); "Grundlagen der allgemeinen Funktionentheorie," in *Encyklopädie der mathematischen Wissenschaften*, II, pt. 1, fasc. 1 (1899), 1–52; "Über den Goursat'schen Beweis des Cauchy'schen Integralsatzes," in *Transactions of the American Mathematical Society*, **2** (1901), 413–421; "Elementare Theorie der ganzen transcendenten Funktionen von endlicher Ordnung," in *Mathematische Annalen*, **58** (1904), 257–342; "Über Wert und angeblichen Unwert der Mathematik," in *Jahresbericht der Deutschen Mathematiker-Vereinigung*, **13** (1904), 357–382; "Algebraische Analysis," in *Encyklopädie der mathematischen Wissenschaften*, II, pt. 3, fasc. 1 (1908), 1–46; "Table générale," in *Acta mathematica* (1913), 164, with portrait; and *Vorlesungen über Zahlen- und Funktionenlehre*, 2 vols. in 5 pts. (Leipzig–Berlin, 1916–1932).

An obituary is O. Perron, "Alfred Pringsheim," in *Jahresbericht der Deutschen Mathematiker-Vereinigung*, **56** (1952), 1–6.

HANS FREUDENTHAL

PRIVALOV, IVAN IVANOVICH (*b.* Nizhniy Lomov, Penza guberniya [now oblast], Russia, 11 February 1891; *d.* Moscow, U.S.S.R., 13 July 1941)

Privalov, son of Ivan Andreevich Privalov, a merchant, and Eudokia Lvovna Privalova, graduated from the Gymnasium in Nizhniy Novgorod (now Gor'kiy) in 1909 and in the same year entered the department of physics and mathematics of Moscow University. He graduated in 1913 and remained at the university to prepare for an academic career. His scientific supervisor was D. F. Egorov, and his work was greatly influenced by N. N. Lusin. In 1916 he passed the examinations for the master's degree and began teaching at Moscow University as lecturer; in 1917 he became professor at Saratov University. Privalov returned to Moscow in 1922 and for the rest of his life was professor of the theory of functions

of a complex variable; from 1923 he also taught at the Air Force Academy. He received his doctorate in physics and mathematics in 1935 without defending a dissertation. He was an active member of the Moscow Mathematical Society, of which he was vice-president from 1936. He was elected a corresponding member of the Soviet Academy of Sciences in 1939.

Privalov's first works, dealing with orthogonal series and integral equations, appeared in 1914; he then turned to the study of properties of Fourier series. His principal interests soon concentrated, however, upon boundary properties of analytic functions, that is, their properties in the vicinity of the set of their singular points; a considerable part of his seventy-nine published works is concerned with these problems. Privalov was closely preceded in this field by V. V. Golubev, another Moscow mathematician who taught at Saratov University and in 1916 published his master's degree thesis on analytic functions with a perfect set of singular points.

In 1917 Privalov and Lusin established a wide-ranging program of studies on the theory of analytical functions by means of the theory of measure and Lebesgue integrals, and began to put it into effect at once. In "Cauchy Integral" (1918), which continued the works of Pierre Fatou (1906) and Golubev (1916) and was initially intended as a master's degree thesis, Privalov described many new discoveries in the theory of boundary properties of analytic functions defined in the domain bounded by one rectifiable curve. Thus it was proved that under conformal mapping of such domains the angles are preserved on the boundary almost everywhere. Privalov and Lusin established the invariance of a point set with a measure equal to zero on the boundary; and Privalov solved many problems on the unicity of analytical functions, proved the existence almost everywhere of the Cauchy type of integral, established its boundary properties, and investigated in detail the problem of determining the analytical function with its values on the boundary by means of the Cauchy type of integral. Because "Cauchy Integral" appeared at a time when scientific contacts between Russia and other countries were almost nonexistent, it did not attract attention abroad. In 1924–1925 some of the results obtained in that work were reported by Privalov in two articles in French, the second of which was written with Lusin. These results were considerably supplemented here by the solution of a number of new and difficult problems of unicity of analytic functions determined by the set of their values on the boundary.

In 1934 Privalov began to study subharmonic functions, which had been introduced as early as 1906 and became the subject of Riesz's works in

1925–1930. In *Subgarmonicheskie funktsii* Privalov presented an original systematic construction of the general theory of this class of functions in close connection with the theory of harmonic functions. He also elaborated the ideas of his work on Cauchy's integral. Shortly before his death Privalov summarized many studies in *Granichnye svoystva odnoznachnykh analiticheskikh funktsy*.

Some of Privalov's manuals, especially university-level courses on the theory of functions of complex variables and a manual of analytical geometry for technological colleges, became very widely used in the Soviet Union.

BIBLIOGRAPHY

I. Original Works. Privalov's writings include "Cauchy Integral," in *Izvestiya Saratovskogo gosudarstvennogo universiteta*, **11** (1918), 1–94; "Sur certaines propriétés métriques des fonctions analytiques," in *Journal de l'École polytechnique*, **24** (1924), 77–112; "Sur l'unicité et la multiplicité des fonctions analytiques," in *Annales scientifiques de l'École normale supérieure*, **42** (1925), 143–191, written with N. N. Lusin; *Analiticheskaya geometria* (Moscow, 1927; 30th ed., 1966); *Vvedenie v teoriyu funktsy kompleksnogo peremennogo* ("Introduction to the Theory of Functions of a Complex Variable"; Moscow, 1927; 11th ed., 1967); *Subgarmonicheskie funktsii* (Moscow–Leningrad, 1937); and *Granichnye svoystva odnoznachnykh analiticheskikh funktsy* ("The Boundary Properties of the Single-Valued Analytic Functions"; Moscow, 1941).

II. Secondary Literature. For bibliographies of Privalov's works see *Matematika v SSSR za tridtsat let* ("Mathematics in the U.S.S.R. During the [Last] Thirty Years"; Moscow–Leningrad, 1948); and V. Stepanov, "Ivan Privalov. 1891–1941," in *Izvestiya Akademii nauk SSSR*, Ser. math., **6** (1941), 389–394.

A. P. Youschkevitch
A. T. Grigorian

PRIVAT DE MOLIÈRES, JOSEPH (*b*. Tarascon, Bouches-du-Rhône, France, 1677; *d*. Paris, France, 12 May 1742)

The son of Charles Privat de Molières and Martine de Robins de Barbantane, Privat de Molières was born into a prominent Provençal family. He showed an early aptitude for philosophical and scientific studies and received an excellent education at Oratorian schools at Aix, Marseilles, Arles, and, finally, Angers, where he studied under the mathematician Charles-René Reyneau during 1698–1699. Against his parents' wishes, Privat de Molières chose an ecclesiastical life and entered the Congregation of the Oratory. He taught at the order's colleges at Saumur,

Juilly, and Soissons but left in 1704 to pursue a more active scientific career in Paris. There he became an intimate of Malebranche, studying mathematics and metaphysics with him until the latter's death in 1715. Elected to the Académie Royale des Sciences as *adjoint mécanicien* in 1721, Privat de Molières succeeded to the chair of philosophy at the Collège Royal in 1723, following the death of Varignon. He was raised to the rank of *associé* in the Academy in 1729 and became fellow of the Royal Society of London in the same year.

A major figure in the protracted struggle against the importation of Newtonian science into France, Privat de Molières devoted his career to developing and improving Cartesian physics. Cognizant of the superiority of Newtonian precision in comparison with Cartesian vagueness in the explication of natural phenomena, he was nonetheless convinced of the rectitude of Descartes's ideal of a purely mechanical science. In a series of memoirs read to the Academy, in articles in the *Journal de Trévoux*, and in the published version of his lectures at the Collège Royal, the four-volume *Leçons de physique, contenant les éléments de la physique déterminés par les seules lois des mécaniques* (1734–1739), Privat de Molières offered an emended Cartesian program which, by incorporating Newton's calculations and mathematical techniques, would accord with exact experimental and observational data. Central to his system was the existence of small vortices (*petits tourbillons*), an idea borrowed from Malebranche to replace the discredited Cartesian theory of matter. Unlike Descartes's elements, the *petits tourbillons* were elastic rather than hard particles and constituted the basic structural units of the universe.

The hypothesis of *petits tourbillons* was adopted to establish the superiority of the concepts of the plenum and impulsion over the rival ideas of the void and attraction. Privat de Molières sought to answer Newton's refutation of the vortex theory (propositions LII and LIII of book II of the *Principia*) by obviating the objection that planetary vortices were incompatible with Kepler's laws. He offered an elaborate mathematical demonstration showing that the subtle movements of *petits tourbillons* within the larger planetary vortices could produce the motion of the planets required by astronomical data. His system, extended to include electrical and chemical phenomena, was influential in France and was cited by Fontenelle, secretary of the Academy, as one of the most effective rehabilitations of Cartesian science. Privat de Molières's ingenious use of the vortex hypothesis, intended as a reconciliation between Cartesian and Newtonian ideas, succumbed, however, to the cogent attacks by French Newtonians, notably Pierre Sigorgne.

BIBLIOGRAPHY

I. ORIGINAL WORKS. Privat de Molières's major books include *Leçons de mathématiques, nécessaires pour l'intelligence des principes de physique qui s'enseignent actuellement au Collège royal* (Paris, 1725), trans. into English by T. Haselden as *Mathematic Lessons . . . Delivered at the College Royal of Paris . . .* (London, 1730); *Leçons de physique, contenant les éléments de la physique déterminés par les seules lois des mécaniques*, 4 vols. (Paris, 1734–1739); and *Traité synthétique des lignes du premier et du second genre, ou éléments de géométrie dans l'ordre de leur génération* (Paris, 1740). Among his more important memoirs presented to the Academy are "Loix générales du mouvement dans le tourbillon sphérique," in *Mémoires de l'Académie royale des sciences* (1728), 245–267; and "Problème physico-mathématique, dont la solution tend à servir de réponse à une des objections de M. Newton contre la possibilité des tourbillons calesses," *ibid.* (1729), 235–244.

II. SECONDARY LITERATURE. For biographical details consult Jean-Jacques Dortous de Mairan, *Éloges des académiciens de l'Académie royale des sciences, morts dans les années 1741, 1742, 1743* (Paris, 1747), 201–234; F. Hoefer, ed., *Nouvelle biographie générale*, XXXV (Paris, 1861), 887–889; and Alexandre Savérien, *Histoire des philosophes modernes*, VI (Paris, 1773), 217–248. The best recent study of Privat de Molières's physics is Pierre Brunet, *L'introduction des théories de Newton en France au XVIIIe siècle. I: Avant 1738* (Paris, 1931), 157–165, 240–262, 327–338. Also useful is E. J. Aiton, *The Vortex Theory of Planetary Motions* (London–New York, 1972), 209 ff. A brief discussion of the use of *petits tourbillons* in chemistry is Hélène Metzger, *Les doctrines chimiques en France du début du XVIIe à la fin du XVIIIe siècle*, I (Paris, 1923), 462–467.

MARTIN FICHMAN

PROCLUS (*b.* Byzantium, 410 [412?]; *d.* Athens, 485)

Proclus' parents, Patricius and Marcella, were wellborn citizens of Lycia; and his father had attained eminence as an advocate in the courts of Byzantium. Proclus received his early education at the grammar school of Xanthus, a city on the southern coast of Lycia. He was later sent to Alexandria, where he began the study of rhetoric and Latin in preparation for following his father's career. But on a visit to Byzantium during these years he experienced a "divine call," as his biographer Marinus tells us (chs. 6, 9, 10), to devote himself to philosophy. Returning to Alexandria, Proclus studied Aristotle with Olympio-

dorus the Elder and mathematics with a certain Heron, otherwise unknown. But these teachers did not satisfy him; and before he was twenty, he moved to Athens, where the Platonic Academy had recently undergone a notable revival under the headship of Plutarch of Athens. From this time until his death in 485 Proclus was a member of the Academy, first as student, then as a teacher, and finally as its head— whence the title Diadochus (Successor) which is usually attached to his name.

Proclus was the last great representative of the philosophical movement now called Neoplatonism. The first notable exponent of this Hellenistic form of Platonism was Plotinus, from whom the doctrine had been transmitted, through Porphyry and Iamblichus, to Plutarch and Syrianus, Proclus' teachers at Athens. During these two centuries Neoplatonism had taken on a more pronounced religious coloration and had acquired a tincture of the Eastern predilection for magic, or "theurgy," as Iamblichus called it; on the other hand, its logical structure had become more precise and systematic, and its exponents had turned increasingly to scholarly examination and exposition of the writings of Plato and Aristotle.

Proclus had an extraordinarily acute and orderly mind. Because of his religious temperament he enthusiastically espoused Neoplatonism and devoted his talents and energies to perfecting it by systematizing and extending the views of his predecessors, strengthening their logical structure, and showing in detail their derivation from the teaching of Plato, who was taken as the source and final authority. But Proclus was more than a systematic metaphysician. He had a broad interest in all products of Greek culture, in religion, literature, science, and philosophy. His literary production was tremendous. Many of his writings have been lost, but those remaining constitute a priceless source of information regarding this last stage of Greek culture; and because of their underlying philosophy they embody an impressive restatement of Greek rationalism in its last confrontation with Christian thought.

The goal of philosophy, according to the Neoplatonists, was to attain a vision of and contact with the transcendent and ineffable One, the principle from which all things proceed and to which they all, according to their several natures and capacities, endeavor to return. But this synthesizing insight was to be attained only by the hard labor of thought. Proclus believed that a prerequisite to the study of philosophy was a thorough grounding in logic, mathematics, and natural science. One of the most important of his extant writings is the *Commentary on the First Book of Euclid's Elements*, in part certainly a product of his lectures at the Academy. Proclus was not a creative mathematician; but he was an acute expositor and critic, with a thorough grasp of mathematical method and a detailed knowledge of the thousand years of Greek mathematics from Thales to his own time. Because of his interest in the principles underlying mathematical thought and their relation to ultimate philosophical principles, Proclus' commentary is a notable—and also the earliest—contribution to the philosophy of mathematics. Its numerous references to the views of Euclid's predecessors and successors, many of them otherwise unknown to us, render it an invaluable source for the history of the science.

In the same vein but of more limited interest today is Proclus' *Hypotyposis* [Outline] *of the Hypotheses of the Astronomers*, an elaborate exposition of the system of eccentrics and epicycles assumed in Ptolemy's astronomy. This Ptolemaic system had arisen out of an effort to provide a mathematical explanation of the anomalies in the motions of the heavenly bodies as observed from the earth. Proclus approved the motives that led to its construction, and thought a knowledge of it desirable for his students; but he was understandably critical of its complexity as a whole and of the ad hoc character of its individual hypotheses. Several other writings on astronomy are attributed to Proclus: an elementary treatise entitled *Sphaera*, which appeared in more than seventy editions or translations during the early Renaissance; a paraphrase of Ptolemy's astrological *Tetrabiblos*; and another astrological essay entitled *Eclipses*, extant in two different Latin translations. Finally, his *Elements of Physics* offered a summary of books VI and VII of Aristotle's *Physics* and the first book of *De caelo*, arranged in geometrical form with propositions and proofs.

Proclus' most systematic philosophical work is his *Elements of Theology*, which presented in geometrical form, in a series of propositions, each supported by its proof, the successive grades of being that proceed from the superexistent and ineffable One downward to the levels of life and soul. The treatise *Platonic Theology*, probably a later work, presented this hierarchy of divine principles as they were revealed in Plato's dialogues, particularly in the *Parmenides*. Planned on a grandiose scale, this work either was not completed or has been imperfectly transmitted to us.

Better known is the impressive series of commentaries on Platonic dialogues: a lengthy commentary on the *Timaeus*—which, Marinus tells us (ch. 38), was Proclus' favorite—another equally long commentary on the *Parmenides*, another on the *First Alcibiades*, and still another on the *Republic*. The texts of all these have been preserved. His commentary on the *Cratylus* survives only in fragments, and those on the *Philebus*, the *Theaetetus*, the *Sophist*, and the *Phaedo* have been completely lost, as have those he is reported to have written on Aristotle. We possess only a fragment of Proclus' commentary on the *Enneads* of Plotinus, and we know of his *Eighteen Arguments for the Eternity of the World*, a tract against the Christians, only because it is extensively quoted in Philoponus' book written to refute it. His treatises *On Providence and Fate* and *On the Subsistence of Evils* were long known only in Latin translations, but large portions of the Greek text have recently been recovered and edited.

Of Proclus' numerous works on religion, none survives except in fragments. Like Aristotle, he believed that ancient traditions often contain truth expressed in mythical form. Orphic and Chaldean theology engaged his attention from his earliest years in Athens. He studied Syrianus' commentary on the Orphic writings along with the works of Porphyry and Iamblichus on the Chaldean Oracles; and he undertook a commentary of his own on this collection, which, Marinus states (ch. 26), took five years to write. Proclus himself was a devout adherent of the ancient faiths, scrupulously observing the holy days of both the Egyptian and Greek calendars—for, he said, it behooves the philosopher to be the hierophant of all mankind, not of one people only (Marinus, ch. 19).

Proclus never married and made liberal use of his apparently ample means for the benefit of his relatives and friends. His diet was abstemious but not ascetic, although he customarily refrained, in Pythagorean fashion, from eating meat. He composed many hymns to the gods, of which seven survive, written in Homeric language and marked by literary quality as well as religious feeling. We are told that he lived in constant communication with the divine world, addressing his adoration and aspiration in prayers and ritual observances and receiving messages from the gods in dreams. His pious biographer also presents him as something of a wonder-worker who, having been initiated into the secrets of the hieratic art, practiced necromancy and other forms of divination and who was able by his arts to produce rain and to heal disease. Such beliefs, like the belief in astrology which both he and Ptolemy held, were almost universal in that age.

Proclus deserves to be remembered, however, not for these beliefs that he shared with almost all his contemporaries, but for the qualities he possessed that are exceedingly rare in any age and were almost unique in his: the logical clarity and firmness of his thought, the acuteness of his analyses, his eagerness to understand and his readiness to present the views of his predecessors on controversial issues, the sustained coherence of his lengthy expositions, and the large horizon, as broad as the whole of being, within which his thinking moved.

Proclus' thought indirectly exercised considerable influence in the early Middle Ages through the writings of the so-called Dionysius the Areopagite, whose teachings were a thinly disguised version of Proclus' doctrines. With the revival of learning in the fifteenth century and the desire of Renaissance thinkers to throw off the yoke of medieval Aristotelianism, Proclus' Platonism had a great vogue in the Florentine Academy and strongly influenced Nicholas of Cusa and Johannes Kepler. Modern criticism has tended, rather hastily, to discredit his interpretation of Plato; and with the decline of interest in speculative philosophy, his writings have fallen into neglect. But it is fair to say that the wealth of learning and insight in his works does not deserve to be neglected, and that the constructive philosophy they contain still awaits adequate appraisal and appreciation by modern philosophers.

BIBLIOGRAPHY

I. ORIGINAL WORKS. *Procli philosophi Platonici opera inedita*, Victor Cousin, ed., 2nd ed. (Paris, 1864), contains text of *Commentary on the Parmenides*, French trans. by A. Chaignet, 3 vols. (Paris, 1901–1903).

Separate eds. of other texts are: *Commentary on the First Alcibiades of Plato*, L. G. Westerink, ed. (Amsterdam, 1959), English trans. by William O'Neill (The Hague, 1965); *Commentary on the Timaeus*, Ernst Diehl, ed., 3 vols. (Leipzig, 1903–1906), French trans. by A. J. Festugière, 5 vols. (Paris, 1966–1968); *Commentary on the Republic*, Wilhelm Kroll, ed., 2 vols. (Leipzig, 1899–1901), French trans., by A. J. Festugière, 3 vols. (Paris, 1970); *Elements of Physics*, Albert Ritzenfeld, ed., with a German trans. (Leipzig, 1911); *Hypotyposis*, Charles Manitius, ed., with a German trans. (Leipzig, 1909); *Commentary on the First Book of Euclid's Elements*, Gottfried Friedlein, ed. (Leipzig, 1873), German trans. by Leander Schönberger (Halle, 1945), French trans. by Paul ver Eecke (Bruges, 1949), English trans. by Thomas Taylor, 2 vols. (London, 1792), and Glenn R. Morrow (Princeton, 1970); *Commentary on the Cratylus*, G. Pasquali, ed. (Leipzig, 1908); *Elements of Theology*, E. R. Dodds, ed., with an English trans., 2nd ed. (Oxford, 1963); *Platonic Theology*, H. D. Saffrey and L. G. Westerink, eds., with a French trans. (Paris, 1968), English trans. by Thomas Taylor (London, 1816); *Providence and Fate* and *Subsistence of Evils*, Helmut Boese, ed. (Berlin, 1960); and *Hymns*, E. Vogt, ed. (Wiesbaden, 1957), Thomas Taylor, ed., with an English trans. (London, 1793).

For a complete list of Proclus' writings, with a bibliography of eds. and translations of individual items during

the modern period to 1940, see Rosán (below), 245–254.

II. SECONDARY LITERATURE. An ancient biography is *Vita Procli*, by his pupil and successor Marinus, J. F. Boissonade, ed. (Leipzig, 1814), repr. in Cousin, *Procli . . . Platonici opera inedita*. See W. Beierwaltes, *Proklos* (Frankfurt am Main, 1965); Rudolf Beutler, "Proklos (4)," in Pauly-Wissowa, *Real-Encyclopädie der classischen Altertumswissenschaft*, XXIII (1957), 186–247; Raymond Klibansky, "Ein Proklus-fund und seine Bedeutung," which is *Sitzungsberichte der Heidelberger Akademie der Wissenschaften*, **19**, no. 5 (1929); Laurence J. Rosán, *The Philosophy of Proclus* (New York, 1949); A. E. Taylor, "The Philosophy of Proclus," in *Proceedings of the Aristotelian Society*, **18** (1918), 600–635; Friedrich Ueberweg, *Grundriss der Geschichte der Philosophie*, I, *Die Philosophie des Altertums*, 12th ed., Karl Praechter, ed. (Berlin, 1926), 621–631; Thomas Whittaker, *The Neo-Platonists*, 2nd ed. (Cambridge, 1928), 155–184, 231–314; and E. Zeller, *Die Philosophie der Griechen*, 5th ed., III, sec. 2 (Leipzig, 1921), 834–890.

GLENN R. MORROW

PTOLEMY (or **Claudius Ptolemaeus**) (*b. ca.* A.D. 100; *d. ca.* A.D. 170)

Our meager knowledge of Ptolemy's life is based mostly on deductions from his surviving works, supplemented by some dubious information from authors of late antiquity and Byzantine times. The best evidence for his dates is the series of his observations reported in his major astronomical work, the *Almagest*: these are all from the reigns of the Roman emperors Hadrian and Antoninus, the earliest 26 March 127 and the latest 2 February 141.[1] Since he wrote several major works after the *Almagest*, this evidence fits well with the statement of a scholiast attached to works of Ptolemy in several late manuscripts—that he flourished under Hadrian and lived until the reign of Marcus Aurelius (161–180).[2] The only other explicit date is that of the "Canobic Inscription": this is found in manuscripts of Ptolemy's astronomical works and purports to be a copy of an inscription dedicated by Ptolemy to the "Savior God" at Canopus, a town at the western mouth of the Nile, in the tenth year of Antoninus (A.D. 147/148).[3] It consists mostly of lists of astronomical parameters determined by Ptolemy; although most of its contents are extracted from the *Almagest* and other genuine works of Ptolemy, I doubt its authenticity. A statement by the sixth-century philosophical commentator Olympiodorus that Ptolemy practiced astronomy for forty years in "the so-called wings at Canopus," and hence set up there the inscription commemorating his astronomical discoveries,[4] is probably a fictional elaboration on the "Canobic Inscription." In fact the only place mentioned in any of Ptolemy's observations is Alexandria, and there is no reason to suppose that he ever lived anywhere else. The statement by Theodore Meliteniotes that he was born in Ptolemais Hermiou (in Upper Egypt) could be correct,[5] but it is late (ca. 1360) and unsupported. The belief that he came from Pelusium is a Renaissance misinterpretation of the title "Phelud(i)ensis" attached to his name in medieval Latin texts, which in turn comes from a corruption of the Arabic "qalūdī," a misunderstanding of Κλαύδιος.[6] His name "Ptolemaeus" indicates that he was an inhabitant of Egypt, descended from Greek or hellenized forebears, while "Claudius" shows that he possessed Roman citizenship, probably as a result of a grant to an ancestor by the emperor Claudius or Nero.

It is possible to deduce something about the order of composition of Ptolemy's surviving works from internal evidence. The *Almagest* is certainly the earliest of the major works: it is mentioned in the introductions to the *Tetrabiblos*, *Handy Tables*, and *Planetary Hypotheses*, and in book VIII, 2, of the *Geography*; a passage of the *Almagest* looks forward to the publication of the *Geography*.[7] One can occasionally trace development: in the *Handy Tables* many tables are presented in a form more convenient for practical use than the corresponding sections of the *Almagest*, and some parameters are slightly changed. The *Planetary Hypotheses* exhibits considerably more change in parameters, and introduces a notable improvement in the theory of planetary latitudes and an entirely new system for calculating the absolute sizes and distances of the planets. The prime meridian of the *Geography* is not Alexandria, as is promised in the *Almagest*, but a meridian through the "Blessed Isles" (the Canaries) at the extreme west of the ancient known world (which had the advantage that all longitudes were counted in the same direction). The phenomenon of the apparent enlargement of heavenly bodies when they are close to the horizon is explained in the *Almagest* as due to physical causes (the dampness of the atmosphere of the earth),[8] whereas in the *Optics* Ptolemy gives a purely psychological explanation.[9] Presumably in the interval between the composition of the two works he had discovered that there is no measurable enlargement. Similarly the *Optics* discusses the problem of astronomical refraction,[10] which is never considered in the *Almagest* despite its possible effect on observation. It is hardly possible, however, to trace Ptolemy's scientific development, except in his astronomical work; and even there the later works contribute only minor modifications to the masterly synthesis of the *Almagest*.

We know nothing of Ptolemy's teachers or associates, although it is a plausible conjecture that the Theon who is said in the *Almagest* to have "given" Ptolemy observations of planets from between 127 and 132 was his teacher.[11] Many of the works are addressed to an otherwise unknown Syrus. It would be hasty, but not absurd, to conclude from the fact that the *Geography* and the *Harmonica* are not addressed to Syrus that they are later than all the works so addressed (that is, all the other extant works except for the dubious Περὶ κριτηρίου and possibly the *Optics* and the *Phaseis*, the relevant sections of which are missing). Living in Alexandria must have been a great advantage to Ptolemy in his work (and perhaps his education). Although much declined from its former greatness as a center of learning, the city still maintained a scholarly tradition and must at the least have provided him with essential reference material from its libraries.

Ptolemy's chief work in astronomy, and the book on which his later reputation mainly rests, is the *Almagest*, in thirteen books. The Greek title is μαθηματικὴ σύνταξις, which means "mathematical [that is, astronomical] compilation." In later antiquity it came to be known informally as ἡ μεγάλη σύνταξις or ἡ μεγίστη σύνταξις ("the great [or greatest] compilation"), perhaps in contrast with a collection of earlier Greek works on elementary astronomy called ὁ μικρὸς ἀστρονομούμενος ("the small astronomical collection").[12] The translators into Arabic transformed ἡ μεγίστη into "al-majistī," and this became "almagesti" or "almagestum" in the medieval Latin translations. It is a manual covering the whole of mathematical astronomy as the ancients conceived it. Ptolemy assumes in the reader nothing beyond a knowledge of Euclidean geometry and an understanding of common astronomical terms; starting from first principles, he guides him through the prerequisite cosmological and mathematical apparatus to an exposition of the theory of the motion of those heavenly bodies which the ancients knew (sun, moon, Mercury, Venus, Mars, Jupiter, Saturn, and the fixed stars, the latter being considered to lie on a single sphere concentric with the earth) and of various phenomena associated with them, such as eclipses. For each body in turn Ptolemy describes the type of phenomena that have to be accounted for, proposes an appropriate geometric model, derives the numerical parameters from selected observations, and finally constructs tables enabling one to determine the motion or phenomenon in question for a given date.

In order to appreciate Ptolemy's achievement in the *Almagest*, we ought to know how far Greek astronomy had advanced before his time. Unfortunately the most significant works of his predecessors have not survived, and the earlier history has to be reconstructed almost entirely from secondary sources (chiefly the *Almagest* itself). Much remains uncertain, and the following sketch of that history is merely provisional.

The first serious attempt by a Greek to describe the motions of the heavenly bodies by a mathematical model was the system of "homocentric spheres" of Eudoxus (early fourth century B.C.). Although mathematically ingenious, this model was ill-suited to represent even the crude data on which it was based; and the approach proved abortive (it would have vanished from history had it not been adopted by Aristotle).[13] Equally insignificant for the development of astronomy were works on "spherics" that treat phenomena such as the risings and settings of stars in terms of spherical geometry (these appear from the fourth century B.C. on). The heliocentric theory of Aristarchus of Samos (early third century B.C.), perhaps developing ideas of Heraclides Ponticus (*ca.* 360 B.C.), was purely descriptive and also without consequence. After Eudoxus, however, the epicyclic and eccentric models of planetary motion were developed; and the equivalence of the two was proved by Apollonius of Perga (*ca.* 200 B.C.), if not earlier. Apollonius made an elegant application of these models to the problem of determining the stationary points of a planet.[14]

Meanwhile astronomical observations were being made in the Greek world from the late fifth century B.C. The earliest were mostly of the dates of solstices, but by the early third century Aristyllus and Timocharis in Alexandria were attempting to determine the positions of fixed stars and observing occultations. These observations, however, were few and unsystematic; no firmly based theory was possible until records of the observers in Babylon and other places in Mesopotamia, reaching back to the eighth century, became available to Greeks. It seems likely that period relations derived by the Babylonian astronomers from these observations were known as early as Eudoxus, but the first Greek who certainly used the observations themselves was Hipparchus; and it is no accident that Greek astronomy was established as a quantitative science with his work. Hipparchus (active from *ca.* 150 to 127 B.C.) used Babylonian eclipse records and his own systematic observations to construct an epicyclic theory of the sun and moon that produced reasonably accurate predictions of their positions. Hence he was able to predict eclipses. He measured the lunar parallax and evolved the first practical method for determining the distances of sun and moon. By comparing his own observations of the position of the star Spica with those of Timocharis 160 years earlier,

he discovered the precession of the equinoxes. He employed plane trigonometry and stereographic projection. In the latter techniques and in the observational instruments he used he may have been a pioneer, but we know too little of his predecessors to be sure. Ptolemy expressly informs us that Hipparchus did not construct a theory of the five planets but contented himself with showing that existing theories did not satisfy the observations.[15] Between Hipparchus and Ptolemy the only advance was the work of Menelaus (*ca.* A.D. 100) on spherical trigonometry.

Greek astronomy, then, as Ptolemy found it, had evolved a geometric kinematic model of solar and lunar motion that successfully represented the phenomena, at least as far as the calculation of eclipses was concerned, but had produced only unsatisfactory planetary models. It had developed both plane and spherical trigonometry and had adopted the Babylonian sexagesimal place-value system not only for the expression of angles but also (although not systematically) for calculation. As a mathematical science it was already sophisticated. From the point of view of physics it was not a science at all: such physical theories as were enunciated were mere speculation. But there was available a fairly large body of astronomical observations, of which the most important, both for completeness and for the length of time it covered, was the series of eclipses observed in Mesopotamia. Ptolemy made no radical changes in the system he took over; but by intelligent use of available observations and ingenious modification of the basic principle of all existing kinematic models (uniform circular motion), he extended that system to include the five planets and significantly improved the lunar model.

Books I and II of the *Almagest* are devoted to preliminaries. Ptolemy begins by stating and attempting to justify his overall world picture, which is that generally (although not universally) accepted from Aristotle on: around a central, stationary, spherical earth the sphere of the fixed stars (situated at a distance so great that the earth's diameter is negligible in comparison) revolves from east to west, making one revolution per day and carrying with it the spheres of sun, moon, and planets; the latter have another, slower motion in the opposite sense, in or near a plane (the ecliptic) inclined to the plane of the first motion. He then develops the trigonometry that will be used throughout the work. The basic function is the chord (which we denote Crd) subtended by the angle at the center of a circle of radius 60. This is related to the modern sine function by

$$\sin \alpha = \frac{1}{2 \cdot 60} \operatorname{Crd} 2\alpha.$$

The values of some chords (for instance, Crd 60°) are immediately obtainable by elementary geometry. By geometrically developing formulas for Crd $(\alpha + \beta)$, Crd $(\alpha - \beta)$, Crd $\frac{1}{2}\alpha$, where Crd α and Crd β are known, and then finding Crd 1° by an approximation procedure, Ptolemy produces a table of chords, at intervals of 1/2° and to three sexagesimal places, which serves for all trigonometric calculations. There was probably nothing new in his procedure (Hipparchus had constructed a similar table).[16]

Since the sine function is sufficient for the solution of all plane triangles, the chord function too was sufficient, although the lack of anything corresponding to a tangent table often made the solution laborious, involving the extraction of square roots. For trigonometry on the surface of the sphere Ptolemy uses a figure that we call a Menelaus configuration. It is depicted in Figure 1, where all the arcs *AB*, *BE*, and

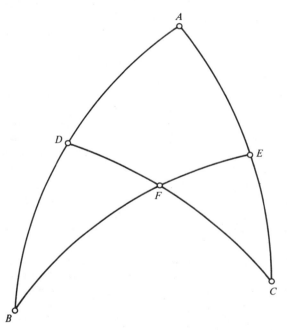

FIGURE 1

so on are segments of a great circle less than 90°. Ptolemy proves (following Menelaus) that

$$(1) \qquad \frac{\text{Crd } 2EC}{\text{Crd } 2EA} = \frac{\text{Crd } 2CF}{\text{Crd } 2FD} \cdot \frac{\text{Crd } 2DB}{\text{Crd } 2BA},$$

$$(2) \qquad \frac{\text{Crd } 2AC}{\text{Crd } 2AE} = \frac{\text{Crd } 2CD}{\text{Crd } 2DF} \cdot \frac{\text{Crd } 2FB}{\text{Crd } 2BE}.$$

It can be shown that the four basic formulas used in modern trigonometry for the solution of right spherical triangles are directly derivable from (1) and (2). Hence all problems soluble by means of the former

can also be solved by the use of Menelaus configurations. Thus Ptolemaic trigonometry, although sometimes cumbersome, is completely adequate.

This trigonometry is applied in books I and II to various phenomena connected with the annual variation in solar declination. The sole numerical parameter used is the inclination of the ecliptic (ϵ). This is also the amount of the greatest declination of the sun from the equator, and that is the basis of the two simple instruments for measuring ϵ which Ptolemy describes (I, 12). He reports that he measured 2ϵ as between 47; 40° and 47; 45°. Since the estimation of Eratosthenes and Hipparchus, that 2ϵ is 11/83 of a circle, also falls between these limits, Ptolemy too adopts the latter, taking ϵ as 23; 51, 20°. His failure to find a more accurate result, and hence to discover the slow decrease in the inclination, is explained by the crudity of his instruments. He can now construct a table of the declination of the sun as a function of its longitude, which is a prerequisite for solving problems concerning rising times. The rising time of an arc of the ecliptic is the time taken by that arc to cross the horizon at a given terrestrial latitude. Most of book II is devoted to calculating tables of rising times for various latitudes. Such tables are useful astronomically, for instance, for computing the length of daylight for a given date and latitude (important in ancient astronomy, since the time of day or night was reckoned in "civil hours," one civil hour being 1/12 of the varying length of day or night); but the space devoted to the topic is disproportionate to its use in the *Almagest*. It is essential in astrology, however (for example, in casting horoscopes); and this is one of the places where astrological requirements may have influenced the *Almagest* discussion (although they are never explicitly mentioned).

Book III treats the solar theory. By comparing his own observations of the dates of equinoxes with those of Hipparchus, and his observation of a solstice with one made by Meton and Euctemon in 432 B.C., Ptolemy confirms Hipparchus' estimate of the length of the tropical year as 365 1/4 − 1/300 days. This estimate is notoriously too long (the last fraction should be about 1/128), and the error was to have multiple consequences for Ptolemaic astronomy. It is derivable from the data only because Ptolemy made an error of about one day in the time of each of his observations. This is a gross error even by ancient standards and is the strongest ground of those modern commentators (such as Delambre) who maintain that Ptolemy slavishly copied Hipparchus, to the point of forging observations to obtain agreement with Hipparchus' results. The conclusion is implausible, but it is likely that in this case Ptolemy was influenced by his knowledge of Hipparchus' value to select such of his own observations as best agreed with it. For Hipparchus' solar and lunar theory represented the known facts (that is, eclipse records) very well, and Ptolemy would be reluctant to tamper with those elements of it that would seriously affect the circumstances of eclipses. Using the above year length, Ptolemy constructs a table of the mean motion of the sun that is the pattern for all other mean motion tables: the basis is the Egyptian calendar, in which the year has an unvarying length of 365 days (twelve thirty-day months plus five epagomenal days). The motion is tabulated to six sexagesimal places, for hours, days, months, years, and eighteen-year periods.

The main problem in dealing with all planets is to account for their "anomaly" (variation in velocity). In the case of the sun this variation is apparent from the fact that the seasons are of unequal length—for instance, in Ptolemy's day the time from spring equinox to summer solstice was longer than that from summer solstice to autumn equinox. Ptolemy proposes a general model for representing anomalistic motion. The "eccentric" version is depicted in Figure 2, where

fastest at its least distance, the perigee Z. The angle κ which P has traveled from the apogee is derivable from its mean motion $\bar{\kappa}$ by the formula

$$\kappa = \bar{\kappa} \pm \delta.$$

δ is called by Ptolemy the $\pi\rho\sigma\theta\alpha\varphi\alpha\acute{\iota}\rho\epsilon\sigma\iota\varsigma$ and by us, following medieval usage, the "equation." The same motion can also be represented by an epicyclic model. In Figure 3 an epicycle, center C, moves with uniform

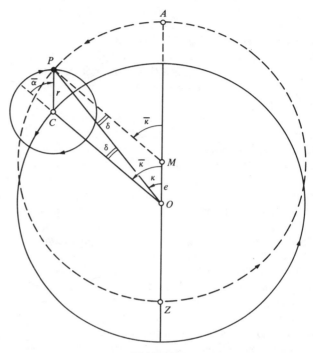

FIGURE 3

angular velocity on the circle (known as the deferent) about O, while the body P moves uniformly about C in the opposite sense. Provided that the angular velocities of body and epicycle are equal and the radius of the epicycle equals the eccentricity, the two models are completely equivalent, as can be seen from Figure 3, where $\bar{\alpha} = \bar{\kappa}$ and $r = e$. Such is the case of Ptolemy's solar model. But the angular velocity of P may be different from that of C, as in the lunar theory (this is equivalent to a rotation of the apogee in the eccentric model); or the rotation of P may be in the same sense as C, as in Ptolemy's planetary theory. The general model is, therefore, extremely versatile.

From his observations of solstices and equinoxes Ptolemy found the same length of seasons as Hipparchus. He therefore concluded that the apogee of the sun is tropically fixed and that its motion can be represented by the simple eccentric of Figure 2. He determined its parameters, as Hipparchus had, from the observed length of the seasons. In Figure 4

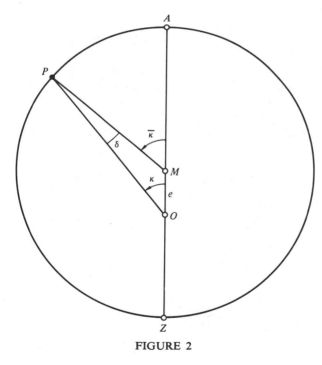

FIGURE 2

O represents the central earth. The body P moves with uniform angular velocity on a circle whose center M is distant from O by an amount e (the eccentricity). It is clear that if the motion of P appears uniform from M, it will appear nonuniform from O, being slowest at its greatest distance, the apogee A, and the sun is in T at spring equinox, in X at summer solstice, and in Y at autumn equinox. Ptolemy states that it moves from T to X in 94 1/2 days and from X to Y in 92 1/2 days. Thus the angles at M (the center of uniform motion), TMX and XMY, can be calculated from the mean motion of the sun; and the angles at O, the earth, are right. Hence one can determine the eccentricity OM and the longitude of the apogee, $<TOA$. Since Ptolemy uses the same data and method as Hipparchus, he gets the same results: an eccentricity of 2;30 (where R, the standard radius, is 60) and an apogee longitude of 65;30°. In fact the eccentricity had decreased and the apogee longitude increased since Hipparchus' time, but this could not be detected through equinox and solstice observations made with crude ancient instruments.

Using the parameters determined, Ptolemy shows how the equation δ can be calculated trigonometrically for a given mean anomaly $\bar{\kappa}$ and sets up a table giving δ as a function of $\bar{\kappa}$. The only thing now lacking in order to calculate the position of the sun at any date is its mean position at some given date. From his equinox observation of A.D. 132 Ptolemy calculates its position at the date he has chosen as epoch, Thoth 1 (first day of the Egyptian year), year 1 of the Babylonian king Nabonassar (26 February 747 B.C.). To complete the solar theory he discusses the equation of time. Since the sun travels in a path inclined to the equator and with varying velocity, the interval between two successive meridian transits of the sun (the true solar day) will not be uniform but will vary slightly throughout the year. Since astronomical calculations employ uniform units

(that is, mean solar days), whereas local time, in an age when the sundial is the main chronometer, is reckoned according to the true solar day, one must be able to convert one to the other. This conversion is done by means of the equation of time, the calculation of which Ptolemy explains.

The lunar theory is the subject of books IV and V. According to Ptolemy one must distinguish three periods connected with the moon: the time in which it returns to the same longitude, the time in which it returns to the same velocity (period of anomaly), and the time in which it returns to the same latitude. In addition one must consider the synodic month, the time between successive conjunctions or oppositions of the sun and moon. He quotes a number of previous attempts to find a period containing an integer number of each of the above (such a period would, clearly, be an eclipse cycle); in particular, from Hipparchus:

(1) In 126,007 days, 1 hour, there occur 4,267 synodic months, 4,573 returns in anomaly, and 4,612 sidereal revolutions less 7 1/2° (hence the length of a mean synodic month is 29; 31, 50, 8, 20 days).
(2) In 5,458 synodic months there occur 5,923 returns in latitude.

Ptolemy says that Hipparchus established these "from Babylonian and his own observations." We now know from cuneiform documents that these parameters and period relations had all been established by Babylonian astronomers.[17] At best Hipparchus could have "confirmed" them from his own observations. Such confirmation could be carried out only by comparison of the circumstances of eclipses separated by a long

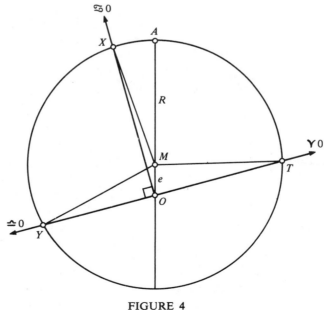

FIGURE 4

interval. Ptolemy gives an acute analysis of the conditions that must then obtain in order for one to detect an exact period of return in anomaly. On the basis of his own comparison of eclipses he accepts the above relations, with very slight modifications to the parameters for returns in anomaly and latitude (justified later). Thus he is able to construct tables of the lunar mean motion in longitude, anomaly, argument of latitude (motion with respect to the nodes in which the orbit of the moon intersects the ecliptic), and elongation (motion with respect to the mean sun).

The next task is to determine the numerical parameters of the lunar model. Ptolemy first assumes (although he knows better) that the moon has a single anomaly, that is, that its motion can be represented by a simple epicycle model (or eccenter with rotating apogee); this was the system of Hipparchus. To determine the size of the epicycle he adopts a method invented by Hipparchus. He takes a set of three lunar eclipses: the time of the middle of each eclipse can be calculated from the observed circumstances. Hence the true longitude of the moon at eclipse middle is known, since it is exactly 180° different from the true longitude of the sun (calculated from the solar theory). Furthermore, the time intervals between the three eclipses are known; hence one can calculate the travel in mean longitude and mean anomaly between the three points. Thus one has the situation of Figure 5: P_1, P_2, P_3 represent the positions of the moon on the epicycle at the three eclipses. The angles δ_1, δ_2 (the equational differences as seen from the earth O) are found by comparing

the intervals in true longitude with the intervals in mean longitude; the angles θ_1, θ_2 are found by taking the travel in mean anomaly modulo 360°. From these one can calculate trigonometrically the size of the epicycle radius r in terms of the deferent radius $R = OC$, and the angle ACP_1 (which gives an epoch value for the anomaly). Ptolemy makes calculations for two sets of eclipses—the first early Babylonian, the second observed by himself—and gets almost identical results. He finally adopts the value $r = 5; 15$, and on this basis he constructs an equation table. Although he borrowed the above procedure from Hipparchus, Ptolemy's result seems to be a distinct improvement on his predecessor's. He tells us that through small slips in calculating intervals Hipparchus found two discrepant results from two eclipse triples—namely, 327 2/3 : 3144 and 247 1/2 : 3122 1/2. Independent evidence shows that Hipparchus adopted the latter eccentricity, although it is a good deal too small.[18]

In the preceding calculations the moon has been treated as if it lay in the plane of the ecliptic. In fact its orbit is inclined to that plane, but the angle of inclination is so small that one is justified in neglecting it in longitude calculations. Accurate knowledge of the latitude is, however, essential for eclipse calculations. The inclination of 5° which Ptolemy accepts was probably an established value. But his procedure for finding the epoch value and mean motion in argument of latitude from two carefully selected eclipses is both original and a great improvement over Hipparchus' method, which involved estimating the apparent diameter of the moon and of the shadow

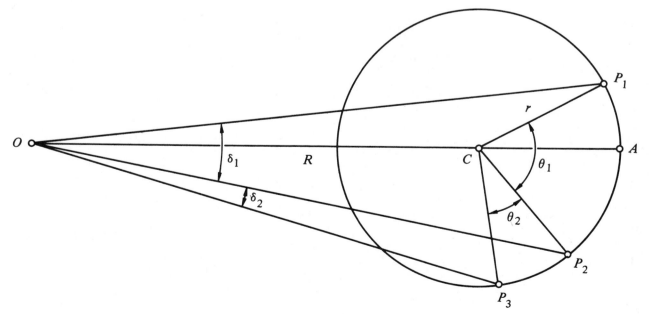

FIGURE 5

of the earth at eclipse, both of which are difficult to measure accurately.

The simple lunar model of book IV is essentially that of Hipparchus. When Ptolemy compared observed positions of the moon with those calculated from the model, he found good agreement at conjunction and opposition (when elongation of the moon from the sun is 0° or 180°); this agreement was to be expected, since the model was derived from eclipse observations. But he found serious discrepancies at intermediate elongations. Hipparchus had already mentioned such discrepancies but failed to account for them. In book V Ptolemy develops his own lunar theory. Analyzing his observations, he finds that they seem to indicate an increase in the size of the epicycle between opposition and conjunction that reaches a maximum at quadrature (90° elongation). This increase he represents by incorporating in the model a "crank" mechanism that "pulls in" the epicycle as it approaches quadrature, thus making it appear larger. Compare Figures 6A and 6B, which depict the same situation according to the simple and refined models, respectively. In the latter the epicycle center C continues to move uniformly about the earth O, but it now moves on a circle the center of which is not O but M. M moves about O in the opposite sense to C, so that its elongation $\bar{\eta}$ from the mean sun is equal to that of C. Since $OM + MC$ of Figure 6B is equal to OC of Figure 6A, it is clear that the two models are identical when $\bar{\eta} = 0°$ or 180°, that is, at mean conjunction and opposition. At intermediate elongations, however, the refined model pulls the epicycle closer to 7;40° at quadrature, and hence e in Figure 6B is

to O, thus increasing the effect of the anomaly. This increase is greatest at quadrature ($\bar{\eta} = 90°$). From two observations of the moon near quadrature by himself and Hipparchus, Ptolemy finds that the maximum equation increases from about 5° at conjunction 10;19 (where $R = 60$). As a further refinement he shows that one can obtain better agreement with observation if one reckons the anomaly $\bar{\alpha}$ not from the true epicycle apogee A but from a mean apogee $\bar{A}$ opposite the point B (B in turn being opposite M on the small circle about O). Thus a third inequality is introduced, also varying with the elongation but reaching its maximum near the octants ($\bar{\eta} = 45°$ and 135°). Ptolemy can now construct a table to compute the position of the moon. In contrast with previous tables, the tabulated function depends on two variables ($\bar{\alpha}$ and $2\bar{\eta}$). Ptolemy's solution to tabulating such a function (which may have been his own invention) became standard: he computes the equation at extreme points (in this case at conjunction and quadrature) and introduces an interpolation function (here varying with $2\bar{\eta}$) to be used as a coefficient for intermediate positions.

Ptolemy's refined lunar model represents the longitudes of the moon excellently. It is a major improvement on Hipparchus' model, and yet it does not disturb it at the points where it was successful—namely, where eclipses occur. But one effect of the crank mechanism is to increase greatly the variation in the distance of the moon from the earth, so that its minimum distance is little more than half its maximum. If correct, this should be reflected by a similar variation in the apparent size of the moon, whereas the

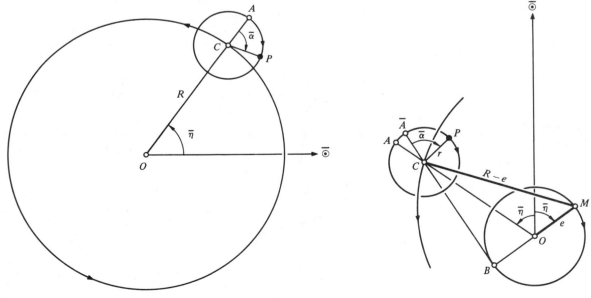

FIGURES 6A AND 6B

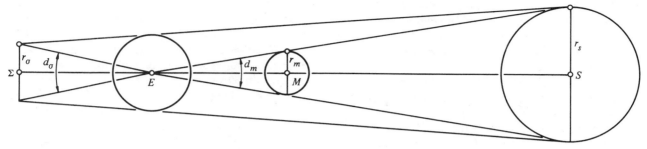

FIGURE 7

observable variation is much smaller. This objection seems not to have occurred to Ptolemy: he treats the crank mechanism not merely as a convenient device for predicting the longitude but also as a real feature of the model (for instance, in his parallax computations). Fortunately the apparent size of the moon is of consequence only at eclipses, when the crank mechanism has no effect.

Having established a complete theory of the motion of sun and moon, Ptolemy can proceed to eclipse theory. But first he must deal with parallax, the angular difference between the true and apparent positions of a body that stems from the fact that we observe it not from the center of the earth but from a point on the surface. In practice only the parallax of the moon is significant, but the misconceptions of the ancients about the distance of the sun led them to estimate solar parallax as well. By comparing a suitable observed position of the moon with its computed position, Ptolemy obtains a value for the parallax. Since this value is equivalent to the angle under which the radius of the earth is seen from the moon in that position, he can immediately calculate the distance of the moon in earth radii, first at that position and then (from his model) at mean distance. His final figure, fifty-nine earth radii, is close to the truth but is reached by a combination of multiple errors in his data and model, which, by pure chance, cancel each other.

Ptolemy knew that solar parallax is too small to measure directly; but he calculates the distance of the sun, and hence its parallax, by a method invented by Hipparchus. The data required are the apparent diameters of moon and sun at distances such that their apparent diameters are equal, that distance for the moon, and the apparent diameter of the shadow of the earth at that distance of the moon. Ptolemy assumes that moon and sun have exactly the same apparent diameter when the moon is at greatest distance (which implies that annular eclipses cannot occur); he determines the apparent diameter of moon and shadow from two pairs of lunar eclipses by an

ingenious method of his own (greatly improving on the figures which Hipparchus had obtained by direct measurement). Then, in Figure 7 he knows EM ($= E\Sigma$), the distance of the moon; d_m, the apparent diameter of moon and sun; and d_σ, the apparent diameter of the shadow. From these data it is simple to calculate r_m and r_s, the radii of moon and sun, and ES, the distance of the sun. His value for the latter is 1,210 earth radii, too small by a factor of twenty. In fact, the method requires much too accurate a measurement of the apparent diameter of the sun to produce a reliable solar distance, but it continued to be used up to and beyond Copernicus. Ptolemy now constructs a table of solar and lunar parallaxes and explains how to compute the parallax for a given situation. This computation is both laborious and mathematically unsatisfactory. Ptolemaic parallax theory is perhaps the most faulty part of the *Almagest*. But it was not significantly improved until the late sixteenth century.

Eclipse theory, the topic of book VI, is easily derived from what precedes. Ptolemy sets up a table for calculating mean syzygies (conjunctions and oppositions), with the corresponding lunar anomaly and argument of latitude. He then determines (from the apparent sizes of the bodies) the eclipse limits, that is, how far from the node the moon can be at mean syzygy for an eclipse still to take place. The eclipse tables proper give the size in digits and duration of eclipses as a function of the distance of the moon from the node. Ptolemy explains minutely how to compute the size, duration, and other circumstances of both lunar and solar eclipses for any given place. But his method does not allow one to compute the path of a solar eclipse (a development of the late seventeenth century).[19]

Books VII and VIII deal with the fixed stars. The order of treatment is a logical one, since it is necessary to establish the coordinates of ecliptic stars to observe planetary positions. Ptolemy compares his own observations with those of Hipparchus and earlier Greeks to show that the relative positions of the fixed stars have not changed and that the sphere of the fixed stars moves about the pole of the ecliptic from east to west 1° in 100 years with respect to the tropical points. He ascribes the discovery of the latter motion (the precession of the equinoxes) to Hipparchus, who had estimated it as *not less than* 1° in 100 years. This figure is too low (1° in seventy years would be more accurate); the error is mostly due to Ptolemy's wrong figure for the mean motion of the sun.[20] The bulk of these two books is composed of the "Star Catalog," a list of 1,022 stars, arranged under forty-eight constellations, with the longitude, latitude, and magnitude (from 1 to 6) of each. To compile this entirely from personal observation would be a gigantic task, and Ptolemy has often been denied the credit. Delambre, for instance, maintained that Ptolemy merely added 2;40° to the longitudes of "Hipparchus' catalog."[21] This particular hypothesis has been disproved.[22] In fact, the evidence suggests that no star catalog in this form had been composed by Hipparchus or anyone else before Ptolemy (the quotations from Hipparchus in *Almagest* VII, 1, show that Ptolemy had before him not a catalog but a description of the constellations with some numerical data concerning distances between stars). Modern computations have revealed numerous errors in Ptolemy's coordinates.[23] In general, the longitudes tend to be too small. This too is explained by the error in his solar mean motion, which is embedded in the lunar theory: the moon was used to fix the position of principal stars (the only practical method for an ancient astronomer).[24] Book VIII ends with a discussion of certain traditional Greek astronomical problems, such as the heliacal risings and settings of stars.

The last five books are devoted to planetary theory. Here, in contrast with the moon and sun, Ptolemy had no solid theoretical foundation to build upon and much less in the way of a body of observations. The most striking phenomenon of planetary motion is the frequent occurrence of retrogradation, which had been explained at least as early as Apollonius by a simple epicyclic model (see Figure 3) in which the sense of rotation of planet and epicycle is the same. Such a model, however, would produce a retrogradation arc of unvarying length and occurring at regular intervals, whereas observation soon shows that both arc and time of retrogradation vary. No geometric model had been proposed that would satisfactorily account for this phenomenon. Certain planetary periods, however, were well established, and so was the law for outer planets that

$$Y = L + A,$$

where (in integer numbers) Y stands for years, L for returns to the same longitude, and A for returns in anomaly (Venus and Mercury have the same period of return in longitude as the sun, hence for them $Y = L$). Ptolemy quotes from Hipparchus such a period relation for each planet—for instance, for Saturn: "In 59 years occur 57 returns in anomaly and 2 returns in longitude." We now know that all the period relations quoted are in fact Babylonian in origin. From these Ptolemy constructs tables of mean motion in longitude and anomaly, first applying small corrections; it turns out, however, that the latter are in part based on the models he is going to develop, so he must have used the uncorrected period relations in the original development.

Analysis of observations revealed that each planet has two anomalies; the first varying according to the planet's elongation from the sun and a second varying according to its position in the ecliptic. Ptolemy isolated the first by comparing different planet-sun configurations in the same part of the ecliptic and the second by comparing the same planet-sun configurations in different parts of the ecliptic. He thus found that the first could be represented by an epicycle model in which the sense of rotation of planet and epicycle are the same, while the second was best represented by an eccenter (to avoid a double epicycle). The model he finally evolved is depicted in Figure 8. The planet P moves on an

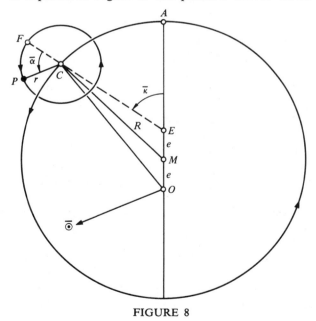

FIGURE 8

epicycle, center C. C moves in the same sense on a circle the center of which, M, is distant from the earth O by the eccentricity e. The uniform motion of C, however, takes place not about M but about another point E on the opposite side of M from O

and distant from M by the same amount e. The mean motion in anomaly is counted from a point F on the epicycle opposite to E. Figure 8 depicts the situation for an outer planet, in which the line CP always remains parallel to the line from O to the mean sun (thus preserving the law $Y = L + A$). Except for this feature the model for Venus is identical. The Mercury model has an additional mechanism to produce a varying eccentricity but is otherwise the same as that for Venus.

The most original element in this model is the introduction of the point E (known as the equant from medieval times). This element disturbed later theoreticians (including Copernicus), since it violated the philosophical principle that uniform motion should take place about the center of the circle of revolution. But it enabled Ptolemy to construct the first satisfactory planetary model. In heliocentric theory a Ptolemaic equant model with eccentricity e produces planetary longitudes differing from those of a Kepler ellipse with the same eccentricity by less than $10'$ (even for the comparatively large eccentricity of Mars).[25] Ptolemy deduces the existence of the eccenter directly from observations only in the case of Venus. For the other planets he merely assumes it and regards this as justified by the resulting agreement between observed and computed positions.

The determination of the parameters of the model for the individual planets, which occupies most of books IX–XI, reveals Ptolemy's brilliance. In his mastery of the choice and analysis of observations in conjunction with theory he has no peer until Kepler. For Venus and Mercury the problem is comparatively simple: the center of their epicycles coincides with the mean sun, and so one "sees" the epicycle by observing maximum elongations. The position of the apsidal line ($OMEA$ in Figure 8) can be determined by observing symmetrical positions of the epicycle, and then it is simple to calculate the size of epicycle and eccentricity. For the outer planets such "direct observation" of the epicycle is not possible. So Ptolemy eliminates the effect of the epicycle by choosing three observed oppositions; this choice gives him three positions of C as seen from O. The problem of finding the eccentricity and apogee then resembles the problem of finding the size of the epicycle of the moon in book IV, but it is complicated by the existence of the equant. Ptolemy meets this complication with an ingenious iterative process: he first assumes that the equant coincides with the center of the eccentric; this produces an approximative apsidal line and eccentricity, which are used to compute corrections to the initial data; then the whole process is repeated as many times as is necessary for the results to converge. Such a procedure

is alien to classical Greek mathematics, although not unique in the *Almagest*.

Book XII is devoted to establishing tables for computing the arcs and times of retrogradation and (for Venus and Mercury) the greatest elongation. In connection with the former, a theorem of Apollonius on stationary points is adapted to fit Ptolemy's refined planetary model. In book XIII he deals with planetary latitudes. All five planets have orbits slightly inclined to the ecliptic. From a heliocentric point of view the situation is simple, but a geocentric theory encounters considerable difficulties. The simplest approximation in Ptolemaic terms would be as follows: For an outer planet set the plane of the deferent at an inclination to the ecliptic equal to that of the heliocentric orbit of the planet, and keep the plane of the epicycle parallel to the ecliptic; for an inner planet keep the plane of the deferent in the ecliptic, and set the inclination of the epicycle to the deferent equal to the inclination of the heliocentric orbit of the planet. Ptolemy eventually reaches that solution in the *Planetary Hypotheses* (except that the deferents of Venus and Mercury are inclined to the ecliptic at a very small angle); but in the *Almagest*, misled by faulty observations and the eccentricity of the orbit of the earth, he devises a much more complicated theory in which the epicycles of outer planets and both epicycles and deferents of inner planets undergo varying inclinations as the epicycle moves round the deferent. The resultant tables do, however, represent the actual changes in latitude fairly well and are no mean achievement. The work ends with a discussion of the traditional problem of the heliacal risings and settings of the planets.

As a didactic work the *Almagest* is a masterpiece of clarity and method, superior to any ancient scientific textbook and with few peers from any period. But it is much more than that. Far from being a mere "systematization" of earlier Greek astronomy, as it is sometimes described, it is in many respects an original work. Without minimizing Ptolemy's debt to Hipparchus (which Ptolemy himself admiringly acknowledges), we may say confidently that Hipparchus' pioneering work would have had very little effect had it not found its completion in the *Almagest*. The Ptolemaic system is indeed named after the right man.

The *Almagest* contains all the tables necessary for astronomical computations, but they are scattered throughout the work. At a later date Ptolemy published the tables separately, together with an introduction explaining their use, under the title Πρόχειροι κανόνες (*Handy Tables*). The tables themselves are extant only in the revised version of Theon of Alexandria (*fl.* 360), but from Ptolemy's introduction it is clear that Theon changed nothing essential. Ptolemy himself is responsible for the numerous differences from the *Almagest*. There are additions (such as a table of the longitudes and latitudes of principal cities, to enable one to convert from the meridian and latitude of Alexandria), changes in layout to facilitate computation, and even occasional improvements in basic parameters. The epoch is changed from era Nabonassar to era Philip (Thoth 1 = 12 November 324 B.C.). The tables became the standard manual in the ancient and Byzantine worlds, and their form persisted beyond the Middle Ages.

Later still Ptolemy published a "popular" résumé of the results of the *Almagest* under the title Ὑποθέσεις τῶν πλανωμένων (*Planetary Hypotheses*), in two books. Only the first part of book I survives in Greek, but the whole work is available in Arabic translation. It goes beyond the *Almagest* in several respects. First, it introduces changes in some parameters and even in the models, notably in the theory of planetary latitude already mentioned. Second, in accordance with Ptolemy's declaration in the introduction that one purpose of the work is to help those who aim to represent the heavenly motions mechanically (that is, with a planetarium), the models are made "physical," whereas in the *Almagest* they had been purely geometric. Ptolemy describes these physical models in detail in book II (most of book I is devoted to listing the numerical parameters). He argues that instead of assigning a whole sphere to each planet, it is sufficient to suppose that the mechanism is contained in a segment of a sphere consisting of a drum-shaped band extending either side of its equator. The most portentous innovation, however, is the system proposed at the end of book I for determining the absolute distances of the planets.

In the *Almagest* Ptolemy had adopted the (traditional) ascending order: moon, Mercury, Venus, sun, Mars, Jupiter, Saturn; but he admitted that this order was arbitrary as far as the planets are concerned, since they have no discernible parallax.[26] This order has no consequences, since the parameters of each planet are determined independently in terms of a conventional deferent radius of 60. In the *Planetary Hypotheses* Ptolemy proposes a system whereby the greatest distance from the earth attained by each body is exactly equal to the least distance attained by the body next in order outward (that is, the planetary spheres are touching, and there is no space wasted in the universe; this system conforms to Aristotelian thinking). He takes the distance of the moon in earth radii derived in *Almagest* V: its greatest distance is equal to the least distance of Mercury (if one assumes the above order of the planets). Using the previously determined parameters of the model

for Mercury, he now computes the greatest distance of Mercury, which is equal to the least distance of Venus, and so on. By an extraordinary coincidence the greatest distance of Venus derived by this procedure comes out very close to the least distance of the sun derived by an independent procedure in *Almagest* V. Ptolemy takes this finding as a striking proof of the correctness of his system (and incidentally of the assumption that Mercury and Venus lie below the sun). He goes on to compute the exact distances of all the bodies right out to the sphere of the fixed stars in earth radii and stades (assuming the circumference of the earth to be 180,000 stades). Furthermore, taking some "observations" by Hipparchus of the apparent diameters of planets and first-magnitude stars, he computes their true diameters and volumes. This method of determining the exact dimensions of the universe became one of the most popular features of the Ptolemaic system in later times.

A work in two books named *Phases of the Fixed Stars* (Φάσεις ἀπλανῶν ἀστέρων) dealt in detail with a topic not fully elaborated in the *Almagest*, the heliacal risings and settings of bright stars. Only book II survives; and the greater part of this book consists of a "calendar," listing for every day of the year the heliacal risings and settings, as well as the weather prognostications associated with them by various authorities. Predicting the weather from the "phases" of well-known stars long predates scientific astronomy in Greece, and calendars like this were among the earliest astronomical publications (Ptolemy quotes from authorities as early as Meton and Euctemon). The chief value of the Φάσεις today is the information it contains on the history of this kind of literature.

Much greater scientific interest attaches to two small works applying mathematics to astronomical problems. The first is the *Analemma* (Περὶ ἀναλήμματος), surviving, apart from a few palimpsest fragments, only in William of Moerbeke's Latin translation from the Greek. It is an explanation of a method for finding angles used in the construction of sundials, involving projection onto the plane of the meridian and swinging other planes into that plane. The actual determination of the angles is achieved not by trigonometry (although Ptolemy shows how that is theoretically possible) but by an ingenious graphical technique which in modern terms would be classified as nomographic. Although the basic idea was not new (Ptolemy criticizes his predecessors, and a similar procedure is described by Vitruvius *ca.* 30 B.C.),[27] the sophisticated development is probably Ptolemy's. The other treatise is the *Planisphaerium* (the Greek title was probably Ἅπλωσις ἐπιφανείας σφαίρας).[28] This treatise survives only in Arabic translation; a revision of this translation was made by the Spanish Islamic astronomer Maslama al-Majrīṭī (d. 1007/1008) and was in turn translated into Latin by Hermann of Carinthia in 1143. It treats the problem of mapping circles on the celestial sphere onto a plane. Ptolemy projects them from the south celestial pole onto the plane of the equator. This projection is the mathematical basis of the plane astrolabe, the most popular of medieval astronomical instruments. Since the work explains how to use the mapping to calculate rising times, one of the main uses of the astrolabe, it is highly likely that the instrument itself goes back to Ptolemy (independent evidence suggests that it goes back to Hipparchus).[29] These two treatises are an important demonstration that Greek mathematics consisted of more than "classical" geometry.

To modern eyes it may seem strange that the same man who wrote a textbook of astronomy on strictly scientific principles should also compose a textbook of astrology ('Ἀποτελεσματικά, meaning "astrological influences," or Τετράβιβλος, from its four books). Ptolemy, however, regards the *Tetrabiblos* as the natural complement to the *Almagest*: as the latter enables one to predict the positions of the heavenly bodies, so the former expounds the theory of their influences on terrestrial things. The introductory chapters are devoted to a defense of astrology against charges that it cannot achieve what it claims and that even if it can, it is useless. Ptolemy regards the influence of heavenly bodies as purely physical. From the obvious terrestrial physical effects of the sun and moon, he infers that all heavenly bodies must produce physical effects (that such an argument could be seriously advanced reflects the poverty of ancient physical science). By careful observation of the terrestrial manifestations accompanying the various recurring combinations of celestial bodies, he believes it possible to erect a system which, although not mathematically certain, will enable one to make useful predictions. Ptolemy is not a fatalist: at least he regards the influence of the heavenly bodies as only one of the determinants of terrestrial events. But, plausible as this introduction might appear to an ancient philosopher, the rest of the treatise shows it to be a specious "scientific" justification for crude superstition. It is difficult to see how most of the astrological doctrines propounded could be explained "physically" even in ancient terms, and Ptolemy's occasional attempts to do so are ludicrous. Astrology was almost universally accepted in the Roman empire, and even superior intellects like Ptolemy and Galen could not escape its dominance.

Book I explains the technical concepts of astrology;

book II deals with influences on the earth in general ("astrological geography" and weather prediction), and books III and IV with influences on human life. Although dependent on earlier authorities, Ptolemy often develops his own dogma. The discussion in books III and IV is confined to what can be deduced from a man's horoscope: Ptolemy ignores altogether the branch of astrology known as catarchic, which answers questions about the outcome of events or the right time to do something by consulting the aspect of the heavens at the time of the question. This omission helps to explain why the *Tetrabiblos* never achieved an authority in its field comparable with that of the *Almagest* in astronomy.

The *Geography* (Γεωγραφικὴ ὑφήγησις), in eight books, is an attempt to map the known world. The bulk of it consists of lists of places with longitude and latitude, accompanied by very brief descriptions of the chief topographical features of the larger land areas. It was undoubtedly accompanied in Ptolemy's own publication by maps like those found in several of the manuscripts. But knowing how easily maps are corrupted in copying, Ptolemy takes pains to ensure that the reader will be able to reconstruct the maps on the basis of the text alone: he describes in book I how to draw a map of the inhabited world and lists longitudes and latitudes of principal cities and geographical features in books II–VII. Book VIII describes the breakdown of the world map into twenty-six individual maps of smaller areas. Ptolemy tells us that the *Geography* is based, for its factual content, on a similar recent work by Marinus of Tyre. But it seems to have improved on Marinus' work (for which the *Geography* is the sole source of our knowledge) in several ways. From I, 7–17 (in which various factual errors of Marinus are corrected), it appears that the bulk of Marinus' text was topographical description (giving, for instance, distances and directions between places), and that this was supplemented by lists of places with the same longest daylight and of places the same distance (in hours) from some standard meridian (book VIII of the *Geography*, which looks as if it is a remnant of an earlier version, uses a system similar to the latter). Ptolemy was probably the first to employ systematically listings by latitude and longitude. Here, as always, he shows a sound sense of what would be of most practical use to the reader.

Ptolemy also criticizes Marinus' map projection, a system of rectangular coordinates in which the ratio of the unit of longitude to that of latitude was 4:5. Ptolemy objects that this system distorts distances except near the latitude of Rhodes (36°). While accepting such a system for maps covering a small

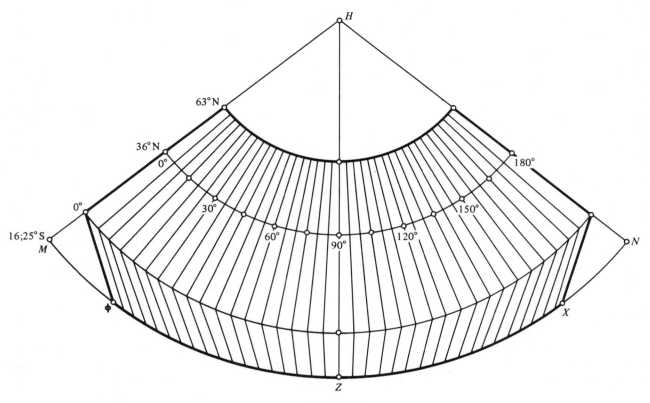

FIGURE 9

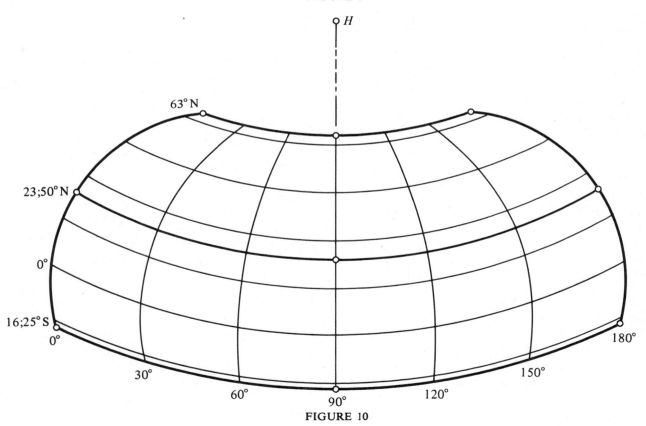

FIGURE 10

area, for the world map he proposes two alternative projection systems (I, 21–24). The known world, according to Ptolemy, covers 180° in longitude from his zero meridian (the Blessed Isles) and in latitude stretches from 16;25° south to 63° north. In his first projection (see Figure 9) the meridians are mapped as radii meeting in a point H (*not* the north pole), the parallels of latitude as circular arcs with H as center. Distances are preserved along the meridians and along the parallel of Rhodes, and the ratio of distances along the parallel of 63° to those along the parallel of the equator is preserved. These conditions completely determine the projection. Ptolemy modifies it south of the equator by dividing the parallel MZN as if it lay at 16;25° *north*, thus avoiding distortion at the expense of mathematical consistency. The second projection aims to achieve more of the appearance of a globe (see Figure 10). The parallels of latitude are again constructed as circular arcs, but now distances are preserved along three parallels: 63° north, 23;50° north, and 16;25° south. The meridians are constructed by drawing circular arcs through the points on these three parallels representing the same angular distance from the central meridian, which is mapped as a straight line along which distances are preserved. The first projection is (except for the modification south of the equator) a true conic projection; the second is not, but for the segment covered by the map is a remarkably good approximation to the true conic projection that was later developed from it (the Bonne projection, which preserves distances along all parallels). Ptolemy took a giant step in the science of mapmaking, but he had no successor for nearly 1,400 years.

The factual content of the *Geography* naturally is inaccurate. Only the Roman empire was well known; and Ptolemy's idea of the outline of, for instance, southern Africa or India is grossly wrong. Even within the boundaries of the empire there are some serious distortions. This was inevitable: although the latitude of a place could be fixed fairly accurately by astronomical observation, very few such observations had been made. Ptolemy says (I, 4) that of his predecessors only Hipparchus had given the latitudes of a few cities. Longitudinal differences could be determined from simultaneous observations of an eclipse at two places, but again almost no such observations existed. Ptolemy seems to have known only one, the lunar eclipse of 20 September 331 B.C., observed at Arbela in Assyria and at Carthage. Unfortunately an error in the observation at Arbela led Ptolemy to assume a time difference of about three hours between the two places instead of about two; this error was probably a major factor in the most notorious distortion in his map, the excessive length of the Mediterranean. In the absence of anything resembling a modern survey, Ptolemy, like his predecessors, had to rely on "itineraries" derived from milestones along the main roads and the reports of merchants and soldiers. In view of the inaccuracies in lengths, and especially directions, inevitable in such works, the *Geography* is a remarkable factual as well as scientific achievement.

The *Optics*, in five books, is lost in Greek. An Arabic translation was made from a manuscript lacking book I and the end of book V; from this translation, which is also lost, Eugenius of Sicily produced the extant Latin translation in the twelfth century. Despite the incompleteness and frequent obscurity of the text, the outlines of Ptolemy's optical theory are clear enough. The lost book I dealt with the general theory of vision. Like most ancient theoreticians Ptolemy believed that vision takes place by means of a "visual flux" emanating from the eye in the form of a cone-shaped bundle of "visual rays," the apex of which lies within the eyeball; this flux produces sensations in the observer when it strikes colored objects. References back in the surviving books show that besides enunciating the above theory, Ptolemy demonstrated that vision is propagated in a straight line and determined the size of the visual field (both probably by experiments).

In book II he deals with the role of light and color in vision (he believes that the presence of light is a "necessary condition" and that color is an inherent quality of objects); with the perception of the position, size, shape, and movement of objects; and with various types of optical illusion.

Books III and IV treat the theory of reflection ("catoptrics," to use the ancient term). First, three laws are enunciated: (1) the image appears at some point along the (infinite) line joining the eye to the point of reflection on the mirror. (2) The image appears on the perpendicular from the object to the surface of the mirror. (3) Visual rays are reflected at equal angles. The laws are then demonstrated experimentally. There follows a remarkable discussion on the propriety of assimilating binocular to monocular vision in geometric proofs. Ptolemy incidentally determines the relationships between the images seen by the left and right eyes and the composite image seen by both, using an ingenious experimental apparatus with lines of different colors. He then develops from the three laws a series of theorems on the location, size, and appearance of images, first for plane mirrors, then for spherical convex mirrors, then (in book IV) for spherical concave mirrors and various types of "composite" (such as cylindrical) mirrors.

Book V deals with refraction. The phenomenon is demonstrated by the experiment (at least as old as Archimedes) of the coin in the vessel that appears when water is poured in. There follows a very interesting experiment to determine the magnitude of refraction from air to glass, from water to glass, and from air to water. Ptolemy does this experiment by means of a disk with a graduated circumference. For each pair of media he tabulates the angles of refraction corresponding to angles of incidence of 10°, 20°, $\cdots$, 80°. The results cannot be raw observations, since the second differences are constant in all cases; but they are remarkably close to what one can derive from Snell's law $\dfrac{\sin i}{\sin \rho} = $ const., with a suitable index of refraction. The rest of the surviving part of the book is devoted to discussion of astronomical refraction, the relationship between the amount of refraction and the density of the media, and the appearance of refracted images.

It is difficult to evaluate Ptolemy's achievement in the *Optics* because so little remains of his predecessors' work. In "pure optics" we have only the work of Euclid (*ca.* 300 B.C.), consisting of some elementary geometrical theorems derived from a few postulates that are a crude simplification of the facts of vision. In catoptrics we have a corrupted Latin version of the work of Hero (*ca.* A.D. 60) and a treatise compiled in late antiquity from authors of various dates, falsely attributed to Euclid. From these we get only an occasional glimpse of Archimedes' catoptrics, which was probably highly original, particularly in its use of experiment. The establishment of theory by experiment, frequently by constructing special apparatus, is the most striking feature of Ptolemy's *Optics*. Whether the subject matter is largely derived or original, the *Optics* is an impressive example of the development of a mathematical science with due regard to the physical data, and is worthy of the author of the *Almagest*.

A work on music theory (Ἁρμονικά), in three books, deals with the mathematical intervals (on a stretched string) between notes and their classification according to various traditional Greek systems. It seeks a middle ground between the two schools of the Pythagoreans and the followers of Aristoxenus, of whom the former, according to Ptolemy (I, 2), stressed mathematical theory at the expense of the ear's evidence, while the latter did the reverse. Again we see Ptolemy's anxiety to erect a theory that is mathematically satisfactory but also takes due account of the phenomena. According to the commentary of Porphyry (late third century), the *Harmonica* is mostly derivative, especially from the work of one Didymus

(first century).[30] We have no means of checking this statement.

Ptolemy's philosophical standpoint is Aristotelian, as is immediately clear from the preface to the *Almagest*. But it is clear from his astronomy alone that he does not regard Aristotle as holy writ; and influences from later philosophy, notably Stoicism, have been detected. An insignificant philosophical work entitled Περὶ κριτηρίου καὶ ἡγεμονικοῦ ("On the Faculties of Judgment and Command") goes under his name. There is nothing in its contents conflicting with Ptolemy's general philosophical position, but the style bears little resemblance to his other works; and the ascription, while generally accepted, seems dubious. Ptolemy's high reputation in later times caused a number of spurious works, mostly astrological, to be foisted on him. An example is the Καρπός (*Centiloquium*, in its Latin translation), a collection of 100 astrological aphorisms.

Ptolemy was active in almost every mathematical science practiced in antiquity, but several of his works are known to us only from references in ancient authors. These are a work on mechanics (Περὶ ῥοπῶν), in three books; a work in which he attempted to prove Euclid's parallel postulate; *On Dimension* (Περὶ διαστάσεως), in one book, in which he "proved" that there can be no more than three dimensions; and *On the Elements* (Περὶ τῶν στοιχείων).

In estimating Ptolemy's stature and achievement as a scientist, it is unfortunately still necessary to react against the general tendency of nineteenth-century scholarship to denigrate him as a mere compiler of the scientific work of his predecessors. This extreme view, exemplified in the writings of Delambre,[31] is no longer held by anyone competent but still persists in handbooks. It need not be refuted in detail. With a candor unusual in ancient authors Ptolemy freely acknowledges what parts of his theory he owes to Hipparchus. To say that he is lying when he claims other parts as his own work is a gratuitous slander, which, when it can be tested by independent evidence (which is rare), has proved false. It is certain that a great part of the theory in the *Almagest* is his personal contribution, and it is unlikely that the situation was radically different in all his other scientific work. On the other hand, his was not an original genius: his method was to take existing theory and to modify and extend it so as to get good agreement with observed facts. In this method, however, Ptolemy was no different from the vast majority of scientists of all periods; and he in no way deserves the reputation of a hack. His work is remarkable for its blend of knowledge, ingenuity, judgment, and clarity. The authority that it achieved in several fields is not surprising.

The *Almagest* was the dominant influence in theoretical astronomy until the end of the sixteenth century. In antiquity it became the standard textbook almost immediately. Commentaries to it were composed by Pappus (*fl.* 320) and Theon of Alexandria, but neither they nor any other Greek advanced the science beyond it. It was translated into Arabic about 800; and improved translations were made during the ninth century, notably in connection with the astronomical activity patronized by Caliph al-Ma'mūn. The Islamic astronomers soon recognized its superiority to what they had derived from Persian and Hindu sources; but since they practiced observation, they also recognized the deficiencies in its solar theory. An example of the influence of Ptolemy on Islamic astronomy and its improvements on his theory is the *Zij* of al-Battānī (*ca.* 880). The first part of this work is closely modeled on the *Almagest*, the second on the *Handy Tables* (also translated earlier). Al-Battānī greatly improves on Ptolemy's values for the obliquity of the ecliptic, the solar mean motion (and hence precession), the eccentricity of the sun, and the longitude of its apogee. He substitutes the sine function (derived from India) for the chord function. Otherwise his work is mostly a restatement of Ptolemy's. This is typical of Islamic astronomy: the solar theory was refined (so that even the proper motion of the apogee of the sun was enunciated by al-Zarqāl *ca.* 1080), but Ptolemy's lunar and planetary theories were accepted as they stood. Such attempts as were made to revise them were based not on observation but on philosophical objections, principally to the equant. Alternative systems, preserving uniform circular rotation, were devised by Naṣīr al-Dīn al-Ṭūsī (*fl.* 1250) and his followers at Maragha, and also by Ibn al-Shāṭir (*fl.* 1350). The latter's lunar model is in one sense a real improvement over Ptolemy's, since it avoids the exaggerated variation in the lunar distance. But the influence of these reformers was very small (except for a hypothetical transmission from Ibn ash-Shāṭir to Copernicus, who adopted almost identical models).

The *Almagest* became known in western Europe through Gerard of Cremona's Latin translation from the Arabic in 1175 (a version made in Sicily from the Greek *ca.* 1160 seems to have been little known). The arrival from Islamic sources of this and other works based on Ptolemy led to a rise in the level of Western astronomy in the thirteenth century, but until the late fifteenth serious attempts to make independent progress were sporadic and insignificant. The first major blow at the Ptolemaic system was Copernicus' *De revolutionibus* (1543). Yet even this work betrays in its form and in much of its content the overwhelming influence of the *Almagest*. However

great the cosmological implication of the change to a heliocentric system, Copernican astronomy is cast in a firm Ptolemaic mold. This influence was not broken until Tycho Brahe realized that the "reform of astronomy" must be based on systematic accurate observation. So he compiled the first star catalog since Ptolemy based entirely on independent observation (earlier star catalogs, such as the famous one of al-Ṣūfī, epoch 964, had been mostly repetitions of Ptolemy's with the addition of a constant of precession; star coordinates independent of Ptolemy, such as those in the list of the *Zij al-Mumtaḥan* compiled at the order of al-Ma'mūn, are very few in number); Brahe was also able to make the first real improvements in lunar theory since Ptolemy. Most important, he provided Kepler with the essential material for his treatise on Mars, justifiably entitled *Astronomia nova*. Kepler's work finally made the *Almagest* obsolete except as a source of ancient observations.

Ptolemy's system for establishing the exact distances and sizes of the heavenly bodies was also enthusiastically adopted in Islamic astronomy. One of the numerous adaptations of it found its way to the West in the twelfth-century Latin translation of the epitome of the *Almagest* by al-Farghānī (*fl.* 850). In this version it became part of the standard world picture of the later Middle Ages (for instance, in Dante's *Divina commedia*) and persisted into the sixteenth century, although its basis was removed by Copernicus.

The *Tetrabiblos* went through a process of transmission to the Islamic world and then to western Europe similar to that of the *Almagest* and also enjoyed an immense reputation in both, although never so unrivaled. The *Geography* was also translated into Arabic early in the ninth century. Its inadequacy for much of the territory subject to Islam was immediately obvious, and so it was soon replaced by revisions more accurate for those parts. The earliest is the *Kitāb Ṣūrat al-Arḍ* of al-Khwārizmī (*ca.* 820). The original Arabic translation of the *Geography* is lost, but its direct and indirect influence on Islamic geographical works is considerable. The *Geography* did not reach western Europe until the fifteenth century (in a Latin translation from the Greek by Jacobus Angelus, *ca.* 1406), when exploration was already making it obsolete. Nevertheless it became very popular, since it was still the best guide to much of the known world; most cartographic publications of the fifteenth and sixteenth centuries are based on it. Ptolemy's two map projections were an important stimulus to the development of cartography in the sixteenth century. The first is reflected in Mercator's map of Europe (1554), the second in various maps beginning with one by Bernardus Sylvanus in his 1511 edition of the *Geography*, which uses an equivalent of the Bonne projection.[32]

The *Optics* had little direct influence on western Europe. Eugenius' version was known to Roger Bacon and probably to Witelo in the later thirteenth century, but they are exceptions. It did however, inspire the great optical work of Ibn al-Haytham (*d.* 1039). The latter was an original scientist who made some notable advances (of which the most important was his correct explanation of the role of light in vision), but the form and much of the content of his *Kitāb al-Manāẓir* are taken from Ptolemy's work; and the inspiration for his remarkable experiments with light must surely also be attributed to Ptolemy. His treatise was translated into Latin and is the basis of the *Perspectiva* of Witelo (*ca.* 1270), which became the standard optical treatise of the later Middle Ages. The indirect influence of the *Optics* persisted until the early seventeenth century.

Ptolemy's treatise on musical theory never attained the authority of his other major works, since rival theories continued to flourish. But it was extensively used by Boethius, whose work was the main source of knowledge of the subject in the Latin West; and hence some of Ptolemy's musical doctrine was always known. When it became available to western Europe in Greek, it was no more than a historical curiosity. But it had a strange appeal for one great scientist. The last three chapters of book III of the *Harmonica* are missing; they dealt with the relationships between the planetary spheres and musical intervals. Kepler intended to publish a translation of book III, with a "restoration" of the last chapters and a comparison with his own kindred speculations, as an appendix to his *Harmonice mundi*. The appendix never appeared, but the whole work is a tribute to his predecessor.

NOTES

1. *Almagest* XI, 5; IX, 7 (Manitius, II, 228, 131).
2. Boll, "Studien," p. 53.
3. *Opera astronomica minora*, p. 155. An alternative MS reading is "the fifteenth year" (152/153).
4. Olympiodorus, . . . *In Platonis Phaedonem* . . ., Norwin ed., p. 59, l. 9.
5. Boll, *op. cit.*, pp. 54–55.
6. Buttmann, "Ueber den Ptolemäus in der Anthologie . . .," pp. 483 ff.
7. II, 13 (Manitius, I, 129).
8. I, 3 (Manitius, I, 9).
9. III, 59; Lejeune ed., p. 116.
10. V, 23–30; Lejeune ed., pp. 237–242.
11. E.g., X, 1 (Manitius, II, 156).
12. See Pappus, *Collectio*, VI, intro.; Hultsch ed., p. 474, with Hultsch's note *ad. loc.*
13. Aristotle, *Metaphysica*, Λ, 1073b17 ff.; Simplicius, *In Aristotelis De caelo*, Heiberg ed., pp. 491 ff.

14. *Almagest* XII, 1 (Manitius, II, 267 ff.).
15. *Almagest* IX, 2 (Manitius, II, 96–97).
16. Theon, *Commentary on the Almagest*, I, 10; Rome ed., p. 451. See Toomer, "The Chord Table . . .," pp. 6–16, 19–20.
17. Kugler, *Die Babylonische Mondrechnung*, pp. 4 ff.
18. See Toomer, "The Size of the Lunar Epicycle . . .," pp. 145 ff.
19. The first to compute and draw the path of an eclipse seems to have been Cassini I in 1664; see Lalande, *Astronomie*, II, 358.
20. Shown by A. Ricius, *De motu octavae sphaerae*, f. 39 (following Levi ben Gerson); see also Laplace, *Exposition*, p. 383.
21. Delambre, *Histoire de l'astronomie ancienne*, II, 250 ff.
22. By Vogt in "Versuch einer Wiederherstellung von Hipparchs Fixsternverzeichnis."
23. E.g., Peters and Knobel, *Ptolemy's Catalogue of Stars*, *passim*.
24. See *Almagest* VII, 4 (Manitius, II, 30).
25. See Caspar's intro. to his trans. of Kepler's *Neue Astronomie*, pp. 60*–61*.
26. IX, 1 (Manitius, II, 93–94).
27. Vitruvius, *De architectura* IX, 7.
28. Suidas, "Πτολεμαῖος ὁ Κλαύδιος"; Adler ed., IV, 254.
29. Synesius, *Opuscula*, Terzaghi ed., p. 138.
30. Porphyry, *Commentary on the Harmonica*; Düring ed., p. 5.
31. E.g., *Histoire de l'astronomie ancienne*, II, *passim*.
32. See Hopfner in Mžik, *Des Klaudios Ptolemaios Einführung*, p. 105.

BIBLIOGRAPHY

I. ORIGINAL WORKS. *Almagest*: The standard text is that of J. L. Heiberg, *Claudii Ptolemaei Opera quae exstant omnia*, I, *Syntaxis mathematica*, 2 pts. (Leipzig, 1898–1903). The only reliable trans. is the German one by K. Manitius: *Ptolemäus, Handbuch der Astronomie*, 2nd ed. (with corrections by O. Neugebauer), 2 vols. (Leipzig, 1963). For detailed discussion of the contents the best guide is still J. B. J. Delambre, *Histoire de l'astronomie ancienne*, II (Paris, 1817; repr. New York–London, 1965). Delambre's notes in the otherwise antiquated edition by N. Halma, *Composition mathématique de Claude Ptolémée*, 2 vols. (Paris, 1813–1816), are also useful. Pappus' lemmas to the Μικρὸς ἀστρονομούμενος are in Bk. VI (474–633) of his Συναγωγή, *Pappi Alexandrini Collectionis quae supersunt*, F. Hultsch, ed., 3 vols. (Berlin, 1875–1878; repr. Amsterdam, 1965). No satisfactory account exists of the early history of Greek astronomy; the best available is P. Tannery, *Recherches sur l'histoire de l'astronomie ancienne* (Paris, 1893). On the astronomical system of Eudoxus see G. V. Schiaparelli, "Le sfere omocentriche di Eudosso, di Calippo e di Aristotele," in *Memorie dell'Istituto lombardo di scienze e lettere*, Classe di Scienze Matematiche e Naturali, **13**, no. 4 (1877), repr. in his *Scritti sulla storia della astronomia antica*, II (Bologna, 1926), 5–112. The account by Simplicius is in his commentary on Aristotle's *De Caelo*, *Commentaria in Aristotelem Graeca*, J. L. Heiberg, ed., VII (Berlin, 1894), 491–510. Examples of early works on "spherics" are those by Autolycus (late fourth century B.C.), edited by J. Mogenet, *Autolycus de Pitane*, which is *Université de Louvain, Recueil de travaux* *d'histoire et de philologie*, 3rd ser., fasc. 37 (Louvain, 1950); and Menelaus' *Spherics* (available only in Arabic translation), M. Krause, ed., in *Abhandlungen der Akademie der Wissenschaften zu Göttingen*, Phil.-hist. Kl., 3rd ser., **17** (1936).

On the trigonometry of Ptolemy and Hipparchus see G. J. Toomer, "The Chord Table of Hipparchus and the Early History of Greek Trigonometry," in *Centaurus*, **18** (1973), 6–28. The cuneiform evidence for the Babylonian origin of Hipparchus' lunar periods is given in F. X. Kugler, *Die Babylonische Mondrechnung* (Freiburg im Breisgau, 1900), pp. 4–46. On the difference between the maximum lunar equations of Ptolemy and Hipparchus see G. J. Toomer, "The Size of the Lunar Epicycle According to Hipparchus," in *Centaurus*, **12** (1967), 145–150. On Hipparchus' determination of the lunar and solar distances see N. Swerdlow, "Hipparchus on the Distance of the Sun," in *Centaurus*, **14** (1969), 287–305. Information on the earliest mappings of the path of a solar eclipse is in Jérôme le Français (Lalande), *Astronomie*, 3rd ed., II (Paris, 1792), 357 ff. Augustinus Ricius gave the correct explanation of the error in Ptolemy's determination of the amount of precession in his *De motu octavae sphaerae*, 2nd ed. (Paris, 1521), f. 39. The same explanation was given independently by P. S. Laplace in his *Exposition du système du monde*, 4th ed. (Paris, 1813), p. 383.

A critical trans. of Ptolemy's star catalog containing detailed comparisons with modern computed positions was made by C. H. F. Peters and E. B. Knobel, *Ptolemy's Catalogue of Stars, a Revision of the Almagest* (Washington, D.C., 1915). This adopts Delambre's erroneous conclusion about Ptolemy's dependence on the (hypothetical) star catalog of Hipparchus, which was refuted by H. Vogt in "Versuch einer Wiederherstellung von Hipparchs Fixsternverzeichnis," in *Astronomische Nachrichten*, **224** (1925), 17–54. The star catalog of al-Ṣūfī was published by the Osmania Oriental Publications Bureau: Abu'l-Ḥusayn 'Abd al-Raḥmān al-Ṣūfī, *Ṣuwaruʾ l-Kawākib* (Hyderabad-Deccan, 1954). A French trans. was made by H. C. F. C. Schjellerup, *Description des étoiles fixes* (St. Petersburg, 1874). The star list of the *Zīj al-Mumtaḥan*, containing 24 items, was published in J. Vernet, "Las 'Tabulae probatae,' " in *Homenaje a Millás-Vallicrosa*, II (Barcelona, 1956), 519. For derivatives from this list see P. Kunitzsch, "Die arabische Herkunft von zwei Sternverzeichnissen," in *Zeitschrift der Deutschen morgenländischen Gesellschaft*, **120** (1970), 281–287.

A description of the Ptolemaic system is given by O. Neugebauer, *The Exact Sciences in Antiquity*, 2nd ed. (Providence, R.I., 1957), pp. 191–206. This should be consulted for such omissions from my account as the details of the Mercury model. Literature comparing Ptolemaic with modern theory will be found *ibid.*, pp. 182–183. A good mathematical presentation of Ptolemy's theory of celestial motion is given by N. Herz, *Geschichte der Bahnbestimmung von Planeten und Kometen*, I (Leipzig, 1887), 86–169. A mathematical comparison between the Kepler ellipse and a Ptolemaic equant model for Mars was made by M. Caspar in the intro. to his trans. of Kepler's

Astronomia nova: Johannes Kepler, *Neue Astronomie* (Munich–Berlin, 1929). For an analysis of the problem of determining the eccentricity from three observations in an equant model see G. W. Hill, "Ptolemy's Problem," in *Astronomical Journal*, **21** (1900), 33–35. An account of the astronomical instruments described by Ptolemy in the *Almagest*, and also of the astrolabe, is given by D. J. Price in *A History of Technology*, C. Singer and E. J. Holmyard, eds., III (Oxford, 1957), 582–609.

For details of the Arabic translations of the *Almagest* and other works of Ptolemy see M. Steinschneider, *Die arabischen Übersetzungen aus dem Griechischen* (Graz, 1960), (191)–(211). An extensive work by P. Kunitzsch on the history of the *Almagest* in Arabic and Latin translation is *Der Almagest—Die Syntaxis Mathematica des Claudius Ptolemäus in arabische-lateinischer Überlieferung* (Wiesbaden, 1974). The astronomical treatise of al-Battānī was published in a masterly ed. by C. A. Nallino, "Al-Battani sive Albatenii Opus astronomicum," *Pubblicazioni del R. Osservatorio astronomico di Brera in Milano*, **40**, 3 pts. (1899–1907). An account of the "improvements" to the Ptolemaic system made by al-Ṭūsī and other late Islamic astronomers, with references to further literature, is given by E. S. Kennedy in *The Cambridge History of Iran*, V (Cambridge, 1968), 668–670. The earliest Latin version of the *Almagest* is discussed in C. H. Haskins, *Studies in the History of Mediaeval Science* (Cambridge, Mass., 1924; repr. New York, 1960), pp. 157–165. Other versions are mentioned *ibid.*, pp. 103–112. An ed. of Copernicus' major work was published by F. and C. Zeller, *Nikolaus Kopernikus Gesamtausgabe*, 2 vols. (Munich, 1944–1949)— vol. I is a facsimile of the MS of the *De revolutionibus* in Copernicus' own hand; vol. II an unreliable "critical" ed. of the text. Brahe's star catalog of 1598 (published only after his death) is in *Tychonis Brahe Opera omnia*, J. L. E. Dreyer, ed., III (Copenhagen, 1916), 335–389. For details of Brahe's other star catalogs refer to the index, *ibid.*, XV (1929). His improvements to the lunar theory are discussed in V. E. Thoren, "Tycho Brahe's Discovery of the Variation," in *Centaurus*, **12** (1968), 151–166. For Kepler's *Astronomia nova* see the ed. by M. Caspar, pub. as vol. III of Johannes Kepler, *Gesammelte Werke*, W. von Dyck and Caspar, eds. (Munich, 1937).

The remains of Pappus' commentary on the *Almagest* were published by A. Rome, *Commentaires de Pappus et de Théon d'Alexandrie sur l'Almageste*, I (Rome, 1931), Studi e Testi, no. 54. He also published Theon's commentary to Bks. I and II, and that to Bks. III and IV, in the same series: no. 72 (1936) and no. 106 (1943). For the remainder of Theon's commentary one must still consult the *editio princeps* of the Greek text of the *Almagest: Claudii Ptolemaei Magnae constructionis . . . lib. xiii, Theonis Alexandrini in eosdem commentariorum lib. xi* (Basel, 1538).

Handy Tables: The only printed version—except for Ptolemy's intro., which is on pp. 159–185 of Heiberg's ed. of *Claudii Ptolemaei Opera quae exstant omnia*, II, *Opera astronomica minora* (Leipzig, 1907)—is the execrable ed. by N. Halma, *Tables manuelles astronomiques de Ptolémée et de Théon*, 3 pts. (Paris, 1822–1825). Pt. 1 contains Theon's smaller commentary on the tables (a larger one exists only in MS). B. L. van der Waerden makes some useful remarks on the parameters and use of the tables in "Bemerkungen zu den Handlichen Tafeln des Ptolemaios," in *Sitzungsberichte der Bayerischen Akademie der Wissenschaften zu München*, Math.-nat. Kl., **23** (1953), 261–272; and "Die Handlichen Tafeln des Ptolemaios," in *Osiris*, **13** (1958), 54–78.

Planetary Hypotheses: The Greek text was published by Heiberg in Ptolemy's *Opera astronomica minora*, pp. 70–106, together with a German trans. of the Arabic by L. Nix, *ibid.*, pp. 71–145. By a strange oversight this omits the end of Bk. I (missing from the Greek), which contains Ptolemy's theory of the absolute distances of the heavenly bodies; and thus Ptolemy's authorship of the latter theory remained unknown in modern times until the complete Arabic text (with English trans. of the part omitted by Nix) was published by B. Goldstein, "The Arabic Version of Ptolemy's Planetary Hypotheses," in *Transactions of the American Philosophical Society*, n.s. **57**, no. 4 (1967), 3–55. For an account of that theory and its medieval developments see N. Swerdlow, "Ptolemy's Theory of the Distances and Sizes of the Planets," Ph.D. thesis (Yale University, 1968). The text through which it reached the West was published, in its most widespread version, by F. J. Carmody, "Alfragani differentie in quibusdam collectis scientie astrorum" (Berkeley, 1943), multigraphed.

Phaseis, Analemma, Planisphaerium: The texts are printed in *Opera astronomica minora*, pp. 3–67, 189–223, and 227–259, respectively. On the *Phaseis* see H. Vogt, "Der Kalender des Claudius Ptolemäus (Griechische Kalender, ed. F. Boll, V)," in *SB Heidelberg. Akad. d. Wiss.*, in Phil.-hist. Kl. (1920), 15. Because of its excellent commentary, the *editio princeps* of the *Analemma* is still worth consulting: *Claudii Ptolemaei liber de Analemmate a Federico Commandino Urbinate instauratus* (Rome, 1562). See especially P. Luckey, "Das Analemma von Ptolemäus," in *Astronomische Nachrichten*, **230** (1927), 17–46. Vitruvius' description of an *Analemma* construction is in his *De architectura* IX, 7; V. Rose, ed. (Leipzig, 1899), pp. 230–233. The Arabic text of the *Planisphaerium* has never been printed (the *Opera astronomica minora* contains only the medieval Latin trans.); but it exists, in a version prior to Maslama's revision, in MS Istanbul, Aya Sofya 2671₈. There are related texts in MS Paris, Bibliothèque Nationale Ar. 4821, 69v ff.; see G. Vajda, "Quelques notes sur le fonds des manuscrits arabes de la Bibliothèque nationale," in *Rivista degli studi orientali*, **25** (1950), 7–9. On the relevance of the *Planisphaerium* to the astrolabe see O. Neugebauer, "The Early History of the Astrolabe," in *Isis*, **40** (1949), 240–256. The work of Synesius referring to Hipparchus and the astrolabe is in *Synesii Cyrenensis Opuscula*, N. Terzaghi, ed. (Rome, 1944), pp. 132–142.

Tetrabiblos: Critical text by F. Boll and A. Boer, *Claudii Ptolemaei Opera quae exstant omnia*, III, 1, ΑΠΟΤΕΛΕΣΜΑΤΙΚΑ (Leipzig, 1957). There is a text with English trans. by F. E. Robbins in Loeb Classical Library (Cambridge, Mass., 1940). On various aspects of the *Tetrabiblos*, Boll, "Studien," pp. 111–218, is useful. For

the content A. Bouché-Leclercq, *L'astrologie grecque* (Paris, 1899; repr. Brussels, 1963), remains unsurpassed.

Geography: There is no complete modern ed. For a complete text one must still use C. F. A. Nobbe, *Claudii Ptolemaei Geographia*, 2 vols. (Leipzig, 1843–1845; repr. in 1 vol., Hildesheim, 1966); but more satisfactory for the parts they contain are the eds. by F. W. Wilberg and C. H. F. Grashof, 6 fascs. (Essen, 1838–1845), Bks. I–VI; and by C. Müller, 2 vols. (Paris, 1883–1901), Bks. I–V. For other partial eds. see the article by E. Polaschek in Pauly–Wissowa (see below) and W. H. Stahl, *Ptolemy's Geography: A Select Bibliography* (New York, 1953). A German trans. of Bk. I by H. von Mžik, *Des Klaudios Ptolemaios Einführung in die darstellende Erdkunde*, Klotho 5 (Vienna, 1938), contains a good study of the projections by F. Hopfner, pp. 87–105. The geographical work of al-Khwārizmī was edited by H. von Mžik, *Das Kitāb Ṣūrat al-Arḍ des abū Ǧaʿfar Muḥammad ibn Mūsā al-Ḫuwārizmī* (Leipzig, 1926). C. A. Nallino gave a classic account of its relationship to Ptolemy in "Al-Khuwārizmī e il suo rifacimento della Geografia di Tolomeo," in *Atti dell' Accademia nazionale dei Lincei. Memorie*, Classe di Scienze Morali, Storiche e Filologiche, 5th ser., **2**, no. 1 (1894), 3–53, repr. in his *Raccolta di scritti editi e inediti*, V (Rome, 1944), 458–532. Excellent reproductions of maps found in MSS of the *Geography* were published in *Claudii Ptolemaei Geographiae codex Urbinas graecus 82 phototypice depictus*, pts. I, 2, and II (Leiden–Leipzig, 1932). Pt. I, 1, by J. Fischer, contains (pp. 290–415) an account of early European cartographic publications influenced by the *Geography*. Bernardus Sylvanus' map is at the end of his *Claudii Ptholemaei Alexandrini liber geographiae* (Venice, 1511).

Optics: This was first printed by G. Govi, *L'Ottica di Claudio Tolomeo* (Turin, 1885). A. Lejeune provided an excellent critical ed.: *L'Optique de Claude Ptolémée*, Université de Louvain, Receuil de travaux d'histoire et de philologie, 4th ser., fasc. 8 (Louvain, 1956). The same author gave a good analysis of most parts of the work in two publications: *Euclide et Ptolémée, deux stades de l'optique géométrique grecque*, *ibid.*, 3rd ser., fasc. 31 (Louvain, 1948); and "Recherches sur la catoptrique grecque," in *Mémoires de l'Académie r. de Belgique. Classe des sciences*, **52**, no. 2 (1957). Euclid's *Optics* and the pseudo-Euclidean *Catoptrics* are in *Euclidis opera omnia*, J. L. Heiberg, ed., VII (Leipzig, 1895). The Latin trans. of Hero's *Catoptrics* was edited by W. Schmidt in *Heronis Alexandrini Opera quae supersunt omnia*, II, 1 (Leipzig, 1900). The Arabic text of Ibn al-Haytham's *Optics* has never been printed (an English trans. and ed. are being prepared by A. Sabra). The Latin trans. is in *Opticae thesaurus*, F. Risner, ed. (Basel, 1572), which also contains Witelo's optical work. For Ibn al-Haytham's experiments see M. Schramm, *Ibn al-Haythams Weg zur Physik*, which is *Boethius*, I (Wiesbaden, 1963). References to Ptolemy's *Optics* by Roger Bacon are found in several parts of his *Opus maius*, J. H. Bridges, ed., 2 vols. (Oxford, 1900), see index under "Ptolemaeus."

Harmonica: Text published by I. Düring, "Die Harmonielehre des Klaudios Ptolemaios," which is *Göteborgs högskolas årskrift*, **36**, no. 1 (1930). The same author published Porphyry's commentary, *ibid.*, **38**, no. 2 (1932); and a German trans. of Ptolemy's work, with commentary on both works, "Ptolemaios und Porphyrios über die Musik," *ibid.*, **40**, no. 1 (1934). Boethius' *De institutione musica* was edited by G. Friedlein together with his *De institutione arithmetica* (Leipzig, 1877; repr. Frankfurt, 1966). Kepler's *Harmonice mundi* was published as vol. VI of his *Gesammelte Werke* by M. Caspar (Munich, 1940).

Doubtful, spurious, and lost works: Περὶ κριτηρίου καὶ ἡγεμονικοῦ was published by F. Lammert in *Claudii Ptolemaei Opera quae exstant omnia*, III, 2 (Leipzig, 1961). The same vol. contains an ed. of the Καρπός by A. Boer. On Ptolemy's philosophical position see Boll, "Studien," pp. 66–111. Fragments and testimonia to the lost works are printed in Heiberg's ed. of the *Opera astronomica minora*, pp. 263–270.

II. SECONDARY LITERATURE. *General*: B. L. van der Waerden *et al.*, "Ptolemaios 66," in Pauly-Wissowa, XXIII, 2 (Stuttgart, 1959), 1788–1859, is a good guide. The supplementary article on the *Geography* by E. Polaschek, *ibid.*, supp. X (1965), 680–833, is useful only for its bibliography.

Life: The evidence is assembled and discussed by F. Boll, "Studien über Claudius Ptolemäus," in *Jahrbücher für classische Philologie*, supp. **21** (1894), 53–66. This takes some note of the Arabic sources, which I omitted since they add nothing credible to the Greek evidence. The only formal biographical notice (wretchedly incomplete) is in the tenth-century Byzantine lexicon of Suidas ("the Suda"), *Suidae Lexicon*, Ada Adler, ed., IV (Leipzig, 1935), 254, no. 3033. The "Canobic Inscription" is printed in Heiberg's ed. of the *Opera astronomica minora*, pp. 149–155. The work of Olympiodorus was published by W. Norvin, *Olympiodori philosophi in Platonis Phaedonem commentaria* (Leipzig, 1913). The origin of the appellation "Phelud(i)ensis" was first correctly explained by J. J. Reiske in the German trans. of B. d'Herbelot's *Bibliothèque orientale: Orientalische Bibliothek*, II (Halle, 1787), 375. It was thence repeated by Philip Buttmann, "Ueber den Ptolemäus in der Anthologie und den Klaudius Ptolemäus," in *Museum der Alterthums-Wissenschaft*, **2** (1810), 455–506. An exhaustive discussion is given by P. Kunitzsch, *Der Almagest* (above).

G. J. TOOMER

PUISEUX, VICTOR (*b.* Argenteuil, Val-d'Oise, France, 16 April 1820; *d.* Frontenay, Jura, France, 9 September 1883)

Puiseux spent his youth in Lorraine, where his father, a tax collector, was posted in 1823. He was educated at the Collège de Pont-à-Mousson and, from 1834, at the Collège Rollin in Paris, where he attended C. Sturm's course in special mathematics. After winning the grand prize in physics (1836) and mathe-matics (1837) in the *concours général*, he was admitted in 1837 to the École Normale Supérieure. There he became friends with his future colleagues Briot and Bouquet. In 1840 Puiseux placed first in the *agrégation* in mathematics and then spent an additional year at the École Normale Supérieure as *chargé de conférences*, completing his training and preparing a dissertation in astronomy and mechanics, which he defended 21 August 1841.

Puiseux was professor of mathematics at the royal college of Rennes (1841–1844) and at the Faculty of Sciences of Besançon (1844–1849). During this period he published about ten articles on infinitesimal geometry and mechanics in Liouville's *Journal de mathématiques pures et appliquées*. In 1849 he was called to Paris as *maître de conférences* of mathematics at the École Normale Supérieure, a post he held until 1855 and again from 1862 to 1868.

In addition to his teaching duties, for several years Puiseux attended Cauchy's courses and became one of his closest followers. Under this fruitful influence, Puiseux wrote several important memoirs on the theory of functions of a complex variable before turning to celestial mechanics. In 1857, having substituted for various professors, including the astronomer Jacques Binet at the Collège de France and Sturm and Le Verrier at the Faculty of Sciences, Puiseux succeeded Cauchy in the chair of mathematical astronomy at the latter institution. He retained this post until 1882, publishing several important memoirs. Brief tenures as director of the Bureau de Calculs at the Paris observatory (1855–1859) and at the Bureau des Longitudes (1868–1872) permitted him to display his mastery of the techniques of astronomical computation. In 1871 he became a member of the mathematics section of the Académie des Sciences, succeeding Lamé.

In 1849 Puiseux married Laure Jeannet; of their six children only Pierre and André survived childhood; both became astronomers. An austere teacher and tireless worker, Puiseux devoted himself to the education of his children, was active in various catholic organizations, and took a passionate interest in botany and alpinism. He was, in fact, a pioneer in the latter sport and in 1848 was the first to scale one of the peaks (now bearing his name) of Mount Pelvoux.

Puiseux's scientific work encompassed infinitesimal geometry, mechanics, mathematical analysis, celestial mechanics, and observational astronomy. His first publication (1841), his doctoral dissertation, dealt with the invariability of the major axes of the planetary orbits and with the integration of the equations of motion of a system of material points. Although well-executed, the work lacked great originality. Similarly, his papers on infinitesimal geometry, most of which were published at the beginning of his career, attested his analytic virtuosity but constituted a rather limited contribution to the subject—notwithstanding his discovery of new properties of evolutes and involutes. The most interesting among these papers pertain to questions related to mechanics: the motion of the conical pendulum, tautochrones, a generalization of the top problem, and the study of the apparent movements of the surface of the earth.

In 1850 and 1851, however, Puiseux accomplished much more original work, developing, correcting, and completing major aspects of the theory of functions of a complex variable that had been elaborated by Cauchy. Examining functions of a complex variable z defined by an algebraic equation of the form $f(u,z) = 0$, Puiseux succeeded in separating the various branches and in formulating the expansions in corresponding series. He clearly distinguished, for the first time, the different types of singular points (poles, essential points, and branch points); determined the integrals of algebraic differentials over the paths of integration; specified the "mode of existence of non-uniform functions" (C. Hermite); and pointed out the applications of series containing fractional powers of the variable. Despite its intrinsic interest, Puiseux's theory was surpassed in 1857 when Riemann, in his *Theorie der Abelschen Funktionen*, approached the topic from a topological point of view and introduced the famous "Riemann surfaces." Puiseux subsequently turned to the study of celestial mechanics and astronomy and virtually never returned to his theory.

Following Cauchy, Puiseux sought to apply the most recent mathematical methods to the fundamental problems of celestial mechanics. His papers on the series expansions of the perturbation function, on long-term inequalities in planetary motions, and on related questions constitute an elaboration and refinement of earlier work by Cauchy. After presenting the lucid exposition "Sur les principales inégalités du mouvement de la lune" (*Annales scientifiques de l'École Normale Supérieure*, 1 [1864], 39–80), Puiseux took up the difficult problem of the acceleration of the mean motion of the moon. Although Laplace (1787) thought he could explain this phenomenon by the secular decrease in the eccentricity of the orbit of the earth, J. Adams showed in 1853 that Laplace's theory accounted for only half of the observed effect. After extensive calculations, Puiseux established (*Journal de mathématiques pures et appliquées*, 2nd ser., 15 [1870], 9–116) that the secular displacement of the ecliptic had no significant influence on the acceleration. Although a purely negative conclusion, Puiseux's finding led to a better delimitation of the problem, which was investigated by G. Hill in 1877.

Puiseux was also concerned with improving the computational methods employed in basic astronomy. At the Bureau de Calculs, he directed the reduction of both the lunar observations made at Paris from 1801 to 1829 and the meridional observations of 1837–1838. After comparing the different methods available for deducing the solar parallax from the observation of the transits of Venus, Puiseux participated in the preparations carried out for the observation of the 1874 and 1882 transits; he also worked on the observations made in 1874 by French astronomers. During his brief tenure at the Bureau des Longitudes, he served as principal editor of the *Connaissance des temps ou des mouvements célestes*.

BIBLIOGRAPHY

I. ORIGINAL WORKS. Puiseux's only separately printed publication was his dissertations, *Sur l'invariabilité des grands axes des orbites des planètes, thèse d'astronomie . . . Sur l'intégration des équations du mouvement d'un système de points matériels, thèse de mécanique* (Paris, 1841).

Forty-one articles and memoirs published between 1842 and 1880 are cited in the Royal Society *Catalogue of Scientific Papers*, V, 39–40; VIII, 672–673; IX, 77; and XII, 592. Most of these are also listed in Poggendorff, II, 542; and III, 1076. A summary of Puiseux's first publications is given in his *Notice sur les travaux scientifiques de M. Victor Puiseux* (Paris, 1856) and in two later, undated eds., the latter of which appeared in 1871.

II. SECONDARY LITERATURE. The chief biographical accounts of Puiseux are E. Glaeser, in *Biographie nationale des contemporains* (Paris, 1878), 620; C. Vapereau, in *Dictionnaire universel des contemporains*, 5th ed. (Paris, 1880), 1485; P. Gilbert, in *Revue des questions scientifiques*, 15 (1884), 5–37; J. Bertrand, "Notice lue à l'Académie des Sciences le 5 mai 1884," in *Bulletin des sciences mathématiques*, 2nd ser., 8, pt. 1 (1884), pp. 227–234, repr. in *Mémoires de l'Académie des sciences de l'Institut de France*, 2nd ser., 44 (1888), lxvii–lxxviii; and in J. Bertrand, *Éloges académiques* (Paris, 1890), 275–285; J. Tisserand, in *Bulletin des sciences mathématiques*, 2nd ser., 8, pt. 1 (1884), 234–245; and M. d'Ocagne, in *Histoire abrégée des sciences mathématiques* (Paris, n.d. [1955]), 283–284.

Information on certain aspects of Puiseux's career and work can be found in M. Chasles, *Rapport sur les progrès de la géométrie* (Paris, 1870), 180–182; and in J. Tannery, "L'enseignement des mathématiques à l'École," in *Le centenaire de l'École normale (1795–1895)* (Paris, 1895), 391–392.

RENÉ TATON

PYTHAGORAS OF SAMOS (*b*. Samos, *ca*. 560 B.C.; *d*. Metapontum, *ca*. 480 B.C.)

Most of the sources concerning Pythagoras' life, activities, and doctrines date from the third and fourth centuries A.D., while the few more nearly contemporary (fourth and fifth centuries B.C.) records of him are often contradictory, due in large part to the split that developed among his followers soon after his death. Contemporary references, moreover, scarcely touch upon the points of Pythagoras' career that are of interest to the historian of science, although a number of facts can be ascertained or surmised with a reasonable degree of certainty.

It is, for example, known that in his earlier years Pythagoras traveled widely in Egypt and Babylonia, where he is said to have become acquainted with Egyptian and Babylonian mathematics. In 530 B.C. (or, according to another tradition, 520 B.C.) he left Samos to settle in Croton, in southern Italy, perhaps because of his opposition to the tyrant Polycrates. At Croton he founded a religious and philosophical society that soon came to exert considerable political influence throughout the Greek cities of southern Italy. Pythagoras' hierarchical views at first pleased the local aristocracies, which found in them a support against the rising tide of democracy, but he later met strong opposition from the same quarter. He was forced to leave Croton about 500 B.C., and retired to Metapontum, where he died. During the violent democratic revolution that occurred in Magna Graecia in about 450 B.C., Pythagoras' disciples were set upon, and Pythagorean meetinghouses were destroyed. Many Pythagoreans thereupon fled to the Greek mainland, where they found a new center for their activities at Phleius; others went to Tarentum, where they continued as a political power until the middle of the fourth century B.C.

The political vicissitudes of Pythagoras and his followers are significant in the reconstruction of their scientific activities. True to his hierarchical principles, Pythagoras seems to have divided his adherents into two groups, the ἀκουσματικοί, or "listeners," who were enjoined to silence, in which they memorized the master's words, and the μαθηματικοί, who, after a long period of training, were allowed to ask questions and express opinions of their own. (The term μαθηματικοί originally meant merely those who had attained a somewhat advanced degree of knowledge, although it later came to imply "scientist" or "mathematician.")

A few decades after Pythagoras' death, these two groups evolved into sharp factions and began a controversy over which of them was most truly Pythagorean. The ἀκουσματικοί based their claim on their literal adherence to Pythagoras' own words (αὐτὸς ἔφα, "he himself has spoken"); the μαθηματικοί, on the other hand, seem to have developed Pythagoras' ideas to such an extent that they were no longer in complete agreement with their originals. The matter was further complicated because, according to ancient tradition, Pythagoras chose to reveal his teachings clearly and completely to only his most advanced disciples, so that the ἀκουσματικοί received only cryptic, or even mysterious, hints. The later Pythagorean tradition thus includes a number of strange prescriptions and doctrines, which the ἀκουσματικοί interpreted with absolute literalness; the more rationalistic group (led at one time by Aristoxenus, who was also a disciple of Plato and Aristotle) preferred a symbolic and allegorical interpretation.

This obscurity concerning Pythagoras' intent has led historians of science into differences of opinion as to whether Pythagoras could really be considered a scientist or even an initiator of scientific ideas. It is further debatable whether those ancient authors who made real contributions to mathematics, astronomy, and the theory of music can be considered to have been true Pythagoreans, or even to have been influenced by authentically Pythagorean ideas. Nonetheless, apart from the theory of metempsychosis (which is mentioned by his contemporaries), ancient tradition assigns one doctrine to Pythagoras and the early Pythagoreans that can hardly have failed to influence the development of mathematics. This is the broad generalization, based on rather restricted observation (a procedure common in early Greek science), that all things are numbers.

Pythagoras' number theory was based on three observations. The first of these was the mathematical relationships of musical harmonies—that is, that when the ratio of lengths of sound-producing instruments (such as strings or flutes) is extended to other instruments in which one-dimensional relations are involved, the same musical harmonies result. Secondly, the Pythagoreans noted that any triangle formed of three sticks in the ratio 3:4:5 is always a right triangle, whatever the length of its segments. Their third important observation derived from the fixed numerical relations of the movements of heavenly bodies. It was thereby apparent to them that since the same musical harmonies and geometric shapes can be produced in different media and sizes by the same combination of numbers, the numbers themselves must express the harmonies and shapes and even the things having those harmonies and shapes. It could thus be said that these things—or, as they were later called, the essences (οὐσίαι) of these things—actually were numbers. The groups of numbers that embodied the essence of a thing, and by which it might be reproduced, were called λόγοι ("words"), a term that later came to mean "ratio."

The translation of philosophical speculation into mathematics is thus clear. This speculation about numbers as essences was extended in several directions; as late as the end of the fifth century B.C., philosophers and mathematicians were still seeking the number of justice, or marriage, or even of a specific man or horse. (Attempts were made to discover the number of, for example, a horse, by determining the number of small stones necessary to produce something like the outline of it.) By this time, however, the Pythagoreans had split into a set of groups holding highly differing viewpoints, so it would be inaccurate to assume that all Pythagorean speculations about numbers were of this primitive, unscientific kind.

The theory of special types of numbers, which lay somewhere between these mystical speculations and true science, was developed by the Pythagoreans during the fifth century B.C. The two aspects of the theory are apparent in that the Pythagoreans distinguished between two types of "perfect" numbers. The number ten was the only example of the first group, and its perfection derived from its fundamental role in the decimal system and in its being composed of the sum of the first four numbers, $1 + 2 + 3 + 4 = 10$. Because of this second quality it was called the tetractys, and represented by the figure ∴∴ ; it was considered holy, and the Pythagoreans swore by it. The second type of perfect numbers consisted of those equal to the sum of their factors, as, for example, six $(1 + 2 + 3)$ or twenty-eight $(1 + 2 + 4 + 7 + 14)$. Euclid, in the *Elements* (IX. 36) gave the general theory for this numerical phenomenon, stating that if $2^n - 1$ is a prime number, then $(2^n - 1)2^{n-1}$ is a perfect number.

Similar speculations prompted the search for "amicable" numbers—that is, numbers of which each equals the sum of the factors of the other—and for integers satisfying the Pythagorean formula $a^2 + b^2 = c^2$ (as, for example, $3^2 + 4^2 = 5^2$, or $5^2 + 12^2 = 13^2$). Only one pair of amicable numbers, 284 and 220, was known by the end of antiquity, and its discovery is attributed by Iamblichus to Pythagoras himself, who is said to have derived it from the saying that a friend is an alter ego. Proclus (in Friedlein's edition of Euclid's *Elements*, p. 426) also attributes to Pythagoras himself the general formula by which any number of integers satisfying the equation $a^2 + b^2 = c^2$ may be found,

$$n^2 + \left(\frac{n^2 - 1}{2}\right)^2 = \left(\frac{n^2 - 1}{2} + 1\right)^2,$$

where n is an odd number. If this tradition is correct (and it is doubtful), Pythagoras must have learned the formula in Babylonia, where it was known,

according to O. Neugebauer and A. Sachs (in *Mathematical Cuneiform Texts* [New Haven, 1945], p. 38).

Figured numbers were of particular significance in Pythagorean arithmetic. These included triangular numbers, square numbers, and pentagonal numbers, as well as *heteromeke* numbers (numbers forming rectangles with unequal sides), stereometric numbers (pyramidal numbers forming pyramids with triangular or square bases), cubic numbers, and altar numbers (stereometric numbers corresponding to *heteromeke* numbers). These numbers were represented by points, with ., ∴, ∴⋅, ∴⋅⋅, ∴⋅⋅⋅, for example, for the triangular numbers, and ⊡ for the square numbers. The triangular numbers thus occur in the series 1, 3, 6, 10, 15, ⋯, which can be expressed by the formula $n(n + 1)/2$, while square numbers have the value n^2 and pentagonal numbers may be given the value $n(3n - 1)/2$. *Heteromeke* numbers may be expressed as $n(n + 1)$, $n(n + 2)$, and so on; pyramidal numbers with triangular bases are formed by the successive sums of the triangular numbers 1, 4, 10, 20, 35, ⋯. Pythagorean authors gave only examples of the various kinds of figured numbers until the second century A.D., and it was only in the third century A.D. that Diophantus developed a systematic mathematical theory based upon Pythagorean speculations.

The theory of μεσότητες, or "means," is also undoubtedly Pythagorean and probably of considerable antiquity. Iamblichus asserts (in Pistelli's edition of Iamblichus' commentary on Nicomachus' *Introductio arithmetica*, p. 118) that Pythagoras learned of arithmetic means during his travels in Babylonia, but this cannot be definitely proved. The theory was at first concerned with three means; the arithmetic, of the form $a - b = b - c$; the geometric, of the form $a:b = b:c$; and the harmonic, of the form $(a - b):a = (b - c):c$. Other means were added at later dates, particularly by the Pythagorean Archytas of Tarentum, in the first half of the fourth century B.C.

It would seem likely, as O. Becker (in *Quellen und Studien zur Geschichte der Mathematik*, III B, pp. 534 ff.) and B. L. van der Waerden have pointed out, that Euclid took the whole complex of theorems and proofs that are based upon the distinction between odd and even numbers from the Pythagoreans, and that these reflect the Pythagorean interest in perfect numbers. This adaptation would seem to be particularly apparent in the *Elements*, IX. 30, and IX. 34, which lay the groundwork for the proof of IX. 36, the general Euclidean formula for perfect numbers. The proofs given in Euclid are strictly deductive and scientific, however, and would indicate that one group of Pythagoreans had quite early progressed from mysticism to true scientific method.

Although the contributions made by Pythagoras and his early successors to arithmetic and number theory can be determined with some accuracy, their contributions to geometry remain problematic. O. Neugebauer has shown (in *Mathematiker Keilschrifttexte*, I, 180, and II, 53) that the so-called Pythagorean theorem had been known in Babylonia at the time of Hammurabi, and it is possible that Pythagoras had learned it there. It is not known whether the theorem was proved during Pythagoras' lifetime, or shortly thereafter. The pentagram, which played an important role in Pythagorean circles in the early fifth century B.C., was also known in Babylonia, and may have been imported from there. This figure, a regular pentagon with its sides extended to intersect in the form of a five-pointed star, has the interesting property that its sides and diagonals intersect everywhere according to the golden section; the Pythagoreans used it as a symbol by which they recognized each other.

Of the mathematical discoveries attributed by ancient tradition to the Pythagoreans, the most important remains that of incommensurability. According to Plato's *Theaetetus*, this discovery cannot have been made later than the third quarter of the fifth century B.C., and although there has been some scholarly debate concerning the accuracy of this assertion, there is no reason to believe that it is not accurate. It is certain that the Pythagorean doctrine that all things are numbers would have been a strong incentive for the investigation of the hidden numbers that constitute the essences of the isosceles right-angled triangle or of the regular pentagon; if, as the Pythagoreans knew, it was always possible to construct a right triangle given sides in the ratio $3 : 4 : 5$, then it should by analogy be possible to determine the numbers by which a right-angled isosceles triangle could be constructed.

The Babylonians had known approximations to the ratio of the side of a square to its diagonal, but the early Greek philosophers characteristically wished to know it exactly. This ratio cannot be expressed precisely in integers, as the early Pythagoreans discovered. They chose to approach the problem by seeking the greatest common measure—and hence the numerical ratio of two lengths—through mutual subtraction. In the case of the regular pentagon, it may easily be shown that the mutual subtraction of its diagonals and sides can be continued through an infinite number of operations, and that its ratio is therefore incommensurable. Ancient tradition credits this discovery to Hippasus of Metapontum, who was living at the period in which the discovery must have been made, and who could easily have made it by the method described. (Hippasus, one of the μαθηματικοί,

who is said to have been set apart from the other Pythagoreans by his liberal political views, is also supposed to have been concerned with the "sphere composed by regular pentagons," that is, the regular dodecahedron.)

An appendix to book X of the *Elements* incorporates a proof of the incommensurability of the diagonal of a square with its side. This proof appears to be out of its proper order, and is apparently much older than the rest of the theorems contained in book X; it is based upon the distinction between odd and even numbers and closely resembles the theorems and proofs of book IX. Like the proofs of book IX, the proof offered in book X is related to the Pythagorean theory of perfect numbers; an ancient tradition states that it is Pythagorean in origin, and it would be gratuitous to reject this attribution simply because other members of the same sect were involved in nonscientific speculations about numbers. It is further possible that the ingenious process by which the theory of proportions (which had been conceived in the form of ratios of integers) had been applied to incommensurables—that is, by making the process of mutual subtraction itself the criterion of proportionality—was also a Pythagorean invention. But it is clear that the later elaboration of the theory of incommensurability and irrationality was the work of mathematicians who no longer had any close ties to the Pythagorean sect.

Pythagoras (or, according to another tradition, Hippasus) is also credited with knowing how to construct three of the five regular solids, specifically the pyramid, the cube, and the dodecahedron. Although these constructions can hardly have been identical to the ones in book XIII of the *Elements*, which a credible tradition attributes to Theaetetus, it is altogether likely that these forms, particularly the dodecahedron, had been of interest not only to Hippasus (as has been noted) but also to even earlier Pythagoreans. Their curiosity must have been aroused by both its geometrical properties (since it is made up of regular pentagons) and its occurrence in nature, since iron pyrite crystals of this form are found in Italy. An artifact in the form of a carved stone dodecahedron, moreover, dates from the tenth century B.C., and would seem to have played some part in an Etruscan cult.

The notion that all things are numbers is also fundamental to Pythagorean music theory. Early Pythagorean music theory would seem to have initially been of the same speculative sort as early Pythagorean mathematical theory. It was based upon observations drawn from the lyre and the flute, the most widely used instruments; from these observations it was concluded that the most beautiful musical harmonies corresponded to the most beautiful (because simplest) ratios or combinations of numbers, namely the octave (2:1), the fifth (3:2), and the fourth (4:3). It was thus possible to assign the numbers 6, 8, 9, and 12 to the four fixed strings of the lyre, and to determine the intervals of the diatonic scale as 9:8, 9:8, and 256:243. From these observations and speculations the Pythagoreans built up, as van der Waerden has pointed out, a deductive system of musical theory based on postulates or "axioms" (a term that has a function similar to its use in mathematics). The dependence of musical intervals on mathematical ratios was thus established.

The early music theory was later tested and extended in a number of ways. Hippasus, perhaps continuing work begun by the musician Lasos of Hermione, is said to have experimented with empty and partially filled glass vessels and with metal discs of varying thicknesses to determine whether the same ratios would produce the same harmonies with these instruments. (Contrary to ancient tradition, it would have been impossible to achieve sufficient accuracy by these means for him to have been altogether successful in this effort.) The systematic deductive theory was later enlarged to encompass the major and minor third (5:4 and 6:5), as well as the diminished minor third (7:6) and the augmented whole tone (8:7). The foundation for the enharmonic and chromatic scales was thus laid, which led to the more complex theory of music developed by Archytas of Tarentum in the first half of the fourth century B.C.

In addition to its specifically Pythagorean elements, Pythagorean astronomy would seem to have comprised both Babylonian observations and theories (presumably brought back by Pythagoras from his travels) and certain theories developed by Anaximander of Miletus, whose disciple Pythagoras is said to have been. It is not known precisely when Babylonian astronomy had begun, or what state it had reached at the time of Pythagoras, although ancient documents indicate that regular observations of the appearances of the planet Venus had been made as early as the reign of King Amisadaqa (about 1975 B.C.). The *mul apin* texts of about 700 B.C. give a summary of Babylonian astronomy up to that time, moreover, and contain divisions of the heavens into "roads of the fixed stars" (similar to the divisions of the zodiac), statements on the courses of the planets, and data on the risings and settings of stars that are obviously based on observations carried out over a considerable period of time. In addition, Ptolemy stated that regular observations of eclipses had been recorded since the time of King Nabonassar, about 747 B.C. The Baby-

lonians of this time also knew that lunar eclipses occur only at full moon and solar eclipses at new moon, and that lunar eclipses occur at intervals of approximately six months; they knew seven "planets" (including the sun and moon), and therefore must have known the morning and evening star to be identical.

The Babylonians also knew that the independent motions of the planets occur in a plane that intersects the equator of the heavenly sphere at an angle. Greek tradition attributes the determination of this angle as 24° to Pythagoras, although the computation was actually made by Oenopides of Chios, in the second half of the fifth century B.C. Oenopides was not a Pythagorean, but he obviously drew upon Pythagorean mathematics and astronomy, just as the Pythagoreans drew upon the body of Babylonian knowledge.

Anaximander's contributions to Pythagorean astronomy were less direct. The Pythagoreans rejected his chief theory, whereby the stars were in fact rings of fire that encircled the entire universe; according to Anaximander these fiery rings were obscured by "dark air," so that they were visible only through the holes through which they breathed. Pythagoras and his adherents, on the other hand, accepted the Babylonian notion of the stars as heavenly bodies of divine origin. They did, however, make use of Anaximander's assumption that the planets (or, rather, the rings in which they appear) are at different distances from the earth, or at any rate are nearer to the earth than are the fixed stars. This idea became an important part of Pythagorean astronomy (see Heiberg's edition, Eudemus of Rhodes in Simplicius' *Commentary* on Aristotle's *De caelo*, p. 471, and Diels and Kranz's edition of *Die Fragmente der Vorsokratiker*, sec. 12, 19).

Their knowledge of the periodicity of the movements of the stars undoubtedly strengthened the Pythagoreans in their belief that all things are numbers. They attempted to develop astronomical theory by combining it with this general principle, among others (including the principle of beauty that had figured in their axiomatic foundations of the theory of music). Their concern with musical intervals led them to try to determine the sequence of the planets in relation to the position of the earth (compare Eudemus, in the work cited, and Ptolemy, *Syntaxis*, IX, 1). According to their theory, probably the earliest of its kind, the order of the planets, in regard to their increasing distance from the earth, was the moon, Mercury, Venus, the sun, Mars, Jupiter, and Saturn—a sequence that was later refined by placing Mercury and Venus above the sun, since no solar transits of these bodies had been observed.

Further theories by which the distances and periods

of revolution of the heavenly bodies are correlated with musical intervals are greatly various, if not actually contradictory. Indeed, according to van der Waerden (in "Die Astronomie der Pythagoreer," pp. 34 ff.), a number of them make very little sense in the context of musical theory. It is almost impossible to tell what the original astronomical-musical theory on which these variants are based actually was, although it was almost certainly of considerable antiquity. It may be assumed, however, that in any original theory the celestial spheres were likened to the seven strings of a lyre, and were thought to produce a celestial harmony called the music of the spheres. Ordinary mortals could not hear this music (Aristotle suggested that this was because they had been exposed to it continuously since the moment of their birth), but later Pythagoreans said that it was audible to Pythagoras himself.

Another mystical notion, this one adopted from the Babylonians, was that of the great year. This concept, which was used by the Pythagoreans and probably by Pythagoras, held that since the periods of revolution of all heavenly bodies were in integral ratio, a least common multiple must exist, so that exactly the same constellation of all stars must recur after some definite period of time (the "great year" itself). It thereupon followed that all things that have occurred will recur in precisely the same way; Eudemus is reported to have said in a lecture (not without irony) that "then I shall sit here again with this pointer in my hand and tell you such strange things."

Pythagorean ideas of beauty required that the stars move in the simplest curves. This principle thus demanded that all celestial bodies move in circles, the circle being the most beautiful curve, a notion that held the utmost importance for the development of ancient astronomy. If van der Waerden's ingenious interpretation of the difficult ancient texts on this subject is correct (in "Die Astronomie der Pythagoreer," pp. 42 ff.), there may have been—even before Plato asked the non-Pythagorean mathematician Eudoxus to create a model showing the circular movements of all celestial bodies—a Pythagorean theory that explained the movements of Mercury and Venus as epicycles around the sun, and thus represented the first step toward a heliocentric system.

Ancient tradition also refers to an entirely different celestial system, in which the earth does not rest in the center of the universe (as in the theories of Anaximander, the Babylonians of the fifth century B.C., and the other Pythagoreans), but rather revolves around a central fire. This fire is invisible to men, because the inhabited side of the earth is always turned away from it. According to this theory, there is also a counter-earth on the opposite side of the fire. Pythagorean principles of beauty and of a hierarchical order in nature are here fundamental; fire, being more noble than earth, must therefore occupy a more noble position in the universe, its center (compare Aristotle, *De caelo*, II, 13). This theory is sometimes attributed to Philolaus, a Pythagorean of the late fifth century B.C., and he may have derived the epicyclic theory from it, although the surviving fragments of Philolaus' work indicate him to have been a man of only modest intellectual capacities, and unlikely to have been the inventor of such an ingenious system. Other ancient sources name Hicetas of Syracuse, a Pythagorean of whom almost nothing else is known, as its author.

The decisive influence of this theory in the history of astronomy lies in its explanation of the chief movements of the celestial bodies as being merely apparent. The assumption that the solid earth, on which man lives, does not stand still but moves with great speed (since some Pythagoreans according to Aristotle explained the phenomenon of day and night by the movement of the earth around the central fire) was a bold one, although the paucity and vagueness of ancient records make it impossible to determine with any certainty how far this notion was applied to other celestial phenomena. Further details on this theory are also difficult to ascertain; van der Waerden (in "Die Astronomie der Pythagoreer," pp. 49 ff.) discusses the problem at length. It is nevertheless clear that this daring, and somewhat unscientific, speculation was a giant step toward the development of a heliocentric system. Once the idea of an unmoving earth at the center of the universe had been overcome, the Pythagorean Ecphantus and Plato's disciple Heraclides were, in about 350 B.C., able to teach that the earth revolves about its own axis (*Aetius*, III, 13). A fully heliocentric system was then presented by Aristarchus of Samos, in about 260 B.C., although it was later abandoned by Ptolemy because its circular orbits did not sufficiently agree with his careful observations.

It is thus apparent that the tendency of some modern scholars to reject the unanimous and plausible ancient tradition concerning the Pythagoreans and their discoveries—and to attribute these accomplishments instead to a number of unknown, cautious, and pedestrian observers and calculators—obscures one of the most interesting aspects of the early development of Greek science.

BIBLIOGRAPHY

I. ORIGINAL WORKS. The most complete collection of ancient Pythagorean texts, with critical apparatus, Italian trans., and commentary, is M. Timpanaro-Cardini, *Pitagorici. Testimonianze e frammenti*, 3 vols. (Florence, 1958–1964). See also H. Diels and W. Kranz, eds., *Die Fragmente der Vorsokratiker*, 7th ed. (Berlin, 1954), sec. 14 (Pythagoras) and secs. 37–58 (early Pythagoreans); K. Freeman, *Ancilla to the Presocratic Philosophers*, a *Complete Translation of the Fragments in Diels, Fragmente der Vorsokratiker* (Cambridge, Mass., 1948), which translates only the fragments but not the very important testimonies; and *The Pre-Socratic Philosophers*, a *Companion to Diels* (Oxford, 1946). A good selection of texts and testimonies is Cornelia J. de Vogel, *Greek Philosophy. A Collection of Texts, Selected and Supplied With Notes*. Vol. I, *From Thales to Plato* (Leiden, 1950).

II. SECONDARY LITERATURE. The modern literature on Pythagoras and the early Pythagoreans is enormous. A more complete selection than the following is found in Timpanaro-Cardini (chs. 11–19). The most important recent contributions to the history of Pythagorean science are B. L. van der Waerden, "Die Arithmetik der Pythagoreer," in *Mathematische Annalen*, **120** (1947–1949), 127–153, 676–700; "Die Harmonielehre der Pythagoreer," in *Hermes*, **78** (1943), 163–199; "Die Astronomie der Pythagoreer," in *Verhandelingen der K. akademie van wetenschappen*, Afdeeling Natuurkunde, eerste Reeks, pt. 20 (1954), art. 1; "Das Grosse Jahr und die Ewige Wiederkehr," in *Hermes*, **80** (1952), 129–155; *Ontwakende Wetenschap* (Groningen, 1954), trans. by A. Dresden as *Science Awakening* (New York, 1963); *Erwachende Wissenschaft*, II, *Die Anfänge der Astronomie* (Groningen, 1967), for the Babylonian antecedents of Pythagorean astronomy.

See also the extensive articles on Pythagoras and the Pythagoreans by B. L. van der Waerden, K. von Fritz, and H. Dörrie in Pauly-Wissowa, *Real-Encyclopädie der classischen Altertumswissenschaft*, XXIV, pt. 1 (Stuttgart, 1963), cols. 171–300. Other important recent works are: Cornelia J. de Vogel, *Pythagoras and Early Pythagoreanism* (Assen, 1966); W. Burkert, *Weisheit und Wissenschaft, Erlanger Beiträge zur Sprach- und Kunstwissenschaft* (Nuremberg, 1962); W. K. C. Guthrie, *A History of Greek Philosophy*, I (Cambridge, 1962), 146–340; and E. Zeller and R. Mondolfo, *La filosofia dei Greci nel suo sviluppo storico*, II (Florence, 1938), 288–685.

For important special problems see R. Mondolfo, "Sui frammenti di Filolao," in *Rivista di filologia e d'istruzione classica*, n. s. **15** (1937), 225–245; O. Neugebauer, *The Exact Sciences in Antiquity* (Copenhagen, 1951), for the oriental antecedents of Pythagorean astronomy; and K. von Fritz, "Mathematiker und Akusmatiker bei den alten Pythagoreern," in *Sitzungsberichte der Bayerischen Akademie der Wissenschaften zu München*, Phil.-hist. Kl., no. 11 (1960).

See further Paul-Henri Michel, *De Pythagore à Euclide, Contribution à l'histoire des mathématiques préeuclidiennes* (Paris, 1950); A. Rostagni, *Il verbo di Pitagora* (Turin, 1924); J. A. Philip, *Pythagoras and Early Pythagoreanism* (Toronto, 1966); Erich Frank, *Platon und die sogenannten Pythagoreer* (Halle, 1923); and G. Sarton, *A History of*

Science (Cambridge, Mass., 1952), 199–217, 275–297.

KURT VON FRITZ

QĀḌĪ ZĀDA AL-RŪMĪ (more properly **Salah al-Din Mūsā Pasha**) (*b.* Bursa, Turkey, *ca.* 1364; *d.* Samarkand, Uzbekistan, *ca.* 1436)

Most historians of science have erred concerning Qāḍī Zāda. A. Sédillot, for example, called him Hassan Tchélebī; and Montucla, in his history of mathematics, said that he was a Greek convert to Islam. Montucla may have been deceived by the surname Rūmī, for the peoples who lived in Asia Minor were called Rūm, meaning Roman (not Greek), because Asia Minor was once Roman. Qāḍī Zāda means "son of the judge."

After completing his secondary education at Bursa, Qāḍī Zāda became a student of the theologian and encyclopedist Mullā Shams al-Dīn Muḥammad al-Fanārī (1350–1431), who taught him geometry and astronomy. Sensing the great talent of his student, al-Fanārī advised him to go to Transoxiana, then a great cultural center, to continue his training in mathematics and astronomy. According to several historians, al-Fanārī gave Qāḍī Zāda letters of recommendation and one of his works (*Enmuzeğ al-ulum*, "Types of Sciences") to present to the scholars of Khurasan and Transoxiana.

The year of Qāḍī Zāda's departure from Bursa is not known. It must have been after 1383, however, for in that year, still at Bursa, he had composed a work on arithmetic, *Risāla fī'l-ḥisāb*. When he presented himself to Ulugh Beg in Samarkand (*ca.* 1410),[1] he had spent some time in Iran, Jurjan, and Khorasan. At Jurjan he had met the philosopher-theologian Seyyid al-Sharif al-Jurjānī. Therefore, the year of departure from Bursa probably falls between 1405 and 1408.

In 1421 Ulugh Beg ordered the construction of a university at Samarkand and named Qāḍī Zāda as its rector. Serving in addition as professor of mathematics and astronomy, Qāḍī Zāda frequently had Ulugh Beg as a student in his classes. Also in 1421, under the direction of the young Persian astronomer and mathematician al-Kāshī, the construction of the observatory at Samarkand was completed. Astronomical observations had been made and the composing of astronomical tables had been begun. These tables were composed to correct and complete the tables of Naṣir al-Dīn al-Ṭūsī. Ulugh Beg made al-Kāshī director of the observatory; and after his death in 1429, Qāḍī Zāda took his place. Qāḍī Zāda died before the astronomical tables were completed. 'Alī

Kūshjī succeeded him, and was director when the Jurjanian Tables were published.

Qāḍī Zāda married in Samarkand and had a son named Shams al-Dīn Muḥammad, who married a daughter of 'Alī Kūshjī; from this marriage was born Quṭb al-Dīn, father of the Turkish mathematician Mīram Chelebi.

One of Qāḍī Zāda's calculations is presented below as an example of his approach to a geometrical-algebraic problem. It concerns determining the value of sin 1°. The example is drawn from the *Dastūr al-'amal wa-taṣḥīḥ al-jadwal* ("Practical Formula and Correction of the Table") of Mīram Chelebi, who states that Qāḍī Zāda wrote it.

Qāḍī Zāda, finding al-Kāshī's work on the approximate determination of the value of sin 1° to be very precise, commented upon it and gave further explanation in his *Risāla fi'l-jayb*.[2]

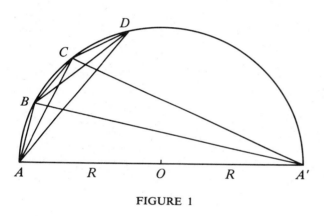

FIGURE 1

Like al-Kāshī, Qāḍī Zāda supposed that an arc *ABCD* taken on a circle with center *O* and diameter $\overline{AA'}$ is divided by the points *C* and *B* into three equal parts. Also like al-Kāshī, he was well aware of the impossibility of geometrically dividing an arc into three equal parts in order to obtain the chords $\overline{AB}$, $\overline{BC}$, $\overline{CD}$, $\overline{AC}$, $\overline{BD}$, and $\overline{AD}$. Applying Ptolemy's theorem to the inscribed quadrilateral *ABCD* thus constructed, he wrote the following equation:

(1) $\qquad \overline{AB} \cdot \overline{CD} + \overline{BC} \cdot \overline{AD} = \overline{AC} \cdot \overline{BD}.$

Considering the equalities

$$\overline{AB} = \overline{BC} = \overline{CD} \quad \text{and} \quad \overline{AC} = \overline{BD}$$

according to the hypothesis, equation (1) becomes

(2) $\qquad \overline{AB}^2 + \overline{AB} \cdot \overline{AD} = \overline{AC}^2.$

Qāḍī Zāda also supposed that arc *ABCD* is equal to

6°; therefore the chords $\overline{AB}$, $\overline{BC}$, and $\overline{CD}$ will belong to arcs of 2°.

Qāḍī Zāda next applied the iterative method of al-Kāshī to the determination of the chord belonging to the arc of 2°. That is, he algebraically divided the arc of 6°, the chord of which was known, into three equal parts. In taking as unknown (as a function of the parts of the radius) the chord belonging to the arc of 2° (that is, $\overline{AB} = x$) he obtained the equation

(3) $\qquad x^2 + x \cdot \overline{AD} = \overline{AC}^2,$

which is the equivalent of (2).

Since the chord $\overline{AD}$ belongs to the arc of 6°, Qāḍī Zāda (like al-Kāshī) obtained the following value of $\overline{AD}$ (in the sexagesimal system):

$$6^p.16.49.07.59.08.56.29.40$$

(where $\overline{OA} = R = 60^p$). This value of $\overline{AD}$ (in both authors) was determined by means of the arc of 72° and 60°, the chords of which were known geometrically. Knowing the chords of the arcs of 72° (the side of a regular pentagon) and of 60° (the side of a regular hexagon), they obtained the chord belonging to the arc of 72° − 60° = 12°. Then, applying the formula that gives the value of the chord belonging to half of an arc of which the chord is known, Qāḍī Zāda obtained the value of $\overline{AD}$. To find the value of $\overline{AC}$, which appears on the right-hand side of (1), he used the theorem discussed below (already utilized by al-Kāshī in his *Risāla al-muḥīṭiyya* ["Treatise on the Circumference"] for determining the value of π).

The theorem is that the ratio of the difference between the diameter of a circle and the chord belonging to any arc (when the arc is taken on this circle and one of its extremities passes through the extremity of the diameter) to the chord belonging to half of the supplement of this arc is equal to the ratio of this same chord to the radius of the circle.

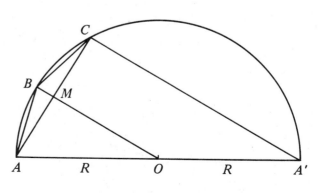

FIGURE 2

Taking $A'C$ as the arc, the theorem can be written in the following manner:

$$(4) \qquad \frac{\overline{AA'} - \overline{CA'}}{\overline{AB}} = \frac{\overline{AB}}{\overline{OA}} \, .$$

In equation (4)[3] one first separates $\overline{CA'}$, then for the value of $\overline{CA'}^2$ obtains (replacing $\overline{OA}$ with R and $\overline{AA'}$ with $2R$):

$$(5)$$
$$\overline{CA'}^2 = 4R^2 - 4\overline{AB}^2 + \frac{\overline{AB}^4}{R^2} = 4R^2 - 4x^2 + \frac{x^4}{R^2} \, .$$

From the right triangle ACA' one obtains

$$(6) \qquad \overline{CA'}^2 = 4R^2 - \overline{AC}^2 \, ;$$

and in equating the two values of $\overline{CA'}^2$ given by (5) and (6), one arrives at the equation

$$\overline{AC}^2 = 4x^2 - \frac{x^4}{R^2} \, .$$

Placing this value of $\overline{AC}^2$ in equation (3), one obtains (after simplifications) the equation

$$(7) \qquad 3x = \overline{AD} + \frac{x^3}{R^2} \, .$$

The value of $\overline{AD}$ having been determined, the above equation can be written in the sexagesimal system as

$$3x = (6^p.16.49.07.59.08.56.29.40) + x^3 \, .$$

Qāḍī Zāda, applying al-Kāshī's iterative method to this last equation, found for the unknown x (the value of the chord relative to 2°) the value

$$x = 2^p.05.39.26.22.19.28.32.52.33 \, .$$

Half of this value would yield approximately the sine of 1°:

$$1^p.02.49.43.11.14.44.16.26.16.30 \, .$$

This value is equal to that found by al-Kāshī. The value of sin 1° in the decimal system thus would be 0.017452406437, which is exact to within 10^{-12}, a degree of precision also achieved by al-Kāshī.[4]

NOTES

1. At this time Ulugh Beg was seventeen years old and was governor of Samarkand. He had appointed Qāḍī Zāda as private professor of mathematics and astronomy. *Qāmūs al-a'lam,* 2, 1023.
2. The full title of this work by Qāḍī Zāda is *Risāla fī istikhrāj jayb daraja wāḥida bi'l-a'māl al-mu'assasa 'alā qawā'id ḥisābiyya wa-handasiyya* ("Treatise on the Determination of sin 1°, With the Aid of the Rules of Computation and of Geometry"). It is in the *Dastūr al-'amal wa-taṣḥiḥ al-jadwal*

of Mīram Chelebi: Süleymaniyye Library, Istanbul, Hassan Hüsnü 1284; and in the same library, Tchorloulou Ali Pasha 342. Also in the Bibliothèque Nationale, in Paris, MSS Thévenol, Anc. Fonds 171.

3. Although the equation (4) that expresses the theorem is not in Euclid's *Elements,* it can readily be verified. From the obvious equalities $\overline{A'C} = 2\overline{OM}$ and $\overline{OM} = R - \overline{MB}$, one immediately derives the relations $\overline{A'C} = 2R - 2\overline{MB}$ and $\overline{AA'} - \overline{A'C} = 2\overline{MB}$. Demonstrating the theorem thus reduces to verifying

$$\frac{2\overline{MB}}{\overline{AB}} = \frac{\overline{AB}}{R}, \text{ or } (4') \ \overline{AB}^2 = 2R \cdot \overline{MB}.$$

On the other hand, from the triangles (see Figure 2) AMB and OAM one can write the equations

$$\overline{AM}^2 = \overline{AB}^2 - \overline{MB}^2; \ \overline{AM}^2 = R^2 - \overline{OM}^2.$$

Then, from the fact that $\overline{OM} = R - \overline{MB}$, one obtains

$$AB^2 - MB^2 = R^2 - (R - \overline{MB})^2,$$

which, after simplification, gives equation (4').

4. Abu'l Wafa' had found sin 1° $\cong$ 0.017452414587, which is exact to within 10^{-7}. Bibliothèque Nationale, Paris, MS 1138.

BIBLIOGRAPHY

I. ORIGINAL WORKS. *Risāla fi'l-ḥisāb* ("Treatise on Arithmetic"), which covers arithmetic, algebra, and measures, was written at Bursa in 1383. It is now in Šehid Ali Paša, Šehzada Ğami, Istanbul.

Sharḥ al-Mulaḥḥaṣ fi'l-hay'a, a commentary on the *Mulaḥḥaṣ* ("Compendium") of the astronomer 'Umar al-Jaghmīnī (d. 1444/1445), was written at Samarkand in 1412–1413 for Ulugh Beg. Several copies of the work are at Istanbul and in various European libraries. It has been printed at Delhi, Lucknow, and Teheran.

Sharḥ Ashkāl al-ta'sīs, a commentary on the *Ashkāl al-ta'sīs* ("Fundamental Theorems") of Shams al-Dīn al-Samarqandī, was written at Samarkand in 1412. It contains 35 propositions from Euclid's *Elements.* It is now in the Ayasofya (Süleymaniyya) Library, Istanbul, MS 2712. An author's autograph copy is at Bursa, Haradji-oğlou Library, no. 21. A Turkish trans. of *Ashkāl al-ta'sīs* by Muftu Zāda 'Abd al-Raḥīm Effendi (1795) is in the library of the Technical University of Istanbul, No. (4316–5075).

Risāla fi'l-hay'a wa 'l-handasa ("Treatise on Astronomy and Geometry"), in an author's autograph copy, is in Iné Bey Library, Bursa, MS 25.

Risāla fī samt al-qibla ("Treatise on the Azimuth of Qibla"), dealing with facing Mecca during prayer, is in Bursa, Iné Bey Library, MS 12. It also contains a short work by Mīram Chelebi, *Risāla fī taḥqīq samt al-qibla wa-barāhiniha* ("Treatise on the Verification and Proof of the Azimuth of Qibla").

Risālat al-jayb ("Treatise on the Sine"), Qāḍī Zāda's most original work, was written at Samarkand at the time of al-Kāshī. See Mīram Chelebi, *Dastūr al-'amal wa-taṣḥiḥ al-jadwal,* Süleymaniyya Library, Istanbul, Hassan Hüsnü

1284 and Tchorloulou Ali Pasha 342.

II. SECONDARY LITERATURE. See Adnan Adivar, *Osmanli Türklarinde Ilim* (Istanbul, 1943), 4; B. A. Rozenfeld and A. P. Youschkevitch, "Primechania k traktatu Kazi-Zade Ar-Rumi" ("Notes on a Treatise of Qāḍī Zāda"), in *Istoriko-matematicheskie issledovania*, **13** (1960), 552–556; Süheyl Ünver, *Ali Kuschdju* (Istanbul, 1948), 73; and Sälih Zeki, *Assār-i Bāqiyya*, I (Istanbul, 1913), 186.

HÂMİT DİLGAN

AL-QALAṢĀDĪ (or **AL-QALṢĀDĪ**), **ABU 'L-ḤASAN ʿALĪ IBN MUḤAMMAD IBN ʿALĪ** (*b*. Basṭa [now Baza], Spain, 1412; *d*. Béja, Tunisia, December 1486)

Al-Qalaṣādī, the last known Spanish-Muslim mathematician, is also known by the epithets al-Qurashī and al-Basṭi, the latter referring to his place of birth. He remained in Basṭa until the city was taken by the Christians, at which time he began his journey through the Islamic world and studied with learned men.

Several books on arithmetic and one on algebra are attributed to al-Qalaṣādī. The one on algebra is a commentary on the *al-urjūzā al-Yāsmīnīya* of Ibn al-Yāsmīnī (*d*. 1204), which gave algebraic rules in verse. This *urjūzā* (poem) had been commented upon by several Western Muslims before al-Qalaṣādī.

One of his arithmetical works is a commentary on the *Talkhīṣ aʿmāl al-ḥisāb* ("Summary of Arithmetical Operations") of Ibn al-Bannā'; several summaries and extracts of this commentary have reached us. Al-Qalaṣādī's original work began with *al-Tabṣira fī'lm al-ḥisāb* ("Clarification of the Science of Arithmetic"); it proved to contain difficult material, and he therefore simplified it in *Kashf al-jilbāb 'an ʿilm al-ḥisāb* ("Unveiling the Science of Arithmetic"). A shorter version of the same work is *Kashf al-asrār ʿan waḍ ʿḥurūf al-ghubār* ("Unfolding the Secrets of the Use of Dust Letters [Hindu Numerals]"). The last two are said to have been used in some schools of North Africa for several generations, and the last is the work studied by F. Woepcke in his "Traduction du traité d'arithmétique d'Aboûl-Haçan Alî Ben Mohammed Alklçadî" (*Atti dell'Accademia pontificia de' nuovi lincei*, **12** [1858-1859], 399-438).

Since the 1850's al-Qalaṣādī has been credited with the following:

Dealing with the sequences $\sum n^2$ and $\sum n^3$.

Using the method of successive approximations for obtaining the roots of imperfect squares.

Using symbols in algebraic equations.

In the light of our present knowledge, the following can be stated:

First, al-Qalaṣādī has no claim to priority in the field of sequences. Those that he treated and more advanced ones, such as those of polygonal and pyramidal numbers, had been treated by Abū Manṣūr al-Baghdādī (*d*. 1037) and al-Umawī al-Andalusī (*fl*. fourteenth century).

Second, the method of finding square roots by successive approximation had been known to the Greeks and, probably, the Babylonians. In principle, it states that if r_1 is an approximation of $\sqrt{n}$, then let $r_2 = n/r_1$ and a better approximation is $r_3 = \frac{1}{2}(r_1 + r_2)$.

This method must have been known to the arithmeticians of eastern Islam, but they seem to have preferred to find roots expressed in sexagesimal fractions in almost the same way we use to find them to any desired decimal place. Al-Qalaṣādī, however, is the first mathematician known to have stressed it.

Third, al-Qalaṣādī used both short Arabic words and letters as symbols. The short words are

> *wa* (and) for addition
> *illā* (less) for subtraction
> *fī* (times) for multiplication
> *ʿalā* (over) for division.

Letters were also used to designate certain terms; these correspond to:

> *j* for *jadhr* (root)
> *sh* (from *shay'*, "thing"), or ∴ (the diacritical points from *shay'*) for *x*.
> *m* for *māl* (x^2)
> *k* for *kaʿb* (x^3)
> *mm* for *mal mal* (x^4)
> *l* (from the verb *yaʿdilu*) for equality.

The letters, more than the words, indicate a sense of symbolism. But al-Qalaṣādī has no claim to priority here, either; the same symbols were used in the same way by Ibn Qunfudh of Algiers (*d*. 1407/1408) and Yaʿqūb Ibn Ayyūb of Morocco (*fl. ca.* 1350), and many earlier writers in the East.

Like similar works from the thirteenth century on, al-Qalaṣādī's writings show Arabic arithmetic and algebra when their constituents—ancient manipulational tradition, Hindu techniques, and Greek number theory—are combined to form one entity. But they also reflect a civilization on the wane, for most of them are commentaries, summaries, or summaries of summaries of works by al-Qalaṣādī himself or by others.

BIBLIOGRAPHY

See C. Brockelmann, *Geschichte der arabischen literatur*, II, pt. 2 (Leiden, 1949), 343–344, and supp. II (Leiden,

1938), 363–369; al-Maqqarī, *Nafḥ al-ṭib*, Iḥsān 'Abbās, ed., II (Beirut, 1968), 692–694; and H. Suter, *Die Mathematiker und Astronomen der Araber und ihre Werke* (Leipzig, 1900), no. 444, pp. 180–182. The best Arabic biography of al-Qalaṣādī is perhaps that written by M. Souissi of the University of Tunisia in the University periodical, **9** (1972), 33–49.

A. S. SAIDAN

QUETELET, LAMBERT-ADOLPHE-JACQUES (*b*. Ghent, Belgium, 22 February 1796; *d*. Brussels, Belgium, 17 February 1874)

Adolphe Quetelet was the son of François-Augustin-Jacques-Henri Quetelet and Anne-Françoise Vandervelde. After graduating from the *lycée* in Ghent he spent a year as a teacher in Oudenaarde. In 1815 he was appointed professor of mathematics at the Collège of Ghent. He wrote an opera, together with his friend G. P. Dandelin (better known for a theorem on conics); he also published poems and essays. Quetelet was the first to receive a doctorate (1819) from the newly established University of Ghent, with a dissertation on geometry. The same year he was appointed professor of *mathématiques élémentaires* at the Athénée of Brussels. In 1820 he was elected a member of the Académie Royale des Sciences et Belles-Lettres of Brussels. During the next years he worked in geometry. His papers were published by the Academy and in the periodical *Correspondance mathématique et physique*, which he founded and coedited with J. G. Garnier, a professor at Ghent who had guided Quetelet's first steps in higher mathematics. From 1824 Quetelet taught higher mathematics at the Athénée and physics and astronomy at the Musée, which later became the Université Libre. His wife, whom he married in 1825, was a daughter of the French physician Curtet and a niece of the chemist van Mons; she bore him a son and a daughter. In 1826 he published popular books on astronomy and on probability.

From 1820 Quetelet had proposed founding an observatory, and in 1823 the government sent him to Paris to gain experience in practical astronomy. Here he met famous scientists. His increasing interest in probability was possibly due to the influence of Laplace and Fourier. In 1827 he went to England to buy astronomical instruments and to visit universities and observatories. The following year he was appointed astronomer at the Brussels Royal Observatory, which was not completed until 1833. Meanwhile he traveled extensively. In 1834 he was elected permanent secretary of the Brussels Academy.

From 1832 Quetelet lived at the observatory. His research there was more meteorological and geophysical than astronomical, with an emphasis on statistics. He had turned to statistics as early as 1825, and until 1835 he wrote a considerable number of papers on social statistics. In that year he published *Sur l'homme et le développement de ses facultés, essai d'une physique sociale*, which made him famous throughout Europe. Subsequently a great part of his activity consisted in organizing international cooperation in astronomy, meteorology, geophysics, and statistics. His work after 1855 was impaired by the consequences of a stroke he had suffered in that year.

Quetelet was an honorary member of a great many learned societies and received many decorations. His funeral was a gathering of princes and famous scientists, and his memory was honored by a monument, unveiled in Brussels in 1880.

By his contemporaries his personality has been described as gay, charming, enthusiastic, and gifted with wide intellectual interests. Though he exerted a tremendous influence in his lifetime, his fame hardly survived him. His work has not been republished since his death.

The word "*Statistik*," first printed in 1672, meant *Staatswissenschaft* or, rather, a science concerning the states. It was cultivated at the German universities, where it consisted of more or less systematically collecting "state curiosities" rather than quantitative material. The actual predecessor of modern statistics was the English school of political arithmetic; the first effort to describe society numerically was made by Graunt in 1661. This school, however, which included Malthus, suffered from a lack of statistical material. In 1700 Napoleon, influenced by Laplace and fond of numerical data, established the Bureau de Statistique. In 1801 the first general censuses were held in France and England. Statistics became a fashionable subject, but nobody knew what kind of data to collect or how to organize the material. Nothing was done to justify Fourier's plea:

"Statistics will not make any progress until it is trusted to those who have created profound mathematical theories."

With Quetelet's work of 1835 a new era in statistics began. It presented a new technique of statistics or, rather, the first technique at all. The material was thoughtfully elaborated, arranged according to certain preestablished principles, and made comparable. There were not very many statistical figures in the book, but each figure reported made sense. For every number, Quetelet tried to find the determining influences, its natural causes, and the perturbations caused by man. The work gave a description of the average man as both a static and a dynamic phenomenon.

This work was a tremendous achievement, but Quetelet had aimed at a much higher goal: social physics, as the subtitle of his work said; the same title under which, since 1825, Comte had taught what he later called sociology. Terms and analogies borrowed from mechanics played a great part in Quetelet's theoretical exposition. To find the laws that govern the social body, said Quetelet, one has to do what one does in physics: to observe a large number of cases and then take averages. Quetelet's average man became a slogan in nineteenth-century discussions on social science. The use of mathematics and physics in social sciences was praised, although none of the parties to the discussions knew what it should really mean.

The above statement also applied to Quetelet himself. There is not much more mathematics contained in his work than the vague idea that the reliability of an average increases with the size of the population—and even this idea was not understood by many of his contemporaries. It is evident that Quetelet knew more about mathematical statistics, but he never thought to apply it in his social statistics. Neither did he make significance tests, although as early as 1840 they came into use in medical statistics. He often urged that one should consider not only the average but also the deviation in order to know whether the latter is accidental or not, but he never followed up this suggestion. He always judged intuitively whether a statistical figure was constant or variable under different conditions.

In more theoretical work about 1845, Quetelet approached mathematical statistics more closely. For the first time he mentioned the normal distribution, or, rather, a binomial distribution of a high degree. As an example, he explained the error distribution by the theory of elementary errors. Possibly he made this discovery independently of Thomas Young, G. Hagen, and Bessel. In any case it was clearly Quetelet's own achievement to unveil the normal distribution of the heights of a population of soldiers. The normal distribution, not only as a law of observation errors but also as a genuine natural law, was indeed an important discovery, although Quetelet's examples were not convincing.

Quetelet's impact on nineteenth-century thinking can in a certain sense be compared with Descartes's in the seventeenth century. He certainly gave science new aims and tools, although his philosophy was rather pedestrian and his thinking in somewhat sophisticated matters was rather confused. There was a strong emotional component in Quetelet's influence. In fact, he became famous for a passage, quoted again and again from *Sur l'homme*, in which he draws his conclusions from the statistics of the French criminal courts from 1826 to 1831:

> The constancy with which the same crimes repeat themselves every year with the same frequency and provoke the same punishment in the same ratios, is one of the most curious facts we learn from the statistics of the courts; I have stressed it in several papers; I have repeated every year: *There is an account paid with a terrifying regularity; that of the prisons, the galleys, and the scaffolds. This one must be reduced.* And every year the numbers have confirmed my prevision in a way that I can even say: there is a tribute man pays more regularly than those owed to nature or to the Treasury; the tribute paid to crime! Sad condition of human race! We can tell beforehand how many will stain their hands with the blood of their fellow-creatures, how many will be forgers, how many poisoners, almost as one can foretell the number of births and deaths.

> Society contains the germs of all the crimes that will be committed, as well as the conditions under which they can develop. It is society that, in a sense, prepares the ground for them, and the criminal is the instrument . . . .

This observation, which seems discouraging at first sight, is comforting at closer view, since it shows the possibility of improving people by modifying their institutions, their habits, their education, and all that influences their behaviour. This is in principle nothing but an extension of the law well-known to philosophers: as long as the causes are unchanged, one has to expect the same effects.

H. T. Buckle, in England, and Adolph Wagner, in Germany, were Quetelet's most fervent supporters in social science. Florence Nightingale considered his work a new Bible.

BIBLIOGRAPHY

I. ORIGINAL WORKS. Quetelet's writings include *Sur l'homme et le développment de ses facultés, essai d'une physique sociale* (Paris, 1835); "Sur l'appréciation des documents statistiques . . .," in *Bulletin de la Commission de Statistique* (de Belgique) (1845), 205–286; *Lettres à S. A. R. le duc régnant de Saxe-Cobourg et de Gotha* (Brussels, 1846); and *Du système social et des lois qui le régissent* (Paris, 1848).

II. SECONDARY LITERATURE. On Quetelet and his works, see Hans Freudenthal, "De eerste ontmoeting tussen de wiskunde en de sociale wetenschappen," in *Verhandelingen van de K. vlaamse academie voor wetenschappen, letteren en schone kunsten van België*, **28**, no. 88 (1966); Maurice Halbwachs, *La théorie de l'homme moyen* (Paris, 1912); F. H. Hankins, *Adolphe Quetelet as Statistician* (New York, 1908); G. F. Knapp, "Bericht über die Schriften Quetelets zur Socialstatistik und Anthropologie," in *Jahrbücher für*

Nationalökonomie und Statistik, **17** (1871), 106–174, 342, 358; J. Lottin, *Quetelet statisticien et sociologue* (Paris, 1912); and E. Mailly, *Essai sur la vie et les ouvrages de L.-A.-J. Quetelet* (Brussels, 1875).

HANS FREUDENTHAL

AL-QŪHĪ (or AL-KŪHĪ), ABŪ SAHL WAYJAN IBN RUSTAM (*fl.* Baghdad, *ca.* 970–1000)

Al-Qūhī's names indicate his Persian origin: al-Qūhī means "from Quh," a village in Tabaristan; and Rustam is the name of a legendary Persian hero. At the peak of his scientific activity he worked in Baghdad under the Buwayhid caliphs ʿAḍud al-Dawla and his son and successor Sharaf al-Dawla.

In 969/970 al-Qūhī assisted at the observations of the winter and summer solstices in Shiraz. These observations, ordered by ʿAḍud al-Dawla, were directed by Abūʾl Ḥusayn ʿAbd al Raḥmān ibn ʿUmar al-Ṣūfī; Aḥmad ibn Muḥammad ibn ʿAbd al Jalīl al Sijzī and other scientists were also present. In 988 Sharaf al-Dawla instructed al-Qūhī to observe the seven planets, and al-Qūhī constructed a building in the palace garden to house instruments of his own design. The first observation was made in June 988 in the presence of al-Qūhī, who was director of the observatory; several magistrates (*quḍāt*); and the scientists Abūʾl Wafāʾ, Aḥmad ibn Muḥammad al-Ṣāghānī, Abūʾl Ḥasan Muḥammad al-Sāmarrī, Abūʾl Ḥasan al-Maghribī, and Abū Isḥāq Ibrāhīm ibn Hilāl ibn Ibrāhīm ibn Zahrūn al Ṣābī. Correspondence between Abū Isḥāq and al-Qūhī still exists. They very accurately observed the entry of the sun into the sign of Cancer and, about three months later, its entry into the sign of Libra. Al-Bīrūnī related that activity at al-Qūhī's observatory ceased with the death of Sharaf al-Dawla in 989.

Al-Qūhī, whom al-Khayyāmī considered to be an excellent mathematician, worked chiefly in geometry. In the writings known to us he mainly solved geometrical problems that would have led to equations of higher than the second degree. Naṣīr al Dīn al Ṭūsī adds to his edition of Archimedes' *Sphere and Cylinder* the following note by al-Qūhī: "To construct a sphere segment equal in volume to a given sphere segment, and equal in surface area to a second sphere segment —a problem similar to but more difficult than related problems solved by Archimedes—Al-Qūhī constructed the two unknown lengths by intersecting an equilateral hyperbola with a parabola and rigorously discussed the conditions under which the problem is solvable."

The same precision is found in *Risāla fī istikhrāj ḍilʿ al-musabbaʿ al-mutasāwīʾlʿ-aḍlāʿ fīʾd-dāʾira* ("Con-

struction of the Regular Heptagon"), a construction more complete than the one attributed to Archimedes. Al-Qūhī's solution is based on finding a triangle with an angle ratio of 1:2:4. He constructed the ratio of the sides by intersecting a parabola and a hyperbola, with all parameters equal. Al-Sijzī, who claimed to follow the method of his contemporary Abū Saʿd al-ʿAlā ibn Sahl, used the same principle. The latter, however, knew al-Qūhī's work, having written a commentary on the treatise *Kitāb ṣanʿat al-asṭurlāb* ("On the Astrolabe"). Another method used by al-Qūhī is found in al-Sijzī's treatise *Risāla fī qismat al-zāwiya* ("On Trisecting an Angle").

Again, in *Risāla fī istikhrāj misāḥat al-mujassam al-mukāfī* ("Measuring the Parabolic Body"), al-Qūhī gave a somewhat simpler and clearer solution than Archimedes had done. He said that he knew only Thābit ibn Qurra's treatise on this subject, and in three propositions showed a shorter and more elegant method. Neither computed the paraboloids originating from the rotation of the parabola around an ordinate. That was first done by Ibn al-Haytham, who was inspired by Thābit's and al-Qūhī's writings. Although he found al-Qūhī's treatment incomplete, Ibn al-Haytham was nevertheless influenced by his trend of thought.

Analyzing the equation $x^3 + a = cx^2$, al-Qūhī concluded that it had a (positive) root if $a \leqslant 4c^3/27$. This result, already known to Archimedes, apparently was not known to al-Khayyāmī, whose solution is less accurate. Al-Khayyāmī also stated that al-Qūhī could not solve the equation $x^3 + 13.5x + 5 = 10x^2$ while Abūʾl Jūd was able to do so. (Abūʾl Jūd, a contemporary of al-Bīrūnī, worked on geometric problems leading to cubic equations; his main work is not extant.)

In connection with Archimedean mathematics, Steinschneider stated that al-Qūhī also wrote a commentary to Archimedes' *Lemmata*. In I. A. Borelli's seventeenth-century Latin edition of the *Lemmata* (or *Liber assumptorum*), there is a reference to al-Qūhī.

Al-Qūhī was the first to describe the so-called conic compass, a compass with one leg of variable length for drawing conic sections. In this clear and rather general work, *Risāla fīʾl birkar al-tāmm* ("On the Perfect Compass"), he first described the method of constructing straight lines, circles, and conic sections with this compass, and then treated the theory. He concluded that one could now easily construct astrolabes, sundials, and similar instruments. Al-Bīrūnī asked his teacher Abū Naṣr Manṣūr ibn ʿIrāq for a copy of the work; and in al-Bīrūnī, Ibn al-Ḥusayn found a reference to al-Qūhī's treatise. Having tried in vain to obtain a copy, Ibn al-Ḥusayn wrote a somewhat inferior work on the subject (H. Suter, *Die Mathematiker und Astronomen der Araber und ihre Werke* [Leipzig, 1900], p. 139).

Al-Qūhī also produced works on astronomy (Brockelmann lists a few without titles), and the treatise on the astrolabe mentioned above. Abū Naṣr Manṣūr ibn ʿIrāq, who highly esteemed al-Qūhī, gave proofs for constructions of azimuth circles by al-Qūhī in his *Risāla fī dawāʾir as-sumūt fī al-asṭurlāb* ("Azimuth Circles on the Astrolabe").

BIBLIOGRAPHY

I. ORIGINAL WORKS. C. Brockelmann, *Geschichte der arabischen Literatur*, 2nd ed., I (Leiden, 1943), 254 and Supp. I (Leiden, 1937), 399, list most of the available MSS of al-Qūhī. See also G. Vajda, "Quelques notes sur le fonds de manuscrits arabes de la bibliothèque nationale de Paris," in *Rivista degli studi orientali*, **25** (1950), 1–10.

Translations or discussions of al-Qūhī's work are in A. Sayili, "A Short Article of Abū Sahl Waijan ibn Rustam al-Qūhī on the Possibility of Infinite Motion in Finite Time," in *Actes du VIII Congrès international d'histoire des sciences* (Florence–Milan, 1956), 248–249; and "The Trisection of the Angle by Abū Sahl Wayjan ibn Rustam al Kūhī," in *Proceedings of the Tenth International Congress of History of Science* (Ithaca, 1962), 545–546; Y. Dold-Samplonius, "Die Konstruktion des regelmässigen Siebenecks nach Abū Sahl al-Qūhī Waiǧan ibn Rustam," in *Janus*, **50** (1963), 227–249; H. Suter, "Die Abhandlungen Thābit ben Ḳurras und Abū Sahl al-Kūhīs über die Ausmessung der Paraboloide," in *Sitzungsberichte der Physikalisch-medizinischen Sozietät in Erlangen*, **49** (1917), 186–227; and F. Woepcke, *L'algèbre d'Omar Alkhayyāmī* (Paris, 1851), 96–114, 118, 122, 127; and "Trois traités arabes sur le compas parfait," in *Notices et extraits de la Bibliothèque nationale*, **22**, p. 1 (1874), 1–21, 68–111, 145–175.

Edited by the Osmania Oriental Publications Bureau are *Risāla fī misāḥat al mujassam al mukāfī* ("On Measuring the Parabolic Body") (Hyderabad, 1948) and *Min kalāmi Abī Sahl fī mā zāda min al ashkāl fī amr al maqālat al ṣāniyati* ("Abū Sahl's Discussion on What Extends the Propositions in the Instruction of the Second Book") (Hyderabad, 1948).

II. SECONDARY LITERATURE. Ibn al-Qifṭī, *Taʾrīkh al-ḥukamāʾ*, J. Lippert, ed. (Leipzig, 1903), 351–354. Information on al-Qūhī the mathematician is also in Woepcke, *L'algèbre ...*, 54–56; and A. P. Youschkevitch, *Geschichte der Mathematik im Mittelalter* (Basel, 1964), 258–259, 292. On the observations in Shirāz, see al-Bīrūnī, *Taḥdīd nihāyāt al-amākin li-taṣḥīḥ masāfāt al-masākin* (Cairo, 1962), 99–100; on the observations at Baghdad, A. Sayili, *The Observatory in Islam* (Ankara, 1960), 112–117; M. Steinschneider, "Die mittleren Bücher der Araber und ihre Bearbeiter," in *Zeitschrift für Mathematik und Physik*, **10** (1865), 480.

YVONNE DOLD-SAMPLONIUS

RADEMACHER, HANS (*b.* Wandsbeck, Schleswig-Holstein, Germany, 3 April 1892; *d.* Haverford, Pennsylvania, 7 February 1969)

Rademacher attended the University of Göttingen, where he studied real functions and the calculus of variations with Constantin Carathéodory and number theory with Edmund Landau. He received the doctorate in 1916 with a dissertation on single-valued mappings and mensurability. After teaching at a school in Thuringia run by teachers with modern ideas, Rademacher became *Privatdozent* at the University of Berlin in December 1916. There he was influenced by Erhard Schmidt, Issai Schur, and Hans Hamburger. In 1922 he was appointed associate professor with tenure at Hamburg. Under the influence of Erich Hecke he turned to number theory, writing at first on the method devised by Viggo Brun and later on the additive prime-number theory of algebraic numbers.

Rademacher's chief field of interest for forty years was analytic number theory, particularly additive problems. At Easter 1925, after long hesitation, he went to Breslau. (Hecke had vainly attempted to procure a corresponding position for him at Hamburg.) There he was concerned in particular with the behavior of the logarithm of the function

$$\eta(\tau) = e^{\frac{2\pi i\tau}{24}} \prod_n (1 - e^{2\pi i\tau n}), \qquad \mathrm{Im}(\tau) > 0$$

with respect to modulus substitutions. The function $\eta(\tau)$ had appeared, in its essential aspects, in the writings of Euler. Dedekind had later treated it in the course of his comments on a fragment of Riemann's (see Riemann, *Gesammelte ... Werke*, R. Dedekind and H. Weber, eds. [1876], 438–447). Rademacher devised a new proof of the results obtained with the function, utilizing the connection between modular functions and Dirichlet series over the Mellin integral (Hecke's method).

During this period Rademacher wrote, in collaboration with Otto Toeplitz, *Von Zahlen und Figuren*, addressed to a broad, nonprofessional audience. In many of his lectures Rademacher discussed fundamental problems in extremely diverse fields and the ways in which they had been treated. Forced to flee Germany in 1933 because of his pacifist views, he went to Swarthmore College and later to the University of Pennsylvania, all the while continuing his research on analytic number theory. His most outstanding achievement was the proof of his asymptotic formula for the growth of the function $p(n)$, which yields the number of representations of a natural number n as a sum of natural numbers. The question had been raised much earlier by Leibniz (see his *Mathematische Schriften*, C. I. Gerhardt, ed., III). Then Euler found that

$$\prod_{n=1}^{\infty} (1 - x^n)^{-1} = \sum_{\kappa=0}^{\infty} p(\kappa)\, x^{\kappa}.$$

The first asymptotic formula for $p(n)$ originated with Hardy and Ramanujan (*Proceedings of the London Mathematical Society*, 2nd ser., **17** [1918], 75–115); Rademacher proposed a simpler formula for $p(n)$ that led to remarkable results. As an example he calculated $p(599)$, a number that consists of twenty-four digits in the decimal system. Rademacher's asymptotic formula deviated from this by only about 0.5.

BIBLIOGRAPHY

A detailed bibliography of Rademacher's works is in *Jahresberichte der Deutschen Mathematiker-Vereinigung*, **71** (1969), 204–205. His writings include "Eindeutige Abbildung und Messbarkeit," in *Monatshefte für Mathematik und Physik*, **27** (1916), 183–290; "Über streckentreue und winkeltreue Abbildungen," in *Mathematische Zeitschrift*, **4** (1919), 131–138; "Über partielle und totale Differenzierbarkeit von Funktionen mehrerer Variablen," in *Mathematische Annalen*, **79** (1919), 340–359, and **81** (1920), 52–63, his *Habilitationsschrift*; "Beiträge zur Viggo Brunschen Methode in der Zahlentheorie," in *Abhandlungen aus dem Mathematischen Seminar, Universität Hamburg*, **3** (1924), 12–30; "Zur additiven Primzahltheorie algebraischer Zahlkörper," *ibid.*, 109–163, 331–337, and *Mathematische Zeitschrift*, **27** (1927), 324–426; "Zur Theorie der Modulfunktionen," in *Journal für die reine und angewandte Mathematik*, **167** (1932), 312–336; *Von Zahlen und Figuren* (Berlin, 1933; repr. 1968), written with Otto Toeplitz, also trans. into English as *The Enjoyment of Mathematics* (Princeton, 1957); "On the Partition Function $p(n)$," in *Proceedings of the London Mathematical Society*, 2nd ser., **43** (1937), 241–254; "On the Expansion of the Partition Function in a Series," in *Annals of Mathematics*, 2nd ser., **44** (1943), 416–422; "Zur Theorie der Dedekindschen Summen," in *Mathematische Zeitschrift*, **63** (1956), 445–463; and "A Proof of a Theorem on Modular Functions," in *American Journal of Mathematics*, **82** (1960), 338–340.

A short account of Rademacher's life appears in Max

Pinl, "Kollegen in einer dunkeln Zeit," in *Jahresberichte der Deutschen Mathematiker-Vereinigung*, **71** (1969), 205 ff.

HEINRICH BEHNKE

RADÓ, TIBOR (*b.* Budapest, Hungary, 2 June 1895; *d.* New Smyrna Beach, Florida, 12 December 1965)

The son of Alexander Radó and Gizella Knappe, Radó began his university studies in civil engineering at the Technical University in Budapest. In 1915 he enlisted in the Royal Hungarian Army, was trained, and then commissioned a second lieutenant in the infantry. He took part in two major battles on the Russian front before being captured on a scouting mission. Of his capture, Radó recounted: "I had spent six months traveling back and forth through the Russian lines, picking up information, cutting telephone wires and holding up supply trains. Then one day I was surrounded by Russians—I wasn't surprised."

His four years in prison camps read like a dramatic scenario. As an officer he found the camp in Tobolsk, Siberia, relatively comfortable in the period preceding the Revolution. Food was plentiful and cheap, but reading material was not readily available. The only books he could obtain happened to be on mathematics.

After the Revolution, the prisoners' life changed drastically. They were packed into boxcars and transported thousands of miles under harrowing conditions, in order to get them out of the fighting zone. During the confusion he and three fellow officers traded names with four private soldiers. As far as his family knew, Radó was dead. He spent the next year working as a laborer in railroad yards. He and a group of prisoners escaped by hijacking a train. Finally, in 1920 he returned to Budapest on an American financed boat which was assisting in the return of war prisoners. Back at the University of Szeged, he re-enrolled, this time as a mathematics major, and in 1922 he received his Ph.D. under Frigyes Riesz.

From 1922 to 1929 Radó was *Privatdozent* at the University of Szeged and also adjunct at the Mathematical Institute in Budapest. He was awarded an international research fellowship of the Rockefeller Foundation to study at Munich during 1928–1929. In 1929 Radó went to the United States as a visiting lecturer, first at Harvard (fall semester, 1929–1930) and then at Rice Institute (spring semester, 1930). In 1930 he moved to Ohio State University as full professor of mathematics.

In 1944–1945 Radó was a fellow at the Institute for Advanced Studies at Princeton. At the end of World War II, he went to Europe as a scientific consultant with the Army Air Force to recruit German scientists needed by the United States. He returned to Ohio State as chairman of the mathematics department in 1946. He resigned this post in 1948, when he was appointed the first Ohio State University research professor, a position created to enable distinguished faculty members to pursue creative activity.

Radó's research interests and contributions span a wide range of topics: conformal mapping, real variables, calculus of variations, partial differential equations, measure and integration theory, point-set and algebraic topology, rigid surfaces (very thin shells), logic, recursive functions, and what he called "Turing programs."

Radó's first major original contribution concerned Plateau's problem, finding the surface of minimal area bounded by a given closed contour in space. The problem, which originated in the initial phases of the calculus of variations, is named for Joseph Plateau, who conducted experiments on certain shapes with soap bubbles. The existence and uniqueness of solutions in the general case remained to be solved independently by Radó and Jesse Douglas in the early 1930's. Radó's interest in problems relating to surface measure dated from his work under Riesz's guidance on problems raised by Zoard de Geöcze. It was on the basis of the theory of functions of real variables of Lebesgue and Riesz that Radó was able to simplify and generalize Geöcze's results and help to create a modern theory of surface area measure.

Radó was active in mathematical societies. He was invited to give the American Mathematical Society Colloquim Lectures in 1945, and in 1952 he gave the first Mathematical Association of America Hedrick Memorial Lecture. He was also an editor of the *American Journal of Mathematics* and served as vice-president of the American Association for the Advancement of Science in 1953.

BIBLIOGRAPHY

I. ORIGINAL WORKS. Radó's major works include "On the Problem of Plateau," in *Ergebnisse der Mathematik und Ihrer Grenzgebiete*, **2** (Leipzig, 1933; repr. New York, 1951); *Sub-Harmonic Functions, Ergebnisse der Mathematik under Ihrer Grenzgebiete*, V (Leipzig, 1937; repr. New York, 1949); *Length and Area*, American Mathematical Society Colloquium Publication, XXX (New York, 1948); and *The Mathematical Theory of Rigid Surfaces: An Application of Modern Analysis* (Chapel Hill, N.C., 1954), a collection of lectures presented at a summer conference at the University of North Carolina in 1954.

II. SECONDARY LITERATURE. Antonio Mambriana, "Una visione dell'opera scientifica di Tibor Radó," in *Rivista di matematica della Università di Parma*, **1** (1950), 239–273, with portrait, covers in considerable detail Radó's contributions in conformal mapping, the Plateau problem, harmonic functions, and work related to surface area and the problems of Geöcze. It also contains an 83-item bibliography of Radó's work through 1949. Alice Holton, "Professor Recalls Siberian Prison Camp," in Columbus (Ohio) *Dispatch* (4 Dec. 1939), and Gwendolyn Riggle, "Years in Russian Concentration Camp Led Him to Professor's Post at O.S.U.," *ibid.*, (2 Mar. 1941), are descriptive interviews with Radó that cover his early life in some detail. The Ohio State University News and Information Service has prepared a short biography as well as a more complete bibliography of 102 items that was drawn up by Radó in 1960. At his death he had written more than 140 papers and books, for which no single complete bibliography exists.

HENRY S. TROPP

RADON, JOHANN (*b.* Tetschen, Bohemia [now Decin, Czechoslovakia], 16 December 1887; *d.* Vienna, Austria, 25 May 1956).

Radon entered the Gymnasium at Leitmeritz (now Litomerice), Bohemia, in 1897 and soon showed a talent for mathematics and physics. In 1905 he enrolled at the University of Vienna to study those subjects and was subsequently influenced by Gustav von Escherich, who introduced him to the theory of real functions and the calculus of variations. His doctoral dissertation (1910), on the latter subject, was also his first published paper. Radon spent the winter semester of 1911 at the University of Göttingen, served for a year as assistant professor at the University of Brünn (now Brno), then went to the Technische Hochschule of Vienna in the same capacity. He became *Privatdozent* at the University of Vienna in 1914 and achieved the same rank a year later at the Technische Hochschule.

In 1919 Radon was appointed associate professor at the University of Hamburg; he became full professor at Greifswald in 1922, at Erlangen in 1925, and at Breslau in 1928. He left Breslau in 1945 and in 1947 obtained a full professorship at Vienna, where he spent the rest of his life. In the same year he became a full member of the Austrian Academy of Sciences.

The calculus of variations remained Radon's favorite field because of its close connections with so many areas of analysis, geometry, and physics. His most important paper in this field (1927) greatly influenced its further development, especially of the difficult Lagrange problem. In 1928, in lectures at Hamburg, Radon presented his results in an expanded form. He was deeply interested in the applications of the calculus of variations to differential geometry and discovered the so-called Radon curves, which have found applications in number theory. In addition to his work in affine differential geometry (1918–1919), in conformal differential geometry (1926), and in Riemannian geometry, Radon treated mathematical problems of relativity theory. His important paper on algebra, "Lineare Scharen orthogonaler Matrizen," was inspired by his work on the calculus of variations and proved to have many applications.

Radon's best-known work, "Theorie und Anwendungen der absolut additiven Mengenfunktionen," which exerted a great influence, essentially combined the integration theories of Lebesgue and Stieltjes. Led to his research by physical considerations, he studied the most general distributions of masses in space and developed the concept of the integral, now known as the Radon integral. A continuation of this work is the paper "Über lineare Funktionaltransformationen und Funktionalgleichungen."

An important theorem in the calculus of variations, later generalized by Otton Nikodym, is the Radon-Nikodym theorem. Radon himself applied this theory to the Dirichlet problem of the logarithmic potential. He also developed a technique now known as the Radon transformation (1917), which has many applications. Radon's interest in the philosophy of mathematics was reflected in his paper "Mathematik und Wirklichkeit."

BIBLIOGRAPHY

Radon published 45 papers which still are of great importance. Among them are "Über das Minimum des Integrales $\int_{s_0}^{s_1} \mathfrak{F}\ (x,y,\theta,\chi)\ ds$," in *Sitzungsberichte der Akademie der Wissenschaften in Wien*, **119** (1910), 1257–1326; "Theorie und Anwendungen der absolut additiven Mengenfunktionen," *ibid.*, **122** (1913), 1295–1438, his *Habilitationsschrift*; "Über die Bestimmung von Funktionen durch ihre Integralwerte längs gewisser Mannigfaltigkeiten," in *Berichte über die Verhandlungen der Königlich Sächsischen Gesellschaft der Wissenschaften in Leipzig*, **69** (1917), 262–277; "Über lineare Funktionaltransformationen und Funktionalgleichungen," in *Sitzungsberichte der Akademie der Wissenschaften in Wien*, **128** (1919), 1083–1121; "Über die Randwertaufgaben beim logarithmischen Potential," *ibid.*, 1123–1167; "Lineare Scharen orthogonaler Matrizen," in *Abhandlungen aus dem Mathematischen Seminar, Universität Hamburg*, **1** (1921), 1–14; "Über statische Gravitationsfelder," *ibid.* (1922), 268–288; "Mathematik und Wirklichkeit," in *Sitzungsberichte der Physikalisch-medizinischen Sozietät in Erlangen*, **58–59** (1926–1927), 181–190; "Oszillationstheoreme der Konjugierten Punkte beim Problem von Lagrange," in *Sitzungsberichte der Bayerischen Akademie der Wissenschaften zu München*, **7** (1927), 243–257; and "Zum Problem von Lagrange," in *Abhandlungen aus dem Mathematischen Seminar, Universität Hamburg*, **6** (1928), 273–299, his lectures.

A monograph on the Radon transformation as well as applications to differential equations can be found in the book of F. John, *Plane Waves and Spherical Means* (New York, 1955). Obituaries can be found amongst others in *Monatshefte für Mathematik*, **62** (1958), 189–199, and in *Almanach. Österreichische Akademie der Wissenschaften*, **107** (1958), 363–368.

E. HLAWKA

RAMANUJAN, SRINIVASA AAIYANGAR (*b*. Erode, near Kumbakonam, Tanjore district, Madras province, India, 22 December 1887; *d*. Chetput, near Madras, India, 26 April 1920)

Ramanujan belonged to a Brahman family, but his father was poor and served as a bookkeeper in the firm of a cloth merchant in Kumbakonam. At the age of seven, after two years in elementary school, he transferred to the high school at Kumbakonam. In 1897 he placed first in the Tanjore primary examination. Ramanujan early studied some trigonometry on his own; but his real enthusiasm for the subject arose in 1903, when he was able to borrow an English text, Carr's *Synopsis of Pure Mathematics*. From then on, mathematics was nearly his only interest. He jotted down his results in a notebook which he carried with him and showed to people who were interested.

Quiet and meditative, Ramanujan was very fond of numerical calculations and had an unusual memory for numbers. In 1904 he won a fellowship at Government College, Kumbakonam. His excessive devotion to mathematics and neglect of English, a fundamental subject, led to his failure to be promoted. He returned to the college after traveling but could not graduate. He briefly attended a college in Madras, then returned to Kumbakonam, where he again failed. For several years he had no definite occupation but continued to record his mathematical results.

In 1909 Ramanujan married and was compelled to earn a living. He went to Ramaswami Aiyar, the founder of the Indian Mathematical Society, then deputy collector in the little town of Tirukkoyilur, to ask for a minor clerical job. He was sent on to Seshu Aayar, one of Ramanujan's former teachers, and obtained a substitute office job for a few months. He was then recommended to Ramachaudra Rao, collector of Nellore, eighty miles north of Madras, who was interested in mathematics; he later described Ramanujan at the time of the interview:

A short uncouth figure, stout, unshaved, not overclean, with one conspicuous feature—shining eyes—walked in with a frayed notebook under his arm. He was miserably poor.—He opened his book and began to explain some of his discoveries. I saw quite at once that there was something out of the way; but my knowledge did not permit me to judge whether he talked sense or nonsense. Suspending judgment, I asked him to come over again, and he did. And then he had gauged my ignorance and shewed me some of his simpler results. These transcended existing books, and I had no doubt he was a remarkable man. Then, step by step, he led me to elliptic integrals and hypergeometric series and at last his theory of divergent series not yet announced to the world converted me. I asked him what he wanted. He said he wanted a pittance to live on so that he might pursue his researches."

Rao was convinced that a job as a clerk was not the answer to Ramanujan's troubles and sent him back to Madras, where Rao supported him for a while and tried unsuccessfully to get a fellowship for him. When this did not succeed, Ramanujan in 1912 found a job in the office of the Madras Port Trust. At this time he began his mathematical publication in the *Journal of the Indian Mathematical Society*. His first paper, "Some Properties of Bernoulli's Numbers," was followed by a number of brief communications on series and infinite products and a geometric approximate construction of π.

Encouraged by influential friends interested in his mathematical work, Ramanujan began a correspondence with G. H. Hardy of Cambridge, one of the world's foremost specialists in analytic number theory. In his first letter Ramanujan mentioned his investigations on the distribution of primes and then added more than 100 theorems he had found in various parts of mathematics. Hardy was duly impressed and invited Ramanujan to come to England but, being a Brahman, he had scruples about leaving India. Instead a two-year fellowship was arranged for him at the University of Madras.

Hardy was disappointed and continued to attempt to persuade Ramanujan to come to Cambridge. When his colleague E. H. Neville lectured in Madras, he approached the young man and this time obtained his consent. Very favorable fellowship arrangements were made, and Ramanujan was admitted to Trinity College in 1914. He developed rapidly under the guidance of Hardy and Littlewood, who also helped him to publish his papers in English periodicals. Aside from the dozen papers in the *Journal of the Indian Mathematical Society*, questions proposed, and notes from the proceedings of meetings, Ramanujan published twenty-one papers during his five-year stay in Europe, several of them in collaboration with Hardy.

It was inevitable that a large portion of Ramanujan's results from his notebooks consisted of rediscoveries; he had never had systematic training in mathematics or access to a good library. To quote

Hardy: "What was to be done in the way of teaching him modern mathematics? The limitations of his knowledge were as startling as its profundity." He worked with modular equations and theorems of complex multiplication, yet had no notion of doubly periodic functions; he worked with analytic number theory and had only the vaguest idea of what a function of a complex variable was. Most of the theorems in the notebooks were not proved in the standard sense but were only made plausible: "His ideas as to what constituted a mathematical proof were of the most shadowy description. All his results, new or old, right or wrong, had been arrived at by a process of mingled argument, intuition and induction, of which he was entirely unable to give any coherent account." Ramanujan's investigations on the distribution of primes suffered particularly from these weaknesses and therefore contributed little to the development of the general theory.

Ramanujan's first paper published in Europe, "Modular Equations and Approximations to π," contained a number of peculiar and very good approximations to π, many of them by means of square root expressions. Of greater systematic interest is his long memoir "Highly Composite Numbers," in which he derived some important properties of these numbers. Ramanujan returned to the question of the average number of prime divisors of a number in a paper written with Hardy, "The Normal Number of Prime Factors of a Number n."

The part of Ramanujan's work that stimulated most contributions from later mathematicians is probably his study of the partition of numbers into summands. From MacMahon's extensive numerical calculations of the number $p(n)$ of partitions of a number n, Ramanujan conjectured that these integers must have simple congruence properties with respect to small primes and their powers. He was able to prove some of these results by means of formulas from the theory of elliptic functions; others have been derived later. These papers by Ramanujan on partitions were followed by a joint paper with Hardy on the asymptotic value of $p(n)$. Their result was remarkable, since not only did their formula give good approximations to the values already calculated but also seemed to give an exact expression for $p(n)$; Rademacher later established that this was correct.

Ramanujan's other work comprised a variety of topics, mainly of a combinatorial nature. He wrote on the representation of integers as the sum of squares and on the lattice points inside a circle; in function theory he produced several papers on definite integrals, as well as on elliptic, hypergeometric, and modular functions.

In 1917 Ramanujan fell ill, possibly with tuberculosis; and the remainder of his stay in England was spent in several sanatoriums. In 1918 he was elected a fellow of the Royal Society and in the same year a fellow of Trinity College. These high distinctions seemed to improve his health and stimulate his mathematical production. Nevertheless, since the English climate did not seem to be beneficial, it was decided to send him back to India. An annual allowance of £250 for five years was awarded him by the University of Madras, with prospects of a later professorship.

Ramanujan returned to Madras in April 1919 in a precarious state of health. A difficult patient who refused medical aid, he went for a while to his home district but was prevailed upon to return to Madras for treatment. Until his last days he continued his mathematical research.

BIBLIOGRAPHY

Ramanujan's works have been brought together in *Collected Papers of Srinivasa Ramanujan*, G. H. Hardy, P. V. Seshu Aiyar, and B. M. Wilson, eds. (Cambridge, 1927), and *Notebooks of Srinivasa Ramanujan*, 2 vols. (Bombay, 1957).

See also G. H. Hardy, *Ramanujan. Twelve Lectures on Subjects Suggested by His Life and Work* (Cambridge, 1940).

OYSTEIN ORE

RAMSDEN, JESSE (*b.* Halifax, England, October 1735; *d.* Brighton, England, 5 November 1800)

Ramsden was acknowledged to be the most skillful and capable instrument maker of the eighteenth century. He developed techniques that permitted him to increase greatly the precision of astronomical, surveying, and navigational equipment.

He was the son of a Halifax innkeeper and the great-nephew of Abraham Sharp, mathematician, instrument maker, and assistant to the Astronomer Royal, John Flamsteed. Ramsden's education included three years at the Halifax free school and four years' study of mathematics under the Reverend Mr. Hall. He was apprenticed at sixteen to a clothworker in Halifax. In 1755, upon finishing this service, he moved to London, where he worked as a clerk in a cloth warehouse. In 1758 he apprenticed himself to the mathematical instrument maker Burton. Ramsden opened his own shop in the Haymarket in 1762, moving to larger quarters at 199 Piccadilly in 1775. His great skill brought him commissions from the foremost practitioners of the period, including J. Sisson, J. Adams, J. Dollond, and E. Nairne. In 1765

he married Dollond's youngest daughter and for her dowry received a share of Dollond's patent on achromatic lenses.

In 1774 Ramsden published *Description of a New Universal Equatorial Instrument*, which improved on the design of Short's portable telescope mounting. Ramsden's mounting was quickly accepted and served to enhance his growing reputation. A passion for precision was the motivating force behind Ramsden's development of the dividing engine, his greatest contribution to the technology of the era. His first machine, built around 1766, produced only moderate improvement in the accuracy he sought, but the machine constructed in 1775 reduced the error to less than one-half second of arc as compared to the three seconds of arc of the first machine. This achievement earned him a grant from the Commissioners of the Board of Longitude in 1777.

Ramsden's shop grew until the staff numbered about sixty workmen. At no time, however, did he permit the quality of his output to diminish. By 1789 he had produced some one thousand sextants, as well as theodolites, micrometers, balances, barometers, and the many philosophical instruments required by the physicists of the period. It appears that the demand far exceeded his capacity for production. In 1784 William Roy, who was conducting the trigonometric survey that linked England with the Continent, ordered a three-foot-diameter theodolite from Ramsden, who took three years to complete it.

Ramsden also supplied many of the observatories of Europe with new achromatic telescopes equipped with accurately divided circles. The altazimuth instrument he built for Piazzi for the observatory at Palermo was equipped with a five-foot-diameter vertical circle. Its graduations were read by means of the micrometer microscope that Ramsden had developed. This instrument was completed in 1789, only a year late, probably because Piazzi personally expedited the project.

Ramsden was elected fellow of the Royal Society on 12 January 1786, and in 1794 he was made a member of the Imperial Academy of St. Petersburg. The Royal Society awarded him the Copley Medal (1795) for "various inventions and improvements in philosophical instruments."

Many of Ramsden's instruments have been preserved and may be seen at the Smithsonian Institution, the Science Museum and the National Maritime Museum in London, the Museum of the History of Science in Florence, Teyler's Museum in Haarlem, the Conservatoire National des Arts et Métiers in Paris, and in many other museums. His portrait is in the Science Museum in London.

BIBLIOGRAPHY

I. ORIGINAL WORKS. Ramsden's works include *Description of a New Universal Equatorial Instrument* (London, 1774; 2nd ed., 1791); *Description of an Engine for Dividing Mathematical Instruments* (London, 1777); *Description of an Engine for Dividing Straight Lines on Mathematical Instruments* (London, 1779); "Description of Two New Micrometers," in *Philosophical Transactions of the Royal Society*, **69** (1779), 419–431; and "A New Construction of Eyeglasses for Such Telescopes as May Be Applied to Mathematical Instruments," *ibid.*, **73** (1782), 94–99.

II. SECONDARY LITERATURE. On Ramsden and his work, see Maurice Daumas, *Les instruments scientifiques au XVII et XVIII siècles* (Paris, 1953), 318; Nicholas Goodison, *English Barometers, 1680–1860* (New York, 1968), 202–204; Henry C. King, *The History of the Telescope* (London, 1955), 162–172, 230–231; W. E. Knowles Middleton, *The History of the Barometer* (Baltimore, 1968), 196–198, 452–453; J. A. Repsold, *Zur Geschichte der astronomischen Messwerkzeuge, 1450–1830* (Leipzig, 1908), 82–87; Leslie Stephen and Sidney Lee, eds., *Dictionary of National Biography*, XVI (London, 1917), 708–710; and E. G. R. Taylor, *The Mathematical Practitioners of Hanoverian England* (London, 1966), 57–59, 244–245.

RODERICK S. WEBSTER

RAMSEY, FRANK PLUMPTON (*b.* Cambridge, England, 22 February 1903; *d.* Cambridge, 19 January 1930)

Ramsey, the elder son of A. S. Ramsey, president of Magdalene College, Cambridge, was educated at Winchester and Trinity colleges, Cambridge. After graduation in 1923 he was elected a fellow of King's College, Cambridge, where he spent the rest of his short life. His lectures on the foundations of mathematics impressed young students by their remarkable clarity and enthusiasm, and his untimely death deprived Cambridge of one of its most brilliant thinkers.

Whitehead and Russell, in their system of mathematical logic, *Principia Mathematica* (1910–1913), had avoided the antinomies (paradoxes) by creating both a theory of types, which dealt with the nature of propositional functions, and an axiom of reducibility. Ramsey accepted the Whitehead-Russell view of mathematics as part of logic but said of the axiom of reducibility that it is "certainly not self-evident and there is no reason to suppose it true." In his first paper (1926) he took up Wittgenstein's work on tautologies and truth functions, reinterpreting the concept of propositional functions and thus obviating the need for the axiom of reducibility. He also drew an important distinction between the logical antinomies, for example, that concerning the class of all classes not members of themselves, and those antinomies that cannot be stated in logical terms alone, for example, "I am lying." For the first class, he accepted Russell's solution; for the second, which are not formal but involve meaning, he applied his reinterpretation of the *Principia Mathematica*.

In a paper "On a Problem of Formal Logic" (1930) Ramsey discussed the *Entscheidungsproblem*—the search for a general method for determining the consistency of a logical formula—using some ingenious combinatorial theorems. To the Oxford meeting of the British Association in 1926, he described the development of mathematical logic subsequent to the publication of *Principia Mathematica*; this address was printed in the *Mathematical Gazette* (1926).

Two papers on the mathematical theory of economics appeared in the *Economic Journal*. In a biographical essay on Ramsey, J. M. Keynes described Ramsey's interest in economics, the importance of his two papers, and the way in which Cambridge economists made use of his critical powers to test their theories. An interesting, if not altogether convincing, study of the bases of probability theory was published posthumously in a collection of Ramsey's essays.

BIBLIOGRAPHY

I. ORIGINAL WORKS. Ramsey's works include "The Foundations of Mathematics," in *Proceedings of the London Mathematical Society*, 2nd ser., **25** (1926), 338–384; "Mathematical Logic," in *Mathematical Gazette*, **13** (1926), 185–194; "A Contribution to the Theory of Taxation," in *Economic Journal* (Mar. 1927); "A Mathematical Theory of Saving," *ibid.* (Dec. 1928); and "On the Problem of Formal Logic," in *Proceedings of the London Mathematical Society*, 2nd ser., **30** (1930), 264–286.

A convenient source is the posthumous volume *Foundations of Mathematics and Other Essays*, R. B. Braithwaite, ed. (London, 1931); this work contains Ramsey's published papers, excluding the two on economics, and a number of items from his unpublished manuscripts.

II. SECONDARY LITERATURE. An obituary notice by Braithwaite is in *Journal of the London Mathematical Society*, **6** (1931), 75–78. The essay on Ramsey by J. M. Keynes, in *Essays in Biography* (London, 1933), is valuable for Ramsey's work in economics and in philosophy.

T. A. A. BROADBENT

RAMUS, PETER, also known as **Pierre de La Ramée** (*b.* Cuts, Vermandois, France, 1515; *d.* Paris, France, 26 August 1572)

Born into a family that had lost its wealth but not its title of nobility with the sack of Liège in 1468, Ramus was the son of Jacques de La Ramée, a laborer, and Jeanne Charpentier. After a primary education at home, in 1527 he entered the University of Paris (Collège de Navarre), where he met his costs by working as a manservant. Apparently an outstanding student, he first drew widespread attention in 1536 with his defense of an M.A. thesis, "Quaecumque ab Aristotele dicta essent, commentitia esse," in which he attacked not only the accuracy but also the authenticity of traditional Aristotelian philosophy. The precise meaning of the thesis, of which there is no extant text, hinges on the term *commentitia*. Translated by some as "false," the word connotes, rather, something made up as opposed to factual. Ong[1] has analyzed the question closely and has argued for a meaning close to "badly organized, unmethodical."

Ramus' teaching career began at the Collège du Mans, from which he soon moved, together with Omer Talon and Bartholomew Alexandre, to the Collège de l'Ave Maria. Attracted by Johannes Sturm to the rhetorical logic and pedagogical ideas of Rudolf Agricola, Ramus undertook a program of critical reeducation that in 1543 culminated in a broad-scale attack on Aristotelian logic, *Aristotelicae animadversiones*, and plans for a new arts curriculum. A counterattack led by Antoine de Govéa soon succeeded in obtaining a royal edict forbidding Ramus to teach or write on philosophical topics. Consequently Ramus turned to rhetoric and mathematics, in part for their inherent importance but also as guises for his logical theories.

Ramus' fortunes began to improve in 1545 when, as a result of staff shortages caused by the plague, he was called to the Collège de Presles. Shortly thereafter he became principal of the college, a position he held, with some interruptions, until his death. Through the intercession of his patron, Charles Cardinal de Guise (later Cardinal de Lorraine), Ramus was released from the 1544 teaching ban upon the accession of Henry II in 1547. The release did not, however, still the controversy Ramus had aroused and was continuing to enflame through the popularity of his lectures at Presles. Moreover, the position of royal lecturer, to which Ramus was appointed in 1551, gave him even greater freedom to attack his scholastic opponents and to espouse his often radical ideas.

Beginning in 1562 Ramus' intellectual positions became increasingly fused with religious and political issues. A defense of the Roman church by the Cardinal de Lorraine at Poissy in 1561 had the unintended consequence of leading Ramus to embrace Calvinism, which he then pursued with his usual enthusiasm. In 1562 Ramus published a plan of reform for the University of Paris. This plan grew out of the work of a commission appointed by Henry II in 1557, to which Ramus had been recommended by a vote of the university faculty. Although the text appeared anonymously, internal evidence[2] makes clear Ramus' authorship but not whether the commission was defunct and, therefore, whether Ramus was acting largely on his own. He suggested a reduction of the teaching staff, the abolition of student fees, and the financing of the institution with income from monasteries and bishoprics. He also proposed a chair of mathematics, which he later endowed from his own estate; a year of physics in the arts curriculum; the teaching of civil law in the law faculty; chairs of botany, anatomy, and pharmacy, and a year of clinical practice in the medical faculty; and the study of the Old Testament in Hebrew and the New Testament in Greek in the theological faculty.[3] The plan hardly endeared him to some of his academic colleagues, who were quick to suggest a link between it and Ramus' religious persuasion. Hence, late in 1562, when Calvinists were ordered out of Paris, Ramus fled to Fontainebleau, where he found refuge for a time with the Queen Mother, Catherine de Medicis.

On his return to Paris under the Peace of Amboise in 1563, Ramus resolved to avoid controversy; but by 1565 he was leading opposition to the naming of Jacques Charpentier (no relation), a long-time adversary, to the royal chair of mathematics. Charpentier, who had by then succeeded Ramus as the Cardinal de Lorraine's protégé and who enjoyed Jesuit support, kept his chair; and Ramus, ever more threatened, in 1567 again fled Paris, taking refuge with the Prince de Condé.

Sensitive to the worsening political situation, in 1568 Ramus returned to Paris, where he found his library ransacked. He stayed just long enough to ask leave of the king to travel in Germany. From 1568 to 1570 he toured the Protestant centers of Switzerland and Germany, where he encountered an enthusiastic welcome strangely coupled with opposition to his permanent settlement in a teaching post because of his non-Aristotelian doctrines. Lured back to Paris in 1570 by promises of tolerance, Ramus soon found himself with titles and salaries, but banned from teaching. In the midst of a vast publication project, he was caught by the St. Bartholomew's Day Massacre and, despite explicit royal protection, was cruelly murdered, apparently by hired assassins.[4]

Ramus' general intellectual stance, from which his thoughts on the sciences derived, was the complex result of two distinct educations and of a life spent entirely within an academic setting. As Ong has emphasized,[5] Ramus was primarily a pedagogue, whose views on the content of philosophy were shaped by the exigencies of teaching in the arts faculty. Having received first a traditional scholastic education, with its emphasis on the Aristotelian corpus, he then immersed himself in the humanist teaching of Rudolf Agricola, who focused on Ciceronian rhetoric and dialectic and on the revival of the seven liberal arts of classical antiquity. The tensions brought about by Ramus' attempt to reconcile and combine these two traditions is best reflected in his attitude toward Aristotle. Like many "anti-Aristotelians" of his day, he aimed his criticism not so much at Aristotle himself, for whom he had genuine respect, but at contemporary Aristotelians. To concentrate solely on Aristotle's works was to ignore or to fail to appreciate a whole body of equally classical material that was often better adapted to the purposes of education.

Aristotelians, Ramus argued, had lost sight of the proper goal of teaching and had become entangled in a sterile web of logical subtleties. In concentrating on forms of the syllogism, for example, scholastics forsook the main purpose of logic, to wit, the finding of arguments and their presentation in a manner designed to convince an audience.[6] By illustrating precisely this use of logic, the works of rhetoricians and dialecticians both before and after Aristotle (most notably, Cicero) provided a more effective means of teaching the subject.

Ramus' attitude reflected a basic epistemology quite close to Aristotle's, as Ramus himself realized. Reason was a natural faculty of man which, like all natural faculties, revealed itself in its actual exercise.[7] Just as general physical principles were the product of induction from particular phenomena of nature, so too the principles of logic should be derived from examples of its effective use by orators, rhetoricians, and dialecticians. Indeed, Ramus maintained, all teaching should be rooted in examples of the use of the subject, from which students could move more easily and naturally to the general precepts underlying that use. It is a mark of Ramus' continuing commitment to Aristotle that he sought the theoretical underpinnings of this method of teaching in the *Posterior Analytics*, and his attacks on Aristotle and his followers were generally based on supposed violations of the precepts contained in that text. Ramus borrowed from the *Posterior Analytics* his three "laws of method"—*kata pantos, kat' auto*, and *kath' holou prōton*—which required that all material taught should be in the form of propositions that are universally true, demonstrable within the strict confines of the subject, and as general as possible. Although trivial in content, the "laws" became a touchstone for Ramists.[8]

Thus "method" was for Ramus primarily a pedagogical concept; accordingly, his contributions to the sciences were essentially pedagogical and propagandistic in nature. In seeking a return to the curriculum of the seven liberal arts, he sought in particular to retrieve arithmetic, geometry, astronomy, and physics (the quadrivium[9]) from the neglect into which they had fallen. As taught (when they were taught at all) they suffered from a form of intellectual detachment that made them appear more abstruse, and hence less important, than they were. Ramus' solution to this problem was twofold: first, to make clear in a series of commentaries *(scholae)* where the teaching of the sciences had gone astray and, second, to reorganize the subjects according to his own method. The result was a series of textbooks which, together with his texts on grammar, rhetoric, and dialectic, circulated widely for the next hundred years.

Ramus' twofold approach emerges most clearly from his *Scholae mathematicae* (1569) and his texts on arithmetic (1555) and geometry (1569). In the first three books of the *Scholae*, which appeared separately in 1567 under the title *Prooemium mathematicum*, he sought first to defend mathematics against charges of its lack of utility and its obscurity. Surveying the history of Greek mathematics (largely on the basis of Proclus' summary), Ramus insisted on the practical origins of the subject and on the use to which the ancients had put it, both as a theoretical foundation for natural philosophy and as a practical tool in areas like astronomy and mechanics. A mere look at the contemporary scene, he argued, revealed the continuing utility of mathematics in commerce and industry; moreover, recent developments in astronomy and mechanics showed by contrast the sterility of a scholastic natural philosophy devoid of mathematics. The blame for the neglect of mathematics lay first with Plato for having shunned its practical application (a fault Archimedes shared for not having written about his engineering feats and mechanical inventions) and then with Euclid for having severed the precepts of geometry from their use and for having written the *Elements* in an obscure syllogistic form, ostensibly following Aristotle's precepts. The remaining books of the *Scholae* are devoted to analyzing in exhaustive detail the methodological faults of the *Elements*.

The cure for obscurity lay in a return to teaching mathematics on the basis of its application to practical problems. Arithmetic should deal with computational problems occurring in the market place and in the law courts; geometry should be concerned with measurement of distances, areas, volumes, and angles, and with the types of mechanical problems to which Aristotle had applied the properties of the circle in his treatise on mechanics; the theory of proportion should be rooted in pricing and exchange problems and in applications of the law of the lever. Ramus' textbooks on arithmetic and geometry sought to effect this cure by rearranging the content of traditional arithmetical texts and of Euclid's *Elements* (together with scraps from Archimedes, Apollonius, and Pappus) in terms of the bodies of related problems that the theorems helped to solve. Apparently Ramus was perplexed about the proper role of algebra, and a text attributed to him was published only some years after his death. At one point in the *Scholae mathematicae*, however, he did suggest a link between algebra and Greek geometrical analysis, a notion that was picked up and developed by Viète and Descartes.[10]

The same separation of theory and practice led Ramus to discard completely Aristotle's *Physics* as a suitable text for natural philosophy. In terms that Bacon would later echo, Ramus argued that the *Physics* dealt not with natural phenomena but with logical analysis addressed to concepts rooted in the mind alone. Far more revealing of Aristotle's philosophy of nature were his *Mechanical Problems*, his *Meteorologica*, and his biological texts. Beyond Aristotle, Hippocrates, Plato, Theophrastus, Virgil, Pliny, Witelo, Copernicus, and Georgius Agricola all belonged in the physics curriculum; in particular, despite Aristotle's strictures, astronomy, optics, and mechanics formed an integral part of physics, even if it was more convenient to teach them separately or as subtopics of geometry. Ramus' broad view of this subject remained largely programmatic. His *Scholae physicae* appeared in 1565; but he never did write a textbook, and his lectures suggest that he lacked the technical command necessary to do so.[11] As presented to his students, Ramus' physics consisted primarily of agricultural maxims and natural history culled from Virgil and Pliny.

Ramus turned to astronomy late in his career, and apparently the subject perplexed him. Filled with admiration for this most obviously useful and practical application of mathematics, he nonetheless felt that both Ptolemy and Copernicus had succumbed to the lure of Aristotelian metaphysics in their reliance on such "hypotheses" as the principle of uniform motion on circles. In a letter written to Rheticus in 1563[12] Ramus urged a return to the observational astronomy of the Babylonians and Egyptians in an attempt to determine the nonhypothetical, directly observable regularities of the heavens and to build astronomy on them. It is unclear from his letter and from other statements whether Ramus would have accepted as "nonhypothetical" a system based on sun-centered measurements (that is, the Copernican system), although Kepler did later claim to have met Ramus' demands.[13]

Although the problem of Ramus' influence, especially in the sciences, still requires much study, it is clear that he and his works enjoyed widespread popularity both during his lifetime and in the century following his death. If that popularity was concentrated in the Protestant areas of the Rhineland, the Low Countries, England, and New England, it also filtered back to France, particularly after the accession of Henry IV. The Latin and French editions of Ramus' *Dialectics* went through a hundred printings in as many years, and his other texts seem to have been only slightly less well known. For example, through Rudolph Snellius and his son Willebrord, Ramus' mathematical works became part of the Dutch curriculum by the early 1600's, and Ramist texts in mathematics and physics spread rapidly.[14]

In particular, however, Ramus and Ramism became almost synonymous with the term "method," and all writers who dealt with the subject in the early seventeenth century, including Bacon and Descartes, felt it necessary to come to terms with Ramus' ideas. Indeed, as Ong[15] points out, the lack of reference to Ramus in the seventeenth century often means not that he had been forgotten but, rather, that the content of his thought was so well known as to obviate the need of naming the source. By emphasizing the central importance of mathematics and by insisting on the application of scientific theory to practical problem-solving, Ramus helped to formulate the quest for operational knowledge of nature that marks the Scientific Revolution.

NOTES

1. Ong, *Ramus, Method, and the Decay of Dialogue*, 45–47.
2. Cf. Waddington, *Ramus*, 141.
3. *Ibid.*, 144 ff.
4. Waddington, in *Ramus*, ch. 10, lays the blame squarely on Charpentier; but Ong (*Ramus*, 29) feels the evidence is insufficient.
5. Ong, *Ramus, passim* but esp. ch. VII, emphasizes as a main theme the continuity of pedagogical concerns within the scholastic tradition and sees many of Ramus' ideas as new solutions to old problems.
6. Here Ramus contributed decisively to a Renaissance concept that largely erased Aristotle's careful distinction between scientific logic and rhetorical dialectic. For a careful analysis of the concept, see Ong, *Ramus*, ch. IV, esp. 59–63.
7. Cf. Hooykaas, *Humanisme, science et réforme*, ch. 5.
8. Cf. Ong, *Ramus*, 258–262.
9. The traditional quadrivium made music the fourth subject, but Ramus believed music, like astronomy and optics, belonged to the wider subject of physics.

10. Cf. M. S. Mahoney, "Die Anfänge der algebraischen Denkweise im 17. Jahrhundert," in *Rete*, **1** (1971), 15–30.
11. Apparently Ramus relied heavily on the work of his students, notably Henri de Monantheuil and Risner.
12. First published in the preface to *Professio regia* (1576).
13. Cf. Hooykaas, *op cit.*, ch. 9.
14. Viète clearly knew Ramus' works, and Descartes almost certainly learned of them through Beeckman, who had studied with Rudolph Snellius.
15. Ong, *Ramus*, 9.

BIBLIOGRAPHY

I. ORIGINAL WORKS. Ramus published extensively. Waddington (see below) provides an initial survey, which has been extensively supplemented by Walter J. Ong, *Ramus and Talon Inventory. A Short-Title Inventory of the Published Works of Peter Ramus (1515–1572) and of Omer Talon (ca. 1510–1562) in Their Original and in Their Variously Altered Forms* (Cambridge, Mass., 1958). There is no modern edition of Ramus' works, although recently some have been reprinted photostatically from the originals. Ramus' most important writings include *Dialecticae partitiones sive institutiones* (Paris, 1543), later replaced by *Dialectique de Pierre de la Ramée* (Paris, 1555) and *Dialecticae libri duo, Audomari Talaei praelectionibus illustrati* (Paris, 1556); *Aristotelicae animadversiones* (Paris, 1543); *Oratio de studiis philosophiae et eloquentiae conjungendis, Lutetiae habita anno 1546* (Paris, 1547); *Arithmeticae libri duo* (Paris, 1555); *Grammaticae libri quatuor* (Paris, 1559); *Scholae grammaticae* (Paris, 1559); and *Prooemium reformandae Parisiensis Academiae, ad regem* (Paris, 1562).

Subsequent writings are *Scholarum physicarum libri octo, in totidem acroamaticos libros Aristotelis* (Paris, 1565); *Scholarum metaphysicarum libri quatuordecim, in totidem metaphysicos libros Aristotelis* (Paris, 1566); *Actiones duae habitae in senatu, pro regia mathematicae professionis cathedra* (Paris, 1566); *Prooemium mathematicum* (Paris, 1567), which is bks. I–III of *Scholae mathematicae; Geometriae libri septem et viginti* (Basel, 1569); and *Scholarum mathematicarum libri unus et triginta* (Basel, 1569).

Three important writings appeared posthumously: *Testamentum* (Paris, 1576), which endowed a chair of mathematics at the Collège Royal; *Professio regia. Hoc est, Septem artes liberales, in Regia cathedra, per [Ramum] Parisiis apodictico docendi genere propositae . . .* (Basel, 1576); and *Collectaneae Praefationes, Epistolae, Orationes* (Paris, 1577). A work on optics is also attributed to Ramus, both by its title and by references in his letters, although his precise role in it is not clear: *Opticae libri quatuor ex voto Petri Rami novissimo per Fridericum Risnerum ejusdem in mathematicis adjutorem olim conscripti* (Cassel, 1606). Similarly, Lazarus Schoner published in Frankfurt in 1586 an *Algebrae libri duo*, which he attributed to Ramus. Ramus also appears to have had some hand in Henri de Monantheuil's edition of Aristotle's *Mechanical Problems* (Paris, 1557).

II. SECONDARY LITERATURE. Two major nineteenth-century studies, Charles Desmazes' *P. Ramus: Sa vie, ses écrits, sa mort (1515–1572)* (Paris, 1864) and Charles Waddington's *Ramus (Pierre de la Ramée), sa vie, ses écrits et ses opinions* (Paris, 1855), have been updated, but not entirely superseded, by Walter J. Ong's *Ramus, Method, and the Decay of Dialogue: From the Art of Discourse to the Art of Reason* (Cambridge, Mass., 1958), which contains the best scholarly account of Ramus' theories of logic and method.

For Ramus' influence in England, see Wilbur S. Howell, *Logic and Rhetoric in England, 1500–1700* (Princeton, 1956); for his influence in New England, see Perry Miller, *The New England Mind: The Seventeenth Century* (New York, 1939); for his influence in the Low Countries, see Paul Dibon, "L'influence de Ramus aux universités néerlandaises du XVIIe siècle," *Actes du XIe Congrès international de philosophie*, XIV (Louvain, 1953), 307–311.

For a general survey of Ramus' scientific thought, see R. Hooykaas, *Humanisme, science et réforme. Pierre de la Ramée (1515–1572)* (Leiden, 1958); for his mathematics, see J. J. Verdonk, *Petrus Ramus en de wiskunde* (Assen, 1966), with extensive bibliography of his mathematical writings. Other, more specialized studies include P. A. DuHamel, "The Logic and Rhetoric of P. Ramus," in *Modern Philology*, **46** (1949), 163–171; N. W. Gilbert, *Renaissance Concepts of Method* (New York, 1960); F. P. Graves, *P. Ramus and the Educational Reform of the 16th Century* (London 1912); Henri Lebesgue, "Les professeurs de mathématique du collège de France: Humbert et Jordan; Roberval et Ramus," in *Revue scientifique*, **59** (1922), 249–262; and N. E. Nelson, *Peter Ramus and the Confusion of Logic, Rhetoric and Poetry* (Ann Arbor, 1947).

See also W. J. Ong, "P. Ramus and the Naming of Methodism," in *Journal of the History of Ideas*, **14** (1953), 235–248; Edward Rosen, "The Ramus-Rheticus Correspondence," *ibid.*, **1** (1940), 363–368; Paolo Rossi, *Francesco Bacone. Dalla magia alla scienza* (Bari, 1957); "Ramismo, logica e retorica nei secoli XVI e XVII," in *Rivista critica di storia della filosofia*, **12** (1957), 357–365, with extensive critical bibliography; *Clavis universalis. Arti mnemoniche e logica combinatoria da Lullo a Leibniz* (Milan–Naples, 1960); L. A. Sédillot, "Les professeurs de mathématiques et de physique générale au Collège de France," in *Bollettino Boncompagni*, **2** (1869), 389–418; and J. A. Vollgraff, "Pierre de la Ramée (1515–1572) et Willebrord Snel van Royen (1580–1626)," in *Janus*, **18** (1913), 595–625.

MICHAEL S. MAHONEY

RAZMADZE, ANDREI MIKHAILOVICH (*b.* Chkhenisi, Russia [now Samtredia district, Georgian S.S.R.], 11 August 1889; *d.* Tbilisi, U.S.S.R., 2 October 1929)

Razmadze was a son of a railway employee, Mikhail Gavrilovich Razmadze, and of the former Nino Georgievna Nodia. In 1906 he graduated from high school in Kutaisi and in 1910 from the mathematics department of the University of Moscow, then taught mathematics in high schools for several years. In 1917 he passed the examinations for the master's degree and for a short time was a lecturer at Moscow University. At the end of 1917 Razmadze returned to Georgia and became one of the most prominent organizers of higher education and scientific research there. He was one of the founders of Tbilisi University, opened in 1918, particularly of the Physics and Mathematics Faculty; and he spent the rest of his life as a professor there. Razmadze also had a major role in the elaboration of Georgian mathematical terminology and textbooks. He wrote texts in Georgian on infinitesimal calculus, on the introduction to analysis (1920), and on the theory of indefinite integrals (1922). These works were to have been parts of a complete course of analysis, which Razmadze was unable to complete.

Razmadze's investigations covered the calculus of variations. In this field he followed the classical direction of Weierstrass, and partly that of David Hilbert. In his first paper, published in 1914, he considered the problem of determining the plane curve minimizing the integral $\int_{t_1}^{t_2} F\left(x, y, \dfrac{dx}{dt}, \dfrac{dy}{dt}\right) dt$, when one end point of the curve is fixed and the other is absolutely free; he established the necessary and sufficient conditions of the existence of a minimum. Razmadze next largely generalized the so-called fundamental lemma of the calculus of variations; from Razmadze's lemma, Euler's differential equation for extremals of the integral $\int_a^b F\left(x, y, \dfrac{dy}{dx}\right) dx$ is deduced very simply and without partial integration.

Razmadze obtained his most important results when investigating discontinuous solutions. The first problems of the calculus of variations to be studied were those in which solutions are represented by smooth curves with continuously changing tangents. But there are problems which do not have such solutions and may be solved, for instance, by means of continuous curves with corners, where a slope of the tangent line has a jump. Such solutions, systematically studied by G. Erdmann and later by Carathéodory, were called discontinuous; but Razmadze designated them more properly as angular solutions. Proceeding further, Razmadze developed a comprehensive theory of the solutions represented by curves with a finite number of finite jumps. He presented a report on his research to the International Congress of Mathematicians at Toronto in 1924, and for that paper he received the doctorate in mathematics from the Sorbonne in 1925.

BIBLIOGRAPHY

I. ORIGINAL WORKS. Razmadze's writings) include "Über Lösungen mit einem variablen Endpunkt in der Variationsrechnung," in *Mathematische Annalen*, **75** (1914), 380–401; "Deux propositions du calcul des variations," in *Bulletin de l'Université de Tiflis*, **1** (1919–1920), 157–172; *Introduction to Analysis* (Tbilisi, 1920), in Georgian; "Über das Fundamentallemma der Variationsrechnung," in *Mathematische Annalen*, **84** (1921), 115–116; *Theory of Indefinite Integrals* (Tbilisi, 1922), in Georgian; "Über unstetige Lösungen mit einem Unstetigkeitspunkt in der Variationsrechnung," in *Bulletin de l'Université de Tiflis*, **2** (1922–1923), 282–312; "Sur une condition de minimum nécessaire pour solutions anguleuses dans le calcul des variations," in *Bulletin de la Société mathématique de France*, **51** (1923), 223–235; and "Sur les solutions discontinues dans le calcul des variations," in *Mathematische Annalen*, **94** (1925), 1–52.

II. SECONDARY LITERATURE. See L. P. Gokieli, "A. M. Razmadze," in *Trudy Tbilisskogo matematicheskogo instituta*, **1** (1937), 6–10, with bibliography of Razmadze's works on 10; and L. Tonelli, "Andrea Razmadzé," *ibid.*, 11–13.

A. P. YOUSCHKEVITCH

RÉAUMUR, RENÉ-ANTOINE FERCHAULT DE (*b.* La Rochelle, France, 28 February 1683; *d.* near St.-Julien-du-Terroux, France, 18 October 1757)

Réaumur was of an illustrious Vendée family, the Ferchaults, who prospered in trade and purchased the ancient Réaumur estate in the early seventeenth century. Through a protracted lawsuit Réaumur's grandfather, Jean Ferchault, obtained half the seignorial rights over his newly acquired fiefdom and thus entered into the ranks of the lesser French nobility. René Ferchault, Réamur's father, was a *conseiller au présidial* at La Rochelle, a position corresponding to an appellate judge in an intermediate provincial court. He married Geneviève Bouchel, the youngest daughter of a municipal magistrate from Calais, in April 1682; René-Antoine was born the following February. Réaumur's father died nineteen months later. A second son, Jean-Honoré, was born posthumously. Réamur and his brother were reared by their mother with the aid of several aunts and uncles.

Concerning Réaumur's early education, nothing is known with certainty. Probably he studied with either the Oratorians or the Jesuits at La Rochelle. Then, in accordance with established custom among the bourgeoisie and lesser nobility of the region, he would most likely have been sent to study with the Jesuits at Poitiers. In any case, Réaumur's early education probably included very little physics or mathematics. In 1699 his uncle, Gabriel Bouchel, summoned him to Bourges to study law. He went there with his younger brother and stayed for three years.

In 1703 Réaumur went to live in Paris, where he met a cousin on his mother's side, Jean-François Hénault, the future *président*.[1] Hénault was studying mathematics with a certain M. Guisnée, an obscure "student geometer" of the Academy of Sciences.[2] Réaumur decided to take lessons from Guisnée and, according to Hénault, after only three sessions knew more than his cousin and as much as his instructor. It was probably through Guisnée that Réaumur became acquainted with the great mathematician Pierre Varignon. Varignon became Réaumur's friend, teacher, and guide; and in March 1708 he nominated him to be his "student geometer" at the Academy of Sciences.

Réaumur's first three communications to the Academy, on geometrical subjects, were presented in 1708 and 1709, and demonstrate a degree of mathematical sophistication worthy of a student of Varignon. Had Réaumur decided to remain a mathematician, he might well have been one of the greatest geometers of his age. In November 1709, however, he quite suddenly changed the course of his scientific career by reading a paper on the growth of animal shells. From then on, Réaumur's work would be characterized by its extraordinary richness and diversity, but never again would he devote himself to the pure mathematical researches that had so fascinated him in his youth.

Technology and Instrumentation. Shortly after the formation of the Paris Academy of Sciences, Louis XIV's finance minister, Colbert, charged it with the task of collecting a description of all the arts, industries, and professions. This work was intended to be a sort of industrial encyclopedia which was to present the secret processes of industrial technology so that they might be better examined and improved. The French Academy, unlike the English Royal Society, was an integral part of the French bureaucratic system. This governmental role of the Academy became more and more pronounced throughout the eighteenth century as academicians assumed administrative control of French technology as consultants, inspectors, and even directors of industry.[3] Réaumur was one of the earliest and most enthusiastic supporters of this technocratic function of the Academy, and perhaps it was for this reason that he was given charge of writing the vast industrial encyclopedia that Colbert had projected.

Réaumur began this enormous task in 1713 with his "Description de l'art du tireur d'or," a paper on the art of drawing gold into thread and wire. Two years later he published his investigations of the arts dealing with precious stones, in which he showed that certain turquoise stones were actually fossilized animal teeth. His most significant and original contribution to industrial technology was unquestionably his investigation of the iron and steel industry, the results of which he presented in a series of memoirs read before the Academy in 1720, 1721, and 1722.[4] Réaumur was not a trained engineer or metallurgist and knew only a little chemistry; but he did bring to these researches a profound mathematical ability, an extraordinarily keen power of observation, a lively experimental imagination, and a fine rational intellect.

The French government, especially the regent, Philippe II, duke of Orléans, took great interest in Réamur's work. It was primarily through the duke's good offices that Réaumur was able to obtain documentation concerning the iron and steel industries of foreign countries. The regent also subsidized Réaumur's researches by granting him a pension of 12,000 *livres* on the postal farm. All this generosity was based on the mercantilistic policy of the French government, which encouraged and subsidized native industries in hopes of improving the balance of trade. The French ferrous metals industry was technologically backward, and it was hoped that Réaumur's study would help to remedy the situation.

The first part of Réaumur's investigation concerns the production of steel. This was usually accomplished in the eighteenth century by the lengthy and expensive process of cementation. Small pieces of wrought iron were mixed with charcoal and heated for two or three weeks, until the iron was carburized or case-hardened into blister steel. In the first part of his study, Réaumur was concerned to find the best possible cement, that is, the best combination of substances to mix with the iron. His procedure was experimental and crudely empirical, although of course he knew from the experience of generations of ironmasters what kinds of substances to try. He made dozens of tiny, earthen crucibles of equal size and shape and capable of holding about half a pound of iron. This way he could make about forty trials at once in the ovens that were available to him. The experiments were rigidly controlled in such a way as to insure that the only variable would be the cement. After innumerable experiments of this nature, Réaumur concluded that the best mixture was a specific combination of chimney soot, charcoal, ashes, and common salt.

This result, however, is less significant than Réaumur's conclusion concerning the nature of steel. He recognized that steel, far from being a more refined form of iron, as most people thought, was in fact impure iron the small parts of which were interpenetrated with "sulfurous and saline particles." Réaumur is sometimes taken to task for not having recognized that steel is iron combined with a small quantity of carbon; but given the relatively primitive state of early eighteenth-century chemistry, he could hardly have reached such a conclusion. Also, it should be remembered that the "sulfurous particles" he believed to be one of the constituents of steel were not particles of common sulfur. In the parlance of eighteenth-century chemistry, the term "sulfurous" usually referred to an inflammable or oily principle that was present in combustible bodies, such as charcoal, chimney soot, and other carboniferous substances. Thus Réaumur was closer to realizing the truth about the nature of steel than many people give him credit for.

Réaumur also investigated the treatment of steel after it was manufactured. He was especially interested in the tempering process, for which he attempted, without much success, to give a scientific explanation. He also noted that by rupturing a steel sample and examining the texture of the grain at the point of breakage, one could determine the quality of the steel. The better to determine the relative hardness of metals, Réaumur set up a scale of seven substances not unlike the hardness scale contrived by Mohs a century later and still in use by mineralogists. He also invented an apparatus for measuring the flexibility of tempered steel wire.

The second part of Réaumur's study concerns his attempts to produce a malleable (nonbrittle) cast iron. In the eighteenth century cast iron was made by heating iron ore in a blast furnace at temperatures high enough to produce the metal in a molten state. The resulting iron always had a high carbon content, which had the advantage of lowering its melting point and thus making it suitable for casting, but the disadvantage of making it brittle and thus unsuitable for objects that had to withstand severe strain. Guns were often cast of iron instead of the preferred bronze; but they were liable to fracture and explode, causing more deaths among the friends at the firing end than among the enemies at the receiving end. It was of the greatest importance, not only to the art of war but also to the arts of peace, that a cast iron be produced that had the strength of steel and the resilience of bronze. This was the ultimate goal of Réaumur's entire study.

Although the composition of cast iron is fairly complex and the chemical tools available to Réaumur were quite primitive, he nonetheless came surprisingly close to identifying its true nature. Just as steel is made harder and more brittle than iron by the penetration between its parts of sulfurous and saline particles, so,

Réaumur thought, cast iron is made harder and more brittle than steel by the interpenetration of its parts by still more sulfurous and saline particles. If one substitutes "carbon" for "sulfurous and saline particles," then one has the modern notion of what constitutes the basic differences between wrought iron, steel, and cast iron.

To remove the brittleness of cast iron, Réaumur reasoned, it was necessary to remove at least some of the sulfurous and saline particles. Heat would open the pores of the metal and force out many of the offending particles; but it was necessary to find a substance that would combine with them, thus preventing their reentry into the body of the metal. Again Réaumur's method for finding the best substance to achieve this end was largely inspired guesswork. At first he tried bone ash and powdered chalk, but the results were not entirely satisfactory.

He then turned his attention to an interesting substance that had appeared as a by-product of some of his experiments. He had noticed that when cast iron plaques were heated in his oven for several days, a thick layer of reddish powder formed on them. This substance was known to chemists as "saffron of Mars," and it was believed to be a calcined or burned iron. Réaumur reasoned that iron in this state was divested by fire of all its oily, sulfurous, and saline particles, and that therefore it would be a substance most fit to reabsorb those same particles, like a chemical sponge. He entirely surrounded pieces of cast iron with this powder, placed the mixture in a crucible, and heated it to bright red. After several days Réaumur discovered that the iron had become soft, resilient, and malleable, rather like wrought iron. Unwittingly, he had found the process for making European malleable castings or "whiteheart." Unfortunately for the French iron industry, Réaumur did not fully realize the importance of this discovery, and did not emphasize it sufficiently. The reason seems to be that he thought that the saffron of Mars (the red oxide of iron) was a particular substance obtained only through the firing of manufactured iron and that it was, therefore, quite uncommon, relatively expensive to produce, and thus unsuitable for large-scale enterprise. In fact it is, as we now know, the same substance as the common and inexpensive red ore of iron. Of so little importance did Réaumur consider this process that when he returned to the subject in his *Nouvel art d'adoucir le fer fondu* (1726), he neglected altogether to mention it. Only in the nineteenth century was the "Réaumur process" exploited on a large commercial scale.

Réaumur also studied and worked in the tinplate industry. Once encouraged and subsidized by the government, the French tinplate industry had fallen into a state of utter ruin during the early part of the eighteenth century. At the public assembly of the Academy of Sciences on 11 April 1725, Réaumur delivered a paper in which he revealed the basic industrial secrets of tin-plating. It was believed that once the essential processes of the industry became known, anyone possessing the necessary capital could set up a tinplate factory in France. Indeed, Réaumur helped to found such an operation at Cosne-sur-Loire; but the costs of production proved too great to meet competition from imported German tinplate.

From about 1717 Réaumur undertook a lengthy and intensive investigation of the porcelain industry. China porcelain was in great demand in Europe because of its delicate beauty and its soft, appealing translucence. European workmen had attempted to imitate it, but they were deceived by its vitrified texture into believing that common glass entered into its composition. In France factories were set up at Rouen (1673) and St. Cloud (1677) to manufacture an artificial porcelain made with a previously fired glassy mixture or frit of the type known as soft paste (*pâte tendre*) to distinguish it from hard paste, from which true porcelain is made. In Germany a technique for making true, hard-paste porcelain was discovered by Johann Friederich Böttger in association with Tschirnhausen; and as early as 1708 their factory at Dresden began to turn out a hard, red stoneware in almost every way comparable with a type of true china.

What seems to have initiated Réaumur's interest in porcelain was a letter published in 1717, from a Jesuit missionary to China, Father François-Xavier Entrecolles, in which he described in detail the processes used to manufacture porcelain in the famous Chinese factory at Ching-te-chen (Fou-liang). Along with his letter Father Entrecolles sent samples of the two substances used in the making of china. One of these substances, petuntse, was a feldspar; the other, kaolin, was a clay. Réaumur obtained the samples from Entrecolles's correspondent and began a two-year effort to identify them. The regent ordered intendants all over France to send specimens of all manner of sands, stones, earths, and other mineral substances found in their districts. Although large numbers of samples were collected, Réaumur was not able to identify the two Chinese specimens or to find their French equivalents.

Réaumur did, however, discover and make public, in a series of memoirs delivered before the Academy of Sciences, the secret processes for making soft-paste porcelain from glass. He confirmed by experiment that, despite their similar appearances, true China porcelain and the French imitation were quite differently composed. During the course of his experiments Réaumur invented a new type of crystalline ceramic that has proved useful in the twentieth century in protecting rocket nose cones from overheating.

Although Réaumur was unsuccessful in his attempts to discover the secret of making hard-paste porcelain, he did prepare the way for later investigators. His pupil Jean-Étienne Guettard discovered French sources of the two substances, kaolin and petuntse, necessary for the manufacture of porcelain. Later chemists and academicians, such as Pierre-Joseph Macquer, Jean Hellot, and the count of Milly, built on his pioneer researches a complete and detailed technological structure that was to make French porcelain among the finest in the world.

Réaumur was perhaps best known for the thermometer scale that he invented and that bears his name. Thermometers had been in use for about a century when he became interested in them, but there were not yet any universally accepted scales that would allow scientists who were not in the same place to compare their thermometric findings. Fahrenheit's scale was beginning to be adopted both in England and in Holland; but with its two fixed points and its scale divided linearly into a given number of degrees, it was accurate only if the inside diameter of the hollow thermometer tube was perfectly regular.

Réaumur sought to avoid this difficulty by constructing a thermometer with a single fixed point and a degree defined volumetrically (instead of linearly) in terms of some fraction of the total volume of liquid in the thermometer bulb. To fashion his thermometer according to these principles, he made a series of pipettes, the smallest equal to the volume of a single degree and the others equal to 25, 50, or 100 times the volume of the smallest. Then, using these pipettes, he filled a thermometer with 1,000 measures of liquid. Since it was not necessary to use the thermometric liquid itself when graduating the thermometer, Réaumur first used water and then switched to mercury, which he found more convenient. The place on the thermometer tube reached by 1,000 measures of liquid was marked 0°, and each degree above and below that single and arbitrary fixed point was equal to 1/1,000 the volume of the liquid at 0°. Then the graduated thermometer was emptied and refilled to a point just below the 0° mark with the thermometric liquid—in this case alcohol. The thermometer was then placed in ice water and alcohol was carefully added until it reached the 0° mark. Then the tube was hermetically sealed.

The one serious drawback to Réaumur's thermometer was that different strengths of alcohol have different coefficients of dilation, so that while one type of alcohol might expand one degree after the application of a certain amount of heat, another might expand two degrees under the same conditions. It was vital that all thermometers scaled according to his system have the same grade of alcohol. Réaumur suggested that the alcohol used in his thermometers be of a type that would dilate 80 degrees—that is, 8 parts in 100—between the temperature of ice and the temperature at which the alcohol began to boil in an open thermometer tube. Owing to an unfortunate confusion of language in his article on the thermometer, however, nearly everyone believed that 80° on his scale was the temperature of boiling water; and as a result, when so-called Réaumur thermometers began to be made by the artisans of Paris, they were nearly all scaled linearly with respect to two fiducial points, 0° for ice and 80° for boiling water. Scientists using mercury for their thermometers and basing their degree on the same value as Réaumur (1/1,000 the volume of the liquid at 0°) found the boiling point somewhere between 100° and 110°. In short, while there were many types of thermometers named for Réaumur, few were constructed in accordance with his specific instructions. As a result, it is often impossible to tell from the text of an eighteenth-century author claiming to use a Réaumur thermometer exactly what scale he is referring to, unless he happens to mention a universal fixed point, such as the temperature of boiling water.

Natural History. Réaumur was among the greatest naturalists of his or any age. In the breadth and range of his researches, in the patient detail of his observations, and in the brilliant ingenuity of his experiments, it would be difficult to name his equal. Thomas Henry Huxley has compared him favorably with Darwin.[5]

Réaumur's motives in pursuing natural history were a strange mixture of hardheaded practicality and frivolous delight in the curiosities of nature. In 1715 his investigation of artificial pearls led him to study the substance that gave luster to the scales of fishes. These researches were in turn linked to inquiries that he had undertaken since 1709 into the formation of mollusk shells, which he showed to grow by the addition of successive layers rather than by the incorporation of new matter into an already existing structure. In 1717 he attempted artificially to stimulate pearl formation in bivalves, and in 1711 he rediscovered the secret of making the purple dye of the ancient Romans from the substance produced by a particular species of mollusk. Réaumur also investigated the means by which mollusks, starfish, and various other invertebrates move about. He was the first to describe ambulacral feet. In 1710 he published a memoir on the fabric he had made from spiders' silk. He presented the duke of Noailles with a pair of spiders' silk stockings, and he gave Jean-Paul Bignon some spiders' silk gloves. His memoir on spiders' silk was translated into Italian, English (it was inserted into the *Philosophical Transactions of the Royal Society*), and Chinese (by request of the Manchu emperor).

Réaumur's greatest work in natural history was his *Mémoires pour servir à l'histoire des insectes*, published in six volumes between 1734 and 1742. He had originally intended to publish ten volumes on insects; but after the six published during his lifetime, nothing remained of the project but fragments in manuscript, some of which were not published until the twentieth century.[6] It is not altogether clear why Réaumur stopped writing his great work at such an early date. There is some evidence, however, that he may have been discouraged by the jealous rivalry with his younger and more popular contemporary Buffon.[7]

The term "insect" was used in the early eighteenth century to designate almost any small invertebrate —not just hexapods or six-legged arthropods. The word refers primarily to creatures possessing segmented bodies; thus spiders, myriopods, and worms were usually included in the class. Réaumur's concept of the insects was even broader; he included polyps, mollusks, crustaceans, and even reptiles and amphibians. "The crocodile is certainly a fierce insect," he once proclaimed, "but I am not in the least disturbed about calling it one."[8]

Because of their large numbers and great diversity, insects were difficult to classify. Taxonomical schemata had been formulated by Aldrovandi and Vallisnieri which relied on superficial physiological and ethological, as well as morphological, characteristics. Swammerdam made things even more complicated by taking into consideration developmental characteristics. It is typical of Réaumur's approach that he tended to neglect morphology (which has since been used as the basis for insect classification) and concentrated instead on ethological characteristics. As a result, it is difficult at times to determine exactly what insect he was discussing. He seemed fascinated above all with insect behavior, obviously admiring the industry, diligence, ingenuity, organization, and skill of those small creatures. There is something almost of the eighteenth-century *bon bourgeois* in his description of the bees and the ants; and just as middle-class humans are categorized according to their professions, so, Réaumur thought, the insects might be classified according to their industries and occupations:

. . . the portion of the history of insects to which I am most sensitive is that which concerns their ingenuity [*génie*],[9] their industries; also their industries will often decide the order in which I shall treat them. I have thought, for example, that one would prefer to see together all the insects that know how to clothe themselves, and which are above all remarkable for that, than to find them dispersed in different classes as they necessarily would be according to the methods of Swammerdam and Valisnieri.[10]

Another characteristic of Réaumur's approach to the natural history of insects is his persistent utilitarianism. There is in him little of the gimcrack virtuosity which seeks to know petty and useless details merely for the sake of knowing them. He doubtless admired the cunning practicality of the insects because it reflected his own turn of mind. He sought always to justify his researches by emphasizing their usefulness. Near the beginning of the first volume of his monumental study on insects he discussed at some length the economic value of entomological research. Silk, wax, honey, lacquer, and cochineal, to name just a few, are products of economic importance derived from the "industries" of insects.[11] Réaumur apparently believed that it might be possible to derive useful technological procedures from the observation of insect activities. He sought, for example, to mimic the industry of the bees by attempting to make wax from pollen.[12] He seemed to imply that perhaps the caterpillars and the spiders have something to teach us about weaving, that perhaps the useful resins manufactured by the ants could be made artificially.

The study of insects is profitable from another point of view as well—pest control. As early as 1728, Réaumur had investigated the life cycle of clothes moths in order to determine the best means of eradicating them. Again, at the beginning of his first volume on the natural history of insects he stressed the utility of this aspect of his research.

An infinity of these tiny animals defoliate our plants, our trees, our fruits. . . . they attack our houses, our fabrics, our furniture, our clothing, our furs. . . . He who in studying all the different species of insects that are injurious to us, would seek means of preventing them from harming us, would seek to cause them to perish, to cause their eggs to perish, proposes for his goal important tasks indeed.[13]

Réaumur, in short, was a pioneer in applied entomological research.

The most widely read portion of Réaumur's natural history of insects is probably the nine memoirs of volume V on the history of the bees. Réaumur lavished an enormous amount of time and observational and experimental skill on these productive social insects. His descriptions were minute and exacting in every detail, and his experiments were among the most ingenious he ever contrived. Réaumur was one of the first to undertake extensive quantitative research on insects. He discovered that by immersing a hive in cold water he could, in effect, anesthetize the insects for a time, thus enabling him to separate the members of the bee community into their various classes and to count them. He carefully kept track of the number of bees leaving the hive in the course of a day, measured the average amount of pollen brought back by each, and from this estimated the weight of a single day's harvest. Réaumur also counted cells and larvae in a hive relative to its adult population; estimated the prodigious number of eggs laid by a single queen; weighed a swarm of bees in order to determine their number; measured the temperature of the hive and kept track of its variations in relation to both the season and the number and density of its inhabitants; and even made very careful investigations of the geometric form of the honey cells.

With regard to the position and function of the queen in bee society, Réaumur's researches were extensive and original. He discovered that all hives, even those very close to swarming, have only one queen; if others are introduced, they will be rejected or even killed. He found that if a colony is deprived of its queen, it must make a new one (by feeding a special substance called royal jelly to a developing larva) or it will die. He discovered that a hive without a queen will (under certain conditions) accept an exogenous ruler.

Réaumur kept track of individual bees by tinting them with various dyes. He dissected bees and their larvae and had detailed plates made to accompany his treatise. He made some of the first tentative studies of communication among the bees. In short, there was no aspect of the life cycle or behavior of bees too minute or too unimportant to escape his attention. He took every pain, every precaution to make his study as complete and exhaustive as possible. And so it was with the other insects he studied.

Biology and Genetics. Réaumur's biological and genetical notions were dominated by the ideas of the preformationists. Given the prevalence of the mechanical philosophy at the beginning of the eighteenth century, it was very difficult to imagine ways in which new biological forms could arise from undifferentiated matter. To deal with this problem, the preformationists went so far as to deny that there had ever been generation of any kind, whether of biological individuals or of members or parts. Thus when Leeuwenhoek peered through his microscope at semen, he fancied that he observed a tiny fetus encased in the head of each sperm. When properly "planted" in the female womb, these tiny creatures would simply enlarge into infants. Swammerdam believed that each structure of the adult butterfly was present in the infant caterpillar. All that was needed to change the latter into the former was that the caterpillar slough off its skin and allow the preexisting butterfly parts to unfold and grow. There was neither metamorphosis nor generation, only unfolding and growth. It follows, then, that every living creature that ever will exist actually exists now, with all its mature parts, in seeds or in seeds of seeds. The unborn are indescribably small, but they are nonetheless there, even though we may not be able to see them. In the biology of the preformationists there was literally nothing new under the sun and Adam was, in the realest of senses, the father of us all, or perhaps (because eighteenth-century opinion was divided on the matter) Eve was the universal mother.

Réaumur gave his cautious support to some of the ideas of the preformationists, largely because the alternative—the outmoded Aristotelian notions of epigenesis—seemed, in an era insistent upon mechanism, absurd and without foundation. For example, in his discussion of caterpillars and butterflies, which takes up the first two volumes of his natural history of the insects, Réaumur repeated Swammerdam's observations on the development of the chrysalis and came to the same conclusion—the parts of the adult butterfly are simply enlargements of structures preexistent beneath the skin of the caterpillar. It is indicative of the power of these preformationist conceptions that when he was unable to find certain preexistent structures in the caterpillar, he asserted that they were there nonetheless, although invisible.

Others of Réaumur's observations lent support to the ideas of preformation. For example, he discovered that different degrees of heat could retard or accelerate the growth of the butterfly chrysalis. This experiment showed that conditions in the environment played an important role in the rate of biological development. The implication was that preformed biological structures could, like the chrysalis, remain in a state of suspended animation until the conditions became suitable for their development.

Another observation that seemed to lend credence to preformationism was the discovery of parthenogenesis among the aphids. It had been noticed long before that female aphids seemed capable of producing abundant offspring even when there were no males around to fertilize them. Furthermore, no one had ever observed aphids in the act of mating. Réaumur suggested that one could discover whether it was possible for aphids to reproduce without sexual contact by raising them in isolation from the time of their birth. He attempted the experiment himself, but his aphids died before reaching sexual maturity. His student, the young Genevan naturalist Charles Bonnet, repeated the experiment at Réaumur's suggestion and succeeded in producing aphids parthenogenetically. To Bonnet the experiment seemed to show that the preformed fetus was in the female egg rather than in the male sperm, and he became a leader of the "ovist" school of preformationism.

Réaumur never accepted all the ideas of preformationism, for he was too aware of the difficulties some aspects of the theory entrained. How can it be, for example, that offspring resemble both of their parents, since the preformed infant would have to originate in the seed of only one of them? In the second edition of his study of the technique of artificial incubation, Réaumur included an account of the inheritance of human polydactyly showing that the trait is passed to the offspring through male and female parents alike. It was precisely this kind of observation of biparental inheritance that led many biologists in the middle of the eighteenth century to abandon the notions of preformationism altogether and adopt pangenetic theories instead.

As early as 1712, Réaumur had apparently rejected the idea of *emboîtement* (the "encasement" of germs within germs). In that year he published a paper in which he demonstrated that certain crustaceans had the power to regenerate missing legs or parts of legs lost through misadventure. A preformationist account of this type of regeneration posed serious difficulties. Presumably any given place on the leg would have to possess a germ containing a preformed leg or a preformed section of leg similar to the section below the place where the germ was located. Furthermore, to account for secondary regenerations, one would have to assume that each of these tiny preformed legs contained multitudes of yet tinier preformed legs and sections of legs, and so on ad infinitum. Yet if the germs were not preformed, where did they come from? Were they, then, truly generated from undifferentiated matter? Réaumur was at a loss to explain the phenomenon. The preformationist account of regeneration was manifestly absurd; but then, so it seemed, were the alternative explanations.

If the discovery of regenerated animal members posed serious difficulties for preformationism, the discovery of regeneration in the fresh-water hydra nearly devastated the theory and many others as well. It was a cousin of Charles Bonnet, Abraham Trembley, who collected some of these tiny creatures from a stagnant pool in the summer of 1740 and observed that they had animallike powers of locomotion, extension, and contraction. Uncertain whether to classify them as animals or plants, he communicated his findings to Réaumur and asked for his opinion. After observing the creatures, Réaumur was convinced that they were indeed animals. Trembley had also cut one of his "polyps," as they were to be called, transversely in two and noted, to his great astonishment, that each part continued to manifest signs of life and that at the end of about nine days each had regenerated its other half. Later it was found that one could divide hydras into almost as many pieces as one pleased and each part would live independently and, after a time, regenerate the whole. It was Réaumur who announced these remarkable facts to a startled and somewhat incredulous scientific community in March and April 1741. The following summer his student Guettard went to the coast to test the regenerative powers of several marine animals.

The discovery of the hydra and its peculiar ability to sustain life even when divided into a number of small parts caused a profound shock among European naturalists. The observation of analogous regenerative powers in starfish, sea anemones, and worms was likewise highly disturbing to the commonly received notions of biology. Many of the materialist biological theories that arose in the middle of the eighteenth century were founded upon observations such as these.[14]

Réaumur also made a significant contribution to physiology in his brilliantly conceived experimental investigation of the process of digestion in birds. He demonstrated the enormous power of the gizzard by forcing several grain-eating birds to swallow tubes of glass and tin. When the animals were opened after two days, the glass tubes were found shattered, the pieces of glass smoothed and polished by the action of the gizzard; the tin tubes were crushed and flattened. In carnivorous birds he showed that digestion was more chemical than mechanical. He enclosed pieces of meat in a tube, the ends of which were closed with fine gratings, and forced a kite to swallow it. When the bird later regurgitated the tube, Reaumur found that the meat had been partially digested. There was no sign of putrefaction. Vegetable matter introduced into the bird's stomach in the same manner underwent little change.

Academic Activities and Death of Réaumur. Réaumur was perhaps the most prestigious member of the Academy of Sciences during the first half of the eighteenth century. Through his incessant labors and voluminous publications, through his extensive correspondence with scientists both in France and abroad, and through the reflected brilliance of his students, he acquired enormous authority and renown in the European scientific community. Many of the im-

portant discoveries of the day were announced by him—for instance, the discoveries of the parthenogenesis of aphids and of the regenerative powers of the hydra. It was also he who announced Musschenbroeck's discovery of the Leyden jar in 1746.

Réaumur rose quickly in the ranks of the Academy. He was elected *pensionnaire mécanicien* in May 1711; he was also made director of the Academy twelve times and subdirector nine times. He was elected to the Royal Society of London, to the Academies of Science of Prussia, Russia, and Sweden, and to the Institute of Bologna.

Réaumur never married, but devoted all his time to his scientific and academic career. From a needy relative he bought the title of commander and intendant of the Royal Military Order of Saint Louis, an honorific office possessing the dignity of a count. Two years before his death he inherited the castle and lordship of La Bermondière in Maine. There in October 1757 he suffered a fall from his horse while returning from Mass and died. He was buried in the parish church of the nearby village, St.-Julien-du-Terroux. An inscription dedicated to his memory was placed in the church at the time of its restoration in 1879.

NOTES

1. A *président* is a chief justice. Hénault was *président* of the most prestigious court in France, the Parlement of Paris.
2. No *éloge* was ever published for Guisnée; thus neither his first names nor the date and place of his birth are known.
3. For a discussion of the French Academy of Science's role in the bureaucracy of the *ancien régime*, see Roger Hahn, *The Anatomy of a Scientific Institution: The Paris Academy of Sciences, 1666–1803* (Berkeley, Calif., 1971).
4. They were collected and published under the title *L'Art de convertir le fer forgé en acier, et l'art d'adoucir le fer fondu, ou de faire des ouvrages de fer fondu aussi finis que de fer forgé* (Paris, 1722).
5. "From the time of Aristotle to the present day I know of but one man who has shown himself Mr. Darwin's equal in one field of research—and that is Réaumur." Quoted in Leonard Huxley, *Life and Letters of Thomas Henry Huxley*, I (New York, 1901), 515.
6. *The Natural History of Ants*, William Morton Wheeler, trans. and ed. (New York, 1926), French text included; *Histoire des fourmis*, Charles Perez, ed., with intro. by E. L. Bouvier; *Encyclopédie entomologique*, ser. A, XI (Paris, 1928); *Histoire des scarabés*, P. Lesne and F. Picard, eds., XXXII (Paris, 1955); *Les papiers laissés par de Réaumur et le tome VII des Mémoires pour servir à l'histoire des insectes . . . Introduction du tome VII des Mémoires pour servir à l'histoire des insectes*, Maurice Caullery, ed., *Encyclopédie entomologique*, ser. A, XXXIIa (Paris, 1929).
7. Jean Torlais, "Une rivalité célèbre: Réaumur et Buffon," in *Presse médicale*, **65** (11 June 1958), 1057–1058.
8. Quoted by Wheeler in *Natural History of Ants*, 29.
9. It is difficult to give an exact English equivalent for the word *génie* in this context. Réaumur seems to have had in mind their characteristic skills. The older English word "ingeniosity" would be etymologically nicer.

10. Réaumur, *Mémoires pour servir à l'histoire des insectes*, I, 42.
11. *Ibid.*, 4–5.
12. Réaumur did not know that the wax is made from special secretions and not directly from the pollen collected by the bee.
13. Réaumur, *Mémoires* . . ., I, 8.
14. See Aram Vartanian, "Trembley's Polyp, La Mettrie, and Eighteenth-Century French Materialism," in *Journal of the History of Ideas*, **11** (1950), 259–286.

BIBLIOGRAPHY

I. ORIGINAL WORKS. Complete lists of Réaumur's works are in William Morton Wheeler's trans. of Réaumur's *The Natural History of Ants* (New York, 1926), 263–274; and Jean Torlais, "Chronologie de la vie et des oeuvres de René-Antoine Ferchault de Réaumur," in *Revue d'histoire des sciences et de leurs applications*, **11** (1958), 1–12, with portrait.

Réaumur's major works are *L'art de convertir le fer forgé en acier, et l'art d'adoucir le fer fondu, ou de faire des ouvrages de fer fondu aussi finis que de fer forgé* (Paris, 1722), English trans. by Annelie Grünhaldt Sisco, with notes and intro. by Cyril Stanley Smith, *Réamur's Memoirs on Steel and Iron* (Chicago, 1956); *Mémoires pour servir à l'histoire des insectes*, 6 vols. (Paris, 1734–1742); *Art de faire éclorre et d'élever en toute saison des oiseaux domestiques de toutes espèces, soit par le moyen de la chaleur du fumier, soit par le moyen de celle du feu ordinaire*, 2 vols. (Paris, 1749), 2nd ed. entitled *Practique de l'art de faire éclore et d'élever en toute saison des oiseaux domestiques* . . . (Paris, 1751), also an English trans. of the 1st ed., *The Art of Hatching and Bringing up Domestic Fowls* . . . (London, 1750); and 3 vols. in the Paris Academy of Sciences' series Description des Arts et Métiers: *Art de l'épinglier . . . avec des additions de M. Duhamel du Monceau* . . . (Paris, 1761); *Fabrique des ancres . . . avec des notes et additions de M. Duhamel* (Paris, 1761); and *Nouvel art d'adoucir le fer fondu aussi finis que de fer forgé* . . ., with intro. by Duhamel du Monceau (Paris, 1762). Also see the works cited in note 6.

In addition see *Abhandlungen über Thermometrie, von . . . Réaumur* . . ., A. J. von Oettingen, trans., in *Ostwalds Klassiker der exakten Wissenschaften*, **57** (1894); and *Correspondance inédite entre Réaumur et Abraham Trembley*, Émile Guyenot, ed. (Geneva, 1943).

II. SECONDARY LITERATURE. For general biographical information see Jean-Paul Grandjean de Fouchy's *éloge* in *Histoire de l'Académie royale des sciences* . . . for 1757 (1762), 201–216; Frédéric Lusson, *Étude sur Réaumur* (La Rochelle, 1875); and Jean Torlais, *Réaumur et Ch. Bonnet d'après leur correspondance inédite* (Bordeaux, 1932); *Réaumur et sa société* (Bordeaux, 1932); and *Un esprit encyclopédique en dehors de "l'Encyclopédie": Réaumur, d'après des documents inédits* (Paris, 1936; 2nd ed., rev. and enl., 1961).

On Réaumur's mathematical papers, see René Taton, "Réaumur mathématicien," in *Revue d'histoire des sciences et de leurs applications*, **11** (1958), 130–133. On Réaumur's work on iron and steel technology, see A. Birembaut, "Réaumur et l'élaboration des produits ferreux," in *Revue d'histoire des sciences* . . ., **11** (1958), 138–166; and A. Portevin, "Réaumur, métallurgiste et chimiste," in *Archives internationales d'histoire des sciences*, **13** (1960), 99–103. On Réaumur's thermometer, A. Birembaut, "La contribution de Réaumur à la thermométrie," in *Revue d'histoire des sciences* . . ., **11** (1958), 302–329.

On Réaumur as a naturalist, see Pierre Grasse, *Réaumur et l'analyse des phénomènes instinctives*, Conférences du Palais de la Découverte, ser. D, no. 48 (Paris, 1957); Jean Torlais, "Réaumur et l'histoire des abeilles," in *Revue d'histoire des sciences* . . ., **11** (1958), 51–67; A. Davy de Virville, "Réaumur botaniste," *ibid.*, 134–137; Jean Rostand, "Réaumur et les premiers essais de léthargie artificielle," *ibid.*, **15** (1962), 69–71; and "Réaumur et la résistance des insectes à la congélation," *ibid.*, 71–72; and Jean Théodoridès, "Réaumur (1683–1757) et les insectes sociaux," in *Janus*, **48** (1959), 62–76.

On Réaumur's biology and genetics, see Jean Torlais, "Réaumur philosophe," in *Revue d'histoire des sciences* . . ., **11** (1958), 13–33; Jean Rostand, "Réaumur embryologiste et généticien," *ibid.*, 33–50. For general background on the problem of preformation, see Jacques Roger, *Les sciences de la vie dans la pensée française du XVIIIᵉ siècle* (Paris, 1971), 326–453, and Réaumur and preformation, 380–384. On Réaumur and polydactyly, see Bentley Glass, "Maupertuis, Pioneer of Genetics and Evolution," in Bentley Glass, ed., *Forerunners of Darwin: 1745–1859* (Baltimore, 1959), 63–66.

On Réaumur's correspondence, see Pierre Speziali, "Réaumur et les savants genevois. Lettres inédites," in *Revue d'histoire des sciences* . . ., **11** (1958), 68–80 (which contains eight letters to Gabriel Cramer, Théodore Tronchin, and André Roger); Jean Chaia, "Sur une correspondance inédite de Réaumur avec Arthur, premier médecin du roy à Cayenne," in *Episteme*, **2** (1968), 37–57, (which contains twelve letters); and Peeter Müürsepp, "Rapports entre le célèbre savant français Réaumur et le Tzar Pierre I," in *Actes du XIIᵉ Congrès internationale d'histoire des sciences*, XI (Paris, 1971), 95–101.

On Réaumur's last years, see A. Davy de Virville, "Réaumur dans la Mayenne," in *Revue d'histoire des sciences* . . ., **11** (1958), 81–82. The articles on Réaumur in *Revue d'histoire des sciences et de leurs applications*, **11** (1958), have been collected and published as *La vie et l'oeuvre de Réaumur (1683–1757)* (Paris, 1962).

J. B. GOUGH

RECORDE, ROBERT (*b.* Tenby, Pembrokeshire, Wales, *ca.* 1510; *d.* London, England, 1558)

Recorde was the second son of Thomas Recorde, whose father had come to Wales from Kent, and of Rose Johns of Montgomeryshire. He graduated B.A. from Oxford in 1531 and was elected a fellow of All Souls College in the same year. All Souls was a chantry and graduate foundation for the study and training of clerks in theology, civil and canon law, and medicine. At some time he removed to Cambridge and there received the M.D. degree in 1545. According to the Cambridge records he had been licensed in medicine at Oxford some twelve years earlier, and the B.M. usually went with the Oxford license. Tradition has it that he lectured on mathematics at Oxford and Cambridge; but details of his university career, and of any degrees other than the B.A. and M.D., are lacking.

Recorde was in London by 1547, probably practicing medicine. There is no evidence that he acted as physician to any of the Tudors, although he served the government in other capacities. In January 1549 he was appointed comptroller of the Bristol mint. In October 1549, at the time of Somerset's first fall, he sided with the protector, refusing to divert money intended for King Edward to the armies of the west under Lord John Russell and Sir William Herbert. He was accused of treason by Herbert (later earl of Pembroke) and was confined at court for sixty days while the mint ceased production. This was the beginning of a permanent quarrel with Herbert which had serious consequences for Recorde's later career.

From 1551 to 1553 Recorde was surveyor of the mines and monies in Ireland, in charge of the abortive silver mines at Wexford and, technically, supervisor of the Dublin mint. The venture was unsuccessful from the start. In addition to differences with the German miners over technology, and the personal animosity of Pembroke, the treasury was not able to bear the great expenses of the mines and their lack of profits. The work stopped in 1553 and Recorde was recalled. Not until 1570 was his estate compensated for some £ 1,000 due him for his services there.

In 1556 Recorde attempted to regain a position at court and laid charges of malfeasance as commissioner of the mints against Pembroke. Regardless of the merits of the case, it was a serious error in judgment on his part; Pembroke had the complete confidence of Queen Mary and King Philip, and it was impossible for a minor civil servant, whose last post had ended in failure, to survive the clash with the "politic old earl." Pembroke sued for libel in a bill of 16 October 1556. The hearing was held in January 1557, with a judgment of £ 1,000 damages against Recorde awarded 10 February. Presumably Recorde was imprisoned for failure to pay this sum. His will was written in King's Bench prison and was admitted to probate 18 June 1558.

Recorde has been justly called the founder of the English school of mathematical writers. He envisioned a course of instruction in elementary mathematics and its applications for mathematical practitioners. Deliberately choosing the vernacular, he wrote simple, clear English prose of a higher quality than his scientific contemporaries or immediate successors. Recorde made a special effort to find English equivalents for Latin and Greek technical terms, but very few of his innovations were adopted by later writers. His books indicate great skill as a teacher. His use of dialogue enabled him to carry a student step by step through the mastery of techniques, and to emphasize the proper order and method of instruction. Difficult questions were deferred until an understanding of fundamentals was achieved. Recorde took a rational view of his sources and was refreshingly critical of unquestioning acceptance of established authority. The mathematical books were written in the order in which he intended them to be studied: arithmetic, plane geometry, practical geometry, astronomy, and theoretical arithmetic and algebra. Projected works on advanced astronomy, navigation, and a translation of Euclid's *Elements* probably were never completed.

The arithmetic, *The Ground of Artes* (1543, enlarged in 1552), was the most popular of all Recorde's works. The first edition dealt only with whole numbers, covering the fundamental operations, reduction, progression, golden rule, and counter reckoning. In 1552 it was enlarged to include the same operations with fractions, and false position and alligation. There are three editions of the first version: 1543, 1549, and 1550[?]. The third has been dated formerly 1542[?] or 1545[?]; but bibliographers, on the basis of the state of the title-page border, now place it between the editions of 1549 and 1552.

The Pathway to Knowledge (1551) is a translation and rearrangement of the first four books of Euclid's *Elements*. Like Proclus before him, and Ramus later, Recorde separated the constructions ("things to be done") from the theorems ("things to be proved"). Proofs are not given, but explanations and examples are provided. Pedagogically, Recorde felt that it is not easy for a student to understand at the beginning both the thing that is taught and the reason why it is so.

The Gate of Knowledge dealt with measurement and the use of the quadrant. It has been lost and possibly was never published, although in the *Castle* it is referred to as complete.

The Castle of Knowledge (1556), on the construction and use of the sphere, is an elementary Ptolemaic astronomy with a brief, favorable reference to the Copernican theory. The often-cited edition of 1551 is a "ghost." The *Castle* is based chiefly on Ptolemy, Proclus, Sacrobosco, and Oronce Fine, but is much more than a synthesis of earlier writers. More than in any other of his books, Recorde was concerned here with sources. He devoted considerable space to a critical examination of the standard authorities, offering corrections of textual errors in the Greek authors and suggesting that the mistakes of Sacrobosco and others were caused by their lack of knowledge of Greek.

The Whetstone of Witte (1557) was the only one of Recorde's book not to have seen at least two editions, no doubt because it was less immediately useful to the London craftsmen than were his other works. It contains the "second part of arithmetic" promised in *The Ground of Artes* (from the arithmetic books of Euclid) and elementary algebra through quadratic equations. It is based on German sources, especially Johann Scheubel and Michael Stifel, and the algebra uses the German cossic notation. With Recorde's addition of the "equal" sign this algebra became completely symbolic. Although it is derivative, there are several noteworthy features: the use of zero coefficients in algebraic long division; the use of arbitrary numbers to check algebraic operations rather than the check by inverse operations; and the treatment of quadratics. Recorde did not admit negative roots but did use negative coefficients in equations. All quadratics are written with the square term equal to roots plus or minus numbers, or numbers minus roots. He still had to give the three usual rules of solution; but, in the case of an equation with two positive roots, $x^2 = px - q$, he stressed the solution using the relation between the roots and coefficients: $r_1 + r_2 = p$, $r_1 r_2 = q$.

In addition to his mathematical works, Recorde published *The Urinal of Physick* (1547), dedicated to the Company of Surgeons. A promised anatomy has not survived. A traditional medical work on the judgment of urines, full of sensible nursing practice, the *Urinal* is less modern than his mathematical works and less critical of authority.

Recorde was not only an able teacher and a skillful textbook writer but was also one of the outstanding scholars of mid-sixteenth-century England. He was well trained in mathematics, and was familiar with Greek and medieval texts as well as contemporary developments. His intelligent attitude toward authority, and his appeals to reason and observation, anticipated in a more moderate manner the anti-Aristotelianism of Petrus Ramus. Recorde was learned in medicine and the law. He was an able Greek scholar who stressed the importance of a knowledge of that language for an accurate understanding of sources. He had a wide range of learning in various fields: he was a historian interested in the antiquities of Britain, a collector of manuscripts, and one of the first students of the Anglo-Saxon language.

Recorde had no international reputation because all of his works were in English and on an elementary level. In England, however, his books remained the standard texts throughout the Elizabethan period. A generation of English scientists, especially the non-university men, stated that Recorde's books had been their first tutors in the mathematical sciences. The excellence of the English school of mathematical practitioners, fostered by growing geographical interests, has been attributed to the high quality of the vernacular movement in applied science begun by Recorde.

BIBLIOGRAPHY

I. ORIGINAL WORKS. Recorde's published works are *Ground of Artes* (London, 1543, 1549, 1550[?]; enl. ed., 1552, 1558, and many later eds.; last ed., 1699); *Urinal of Physick* (London, 1547, 1548, and others; last ed., 1665); *Pathway to Knowledge* (London, 1551, 1574, 1602); *Castle of Knowledge* (London, 1556, 1596); and *Whetstone of Witte* (London, 1557).

John Bale's contemporary autograph notebook lists other, unpublished, works by Recorde as well as MSS from his library. Bale's work has been published as *Index Britanniae scriptorum*, R. L. Poole, ed. (Oxford 1902).

II. SECONDARY LITERATURE. W. G. Thomas of Tenby, Pembrokeshire, who discovered the King's Bench records concerning Recorde and the Earl of Pembroke, is publishing a full account of the case.

For details on specific books see J. B. Easton, "The Early Editions of Robert Recorde's *Ground of Artes*," in *Isis*, **58** (1967), 515–532; and "A Tudor Euclid," in *Scripta mathematica*, **27** (1966), 339–355; L. D. Patterson, "Recorde's Cosmography, 1556," in *Isis*, **42** (1951), 208–218 (which must be read with caution); F. R. Johnson, "Astronomical Textbooks in the Sixteenth Century," in E. A. Underwood, ed., *Science, Medicine and History* (Oxford, 1953), 285–302; and L. C. Karpinski, "The Whetstone of Witte," in *Bibliotheca mathematica*, 3rd ser., **13** (1912–1913), 223–228.

Recorde's place in Renaissance science is discussed in F. R. Johnson and S. V. Larkey, "Robert Recorde's Mathematical Teaching and the Anti-Aristotelian Movement," in *Huntington Library Bulletin*, no. 7 (1935), 59–87; F. R. Johnson, *Astronomical Thought in Renaissance England* (Baltimore, 1937); and Edward Kaplan, "Robert Recorde (c. 1510–1558): Studies in the Life and Works of a Tudor Scientist," Ph.D. diss. (New York University, 1960), available on University Microfilms (Ann Arbor, Mich., 1967).

JOY B. EASTON

REGIOMONTANUS, JOHANNES (*b.* Königsberg, Franconia, Germany, 6 June 1436; *d.* Rome, Italy, *ca.* 8 July 1476)

Nothing is known of Regiomontanus before he enrolled in the University of Vienna on 14 April 1450 as "Johannes Molitoris de Künigsperg."[1] Since the name of his birthplace means "King's Mountain," he sometimes Latinized his name as "Joannes de Regio monte," from which the standard designation Regiomontanus was later derived. He was awarded the bachelor's degree on 16 January 1452 at the age of fifteen; but because of the regulations of the university, he could not receive the master's degree until he was twenty-one. On 11 November 1457 he was appointed to the faculty, thereby becoming a colleague of Peuerbach, with whom he had studied astronomy. The two men became fast friends and worked closely together as observers of the heavens.

The course of their lives was deeply affected by the arrival in Vienna on 5 May 1460 of Cardinal Bessarion (1403–1472), the papal legate to the Holy Roman Empire.[2] Bessarion's native tongue was Greek (he was born in Trebizond), and as part of his ardent campaign to bring ancient Greek authors to the attention of intellectuals in the Latin West, he persuaded Peuerbach to undertake a "briefer and more comprehensible" condensation, in Latin, of the *Mathematical Syntaxis* of Ptolemy, whose Greek style was formidable and whose ideas were far from simple. In those days Greek was not taught at the University of Vienna,[3] and Peuerbach did not know it. He had, however, made his own copy of Gerard of Cremona's Latin translation of Ptolemy's *Syntaxis*. Using this twelfth-century version, Peuerbach reached the end of book VI just before he died on 8 April 1461. On his deathbed he pledged Regiomontanus to complete the project.

Complying with Peuerbach's last wish, Regiomontanus accompanied Bessarion on his return trip to Rome, where they arrived on 20 November 1461.[4] When Regiomontanus finished the *Epitome*, as he entitled the translation by Peuerbach and himself, he dedicated it to Bessarion. In the parchment manuscript, which still survives, he did not address Bessarion as titular Patriarch of Constantinople, an honor bestowed on him on 28 April 1463,[5] a decade after the capital of the Byzantine Empire had been captured by the Turks. Thus, sometime before that date the Peuerbach-Regiomontanus *Epitome* was ready to go to press; but it was not actually printed until 31 August 1496, twenty years after the death of Regiomontanus.

At the end of the fifteenth century, Ptolemy's achievement remained at the pinnacle of astronomical thought; and by providing easier access to Ptolemy's complex masterpiece, the Peuerbach-Regiomontanus *Epitome* contributed to current scientific research rather than to improved understanding of the past. Moreover, the *Epitome* was no mere compressed translation of the *Syntaxis*, to which it added later observations, revised computations, and critical reflections—one of which revealed that Ptolemy's lunar theory required the apparent diameter of the moon to vary in length much more than it really does. This passage (book V, proposition 22) in the *Epitome*, which was printed in Venice, attracted the attention of Copernicus, then a student at the University of Bologna. Struck by this error in Ptolemy's astronomical system, which had prevailed for over 1,300 years, Copernicus went on to lay the foundations of modern astronomy and thus overthrow the Ptolemaic system.

Ptolemy was not only the foremost astronomer of antiquity but also its leading geographer; and Jacopo Angeli's widely used Latin translation (1406–1410)[6] of Ptolemy's *Geography* was condemned by Regiomontanus because the translator "had an inadequate knowledge of the Greek language and of mathematics."[7] Many of the obscure passages in Angeli's translation could not be explained by Peuerbach, who, as noted above, had not learned Greek. Hence Regiomontanus determined to master the language of Ptolemy. He acquired a remarkable fluency in Greek from his close association with Bessarion, and armed with a thorough comprehension of Ptolemy's language, he announced his intention to print an attack on Angeli's translation. But he died before completing this work. Nevertheless, "Johannes Regiomontanus' Notes on the Errors Committed by Jacopo Angeli in His Translation" formed the appendix (sig. P1r–Q8r) to a new version of Ptolemy's *Geography* (Strasbourg, 1525) by a scholar who had access to Regiomontanus' literary remains.

In a letter written not long after 11 February 1464 to the Italian mathematician Giovanni Bianchini, Regiomontanus reported that he had found an incomplete manuscript of Diophantus and, if he had the whole work, he would undertake to translate it into Latin—"since for this purpose the Greek I have learned in the home of my most revered master would be adequate."[8] Regiomontanus never translated Diophantus nor did he ever find a complete manuscript; nor did anyone else. Nevertheless, the recovery of Diophantus in modern times began with Regiomontanus' discovery of the incomplete manuscript.

When Bessarion was designated papal legate to the Venetian Republic, Regiomontanus left Rome with him on 5 July 1463.[9] In the spring of 1464[10] at the University of Padua, then under Venetian control, Regiomontanus lectured on the ninth-century Muslim scientist al-Farghānī. Although the main body of these lectures has not survived, "Johannes Regiomontanus' Introductory Discourse on All the Mathematical Disciplines, Delivered at Padua When He was Publicly Expounding al-Farghānī" was later published in *Continentur in hoc libro Rudimenta astronomica Alfragani . . .*, whose first item was John of Seville's twelfth-century Latin translation of al-Farghānī's *Elements of Astronomy* (Nuremberg, 1537).

Also included in this volume was Plato of Tivoli's twelfth-century Latin version, "together with geometrical proofs and additions by Johannes Regiomontanus," of al-Battānī's *The Motions of the Stars*. One such addition (to al-Battānī's chapter 11, although the printed edition misplaced it in the middle of chapter 12) may have been the germ from which Regiomontanus subsequently developed the earliest statement of the cosine law for spherical triangles. Although he employed the versed sine $(1 - \cos)$ rather than the cosine itself and used the law only once, he was the first to formulate this fundamental proposition of spherical trigonometry. He enunciated it as theorem 2 in book V of his treatise *On All Classes of Triangles* (*De triangulis omnimodis*).

The urgent need for a compact and systematic treatment of the rules governing the ratios of the sides and angles in both plane and spherical triangles had become apparent to Peuerbach and Regiomontanus while they were working on the *Epitome*. At the close of the dedication of that work Regiomontanus stated that he would write a treatise on trigonometry. The manuscript of the last four books contains many blank spaces, which, despite Regiomontanus' intentions, were never completed. Part of the volume had been written before he left Rome on 5 July 1463. At the end of that year or at the beginning of 1464 he told a correspondent: "I do not have with me the books which I have written about triangles, but they will soon be brought from Rome."[11] It may have been in Rome that Regiomontanus propounded, in theorem 1 of book II, the proportionality of the sides of a plane triangle to the sines of the opposite angles (or, in modern notation $a/\sin A = b/\sin B = c/\sin C$, the sine law). The corresponding proposition for spherical triangles appears in book IV, theorem 17. Theorem 23 in book II solves, for the first time in the Latin West, a trigonometric problem by means of algebra (here called the *ars rei et census*). Regiomontanus' monumental work on *Triangles*, the first publication of which was delayed until

12 August 1533, attracted many important readers and thereby exerted an enormous influence on the later development of trigonometry because it was the first printed systematization of that subject as a branch of mathematics independent of astronomy.

Regiomontanus dedicated his *Triangles* to Bessarion, whom Pius II, in 1463, had named titular Patriarch of Constantinople. When the pope died, Bessarion returned to Rome in August 1464 to take part in the election of a successor. Regiomontanus accompanied him and while in Rome composed a dialogue between a Viennese named Johannes (evidently himself) and an unnamed scholar from Cracow. The subject of their conversation was a thirteenth-century planetary theory that was still very popular. Some of its defects were discussed in the dialogue, which was printed by Regiomontanus when he later acquired his own press. Although he published the dialogue without a title, it was often reprinted under some such heading as *Johannes Regiomontanus' Attack on the Absurdities in the Planetary Theory of Gerard of Cremona* (Gerard's pupils did not list this *Theorica planetarum* in the catalog of their teacher's productions).[12]

After an observation on 19 June 1465,[13] presumably in Viterbo, a favorite resort of Bessarion's, Regiomontanus' activities during the next two years are not known. In 1467, however, he was firmly established in Hungary, where the post of astronomer royal was held by Martin Bylica of Olkusz (1433–1493), who was also present in Rome during the papal election and in all likelihood is the unnamed interlocutor in Regiomontanus' dialogue on planetary theory.

In 1467, with Bylica's assistance, Regiomontanus computed his *Tables of Directions*, which consisted of the longitudes of the celestial bodies in relation to the apparent daily rotation of the heavens. These *Tables*, computed for observers as far north of the equator as 60°, were first published in 1490 and very frequently thereafter.[14] Regiomontanus wrote accompanying problems and in problem 10 he indicated the desirability of abandoning the sexagesimal character of the table of sines by putting $\sin 90° = 100{,}000$ (10^5) instead of $60{,}000$ (6×10^4), the base he had used in *Triangles* (book IV, theorem 25). In that work he had not employed the tangent function; but in *Tables of Directions* he included a table of tangents (although he did not use this term) for angles up to 90°, the interval being 1° and $\tan 45° = 100{,}000$, thereby providing the model for our modern tables.

In 1468 in Buda, then the capital of the kingdom of Hungary, Regiomontanus computed a table of sines with $\sin 90° = 10{,}000{,}000$ (10^7). But before he realized the advantage of the decimal base, he had prepared a sexagesimal sine table, to which he had referred in the dedication of his *Triangles* and which he had used in computing his *Tables of Directions*, with sin 90° = 6,000,000 (6 × 10⁶), the interval being 1' and the seconds being found by an auxiliary table of proportional parts. Both of Regiomontanus' major sine tables, the sexagesimal and the decimal, were first published at Nuremberg in 1541, together with his essay on the *Construction of Sine Tables*.

While still in Italy, Regiomontanus began to compute his *Table of the First Movable* [*Sphere*], or of the apparent daily rotation of the heavens. He completed this work, together with an explanation of its use, in Hungary and dedicated it to his friend King Matthias I Corvinus. He also expounded the geometrical basis of this *Table*. These three related works constituted an item in the list of his own writings that Regiomontanus intended to print on his own press, an intention he could not carry out. Of these three works, the first two were published in Vienna in 1514, and the third in Neuburg in 1557. Regiomontanus wrote each of these works for the purpose of facilitating astronomical computations. But whatever use was made of them ended with the advent of logarithms.

In 1471 Regiomontanus left Hungary. "Quite recently I have made [observations] in the city of Nuremberg . . . for I have chosen it as my permanent home," he informed a correspondent on 4 July 1471, "not only on account of the availability of instruments, particularly the astronomical instruments on which the entire science of the heavens is based, but also on account of the very great ease of all sorts of communication with learned men living everywhere, since this place is regarded as the center of Europe because of the journeys of the merchants."[15] On 29 November 1471 the City Council of Nuremberg granted Regiomontanus residence in the city until Christmas of the following year. He installed a printing press in his own house in order to publish scientific writings, a class of books in which the existing establishments were reluctant to invest their capital, partly because the necessary diagrams required special craftsmen and additional expense.

Regiomontanus was the first publisher of astronomical and mathematical literature, and he sought to advance the work of scientists by providing them with texts free of scribal and typographical errors, unlike the publications then in circulation. His emphasis on correct texts was aided by his introduction into Nuremberg printing of the Latin alphabet and, for writings in the German language, rounded and simplified letters that approached the Latin alphabet in legibility.

Regiomontanus' first publication, a mark of his deep affection for his former teacher, colleague, and collaborator, was Peuerbach's *New Theory of the Planets*. This work was the first item in the catalog which Regiomontanus sent out in the form of a broadside, listing his publications, issued or projected, written by himself or others. The second item in the list of his own publications was the *Ephemerides*, which he issued in 1474 and which was the first such work to be printed. It gave the positions of the heavenly bodies for every day from 1475 to 1506. Of all the books written and published by Regiomontanus, this is perhaps the most interesting from the standpoint of general history: Columbus took a copy on his fourth voyage and used its prediction of the lunar eclipse of 29 February 1504 to frighten the hostile Indians in Jamaica into submission.[16]

The geographer Martin Behaim "boasted that he was a pupil of Regiomontanus"[17] in Nuremberg. More credit is given to the statement that Regiomontanus attracted Bernhard Walther as a pupil. Walther, who was born in Memmingen, in 1467 became a citizen of Nuremberg, where he helped Regiomontanus with his observations and continued them after his teacher left for Rome in the summer of 1475. Regiomontanus' last observation in Nuremberg is dated 28 July 1475 and Walther's observations begin five days later.[18]

According to a Nuremberg chronicler, Regiomontanus went to Rome in response to a papal invitation to emend the notoriously incorrect ecclesiastical calendar. If this report is true, nothing positive resulted from his trip, for he died in less than a year.

In all probability Regiomontanus fell victim to the plague that spread through Rome after the Tiber overflowed its banks in January 1476. But a more sensational rumor concerning the cause of his death surfaced in a laudatory poem that served as the title page of a posthumous edition of his *Latin Calendar* (Venice, 1482). The rumor gained currency by being repeated in 1549 in Reinhold's commemorative eulogy of Regiomontanus and again in 1654[19] in Gassendi's biography of the astronomer. In his catalog Regiomontanus had announced his intention to publish an extensive polemic against George of Trebizond, whose "commentary on the *Syntaxis* he will show with the utmost clarity to be worthless and his translation of Ptolemy's work not to be free of faults." Although Regiomontanus never actually published his attack, which still remains in manuscript in Leningrad, George's sons poisoned him, according to the rumor. Yet Bessarion died unmolested on

18 November 1472, three years after his own devastating attack on George of Trebizond as a *Calumniator of Plato* was published in Rome (1469).

"The motion of the stars must vary a tiny bit on account of the motion of the earth." This portentous statement in the handwriting of Regiomontanus was excerpted from one of his letters by Georg Hartmann, the discoverer of the vertical dip of the magnetic needle and an early supporter of the Copernican cosmology. Hartmann regarded the excerpt as a treasure, undoubtedly because to his mind it provided clear proof that Regiomontanus, the greatest astronomer of the fifteenth century, had accepted the concept of the moving earth and realized one of its numerous implications; Regiomontanus was therefore a Copernican before Copernicus.

The letter from which Hartmann took this excerpt has not survived, nor has the excerpt itself. But it was copied by a professor onto the margin of his unpublished lecture in 1613 on Copernicus' planetary theory, with the explanation that Hartmann "recognized Regiomontanus' handwriting because he was also familiar with his features." Yet Hartmann was not even born until 1489, thirteen years after the death of Regiomontanus.

Nevertheless, it has been suggested that the letter in question may have been sent by Regiomontanus to Novara, who, in an unpublished essay on the duration of pregnancy, called Regiomontanus his teacher. Novara in turn became the teacher of Copernicus. Thus it can be inferred that the concept of the revolutionary geokinetic doctrine was first conceived by Regiomontanus and communicated to Novara, who then passed it to Copernicus. Nevertheless, in the voluminous published and unpublished writings of Regiomontanus, no other reference to the earth in motion has ever been found.

NOTES

1. *Die Matrikel der Universität Wien*, I (Graz–Cologne, 1954), 275. The Johannes Molitoris who entered the University of Leipzig on 15 October 1447 has been identified with Regiomontanus by Zinner, *Leben und Wirken des . . . Regiomontanus*, 13. The Leipzig rector, however, did not associate his namesake with any particular place and Molitoris, as a Latinized form of the surname Müller, was extremely common.
2. Ludwig Mohler, *Kardinal Bessarion als Theologe, Humanist und Staatsman*, Quellen und Forschungen aus dem Gebiete der Geschichte, no. 20 (Paderborn, 1923), 298.
3. Joseph Aschbach, *Geschichte der Wiener Universität im ersten Jahrhunderte ihres Bestehens* (Farnborough, 1967; repr. of Vienna, 1865), 539.
4. Mohler, *op. cit.*, 303.
5. Conrad Eubel, *Hierarchia catholica medii aevi*, II (Padua, 1960; repr. of 2nd ed., Münster, 1913–1923), 150. Bessarion's elevation is dated in April 1463, but the exact day is marked

as unknown. However, Bessarion's predecessor, Isidore of Kiev, died on 27 April 1463 (Eubel, II, 36, n. 199).
6. Robert Weiss, "Jacopo Angeli da Scarperia," in *Medioevo e rinascimento, studi in onore di Bruno Nardi*, Pubblicazioni dell'Istituto di filosofia dell'Università di Roma (Florence, 1955), 824.
7. Regiomontanus' catalog of the books to be printed on his press; reproduced by Zinner, "Die wissenschaftlichen Bestrebungen Regiomontans," in *Beiträge zur Inkunabelkunde*, **2** (1938), 92.
8. Silvio Magrini, "Joannes de Blanchinis Ferrariensis e il suo carteggio scientifico col Regiomontano (1463–64)," in *Atti e memorie della deputazione ferrarese di storia patria*, **22**, fasc. 3, no. 2, (1915–1917), lvii.
9. Mohler, *op. cit.*, 312.
10. The total eclipse of the moon on 21 April 1464 was observed by Regiomontanus in Padua; see *Scripta clarissimi mathematici M. Ioannis Regiomontani* (Nuremberg, 1544), fol. 41r–42r; or Willebrord Snell, *Coeli et siderum . . . observationes Hassiacae* (Leiden, 1618), Ioannis de Monteregio . . . observationes, fol. 20v.
11. Maximilian Curtze, "Der Briefwechsel Regiomontan's mit Giovanni Bianchini, Jacob von Speier und Christian Roder," in *Abhandlungen zur Geschichte der Mathematik*, **12** (1902), 214.
12. Olaf Pedersen, "The Theorica Planetarum Literature of the Middle Ages," in *Ithaca, Proceedings of the Tenth International Congress of History of Science* (Paris, 1964), 617.
13. *Scripta . . . Regiomontani*, fol. 42r; Snell, fol. 21v.
14. The manuscript of Regiomontanus' *Tables of Directions* that Bylica presented to Cracow University is still preserved there; see Władysław Wisłocki, *Katalog rękopisów biblioteki uniwersytetu jagiellońskiego* (Cracow, 1877–1881), 188; and Jerzy Zathey *et al.*, *Historia biblioteki jagiellońskiej* (Cracow, 1966), 154, n. 64.
15. Curtze, *op. cit.*, 327. The lunar eclipse on 2 June 1471 was observed by Regiomontanus in Nuremberg—*Scripta*, fol. 42v; Snell, fol. 22r.
16. Samuel Eliot Morison, *Admiral of the Ocean Sea*, II (Boston, 1942), 400–403.
17. João de Barros, *Asia*, I, decade I, bk. 4, ch. 2 (Lisbon, 1945), 135. If Behaim's claim was correct, he was at most 16 years old when Regiomontanus left Nuremberg; see Richard Hennig, *Terrae incognitae*, 2nd ed., IV, (Leiden, 1944–1956), 434.
18. *Scripta*, fol. 27v; Snell, fol. 1v; Donald Beaver, "Bernard Walther: Innovator in Astronomical Observation," in *Journal for the History of Astronomy*, **1** (1970), 39–43.
19. Gassendi, *Tychonis Brahei . . . vita . . . accessit . . . Regiomontani . . . vita* (Paris, 1654), app., 92; and *Opera omnia*, V (Stuttgart-Bad Cannstatt, 1964; repr. of Lyons, 1658 ed.), 532.

BIBLIOGRAPHY

Regiomontanus' works were reprinted in *Joannis Regiomontari opera collectanea* (Osnabrück, 1972) with a biography by the ed. Felix Schmeidler. An older work is Ernst Zinner, *Leben und Wirken des Johannes Müller von Königsberg genannt Regiomontanus*, 2nd ed., rev. and enl. (Osnabrück, 1968). A recent trans. of Regiomontanus' *De triangulis omnimodis* is Barnabas Hughes, *Regiomontanus on Triangles* (Madison, Wis., 1967).

On Regiomontanus and his work, see the anonymous "Regiomontanus's Astrolabe at the National Maritime Museum," in *Nature*, **183** (1959), 508–509; and Edward

Rosen, "Regiomontanus's Breviarium," in *Medievalia et Humanistica*, **15** (1963), 95–96.

EDWARD ROSEN

REICHENBACH, HANS (*b.* Hamburg, Germany, 26 September 1891; *d.* Los Angeles, California, 9 April 1953)

Reichenbach was one of five children of Bruno Reichenbach, a prosperous wholesale merchant, and the former Selma Menzel. Both parents were members of the Reformed Church; his paternal grandparents were Jewish. The family was cultured, with a lively interest in music, chess, books, and the theater.

From 1910 to 1911 Reichenbach studied engineering in Stuttgart but, dissatisfied, turned to mathematics, physics, and philosophy, attending the universities of Berlin, Munich, and Göttingen. Among his teachers were Planck, Sommerfeld, Hilbert, Born, and Cassirer. He took his doctorate in philosophy at the University of Erlangen in 1915, and another degree by state examination in mathematics and physics at Göttingen in 1916. His doctoral dissertation was on the validity of the laws of probability for physical reality. He wrote it without academic guidance, for he could find no professor interested in the topic. The completed dissertation consisted of an epistemological treatise and a mathematical calculus. After traveling in vain to several universities in search of a sponsor willing and able to read both parts, Reichenbach found at Erlangen a philosopher and a mathematician, each willing to sponsor the part within his competence and together willing to accept the dissertation as a whole. Decades later he would chuckle when he cited their decision as a fallacy of composition, adding: "But I did not point that out to the good professors at that time!"

Reichenbach served for two and a half years in the Signal Corps of the German army, contracting a severe illness at the Russian front. Throughout his life he regarded war as catastrophe and considered it a duty of intellectuals to combat the attitudes from which wars arise. From 1917 to 1920 he worked in the radio industry, continuing his studies in the evening. He was one of the five to attend Einstein's first seminar in relativity theory at the University of Berlin. From 1920 to 1926 he taught surveying, radio techniques, the theory of relativity, philosophy of science, and history of philosophy at the Technische Hochschule in Stuttgart.

In 1926 Reichenbach obtained a professorial appointment at the University of Berlin. Opposition to his appointment, due in part to his social activism during his student days and in part to his outspoken disrespect for many traditional metaphysical systems, was overcome by Einstein's persistent and witty pleading. In 1930 Reichenbach and Rudolf Carnap founded and edited the journal *Erkenntnis*, which for many years was the major organ of the Vienna Circle of logical positivists, of the Berlin Group for Empirical Philosophy, and of the International Committee for the Unity of Science. He also broadcast over the German state radio the lectures published in 1930 as *Atom und Kosmos*.

Within a few days of Hitler's election to power in 1933, Reichenbach was dismissed from the University of Berlin and from the state radio. Anticipating this action, he was on his way to Turkey before the dismissal notices were delivered. From 1933 to 1938 he taught philosophy at the University of Istanbul, where he was charged with reorganizing instruction in that subject. He was delighted to find that among his students there were many excellent young teachers, who had been given paid leave of absence by Ataturk's government so that they might profit from the presence in Turkey of German refugee professors.

In 1938 Reichenbach received his immigration permit to enter the United States, and from then until his death in 1953 was professor of philosophy at the University of California at Los Angeles, frequently lecturing at other universities and at congresses in the United States and Europe. Shortly before his death a volume was planned for the Library of Living Philosophers (edited by P. A. Schilpp) to include both Carnap and Reichenbach, but his death prevented fulfillment of the project.

As a teacher Reichenbach was extraordinarily effective. Carl Hempel, who studied under him at Berlin, stated: "His impact on his students was that of a blast of fresh, invigorating air; he did all he could to bridge the wide gap of inaccessibility and superiority that typically separated the German professor from his students." His pedagogical technique consisted of deliberately oversimplifying each difficult topic, after warning students that the simple preliminary account would be inaccurate and would later be corrected. Students who pursued advanced work with him found him kindly, witty, morally courageous, and loyal. Those whose interests or convictions differed from his sometimes found him arrogant and intolerant.

Reichenbach never substantially altered his epistemological stance, which can be briefly characterized as anti-Kantian, antiphenomenalistic empiricism. In his first book, *Relativitätstheorie und Erkenntnis apriori* (1920), he began his attack upon the Kantian doctrine of synthetic a priori knowledge, although at that time he still regarded the "concept of an object" as a priori. He declared, however, that this concept is a priori only in the sense of being a conceptual construction contributed by the mind to sense data, and not also, as Kant had believed, a priori in the sense of necessarily true for all minds. By 1930 Reichenbach had replaced this view with the thesis that the concept of a physical object results from a projective inductive inference. From that time on, he maintained that there is no synthetic a priori knowledge, defending this thesis by showing that every knowledge claim held by Kant to be a synthetic a priori truth could be classified as analytic a priori, synthetic a posteriori, or decisional. In accord with Helmholtz, Frege, and Russell, Reichenbach regarded the axioms and theorems of arithmetic as analytic a priori. He classified the parallel postulate and the theorems of Euclidean geometry as synthetic a posteriori if, in combination with congruence conventions, they are taken as descriptive of physical spatial relations. The Kantian principle of universal causality was also classified as synthetic a posteriori. In his later work, after reformulating the principle of causality in terms of inductive inference, Reichenbach denied that it applies to the subatomic realm of quantum theory. As for the Kantian moral synthetic a prioris, he regarded them as volitional decisions, neither true nor false.

By 1924 Reichenbach had developed his theory of "equivalent descriptions," a central tenet of his theory of knowledge. It is formulated in his *Axiomatik der relativistischen Raum-Zeit-Lehre* (1924), in *Philosophie der Raum-Zeit-Lehre* (1928), in *Atom und Kosmos* (1930), in *Experience and Prediction* (1938), and in the less technical *Rise of Scientific Philosophy* (1951); and it is developed with new applications in his works on quantum mechanics and time. This theory attributes an indispensable role in physical theory to conventions but rejects the extreme conventionalism of Poincaré and his school. Reichenbach insisted that a completely stated description or physical theory must include conventional elements, in particular such "coordinating definitions" as equal lengths and simultaneous times. These definitions are not bits of knowledge, for such questions as whether or not two rods distant from each other have the same length are not empirically answerable. Hence such coordinations must be regarded as conventions, as definitions, as neither true nor false.

Physical theory contains much more than these conventional elements, however. The truth of a theory, the complete statement of which must include a set of coordinating definitions, is not a matter of convention but of empirical confirmation. Furthermore, one theory using one set of congruence conventions may be empirically equivalent to another theory using another set of conventions. For example, Riemannian geometry combined with the usual coordinating definitions of equal times, equal lengths, and straight lines yields a description of physical space equivalent to Euclidean geometry combined with coordinating definitions which attribute systematic changes to lengths of rigid rods.

This equivalence Reichenbach explicated as follows: When all possible observations confirm to the same degree two descriptions, one of which uses one set of congruence conventions and the other another set, the two descriptions are equivalent, that is, have the same knowledge content or cognitive meaning.

Theories of meaning had long been a focal concern of logical positivists, to whose work Reichenbach acknowledged indebtedness, offering his own theory of meaning as a development and correction of the positivists' verifiability theory. He disagreed with the positivists on two crucial points. First, their theory made complete verifiability (as true or false) a condition of cognitive meaningfulness. This, Reichenbach pointed out, denies that statements confirmed with probability have cognitive meaning, and hence consigns to the category "meaningless" all generalizations and all predictions of science. The strictness of their limitation on cognitive meaning had forced the positivists into a phenomenalism which equated the conclusions of physical science with statements about sensory data. Reichenbach proposed to give the neglected but all-important concept of probability the central role in theory of meaning which it actually plays in scientific method. He regarded the relation between observational data and physical theory as a probability inference, not a logical equivalence. This permits a "realistic" (as opposed to the positivists' phenomenalistic) view of the objects of scientific knowledge.

Reichenbach's second disagreement with the positivists' theory of knowledge involved the logical status of any criterion of cognitive meaningfulness. The positivists assumed that their theory was itself an item of knowledge, a description of the class of meaningful statements. Reichenbach declared that any definition of "knowledge" or of "cognitive meaning" is a volitional decision without truth character (see *Experience and Prediction*, ch. 1, esp. pp. 41, 62). He continued to use the label "theory of meaning" because each decision concerning what is to be accepted as cognitively meaningful is connected with two cognitive questions: whether the decision accords with the actual practice of scientists, and what subordinate decisions are logically entailed by the definition of meaning.

Reichenbach formulated his own decision concerning cognitive meaning in two principles: a proposition has meaning if it is possible to determine a degree of probability for it; and two sentences have the same meaning if they obtain the same degree of probability through every possible observation (for complete formulation, see *Experience and Prediction*, p. 54). The second of these principles he regarded as a modern version of Ockham's razor, core of the antimetaphysical attitude of every consistent empiricism. As examples of its application he cited Mach's criticism of the concept of force and Einstein's principle of the equivalence of gravitation and acceleration.

Throughout his life Reichenbach maintained that the mathematical or frequency concept of probability suffices and needs no supplementation by a priori equal probabilities or by such concepts as "degree of credibility." For prediction of individual events the probability was the "best wager," determined by the frequency of the narrowest class for which there were reliable statistics. He applied the frequency concept of probability to general hypotheses by regarding them as members of classes of hypotheses having known success ratios. These views were opposed by Russell in *Human Knowledge, Its Scope and Limits*, and were supported by Wesley Salmon in *Foundations of Scientific Inference*.

Reichenbach's work on induction was closely connected with his theory of probability, for it introduced the distinction between appraised and unappraised (or "blind") posits. The former have frequency probabilities attached to them; the latter admit of no probability estimate. One blind posit is involved in every inductive inference: the posit that frequencies of series of events converge toward limits. (Causal or one-to-one regularities are simply one case of statistical regularities.) With this thesis Reichenbach reopened the old question of the justification of induction. He accepted Hume's argument that inductive inferences admit of neither deductive (demonstrative) justification nor inductive justification (at pain of circularity). Thus there can be no proof of any sort that inductive inferences will ever succeed in the future, let alone succeed more often than they fail.

Nevertheless, Reichenbach offered the following "pragmatic justification" of our use of inductive inferences. He showed that if the world becomes such that inductive inferences usually fail, as would happen if no past regularities were to continue into the future, then no principles of predictive inference could succeed. Hence inductive procedures offer us our only chance of making successful predictions, although we cannot know whether they will succeed or not. If there are series of events with frequencies which converge toward limits, inductive methods will lead to increasingly successful predictions as observed frequencies approach those limits; if this condition does not obtain, no method whatsoever of making predictions will succeed. Since we cannot know that this necessary condition of successful prediction will not obtain, it would be unreasonable to renounce the method which will yield success if it does obtain. The choice is between certain cognitive failure and our only chance of success. Hence, Reichenbach concluded, it is reasonable to make inductive inferences—that is, to adopt and act on the blind posit that frequencies of series of events will converge toward limits (see *Experience and Prediction*, secs. 38–40).

In "Philosophy: Speculation or Science?" (1947) and in *The Rise of Scientific Philosophy* (1951) Reichenbach drew the corollaries for ethics of his theory of knowledge. His definition of cognitive meaning precluded any extrascientific kinds of knowledge. Hence moral principles and ethical aims are volitional decisions, not items of knowledge. He condemned traditional philosophical systems for conflating cognition and volition in the mistaken hope of establishing knowledge of ultimate values, and he also rejected John Dewey's attempt to test moral judgments by scientific methods. "There is no such thing as 'the good' in the sense of an object of knowledge" ("Philosophy: Speculation or Science?" p. 21). In his brief writings on the nature of moral judgments, his style and tone are as dogmatic as the style and tone of other ethical noncognitivists of the era. He does not mention that his classification of moral judgments as volitional decisions is a classification dependent upon his own decisional definition of cognitive meaning.

The Direction of Time, nearly completed before Reichenbach's death and published posthumously, is the culmination of his epistemological investigations of relativity physics and quantum theory. In it he applied his analyses of conventions, equivalent descriptions, probability inferences, and three-valued logic to subjective (experienced) time, to the time concepts of macrophysics, and to the possibility of establishing time order and time direction among subatomic events. He found that among the equivalent descriptions of the "interphenomena" of quantum theory, every possible description contains causal anomalies, reversals of time direction, or both. He concluded that both time order and time direction are statistical macrocosmic properties which cannot be traced to microcosmic events. To the question "Why is the flow of psychological time identical with the direction of increasing entropy?" his answer was "Man is a part of nature, and his memory is a registering instrument subject to the laws of information theory" (*The Direction of Time*, p. 269).

BIBLIOGRAPHY

I. ORIGINAL WORKS. A complete bibliography is in *Modern Philosophy of Science* (below). Reichenbach's earlier writings include *Der Begriff der Wahrscheinlichkeit für die mathematische Darstellung der Wirklichkeit* (Leipzig, 1915), his inaugural dissertation, also in *Zeitschrift für Philosophie und philosophische Kritik*, **161** (1916), 210–239, and **162** (1917), 98–112, 223–253, and summarized in "Der Begriff der Wahrscheinlichkeit für die mathematische Darstellung der Wirklichkeit," in *Naturwissenschaften*, **7**, no. 27 (1919), 482–483; *Relativitätstheorie und Erkenntnis apriori* (Berlin, 1920), trans. with an intro. by Maria Reichenbach as *The Theory of Relativity and A Priori Knowledge* (Berkeley–Los Angeles, 1965); *Axiomatik der relativistischen Raum-Zeit-Lehre*, no. 72 in the series Die Wissenschaft (Brunswick, 1924; repr. Brunswick, 1965), trans. by Maria Reichenbach with an intro. by W. C. Salmon as *Axiomatization of the Theory of Relativity* (Berkeley–Los Angeles, 1969); *Von Kopernikus bis Einstein* (Berlin, 1927), trans. by R. B. Winn as *From Copernicus to Einstein* (New York, 1942; paperback ed., 1957); *Philosophie der Raum-Zeit-Lehre* (Berlin–Leipzig, 1928), trans. by Maria Reichenbach and John Freund, with intro. by Rudolf Carnap, as *The Philosophy of Space and Time* (New York, 1958); *Atom und Kosmos. Das physikalische Weltbild der Gegenwart* (Berlin, 1930), trans. by E. S. Allen, rev. and updated by Reichenbach, as *Atom and Cosmos. The World of Modern Physics* (London, 1932; New York, 1933; repr. New York, 1957); and *Experience and Prediction. An Analysis of the Foundations and the Structure of Knowledge* (Chicago, 1938).

Later works include "On the Justification of Induction," in *Journal of Philosophy*, **37**, no. 4 (1940), 97–103, repr. in Herbert Feigl and Wilfried Sellars, eds., *Readings in Philosophical Analysis* (New York, 1949), 324–329; *Philosophic Foundations of Quantum Mechanics* (Berkeley–Los Angeles, 1944); "Bertrand Russell's Logic," in P. A. Schilpp, ed., *The Philosophy of Bertrand Russell*, vol. 5 in Library of Living Philosophers (Evanston, Ill., 1944), 23–54; *Elements of Symbolic Logic* (New York, 1947); "Philosophy: Speculation or Science?" in *The Nation*, **164**, no. 1 (4 Jan. 1947), 19–22, repr. as "The Nature of a Question," in I. J. Lee, ed., *The Language of Wisdom and Folly* (New York, 1949), 111–113; *The Theory of Probability. . . .*, trans. by Maria Reichenbach and E. H. Hutten, 2nd ed. (Berkeley–Los Angeles, 1949); "The Philosophical Significance of the Theory of Relativity," in P. A. Schilpp, ed., *Albert Einstein: Philosopher-Scientist*, vol. 7 in Library of Living Philosophers (Evanston, Ill., 1949), 287–311, repr. in Herbert Feigl and May Brodbeck, eds., *Readings in the Philosophy of Science* (New York, 1953), 195–211, and in P. P. Wiener, *Readings in Philosophy of Science* (New York, 1953), 59–76; "Philosophical Foundations of Probability," in *Proceedings of the Berkeley Symposium on Mathematical Statistics and Probability* (Berkeley–Los Angeles, 1949), 1–20; *The Rise of Scientific Philosophy* (Berkeley–Los Angeles, 1951; 1954; paperback ed., 1956); *Nomological Statements and Admissible Operations*, in Studies in Logic and the Foundations of Mathematics (Amsterdam, 1954); *The Direction of Time*, Maria Reichenbach, ed. (Berkeley–Los Angeles, 1956); and *Modern Philosophy of Science: Selected Essays*, Maria Reichenbach, ed. and trans. (London, 1959).

II. SECONDARY LITERATURE. See A. Grünbaum, *Philosophical Problems of Space and Time* (New York, 1963), ch. 3; A. Grünbaum, W. C. Salmon, *et al.*, "A Panel Discussion of Simultaneity by Slow Clock Transport in the Special and General Theories of Relativity," in *Philosophy of Science*, **36**, no. 1 (Mar. 1969), 1–81; Ernest Nagel, "Review of Philosophical Foundations of Quantum Mechanics," in *Journal of Philosophy*, **42** (1945), 437–444; and "Probability and the Theory of Knowledge," in his *Sovereign Reason* (Glencoe, Ill., 1954); *Probability in Philosophy and Phenomenological Research*, V–VI (1945), which contains papers by Reichenbach, D. C. Williams, Ernest Nagel, Rudolf Carnap, Henry Margenau, and others; Hilary Putnam, review of *The Direction of Time*, in *Journal of Philosophy*, **59** (1962), 213–216; W. V. Quine, review of *Elements of Symbolic Logic, ibid.*, **45** (1948), 161–166; Bertrand Russell, *Human Knowledge, Its Scope and Limits* (New York, 1948), *passim*; W. C. Salmon, "Should We Attempt to Justify Induction?" in *Philosophical Studies*, **8** (1957), 33–48; and *Foundations of Scientific Inference* (Pittsburgh, 1966), 1–15 and *passim*.

CYNTHIA A. SCHUSTER

REIDEMEISTER, KURT WERNER FRIEDRICH (*b.* Brunswick, Germany, 13 October 1893; *d.* Göttingen, Germany, 8 July 1971)

The son of Hans Reidemeister and the former Sophie Langerfeldt, Reidemeister attended school in Brunswick. His student years at the universities of Freiburg, Munich, and Göttingen were interrupted by four years of military service during World War I. He passed the *Staatsexamen* in mathematics (Edmund Landau was his examiner), philosophy (at Freiburg H. Rickert had been his teacher), physics, chemistry, and geology in 1920. After having accepted an assistantship with E. Hecke at the University of Hamburg, he earned his doctorate in 1921 with a dissertation on algebraic number theory, "Über die Relativklassenzahl gewisser relativquadratischer Zahlkörper" (published in *Abhandlungen aus dem Mathematischen Seminar, Universität Hamburg*, **1** [1921]). At the same time he studied affine geometry, published several papers, and assisted Wilhelm Blaschke in editing the second volume of his *Vorlesungen über Differentialgeometrie*, entitled *Affine Differentialgeometrie* (Berlin, 1923).

In 1923 Kurt Reidemeister accepted an associate professorship in Vienna, where he came in close contact with Hans Hahn, with research on the foundations of mathematics, and with the Vienna philosophical circle. Two years later he accepted a full professorship at Königsberg, where he worked with other young mathematicians, notably Ruth Moufang, Richard Brauer, and Werner Burau. His interest at this time was in the foundations of geometry and combinatorial topology. He wrote books and articles in both fields. His *Knotentheorie* (Berlin, 1932; repr. New York, 1948) remained the standard work on knot theory for several decades.

In April 1933 Reidemeister was expelled from his Königsberg professorship because he opposed the Nazis. In 1934 he became professor at the University of Marburg, in the chair of Kurt Hensel. He remained there—except for a two-year visit to the Institute for Advanced Study at Princeton in 1948–1950—until he moved to the University of Göttingen in 1955. While at Marburg he collaborated with F. Bachmann, laying the foundations of a development which culminated in Bachmann's *Aufbau der Geometrie aus dem Spiegelungsbegriff* (1959), and with Helene Braun.

The foundations of geometry and topology, established on a purely combinatorial and group-theoretical basis without introduction of a limit concept, always held a prominent place in Reidemeister's mathematical research. He was convinced that problems in mathematics that are original should arise from vivid perception, and even from the beauty of geometrical objects, and that abstraction should only be the result of intensive thought, which justifies the lack of immediate visualization. In accordance with this view he was critical of the modern trend of replacing traditional geometry by linear algebra. He had worked out a modern course along the lines of Felix Klein's "Erlanger Programm," classifying the various geometries by their related groups. His book *Raum und Zahl* (Berlin–Göttingen–Heidelberg, 1957) gave an idea of this concrete approach to mathematics in which mathematical thinking and reflections on thought are to illuminate each other.

Besides mathematics it was the historical origin of mathematical and rational thought that fascinated Reidemeister most—the Greeks in particular and philosophy in general. Three of his historical articles were republished in 1949 under the title *Das exakte Denken der Griechen*. In several publications he expounded his own philosophical position, one of critical rationalism. Reidemeister was strongly opposed to existentialism, which came into vogue in Germany after 1945. He reproached it for lack of objectivity and logical reasoning (*Die Unsachlichkeit der Existenzphilosophie* [Berlin, 1954; 2nd ed., 1970]). Although an advocate of enlightenment and rationality, Reidemeister was highly sensitive and responsive to beauty and symmetry. Among his publications are two small volumes of essays and poems: *Figuren* (Frankfurt, 1946) and *Von dem Schönen* (Hamburg, 1947). His last book was a memorial to Hilbert: *Hilbert-Gedenkband* (Berlin–Heidelberg–New York, 1971).

Reidemeister was married to Elisabeth Wagner, a photographer and the daughter of a Protestant minister at Riga.

BIBLIOGRAPHY

Reidemeister's publications are listed in Poggendorff, VI, 2144; and VIIa, 714.

Obituaries include R. Artzy, "Kurt Reidemeister, 13. 10. 1893–8. 7. 1971," in *Jahresbericht der Deutschen Mathematiker-Vereinigung*, **74** (1972), 96–104, with bibliography; and F. Bachmann, H. Behnke, W. Franz, "In Memoriam Kurt Reidemeister," in *Mathematische Annalen*, **199** (1972), 1–11.

CHRISTOPH J. SCRIBA

RÉNYI, ALFRÉD (*b*. Budapest, Hungary, 30 March 1921; *d*. Budapest, 1 February 1970)

Rényi was the son of Artur Rényi, an engineer and linguist, and of Barbara Alexander, both of whom were Jewish. Rényi's paternal grandfather, originally named Rosenthal, left Germany and settled in Hungary under the name of Rényi after an adventurous interlude of sheep farming in Australia. In Budapest he founded a walking-stick factory and made a modest fortune. Rényi's maternal grandfather, Bernát Alexander, was professor of philosophy at the University of Budapest and a literary critic.

At school Rényi excelled in classical Greek. From early on, he was interested in astronomy, and that led him to physics, which in turn sparked his interest in mathematics. His university studies (1940–1944) were in mathematics and physics. In 1944 he was called up for forced labor service, but he managed to escape and lived in hiding. When conditions normalized, he obtained a Ph.D. in mathematics at Szeged (1945) under Frigyes (Friedrich) Riesz for work on Cauchy-Fourier series. Among his other teachers were Rózsa Péter (in high school) and Lipót Féjér (at Budapest). In 1946 he was awarded a scholarship that made it possible for him to go to Leningrad with his wife, Katalin Schulhof, whom he had married earlier that year. In Leningrad he worked with Yuri V. Linnik and made spectacular discoveries in the theory of numbers, which he expounded in his 1947 paper on the representation of an even number as the sum of a prime and an almost prime. There he also encountered the theory of probability, and he returned to Hungary already embarked on his brilliant career as a probabilist.

Rényi was the acknowledged founder of the school of probabilists centered at the Mathematical Research Institute of the Hungarian Academy of Sciences in Budapest, of which he was the director from 1950 to 1970. Among his Ph.D. students were many who subsequently made their mark in probability theory, including A. Prékopa, P. Révész, J. Mogyorodi, J. Kumlós, G. Tusnády, G. Katona, and D. Szász. His interest in the theory of numbers persisted throughout his life and (often in probabilistic contexts) found expression in his regular collaboration with Pál (Paul) Erdös and Pál (Paul) Turán. He held many important and influential positions—professor of mathematics at the universities of Debrecen (1949–1950) and of Budapest (1952–1970), general secretary of the Bolyai János Mathematical Society (1949–1955), and secretary of the Mathematical Section of the Hungarian Academy of Sciences (1949–1953)—and soon was recognized worldwide as one of the leaders in probability theory. Indications of the geographical range of this influence are his publication of a paper in Chinese and his receipt of an Overseas Fellowship from Churchill College, Cambridge, where he gave the prestigious Rouse Ball lecture in 1966. His publications and occasional writings, 355 in number, are listed in his *Selected Papers* (1976), which contains English translations of many of the most important items.

In the hands of writers like Linnik, Erdös, and Rényi, the theory of numbers is not clearly distinguished from the theory of probability. Each lends techniques to the other, and important problems lie along their common frontier. Thus, when Rényi is referred to as a great applied probabilist, this is partly because of his interest in probability applied to other parts of mathematics. A joint paper with Erdös, "On the Evolution of Random Graphs" (1960), illustrates this interest very well. A set of points called vertices is given, and "edges" joining pairs of vertices are then created by some specific time-dependent random mechanism. What results is an evolving "random graph." This is truly applied mathematics, important, for example, in studies of the spread of disease.

Another illustration is "random space-filling," which at first may be seen as a problem in stochastic geometry but turns out to be very important in chemistry, in physics, and in such applications as the design of parking lots. A careful study of the complete bibliography in Rényi's *Selected Papers* reveals (especially in the titles of the shorter notes, usually published in Hungarian) the practical origin of many of Rényi's more famous "pure" papers. An example of an explicitly practical paper is "On Two Mathematical Models of the Traffic on a Divided Highway" (1969).

Rényi was, however, an important contributor to fundamentals. In 1954, at the International Congress of Mathematicians in Amsterdam, he announced a new system of axioms for probability (for a later account, see "On a New Axiomatic Theory of Probability" [1955]), based on conditionality as a fundamental concept. The full impact of this has yet to be absorbed. He also made seminally important contributions to the foundations of information technology.

Rényi's most famous single achievement was his proof of the representability of each even number as the sum of a prime and an "almost prime"; in the best contemporary improvement (by Chen Jingrun), "almost prime" has been refined to "integer with at most two prime factors."

Rényi wrote many books; among them, *Foundations of Probability* (1970) is perhaps the most beautiful text ever written on the subject. He had an exceptionally clear and lucid style, and his longer papers are full of comments and insights that enhance their value. His great interest in the history of ideas found expression in fictitious dialogues and letters (*Dialogues on Mathematics* [1967] and *Letters on Probability* [1972]), which combine great depth with astonishing artistry. *A Diary on Information Theory* (1984), published after his death, is a natural successor to these two remarkable works.

Rényi traveled widely, especially in Europe, and did much to reunify the mathematical community after World War II. One of his sayings, now widely current, defined a mathematician as "a machine for converting coffee into theorems." (Turán improved on this by a remark, prompted by a cup that was too weak: "This coffee is fit only for lemmas.") These anecdotes show that for Rényi, mathematics was a social activity through which he generated a great number of friends.

In 1969 Rényi's wife, also a distinguished mathematician, with whom he had written "The Prüfer Code for *k*-Trees," died; and less than six months later, Rényi died at the age of forty-eight.

BIBLIOGRAPHY

I. Original Works. *Selected Papers of Alfréd Rényi*,

Pál Turán, ed., 3 vols. (Budapest, 1976), lists 355 publications and manuscripts, and reprints a great many of these, in English translation where necessary, together with valuable commentaries. Vol. I contains a portrait and a short biography by Turán. Bibliographies are in *Studia scientiarum mathematicarum Hungarica*, **6** (1971), 3–22, with addition in *ibid.*, **7** (1972), 477; and by B. Gyires, in *Universitatis Debreceniensis, Institum mathematicum, Publicationes mathematicae*, **17** (1970), 1–17.

Among Rényi's works are "O predstavlenii chetnvikh chisel v vide summ'e odnogo prostogo i odnogo prochtiprostogo chisla" ("On the Representation of an Even Number as the Sum of a Prime and an Almost Prime," in *Doklady Akademii nauk USSR*, **56** (1947), 455–458, English trans. in *American Mathematical Society Translations*, 2nd ser., **19** (1962), 299–321; "On a New Axiomatic Theory of Probability," in *Acta mathematica Academiae scientiarum Hungaricae*, **6** (1955), 285–335; "Egy egydimenziós véletlen térkitöltési problémáról" ("On a One-Dimensional Random Space-Filling Problem"), in *Magyar tudományos Akadémia matamatikai kutató intézetének közleményei*, **3** (1958), 109–127; "On the Dimenand Entropy of Probability Distributions," in *Acta mathematica Academiae scientiarum Hungaricae*, **10** (1959), 193–215; "On the Evolution of Random Graphs," in *Magyar tudományos Akadémia matamatikai kutató intézetének közleményei*, **5** (1960), 17–61, written with Paul Erdős; "On Measures of Entropy and Information," in *Proceedings of the 4th Berkeley Symposium on Mathematical Statistics and Probability*, vol. I (1961), 547–561; "Über die konvexe Hülle von n zufällig gewählten Punkten," in *Zeitschrift für Wahrscheinlichkeitstheorie*, **2** (1963–1964), 75–84, and **3** (1964–1965), 138–147, and "Zufällige konvexe Polygone in einem Ringgebiet," *ibid.*, **9** (1968), 146–157, written with R. Sulanke; "On Two Mathematical Models of the Traffic on a Divided Highway," in *Journal of Applied Probability*, **1** (1964), 311–320; "On the Theory of Random Search," in *Bulletin of the American Mathematical Society*, **71** (1965), 809–828; *Dialogues on Mathematics* (San Francisco, 1967); "Applications of Probability Theory to Other Areas of Mathematics," in *12th Biennial International Seminar of the Canadian Mathematical Congress* (Vancouver, 1970), 177–295; *Foundations of Probability* (San Francisco, 1970); "The Prüfer Code for k-Trees," in *Combinatorial Theory and Its Applications*, vol. III (Amsterdam, 1970), 945–971, written with Kató Rényi; *Letters on Probability*, Laszló Vekerdi, trans. (Detroit, 1972); "On Some Applications of Probability Methods to Additive Number Theoretic Problems," in *Contributions to Ergodic Theory and Probability* (Berlin, 1970), 37–44, written with Paul Erdős; and *A Diary on Information Theory*, Louis Sucheston, ed. (Budapest, 1984; repr. New York, 1987).

II. SECONDARY LITERATURE. Obituaries include those by David G. Kendall in *Journal of Applied Statistics*, **7** (1970), 509–522; and by P. Révész and I. Vincze, in *Annals of Mathematical Statistics*, **43**, no. 6 (1972), i–xvi. There is a group of articles in *Matematikai lapok. Bolyai János Matematikai tórsulat*, **21** (1970): by Pál Turán, 199–210, by P. Révész, 211–231, by I. Csiszár, 233–241, by G. Katona *et al.*, 243–244, and by V. B. Mészáros, 245–248.

DAVID G. KENDALL

REYE, THEODOR (*b.* Ritzebüttel, near Cuxhaven, Germany, 20 June 1838; *d.* Würzburg, Germany, 2 July 1919)

After schooling in Hamburg, Reye studied mechanical engineering and then mathematical physics at Hannover, Zurich, and Göttingen. He received his doctorate at Göttingen in 1861 with a dissertation on gas dynamics. After qualifying as lecturer at Zurich in 1863, he remained there until 1870 as a *Privatdozent* in mathematical physics. Following a short stay in Aachen came his most productive years 1872–1909, when he was professor of geometry at the University of Strasbourg. He remained in Strasbourg until after World War I, when he moved to Würzburg.

In his younger years Reye published works on physics and meteorology—for example, a book on cyclones (1872). The two-volume first edition of his *Geometrie der Lage* appeared in 1866 and 1868. He remained faithful throughout his life to the synthetic geometry presented in this work. His interest in geometry had been stimulated by analytical mechanics, and Culmann, the founder of graphic statics, had drawn his attention to Staudt's works on geometry. Staudt's books were considered very difficult to read; Reye's *Geometrie der Lage*, the fifth edition of which appeared in 1923, was easily comprehended.

Reye treated in detail the theory of conics and quadrics and of their linear systems, that of third-degree surfaces and some of the fourth degree, as well as many quadratic congruences and aggregates taken from line geometry. He was one of the leading geometers of his time, and he published a great deal on synthetic geometry. His name is linked to the axial complex of a second-degree surface, and he generalized the polarity theory of algebraic curves and surfaces, introducing the concept of apolarity.

Reye was the founder of that portion of projective geometry that E. A. Weiss later called point-series geometry. In a series of writings, Reye treated linear manifolds of projective plane pencils and of collinear bundles or spaces. Later these investigations were easily interpreted multidimensionally by means of the geometry of Segre manifolds. Reye refused to speak of true geometry when dealing with spaces of more than three dimensions. He was satisfied to interpret multidimensional relations in P_2 and P_3, that is, he treated the geometries of lines and spheres in P_3 as four-dimensional geometries. In 1878 Reye published a short work on spherical geometry, the only one of his mathematical writings, besides the *Geometrie der Lage*, to appear as a separate publication. An important configuration of twelve points, twelve planes, and sixteen lines in P_3 is named for Reye.

BIBLIOGRAPHY

I. ORIGINAL WORKS. Reye's writings include *Die Geometrie der Lage*, 2 vols. (Leipzig, 1866–1868), 5th ed., 3 vols. (Leipzig, 1923); *Synthetische Geometrie der Kugeln* (Leipzig, 1879); "Über algebraische Flächen, die zueinander apolar sind," in *Journal für die reine und angewandte Mathematik*, **79** (1874), 159–175; and "Über lineare Mannigfaltigkeiten projektiver Ebenenbüschel und kollinearer Bündel oder Räume," *ibid.*, **104** (1889), 211–240; **106** (1890), 30–47, 315–329; **107** (1891), 162–178; **108** (1891), 89–124.

II. SECONDARY LITERATURE. See C. F. Geiser, "Zur Erinnerung an Theodor Reye," in *Vierteljahrsschrift der Naturforschenden Gesellschaft in Zürich*, **66** (1921), 158–160; C. Segre, "Cenno commemorativo di Reye," in *Atti dell' Accademia nazionale dei Lincei. Rendiconti*, 5th ser., **31** (1922), 269–272; and H. E. Timerding, "Theodor Reye," in *Jahresbericht der Deutschen Mathematiker-Vereinigung*, **31** (1922), 185–203.

WERNER BURAU

REYNEAU, CHARLES RENÉ (*b.* Brissac, Maine-et-Loire, France, 11 June 1656; *d.* Paris, France, 24 February 1728)

Reyneau is important historically as the author of a textbook, written at the request of Malebranche, that was designed to provide instruction in the new mathematics developed at the beginning of the eighteenth century. The son of a surgeon, he studied at the Oratorian *collège* in Angers. Attracted by the order, on 17 October 1676 he entered the Maison d'Institution in Paris, where, besides Malebranche, he met Jean Prestet, who had just published his *Élémens des mathématiques*. In 1679 Reyneau was sent to the Collège de Toulon, and in March 1681 he was ordained a priest there. In October 1682 he went to the University of Angers to replace Prestet as professor of mathematics, a post he held for twenty-three years. Suffering from deafness, he had former students substitute for him for several years but was finally obliged to give up teaching in 1705. Reyneau spent the rest of his life in Paris, at the Oratorian house on rue Saint-Honoré, and published his textbooks there. He was named an *associé libre* of the Académie Royale des Sciences on 12 February 1716.

Many surviving manuscripts reveal Reyneau's pedagogical ability and are a valuable source for the study of mathematics in France at the end of the seventeenth century. Reyneau was only slightly aware of the projects of Malebranche and L'Hospital in 1690–1691 and of the revolution resulting from Johann Bernoulli's stay in Paris in 1692. As late as 1694 all that Malebranche had for Reyneau to do was edit Prestet's posthumous *Géométrie*. But, after abandoning the last shred of Cartesian mathematics, Malebranche chose Reyneau to write the entirely new textbook required by this turnabout (1698).

Reyneau worked with two other Oratorians, Louis Byzance and Claude Jaquemet, who were better mathematicians than he. Reyneau had some difficulty in assimilating the differential and integral calculus and was very interested in the debates, beginning in 1700, provoked by Rolle on this subject. Reyneau's editorial efforts were frustrated in various ways, and the textbook was not published until 1708.

In 1705 Reyneau came into possession of Byzance's papers, which included a copy of the "Leçons" that Bernoulli had prepared for L'Hospital. Unfortunately, Reyneau lent some of the documents to Montmort, who lost them. On the whole, however, he preserved as well as possible the manuscripts of the group around Malebranche; and from them he drew the inspiration for a second didactic work, published in 1714. This work, which attempted to preserve the central conceptions of the Oratorian mathematics of the end of the preceding century, was less successful than the first.

Reyneau's most notable contribution to mathematical education was *Analyse démontrée* (1708). It was from the second edition of this work that d'Alembert learned the fundamentals of the subject.

BIBLIOGRAPHY

I. ORIGINAL WORKS. Reyneau's writings include *Analyse démontrée ou la méthode de résoudre les problèmes des mathématiques et d'apprendre facilement ces sciences, expliquée et démontrée . . . et appliquée . . . à découvrir les propriétés des figures de la géométrie simple et composée, à résoudre les problèmes . . . en employant le calcul ordinaire de l'algèbre, le calcul différentiel et le calcul intégral . . .*, 2 vols. (Paris, 1708; 2nd ed., enl., 1736–1738); *La science du calcul des grandeurs en général . . .*, 2 vols. (Paris, 1714–1735); *La logique ou l'art de raisonner juste à l'usage des dames* (Paris, 1744); and "Traité de la marine ou l'art de naviguer," MS no. 3729, Bibliothèque Mazarine, Paris.

II. SECONDARY LITERATURE. See an unsigned review of *L'analyse démontrée* in *Mémoires pour l'histoire des sciences et des beaux-arts*, **3** (1708), 1438–1452; Bernard de Fontenelle, "Éloge du Père Reyneau," in *Histoire de* *l'Académie royale des sciences pour l'année 1728 . . . avec les mémoires . . .* 112–116; and Pierre Costabel, "Deux inédits de la correspondance indirecte Leibniz–Reyneau," in *Revue d'histoire des sciences et de leurs applications,* **2** (1949), 311–332; "Rectification et compléments . . .," *ibid.,* **19** (1966), 167–169; and *Oeuvres de Malebranche,* XVII, pt. 2, *Malebranche et la réforme mathématique en France de 1689 à 1706* (Paris, 1968).

PIERRE COSTABEL

REY PASTOR, JULIO (*b.* Logroño, Spain, 16 August 1888; *d.* Buenos Aires, Argentina, 21 February 1962)

Rey Pastor, a poet in his youth, studied science at the University of Zaragoza. In 1905 he published his first monograph, *Sobre los números consecutivos cuya suma es a la vez cuadrado y cubo perfecto.* Appointed professor of mathematical analysis at the University of Oviedo in 1911, Rey Pastor wrote the inaugural address for the academic year 1913–1914, *Los matemáticos españoles del siglo XVI* (enlarged and reprinted in 1925 and 1934). In this work he described the deplorable state of science in Spain under the Hapsburgs and, as a consequence, was accused of being unpatriotic. The following year he was professor at Madrid. A series of trips to Germany resulted in the monograph *Estudio geométrico de la polaridad* (Madrid, 1912) and his *Fundamentos de la geometría proyectiva superior* (Madrid, 1916). In the latter work Rey Pastor expounded the synthetic geometry of space in *n* dimensions, introducing concepts of great generality (for example, the definition of the curve) and developing them in all their consequences.

In 1915 Rey Pastor gave a series of lectures at the Institut d'Estudis Catalans in Barcelona on conformal mapping, in which he expounded and developed the work of H. A. Schwarz. Notes from those lectures by Esteban Terrades were published in Catalan. In 1917 Rey Pastor gave an extension course at the University of Buenos Aires and accepted a contract "to direct the advanced study of the exact sciences" in Argentina, spending half of the school year there and half in Spain.

Rey Pastor founded a mathematics laboratory, the Seminario Matemático de Madrid (1916), and the *Revista matemática hispanoamericana* (1919), and published the now-classic *Elementos de análisis algebraico* (Madrid, 1917), in which he introduced his own discoveries and innovations. Besides his mathematical work he studied the history of Spanish cartography, which led to publication of *La cartografía mallorquina,* written with E. García Camarero (Madrid, 1960).

BIBLIOGRAPHY

See Juan José González Covarrubia, *Julio Rey Pastor* (Buenos Aires, 1964); and Esteban Terrades, "Julio Rey Pastor como hombre e investigador," in *Homenaje a Rey Pastor,* I (Santa Fé, Argentina, 1945).

J. VERNET

RHETICUS, GEORGE JOACHIM (*b.* Feldkirch, Austria, 16 February 1514; *d.* Kassa, Hungary [now Košice, Czechoslovakia], 4 December 1574)

Rheticus was the son of George Iserin, the town physician of Feldkirch, and Thomasina de Porris, an Italian lady. After Rheticus' father was beheaded for sorcery in 1528, his surname could no longer be used. Hence his widow reverted to her maiden name, de Porris, for herself and her two children. Our George Joachim de Porris tacked on "Rheticus" to indicate that he came from a place in what had been the ancient Roman province Rhaetia. Since he had not been born in Italy, he converted "de Porris" (meaning "of the leeks") into the German equivalent "von Lauchen." Then as a mature man he dropped both references to leeks, thereby transforming "Rheticus" from a geographical designation into an adopted surname. This fifth stage remained the name by which he is commonly known.

Rheticus' first teacher was his father. After the execution of his father Rheticus studied at Zurich, where Gesner was a schoolmate. He also met Paracelsus "and in the year 1532 had a conversation with him, a great man who published famous works."[1] In 1532 Rheticus matriculated at the University of Wittenberg, where he obtained his M.A. on 27 April 1536; ten days earlier he had publicly defended the thesis that Roman law did not absolutely prohibit all forms of astrological predictions, since predictions based on physical causes were permitted, like medical predictions.

In the same year Rheticus was appointed to teach elementary arithmetic and geometry at the University of Wittenberg. On 18 October 1538 he took a leave of absence for the purpose of visiting such leading astronomers as Johannes Schöner of Nuremberg, Peter Apian of Ingolstadt, and Philip Imser of Tübingen. At Feldkirch on 27 November 1538 he presented an edition of Sacrobosco (published earlier that year at Wittenberg) to Achilles Pirmin Gasser (1505–1577), who was his father's successor, twice removed, as town physician.[2] In the summer of 1539 Rheticus arrived in Frombork (Frauenburg) in order to learn from Copernicus himself about the rumored new and revolutionary cosmology.

The momentous meeting between Rheticus and Copernicus precipitated the beginning of modern astronomy. The reviver of the geokinetic system had long resisted friendly entreaties to release his masterpiece for publication, but permitted Rheticus to write a *Narratio prima* (*First Report*) about *De revolutionibus*. On 23 September 1539 Rheticus completed the *First Report*, which was published at Gdańsk in early 1540. The work was the earliest printed announcement to the educated public of a rival to the Ptolemaic system, which had dominated men's minds for fourteen hundred years. Rheticus immediately sent a copy of the *First Report* to Gasser, who promptly wrote a foreword for the second edition, which was published at Basel in 1541.[3] The first two editions of Rheticus' *First Report* did not detonate any such hostile explosion as Copernicus had feared would be the instant reaction to his geokineticism. Hence he finally made up his mind (perhaps by 9 June 1541) to let *De revolutionibus* be printed and began putting the final touches to his manuscript.

To the *First Report* Rheticus appended an *Encomium Borussiae*, a praise of Prussia based on his travels throughout that region. Presumably utilizing also Copernicus' earlier and incomplete geographical studies, Rheticus drew up a "Tabula chorographica auff Preussen und etliche umbliegende lender," which he presented to Duke Albert of Prussia on 28 August 1541. While Rheticus' "Topographical Survey of Prussia and Several Neighboring Lands" has not survived, it may have provided the foundation for the map of Prussia that was printed at Nuremberg in 1542 as the work of Rheticus' editorial assistant, Heinrich Zell. Rheticus' theoretical discussion of mapmaking, *Chorographia tewsch*, the first work he wrote in German, using his native Vorarlberg dialect,[4] was likewise dedicated to Duke Albert as a companion piece to the "Tabula chorographica." Since the duke had tried in vain to learn from other mathematicians how to anticipate the time of daily sunrise, Rheticus constructed a "small instrument for ascertaining the length of the day throughout the year." In transmitting his "Instrumentlin" to the duke on 29 August 1541, Rheticus asked Albert to recommend to both the Elector of Saxony and the University of Wittenberg that he be permitted to publish Copernicus' *De Revolutionibus*. Three days later Duke Albert complied, further requesting that Rheticus be retained in his professorship.

When Rheticus returned to Wittenberg for the opening of the winter semester, he was elected dean of the liberal arts faculty on 18 October 1541. In early 1542 he separately published—under the title *De lateribus et angulis triangulorum*[5]—the section on plane and spherical trigonometry in Copernicus' *De revolutionibus*. To this brief discussion of the *Sides and Angles of Triangles* Rheticus added a table of half-chords subtended in a circle. Such a half-chord is actually a sine, although both Copernicus and Rheticus studiously avoided the use of that term. The table of sines in the *Sides and Angles of Triangles* differs from the corresponding table in *De revolutionibus* by increasing the length of the radius from one hundred thousand to ten million and by diminishing the interval of the central angle from 10′ to 1′. Furthermore, by indicating the complementary angle at the foot of the columns and at the right-hand side of the page, the 1542 table became the first to give the cosine directly, although that term is not mentioned. Rheticus did not ascribe the authorship of this table to Copernicus nor, presumably out of modesty, to himself. Nevertheless, the table was undoubtedly his doing. His independent place in the history of mathematics is due precisely to his computation of innovative and monumental trigonometrical tables.

Although such a purely technical work as Copernicus' *Sides and Angles of Triangles* could be published without opposition in Wittenberg, that citadel of Lutheran orthodoxy was no place to print Copernicus' *De revolutionibus*, with its far-reaching cosmological implications. Hence, shortly after the end of the winter semester on 30 April 1542, Rheticus left for Nuremberg, where on 1 August 1540 a printer had dedicated to him an astrological tract. Rheticus could not remain in Nuremberg long enough to supervise the entire printing of *De revolutionibus*, since he had been appointed professor of mathematics at the University of Leipzig, where he had to be present in mid-October 1542.

After teaching three years at Leipzig, Rheticus obtained a leave of absence. He went back to Feldkirch and then on to Milan, where he spent some time with Cardano. In Lindau, during the first five months of 1547, he suffered a severe mental disorder, which gave rise to rumors that he had gone mad and died. But he recovered well enough to teach mathematics at Constance for more than three months in the latter half of 1547. Then he moved to Zurich, where he studied medicine with his old classmate Gesner, who was now a widely recognized authority. On 13 February 1548 Rheticus reported to the University of Leipzig that on the advice of his doctors he would leave at Easter to undergo hydrotherapeutic treatment and thereafter return to his post.

At the beginning of the winter semester of 1548 Rheticus was back in harness, having been elected dean. In 1549 he became involved in a legal dispute with a goldsmith and then in April 1551 in a drunken homosexual encounter with a student, on account of which he had to run away from Leipzig.

Seeking to build a new career, Rheticus resumed the study of medicine at the University of Prague in 1551–1552. Although he was invited to teach mathematics at the University of Vienna in 1554, in the spring of that year he settled down at Cracow, where he practiced medicine for two full decades. On 12 April 1564 he wrote to a friend that he had not accepted an unofficial invitation by Peter Ramus to teach at the University of Paris. In Cracow, Rheticus' lifelong interest in astrology attained its greatest success. He had followed up his master's thesis of 1536 by inserting in 1539 an astrological section in his *First Report*, although Copernicus' astronomy was entirely free of that pathetic delusion. As late as 1 March 1562 Rheticus was still contemplating—on the basis of his astrological version of Copernicus[6]—the construction of a chronology of the world from creation to dissolution. But by correctly predicting in 1571 that the successor of King Sigismund Augustus of Poland "will reign only a very short time," Rheticus acquired immense renown as a seer.[7]

L. Valentine Otho, a student of mathematics at the University of Wittenberg, was deeply impressed by Rheticus' *Canon of the Doctrine of Triangles* (Leipzig, 1551), the first table to give all six trigonometric functions, including the first extensive table of tangents and the first printed table of secants (although such modern designations were eschewed by Rheticus as "Saracenic barbarisms"). Without any recourse to arcs, Rheticus' *Canon* defined the trigonometrical functions as ratios of the sides of a right triangle and related these ratios directly to the angles. By equating the functions of angles greater than 45° with the corresponding cofunctions of the complementary angles smaller than 45°, Rheticus reduced the length of his table by half.

When Otho went to visit Rheticus in 1574, he found him in Košice, where he had gone on the invitation of a local magnate. In the arrival of the youthful student to help him publish his life's work, Rheticus recognized a replay of the scenario he himself had enacted with Copernicus a generation earlier. But unfortunately the outcome was different, for Rheticus died on 4 December 1574, leaving his books and manuscripts to Otho, who faithfully promised to see his master's massive tables through the press.

These tables were a "labor of twelve years, while I always had to support a certain number of arithmeticians for these computations," Rheticus had informed Ramus in 1568.[8] Nevertheless Otho had to cope with enormous difficulties before he succeeded in fulfilling his promise to Rheticus. Through his deceased teacher's local patron, he obtained financial support from the Holy Roman Emperor, but within two years this ruler died. On 7 September 1576 Otho appealed from Košice to the Elector of Saxony, who consented to have him appointed as professor of mathematics at the University of Wittenberg. But in January 1581 Otho refused to sign a religious formula required of all the Wittenberg professors, and therefore he had to turn elsewhere.

He found his last patron in the count palatine, Frederick IV, with whom he signed a contract on 24 August 1587. Designated the count's official mathematician, permitted to eat at the table of the professors of the University of Heidelberg, and granted the aid of four students as computers, Otho was finally able to complete and publish in 1596 Rheticus' immense *Opus Palatinum de triangulis*, as Otho entitled it in gratitude to his backer.

The foundation of the Rheticus-Otho *Opus Palatinum* is the table of sines for the first quadrant 0° to 90°, the interval being 45″ and the radius 10^{15}. For purposes of interpolation, a process of successive halving was relentlessly pursued in order to find the small angle the sine of which is 1 in the fifteenth decimal place as the first significant figure. Then, with a radius of 10^{10}, the sines and cosines were computed for intervals of 10″. The functions of each degree occupy six full pages, so enormous was the labor expended in these computations.

After Otho's death, among his papers were found additional Rheticus manuscripts, which were published by Pitiscus in his *Thesaurus mathematicus* (Frankfurt am Main, 1613). These manuscripts included a table of sines for a radius of 10^{15} and intervals of 10″, but an interval of only 1″ for the two special cases of 1° and 89°. Although Rheticus' trigonometrical tables were understandably far from perfect, modern recomputations have found them accurate to a relatively high degree.

NOTES

1. Rheticus to Joachim Camerarius, 29 May 1569 (Burmeister, *Rhetikus*, III, 191).
2. *Bibliotheca apostolica vaticana, inventario dei libri stampati palatino-vaticani*, Enrico Stevenson, ed., vol. I, pt. 1 (Rome, 1886), libri latini, no. 2195.
3. Stevenson, no. 1532.
4. Part of it was translated into modern German, and the rest summarized by Heinz Balmer, *Beiträge zur Geschichte der Erkentniss des Erdmagnetismus* (Aarau, 1956), pp. 279–286.
5. For the copy presented by Rheticus to Gasser on 20 June 1542 in Feldkirch, see Stevenson, no. 1528.
6. Burmeister, *Rhetikus*, III, 162.
7. *Ibid.*, III, 198.
8. *Ibid.*, III, 187.

BIBLIOGRAPHY

I. ORIGINAL WORKS. Rheticus' publications are listed in Karl Heinz Burmeister, *Georg Joachim Rhetikus 1514–1574, eine Bio-Bibliographie*, II (Wiesbaden, 1967–1968), 55–83; the extant MSS: II, 18–31; and correspondence: II, 32–39; III, 15–200.

II. SECONDARY LITERATURE. On Rheticus and his work, see the following references by K. H. Burmeister: *G. J. Rhetikus*, II, 84–92; III, 201; "G. J. Rhetikus und A. P. Gasser," in *Schriften des Vereins für Geschichte des Bodensees*, **86** (1968), 217–225; "G. G. Porro Retico," in *Archivio storico lombardo*, **7** (1968), 3–11; and "G. J. Rheticus as a Geographer," in *Imago mundi*, **23** (1969), 73–76. See also Edward Rosen, "Rheticus's Earliest Extant Letter to Paul Eber," in *Isis*, **61** (1970), 384–386, with commentary by K. H. Burmeister; and "Rheticus as Editor of Sacrobosco" (in press).

EDWARD ROSEN

RIBAUCOUR, ALBERT (*b.* Lille, France, 28 November 1845; *d.* Philippeville [now Skikda], Algeria, 13 September 1893)

Ribaucour was the son of Placide François Charles Ribaucour, a teacher of mathematics, and Angélique Françoise Devemy. In 1865 he entered the École Polytechnique in Paris and in 1867 began studying at the École des Ponts et Chaussées, which he left in 1870 to become an engineer at the Rochefort naval base. At Rochefort he showed an exceptional aptitude for engineering, which also distinguished him after transfer, in 1873, to Draguignan (Var), where from 1874 to 1876 he was in charge of road construction in Var. The bridges that he designed were remarkable because of their combination of maximum strength with minimum material. From 1878 to 1885 he stayed at Aix-en-Provence, where his skills displayed in the construction works on the canal of the Durance earned him a Légion d'Honneur and a gold medal at the Paris Exposition of 1889. Ribaucour's suspension bridge of Mallemort-sur-Corrège and his construction of the reservoir of Saint-Christophe (near Rognes, Bouches-du-Rhône) were especially praised.

After a short stay at Vesoul (Haute-Saône) in order to receive the title of chief engineer, Ribaucour was sent to Algeria, where from 1886 until his death he stayed at Philippeville and worked on the construction of railroads and harbor works.

Ribaucour's mathematical work—to which he dedicated himself especially under the influence of Mannheim—belonged to his spare time, except for a short period during 1873 and 1874, when he was *répétiteur* in geometry at the École Polytechnique. His main field was differential geometry, and his work

was distinguished enough to earn him the Prix Dalmont in 1877 and a posthumous Prix Petit d'Ormoy in 1895, awarded by the Paris Academy. His most elaborate work was a study of minimal surfaces, *Étude des élassoïdes ou surfaces à courbure moyenne nulle*, presented to the Belgian Academy of Sciences in 1880 (in *Mémoires couronnés et mémoires des savants étrangers. Académie royale des sciences, des lettres et des beaux-arts de Belgique*, **44** [1881]). In the work he explained his method called *périmorphie*, which utilized a moving trihedron on a surface. The approach to minimal surfaces was to consider them as the envelope of the middle planes of isotropic congruences; this approach led Ribaucour to a wealth of results.

Many of Ribaucour's papers deal with congruences of circles and spheres. Special attention was devoted to those systems of circles that are orthogonal to a family of surfaces. Such systems form *systèmes cycliques*, and it is sufficient for the circles to be orthogonal to more than two surfaces for them to be orthogonal to a family. Ribaucour's research thus led him to envelopes of spheres, to triply orthogonal systems, cyclides, and surfaces of constant curvature.

BIBLIOGRAPHY

I. ORIGINAL WORKS. Ribaucour reported most of his results in *Comptes rendus hebdomadaires des séances de l'Académie des sciences*, **67** (1868), to **113** (1891); also in the *Nouvelles annales de mathématiques*, 2nd ser., **4** (1865), to **10** (1871); and the *Bulletin de la Société philomathique in Paris* (1867–1871). See also "Sur deux phénomenes d'hydrodynamique observés au bassin de Saint Christophe," in *Compte rendu de la 14e session de l'Association française pour l'avancement des sciences*, pt. 2 (1885), 252–255; and M. Salva, *Notice sur le port de Philippeville* (Paris, 1892), esp. chs. 5 and 6.

II. SECONDARY LITERATURE. A good approach to Ribaucour's work is through Gaston Darboux, *Leçons sur la théorie générale des surfaces et les applications géométriques du calcul infinitésimal*, 4 vols. (Paris, 1887–1896); see also L. Bianchi, *Lezioni di geometria differenziale*, 3rd ed., II (Pisa, 1923), esp. chs. 17, 19, 20, 21. Other works include P. Mansion, "Ribaucour," in *Mathésis*, 2nd ser., **3** (1893), 270–272; and P. M. d'Ocagne, "Un ingénieur et géomètre polytechnicien: Albert Ribaucour," *Bulletin de la Société des amis de l'École Polytechnique* (July, 1913). (A. Brunot in Paris and E. de Zelicourt in Aix have also provided data for this article.)

D. J. STRUIK

RICCATI, JACOPO FRANCESCO (*b.* Venice, Italy, 28 May 1676; *d.* Treviso, Italy, 15 April 1754)

Riccati was the son of a noble family who held

land near Venice. He received his early education at the school for the nobility in Brescia then entered the University of Padua where, to please his father, he began to study law. He took the degree on 7 June 1696. At Padua he became a friend of Stefano degli Angeli, who encouraged him in the pursuit of mathematics; Riccati's detailed study of recent methods of mathematical analysis enabled him to solve, in 1710, a difficult problem posed in the *Giornale de' letterati d'Italia*. He soon embarked on the extensive series of mathematical publications that brought him contemporary fame. His renown was such that Peter the Great invited him to come to Russia as president of the St. Petersburg Academy of Sciences; he was also asked to Vienna as an imperial councillor and offered a professorship at the University of Padua. He declined all these offers, since he preferred to stay in Italy and devote himself to his studies privately, in his own family circle. He was often consulted by the senate of Venice, particularly on the construction of dikes along rivers and canals, and his expertise was deferred to on this and other topics. In addition to his works in mathematics and hydraulics, he published a number of studies on central forces that are marked by his enthusiastic advocacy of Newton's ideas.

Riccati's mathematical work dealt chiefly with analysis and, in particular, with differential equations. He achieved notable results in lowering the order of equations and in the separation of variables. In 1722–1723 he was engaged to teach infinitesimal calculus to two young noblemen, Lodovico Riva and Giuseppe Suzzi, and his lectures to them, subsequently published, demonstrate the technique he employed. In expounding the known methods of integration of first-order differential equations, Riccati studied those equations that may be integrated with appropriate algebraic transformation before considering those that require a change of variables. He then discussed certain devices suggested by Johann I Bernoulli and expounded the method used by Gabriele Manfredi to integrate homogeneous equations. He further pointed out that in order to determine a curve endowed with an assigned property, it may at times be useful to relate it to some system of coordinates other than the usual one.

Riccati then discussed, with many examples, the integration methods that he himself had devised. Of these, one involves the reduction of the equation to a homogeneous one, while another, more interesting method is that of "halved separation," as Riccati called it. The technique of halved separation comprises three operations. In the first, the entire equation is multiplied or divided by an appropriate function of the unknown so that it becomes integra-

ble; second, after this integration has been carried out, the result is considered to be equal to a new unknown, and one of the original variables is thus eliminated; and finally, the first two procedures are applied to the result until a new and desired result is attained. Riccati communicated this method to Bernardino Zendrini, a mathematician who was also superintendent of waterworks for the Venetian state; Zendrini passed it on to Leibniz, who considered it highly ingenious and wrote Riccati an encouraging letter. Riccati first published it as "Contrarisposta alle annotazioni del Sig. Niccolò Bernoulli" in *Giornale de' letterati d'Italia*, in 1715.

At a later point in his lectures, Riccati also dealt with higher-order equations, indicating how some of the techniques implicit in them may be further applied. He also took up the methods used by other mathematicians, of which he is occasionally critical.

In an earlier work, published in the *Giornale de' letterati d'Italia* in 1712, Riccati had already given the solutions to a number of problems related to plane curves determined by curvature properties, for which the integration of second-order differential equations is required. His results were widely known and used by other mathematicians (indeed, they were sometimes republished without mention of his name), and he himself repeated them in his lectures. The earlier memoir also contains Riccati's important statement that the method he had used will lead to the integration of all differential equations of the type

$$f = \left(y, \frac{dy}{dx}, \frac{d^2y}{dx^2} \right) = 0,$$

which he was the first to consider in their generality.

Riccati also provided, in a memoir communicated to Zendrini in 1715 (and intended for publication in the *Giornale*, although it was not actually published until 1747, when it appeared in the *Comentarii* of the Bologna Academy of Sciences), the integration of an equation of the type $r = f(s)$, in which r is the radius of curvature and s the length of the arc. His result is significant because it bears upon the search for the Cartesian equation of a curve determined by its intrinsic equation. Riccati had already solved a general problem of the same type, in determining a curve of which the expression for the radius of curvature is known at any point whatever as a function of the radius vector ("Soluzione generale del problema inverso intorno ai raggi osculatori," published in the *Giornale* in 1712).

In his "Animadversiones in aequationes differentiales secundi gradus," published in *Acta eruditorum* in 1724, Riccati suggested the study of cases of integrability of the equation

$$X^m dx = dy + \frac{y^2\, dx}{X^n},$$

which is now known by his name. In response to this suggestion Nikolaus II Bernoulli wrote an important treatise on the equation and Daniel Bernoulli presented, in his *Exercitationes quaedam mathematicae*, the conditions under which it may be integrated by the method of separation of the variables. Euler also integrated it.

Riccati also drew upon the integration of differential equations in the context of his work in Newtonian mechanics. Thus, he studied the motion of cycloidal pendulums under the hypothesis that the force of resistance varies as the square of the velocity, and, in the results that he communicated to his former student Suzzi (on 5 March 1732), included the integration, by means of halved separation, of an equation in two variables, namely the arc *s* and the velocity *u*. In a memoir on the laws of resistance governing the retardation of the motion of bodies by a fluid medium he integrated, using a procedure different from that used by Manfredi, the homogeneous equation $ydy + 2\,budy = udu$.

In differential geometry, Riccati demonstrated that the segment lying between an arc and a tangent at point *P* of the ordinate at the point of the curve following *P* is an infinitesimal of the second order. In addition, he also studied a problem that had interested Descartes and Fermat—how to determine the algebraic curves of the minimum degree that must be employed to solve a geometric problem of a given order.

Riccati carried on an extensive correspondence with mathematicians all over Europe. His works were collected and published, four years after his death, by his sons, of whom two, Vincenzo and Giordano, were themselves eminent mathematicians.

BIBLIOGRAPHY

I. ORIGINAL WORKS. Riccati's complete works were published as *Opere del conte Jacopo Riccati*, 4 vols. (Lucca, 1761–1765). Vol. I contains an essay on the system of the universe and a treatise on the indeterminates in differential equations of the first order, and the reduction of those of the second and of higher orders. Vol. II deals with the principles and methods of physics; vol. III, with physiomathematical subjects; and vol. IV, with philosophical, ecclesiastical, rhetorical, practical, and scholarly topics.

II. SECONDARY LITERATURE. On Riccati and his work, see A. Agostini, "Riccati," in *Enciclopedia italiana*, XXIX (1936), 241; L. Berzolari, G. Vivanti, and D. Gigli, eds., *Enciclopedia delle matematiche elementari*, I, pt. 2 (Milan, 1932), 527; A. Fabroni, *Vitae italorum doctrina excellentium*, XVI (Pisa, 1795), 376 ff.; and G. Loria, *Curve piane speciali algebriche e trascendenti*, II (Milan, 1930), 168, 170; and *Storia delle matematiche*, 2nd ed. (Milan, 1950), 630, 631, 659 ff., 667, 701.

A. NATUCCI

RICCATI, VINCENZO (*b.* Castelfranco, near Treviso, Italy, 11 January 1707; *d.* Treviso, 17 January 1775)

Riccati was the second son of the mathematician Jacopo Francesco Riccati. He received his early education at home and under the auspices of the Jesuits, whose order he entered on 20 December 1726. In 1728 he went to teach literature in the Jesuit college in Piacenza; the following year he was sent to the college in Padua, where he remained until he was transferred to Parma in 1734. At some subsequent date he went to Rome to study theology, then, in 1739, returned to Bologna, where for the next thirty years he taught mathematics in the College of San Francesco Saverio. Like his father, Riccati was also skilled in hydraulic engineering and, under government commissions, carried out flood control projects along the Reno, Po, Adige, and Brenta rivers. He was much honored for this work, which saved the Venetian and Bolognan regions from disastrous flooding, and was made one of the first members of the Società dei Quaranta. When Pope Clement XIV suppressed the Society of Jesus in 1773, Riccati retired to his family home in Treviso, where he died two years later.

Riccati further followed his father's example in studying the integration of differential equations, including some derived from geometrical problems. He, too, was well informed concerning pre-Eulerian mathematical analysis, and took his topics from other eminent mathematicians. Thus, a memoir by Johann I Bernoulli led him to consider the relationship between the lengths of two curves and a treatise by Jakob Hermann prompted him to suggest some methods whereby the conic equations of Cartesian coordinates might be discussed. He was also concerned with the rectification of conic sections and studied elliptic integrals as an introduction to the theory of elliptic functions.

Riccati's principal works in mathematics and physics were published in his two-volume *Opusculorum ad res physicas et mathematicas pertinentium* (1757–1762). He here introduced the use of hyperbolic functions to obtain the roots of certain types of algebraic equations, particularly cubic equations. He discussed this method further in the three-volume *Institutiones analyticae* (1765–1767), which he wrote in collaboration with Girolamo Saladini. In the latter work Riccati for the first time used the term "trigonometric lines" to indicate circular functions. He demonstrated that just as in a circle of radius 1, the coordinates of the extremity of an arc of φ length may be considered to be functions of twice the area of the sector determined by the arc $x = \cos \varphi$, $y = \sin \varphi$, so in an equilateral hyperbola, the coordinates of a point may be expressed as a function of twice the area of a hyperbolic sector w. He thus was able to make use of hyperbolic functions possessing properties similar to those of circular functions, obtaining (in modern notation)

$$\cosh w = \frac{e^w + e^{-w}}{2}, \quad \sinh w = \frac{e^w - e^{-w}}{2},$$

from which the relations $\cosh^2 w - \sinh^2 w = 1$; $\sinh w + \cosh w = e^w$; and $\cosh 0 = 1$; $\sinh 0 = 0$.

Riccati and Saladini (who published a commentary on the process in Italian) then went on, in the second volume, to establish the formulas for the addition and subtraction of hyperbolic functions as well as the general formulas $2 \sinh nw = (\cosh w + \sinh w)^n - (\cosh w - \sinh w)^n$; $2 \cosh nw = (\cosh w + \sinh w)^n + (\cosh w - \sinh w)^n$. They were then able to calculate the derivatives of $\sinh w$ and $\cosh w$, which they deduced from the geometric properties of the hyperbola. Riccati and Saladini thus anticipated Lambert in his study of hyperbolic functions, although Lambert, who published his findings in 1770, is often cited as having been the first to mention them.

Riccati and Saladini also considered the principle of the substitution of infinitesimals in the *Institutiones analyticae*, together with the application of the series of integral calculus and the rules of integration for certain classes of circular and hyperbolic functions. Their work may thus be considered to be the first extensive treatise on integral calculus, predating that of Euler. Although both Newton and Leibniz had recognized that integration and derivation are inverse operations, they had defined the integral of a function as a second function from which the former function is derived; Riccati and Saladini, on the other hand, considered differentiation to be the division of a quantity into its elements and integration to be the addition of these elements and offered examples of direct integrations.

Riccati's geometrical work includes a study, published in 1755 as "De natura et proprietatibus quarundam curvarum quae simul cum tractrice generantur, quaeque proinde syntractoriae nominabuntur," in which he examined the location of the points that divide the tangents of a tractrix in a certain relationship. Leibniz and Huygens also studied this curve,

which may be defined as the locus of points so taken that the segment of the tangent between the point of contact and the intersection with a fixed straight line will be of constant length. Thus, given a cone of revolution with vertex V and a generator g, let t be a tangent perpendicular to g; each plane π passing through t will cut the cone in a conic, Γ, of which F_1 and F_2 are the foci. Rotating the plane π around the tangent t produces a curve called the strophoid, which had been discovered in France, possibly by Roberval. This curve was further studied by De Moivre, in 1715, and later by Gregorio Casali; Riccati and Saladini discussed it in the first volume of *Institutiones analyticae*.

Riccati and Saladini also considered the figure of the four-leaf rose, introduced by Guido Grandi, and further discussed the problem posed by Ibn al-Haytham in which given two points, A and B, it is required to find on a circular mirror a point C so located that a ray of light starting from A and reflected by the mirror at C passes through B. Ibn al-Haytham himself offered only a tortuous and confused solution to this problem, but in 1676 a simple geometrical solution was stated by Huygens, whose result Riccati and Saladini refined and further simplified. In the second volume of their work, they generalized a problem that was proposed to Descartes by Debeaune, then solved by Johann I Bernoulli and by L'Hospital.

BIBLIOGRAPHY

I. ORIGINAL WORKS. Riccati's works include *Opusculorum ad res physicas et mathematicas pertinentium*, 2 vols. (Bologna, 1757–1762); and *Institutiones analyticae*, 2 vols. (Bologna, 1765–1767), written with G. Saladini.

II. SECONDARY LITERATURE. On Riccati and his work, see Amedeo Agostini, "Riccati," in *Enciclopedia italiana*, XXIX (1936), 241; L. Berzolari, G. Vivanti, and D. Gigli, eds., *Enciclopedia delle matematiche elementari*, I, pt. 2 (Milan, 1932), 389, 478, 491; III, pt. 2 (1950), 826; and Gino Loria, *Curve piane speciali algebriche e trascendenti* (Milan, 1930), I, 72, 231, 427 and II, 153; and *Storia delle matematiche*, 2nd ed. (Milan, 1950), 663, 681, 706, 725.

A. NATUCCI

RICCI, MATTEO (*b.* Macerata, Italy, 6 October 1552; *d.* Peking, China, 11 May 1610)

Ricci was the son of Giovanni Battista Ricci, a pharmacist, and Giovanna Angiolelli. In 1568 he went to Rome to study law, but in 1571 he joined the Jesuits and in 1572 was enrolled at the Collegio

Romano, where he studied until 1577. One of his professors was the renowned Clavius. Ricci left Rome in 1577 when he was ordered to the missions in the Orient. He sailed from Lisbon for Goa, and from there moved on to Macao in 1582. In 1583 he entered the Chinese Empire, settling at Ch'ao-ching (Shiuhing), in Kwantung province. This expedition was the beginning of modern Catholic missions in China. After establishing missions in different parts of the empire, in 1601 Ricci finally settled in Peking, where, under the protection of the Emperor Wan-li, he remained until his death.

The success of Ricci's missionary activity was due not only to his personal high qualities and to his complete adaptation to China, both in customs and in language, but also to his authoritative knowledge of the sciences, especially mathematics, astronomy, and geography. He disseminated Western science by lecturing, publishing books and maps, and making instruments.

Besides his books in Chinese on religious and moral topics (including *Basic Treatise on God*; *Christian Doctrine*; *Treatise on Friendship*; and *Ten Paradoxes*), Ricci is remembered for his Chinese works in the sciences, generally translations or shortened versions of works of Clavius. His Chinese pupils helped him with the Chinese literary style. These works comprised the *Astrolabe*, *Sphere*, *Arithmetic*, *Measures*, and *Isoperimeters*. But especially important was his Chinese version of the first six books of Euclid's *Elements*, also from the Latin text of Clavius. Entitled *A First Textbook of Geometry*, this work assures Ricci an important place in the history of mathematics. Written in collaboration with his pupil Hsu Kuang-ch'i, it was published at Peking in 1607. In about 1672 it was translated into Tatar at the suggestion of the Emperor K'ang Hsi. The work was completed in 1865, with the translation of the remaining books of Euclid, by the English Protestant missionary Alexander Wylie and the Chinese mathematician Li Shan-lan.

Ricci's map of the world is important in the history of geography. It was published at Ch'ao-ching in 1584 and at Nanking in 1600; later editions, one issued at the special request of the emperor, appeared at Peking. For the first time the Chinese had a complete idea of the distribution of the oceans and landmasses. Very few authentic copies of the map are known today. The copy at the Vatican Library (Peking, 1602) is entitled "Complete Geographical Map of All Kingdoms." It is an oval planisphere, on a folding screen of six panels, each seventy-and-a-half inches (1.79 meters) high and twenty-seven inches (0.69 meters) wide, with numerous illustrations and legends.

Ricci's other important contributions to geography were his calculation of the breadth of China in latitude (three-quarters the breadth assumed by Western geographers) and his identification of China and Peking with the Cathay and Cambaluc of Marco Polo. He shares the latter recognition with another Jesuit, Benedetto de Góis, who made a journey from India to China (1602–1605).

Ricci's life and activities are also documented in his letters, written in Italian and Portuguese, and in an extensive report, *Della entrata della compagnia di Giesù e Christianità nella Cina*. He was proposed for beatification in 1963 at the Second Ecumenical Vatican Council.

BIBLIOGRAPHY

I. ORIGINAL WORKS. For a bibliography of Ricci's works, see Louis Pfister, *Notices biographiques et bibliographiques sur les Jésuites de l'ancienne mission de Chine 1552–1773*, 2 vols. (Shanghai, 1932–1934), I, 22–42; II, 9*–10*; Henri Bernard, "Les adaptations chinoises d'ouvrages européens: bibliographie chronologique depuis la venue des Portugais à Canton jusqu'à la mission française de Pekin 1514–1688," in *Monumenta serica*, **10** (1945), 1–57, 309–388; and Pasquale M. D'Elia, *Fonti Ricciane* (cited below), esp. III, 239–243.

Modern eds. of Ricci's works are Pietro Tacchi Venturi, *Opere storiche del P. Matteo Ricci S.I.*, 2 vols.: I. *I commentarj della Cina*, II. *Le lettere dalla Cina* (Macerata, 1911–1913), with intros., notes, tables, and a bibliography of Ricci's Chinese works compiled by Giovanni Vacca, II, 544–548; Pasquale M. D'Elia, *Il mappamondo cinese del P. Matteo Ricci S.I.* (Vatican City, 1938), a facs. ed. based on the 3rd ed. of the map (Peking, 1602), with trans., intro., and commentary; and Pasquale M. D'Elia, *Fonti Ricciane* (Rome, 1942–1949), the first three vols. of the planned national ed. of Ricci's works, which contain *Storia dell'introduzione del cristianesimo in Cina*.

Tacchi Venturi's ed. of the *Commentarj* and the *Storia* in D'Elia's ed. reproduce the autograph text of *Dell'entrata...*, cited in the text of the article. This MS discovered by Tacchi Venturi in 1910 (Archivio Romano della Compagnia di Gesù, *Jap.-Sin.*, n. 106a), was known in the Latin trans. of Nicolas Trigault, *De Christiana expeditione apud Sinas a Societate Iesu suscepta* (Augsburg, 1615). There are several eds. and trans. of this work, including L. J. Gallagher, *The China That Was: China As Discovered by the Jesuits at the Close of the Sixteenth Century* (Milwaukee, Wis., 1942).

D'Elia has edited other works by Ricci: "Il trattato sull'amicizia. Primo libro scritto in cinese da Matteo Ricci S.I. (1595)," in *Studia missionalia*, **7** (1952), 449–515, contains Ricci's Chinese text, an Italian trans., and commentary; "Musica e canti italiani a Pechino," in *Rivista degli studi orientali*, **30** (1955), 131–145, includes the

Chinese text of eight songs by Ricci with Italian trans. and commentary; and "Presentazione della prima traduzione cinese di Euclide," in *Monumenta serica*, **15** (1956), 161–202, which gives an Italian trans., with commentary, of Chinese texts of Ricci and Hsu Kuang-ch'i.

II. SECONDARY LITERATURE. One of the most prolific writers on Ricci and his work was Pasquale D'Elia; see the bibliography of his publications (1913–1959), in *Studia missionalia*, **10** (1960), 90–112. In his *Fonti Ricciane* D'Elia collected a rich bibliography on Ricci. See also Giovanni Vacca, "L'opera di Matteo Ricci," in *Nuova antologia*, 5th ser., **149** (1910), 265–275; and "Sull'opera geografica del P. Matteo Ricci," in *Rivista geografica italiana*, **48** (1941), 66–74.

Other sources are Arnaldo Masotti, "Sull'opera scientifica di Matteo Ricci," in *Rendiconti dell' Istituto lombardo di scienze e lettere*, **85** (1952), 415–445; Joseph Needham, *Science and Civilization in China*, 4 vols. (Cambridge, 1954–1971); and *Clerks and Craftsmen in China and the West* (Cambridge, 1970), 21, 205, 397. Two recent biographies are Vincent Cronin, *The Wise Man from the West* (Glasgow, 1961); and Fernando Bortone, *P. Matteo Ricci S.I., il "Saggio d'Occidente"* (Rome, 1965).

ARNALDO MASOTTI

RICCI, MICHELANGELO (*b.* Rome, Italy, 30 January 1619; *d.* Rome, 12 May 1682)

Although he was never ordained, Ricci served the papal court in various capacities and on 1 September 1681 was made a cardinal by Pope Innocent XI. He was a member of the school of Galileo, although not a direct disciple; his teacher was Benedetto Castelli, whose students also included Torricelli. Torricelli himself was later a close friend of Ricci, and exerted a marked influence on Ricci's geometrical researches.

Ricci's only extant mathematical work is a nineteen-page printed booklet entitled *Geometrica exercitatio* (but more usually called by a later subtitle, *De maximis et minimis*), published in Rome in 1666. It enjoyed a wide circulation and was reprinted as an appendix to Nicolaus Mercator's *Logarithmo-technia*, issued in London in 1668. The work deals primarily with two problems: finding the maximum of the product $x^m(a - x)^n$, m and n being positive integers; and applying this result to the determination of the lines tangential to the parabolas $y^m = kx^n$. It thus represents a generalization of the property by which a tangent of the ordinary second-order parabola $y^2 = kx$ ($m = 2$, $n = 1$) meets the x-axis at a point of which the distance from the vertex (changing its sign) equals the abscissa of the point of contact. It has been suggested that Ricci's method anticipates the so-called method of induction from n to $n + 1$, since he begins

with the values of $m = n = 1$, which he subsequently increases. The first explicit use of the method is, perhaps, the one set out in Pascal's posthumous *Traité du triangle arithmétique* of 1665, although some possibility exists that Ricci may not have been familiar with it.

Ricci's other mathematical contributions are contained in his numerous letters. These include his study of spirals (1644), his investigation of a family of curves more general than ordinary cycloids (1674), and the methods by which he recognized fairly explicitly that the treatment of tangents is an operation inverse to that of the calculation of areas (1668). His demonstrated competence in algebra was somewhat exceptional among the followers of Galileo, most of whom were more deeply concerned with geometrical speculation.

Ricci's extensive correspondence with both Italian and foreign scholars (including physicists and astronomers, as well as mathematicians) brought him considerable contemporary fame. Through such correspondence Ricci participated in the activities of the Florentine Accademia del Cimento, particularly in the final editing of its *Saggi*, published in 1667. He also served as an editor of the *Giornale dei letterati*, which was founded in Rome in the following year. As a cardinal, he discussed with Vincenzo Viviani the life of Galileo that the latter was preparing, advising him on matters that the church felt to be of some delicacy.

A curious aspect of Ricci's career was his refusal to edit the manuscript remains of his friend and master Torricelli, who had in his will requested that Cavalieri and Ricci do so. Cavalieri died soon after Torricelli, so that the entire task devolved upon Ricci. Stating that he had too many other occupations—and that he had been away from mathematics too long—Ricci declined the undertaking. His action has been subjected to various interpretations; as a result of it, Torricelli's complete works were published only in the twentieth century.

BIBLIOGRAPHY

I. ORIGINAL WORKS. *Geometrica exercitatio* [*De maximis et minimis*] (Rome, 1666) was summarized in *Philosophical Transactions of the Royal Society*, **3** (1668), 738–740; and was reprinted in Nicolaus Mercator, *Logarithmotechnia* (London, 1668); and in Carlo Renaldini, *Geometra promotus* (Padua, 1670).

Ricci's correspondence was published in the following: *Bullettino di bibliografia e storia delle scienze matematiche e fisiche*, **18** (1885), see index; Raffaello Caverni, *Storia del metodo sperimentale in Italia*, V (Florence, 1898); C. R.

Dati, *Lettera a Filaleti di Timauro Antiate della vera storia della cicloide* . . . (Florence, 1663), repr. in *Opere di Evangelista Torricelli*, G. Loria and G. Vassura, eds., I, pt. 2 (Faenza, 1919), 441–482; Angelo Fabroni, *Lettere inedite di uomini illustri*, 2 vols. (Florence, 1773–1775); Christiaan Huygens, *Oeuvres complètes*, 22 vols. (The Hague, 1888–1950); Ferdinando Jacoli, *Una lettera inedita del Cardinale Michelangelo Ricci a Gio. Domenico Cassini*, 1895, cited in P. Riccardi, *Biblioteca matematica italiana*, II, sec. 7, col. 82; Giovanni Lami, ed., *Novelle letterarie publicate in Firenze*, XIII (Florence, 1740–1769), col. 35; Giambattista Clemente de' Nelli, *Saggio di storia letteraria fiorentina del secolo XVII* (Lucca, 1759), 190; Carlo Renaldini, *Commercium epistolicum ab eodem cum viris eruditione* (Padua, 1682); Giovanni Targioni-Tozzetti, *Atti e memorie inedite dell'Accademia del cimento*, 3 vols. (Florence, 1780); Luigi Tenca, "Relazione fra Vincenzo Viviani e Michel Angelo Ricci," in *Rendiconti dell'Istituto lombardo di scienze e lettere*, Cl. di scienze, **87** (1954), 212–228; "M. A. Ricci," in *Atti e memorie dell'Accademia patavina di scienze, lettere ed arti*, **68** (1956), 1–8; and "Michel Angelo Ricci," in *Torricelliana*, **11** (1960), 5–13; Girolamo Tiraboschi, *Storia della letteratura italiana*, VIII (Venice, 1825), 554; and V. P. Zubov, "Iz perepiski mezhdu Evandzhelista Torrichelli i Mikelandzhelo Richi" ("From the Correspondence Between Evangelista Torricelli and Michelangelo Ricci"), in *Voprosy istorii estestvoznaniya i tekhniki*, **8** (1959), 95–101, which includes three letters, in Russian.

Fragments of Ricci's correspondence were also published in association with the following eds. of *Saggi di naturali esperienze fatte nell'Accademia del cimento:* Vincenzio Antinori, ed., 3rd ed. (Florence, 1841); and Giorgio Abetti and Pietro Pagnini, eds., *Le opere dei discepoli di Galileo Galilei, Edizione nazionale*, I, *L'Accademia del Cimento*, pt. 1 (Florence, 1942).

There does not appear to be any systematic study of Ricci's MS remains. There are quite possibly some fragments at the Bibliothèque Municipale, Toulouse; see the article by Costabel cited below. Other MSS are at the Biblioteca Apostolica Vaticana, Vatican City; Biblioteca Comunale and Museo Torricelliano, Faenza; and in the Galileiana MSS at the Biblioteca Nazionale Centrale, Florence. A substantial portion of the published correspondence derives from the Faenza and Florence collections; see esp.: Angiolo Procissi, "I Mss. Torricelliani conservati a Firenze," in *Evangelista Torricelli nel terzo centenario della morte* (Florence, 1951), 77–112. Indirect citations of Ricci and clues to the locations of other MSS can be found in various published collections of seventeenth-century correspondence, esp. B. Boncompagni, "Intorno ad alcune lettere di Evangelista Torricelli, del P. Marino Mersenne e di Francesco di Verdus," in *Bullettino di bibliografia e storia delle scienze matematiche e fisiche*, **8** (1875), 353–456; *Correspondance du P. Marin Mersenne* (Paris, 1932–); and M. C. Le Paige, "Correspondance de René-François de Sluse publiée pour la première fois et précédée d'une introduction," in *Bullettino di bibliografia e storia delle scienze matematiche e fisiche*,

17 (1884), 427–554, 603–726.

II. SECONDARY LITERATURE. On Ricci and his work, see the following: Amedeo Agostini, "Massimi e minimi nella corrispondenza di E. Torricelli con M. Ricci," in *Atti del IV Congresso dell'Unione matematica italiana*, II (Rome, 1953), 629–632; Davide Besso, "Sopra un opusculo di Michelangelo Ricci," in *Periodico di matematica per l'insegnamento secondario*, 8 (1892), 1–16; Pierre Costabel, "Un registre de manuscrits témoin de l'activité de Mersenne en Italie en 1645," in *Revue d'histoire des sciences et de leurs applications*, **22**, no. 2 (1969), 155–162; Angelo Fabroni, *Vitae italorum doctrina excellentium*, II (Pisa, 1778), 200–221; Mario Gliozzi, "Origini e sviluppi dell'esperienza torricelliana," in *Opere di Evangelista Torricelli*, IV (Faenza, 1919), 231–294; Josef E. Hofmann, "Über die 'Exercitatio geometrica' des M. A. Ricci," in *Centaurus*, 9 (1964), 139–193; and Ferdinando Jacoli, "Evangelista Torricelli ed il metodo delle tangenti detto 'metodo del Roberval,' " in *Bullettino di bibliografia e storia delle scienze matematiche e fisiche*, 8 (1875), 265–304.

Two collections published in Faenza that deal primarily with Torricelli also include material on Ricci: *Torricelliana, pubblicate dalla commissione per le onoranze a Evangelista Torricelli, III centenario della scoperta del barometro*, 2 vols. (1945–1946); and the annual *Torricelliana, Bollettino della Società Torricelliana di scienze e lettere* (1949–). Every issue through **15** (1964) has articles mentioning Ricci.

Other sources on Ricci include Étienne Charavay, *Lettres autographes composant la collection de M. Bovet Alfred* (Paris, 1885); Mario Guarnacci, *Vita et res gestae pontificum Romanorum*, I (Rome, 1751), cols. 189–194; Prospero Mandosio, *Biblioteca romana*, I (Rome, 1682), 344; Gabriel Maugain, *Étude sur l'évolution intellectuelle de l'Italie de 1657 à 1750 environ* (Paris, 1909); and Gaetano Moroni, *Dizionario di erudizione storico-ecclesiastica*, LVII (Venice, 1852), 177.

LUIGI CAMPEDELLI

RICCI, OSTILIO (*b.* Fermo, Italy, 1540; *d.* Florence [?], Italy, 15 January 1603)

Ricci was the son of Orazio Ricci and Elisabetta Gualteroni, patricians of Fermo. It is not known with any certainty where he studied mathematics, but some of his intellectual influences perhaps may be conjectured: Leonardo Olschki has likened his teaching to that of Niccolò Tartaglia, and Thomas Settle has pointed out a remarkable connection of Ricci with Leon Battista Alberti (see below). Ricci began, probably in 1580, to teach mathematics and likely military engineering to the pages of Francesco de' Medici, grand duke of Tuscany. In 1583, he also gave instruction to Galileo, the son of his friend Vincenzo Galilei, who was then nineteen years old and a medical student at the University of Pisa. Under Ricci's tutelage, Galileo studied

Euclid and, later, Archimedes (a set of whose works Ricci gave to Galileo). Galileo also attended, with Ludovico Cardi da Cigoli and Giovanni de' Medici, the lessons on perspective that Ricci gave at the house of Bernardo Buontalenti in Florence, presumably around 1585. When Galileo applied for a chair at the University of Bologna in 1587, Ricci recommended him; he was also helpful in attaining for Galileo the chair of mathematics at the University of Pisa two years later.

Ricci was also active as an engineer. Around 1590 he was in Ferrara to study the courses of streams in that region and in the area of Bologna, a subject on which he wrote a report. He returned to Florence (from 1593 he taught at the Academy of Design) and in 1597, during a conflict between Tuscany and France, he directed the construction of fortifications on the islands off Marseilles. Later, according to his biographer Carlo Promis, he worked as a military engineer in Ferrara during the controversy between Pope Clement VIII and Cesare d'Este in 1597–1598.

Although he wrote on both mathematics and engineering, Ricci did not publish his works. Of the manuscripts that remain, two are of particular importance in establishing Ricci's influence on Galileo. One of these, a mathematical manuscript attributed to Ricci and probably used by him in his teaching, has been identified by Thomas Settle as a copy of Alberti's *Ludi matematici*. Settle emphasizes Ricci's role as the spiritual intermediary between Alberti and Galileo; Alberti's influence, transmitted by Ricci, is apparent in Galileo's thought and experimental methods, and in some of his specific works, particularly *La bilancetta*. The other, a tract entitled "Libro primo delle fortificationi di M. Hostilio Ricci da Fermo," was discovered in Pesaro by Promis, who, in his biography of Ricci, noted the similarity between it and the treatise on fortifications by Galileo, and suggested that Galileo had probably been instructed in this subject by Ricci.

Of the few other manuscripts by Ricci, there may be mentioned a brief treatise taken from one of the Florentine manuscripts; it was published in 1929 by Federico Vinci under the title "L'uso dell'archimetro ovvero del modo di misurare con la vista." The manuscript is dated 1590, and deals with the use of the "archimeter," a simple instrument for the visual measurement of inaccessible distances, heights, and depths through the properties of similar triangles. Another manuscript, of which there is mention under the title "Intorno ad una leva ad argano," is now apparently lost. A manuscript of Giorgio Vasari (Rome, Biblioteca Angelica, n. 2220) mentions Ricci as solver of a peculiar geometrical question.

BIBLIOGRAPHY

I. ORIGINAL WORKS. "L'uso dell'archimetro" exists in two MSS at the National Library in Florence: Codici Magliabechiani II, 57, and VII, 380; the former was published in Federico Vinci, *Ostilio Ricci da Fermo, maestro di Galileo Galilei* (Fermo, 1929), 23–29, with nine facsimile figures. This is presumably the same work mentioned by Targioni-Tozzetti (p. 298) and Promis (p. 349) under the title *L'uso dell'aritmetica*; it is likely also the work described as concerning "il modo di misurare colla vista" by Nelli (p. 35), Fracassetti (pp. 30, 103), and Promis (p. 349), for which see below.

MS Gal. 10 (div. 1, anteriori, vol. X) in the Galilean Collection of the National Library, Florence, is entitled "Ricci Ostilio. Problemi geometrici." It is described in Angiolo Procissi, *La collezione Galileiana nella Biblioteca nazionale di Firenze*, I (Rome, 1959), 10. Fols. 1a–16a are derived from Alberti (Settle, pp. 121, 124). Settle also cites (p. 125, notes 6, 8, 9) various biographical documents on Ricci in the state archives of Florence, one of which gives the date of Ricci's death.

For Ricci's works on military fortifications, see Promis (pp. 341, 347–348) and the catalogs of the Campori collection, which is now at the Estense Library, Modena: Luigi Lodi, *Catalogo dei codici e degli autografi posseduti dal marchese Giuseppe Campori* (Modena, 1875), 273, art. 622; and Raimondo Vandini, *Appendice prima al catalogo dei codici e manoscritti posseduti dal marchese Giuseppe Campori* (Modena, 1886), 250, art. 753.

On Ricci's report on the waters of the Ferrara–Bologna region, see Frizzi, V, 28; and Promis, p. 343.

II. SECONDARY LITERATURE. Publications concerning Ricci's relations with Galileo are of particular interest. Mentions of Ricci in Galileo's application of 1587 and in the biographies of Galileo by Vincenzo Viviani and Niccolò Gherardini are in *Le opere di Galileo Galilei*, Antonio Favaro, ed., XIX (Florence, 1907), 36, 604–605, 636–638; Gherardini mistakenly called Ricci a priest, and Libri later called him an abbé. Ricci as a teacher is mentioned in a biography of Cigoli written in 1628 by his nephew Giovan Battista Cardi and published by Guido Battelli, *Vita di Lodovico Cardi Cigoli* (Florence, 1913), 14.

An early biography of Ricci is Giuseppe Santini, *Picenorum mathematicorum elogia* (Macerata, 1779), 51–52. In 1830 Giuseppe Fracassetti delivered to the Accademia Tiberina of Rome his *Elogio di Messer Ostilio Ricci da Fermo* (Fermo, 1830); Fracassetti later contributed a biography of Ricci to Antonio Hercolani, ed., *Biografie e ritratti di uomini illustri Piceni*, I (Forli, 1837), 97–106. See also Carlo Promis' biography of Ricci in "Gli ingegneri militari della Marca d'Ancona . . .," in *Miscellanea di storia italiana*, 6 (1865), 339–349. Vinci (see above) includes a biography of Ricci (pp. 7–21), his coat of arms, and notes on his family; there are also citations of biographical works on Ricci by Mistichelli (1844) and Giannini (1874), and of unpublished MSS by Eufemio Vinci on the nobility and leading men of Fermo, in the historical archives of the Vinci family in Fermo.

See also Giovan Battista Clemente de' Nelli, *Vita e commercio letterario di Galileo Galilei* (Florence, 1793), 35–36, 46, 797; Antonio Favaro, *Galileo Galilei e lo Studio di Padova* (Florence, 1883), I, 16–19, 23, 31—new ed. (Padua, 1966), I, 13–15, 18, 24; Antonio Frizzi, *Memorie per la storia di Ferrara*, V (Ferrara, 1809), 28; Riguccio Galluzzi, *Istoria del Granducato di Toscana sotto il governo della Casa Medici* (Florence, 1781), III, 291; also in Capolago, 1841 ed., V, 67; Guillaume Libri, *Histoire des sciences mathématiques en Italie*, IV (Paris, 1841; 2nd ed., Halle, 1865; repr. Bologna, 1967), 173–174; Ernan McMullin, ed., *Galileo, Man of Science* (New York, 1967), 53, 122, 234–235; Leonardo Olschki, *Geschichte der neusprachlichen wissenschaftlichen Literatur*, III, *Galilei und seine Zeit* (Halle, 1927; repr. Vaduz, 1965), 141–153; Thomas B. Settle, "Ostilio Ricci, A Bridge Between Alberti and Galileo," in *Acts of the Twelfth International Congress on the History of Sciences*, IIIB (Paris, 1971), 121–126; and Giovanni Targioni-Tozzetti, *Notizie sulla storia delle scienze fisiche in Toscana* (Florence, 1832), 298, 300.

ARNALDO MASOTTI

RICCI-CURBASTRO, GREGORIO (*b.* Lugo, Italy, 12 January 1853; *d.* Bologna, Italy, 6 August 1925)

Ricci-Curbastro[1] was the son of a noble family situated in the province of Ravenna. His father, Antonio Ricci-Curbastro, was a well-known engineer; his mother was Livia Vecchi. With his brother Domenico, Ricci received his elementary and secondary education from private teachers; he then, in 1869, entered the University of Rome to study philosophy and mathematics. After a year of study he returned home, and it was only in 1872 that he enrolled at the University of Bologna. The following year transferred to the Scuola Normale Superiore of Pisa, where he attended the courses of Betti, Dini, and Ernesto Padova. In 1875 Ricci defended a thesis entitled "On Fuchs's Research Concerning Linear Differential Equations," for which he received the degree of doctor of physical and mathematical sciences. The following year—in conformity with the then existing requirements for teaching—he presented a paper "On a Generalization of Riemann's Problem Concerning Hypergeometric Functions."[2] Betti then asked Ricci to write a series of articles on electrodynamics, particularly Maxwell's theory, for *Nuovo Cimento*. Under the influence of Dini, Ricci took up Lagrange's problem of a linear differential equation, on which he contributed a nineteen-page article to the *Giornale di matematiche di Battaglini*. Shortly afterward, having won a competition for a scholarship to study abroad, he spent a year (1877–1878) in Munich, where he attended the lectures of Felix Klein and A.

Brill. Ricci greatly admired Klein, and his esteem was soon reciprocated; nevertheless, Ricci does not seem to have been decisively influenced by Klein's teaching. It was, rather, Riemann, Christoffel, and Lipschitz who inspired his future research. Indeed, their influence on him was even greater than that of his Italian teachers.

In 1879 Ricci worked as Dini's assistant in mathematics at Pisa. Then, on 1 December 1880, he was named professor of mathematical physics at the University of Padua, a position that he held without interruption for forty-five years. In 1891 he also began to teach higher algebra.

Ricci is best known for the invention of absolute differential calculus, which he elaborated over ten years of research (1884–1894). With this new calculus he was able to modify the usual procedures of the differential calculus in such a way that the formulas and results retain the same form whatever the system of variables used. This procedure requires the employment of systems of functions that behave, when a change of variables is made, like coefficients of expressions that are themselves independent (whether by nature or by convention) of the choice of variables. A further requirement is the introduction of an invariant element (called an absolute, from which the calculus takes its name), that is to say, an element that can also be used in dealing with other systems. The absolute that best lends itself to this operation is the quadratic differential form, which expresses, geometrically, the elementary distance between two points.

Ricci's attention was first drawn to the theory of the invariants of algebraic forms, which had been developed principally after Riemann wrote his thesis,[3] and to the works of Christoffel and of Lipschitz on the quadratic forms.[4] But it was essentially Christoffel's idea of covariant derivation that allowed Ricci to make the greatest progress. This operation, which possesses the characteristics of ordinary derivation, has the additional property of preserving, with respect to any change of variables, the invariance of the systems to which it is applied. Ricci realized that the methods introduced and utilized by these three authors required fuller development and were capable of being generalized. Their methods furnished the basis of Ricci's works on the quadratic differential forms (1884 and 1888) and on the parameters and the differential invariants of the quadratics (1886), which Ricci reduced to a problem of algebra. The method he used to demonstrate their invariance led him to the technique of absolute differential calculus, which he discussed in its entirety in four publications written between 1888 and 1892.

In 1893 Ricci revealed the first applications of his algorithm, to which he gave its specific name for the first time. Two years later, Klein urged him to make his methods more widely available in a complete exposition, but Ricci did not do so until five more years had passed. Meanwhile, he prepared a long paper on intrinsic geometry (published in the *Memorie dell'Accademia dei Lincei* in 1896), in which he examined the congruences of lines on an arbitrary Riemannian variety. He applied the absolute calculus to these problems by means of a special form given to the differential equations of the congruences, which appear with their covariant and contravariant systems and in this way arrived at the notion of a canonical orthogonal system of a given congruence. (In this case the coefficients of rotation replace the Christoffel symbols of absolute calculus.) Ricci next utilized the Riemann symbols to find the contract tensor (today called Ricci's tensor) that plays a fundamental role in the general theory of relativity. He also discovered invariants that occur in the theory of the curvature of varieties.[5]

This intrinsic geometry completed one stage in the development of absolute calculus, and Ricci was now in a position to fulfill Klein's earlier request. In collaboration with Levi-Civita, he published a seventy-seven-page memoir entitled "Méthodes de calcul différentiel absolu et leurs applications." The following brief discussion of the paper is, of necessity, limited to the simplest expressions used by Ricci and Levi-Civita.[6]

Given a change of variables $x_1, ..., x_n$ into $y_1, \cdots, y_n$:

$$a_1 \, dx_1 + \cdots + a_n \, dx_n = b_1 \, dy_1 + \cdots + b_n \, dy_n,$$

one also has

$$b_i = \sum_j a_j \frac{\partial x_j}{\partial y_i}.$$

The system a_j is then said to be covariant of order 1. This will be the case if the a_j are the derivatives of a function $\varphi(x_1, ..., x_n)$. A system of arbitrary order m can then be generalized, from which a system

$$Y_{r_1 r_2 \cdots r_m}$$

may be obtained. The elements $dx_1, ..., dx_n$ form a contravariant system of order 1, which is written

$$dy_i = \sum_k \frac{\partial y_i}{\partial x_k} \cdot dx_k.$$

From this expression a system of order m,

$$Y^{(r_1 r_2 \cdots r_m)}$$

may be derived.

Next, a quadratic form is selected. Called the fundamental form,

$$\varphi = \sum a_{rs} \cdot dx_r \, dx_s,$$

this is an n-dimensional linear element of a variety V_n, with the a_{rs} forming a covariant system of order 2. The a^{rs} is established and generalized to

$$X^{(r_1 r_2 \cdots r_m)},$$

which is called reciprocal to the covariant system $X_{s_1 s_2 \cdots s_m}$ with respect to φ. With the equalities established by Christoffel,[7] it is possible to find formulas for deriving, from any covariant system of order m, a covariant system of order $m + 1$. This is what Ricci called covariant derivation based on φ. The contravariant derivation of a contravariant system is then defined by passing to the reciprocal system, which is derived, and returning again to the reciprocal system.

A chapter on intrinsic geometry as an instrument of computation deals with normal congruences, geodesic lines, isothermal families of surfaces, the canonical system with respect to a given congruence, and the canonical forms of the systems associated with the fundamental form. With regard to the last problem, Ricci started with a system X_r to which he associated a congruence defined by the equations

$$\frac{dx_1}{X^{(1)}} = \frac{dx_2}{X^{(2)}} = \cdots \frac{dx_n}{X^{(n)}},$$

whose covariant coordinated system will result from the elements $\lambda_{n/r} = x_r : \rho$ with $\rho^2 = \sum_1^n r X^{(r)} X_r$. The formulas $X_r = \rho \cdot \lambda_{n/r}$ furnish the canonical expressions of the X_r.

The authors then show how to proceed in order to arrive at general rules. The succeeding chapters are devoted to analytical, geometric, mechanical, and physical applications.

Analytical applications include classification of the quadratic forms of differentials; absolute invariants and fundamental invariants of the form φ; and differential parameters.

Geometric applications cover a study of two-dimensional varieties; remarks on surfaces of ordinary space; an extension of the theory of surfaces to linear spaces of n dimensions; groups of motions in an arbitrary variety; a complete study of the groups of motions of a three-dimensional variety; and comments on the relationship of this research with that done by Lie and Bianchi.

Mechanical applications include first integrals of

the equations of dynamics. Here Ricci solved the Lagrange equations with respect to the second derivatives of the coordinates and found that

$$x_i'' = X^{(i)} - \sum_1^n rs \begin{Bmatrix} rs \\ i \end{Bmatrix} x_r' x_s'.$$

This is the form best suited to the question under examination. If, in seeking a function f of the x's and of the x''s, it is desired that $f =$ constant be a first integral of the equations, then certain conditions must be satisfied. The latter, applied to the case in which there are no forces, yield the homogeneous integrals of the geodesics of the variety V_n, whose length ds^2 is expressed by $2T\,dt^2$.

Linear integrals, the quadratics, and the conditions of existence are then considered. Finally, Ricci and Levi-Civita took up surfaces whose geodesics possess a quadratic integral and the transformation of the equations of dynamics.

In their treatment of physical applications Ricci and Levi-Civita first examined the problem of the reducibility to two variables of the equation $\Delta u = 0$ (binary potentials), then went on to consider vector fields, and finally, equations in general coordinates of electrodynamics, of the theory of heat, and of elasticity.

The authors set forth a general statement of their work in their preface:

> The algorithm of absolute differential calculus, the *instrument matériel* of the methods,. . . can be found complete in a remark due to Christoffel. But the methods themselves and the advantages they offer have their *raison d'être* and their source in the intimate relationships that join them to the notion of an *n*-dimensional variety, which we owe to the brilliant minds of Gauss and Riemann. . . . Being thus associated in an essential way with V_n, it is the natural instrument of all those studies that have as their subject such a variety, or in which one encounters as a characteristic element a positive quadratic form of the differentials of *n* variables or of their derivatives.

In mechanics this is the case for kinetic energy, and it later proved to be the case, in general relativity, for the elementary interval between two events in space-time. Meanwhile, however, Ricci's methods—which Beltrami judged important, while adopting a prudent and reserved attitude toward them—were not known beyond the restricted circle of his students, and the memoir in the *Annalen* did not evoke a particularly enthusiastic response.

In 1911 Ricci and Levi-Civita sent to the *Bulletin des sciences mathématiques* a detailed exposition of the absolute calculus. The editors of the journal published it in abridged form with the comment that "essentially, it is only a calculus of differential covariants for a quadratic form," while adding that it was "very interesting."

Ricci was now almost sixty, and more than twenty-seven years had passed since he had begun his initial research. He probably was not aware that at the Zurich Polytechnikum, Marcel Grossmann, a colleague of Albert Einstein, had an intuition that only Ricci's methods could permit the expression of the quadrimensional metric of ds^2. And, indeed, it was by means of absolute differential calculus that Einstein was able to write his gravitational equations,[8] and on more than one occasion he paid tribute to the efficacy of this tool and to Ricci.[9]

In 1917 Levi-Civita, Ricci's brilliant student, introduced, with his new concept of parallel transport,[10] the geometric foundation of the algorithms of invariance, and Ricci's calculus gave rise to a series of developments and generalizations that confirmed its validity.

Ricci's other publications include a book on higher algebra (containing material from his course at Padua), a book on infinitesimal analysis, and papers on the theory of real numbers, an area in which he extended the research begun by Dedekind. Between 1900 and 1924 he published twenty-two items, most of which dealt with absolute differential calculus. His last work was a paper on the theory of Riemannian varieties, presented to the International Congress of Mathematics held at Toronto in August 1924.

Ricci was a member of the Istituto Veneto (admitted in 1892, president 1916–1918), the Reale Accademia of Turin (1918), the Società dei Quaranta (1921), the Reale Accademia of Bologna (1922), and the Accademia Pontificia (1925). He became a corresponding member of the Paduan Academy in 1905 and a full member in 1915. The Reale Accademia dei Lincei, which elected him a corresponding member in 1899 and a national associate member in 1916, published many of Ricci's works.

In addition to his activities in research and teaching, Ricci held a number of civic posts. He served as provincial councillor and assisted in public works projects, including water supply and swamp drainage, at Lugo. He was elected communal councillor of Padua, where he was concerned with public education and finance, although he declined the post of mayor. In 1884 he married Bianca Bianchi Azzarani, who died in 1914; they had two sons and one daughter.

NOTES

1. This is his complete name. It is also the way in which he

signed all his works, except for the one he published with his former student Levi-Civita in 1900 in the *Mathematische Annalen*, where he kept only the first part of his name. This memoir, written in French, made its senior author famous under the simple name of Ricci, and we shall keep to this usage.

2. These first two works by Ricci have never been published.

3. B. Riemann, "Ueber die Hypothesen, welche der Geometrie zu Grunde liegen," in *Gesammelte Werke*, 2nd ed. (Leipzig, 1892), 272–287.

4. See E. B. Christoffel, "Ueber die Transformation der homogenen Differentialausdrücke zweiten Grades," in *Journal für die reine und angewandte Mathematik*, 70 (1869), 46–70, 241–245; and R. Lipschitz, "Untersuchungen in Betreff der ganzen homogenen Funktionen von *n* Differentialen," *ibid.*, 71–102.

5. Concerning the curvature of surfaces in hyperspaces, Ricci mentions, in his "Méthodes de calcul différentiel absolu" of 1900 (p. 156), a paper by Lipschitz that he considers fundamental: "Entwickelungen einiger Eigenschaften der quadratischen Formen von *n* Differentialen," in *Journal für die reine und angewandte Mathematik*, 71 (1870), 274–295. Compare also, for these questions of intrinsic geometry, F. Schur, "Ueber den Zusammenhang der Räume constanten Riemann'schen Krümmungsmaasses mit den projectiven Räumen," in *Mathematische Annalen*, 27 (1886), 537–567.

6. It should be noted that Ricci puts the upper indices (of the contravariants) in parentheses and that he always uses the sign Σ for summations.

7. $\dfrac{\partial a_{ik}}{\partial x_l} = \begin{bmatrix} i\,l \\ k \end{bmatrix} + \begin{bmatrix} k\,l \\ i \end{bmatrix}$ and $\begin{bmatrix} i\,k \\ l \end{bmatrix} = \sum\limits_{p} a_{lp} \begin{Bmatrix} i\,k \\ p \end{Bmatrix}$

8. These are the well-known equations:

$$G_{\mu\nu} - \tfrac{1}{2}g_{\mu\nu}G = -\kappa T_{\mu\nu}\,.$$

Ricci's theorem shows that the covariant derivation cancels the effects of the variation of the metric tensor (Ricci does not use the term "tensor") and operates intrinsically on geometric entities. With the aid of this theorem and of the rules of tensor contraction one can write:

$$\nabla_\lambda \cdot S_\sigma^\lambda = 0,$$

where ∇_λ is the covariant derivation with respect to x^λ and S_σ^λ is the Einstein tensor. This relationship, which is fundamental in general relativity, serves to express the principle of the conservation of energy.

9. Compare, for example, "Entwurf einer verallgemeinerten Relativitätstheorie und einer Theorie der Gravitation. I. Physikalischer Teil von Albert Einstein. II. Mathematischer Teil von Marcel Grossmann," in *Zeitschrift für Mathematik und Physik*, 62 (1913), 225–261.

10. T. Levi-Civita, "Nozione di parallelismo in una varietà qualunque," in *Rendiconti del Circolo matematico di Palermo*, 42 (1917), 173.

BIBLIOGRAPHY

I. Original Works. The obituary of Ricci by Levi-Civita contains a complete list of his scientific publications, running to sixty-one titles.

Ricci's early works include "Sopra un sistema di due equazioni differenziali lineari, di cui l'una è quella dei fattori integranti dell'altra," in *Giornale di matematiche di Battaglini* (Naples), 15 (1877), 135–153; "Sopra la deduzione di una nuova legge fondamentale di elettro-dinamica," in *Nuovo cimento*, 3rd ser., 1 (1877), 58–72; "Sopra il modo di agire delle forze pondero- ed elettromotrici fra due conduttori filiformi secondo R. Clausius," *ibid.*, 2 (1877), 5–27; "Sulla teoria elettrodinamica di Maxwell," *ibid.*, 93–116; "Sulla funzione potenziale di conduttori di correnti galvaniche costanti," in *Atti del Istituto veneto di scienze, lettere ed arti*, 5th ser., 8 (1882), 1025–1048; "Sulla integrazione della equazione $\Delta U = f$," *ibid.*, 6th ser., 2 (1885), 1439–1444; "Sulla classificazione delle forme differenziali quadratiche," in *Atti dell' Accademia nazionale dei Lincei Rendiconti*, 4th ser., 4 (1888), 203–207.

Ricci laid the basis of absolute differential calculus in the following four articles: "Delle derivazioni covarianti e del loro uso nella analisi applicata," in *Studi editi dalla Università Padovana a commemorare l'ottavo centenario dalla origine della Università di Bologna*, III (Padua, 1888); "Sopra certi sistemi di funzioni," in *Atti dell' Accademia nazionale dei Lincei Rendiconti*, 4th ser., 5 (1889), 112–118; "Di un punto della teoria delle forme differenziali quadratiche," *ibid.*, 643–651; and "Résumé de quelques travaux sur les systèmes variables de fonctions," in *Bulletin des sciences mathématiques*, 16 (1892), 167–189.

On the applications of absolute calculus, intrinsic geometry, varieties, and groups see "Di alcune applicazioni del calcolo differenziale assoluto alla teoria delle forme differenziali quadratiche e dei sistemi a due variabili," in *Atti del Istituto veneto di scienze, lettere ed arti*, 7th ser., 4 (1893), 1336–1364; "Dei sistemi di coordinate atti a ridurre l'elemento lineare di una superficie alla forma $ds^2 = (U + V)(du^2 + dv^2)$," in *Atti dell'Accademia nazionale dei Lincei. Rendiconti*, 5th ser., 2 (1893), 73–81; "Sulla teoria delle linee geodetiche e dei sistemi isotermi di Liouville," in *Atti del Istituto veneto di scienze, lettere ed arti*, 7th ser., 5 (1894), 643–681; "Dei sistemi di congruenze ortogonali in una varietà qualunque," in *Atti dell' Accademia nazionale dei Lincei. Memorie*, 5th ser., 2 (1896), 275–322; and "Sur les groupes continus de mouvements d'une variété quelconque à trois dimensions," in *Comptes rendus . . . de l'Académie des sciences de Paris*, 127 (1898), 344–346, 360–361.

Ricci's articles on number theory are "Saggio di una teoria dei numeri reali secondo il concetto di Dedekind," in *Atti del Istituto veneto di scienze, lettere ed arti*, 7th ser., 4 (1893), 233–281; and "Della teoria dei numeri reali secondo il concetto di Dedekind," in *Giornale di matematiche di Battaglini*, 35 (1897), 22–74.

Ricci's memoir written with Levi-Civita, "Méthodes du calcul différentiel absolu et leurs applications," in *Mathematische Annalen*, 54 (1900), 125–201, appeared in a Polish trans., in *Praec matematyczno-fizyczne*, 12 (1901), 11–94, and was reprinted in Collection de Monographies Scientifiques Étrangères (Paris, 1923).

Ricci's books are *Lezioni di algebra complementare* (Padua–Verona, 1900); and *Lezioni di analisi infinitesimale. Funzioni di una variabile* (Padua, 1926).

His last publications include "Sulla determinazione di varietà dotate di proprietà intrinseche date a priori," in

Atti dell'Accademia nazionale dei Lincei. Rendiconti, 5th ser., **19** (1910), 181–187 (first semester), and 85–90 (second semester); "Di un metodo per la determinazione di un sistema completo di invarianti per un dato sistema di forme," in *Rendiconti del Circolo matematico di Palermo*, **33** (1912), 194–200; "Sulle varietà a tre dimensioni dotate di terne principali di congruenze geodetiche," in *Atti dell'Accademia nazionale dei Lincei. Rendiconti*, 5th ser., **27** (1918), 21–28, 75–87; "Riducibilità delle quadriche differenziali e ds^2 della statica einsteiniana," *ibid.*, **31** (1922), 65–71; and "Di una proprietà delle congruenze di linee tracciate sulla sfera di raggio eguale ad 1," *ibid.*, **32** (1923), 265–267.

See also L'Unione Matematica Italiana, ed., *Opere de Ricci*, 2 vols. (1956–1957).

II. SECONDARY LITERATURE. The first account of Ricci's life and works is the excellent one by Levi-Civita, "Commemorazione del socio nazionale prof. Gregorio Ricci-Curbastro, letta dal socio T. L.-C. nella seduta del 3 gennaio 1925," in *Atti dell'Accademia nazionale dei Lincei. Memorie*, 6th ser., **1** (1926), 555–567. Angelo Tonolo, another disciple of Ricci, "Commemorazione di Gregorio Ricci-Curbastro nel primo centenario della nascita," in *Rendiconti del Seminario matematico della Università di Padova*, **23** (1954), 1–24, contains a beautiful portrait of Ricci and a partial bibliography. See also A. Natucci in *Giornale di matematiche di Battaglini*, 5th ser., **2** (1954), 437–442; and two articles in *Enciclopedia italiana*, on absolute differential calculus, XII, 796–798; and on Ricci's life and work, XXIX, 250.

Reports on almost all of Ricci's publications were published in *Bulletin des sciences mathématiques*; although sometimes very detailed, they often appeared only after a considerable delay. For the report on "Méthodes de calcul différentiel absolu," see **35** (1911), 107–111.

The most important works on absolute calculus and related questions are H. Weyl, *Raum, Zeit und Materie* (Berlin, 1918); G. Juvet, *Introduction au calcul tensoriel et au calcul différentiel absolu* (Paris, 1922); J. A. Schouten, *Der Ricci-Kalkül* (Berlin, 1924); A. S. Eddington, *The Mathematical Theory of Relativity*, 2nd ed. (Cambridge, 1924); L. P. Eisenhart, *Riemannian Geometry* (Princeton, N.J., 1926); and *Non-Riemannian Geometry* (New York, 1927); and É. Cartan, *Leçons sur la géométrie des espaces de Riemann* (Paris, 1928).

PIERRE SPEZIALI

RICHARD, JULES ANTOINE (*b.* Blet, Cher, France, 12 August 1862; *d.* Châteauroux, Indre, France, 14 October 1956)

Richard taught in several provincial *lycées*, including those at Tours, Dijon, and Châteauroux. He defended a doctoral thesis, on the surface of Fresnel waves, at the Faculté des Sciences of Paris on 22 November 1901. Of an eminently philosophical cast of mind, Richard published a work on the philosophy of mathematics at Paris in 1903. He collaborated on several scientific journals, most notably *Enseignement mathématique* (1905–1909), in which he was able to give free reign to his critical mind.

In an article published in *Enseignement mathématique*, "Sur une manière d'exposer la géométrie projective" (1905), Richard cited Staudt, David Hilbert, and Charles Méray. He based his exposition on the theorem of homological triangles, that is, on an implicit axiomatics very close to that of Staudt.

In a philosophical and mathematical article, "Sur la nature des axiomes de la géométrie" (1908), Richard distinguished four attitudes displayed by theoreticians and submitted them successively to critical analysis: (1) Geometry is founded upon arbitrarily chosen axioms or hypotheses; there are an infinite number of equally true geometries; (2) Experience provides the axioms; the basis of science is experimental, and its development is deductive; (3) Axioms are definitions —this third point of view is totally different from the first; (4) Axioms are neither experimental nor arbitrary; they force themselves upon us because without them experience would be impossible (this is the Kantian position). Richard found something unacceptable in each of these attitudes. He observed that the notions of the identity of two objects or of an invariable object are vague and that it is essential to make them precise; it is the role of axioms to do this. "Axioms are propositions the task of which is to make precise the notion of identity of two objects preexisting in our mind." Further on he asserted, "To explain the material universe is the goal of science."

Utilizing the group of anallagmatic spatial transformations and taking a subgroup that leaves a sphere invariant, Richard later remarks in the article that for a real sphere the subgroup is Lobachevskian, for a point sphere it is Euclidean, and for an imaginary sphere it is Riemannian. "One sees from this that, having admitted the notion of angle, one is free to choose the notion of the straight line in such a way that one or another of the three geometries is true." Hence, for Richard, difficulties persist, since "to study these groups we are obliged to assume that ordinary geometry has in fact been established." This article gave rise to several polemics, and Richard, having received a letter from Giuseppe Peano, returned to the question the following year.

In an article on mechanics, Richard took a mild swipe at Poincaré: "The consistent relativist will say not only that it is convenient to suppose that the earth revolves; he will say that it is convenient to suppose that the earth is round, that it has an invariable shape, and that it is greater than a billiard ball not contained in its interior."

"Richard's paradox or antinomy" was first stated in 1905 in a letter to Louis Olivier, director of the *Revue générale des sciences pures et appliquées*. Richard wrote, in substance:

The Revue has pointed out certain contradictions encountered in the general theory of sets.

It is not necessary to go as far as the theory of ordinal numbers to find such contradictions. Let E be the set of real numbers that can be defined by a finite number of words. This set is denumerable. One can form a number not belonging to this set.

"Let p be the nth decimal of the nth number of the set E; we form a number N having zero for the integral part and $p + 1$ for the nth decimal, if p is not equal to either 8 nor 9, and unity in the contrary case." This number does not belong to the set E. If it were the nth number of this set, its nth cipher would be the nth decimal numeral of this number, which it is not. I call G the group of letters in quotation marks [above]. The number N is defined by the words of the group G, that is to say by a finite number of words. It should therefore belong to the set E. That is the contradiction.

Richard then attempted to remove the contradiction by noting that N is not defined until after the construction of the set E. After having received some comments from Peano, he returned to the problem for the last time in 1907. Richard never presented his antinomy in any other form, although certain variants and simplifications falsely bearing his name are found in the literature.

BIBLIOGRAPHY

On Richard's paradox, see "Les principes des mathématiques et le problème des ensembles," in *Revue générale des sciences pures et appliquées*, **16**, no. 12 (30 June 1905), 541–543, which includes Richard's letter and Olivier's comments. The letter alone is reproduced in *Acta mathematica*, **30** (1906), 295–296. Richard returned to the question in "Sur un paradoxe de la théorie des ensembles et sur l'axiome de Zermelo," in *Enseignement mathématique*, **9** (1907), 94–98.

Sur la philosophie des mathématiques (Paris, 1903) was reviewed by P. Mansion, in *Mathésis*, 3rd ser., **3** (1903), 272; and *Notions de mécanique* (Paris, 1905) was reviewed by G. Combeliac, in *Enseignement mathématique*, **8** (1906), 90. Articles published in *Enseignement mathématique* include "Sur une manière d'exposer la géométrie projective," **7** (1905), 366–374; "Sur les principes de la mécanique," **8** (1906), 137–143; "Considérations sur l'astronomie, sa place insuffisante dans les divers degrés de l'enseignement," **8** (1906), 208–216; "Sur la logique et la notion de nombre entier," **9** (1907), 39–44; "Sur la nature des axioms de la géométrie," **10** (1908), 60–65; and "Sur les translations," **11** (1909), 98–101.

JEAN ITARD

RICHARD, LOUIS PAUL ÉMILE (*b*. Rennes, France, 31 March 1795; *d*. Paris, France, 11 March 1849)

Richard, the son of a lieutenant colonel in the artillery, was the eldest of four children. A physical impediment resulting from an accident prevented him from pursuing a military career, and he began teaching in 1814 as *maître d'étude* at the *lycée* in Douai. There he became friendly with the student A. J. H. Vincent, who became a historian of Greek mathematics and member of the Académie des Inscriptions et Belles-Lettres. The two friends later met again in Paris, where they held similar posts.

In 1815 Richard was appointed professor of the *sixième* at the Collège de Pontivy. He became professor of special mathematics the following year. In 1820 he was called to Paris to teach elementary mathematics at the Collège Saint-Louis. From there he went to the Collège Louis-le-Grand, and in 1822 he was given a chair of special mathematics, which he held until his death.

During this period virtually the only concern of secondary-school mathematics teachers in France was to prepare students for the entrance examination for the École Polytechnique. For this purpose, three classes were sufficient: preparatory, elementary, and, finally, special classes. Richard taught the latter class with extraordinary distinction. No program was imposed. Richard, rising above the routine, gave instruction in the principal modern theories, including the new geometry introduced by Poncelet. He was one of Poncelet's most fervent supporters, and when, in 1846, a chair of higher geometry was created at the Sorbonne for Michel Chasles, Richard was one of his most diligent auditors.

Richard stayed abreast of advances in mathematics, with which he constantly enriched his courses. The exercises he propounded were zealously investigated by his students. Of the many distinguished scientists whom he trained, the most famous, Evariste Galois, attended his class in 1828–1829. His students also included Le Verrier, J. A. Serret, and especially Hermite, to whom Richard entrusted the manuscripts of Galois's student exercises.

Richard never married.

BIBLIOGRAPHY

Despite the entreaties of his friends, Richard published nothing. On his life and work, see the notice by Olry Terquem, in *Nouvelles annales de mathématiques*, **8** (1849), 448–451.

JEAN ITARD

RICHARD OF WALLINGFORD (*b.* Wallingford, Berkshire, England, *ca.* 1292; *d.* St. Albans, Hertfordshire, England, 23 May 1336)

Since Richard of Wallingford was for nine years abbot of St. Albans, the best chronicled monastery in England, much more is known about his personal life than about most medieval writers. From the *Gesta abbatum Monasterii Sancti Albani* (H. T. Riley, ed., Rolls Series, II [London, 1867], 181–183), we learn that he was the son of William, a blacksmith, and his wife, Isabella; the family was moderately prosperous. When his father died, Richard was adopted by the prior of Wallingford, William of Kirkeby, who in due course sent him to Oxford (*ca.* 1308).

Having determined in arts before he was twenty-three years of age, Richard left for St. Albans, where he assumed the monastic habit. He was ordained deacon (18 December 1316) and then priest (28 May 1317). His abbot sent him back to Oxford—probably to Gloucester College, a Benedictine establishment—where he studied philosophy and theology for nine years. Having determined as B.Th. in 1327, he returned once again to St. Albans to ask for the festive expenses of his graduation. While he was there the abbot died, and Richard was elected in his place. He visited Avignon for the papal confirmation, which was at length obtained, despite some legal difficulties.

Once back at St. Albans Richard found himself oppressed by three great burdens: the abbey was deeply in debt; the townsmen of St. Albans were in revolt, objecting to the abbot's feudal privileges; and he himself had contracted leprosy. Before he died of this disease, in 1336, he had cleared most of the debts and put down the revolt in the town. He had also kept control of a difficult internal situation, several of his monks having objected to his holding office, and one having gone so far as to instigate a papal inquisition. He skillfully negotiated these difficulties; and when he died in office, he left a reputation not only for moral firmness, but for intellectual and practical genius. He was especially remembered at St. Albans for the vast and intricate astronomical clock that he designed, and which in its final form was completed after his death.

Richard's first essay in mathematical or astronomical writing seems to have been a product of the early years in his second period at Oxford and was a set of instructions (canons) for the use of the tables that had been drawn up by John Maudith, the Merton College astronomer, in the approximate period 1310–1316. Richard followed this essay with *Quadripartitum*, a work on such of the fundamentals of trigonometry as were required for the solution of problems of spherical astronomy. The first part of this work has the appearance of a theory of trigonometrical identities, but at the time it was written it was regarded as a basis for the calculation of sines and cosines, and chords and versed chords. The next two parts of the *Quadripartitum* deal with a systematic and rigorous exposition of Menelaus' theorem, in the so-called "eighteen modes" of Thābit ibn Qurra. Finally, the work ends with an application of the foregoing principles to astronomy. The main sources of the work were Ptolemy's *Almagest*, the canons to the Toledan tables, and a short treatise that was possibly by Campanus of Novara. The *Quadripartitum* may reasonably be claimed as the first comprehensive medieval treatise on trigonometry to have been written in Europe, at least outside Spain and Islam. When Richard was abbot of St. Albans, he revised the work, taking into account the *Flores* of Jābir ibn Aflaḥ, but only one copy of the later recension is known.

Before finally leaving Oxford in 1327, Richard wrote three other works. The *Exafrenon pronosticacionum temporis* was a treatise on astrological meteorology. There is no good reason to doubt that it was his. Richard's most important finished treatise, *Tractatus albionis*, dealt with the theory, construction, and use of his instrument, the "Albion" ("all by one"), which was a highly original equatorium to assist in calculating planetary positions, together with ancillary instruments concerned with eclipse calculation, ordinary astrolabe practice, and a *saphea Arzachelis*. The Albion earned considerable renown in England, where Simon Tunsted produced a new version differing slightly from the original. John of Gmunden's recension included some new parameters, drawn from the Alphonsine tables, in place of the Toledan parameters. His version was much copied in southern Europe, and the instrument continued in vogue until the sixteenth century, influencing Schöner and Apian. The original treatise provides very few clues as to its sources, and many of its best parts are undoubtedly original. Regiomontanus drafted a much debased version.

While writing *Albion* (1326–1327) Richard composed a treatise on another new instrument he had designed, the "rectangulus." This instrument was meant as a substitute for the armillary sphere and was intended for observation and calculation. The chief advantage it was supposed to have was simplicity of construction: it was made from seven straight pivoted rods. Nevertheless, there were certain inherent disadvantages in its design. In connection with the treatise on the rectangulus, we note a table of an inverse trigonometrical function.

At St. Albans, where he was able to direct relatively

large sums of money, Richard embarked on the task of building his astronomical clock. It seems that a sound mechanical escapement had been known for more than forty years when he began his work, but his clock is the first entirely mechanical clock of which we have detailed knowledge. It had a mechanism for hour-striking and an escapement older than (and in some ways superior to) the better-known verge and foliot as used with a contrate wheel. But the true originality of the design relates to its astronomical trains, with, for example, an oval wheel to give a variable velocity for the solar motion, correcting trains for the moon (leading to a theoretical error of only 7 parts in 10^6), and a lunar phase and eclipse mechanism. No mechanism of comparable complexity is known from any earlier time. The clock was lost to history after the dissolution of the monasteries in the sixteenth century. John Leland reported that it included planetary trains and a tidal dial. It had, of course, an astrolabe face, which, like the works, was probably ten feet across. The solitary treatise from which the details of the mechanism are known is now bound out of sequence, added to which it seems to have been copied from a pile of disordered drafts, with duplication of subject matter. It originally belonged to the subsacristan of the abbey.

BIBLIOGRAPHY

I. ORIGINAL WORKS. Transcripts of parts of *Albion*, *Rectangulus*, and *Quadripartitum* have appeared in print. See R. T. Gunther, *Early Science in Oxford*, II (Oxford, 1926), 337–370, for parts of the first two works by H. H. Salter. J. D. Bond printed the first book only of *Quadripartitum*, from an inferior MS, in *Isis*, **5** (1923), 99–115, with English trans. (*ibid.*, 339–363). The bulk of Richard's writings are available only in MSS, but J. D. North has in the press a complete ed. of all the known writings, including translations and commentaries, and a discussion of conjectured and spurious works not mentioned above.

II. SECONDARY LITERATURE. For the best bibliographical guide before the work by J. D. North, see Thomas Tanner, *Bibliotheca Britannico-Hibernica* (London, 1748), 628–629. Bishop Tanner drew heavily on the sixteenth-century antiquary John Leland. The most fundamental biographical source is *Gesta abbatum*, referred to in the text above.

JOHN D. NORTH

RIEMANN, GEORG FRIEDRICH BERNHARD (*b.* Breselenz, near Dannenberg, Germany, 17 September 1826; *d.* Selasca, Italy, 20 July 1866)

Bernhard Riemann, as he was called, was the second of six children of a Protestant minister, Friedrich Bernhard Riemann, and the former Charlotte Ebell. The children received their elementary education from their father, who was later assisted by a local teacher. Riemann showed remarkable skill in arithmetic at an early age. From Easter 1840 he attended the Lyceum in Hannover, where he lived with his grandmother. When she died two years later, he entered the Johanneum in Lüneburg. He was a good student and keenly interested in mathematics beyond the level offered at the school.

In the spring term of 1846 Riemann enrolled at Göttingen University to study theology and philology, but he also attended mathematical lectures and finally received his father's permission to devote himself wholly to mathematics. At that time, however, Göttingen offered a rather poor mathematical education; even Gauss taught only elementary courses. In the spring term of 1847 Riemann went to Berlin University, where a host of students flocked around Jacobi, Dirichlet, and Steiner. He became acquainted with Jacobi and Dirichlet, the latter exerting the greatest influence upon him. When Riemann returned to Göttingen in the spring term of 1849, the situation had changed as a result of the physicist W. E. Weber's return. For three terms Riemann attended courses and seminars in physics, philosophy, and education. In November 1851 he submitted his thesis on complex function theory and Riemann surfaces (*Gesammelte mathematische Werke. Nachträge*, pp. 3–43), which he defended on 16 December to earn the Ph.D.

Riemann then prepared for his *Habilitation* as a *Privatdozent*, which took him two and a half years. At the end of 1853 he submitted his *Habilitationsschrift* on Fourier series (*ibid.*, pp. 227–271) and a list of three possible subjects for his *Habilitationsvortrag*. Against Riemann's expectation Gauss chose the third: "Über die Hypothesen, welche der Geometrie zu Grunde liegen" (*ibid.*, pp. 272–287). It was thus through Gauss's acumen that the splendid idea of this paper was saved for posterity. Both papers were posthumously published in 1867, and in the twentieth century the second became a great classic of mathematics. Its reading on 10 June 1854 was one of the highlights in the history of mathematics: young, timid Riemann lecturing to the aged, legendary Gauss, who would not live past the next spring, on consequences of ideas the old man must have recognized as his own and which he had long secretly cultivated. W. Weber recounts how perplexed Gauss was, and how with unusual emotion he praised Riemann's profundity on their way home.

At that time Riemann also worked as an assistant, probably unpaid, to H. Weber. His first course as a

Privatdozent was on partial differential equations with applications to physics. His courses in 1855–1856, in which he expounded his now famous theory of Abelian functions, were attended by C. A. Bjerknes, Dedekind, and Ernst Schering; the theory itself, one of the most notable masterworks of mathematics, was published in 1857 (*ibid.*, pp. 88–144). Meanwhile he had published a paper on hypergeometric series (*ibid.*, pp. 64–87).

When Gauss died early in 1855, his chair went to Dirichlet. Attempts to make Riemann an extraordinary professor failed; instead he received a salary of 200 taler a year. In 1857 he was appointed extraordinary professor at a salary of 300 taler. After Dirichlet's death in 1859 Riemann finally became a full professor.

On 3 June 1862 Riemann married Elise Koch, of Körchow, Mecklenburg-Schwerin; they had a daughter. In July 1862 he suffered an attack of pleuritis; in spite of periodic recoveries he was a dying man for the remaining four years of his life. His premature death by "consumption" is usually imputed to that illness of 1862, but numerous early complaints about bad health and the early deaths of his mother, his brother, and three sisters make it probable that he had suffered from tuberculosis long before. To cure his illness in a better climate, as was then customary, Riemann took a leave of absence and found financial support for a stay in Italy. The winter of 1862–1863 was spent on Sicily; in the spring he traveled through Italy as a tourist and a lover of fine art. He visited Italian mathematicians, in particular Betti, whom he had known at Göttingen. In June 1863 he was back in Göttingen, but his health deteriorated so rapidly that he returned to Italy. He stayed in northern Italy from August 1864 to October 1865. He spent the winter of 1865–1866 in Göttingen, then left for Italy in June 1866. On 16 June he arrived at Selasca on Lake Maggiore. The day before his death he was lying under a fig tree with a view of the landscape and working on the great paper on natural philosophy that he left unfinished. He died fully conscious, while his wife said the Lord's Prayer. He was buried in the cemetery of Biganzole.

Riemann's evolution was slow and his life short. What his work lacks in quantity is more than compensated for by its superb quality. One of the most profound and imaginative mathematicians of all time, he had a strong inclination to philosophy, indeed, was a great philosopher. Had he lived and worked longer, philosophers would acknowledge him as one of them. His style was conceptual rather than algorithmic—and to a higher degree than that of any mathematician before him. He never tried to conceal his thought in a thicket of formulas. After more than a century his papers are still so modern that any mathematician can read them without historical comment, and with intense pleasure.

Riemann's papers were edited by H. Weber and R. Dedekind in 1876 with a biography by Dedekind. A somewhat revised second edition appeared in 1892, and a supplement containing a list of Riemann's courses was edited by M. Noether and W. Wirtinger in 1902. A reprint of the second edition and the supplement appeared in 1953. It bears an extra English title page and an introduction in English by Hans Lewy. The latter consists of a biographical sketch and a short analysis of part of Riemann's work. There is a French translation of the first edition of Dedekind and Weber. Riemann's style, influenced by philosophical reading, exhibits the worst aspects of German syntax; it must be a mystery to anyone who has not mastered German. No complete appreciation of Riemann's work has ever been written. There exist only a few superficial, more or less dithyrambic, sermons. Among the rare historical accounts of the theory of algebraic functions in which Riemann's contributions are duly reported are Brill and Noether's "Die Entwicklung der Theorie der algebraischen Functionen . . ." (1894) and the articles by Wirtinger (1901) and Krazer and Wirtinger (1920) in *Encyclopädie der mathematischen Wissenschaften*. The greater part of *Gesammelte mathematische Werke* consists of posthumous publications and unpublished works. Some of Riemann's courses have been published. *Partielle Differentialgleichungen* . . . and *Schwere, Electricität und Magnetismus* are fairly authentic but not quite congenial editions; H. Weber's *Die partiellen Differentialgleichungen* is not authentic; and it is doubtful to what degree *Elliptische Funktionen* is authentic.

People who know only the happy ending of the story can hardly imagine the state of affairs in complex analysis around 1850. The field of elliptic functions had grown rapidly for a quarter of a century, although their most fundamental property, double periodicity, had not been properly understood; it had been discovered by Abel and Jacobi as an algebraic curiosity rather than a topological necessity. The more the field expanded, the more was algorithmic skill required to compensate for the lack of fundamental understanding. Hyperelliptic integrals gave much trouble, but no one knew why. Nevertheless, progress was made. Despite Abel's theorem, integrals of general algebraic functions were still a mystery. Cauchy had struggled with general function theory for thirty-five years. In a slow progression he had discovered fundamentals that were badly needed but still inadequately appreciated. In 1851, the year in which Riemann defended his thesis, he had reached the height of his own understanding of complex functions. Cauchy had early hit upon the sound definition of the subject functions, by differentiability in the complex domain rather than by analytic expressions. He had characterized them by what are now called the Cauchy-Riemann differential equations. Riemann was the first to accept this view wholeheartedly. Cauchy had also discovered complex integration, the integral theorem, residues, the integral formula, and the power series development; he had even done work on multivalent functions, had dared freely to follow functions and integrals by continuation through the plane, and consequently had come to understand the periods of elliptic and hyperelliptic integrals, although not the reason for their existence. There was one thing he lacked: Riemann surfaces.

The local branching behavior of algebraic functions had been clearly understood by V. Puiseux. In his 1851 thesis (*Gesammelte mathematische Werke. Nachträge*, pp. 3–43) Riemann defined surfaces branched over a complex domain, which, as becomes clear in his 1857 paper on Abelian functions (*ibid.*, pp. 88–144), may contain points at infinity. Rather than suppose such a surface to be generated by a multivalued function, he proved this generation in the case of a closed surface. It is quite credible that Riemann also knew the abstract Riemann surface to be a variety with a complex differentiable structure, although Friedrich Prym's testimony to this, as reported by F. Klein, was later disclaimed by the former (F. Klein, *Über Riemann's Theorie der algebraischen Funktionen und ihrer Integrale*, p. 502). Riemann clearly understood a complex function on a Riemann surface as a conformal mapping of this surface. To understand the global multivalency of such mappings, he analyzed Riemann surfaces topologically: a surface T is called "simply connected" if it falls apart at every crosscut; it is $(m + 1)$ times connected if it is turned into a simply connected surface T' by m crosscuts. According to Riemann's definition, crosscuts join one boundary point to the other; he forgot about closed cuts, perhaps because originally he did not include infinity in the surface. By Green's theorem, which he used instead of Cauchy's, Riemann proved the integral of a complex continuously differentiable function on a simply connected surface to be univalent.

A fragment from Riemann's papers reveals sound ideas even on higher-dimensional homology that subsequently were worked out by Betti and Poincaré. There are no indications that Riemann knew about homotopy and about the simply connected cover

of a Riemann surface. These ideas were originated by Poincaré.

The analytic tool of Riemann's thesis is what he called Dirichlet's principle in his 1857 paper. He had learned it in Dirichlet's courses and traced it back to Gauss. In fact it is due to W. Thomson (Lord Kelvin) ("Sur une équation aux dérivées partielles . . ."). It says that among the continuous functions u defined in a domain T with the same given boundary values, the one that minimizes the surface integral

$$\iint | \operatorname{grad} u |^2 \, dT$$

satisfies Laplace's equation

$$\Delta u = 0$$

(is a potential function); it is used to assure the existence of a solution of Laplace's equation which assumes reasonable given boundary values—or, rather, a complex differentiable function if its real part is prescribed on the boundary of T and its imaginary part in one point. (Since Riemann solved this problem by Dirichlet's principle, it is often called Dirichlet's problem, which usage is sheer nonsense.) Of course, if T is not simply connected, the imaginary part can be multivalued; or if it is restricted to a simply connected T', it may show constant jumps (periods) at the crosscuts by which T' was obtained.

In his thesis Riemann was satisfied with one application of Dirichlet's principle: his celebrated mapping theorem, which states that every simply connected domain T (with boundary) can be mapped one-to-one onto the interior of a circle by a complex differentiable function (conformal mapping). Riemann's proof can hardly match modern standards of rigor even if Dirichlet's principle is granted.

Riemann's most exciting applications of Dirichlet's principle are found in his 1857 paper. Here he considers a closed Riemann surface T. Let n be the number of its sheets and $2p + 1$ the multiplicity of its connection (that is, in the now usual terminology, formulated by Clebsch, of genus p). Dirichlet's principle, applied to simply connected T', yields differentiable functions with prescribed singularities, which of course show obligatory imaginary periods at the crosscuts. Riemann asserted that he could prescribe periods with arbitrary real parts along the crosscuts. This is true, but his argument, as it stands, is wrong. The assertion cannot be proved by assigning arbitrary boundary values to the real part of the competing functions at one side of the crosscut, since this would not guarantee a constant jump of the imaginary part. Rather one has to prescribe the constant jump of the real part combined with the continuity of the normal derivative across the crosscut, which would require another sort of Dirichlet's principle. No doubt Riemann meant it this way, but apparently his readers did not understand it. It is the one point on which all who have tried to justify Riemann's method have deviated from his argument to circumvent the gap although the necessary version of Dirichlet's principle would not have been harder to establish than the usual one.

If Riemann's procedure is granted, the finite functions on T (integrals of the first kind) form a linear space of real dimension $2p + 2$. By admitting enough polar singularities Riemann removed more or fewer periods. The univalent functions with simple poles in m given general points form an $(m - p + 1)$-dimensional linear variety. Actually, for special m-tuples the dimension may be larger—this should be recognized as Gustav Roch's contribution to Riemann's result.

The foregoing results stress the importance of the genus p, which Abel had come across much earlier in a purely algebraic context. By analytic means Riemann obtained the well-known formula that connects the genus to the number of branchings, although he also mentioned its purely topological character.

It is easily seen that the univalent functions w on T with m poles fulfill an algebraic equation $F(w, z) = 0$ of degrees n and m in w and z. It is a striking feature that these functions were secured by a transcendental procedure, which was then complemented by an algebraic one. In a sense this was the birth of algebraic geometry, which even in the cradle showed the congenital defects with which it would be plagued for many years—the policy of stating and proving that something holds "in general" without explaining what "in general" means and whether the "general" case ever occurs. Riemann stated that the discriminant of $F(w, z)$ is of degree $2m(n - 1)$, which is true only "in general." The discriminant accounts for the branching points and for what in algebraic geometry were to be called the multiple points of the algebraic curve defined by $F(w, z) = 0$. The general univalent function on T with m poles, presented as a rational quotient $\varphi(w, z)/\psi(w, z)$, must be able to separate the partners of a multiplicity, which means that both φ and ψ must vanish in the multiple points—or, in algebraic geometry terms, that they must be adjoint. An enumeration shows that such functions depend on $m - p + 1$ complex parameters, as they should. In this way the integrands of the integrals of the first kind are presented by $\varphi/(\partial F/\partial w)$, where the numerator is an adjoint function.

The image of a univalent function on T was considered as a new Riemann surface T^*. Thus Riemann was led to study rational mappings of Riemann surfaces and to form classes of birationally equivalent surfaces. Up to birational equivalence Riemann counted $3p - 3$ parameters for $p > 1$, the "modules." The notion, the character, and the dimension of the manifold of modules were to remain controversial for more than half a century.

To prepare theta-functions the crosscuts of T are chosen in pairs a_j, b_j $(j = 1, \cdots, p)$, where b_j crosses a_j in the positive sense and no crosscut crosses one with a different subscript. Furthermore, the integrals of the first kind u_j $(j = 1, \cdots, p)$ are chosen with a period πi at the crosscut a_j and 0 at the other, a_k. The period of u_j at b_k is then called a_{jk}. By the marvelous trick of integration of $u_j \, dw_k$ over the boundary, the symmetry of the system a_{jk} is obtained; and integration of $w d\bar{w}$ with $w = \sum m_j u_j$ yields the result that the real part of $\sum a_{kl} m_k m_l$ is positive definite.

As if to render homage to his other master, Riemann now turned from the Dirichlet integral to the Jacobi inversion problem, showing himself to be as skillful in algorithmic as he was profound in conceptual thinking.

When elliptic integrals had been mastered by inversion, the same problem arose for integrals of arbitrary algebraic functions. It was more difficult because of the paradoxical phenomenon of more than two periods. Jacobi saw how to avoid this stumbling block: instead of inverting one integral of the first kind, he took p independent ones $u_1, \cdots, u_p$ to formulate a p-dimensional inversion problem—namely, solving the system $(i = 1, \cdots, p)$

$$u_i(\eta_1) + \cdots + u_i(\eta_p) = e_i \text{ mod periods.}$$

This problem had been tackled in special cases by Göpel (1847) and Rosenhain (1851), and more profoundly by Weierstrass (1856). With tremendous ingenuity it was now considered by Riemann.

The tool was, of course, a generalization of Jacobi's theta-function, which had proved so useful when elliptic integrals must be inverted. Riemann's insight into the periods of functions on the Riemann surface showed him the way to find the right theta-functions. They were defined by

$$\vartheta(v_1, \cdots, v_p) = \sum_m \exp(\sum_{jk} a_{jk} m_j m_k + 2 \sum_j v_j m_j),$$

where the a_{jk} are the periods mentioned earlier and m runs through all systems of integer $m_1, \cdots, m_p$. Thanks to the negative definiteness of the real part of $\sum_{jk} a_{jk} m_j m_k$ this series converges. It is also characterized by the equations

$$\vartheta(v) = \vartheta(v_1, \cdots, v_j + \pi i, \cdots, v_p),$$

$$\vartheta(v) = \exp(2v_h + a_{hk}) \cdot \vartheta(v_j + a_{jk}).$$

The integrals of the first kind $u_j - e_j$ are now substituted for v_j. $\vartheta(u_1 - e_1, \cdots, u_p - e_p)$ is a function of $x \in T'$, which passes continuously through the crosscuts a_j and multiplies by $\exp(-2[u_j - e_j])$ at b_j. The clever idea of integration of $d \log \vartheta$ along the boundary of T' shows ϑ, if not vanishing identically, to have exactly p roots $\eta_1, \cdots, \eta_p$ in T'. Integrating $\log \vartheta \, du_j$ again yields

$$e_j = \sum_k u_j(\eta_k)$$

up to periods and constants that can be removed by a suitable norming of the u_j. This solves Jacobi's problem for those systems $e_1, \cdots, e_p$ for which $\vartheta(u_j - e_j)$ does not vanish identically. Exceptions can exist and are investigated. In *Gesammelte mathematische Werke. Nachträge* (pp. 212–224), Riemann proves that $\vartheta(r) = 0$ if and only if

$$r_j = \sum_{k=1}^{p-1} u_j(\eta_k) \bmod \text{periods}$$

for suitable systems $\eta_1, \cdots, \eta_{p-1}$ and finds how many such systems there are. Riemann's proofs, particularly for the uniqueness of the solution of $e_j = \sum_k u_j(\eta_k)$, show serious gaps which are not easy to fill (see C. Neumann, *Vorlesungen über Riemann's Theorie. . .*, 2nd ed., pp. 334–336).

The reception of Riemann's work sketched above would be an interesting subject of historical study. But it would not be enough to read papers and books related to this work. One can easily verify that its impact was tremendous and its direct influence both immediate and long-lasting—say thirty to forty years. To know how this influence worked, one should consult other sources, such as personal reminiscences and correspondence. Yet no major sources of this sort have been published. We lack even the lists of his students, which should still exist in Göttingen. One important factor in the dissemination of Riemann's results, if not his ideas, must have been C. Neumann's *Vorlesungen über Riemann's Theorie . . .*, which, according to people around 1900, "made things so easy it was affronting"—indeed, it is a marvelous book, written by a great teacher. Riemann needed an interpreter like Neumann because his notions were so new. How could one work with concepts that were not accessible to algorithmization, such as Riemann surfaces, crosscuts, degree of connection, and integration around rather abstract domains?

Even Neumann did not fully succeed. Late in the 1850's or early 1860's the rumor spread that Weierstrass had disproved Riemann's method. Indeed, Weierstrass had shown—and much later published—that Dirichlet's principle, lavishly applied by Riemann, was not as evident as it appeared to be. The lower bound of the Dirichlet integral did not guarantee the existence of a minimizing function. Weierstrass' criticism initiated a new chapter in the history of mathematical rigor. It might have come as a shock, but one may doubt whether it did. It is more likely that people felt relieved of the duty to learn and accept Riemann's method—since, after all, Weierstrass said it was wrong. Thus investigators set out to reestablish Riemann's results with quite different methods: nongeometric function-theory methods in the Weierstrass style; algebraic-geometry methods as propagated by the brilliant young Clebsch and later by Brill and M. Noether and the Italian school; invariant theory methods developed by H. Weber, Noether, and finally Klein; and arithmetic methods by Dedekind and H. Weber. All used Riemann's material but his method was entirely neglected. Theta-functions became a fashionable subject but were not studied in Riemann's spirit. During the rest of the century Riemann's results exerted a tremendous influence; his way of thinking, but little. Even the Cauchy-Riemann definition of analytic function was discredited, and Weierstrass' definition by power series prevailed.

In 1869–1870 H. A. Schwarz undertook to prove Riemann's mapping theorem by different methods that, he claimed, would guarantee the validity of all of Riemann's existence theorems as well. One method was to solve the problem first for polygons and then by approximation for arbitrary domains; the other, an alternating procedure which allowed one to solve the boundary problem of the Laplace equation for the union of two domains if it had previously been solved for the two domains separately. From 1870 C. Neumann had tackled the boundary value problem by double layers on the boundary and by integral equations; in the second edition (1884) of his *Vorlesungen über Riemann's Theorie . . .* he used alternating methods to reestablish all existence theorems needed in his version of Riemann's theory of algebraic functions. Establishing the mapping theorem and the boundary value theorem for open or irregularly bounded surfaces was still a long way off, however. Poincaré's *méthode de balayage* (1890) represented great progress. The speediest approach to Riemann's mapping theorem in its most general form was found by C. Carathéodory and P. Koebe. Meanwhile, a great thing had happened: Hilbert had saved Dirichlet's principle (1901), the most direct approach to Riemann's results. (See A. Dinghas, *Vorlesungen über Funktionentheorie*, esp. pp. 298–303.)

The first to try reviving Riemann's geometric methods in complex function theory was Klein, a student of Clebsch's who in the late 1870's had discovered Riemann. In 1892 he wrote a booklet to propagate his own version of Riemann's theory, which was much in Riemann's spirit. It is a beautiful book, and it would be interesting to know how it was received. Probably many took offense at its lack of rigor; Klein was too much in Riemann's image to be convincing to people who would not believe the latter.

In the same period Riemann's function theory first broke through the bounds to which Riemann's broad view was restricted; function theory, in a sense, took a turn that contradicted Riemann's most profound work. (See H. Freudenthal, "Poincaré et les fonctions automorphes.") Poincaré, a young man with little experience, encountered problems that had once led to Jacobi's inversion problem, although in a different context. It was again the existence of (multivalent) functions on a Riemann surface that assume every value once at most—the problem of uniformization, as it would soon be called. Since the integrals of the first kind did not do the job, Jacobi had considered the system of p of such functions, which should assume every general p-tuple of values once. Riemann had solved this Jacobi problem, but Poincaré did not know about Jacobi's artifice. He knew so little about what had happened in the past that instead of trying functions that behave additively or multiplicatively at the crosscuts, as had always been done, he chose the correct ones, which at the crosscuts undergo fractional linear changes but had never been thought of; when inverted, they led to the automorphic functions, which at the same time were studied by Klein.

This simple, and afterward obvious, idea rendered Jacobi's problem and its solution by Riemann obsolete. At this point Riemann, who everywhere opened new perspectives, had been too much a slave to tradition; nevertheless, uniformization and automorphic functions were the seeds of the final victory of Riemann's function theory in the twentieth century. It seems ironic, since this chapter of function theory went beyond and against Riemann's ideas, although in a more profound sense it was also much in Riemann's spirit. A beautiful monograph in that spirit was written by H. Weyl in 1913 (see also J. L. V. Ahlfors and L. Sorio, *Riemann Surfaces*).

The remark that nobody before Poincaré had thought of other than additive or multiplicative behavior at the crosscuts needs some comment. First, there were modular functions, but they did not pose a problem because from the outset they had been known in the correctly inverted form; they were linked to uniformization by Klein. Second, Riemann was nearer to what Poincaré would do than one would think at first sight. In another paper of 1857 (*Gesammelte mathematische Werke. Nachträge*, pp. 67–83) he considered hypergeometric functions, which had been dealt with previously by Gauss and Kummer, defining them in an axiomatic fashion which gave him all known facts on hypergeometric functions with almost no reasoning. A hypergeometric function $P(x; a, b, c; \alpha, \beta, \gamma; \alpha', \beta', \gamma')$ should have singularities at a, b, c, where it behaves as $(x - a)^\alpha Q(x) + (x - a)^{\alpha'} R(x)$, and so on, with regular Q and R; and between three arbitrary branches of P there should be a linear relation with constant coefficients.

Riemann's manuscripts yield clear evidence that he had viewed such behavior at singularities in a much broader context (*ibid.*, pp. 379–390). He had anticipated some of L. Fuchs's ideas on differential equations, and he had worked on what at the end of the century became famous as Riemann's problem. It was included by Hilbert in his choice of twenty-three problems: One asks for a k-dimensional linear space of regular functions, with branchings at most in the points $a_1, \cdots, a_l$, which undergoes given linear transformations under circulations around the $a_1, \cdots, a_l$. Hilbert and Josef Plemelj tackled this problem, but the circumstances are so confusing that it is not easy to decide whether it has been solved more than partially. (See L. Bieberbach, *Theorie der gewönlichen Differentialgleichungen*, esp. pp. 245–252.)

If there is one paper of Riemann's that can compete with that on Abelian functions as a contributor to his fame, it is that of 1859 on the ζ function.

The function ζ defined by

$$\zeta(s) = \sum_{n=0}^{\infty} n^{-s}$$

is known as Riemann's ζ function although it goes back as far as Euler, who had noted that

$$\sum n^{-s} = \prod (1 - p^{-s})^{-1}$$

where the product runs over all primes p. This relation explains why the ζ function is so important in number theory. The sum defining ζ converges for $Re\, s > 1$ only, and even the product diverges for $Re\, s < 1$. By introducing the Γ function Riemann found an everywhere convergent integral representation. That in turn led him to consider

$$\eta(s) = \zeta(s) \, \Gamma(\tfrac{1}{2}s) \, \pi^{-\frac{1}{2}s},$$

which is invariant under the substitution of $1 - s$, for s. This is the famous functional equation for the ζ function. Another proof via theta-functions gives the same result.

It is easily seen that all nontrivial roots of ζ must have their real part between 0 and 1 (in 1896 Hadamard and de la Vallée-Poussin succeeded in excluding the real parts 0 and 1). Without proof Riemann stated that the number of roots with an imaginary part between 0 and T is

$$\frac{1}{2\pi} T \log T - \frac{1 + \log 2\pi}{2\pi} T + O(\log T)$$

(proved by Hans von Mangoldt in 1905) and then, with no fuss he said that it seemed quite probable that all nontrivial roots of ζ have the real part 1/2, although after a few superficial attempts he had shelved this problem. This is the famous Riemann hypothesis; in spite of the tremendous work devoted to it by numerous mathematicians, it is still open to proof or disproof. It is even unknown which arguments led Riemann to this hypothesis; his report may suggest that they were numerical ones. Indeed, modern numerical investigations show the truth of the Riemann hypothesis for the 25,000 roots with imaginary part between 0 and 170,571.35 (R. S. Lehman, "Separation of Zeros of the Riemann Zeta-Functions"); Good and Churchhouse ("The Riemann Hypothesis and the Pseudorandom Features of the Möbius Sequence") seem to have proceeded to the 2,000,000th root. In 1914 G. H. Hardy showed that if not all, then at least infinitely many, roots have their real part 1/2.

Riemann stated in his paper that ζ had an infinite number of nontrivial roots and allowed a product presentation by means of them (which was actually proved by Hadamard in 1893).

The goal of Riemann's paper was to find an analytic expression for the number $F(x)$ of prime numbers below x. Numerical surveys up to $x = 3,000,000$ had shown the function $F(x)$ to be a bit smaller than the integral logarithm $Li(x)$. Instead of $F(x)$ Riemann considered

$$f(x) = \sum \frac{1}{n} F(x^{1/n})$$

and proved a formula which, duly corrected, reads

$$f(x) = \log 1/2 + Li(x) - \sum_{\alpha} Li(x^{\alpha})$$

$$+ \int_{x}^{\infty} \frac{dx}{x(x^2 + 1) \log x},$$

where α runs symmetrically over the nontrivial roots of ζ. For $F(x)$ this means

$$F(x) = \sum \mu(n) n^{-1} \, Li(x^{1/n}),$$

where μ is the Möbius function.

For an idea of the subsequent development and the enormous literature related to Riemann's paper, one is advised to consult E. Landau, *Handbuch der Lehre von der Verteilung der Primzahlen* (esp. I, 29–36) and E. C. Titchmarsh, *The Theory of the Zeta-Function*.

Riemann taught courses in mathematical physics. A few have been published: *Partielle Differentialgleichungen und deren Anwendung auf physikalische Fragen* and *Schwere, Electricität und Magnetismus*. The former in particular was so admired by physicists that its original version was reprinted as late as 1938. Riemann also made original contributions to physics, even one to the physics of hearing, wherein no mathematics is involved. A great part of his work is on applications of potential theory. He tried to understand electric and magnetic interaction as propagated with a finite velocity rather than as an *actio in distans* (*Gesammelte mathematische Werke. Nachträge*, pp. 49–54, 288–293; *Schwere, Electricität und Magnetismus*, pp. 326–330). Some historians consider this pre-Maxwellian work as important (see G. Lampariello, in *Der Begriff des Raumes in der Geometrie*, pp. 222–234). Continuing work of Dirichlet, in 1861 Riemann studied the motion of a liquid mass under its own gravity, within a varying ellipsoidal surface (*Gesammelte mathematische Werke. Nachträge*, pp. 182–211), a problem that has been the subject of many works. One of Riemann's classic results deals with the stability of an ellipsoid rotating around a principal axis under equatorial disturbances. A question in the theory of heat proposed by the Académie des Sciences in 1858 was answered by Riemann in 1861 (*ibid.*, pp. 391–423). His solution did not win the prize because he had not sufficiently revealed his arguments. That treatise is important for the interpretation of Riemann's inaugural address.

Riemann's most important contribution to mathematical physics was his 1860 paper on sound waves (*ibid.*, pp. 157–175). Sound waves of infinitesimal amplitude were well-known; Riemann studied those of finite amplitude in the one-dimensional case and under the assumption that the pressure p depended on the density ρ in a definite way. Riemann's presentation discloses so strong an intuitive motivation that the reader feels inclined to illustrate every step of the mathematical argumentation by a drawing. Riemann shows that if u is the gas velocity and

$$\omega = \int_{\rho_0}^{\rho} (dp/d\rho)^{1/2} \rho^{-1} \, d\rho,$$

then any given value of $\omega + u$ moves forward with the velocity $(dp/d\rho)^{1/2} + u$ and any $\omega - u$ moves backward with the velocity $-(dp/d\rho)^{1/2} + u$. An original disturbance splits into two opposite waves. Since phases with large ρ travel faster, they should overtake their predecessors. Actually the rarefaction waves grow thicker, and the condensation waves thinner—finally becoming shock waves. Modern aerodynamics took up the theory of shock waves, although under physical conditions other than those admitted by Riemann.

Riemann's paper on sound waves is also very important mathematically, giving rise to the general theory of hyperbolic differential equations. Riemann introduced the adjoint equation and translated Green's function from the elliptic to the hyperbolic case, where it is usually called Riemann's function. The problem to solve

$$L(u) = \frac{\partial^2 w}{\partial x \, \partial y} + a \frac{\partial w}{\partial x} + b \frac{\partial w}{\partial y} + cw = 0,$$

if w and $\partial w / \partial n$ are given on a curve that meets no characteristic twice, is reduced to that of solving the adjoint equation by a Green function that fulfills

$$\partial G / \partial y = aG, \qquad \partial G / \partial x = bG,$$

along the characteristics $x = \xi$ and $y = \eta$ and assumes the value 1 at $\ulcorner \xi, \eta \urcorner$.

Riemann's method was generalized by J. Hadamard (see *Lectures on Cauchy's Problem in Linear Partial Differential Equations*) to higher dimensions, where Riemann's function had to be replaced by a more sophisticated tool.

A few other contributions, all posthumous, by Riemann to real calculus should be mentioned: his first manuscript, of 1847 (*Gesammelte mathematische Werke. Nachträge*, pp. 353–366), in which he defined derivatives of nonintegral order by extending a Cauchy formula for multiple integration; his famous *Habilitationsschrift* on Fourier series of 1851 (*ibid.*, pp. 227–271), which contains not only a criterion for a function to be represented by its Fourier series but also the definition of the Riemann integral, the first integral definition that applied to very general discontinuous functions; and a paper on minimal surfaces—that is, of minimal area if compared with others in the same frame (*ibid.*, pp. 445–454). Riemann noticed that the spherical mapping of such a surface by parallel unit normals was conformal; the study of minimal surfaces was revived in the 1920's and 1930's, particularly in J. Douglas' sensational investigations.

Riemann left many philosophical fragments—which, however, do not constitute a philosophy.

Yet his more mathematical than philosophical *Habilitationsvortrag*, "Über die Hypothesen, welche der Geometrie zu Grunde liegen" (*ibid.*, pp. 272–287), made a strong impact upon philosophy of space. Riemann, philosophically influenced by J. F. Herbart rather than by Kant, held that the a priori of space, if there was any, was topological rather than metric. The topological substratum of space is the n-dimensional manifold—Riemann probably was the first to define it. The metric structure must be ascertained by experience. Although there are other possibilities, Riemann decided in favor of the simplest: to describe the metric such that the square of the arc element is a positive definite quadratic form in the local differentials,

$$ds^2 = \sum g_{ij} \, dx^i dx^j.$$

The structure thus obtained is now called a Riemann space. It possesses shortest lines, now called geodesics, which resemble ordinary straight lines. In fact, at first approximation in a geodesic coordinate system such a metric is flat Euclidean, in the same way that a curved surface up to higher-order terms looks like its tangent plane. Beings living on the surface may discover the curvature of their world and compute it at any point as a consequence of observed deviations from Pythagoras' theorem. Likewise, one can define curvatures of n-dimensional Riemann spaces by noting the higher-order deviations that the ds^2 shows from a Euclidean space. This definition of the curvature tensor is actually the main point in Riemann's inaugural address. Gauss had introduced curvature in his investigations on surfaces; and earlier than Riemann he had noticed that this curvature could be defined as an internal feature of the surface not depending on the surrounding space, although in Gauss's paper this fundamental insight is lost in the host of formulas.

A vanishing curvature tensor characterizes (locally) Euclidean spaces, which are a special case of spaces with the same curvature at every point and every planar direction. That constant can be positive, as is the case with spheres, or negative, as is the case with the non-Euclidean geometries of Bolyai and Lobachevsky—names not mentioned by Riemann. Freely moving rigid bodies are feasible only in spaces of constant curvature.

Riemann's lecture contains nearly no formulas. A few technical details are found in an earlier mentioned paper (*ibid.*, pp. 391–423). The reception of Riemann's ideas was slow. Riemann spaces became an important source of tensor calculus. Covariant and contravariant differentiation were added in G. Ricci's absolute differential calculus (from

1877). T. Levi-Civita and J. A. Schouten (1917) based it on infinitesimal parallelism. H. Weyl and E. Cartan reviewed and generalized the entire theory.

In the nineteenth century Riemann spaces were at best accepted as an abstract mathematical theory. As a philosophy of space they had no effect. In revolutionary ideas of space Riemann was eclipsed by Helmholtz, whose "Über die Thatsachen, die der Geometrie zum Grunde liegen" pronounced his criticism of Riemann: facts versus hypotheses. Helmholtz' version of Kant's philosophy of space was that no geometry could exist except by a notion of congruence—in other words, geometry presupposed freely movable rigid bodies. Therefore, Riemann spaces with nonconstant curvature were to be considered as philosophically wrong. Helmholtz formulated a beautiful space problem, postulating the free mobility of solid bodies; its solutions were the spaces with constant curvature. Thus Helmholtz could boast that he was able to derive from facts what Riemann must assume as a hypothesis.

Helmholtz' arguments against Riemann were often repeated (see B. Erdmann, *Die Axiome der Geometrie*), even by Poincaré, who later admitted that they were entirely wrong. Indeed, the gist of Riemann's address had been that what would be needed for metric geometry is the congruence not of solids but of (one-dimensional) rods. This was overlooked by almost everyone who evaluated Riemann's address philosophically. Others did not understand the topological substrate, arguing that it presupposed numbers and, hence, Euclidean space. The average level in the nineteenth-century discussions was even lower. Curvature of a space not contained in another was against common sense. Adversaries as well as champions of curved spaces overlooked the main point: Riemann's mathematical procedure to define curvature as an internal rather than an external feature. (See H. Freudenthal, "The Main Trends in the Foundations of Geometry in the 19th Century.")

Yet there was more profound wisdom in Riemann's thought than people would admit. The general relativity theory splendidly justified his work. In the mathematical apparatus developed from Riemann's address, Einstein found the frame to fit his physical ideas, his cosmology, and cosmogony; and the spirit of Riemann's address was just what physics needed: the metric structure determined by physical data.

General relativity provoked an accelerated production in general differential geometry, although its quality did not always match its quantity. But the gist of Riemann's address and its philosophy have been incorporated into the foundations of mathe-matics.

According to Riemann, it was said, the metric of space was an experience that complemented its a priori topological structure. Yet this does not exactly reproduce Riemann's idea, which was infinitely more sophisticated:

> The problem of the validity of the presuppositions of geometry in the infinitely small is related to that of the internal reason of the metric. In this question one should notice that in a discrete manifold the principle of the metric is contained in the very concept of the manifold, whereas in a continuous manifold it must come from elsewhere. Consequently either the entity on which space rests is a discrete manifold or the reason of the metric should be found outside, in the forces acting on it [Neumann, *Vorlesungen über Riemanns Theorie*].

Maybe these words conceal more profound wisdom than we yet can fathom.

BIBLIOGRAPHY

I. ORIGINAL WORKS. Riemann's writings were collected in *Gesammelte mathematische Werke und wissenschaftlicher Nachlass*, R. Dedekind and H. Weber, eds. (Leipzig, 1876; 2nd ed., 1892). It was translated into French by L. Laugel as *Oeuvres mathématiques* (Paris, 1898), with a preface by Hermite and an essay by Klein. A supplement is *Gesammelte mathematische Werke. Nachträge*, M. Noether and W. Wirtinger, eds. (Leipzig, 1902). An English version is *The Collected Works*, H. Weber, ed., assisted by R. Dedekind (New York, 1953), with supp. by M. Noether and Wirtinger and a new intro. by Hans Lewy; this is based on the 1892 ed. of *Gesammelte . . . Nachlass* and the 1902 . . . *Nachträge*.

Individual works include *Partielle Differentialgleichungen und deren Anwendung auf physikalische Fragen. Vorlesungen*, K. Hattendorff, ed. (Brunswick, 1896; 3rd ed., 1881; repr., 1938); *Schwere, Electricität und Magnetismus, nach Vorlesungen*, K. Hattendorff, ed. (Hannover, 1876); and *Elliptische Funktionen. Vorlesungen mit Zusätzen*, H. Stahl, ed. (Leipzig, 1899).

See also H. Weber, *Die partiellen Differentialgleichungen der mathematischen Physik. Nach Riemann's Vorlesungen bearbeitet* (4th ed., Brunswick, 1901; 5th ed., 1912); and P. Frank and R. von Mises, eds., *Die Differential- und Integralgleichungen der Mechanik und Physik*, 2 vols. (Brunswick, 1925), the 7th ed. of Weber's work (see above)—the 2nd, enl. ed. (Brunswick, 1930) is the 8th ed. of Weber's work.

II. SECONDARY LITERATURE. Reference sources include J. L. V. Ahlfors and L. Sario, *Riemann Surfaces* (Princeton, 1960); L. Bieberbach, *Theorie der gewöhnlichen Differentialgleichungen* (Berlin, 1953), esp. pp. 245–252; A. Brill and M. Noether, "Die Entwicklung der Theorie der algebraischen Functionen in älterer und neuerer Zeit," in *Jahresbericht der Deutschen Mathematiker Vereinigung*, **3** (1894), 107–566; E. Cartan, *La géométrie des espaces de Riemann*, Mémorial des sciences mathématiques, no. 9 (Paris, 1925); and *Leçons sur la géométrie des espaces de Riemann* (Paris, 1928); R. Courant, "Bernhard Riemann und die Mathematik der letzten hundert Jahre," in *Naturwissenschaften*, **14** (1926), 813–818, 1265–1277; A. Dinghas, *Vorlesungen über Funktionentheorie* (Berlin, 1961), esp. pp. 298–303; J. Douglas, "Solution of the Problem of Plateau," in *Transactions of the American Mathematical Society*, **33** (1931), 263–321; B. Erdmann, *Die Axiome der Geometrie* (Leipzig, 1877); H. Freudenthal, "Poincaré et les fonctions automorphes," in *Livre du centenaire de la naissance de Henri Poincaré, 1854–1954* (Paris, 1955), pp. 212–219; and "The Main Trends in the Foundations of Geometry in the 19th Century," in *Logic, Methodology and Philosophy of Science* (Stanford, Calif., 1962), pp. 613–621; I. J. Good and R. F. Churchhouse, "The Riemann Hypothesis and Pseudorandom Features of the Möbius Sequence," in *Mathematics of Computation*, **22** (1968), 857–862; J. Hadamard, *Lectures on Cauchy's Problem in Linear Partial Differential Equations* (New Haven, 1923; repr. New York, 1952); H. von Helmholtz, "Über die Thatsachen, die der Geometrie zum Grunde liegen," in *Nachrichten von der Gesellschaft der Wissenschaften zu Göttingen* (1868), 193–221, also in his *Wissenschaftliche Abhandlungen* II (Leipzig, 1883), 618–639; F. Klein, *Über Riemann's Theorie der algebraischen Funktionen und ihrer Integrale* (Leipzig, 1882), also in his *Gesammelte mathematische Abhandlungen*, III (Leipzig, 1923), 501–573; and "Riemann und seine Bedeutung für die Entwicklung der modernen Mathematik," in *Jahresbericht der Deutschen Mathematiker-vereinigung*, **4** (1897), 71–87, also in his *Gesammelte mathematische Abhandlungen*, III, 482–497; A. Krazer and W. Wirtinger, "Abelsche Funktionen und allgemeine Funktionenkörper," in *Encyklopädie der mathematischen Wissenschaften*, IIB, **7** (Leipzig, 1920), 604–873; E. Landau, *Handbuch der Lehre von der Verteilung der Primzahlen*, 2 vols. (Leipzig, 1909), esp. I, 29–36; R. S. Lehman, "Separation of Zeros of the Riemann Zeta-Function," in *Mathematics of Computation*, **20** (1966), 523–541; J. Naas and K. Schröder, eds., *Der Begriff des Raumes in der Geometrie—Bericht von der Riemann-Tagung des Forschungsinstituts für Mathematik*, Schriftenreihe des Forschungsinstituts für Mathematik, no. 1 (Berlin, 1957), esp. K. Schröder, pp. 14–26; H. Freudenthal, pp. 92–97; G. Lampariello, pp. 222–234; and O. Haupt, pp. 303–317; C. Neumann, *Vorlesungen über Riemann's Theorie der Abelschen Integrale* (Leipzig, 1865; 2nd ed., 1884); and "Zur Theorie des logarithmischen und des Newton'schen Potentials," in *Mathematische Annalen*, **11** (1877), 558–566; M. Noether, "Zu F. Klein's Schrift 'Über Riemann's Theorie der algebraischen Funktionen,'" in *Zeitschrift für Mathematik und Physik*, Hist.-lit. Abt., **27** (1882), 201–206; and "Übermittlung von Nachschriften Riemannscher Vorlesungen," in *Nachrichten von der Gesellschaft der Wissenschaften zu Göttingen*, Geschäftliche Mitteilungen (1909), 23–25; E. Schering,

"Bernhard Riemann zum Gedächtnis," in *Nachrichten von der Gesellschaft der Wissenschaften zu Göttingen* (1867), 305–314; and *Gesammelte mathematische Werke*, R. Haussner and K. Schering, eds., 2 vols. (Berlin, 1902–1909); H. A. Schwarz, *Gesammelte mathematische Abhandlungen*, II (Berlin, 1890), 108–210; W. Thomson, "Sur une équation aux dérivées partielles qui se présente dans plusieurs questions de mathématique physique," in *Journal de mathématiques pures et appliquées*, **12** (1847), 493–496; E. C. Titchmarsh, *The Theory of the Zeta-Function* (Oxford, 1951); H. Weyl, *Die Idee der Riemannschen Fläche* (Leipzig, 1913; 2nd ed., 1923); and *Raum, Zeit und Materie. Vorlesungen über allgemeine Relativitätstheorie* (Berlin, 1918); and W. Wirtinger, "Algebraische Funktionen und ihre Integrale," in *Encyklopädie der mathematischen Wissenschaften*, IIB, 2 (Leipzig, 1901), 115–175.

HANS FREUDENTHAL

RIES (or **RISZ, RIESZ, RIS,** or **RIESE**), **ADAM** (*b.* Staffelstein, upper Franconia, Germany, 1492; *d.* Annaberg-Buchholz, Germany, 30 March 1559)

The son of Contz and Eva Riese, Adam (who always signed himself simply "Risz" or "Ries"[1]) came from a wealthy family. Little is known about his youth and nothing about his education. In 1509 he was at Zwickau, where his younger brother Conradus was attending the famous Latin school, and in 1515 he was living in Annaberg, a mining town. Ries finally settled at Erfurt in 1518, working there until 1522 or 1523 as a *Rechenmeister*. He benefited greatly from his contact with the university humanists, who gathered at the house of Georg Sturtz, a rich physician from Annaberg.

Ries wrote his first two books while at Erfurt: *Rechnung auff der linihen* (1518), of which no copy of the first edition is known, and *Rechenung auff der linihen vnd federn* (1522), which had gone through more than 108 editions by 1656. Sturtz encouraged Ries to study algebra—or *Coss*, as it was then called—which had slowly become known in Germany during the second half of the fifteenth century. Sturtz also recommended certain authors: Johann Widman, who had given the first lecture on algebra in Germany (at Leipzig in 1486), and Heinrich Schreiber (or Grammateus, who taught Rudolff at Vienna), whose arithmetic book of 1518 contained sections on algebra incorporating an improved symbolism. Among the books that Sturtz made available to his friend was an old one—and, as Ries stated, "cast-off" (in the sense of "disordered" or "uncared-for")—containing a group of essays on algebraic topics.[2] Ries was therefore able to compose a *Coss* while still at Erfurt. He completed the book in Annaberg, where he had resettled about 1523, and dedicated the manuscript to Sturtz.[3]

In 1525 Ries married Anna Leuber, by whom he had eight children. He then purchased his own home and became a citizen of Annaberg. He held important positions in the ducal mining administration: *Rezessschreiber* (recorder of mine yields, from 1525), *Gegenschreiber* (recorder of ownership of mining shares from 1532), and *Zehnter auf dem Geyer* (calculator of ducal tithes, 1533–1539). While fulfilling his official responsibilities he still found time to continue teaching arithmetic. He ran a highly regarded school, and improved and revised his books. During this period he wrote a comprehensive work, *Rechenung nach der lenge, auff den Linihen vnd Feder*, which far surpassed his books written at Erfurt, especially in the number of examples. Most of the work had been completed by 1525; but it was not published until 1550, after Elector Maurice of Saxony had advanced the printing costs. Because the expense was so great, the book was reprinted only once, in 1616.

The year 1539 was decisive for Ries. Duke Georg, an intransigent defender of Catholicism, was succeeded by his brother Heinrich, who favored the Lutherans. The change in rulers ended the religious troubles with which Annaberg, like so many other German cities, had been afflicted.[4] In the same year Ries received the title "Churfürstlich Sächsischer Hofarithmeticus." During this period Ries prepared a revised edition of his *Coss*, in which he referred to the achievements of his contemporaries Rudolff, Stifel, and Cardano.[5] This was his last work.

In all his arithmetic books (but with greatest detail in the one of 1550) Ries described how the computations were done, both on the abacus and with the new Indian methods. He employed the rule of three to solve many problems encountered in everyday life. While asserting that he had found "proper instruction in only a few places" in the arithmetic of his predecessors, Ries failed to set forth the logical foundations of the subject. Instead, he simply presented formulas with the command "Do it this way."

Ries did, however, furnish the student with a great number of exercises. The steps to be followed were presented in detail, and the reader could check the correctness of answers by following the procedure used to obtain them. Ries surpassed his predecessors in the presentation of his material: it was clear and orderly, and proceeded methodically from the simpler to the more difficult.

Besides the section on gauging, the *Rechenung nach der lenge* contains an extensive section entitled "Practica," in which Ries solves problems according to the "Welsh practice" through the use of pro-

portional parts.[6] In addition he treats problems taken from recreational mathematics, solving them according to the *regula falsi*. Particularly noteworthy is the fact that in his table of square roots the fractions are repeated in a manner that prepared the way for the use of decimal fractions.[7]

In the *Coss*, too, Ries proves to be a good mathematician. He recognized that the Cossists employed a superfluous number of distinct types of equations. He knew about negative quantities and did compute with them.

Ries composed a work that was commissioned by the city of Annaberg, *Ein Gerechnet Büchlein auff den Schöffel, Eimer vnd Pfundtgewicht* . . . (1533), which contains tables of measures and prices from which one could immediately determine the cost of more than one of an item for which a unit price was given, and a *Brotordnung*. From the latter one could directly read off the correct weight for loaves of bread when grain prices varied and the price of an individual loaf was held constant.

It is not known how Ries learned Latin. While in the Erzgebirge he gained a thorough knowledge of mining and of mining problems that lend themselves to computation. At Erfurt he obtained the mathematics books of Widman, Köbel, and Grammateus, and he also saw the book from which Widman had taken his examples, which ultimately stem from the *Algorismus Ratisbonensis*.[8]

Ries furnished precise information on the sources of his *Coss*. As early as 1515 he had solved algebraic problems in Annaberg with a coin assayer named Conrad.[9] Later he studied a revision of al-Khwārizmī's *Algebra* prepared by Andreas Alexander.[10] His principal source, however, was the old book he had received from Sturtz.[11] The contents of this work included al-Khwārizmī's *Algebra* in the translation by Robert of Chester, the *De numeris datis* of Jordanus de Nemore, the *Liber augmenti et diminutionis* of "Abraham," and a Latin and a German algebra (1481).

Because Ries's *Coss* was never printed it had little influence on the development of mathematics.[12] His arithmetic books enjoyed a different fate. Between 1518 and 1656 they went through more than 100 editions in cities from Stettin to Augsburg and from Breslau to Zurich.[13] Ries did more than any previous author to spread knowledge of arithmetic, the branch of mathematics most useful in arts and trade. He was a pioneer in the use of Indian numerals. Ries soon became synonymous with "arithmetic"; to this day, "nach Adam Ries" signifies the accuracy of a calculation.

NOTES

1. See F. Deubner, *Nach Adam Ries*, p. 109; and Roch, *Adam Ries*, p. 79.
2. The book, now Codex Dresdensis C 80, once belonged to Widman.
3. It was partially published by Berlet in 1860 and again in 1892.
4. Ries's name appeared on the list of Lutheran citizens of Annaberg that Duke Georg requested city officials to prepare. He was not persecuted for his religion, however; obviously his services were needed. See Roch, *op. cit.*, p. 21.
5. No study has yet been made of the extent to which Ries utilized the new knowledge in preparing this revision, which exists, in Ries's own handwriting, in an incomplete MS volume in the Erzgebirgsmuseum, Annaberg-Buchholz. This volume also contains an introduction to arithmetic, the old *Coss*, and a German translation of the *Data*. See Berlet, p. 27.
6. In *Regula proportionum*, Ries alludes to their relationship to the rule of three. See 121r.
7. For example, $\sqrt{19} = $ "4 gantze und 358 tausend-teil." See the arithmetic book of 1550, fols. Aa IIIv and Bb IIr ff, and the arithmetic book of 1574 (available in facsimile), fols. 84v ff.
8. See Berlet, p. 34. Widman also took examples from the Bamberg arithmetic book of 1483, which had borrowed problems from the *Algorismus Ratisbonensis*. See Kaunzner, pp. 26, 102 ff.
9. See Berlet, p. 53.
10. On Andreas Alexander, see *Neue deutsche Biographie*, I (1953), 195 f. The original MS of this revision is lost, but there are four copies done by Ries and his sons Jakob and Abraham. See Curtze's ed. in *Abhandlungen zur Geschichte der Mathematik*, **13** (1902), 435–651.
11. For the marginal notations made by Ries, see Kaunzner, p. 35.
12. Three extracts written later can be found in the Sächsische Landesbibliothek, Dresden. On this matter see Roch, *Adam Ries*, p. 62. Stifel admired Ries's examples and incorporated many of them in his *Deutsche Arithmetica*.
13. For the printing history, see Smith, p. 139; and F. Deubner, "Adam Ries."

BIBLIOGRAPHY

A complete bibliography of Ries's works, including MSS, is in F. Deubner, "Adam Ries" (see below); most of them also are listed in D. E. Smith, *Rara arithmetica* (see below).

Secondary literature includes Bruno Berlet, *Adam Riese, sein Leben, seine Rechenbücher und seine Art zu rechnen . . .* (Leipzig–Frankfurt, 1892); Moritz Cantor, *Vorlesungen über Geschichte der Mathematik*, II, pt. 2 (1900), 420–429; Dorothy I. Carpenter, "Adam Riese," in *Mathematics Teacher*, **58** (Oct. 1965), 538–543; Fritz Deubner, *Nach Adam Riese. Leben und Wirken des grossen Rechenmeisters* (Leipzig–Jena, 1959); and "Adam Ries, der Rechenmeister des deutschen Volkes," in *Zeitschrift für Geschichte der Naturwissenschaften, der Technik und der Medizin*, **1**, no. 3 (1964), 11–44; Hildegard Deubner, "Adam Ries— Rechenmeister des deutschen Volkes. Teil II, 1," in *Schriftenreihe für Geschichte der Naturwissenschaften, Technik und Medizin*, **7**, no. 1 (1970), 1–22; Wolfgang Kaunzner, "Über Johannes Widmann von Eger . . .," in *Veröffent-* lichungen des Forschungsinstituts des Deutschen Museums für die Geschichte der Naturwissenschaften und der Technik, ser. C, no. 4 (1968); Willy Roch, *Adam Ries. Ein Lebensbild des grossen Rechenmeisters* (Frankfurt, 1959); and *Die Kinder des Rechenmeisters Adam Ries*, vol. I of Veröffentlichungen des Adam-Ries-Bundes (Staffelstein, 1960); D. E. Smith, *Rara arithmetica*, 4th ed. (New York, 1970), 138–140, 250 ff.; F. Unger, *Die Methodik der praktischen Arithmetik in historischer Entwicklung* (Leipzig, 1888), 48–53; Kurt Vogel, "Adam Riese, der deutsche Rechenmeister," in *Deutsches Museum. Abhandlungen und Berichte*, **27**, no. 3 (1959), 1–37; and "Nachlese zum 400. Todestag von Adam Ries(e)," in *Praxis der Mathematik*, **1** (1959), 85–88; and H. E. Wappler, "Zur Geschichte der deutschen Algebra im 15. Jahrhundert," in *Programm Gymnasium Zwickau* (1887).

Additional articles on Ries are cited in all works on the history of mathematics; for literature from the period 1544–1900, see especially the article by H. Deubner cited above.

KURT VOGEL

RIESZ, FRIGYES (FRÉDÉRIC) (*b*. Györ, Hungary, 22 January 1880; *d*. Budapest, Hungary, 28 February 1956)

Riesz's father, Ignacz, was a physician; and his younger brother Marcel was also a distinguished mathematician. He studied at the Polytechnic in Zurich and then at Budapest and Göttingen before taking his doctorate at Budapest. After further study at Paris and Göttingen and teaching school in Hungary, he was appointed to the University of Kolozsvár in 1911. In 1920 the university was moved to Szeged, where, in collaboration with A. Haar, Riesz created the János Bolyai Mathematical Institute and its journal, *Acta scientiarum mathematicarum*. In 1946 he went to the University of Budapest, where he died ten years later after a long illness.

Riesz's output is most easily judged from the 1,600-page edition of his writings (cited in the text as *Works*). He concentrated on abstract and general theories connected with mathematical analysis, especially functional analysis. One of the theorems for which he is best remembered is the Riesz-Fischer theorem (1907), so called because it was discovered at the same time by Emil Fischer. Riesz formulated it as follows (*Works*, 378–381; cf. 389–395). Let $\{\phi_i(x)\}$ be a set of orthogonal functions over $[a, b]$ of which each member is summable and square-summable. Associate with each ϕ_i a real number a_i. Then $\sum_{i=1}^{\infty} a_i^2$ is convergent if and only if there exists a function f such that

$$a_i = \int_a^b f(x)\, \phi_i(x)\, dx, \qquad i = 1, 2, \cdots. \qquad (1)$$

In this form the theorem implies that the $\{a_i\}$ are the coefficients of the expansion of f in terms of the $\{\phi_i\}$ and that f itself is square-summable. This result, the converse of Parseval's theorem, immediately attracted great interest and soon was being re-proved.

Riesz had been motivated to discover his theorem by Hilbert's work on integral equations. Under the influence of Maurice Fréchet's abstract approach to function spaces, such studies became associated with the new subject of functional analysis. Riesz made significant contributions to this field, concentrating on the space of L^p functions (functions f for which $|f^p|$, $p > 1$, is Lebesgue integrable). He provided much of the groundwork for Banach spaces (*Works*, esp. 441–489) and later applied functional analysis to ergodic theory.

Riesz's best-known result in functional analysis has become known as the Riesz representation theorem. He formulated it in 1909, as follows (*Works*, 400–402). Let A be a linear (distributive, continuous) functional, mapping real-valued continuous functions f over [0,1] onto the real numbers. Then A is bounded, and can be represented by the Stieltjes integral

$$A(f) = \int_0^1 f(x)\, d\alpha(x), \tag{2}$$

where α is a function of bounded variation. The theorem was a landmark in the subject and has proved susceptible to extensive generalizations and applications.

Another implication of Hilbert's work on integral equations that Riesz studied was its close connection with infinite matrices. In *Les systèmes d'équations linéaires à une infinité d'inconnues* (1913; *Works*, 829–1016), Riesz tried not only to systematize the results then known into a general theory but also to apply them to bilinear and quadratic forms, trigonometric series, and certain kinds of differential and integral equations.

Functional analysis and its ramifications were Riesz's most consistent interests; and in 1952 he published his other book, a collaboration with his student B. Szökefnalvy-Nagy, *Leçons d'analyse fonctionnelle*. A classic survey of the subject, it appeared in later French editions and in German and English translations.

In much of his work Riesz relied on the Lebesgue integral, and during the 1920's he reformulated the theory itself in a "constructive" manner independent of the theory of measure (*Works*, 200–214). He required only the idea of a set of measure zero and built up the integral from "simple functions" (effectively, step functions) to more general kinds. He also re-proved some of the basic theorems of the Lebesgue theory.

In the topics so far discussed, Riesz was a significant contributor in fields that had already been developed. But a topic he created was subharmonic functions. A function f of two or more variables is subharmonic if it is bounded above in an open domain D; is continuous almost everywhere in D; and, on the boundary of any subdomain D' of D, is not greater than any function F that is continuous there and harmonic within. The definition is valuable for domains in which the Dirichlet problem is solvable and F is unique, for then $f \leqslant F$ within D and $f = F$ on its boundary. By means of a criterion for subharmonicity given by

$$f(x_0, y_0) \tag{3}$$
$$\leqslant \frac{1}{2\pi} \int_0^{2\pi} F(x_0 + r \sin p, y_0 + r \cos p)\, dp,$$

where r is the radius and (x_0, y_0) the center of a small circle within D, Riesz was able to construct a systematized theory (see esp. *Works*, 685–739) incorporating applications to the theory of functions and to potential theory.

Among Riesz's other mathematical interests, some early work dealt with projective geometry. Soon afterward he took up matters in point set topology, such as the definition of continuity and the classification of order-types. He also worked in complex variables and approximation theory.

BIBLIOGRAPHY

I. ORIGINAL WORKS. Riesz's writings were collected in *Összegyűjtött munkái—Oeuvres complètes—Gesammelte Arbeiten*, Á. Császár, ed., 2 vols. (Budapest, 1960), with illustrations and a complete bibliography but little discussion of his work. *Leçons d'analyse fonctionnelle* (Budapest, 1952; 5th ed., 1968), written with B. Szökefnalvy-Nagy, was translated into English by L. F. Boron as *Functional Analysis* (New York, 1955).

II. SECONDARY LITERATURE. On Riesz's work in functional analysis and on the Riesz-Fischer theorem, see M. Bernkopf, "The Development of Functional Spaces With Particular Reference to Their Origins in Integral Equation Theory," in *Archive for History of Exact Sciences*, **3** (1966–1967), 1–96, esp. 48–62. See also E. Fischer, "Sur la convergence en moyenne," in *Comptes rendus . . . de l'Académie des sciences*, **144** (1907), 1022–1024; and J. Batt, "Die Verallgemeinerungen des Darstellungssatzes von F. Riesz und ihre Anwendungen," in *Jahresbericht der Deutschen Mathematiker-vereinigung*, **74** (1973), 147–181.

I. GRATTAN-GUINNESS

RIESZ, MARCEL (*b.* Györ, Hungary, 16 November 1886; *d.* Lund, Sweden, 4 September 1969)

Marcel Riesz, the younger brother of Frigyes Riesz and the son of Ignácz Riesz, a physician, showed his talent for mathematics early by winning the Loránd Eötvös competition in 1904. After studying at the University of Budapest, he worked on trigonometric series under the influence of Lipót (Leopold) Fejér. One of Fejér's theorems states that the first order Cesàro sums of the Fourier series of a continuous function tend to $f(x)$ at every point x. Fejér also pointed out that a trigonometric series can be $(C,1)$-summable to zero at each point $x \neq 2k\pi$ ($k = 0, \pm 1, \ldots$) without the coefficients being all zero. Riesz generalized Fejér's theorem, replacing $(C,1)$-summability with (C,α)-summability with any $\alpha > 0$. In his doctoral dissertation, "Über summierbare trigonometrische Reihen" (1912), Riesz gave a condition implying that if a trigonometric series is $(C,1)$-summable to zero everywhere, then all its coefficients are zero. This result was later sharpened by A. Rajchman, Antoni Zygmund, and S. Verblunsky.

Pierre Fatou's dissertation, "Séries trigonométriques et séries de Taylor" (1906), influenced both Riesz brothers. One of Fatou's theorems asserts that if the power series $\sum_{n=0}^{\infty} c_n z^n$ represents a holomorphic function $f(z)$ in the unit disk $|z| < 1$ and $\lim_{n\to\infty} c_n = 0$, then the power series converges at each point of the circle $|z| = 1$ where $f(z)$ is regular. Riesz improved the result in two directions: first, if $f(z)$ is regular on a closed arc, then the power series converges uniformly on the arc; second, if $\lim_{n\to\infty}(c_n/n^k) = 0$, then (C,k)-summability replaces convergence.

It was the typical means (now also called Riesz means) that made Riesz internationally known. Given a sequence $0 < \lambda_0 < \lambda_1 \ldots < \lambda_n < \ldots$, the means of type (λ_n) and order k of the series $\sum u_n$ are given by $R(\omega; \lambda, k) = \sum_{\lambda_j \leq \omega} \left(1 - \frac{\lambda_j}{\omega}\right) k_{u_j}$, and they are tailormade for the Dirichlet series $\sum_{n=0}^{\infty} d_n e^{-\lambda_n s}$. An exposition can be found in a Cambridge Tract written jointly with G. H. Hardy.

Like most young Hungarian mathematicians of the period, Riesz visited Göttingen regularly; he also spent the year 1910 to 1911 in Paris. There he received an invitation from Gustav Mittag-Leffler, whom he had met at the 1908 International Congress of Mathematicians in Rome, to deliver three lectures in Stockholm. Riesz accepted, and spent the rest of his life in Sweden. Some of the most distinguished Swedish mathematicians were his doctoral students.

After his arrival in Sweden, Riesz proved an interpolation formula from which S. N. Bernstein's inequality between a polynomial and its derivative follows. During World War I he wrote his only joint paper with his brother, on the boundary behavior of an analytic function. Their theorem, with its many variants and generalizations, became central in several branches of mathematics.

In the 1920's Riesz's interests, which until then had been concentrated on classical analysis, broadened. Under the influence of his brother, he turned to functional analysis. In three notes on the moment problem of Thomas Stieltjes and Hans Hamburger, he proved and applied a result on the extension of positive linear operators similar to the Hahn-Banach theorem. He also introduced a class of orthogonal polynomials to investigate the existence and the uniqueness of the solutions of the moment problem. He never published detailed proofs because others became interested in these questions, and he did not wish to compete with them.

In 1927 Riesz published his two most often quoted results: his theorem on conjugate functions and his convexity theorem. The former states that if the function f belongs to $L^p(-\infty, \infty)$ and $1 < p < \infty$, then the conjugate

$$\bar{f}(x) = \lim_{\varepsilon \to 0+} \frac{1}{\pi} \int_{|t-x| \geq \varepsilon} \frac{f(t)}{t-x} dt$$

also belongs to $L^p(-\infty, \infty)$, and the map that associates $\bar{f}$ with f is continuous. Conjugate functions originated in the theory of Fourier series, and Riesz's theorem solved a problem that had been open for some time. The generalization of his result to several variables by A. P. Calderón and Antoni Zygmund led to singular integrals and pseudo-differential operators, which play a fundamental role in the theory of partial differential equations.

The convexity theorem asserts that if a linear map is continuous from L^{p_0} to L^{q_0} and from L^{p_1} to L^{q_1}, then it is also continuous from L^p to L^q, where $p^{-1} = (1-\theta)p_0^{-1} + \theta p_1^{-1}$, $q^{-1} = (1-\theta)q_0^{-1} + \theta q_1^{-1}$, $0 \leq \theta \leq 1$. The theorem has earlier results of Felix Hausdorff and William H. Young on Fourier series and integrals, and of Frigyes Riesz on orthonormal series as a consequence. A simple proof was later found by Riesz's student Olof Thorin, and the theorem is now attributed to both. It became the starting point of abstract "interpolation theorems" developed mainly by E. M. Stein, A. P. Calderón, J. L. Lions, and J. Peetre.

In 1926 Riesz obtained a professorship at the University of Lund, where he became interested in partial differential equations, mathematical physics, number theory, and (through the *Moderne algebra* of B. L. van der Waerden) abstract algebra. At the Oslo International Congress of Mathematicians in 1936 he presented four short communications: one on mixed volumes in the theory of modules, one on reciprocal modules, and two on generalizations of the Riemann-Liouville integral.

The Riemann-Liouville integral, which generalizes differentiation and integration on the real line to fractional orders, figured in the theory of typical means. Its analogue, defined by Riesz on n-dimensional Euclidean space—the Riesz potential of fractional order—has properties that, among other things, prove that the kernel of the Newtonian potential is a positive function. This observation, used in the 1935 dissertation of Riesz's student Otto Frostman, led to a renewal of potential theory by M. Brelot, H. Cartan, J. Deny, G. Choquet, and others.

The Riemann-Liouville integral defined on an n-dimensional space with the Lorentz metric $\|x\|^2 = x_1^2 - x_2^2 - \ldots - x_n^2$ yields a new approach to the Cauchy problem for the wave equation and, more generally, for hyperbolic partial differential equations with variable coefficients in which Jacques Hadamard's concept of finite parts of integrals is replaced by analytic continuation. Riesz found these results between 1933 and 1936, but his monumental paper did not appear until 1949.

Riesz was a visiting professor at the University of Chicago in 1947 and 1948. After his retirement in 1952, he spent much time in the United States, mainly at the Courant Institute in New York, the University of Washington, Stanford University, the University of Maryland, and Indiana University. In 1960 illness forced him to return to Lund. Riesz was a member of the Swedish Academy of Sciences and in 1950 received an honorary doctorate from the University of Copenhagen.

BIBLIOGRAPHY

I. ORIGINAL WORKS. Lists of Riesz's writings are in the articles by Gårding and Horváth (see below). Among his works are "Sur les séries de Dirichlet," in *Comptes rendus . . . de l'Académie des sciences*, **148** (1909), 1658–1660; "Sur la sommation des séries de Dirichlet," *ibid.*, **149** (1909), 18–21; "Sur les séries de Dirichlet et les séries entières," *ibid.*; "Une méthode de sommation équivalente à la méthode des moyennes arithmétiques," *ibid.*, **152** (1911), 1651–1654; "Über summierbare trigonometrische Reihen," in *Mathematische Annalen*, **71** (1912), 54–75; *General Theory of Dirichlet Series* (Cambridge, 1915; repr. 1952), written with G. H. Hardy; "Sur les maxima des formes bilinéaires et sur les fonctionnelles linéaires," in *Acta Mathematica*, **49** (1927), 465–497; "Sur les fonc-tions conjugées," in *Mathematische Zeitschrift*, **27** (1927), 218–244; and "L'intégrale de Riemann-Liouville et le problème de Cauchy," in *Acta Mathematica*, **81** (1949), 1–223.

His works have been gathered in *Collected Papers of Marcel Riesz* (Berlin and New York, 1988).

II. SECONDARY LITERATURE. See Jöran Bergh and Jörgen Löfström, *Interpolation Spaces* (Berlin, 1976); Lars Gårding, "Marcel Riesz in Memoriam," in *Acta Mathematica*, **124** (1970), i–xi; and John Horváth, "Riesz Marcel matematikai munkássága" (The mathematical works of Marcel Riesz), in *Matematikai lapok*, **26** (1975), 11–37, and **28** (1980), 65–100, French trans. in *Cahiers du Séminaire d'histoire de mathématique*, **3** (1982), 83–121, and **4** (1983), 1–59. Two writings that influenced Riesz's early work are Pierre Fatou, "Séries trigonométriques et séries de Taylor," in *Acta Mathematica*, **30** (1906), 335–400; and Lipót Fejér, "Sur les fonctions bornées et intégrables," in *Comptes rendus . . . de l'Académie des sciences*, **131** (1900), 984–987.

JOHN HORVÁTH

RISNER, FRIEDRICH (*b.* Herzfeld, Hesse, Germany; *d.* Herzfeld, *ca.* 1580)

Risner spent most of his scholarly life as the protégé and colleague of Peter Ramus, the renowned anti-Aristotelian humanist and educational reformer, who was accustomed to collaborating with younger scholars on mathematical subjects. Risner's mathematical ability is evident from Ramus' reference to his "assistant in mathematical studies, . . . Friedrich Risner, so well versed in mathematics" (Hooykaas, *Humanisme*, p. 45). In his will Ramus established a chair in mathematics at the Collège Royal de France and specified that Risner should be its first occupant. When legal disputes over the chair were settled in 1576, Risner accepted the salary but never lectured; he resigned a few months later and returned to his native Hesse, where he died after a long illness.

The most noteworthy result of the collaboration between Ramus and Risner was the immensely influential edition (1572) of the optical works of Ibn al-Haytham and Witelo. Risner produced the *editio princeps* of Ibn al-Haytham's *Optics (De aspectibus)* from two manuscripts discovered by Ramus, adding citations and subdividing the book into propositions. Witelo's *Perspectiva* had already been published twice; but Risner improved the text by comparing several manuscripts, redrafted the figures, and added citations to corresponding propositions in Ibn-al Haytham's *Optics*.

The collaboration of Ramus and Risner also resulted in the posthumous publication of Risner's *Opticae libri quatuor*, which later influenced Snell. It seems that the book was begun during the early years of Ramus and Risner's association; and it is probable that the basic outline was Ramus', while Risner was given the task of providing appropriate demonstrations and discussion. Only the first of the four books is complete, however, and the final two consist of little more than the enunciations of the propositions. The work depends primarily on Witelo, although other ancient and medieval authors are also cited.

BIBLIOGRAPHY

I. Original Works. Risner edited *Opticae thesaurus Alhazeni Arabis libri septem, nunc primum editi. Eiusdem liber de crepusculis et nubium ascensionibus. Item Vitellonis thuringopoloni libri X. Omnes instaurati, figuris illustrati et aucti, adiectis etiam in Alhazenum commentariis, a Federico Risnero* (Basel, 1572). Risner's own *Optica* has been published as *Opticae libri quatuor ex voto Petri Rami novissimo per Fridericum Risnerum ejusdem in mathematicis adjutorem, olim conscripti* (Kassel, 1606); and *Risneri optica cum annotationibus Willebrordi Snellii*, J. A. Vollgraff, ed. (Ghent, 1918).

II. Secondary Literature. On Risner's life and works, see Bernardino Baldi, "Vite di matematici Arabi," in *Bullettino di bibliografia e di storia delle scienze matematiche e fisiche*, V (1872), 461–462; R. Hooykaas, *Humanisme, science et réforme: Pierre de la Ramée* (Leiden, 1958); J. J. Verdonk, *Petrus Ramus en de wiskunde* (Assen, 1966), 66–73; and Charles Waddington, *Ramus (Pierre de la Ramée), sa vie, ses écrits et ses opinions* (Paris, 1855).

David C. Lindberg

RITT, JOSEPH FELS (*b.* New York, N.Y., 23 August 1893; *d.* New York, 5 January 1951)

After two years of study at the College of the City of New York, Ritt obtained the B.A. from George Washington University in 1913. He received the Ph.D. from Columbia University in 1917 for a work on linear homogeneous differential operators with constant coefficients. He was colloquium lecturer of the American Mathematical Society (1932), a member of the National Academy of Sciences, and vice-president of the American Mathematical Society from 1938 to 1940.

Ritt's early work was highly classical. Papers entitled "On Algebraic Functions Which Can Be Expressed in Terms of Radicals," "Permutable Rational Functions," and "Periodic Functions With a Multiplication Theorem" were the result of a thorough study of classic masters. His work on elementary functions took its inspiration directly from Liouville.

Ritt also investigated the algebraic aspects of the theory of differential equations, considering differential polynomials or forms in the unknown functions $y_1, ..., y_n$ and their derivatives with coefficients that are functions meromorphic in some domain. Given a system Σ of such forms, he shows that there exists a finite subsystem of Σ having the same set of solutions as Σ. Furthermore, if a form G vanishes for every solution of the system of forms $H_1, ..., H_r$, then some power of G is a linear combination of the H_i and their derivatives. These arguments lead to the statement that every infinite system of forms has a finite basis.

In considering reducibility Ritt concluded that the perfect differential ideal generated by a system of forms equals the intersection of the prime ideals associated with its irreducible components. The purpose of this work was to advance knowledge of "general" and "singular" solutions, which in the preceding literature (Laplace, Lagrange, and Poisson, for example) had been very unsatisfactory.

Contributions to algebraic differential equations and algebraic difference equations were made by many of Ritt's students after 1932, in particular, by E. R. Kolchin, W. Strodt, H. W. Raudenbush, and H. Levi. Differential algebra, a new branch of modern algebra, also owes much to these early researches.

BIBLIOGRAPHY

The most important aspects of Ritt's work are summed up in two books published in the Colloquium Publications series of the American Mathematical Society: *Differential Equations From the Algebraic Standpoint* (New York, 1932) and *Differential Algebra* (New York, 1950).

Complete bibliographies of Ritt's writings are included in the notices by E. R. Lorch, in *Bulletin of the American Mathematical Society*, **57** (1951), 307–318; and by Paul A. Smith, in *Biographical Memoirs. National Academy of Sciences*, **29** (1956), 253–264.

Edgar R. Lorch

ROBERVAL, GILLES PERSONNE (or **PERSONIER**) **DE** (*b.* near Senlis, France, 10 August 1602;[1] *d.* Paris, France, 27 October 1675)

Very little is known about Roberval's childhood and adolescence. His parents seem to have been simple farmers. He stated that he was born and educated among the people (*inter multos*). J.-B. du Hamel reports that he devoted himself to mathematical studies beginning at the age of fourteen. Having left his family at an unknown date, Roberval traveled through various regions of the country, earning a living from private lessons and continuing to educate himself. In 1628 he arrived in Paris and put himself in touch with the scientists of the Mersenne circle: Claude Mydorge, Claude Hardy, and Étienne and Blaise Pascal. Mersenne, especially, always held Roberval in the highest esteem. In 1632 Roberval became professor of philosophy at the Collège de Maître Gervais. On 24 June 1634, he was proclaimed the winner in the triennial competition for the Ramus chair (a position that he kept for the rest of his life) at the Collège Royal in Paris, where at the end of 1655 he also succeeded to Gassendi's chair of mathematics. In 1666 Roberval was one of the charter members of the Académie des Sciences in Paris.

Roberval's tendency to keep his own discoveries secret has been attributed to his desire to profit from them in order to retain the Ramus chair. But this habit also resulted in his tardy and rather frequent claims to priority. He himself published only two works: *Traité de méchanique* (1636) and *Aristarchi Samii de mundi systemate* (1644). A rather full collection of his treatises and letters was published in the *Divers ouvrages de mathématique et de physique par messieurs de l'Académie royale des sciences* (1693), but since few of his other writings were published in the following period, Roberval was for long eclipsed by Fermat, Pascal, and, above all, by Descartes, his irreconcilable adversary. Serious research on Roberval dates from approximately the end of the nineteenth century, and many of his writings still remain unpublished.

In the field of elementary geometry, a collection of Roberval's manuscripts includes some remarkable constructions of isoperimetric figures,[2] of which at least two are earlier than October 1636.[3] In addition, in 1644 Mersenne reported, without indicating the procedure employed, several problems solved by Roberval under the condition of the *extrema*.[4]

Roberval was one of the leading proponents of the geometry of infinitesimals, which he claimed to have taken directly from Archimedes, without having known the work of Cavalieri. Moreover, in supposing that the constituent elements of a figure possess the same dimensions as the figure itself, Roberval came closer to the integral calculus than did Cavalieri, although Roberval's reasoning in this matter was not free from imprecision. The numerous results that he obtained in this area are collected in the *Divers ouvrages*, under the title of *Traité des indivisibles*. One of the first important findings was, in modern terms, the definite integration of the rational power, which he most probably completed around 1636, although by what manner we are not certain. The other important result was the integration of the sine, and he formulated by virtue of it the problem of which he was so proud: Trace on a right cylinder, with a single

motion of the compass, a surface equal to that of a given square, or, except for the bases, of an oblique cylinder. Furthermore, in 1644 Mersenne recounts —but again without saying how—that Roberval was the first to square the surface of the oblique cone. Yet the most famous of his works in this domain concerns the cycloid. Roberval introduced the "compagne" ("partner") ($x = r\theta$, $y = r - r \cos \theta$) of the original cycloidal curve and appears to have succeeded, before the end of 1636, in the quadrature of the latter and in the cubature of the solid that it generates in turning around its base. But the cubature of the solid of revolution around its axis (presented in the treatise *Ad trochoidem, ejusque solida*),[5] must have been achieved between May 1644 and October 1645. Roberval, moreover, knew how to extend all these results to the general case:

$$x = a\theta - b \sin \theta, \quad y = a - b \cos \theta.$$

On account of his method of the "composition of movements" Roberval may be called the founder of kinematic geometry. This procedure had three applications—the fundamental and most famous being the construction of tangents. "By means of the specific properties of the curved line," he stated, "examine the various movements made by the point which describes it at the location where you wish to draw the tangent: from all these movements compose a single one; draw the line of direction of the composed movement, and you will have the tangent of the curved line."[6]

Roberval conceived this remarkably intuitive method during his earliest research on the cycloid (before 1636). At first, he kept the invention secret, but he finally taught it between 1639 and 1644; his disciple François du Verdus recorded his lessons in *Observations sur la composition des mouvemens, et sur le moyen de trouver les touchantes des lignes courbes*.[7] Jean-Marie-Constant Duhamel's criticism of this method (1838) applied only to the abuse some others had made of the parallelogram or parallelepiped of velocities; Roberval himself employed, in his own fashion, the rule advanced by Duhamel. In the last analysis, the latter failed to recognize that Roberval's method had to do with the moving system of coordinates.

In the second place, he also applied this procedure to comparison of the lengths of curves, a subject almost untouched since antiquity. In the winter of 1642–1643, Roberval equated not only the spiral and the parabola in their ordinary forms, but also the curves $r = k\theta^n$ and $y^{n+1} = k'x^n$ (n being any whole number).[8] He accomplished this equation by purely kinematic considerations, probably without making any computations at all (according to an unpublished work, preserved in the archives of the Academy of Sciences). In addition, he declared that he had carried out the rectification of the simple cycloid before 1640, by reducing it kinematically to the integration of the sine—a serious claim that would deprive Torricelli of the glory of having first rectified a curve (1644 or 1645), but for which there is not yet any objective proof. It is possible, however, that Roberval discovered before August 1648 the equality in length of the generalized cycloid and the ellipse, which was established by Pascal in 1659.[9]

The third application consisted in determining extrema, and four problems of this type are solved in an unpublished manuscript.[10] The solution is certainly ingenious, but we know of no other writings by Roberval that treat more difficult problems of the same type in this fashion. It was quadrature that, in accord with the general trend of mathematics in his century, Roberval pursued as the principal goal of his kinematics; but his efforts in this direction were not fruitful. Lacking the aid of analysis, his kinematics was still far from the Newtonian method of fluxions.

Roberval composed a treatise on algebra, *De recognitione aequationum*, and another on analytic geometry, *De geometrica planarum et cubicarum aequationum resolutione*.[11] Before 1632, he had studied the "logistica speciosa" of Viète; but the first treatise, which probably preceded Descartes's *Géométrie*, contains only the rudiments of the theory of equations. On the other hand, in 1636 he had already resorted to algebra in search of a tangent. By revealing the details of such works, he would have assured himself a more prominent place in the history of analytic geometry, and even in that of differential calculus. But the second treatise cited above was written later than the *Géométrie*, and therefore contributed nothing of particular interest, except for a thorough discussion of the "ovale optique," the style of which, however, is that of elementary geometry.

Turning now to mechanics, his *Traité* of 1636 led to the law of the composition of forces through a study—like the one in the *Beghinselen der weegconst* of Stevin—of the equilibrium of a body supported at first on an inclined plane, then suspended by two cords. But when Roberval reduced the equilibrium on the inclined plane to that of the balance, he was very close to Galileo, whose *Le meccaniche* he no doubt knew through the efforts of Mersenne. This treatise of Roberval contains, however, a clear notion of the pressure that the body exerts on the plane, and of the equivalent resistance that the latter opposes to the former. Moreover, Roberval stated that the treatise "is only a sample of a greater work on Mechanics which cannot so soon make its appearance."

Perhaps he meant the French version of a booklet in Latin, now lost, which he had written before 1634, and from which he had just taken this treatise on statics.

Roberval's ambition did not cease to grow. In 1647 he wrote to Torricelli: "We have constructed a mechanics which is new from its foundations to its roof, having rejected, save for a small number, the ancient stones with which it had been built."[12] Roberval indicated the materials for this work: book I, on the center of action of forces (*de centro virtutis potentiarum*) in general; book II, on the balance; book III, on the center of action of particular forces; book IV, on the cord; book V, on instruments and machines; book VI, on the forces that act within certain media; book VII, on compound movements; and book VIII, on the center of percussion of moving forces. This great treatise has not come down to us; the most we can do is to find some traces of its content among Roberval's surviving papers. The "Tractatus mechanicus, anno 1645,"[13] treating of the composition of parallel forces, might have been the beginning of book I. The "demonstratio mechanica,"[14] establishing the law of the balance in the manner of Stevin and Galileo,[15] was undoubtedly destined for book II. Since book III was to deal with the center of gravity, the "Theorema lemmaticum"[16] would have served as its basis; this unpublished manuscript demonstrates the general equation of moments in space of three dimensions. As for book IV, the booklet mentioned above would already have furnished the material for it. The "Proposition fondamentale pour les corps flottants sur l'eau"[17] would have been included in book VI. With regard to book VII, we may refer to the preceding paragraphs on kinematic geometry. And yet around 1669, Roberval wrote *Projet d'un livre de mechanique traitant des mouvemens composez*.[18] Book VII would therefore not have been completed; Roberval dreamed, certainly with too great temerity, of a vast physical theory based uniquely on the composition of motions. Concerning book VIII, a part of it is in the unpublished manuscript "De centro percussionis,"[19] as well as three texts of 1646 in the *Oeuvres de Descartes*.[20] The problem of the center of oscillation of the compound pendulum provoked in 1646 a new polemic between Descartes and Roberval. Although Descartes had a better idea of the center of oscillation, nevertheless he was wrong in neglecting the directions of the forces. Roberval well knew how to rectify this error. But he did not consider it necessary to locate the center of oscillation on the right line linking the point of suspension and the center of gravity of the body under consideration; he doubted that, even located on this right line, the point that he determined was precisely the center of oscillation.

On 21 August 1669 Roberval presented to the Royal Academy of Sciences the plans for a particular type of balance, which today bears his name. Although the notion of virtual work is clearly contained and expressed therein under the name "momentum," he probably considered only the finite path of the weight.

In mechanics, no less than in mathematics, Roberval displayed a great concern for rigor. For example, he began the "Tractatus mechanicus, anno 1645" by postulating the possibility of the movement of a point along an arbitrary curve. It is not the case, however, that he failed to appreciate the importance of experiment in mechanics; and positivism is even more evident in his work in physics. In this regard, it is also useful to consult his philosophical reflections, such as "Les principes du debvoir et des cognoissances humaines,"[21] *L'évidence—le fait avéré—la chymère*,[22] and the unpublished manuscript "Quelle créance l'homme doit avoir à ses sens et à son entendement" (in Archives of the Academy of Sciences).

Roberval's positivism appears in a particularly nuanced form in the book *De mundi systemate* of 1644, where he claimed to have translated an Arabic manuscript of Aristarchus, to which he had added his own notes, all of them favorable to the author. Yet he did not adhere to the system of Aristarchus to the exclusion of those of Ptolemy and Tycho Brahe. In the dedication of the work, Roberval wrote: "Perhaps all three of these systems are false and the true one unknown. Still, that of Aristarchus seemed to me to be the simplest and the best adapted to the laws of nature." It is with this reservation that Roberval expressed his opinion on the great system of the world (the solar system), the minor systems (planetary), the motions of the sun and the planets, the declination of the moon, the apogees and perigees, the agitation of the oceans, the precession of the equinoxes, and the comets. Despite this reservation, Roberval appeared convinced of the existence of universal attraction, which—under the inspiration of Kepler—he put forth as the foundation of his entire astronomy: "In all this worldly matter [the fluid of which the world is composed, according to our author], and in each of its parts, resides a certain property, or accident, by the force of which this matter contracts into a single continuous body."[23]

On the problem of the vacuum, which had been agitating French scientific circles since 1645, Roberval composed two *Narrationes*.[24] In the first of them (dated 20 September 1647), he reported Pascal's experiments at Rouen and the experiments he himself subsequently had undertaken. Roberval agreed with his friend, concluding that if the space at the top of the barometric tube was not absolutely empty, it was free of all the elements alleged by the philosophers. But the second *Narratio*—probably composed in May–June and October 1648—is much more important. In this work Roberval proved himself to be a very skillful and scrupulous experimenter. He explained the suspension of the mercury in the tube by the pressure of the air on the exterior mercury. Moreover, a very ingenious apparatus that he had invented to support this thesis later served as the prototype for the one in Pascal's experiment of "the vacuum in the vacuum," described in the *Traité de l'équilibre des liqueurs et de la pesanteur de la masse de l'air*. Roberval thus remained in agreement with his friend, save that he attributed the equilibrium of the liquids to the universal attraction mentioned in the discussion of his astronomical work. But, on the other hand, he did deliberately assert the existence of rarefied air in the top of the tube. He showed in particular that an exhausted carp bladder placed in the empty space of the tube became inflated by virtue of the spontaneous dilation of the air. And that, in principle, is all he wished to do. He refrained from tackling the ancient question of whether a vacuum existed in nature. While ironically returning the problem to the schools, he did not at all tolerate the Cartesian confusion of space and matter.

The same positivism is evident in book II of *L'optique et la catoptrique de Mersenne* (1651), in which proposition 4 is particularly remarkable for its disdainful rejection of all speculation on the nature of light. Roberval promised himself to "join experiment to reasoning" in the study of the phenomenon of reflection. In the same spirit, he rewrote the "Livre troisiesme de la dioptrique, ou des lunettes,"[25] where we find again his cherished geometric dissertation on the oval.

NOTES

1. According to Pierre Desnoyers, secretary to the queen of Poland and correspondent of Roberval.
2. Bibliothèque Nationale, fonds latin, nouvelle acquisition 2340, 1_r–6_v, 196_r–214_r.
3. Given two cones of unequal bases or heights of two cones of equal volume and surface area (the bases included or excluded), find the cones. See *Oeuvres de Fermat*, II, 82–83.
4. M. Mersenne, "Phaenomena hydraulica," in *Cogitata physico-mathematica*, 55–77.
5. *Divers ouvrages*, 257–274.
6. *Ibid.*, 80.
7. *Ibid.*, 69–111.
8. One determines k, k' in such a manner that the two curves will have equal subtangents for any given pair of equal values of r and y.
9. The arc corresponding to the interval $[\theta_1, \theta_2]$ of the generalized cycloid (see end of fourth paragraph) is double the arc

corresponding to the interval $[\theta_1/2, \theta_2/2]$ of the ellipse $x = (a + b) \cos \theta,\ y = (a - b) \sin \theta$.

10. Bibliothèque Nationale, fds. fr. 9119, 464v–470r.
11. *Divers ouvrages*, 114–189.
12. The original is in Latin, in *Divers ouvrages*, 301.
13. Bibliothèque Nationale, fds. lat. 7226, 2r–27r.
14. *Ibid.*, 31r–33v.
15. *The Principal Works of Simon Stevin*, I (Amsterdam, 1955), 116–125; *Le opere di Galileo Galilei*, VIII, 152–153.
16. Bibliothèque Nationale, fds. lat. 7226, 59r–82r.
17. *Ibid.*, 207v–210r.
18. *Divers ouvrages*, 112–113.
19. Bibliothèque Nationale, fds. lat. nouv. acq. 2341, 41r–45r.
20. *Oeuvres de Descartes*, IV, 420–428, 502–508.
21. In Victor Cousin, *Fragments de philosophie cartésienne*, 242–261.
22. *Oeuvres de Blaise Pascal*, II, 49–51.
23. *Op. cit.*, 2–3.
24. *Oeuvres de Blaise Pascal*, II, 21–35, 310–340.
25. Bibliothèque Nationale, fds. fr. 12279, 1r–108r.

BIBLIOGRAPHY

I. ORIGINAL WORKS. Works published during Roberval's lifetime include *Traité de mechanique. Des poids soustenus par des puissances sur les plans inclinez à l'horizon. Des puissances qui soustiennent un poids suspendu à deux chordes* (Paris, 1636), repr. in Mersenne, *Harmonie universelle* (see below); and *Aristarchi Samii de mundi systemate, partibus et motibus ejusdem libellus. Adjectae sunt AE. de Roberval . . . notae in eundem libellum* (Paris, 1644), repr. with some modifications in Mersenne, *Novarum observationum . . .* (see below). The extract of a letter to Mersenne and of another to Torricelli is in Dati (see below), pp. 8, 12–14. Two anti-Cartesian letters and an annexed fragment were published by C. Clerselier in *Lettres de M. Des-Cartes*, III (Paris, 1667), 313–321, 498–505. See also *L'optique et la catoptrique du R. P. Mersenne, mise en lumière après la mort de l'autheur*, (Paris, 1651), of which propositions 4–16 (pp. 88–131) of bk. II are actually the work of Roberval.

Posthumous publications before the end of the nineteenth century include 4 letters to Fermat, in *Varia opera mathematica D. Petri de Fermat Senatoris Tolosani* (Toulouse, 1679), 124–130, 138–141, 152–153, 165–166; 6 treatises (one of which is completely fragmentary) and 2 letters in *Divers ouvrages de mathématique et de physique par messieurs de l'Académie royale des sciences* (Paris, 1693), 69–302, repr. in *Mémoires de l'Académie royale des sciences, depuis 1666 jusqu'à 1699*, VI (Paris, 1730), 1–478; "Avant-propos sur les mathématiques," in Cousin (see below), 236–239; and "Les principes du debvoir et des cognoissances humaines," *ibid.*, 242–261.

Letters and other minor writtings of Roberval have been published or reprinted in the following works, in which one may also find various information about him: Charles Henry, *Huygens et Roberval* (Leiden, 1880), 35–41; *Oeuvres de Blaise Pascal*, I–II (see below); *Oeuvres complètes de Christiaan Huygens, publiées par la Société Hollandaise des Sciences*, I (The Hague, 1888); *Oeuvres de Fermat*, Charles Henry and Paul Tannery, eds., II, IV (Paris, 1894, 1912), with supp. by Cornelis de Waard (Paris, 1922); *Oeuvres de Descartes*, C. Adam and P. Tannery, eds., II, IV (Paris, 1898, 1901); *Opere di Evangelista Torricelli*, G. Loria and G. Vassura, eds., III (Faenza, 1919); Mersenne's *Correspondance*, C. de Waard, R. Pintard, and B. Rochet, eds., III–XII (Paris, 1946–1973) and L. Auger, *Un savant méconnu* (see below), 179–202, which presents two new documents on gravity (*pesanteur*) and on the so-called Roberval balance.

The Bibliothèque Nationale in Paris possesses numerous unpublished MSS of Roberval, cataloged as follows: fonds latins 7226, 11195, 11197; fds lat. nouvelles acquisitions 2338, 2340, 2341; fds. français 9119, 9120, 12279; and fds. fr. nouv. acq. 1086, 2340, 5161, 5175, 5856. The Archives of the Académie des Sciences also preserve a good number of Roberval's papers, almost all of which are unpublished and poorly classified. Besides the writings dealing with mathematics and mechanics, one may find items such as "Cours d'astronomie," "L'aere chrestienne," "Tractatus de architectura," "Geographie physique sur les golfes," "L'arpentage," and "Du nivelage." The Bibliothèque Sainte Geneviève possesses, according to Auger, "Trois tables de la grandeur des parties d'une fortification royale, dédiées à M. le Duc de Buckingham par M. Roberval, Paris, 1645."

Many of Roberval's papers preserved in the archives of the Académie des Sciences have been classified by Alan Gabbey and are described in a catalog (deposited in the archives of the Academy), which he prepared in 1966, and which covers MSS and documents by or relating to the founding members of the Academy, other than Huygens. The present author was not able to consult the catalog at the time of the composing of this article.

II. SECONDARY LITERATURE. On Roberval and his work, see Léon Auger, "Les idées de Roberval sur le système du monde," in *Revue d'histoire des sciences et de leurs applications*, 10, no. 3 (1957), 226–234, and *Un savant méconnu: G. P. de Roberval, son activité intellectuelle dans les domaines mathématique, physique, mécanique et philosophique* (Paris, 1962); Adrien Baillet, *La vie de Monsieur Des-Cartes*, 2 vols. (Paris, 1691); Le Marquis de Condorcet, "Éloge de Roberval" (1773), republished in Oeuvres de Condorcet, II (Paris, 1847), 5–12; Pierre Costabel, "La controverse Descartes–Roberval au sujet du centre d'oscillation," in *Revue des sciences humaines*, n.s. 61, fasc. 61 (Lille–Paris, 1951), 74–86; Victor Cousin, "Roberval philosophe," in *Fragments de philosophie cartésienne* (Paris, 1845), 229–261; Carlo Dati, *Lettera a Filaleti di Timauro Antiate della vera storia della cicloide, e della famosissima esperienza dell'argento vivo* (Florence, 1663); Jean-Marie-Constant Duhamel, "Note sur la méthode des tangentes de Roberval," in *Mémoires présentés par divers savants à l'Académie des sciences de l'Institut de France*, 5 (1838), 257–266; Pierre Duhem, *Les origines de la statique*, 2 vols. (Paris, 1905–1906), and *Études sur Léonard de Vinci*, I (Paris, 1955); Marie-Antoinette Fleury and Georges Bailhache, "Le testament, l'inventaire après décès . . . de Gassendi," in *Tricentenaire de Gassendi*, Actes du Congrès de Digne, 1955 (Paris–

Digne, 1957), 21–68; Kokiti Hara, "Étude sur la théorie des mouvements composés de Roberval" (*thèse de troisième cycle*, defended in 1965 at the Faculté des lettres et sciences humaines de l'Université de Paris), and "Remarque sur la quadrature de la surface du cône oblique," in *Revue d'histoire des sciences et de leurs applications*, **20**, no. 4 (1967), 317–332; J. E. Hofmann and P. Costabel, "A propos d'un problème de Roberval," *ibid.*, **5**, no. 4 (1952), 312–333; Jean Itard, "Autre remarque sur la quadrature de la surface du cône oblique," *ibid.*, **20**, no. 4 (1967), 333–335; Robert Lenoble, "Roberval éditeur de Mersenne et du P. Niceron," *ibid.*, **10**, no. 3 (1957), 235–254; and M. Mersenne, *Harmonie universelle*, . . . 2 vols. (Paris, 1636), reprinted in facsimile (Paris, 1963), *Cogitata physico-mathematica* (Paris, 1644), and *Novarum observationum physico-mathematicarum tomus III* (Paris, 1647); Blaise Pascal, *Histoire de la roulette . . .* (10 Oct. 1658), also in Latin, *Historia trochoidis* (same date), republished in *Oeuvres de Blaise Pascal*, L. Brunschvicg, P. Boutroux, and F. Gazier, eds., VIII (1914), 195–223; Bernard Rochot, "Roberval, Mariotte et la logique," in *Archives internationales d'histoire des sciences*, **22** (1953), 38–43; Paul Tannery, *La correspondance de Descartes dans les inédits du fonds Libri* (Paris, 1893), republished in *Mémoires scientifiques*, **6** (1926), 153–267; Cornelis de Waard, "Une lettre inédite de Roberval du 6 janvier 1637 contenant le premier énoncé de la cycloïde," in *Bulletin des sciences mathématiques*, 2nd ser., **45** (1921), 206–216, 220–230; and Evelyn Walker, *A Study of the Traité des indivisibles de G. P. de Roberval* (New York, 1932).

KOKITI HARA

ROBINS, BENJAMIN (*b.* Bath, England, 1707; *d.* Fort St. David, India, 29 July 1751)

Robins probably is best known as the inventor of the ballistic pendulum. Today the device is used to demonstrate conservation of momentum as well as for the purpose to which Robins put it: to determine the muzzle velocity of bullets. Robins needed experimental confirmation of his theoretical computations.

Born of Quaker parents, Robins never showed an inclination for pacifism. Trained as a teacher, he soon left that profession for mathematics and for ballistics and fortifications. In 1727 he published an article in the *Philosophical Transactions of the Royal Society*, a demonstration of the eleventh proposition of Newton's *Treatise on Quadratures*. Although the *Dictionary of National Biography* asserts that he accomplished the work without help, it is doubtful that Newton missed passing on it. Robins became one of Newton's most adamant defenders, often to the point of indelicacy. Much of his writing was devoted to attacks on Newton's enemies—Leibniz, the Bernoullis, Berkeley, and James Jurin. Robins took part in the celebrated *vis viva* controversy, the subject of most of his polemics.

Robins' best-known work, *New Principles of Gunnery*, appeared in 1742. Euler translated it into German in 1745, adding his own commentary. It was also translated into French in 1751. It was there that Robins described the ballistic pendulum. His other work on ballistics was far from trivial, including studies of the resistance of fluid media to high-speed objects, pressures on projectiles inside a gun barrel, the rifling of barrel pieces, and the shape of actual, as opposed to ideal, trajectories. For his service he was awarded the Copley Medal in 1747. His last work consisted of investigations of rockets for the purpose of military signaling.

Robins never married. He died in India, where he had gone to assist the British East India Company in renovating fortifications.

BIBLIOGRAPHY

I. ORIGINAL WORKS. Robins published only two articles in the *Philosophical Transactions of the Royal Society*: "Demonstration of the Eleventh Proposition of Sir I. Newton's Treatise of Quadratures," **34** (1727), 230–236; and "On the Height to Which Rockets Will Ascend," **46** (1749), 131–133; and participated in the research for John Ellicott, "An Account of Some Experiments . . . to Discover the Height to Which Rockets May Be Made to Ascend," **46** (1750), 578–584. His major work remains *New Principles of Gunnery* (London, 1742). The most valuable collection of his writings was published by a friend ten years after his death: *Mathematical Tracts of the Late Benjamin Robins*, James Wilson, ed., 2 vols. (London, 1761). This collection contains Robins' book on gunnery, the polemics on the *vis viva* controversy and other articles read to the Royal Society but until then unpublished, reprints of the published articles, and Wilson's personal comments on the life and character of his old friend.

II. SECONDARY LITERATURE. There is almost nothing except occasional mention of Robins in general histories. There are accounts of his life in British biographical series, most notably the *Dictionary of National Biography*. No full biography has been published.

J. MORTON BRIGGS, JR.

ROBINSON, ABRAHAM (*b.* Waldenburg, Germany [now Walbrzych, Poland], 6 October 1918; *d.* New Haven, Connecticut, 11 April 1974)

Abraham Robinson was the second son of Hedwig Lotte Bähr and Abraham Robinsohn. His father, a scholar and secretary to the Zionist leader David

Wolffsohn (and curator of the papers of Wolffsohn and Theodor Herzl), died in 1918 before Abraham was born. His mother, a teacher, moved to her parent's home in Waldenburg and later settled in Breslau, where she found work with the Keren Hayesod (the Zionist organization set up to aid the emigration and settlement of Jews in Palestine).

In 1933, as the National Socialists were beginning their attacks on Jews in all walks of life, the Robinsohns emigrated to Palestine. There, in Jerusalem, Robinson finished his secondary education and entered Hebrew University in 1936, where he studied mathematics with Abraham Fraenkel and Jakob Levitzki, as well as physics with S. Sambursky and philosophy (especially Leibniz) with L. Roth. In 1939 Robinson won a French government scholarship to the Sorbonne, where he studied in the spring of 1940 until the German invasion of France in June forced him to flee. Making his way to the coast on foot and by train, he managed to reach Bordeaux, where he embarked on one of the last boats to leave France with refugees for England.

Having resettled in London, Robinson soon changed the spelling of his name (dropping the "h" from Robinsohn). In 1940 he enlisted with the Free French Air Force, and from 1942 to 1946 served with the Royal Aircraft Establishment in Farnborough, where he was a scientific officer specializing in aircraft structures and aerodynamics, particularly in supersonic wing theory. During the war he met Renée Kopel, an actress and fashion designer from Vienna; they were married on 30 January 1944, exactly one year after they met.

In light of the success of his work in aerodynamics at Farnborough, Robinson was offered a position in 1946 as senior lecturer in mathematics at the newly founded College of Aeronautics at Cranfield. Later that year Hebrew University awarded him an M.Sc. degree, primarily for the high-level scientific research he had done during the war. By then, thanks to his technical publications, Robinson had come to be regarded as one of the world's authorities on supersonic aerodynamics and wing theory. As a result, he was invited to serve as a member of the Fluid Motion Committee of the Aeronautical Research Council of Great Britain.

Robinson returned to the study of advanced mathematics in the late 1940's, enrolling as a graduate student at Birkbeck College, University of London. Working with Roger Cooke, Paul Dienes, and others, he received his Ph.D. in 1949 for a dissertation on the metamathematics of algebraic systems (published as a book in 1951). This was a pioneering work in model theory. Subsequently Robinson's many contributions to the study of relations between axiom systems and mathematical structures helped to provide the classic foundations for the subject.

It was largely on the strength of his work in aerodynamics that Robinson was offered a position in 1951 as associate professor of applied mathematics at the University of Toronto, where he succeeded Leopold Infeld. Increasingly, however, Robinson's research concentrated on pure mathematics. One of the most important early successes of his application of model theory to algebra was a model-theoretic solution (published in 1955) of Hilbert's seventeenth problem, for which he achieved a considerably simpler solution than the original algebraic one given by Emil Artin in 1927.

After six years in Canada, Robinson received an offer of the chair of his former professor, Abraham Fraenkel, at Hebrew University in Jerusalem. This proved irresistible, and the Robinsons left Canada for Israel in 1957. There Robinson's work was increasingly devoted to algebra and model theory. It was during this period that Robinson found a model completion for the axioms of differential fields, which then served as models of the "closure" axioms associated with this completion. Angus Macintyre said of this accomplishment, "It would be appropriate to say that he *invented* differentiably closed fields." [1]

Robinson spent the academic year 1960–1961 as a visiting professor in the department of mathematics at Princeton University, where he had the inspiration for his best-known discovery, nonstandard analysis. In the spring of 1961 he also visited the department of philosophy at the University of California at Los Angeles; a year later UCLA succeeded in negotiating a joint appointment for Robinson as professor of mathematics and philosophy, a position he held from 1962 to 1967. There the chance to build a program in logic where he could teach graduate students and interact with a large faculty having diverse interests proved extremely productive for Robinson. While he was at UCLA, he began to develop in earnest the basic features of nonstandard analysis.

The last academic move Robinson made was in 1967, when Yale University appointed him professor of mathematics; after 1971 he was Sterling professor. There the department of mathematics provided a congenial and stimulating environment where Robinson's talents as a teacher flourished, as did his publications. Late in 1973, at the height of his career, he was diagnosed as suffering from incurable cancer of the pancreas. In less than six months, at the age of fifty-five, Robinson died at Yale University Hospital.

In the course of his prematurely curtailed career, Robinson wrote more than 135 articles and 9 books. He held a number of visiting positions, including appointments at Paris, Princeton, Heidelberg, Rome, and Tübingen, as well as at the California Institute of Technology, the Weizmann Institute, and St. Catherine's College, Oxford. From 1968 to 1970 he served as president of the Association for Symbolic Logic. In 1972 Robinson was made a fellow of the American Academy of Arts and Sciences, and in 1973 he was awarded the Brouwer Medal by the Dutch Mathematical Society. The following year he was elected (posthumously) to membership in the U.S. National Academy of Sciences.

Aerodynamics. At the Royal Aircraft Establishment in Farnborough, Robinson not only tutored himself to pass examinations in aeronautical engineering but also took flying lessons in order to complement his theoretical knowledge of structures and aerodynamics with some hands-on experience. At first he dealt with fundamental problems related to structural weaknesses in aircraft design; development of the jet engine toward the end of the war, however, not only greatly increased aircraft speeds but also made questions of supersonic flow of considerable theoretical and practical interest. In the latter field Robinson made essential contributions to the understanding of delta-form wings.

After the war, having established himself as an expert on aerodynamics, Robinson was invited to join the staff of the newly founded College of Aeronautics at Cranfield, just outside London. There he taught mathematics, and by 1950 had been named deputy head of the department of aerodynamics. Although he had just begun to write a book on wing theory with a recent graduate of the college, J. A. Laurmann, Robinson left Cranfield in 1951 to accept an offer from the University of Toronto. From then on, although his interests were drawn more and more to logic and model theory, he continued to read papers at aerodynamics symposia in Canada, and to publish papers of considerable interest and sophistication on wave propagation and structural analysis. In 1956 Robinson was promoted to professor, the same year in which his book on *Wing Theory* (coauthored with Laurmann), was published.

Algebra. Robinson's career as a mathematician was typified primarily, but not exclusively, by deep research into the interconnections between algebra and symbolic logic. The first two papers he wrote (while still a student at Hebrew University) were on the independence of the axiom of definiteness in Zermelo-Fraenkel set theory and on nil-ideals in ring theory. His first book, based upon his dissertation (University of London, 1949), *On the Metamathematics of Algebra* (1951), was a pioneer in model theory and the application of mathematical logic to algebra. Many of Robinson's most important contributions to modern mathematics concern fertile hybridizations of algebra and model theory. In algebra, for example, he introduced model completeness, and in model theory he developed the idea of differentially closed fields.

Model Theory. Model theory studies the relationship between a set of axioms and various models that may satisfy the axioms in question. Among early-twentieth-century proponents of model theory, Löwenheim, Skolem, Gödel, Malcev, Tarski, and Henkin all made important contributions before Robinson's first book, *On the Metamathematics of Algebra*, appeared in 1951. This book set the tone for much of Robinson's later work, and served as a guiding force in the development of model-theoretic algebra in the decades after it was written.

One of the major tools Robinson developed was model completeness, which he introduced in 1955. This is basically an abstract form of elimination of quantifiers. It may also be regarded, in the study of algebraically closed fields, as a generalization of Hilbert's *Nullstellensatz*. Robinson's book *Complete Theories* (1956) developed the notion of the theory of algebraically closed fields and showed that real closed fields and modules over a field, among other familiar algebraic theories, are model complete. One of the most important examples of model completion in algebra is Robinson's 1959 discovery that the theory of differential fields of characteristic zero has a model completion: differentially closed fields of characteristic zero.

In 1970 Robinson developed another important method of constructing models based upon an extension of the earlier idea of model completion. This method, known as Robinson forcing, bears a close similarity to the method of forcing in set theory introduced by Paul Cohen in 1963. The paper "Model Theory as a Framework for Algebra" provided an excellent introduction to the subject of forcing. Closely related, and also influential in the work of later mathematicians, was Robinson's development of generic and existentially closed models.

Nonstandard Analysis. Robinson's best-known discovery is nonstandard analysis, which provides a means of introducing infinitesimals, or "infinitely small" quantities, rigorously into the body of mathematics. The basic idea of nonstandard analysis makes use of model-theoretic concepts that provide for the first time, 300 years after its invention by Newton and Leibniz, a rigorous foundation for the differential and integral calculus using infinitesimals. But the great interest of nonstandard analysis for mathematicians is not foundational, nor is it due to the intuitiveness with which infinitesimals can be taught to students (which is considerable). What is impressive and of great utility is the power non-standard analysis brings to the solution of difficult and significant mathematical problems.

The source of this strength is not merely the addition of infinitesimals to mathematics but lies in Robinson's use of model theory, which makes it possible to establish a fundamental connection between the set of real numbers $\mathbf{R}$ and the nonstandard model $\mathbf{R}^*$ of $\mathbf{R}$ that contains the infinitesimals (as well as infinitely large nonstandard numbers). What Robinson established is the fact that $\mathbf{R}^*$ is an elementary extension of $\mathbf{R}$. In terms of Robinson's transfer principle, this means that the infinitesimals in $\mathbf{R}^*$ behave like the real numbers in $\mathbf{R}$.

Because of the extraordinary breadth of Robinson's knowledge, he was able from the beginning to apply nonstandard analysis with impressive results in many areas of mathematics. In the years following his death, more and more mathematicians have found that nonstandard analysis can be applied to great advantage in an increasingly large number of special areas. For example, important applications have already been made to functional analysis, number theory, mathematical economics, and quantum physics. Much of this work was first done by Robinson with colleagues or graduate students, many of whom have gone on to establish significant reputations in model theory and mathematical logic, including nonstandard analysis.

Arithmetic. Class field theory and Diophantine geometry were areas in which Robinson made especially significant contributions through applications of nonstandard methods. Here "enlargements" of algebraic number fields were the key insight—"enlargements" being considered as completions in a universal sense. Thus, in terms of mathematical logic, transfer principles are extremely powerful, and consequently they prove to be of great utility, as well as of great generality, in dealing with problems of arithmetic.

In the last decade of his life Robinson became increasingly interested in these questions, especially the extent to which nonstandard methods could serve to establish new results or improve old ones. His last major work was a nonstandard treatment, developed with Peter Roquette, of the finiteness theorem on Diophantine equations of Siegel and Mahler.

Computers. Robinson spent several summers in the early 1960's at the IBM Watson Research Center in Yorktown Heights, New York. There he collaborated with Calvin C. Elgot on a paper that developed a more realistic model of a digital computer (using programming languages with semantics) for random-access stored program (RASP) machines than that provided by a Turing machine. One major result they were able to establish was a proof that particular RASP machines could compute all partial recursive functions. This work was later extended to multiple-control RASP's with the capacity for parallel processing with programs able to handle computations in partial rather than serial order. Robinson coauthored a paper on the subject of "multiple control" with Elgot and J. E. Rutledge that was a pioneering work on the subject of parallel programming when it was published in 1967. Here the problem of programming highly parallel computers was treated formally, based upon a mathematical model of a parallel computer.

Character and Influence. Again and again, those who knew Abraham Robinson remarked on his capacity for "organic growth," especially his ability to bring together vastly different areas of mathematics and respond to new ideas and techniques that united them in his mind to produce fruitful and stimulating results. As Simon Kochen put it, ". . . his viewpoint was that of an applied mathematician in the original and best sense of that phrase; that is, in the sense of the 18th and 19th century mathematicians, who used the problems and insights of the real world (that is, physics) to develop mathematical ideas."[2]

Robinson was a man of great simplicity, modesty, and charm. He loved to travel and enjoyed meeting people. He studied ancient Greek, and was fluent in French, German, Hebrew, English, and several other languages. On various occasions he lectured in Italian, Portuguese, and Spanish.

Perhaps Robinson's overall character and significance as a mathematician were best captured by the logician Kurt Gödel, who at the time of Robinson's death said that he was a mathematician "whom I valued very highly indeed, not only as a personal friend, but also as the one mathematical logician who accomplished incomparably more than anybody else in making this logic fruitful to mathematics."[3]

NOTES

1. As reported by George B. Seligman in his "Biography of Abraham Robinson," in *Selected Papers of Abraham Robinson*, H. J. Keisler *et al.*, eds. (New Haven, 1979), I, xxiv.
2. Simon Kochen, "The Pure Mathematician. On Abraham Robinson's Work in Mathematical Logic," in *Bulletin of the London Mathematical Society*, **8** (1976), 313.

3. Kurt Gödel, in a letter to Mrs. Abraham Robinson, 10 May 1974; Robinson Papers, Sterling Library, Yale University.

BIBLIOGRAPHY

I. ORIGINAL WORKS. A selection of Robinson's most important publications, including one of his earliest papers not previously published ("On Nil-ideals in General Rings," 1939), is in *Selected Papers of Abraham Robinson*, H. J. Keisler, S. Körner, W. A. J. Luxemburg, and A. D. Young, eds., 3 vols. (New Haven, 1979). Readers should also consult the special historical and critical introductions in each volume. Robinson's papers, including correspondence and lecture notes, are in the archives of Yale University, Sterling Library, New Haven.

II. SECONDARY LITERATURE. Joseph W. Dauben, "Abraham Robinson and Nonstandard Analysis: History, Philosophy, and Foundations of Mathematics," in William Aspray and Philip Kitcher, eds., *History and Philosophy of Mathematics* (Minneapolis, 1988), 177–200; Martin Davis, *Applied Nonstandard Analysis* (New York, 1977); W. A. J. Luxemburg, *Non-standard Analysis. Lectures on A. Robinson's Theory of Infinitesimals and Infinitely Large Numbers*, 2nd, rev. ed. (Pasadena, Calif. 1964), and *Introduction to the Theory of Infinitesimals* (New York, 1976), with K. D. Stroyan; Angus J. Macintyre, "Abraham Robinson, 1918–1974," in *Bulletin of the American Mathematical Society*, **83** (1977), 646–666; George B. Seligman, "Biography of Abraham Robinson," in Robinson's *Selected Papers* (see Notes); and Alec D. Young, Simon Kochen, Stephan Körner, and Peter Roquette, "Abraham Robinson," in *Bulletin of the London Mathematical Society*, **8** (1976), 307–323.

JOSEPH W. DAUBEN

ROHN, KARL (*b.* Schwanheim, near Bensheim, Hesse, Germany, 28 January 1855; *d.* Leipzig, Germany, 4 August 1920)

Rohn entered the Polytechnikum at Darmstadt in 1872, studying engineering and then mathematics. He continued his work in the latter at the universities of Leipzig and Munich, receiving his doctorate at Munich in 1878 and qualifying as lecturer at Leipzig a year later. In 1884 he became an assistant professor at Leipzig, and in 1887 full professor of descriptive geometry at the Technische Hochschule in Dresden. From 1904 until his death he was full professor at the University of Leipzig.

In his dissertation and in his *Habilitationsschrift* Rohn, stimulated by F. Klein, examined the relationship of Kummer's surface to hyperelliptic functions. In these early writings he demonstrated his ability to work out the connections between geometric and algebraic-analytic relations. In the following years

Rohn further developed these capacities and became an acknowledged master in all questions concerning the algebraic geometry of the real P_2 and P_3, where it is possible to overlook the different figures. This concerns forms of algebraic curves and surfaces up to degree 4, linear and quadratic congruences, and complexes of lines in P_3. Gifted with a strong spatial intuition, Rohn possessed outstanding ability to select geometric facts from algebraic equations.

In several instances no decisive advance has been made on the results that Rohn obtained. This is especially true of his investigations on fourth-degree surfaces having one triple point or having finitely many isolated singular points. Most later studies concerning fourth-degree surfaces with only isolated singularities have been devoted to Kummer surfaces, which possess the greatest number of singular points (sixteen). Early in his career Rohn also constructed spatial models of the surfaces and space-curves he was studying. Rohn was the first to solve the difficult problem concerning the possible positions of the eleven ovals that the real branch of a sixth-degree plane curve can maximally possess. These problems were of great interest to Hilbert, but he did not succeed in resolving them.

BIBLIOGRAPHY

I. ORIGINAL WORKS. Rohn's writings include "Über Flächen 4. Ordnung mit dreifachem Punkte," in *Mathematische Annalen*, **24** (1884), 55–151; "Über Flächen 4. Ordnung mit 8–16 Knotenpunkten," in *Berichte über die Verhandlungen der Sächsischen Akademie der Wissenschaften zu Leipzig*, **36** (1884), 52–60; *Lehrbuch der darstellenden Geometrie*, 2 vols. (Leipzig, 1893–1896), written with E. Papperitz; and "Die ebene Kurve 6. Ordnung mit 11 Ovalen," in *Berichte über die Verhandlungen der Sächsischen Akademie der Wissenschaften zu Leipzig*, **63** (1911), 540–555.

II. SECONDARY LITERATURE. See O. Hölder, "Nekrolog für K. Rohn," in *Leipziger Berichte*, **72** (1920), 107–127; and F. Schur, "Karl Rohn," in *Jahresbericht der Deutschen Mathematiker-vereinigung*, **32** (1923), 201–211.

WERNER BURAU

ROLLE, MICHEL (*b.* Ambert, Basse-Auvergne, France, 21 April 1652; *d.* Paris, France, 8 November 1719)

The son of a shopkeeper, Rolle received only a very elementary education. He worked first as a transcriber for a notary and then for various attorneys in his native region. At the age of twenty-three he moved to Paris. Married early and burdened with a family, he had difficulty earning sufficient money as master scribe and reckoner. But by independent study he learned algebra and Diophantine analysis. In the *Journal des sçavans* of 31 August 1682 Rolle gave an elegant solution to a difficult problem publicly posed by Ozanam: to find four numbers the difference of any two of which is a perfect square as well as the sum of the first three. Ozanam had stated that the smallest of the four numbers would have at least fifty figures. Rolle provided a solution in which the four numbers were expressed by homogeneous polynomials in two variables and of degree twenty. The smallest numbers found in this fashion each had only seven figures.

This brilliant exploit brought Rolle public recognition. Colbert took an interest in him and obtained for him a reward and, it was said, a pension. Rolle later enjoyed the patronage of the minister Louvois. He gave lessons in elementary mathematics to the latter's fourth son, Camille Le Tellier, abbé de Louvois (1675–1718). Rolle even received an administrative post in the ministry of war, from which he soon resigned.

Rolle entered the Académie des Sciences in 1685 with the title—rather disconcerting for us—of *élève astronome*. When the Académie was reorganized in 1699 he became *pensionnaire géomètre*, a post that assured him a regular salary. In 1708 he suffered an attack of apoplexy. He recovered, but a second attack in 1719 proved fatal.

Although it was his skill in Diophantine analysis that made Rolle's reputation, his favorite area was the algebra of equations, in which he published *Traité d'algèbre* (1690), his most famous work. In this book he designated, following Albert Girard (1629), the *n*th root of a number a, $\sqrt[n]{a}$, not as $\sqrt{na}$, as was usually done before him. His notation soon became generally accepted. He retained the Cartesian equality sign ∞ until 1691, when he adopted the equal sign ($=$), which originated with Robert Recorde (1557).

In 1691, Rolle adopted, in advance of many of his contemporaries and in opposition to Descartes, the present order relation for the set of the real numbers: "I take $-2a$ for a greater quantity than $-5a$."

Rolle's *Algèbre* contains interesting considerations on systems of affine equations. Following the techniques established by Bachet de Méziriac (1621), Rolle utilized the Euclidean algorithm for resolving Diophantine linear equations. He employed the same algorithm to find the greatest common divisor of two polynomials, and in 1691 he was able to eliminate one variable between two equations.

The *Traité d'algèbre*, the language of which is so special, has remained famous, thanks notably to the method of "cascades." Rolle used this method to separate the roots of an algebraic equation. He justified it by showing (1691) that if $P(x) = 0$ is the given equation, and if it admits two reals roots a and b, then $P'(b) = (b - a) Q(b)$, where Q is a polynomial. $P'(x)$, a polynomial derived from $P(x)$, is what Rolle called the "first cascade" of the polynomial $P(x)$. The second cascade is our second derivative, and so on.

Arranging the real roots in ascending order, Rolle showed that between two consecutive roots of $P(x)$ there exists a root of $P'(x)$. His methods of demonstration are elaborations of the method utilized by Jan Hudde in his search for extrema (1658).

In 1846 Giusto Bellavitis gave Rolle's name to the present theorem: if the function $f(x)$ is defined and continuous on the segment $[ab]$, if $f(a) = f(b)$, and if $f'(x)$ exists in the interior of the segment, then $f'(x)$ is equal to zero at least once in the segment.

In 1699 the three pensionary geometers of the Academy were the Abbé Jean Gallois, a partisan of Greek mathematics; Rolle, an autodidact but very well versed in Cartesian techniques; and Pierre Varignon, who favored the ideas of Leibniz. L'Hospital was an honorary academician; in 1696 he had published *Analyse des infiniment petits*. The Academy was very divided over infinitesimal analysis. Rolle—incited, it was said, by influential persons—vigorously attacked infinitesimal analysis and strove to demonstrate that it was not based on solid reasoning and led to errors. Among the examples he chose were the curves

$$y - b = (x^2 - 2ax + a^2 - b^2)^{2/3} \text{ and}$$
$$y = 2 + \sqrt{(4 + 2x)} + \sqrt{(4x)}.$$

Varignon defended the new methods and pointed out the paralogisms that Rolle displayed in discussing these examples. The latter, too plebeian to control himself, created an uproar. A commission established to resolve the matter was unable to come to a decision. The dispute lasted from 1700 to 1701, and then continued in the *Journal des sçavans* in the form of exchanges between Rolle and a newcomer, Joseph Saurin. The Academy again intervened, and in the fall of 1706 Rolle acknowledged to Varignon, Fontenelle, and Malebranche that he had given up and fully recognized the value of the new techniques.

Rolle also displayed a certain vigor in the field of Cartesian geometry. In 1693, in the *Journal des sçavans*, he offered a prize of sixty pistoles for the solution, without the use of his methods, of the following problem: construct the roots of an equation by utilizing a given arc of an algebraic curve. Before leaving Paris, Johann I Bernoulli had given a solution to this problem in Latin to L'Hospital and had requested him to submit a French translation to the

Journal. The solution did not meet with Rolle's approval, and the resulting polemic lasted for five numbers of the *Journal*; the sixty pistoles remained in the donor's coffers.

Another of Rolle's achievements is an observation that, though initially paradoxical, was recognized as correct by Saurin: two arcs of algebraic curves the convexity of which is in the same direction can have a large number of common points.

Rolle was a skillful algebraist who broke with Cartesian techniques; and his opposition to infinitesimal methods, in the final analysis, was beneficial.

BIBLIOGRAPHY

I. ORIGINAL WORKS. Rolle's books are *Traité d'algèbre, ou principes généraux pour résoudre les questions de mathématique* (Paris, 1690); *Démonstration d'une méthode pour resoudre les egalitez de tous les degrez; suivie de deux autres méthodes dont la première donne les moyens de résoudre ces mêmes égalitez par la géométrie, et la seconde pour résoudre plusieurs questions de Diophante qui n'ont pas encore esté resoluës* (Paris, 1691); and *Méthode pour résoudre les équations indéterminées de l'algèbre* (Paris, 1699). See also two papers in *Mémoires de l'Académie royale des Sciences:* "Règles pour l'approximation des racines des cubes irrationnels" (read 31 Jan. 1692), **10**; and "Méthode pour résoudre les égalités de tous degrés qui sont exprimés en termes généraux" (read 15 Mar. 1692), *ibid.*, 26–33.

Rolle's later papers in the Mémoires of the Académie des Sciences include "Remarques sur les lignes géométriques" (1702), 171–175, (1703), 132–139; "Du nouveau système de l'infini" (1703), 312–336; "De l'inverse des tangents" (1705), 222–225; "Méthode pour trouver les foyers des lignes géométriques de tous les genres" (1706), 284–295; "Recherches sur les courbes géométriques et mécaniques, où l'on propose quelques règles pour trouver les rayons de leurs développées" (1707), 370–381; "Éclaircissements sur la construction des égalitez" (1708), 339–374 (1709), 320–350; "De l'évanouissement des quantités inconnues" (1709), 419–451; "Règles et remarques pour la construction des égalités" (1711), 86–100; "Remarque sur un paradoxe des effections géométriques" (1713), 243–261, read 12 July 1713; and "Suite des remarques sur un paradoxe des effections géométrique" (1714), 5–22, read 10 Jan. 1714.

Rolle also published many articles in the *Journal des sçavans* beginning in 1682.

II. SECONDARY LITERATURE. See the *éloge* by Fontenelle, read at the Académie des Sciences on 10 Apr. 1720, Niels Nielsen, *Géomètres français du dix-huitième siècle* (Copenhagen, 1935), 382–390; Gino Loria, *Storia delle matematiche*, 2nd ed. (Milan, 1950), 670–673; J. E. Montucla, *Histoire des mathématiques*, II (Paris, 1758), 361–368, 2nd. ed., III (Paris, 1802; repr. 1960), 110–116, (which contains a detailed account of the polemic over the infinitesimal calculus—Montucla had access to Varignon's MSS); Cramer, ed., *Virorum Celebrium G. G. Leibnitii et Johan Bernoullii commercium philosophicum et mathematicum*, 2 vols. (Lausanne, 1745)—see index and II, 148 for Cramer's note containing a list of the articles in the *Journal des sçavans* concerning the dispute between Rolle and Saurin; O. Spiess, ed., *Der Briefwechsel von Johann I Bernoulli* (Basel, 1955)—see index and p. 393 for a note on the articles in the *Journal des sçavans* concerning the prize offered by Rolle and claimed by Johann I Bernoulli; Malebranche, *Oeuvres complètes*, XVII, pt. 2 (Mathematica) (Paris, 1968); Pierre Costabel, *Pierre Varignon (1654–1722) et la diffusion en France du calcul différentiel et intégral*, in the series Conférences du Palais de la Découverte (Paris, 1965); Petre Sergescu, *Un episod din batalia pentru triumful calculului diferential: polemica Rolle-Saurin 1702–1705* (Bucharest, 1942), repr. in *Essais scientifiques* (Timisoara, 1944); D. E. Smith, *A Source Book in Mathematics* (1929; repr. New York, 1959), 253–260, which contains Rolle's theorem and partial English translations of the works of 1690 and 1691; L. E. Dickson, *History of the Theory of Numbers*, II (New York, 1934), 45 (on linear Diophantine equations) and p. 447 (on the problem posed by Ozanam that Rolle solved); Dickson nowhere cites the passage of the 1691 work concerning Diophantine analysis; Jean Prestet, *Nouveaux élémens des mathématiques*, II (Paris, 1689), 238, a solution, by a different procedure, of Ozanam's problem and a criticism of Rolle's method—this work is not cited in Dickson; and Jakob Hermann, "Observationes in schediasma quod Dn. Rolle cum hac inscriptione: Éclaircissements sur la construction des égalitez," in *Commentariis Academiae Regiae Scientiarum* (1708, published in 1727), *Miscellanea Berolinensia*, III (Berlin, 1927), 131–146.

JEAN ITARD

ROOMEN, ADRIAAN VAN (*b.* Louvain, Belgium [?], 29 September 1561; *d.* Mainz, Germany, 4 May 1615)

Roomen's father, for whom he was named, was a merchant; his mother was Maria van den Daele. According to the dedication of his *Ideae mathematicae* (1593), he studied mathematics and philosophy at the Jesuit College in Cologne. In 1585 he spent some time in Rome, where he met Clavius. From about 1586 to 1592 van Roomen was professor of medicine and mathematics at Louvain. He then became professor of medicine at Würzburg, where on 17 May 1593 he gave his first lecture. From 1596 to 1603 he was also "mathematician" of the chapter in Würzburg; his duties included drawing up the calendar each year. In 1598 van Roomen was at Prague, where the Emperor Rudolf II very probably bestowed the titles of count palatine and imperial court physician upon him. In

1601 he was in France for three months to recover his health, and during his stay he visited Viète. Between 1603 and 1610 he lived in both Würzburg and Louvain; he was ordained a priest in the latter city at the end of 1604 or the beginning of 1605.

In 1610 van Roomen was invited to teach mathematics in Zamosc, Poland; his pupil was most likely Thomas Zamojski, son of the founder of the college in that town. During his sojourn there (September 1610–July 1612) he became acquainted with the Polish mathematician Jan Brożek, whom he met several times and with whom he conducted a correspondence. In one of his letters to van Roomen, Brożek posed two questions. The first concerned the dispute between the astronomers Giovanni Antonio Magini and David Origanus, and the second concerned a theorem on isoperimetric figures from the *Geometria* of Petrus Ramus. Van Roomen's answer to the latter question forms the most interesting part of the correspondence and was published by Brożek in his *Epistolae* (Cracow, 1615) and in his *Apologia* (Danzig, 1652).

An important part of van Roomen's works dealt with mathematical subjects, especially trigonometry and the calculation of chords in a circle. His first known work, *Ouranographia* (Louvain or Antwerp, 1591), is a speculative consideration on nature, specifically the number and the motion of the heavenly spheres. His *Ideae mathematicae pars prima* (Antwerp, 1593), dedicated to Clavius, was intended to be the first part of a great work on the calculation of chords in a circle and on the quadrature of the circle. In it van Roomen hoped to publish his discoveries on regular polygons; but except for some fragments, the remainder of the work did not appear. In the introduction van Roomen states that for some years he had tried to find a general rule to calculate the sides of all regular polygons. He discovered three methods, one of which used algebraic equations. For all regular polygons from the triangle up to the eighty-sided polygon he derived the equations and sent them to Ludolph van Ceulen, to whom he left the calculation of the solutions. In his work van Roomen gives, without any proof, the calculation to thirty-two decimal places of the sides of regular three-, four-, five-, and fifteen-sided polygons and of the polygons arising from the preceding by a continuous doubling of the number of the sides. He continued his calculations up to the polygon with $15 \cdot 2^{60}$ sides, and with the help of the side of the regular 251,658,240-sided polygon he calculated π to sixteen decimal places.

At the beginning of his treatise van Roomen propounded to all the geometers the famous equation of the forty-fifth degree. An ambassador from the Netherlands told Henry IV that France did not possess a single geometer capable of solving the problem. Henry sent for Viète, who at once gave a solution and, the next day, twenty-two more. In his turn Viète proposed to van Roomen the Apollonian problem: to draw a circle touching three given circles. Van Roomen published his answer in *Problema Apolloniacum* (Würzburg, 1596). He solved the problem by the intersection of two hyperbolas, but he did not give a construction in the proper sense. Viète published his own geometrical solution in his *Apollonius Gallus* (Paris, 1600).

In 1594 Scaliger published his *Cyclometrica elementa duo*, in which he tried to prove that Archimedes' approximation of π was incorrect. At once he was attacked by several mathematicians, among them Viète and van Ceulen, as well as van Roomen in his *In Archimedis circuli dimensionem* (Geneva, 1597). The first part of this tract contained a reedition of the Greek text of Archimedes' *On the Measurement of the Circle*, with a Latin translation and an elaborate analysis. In the second part, "Apologia pro Archimede ad clarissimum virum Josephum Scaligerum," van Roomen refuted Scaliger's objections to Archimedes' tract. In the third part he refuted, in ten dialogues, the quadratures of the circle of Oronce Finé, Simon van der Eycke, Raymarus Ursus, and Scaliger.

Van Roomen also wrote a commentary on al-Khwārizmī's *Algebra*, "In Mahumedis Algebram prolegomena," which is now lost, the copy at the University of Louvain having been destroyed in 1914 and that at Douai in 1944. Van Roomen was partial to extensive calculations, as can be seen in his *Chordarum arcubus circuli* (Würzburg, 1602). In this work he gave, to 220 or 300 decimal places, the square roots needed for the calculation of the side of the regular thirty-sided polygon. He also wrote several works on plane and spherical trigonometry, including the *Speculum astronomicum* (Louvain, 1606) and the *Canon triangulorum sphaericorum* (Mainz, 1609). These works contain the first systematic use of a trigonometric notation.

In his terminology van Roomen imitated Viète, using the expressions "prosinus" and "transinuosa" for tangent and secant, respectively. The tables for sines, tangents, and secants, together with their cofunctions, in the *Canon triangulorum* were borrowed from Clavius. A last contribution to the project developed in his *Ideae mathematicae* is in van Roomen's *Mathematicae analyseos triumphus* (Louvain, 1609). In this work he calculated the sides of the nine-sided and eighteen-sided regular polygons to 108 decimal places.

Besides his printed works there were manuscripts,

now lost, containing unpublished works by van Roomen: the "Tractatus de notatione numerorum" and the "Nova multiplicandi, dividendi, quadrata componendi, radices extrahendi ratio." The last, dealing with his methods for calculating with large numbers, was published in 1904 by H. Bosmans.

BIBLIOGRAPHY

The best survey of van Roomen's life and works is the article by P. Bockstaele in *Nationaal biografisch woordenboek* (Brussels, 1966), cols. 751–765, which also contains an extensive bibliography.

H. L. L. BUSARD

ROSANES, JAKOB (*b*. Brody, Austria-Hungary [now Ukrainian S.S.R.], 16 August 1842; *d*. Breslau, Germany [now Wrocław, Poland], 6 January 1922)

Rosanes was the son of Leo Rosanes, a merchant. From 1860 until 1865 he studied at the universities of Berlin and Breslau; having taken the Ph.D. at the latter in 1865, he remained there for the rest of his career. In 1870 he became *Privatdozent*, in 1873 professor extraordinarius, and in 1876 ordinary professor; he also served the university as its rector during the academic year 1903–1904.

Rosanes' mathematical papers concerned the various questions of algebraic geometry and invariant theory that were current in the nineteenth century. One of his first papers, written with Moritz Pasch, discussed a problem on conics in closure-position. In 1870 he provided a demonstration that each plane Cremona transformation can be factored as a product of quadratic transformations, a theorem that M. Noether also proved independently at about the same time. Both demonstrations were, however, incomplete and were put into final form by G. Castelnuovo some thirty years later.

Rosanes' contributions to the theory of invariants were made in the 1870's and 1880's. He gave conditions for a form to be expressed as a power-sum of other forms, then, in a series of papers, treated linearly dependent point systems in a plane and in space. In later years his scientific productivity declined, but his rector's lecture of 1903, on the characteristic features of nineteenth-century mathematics, is noteworthy. Like a number of other mathematicians, Rosanes was also interested in chess and published a book on *Theorie und Praxis des Schachspiels*. He retired from the university in 1911 and spent the rest of his life in Breslau. In 1876 he married Emilie Rawitscher.

BIBLIOGRAPHY

Rosanes' works, cited in the text, are "Über das einem Kegelschnitt umbeschriebene und einem anderen einbeschriebene Polygon," in *Journal für die reine und angewandte Mathematik*, **64** (1865), 126–166, written with M. Pasch; "Über diejenigen rationalen Substitutionen, welche eine rationale Umkehrung zulassen," *ibid.*, **73** (1871), 97–111; "Über linear abhängige Punktsysteme," *ibid.*, **88** (1880), 241–273; and "Charakteristische Züge in der Entwicklung der Mathematik des 19. Jahrhunderts," in *Jahresbericht der Deutschen Mathematische-Vereinigung*, **13** (1904), 17–30.

WERNER BURAU

ROSENHAIN, JOHANN GEORG (*b*. Königsberg, Prussia, 10 June 1816; *d*. Königsberg, 14 May 1887)

Rosenhain studied at the University of Königsberg, where he earned the Ph.D. In 1844 he qualified as lecturer at the University of Breslau and remained there as a *Privatdozent* until 1848. His participation in the revolutionary activities of 1848 deprived him of any chance to further his career at Breslau. He therefore qualified as lecturer again in 1851, this time at the University of Vienna. In 1857 he returned to Königsberg, where he was an associate professor until a year before his death.

While studying at Königsberg, Rosenhain was especially close to Jacobi; and while still a student in the 1830's he edited some of Jacobi's lectures. His own scientific activity was mainly inspired by Jacobi, who had enriched the theory of elliptic functions with many new concepts and had formulated, on the basis of Abel's theorem, the inverse problem, named for him, for an Abelian integral on a curve of the arbitrary genus p. The next step was to solve this problem for $p = 2$.

In 1846 the Paris Academy had offered a prize for the solution of that problem, and Rosenhain won it in 1851 for his work entitled "Sur les fonctions de deux variables à quatre périodes, qui sont les inverses des intégrales ultra-elliptiques de la première classe." Göpel had solved this problem at almost the same time, but he did not enter the competition. Rosenhain's work followed Jacobi even more closely than did Göpel's.

In his unpublished dissertation Rosenhain had already treated triple periodic functions in two variables. The solution of the inverse problem for $p = 2$ presented him with considerable difficulties, as can be seen in his communications to Jacobi published in Crelle's *Journal*. It was not until chapter 3 of his prize essay that he introduced, in the same manner as

Göpel, the sixteen θ functions in two variables and examined in detail their periodic properties and the algebraic relations.

Most important, Rosenhain demonstrated (in modern terminology) that the squares of the quotients of these sixteen θ functions can be conceived of as functions of the product surface of a hyperelliptic curve of $p = 2$ with itself. Starting from this point and employing the previously derived addition theorem of the θ quotients, Rosenhain succeeded in demonstrating more simply than Göpel that these quotients solve the inverse problem for $p = 2$. Rosenhain never fulfilled the expectations held for him in his younger years, and published nothing after his prize essay.

BIBLIOGRAPHY

Extracts from most of Rosenhain's letters to Jacobi concerning hyperelliptic transcendentals are in *Journal für die reine und angewandte Mathematik*, **40** (1850), 319–360. Rosenhain's prizewinning work is "Sur les fonctions de deux variables à quatre périodes, qui sont les inverses des intégrales ultra-elliptiques de la première classe," in *Mémoires présentés par divers savants*, 2nd ser., **11** (1851), 361–468; also translated into German as *Abhandlung über die Functionen zweier Variabler mit vier Perioden*, Ostwalds Klassiker der Exakten Wissenschaften, no. 65 (Leipzig, 1895).

WERNER BURAU

ROWNING, JOHN (*b.* Ashby, Lincolnshire, England, 1701[?]; *d.* London, England, November 1771)

Educated in local schools, Rowning may then have worked with his father, also John Rowning (probably a watchmaker, as another son entered that trade, and John was credited with mechanical abilities). He was admitted as sizar to Magdalene College, Cambridge, in 1721. He gained the B.A. in 1724, a fellowship in 1725, and the M.A. in 1728. A college tutor for some years, he joined William Deane, an instrument-maker in London, about 1733 in giving courses of lectures in experimental philosophy. In 1733 he wrote a paper describing a barometer with a changeable scale of variation.

In 1734 Rowning became rector of Westley Waterless, Cambridgeshire, and by 1738, rector of Anderby, Lincolnshire, one of six livings in gift of Magdalene College. He became a member of the Gentleman's Society of Spalding, which was founded in 1710 and was the oldest provincial learned society in England. Under his urging, the Society temporarily forgot its antiquarian pursuits in the study of experimental philosophy. In 1756 he published the preliminaries to a projected text (never printed) in which he outlines his method of teaching fluxions and denies the "Analyst's" (George Berkeley) objections to the subject. His second, and last, mathematical work was a paper describing an analogue machine for the graphical solution of equations.

His most significant work was the *Compendious System of Natural Philosophy*, one of the most popular texts throughout the eighteenth century. The work was used at Cambridge and Oxford, at the College of William and Mary in Virginia, at many dissenting academies, and by John Wesley as a text for his itinerant preachers, it was also mentioned in the correspondence of people as various as John Adams, William Beckford, and Joseph Priestley. Chiefly distinguished for its clarity, the work should also be noted for its explicit rejection of Newtonian ether, its explanation of forces as the continuing action of God upon matter, and its proposal of alternating spheres of attraction and repulsion some twenty years before Boškovič's *Philosophiae*.

Rowning died at his London lodgings late in November 1771; he left a daughter, Mrs. Thomas Brown of Spalding, his heiress and executrix.

BIBLIOGRAPHY

I. ORIGINAL WORKS. Rowning's works are "A Description of a Barometer, Wherein the Scale of Variation May Be Increased at Pleasure," in *Philosophical Transactions of the Royal Society*, **38** (1733–1734), 39–42; the barometer is also illustrated and described in "Barometer," in *Encyclopaedia Britannica*, 3rd ed., III (1797), 25, with plate on facing page; *A Compendious System of Natural Philosophy: With Notes Containing the Mathematical Demonstrations, and Some Occasional Remarks*, pt. 1 (Cambridge, 1735); pt. 2 (London, 1736); pt. 3 (London, 1737); pt. 4 (London, 1742–1743). Each pt. was also revised and republished as successive pts. were issued, and any extant set may consist of varying eds. of pts. and secs. within pts. The 6th, 7th, and 8th eds. appear to be all of the same years: 1767, 1772, and 1779 respectively; *A Preliminary Discourse to an Intended Treatise on the Fluxionary Method* (London, 1756), reviewed by William Bewley, in *Monthly Review*, **14** (1756), 286–289; "Directions for Making a Machine for Finding the Roots of Equations Universally, With the Manner of Using It," in *Philosophical Transactions of the Royal Society*, **60** (1770), 240–256; and a copy of the syllabus of Rowning's course, *A Compleat Course of Experimental Philosophy and Astronomy*, is in the Science Museum, Oxford, MS Radcliffe 29.

II. SECONDARY LITERATURE. On Rowning and his work, see John Nichols, *Literary Anecdotes of the Eighteenth*

Century, VI, pt. 1 (London, 1812), 109, 124; Robert E. Schofield, *Mechanism and Materialism* (Princeton, 1970), 34–39; and John Venn and J. A. Venn, *Alumni Cantabrigienses*, III, pt. 1 (Cambridge, 1927).

ROBERT E. SCHOFIELD

RUDIO, FERDINAND (*b.* Wiesbaden, Germany, 2 August 1856; *d.* Zurich, Switzerland, 21 June 1929)

Rudio completed his secondary schooling in Wiesbaden, then, in 1874, entered the Zurich Polytechnic to study physics and mathematics. From 1877 until 1880 he studied at the University of Berlin, from which he received the doctorate *magna cum laude* with a dissertation on Kummer's problem of determining all surfaces of which the centers of curvature form second-order confocal surfaces. Rudio's solution utilized reduction to a differential equation. He also worked in group theory, algebra, and geometry. In 1881 he returned to Zurich as lecturer at the Polytechnic; he was appointed professor of mathematics there in 1889 and served in that post until 1928. He also administered the Polytechnic's library from 1893 to 1919.

Rudio wrote on a number of topics in the history of mathematics, including the quadrature of the circle, Simplicius' work on quadratures, and Hippocrates' lunes. He also composed biographies of contemporary mathematicians, and wrote a history of the Zurich Naturforschende Gesellschaft for the years 1746 to 1896.

Of particular importance was Rudio's project for editing the collected works of Euler. He first proposed this edition in 1883, on the occasion of the centenary of Euler's death, then brought it up again before the meeting of the first International Congress of Mathematicians at Zurich in 1897, and finally suggested it as an appropriate memorial for the bicentennial of Euler's birth in 1907. His efforts bore fruit in 1909, when the Naturforschende Gesellschaft decided to undertake the work, and named Rudio general editor. He himself edited two volumes (the *Commentationes arithmeticae*) and brought out an additional three in collaboration, including the *Introductio in analysin infinitorum*. In all, he supervised the production of some thirty volumes.

BIBLIOGRAPHY

I. ORIGINAL WORKS. Rudio's publications include "Zur Theorie der Flächen, deren Krümmungsmittelpunktsflächen confocale Flächen zweiten Grades sind," an abstract of his inaugural dissertation (Berlin, 1880), published in *Journal für die reine und angewandte Mathematik*, **95** (1883), 240–246; *Archimedes, Huygens, Lambert, Legendre. Vier Abhandlungen* (Leipzig, 1892); "Die Möndchen des Hippokrates," in *Vierteljahrsschrift der Naturforschenden Gesellschaft in Zürich*, **50** (1905), 177–200; and "Der Bericht des Simplicius über die Quadraturen des Antiphon und des Hippokrates," in *Bibliotheca mathematica*, 3rd ser., **3** (1902), 7–62.

II. SECONDARY LITERATURE. See G. Pólya, obituary, in *Vierteljahrsschrift der Naturforschenden Gesellschaft in Zürich*, **74** (1929), 329–330; Alice Rudio, "F. Rudio," in *Biographisches Lexikon verstorbener Schweizer*, II (Zurich, 1948), 230; and C. Schröter and R. Fueter, "Ferdinand Rudio zum 70. Geburtstag," in *Vierteljahrsschrift der Naturforschenden Gesellschaft in Zürich*, **71** (1926), 115–135, with portrait and bibliography of his works.

J. J. BURCKHARDT

RUDOLFF (or **RUDOLF**), **CHRISTOFF** (*b.* Jauer, Silesia [now Jawor, Poland], end of the fifteenth century; *d.* Vienna, Austria, first half of the sixteenth century)

Virtually nothing is known about Rudolff's life.[1] It was formerly thought that he was born in 1499 and died in 1545, but these dates are not confirmed by any documentary evidence.[2] The earliest reliable information attests his presence in Vienna in 1525, the year in which he dedicated his *Coss* to the bishop of Brixen (now Bressanone, Italy). This book was the first comprehensive work in German on algebra, or *Coss*, as it was then called. Rudolff learned the subject from Grammateus, who taught at the University of Vienna from 1517 to 1521. In 1521 Grammateus went to Nuremberg and then Erfurt, not returning to Vienna until the summer semester of 1525.[3] Consequently, Rudolff must have been in Vienna before 1521. He supported himself by giving private lessons; and although he was not affiliated with the university, he was able to use its library. Some critics accused him of stealing the examples for his *Coss* from the Vienna Library, an accusation against which he was defended by Michael Stifel in the preface to the new edition of the *Coss*. In 1526 Rudolff published an arithmetic book entitled *Künstliche Rechnung mit der Ziffer und mit den Zahlpfennigen*, and in 1530 an *Exempelbüchlin*; which was reprinted as "exempelbüchle" in later editions of the *Künstliche Rechnung*. He stated his intention to publish an improved, Latin version of his *Coss* containing new examples, but he never did so.[4]

The *Coss* is divided into two parts. In the first, Rudolff devotes twelve chapters to the topics that the reader must master before taking up the study of algebra (the solution of equations). In chapters 1–4 he presents the basic operations and the rule of three, giving examples with whole numbers and fractions, and then treats the extraction of square and cube roots. In the section "Progredieren" he states in the style of recipes the summation formulas of arithmetic and geometric series. By relating the geometric series, the "Progredieren in Proportz" (*proportio dupla, tripla,* and so forth), to the series of natural numbers, he obtains the configuration

0	1	2	3	4	5	· · ·
1	2	4	8	16	32	· · · ·

This procedure enables him to determine an arbitrarily high member of the geometric series.

In chapters 5 and 6 Rudolff carries out the four operations and the rule of three on algebraic polynomials,[5] after first setting forth the names and symbols of the powers of the unknowns. The schema

0	1	2	3	4	5	6	7	8	9
r	z	c	zz	β	zc	$b\beta$	zzz	cc	

shows that he considers the proper designation of a member without x to be $x^0 = 1$. (Grammateus still used N (for *numerus*) in such cases instead of 0.) Chapters 7–11 are devoted to roots, binomials, and residues. Rudolff distinguishes three types of roots: rational, irrational, and communicant. Two roots are communicant if they have a common rational factor: for example, $\sqrt[3]{16}$ and $\sqrt[3]{54}$. If a factor is brought under the radicals, then the "denominierte" number is formed; for example, $5\sqrt{18}$ gives rise to $\sqrt{450}$. Rudolff computes $\sqrt{a + \sqrt{b}} = \sqrt{c} + \sqrt{d}$, using letters instead of numbers.[6] The first part of the book concludes with a short explanation of the five types of "proportioned" numbers (*multiple, super-particular,* and so forth).

In part two of the *Coss* (which is divided into three sections) Rudolff discusses first- and second-degree equations and their variations of higher degree. He assumes the existence of only eight distinct *equationen* or "rules of the coss," not the twenty-four distinguished by earlier cossists. In his presentation of the sixth rule ($ax^2 + c = bx$) he deliberately admits only the one solution that fits the conditions of the problem under study. Later he recognized his error.[7] The second section offers rules (*cautelae*) for solving equations, and the third is a collection of problems containing over 400 examples. Some of the problems involve abstract numbers; others, taken from daily life, are presented in fantastic forms similar to those of the *Enigmata* of recreational mathematics. In some of the problems Rudolff introduces a second unknown, q (for *quantitas*). If there are more unknowns than equations, the problem is considered indeterminate.

For several such problems concerned with "splitting the bill" (*Zechenaufgaben*) Rudolff supplied all the possible solutions.[8]

The *Coss* ends with three cubic problems. Rudolff does not work out their solutions because, as he stated, he wanted to stimulate further algebraic research.[9] In an "addendum" he presents still another "verbal computation" and a drawing of a cube with edge $3 + \sqrt{2}$. According to Stifel, with this illustration Rudolff sought to hint at the solution of the cubic equation, which was then unknown.[10]

Rudolff's other major work, *Künstliche Rechnung mit der Ziffer und mit den Zahlpfennigen*, consists of three parts: a "Grundbüchlein," in which the beginner is introduced to computing with whole numbers and fractions; a "Regelbüchlein," which treats the rule of three and the "Welsh practice"; and an "Exempelbüchlein," some 300 problems that vividly evoke the commerce and manufacturing of the period. Rudolff also includes several *Enigmata*, termed "amusing calculations." Examples of this type are the rule of Ta-Yen, hound and hare, or the "horse sale," in which the price of thirty-two horseshoe nails is expressed in a geometric sequence. As in the *Coss*, the two number sequences are related to each other, with the first sequence again beginning with 0.[11]

The *Exempelbüchlin* that Rudolff published in 1530 contains 293 problems, as well as tables of measurements for many regions, a list of symbols used in gauging, and numerous hints for solving problems. Decimal fractions appear in the computation of compound interest.[12]

Rudolff's importance in the history of mathematics lies in his having written the first comprehensive book on algebra in German. In this work he went far beyond his teacher Grammateus, especially concerning calculation with rational and irrational polynomials. Rudolff was aware of the double root of the equation $ax^2 + b = cx$ and gave all the solutions to indeterminate first-degree equations. His writings are remarkable both for the occasional appearance of decimal fractions and for improvements in symbolism. Adding a diagonal stroke to the points used by earlier cossists, Rudolff introduced the signs $\sqrt{}$, $\sqrt[3]{}$, $\sqrt[4]{}$ for the second, third, and fourth roots.[13] His work also gives a hint of the beginnings of exponential arithmetic and the fundamental idea of logarithms—that is, setting x^0 equal to 1. His methodical hints on using the *Coss* are worth noting as well. In brief, Rudolff's role in the development of mathematical studies in Germany was analogous to that of Fibonacci in Italy.[14]

Rudolff learned arithmetic from early printed books

on the subject, some of which he cited.[15] It is obvious that he thoroughly studied Johannes Widman's arithmetic book (1489).[16] He also obtained information from other writings on algebra. He mentioned earlier books in which the solutions to problems are introduced by the words "ponatur una res,"[17] and in which the second power of the unknown is designated by the word "substantia" instead of "zensus." These remarks indicate Robert of Chester's translation of the *Algebra* of al-Khwārizmī, which exists in a fourteenth-century manuscript.[18] In particular, Rudolff used an algebraic treatise included in a volume compiled at Vienna by Johann Vögelin.[19] Further, he was acquainted, directly or indirectly, with the Regensburg algebra (1461), from which he took a problem involving computation of compound interest; this problem, the solution to which was $\sqrt{600} - 20$, was earlier used by Widman in his arithmetic book of 1489.[20]

Rudolff's *Künstliche Rechnung* was widely read and was reprinted as late as 1588, at Augsburg. The importance of the *Coss* was recognized by Gemma Frisius and Stifel, but it soon went out of print. In 1553 Stifel brought out a new edition of the *Coss* containing supplementary material.

NOTES

1. J. E. Scheibel, who, like Rudolff, came from Silesia, sought information about his compatriot. See *Einleitung zur mathematischen Bücherkenntnis*, I (Breslau, 1769–1775), 313. As late as 1850 nothing was known in Vienna concerning the circumstances of Rudolff's life. See *Zeitschrift für Slawistik*, **1** (1956), 132.
2. R. Wolf, *Geschichte der Astronomie* (Munich, 1877), 340.
3. On Grammateus see W. Kaunzner, "Über die Algebra bei Heinrich Schreyber," in *Verhandlungen des Historischen Vereins für Oberpfalz und Regensburg*, **110** (1970), 227–239; and *Neue deutsche Biographie*, VI (1964), 738–739.
4. See *Coss*, A_{II}r and *Künstliche Rechnung*, fol. s_4v.
5. The division by a polynomial was only an attempt at this operation; see *Coss*, fol. E_1r.
6. See *Coss*, fols. G_{III}r, P_7v, P_8r.
7. On the ambiguous wording of the sixth rule see *Künstliche Rechnung*, fol. s_4v f.
8. See *Coss*, R_{VI}r f.
9. The third of these problems—cited by Cantor (*Vorlesungen über Geschichte der Mathematik*, II, pt. 2, 426) and Smith (*History of Mathematics*, II, 458)—and the suggested method for solving it both derive from Stifel.
10. The drawing is in P. Treutlein, p. 89.
11. See *Künstliche Rechnung*, fol. s_2v.
12. The decimal fractions are separated by a stroke; for example: 393|75. See *Exempelbüchlin*, fol. x_1v.
13. See H. E. Wappler, "Zur Geschichte der deutschen Mathematik im 15. Jahrhundert," p. 13, n. 1.
14. On this point see M. Terquem, "Christophe Rudolff," p. 326.
15. See *Coss*, C_Vr.
16. The problem of "splitting the bill" (*Zechenaufgabe*) that Rudolff found in "an arithmetic book"—see *Coss*, R_{VI}v—

appeared earlier in the work by Widman. A comparison between Rudolff's problems and Widman's is given by Treutlein, pp. 120 f.

17. The solutions to problems in both the Regensburg algebra of 1461 and the Latin algebra of Codex Dresdensis C 80 begin with words such as "Pono quod lucrum sit una res" or "Pono quod A 1 r[em] habeat." See, respectively, M. Curtze, "Ein Beitrag zur Geschichte der Algebra in Deutschland im fünfzehnten Jahrhundert," pp. 58 ff.; and Wappler, *op. cit.*, p. 19.
18. Vienna, Cod. Vind. 4770; see L. C. Karpinski, *Robert of Chester's Latin Translation of the Algebra of al-Khowarizmi* (Ann Arbor, Mich., 1915), repr. as pt. I of Karpinski and J. G. Winter, *Contributions to the History of Science* (Ann Arbor, 1930).
19. This volume is Cod. Vind. 5277. See Wappler, *op. cit.*, p. 3, n. 2. Cod. Lat. Mon. 19691 is a copy of Cod. Vind. 5277. The marginal notes in the Vienna MS were incorporated into the text of the Munich MS. They both contain the 24 old rules of the cossists, as did Widman's Latin algebra. Widman's work had many problems in common with Cod. Lat. Mon. 26639. The relationships among all these texts have not yet been determined; on this question see W. Kaunzner, *Über Christoff Rudolff und seine Coss*, p. 2 and n. 28.
20. Problem 16 of the "Fünfften regl" in Rudolff's *Coss* (fol. X_{VI}r) appears in the following works: Cod. Dresd. C 80, fol. 356v (see Wappler, *op. cit.*, p. 21); the Regensburg algebra in Cod. Lat. Mon. 14908, fol. 149v (see Curtze, *op. cit.*, p. 61); and Widman's arithmetic of 1489, 127v.

BIBLIOGRAPHY

I. ORIGINAL WORKS. Rudolff's writings are *Behend und hübsch Rechnung durch die künstreichen Regeln Algebre so gemeincklich die Coss genent werden* (Strasbourg, 1525), new ed. by M. Stifel (Königsberg, 1553—the colophon is dated 1554); *Künstliche rechnung mit der ziffer vnd mit den Zal pfenningen sampt der Wellischen Practica vnnd allerley fortheil auff die Regel de Tri* (Vienna, 1526)—Smith, *Rara arithmetica*, p. 152, cites 11 eds. (there are some other eds., but here the 1550 ed. was used); and *Exempelbüchlin* (Augsburg, 1530, 1538, 1540), also included in later eds. of *Künstliche Rechnung*.

II. SECONDARY LITERATURE. See *Allgemeine deutsche Biographie*, XXIX, 571–572; M. Cantor, *Vorlesungen über Geschichte der Mathematik*, II, 2nd ed. (Leipzig, 1913), 397–399, 425–429; M. Curtze, "Ein Beitrag zur Geschichte der Algebra in Deutschland im fünfzehnten Jahrhundert," in *Abhandlungen zur Geschichte der Mathematik*, **7** (1895), 31–74; A. Drechsler, *Scholien zu Christoph Rudolphs Coss* (Dresden, 1851); C. J. Gerhardt, *Geschichte der Mathematik in Deutschland* (Munich, 1877), 54–59; W. Kaunzner, *Über Christoff Rudolff und seine Coss*, no. 67 in Veröffentlichungen des Forschungsinstituts des Deutschen Museums für die Geschichte der Naturwissenschaften und der Technik, ser. A (Munich, 1970); and *Deutsche Mathematiker des 15. und 16. Jahrhunderts und ihre Symbolik*, no. 90 in the same series (Munich, 1971); C. F. Müller, "Henricus Grammateus und sein *Algorismus de integris*," in *Programm Gymnasium Zwickau* (1896); D. E. Smith, *Rara arithmetica* (Boston–London, 1908), 151 ff.; and *History of Mathematics*, 2 vols. (New York, 1923–1925),

I, 328 f., and II, 721; M. Terquem, "Christophe Rudolf," in *Annali di scienze matematiche e fisiche*, **8** (1857), 325–338; P. Treutlein, "Die deutsche Coss," in *Abhandlungen zur Geschichte der Mathematik*, **2** (1879), 15 ff., 44 ff.; F. Unger, *Die Methodik der praktischen Arithmetik* (Leipzig, 1888), 238; and H. E. Wappler, "Zur Geschichte der deutschen Mathematik im 15. Jahrhundert," in *Programm Gymnasium Zwickau* (1887); and "Zur Geschichte der deutschen Algebra," in *Abhandlungen zur Geschichte der Mathematik*, **9** (1899), 537–554.

KURT VOGEL

RUFFINI, PAOLO (*b*. Valentano, Italy, 22 September 1765; *d*. Modena, Italy, 10 May 1822)

Ruffini was the son of Basilio Ruffini, a physician, and Maria Francesca Ippoliti. While he was in his teens, his family moved to Modena, where he spent the rest of his life. At the University of Modena he studied medicine, philosophy, literature, and mathematics, including geometry under Luigi Fantini and infinitesimal calculus under Paolo Cassiani. When Cassiani was appointed councillor of the Este domains, Ruffini, while still a student, was entrusted with his course on the foundations of analysis for the academic year 1787–1788. Ruffini obtained his degree in philosophy and medicine on 9 June 1788 and, soon afterward, that in mathematics. On 15 October 1788 he was appointed professor of the foundations of analysis, and in 1791 he replaced Fantini, who had been obliged by blindness to give up teaching, as professor of the elements of mathematics. Also in 1791 Ruffini was licensed by the Collegiate Medical Court of Modena to practice medicine. His exceptional versatility was reflected in his simultaneous activity as physician and researcher and teacher in mathematics—especially at a time when scientific specialization predominated.

Following the occupation of Modena by Napoleon's troops in 1796, Ruffini was appointed, against his wishes, representative from the department of Panaro to the Junior Council of the Cisalpine Republic. Relieved of these duties, he resumed his scientific activity at the beginning of 1798. His subsequent refusal, on religious grounds, to swear an oath of allegiance to the republic resulted in his exclusion from teaching and from holding any public office. Ruffini accepted the experience calmly, continuing to practice medicine and to pursue mathematical research. It was during this period that he published the mathematical theorem known as the Abel-Ruffini theorem: a general algebraic equation of higher than the fourth degree cannot be solved by means of radical-rational operations.

A preliminary demonstration of this result appeared in *Teoria generale delle equazioni* (1799). Discussions with mathematicians such as Malfatti, Gregorio Fontana, and Pietro Paoli led to publication of the theorem in refined form in *Riflessioni intorno alla soluzione delle equazioni algebriche generali* (1813). Ruffini's results were received with extreme reserve and suspicion by almost every leading mathematician. Only Cauchy accorded them full credence, writing to Ruffini in 1821: "Your memoir on the general resolution of equations is a work that has always seemed to me worthy of the attention of mathematicians and one that, in my opinion, demonstrates completely the impossibility of solving algebraically equations of higher than the fourth degree." Following its independent demonstration by Abel in 1824, the theorem eventually took its place in the general theory of the solubility of algebraic equations that Galois constructed on the basis of the theory of permutation groups.

Ruffini's methods began with the relations that Lagrange had discovered between solutions of third- and fourth-degree equations and permutations of three and four elements; and Ruffini's development of this starting point contributed effectively to the transition from classical to abstract algebra and to the theory of permutation groups. This theory is distinguished from classical algebra by its greater generality: it operates not with numbers or figures, as in traditional mathematics, but with indefinite entities, on which logical operations are performed.

Ruffini also developed the basic rule, named for him, for determining the quotient and remainder that result from the division of a polynomial in the variable x by a binomial of the form $x - a$. He treated the problem of determining the roots of any algebraic equation with a preestablished approximation by means of infinite algorisms (continuous fractions, development in series).

Ruffini was a staunch advocate of rigor in infinitesimal processes, a requirement that had assumed special importance toward the turn of the nineteenth century. Despite the success obtained following the algorismic systematization of calculus by Newton and Leibniz, there was an increasing awareness of the uncertainty of the foundations of infinitesimal analysis and of the lack of rigor of demonstrations in this field. A critical detail of the issue concerned the use of divergent and indeterminate series. As president of the Società Italiana dei Quaranta, Ruffini refused to approve two papers by Giuliano Frullani, presented by Paoli, because they used series of which the convergence had not been demonstrated. Although Frullani cited Euler and Laplace as having remained unconcerned about convergence in treating similar problems, Ruffini remained firm in his own demand for rigor. His position was supported by Cauchy in his *Analyse algébrique* (1821) and by Abel in a letter to Holmboe in 1826.

The application of Ruffini's mathematical outlook to philosophical questions is reflected in *Della immaterialità dell'anima* (1806), in which he enunciated the "theorem" that a being endowed with the faculty of knowledge is necessarily immaterial. His extremely detailed argument is developed by showing irresolvable differences between the properties of material beings and of beings endowed with the faculty of knowledge—such as the human soul. In another philosophical work, *Riflessioni critiche sopra il saggio filosofico intorno alla probabilità del signor Conte Laplace* (1821), Ruffini attempted to refute certain theses in Laplace's *Essai philosophique sur les probabilités* (1812) that he considered contrary to religion and morality. He began by rejecting the conception of Laplace's intelligence, which was inspired by the hypothesis of a rigid universal determinism. Ruffini argued from the basis of man's direct psychological experience of the exercise of his free will, which effects a change not only in states of consciousness but also in the physical world. Citing Jakob Bernoulli's theorem on probability and frequency, Ruffini developed a criticism of the applicability of the urn model to problems concerning the probability of natural events and attempted to determine to what extent the analogy between the two types of considerations holds true. In contrast with Laplace, who attempted to apply his calculus indiscriminately to moral actions, Ruffini observed that since the faculties of the soul are not magnitudes, they cannot be measured quantitatively.

The mathematician and physician converged in Ruffini to consider the probability that a living organism is formed by chance. He examined probability in relation to the truthfulness of evidence, showing that Laplace's solution applied to a different problem than that under consideration and that it represented a faulty application of Bayes's theorem. Ruffini thus anticipated the thinking of certain modern writers on the calculus of probability (see G. Castelnuovo, *Calcolo della probabilità*, I [Bologna, 1947], 150).

With the fall of Napoleon and the return of the Este family to Modena, Ruffini was appointed rector of the restored university in 1814. The contemporary political climate rendered his rectorship especially difficult, despite his enthusiasm, discretion, and honesty. He also held the chairs of applied mathematics and practical medicine until his death, but poor health forced him to relinquish the chair of clinical medicine in 1819.

Ruffini's patients included the destitute, as well as the duchess, of Modena. While tending to the victims of the typhus epidemic of 1817–1818 he contracted a serious form of the disease. In "Memoria del tifo contagioso" (1820), written after his recovery, he dealt with the symptoms and treatment of typhus on the basis of his own experience. Despite advice that he moderate his activities, he resumed his scientific and medical work. His strength gradually ebbed; and in April 1822, after a visit to one of his patients, he was struck by a raging fever, which obliged him to give up his activities. This last illness (chronic pericarditis) led to his death.

He was almost completely forgotten after his death, because of political and ideological reasons as well as the difficulty of interpreting his writings. His research bore precious fruit, however, largely through the work of Cauchy.

BIBLIOGRAPHY

I. ORIGINAL WORKS. Ruffini's writings include *Teoria generale delle equazioni in cui si dimostra impossibile la soluzione algebrica delle equazioni generali di grado superiore al quarto*, 2 vols. (Bologna, 1799); "Della soluzione delle equazioni algebriche determinate particolari di grado superiore al quarto," in *Memorie di matematica e di fisica della Società italiana delle scienze*, **9** (1802), 444–526; "Riflessioni intorno alla rettificazione, ed alla quadratura del circolo," *ibid.*, 527–557; "Della insolubilità delle equazioni algebriche generali di grado superiore al quarto," *ibid.*, **10**, pt. 2 (1803), 410–470; *Sopra la determinazione delle radici delle equazioni numeriche di qualunque grado* (Modena, 1804); "Risposta . . . ai dubbi propostigli dal socio Gianfrancesco Malfatti sopra la insolubilità delle equazioni di grado superiore al quarto," in *Memorie di matematica e di fisica della Società italiana delle scienze*, **12**, pt. 1 (1805), 213–267; "Riflessioni . . . intorno al metodo proposto dal consocio Gianfrancesco Malfatti per la soluzione delle equazioni di quinto grado," *ibid.*, 321–336: *Della immaterialità dell'anima* (Modena, 1806); and "Della insolubilità delle equazioni algebriche generali di grado superiore al quarto qualunque metodo si adoperi algebrico esso siasi o trascendente," in *Memorie dell'Istituto nazionale italiano*, Classe di fisica e di matematica, **1**, pt. 2 (1806), 433–450.

Subsequent works are "Alcune proprietà generali

delle funzioni," in *Memorie di matematica e di fisica della Società italiana delle scienze*, **13**, pt. 1 (1807), 292–335; *Algebra e sua appendice*, 2 vols. (Modena, 1807–1808); "Di un nuovo metodo generale di estrarre le radici numeriche," in *Memorie di matematica e di fisica della Società italiana delle scienze*, **16**, pt. 1 (1813), 373–429; *Riflessioni intorno alla soluzione delle equazioni algebriche generali* (Modena, 1813); "Memoria del tifo contagioso," in *Memorie della Società italiana delle scienze*, Phys. sec., **18**, pt. 1 (1820), 350–381; "Intorno al metodo generale proposto dal Signor Hoêne Wronscki onde risolvere le equazioni di tutti i gradi," *ibid.*, Math. sec., **18**, fasc. 1 (1820), 56–68; and "Opuscolo I e II della classificazione delle curve algebriche a semplice curvatura," *ibid.*, 69–142, 269–396.

See also *Riflessioni critiche sopra il saggio filosofico intorno alla probabilità del signor Conte Laplace* (Modena, 1821); "Elogio di Berengario da Carpi," in *Fasti letterari della città di Modena e Reggio*. III (Modena, 1824); "Alcune proprietà delle radici dell'unità," in *Memorie dell'I.R. Istituto del regno lombardo-veneto*, **3** (1824), 67–84; "Riflessioni intorno alla eccitabilità, all'eccitamento, agli stimoli, ai controstimoli, alle potenze irritative, alle diatesi sì ipersteniche che iposteniche," in *Memorie della R. Accademia di scienze, lettere ed arti in Modena*, **1** (1833), 1–55; "Osservazioni intorno al moto dei razzi alle Congreve," *ibid.*, 56–78; "Intorno alla definizione della vita assegnata da Brown," *ibid.*, 319–333; and *Opere matematiche*. E. Bortolotti, ed., 3 vols. (Rome, 1953–1954).

MSS, letters, and documents relating to Ruffini are in the Academy of Science, Letters, and Arts of Modena.

II. SECONDARY LITERATURE. See the following, listed chronologically: A. Lombardi, *Notizie sulla vita e sugli scritti del prof. Paolo Ruffini* (Modena, 1824); H. Burkhardt, "Die Anfänge der Gruppentheorie und Paolo Ruffini," in *Zeitschrift für Mathematik und Physik*, **37** (1892), supp., 119–159; and "Paolo Ruffini e i primordi della teoria dei gruppi," in *Annali di matematica*, 2nd ser., **22** (1894), 175–212; E. Bortolotti, "Influenza dell'opera matematica di Paolo Ruffini sullo svolgimento delle teorie algebriche," in *Annuario della R. Università di Modena* (1902–1903), 21–77; "Un teorema di Paolo Ruffini sulla teoria delle sostituzioni," in *Rendiconti dell' Accademia dei Lincei*, ser. 5a, **22** (1913), 1st sem., pp. 679–683; and "I primordi della teoria generale dei gruppi di operazioni e la dimostrazione data da Paolo Ruffini della impossibilità di risolvere con funzioni trascendenti esatte le equazioni generali di grado superiore al quarto," in *Memorie della R. Accademia di scienze, lettere ed arti in Modena*, ser. 3a, **12** (1913), 179–195; G. Barbensi, *Paolo Ruffini nel suo tempo* (Modena, 1955), with complete bibliography of Ruffini's writings; G. Varoli, "Su un'opera pressochè sconosciuta di Paolo Ruffini," in *Statistica* (Bologna) (July–Sept. 1957), 421–442; and E. Carruccio, "Paolo Ruffini matematico e pensatore," in *Memorie della R. Accademia di scienze, lettere ed arti in Modena*, 6th ser., **8** (1966), liii–lxix.

ETTORE CARRUCCIO

RUMOVSKY, STEPAN YAKOVLEVICH (*b.* Stary Pogost, near Vladimir, Russia, 9 November 1734; *d.* St. Petersburg, Russia, 18 July 1812)

Rumovsky was the son of a priest. In 1739, after the family moved to St. Petersburg, he entered the Aleksander Nevsky Seminary, where he studied for nine years. In 1748 Rumovsky was one of four students chosen to study at the university of the St. Petersburg Academy of Sciences, where he heard Lomonosov lecture in chemistry, Richmann in mathematics and physics, and Nikita Popov in astronomy. In 1750 Rumovsky decided to specialize in mathematics and two years later presented a work that dealt with the use of tangents to find a straight line equal to the arc of an ellipse. In 1753 Rumovsky became adjunct of the Academy of Sciences after having submitted to it a work in which he offered a solution to the problem, posed by Kepler, of finding a semiordinate for a given sector. In his review of this paper, Euler noted the author's gift for mathematics. Rumovsky continued his mathematical education under Euler for two years, living in his house in Berlin and working under his direction.

After returning to St. Petersburg, Rumovsky held various posts at the Academy of Sciences. In 1760 he was sent to A. N. Grischow. He lived with Grischow in St. Petersburg and in his well-furnished observatory "became skilled in astronomical practice." In 1761 he took part in an expedition to Selenginsk in Transbaikalia, to observe the transit of Venus.

After Lomonosov's death, Rumovsky succeeded him as director of the geographical department of the St. Petersburg Academy, holding the post from 1766 to 1805; he also headed the astronomical observatory of the Academy from 1763. An active participant in the expedition to observe the 1769 transit of Venus, Rumovsky supervised the preparations of the observers, the choice of sites, and the building of temporary observatories. In connection with the latter problem he corresponded with James Short and with Euler. Rumovsky himself observed the transit on the Kola Peninsula. Having analyzed all the observations from both transits, he calculated the value of the solar parallax as 8.67"—he came nearer than any of his contemporaries to the presently accepted value (8.79").

Participating in a number of expeditions, Rumovsky determined the longitude and latitude of various sites, then compiled the first summary catalog of the astronomically determined coordinates of sixty-two sites in Russia. The *Berliner astronomisches Jahrbuch* for 1790 published fifty-seven determinations from Rumovsky's catalog—thirty-nine for European Russia and eighteen for Siberia. Prior to Rumovsky's work, only seventeen complete determinations had been made. According to W. Struve, Rumovsky's determinations were "distinguished by a precision remarkable for that time, the probable error in longitude not exceeding 32 seconds or 8' of arc."

Rumovsky's more than fifty basic scientific works cover astronomy, geodesy, mathematics, and physics. Like Lomonosov, his interests included a profound study of the Russian language and literature. In 1783 he became a member of the Russian Academy. Especially valuable was his activity in the translation and compilation of the first etymological dictionary of the Russian Academy (6 vols., 1789–1794), for which he received its gold medal.

Rumovsky began teaching in 1757 at the university of the St. Petersburg Academy, where he lectured in mathematics and in theoretical and practical astronomy. In 1763 he was appointed extraordinary professor of astronomy and, in 1767, professor of astronomy and an honorary member of the Academy of Sciences. From 1800 to 1803 he was a vice-president of the Academy of Sciences. In 1803 he became a member of the Main School Administration Board, which was charged with introducing educational reforms. In the same year Rumovsky also became superintendent of the Kazan educational district. In his effort to create a university at Kazan and, more specifically, to establish a physics and mathematics faculty, he recruited J. J. von Littrow from Austria for the department of astronomy. The university was opened in 1804.

BIBLIOGRAPHY

I. Original Works. Rumovsky's basic writings are "Rassuzhdenie o kometakh (v svyazi s poyavleniem komety Galleya)" ("Reflections on Comets [in Connection With the Appearance of Halley's Comet]"), in *Ezhemesyachnye sochinenia k polze i uveseleniyu sluzhashchie*, 6 (1757), 40–53; *Sokrashchenia matematiki . . . (rukovodstvo dlya gimnazistov)* ("Abridged Mathematics [Text for Gymnasium Students]"; St. Petersburg, 1760); *Rech o nachale i prirashchenii optiki do nyneshnikh vremen . . .* ("Speech on the Beginning and Growth of Optics to Our Time . . ."; St. Petersburg, 1763); *Investigatio parallaxeos solis ex observatione transitus Veneris per discum solis Selenginski habita . . .* (St. Petersburg, 1764); the translation of Euler's *Pisma o raznykh fizicheskikh i filosofskikh materiakh . . .* ("Letters on Various Physical and Philosophical

Matters . . ."), 3 vols. (St. Petersburg, 1768–1774); and "Nablyudenia nad prokhozhdeniem Venery cherez disk solntsa 23 maya v Kole . . ." ("Observations on the Transit of Venus Across the Sun's Disk 23 May in Kola . . ."), in *Novye Kommentarii Peterburgskoy Akademii nauk* (1769), 111–153.

See also *Yavlenia Venery v solntse v Rossyskoy imperii v 1769 godu uchinennye s istoricheskim preduvedomleniem* ("Observations on the Phenomenon of Venus and the Sun, Made in the Russian Empire in 1769, With Historical Notice"; St. Petersburg, 1771); *Tablitsy s pokazaniem shiroty i dolgoty mest Rossyskoy imperii cherez nablyudenia [astronomicheskie] opredelennye . . .* ("Tables With Indications of the Latitude and Longitude of Places in the Russian Empire Determined Through [Astronomical] Observations . . ."; St. Petersburg, 1780); translation of F. T. Schubert, *Rukovodstvo k astronomicheskim nablyudeniam, sluzhashchim k opredeleniyu dolgoty i shiroty mest* ("Handbook for Astronomical Observations Used for the Determination of Longitude and Latitude of Places"; St. Petersburg, 1803); and *Letopis Kornelia Tatsita* ("Chronicles of Cornelius Tacitus"), 4 pts. (St. Petersburg, 1806–1809), containing a Latin text and Russian trans. of Tacitus' *Annals* and two articles by Rumovsky: "Izvestia o zhizni Tatsita" ("Notes on the Life of Tacitus") and "Kratkoe izyasnenie nekotorykh slov, vstrechayushchikhsya v *Letopisi* Kornelia Tatsita" ("Brief Explanation of Certain Words Encountered in the *Annals* of Cornelius Tacitus").

II. Secondary Literature. See V. V. Bobylin, "S. Y. Rumovsky," in *Russky biografichesky slovar* ("Russian Biographical Dictionary"), XVII (1918), 441–450; V. L. Chenakal, "James Short i russkaya astronomia XVIII v." ("James Short and Russian Astronomy in the Eighteenth Century"), in *Istoriko-astronomicheskie issledovania* (1959), no. 5, 76–82; S. F. Ogorodnikov, "Tri astronomicheskie observatorii v Laplandii" ("Three Astronomical Observatories in Lapland"), in *Russkaya starina*, 33 (Jan. 1882), 177–187; V. E. Prudnikov, *Russkie pedagogi-matematiki XVIII–XIX vekov* ("Russian Teacher-Mathematicians of the Eighteenth and Nineteenth Centuries"; Moscow, 1956), 84–101; W. Struve, "Obzor geograficheskikh rabot v Rossii" ("Survey of Geographical Work in Russia"), in *Zapiski Russkogo geograficheskogo obshchestva* (1849), nos. 1–2, 23–35; and A. P. Youschkevitch, "Euler i russkaya matematika v XVIII veke" ("Euler and Russian Mathematics in the Eighteenth Century"), in *Trudy Instituta istorii estestvoznania*, 3 (1949), 104–108.

P. G. Kulikovsky

RUNGE, CARL DAVID TOLMÉ (*b.* Bremen, Germany, 30 August 1856; *d.* Göttingen, Germany, 3 January 1927)

Runge was the third son of Julius Runge and his

wife Fanny. His father, of a Bremen merchant family, had accumulated a comfortable capital during some twenty years in Havana, then retired to Bremen a few years before his early and unexpected death in 1864. Fanny Runge was herself the daughter of a foreign merchant in Havana, an Englishman of Huguenot descent, Charles David Tolmé. English was the language of choice between Runge's parents, and three of his four elder siblings eventually settled in England. There was thus a strong British element in his upbringing, particularly an emphasis upon sport, self-reliance, and fair play that, in combination with the civic traditions of the Hanseatic town, influenced his political and social views. All three of his brothers pursued commercial careers; but Runge, the most closely attached to his mother and an excellent student, pointed from his youth toward a more intellectual career.

At nineteen, after completing the Gymnasium, Runge spent six months on a pilgrimage with his mother to the cultural shrines of Italy. On his return at Easter of 1876, he enrolled at the University of Munich, registering for four courses on literature and philosophy and only one in science (taught by Jolly). But six weeks after the start of the semester, Runge had made up his mind to concentrate upon mathematics and physics. In his three semesters at Munich he attended several courses with Max Planck; they became warm friends and remained in close personal contact throughout Runge's life.[1] In the fall of 1877 Planck and Runge went to Berlin together; but Runge, not much attracted by the lectures of Kirchhoff and Helmholtz that he heard, turned to pure mathematics, becoming one of Weierstrass' disciples. In the winter semester 1878–1879 Runge also attended Friedrich Paulsen's seminar course on Hume.[2] A close and lasting personal friendship developed with Paulsen, whom Runge, upon the completion of his doctorate, placed alongside Weierstrass as one of the two men "to whom I owe the best of my knowledge and ability." The dissertation, submitted in the spring of 1880, dealt with differential geometry, a topic unrelated to Weierstrass' interest (or his own subsequent work). It stemmed from an independent study of Gauss's *Disquisitiones generales circa superficies curvas* and was stimulated by the discussion of these questions in the Mathematischer Verein, the student mathematical society, in which Runge played an active role.

Although he had resolved upon an academic career, Runge, as was customary, spent the year following his doctorate preparing for the *Lehramts-examen* for secondary school teachers. In the fall of 1881 he returned to Berlin to continue his education, largely transferring his allegiance to Leopold Kronecker. In his *Habilitationsschrift* (February 1883), influenced by Kronecker, Runge obtained a general procedure for the numerical solution of algebraic equations in which the roots were expressed as infinite series of rational functions of the coefficients, and the three traditional procedures for numerical solution of Newton, Bernoulli, and Gräffe were derived as special cases from a single function-theoretic theorem. This problem, which he treated as one in pure mathematics, was indeed to become Runge's characteristic *Fragestellung*— but only after his defection (1887) to "applied mathematics," and then from the diametrically opposite perspective, namely as a problem in numerical computation.

Meanwhile, accepted into Kronecker's circle in Berlin, Runge continued to work on a variety of problems in algebra and function theory. The feeling of being at the very center of the mathematical world dampened the urge to publish, and it was only after the promising young pure mathematician visited Mittag-Leffler in Stockholm for two weeks in September 1884 that his results were released in a spate in Mittag-Leffler's *Acta mathematica* (1885).

Runge—tall, lean, with a large and finely sculptured head—had developed exceptional skill as an ice skater in his youth; and in Berlin in the early 1880's, when that activity was becoming extremely fashionable, he cut a striking figure. He drew the attention of the children of Emil du Bois-Reymond; and, after three years of close friendship with that sporty clan, in 1885 Runge was betrothed to one of the daughters, Aimée. The precondition of the marriage—which took place in August 1887 and produced two sons and four liberated daughters—was a professorship. The first call, to the Technische Hochschule at Hannover, came in March 1886. Runge took up his duties immediately and remained there for eighteen years.

Within a year of his arrival at Hannover, Runge had undergone a thorough reorientation in his research interests and his attitude toward mathematics, a reorientation viewed by his former teachers and fellow students almost as treason. The initial step was Runge's immersion in the problem of constructing formulas, analogous to that which J. J. Balmer had recently found for hydrogen, giving the wavelengths of the spectral lines of other elements. Curiously, the stimulus for this investigation originated only very indirectly from the spectroscopist

Heinrich Kayser, who had come to Hannover as professor of physics in the fall of 1885 and who was then lunching daily with Runge. Rather, Runge's attention was first drawn to these questions late in 1886 by his future father-in-law, who had been stimulated by a lecture and subsequent conversation with Kayser in Berlin in June 1885.[3] All three men became interested in the problem primarily because of its fundamental physical importance: "affording a much deeper insight into the composition and nature of the molecules [atoms] than any other physical process."[4] Runge set himself the goal of finding for each element a single formula giving all its spectral lines; "then the constants of this formula would be just as characteristic of the element as, let's say, the atomic weight."[5]

Runge began his investigations by using published data, especially those of G. D. Liveing and J. Dewar on the spectra of lithium, sodium, potassium, calcium, and zinc; he found many series of lines that could be represented by adding to Balmer's formula $- 1/\lambda = A - B/m^2 -$ a third term, either C/m or C/m^4.[6] The inaccuracy of the available measurements made it uncertain what significance to attach to these formulas. Kayser, who had abandoned his spectroscopic researches in favor of the expansion of gases when he left Berlin, now responded to Runge's passion. He proposed "to make no use whatsoever of the available data, and . . . to determine anew the spectra of the elements from one end to the other"[7] with at least an order of magnitude greater accuracy.

This proposal was feasible with the photographic techniques and Rowland gratings that had become available in the preceding five years. Kayser's first spectrograms were made in May 1887; and for the next seven years, until his call to Bonn, he and Runge worked together at this task—Runge doing all the calculations of series and gradually taking a large role in the experimental work. They were aided by a number of grants for equipment from the Berlin Academy of Sciences (through the influence first of Helmholtz and subsequently of Planck).[8] Their results, published in seven *Abhandlungen der Preussischen Akademie der Wissenschaften*, ran to more than 350 pages.[9]

As the work progressed, the ultimate goal of unraveling atomic structure receded into the background, and was replaced by an overriding concern with precision of the data, of the methods of data reduction, and of the determination of the constants in the series formulas, without regard to their physical interpretation. Although Runge's approach to the problem of spectral series was thus far more "scientific" than that of Rydberg, whose treatise appeared simultaneously with Kayser and Runge's, by the turn of the century it was clear that Runge's formulas were physically rather barren while Rydberg's proved ever more fruitful.

After Kayser's departure Runge struggled on alone for six months. His second seven-year collaboration began early in 1895, when, following Ramsay's discovery of terrestrial helium, Runge induced Friedrich Paschen to join him in an investigation of the spectrum of that substance. Paschen, an experimentalist of extraordinary virtuosity, had come to Hannover in 1891 as Kayser's teaching assistant but had thus far not participated in spectroscopic work. With great speed and accuracy Runge and Paschen now identified all the chief lines due to helium and, surprisingly, were able to arrange them all into two systems of spectral series.[10] This was the first instance of either achievement. The latter was taken as evidence that helium was a mixture of two elements until 1897, when Runge and Paschen, continuing the Kayser-Runge program of measurements, showed that oxygen too had more than one system of series.[11]

The final substantial collaboration with Paschen, and Runge's most important contribution to theoretical spectroscopy, occurred in 1900–1902, after Thomas Preston had presented evidence for a close connection between the type of splitting of spectral lines in a magnetic field and the type of series to which they belong. In part through contact with Paschen and in part through recognition of Rydberg's unreasonable success in extracting the "right" formulas from "inadequate" data, but perhaps also in part reflecting the changing methodological ideals in the exact sciences circa 1900, Runge had gradually come to allow a freer rein to fantasy and speculation in his own work. Now, analyzing their magnetic splitting data, Runge found not only that the splitting was characteristic of the series, and quantitatively as well as qualitatively identical for analogous series in the spectra of different elements, but also that all the splittings were rational fractions of the "normal" splitting given by the Lorentz theory of the Zeeman effect.[12] This last result, known as Runge's rule, brought him great applause and for twenty years remained an incitement to both theoretical and experimental spectroscopists. Eventually, however, it proved to be largely misleading.

The exceedingly solid work with Kayser and the brilliant work with Paschen drew the attention and approval of the numerous British and American spectroscopists and astrophysicists (but not of the

German physicists, who on the whole showed remarkably little interest in spectroscopy). On visits to England (1895) and America (1897), Runge became acquainted with, and was found particularly congenial by, many physicists—including the two contemporaries whom Runge most admired, Lord Rayleigh and A. A. Michelson. Following Runge's visit to Yerkes Observatory, George E. Hale was moved to offer him a research professorship there.

After Paschen's departure for Tübingen in 1901, Runge continued his experimental spectroscopic work in collaboration with Julius Precht. When Runge transferred to Göttingen in October 1904, it was intended that his work on the Zeeman effect be continued there; and for this purpose extensive facilities were provided in Woldemar Voigt's new physical institute.[13] In fact, however, Runge never used them until after his retirement in 1925; his only experimental work in those two decades was performed with Paschen at Tübingen in October 1913.

First Kayser, then Paschen had been called to chairs at first-class universities, but Runge remained stranded at the Technische Hochschule. Planck tried more than once to arrange a call to Berlin, but could never persuade his colleagues to propose a man whom the mathematicians refused to recognize as a mathematician, nor the physicists as a physicist. In 1904, however, Klein, doubtless seconded by Woldemar Voigt, managed to persuade his Göttingen colleagues to include Runge among three nominees, albeit in last place. He then used his great influence with Friedrich Althoff, the head of the university section of the Prussian Ministry of Education, in order to have the position offered to Runge on most generous terms: 11,000 marks per year income and an independent institute comprising some fifteen rooms.[14]

Runge went to Göttingen as the first (and last) occupant of the first full professorship for "angewandte Mathematik" in Germany. It was as the leading practitioner—indeed, in a sense as the inventor and sole practitioner—of this discipline that he was best known among his contemporaries. Although the bulk of his publications had been in spectroscopy, Runge had never ceased to regard himself as a mathematician. The laborious reductions of spectroscopic observations and computations with spectral formulas, as well as his preparation of courses for engineering students, had led him to conceive an "executive" branch of mathematics to be joined to the "legislative," or pure, branch of the discipline.

"Applied mathematics" as understood and practiced by Runge was not at all concerned with the rigorous mathematical treatment of models derived from the physical world, and very little concerned with the mathematical methods useful in physics and technology. Primarily it treated the theory and practice of numerical and graphical computation—with a great deal of emphasis on the teaching of the practice.[15] Some of the methods that Runge developed, notably the Runge-Kutta procedure for the numerical integration of differential equations,[16] have remained current or have gained in currency because they are suited for execution upon modern digital computers. On the whole, however, Runge's work belongs rather more to mathematical *Zeitgeschichte* than to mathematical history: it formed one wing of a broad movement in pre-World War I Germany toward applied mathematics, of which Felix Klein was the chief ideologist and strategist, but which did not survive Germany's defeat.

Runge, whose talent and pleasure in grasping and discussing the other fellow's problems had been largely frustrated since leaving Berlin,[17] threw himself fully into the lively scientific (and sporting) life of Göttingen. The number and importance of his publications declined. His interest and energies were absorbed in the development of an instructional program in "applied mathematics"; in regularly attending the mathematical, physical, and astronomical colloquiums, as well as the Academy of Sciences; in mediating between the younger mathematicians and physicists and king Klein; and in service as Klein's lieutenant in the movement for reform of mathematical curricula in Germany. Although Runge made no contributions to the quantum theory of spectra built upon Bohr's model, he followed this work fairly closely and sympathetically.

Despite his liberal political views—open opposition to the annexationists during World War I and membership in the Democratic Party afterward—Runge retained the confidence of his colleagues and his influence within the university. When Peter Debye vacated his chair in the spring of 1920 without a successor having been appointed, he urged that Runge, "because of his authority and his great knowledge of physics, is in my opinion the only person in Göttingen" capable of managing the affairs of the physical institute.[18] And late in that year, when the Göttingen Academy was charged with forming the physics review committee of the Notgemeinschaft der Deutschen Wissenschaft, it elected Runge, its presiding secretary, as chairman—which immediately brought protests from physicists outside Göttingen, to whom he remained a "mathematician."[19]

Runge reached the obligatory retirement age of sixty-eight in 1923, but continued to examine and to administer his institute until his successor, Gustav Herglotz, arrived in 1925. The chair then ceased to be one of applied mathematics in any sense, least of all in Runge's sense; Runge had never even had any really talented students who had wished to be applied mathematicians in his sense. His scientific activity and his self-conception were too idiosyncratic, too heedless of conventional disciplinary boundaries and ideologies, too fully the free expression of his own broad mind and pleasure in scientific exchange. In excellent health at his seventieth birthday—doing handstands to amuse his grandchildren—he had several ambitious projects under way when he died suddenly of a heart attack six months later.

NOTES

1. Max Planck, "Persönliche Erinnerungen aus alten Zeiten" (1946), in his *Vorträge und Erinnerungen* (Stuttgart, 1949), 4.
2. F. Paulsen, *An Autobiography,* Theodor Lorenz trans. and ed. (New York, 1938), 278.
3. H. Kayser, "Erinnerungen aus meinem Leben," typescript (dated 1936, presented by Kayser to W. F. Meggers and by Meggers to the Library of the American Philosophical Society, Philadelphia), 144–147, 164, represents Runge as having been "inoculated" by du Bois-Reymond before his arrival in Hannover, but otherwise gives an account agreeing essentially with Iris Runge, *Carl Runge* (1949). I have drawn upon Kayser's "Erinnerungen" for information about the origins and style of the Kayser-Runge collaboration.
4. Kayser and Runge, "Über die Spectren der Elemente" [1st part], in *Abhandlungen der Preussischen Akademie der Wissenschaften* (1888), 4–5.
5. *Ibid.,* 7.
6. Runge, "On the Harmonic Series of Lines in the Spectra of the Elements," in *Report of the British Association for the Advancement of Science* (1888), 576–577.
7. Kayser and Runge, *op. cit.,* 9.
8. *Abhandlungen der Preussischen Akademie der Wissenschaften* (1891), xxi; (1893), xxii; Runge to Kayser, 22 Dec. 1894. Subsequently the Academy supported Runge's researches with Paschen (*Sitzungsberichte der Preussischen Akademie der Wissenschaften zu Berlin* [1900], 928) and Precht (*ibid.* [1903], 648).
9. The principal discussion of Runge's series formulas is in the "Dritter Abschnitt," dealing with the first column of the periodic table: *Abhandlungen der Preussischen Akademie der Wissenschaften* (1890); Runge to E. du Bois-Reymond, 27 May 1890.
10. Runge and Paschen, "Über das Spectrum des Heliums," in *Sitzungsberichte der Preussischen Akademie der Wissenschaften zu Berlin* (1895), 593, 639–643, presented 20 June 1895; "Über die Bestandtheile des Cleveit-Gases," *ibid.,* 749, 759–763, presented 11 July 1895; Runge to Kayser, 15 May 1895 and 13 July 1895.
11. Runge and Paschen, "Über die Serienspectra der Ele-

mente. Sauerstoff, Schwefel und Selen," in *Annalen der Physik,* 61 (1897), 641–686.
12. Runge to Kayser, 5 June 1900, 1 May 1901, 17 July 1901; Runge and Paschen, "Über die Strahlung des Quecksilbers im magnetischen Felde," in *Abhandlungen der Preussischen Akademie der Wissenschaften* (1902), presented 6 Feb. 1902; "Über die Zerlegung einander entsprechender Serienlinien im magnetischen Felde," in *Sitzungsberichte der Preussischen Akademie der Wissenschaften* (1902), 349, 380–386, presented 10 Apr. 1902; and "Über die Zerlegung . . . Zweite Mitteilung," *ibid.,* 705, 720–730, presented 26 June 1902. All three papers were translated immediately in *Astrophysical Journal,* 15 (1902), 335–351, and 16 (1902), 123–134. In Apr. 1907 Runge extended his rule to the particularly multifarious Zeeman effects of neon: "Über die Zerlegung von Spektrallinien im magnetischen Felde," in *Physikalische Zeitschrift,* 8 (1907), 232–237.
13. Runge to Voigt, 10 July 1904; Göttinger Vereinigung . . ., *Die physikalischen Institute der Universität Göttingen . . .* (Leipzig, 1906), 43–47, 197–198.
14. Personalakten Runge, Universitätsarchiv. Göttingen; *Die physikalischen Institute der Universität Göttingen,* 95–111.
15. The most important of Runge's textbooks of "applied mathematics" are *Graphical Methods* (New York, 1912), his lectures as exchange professor at Columbia in 1909–1910; and *Vorlesungen über numerisches Rechnen* (Berlin, 1924), written with Hermann König. See Runge, "Was ist 'angewandte Mathematik'?" in *Zeitschrift für den mathematischen und naturwissenschaftlichen Unterricht,* 45 (1914), 269–271, and Wilhelm Lorey, *Das Studium der Mathematik an den deutschen Universitäten seit Anfang des 19. Jahrhunderts* (Leipzig–Berlin, 1916), 253–254, and *passim,* for the applied movement in general.
16. Runge, "Über die numerische Auflösung von Differentialgleichungen," in *Mathematische Annalen,* 46 (1895), 167–178.
17. Important exceptions are Runge's suggestions to Paschen and Planck for, respectively, the experimental discovery and the theoretical deduction of the blackbody radiation law. See Hans Kangro, *Vorgeschichte des Planckschen Strahlungsgesetzes* (Wiesbaden, 1970), esp. the letter from Planck to Runge, 14 Oct. 1898, located by Kangro in the Stadtbibliothek, Dortmund.
18. Debye to Kurator, 29 Mar. 1920 (Personalakten Runge).
19. Steffen Richter, "Forschungsförderung in Deutschland, 1920–1936" (Ph.D. diss., University of Stuttgart, 1971), 37.

BIBLIOGRAPHY

I. ORIGINAL WORKS. The most complete bibliography of Runge's publications is that in the biography by I. Runge (see below), 201–205. The following further items include the additional citations in Poggendorff, IV, 1286–1287; V, 1078–1079; VI, 2244; and in the bibliography published by Runge's son-in-law, Richard Courant, in *Zeitschrift für angewandte Mathematik und Mechanik,* 7 (1927), 416–419; "On the Line Spectra of the Elements," in *Nature,* 45 (1892), 607–608, and 46 (1892), 100, 200, 247; "On a Certain Law in the Spectra of Some of the Elements," in *Astronomy and Astrophysics,* 13 (1894), 128–130; "Spektralanalytische Untersuchungen," in *Unterrichtsblätter für Mathematik und Naturwissenschaften,* 5 (1899), 69–72; "Über das Zeemansche Phänomen" (abstract only), in *Sitzungsberichte der Preussischen Akademie der Wissenschaften*

(1900), 635, written with F. Paschen; "Schwingungen des Lichtes im magnetischen Felde," in H. Kayser, ed., *Handbuch der Spectroscopie*, II (Leipzig, 1902), 612–672; "Über die spektroskopische Bestimmung des Atomgewichtes," in *Verhandlungen der Deutschen physikalischen Gesellschaft*, **5** (1903), 313–315; *Rechnungsformular zur Zerlegung einer empirisch gegebenen Funktion in Sinuswellen* (Brunswick, 1913), written with F. Emde; and "Method for Checking Measurements of Spectral Lines," in *Astrophysical Journal*, **64** (1926), 315–320.

When preparing the biography of her father, Iris Runge had available to her an exceedingly full *Nachlass*, including correspondence, diaries, programs of meetings, and newspaper clippings. In 1948 she deposited at the Deutsches Museum, Munich, a collection of letters, almost all to Runge, which cannot have been more than a small fraction of even the scientific correspondence in that *Nachlass*. The other materials presumably no longer exist (letter to the author from Wilhelm T. Runge, 8 May 1972), and may not have existed in 1948. The letters by Runge at the Deutsches Museum, and some six letters by Runge in other collections, are listed in T. S. Kuhn *et al.*, *Sources for History of Quantum Physics* (Philadelphia, 1967), 80.

The largest group of letters by Runge is in the Darmstädter collection, H 1885, at the Staatsbibliothek Preussischer Kulturbesitz, Berlin-Dahlem: to Emil du Bois-Reymond, 12 Jan. 1885, 24 June 1885, 27 May 1890, 30 Apr. 1892; to René du Bois-Reymond, 29 Dec. 1903, 15 Jan. 1906; to Hans Geitel, 1 July 1899, 29 July 1899; to Heinrich Kayser, 22 Dec. 1894, 20 Jan. 1895, 17 Mar. 1895, 15 May 1895, 13 July 1895, 22 July 1895, 27 July 1895, 24 Nov. 1895, 28 Nov. 1895, 8 May 1897, 30 Oct. 1899, 5 June 1900, 9 Oct. 1900, 28 Dec. 1900, 1 May 1901, 17 July 1901, 9 Jan. 1902, 17 Jan. 1902, 22 Jan. 1902, 14 June 1902, 2 May 1903, 11 May 1903, 15 Nov. 1903, 15 Sept. 1905, 12 Apr. 1913, 29 July 1913, 31 July 1913; to Johannes Knoblauch, 15 Sept. 1886. The Nachlass Stark in the same depository includes letters from Runge to Stark of 10 Aug. 1906, 31 Aug. 1906, 25 Apr. 1907, 27 June 1907, 6 July 1910, 29 Oct. 1911, 7 Dec. 1911; and copies of Stark's letters to Runge of 25 July 1906, 2 Aug. 1906, 27 Aug. 1906, 20 Nov. 1906, 25 Apr. 1907.

Runge's MS "Ausarbeitungen" of Weierstrass' lectures on the calculus of variations and on elliptic functions are in Stockholm: I. Grattan-Guinness, "Materials for the History of Mathematics in the Institut Mittag-Leffler," in *Isis*, **62** (1971), 363–374. Three letters regarding a plaque for Runge on his seventieth birthday are in the Hale Papers, California Institute of Technology Archives, Pasadena; a letter to William F. Meggers, 8 Dec. 1921, is in the Meggers Papers, American Institute of Physics, New York.

II. SECONDARY LITERATURE. Iris Runge, *Carl Runge und sein wissenschaftliches Werk* (Göttingen, 1949), which is *Abhandlungen der Akademie der Wissenschaften zu Göttingen*, Math.-phys. Kl., 3rd ser., no. 23, is by

far the fullest and most authoritative source. Biographical data of which the source is not otherwise indicated are derived from this work. Runge's early spectroscopic work is discussed in William McGucken, *Nineteenth-Century Spectroscopy* (Baltimore, 1969); and his later magneto-optic work in James Brookes Spencer, *An Historical Investigation of the Zeeman Effect (1896–1913)* (Ann Arbor, Mich., 1964), issued by University Microfilms; and P. Forman, "Alfred Landé and the Anomalous Zeeman Effect, 1919–1921," in *Historical Studies in the Physical Sciences*, **2** (1970), 153–262.

Useful evaluations of Runge's work and personality are Ludwig Prandtl, "Carl Runge," in *Jahrbuch der Akademie der Wissenschaften zu Göttingen* (1926–1927), 58–62; and "Carl Runge," in *Naturwissenschaften*, **15** (1927), 227–229; Richard Courant, "Carl Runge als Mathematiker," *ibid.*, 229–231, and 473–474 for the ensuing exchange with Richard von Mises over the status of "angewandte Mathematik" in Germany; Friedrich Paschen, "Carl Runge als Spectroskopiker," *ibid.*, 231–233; and "Carl Runge," in *Astrophysical Journal*, **69** (1929), 317–321; Walther Lietzmann, "Carl Runge," in *Zeitschrift für den mathematischen und naturwissenschaftlichen Unterricht*, **58** (1927), 482–483; Hans Kienle, "Carl Runge," in *Vierteljahrsschrift der Astronomischen Gesellschaft* (Leipzig), **62** (1927), 173–177; Erich Trefftz, "Carl Runge," in *Zeitschrift für angewandte Mathematik und Mechanik*, **6** (1926), 423–424; H. L., "Prof. Carl Runge," in *Nature*, **119** (1927), 533–534; and Oliver Lodge, "Prof. Carl Runge," *ibid.*, 565.

PAUL FORMAN

RUSSELL, BERTRAND ARTHUR WILLIAM (*b.* Trelleck, Monmouthshire, England, 18 May 1872; *d.* Plas Penrhyn, near Penrhyndeudraeth, Wales, 2 February 1970)

The Russell family has played a prominent part in the social, intellectual, and political life of Great Britain since the time of the Tudors; Russells were usually to be found on the Whig side of politics, with a firm belief in civil and religious liberty, as that phrase was interpreted by the Whigs. Lord John Russell (later first earl Russell), the third son of the sixth duke of Bedford, was an important figure in nineteenth-century politics: He was a leader in the struggle to establish the great Reform Act of 1832, held several high offices of state, and was twice prime minister in Whig and Whig-Liberal administrations. His eldest son, known by the courtesy title of Viscount Amberley, married Katherine Stanley, of another famous English family, the Stanleys of Alderley. The young couple were highly intelligent and were in strong sympathy with most of the reforming and progressive movements of their time, a stance that made them far from popular with the conservative section of the aristocracy. Unhappily, neither enjoyed good health; the wife died in 1874 and the husband in 1876. There were two children, Frank and Bertrand, the latter the younger by about seven years.

The Russell family did not approve of the arrangements made by Viscount Amberley for the upbringing of the two children in the event of his death. When this occurred, the boys were made wards in chancery and placed in the care of Earl Russell and his wife, who were then living at Pembroke Lodge in Richmond Park, a house in the gift of the Crown. Bertrand's grandfather died in 1878, but his grandmother lived until 1898 and had a strong influence on his early life.

Like many Victorian children of the upper class, the boy was educated at home by a succession of tutors, so that when he entered Trinity College, Cambridge, as a scholar in 1890, he had had no experience of communal life in an educational establishment save for a few months in a "cramming" school in London. At Trinity he was welcomed into a society that for intellectual brilliance could hardly have been bettered anywhere at that time. He obtained a first class in the mathematical tripos and in the moral sciences tripos, although the formality of examinations seems not to have appealed to him. He remarks in his autobiography that the university teachers "contributed little to my enjoyment of Cambridge," and that "I derived no benefits from lectures."

A great stimulus to Russell's development was his election in 1892 to the Apostles. This was a small, informal society, founded about 1820, that regarded itself—not without some justification—as composed of the intellectual cream of the university; its main object was the completely unfettered discussion of any subject whatsoever. One member was A. N. Whitehead, then a mathematical lecturer at Cambridge, who had read Russell's papers in the scholarship examination and had in consequence formed a high opinion of his ability. Through the society Russell acquired a circle of gifted friends: the philosophers G. E. Moore and Ellis McTaggart, the historian G. M. Trevelyan and his poet brother R. C. Trevelyan, the brilliant brothers Crompton and Theodore Llewelyn Davies, and later the economist J. M. Keynes and the essayist Lytton Strachey.

In the latter part of the nineteenth century, progressive opinion at Cambridge had begun to maintain that university dons should regard research as a primary activity, rather than as a secondary pursuit for leisure hours after teaching duties had been performed. This opinion was particularly strong in Trinity, where A. R. Forsyth, W. W. Rouse Ball, and Whitehead encouraged the researches of younger men such as E. W. Barnes, G. H. Hardy, J. H. Jeans, E. T. Whittaker, and Russell; these themselves exercised a great influence on the next generation, the remarkable set of Trinity mathematicians of the period 1900–1914.

One mode of encouragement was the establishment of prize fellowships, awarded for original dissertations; such a fellowship lasted for six years and involved no special duties, the object being to give a young man an unhindered opportunity for intellectual development. Russell was elected in 1895, on the strength of a dissertation on the foundations of geometry, published in 1897. During the later part of his tenure and after it lapsed, he was not in residence; but in 1910 the college appointed him to a special lectureship in logic and the philosophy of mathematics.

During World War I pacifism excited emotions much more bitter than was the case in World War II. Russell's strongly held views made him unpopular in high places; and when in 1916 he published a leaflet protesting against the harsh treatment of a conscientious objector, he was prosecuted on a charge of making statements likely to prejudice recruiting for and discipline in the armed services, and fined £100. The Council, the governing body of Trinity, then dismissed him from his lectureship, and Russell broke all connection with the college by removing his name from the books. In 1918 another article of his was judged seditious, and he was sentenced to imprisonment for six months. The sentence was carried out with sufficient leniency to enable him to write his very useful *Introduction to Mathematical Philosophy* in Brixton Prison.

Many members of Trinity felt that the Council's action in dismissing Russell in 1916 was excessively harsh. After the war the breach was healed: in 1925 the college invited Russell to give the Tarner lectures, later published under the title *The Analysis of Matter*; and from 1944 until his death he was again a fellow of the college.

In the prologue to his *Autobiography* Russell tells us that three strong passions have governed his life: "the longing for love, the search for happiness, and unbearable pity for the suffering of mankind." His writings and his actions testify to the perseverance with which he pursued his aims from youth to extreme old age, undeterred by opposition and regardless of obloquy. Russell's perseverance did not necessarily imply obstinacy, for his mind was never closed; and if his acute sense of logic revealed to him a fallacy in his argument, he would not cling to a logically indefensible view but would rethink his position, on the basis of his three strong principles. But it was also his devotion to logic that led him frequently to reject the compromises so often forced on the practical politician.

Russell—not surprisingly, in view of his ancestry—was always ready to campaign for "progressive" causes. About 1907 he fought hard for women's suffrage, a cause that provoked more opposition and rowdyism in the United Kingdom than any other political question during this century—even more than the pacifism for which Russell was prosecuted in World War I. After the war Russell continued his search for a genuine democracy, in which freedom for the individual should be compatible with the common good; his experiments in education were designed to contribute to this end. Never insular, he would expose what he saw as the faults of his own country or of the English-speaking nations as caustically as he would those of the totalitarian regimes; but that the growth of the latter could be met only by war was a conclusion to which he came very reluctantly. At the close of World War II, his vision of humanity inevitably destroying itself through the potency of nuclear weapons caused him to lead a long campaign for nuclear disarmament.

A long list of books bears witness to Russell's endeavor to encourage human beings to think clearly, to understand the new scientific discoveries and to realize some of their implications, and to abhor injustice, violence, and war. *The Impact of Science on Society, History of Western Philosophy, Common Sense and Nuclear Warfare, Marriage and Morals, Freedom and Organisation*, and *Prospects of Industrial Civilisation*, to name only a few, show how earnestly he sought to promote his ideals. All were written in an English that was always clear and precise, and often beautiful. Critics might disagree with his opinions but seldom could misunderstand them. An occasional didactic arrogance might offend, but it could be forgiven in view of the author's manifest sincerity.

A few of Russell's many honors were fellowship of the Royal Society in 1908, the Order of Merit in 1949, and the Nobel Prize for literature in 1950.

Russell has told us in his autobiography how he began the study of geometry, with his elder brother as tutor, at the age of eleven. Like almost every other English boy of his time, he began on Euclid; unlike almost every other English boy, he was entranced, for he had not known that the world contained anything so delicious. His brother told him that the fifth proposition of book I, the notorious *pons asinorum*, was generally considered difficult; but Russell found it no trouble. Having been told, however, that Euclid proved things, he was disappointed at having to begin by assimilating an array of axioms and would not accept this necessity until his brother told him that unless he did so, his study of geometry could not proceed, thus extorting a reluctant acceptance. The anecdote is not irrelevant; Russell's mathematical work, which occupied him until he was over forty, was almost entirely concerned with probing and testing the foundations of mathematics, in order that the superstructure might be firmly established.

Russell's fellowship thesis was revised for publication in 1897 as *An Essay on the Foundations of Geometry*. Its basic theme was an examination of the status assigned to geometry by Kant in his doctrine of synthetic a priori judgments. Analytic propositions are propositions of pure logic; but synthetic propositions, such as "New York is a large city," cannot be obtained by purely logical processes. Thus all propositions that are known through experience are synthetic; but Kant would not accept the converse, that only such propositions are synthetic. An empirical proposition is derived from experience; but an a priori proposition, however derived, is eventually recognized to have a basis other than experience.

Kant's problem was to determine how synthetic a priori judgments or propositions are possible. He held that Euclidean geometry falls into this category, for geometry is concerned with what we perceive and thus is conditioned by our perceptions. This argument becomes dubious when the full implication of the existence of non-Euclidean geometries is appreciated; but although these geometries were discovered about 1830, the philosophical implications had hardly been fully grasped by the end of the nineteenth century. One considerable step was taken by Hilbert when he constructed his formal and abstract system based on his epigram that in geometry it must be possible to replace the words "points," "lines," and "planes" by the words "tables," "chairs," and "beer mugs"; but his *Grundlagen der Geometrie* was not published until 1899.

To Russell, non-Euclidean spaces were possible, in the philosophical sense that they are not condemned by any a priori argument as to the necessity of space for experience. His examination of fundamentals led him to conclude that for metrical geometry three axioms are a priori: (1) the axiom of free mobility, or congruence: shapes do not in any way depend on absolute position in space; (2) the axiom of dimensions: space must have a finite integral number of dimensions; (3) the axiom of distance: every point must have to every other point one and only one relation independent of the rest of space, this relation being the distance between the two points.

For projective geometry the a priori axioms are (1) as in metrical geometry; (2) space is continuous and infinitely divisible, the zero of extension being a point; (3) two points determine a unique figure, the straight line. For metrical geometry an empirical element enters into the concept of distance, but the two sets are otherwise equivalent. In the light of modern views on the nature of a geometry, these investigations must be regarded as meaningless or at least as devoted to the wrong kind of question. What remains of interest in the *Foundations of Geometry* is the surgical skill with which Russell can dissect a corpus of thought, and his command of an easy yet precise English style.

Following the publication of the *Foundations of Geometry*, Russell settled down to the composition of a comprehensive treatise on the principles of mathematics, to expound his belief that pure mathematics deals entirely with concepts that can be discussed on a basis of a small number of fundamental logical concepts, deducing all its propositions by means of a small number of fundamental logical principles. He was not satisfied with his first drafts, but in July 1900 he went to Paris with Whitehead to attend an International Congress of Philosophy. Here his meeting with Peano brought about, in his own phrase, "a turning point in my intellectual life." Until then he had had only a vague acquaintance with Peano's work, but the extraordinary skill and precision of Peano's contributions to discussions convinced Russell that such mastery must be to a large extent due to Peano's knowledge of mathematical logic and its symbolic language.

The work of Boole, Peirce, and Schröder had constructed a symbolic calculus of logic; and their success contributed to Peano's systematic attempt to place the whole of mathematics on a purely formal and abstract basis, for which purpose he utilized a symbolism of his own creation. This enabled him and his disciples to clarify distinctions hitherto obscured by the ambiguities of ordinary language, and to analyze the logic, basis, and structure of such mathematical concepts as the positive

integers. The apparently trivial symbolism that replaces "The entity x is a member of the class A" with "$x \in A$" leads not only to brevity but, more importantly, to a precision free from the ambiguities lurking in the statement "x is A." One result of Peano's work was to dispose of Kant's synthetic a priori judgments.

Russell rapidly mastered Peano's symbolism and ideas, and then resumed the writing of his book on principles; the whole of the first volume was completed within a few months of his meeting with Peano. Some sections were subjected to a thorough rewriting, however; and volume I of *Principles of Mathematics* was not published until 1903. The second edition (1937) is perhaps more valuable for the study of the development of Russell's ideas, for it both reprints the first edition and contains a new introduction in which Russell gives his own opinion on those points on which his views had changed since 1903; but in spite of Hilbert and Brouwer, he is still firm in his belief that mathematics and logic are identical.

The second volume of the *Principles,* to be written in cooperation with Whitehead, never appeared because it was replaced by the later *Principia Mathematica.* It was to have been a completely symbolic account of the assimilation of mathematics to logic, of which a descriptive version appears in volume I. The main sections of volume I treat indefinables of mathematics (including a description of Peano's symbolic logic), number, quantity, order, infinity and continuity, space, and matter and motion. On all these topics Russell's clarity of thought contributed to the establishment of precision; thus his analysis of the words "some," "any," "every," for instance, is very searching. In two places, at least, he was able to throw light on familiar but vexed topics of mathematical definition and technique.

That the positive integer 2 represents some property possessed by all couples may be intuitively acceptable but does not supply a precise definition, since neither existence nor uniqueness is guaranteed in this way. Russell's definition of a number uses a technique of equivalence that has had many further applications. The definition had already been given by Frege, but his work was not then known to Russell;[1] indeed, it was known to hardly any mathematician of the time, since Frege's style and symbolism are somewhat obscure. Two classes, A and B, are said to be similar ($A \sim B$) if each element of either class can be uniquely mated to one element of the other class; clearly A is similar to itself. Similarity is a transitive and symmetrical relation; that is, if $A \sim B$ and $B \sim C$, then $A \sim C$, and if $A \sim B$, then $B \sim A$. The (cardinal) number of a class A is, then, the class consisting of all classes similar to A. Thus every class has a cardinal number, and similar classes have the same cardinal number. The null class φ is such that $x \, \epsilon \, \varphi$ is universally false, and its cardinal is denoted by 0. A unit class contains some term x and is such that if y is a member of this class, then $x = y$; its cardinal is denoted by 1. The operations of addition and multiplication are then readily constructed. We thus have a workable definition with no difficulties about existence or uniqueness; but—and this is a considerable concession—the concept of "class" must be acceptable.

A similar clarification of the notion of a real number was also given by Russell. Various methods of definition were known, one of the most popular being that of Dedekind. Suppose that p and q are two mutually exclusive properties, such that every rational number possesses one or the other. Further, suppose that every rational possessing property p is less than any rational possessing property q. This process defines a section of the rationals, giving a lower class L and an upper class R. If L has a greatest member, or if R has a least member, the section corresponds to this rational number. But if L has no greatest and R no least member, the section does not determine a rational. (The case in which L has a greatest and R has a least member cannot arise, since the rationals are dense.) Of the two possible cases, to say that the section in one case corresponds to a rational number and in the other it corresponds to or represents an irrational number is—if instinctive—not to define the irrational number, for the language is imprecise. Russell surmounts this difficulty by simply defining a real number to be a lower section L of the rationals. If L has a greatest member or R a least member, then this real number is rational; in the other case, this real number is irrational.

These are two of the outstanding points in the *Principles*. But the concept of "class" is evidently deeply involved, and the "contradiction of the greatest cardinal" caused Russell to probe the consequences of the acceptance of the class concept more profoundly, particularly in view of Cantor's work on infinite numbers. Cantor proved that the number of subclasses that can be formed out of a given class is greater than the number of members of the class, and thus it follows that there is no greatest cardinal number.

Yet if the class of all objects that can be counted is formed, this class must have a cardinal number that is the greatest possible. From this contradiction Russell was led to formulate a notorious antinomy: A class may or may not be a member of itself. Thus, the class of men, mankind, is not a man and is not a member of itself; on the other hand, the class consisting of the number 5 is the number 5, that is, it is a member of itself. Now let W denote the class of all classes not members of themselves. If W is not a member of itself, then by definition it belongs to W—that is, it is a member of itself. If W is a member of W, then by definition it is not a member of itself—that is, it is not a member of W. In the main text this contradiction is discussed but not resolved. In an appendix, however, there is a brief anticipation of an attempt to eliminate it by means of what Russell called the "theory of types," dealt with more fully in *Principia Mathematica*.

A commonsense reaction to this contradiction might well be a feeling that a class of objects is in a category different from that of the objects themselves, and so cannot reasonably be regarded as a member of itself. If x is a member of a class A, such that the definition of x depends on A, the definition is said to be impredicative; it has the appearance of circularity, since what is defined is part of its own definition. Poincaré suggested that the various antinomies were generated by accepting impredicative definitions,[2] and Russell enunciated the "vicious circle principle" that no class can contain entities definable only in terms of that class. This recourse, however, while ostracizing the antinomies, would also cast doubt on the validity of certain important processes in mathematical analysis; thus the definition of the exact upper bound is impredicative.

To meet the difficulty, Russell devised his theory of types. Very crudely outlined, it starts with primary individuals; these are of one type, say type 0. Properties of primary individuals are of type 1, properties of properties of individuals are of type 2, and so on. All admitted properties must belong to some type. Within a type, other than type 0, there are orders. In type 1, properties defined without using any totality belong to order 0; properties defined by means of a totality of properties of a given order belong to the next higher order. Then, finally, to exclude troubles arising from impredicative definitions, Russell introduced his axiom of reducibility: for any property of order other than 0, there is a property over precisely the same range that is of order 0; that is, in a given type any impredicative definition is logically equivalent to some predicative definition.

Whitehead and Russell themselves declared that they were not entirely happy about this new axiom. Even if an axiom may well be arbitrary, it should, so one feels, at least be plausible. Among the other axioms this appears as anomalous as, for instance, the notorious axiom of parallels seems to be in Euclidean geometry.

F. P. Ramsey showed that the antinomies could be separated into two kinds: those which are "logical," such as Russell's, and those which are "semantical," such as that involved in the assertion "I am lying."[3] The first class can then be eliminated by the simpler theory of types, in which the further classification into orders is not required. But even so, Ramsey did not regard this reconstruction of the Whitehead-Russell position as altogether satisfactory. Weyl pointed out that one might just as well accept the simpler axiomatic set theory of Zermelo and Fraenkel as a foundation, and remarked that a return to the standpoint of Whitehead and Russell was unthinkable.[4]

Before leaving the *Principles,* some other matters are worthy of note. First, the important calculus of relations, hinted at by De Morgan and explored by C. S. Peirce, is examined in detail.[5] Second, Russell was not concerned merely with foundations; he took the whole mathematical world as his parish. There is thus a long examination of the nature of space and of the characteristics of projective, descriptive, and metrical geometries. Third, there is an analysis of philosophical views on the nature of matter and motion. Finally, he draws, possibly for the first time, a clear distinction between a proposition, which must be true or false, and a propositional function, which becomes a proposition, with a truth value, only when the argument is given a determinate value; the propositional function "x is a prime number" becomes a proposition, which may be true or false, when x is specified.

In the three volumes of *Principia Mathematica* (1910–1913) Whitehead and Russell took up the task, attempted in Russell's uncompleted *Principles,* of constructing the whole body of mathematical doctrine by logical deduction from the basis of a small number of primitive ideas and a small number of primitive principles of logical inference, using a symbolism derived from that of Peano but considerably extended and systematized.

Associated with elementary propositions p, q, the primitive concepts are (1) negation, the contradictory of p, not-p, denoted by $\sim p$; (2) disjunction, or logical sum, asserting that at least one of p and q is true, denoted by $p \vee q$; (3) conjunction, or logical product, asserting that both p and q are true, denoted by $p \cdot q$; (4) implication, p implies q, denoted by $p \supset q$; (5) equivalence, p implies q and q implies p, denoted by $p \equiv q$. If a proposition is merely to be considered, it may be denoted simply by p; but if it is to be asserted, this is denoted by $\vdash p$, so that $\vdash$ may be read as "It is true that. . . ." The assertion of a propositional function for some undetermined value of the argument is denoted by $\exists$, which may be read as "There exists a . . . such that. . . ."

Dots are used systematically in place of brackets; the rule of operation is that the more dots, the stronger their effect. An example will show the way in which the dots are used. The proposition "if either p or q is true, and either p or 'q implies r' is true, then either p or r is true" may be written as

$$\vdash : \cdot p \vee q : p \cdot \vee \cdot q \supset r : \supset \cdot p \vee r.$$

The five concepts listed above are not independent. In the *Principia* negation and disjunction are taken as fundamental, and the other three are then defined in terms of these two. Thus conjunction, $p \cdot q$, is defined as $\sim (\sim p \vee \sim q)$; implication, $p \supset q$, as $\sim p \vee q$; and equivalence, $p \equiv q$, as $(p \supset q) \cdot (q \supset p)$, which can of course now be expressed entirely in terms of the symbols $\sim$ and $\vee$. Another elementary function of two propositions is incompatibility; p is incompatible with q if either or both of p and q are false, that is, if they are not both true; the symbolic notation is p/q. Negation and disjunction are then definable in terms of incompatibility:

$$\sim p = p/p, \quad p \vee q = p/\sim q.$$

Thus the five concepts (1) − (5) are all definable in terms of the single concept of incompatibility; for instance, $p \supset q = p/(q/q)$. This reduction was given by H. M. Sheffer in 1913,[6] although Willard Quine points out that Peirce recognized the possibility about 1880.

The primitive propositions first require two general principles of deduction—anything implied by a true proposition is true, and an analogous statement for propositional functions: when $\phi (x)$ and "$\phi (x)$ implies $\psi (x)$" can be asserted, then $\psi (x)$ can be asserted. There are then five primitive propositions of symbolic logic:

(1) Tautology. If either p is true or p is true, then p is true:

$$\vdash : p \vee p \cdot \supset \cdot p.$$

(2) Addition. If q is true, then "p or q" is true:

$$\vdash : q \cdot \supset \cdot p \lor q.$$

(3) Permutation. "p or q" implies "q or p":

$$\vdash : p \lor q \cdot \supset \cdot q \lor p.$$

(4) Association. If either p is true or "q or r" is true, then either q is true or "p or r" is true:

$$\vdash : p \lor (q \lor r) \cdot \supset \cdot q \lor (p \lor r).$$

(5) Summation. If q implies r, then "p or q" implies "p or r":

$$\vdash : \cdot q \supset r \cdot \supset : p \lor q \cdot \supset \cdot p \lor r.$$

Following up Sheffer's use of incompatibility as the single primitive concept, Nicod showed that the primitive propositions could be replaced by a single primitive proposition of the form

$$p \cdot \supset \cdot q \cdot r : \supset \cdot t \supset t \cdot s | q \supset p | s,$$

which, since $p \supset q = p|(q|q)$, can be expressed entirely in terms of the stroke symbol for incompatibility.[7]

The second edition of the *Principia* (1925–1927) was mainly a reprint of the first, with small errors corrected; but its worth to the student is considerably increased by the addition of a new introduction, of some thirty-four pages, in which the authors give an account of modifications and improvements rendered possible by work on the logical bases of mathematics following the appearance of the first edition—for instance, the researches of Sheffer and Nicod just mentioned. The authors are mildly apologetic about the notorious axiom of reducibility; they are not content with it, but are prepared to accept it until something better turns up. In particular, they refer to the work of Chwistek and of Wittgenstein, without, however, being able to give wholehearted approval.[8] Much of the introduction is devoted to Wittgenstein's theory and its consequences. Here they show that the results of volume I of the *Principia* stand, although proofs have to be revised; but they cannot, on Wittgenstein's theory, reestablish the important Dedekindian doctrine of the real number, nor Cantor's theorem that $2^n > n$, save for the case of n finite. The introduction was also much influenced by the views of Ramsey, whose death in 1930, at the age of twenty-seven, deprived Cambridge of a brilliant philosopher.

The publication of the *Principia* gave a marked impulse to the study of mathematical logic. The deft handling of a complicated but precise symbolism encouraged workers to use this powerful technique and thus avoid the ambiguities lurking in the earlier employment of ordinary language. The awkwardness and inadequacy of the theory of types and the axiom of reducibility led not only to further investigations of the Whitehead-Russell doctrine but also to an increased interest in rival theories, particularly Hilbert's formalism and Brouwer's intuitionism. Perhaps because none of these three competitors can be regarded as finally satisfactory, research on the foundations of mathematics has produced new results and opened up new problems the very existence of which could hardly have been foreseen in the early years of this century. Whitehead and Russell may have failed in their valiant attempt to place mathematics once and for all on an unassailable logical basis, but their failure may have contributed more to the development of mathematical logic than complete success would have done.

The *Introduction to Mathematical Philosophy* (1919), written while Russell was serving a sentence in Brixton Prison, is a genuine introduction but certainly is not "philosophy without tears"; it may perhaps best be described as *une oeuvre de haute vulgarisation*. The aim is to expound work done in this field, particularly by Whitehead and Russell, without using the complex symbolism of *Principia Mathematica*. Russell's mastery of clear and precise English stood him in good stead for such a task, and many young students in the decade 1920–1930 were first drawn to mathematical logic by a study of this efficient and readable volume.

To explain the arrangement of the book, Russell remarks, "The most obvious and easy things in mathematics are not those that come logically at the beginning: they are things that, from the point of view of logical deduction, come somewhere near the middle." Taking such things as a starting point, a close analysis should lead back to general ideas and principles, from which the starting point can then be deduced or defined. This starting point is here taken to be the familiar set of positive integers; the theory of these, as shown by Peano, depends on the three primitive ideas of zero, number, and successor, and on five primitive propositions, one of which is the principle of mathematical induction. The integers themselves are then defined by the Frege-Russell method, using the class of all similar classes, and the relation between finiteness and mathematical induction is established. Order and relations are studied next, to enable rational, real, and complex numbers to be defined, after which the deeper topics of infinite cardinals and infinite ordinals can be broached. It is then possible to look at certain topics in analysis, such as limit processes and continuity.

The definition of multiplication when the number of factors may be infinite presents a subtle difficulty. If a class A has m members and a class B has n members, the product $m \times n$ can be defined as the number of ordered couples that can be formed by choosing the first term of the couple from A and the second from B. Here m or n or both may be infinite, and the definition may readily be generalized further to the situation in which there is a finite number of classes, $A, B, \cdots, K$. But if the number of classes is infinite, then in defect of a rule of selection, we are confronted with the impossible task of making an infinite number of arbitrary acts of choice.

To turn this obstacle, recourse must be had to the multiplicative axiom, or axiom of selection: given a class of mutually exclusive classes (none being null), there is at least one class that has exactly one term in common with each of the given classes. This is equivalent to Zermelo's axiom that every class can be well-ordered, that is, can be arranged in a series in which each subclass (not being null) has a first term.[9] This matter is dealt with in *Principia Mathematica,* but here Russell offers a pleasant illustration provided by the arithmetical perplexity of the millionaire who buys a pair of socks whenever he buys a pair of boots, ultimately purchasing an infinity of each. In dealing with the number of boots, the axiom is not required, since we can choose, say, the right boot (or the left) from every pair. But no such distinction is available in counting the socks, however, and here the axiom is needed.

The last six chapters of the *Introduction* are concerned with the theory of deduction and the general logical bases of mathematics, including an analysis of the use and nature of classes and the need, in Russell's theory, for a doctrine of types.

Among the essays collected in *Mysticism and Logic* (1921) are some that deal, in popular style, with Russell's views on mathematics and its logical foundations. One of these, "Mathematics and the Metaphysicians," written in 1901, had appeared in *International Monthly.* The editor had asked Russell to make the article "as romantic as possible," and hence it contains a number of quips, some now famous, in which the air of paradox masks a substantial degree of truth. To say that pure mathematics was discovered by George Boole in 1854 is merely Russell's way of stating that Boole was one of the first to recognize the identity of formal logic with mathematics, a point of view firmly held by

Russell. In emphasizing that pure mathematics is made up of logical steps of the form "If p, then q" —that is, if such and such a proposition is true of anything, then such and such another proposition is true of that thing—Russell remarks that it is essential not to discuss whether the first proposition is really true, and not to mention what the anything is, of which it is supposed to be true. He is thus led to his oft-quoted description of mathematics as "the subject in which we never know what we are talking about, nor whether what we are saying is true." He comments that many people may find comfort in agreeing that the description is accurate.

Russell's gifts as a popularizer of knowledge are shown in a number of his other books, such as *The Analysis of Matter* and *The ABC of Relativity,* in which problems arising from contemporary physics are discussed. He never wholly divorced mathematics from its applications; and even his first book, on the foundations of geometry, had its origin in his wish to establish the concept of motion and the laws of dynamics on a secure logical basis. In these later books his critical skill is exercised on the mathematical foundations of physics and occasionally is used to provide alternatives to suggested theories.

For instance, the advent of relativity, bringing in the notion of an event as a point in the space-time continuum, had encouraged Whitehead to deal with the definition of points and events by the application of his principle of extensive abstraction, discussed in detail in his *An Enquiry Concerning the Principles of Natural Knowledge* (1919). This principle has a certain affinity with the Frege-Russell definition of the number of a class as the class of all similar classes. To state the application very crudely, a point is defined as the set of all volumes that enclose that point; Whitehead is of course careful to frame the principle in such a way as to avoid the circularity suggested in this crude statement. This idea is then used to define an event. In *The Analysis of Matter,* Russell argues that while logically flawless, this definition, in the case of an event, does not seem genuinely to correspond to the nature of events as they occur in the physical world, and that it makes the large assumption that there is no minimum and no maximum to the time extent of an event. He develops an alternative theory involving an ingenious application of Hausdorff's axioms for a topological space.[10]

Whatever the final verdict on Russell's work in symbolic logic may be, his place among the outstanding leaders in this field in the present century must be secure.

NOTES

1. G. Frege, *Die Grundlagen der Arithmetik* (Breslau, 1884), also in English (Oxford, 1953); *Grundgesetze der Arithmetik, begriffsschriftlich abgeleitet*, 2 vols. (Jena, 1893–1903), vol. I also in English (Berkeley–Los Angeles, 1964).
2. H. Poincaré, "La logique de l'infini," in *Scientia*, 12 (1912).
3. F. P. Ramsey, "The Foundations of Mathematics," in *Proceedings of the London Mathematical Society*, 2nd ser., 25 (1926).
4. H. Weyl, "Mathematics and Logic," in *American Mathematical Monthly*, 53 (1946); and "David Hilbert and His Mathematical Work," in *Bulletin of the American Mathematical Society*, 50 (1944).
5. A. De Morgan, "On the Logic of Relations," in *Transactions of the Cambridge Philosophical Society*, 10 (1864); C. S. Peirce, "On the Algebra of Logic," in *American Journal of Mathematics*, 3 (1880).
6. H. M. Sheffer, "A Set of Five Independent Postulates of Boolean Algebra," in *Transactions of the American Mathematical Society*, 14 (1913).
7. Jean Nicod, "A Reduction in the Number of the Primitive Propositions of Logic," in *Proceedings of the Cambridge Philosophical Society. Mathematical and Physical Sciences*, 19 (1919).
8. Leon Chwistek, "The Theory of Constructive Types," in *Annales de la Société mathématique de Pologne* (1924); L. Wittgenstein, *Tractatus Logico-Philosophicus* (London, 1922).
9. E. Zermelo, "Beweis, dass jede Menge wohlgeordnet werden kann," in *Mathematische Annalen*, 59 (1904); see also *ibid.*, 65 (1908).
10. F. Hausdorff, *Grundzüge der Mengenlehre* (Leipzig, 1914).

BIBLIOGRAPHY

I. ORIGINAL WORKS. Russell's contributions to mathematical logic are best studied through *An Essay on the Foundations of Geometry* (London, 1897); *The Principles of Mathematics*, I (London, 1903; 2nd ed. with new intro., 1937); *Principia Mathematica*, 3 vols. (London, 1910–1913; 2nd ed., with new intro., 1925–1927), written with A. N. Whitehead; and *Introduction to Mathematical Philosophy* (London, 1919).

The Autobiography of Bertrand Russell, 3 vols. (London, 1967–1969), contains a nontechnical account of his mathematical work in vol. I and early chs. of vol. II. *Mysticism and Logic* (London, 1917) contains some essays of a popular nature.

II. SECONDARY LITERATURE. The primary authority for Russell's life in his *Autobiography*, cited above. G. H. Hardy, *Bertrand Russell and Trinity* (London, 1970), clears away some misconceptions concerning Russell's relations with the college. An able and witty criticism of Russell's logical ideas is presented by P. E. B. Jourdain, given in *The Philosophy of Mr. B*rtr*nd R*ss*ll* (London, 1918).

For useful surveys of the doctrine of *Principia Mathematica*, see S. K. Langer, *An Introduction to Symbolic Logic* (New York, 1937); S. C. Kleene, *Introduction to Metamathematics* (New York, 1952), which has a valuable selected bibliography; and, by F. P. Ramsey, several items in *The Foundations of Mathematics and Other Logical Essays* (London, 1931). *The Philosophy of Bertrand Russell*, P. A. Schilpp, ed. (Chicago, 1944), contains a section by Gödel on Russell's mathematical logic.

To trace the many publications related directly or indirectly to Russell's work, see A. Church, "A Bibliography of Symbolic Logic," in *Journal of Symbolic Logic*, 1 (1936) and 3 (1938); it is also available as a separate volume. For the literature since 1935, the reader is advised to consult the volumes and index parts of the *Journal of Symbolic Logic*.

T. A. A. BROADBENT

RYDBERG, JOHANNES (JANNE) ROBERT (*b.* Halmstad, Sweden, 8 November 1854; *d.* Lund, Sweden, 28 December 1919)

Rydberg was the son of Sven R. and Maria Anderson Rydberg. After completing the Gymnasium at Halmstad in 1873, he entered the University of Lund, from which he received a bachelor's degree in philosophy in 1875. He continued his studies at Lund and was granted a doctorate in mathematics in 1879 after defending a dissertation on the construction of conic sections. In 1880 Rydberg was appointed a lecturer in mathematics. After some work on frictional electricity, he was named lecturer in physics in 1882 and was promoted to assistant at the Physics Institute in 1892. Rydberg married Lydia E. M. Carlsson in 1886; they had two daughters and a son. After provisionally occupying the professorship in physics at Lund from 1897, he was granted the appointment permanently in March 1901 and held it until November 1919. He was elected a foreign member of the Royal Society in 1919.

Rydberg's most significant scientific contributions were to spectroscopy; but his involvement with spectra had its origin in his interest in the periodic system of the elements, an interest that endured throughout his professional life. His earliest published papers in physics dealt with the periodic table. In the introduction to his major work on spectra (1890), he stated that he considered it only a part of a broader investigation, the goal of which was to achieve a more exact knowledge of the nature and constitution of the chemical and physical properties of the elements. He held that the effective force between atoms must be a periodic function of their atomic weights and that the periodic motions of the atoms, which presumably gave rise to the spectral lines and were dependent on the effective force, thus might be a fruitful study leading to a better knowledge of the mechanics, nature, and structure of atoms and molecules and to a deeper understanding of the periodic system of the other physical and chemical properties of the elements. In line with contemporary conceptions, Rydberg's view was that each individual line spectrum was the product of a single fundamental system of vibrations.

His major spectral work, "Recherches sur la constitution des spectres d'émission des éléments chimiques," published in 1890, mapped out Rydberg's total approach with remarkable clarity. He conceived of the spectrum of an element as composed of the superposition of three different types of series—one in which the lines were comparatively sharp, one in which the lines were more diffuse, and a third that he called principal series even though they consisted mostly of lines in the ultraviolet. The first lines were located in the visible spectrum and were usually the most intense. The members of each series might be single, double, triple, or of higher multiplicity. Any particular elementary spectrum might contain any number (even zero) of series of each of the basic types.

While Rydberg observed and measured some spectral lines on his own, he was not particularly noted as an experimental physicist and did not publish any of his experimental investigations or spectroscopic measurements. Most of the data he needed were already available in the voluminous literature. While T. R. Thalén and Bernhard Hasselberg, Rydberg's major Swedish contemporaries in spectral studies, concentrated upon accurate measurements of the spectra of the elements, Rydberg's major spectral contributions were to theory and mathematical form, and those to form were the ones of enduring value.

Unlike most others, Rydberg used wave numbers (the number of waves per unit length) instead of a correlated reciprocal, the directly measured wavelengths. This enabled him to manipulate his final formula into a particularly useful form.

Rydberg concluded that each series could be expressed approximately by an equation of the form

$$n = n_0 - \frac{N_0}{(m+\mu)^2},$$

where n was the wave number of a line; $N_0 = 109,721.6$, a constant common to all series and to all elements; n_0 and μ constants peculiar to the series; and m any positive integer (the number of the term). The lines of a series were generated by allowing m to take on integer values sequentially; n_0 defined the limit of the series that the wave number n approached when m became very large.

Just when he became occupied with confirming this relationship, Rydberg learned about Balmer's formula, which represented the observed lines of the hydrogen spectrum with extraordinary accuracy. He arranged Balmer's formula into its wave-number form and noted that, with appropriately selected constants, it was then a special form of his own more general formula. He felt that the success of Balmer's formula strengthened the justification of his own form. Thus encouraged, Rydberg proceeded to use the latter with sufficient success to propose it as the general formula for all series in all elementary line spectra, and to conclude that N_0 was indeed a universal constant, which has since become known as Rydberg's constant.

Spectroscopy had been a major developed field of physical study for several decades, but its most pressing need near the end of the nineteenth century was for the organization of its vast amount of data into some mathematically ordered form that theoreticians might find useful in their attempts to understand the underlying significance of spectra. Rydberg's general formula was the most important presentation of this type. Many others groped in the same general direction, mostly with ephemeral results. Rydberg's most significant competitors in this regard were Heinrich Kayser and Carl Runge, but their general formulas were of significantly different form.

The scope and structure of Rydberg's formula allowed him to note some important relationships. For example, he found not only that certain series with different values of μ exhibited the same value of n_0 but also that the value of the constant term n_0 in any series coincided with a member of the sequence of variable terms in some other series of the element. In particular, he discovered that the difference between the common limit of the diffuse and sharp series and the limit of the corresponding principal series gave the wave number of the common first-member term of the sharp and principal series, a relationship independently noted by Arthur Schuster and commonly known as the Rydberg-Schuster law.

Along this same line, Rydberg speculatively suggested as a comprehensive formula for every line of an element the relationship

$$\pm n = \frac{N_0}{(m_1 + \mu_1)^2} - \frac{N_0}{(m_2 + \mu_2)^2},$$

with which he hoped to represent a series according to whether he assumed either m_1 or m_2 to be variable. Thus, he viewed every spectral series as a set of differences between two terms of the type $N_0/(m + \mu)^2$ — that is, every spectral line would be expressed as $n = T_1 - T_2$, where T_1 and T_2 are two members of a set of terms characteristic of the element. This aspect, little appreciated at the time, was stated independently in 1908 by Walther Ritz and is commonly known as the Ritz combination principle.

The combination principle revealed several significant features about spectra. First, the wave number of each line could be conveniently represented as the difference between two numbers, called terms. Second, the terms could be naturally grouped into ordered sequences — the terms of each sequence converging toward zero. Third, the terms could be combined in various ways to give the wave numbers of the spectral lines. Fourth, a series of lines all having similar character resulted from the combination of all terms of one sequence taken in succession with a fixed term of another sequence. Thus, fifth, a large number of spectral lines could be expressed as the differences of a much smaller number of terms that in some way were characteristic of the atom and therefore, from a theoretical perspective, were more important than the lines themselves when speculating on atomic structure. Now it was these terms, rather than the lines, for which a direct physical interpretation should be found. This last point was widely overlooked by most contemporary physicists, including Rydberg.

As deeply as the notion of the existence of some fundamental mechanism might be stimulated by them, all the regularities noted by Rydberg were in themselves only empirical generalizations. His own theoretical concepts on atomic structure were still based on an analogy to acoustics. Therefore, Rydberg did not reach the final goal he had set for his work: an adequate insight into the nature and structure of the atom. His work did, however, provide a basis for the later development of successful ideas on atomic structure.

Some radically new ideas concerning the structure of the atom resulted from the development of other lines of evidence. In 1913 Niels Bohr proposed his theory of atomic structure based on Ernest Rutherford's nuclear atomic model and on Max Planck's quantum theory of radiation. These conceptions led to the first reasonably successful theoretical account of spectral data.

Bohr's view provided an immediate interpretation of the combination principle by identifying each Rydberg spectral term multiplied by hc (Planck's constant times the speed of light) with the energy of an allowable stationary state of the atom. The difference between two such states equaled the energy in the light quantum emitted in the transition from a higher allowable atomic-energy state to a lower one.

On this basis, spectral series were used to determine the excitation energies and ionization potentials of atoms. The further elaboration of these views led to a classification of the states of electron binding in a shell structure of the atoms that accounted for the periodic relationships of the properties of the elements, thereby fully justifying Rydberg's earlier faith that spectral studies could assist in attaining this goal. Rydberg played no role in this elaboration, however.

But earlier, along similar lines, Rydberg's study of the periodic properties of the elements led him in 1897 to suggest that certain characteristics of the elements could be more simply organized by using an atomic number instead of the atomic weights. This atomic number was to be identified with the ordinal index of the element in the periodic table. In 1906 Rydberg stated for the first time that 2, 8, and 18 (that is, $2n^2$, where $n = 1,2,3$) represented the number of elements in the early periods of the system. In 1913 he went further, correcting an earlier error about the number of rare earths from 36 to 32, thus allowing the $n = 4$ group to be included in the pattern.

Rydberg presented a spiral graph arrangement of the periodic table in which earlier holes in his system were corrected so that atomic numbers from helium on were two greater than at present. He maintained that there were two elements, nebulium and coronium, between hydrogen and helium in the system, supporting their existence by evidence from both spectra and graphical symmetry.

In 1913, H. G. J. Moseley published his paper based on researches on the characteristic X-ray spectra of the elements that strongly supported the fundamental importance of atomic numbers and Rydberg's basic expectations about the lengths of the periods of the periodic table. The physical reality that underlay Rydberg's atomic-number proposal was later interpreted as the positive charge on the atomic nucleus expressed in elementary units of charge.

Rydberg received a copy of Moseley's paper in manuscript form before publication. In a note written in 1914, he expressed satisfaction at the confirmation of his ideas on atomic numbers and the details of the periodic system, but he still maintained his conviction of the existence of the two elements between hydrogen and helium and the resulting difference of two in most atomic numbers. Later the nebulium spectrum was attributed to ionized oxygen and nitrogen, and the coronium lines to highly ionized iron.

Rydberg's health did not permit him to follow subsequent developments. In 1914 he became seriously ill. He went on an extended leave of absence that lasted until his formal retirement in 1919, a month before his death.

BIBLIOGRAPHY

I. ORIGINAL WORKS. Rydberg's most important spectral publication was "Recherches sur la constitution des spectres d'émission des éléments chimiques," in *Kungliga Svenska vetenskapsakademiens handlingar*, n.s. **23**, no. 11 (1890). Some of his other spectral works of significance are "On the Structure of the Line-Spectra of the Chemical Elements," in *Philosophical Magazine*, 5th ser., **29** (1890), 331–337; "Contributions à la connaissance des spectres linéaires," in *Ofversigt af K. Vetenskapsakademiens förhandlingar*, **50** (1893), 505–520, 677–691; "The New Elements of Cleveite Gas," in *Astrophysical Journal*, **4** (1896), 91–96; "The New Series in the Spectrum of Hydrogen," *ibid.*, **6** (1897), 233–238; "On the Constitution of the Red Spectrum of Argon," *ibid.*, 338–348; and "La distribution des raies spectrales," in *Rapports présentés au Congrès international de physique, Paris*, II (1900), 200–224.

Concerning his other work related to the periodic table, significant articles are "Die Gesetze der Atomgewichtszahlen," in *Bihang till K. Svenska vetenskapsakademiens handlingar*, **11**, no. 13 (1886); "Studien über die Atomgewichtszahlen," in *Zeitschrift für anorganische Chemie*, **14** (1897), 66–102; *Elektron der erste Grundstoff* (Berlin, 1906); "Untersuchungen über das System der Grundstoffe," in *Acta Universitatis lundensis*, Avd. 2, n.s. **9**, no. 18 (1913); and "The Ordinals of the Elements and the High-Frequency Spectra," in *Philosophical Magazine*, 6th ser., **28** (1914), 144–148.

II. SECONDARY LITERATURE. A short biography of value is Manne Siegbahn, in *Swedish Men of Science 1650–1950*, Sten Lindroth, ed., Burnett Anderson, trans. (Stockholm, 1952), 214–218. Siegbahn was a student at the University of Lund from 1906 to 1911 and an assistant at the Physics Institute from 1911 to 1914 while Rydberg was there. In the autumn of 1915 Siegbahn was appointed to fulfill Rydberg's duties while the latter went on an extended leave. In early 1920 Siegbahn permanently succeeded Rydberg in the chair of physics at Lund.

On the centenary of Rydberg's birth, an important collection of papers was presented at Lund: "Proceedings of the Rydberg Centennial Conference on Atomic Spectroscopy," in *Acta Universitatis lundensis*, Avd. 2, n.s. **50**, no. 21 (1954). Biographically, the two most significant articles are Niels Bohr, "Rydberg's Discovery of the Spectral Laws," 15–21; and Wolfgang Pauli, "Rydberg and the Periodic System of the Elements," 22–26.

Another biographical essay of merit is Sister St. John Nepomucene, "Rydberg: The Man and the Constant," in *Chymia*, **6** (1960), 127–145. Two brief biographical obituaries are in *Physikalische Zeitschrift*, **21** (1920), 113; and *Nature*, **105** (1920), 525.

C. L. MAIER

SACCHERI, (GIOVANNI) GIROLAMO (*b.* San Remo, Italy, 5 September 1667; *d.* Milan, Italy, 25 October 1733)

Saccheri is sometimes confused with his Dominican namesake (1821–1894), a librarian at the Biblioteca Casanatense of Rome. In 1685 Saccheri entered the Jesuit novitiate in Genoa and after two years taught at the Jesuit college in that city until 1690. Sent to Milan, he studied philosophy and theology at the Jesuit College of the Brera, and in March 1694 he was ordained a priest at Como. In the same year he was sent to teach philosophy first at Turin and, in 1697, at the Jesuit College of Pavia. In 1699 he began teaching philosophy at the university, where until his death he occupied the chair of mathematics.

One of Saccheri's teachers at the Brera was Tommaso Ceva, best known as a poet but also well versed in mathematics and mechanics. Through him Saccheri met his brother Giovanni, a mathematician living at the Gonzaga court in Mantua. This Ceva is known for his theorem in the geometry of triangles (1678). Under Ceva's influence Saccheri published his first book, *Quaesita geometrica* (1693), in which he solved a number of problems in elementary and coordinate geometry. Ceva sent this book to Vincenzo Viviani, one of the last surviving pupils of Galileo, who in 1692 (*Acta eruditorum*, 274–275) had challenged the learned world with the problem in analysis known as the window of Viviani. Although it had been solved by Leibniz and others, Viviani published his own solution and sent it to Saccheri in exchange for the *Quaesita*. Two letters from Saccheri to Viviani (1694) are preserved, one containing Saccheri's own solution (without proof).

While in Turin, Saccheri wrote *Logica demonstrativa* (1697), important because it treats questions relating to the compatibility of definitions. During his years at Pavia he wrote the *Neo-statica*

(1708), inspired by and partly a polemic against T. Ceva's *De natura gravium* (Milan, 1669). This book seems of little importance now, being well within the bounds of Peripatetic statics. *Euclides ab omni naevo vindicatus* (1733), also written at Pavia, contains the classic text that made Saccheri a precursor of the discoverers of non-Euclidean geometry.

Saccheri's two most important books, the *Logica* and the *Euclides,* were virtually forgotten until they were rescued from oblivion—the *Euclides* by E. Beltrami in 1889 and the *Logica* by G. Vailati in 1903. They show that Euclid's fifth postulate (equivalent to the parallel axiom) intrigued Saccheri throughout his life. In the *Logica* it led him to investigate the nature of definitions and in the *Euclides* to an attempt to apply his logic to prove the correctness of the fifth postulate. Although the fallacy in this attempt is now apparent, much of Saccheri's logical and mathematical reasoning has become part of mathematical logic and non-Euclidean geometry.

The *Logica demonstrativa* is divided into four parts corresponding to Aristotle's *Analytica priora, Analytica posteriora, Topica,* and *De sophisticis Elenchis.* It is an attempt, probably the first in print, to explain the principles of logic *more geometrico.* Stress is placed on the distinction between *definitiones quid nominis* (nominal definitions), which simply define a concept, and *definitiones quid res* (real definitions), which are nominal definitions to which a postulate of existence is attached. But when we are concerned with existence, the question arises whether one part of the definition is compatible with another part. This may be the case in what Saccheri called complex definitions. In these discussions he was deeply influenced by Euclid's *Elements,* notably by the definition of parallelism of two lines. He warned against the definition, given by G. A. Borelli (*Euclides restitutus* [Pisa, 1658]), of parallels as equidistant straight lines. Thus Saccheri was one of the first to draw explicit attention to the question of consistency and compatibility of axioms.

To test whether a valid proposition is included in a definition, Saccheri proposed reasoning seemingly analogous to the classical *reductio ad absurdum,* using for his example *Elements* IX, 12: if $1, a_1, a_2, \cdots, a_n$ form a geometric progression and a_n has a prime factor p, then a_1' also contains this factor. There was a difference in Saccheri's proposal, however: his demonstration resulted from the fact that, reasoning from the negation, we obtain exactly the proposition to be proved, so that this

proposition appears as the consequence of its own negation (an example of his reasoning is seen below). As Vailati observed, Saccheri's reasoning had much in common with that of Leibniz (see L. Couturat, *Opuscules et fragments inédits de Leibniz* [Paris, 1903]); but whereas Leibniz's primary inspiration came from algebra and the calculus, Saccheri's came from geometry.

In the *Euclides* Saccheri applied his logical principle to three "blemishes" in the *Elements.* By far the most important was his application of his type of *reductio ad absurdum* to Euclid's parallel axiom. He took as true Euclid's first twenty-six propositions and then assumed that the fifth postulate was false. Among the consequences of this hypothesis he sought a proposition to test the postulate itself. He found it in what is now called the quadri-

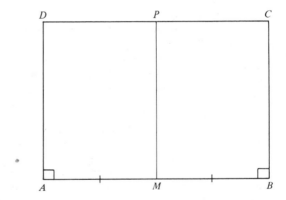

lateral of Saccheri, an isosceles birectangular quadrilateral consisting of a side *AB* and two sides of equal length, *AD* and *BC* at right angles to *AB.* Then without the fifth postulate it cannot be proved that the angles at *C* and *D* are right. One can prove that they are equal, since if a line *MP* is drawn through the midpoint *M* of *AB* perpendicular to *AB,* it intersects *DC* at its midpoint *P.* Thus there are three possibilities, giving rise to three hypotheses:

1. that of the right angle: $\angle C = \angle D = 1$ right angle;

2. that of the obtuse angle: $\angle C = \angle D > 1$ right angle;

3. that of the acute angle: $\angle C = \angle D < 1$ right angle.

Saccheri proceeded to prove that when each of these hypotheses is true in only one case, it is true in every other case. Thus in the first case the sum of the angles of a triangle is equal to, in the second it is greater than, and in the third case it is less than, two right angles.

For the proofs Saccheri needed the axiom of

Archimedes and the principle of continuity. Then came the crucial point: he proved that for both the hypothesis of the right angle and that of the obtuse angle the fifth postulate holds. But the fifth postulate implies the hypothesis of the right angle; hence the hypothesis of the obtuse angle is false. (This argument is not now cogent because in the case of the obtuse angle the existence of the finite length of lines is accepted.) He could not dispose of the hypothesis of the acute angle in this way, but he was able to show that it leads to the existence of asymptotic straight lines, which, he concluded, was repugnant to the nature of the straight line. Saccheri thus thought that he had established the truth of the hypothesis of the right angle and, hence, of the fifth postulate and of Euclidean geometry as a whole.

Several other theorems resulted from Saccheri's three hypotheses, some of which are now established as part of non-Euclidean geometry. The three types of quadrangles had already been studied by al-Khayyāmī and Nasīr-al-Dīn al-Tūsī; the latter was cited by John Wallis (1693) in a book known to Saccheri.

Saccheri's *Euclides*, although it had little direct influence on the subsequent discovery of non-Euclidean geometry, was not so forgotten as is sometimes believed. (See Segre, below.)

BIBLIOGRAPHY

I. ORIGINAL WORKS. Saccheri's writings include *Quaesita geometrica a comite Rugerio De Vigintimilliis* . . . (Milan, 1693), included in *Sphinx geometra, seu quesita geometrica proposita et solida* . . . (Parma, 1694); *Logica demonstrativa quam una cum thesibus ex tota philosophiae decerptis defendendam proposuit J. F. Caselette Graveriarum Comes* (Turin, 1697), 2nd ed. entitled *Logica demonstrativa auctore Hieronym. Saccherio Societatis Jesu* . . . (Pavia, 1701), 3rd ed. entitled *Logica demonstrativa, theologicis, philosophicis et mathematicis disciplinis accomodata* . . . (Cologne, 1735); *Neo-statica* . . . (Milan, 1708); and *Euclides ab omni naevo vindicatus: Sive conatus geometricus quo stabiliuntur prima ipsa universae geometriae principia* . . . (Milan, 1733). Theological works are listed in P. C. Sommervogel, *Bibliothèque des écrivains de la Compagnie de Jésus, VII* (Brussels–Paris, 1897), 360.

Letters by Saccheri to Viviani, Ceva, and Grandi are in A. Favaro, "Due lettere inedite del P. Girolamo Saccheri d. C. d. G. a Vincenzo Viviani," in *Rivista di fisica, matematica e scienze naturali*, **4** (1903), 424–434; A. Pascal, "Sopra una lettera inedita di G. Saccheri," in *Atti del R. Istituto Veneto di scienze, lettere ed arti*, **74** (1914–1915), 813–820; and A. Agostini, "Due lettere inedite di G. Saccheri," in *Memorie della R. Academia d'Italia*, Cl. di Scienze Matematiche e Na- turale, 2, no. 7 (1931), 31–48.

II. SECONDARY LITERATURE. The full text of the *Logica demonstrativa*, with English trans., is in A. F. Emch, "The *Logica demonstrativa* of Girolamo Saccheri" (Ph.D. diss., Harvard, 1933), with a life of Saccheri by F. Gambarana from a MS at the Biblioteca Estense in Modena. The *Logica* is discussed by Emch in articles of the same title as his dissertation in *Scripta mathematica*, **3** (1935–1936), 51–60, 143–152, 221–233. On the *Logica*, see also G. Vailati, "Di un' opera dimenticata del P. Gerolamo Saccheri," in *Rivista filosofica*, **4** (1903), 528–540; with other papers on the book, it is also in *Scritti di G. Vailati (1863–1909)* (Leipzig–Florence, 1911), 477–484, see also 449–453. Also of value is F. Enriques, *Per la storia della logica* (Bologna, 1922), 94–99, also available in French, German, and English.

The *Euclides ab omni naevo vindicatus* has been partially translated (only bk. I with the discussion of the parallel axiom) by P. Stäckel and F. Engel in *Die Theorie der Parallellinien von Euclid bis auf Gauss* (Leipzig, 1895), 31–136, and into English by G. B. Halsted in *Girolamo Saccheri's Euclides vindicatus* (Chicago–London, 1920). See also ten articles by Halsted on non-Euclidean geometry in *American Mathematical Monthly*, **1** (1894), see index, p. 447. There is an unsatisfactory Italian trans. by G. Boccardini, *L'Euclide emendato* . . . (Milan, 1904). Further literature on the *Euclides* (listed chronologically) includes E. Beltrami, "Un precursore italiano di Legendre e di Lobatschewsky," in *Atti della Reale Accademia Lincei, Rendiconti*, 4th ser., **5**, no. 1 (1889), 441–448, also in Beltrami's *Opere*, IV (Milan, 1920), 348–355; P. Mansion, "Analyse des recherches du P. Saccheri S.J. sur le postulatum d'Euclide," in *Annales de la Société scientifique de Bruxelles*, **14** (1889–1890), pt. 2, 46–59, also in *Mathesis*, 2nd ser., **1** (1891), supp. 15–29; C. Segre, "Congettare informo all'influenza di Girolamo Saccheri sulla formazione della geometrica non-euclidea," in *Atti dell'Accademia delle scienze* (Turin), **38** (1902–1903), 535–547; A. Pascal, "Girolamo Saccheri nella vita e nelle opere," in *Giornale di matematica di Battaglini*, **52** (1914), 229–251; and H. Bosmans, "Le géomètre Jérome Saccheri S. J.," in *Revue des questions scientifiques*, 4th ser., **7** (1925), 401–430.

Saccheri's contribution to non-Euclidean geometry is discussed in R. Bonola, *La geometria non-euclidea* (Bologna, 1906), also in English (Chicago, 1911; repr. 1955) and in German (Berlin, 1908). See also article on Saccheri by E. Carruccio, *Enciclopedia italiana di scienze, lettere ed arte*, **30** (Rome, 1936), 389–390.

D. J. STRUIK

SACROBOSCO, JOHANNES DE (or JOHN OF HOLYWOOD)

(*b.* Holywood, Yorkshire, England, end of twelfth century; *d.* Paris, France, 1256 [1244?])

Sacrobosco (also called John or Johannes Halifax, Holyfax, Holywalde, Sacroboscus, Sacrobuschus, de Sacro Bosco, or de Sacro Busto) has been called a Scot, an Irishman, a Frenchman, a Brabançon, a Catalan, and a Jewish convert—all unfounded attributions. Some put his birthplace at Holywood near Dublin, or even at Nithsdale, Scotland. Very little is known of his life. English biographies maintain, and it is commonly held, that he was educated at Oxford.

After his studies Sacrobosco entered into orders and became a canon regular of the Order of St. Augustine at the famous monastery of Holywood in Nithsdale. About 1220 he went to Paris, where he spent most of his life and where he was admitted as a member of the university, on 5 June 1221, under the syndics of the Scottish nation. Elected professor of mathematics soon afterward, he won wide and enduring renown and was among the first exponents in the thirteenth century of the Arab arithmetic and algebra. By 1231 he was the outstanding mathematician and astronomer. He died in either 1244 or 1256 and was buried in the cloisters of the Fathers of Mercy, convent of St. Mathurin, in Paris.

The ambiguity of the year of Sacrobosco's death comes from the epitaph engraved on his tombstone in the convent cloisters: "M. Christi bis C. quarto deno quater anno De Sacro Bosco discrevit tempora ramus Gratia cui dederat nomen divina Joannes." If *quater* modifies only *deno*, then four times ten equals forty, plus four gives forty-four. If *quater* modifies *quarto deno*, then *quarto deno* is fourteen, and four times fourteen is fifty-six. The second interpretation is preferred by Johannes Fabricius, Christopher Saxius, Montucla, Bossut, and G. J. Vossius. An astrolabe decorates the stone, identifying the science to which he was most dedicated.

Sacrobosco's chief extant works are elementary textbooks on mathematics and astronomy: *De algorismo, De computo*, and *De sphaera*. All three are frequently found in the same manuscript, or at least bound together, and may be his only extant books. Prosdocimo de Beldemandis, however, wrote in his fifteenth-century commentary on the *De sphaera* that there were "many other works that it would take too long to enumerate here." A second arithmetic on fractions, *Algorismus de minutiis*, is attributed to Sacrobosco by Prosdocimo, but the opening words are those commonly occurring in a treatise usually ascribed to a Richard of England. Other works dubiously ascribed to him are a brief tract on physical or philosophical

(that is, sexagesimal or astronomical) rather than common fractions, two tracts on the quadrant (one of which is more often ascribed to Campanus of Novara), an *Arithmetica communis*, and perhaps some commentaries on Aristotle.

Sacrobosco's fame rests firmly on his *De sphaera*, a small work based on Ptolemy and his Arabic commentators, published about 1220 and antedating the *De sphaera* of Grosseteste. It was quite generally adopted as the fundamental astronomy text, for often it was so clear that it needed little or no explanation. It was first used at the University of Paris.

There are only four chapters to the work. Chapter one defines a sphere, explains its divisions, including the four elements, and also comments on the heavens and their movements. The revolutions of the heavens are from east to west and their shape is spherical. The earth is a sphere, acting as the middle (or center) of the firmament; it is a mere point in relation to the total firmament and is immobile. Its measurements are also included.

Chapter two treats the various circles and their names—the celestial circle; the equinoctial; the movement of the *primum mobile* with its two parts, the north and south poles; the zodiac; the ecliptic; the colures; the meridian and the horizon; and the arctic and antarctic circles. It closes with an explanation of the five zones.

Chapter three explains the cosmic, chronic, and heliacal risings and settings of the signs and also their right and oblique ascensions. Explanations are furnished for the variations in the length of days in different global zones, namely, the equator, and in zones extending from the equator to the two poles. A discussion of the seven climes ends the chapter.

The movement of the sun and other planets and the causes of lunar and solar eclipses form the brief fourth chapter.

During the Middle Ages the *De sphaera* enjoyed great renown, and from the middle of the thirteenth century it was taught in all the schools of Europe. In the sixteenth century it gained the attention of mathematicians, including Clavius. As late as the seventeenth century it was used as a basic astronomy text, but after 1700 it was completely forgotten.

After Manilius' *Astronomica, The Sphere* was the first printed book on astronomy (Ferrara, 1472). Twenty-four more editions appeared in the following twenty-eight years, and more than forty editions from 1500 to 1547, the last being issued at Leiden. For eighty years after Barocius in 1570 had pointed out some eighty-four errors, *The Sphere* was still studied, and in the seventeenth century it served as a manual of astronomy in some German and Low Countries schools. Often it appeared with commentaries by the most distinguished scholars of the time. There were three Italian editions: by Maurus (Florence, 1550); by Dante de'Rinaldi (Florence, 1571), and by Francesco Pifferi at Sienna in 1537, 1550, 1572, 1579, 1604. Two French editions, by Martin Perer and Guillaume Desbordes, were printed at Paris in 1546 and 1576.

Some claim that *The Sphere* merely paraphrases the elementary ideas of Ptolemy and the Arab astronomers al-Battānī and al-Farghānī, but this is a great exaggeration. Sacrobosco's *Sphere* is far superior in structure and order to that of al-Farghānī. Resemblances should not be surprising, however, since both writers summarized the *Almagest*. Actually Sacrobosco omitted much of what is found in al-Farghānī, condensed what little he did use of it, and restated and rearranged the matter into a more effective plan. Indications are equally strong for his using Macrobius' *Commentary on the Dream of Scipio* as for al-Farghānī's *Elements*, although Macrobius is rarely mentioned.

Commentaries on *The Sphere* were written by Michael Scot between 1230 and 1235; by John Pecham, a Franciscan, sometime before 1279; by the Dominican Bernard of Le Treille between 1263 and 1266; and by Campanus of Novara between 1265 and 1292. Robertus Anglicus gave a course of lectures on Sacrobosco's *Sphere* at either the University of Paris or the University of Montpellier in 1271, which helps to date his own commentary. He stated that for the most part *The Sphere* was so clear it needed no further explanation.

Cecco d'Ascoli was the earliest of the fourteenth-century commentators on *The Sphere* (probably before 1324). The Dominican Ugo de Castello (Ugo di Città di Castello) wrote a commentary on *The Sphere* that was begun at Paris and finished at Florence in 1337. On 19 October 1346, at Ghent, Henry of Sinrenberg, an Augustinian friar, completed a commentary on *The Sphere*, in which he addressed friends and fellow Augustinians in the *studium* of the monastery of Milan. This indicates the wide geographical spread of the use of *The Sphere*, beyond universities to convent schools. Blasius of Parma commented on *The Sphere* in the late fourteenth century.

Fifteenth-century commentators included Prosdocimo de Beldemandis in 1418 and Franciscus Capuanus de Manfredonia about 1475. Their works are quite detailed and concern any subject that might be even remotely connected with *The Sphere*. Other commentators of this period were Jacques Lefèvre d'Étaples, Wenceslaus Faber of Budweis, and Pedro Ciruelo of Daroca (his commentary was published in February 1498). Incunabula editions of Sacrobosco's *Sphere* were brought out by Gasparino Borro (*d.* 1498), a Servite; and by George of Montferrat. Fausto Andrelini, the Italian humanist, lectured on *The Sphere* while at the University of Paris in 1496.

Sixteenth- and seventeenth-century commentators included Joannes Baptista Capuanus, Bartolomaeus Vespuccius, Erasmus Oswald (Schreckenfuchs), Maurus Florentinus, and Christoph Clavius, the Jesuit astronomer whose huge commentary was held in high regard.

Although the university curriculum of the time was based heavily on logic, Sacrobosco's *Sphere* was required reading, and properly so, first at Paris. The Faculty of Arts at Vienna in 1389 made *The Sphere* and the *De algorismo* required for the A.B. degree. At Erfurt in 1420 the matter of the quadrivium consisted solely of *The Sphere*. At Bourges in the fifteenth century, Euclid, various works of Aristotle, and *The Sphere* were required for the licentiate. In 1409 at Oxford it was required for the A.B. degree. At Bologna the Faculty of Arts required the *De algorismo* in the first year of their premedical course and *The Sphere* in the second year.

The *De computo ecclesiastico* or *De anni ratione*, written about 1232 and probably after *The Sphere*, points out the increasing error in the Julian calendar and suggests a remedy markedly similar to the one actually used under Gregory XIII, some 350 years later, in the revision of the calendar. It was printed at Paris in 1538(?), 1550, and 1572, and at Antwerp in 1547 and 1566.

Sacrobosco's *De computo ecclesiastico* deals with the division of time—marked out by the movements of the sun and moon and their interrelationship—into days and years. A discussion of the sun and its influence on the lengths of days, months, and years forms the first half of the work. In the second half, similar considerations are applied to the moon. The solar and lunar years, the solar and lunar cycles, intercalary days, and the movable feasts are examined.

De algorismo discusses the art of calculating with nonnegative integers. The work contains eleven chapters and examines numeration, addition, subtraction, mediation, duplication, multiplication, division, progression, and extraction of both the square and cube roots of numbers. Mediation is the halving of a given number, and duplication is the doubling of a number. Six rules of multiplication are included, depending on what combination of digits and articles are to be multiplied. Natural progression begins with the number one and the difference between adjacent numbers is one. Broken progression begins with the number two and the difference between adjacent terms of the progression is two. Two rules are given for finding the sum of terms in a natural progression, depending on whether the last term is an odd or even number. In the section on extracting roots, lineal, superficial, and solid numbers are first defined and their properties listed. Lastly, methods of extracting the square and cubic roots of a number are discussed.

Throughout the work examples of various arithmetic processes are included, and diagrams are supplied to facilitate understanding the method.

The *De algorismo* or *De arte numerandi* was first printed without date or place (1490[?]). It was later printed at Vienna by Hieronymus Vietor in 1517, at Cracow in 1521 or 1522, at Venice in 1523, and on occasion printed with *The Sphere*. It was the most widely used manual of arithmetic in the Middle Ages. Copies abound in manuscript form: some forty-three are in the Vatican holdings alone. Peter Philomenus of Dacia wrote a commentary on *De algorismo* toward the close of the thirteenth century, a copy of which is included in Holliwell's *Rara mathematica* of 1841.

BIBLIOGRAPHY

I. Original Works. Maximilian Curtze's ed. of Sacrobosco's *Algorismus vulgaris*, with the commentary of Peter Philomenus of Dacia, is *Petri Philomeni de Dacia in Algorismus vulgarem Johannis de Sacrobosco commentarius una cum Algorismo ipso* (Copenhagen, 1897). Robert R. Steele translated Sacrobosco's *De arte numerandi* as "The Art of Nombryng," in R. Steele, ed., *The Earliest Arithmetics in English*, Early English Text Society Extra Ser. no. 118 (London, 1922), 33–51. MSS are McGill University MS 134, fols. 1r–20v; Vaticana Latina 3114, fols. 28–33; and Vaticana Rossi 732, fols. 76–80.

II. Secondary Literature. See Pierre Duhem, *Le système du monde,* 5 vols. (Paris, 1913–1917); J. O. Halliwell-Phillips, *Rara arithmetica* (London, 1839; 2nd ed., 1841); *Histoire littéraire de la France*, XIX (1838), 1–4; and Lynn Thorndike, *History of Magic and Experimental Science,* IV (1941), 560; and *The Sphere of Sacrobosco and Its Commentators* (Chicago, 1949).

JOHN F. DALY, S.J.

SAINT-VENANT, ADHÉMAR JEAN CLAUDE BARRÉ DE (*b.* Villiers-en-Bière, Seine et-Marne, France, 23 August 1797; *d.* St.-Ouen, Loir-et-Cher, France, 6 January 1886)

Saint-Venant entered the École Polytechnique in 1813. Upon graduating he joined the Service des Poudres et Salpêtres and in 1823 transferred to the Service des Ponts et Chaussées, where he served for twenty years. He devoted the remainder of his life to teaching and, especially, to scientific research. In 1868 he was elected to the mechanics section of the Académie des Sciences, succeeding Poncelet.

Saint-Venant's investigations deal chiefly with the mechanics of solid bodies, elasticity, hydrostatics, and hydrodynamics. Closely related to engineering, they frequently had immediate applications to road- and bridge-building, to the control of streams, and to agriculture. On the basis of his work on the torsion of prisms or cylinders of any base and on the equilibrium of elastic beams, Saint-Venant presented a memoir to the Académie des Sciences in 1844 dealing with gauche curves. In it he introduced the term "binormal," which is still used: "This line is, in effect, normal to two consecutive elements at the same time."

In "Mémoire sur les sommes et les différences géométriques et sur leur usage pour simplifier la mécanique" (1845), Saint-Venant set forth a vector calculus displaying certain analogies with the conceptions of H. G. Grassmann. In a subsequent priority dispute Saint-Venant asserted in a letter to Grassmann, written in 1847, that his ideas dated from 1832.

Saint-Venant used this vector calculus in his lectures at the Institut Agronomique, which were published in 1851 as *Principes de mécanique fondés sur la cinématique.* In this book Saint-Venant, a convinced atomist, presented forces as divorced from the metaphysical concept of cause and from the physiological concept of muscular effort, both of which, in his opinion, obscured force as a kinematic concept accessible to the calculus. Although his atomistic conceptions did not prevail, his use of vector calculus was adopted in the French school system.

BIBLIOGRAPHY

I. Original Works. The Royal Society *Catalogue of Scientific Papers,* I, 189–191; VIII, 812–814; and XI, 262, lists 111 works by Saint-Venant and four of which he was coauthor. Among his some 170 published writings are *Leçons de mécanique appliquée faites à l'École des ponts et chaussées* (Paris, 1838); "Mémoire et expériences sur l'écoulement de l'air," in *Journal de l'École polytechnique*, **16** (1839), 85–122, written with Laurent Wantzel; "Mémoire sur les courbes non planes," *ibid.*, **18** (1845), 1–76; "Mémoire sur les sommes et les différences géométriques et sur leur usage pour simplifier la mécanique," in *Comptes rendus . . . de l'Académie des sciences*, **21** (1845), 620–625; *Principes de mécanique fondés sur la cinématique* (Paris, 1851); "De l'interprétation géométrique des clefs algébriques et des déterminants," in *Comptes rendus . . . de l'Académie des sciences*, **36** (1853), 582–585; *Mécanique appliquée de Navier, annotée par Saint-Venant* (Paris, 1858); "Deux leçons sur la théorie générale de l'élasticité," in Chanoine Moigno, *Stratique* (Paris, 1868), lessons 21 and 22; R. Clebsch, *Theorie de l'élasticité des corps solides*, translated by Saint-Venant and Alfred Flamant, with notes by Saint-Venant (Paris, 1883), and "Resistance des fluides: Considérations historiques physiques et pratiques relatives au problème de l'action dynamique mutuelle d'un fluide et d'un solide, spécialement dans l'état de permanence supposé acquis dans leurs mouvements," in *Mémoires de l'Académie des sciences*, **44** (1888), 1–192, 271–273.

II. SECONDARY LITERATURE. See J. Boussinesq and A. Flamant, "Notice sur la vie et les travaux de M. de Saint-Venant," in *Annales des ponts et chaussées*, 6th ser., **12** (1886), 557–595, which includes a very comprehensive bibliography; Michel Chasles, *Rapport sur les progrès de la géométrie* (Paris, 1870), 197–199; Michael J. Crowe, *A History of Vector Analysis* (Notre Dame, Ind., 1967), 81–85; René Dugas, *Histoire de la mécanique* (Paris, 1950), 421–422; and E. Phillips, "Notice sur M. de Saint-Venant," in *Comptes rendus . . . de l'Académie des sciences*, **102** (1886), 141–147.

JEAN ITARD

SAINT VINCENT, GREGORIUS (*b.* Bruges, Belgium, 8 September 1584; *d.* Ghent, Belgium, 27 January 1667)

Nothing is known of Gregorius' origins. He entered the Jesuit *collège* of Bruges in 1595 and from 1601 studied philosophy and mathematics at Douai. In 1605 he became a Jesuit novice at Rome and in 1607 was received into the order. His teacher Christoph Clavius recognized Gregorius' talents and arranged for him to remain in Rome to study philosophy, mathematics, and theology. When Galileo compared his telescope with those of the Jesuits in 1611, Gregorius hinted that he had doubts about the geocentric system, thereby displeasing the scholastically oriented philosophers.

After Clavius died in 1612, Gregorius went to Louvain to complete his theological studies, and in 1613 he was ordained priest. After being assigned to teach Greek for several years, first in Brussels, then in Bois-le-Duc ('s Hertogenbosch, Netherlands [1614]), and in Courtrai (1615), he served for a year as chaplain with the Spanish troops stationed in Belgium. He then became lecturer in mathematics at the Jesuit college in Antwerp, succeeding François d'Aguilon (*d.* 1617). Gregorius' *Theses de cometis* (Louvain, 1619) and *Theses mechanicae* (Antwerp, 1620) were defended by his student Jean Charles de la Faille, who later made them the basis of his highly regarded *Theoremata de centro gravitatis* (1632).

Established as a mathematician at Louvain in 1621, Gregorius elaborated the theory of conic sections on the basis of Commandino's editions of Archimedes (1558), Apollonius (1566), and Pappus (1588). He also developed a fruitful method of infinitesimals. His students Gualterus van Aelst and Johann Ciermans defended his *Theoremata mathematica scientiae staticae* (Louvain, 1624); and two other students, Guillaume Boelmans and Ignaz Derkennis, aided him in preparing the *Problema Austriacum*, a quadrature of the circle, which Gregorius regarded as his most important result. He requested permission from Rome to print his manuscript, but the general of the order, Mutio Vitelleschi, hesitated to grant it. Vitelleschi's doubts were strengthened by the opinion that Christoph Grienberger (Clavius' successor) rendered on the basis of preliminary material sent from Louvain.

Gregorius was called to Rome in 1625 to modify his manuscript but returned to Belgium in 1627 with the matter still unsettled. In 1628 he went to Prague, where he suffered a stroke. Following his recovery, his superiors granted his request that a former student, Theodor Moret, be made his assistant. His poor health forced Gregorius to decline an offer from the Madrid Academy in 1630. The following year he fled to Vienna just ahead of the advancing Swedes, but he was obliged to leave behind his scientific papers, including an extensive work on statics. A colleague, Rodrigo de Arriaga, rescued the studies on the conic sections and on methods of quadrature. Gregorius, who meanwhile had become a mathematician in Ghent (1632), did not receive his papers until 1641. He published them at Antwerp in 1647 as *Opus geometricum quadraturae circuli et sectionum coni*. His *Opus geometricum posthumum ad mesolabium* (Ghent, 1668) is an unimportant work, the first part of which had been printed at the time of his death.

Gregorius' major work is the *Opus geometricum* of 1647, misleadingly entitled *Problema Austria-*

cum; it is over 1,250 folio pages long and badly organized. It treats of four main subjects. Book I contains various introductory theorems on the circle and on triangles as well as geometrically clothed algebraic transformations. Book II includes the sums of geometric series obtained by means of transformation to the differences of the terms. Among the applications presented in this book is the step-by-step approximation of the trisection of an angle through continuous bisection, corresponding to the relationship $1/2 - 1/4 + 1/8 \mp \cdots = 1/3$. Another is the skillful treatment of Zeno of Elea's paradox of Achilles and the tortoise. In book VIII it is shown that if the horn angle is conceived as a quantity, the axiom of the whole and the parts no longer holds.

Books III–VI are devoted to the circle, ellipse, parabola, and hyperbola, and to the correspondence between the parabola and the Archimedean spiral (today expressed as $x = r$, $y = r\phi$). These books contain various propositions concerning the metric and projective properties of conic sections. Their scope far exceeds that found in older treatments, but their presentation is unsystematic. Common properties are based on the figure of the conic section pencil $y^2 = 2\,px - (1 - \epsilon^2)x^2$, where ϵ is the parameter. (This figure had appeared in 1604 in a work by Kepler.) By inscribing and circumscribing rectangles in a geometric series in and about a hyperbola, Gregorius developed a quadrature of a segment bound by two asymptotes, a line parallel to one of them, and the portion of the curve contained between the two parallels. The relation between this procedure and logarithms was first noted by Alfonso Antonio de Sarasa (1649).

Book VII contains Gregorius' remarkable quadrature method. It is a summation procedure—the so-called *ductus plani in planum*—related to the method of indivisibles developed by Bonaventura Cavalieri, although the two are mutually independent. Gregorius' method, however, is somewhat better founded. In modern terms it amounts to the geometric interpretation of cubatures of the form $\int y(x) \cdot z(x) \cdot dx$. It touches on considerations related to the then-unknown *Method* of Archimedes, considerations that, in book IX, are applied to bodies of simple generation. A section of book VII deals with "virtual" parabolas, expressible in modern notation as $y = \sqrt{ax + b} + \sqrt{cx + d}$.

Book X is devoted to the quadrature of the circle, which here is based on cubatures of the following type:

$$X_1 = 2a \int_{x-c}^{x+c} \sqrt{a^2 - t^2}\,dt, \quad X_2 = \int_{x-c}^{x+c} (a^2 - t^2)\,dt,$$

$$X_3 = \int_{x-c}^{x+c} (a^2 - t^2)^2 dt/4a^2$$

$$Y_1 = 2a \int_{y-c}^{y+c} \sqrt{a^2 - t^2}\,dt, \quad Y_2 = \int_{y-c}^{y+c} (a^2 - t^2)\,dt,$$

$$Y_3 = \int_{y-c}^{y+c} (a^2 - t^2)^2 dt/4a^2,$$

given that $x \neq y$ and $0 \leqq x - c < x + c \leqq a$ and $0 \leqq y - c < y + c \leqq a$. The crucial element of the argument is the false assertion that from $X_2/Y_2 = (X_1/Y_1)^n$ it follows that $X_3/Y_3 = (X_2/Y_2)^n$. The result is the appearance in the calculations of an error of integration, first detected by Huygens (1651). The error arose from the geometric presentation of the argument, which made it extraordinarily difficult to get an overall grasp of the problem. This error considerably damaged Gregorius' reputation among mathematicians of the following generation. But their reaction was unfair, for his other results show that he was a creative mathematician with a broad command of the knowledge of his age. Although Gregorius basically despised algebraic terminology, he was, as his students recognized, one of the great pioneers in infinitesimal analysis.

BIBLIOGRAPHY

I. ORIGINAL WORKS. Gregorius' unprinted posthumous papers are in the Bibliothèque Royale Albert Ier, nos. 5770–5793. Nos. 5770–5772, which are partially illustrated with remarkable figures, are discussed in E. Sauvenier-Goffin, "Les manuscrits de Saint-Vincent," in *Bulletin de la Société r. des sciences de Liège*, **20** (1951), 413–436, 563–590, 711–737. See also P. Bockstaele, "Four Letters from Gregorius a S. Vincentio to Christophe Grienberger," in *Janus*, **56** (1969), 191–202. A portrait of Gregorius is in *Opus geometricum posthumum* (1668).

II. SECONDARY LITERATURE. For a biography of Gregorius, see H. Bosmans, "Saint Vincent (Grégoire de)," in *Biographie nationale belge*, XXI, cols. 141–171, which contains an extensive bibliography.

For a discussion of Gregorius' work on conic sections, see K. Bopp, "Die Kegelschnitte des Gregorius a S. Vincentio," in *Abhandlungen zur Geschichte der Mathematik*, no. 20 (1907), 83–314.

Gregorius' work on infinitesimal analysis and its influence on other mathematicians is discussed in J. E. Hofmann, "Das *Opus geometricum* des Gregorius a S. Vincentio und seine Einwirkung auf Leibniz," in *Abhandlungen der Preussischen Akademie der Wissenschaf-*

ten, Math. Naturwiss. Kl. (1941), no. 13.

On the debate over the quadrature of the circle, see A. A. de Sarasa, *Solutio problematis a M. Mersenno propositi* (Antwerp, 1649); C. Huygens, *Exetasis cyclometriae Gregorii a S. Vincentio*, which was appended to *Theoremata de quadratura hyperboles, ellipsis et circuli ex dato portionum gravitatis centro* (Leiden, 1651), repr. in Huygens' *Oeuvres complètes*, XI (The Hague, 1908), 315–337; and *Ad. Fr. X. Ainscom epistola* (The Hague, 1656), repr. in his *Oeuvres complètes*, XII (1910), 263–277; Alexius Sylvius, *Lunae circulares periodi . . ., adjunctum quoque est examen quarundam propositionum quadraturae circuli Gregorii a S. Vincentio* (Lesna, 1651), 374–418; Gottfried Alois Kinner von Löwenthurn, *Elucidatio geometrica problematis Austriaci* (Prague, 1653); Vincent Léotaud, *Examen circuli quadraturae . . .* (Lyons, 1654); and *Cyclomathia . . .* (Lyons, 1663), I, *Quadraturae examen confirmatur ac promovetur*; Marcus Meibom, *De proportionibus dialogus* (Copenhagen, 1655); and Franz X. Aynscom, *Expositio ac deductio geometrica quadraturarum circuli Gregorii a S. Vincentio* (Antwerp, 1656).

J. E. HOFMANN

SAKS, STANISŁAW (*b.* Warsaw, Poland, 30 December 1897; *d.* Warsaw, November 1942)

Saks was a member of the Polish school of mathematics that flourished between the two world wars. The son of Philip and Ann Łabedz Saks, he received his secondary education in Warsaw. In the autumn of 1915 Saks entered the newly established Polish University of Warsaw, from which he received his doctorate in 1921 with a dissertation in topology. From 1921 to 1939 he was an assistant at the Warsaw Technical University and, from 1926 to 1939, he also lectured at the University of Warsaw. In 1942 he was arrested by the Nazi authorities and killed, allegedly while attempting to escape from prison.

Most of Saks's research involved the theory of real functions, such as problems on the differentiability of functions and the properties of Denjoy-Perron integrals. His work also touched upon questions in such related fields as topology and functional analysis. The two mathematicians at the University of Warsaw who exerted the greatest influence upon Saks were the topologist Stefan Mazurkiewicz, from whom Saks acquired a sensitivity to topological problems and methods, and Wacław Sierpiński. Saks, in turn, considerably influenced the development of real analysis within the Polish school.

Saks's contributions to mathematics included two important books. The first, *Théorie de l'inté-*

grale (1933), grew out of his lectures at the University of Warsaw and appeared as the second volume in the series Monografie Matematyczne. A thoroughly revised English edition was published in 1937 as the seventh volume of the series. In this highly original work Saks systematically developed the theory of integration and differentiation from the standpoint of countably additive set functions. Widely read outside Poland, it is now considered a still useful classic. In 1938 Saks collaborated with Antoni Zygmund to produce the ninth volume of Monografie Matematyczne, *Funkcje analityczne*, which received the prize of the Polish Academy of Sciences that year. An English edition, published by Zygmund in 1952, helped make its contents known to a larger audience, for whom it has become a standard reference work on complex analysis.

BIBLIOGRAPHY

I. ORIGINAL WORKS. Saks's papers have not been published in collected form, but many appeared in *Fundamenta mathematicae* and, to a lesser extent, in *Studia mathematica*. His books are *Zarys teorii całki* (Warsaw, 1930); *Théorie de l'intégrale* (Warsaw, 1933), rev. as *Theory of the Integral*, L. C. Young, trans. (Warsaw–Lvov–New York, 1937; repr. New York, 1964); and *Funkcje analityczne* (Warsaw, 1938), written with A. Zygmund, rev. as *Analytic Functions*, E. J. Scott, trans. (Warsaw, 1952; 2nd English ed., 1965).

II. SECONDARY LITERATURE. Apparently nothing has been written on Saks. (The author is indebted to Professor A. Zygmund of the University of Chicago for much helpful information.) For further references concerning the Polish school of mathematics, see M. G. Kuzawa, *Modern Mathematics: The Genesis of a School in Poland* (New Haven, 1968).

THOMAS HAWKINS

SALEM, RAPHAËL (*b.* Saloniki, Greece, 7 November 1898; *d.* Paris, France, 20 June 1963)

Salem was born to Jewish parents of Spanish origin, and the family moved to Paris when he was fifteen. His father, Emmanuel Salem, a well-known lawyer, died in 1940. His mother, Fortunée, and other members of his family died in a concentration camp.

Salem studied law at the University of Paris and mathematics at the Sorbonne, and received the *licence* in each field in 1919. He completed the engineering course at the École Centrale des Arts et

Manufactures, where he studied mathematics under Jacques Hadamard, in 1921. Though he preferred mathematics, Salem went into banking. From 1921 to 1938 he worked for the Banque de Paris et des Pays-Bas, becoming a manager in 1938. He and his wife, Adriana, were married in 1923; they had two sons and a daughter.

Among Salem's avocations were music (he played the violin and liked to join quartets), fine arts, literature (mainly Italian and French), and sports (he skied and rode horseback). His main interest, however, was mathematics. He chose Fourier series, a field rather neglected in France at the time (except by Denjoy and S. Mandelbrojt), worked on special and difficult topics, and wrote a series of short papers published in *Comptes-rendus de l'Académie des sciences*. Denjoy insisted that he write a dissertation, for which Salem received the doctorate in mathematics from the Sorbonne in 1940.

Salem was mobilized in 1939, sent to England as assistant to Jean Monnet, and demobilized in June 1940. He took his family to Cambridge, Massachusetts, after a short stay in Canada. His doctorate enabled Salem to obtain a position at the Massachusetts Institute of Technology, where he taught from 1941 to 1955, achieving a full professorship by the latter year. There he met a number of mathematicians interested in Fourier series: Norbert Wiener, J. D. Tamarkin, D. C. Spencer, and Antoni Zygmund. He and Zygmund became close friends and wrote a number of joint papers.

Salem visited Paris every year after the war and gave a course at the Sorbonne from 1948 to 1955. He became professor there in 1955 and moved to Paris, where he played a major role in the renewal of interest in Fourier series.

An extraordinary teacher, Salem lectured in both English and French in his elementary and research courses. His writings contained nothing superfluous, nothing hidden; they were easy to comprehend even when they dealt with the most intricate mathematics—such as the interplay between harmonic analysis and the theory of algebraic numbers. His work is likely to remain a masterpiece of difficult mathematics and beautiful exposition.

After Salem's death his wife established an international prize, awarded every year to a young mathematician who has made an exceptional contribution to the theory of Fourier series or a related field. The list of those who have received the prize, first awarded in 1968, is impressive and testifies to the explosive activity in this area of mathematics.

Salem's works range over topics in the theory of Fourier series, number theory, geometrical set theory, and probability theory. The following two results of Salem's convey the flavor of his work. The first was discovered by him but was developed with others until the final form was achieved. The second has been the source of considerable research.

The first is related to a problem going back to Heinrich Eduard Heine and Georg Cantor (1870). Given a set E of $[0, 2\pi]$, does the convergence of a trigonometric series out of E imply that all coefficients are 0? If the answer is yes, E is called a U set (set of uniqueness); if not, an M set (set of multiplicity). The fact that the empty set is a U set is not obvious; it was proved by Cantor, together with a number of results from which set theory originated. Now consider a set E of a special type, associated with a given number ξ between 0 and $\frac{1}{2}$: E is closed, and can be decomposed into two disjoint subsets homothetic to E with a ratio ξ. The case $\xi = 1/3$ is the classic triadic Cantor set, which is obtained from a closed interval I by removing the open middle third, then repeating this dissection on the remaining intervals, and so on; what remains is E. From the works of Rajchman and Nina Bari (about 1920) it was known that E is a U set when $1/\xi$ is an integer, and an M set when $1/\xi$ is a nonintegral rational number. What Salem discovered (stated in 1943, proved with Antoni Zygmund in 1955, using a new approach developed by I. I. Piatecki-Shapiro) is a complete and surprising answer: E is a U set if and only if $1/\xi$ is an algebraic integer (that is, a root of a polynomial with integral coefficients, the leading term having the coefficient 1), such that all other roots of the polynomial lie inside the unit circle of the complex plane. This class of numbers is a closed set on the line; the numbers in question were called Pisot-Vijayaraghayan numbers by Salem, and their class was called S (for Salem) by C. Pisot.

The second problem was posed by A. Beurling and solved by Salem in 1950. Given a number α between 0 and 1, does there exist a closed set on the line whose Hausdorff dimension is α and that carries a measure μ whose Fourier transform $_\mu(u)$ is dominated by $|u|^{-\alpha/2}$? From previous results on Hausdorff dimension found by O. Frostman, it was known that $\alpha/2$ is the critical index. The answer is affirmative and the result interesting, but the proof is of greater interest because it contains the first introduction of a random measure into harmonic analysis; no measure is exhibited as an example, but almost all measures (with a convenient probability space) fit the requirement. Today the study of random measures forms an active field in its own right and has provided new proofs of Salem's theorem.

Brownian images, local times, and occupation densities can be studied through the Salem approach and have yielded new results in probability theory.

BIBLIOGRAPHY

Salem's books are *Essais sur les séries trigonométriques* (Paris, 1940); *Algebraic Numbers and Fourier Series* (Belmont, Calif., 1963); *Ensembles parfaits et séries trigonométriques* (Paris, 1963), written with Jean-Pierre Kahane; and *Oeuvres mathématiques* (Paris, 1967), see especially 295–304, 311–315, 481–493, and 590–592 for problems discussed in text. The latter volume also includes a useful preface by Antoni Zygmund and an introduction by Jean-Pierre Kahane and Antoni Zygmund.

JEAN-PIERRE KAHANE

SALMON, GEORGE (*b.* Cork, Ireland, 25 September 1819; *d.* Dublin, Ireland, 22 January 1904)

Salmon's father, Michael Salmon, was a linen merchant; his mother, Helen, was the daughter of the Reverend Edward Weekes. After early schooling in Cork he entered Trinity College, Dublin, in 1833 to read classics and mathematics. He graduated in 1838 as first mathematical moderator. He was elected a fellow of Trinity College in 1841 and, as required by college statutes, took Holy Orders in the Church of Ireland. In 1844 he married Frances Anne, the daughter of the Reverend J. L. Salvador; they had four sons and two daughters.

The main burden of teaching in Trinity College was then borne by the fellows, and Salmon spent twenty-five years as a lecturer and tutor—mainly in the mathematical school, but also to a lesser extent in the divinity school. During this period he published some forty papers in various mathematical journals and wrote four important textbooks.

Over the years Salmon became frustrated by the heavy load of tutoring and lecturing, much of it of an elementary kind, and was disillusioned because he was not made a professor, a promotion that would have relieved him of most of this load and given him more time for his research. It must have been this which influenced him, in about 1860, to turn away from mathematics toward the theological studies in which he had always been interested—and which appeared to offer better prospects of promotion. In fact, in 1866 he was appointed regius professor of divinity and head of the divinity school, a post that he held for twenty-two

years. During this period he published four more books; they earned him a reputation as a theologian that was as great as the one he already had as a mathematician.

In 1888 Salmon was appointed provost of Trinity College. He remained an administrator for the rest of his life. He was a good and much-loved head of his college, although he had become a strong conservative in his old age, so that his provostship was a period of consolidation in the college rather than one of reform.

When Salmon joined the staff of Trinity College in 1841, its mathematical school was already internationally known and his colleagues included the well-known scholars Rowan Hamilton, James MacCullagh, Charles Graves, and Humphrey Lloyd. There was a strong bias toward synthetic geometry in the school, and it was in this field that Salmon began his research work, although he shortly became interested in the algebraic theories that were then being developed by Cayley and Sylvester in England and by Hermite and later Clebsch on the Continent. Salmon soon joined their number, and played an important part in the applications of the theory of invariants and covariants of algebraic forms to the geometry of curves and surfaces. He became a close friend of both Cayley and Sylvester and exchanged a voluminous mathematical correspondence with them for many years. His chief fame as a mathematician, however, rests on the series of textbooks that appeared between 1848 and 1862. These four treatises on conic sections, higher plane curves, modern higher algebra, and the geometry of three dimensions not only gave a comprehensive treatment of their respective fields but also were written with a clarity of expression and an elegance of style that made them models of what a textbook should be. They were translated into every western European language and ran into many editions (each incorporating the latest developments); they remained for many years the standard advanced textbooks in their respective subjects.

Salmon's own most important contributions to mathematics included his discovery (with Cayley) of the twenty-seven straight lines on the cubic surface, his classification of algebraic curves in space, his investigations of the singularities of the ruled surface generated by a line meeting three given directing curves, his solution of the problem of the degree of a surface reciprocal to a given surface, his researches in connection with families of surfaces subjected to restricted conditions, his conditions for repeated roots of an algebraic equation, and his theorem of the equianharmonic ratio of the four tangents to a plane cubic curve from a variable point on it.

When his investigations called for it, Salmon was an indefatigable calculator. The most famous example of this was his calculation of the invariant E of the binary sextic, which he published in the second edition (1866) of his treatise on modern higher algebra and which occupied thirteen pages of text.

BIBLIOGRAPHY

I. ORIGINAL WORKS. The Royal Society *Catalogue of Scientific Papers*, V, 381–382; VII, 819, lists forty-one memoirs by Salmon published between 1844 and 1872. His mathematical textbooks are *A Treatise on Conic Sections* (Dublin, 1848); *A Treatise on the Higher Plane Curves: Intended as a Sequel to a Treatise on Conic Sections* (Dublin, 1852); *Lessons Introductory to the Modern Higher Algebra* (Dublin, 1859); and *A Treatise on the Analytic Geometry of Three Dimensions* (Dublin, 1862).

His most important theological writings are *A Historical Introduction to the Study of the Books of the New Testament* (London, 1885); *The Infallibility of the Church* (London, 1888); *Some Thoughts on the Textual Criticism of the New Testament* (London, 1897); and *The Human Element in the Gospels*, N. J. D. White, ed. (London, 1907), posthumously published.

II. SECONDARY LITERATURE. On Salmon and his work, see the obituary by J. H. Bernard in *Proceedings of the British Academy*, **1** (1903–1904), 311–315; by R. S. Ball in *Proceedings of the London Mathematical Society*, 2nd ser., **1** (1903–1904), xxii–xxviii; the unsigned obituary in *Nature*, **69** (1903–1904), 324–326; and the obituary by C. J. Joly in *Proceedings of the Royal Society*, **75** (1905), 347–355. See also *The Times* (London) (23 Jan. 1904), 13; and *Dictionary of National Biography*.

A. J. McCONNELL

AL-SAMARQANDĪ, SHAMS AL-DĪN MUḤAMMAD IBN ASHRAF AL-ḤUSAYNĪ (*b.* Samarkand, Uzbekistan, Russia, *fl.* 1276)

Al-Samarqandī was a contemporary of Nasīr al-Dīn al-Ṭūsī (1201–1274) and Quṭb al-Dīn al-Shīrāzī (1236–1311). Al-Samarqandī was not among the scientists associated with al-Ṭūsī at the observatory at Marāgha. A noted logician, al-Samarqandī was best known to mathematicians for his famous tract *Kitāb Ashkāl al-ta'sīs* ("Book on the Fundamental Theorems"). This work of twenty pages, probably composed around 1276, summarizes with their abridged demonstrations thirty-five funda-

mental propositions of Euclid's geometry. To write this short work, Samarqandī consulted the writings of Ibn al-Haytham, ʿUmar al-Khayyāmī, al-Jawharī, Naṣīr al-Dīn al-Ṭūsī, and Athīr al-Dīn al-Abharī. Several mathematicians, notably Qāḍī Zāda, commented on this work by al-Samarqandī.

It was chiefly with his book on dialectics that al-Samarqandī became famous. This valuable work, entitled *Risāla fī ādāb al-baḥth* ("Tract on the Methods of Enquiry"), was the subject of several commentaries. Two other works on logic by al-Samarqandī are known: *Mīzān al-Qusṭās* and *Kitāb ʿAyn al-naẓar fīʿilm al-jadal*. Al-Samarqandī was also interested in astronomy. He wrote *Al-Tadhkira fī 'l-hay'a* ("Synopsis of Astronomy") and a star calendar for 1276–1277. His *Ṣaḥā'if al-ilāhiyya* and his *ʿAqā'id* are two works on dogmatic theology.

BIBLIOGRAPHY

MSS of the works of al-Samarqandī are listed in C. Brockelmann, *Geschichte der arabischen Literatur*, **I** (Weimar, 1898), 486; and *ibid.*, supp. 1 (Leiden, 1937), 860. See also H. Suter, *Die Mathematiker und Astronomen der Araber* (Leipzig, 1900), 157; and "Nachträge und Berichtigungen zu 'Die Mathematiker . . .,'" in *Abhandlungen zur Geschichte der Mathematik*, **14** (1902), 176.

Also helpful are Ḥājjī Khalīfa's *Kashf al-ẓunūn*, G. Flügel, ed. (Leipzig, 1835–1855), I, 322; Carra de Vaux's article "Baḥth," in *Encyclopaedia of Islam*, 1st ed., I (1911), 587; and G. Sarton, *Introduction to the History of Science*, II (Baltimore, 1962), 1020–1021.

For a demonstration of Euclid's fifth postulate attributed to al-Samarqandī, see H. Dilgan, "Démonstration du Vᵉ postulat d'Euclide par Shams-ed-Dīn Samarkandī," in *Revue d'histoire des sciences et de leurs applications*, **13** (1960), 191–196. For the attribution of this demonstration to Athīr al-Dīn al-Abharī, see A. I. Sabra, "Thābit ibn Qurra on Euclid's Parallels Postulate," in *Journal of the Warburg and Courtauld Institutes*, **31** (1968), 14, note 9.

HÂMIT DILGAN

AL-SAMAW'AL, IBN YAḤYĀ AL-MAGHRIBĪ (*b.* Baghdad, Iraq; *d.* Marāgha, Iran [?], *ca.* 1180)

Al-Samaw'al was the son of Yehuda ben Abun (or Abu'l-ʿAbbās Yaḥyā al-Maghribī), a Jew learned in religion and Hebrew literature who had emigrated from Fez (Morocco) and settled in Baghdad. His mother was Anna Isaac Levi, an educated woman who was originally from Baṣra (Iraq).

Al-Samaw'al thus grew up in a cultivated milieu; a maternal uncle was a physician, and after studying Hebrew and the Torah the boy was encouraged, when he was thirteen, to take up the study of medicine and the exact sciences. He then began to study medicine with Abu'l-Barakāt, while taking the opportunity to observe his uncle's practice. At the same time he started to learn mathematics, beginning with Hindu computational methods, *zījes* (astronomical tables), arithmetic, and *misāḥa* (practical techniques for determining measure, for use in surveying), then progressing to algebra and geometry.

Since scientific study had declined in Baghdad, al-Samaw'al was unable to find a teacher to instruct him beyond the first books of Euclid's *Elements* and was therefore obliged to study independently. He finished Euclid, then went on to the *Algebra* of Abū Kāmil, the *al-Badī'* of al-Karajī, and the *Arithmetic* of al-Wasīṭī (most probably Maymūn ibn Najīb al-Wasīṭī, who collaborated in making astronomical observations with ᶜUmar al-Khayyāmī between 1072 and 1092). By the time he was eighteen, al-Samaw'al had read for himself all of the works fundamental to the study of mathematics and had developed his own mode of mathematical thinking.

In science, this independence of thought led al-Samaw'al to point out deficiencies in the work of al-Karajī (whom he admired) and to challenge the arrangement of the *Elements*; in religion he was similarly inclined to test the validity of the claims of the various creeds and came to accept those of Islam, although he postponed his conversion for a number of years to avoid distressing his father. His autobiography states that he reached his decision at Marāgha on 8 November 1163 as a result of a dream; four years later he wrote to his father, setting out the reasons for which he had changed his religion, and his father immediately set out to Aleppo to see him, dying en route. Al-Samaw'al himself spent the rest of his life as an itinerant physician in and around Marāgha. His earlier travels had taken him throughout Iraq, Syria, Kūhistān, and Ādharbayjān.

His biographers record that al-Samaw'al was a successful physician, and had emirs among his patients. In his autobiography al-Samaw'al recorded that he had compounded several new medicines, including an almost miraculous theriac, but no other account of them has survived. His only extant medical work is his *Nuzhat al-aṣḥāb* (usually translated as "The Companions' Promenade in the Garden of Love"), which is essentially a treatise on sexology and a collection of erotic stories. The medical content of the first and longer section of the book lies chiefly in descriptions of diseases and sexual deficiencies; the second, more strictly medical, part includes a discussion of states of virile debility and an account of diseases of the uterus and their treatment. This part is marked by al-Samaw'al's acute observation and his interest in the psychological aspects of disease; he provides a detailed description of the condition of being in love without recognizing it, and gives a general prescription for the anguished and melancholic that comprises well-lighted houses, the sight of running water and verdure, warm baths, and music.

It is, however, chiefly as a mathematician that al-Samaw'al merits a place in the history of science. His extant book on algebra, *Al-bāhir* ("The Dazzling"), written when he was nineteen years old, represents a remarkable development of the work of his predecessors. In it al-Samaw'al brought together the algebraic rules formulated by, in particular, al-Karajī and, to a lesser extent, Ibn Aslam and other authors, including al-Sijzī, Ibn al-Haytham, Qusṭā ibn Lūqā, and al-Harīrī. The work consists of four parts, of which the first provides an account of operations on polynomials in one unknown with rational coefficients; the second deals essentially with second-degree equations, indeterminate analysis, and summations; the third concerns irrational quantities; and the fourth, and last, section presents the application of algebraic principles to a number of problems.

It is apparent in the first section of this work that al-Samaw'al was the first Arab algebraist to undertake the study of relative numbers. He chose to treat them as if they possessed an identity proper to themselves, although he did not recognize the significance of this choice. He was thus able, in a truly bold stroke, to subtract from zero, writing that

If we subtract an additive [positive] number from an empty power $(0 \cdot x^n - a \cdot x^n)$, the same subtractive [negative] number remains; if we subtract the subtractive number from an empty power, the same additive number remains $(0 \cdot x^n - [-ax^n] = ax^n)$. . . . If we subtract an additive number from a subtractive number, the remainder is their subtractive sum: $(-ax^n) - (bx^n) = -(a + b) x^n$; if we subtract a subtractive number from a greater subtractive number, the result is their subtractive difference; if the number from which one subtracts is smaller than the number subtracted, the result is their additive difference.

These rules appear in the later European work of Chuquet (1484), Pacioli (1494), Stifel (1544), and Cardano (1545); it is likely that al-Samaw'al reached them by considering the extraction of the square root of a polynomial.

Al-Karajī had conceived the algorithm of extraction, but did not succeed in applying it to the case in which the coefficients are subtractive. His failure may have stimulated al-Samaw⁾al's abilities, since the problem in which these rules are stated in the *Al-bāhir* is that of the extraction of the square root of

$$25x^6 + 9x^4 + 84x^2 + 64 + 100(1/x^2) + 64(1/x^4)$$
$$- 30x^5 - 40x^3 - 116x - 48(1/x) - 96(1/x^3).$$

Since al-Karajī's algebra lacked symbols, so that the numbers had to be spelled out in letters, this operation would have presented an insurmountable obstacle. Al-Samaw⁾al was able to overcome this trial of memory and imagination by using a visualization in which he assigned to each power of x a place in a table in which a polynomial was represented by the sequence of its coefficients, written in Hindu numerals. This technique, a major step in the development of symbolism, was requisite to the progress of algebra because of the increasing complexity of mathematical computations.

Al-Samaw⁾al's rules of subtraction were also important in the division of polynomials; in the interest of obtaining better approximations he pursued division up to negative powers of x, and thereby approached the technique of development in series (although he overlooked the opportunity of unifying the various cases of the second-degree equation and of computation by double error). He computed the quotient of $20x^2 + 30x$ by $6x^2 + 12$, for example, to obtain the result $3\ 1/3 + 5(1/x) - 6\ 2/3(1/x^2) - 10(1/x^3) + 13\ 1/3(1/x^4) + 20(1/x^5) - 26\ 2/3(1/x^6) - 40(1/x^7)$. He then recognized that he could apply the law of the formation of coefficients $a_{n+2} = -2a_n$, which allowed him to write out the terms of the quotient directly up to $54,613 \cdot 1/3$ $(1/x^{28})$.

Al-Samaw⁾al further applied the rules of subtraction to the multiplication and division of the powers of x, which he placed in a single line on both sides of the number 1, to which he assigned the rank zero. The other powers and other constants are displayed on each side of zero, in ascending and descending order:

...	4	3	2	1	0	1	2	3	4	...
						$\frac{1}{x}$	$\frac{1}{x^2}$	$\frac{1}{x^3}$	$\frac{1}{x^4}$	
	x^4	x^3	x^2	x	1	x				

The rules of multiplication and division that al-Samaw⁾al enunciated are, except for their nota-

tion, those still in use.

The second part of the *Al-bāhir* contains the six classical equations ($ax = b$, $ax^2 + bx = c$, and so forth) that were set out by al-Khwārizmī. Interestingly, however, al-Samaw⁾al gave only geometrical demonstrations of the equations, although their algebraic solutions were known to his predecessor al-Karajī, who dedicated a monograph, ᶜ*Ilal ḥisāb al-jabr wa 'l-muqābala*, to them. Al-Samaw⁾al then presented a remarkable calculation of the coefficients of $(a + b)^n$, which al-Karajī discovered after 1007 (for the dating of this and other of al-Karajī's works, see A. Anbouba, ed., *L'algèbre al-Badīᶜ d'al-Karagi* [Beirut, 1964], p. 12). Since al-Karajī's original computation has been lost, al-Samaw⁾al's work is of particular interest in having preserved it; these coefficients are arranged in the triangular table that much later became known in the west as Tartaglia's or Pascal's triangle.

A further, and equally important, part of the second section of the book deals with number theory. This chapter contains about forty propositions, including that among n consecutive integers there is one divisible by n; that

$$1 \cdot 2 + 3 \cdot 4 + \cdots + (2n-1)\ 2n = 1 + 3 + \cdots$$
$$+ (2n-1) + 1^2 + 3^2 + \cdots + (2n-1)^2;$$

and that $1^2 + 2^2 + \cdots + n^2 = n(n+1)(2n+1)/6$. Al-Samaw⁾al was especially proud of having established the last, since neither Ibn Aslam nor al-Karajī had been successful in doing so.

The chief importance of the second part of the *Al-bāhir* lies, however, in al-Samaw⁾al's use of recursive reasoning, which appears in such equations as

$$(n-1)\sum_1^n i = (n+1)\sum_1^{n-1} i \text{ and}$$
$$(n-1)\sum_1^n i = (n-1)\sum_1^{n-3} i + 3(n-1)^2.$$

The third part of *Al-bāhir* is chiefly concerned with the classification of irrationals found in Book X of the *Elements*. Al-Samaw⁾al's account is complete and clear, but contains nothing new or noteworthy except his rationalization of $\sqrt{30} : \sqrt{2} + \sqrt{5} + \sqrt{6}$, which had eluded al-Karajī.

The final section of the work contains a classification of problems by the number of their known solutions, a device used by earlier writers. Al-Samaw⁾al was led by this procedure to solve a varied group of these problems and to master a prodigious system of 210 equations in ten unknowns, a result of his having undertaken the determination of ten numbers of which are given their sums, taken six at a time. He further elucidated the 504 conditions necessary to the compatibility of the system. He overcame the lack of symbolic representation by the expedient of designating the unknown quantities 1, 2, 3, $\cdots$, 10, and was then able to draw up a table that started from

$$123456 \cdots 65$$
$$123457 \cdots 70$$
$$123458 \cdots 75$$
$$123459 \cdots 80.$$

Al-Samaw᾿al's intention in writing the *Al-bāhir* was to compensate for the deficiencies that he found in al-Karajī's work and to provide for algebra the same sort of systematization that the *Elements* gave to geometry. He wrote the book when he was young, then allowed it to remain unpublished for several years; it seems quite possible that he reworked it a number of times. It is difficult to ascertain the importance of the book to the development of algebra in the Arab world, but an indirect and restricted influence may be seen in the *Miftaḥ-al-ḥisab* ("Key of Arithmetic") of al-Kāshī, published in 1427. The book was apparently altogether unknown in the west.

The mathematical counterpart of the *Al-bāhir*, the *Al-zāhir* ("The Flourishing"), has been lost, and of al-Samaw᾿al's mathematical writings only two almost identical elementary treatises remain. These are the *Al-tabṣira* ("Brief Survey") and *Al-mūjiz* ("Summary"). The influence of the Arabic language is seen in their classification of fractions as deaf, Arab, or genitive, and both contain sections on ratios that are clearly derived from the work of al-Karajī. The ratio $80:3\cdot7\cdot9\cdot10$, for example, is expressed as a sum of fractions with numerator 1 and the respective denominators $3\cdot10$, $3\cdot7\cdot9$, and $3\cdot9\cdot10$; this use of the sexagesimal system reflects the continuing importance of the concerns of the commercial and administrative community of Baghdad, since this system was still favored by merchants and public servants. In his account of division, al-Samaw᾿al noted the periodicity of the quotient $5:11$, also calculated in the sexagesimal system. The last section of *Al-mūjiz* exists only in mutilated form, but what remains would indicate that it contained interesting material on abacuses.

In an additional work related to his mathematics al-Samaw᾿al again demonstrated the independence of his thinking. In this, the *Kashf ᾿uwār al-munajjimīn* ("The Exposure of the Errors of the Astrologers"), he refuted the pronouncements of scientific astrology by pointing out the multiple contradictions in its interpretation of sidereal data, as well as the errors of measurement that he found in astrological observations. He then, for the sake of argument, assumed astrology to be valid, but showed that the astrologer could scarcely hope to make a valid prediction since, by al-Samaw᾿al's count, he would have to take into simultaneous consideration 6,817 celestial indicators, a computation that would surely exceed his abilities.

BIBLIOGRAPHY

I. ORIGINAL WORKS. Al-Samaw᾿al wrote at least eighty-five works, of which most have been lost. (It must be remembered, however, that the word *kitāb* may be used to designate either a brief note or a full volume.) A brief autobiographical writing may be found in *Ifḥām ṭā ᾿ifat al-yahūd*, Cairo MS (Cat. F. Sayyid, I, p. 65), fols. 25–26, and in *Al-ajwiba al fākhira raddan ῾ala'l milla 'l-kāfira*, Paris MS 1456, fols. 64–65.

His mathematical works that have been preserved include *Al-bāhir* ("The Dazzling"), Istanbul MS Aya Sofya 2718, 115 ff., and Esat Ef. 3155; extracts are in A. Anbouba, "Mukhtārāt min Kitāb al-Bāhir," in *al-Mashriq* (Jan.-Feb. 1961), 61–108, while a complete modern ed., with notes, a detailed analysis, and French introduction is S. Ahmad and R. Rashed, eds., *Al-bāhir en algèbre d'as-Samaw᾿al* (Damascus, 1972). *Al-tabṣira fi'l ḥisāb* ("Brief Survey") is Berlin MS 5962, 29 ff., Bodleian (Oxford) I, 194, and Ambrosiana (Milan) C. 211 ii; *Al-mūjiz al-mūḍawī* [?] *fi'l ḥisāb* ("Summary") is Istanbul MS Fatih 3439, 15 (consisting of thirty-three pages of thirty-five lines each); and *Kashf ῾uwār al-munajjimīn wa ghalaṭihim fī akthar al-a῾māl wa'l-aḥkām* ("The Exposure of the Errors of the Astrologers") is Leiden MS Cod. Or 98, 100 ff., and Bodleian I, 964, and II, 603, while its preface has been translated into English by F. Rosenthal, "Al-Asṭurlābī and al-Samaw᾿al on Scientific Progress," in *Osiris*, 9 (1950), 555-564.

Al-Samaw᾿al's only surviving medical work, *Nuzhat al-aṣḥāb fī mu῾āsharat al-aḥbāb* ("The Companions' Promenade in the Garden of Love"), is preserved in Berlin MS 6381, Paris MS 3054, Gotha MS 2045, Istanbul MS Aya Sofya 2121, and Escorial MS 1830. His other extant works are apologetics, and include *Ifḥām ṭā'ifat al-yahūd* ("Confutation of the Jews"), Cairo MS Cat. F. Sayyid, I, p. 65, Cairo MS VI, ii, and Teheran MS I, 184, and II, 593, of which the text and an English trans. with an interesting introduction by M. Perlmann are *Proceedings of the American Academy for Jewish Research*, 32 (1964); and *Ghāyat al-maqṣūd fī 'l-radd ῾ala 'l-naṣārā wa 'l-yahūd* ("Decisive Refutation of the Christians and the Jews"), Istanbul MS As'ad 3153 and Asir 545. A last MS, *Badhl al-majhūd fī iqnā῾ al-yahūd* ("The Effort to Persuade the Jews"), formerly in Berlin, has been lost since World War II. See also Perlmann (above), pp. 25–28, 127.

II. SECONDARY LITERATURE. Recent editions of Arabic sources on al-Samaw᾿al and his work include Ibn

Abī Uṣaybiᶜa, ᶜUyūn al anbāʾ, II (Cairo, 1882), 30–31; Ḥājjī Khalīfa, Kashf al-ẓunūn, I (Istanbul, 1941), col. 664, and II (1943), col. 1377; Ibn al ᶜIbrī [Barhebraeus], Taʾrīkh mukhtaṣar al-duwal (Beirut, 1958), 217; Ibn al-Qifṭī, Ikhbār al-ᶜulama (Cairo, 1908), 142; Ibn Ṣāᶜid al-Akfānī, Irshād al-Qāṣid (Beirut, 1904), 123, 125, 127; and Tash Kupri Zadeh, Miftāḥ al-Saᶜāda, I (Hyderabad, 1910), 327, 329.

Works by later authors include A. Anbouba, "Al-Karajī," in Al-Dirāsāt al-Adabiyya (Beirut, 1959); and "Mukhtārāt min Kitāb al-Bāhir," in al-Mashriq (Jan.-Feb. 1961), 61–108; C. Brockelmann, Geschichte der arabischen Literatur, I² (Leiden, 1943), 643, and Supp. I (Leiden, 1937), 892; H. Hirschfeld, "Al-Samawʾal," in Jewish Encyclopedia, I (New York–London, 1901), 37–38; Lucien Leclerc, Histoire de la médecine arabe, II (Paris, 1876), 12–17; S. Perez, Biografías de los mathematicos arabos que florecieron en España (Madrid, 1921), 137; F. Rosenthal, "Al-Asṭurlābī and al-Samawʾal on Scientific Progress," in Osiris, 9 (1950), 555–564; G. Sarton, Introduction to the History of Science, II (Baltimore, 1953), 401, and III (1953), 418, 596; M. Steinschneider, Mathematik bei den Juden (Hildesheim, 1964), 96; and H. Suter, Die Mathematiker und Astronomen der Araber und ihre Werke (Leipzig, 1900), biography, 24.

See also introductions and notes in S. Ahmad and R. Rashed, eds., Al-bāhir en algèbre d'as-Samawʾal (Damascus, 1971); and in A. Anbouba, ed., L'algèbre al-Badīᶜ d'al-Karagi (Beirut, 1964).

ADEL ANBOUBA

SAURIN, JOSEPH (b. Courthézon, Vaucluse, France, 1 September 1659; d. Paris, France, 29 December 1737)

The youngest son of Pierre Saurin, a Calvinist minister of Grenoble, Saurin was educated at home and in 1684 entered the ministry as curate of Eure. Outspoken in the pulpit, he soon had to take refuge in Switzerland, where he became pastor of Bercher, Yverdon. No less combative in exile, he refused at first to sign the Consensus of Geneva (1685). The pressure brought to bear on him as a result apparently weakened his Calvinist persuasion; after discussions with elders in Holland, he had an audience with Bishop Bossuet in France and shortly thereafter, on 21 September 1690, embraced Roman Catholicism. After an adventurous[1] return to Switzerland to fetch his wife, the daughter of a wealthy family named de Crouzas, Saurin settled in Paris for the rest of his life.

Forced to find a new career, Saurin turned to mathematics, which he studied and then taught. By 1702, as mathematics editor for the Journal des sçavans, he was again involved in dispute, most notably with Rolle, over the infinitesimal calculus. Failing to get a satisfactory response from Rolle, Saurin appealed to the Academy of Sciences, of which Rolle was a member. The Academy avoided a direct decision in favor of an outsider by naming Saurin an élève géomètre on 10 March 1707 and a full pensionnaire géomètre on 13 May 1707.

Even this rise to prominence could not keep Saurin out of trouble. Accused by the poet Jean-Baptiste Rousseau of having written libelous poems against him, Saurin spent six months in jail before an arrêt of Parlement (7 April 1712) exonerated him and sent Rousseau into exile. Thereafter, Saurin appears to have retired to his scientific research, working all night and sleeping all day.[2] His active career ended with his being named a vétéran of the Academy in 1731. He died of lethargic fever in 1737, leaving at least one son, Bernard-Joseph (1706–1781), who earned some fame as a dramatic poet.

Saurin made no original contributions to mathematics. Rather, firmly committed to the new infinitesimal calculus, he explored the limits and possibilities of its methods and defended it against criticism based on lack of understanding. Rolle, for example, assumed that the new method of tangents could not handle singularities of multivalued curves where dy/dx took the form $0/0$. In reply (1702, 1703, 1716), Saurin explicated the nature and treatment of such indeterminate expressions on the basis of L'Hospital's theorem (Analyse des infiniment petits [1969], section 9, article 163), by which, for a $f(x) = g(x)/h(x)$ of the form $0/0$ at $x = a$, one determines $f(a)$ by differentiating $g(x)$ and $h(x)$ simultaneously until one of them is nonzero at $x = a$. His further study of multivalued curves (1723, 1725) became the basis for correcting Guisnée's and Crousaz's misunderstanding of the nature of extreme values and of their expression in the new calculus.

Saurin's two papers (1709) on curves of quickest descent represent a solution of a problem first posed by Jakob I Bernoulli—to find which of the infinitely many cycloids linking a given point as origin to a given line is the curve of quickest descent from the point to the line—and then an extension of the problem to any family of similar curves. Saurin followed the differential methods of Johann I Bernoulli, although he studiously avoided taking a position in the brothers' famous quarrel.[3]

Combining his command of infinitesimal methods with a firm understanding of the new dynamics, Saurin offered (1722) a sensitive and subtle explanation of why the infinitesimal path of a simple pendulum must be approximated by the arc of a cycloid rather than by the chord subtending the arc of the circle. Thus he defended Huygens' theory of the pendulum against the attacks of Antoine Parent and the Chevalier de Liouville. Saurin had already provided (1703) rather neat algebraic demonstrations of Huygens' theorems on centrifugal force and the cycloidal path and had done an experimental and theoretical study (1720) of the damping and driving effects of the escapement and weight in a pendulum clock.

Huygens himself became the target of Saurin's rebuttals on the issue of Descartes's vortex theory of gravity. Saurin's first effort (1703)—to explain how a terrestrial vortex with lines of force parallel to the equatorial plane could cause bodies to fall toward the center of the earth—was patently clumsy. In 1709, however, to counter Huygens' objection that the necessarily greater speed of the vortex would sweep objects off the earth, Saurin proposed an attenuated ether that, on the basis of Mariotte's experimental findings on the force of moving fluids, made the ether all but nonresisting while still accounting for gravity by its greater speed of rotation. In Johann I Bernoulli's opinion, it was the best theory of gravity devised up to that time. Although, as Aiton points out,[4] it offered the chance for a reconciliation of Cartesian and Newtonian cosmology, Saurin himself felt that Newtonianism threatened a return to "the ancient shadows of Peripateticism" (*Mémoires de mathématique et physique* [1709], 148).

NOTES

1. The biographical note in Didot speaks of an outstanding charge of theft, while other notices recount the dangers of religious persecution only.
2. Fontenelle, "Éloge de M. Saurin," 120, makes this point and then adds that Saurin had few friends.
3. Saurin did, however, sarcastically reject Johann's claims of priority over L'Hospital in the matter of indeterminate expressions; cf. his 1716 paper and Joseph E. Hofmann, *Geschichte der Mathematik,* III (Berlin, 1957), 11.
4. *Vortex Theory of Planetary Motion,* 176. On Bernoulli's judgment, *ibid.,* 188.

BIBLIOGRAPHY

I. ORIGINAL WORKS. Saurin's works include "Démonstration des théorèmes que M. Hu(y)gens a proposés dans son Traité de la Pendule sur la force centrifuge des corps mûs circulairement," in *Mémoires pour servir à l'histoire des sciences et des beaux-arts (Mém-*oires de Trevoux), 1702 (Addition pour . . . Novembre et Decembre), 27–60; "Réponse à l'écrit de M. Rolle de l'Académie Royale des Sciences inséré dans le Journal du 13. Avril 1702, sous le titre de Règles et Remarques pour le Problème général des Tangentes par M. Saurin," in *Journal des sçavans* (Amsterdam ed.), **30** (3 Aug. 1702), 831–861; "Solution de la principale difficulté proposée par M. Hu(y)gens contre le système de M. Descartes, sur la cause de la pesanteur," *ibid.,* **31** (8 Jan. 1703), 36–47; "Remarques sur les courbes des deux premiers exemples proposés par M. Rolle dans le Journal du jeudi 13. Avril 1702," *ibid.* (15 Jan. 1703), 65–73, (22 Jan. 1703), 78–84; and "Manière aisée de démontrer l'égalité des temps dans les chutes d'un corps tombant par une cycloide de plus ou de moins haut, et de trouver le rapport du temps de la chute par la cycloide au temps de la chute perpendiculaire par son axe," *ibid.* (4 June 1703), 563–570.

In the *Mémoires de mathématique et physique* of the Paris Academy of Sciences, see "Solutions et analyses de quelques problèmes appartenans aux nouvelles méthodes" (1709), 26–33; "Examen d'une difficulté considérable proposée par M. Hu(y)ghens contre le système cartésien sur la cause de la pesanteur" (1709), 131–148; "Solution générale du problème, où parmi une infinité de courbes semblables décrites sur un plan verticale, et ayant un même axe et un même point d'origine, il s'agit de déterminer celle dont l'arc compris entre le point d'origine et une ligne donnée de position, est parcouru dans le plus court temps possible" (1709), 257–266, with addendum in 1710, pp. 208–214; "Remarques sur un cas singulier du problème général des tangentes" (1716), 59–79, 275–289; and "Problème" (1718), 89–92.

In the same journal, see "Démonstration d'une proposition avancée dans un des mémoires de 1709. Avec l'examen de quelques endroits de la *Recherche de la vérité,* qui se trouvent dans la dernière edition, et qui ont rapport à ce mémoire" (1718), 191–199; "Démonstration de l'impossibilité de la quadrature indéfinie du cercle. Avec une manière simple de trouver une suite de droites qui approchent de plus en plus d'un arc de cercle proposé, tant en dessus qu'en dessous" (1720), 15–19; "Remarques sur les horloges à pendule" (1720), 208–230; "Éclaircissement sur une difficulté proposé aux mathématiciens par M. le Chevalier de Liouville" (1722), 70–95; "Sur les figures inscrites et circonscrites au cercle" (1723), 10–11; "Dernières remarques sur un cas singulier du problème des tangentes" (1723), 222–250; "Observations sur la question des plus grandes et des plus petites quantités" (1725), 238–260; and "Recherches sur la rectification des baromètres" (1727), 282–296.

II. SECONDARY LITERATURE. Bernard Fontenelle's "Éloge de M. Saurin," in *Histoire de l'Académie royale des sciences . . .* (1737), 110–120, is the basis for the account in Joseph Bertrand's *L'Académie des sciences et les académiciens de 1666 à 1793* (Paris, 1869), 242–247. The entry in the Didot *Nouvelle biographie générale* provides some additional details from Swiss sources. Saurin earns only passing mention in histories of mathematics, but his vortex theory of gravity receives considerable attention from Eric J. Aiton in *The Vortex Theory of Planetary Motions* (London–New York, 1972), 172–176 and *passim*.

Michael S. Mahoney

SAVAGE, LEONARD JIMMIE (*b*. Detroit, Michigan, 20 November 1917; *d*. New Haven, Connecticut, 1 November 1971)

Jimmie Savage was the eldest son of Louis Savage, descended from a family of orthodox Jews, and Mae Rugawitz Savage. He was educated at Central High School in Detroit, and at the University of Michigan in Ann Arbor, where he obtained a B.S. in 1938, and a Ph.D. in 1941, both in mathematics. He had studied chemistry and physics before turning to mathematics. He was married to Jane Kretschmer in 1938; they had two sons, Sam Linton and Frank Albert. The marriage ended in divorce in 1964, and Savage married Jean Strickland Pearce the same year. Savage enjoyed good health, and was a vigorous walker, swimmer, and talker, although he had poor eyesight, suffering from a combination of nystagmus and extreme myopia.

Savage's doctoral dissertation, written under the direction of S. B. Meyers of the Department of Mathematics, was in the area of metric and differential geometry. Another mathematician at Michigan who influenced Savage was R. L. Wilder. After receiving the doctorate Savage spent an academic year, 1941–1942, at the Institute for Advanced Study in Princeton, still working in pure mathematics. While there he attracted the attention of John von Neumann, who considered Savage to be a highly gifted mathematician, but recognized that his true interests lay elsewhere. In 1944 Savage joined the Statistical Research Group at Columbia University, and it was there that he first became deeply interested in statistics, an interest that continued throughout his life.

Savage was author of two historically significant books: *The Foundations of Statistics* (1954) and *How to Gamble If You Must: Inequalities for Stochastic Processes* (1965, written with Lester Dubins). He also wrote a substantial number of extremely important articles in statistics, probability, and philosophy, centering on two main themes. The first theme concerns the foundations of statistics, how to understand and justify what statistics is about. These questions necessarily led him to ask deep philosophical questions about the various approaches to statistics, the sources of human knowledge, and the process of induction. Savage's second theme concerns the theory of gambling, which he viewed as a stimulating source of problems in probability and decision theory.

Savage's crowning achievement, which grew out of the work of the greatest mathematicians and philosophers, including Blaise Pascal, James Bernoulli, Daniel Bernoulli, the Marquis de Laplace, Carl Friedrich Gauss, Henri Poincaré, Frank Ramsey, John von Neumann, and Bruno de Finetti, was his book *The Foundations of Statistics*. Partly through the influence of von Neumann, who had developed the theory of games and formulated the basic ideas of decision theory, and partly through the influence of the English logician and mathematician Ramsey and the Italian mathematician and philosopher de Finetti, Savage developed in the first five chapters of his book the most complete version of the theory of subjective probability and utility that has yet been developed.

Starting with a set of six basic axioms, each of which he carefully motivated and discussed, Savage demonstrated the existence of both a numerical subjective probability and a utility function. Nothing quite like this had been done before for probability, although there were important predecessors. Von Neumann and Morgenstern in their *Theory of Games and Economic Behavior* (1947) had developed the existence of a utility function for the case in which probability was assumed to be objectively given. De Finetti, beginning in 1937 and culminating with his *Theory of Probability* (1975), had developed a theory of coherence and subjective probability, which, although it was partly axiomatic, did not fully develop utility theory within the system. Ramsey, in his "Truth and Probability" (1926), had developed an axiomatic system with a simultaneous derivation of subjective probability and utility; in spirit his work is very close to the later work of Savage, although with a different formulation of the axioms and a different mode of derivations.

Savage's other main contribution was the book *How to Gamble If You Must*, written with L. Dubins. This is a highly innovative development of probability theory in connection with its ancient origins in gambling, and it uses the finitely additive approach to probability. Savage and de Finetti had been the primary proponents of finitely additive probability, which was all that could be logically derived within their systems of thought.

Savage's articles include extremely important contributions to statistical inference, especially the application of the Bayesian approach. There is space only to mention a few of these. The article "Bayesian Statistical Inference for Psychological Research" (1963), written with W. Edwards and H. Lindman, is possibly the best article ever written relating to serious applications of statistical inference. In particular, the authors give the fullest development of the theory of Bayesian hypothesis tests, as originated by H. Jeffreys in his *Theory of Probability* (1939; 3rd ed., 1961). The article, "Symmetric Measures on Cartesian Products (1955), written with E. Hewitt, was a highly innovative mathematical generalization of de Finetti's theorem. The monograph, *The Foundations of Statistical Inference* (1962), contains Savage's beautiful discussion of Bayesian estimation and hypothesis testing and his theory of precise or stable measurement, which clearly shows the role of so-called uninformative prior distributions. Another important article is "Elicitation of Personal Probabilities and Expectations" (1971), which contains an innovative development of the theory of scoring rules.

Savage exerted an enormous influence upon the development of statistics in the second half of the twentieth century. The resurgence of the subjective Bayesian approach, which Savage insisted was the only foundationally sound and sensible approach, thereby opposing the views of R. A. Fisher and J. Neyman, was largely due to Savage's efforts, especially in the United States. In his last years Savage wrote a number of articles on the philosophy of statistics, emphasizing the "objectivity" of the subjective Bayesian approach, as contrasted with the "subjectivity" of the so-called objectivistic approach. Savage had an intense and spirited curiosity about almost everything. He was extremely generous in dealing with younger researchers, such as myself, who crossed his path and no doubt affected us in multitudinous ways. He was uncompromising, both with himself and with others. In his honor many of his articles have been collected in *The Writings of Leonard Jimmie Savage: A Memorial Selection* (1981), along with reminiscences by several of his friends and colleagues. Savage's honors included the presidency of the Institute of Mathematical Statistics (1957–1958), the Fisher lectureship (1970), and the Wald lectureship (1972). He received an honorary degree from the University of Rochester in 1963.

BIBLIOGRAPHY

I. ORIGINAL WORKS. Savage's two most important books were *The Foundations of Statistics* (New York, 1954; 2nd rev. ed., New York, 1972), and *How to Gamble If You Must: Inequalities for Stochastic Processes* (New York, 1965), the latter written with Lester Dubins. See also *The Foundations of Statistical Inference* (London, 1962; New York, 1962). Many of his articles are collected in *The Writings of Leonard Jimmie Savage: A Memorial Selection* (Washington, D.C., 1981). See, in particular, "Symmetric Measures on Cartesian Products," in *Transactions of the American Mathematical Society*, **80** (1955), 470–501, written with E. Hewitt; "Bayesian Statistical Inference for Psychological Research," in *Psychological Review*, **70** (1963), 193–242, written with W. Edwards and H. Lindman; and "Elicitation of Personal Probabilities and Expectations," in *Journal of the American Statistical Association*, **66** (1971), 783–801, all of which are reprinted in the 1981 anthology of Savage's writings.

II. SECONDARY LITERATURE. *The Writings of Jimmie Savage: A Memorial Selection*, cited above, includes the texts of the memorial service given for Savage at Yale University on 18 March 1972 and the memorial service tributes given by W. Allen Wallis, Frederick Mosteller, William and Esther Sleator, and Francis J. Anscombe; the volume also includes a reprint of D. V. Lindley, "L.J. Savage: His Work in Probability and Statistics," originally published in *Annals of Statistics*, **8** (1980), 1–24, and a bibliography of Savage's writings. See also Lester Dubins' preface to *How to Gamble If You Must*, cited above, and the preface to Bruno de Finetti's *Probability, Induction, and Statistics* (New York, 1972), for evaluations of Savage's work. For further information on his life and work, see D. A. Berry, "Letter to the Editor," in *The American Statistician*, **26**, no. 1 (1972), 47; S. Feinberg and A. Zellner, eds., *Studies in Bayesian Econometrics and Statistics in Honor of Leonard J. Savage* (Amsterdam, 1975); W. Kruskal, "Leonard Jimmie Savage," in W. Kruskal and J. M. Tanur, eds., *Internal Encyclopedia of Statistics* (New York, 1978), 889–892; D. V. Lindley, "L. J. Savage," in *Journal of the Royal Statistical Society*, **A135** (1972), 462–463; and "Savage, Leonard Jimmie," in *International Encyclopedia of the Social Sciences, Biographical Supplement*, **18** (1979).

BRUCE M. HILL

SCHAUDER, JULIUSZ PAWEL (*b*. Lvov, Galicia, Austria-Hungary [now Ukrainian SSR], 21 September 1899; *d*. Lvov, September 1943)

The son of Samuel Schauder, a Jewish lawyer, Schauder was educated in the Austro-Hungarian school system. In 1917 he was drafted into the Austro-Hungarian army, fought in Italy, and was taken prisoner. He joined the new Polish army in France and after his return to Lvov started his studies at the Jan Kazimierz University.

His university studies brought him into contact with the Polish mathematical school, of which he was to become an integral part. Zygmunt Jani-szewski, who had studied in Paris under Henri Poincaré, Henri Lebesgue, and M. Fréchet, played a decisive role in the formation of this school. Schauder received his Ph.D. in 1923 and then worked in insurance and as a secondary-school teacher in Przemyślany. In 1927 he received his *venia legendi*, which entitled him to give courses at the university. In 1928 and 1929 he gave his first course on partial differential equations. He then became an assistant lecturer at the university, and for a time held two jobs, one as an assistant lecturer and one as a teacher in a secondary school. In 1929 he married Emilia Löwenthal, whose grandfather had been expelled from his small Jewish community for being an atheist.

L. E. J. Brouwer published his famous fixed point theorem for finite dimensional spaces in 1911. A fixed point x^* is a point that does not change under a transformation T, that is, for a fixed point we have $T(x^*) = x^*$. Schauder published his fixed point theorem for infinite dimensional spaces (Banach spaces) in 1930, using compactness arguments in the proof. For 1932 and 1933 he was awarded a Rockefeller Fellowship. He spent September 1932 to May 1933 with L. Lichtenstein in Leipzig and the remaining time to September 1933 with Jacques Hadamard in Paris.

With J. Leray he published a paper (1934) considered to be a landmark in topological thinking in connection with partial differential equations. In this paper what is now known as Leray-Schauder degree (a homotopy invariant) is defined. This degree is then used in an ingenious method to prove the existence of solutions to complicated partial differential equations. First the existence of solutions to a simple partial differential equation is proved and then, by deforming this simple partial differential equation in a suitable function space, the existence of solutions to the complicated partial differential equation can be established. Schauder attended conferences at Geneva and Moscow in 1935 and at Oslo in 1936. At about the same time he tried to get an invitation to Princeton University.

Schauder's last paper was published in 1937. It includes a correction to his 1930 fixed point paper and thus completes the proof of his fixed point theorem. After 1934 his papers are mainly concerned with refining his techniques, for instance, by giving detailed estimates for the norm of the solution function for elliptic partial differential equations. In the context of hyperbolic partial differential equations, R. Courant, K. Friedrichs, and H. Lewy had investigated the connection between the original partial differential equation and discrete approximations suitable for numerical solution. Schauder generalized their approach and used inequalities of the Sobolev type to obtain estimates for hyperbolic partial differential equations. In 1938 he and Leray were awarded the Prix Internationaux de Mathématiques Malaxa.

In 1939 the Red Army entered Lvov. Schauder was made a professor at the university and became a member of the Ukrainian Academy of Sciences. This lasted until the Germans occupied Lvov in June 1941 and began the systematic extermination of Jews. A last desperate plea for help, delivered by a Polish student who escaped to Switzerland, reached the topologist Heinz Hopf. Among other things, Schauder wrote that he had many important new results but no paper to write them on. He implored the Swiss mathematicians to ask the German physicist Werner Heisenberg to intervene with the German authorities so that his life would be spared. The Swiss physicist W. Scherrer wrote a letter to Heisenberg, but to no avail. Schauder died in September 1943. According to one version he was betrayed to the Gestapo, was arrested, and disappeared; according to another (more probable) version he was shot after one of the regular roundups. His wife, Emilia, and his daughter, Eva, were hidden by the Polish underground and lived for a while in the sewers of Warsaw. Eva survived the war in a Catholic nunnery. Emilia surrendered to the police and perished in Majdanek (Lublin) concentration camp. After the war Eva went to live with her father's brother in Italy and became an English teacher.

Schauder's fixed point theorem and his skillful use of function space techniques to analyze elliptic and hyperbolic partial differential equations are contributions of lasting quality. Existence proofs for complicated nonlinear problems using his fixed point theorem have become standard. The topological method developed in the 1934 Leray-Schauder paper, known as the continuation or homotopy method, is now utilized not only to obtain qualitative results but also to solve problems numerically on computers.

BIBLIOGRAPHY

I. ORIGINAL WORKS. Schauder's collected works are available in an excellent edition prepared by the Polish Academy of Sciences, *Oeuvres* (Warsaw, 1978). Writings specifically discussed in the article are "Der Fixpunktsatz in Funktionalräumen," in *Studia mathematica*, **2** (1930), 171–180; and "Topologie et équations fonctionelles," in *Annales scientifiques de l'École normale Supérieure*, 3rd ser., **51** (1934), 45–78, written with J. Leray.

II. SECONDARY LITERATURE. Walter Forster, "J. Schauder: Fragments of a Portrait," and J. Leray, "My Friend Julius Schauder," in Walter Forster, ed., *Numerical Solution of Highly Nonlinear Problems* (Amsterdam, 1980), 417–425 and 427–439; and Kazimierz Kuratowski, *A Half Century of Polish Mathematics*, Andrzej Kirkor, trans. (Oxford, 1980).

WALTER FORSTER

SCHEFFÉ, HENRY (*b.* New York City, 11 April 1907; *d.* Berkeley, California, 5 July 1977)

Scheffé was born of German parents living in New York. His father, who had for many years worked as a baker, lost his job during the Depression and was reduced to selling apples at a street corner. The memory of this injustice and of his father's suffering remained with Scheffé throughout his life.

Following some preliminary training and work in engineering, Scheffé studied mathematics at the University of Wisconsin, where he obtained his B.A. in 1931 and his Ph.D. in 1935 with a thesis on differential equations, written under R. E. Langer. After teaching mathematics at Wisconsin (1935–1937), Oregon State University (1937–1939, 1941), and Reed College (1939–1940), he decided to switch from pure mathematics to statistics, and for this purpose in 1941 joined the statistics group assembled by S. S. Wilks at Princeton. As a statistician he taught at Syracuse (1944–1945), U.C.L.A. (1946–1948), and Columbia (1948–1953), and then went to Berkeley as professor of statistics and assistant director of the Statistical Laboratory. Although he soon resigned from his administrative position, he remained in Berkeley until his retirement in 1974. At both Columbia and Berkeley he chaired the statistics department for a number of years.

Scheffé was elected fellow of the Institute of Mathematical Statistics (1944), the American Statistical Association (1952), and the International Statistical Institute (1964). He also served as president of the IMS and vice president of the ASA.

Throughout his life Scheffé enjoyed reading, music (as an adult he learned to play the recorder), and traveling. He was also physically active. At Wisconsin he was an intercollegiate wrestler, and he liked to bicycle, swim, and backpack with his family. (In 1934 he had married Miriam Kott and they had two children, Miriam and Michael.)

As he came to statistics from mathematics, it was natural for Scheffé to become interested in the more mathematical aspects of statistical theory, particularly in optimality properties of statistical procedures. In a series of papers (1942–1955) he supplemented and extended the Neyman-Pearson theory of best similar test, and eventually in joint work with Lehmann developed a general theory containing many of the earlier results as special cases. The central concepts of this approach were those of sufficiency and completeness, which led to a characterization of all similar tests (and all unbiased estimates) when the minimal sufficient statistics are complete.

Scheffé's interest in more applied aspects of statistics grew out of, and was constantly fed by, consulting activities. From 1943 to 1946 he worked as consultant and senior mathematics officer at the Office of Scientific Research and Development under a contract with Princeton University. Later, he became a consultant for Consumers' Union and Standard Oil. Nearly all of Scheffé's research during the second phase of his career, which started in the early 1950's, was concerned with various aspects of linear models, particularly the analysis of variance. By adapting the theory to new situations, he significantly extended its range of applicability. Throughout, this work is characterized by a combination of the mathematical and applied points of view. He insists on clearly defined mathematical models. However, these are not formulated on the basis of mathematical convenience but are carefully grounded in the process generating the obervations.

Perhaps the most important of Scheffé's papers from this period is the 1953 paper in which he develops his S-method of simultaneous confidence intervals for all contrasts (and more generally for all estimable functions in a linear subspace of the parameter space), which permits the testing and estimation of contrasts suggested by the data. While this work had forerunners in Tukey's T-method (and, though not known to Scheffé at the time, in the much earlier work of H. Working and H. Hotelling [1929]), this was the first general procedure, applicable to all linear models. It is an extremely elegant solution of a fundamental problem of statistical practice. That it is the only solution exhibiting certain desirable symmetry properties was shown by Wijsman (1979).

Among other analysis of variance topics treated in this rigorous yet practice-oriented way are paired comparisons with ordered categorical response (1952), mixed models (1956), experiments on mixtures (1958, 1963), and some aspects of calibration (1973). Of these, the work on mixtures initiated a new methodology, which since then has developed a substantial literature.

Scheffé's research extended into his expository writing. In 1943 he published the first comprehensive review of nonparametric statistics, which laid a foundation for the explosive development of this field during the next two decades. His most influential work, however, was his book *The Analysis of Variance* (1959). Its careful exposition of the different principal models, their analyses, and the performance of the procedures when the model assumptions do not hold is exemplary, and the book continues to be a standard text and reference. Scheffé hoped to revise it after retirement. However, a few weeks after returning to Berkeley from a three-year post-retirement position at the University of Indiana, while still in the midst of the revision, he died as the result of a bicycle accident.

BIBLIOGRAPHY

A complete list of Scheffé's publications is given at the end of the obituary by C. Daniel and E. L. Lehmann in *Annals of Statistics*, **7** (1979), 1149–1161. Optimality of Scheffé's *S*-method was proved by Robert A. Wijsman in "Constructing All Smallest Simultaneous Confidence Sets in a Given Class, with Applications to MANOVA," *ibid.*, 1003–1018. The mixture designs introduced by Scheffé constitute the foundation of the later theory, an account of which is provided by John A. Cornell, *Experiments with Mixtures* (New York, 1981).

ERICH LEHMANN

SCHEFFERS, GEORG (*b.* Altendorf, near Holzminden, Germany, 21 November 1866; *d.* Berlin, Germany, 12 August 1945)

Scheffers studied mathematics and physics from 1884 to 1888 at the University of Leipzig, where his father was professor at the Academy of Art. He received the doctorate from Leipzig in 1890 and qualified as a lecturer there the following year. In 1896 he became extraordinary professor at the Technische Hochschule in Darmstadt, and in 1900 he was promoted to full professor. In 1907 he succeeded Guido Hauck as full professor at the Technische Hochschule in Charlottenburg, where he remained until his retirement in 1935.

As a student Scheffers was greatly influenced by Sophus Lie, who was professor at the University of Leipzig from 1886 to 1898. He followed Lie's suggestions in choosing topics for both his doctoral dissertation and his *Habilitationsschrift*, which dealt respectively with plane contact transformations and complex number systems. Scheffers'

most important independent research inspired by Lie was his 1903 paper on Abel's theorem and translation surfaces.

In later years Scheffers' reputation was based largely on his own books. These writings, which grew out of his wide-ranging activities at technical colleges, were directed at a broader audience than the books he edited with Lie; and they all went through several editions. Scheffers' two-volume *Anwendung der Differential- und Integralrechnung auf Geometrie* (1901–1902) was a popular textbook of differential geometry. Also widely used was his revision of Serret's *Lehrbuch der Differential- und Integralrechnung*, the last edition of which appeared in 1924; subsequently it was superseded by books written in a more modern style. Scheffers also published *Lehrbuch der darstellenden Geometrie* and, in 1903, an article entitled "Besondere transzendente Kurven" in the *Encyklopädie der mathematischen Wissenschaften*.

Scheffers' favorite field of study was geometry and, more specifically, the differential geometry of intuitive space. In this area he was a master at discovering many properties of particular curves and surfaces and their representation; he also possessed a gift for giving an easily understandable account of them—although in a much wordier style than is now customary. His exceptional talent for vividly communicating material is also apparent in a later work on the grids used in topographic maps and stellar charts.

BIBLIOGRAPHY

Scheffers' original works are as follows: "Bestimmung einer Klasse von Berührungstransformationsgruppen," in *Acta mathematica*, **14** (1891), 117–178; *Zurückführung komplexer Zahlensysteme auf typische Formen* (Leipzig, 1891); *Anwendung der Differential- und Integralrechnung auf Geometrie*, 2 vols. (Leipzig, 1901–1902; 3rd ed., 1922–1923); "Das Abelsche Theorem und das Lie'sche Theorem über Translationsflächen," in *Acta mathematica*, **28** (1902), 65–91; "Besondere transzendente Kurven," in *Encyklopädie der mathematischen Wissenschaften*, III, pt. 3 (Leipzig, 1903), 185–268; *Lehrbuch der darstellenden Geometrie*, 2 vols. (Berlin, 1919–1920; 2nd ed., 1922–1927); and *Wie findet und zeichnet man Gradnetze von Land- und Sternkarten?* (Leipzig–Berlin, 1934).

Scheffers edited the following volumes by Lie: *Vorlesungen über Differentialgleichungen mit bekannten infinitesimalen Transformationen* (Leipzig, 1891); *Vorlesungen über kontinuierliche Gruppen mit geometrischen und anderen Anwendungen* (Leipzig, 1893); and collaborated with Lie on *Geometrie der Berührungs-*

transformationen, I (Leipzig, 1896). He also revised J. A. Serret's *Lehrbuch der Differential- und Integralrechnung,* A. Harnack, trans., 5th ed., 3 vols. (Leipzig, 1906–1914; I, 8th ed., 1924; II, 7th ed., 1921; III, 6th ed., 1924).

WERNER BURAU

SCHEUCHZER, JOHANN JAKOB (*b.* Zurich, Switzerland, 2 August 1672; *d.* Zurich, 23 June 1733)

A diligent pupil at the age of three, Scheuchzer later became a brilliant student at the Carolinum in Zurich. Devoted to the natural sciences, he decided to study medicine and, having won a scholarship in 1691, was able to enroll in both science and medicine courses at the Altdorf Academy, near Nuremberg. He remained there for two years, then went to Utrecht, where he was awarded the doctorate in 1694. The fossil collection that he began assembling in 1690 soon became famous and brought Scheuchzer to the attention of the scholarly world. In 1694 he returned to Zurich and began systematic exploration of the Alps. His first writings for the Collegium der Wohlgesinnten (1695) were a scientific study of the Helvetic Alps. Scheuchzer then went to Nuremberg, where he studied for a diploma in mathematics, intending to teach this subject. But he was recalled to Zurich to become assistant municipal physician and medical supervisor of the orphanage. A few years later he became head of the Bibliothèque des Bourgeois, a post that he occupied while serving as director of the Museum of Natural History (then called the Kunsthammer).

By the age of thirty Scheuchzer had become prominent in Zurich and was carrying on a voluminous correspondence with many European scholars that has become of great interest to historians of science. A grant from the Zurich government in 1702 enabled him to resume his Alpine excursions, which provided the subject for numerous communications on geology, geophysics, natural sciences, and medicine. The results of his annual excursions to the Alps are presented in *Helvetiae stoicheiographia* (1716–1718), his greatest work in natural history and geophysics. In 1716 he became professor of mathematics at the Carolinum, and a few months before his death he was named *premier médecin* of Zurich, professor of physics at the Academy, and *Chorherr.*

Scheuchzer left the municipal library of Zurich more than 260 folio volumes, which he wrote in less than forty years. The moving force in the establishment of paleontology in Switzerland, he is also considered the founder of paleobotany and his *Herbarium diluvianum* remained a standard through the nineteenth century. His work on a great variety of fossils and notably on *Homo diluvii testis* of Oensingen (1726) makes him generally considered the founder of European paleontology. Scheuchzer became famous for his medical studies on the effects of altitude, published a remarkable topographic map of Switzerland, and took an active part in the military life of his canton as an army doctor.

In addition to his scientific accomplishments, Scheuchzer compiled a twenty-nine-volume *Histoire suisse* and a critical collection of deeds and other documents, entitled *Diploma Helvetiae.*

BIBLIOGRAPHY

I. ORIGINAL WORKS. A complete bibliography of Scheuchzer is in the Steiger article (below) with a list of his correspondence. Among his works are his medical diss., *De surdo audiento* (Zurich, 1694); "De generatione conchitarum," in *Miscellanea curiosa Academiae naturae curiosorum,* IV (Zurich, 1697); *Helvetiae stoicheiographia, orographia et oreographia* (Zurich, 1716); *Homo diluvii testis* (1726); and *Physica sacra,* 3 vols. (Zurich, 1731–1733).

II. SECONDARY LITERATURE. The most complete account of Scheuchzer is R. Steiger, "Johann Jakob Scheuchzer (1672–1733)," in *Beiblatt zur Vierteljahrsschrift der Naturforschenden Gesellschaft in Zurich,* **21** (1933), 1–75, with a complete bibliography. See also C. Walkmeister, "J. J. Scheuchzer und seiner Zeit," in *Bericht der St. Gallischen naturwissenschaft Gesellschaft* (1896), 364–401; F. X. Hoeherl, "J. J. Scheuchzer, der Begrunder der physischen Geographie des Hochgebirges" (diss., University of Munich, 1901); and B. Peyer, "J. J. Scheuchzer im europaischen Geistleben seiner Zeit," in *Gesnerus,* **2** (1945), 23–33.

P. E. PILET

SCHICKARD, WILHELM (*b.* Herrenberg, Germany, 22 April 1592; *d.* Tübingen, Germany, 23 October 1635)

Schickard, a brilliant student, received the B.A. in 1609 and the M.A. in 1611 from the University of Tübingen, where he continued with the study of theology and oriental languages until 1613. He then served as deacon or pastor in several nearby towns. In 1617 he befriended Kepler, who reawakened in him an interest in mathematics and astronomy and with whom he maintained an active correspondence for several years. In 1619 he was named professor of Hebrew at the University of Tübingen. Upon the death in 1631 of his former teacher, Michael Mästlin, Schickard succeeded to the chair of astronomy but continued to lecture on Hebrew.

Schickard was a polymath who knew several Near Eastern languages, some of which he taught himself. He was a skilled mechanic, cartographer, and engraver in wood and copperplate; and he wrote treatises on Semitic studies, mathematics, astronomy, optics, meteorology, and cartography. He invented and built a working model of the first modern mechanical calculator and proposed to Kepler the development of a mechanical means of calculating ephemerides. Schickard's works on astronomy include a lunar ephemeris, observations of the comets of 1618, and descriptions of unusual solar phenomena (meteors and the transit of Mercury in 1631). He also constructed and described a teaching device consisting of a hollow sphere in three segments with the heavens represented on the inside.

Schickard was an early supporter of Kepler's theories; his treatise on the 1631 transit of Mercury called attention to some of Kepler's ideas and works and to the superiority of the *Rudolphine Tables*. Schickard also mentioned Kepler's first two laws of planetary motion; the second law, however, was given only in the inverse-distance, rather than in the correct, equal-areas formulation.

BIBLIOGRAPHY

I. ORIGINAL WORKS. Schickard's unpublished MSS are in the Österreichische Nationalbibliothek of Vienna and in the Württembergische Landesbibliothek in Stuttgart. His chief works (all published in Tübingen) are *Astroscopium pro facillima stellarum cognitione noviter excogitatum* (1623); *Ignis versicolor e coelo sereno delapsus et Tubingae spectatus* (1623); *Weiterer Bericht von der Fliegenden Liecht-Kugel* (1624); *Anemographia, seu discursus philosophicus de ventis* (1631); *Contemplatio physica de origine animae rationalis* (1631); and *Pars responsi ad epistolas P. Gassendi . . . de mercurio sub sole viso et alijs novitatibus uranicis* (1632). Useful collections of his correspondence are in *Epistolae W. Schickarti et M. Berneggeri mutuae* (Strasbourg, 1673); *Johannes Kepler Gesammelte Werke*, **17–18**, Max Caspar, ed. (Munich, 1955, 1959); and the appendix to Schnurrer's biography (see below), pp. 249–274.

II. SECONDARY LITERATURE. The standard biographies remain Johann C. Speidel, in his ed. of Schickard's *Nova et plenior grammatica Hebraica* (Tübingen, 1731) and Christian F. Schnurrer, in *Biographische und litterarische Nachrichten von ehmaligen Lehrern der hebräischen Litteratur in Tübingen* (Ulm, 1792), 160–225. Recent accounts of Schickard's invention of the calculating machine are Franz Hammer, "Nicht Pascal, sondern der Tübinger Professor Wilhelm Schickard erfand die Rechenmaschine," in *Büromarkt-Bibliothek*, **13** (1958), 1023–1025; and René Taton, "Sur l'invention de la machine arithmétique," in *Revue d'histoire des sciences et de leurs applications*, **16** (1963), 139–160.

WILBUR APPLEBAUM

SCHLÄFLI, LUDWIG (*b.* Grasswil, Bern, Switzerland, 15 January 1814; *d.* Bern, Switzerland, 20 March 1895)

Schläfli, the son of Johann Ludwig Schläfli, a citizen of Burgdorf, and Magdalena Aebi, attended primary school in Burgdorf. With the aid of a scholarship he was able to study at the Gymnasium in Bern, where he displayed a gift for mathematics. He enrolled in the theological faculty at Bern but, not wishing to pursue an ecclesiastical career, decided to accept a post as teacher of mathematics and science at the *Burgerschule* in Thun. He taught there for ten years, using his few free hours to study higher mathematics. In the autumn of 1843 Jakob Steiner, who was traveling to Rome with Jacobi, Dirichlet, and Borchardt, proposed that they take Schläfli with them as interpreter. Schläfli thus had an opportunity to learn from the leading mathematicians of his time. Dirichlet instructed him daily in number theory, and Schläfli's later works on quadratic forms bear the mark of this early training. During this period Schläfli translated two works by Steiner and two by Jacobi into Italian.

In 1848 Schläfli became a *Privatdozent* at Bern, where, as he expressed it, he was "confined to a stipend of Fr. 400 and, in the literal sense of the word, had to do without (*darben musste*)." His nomination as extraordinary professor in 1853 did not much improve his situation, and it was not until he became a full professor in 1868 that he was freed from financial concerns. Schläfli's scientific achievements gained recognition only slowly. In 1863 he received an honorary doctorate from the University of Bern; in 1868 he became a corresponding member of the Istituto Lombardo di Scienze e Lettere in Milan and was later accorded the same honor by the Akademie der Wissenschaften in Göttingen (1871) and the Accademia dei Lincei (1883). He won the Jakob Steiner Prize for his geometric works in 1870.

While at Bern, Schläfli was concerned with two major problems, one in elimination theory and the other in n-dimensional geometry, and he brought his results together in two extensive works. The first problem is discussed in "Ueber die Resultante eines Systems mehrerer algebraischer Gleichungen. Ein Beitrag zur Theorie der Elimination" (published in *Denkschriften der Akademie der Wissenschaften*, **4**). Schläfli summarized the first part of this work in a letter to Steiner:

> For a given system of n equations of higher degree with n unknowns, I take a linear equation with literal (undetermined) coefficients $a, b, c, \cdots$ and show how one can thus obtain true resultants without burdening the calculation with extraneous factors. If everything else is given numerically, then the resultant must be decomposable into factors all of which are linear with respect to $a, b, c, \cdots$. In the case of each of these linear polynomials the coefficients of $a, b, c, \cdots$ are then values of the unknowns belonging to a *single* solution.

Drawing on the works of Hesse, Jacobi, and Cayley, Schläfli presented applications to special cases. He then developed the fundamental theorems on class and degree of an algebraic manifold, theorems that attracted the interest of the Italian school of geometers. The work concluded with an examination of the class equation of third-degree curves. Through this publication Schläfli became acquainted with Arthur Cayley, whose paper "Sur un théorème de M. Schläfli" begins: "In §13 of a very interesting memoir by M. Schläfli one finds a very beautiful theorem on resultants." The acquaintance led to an extensive correspondence and opened the way for Schläfli to publish in English journals. In his obituary of Schläfli, F. Brioschi wrote:

> While rereading this important work recently it occurred to me that it displays the outstanding characteristics of Schläfli's work as a whole. These are, first, deep and firsthand knowledge of the writings of other authors; next, a desire and ability to generalize results; and, finally, great penetration in investigating problems from very different points of view.

The second of the two major works, "Theorie der vielfachen Kontinuität," was rejected by the academies of Vienna and Berlin because of its great length and was not published until 1901 (in *Neue Denkschriften der Schweizerischen naturfor-* *schenden Gesellschaft*). For many years only sections of it appeared in print—in the journals of Crelle and Liouville and in the *Quarterly Journal of Mathematics*. The core of this work consisted of the detailed theory of regular bodies in Euclidean space R_n of n dimensions and the associated problems of the regular subdivision of the higher-dimensional spheres. Schläfli based his investigation of regular polytopes on his discovery that such objects can be characterized by certain symbols now known as Schläfli symbols. His definition was recursive: $\{k_1\}$ is the symbol of the plane regular k_1-gon. $\{k_1, \cdots, k_{n-1}\}$ is the Schläfli symbol of that regular polytope the boundary polytopes of which have the symbol $k_1, \cdots, k_{n-2}$ and the vertex polytopes of which have the symbol $\{k_2, \cdots, k_{n-1}\}$.

Schläfli discovered a way of finding all regular polytopes by calculating the numbers $k_1, \cdots, k_{n-1}$ in the following manner: In the plane, for every k_1 there exists a $\{k_1\}$. In considering n-space he started from Euler's theorem on polyhedrons, which he formulated and proved for R_n: assume a polytope with a_0 vertexes, a_1 edges, a_2 faces and so on in higher dimensions until a_{n-1} boundary polytopes of dimension $n-1$, and $a_n = 1$. Then it is true that

$$a_0 - a_1 + a_2 - \cdots (-1)^{n-1} a_{n-1} + (-1)^n a_n = 1.$$

For $n = 3$ the Euler theorem on polyhedrons becomes $a_0 - a_1 + a_2 = 2$. Since, further, for $\{k_1, k_2\}$ it is true that $k_2 \cdot a_0 = 2a_1 = k_1 \cdot a_2$, it follows that

$$a_0 : a_1 : a_2 : 1 = 4k_1 : 2k_1 k_2 : 4k_2 : [4 - (k_1 - 2)(k_2 - 2)].$$

The nature of the problem requires a positive value for $[4 - (k_1 - 2)(k_2 - 2)]$; therefore $(k_1 - 2)(k_2 - 2)$ can take only the values 1,2,3. This yields the following possibilities: $\{3,3\}$ tetrahedron, $\{3,4\}$ octahedron, $\{3,5\}$ icosahedron, $\{4,3\}$ cube, and $\{5,3\}$ dodecahedron. For $n = 4$ the Euler equation $a_0 - a_1 + a_2 - a_3 = 0$ becomes homogeneous and yields only the ratios of the a_i. Schläfli therefore determined the radius of the circumscribed sphere of a $\{k_1, k_2, k_3\}$ of edge length 1. If this radius is to be real, then it must be true that $\sin \frac{\pi}{k_1} \cdot \sin \frac{\pi}{k_3} > \cos \frac{\pi}{k_2}$. This condition yields the six bodies $\{3,3,3\}$, $\{4,3,3\}$, $\{3,3,4\}$, $\{3,4,3\}$, $\{5,3,3\}$, and $\{3,3,5\}$. Schläfli proved further that in every R_n with $n > 4$ there are only three regular solids: $\{3, 3, \cdots, 3\}$, regular simplex; $\{4, 3, \cdots, 3\}$, n-dimensional cube; and $\{3, 3, \cdots, 3, 4\}$, regular n-dimensional octahedron.

Schläfli achieved another beautiful result by considering the unit sphere in R_n and n hyperplanes through the origin $(1) = 0, \cdots, (n) = 0$. Specifically, he found that the inequalities $(1) \geq 0, \cdots, (n) \geq 0$ determine a spherical simplex with surface S_n. Schläfli proved $dS_n = \frac{1}{n-2} \{\Sigma S_{n-2} \, d\lambda\}$, where S_{n-2} is the surface of a boundary simplex of two dimensions less and λ is a suitable angle between two such simplexes, and the summation extends over all such boundary simplexes. Let O_n be the surface of the sphere; then the Schläfli function f_n is defined by $S_n = \frac{1}{2^n} O_n f_n$. It can be proved that $f_{2m+1} = a_0 \Sigma f_{2m} - a_1 \Sigma f_{2m-2} + \cdots$, where a_k is proportional to the $k+1$ Bernoulli number B_k. This equation states that the Schläfli function in a space of odd dimension can be reduced to Schläfli functions in spaces of even dimension. Concerning this discovery Schläfli wrote to Steiner: "I believe I am not overestimating the importance of this general theorem if I set it beside the most beautiful results that have been achieved in geometry."

Besides the theory of Schläfli functions the second section of the paper included a detailed treatment of the decomposition of an arbitrary spherical simplex into right-angled simplexes. The section concluded with a theorem on the sum of the squares of the projections of a ray on the vertex rays of a regular polytope, a question that has interested researchers in recent times.

The third section, headed "Verschiedene Anwendungen der Theorie der vielfachen Kontinuität, welche das Gebiet der linearen und sphärischen übersteigen," contains both applications of theorems of Binet, Monge, Chasles, and Dupin to quadratic continua in R_n and Schläfli's own discoveries. After first determining the midpoint, major axes, and conjugate diameters for a quadratic continuum, he demonstrates the law of inertia of the quadratic forms by means of continuity considerations. Among other results presented is a generalization of a theorem of Binet for a system of conjugate radii: the sum of the squares of all m-fold parallelepipeds constructed out of the conjugate radii of a system is equal to the sum obtained when the system is formed from the major axes. Schläfli then divided the quadratic continua into two classes and generalized Monge's theorem on the director circle, or great circle, of a central conic section. He also examined confocal systems and showed that in R_3 their determination depends on a third-order linear differential equation.

After "Theorie der vielfachen Kontinuität" had appeared in its entirety, P. H. Schoute wrote in 1902:

This treatise surpasses in scientific value a good portion of everything that has been published up to the present day in the field of multidimensional geometry. The author experienced the sad misfortune of those who are ahead of their time: the fruits of his most mature studies cannot bring him fame. And in this case the success of the division of the cubic surfaces was only a small compensation; for, in my opinion, this achievement, however valuable it might be, is far from conveying the genius expressed in the theory of manifold continuity.

Steiner communicated to Schläfli Cayley's discovery of the twenty-seven straight lines on the third-degree surface. Schläfli thereupon found the thirty-six "doubles sixes" on this surface and then the division of the cubic surface into twenty-two species according to the nature of the singularities. Schläfli also solved problems posed by the Italian school of geometers. He gave a condition under which a manifold has constant curvature: its geodesic lines must appear as straight lines in a suitable coordinate system. He also investigated the space of least dimension in which a manifold can be imbedded; his conjecture on this question was demonstrated by M. Janet and E. Cartan (1926–1927). Schläfli's work on the division of third-order surfaces led him to assert the one-sidedness of the projective plane in a letter to Felix Klein in 1874.

Schläfli wrote a work on the composition theory of quadratic forms in which he sought to provide the proof of the associative law that was lacking in Gauss's treatment of the subject. Schläfli's posthumous papers contain extensive tables for the class number of quadratic forms of both positive and negative determinants.

Schläfli's geometric and arithmetical studies were equaled in significance by his work in function theory. Stimulated by C. G. Neumann's investigations (1867) and following up the representation of the gamma function by a line integral, Schläfli gave the integral representation of the Bessel function $J_n(z)$ for arbitrary n, even where n is not integral. He also wrote an outstanding work on elliptic modular functions (1870) that gave rise to the designation "Schläfli modular equation." An examination of his posthumous manuscripts reveals that in 1867, ten years before Dedekind, Schläfli discovered the domain of discontinuity of the modular group and used it to make a careful analysis of the Hermite modular functions from the analytic, number theoretic, and geometric points of view. As early as 1868, moreover, Schläfli employed means that Weber discovered only twenty years later and termed f-functions or class invariants.

Besides his mathematical achievements, Schläfli was an expert on the flora of the canton of Bern and an accomplished student at languages. He possessed a profound knowledge of the *Veda,* and his posthumous manuscripts include ninety notebooks of Sanskrit and commentary on the *Rig-Veda.*

BIBLIOGRAPHY

I. ORIGINAL WORKS. Schläfli's writings were brought together as *Gesammelte mathematische Abhandlungen,* 3 vols. (Basel, 1950–1956). His correspondence with Steiner is in *Mitteilungen der Naturforschenden Gesellschaft in Bern* for 1896 (1897), 61–264. That with Cayley is in J. H. Graf, ed., *Briefwechsel von Ludwig Schläfli mit Arthur Cayley* (Bern, 1905); and that with Borchardt (1856–1877) is in *Mitteilungen der Naturforschenden Gesellschaft in Bern* for 1915 (1916), 50–69. Graf also edited the following: "Lettres de D. Chelini à L. Schläfli," in *Bullettino di bibliografia e di storia delle scienze matematiche e fisiche,* 17 (1915), 36–40; "Correspondance entre E. Beltrami et L. Schläfli," *ibid.,* 81–86, 113–122; and "Correspondance entre Luigi Cremona et Ludwig Schläfli," *ibid.,* 18 (1916), 21–35, 49–64, 81–83, 113–121, and 19 (1917), 9–14. Two letters from Schläfli to P. Tardy (1865) are in G. Loria, "Commemorazione del socio Prof. Placido Tardy," in *Atti dell'Accademia nazionale dei Lincei. Rendiconti,* Cl. fis., 24 (1915), 519–531.

II. SECONDARY LITERATURE. See J. J. Burckhardt, "Der mathematische Nachlass von Ludwig Schläfli, mit einem Anhang: Ueber Schläflis nachgelassene Manuskripte zur Theorie der quadratischen Formen," in *Mitteilungen der Naturforschenden Gesellschaft in Bern* for 1941 (1942), 1–22; and "Ludwig Schläfli," supp. no. 4 of *Elemente der Mathematik* (1948); J. H. Graf, "Ludwig Schläfli," in *Mitteilungen der Naturforschenden Gesellschaft in Bern* for 1895 (1896), 120–203; A. Häusermann, *Ueber die Berechnung singulärer Moduln bei Ludwig Schläfli* (inaugural diss., Zurich, 1943); W. Rytz, "Prof. Ludwig Schläfli als Botaniker," in *Mitteilungen der Naturforschenden Gesellschaft in Bern* for 1918 (1919), 213–220; and O. Schlaginhaufen, "Der Schädel des Mathematikers Ludwig Schläfli," *ibid.* for 1930 (1931), 35–66.

JOHANN JAKOB BURCKHARDT

SCHMIDT, ERHARD (*b.* Dorpat, Germany [now Tartu, E.S.S.R.], 13 January 1876; *d.* Berlin, Germany, 6 December 1959)

Schmidt's most significant contributions to mathematics were in integral equations and in the founding of Hilbert space theory. Specifically, he simplified and extended David Hilbert's results in the theory of integral equations; and he formalized Hilbert's distinct ideas on integral equations into the single concept of a Hilbert space, in the process introducing many geometrical terms. In addition, he made contributions in the fields of partial differential equations and geometry. The most important of these discoveries were the extensions of the isoperimetric inequality, first to *n*-dimensional Euclidean space and then to multidimensional hyperbolic and spherical spaces. Although his methods were classical rather than abstractionist, nevertheless he must be considered a founder of modern functional analysis.

The son of Alexander Schmidt, a medical biologist, Erhard studied at Dorpat, Berlin, and finally at Göttingen, where he was a doctoral candidate under Hilbert. His degree was awarded in 1905 after the presentation of his thesis, "Entwicklung willkürlicher Funktionen nach Systemen forgeschriebener." After short periods as a teacher in Bonn, Zurich, Erlangen, and Breslau (now Wrocław), in 1917 he went to the University of Berlin, where he was to remain the rest of his life. In 1946 he became the first director of the Research Institute for Mathematics of the German Academy of Sciences, a post he held until 1958. He was also one of the founders and first editors of *Mathematische Nachrichten* (1948).

The integral equation on which Schmidt's reputation is based has the form

$$f(s) = \phi(s) - \lambda \int_a^b K(s, t) \, \phi(t) dt. \qquad (1)$$

In (1), $K(s, t)$ – called the kernel – and $f(s)$ are known functions and ϕ is an unknown function that is to be found. This equation has a long history. Interest in it stemmed from its many applications; for example, if (1) can be solved, then the partial differential equation $\Delta u = \partial^2 u / \partial x^2 + \partial^2 u / \partial y^2 = 0$ with the prescribed condition $u(x, y) = b(s)$ of arc length s on the boundary of a given region of the plane can also be solved. This differential equation arises in many problems of physics.

From the early nineteenth century on, there were many attempts to solve equation (1), but only partial results were obtained until 1903. In that year Ivar Fredholm was able to present a complete solution to (1), although in his theory the parameter λ plays no significant role. Fredholm showed that for a fixed λ and K either (1) has a unique solution for every function f, or the associated homogeneous equation

$$\phi(s) - \lambda \int_0^1 K(s, t) \phi(t) dt = 0 \qquad (2)$$

has a finite number of linearly independent solutions; in this case (1) has a solution ϕ only for those f that satisfy certain orthogonality conditions.

In 1904 Hilbert continued the study. He first used a complicated limiting process involving infinite matrices to show that for the fixed but symmetric kernel K ($K(s, t) = K(t, s)$), there would always be values of λ—all real—for which (2) had nontrivial solutions. These λ's he called the *eigenvalues* associated with K, and the solutions he called *eigenfunctions*. He also proved that if f is such that there exists g continuous on [0, 1] with

$$f(s) = \int_a^b K(s, t)g(t)dt,$$

then $f(s)$ can be expanded in a series in eigenfunctions of K, that is,

$$f(s) = \sum_{p=1}^{\infty} a_p\phi_p$$

where $\{\phi_p\}$ is an orthonormal[1] set of eigenfunctions of K.

A year later Hilbert introduced the concept of infinite bilinear forms into both the theory of integral equations and the related topic of infinite matrices. He discovered the concept of complete continuity[2] for such forms and then showed that if $\{a_{ij} : i, j = 1, 2, \cdots\}$ are the coefficients of a completely continuous form, then the infinite system of linear equations

$$x_i + \sum_{j=1}^{\infty} a_{ij}x_j = a_i, \qquad i = 1, 2, \cdots \quad (3)$$

either has a unique square summable[3] solution $\{x_i : i = 1, 2, \cdots\}$ for every square summable sequence $\{a_i\}$ or the associated homogeneous system $x_i + \Sigma\, a_{ij}x_j = 0$ has a finite number of linearly independent solutions. In the latter case, (3) will have solutions only for those sequences $\{a_i\}$ that satisfy certain orthogonality conditions. Hilbert then went on to prove again Fredholm's result converting equation (1) to equation (3) by using Fourier coefficients.

Schmidt's paper on integral equation (1) appeared in two parts in 1907. He began by reproving Hilbert's earlier results concerning symmetric kernels. He was able to simplify the proofs and also to show that Hilbert's theorems were valid under less restrictive conditions. Included in this part of the work is the well-known Gram-Schmidt process for the construction of a set of orthonormal functions from a given set of linearly independent functions.

Schmidt then went on to consider the case of (1) in which the kernel $K(s, t)$ is no longer symmetric. He showed that in this case, too, there always will be eigenvalues that are real. The eigenfunctions, however, now occur in adjoint pairs; that is, ϕ and

ψ are adjoint eigenfunctions belonging to λ if ϕ satisfies

$$\phi(s) = \lambda \int_a^b K(t, s)\psi(t)dt,$$

which is called an eigenfunction of the first kind, and ψ satisfies

$$\psi(s) = \lambda \int_a^b K(s, t)\phi(t)dt,$$

an eigenfunction of the second kind. Moreover, if $\phi = \phi_1 + i\phi_2$, $\psi = \psi_1 + i\psi_2$, then ϕ_1 and ψ_1 are an adjoint pair of eigenfunctions, as are ϕ_2 and ψ_2. Thus, it is only necessary to consider real pairs of eigenfunctions.

Other extensions of the symmetric to the unsymmetric case were also developed by Schmidt. As a broadening of Hilbert's result, Schmidt proved (Hilbert-Schmidt theorem) that if f is such that there is a function g continuous on [a, b] with

$$f(s) = \int_a^b K(s, t)g(t)dt,$$

then f can be represented by an orthonormal series of the eigenfunctions of the first kind of K; and if

$$f(s) = \int_a^b K(t, s)g(t)dt,$$

then f has a representation in a series of the second kind of eigenfunctions. He also proved a type of diagonalization theorem: If $x(s)$ and $y(s)$ are continuous on [a, b], then

$$\int_a^b \int_a^b K(s, t)x(s)y(s)dsdt =$$

$$\sum_v \frac{1}{\lambda_v} \int_a^b x(s)\phi_v(s)ds \int y(t)\psi_v(t)dt$$

where $\{\phi_p\}$ and $\{\psi_p\}$ are orthonormal sets of eigenfunctions of the first or second kinds and λ_v are the associated eigenvalues.

The idea behind Schmidt's work is extremely simple. From the kernel $K(s, t)$ of equation (1) he constructed two new kernels:

$$\overline{K}(s, t) = \int_a^b K(s, r)K(t, r)dr$$

and

$$\underline{K}(s, t) = \int_a^b K(r, s)K(r, t)dr,$$

which are both symmetric. Then ϕ and ψ are an adjoint pair of eigenfunctions belonging to λ if and only if

$$\phi(s) = \lambda^2 \int_a^b \overline{K}(s, t)\, \phi\, (t)dt,$$

and

$$\psi(t) = \lambda^2 \int_a^b \underline{K}(s, t)\psi(t)dt;$$

that is, ϕ is an eigenfunction belonging to λ^2 of $\overline{K}$ and ψ is an eigenfunction belonging to λ^2 of $\underline{K}$. Thus

Schmidt could then apply much of the earlier theory of symmetric kernels.

Schmidt's contributions to Hilbert space theory stem from Hilbert himself. Before Hilbert there had been some attempts to develop a general theory of infinite linear equations, but by the turn of the twentieth century only a few partial results had been obtained. Hilbert focused the attention of mathematicians on the connections among infinite linear systems, square summable sequences, and matrices of which the entries define completely continuous bilinear forms. These equations were of importance since their applications were useful not only in integral equations but also in differential equations and continued fractions.

In 1908 Schmidt published his study on the solution of infinitely many linear equations with infinitely many unknowns. Although his paper is in one sense a definitive work on the subject, its chief importance was the explicit development of the concept of a Hilbert space and also the geometry of such space—ideas that were only latent in Hilbert's own work.

A vector or point z of Schmidt's space H was a square summable sequence of complex numbers, $\{z_n\}$. The inner product of two vectors z and w—denoted by (z, w)—was given by the formula

$$(z, w) = \sum_{p=1}^{\infty} z_p w_p$$

and a norm—denoted by $\|z\|$—was defined by $\|z\| = \sqrt{(z, \bar{z})}$. The vectors z and w were defined to be perpendicular or orthogonal if $(z, w) = 0$, and Schmidt showed that any set of mutually orthogonal vectors must be linearly independent. The Gram-Schmidt orthogonalization process was then developed for linearly independent sets, and from this procedure necessary and sufficient conditions for a set to be linearly independent were derived.

Schmidt then considered convergence. If $\{z^n\}$ is a sequence of vectors of H, then $\{z^n\}$ is defined to converge strongly in H to z if $\lim_{h \to \infty} \|z^n - z\| = 0$, and $\{z^n\}$ is said to be a strong Cauchy sequence if $\lim \|z^p - z^n\| = 0$ independently in p and n. He then showed that every strong Cauchy sequence in H converges strongly to some element of H. Then the nontrivial concept of a closed subspace A of H was introduced. Schmidt showed how such subspaces could be constructed and then proved the projection theorem: If z is a vector H and A is a closed subspace of H, then z has a unique representation $z = a + w$ where a is in A and w is orthogonal to every vector in A. Furthermore, $\|w\| = \min \|z - y\|$ where y is any element of A, and this minimum is

actually assumed only for $y = a$. Finally, these results were used to establish necessary and sufficient conditions under which the infinite system of equations

$$\sum_{p=1}^{\infty} a_{np} z_p = c_n$$

has a square summable solution $\{z_p\}$ where $\{c_n\}$ is a square summable sequence and, for each n, $\{a_{np}\}$ is also square summable. He then obtained specific representations for the solutions.

Schmidt's work on Hilbert space represents a long step toward modern mathematics. He was one of the earliest mathematicians to demonstrate that the ordinary experience of Euclidean concepts can be extended meaningfully beyond geometry into the idealized constructions of more complex abstract mathematics.

NOTES

1. The set $\{\phi_p\}$ is orthonormal if

$$\int_a^b (\phi_p(s))^2 \, ds = 1 \quad (p = 1, 2, \cdots)$$

and

$$\int_a^b \phi_p(s)\phi_q(s) \, ds = 0 \quad (p \neq q).$$

2. The form $K(x, x)$ is completely continuous at a if

$$\lim_{h \to \infty} \epsilon_i^{(h)} \to 0 \quad (i = 1, 2, \cdots)$$

implies that

$$\lim_{h \to \infty} K(a + \epsilon^{(h)}, a + \epsilon^{(h)}) = K(a, a)$$

where $a = (a_1, a_2, \cdots)$ and $\epsilon^{(h)} = (\epsilon_1^{(h)}, \epsilon_2^{(h)}, \cdots)$. In a Hilbert space this is stronger than ordinary continuity (in the norm topology).

3. The sequence of (complex) numbers $\{b_n\}$ is square summable if

$$\sum_{n=1}^{\infty} |b_n|^2 < \infty.$$

BIBLIOGRAPHY

I. ORIGINAL WORKS. A complete bibliography of Schmidt's works can be found in the obituary by Kurt Schröder in *Mathematische Nachrichten*, **25** (1963), 1–3. Particular attention is drawn to "Zur Theorie der linearen und nichtlinearen Integralgleichungen. I," in *Mathematische Annalen*, **63** (1907), 433–476; "Zur Theorie . . . II," *ibid.*, **64** (1907), 161–174; and "Über die Auflösung linearen Gleichungen mit unendlich vielen Unbekannten," in *Rendiconti del Circolo matematico di Palermo*, **25** (1908), 53–77.

II. SECONDARY LITERATURE. On Schmidt and his work, see Ernst Hellinger and Otto Toeplitz, "Integralgleichungen und Gleichungen mit unendlichvielen Unbekannten," in *Encyklopädie der Mathematischen Wis-*

senschaften, IIC, 13 (Leipzig, 1923–1927), 1335–1602. This article, also published under separate cover, is an excellent general treatise, and specifically shows the relationship between integral equation theory and the theory of infinite linear systems.

MICHAEL BERNKOPF

SCHOENFLIES, ARTHUR MORITZ (b. Landsberg an der Warthe, Germany [now Gorzów, Poland], 17 April 1853; d. Frankfurt am Main, Germany, 27 May 1928)

Schoenflies studied with Kummer at the University of Berlin from 1870 to 1875 and received the Ph.D. in 1877. From 1878 he taught at a Gymnasium in Berlin and then, from 1880, in Colmar, Alsace. In 1884 he earned his *Habilitation* as *Privatdozent* at the University of Göttingen, where, in 1892, he was named professor extraordinarius and was given the chair of applied mathematics. (This chair had been created thanks to Felix Klein's initiative.) In 1899 Schoenflies was appointed professor ordinarius at the University of Königsberg and then, in 1911, at the Academy for Social and Commercial Sciences in Frankfurt am Main; this school became a university in 1914. He was later professor ordinarius (1914–1922) at the University of Frankfurt and in 1920–1921 served as rector of the university.

Schoenflies produced an extensive mathematical *oeuvre* consisting of about ninety papers and many reports and books. He started his scientific work with rather traditional geometry and kinematics. This research was published in 1886 (1) and was later translated into French (1a). In the same year, under Klein's influence, Schoenflies turned to Euclidean motion groups and regular space divisions. His investigations culminated in 1891 in his magnum opus (2). The result of this book, the 230 crystallographic groups, was at the same time obtained independently by E. S. Fedorov. During the last phase of this research, Schoenflies corresponded with Fedorov and was thus able to correct some minor errors that he had originally made in his classification. In 1923 Schoenflies reedited his 1891 publication under another title (2a). He also wrote a textbook on crystallography (9).

In the mid-1890's Schoenflies, by then in his forties, turned to topology and set theory. In 1898 he published an article (5) on this subject in the *Encyklopädie der mathematischen Wissenschaften*. He also published extensive reports in *Deutsche Mathematiker-Vereinigung*, which appeared in 1900 and 1908 (6) and were reedited in 1913 (6a). These reports were totally eclipsed by Hausdorff's *Grundzüge der Mengenlehre* (1914). The greater part of Schoenflies' original contributions to topology is contained in three papers (7) and is devoted to plane topology. He proved the topological invariance of the dimension of the square, and he invented the notions and theorems that are connected with the characterization of the simple closed curve in the plane by its dividing the plane into two domains of which it is the everywhere attainable boundary. There are numerous gaps and wrong statements in this part of Schoenflies' work, and these errors led L. Brouwer to some of his startling discoveries.

Schoenflies published four articles in the *Encyklopädie der mathematischen Wissenschaften* (on set theory, kinematics, crystallography, and projective geometry), in part with others (5). With W. Nernst, he wrote a textbook (1895) on calculus (3) that went through at least eleven editions and two Russian translations. He also wrote textbooks on descriptive geometry (8) and analytic geometry (10). In 1895 he edited the work of Julius Plücker (4). Schoenflies was elected a fellow of the Bayerische Akademie der Wissenschaften in 1918.

BIBLIOGRAPHY

I. ORIGINAL WORKS. Schoenflies' works are the following:

(1) *Geometrie der Bewegung in synthetischer Darstellung* (Leipzig, 1886), with French trans. by C. Speckel as (1a) *La géométrie du mouvement—exposé synthétique* (Paris, 1893);

(2) *Kristallsysteme und Kristallstruktur* (Leipzig, 1891); the 2nd ed. appeared as (2a) *Theorie der Kristallstruktur* (Berlin, 1923);

(3) *Einführung in die mathematische Behandlung der Naturwissenschaften—Kurzgefasstes Lehrbuch der Differential- und Integralrechnung* (Munich, 1895; 11th ed., 1931), written with W. Nernst;

(4) Julius Plücker, *Gesammelte Mathematische Abhandlungen*, Schoenflies, ed. (Leipzig, 1895);

(5) "Mengenlehre," in *Encyklopaedie der mathematischen Wissenschaften*, 184–207; "Kinematik," *ibid.*, IV, 190–278, written with M. Grübler; "Kristallographie," *ibid.*, V, pt. 7, 391–492, written with T. Liebisch and O. Mügge; "Projektive Geometrie," *ibid.*, III, pt. 5, 389–480;

(6) "Die Entwicklung der Lehre von den Punktmannigfaltigkeiten. I," in *Jahresbericht der Deutschen Mathematiker-Vereinigung*, **8** (1900). 1–250; "Die Entwicklung . . . II," supp. 2 (1908), 1–331;

(6a) *Entwicklung der Mengenlehre und ihrer Anwendungen* (Leipzig, 1913), written with H. Hahn;

(7) "Beiträge zur Theorie der Punktmengen," in *Mathematische Annalen,* **58** (1903), 195–234; **59** (1904), 152–160; **62** (1906), 286–326;

(8) *Einführung in die Hauptgesetze der zeichnerischen Darstellungsmethoden* (Leipzig, 1908);

(9) *Einführung in die Kristallstruktur—ein Lehrbuch* (Berlin, 1923);

(10) *Einführung in die analytische Geometrie der Ebene und des Raumes,* Grundlehren der Mathematischen Wissenschaften no. 21 (Leipzig, 1925), with 2nd ed. by M. Dehn (Leipzig, 1931).

II. SECONDARY LITERATURE. On Schoenflies and his work, see L. Bieberbach, "Arthur Schoenflies," in *Jahresbericht der Deutschen Mathematiker-Vereinigung,* **32** (1923), 1–6; J. J. Burckhardt, "Zur Entdeckung der 230 Raumgruppen," in *Archives for History of Exact Sciences,* **4** (1967), 235–246; "Der Briefwechsel von E. S. Fedorow mit A. Schoenflies, 1889–1908," *ibid.,* **7** (1971), 91–141; R. von Mises, "Schoenflies," in *Zeitschrift für angewandte Mathematik und Mechanik,* **3** (1923), 157–158; A. Sommerfeld, "A. Schoenflies," in *Jahrbuch der bayerischen Akademie der Wissenschaften* (1928–1929), 86–87; and K. Spangenberg, "A. Schönflies," in *Handwörterbuch der Naturwissenschaften,* 2nd ed., VIII (1933), 1108–1109.

HANS FREUDENTHAL

SCHOOTEN, FRANS VAN (*b.* Leiden, Netherlands, *ca.* 1615; *d.* Leiden, 29 May 1660)

Schooten's father, Frans van Schooten the Elder, succeeded Ludolph van Ceulen at the engineering school in Leiden. The younger Schooten enrolled at the University of Leiden in 1631 and was carefully trained in the tradition of the Dutch school of algebra. In early youth he studied Michael Stifel's edition of Christoph Rudolff's German *Coss.* He was also acquainted with the Dutch and French editions of the works of Simon Stevin, with van Ceulen's *Arithmetische en geometrische Fondamenten,* and with Albert Girard's *Invention nouvelle en l'algèbre.* Schooten studied Girard's edition of the mathematical works of Samuel Marolois and his edition of Stevin's *Arithmétique.* He was of course familiar with Commandino's editions of Archimedes, Apollonius, and Pappus, and with Cavalieri's geometry of indivisibles.

It was probably through his teacher, the Arabist and mathematician Jakob Gool, that Schooten met Descartes, who had just come to Leiden from Utrecht to supervise the printing of the *Discours de la méthode* (1637). Schooten saw the proofs of the *Géométrie* (the third supplement to the *Discours*) by the summer of 1637 at the latest. He recognized the utility of the new notation, but he

had difficulty in mastering the contents of the work. He therefore undertook a more intensive study of literature on the subject and sought to discuss the work with colleagues.

Armed with letters of introduction from Descartes, Schooten went to Paris. Although he was a convinced Arminian, he received an extremely cordial welcome from the Minimite friar Marin Mersenne and his circle. In Paris, Schooten was able to read manuscripts of Viète and Fermat; and, on a commission from the Leiden printing firm of Elzevier, he gathered all the printed works of Viète that he could find. He went next to England, where he met the leading algebraists of the day, and finally to Ireland.

Schooten returned home in 1643 and served as his father's lecture assistant, introducing a number of young people—including Jan de Witt—to mathematics. He also prepared a collected edition of the mathematical writings of Viète (1646). Although Schooten generally followed the original texts closely, he did change the notation in several places to simplify the mathematical statements and to make the material more accessible, for Viète's idiosyncratic presentation and the large number of Greek technical terms rendered the originals quite difficult to read. Unfortunately, because he misunderstood a remark that Viète made concerning the unsuccessful edition of his *Canon mathematicus* (1579), Schooten omitted this work and the interesting explanatory remarks that accompanied it from his edition. Schooten had also brought back copies of Fermat's papers, but he was unable to convince Elzevier to publish them, especially since Descartes had expressed an unfavorable opinion of Fermat's work.

In 1645 Christiaan Huygens and his elder brother Constantijn began to study law at Leiden. They attended Schooten's general introductory course (published by Erasmus Bartholin in 1651), and in advanced private instruction became acquainted with many interesting questions in mathematics. A close friendship developed between Schooten and Christiaan Huygens, as their voluminous correspondence attests. The letters reveal how quickly Huygens outgrew the solicitous guidance of his teacher to become the leading mathematician and physicist of his time.

Schooten's first independent work was a study of the kinematic generation of conic sections (1646). In an appendix he treated the reduction of higher-order binomial irrationals $\sqrt[n]{a + \sqrt{b}}$ to the form $x + \sqrt{y}$ in cases where this is possible, using a development of a procedure of Stifel's. An interesting problem that Schooten considered was how to construct a cyclic quadrilateral of given sides, one of which is to be the diameter—a problem that Newton later treated in the lectures on *Arithmetica universalis* (*Mathematical Papers*, V, 162–181).

After the death of his father in 1645, Schooten took over his academic duties. He also worked on a Latin translation of Descartes's *Géométrie*. Although Descartes was not completely satisfied with Schooten's version (1649), it found a broad and receptive audience by virtue of its more carefully executed figures and its full commentary. It was from Schooten's edition of the *Géométrie* that contemporary mathematicians lacking proficiency in French first learned Cartesian mathematics. In this mathematics they encountered a systematic presentation of the material, not the customary, more classificatory approach that essentially listed single propositions, for the most part in unconnected parallel. Further, in the Cartesian scheme the central position was occupied by algebra, which Descartes considered to be the only "precise form of mathematics."

The great success of Schooten's edition led him to prepare a second, much enlarged one in two volumes (1659–1661), which became the standard mathematical work of the period. A third edition appeared in 1683, and an appendix to the fourth edition (1695) contained interesting remarks by Jakob Bernoulli. In the second edition Schooten not only greatly expanded his commentary, but also added new material including an example of Fermat's extreme value and tangent method (with a reference to Hérigone's *Cursus mathematicus* [*Supplementum*, 1642]) and a peculiar procedure for determining the center of gravity of parabolic segments. Since Fermat was not mentioned in the latter connection, it is likely that Schooten came upon the procedure independently, for he usually cited his sources very conscientiously.

In the first edition (1649) Schooten inserted Debeaune's rather insignificant *Notae breves* to the *Géométrie*. The commentary of the second edition contained valuable contributions by Huygens dealing with the intersections of a parabola with a circle and certain corollaries, as well as on an improved method of constructing tangents to the conchoid. Schooten also included longer contributions by his students: Jan Hudde's studies on equations and the rule of extreme values and Hendrik van Heuraet's rectification method.

Volume II of the second edition of the *Geometria* (1661) commences with a reprinting of Schooten's introductory lectures. This material is followed by Debeaune's work on the limits of roots of equations and then by de Witt's excellent tract on conic sections. The volume concludes with a paper by Schooten's younger half brother Pieter on the algebraic discussion of Descartes's data. This edition shows the great effort Schooten devoted to the training of his students and to the dissemination of their findings. This effort can be seen even more clearly in his wide-ranging correspondence, most of which is reprinted in Huygens' *Oeuvres complètes*. (Unfortunately, not all of Schooten's correspondence has been located.)

Schooten made an original contribution to mathematics with his *Exercitationes mathematicae* (1657). Book I contains elementary arithmetic and geometry problems similar to those found in van Ceulen's collection. Book II is devoted to constructions using straight lines only and Book III to the reconstruction of Apollonius' *Plane Loci* on the basis of hints given by Pappus. Book IV is a revised version of Schooten's treatment of the kinematic generation of conic sections, and Book V offers a collection of interesting individual problems. Worth noting, in particular, is the restatement of Hudde's method for the step-by-step building-up of equations for angular section and the determination of the girth of the folium of Descartes: $x^3 + y^3 = 3\,axy$. Also noteworthy is the determination of Heronian triangles of equal perimeter and equal area (Roberval's problem) according to Descartes's method (1633). As an appendix Schooten printed Huygens' *De ratiociniis in aleae ludo*, which was extremely important in the development of the theory of probability.

Schooten possessed an excellent knowledge of the mathematics of both his own time and earlier periods. Besides being an extraordinarily industrious and conscientious scholar, a skillful commentator, and an inspiring teacher, he was a man of rare unselfishness. He recognized his own limitations and did not seek to overstep them. Fascinated by the personality and ideas of Descartes, he worked hard to popularize the new mathematics; his highly successful efforts assured its triumph.

BIBLIOGRAPHY

I. ORIGINAL WORKS. Schooten's writings include his ed. of Viète's *Opera mathematica* (Leiden, 1646); *De organica conicarum sectionum in plano descriptione* (Leiden, 1646); *Geometria a Renato Descartes anno 1637 gallice edita, nunc autem . . . in linguam latinam versa* (Leiden, 1649; 2nd ed., 2 vols., Amsterdam, 1659–1661; 3rd ed., 1683; 4th ed., Frankfurt, 1695);

Principia matheseos universalis, E. Bartholin, ed. (Leiden, 1651), also included in the 2nd ed. of *Geometria; Exercitationum mathematicarum libri quinque* (Leiden, 1657), also in Flemish as *Mathematische Oeffeningen* (Amsterdam, 1660); and "Tractatus de concinnandis demonstrationibus geometricis ex calculo algebraico," Pieter van Schooten, ed., in the 2nd ed. of *Geometria.*

II. SECONDARY LITERATURE. See J. E. Hofmann, "Frans van Schooten der Jüngere," in *Boethius,* II (Wiesbaden, 1962), with portrait; and C. de Waard, "Schooten, Frans van," in *Nieuw Nederlandsch biographisch woordenboeck,* VII (1927), 1110–1114.

J. E. HOFMANN

SCHOTT, GASPAR (*b.* Königshofen, near Würzburg, Germany, 5 February 1608; *d.* Würzburg, 22 May 1666)

Apart from the place and date of his birth, nothing is known of Schott's origins; almost the only childhood recollection in his works is of a suction pump bursting at Paderborn in 1620, which suggests an early interest in machinery. In 1627 he entered the Society of Jesus and was sent to Würzburg University, where he studied philosophy under Athanasius Kircher. The Swedish invasion of the Palatinate in 1631 forced teacher and pupils to flee. Schott may have first accompanied Kircher to France, for he mentions his travels in that country; but he certainly completed his studies in theology, philosophy, and mathematics at Palermo. He remained in Sicily for twenty years, mostly teaching at Palermo, although he spent two years at Trapani. Nevertheless he was anxious to satisfy a strong thirst for knowledge and to resume his connection with Kircher, whom he always revered as his master. Schott was able to satisfy his desire in 1652, when he was sent to Rome, where for three years he collaborated with Kircher on his researches. Schott decided that since Kircher did not have time to publish all that he knew and all the information communicated to him by Jesuits abroad, he himself would do so. While compiling this material, he returned to Germany in the summer of 1655, first to Mainz and then to Würzburg, where he taught mathematics and physics.

Schott first published what had originally been intended as a brief guide to the hydraulic and pneumatic instruments in Kircher's Roman museum, expanding it into the first version of his *Mechanica hydraulico-pneumatica.* But he added as an appendix a detailed account of Guericke's experiments on vacuums, the earliest published report of this work. This supplement contributed greatly to the success of Schott's compendium; and as a result he became the center of a network of correspondence as other Jesuits, as well as lay experimenters and mechanicians, wrote to inform him of their inventions and discoveries. Schott exchanged several letters with Guericke, seeking to draw him out by suggesting new problems, and published his later investigations. He also corresponded with Huygens and was the first to make Boyle's work on the air pump widely known in Germany. Schott repeated Guericke's experiments, and later those of Boyle, at Würzburg, as well as some medical experiments on the effects of intravenous injections. He does not, however, seem to have attempted any original investigations.

During the last years of his life, Schott was engaged in publishing this mass of material, besides what he had brought with him from Rome, adding his own commentaries and footnotes: he produced some eleven titles over eight years (1658–1666). But although his industry was impressive, these books consist largely of extracts from communications he had received or from books he had used. Schott was so determined to include all possible arguments on every side that it is often hard to discover what he himself thought. While he maintained that the experiments of Guericke, Torricelli, Boyle, and others had not produced a true vacuum, the space exhausted of air being filled with "aether," he accepted the assumption that the phenomena previously attributed to the effects of *horror vacui* were really due to atmospheric pressure or to the elasticity of the air. In a treatise on the then very popular theme of the origin of springs, his own opinion, when finally expressed, amounted to saying that everyone was right: some springs are due to precipitation, some to underground condensation, and some are connected directly to the sea.

Schott's chief works, the *Magia universalis* and the two companion volumes, *Physica curiosa* and *Technica curiosa,* are huge, uncritical collections, mines of quaint information in which significant nuggets must be extracted from a great deal of dross. Like many of his time, Schott believed that the principles of nature and art are best revealed in their exceptions. This makes him a useful source on the history of scientific instruments and mechanical technology; a treatise on "chronometric marvels" (which may be his own, since it is ascribed to "a friend" and often quotes his earlier writings) contains the first description of a universal joint to translate motion and a classification of gear teeth. Although the "natural curiosities" include some useful matter (such as on South American mammals), his syncretic attitude and taste for the abnormal made him far readier than most of his contemporaries to credit tales of ghosts, demons, and centaurs. All this writing about magic, both natural and supernatural, involved him in slight difficulties with the censors.

Schott apparently yearned for the intellectual delights of Rome, and after twenty-five years in Italy he suffered from German winters and had to have his own hypocaust installed. He visited Rome in 1661, and in 1664 he applied for a post to teach mathematics at the Jesuits' Roman college; this was rejected, and instead he was offered the headship of the college at Heiligenstadt, which he rejected, feeling himself unsuited to administration. Exhausted, it was said, by overwork on his books, he died in 1666.

Undoubtedly Schott was extraordinarily productive. But his contribution was essentially that of an editor who prepared the researches of others for the press without adding much of consequence. Still, he did much to popularize the achievements of contemporary physicists, especially—but not exclusively—in Catholic Germany.

BIBLIOGRAPHY

I. ORIGINAL WORKS. Schott's most important writings are *Mechanica hydraulico-pneumatica* (Würzburg, 1657); *Magia universalis,* 4 vols. (Würzburg, 1657–1659); *Physica curiosa,* 2 vols. (Würzburg, 1662); *Anatomia physico-hydrostatica fontium ac fluminum* (Würzburg, 1663); and *Technica curiosa* (Würzburg, 1664).

II. SECONDARY LITERATURE. All later articles are based on N. Southwell [N. Bacon], *Bibliotheca scriptorum Societatis Jesu* (Rome, 1682), 282; and A. de Backer, in *Bibliothèque des écrivains de la Compagnie de Jésus,* K. Sommervogel, ed., VII (Paris, 1896), 904–912. The only later biographer to add further information is G. Duhr, *Geschichte der Jesuiten in den Ländern deutscher Zunge,* III (Munich–Regensburg, 1923), 587–592.

A. G. KELLER

SCHOTTKY, FRIEDRICH HERMANN (*b.* Breslau, Germany [now Wrocław, Poland], 24 July 1851; *d.* Berlin, Germany, 12 August 1935)

After attending the Humanistisches Gymnasium St. Magdalenen in Breslau, Schottky studied mathematics and physics at Breslau University from 1870 to 1874 and continued his studies at Berlin with Weierstrass and Helmholtz. He received the Ph.D. in 1875, was admitted as a *Privatdozent* at Berlin in 1878, and in 1882 was appointed a professor at Zurich—at the university, according to one source, and at the Eidgenössische Technische Hochschule, according to another. In 1892 Schottky was appointed to a chair at Marburg University and in 1902 to one at Berlin, where he remained until 1922. In 1902 he was elected a fellow of the Preussische Akademie der Wissenschaften and, in 1911, a corresponding member of the Akademie der Wissenschaften in Göttingen.

Schottky's thesis [1,3] was an important contribution to the conformal mapping of multiply connected plane domains and was the origin of the famous mapping of a domain bounded by three disjoint circles, which, continued by mirror images, provides an example of an automorphic function with a Cantor set boundary. The dissertation also dealt with the conformal mapping of domains bounded by circular and conic arcs.

A contribution to the realm of Picard's theorem, known as Schottky's theorem [5], is an absolute estimation $C(f(0), |z|)$ for functions $f(z)$ defined in $|z| < 1$ and omitting the values 0,1. Schottky also initiated the study of the oscillation, at the boundary, of regular functions defined in the unit circle [4].

The greater part of Schottky's work concerned elliptic, Abelian, and theta functions, a subject on which he wrote a book [2]. He published some fifty-five papers, most of them in *Journal für die reine und angewandte Mathematik, Mathematische Annalen,* and *Sitzungsberichte der Preussischen Akademie der Wissenschaften zu Berlin.* His work is difficult to read. Although he was a student of Weierstrass, his approach to function theory was Riemannian in spirit, combined with Weierstrassian rigor.

BIBLIOGRAPHY

I. ORIGINAL WORKS. Schottky's writings include [1] "Ueber die conforme Abbildung mehrfach zusammenhängender ebener Flächen," in *Journal für die reine und angewandte Mathematik,* **83** (1877), 300–351, his dissertation; [2] *Abriss einer Theorie der Abel'schen Functionen von drei Variablen* (Leipzig, 1880); [3] "Ueber eine specielle Function, welche bei einer bestimmten linearen Transformation ihres Arguments unverändert bleibt," in *Journal für die reine und angewandte Mathematik,* **101** (1887), 227–272; [4] "Ueber die Werteschwankungen der harmonischen Functionen," *ibid.,* **117** (1897), 225–253; [5] "Ueber den Picardschen Satz und die Borelschen Ungleichungen," in *Sitzungsberichte der Preussischen Akademie der Wissenschaften zu Berlin* (1904), 1244–1262; and "Bemerkungen zu meiner Mitteilung . . . ," *ibid.* (1906), 32–36.

II. SECONDARY LITERATURE. See [6] L. Bieberbach, "Friedrich Schottky zum 80. Geburtstage," in *Forschungen und Fortschritte,* **7** (1931), 300; and [7] "Gedächtnisrede auf Friedrich Schottky," in *Sitzungsberichte der Preussischen Akademie der Wissenschaften zu Berlin,* Math.-phys. Kl. (1936), cv–cvi; and the [8] obituary in *Nachrichten von der Gesellschaft der Wissenschaften zu Göttingen* (1935–1936), 6–7.

Portraits of Schottky are in *Acta mathematica 1882–1913. Table générale des tomes 1–35* (Uppsala, 1913), 168; and *Journal für die reine und angewandte Mathematik,* **165** (1931), frontispiece.

HANS FREUDENTHAL

SCHOUTE, PIETER HENDRIK (*b.* Wormerveer, Netherlands, 21 January 1846; *d.* Groningen, Netherlands, 18 April 1923)

Schoute, whose family were industrialists on the Zaan near Amsterdam, studied at the Polytechnical School at Delft, from which he graduated in 1867 as a civil engineer. He continued his study of mathematics at Leiden, where he received his Ph.D. in 1870 with the dissertation "Homography Applied to the Theory of Quadric Surfaces." While teaching at high schools in Nijmegen (1871–1874) and The Hague (1874–1881), he published two textbooks on cosmography. From 1881 until his death he was professor of mathematics at the University of Groningen.

Schoute was a typical geometer. In his early work he investigated quadrics, algebraic curves, complexes, and congruences in the spirit of nineteenth-century projective, metrical, and enumerative geometry. From 1891 he turned to geometry in Euclidean spaces of more than three dimensions, then a field in which little work had been done. He did extensive research on regular polytopes (generalizations of regular polyhedrons). Some of his almost thirty papers in this field were written in collaboration with Alice Boole Stott (1860–1940), daughter of the logician George Boole.

Schoute was an editor of the *Revue semestrielle des publications mathématiques* from its founding in 1893, and in 1898 he became an editor of the *Nieuw archief voor wiskunde.* He held both positions until his death. In 1886 he became a member of the Royal Netherlands Academy of Sciences.

BIBLIOGRAPHY

I. ORIGINAL WORKS. Much of Schoute's work appeared in *Verhandelingen der Koninklyke nederlandsche akademie van wetenschappen,* Afdeeling Natuurkunde, 1st section; see esp. "Regelmässige Schnitte und Projektionen des Hundertzwanzigzelles und des Sechshundertzelles im vierdimensionalen Raume," **2,** no. 7 (1894); and **9,** no. 4 (1907). Writings on other polytopes are in **2,** no. 2 and 4 (1894), which deal with the 8-cell, the 16-cell, and the 24-cell. See also "Het vierdimensionale prismoïde," **5,** no. 2 (1896); and "Les hyperquadratiques dans l'espace à quatre dimensions," **7,** no. 4 (1900). Several articles appeared in *Archives néerlandaises des sciences exactes et naturelles,* 2nd ser. **5–9** (1896–1904). Many of Schoute's results were collected in his *Mehrdimensionale Geometrie,* 2 vols. (Leipzig, 1902–1905).

II. SECONDARY LITERATURE. See H. S. M. Coxeter, *Regular Polytopes* (New York–London, 1948; 2nd ed., 1963), *passim*; and D. J. Korteweg, "P. H. Schoute," in *Zittingsverslagen der Koninklyke nederlandsche akademie van wetenschappen,* **21** (1912–1913), 1396–1400. Also: H. Fehr, *Enseignement mathématique,* **35** (1913), 256–257.

D. J. STRUIK

SCHOUTEN, JAN ARNOLDUS (*b.* Nieuweramstel [now part of Amsterdam], Netherlands, 28 August 1883; *d.* Epe, Netherlands, 20 January 1971)

A descendant of a prominent family of shipbuilders, Schouten grew up in comfortable surroundings. He became not only one of the founders of the "Ricci calculus" but also an efficient organizer (he was a founder of the Mathematical Center at Amsterdam in 1946) and an astute investor. A meticulous lecturer and painfully accurate author, he instilled the same standards in his pupils.

After studying electrical engineering at what is now the Technische Hogeschool at Delft, Schouten practiced this profession for a few years and then returned to study in Leiden when an inheritance gave him the necessary independence. Upon completion of his doctoral dissertation in 1914, his first contribution to the foundations of tensor analysis, he was appointed professor at Delft. In 1943 Schouten resigned the post, divorced his wife, and remarried. From then on, he lived in semiseclusion at Epe. Although he was a professor at the University of Amsterdam from 1948 to 1953, the Mathematical Center had replaced teaching as his first commitment. He served the Center until 1968 and was its director for about five years.

Schouten attained numerous distinctions during

his lifetime, including membership in the Royal Netherlands Academy of Sciences, the rotating position of *rector magnificus* at Delft, the presidency of the 1954 International Congress of Mathematicians at Amsterdam, several terms as president of the Wiskundig Genootschap (the society of Netherlands mathematicians), and a royal decoration.

Schouten's scientific contributions comprise some 180 papers and six books, virtually all related to tensor analysis and its applications to differential geometry, Lie groups, relativity, unified field theory, and Pfaffian systems of differential equations. Having entered the field when it was in its infancy, he helped develop and perfect the basic techniques of local differential geometry and applied them in numerous ways. He discovered connections ("geodesic displacements") in Riemannian manifolds in 1919, independently of, although later than, Levi-Civita; and he also discovered basic properties of Kähler manifolds in 1931, two years before Kähler. Under the influence of Weyl and Eddington he was led to general linear connections and investigated affine, projective, and conformal manifolds.

Schouten's approach to differential geometry was strongly influenced by Felix Klein's "Erlanger Programm" (1872), which viewed each geometry as the theory of invariants of a particular group. This approach led him to a point of view that handled geometric problems more formally than most other prominent differential geometers of his time, notably Levi-Civita, E. Cartan, Veblen, Eisenhart, and Blaschke. This same point of view underlies his "kernel-index method," a notation of great precision, which he and his pupils used masterfully, but which gained favor elsewhere only in less extreme forms.

Schouten inspired numerous co-workers, including D. J. Struik, D. van Dantzig, J. Haantjes, E. R. van Kampen, V. Hlavaty, S. Gołab, Kentaro Yano, E. J. Post, and A. Nijenhuis. His influence extended as far as Russia and Japan.

BIBLIOGRAPHY

I. ORIGINAL WORKS. Most of Schouten's work on tensor analysis and differential geometry can be found or is referred to in *Der Ricci Kalkül* (Berlin, 1924); *Einführung in die neueren Methoden der Differentialgeometrie*, 2 vols. (Groningen, 1934–1938), I, *Uebertragungslehre*, by Schouten, II, *Geometrie*, by D. J. Struik, also translated into Russian (Moscow, 1939, 1948); and *Pfaff's Problem and Its Generalisations*

(Oxford, 1948), written with W. van der Kulk. *Ricci Calculus* (Berlin, 1954), the 2nd ed. of *Der Ricci Kalkül*, is completely rewritten and contains all that Schouten considered relevant in differential geometry at the end of his career. *Tensor Analysis for Physicists* (Oxford, 1951) is an attempt to spread to sophisticated physicists the subtleties of tensor analysis and its implications for field theory and elasticity.

A collection of Schouten's papers and correspondence has been deposited at the library of the Mathematical Center in Amsterdam.

II. SECONDARY LITERATURE. A short biographical article, concentrating on Schouten's scientific work, is D. J. Struik's *Levensbericht* on Schouten, in *Jaarboek der K. Nederlandsche akademie van wetenschappen* for 1971, pp. 94–100, with portrait. A. Nijenhuis, "J. A. Schouten: A Master at Tensors," in *Nieuw archief voor wiskunde*, 3rd ser., **20** (1972), 1–19, contains a complete list of publications.

ALBERT NIJENHUIS

SCHRÖDER, FRIEDRICH WILHELM KARL ERNST (*b.* Mannheim, Germany, 25 November 1841; *d.* Karlsruhe, Germany, 16 June 1902)

Schröder was the son of Heinrich Schröder, who did much to foster the teaching of science in secondary and college-level schools and also strongly influenced his son to choose a scientific career. Schröder's mother, the former Karoline Walter, was the daughter of a minister. Her father tutored Ernst until he was fifteen, providing him with an excellent basic education, especially in Latin. In 1856 Schröder enrolled at the lyceum in Mannheim, from which he graduated in 1860.

Schröder then attended the University of Heidelberg, where he studied under Hesse, Kirchhoff, and Bunsen. He passed his doctoral examination in 1862 and spent the next two years studying mathematics and physics at the University of Königsberg under Franz Neumann and F. J. Richelot. Soon afterward, at Karlsruhe, he took the examination to qualify for teaching in secondary schools. He then went to the Eidgenössische Polytechnikum in Zurich, where he qualified as a lecturer in mathematics in 1865 and taught for a time. In 1874, after teaching at Karlsruhe, Pforzheim, and Baden-Baden, Schröder was offered, on the basis of his mathematical publications, a full professorship at the Technische Hochschule in Darmstadt. In 1876 he accepted a post at the Technische Hochschule in Karlsruhe, of which he became director in 1890. He most often lectured on arithmetic, trigonometry, and advanced analysis.

Schröder was described as kind and modest. A lifelong bachelor, he was an ardent mountain climber and cyclist, and learned to ski when he was sixty years old.

Schröder published more than forty mathematical works, including seven separately printed essays and books. They deal almost exclusively with the foundations of mathematics, notably with combinatorial analysis; the theory of functions of a real variable; and mathematical logic. Particularly noteworthy was his early support of Cantor's ideas on set theory, which he was one of the first to accept.

Through his writings on theoretical algebra and symbolic logic, especially *Algebra der Logik*, Schröder participated in the development of mathematical logic as an independent discipline in the second half of the nineteenth century. This is his real achievement, although his contribution was not recognized until the beginning of the twentieth century. Three factors accounted for the delay: the immature state of the field during his lifetime; a certain prolixity in his style; and, above all, the isolation imposed by his teaching in technical colleges. As a result he was an outsider, at a disadvantage in choosing terminology, in outlining his argumentation, and in judging what mathematical logic could accomplish.

Despite Schröder's relative isolation, his work was in the mainstream of the conceptual development of mathematical logic, the chief figures in which were Boole, de Morgan, and C. S. Peirce. Other new ideas that Schröder adopted and elaborated were Peano's formulation of the postulates of arithmetic (1889) and the abstract conception of mathematical operations vigorously set forth by Grassmann and Hankel. With respect to the philosophical problems raised in the formation of mathematical logic, Schröder was guided primarily by Lotze and Wundt, who closely followed Aristotle in questions of logic.

The terminology and contents of Schröder's "logical calculus" are now primarily of historical interest. His ideas, however, furnished the fundamental notion of mathematical logic: the partition of objects into classes. His work constituted a transitional stage that helped to prepare the way for the development of mathematical logic in the twentieth century.

BIBLIOGRAPHY

I. ORIGINAL WORKS. Schröder's writings are listed in Poggendorff, III, 1212–1213; IV, 1353–1354; V, 1131–1132. They include *Lehrbuch der Arithmetik und Algebra* (Leipzig, 1872); *Formale Elemente der absoluten Algebra* (Baden-Baden–Stuttgart, 1874); *Operationskreis des Logikkalküls* (Stuttgart, 1877); *Vorlesungen über die Algebra der Logik*, 3 vols. in 4 pts. (Leipzig, 1890–1905; 2nd ed., New York, 1966), II, pt. 2, edited by E. Müller; *Über das Zeichen. Festrede bei dem Direktoratswechsel an der Technischen Hochschule zu Karlsruhe am 22. November 1890* (Karlsruhe, 1890); and *Abriss der Algebra der Logik*: pt. 1, *Elementarlehre* (Leipzig, 1909), and pt. 2, *Aussagentheorie, Funktionen, Gleichungen und Ungleichungen* (Leipzig, 1910), both parts edited by E. Müller.

II. SECONDARY LITERATURE. See J. Lüroth, "Nekrolog auf Ernst Schröder," in *Jahresbericht der Deutschen Mathematiker-Vereinigung*, **12** (1903), 249–265, with portrait and bibliography; and Lüroth's obituary and bibliography in Schröder's *Vorlesungen über die Algebra der Logik*, II, pt. 2 (1905), iii–xix.

H. WUSSING

SCHROETER, HEINRICH EDUARD (*b.* Königsberg, Germany [now Kaliningrad, R.S.F.S.R.], 8 January 1829; *d.* Breslau, Germany [now Wrocław, Poland], 3 January 1892)

The son of a merchant, Schroeter attended the Altstädtische Gymnasium of his native city. In the summer of 1848 he began to study mathematics and physics at the University of Königsberg, and after his military service he continued his studies at Berlin for two years. He earned the doctorate at Königsberg in 1854 and qualified as lecturer in the fall of 1855 at the University of Breslau, where he became extraordinary professor in 1858 and full professor in 1861. He taught at Breslau until his death but was severely handicapped by paralysis during the final years of his life.

As a student at Königsberg, Schroeter attended the mathematics lectures of Friedrich Richelot, a follower of Jacobi. At Berlin his most important teachers were Dirichlet and Jakob Steiner. The influence of Steiner's ideas, on synthetic geometry in particular, was so strong that Schroeter later devoted almost all his research to this branch of mathematics. For his doctoral dissertation (under Richelot) and *Habilitationsschrift*, however, he chose topics from the theory of elliptic functions. Schroeter became more widely known through his association with Steiner—specifically, by editing the second part of Steiner's lectures on synthetic geometry.

The publication of Steiner's lectures ended with this second part, but Schroeter's extensive book of

1880 on the theory of second-order surfaces and third-order space curves can be considered a continuation of Steiner's work. Among the topics Schroeter treated were many metric properties of quadrics and cubic space curves; for unlike Staudt, for example, he did not confine himself to pure projective geometry. Schroeter pursued Steiner's fundamental aim of generating more complicated geometric elements from simpler ones (for instance, generating conic sections from the intersections of corresponding straight lines of projectively related pencils). Schroeter's name has been given to the generation of a third-degree plane curve c starting from six points of the plane, given that c should pass through six points of the plane and that further points are to be obtained using only a ruler; and to two generations of a third-degree surface when only one point and four straight lines in P_3 are given.

In 1888 Schroeter published a book in which he applied his approach to third-order plane curves. His last separately printed publication (1890) was devoted to fourth-order space curves of the first species, that is, to total intersections of two quadrics. Examining this topic from the viewpoint of synthetic geometry, Schroeter obtained many results on these curves, which are closely related to plane cubics. In his last years he studied various plane and spatial configurations, employing—as in all his writings—a purely elementary approach. In his view, all multidimensional considerations were not elementary, as were all those that were later designated by Felix Klein as belonging to higher geometry.

Schroeter's most important student in synthetic geometry was Rudolf Sturm.

BIBLIOGRAPHY

Schroeter's ed. of Steiner's work is . . . *Vorlesungen über synthetische Geometrie. Zweiter Teil: Die Theorie der Kegelschnitte, gestützt auf projectivische Eigenschaften* (Leipzig, 1867; 2nd ed., 1876). His own writings include *Die Theorie der Oberflächen 2. Ordnung und der Raumkurven 3. Ordnung als Erzeugnisse projectivischer Gebilde* (Leipzig, 1880); *Die Theorie der ebenen Kurven 3. Ordnung, auf synthetischem Wege abgeleitet* (Leipzig, 1888); and *Grundzüge einer reingeometrischen Theorie der Raumkurven 4. Ordnung, I. Spezies* (Leipzig, 1890).

A biography is R. Sturm, "Heinrich Schroeter," in *Jahresberichte der Deutschen Mathematikervereinigung,* **2** (1893), 32–41.

WERNER BURAU

SCHUBERT, HERMANN CÄSAR HANNIBAL (*b.* Potsdam, Germany, 22 May 1848; *d.* Hamburg, Germany, 20 July 1911)

Schubert, the son of an innkeeper, attended secondary schools in Potsdam and Spandau. He first studied mathematics and physics in 1867 at the University of Berlin and then went to Halle, where he received the doctorate in 1870. Soon afterward he became a secondary school teacher; his first post was at the Andreanum Gymnasium in Hildesheim (1872–1876). In 1876 he accepted the same post at the Johanneum in Hamburg. He remained there until 1908, having been promoted in 1887 to the rank of professor. Besides this school activity he was engaged by the Hamburg authorities to teach adult courses in which he dealt with various fields of mathematics for teachers already in the profession. In 1905 Schubert began to suffer from circulatory disorders that forced him to retire three years later. He died after a long illness that, toward the end, left him paralyzed. Schubert married Anna Hamel in 1873; they had four daughters.

Schubert published sixty-three works, including several books. His place in the history of mathematics is due chiefly to his work in enumerative geometry. He quickly established a reputation in that field on the basis of his doctoral dissertation, "Zur Theorie der Charakteristiken" (1870), and two earlier papers on the system of sixteen spheres that touch four given spheres. When he was only twenty-six, Schubert won the Gold Medal of the Royal Danish Academy of Sciences for the solution of a prize problem posed by H. G. Zeuthen on the extension of the theory of characteristics in cubic space curves (1874). A member of the Société Mathématique de France and honorary member of the Royal Netherlands Academy of Sciences, Schubert knew and corresponded with such famous geometers as Klein, Loria, and Hurwitz.

Schubert was content to remain in Hamburg, which had no university until 1919. Like Hermann Grassmann, he never became a university teacher and, in fact, declined offers that would have enabled him to do so. Mathematics in Hamburg centered in this period on the Mathematische Gesellschaft (founded in 1690 and still in existence), in the *Mitteilungen* of which Schubert published a number of papers.

In 1879 Schubert was able to present the methods and many individual results of his research in *Kalkül der abzählenden Geometrie.* Many further results were in papers he published until 1903.

Enumerative geometry is concerned with all those problems and theorems of algebraic geometry that involve a finite number of solutions. For example:

1. Bézout's theorem of the plane: two algebraic curves of orders a and b with no common elements have no more than ab points of intersection in common; this number can be reached.

2. Apollonius' theorem, according to which there are eight circles that simultaneously touch three given circles in the plane. Schubert's earliest works dealt with a spatial generalization of this theorem.

3. A somewhat more difficult result of enumerative geometry, Halphen's theorem: two algebraic linear congruences of P_3, one of order a and class b, and the other of order a' and class b', have in general $aa' + bb'$ straight lines in common.

Algebraically, the solution of the problems of enumerative geometry amounts to finding the number of solutions for certain systems of algebraic equations with finitely many solutions. Since the direct algebraic solution of the problems is possible only in the simplest cases, mathematicians sought to transform the system of equations, by continuous variation of the constants involved, into a system for which the number of solutions could be determined more easily. Poncelet devised this process, which he called the principle of continuity; in his day, of course, the method could not be elucidated in exact terms. Schubert's achievement was to combine this procedure, which he called "the principle of the conservation of the number," with the Chasles correspondence principle, thus establishing the foundation of a calculus. With the aid of this calculus, which he modeled on Ernst Schröder's logical calculus, Schubert was able to solve many problems systematically.

In *Kalkül der abzählenden Geometrie* Schubert formulated his fundamental problem as follows: Let C_k be a given set of geometric objects that depend on k parameters. Then, on the model of Bézout's theorem, formulate theorems on the number of common objects of two subsets C_a and C'_{k-a} of C_k. Here C_a (and analogously C'_{k-a} are designated by certain characteristics, that is numbers $\rho_1, \cdots, \rho_s$ of objects that C_a has in common with certain previously designated elementary sets $E^1_{k-a}, \cdots, E^s_{k-a}$ of C_k of dimension $k - a$. The best known of Schubert's investigations are those for the case where C_k is the totality of all subspaces P_d of the projective P_n, where $k = (n - d)(d + 1)$. The appropiate elementary sets have since been known as Schubert sets, defined as follows: Let P_{a_i}

($i = 0, 1, \cdots, d$) be subspaces of P_n, each of them of dimension a_i with $0 \leqslant a_0 < a_1 < \cdots < a_d \leqslant n$ and $P'_{a_0} \subset P'_{a_1} \subset \cdots \subset P'_{a_d}$. Then Schubert designated as $[a_0, a_1, \cdots, a_d]$ the set of those P_d that intersect P'_{a_i} in at least i dimensions ($i = 0, 1, \cdots, d$). If the totality of all P_d in P_n is mapped into the points of the Grassmann-manifold $G_{n,d}$, there corresponds to $[a_0, a_1, \cdots, a_d]$ a subset of dimension $a_0 + a_1 + \cdots + a_d - \binom{d+1}{2}$ on $G_{n,d}$. Later investigations have shown that the Schubert sets are precisely the basic sets of $G_{n,d}$ in Severi's sense.

Another set that Schubert studied is the totality C_6 of all plane triangles. His results on this set were rederived and confirmed from the modern standpoint by J. G. Semple.

Schubert could not rigorously demonstrate the principle of the conservation of number with the means available in his time, and E. Study and G. Kohn showed through counterexamples that it could lead to false conclusions. Schubert avoided such errors through his sure instinct. In 1900, in his famous Paris lecture David Hilbert called for an exact proof of Schubert's principle (problem no. 15). In 1912 Severi published a rigorous proof, but it was little known outside Italy. B. L. van der Waerden independently established the principle in 1930 on the basis of the recently created concepts of modern algebra and topology.

Schubert was known to a broader public as the editor of Sammlung Schubert, a series of textbooks in wide use before World War I. He wrote the first volume of the series, on arithmetic and algebra, and a subsequent volume on lower analysis. He also edited tables of logarithms and collections of problems for schools and published a simple method for computing logarithms.

Schubert was very interested in recreational mathematics and games of all kinds, including chess and skat, and in the mathematical questions that arise in connection with them. In 1897 he published the first edition of his book on recreational mathematics, *Mathematische Mussestunden;* the second edition, expanded to three volumes, appeared in 1900; and a thirteenth edition, revised by J. Erlebach, appeared in 1967. Schubert also was the author of the first article to appear in the *Encyklopädie der mathematischen Wissenschaften:* "Grundlagen der Arithmetik." His article, however, was subjected to severe criticism by the great pioneer in this area, Gottlob Frege.

BIBLIOGRAPHY

I. Original Works. Schubert's writings include

"Zur Theorie der Charakteristiken," in *Journal für die reine und angewandte Mathematik*, 71 (1870), 366–386; *Kalkül der abzählenden Geometrie* (Leipzig, 1879); "Abzählende Geometrie der Dreiecke," in *Mathematische Annalen*, 17 (1880), 153–212; *Mathematische Mussestunden* (Leipzig, 1897; 2nd ed., 3 vols., 1900; 13th ed., enl. by J. Erlebach, 1967); "Grundlagen der Arithmetik," in *Encyklopädie der mathematische Wissenschaften*, I, pt. 1 (1898), 1–29; *Arithmetik und Algebra* (Leipzig, 1898–1904); and *Niedere Analysis* (Leipzig, 1902).

II. SECONDARY LITERATURE. See W. Burau, "Der Hamburger Mathematiker Hermann Schubert," in *Mitteilungen der Mathematischen Gesellschaft in Hamburg*, 9th ser., 3 (1966), 10–20; G. Kohn, "Über das Prinzip von der Erhaltung der Anzahl," in *Archiv der Mathematik und Physik*, 3rd ser., 4 (1902), 312–316; J. G. Semple, "The Triangle as a Geometric Variable," in *Mathematica*, 1 (1954), 80–88; F. Severi, "Sul principio della conservazione del numero," in *Rendiconti del Circolo mathematico di Palermo*, 33 (1912), 313–327; "I fondamenti della geometria numerative," in *Annali di matematica pura ed applicata*, 4th ser., 19 (1940), 153–242; and *Grundlagen der abzählenden Geometrie* (Wolfenbüttel, 1948); and B. L. van der Waerden, "Topologische Begründung des Kalküls der abzählenden Geometrie," in *Mathematische Annalen*, 102 (1930), 337–362.

WERNER BURAU

SCHUR, ISSAI

(*b.* Mogilev, Russia, 10 January 1875; *d.* Tel Aviv, Palestine [now Israel], 10 January 1941)

Schur was one of the most brilliant Jewish mathematicians active in Germany during the first third of the twentieth century. He attended the Gymnasium in Libau (now Liepaja, Latvian S.S.R.) and then the University of Berlin, where he spent most of his scientific career. From 1911 until 1916, when he returned to Berlin, he was an assistant professor at Bonn. He became full professor at Berlin in 1919. Schur was forced to retire by the Nazi authorities in 1935 but was able to emigrate to Palestine in 1939. He died there of a heart ailment two years later. Schur had been a member of the Prussian Academy of Sciences before the Nazi purges. He married and had a son and daughter.

Schur's principal field was the representation theory of groups, founded a little before 1900 by his teacher Frobenius. Schur seems to have completed it shortly before World War I; but he returned to the subject after 1925, when it became important for physics. Further developed by his student Richard Brauer, it is in our time experiencing an extraordinary growth through the opening of new questions. Schur's dissertation (1901) became fundamental to the representation theory of the general linear group; in fact English mathematicians have named certain of the functions appearing in the work "S-functions" in Schur's honor. In 1905 Schur reestablished the theory of group characters—the keystone of representation theory. The most important tool involved is "Schur's lemma." Along with the representation of groups by integral linear substitutions, Schur was also the first to study representation by linear fractional substitutions, treating this more difficult problem almost completely in two works (1904, 1907). In 1906 Schur considered the fundamental problems that appear when an algebraic number field is taken as the domain; a number appearing in this connection is now called the Schur index. His works written after 1925 include a complete description of the rational and of the continuous representations of the general linear group; the foundations of this work were in his dissertation.

A lively interchange with many colleagues led Schur to contribute important memoirs to other areas of mathematics. Some of these were published as collaborations with other authors, although publications with dual authorship were almost unheard of at that time. Here we can only indicate the areas. First there was pure group theory, in which Schur adopted the surprising approach of proving without the aid of characters theorems that had previously been demonstrated only by that means. Second, he worked in the field of matrices. Third, he handled algebraic equations, sometimes proceeding to the evaluation of roots, and sometimes treating the so-called equations without affect, that is, with symmetric Galois groups. He was also the first to give examples of equations with alternating Galois groups. Fourth, he worked in number theory, notably in additive number theory; fifth in divergent series; sixth in integral equations; and lastly in function theory.

BIBLIOGRAPHY

Schur's writings are collected in *Gesammelte Abhandlungen*, A. Brauer and H. Rohrbach, ed., 3 vols. (Berlin, 1973). Moreover, two lectures have been published as *Die algebraischen Grundlagen der Darstellungstheorie der Gruppen: Zürcher Vorlesungen 1936*, E. Stiefel, ed.; and *Vorlesungen über Invariantentheorie*, H. Grunsky, ed. (Berlin, 1968).

On Schur and his work, see *Mathematische Zeitschrift*, 63 (1955–1956), a special issue published to commemorate Schur's eightieth birthday, with forty articles dedicated to his memory by leading mathematicians. See also Alfred Brauer, "Gedenkrede auf Issai Schur, gehalten 1960 bei der Schur-Gedenkfeier an der Humboldt-Universität Berlin," in *Gesammelte Abhandlungen*, I, which contains a detailed report of Schur's life and work.

. H. BOERNER

SCHUSTER, ARTHUR (*b.* Frankfurt, Germany, 12 September 1851; *d.* Yeldall, near Twyford, Berkshire, England, 14 October 1934)

Schuster was the son of Francis Joseph Schuster, a well-to-do Jewish textile merchant with business connections in Great Britain. After the Seven Weeks' War the family firm moved to Manchester, England, when Frankfurt was annexed by Prussia. Schuster, baptized as a young boy, was educated privately and at the Frankfurt Gymnasium. He attended the Geneva Academy from 1868 until he joined his parents at Manchester in the summer of 1870.

By the age of sixteen Schuster had developed an interest in physical science, mainly through Henry Roscoe's elementary textbook on spectrum analysis. His parents saw at once that he lacked enthusiasm for business; and they consulted Roscoe, then professor of chemistry at Owens College, Manchester, who arranged for Schuster to enroll as a day student in October 1871. He studied physics under Balfour Stewart and was directed in research in spectrum analysis by Roscoe. Within a year he produced his first research paper, "On the Spectrum of Nitrogen." Again at Roscoe's suggestion, Schuster enrolled at Heidelberg under Kirchhoff and received his Ph.D. after a less-than-brilliant examination in 1873.

Schuster served at Owens in 1873 as unpaid demonstrator in the new physics laboratory and later, at the request of Lockyer, joined an eclipse expedition to the coast of Siam. Upon his return to England in 1875, Schuster remained at Owens for a semester and then joined Maxwell as a researcher at the Cavendish Laboratory, where he remained for five years, ultimately joining Lord Rayleigh in an absolute determination of the ohm.

In 1879 Schuster applied for a post at Mason Science College, Birmingham, but was rejected in favor of his friend J. H. Poynting. Two years later, when a professorship of applied mathematics was founded at Owens, Schuster was selected for the chair over his former student J. J. Thomson and Oliver Lodge. Subsequently he was rejected as

Rayleigh's successor at the Cavendish in 1884; but after Balfour Stewart's death in 1887 he succeeded in the following year to the chair of physics at Manchester.

At the beginning of his Owens College career, Schuster resumed his interest in what was by then termed "spectroscopy." In an important paper, "On Harmonic Ratios in the Spectra of Gases" (*Proceedings of the Royal Society*, **31** [1881], 337–347), he refuted G. J. Stoney's explanation of spectral lines that used simple harmonic series by demonstrating statistically that the spectra of five chosen elements conform more closely to a random distribution than to Stoney's "law." He concluded, however, that "Most probably some law hitherto undiscovered exists which in special cases resolves itself into the law of harmonic ratios." In 1897 Schuster independently discovered and published the relationship known as the Rydberg-Schuster law, which relates the convergence frequencies of different spectral series of the same substance.

Schuster's interests led him to investigate the spectra produced by the discharge of electricity through gases in otherwise evacuated tubes. Such electrical discharges were imperfectly understood, and he began a series of detailed investigations that led to his Bakerian lectures before the Royal Society in 1884 and 1890. Schuster's findings were of major importance: he showed that an electrical current was conducted through gases by ions and that once a gas was "dissociated" (ionized), a small potential would suffice to maintain a current.

Schuster was also the first to indicate the path toward determining the ratio *e/m* for cathode rays by using a magnetic field, a method that ultimately led to the discovery of the electron. In 1896, shortly after the appearance of Roentgen's researches, he offered the first suggestion that X rays were small-wavelength transverse vibrations of the ether.

Schuster's interests were too wide-ranging to give even a brief account here. His work on terrestrial magnetism, however, deserves special notice. In 1889 he showed that daily magnetic variations are of two kinds, internal and atmospheric. He attributed the latter to electric currents in the upper atmosphere, and the former to induction currents in the earth. In a later estimate of the ionization of the upper atmosphere he helped lay the groundwork for the studies of Heaviside and Kennelly.

In 1907 Schuster resigned his chair at Manchester and secured Ernest Rutherford as his successor, thus reinforcing Manchester's prominence in physical research.

Elected a fellow of the Royal Society in 1879, Schuster served twice on its Council and was secretary from 1912 to 1919. He was founder and first secretary of the International Research Council and served as president of the British Association in 1915. He was knighted in 1920.

A man of remarkable originality and ingenuity, Schuster often pointed the way toward novel areas but left the task of reaching research summits to others, a pattern perhaps inevitable in a period of exploding possibilities for one of such wide interests and perception.

BIBLIOGRAPHY

I. ORIGINAL WORKS. A record of Schuster's scientific papers from 1881 to 1906 is in *The Physical Laboratories of the University of Manchester* (Manchester, 1906), 45–60; papers published to 1901 are listed in the Royal Society *Catalogue of Scientific Papers*, VIII, 899; XI, 359–360; XVIII, 623–625. Schuster's major books include *Spectrum Analysis*, 4th ed. (London, 1885), written with H. E. Roscoe; *Introduction to the Theory of Optics* (London, 1904; 3rd ed., 1924); *The Progress of Physics During 33 Years (1875–1908)* (Cambridge, 1911); and *Biographical Fragments* (London, 1932). With Arthur Shipley he wrote *Britain's Heritage of Science* (London, 1917), a fascinating Victorian view of the history of science.

II. SECONDARY LITERATURE. On Schuster's life and work the following are of special value: G. C. Simpson, "Sir Arthur Schuster, 1851–1934," in *Obituary Notices of Fellows of the Royal Society of London*, 1 (1932–1935), 409–423; "Sir Arthur Schuster, FRS," in *Nature*, 134 (1934), 595–597; and his article in *Dictionary of National Biography*; G. E. Hale, "Sir Arthur Schuster," in *Astrophysical Journal*, 81 (1935), 97–106; R. S. Hutton, *Recollections of a Technologist* (London, 1964), pp. 103–106; and J. G. Crowther, *Scientific Types* (London, 1968), 333–358. See also *Manchester Faces and Places*, IV (1892–1893), 158–159; and *Commemoration of the 25th Anniversary of the Election of Arthur Schuster, F.R.S., to a Professorship in the Owens College* (Manchester, 1906).

On Schuster's work see Edmund Whittaker, *History of the Theories of Aether and Electricity*, I (New York, 1960), pp. 355–360; Norah Schuster, "Early Days of Roentgen Photography in Britain," in *British Medical Journal* (1962), 2, 1164–1166; D. L. Anderson, *The Discovery of the Electron* (Princeton, 1964), pp. 30, 42, 74; and William McGucken, *Nineteenth-Century Spectroscopy* (Baltimore, 1969), *passim*.

On Schuster at Owens, see P. J. Hartog, *The Owens College Manchester* (Manchester, 1900), pp. 54–59; and

H. B. Charlton, *Portrait of a University* (Manchester, 1951), pp. 78–84.

ROBERT H. KARGON

SCHWARZ, HERMANN AMANDUS (*b.* Hermsdorf, Silesia [now Sobiecin, Poland], 25 January 1843; *d.* Berlin, Germany, 30 November 1921)

Schwarz, the son of an architect, was the leading mathematician in Berlin in the period following Kronecker, Kummer, and Weierstrass. He may be said to represent the link between these great mathematicians and the generation active in Germany in the first third of the twentieth century, a group that he greatly influenced. After attending the Gymnasium in Dortmund, he studied chemistry in Berlin at the Gewerbeinstitut (now the Technische Universität) but, under the influence of Kummer and Weierstrass, soon changed to mathematics. Schwarz received the doctorate in 1864 and then completed his training as a *Mittelschule* teacher. Immediately thereafter, in 1867, he was appointed assistant professor at Halle. In 1869 he became a full professor at the Eidgenössische Technische Hochschule in Zurich and in 1875 assumed the same rank at the University of Göttingen. Schwarz succeeded Weierstrass at the University of Berlin in 1892 and lectured there until 1917. During this long period, teaching duties and concern for his many students took so much of his time that he published very little more. A contributing element may have been his propensity for handling both the important and the trivial with the same thoroughness, a trait also evident in his mathematical papers. Schwarz was a member of the Prussian and Bavarian academies of sciences. He was married to a daughter of Kummer.

Schwarz's greatest strength lay in his geometric intuition, which was brought to bear in his first publication, an elementary proof of the chief theorem of axonometry, which had been posed by Karl Pohlke, his teacher at the Gewerbeinstitut. The influence of Weierstrass, however, soon led Schwarz to place his geometric ability in the service of analysis; and this synthesis was the basis of his contribution to mathematics. Schwarz tended to work on narrowly defined, concrete, individual problems, but in solving them he developed methods the significance of which far transcended the problem under discussion.

Schwarz's most important contribution to the history of mathematics was the "rescue" of some of Riemann's achievements. The demonstrations had been justly challenged by Weierstrass. The question centered on the "main theorem" of conformal (similar in the least parts) mapping, which stated that every simply connected region of the plane can be conformally mapped onto a circular area. In order to prove it, Riemann had employed the relation of the problem to the first boundary-value problem of potential theory (Dirichlet's problem), which requires a solution of the partial differential equation $\Delta u = 0$ with prescribed values at the boundary of the region. Dirichlet believed he had disposed of this problem with the observation (Dirichlet's principle) that such a function yields an extreme value for a certain double integral; Weierstrass had objected that the existence of a function which can do that is not at all self-evident but must be demonstrated.

Schwarz first solved the mapping problem explicitly for various simple geometric figures—the square and the triangle—and then in general for polygons. He also treated the conformal mapping of polyhedral surfaces onto the spherical surface. These results enabled him to solve the two problems mentioned, that is, to present the first completely valid proofs for extended classes of regions by approximating the given region by means of polygons. These works contained the first statement of principles that are now familiar to all: the principle of reflection; the "alternating method," which provides a further method for the approximation of solution functions, and "Schwarz's lemma."

Schwarz also worked in the field of minimal surfaces (surfaces of least area), a characteristic problem of the calculus of variation. Such a surface must everywhere have zero mean curvature, and in general all surfaces with this property are termed minimal surfaces. The boundary-value problem requires in this case that a minimal surface be passed through a given closed space curve, a procedure that can be carried out experimentally by dipping a wire loop into a soap solution. Following his preference for concrete geometrical problems, Schwarz first solved the problem explicitly for special space curves, mostly consisting of straight sections, of which the curve composed of four out of six edges of a tetrahedron has become the best known.

In his most important work, a *Festschrift* for Weierstrass' seventieth birthday, Schwarz set himself the task of completely answering the question of whether a given minimal surface really yields a minimal area. Aside from the achievement itself, which contains the first complete treatment of the second variation in a multiple integral, this work introduced methods that immediately became extremely fruitful. For example, a function was constructed through successive approximations that Picard was able to employ in obtaining his existence proof for differential equations. Furthermore, Schwarz demonstrated the existence of a certain number, which could be viewed as the (least) eigenvalue for the eigenvalue problem of a certain differential equation (these concepts did not exist then). This was done through a method that Schwarz's student Erhard Schmidt later applied to the proof of the existence of an eigenvalue of an integral equation—a procedure that is one of the most important tools of modern analysis. In this connection Schwarz also employed the inequality for integrals that is today known as "Schwarz's inequality."

Algebra played the least role in Schwarz's work; his dissertation, however, was devoted to those surfaces developable into the plane that are given by algebraic equations of the first seven degrees. Much later he answered the question: In which cases does the Gaussian hypergeometric series represent an algebraic function? In approaching this matter, moreover, he developed trains of thought that led directly to the theory of automorphic functions, which was developed shortly afterward by Klein and Poincaré.

Of a series of minor works, executed with the same devotion and care as the major ones, two that involve criticism of predecessors and contemporaries remain to be mentioned. Schwarz presented the first rigorous proof that the sphere possesses a smaller surface area than any other body of the same volume. Earlier mathematicians, particularly Steiner, had implicitly supposed in their demonstrations the existence of a body with least surface area. Schwarz also pointed out that in the definition of the area of a curved surface appearing in many textbooks of his time, the method employed for determining the length of a curve was applied carelessly and that it therefore, for example, led to an infinitely great area resulting for so simple a surface as a cylindrical section.

BIBLIOGRAPHY

I. ORIGINAL WORKS. Schwarz's writings were collected in his *Gesammelte mathematische Abhandlungen*, 2 vols. (Berlin, 1890). He also compiled and edited *Nach Vorlesungen und Aufzeichnungen des Hrn. K. Weierstrass*, 12 pts. (Göttingen, 1881–1885), brought together in the 2nd ed. (Berlin, 1893), and also in French

(Paris, 1894).

II. SECONDARY LITERATURE. See *Mathematische Abhandlungen Hermann Amandus Schwarz zu seinem fünfzigjährigen Doktorjubiläum gewidmet von Freunden und Schülern*, C. Carathéodory, G. Hessenberg, E. Landau, and L. Lichtenstein, eds. (Berlin, 1914), with portrait; L. Bieberbach, "H. A. Schwarz," in *Sitzungsberichte der Berliner mathematischen Gesellschaft*, **21** (1922), 47–51, with portrait and list of works not included in *Gesammelte Abhandlungen*; C. Carathéodory, "Hermann Amandus Schwarz," in *Deutsches biographisches Jahrbuch*, III (1921), 236–238; G. Hamel, "Zum Gedächtnis an Hermann Amandus Schwarz," in *Jahresberichte der Deutschen Mathematikervereinigung*, **32** (1923), 6–13, with portrait and complete bibliography; F. Lindemann, obituary in *Jahrbuch der bayerischen Akademie der Wissenschaften* (1922–1923), 75–77; R. von Mises, "H. A. Schwarz," in *Zeitschrift für angewandte Mathematik und Mechanik*, **1** (1921); and E. Schmidt, "Gedächtnisrede auf Hermann Amandus Schwarz," in *Sitzungsberichte der Preussischen Akademie der Wissenschaften zu Berlin* (1922), 85–87.

H. BOERNER

SCHWEIKART, FERDINAND KARL (*b.* Erbach, Germany, 28 February 1780; *d.* Königsberg, Germany [now Kaliningrad, R.S.F.S.R.], 17 August 1859)

Schweikart studied law at the University of Marburg from 1796 to 1798 and received his doctorate in law from Jena in the latter year. After practicing at Erbach from 1800 to 1803, he worked as a private tutor until 1809; his pupils included the prince of Hohenlohe-Ingelfingen. In 1809 Schweikart became extraordinary professor of law at the University of Giessen; from 1812 to 1816 he was full professor at the University of Kharkov; and from 1816 to 1820 he taught at Marburg. From 1821 until his death he was professor of law at Königsberg, where he also earned a doctorate in philosophy.

Schweikart published extensively in his principal field of endeavor, including a work on the relationship of natural and positive law (1801). Early in his life he also became interested in mathematics, and he holds an important place in the prehistory of non-Euclidean geometry. While a student at Marburg, the lectures of J. K. F. Hauff had stimulated him to consider the problem of parallel lines, which provided the subject of his only publication in mathematics (1807). His approach was still completely Euclidean; but later he arrived at the beginnings of a hyperbolic geometry, which he called astral geometry. He made this advance independently of Gauss, Bolyai, and Lobachevsky, as is proved by the correspondence cited by Engel and Stäckel in *Die Theorie der Parallellinien von Euklid bis Gauss*. The astronomer Christian Gerling, a student of Gauss, wrote in a letter to Wolfgang Bolyai, the father of János Bolyai, that in 1819 Schweikart had reported on the basic elements of his "astral geometry" to colleagues at Marburg. Schweikart also wrote on this topic to his nephew Taurinus in Cologne. Stimulated by his uncle's work, Taurinus had virtually discovered hyperbolic trigonometry; but unlike his uncle, he still believed in the sole validity of Euclidean geometry.

The three chief founders of hyperbolic geometry surpassed Schweikart only because of the thoroughness with which they examined specific topics of this subject. The demands of his legal career undoubtedly prevented him from finding sufficient time to undertake similarly extensive research.

BIBLIOGRAPHY

Schweikart's only mathematical work is *Die Theorie der Parallellinien, nebst einem Vorschlag ihrer Verbannung aus der Geometrie* (Jena–Leipzig, 1807).

A secondary source is Friedrich Engel and Paul Stäckel, *Die Theorie der Parallellinien von Euklid bis Gauss* (Leipzig, 1895), 243–252.

WERNER BURAU

SEGNER, JÁNOS-ANDRÁS (JOHANN ANDREAS VON) (*b.* Pressburg, Hungary [now Bratislava, Czechoslovakia], 9 October 1704; *d.* Halle, Germany, 5 October 1777)

Segner was the son of Miklós Segner, a merchant. He was educated in the Gymnasiums of Pressburg and Debrecen and then at the University of Jena (1725–1730), from which he received the M.D. Simultaneously he also studied physics and mathematics and in 1728 he published a work containing a demonstration of Descartes's rule of signs for the determination of the number of positive and negative roots of an algebraic equation when all roots are real; later he devoted another article to the derivation of this rule (1758). Segner practiced medicine in Pressburg and Debrecen for a short time. He went to Jena in 1732 as assistant professor and in 1733 became extraordinary professor of mathematics. In 1735 he was named ordinary professor of mathematics and physics at Göttingen; and from 1755 until his death he held the same chair at the University of Halle. He was a foreign member of the Berlin (1746) and St. Petersburg (1754) academies of science.

Segner's invention of one of the first reaction hydraulic turbines, named for him, was of outstanding importance. It consists of a wheel rotating under the action of water streaming from parallel and oppositely directed tubes. He wrote of this invention in a letter to Euler dated 11 January 1750, and in the same year he described in detail the construction and action of his machine, which he later improved; further improvements in construction were added by Euler. Segner's letters to Euler give detailed evidence of the progress of early work in the theory and construction of reaction hydraulic turbines (Euler's letters to Segner are lost). Segner's wheel is now used for horticultural irrigation and serves as a demonstration device in schools. Segner generally spent much time constructing and perfecting scientific devices, from a slide rule to clocks and telescopes.

While studying the theory of tubes, Segner introduced the three principal axes of rotation (axes of inertia) of a solid body and offered first considerations on this problem. Euler made considerable use of this discovery and, referring motion to principal axes of inertia, deduced his important equations of the motion of a solid body (1765).

Segner also wrote on various problems of physics and mathematics. He defended Newton's theory of the emanation of light (1740), developed an original graphic device for the construction of roots of algebraic equations (1761), and presented a recurrent solution of Euler's famous problem of the number of possible dissections of an n-gon into triangles by means of noncrossing diagonals (1761). In mathematical logic Segner developed Leibniz' ideas and was one of the first to make extensive use of an entire system of symbolic designations to formalize logical conclusions; he did not, however, confine himself to classical syllogistics.

Segner wrote a number of mathematical manuals, proceeding, to a certain extent, from Euler's works and using his advice, which were popular in their time.

BIBLIOGRAPHY

I. ORIGINAL WORKS. Bibliographies of Segner's works are in Poggendorff, II, cols. 892–894; and C. von Wurzbach, ed., *Biographisches Lexikon des Kaiserthums Oesterreich*, XXXIII (1877), 318–320. His writings include *Dissertatio epistolica . . . qua regulam Harriotti, de modo ex aequationum signis numerum radi-*
cum eas componentium cognoscendi demonstrare conatur* (Jena, 1728); *Specimen logicae universaliter demonstratae* (Jena, 1740); *Programma in quo computatio formae atque virium machinae nuper descriptae* (Göttingen, 1750); *Programma in quo theoriam machinae cujusdam hydraulicae praemittit* (Göttingen, 1750); *Specimen theoriae turbinum* (Halle, 1755); *Cursus mathematicus*, 5 vols. (Halle, 1758–1767); and *Elementa analyseos infinitorum*, 2 vols. (Halle, 1761–1763).

II. SECONDARY LITERATURE. See *Allgemeine deutsche Biographie*, XXXIII (1891), 609–610; M. Cantor, *Vorlesungen über Geschichte der Mathematik*, III–IV (Leipzig, 1900–1908), see index; *Leonhardi Euleri Opera omnia*, fourth series, *Commercium epistolicum*, I, A. Juškerič, V. Smirnov, and W. Habicht, eds. (Basel, 1975), 403–426; Jakusc István, "Segner András," in *Fizikai szemle*, 5 (1955), 56–65; N. M. Raskin, "Voprosy tekhniki u Eylera" ("Technical Problems of Euler"), in M. A. Lavrentiev, A. P. Youschkevitch, and A. T. Grigorian, eds., *Leonard Eyler. Sbornik statey . . .* (Moscow, 1958), 509–536; and F. Rosenberger, *Die Geschichte der Physik in Grundzügen*, II (Brunswick, 1884), 345.

A. P. YOUSCHKEVITCH
A. T. GRIGORIAN

SEGRE, CORRADO (*b*. Saluzzo, Italy, 20 August 1863; *d*. Turin, Italy, 18 May 1924)

Segre studied under Enrico D'Ovidio at the University of Turin, where he formed a long friendship with his fellow student Gino Loria. Segre submitted his doctoral dissertation in 1883, when he was only twenty; and in the same year he was named assistant to the professor of algebra and to the professor of analytic geometry. Two years later he became an assistant in descriptive geometry, and from 1885 to 1888 he replaced Giuseppe Bruno in the courses on projective geometry. In 1888 he succeeded D'Ovidio in the chair of higher geometry, a post he held without interruption until his death.

Segre was much influenced by D'Ovidio's course on the geometry of ruled spaces (1881–1882). D'Ovidio started from the ideas of Plücker, which had been taken up and developed by Felix Klein. According to these ideas, the geometry of ruled space is equivalent to the study of a quadratic variety of four dimensions imbedded in a linear space of five dimensions. In his lectures D'Ovidio examined the works of Veronese on the projective geometry of hyperspaces and those of Weierstrass on bilinear and quadratic forms. These topics inspired much of Segre's research, beginning with his thesis. The latter consists of two parts: a study of the quadrics in a linear space of arbitrary dimension and an examination of the geometry of the right line and of its quadratic series. Before completing his thesis, Segre collaborated with Loria on a twenty-two-page article in French that they sent to Klein, who published it in *Mathematische Annalen* (1883). A long and active correspondence between Segre and Klein then ensued.

Segre's mathematical work can be divided into four distinct areas, all of which are linked by a common concern with the problem of space. The first of these areas comprises Segre's articles on the geometric properties that are invariant under linear transformations of space. In this connection Segre showed the value of investigating hyperspaces in the study of three-dimensional space S_3. For example, a ruled surface of S_3, which is composed of right lines, can be represented by a curve in S_5; it thus becomes possible to reduce the classification of surfaces to that of curves. The insufficiencies of the earlier theories proposed by A. Möbius, Grassmann, Cayley, and Cremona were thus soon revealed.

According to Segre, a ruled surface in a space S_n can also be considered a variety of ∞^2 points distributed on ∞^1 right lines. Further, Segre generalized the theory of the loci formed by ∞^1 right lines of S_n to the theory of the loci formed by ∞^1 planes. He took as his point of departure certain problems on bundles of quadrics that Weierstrass and L. Kronecker had treated in a purely algebraic manner.

At this time it was known that the intersection of two quadrics of S_3 is a quartic the projection of which from a point exterior to it onto a plane is a quartic with two double points. John Casey and Gaston Darboux had shown that its study is useful for that of fourth-order surfaces, called cyclides. Segre reexamined and generalized the problem by placing the two quadrics in a space S_4. He also investigated the locus resulting from the intersection of two quadrics of S_5 and discovered that it is no longer a surface but rather a three-dimensional variety that can be interpreted as a complex quadratic of S_3. From this result he confirmed in an elegant manner the famous fourth-order surface with sixteen double points, which had been found by Kummer in 1864 and bear his name. Before Segre's findings, the study of this surface required the use of extremely complicated algebraic procedures.

Segre next began a series of works on the properties of algebraic curves and ruled surfaces subjected to birational transformations. Alfred Clebsch, Paul Gordan, Alexander Brill, and Max Noether had already studied these transformations with a view toward giving a geometric interpretation to the theory of Abelian functions. Segre showed the advantage gained by operating in a hyperspace. His article of 1896 on the birational transformations of a surface contains the invariant that Zeuthen had encountered under another form in 1871, now called the Zeuthen-Segre invariant.

Segre's interest in 1890 in the properties of the Riemann sphere led him to a third area of research: the role of imaginary elements in geometry. He laid the basis of a new theory of hyperalgebraic entities by representing complex points of S_n by means of the ∞^{2n} real points of one of the varieties V_{2n}. (This variety has since been named for Segre.) Certain of Segre's hyperalgebraic transformations possess invariant properties, and he was led to enlarge the concept of a point. To this end, he introduced points that he called bicomplex, which correspond to the ordinary complex points of the real image. Their coordinates are bicomplex numbers constructed with the aid of the two unities i and j, such that:

$$i \cdot j = j \cdot i$$

and

$$i^2 = j^2 = -1.$$

Later, in 1912, Segre returned to this subject, when, utilizing the works of Von Staudt, he studied another type of complex geometry.

Darboux's *Leçons sur la théorie générale des surfaces*, which Segre often used in his courses, inspired him to investigate (from 1907) infinitesimal geometry. Extending the work of Darboux, Segre studied a certain class of surfaces in S_n defined by second-order linear partial differential equations. These surfaces are described by a moving point of which the homogeneous coordinates—functions of two independent parameters u and v—are the solutions of a second-order partial differential equation. Among the surfaces of a hyperspace, Segre was particularly interested in those that lead to a Laplace equation. In an article of 1908 on the conjugate tangents of a surface, he established a relationship between the points of the tangent plane and those of the planes passing through the origin. To establish this relationship he employed infinitesimals of higher order in a problem concerning the neighborhood of a point. This procedure led him to introduce a new system of lines, analogous to those studied by Darboux, traced on the surface: they were named Segre lines, and their differential equation was established by Fubini. It may be noted that Segre's last publication dealt with differential geometry. Segre wrote a long article on hyperspaces for the *Encyklopädie der mathematischen Wissenschaften*, containing all that was then known about such spaces. A model article, it is notable for its clarity and elegance.

Segre became a member of the Academy of Turin in 1889. He long served on the editorial board of the *Annali di matematica pura ed applicata*, on which he was succeeded by his former student Severi of the University of Rome.

Through his teaching and his publications, Segre played an important role in reviving an interest in geometry in Italy. His reputation and the new ideas he presented in his courses attracted many Italian and foreign students to Turin. Segre's contribution to the knowledge of space assures him a place after Cremona in the ranks of the most illustrious members of the new Italian school of geometry.

BIBLIOGRAPHY

I. ORIGINAL WORKS. The complete works of Segre have been published as *Opere*, 4 vols. (1957–1963), but it does not contain the paper "Mehrdimensionale Räume" (see below). A complete list of Segre's publications, 128 titles, is given in G. Loria (see below). A. Terracini lists ninety-eight titles. See also Poggendorff, V, 1151–1152.

Segre's most important works include "Sur les différentes espèces de complexes du 2e degré des droites qui coupent harmoniquement deux surfaces du 2e ordre." in *Mathematische Annalen*, **23** (1883), 213–234, written with G. Loria; "Studio sulle quadriche in uno spazio lineare ad un numero qualunque di dimensioni," in *Memorie dell'Accademia delle scienze di Torino*, **36** (1883), 3–86; "Sulla geometria della retta e delle sue serie quadratiche," *ibid.*, 87–157; "Note sur les complexes quadratiques dont la surface singulière est une surface du 2e degré double," in *Mathematische Annalen*, **23** (1883), 235–243; "Sulle geometrie metriche dei complessi lineari e delle sfere e sulle loro mutue analogie," in *Atti dell'Accademia delle scienze*, **19** (1883), 159–186; "Sulla teoria e sulla classificazione delle omografie in uno spazio lineare ad un numero qualunque di dimensioni," in *Memorie della R. Accademia dei Lincei*, 3rd ser., **19** (1884), 127–148; and "Étude des différentes surfaces du quatrième ordre à conique double ou cuspidale (générale ou décomposée) considérées comme des projections de l'intersection de deux variétés quadratiques de l'espace à quatre dimensions," in *Mathematische Annalen*, **24** (1884), 313–444.

Later writings are "Le coppie di elementi imaginari nella geometria proiettiva sintetica," in *Memorie dell'Accademia delle scienze di Torino*, **38** (1886), 3–24; "Recherches générales sur les courbes et les surfaces réglées algébriques," in *Mathematische Annalen*, **30** (1887), 203–226, and **34** (1889), 1–25; "Un nuovo campo di ricerche geometriche," in *Atti dell'Accademia delle scienze*, **25** (1889), 276–301, 430–457, 592–612, and **26** (1890), 35–71; "Su alcuni indirizzi nelle investigazioni geometriche," in *Rivista di matematica*, **1** (1891), 42–66, with English trans. by J. W. Young as "On Some Tendencies in Geometric Investigations," in *Bulletin of the American Mathematical Society*, 2nd ser., **10** (1904), 442–468; "Le rappresentazioni reali delle forme complesse e gli enti iperalgebrici," in *Mathematische Annalen*, **40** (1891), 413–467; "Intorno ad un carattere delle superficie e delle varietà superiori algebriche," in *Atti dell'Accademia delle scienze*, **31** (1896), 485–501; and "Su un problema relativo alle intersezioni di curve e superficie," *ibid.*, **33** (1898), 19–23.

See also "Intorno ai punti di Weierstrass di una curva algebrica," in *Atti dell'Accademia nazionale dei Lincei. Rendiconti*, 5th ser., **8** (1889), 89–91; "Gli ordini delle varietà che annullano i determinanti dei diversi gradi estratti da una data matrice," *ibid.*, **9** (1900), 253–260; "Su una classe di superficie degli iperspazi, legata con le equazioni lineari alle derivate parziali di 2° ordine," in *Atti dell'Accademia delle scienze*, **42** (1907), 1047–1079; "Complementi alla teoria delle tangenti coniugate di una superficie," in *Atti dell'Accademia nazionale dei Lincei. Rendiconti*, 5th ser., **17** (1908), 405–412; "Mehrdimensionale Räume," in *Encyklopädie der mathematischen Wissenschaften*, III, pt. 3, fasc. 7 (1918), 769–972; "Sulle corrispondenze quadrilineari tra forme di prima specie e su alcune loro rappresentazioni spaziali," in *Annali di matematica pura ed applicata*, 3rd ser., **29** (1920), 105–140; "Sui fochi di 2° ordine dei sistemi infiniti di piani e sulle curve iperspaziali con una doppia infinità di piani plurisecanti," in *Atti dell'Accademia nazionale dei Lincei. Rendiconti*, 5th ser., **30** (1921), 67–71; "Le superficie degli iperspazi con una doppia infinità di curve piane o spaziali," in *Atti dell'Accademia delle scienze*, **56** (1921), 143–157; "Sugli elementi lineari che hanno comuni la tangente e il piano osculatore," in *Atti dell'Accademia nazionale dei Lincei. Rendiconti*, 5th ser., **33** (1924), 325–329; "Le curve piane d'ordine *n* circoscritte ad un $(n + 1) = $ latero completo di tangenti ed una classe particolare di superficie con doppio sistema coniugato di coni circoscritti," in *Atti dell'Accademia delle scienze*, **59** (1924), 303–320.

II. SECONDARY LITERATURE. Obituary notices are L. Berzolari, in *Rendiconti dell'Istituto lombardo di scienze e lettere*, **57** (1924), 528–532; G. Castelnuovo, in *Atti dell'Accademia nazionale dei Lincei. Rendiconti*, 5th ser., **33** (1924), 353–359; E. Pascal, in *Rendiconti dell'Accademia delle scienze fisiche e matematiche*, **30** (1924), 114–116; and V. Volterra, in *Atti dell'Accademia nazionale dei Lincei. Rendiconti*, 5th ser., **33** (1924), 459–461. See also Poggendorff, VI, 2407, for a list of notices.

On Segre and his work, see H. F. Baker's article in

Journal of the London Mathematical Society, **1** (1926), 263–271, with trans. by G. Loria in *Bollettino dell'Unione matematica italiana,* **6** (1927), 276–284; J. L. Coolidge, in *Bulletin of the American Mathematical Society,* **33** (1927), 352–357; G. Loria, in *Annali di matematica pura ed applicata,* 4th ser., **2** (1924), 1–21; and A. Terracini, in *Jahresbericht der Deutschen Mathematikervereinigung,* **35** (1926), 209–250, with portrait. The articles by Loria, Terracini, and Baker are especially helpful.

PIERRE SPEZIALI

SEIDEL, PHILIPP LUDWIG VON (*b.* Zweibrücken, Germany, 24 October 1821; *d.* Munich, Germany, 13 August 1896)

Seidel was the son of Justus Christian Felix Seidel, a post office official, and Julie Reinhold. Because of his father's work he began school in Nördlingen, continued in Nuremberg, and finished in Hof. After passing the graduation examination in the fall of 1839 he took private lessons from L. C. Schnürlein, a teacher of mathematics at the Hof Gymnasium who had studied under Gauss. In the spring of 1840, Seidel entered Berlin University, where he attended the lectures of Dirichlet and Encke, for whom he subsequently carried out calculations at the astronomical observatory. In the fall of 1842 he moved to Königsberg, where he studied with Bessel, Jacobi, and F. E. Neumann. When Jacobi left Königsberg because of his health in the fall of 1843, Seidel, on Bessel's recommendation, moved to Munich and obtained the doctorate with the dissertation "Über die beste Form der Spiegel in Teleskopen" in January 1846. Six months later he qualified as a *Privatdozent* on the basis of his "Untersuchungen über die Konvergenz und Divergenz der Kettenbrüche."

These two works treat two fields investigated by Seidel throughout his life, dioptrics and mathematical analysis. He also produced works in probability theory and photometry, the latter stimulated by his collaboration with Steinheil. In his mathematical investigations he depended on Dirichlet but filled important gaps left by his teacher—for instance, introducing the concept of nonuniform convergence.

Seidel's photometric measurements of fixed stars and planets were the first true measurements of this kind. The precise evaluation of his observations by methods of probability theory, considering atmospheric extinction, are worthy of special mention. At Steinheil's suggestion Seidel derived trigonometric formulas for points lateral to the axis of an optical system; they soon became important for astronomical photography and led to the production of improved telescopes.

Besides the application of probability theory to astronomy, Seidel investigated the relation between the frequency of certain diseases and climatic conditions at Munich. His pioneer work in several fields was acknowledged by Bavaria. In 1847 he became assistant professor, in 1855 full professor, and later royal privy councillor; he also received a number of medals, one of them connected with nobility. Seidel was a member of the Bavarian Academy of Sciences (1851) and corresponding member of the Berlin and Göttingen academies, as well as a member of the Commission for the European Measurement of a Degree and of a group observing a transit of Venus.

Seidel suffered from eye problems and was obliged to retire early. A bachelor, he was cared for by his unmarried sister Lucie until 1889, and later by the widow of a clergyman named Langhans.

Seidel's lectures covered mathematics, including probability theory and the method of least squares, astronomy, and dioptrics. He never accepted Riemannian geometry.

BIBLIOGRAPHY

I. ORIGINAL WORKS. Seidel's earlier works include "Über die Bestimmung der Brechungs- und Zerstreuungs-Verhältnisses verschiedener Medien," in *Abhandlungen der Bayerischen Akademie der Wissenschaften,* Math.-phys. Kl., **5** (1848), 253–268, written with K. A. Steinheil; "Note über eine Eigenschaft der Reihen, welche discontinuierliche Functionen darstellen," *ibid.,* 381–393; "Untersuchungen über die gegenseitigen Helligkeiten der Fixsterne erster Grösse, und über die Extinction des Lichtes in der Atmosphäre," *ibid.,* **6**, no. 3 (1852), 539–660; "Zur Theorie der Fernrohr-Objective," in *Astronomische Nachrichten,* **35** (1852), 301–316; "Zur Dioptrik," *ibid.,* **37** (1853), 105–120; "Bemerkungen über den Zusammenhang zwischen dem Bildungsgesetze eines Kettenbruches und der Art des Fortgangs seiner Näherungsbrüche," in *Abhandlungen der Bayerischen Akademie der Wissenschaften,* Math.-phys. Kl., **7** (1855), 559–602; "Entwicklung der Glieder 3.ter Ordnung, welche den Weg eines ausserhalb der Ebene der Axe gelegenen Lichtstrahles durch ein System brechender Medien bestimmen," in *Astronomische Nachrichten,* **43** (1856), 289–332; "Über den Einfluss der Theorie der Fehler, mit welchen die durch optische Instrumente gesehenen Bilder behaftet sind, und über die mathematischen Bedingungen ihrer Aufhebung," in *Abhandlungen der naturwissenschaftlich-technischen Commission der Bayerisch-*

en *Akademie der Wissenschaften,* **1** (1857), 227–267; and "Untersuchungen über die Lichtstärke der Planeten vergleichen mit den Sternen, und über die relative Weisse ihrer Oberfläche," in *Monumenta saecularum der Bayerischen Akademie der Wissenschaften* (1859), 1–102.

Among his later writings are "Resultate photometrischer Messungen an 208 der vorzüglichsten Fixsterne," in *Abhandlungen der Bayerischen Akademie der Wissenschaften,* Math.-phys. Kl., **9** (1863), 419–607; "Über eine Anwendung der Wahrscheinlichkeitsrechnung, bezüglich auf die Schwankungen in den Durchsichtigkeitsverhältnissen der Luft," in *Sitzungsberichte der Bayerischen Akademie der Wissenschaften zu München* (1863), pt. 2, 320–350; "Trigonometrische Formeln für den allgemeinsten Fall der Brechung des Lichtes an centrirten sphärischen Flächen," *ibid.* (1866), pt. 2, 263–284; "Über ein Verfahren, die Gleichungen, auf welche die Methode der kleinsten Quadrate führt, sowie lineäre Gleichungen überhaupt," in *Abhandlungen der Bayerischen Akademie der Wissenschaften,* Math.-phys. Kl., **11**, no. 3 (1874), 81–108; and "Über eine einfache Entstehungsweise der Bernoulli'schen Zahlen," in *Sitzungsberichte der Bayerischen Akademie der Wissenschaften,* Math.-phys. Kl., n.s. **7** (1877), 157–187.

II. SECONDARY LITERATURE. See F. Lindemann, *Gedächtnisrede auf L. Ph. von Seidel* (Munich, 1898).

H.-CHRIST. FREIESLEBEN

SEKI, TAKAKAZU (*b.* Huzioka[?], Japan, 1642[?]; *d.* Edo [now Tokyo], Japan, 24 October 1708)

Knowledge of Seki's life is meager and indirect. His place of birth is variously given as Huzioka or Edo, and the year as 1642 or 1644. He was the second son of Nagaakira Utiyama, a samurai; his mother's name is unknown. He was adopted by the patriarch of the Seki family, an accountant, whom he accompanied to Edo as chief of the Bureau of Supply. In 1706, having grown too old to fulfill the duties of this office, he was transferred to a sinecure and died two years later.

Seki is reported to have begun the study of mathematics under Yositane Takahara, a brilliant disciple of Sigeyosi Mōri. Mōri is the author of *Warizansyo* ("A Book on Division," 1622), believed to be the first book on mathematics written by a Japanese, but little is known about Takahara. Of particular influence on Seki's mathematics was *Suan-hsüeh ch'i-mêng* ("Introduction to Mathematical Studies," 1299), compiled by Chu Shih-chieh, a collection of problems solved by a method known in Chinese as *t'ien-yuan shu* ("method of the celestial element"); this method makes it possible to solve a problem by transforming it into an algebraic equation with one variable. Kazuyuki Sawaguchi, allegedly the first Japanese mathematician to master this method, used it to solve 150 problems proposed by Masaoki Satō in his *Sanpô Kongenki* ("Fundamentals of Mathematics," 1667). He then organized these problems, together with their solutions, into the seven-volume collection *Kokon sanpōki* ("Ancient and Modern Mathematics," 1670). At the end of the last volume Sawaguchi presented fifteen problems that he believed to be unsolvable by means of *t'ien-yuan shu.*

Seki's solutions to these problems were published in 1674 as *Hatubi sanpō.* Because mathematicians of those days were unable to grasp how the solutions had been accomplished, Katahiro Takebe (1664–1739), a distinguished disciple of Seki, published *Hatubi sanpō endan genkai* ("An Easy Guide to the *Hatubi sanpō*," 1685), the work that made Seki's method known.

In Chinese mathematics operations were performed by means of instruments called *suan-ch'ou* ("calculating rods") and therefore could not treat any algebraic expressions except those with one variable and numerical coefficients. Seki introduced Chinese ideographs and wrote them to the right of a vertical—such as $|a$—where a is used, for typographical reasons, instead of a Chinese ideograph. Seki called this notation *bōsyohō* ("method of writing by the side") and used it as the basis of his *endan zyutu* ("endan method"). *Endan zyutu* enabled him to represent known and unknown quantities by Chinese ideographs and led him to form equations with literal coefficients of any degree and with several variables. The technique was later renamed *tenzan zyutu* by Yosisuke Matunaga (1693–1744), the third licensee of the secret mathematical methods of Seki's school.

The *Hatubi sanpō* did not include Seki's principal theorems, which were kept secret; but in order to initiate students he arranged the theorems systematically. Parts of these works and some more extended theorems were collected and published posthumously by his disciples as *Katuyō sanpō*—which, with *Sekiryū sanpō sitibusyo* ("Seven Books on the Mathematics of Seki's School," 1907), is sufficient to grasp his mathematics.

Seki first treated general theories of algebraic equations. Since his method of side writing was inconvenient for writing general equations of degree n, he worked with equations of the second through fifth degrees. But his treatment was so general that his method could be applied to equations of any degree. Seki attempted to find a means of solving second-degree algebraic equations with numerical coefficients but, having no concept of algebraic solution, directed his efforts at finding an approximate solution. He discovered a procedure, used long before in China, that was substantially the same as Horner's. The notion of a discriminant of an algebraic equation also was introduced by Seki. Although he had no notion of the derivative, he derived from an algebraic expression $f(x)$ another expression that was the equivalent of $f'(x)$ in modern notation. Eliminating x from the pair of equations $f(x) = 0$ and $f'(x) = 0$, he obtained what is now called a discriminant. With the help of this expression Seki found double roots of the equation $f(x) = 0$. He also developed a method similar to Newton's by which an approximate value of the root of a numerical equation can be computed. Seki's *tenzan zyutu* was important in the treatment of problems that can be transformed into the solution of a system of simultaneous equations. In order to solve the problem of elimination, he introduced determinants and gave a rule for expressing them diagrammatically. For third-order equations his formula was basically similar to Sarrus'.

The method that Seki named *syōsahō* was intended to determine the coefficients of the expression $y = a_1 x + a_2 x^2 + \cdots + a_n x^n$, when n values of $x_1, x_2, \cdots, x_n$ of x and the corresponding n values of $y_1, y_2, \cdots, y_n$ of y are given. Since his notation was not suitable for the general case corresponding to an arbitrary n, Seki treated the case that corresponds to the special value of n. His solution was similar to the method of finite difference.

Another method, *daseki zyutu*, also is important in Seki's mathematics. Its purpose is to find values of $s_p = 1^p + 2^p + \cdots + n^p$ for $p = 1, 2, 3, \cdots$. Using the *syōsahō*, Seki calculated $s_1, s_2, \cdots, s_6$ for a particular value of n:

$$s_1 = \frac{n^2}{2} + \frac{n}{2}$$

$$s_2 = \frac{n^3}{3} + \frac{n^2}{2} + \frac{1}{6} \cdot \frac{2n}{2}$$

$$s_3 = \frac{n^4}{4} + \frac{n^3}{2} + \frac{1}{6} \cdot \frac{3n^2}{2}$$

$$s_4 = \frac{n^5}{5} + \frac{n^4}{2} + \frac{1}{6} \cdot \frac{4n^3}{2} - \frac{1}{30} \cdot \frac{4 \cdot 3 \cdot 2n}{2 \cdot 3 \cdot 4}$$

$$s_5 = \frac{n^6}{6} + \frac{n^5}{2} + \frac{1}{6} \cdot \frac{5n^4}{2} - \frac{1}{30} \cdot \frac{5 \cdot 4 \cdot 3n^2}{2 \cdot 3 \cdot 4}$$

$$s_6 = \frac{n^7}{7} + \frac{n^6}{2} + \frac{1}{6} \cdot \frac{6n^5}{2} - \frac{1}{30} \cdot \frac{6 \cdot 5 \cdot 4n^3}{2 \cdot 3 \cdot 4} +$$

$$\frac{1}{42} \cdot \frac{6 \cdot 5 \cdot 4 \cdot 3 \cdot 2n}{2 \cdot 3 \cdot 4 \cdot 5 \cdot 6}.$$

The numbers 1/6, 1/30, 1/42 are Bernoulli numbers, which were introduced in his *Ars conjectandi* (1713).

Enri ("principle of the circle"), one of Seki's important contributions, consists of rectification of the circumference of a circle, rectification of a circular arc, and cubature of a sphere. In the rectification of a circumference, Seki considered a circle of diameter 1 and an inscribed regular polygon of 2^n sides. He believed that the inscribed polygon gradually loses its angularities and finally becomes a circumference of the circle when the number of sides is increased without limit. He therefore calculated the perimeter c_i of the regular polygon of 2^i sides, where i represents any integer not greater than 17, and devised a method by which he was able to obtain a better result from c_{15}, c_{16}, c_{17}. The formula was

$$s = c_{16} + \frac{(c_{16} - c_{15})(c_{17} - c_{16})}{(c_{16} - c_{15}) - (c_{17} - c_{16})},$$

where

$$c_{15} = 3.1415926487769856708,$$
$$c_{16} = 3.1415926523565913571,$$

and

$$c_{17} = 3.1415926532889027755.$$

Therefore, $s = 3.14159265359$, where s is the circumference of the circle; this value is accurate except for the last figure. Also in connection with this problem Seki created a method of approximation called *reiyaku zyutu*, by which he theoretically obtained 355/113 as an approximate value of π, a value found much earlier in China.

In the rectification of a circular arc, Seki considered an arc of which the chord is 8 and the corresponding sagitta is 2. He considered an inscribed open polygon of 2^{15} sides and, using the above formula, calculated the approximate value of the arc as 9.272953. In the cubature of a sphere, Seki calculated the volume of a sphere of diameter 10 and obtained $523\frac{203}{339}$ as an approximate value. Using the approximate value of π as 355/113, Seki observed that if d is the diameter of this sphere,

$$\frac{\pi}{6} d^3 = \frac{355}{678} \times (10)^3 = 523\frac{203}{339}.$$

Certain other geometrical problems, which do not belong among the *enri*, concern ellipses. Seki believed that any ellipse can be obtained through cutting a suitable circular cylinder by a plane. In order to obtain the area of an ellipse, he cut off from a circular cylinder two segments with generatrices of equal length such that one has elliptical bases and the other has circular bases. These two cylinders have the same volume. By equating the volumes of these two pieces of the cylinder, Seki obtained the result that the area of an ellipse is $\pi/4 \times AA' \times BB'$, where AA' and BB' denote, respectively, the major and minor axis of an ellipse. Among the problems of cubature, that of a solid generated by revolving a segment of circle about a straight line that lies on the same plane as the segment is noteworthy. His result in this area had generality, and the theorem that he established was substantially the same as that now called the theorem of Pappus and Guldin.

BIBLIOGRAPHY

I. ORIGINAL WORKS. Seki's published writings are *Hatubi sanpō* (Edo, 1674) and *Katuyō sanpō* (Tokyo–Kyoto, 1709), copies of which are owned by the Mathematical Institute, Faculty of Science, Kyoto University. *Sekiryū sanpō sitibusyo* ("Seven Books on the Mathematics of Seki's School"; Tokyo, 1907), is a collection of Seki's papers (1683–1685) that were transmitted from master to pupils, who were permitted to copy them. An important collection of MS papers, "Sanbusyō" ("Three Selected Papers"), is discussed by Fujiwara (see below). See also *Collected Papers of Takakazu Seki* (Osaka, 1974).

II. SECONDARY LITERATURE. See the following, listed chronologically: Katahiro Takebe, *Hatubi sanpō endan genkai* ("An Easy Guide to the Hatubi sanpō"; n.p., 1685), a copy of which is owned by the Mathematical Institute, Faculty of Science, Kyoto University, with a facs. of the text of *Hatubi sanpō* and an explanation of Seki's method of solution; Dairoku Kikuchi, "Seki's Method of Finding the Length of an Arc of a Circle," in *Proceedings of the Physico-Mathematical Society of Japan*, **8**, no. 5 (1899), 179–198; and Matsusaburo Fujiwara, *Mathematics of Japan Before the Meiji Era*, II (Tokyo, 1956), 133–265, in Japanese. There are many other works that treat Seki's mathematics, such as Yoshio Mikami, *The Development of Mathematics in China and Japan* (Leipzig–New York, 1913; repr. New York, n.d.), but only those of scientific importance are cited here.

AKIRA KOBORI

SEMYONOV-TYAN-SHANSKY, PETR PETROVICH (*b.* near Urusov, Ryazan guberniya, Russia, 14 January 1827; *d.* St. Petersburg, Russia, 11 March 1914)

Semyonov's father, Petr Nikolaevich Semyonov, was a landowner and well-known playwright; his mother, Aleksandra Petrovna Blank, came from a French family that had immigrated to Russia at the end of the seventeenth century. Semyonov was interested in botany and history as a child and was educated at home by private tutors. In 1842 he entered the school for guard cadets at St. Petersburg, from which he graduated with distinction. Three years later he enrolled in the natural sciences section of St. Petersburg University. After graduating in 1848 he was elected a member of the Russian Geographical Society, and by the end of his life he had held honorary memberships in seventy-three Russian and foreign scientific societies and institutions.

In addition to his scientific activity, Semyonov was an expert on Dutch painting and collected 700 pictures and 3,500 prints by Dutch and Flemish masters of the sixteenth and seventeenth centuries; the collection was presented to the Hermitage Museum in 1910. He also published works on seventeenth-century Dutch painting and in 1874 was elected an honorary member of the Academy of Arts in St. Petersburg. His abiding interest in entomology was reflected in his collection of 700,000 specimens, given to the Zoological Museum of the Academy of Sciences.

Semyonov began his geographical research in 1849, when, at the request of the Free Economic Society, he and Nikolai Danilevsky investigated the chernozem zone of European Russia. The botanical material that they collected provided the basis for his master's thesis, defended in 1851, on the flora of the Don basin in relation to the geographical distribution of plants in European Russia. In the same year, at the request of the Russian Geographical Society, he began work on a translation of Karl Ritter's *Die Erdkunde von Asien*, taking into consideration material obtained after 1830. This project stimulated his interest in the then almost unknown Tien Shan. From 1853 to 1855 he lived in Berlin and became acquainted with Ritter.

In preparation for an expedition to Tien Shan, Semyonov attended lectures at Berlin University, studied geography and geology, traveled on foot through the mountainous regions of western Europe and Switzerland, studied volcanic phenomena, and made seventeen ascents of Vesuvius. His acquaintance with Humboldt and study of his scientific work especially influenced his scientific outlook; Humboldt, in turn, enthusiastically encouraged Semyonov to explore Tien Shan.

In 1855 Semyonov returned to Russia, and the following year he published the first volume of his translation of Ritter's *Die Erdkunde von Asien*, devoted to Mongolia, Manchuria, and northern China. Semyonov's extensive additions constituted half the volume, and his edition subsequently acquired the significance of an independent work. In the introduction he emphasized the need for geography to deal with the particulars of nature as they related to agriculture and discussed the importance of developing a Russian orthography—especially for Chinese place names—and geographical terminology; he himself introduced "upland" (*nagore*), "plateau" (*ploskogore*), "hollow" (*kotlovina*), and "foothills" (*predgore*). In his annotations he corrected Ritter's text and also disputed the author's assertion that the junctions of the Caspian with the Aral and Black seas could have occurred only in prehistoric times. This problem is still unresolved. He also corrected Humboldt and accounted for the Caspian depression "by the gradual drying up of the seas and not by a volcanic collapse, as in the Dead Sea."

In 1856 Semyonov reached Tien Shan. He had traveled through the cities of Ekaterinburg (now Sverdlovsk), Omsk, Barnaul, Semipalatinsk, and the fortress of Verny (now Alma-Ata); and en route he had met the geographers G. N. Potanin and C. C. Valikhanov, and the exiled F. Dostoevsky. From Verny he made two excursions to Lake Issyk Kul and one to Kuldja. In 1857 Semyonov wrote to the Russian Geographical Society: "My second long trip to the Chu River exceeded my expectations. I not only succeeded in crossing the Chu but even in reaching Issyk Kul by this route, that is, by its western extremity, on which no European had yet set foot and which no scientific research of any kind had touched."

In 1857 Semyonov crossed the northern chain of the Terskey Ala-Tau range; discovered the upper reaches of the Naryn River—the main source of the Syr Darya; and climbed along the canyon of the Dzhuuk, having observed the hill and valley topography of the elevated watersheds. He then crossed the Tien Shan to the basin of the Tarim, climbed the Khan Tengri group, and discovered broad glaciers in the upper reaches of the Sazydzhas River. On his return he studied the Trans-Ili Ala-Tau range, Dzungarian Ala-Tau, Lake Alakol, and the Tarbagatai range.

Semyonov's route enabled him to trace the over-all configuration of the country and to discover the actual structure of the interior of Asia. He refuted Humboldt's assertion of the volcanic origin of the mountains of central Asia and of the presence of the north-south Bolor (Muztagh Ata) range. His observations provided a basis for refuting Ritter's and Humboldt's assertion that the Chu River arises from Lake Issyk Kul. The river, he discovered, only approaches the lake, which has no outlet and only provisional connections with the Chu along the channel of the Kutemalda. He pointed out the great altitude of the snow line in the mountains of central Asia (from 11,000 to 15,000 feet), convincing Humboldt that "the dryness of the climate elevates the snowline to an unusual extent." He established the existence of extensive glaciation in the Tien Shan, first suggested by Humboldt, and compiled the first orographical scheme of the area. He discussed the tectonics and geological structure, noting the line of east-west elevations and intermontane depressions, in which young sedimentary rock had developed. Semyonov also described the vertical division of the landscape in the mountains of the Trans-Ili Ala-Tau into five zones of vegetation and evaluated their agricultural potential. The vast collection of geological and botanical specimens that he amassed included insects, mollusks, and ethnographical material.

After his return to Russia in 1857 Semyonov became active as a scientific encyclopedist. His thirty-year study of Russian economics and statistics was reflected in publication of the five-volume *Geografichesko-statistichesky slovar* ("Geographical-Statistical Dictionary," 1863–1885), a basic reference work. As head of the Central Statistical Committee from 1864 Semyonov organized important studies and introduced the geographical method into the study of landed property, sowing area, and yields; the material was grouped by districts classified according to their natural and economic features. In 1870 he organized the First All-Russian Statistical Congress. He conducted a classic investigation of the peasant economy in 1880, and the first general census of Russia (1897) was carried out on his initiative. In 1882 Semyonov became a senator, and from 1897 he was a member of the State Council.

In 1860 Semyonov was elected president of the Section of Physical Geography of the Russian Geographical Society, and from 1873 he was vice-president of the Society. He organized many expeditions to central Asia, including those of N. M. Przhevalsky, M. V. Pevtsov, G. N. Potanin, P. K.

Kozlov, and V. A. Obruchev, the results of which substantially altered existing ideas about Asia. He actively assisted the expedition of N. N. Miklu-kho-Maklai and G. Sedov; organized, with Shokal-sky, the Kamchatka expedition of the Russian Geographical Society; and assisted scientists in political exile, including Potanin, A. L. Chekanov-sky, and I. D. Chersky.

In 1888 Semyonov visited central Asia for the second time, passing through Ashkhabad and Bukhara to Samarkand and Tashkent. He traveled up the valley of the Zeravshan River and climbed the mountains of Turkestan and the Gissar range. His descriptions of the natural history and economy of the area are still of scientific value.

As a popularizer of geographical knowledge, Semyonov wrote and edited many works. He translated and supplemented Ritter's *Die Erdkunde von Asien* with sections on the Altai, Sayan, Baikal, and regions around Lake Baikal. He edited the multivolume *Zhivopisnaya Rossia* ("Scenic Russia") and wrote a three-volume history of the Russian Geographical Society. In 1906, on the fiftieth anniversary of his expedition to Tien Shan, the epithet "Tyan-Shansky" was officially added to the family name.

BIBLIOGRAPHY

I. ORIGINAL WORKS. Semyonov's earlier writings include "Neskolko zametok o granitsakh geologicheskikh formatsy v sredney i yuzhnoy Rossii" ("Some Notes on the Boundaries of Geological Formations in Central and Southern Russia"), in *Geograficheskie izvestiya* (1850), 513–518; *Pridonskaya flora v ee otnosheniakh s geograficheskim raspredeleniem rasteny v Evropeyskoy Rossii* ("Flora of the Don in Relation to the Geographical Distribution of Plants in European Russia"; St. Petersburg, 1851), his master's diss.; "Obozrenie Amura v fiziko-geograficheskom otnoshenii" ("Review of the Amur in Its Physical-Geographical Aspects"), in *Vestnik Russkogo geograficheskogo obshchestva*, no. 15 (1855), 227–255; *Zemlevedenie Azii K. Rittera* (Ritter's *Die Erdkunde von Asien*), translated and supplemented by Semyonov, 5 vols. (St. Petersburg, 1856–1879); "Pervaya poezdka na Tyan-Shan ili Nebesny khrebet do verkhoviev r. Yaksarta ili Syr-Dari v 1857 g." ("First Trip to the Tien Shan or Heavenly Range as Far as the Upper Reaches of the Jaxartes or Syr Darya River in 1857"), in *Vestnik Russkogo geograficheskogo obshchestva*, no. 23 (1858), 7–25; "Zapiska po voprosu ob obmelenii Azovskogo morya" ("Note on . . . the Shallowness of the Sea of Azov"), *ibid.*, no. 30 (1860); and *Geografichesko-statistichesky slovar Rossyskoy imperii* ("Geographical-Statistical Dictionary of the Russian Empire"), 5 vols. (St. Petersburg, 1863–1885).

Subsequent works are "Naselennost Evropeyskoy Rossii v zavisimosti ot prichin, obuslovlivayushchikh raspredelenie naselenia imperii" ("Population of European Russia in Relation to the Conditions That Determine the Distribution of the Population of the Empire"), in *Statistichesky vremennik Rossyskoy imperii*, **2**, no. 1 (1871), 125–156; articles in *Statistika pozemelnoy sobstvennosti i naselennykh mest Evropeyskoy Rossii* ("Statistics on Landed Property and Settled Localities of European Russia"), pts. 1–2, 4–5 (St. Petersburg, 1880–1884); "O vozvrashchenii Amu-Dari v Kaspyskom more" ("On the Return of the Amu Darya Into the Caspian Sea"), in *Moskovskie vedomosti*, nos. 45–46 (1881); "Oblast kraynego severa Evropeyskoy Rossii v eyo sovremennom ekonomicheskom sostoyanii" (". . . the Extreme North of European Russia in Its Present Economic Condition"), in Semyonov, ed., *Zhivopisnaya Rossia* ("Scenic Russia"), I (St. Petersburg–Moscow, 1881), 313–336; "Ozernaya oblast v eyo sovremennon ekonomicheskom sostoyanii" ("The Lake Region in Its Present Economic Condition"), *ibid.*, 817–834; "Ermitazh i kartinnye gallerei Peterburga" ("The Hermitage and Picture Galleries of St. Petersburg"), *ibid.*, 687–720; "Obshchy obzor ekonomicheskogo sostoyania Finlyandii" ("A General Survey of the Economic Conditions of Finland"), *ibid.*, II (St. Petersburg–Moscow, 1882), 119–128; "Belorusskaya oblast v eyo sovremennom ekonomicheskom sostoyanii" ("The Belorussian Region in Its Present Economic Condition"), *ibid.*, III (St. Petersburg–Moscow, 1882), 473–490; "Zapadnaya Sibir v eyo sovremennom ekonomicheskom sostoyanii" ("Western Siberia in Its Present Economic Condition"), *ibid.*, IX (St. Petersburg–Moscow, 1884), 349–370; and "Nebesny khrebet i Zailysky kray" ("The Heavenly Range and the Trans-Ili Region"), *ibid.*, X (St. Petersburg–Moscow, 1885), 333–376.

Among his later works are *Kratkoe rukovodstvo dlya sobirania zhukov ili zhestkokrylykh (Coleoptera) i babochek ili cheshuekrylykh (Lepidoptera)* ("A Short Guide to Collecting Beetles . . . and Butterflies . . ."; St. Petersburg, 1882; 2nd ed., 1893); "Turkestan i Zakaspysky kray v 1888 godu" ("Turkestan and the Transcaspian Region in 1888"), in *Izvestiya Russkogo geograficheskogo obshchestva*, **24**, no. 4 (1888), 289–347; *Istoria poluvekovoy deyatelnosti Russkogo geograficheskogo obshchestva 1845–1895* ("History of a Half-Century . . . of the Russian Geographical Society . . ."), 3 vols. (St. Petersburg, 1896); "Kharakternye vyvody iz pervoy vseobshchey perepisi" ("Characteristic Conclusions From the First General Census"), in *Izvestiya Russkogo geograficheskogo obshchestva*, **33** (1897), 249–270; "Sibir" ("Siberia"), in Semyonov, ed., *Okrainy Rossii. Sibir, Turkestan, Kavkaz, i polyarnaya chast Evropeyskoy Rossii* ("Outlying Districts of Russia. Siberia, Turkestan, the Caucasus, and the Polar Part of European Russia"; St. Petersburg, 1900); "Rastitelny i zhivotny mir" ("The

Plant and Animal World"), II, ch. 3; and "Istoricheskie sudby srednerusskoy chernozemnoy oblasti i kulturnye eyo uspekhi" ("The Historical Fate of the Central Russian Chernozem Regions and Their Cultural Progress"), II, ch. 4, written with V. I. Lamansky, in *Rossia* (St. Petersburg, 1899–1914); and *Memuary* ("Memoirs"), 4 vols. (I, III, IV, Petrograd, 1916–1917; II, Leningrad, 1946–1947).

II. SECONDARY LITERATURE. See L. S. Berg, "Petr Petrovich Semyonov-Tyan-Shansky," in his *Ocherki po istorii russkikh geograficheskikh otkryty* ("Sketches in the History of Russian Geographical Discoveries"; Moscow–Leningrad, 1946), 232–272; and *Vsesoyuznoe geograficheskoe obshchestvo za sto let* ("The All-Union Geographical Society for the Last Hundred Years"; Moscow–Leningrad, 1946), 57–77; V. I. Chernyavsky, *P. P. Semyonov-Tyan-Shansky i ego trudy po geografii* ("Semyonov . . . and His Work in Geography"; Moscow, 1955), 296; A. A. Dostoevsky, "P. P. Semyonov-Tyan-Shansky kak issledovatel, geograf i statistik" (". . . Semyonov . . . as Researcher, Geographer, and Statistician"), in *Pamyati P. P. Semyonov-Tyan-Shansky* ("Recollections of Semyonov . . ."; Petrograd, 1914), 9–22; G. Y. Grumm-Grzhimaylo, "P. P. Semyonov-Tyan-Shansky kak geograf" (". . . Semyonov . . . as Geographer"), in A. A. Dostoevsky, ed., *Petr Petrovich Semyonov-Tyan-Shansky, ego zhizn i deyatelnost* (". . . Semyonov . . ., His Life and Work"; Leningrad, 1928), 161–165; V. I. Lavrov, "Petr Petrovich Semyonov-Tyan-Shansky," in *Lyudi russkoy nauki* ("People of Russian Science"; Moscow, 1962), 460–468; S. I. Ognev, "P. P. Semyonov-Tyan-Shansky," in *Byulleten Moskovskogo obshchestva ispytateley prirody*, Biol. ser., **51**, no. 3 (1946), 122–137; and Y. K. Efremov, "Petr Petrovich Semyonov-Tyan-Shansky kak fiziko-geograf" (". . . Semyonov . . . as Physical Geographer"), in *Otechestvennye fiziko-geografy* ("Native Physical Geographers"; Moscow, 1959), 284–293.

VERA N. FEDCHINA

SERENUS (*b.* Antinoupolis, Egypt, *fl.* fourth century A.D. [?])

Serenus was the author of two treatises on conic sections, *On the Section of a Cylinder* and *On the Section of a Cone*, which have survived, and a commentary on the *Conics* of Apollonius, which has not. From a subscription in a later hand to the Vatican archetype of the first-named work and from the title of the second as given in a Paris manuscript from Mount Athos, Serenus' birth can be placed at Antinoupolis, a city founded by Hadrian in A.D. 122. This birthplace gives an upper limit for his date. As Serenus reckoned Apollonius among the "ancient" writers on conics, and

used two lemmas proved by Pappus to transform certain unequal proportions,[1] he is generally thought to have flourished in the fourth century. Certainly his surviving works belonged to an age when Greek geometry had passed its creative phase.[2]

On the Section of a Cylinder, dedicated to an otherwise unknown Cyrus, consists of an introduction, eight definitions, and thirty-three propositions. It counters what is said to have been a prevalent belief—that the curve formed by the oblique section of a cylinder differs from the curve formed by the oblique section of a cone known as the ellipse. In the final five propositions Serenus defended a friend Peithon, who, not satisfied with Euclid's treatment, had defined parallels to be such lines as are cast on a wall or a roof by a pillar with a light behind it. Even in the decline of Greek mathematics this description had been a source of amusement to Peithon's contemporaries.[3]

On the Section of a Cone, also dedicated to Cyrus, consists of an introduction and sixty-nine propositions. It deals mainly with the areas of triangular sections of right or scalene cones made by planes passing through the vertex. Serenus specified the conditions for which the area of a triangle in a certain class is a maximum, those for which two triangles in a particular class may be equal, and so on. In some instances he also evaluated areas.

Serenus himself bore witness to his lost commentary on Apollonius.[4] Certain manuscripts of Theon of Smyrna preserve a fragment that may have come from that work or from a separate collection of lemmas. It is introduced with the words, "From Serenus the philosopher out of the lemmas," and it lays down that if a number of rectilineal angles be subtended at a point on the diameter of a circle (not being its center) by equal arcs of the circle, an angle nearer the center is always less than an angle farther away; this is applied to angles subtended at the center of the ecliptic by equal arcs of the eccentric circle of the sun.

NOTES

1. *De sectione coni*, Prop. XIX, in J. L. Heiberg, *Sereni Antinoensis opuscula*, pp. 160.15–162.11; Pappus, *Collectio* VII. 45 and 47, in F. Hultsch, *Pappi Alexandrini Collectionis quae supersunt*, II (Berlin, 1877), pp. 684.20–686.4, 686.15–27.
2. Halley's beliefs *(Apollonii Pergaei Conicorum libri octo, Praefatio ad finem)* that Serenus was born at Antissa in Lesbos and that a lower date for his life is given by an apparent reference to him in the commentary of Marinus (*fl.* A.D. 425)

on Euclid's *Data* (David Gregory, *Euclidis quae supersunt omnia* [Oxford, 1703], p. 457.3) have been shown philologically by Heiberg in his review of M. Cantor, *Vorlesungen über Geschichte der Mathematik* in *Revue critique d'histoire et de Littérature,* **11** (1881), 381, and by Menge (*Euclidis opera omnia,* J. L. Heiberg and H. Menge, eds., VI [Leipzig, 1896], p. 248.3–4, where there is no mention of Serenus) to be erroneous.

3. J. L. Heiberg, *Sereni Antinoensis opuscula,* p. 96.14–25.
4. *Ibid.,* pp. 26–27.

BIBLIOGRAPHY

I. ORIGINAL WORKS. It seems likely that from the seventh century the two surviving works of Serenus and the commentary of Eutocius were bound with the *Conics* of Apollonius—Theodorus Metochita certainly read them together early in the fourteenth century—and their survival is probably due to these circumstances. A Latin trans. of Serenus' *De sectione cylindri* and *De sectione coni* was published by F. Commandinus at the end of his *Apollonii conicorum libri quatri* (Bologna, 1566). The Greek text was first published by E. Halley in *Apollonii Pergaei Conicorum libri octo et Sereni Antissensis De sectione cylindri et coni libri duo* (Oxford, 1710). A definitive critical ed. with Latin trans. was published by J. L. Heiberg, *Sereni Antinoensis opuscula* (Leipzig, 1896). A German trans. was made by E. Nizze, *Serenus von Antissa: Ueber den Schnitt des Cylinders* (Stralsund, 1860) and *Ueber den Schnitt des Kegels* (Stralsund, 1861); and there is an excellent French trans. with intro. and notes by Paul Ver Eecke, *Serenus d'Antinoë: Le livre De la section du cylindre e le livre De la section du cône* (Paris–Bruges, 1929).

The fragment from the lemmas has been published by T. H. Martin, *Theonis Platonici Liber De astronomia* (Paris, 1849; repr. Groningen, 1971), 340–343, with a Latin trans. and by J. L. Heiberg, *Sereni Antinoensis opuscula,* XVIII–XIX.

II. SECONDARY LITERATURE. See Thomas Heath, *History of Greek Mathematics,* II (Oxford, 1921), 519–526; J. L. Heiberg, "Über der Geburtsort des Serenos," in *Bibliotheca mathematica,* n.s. **8** (1894), 97–98; Gino Loria, *Le scienze esatte nell' antica Grecia,* 2nd ed. (Milan, 1914), 727–735; T. H. Martin, *Theonici Liber De astronomia* (Paris, 1849; repr. Groningen, 1971), 79–81; and Paul Tannery, "Serenus d'Antissa," in *Bulletin des sciences mathématiques et astronomiques,* 2nd ser., **7** (1883), 237–244, repr. in *Mémoires scientifiques,* I (Paris–Toulouse, 1912), 290–299.

IVOR BULMER-THOMAS

SERRET, JOSEPH ALFRED (*b.* Paris, France, 30 August 1819; *d.* Versailles, France, 2 March 1885)

Serret is sometimes confused with Paul Joseph Serret (1827–1898), a mathematician at the Université Catholique in Paris. After graduating from the École Polytechnique in 1840, Serret decided on a life of science and in 1848 became an entrance examiner at the École. After several other academic appointments he was named professor of celestial mechanics (1861) at the Collège de France and then, in 1863, professor of differential and integral calculus at the Sorbonne. In 1873 he joined the Bureau des Longitudes.

With his contemporaries P.-O. Bonnet and J. Bertrand, Serret belonged to that group of mathematicians in Paris who greatly advanced differential calculus during the period 1840–1865, and the fundamental formulas in the theory of space curves bear his name and that of J. F. Frenet. Serret also worked in number theory, calculus, mechanics, and astronomy and wrote several popular textbooks, including *Cours d'algèbre supérieure* (1849) and *Cours de calcul différentiel et intégral* (1867–1868).

In 1860 Serret succeeded Poinsot in the Académie des Sciences. After 1871 Serret's health declined; and he retired to Versailles, where he lived quietly with his family until his death.

BIBLIOGRAPHY

I. ORIGINAL WORKS. The *Journal des mathématiques pures et appliquées* contains several of Serret's papers, including "Mémoire sur les surfaces orthogonales," **12** (1847), 241–254; "Sur quelques formules relatives à la théorie des courbes à double courbure," **16** (1851), 193–207; and "Mémoire sur les surfaces dont toutes les lignes de courbure sont planes ou sphériques," **18** (1853), 113–162. See also "Sur la moindre surface comprise entre des lignes droites données, non situées dans le même plan," in *Comptes rendus hebdomadaire des séances de l'Académie des sciences,* **40** (1855), 1078–1082.

Serret edited the *Oeuvres de Lagrange,* 14 vols. (Paris, 1867–1892), and the fifth ed. of Monge's *Application de l'analyse à la géométrie* (Paris, 1850), with annotations.

II. SECONDARY LITERATURE. An obituary notice is given in *Bulletin des sciences mathématiques,* 2nd ser., **9** (1885), 123–132.

D. J. STRUIK

SERVOIS, FRANÇOIS-JOSEPH (*b.* Mont-de-Laval, Doubs, France, 19 July 1767; *d.* Mont-de-Laval, 17 April 1847)

Servois was the son of Jacques-Ignace Servois, a merchant, and Jeanne-Marie Jolliet. He was ordained a priest at Besançon at the beginning of the

Revolution, but in 1793 he gave up his ecclesiastical duties in order to join the army. In 1794, after a brief stay at the artillery school of Châlons-sur-Marne, he was made a lieutenant. While serving in several campaigns as staff officer, he devoted his leisure time to the study of mathematics. With the support of Legendre, he was appointed professor of mathematics at the artillery school of Besançon in July 1801. A few months later he transferred to the school at Châlons-sur-Marne; in 1802, to the artillery school at Metz; and in 1808, to the school at La Fère. After a brief return to Metz as professor at the artillery and engineering school, he was appointed curator of the artillery museum at Paris in 1816. He held the post until 1827, when he retired to his native village.

Like a number of his colleagues who taught at military schools, Servois closely followed developments in mathematics and sought, at times successfully, to make an original contribution. His first publication was a short work on pure and applied geometry: *Solutions peu connues de différents problèmes de géométrie pratique* . . . (1805). Drawing upon Mascheroni's *Geometria del compasso* and upon Lazare Carnot's *Géométrie de position* (1803), Servois formulated some notions of modern geometry and applied them to practical problems. The book was well received, and Poncelet considered it a "truly original work, notable for presenting the first applications of the theory of transversals to the geometry of the ruler or surveyor's staff, thus revealing the fruitfulness and utility of this theory" (*Traité des propriétés projectives* [Paris, 1822], xliv).

Servois presented three memoirs before the Académie des Sciences. The first was on the principles of differential calculus and the development of functions in series (1805; new version, 1810); the second, which was never published, was devoted to the elements of dynamics (1809; additions in 1811); the third, also never published, dealt with the "determination of cometary and planetary orbits." In 1810 Servois published a study on the principle of virtual velocities in the *Mémoires* of the Turin Academy, but most of his subsequent papers appeared in Gergonne's *Annales de mathématiques pures et appliquées*. In his first contribution to the latter, he solved two construction problems by projective methods and introduced the term *pôle*. His ability in geometry was recognized by Poncelet, who consulted him on several occasions while writing his *Traité des propriétés projectives*.

In a letter to Gergonne of November 1813, Servois criticized, in the name of the primacy of algebraic language, the geometric representation of imaginary numbers that had recently been proposed by J. R. Argand and J. F. Français: "I confess that I do not yet see in this notation anything but a geometric mask applied to analytic forms the direct use of which seems to me simple and more expeditious" (*Annales de mathématiques* . . . , **4**, no. 7 [January 1814], 230). This formalist conception of algebra made Servois one of the chief precursors of the English school of symbolic algebra. It can be seen still more clearly in his "Essai sur un nouveau mode d'exposition des principes du calcul différentiel," which contains the most important aspects of the memoir presented to the Academy in 1805 and 1810. Familiar with the work of Hindenburg's combinatorial school and with L. F. A. Arbogast's *Calcul des dérivations*, Servois sought in the "Essai" to provide differential calculus with a rigorous foundation. In the course of this effort he developed the first elements of what became the calculus of operations. Observing that this calculus is based on the conservation of certain properties of the operations to which it is applied, he introduced the fundamental notions of "commutative property" and "distributive property" (*Annales*, **5**, no. 5 [November 1814], 98). He did not, however, always distinguish between "function" and "operation." Servois's memoir, which more or less directly inspired the work of Robert Murphy and of George Boole, was followed by an interesting critique of the various presentations of the principles of differential calculus, particularly the theory of the infinitely small and the method of Wronski.

Although Servois did not produce a major body of work, he made a number of original contributions to various branches of mathematics and prepared the way for important later developments.

BIBLIOGRAPHY

I. ORIGINAL WORKS. Servois's book on geometry, *Solutions peu connues de différents problèmes de géométrie pratique pour servir de supplément aux traités de cette science* (Metz–Paris, 1805), was followed by *Lettre de S . . . à F . . . professeur de mathématiques sur le Traité analytique des courbes et surfaces du second ordre* (Paris, 1802). He also published "De principio velocitatum virtualium," in *Mémoires de l'Académie impériale des sciences de Turin*, **18** (1809–1810), pt. 2, 177–244.

The following articles appeared in Gergonne's *Annales de mathématiques pures et appliquées:* "Solutions de deux problèmes de construction," **1**, no. 11 (May 1811), 332–335, 337–341; "Démonstrations de quelques formules de trigonométrie sphérique," **2**, no. 3 (Sept. 1811), 84–88; "Remarques relatives à la formule logarithmique" (dated 2 Oct. 1811), **2**, no. 7 (Jan. 1812), 178–179; "Calendrier perpétuel," **4**, no. 3 (Sept. 1813), 84–90; "Sur la théorie des quantités imaginaires. Lettre de M. Servois" (dated 23 Nov. 1813), **4**, no. 7 (Jan. 1814), 228–235, also in J. R. Argand, *Essai sur une manière de représenter les quantités imaginaires . . .*, 2nd ed. (Paris, 1874), 101–109; "Essai sur un nouveau mode d'exposition des principes du calcul différentiel," **5**, no. 4 (Oct. 1814), 93–140; "Réflexions sur les divers systèmes d'exposition des principes du calcul différentiel, et, en particulier, sur la doctrine des infiniment petits" (La Fère, 10 Aug. 1814), **5**, no. 5 (Nov. 1814), 141–170. The last two articles were printed together in a pamphlet (Nîmes, 1814).

See also "Note de M. Servois (Sur la trigonométrie des Indiens)," in *Correspondance sur l'École polytechnique*, **3**, no. 3 (Jan. 1816), 265–266; "Mémoire sur les quadratures," in *Annales de mathématiques . . .*, **8**, no. 3 (Sept. 1817), 73–115; "Lambert (Henri-Jean)," in Michaud, ed., *Biographie universelle*, XXIII (1819), 46–51; "Trajectoire," in *Dictionnaire de l'artillerie*, G.-H. Cotty, ed. (Paris, 1822), 464–471; "Lettre sur la théorie des parallèles" (dated 15 Nov. 1825), in *Annales de mathématiques . . .*, **16**, no. 7 (Feb. 1826), 233–238. Royal Society *Catalogue of Scientific Papers*, V, 665, gives only a portion of this bibliography.

II. SECONDARY LITERATURE. The principal account of Servois's career and writings is J. Boyer, "Le mathématicien franc-comtois François-Joseph Servois, ancien conservateur du Musée d'artillerie d'après des documents inédits," in *Mémoires de la Société d'émulation du Doubs*, 6th. ser., **9** (1894), 5–37, also separately printed as a 26-page pamphlet (Besançon, 1895).

Comments on Servois's work are given by S. F. Lacroix, in *Procès-verbaux des séances de l'Académie des sciences*, V (Hendaye, 1914), 99–101; and in *Traité du calcul différentiel et du calcul intégral*, 2nd ed., III (Paris, 1819), see index; by J. V. Poncelet, in *Traité des propriétés projectives . . .* (Paris, 1822), v–vi, xliv; and in *Applications d'analyse et de géométrie*, II (Paris, 1864), 530–552; by M. Chasles, in *Aperçu historique . . .* (Paris, 1875), see index; by O. Terquem, in *Bulletin de bibliographie, d'histoire et biographie mathématique*, **1**, 84, 93, 110, 185, supp. to *Nouvelles annales de mathématiques*, **14** (1855); and by S. Pincherle, "Équations et opérations fonctionnelles," in *Encyclopédie des sciences mathématiques*, II, pt. 5, fasc. 1 (Paris–Leipzig, 1912), 4–5; and in *Intermédiaire des mathématiciens*, **2** (1895), 58, 220, and **23** (1916), 195. The most recent study, N. Nielsen, *Géomètres français sous la Révolution* (Copenhagen–Paris, 1929), 221–224, analyzes certain aspects of Servois's work in greater detail but contains a number of errors.

RENÉ TATON

SEVERI, FRANCESCO (*b*. Arezzo, Italy, 13 April 1879; *d*. Rome, Italy, 8 December 1961)

From 1898 until his death, Severi published more than 400 books and papers on mathematics, history of science, education, and philosophy. His most outstanding contributions, however, were in the field of algebraic geometry. Severi acquired the taste for elegant synthetic arguments while studying with Segre at the University of Turin, from which he graduated in 1900 under Segre's guidance. At Turin he became interested in algebraic and enumerative problems and developed a broad geometric eclecticism and a formidable dexterity in the projective geometry of higher spaces.

In the latter field Segre published (1894) an interesting reworking of geometry on an algebraic curve. In Italy, Bertini and Castelnuovo also contributed to this field, while in Germany, Brill and Max Noether, in the footsteps of Riemann, made more studies using different methods. A more invariant view, derived from the transformations introduced by Cremona thirty years earlier, led Castelnuovo and Enriques to lay the foundations of a similar theory for algebraic surfaces. This theory anticipated the work of Picard in France on the same subject.

Having served as *assistente* to Enriques at Bologna in 1902 and to Bertini at Pisa in 1903, Severi was drawn to these new developments. He attempted, with great success, to explain important and still unsolved problems along with work in new areas. He perfected the theory of birational invariants of algebraic surfaces and created an analogous (but more complex) theory for algebraic varieties of arbitrary dimension. The completion of this work was to take him another fifty years. Severi's work on algebraic geometry can best be described by dividing it into five sections, rather than maintaining a chronological order.

1. Enumerative and Projective Geometry, Intersections, and Questions on the Foundations of Algebraic Geometry. The proof of the principle of the "conservation of number," established heuristically by Schubert in the nineteenth century, was listed by Hilbert at the Paris Congress of 1900 as one of the fundamental unsolved problems of mathematics. Severi subsequently found and proved the conditions under which this principle is true. Thus he refined Schubert's work and also advanced it through the theory of the base and the theory of characteristics.

Twenty years later this research by Severi inspired several mathematicians, including William V. D. Hodge, Wei L. Chow, and Bartel van der

Waerden. Severi also introduced the important notion of the invariant order of an algebraic variety, which led to the theory of minimal models; and he studied improper double points of algebraic surfaces, characters of embedding of one variety in another, and generalizations of Bezout's theorem from intersections of plane curves to those of arbitrary varieties in higher projective spaces.

2. Series and Systems of Equivalence. This theory, created almost wholly by Severi, added to algebraic geometry many important entities, for example, the canonical varieties of arbitrary dimension—a theory (completed later by Beniamino Segre and J. A. Todd) that has had considerable connections and implications in both algebra and topology. He generalized the theory of linear equivalence to arbitrary subvarieties of a given variety and also made lengthy fundamental studies of rational equivalence, algebraic equivalence, and algebraic correspondences between varieties.

3. Geometry on Algebraic Surfaces. At the beginning of the twentieth century, the geometry of algebraic surfaces had reached a dead end. Although Castelnuovo and Enriques had defined the genera, irregularity, and plurigenera of surfaces and had characterized those surfaces that are birationally equivalent to a plane or to a ruled surface, there were still several unsolved problems; and Picard's introduction of three types of integrals on a surface suggested many additional questions, a large number of which were successfully explained by Severi. Also, Severi reduced Picard's three types of integrals to normal form and found conditions of integrability for certain linear differential equations on a surface.

Severi introduced the notion of semiexact differentials of the first type and, using Hodge's findings, surprisingly showed that they are always exact. An important property utilized in these investigations was the completeness of the characteristic series of a continuous complete system. Much effort was later required to establish this result in its correct generality.

4. Geometry on Algebraic Varieties. The extension from surfaces to varieties of three or more dimensions is no less difficult than that from curves to surfaces. In an early memoir (1909), Severi established the basis for the extended theory with his study of linear systems of hypersurfaces. He gave various definitions of the arithmetic genus of a variety and proved their equivalence, thus partially extending the Riemann-Roch theorem and also Picard's theorem on the regularity of the adjoint.

Besides his work on the foundations of the general theory of algebraic varieties, Severi established the theory of irregularity and made important studies of continuous systems of curves in the plane and in higher projective spaces.

5. Abelian and Quasi-Abelian Varieties. The theory of Abelian varieties V_p, of dimension p, originated in 1889 with Picard, who investigated algebraic V_p possessing a continuous, transitive, Abelian group of ∞^p birational automorphisms. The infinitesimal transformations of the group led to p independent integrals. Picard maintained that these integrals were all of the first type, but Severi showed that this is not true for $p = 2$ if the group is not absolutely transitive.

The study of these V_p is connected with that of a particular type of functions of several complex variables—a generalization of elliptic functions. These functions are related to particular varieties, called Picard and Albanese varieties, to which Severi devoted several works. When the group of the V_p is transitive, but not necessarily absolutely transitive, V_p is called quasi-Abelian. Severi discussed these V_p in a lengthy paper written during the turbulent period October 1944–May 1945.

Algebraic geometry has undergone several revolutionary changes in the twentieth century that have led to many schools and to several widely differing methods of approach. Severi's work remains not merely a monument to him but also a valuable source from which all algebraic geometers continue to draw ideas. He himself characterized his approach to mathematical research with the following admonition:

> Let us not pride ourselves too much on perfect rigour, which we today believe to be capable of reducing so large a part of mathematics to nothing, and let us not discard what does not appear quite as rigorous, for tomorrow we will certainly find imperfections in our perfection and from some brilliant, intuitive thought which had not yet the blessing of rigour will be drawn unthinkable results [Severi, "Intuizionismo e astrattismo nella matematica contemporanea," in *Atti del congresso. Unione matematica italiana* (Sept. 1948), p. 30].

BIBLIOGRAPHY

I. ORIGINAL WORKS. Severi's works include *Vorlesungen über algebraische Geometrie*, L. Löffler, ed. and trans. (Leipzig, 1921; repr., New York–London, 1968); "Geometria delle serie lineari," in *Trattato di geometria algebrica*, 1, pt. 1 (1926), 145–169; *Serie, sistemi d'equivalenza e corrispondenze algebriche sulle varietà algebriche*, F. Conforto and E. Martinelli, eds. (Rome, 1942); *Funzioni quasi abeliane* (Vatican City, 1947); *Memorie scelte*, B. Segre, ed. (Bologna, 1950);

Geometria dei sistemi algebrici sopra una superficie e sopra una varietà algebrica, II (Rome, 1957), III (Rome, 1959); and *Il teorema di Rimann-Roch per curve, superficie e varietà* (Berlin, 1958). Severi's mathematical papers, collected in seven volumes, will soon be published by the Lincei Academy (vols. I and II have already appeared in 1971 and 1974).

II. SECONDARY LITERATURE. On Severi and his work, see B. Segre, *L'opera scientifica di Francesco Severi* (Rome, 1962), with complete bibliography.

BENIAMINO SEGRE

SEZAWA, KATSUTADA (*b.* Yamaguchi, Japan, 21 August 1895; *d.* Tokyo, Japan, 23 April 1944)

The son of a judge, Sezawa entered the Imperial University of Tokyo in 1918 and graduated as a shipbuilding engineer in 1921. He was then appointed assistant professor of engineering at the university and became a full professor in 1928. He first worked on problems of shipbuilding engineering and of vibration, in which he acquired a considerable reputation. In 1925 he started a lifelong association with the Earthquake Research Institute of the university, becoming its director in 1943. In 1932 he visited Britain, Germany, and the United States to further his studies in theoretical seismology, the field in which he is now best known. Sezawa was associated with many Japanese research organizations, including the Seismological Society of Japan, the Aeronautical Research Institute, and the Aviation Council. During World War II his responsibilities were greatly extended: he was supervisor of research projects at the Admiralty and a member of the Air Force Weapons Research Committee and was closely connected with army research.

When Sezawa began his research career, the new science of seismology presented challenging problems requiring sophisticated mathematical analysis. Sezawa's pioneering work on many of these problems provided the basis for important later developments both in Japan and elsewhere, and his mathematical ability was a significant factor in raising the world standard of seismological research. Much of this work was carried out in collaboration with his brilliant former pupil Kiyoshi Kanai.

Sezawa is particularly noted for his contributions to the theory of seismic surface waves, one of the main wave types generated by earthquakes. These waves tend to become increasingly regular in form as they move away from an earthquake source. Mathematical analysis of this property throws light on the structure of the outer part of the earth. By this means Sezawa derived useful estimates of layering in the earth's crust and produced evidence indicating that the Pacific crust is thinner than the Eurasian. More profoundly, his work pointed the way to important developments of the existing mathematical theory of seismic surface waves.

Sezawa produced a body of theory important to such seismological problems as seiches in lakes and tsunami (seismic sea waves) generated by large earthquakes, and the mechanism of earthquake generation. He applied his earlier studies of vibration theory to the problems of vibrations excited in buildings and bridges by strong earthquakes, contributed to the theory of designing structures to withstand earthquakes, and participated in related experimental work.

Although he was often unwell, Sezawa drove himself hard and lived very austerely. His health deteriorated seriously during the war, and he died at the age of forty-eight. The Imperial Academy of Sciences of Japan awarded him its highest honor, the Imperial Order of Merit, in 1931 and elected him a member in 1943.

BIBLIOGRAPHY

Most of Sezawa's 140 research papers on seismology and earthquake engineering were published as *Bulletins* of the Earthquake Research Institute of Tokyo Imperial University. Forty-six of his more important papers are listed in W. M. Ewing, W. S. Jardetzky, and F. Press, *Elastic Waves in Layered Media* (New York, 1957). He also wrote 50 papers on aeronautics, published in *Reports of the Aeronautical Research Institute, Tokyo University*; and 20 papers on ship construction, published as Reports of the Society of Naval Architecture of Japan.

An obituary was published in Japanese in *Jishin,* **16,** no. 5 (May 1944), 1–2.

K. E. BULLEN

SHANKS, WILLIAM (*b.* Corsenside, Northumberland, England, 25 January 1812; *d.* Houghton-le-Spring, Durham, England, 1882)

Shanks's contributions to mathematics lie entirely in the field of computation, in which he was influenced by William Rutherford of Edinburgh. From 1847 his life was spent in Houghton-le-Spring, a small town in the coal-mining area of County Durham. There he kept a boarding school, and carried out his laborious and generally reliable calculations, most of which concerned the constant π, the ratio of the circumference of a circle to its diameter.

Modern methods for the calculation of π rely mainly on the formula

$$\text{arc tan } x = x - \frac{x^3}{3} + \frac{x^5}{5} - \cdots,$$

discovered independently by James Gregory (1670) and Leibniz (1673). With $x = 1$ it yields

$$\frac{1}{4}\pi = 1 - \frac{1}{3} + \frac{1}{5} - \cdots;$$

but the series converges too slowly to be of use, and more rapid processes may be obtained by using the Gregory series in formulas derived from the addition theorem

$$\text{arc tan } x + \text{arc tan } y = \text{arc tan } \{(x+y)/(1-xy)\}.$$

By repeated application of this theorem, John Machin (1706) found the convenient formula

$$\frac{1}{4}\pi = 4 \text{ arc tan } \left(\frac{1}{5}\right) - \text{arc tan } \left(\frac{1}{239}\right),$$

and calculated π to 100 decimal places.

This and similar formulas encouraged more extended calculations: here it is enough to note that in 1853 Rutherford gave 440 decimal places; and in the same year Shanks, in conjunction with Rutherford, gave 530 places, which proved to be his most accurate value. Also in 1853 Shanks gave 607 places, and the value to 500 places was independently checked. Some errors were corrected in 1873; and by that year Shanks, using Machin's formula, carried his calculations to 707 decimal places. There the matter rested for a considerable period. Subsidiary calculations provided the natural logarithms of 2, 3, 5, 10 to 137 decimal places and the values of 2^n, with $n = 12m + 1$ for $m = 1, 2, \cdots, 60$. Shanks also computed the value of e and of Euler's constant γ to a great many decimal places, and prepared a table of the prime numbers less than 60,000.

In 1944 D. F. Ferguson of the Royal Naval College, Dartmouth, attracted by the formula

$$\frac{1}{4}\pi = 3 \text{ arc tan } \left(\frac{1}{4}\right) + \text{arc tan } \left(\frac{1}{20}\right) + \text{arc tan } \left(\frac{1}{1985}\right),$$

proceeded to calculate π and compare his value with that given by Shanks. At the 528th decimal place there was a disagreement that was not reduced when Ferguson rechecked his own work, which he eventually carried to 710 decimal places. This discrepancy was communicated to R. C. Archibald, editor of *Mathematical Tables and Aids to Computation,* who suggested to J. W. Wrench,

Jr., and L. B. Smith that they might recalculate π by Machin's formula; their value, to 808 decimal places, confirmed Ferguson's result and his identification of two terms omitted by Shanks, which had caused the latter's errors. Modern computing machinery has carried the calculation of π to great lengths: in 1949 the first such determination, by ENIAC, went to 2,000 decimal places; by 1960 at least 100,000 places were known.

BIBLIOGRAPHY

I. ORIGINAL WORKS. Shanks's book was *Contributions to Mathematics, Comprising Chiefly the Rectification of the Circle* . . . (London–Cambridge–Durham, 1853). His papers are listed in Royal Society *Catalogue of Scientific Papers,* V, 672; VIII, 941; and XI, 401; and include nine memoirs published in *Proceedings of the Royal Society,* **6–22** (1854–1874).

II. SECONDARY LITERATURE. Poggendorff mentions Shanks briefly, in III, 1241; but his reference in IV, 1390, to an obituary by J. C. Hoffmann in *Zeitschrift für mathematischen und naturwissenschaftlichen Unterricht,* **26** (1895), is misleading; this item merely reproduces Shanks's 1873 figures, with a little comment. Local sources could supply only the information that Shanks kept a school. A. Fletcher, J. C. P. Miller, and L. Rosenhead, *An Index of Mathematical Tables,* 2nd ed. (London, 1962), gives full bibliographical details and critical notes. A concise history of the evaluation of π is given by E. W. Hobson, *Squaring the Circle* (London, 1913; repr. 1953).

Ferguson's two notes on his evaluation of π are in *Mathematical Gazette,* no. 289 (May 1946), 89–90; and no. 298 (Feb. 1948), 37. A note by R. C. Archibald, J. W. Wrench, Jr., L. B. Smith, and D. F. Ferguson, in *Mathematical Tables and Other Aids to Computation,* **2** (Apr. 1947), gives agreed figures (as in Ferguson's second note) and adds some details.

T. A. A. BROADBENT

SHATUNOVSKY, SAMUIL OSIPOVICH (*b.* Znamenka, Melitopol district, Tavricheskaya guberniya, Russia, 25 March 1859; *d.* Odessa, U.S.S.R., 27 March 1929)

Shatunovsky was the ninth child in the family of an impoverished artisan. In 1877 he graduated from a technological high school in Kherson and the following year completed a specialized supplementary course at Rostov. He then studied for a short time at the Technological College and the College of Transport in St. Petersburg. Shatunovsky, however, was interested in mathematics rather than technology; instead of following the curriculum at the college, he attended the lectures of Chebyshev and his disciples at St. Petersburg University. Unable to enroll at the university (he did not have the prerequisite diploma from a classical high school), Shatunovsky attempted to acquire a higher mathematical education in Switzerland. In 1887 lack of money forced him to return to Russia, where he was a private teacher in small towns in the south. One of his works that was sent to Odessa was well received by local mathematicians, who invited him to move there. He was elected a member (1897) and secretary (1898) of the mathematical department of the Novorossysky (Odessa) Society of Natural Scientists, and for some time taught school. In 1905 Shatunovsky passed the examinations for the master's degree and became assistant professor at Novorossysky (Odessa) University, where he worked until his death, becoming professor in 1920. In 1906–1920 he also taught at the Women's School for Higher Education.

Shatunovsky's principal works concern the foundations of mathematics. Independently of Hilbert he elaborated an axiomatic theory of the measurement of areas of rectilinear figures and reported on the subject to the Society of Natural Scientists in Odessa (1897) and at the Tenth Congress of the All-Russian Society of Natural Scientists and Physicians (1898). Publication of Hilbert's *Die Grundlagen der Geometrie* (1899) probably kept Shatunovsky from stating his theory, which was almost identical with Hilbert's, in print. From 1898 to 1902 Shatunovsky developed his theory for measuring the volumes of polyhedrons. In his theory of areas the principal concept is that of the invariant of one triangle (the product of base times corresponding height), and in the theory of volumes the principal notion is the invariant of the tetrahedron (the product of the area of some face times corresponding height). These studies led Shatunovsky to an axiomatic general theory of scalar quantities.

From 1906 Shatunovsky taught introduction to analysis; his lectures contain an original description of the theory of sets and functions, particularly of the definition of irrational and real numbers. The generalization of the concept of limit suggested in them is close to that introduced by E. H. Moore in 1915 ("Definition of Limit in General Integral Analysis," in *Proceedings of the National Academy of Sciences* [1915], no. 12). For a long time Shatunovsky's *Vvedenie v analiz* could be obtained only as a lithograph (Odessa, 1906–1907), however, and was not printed until 1923.

In a report to the Society of Natural Scientists in Odessa (1901), Shatunovsky critically approached the problem of applying the logical law of the excluded third to the elements of infinite sets. He discussed the subject in print in the introduction to his master's thesis, published in 1917. Pointing out the logical inadmissibility of the purely formal use of the logical law of the excluded third, the applicability of which needs special verification every time, Shatunovsky did not reach conclusions as radical as those presented by L. E. J. Brouwer in his works on intuitionism. Shatunovsky's thesis contains a new construction of Galois's theory that does not presuppose the existence of the roots of algebraic equations, which is demonstrated only in the final part of this work.

Shatunovsky also wrote articles and books on elementary mathematics. In them, for example, he stated a general principle for solving trigonometrical problems and a classification of problems connected with this principle.

BIBLIOGRAPHY

I. ORIGINAL WORKS. Shatunovsky's writings include "Ob izmerenii obemov mnogogrannikov" ("On the Measurement of Volumes of Polyhedrons"), in *Vestnik opytnoi fiziki i elementarnoi matematiki* (1902), 82–87, 104–108, 127–132, 149–155; "Über den Rauminhalt der Polyeder," in *Mathematische Annalen*, 57 (1903), 496–508; "O postulatakh lezhashchikh v osnovanii ponyatia o velichine" ("On the Basic Postulates of the Concept of Quantity"), in *Zapiski Matematicheskago otdeleniya Novorossiiskago obshchestva estestvoispytatelei*, 26 (1904); *Algebra kak uchenie o sravnenyakh po funktsionalnym modulyam* ("Algebra as the Theory of Congruences With Respect to the Functional Modulus"; Odessa, 1917); *Vvedenie v analiz* ("Introduction to Analysis"; Odessa, 1923); and *Metody reshenia zadach pryamolineynoy trigonometrii* ("Methods of Solving Problems in Rectilinear Trigonometry"; Moscow, 1929).

II. SECONDARY LITERATURE. See E. Y. Bakhmutskaya, "O rannikh rabotakh Shatunovskogo po osnovaniam matematiki" ("On Shatunovsky's First Research on the Foundations of Mathematics"), in *Istoriko–matematicheskie issledovaniya*, 16 (1965), 207–216; N. G. Chebotarev, "Samuil Osipovich Shatunovsky," in *Uspekhi matematicheskikh nauk*, 7 (1940), 316–321; V. F. Kagan, "S. O. Shatunovsky," in Shatunovsky's *Metody . . . trigonometrii* (above); and "Etudy po osnovaniam geometrii" ("Essays on the Foundations of Geometry"), in *Vestnik opytnoi fiziki i elementarnoi matematiki*, (1901), 286–292, also in Kagan's book *Ocherki po geometrii* ("Geometrical Essays"; Moscow, 1963), 147–154; *Matematika v SSSR za tridtsat let* ("Mathematics in the U.S.S.R. for Thirty Years"; Moscow–Leningrad, 1948), see index; F. A. Medvedev, "O formirovanii ponyatia obobshchennogo predela" ("On the Development of the Concept of the Generalized Limit"), in *Trudy Instituta istorii estestvoznaniya i tekhniki. Akademiya nauk SSSR*, **34** (1960), 299–322; *Nauka v SSSR za pyatnadtsat let. Matematika* ("Science in the U.S.S.R. During Fifteen Years. Mathematics"; Moscow–Leningrad, 1932), see index; J. Z. Shtokalo, ed., *Istoria otechestvennoy matematiki*, 4 vols. ("A History of [Russian] Mathematics"; Kiev, 1966–1970), see index; and A. P. Youschkevitch, *Istoria matematiki v Rossii do 1917 goda* ("History of Mathematics in Russia Until 1917"; Moscow, 1968), see index.

A. P. YOUSCHKEVITCH
A. T. GRIGORIAN

SHEN KUA[1] (*b.* 1031, registered at Ch'ien-t'ang[2] [now Hangchow, Chekiang province], China; *d.* Ching-k'ou, Jun prefecture[3] [now Chinkiang, Kiangsu province], China, 1095)

Shen was the son of Shen Chou[4] (*ca.* 978–1052) and his wife, whose maiden name was Hsu.[5] Shen Chou came of a gentry family with neither large landholdings nor an unbroken tradition of civil service. He spent his life in minor provincial posts, with several years in the capital judiciary. Shen Kua apparently received his early education from his mother. A native of Soochow (the region of which was known for its flourishing manufactures, commerce, and agriculture), she was forty-four or forty-five years old when he was born. Shen's background made possible his entry into the imperial bureaucracy, the only, conventional road to advancement for educated people of his time. Unlike colleagues who came from the ancient great clans, he could count on few advantages save those earned by his striving and the full use of his intellectual talents. Shortly after he was assigned to the court, he became a confidant of the emperor and played a brilliant part in resolving the crises of the time. But within slightly over a decade his career in the capital was ended by impeachment. After a provincial appointment and five years of meritorious military accomplishment, he was doubly disgraced and politically burned out. The extremes of Shen's career and the shaping of his experience and achievement in science and technology become comprehensible only if the pivotal circumstances of his time are first considered.

Historical Background. Shen's time was in many senses the climax of a major transition in the Chinese polity, society, and economy.

Three centuries earlier the center of gravity in all these respects still lay in the north, the old center of civilization of the Han people. Wealth and power rested in the hands of the old aristocratic landowning families. Governmental institutions incorporated the tension between their private interests and the inevitable desire of their foremost peer, the emperor, to concentrate authority. The civil service examination system was beginning to give the central government a means to shape a uniform education for its future officials; but since birth or local recommendation determined who was tested, the mass of commoners remained uninvolved. The social ideals prevalent among the elite were static; the ideal past was cited to discourage innovation; and the moral example of those who ruled, rather than responsive institutions or prescriptive law, was held to be the key to the healthy state. The classicist's paradigm of a two-class society—self-sufficient agriculturalists ruled and civilized by humane generalists, with land as the only true wealth—did not encourage commerce, industry, or the exploitation of natural resources. The wants of the great families, whose civil servant members were becoming city dwellers by the middle of the eighth century, nonetheless gave momentum to all of these activities; but the majority of the population still took no part in the rudimentary money economy.

The T'ang order began a long, slow collapse about 750, until in the first half of the tenth century the empire of "All Under Heaven" was reduced to a succession of ephemeral and competing kingdoms. When the universal state was reconstructed in the Northern Sung (960–1126), its foundations were in many important respects different from those of the early T'ang. A new dynasty was not only, as classical monarchic theory had it, a fresh dispensation of the cosmos; it was also the occasion for institutionalizing a new distribution of power in society. The cumulative result of changes in taxation had been to make the old families accountable for their estates as they had not been earlier, and to encourage smaller landholdings—and, thus, a wider diffusion of wealth.

The center of vitality had moved southeast to the lower Yangtze valley, which had long before emerged as the major rice-yielding region. By this time its fertility, combined with its relative freedom from restrictive social arrangements, had bred a new subculture that was more productive in industry than elsewhere and hospitable to the growth of commerce and stable markets, the beginnings of a uniform money economy, and the great broadening of education that printing had just made possible. The new southern elite was, on the whole, small gentry, and lacked the military traditions of the ancient northern clans and of power holders in the period of disunion. Their families were often too involved in trade for them to despise it. Although conservative, as all Chinese elites have been, they were prepared to think of change as a useful tool. The novelties of attitude and value were often slighter or subtler than such a brief account can convey, but within the established limits of Chinese social ideals their consequences were very considerable.

In Shen Kua's time the old families still provided many of the very highest officials and thus wielded great influence, positive or obstructive, in discussions about the future of China. But they had become merely influential members of a new political constellation that brought a variety of convictions and interests to that perennial debate. An especially obvious new element was that many southern small gentry families like Shen's established traditions of civil service, either as a main means of support or to protect and further their other concerns. Once a family's social standing was achieved, one or more members could enter the bureaucracy freely because of experience as subordinates in local administration or because they were amply prepared by education for the examinations. Their sons could enter still more freely because special access to both direct appointment and examination was provided to offspring of officials.

Not sharing the old vision of a virtue-dominated social order fixed by precedent, men of the new elite were willing to sponsor institutional renovation in order to cope directly with contemporary problems. Dependent on their own talents and often needing their salaries, they were dedicated to building a rational, systematic, and in most respects more centrally oriented administration. They were willing to make law an instrument of policy, and insisted that local officials be rated not only on the moral example they set but also quantitatively—on how effectively they made land arable and collected taxes. In the name of efficiency they devoted themselves to removing customary curbs on imperial authority and (with only partial success in the Sung) to dismantling the structures of privilege that underlay regional autonomy. Only later would it become clear that they were completing the metamorphosis of the emperor from paramount aristocrat to autocrat. At the same time they were successfully demanding more policy-making authority as the emperor's surrogates, although at the cost to themselves of greater conformity than officials of the old type had willingly accepted.

This irreversible transition did not lead to a modern state, but only to a new and ultimately stagnant pattern. The most accelerated phase of change was the activity of what is called the New Policies[6] group (actually a shifting coalition) between 1069 and 1085. Its leader, Wang An-shih[7] (1021–1086), was brought to the capital in 1068 by the young emperor Shen-tsung, who had just taken the throne. Within two years Wang had become first privy councillor. He resigned for nine months in 1074, when pressure from his antagonists persuaded the emperor to be less permissive, and returned permanently to private life in 1076. The New Policies continued to be applied and extended, but with less and less attention to their founding principles, until Shen-tsung's death in 1085. Under the regency of the empress dowager, enemies of the reform attempted for eight years to extirpate Wang's influence and take revenge upon his adherents. When Emperor Che-tsung came of age in 1093, the New Policies were revived, but were so bent toward selfish ends and administered so disastrously that the word "reform" is hardly applicable.

Wang An-shih's opponents were many: the old aristocrats, career bureaucrats of the sort who would oppose any change as disruptive, officials whose individual or group interests ran in other directions —and men of high ideals who found his proposals ill-advised and his personal style too intolerant.*

No institution had evolved through Chinese history to work out and resolve conflicts of political viewpoint. This lack was filled by cliques, intrigues, and appeals to imperial intervention. Division and corruption among active supporters of the New Policies also had been a problem from the start. The scope of Wang's program was so large that he had to take competent support where he found it. The new access to power that he offered attracted ambitious men, many of whom had little real sympathy for his convictions and dedicated themselves primarily to manipulation and graft.

*In the successive reform movements of the Northern Sung there were considerable differences in the alignment of men with different beliefs and backgrounds. See the discussion in James T. C. Liu, "An Early Sung Reformer: Fan Chung-yen," in John K. Fairbank, ed., *Chinese Thought and Institutions* (Chicago, 1957), 105–131, esp. 107–109. The generalizations of the present article and of current scholarship as a whole are crude and tentative, pending the "comparative analysis of the interrelationships between ideology and family, class, status-group, and regional interests" that Robert M. Hartwell has called for in "Historical Analogism, Public Policy, and Social Science in Eleventh- and Twelfth-Century China," in *American Historical Review*, **76** (1971), 690–727.

Once Wang was gone, the leadership of his group tended to become a battleground for aspirations of this kind. The internal and external enemies of the New Policies left the program a shambles by the time the Chin Tartars drove the Sung south in 1127.

A primary aim of the reforms was financial security of the state, which prompted initiatives in water control and land reclamation, encouragement of extractive industries and agriculture, intervention in commerce, and rationalization of taxes. Another goal, particularly at the emperor's insistence, was military strength. There had been a long confrontation between the Chinese and the powerful Khitan empire, pastoral masters of mounted combat to the north (renamed Liao in 1066). Seventy years of fitful peace were punctuated by humiliating Chinese failures to recapture territory south of the Great Wall and maintained by large annual bribes. For three decades the Tangut people of the northwest had posed an almost equally unpalatable demand for appeasement. Victory or détente through strength, the emperor hoped, could be bought on both fronts with the wealth that the New Policies generated from man's exploitation of nature. Here too expertise was needed in cartography, strategic theory and tactical doctrine (both of which contained cosmological elements), design and manufacture of war matériel, fortification, troop organization and training, and development of a stable economy in border regions.

Shen Kua contributed to nearly every field of New Policies activity, both civil and military. His social background and political commitments cannot be considered responsible for his scientific talent or curiosity; the antecedents and loyalties of other major contemporary scientific figures were very different from his. But a review of his career and of his work will show how regularly his involvement with particular technical themes and problems grew out of his activities in government.

Life. From about 1040 Shen traveled with his father to successive official posts from Szechwan in the west to the international port of Amoy. He was exposed not only to the geographical diversity of China but also to the broad range of technical and managerial problems—public works, finance, improvement of agriculture, maintenance of waterways—that were among the universal responsibilities of local administrators. Because his physical constitution was weak, he became interested in medicine at an early age.

Late in 1051, when Shen was twenty, his father died. As soon as the customary inactivity of the mourning period ended in 1054, Shen received the first of a series of minor local posts; his father's service exempted him from the prefectural examination. His planning ability became almost immediately apparent when he designed and superintended a drainage and embankment system that reclaimed some hundred thousand acres of swampland for agriculture. This was the first of a series of projects that established his reputation for skill in water control. In 1061, as a subprefect in Ning-kuo[8] (now Fu-hu,[9] Anhwei province), after a cartographic survey and a historical study of previous earthworks in the region, he applied the labor of fourteen thousand people to another massive land reclamation scheme that won the recognition of the emperor. In a series of floods four years later, Shen noted, it was the only such project not overwhelmed. He wrote characteristically that in the first year it returned the cost of the grain used, and that there was more than a tenfold profit on cash expended. In 1063 he passed the national examinations. Posted to Yangchow, he impressed the fiscal intendant (a post then equivalent to governor), Chang Ch'u[10] (1015–1080), who recommended him for a court appointment leading to a career in the professional financial administration.*

Shen apparently used the time not occupied by his early metropolitan appointments, which were conventional and undemanding, to study astronomy. In reply to the informal questions of a superior he set down clear explanations, still extant, of the sphericity of the sun and moon as proved by lunar phases, of eclipse limits, and of the retrogradation of the lunar nodes. They demonstrate an exceptional ability to visualize motions in space, which were at best implicit in the numerical procedures of traditional astronomy and seldom were discussed in technical writing. In 1072 Shen was given an additional appointment as director of the Astronomical Bureau. With the collaboration of his remarkable commoner protégé Wei P'u[11] and the aid of other scholarly amateurs, using books gathered from all over the country, he undertook a major calendar reform. He planned an ambitious series of daily observations to extend over five years, using renovated and redesigned instruments. When he took office, the bureau was staffed with incompetents. He forced the dismissal of six whom he caught falsifying records of phenomena, but the obstruction of those who remained doomed his

---

*The succession of fiscal posts that often led to a seat on the Council of State in the eleventh century has been documented by Robert M. Hartwell in "Financial Expertise, Examinations, and the Formulation of Economic Policy in Northern Sung China," in *Journal of Asian Studies*, **30**, 281–314.

program of observations and kept his new system of ephemerides computation from being among the two or three most securely founded before modern times. Shen's personal involvement in later stages of the reform undoubtedly was limited by his gradual movement into the vortex of factional politics.

Shen was early known to Wang An-shih, who composed his father's epitaph while a young provincial official; Shen eventually came to be publicly identified by enemies of the New Policies as among the eighteen members of Wang's intimate clique. In late 1072, in support of Wang's program, Shen surveyed the silting of the Pien Canal near the capital by an original technique, dredged it, and demonstrated the value of the silt as fertilizer. Until mid-1075 he spent much time traveling as a troubleshooter of sorts, inspecting and reporting on water control projects, military preparations, and local administrations—and, it has been conjectured, providing encouragement to Wang's provincial supporters. Shen was put in charge of arsenal activities and, in 1075, was sponsored by Wang (then head of government) to revise defensive military tactics, a task the throne had proposed for Wang himself.

In 1074 the Khitan were pressing negotiations to move their borders further south. Incompetent and timorous Chinese negotiators were conceding unfounded Liao assertions about the language and substance of previous agreements. Shen built a solid Chinese case by going to the archives, as no one had bothered to do before. His embassy in mid-1075 to the camp of the Khitan monarch on Mt. Yung-an[12] (near modern P'ing-ch'üan,[13] Hopei) was triumphant. He described himself surrounded by a thousand hostile onlookers, calling on his staff, who had memorized the old documents of the Khitan themselves, to cite without pause or flurry the exact reference to refute one historical claim after another.

Shen returned to China—with biological specimens and maps of the territories he had passed through—to become a Han-lin academician, to be given charge of a large-scale water control survey in the Yangtze region, and then to become head of the Finance Commission. While in this very powerful position he untangled a variety of contradictory policies, producing in the process some of the most penetrating writings before modern times on the operation and regulation of supply and demand, on methods of forecasting prices in order to intervene effectively in the market, and on factors that affect the supply of currency (varying through hoarding, counterfeiting, and melting) as

the value of the metal in it fluctuates about its controlled monetary value. In the autumn of 1077, just as his revision of critical fiscal measures was well launched, he was impeached by the corrupt and vindictive censor Ts'ai Ch'üeh[14] (1036–1093). The charge was that Shen had opposed a New Policies taxation measure in an underhanded, inconsistent, and improper way. It was credited by historians for centuries, but its truth has been refuted in every detail by recent Chinese research. His protector Wang An-shih had just left government; it is believed, given the mood of the time, that by threatening an established budget item in order to ease the burdens of the poor, Shen became an easy victim of factional maneuvering.

The emperor was not only the ritual synapse between the political and natural orders; he was a human being whose likes and dislikes were indulged within broad limits that could be further widened by force of his personal charisma and will. The closer to him an official penetrated, the more achievement and even survival became subject to imperial whim and the intrigue of colleagues. Although the record is fragmentary, it gives the impression that Shen Kua was maneuvered by Wang An-shih into the proximity of the throne because of his brilliance, judgment, and effectiveness at complicated tasks. Nothing indicates that he was adept at protecting himself. He attracted the most damaging animosity not from opponents of the New Policies but from designing members of his coalition. Once the emperor qualified his support of the New Policies in 1074, the risk of debacle remained great and imminent. Many officials who had risen with Wang fought furiously for the power that would keep them afloat even though the program sank. They did not wish to be deterred by a colleague who judged issues on their own merits. They probably also felt, as others did, that a man of Shen's age and rank did not deserve the emperor's confidence.

Ts'ai Ch'üeh was rising into the vacuum that Wang's retirement had left. The emperor depended increasingly on Ts'ai's monetary counsel and could not easily disregard what he insisted upon. For three years it was impossible to overcome his objections and those of another censor, and to rehabilitate Shen. Finally Shen was sent to Yen-chou[15] (now Yenan, Shensi province), on the necessary route for military operations by or against the Tanguts, as commissioner for prefectural civil and military affairs.[16] The Tanguts were then divided and weakened, minor Chinese conquests around 1070 had set the stage for a war, and the treasury had ample funds. Shen played an important part in organizing and fortifying for the victorious offensive of the autumn of 1081. In extending Sung control he showed a practical as well as a theoretical mastery of the art of warfare. He was cited for merit and given several honorary appointments. It was probably at the same time that he was ennobled as state foundation viscount.[17] In his sixteen months at Yen-chou, Shen received 273 personal letters from the emperor. His standing at the court was in principle reestablished. Whether he had become shrewd enough to survive there was never tested.

Shen and a colleague followed up the victory by proposing fortifications to close another important region to the Tanguts. The emperor referred the matter to an ambitious and arrogant official who, ignoring the proposal, changed the plan to provide defenses for what Shen argued was an indefensible and strategically useless location. Shen was commanded to leave the vicinity of the new citadel so as not to share in the credit for the anticipated victory. When the Tangut attack came, the emissary's force was decimated while Shen, with imperial permission, was successfully defending a key town on the enemy invasion route to Yen-chou. The campaign thus provided the Tanguts with no opening for advance—but Ts'ai Ch'üeh was now a privy councillor. As titular military commander Shen was held responsible for the defeat and considerable loss of life. At the age of fifty-one his career was over. The towns he saved were later abandoned by the anti–New Policies regime to no advantage, just as the lands he had saved from the Khitan through diplomacy had since been lost by another negotiator.

Shen spent six years in fixed probationary residence, forbidden to engage in official matters. He used at least two of these years to complete a great imperially commissioned atlas of all territory then under Chinese control. He had been working on this atlas intermittently since, as finance commissioner a decade earlier, he had had access to court documents. His reward included the privilege of living where he chose.

Ten years earlier Shen had bought, sight unseen, a garden estate on the outskirts of Ching-k'ou. In 1086, visiting it for the first time, he recognized it as a landscape of poignant beauty that he had seen repeatedly in dreams, and named it Dream Brook (*Meng ch'i*,[18] alternately read *Meng hsi*). He moved there in 1088. Despite a pardon and the award of sinecures to support him in his old age, he spent seven years of leisure, isolation, and illness until his death there.*

Shen's writings, of which only a few are extant even in part, include commentaries on Confucian classics, two atlases, reports on his diplomatic missions, a collection of literary works, and monographs on rituals, music, mathematical harmonics, administration, mathematical astronomy, astronomical instruments, defensive tactics and fortification, painting, tea, medicine, and poetry. Of three books compiled during his last years at Dream Brook, one, "Good Prescriptions" (*Liang fang*[19]), was devoted to medical therapy, theory, and philology; the other two belong to particularly Chinese genres. "Record of Longings Forgotten" (*Wang huai lu*[20]), a collection of notes on the life of the gentleman farmer in the mountains, contains useful information on implements and agricultural technique and, unlike more conventional agricultural treatises up to that time, on the culture of medicinal plants.

"Brush Talks From Dream Brook" (*Meng ch'i pi t'an*[21]) and its sequels, extant and well-edited in modern times, is by any reckoning one of the most remarkable documents of early science and technology. It is a collection of about six hundred recollections and observations, ranging from one or two sentences to about a page of modern print— "because I had only my writing brush and ink slab to converse with, I call it Brush Talks." They are loosely grouped under topics (seventeen in all current versions), of which seven contain considerable matter of interest in the study of nature and man's use of it: "Regularities Underlying the Phenomena"[22] (mostly astronomy, astrology, cosmology, divination), "Technical Skills"[23] (mathematics and its applications, technology, medicine), "Philology"[24] (including etymology and meanings of technical terms), "Strange Occurrences"[25] (incorporating various natural observations), "Artifacts and Implements"[26] (techniques reflected in ancient objects), "Miscellaneous Notes"[27] (greatly overlapping other sections), and "Deliberations on Materia Medica"[28] (most of it on untangling historic and regional confusions in identities of medical substances).

Notices of the highest originality stand cheek by jowl with trivial didacticisms, court anecdotes, and ephemeral curiosities under all these rubrics; other sections were given to topics conventional in collections of jottings—memorable people, wisdom in emergencies, and so on. Shen's theoretical discussions of scientific topics employed the abstract

*For a translation that conveys the flavor of Shen's autobiography, see Donald Holzman, "Shen Kua," 275–276.

concepts of his time—yin-yang, the Five Phases (*wu-hsing*[29]), *ch'i*,[30] and so on. A large fraction of the book's contents is devoted to fate, divination, and portents, his belief in which has been ignored by historians seeking to identify in him the prototype of the modern scientist. The author of "Brush Talks" has been compared with Leibniz; and in an era of happier relations with the Soviet Union, Hu Tao-ching, the foremost authority on Shen, referred to him as the Lomonosov of his day. But Shen was writing for gentlemen of universal curiosity and humanistic temperament; custom, wisdom, language, and oddity were as important themes as nature and artifice.

Because Shen's interests were multifarious, the record unsystematic, and its form too confining for anything but fragmentary insight, only accumulation can provide a fair impression of what constitutes his importance. What follows is the mere sample that space allows of his attempts to deepen the contemporary understanding of nature, his observations that directed the attention of his educated contemporaries to important phenomena or processes, and his own technical accomplishments. They are grouped to bring out contiguity of subject matter without interposing the radically different disciplinary divisions of modern science. These samples will become the basis of discussion—which, given the state of research, must be highly tentative—of the epistemological underpinnings of Shen's work, and of the unity of his scientific thought with elements that today would be considered unscientific, primitive, or superstitious. Finally, it will be possible to evaluate Shen's life as a case study in the reconcilability of Confucianism and science, which the conventional wisdom among sinologists for over a generation has tended to place in opposition.

Quantity and Measure. Mathematics was not the queen of sciences in traditional China. It did not exist except as embodied in specific problems about the physical world. Abstract thought about numbers was always concerned with their qualities rather than their properties, and thus remained numerology. This art, although it blended into arithmetic, was only partly distinct from other symbolic means (in the anthropologist's sense: magical, ritual, religious, divinatory) for exploring the inherent patterns of nature and man's relation to it. Computation, on the other hand, was applied to a great variety of mensurational, accounting, and other everyday tasks of the administrator in a coherent tradition of textbooks. Occasionally curiosity and skill pushed beyond these pragmatic lim-

its, but never very far. Some of the problems that Shen presented in "Brush Talks" had no application, but his enthusiasm for them was in no way qualified.

In addition to this accumulation of individual problems there were two exact sciences, in which mathematics served theory to advance knowledge of the patterns underlying the phenomena. One was mathematical harmonics (*lü lü*[31]), which explored the relations between musical intervals and the dimensions of instruments that produced them, in ways analogous to the Pythagorean art. Its appeal was much the same in both China and Greece: it demonstrated how deeply the power of number was grounded in nature. For this reason in China mathematical harmonics was often put into the same category as mathematical astronomy, which also had foundations in metaphysics. Astronomy, by far the more technically sophisticated of the two exact sciences, was normally employed on behalf of the monarch. Unpredictable phenomena and failures of prediction were either good or bad omens. Bad omens were interpreted as warnings that the emperor's mediating virtue, which maintained concord between the cosmic and political orders, was deficient. Successful prediction of celestial events was symbolic preservation or enhancement of the charisma of the ruling dynasty.

The annual calendar (or almanac) issued by authority of the throne was thus of great ceremonial importance. It encompassed all predictable phenomena, including planetary phenomena and eclipses. The utilitarian calendrical aspects—lunar months and solar years—had long since been refined past any practical demand for accuracy, but astronomical reinforcement of the Mandate of Heaven called forth endless attempts at greater precision of constants. As it became conventional to institute a complete new system for computing these ephemerides when a new emperor was enthroned, technical novelty was at a premium. When new ideas were unavailable, trivial recasting of old techniques was usually substituted. Repeated failures of prediction were another motive for reform of the astronomical system. In such cases too the system was in principle replaced as a unit rather than repaired. Most systems survived or fell on their ability to predict eclipses, particularly solar eclipses. These were the least amenable of all celestial phenomena to the algebraic, nongeometric style of mathematics. Prior to Shen's time little effort had gone into predicting the apparent motions of the planets, which lacked the immediacy of solar and lunar phenomena. This was, in fact, an omission that Shen seems to have been the first to confront.

General Mathematics. As wood-block printing became widespread, the government used it to propagate carefully edited collections of important ancient textbooks for use in education. This was being done in medicine at the time Shen entered the capital bureaucracy. In 1084 a collection of ten mathematical manuals, made four centuries earlier and reconstituted as well as extant texts allowed, was printed. The authority of these projects served both to fix textual traditions, preserving selected treatises from further attrition, and passively to encourage the fading into oblivion of books left out. Shen thus lived at a pivotal period in the development of mathematics, and his judgments on lost techniques and disused technical terms (such as 300, 306) have played an important part in later attempts to interpret them.*
"Brush Talks" is also an essential source for the study of pre-Sung metrology, currency, and other subjects related to computation.

Shen used mathematics in the formulation of policy arguments more consistently than most of his colleagues; examples are his critique of military tactics in terms of space required for formations (579) and his computation that a campaign of thirty-one days is the longest that can feasibly be provisioned by human carriers (205). But of the computational methods discussed in his "Technical Skills" chapter, those not related to astronomy are almost all abstractly oriented.

This original bent emerges most clearly in two problems. One departs from earlier formulas for computing the frustum of a solid rectangular pyramid. Shen worked out the volume of the same figure if composed of stacked articles (he mentioned *go* pieces, bricks, wine vats) that leave interstices (301). Since Shen intended this "volume with interstices" (*ch'i chi*[32]) method to be applicable regardless of the shape of the objects stacked, what he gave is a correct formula for the number of objects, which are thus to be considered of unit volume. His presentation has several interesting features. Needham has suggested that the concern

with interstices (and, one would add, unit volumes) may have been a step in the direction of geometric exhaustion methods (III, 142–143)—although it was tentative and bore fruit only in seventeenth-century Japan. Second, instead of the worked-out problem with actual dimensions that is conventional in early textbooks, Shen simply gave a generalized formula: "double the lower length, add to the upper length, multiply by the lower width," and so on. Third, this was the earliest known case in China of a problem involving higher series. Built on earlier numerical approaches to arithmetical progressions, it provided a basis for more elaborate treatment by Yang Hui[33] (1261) and Chu Shih-chieh[34] (1303).

The second problem of interest was said "in a story" to have been solved by one of China's greatest astronomers, the Tantric Buddhist patriarch I-hsing[35] (682–727): the number of possible situations on a *go* board, with nineteen by nineteen intersections on which any number of black or white pieces may be placed. Whether I-hsing actually solved this problem we do not know; Shen's single paragraph was the first and last known discussion of permutations in traditional mathematics. It stated the order of magnitude of the answer—"approximately speaking one must write the character *wan*[36] (10,000) fifty-two times in succession"—adding exact answers for smaller arrays, three methods of solution, and a note on the limited traditional notation for very large numbers (304).*

Mathematical Harmonics. The Pythagoreans were fascinated by the relations of concordant intervals to the plucked strings that produced them, since the lengths between stops were proportionate to simple ratios of integers. The Chinese built up a similar science on a gamut of standard pipes. Beginning with a pipe eight inches long and 0.9 inch in diameter, they generated the lengths of subsequent pipes by multiplying the previous length alternately by 2/3 and 4/3, making twelve pipes within an approximate octave. The dozen were then related to such categories as the twelve divisions of the tropical year, in order to provide a cosmic basis for the system of modes that the pipes determined. A pentatonic scale, which could be used in any of the twelve modes, provided similar associations with the Five Phases. This basis was extended to metrology by defining the lengths and capacities of

---

*Numbers in parentheses are item numbers in the Hu Tao-ching edition of *Meng ch'i pi t'an* (the latter is referred to hereafter as "Brush Talks"). Roman volume numbers followed by page numbers refer to translations in Joseph Needham *et al.*, *Science and Civilisation in China.* Where my own understanding differs considerably from Needham's, an asterisk follows the page reference. All quotations below are from Shen, and all translations are my own. Full bibliographical data are given in the notes only for sources of too limited pertinence to be included in the bibliography. Chinese and Japanese family names precede personal names throughout this article.

*This was translated in part by Needham (III, 139). The extant text, even in Hu's edition, is very corrupt. It has been edited and considerably emended by Ch'ien Pao-tsung in *Sung Yuan shu-hsueh-shih lun-wen-chi,* 266–269.

the pipes in terms of millet grains of standard dimensions. Shen provided a lucid and concise explanation of these fundamentals of mathematical harmonics, and corrected grotesque complications that had crept into a canonic source through miscopying of numbers (143, 549). He also experimentally studied stringed instruments. By straddling strings with paper figures, he showed that strings tuned to the same notes on different instruments resonate, as do those tuned an octave apart on the same instrument (537; cf. IV.1, 130). His two chapters on music and harmonics[37] are also a trove of information on composition and performance.

Astronomy. Shen's major contributions in astronomy were his attempts to visualize celestial motions spatially, his arc-sagitta methods that for the first time moved algebraic techniques toward trigonometry, and his insistence on daily observational records as a basis for his calendar reform. The first had no direct application in computation of the ephemerides, although it may well have inspired (and at the same time have been inspired by) the second, which grew out of traditional mensurational arithmetic. It has been suggested that the clarity of Shen's cosmological explanations led to his appointment to the Astronomical Bureau, which provided opportunity for his contributions in the second and third areas. But circumstances that arose from the bureaucratic character of mathematical astronomy made these contributions futile in his lifetime.

Shen's discussions of solar, lunar, and eclipse phenomena (130–131; excerpts, III, 415–416) have been mentioned. By far the most remarkable of his cosmological hypotheses attempted to account for variations in the apparent planetary motions, including retrogradation. This concern is not to be taken for granted, since traditional astronomers preferred purely numerical approaches to prediction, unlike the spatial geometric models of Greek antiquity, and showed little interest in planetary problems. Noting that the greatest planetary anomaly occurred near the stationary points, Shen proposed a model in which the planet traced out a figure like a willow leaf attached at one side to the periphery of a circle (see Figure 1). The change in direction of the planet's motion with respect to the stars was explained by its travel along the pointed ends of the leaf (148).* The willow leaf, in other

*Translated by N. Sivin, *Cosmos and Computation in Early Chinese Mathematical Astronomy* (Leiden, 1969), also published in *T'oung Pao,* **55** (1969), 1–73 (see 71–73), from which the figure is reproduced with permission of E. J. Brill.

words, served one of the same functions that the epicycle served in Europe. It is characteristic that, having taken a tack that in the West was prompted entirely by geometric reasoning, Shen's first resort should have been a familiar physical object. Use of a pointed figure doubtless would not have survived a mathematical analysis of observational data, but this remained an offhand suggestion.

Another early outcome of Shen's service at the court was a series of proposals for the redesign of major astronomical instruments: the gnomon, which was still employed to measure the noon shadow and fix the solstices; the armillary sphere, with which angular measurements were made; and the clepsydra, used to determine the time of observations (and to regulate court activities). Shen's improved versions of the latter two apparently were not built until late 1073, after he had taken charge of the Astronomical Bureau. The armillary at least was discarded for a new one in 1082, a casualty of his personal disgrace.

Shen's clepsydra proposals represent a new design of the overflow-tank type (Needham's Type B; III, 315–319, 325), but the most significant outcome of his work on this instrument was a jotting on problems of calibration. Day and night were by custom separately divided into hours, the length of which varied with the season. The time was read off graduated float rods, day and night sets of which were changed twenty-four times a year. Shen pointed out that this crude and inadequate scheme amounted to linear interpolation, "treating the ecliptic as a polygon rather than a circle," and argued for the use of higher-order interpolation (128).

The best armillary sphere available in the central administration when Shen first worked there was based on a three-hundred-year-old design "and lacked ease of operation" (150). The most interesting of Shen's improvements was in the diameter of the naked-eye sighting tube. At least from the first millennium B.C. a succession of stars had been taken up and abandoned as the pole star. In the late fifth century of the current era Tsu Keng[38] discovered that the current polestar, 4339 Camelopardi, rotated about a point slightly more than a degree away. This determination of the true pole was incorporated in subsequent instruments by making the radius of their sighting tubes 1.5 Chinese degrees (each 360/365.25°). The excursion of the pole star just inside the field of view thus provided a nightly check on orientation. Six hundred years later Shen found that the polestar could no longer be kept in view throughout the night. He

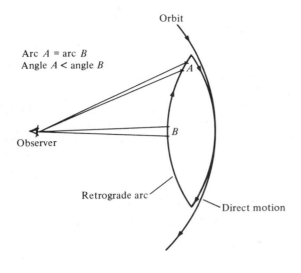

Arc *A* = arc *B*
Angle *A* < angle *B*

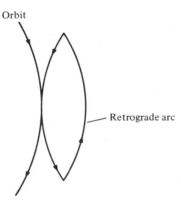

FIGURE 1. Shen Kua's explanation of planetary anomaly. He suggested that the "willow leaf" could be either inside or outside the orbit. No drawings appear with the text in "Brush Talks."

gradually widened the tube, using plots of the pole-star's position made three times each night for three months to adjust aim, until his new calibration revealed that the distance of the star from "the unmoving place at the celestial pole" was now slightly over three degrees (127; III, 262). Shen's successors followed him in treating the distance as variable, although the relation of this secular change to the equinoctial precession was not explored. Aware of the periodic retrogradation of the lunar nodes, Shen also discarded the armillary ring representing the moon's path, which could not reflect this motion; it was never used again.

Calendar Reform. On the accession of Shen-tsung in 1068, a new computational system was expected. The inability of the incumbent specialists to produce one left Shen with a clear mandate when he took over the Astronomical Bureau in 1072. The situation became even more awkward

when he was forced to bring in Wei P'u and others from outside the civil service, although few of the incompetents already in the bureau could be dislodged, in order to begin work on the calendar reform. It is not yet possible to tell what part of the work was done by Shen and what part by his assistants, although it is clear that Wei took responsibility for compiling the system as Shen became increasingly occupied elsewhere in government. Wei, a commoner whose connection with Shen was first reported in 1068, bore the brunt of fervent opposition within the bureau. He was even formally accused of malfeasance.

Shen knew that previous Sung astronomical systems had suffered greatly from reliance on old observations, and had a clear conception of what new data were needed for the first major advance in centuries. Unabating opposition within the bureau and his own demanding involvements outside it limited the number of innovations of lasting importance in his Oblatory Epoch (*Feng-yuan*[39]) system. It was the official basis of calendar computation from 1075, the year of its completion, to 1094, a period very close to the average for systems of the Northern Sung. That the system was not used longer has little to do with its merits, since except in cases of spectacular failure, Sung astronomical systems changed as rulers changed. Shen's was replaced when a new era was marked by the coming of age of Che-tsung. The immediate vicissitudes and long-term influence of three special features will give a general idea of the limits that historical actuality set upon Shen's astronomical ambitions.

The boldest aspect of Shen's program was the attempt to master the apparent motions of the planets—not merely their mean speeds and prominent phenomena—for the first time. This could not be done with a few observations of stationary points, occultations, and maximum elongations. Shen and Wei therefore planned a series of observations of a kind not proposed in Europe until the time of Tycho Brahe, five centuries later: exact coordinates read three times a night for five years. Similar records were to be kept for the moon's positions, since previous Sung systems had still used the lunar theory of I-hsing, which after 350 years had accumulated considerable error. These records were the most unfortunate casualty of the antagonism within the Bureau. Shen and Wei had no recourse but to produce a conventional planetary theory based mainly on old observations. They were able to correct the lunar error, but even this proposal provoked such an outcry that it could be vindicated only by a public demonstration using a gnomon (116).

A second issue was the central one of eclipse prediction. Previous attempts to add or subtract correction factors showed the futility of this approach. It was Wei P'u who "realized that, because the old eclipse technique used the mean sun, [the apparent sun] was ahead of it in the accelerated phase of its motion and behind it in the retarded phase." He therefore incorporated apparent solar motion into the eclipse theory (139). This had been done centuries earlier but abandoned.

A major obstacle in eclipse prediction, as well as in such workaday problems as the projection of observations in equatorial coordinates onto the ecliptic, was the absence of spherical geometry. Shen's evolution of arc-chord-sagitta relations out of some inferior approximations for segment areas given in the arithmetical classics was a first step toward trigonometry, making it possible in effect to apply sine relations and a fair approximation of cosine relations (301; III, 39, with diagram). The great remaining lack, as in planetary theory, was a mass of fresh observations on which to base new parameters. That this weakness could threaten the continuance of the system became clear the year after it was adopted (1076), when the failure of a predicted lunar eclipse to occur left Shen and his associates open to attack. Shen parried with a successful request that astronomical students at the Han-lin Academy observatory be ordered to carry out his observational program "for three or five years" and to communicate the results to the original compilers. Whether this attempt to bypass the stalemate at the Astronomical Bureau's observatory was well-conceived remains unknown, for in the next year Shen's impeachment aborted it.

In sum, the immediate outcome of the Oblatory Epoch calendar reform was undistinguished, and within half a century the official documents embodying it had been lost. It is impossible to be sure, for instance, to what extent arc-sagitta relations had been incorporated after Shen invented them. But enough information survived in proposals, reports, Shen's writings, and compendiums of various sorts for his astronomical system to play a considerable part in the highest achievement of traditional Chinese mathematical astronomy, the Season-Granting (Shou shih[40]) system of Kuo Shou-ching[41] (1280). Kuo carried out a sustained program of observation using instruments that incorporated Shen's improvements. He took up Shen's arc-sagitta formula, greatly improving the cosine approximation, and applied it to the equator-ecliptic transform. Aware of Shen's emphasis on the continuous variation of quantities in nature, and of his criticism of linear interpolation in clepsydra design, Kuo used higher-order interpolation to an unprecedented extent in his calendar reform.

Shen recorded another scheme for reform of the civil calendar that was most remarkable for his time and place. It almost certainly occurred to him in the last decade of his life. The traditional lunisolar calendar was a series of compromises in reconciling two incommensurable quantities. The modern value for the tropical year is 365.2422 days, and that for the synodic month 29.53059 days, so that there are roughly 12.37 lunar months per solar year. The practical problem was to design a civil calendar with an integral number of days each month, and an integral number of months each year, in such a way that the long-term averages approach the astronomical constants. Hardly two of the roughly one hundred computational systems recorded in early China solved this problem in exactly the same way, just as there was endless tactical variety in other traditional societies, but strategy was generally the same. Months of twenty-nine and thirty days alternated, with occasional pairs of long months to raise the average slightly. Intercalary thirteenth months were inserted roughly seven times every nineteen years, which comes to 0.37 additional months per year.

By a millennium before Shen's time the calendar was more than adequate in these respects for every civil need, although attempts to further refine the approximation led to endless retouching. The rhythms of administration, and to some extent of commerce, were of course paramount in the design of the lunisolar calendar, despite pieties about imperial concern for agriculture. It is most unlikely that Chinese peasants ever needed a printed almanac by which to regulate their activity; what they consulted, if anything, was its notations of lucky and unlucky days. Division of the year by lunar months is, in fact, useless for agriculture, since the seasons that pace the farmer's work vary with the sun alone. The Chinese calendar also incorporated twelve equal divisions of the tropical year (ch'i[30], like the Babylonian tithis), further subdivided into twenty-four periods with such names as Spring Begins, Grain Rains, and Insects Awaken. These provided a reliable notation for seasonal change in the part of northern China in which the series originated.

Shen's suggestion was a purely solar calendar, based on the twelve divisions of the tropical year (average 30.43697 days in his system) instead of on the lunation. The civil calendar would thus alternate months of thirty and thirty-one days, with pairs of short months as necessary to approach the average. This would provide truly seasonal months and at the same time do away with "that goitrous excrescence" the intercalary month. "As for the waxing and waning of the moon, although some phenomena such as pregnancy and the tides are tied to them, they have nothing to do with seasons or changes of climate; let them simply be noted in the almanac" (545). Shen was aware that because the lunisolar calendar went back to hoary antiquity "it is by no means appropriate to criticize it." He predicted that his discussion "will call forth offense and derision, but in another time there will be those who use my arguments." This proposal was in fact considered by later scholars the greatest blemish on Shen's astronomical talent. His posterity appeared in the mid-nineteenth century, with the even more radical solar calendar enacted for a few years by the T'ai-p'ing rebels.* His work was cited to justify historically more respectable proposals between that time and the adoption of the Gregorian calendar in 1912.

Configuration and Change. Chinese natural philosophers, unlike the majority in the postclassical West, did not dismiss the possibility that terrestrial phenomena could conform to mathematical regularities. But given the strength of Chinese quantitative sciences in numerical rather than geometric approaches, the very late and partial development of mathematical generalization, and the complete absence of notions of rigor, it is only consistent that much of the effort to discover such regularities produced numerology. Thus the most obvious of Shen's contributions to understanding of the earth and its phenomena are qualitative.

Magnetism. For more than a millennium before Shen's time, south-pointing objects carved from magnetite had been used from time to time in ceremonial and magic, and in 1044 objects cut from sheet iron and magnetized by thermoremanence were recommended for pathfinding in a book on military arts. Shen took up the matter of needles rubbed against lodestone by contemporary magi, discussed floating and other mountings, recommended suspension, noted that some needles point north and some south, and asserted that "they are

always displaced slightly east rather than pointing due south"—all in about a hundred characters (437; IV.1, 249–250). This recognition of magnetic declination depended not only on consideration of a suspended needle but also on the improved meridian determined by Shen's measurement of the distance between the polestar and true north; declination in his part of China at the time has been estimated as between five and ten degrees (Needham and Peter J. Smith, "Magnetic Declination in Mediaeval China," in *Nature* [17 June 1967], 1213–1214. See the historical table in *Science and Civilisation in China*, IV.1, 310).

Shen may have been anticipated by geomancers, who practiced a sophisticated protoscience of land configuration and siting, but the dates of texts on which such claims have been based are questionable. The use of compass needles in navigation is recorded shortly after Shen's death, and later descriptions provide enough detail to show that the twenty-four-point rose that Shen substituted for the old eight compass points (perhaps also under the stimulus of the better meridian, if not of geomantic practice) had become widely used. He apparently was unaware of the polarity of magnetite itself, since in another article he explained the difference between north-pointing and south-pointing needles as "perhaps because the character of the stone also varies" (588; IV.1, 250).

Cartography. It has been conjectured that Shen was the first to use a compass in mapmaking, although traditional methods would have sufficed. Neither his early maps of Khitan territory nor the atlas of China completed in 1087 have survived to answer this question. But in an enclosure to the latter he did separately record bearings between points using his twenty-four-point compass rose, as well as rectilinear distances rather than, as customary, distances along established routes (he calls the use of distances "as the bird flies" ancient, but we have no earlier record). "Thus although in later generations the maps may be lost, given my book the territorial divisions may be laid out according to the twenty-four directions, and the maps speedily reconstructed without the least discrepancy" (575; III, 576). His great atlas included twenty-three maps drawn to a uniform scale of 1:900,000; the general map was ten by twelve Chinese feet. There is no evidence that the handbook outlasted the maps.

Three-dimensional topographic maps go back at least to Hsieh Chuang[46] (421–466), who had a demountable wooden model carved, apparently on the basis of an ancient map. In 1075, while in-

---

*Kuo T'ing-i,[42] *T'ai-p'ing t'ien kuo li-fa k'ao-ting*[43] ("Review of the Calendrical Methods of the T'ai-p'ing Heavenly Kingdom," 1937; reprinted Taipei, 1963); Lo Erh-kang,[44] *T'ien li k'ao chi t'ien li yü yin yang li jih tui-chao-piao*[45] ("On the T'ai-p'ing Calendar, With a Concordance Table for the Lunar and Gregorian Calendars": Peking, 1955).

specting the Khitan border, Shen embodied information gathered from the commander and the results of his own travels in a series of relief maps modeled, for the sake of portability, in plastic media—wheat paste and sawdust until the weather turned freezing, then beeswax—on wooden bases. These were carried to the capital and duplicated in wood; similar models were thenceforth required from other frontier regions (472; III, 580).

Shen's regular use of both historical research and special on-the-ground surveys to solve such cartographic problems as tracing changes in watercourses also is noteworthy (431). Typical of his ingenious topographic survey methods were those used in 1072 to measure the slope of the Pien Canal near the capital. There he built a series of dikes in temporary, narrow parallel channels to measure incremental changes in water level (457; III, 577*).

Formation of the Earth. In 1074, in the T'ai-hang mountain range (Hopei), Shen noticed strata of "bivalve shells and ovoid rocks running horizontally through a cliff like a belt. This was once a seashore, although the sea is now hundreds of miles east. What we call our continent is an inundation of silt. . . . This mud year by year flows eastward, forming continental land." A similar stratum had been observed long before by Yen Chen-ch'ing[47] (708–784), who vaguely suggested its origin in the sea; but Shen—whose duties had made him intimately familiar with the process of silting—opened a new line of investigation by proposing a mechanism (430; III, 604).

Probably on his southward drought survey earlier in the same year, Shen saw the Yen-tang range (Chekiang), a series of fantastic rock formations "invisible from beyond the ridgeline [opposite], but towering to the sky when seen from the valleys. If we trace the underlying pattern, it must be that great waters in the valleys have attacked and washed away all the sand and earth, leaving only the great rocks erect and looming up." His explanation proceeded to generalize the shaping role of erosion, and then to apply it to the hills that divide streams in the loess country of northwest China—"miniatures of the Yen-tang mountains, but in earth rather than stone" (433; III, 603–604).

Shen reported a variety of contemporary finds of petrified plants and animals (373–374; III, 614–618). He remarked particularly on a stony formation he identified as originally a grove of interconnected bamboo roots and shoots, found dozens of feet below ground level at Yenan (Shensi). He knew from his military service there that the climate was too dry to grow bamboo: "Can it be that in earliest times [literally, 'before antiquity'] the land was lower and the climate moister, suitable for bamboo?" (373). About a century later the great philosopher and polymath Chu Hsi[48] (1130–1200), who knew Shen's jottings well and often extended ideas from them in his teaching, suggested that the stone of certain mountains was itself petrified silt deposits. But Shen's notion of prehistoric climatic change, like that of the reshaping of land by erosion, was not pushed further soon after his lifetime.

Atmospheric Phenomena. Although Shen did not report important original discoveries of his own, he preserved a number of interesting observations not recorded elsewhere. Perhaps the most important is a vivid description of a tornado (385; translated in Holzman, "Shen Kua," 286), the veracity of which was questioned by modern meteorologists until, in the first decade of the twentieth century, the Sikawei Observatory in Shantung reported phenomena of the same kind, previously thought restricted to the western hemisphere. Shen was also responsible for transmitting an explanation of the rainbow by Sun Ssu-kung,[49] an elder contemporary in the court who was also considered one of the best mathematical astronomers of his era. "The rainbow is the image [literally, 'shadow'] of the sun in rain, and occurs when the sun shines upon it." This sentence does not, as often claimed, adduce refraction (pinhole or mirror images were regularly called "shadows"; see 44). Shen was prompted to determine by experiment that the rainbow is visible only opposite the sun (357). Later Chu Hsi, aware of Shen's account, added that by the time the rainbow appears "the rain ch'i[30] has already thinned out; this in turn is because sunlight has shone on and attenuated the rain ch'i."[30] *Ch'i* must mean vapor here; the notion of reflections off individual drops is, as in Sun's explanation, implicit at best. Shen also recorded the fall of a fist-sized meteorite in more detail and with less mystification than previous reports. The particulars of its fall came from a careful account by another of Wang An-shih's associates. The object was recovered and exhibited, but Shen did not claim that he himself had observed that "its color is like that of iron, which it also resembles in weight" (340; III, 433–434).

Products of the Earth. Responsibilities with respect to fiscal policy gave Shen a detailed knowledge of important commodities, their varieties, and the circumstances of their production, as may be seen from his descriptions of tea (208) and salt

(221). Inflammable seepages from rock had been known a millennium before Shen's time, and for centuries had been used locally as lamp fuel and lubricant. While civil and military commissioner near Yen-chou, he noted the blackness of soot from petroleum and began an industry to manufacture the solid cakes of carbon ink used for writing and painting throughout China. Good ink was then made by burning pine resin, but Shen knew that North China was being rapidly deforested. He remarked that, in contrast with the growing scarcity of trees, "petroleum is produced inexhaustibly within the earth." The name Shen coined for petroleum[50a] is the one used today, and the source in Shensi province that he developed is still exploited. In the same article he quoted a poem of his that is among the earliest records of the economic importance of coal, then beginning to replace charcoal as a fuel (421; III, 609, partial).

Optical Phenomena. Shen's interest in image formation was not directly connected with his worldly concerns. His motivation is more plausibly traced to the play of his curiosity over old artifacts than to the improvement of naked-eye astronomical instruments.

In the canons of the Mohist school (*ca.* 300 B.C.) is a set of propositions explaining the formation of shadows and of optical images (considered a kind of shadow) in plane, convex, and concave mirrors. One proposition is widely believed to concern pinhole images, although textual corruption and ambiguity make this uncertain. These propositions are in many respects correct, although very schematic, and rays of light are not presupposed. Shen concerned himself with the single question of why a concave mirror forms an inverted image. He posited an "obstruction" (*ai*[50]), analogous to an oarlock, that constricts the "shadow" to a shape like that of a narrow-waisted drum—or, as we would put it, to form two cones apex to apex, the second constituting the inverted image. Like the Mohists, Shen clearly believed that inversion takes place before the image is reflected. He expressly likened the inverted image to that of a moving object formed on the wall of a room through a small opening in a paper window. Aware for the first time that there is a range of distances from a concave mirror within which no image is formed (that is, between the center of curvature and the focal point), he explained that this blank region, corresponding to the pinhole, is the locus of "obstruction" (44; translated in A. C. Graham and N. Sivin, "A Systematic Approach to the Mohist Optics," in S. Nakayama and N. Sivin, eds., *Chinese Science:*

Explorations of an Ancient Tradition [Cambridge, Mass., 1973], 145–147). His pinhole observation was adventitious, but his approach to the burning-mirror was experimental in its details.

Two other observations of optical interest are found under the rubric "Artifacts and Implements." The first, in the "Sequel to Brush Talks," noted that when the ancients cast bronze mirrors, they made the faces just convex enough that, regardless of size, every mirror would reflect a whole face. By Shen's time this refinement had been abandoned and the reasoning behind the curvature forgotten, so that collectors were having the faces of old mirrors scraped flat (327; IV.1, 93).

The second jotting is the oldest record of a Far Eastern curiosity still being investigated: "magic mirrors," or, as Shen called them, "transparent mirrors." Shen described a bronze mirror with a smooth face and an integrally cast inscription in relief on its back (both conventional features). When the mirror was used to reflect the sun onto a wall, the inscription was duplicated within the image. Shen cited with approval an anonymous explanation: "When the mirror is cast, the thinner parts cool first; the raised design on the back, being thicker, cools later and the shrinkage of the bronze is greater. Although the inscription is on the obverse, there are imperceptible traces of it on the face, so that it becomes visible within the light." He then qualified this explanation as incomplete, because he had tried mirrors in his own and other collections that were physically indistinguishable from the "transparent" ones and found that they did not cast images (330; IV.1, 94*). His doubt was justified, although the approach taken by his informant was at least as good as those of some modern metallurgists. Although cooling rate plays no discernible part, the variation in thickness is indeed responsible for the image in this sort of mirror, the most common among several types extant. Filing considerable bronze off the face of the mirror after casting is the key. This releases tensions in the metal and gives rise to slight deformations that produce the image.

Productive Techniques and Materials. The technologies of Shen's time were not cumulative and linked to science, but independent artisanal traditions transmitted from master to pupil. Shen left so many unique and informative accounts of ancient and contemporary processes among his jottings that "Brush Talks" has become a major source for early technology. Shen's interests in contemporary techniques can in most cases be linked to broad concerns of his official career; but the exceptional richness of his record bespeaks a rare curiosity, and the trenchancy of his descriptions a seriousness about mechanical detail unusual among scholar-officials. His notes on techniques lost by his time reflect the application of this technical curiosity and seriousness to archaeology, which was just becoming a distinct branch of investigation in the eleventh century.

Most of Shen's cultured contemporaries had a keen appreciation for good workmanship but considered the artisans responsible for it beneath notice except for occasional condescension. Shen wrote about resourceful craftsmen and ingenious laborers with much the same admiration he gave to judicious statesmen. He did not lose sight of the social distance between himself and members of the lower orders, but in his writing there is no snobbishness about the concert of hand, eye, and mind.

Contemporary Techniques. The most famous example is Shen's account of the invention of movable-type printing by the artisan Pi Sheng[51] (*fl.* 1041–1048). Shen described the carving and firing of ceramic type and the method of imbedding and leveling them in a layer of resin, wax, and paper ash in an iron form, one form being set as a second is printed. As in xylography, water-base ink was used. Since the porous, thin paper took it up with little pressure, no press was needed. Shen also remarked, with his usual acumen, that the process could become faster than carving wood blocks only with very large editions[52] (the average then has been estimated at between fifty and a hundred copies). Unevenness of the surface and absorption of ink by the fired clay must have posed serious problems. Abandonment of the process after Pi died was probably due to the lack of economic incentive that Shen noted. The long series of royally subsidized Korean experiments in the fifteenth century that perfected cast-metal typesetting still began with Pi Sheng's imbedding technique as described by Shen. Whether he knew Pi is unclear, but Shen's cousins preserved Pi's original font (307; translated in full, but not entirely accurately, in T. F. Carter, *The Invention of Printing in China and Its Spread Westward*, L. C. Goodrich, ed., 2nd ed. [New York, 1955], 212).

Shen left a number of descriptions of metallurgical interest—for instance, an account of the recovery of copper from a mineral creek by replacement of iron, a process then being carried out on an industrial scale to provide metal for currency (455; II, 267); observations of two of the three steelmaking processes used in early China (56; translated

in Needham, *The Development of Iron and Steel Technology in China* [London, 1958], 33–34; the book was reprinted at Cambridge, England, in 1964); and remarks on a little-known cold-working method used by smiths of the Ch'iang[53] people of western China to make extremely tough steel armor (333). Water control techniques of which he records details include pound-locks with double slipways (213; IV.3, 351–352), piles for strengthening embankments (210; IV.3, 322–323), and sectional gabions for closing gaps after embankment repairs (207; IV.3, 342–343).

Ancient Techniques. The concern for understanding ancient techniques began with the commentators on the Confucian and other classics more than a millennium earlier. Exegesis remained an important activity in China, and the productive methods of golden antiquity were investigated with the same assiduity as anything else mentioned in its literary remains. For various reasons—among them the recovery of ancient artifacts in large numbers for the first time, the growth of collecting, and the elaboration of a conscious aesthetics—archaeology began to emerge from the footnotes less than a century before Shen's time, especially in monographs on ancient implements and ritual institutions. He was familiar with this literature and responded to it critically. Much of his writing in the "Artifacts and Implements" chapter falls squarely in this tradition, drawing on the testimony of both objects and books.

Shen's vision of the past as a repertory of lost processes introduced an influential new theme. A constant concern in his writing was not only that the workmanship of the past be esteemed for its excellence, but also that the present be enriched through understanding what the practical arts had been capable of. Although the belief was still current that the inventions that first made civilization possible were all due to semidivine monarchs of archaic times, in a letter Shen saw the technological past as successful for just the opposite reason: "How could all of this have come from the Sages? Every sort of workman and administrator, the people of the towns and those of the countryside—none failed to take part" (*Ch'ang-hsing chi* [1718 ed.], 19:53b).

Shen's remarks on magic mirrors are typical of his effort to understand lost processes. Another example is his reconstruction (and personal trial) of ancient crossbow marksmanship, interpreting a gnomic aiming formula in an ancient footnote with the aid of a graduated sight and trigger assembly that he examined after it was unearthed (331;

III, 574–575). The most famous instance of Shen's use of literary sources for the study of techniques has to do with the remarkable modular system of architecture used in public buildings. The set of standard proportions is well-known from an official compilation printed about a decade after Shen's death. Shen, by describing the proportion system of the Timberwork Canon (*Mu ching*[54]), attributed to a great builder of about 1000 and already falling out of use, demonstrates the antiquity of this art (299; IV.3, 82–83).

Medicine. By Shen's time medicine, which from the start drew heavily upon natural philosophy for its conceptual underpinnings, had accumulated a classical tradition. Not only was each new treatise consciously built upon its predecessors, but a major goal of new work was restoring an understanding that medical scholars believed was deepest in the oldest writings. The revealed truth of the archaic canons was too concentrated for ordinary latter-day minds, who could hope to recapture it only as the culmination of a lifetime of study. Writers in the intervening centuries referred to the early classics as the ultimate source of significance even while aware that empirical and practical knowledge had considerably advanced since antiquity. The major contribution of the continuous tradition of medical writing was to fit new experiences into the old framework and, when necessary, to construct new frameworks in the spirit of the old. As woodblock printing became feasible, standard editions of the chief classics were compiled and disseminated by government committees. This increased the respectability of the curing arts as a field of study. Large numbers of men from the scholar-official class began to take up medicine, not in competition with those who made a living by it but as a means of self-cultivation allied to cosmology and occasionally useful. The initial motivations commonly were personal ill health and the desire to serve one's sick parents.

Shen, as noted earlier, began the study of medicine early, for the former reason. One of his two therapeutic compilations survives in somewhat altered form. Its preface is a long disquisition on the difficulty of adequate diagnosis and therapy, as well as on the proper selection, preparation, and administration of drugs. His criticisms of contemporary trends toward simplification remind us that the development of urban culture and education in Sung China had led to increased medical practice among ordinary people as well as study by the literati. As protoscientific medicine began to displace magico-ritual folk remedies (at least in the cities),

there were more half-educated physicians to be criticized by learned amateurs such as Shen. Shen's most characteristic contribution was undoubtedly his emphasis on his own experience, unusual in a tradition whose literature in the Sung still tended to depend heavily on copying wholesale from earlier treatises. Shen not only omitted any prescription the efficacy of which he had not witnessed, but appended to most a description of the circumstances in which it had succeeded. He provided many precise descriptions of medicinal substances of animal, vegetable, and mineral origin. Although he had no more interest in general taxonomic schemes than other pharmacognostic scholars of his time, his concern for exact identification and for philological accuracy gave his critical remarks enduring value. Many were incorporated into later compilations on materia medica, and Shen's writing also served as a stimulus to the work a few decades later of the great pharmacognostic critic K'ou Tsung-shih[55] in his "Dilatations Upon the Pharmacopoeias" (*Pen-ts'ao yen i,*[56] 1116).

A recent discovery of considerable interest is that certain medical preparations from human urine collectively called "autumn mineral" (*ch'iu shih*[57]), which have a long history in China, contain high concentrations of steroid hormones and some protein hormones as well. In "Good Prescriptions" Shen gives one of the earliest accounts, in the form of detailed instructions for two such preparations that he performed in 1061 (other accounts by contemporaries are harder to date).*

Perhaps Shen's most famous writing on general medical matters is one in which he refutes the common belief that there are three passages in the throat — as shown, for instance, in the first book of drawings of the internal organs based directly on dissection (1045).† His supporting argument is not from independent dissection but from sufficient reason — "When liquid and solid are imbibed to-

*See Lu Gwei-djen and Joseph Needham, "Medieval Preparations of Urinary Steroid Hormones," in *Medical History,* **8** (1964), 101–121; Miyashita Saburō,[58] *Kanyaku shūseki no yakushigakuteki kenkyū*[59] ("A Historical Pharmaceutical Study of the Chinese Drug 'Autumn Mineral' the *Ch'iu-shih*"; Osaka, 1969), esp. 9–12.

†Persons untrained in medicine performed the dissection upon executed bandits in 1045 and recorded what was found under the direction of an enthusiastic amateur. Another episode of the same kind, undertaken explicitly to correct the earlier drawings, took place at the beginning of the twelfth century. There is no reliable account of either in any European language, but see Watanabe Kōzō,[60] "Genson suru Chūgoku kinsei made no gozō rokufu zu no gaisetsu"[61] ("A Survey of Extant Chinese Anatomical Drawings Before Modern Times"), in *Nihon ishigaku zasshi,* 7 (1956), 88.

gether, how can it be that in one's mouth they sort themselves into two throat channels?" He thus saw the larynx as the beginning of a network for distributing throughout the body the vital energy carried in atmospheric air, and the esophagus as carrying nutriment directly to the stomach cavity, where its assimilation begins. This was a significant increase in clarity as well as accuracy (480).

A passage that has been praised for its simple but beautiful language takes issue with the ancient principle that medicinal plants should be gathered in the second and eighth lunar months (when they were thought easiest to identify). In a few hundred words it epitomizes the variation of ripening time with the identity and variety of the plant; the part used in therapy; the physiological effect needed for the application; altitude; climate; and, for domesticated medicinal plants, variation with planting time, fertilization, and other details of horticulture. The sophistication of this passage reflects not only increasing domestication (exceptional in earlier eras) but also the integration of drugs from every corner of China into the expanding commercial network.

Conclusion. The expansiveness of Northern Sung society and its relative openness to talent, not to mention increasing government sponsorship of learning, made this an important period in the history of every branch of science and technology. Shen was not the first polymath it produced. There was also Yen Su[62] (*fl.* 1016), who designed an odometer and south-pointing chariot (in which a differential gear assembly kept figures pointing in a constant direction as the chariot turned), improved the design of the water clock and other astronomical instruments, and wrote on mathematical harmonics and the tides. In Shen's lifetime there was Su Sung[63] (1020–1101), who was first privy councillor during the last part of the reaction against the New Policies (1092–1093). Through the 1060's he played a major part in a large imperially sponsored compilation of materia medica, and in the editing and printing of ancient medical classics. In 1088 a group that he headed completed a great water-driven astronomical clock incorporating an escapement device. Their detailed description of the mechanism included the oldest star map extant in printed form, based on a new stellar survey. (The book has been studied and translated in Wang Ling, Joseph Needham, Derek J. de Solla Price, *et al., Heavenly Clockwork* [Cambridge, England, 1960].) That Yen, Su, and Shen were all in the central administration is not surprising. The projects on which they were trained and those in

which they worked out many of their ideas were of a scale that only the imperial treasury could (or at least would) support.

Breadth of interest alone does not account for Shen's importance for the study of the Chinese scientific intellect. Another aspect is his profound technical curiosity. A number of the phenomena he recorded were mentioned by others; but even when others' descriptions happen to be fuller, they usually are of considerably less interest because their subject matter is treated as a mere curiosity or as an occasion for anecdote rather than as a challenge to comprehension. Above all, one is aware in Shen, as in other great scientific figures, of a special directness. A member of a society in which the weight of the past always lay heavily on work of the mind, he nevertheless often cut past deeply ingrained structures and assumptions. This was as true in his program of astronomical observations and his audacious solar calendar as in his work on government policies. People in the Sung were aware that man's world had greatly expanded since antiquity, and questioning of precedent (in the name of a return to classical principles) was inherent in the New Policies. Shen's commitment to this political point of view can only have reinforced the sense of cumulative improvement of techniques and increasing accuracy over time that one finds in major Chinese astronomers. But given these predispositions and opportunities, Shen remains in many senses an atypical figure, even in his time and among his associates.

There certainly is much that a modern scientist or engineer finds familiar, not only in the way Shen went about making sense of the physical world but also in the temper of his discourse, despite the profoundly antique nature of the concepts he used. One comes away from his writings confident that he would see much of modern science as a culmination (not the only possible culmination) of his own investigations—more confident than after reading Plato, Aristotle, or St. Thomas Aquinas. But does Shen's special configuration of abilities and motivations suggest that a genetic accident produced, out of time, a scientific rationalist-empiricist of essentially modern type? To answer this question it is necessary to look at Shen's larger conception of reality, of which his scientific notions compose only a part but from which they are inseparable.

The Relation of Scientific Thought to Reality. The sense of cumulative enterprise in mathematical astronomy did not imply the positivistic conviction that eventually the whole pattern could be mastered. Instead, from the earliest discussions there was a prevalent attitude that scientific explanation—whether in terms of number or of abstract qualitative concepts, such as yin-yang—merely expresses, for human purposes, limited aspects of a pattern of constant relations too subtle to be understood directly. No one expressed this attitude more clearly than Shen. In instance after instance he emphasized the inability of secular knowledge to encompass phenomena: the reason for magnetic declination (437), why lightning striking a house can melt metal objects without burning the wooden structure (347), and so on.

Shen made this point most clearly in connection with astronomy. In one passage he discussed the fine variations that astronomers must, in the nature of their work, ignore. Every constant, every mean value obscures continuous variation of every parameter (123). In his official proposals on the armillary sphere,[64] he argued that measure is an artifact, that it allows particular phenomena to be "caught" (po[65]) in observational instruments, where they are no longer part of the continuum of nature. That Shen saw as the condition of their comprehensibility. This and similar evidence amount not merely to an appreciation of the role of abstraction in science, but also to the steady conviction that abstraction is a limited process incapable of producing universal and fundamental knowledge of the concrete phenomenal world. Nature is too rich, too multivariant, too subtle (wei[66]). This limitation did not detract from the interest or worth of theoretical inquiry, and did not lead intellectuals to question whether learning could contribute to the satisfaction of social needs; but the ambit of rationalism in traditional scientific thought was definitely circumscribed.

In this light Shen's explanatory metaphors become more comprehensible. In his remarkable suggestion that variations in planetary speed may be represented by a compounded figure, he chose to fasten to the periphery of his circle a willow leaf, whereas in Europe no figure but another circle was thinkable (148). When explaining optical image inversion in terms of converging and diverging rays, the images of the oarlock and waisted drum occurred to him (44). The variation in polarity of different magnetized needles was likened to the shedding of antlers by two species of deer in opposite seasons (588; IV.1, 250), and so on. Geometric figures, numbers, and quantities were useful for computation but had very limited value, not so great as cogent metaphors from the world of experience, in understanding the pattern inherent in physical reality.

Many Chinese thinkers, even in the Sung, did believe in number as a key to the pattern of physical reality; but their search was concentrated in numerology (especially as founded on the "Great Commentary" to the *Book of Changes*) rather than in mathematics. This is not to imply that numerology was a distraction from mathematics. The two were not considered alternate means to the same goal.

Other Kinds of Knowledge. Did Shen believe that other ways of knowing complemented and completed empirical and theoretical investigation? Aside from its scientific aspects, Shen's thought has been so little studied that only some tentative suggestions can be offered. Contemplation and disciplined self-examination were ancient themes in Confucianism, and by Shen's time illumination was widely considered among the learned as a source of knowledge complementary to that given by experience of the external world. The domestication and secularization of Buddhist and Taoist meditation were gradually leading to a more introspective and less ritualistic approach to self-realization. This tendency was later elaborated with great variety of emphasis and weight in the schools of neo-Confucianism.

To understand what part contemplation and meditation played in the thought of Shen Kua requires a clearer view than we now have of their currency and coloring in his time, of the considerable role of Wang An-shih's thought in his intellectual development, and of Shen's own attitudes as indirectly expressed in his literary remains. There is as yet no sound basis for evaluating his interest in Taoist arcana that seems to have peaked in his thirties, his public remarks that express sympathetic interest in illuminationist (Ch'an, Japanese "Zen") Buddhism, and his statement in an autobiographical fragment that Ch'an meditation was one of the things to which he turned his attention after retirement. In any case these involvements refract aspects of his epistemology that cannot be overlooked without badly distorting our recognition of the whole.

Teraji Jun has recently demonstrated this point in examining how strong a factor in Shen's motivation and individuality was his belief in destiny and prognostication. There are crucial passages, especially in his commentary on Mencius, where Shen spoke of the necessity for choosing what is true and holding to it, and called the rule of the heart and mind by sensory experience "the way of the small man." The basis of moral choice was an autonomous inner authority defined in an original way but largely in Mencian terms, a centeredness "filling the space between sky and earth," unquestionably linked with the self-reliance that marked his unhappy career.

It is not immediately obvious why someone who so valued individual responsibility should have been fascinated by fate and divination, which in fact are the themes of whole chapters of "Brush Talks." Shen does not seem to have viewed these enthusiasms as in conflict with his scientific knowledge. His delight in strange occurrences and his tendency to place matters of scientific interest under that rubric begin to make sense under the hypothesis that he accepted the odd, the exceptional, and the affront to common sense as a challenge for explanation at another time, or by someone else—without assuming that explanation was inevitable. In his hundreds of jottings on people, the person he chose to praise is most often the one who did not do the obvious thing, even when it seemed the sound thing to do.

At one point Shen provided a thoroughly rational explanation of the relations between fate and prognostication. The future can of course be foreknown by certain people, he said, but it is a mistake to conclude that all matters are preordained. The vision of the future is always experienced in present time; the years in the interim also become simultaneous. One can do nothing to avoid an undesirable future so glimpsed. Authentic foreknowledge would have witnessed the evasive measures; a vision that failed to see them could not be authentic foreknowledge (350).

In addition to the visionary ability of certain minds, Shen pondered universally accessible methods of divination, which (he seems to have believed) do not describe the future or the spatially distant so much as provide counsel about them or aid thought about them. In one of his chapters, "Regularities Underlying the Phenomena," he explained why the same divinatory technique gives different outcomes when used by different people, and thus has no inherent verifiability. He quoted the "Great Commentary" to the *Book of Changes* to the effect that understanding is a matter of the clarity and divinity (in a very abstract sense) within one's mind. But because the mind is never without burdens that hinder access to its divinity, Shen reasoned, one's communion with it may take place through a passive mediating object or procedure (144, 145). This divinity is, for Shen's sources, the moral center of the individual. Prognostication, however ritualized (as we would

put it), thus draws indirectly upon the power of self-examination. Access to the future, whether by vision or by divination, is a perfectly natural phenomenon that is imperfectly distinct, on the one hand, from the moral faculties, the choices of which condition the future, and, on the other, from science, the rational comprehension of the natural order as reflected in all authentic experience.

Thus it appears that introspection supplemented by divinatory procedures was a legitimate means to knowledge in Shen Kua's eyes, just as painstaking observation and measurement of natural phenomena were another. He neither confused the two approaches nor attempted to draw a clear line between them. Nor was he inclined to assess the comparative importance of these ways of knowing.

The complementarity in Shen's attitudes toward knowledge is echoed by another in the external world of his work. Computational astronomy and divination of various kinds (including judicial astrology) were equally weighty functions carried out by the central government on the emperor's behalf, for both kinds of activity were established supports of his charisma. The need to combine science with ritual in this sphere is implied in an important memorial of Wang An-shih: because the monarch acts on behalf of the natural order, he can safeguard the empire and command the assent of the governed only through knowledge of nature. Ritually expressed awe of that order, without knowledge, is not enough (*Hsu tzu chih t'ung chien ch'ang pien*[67] ["Materials for the Sequel to the Comprehensive Mirror for Aid in Government"], presented to the throne 1168 [1881 ed.], 236:16b). Teraji has acutely pointed out that this is precisely the political justification for Shen's research, and the reason that traditional bureaucrat-scientists who were concerned mainly with maintaining ancient practices were not what Wang wanted.

Confucianism and Science. Recent attempts in both East and West to construct a historical sociology of Chinese science have in large part been built around a contrast between Confucianist and Taoist ideology. The values of the Confucian elite are often described as oriented toward stasis, hierarchy, bureaucracy, and bookishness. These characteristics are seen as perennially in tension with the appetite of socially marginal Taoists for novelty and change, their tendency to contemplate nature and the individual in it as a system, and their fascination with techniques, which kept them in touch with craftsmen and made them willing to engage in manual work themselves. It will no doubt be possible eventually to excavate a falsifiable, and thus historically testable, hypothesis from the mound of observations and speculations in this vein that have accumulated over the last half-century. For the moment, all one can do is point out how relentlessly unsociological this discussion has been.

Sociology is about groups of people. Doctrines are germane to sociology to the extent that their effect on what groups of people do, or on how they form, can be demonstrated. Generalizations about people who accept a certain doctrine have no sociological significance unless such people can be shown to act as a group, or at least to identify themselves as a group. The term "Confucian" is commonly used indifferently even by specialists to refer to a master of ceremonial, a professional teacher of Confucian doctrines, a philosopher who contributes to their elaboration, someone who attempts to live by Confucius' teachings, any member of the civil service, any member of the gentry regardless of ambition toward officialdom, or any conventional person (since it was conventional to quote Confucian doctrines in support of conventional behavior). A "Taoist" can be anyone from a hereditary priest ordained by the Heavenly Master to a retired bureaucrat of mildly unconventional tastes living on a city estate. Either group, by criteria in common use, includes people who would make opposite choices on practically any issue. This being so, the proposition "Taoists were more friendly toward science and technology than Confucians" reduces to "Educated individuals who hold unconventional sentiments are more inclined to value activities unconventional for the educated than are educated people who hold conventional sentiments." That is probably not quite a tautologous statement, but it is sociologically vacuous and historically uninteresting.

Unease of this sort is probably the most obvious outcome of reflection on Shen Kua's career. By sentimental criteria he can be assigned to Confucianism, Taoism, or Buddhism, to suit the historian's proclivities.* He was a member of the elite, a responsible official, a writer of commentaries on several of the Confucian classics, and a user of the concepts of Confucius' successor Mencius to explore the depths of his own identity. He spoke well and knowledgeably of Buddhism. He practiced arcane disciplines, such as breath control, that he called Taoist.

As for his allegiances, Shen was prominently associated with a powerful but shifting group of background very generally similar to his own. Social stasis and institutional fixity were impediments to their aims in reshaping government. At the same time, the new balance of power toward which they strove was more authoritarian than the old. Underlying their common effort was an enormous disparity of motivation, from the well-intentioned (Shen) to the simultaneously manipulative and corrupt (Ts'ai Ch'ueh).

Were these Confucians more or less Confucian than their Confucian opponents? Wang An-shih earned enduring stature for his commentaries on the classics and his thought on canonic themes. His followers seem to have found inspiration in the classics as often as their enemies and as those who avoided taking a political position. This is not to say that everyone understood the Confucian teachings in the same way. The latter were not, from the viewpoint of intellectual history, a set of tightly linked ideas that set fixed limits on change; rather, they were a diverse and fragmentary collection of texts reinterpreted in every age. They were understood differently by every individual and group who looked to them for guidance when coping with problems of the moment.

The major commentaries, which attempted to define the meanings of Confucian teachings philologically, carried enormous authority; and governments (that of Wang An-shih, for instance) repeatedly attempted to make one interpretation orthodox. But the urge to pin down meanings was always in conflict with precisely what made these books classic. Their unlimited depth of significance depended more on what could be read into them than on precisely what their authors had meant them to say. That depth made them applicable to an infinity of human predicaments and social issues, unprecedented as well as perennial. Late neo-Confucian philosophers striking out in new directions demonstrated again and again how little the bounded intellectual horizons and social preju-

---

*A new element was introduced in 1974 in a book issued as part of the "anti-Confucius anti-Lin Piao" campaign against current ideological trends. Two of its essays (pp. 118–140) portray Shen as a legalist and a relentless opponent of Confucianism. "Legalist" is a term applied to writers on government and administration concentrated in the last centuries before the Christian era, especially those who argued that polity must be built on law and regulation, in contrast with the traditionalist faith of Confucius in rites and moral example. Although the arguments in this book are too distorted and too selective in their use of sources to be of interest as history, they become intelligible when "legalism" and "Confucianism" are understood as code words for the political convictions of two contending power groups in China today, as portrayed by spokesmen for one of the two. The book is *Ju-Fa tou-cheng yü wo kuo ku-tai k'o-hsueh chi-shu ti fa-chan*[6K] ("The Struggle Between Confucianism and Legalism and the Development of Science and Technology in Our Country in Ancient Times"; Peking, 1974). The first printing was 31,000 copies.

dices of the classics' authors objectively limited what may be drawn from them.

In other words, the Confucian canon had the influence it did because it provided a conceptual language that over the centuries educated people used and redefined in thinking out decisions and justifying action and inaction. The classics were often cited as a pattern for static social harmony and willing subordination in arguments against the New Policies. Shen, on the other hand, used them to argue for flexibility in social relations and for greater receptivity toward new possibilities than was usual in his time. Either as a social institution or as an ideology, Confucianism is too protean and thus too elusive a base for generalizations about the social foundations of science and techniques in China.

Institutions also changed constantly, but at least they were tangible entities. It is essential to consider them when tracing the social connections of science. Very little is known about how scientists were educated in the Northern Sung period; the obvious next step is a collective study of a great many biographies. In Shen's case we can see a pattern that certainly was not unique. He was, so far as we know, self-educated in astronomy, but with many learned associates to draw upon. In medicine and breath control he probably received teaching in the traditional master-disciple relationship. Defined in the ages before printing made possible access to large collections of books, this relationship involved the student's memorizing the classics (more often one than several) that the teacher had mastered. This verbatim transmission of a text was supplemented by the teacher's oral explanations. The relation was deepened by ceremonial formality; the master took on the obligation to monitor the disciple's moral as well as intellectual growth, and the disciple accepted the responsibility of becoming a link in an endless chain of transmission. Schools were largely communities of masters and disciples. The scale of government-sponsored elementary schools in the provinces was small in Shen's youth, and began to compete with private academies only in the New Policies period. The two sorts together did not serve more than a small minority of youth.

By the eighth century there were small schools in the central government to train technical specialists. The masters, usually several in number, were functionaries, representing the departments of the bureau that the disciples were being trained to staff. The schools for medicine and astronomy could not lead to the top of government, but guaranteed steady advancement between minor sinecures. Very few of the great physicians or astronomers of traditional China began in these schools.

In the absence of evidence to the contrary, there is no reason to believe that Shen Kua ever attended a school of any sort, nor does that make him untypical. His early education by his mother, his training in medicine by an obscure physician and others who remain unknown, and his catch-as-catch-can studies of most other matters do not set him apart from his contemporaries. With no knowledge of particulars one cannot even guess how his personal style in technical work was formed. But to say that we are ignorant is not to say everything. The intimate relations of master and teacher and the isolation of the autodidact were themselves important institutions in the Northern Sung, institutions of a sort that did not discourage the emergence of unforeseen abilities in the small number of people who had the opportunity to be educated. Shen did not have to cope with a standard curriculum, for better or worse. If we are searching for the decisive curriculum of science and technology, it is necessary to look outside the realm of education.

The Civil Service and Science. One institution above all others influenced the mature ideas and attitudes of the ruling stratum: the bureaucracy. What can be said about its influence on science and technology in the life of Shen Kua? First, like every bureaucracy, it depended upon science and technology. It supported both sorts of activity on a scale otherwise unattainable, and unheard of in Europe at the time. Shen's curiosity, experience, and skills were so largely shaped by the civil service that it is absurd to ask what he would have become had he lived as a country gentleman or a Taoist priest. On the other hand, as elsewhere, technicians were certainly less important to the priorities of the state than administrators. The responsibility of the former was to provide the emperor and his administrators with wealth and other tools for the realization of policy. Specialist positions in science and engineering did not often serve as the beginnings of great careers.

By the New Policies period a career stream for economic experts had been established. It could assimilate people who combined technological acumen with fiscal skills, and carry them to the central councils of the empire. Shen's early technical feats were performed in general administrative posts, but his talents came to be valued and he rose quickly through formal and informal structures. It is not irrelevant that his directorship of the Astronomical Bureau was never more than a concurrent position. His attempt to combine an effective voice in the shaping of change with scientific contributions ended in personal disaster. He was ruined by men of his own faction, apparently for his political seriousness and naïveté. His astronomical work was rendered futile by subordinates because of his professional demands upon them. The bureaucracy was not neutral; it was a two-edged sword.

The civil service provided a form for great projects in science and technology, and practically monopolized certain disciplines, such as mathematical astronomy and observational astrology. Printing gave it the wherewithal to determine much of the content of elementary technical education (as in medicine and mathematics). A man of Wei P'u's genius, who had not had the opportunity to enter the bureaucracy by a regular route, was looked down upon and deliberately frustrated. Had Shen himself chosen to be a mere technician, his standing in the civil service would have been sufficient to protect him from personal attack. He would have had more time but less power. It would be rash indeed to speculate that his calendar reform would not have failed. But there is a larger issue.

Shen's mind was shaped for the civil service, as were those of his ancestors and peers, by an early education centered in moral philosophy and letters. He was a generalist. The development of depth in thought and work was left to his own proclivities. Only a superficial knowledge of technical matters was expected of him as a youth—a situation not very different from that of the British civil service generalist of some decades ago. Shen's growing responsibilities in fiscal affairs were the one aspect of his career that we can be sure encouraged him to draw coherence out of his varied experiences and studies. For this reason and others of which we are still ignorant, the great breadth of his knowledge was accompanied by enough depth to let him write monographs of some importance and, even through his brief jottings, to reshape Chinese knowledge of certain phenomena. But distraction is a theme that runs through his writings: promising studies laid aside; endless skirmishes to defend administratively measures that spoke for themselves technically and strategically; proposals negated by political setbacks. Regardless of his capacity for scientific depth and his willingness to find his way to it, the sheer busyness of his career drastically limited him. The works of his final leisure, however valuable, were all superficial in

form. Was this the result of habit, of distance necessitated by disillusion, or of an aesthetic choice of the style appropriate for conversing with one's brush and ink slab in a silent garden? That remains for deeper study to decide.

What, then, was responsible for Shen Kua's scientific personality? We do not know the answers to all sorts of prior questions. The greatest difficulty comes in learning what these questions should be—in isolating the important issues, in coming to terms with the paucity and partiality of the sources, and in doing justice to a rich mind that, despite its absorption in a quest that transcends people and eras, partook fully of its time and place. It is not a matter of mechanically juxtaposing the usual factors: intelligence, subjectivity, philosophical convictions, social background, career, and other experiences. We have already seen how problematic the last three are. The most conspicuous traits of Shen's consciousness were open curiosity, mental independence (without the intolerance for intellectual disagreement that was a major limitation of Wang An-shih), sympathy for the unconventional, ambition, loyalty, and lack of snobbishness. The first four are considered marks of promise among technical people today, although one often meets great scientists who lack one or more of them. Were these characteristics in Shen due to heredity, to early experiences and education, or to influences encountered in adult life? This is an example of the sort of question that bars understanding; surely Shen was the sum of all three. The secret of his uniqueness will not yield itself to historical method, however powerful, unless it is applied with imagination, artifice, and awareness of the springs of human complexity.

Attitudes Toward Nature. When examined closely, attitudes toward nature in the late eleventh century become as elusive as attitudes toward Confucian humanism. The richly articulated philosophic vision of man in harmony with his physical surroundings was proving quite incapable of preventing the deforestation of northern China, which was virtually complete a generation after Shen's death. One cannot even speak of the defeat of that vision in an encounter of ideas, for no intellectual confrontation is recorded. What happened? The most obvious part of the answer is that the people who were chopping down the trees for charcoal were not the people who were seeking union with the ineffable cosmic Tao. Since that social difference was of very long standing, however, it does not explain the crescendo of exploitation in the Northern Sung. The coincidence of that fateful shift with the rise of large-scale industry and market networks is again obvious enough.* What needs to be explained, in fact, is the survival of the naturalist ideal until modern times.

The dilemma emerges clearly in the attitudes of Shen Kua and Wang An-shih toward nature. The orientations that pervade "Brush Talks" are in most respects the same as those of literati thinking about nature a millennium earlier. Philosophical pigeonholes are largely beside the point. Some "Confucians" thought about nature a great deal, and some, convinced that human society is the sole proper object of reflection and action, as little as possible; but their perspectives were, on the whole, the ones common to all Chinese who could read and write. Nature was an organismic system, its rhythms cyclic and governed by the inherent and concordant pattern uniting all phenomena.

It comes as a shock to see Shen's definition of salt in a memorial: "Salt is a means to wealth, profit without end emerging from the sea" (*Hsu tzu chih t'ung chien ch'ang pien*, 280:17b–21b). This was not a slip, nor is it difficult to find philosophical precedents. Shen saw the fiscal function of the state (for which he briefly had supreme responsibility) as the provision of wealth from nature. His recommendations encouraged extractive industries and manufactures, and mobilization of the popular strength for land reclamation, in order to increase national wealth. In that respect he was faithful to the priorities of Wang An-shih. This is a far cry from the senior civil servant in China in the 1960's designing a campaign to convince farmers that nature is an enemy to be conquered, tamed, and remolded to social ends. But neither is it the pastoral ideal.

Why this discrepancy between nature as the ideal pattern to which man adjusts and nature as a (still beneficent) means of enrichment? Why does Shen seem not to be conscious of it as contradictory? These are questions on which the research has yet to be done. But Shen Kua's career, considered in the round, suggests a working hypothesis. Such notions as yin-yang, the Five Phases, and certain related ideas associated with the *Book of Changes*

are often considered to have been hindrances to an autochthonous scientific revolution in traditional China. This is, of course, an elementary fallacy, comparable to considering the railroad, because it filled a need satisfactorily for so long, an impediment to the invention of the airplane. The old Chinese world view had much in common with cosmological ideas practically universal in Europe until the consummation of the Scientific Revolution—the four elements and so on—but that gave way soon enough. Historically speaking, Chinese organismic naturalism was not a rigid framework of ideas that barred change; rather, it was the only conceptual language available for thinking about nature and communicating one's thoughts, new or old, to others. Like any language, it imposed form and was itself malleable. Its historical possibilities were less a matter of original etymology or definition than of the ambiguity and extensibility that let people in later ages read new and often drastically changed import into old words. There is no true paradox in appeals to the harmony of man and nature by Shen and others before and after him who favored the exploitation of nature in the interests of the state. Although such activist thinkers stretched the old pattern of understanding, its fabric remained seamless. Their definition of what they wanted could not transcend it. Only the more desperate urgencies of another time could finally stretch it until it tore.

BIBLIOGRAPHY

I. ORIGINAL WORKS. The best attempt at a complete list of Shen's writings is in an appendix to Hu Tao-ching's standard ed. of "Brush Talks," *Meng ch'i pi t'an chiao cheng*[69] ("Brush Talks From Dream Brook, a Variorum Edition"), rev. ed., 2 vols. (Peking, 1960 [1st ed., Shanghai, 1956]), 1151–1156. There are forty titles, including some only mentioned in early writings about Shen. A portion of the list belongs to parts or earlier versions of larger writings. It has been suggested that the high rate of attrition was due to the campaign of Ts'ai Ching[70] (1046–1126), virtual dictator during the revival of the New Policies in the first quarter of the twelfth century, to obliterate the literary remains of his predecessors as well as their enemies. (See Ch'en Teng-yuan,[71] *Ku-chin tien-chi chü-san k'ao*[72] ["A Study of the Collection and Dispersion of Classical Writings in Ancient and Modern Times"; Shanghai, 1936], 54.) Six works are extant, although only two appear to be substantially unaltered, and considerable fragments of four others exist. Those of scientific interest are described below:

---

*It was made obvious in a brilliant series of papers by Robert M. Hartwell: "A Revolution in the Chinese Iron and Coal Industries During the Northern Sung, 960–1126 A.D.," in *Journal of Asian Studies*, 21 (1962), 153–162; "Markets, Technology, and the Structure of Enterprise in the Development of the Eleventh-Century Chinese Iron and Steel Industry," in *Journal of Economic History*, 26 (1966), 29–58; "A Cycle of Economic Change in Imperial China: Coal and Iron in Northeast China, 750–1350," in *Journal of the Economic and Social History of the Orient*, 10 (1967), 102–159.

1. *Meng ch'i pi t'an*[21] ("Brush Talks From Dream Brook"), written over the greater part of Shen's retirement and possibly printed during his lifetime. It was first quoted in a book dated 1095. Originally it consisted of thirty *chüan* (a chapterlike division); but all extant versions, descended from a xylograph of 1166, follow an unknown prior editor's rearrangement into twenty-six *chüan*. The editor of the 1166 reprint noted a number of errors already in the text that he could not correct for want of variants. There are 587 jottings.

The practically definitive ed. of this book and its sequels (items 2 and 3 below), and in many other respects the foundation of future studies, is the Hu Tao-ching recension mentioned two paragraphs above. It includes a carefully collated and corrected text with variorum notes and modern (but occasionally faulty) punctuation, based on all important printed versions and on five previous sets of notes on variants. It also provides exegetic and explanatory notes and generous quotations from documents concerning Shen, from his other books, from the reflections of other early writers on his subject matter, and from modern Chinese (and to some extent Japanese and Western) scholarship. Appendixes include thirty-six additional jottings or fragments that have survived only in the writings or compilations of others; all known prefaces and colophons; notes on eds. by early bibliographers and collators; a chronological biography; a list of Shen's writings; and an index to names and variant names of all persons mentioned in "Brush Talks" (a tool still very rare in Chinese publications). A 1-vol. version of the text with minimal apparatus was published by Hu as *Hsin chiao cheng Meng ch'i pi t'an*[73] ("Brush Talks From Dream Brook, Newly Edited"; Peking, 1957).

2. *Pu pi t'an*[74] ("Supplement to Brush Talks"), listed in most early bibliographies as two *chüan* but rearranged into three *chüan* with some alteration of order in the 1631 ed. Ninety-one jottings. Hu suggests that this and the next item were edited posthumously from Shen's notes. There is even stronger evidence for this hypothesis than he adduces, for some articles appear to be rejected drafts of jottings in "Brush Talks" (compare 588 with 437, 601 with 274).

3. *Hsu pi t'an*[75] ("Sequel to Brush Talks"), eleven jottings in one *chüan*, mostly on literature.

4. *Hsi-ning Feng-yuan li*[76] ("The Oblatory Epoch Astronomical System of the Splendid Peace Reign Period," 1075), lost, but listed in a Sung bibliography as seven *chüan*. This was the official report embodying Shen's calendar reform. It would have followed the usual arrangement, providing lists of constants and step-by-step instructions for computation, with tables as needed, so that the complete ephemerides could be calculated by someone with no knowledge of astronomy. Since a *Hsi-ning Feng-yuan li ching*[77] ("Canon of the Oblatory Epoch Astronomical System . . .") in three *chüan* is separately recorded, the remaining four *chüan* may have been, as in other instances, an official critique (*li i*[78]) outlining the observational basis of the system and reporting on tests of its accuracy. The Sung standard

history also records a ready reckoner (*li ch'eng*[79]) in fourteen *chüan*, used to simplify calculations, and a detailed explanation of the mathematics with worked-out examples (*pei ts'ao*[80]) in six *chüan*. Surviving fragments of the basic document have been gathered by the great student of ancient astronomy Li Jui[81] (1765–1814) under the title *Pu hsiu Sung Feng-yuan shu*[82] ("Restoration of the Sung Oblatory Epoch Techniques"), printed in his *Li shih i shu*[83] ("Posthumous works of Mr. Li," 1823).

5. *Liang fang*[19] ("Good Prescriptions"), a work of ten or fifteen *chüan* compiled during Shen's retirement. In the Sung it was combined with a smaller medical miscellany by the greatest literary figure of Shen's time, Su Shih[84] (1036–1101), a moderate but influential opponent of the New Policies. The conflation is called *Su Shen nei-han liang fang*[85] ("Good Prescriptions by the Hanlin Academicians Su and Shen"), often referred to as *Su Shen liang fang*. The most broadly based text is that in the *Chih pu-tsu chai ts'ung-shu*[86] collection and modern reprints descended from it. One copy of an illustrated Ming ed. still exists. Shen's original compilation was lost sometime after 1500. There is some overlap between *chüan* 1 of *Su Shen liang fang* and jottings in *chüan* 26 of *Meng ch'i pi t'an*; see the comparison in Hu's *Chiao cheng*, pp. 880–882. A lost collection of prescriptions in twenty *chüan*, *Ling yuan fang*[87] ("Prescriptions From the Holy Garden"), is quoted in Sung treatises on materia medica. Hu has shown that it was written before *Liang fang* (*Meng ch'i pi t'an chiao cheng*, pp. 830–831).

6. *Wang huai lu*[20] ("Record of Longings Forgotten"), three *chüan*, compiled during Shen's retirement. It incorporates a lost book of observations on mountain living written (or at least begun) in Shen's youth and entitled *Huai shan lu*[88] ("Record of Longings for the Mountains"). His retirement to Dream Brook satisfied his early longings, hence the title of the later collection. It was lost soon after his death. The only well-known excerpts, in the *Shuo fu*[89] collection, are on implements useful to the well-born mountain dweller, but Hu Tao-ching in a recent study has shown that the book was correctly classified by early bibliographers as agricultural. See "Shen Kua ti nung-hsueh chu-tso *Meng ch'i Wang huai lu*"[90] ("Shen Kua's Agricultural Work . . ."), in *Wen shih*,[91] 3 (1963), 221–225. Hu's collection of all known fragments has not yet appeared.

7. *Ch'ang-hsing chi*[92] ("Collected Literary Works of [the Viscount of] Ch'ang-hsing"), originally forty-one *chüan*, almost certainly a posthumous compilation. Includes prose, poetry, and administrative documents prized for their language. By the time this work was reprinted in the Ming (*ca.* fifteenth century), only nineteen *chüan* of the Sung version remained. An additional three *chüan* were collected from other works and printed at the head of the recension in *Shen shih san hsien-sheng wen chi*[93] (1718). This is now the best ed. available. The collection includes important astronomical documents and a great deal of information on Shen's intellectual formation, in particular his commentary on

Mencius (*Meng-tzu chieh*[94]) in *chüan* 23.

The only book in any Western language that translates more than a few examples of Shen's writings is Joseph Needham *et al.*, *Science and Civilisation in China*, 7 vols. projected (Cambridge, 1954–   ), particularly from vol. III on. The translations always occur in context, usually with fuller historical background than given in Chinese publications. Occasionally the English version is extremely free, as when "Meng ch'i" is translated "Dream Pool." Translations into modern Chinese are sprinkled through Chang Chia-chü,[95] *Shen Kua* (Shanghai, 1962). A complete Japanese trans. of "Brush Talks" and its sequels is an ongoing project of the History of Science Seminar, Research Institute for Humanistic Studies (Jimbun Kagaku Kenkyūsho[96]), Kyoto University. A representative selection of English translations will be included in a sourcebook of Chinese science being compiled by N. Sivin.

II. SECONDARY LITERATURE. There is no bibliography devoted to studies of Shen's life or work, but most primary and secondary sources in Chinese have been cited in Hu's ed. or in the footnotes to the biography of Shen by Chang Chia-chü (see above). The latter is the fullest and most accurate account of Shen's life, and pays attention to the whole range of his work. It is generally critical in method, but sometimes careless. Like other recent Chinese accounts, it is extremely positivistic, patronizing toward "feudal" aspects of Shen's mentality, and inclined to exaggerate his sympathies toward the common people. A concise survey of Shen's life and positive contributions by a great historian of mathematics is Ch'ien Pao-tsung,[97] "Shen Kua," in Seminar in the History of the Natural Sciences, ed., *Chung-kuo ku-tai k'o-hsueh-chia*[98] ("Ancient Chinese Scientists"; Peking, 1959), 111–121. Another work of interest by Hu Tao-ching, overlapping to some extent the preface to his ed. of "Brush Talks," is "Shen Kua ti cheng-chih ch'ing-hsiang ho t'a tsai k'o-hsueh ch'eng-chiu-shang ti li-shih t'iao-chien"[99] ("Shen Kua's Political Tendencies and the Historical Conditions Bearing on His Scientific Accomplishments"), in Li Kuang-pi and Ch'ien Chün-yeh,[100] eds., *Chung-kuo li-shih jen-wu lun-chi*[101] ("Essays on Chinese Historical Figures"; Peking, 1957), 330–347. Its summary of scientific and technical accomplishments in the Northern Sung period from 960 to *ca.* 1100 is especially useful.

In addition to discursive biographical studies, Shen's life has been the subject of four chronologies (*nien-p'u*[102]), an old form in which individual events are simply listed year by year along with related data. The fullest in print (although obsolete in a number of respects) is Chang Yin-lin,[103] "Shen Kua pien nien shih chi"[104] ("A Chronicle of Shen Kua"), in *Ch'ing-hua hsueh-pao*,[105] 11 (1936), 323–358. That appended to the 2-vol. Hu Tao-ching ed. of "Brush Talks," 1141–1156, is especially handy because of its references to jottings and to sources cited in the book's notes. The most up-to-date and accurate chronology is the one at the end of Chang Chia-chü, *Shen Kua*, 235–259. Hu Tao-ching, in his colophon to the 1960 ed. of "Brush Talks," remarked that his own book-length chronology was in the press, but it has not yet appeared.

Yabuuchi Kiyoshi,[106] Japan's leading historian of science, has provided a characteristically reflective discussion of the historic circumstances of Shen's career in "Shin Katsu to sono gyōseki,"[107] ("Shen Kua and His Achievements"), in *Kagakushi kenkyū*,[108] 48 (1958), 1–6. The most stimulating contribution to the study of Shen in the past decade is Teraji Jun,[109] "Shin Katsu no shizen kenkyū to sono haikei"[110] ("The Natural Investigations of Shen Kua and Their Background"), in *Hiroshima daigaku bungakubu kiyō*,[111] 27, no. 1 (1967), 99–121. Rejecting the prevalent tendency to prove Shen's greatness by citing anticipations of European science and technology, the author has made a fruitful and original effort to grasp the inner coherence of his thought and work. This article provided a point of departure for the first two sections of the "Conclusion" of the present article.

The first, and so far the only, European introduction to Shen's life is Donald Holzman, "Shen Kua and his *Meng-ch'i pi-t'an*," in *T'oung Pao* (Leiden), 46 (1958), 260–292, occasioned by the first publication of Hu's ed. of "Brush Talks." In addition to providing a critical and well-proportioned biographical sketch, Holzman has paid more attention to Shen's humanistic scholarship than has any other author discussed in this section. He also considers some of the evidence for Shen's position in the history of science, but reaches no conclusion. He tends to ask whether Shen's ideas are correct from today's point of view rather than what they contributed to better understanding of nature in the Sung. The most reliable and compendious introduction to the New Policies is James T. C. Liu, *Reform in Sung China. Wang An-shih (1021–1086) and His New Policies* (Cambridge, Mass., 1959). A full-length intellectual biography of Shen is under way by N. Sivin.

The first modern study of any aspect of Shen's interests, largely responsible for the attention paid him by Chinese educated in modern science, is Chu K'o-chen,[112] "Pei Sung Shen Kua tui-yü ti-hsueh chih kung-hsien yü chi-shu"[113] ("Contributions to and Records Concerning the Earth Sciences by Shen Kua of the Northern Sung Period"), in *K'o-hsueh*,[114] 11 (1926), 792–807. Chu's erudite and broadly conceived article has influenced much of the later writing on the subject. A great number of observations on Shen's scientific and technical ideas are distributed through Needham *et al.*, *Science and Civilisation in China*, as well as through the topical studies by leading Japanese specialists in Yabuuchi Kiyoshi, ed., *Sō Gen jidai no kagaku gijutsu shi*[115] ("History of Science and Technology in the Sung and Yuan Periods"; Kyoto, 1967).

There is no recent investigation in depth of Shen's astronomical activities, but a good technical description of what were traditionally considered his most important contributions is found in Juan Yuan,[116] *Ch'ou jen chuan*[117] ("Biographies of Mathematical Astronomers"

[1799]; Shanghai, 1935), 20:238–243. Shen's most noteworthy mathematical problems have been studied in the various articles in Ch'ien Pao-tsung, ed., *Sung Yuan shu-hsueh-shih lun-wen-chi*[118] ("Essays in the History of Mathematics in the Sung and Yuan Periods"; Peking, 1966). The considerable portion of "Brush Talks" devoted to music is evaluated and used in Rulan C. Pian, *Sonq [sic] Dynasty Musical Sources and Their Interpretation* (Cambridge, Mass., 1967), esp. 30–32. Shen's ideas concerning economic theory, the circulation of money, and similar topics have been related to traditions of thought on these subjects in an unpublished study by

Robert M. Hartwell. A number of interesting ideas are found in Sakade Yoshinobu's[119] positivistic discussion of Shen's use of theory, "Shin Katsu no shizenkan ni tsuite"[120] ("On Shen Kua's Conception of Nature"), in *Tōhōgaku*,[121] **39** (1970), 74–87. Shen's remarks on ancient techniques are elucidated in Hsia Nai,[122] "Shen Kua ho k'ao-ku-hsueh"[123] ("Shen Kua and Archaeology"), in *K'ao-ku*,[124] no. 5 (1974), 277–289, also in *K'ao-ku hsueh-pao*,[125] no. 2 (1974), 1–14, with English summary, 15–17.

N. SIVIN

NOTES

1. 沈括	29. 五行	53. 羌	筆談	和他在科学成就	119. 坂出祥伸
2. 錢塘	30. 氣	54. 木經	74. 補筆談	上的历史条件	120. 沈括の自然觀に
3. 潤州京口	31. 律呂	55. 寇宗奭	75. 續筆談	100. 李光璧, 錢君曄	ついて
4. 沈周	32. 隙積	56. 本草衍義	76. 熙寧奉元曆	101. 中國歷史人物	121. 東方學
5. 許	33. 楊輝	57. 秋石	77. 曆經	論集	122. 夏鼐
6. 新法	34. 朱世傑	58. 宮下三郎	78. 曆議	102. 年譜	123. 沈括和考古学
7. 王安石	35. 一行	59. 漢薬秋石の薬	79. 立成	103. 張蔭麟	124. 考古
8. 寧國	36. 萬	史学的研究	80. 備草	104. 編年事輯	125. 学報
9. 蕪湖	37. 樂律	60. 渡辺幸三	81. 李銳	105. 清華學報	
10. 張蒭	38. 祖暅	61. 現存する中國	82. 補修宋奉元術	106. 藪內清	
11. 衛朴	39. 奉元	近世までの五	83. 李氏遺書	107. 沈括とその業績	
12. 永安	40. 授時	藏六府図の概	84. 蘇軾	108. 科学史研究	
13. 平泉	41. 郭守敬	説	85. 蘇沈內翰良方	109. 寺地遵	
14. 蔡確	42. 郭廷以	62. 燕肅	86. 知不足齋叢書	110. 沈括の自然研	
15. 延州	43. 太平天国曆法	63. 蘇頌	87. 靈苑方	究とその背景	
16. 經略安撫使	考訂	64. 渾儀議	88. 懷山錄	111. 広島大学文学	
17. 開國子	44. 羅爾綱	65. 搏	89. 說郛	部紀要	
18. 夢溪	45. 天曆考及天曆	66. 微	90. 沈括的農學著	112. 竺可楨	
19. 良方	與陰陽曆日對	67. 續資治通鑑長編	作《夢溪忘懷錄》	113. 北宋沈括對於	
20. 忘懷錄	照表	68. 儒法斗争与我	91. 文史	地學之貢獻與	
21. 夢溪筆談	46. 謝莊	国古代科学技	92. 長興集	紀述	
22. 象數	47. 顏眞卿	术的发展	93. 沈氏三先生文集	114. 科學	
23. 技藝	48. 朱熹	69. 胡道靜, 校證	94. 孟子解	115. 宋元時代の科	
24. 辯證	49. 孫思恭	70. 蔡京	95. 張家駒	学技術史	
25. 異事	50. 磁	71. 陳登原	96. 人文科學研究所	116. 阮元	
26. 器用	50a. 石油	72. 古今典籍聚	97. 錢宝琮	117. 疇人傳	
27. 雜識	51. 畢昇	散考	98. 中国古代科学家	118. 宋元数学史论	
28. 藥議	52. 十百千	73. 新校證夢溪	99. 沈括的政治傾向	文集	

SHEWHART, WALTER ANDREW (*b.* New Canton, Illinois, 18 March 1891; *d.* Troy Hills, New Jersey, 11 March 1967)

Shewhart, the "father" of statistical quality control, was the son of Anton and Esta Barney Shewhart. He received an A.B. from the University of Illinois in 1913 and an A.M. in 1914. On 4 August 1914 he married Edna Hart. He received a Ph.D. in physics from the University of California in 1917, having been an assistant in physics (1914–1915) and a Whiting Fellow (1914–1916).

Following receipt of his doctorate, Shewhart was an assistant in physics at the University of Illinois (1916–1917), then head of the physics department at the Wisconsin Normal School in Lacrosse (1917–1918). The rest of his professional career was spent in the Bell System, initially with the Western Electric Company (1918–1924), then in the Bell Telephone Laboratories from their incorporation in 1925 until his retirement in 1956.

Sometime around 1920, the Western Electric Company, manufacturer of telephone equipment for the Bell Telephone System, learned from experience that repeated adjustment of a manufacturing process to compensate for observed departures from the process average can result in greater variability. (A mathematical explanation was provided by Preston C. Hammer in 1950.) On the other hand, a ''large'' deviation from, or a succession of values above (or, below), the process average may indicate a need for corrective action. An answer was needed to the question of how to distinguish situations that call for corrective action from situations in which the process should be left alone. The problem of finding an answer was handed to Shewhart. He devised (1924) a new statistical tool, known today as the control chart, that signals when search for a cause of variation, and removal of this cause, will indeed reduce variation; and when search for a cause of variation, accompanied by action on the system, will only intensify the variation.

A control chart is a graph showing repeated determinations of some characteristic of a production process plotted in chronological order, with a horizontal center line corresponding to the average value of the characteristic, and upper and lower control limits such that plotted points outside these limits will tend to indicate the presence of a cause (or causes) of variation in addition to the random variation inherent in the process. Points outside these action limits are deemed to signal the need for a special investigation of the process to identify the disturbing cause(s). The plot of observed or measured values *in chronological order* is the essential feature of a control chart; and it marked an important departure from traditional statistical practice, in which observed or measured values are lumped together without regard to their chronological order to form a sample for which measures of location (average, median, mode), measures of dispersion (average deviation, standard deviation, range), and so on are then evaluated.

During the 1920's, Shewhart published a series of articles in the *Bell System Technical Journal* on the construction, application, and usefulness of control charts of various kinds, culminating in his definitive exposition of statistical quality control, *Economic Control of Quality of Manufactured Product* (1931), in which he recognized two distinct causes of variation: (a) chance causes, producing random variation intrinsic to the process, and (b) assignable causes (now sometimes called special causes), the kind that one should search for, try to identify, and eliminate. He noted that when all assignable causes have been removed, the variation of the outputs of the process will be stable, the process will be in ''a state of statistical control,'' and its variation cannot be further reduced. Hence, if less variation is desired, this can be attained only by introducing a new process. A control chart is thus a triple-valued statistical tool: (1) it serves to define the goal of process performance that management might strive to achieve; (2) it is an instrument for attaining this goal; and (3) it is a tool for judging whether the goal of statistical control has been attained.

For action limits separating when to look from when to not look for assignable causes, Shewhart recommended ''three-sigma'' control limits, that is, horizontal lines at distances 3σ above and below the center line, with σ being the standard deviation of the plotted values implied by the inherent random variation of the process under study. From experience with a wide range of industrial processes, he had found that 3σ limits provided an approximate economic balance between the costs of mistakenly signaling the presence of nonexistent assignable causes and the costs of failure to signal the presence of existent assignable causes. Adopted by the American Society for Testing Materials in its *1933 A.S.T.M. Manual on Presentation of Data*, and with the coming of World War II recommended also in the American Standards Association's American War Standards Z1.1-1941, Z1.2-1941, and Z1.3-1942, 3σ limits became, and have largely remained, the standard practice in American industry.

In 1935 the British Standards Institution adopted Shewhart control chart techniques with two changes. First, instead of 3σ control limits, it recommended an outer pair of .001-probability action limits such that, when inherent chance causes alone are operative, the probability of a plotted point falling above the upper action limit (or below the lower action limit) would be .001. Second, it recommended an inner pair of .025-probability warning limits similarly determined, with the appearance of a succession of plotted values above the upper (or below the lower) inner limit to be taken as a warning, if not as a positive indication, of lack of control. The aim of the inner warning limits was to aid in identifying the onset of trouble.

Whereas the 3σ and .001-probability control limits are very nearly the same in the case of control charts for averages of successive sets of n (≥ 4) individual values, such is not the case for control charts for product variation, that is, charts for standard deviations or ranges of sets of n individual values, or for defects per unit area (or failures per unit time). The sampling distributions of these measures are skewed with the long "tail" to the right. Consequently, in these cases the upper 3σ limit will lie below the upper .001-probability limit, so that the risk of looking for assignable causes of increased product variation (or increased rate of defects or failures) will be greater than .001 when no change has occurred. The situation will be the opposite in the case of the lower limits, but to a lesser degree. The net result of using 3σ limits will be an increased risk of looking for trouble when there is none, the actual increase depending on the degree of skewness.

Although the foregoing reasoning seems to favor the probability limits, Shewhart remained firm in support of 3σ limits on at least two grounds. First, as noted above, he had found from extensive experience that 3σ limits yielded an approximate economic balance between the costs of failure to notice real trouble when present, and the costs of crying, "Wolf! Wolf!" when there was no trouble. Second, 3σ limits are computationally defined and do not depend, as do probability limits, on the assumed mathematical form of the random variation of product characteristics (or on the assumed mathematical form of the sampling distributions of standard deviations, ranges, and so on, evaluated from small sets of measurements).

Instead of inner warning limits, Shewhart (1941) recommended looking for warnings in nonrandom patterns of the plotted points: a "long run" of, say, seven or more consecutive points above (or below) the center line would suggest the possibility of a shift up (down) of average performance; a "long run up" ("down") of, say, seven or more consecutive increases (decreases) would suggest the onset of a trend; and when there are no significantly long runs above or below the center line (or up or down), if, nonetheless, the total number (N) of runs above and below (or up and down) is exceptionally small (say $N \leq N_{.005}$), or excessively large (say, $N \geq N_{.995}$), or there are a great many short runs above and below (or up and down), these departures from randomness may be indicative of erratic or oscillatory behavior calling for investigation.

As Shewhart stressed (1939, Chap. 2), bringing a production process into a state of statistical control and keeping it in control (or restoring it to control) are necessary for prediction of performance of future product. Without statistical control, such prediction is not logically possible. For a production process that has been in control for a substantial period, he showed (ibid.), with the aid of empirical sampling experiments, how to construct prediction limits bounding a statistical tolerance range (or interval) within which a prescribed percentage of future product performance may be expected to fall as long as the process remains in control; he emphasized that such statistical tolerance intervals (limits) differ markedly from the statistician's confidence intervals (limits). Others promptly provided mathematical theory and tables for determining statistical tolerance limits of various kinds.

Whereas Shewhart's early writings and first book (1931) were focused on statistical control of industrial production processes, in his second book (1939) he extended the applications of statistical process control to the measurement processes of science, and stressed the importance of operational definitions of basic quantities in science, industry, and commerce.

In 1950, W. Edwards Deming, at the request of the Union of Japanese Scientists and Engineers, give a series of lectures in Japan on Shewhart's statistical quality control of industrial processes. These lectures were the catalyst that gave birth to Japan's industrial efficiency and emphasis on highest attainable quality of manufactured products.

Shewhart was a founding member and fellow of the Institute of Mathematical Statistics (president, 1937, 1944); founding member of the American Society for Quality Control (first honorary member, 1947; first Shewhart Medalist, 1948); a fellow of the American Statistical Association (president, 1945), International Statistical Institute, Royal Statistical Society (honorary fellow, 1954), Econometric Society, Royal Economic Society, American Association for the Advancement of Science (Council member, 1942–1949), and New York Academy of Science; and a member of the American Mathematical Society, Mathematical Association of America, American Physical Society, American Society for Testing Materials, Psychometric Society, Acoustical Society of America, Philosophy of Science Association, and Association for Symbolic Logic. In 1954, Shewhart was awarded the Holley Medal by the American Society of Mechanical Engineers, and in 1962 he received an honorary doctorate from the Indian Statistical Institute of Calcutta.

BIBLIOGRAPHY

I. ORIGINAL WORKS. Shewhart's most important publications are his two books: *Economic Control of Quality of Manufactured Product* (New York, 1931; repr. 1980) and *Statistical Method from the Viewpoint of Quality Control* (Washington, D.C., 1939; repr. New York, 1986). The first is a complete and thorough exposition of basic principles and techniques of quality control of manufactured products through statistical control of industrial processes. The second, based on his four lectures in March 1938 at the Graduate School of the U.S. Department of Agriculture in Washington, edited by W. Edwards Deming, has profoundly influenced statistical methods of research in the behavioral, biological, and physical sciences and in engineering by bringing his ideas and procedures to the attention of users of statistical methods. For a fuller appreciation of Shewhart's greatness, see his "Nature and Origin of Standards of Quality," in *Bell System Technical Journal*, **37** (1958), 1–22, written in 1935.

During the 1920's and early 1930's, Shewhart wrote a series of papers that reveal the evolution of his thinking and methods that jelled in his 1931 book: "On the Measurement of a Physical Quantity Whose Magnitude Is Influenced by Primary Causes Beyond the Control of the Observer and on the Method of Determining the Relation Between Two Such Quantities," in *Proceedings of the National Academy of Sciences*, **8** (1922), 248–251; "Some Applications of Statistical Methods to the Analysis of Physical and Engineering Data," in *Bell System Technical Journal*, **3** (1924), 43–87; "The Application of Statistics as an Aid in Maintaining Quality of a Manufactured Product," in *Journal of the American Statistical Association*, **20** (1925), 546–548; "Correction of Data for Errors of Measurement," in *Bell System Technical Journal*, **5** (1926), 11–26; "Correction of Data for Errors of Averages Obtained from Small Samples," *ibid.*, 308–319; "Finding Causes of Quality Variations," in *Manufacturing Industries*, **11**, no. 2 (1926), 125–128; "Quality Control Charts," in *Bell System Technical Journal*, **5** (1926), 593–603; "Quality Control," *ibid.*, **6** (1927), 722–735; "Economic Aspects of Engineering Applications of Statistical Methods," in *Journal of the Franklin Institute*, **205** (1928), 395–405; "Note on the Probability Associated with the Error of a Single Observation," in *Journal of Forestry*, **26** (1928), 600–607; "Small Samples: New Experimental Results," in *Journal of the American Statistical Association*, **23** (1928), 144–153, written with F. W. Winters; "Significance of an Observed Range," in *Journal of Forestry*, **26** (1928), 899–905; "Basis for Analysis of Test Results of Die-Casting Alloy Investigation," in *American Society for Testing Materials, Proceedings*, **29** (1929), 200–210; "Economic Quality Control of Manufactured Product," in *Bell System Technical Journal*, **9** (1930), 364–389; "Applications of Statistical Method in Engineering," in *Journal of the American Statistical Asso-*

ciation, **26** (1931), March supp., 214–221; "Random Sampling," in *American Mathematical Monthly*, **38** (1931), 245–270; and "Statistical Method from an Engineering Viewpoint," in *Journal of the American Statistical Association*, **26** (1931), 262–269.

After his 1931 book Shewhart published "The Rôle of Statistical Method in Economic Standardization," in *Econometrica*, **1** (1933), 23–35; "Annual Survey of Statistical Technique. Developments in Sampling Theory," *ibid.*, 225–237; "Some Aspects of Quality Control," in *Mechanical Engineering*, **56** no. 12 (1934), 725–730; "Applications of Statistical Methods to Manufacturing Problems," in *Journal of the Franklin Institute*, **226** (1938), 163–186; "The Future of Statistics in Mass Production," in *Annals of Mathematical Statistics*, **10** (1939), 88–90; "Contribution of Statistics to the Science of Engineering," in Hugh Dryden *et al.*, *Fluid Mechanics and Statistical Methods in Engineering* (Philadelphia, 1941), 97–124, in which he recommends augmenting his former control chart techniques with examination of the statistical significance of observed "runs above and below average" and "runs up and down"; "Statistical Control in Applied Science," in *Transactions of the American Society of Mechanical Engineers*, **65** (1943), 222–225; and "The Advancing Statistical Front," in *Journal of the American Statistical Association*, **41** (1946), 1–15.

II. SECONDARY LITERATURE. W. Edwards Deming, "Walter A. Shewhart, 1891–1967," in *Review of the International Statistical Institute*, **36** (1968), 372–375, a slightly abridged version of which appeared in *The American Statistician*, **21**, no. 2 (1967), 39–40, and "Shewhart, Walter A.," in *International Encyclopedia of Statistics*, II (New York, 1978), 942–944; Harold F. Dodge, obituary in *International Quality Control*, **23** (1967), 529; and L. H. C. Tippett, obituary in *Journal of the Royal Statistical Society*, **A130**, pt. 4 (1967), 593–594.

Seven articles on Shewhart and his impact on industrial production and quality control in *Industrial Quality Control*, **24** (1967) are rich sources of further information, insight, and perspective: "The First Shewhart Control Chart" (a facsimile of the chart and memorandum of transmittal dated 16 May 1924), 72; Paul S. Olmsted, "Our Debt to Walter Shewhart," 73; "The Shewhart Medal," 74; E. S. Pearson, "Some Notes on W. A. Shewhart's Influence on Application of Statistical Methods in Great Britain," 81–83; William A. Golomski, "Walter A. Shewhart, Man of Quality: His Work, Our Challenge," 83–85; "Highlights in the Life of Walter A. Shewhart," 109–110; "Tributes to Walter A. Shewhart," 111–122. A brief letter from Edna Shewhart and two more tributes are in *ibid.*, 332–333. See also Lloyd S. Nelson, "The Legacy of Walter Shewhart," in *Quality Progress*, **12**, no. 7 (1979), 26–28; and "Walter A. Shewhart, Father of Statistical Quality Control," *ibid.*, **19**, no. 1 (1986), 50–51.

For the background, philosophical basis, intent, and early history of Shewhart's control chart, see M. D. Fagen, ed., *A History of Engineering and Science in the Bell System* (New York, 1975), chap. 9, esp. sec. 5, which includes a facsimile of the first chart and accompanying memorandum (Fig. 9-6, p. 879).

See also American Society for Testing Materials, *1933 A.S.T.M. Manual on Presentation of Data* (Philadelphia, 1933; 4th rev., 1976); American Standards Association, *Guide for Quality Control*, American War Standard Z1.1-1941 (New York, 1941; also ANSI/ASQC Standard Z1.1-1985), *Control Chart Method of Analyzing Data*, American War Standard Z1.2-1941 (New York, 1941; also ANSI/ASQC Standard Z1.2-1985), and *Control Chart Method for Controlling Quality During Production*, American War Standard Z1.3-1942 (New York, 1942; also ANSI/ASQC Standard Z1.3-1985); Preston C. Hammer, "Interference with a Controlled Process," in *Journal of the American Statistical Association*, **45** (1950), 249–256; and E. S. Pearson, *The Application of Statistical Methods to Industrial Standardization and Quality Control* (London, 1935).

CHURCHILL EISENHART

SHIRAKATSÍ, ANANIA (also known as Ananias of Shirak) (*b.* Shirakavan [now Ani], Armenia, *ca.* 620; *d.* shortly after 685)

A representative of the progressive Armenian scholars of the seventh century and a follower of the best traditions of Hellenistic science and culture, Shirakatsí lived during the period when Armenia had lost her political independence; the western part being ruled by Byzantium and the eastern by Persia. He received his basic education at a local monastery school. After several journeys in search of a teacher of mathematics, which he considered the "mother of all sciences," Shirakatsí reached Trebizond and entered the school of the Greek scientist Tychicus, who taught the children of many Byzantine nobles. During the next eight years he studied mathematics, cosmography, philosophy, and several other sciences, before returning to his native region of Shirak, where he opened a school. In addition to teaching, he conducted scientific research and wrote works on astronomy, mathematics, geography, history, and other sciences. He possessed truly encyclopedic knowledge and the ability to reach the essence of matters.

Shirakatsí produced his most important scientific work from the 650's through the 670's. In 667–669 he was concerned with the reform of the Armenian calendar, anticipating the modern desire for an "immovable" calendar.

Shirakatsí's scientific works are known through manuscripts of the eleventh through seventeenth centuries that are scattered in the Soviet Union, Italy, Great Britain, Austria, Israel, and perhaps other countries. His advanced philosophical and cosmological views brought him to the attention of official circles, and he was persecuted by both lay and ecclesiastical authorities.

Like the scientists of antiquity, Shirakatsí believed that the world consists of four elements: earth, water, air, and fire. The world, in which he included plants, animals, and man, is a "definite composition of intermixed elements."

All things in nature move and are subject to change. Old substances decompose in due course, and new forms arise in their place. Creation, wrote Shirakatsí, is the basis of destruction; and destruction in its turn is the basis of creation; "as a consequence of this harmless contradiction, the world acquires its eternal existence."

On the form of the earth, Shirakatsí wrote: "The earth seems to me to have an egg-shaped form: as the yolk in spherical form is in the middle, the white around it, and a shell surrounds it all, so the earth is in the center like the yolk, the air around it like the white, and the sky surrounds it all like the shell." In the early Middle Ages such ideas were very daring.

In connection with the spherical form of the earth, Shirakatsí spoke of the mountains and canyons "on the other side" of the earth. He wrote about the antipodes, of animals and people "like a fly, moving on an apple equally well on all sides. When it is night on one side of the earth, the sun lights the other half of the earth's sphere."

Shirakatsí believed that the earth is in equilibrium in space because the force of gravity, which pulls it down, is opposed by the force of the wind, which tries to raise it.

Criticizing numerous legends that explained the Milky Way, Shirakatsí gave an explanation that was correct and bold for the time: "The Milky Way is a mass of thickly clustered and weakly shining stars."

The moon, in Shirakatsí's opinion, does not emit its own light but reflects that of the sun. He associated the phases of the moon, which proceed from changes in the mutual positions of the sun and moon, with this reflection of the sun's light.

Shirakatsí gave a correct explanation for solar and lunar eclipses and composed a special table for calculating their occurrence, using the nineteen-year "lunar cycle."

In his *Geometry of Astronomy* Shirakatsí tried to determine the distance from the earth to the sun, the moon, and the planets, and to estimate the true dimensions of the sun. Such a problem was of course beyond the observational techniques of his time.

Shirakatsí's works on the calendar were of great importance. He studied and compared the calendar systems of fourteen nations, among them the Agvancians (ancient inhabitants of Azerbaidjan), who did not leave any written records, and the Cappadocians.

Of special interest is his *Tables of the Lunar Cycle*, the authorship of which was established in the mid-twentieth century. The Yerevan Matenadaran, a repository of ancient manuscripts and books, possesses ten records that contain this work, which was based on his own observations. He wrote in his foreword:

> I, Anania Shirakatsí, have faithfully studied the course and changes in the appearance of the moon through all the days of its passage and, noting them, have fixed this information in tables, wishing to lighten the work of those who are interested. And I have drawn first the newborn moon, and then the full moon, on what day it takes place, at what time—in the night or in the day, at what hour and what minute.

Shirakatsí considered not only the days of the various phases of the moon but also the hours, which had not been done in any previous calendar. A comparison of his lunar tables with modern data shows the former's great precision.

Shirakatsí's textbook of arithmetic is one of the oldest known Armenian textbooks. Its mathematical tables—of multiplication and of arithmetical and geometrical progression—also are the oldest.

BIBLIOGRAPHY

I. ORIGINAL WORKS. Shirakatsí's writings include *Ananiayi Širakunwoy mnatsordk' panic'* ("Collected Works of Anania Shirakatsí"), K. P. Patkanian, ed. (St. Petersburg, 1877), in classical Armenian; his autobiography in English, in F. C. Conybeare, "Ananias of Širak," in *Byzantinische Zeitschrift*, 11 (1897), 572–584, also translated into French by H. Berberian in *Revue des Études Arméniennes*, n.s. 1 (1964), 189; *T'uabanut'iwn* ("Arithmetic"), A. G. Abrahamean, ed. (Erevan, 1939); *Tiezeragitut'iwn ew Tomar* ("Cosmography and Chronology"), A. G. Abrahamean, ed. (Erevan, 1940), also in Armenian; *Tablitsy lunnogo kruga* ("Tables of the Motions of the Moon"), A. G. Abrahamean, ed. (Erevan, 1962), in Russian and Armenian; and a collection of Shirakatsí's other works, *Anania Širakac'u matenadrut'iwn* ("The Works of Anania Shirakatsí"), A. G. Abrahamean, ed. (Erevan, 1944), in Armenian.

II. SECONDARY LITERATURE. See A. G. Abrahamean and G. B. Petrosian, *Ananias Shirakatsy* (Erevan, 1970), in Russian; F. C. Conybeare, "Ananias of Shirak, 'On Christmas,' " in *Expositor* (London), 5th ser., 4 (1896), 321–337; R. H. Hewsen, "Science in VIIth Century Armenia: Ananias of Širak," in *Isis*, 59 (1968), 32–45; I. A. Orbely, *"Voprosy i reshenia" Ananii Shirakatsi* ("The Problems and Solutions of Anania Shirakatsi") (Petrograd, 1918); W. Petri, "Anania Shirakazi—ein armenischer Kosmograph des 7. Jahrhunderts," in *Zeitschrift der Deutschen morgenländischen Gesellschaft*, 114, no. 2 (1964), 269–288, also in *Mitteilungen der Sternwarte München*, 1, no. 14 (1964), 269–288; G. Ter-Mkrtchian, "Anania Shirakatsy," in *Ararat* (1896), 96–104, 143–152, 199–208, 292–296, 336–344; and B. E. Tumanian and R. A. Abramian, "Ob astronomicheskikh rabotakh Ananii Shirakatsi" ("On the Astronomical Works of Anania Shirakatsi"), in *Istoriko-astronomicheskie issledovaniya*, no. 2 (1956), 239–246.

P. G. KULIKOVSKY

SHNIRELMAN, LEV GENRIKHOVICH (*b.* Gomel, Russia, 2 January 1905; *d.* Moscow, U.S.S.R., 24 September 1938)

The son of a teacher, Shnirelman displayed remarkable mathematical abilities even as a child. In his twelfth year he studied an entire course of elementary mathematics at home; and in 1921 he entered Moscow University, where he attended courses taught by N. N. Lusin, P. S. Uryson, and A. Y. Khinchin. While still a student he obtained several interesting results in algebra, geometry, and topology that he did not wish to publish, considering them of insufficient importance. After two and a half years Shnirelman graduated from the university, then remained for further study. Having completed his graduate work, he became professor and head of the department of mathematics at the Don Polytechnical Institute in Novocherkassk (1929). In the following year Shnirelman returned to Moscow and taught at the university. He was elected a corresponding member of the Soviet Academy of Sciences in 1933, and from 1934 he worked in the Mathematical Institute of the Academy.

In 1927–1929 Shnirelman, with his friend L. A. Lyusternik, made important contributions to the qualitative (topological) methods of the calculus of variations. Their starting point was Poincaré's problem of the three geodesics, which they first solved completely and generally by showing the existence of three closed geodesics on every simply connected surface (every surface homeomorphic to a sphere). For the proof of this theorem the authors used a method, which they broadly generalized, that had been devised by G. Birkhoff, who in 1919 showed the existence of one closed geodesic. Shnirelman and Lyusternik also applied their "principle of the stationary point" to other problems of geometry "im Grossen." They also presented a new topological invariant, the category of point sets.

In 1930 Shnirelman introduced an original and profound idea into number theory, using the concept of the compactness α of the sequence of natural numbers, $n_1, n_2, n_3, \ldots$ so that $\alpha = \inf \dfrac{N(x)}{x}$ ($x \geq 1$) where $N(x)$ is a number of the members of the sequence not exceeding x, and proving that every natural number n is representable as the sum of a finite (and independent of n) number of members of the sequences with a positive compactness. This allowed Shnirelman to prove, in particular, that any natural number is the sum of a certain finite number k of prime numbers—the Goldbach hypothesis in a less rigid form. According to the Goldbach hypothesis $k = 3$; by Shnirelman's method it is now possible to show that k is not greater than 20. Shnirelman also stated several arithmetical propositions, among them a generalization of Waring's theorem.

BIBLIOGRAPHY

I. ORIGINAL WORKS. Shnirelman's writings include "Sur un principe topologique en analyse," in *Comptes rendus . . . de l'Académie des sciences*, **188** (1929), 295–297, written with L. A. Lyusternik; "Existence de trois géodésiques fermées sur toute surface de genre 0," *ibid.*, 534–536, written with Lyusternik; "Sur le problème de trois géodésiques fermées sur les surfaces de genre 0," *ibid.*, **189** (1929), 269–271, written with Lyusternik; "Ob additivnykh svoystavakh chisel" ("On the Additive Properties of Numbers"), in *Izvestiya Donskogo politekhnicheskogo instituta v Novocherkasske*, **14**, nos. 2–3 (1930), 3–28, also in *Uspekhi matematicheskikh nauk*, **6** (1939), 9–25; "Über eine neue kombinatorische Invariante," in *Monatshefte für Mathematik und Physik*, **37** (1930), 131–134; *Topologicheskie metody v variatsionnykh zadachakh* ("Topological Methods in Variational Problems"; Moscow, 1930), written with Lyusternik; "Über additive Eigenschaften von Zahlen," in *Mathematische Annalen*, **107** (1933), 649–690; "Ob additivnykh svoystvakh chisel" ("On the Additive Properties of Numbers"), in *Uspekhi matematicheskikh nauk*, **7** (1940), 7–46; and "O slozhenii posledovatelnostey" ("On Addition of Sequences"), *ibid.*, 62–63.

II. SECONDARY LITERATURE. See "L. G. Shnirelman (1905–1938)," in *Uspekhi matematicheskikh nauk*, **6** (1939), 3–8; *Matematika v SSSR za pyatnadtsat let* ("Mathematics in the U.S.S.R. for Fifteen Years"; Moscow–Leningrad, 1932); *Matematika v SSSR za tridtsat let* ("Mathematics in the U.S.S.R. for Thirty Years"; Moscow–Leningrad, 1948); and *Matematika v SSSR za sorok let* ("Mathematics in the U.S.S.R. for Forty Years"), 2 vols. (Moscow, 1959), esp. II, 781–782.

A. P. YOUSCHKEVITCH

SIEGEL, CARL LUDWIG (*b.* Berlin, Germany, 31 December 1896; *d.* Göttingen, Federal Republic of Germany, 4 April 1981)

The son of a postal worker, Siegel studied at the University of Berlin from 1915 to 1917, attending lectures by Georg Frobenius that introduced him to the theory of numbers. Called into military service in 1917, he could not adapt to army life and was discharged. He then went to the University of Göttingen (1919–1920), where he worked on his inaugural dissertation and *Habilitationsschrift* under the guidance of Edmund Landau, a specialist in analytic number theory. Siegel was a professor at the University of Frankfurt from 1922 to 1937 and at the University of Göttingen from 1938 to 1940.

Siegel despised the Nazi regime. After lecturing in Denmark and Norway in 1940, he left Norway for the United States just a few days before the Nazi invasion. From 1940 to 1951 he worked at the Institute for Advanced Study at Princeton, where he had spent the year 1935. In 1946 he was appointed to a permanent professorship at the institute. Five years later he returned to Göttingen, where he spent the rest of his life.

Siegel was one of the leaders in the development of the theory of numbers, but he also proved important theorems in the theory of analytic functions of several complex variables and in celestial mechanics.

Siegel's inaugural dissertation (1920) was a landmark in the history of Diophantine approximations. Joseph Liouville had been the first to observe that algebraic numbers of degree $n > 1$ are "badly" approximated by rational numbers: for any such number ξ there is a constant $C(\xi)$ such that, for every rational number p/q with greatest common divisor $(p, q) = 1$, one has

$$\left|\xi - \frac{p}{q}\right| > C(\xi) \cdot \frac{1}{q^n}. \tag{1}$$

The proof is almost trivial, but the improved result obtained by Axel Thue in 1908 was more difficult to prove: the inequality

$$\left|\xi - \frac{p}{q}\right| \leq \frac{1}{q^2 + 1 + \epsilon} \tag{2}$$

(where $\epsilon > 0$ is arbitrary) is possible only for a finite number of values of p/q. Siegel obtained a still better result, which was crucial for his work of 1929 on Diophantine equations: there are only a finite number of rational numbers p/q such that

$$\left|\xi - \frac{p}{q}\right| \leq \frac{1}{q^{2\sqrt{n}}}. \tag{3}$$

The proof was very ingenious. In fact, Siegel did not directly prove that (3) has only a finite number of solutions p/q, but he showed that this is true for the inequality

$$\left|\xi - \frac{p}{q}\right| \leq \frac{1}{q^\beta}, \tag{4}$$

where $\beta = \dfrac{n}{s+1} + s + \dfrac{1}{2}$, s being any integer such that $0 \leq s \leq n - 1$; from that (3) is easily deduced by a suitable choice of s. The proof was by contradiction. If it is assumed that (4) has infinitely many solutions, it is possible to choose two of them, p_1/q_1 and p_2/q_2, such that q_1 and $r = [\log q_2/\log q_1]$ are arbitrarily large.

Siegel introduced two integers:

$$p < \frac{r}{16n} + n^2 \tag{5}$$

and m, which is the integral part of

$$\left(\frac{n + \dfrac{1}{16n}}{s+1} - 1\right)r.$$

He considered the two numbers

$$E_1 = C^r q_1^{m+r} q_2^s \left|\xi - \frac{p_1}{q_1}\right|^{r-p},$$

$$E_2 = C^r q_1^{m+2} q_2^s \left|\xi - \frac{p_2}{q_2}\right|,$$

and showed that there is a constant C, depending

only on ξ, such that $E_1 < 1$ and $E_2 < 1$. On the other hand, using the fact that ξ is an algebraic number of degree n, he constructed, by very intricate arguments, for each value of p satisfying (5) a polynomial $R_p(x, y)$ of degree $m + r - p$ in x, and degree s in y, with integral coefficients $\leq C''$ (with a constant C' depending only on ξ). Then, using Gustav Dirichlet's pigeonhole principle, he could show that there is a degree p satisfying (5) for which

$$q_1^{m+r-p} q_2^s R_p\left(\frac{p_1}{q_1}, \frac{p_2}{q_2}\right) \neq 0, \text{ and hence an integer} \geq$$

1; and that number, compared with the sum $E_1 + E_2$, implies that one of these two numbers must be ≥ 1, yielding the required contradiction.

In 1955 Siegel's result (3) was drastically improved by K. F. Roth: there are only a finite number of rational numbers p/q such that

$$\left|\xi - \frac{p}{q}\right| \leq \frac{1}{q^{2+\varepsilon}}, \tag{6}$$

where ε is any number > 0; this result is the best possible because there is an infinity of rational numbers p/q such that

$$\left|\xi - \frac{p}{q}\right| \leq \frac{1}{q^2}.$$

In 1929 Siegel published a long paper in two parts that is probably his deepest and most original. The first part (contemporary with Aleksandr Gelfond's proof of the transcendence of e^π) contains an entirely new result on transcendental numbers: he proved that if J_0 is the Bessel function of index 0, then $J_0(\xi)$ is transcendent for any algebraic value of $\xi \neq 0$. More precisely, let $g(y, z)$ be a polynomial of total degree $p > 0$ whose coefficients are integers of absolute value $\leq G$; if ξ is an algebraic number of degree m and $\neq 0$, then

$$|g(J_0(\xi), J_0'(\xi))| \geq cG^{-123p^2m^3}, \tag{7}$$

where c depends only on p and ξ.

Siegel's method differed from those used earlier in the theory of transcendental numbers. He starts with an analytic study, in the manner of Liouville, of the algebraic relations between x, $J_0(x)$ and $J_0'(x)$. The main result was the following: let

$$\phi(x) = \sum_\beta \sum_{\alpha=0}^\beta f_{\alpha\beta}(x)(J_0(x))^\alpha J_0'(x)^{\beta-\alpha}, \tag{8}$$

where the $f_{\alpha\beta}$ are polynomials in x with real coefficients, which are $\neq 0$ for q values of the pair $(\alpha, \beta - \alpha)$; then ϕ and its derivatives up to order $q -$

1 are q linear forms in the $J_0(x)^\alpha J_0'(x)^{\beta-\alpha}$, whose determinant is a polynomial in x that is not 0.

Let $l > p$ be an integer, and $k = \frac{1}{2}(l + 1)(l + 2)$; let $n \geq 2k^2$ be an arbitrary integer and $\varepsilon > 0$ an arbitrary real number. The center of the proof consisted in constructing a function (8) with the following properties: (1) the k polynomials $f_{\alpha\beta}$ for $\beta \leq l$ have a degree $\leq 2n - 1$, with integer coefficients at most $(n!)^{2+\varepsilon}$; (2) the Maclaurin series of ϕ begins with a term in $x^{(2k-1)n}$, and its coefficients are majorized in absolute value by those of the series

$$Cn! \sum_{\nu=(2k-1)n}^{\infty} \frac{|x|^\nu}{(\nu!)^{1-\varepsilon}}.$$

Let $T_j(x)$ for $1 \leq j \leq k$ be the functions $J_0(x)^\alpha J_0'(x)^{\beta-\alpha}$ for $\beta \leq l$ and $\alpha \leq \beta$, with $T_1 = 1$. As J_0 satisfies the second-order Bessel differential equation, the function ϕ and its derivatives can be written in the form

$$x^a \phi^{(a)}(x) = \sigma_{a1} T_1(x) + \cdots + \sigma_{ak} T_k(x), \qquad (9)$$

where $\sigma_{ab}(x)$ is a polynomial of degree $2n + a - 1$, with coefficients that are integers $0((n!)^{3+2\varepsilon})$ for $a < n + k^2$. The essential part of the proof involved showing that for $a \leq n + k^2 - 1$ and for every real number $\xi \neq 0$, the matrix $(\sigma_{aj}(\xi))$ has rank equal to k.

It is then possible to choose k integers

$$h_\nu \leq n + k^2 - 1$$

such that the k functions

$$\phi_\nu(x) = \sigma_{h_\nu 1}(\xi) T_1(x) + \cdots + \sigma_{h_\nu k}(\xi) T_k(x) \qquad (10)$$

are linearly independent. Let $r = l - p$, $v = (r + 1)(r + 2)/2$, and consider the v functions

$$J_0(x)^p J_0'(x)^\sigma g(J_0(x), J_0'(x)) \qquad (11)$$

for $p + \sigma \leq r$; they can be written

$$\psi_\mu(x) = c_{\mu 1} T_1(x) + \cdots + c_{\mu k} T_k(x) \qquad (12)$$

for $1 \leq \mu \leq v$, where the $c_{\mu j}$ are integers whose absolute value is $\leq G$; the v functions ψ_μ are linearly independent and can be completed by $w = k - v$ functions ϕ_ν in order to have k linearly independent linear combinations of the T_j. It can then be shown that the determinant Δ of the coefficients of these k linear forms is a polynomial in ξ of degree $w(3n + k^2 - 2)$ with integer coefficients all $0((n!)^{3w+2\varepsilon Gv})$. This finally proves that $|\Delta|$ is majorized by

$$K(n!)^{3w+2\varepsilon Gv}\left(\frac{g(J_0(\xi), J_0'(\xi))}{G} + (n!)^{1-2k}\right), \qquad (13)$$

where $K \geq 1$ is independent of n.

All this is true for any real number $\xi \neq 0$. But now suppose $\xi \neq 0$ is an algebraic number of degree m; if c is an integer such that $c\xi$ is an algebraic integer, then $c^{w(3n+k^2-2)}\Delta$ is an algebraic integer $\neq 0$. It is then enough to write that the norm of that algebraic integer is ≥ 1 to obtain (7) after having chosen conveniently n as a function of G.

Shidlovskii later generalized Siegel's transcendence theorem to what Siegel had called E-functions (he had introduced them as auxiliaries in his proof). They are series defined by arithmetic conditions on their coefficients.

The second part of Siegel's 1929 paper was even more startling, since it contained the first general result on Diophantine equations

$$f(x, y) = 0, \qquad (14)$$

where f is a polynomial with integer coefficients. Until then the best result had been Thue's theorem for the special type of equations (14), written $g(x, y) - a = 0$, where $a \neq 0$ and g is a homogeneous polynomial of degree ≥ 3. Thue had shown that such equations have only a finite number of solutions (x, y) consisting of integers. What Siegel showed is that the same thing may be said of all equations (14) except those for which the curve Γ having (14) for equation possesses a parametric representation by rational functions with denominators of degree 1 or 2 (this implies that Γ has genus 0 and at most two points at infinity).

The least difficult part of the proof concerned the case when Γ has genus 1. Let L be the field of rational functions on Γ and F a function in L of order m, and suppose there are infinitely many pairs $(x/z, y/z)$ with x, y, z integers having no common factor, such that (1) $F(x/z, y/z) = 0$; (2) $F(x/z, y/z)$ is an integer. Then one can extract from that set of pairs $(x/z, y/z)$ a sequence that converges to a point of Γ that is a pole of F; if r is the order of that pole, then for every function $\phi \in L$ that vanishes at that pole and every $\varepsilon > 0$ there is a constant $C(\phi, \varepsilon)$ such that

$$|\phi(x/z, y/z)| \leq C(\phi, \varepsilon)(|x| + |y| + |z|)^{-(m/hr)+\varepsilon} \quad (15)$$

(where h is the degree of f) for every point in the convergent sequence.

Since Γ has genus 1, there is a parameterizing of

Γ by elliptic functions $x = w(s)$, $y = v(s)$. Let r be the number of roots of the equation $w(s) = a$ in a parallelogram of periods. Siegel made essential use of a theorem proved by Louis J. Mordell in 1922: If M is the Z-module of complex numbers s such that both $w(s)$ and $v(s)$ are rational numbers, then M has a finite basis $s_1, \ldots s_q$. Let n be an arbitrary integer (later allowed to be arbitrarily large); using the euclidean algorithm, one can write every element of M in the form

$$s = n\sigma + c, \qquad (16)$$

where $\sigma \in M$ and $c \in M$ takes only a finite number of values. The proof used contradiction (as in Thue's theorem). Suppose equation (14) has infinitely many solutions in integers. There is therefore an infinity of these solutions for which, in the expression of the parameter s, the number $c \in M$ is the same. Apply inequality (15) to $F(x/z, y/z) = x$. From the addition theorem of elliptic functions, it follows that $s \mapsto w(ns + c)$ belongs to the field L and has order n^2m, and its n^2m poles have coordinates that are algebraic numbers of degree $\leq n^2m$.

From (14) it follows that one of these poles is the limit of a sequence of points $(\xi/\zeta, \eta/\zeta)$ of Γ, where ξ, η, and ζ are integers with no common factor. If the sequence of the numbers ξ/ζ has a finite limit p, it is an algebraic number of degree $\leq n^2m$, and the inequality (15) shows that

$$\left| \frac{\xi}{\zeta} - p \right| \leq C(|\xi| + |\zeta|)^{-kn^2m}, \qquad (17)$$

where $k > 0$ does not depend on n. On the other hand, the inequality (3) proved by Siegel in his dissertation showed that, except for a finite number of numbers ξ/ζ of the sequence, one has

$$\left| \frac{\xi}{\zeta} - p \right| \geq C'(n)(|\xi| + |\zeta|)^{-n\sqrt{m}}, \qquad (18)$$

where $C'(n)$ depends only on n. Comparing (17) and (18) yields

$$(|\xi| + |\zeta|)^{kn^2m - n\sqrt{m}} \leq \frac{C}{C'(n)}. \qquad (19)$$

But it is clear that, when $n > \dfrac{1}{k\sqrt{m}}$, the relation (19) can be verified only for finitely many pairs of integers (ξ, ζ), which yields the desired contradiction. The argument is similar and simpler when the se-

quence of the $|\xi/\zeta|$ tends to $+\infty$.

Siegel was able to construct a similar but much more intricate proof when Γ has genus ≥ 2, by making use of André Weil's generalization of Mordell's theorem. But instead of the curve Γ the Jacobian of Γ must be used, which causes complications. Until very recently Siegel's theorem remained the most powerful of its kind. In 1983, however, G. Faltings obtained a more profound result: for curves (14) of genus ≥ 2, there are only finitely many points of the curve that have rational coordinates, a theorem that had been conjectured by Mordell.

In 1934, H. Heilbronn had proved a conjecture of Carl Friedrich Gauss: if $h(-d)$ is the number of ideal classes in an imaginary quadratic field of discriminant $-d$, then $h(-d)$ tends to $+\infty$ with d. In 1935 Siegel, using the relation between the zeta functions of two quadratic fields and the zeta function of their "compositum," was able significantly to improve Heilbronn's theorem: when d tends to $+\infty$,

$$\log h(-d) \sim \tfrac{1}{2}\log d.$$

From 1935 on, most of Siegel's papers in the theory of numbers were concerned with the arithmetic theory of quadratic forms in an arbitrary number n of variables, with integer coefficients. The theory had been stated by Joseph Lagrange and Gauss for $n = 2$ and $n = 3$, and developed during the nineteenth century for arbitrary dimension n by Adrien-Marie Legendre, Ferdinand Eisenstein, Charles Hermite, Henry J. S. Smith, and Hermann Minkowski. The work of Siegel in this domain may be considered the crowning achievement of the theory; but at the same time, he broadened it considerably and prepared its modern versions by connecting it with the theory of Lie groups and automorphic functions.

In three long papers published between 1935 and 1937, Siegel tackled the general problem of using linear transformations with integer coefficients to transform a quadratic form Q in m variables with integer coefficients into a quadratic form R in $n \leq m$ variables with integer coefficients. It is easier to express the problem in terms of matrices with integer coefficients: Given two symmetric matrices, an $m \times m$ matrix S and an $n \times n$ matrix T, one must study the $m \times n$ matrices X such that

$$'X.S.X = T. \qquad (20)$$

The first paper deals with the case in which S and T are positive definite, which had been most studied by Siegel's predecessors. The number $A(S, T)$ of matrices X satisfying (20) is then finite. The number

$E(S) = A(S, S)$ is the order of the subgroup of $GL(m, Z)$ leaving S invariant (called the group of "units" of S). Gauss had defined the concepts of class and of genus for binary quadratic forms. They can be extended to any number of variables. Two $n \times n$ matrices S, S_1 with integer coefficients belong to the same class if there exists an invertible $n \times n$ matrix Y with integer coefficients, such that

$$'Y.S.Y = S_1; \qquad (21)$$

when $A(S, T)$ is finite, it depends only on the classes of S and T. The definition of genus was simplified by Henri Poincaré and Minkowski: S and S_1 are in the same genus if, on the one hand, there is an $n \times n$ invertible matrix Y with real terms satisfying equation (21) and, on the other hand, for every integer q, there is an $n \times n$ matrix Y_q with integer coefficients and a determinant invertible mod. q, such that

$$'Y_q.S.Y_q = S_1 \qquad (\text{mod. } q). \qquad (22)$$

Hermite's reduction process showed that, for positive definite matrices, a genus contains only a finite number of classes. Suppose a genus contains h classes, and let S_j be matrices chosen in these classes ($1 \le j \le h$). Eisenstein and Smith had associated to the genus its "mass"

$$\frac{1}{E(S_1)} + \frac{1}{E(S_2)} + \cdots + \frac{1}{E(S_h)}, \qquad (23)$$

and Smith (and independently Minkowski) had expressed (23) with the help of the "characters" of the genus.

Siegel's first paper on quadratic forms was concerned, more generally, with the expression

$$M(S, T) = \frac{\dfrac{A(S_1 T)}{E(S_1)} + \dfrac{A(S_2, T)}{E(S_2)} + \cdots + \dfrac{A(S_h, T)}{E(S_h)}}{\dfrac{1}{E(S_1)} + \dfrac{1}{E(S_2)} + \cdots + \dfrac{1}{E(S_h)}}, \qquad (24)$$

where S and T are positive definite, and $S_1, \cdots, S_h$ are representatives of the classes in the genus of S. The main result was the value of $M(S, T)$ as an infinite product

$$M(S, T) = A_\infty(S, T) \prod_p d_p(S, T). \qquad (25)$$

In (25) p varies in the set of all prime numbers. Let $A_q(S, T)$ be the number of solutions mod. q of the

congruence in matrices with integer coefficients

$$'X.S.X \equiv T \qquad (\text{mod. } q); \qquad (26)$$

$d_p(S, T)$ is the limit of $A_q(S, T)/q^{mn - \frac{1}{2}n(n+1)}$ when, for $q = p^N$, N tends to $+\infty$ [a "p-adic mean value" of $A(S, T)$]. Finally, $A_\infty(S, T)$ is also a kind of "mean value": when $m > n$ and $m \ne 2$, consider a neighborhood V of T in the space of $n \times n$ symmetric real matrices (an open set in $R^{\frac{1}{2}n(n+1)}$); $A_\infty(S, T)$ is the limit, when V tends to T, of the ratio of the volume of the inverse image of V by $X \mapsto 'X.S.X$ in R^{mn}, to the volume of V. The proof is by induction on m and a very subtle adaptation of the methods used by Gauss, Dirichlet, and Minkowski.

Siegel's second paper on quadratic forms dealt with "indefinite" quadratic forms of arbitrary signature. He first proved that the right-hand side of (25) is still meaningful except in two particular cases (when $m = 2$ and $-\det S$ is a square, and when $m - n = 2$ and $-\det S.\det T$ is a square). However, (23) and (24) are meaningless because the subgroup of $GL(m, Z)$ leaving S invariant is infinite. Finding what should replace the left-hand side of (25) was a problem that had been tackled by Georges Humbert only in a very particular case, the ternary forms.

Siegel was able to solve it in general: in the space of symmetric $m \times m$ matrices of given signature, let B be a neighborhood of S, and let B_1 be its inverse image in the space R^{mn} by the map $X \mapsto 'X.S.X$. B_1 is invariant by the group of "units" of S acting by left multiplication. There is a fundamental domain D for that action on B_1. If the volume $v(B)$ is finite, then the volume $v(D)$ is also finite and the limit

$$p(S) = \lim v(D/v(B)$$

exists when B tends to S. In a genus containing S there are again only a finite number of classes. Let $S_1, \cdots, S_h$ be representatives of those classes. The number

$$\mu(S) = p(S_1) + p(S_2) + \cdots + p(S_h) \qquad (27)$$

replaces the "mass" of the genus of S. There is a similar, more complicated definition of a number $\mu(S, T)$ that replaces the numerator of (24). Finally, Siegel's formula (25) is valid when the left-hand side is replaced by $\mu(S, T)/\mu(S)$. Siegel improved that formula in 1944, showing that in some cases the terms in the expression of $\mu(S, T)$ are the same for all classes of a genus.

In the third paper (1937) on quadratic forms, Siegel

considered quadratic forms in which the coefficients belong to a field of algebraic numbers, which nobody had studied before him. There are new difficulties in the theory, but he is able to overcome them.

Siegel's results on positive definite quadratic forms warrant further discussion. When a genus contains only one class, the left-hand side of (25) is $A(S, T)$; this is true for $m \leq 8$ when S is the unit matrix; if, in addition, $n = 1$, then (25) gives back the formulas of Carl C. J. Jacobi, Eisenstein, Smith, and Minkowski for the number of representations of an integer as a sum of m squares for $4 \leq m \leq 8$. Jacobi's proof relied on his study of theta functions and their relations with the modular group $SL(2, Z)$, which proceed from the formula (found independently by Gauss, Augustin-Louis Cauchy, and Siméon-Denis Poisson)

$$\theta(z) = \frac{1}{\sqrt{z}}\theta\left(\frac{1}{z}\right) \qquad (28)$$

for the simplest of theta functions

$$\theta(z) = \sum_{n=-\infty}^{+\infty} e^{-\pi n^2 z} \qquad (\text{where } \operatorname{Re} z \geq 0). \qquad (29)$$

In his first paper on positive definite quadratic forms, Siegel observed that (25) is equivalent to a remarkable identity between functions that generalize modular forms. The space of the variables is what is now called "Siegel's half-space," a generalization of "Poincaré's half-plane." It consists of the symmetric complex $n \times n$ matrices Z, whose imaginary part is positive definite. For any symmetric $m \times m$ matrix S with integer coefficients, Siegel considered the following function of Z that is a generalization of theta functions—

$$f(S,Z) = \sum_{C} \exp(\pi i. \operatorname{Tr}({}'C.S.C.Z)\text{---} \qquad (30)$$

where C takes all values in the space Z^{mn} of $m \times n$ matrices with integer coefficients; this series is absolutely convergent when Z is in the Siegel half-space. It is easy to see that

$$f(S,Z) = \sum_{T} A(S,T)\exp(\pi i. \operatorname{Tr}(T.Z)) \qquad (31)$$

where T takes all values in the space of $n \times n$ symmetrical matrices with integer coefficients. Now, if

$$F(S,Z) = \frac{\dfrac{f(S_1,Z)}{E(S_1)} + \cdots + \dfrac{f(S_h,Z)}{E(S_h)}}{\dfrac{1}{E(S_1)} + \cdots + \dfrac{1}{E(S_h)}}, \qquad (32)$$

then (25) is equivalent (for large enough m) to an expression for $F(S, Z)$ as a convergent series

$$F(S,Z) = \sum_{K,L} c_{K,L} \det(KZ + L)^{-m/2} \qquad (33)$$

where K and L are $n \times n$ matrices with integer coefficients satisfying additional arithmetic conditions. The series (33) is clearly similar to the Eisenstein series (for $n = 1$); this led Siegel, in several later papers, to make a systematic study of what he called modular forms of degree n. They are holomorphic functions defined in the Siegel half-space D; the symplectic group $\operatorname{Sp}(2n, R)$, consisting of $2n \times 2n$ matrices $U = \begin{pmatrix} A & B \\ C & D \end{pmatrix}$ such that ${}'U.J.U = J$ for $J = \begin{pmatrix} 0 & I \\ -I & 0 \end{pmatrix}$, acts on D by

$$Z \mapsto (AZ + B)(CZ + D)^{-1}.$$

In a 1939 paper Siegel considered the subgroup $\operatorname{Sp}(2n, Z)$ of $\operatorname{Sp}(2n, R)$, which is the group of transformations of the systems of $2n$ periods of a linearly independent system of abelian integrals of the first kind on a Riemann surface of genus n. That subgroup acts on D in a properly discontinuous way. Siegel described a fundamental domain for that action, using Minkowski's reduction of quadratic forms. The modular forms of degree n and weight r are the holomorphic functions defined in D that transform under $\operatorname{Sp}(2n, Z)$ according to the relation

$$\psi_r((AZ + B)(CZ + D)^{-1}) = \det(CZ + D)^r \psi_r(Z) \qquad (34)$$

(for even r). Siegel could express these forms by series generalizing Eisenstein's series. He next considered modular functions, which are meromorphic in D and invariant under the action of $\operatorname{Sp}(2n, Z)$. A quotient of two modular forms of the same weight is such a function, and in 1960 Siegel proved that all modular functions can be obtained in that way. He also showed that the set of all modular functions is a field having transcendence degree $n(n + 1)/2$ over C.

Siegel thus inaugurated the general theory of automorphic functions in any number of variables, which since Poincaré had not gone beyond the consideration of some very particular cases. In a paper of 1943, Siegel studied other subgroups of $\mathrm{Sp}(2n, R)$ also acting in a properly discontinuous way on the Siegel half-space D. He linked this question to the theory of Lie groups, showing that D is isomorphic to a bounded domain in C^n that is a symmetric space in the sense of Élie Cartan (who had determined all bounded domains in C^n that are symmetric spaces). Since then the study of automorphic functions has been developed for groups acting in a properly discontinuous way in these domains.

In 1903 Paul Epstein had defined "zeta functions" for a positive definite quadratic form $Q(x_1, x_2, \cdots, x_n)$ with integer coefficients, the simplest of which is

$$\zeta_Q(s) = \sum (Q(x_1, x_2, \cdots, x_n))^{-s} \qquad (35)$$

where the summation is over $Z^n - \{0\}$. The series converges for Re $s > n/2$, and Epstein had shown that it can be continued to a meromorphic function in the whole complex plane, satisfying a functional equation similar to those satisfied by zeta functions of number fields. Definitions such as (35) were of course meaningless for indefinite quadratic forms.

In two papers of 1938 and 1939, Siegel showed what to do in that case. Let S be the symmetric matrix of a quadratic form of signature $(n, m - n)$, and let $\Gamma(S)$ be its group of "units." It acts properly on the open subset U of the Grassmannian $G_{m.n}$ consisting of the n-dimensional subspaces of R^m in which the quadratic form is positive definite; there is in U a fundamental domain of finite volume $\mu(S)$ for that action. For a vector $a \in Z^m$, let $\Gamma(S, a)$ be the subgroup of $\Gamma(S)$ leaving a fixed; for $m \geq 3$, $\Gamma(S, a)$ has in U a fundamental domain of finite volume $\mu(S, a)$. For every integer $t > 0$ such that the equation $'a.S.a = t$ has at least a solution $a \in Z^m$, Siegel wrote

$$M(S, t) = \sum_a \mu(S, a),$$

where the sum is extended to a set of representatives of the orbits of $\Gamma(S)$ in the set of solutions of $'a.S.a = t$. Siegel's zeta function is then

$$\zeta(S, s) = \sum_{t > 0} M(S, t) t^{-s}. \qquad (36)$$

He showed that the series converges for Re $s > m/2$ and is continued in the whole complex plane as a meromorphic function satisfying a functional equation. His proof is a generalization of Riemann's proof of the functional equation for the usual zeta

function, using a theta function, which depends on a parameter varying in a fundamental domain in U of the group $\Gamma(S)$.

In the year 1951–1952 Siegel returned to the theta function and its transformations by the modular group, and gave an expression for its "mean value" in a fundamental domain of $\Gamma(S)$. From that he deduced another proof for his fundamental result of 1936 on indefinite quadratic forms. He also stated without proof that his mean value formula could be extended to quadratic forms in which both coefficients and variables belong to a simple algebra over the rational field Q, equipped with an involution.

A central theme in all these works is the computation of "volumes" of fundamental domains or, equivalently, of quotients of Lie groups by discrete subgroups. These computations have led to general views on "measures" on Lie groups or on p-adic groups, the outcome of which was the discovery by Tamagawa of a privileged measure on a group of "adeles" of an algebraic group defined on a number field. Tamagawa showed that the properties of that measure implied Siegel's theorems on quadratic forms; Weil similarly interpreted the mean value formula Siegel had proved in 1951 on such groups of "adeles."

In another area, in 1935 Siegel had deduced from his formula (25) the remarkable fact that the zeta function of a number field takes rational values at integers <0. Later he improved that result, using the theory of modular forms. These results form the basis of numerous papers on that subject published in recent years.

The papers we have analyzed are those which have given Siegel his eminent position in the theory of numbers. But they are far from exhausting his scientific production, which includes many results of lesser scope although none of them is trivial. They cover a wide range of topics: geometry of numbers, Pisot numbers, mean values of arithmetic functions, sums of squares and Waring's problem in number fields, zeros of Dirichlet's L-functions, iteration of holomorphic functions, meromorphic functions on a compact kählerian manifold, groups of isometries in non-euclidean geometries, abelian functions, differential equations on the torus, and calculus of variations. After the theory of numbers, Siegel's favorite subjects were celestial mechanics and analytic differential equations, particularly hamiltonian systems.

Siegel had few students working under his guidance; the perfection and thoroughness of his papers, which did not leave much room for improvement with the same technique, discouraged many research students because to do better than he required new methods. Siegel enjoying teaching, however, even elementary courses, and he published textbooks on the theory of numbers, celestial mechanics, and the theory of functions of several complex variables.

Siegel, who never married, devoted his life to research. He traveled and lectured in many countries, particularly at the Tata Institute in Bombay. His mental powers remained unabated in his old age, and he published important papers when he was in his seventies. He was the recipient of many honorary doctorates, and a member of the most renowned academies. In 1978, when the Wolf Prize for mathematics was awarded for the first time, he and Izrail Moiseevich Gelfand were selected for this honor.

BIBLIOGRAPHY

Siegel's writings are collected in *Gesammelte Abhandlungen*, K. Chandrasekharan and H. Maass, eds., 4 vols. (Berlin and New York, 1966).

JEAN DIEUDONNÉ

SIERPIŃSKI, WACŁAW (*b.* Warsaw, Poland, 14 March 1882; *d.* Warsaw, 21 October 1969)

Sierpiński was the son of Constantine Sierpiński, a prominent physician, and Louise Łapińska. He entered the University of Warsaw in 1900 and studied under G. Voronoi, an outstanding expert on number theory who influenced his scientific career for the next decade or more. Sierpiński's important contributions to number theory (for instance, in the theory of equipartitions) were continued and developed in G. H. Hardy, Edmund Landau, and H. Weyl. In 1903 the university awarded Sierpiński a gold medal for mathematics; his abilities in this area were evident from childhood. He received his degree the following year.

Sierpiński's most important work, however, was in set theory, and in 1908 he was the first to teach a systematic course on that subject. He investigated set theory and related domains (point-set topology, theory of functions of a real variable) for fifty years; he devoted the last fifteen to number theory. He also served as editor in chief of *Acta arithmetica*.

Sierpiński published some six hundred papers on set theory and a hundred on number theory. The most important of his books and monographs on set theory are *Hypothèse du continu* (1934) and *Cardinal and Ordinal Numbers* (1958). His chief work on number theory was *Elementary Theory of Numbers* (1964). His papers contained new and important theorems (some of which bear his name), geometrical constructions (Sierpiński curves), concepts, and original and improved proofs of earlier theorems. His findings stimulated further research by his students and by mathematicians throughout the world.

Sierpiński was a foreign member of twelve academies of science (among them the French, the Lincei, and Pontifical), and he received honorary doctorates from ten universities (including Paris, Moscow, and Amsterdam). He was also elected vice-president of the Polish Academy of Sciences and was awarded the scientific prize of the first degree (1949) and the Grand Cross of the Order of Polonia Restituta (1958).

Sierpiński's career spanned more than sixty years; he lectured at the University of Lvov until 1914 and then, after World War I, at the University of Warsaw. He was considered an excellent and stimulating teacher. About 1920 Sierpiński, Janiszewski, and Mazurkiewicz created a Polish school of mathematics centered on foundations, set theory, and applications, and also founded in 1919 a periodical to specialize in these areas, *Fundamenta mathematicae*. The first editor in chief was Janiszewski, and after his death in 1920 Sierpiński and Mazurkiewicz carried on the work for decades.

BIBLIOGRAPHY

I. ORIGINAL WORKS. Sierpiński's most important works are *Hypothèse du continu* (Warsaw, 1934); *Cardinal and Ordinal Numbers* (Warsaw, 1958); and *Elementary Theory of Numbers* (Warsaw, 1964).

II. SECONDARY LITERATURE. Works on Sierpiński and his work are M. Fryde, "Wacław Sierpiński-Mathematician," in *Scripta mathematica*, 27 (1964), 105–111; S. Hartman, "Les travaux de W. Sierpiński sur l'analyse," in *Oeuvres choisies*, I (1974), 217–221; S. Hartman, K. Kuratowski, E. Marczewski, A. Mostowski, "Travaux de W. Sierpiński sur la théorie des ensembles et ses applications," *ibid.*, II (1975), 9–36; K. Kuratowski, "Wacław Sierpiński (1882–1969)," in *Acta arithmetica*, 21 (1972), 1–5; A. Schinzel, "Wacław Sierpiński's Papers on the Theory of Numbers," *ibid.*, 7–13.

KAZIMIERZ KURATOWSKI

SIGÜENZA Y GÓNGORA, CARLOS DE (*b.* Mexico City, 20 August 1645; *d.* Mexico City, 22 August 1700)

Sigüenza's father was tutor to Prince Baltazar before going to New Spain. After receiving his first education at home, Sigüenza entered the Jesuit Colegio de Tepozotlán and took his first vows in 1662. He continued his studies at the Colegio del Espíritu Santo at Puebla until 1667, when he was expelled for disciplinary reasons; he remained a secular priest. During the following years Sigüenza was a student at the University of Mexico and chaplain at Amor de Dios Hospital. In 1672 he was awarded the chair of astrology and mathematics at the university and occupied it for more than twenty years.

In 1680, to calm the fears aroused by a comet, Sigüenza wrote *Manifiesto filosófico contra los cometas* (1681), which drew a reply from Martín de la Torre the same year. To answer it Sigüenza wrote *El Belerofonte matemático* (now lost), which aroused the antagonism of Father Eusebio Kino, a Jesuit missionary who was a renowned mathematician and astronomer, leading him to publish a strong response to Sigüenza's arguments: *Exposición astronómica del cometa* (1681). Kino's book gave Sigüenza the opportunity to publish in 1690 *Libra astronómica y philosóphica*, a short book of great significance for its sound mathematical background, anti-Aristotelian outlook, and familiarity with modern authors: Copernicus, Galileo, Descartes, Kepler, and Tycho Brahe.

As royal cosmographer, Sigüenza made valuable observations and drew good charts. These included a general map of New Spain, probably the first by a Mexican, best known through a reproduction by Beaumont in 1873–1874; a map of the lakes of the Valley of Mexico, probably made in 1691, but not published until 1748, and reprinted in 1768, 1783, and 1786; and a map of the bay of Santa María de Galve (Pensacola), 1693. In 1692 the viceroy's palace was set on fire during a riot and Sigüenza risked his life to save valuable papers in the archives.

Sigüenza projected writing a history of ancient Mexico and collected much material, but little was published. His manuscripts, now lost, were considered by contemporaries of great value. He assembled a large library, said to be the best in the realm. In 1693 Sigüenza was sent with Admiral Andrés de Pez to reconnoiter Pensacola Bay; he kept an interesting diary and made valuable charts.

BIBLIOGRAPHY

I. ORIGINAL WORKS. Besides those works cited in text, Sigüenza wrote *Piedad heróica de don Fernando Cortes* (Mexico City, 1689); *Trofeo de la justicia española* (Mexico City, 1691); *Mercurio volante* (Mexico City, 1693), and several unpublished MSS.

II. SECONDARY LITERATURE. See F. Pérez Salazar, *Obras de Carlos de Sigüenza y Góngora con una biografía* (Mexico City, 1928); J. Rojas Garcidueñas, *Don Carlos de Sigüenza y Góngora. Erudito barroco* (Mexico City, 1945); I. A. Leonard, *Don Carlos de Sigüenza y Góngora. A Mexican Savant of the Seventeenth Century* (Berkeley, 1929).

ENRIQUE BELTRÁN

AL-SIJZĪ, ABŪ SAʿĪD AḤMAD IBN MUḤAMMAD IBN ʿABD AL-JALĪL (*b.* Sijistān, Persia, *ca.* 945; *d. ca.* 1020)

Al-Sijzī is also known as al-Sijazī, al-Sijizī, or al-Sijarī. The following evidence indicates that he was an older contemporary of al-Bīrūnī (973 – *ca.* 1050): he is not mentioned in Ibn al-Nadīm's *Fihrist* (987), but al-Bīrūnī quoted him in his *Chronology*. Al-Bīrūnī wrote to al-Sijzī on the determination of the *qibla* (direction of Mecca, for prayer) and on a proof by his teacher Mansūr ibn ʿIrāq for the theory of the transversal figure. Conversely, al-Sijzī quoted three propositions by al-Bīrūnī in his treatise on trisecting an angle, which he ended with five problems of al-Bīrūnī. Around 969 al-Sijzī had written and copied mathematical works at Shīrāz, a later version of which is in Paris (Bib. Nat. arabe 2457). Presumably around the same time (*ca.* 967) he composed his *Kitāb al-qirānāt* ("Book of the Conjunctions"), which contains references to an even earlier work of his, *Muntakhab Kitāb al-ulūf* ("Summary of the Thousands of Abū Maʿshar"). In 969–970 al-Sijzī assisted at the observations of the meridian transits in Shīrāz conducted by ʿAbd al-Raḥmān al-Ṣūfī.

Al-Sijzī may have spent some time in Khurāsān, since he answered questions by mathematicians of that region. He dedicated works to the Sayyid Amīr Abū Jaʿfar Aḥmad ibn Muḥammad, a prince of Balkh (*d.* 1019) (L. Massignon, *Opera omnia*, I [Beirut, 1963], 650–666), and to the Buwayhid Caliph ʿAḍud al-Dawla (Shīrāz – Baghdad, 949 – 983).

Al-Sijzī's main scientific activity was in astrology, and he had a vast knowledge of the older literature. He usually compiled and tabulated, adding his own critical commentary. Al-Sijzī summarized three works by Abū Maʿshar and wrote on the second of the five books ascribed to Zoroaster in his *Kitāb Zarādusht ṣuwar darajāt al-falak* ("The Book of Zoroaster on the Pictures of the Degrees of the Zodiac"). In his *Kitāb al-qirānāt*, which treats general astrology and its history, he used Sassanid material and sources from the time of Hārūn al-Rashīd and from the late Umayyad period. In *Zāʾirjāt*, a book on horoscopes, he gave tables based on Hermes, Ptolemy, Dorotheus, and "the moderns." Al-Sijzī's tables, together with those of Ptolemy, are quoted by Iḥtiyāzuʿ l'Dīn Muḥammad in his *Judicial Astrology* (Trinity College, Cambridge). Al-Bīrūnī described in his *Kitāb fī istīʿāb* three degenerate astrolabes constructed by al-Sijzī: one fish-shaped, one anemone-shaped, and one skiff-shaped.

Al-Sijzī's mathematical papers are less numerous but more significant than his astrological ones, and he is therefore better known as a geometer. He wrote original treatises on spheres and conic sections, the construction of a conic compass, and the trisection of an angle by intersecting a circle with an equilateral hyperbola. This method became widely accepted: Abū'l-Jūd, for example, describes it in the Leiden manuscript Or 168(13). Al-Sijzī mentioned several other methods for solving this problem, including one by "mobile geometry," which he ascribed to the ancients; but he omitted any reference to Pappus. His treatise on proportions in the transversal figure is especially useful for astronomy, and his emphasis on the position of the lines was new and important. Al-Sijzī constructed the regular heptagon according to the same principle as that used by al-Qūhī. He also wrote articles on subdividing segments and several letters on problems related to the work of Euclid and Archimedes.

BIBLIOGRAPHY

I. ORIGINAL WORKS. Al-Sijzī's available mathematical MSS are listed in F. Sezgin, *Geschichte des arabischen Schrifttums*, V (Leiden, 1974), 331–334. On the astrological MSS see M. Krause, "Stambuler Handschriften islamischer Mathematiker," in *Quellen und Studien zur Geschichte der Mathematik, Astronomie und Physik*, B.3 (1934), 468–472; and W. Thomson and G. Junge, *The Commentary of Pappus on Book X of Euclid's Elements* (Cambridge, 1930), 48–51. C. Brockelmann, *Geschichte der arabischen Literatur*, I (Leiden, 1943), 246–247; and supp. I (Leiden, 1937), 388–389, lists a few more MSS and additional copies. Neither mentions *Kitāb al-qirānāt wa tahāwīl sinī al-ʿālam*, a MS that David Pingree dealt with in *The Thousands of Abū Maʿshar* (London, 1968). In this work Pingree also discusses the *Muntakhab Kitāb al-ulūf*, which was partly translated by E. S. Kennedy in "The World-Year of the Persians," in *Journal of the American Oriental Society*, **83**, no. 3 (1963), 315–327. Translations or discussions of mathematical treatises are found in: F. Woepcke, *L'Algèbre d'Omar Alkhayāmī* (Paris, 1851), 117–127; and "Trois traités arabes sur le compas parfait," in *Notices et extraits de la Bibliothèque nationale*, **22**, part 1 (1874), 112–115; C. Schoy, "Graecoarabische Studien," in *Isis*, **8** (1926), 21–40; H. Bürger and K. Kohl, "Thabits Werk über den Transversalensatz," in *Abhandlungen zur Geschichte der Naturwissenschaften und der Medizin*, **7** (1924), 49–53; and L. A. Sédillot, "Notice de plusieurs opuscules mathématiques," in *Notices et extraits de la Bibliothèque nationale*, **13** (1838), 136–145. Edited by the Osmania Oriental Publications Bureau is *Risāla fī 'l-shakl al-qaṭṭāʿ* ("On the Transversal-Theorem"; Hyderabad, 1948).

II. SECONDARY LITERATURE. There are few biographical references to al-Sijzī. On the observations in Shīrāz see al-Bīrūnī, *Taḥdīd nihāyāt al-amākin li-taṣḥīḥ masāfāt al-masākin* (Cairo, 1962), 99; and E. S. Kennedy, *A Commentary Upon Bīrūnī's Kitāb Taḥdīd al-Amākin* (Beirut, 1973), 42. On al-Sijzī as an astrologer see Pingree (see above), 21–26, 55, 63–67, 70–127. On his mathematics consult Sezgin (see above), 46–47, 329–334; Thomson and Junge (see above), 43–51; and the notes of G. Bergsträsser in "Pappos Kommentar zum Xten Buch von Euklid's Elementen," in *Islam*, **21** (1938), 195–198. On his astrolabes see Josef Frank, "Zur Geschichte des Astrolabs," in *Sitzungsberichte der Physikalisch-medizinischen Sozietät in Erlangen*, **50–51** (1918–1919), 290–293; and al-Bīrūnī, *Al-Qānūn al Masʿūdī*, I (Hyderabad, 1954), introduction, 17–18.

YVONNE DOLD-SAMPLONIUS

SIMPSON, THOMAS (*b.* Market Bosworth, Leicestershire, England, 20 August 1710; *d.* Market Bosworth, 14 May 1761)

Simpson's father, a weaver, wanted him to take up the same trade. After limited education the son moved to Nuneaton, where he was influenced by the 1724 eclipse and by a visiting peddler, who lent him a copy of Cocker's *Arithmetic* and a work by Partridge on astrology. Young Simpson made such progress with his studies that he acquired a local reputation as a fortune-teller. He was able to leave his weaving and marry his landlady, a widow Swinfield, whose son was a little older than her new husband. About 1733 an unfortunate incident obliged him to move to Derby, where he taught at an evening school and resumed his trade as a weaver during the day.

By the beginning of 1736 Simpson had moved to London and settled in Spitalfields, where the

Mathematical Society had flourished for two decades. In 1736 his first mathematical contributions were published in the well-known *Ladies' Diary*. One of these showed that he was already versed in the subject of fluxions, which had elicited a growing interest, as illustrated by the famous controversy sparked by Bishop George Berkeley in 1734.[1] In December 1735 Simpson had issued proposals[2] for publishing his first book, *A New Treatise of Fluxions*, which appeared in 1737. Although publication may have been delayed by the author's teaching duties, it indicated his success, which enabled him to bring his family from Derby, and his future career as a mathematics teacher, editor, and textbook writer.

Robert Heath's accusation of plagiarism probably brought Simpson useful publicity, which was supplemented by the publication in 1740 of *The Laws of Chance* and *Essays on Several Subjects*. They were rapidly followed by *Annuities and Reversions* (1742) and *Mathematical Dissertations* (1743), the latter being dedicated to Martin Folkes, then president of the Royal Society, with whom he had been in correspondence for some months. Apart from Francis Blake, Simpson's other correspondents were relatively humble philomaths. Largely through Folkes's support, Simpson was appointed second mathematical master at the Royal Military Academy, Woolwich, in August 1743 and was elected fellow of the Royal Society two years later.

Simpson seems to have been quite successful as a teacher, and his duties left him time for other activities. Three subsequent textbooks were best-sellers, partly because of his position and partly because of their scope: *Algebra*, with ten English editions in 1745–1826, besides American and German versions; *Geometry*, six London editions between 1747 and 1821, five at Paris, and one at Amsterdam; and *Trigonometry*, five London editions in 1748–1799, besides French and American versions. *Geometry*, which led to an argument with Robert Simson (whose editions of Euclid became very popular), represented a significant revision of the original Greek treatment along the lines of Clairaut and other Continental mathematicians.

Simpson's influence on English mathematics was extended by his editorship of the annual *Ladies' Diary* from 1754.[3] This post demanded an extensive correspondence with contributors throughout the country, in addition to the normal responsibility of seeing the work through the press; and Simpson seems to have worn himself out with his many activities and aged prematurely. In 1760 he be-

came involved as a consultant on the best form for a new bridge across the Thames at Blackfriars.[4] The intense work on this project accelerated his death.

Simpson obtained a reputation as "the ablest Analyst (if we regard the useful purposes of Analytical Science) that this country [Britain] can boast of" and as author of one of the two best treatises "on the Fluxionary Calculus."[5] He was aware of the importance of Continental mathematicians, for the first book on the subject he read was a translation from the French of L'Hospital's *Analyse des infiniment petits*; and the final paragraph of the preface to his last work, *Miscellaneous Tracts* (1757), was by nature of a testament. Having mentioned in the latter that he had "chiefly adhered to the analytic method of Investigation," he warned that "by a diligent cultivation of the Modern Analysis, . . . Foreign Mathematicians have, of late, been able to push their Researches farther, in many particulars, than Sir Isaac Newton and his Followers here, have done. . . ."

Although Simpson clearly was more interested in the applications to problems in series and mechanics[6] than in the foundations of analysis, he avoided the difficulties of infinitesimals by his definition: "The Fluxions of variable Quantities are always measured by their Relation to each other; and are ever expressed by the finite spaces that would be uniformly described in equal Times, with the Velocities by which those Quantities are generated." F. M. Clarke has detailed the correspondence with Francis Blake, author of an anonymous but influential pamphlet, *Explanation of Fluxions* (1741), which clarified his and Simpson's ideas on the subject before the appearance, in an enlarged and revised form, of Simpson's *Doctrine and Applications of Fluxions* (1750); this work inspired another polemic.

Until his death in 1754, one of the leading mathematicians in England was Abraham De Moivre, whose well-known *Doctrine of Chances* (1718) included work on annuities. In *Laws of Chance* (1740) Simpson wrote approvingly of De Moivre but claimed to have investigated two problems in probability for which the latter had given only the results; two years later he issued *Annuities and Reversions*. The latter was criticized by De Moivre, and Simpson replied immediately with an appendix that seems to have effectively terminated the dispute. In 1752 Simpson issued a supplementary essay that included his much-quoted tables on the valuation of lives according to London bills of mortality. Paradoxically he is now best remembered for Simpson's rule, discovered long before him, for determining the area under a curve,

$$\frac{Aa + 4Bb + Cc}{3} \times AB,$$

obtained by replacing the curve by a parabola with vertical axis going through the points a, b, and c.[7] Fifty years after Simpson's death Robert Woodhouse and his disciples achieved Simpson's aim with the reform of mathematical analysis at Cambridge, which brought English mathematics once more into the front rank of European developments.

NOTES

1. Details are in F. Cajori, *A History of the Conceptions of Limits and Fluxions in Great Britain From Newton to Woodhouse* (Chicago, 1919), chs. 3, 4.
2. D. F. McKenzie and J. C. Ross, *A Ledger of Charles Ackers* (Oxford, 1968), no. 398, quotes 750 copies costing £1 each. The only known copy is that in the Simpson papers, IV.
3. Simpson also contributed to other periodicals. See R. C. Archibald, "Notes on Some Minor English Mathematical Serials," in *Mathematical Gazette*, 14, no. 200 (Apr. 1929), 379–400.
4. A brief account in F. M. Clarke, *Simpson and His Times*, can be supplemented by J. Nichols, *The History and the Antiquities of the County of Leicester*, IV (London, 1811), 510–514.
5. The assessments by R. Woodhouse and J. Playfair are quoted in Simpson's *Fluxions* (1823), iv.
6. See I. Todhunter, *A History of the Mathematical Theories of Attraction* (London, 1873), ch. 10, for an estimate of Simpson's contributions to this subject and (sec. 294) his estimate that Simpson was "at the head of the non-academical body of English mathematicians" and second only to Newton.
7. Given in *Mathematical Dissertations* (1743), p. 110, for the equidistant ordinates Aa, Bb, and Cc.

BIBLIOGRAPHY

I. ORIGINAL WORKS. Clarke (see below) gives the full titles, but not details of the eds., of Simpson's works except the last: *Miscellaneous Tracts on Some Curious and Very Interesting Subjects in Mechanics, Physical-Astronomy and Speculative Mathematics; Wherein the Precessions of the Equinox, the Nutation of the Earth's Axis, and the Motion of the Moon in Her Orbit, Are Determined* (London, 1757). Simpson's books reprinted many of his *Philosophical Transactions* articles, listed in Poggendorff, II, 937.

II. SECONDARY LITERATURE. The main source for this article is Frances M. Clarke, *Thomas Simpson and His Times* (New York, 1929), based on her 1929 Columbia University thesis but incompletely documented and unindexed. This often quotes from the 8 vols. of Simpson papers in Columbia University Library, which kindly sent a microfilm to the writer. Most other biographies depend on Charles Hutton, "Memoirs of the Life and Writings of the Author," prefixed to Simpson's *Select Exercises* (London, 1792), itself an extended version of an account in the *Annual Register* (1764), 29–38.

P. J. WALLIS

SIMSON, ROBERT (*b.* West Kilbride, Ayrshire, Scotland, 14 October 1687; *d.* Glasgow, Scotland, 1 October 1768)

Simson's father, Robert, was a prosperous merchant in Glasgow who had acquired the small estate of Kirktonhall in West Kilbride; his mother, Agnes, whose maiden name was also Simson, came from a family that had provided parish ministers for the Church of Scotland from the time of the Reformation. It was with the intention of training for the Church that Simson matriculated at the University of Glasgow in 1701. He followed the standard course in the faculty of arts (Latin, Greek, logic, natural philosophy) and then devoted himself to the study of theology and Semitic languages. During these years, one of his teachers was his maternal uncle, John Simson, professor of divinity. He also acquired a knowledge of natural history that was a source of pleasure to him throughout his life; it is interesting to note that until his death he was held by his contemporaries to be one of the best botanists of his time.

At this time no instruction in mathematics was given at the University of Glasgow. The chair of mathematics had been revived in 1691 and during the years 1691–1696 it was occupied by George Sinclair, a mathematician and engineer of some repute. On his death Sinclair was succeeded by his son, Robert, who flagrantly neglected the duties of his chair. Thus Simson had no formal tuition in mathematics. It would appear to have been through reading George Sinclair's *Tyrocinia Mathematica in Novem Tractatus* (Glasgow, 1661) that Simson's interest in the subject was first aroused and it was this work that encouraged him to read Euclid's *Elements* (in the edition of Commandinus). He soon became absorbed in the study of geometry and acquired such a reputation as an "amateur" mathematician that in 1710 the senate of the university, having relieved Sinclair of his office, offered Simson the chair of mathematics. Simson declined the invitation on the grounds that he had received no formal training in mathematics; when the senate reaffirmed its confidence in his ability to discharge the duties of the chair, Simson suggested that the appointment be left open for a year, during which he would devote himself entirely to the study of mathematics.

Simson chose to spend the academic year 1710–1711 in London. He had originally intended to study in Oxford, but his efforts to make contact with mathematicians there were unsuccessful; so he spent the year at Christ's Hospital (the Blue Coat school), where, under the aegis of Samuel Pepys, a mathematical school had been founded for the purpose of training navigation officers for the Royal Navy. More important than the formal instruction that Simson received there were the personal relationships he established with several prominent mathematicians: John Caswell, James Jurin (secretary of the Royal Society), and Humphrey Ditton. He was most profoundly influenced by Halley, who had recently been appointed Savilian professor of geometry at Oxford while still a captain in the Royal Navy; not only was Halley regarded as second only to Newton in the field of scientific research, he was also a distinguished scholar (and editor) of the works of the Greek mathematicians.

While Simson was still in London the senate of the University of Glasgow elected him (on 11 March 1711) to the chair of mathematics on the condition that "he give satisfactory proof of his skill in mathematics previous to his admission." On his return to Glasgow he submitted to a simple test and was duly admitted professor of mathematics on 20 November 1711.

At Glasgow, Simson's first task was to design a proper course in mathematics. The course extended over two complete academic years, each of seven months' duration; to each class he lectured for five hours a week. Although his own interest was entirely in geometry, he lectured on Newton's theory of fluxions; on Cartesian geometry, algebra, and the theory of logarithms; and on mechanics and geometrical optics. Among his students were Maclaurin, Matthew Stewart, and William Trail, all of whom subsequently occupied chairs of mathematics in Scottish universities.

Simson lived the rest of his life in rooms within the College of Glasgow; outwardly his life gave every appearance of being uneventful—so much so that it was highlighted only by the conferment upon him in 1746 of the M.D. (honoris causa) by the University of St. Andrews. In 1761 John Williamson was appointed his assistant and successor.

Simson's lifework was devoted to the restoration of "lost" works of the Greek geometers and to the preparation of definitive editions of those works that had survived. Halley had encouraged this predilection for the works of the Greek geometers.

(Simson's classical education and his knowledge of oriental languages were especially useful to him.) He first turned his attention to the restoration of Euclid's porisms, which are known only from the scant account in Pappus' *Mathematical Collections*. Although Fermat claimed to have restored Euclid's work, and Halley had edited the Greek text of the preface to Pappus' seventh book, Simson is usually regarded as the first to have thrown real light on the matter. In a paper, "Two General Propositions of Pappus, in Which Many of Euclid's Porisms Are Included" (*Philosophical Transactions of the Royal Society*, **32** [1723], 330), Simson elucidated two general propositions of Pappus and showed that they contained several of the porisms as special cases. He continued to work on this topic throughout his life, but nothing further was published until *De porismatibus tractatus* appeared posthumously in 1776. Simson's only other genuine research paper, "An Explanation of an Obscure Passage in Albert Girard's Commentary on Simon Stevin's Works, p. 169, 170," appeared in 1753 (*Philosophical Transactions of the Royal Society*, **48**, 368).

Simson's book on conic sections (1735) used only geometrical methods. Although he was familiar with the methods of coordinate geometry—and lectured upon them—he developed the subject in the style of the classical Greek authors. His authoritative account of the *loci plani* of Apollonius appeared in 1749. But his most influential work was his definitive edition (1756) of Euclid's *Elements*. This edition was the basis of every subsequent edition of the *Elements* until the beginning of the twentieth century. Simson adopted the perhaps naive view that Euclid's treatise in its original form had been free from logical faults—any blemishes were regarded by him as being due to the bungling of editors such as Theon. Simson's restoration of Euclid's *Data* was added to his second edition of the *Elements* (1762).

A posthumous edition of Simson's unpublished mathematical works was published as *Opera Quaedam Reliqua R. Simson* (1776) at the expense of Philip Stanhope, second earl of Stanhope. It consists of four books: *De porismatibus tractatus*; *De sectione determinata*; *De logarithmis liber*; and *De limitibus quantitatum et rationum, fragmentum*. The last two books are based on his lectures to students; *De logarithmis* is a purely geometrical theory of logarithms. *De limitibus* is of great interest because it shows that Simson perceived that the fluxionary calculus of Newton rested on insecure foundations; accordingly, he attempted to place the theory of limits on a rigorous foundation. His failure lies probably in the fact that he tried to formulate the theory entirely in terms that would have been intelligible to a Greek geometer of the Alexandrian School.

Simson's manuscripts contain a great variety of miscellaneous geometrical propositions and many interesting reflections on various aspects of mathematical teaching and research, but none of it in a state for publication. He also prepared a draft of an edition of the complete works of Pappus that was based on material he had received from Halley many years earlier, and it is perhaps for this reason that a transcript was obtained by the Clarendon Press at Oxford.

On his death Simson bequeathed to the University of Glasgow his collection of mathematical books—at that time recognized as the most complete in the British Isles. They are preserved as the Simson Collection of the university library.

BIBLIOGRAPHY

I. ORIGINAL WORKS. Simson's works include *Sectionum Conicarum Libri V* (Edinburgh, 1735; 2nd ed., enlarged, 1750); *Apollonii Pergaei Locorum Planorum Libri II, restituti a R. Simson* (Glasgow, 1749); *Elements of Euclid* (Glasgow, 1756), of which the 2nd ed. (1762) contained Euclid's *Data*; and *Opera Quaedam Reliqua R. Simson*, James Clow, ed. (Glasgow, 1776).

II. SECONDARY LITERATURE. The best source is William Trail, *Life and Writings of Robert Simson* (Bath, 1812).

IAN N. SNEDDON

SINĀN IBN THĀBIT IBN QURRA, ABŪ SAʿĪD (*b. ca.* 880; *d.* Baghdad, 943)

The son of Thābit ibn Qurra al-Ḥarrānī (*ca.* 830–901), and the father of Ibrāhīm ibn Sinān ibn Thābit (908–946), Sinān belonged to the sect of the Sabians originating in Ḥarrān. One of the most famous physicians of his time, Sinān worked mainly in Baghdad. He was born probably around 880: al-Masʿūdī mentions a description by Sinān of the life at the court of Caliph al-Muʿtaḍid (892–902), his father's protector. Apparently, Sinān held no position before 908. He was then physician to the caliphs al-Muqtadir (908–932), al-Qāhir (932–934), and al-Rāḍī (934–940).

Under al-Muqtadir, Sinān brilliantly directed the hospitals and medical administration of Baghdad. He was not a Muslim, and he cared for the faithful and unfaithful without discrimination. In 931, after a fatal malpractice, every Baghdad doctor, except a few famous ones, had to pass a test before Sinān.

Under al-Qāhir, Sabians were persecuted, and Sinān had to become Muslim and later fled to Khurāsān, returning under al-Rāḍī. After the latter's death he served Amīr Abu 'L-Ḥusayn Baḥkam in Wāsiṭ, looking after his character and physical health.

None of Sinān's work is extant. As listed by Ibn al-Qifṭī, it can be divided into three categories: historical-political, mathematical, and astronomical; no medical texts are mentioned. A treatise of the first kind contained the already mentioned description of life at the court of al-Muʿtaḍid, and, among other things, a sketch for a government according to Plato's *Republic*. Al-Masʿūdī criticizes it, adding that Sinān should rather have occupied himself with topics within his competence, such as the science of Euclid, the *Almagest*, astronomy, the theories of meteorological phenomena, logic, metaphysics, and the philosophical systems of Socrates, Plato, and Aristotle.

Four mathematical treatises are listed: one addressed to ʿAḍud al-Dawla; a correction of a commentary on his entire work by Abū Sahl al-Qūhī, made on the latter's request; one connected with Archimedes' *On Triangles*; and a correction, with additions, of Aqāṭun's *On Elements of Geometry* (Is this the Aya Sofya MS 4830, 5, *Kitāb al-Mafrūḍāt* by Aqāṭun?). The first two treatises cannot be Sinān's, since the addressees were active in the second half of the tenth century.

As to the third category, only the content of the *Kitāb al-Anwāʾ* (dedicated to al-Muʿtaḍid) is somewhat known through excerpts by al-Bīrūnī; it is probably identical with *Kitāb al-Istiwāʾ* listed in the *Fihrist* and Ibn al-Qifṭī. The *anwāʾ* are the meteorological qualities of the individual days. Scholars disagree on their cause. Some scholars deduce them from the rising and setting of the fixed stars, others by comparing the weather in the past. Sinān maintains the latter opinion and disapproves of Galen, who wants to decide between the two only after prolonged experimental examination. Sinān agrees on the difficulty of testing them in a short period. He advises to verify whether the Arabs and Persians agree on a *nawʾ* (singular form of *anwāʾ*); if they do, it is most probable. According to al-Bīrūnī, Sinān also relates an Egyptian theory and one by Hipparchus, on where to fix the beginnings of the seasons.

One of the other astronomical treatises, directed to the Sabian Abū Isḥāq Ibrāhīm ibn Hilāl (*ca.*

924–994), is on the assignment of the planets to the days of the week. The seven planets were important in Sabian religion; each one had its own temple. Ibn al-Qiftī lists several works on Sabian rites and religion.

BIBLIOGRAPHY

I. ORIGINAL WORKS. Fuat Sezgin, *Geschichte des arabischen Schrifttums*, V (Leiden, 1974), 291; Ibn al-Qiftī, *Ta'rīkh-al-ḥukamā'*, J. Lippert, ed. (Leipzig, 1903), 195 and the Ibn Abī Uṣaybi'a, *Ṭabaqāt al-aṭibbā'*, I. A. Müller, ed. (Cairo, 1882), 224, list Sinān's work, of which nothing is extant. Al-Bīrūnī gives excerpts from the *Kitāb al-anwā'* in his *Chronology of Ancient Nations*, C. E. Sachau, ed. (London, 1879), 232, 233, 262, 322; see on this subject also O. Neugebauer, "An Arabic Version of Ptolemy's Parapegma From the 'Phaseis,'" in *Journal of the American Oriental Society*, **91**, no. 4 (1971), 506. A translation of the Aya Sofya MS 4830, 5, of which Sinān might be the author, is in preparation by the writer of this article.

II. SECONDARY LITERATURE. Biographical references can be found in Ibn al-Qiftī, *Ta'rīkh al-ḥukamā'*, J. Lippert, ed. (Leipzig, 1903), 190–195; Ibn Abī Uṣaybi'a, *Ṭabaqāt al-aṭibbā'*, I. A. Müller, ed. (Cairo, 1882), 220–224; and C. Brockelmann, *Geschichte der arabischen Literatur*, I (Leiden, 1943), 244–245 and supp. I (Leiden, 1937), 386. Ya'qub al-Nadīm, *Kitāb al-Fihrist*, G. Flügel, ed. (Leipzig, 1871–1872), 272, 302, mentions Sinān, without giving much information. D. Chwolson, *Die Ssabier und der Ssabismus*, I (St. Petersburg, 1856; repr., Amsterdam, 1965), 569–577, elucidates Sinān's biography and Sabian religion. L. Leclerc, *Histoire de la médecine arabe* (Paris, 1876), 365–368, emphasizes Sinān the physician. Al-Mas'ūdī's description and criticism is to be found in al-Mas'ūdī, *Murūj al-dhahab wa ma'ādin al-jawhar, Les prairies d'or*, I, Arabic text and French translation by C. Barbier de Meynard and Pavet de Courteille (Paris, 1861), 19–20.

YVONNE DOLD-SAMPLONIUS

SKOLEM, ALBERT THORALF (*b.* Sandsvaer, Norway, 23 May 1887; *d.* Oslo, Norway, 23 March 1963)

Skolem was the son of Even Skolem, a teacher, and Helene Olette Vaal. He took his *examen artium* in Oslo in 1905 and then studied mathematics (his preferred subject), physics, chemistry, zoology, and botany. In 1913 he passed the state examination with distinction.

In 1909 Skolem became an assistant to Olaf Birkeland and in 1913–1914 traveled with him in the Sudan to observe the zodiacal light. Then, in 1915–1916, he studied in Göttingen. In the latter year he returned to Oslo, where he was made *Dozent* in 1918. He received his doctorate in 1926.

Skolem conducted independent research at the Christian Michelsens Institute in Bergen from 1930 to 1938, when he returned as full professor to the University of Oslo. He retired in 1950. On several occasions after 1938 he was a visiting professor in America. Skolem served as editor of various mathematical periodicals and was a member of several learned societies. In 1962 he received the Gunnerus Medal in Trondheim.

Skolem published more than 175 works. His main field of research was the foundations of mathematics; but he also worked on algebra, number theory, set theory, algebraic topology, group theory, lattice theory, and Dirichlet series. Half of his works are concerned with Diophantine equations, and in this connection he developed a *p*-adic method. In 1920 he stated the Skolem-Löwenheim theorem: If a finite or denumerably infinite sentential set is formulable in the ordinary predicate calculus, then it is satisfiable in a denumerable field of individuals.

Skolem freed set theory from Cantor's definitions. In 1923 he presented the Skolem-Noether theorem on the characterization of the automorphism of simple algebras. According to this theorem, it is impossible to establish within a predicate calculus a categorical axiom system for the natural numbers by means of a finite or denumerably infinite set of propositions (1929).

Most of Skolem's works appeared in Norway, although his monograph *Diophantische Gleichungen* (1938) was published in Berlin. With Viggo Brun, he brought out a new edition (1927) of Netto's textbook on combinatorial analysis, for which he wrote all the notes and an important addendum.

Skolem also investigated the formal feasibility of various theories and concerned himself with the discovery of simpler, more constructive demonstrations of known theorems. He was especially influenced by the mathematicians Sylow and Thue.

BIBLIOGRAPHY

For a bibliography of Skolem, see T. Nagell, "Thoralf Skolem in Memoriam," in *Acta mathematica*, **110** (1963), which lists 171 titles. On his life, see also Erik Fenstadt, "Thoralf Albert Skolem in Memoriam," in *Nordisk Mathematisk Tidsskrift*, **45** (1963), 145–153, with portrait; and Ingebrigt Johansson, "Minnetale over Professor Thoralf Skolem," in *Norske Videnskåps-Akademi i Oslo Arbok 1964* (1964), 37–41.

H. OETTEL

SLUSE, RENÉ-FRANÇOIS DE (*b.* Visé, Principality of Liège [now Belgium], 2 July 1622; *d.* Liège, 19 March 1685)

Although the family name is variously spelled in the archives and documents, its correct form is de Sluse in French and Slusius in Latin. Sluse was a nephew of Gualthère Waltheri, secretary of papal briefs to Innocent X. Destined by his well-to-do family for an ecclesiastical career, Sluse went to Louvain in the fall of 1638 and remained through the summer of 1642. In 1643 he obtained a doctorate in law from the University of Rome. He lived in Rome for ten years more, becoming proficient in Greek, Hebrew, Arabic, Syriac, and astronomy. But his natural gifts led him to mathematics and a thorough study of the teachings of Cavalieri and Torricelli on the geometry of indivisibles.

On 8 October 1650, Innocent X appointed Sluse canon of the cathedral of Liège. His understanding of law and his great knowledge brought him many high positions. But his success in the administration of a small state severed him from the life he had known in Rome and thrust him into an intellectual vacuum; and his administrative duties left him little leisure for scientific work, particularly after 1659, when he became a member of the Privy Council of Prince-Bishop Maximilian Henry, who was also elector of Cologne. The only way that Sluse could survive as a scientist was, according to the practice of the time, to conduct an extensive correspondence with the leaders of mathematical studies: Blaise Pascal, Huygens, Oldenburg, Wallis, and M. A. Ricci.

In June 1658, Pascal, under the name of A. Dettonville, challenged mathematicians to solve a number of problems related to the cycloid. The evaluation of the area between a cycloid and a line parallel to its base, and the calculation of the volume generated by a rotation of this area around the base or around a line parallel to the base, were among the problems proposed, and already solved, by Pascal. In his work on the cycloid (1658) Pascal paid homage to the elegance of the solutions Sluse had sent to him, and the two remained regular correspondents. In his correspondence with Pascal, Sluse discussed the areas limited by curves corresponding to the equation

$$Y^m = Kx^p (a-x)^n$$

and the cubature of various solids; and as an example he found the volume generated by the rotation of a cissoid around its asymptote. These questions were discussed in his *Miscellanea*, published in 1668 as a section of the second edition of his *Mesolabum*.

One of the questions widely studied by the geometers of Greek antiquity was the duplication of the cube, that is, the construction of a cube of a volume double that of a given cube. This led to the solution of a cubic. More generally, Sluse discussed the solutions of third- and fourth-degree equations. Descartes had shown that their solution corresponds to the intersection of a parabola and a circle, and Sluse demonstrated that any conic section can be substituted for the parabola. He developed his method in *Mesolabum* (1659), particularly in the second edition.

In his *Géométrie*, Descartes had demonstrated the application of geometrical loci to the solution of equations of higher degrees. Sluse was among those who perfected the methods of Descartes and Fermat to draw tangents and determine the maxima and minima. By completing Descartes's construction for the solution of third- and fourth-degree equations and using a circle and any conic section, Sluse generalized the method for the solution of equations through the construction of roots by means of curves. In 1673 he published a digest of the results of his work in the *Philosophical Transactions* and became a member of the Royal Society in the following year.

The discovery of a general method for the construction of tangents to algebraic curves places Sluse among the pioneers in the discovery of the calculus. At Huygens' suggestion, Leibniz learned analytical geometry through the writings of Sluse and Descartes. Sluse deserved the judgment formulated by Huygens in a letter to Oldenburg: "(Slusius) est geometrarum, quos novi, omnium doctissimus candidissimusque."

Sluse was also a historian and wrote a book on the death of St. Lambert, the bishop of Tongres, who was killed on the spot to which St. Hubert, his successor, transferred the seat of his bishopric (which became Liège). Another historical study concerns the famous bishop of Maastricht, St. Servatius. Among his unpublished manuscripts is a history of Cologne.

The breadth of Sluse's interests is attested by the variety of subjects covered in the hundreds of pages of his unpublished manuscripts now preserved at the Bibliothèque Nationale, Paris. Although concerned mainly with mathematics, they also treat astronomy, physics, and natural history.

BIBLIOGRAPHY

Sluse's writings include *Mesolabum seu duae mediae proportionales inter extremas datas per circulum et el-*

lipsim vel hyperbolam infinitis modis exhibitae (Liège, 1659; 2nd ed., enl., 1668); "An Extract of a Letter From the Excellent Renatus Franciscus Slusius, Canon of Liège and Counsellor of His Electoral Highness of Collen [Cologne], Written to the Publisher in Order to Be Communicated to the R. Society, Concerning His Short and Easier Method of Drawing Tangents to All Geometrical Curves Without Any Labour of Calculation," in *Philosophical Transactions of the Royal Society*, **7** (1672), 5143–5147; "Illustrissimi Slusii modus, quo demonstrat methodum suam ducendi tangentes ad quaslibet curvas . . .," ibid., **8** (1673), 6059; *De tempore et causa martyrii B. Lamberti, Tungrensis episcopi, diatriba chronologica et historica* (Liège, 1679); and *De S. Servatio episcopo Tungrensi, ejus nominis unico: Adversus nuperum de sancto Arvatio vel duobus Servatiis commentum* (Liège, 1684).

M. C. Le Paige published more than 100 letters from Sluse to Pascal, Huygens, Oldenburg, Lambeck, Sorbière, and Pacichelli in "Correspondance de René-François de Sluse publiée pour la première fois," in *Bullettino di bibliografia e di storia delle scienze matematiche e fisiche*, **17** (1884), 494–726, and his introduction is the best available biography of Sluse. Secondary literature also includes C. Le Paige, "Notes pour servir à l'histoire des mathématiques dans l'ancien Pays de Liège," in *Bulletin de l'Institut archéologique liègeois*, **21** (1890), 457–565; P. Gilbert, *René de Sluse* (Brussels, 1886); F. Van Hulst, *René Sluse* (Liège, 1842); and L. Godeaux, *Esquisse d'une histoire des sciences mathématiques en Belgique* (Brussels, 1943).

Marcel Florkin

SLUTSKY, EVGENY EVGENIEVICH (*b.* Novoe, Yaroslavskaya guberniya, Russia, 19 April 1880; *d.* Moscow, U.S.S.R., 10 March 1948)

Slutsky's father was an instructor at a teachers' seminary and, from 1886, director of a school in Zhitomir. After graduating from a classical Gymnasium, Slutsky enrolled in the mathematics department of Kiev University in 1899. He participated in student disturbances there and consequently was inducted into the army in 1901; readmitted to the university shortly thereafter, he was again expelled in 1902. He then studied for three years at the Munich Polytechnikum.

In 1905 Slutsky received permission to continue his studies in Kiev. His interest in political economy led him to enroll at the Faculty of Law, from which he graduated in 1911 with a gold medal. From 1913 he taught at the Kiev Institute of Commerce, and from 1926 he worked in Moscow in the government statistical offices. He began teaching at Moscow University in 1934 and, in 1938, at the Institute of Mathematics of the Academy of Sciences of the U.S.S.R.

Slutsky belonged to the generation of Russian statisticians that developed under the influence of Pearson and his school. His interest in both practical statistical problems (economics and later the natural sciences) and their theoretical background led Slutsky into purely mathematical studies, which although sometimes not fully extended in their generality, nevertheless contained fundamental new ideas.

A pioneer of the theory of random functions, Slutsky generalized or introduced stochastic concepts of limits, derivative, and integral (1925-1928), and obtained the conditions of measurability of functions (1937). In 1927 he discovered that multiple moving averages obtained from a series of independent random variables generate series close to periodic ones; this finding stimulated the creation of the theory of stationary stochastic processes and constituted an important contribution to business cycle theory. An important group of Slutsky's papers is devoted to the classical theory of correlations of related series for a limited number of trials. In 1915 he contributed to economics what is now known as the fundamental equation of value theory, which partitions the effect of a change in the price of a commodity into the income and substitution effects.

Slutsky's applied work included studies of the pricing of grain, the mean density of population, the periodicity of solar activity (using information on aurorae boreales from 500 B.C.), and statistical studies of chromosomes.

BIBLIOGRAPHY

Slutsky's basic writings were collected in *Izbrannye trudy. Teoria veroyatnostey i matematicheskaya statistika* ("Selected Works. Probability Theory and Mathematical Statistics"; Moscow, 1960). Separately published works include *Teoria korrelyatsii i elementy uchenia o krivykh raspredelenia* ("Correlation Theory and Elements of the Theory of Distribution Curves"; Kiev, 1912); *Ser Viliam Petty. Kratky ocherk ego ekonomicheskikh vozzreny* ("Sir William Petty. A Short Essay on His Economic Views"; Kiev, 1914); *Tablitsy dlya vychislenia nepolnoy Γ-funktsii i funktsii veroyatnosti χ²* ("Tables for the Calculation of an Incomplete Γ-Function and the Probability Function χ^2"; Moscow–Leningrad, 1950); and "Sulla teoria del bilancio del consumatore," in *Giornale degli economisti*, **51** (1915), 1–26, trans. by American Economic Association, as "On the Theory of the Budget of the Consumer," in *Readings in Price Theory* (Chicago, 1952), 27–56.

On Slutsky and his work, see A. N. Kolmogorov, in *Uspekhi matematicheskikh nauk*, **3**, no. 4 (July – Aug. 1948), 143 – 151, with bibliography of 47 works by Slutsky (1912 – 1946); and N. V. Smirnov's obituary in *Izvestiya Akademii nauk SSSR*, Seria mat., **12** (1948), 417 – 420.

A. A. YOUSCHKEVITCH

SMITH, HENRY JOHN STEPHEN (*b.* Dublin, Ireland, 2 November 1826; *d.* Oxford, England, 9 February 1883)

Smith's contributions to mathematics, although relatively few, were not slight in importance. His best work was done in number theory, but he also wrote on elliptic functions and geometry.

Smith was the youngest of four children of John Smith, an Irish barrister, and the former Mary Murphy. His mother's family were country gentry from near Bantry Bay. After his father's death in 1828, Smith's mother took the family to the Isle of Man in 1829 and to the Isle of Wight in 1831. Smith was taught entirely by his mother until 1838, when he was given instruction by a Mr. R. Wheler. In 1840 the family moved to Oxford, and Henry Highton was engaged as tutor. When Highton went to teach at Rugby School in 1841, Smith accompanied him as a pupil but was soon removed, following his brother's death, and spent some time in France and Switzerland. He won a scholarship to Balliol College, Oxford, in 1844. Benjamin Jowett later described his natural abilities as greater than those of anyone he had ever known at Oxford, and T. H. Huxley made a similar comment. While on a visit to Rome, Smith was obliged by illness to interrupt his studies at Oxford between 1845 and 1847; but during his convalescence in Paris he attended the lectures of Arago and Milne-Edwards. After returning to Oxford he won the Dean Ireland scholarship in classical learning in 1848, and took a first class in the schools of both mathematics and *literae humaniores* in 1849. He was elected a fellow of Balliol and in 1851 was senior mathematical scholar in the university. Smith was long undecided between a career in classics and one in mathematics. He was elected Savilian professor of geometry in 1860, fellow of the Royal Society in 1861, and president of the Mathematical Section of the British Association and fellow of Corpus Christi College, Oxford, in 1873; from 1874 he was keeper of the University Museum, and in 1877 he became first chairman of the Meteorological Council in London. Smith devoted considerable effort to educational administration and reform, and was appointed an Oxford University commissioner in 1877. Smith was an unsuccessful Liberal candidate for Parliament. He died unmarried. The many eulogies to his powers and character are tempered with hints that he was lacking in ambition; and this was, no doubt, the secret of his undoubted popularity.

After graduating, Smith published a few short papers on number theory and geometry but soon turned to an intensive study of Gauss, Dirichlet, Eisenstein, and other writers on number theory. His reports to the British Association between 1859 and 1865, which contain much original work, were the outcome of this study. He presented important papers to the Royal Society on systems of linear indeterminate equations and congruences, and established a general theory of n-ary quadratics permitting the derivation of theorems on expressing any positive integer as the sum of five and seven squares. (Eisenstein had proved the theorem for three squares, and Jacobi for two, four, and six.) Smith's general theory with n indeterminates has been described by J. W. L. Glaisher as possibly the greatest advance made between the publication of Gauss's *Disquisitiones arithmeticae* (1801) and Smith's time.

Smith gave only an abstract of his results in 1864, and in 1868 he provided the general formulas without proofs. In 1882 the French Academy, not knowing of his work, set the problem of five squares for its Grand Prix des Sciences Mathématiques; the last of his published memoirs contains his entry, with proofs of the general theorems so far as they were needed. The prize of 3,000 francs was awarded to Smith posthumously in March 1883. An apology was subsequently made for awarding the prize jointly to a competitor (Minkowski), who seems to have followed Smith's published work.

Smith extended many of Gauss's theorems for real quadratic forms to complex quadratic forms. During the last twenty years of his life he wrote chiefly on elliptic functions; in a field marred by an excessive number of alternative methods and notations, his work is especially elegant. At the time of his death Smith had almost completed his "Memoir on the Theta and Omega Functions," which was written to accompany Glaisher's tables of theta functions. The memoir is a very substantial work running to 208 large quarto pages in the second volume of Smith's collected papers. As an appendix to the same volume there is an introduction written by Smith for the collected papers of

W. K. Clifford, and papers written for the South Kensington Science Museum on arithmetical and geometrical instruments and models. Smith was one of the last mathematicians to write an original and significant memoir in Latin, "De fractionibus quibusdam continuis" (1879).

BIBLIOGRAPHY

Smith's mathematical works are assembled in *The Collected Mathematical Papers of Henry John Stephen Smith*, J. W. L. Glaisher, ed., 2 vols. (Oxford, 1894). This collection includes a comprehensive mathematical introduction by the editor (I, lxi–xcv), a portrait, and biographical sketches containing references to nonmathematical writings and to forty mathematical notebooks, more than a dozen of which include unpublished works.

Apart from the introduction to the collected papers, the best biographical notice is the obituary by J. W. L. Glaisher, in *Monthly Notices of the Royal Astronomical Society*, **44** (1884), 138–149. For references to similar notices by P. Mansion, L. Cremona, W. Spottiswoode, and others, see G. Eneström, "Biobibliographie der 1881–1900 verstorbenen Mathematiker," in *Bibliotheca mathematica*, 3rd ser., **2** (1901), 345. For a different collection of references, see A. M. Clerke's article on Smith in *Dictionary of National Biography*. See also A. Macfarlane, *Lectures on Ten British Mathematicians of the Nineteenth Century* (New York, 1916), 92–106.

The introductory material for *Collected Mathematical Papers*, by C. H. Pearson, Benjamin Jowett, Lord Bowen, J. L. Strachan-Davidson, Alfred Robinson, and J. W. L. Glaisher, is reprinted without change in *Biographical Sketches and Recollections (With Early Letters) of Henry John Stephen Smith* (Oxford, 1894). It includes new material in the form of fifteen early letters, one to Smith's mother and the rest to his sister Eleanor.

J. D. NORTH

SNEL (Snellius or Snel van Royen), WILLEBRORD (*b.* Leiden, Netherlands, 1580; *d.* Leiden, 30 October 1626)

Snel was the son of Rudolph Snellius, or Snel van Royen, professor of mathematics at the new University of Leiden, and of Machteld Cornelisdochter. He studied law at the university but became interested in mathematics at an early age. Through the influence of Van Ceulen, Stevin, and his father, he received permission in 1600 to teach mathematics at the university. Soon afterward he left for Würzburg, where he met Van Roomen. He then went to Prague to conduct observations under Tycho. He also met Kepler, and traveled to Altdorf and Tübingen, where he saw Mästlin, Kepler's teacher. In 1602 Snel studied law in Paris. He returned home in 1604, after having traveled to Switzerland with his father, who was then in Kassel at the court of the learned Prince Maurice of Hesse.

At Leiden, Snel prepared a Latin translation of Stevin's *Wisconstighe Ghedachtenissen*, which was then being published; Snel's translation appeared as *Hypomnemata mathematica* (1608). He also busied himself with the restoration of the two books of Apollonius on plane loci, preserved only in abstract by Pappus. Related tasks on other books of Apollonius also occupied Viète (*Apollonius gallus* [1600]) and Ghetaldi (*Apollonius redivivus* [1607–1613]). Snel's work was in three parts: the first remained in manuscript and is preserved at the library of the University of Leiden; the second appeared under the title Περὶ λόγου ἀποτομῆς καὶ περὶ χωρίου ἀποτομῆς *resuscita geometria* (1607); and the third was published as *Apollonius batavus* (1608).

In 1608 Snel received the M.A. and married Maria De Lange, daughter of a burgomaster of Schoonhoven; only three of their eighteen children survived. After his father's death in March 1613, Snel succeeded him at the university, and two years later he became professor. He taught mathematics, astronomy, and optics, using some instruments in his instruction.

Sharing the admiration of his father and of Maurice of Hesse for Ramus, Snel published Ramus' *Arithmetica*, with commentary, in 1613. He later published *P. Rami Meetkonst* (1622), an annotated Dutch translation by Dirck Houtman of Ramus' *Geometria*. It was the only one of Snel's works to be published in Amsterdam; all the others appeared at Leiden. Snel's *De re numeraria* (dedicated to Grotius), a short work on money in Israel, Greece, and Rome, also dates from 1613.

During this period Snel prepared the Latin translation of two books by Van Ceulen, probably at the request of his widow, Adriana Symons. His rather careless translation of *Van den Circkel* includes some notes by Snel, among them the expression $\sqrt{(s-a)(s-b)(s-c)(s-d)}$ for the area of a cyclic quadrilateral. Although this expression had already appeared in the work of Brahmagupta, it seems to be the first time that it was used in Europe.

Snel's lack of attention to this translation may have been due to preoccupation with geodetic work. In 1615 he became deeply involved in the determination of the length of the meridian, selecting for this work the method of triangulation, first proposed by Gemma Frisius in 1533 and also used by Tycho. Snel developed it to such an extent that he may rightfully be called the father of triangulation. Starting with his house (marked by a memorial plaque in 1960), he used the spires of town churches as points of reference. Thus, through a net of triangles, he computed the distance from Alkmaar to Bergen-op-Zoom (around 130 kilometers). The two towns lie on approximately the same meridian. Snel used the distance from Leiden to Zoeterwoude (about 5 kilometers) as a baseline. His instruments were made by Blaeu; and the huge, 210-centimeter quadrant used for his triangulations is suspended in the hall of the Leiden astronomical observatory. The unit of measure was the Rhineland rod (1 rod = 3.767 meters), recommended by Stevin to the States General in 1604 (Stevin, *Principal Works*, IV [1964], 24); and, following Stevin, the rod was divided into tenths and hundredths. The results were presented in *Eratosthenes batavus* (1617).

In order to locate his house with respect to three towers in Leiden, Snel solved the so-called recession problem for three points. The problem is often named after Snel, as well as after L. Pothenot (1692); and claims have been made for Ptolemy.

Dissatisfied with his geodetic work, Snel began to correct it, aided by his pupils, and extended his measurements to include the distance from Bergen-op-Zoom to Mechelen. Unaided by logarithms, he continued this work throughout his life. His early death in 1626 prevented him from publishing his computations, which are preserved in his own copy of *Eratosthenes batavus* at the Royal Library in Brussels. They were recently checked by N. D. Haasbroek and were found to be conscientious and remarkably accurate. Haasbroek could not say as much for the way in which Musschenbroek handled these notes in his "De magnitudine terrae," in *Physicae experimentales . . .* (1729).

Snel published some observations by Bürgi and Tycho in 1618, and his descriptions of the comets of 1585 and 1618, published in 1619, show Snel to be a follower of the Ptolemaic system. Although he demonstrated from the parallax that the comet was beyond the moon and therefore could not consist of terrestrial vapors, he still believed in the character of comets as omina.

In the *Cyclometricus* (1621) π was found, by Van Ceulen's methods, to thirty-four decimals; and the thirty-fifth decimal, found in Van Ceulen's papers, was added. Snel also explained his own shorter method, following and improving on Van Lansberge's *Cyclometria nova* (1616), establishing the inequality

$$\frac{3\sin\varphi}{2+\cos\varphi} < \varphi < \tan\frac{\varphi}{3} + 2\sin\frac{\varphi}{3},$$

of which the inequality to the left agrees with Cusa's result in *Perfectio mathematica* (1458).

In 1624 Snel published his lessons on navigation in *Tiphys batavus* (Tiphys was the pilot of the *Argo*). The work is mainly a study and tabulation of Pedro Nuñez' so-called rhumb lines (1537), which Snel named "loxodromes." His consideration of a small spherical triangle bounded by a loxodrome, a parallel, and a meridian circle as a plane right triangle foreshadows the differential triangle of Pascal and later mathematicians.

The last works published by Snel himself were *Canon triangulorum* (1626) and *Doctrina triangulorum* (1627), the latter completed by his pupil Hortensius. The *Doctrina*, which comprise a plane and spherical trigonometry, includes the recession problem for two points, often named after P. A. Hansen (1841). It uses the polar triangle for the computation of the sides of a spherical triangle.

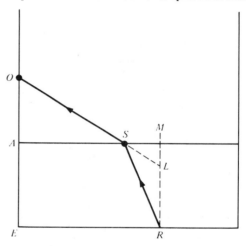

FIGURE 1

Snel's best-known discovery, the law of refraction of light rays, which was named after him, was formulated probably in or after 1621, and was the result of many years of experimentation and of the study of such books as Kepler's *Ad Vitellionem paralipomena* (1604) and Risner's *Optica* (1606), both of which quote Ibn al-Haytham and Witelo. Snel's manuscript, which contained his results, has disappeared, but it was examined by Isaac Vossius (1662) and by Huygens, who commented on it in his *Dioptrica* (1703, 1728). Snel's wording of his law has been preserved in what C. De Waard considered to be an index of the manuscript preserved in Amsterdam, and it checks with the account of

Snel's law given by Vossius: If the eye O (in the air) receives a light ray coming from a point R in a medium (for example, water) and refracted at S on the surface A of the medium, then O observes the point R as if it were at L on the line $RM \perp$ surface A. Then $SL:SR$ is constant for all rays. This agrees with the present formulation of the law, which states that $\sin r : \sin i$ is constant, where i and r are the angles that OS and SR make with the normal to A at S.

The priority of the publication of the law remains with Descartes in his *Dioptrique* (1637), stated without experimental verification. Descartes has been accused of plagiarism (for example, by Huygens), a fact made plausible by his visits to Leiden during and after Snel's days, but there seems to be no evidence for it.

Snel was buried in the Pieterskerk in Leiden. The monument erected to him and his wife, who died in 1627, is still there.

BIBLIOGRAPHY

Snel's works are cited in the text. On his life and work see C. De Waard, in *Nieuw nederlandsch biographisch woordenboek*, 7 (1927), 1155–1163; and P. van Geer, "Notice sur la vie et les travaux de Willebrord Snellius," in *Archives néerlandaises des sciences exactes et naturelles*, 18 (1883), 453–468. On his trigonometric work, see A. von Braunmühl, *Geschichte der Trigonometrie*, I (Leipzig, 1900), 239–246. On his geodetic work, see H. Bosmans, "Le degré du méridien terrestre mesuré par la distance de Berg-op-Zoom et de Malines," in *Annales de la Société scientifique de Bruxelles*, 24, pt. 2, 113–134; N. D. Haasbroek, *Gemma Frisius, Tycho Brahe and Snellius, and Their Triangulations* (Delft, 1968), with references to three previous papers by Haasbroek, in *Tydschrift voor kadaster en landmeetkunde* (1965–1967); and J. J. Delambre, *Histoire de l'astronomie moderne*, II (Paris, 1821), 92–110.

On the recession problem, see J. Tropfke, *Geschichte der Elementarmathematik*, 2nd ed., V (Berlin 1923), 97; and J. A. Oudemans, "Het problema van Snellius, opgelost door Ptolemaeus," in *Verslagen en mededeelingen der K. Akademie van wetenschappen*, 2nd ser., 19 (1884), 436–440.

For Snel's formulation of the law of refraction, see E. J. Dyksterhuis, *The Mechanization of the World Picture*, pt. 4, sec. 170 (Oxford, 1961), also in Dutch and German; this follows the text of Isaac Vossius, *De lucis natura et proprietate* (Amsterdam, 1662), 36 (see J. A. Vollgraff's ed. of *Risneri optica cum annotationibus W. Snellü pars I liber I* [Ghent, 1918], 216). Other works are D. J. Korteweg, "Descartes et les manuscrits de Snellius," in *Revue de métaphysique et de morale*, 4 (1896), 489–501; C. de Waard, "Le manuscript perdu de Snellius sur la réfraction," in *Janus*, 39 (1935), 51–75;

J. A. Vollgraff, "Snellius' Notes on the Reflection and Refraction of Rays," in *Osiris*, 1 (1936), 718–725; and Huygens' remarks in *Oeuvres complètes de Christiaan Huygens, publiées par la Société Hollandaise des Sciences*, XIII, and esp. X (1903), 405–406.

DIRK J. STRUIK

SOKHOTSKY, YULIAN-KARL VASILIEVICH (*b.* Warsaw, Poland, 5 February 1842; *d.* Leningrad, U.S.S.R., 14 December 1927)

Sokhotsky was the son of Vasili Sokhotsky, a clerk, and Iozefa Levandovska. After graduating from the Gymnasium in Warsaw, he joined the department of physics and mathematics of St. Petersburg University in 1861 but returned to Poland the following year to study mathematics independently. In 1865 he passed the examinations at the mathematics department of the University of St. Petersburg and received the bachelor of mathematics degree in 1866. After defending his master's thesis in 1868, Sokhotsky began teaching at the university as assistant professor and in 1869–1870 delivered the first course taught there on the theory of functions of a complex variable. He defended his doctoral thesis in 1873 and was elected extraordinary professor, becoming professor in 1883; from 1875 he also taught at the Institute of Civil Engineers. His lectures, especially on higher algebra, the theory of numbers, and the theory of definite integrals, were extremely successful. Sokhotsky was elected vice-president of the Mathematical Society at its founding in St. Petersburg in 1890 and succeeded V. G. Imshenetsky as president in 1892. He taught at the university until 1923.

Sokhotsky belonged to the school of P. L. Chebyshev; and the latter's influence, while not exceptional, is strong throughout his work. Thus, in his master thesis, which was devoted to the theory of special functions, Sokhotsky, besides employing expansions into an infinite series and continued fractions, made wide use of the theory of residues. (Chebyshev avoided the use of functions of a complex variable.) Elaborating the foundations of the theory of residues, Sokhotsky discovered and demonstrated one of the principal theorems of the theory of analytical functions. According to this theorem, a single-valued analytical function assumes in every vicinity of its essential singular point all complex values. This result was simultaneously published by Felice Casorati, but the theorem attracted attention only after its independent formulation and strict demonstration by Weierstrass in 1876. In his doctoral thesis Sokhotsky continued his studies on special functions, particularly on Jacobi polynomials and Lamé functions. One of the first to approach problems of the theory of singular integral equations, Sokhotsky in this work considered important boundary properties of the integrals of the type of Cauchy and, essentially, arrived at the so-called formulas of I. Plemel (1908).

Sokhotsky also gave a brilliant description of E. I. Zolotarev's theory of divisibility of algebraic numbers and wrote several articles on the theory of elliptic functions and theta functions.

BIBLIOGRAPHY

I. ORIGINAL WORKS. There is no complete bibliography of Sokhotsky's writings. His principal works include *Teoria integralnykh vychetov s nekotorymi prilozheniami* ("The Theory of Integral Residues With Some Applications"; St. Petersburg, 1868), his master's thesis; *Ob opredelennykh integralakh i funktsiakh upotreblyaemykh pri razlozheniakh v ryady* ("On Definite Integrals and Functions Used for Serial Expansion"; St. Petersburg, 1873), his doctoral dissertation; and *Nachalo naibolshego delitelia v primenenii k teorii delimosti algebraicheskikh chisel* ("The Application of the Principle of the Greatest Divisor to the Theory of Divisibility of Algebraic Numbers"; St. Petersburg, 1898).

II. SECONDARY LITERATURE. See the following (listed chronologically): S. Dickstein, "Wspomnienie pośmiertne o prof. J. Sochoskim," in *Wiadomości matematyczne*, **30** (1927–1928), 101–108; A. I. Markushevich, "Vklad Y. V. Sokhotskogo v obshchuyu teoriyu analiticheskikh funktsy" ("Y. V. Sokhotsky and the Development of the General Theory of Analytic Functions"), in *Istoriko-matematicheskie issledovaniya*, **3** (1950), 399–406; and *Skizzen zur Geschichte der analytischen Funktionen* (Berlin, 1955)—see index; I. Y. Depman, "S.-Peterburgskoe matematicheskoe obshchestvo" ("The St. Petersburg Mathematical Society"), in *Istoriko-matematicheskie issledovaniya*, **13** (1960), 11–106, esp. 33–38; and I. Z. Shtokalo, ed., *Istoria otechestvennoy matematiki* ("A History of Native Mathematics"), II (Kiev, 1967)—see index.

A. P. YOUSCHKEVITCH

SOMERVILLE, MARY FAIRFAX GREIG (*b.* Jedburgh, Roxburghshire, Scotland, 26 December 1780; *d.* Naples, Italy, 29 November 1872)

One of the foremost women of science of the nineteenth century, Mrs. Somerville was through her writings and example influential in gaining wider acceptance among a literate public for various nineteenth-century scientific ideas and practices and in opening new opportunities to women. Her notable career, spanning more than half a century, brought her in contact with many of the foremost scientific, literary, and political personages of Europe and America. Public recognition accorded her had profound and beneficial effects in advancing the cause of science and of women's education and emancipation.

Through her father, Vice-Admiral Sir William George Fairfax, R.N., a hero of the Battle of Camperdown, she was connected with the distinguished Fairfax family of England that produced the great Cromwellian general Sir Thomas Fairfax and the Fairfaxes of the Virginia Colony. Through her mother, Margaret Charters, his second wife, daughter of Samuel Charters, solicitor of customs for Scotland, she was related to several ancient Scottish houses, among them the Murrays of Philiphaugh, the Douglases of Friarshaw, the Douglases of Springwood Park, the Charterises of Wemyss, and John Knox.

Fifth of their seven children (only three of whom survived to majority), Mary Fairfax was born in the manse at Jedburgh, the home of an aunt, Martha Charters Somerville, who later became her mother-in-law. Her childhood was spent in Burntisland, a small seaport on the Firth of Forth opposite Edinburgh. In a house sold to the Fairfaxes by Samuel Charters and still standing, her easygoing, indulgent mother thriftily reared four children—the eldest surviving son Samuel, Mary, and two younger ones, Margaret and Henry—on slim navy pay. Customarily in the Charters, as in many well-connected Scottish families, sons received excellent educations, attending university and entering the kirk, the legal profession, or service in the East India Company. For daughters, mastery of social and domestic arts and a minimum of formal book learning was considered sufficient. Mary's father, returning from a long period of sea duty, was "shocked to find . . . [his daughter] such a savage," hardly able to read, unable to write, and with no knowledge of language or numbers. He dispatched her, at the age of ten, to a fashionable, expensive boarding school at Musselburgh—a drastic step for a man of such strong Tory convictions. There for twelve months she had the only full-time instruction of her long life, emerging from the experience, she recounts in her autobiography, "like a wild animal escaped out of a cage" but with a taste for reading, some notion of simple arithmetic, a smattering of grammar and French, poor handwriting, and abominable spelling.

Over the next years she had occasional lessons in ballroom dancing, pianoforte playing, fine cookery, drawing and painting (under Alexander Nasmyth), penmanship, needlework, and the use of the globes. A lively and persistent mind, immense curiosity and eagerness to learn, supported by a robust constitution and quiet, unswerving determination, enabled her to take advantage of every opportunity for enlightenment. At Burntisland she had freedom to roam the Scottish countryside and seashore, observing nature at first hand. She read through the small family library, teaching herself enough Latin for Caesar's *Commentaries.* In Edinburgh during the winter months, family position brought her in contact with intellectual and professional circles and the rich artistic life of the Scottish capital. A charmingly shy, petite, and beautiful young woman—Edinburgh society dubbed her the "Rose of Jedburgh"—she delighted in the parties, visits, balls, theaters, concerts, and innocent flirtations that, with domestic and daughterly duties, filled the days of popular Edinburgh belles at the turn of the century.

Another and less conventional interest absorbed her during these years. Between the ages of thirteen and fifteen, the chance glimpse in a ladies' fashion magazine of some strange symbols, said to be "algebra," aroused her curiosity. None of her close relatives or acquaintances could have told her anything of the subject, even had she the courage to ask. Mrs. Somerville, in contrast to other scientific women of the nineteenth century, had no family incentive to investigate science or mathematics and no household exposure to these subjects. Her unguided efforts to learn something of this mysterious but strangely attractive "algebra" were fruitless until, overhearing a casual remark by Nasmyth, she was led to persuade her younger brother's tutor to buy for her copies of Bonnycastle's *Algebra* and Euclid's *Elements,* which she then began to study on her own. Discovering her reading mathematics, her father instantly forbade it, fearing that the strain of abstract thought would injure the tender female frame. This view was widely and long held and shared to a degree by Mrs. Somerville herself: she believed her injudicious encouragement of her oldest daughter's intellectual precocity had been a factor in the child's death at age ten. In the late 1790's Captain Fairfax's strictures against arduous mental effort, combined with outspoken criticism of "unwomanly behavior" by aunts and female cousins, drove Mary Fairfax to secret, intermittent application to

mathematics but sharpened her resolve to learn the subject.

In May 1804 she married a cousin, Samuel Greig, commissioner of the Russian navy and Russian consul general in Great Britain. Greig's father, Admiral Sir Samuel Greig, a nephew of her grandfather Charters, had been one of five young British naval officers who, at the request of Empress Catherine II, went to Russia in 1763 to reorganize her navy and had been chiefly responsible for the success of that undertaking. He and his English wife reared their children in Russia: their sons made careers in Russian service, and their daughters married into Russian families, but ties with Britain were never broken. Young Samuel Greig, a captain in the Russian navy, trained aboard Admiral Fairfax's ship and, on his marriage to the admiral's daughter, was given an appointment in London, where he and his bride lived until his death in September 1807, at the age of twenty-nine. For Mary Greig, this period in London—away for the first time from family and Scotland—was a difficult one. She was much alone, and although she could read and study more freely than ever before, her husband had, in her words, "a low opinion of the capacity of . . . [the female] sex, and had neither knowledge of nor interest in science of any kind." After his death she returned with their two young sons to her parents' home in Scotland.

With the newly acquired independence of widowhood and a modestly comfortable fortune, she set out openly to educate herself in mathematics, ignoring the ridicule of relations and acquaintances. The greater part of each day was occupied with her children, and her evenings with social and filial obligations; yet she read Newton's *Principia* and began the study of higher mathematics and physical astronomy. Moreover, she found help and encouragement among Edinburgh intellectuals. John Playfair gave her useful hints on study. A group of young Whigs in her social circle, among them Henry Brougham, Francis Jeffrey, the Horner brothers, and Sydney Smith—who had some years earlier launched the successful *Edinburgh Review* and who urged, as social reforms, widened educational opportunities—became and remained her champions, finding in this pretty, quiet, and liberal-minded young widow the capacity and zest for learning that they asserted for her sex. Mrs. Somerville's most helpful mentor in these days was William Wallace, later professor of mathematics at Edinburgh. Wallace advised her by correspondence and rewarded her efforts with a silver medal for solving, in his *Mathematical Repository*, a prize problem, the first of many awards she would receive over the next sixty years.

In May 1812 Mary Greig married, as his second wife, her first cousin, William Somerville, son of the historian and minister at Jedburgh, Thomas Somerville. A cosmopolitan army doctor who had served in Canada, Sicily, and South Africa, and an affable, generous, and intelligent man of liberal convictions, William Somerville, from the first, staunchly supported his wife's aspirations. Throughout their half century of marriage, until his death in 1860 in his ninetieth year, he was her invaluable aide, taking great pride and satisfaction in her fame. Soon after their marriage she began, at age thirty-three, to continue on her own a rigorous course of readings (laid out by Wallace) in French higher mathematics and astronomical science. At her husband's urging she also devoted an hour each morning to Greek and, when the young naturalist George Finlayson became tutor to her son Woronzow Greig, she commenced the systematic study of botany. Together she and Somerville interested themselves in geology and mineralogy under the casual tutelage of their friends John Playfair, Robert Jameson, and James Hall. Among their other Edinburgh intimates were Sir James Mackintosh, Sir Walter Scott, John Leslie, James Gregory, and David Brewster.

When in 1816 William Somerville was named to the Army Medical Board, the family moved from Edinburgh to London, their chief residence for the next twenty years. Through Scottish friends and connections they were immediately introduced into the best intellectual society of the British capital, where they were soon popular figures. Dr. Somerville became a Fellow of the Royal Society. Mrs. Somerville's mathematical and scientific pursuits made her a minor lioness. In 1817 on their first tour abroad, Biot and Arago, who had been charmed by her in London, introduced them to Laplace, Gay-Lussac, Bouvard, Poisson, Cuvier, Haüy, and other French savants, who received them both as colleagues, entertained them during their stay in Paris, and afterward maintained friendly correspondences with the couple. In Switzerland the Somervilles were welcomed by Candolle, de La Rive, Prevost, and Sismondi; and in Italy by the English colony and various celebrated Italians. Many of Mrs. Somerville's friendships with scientific, literary, and political personages date from this time.

In London their familiar circle included the Henry Katers, the Thomas Youngs, the Alexander Marcets (Mary Somerville and Jane Marcet always held each other in affectionate esteem), Sir Humphry and Lady Davy (whom Mrs. Somerville had known in Edinburgh as Mrs. Apreece), the poets Thomas Campbell, Samuel Rogers, and Thomas Moore, Maria Edgeworth, John Allen, the Misses Berry, Harriet Martineau, Joanna Baillie and her family, Francis Chantrey, John Saunders Sebright, Henry Warburton, and, above all, William Hyde Wollaston. From such natural philosophers she learned science directly, as they discussed their latest findings, described and demonstrated their newest apparatus, and shared their enthusiasms and ideas with fellow guests at the small, convivial gatherings typical of the day. In an age of gentleman amateurs, Mrs. Somerville's informal apprenticeship to these scientific masters was in many respects identical with the nurture of male scientists.

Her first paper, a report in *Philosophical Transactions* of some experiments she designed and carried out on magnetizing effects of sunlight, appeared in 1826; it was communicated to the Royal Society by her husband. This work, widely praised and accepted for some years, although its conclusions were later disputed and disproved, had a vitalizing effect on investigations of the alleged phenomenon. Ten years later Arago presented to the Académie des Sciences an extract from one of her letters as a paper entitled "Experiments on the Transmission of Chemical Rays of the Solar Spectrum Across Different Media," which appeared in the *Comptes rendus*. Her third and final experimental paper, "On the Action of Rays of the Spectrum on Vegetable Juices" (1845), came out in *Abstracts of the Philosophical Transactions*. All her experimental work is characterized by rationality in approach, delicacy and simplicity in execution, and clarity in presentation. Her only essay for a popular journal was a long one on comets in the December 1835 issue of *Quarterly Review*, soon after Halley's comet had been seen.

Research, writing, and study were always unobtrusively carried on in the midst of a full social life and numerous maternal and domestic responsibilities. In 1824 William Somerville was appointed physician to the Royal Hospital, Chelsea; and, with three children, they moved to Chelsea College, on the outskirts of London. Margaret, their oldest daughter, had died the previous year. In 1814 they had lost two children: the younger Greig boy at the age of nine, and their own only son, an infant. Of Mrs. Somerville's remaining offspring, her son Woronzow Greig, a successful and esteemed barrister, graduate of Trinity College, Cambridge, died in 1865 at the age of sixty, while her two daughters, Martha and Mary Somerville, both unmarried, survived their mother. She herself supervised the education of the girls, determined that they should not lack, as she did, for systematic learning. At the behest of Lady Byron, widow of the poet, Mrs. Somerville directed also the early mathematical studies of Ada Byron, later Lady Lovelace; the Byron and Somerville families were, from the mid-1820's onward, intimate friends.

In 1827 Henry Brougham wrote William Somerville to ask him to persuade his wife to put Laplace's *Mécanique céleste*, which she had studied in Edinburgh, into English for the Library of Brougham's Society for the Diffusion of Useful Knowledge. Unsure of her ability, she finally gave in to their urgings, provided the manuscript, if unsatisfactory, would be destroyed. A rendition rather than mere translation—since full mathematical explanations and diagrams were added to make Laplace's work comprehensible to most of its English readers—her treatise when completed in 1830 was too long for the Library series. Somerville, however, submitted it to their great friend J. F. W. Herschel, who urged the publisher John Murray to bring it out. Dubious of the success of a book on such a subject, Murray printed 750 copies in 1831. To his and Mrs. Somerville's amazement, *The Mechanism of the Heavens* sold well and won praise for her. It was put to use in advanced courses at Cambridge. Its preface—the necessary mathematical background—was reprinted in 1832 as *A Preliminary Dissertation on the Mechanism of the Heavens*; both it and the previous volume were immediately pirated in the United States and were used in Britain as textbooks for almost a century. The Royal Society hailed the work by voting to place a portrait bust of Mrs. Somerville in their Great Hall. Acclaim came also from the younger generation of British scientists, including Babbage, Brewster, Buckland, Faraday, Herschel, Lyell, Murchison, Sedgwick, and Whewell, who gave her the same unstinting admiration, respect, and assistance their elders had bestowed, regarding her as the spokeswoman for science and offering her honors and opportunities unique for a woman.

Thus at age fifty-one Mary Somerville embarked on a professional career as a scientific expositor. Her gift for clear and cogent explanation, a quick and lively mind, access to the best scientific thought of the times, patience and perseverance, together with a sweet simplicity and charm of manner and a "womanliness," which demonstrated that learning and comfortable domesticity could successfully

be combined, sustained this career for the next four decades. Mrs. Somerville was fortunate too in her times: industrialization had popularized notions of self-help, expanding opportunities, changes, and new freedoms. Her second book, *On the Connexion of the Physical Sciences*, a synthetical consideration of the mutual dependence of the physical sciences, came out in 1834 to even greater acclaim. The Royal Astronomical Society (1835) elected her and Caroline Herschel their first female honorary members. Sir Robert Peel awarded her a civil pension of £200 annually (later increased to £300 by Lord Melbourne) in recognition of her work. The Royal Academy of Dublin (1834), the Société de Physique et d'Histoire Naturelle (Geneva, 1834), and the Bristol Philosophical Institution (1835?) voted her honorary memberships. In the ten editions of this work Mrs. Somerville put forward the newest, most penetrating, and authoritative ideas and practices, avoiding fads and gimcrackery. Clerk Maxwell, forty years afterward, classed the work as one important in advancing scientific thought through its insistence on viewing physical science as a whole. J. C. Adams attributed his first notions about the existence of Neptune to a passage he read in its sixth edition.

In the late 1830's her husband's health failed, and the family migrated to Italy, where Mrs. Somerville spent the remaining thirty-six years of her long life, a valued guest and brilliant part of the Italian scene during the Risorgimento. Not only was she offered access to Italian libraries and scientific facilities, but she was given membership in six of the leading Italian scientific societies (1840–1845). Although, as the years passed, it became more and more difficult to stay abreast of British science, she managed through letters, visits, journals, and books to keep in touch with major developments. In 1848, at age sixty-eight, she published her third and most successful book, *Physical Geography*, a subject which had always interested her deeply. Its seven editions brought her numerous honors: the Victoria Gold Medal of the Royal Geographical Society (1870); election to the American Geographical and Statistical Society (1857), to the Italian Geographical Society (1870), and to five additional provincial Italian societies (1853–1857); several medals; and praise from Humboldt. In this book, as in the *Connexion of the Physical Sciences*, Mrs. Somerville strongly endorsed the new geology of Lyell, Murchison, Buckland, and their school—a stand that brought her some public criticism.

Twenty-one years later, when she was eighty-nine, her final work, *On Molecular and Microscop-*

ic Science, appeared in two volumes. It deals with the constitution of matter and the structure of microscopic plants. At this date its science was considered old-fashioned, but young John Murray published it out of loyalty to and affection for its author, on the recommendation of Sir John Herschel, who had also been instrumental in persuading Mrs. Somerville to bring out her *Physical Geography*. The public received it with kindly interest and deference to its venerable creator. In the same year she was made a member of the American Philosophical Society (she had warm regard for Americans) and completed her autobiography—a vivid and spritely account of her life in Scotland, England, and Italy; of her visits to Switzerland, France, and Germany; and of the many interesting personages she had known. After her death her elder surviving daughter, Martha, published parts of this manuscript as *Personal Recollections From Early Life to Old Age of Mary Somerville* (1873).

In her later years Mrs. Somerville gave powerful but always temperate support to the cause of the education and emancipation of women. Hers was the first signature on John Stuart Mill's great petition to Parliament for women's suffrage, solicited by Mill himself. An early advocate of higher education for women, many of her books were given after her death to the new Ladies College at Hitchin (now Girton College, Cambridge). Somerville College (1879), one of the first two colleges for women at Oxford, is named after her. Although frail and deaf in her last years, Mary Somerville's spirit and intelligence, her interest in friends, in the cause of women, and in science never faltered. At the time of her death, at ninety-two, she was revising a paper on quaternions.

BIBLIOGRAPHY

I. ORIGINAL WORKS. The Somerville Collection (MSS, papers, letters, documents, diplomas, and memorabilia owned by Mrs. Somerville's heir) is deposited in the Bodleian Library, Oxford.

Mary Somerville's works are "On the Magnetizing Power of the More Refrangible Solar Rays," in *Philosophical Transactions of the Royal Society*, **116** (1826), 132; *The Mechanism of the Heavens* (London, 1831); *A Preliminary Dissertation on the Mechanism of the Heavens* (London, 1832); *On the Connexion of the Physical Sciences* (London, 1834; 2nd ed., 1835; 3rd ed., 1836; 4th ed., 1840; 5th ed., 1842; 6th ed., 1846; 7th ed., 1848; 9th ed., 1858; 10th ed., A. B. Buckley, ed., 1877); "Art. VII.-1. Ueber den Halleyschen Cometen . . .," in *Quarterly Review*, **105** (1835), 195–233; and "Experiments on the Transmission of Chemical Rays of the So-

lar Spectrum Across Different Media," in *Comptes rendus hebdomadaires des séances de l'Académie des sciences*, **3** (1836), 473–476.

See also the extract from a letter by Mrs. Somerville to Sir John Herschel, Bart., F.R.S., dated Rome, 20 September 1845, entitled "On the Action of the Rays of the Spectrum on Vegetable Juices," in *Philosophical Transactions of the Royal Society*, **5** (1845), 569; *Physical Geography* (London, 1848; 2nd ed., 1849; 3rd ed., 1851; 4th ed., 1858; 5th ed., 1862; 6th [1870] and 7th [1877] eds. revised by H. W. Bates); and *On Molecular and Microscopic Science* (London, 1869).

II. SECONDARY LITERATURE. On Mary Somerville and her work, see the following works by Elizabeth C. Patterson: "Mary Somerville," in *British Journal for the History of Science*, **4** (1969), 311–339; "A Washington Letter," in *Bodleian Library Record*, **8** (1970), 201–205; and "The Case of Mary Somerville: An Aspect of Nineteenth-Century Science," in *Proceedings of the American Philosophical Society*, **118** (1974), 269–275. See also Martha Somerville, ed., *Personal Recollections From Early Life to Old Age of Mary Somerville, With Selections From Her Correspondence* (London, 1873).

ELIZABETH C. PATTERSON

SOMMERVILLE, DUNCAN MCLAREN YOUNG (*b.* Beawar, Rajasthan, India, 24 November 1879; *d.* Wellington, New Zealand, 31 January 1934)

Sommerville, the son of Rev. James Sommerville of Jodhpur, India, was educated in Scotland, first at the Perth Academy, then at the University of St. Andrews, where he was awarded Ramsay and Bruce scholarships and in the mathematics department of which he served as lecturer from 1902 to 1914. During that time he met, and in 1912 married, Louisa Agnes Beveridge, originally of Belfast, Ireland. From 1915 on Sommerville was professor of pure and applied mathematics at Victoria University College, Wellington, New Zealand. He was active in the Edinburgh Mathematical Society, to whose presidency he was elected in 1911. He helped to found the Royal Astronomical Society of New Zealand and became its first executive secretary. Sommerville presided over the mathematics section at the Adelaide meeting (1924) of the Australasian Association for the Advancement of Science. In 1928 the Institute (Royal Society) of New Zealand awarded him its Hector Medal.

Although primarily a mathematician, Sommerville was interested in other sciences, particularly astronomy, anatomy, and chemistry. Crystallography held special appeal for him, and crystal forms doubtless motivated his investigation of repetitive space-filling geometric patterns. Also, his abstract conceptions called for the construction of clarifying models, which revealed an artistic skill that was even more evident in his many watercolors of New Zealand scenes.

Sommerville contributed to mathematics both as a teacher and as an original researcher. His biographer, H. W. Turnbull, who considered him (in 1935) Scotland's leading geometer of the twentieth century, stated that his pedagogic style was scholarly, unobtrusive, and much appreciated at St. Andrews. One of his most distinguished pupils, A. C. Aitken, revealed that when the New Zealand University of Otago was without a mathematics professor, Sommerville willingly provided a sort of "correspondence course" in higher mathematics. Further evidence of his teaching ability is reflected in his four textbooks, which are models of deep, lucid exposition. Among them are *The Elements of Non-Euclidean Geometry* and *An Introduction to the Geometry of n Dimensions*, books whose titles indicate his two major research specialties and whose contents develop geometric concepts that Sommerville himself created. In addition to his texts, his *Bibliography of Non-Euclidean Geometry* is also a bibliography of *n*-dimensional geometry.

Sommerville wrote over thirty original papers, almost all on geometric topics. Notable exceptions were his 1928 "Analysis of Preferential Voting" (geometrized, however, in his 1928 "Certain Hyperspatial Partitionings Connected With Preferential Voting") and two 1906 papers that gave pure mathematical treatment to statistical questions arising from notions in Karl Pearson's biometric research.

In his texts Sommerville explained how non-Euclidean geometries arose from the use of alternatives to Euclid's parallel postulate. Thus, in the Lobachevskian or hyperbolic geometry, it is assumed that there exist two parallels to a given line through an outside point. In Riemannian or elliptic geometry, the assumption of no parallels is made. By suitable interpretation Klein, Cayley, and then Sommerville showed that Euclidean and non-Euclidean geometries can all be considered as subgeometries of projective geometry. For Klein any geometry was the study of invariants under a particular transformation group. From his point of view, projective geometry is the invariant theory associated with the group of linear fractional transformations. Those special plane projective transformations leaving invariant a specified conic section, Cayley's "absolute," constitute a subgroup of the plane projective group; and the corresponding geometry is hyperbolic, elliptic, or Euclidean according to whether the conic is real (an ellipse, for example), imaginary, or degenerate. This conception makes it possible in all three geometries to express distance and angle measure in terms of a cross ratio, the fundamental invariant under projective transformation.

Even in two of his earliest investigations, namely, "Networks of the Plane in Absolute Geometry" (1905) and "Semi-Regular Networks of the Plane in Absolute Geometry" (1906), Sommerville used the Cayley-Klein notion of non-Euclidean geometries, in particular the projective measurement of lengths and angles. These two papers indicated a trend that he was to follow in much of his research, namely, the study of tesselations of Euclidean and non-Euclidean spaces, a theme suggested by the repetitive designs on wallpaper or textiles and by the arrangement of atoms in crystals. Sommerville showed that whereas there are only three regular tesselations in the Euclidean plane (its covering by congruent equilateral triangles, squares, or regular hexagons), there are five mosaics of congruent regular polygons of the same kind in the elliptic plane, and an infinite number of such patterns in the hyperbolic plane. In all cases the variety is greater if "semi-regular" networks of regular polygons of different kinds are permitted. Moreover, as Sommerville pointed out, still further variations are attainable because the regular patterns are topologically equivalent, if not aesthetically so, to nonregular designs. In several papers and in his text on *n*-dimensional geometry, he generalized his earlier results and methods to include honeycombs of polyhedrons in three-dimensional spaces and "honeycombs" of polytopes in spaces (Euclidean and non-Euclidean) of 4, 5, $\cdots$, *n* dimensions.

Many of Sommerville's geometric concepts have algebraic counterparts in the theory of groups. Thus, since his repetitive patterns can be considered as the result of moving a single basic design to different positions, it is possible to asssociate with each tesselation or honeycomb one or more "crystallographic groups," each a set of motions that displace a fundamental region so that it will cover an entire plane, space, or hyperspace. Thus, if a square (with sides horizontal and vertical) is the fundamental region in a Euclidean plane, one can cover that plane with duplications of the square by two basic motions or their inverses, namely translation of the square one side-length to the right, and a similar translation upward. Those two motions are said to "generate" a crystallographic group corresponding to the network of squares. For that same network a different crystallographic group is generated by three basic motions—the two reflections of the square in its vertical sides, and the translation of the square one side-length upward.

There are also associations with group theory in Sommerville's "On Certain Projective Configurations in Space of n Dimensions and a Related Problem in Arrangements" (1906), in which he showed interrelationships between certain finite groups and the finite projective geometries of Veblen and Bussey. Such groups also played a role in his "On the Relation Between the Rotation-Groups of the Regular Polytopes and Permutation Groups" (1933).

BIBLIOGRAPHY

I. ORIGINAL WORKS. Among Sommerville's many research papers are "Networks of the Plane in Absolute Geometry," in *Proceedings of the Royal Society of Edinburgh*, 25 (1905), 392–394; "Semi-Regular Networks of the Plane in Absolute Geometry" in *Transactions of the Royal Society of Edinburgh*, 41 (1906), 725–747; "On the Distribution of the Proper Fractions," in *Proceedings of the Royal Society of Edinburgh*, 26 (1906), 116–129; "On the Classification of Frequency Ratios," in *Biometrika*, 5 (1906), 179–181; "On Links and Knots in Euclidean Space of n Dimensions," in *Messenger of Mathematics*, 2nd ser., 36 (1906), 139–144; "On Certain Projective Configurations in Space of n Dimensions and a Related Problem in Arrangements," in *Proceedings of the Edinburgh Mathematical Society*, 25 (1906), 80–90; "The Division of Space by Congruent Triangles and Tetrahedra," in *Proceedings of the Royal Society of Edinburgh*, 43 (1923), 85–116; "The Regular Divisions of Space of n Dimensions and Their Metrical Constants," in *Rendiconti del Circolo matematico di Palermo*, 48 (1924), 9–22; "The Relations Connecting the Angle-Sums and Volume of a Polytope in Space of n Dimensions," in *Proceedings of the Royal Society of London*, A115 (1927), 103–119; "An Analysis of Preferential Voting," in *Proceedings of the Royal Society of Edinburgh*, 48 (1928), 140–160; "Certain Hyperspatial Partitionings Connected With Preferential Voting," in *Proceedings of the London Mathematical Society*, 2nd ser., 28 (1928), 368–382; "Isohedral and Isogonal Generalizations of the Regular Polyhedra," in *Proceedings of the Royal Society of Edinburgh*, 52 (1932), 251–263; and "On the Relations Between the Rotation-Groups of the Regular Polytopes and Permutation-Groups," in *Proceedings of the London Mathematical Society*, 2nd ser., 35 (1933), 101–115.

Sommerville's books are *Bibliography of Non-Euclidean Geometry* (London, 1911); *The Elements of Non-Euclidean Geometry* (London, 1914, 1919); *Analytical Conics* (London, 1924); *An Introduction to the Geometry of n Dimensions* (London, 1929); and *Analytical Geometry of Three Dimensions* (Cambridge, 1934).

II. SECONDARY LITERATURE. On Sommerville and his work, see H. W. Turnbull, "Professor D. M. Y. Sommerville," in *Proceedings of the Edinburgh Mathematical Society*, 2nd ser., 4 (1935), 57–60.

EDNA E. KRAMER

SOMOV, OSIP IVANOVICH (*b*. Otrada, Moscow gubernia [now Moscow oblast], Russia, 1 June 1815; *d*. St. Petersburg, Russia [now Leningrad, U.S.S.R.], 26 April 1876)

Somov graduated from the Gymnasium in Moscow and enrolled at the Faculty of Physics and Mathematics of Moscow University. After graduating in 1835, he published a work on the theory of determinate algebraic equations of higher degree (1838), in which he manifested not only deep knowledge but also extraordinary skill in presenting the newest achievements of algebraic analysis.

Somov's pedagogic career began in 1839 at the Moscow Commercial College. After defending his master's dissertation in Moscow, he was invited to St. Petersburg University in 1841 and taught various courses in mathematics and mechanics there for the next twenty-five years. Somov defended his doctoral dissertation at St. Petersburg and was awarded the title of professor of applied mathematics.

In 1857 Somov was elected an associate member of the St. Petersburg Academy of Sciences, and in 1862 he succeeded Ostrogradsky as academician.

Turning his attention to problems of theoretical mechanics, Somov applied results obtained in analytical mechanics to specifically geometric problems. He is rightfully considered the originator of the geometrical trend in theoretical mechanics in Russia during the second half of the nineteenth century. In the theory of elliptical functions and their application to mechanics, he completed the solution of the problem concerning the rotation of a solid body around an immobile point in the Euler-Poinsot and Lagrange-Poisson examples.

The first in Russia to deal with the solution of kinematic problems, Somov included a chapter on this topic in his textbook on theoretical mechanics. His other kinematic works include studies of a point in curvilinear coordinates. Somov's theory of higher-order accelerations of a point, and of an unchanging system of points, was a significant contribution. His works were the first special studies in Russia of *n*th-order accelerations of both absolute and relative motions of points. His studies of small oscillations of a system around the position of equilibrium are also important.

BIBLIOGRAPHY

I. ORIGINAL WORKS. In addition to more than fifty papers on mechanics and mathematics, Somov published *Teoria opredelennykh algebraicheskikh uravneny vysshikh stepeny* ("Theory of Determinate Algebraic Equations of Higher Degree"; Moscow, 1838); *Analiticheskaya teoria volnoobraznogo dvizhenia efira* ("Analytic Theory of the Undulatory Motion of the Ether"; St. Petersburg, 1847); *Osnovania teorii ellipticheskikh funktsy* ("Foundations of the Theory of Elliptical Functions"; St. Petersburg, 1850); *Kurs differentsialnogo ischislenia* ("Course in Differential Calculus"; St. Petersburg, 1852); *Analiticheskaya geometria* ("Analytic Geometry"; St. Petersburg, 1857); *Nachalnaya algebra* ("Elementary Algebra"; St. Petersburg, 1860); *Nachertatelnaya geometria* ("Descriptive Geometry"; St. Petersburg, 1862); and *Ratsionalnaya mekhanika* ("Rational Mechanics"), 2 pts. (St. Petersburg, 1872–1874), translated into German by A. Ziwet as *Theoretische Mechanik* (Leipzig, 1878).

II. SECONDARY LITERATURE. Bibliographies of Somov's works are included in Y. L. Geronimus, *Ocherki o rabotakh korifeev russkoy mekhaniki* ("Essays on the Works of Leading Russian Mechanists"; Moscow, 1952), 58–96; T. R. Nikiforova, *Osip Ivanovich Somov* (Moscow–Leningrad, 1964); and E. I. Zolotarev, "Ob uchenykh trudakh akademika O. I. Somova," in *Zapiski Imperatorskoi akademii nauk*, **31** (1878), 248–266.

A. T. GRIGORIAN

SONIN, NIKOLAY YAKOVLEVICH (*b*. Tula, Russia, 22 February 1849; *d*. Petrograd [now Leningrad], Russia, 27 February 1915)

The son of a state official who later became a lawyer, Sonin received his higher education at the Faculty of Physics and Mathematics of Moscow University (1865–1869). His first scientific work was a report on differentiation with arbitrary complex exponent (1869). After defending his master's thesis in 1871, Sonin was appointed *Dozent* in mathematics at Warsaw University in 1872 and, after defending his doctoral dissertation in 1874, was promoted to professor in 1877. He taught at

Warsaw for more than twenty years, was twice elected dean of the Faculty of Physics and Mathematics, and was an organizer of the Society of Natural Scientists. In 1891 Sonin was elected corresponding member of the Russian Academy of Sciences and, in 1893, academician in pure mathematics. In connection with the latter rank he moved to St. Petersburg, where from 1894 to 1899 he was professor at the University for Women, from 1899 to 1901 superintendent of the Petersburg Educational District, and from 1901 to 1915 president of the Scientific Committee of the Ministry of National Education. With A. A. Markov, Sonin prepared a two-volume edition of the works of Chebyshev in Russian and French (1899–1907).

Sonin made a substantial contribution to the theory of special functions; the unifying idea of his researches was to establish a few convenient definitions of initial notions and operations leading to broad and fruitful generalizations of these functions. Especially important were his discoveries in the theory of cylindrical functions, which he enriched both with general principles and with many particular theorems and formulas that he introduced into the contemporary literature. He also wrote on Bernoullian polynomials, and his works on the general theory of orthogonal polynomials were closely interwoven with his research on the approximate computation of definite integrals and on the various integral inequalities; in the latter area he continued Chebyshev's research. Also noteworthy are Sonin's works on the Euler-Maclaurin sum formula and adjacent problems.

BIBLIOGRAPHY

I. ORIGINAL WORKS. Sonin's writings include "O razlozhenii funktsy v beskonechnye ryady" ("On the Expansion of Functions in Infinite Series"), in *Matematicheskii sbornik*, **5** (1871), 271–302, his master's thesis; "Ob integrirovanii uravneny s chastnymi proizvodnymi vtorogo poryadka" ("On the Integration of Partial Differential Equations of the Second Order"), *ibid.*, **7** (1874), 285–318, translated into German in *Mathematische Annalen*, **49** (1897), 417–447, his doctoral dissertation; "Recherches sur les fonctions cylindriques et le développement des fonctions continues en séries," *ibid.*, **16** (1880), 1–80; "Sur les termes complémentaires de la formule sommatoire d'Euler et de celle de Stirling," in *Annales scientifiques de l'École normale supérieure*, **6** (1889), 257–262; "Sur les polynômes de Bernoulli," in *Journal für die reine und angewandte Mathematik*, **116** (1896), 133–156; "Sur les fonctions cylindriques," in *Mathematische Annalen*, **59** (1904), 529–552; see also *Issledovania o tsilindricheskikh funktsiakh i o spetsial-*

nykh polinomakh ("Research on Cylindrical Functions and on Special Polynomials"), N. I. Akhiezer, ed. (Moscow, 1954).

II. SECONDARY LITERATURE. See N. I. Akhiezer, "Raboty N. Y. Sonina po priblizhennomu vychisleniyu opredelennykh integralov" ("The Works of N. Y. Sonin on the Approximate Computation of Definite Integrals"), in Sonin's *Issledovania o tsilindricheskikh funktsiakh*, 220–243; A. I. Kropotov, *Nikolay Yakovlevich Sonin* (Leningrad, 1967), with complete bibliography of Sonin's works, pp. 126–130; and G. N. Watson, *A Treatise on the Theory of Bessel Functions* (Cambridge, 1922).

A. P. YOUSCHKEVITCH

SPORUS OF NICAEA (*fl.* second half of third century)

Little is known of Sporus. The juxtaposition of available historical data makes it likely that he came from Nicaea, was a pupil of Philo of Gadara, and was either the teacher or a slightly older fellow student of Pappus of Alexandria. Our knowledge of Sporus' activities stems only from such secondary sources as the works of Pappus and the writings of various commentators, among them Eutocius and Leontius, a seventh-century engineer.[1] Most historians, with the notable exception of J. L. Heiberg, agree that Sporus was the author of a work entitled Κηρία, noted by Eutocius.[2] They interpret a second reference by Eutocius to an anonymous Κηρία Ἀριστοτελικά[3] as a subsection of Sporus' work, but Heiberg believes this to be a reference to Aristotle's *De sophisticis elenchis*.

From the above sources it appears that Sporus concerned himself intensively with two mathematical problems: that of squaring the circle and that of doubling the cube.[4] Like many Greek mathematicians who attempted to solve them, he was aware that neither has a solution by means of ruler and compass alone. The close relationship of both problems to limiting processes[5] suggests that Sporus was also interested in questions dealing with approximation, since he reportedly criticized Archimedes for having failed to approximate the value of π more accurately.[6]

The value of the ancient Greeks' preoccupation with special mathematical problems of this type clearly lies in the by-products that this study produced. The squaring problem led to the development of special curves, the quadratrix of Hippias, for example; and the doubling-of-the-cube problem resulted in Menaechmus' discovery of the theory of conic sections and produced a refinement of the theory of proportions. Sporus seems to have contributed to the study of these problems chiefly through his constructive criticism of existing solutions. Indeed, his own solution of the doubling-of-the-cube problem essentially coincides with that of Pappus.

Sporus' writings seem to have been a fruitful source of information for Pappus and later scholars. Pappus, in particular, appears to have valued Sporus' reputation and judgment, since he quoted Sporus in support of his own criticism of the use of the quadratrix in the solution of the squaring problem.

Sporus' nonmathematical writings are known essentially only by topics, through references to them in Maass's *Analecta Eratosthenica* and *Commentariorum in Aratum reliquiae*. They consist of scientific essays on subjects such as the polar circle, the size of the sun, and comets. His literary achievements are reported to include a critical edition of the Φαινομενά of Aratus of Soli.

NOTES

1. E. Maass, *Analecta Eratosthenica*, pp. 45, 47–49, 1939, and *Commentariorum in Aratum reliquiae*, p. lxxi.
2. J. L. Heiberg, *Archimedis opera omnia*, 2nd ed., III, p. 258.
3. *Ibid.*, p. 228.
4. T. L. Heath, *A History of Greek Mathematics*, I, pp. 226, 229–230, 234, 266–268.
5. *Ibid.*, pp. 230, 269.
6. J. L. Heiberg, *Archimedis opera omnia*, 2nd ed., III, p. 258.

BIBLIOGRAPHY

See T. L. Heath, *A History of Greek Mathematics*, I (Oxford, 1921), 226, 229–230, 234, 266–268; J. L. Heiberg, ed., *Archimedis opera omnia*, 2nd ed., III (Leipzig, 1915), 228, 258; F. Hultsch, ed., *Pappus, Collectionis quae supersunt*, I (Berlin, 1878), 252; *Lexikon der alten Welt* (Zurich, 1965), 2863; E. Maass, *Analecta Eratosthenica* (Berlin, 1883), 45–49, 139; and *Commentariorum in Aratum reliquiae* (Berlin, 1898), lxxi; Pauly-Wissowa, *Real-Encyclopädie der classischen Altertumswissenschaft*, 2nd ser., III, 1879–1883; G. Sarton, *Introduction to the History of Science*, I (Baltimore, 1927), 331, 338; P. Tannery, "Sur Sporos de Nicée," in *Annales de la Faculté des lettres de Bordeaux*, 4 (1882), 257–261.

MANFRED E. SZABO

ŚRĪDHARA (*fl.* India, ninth century)

Śrīdhara, of whose life nothing is known save that he was a devotee of Śiva, wrote two works on arithmetic, the *Pāṭīgaṇita* and the *Pāṭīgaṇitasāra* or *Triśatikā*, and one work, now lost, on algebra. Since he seems to refer to the views of Mahāvīra (*fl.* ninth century), and was used by Āryabhaṭa II (*fl.* between *ca.* 950 and 1100) and cited by Abhayadeva Sūri (*fl.* 1050), it can be concluded that he flourished in the ninth century.

The *Pāṭīgaṇita* is divided into two sections. The first, after metrological definitions, covers the mathematical operations of addition, subtraction, multiplication, and division; finding squares and square roots; finding cubes and cube roots; fractions; and proportions; the second gives solutions for problems involving mixtures, series, plane figures, volumes, shadows, and zero. The text, preserved in a unique manuscript in Kashmir, breaks off in the middle of the rules for determining the areas of plane figures in the second section. The *Triśatikā* summarizes much of the material in the *Pāṭīgaṇita*, including the parts no longer available to us. In the Kashmir manuscript there is an anonymous commentary on the *Pāṭīgaṇita*, and the *Triśatikā* was commented on by Śrīdhara himself and in Kannaḍa (Kanarese), Telugu (by Vallabha), and Gujarātī; the commentaries on the *Triśatikā* ascribed to Śambhūnātha or Śambhūdāsa (*fl.* 1428; *Gaṇitapañcaviṃśatikā* or *Gaṇitasāra* and to Vṛndāvana Śukla (*Pāṭīsāraṭīkā*) are still uncertain, pending an investigation of the manuscripts.

BIBLIOGRAPHY

The best work on Śrīdhara is the introduction to K. S. Shukla's valuable ed. and trans., *The Patiganita of Sridharacarya* (Lucknow, 1959). There is also a Russian trans. and study of the *Pāṭīgaṇita* by A. I. Volodarsky and O. F. Volkovoy in *Fiziko-matematicheskie nauki v stranakh vostoka* (Moscow, 1966), 141–246. The *Triśatikā* was edited by Sudhākara Dvivedin (Benares, 1899) and was largely translated into English by N. Ramanujacharia and G. R. Kaye, "The *Triśatikā* of Śrīdharācarya," in *Bibliotheca mathematica*, 3rd ser., **13** (1912–1913), 203–217.

DAVID PINGREE

ŚRĪPATI (*fl.* Rohiṇīkhaṇḍa, Mahārāṣṭra, India, 1039–1056)

Śrīpati, who was the son of Nāgadeva (or Nāmadeva) and the grandson of Keśava of the Kāśyapagotra, is one of the most renowned authorities on astrology in India, although his works on astronomy and mathematics are not negligible; in many he follows the opinions of Lalla (*fl.* eighth century; see essay in Supplement). His numerous works include not only Sanskrit texts but also one of the earliest examples of Marāṭhī prose extant. They include the following:

1. The *Dhīkoṭidakaraṇa*, written in 1039, a work in twenty verses on solar and lunar eclipses. There are commentaries by Harikṛṣṇa (*fl.* 1708–1714 at Delhi) and Dinakara. The *Dhīkoṭidakaraṇa* was edited by N. K. Majumdar in *Calcutta Oriental Journal*, **1** (1934), 286–299 — see also his "Dhikoti-Karaṇam of Śrīpati," in *Journal of the Asiatic Society of Bengal*, n.s. **17** (1921), 273–278 — and by K. S. Shukla, in *Ṛtam*, **1** (1969), supp.

2. The *Dhruvamānasa*, written in 1056, is a short treatise in 105 verses on calculating planetary longitudes, on gnomon problems, on eclipses, on the horns of the moon, and on planetary transits. It is very rare and has not been published.

3. The *Siddhāntaśekhara*, a major work on astronomy in nineteen chapters, follows, in general, *the Brāhmapakṣa*. The chapters are on the following subjects:

    1. Fundamentals.
    2. Mean motions of the planets.
    3. True longitudes of the planets.
    4. On the three questions relating to the diurnal rotation.
    5. Lunar eclipses.
    6. Solar eclipses.
    7. On the syzygies.
    8. On the *pātas* of the sun and moon.
    9. On first and last appearances.
    10. On the moon.
    11. On transits of the planets.
    12. On conjunctions of the planets with the constellations.
    13. Arithmetic.
    14. Algebra.
    15. On the sphere.
    16. On the planetary spheres.
    17. On the cause of eclipses.
    18. On the projection of eclipses.
    19. On astronomical instruments.

A commentary on this work, the *Gaṇitabhūṣaṇa*, was composed by Makkibhaṭṭa (*fl.* 1377); unfortunately, only the portion on the first four chapters survives. The *Siddhāntaśekhara*, with Makkibhaṭṭa's commentary on chapters 1–4 and the editor's on chapters 5–19, was edited by Babuāji Miśra, 2 vols. (Calcutta, 1932–1947).

4. The *Gaṇitatilaka* is a mathematical treatise apparently based on the *Pāṭīgaṇita* or *Triśatikā* of Srīdhara; there is a commentary by Siṃhatilaka Sūri (*fl.* 1269 at Bijāpura, Mysore). Both text and

commentary were published by H. R. Kapadia (Baroda, 1937).

5 and 6. The *Jyotiṣaratnamālā*, in twenty chapters, is the most influential work in Sanskrit on *muhūrta* or catarchic astrology, in which the success or failure of an undertaking is determined from the time of its inception. It is based largely on the *Jyotiṣaratnakośa* of Lalla. Śrīpati himself wrote a Marāṭhī commentary on this (edited and studied for its linguistic content by M. G. Panse [Poona, 1957]); but of much greater historical importance is the commentary *Gautamī* composed by Mahādeva in 1263, for it contains numerous citations from lost or little-known astronomical and astrological texts. There are also commentaries by Dāmodara (*Bālāvabodha*), Paramakāraṇa (*Bālabodhinī* in Prākṛt), Śrīdhara (*Śrīdharīya*), and Vaijā Paṇḍita (*Bālāvabodhinī*). The *Jyotiṣaratnamālā* was published twice with Mahādeva's *Gautamī*: at Bombay in 1884 and by Rasikamohana Caṭṭopādhyāya (2nd ed., Calcutta, 1915). The first six chapters were edited by P. Poucha, "La Jyotiṣaratnamālā ou Guirlande des joyaux d'astrologie de Śrīpatibhaṭṭa," in *Archiv orientální*, **16** (1949), 277–309.

7. The *Jātakapaddhati* or *Śrīpatipaddhati*, in eight chapters, is one of the fundamental textbooks for later Indian genethlialogy, contributing an impressive elaboration to the computation of the strengths of the planets and astrological places. It was enormously popular, as the large number of manuscripts, commentaries, and imitations attests. The more important of these commentaries are Sūryadeva Yajvan (b. 1191), *Jātakālaṅkāra*; Parameśvara (ca. 1380–1460); Acyuta (fl. 1505–1534), *Bhāvārthamañjarī*—see D. Pingree, *Census of the Exact Sciences in Sanskrit*, ser. A, I (Philadelphia, 1970), 36a–36b; Kṛṣṇa (fl. 1600–1625), whose *udāharaṇa* was edited by J. B. Chaudhuri (Calcutta, 1955)—see also D. Pingree, *Census*, II (Philadelphia, 1971), 53a–55b; Sumatiharṣa Gaṇi (fl. 1615); Mādhava; and Raghunātha. Acyuta Piṣāraṭi (ca. 1550–1621; see D. Pingree, *Census*, I, 36b–38b) wrote an imitation, the *Horāsāroccaya*. The *Jātakapaddhati* was edited with an English translation by V. Subrahmanya Sastri (Bombay, 1903; 4th ed., Bangalore, 1957).

8. A *Daivajñavallabha* on astrology, in fifteen chapters, sometimes is attributed to Śrīpati and sometimes to Varāhamihira (fl. ca. 550); its real author remains unknown. It was published with the Hindī translation, *Subodhinī*, of Nārāyaṇa (fl. 1894) at Bombay in 1905, in 1915–1916, and in 1937.

There is no reliable discussion of Śrīpati or study of his works.

DAVID PINGREE

STÄCKEL, PAUL GUSTAV (*b.* Berlin, Germany, 20 August 1862; *d.* Heidelberg, Germany, 12 December 1919)

Stäckel studied at Berlin and defended his dissertation in 1885. He wrote his *Habilitationsschrift* at Halle in 1891 and then held chairs at various German universities, teaching finally at Heidelberg. His interests were varied, for he worked with equal ease in both mathematics and its history. The chief influence was the work of Weierstrass. He specialized in analytical mechanics (particularly in the use of Lagrangians in problems concerning the motion of points in the presence of given fields of force), related questions in geometry, and properties of analytical functions. A linking problem for these fields was the solution of linear differential equations; Stäckel also explored the existence theorems for such solutions. His other interests in mathematics included set theory and, in his later years, problems concerning prime numbers. He was renowned among his students for delivering new sets of lectures every academic year, and he wrote on problems in mathematical education.

In the history of mathematics Stäckel's interests centered on the eighteenth and early nineteenth centuries. He was especially noted for his role in instituting the publication of Euler's *Opera omnia*; and he also published editions of works, manuscripts, and correspondence of J. H. Lambert, F. and J. Bolyai, Gauss, and Jacobi. In addition, he edited several volumes in Ostwald's *Klassiker der Exacten Wissenschaften*. His interpretive articles dealt largely with the history of the theory of functions and of non-Euclidean geometry. From indications in his and others' writings, it seems clear that locating his *Nachlass* is highly desirable.

BIBLIOGRAPHY

The most comprehensive list of Stäckel's works is in Poggendorff, IV, 1427–1428, and V, 1194–1195.

For a sympathetic obituary, see O. Perron, "Paul Stäckel," *Sitzungsberichte der Heidelberger Akademie der Wissenschaften*, Math.-naturwiss. Kl., Abt. A (1920), no. 7.

I. GRATTAN-GUINNESS

STAMPIOEN, JAN JANSZ, DE JONGE (*b.* Rotterdam, Netherlands, 1610; *d.* The Hague, Netherlands [?], after 1689)

Stampioen's father (of the same name, whence the cognomen *de Jonge*) made astronomical instruments and was an official surveyor and gauger until his removal from office in 1660 for breach of trust.[1] The son began his own career in 1632 with an edition of Frans van Schooten the Elder's sine tables, to which Stampioen appended his own fully algebraic treatment of spherical trigonometry.

In 1633, while a mathematics teacher in Rotterdam, Stampioen took part in a public competition, during which he challenged Descartes to resolve a quartic problem involving a triangle with inscribed figures. Descartes derived the correct equation but did not solve it explicitly, and Stampioen rejected the solution as incomplete.[2] The issue was dropped for the moment, but Stampioen had made an enemy of Descartes and would soon feel the effects.

After being named tutor to Prince William (II) in 1638, Stampioen moved to The Hague, where he opened up a printing shop and in 1639 published his *Algebra ofte nieuwe stelregel* (*Algebra, or the New Method*), which he had completed in 1634. Despite the general title, the work focused on a new method of determining the cube root of expressions of the form $a + \sqrt{b}$ and on the method's application to the solution of cubic equations. In order to attract attention to his forthcoming book, he assumed in 1638 the alias Johan Baptista of Antwerp and posed two public challenges, the more difficult of which demanded the calculation of a traversing position for a siege gun (as stated, a cubic problem). Then he immediately published a solution under his own name. Soon thereafter, he presented another challenge requiring the determination of the position of the sun from the condition that three poles of given heights placed vertically in the ground each cast shadows reaching to the feet of the other two.[3]

A young surveyor in Utrecht, Jacob van Waessenaer, also published a solution to the first, or Antwerp, challenge, employing the methods of Descartes's *Geometry*. Stampioen's rejection of this solution prompted Waessenaer to publish a broad-scale critique of Stampioen's mathematics, emphasizing the inadequacies of the "new methods."[4] The exchange of pamphlets lasted two years and soon involved Descartes, who may in fact have been behind Waessenaer from the beginning.[5] With a wager of 600 gulden riding on the outcome, the issue was adjudicated in 1640 by Van Schooten and Jacob Gool, who found in Waessenaer's favor.[6]

Judging from their correspondence, Constantijn Huygens agreed with Descartes that Stampioen behaved badly during the dispute. Nonetheless, in 1644 Huygens engaged Stampioen for a year as mathematics tutor for his two elder sons, Constantijn, Jr., and Christiaan.[7] Thereafter, Stampioen faded from public notice. A brief reprise of the Waessenaer dispute in 1648, a topographical map published in 1650, and a mention of his having served in 1689 as an expert in a test of a method for determining longitude at sea are the only traces left of Stampioen's later life.

NOTES

1. The British Museum Catalogue (Ten-year supplement, XXI, col. 148) lists a copy of the *Sententien, by den Hove van Hollant gearresteert, jegens Ian Ianssz Stampioen en Quirijn Verblas. Gepronuncieert den acht en twintichsten Iulij Anno 1660.* For further details, see Bierens de Haan's "Bouwstoffen," cited in the bibliography.

2. For details, see the letter from Descartes to Stampioen in Charles Adam and Paul Tannery, eds., *Oeuvres de Descartes*, I (Paris, 1897), 275–280, and the editorial note in *ibid.* 573–578.

3. Newton, in his deposited lectures on algebra, published in *Universal Arithmetick* (London, 1707), states the problem as follows: "When, somewhere on Earth, three staves are erected perpendicular to the horizontal plane at points A, B, and C—that at A being 6 feet, that at B 18 feet and that at C 8 feet, with the line AB 33 feet in length—, it happens on a certain day that the tip of stave A's shadow passes through the points B and C, that of stave B, however, through A and C, and that of stave C through the point A. What is the sun's declination and the polar elevation? in other words, on what day and at what place do these events occur?" (Derek T. Whiteside, ed., *The Mathematical Papers of Isaac Newton*, V [Cambridge, 1972], 267.) Newton's complete solution of this problem, which involves conic sections, occupies pp. 266–278 of this edition.

4. Waessenaer's two major tracts are *Aanmerckingen op den nieuwen Stel-Regel van J. Stampioen, d'Jonge* (Leiden, 1639); and *Den On-wissen Wis-konstenaer I. I. Stampioen ontdeckt Door sijne ongegronde Weddinge ende mis-lucte Solutien van sijne eygene questien. Midtsgaders Eenen generalen Regel om de Cubic-wortelen ende alle andere te trecken uyt twee-namighe ghetallen: dewelcke voor desen niet bekent en is geweest. Noch De Solutien van twee sware Geometrische Questien door de Algebra: dienstich om alle te leeren ontbinden* (Leiden, 1640).

5. That is the conclusion of Bierens de Haan in his "Bouwstoffen," cited in the bibliography below, 79ff.

6. Stampioen published the judgment, entitling it so as to make himself appear the winner: *Verclaringe over het gevoelen by de E. H. professoren matheseos der Universiteit tot Leyden uyt-ghesproken, nopende den Regel fol. 25 van J. Stampioen, Welcke dese Verclaeringhe soodanigh ghetstelt is, dat yeder een daer uyt can oordeelen dat den Regel fol. 25 beschreven van Johan Stampioen de Jonge in sijnen Nieuwen Stel-Regel, seer licht, generael, ende der waerheydt conform is, om daer door den Teerling-wortel te trecken uyt twee-naemighe ghetallen* (The Hague, 1640). Judging by Descartes's complaints to Henricus Regius (Bierens de Haan, "Bouwstoffen," 99), the decision was formulated in a manner vague enough to permit such a contrary reading.

7. See Christiaan Huygens, *Oeuvres complètes*, XXII (The Hague, 1950), 399ff., and *ibid.*, I (The Hague, 1888), 15, for the list of mathematical works suggested by Stampioen as a syllabus for Huygens' sons.

BIBLIOGRAPHY

I. ORIGINAL WORKS. Stampioen's major works include his *Kort byvoeghsel der sphaerische triangulen* appended to his edition of Frans van Schooten, *Tabula sinuum* (Rotterdam, 1632): and his *Algebra, ofte Nieuwe stel-regel, waer door alles ghevonden wordt inde wisconst, wat vindtbaer is* . . . (The Hague, 1639).

The challenges and disputes of 1633 and 1638–1640 gave rise to several polemic pamphlets, a complete listing of which can be found in either of Bierens de Haan's articles listed below. The more important items are "Solutie op alle de questien openbaer angeslagen ende voorgestelt door Ez. de Decker" (Rotterdam, 1634); "Questie aen de Batavische Ingenieurs, Voor-gestelt door Johan Baptista Antwerpiensis. Volghens het spreeckwordt: Laet const blijken, Met goet bewys" (1638: for a more easily accessible statement of the problem, see *Oeuvres de Descartes*, C. Adam and P. Tannery, eds., II [Paris, 1898], 601ff.); "Wiskonstige Ontbinding. Over het Antwerpsch Vraegh-stuck toe-ge-eyghent alle Lief-Hebbers der Wis-Const" (The Hague, 1638); and "Wis-Konstigh Ende Reden-Maetigh Bewijs. Op den Reghel Fol. 25, 26 en 27. Van sijn Boeck ghenaemt den Nieuwen Stel-Regel" (The Hague, 1640).

Bibliographical details of Stampioen's map are given by Bierens de Haan in his "Bouwstoffen" (see below), 114.

II. SECONDARY LITERATURE. The most complete biography is that of Cornelis de Waard in *Nieuw Nederlandsch Biografisch Woordenboek*, II (Leiden, 1912), cols. 1358–1360. See also David Bierens de Haan, "Bouwstoffen voor de geschiedenis der wis- en natuurkundigen weteschappen en de Nederlanden, XXX: Jan Jansz. Stampioen de Jonge en Jacob à Waessenaer," in *Verslagen en Mededeelingen der koninklijke Akademie van Wetenschappen, Afdeeling Natuurkunde*, 3rd ser., III (Amsterdam, 1887), 69–119; and "Quelques lettres inédites de René Descartes et de Constantyn Huygens," in *Zeitschrift für Mathematik und Physik*, **32** (1887), 161–173. Further bibliography can be found in these three articles.

MICHAEL S. MAHONEY

STAUDT, KARL GEORG CHRISTIAN VON (*b.* Rothenburg-ob-der-Tauber, Germany, 24 January 1798; *d.* Erlangen, Germany, 1 June 1867)

Staudt was the son of Johann Christian von Staudt, a municipal counsel, and Maria Albrecht. Rothenburg, famous for its many antiquities, was then a free imperial German city. The family had settled in Rothenburg as craftsmen as early as 1402. Various members became municipal councilmen in the sixteenth century and received a coat of arms. In 1700 Leopold I ennobled the family. Staudt's maternal ancestors, the Albrechts, also served as councilmen and burgomasters in the seventeenth and eighteenth centuries. Staudt's father was appointed a municipal legal officer by the Bavarian government in 1805, the year Rothenburg became part of the Kingdom of Bavaria.

After carefully supervising his early education, Staudt's parents sent him to the Gymnasium in Ansbach from 1814 to 1817. Then, drawn by the great reputation of Gauss, Staudt attended the University of Göttingen from 1818 to 1822. As a student he was surely well acquainted with Gauss's studies in number theory. His chief concern in these years, however, was theoretical and practical astronomy, to which he was also introduced by Gauss, who was then director of the observatory. As early as 1820 Staudt observed and computed the ephemerides of Mars and Pallas. His most comprehensive work in astronomy was the determination of the orbit of the comet discovered by Joseph Nicollet and Jean-Louis Pons in 1821. His precise calculations were highly praised by Gauss, and later observations led to only minor improvements. Staudt never returned to the field of astronomy, but it was on the basis of this early work that he received the doctorate from the University of Erlangen in 1822.

In the same year Staudt qualified at Munich as a mathematics teacher. His first assignment was at the secondary school in Würzburg. But with Gauss's intervention he was also able to lecture at the University of Würzburg. His lectures dealt with rather elementary topics. Because of insufficient support from the university, he transferred in 1827 to the secondary school in Nuremberg and taught there and at the Nuremberg polytechnical school until 1835. He finally achieved his primary goal when, on 1 October 1835, he was appointed full professor of mathematics at the University of Erlangen, where he remained until his death. He was unquestionably the leading mathematician at Erlangen, not least because of his outstanding human qualities. The latter, indeed, brought him many honorary posts in the university administration.

As at most German universities during this period, the level of mathematics instruction at Erlangen was not high, nor did the subject attract many students. It was not yet customary for mathematicians to discuss their own research in the classroom—a practice first introduced by Jacobi, at Königsberg. Accordingly, it was not until 1842–1843 that Staudt gave special lectures on his new geometry of position.

In 1832 Staudt married Jeanette Drechsler. They had a son, Eduard, and a daughter, Mathilde, who became the wife of a burgomaster of Erlangen. Staudt's wife died in 1848, and he never remarried. In his last years he suffered greatly from asthma.

Staudt was not a mathematician who astounded his colleagues by a flood of publications in a number of fields. He let his ideas mature for a long period before making them public, and his research was confined exclusively to projective geometry and to the only distantly related Bernoullian numbers. His fame as a great innovator in the history of mathematics stems primarily from his work in projective geometry, which he still called by the old name of "geometry of position," or *Geometrie der Lage*, the title of his principal publication (1847). This work was followed by three supplementary *Beiträge zur Geometrie der Lage* (1856–1860), which together contain more pages than the original book (396 as compared with 216).

After centuries of dominance, Euclidean geometry was challenged by Poncelet and Gergonne, who created projective geometry during the first third of the nineteenth century. These two mathematicians found that, through the use of perspective, circles and squares and other figures could be transformed into arbitrary conic sections and quadrilaterals and that a metric theorem for, say, the circle could be transformed into a metric theorem for conic sections. The most important contributions made by Poncelet (whose main writings appeared between 1813 and 1822) and Gergonne were the polarity theory of the conic sections and the principle of duality. Jakob Steiner, in his fundamental work *Systematische Entwicklung der Abhängigkeit geometrischer Gestalten voneinander* (1832), then introduced the projective production of conic sections and second-degree surfaces that is now named for him.

In their writings, however, all three of these pioneers failed to adhere strictly to the viewpoint of projective geometry, which admits only intersection, union, and incidence of points, straight lines, and planes. Staudt, in his 1847 book, was the first to adopt a fully rigorous approach. Without exception, his predecessors still spoke of distances, perpendiculars, angles, and other entities that play no role in projective geometry. Moreover, as the name of that important relationship indicates, in accounting for the cross ratio of four points on a straight line, they all made use of line segments. In contrast, Staudt stated in the preface to his masterpiece his intention of establishing the "geometry of position" free from all metrical considerations, and in the body of the book he constructed a real projective geometry of two and three dimensions.

Naturally, in Staudt's book these geometries are not founded on a complete axiom system in the modern sense. Rather, he adopted from Euclid's system everything that did not pertain to interval lengths, angles, and perpendicularity. Although it was not necessary, he also retained Euclid's parallel postulate and was therefore obliged to introduce points at infinity. This decision, while burdening his treatment with a constant need to consider the special positions of the geometric elements at infinite distance, altered nothing of the basic structure of geometry without a metric. Using only union and intersection of straight lines in the plane, Staudt constructed the fourth harmonic associated with three points on a straight line. Correspondingly, with three straight lines or planes of a pencil he was able to construct the fourth harmonic element. Although he did not give the theorem that name, he used Desargues's theorem to prove that his construction was precise.

Using the relationship of four points in general position on a plane to four corresponding points or straight lines on another plane or on the same plane, Staudt defined a collineation—or, as the case may be, a correlation—between these planes. Analogously he also pointed out spatial collineations and correlations. In this instance he made use of Möbius' network construction, which enabled him to obtain, from four given points of a plane, denumerably many points by drawing straight lines through point pairs and by making straight lines intersect. He then associated the points derived in this way with correspondingly constructed points and straight lines of the other plane. Felix Klein later noted that a continuity postulate is still required in order to assign to each of the infinitely many points of the first plane its image point (or image lines) on the other plane.

From the time of his first publications, Staudt displayed a grasp of the importance of the principle of duality. For every theorem he stated its converse. (As was customary, he generally gave the theorem on one half of the page and its converse on the other half.) In discussing the autocorrelations of P_2 and P_3, he succeeded in obtaining the polarities and also the null correlations that had previously been discovered by Gaetano Giorgini and Möbius. For example, he described a plane polarity as a particular type of autocorrelation that yields a triangle in which each vertex is associated with the side opposite. On this basis, Staudt formulated the definition of the conic sections and quadrics that bears his name: they are the loci of those points that, through a polarity, are incident with their assigned straight lines or planes. This definition is superior to the one given by Steiner. For instance, in Staudt's definition the conic section appears as a point locus together with the totality of its tangents. Steiner, in contrast, required two different productions: one for the conic section K and another for the totality of its tangents, that is, for the dual figures associated with K. A conic section defined in Staudt's manner can consist of the empty set; that is, it can contain no real points—accordingly, Klein applied the term *nullteilig* to it.

In a coordinate geometry it is easy to extend the domain of the real points to the domain of the complex points with complex coordinates. Employing the concepts of real geometry, Staudt made an essential contribution to synthetic geometry through his elegantly formulated introduction of the complex projective spaces of one, two, and three dimensions. This advance was the principal achievement contained in his *Beiträge zur Geometrie der Lage*. He conceived of the complex points of a straight line P_1 by means of the so-called elliptic involution of the real range p_1 of P_1, which can also be described as those involuted autoprojectivities of p_1 among which pairs of corresponding points intersect each other. It can be shown by calculation that such an elliptic involution has two complex, conjugate fixed points; and Staudt had to furnish the elliptic involutions with two different orientations, so that ultimately he could interpret the oriented elliptic involutions on the real range of P_1 as points of P_1. The degenerate parabolic involutions are to be associated with the real points of P_1. In this way he also extended the real projective planes p_2 and p_3 to complex P_2 and P_3. He then showed—not an easy feat—that P_2 and P_3 satisfy the connection axioms of projective geometry. Among the lines P_1 of P_3 he found three types: those with infinitely many real points, those with only one real point, and those with no real point. He carefully classified the quadrics of P_3 according to the way in which straight lines of these three types lie on them.

Staudt favored the use of the second type of complex line of P_3 as a model of the complex numbers P_1. He applied the term *Wurf* ("throw") to a point quadruple and gave the procedure for finding sums and products in the set of these throws—or, more precisely, the set of the equivalence classes of projectively equivalent throws. Here he approached the projective foundation of the complex

number field and the projective metric determination. Staudt termed certain throws neutral: those with real cross ratio, a property that can be determined computationally. Then, for three given points—A, B, C, in P_1—he designated as a chain the set of all those points of P_1 that form a neutral throw with A, B, C. These sets and their generalization to complex P_n are called "Staudt chains." In part three of the *Beiträge*, Staudt also dealt with third- and fourth-order spatial curves in the context of the theory of linear systems of equations.

At the time of their publication, Staudt's books were considered difficult. This assessment arose for several reasons. First, since he sought to present a strictly systematic construction of synthetic geometry, he did not present any formulas; moreover, he refused to employ any diagrams. Second, he cited no other authors. Finally, although his theory of imaginaries was remarkable, it was extremely difficult to manipulate in comparison with algebraic equations. Accordingly, little significant progress could have been expected from its adoption in the study of figures more complicated than conic sections and quadrics.

Staudt is also known today for the Staudt-Clausen theorem in the theory of Bernoulli numbers. These numbers—B_n ($n = 1, 2, \cdots$)—appear in the summation formulas of the nth powers of the first h natural numbers; they also arise in analysis, for example, in the series expansion $x \cot x$. The B_n are rational numbers of alternating sign, and the Staudt-Clausen theorem furnished the first significant indication of the law of their formation. In formulating the theorem, for the natural number n there is a designated uneven prime number, p, called Staudt's prime number, such that $p - 1$ divides the number $2n$. Then, according to the theorem, $(-1)^n B_n$ is a positive rational number, which, aside from its integral component, is a sum of unit fractions, among the denominators of which appear precisely the number 2 and all Staudt prime numbers for n. Staudt published his theorem in 1840; it was also demonstrated, independently, in the same year by Thomas Clausen, who was working in Altona. Staudt published two further, detailed works in Latin on the theory of Bernoulli numbers (Erlangen, 1845); but these writings never became widely known and later authors almost never cited them.

BIBLIOGRAPHY

I. ORIGINAL WORKS. Staudt's major works are "Beweis eines Lehrsatzes, die Bernoullischen Zahlen betreffend," in *Journal für die reine und angewandte Mathe-*

matik, **21** (1840), 372–374; *Geometrie der Lage* (Nuremberg, 1847), with Italian trans. by M. Pieri (see below); and *Beiträge zur Geometrie der Lage*, 3 vols. (Nuremberg, 1856–1860).

II. SECONDARY LITERATURE. See G. Böhmer, *Professor Dr. K. G. Chr. von Staudt, Ein Lebensbild* (Rothenburg-ob-der-Tauber, 1953); M. Noether, "Zur Erinnerung an Karl Georg Christian von Staudt," in *Jahresbericht der Deutschen Mathematikervereinigung*, **32** (1923), 97–119; "Nekrolog auf K. G. Chr. von Staudt," in *Sitzungsberichte der Bayerischen Akademie der Wissenschaften zu München*, **1** (1868), repr. in *Archiv der Mathematik*, **49** (1869), 1–5; and C. Segre, "C. G. C. von Staudt ed i suoi lavori," in *Geometria di posizione de Staudt*, M. Pieri, ed. and trans. (Turin, 1888), 1–17.

WERNER BURAU

STEINER, JAKOB (*b.* Utzensdorf, Bern, Switzerland, 18 March 1796; *d.* Bern, Switzerland, 1 April 1863)

Life. Steiner was the youngest of the eight children of Niklaus Steiner (1752–1826), a small farmer and tradesman, and the former Anna Barbara Weber (1757–1832), who were married on 28 January 1780. The fourth child, Anna Barbara (1786–1870), married David Begert; and their daughter Elisabeth (*b.* 1815) married Friedrich Geiser, a butcher, in 1836. To this marriage was born the mathematician Karl Friedrich Geiser (1843–1934), who was thus a grandnephew of Steiner.[1]

Steiner had a poor education and did not learn to write until he was fourteen. As a child he had to help his parents on the farm and in their business; his skill in calculation was of great assistance. Steiner's desire for learning led him to leave home, against his parents' will, in the spring of 1814 to attend Johann Heinrich Pestalozzi's school at Yverdon, where he was both student and teacher. Pestalozzi found a brilliant interpreter of his revolutionary ideas on education in Steiner, who characterized the new approach in an application to the Prussian Ministry of Education (16 December 1826):

> The method used in Pestalozzi's school, treating the truths of mathematics as objects of independent reflection, led me, as a student there, to seek other grounds for the theorems presented in the courses than those provided by my teachers. Where possible I looked for deeper bases, and I succeeded so often that my teachers preferred my proofs to their own. As a result, after I had been there for a year and a half, it was thought that I could give instruction in mathematics.[2]

Steiner's posthumous papers include hundreds of pages of manuscripts containing both courses given by his fellow teachers and his own ideas. These papers include the studies "Einige Gesetze über die Teilung der Ebene und des Raumes," which later appeared in the first volume of Crelle's *Journal für die reine und angewandte Mathematik*. Steiner stated that they were inspired by Pestalozzi's views.

In the application of 1826 Steiner also wrote:

> Without my knowing or wishing it, continuous concern with teaching has intensified by striving after scientific unity and coherence. Just as related theorems in a single branch of mathematics grow out of one another in distinct classes, so, I believed, do the branches of mathematics itself. I glimpsed the idea of the organic unity of all the objects of mathematics; and I believed at that time that I could find this unity in some university, if not as an independent subject, at least in the form of specific suggestions.

These two statements provide an excellent characterization of Steiner's basic attitude toward teaching and research. The first advocates independent reflection by the students, a practice that was the foundation of Steiner's great success as a teacher. At first, in Berlin, he was in great demand as a private teacher; among his students was the son of Wilhelm von Humboldt. Steiner often gave his courses as colloquiums, posing questions to the students. This direct contact with the students was often continued outside the classroom. The second statement expresses the idea that guided all his work: to discover the organic unity of all the objects of mathematics, an aim realized especially in his fundamental research on synthetic geometry. Steiner left Yverdon in the autumn of 1818 and went to Heidelberg, where he supported himself by giving private instruction. His most important teacher there was Ferdinand Schweins, whose lectures on combinatorial analysis furnished the basis for two of Steiner's works.[3]

At this time Steiner also studied differential and integral calculus and algebra. In addition, lectures at Heidelberg stimulated the careful work contained in manuscripts on mechanics from 1821, 1824, and 1825, upon which Steiner later drew for investigations on the center of gravity.[4]

Following a friend's advice, Steiner left for Berlin at Easter 1821. Not having passed any academic examinations, he was now obliged to do so in order to obtain a teaching license. He was only partially successful in his examinations and therefore received only a restricted license in mathematics, along with an appointment at the Werder Gymnasium. The initially favorable judgment of his teaching was soon followed by criticism that led to his dismissal in the autumn of 1822. From November 1822 to August 1824 he was enrolled as a student at the University of Berlin, at the same time as C. G. J. Jacobi. He again earned his living by giving private instruction until 1825, when he became assistant master (and in 1829 senior master) at the technical school in Berlin. On 8 October 1834 he was appointed extraordinary professor at the University of Berlin, a post he held until his death.

Steiner never married. He left a fortune of about 90,000 Swiss francs, equivalent to 24,000 thaler.[5] He bequeathed a third of it to the Berlin Academy for establishment of the prize named for him,[6] and 60,000 francs to his relatives. In addition he left 750 francs to the school of his native village, the interest on which is still used to pay for prizes awarded to students adept at mental computations.[7] Steiner, with a yearly income of between 700 and 800 thaler, amassed this fortune by giving lectures on geometry.[8]

Students and contemporaries wrote of the brilliance of Steiner's geometric research and of the fiery temperament he displayed in leading others into the new territory he had discovered. Combined with this were very liberal political views. Moreover, he often behaved crudely and spoke bluntly, thereby alienating a number of people. Thus it is certain that his dismissal from the Werder Gymnasium cannot have been merely a question of his scholarly qualifications. Steiner attributed this action to his refusal to base his course on the textbook written by the school's director, Dr. Zimmermann. The latter, in turn, reproached Steiner for using Pestalozzi's methods, claiming that they were suitable only for elementary instruction and therefore made Steiner's teaching deficient. Steiner also experienced difficulties at the technical school, where he was expected to follow, without question, the orders of the director, K. F. von Klöden. Klöden, however, felt that Steiner did not treat him with proper respect, and made exacting demands of him that were of a magnitude and severity that even a soldier subject to military discipline could hardly be expected to accept.

Steiner's scientific achievements brought him an honorary doctorate from the University of Königsberg (20 April 1833) and membership in the Prussian Academy of Sciences (5 June 1834). He spent the winter of 1854–1855 in Paris and became a corresponding member of the French Academy of Sciences. He had already been made a corresponding member of the Accademia dei Lincei in 1853. A kidney ailment obliged him to take repeated cures in the following years, and he lectured only during the winter terms.

Mathematical Work. Having set himself the task of reforming geometry, Steiner sought to discover simple principles from which many seemingly unrelated theorems in the subject could be deduced in a natural way. He formulated his plan in the preface to *Systematische Entwicklung der Abhängigkeit geometrischer Gestalten voneinander, mit Berücksichtigung der Arbeiten alter und neuer Geometer über Porismen, Projections-Methoden, Geometrie der Lage, Transversalen, Dualität und Reciprocität* (1832), dedicated to Wilhelm von Humboldt:

The present work is an attempt to discover the organism [*Organismus*] through which the most varied spatial phenomena are linked with one another. There exist a limited number of very simple fundamental relationships that together constitute the schema by means of which the remaining theorems can be developed logically and without difficulty. Through the proper adoption of the few basic relations one becomes master of the entire field. Order replaces chaos; and one sees how all the parts mesh naturally, arrange themselves in the most beautiful order, and form well-defined groups. In this manner one obtains, simultaneously, the elements from which nature starts when, with the greatest possible economy and in the simplest way, it endows the figures with infinitely many properties. Here the main thing is neither the synthetic nor the analytic method, but the discovery of the mutual dependence of the figures and of the way in which their properties are carried over from the simpler to the more complex ones. This connection and transition is the real source of all the remaining individual propositions of geometry. Properties of figures the very existence of which one previously had to be convinced through ingenious demonstrations and which, when found, stood as something marvelous are now revealed as necessary consequences of the most common properties of these newly discovered basic elements, and the former are established a priori by the latter.[9]

Also in the preface Steiner asserted that this work would contain "a systematic development of the problems and theorems concerning the intersection and tangency of the circle in the plane and on spherical surfaces and of spheres." The plan was not carried out, and the manuscript of this part was not published until 1931.[10] But many of the observations, theorems, and problems included in it appeared in "Einige geometrische Betrachtungen" (1826), Steiner's first long publication.[11]

The earliest detailed account of some of the sources of Steiner's concepts and theorems can be found in the posthumously published *Allgemeine Theorie über das Berühren und Schneiden der Kreise und der Kugeln, worunter eine grosse Anzahl neuer Untersuchungen und Sätze, in einem systematischen Entwicklungsgange dargestellt.* . . .[12] The headings of the sections describe its contents: "I. Of Centers, Lines, and Planes of Similitude in Circles and Spheres. II. Of the Power and the Locus of Equal Powers With Respect to Circles and Spheres. III. Of the Common Power in Circles and in Spheres. IV. Of Angles at Which Circles and Spheres Intersect."

In the foreword to *Allgemeine Theorie*, F. Gonseth stated in current terminology the basic principle on which many of Steiner's theorems and constructions are founded: the stereographic projection of the plane onto the sphere.[13] Section 4 of this work contains the following problem (§ 29, X, p. 167): "Draw a circle that intersects at equal angles four arbitrary circles of given size and position." The new methods were applied to the solution of Apollonius' problem (§ 31, II, p. 175): "Find a circle tangent to three arbitrary circles of given size and position." Another problem (§ 31, III, p. 182) reads: "Find a circle that intersects three arbitrary circles of given size and position at the angles α_1, α_2, α_3." Analogous problems for spheres are given in chapter 2, where the theorems and problems are presented systematically according to the number of spheres involved (from two to eight), with size and position again given—for example (p. 306): "Draw a sphere that intersects five arbitrary spheres of given size and position at one and the same angle" and (p. 333) "Find a sphere that is tangent to a sphere M_1 of given size and position and that cuts at one and the same angle three pairs of spheres, of given size and position, M_2 and M_3, M_4 and M_5, M_6 and M_7, each pair taken singly."

At Berlin, Steiner became friendly with Abel, Crelle, and Jacobi; and together they introduced a fresh, new current into mathematics. Their efforts were considerably aided by Crelle's founding of the *Journal für die reine und angewandte Mathematik*, to which Steiner contributed sixty-two articles. In the first volume (1826) he published his

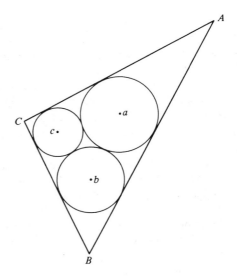

FIGURE 1

great work "Einige geometrische Betrachtungen."[14] It contains a selection from the *Allgemeine Theorie* and the first published systematic development of the theory of the power of a point with respect to a circle and of the points of similitude of circles; in his account Steiner mentions Pappus, Viète, and Poncelet. As the first application of these concepts Steiner states, without proof, his solution to Malfatti's problem (§ IV, no. 14). In a given triangle ABC draw three circles a, b, and c that are tangent to each other and such that each is

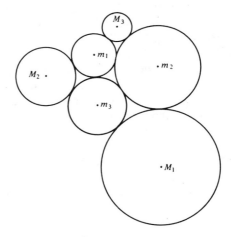

FIGURE 2

tangent to two sides of the triangle (Figure 1). Steiner then remarks that this is a special case of the next problem (no. 15): "Given three arbitrary circles, M_1, M_2, M_3, of specified size and position, to find three other circles m_1, m_2, m_3 tangent to each other and such that each is tangent to two of the given circles, and that each of the given circles M_i is tangent to two of the circles m_k that are to be found" (Figure 2).

Steiner did not prove his solution. Examination of his posthumous papers shows that he knew of the principle of inversion and that he used it in finding and proving the above and other theorems.[15]

It was likewise by means of an inversion that Steiner found and proved his famous theorem on series of circles (§ IV, no. 22; see Figure 3):

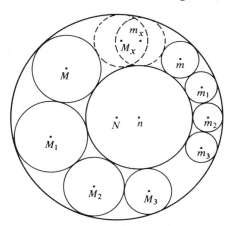

FIGURE 3

Two circles n, N of assigned size and position, lying one within the other, are given. If, for a definite series of circles M, M_1, $\cdots$, M_x, each of which is tangent to n and N unequally and that are tangent to each other in order, the interval between n and N is *commensurable*, that is, if the series consists of $x + 1$ members forming a sequence of u circuits such that the last circle M_x is tangent to the first one M: then this interval is commensurable for any series of circles m, m_1, $\cdots$, m_x; and the latter series also consists of $x + 1$ members forming u circuit, as in the first series.

In this same work (§ VI; see Figure 4), he proves a theorem of Pappus, in the following form:

Given two circles M_1, M_2, of assigned size and position that are tangent to each other in B. If one draws two arbitrary circles m_1, m_2 that are tangent to each other externally in b and each of which is tangent to the two given circles, and if one drops the perpendiculars m_1P_1, m_2P_2 from the centers m_1, m_2 on the axis M_1M_2 of the given circles and divides these perpendiculars by the radii r_1, r_2 of the circles m_1, m_2: then the quotient corresponding to the circle m_2 is greater by 2 than that corresponding to the former; that is, $\dfrac{m_1P_1}{r_1} + 2 = \dfrac{m_2P_2}{r_2}$. Or, as Pappus expressed it: the perpendicular m_1P_1 plus the diameter of the corresponding circle m_1 is to that diameter as the per-

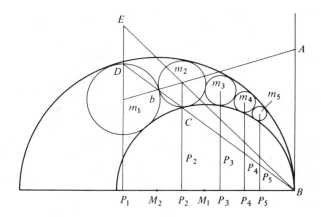

FIGURE 4

pendicular m_2P_2 is to the diameter of the corresponding circle m_2 — that is, $\dfrac{m_1P_1 + 2r_1}{2r_1} = \dfrac{m_2P_2}{2r_2}$.

Steiner furnishes a proof of this proposition, which consists, essentially, of the following steps:

1. The straight line $AB \perp BM_1$ is the line of equal powers with respect to the circles M_1 and M_2.

2. AB passes through the exterior center of similitude A of the circles m_1 and m_2.

3. $Am_2 : Am_1 = r_2 : r_1 = BP_2 : BP_1$ and $AB = Ab$.

4. The points B, C, b, D lie on one straight line.

5. The assertion follows from similarity considerations. In a later paper Steiner applied this "ancient" theorem of Pappus to the sphere.[16]

Also in the first volume of Crelle's *Journal*, Steiner published an expanded version of considerations that stemmed from the period that he was in Yverdon: "Einige Gesetze über die Teilung der Ebene und des Raumes."[17] In it he expressly stated that his ideas were inspired by Pestalozzi's ideas. The simplest result in this paper was presented in the following form:

A plane is divided into two parts by a straight line lying within it; by a second straight line that intersects the first, the number of parts of the plane is increased by 2; by a third straight line that intersects the two first lines at two points, the number is increased by 3; and so forth. That is, each successive straight line increases the number of parts by the number of parts into which it was divided by the preceding straight lines. Therefore, a plane is divided by n arbitrary straight lines into at most $2 + 2 + 3 \cdots + (n-1) +$

$$n = 1 + \frac{n(n+1)}{2} = 1 + n + \frac{n(n-1)}{1 \cdot 2} \text{ parts.}$$

He then subdivided space by means of planes and spherical surfaces.

In the following years Crelle's *Journal* and Gergonne's *Annales de mathématiques* published many of Steiner's papers, most of which were either problems to be solved or theorems to be proved.[18] In this way Steiner exerted an exceptionally stimulating influence on geometric research that was strengthened by the publication of his first book, *Systematische Entwicklung* (1832).[19] It was originally supposed to consist of five sections, but only the first appeared. Some of the remaining sections were published in the *Vorlesungen*.[20]

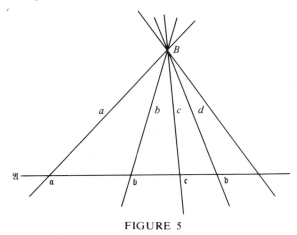

FIGURE 5

Steiner believed that the fundamental concepts of plane geometry are the range of points considered as the totality of points $\mathfrak{a}$, $\mathfrak{b}$, $\mathfrak{c}$, $\cdots$ of a straight line $\mathfrak{A}$ and the pencil of lines a, b, c, $\cdots$ through a point B (Figure 5). Since the latter are the intersection points of a, b, c, $\cdots$ with straight line $\mathfrak{A}$, an unambiguous relationship is established between the pencil of lines and the range, a relationship that he called projectivity. In volume II, § 2, of the *Vorlesungen über synthetische Geometrie* (1867), Steiner expressed this property through the statement that the two constructs are of the same *cardinality*, an expression that Georg Cantor adopted and generalized.[21]

In the first chapter of this part of the *Vorlesungen*, Steiner discusses the elements of projectivity, emphasizing the duality between point and straight line. In particular he proves the harmonic properties of the complete quadrangle and of the complete quadrilateral. In the second chapter he treats the simple elements of solid geometry. At the center of the epochal work stands the theory of conic sections in the third book. Here Steiner proved his fundamental theorem: The intersection points of corresponding lines of two projective pencils of

lines form a conic section. In its metric formulation this theorem was essentially known to Jan de Witt and Newton.[22] Steiner, however, was the first to recognize that it was a theorem of projective geometry, and he made it the cornerstone of the projective treatment of the theory of conic sections.

Steiner knew of the significance of his discovery.

The above investigation of projective figures, by placing them in oblique positions deliberately avoided closer research into the laws that govern the projective rays for two straight lines A, A_1 [Figure 6]. We shall now proceed to this examination. It leads, as will be seen, to the most interesting and fruitful properties of curves of the second order, the so-called conic sections. From these almost all other properties of the conics can be developed in a single, comprehensive framework and in a surprisingly simple and clear manner. This examination shows the necessary emergence of the conic sections from the elementary geometric figures; indeed, it shows, at the same time, a very remarkable double production of these [sections] by means of projective figures. . . . When one considers with what ingenuity past and present mathematicians have investigated the conic sections, and the almost countless number of properties that remained hidden for so long, one is struck that, as will be seen, almost all the known properties (and many new ones) flow from their projective generation as from a spring; and this generation also reveals the inner nature of the conic sections to us. For even if properties are known that are similar to those named here, the latter have never, in my opinion, been explicitly stated; in no case, however, has anyone until now recognized the importance that they derive from our development of them, where they are raised to the level of fundamental theorems.[23]

In proposition no. 37 of this volume, Steiner stated and proved his fundamental theorem for the circle (Figure 6): "Any two tangents A, A_1 are projective with respect to the corresponding pairs of points in which they are cut by the other tangents; and the point of intersection $\mathfrak{b}$, e_1, of the tangents corresponds to the points $\mathfrak{b}_1$, e, where they touch the circle." He also gave the dual of this theorem (Figure 7): "Any two points $\mathfrak{B}$, $\mathfrak{B}_1$ of a circle are the centers of two projective pencils of lines, the corresponding lines of which intersect in the remaining points of the circle; and the reciprocal tangents d_1, e at the points $\mathfrak{B}$, $\mathfrak{B}_1$ correspond to the lines d, e_1." Applying these theorems to the second-degree cone, Steiner obtained the following result: "Any two tangents of a conic section are projective with respect to the pair of points in which they are intersected by the remaining tangents; and conversely."

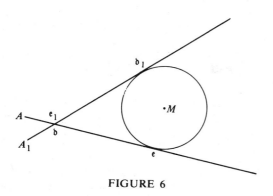

FIGURE 6

Steiner emphasized here that "these new theorems on the second-degree cone and its sections are more important for the investigation of these figures than all the theorems previously known about them, for they are, in the strict sense, the true fundamental theorems."

From these fundamental theorems, Steiner derived consequences ranging from the known theorems on conic sections to the Braikenridge-Maclaurin theorem. Propositions 49–53 deal with the production of projective figures in space. An important group of propositions (54–58) contains previously known "composite theorems and problems" that Steiner was the first to derive in a uniform manner from one basic principle. An example is the following problem taken from Möbius: "Given an arbitrary tetrahedron, draw another the vertices of which lie in the faces of the first and the faces of which pass through the vertices of the

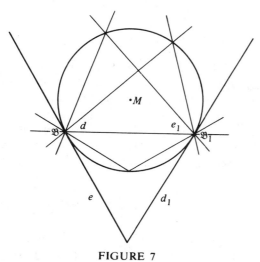

FIGURE 7

first, two vertices of the second tetrahedron being given." Proposition 59, labeled "general observation," contains the "skew projection," a quadratic relationship in space, sometimes called the "Steiner

relationship," which had been noted by Poncelet.[24]

The eighty-five "Problems and Theorems" that Steiner appended in a supplement proved especially stimulating to a generation of geometers. They are discussed in the dissertation of Ahmed Karam,[25] who found that, as of 1939, only three problems remained unsolved: no. 70, "What are the properties of a group of similar quadratic surfaces that pass through four or five points of space?"; no. 77, "Does a convex polyhedron always have a topological equivalent that can be either circumscribed about or inscribed in a sphere?"; and no. 76, "If polyhedra are distinguished solely according to their boundary surfaces, there exist only one with four faces, two with five faces, and seven with six faces. How many different bodies are possible with 7, 8, ···, n faces?"

The last problem was posed by Steiner's teacher at Heidelberg, Ferdinand Schweins.[26] It was partially solved by Otto Hermes in 1903, and further elements of it have been solved by P. J. Frederico.[27]

Of Steiner's work Jacobi stated:

> Starting from a few spatial properties Steiner attempted, by means of a simple schema, to attain a comprehensive view of the multitude of geometric theorems that had been rent asunder. He sought to assign each its special position in relation to the others, to bring order to chaos, to interlock all the parts according to nature, and to assemble them into well-defined groups. In discovering the organism [*Organismus*] through which the most varied phenomena of space are linked, he not only furthered the development of a geometric synthesis; he also provided a model of a complete method and execution for all other branches of mathematics.[28]

Only a year after the appearance of *Systematische Entwicklung*, Steiner published his second book: *Die geometrischen Konstruktionen ausgeführt mittelst der geraden Linie und eines festen Kreises, als Lehrgegenstand auf höheren Unterrichtsanstalten und zur praktischen Benützung* (1833).[29] He took as his point of departure Mascheroni's remark that all constructions made with straightedge and compass can be carried out using compass alone. As a counterpart to this statement, Steiner proved that all such constructions can also be carried out with the straightedge and one fixed circle. To this end he devoted the first chapter to rectilinear figures and especially to the harmonic properties of the complete quadrilateral. In the third chapter he proved his assertion in a way that enabled him to solve eight fundamental problems, to which all others can be reduced. For example (no. 1): "Draw the parallel to a straight line through a point" and (no. 8) "Find the intersection point of two circles." In the intervening chapter 2, he considered centers of similitude and the radical axis of a pencil of circles. This work, which enjoyed great success, contained an appendix of twenty-one problems that were partly taken from *Systematische Entwicklung.* The first one, for example, was "Given two arbitrary triangles, find a third that is simultaneously circumscribed about the first and inscribed in the second."

At this point we shall present a survey of Steiner's further research, published in volume II of the *Gesammelte Werke* (the page numbers in parentheses refer to that volume). A fuller description of its contents can be found in Louis Kollros' article on Steiner, cited in the bibliography.

Steiner pursued the investigation of conic sections and surfaces in some dozen further publications. Sometimes he merely presented problems and theorems without solutions or proofs. In part the material follows from the general projective approach to geometry; but some of it contains new ideas, as the examination of the extreme-value problem: "Determine an ellipse of greatest surface that is inscribed in a given quadrangle" (333 f.) and "Among all the quadrangles inscribed in an ellipse, that having the greatest perimeter is the one the vertices of which lie in the tangent points of the sides of a rectangle circumscribed about the ellipse. There are infinitely many such quadrangles. . . . All have the same perimeter, which is equal to twice the diagonal of the rectangle. All these quadrangles of greatest perimeter are parallelograms; and they are, simultaneously, circumscribed about another ellipse the axes of which fall on the corresponding axes of the given ellipse and that is confocal with the latter. . . . Among all the quadrangles circumscribed about a given ellipse, the one with least perimeter is that in which the normals at the tangent points of its sides form a rhombus" (411–412).

In a paper on new methods of determining second-order curves, Steiner considered pairs of such curves and demonstrated propositions of the following type: "If two arbitrary conic sections are inscribed in a complete quadrilateral, then the eight points in which they are tangent to the sides lie on another conic section" (477 f.). To the theory of second-degree surfaces, he contributed the geometric proof of Poisson's theorem: The attraction of a homogeneous elliptical sheet falls on a point P

in the axis of the cone that has P as vertex and is tangent to the ellipsoid.

Steiner dealt on several occasions with center-of-gravity problems. One of the simplest follows.

If, in a given circle $ADBE$, one takes an arc AB, of which one end point, A, is fixed, and lets it increase steadily from zero, then its center of gravity C will describe a curved line ACM. What properties will this barycentric curve possess? . . . The same question can be phrased generally, if instead of the circle an arbitrary curve is given. . . . Questions like those of the above problem occur if one considers the center of gravity of the segment (instead of the arc) ADB. Other questions of the same sort arise regarding the center of gravity of a variable sector AMB, if M is an arbitrary fixed pole and one arm of the sector is fixed, while the other, MB, turns about the pole M [p. 30; see Figure 8].

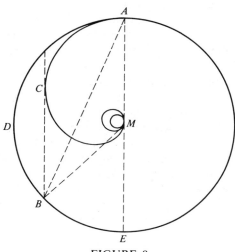

FIGURE 8

Steiner developed a general theory of the center of gravity of mass points in "Von dem Krümmungsschwerpunkt ebener Kurven" (97–159). It led to the pedal curve of a given curve and its area, and was followed by the important memoir "Parallele Flächen" (171–176), which generalized a theorem proved in the preceding paper for plane curves: Let A and B be two parallel polyhedra (surfaces) separated by a distance h. Then it is true for A and B that $B = A + hk + h^2e$; and for the volume I between A and B that $I = hA + h^2k/2 + h^3e/3$, where k is "the sum of the edge curvature" and e "the sum of the vertex curvature."

Steiner's great two-part paper "Ueber Maximum und Minimum bei den Figuren in der Ebene, auf der Kugelfläche und im Raume überhaupt" (177–308, with 36 figures) was written in Paris during the winter of 1840–1841. It shows the tremendous achievements of which he was still capable—given the necessary time and freedom from distractions. His basic theorem states: "Among all plane figures of the same perimeter, the circle has the greatest area (and conversely)." He gives five ways of demonstrating it, in all of which he assumes the existence of the extremum. All five, moreover, are based on the inequalities of the triangle and of polygons. The first proof proceeds indirectly: Assume that among all figures of equal perimeter the convex figure $EFGH$ possesses the greatest area and that it is not a circle (Figure 9).

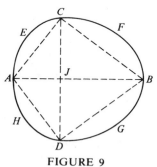

FIGURE 9

Let A and B be two points that bisect the perimeter. Then the surfaces $AEFB$ and $AHGB$ are equal. For if one of them were smaller, then the other could be substituted for it, whereby the perimeter would remain equal and the surface would be increased. These two surfaces should be considered to have the same form; for if they were different, the mirror image of AB could be substituted for one, whereby the perimeter and area would remain the same. According to "Fundamental Theorem II" on triangles, for the extremal figure the angles at C and D must be right angles. Since this consideration holds for every point A of the perimeter, the figure sought is a circle. This is the first occasion on which Steiner employed his principle of symmetrization.

In the fifth proof the basic theorem takes the form that among all plane figures of the same area, the circle has the least perimeter. The principle of the proof is again symmetrization with respect to the axis X.

Steiner next effects the transformation of the pentagon $ABCDE$ (Figure 10) into the pentagon of equal area $abcde$ in such a way that each line segment $B_1B = b_1b$; and bb_1 is bisected by X. As a result, the perimeter decreases. Steiner then turns to the extremal properties of prisms, pyramids, and the sphere (269–308).

In 1853, while investigating the double tangents of a fourth-degree curve, Steiner encountered a

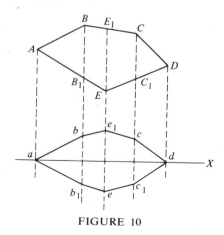

FIGURE 10

combinatorial problem (435–438): What number N of elements has the property that the elements can be ordered into triplets (t-tuples) in such a way that each two (each t-1) appear in one and only one combination? For the Steiner triple system, N must have the form $6n + 1$ or $6n + 3$, and there exist $\dfrac{N(N-1)}{2 \cdot 3}$ triples, $\dfrac{N(N-1)(N-3)}{2 \cdot 3 \cdot 4}$ quadruples, and so on. For example, for $N = 7$ there is only one triple system: 123, 145, 167, 246, 257, 347, 356. For $N = 13$ there are two different triple systems. Steiner was unaware of the work on this topic done by Thomas Kirkman (1847).[30]

In a short paper of fundamental importance, published in 1848 and entitled "Allgemeine Eigenschaften der algebraischen Kurven" (493–500), Steiner first defined and examined the various polar curves of a point with respect to a given curve. He then introduced the "Steiner curves" and discussed tangents at points of inflection, double tangents, cusps, and double points. In particular he indicated the resulting relationships for the twenty-eight double tangents of the fourth-degree curve. Luigi Cremona proved the results and continued Steiner's work in his "Introduzione ad una teoria geometrica delle curve piane."[31]

The desire to find, with the methods of pure geometry, the proofs of the extremely important theorems stated by the celebrated Steiner in his brief memoir "Allgemeine Eigenschaften der algebraischen Kurven" led me to undertake several studies, a sample of which I present here, even though it is incomplete.

In 1851 Steiner wrote "Über solche algebraische Kurven, die einen Mittelpunkt haben . . ." (501–596), a version of which he published in Crelle's *Journal*. In the *Gesammelte Werke* this paper is followed by "Problems and Theorems" (597–601). Steiner's results include the following example: "Through seven given points in the plane there pass, in general, only nine third-degree curves possessing a midpoint." Next follows a discussion of the twenty-eight double tangents of the fourth-degree curve (603–615). In January 1856 Steiner delivered a lecture at the Berlin Academy, "Ueber die Flächen dritten Grades" (649–659), in which he offered four methods of producing these cubic surfaces. The first states: "The nine straight lines in which the surfaces of two arbitrarily given trihedra intersect each other determine, together with one given point, a cubic surface." Aware that Cayley already knew the twenty-seven straight lines of this surface, Steiner introduced the concept of the "nuclear surface" and investigated its properties (656).

Steiner's correspondence with Ludwig Schläfli reveals that the latter discovered his "Doppelsechs" in the course of research on this topic undertaken at Steiner's request.[32] Again, it was Cremona who proved Steiner's theorems in his "Mémoire de géométrie pure sur les surfaces du troisième ordre" (1866).[33] Cremona began his memoir by declaring that "This work . . . contains the demonstration of all the theorems stated by this great geometer [Steiner] in his memoir *Ueber die Flächen dritten Grades*."

A second treatment of Steiner's theorems appeared in Rudolf Sturm's *Synthetische Untersuchungen über Flächen dritter Ordnung* (Leipzig 1867). In the preface Sturm wrote: "Steiner's paper contains a wealth of theorems on cubic surfaces, although, as had become customary with this celebrated geometer, without any proofs and with only few hints of how they might be arrived at." The works of both Cremona and Sturm were submitted in 1866 as entries in the first competition held by the Berlin Academy for the Steiner Prize, which was divided between them.

During his stay at Rome in 1844, Steiner investigated a fourth-order surface of the third class (721–724, 741–742), but it became known only much later through a communication from Karl Weierstrass (1863).[34] The surface, since called the Roman surface or Steiner surface, has the characteristic property that each of its tangent planes cuts it in a pair of conics. On the surfaces there lie three double straight lines that intersect in a triple point of the surface. The surface was the subject of many studies by later mathematicians.

NOTES

1. See F. Bützberger, "Biographie Jakob Steiners."
2. J. Lange, "Jacob Steiners Lebensjahre in Berlin 1821–1863. Nach seinen Personalakten dargestellt"; E. Jahnke, "Schreiben Jacobis . . .," in *Archiv der Mathematik und Physik*, 3rd ser., **4** (1903), 278.
3. *Jacob Steiner's Gesammelte Werke*, K. Weierstrass, ed., I, 175–176, and II, 18.
4. *Ibid.*, II, 97–159.
5. E. Lampe, "Jakob Steiner"; J. H. Graf, "Beiträge zur Biographie Jakob Steiners."
6. K.-R. Biermann, "Jakob Steiner."
7. *Ibid.*
8. J. Lange, *op. cit.*
9. *Gesammelte Werke*, I, 233–234.
10. Steiner, *Allgemeine Theorie über das Berühren und Schneiden der Kreise und der Kugeln*; B. Jegher, "Von Kreisen, die einerlei Kugelfläche liegen. Jakob Steiners Untersuchungen über das Schneiden und Berühren von Kegelkreisen. . . ."
11. *Gesammelte Werke*, I, 17–76.
12. Steiner, *Allgemeine Theorie*.
13. *Ibid.*, xiv–xvi.
14. *Gesammelte Werke*, I, 17–76.
15. See F. Bützburger, "Jakob Steiners Nachlass aus den Jahren 1823–1826," § 11, "Die Erfindung der Inversion"; A. Emch, "The Discovery of Inversion"; and Mautz, *op. cit.*
16. *Gesammelte Werke*, I, 133.
17. *Ibid.*, 77–94.
18. *Ibid.*, 121–228.
19. *Ibid.*, 229–460.
20. The MS material is in Steiner, *Allgemeine Theorie*, and in Jegher, *op. cit.*
21. See G. Cantor, *Gesammelte Abhandlungen* (Berlin, 1932), 151.
22. See W. L. Schaaf, "Mathematicians and Mathematics on Postage Stamps," in *Journal of Recreational Mathematics*, **1** (1968), 208; and I. Newton, *Principia mathematica*, 2nd ed. (Cambridge, 1713), Bk. I, 72; and *Universal Arithmetick* (London, 1728), probs. 57, 95.
23. *Vorlesungen*, II, no. 35.
24. V. Poncelet, *Traité des propriétés projectives des figures* (Paris–Metz, 1822), sec. III, ch. 2.
25. A. Karam, *Sur les 85 problèmes de la "dépendance systématique" de Steiner*. See also L. Kollros, "Jakob Steiner," p. 10.
26. F. Schweins, *Skizze eines Systems der Geometrie* (Heidelberg, 1810), 14–15.
27. See R. Sturm, "Zusammenstellung von Arbeiten, welche sich mit Steinerschen Aufgaben beschäftigen," in *Bibliotheca mathematica*, 3rd ser., **4** (1903), 160–184; P. J. Frederico, "Enumeration of Polyhedra," in *Journal of Combinatorial Theory*, 7 (1969), 155–161.
28. See F. Bützberger, "Biographie Jakob Steiners," 109; and K.-R. Biermann, *op. cit.*, 38.
29. *Gesammelte Werke*, I, 469–522.
30. T. Kirkman, in *Cambridge and Dublin Mathematical Journal*, **2** (1847), 191–204.
31. *Opere matematiche di Luigi Cremona*, I (Milan, 1914), 313–466.
32. See J. H. Graf, *Der Briefwechsel Steiner-Schläfli*.
33. *Opere matematiche di Luigi Cremona*, III (Milan, 1917), 1–121.
34. In *Monatsberichte der Deutschen Akademie der Wissenschafter. zu Berlin* (1863), 339, repr. in *Mathematische Werke von Karl Weierstrass*, III (Berlin, 1902), 179–182.

BIBLIOGRAPHY

I. ORIGINAL WORKS. Many of Steiner's writings are in *Jacob Steiner's Gesammelte Werke*, K. Weierstrass, ed., 2 vols. (Berlin, 1881–1882). The major ones include *Jacob Steiners Vorlesungen über synthetische Geometrie: I, Die Theorie der Kegelschnitte in elementarer Darstellung*, C. F. Geiser, ed. (Leipzig, 1867; 3rd ed., 1887), and II, *Die Theorie der Kegelschnitte gestützt auf projektive Eigenschaften*, H. Schröter, ed. (Leipzig, 1867; 3rd ed., 1898); *Allgemeine Theorie über das Berühren und Schneiden der Kreise und der Kugeln*, R. Fueter and F. Gonseth, eds. (Zurich–Leipzig, 1931); and Barbara Jegher, "Von Kreisen, die in einerlei Kugelfläche liegen. Jakob Steiners Untersuchungen über das Schneiden und Berühren von Kugelkreisen . . .," in *Mitteilungen der Naturforschenden Gesellschaft in Bern*, n.s. 24 (1967), 1–20.

Two letters from Steiner to Rudolf Wolf, dated 25 July 1841 and 5 Aug. 1848, are in the autograph collection of the Schweizerische Naturforschende Gesellschaft, at the Bern Burgerbibliothek (nos. 110 and 588 under MSS Hist. Helv. XIV, 150).

The following works by Steiner appeared in Ostwald's Klassiker der Exakten Wissenschaften: *Die geometrischen Konstruktionen, ausgeführt mittels der geraden Linie und eines festen Kreises* (1833), no. 60 (Leipzig, 1895), which contains a short biography of Steiner by the editor, A. J. von Oettingen, pp. 81–84; *Systematische Entwicklung der Abhängigkeit geometrischer Gestalten voneinander* (1832), nos. 82–83 (Leipzig, 1896); and *Einige geometrische Betrachtungen* (1826), no. 123, R. Sturm, ed. (Leipzig, 1901).

II. SECONDARY LITERATURE. Undated MS material is F. Bützberger, "Kleine Biographie über Jakob Steiner," Bibliothek der Schweizerischen Naturforschenden Gesellschaft, in the Bern Stadt und Universitätsbibliothek, MSS Hist. Helv. XXIb, 347; "Biographie Jakob Steiners," in the same collection, MSS Hist. Helv. XXIb, 348; and "Jakob Steiners Nachlass aus den Jahren 1823–1826," Bibliothek der Eidgenössischen Technischen Hochschule, Zurich, Hs. 92, pp. 30–223.

On Steiner's youth and years in Yverdon, see especially F. Bützberger, "Zum 100. Geburtstage Jakob Steiners," in *Zeitschrift für mathematischen und naturwissenschaftlichen Unterricht*, 27 (1896), 161 ff.; on the years in Berlin see Felix Eberty, *Jugenderinnerungen eines alten Berliners* (Berlin, 1878; repr. 1925), 238–243; and Julius Lange, "Jacob Steiners Lebensjahre in Berlin 1821–1863. Nach seinen Personalakten dargestellt," in *Wissenschaftliche Beilage zum Jahresbericht der Friedrichs-Werderschen Oberrealschule zu Berlin, Ostern 1899*, Program no. 116 (Berlin, 1899). See also three short obituary notices: C. F. Geiser, "Nekrolog J. Steiner," in *Die Schweiz: Illustrierte Zeitschrift für Literatur und Kunst* (Nov. 1863), 350–355; Otto Hesse, "Jakob Steiner," in *Journal für die reine und angewandte Mathematik*, 62 (1863), 199–200; and Bernhard Wyss, "Nekrolog J. Steiner," in *Bund* (Bern) (9 Apr. 1863).

The first detailed biography of Steiner was written by his grandnephew: Carl Friedrich Geiser, *Zur Erinnerung an Jakob Steiner* (Schaffhausen, 1874). Steiner's correspondence with Schläfli was edited by Schläfli's student J. H. Graf: *Der Briefwechsel Steiner-Schläfli* (Bern, 1896); see also the following three works by Graf: *Der Mathematiker Steiner von Utzensdorf* (Bern, 1897); "Die Exhuminierung Jakob Steiners und die Einweihung des Grabdenkmals Ludwig Schläflis . . . am 18. März 1896," in *Mitteilungen der Naturforschenden Gesellschaft in Bern* (1897), 8–24; and "Beiträge zur Biographie Jakob Steiners," *ibid.* (1905). Another of Schläfli's students, F. Bützberger, examined Steiner's posthumous MSS and reported on them in "Zum 100. Geburtstage Jakob Steiners" (see above) and in his long MS "Jakob Steiners Nachlass aus den Jahren 1823–1826" (see above).

Recent accounts of Steiner's life and work are Louis Kollros, "Jakob Steiner," supp. 2 of *Elemente der Mathematik* (1947), 1–24; and J.-P. Sydler, "Aperçus sur la vie et sur l'oeuvre de Jakob Steiner," in *Enseignement mathématique*, 2nd ser., 11 (1965), 240–257. Valuable corrections of errors in earlier accounts are given by Kurt-R. Biermann, "Jakob Steiner," in *Nova acta Leopoldina*, n.s. 27, no. 167 (1963), 31–47.

For further information see the following: F. Bützberger, "Jakob Steiner bei Pestalozzi in Yverdon," in *Schweizerische pädagogische Zeitschrift*, 6 (1896), 19–30; and *Bizentrische Polygone, Steinersche Kreis- und Kugelreihen und die Erfindung der Inversion* (Leipzig, 1913); Moritz Cantor, "Jakob Steiner," in *Allgemeine deutsche Biographie*, XXXV (1893), 700–703; A. Emch, "Unpublished Steiner Manuscripts," in *American Mathematical Monthly*, 36 (1929), 273–275; and "The Discovery of Inversion," in *Bulletin of the American Mathematical Society*, 20 (1913–1914), 412–415, and 21 (1914–1915), 206; R. Fueter, *Grosse schweizer Forscher* (Zurich, 1939), 202–203; C. Habicht, "Die Steinerschen Kreisreihen" (Ph.D. diss., Bern, 1904); A. Karam, *Sur les 85 problèmes de la "dépendance systématique" de Steiner* (Ph.D. diss., Eidgenössische Technische Hochschule, Zurich, 1939); E. Kötter, "Die Entwicklung der synthetischen Geometrie. Dritter Teil: Von Steiner bis auf Staudt," in *Jahresbericht der Deutschen Mathematikervereinigung*, 5, no. 2 (1898), 252 ff.; Emil Lampe, "Jakob Steiner," in *Bibliotheca mathematica*, 3rd ser., 1 (1900), 129–141; Otto Mautz, "Ebene Inversionsgeometrie," in *Wissenschaftliche Beilage zum Bericht über das Gymnasium Schuljahr 1908–1909* (Basel, 1909); R. Sturm, "Zusammenstellung von Arbeiten, welche sich mit Steinerschen Aufgaben beschäftigen," in *Bibliotheca mathematica*, 3rd ser., 4 (1903), 160–184; and a series of articles by Rudolf Wolf in *Vierteljahrsschrift der Naturforschenden Gesellschaft in Zürich*: 9 (1864), 145 ff.; 13 (1868), 110 ff.; 19 (1874), 325 ff.; 25 (1880), 215 ff.; and 35 (1890), 428 ff.

JOHANN JAKOB BURCKHARDT

STEINITZ, ERNST (*b*. Laurahütte, Silesia, Germany [now Huta Laura, Poland], 13 June 1871; *d*. Kiel, Germany, 29 September 1928)

Steinitz began the study of mathematics in 1890 at the University of Breslau (now Wrocław, Poland). A year later he went to Berlin and in 1893 returned to Breslau, where he received the Ph.D. in 1894. Two years later he began his teaching career as *Privatdozent* in mathematics at the Technical College in Berlin-Charlottenburg. In 1910 he was appointed professor at the Technical College in Breslau. He assumed a similar post in 1920 at the University of Kiel, where his friend Otto Toeplitz was teaching, remaining there until his death.

In his most important publication, "Algebraische Theorie der Körper" (1910), Steinitz gave an abstract and general definition of the concept of a "field" (*Körper*) as a system of elements with two operations (addition and multiplication) that satisfy associative and commutative laws (which are joined by the distributive law), the elements of which admit unlimited and unambiguous inversion up to division by zero. Steinitz sought to discuss all possible types of fields and to ascertain their relationships. By means of a systematic development of the consequences of the axioms for commutative fields, he introduced a series of fundamental concepts: prime field, separable elements, perfect fields, and degree of transcendence of an extension. His most important achievement was undoubtedly the proof that for every base field K there exist extension fields L in which all polynomials with coefficients in K decompose into linear factors, and that the smallest possible such field is virtually determined up to isomorphism. Because this smallest field possesses no genuine algebraic extension, Steinitz called it algebraically closed, proving its existence with the aid of the axiom of choice; this is now done by means of Zorn's lemma.

In his basic approach Steinitz was influenced primarily by Heinrich Weber and, in his methods, by Leopold Kronecker; Hensel's discovery in 1899 of the field of p-adic numbers provided the direct stimulus for his work. His polished and fully detailed treatment of the subject was the starting point for many far-reaching studies in abstract algebra, including those by E. Artin, H. Hasse, W. Krull, E. Noether, and B. L. van der Waerden. The general concept of the derivative or of differentiation, which Steinitz introduced in special cases, is essential in modern algebraic geometry.

In addition to his epochal paper, Steinitz wrote on the theory of polyhedra, a topic of lifelong interest. He gave two lectures on it at Kiel and prepared a comprehensive treatment during his last years. An almost complete manuscript of a planned book was found among his papers; it was completed and edited by Rademacher in 1934. Dealing chiefly with convex polyhedra and their topological types, the book also includes a detailed historical survey of the development of the theory of polyhedra.

BIBLIOGRAPHY

Steinitz' works are listed in Poggendorff, IV, 1435; V, 1203; and VI, 2534. His most important writings are "Algebraische Theorie der Körper," in *Journal für die reine und angewandte Mathematik*, **137** (1910), 137–309, which was also separately published, R. Baer and H. Hasse, eds. (Berlin–Leipzig, 1930; New York [in German], 1950); and *Vorlesungen über die Theorie der Polyeder, unter Einschluss der Elemente der Topologie*, Hans Rademacher, ed. (Berlin, 1934; repr. Ann Arbor, Mich., 1945).

BRUNO SCHOENEBERG

STEKLOV, VLADIMIR ANDREEVICH (*b*. Nizhni Novgorod [now Gorky], Russia, 9 January 1864; *d*. Gaspra, Crimea, U.S.S.R., 30 May 1926)

Steklov's father, Andrey Ivanovich Steklov, a clergyman, taught history and was rector of the Nizhni Novgorod seminary; his mother, Ekaterina Aleksandrovna Dobrolyubov, was a sister of the revolutionary-democratic literary critic Nikolay Dobrolyubov. In 1874–1882 Steklov studied at the Alexander Institute in Nizhni Novgorod; after graduation he entered the department of physics and mathematics at Moscow University, transferring a year later to Kharkov. A. M. Lyapunov, who had been lecturing there since 1885, soon became his scientific supervisor. In 1887 Steklov passed his final examinations, and the following summer it was suggested that he remain at the university to prepare for an academic career. He was appointed university lecturer in mechanics in 1891; two years later he presented his master's thesis, and in 1896 he was named extraordinary professor of mechanics. After defending his doctoral dissertation in 1902, Steklov was elected professor; Lyapunov then moved to St. Petersburg, and Steklov obtained the chair of applied mathematics. An active member of the Kharkov Mathematical Society, he served successively as secretary (1891), deputy chairman (1899), and chairman (1902–1906).

In 1906 Steklov transferred to the chair of mathematics at St. Petersburg University. His profound lectures, open sympathy with the aims of progressive students, and acute criticism of the tsarist order—especially at the universities—added new dimensions to the scientific and educational activity of the department of physics and mathematics and attracted numerous students. In St. Petersburg, Steklov laid the foundations of the school of mathematical physics that achieved considerable distinction, particularly after the October Revolution. Among his pupils were such prominent scientists as A. A. Friedmann, V. I. Smirnov, and Y. D. Tamarkin.

In 1910 V. Steklov was elected a member of the Academy of Sciences (he had been a corresponding member since 1902), and in 1916 he became a member of its board of directors. From then on, especially after becoming vice-president of the Academy in 1919, Steklov devoted most of his time to that organization. During the civil war, military conflicts, economic decline, and the early phases of reconstruction, he proved to be a brilliant scientific administrator. For eight years he worked tirelessly to maintain, and later to enlarge, the activity of the Academy and to reorganize it in order to bring science and practical requirements closer together. This work embraced all aspects of academic activity, from repairing old buildings and restoring the network of seismic stations to publishing academic proceedings and books, providing foreign periodicals for libraries, and organizing new institutes within the Academy. The Institute of Physics and Mathematics was organized in 1921 on Steklov's suggestion, and he served as its director until his death. In 1934 this institute was divided into the P. N. Lebedev Institute of Physics and the V. A. Steklov Mathematical Institute, both of which became centers of scientific activity.

Along with organizational work, Steklov continued his scholarly pursuits. In his later years he produced a series of articles on the theory of quadratures and on Chebyshev's polynomials, a monograph on mathematical physics, a popular book on the importance of mathematics for mankind, and biographies of Galileo and Newton.

Steklov's early works were devoted mostly to mechanics. In his master's thesis he pointed out the third case in which the integration of equations of a solid body moving in an ideal nonviscous fluid (under certain suppositions) is reduced to quadratures. The two earlier cases were described in 1871 by Rudolf Clebsch, and the fourth (and last) by Lyapunov in 1893. Steklov also treated prob-

lems of hydromechanics.

Steklov's principal field of endeavor, however, was mathematical physics and corresponding problems of analysis. Many problems of potential theory, electrostatics, and hydromechanics are reduced to the boundary-value problems of Dirichlet and Neumann when it is necessary to find a solution of Laplace's differential equation satisfying some boundary conditions on a surface S enclosing the region under consideration. Although Neumann, Hermann Schwarz, Poincaré, G. Robin, E. Le Roy, and others had suggested methods of solving such problems, they did not elaborate their rigorous grounding, and their methods were applied to relatively restricted classes of surfaces. The precision of analysis in the general investigation of the problem was first achieved by Lyapunov and Steklov. Steklov presented the first summary of his studies in this field in his doctoral thesis and in the articles "Sur les problèmes fondamentaux de la physique mathématique" and "Théorie générale des fonctions fondamentales." He made a valuable contribution to the theory of fundamental functions (Poincaré's term) or, to use a contemporary expression, the theory of eigen functions depending in a particular way upon the character of the surface S and forming on the surface a normal and orthogonal system; the solution of the boundary-value problems of Dirichlet and Neumann is expressed in terms of these eigen functions. Steklov was the first to demonstrate strictly for a very broad class of surfaces the existence of an infinite sequence of (proper) eigen values and corresponding eigen functions defining them in a way different from Poincaré's. Using a method going back to Fourier, Steklov also solved new problems of the theory of heat conduction subject to some boundary, and initial conditions.

When boundary value problems are considered, an especially difficult problem arises when one wishes to expand an arbitrary function, for example, $f(x)$, subject to certain restrictions, into a convergent series of the form $\sum_{k=0}^{\infty} A_k U_k(x)$ where each A_k is a constant and the eigen functions $U_k(x)$ form a normal and orthogonal system. Particular cases of this kind had occurred since the latter half of the eighteenth century. From 1896, Steklov devoted numerous works to the elaboration of a general method of solving this problem in one, two, and three dimensions; this work resulted in the creation of the general "theory of closedness," the term he introduced in 1910. The condition of closedness established by Steklov is the generalization of Parseval's equality (1805) in the theory of Fourier series. The closed systems are "complete": they cannot be extended by adding new functions without loss of orthogonality; only closed systems may be used for solving the mentioned problem. In the simplest case, when it is necessary to expand a continuous function $f(x)$ on the segment (a, b) into a series of functions of one normal and orthogonal system $\{U_k(x)\}$ with respect to a weight $p(x) \geq 0$, so that $f(x) = \sum_{k=0}^{\infty} A_k U_k$ and the coefficients $A_k = \int_a^b p(x)f(x)U_k(x)dx$, the condition of closedness takes the form $\sum_{k=0}^{\infty} a_k^2 = \int_a^b p(x)f^2(x)dx$. Steklov investigated the closedness of diverse concrete systems and defined certain conditions under which the expansions in question really occur. In 1907 he began to use in the theory of closedness an important "smoothing method," which consisted of replacing the function under study—for example, $f(x)$—with some other mean function—$F_h(x) = \frac{1}{h}\int_x^{x+h} f(t)dt$—that in some sense has more convenient characteristics. For example, it is continuous, whereas $f(x)$ is only integrable. This device is now widely used in mathematical physics. Steklov investigated expansions into series not only with the theory of closedness but also by means of asymptotic methods or by direct evaluation of the remainder term in the series.

The rise of the theory of integral equations at the beginning of the twentieth century, which led to new, general, and effective methods of solving the problems of mathematical physics and expansions of functions on orthogonal systems, inspired Steklov to improve the theory of closedness, although he did not participate in the elaboration of the theory of integral equations itself.

BIBLIOGRAPHY

I. ORIGINAL WORKS. Steklov produced 154 works. Bibliographies are in *Pamyaty V. A. Steklova*, G. I. Ignatius, *Steklov* and (most complete) in V. S. Vladimirov and I. I. Markush, *Akademik V. A. Steklov* (see below). Among his writings are *O dvizhenii tverdogo tela v zhidkosti* ("On the Motion of a Solid Body in a Fluid"; Kharkov, 1893), his master's thesis; *Obshchie metody reshenia osnovnykh zadach matematicheskoy fiziki* ("General Methods of Solving Fundamental Problems of Mathematical Physics"; Kharkov, 1901), his doctoral dissertation; "Sur les problèmes fondamentaux de la physique mathématique," in *Annales de l'École normale supérieure*, 3rd ser., **19** (1902), 191–259, 455–490; "Théorie générale des fonctions fondamentales," in *Annales de la Faculté des sciences de Toulouse*, 2nd ser., **6** (1905), 351–475; "Sur les expressions asymptotiques des certaines fonctions définies par les équations différentielles du second ordre et leurs applications au problème du développement d'une fonction arbitraire en série procédant suivant les dites fonctions," in *Soobshchenia Kharkovskogo matematicheskogo obshchestva*, **10** (1907), 97–201; "Problème du mouvement d'une masse fluide incompressible de la forme ellipsoïdale dont les parties s'attirent suivant la loi de Newton," in *Annales scientifiques de l'Ecole normale supérieure*, 3rd ser., **25** (1908), 469–528, and **26** (1909), 275–336; "Une application nouvelle de ma méthode de développement suivant les fonctions fondamentales," in *Comptes rendus . . . de l'Académie des sciences*, **151** (1910), 974–977; "Sur le mouvement d'un corps solide ayant une cavité ellipsoïdale remplie par un liquide incompressible et sur les variations des latitudes," in *Annales de la Faculté des sciences de Toulouse*, 3rd ser., **1** (1910), 145–256; *Osnovnye zadachi matematicheskoy fiziki* ("Fundamental Problems of Mathematical Physics"), 2 vols. (Petrograd, 1922–1923); and *Matematika i ee znachenie dlya chelovechestva* ("Mathematics and Its Importance for Mankind"; Berlin–Petrograd, 1923).

II. SECONDARY LITERATURE. See G. I. Ignatius, *Vladimir Andreevich Steklov* (Moscow, 1967); V. S. Vladimirov and I. I. Markush, *Akademik V. A. Steklov* (Moscow, 1973); *Istoria otechestvennoy matematiki* ("History of Native Mathematics"), I. Z. Shtokalo, ed., II and III (Kiev, 1967–1968), see index; *Pamyaty V. A. Steklova* ("Memorial to . . . Steklov"; Leningrad, 1928), with articles by N. M. Gyunter, V. I. Smirnov, B. G. Galiorkin, I. V. Meshchersky, and R. O. Kuzmin—Gyunter's article, "Trudy V. A. Steklova po matematicheskoy fizike" ("Steklov's Works on Mathematical Physics") is reprinted in *Uspekhi matematicheskikh nauk*, **1**, nos. 3–4 (1946), 23–43; Y. V. Uspensky, "Vladimir Andreevich Steklov," in *Izvestiya Akademii nauk SSSR*, 6th ser., **20**, nos. 10–11 (1926), 837–856; and A. Youschkevitch, *Istoria matematiki v Rossii do 1917 goda* ("History of Mathematics in Russia Before 1917"; Moscow, 1968), see index.

A. P. YOUSCHKEVITCH

STEPANOV, VYACHESLAV VASSILIEVICH (*b.* Smolensk, Russia, 4 September 1889; *d.* Moscow, U.S.S.R., 22 July 1950)

Stepanov was the son of Vassily Ivanovich Stepanov, who taught history and geography at high schools in Smolensk; his mother, Alexandra Yakovlevna, was a teacher at a girls' school. An honor graduate of Smolensk high school in 1908, Stepanov entered the department of physics and mathematics of Moscow University later that year; his scientific supervisor was Egorov. In 1912, when he was about to graduate, it was suggested that he remain at the university to prepare for a professorship. After spending some time at Göttingen, where he attended lectures by Hilbert and E. Landau, Stepanov returned to Moscow and became lecturer at Moscow University in 1915. At that time he published his first scientific work, an article on Paul du Bois-Reymond's theory of the growth of functions.

From the first Soviet years, Stepanov participated in the organization of new types of university work, especially in the training of young scientists at the Research Institute of Mathematics and Mechanics, established at Moscow University in 1921. He was director of the Institute from 1939 until his death. He was also one of the most influential and active leaders of the Moscow Mathematical Society, owing, among other things, to his exceptional erudition and memory. In 1928 Stepanov became a professor, and in 1946 he was elected corresponding member of the Academy of Sciences of the U.S.S.R.

Stepanov's scientific interests were formed first under the influence of Egorov and Luzin, founders of the Moscow school of the theory of functions of a real variable. In works published in 1923 and 1925 Stepanov established the necessary and sufficient conditions under which a function of two variables, defined on a measurable plane set of finite measure greater than zero, possesses a total differential almost everywhere on that set. These works laid the foundations for the studies of I. Y. Verchenko, A. S. Cronrod, and G. P. Tolstov in the theory of functions of n variables. In his most widely known works, Stepanov treated the theory of almost periodic functions, introduced a short time earlier by H. Bohr; he also constructed and investigated new classes of generalized almost periodic functions.

Stepanov's interest in applications of mathematics and his work at the State Astrophysical Institute in 1926–1936 led him to study the qualitative theory of differential equations. In this field his principal works are related to the general theory of dynamic systems that G. D. Birkhoff elaborated, extending the work of Poincaré. Besides writing articles on the study of almost periodic trajectories and on generalization of Birkhoff's ergodic theorem (which found an important application in statistical physics), Stepanov organized a seminar on the qualitative methods of the theory of differential

equations (1932) that proved of great importance for the creation of the Soviet scientific school in this field.

BIBLIOGRAPHY

I. ORIGINAL WORKS. Stepanov's writings include "Über totale Differenzierbarkeit," in *Mathematische Annalen*, **90** (1923), 318–320; "Sur les conditions de l'existence de la différentielle totale," in *Matematicheskii sbornik*, **32** (1925), 511–527; "Über einige Verallgemeinerungen der fast periodischen Funktionen," in *Mathematische Annalen*, **95** (1925), 473–498; also in French in *Comptes rendus . . . de l'Académie des sciences*, **181** (1925), 90–94; "Über die Räume der fast periodischen Funktionen," in *Matematicheskii sbornik*, **41** (1934), 166–178, written with A. N. Tikhonov; "Sur une extension du théorème ergodique," in *Compositio mathematica*, **3** (1936), 239–253; *Kachestvennaya teoria differentsialnykh uravneny* (Moscow, 1947; 2nd ed., 1949), written with V. V. Nemytsky, translated into English as *Qualitative Theory of Differential Equations* (2nd ed., Princeton, 1960, 1964); and *Kurs differentsialnykh uravneny* ("Lectures on Differential Equations"; Moscow, 1936; 6th revised ed., 1953), translated into German by J. Auth *et al.* as *Lehrbuch der Differentialgleichungen* (Berlin, 1956).

II. SECONDARY LITERATURE. See P. S. Aleksandrov and V. V. Nemytsky, *Vyacheslav Vassilievich Stepanov* (Moscow, 1956); *Istoria otechestvennoy matematiki* ("History of Native Mathematics"), I. Z. Shtokalo, ed., III–IV (Kiev, 1968–1970), see index; *Matematika v SSSR za sorok let* ("Forty Years of Mathematics in the U.S.S.R."), 2 vols. (Moscow, 1959), see index; and *Matematika v SSSR za tridtsat let* ("Thirty Years of Mathematics in the U.S.S.R."; Moscow–Leningrad, 1948), see index.

A. P. YOUSCHKEVITCH

STEPHANUS (or **STEPHEN**) **OF ALEXANDRIA** (*fl.* first half of seventh century A.D.)

Stephanus was a public lecturer in Constantinople at the court of Emperor Heraclius (A.D. 610–641). Although primarily a mathematician, he apparently also taught philosophy, astronomy, and music in addition to arithmetic and geometry. Commentaries on Aristotle have come down to us under his name, but Stephanus is also reported to have written on other subjects, including astronomy. He has been identified, probably incorrectly, by some authorities with Stephanus of Athens, a medical writer; and commentaries on Galen and Hippocrates have been attributed to both these authors. The *Opusculum apotelesmaticum*, ascribed to Stephanus of Alexandria but probably dating from the eighth century, deals with Islam in astrological terms.

Considerable attention has been given to a long Greek treatise on alchemy, *De chrysopoeia*, which has been ascribed to Stephanus and which was much praised by later alchemists. Consisting of nine mystical lectures, this uncritical, rhetorical, and theoretical document gives no evidence of experimental work. Indeed, in the first lecture the author writes, "Put away the material theory so that you may be deemed worthy to see the hidden mystery with your intellectual eyes." The work may be dated later than the seventh century, but it is mentioned in an Arabic bibliography of A.D. 987, *Kitāb-al-Fihrist*, where the author is known as Stephanus the Elder, who is said to have "translated for Khālid ibn Yāzid alchemical and other works." This Umayyad prince, much interested in science and especially alchemy, died in A.D. 704.

BIBLIOGRAPHY

I. ORIGINAL WORKS. See *Democritus Abderita, De arte magna, sive de rebus naturalibus. Nec non Synesii, et Pelagii, et Stephani Alexandri, et Michaelis Pselli in eundem commentaria*, Dominic Pizimentus, ed. (Padua, 1573); "De chrysopoeia," Julius L. Ideler, ed., in *Physici et medici graeci minores*, II (Berlin, 1842), 199–253; *Opusculum apotelesmaticum*, Hermann Usener, ed. (Bonn, 1879); "In librum Aristotelis de interpretatione commentarium," Michael Hayduck, ed., in *Commentaria in Aristotelem graeca*, XVIII, 3 (Berlin, 1885); "Anonymi et Stephani in artem rhetoricam commentaria," H. Rabe, ed., *ibid.*, XXI, 2 (Berlin, 1896); and "The Alchemical Works of Stephanos of Alexandria," trans. and commentary by F. Sherwood Taylor, in *Ambix, the Journal of the Society for Study of Alchemy and Early Chemistry*, 1 (1937), 116–139; 2 (1938), 38–49.

II. SECONDARY LITERATURE. See Marcellin P. E. Berthelot, *Les origines de l'alchemie* (Paris, 1885), 199–201 and *passim; Introduction à l'étude de la chimie des anciens et du moyen age* (Paris, 1938), 287–301 and *passim;* Lucien Leclerc, *Histoire de la médecine arabe* (Paris 1876; New York, 1961); Hermann Usener, *De Stephano Alexandrino* (Bonn, 1880); Edmund O. von Lippmann, *Enstehung und Ausbreitung der Alchemie* (Berlin, 1919), 103–105; and George Sarton, *Introduction to the History of Science*, I (Baltimore, 1927), 472–473.

KARL H. DANNENFELDT

STEPLING, JOSEPH (*b*. Regensburg, Germany, 29 June 1716; *d*. Prague, Bohemia [now Czechoslovakia], 11 July 1778)

Stepling's father came from Westphalia and was a secretary to the Imperial Embassy at Ratisbon (Regensburg). His mother's homeland was Bohemia. After his father's early death, the family moved to Prague. There Stepling began his studies at the Gymnasium run by the Jesuits. He soon demonstrated an extraordinary gift for mathematics, and a certain Father Sykora successfully endeavored to bring out his protégé's talent. When Stepling was only seventeen he calculated with great accuracy the lunar eclipse of 28 May 1733.

Despite a frail physical constitution, Stepling was admitted to the Jesuit order in 1733. After a biennial novitiate at Brno, he attended a three-year course of philosophy (1735 to 1738). His pupil, and later biographer, Stanislaus Wydra, states that Stepling, even in his early studies, transposed Aristotelian logic into mathematical formulas, thus becoming an early precursor of modern logic. Having already adopted the atomistic conception of matter (hyle), he radically refused to accept Aristotelian metaphysics and natural philosophy (the hylomorphic system). From 1738 to 1741 Stepling was a teacher at the Gymnasiums of Glatz (now Kłodzko) and Schweidnitz (now Świdnica). During the period 1741–1743, he devoted himself to special studies in mathematics, physics, and astronomy in Prague. From 1743 to 1747 he studied theology there and in 1745 took holy orders. The last year of his training began a tertianship (special studies of the law of the Jesuit order) in Gitschin (now Jičín), after which he declined a professorship of philosophy at the University of Prague in favor of the chair of mathematics. In 1748, at the request of the Berlin Academy, he carried out an exact observation of a solar and lunar eclipse in order to determine the precise location of Prague.

During Stepling's long tenure at Prague, he set up a laboratory for experimental physics and in 1751 built an observatory, the instruments and fittings of which he brought up to the latest scientific standard. In 1753 the Empress Maria Theresia, as part of her reform of higher education, appointed Stepling director of the faculty of philosophy at Prague. In this capacity he modernized the entire philosophical curriculum, which in those days embraced the natural sciences. He was particularly intent on cultivating the exact sciences, including physics and astronomy; and, following the example of the Royal Society in London, he founded a scientific study group. In their monthly sessions, over which he presided until his death, the group carried out research work and investigations in the field of pure mathematics and its application to physics and astronomy. A great number of treatises of this academy were published.

Stepling corresponded with the outstanding contemporary mathematicians and astronomers: Christian Wolf, Leonhard Euler, Christopher Maire, Nicolas-Louis de Lacaille, Maximilian Hell, Joseph Franz, Rudjer Bošković, Heinrich Hiss, and others. Also, Stepling was particularly successful in educating many outstanding scientists, including Johann Wendlingen, Jakob Heinisch, Johannes von Herberstein, Kaspar Sagner, Stephan Schmidt, Johann Körber, and Joseph Bergmann. After his death, Maria Theresia ordered a monument erected in the library of the University of Prague.

BIBLIOGRAPHY

I. ORIGINAL WORKS. Stepling's works include *Eclipsis lunae totalis Pragae octava Augusti 1748 observata* (Prague, 1748); *De actione solis in diversis latitudinibus* (Prague, 1750); *Exercitationes geometrico-analyticae de angulis aliisque frustis cylindrorum, quorum bases sunt sectiones conicae infinitorum generum* (Prague, 1751); *Observationes baroscopicae, thermoscopicae, hyetometricae* (Prague, 1752); *De pluvia lapidea anni 1753 ad Strkow et ejus causis* (Prague, 1754); *Brevicula descriptio speculae astronomicae Pragae instructae* (Wittenberg, 1755); *De terrae motus causa discursus* (Prague, 1756); *Liber II. Euclidis algebraice demonstratus* (Prague, 1757); *Solutio directa problematis de inveniendo centro oscillationis* (Prague, 1759); *Contra insignem superficiei oceani et marium cum eo communicantium inaequalitatem a V. Cl. Henrico Kuehnio assertam* (Prague, 1760); *Beantwortung verschiedener Fragen über die Beschaffenheit der Lichterscheinung Nachts den 28 Hornungstage, und über die Nordlichter* (Prague, 1761); *De aberratione astrorum et luminis; item de mutatione axis terrestris historica relatio* (Prague, 1761); *Adnotationes in celebrem transitum Veneris per discum solis anno labente 6. Jun. futurum* (Prague, 1761); *De terrae motibus . . . adnexa est meditatio de causa mutationis Thermarum Töplicensium . . .* (Prague, 1763); *Vergleichungstafeln der altböhmischen Maasse und deren Preis mit den neu Oestreichischen und deren Preis* (Prague, 1764); *Differentiarum minimarum quantitatum variantium calculus directus, vulgo differentialis* (Prague, 1765); and *Clarissimi ac magnifici viri Iosephi Stepling . . . litterarum commercium eruditi cum primum argumenti* (Prague, 1782).

Stepling published many papers in *Nova acta eruditorum* (1750, 1761), and *Abhandlungen einer Privatgesellschaft in Böhmen zur Aufnahme der Mathematik, der vaterländischen Geschichte, und der Naturgeschichte* (1775–1784).

A bibliography appears in Poggendorff, II, 1004.

II. SECONDARY LITERATURE. On Stepling and his work, see Ludwig Koch, S.J., *Jesuitenlexikon* (Paderborn, 1934), cols. 1692–1693; Franz Martin Pelzel, *Boehmische, Maehrische und Schlesische Gelehrte und Schriftsteller aus dem Orden der Jesuiten* (Prague, 1786), 227–230; Carlos Sommervogel, S.J., *Bibliothèque de la Compagnie de Jésus*, VII (Brussels, 1896), cols. 1564–1568; Stanislaus Wydra, *Laudatio funebris Jos. Stepling coram senatu populoque academico . . . dicta* (Prague, 1778); *Vita Admodum Reverendi ac magnifici viri Iosephi Stepling* (Prague, 1779); and *Oratio ad monumentum a Maria Theresia Aug. Josepho Stepling erectum . . .* (Prague, 1780); and *Abbildungen böhmischer und Mährischer Gelehrter und Künstler nebst kurzen Nachrichten von ihren Leben und Werken*, IV (Prague, 1782), 164–172, which appeared without the name of the author but has the printed signature "Franz Martin Pelzel und die übrigen Verfasser" on the dedication page.

D. ANTON PINSKER, S.J.

STEVIN, SIMON (*b.* Bruges, Netherlands [now Belgium], 1548; *d.* The Hague, Netherlands, *ca.* March 1620)

Stevin was the illegitimate son of Antheunis Stevin and Cathelijne van de Poort, both wealthy citizens of Bruges. There is little reliable information about his early life, although it is known that he worked in the financial administration of Bruges and Antwerp and traveled in Poland, Prussia, and Norway for some time between 1571 and 1577. In 1581 he established himself at Leiden, where he matriculated at the university in 1583. His religious position is not known, nor is it known whether he left the southern Netherlands because of the persecutions fostered by the Spanish occupation. At any rate, in the new republic of the northern Netherlands Stevin found an economic and cultural renaissance in which he at once took an active part. He was first classified as an "engineer," but after 1604 he was quartermaster-general of the army of the States of the Netherlands. At the same time he was mathematics and science tutor to Maurice of Nassau, prince of Orange, for whom he wrote a number of textbooks. He was often consulted on matters of defense and navigation, and he organized a school of engineers at Leiden and served as administrator of Maurice's domains. In 1610 he married Catherine Cray; they had four children, of whom one, Hendrick, was himself a gifted scientist who, after Stevin's death, published a number of his manuscripts.

Stevin's work is part of the general scientific revival that resulted from the commercial and industrial prosperity of the cities of the Netherlands and northern Italy in the sixteenth century. This development was further spurred by the discovery of the principal works of antique science—especially those of Euclid, Apollonius, Diophantus, and Archimedes—which were brought to western Europe from Byzantium, then in a state of decline, or from the Arabic centers of learning in Spain. A man of his time, Stevin wrote on a variety of topics. A number of his works are almost wholly original, while even those that represent surveys of science as it existed around 1600 contain his own interpretations; all are characterized by a remarkably lucid and methodical presentation. Stevin chose to write almost all of his books in the vernacular, in accordance with the spirit of self-confidence of the newly established republic. In the introduction to his *De Beghinselen der Weeghconst* of 1586, he stated his admiration for Dutch as a language of wonderful power in shaping new terms; and a number of the words coined by Stevin and his contemporaries survive in the rich Dutch scientific vocabulary.

Stevin's published works include books on mathematics, mechanics, astronomy, navigation, military science, engineering, music theory, civics, dialectics, bookkeeping, geography, and house building. While many of these works were closely related to his mercantile and administrative interests, a number fall into the realm of pure science. His first book, the *Tafelen van Interest* (1582), derives entirely from his early career in commerce; in it Stevin set out the rules of single and compound interest and gave tables for the rapid computation of discounts and annuities. Such tables had previously been kept secret by big banking houses, since there were few skilled calculators, although after Stevin's publication interest tables became common in the Netherlands.

In *De Thiende*, a twenty-nine-page booklet published in 1585, Stevin introduced decimal fractions for general purposes and showed that operations could be performed as easily with such fractions as with integers. He eliminated all difficulties in handling decimal fractions by interpreting 3.27, for example, as 327 items of the unit 0.01. Decimal fractions had previously found only occasional use in trigonometric tables; although Stevin's notation was somewhat unwieldy, his argument was convincing, and decimal fractions were soon generally

adopted. At the end of the tract, Stevin went on to suggest that a decimal system should also be used for weights and measures, coinage, and divisions of the degree of arc.

In *L'arithmétique*, also published in 1585, Stevin gave a general treatment of the arithmetic and algebra of his time, providing geometric counterparts. (An earlier work, the *Problemata geometrica* of 1583 had been entirely devoted to geometry; strongly marked by the influence of Euclid and Archimedes, it contained an especially interesting discussion of the semi-regular bodies that had also been studied by Dürer.) Stevin was of the opinion that all numbers—including squares, square roots, and negative or irrational quantities—were of the same nature, an opinion not shared by contemporary mathematicians but one that was vindicated in the development of algebra. Stevin introduced a new notation for polynomials and gave simplified and unified solutions for equations of the second, third, and fourth degrees; in an appendix published at a later date he showed how to approximate a real root for an equation of any degree.

De Deursichtighe is a mathematical treatment of perspective, a subject much studied by artists and architects, as well as mathematicians, in the fifteenth and sixteenth centuries. Stevin's book gives an important discussion of the case in which the plane of the drawing is not perpendicular to the plane of the ground and, for special cases, solves the inverse problem of perspective, that is, of finding the position of the eye of the observer, given the object and the perspective drawing of it. A number of other works are also concerned with the application of mathematics to practical problems, and in these the instances in which Stevin had to perform what amounts to an integration are particularly interesting. While mathematicians up to his time had followed the Greek example and given each proof by *reductio ad absurdum*, Stevin introduced methods that, although still cumbersome, paved the way toward the simpler methods of the calculus.

De Beghinselen der Weeghconst is Stevin's chief work in mechanics. Published in 1586, some fifty years before Galileo's discoveries, it is devoted chiefly to statics. From the evidence that it provides, Stevin would seem to be the first Renaissance author to develop and continue the work of Archimedes. The book contains discussions of the theory of the lever, the theorems of the inclined plane, and the determination of the center of gravity; but most particularly it includes what is perhaps the most famous of Stevin's discoveries, the law of the inclined plane, which he demonstrated with the *clootcrans*, or wreath of spheres.

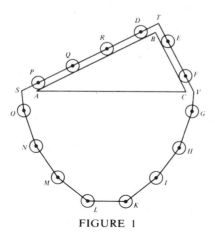

FIGURE 1

The *clootcrans*, as conceived by Stevin, consists of two inclined planes (*AB* and *BC*), of which one is twice the length of the other. A wreath of spheres placed on a string is hung around the triangle *ABC*, all friction being disregarded. The wreath will not begin to rotate by itself, and the lower section *GH* ⋯ *MNO*, being symmetrical, may be disregarded. It is thus apparent that the pull toward the left exerted by the four spheres that lie along *AB* must be equal to the pull to the right exerted by the two spheres that lie along *BC*—or, in other words, that the effective component of gravity is inversely proportional to the length of the inclined plane. If one of the inclined planes is then placed vertically, the ratio between the component along the inclined plane and the total force of gravity becomes obvious. This is, in principle, the theory of the parallelogram of forces.

Beneath his diagram of the *clootcrans* Stevin inscribed a cherished maxim, "Wonder en is gheen wonder"—"What appears a wonder is not a wonder" (that is, it is actually understandable), a rallying cry for the new science. He was so delighted with his discovery that he used the diagram of his proof as a seal on his letters, a mark on his instruments, and as a vignette on the title pages of his books; the device also appears as the colophon of this *Dictionary*.

Stevin's next work on mechanics, *De Beghinselen des Waterwichts*, is the first systematic treatise on hydrostatics since Archimedes. In it, Stevin gave a simple and immediately comprehensible explanation for the Archimedean principle of displacement; before a body *C* is immersed, consider a volume of water equal to that of *C*. Since the lat-

ter body was at rest, it must have experienced, on displacement, an upward force equal to its weight, while *C* itself will, upon being placed in the water, experience the same degree of buoyancy. Stevin similarly chose to explain the hydrostatic paradox by imagining parts of the water to be solidified, so that neither equilibrium nor pressure was disturbed. He also wrote a number of shorter works in which he applied the principles of mechanics to practical problems of simple machines, balances, the windlass, the hauling of ships, wheels powered by men, the block-and-tackle, and the effect of a bridle upon a horse.

Stevin's chief book on astronomy, *De Hemelloop*, was published in 1608; it is one of the first presentations of the Copernican system, which Stevin unconditionally supported, several years before Galileo and at a time when few other scientists could bring themselves to do likewise. Calling the Copernican hypothesis "the true theory," Stevin demonstrated that the motions of the planets can be inductively derived from observations; since there were no complete direct observations, he used the ephemerides of Johann Stadius in their stead. He first explained the Ptolemaic model (in which the earth is at the center and the sun and planets move in epicycles) by this means, then offered a similar explanation of the Copernican system, in which he improved on the original theory in several minor points.

In a seafaring nation like the Dutch republic matters of navigation were, of course, of great importance. In addition to his astronomical works, Stevin gave a theory of the tides that was—as it must have been, fifty years before Newton—purely empirical. He also, in a short treatise entitled *De Havenvinding*, approached the subject of determining the longitude of a ship, a problem that was not fully solved until the nineteenth century. Several previous authors had suggested that longitude might be determined by measuring the deviation of the magnetic needle from the astronomical meridian, a suggestion based on the assumption that the earthwide distribution of terrestrial magnetism was known. Since the determination of latitude was well known, such a measurement would allow the sailor to chart longitudinal position against the latitudinal circle.

Stevin, in his booklet, gave a clear explanation of this method; he differed from Petrus Plancius and Mercator in that he did not rely upon a priori conceptions of the way in which geomagnetic deviation depends upon geographical position. Although he was willing to offer a conjecture about this dependence, Stevin insisted on the necessity of collecting actual measurements from all possible sources and urged the establishment of an empirical, worldwide survey. His method was sound, although as data began to accumulate it became clear that the magnetic elements were subject to secular variation. The problem of determining longitude was at last solved more simply by the invention of the ship's chronometer.

In *Van de Zeijlstreken*, Stevin set out a method, based on one proposed by Nuñez in 1534, of steering a ship along a loxodrome, always keeping the same course, to describe on the globe a line cutting the meridians at a constant angle. Although the feat was beyond the grasp of the seaman of Stevin's time, his exposition nonetheless contributed to a clear formulation of the principles upon which it was based and helped make the method itself better known both in the Netherlands and abroad.

A considerable body of Stevin's other work developed from his military duties and interests. The Dutch army had been completely reorganized through the efforts of Maurice and counts William Louis and John of Nassau; their innovations, which were widely adopted by other countries, included the establishment of regular drills and maneuvers, the development of fortifications (combined with new methods of attacking a besieged city), and army camps planned after those of the Romans. As quartermaster general, Stevin observed these reforms, as well as actual battles, and wrote in detail, in his usual lucid and systematic style, of sieges, camps, and military equipment.

Stevin's *De Sterctenbouwing* is a treatise on the art of fortification. Although cost prohibited the implementation of the ideas Stevin set out in it, these notions were put to practical effect a century later by Vauban and Coehoorn. *De Legermeting* is a less theoretical work, a description of field encampment during Maurice's campaigns, with the encampment before the Battle of Juliers (in 1610) as a particular example. Stevin gave an account of the layout of the camp, inspired by the writings of Polybius (since later Roman authors were not then known), together with the modifications made by Maurice. He listed all the equipment required in the campaign, and gave detailed instructions concerning the building of huts and the housing of dependents and suppliers. In the last section of the work he made a comparative study of the different methods of deploying soldiers in files and companies, and again recommended distribution by a decimal system. All told, his book gives a vivid impression of the army life of his period.

Of his works on engineering, two books are devoted to the new types of sluices and locks that Stevin himself had helped to devise. He cites their particular usefulness in scouring canals and ditches through the use of tidal action, and cites their application for the waterways of Danzig and other German coastal cities. In these short works he also discusses the formation of sandbanks, peat and quicksand, and the modifications of the course of a river; his explanation of the changes of the surface of the earth, which he attributes to natural forces only, is quite modern.

In *Van de Molens*, Stevin discusses wind-driven drainage mills, crucially important to the flat regions of the Netherlands. Stevin proposed the construction of a new type of mill with more slowly revolving scoop wheels and a smaller number of wider floats, and he further modified the means of transmission of power by making use of conical toothed wheels. A number of mills were built or rebuilt according to his specifications; that they were not completely successful may lie in imperfections in the execution of his design. Stevin also applied the principles of mechanics to windmills, in a series of computations that allowed him to determine, given the size and the number of the cogs, both the minimum wind pressure required on each square foot of the sails to lift the water to the necessary height and how much water is raised by each revolution of the sails. He gave the results of his measurement of fifteen mills.

In another book, *Van de Spiegeling der Singconst*, Stevin turned to the theory of musical tuning, a subject that had enthralled mathematicians from antiquity on. Musicians had also long been concerned with devising a scale in which the intervals of the pure octave (2:1), the pure fifth (3:2), and the pure third (5:4) could be rigorously combined. The chief problem lay in the resolution of the progression by four fifths (96:144:216:324:486) and the interval with the double octave ($96 \times 2 \times 2 = 384$); this ratio, which should be the third, 480:384, is rather the imperfect ratio 486:384. While a number of other mathematicians and musicians had attempted to reach a resolution by minor modifications in the scale, Stevin boldly rejected their methods and declared that all semitones should be equal and that the steps of the scale should each correspond to the successive values of $2^{n/12}$; he dismissed the difference between the third and the fifth as unimportant. Stevin's scale is thus the "equal temperament" now in general use; at the time he proposed it he had been anticipated only by Vincenzio Galilei (1581) and the Chinese prince Chi Tsai-Yü (1584). It is unlikely that Stevin knew the latter's work.

Another of Stevin's many publications was a book on civic life, *Het Burgherlick Leven*. The work is a handbook designed to guide the citizen through periods of civil disorder, a matter of some concern in a nation that had only recently won its freedom through rebellion, and in which religious freedom was still a matter for discussion. Stevin only rarely refers to these circumstances in his book, however; he rather presents his precepts as being completely objective and derived from common sense. The first of his tenets is that the citizen should obey anyone in a position of *de facto* authority, no matter how this authority has been obtained. Since history consists of a succession of princes, Stevin questions how historical rights can be established, then goes on to state that the citizen's duty is to obey the laws, no matter if they appear wrong or unjust. He cites the necessity of religion as a means of instilling virtue in children, but adds that if a man's religion is different from that of his countrymen, the dissenter should either conform or leave. All told, his views are typical of those current in a post-revolutionary period in which consolidation was more important than individual freedoms.

In the last years of his life, Stevin returned to the study of mathematics. He reedited his mathematical works and collected them into the two folio volumes of his *Wisconstighe Ghedachtenissen* (published in 1605–1608). These mathematical memoirs were also published, at almost the same time, in Latin and French translations.

Stevin's writings in general are characterized by his versatility, his ability to combine theory and practice, and the clarity of his argument. They demonstrate a mind confident of the prevalence of reason and common sense and convinced of the comprehensibility of nature. His style, especially the personal way in which he addresses the reader, is particularly charming.

BIBLIOGRAPHY

I. ORIGINAL WORKS. A committee of Dutch scientists has edited *The Principal Works of Simon Stevin*, 5 vols. (Amsterdam, 1955–1968), which contains a bibliography and extensive introductions to each of the works.

Stevin's major works include *Tafelen van Interest* (Antwerp, 1582; Amsterdam, 1590), a French trans. of which appears in *De Thiende* (Leiden, 1585); *Problematum geometricorum-Libri V* (Antwerp, 1583); and *De Thiende* (Leiden, 1585; Gouda, 1626, 1630; Antwerp–

The Hague, 1924). Translations of *De Thiende* are H. Gericke and K. Vogel, *De Thiende von Simon Stevin* (Frankfurt am Main, 1965); Robert Norton, *Disme, the Art of Tenths* (London, 1608); J. Tuning, "La disme," in *Mémoires mathématiques* (Leiden, 1608), also reprinted in *Isis*, 23 (1925); Henry Lyte, *The Art of Tenths* (London, 1619), and "The Disme of Simon Stevin," in *Mathematics Teacher*, 14 (1921), 321, also in D. E. Smith, *Source Book of Mathematics* (New York–London, 1929).

Subsequent writings include *L'arithmétique* (Leiden, 1585, 1625), which contains French translations of *Tafelen van Interest* and *De Thiende*; *Vita Politica, Het Burgherlick Leven* (Leiden, 1590; Amsterdam, 1939); *De Stercktenbouwing* (Leiden; 1594; Amsterdam, 1624), also trans. by G. A. von Dantzig (Frankfurt, 1608, 1623), and by Albert Girard, *Les oeuvres mathématiques de Simon Stevin* (Leiden, 1634); *Castrametatio, Dat is legermeting. Nieuwe Maniere van Sterctebou door Spilseuysen* (Rotterdam, 1617), trans. in French (Leiden–Rotterdam, 1618) and in Albert Girard, trans., *Les oeuvres mathématiques de Simon Stevin* (Leiden, 1634), and in German (Frankfurt, 1631); *Van de Spiegeling der Singconst. Van de Molens* (Amsterdam, 1884).

II. SECONDARY LITERATURE. A bibliography of Stevin's works is in *Bibliotheca Belgica. Bibliographie générale des Pays-Bas*, ser. 1, XXIII (Ghent–The Hague, 1880–1890). On Stevin and his work, see R. Depau, *Simon Stevin* (Brussels, 1942), which is in French and contains a bibliography of the articles on Stevin; E. J. Dijksterhuis, *Simon Stevin* (The Hague, 1943), in Dutch, with bibliography of Stevin's works, and which is in an abbreviated English version: R. Hooykaas and M. G. J. Minnaert, eds., *Simon Stevin: Science in the Netherlands Around 1600* (The Hague, 1970); and A. J. J. van de Velde, "Simon Stevin 1548–1948," in *Mededelingen Kongelige Vlaamse Academie*, 10 (1948), 10.

M. G. J. MINNAERT

STEWART, MATTHEW (*b.* Rothesay, Isle of Bute, Scotland, January 1717; *d.* Catrine, Ayrshire, Scotland, 23 January 1785)

Stewart's father, Dugald, was minister of the parish of Rothesay; his mother was Janet Bannatyne. Intending to follow his father's career, he entered the University of Glasgow in 1734, soon coming under the influence of Robert Simson, professor of mathematics, and Francis Hutcheson, professor of moral philosophy.

Simson was then attempting to reconstruct Euclid's lost book on porisms; and he communicated his enthusiasm for this project—and for the study of Greek mathematics in general—to Stewart, who soon developed his own approach to the subject. Aware that new horizons were opening in mathematics, Simson conscientiously instructed his students in the newer subjects of calculus and analytical geometry. It was at his suggestion that Stewart went to the University of Edinburgh to work under Colin Maclaurin, himself a pupil of Simson's. Although he was studying calculus, higher plane curves, and cosmogony with Maclaurin, Stewart continued to correspond with Simson and, under his general direction, to carry on his work in pure geometry.

Simson's investigations were slow and laborious, and he was disinclined to publish findings that he regarded as incomplete—after the publication of a paper on porisms in 1723, nothing by him on the subject was published until eight years after his death—but he made his work freely available to Stewart. He actively encouraged Stewart to publish his celebrated series of geometrical propositions, General Theorems, in 1746 because the chair of mathematics at Edinburgh was vacant as a result of Maclaurin's service with the government troops in the Jacobite Rebellion of 1745 and subsequent death from an illness contracted during that campaign. Stewart was then largely unknown in Scottish academic circles; and the chair was offered to James Stirling, who already enjoyed a European reputation as a mathematician of distinction. Stirling declined the invitation; and when the electors to the chair re-assessed the situation at the end of 1746, the reception accorded the publication of Stewart's book had been so favorable that they were encouraged to offer him the chair. Stewart had only recently (May 1745) been ordained minister of the parish of Roseneath, Dunbartonshire, on the nomination of the Duke of Argyll; but he had no hesitation in changing his career and was duly elected to the chair of mathematics at Edinburgh in September 1747.

Stewart's reputation as a mathematician was established overnight by the publication of the General Theorems. John Playfair, himself a scientist of distinction, claimed that Stewart's results were "among the most beautiful, as well as most general propositions known in the whole compass of geometry, and are perhaps only equalled by the remarkable locus to the circle in the second book of Apollonius, or by the celebrated theorems of Mr. Cotes. . . . The unity which prevails among them is a proof that a single though extensive view guided Mr. Stewart in the discovery of them all" ("Memoir of Matthew Stewart," 59–60). Simson's influence is obvious throughout the work. Several of Stewart's theorems are in fact porisms, although he refrains from calling them by that name, probably through fear of seeming to anticipate Simson. Several of their contemporaries assert in their memoirs that Simson, singularly lacking in personal ambition, was so keen for Stewart to succeed to Maclaurin's chair that he allowed him to incorporate in his book results that were originally Simson's; it is fairly clear that what is usually described as "Stewart's theorem" was demonstrated in lectures by Simson several years before the publication of Stewart's book.

After his election to the chair, Stewart's interests turned to astronomy and natural philosophy; and he displayed great ingenuity in devising purely geometrical proofs of results in these subjects that had previously been established by the use of algebraic and analytical methods. Examples of this kind are to be seen in his Tracts, Physical and Mathematical (1761). In a work published in 1763 he extended these methods to provide a basis for the approximate calculation of the distance of the earth from the sun. He derived a value of 29,875 radii of the earth for this distance—a result that was shown shortly afterward (1768) by John Dawson to be greatly in error; Stewart's mistake had been his failure to realize that his geometrical methods did not indicate how small arithmetical errors could grow in the course of his calculation.

Stewart bore the attacks on this work rather badly, and as a result his health began to fail. In 1772 he retired to his country estate at Catrine in Ayrshire, leaving the duties of his chair to his son Dugald, who was elected joint professor with him in 1775.

BIBLIOGRAPHY

I. ORIGINAL WORKS. Stewart's books include General Theorems of Considerable Use in the Higher Parts of Mathematics (Edinburgh, 1746); Tracts, Physical and Mathematical . . . (Edinburgh, 1761); Distance of the Sun From the Earth . . . (Edinburgh, 1763); and Propositiones geometricae more veterum demonstratae ad geometriam antiquam illustrandam et promovendam idoneae (Edinburgh, 1763).

II. SECONDARY LITERATURE. See John Playfair, "Memoir of Matthew Stewart," in Transactions of the Royal Society of Edinburgh, 1 (1788), 57–76; and Matthew Stewart, Memoir of Dugald Stewart (Edinburgh, 1838).

IAN N. SNEDDON

STIELTJES, THOMAS JAN (b. Zwolle, Netherlands, 29 December 1856; d. Toulouse, France, 31 December 1894)

To the majority of mathematicians, Stieltjes' name is remembered in association with the Stieltjes integral,

$$\int_a^b f(u)\,dg(u),$$

a generalization of the ordinary Riemann integral with wide applications in physics. Yet in his own day, he was renowned as a versatile mathematician whose publications include papers in almost every area of analysis. He is the father of the analytic theory of continued fractions, and his integral was developed as a tool for its study.

Stieltjes, the son of a distinguished Dutch civil engineer, received his principal schooling at the École Polytechnique in Delft. He left the École in 1877 to take up a post at the observatory in Leiden, where he served six years. Evidently he kept up his mathematical studies, since he left Leiden to accept a chair in mathematics at the University of Groningen. Honors came to Stieltjes early. In 1884 the University of Leiden awarded him an honorary doctorate, and in 1885 he was elected to membership in the Royal Academy of Sciences of Amsterdam. Disappointed at Groningen, Stieltjes went to live in Paris, where he received his doctorate of science in 1886. In the same year he was appointed to the faculty at the University of Toulouse, where he remained until his death eight years later. Although not elected to the Academy of Sciences in Paris, Stieltjes was considered for membership in 1892 and won its Ormoy Prize in 1893 for his work on continued fractions.

Stieltjes' published work encompasses almost all of analysis of his time. He made contributions to the theory of ordinary and partial differential equations, studied gamma functions and elliptical functions, and worked in interpolation theory. His thesis was on asymptotic series. A special and increasing interest was the evaluation of particular integrals such as

$$\int_0^\infty \frac{\sin(xu)}{1+u^2}\,du$$

or

$$\int_0^\infty \frac{u\cos(xu)}{1+u^2}\,du$$

and series of the general form $\overset{\infty}{\Sigma}\, a_n/x^n$, which arise in a natural way from such integrals. These series

also occur in the study of continued fractions, and this may have led Stieltjes to analytic continued fraction theory.

His first paper on continued fractions, published in 1884, proves the convergence of

$$\cfrac{2}{z-\cfrac{1\cdot1}{1\cdot3}-\cfrac{}{z-\cfrac{3\cdot3}{5\cdot7}-\cfrac{}{z-\cfrac{4\cdot4}{7\cdot9}-\cfrac{}{z-\cdots}}}}$$

in the slit complex z-plane excluding the interval $(-1,1)$, with use of the series in decreasing powers of z. This convergence, which is locally uniform, was established by transforming the fraction into a definite integral.

Yet Stieltjes' monument is his last memoir, "Recherches sur les fractions continues," written just before he died, and published in two parts (*Annales de la Faculté des sciences de l'Université de Toulouse pour les sciences mathématiques et physiques*, **1**, ser. 1 [1894], 1–122; **1**, ser. 9 [1895], 5–47), the second posthumously. In it he polished and refined all of his previous work on the subject, and here is the first appearance of his integral. The memoir is a beautiful piece of mathematical writing—clear, self-contained, almost lyric in its style.

In this paper the fraction

$$\cfrac{1}{a_1 z+\cfrac{1}{a_2+\cfrac{1}{a_3 z+\cfrac{1}{a_4+\cfrac{1}{\ddots\cfrac{1}{a_{2n-1}z+\cfrac{1}{a_{2n}+\cdot}}}}}}} \qquad (1)$$

is considered. The a_i's are assumed to be known real positive quantities, and z is a complex variable. Fraction (1) will be said to converge, or otherwise, according to the convergence or not of the sequence of "approximates" $P_n(z)/Q_n(z)$. Each approximate where in (2) $\{x_1, x_2, \cdots, x_n\}$ are the (positive) roots of $Q_{2n}(-z)$ and in (3) $\{0, y_1, y_2, \cdots, y_n\}$ are the roots of $Q_{2n+1}(-z)$.

Next Stieltjes was able to show that

$$\frac{P_n(z)}{Q_n(z)} = \sum_{k=1}^{n} (-1)^{k-1} \frac{c_{k-1}}{z^k} + \sum_{k=n+1}^{\infty} \frac{\alpha_{n,k-1}}{z^k}, \quad (4)$$

where the $\{c_k : k = 1, 2, \cdots, n\}$ depend only upon the original fraction (1) and not upon n. Formula (4) led to the definition of the development of (1) in decreasing powers of z:

$$\sum_{k=1}^{\infty} (-1)^{k-1} \frac{c_{k-1}}{z^k} \quad (5)$$

The c_k are all real and positive, and

$$\frac{c_{n+1}}{c_n} < \frac{c_{n+2}}{c_{n+1}}. \quad (6)$$

Either the sequences of ratios is unbounded, in which case (5) diverges for all z, or (6) is bounded, in which case there is a $\lambda > 0$ with the property that (5) converges for all z satisfying $|z| > \lambda$. Stieltjes then proved that, in the latter case, if the (necessarily positive) roots of $Q_n(-z)$ are ordered according to size, and if the largest is, say, $x_{n,k}$, then $\lim_{n\to\infty} x_{n,k} = \lambda$.

oscillation of (1). Here Stieltjes showed that for all z with positive real part,

$$\lim_{n\to\infty} \frac{P_{2n+1}(z)}{Q_{2n+1}(z)} = F_1(z) \quad (7)$$

and

$$\lim_{n\to\infty} \frac{P_{2n}(z)}{Q_{2n}(z)} = F(z). \quad (8)$$

Furthermore, for z real $(=x)$, $F(x)$ and $F_1(x)$ are real, and $F_1(x) \geq F(x)$. Equality in the right half plane, including the positive real axis, was proved to hold if and only if the series

$$\sum_{k=1}^{\infty} a_k \quad (9)$$

formed from the terms of fraction (1) is divergent. (Recall that the a_k are all positive.) Also, since the convergence of (7) and (8) is locally uniform, the functions $F(z)$ and $F_1(z)$ are analytic in the right half plane. Thus, to sum up, Stieltjes had shown that the continued fraction (1) was convergent when and only when the series (9) diverged; otherwise the fraction oscillated. The remaining problem was

in the rational function formed by considering only the first n terms of (1) and simplifying the resulting compound fraction. Thus, $Q_{2n}(z)$ and $P_{2n+1}(z)$ are polynomials of degree n in z, while P_{2n} is of degree $n-1$, and Q_{2n+1} is of degree $n+1$.

Stieltjes began by studying the roots of the polynomials $P_n(z)Q_n(z)$, which are all real. He proved a whole series of theorems concerning the interlacing of their roots; for example, the roots of $Q_{2n}(z)$ separate the roots of $Q_{2n-2}(z)$. This was then used to prove that the roots of $P_n(z)$ and $Q_n(z)$ $(n = 1, 2, \cdots)$ are all nonpositive and distinct. Thus, the approximates have the following partial fraction decomposition:

$$\frac{P_{2n}(z)}{Q_{2n}(z)} = \sum_{k=1}^{n} \frac{M_k}{z + x_k} \quad (2)$$

$$\frac{P_{2n+1}(z)}{Q_{2n+1}(z)} = \frac{N_0}{z} + \sum_{k=1}^{n} \frac{N_k}{z + y_k}, \quad (3)$$

to extend this result to the z in the left half plane, except for certain points on the negative real axis.

To this end, Stieltjes showed that the limits

$$\lim_{n\to\infty} P_{2n}(z) = p(z) \qquad \lim_{n\to\infty} P_{2n+1}(z) = p_1(z)$$

$$\lim_{n\to\infty} Q_{2n}(z) = q(z) \qquad \lim_{n\to\infty} Q_{2n+1}(z) = q_1(z)$$

all exist, that p, q, p_1, q_1 are all analytic, and that

$$p_1(z)q(z) - p(z)q_1(z) \equiv 1.$$

Then, again he supposed that the roots $\{x_{n,1}, x_{n,2}, \cdots, x_{n,n}\}$ of $Q_{2n}(-z)$ were ordered according to increasing size for each n. Stieltjes then proved that $\lim_{n\to\infty} x_{nk} = \lambda k$, that $\{\lambda_k; k = 1, 2, \cdots\}$ are all distinct real and positive, and that the λ_k are the only zeros of $q(z)$. Similar results hold for $q_1(z)$, $p(z)$, and $p_1(z)$. Next, μ_k is defined by

$$\mu_k = \frac{p(-\lambda_k)}{q'(-\lambda_k)}, \quad (10)$$

and it was proved that $\mu_k = \lim_{n\to\infty} M_k$ $(k = 1, 2, \cdots)$, where the M_k are from expression (2). Furthermore,

$$S(z) = \sum_{k=1}^{\infty} \frac{\mu_k}{z + x_k} \quad (11)$$

is meromorphic in the plane, $S(z) = F(z)$ (see [8]), and finally that for each i

$$c_i = \sum_{k=1}^{\infty} \mu_k \lambda_k^{i}, \quad (12)$$

where the c_i's are from (5).

In precisely the same way, an infinite set of pairs of positive real numbers similar to $\{(\mu_k, \lambda_k)\}$ above was associated with the sequence $\{p_{2n+1}(z)/Q_{2n+1}(z)\}$. In particular $F_1(z)$ was shown to be meromorphic, and if $\nu_k = \lim_{n \to \infty} N_k ((k=0, 1, 2, \cdots); \text{see [3]})$, and if $\theta_k = \lim_{n \to \infty} y_{n,k} (k=1, 2, \cdots)$, then

$$c_0 = \sum_{k=0}^{\infty} \nu_k \text{ and } c_i = \sum_{k=1}^{\infty} \nu_k \theta_k^i \ (i=1, 2, \cdots), \text{ and}$$

$$F(z) = \frac{\nu_0}{z} + \sum_{k=1}^{\infty} \frac{\nu_k}{z + \theta_k}. \tag{13}$$

In this way he established the analyticity of $F_1(z)$ and $F(z)$ in the slit plane.

Observe that the above systems (12) (or [13]) can be considered as the equations of the moments of all orders of a system of masses μ_k (or ν_k) placed at a distance λ_k (or θ_k) from the origin, and that in either case the ith moment is c_i. Of course, if Σa_k is divergent, $\nu_k = \mu_k$ and $\lambda_k = \theta_k$ for all k, since $F(z)$ and $F_1(z)$ are the same function. But if Σa_k is convergent, the equalities do not hold, even though the c_i are the same in each case.

The further study of the nature of $F_1(z)$ and $F(z)$ in more detail led Stieltjes to the "moment problem": that is, to find a distribution of mass (an infinite set of ordered pairs of positive numbers) whose moments of all orders are known. If this problem can be solved, then $F_1(z)$ and $F(z)$ will be known, since the c_i's can be calculated from the a_k's of fraction (1). However, it is immediately evident that if Σa_k is convergent, there can be no unique solution, as there are at least two. But Stieltjes was able to show (later on) that if Σa_k diverges, there is a unique solution.

It was to solve the moment problem that Stieltjes introduced his integral. First he considered an increasing real-valued function φ defined on the positive real axis, and gave a lengthy discussion of one-sided limits. For example, he showed that φ is continuous at x, if and only if $\varphi^+(x) = \varphi^-(x)$. Only bounded functions with countably many discontinuities on the positive axis were considered. Next he supposed that φ was a step function, with $\varphi(0) = 0$. Then a finite mass condensed at each point of discontinuity can be given by $\varphi^+(x) - \varphi^-(x)$, and $\varphi(b) - \varphi(a)$ is the total mass between a and b; in particular $\varphi(x)$ is the total mass between x and the origin. Also, changing the value of φ at a point of discontinuity does not change the associated mass distribution there.

Stieltjes then defined the integral

$$\int_a^b f(x) d\varphi(x) \tag{14}$$

to be the limit, as max $(x_{i+1} - x_i) \to 0$ of

$$\sum_{i=1}^n f(\zeta_i)[\varphi(x_i) - \varphi(x_{i-1})], \tag{15}$$

where $a = x_0 < x_i < \cdots < x_n = b$ and $x_{i-1} \leq \zeta_i \leq x_i$. Stieltjes then established the formula for integration by parts

$$\int_a^b f(x) d\varphi(x) =$$

$$f(b)\varphi(b) - f(a)\varphi(a)$$

$$- \int_a^b \varphi(x) df(x),$$

defined the improper integral $\int_a^\infty f(a) d\varphi(x)$ in the usual way, and established many properties of the integral.

Next he considered the function φ_n defined from the even-order approximates by

$$\varphi_n(0) = 0 \quad 0 \leq u < x_1$$

$$\varphi_n(u) = \sum_{i=1}^k M_i \quad x_k \leq u < x_{k+1} (1 \leq k \leq n-1)$$

$$\varphi_n(u) = \sum_{i=1}^n M_i = \frac{1}{a_1} \quad x_n \leq u < \infty,$$

where the M_i and the x_k are defined as in (2), and where a_1 is the first term of (1). After a lengthy discussion of "lim inf" and "lim sup" (the ideas were new then), he defined, for each u: $\psi(u) = \lim$ sup $\varphi_n(u)$, $\chi(u) = \lim \inf \varphi_n(u)$, and $\Phi(u) = \frac{1}{2}(\psi(u) + \chi(u))$. Φ was shown to have the property that

$$F(z) = \int_0^\infty \frac{d\Phi(u)}{z + u}$$

and also that the distribution of mass represented by Φ solved the moment problem, since

$$c_k = \int_0^\infty u^k d\Phi(u).$$

A function $\Phi_1(u)$ with similar properties was constructed from the odd-order approximates. He also undertook the study of the inverse problem; that is, given an increasing function $\psi(u)$, with $\psi(0) = 0$, then, by setting

$$c_k = \int_0^\infty u^k d\varphi(x)$$

a fraction like (1) can be determined with the property that

$$F(x) \le \int_0^\infty \frac{d\psi(u)}{x+u} \le F_1(x).$$

Stieltjes' paper, of which only a portion has been summarized here, is a mathematical milestone. The work represents the first general treatment of continued fractions as part of complex analytic function theory; previously, only special cases had been considered. Moreover, it is clearly in the historical line that led to Hilbert spaces and their generalizations. In addition, Stieltjes gave a sort of respectability to discontinuous functions and, together with some earlier work, to divergent series. All together these were astonishing accomplishments for a man who died just two days after his thirty-eighth birthday.

BIBLIOGRAPHY

All Stieltjes' published papers, with some letters, notes, and incomplete works found after his death, are in *Oeuvres complètes de Thomas Jan Stieltjes* (Groningen, 1914–1918). An annotated bibliography of his published works appears with his obituary in *Annales de la Faculté des sciences de l'Université de Toulouse pour les sciences mathématiques et physiques*, **1**, ser. 1 (1895), 1–64.

MICHAEL BERNKOPF

STIFEL (STYFEL, STYFFEL, STIEFFELL, STIFELIUS, or STIEFFEL), MICHAEL (*b*. Esslingen, Germany, *ca*. 1487; *d*. Jena, Germany, 19 April 1567)

Stifel was the son of Conrad Stifel. Nothing is known about his education except that, on his own testimony, he knew no Greek.[1] He was a monk at the Augustinian monastery of Esslingen, where he was ordained priest in 1511. Reacting to the declining morality of the clergy and the abuses committed in the administration of indulgences, Stifel became an early follower of Luther. While studying the Bible he came upon the numbers in Revelation and in the Book of Daniel.[2]

After 1520 he became increasingly preoccupied with their cabalistic interpretation, for which he used a "word calculus" (*Wortrechnung*). In the malevolent great beast designated in Revelation by the number 666 he saw Pope Leo X.[3] Stifel aroused the suspicion of the bishop of Constance and of his vicar-general by giving absolution without receiving indulgence money and by composing a song in honor of Luther.[4] Realizing that his life was in danger, Stifel escaped in 1522 to Kronberg in the Taunus Mountains, seeking refuge in the castle of a knight named Hartmut, a relative of Franz von Sickingen. He soon had to flee again[5] and went to Wittenberg, where Luther lodged him in his own house. The two became friends, and in 1523 Luther obtained Stifel a post as pastor at the court of the count of Mansfeld. Two years later Stifel became pastor and tutor at Castle Tollet in Upper Austria, in the service of the widow of a nobleman, Wolfgang Jörger.[6] The persecution unleashed by Ferdinand I of Bohemia against the new religious teaching forced Stifel to return to Luther, who procured him a parish at Annaberg. Luther accompanied Stifel there on 25 October 1528 and married him to the widow of the previous incumbent.

At Annaberg, Stifel resumed his dabbling in number mysticism, an activity that, if nothing else, revealed his skill in detecting number-theory relationships. From his reading of the Bible, he thought that he had discovered the date of the end of the world; and in *Ein Rechen-büchlin Vom End Christ* (1532) he prophesied that the event would occur at 8 o'clock on 18 October 1533.[7] On 28 September 1533 Luther implored him not to spread his fantastic notions. Stifel could not be dissuaded, however; and as he vainly warned his assembled congregation of the coming of the end, he was arrested and subsequently dismissed from his post.[8] Through the intervention of Luther—who forgave his "little temptation" (*kleine Anfechtlein*)—and Melanchthon, he finally received another parish, at nearby Holzdorf, in 1535.

Now cured of prophesying, Stifel devoted himself to mathematics. He enrolled at, and received his master's degree from, the University of Wittenberg, where Jacob Milich was lecturer on mathematics.[9] Stifel gave private instruction in mathematics, and among his pupils was Melanchthon's son-in-law Kaspar Peucer. The years at Holzdorf were Stifel's most productive period. At the urging of Milich he wrote *Arithmetica integra* (1544), in which he set forth all that was then known about arithmetic and algebra, supplemented by important original contributions.[10] In his next work, *Deutsche arithmetica* (1545), Stifel sought to make his favorite branch of mathematics, the coss (algebra) or "artful calculation" (*Kunstrechnung*), more accessible to German readers by eliminating foreign words.[11] His last book written at Holzdorf was *Welsche Practick* (1546).[12]

The peaceful years in Holzdorf ended suddenly after the Schmalkaldic War (1547), for the "Hispanier" drove off all the inhabitants.[13] Stifel fled to Prussia, where he finally found a position in 1551 as pastor at Haberstroh, near Königsberg.[14] He lectured on theology and mathematics at the University of Königsberg and brought out a new edition of Christoph Rudolff's *Coss*, which first appeared in 1525 and had since become unavailable. He undertook the republication at the request of a businessman named Christoff Ottendorffer, who paid the printing costs. Stifel reproduced Rudolff's text in its entirety, as well as all 434 problems illustrating the eight rules of the *Coss*. To each chapter of the original text he appended critical notes and additional developments, most of which he drew from his *Arithmetica integra*.[15] Stifel's additions are much longer than the corresponding sections of Rudolff's book.[16]

Stifel returned to playing with numbers, as is evident from his next published book, *Ein sehr wunderbarliche Wortrechnung* (1553).[17] At odds with his colleagues, especially Andreas Osiander, as a result of theological controversies, and urged to return to Holzdorf by his former congregation, he returned to Saxony in 1554. His first post there was as pastor at Brück, near Wittenberg. He then went to Jena, following his friend Matthias Flacius,[18] and lectured on arithmetic and geometry at the university. In 1559 he was mentioned in the register as "senex, artium Magister et minister verbi divini."[19] By this time he apparently had given up his pastorate. Stifel's life in Jena was made difficult by theological disputes until Flacius, from whom Stifel had become alienated, found a successor (Nikolaus Selnecker) for him in 1561.[20] Stifel bequeathed the latter a long work on *Wortrechnung* that was never printed.[21]

In his books Stifel offered more than a methodical exposition of existing knowledge of arithmetic and algebra:[22] he also made original contributions that prepared the way for further progress in these fields. A principal concern was the establishment of generally valid laws. He contended that to improve algebra, it was necessary to formulate rules the validity of which was not limited to special cases, and which therefore could advance the study of the entire subject.[23] He was, in fact, the first to present a general method for solving equations, one that replaced the twenty-four rules traditionally given

by the cossists (and the eight that appeared in Rudolff's *Coss*).[24] For example, he pointed out that basically there was nothing different about problems with several unknowns, a type for which Rudolff had introduced a special name.[25] Similarly, he asserted that the symbol "dragma" for the linear member could simply be omitted.[26] Stifel introduced into western mathematics a general method for computing roots that required, however, the use of binomial coefficients. He had discovered these coefficients only with great difficulty, having found no one to teach them to him nor any written accounts of them.[27] Stifel also surpassed his predecessors in the division of general polynomials and extraction of their roots, as well as in computing with irrational numbers.

The second chapter of *Arithmetica integra* is devoted entirely to the numerical treatment of Euclidean irrationals (binomials, residues, and so forth), a topic that Fibonacci had planned to discuss.[28] Stifel's exceptional skill in number theory is evident in his investigation of numerical relationships in number sequences, polygonal numbers, and magic squares.[29] Particularly noteworthy is his contribution to the preliminary stages of logarithmic computation. The starting point for this type of computation was attained by correlating a geometric series with an arithmetic series. This can be seen in Stifel's explanation of the cossists' symbols:

$$0 \cdot 1 \cdot 2 \cdot 3 \cdot 4 \cdot 5 \cdot 6 \cdot 7$$
$$1 \cdot 1x \cdot 1z \cdot 1c \cdot 1zz \cdot 1\beta \cdot 1zc \cdot 1b\beta.$$

On this occasion Stifel introduced the term "exponent" for the numbers of the upper series.[30] In correlating the two number sequences he extended the use of exponents to the domain of the negative numbers in the manner shown below.

−3	−2	−1	0	1	2	3	4	5	6
1/8	1/4	1/2	1	2	4	8	16	32	64

Stifel suspected the importance of his innovation, stating: "A whole book might be written concerning the marvellous things relating to numbers, but I must refrain and leave these things with eyes closed."[31] He did, however, provide a table that made it possible to carry out logarithmic calculations. Stifel approached the concept of the logarithm from another direction as well. He was aware of both inversions of the power, the root, and the "logarithmus." He discussed "division" of a ratio by a number, obtaining, for example, in the case of (27:8) "divided" by 3/4: $\sqrt[3/4]{27:8}$ $= \sqrt[3]{(27:8)^4} = 81:16$.[32] In contrast, Stifel saw the "division" of a ratio by a ratio as a way of finding exponents. Thus, by means of continuous "subtraction," he obtained from the equality $(729:64) = (3:2)^x$ the "quotient" $x = 6$; and in the case of $(2187:128) = (27:8)^x$, the result was $x = 2\ 1/3$.[33]

Stifel was also a pioneer in the development of algebraic symbolism. To designate the unknowns he used A, B, C, D, and F, as well as the traditional x.[34] For the powers he employed Az, $x^3 = AAA$, $x^4 = FFFF$, and so forth—not just the traditional z (census).[35] He simplified the square root sign from $\sqrt{z}$ to $\sqrt{.}$, and later to $\sqrt{}$ alone.[36] In one instance he closely approached modern symbolism, writing $\sqrt[11]{38}$ as $11\sqrt{38}$.[37] Other, more cumbersome designations for unknowns and the root used in *Deutsche arithmetica* were not adopted by later mathematicians.[38] The only operational signs that Stifel employed were $+$ and $-$; other operations were indicated verbally. Equality was designated either in words or by a point, as in $1x. \sqrt{48}$.[39]

Stifel made a thorough study of magic squares and polygonal numbers for a nonmathematical purpose.[40] He correlated the twenty-three letters of the alphabet with the first twenty-three triangular numbers, thereby establishing connections between words and numbers.[41] He called such *Wortrechnung* "the holy arithmetic of numbers."[42] For example, from the number 666 he derived the sentence "Id bestia Leo"; and the equality 2.5 ages = 1,260 days that he found in the book of Daniel yielded the sentence "Vae tibi Papa, vae tibi." Although Stifel's work at Holzdorf is most admired today, he declared that he valued his "word calculus" above all the computations he had ever made.[43]

The development of Stifel's scientific ideas was decisively influenced by Jacob Milich, who recommended that he study Campanus of Novara's translation of Euclid.[44] He also proposed that Stifel write a comprehensive work on arithmetic and algebra (which became *Arithmetica integra*).[45] To prepare for the latter project Stifel worked through Rudolff's *Coss* without assistance.[46] He had already studied proportions in the writings of Boethius, and had long been acquainted with contemporary arithmetic books, such as the *Margarita phylosophica* of Gregor Reisch (1503) and the works of Peter Apian (*Eyn newe unnd wolgegründete Underweysung aller Kauffmanns Rechnung*, 1527) and Adam Ries (*Rechnung auf der Lynihen un Federn in Zalmass und gewicht auff allerley handierung gemacht*, 1522).[47] (He espe-

cially admired Ries's book.)[48] Stifel conscientiously named the authors from whom he had taken examples and never neglected to express his appreciation.[49] The enthusiasm with which he followed Milich's advice[50] to collect mathematical writings is obvious from the large number of authors he cited.[51]

Stifel's achievements were respected and adopted by contemporary mathematicians, although, like Clavius, they often did not cite him.[52] The last edition of *Arithmetica integra* appeared in 1586, and the last of the *Coss* in 1615. After that, mathematicians surpassed Stifel's level of knowledge in symbolism and logarithms, and they opened new fields of research. It is for both these reasons that his work fell into neglect. He was, in fact, the greatest German algebraist of the sixteenth century.

NOTES

1. Stifel admitted that he was "ignarus linguae graecae." Since he knew Euclid only from the translations of Campanus and Zamberti, he turned to other scholars for assistance. See *Arithmetica integra* (cited below as *AI*), fol. 143v.
2. In these numbers Stifel saw "sealed words" (*versiegelte Worte*). See *Wortrechnung* (cited below as *WR*), fol. B2ʳ.
3. The numbers (LDCIMV) that Stifel obtained from the name "Leo DeCIMVs" yielded 1656, 1,000 too much and 10 too little; but he manipulated them to obtain 666 by the addition of *decimus* = 10 and by setting M = *Mysterium*.
4. "Von der Christförmigen rechtgegründten leer Doctoris Martini Luthers . . ." (1522).
5. The castle was besieged by Franz von Sickingen's enemies and was taken on 15 Oct. 1522. A sermon that Stifel gave on 8 Sept. is still preserved; see J. E. Hofmann, "Michael Stifel, 1487?–1567," n. 14.
6. In the Grieskirchen congregation; see Ritter's *Geographisch-statistisches Lexicon*, II (Leipzig, 1906), 1051.
7. On the Biblical passages see J. E. Hofmann, "Michael Stifel," in n. 43. Other dates also were mentioned: 3 Oct. (J. H. Zedler, *Universallexikon*, XL [1744], 22); 16 Oct. (see Treutlein, p. 17, and Poggendorff, II, 1010–1011); and 19 Oct. (Giesing, p. 11). *Der Biograph*, p. 473, mentions the 282nd day and the 42nd week of the year.
8. For an eyewitness report in a letter from Petrus Weller to Ioannes Briessmann, see Strobel, pp. 74–84; the German trans. of the letter is given by Grosse, p. 19 ff.
9. With Luther and Melanchthon, Milich was also friendly with Stifel at Annaberg and acted as the family's physician. See *AI*, fol. (α4)r, entry of 25 Oct. 1541, *Album der Universität Wittenberg*, I (Leipzig, 1841), 195a: "Gratis inscripti . . . Michael Stifel pastor in Holtzdorff."
10. A detailed description of the contents of the book can be found in Kaestner, *Geschichte der Mathematik*, I, 112 ff.; and in Treutlein; in Cantor; and in Hofmann, *op. cit.*
11. Stifel stated that the *regula falsi* is related to the coss as a point is to a circle. *AI*, 227r.
12. In the *Welsche Practick* (cited below as *WP*) Stifel objected to Apian's problems, which were correct but not comprehensible to everyone. He did not wish to blame Apian but to "diligently expound" his work (see pp. 293, 337). Stifel also drew on the "*praxis italica*" in *AI*, fols. 83v ff.
13. See *WR*. fol. A(1)v.
14. He went to Memel in 1549 and to Eichholz in 1550.
15. The title page bears the date 1553, the preface 1552, and

the *explicit* 1554. Stifel made changes in the course of the printing, and thus the table of contents must be corrected. See *Coss*, fol. 179r.

16. Rudolff's 208 pages grew to 494 in Stifel's edition.

17. Osiander wrote on 19 Feb. 1549: ". . . Commentus est novos alphabeti numeros scil. triangulares et delirat multo ineptius quam antea" ("He has devised new numbers for the alphabet, namely the triangular numbers, and his fantasies are more absurd than before"). See B. F. Hummel, *Epistolarum historico-ecclesiasticarum saeculo XVI a celeberrimis viris scriptorum semicenturia altera* (Halle, 1780), 70 ff.

18. Like Stifel and Ottendorffer, Flacius was an opponent of Osiander.

19. Entry in *Die Matrikel der Universität Jena*, I (Jena, 1944), 320.

20. See J. E. Hofmann, "Michael Stifel," p. 59.

21. The MS, "Explicatio apocalypseos," is now in the Karl Marx University Library, Leipzig. The Lutheran congregation of Kronberg possesses a microfilm copy of the work. See W. Meretz, "Aus Stiefels Nachlass," p. 5.

22. The first book of *AI* is devoted to the fundamental operations—including roots, properties of numbers, series, magic squares, proportions, the rule of three, false substitution, and the Welsh practice; the second book treats computation with irrationals, corresponding to the tenth book of Euclid; the third book takes up algebra and equations of higher degree, such as were found in the work of Rudolff and Cardano and that could be solved by employing certain devices.

The first part of the *Deutsche arithmetica* (cited below as *DA*) is devoted to "household computations" (*Hausrechnung*): carrying out on the abacus fundamental operations and the rule of three using whole numbers. The second part is concerned with computation with fractions, with the German *Coss* or "Kunstrechnung," and with extracting roots on the abacus. The third part, on "church computations" (*Kirchrechnung*), treats the division of the church year.

The division of the *Coss* is the same as in Rudolff's original edition. Stifel also reproduced Rudolff's *Wortrechnung*, but he did not agree with its contents. Among the new elements that he added were remarks on the higher-degree equations that Rudolff had presented; on the rules of the *Cubicoss* formulated by Scipione dal Ferro and Cardano that had been published in the meantime; and a procedure for computing

$$\sqrt[3]{a+\sqrt{b}}$$

Stifel's edition of the *Coss* also contained diagrams for verifying solutions. These had been drawn by Rudolff but did not appear in the original edition. Stifel obtained them from Johann Neudörfer, a brother-in-law of the printer Johannes Petrejus. See *Coss*, fol. 172r.

23. *DA*, fol. 72v.

24. Stifel reduced the three cases of the quadratic equation, $x^2 + a = b$, $x^2 + b = ax$, and $x^2 = ax + b$, to the standard form $x^2 = \pm ax \pm b$. By "extracting roots with cossic numbers" he obtained his rule called AMASIAS: $x = \sqrt{\left(\frac{a}{2}\right)^2 \pm b} \pm \frac{a}{2}$, where the plus and minus signs correspond to those of the standard form. See *AI*, fols. 240r f.; and Treutlein, *op. cit.*, 79. Stifel knew of the double solution only for $x^2 = ax$ (*AI*, fol. 243v). He avoided negative solutions, although he recognized negative numbers as those less than zero. (*AI*, fol. 48r). An equation of which the solution happened to be zero can be found in *AI*, fol. 283r.

25. For the term *quantitas*, see *AI*, fol. 257v; it was also used by Cardano (see *AI*, fol. 252r).

26. *DA*, fol. 17v.

27. *Ibid.*, fol. 72v. The table with binomial coefficients can be found in *AI*, fol. 44v; *DA*, fol. 71v; and *Coss*, fol. 168r.

28. See article on Fibonacci in this Dictionary, IV, 612, n. 7.

29. A detailed account is given by Hofmann in "Michael Stifel 1487?–1567," 13 ff.

30. *AI*, fol. 235.

31. "Posset hic fere novus liber integer scribi de mirabilibus numerorum sed oportet ut me hic subducam et clausis oculis abeam" (*AI*, fol. 249v). Translation from D. E. Smith, *History of Mathematics*, II (New York, 1925), 521.

32. Stifel distinguished between fraction (*Bruch*) and ratio (*Verhältnis*), and wrote the latter as a fraction without a fraction line. Nevertheless, he conceived of the ratio as a fraction; the quotient was its "name." Thus, 4:3 had the name 1 1/3. See *WP*, pp. 36 ff.; and *Coss*, fol. 135v.

33. First Stifel obtained, as the result of two "subtractions," $(2187:128) = (27:8)^2 (3:2)$ and then, because $(3:2) = (27:8)^{1/3}$, $(2187:128) = (27:8)^{2\,1/3}$. The details are in *AI*, fols. 53v ff. On computation with fractional power exponents and fractional radical indices, see *Coss*, fols. 138r f.

34. *AI*, fol. 254r.

35. *DA*, fol. 74v.

36. As Rudolff originally had it in the *Coss*.

37. *DA*, fol. 71r.

38. See *DA*, fol. 61v. Stifel extended the cumbersome symbols for the square root ($\sqrt{}$) and cube root ($\sqrt[3]{}$) as far as the sixth root (*DA*, fol. 62r). The designations for the unknowns in the *DA* (see fols. 20 ff.) are $x = 1$ Sum:or 1 Sum *A*:, $x^2 = 1$ Sum:Sum; and so on, up to x^{11} (*DA*, fol. 70v).

39. *Coss*, fol. 351v. He also uses points to indicate inclusion of several elements in the same operation, as in $\sqrt{z. 6 + \sqrt{z}2.} = \sqrt{6 + \sqrt{2}}$. *AI*, fol. 112v.

40. The number 666 of the "great beast" appeared in *Ein Rechen Büchlin vom End Christ* (fols., H 4v and 5r) as the sum of all the cells of a magic square.

41. See *WR*, fol. D2r. For Stifel, i = j and u = v = w; Rudolff's alphabet, however, had twenty-four letters, since he included w.

42. See *WR*, fol. A(1)r.

43. See *Coss*, fol. 487v.

44. See *AI*, fol. 226v.

45. *AI*, fols. (α4)v.

46. See *WR*, fol. B(1)r; *Coss*, fol. A2r.

47. *AI*, fols. 55 f., 250r: *Coss*, fol. 23r; *AI*, fol. 102r; *WP*, fol. A2v.

48. *AI*, fol. 226v; *DA*, fol. 31r.

49. The problems come from Peter Apian, Cardano, Johann Neudörfer, Adam Ries, Adamus Gigas, Rudolff, and Widmann.

50. *AI*, fol. (α4)v.

51. Stifel names the following: Apian, Boethius, Campanus, Cardano, Nicholas Cusa, Dürer, Euclid, Gemma Frisius, Faber Stapulensis, Jordanus de Nemore, Neudörfer, Ptolemy, Reisch, Ries, Rudolff, Sacrobosco, Schöner, Theon of Alexandria, Zamberti, and Widmann.

52. See Hofmann, "Michael Stifel 1487?–1567," 31, n. 94.

BIBLIOGRAPHY

I. ORIGINAL WORKS. Stifel's works include *Ein Rechen Büchlin vom End Christ, Apocalypsis in Apocalypsin* (Wittenberg, 1532); *Arithmetica integra*, with preface by Melanchthon (Nuremberg, 1544; 1545; 1546; 1548; 1586); *Deutsche arithmetica, inhaltend Haussrechnung, deutsche Coss, Kirchrechnung* (Nuremberg, 1545); *Rechenbuch von der welschen und deutschen Practick* . . . (Nuremberg, 1546); *Ein sehr wunderbarliche Wortrechnung. Sampt einer mercklichen Erklärung ettlicher Zahlen Danielis unnd der Offenbarung Sanct Iohannis* ([Königsberg], 1553); and *Die Coss Christoffs Rudolffs.*

Die schönen Exempeln der Coss. Durch Michael Stifel gebessert und sehr gemehrt (Königsberg, 1552–1553 [colophon dated 1554], 1571; Amsterdam, 1615).

Lists of Stifel's theological writings and songs are in J. E. Hofmann, "Michael Stifel 1487?–1567" (see below), and in the articles by G. Kawerau and W. Meretz cited below. Illustrations of the title pages of Stifel's books are given by Hofmann and Meretz.

II. SECONDARY LITERATURE. See *Allgemeine deutsche biographie*, VI (1893), 208–216; *Der Biograph*, VI (Halle, 1807), 458–488; F. J. Buck, *Lebensbeschreibung der preussischen Mathematiker* (Königsberg, 1764), 34–38; M. Cantor, *Vorlesungen über Geschichte der Mathematik*, 2nd ed., II (Leipzig, 1913), 430–449; C. J. Gerhardt, *Geschichte der Mathematik in Deutschland* (Munich, 1877), 60–74; J. Giesing, *Stifels Arithmetica integra* (Döbeln, 1879); J. Grosse, "Michael Stiefel, der Prophet," in *Westermanns Monatshefte*, no. 85 (Oct. 1863), 1–40; J. E. Hofmann, "Michael Stifel 1487?–1567," *Sudhoffs Archiv . . .*, supp. no. 9 (1968); and "Michael Stifel," in *Jahrbuch für Geschichte der Oberdeutschen Reichsstädte*, Esslinger Studien, **14** (1968), 30–60; G. Kawerau, "Stiefel (Styfel)," in *Realencyclopädie für protestantische Theologie und Kirche*, 3rd ed., X (Leipzig, 1907), 74–88, and XXIV (Leipzig, 1913), 529; A. G. Kaestner, *Geschichte der Mathematik*, I (Göttingen, 1796), 112–128, 163–184; W. Kaunzner, "Deutsche Mathematiker des 15. und 16. Jahrhunderts und ihre Symbolik," *Veröffentlichungen des Forschungsinstitutes des Deutschen Museums für die Geschichte der Naturwissenschaften und der Technik*, ser. A, no. 90 (1971); W. Meretz, "Uber die erste Veröffentlichung von Kronbergs erstem Pfarrer Michael Stiefel," in *Jahresberichte des Kronberger Gymnasiums, die Altkönigsschule* (Jan. 1969), 15–20; and "Aus Stiefels Nachlass," *ibid.* (Feb. 1969), 5–6; J. E. Montucla, *Histoire des mathématiques*, 2nd ed., I (Paris, 1799), 614; G. C. Pisansky, *Historia litteraria Prussiae* (Königsberg, 1765), 228; G. T. Strobel, *Neue Beiträge besonders zur Literatur des 16. Jahrhunderts*, I, pt. 1 (Nuremberg–Altdorf, 1790), 3–90; P. Treutlein, "Das Rechnen im 16. Jahrhundert," in *Abhandlungen zur Geschichte der Mathematik*, **2** (1879), 1–124, esp. 17 f., 33 ff., 42 f., 48 ff., 77 ff.; and F. Unger, *Die Methodik der praktischen Arithmetik* (Leipzig, 1888), see index, 239. Concerning a MS from 1599 with solutions to problems from the *Coss*, see D. E. Smith, *Rara arithmetica* (Boston–London, 1908), 493.

For further bibliographical information, see especially Hofmann, Kawerau, and Meretz.

KURT VOGEL

STIRLING, JAMES (*b.* Garden, Stirlingshire, Scotland, 1692; *d.* Edinburgh, Scotland, 5 December 1770)

Stirling was the third son of Archibald Stirling and his second wife, Anna Hamilton, and grandson of Lord Garden of Keir. The whole family supported the Jacobite cause, and Archibald Stirling was in prison on a charge of high treason (of which he was later acquitted) while his son attended Glasgow University. James Stirling matriculated at Balliol College, Oxford, in 1711, without taking the oath. He himself was acquitted of the charge of "cursing King George" at the assizes. He seems to have left Oxford in 1716, after refusing to take the oaths needed to continue his scholarship. He did not graduate.

The previous year John Keill had mentioned Stirling's achievements in a letter to Newton, and at about the same time Stirling became acquainted with John Arbuthnot, the well-known mathematician, physician, and satirist. Such connections enabled him to publish (in Oxford) his first book, *Lineae tertii ordinis Neutonianae, sive illustratio tractatus D. Neutoni de enumeratione linearum tertii ordinis* (1717). The eight-page subscription list included Newton himself, besides many Oxford men. The book was dedicated to Nicholas Tron, the Venetian ambassador, who had become a fellow of the Royal Society in 1715, the same year in which Newton's correspondent, the Abbé Conti, was also elected. Stirling may then have held a teaching appointment in Edinburgh,[1] but the fame brought him by his book and the influence of his Venetian friends soon secured him a post in Venice. In 1718 Stirling submitted, through Newton, his first Royal Society paper, "Methodus differentialis Newtoniana illustrata," and in August 1719 he wrote from Venice thanking Newton for his kindness and offering to act as intermediary with Nikolaus I Bernoulli.

Little else is known about Stirling's stay in Venice, although his return to Britain is supposed to have been hastened because he had learned some secrets of the glass industry and may have feared for his life. By mid-1724 he had returned to Scotland, and a few months later he settled in London. In 1726 Newton helped secure Stirling's fellowship in the Royal Society and at about this time Stirling succeeded Benjamin Worster as one of the partners of the Little Tower Street Academy,[2] conducted by William Watts. This was one of the most successful schools in London; and, although he had to borrow money to pay for the mathematical instruments he needed, Stirling's finances improved. He helped to prepare *A Course of Mechanical and Experimental Philosophy* (to give it the title of a syllabus published in 1727) that included mechanics, hydrostatics, optics, and astronomy, a course very much in the tradition of Keill and Desaguliers, the leading scientific lecturer at that time. Stirling gave up some of his leisure to write his main work, *Methodus differentialis*, which appeared in 1730. A little later, through his friend Arbuthnot, Stirling was brought in as an adviser to Henry St. John, Lord Bolingbroke, since he was considered to be one of the few persons capable of understanding the financial calculations of Sir Robert Walpole. The latter's electoral victory of 1734 led to Bolingbroke's retirement to France.[3]

Given his reputation it was not surprising that Stirling was asked to reorganize the work of the Scottish Mining Company in the lead mines at Leadhills, Lanarkshire, near the border with Dumfries. Stirling was a successful administrator and spent most of his time after 1735 in the remote village. He married Barbara Watson of Thirtyacres, near Stirling; their only child, a daughter, married her cousin Archibald Stirling, who succeeded Stirling as manager at Leadhills.

Although Stirling continued his mathematical correspondence—with John Machin, Alexis-Claude Clairaut, Leonhard Euler, and Martin Folkes, among others—it is clear that most of his energy was spent in mining affairs. His most influential mathematical correspondent, Colin Maclaurin, died in 1746, largely as a result of his efforts in defending Edinburgh against the Jacobite rebellion of the preceding year; Stirling's own political principles prevented him from succeeding to the Edinburgh chair left vacant at Maclaurin's death.[4] In 1748 Stirling was elected to the Berlin Academy of Sciences, even though his directly mathematical activities had ceased; he resigned his fellowship in the Royal Society in 1754. In 1752 he was presented with a silver teakettle for conducting the first survey of the Clyde by the town council of Glasgow, where he also apparently acted as a teacher of bookkeeping, navigation, geography, practical mathematics, and French.[5] In his later years he became too frail to move about easily; he died on a visit to Edinburgh for medical treatment.

Stirling's *tractatus* of 1717 won him a considerable reputation. In it, after a considerable amount of introductory material, Stirling proved Newton's enumeration of seventy-two species of cubic curves and added four more. François Nicole and Nikolaus I Bernoulli then added two more curves, in 1731 and 1733, respectively, the latter in a letter to Stirling.

Stirling next turned from cubics to differences,

the other main topic of Newton's *Analysis* (1711). But these studies were interrupted by his moving from Oxford to Venice, from which he wrote to give permission for publication (without an intended supplement) of his 1719 paper "Methodus differentialis." This paper should not be confused with a later book of similar title, but it may be considered a precursor to it, since the book represents the further development and fuller treatment of the same ideas. Some of the same results are given in both; the so-called Newton-Stirling central difference formula,[6] which was also discussed by Cotes, is especially noteworthy.

The *Methodus differentialis: sive tractatus de summatione et interpolatione serierum infinitarum* of 1730 consists of a relatively brief introduction followed by two parts, on summation and interpolation. The work was sufficiently important to be reprinted twice during Stirling's lifetime, in 1753 and 1764, and to be published in an English translation in 1749.[7] The translation was made by Francis Holliday, who was then master of a grammar school near Retford, Nottinghamshire, as well as editor of *Miscellanea curiosa mathematica*, one of a number of relatively short-lived popular mathematical serials[8] published during the mid-eighteenth century. (The translator's preface shows that Holliday had originally intended to publish the translation in his serial and indicates that he planned to follow *The Differential Method* with other translations of Stirling's work as well; perhaps the reception of the book was insufficiently favorable for these other plans to materialize.)

In his preface, Stirling indicated that Newton, too, had considered the problem of speeding the convergence of series by transformations involving differences. De Moivre had made progress with a recurring series, but his methods could be generalized to other series in which "the relation of the terms is varied according to some regular law." The most useful representation of terms was in a series of factorials, positive or negative. Manipulation often required conversion of factorials into powers, and Stirling gave tables of the coefficients for this conversion. He then showed that the columns of the tables gave the coefficients for the inverse expressions, of powers in factorials; those for positive (negative) powers are now called "Stirling Numbers of the first [or second] kind" in his honor.[9] The so-called Stirling series

$$\frac{1}{x-a}=\frac{1}{x}+\frac{a}{x(x+1)}+\frac{a(a+1)}{x(x+1)(x+2)+\cdots}$$

is equivalent to the expansion of $(z^2 + nz)^{-1}$ in negative factorials, which is the last example given in his introduction.

Stirling explained that part one of the *Methodus differentialis*, "on the summation of series," was designed to show how to transform series in order to make them converge more rapidly and so to expedite calculation. As an example[10] he gave the series

$$\sum_1^\infty 1/(2n-1)2n,$$

studied by Brouncker in connection with the quadrature of the hyperbola; Stirling concluded that "if anyone would find an accurate value of this series to nine places . . . they would require one thousand million of terms; and this series converges much swifter than many others. . . ." Another example[11] was the calculation—"which Mr. Leibnitz long ago greatly desired"—of

$$\frac{\pi}{4} = 1 - \frac{1}{3} + \frac{1}{5} - \frac{1}{7} + \cdots.$$

Stirling's sixth proposition was effectively an early example of a test for the convergence of an infinite product; he gave many examples of problems, now solved by the use of gamma functions, that illustrated his aim. The last section of the first part of the book contains an incomplete development of De Moivre's principles used in recurring series; for linear relations with polynomial coefficients connecting a finite number of terms, Stirling reduced the solution to that of a corresponding differential equation.

Stirling continued to show his analytical skill in part two, on the interpolation of series. As an example[12] of interpolation at the beginning of a series, he took the gamma series $T_{n+1} = nT_n$, with $T_1 = 1$, to find the term $T_{3/2}$ intermediate between the two terms T_1 and T_2 and calculated the result to ten decimal places: his result is now written $\Gamma(1/2) = \sqrt{\pi}$. Stirling's other results are now expressed using gamma functions or hypergeometric series. He also discussed[13] the sum of any number of logarithms of arguments in arithmetical progression and obtained the logarithmic equivalent of the result, sometimes called Stirling's theorem, that

$$n! \sim n^{n+1/2}e^{-n}.$$

Just before leaving London, Stirling contributed a short article to the *Philosophical Transactions of the Royal Society* entitled "Of the Figure of the Earth, and the Variation of Gravity on the Sur-face." In it he stated, without proof, that the earth was an oblate spheroid, supporting Newton against the rival Cassinian view. This paper was unknown to Clairaut, who submitted a paper partly duplicating it from Lapland, where he was part of the expedition under Maupertuis that proved Newton's hypothesis.[14] Although Stirling contributed another technical paper ten years later, it is clear that his new post in Scotland did not give him an opportunity to pursue his mathematical activities in any depth and that his significant work was confined to the 1720's and 1730's.

NOTES

1. W. Steven, *History of George Heriot's Hospital*, F. W. Bedford, ed. (Edinburgh, 1859), 307, mentions James Stirling as assistant master, elected 12 August 1717.
2. N. Hans, *New Trends in Education in the Eighteenth Century* (London, 1951), 82–87, gives the best account of the Academy, but his dates for Stirling and Patoun are unreliable.
3. The connection with Bolingbroke is given by Ramsay (see bibliography), 308–309, but is ignored in most accounts.
4. A. Grant, *The Story of the University of Edinburgh*, II (London, 1884), 301.
5. Glasgow City Archives and *Glasgow Courant*, Nov. 1753, Nov. 1754, and Nov. 1755, reported by M. J. M. McDonald and J. A. Cable respectively.
6. D. T. Whiteside, ed., *The Mathematical Papers of Isaac Newton*, IV (Cambridge, 1971), 58, n. 19.
7. The Latin and English versions had 153 and 141 pages, respectively; references in Tweedie to the Latin ed. can be converted to those to the latter, given here, by subtracting about ten.
8. R. C. Archibald, "Notes on some Minor English Mathematical Serials," in *Mathematical Gazette*, 14, no. 200 (April 1929), 379–400.
9. Stirling, *Differential Method*, 17, 20. A useful, modern textbook, C. Jordan's *Calculus of Finite Differences*, 2nd ed. (New York, 1947), devotes ch. 4 to Stirling's numbers. Jordan and Tweedie give details of the articles by N. Nielsen that stress the significance of Stirling.
10. *Differential Method*, 23–25.
11. *Ibid.*, 27–28.
12. *Ibid.*, 99–103.
13. *Ibid.*, 123–125.
14. I. Todhunter, *A History of the Mathematical Theories of Attraction*, I (London, 1873), ch. 4.

BIBLIOGRAPHY

I. ORIGINAL WORKS. Stirling's works are listed in the text. His major work is *Methodus differentialis: sive tractatus de summatione et interpolatione serierum infinitarum* (London, 1730). The family papers are at the General Register House, Edinburgh; they contain disappointingly few mathematical papers, but more about Stirling's mining activities.

II. SECONDARY LITERATURE. The main authority is the unindexed volume C. Tweedie, *James Stirling: A Sketch of His Life and Works Along With His Scientific Correspondence* (Oxford, 1922); also J. O. Mitchell's

Old Glasgow Essays (Glasgow, 1905), repr. from "James Stirling Mathematician," *Glasgow Herald* (1886); and J. Ramsay's *Scotland and Scotsmen in the Eighteenth Century*, A. Allardyce, ed., II (Edinburgh, 1888), 306–326. Other works are detailed in the notes and in Tweedie.

P. J. WALLIS

STOKES, GEORGE GABRIEL (*b.* Skreen, County Sligo, Ireland, 13 August 1819; *d.* Cambridge, England, 1 February 1903)

Stokes was born into an Anglo-Irish family that had found its vocation for a number of generations in the established Church of Ireland. His father, Gabriel Stokes, was the rector of the parish of Skreen in County Sligo. His mother, Elizabeth Haughton, was the daughter of a rector. The youngest of six children, Stokes had three brothers, all of whom took holy orders, and two sisters. He received his earliest education from his father and the parish clerk in Skreen. Stokes then attended school in Dublin before going to Bristol College in Bristol, England, to prepare to enter university. Later in life Stokes recalled that one of his teachers at Bristol, Francis William Newman, a classicist and mathematician, had influenced him profoundly. In 1837 Stokes entered Pembroke College, Cambridge, where during his second year he began to read mathematics with William Hopkins, an outstanding private tutor whose influence on Stokes probably far outweighed that of the official college teaching. When he graduated as senior wrangler and first Smith's prizeman in 1841, Pembroke College immediately elected him to a fellowship.

Stokes became the Lucasian professor at Cambridge in 1849, rescuing the chair from the doldrums into which it had fallen, and restoring it to the eminence it had when held by Newton. Since the Lucasian chair was poorly endowed, Stokes taught at the Government School of Mines in London in the 1850's to augment his income. He held the Lucasian chair until his death in 1903. In 1857 he married Mary Susanna, daughter of the Reverend Thomas Romney Robinson, the astronomer at Armagh Observatory in Ireland. Stokes had to relinquish his fellowship to marry, but under new regulations he held a fellowship again from 1869 to 1902. A very active member of the Cambridge Philosophical Society, he was president from 1859 to 1861. Always willing to perform administrative tasks, Stokes became a secretary for the Royal Society of London in 1854, conscientiously carrying out his duties until 1885 when he became president of the society, a post he held until 1890. The society awarded him the Copley Medal in 1893. From 1887 to 1891 he represented the University of Cambridge in Parliament at Westminster; and from 1886 to 1903 he was president of the Victoria Institute of London, a society founded in 1865 to examine the relationship between Christianity and contemporary thought, especially science. Stokes was universally honored, particularly in later life, with degrees, medals, and membership in foreign societies. He was knighted in 1889. The University of Cambridge lavishly celebrated his jubilee as Lucasian professor in 1899, and three years later Pembroke College bestowed on him its highest honor by electing him master.

As William Thomson commented in his obituary of Stokes, his theoretical and experimental investigations covered the entire realm of natural philosophy. Stokes systematically explored areas of hydrodynamics, the elasticity of solids, and the behavior of waves in elastic solids including the diffraction of light, always concentrating on physically important problems and making his mathematical analyses subservient to physical requirements. His few excursions into pure mathematics were prompted either by a need to develop methods to solve specific physical problems or by a desire to establish the validity of mathematics he was already employing. He also investigated problems in light, gravity, sound, heat, meteorology, solar physics, and chemistry. The field of electricity and magnetism lay almost untouched by him, however; he always regarded that as the domain of his friend Thomson.

After graduating, Stokes followed Hopkins' advice to pursue hydrodynamics, a field in which George Green and James Challis had recently been working at Cambridge. Thus in 1842 Stokes began his investigations by analyzing the steady motion of an incompressible fluid in two dimensions. In one instance, for motion symmetrical about an axis, he was able to solve the problem in three dimensions. In the following year he continued this work. Some of the problems that Stokes tackled had already been solved by Duhamel in his work on the permanent distribution of temperature in solids. Despite this duplication, which Stokes mentioned, he deemed the application of the formulas to fluid flow instead of heat flow sufficiently different to warrant publication. Stokes had not yet analyzed the motion of a fluid with internal friction, later known as viscosity, although references to the effects of friction continually appear in his papers. The problem, however, of the motion of a fluid in a closed box with an interior in the shape of a rectangular parallelepiped, which Stokes solved in 1843, was attacked partly with an eye to possible use in an experiment to test the effects of friction. By 1846 he had performed the experiment, but to Stokes's disappointment the differences between the experimental results and the theoretical calculations that excluded friction were too small to be useful as a test of any theory of internal friction.

Stokes's analysis of the internal friction of fluids appeared in 1845. Navier, Poisson, and Saint-Venant had already derived independently the equations for fluid flow with friction, but in the early 1840's Stokes was not thoroughly familiar with the French literature of mathematical physics, a common situation in Cambridge. Stokes said that he discovered Poisson's paper only after he had derived his own equations. He insisted, however, that his assumptions differed sufficiently from Poisson's and Navier's to justify publishing his own results. One novel feature of Stokes's derivation was that instead of using the Frenchmen's ultimate molecules he assumed that the fluid was infinitely divisible, for he was careful not to commit himself to the idea that ultimate molecules existed. Another novel feature was his treatment of the relative motion of the parts of the fluid. He was able also to use these equations and the principles behind them to deduce the equations of motion for elastic solids, although he introduced two independent constants for what were later called the moduli of compression and rigidity, instead of one independent constant to describe elasticity as Poisson had. Stokes noted that the equations of motion he obtained for an elastic solid were the same as those that others had derived for the motion of the luminiferous ether in a vacuum. He then justified the applicability of these equations to the ether partly on the basis of the law of continuity, which permitted no sharp distinction between a viscous fluid and a solid, and which he believed held throughout nature.

Stokes became well known in England through a report on recent developments in hydrodynamics, which he presented in 1846 to the British Association for the Advancement of Science. So perceptive and suggestive was his survey that it immediately drew attention to his abilities and further enhanced his reputation as a promising young man. The report shows Stokes's increasing familiarity with the French literature on hydrodynamics and reveals his admiration for the work of George Green.

Stokes then pursued (1847) the topic of oscillatory waves in water, which he had suggested in his report merited further investigation. Poisson and Cauchy had already analyzed the complicated situation in which waves were produced by arbitrary disturbances in the fluid, but Stokes ignored the disturbances to examine the propagation of oscillatory waves the height of which is not negligible compared with their wavelength. Much later, in 1880, Stokes examined the shape of the highest oscillatory waves that could be propagated without changing their form. He showed that the crest of these waves enclosed an angle of 120°, and proposed a method for calculating the shape of the waves.

In one of his most important papers on hydrodynamics, presented in 1850, Stokes applied his theory of the internal friction of fluids to the behavior of pendulums. Poisson, Challis, Green, and Plana had analyzed in the 1830's the behavior of spheres oscillating in fluids, but Stokes took into account the effects of internal friction, including both spherical bobs and cylindrical pendulums. He then compared his theoretical calculations with the results of experiments conducted by others, including Coulomb, Bessel, and Baily. In the same paper he showed that the behavior of water droplets in the atmosphere depended almost completely on the internal friction of air and so explained how clouds could form in the atmosphere of the earth.

On account of his theoretical analysis and experimental observations of pendulums combined with his study of gravity at the surface of the earth, Stokes became the foremost British authority on the principles of geodesy. In his study of 1849 he related the shape of the surface of the earth to the strength of gravity on it without having to adopt any assumptions whatsoever about the interior of the earth. He obtained Clairaut's theorem as a particular result. Stokes assumed merely that the earth has a surface of equilibrium, one perpendicular to the gravity on it, whereas previously assumptions about the distribution of matter in the earth were always introduced to derive Clairaut's theorem. One result of his analysis was an explanation of the well-known observation that gravity is less on a continent than on an island. When the pendulum observations for the Great Trigonometrical Survey of India were conducted from 1865 to 1873, his expertise, together with his position as secretary to the Royal Society, made him an obvious person for the surveyors to turn to for advice, even though numerical calculations based on some of Stokes's own formulas would have been too laborious to carry out.

Occasionally Stokes studied problems in sound, which he considered a branch of hydrodynamics. In 1848 and 1849 he replied to Challis' claim of a contradiction in the commonly accepted theory, and in doing so Stokes introduced surfaces of discontinuity in the velocity and density of the medium. But later, on the basis of the argument by William Thomson and Lord Rayleigh that the proposed motion violated the conservation of energy, he retracted the idea that such motion, later called shock waves, could take place. (Stokes frequently crossed swords with Challis publicly in the *Philosophical Magazine.* They disagreed over the basic equations of fluid flow [1842, 1843, 1851], the theory of aberration [1845, 1846, 1848], and the theory of colors [1856].) In 1857 Stokes explained succinctly the effect of wind on the intensity of sound. Also, using a sphere to represent a bell and an infinite cylinder to represent a string or wire, he analyzed mathematically the production of sound by the transmission of motion from a vibrating body to a surrounding gas (1868). Poisson had already solved the case of the sphere, but Stokes was quick to point out that Poisson had examined a different problem. Stokes's analysis explained John Leslie's observation that hydrogen or a mixture of hydrogen and air transmitted the sound of a bell feebly, and why sounding boards were necessary for stringed instruments to be heard, the vibrations being communicated to the board and then to the air. In a manner typical of Stokes, he then proceeded to explain how sound was produced by telegraph wires suspended tightly between poles.

The wave theory of light was well established at Cambridge when Stokes entered the university, and he seems to have embraced it right from the beginning of his studies. His earliest investigations in this field centered on the nature of the ether, beginning in 1845 with a proof that the wave theory was consistent with a theory of aberration in which the earth dragged along the ether instead of passing freely through it, as Fresnel had suggested. In 1846 Stokes showed that when the motion of the earth through the ether was not ignored, the laws of reflection and refraction remained unchanged in his own theory as well as in Fresnel's theory, thus offering no way to decide between the two theories of the interaction of the ether with the earth. In 1848 Stokes examined mathematically the properties of the ether, and by analogy with his own theory of the motion of fluids with internal friction he combined in his ether the seemingly contradictory properties of fluidity and solidity. He maintained that to examine the motion of the earth, the ether must be viewed as a very rarefied fluid, but to examine the propagation of light the same ether must be regarded as an elastic solid. To illustrate his view Stokes suggested that the ether is related to air in the same way as thin jelly is to water. Also in 1848 Stokes employed the wave theory of light to calculate the intensity of the central spot in Newton's rings beyond the critical angle of the incident light at which the rings vanish, leaving only the central black spot. He also examined the perfectly black central spot that results when the rings are formed between glasses of the same material. Fresnel had already analyzed this phenomenon, but Stokes's assumptions and derivation differed from his.

In a major paper on the dynamical theory of diffraction (1849), Stokes treated the ether as a sensibly incompressible elastic medium. Poisson had already calculated the disturbance at any point at any time resulting from a given initial disturbance in a finite portion of an elastic solid; but Stokes presented a different derivation, which he deemed simpler and more straightforward than Poisson's. Stokes also determined the disturbance in any direction in secondary waves, upon which the dynamical theory of diffraction depends, not limiting himself, as others had, to secondary waves in the vicinity of the normal to the primary wave. Moreover, by comparing his theory with the results of diffraction experiments that he conducted with a glass grating, Stokes answered the vexing question about the direction of vibrations of plane-polarized light by concluding that they were perpendicular to the plane of polarization.

At this time, both Stokes's theoretical analyses and his experiments covered a broad area of optics. In addition to his experiments on diffraction, he conducted experiments on Talbot's bands (1848), on the recently discovered Haidinger's brushes (1850), on phase differences in streams of plane-polarized light reflected from metallic surfaces (1850), and on the colors of thick plates (1851). Occasionally he invented and constructed his own instruments, as he did to facilitate measurements of astigmatism in the human eye (1849). In 1851 Stokes devised and largely constructed an instrument for analyzing elliptically polarized light. Here we see an excellent example of his theoretical studies complementing his experimental and instrumental work. In 1852 he published a mathematical analysis of the composition and resolution of streams of polarized light originating from different sources; the four parameters by which he characterized polarized light in this study became known as the Stokes parameters.

Stokes's explanation of fluorescence, published in 1852, for which the Royal Society awarded him the Rumford Medal, arose from his investigations begun the previous year into the blue color exhibited at the surface of an otherwise colorless and transparent solution of sulfate of quinine when viewed by transmitted light. Sir John Herschel had described this phenomenon in 1845, and Sir David Brewster had also examined it. Stokes, who had started by repeating some of Herschel's experiments and then had devised his own, rapidly concluded that light of a higher refrangibility, which corresponded to light of a higher frequency, produced light of lower refrangibility in the solution. Thus the invisible ultraviolet rays were absorbed in the solution to produce blue light at the surface. Stokes named this phenomenon fluorescence. Always looking for applications of optics, he quickly devised a method for exhibiting the phenomenon that did not require direct sunlight and so would render a chemist independent of the fickle British weather in utilizing fluorescence to distinguish between various chemicals. In opening up the entire field of fluorescence to investigation, Stokes showed how it could be used to study the ultraviolet segment of the spectrum. By 1862 Stokes was using the spark from an induction coil to generate the spectra of various metals employed as electrodes. The invisible rays of the spectra were then examined and recorded systematically by means of fluorescence, although Stokes knew that photography was already beginning to replace fluorescence as a tool for mapping out spectra. Through his studies on fluorescence Stokes in 1862 began to collaborate with the Reverend W. Vernon Harcourt, who was one of the few people at that time attempting to vary the chemical composition of glass to produce new glasses with improved optical properties. Hoping to make glasses that would allow them to construct a perfectly achromatic combination, they collaborated until Harcourt's death in 1871.

While studying spectra by means of fluorescence, Stokes speculated on the physical principles of spectra, a topic of growing interest in the 1850's. Although Stokes always disclaimed priority in developing the principles of spectrum analysis, William Thomson insisted vigorously that Stokes taught him the principles in their conversations no later than 1852. They were discussing the topic in their correspondence in 1854 and speculating on the possibility of employing spectra to iden-

tify the chemical constituents of the sun. But Stokes did not publish anything on these ideas at that time, so the credit for the development of the principles of spectrum analysis went later to Kirchhoff and Bunsen.

Stokes's use of fluorescence in the 1850's as a tool for investigation typified his increasing emphasis on the exploitation of light to study other aspects of nature than light itself. In the 1860's, for instance, he drew the attention of chemists to the value of optical properties such as absorption and colored reflection as well as fluorescence in discriminating between organic substances. He was also a pioneer in combining spectrum analysis with chemical reactions to study blood.

Stokes's final major mathematical study on light was his classic report of 1862 on the dynamical theory of double refraction, presented to the British Association. He reviewed the theories of Fresnel, Cauchy, Neumann, Green, and MacCullagh, showing his preference for the ideas of Green and pointing out that he thought the true dynamical theory had not yet been discovered. Continuing his study of the dynamical theories, Stokes later showed experimentally that double refraction could not depend on differences of inertia in different directions, an idea W. J. M. Rankine, Lord Rayleigh, and Stokes had all entertained. He concluded that Huygens' construction for the wave fronts should be followed. A very brief summary of his experiments and conclusion was published in 1872, but a detailed account that he promised to present to the Royal Society was never published.

Stokes's papers on pure mathematics were tailored to his requirements for solving physical problems. His paper on periodic series (1847) consisted of an examination of various aspects of the validity of the expansion of an arbitrary function in terms of functions of known form. The expansions are now called Fourier series. In the paper Stokes applied his findings to problems in heat, hydrodynamics, and electricity. In 1850 he calculated the value of $\int_0^\infty \cos \frac{\pi}{2}(x^3 - mx)dx$, when m is large and real, an integral that had arisen in the optical studies of G. B. Airy. The method employed by Stokes for expanding the integral in the form of power series that initially converge rapidly and ultimately diverge rapidly was the one he afterward used in 1850 to determine the motion of a cylindrical pendulum in a fluid with internal friction. In 1857 he solved the equation $\frac{d^2w}{dz^2} - 9zw = 0$ in the complex z-plane, which was equivalent to calculating the definite integral above. He also showed that the arbitrary constants forming the coefficients of the linear combination of the two independent asymptotic solutions for large $|z|$ were discontinuous, changing abruptly when the amplitude of z passed through certain values. The discontinuous behavior became known as the Stokes phenomenon, and the lines for which the amplitude of z has a constant value at which the discontinuities occur became known as the Stokes lines. He later examined (1868) a method of determining the arbitrary constants for the asymptotic solutions of the Bessel

equation, $\dfrac{d^2y}{dx^2} + \dfrac{1}{x}\dfrac{dy}{dx} - \dfrac{n^2}{x^2}y = y$, where n is a real

constant. These studies in mathematics, however, formed only one small area of Stokes's publications.

In the early years of his career, through the Cambridge Philosophical Society, his teaching, and the examinations he composed, Stokes was a pivotal figure in furthering the dissemination of French mathematical physics at Cambridge. Partly because of this, and because of his own researches, Stokes was a very important formative influence on subsequent generations of Cambridge men, including Maxwell. With Green, who in turn had influenced him, Stokes followed the work of the French, especially Lagrange, Laplace, Fourier, Poisson, and Cauchy. This is seen most clearly in his theoretical studies in optics and hydrodynamics; but it should also be noted that Stokes, even as an undergraduate, experimented incessantly. Yet his interests and investigations extended beyond physics, for his knowledge of chemistry and botany was extensive, and often his work in optics drew him into those fields.

Stokes's output of papers dropped rapidly in the 1850's, while his theoretical studies gradually gave way to experimental investigations. This occurred partly when he became a secretary to the Royal Society in 1854 and partly after he married in 1857. He often took on heavy administrative duties, which prevented him from conducting any research; and so from the 1860's many of his publications related to points arising from his official duty of reading papers submitted to the Royal Society. Stokes's papers eventually became a guide to other people's problems and interests. This is also seen in his correspondence with Thomson, for whom Stokes was a lifelong sounding board.

Throughout his life Stokes invariably took time to reply in detail to private as well as official requests for aid in solving problems, a frequent occurrence. A good example is his paper (1849) on the solution of a differential equation representing the deflection of iron railroad bridges, which Robert Willis, who was on a royal commission looking into the behavior of iron in various structures, had asked him to examine.

Although Stokes never fulfilled the expectations of his contemporaries by publishing a treatise on optics, his Burnett lectures on light, delivered at the University of Aberdeen from 1883 to 1885, were published as a single volume. The Gifford lectures on natural theology, which he delivered at Edinburgh in 1891 and 1893, were also published. A devoutly religious man, Stokes was deeply interested in the relationship of science to religion. This was especially true toward the end of his life, although he did not feel qualified to do justice to his Gifford lectureship.

BIBLIOGRAPHY

I. ORIGINAL WORKS. A comprehensive list of Stokes's papers appears in the Royal Society *Catalogue of Scientific Papers*, V, 838–840; VIII, 1022–1023; XI, 505–506; XVIII, 977. Almost all of his published papers are included in *Mathematical and Physical Papers*, 5 vols. (Cambridge, 1880–1905); vols. I–III were edited by Stokes, and vols. IV–V posthumously by Sir Joseph Larmor. Vol. V also contains a previously unpublished MS on waves in water, as well as Smith's Prize examination papers and mathematical tripos papers set by Stokes at Cambridge.

A list of lectures and addresses on scientific topics, which were not printed in *Mathematical and Physical Papers*, is included in Larmor's preface to vol. V. A second ed. with a new preface by C. Truesdell appeared as *Mathematical and Physical Papers by the Late Sir George Gabriel Stokes, Bart. . . . Second Edition, Reprinting the Former of 1880–1905, Prepared by the Author (Volumes 1–3) and Sir J. Larmor (Volumes 4–5). With Their Annotations and the Obituary Notices by Lord Kelvin and Lord Rayleigh, and Also Including the Portions of the Original Papers Which Were Omitted From the Former Edition . . . ,* 5 vols. (New York–London, 1966). *Memoirs and Scientific Correspondence of the Late Sir George Gabriel Stokes . . . Selected and Arranged by Joseph Larmor . . . ,* 2 vols. (Cambridge, 1907; repr., New York–London, 1971), contains selected correspondence of Stokes, memoirs by his daughter Mrs. Laurence Humphrey and some of his colleagues, and miscellaneous material about Stokes's life and work.

Cambridge University Library, England, holds an extensive collection of Stokes's MSS, especially the Stokes Papers, which include his scientific, miscellaneous, family, Royal Society, and religious correspondence; notes for lectures; notes taken in lectures; and material concerning university administration. Add. MS 7618 at Cambridge contains the Stokes-Kelvin correspondence. The Scientific Periodicals Library, Cambridge, holds a number of Stokes's notebooks, some containing records of his experiments.

From the journal's inception in 1857 to 1878, Stokes, with A. Cayley and M. Hermite, assisted editors J. J. Sylvester and N. M. Ferrers of the *Quarterly Journal of Pure and Applied Mathematics* (London). He contributed articles, mostly on physical optics, and revised others on physical topics taken from the *Penny Cyclopaedia*, for *The English Cyclopaedia. A New Dictionary of Universal Knowledge. Conducted by Charles Knight. Arts and Sciences*, 8 vols. (London, 1859–1861). The three series of Burnett lectures were issued separately, and then published together as *Burnett Lectures. On Light. In Three Courses Delivered at Aberdeen in November, 1883, December, 1884, and November, 1885* (London–New York, 1887; 2nd ed., 1892), with a German trans. by O. Dziobek appearing as *Das Licht* (Leipzig, 1888).

Apart from his contributions to the *Journal of the Transactions of the Victoria Institute* (London), Stokes's principal writings on religion and on aspects of its relationship to science are *Natural Theology. The Gifford Lectures Delivered Before the University of Edinburgh in 1891* (London, 1891), *Natural Theology. The Gifford Lectures . . . 1893* (London, 1893), and *Conditional Immortality. A Help to Sceptics. A Series of Letters Addressed . . . to James Marchant (With a Prefatory Note by the Latter)* (London, 1897).

The *Transactions of the Cambridge Philosophical Society*, **18** (1900), consists of memoirs presented to the society to celebrate Stokes's jubilee as Lucasian professor.

II. SECONDARY LITERATURE. The two most important obituaries assessing Stokes's scientific work are Lord Kelvin, in *Nature*, **67** (1903), 337–338, also in *Mathematical and Scientific Papers*, 2nd ed., V, xxvii–xxxii, and Lord Rayleigh, *Proceedings of the Royal Society*, **75** (1905), 199–216, repr. in both eds. of *Mathematical and Physical Papers*, V, ix–xxv.

Since these obituaries and Larmor's *Memoir and Scientific Correspondence . . .*, little has been published on Stokes's scientific work. A few recent accounts are Truesdell's preface to the *Mathematical and Physical Papers*, 2nd ed., I, IVA–IVL; I. Grattan-Guinness, *The Development of the Foundations of Mathematical Analysis From Euler to Riemann* (Cambridge, Mass.–London, 1970), 113–120; and David B. Wilson, "George Gabriel Stokes on Stellar Aberration and the Luminiferous Ether," in *British Journal for the History of Science*, **6** (1972–1973), 57–72.

E. M. PARKINSON

STOLZ, OTTO (*b.* Hall [now Solbad Hall in Tirol], Austria, 3 July 1842; *d.* Innsbruck, Austria, 25 October 1905)

Stolz was the son of a physician who later achieved some prominence as a psychiatrist. After graduating from the Gymnasium at Innsbruck, he studied mathematics and natural sciences at the University of Innsbruck and later at Vienna. In 1864 he received the Ph.D. at the University of Vienna, where he was subsequently a *Privatdozent* until 1869, when he obtained a scholarship for further study at Berlin and Göttingen.

From 1869 to 1871 Stolz attended courses given by Weierstrass, Kummer, and Kronecker at Berlin and by Clebsch and Klein at Göttingen. Weierstrass made the greatest impression on him and led him to extend his research from geometry to analysis.

In July 1872 Stolz was appointed associate professor at the University of Innsbruck. He became a full professor in 1876 and married in the same year. He remained in Innsbruck for the rest of his life.

Stolz's earliest papers were concerned with analytic or algebraic geometry, including spherical trigonometry. He later dedicated an increasing part of his research to real analysis, in particular to convergence problems in the theory of series, including double series; to the discussion of the limits of indeterminate ratios; and to integration. Stolz was the first to formulate the counterpart, for double series, of Cauchy's necessary and sufficient condition for convergence. He also generalized Abel's theorem on the behavior of a power series in radial approach to the circle of convergence ("regularity of Abelian summability") to approach in an angular region with a vertex on the circle of convergence.

During his lifetime, and for some time afterward, Stolz was known as the author of several carefully written textbooks, of which *Vorlesungen über allgemeine Arithmetik* (1885–1886) and *Theoretische Arithmetik* (1900–1902) in particular gained wide recognition. The latter work was written with his student J. A. Gmeiner. Stolz is known today for his contributions to many questions of detail rather than for any major single achievement. For example, he is credited by K. Knopp with having been the first to show that every irrational number has a unique representation in decimal notation.

Stolz was greatly interested in the history of mathematics. After the Weierstrass ϵ, δ approach had found general acceptance in the early 1870's, he was the first to point out that Bolzano had suggested essentially the same approach even before

Cauchy introduced his own, less rigorous method. Under the influence of P. du Bois-Reymond, Stolz also reexamined the theory of infinitely small and infinitely large quantities that had been used, on shaky foundations, until the advent of Weierstrass' method.

BIBLIOGRAPHY

I. ORIGINAL WORKS. Stolz's writings include "Beweis einiger Sätze über Potenzreihen," in *Zeitschrift für Mathematik und Physik*, **20** (1875), 369–376; "B. Bolzano's Bedeutung in der Geschichte der Infinitesimalrechnung," in *Mathematische Annalen*, **18** (1881), 255–279; *Vorlesungen über allgemeine Arithmetik*, 2 vols. (Leipzig, 1885–1886); and *Theoretische Arithmetik*, 2 vols. (Leipzig, 1900–1902), written with J. A. Gmeiner.

II. SECONDARY LITERATURE. See J. A. Gmeiner, "Otto Stolz," in *Jahresberichte der Deutschen Mathematikervereinigung*, **15** (1906), 309–322; and K. Knopp, *Theorie und Anwendung der unendlichen Reihen*, Grundlehren der mathematischen Wissenschaften in Einzeldarstellungen, no. 2 (Berlin, 1922).

ABRAHAM ROBINSON

STONEY, GEORGE JOHNSTONE (*b.* Oakley Park, Kingstown [now Dún Laoghaire], County Dublin, Ireland, 15 February 1826; *d.* London, England, 5 July 1911)

Stoney was the eldest son of George Stoney and his wife, Anne, who were Protestant landowners. The family was a talented one: Stoney's younger brother, Bindon Blood Stoney (1828–1909); his son, George Gerald Stoney (1863–1942); and his nephew, George Francis Fitzgerald (1851–1901), made significant contributions to science and technology, and were fellows of the Royal Society.

Stoney graduated from Trinity College, Dublin, in 1848 and became assistant to Lord Rosse in his observatory at Parsonstown (now Birr). After failing to obtain a fellowship at Trinity College, he obtained the chair of natural philosophy at Queen's College, Galway, which he held for five years. In 1857 he returned to Dublin as secretary to Queen's University, in which post he spent the rest of his working life. Stoney was a member of the Royal Irish Academy and the Royal Dublin Society, and was secretary of the latter for over twenty years. In 1893 he moved to London and became involved in the affairs of the Royal Society, of which he had been elected a fellow in 1861; in 1898 he was vice-president and a member of the Council.

Stoney had an interest in all fields of science and, like many of his Irish contemporaries, applied mathematics to the solution of scientific problems. He was particularly interested in spectrum analysis. A paper he wrote in 1868 suggested that spectral lines were due to periodic motions inside the atom rather than to the translational motion of molecules. Stoney continued this line of thought for a number of years and, as a result, put forward important ideas on atomic structure. In 1891 he explained the presence of double and triple lines in spectra by apsidal and precessional motions of orbital electrons.

Since his early work in Rosse's observatory, Stoney maintained an interest in astronomy and wrote many papers on the subject. Using the kinetic theory as a basis of his work, he reached certain conclusions concerning the atmospheres of planets. Stoney's paper of 1897 suggested that if the velocity of molecules exceeded a limit set by the force of gravity, then the molecules would fly off into space. By this means he explained the absence of an atmosphere on the moon.

Stoney probably is best-known for having coined the term "electron." He hoped that by a careful choice of fundamental units, science would be simplified; and at the 1874 meeting of the British Association, he presented the paper "On the Physical Units of Nature." One of the basic units he suggested was the charge carried on a hydrogen ion, which he determined from experimental data. The weight of hydrogen liberated on electrolysis by a given quantity of electricity was known; and by calculating the number of atoms associated with this weight of hydrogen, Stoney found the electric charge associated with each atom. A similar theory of electrical atomicity was advanced by Helmholtz in his Faraday lecture in 1881, and ten years later Stoney introduced the word "electron" for this fundamental unit. The term later came to be used for the "corpuscles" discovered by J. J. Thomson.

BIBLIOGRAPHY

I. ORIGINAL WORKS. Stoney's writings include "The Internal Motions of Gases Compared With the Motions of Waves of Light," in *Philosophical Magazine*, 4th ser., **36** (1868), 132–141; "On the Physical Units of Nature," *ibid.*, 5th ser., **11** (1881), 381–389; "On the Cause of Double Lines and of Equidistant Satellites in the Spectra of Gases," in *Scientific Transactions of the Royal Dublin Society*, **4** (1891), 563–608; "Of the 'Electron' or Atom of Electricity," in *Philosophical Magazine*, 5th ser., **38** (1894), 418–420; and "Of Atmospheres Upon Planets and Satellites," in *Scientific Transactions of the Royal

Dublin Society, **6** (1897), 305–328.

II. SECONDARY LITERATURE. Biographies are by F. T. Trouton in *Nature*, **87** (1911), 50–51; and by an anonymous author in *Proceedings of the Royal Society*, **86** (1912), xx–xxv.

BRIAN B. KELHAM

STØRMER, FREDRIK CARL MÜLERTZ (*b.* Skien, Norway, 3 September 1874; *d.* Oslo, Norway, 13 August 1957)

Størmer's father, Georg Størmer, was a pharmacist; his mother was the former Elisabeth Mülertz. When he was twelve, the family moved to Oslo (then Christiania). As a young boy he was interested in botany, which remained a lifelong hobby. During his high school years, Størmer's interest and ability in mathematics became apparent; and through a friend of the family, who was a professor of mathematics at the University of Oslo, he received instruction in that science. His first publication was published while he was still in high school (1892). Størmer entered the University of Oslo in 1892, received the master's degree in 1898, and was awarded the doctorate in 1903. In the latter year he became professor of pure mathematics, a post he held until his retirement in 1944.

Størmer's first papers were on number theory; but in 1903 he met the physicist Kristian Birkeland, who studied the polar aurora. Birkeland approached the problem experimentally, by bombarding a magnetic sphere in a vacuum with cathode rays. In this way it was possible to observe phenomena resembling the polar aurora. Størmer made the field observations and the theoretical calculations of the charged particles. The observations of the polar aurora were made photographically, by taking parallactic pictures along a base line. Størmer thus accumulated an enormous amount of observational material, not only on the altitude but also on the size, shape, and periodicity of the polar aurora. In the course of this work he also acquired interesting information on noctilucent and mother-of-pearl (nacreous) clouds. He constructed the instruments and worked out the procedures for these observations himself, showing a gift for experimentation that is rare among pure mathematicians.

Størmer's other approach to the study of the polar aurora was a mathematical analysis of the trajectories of charged particles in the earth's dipole magnetic field. It included the numerical integration of series of differential equations—an enormous task before the advent of electronic computers—in which Størmer was assisted by many of his students. His analysis showed that only some trajectories are possible, others being "forbidden." Størmer was also led to postulate a circular electric current in the equatorial plane of the earth and showed that electrons may be trapped into oscillatory trajectories in the earth's dipole field. Although his calculations were made in the course of studying the polar aurora, they became important for other areas of cosmic geophysics. When the latitudinal variation in cosmic radiation was discovered in the 1930's, it could be explained by Størmer's calculations; and the discovery of the Van Allen belts confirmed, to a surprising degree, his theoretical analysis of the trajectories of charged particles from the sun in the dipole field of the earth.

Størmer was an old-fashioned scientist who worked by himself. He mastered the field and often did the manual labor connected with his experiments and calculations. His last book, *The Polar Aurora* (1955), is not only his final summary, but also an up-to-date and authoritative study. Størmer had no direct followers; but he exerted a profound influence during his forty-one-year teaching career. He also was an excellent popularizer.

BIBLIOGRAPHY

Most of Størmer's scientific publications appeared in the *Norske Videnskabsakademiets Skrifter*; lists can be found in *Årbok. Norske videnskapsakademi i oslo* (1892–1953). His books include *Fra verdensrummets dybder til atomenes indre* (Oslo, 1923), which went through 4 eds. in Norwegian and was translated into 5 foreign languages; and *The Polar Aurora* (Oxford, 1955).

An obituary is L. Harang, "Minnetale over professor Carl Størmer," in *Årbok. Norske videnskapsakademi i Oslo* (1958), 81–85.

NILS SPJELDNAES

STUDY, EDUARD (*b.* Coburg, Germany, 23 March 1862; *d.* Bonn, Germany, 6 January 1930)

Study, the son of a Gymnasium teacher, studied mathematics and science, beginning in 1880, at the universities of Jena, Strasbourg, Leipzig, and Munich. One of his favorite subjects was biology, and even late in life he investigated entomological questions and assembled an imposing butterfly collection. He received the doctorate from the University of Munich in 1884 and the following year became a *Privatdozent* in mathematics at Leipzig, where he was influenced chiefly by Paul Gordan, an expert in invariant theory.

In 1888 Study left this post to take a similar one at Marburg. From July 1893 to May 1894 he lectured in the United States, mainly at the Johns Hopkins University. He was appointed extraordinary professor at Göttingen in 1894 and full professor at Greifswald in 1897. In 1904 he succeeded Lipschitz at Bonn, where he remained until his retirement in 1927; he died of cancer three years later.

Study was largely self-taught in mathematics, and his writings reflect a highly individual way of thinking. He worked in many areas of geometry but did not accept the geometric axiomatics that Pasch and Hilbert were then developing. (On this point see Study's remarks in his more philosophical writings [1, 2].) Study mastered Grassmann's *Ausdehnungslehre*, Lie's theory of continuous groups, and the calculus of invariant theory; he was highly skilled at employing related algebraic techniques in the solution of geometric questions.

It was then usual for geometers to state their findings with little concern for exactitude in individual aspects of problems, and many theorems were labeled simply "in general," without any indication of the scope of their validity. Questions concerning real numbers, for example, were not carefully distinguished from those concerning complex numbers. Many of Study's papers were addressed to drawing such distinctions. His objections, buttressed by counterexamples, to Schubert's principle of the conservation of number were particularly well known, and the principle was eventually firmly established with suitable restrictions on its range of applicability [3].

In his own work Study demonstrated what he considered to be a thorough treatment of a problem. Moreover, a number of the problems he chose to discuss—for example, Apollonius' tangent problem [4] and Lie's straight-line–sphere transformation [5]—had long been thought resolved. Study was the first to show how the totality of the conic sections of the plane—that is, the conic sections considered as unions of elements—can be mapped into a point set M_5 of P_{27} [6].

With Corrado Segre, Study was one of the leading pioneers in the geometry of complex numbers. He systematically constructed the analytic geometry of the complexly extended Euclidean spaces R_2 and R_3; and, with Fubini, he was the first to introduce metrics for these spaces [7]. His contributions to complex differential geometry include the first systematic studies of isotropic curves and the introduction of isotropic parameters [8].

Adept in the methods of invariant theory—which are almost completely forgotten today—Study, employing the identities of the theory, sought to demonstrate that geometric theorems are independent of coordinates. This undertaking was not a simple one, but he achieved a number of successes. In a long work [9] he derived the formulas of spherical trigonometry from a new point of view, and in the process created many links between trigonometry and other branches of mathematics. He wrote other works on invariant theory, but they provoked little response even at the time of their publication [10].

Study was the first to investigate systematically all algebras possessing up to four generators over R and C [11], including W. R. Hamilton's quaternions, which interested him chiefly because of their applications to geometry and Lie groups. In his long work *Geometrie der Dynamen* [12] Study made a particularly thorough examination of Euclidean kinematics and the related subject of the mechanics of rigid bodies. Unfortunately, because of its awkward style and surfeit of new concepts, this work has never found the public it merits.

BIBLIOGRAPHY

I. ORIGINAL WORKS.

[1] *Die realistische Weltansicht und die Lehre vom Raume* (Brunswick, 1914; 2nd ed. 1923).

[2] *Denken und Darstellung in Mathematik und Naturwissenschaften*, 2nd ed. (Brunswick, 1928).

[3] "Über das sogenannte Prinzip von der Erhaltung der Anzahl," in *Archiv der Mathematik und Physik*, 3rd ser., **8** (1905), 271–278.
"Das Prinzip der Erhaltung der Anzahl," in *Berichte über die Verhandlungen der K. Sächsischen Gesellschaft der Wissenschaften zu Leipzig*, Math.-phys. Kl., **68** (1916), 65–92.

[4] "Das Apollonische Problem," in *Mathematische Annalen*, **49** (1897), 497–542.

[5] "Vereinfachte Begründung von Lie's Kugelgeometrie," in *Sitzungsberichte der Preussischen Akademie der Wissenschaften zu Berlin*, **27** (1926), 360–380.

[6] "Über die Geometrie der Kegelschnitte, insbesondere Charakteristikenproblem," in *Mathematische Annalen*, **27** (1886), 58–101.

[7] "Kürzeste Wege im komplexen Gebiet," *ibid.*, **60** (1905), 327–378.

[8] "Zur Differentialgeometrie der analytischen Kurven," in *Transactions of the American Mathematical Society*, **10** (1909), 1–49.

[9] "Sphärische Trigonometrie, orthogonale Substitutionen und elliptische Funktionen," in *Abhandlungen der Sächsischen Akademie der Wissenschaften*, **20** (1893), 83–232.

[10] *Methoden zur Theorie der ternären Formen* (Leipzig, 1889); and *Einleitung in die Theorie der invarianten linearer Transformationen auf Grund der Vektorrechnung* (Brunswick, 1923).

[11] "Theorie der gemeinen und höheren komplexen Grössen," in *Encyklopädie der mathematischen Wissenschaften*, I, pt. 4 (Leipzig).

[12] *Geometrie der Dynamen . . .* (Leipzig, 1903).

II. SECONDARY LITERATURE. See F. Engel, "Eduard Study," in *Jahresberichte der Deutschen Mathematikervereinigung*, **40** (1931), 133–156; and E. A. Weiss, "Eduard Study, ein Nachruf," in *Sitzungsberichte der Berliner mathematischen Gesellschaft*, **10** (1930), 52–77; "Eduard Study's mathematischen Schriften," in *Jahresberichte der Deutschen Mathematikervereinigung*, **43** (1934), 108–124, 211–225.

WERNER BURAU

STURM, CHARLES-FRANÇOIS (*b.* Geneva, Switzerland, 29 September 1803; *d.* Paris, France, 18 December 1855)

Sturm's family, originally from Strasbourg, had lived in Geneva since the middle of the eighteenth century. He was the elder son of Jean-Henri Sturm, a teacher of arithmetic, and Jeanne-Louise-Henriette Gremay. Sturm at first studied classics, a field in which he displayed considerable ability. For example, at age sixteen he improvised Greek and Latin verses without the aid of a dictionary. In order to perfect his German, he attended the Lutheran church to hear sermons given in that language. In 1819, the year of his father's death, Sturm abandoned his literary studies and devoted himself to mathematics. At the Geneva Academy he attended the mathematics lectures of Simon L'Huillier and the physics lectures of Marc-Auguste Pictet and Pierre Prevost. L'Huillier, who in 1821 was preparing to retire, soon discovered Sturm's abilities; he encouraged Sturm, offered him advice, and lent him books. His influence, however, was less decisive than that of his successor, Jean-Jacques Schaub.[1] Sturm also attended a course in mathematics given by Baron Jean-Frédéric-Théodore Maurice and one in astronomy taught by Alfrède Gautier. Among Sturm's fellow students were Auguste de La Rive, Jean-Baptiste Dumas, and Daniel Colladon, his best friend.[2]

Having completed his studies at the Academy, Sturm moved early in May 1823 to the château of Coppet, about fifteen kilometers from Geneva, as tutor to the youngest son of Mme de Staël.[3] About ten people lived at the château, including Duke Victor de Broglie, his wife, the former Albertine de Staël, and their three children. Sturm's duties as tutor left him sufficient free time to write his first articles on geometry, which were published immediately in *Annales de mathématiques pures et appliquées*, edited by J. D. Gergonne. Toward the end of the year, he accompanied the duke's family to Paris for a stay of approximately six months. Through de Broglie's assistance he was able to enter the capital's scientific circles.

During this period Sturm wrote to Colladon: "As for M. Arago, I have two or three times been among the group of scientists he invites to his house every Thursday, and there I have seen the leading scientists, MM Laplace, Poisson, Fourier, Gay-Lussac, Ampère, etc. Mr de Humboldt, to whom I was recommended by Mr de Broglie, has shown an interest in me; it is he who brought me to this group. I often attend the meetings of the Institut that take place every Monday."[4]

In May 1824 Sturm returned to Coppet with the de Broglie family, but toward the end of that year he gave up teaching in order to devote himself to scientific research. With Colladon he undertook a study of the compression of liquids, which had just been set by the Paris Academy as the subject of the grand prize in mathematics and physics for the following year. They decided to measure the speed of sound in water—Lake Geneva was nearby—and then to seek the coefficient of compressibility of water, introduce this coefficient into Poisson's formula for the speed of sound, and compare their results with those predicted by the formula. The project did not, however, yield the desired results. In addition, Colladon seriously injured his hand during the tests.

On 20 December 1825 Sturm and Colladon left for Paris with the intention of attending physics courses and of finding the instruments needed for the experiments that would enable them to complete their memoir. Arago often invited them to his house, and for a time Sturm gave mathematics lessons to his eldest son. In addition, Ampère offered them the use of his physics laboratory.

At the Sorbonne and at the Collège de France, Sturm and Colladon attended the lectures of Ampère and Gay-Lussac in physics and of Cauchy and Lacroix in mathematics. They also were present during the tests on steam engines that Arago and Dulong conducted near the Paris observatory. In addition they visited Fourier, who at this time was engaged in research on heat. Fourier asked Colladon to measure the thermal conductivity of various substances and, recognizing Sturm's inclination and talent for theoretical work, suggested that the latter make a thorough study of a certain procedure in analysis, later called harmonic analysis, that Fourier believed would be of great use in theoretical physics.

Sturm and Colladon finished their paper on the compression of liquids and submitted it to the Academy, which eventually decided that none of the memoirs it had received merited the prize and that the the same subject would be set for the 1827 award. Meanwhile, Sturm and Colladon had been appointed assistants to Ampère, who suggested that they collaborate on a major treatise on experimental and theoretical physics (the project was never undertaken). In November 1826 Colladon returned to Geneva and measured the speed of sound in water between Thonon and Rolle, situated on opposite banks of Lake Geneva. He obtained a value of 1,435 meters per second. The agreement was good with the theoretical speed determined by Poisson's formula, which gave 1,437.8 meters per second. Upon his return to Paris, he and Sturm completed the new version of their memoir. This time it won the grand prize of 3,000 francs, a sum that enabled them to pay the costs of their experiments and to prolong their stay in Paris.

Henceforth their scientific careers diverged. Even in his physical research, however, Sturm continued to obtain interesting results in geometry, notably on the theory of caustic curves of reflection, the poles and polars of conic sections, Desargues's theorem, and involutions.

In 1829, through Ampère's influence, Sturm was appointed chief editor for mathematics of the *Bulletin des sciences et de l'industrie*. On 13 May of that year he presented to the Academy "Mémoire sur la résolution des équations numériques," containing the famous theorem that perhaps did more to assure his reputation than the rest of his writings together. The founder of the *Bulletin*, André Étienne, Baron d'Audebard de Férussac, invited his principal collaborators to assemble at his Paris residence once a week; and it is possible that Sturm met Niels Abel and Évariste Galois there, as well as Cournot, Coriolis, Duhamel, Hachette, and Lacroix.[5]

Sturm and Colladon wished to obtain posts in the state school system; but even though they had the backing of several influential members of the Academy, they were unsuccessful because they were foreigners and Protestants. The revolution of July 1830 proved beneficial to their cause: Arago was able to have Sturm named professor of *mathématiques spéciales* at the Collège Rollin and Colladon, professor of mechanics at the École Centrale des Arts et Manufactures. (Colladon returned to Geneva in 1839.) It is interesting that the minister of public education after the revolution was Duke Victor de Broglie.[6]

Sturm became increasingly interested in the theory of differential equations; and in September 1833, six months after he had acquired French citizenship, he read a memoir on this subject before the Academy. About this time the Geneva Academy considered offering him a post, and in October 1833 he received official notification through La Rive. But Sturm declined it, for his decision to remain in France was irrevocable. He also rejected an offer from the University of Ghent.

Upon the death of Ampère, a seat in the Académie des Sciences became vacant. On 28 November 1836 Sturm was nominated to it by Lacroix; the other candidates were Liouville, Duhamel, Lamé, and Jean-Louis Boucharlat. At the following meeting, it was announced that Liouville and Duhamel had withdrawn their names, considering it right that the seat go to Sturm; he was elected by forty-six of the fifty-two votes cast.

Sturm's career now progressed rapidly; in 1838 he was named *répétiteur* of analysis in Liouville's course at the École Polytechnique, where he became professor of analysis and mechanics in 1840. Also that year he assumed the chair of mechanics formerly held by Poisson at the Faculty of Sciences. In 1837 Sturm became *chevalier* of the Legion of Honor, and in 1840 he won the Copley Medal of the Royal Society and was elected a member of that body. He was already a member of the Berlin Academy (1835) and the Academy of St. Petersburg (1836).

Sturm was obliged to spend much time preparing his courses on differential and integral calculus and on rational mechanics. An excellent lecturer, he was admired for both his personal qualities and his knowledge. Sturm dedicated his remaining time to research. From analysis he turned to optics, particularly to vision, and to mechanics, in which, independently and by a new method, he derived one of Duhamel's theorems on the variation in *vis viva* resulting from a sudden change in the links of a moving system.

Around 1851 Sturm's deteriorating health obliged him to arrange for a substitute at the Sorbonne and at the École Polytechnique. He became obese, had a nervous breakdown, and no longer derived pleasure from intellectual work. His doctors ordered him to walk a great deal and to move to the country. Two years later Sturm resumed some of his teaching duties, but the illness returned—probably with other complications, the nature of which is not known—and it slowly took his life.

On 20 December 1855 a crowd of scientists, friends, and students accompanied Sturm's body to the cemetery of Montparnasse. Moving speeches were given by a Protestant minister and by Liouville, who called Sturm "a second Ampère: candid like him, indifferent to wealth and to the vanities of the world."[7]

Sturm's moral qualities, his innate sense of duty and of honor, and his devotion to the ideals of friendship brought him the esteem and affection of all who knew him. His life, like his writings, was a model of clarity and rigor. Favorable circumstances smoothed the way and permitted him to display his genius; but his long friendship with Colladon and the patronage of such highly placed persons as de Broglie, Arago, and Ampère are also inseparable from his career and should be taken into account in explaining his success.

In the rest of the article we shall not consider Sturm's earliest works nor, in particular, his many articles on plane geometry—in each of which he made a valuable, original contribution. The essential features of his work in this area were incorporated in later works on geometry, often without mention of their origin. We shall, instead, examine rather closely three other important aspects of his work.

Sturm's Theorem. Although the problem of finding the number of real roots of the equation $f(x) = 0$ had already been encountered by Descartes and by Rolle, it was not investigated systematically until the mid-eighteenth century. Gua de Malves made the first significant attempts in 1741, and in 1767 Lagrange approached the problem by forming the transform with the squares of the differences of the zeroes of the polynomial. Later, Fourier considered the sequence formed by the first member of the equation and its successive derivatives. Poisson suggested the problem to Cauchy, who in 1813 sent three notes on the subject to the Academy and in 1815 discussed it at length in his "Mémoire sur la détermination du nombre de racines réelles dans les équations algébriques."[8] By successive eliminations, Cauchy established a system of rational functions of the coefficients of the given polynomial; and from the sign of these functions he deduced the number of zeroes. His was the first complete solution, but the calculations involved are so long and laborious that it was never adopted.

Sturm used Fourier's method, as well as some unpublished results that Fourier had communicated to him. (Sturm credited Fourier for these in the article published in *Bulletin des sciences et de l'industrie*.) But instead of working with the successive derivatives, he was able to develop his method by using only the first derivative. The essential part of the argument is as follows:[9]

Let $V = 0$ be an equation of arbitrary degree with distinct roots, and let V_1 be the derivative of V. One proceeds as in finding the greatest common divisor of V and V_1, the sole difference being that it .is necessary to change the signs of all the remainders when they are used as divisors. Let $Q_1, \cdots, Q_{r-1}$ be the quotients and $V_2, \cdots, V_{r-1}$ the remainders, V_r being a constant. One therefore has

$$V = V_1 Q_1 - V_2$$
$$V_1 = V_2 Q_2 - V_3$$
$$\cdots \cdots$$
$$V_{r-2} = V_{r-1} Q_{r-1} - V_r.$$

The statement of the theorem then reads:

Let us substitute two arbitrary numbers a and b, positive or negative, for x in the sequence of functions $V, V_1, V_2, \cdots, V_{r-1}, V_r$. If a is smaller than b, the number of the variations in the sequence of the signs of these functions for $x = b$ will, at most, be equal to the number of the variations in the sequence of the signs of these same functions for $x = a$. And if it is less, the difference will be equal to the number of real roots of the equation $V = 0$ between a and b.

"Variation" in this statement means "change of sign." The demonstration, which includes an examination of two cases, a scholium, and two corollaries, requires several pages. Sturm's discovery elicited great excitement, and he became famous as the mathematician who had filled a lacuna in algebra. It was not long, however, before voices were raised in support of Cauchy—that, for example, of Olry Terquem, editor of the *Nouvelles annales de mathématiques*, who accorded priority to Cauchy while recognizing that Sturm had found a simpler method. Cauchy himself later asserted his priority. As for Sturm, he was satisfied to speak of the "theorem of which I have the honor to bear the name." Charles Hermite made the following assessment: "Sturm's theorem had the good fortune of immediately becoming classic and of finding a place in teaching that it will hold forever. His demonstration, which utilizes only the most elementary considerations, is a rare example of simplicity and elegance."[10]

Cauchy subsequently found a way to determine the number of imaginary roots of an equation; but here, too, Sturm arrived at the same results by a shorter and more elementary method. The proof of this "Cauchy theorem" was published in *Journal de mathématiques pures et appliquées* for 1836 in an article signed by Sturm and Liouville.

The functions $V, V_1, \cdots, V_r$ are called Sturm functions. J. J. Sylvester discussed them in two articles and expressed them by means of the roots of the given equation.[11]

Differential Equations and Infinitesimal Geometry. On 28 September 1833 Sturm presented a memoir on second-order differential equations to the Académie des Sciences, but it was not published until three years later, in *Journal de mathématiques*. In this work Sturm studied equations of the form

$$L\frac{d^2V}{dx^2} + M\frac{dV}{dx} + N \cdot V = 0,$$

where L, M, and N are given functions of x, and V is the unknown function. The integration is, in general, impossible. Sturm's insight was to determine the properties of V without assigning it in advance to any class. Although used today, this method of proceeding was not at all common at that time. Sturm started by writing the given equation as

$$\frac{d}{dx}\left(K\frac{dV}{dx}\right) + G \cdot V = 0,$$

where K and G are new functions of x that can be determined subsequently. This type of differential equation is encountered in several problems of mathematical physics.

Liouville maintained a special interest in this area of Sturm's research, to which he himself made several important additions in two notes to the Academy in 1835 and 1836. Further, in his *Journal* he published a work written with Sturm on the expansion of functions in series; their paper begins with the differential equation

$$\frac{d}{dx}\left(K\frac{dV}{dx}\right) + (gV - l) = 0.$$

Maxime Bôcher, professor at Harvard University, gave a series of lectures at the Sorbonne in the winter of 1913–1914 on the use of Sturm's methods in the theory of differential equations.

In infinitesimal geometry, Sturm examined the problem of finding the surface of revolution that is at the same time a minimal surface. Delaunay had demonstrated that it is generated by the rotation of the curve described by the focus of an ellipse or of a hyperbola that rolls without sliding on a straight line. His method consisted in imposing on the differential equation of minimal surface the condition that it be a surface of revolution. Sturm handled the problem in another way. He began with an arbitrary surface of revolution; calculated its volume; and sought to determine, with the aid of the calculus of variations, in which cases this volume could become minimum. He thus arrived at the differential equation of the meridian and showed that it is indeed that of the curve described by the focus of a conic section. Furthermore, he demonstrated that in the case of the parabola, the meridian is a catenary curve. He then generalized the question and determined the curve that must be rolled on a straight line in order for a certain point of the plane of this curve to describe another curve the differential equation of which is known. Sturm's solution appeared in Liouville's *Journal* of 1841.

Experimental and Mathematical Physics. Sturm and Colladon's prizewinning "Mémoire sur la compression des liquides et la vitesse du son dans l'eau" consists of three parts. The first contains a description of the apparatus used to measure the compression of liquids, an account of the experiments concerning the compressibility of glass, and the tables of the results for mercury, pure water and water saturated with air, alcohol, sulfuric ether, ethyl chloride, acetic ester, nitrous ester, sulfuric acid, nitric acid, acetic acid, essence of turpentine, carbon disulfide, water partially saturated with ammonia gas, and seawater. The second part records the experiments to measure the heat emitted by liquids following the application of strong and sudden pressures, as well as tests made to determine the influence of mechanical compression on the electrical conductivity of several highly conductive liquids. The third part gives the details of Colladon's experiments on the propagation of sound in water and compares the values obtained experimentally with those resulting from the insertion of the measurements of compressibility in Poisson's formula.

Sturm also published many articles on mechanics and analytical mechanics. Three of the most important deal, respectively, with a theorem of Sadi Carnot's on the loss of *vis viva* in a system of which certain parts are inelastic and undergo sudden changes in velocity; with the motion, studied by Poinsot, of a solid about a fixed point; and with a way of shortening the calculations of W. R. Hamilton and Jacobi for integrating the equations of motion. Further, Sturm's *Cours de mécanique*, like his *Cours d'analyse*, was used by many students and remained a classic for half a century.

In addition to the memoir of 1838 on optics, Sturm earlier wrote many articles and notes on caustics and caustic surfaces. His studies on vision culminated in a long work that displayed a profound knowledge of physiology.

Fourier's influence on Sturm is reflected in a memoir of 1836 on a class of partial differential equations. In it Sturm considers the distribution of heat in a bar, either straight or curved, that is composed of a homogeneous or nonhomogeneous substance, and is of constant or variable thickness but of small dimensions. Under these conditions it may be assumed that all the points of a plane section perpendicular to the axis of the bar are at the same temperature at the same instant. In this work, one of his longest and most important, Sturm exhibits such a richness of ideas and skill in handling mathematics as an instrument for solving a problem in theoretical physics that he may unhesitatingly be placed on the same level as his teacher Fourier.

Sturm, who was so adept at combining mathematics with physics in his work, appears today, by virtue of his modes of thinking, as a very modern scientist. Since 1900 there has been growing interest in his mathematical work, especially in the United States. His contribution to physics, on the other hand, has not yet received the examination it merits. There is still no thorough, full-scale study of his life and work based on the unpublished documents.

NOTES

1. Jean-Jacques Schaub (1773–1825) left MSS on the theory of numerical approximations and on the elementary concepts of the calculus of quaternions. His greatest importance for the history of mathematics is that he was the teacher and patron of Sturm, whose family found itself in financial difficulties after the death of the father.
2. Daniel Colladon (1802–1893), who studied law before turning to physics, played an important role in Sturm's life. A skillful experimenter and brilliant inventor, he conceived the idea of illuminated fountains, which were immediate successes in Paris, London, and Chicago. His research on the action of compressed air led him to construct drilling machines for boring tunnels, and he participated in the cutting of the Mont Cenis and St. Gotthard tunnels. He also was an expert in the building of gasworks.
3. See Countess Jean de Pange, *Le dernier amour de Madame de Staël* (Geneva, 1944). The author, who died at Paris in 1972, at the age of eighty-four, was the sister of Louis de Broglie.

4. This six-page letter of 26 Apr. 1824 is reproduced in D. Colladon, *Souvenirs et mémoires* (Geneva, 1893). The original is at the Bibliothèque Publique et Universitaire, Geneva, MS 3255, fols. 219–222.
5. See R. Taton, "Les mathématiques dans le *Bulletin de Férussac*," in *Archives internationales d'histoire des sciences*, 1 (1947), 100–125.
6. There is a passage concerning Sturm in *Souvenirs du duc de Broglie* (Paris, 1886), II, 454. published by his son, C. J. V. A. Albert de Broglie.
7. The complete text of Liouville's speech is in E. Prouhet, "Notice sur la vie et les travaux de Ch. Sturm." On the same day Colladon, who hurriedly left Geneva to attend his friend's funeral, sent Auguste de La Rive a long letter containing much information on Sturm; this unpublished letter is MS fr. 3748, fols. 206–207, at the Bibliothèque Publique et Universitaire, Geneva.
8. *Journal de l'École polytechnique*, 10 (1815), 457–548; see also *Oeuvres de Cauchy*, 2nd ser., I, 170–257; II, 187–193; XV, 11–16.
9. The statement of the theorem and the notation we follow is Mayer and Charles Choquet, *Traité élémentaire d'algèbre* (Paris, 1832). Sturm had given them permission to publish the results of his research.
10. A full study, already outdated, of Sturm's theorem is in Charles de Comberousse, *Cours de mathématiques*, 2nd ed., IV (Paris, 1890), pt. 2, 442–460.
11. "Memoir on Rational Derivation From Equations of Coexistence, That Is to Say, a New and Extended Theory of Elimination," in *Philosophical Magazine*, 15 (July–Dec. 1839), 428–435; and "On a Theory of the Conjugate Relations of Two Rational Integral Functions, Comprising an Application to the Theory of Sturm's Functions, and That of the Greatest Algebraic Common Measure," in *Abstracts of Papers Communicated to the Royal Society of London*, 6 (1850–1854), 324–327.

BIBLIOGRAPHY

I. ORIGINAL WORKS. Sturm's books, both published posthumously, are *Cours d'analyse de l'École polytechnique*, 2 vols. (Paris, 1857–1859), prepared by E. Prouhet, 8th and subsequent eds. prepared by A. de Saint-Germain—the 14th ed. appeared in 1909—translated into German by Theodor Fischer as *Lehrbuch der Analysis* (Berlin, 1897–1898); and *Cours de mécanique de l'École polytechnique*, 2 vols. (Paris, 1861), prepared by E. Prouhet, 5th ed. rev. and annotated by A. de Saint-Germain (Paris, 1905).

Sturm's articles, notes, memoirs, and reports are listed below according to the journal in which they appeared.

In *Annales de mathématiques pures et appliquées*, edited by J. D. Gergonne: "Extension du problème des courbes de poursuite," 13 (1822–1823), 289–303. In *Mémoires présentés par divers savants à l'Académie royale de France*: "Mémoire sur la compression des liquides," 2nd ser., 5 (1838), 267–347, written with D. Colladon, who republished it thirty-two years after Sturm's death with his own paper of 1841, "Sur la transmission du son dans l'eau," as *Mémoire sur la compression des liquides et la vitesse du son dans l'eau* (Geneva, 1887); and "Mémoire sur la résolution des équations numériques," 6 (1835), 271–318, the complete text of the work containing the statement and demonstration of Sturm's theorem.

In *Nouvelles annales de mathématiques* or *Journal des candidats aux écoles polytechnique et normale*, edited by Orly Terquem and Camille Christophe Gerono: "Sur le mouvement d'un corps solide autour d'un point fixe," **10** (1851), 419–432.

The Bibliothèque Publique et Universitaire, Geneva, has nine original letters (plus one copy) sent by Sturm to Colladon, La Rive, and other Genevans. Colladon's correspondence contains sixteen letters directly concerning Sturm; among recipients are J. Liouville, Baron J.-F.-T. Maurice, Louis-Albert Necker, and Sturm's sister. All these documents are unpublished, except for two letters from Sturm to Colladon.

II. SECONDARY LITERATURE. The first work on Sturm, appearing a year after his death, was E. Prouhet, "Notice sur la vie et les travaux de Ch. Sturm," in *Bulletin de bibliographie, d'histoire et de biographie mathématiques*, **2** (May–June 1856), 72–89; repr. in *Cours d'analyse*, 5th ed. (1877), I, xv–xxix. This article leaves much to be desired: the biographical data are incomplete and the analysis of Sturm's work is superficial; and although the list of writings is complete, it contains many errors. A fuller source is the autobiography of Daniel Colladon, *Souvenirs et mémoires* (Geneva, 1893), which contains long passages on Sturm's life and on their joint work, as well as the complete text of two long letters from Sturm (Coppet, 1823; Paris, 1824).

See also M. B. Porter, "On the Roots of Functions Connected by a Linear Recurrent Relation of the Second Order," in *Annals of Mathematics*, 2nd ser., **3** (1901), 55–70, in which the author discusses Sturm's first memoir on second-order homogeneous differential equations (which appeared in *Journal de mathématiques pures et appliquées*, **1** [1836], 106–186); J. E. Wright, "Note on the Practical Application of Sturm's Theorem," in *Bulletin of the American Mathematical Society*, **12** (1906), 246–347; and F. H. Safford, "Sturm's Method of Integrating $dx/\sqrt{X} + dy/\sqrt{Y} = 0$," *ibid.*, **17** (1910–1911), 9–15. With respect to the last article, it may be noted that one of the simplest methods for obtaining the addition theorem for the elliptic integrals of the first type is based on a procedure that appears in Sturm's *Cours d'analyse*, 5th ed., II (1877), 340–343.

Maxime Bôcher, "The Published and Unpublished Work of Charles Sturm on Algebraic and Differential Equations," in *Bulletin of the American Mathematical Society*, **18** (1911–1912), 1–18, is the best study on this subject. See also Bôcher's "Charles Sturm et les mathématiques modernes," in *Revue du mois*, **17** (Jan.–June 1914), 88–104; and *Leçons sur les méthodes de Sturm dans la théorie des équations différentielles linéaires et leurs développements modernes*, Gaston Julia, ed. (Paris, 1917). Gaspare Mignosi, "Theorema di Sturm e sue estensioni," in *Rendiconti del Circulo matematico di Palermo*, **49** (1925), 1–164, is the most complete study of Sturm's theorem from both the theoretical and the historical points of view. It includes a long historical and critical introduction on works concerning the theorem and a chronological list of 65 notes and memoirs (pp. 152–158).

Gino Loria, "Charles Sturm et son oeuvre mathématique," in *Enseignement mathématique*, **37** (1938), 249–274, with portrait, is very good and, despite its title, also deals with Sturm's works on mechanics, optics, and the theory of vision. Loria's chronological list of Sturm's works is partly based on that of Prouhet; although superior, it still contains several errors. Giorgio Vivanti, "Sur quelques théorèmes géométriques de Charles Sturm," *ibid.*, 275–291, was inspired by Sturm's article on regular polygons in *Annales mathématiques*, **15** (1825), 250–256. The first of the three theorems treated was developed by L'Huillier.

See also Henri Fehr, "Charles Sturm 1803–1855," in *Pionniers suisses de la science* (Zurich, 1939), 210–211, with portrait; and Pierre Speziali, *Charles-François Sturm (1803–1855). Documents inédits*, Conférences du Palais de la Découverte, ser. D, no. 96 (Paris, 1964). The latter is fully documented, especially with regard to Sturm's biography; it includes a reproduction of a profile of Sturm at age nineteen, based on a pencil drawing by Colladon. The portrait in the articles by Loria and Fehr was based on this drawing. There are no other likenesses of Sturm.

One may also consult the chapter on the Sturm-Liouville theory of differential equations in Garrett Birkhoff, *A Source Book in Classical Analysis* (Cambridge, Mass., 1973), 258–281.

PIERRE SPEZIALI

STURM, FRIEDRICH OTTO RUDOLF (*b*. Breslau, Germany [now Wrocław, Poland], 6 January 1841; *d*. Breslau, 12 April 1919)

The son of a Breslau businessman, Sturm attended the St. Maria Magdalena Gymnasium. In the winter semester of 1859 he began to study mathematics and physics at the University of Breslau, where in the summer of 1863 he received his doctorate of philosophy. From then until 1872 he worked as a teaching assistant, part-time teacher, and (from 1866) science teacher in Bromberg (now Bydgoszcz, Poland). With the Easter semester of 1872 he became professor of descriptive geometry and graphic statics at the Technical College in Darmstadt. In 1878 he was appointed full professor at Münster, and in 1892 he accepted a similar post at Breslau, where he taught until his death.

Sturm's principal interest was in pure synthetic geometry. Following Poncelet, Steiner, and von Staudt, the practitioners of this field sought to work with very few or no formulas. At Breslau,

Sturm had the good fortune to be taught by Heinrich Schroeter, who, as a student of Steiner, strongly encouraged Sturm to take up this type of geometry. Since at Darmstadt, Sturm was required to teach descriptive geometry and graphic statics, he directed his efforts to these subjects and as early as 1874 wrote *Elemente der darstellenden Geometrie* (Leipzig, 1874, 1900), a textbook on descriptive geometry for his students. Except for this book and another such textbook that he published later, *Maxima und Minima in der elementaren Geometrie* (Leipzig–Berlin, 1910), his work was devoted entirely to synthetic geometry. His first studies in this area concerned the theory of third-degree surfaces in their various projective representations. In his dissertation, "De superficiebus tertii ordinis disquisitiones geometricae," Sturm proved a number of properties of these representations that Steiner had stated without proof. In 1864 Sturm shared with Luigi Cremona the Steiner Prize of the Berlin Academy for further investigations of surfaces, all of which are collected in *Synthetische Untersuchungen über Flächen*, his first textbook on the subject.

Sturm was a prolific writer, but there is no need to mention his many journal articles individually, since he later collected almost all of them in two multivolume textbooks (*Die Lehre von den geometrischen Verwandtschaften*, I, II [Leipzig 1908], III, IV [Leipzig, 1909]) on line geometry and geometric transformations. The three-volume work on line geometry is the most extensive ever written on this specialty. Like Plücker, the author of the first systematic treatment of line geometry in algebraic form, Sturm sought to develop subsets of straight lines of P_3. Accordingly, in the first two volumes Sturm treated linear complexes, congruences, and the simplest ruled surfaces up to tetrahedral complexes, all of which can be particularly well handled in a purely geometric fashion. He did not systematically investigate the remaining quadratic complexes until volume three, where the difficulties of his approach—as compared with an algebraic treatment—place many demands on the reader. Sturm rejected as "unintuitive" the interpretation proposed in the nineteenth century by Felix Klein and C. Segre, who held that the line geometry of P_3 could be considered a point geometry of a quadric of P_5.

Sturm's *Lehre von den geometrischen Verwandtschaften*, which appeared in four volumes with more than 1,800 pages, was even larger than *Liniengeometrie*. In Sturm's use of the expression, geometric relationships encompassed, first, all collineations and correlations of projective spaces (extended to both real and complex numbers) of three dimensions at the most. The work, however, is much more than a textbook of projective geometry; it also contains many chapters on algebraic geometry, and among "geometric relationships," Sturm included correspondences, Cremona transformations, and plane projections of the simplest types of rational surfaces. Volume I deals with (1,1) relationships and also with (a,b) correspondences on straight lines, spheres, and the constructs generated from them. Volume II contains a description of collineations and correlations between two-step constructs; Volume III provides a similar treatment for three-step constructs; and Volume IV is devoted to Cremona transformations, several plane projections of rational surfaces, and a number of spatial correspondences. Frequently in the work Sturm touches upon questions related to Schubert's enumerative geometry, for example in the treatment of problems of plane and spatial projectivities.

In *Lehre von den geometrischen Verwandtschaften* synthetic geometry in the style of Sturm and his predecessors was developed virtually as far as it could be. During the final years of Sturm's life, mathematicians became markedly less interested in the large number of detailed geometric questions that are discussed in his writings. Consequently, although he trained many doctoral candidates in the course of his career, Sturm had no successor to continue his mathematical work.

BIBLIOGRAPHY

I. Original Works. A list of Sturm's works is in Poggendorff III, 1312–1313; IV, 1462; V, 1227–1228; VI, 2576.

Sturm's major works are "De superficiebus tertii ordinis disquisitiones geometricae" (Ph.D. diss., Bratislava, 1863); *Synthetische Untersuchungen über Flächen* (Leipzig, 1867); *Elemente der darstellenden Geometrie* (Leipzig, 1874, 1900); *Die Gebilde 1. und 2. Grades der Liniengeometrie in synthetischer Behandlung*, 3 vols. (1892–1896); *Die Lehre von dem geometrischen Verwandtschaften*, I, II (Leipzig, 1908), III, IV (Leipzig, 1909); and *Maxima und Minima in der elementaren Geometrie* (Leipzig–Berlin, 1910).

II. Secondary Literature. For works about Sturm, see W. Lorey, "Rudolf Sturm zum Gedenken," in *Zeitschrift für mathematischen und naturwissenschaftlichen Unterricht*, **50** (1919), 289–293; and W. Ludwig, "Rudolf Sturm," in *Jahresbericht der Deutschen Mathematikervereinigung*, **34** (1926), 41–51.

Werner Burau

SUBBOTIN, MIKHAIL FEDOROVICH (*b*. Ostrolenka [now Ostroleka], Lomzhinsk province, Russia [now Poland], 29 June 1893; *d*. Leningrad, U.S.S.R., 26 December 1966)

Subbotin was the son of an army officer. In 1910 he entered the mathematics section of the Faculty of Physics and Mathematics of Warsaw University, where he received the Copernicus stipend, awarded in competition for works on a subject set by the department. In 1912, while still a student, Subbotin worked as a supernumerary calculator at the university astronomical observatory; and after graduating in 1914, he was promoted to junior astronomer. The following year Subbotin was evacuated with the university to Rostov-on-Don; and from there he went to the Polytechnic Institute in Novocherkassk, where he worked until 1922, first as an assistant, then as a docent, and, finally, as professor of mathematics. His first scientific works of this period are mathematical. In 1917 Subbotin passed his master's examination at Rostov-on-Don.

In 1921 Subbotin was invited to work at the Main Russian Astrophysical Observatory, which soon became the State Astrophysical Institute, in Moscow. Ten years later this institute became part of the P. K. Sternberg Astronomical Institute. Subbotin moved to Tashkent in 1922 and became director of the Tashkent division of the State Astrophysical Institute, created on the basis of the old Tashkent observatory. In 1925 the observatory again became independent, with Subbotin as its director; and until 1930 he did much to revitalize and equip it. On his initiative the Kitab international latitude station was created.

From 1930 Subbotin directed the department of astronomy at Leningrad University. From 1935 to 1944 he was chairman of the department of celestial mechanics; from 1931 to 1934, head of the theoretical section of Pulkovo observatory; and from 1934 to 1939, head of the astronomical observatory at Leningrad University. Seriously ill and emaciated from hunger, Subbotin was evacuated in February 1942 from besieged Leningrad to Sverdlovsk, where, after treatment and convalescence, he accepted an invitation to work at the Sternberg Institute, which had been evacuated from Moscow. He traveled several times to Saratov to lecture and consult at Leningrad University, which had been evacuated there. At the end of 1942 Subbotin was named director of the Leningrad Astronomical Institute, which on his recommendation was reorganized in 1943 as the Institute of Theoretical Astronomy of the U.S.S.R. Academy of Sciences and became the main scientific institution in the Soviet Union for problems of celestial mechanics and ephemerides. On his return to Leningrad, Subbotin continued his professorial activity at the university and also taught at the Institute of Theoretical Astronomy.

From 1928 Subbotin was a member of the International Astronomical Union and, from 1933, president of the Commission on Theoretical Astronomy of the Astronomical Council of the U.S.S.R. Academy of Sciences. In 1946 he was elected corresponding member of the Academy of Sciences of the U.S.S.R. In 1963 he was awarded the Order of Lenin.

Subbotin's first scientific work was devoted to the theory of functions and the theory of probability. Several early articles deal with astrometry, particularly the creation of a catalog of faint stars. Later, however, his attention was devoted entirely to celestial mechanics and theoretical astronomy and to related areas of mathematics. He also wrote valuable works in the history of astronomy.

Subbotin began research on celestial mechanics by dealing with the theory of unperturbed motion. His new and original method of computing elliptical orbits from three observations was based on the solution of the Euler-Lambert equation. The solution of the modified equation yielded a semimajor axis, and then the remaining orbital elements were found. A number of Subbotin's works were devoted to the improvement of orbits on the basis of extensive observations. The last of these works included calculations destined to be carried out by electronic computers. In other writings Subbotin not only showed the possibility of improving the convergence of the trigonometric series by which the behavior of perturbing forces is represented, but also gave an expression for determining Laplace coefficients and presented formulas for computing the coefficients of the necessary members of the trigonometric series.

Subbotin also proposed a new, two-parameter form of equation of the Kepler ellipse, the various values of which lead to a number of anomalies, including one that changes with time more uniformly than the true and eccentric anomalies. This greatly simplified the computational integration of the equation of motion, which was particularly important for comets having large orbital eccentricities.

Subbotin's important three-volume course in celestial mechanics embraced all the basic problems of this science: unperturbed movement, the theory of perturbation and lunar theory, and the theory of figures of celestial bodies.

BIBLIOGRAPHY

I. ORIGINAL WORKS. Subbotin's writings include "Ob opredelenii osobykh tochek analiticheskikh funktsy" ("On the Determination of Singular Points of Analytic Functions"), in *Matematicheski sbornik*, **30** (1916), 402–433; "Sur les points singuliers de certaines équations différentielles," in *Bulletin des sciences mathématiques*, 2nd ser., **40**, no. 1 (1916), 339–344, 350–355; "O forme koeffitsientov stepennykh razlozheny algebraicheskikh funktsy" ("On the Form of Coefficients of Exponential Expansion of Algebraic Functions"), in *Izvestiya Donskogo politekhnicheskogo instituta, Novocherkassk*, **7** (1919); "Determination of the Elements of the Orbit of a Planet or Comet by Means of the Variation of Two Geocentric Distances," in *Monthly Notices of the Royal Astronomical Society*, **82** (1922), 383–390; "On the Law of Frequency of Error," in *Matematicheski sbornik*, **31** (1923), 296–300, in English; "On the Solar Rotation Period From Greenwich Sunspot Measures 1886–1909," in *Astronomische Nachrichten*, **218** (1923), 5–12; "Novaya forma uravnenia Eylera-Lamberta i ee primenenie pri vychislenii orbit" ("New Form of the Euler-Lambert Equation and Its Application in the Calculation of Orbits"), in *Russkii astronomicheskii zhurnal*, **1**, no. 1 (1924), 1–28; "A Proposal for a New Method of Improving the Fundamental Starplaces and for Determining the Constant of Aberration," in *Astronomische Nachrichten*, **224** (1925), 163–172; and "Proper Motions of 1186 Stars of the Cluster NGC 7654 (M52) and the Surrounding Region (First Catalogue)," in *Trudy Tashkentskogo gosudarstvennogo universiteta*, 5th ser. (1927), no. 1, 3–32.

Later works are "Sur les propriétés-limites du module des fonctions entières d'ordre fini," in *Mathematische Annalen*, **104** (1931), 377–386; "O chislennom integrirovanii differentsialnykh uravneny" ("On the Numerical Integration of Differential Equations"), in *Izvestiya Akademii nauk SSSR*, Otd. matem. i estest. nauk, 7th ser. (1933), no. 7, 895–902; *Nebesnaya mekhanika* ("Celestial Mechanics"), 3 vols. (Leningrad–Moscow, 1933–1949; I, repr. 1941), also *Prilozhenie: Vspomogatelnye tablitsy dlya vychisleny orbit i efemerid* ("Appendix: Supplementary Tables for Computation of Orbits and Ephemerides"; 1941); "O novoy anomalii, zaklyuchayushchey kak chastnye sluchai ekstsentricheskuyu, istinnuyu i tangentsialnuyu anomalii" ("On a New Anomaly, Including Particular Cases of Eccentric, True, and Tangential Anomalies"), in *Doklady Akademii nauk SSSR*, n.s. **4**, no. 4 (1936), 167–169, also in *Trudy Astronomicheskoi observatorii Leningradskogo gosudarstvennogo universiteta*, **7** (1937), 9–20; "Astronomicheskie raboty Lagranzha" ("Astronomical Work of Lagrange"), in A. N. Krylov, ed., *Zhozef Lui Lagranzh (1736–1813). K 200-letiyu so dnya rozhdenia* (". . . Lagrange. . . . On the 200th Anniversary of His Birth"; Moscow–Leningrad, 1937), 47–84; and "Nekotorye soobrazhenia po voprosu o postroenii fundamentalnogo kataloga" ("Some Considerations on the Question of the Structure of the Fundamental Catalog"), in *Astronomicheskii zhurnal*, **14**, no. 3 (1937), 228–245.

Other works are *Mnogoznachnye tablitsy logarifmov* ("Multidigit Tables of Logarithms"; Moscow–Leningrad, 1940); "O nekotorykh svoystvakh dvizhenia v zadache *n*-tel" ("On Certain Properties of Motion in the *n*-Body Problem"), in *Doklady Akademii nauk SSSR*, **27**, no. 5 (1940), 441–443; "K voprosu ob orientirovke fundamentalnogo kataloga slabykh svezd" ("Toward the Question of the Orientation of the Fundamental Catalog of Faint Stars"), in *Uchenye zapiski Kazanskogo gosudarstvennogo universiteta*, **100**, no. 4 (1940), 138–141; "Sur le calcul des inégalités séculaires. I. Solution nouvelle du problème de Gauss," in *Journal astronomique de l'URSS*, **18**, no. 1 (1941), 35–50; "Ob odnom sposobe uluchshenia skhodimosti trigonometricheskikh ryadov, imeyushchikh osnovnoe znachenie dlya nebesnoy mekhaniki" ("On One Method of Improving the Convergence of Trigonometric Series of Basic Importance for Celestial Mechanics"), in *Doklady Akademii nauk SSSR*, **40**, no. 8 (1943), 343–347; *Proiskhozhdenie i vozrast Zemli* ("Origin and Age of the Earth"; Moscow, 1945; 1947; 1950); and "Uluchshenie skhodimosti osnovnykh razlozheny teorii vozmushchennogo dvizhenia" ("Improvement in the Convergence of the Basic Expansions of the Theory of Perturbed Motion"), in *Byulleten Instituta teoreticheskoi astronomii*, **4**, no. 1 (1947), 1–16.

Writings from late in Subbotin's life are "Differentsialnoe ispravlenie orbity s ekstsentrisitetom, malo otlichayushchimsya ot edinitsy" ("Differential Correction of the Orbit With an Eccentricity Slightly Different From Unity"), in *Byulleten Instituta teoreticheskoi astronomii*, **7**, no. 6 (1959), 407–415; "O vychislenii parabolicheskikh orbit" ("On the Calculation of Parabolic Orbits"), *ibid.*, 416–419; "Raboty Mukhammeda Nasireddina po teorii dvizhenia solntsa i planet" ("Work of Muhammed Nasīr al-Dīn on the Theory of Motion of the Sun and Planets"), in *Izvestiya Akademii nauk Azerbaidzhanskoi SSR* (1952), no. 5, 51–58; "Astronomicheskie i geodezicheskie raboty Gaussa" ("Astronomical and Geodesical Works of Gauss"), in *100 let so dnya smerti (1855–1955)* ("100th Anniversary of His Death . . ."; Moscow, 1956), 241–310; "Raboty Anri Paunkare v oblasti nebesnoy mekhaniki" ("Works of Henri Poincaré in the Area of Celestial Mechanics"), in *Voprosy istorii estestvoznaniya i tekhniki* (1956), no. 2, 114–123; and "Astronomicheskie raboty Leonarda Eylera" ("Astronomical Works of Leonhard Euler"), in *Leonard Eyler. K 250-letiyu so dnya rozhdenia* (". . . Euler. On the 250th Anniversary of His Birth"; Moscow, 1958), 268–376.

II. SECONDARY LITERATURE. See G. A. Merman, "Ocherk matematicheskikh rabot Mikhaila Fedorovicha Subbotina" ("Sketch of the Mathematical Works of . . . Subbotin"), in *Byulleten Instituta teoreticheskoi astronomii*, **7**, no. 3 (1959), 233–255, with a bibliography; and N. S. Yakhontova, "Mikhail Fedorovich Subbotin (k 70-letiyu so dnya rozhdenia)" (". . . Subbotin [on the 70th Anniversary of His Birth]"), *ibid.*, **10**, no. 1 (1965), 2–5.

P. G. KULIKOVSKY

SUTER, HEINRICH (*b.* Hedingen, Zurich canton, Switzerland, 4 January 1848; *d.* Dornach, Switzerland, 17 March 1922)

Suter was the son of a farmer and a keeper of posthorses. In 1875 he married Hermine Frauenfelder, sister of a famous philanthropist and preacher of Schaffhausen cathedral, Eduard Frauenfelder; they had three daughters.

Beginning in 1863 Suter attended the Zurich cantonal school, where he learned Latin and Greek. At the University of Zurich and at the Eidgenössische Technische Hochschule he studied mathematics, physics, and astronomy under Christoffel, K. T. Reye, C. F. Geiser, and Rudolf Wolf; he then completed his training under Kronecker, Kummer, and Weierstrass at the University of Berlin, where he also attended lectures on history and philology. Suter received the doctorate from the University of Zurich in 1871 for the dissertation *Geschichte der mathematischen Wissenschaften, I; Von den ältesten Zeiten bis Ende des 16. Jahrhunderts,* in which the significance of mathematics for cultural history was emphasized. Although Suter set forth the goal of treating the history of mathematics in terms of the history of ideas, he was prevented from attaining it because of the paucity of available data.

Following a temporary appointment at the Wettingen teachers' training college (Aargau canton) and as a part-time teacher at the Gymnasiums in Schaffhausen (1874) and St. Gall (1875), Suter taught mathematics and physics at the cantonal schools of Aargau (1876) and Zurich (1886–1918). At the latter he acquired a thorough knowledge of Arabic under the Orientalists Steiner and Hausheer. His chief studies, in addition to numerous minor publications that appeared mainly in *Bibliotheca mathematica* (1889–1912), are "Das Mathematiker-Verzeichnis im Fihrist des . . . an-Nadîm" and "Die Mathematiker und Astronomen der Araber und ihre Werke." The outstanding expert of his time on Muslim mathematics, Suter was awarded an honorary doctorate of philosophy by the University of Zurich shortly before his death.

BIBLIOGRAPHY

I. ORIGINAL WORKS. Suter's writings include *Geschichte der mathematischen Wissenschaften, I, Von den ältesten Zeiten bis Ende Des 16. Jahrhunderts* (2nd rev. ed., Zurich, 1873), and II, *Vom Anfange des 17. bis gegen Ende des 18. Jahrhunderts* (Zurich, 1875); "Die Mathematiker auf den Universitäten des Mittelalters," in *Wissenschaftliche Beilage zur Programm der Kan-*tonsschule (Zürich, 1887); "Das Mathematiker-Verzeichnis im Fihrist des . . . an-Nadîm," in *Abhandlungen zur Geschichte der mathematischen Wissenschaften,* 6 (1892); "Die Mathematiker und Astronomen der Araber und ihre Werke," *ibid.,* 10 (1900); his edition of "Die astronomischen Tafeln des Muhammad ibn Mûsâ al-Khwârizmî," in *Kongelige Danske Videnskabernes Selskabs Skrifter,* 7th ser., 3, no. 1 (1914); and "Beiträge zur Geschichte der Mathematik bei den Griechen und Arabern," J. Frank, ed., in *Abhandlungen zur Geschichte der Naturwissenschaften und der Medizin* (1922), no. 4, with autobiographical sketch.

II. SECONDARY LITERATURE. See E. Beck, "Heinrich Suter," in *Jahresberichte des Gymnasiums Zürich* for 1921–1922; J. Ruska, "Heinrich Suter," in *Isis,* 5 (1923), 408–417, with portrait and bibliography; and C. Schoy, "Heinrich Suter," in *Neue Zürcher Zeitung* (8 Apr. 1922), also in *Vierteljahrsschrift der Naturforschenden Gesellschaft in Zürich,* 67 (1922), 407–413, with bibliography.

J. E. HOFMANN

SWINESHEAD (**Swyneshed, Suicet,** etc.), **RICHARD** (*fl. ca.* 1340–1355)

The name Richard Swineshead is best known to the modern historian of science as that of the author of the *Liber calculationum,* a work composed probably about 1340–1350 and famous later for its extensive use of mathematics within physics. Very little is known about this Richard Swineshead, and furthermore it appears almost certain that the little biographical data that are available about any fourteenth-century Swineshead cannot all be apportioned to one man, but that there were at least two or three men named Swineshead who may have left works in manuscript. In the early twentieth century, Pierre Duhem settled this confusion of Swinesheads to his own satisfaction by asserting that there was a John Swineshead who wrote some extant logical works, *De insolubilibus* and *De obligationibus,* and a Roger Swineshead who wrote a work on physics (found in MS Paris, Bibliothèque Nationale lat. 16621)—variously titled *De motibus naturalibus, Descriptiones motuum,* and *De primo motore* (the latter by Duhem). Duhem concluded that the famous "Calculator," as the author of the *Liber calculationum* was often called, was not really named Swineshead at all, but was rather one Richard of "Ghlymi Eshedi," as he is called in the explicit of the *Liber calculationum* in MS Paris, Bibliothèque Nationale lat. 6558, f. 70v. Since Duhem's time, historians have rejected the supposed name "Ghlymi Eshedi" as a scribal error and have restored the *Liber calculationum* to

Swineshead. They have not, however, completely unraveled the problem of the existence of two or three Swinesheads as authors of several logical and natural philosophical works.

The most satisfactory theory so far proposed would seem to be that of James Weisheipl, according to whom there were three fourteenth-century Swinesheads of note. One, named John Swineshead, was a fellow of Merton College from at least 1343 and pursued a career in law; he died in 1372, leaving no extant works. A second, named Roger Swineshead, was also at Oxford, but there is no record of his having been at Merton College. This Roger Swineshead wrote the logical works *De insolubilibus* and *De obligationibus* and the physical work *De motibus naturalibus*. He may have been a Benedictine monk and a master in sacred theology and may have died about 1365. The third Swineshead, Richard Swineshead, was, like John, associated with Merton College in the 1340's and was the author of the famous *Liber calculationum*, and possibly also of two extant *opuscula*, *De motu* and *De motu locali*, and of at least a partial *De caelo* commentary.

Given the uncertainty of the biographical data, it seems proper that all the extant physical works ascribed to any Swineshead should be included in this article. This includes, most importantly, the *Liber calculationum*, but also the *opuscula* ascribed by Weisheipl to Richard Swineshead and the *De motibus naturalibus* ascribed by Weisheipl to Roger Swineshead. All of these works can be said to fall within the "Oxford calculatory tradition," if not with the works of the so-called Merton school. The *De motibus naturalibus*, as the earliest work, will be described first (with folio references to MS Erfurt, Amplonian F 135), followed by the *Liber calculationum* (with folio references to the 1520 Venice edition), to be described in much greater detail, and finally by the fragmentary *opuscula* (with folio references to MS Cambridge, Gonville and Caius 499/268), which, although they most probably were written before the *Liber calculationum*, can more easily be described after that work. Weisheipl's hypothesis will be followed as to the correct names of the authors of these works.

De motibus naturalibus

The *De motibus naturalibus* was written at Oxford after the *De proportionibus* of Thomas Bradwardine and at about the same time (ca. 1335) as the *Regule solvendi sophismata* of William Heytesbury. In the material covered, it is similar to the latter work, and, in fact, both works treat topics that were to become standard in treatises *de motu* in the mid- and late fourteenth century. The *De motibus naturalibus* has eight parts, called *differentiae*: I. Introduction; II. Definitions of Motion and Time; III. Generation; IV. Alteration; V. Augmentation; VI. Local Motion; VII. Causes of Motion; and VIII. Maxima and Minima. In contrast to Heytesbury's work and to later treatises *de motu*, however, the *De motibus naturalibus* includes large sections of traditional natural philosophy as well as the logicomathematical natural philosophy typical of the later treatises. It contains many more facts about the natural world (climates, burning mirrors, tides, comets, milk, apples, frogs, worms, etc.) and lacks the strong sophismata character of some of the later works. It represents, therefore, to some extent, a stage halfway between thirteenth-century cosmological and fourteenth-century logicomathematical natural philosophy.

This position, halfway between two traditions, is represented quite strongly in the organization of the work: the treatise is fairly clearly divided into metaphysical-physical discussions and logicomathematical treatments. Thus, for example, the three parts discussing motion in the categories of quality, quantity, and place (parts IV, V, VI) each contain two parts, a first dealing with the physics of the situation and a second dealing with the quantification of motion in that category. Although the logicomathematical topics that Roger discusses are generally those discussed by the later authors *de motu*, the order of topics in his work still reflects an Aristotelian or medical base. Whereas later authors, especially Parisian-trained authors such as Albert of Saxony, generally discussed the measures of motion with respect to cause first (*penes quid attenditur motus tanquam penes causam*) and then discussed the measures of motion with respect to effect (*tanquam penes effectum*), Roger begins with the effects of motion (as, indeed, does the Calculator after him). Furthermore, among effects, he begins with the effects of alteration rather than with the effects of local motion. In accordance with this order of treatment, Roger's basic notions of the measurement of motion come from the category of quality rather than from causes or from locomotion, as was to be the case in seventeenth-century physics. In line with the earlier medical theory of the temperate, Roger places emphasis on mean degrees, and he considers intension at the same time as remission. When he then goes on to talk about possible mean degrees of local motion, and motions being just as fast as they are slow, and so forth, there seems to be no reasonable explanation except that he has taken "measures" which fit with the then current notions of quality and alteration and has applied them by analogy to local motion, even though the result has no apparent basis in the then current notions of local motion. Finally, to all of this, must be added the fact that Roger's basic theoretical terms for his measurements, namely "latitude," "degree," and the like, are earlier found most prominently in medical theory.

From among all the material in the *De motibus naturalibus* concerned with the "measurement" of motion and therefore most closely related to the work of the Calculator perhaps the two points of greatest interest have to do with two idiosyncratic positions which Roger takes, the first having to do with the function relating forces, resistances, and velocities in motion, the second with the relation of latitudes and degrees.

First, in parts VI and VII, Roger rejects the Aristotelian position that velocity is proportional to force and inversely proportional to resistance. Thus in the first chapter of part VI Roger states five conclusions concerning natural local motion which are all aimed at showing that resistance is not required for natural motion (41va–41vb). In part VII, Roger again repeats this view (43vb–44vb). In fact, he says, the equality or inequality of velocities is caused by the equality or inequality of the proportion of proportions of the mover to the moved, where the moved need not resist. Although Roger then accepts the mathematical preliminaries (for example, definitions of the types of proportionalities) that Bradwardine had set down as requisite for investigating velocities, forces, and resistances, he rejects Bradwardine's function relating these variables (see the article on Bradwardine for a description of his logarithmic-type function). Where there is no resistance, Roger asserts, the proportion of velocities is the same as the proportion of moving powers. Where there are resistances, then the proportion of velocities is the same as the proportion of latitudes of resistance between the degrees of resistance equal to the motive powers and the degrees of the media (this conclusion is equivalent in modern terms to stating that velocity is proportional to the difference between the force and resistance). Concerning cases where one motion is resisted and the other is not, Roger says that the proportion of velocities follows no other proportion, or, in modern terms, that he can find no function relating the velocities to forces and resistances. Although there are some obvious resemblances between Roger's position and the position of Ibn

Bājja (Avempace) and the young Galileo, it is not a position at all common in the early fourteenth century.

Second, Roger's combinations of latitudes and degrees for measuring motion are also unique to him, so far as is known. Like the latitudes of earlier authors, Roger's latitudes are ranges within which a given quality, motion, or whatever, may be supposed to vary. Thus in part IV he posits the existence of three latitudes for measuring alteration, each distinguishable by reason into two other latitudes (39ra–39rb). In modern terms the first of these latitudes expresses the range within which the intensities of a quality may vary, the second expresses the range within which velocities of alteration may vary, and the third the range within which accelerations and decelerations of alteration may vary. Similarly, in part VI Roger posits five latitudes for measuring locomotion, all of them distinct from one another only in reason (43ra). In modern terms the first three of these latitudes are the ranges within which velocity or speed may vary and the last two are ranges within which accelerations and decelerations, respectively, may vary. All of these are similar to latitudes posited by the other Oxford calculators, although later there was a tendency to dispense with the latitudes of remissness and tardity that Roger posited (see below).

What is different about Roger's system is his postulation of so-called uniform degrees. Thus Roger defines two types of degrees of heat or any other quality (38rb). One type, the "uniformly difform degree," is a component, divisible part of a latitude of quality and is like the degrees hypothesized by later authors including the Calculator. In calling these degrees "uniformly difform," Roger imagines that each such degree will contain within itself a linearly increasing series of degrees above some minimum and below some maximum, as indeed any segment of a latitude would contain. The other type, the "uniform degree," is not a component part of a latitude, but rather is equally intense throughout, whereas in any part of a latitude the intensity varies. Among the Oxford calculators, only Roger makes such a distinction. Uniform degrees appear again when Roger goes on to discuss the measurement of the velocity of alteration. In the motion of intension of a quality, he says, two velocities of intension can have no ratio to one another if one subject gains a single uniform degree more than the other (39ra). Similarly Roger concludes that some local motions are incomparable to others, and that one latitude of local motion can differ from another by a single uniform degree (43va).

Roger's postulation of uniform degrees having no proportion to latitudes does not seem to be the result of intentional atomism. Rather, the case seems to be that as a pioneer in the effort to find mathematical descriptions and comparisons of concrete distributions of qualities and velocities, he could not devise measures applicable to all cases. Earlier authors had made little attempt to deal with nonuniform distributions of qualities. Roger does try to deal with them, but he has one measure for uniform distributions (the uniform degree), and another for uniformly difform (linearly varying) distributions (the latitude), and none at all for difformly difform (nonlinearly varying) distributions. Rather than stating that he is unable to compare motions or distributions of quality that fall into different categories (which would be, from a modern point of view, the justifiable statement), he says that the motions or distributions themselves have no proportion. It seems very likely that it was exactly the kind of effort to "measure" motion represented by the *De motibus naturalibus* that motivated the Calculator to try to straighten things out in his mathematically much more sophisticated work.

Liber calculationum

The *Liber calculationum* is by far the most famous work associated with the name Swineshead. As it appears in the 1520 Venice edition the *Liber calculationum* contains sixteen parts or *tractatus*. Some of these treatises may have been composed later than others, since they are lacking from some of the extant manuscripts. The emphasis in the *Liber calculationum* is on logicomathematical techniques rather than on physical theory. What it provides are techniques for calculating the values of physical variables and their changes, or for solving problems or sophisms about physical changes. Thus, the order of the treatise is one of increasing complexity in the application of techniques rather than an order determined by categories of subject matter, and the criteria for choosing between competing positions on various topics are often logicomathematical criteria. Thus, it is considered important that theory be complete — that it be able to handle all conceivable cases. Similarly, it is considered important that the mathematical measurements of a given physical variable be continuous, so that, for instance, the mathematical measure of an intensity should not jump suddenly from zero to

four degrees (unless there is reason to believe that an instantaneous change occurs physically).

As stated above, as late as the beginning of the fourteenth century natural philosophers dealing with the qualities of subjects (for instance, Walter Burley in his treatises on the intension and remission of forms) assumed tacitly that the individual subjects they dealt with were uniformly qualified. Thus, as in the pharmaceutical tradition, they could talk of a subject hot in the second degree or cold in the third degree (and perhaps about what the result of their combination would be) without questioning whether the individual subjects had qualitative variations within themselves. Roger Swineshead in the *De motibus naturalibus* attempted to deal with variations in distribution, but managed only to establish criteria for uniform and for uniformly varying (*uniformiter difformis*) distributions. Richard Swineshead in his *opuscula De motu* and *De motu locali* declared that difform distributions are too diverse to deal with theoretically (212ra, 213rb). In the *Liber calculationum*, however, he manages to deal with a good number of more complicated (*difformiter difformis*) distributions.

The overall outline of the *Liber calculationum* is as follows. It begins with four treatises dealing with the qualitative degrees of simple and mixed subjects insofar as the degrees of the subjects depend on the degrees in their various parts. Treatise I considers measures of intensity (and, conversely, of remissness, that is, of privations of intensity) per se. Treatise II, on difform qualities and difformly qualified bodies, considers the effects of variations in two dimensions — intensity and extension — on the intensity of a subject taken as a whole. Treatise III again considers two variables in examining how the intensities of two qualities, for example, hotness and dryness, are to be combined in determining the intensity of an elemental subject (this, of course, being related to the Aristotelian theory that each of the four terrestrial elements — earth, air, fire, and water — is qualified in some degree by a combination of two of the four basic elemental qualities — hotness, coldness, wetness, and dryness). Treatise IV then combines the types of variation involved in treatises II and III to consider how both the intensity and extension of two qualities are to be combined in determining the intensity of a compound (mixed) subject. Treatises I–IV, then, steadily increase in mathematical complexity.

In treatises V and VI the Calculator introduces a new dimension, that of density and rarity, and determines how density, rarity, and augmentation are to be measured. Density and rarity are mathematically somewhat more complex than qualitative intensity because, even in the simplest cases, they depend on two variables, amount of matter and quantity, rather than on one. Treatises VII and VIII, then, which consider whether reaction is possible and, in order to answer that question, discuss how powers and resistances are to be measured mathematically, involve all of the variables introduced in the preceding six parts. Treatise IX, on the difficulty of action, and treatise X, on maxima and minima, complete the discussion of the measurement of powers by determining that the difficulty of an action is proportional to the power acting and by considering how the limits of a power are determined with respect to the media it can traverse in a limited or unlimited time. Treatise IX is apparently intended to apply to all types of motion, although the examples discussed nearly all have to do with local motion. In treatise X the preoccupation with local motion becomes complete. This direction of attention to local motion is continued in treatise XI, on the place of the elements, where the contributions of the parts of a body to its natural motion are discussed. Up through treatise XI, then, the three usual categories of motion according to the medieval and Aristotelian view—alteration, augmentation, and local motion—are discussed. It is significant and typical of medieval Aristotelianism that alteration is discussed first as, so to speak, the fundamental type of motion. In treatises XII and XIII the field of attention is extended to include light, treatise XII considering the measure of power of a light source and treatise XIII considering the distribution of illumination in media.

Beginning at about treatise X the tone of the *Liber calculationum* seems to change. Whereas in the first six treatises and again in the ninth several positions are compared, in treatises X through XVI, on the whole (except perhaps for treatise XIII, which is in question form), a single view is expounded. Beginning with treatise XII and continuing at an accelerating pace to the end of the work, the parts consist mostly of long strings of conclusions concerning all the variations on the basic functions of action that can be elicited by Swineshead's mathematical techniques. Treatise XIV consists of conclusions concerning local motion and how its velocity varies depending on the variations of forces and resistances. Treatise XV concerns what will happen if the resistance of the medium varies as the mobile is moving, or if, in a medium with uniformly increasing (*uniformiter*

difformis) resistance, an increasing power begins to move. Treatise XVI concerns the various rates at which the maximum degree of a quality will be introduced into a subject depending on its initial state and the varying rate of its alteration, or on the rarefaction of the subject. Why the later treatises of the *Liber calculationum* should differ in tone from the earlier ones is, of course, not explained. It may be simply that the greater complexity involved in the later treatises prevented their being presented in the more usual scholastic question form. But another hypothesis might be that the earlier treatises bear the traces of having been used in university teaching, whereas the later treatises, although in a sense prepared for a similar purpose, never saw actual classroom use. At least the form in which we have them does not seem to reflect that use.

With this sketch of the overall structure of the *Liber calculationum* in hand, a more detailed look at the individual treatises is now in order. Although the *Liber calculationum* is fairly well known to historians of science by title, its contents are to date only very sketchily known, evidently (*a*) because the work is quite difficult and technical and (*b*) because it is not a work known to have influenced Galileo or other figures of the scientific revolution very significantly.

Treatise I: On Intension and Remission. In its structure, treatise I has three basic parts. First, it discusses three positions about the measures of intensity and remissness of qualities; second, it discusses whether and in what way degrees of intensity and remissness of a quality are comparable to each other; and third, it raises and replies to three doubts about rates of variation of quality considered, for instance, as loss of intensity versus increase of remissness or as gain of intensity versus decrease of remissness.

Why should these have been topics of primary interest to Swineshead? Although historians have yet to reveal very much about the connections of the *Liber calculationum* to previous tradition, it is hardly questionable that Richard Swineshead's mathematical inquiries here, like those of Roger Swineshead before him, take place against the background of Aristotelian and medical discussions of qualitative changes, especially changes in hotness, coldness, wetness, and dryness. As in the case of Roger Swineshead, Aristotelian and medical backgrounds may explain why Richard Swineshead starts from the assumption of double measures of quality in terms of intensity and remissness, as related, for instance, to hot and cold, rather than beginning simply from one scale of degrees. And again the medical theory of the temperate, representing health, and of departures from it leading to illness, may similarly explain Richard Swineshead's attention in treatise I to middle or mean degrees of whole latitudes and to degrees which might be said to be "just as intense as they are remiss."

But, furthermore, in the more immediate background of Richard Swineshead's inquiries may have been precisely Roger Swineshead's mathematization of the intensities of qualities, on the one hand, and Richard's own reasoning about the defects of some of Roger's conclusions on the other. Thus, the positions concerning the measures of intensity and remissness that Richard Swineshead considers are (1) that the intensity of any quality depends upon its nearness to the maximum degree of that quality and that remissness depends on distance from that maximum degree; (2) that intensity depends upon the distance from zero degree of a quality and remissness on distance from the maximum degree; and (3) that intensity depends upon the distance from zero degree and remissness upon the nearness to zero degree (2ra–vb). In fact, in the *De motibus naturalibus*, Roger Swineshead had held the second of these positions, and this had led him to various, sometimes peculiar, conclusions comparing the intensity and remissness of degrees (for example, 38va). Thus, Richard Swineshead may well have questioned the wisdom of a position which led to such conclusions and have looked for a better position. Beyond the earlier Aristotelian and medical theories, mathematics might have led him to refer to zero degree and to some small unit as the proper basis for a measurement of intensity. Metaphysics, however, might have led him to refer to the maximum degree of a quality, because any species may be supposed to be defined by its maximum or most perfect exemplar. Mostly on the basis of mathematical considerations, Richard concludes that both intensity and remissness ought to be measured with respect to zero degree (that is, he chooses the third position). (*Tertia positio dicit quod intensio attenditur penes distantiam a non gradu et remissio penes appropinquationem ad non gradum* [2ra].)

A result of Richard's conclusion is that intensity and remissness are no longer symmetrical concepts. Thus, although there can be remission *in infinitum* before zero degree of a quality is reached, there cannot be intension *in infinitum* before the maximum degree of the latitude is reached. This follows as in the case of a finite line (lines often appear in the medieval manuscripts as representations of latitudes), where one can get closer to one extreme *in infinitum* (one can get halfway there, three-fourths of the way there, seven-eighths of the way there, continually halving the distance left), but one cannot get farther and farther from the same end *in infinitum* because one reaches the other end of the line. Consequently, if intensity is measured by distance from zero degree, the maximum degree of a quality must be remiss, which Richard admits (2vb).

In further sections, Swineshead elaborates the concept that remission is a privation with respect to intensity (4rb–4va), and then discusses in more detail the correlations between the latitudes of intensity and remissness and motions of intension and remission. Since remissness is measured by closeness to zero degree, the scale of remissness is an inverse scale (values of remissness are proportional to the inverse of the distance from zero degree) and smaller and smaller distances on the latitude close to zero degree correspond to greater and greater differences in degree of remissness. Swineshead apparently decides in this connection that the easiest solution to the problem of remissness is to label degrees of remissness by the same numbers as the degrees of intensity and merely to say that a degree of two corresponds to twice the remissness of the degree four (5ra). Again, since remission is a privation, if one allowed in imagination intensities beyond the maximum natural degree of the given quality, there would be an infinite latitude between any degree of remission and zero remissness, even though there is only a finite latitude of intensity between any degree of remission and infinite remissness.

Thus, although it is not stated this way, the net effect of treatise I is to dispense with the need for talking about remissness at all: one can deal with all cases of interest while only considering intensity, and furthermore the intensities one is dealing with will be additive. In this way Richard Swineshead removes what now seems the needless complexity of double measures of quality and at the same time ends up with an additive measure. The treatise by no means provides a complete basis for actual measurements of qualities, but it does help to move in that direction by emphasizing measures of quality that are additive. For the Oxford calculators qualities were not, to use the modern terminology, "intensive magnitudes," but were, even in their intensity, "extensive magnitudes," again to use the modern terminology. In fact, it may be somewhat startling to the modern historian to realize that fourteenth-century authors developed their concept of "dimension" or of additive magnitude in the abstract more often through the discussion of qualitative latitudes than through the discussion of spatial extension, as was to be the case in later science.

It should be noted that treatise I, in addition to determining the proper measures of intensity of qualities, also introduces many of the basic technical terms of the rest of the work. Like the *De motibus naturalibus*, it assumes that any physical variable has a continuous range, called a "latitude," within which it can vary. In the case of qualities, this latitude starts from zero degree (*non gradus*), zero being considered as an exclusive terminus, and goes up to some determinate maximum degree, the exact number of which is usually left vague, but which is commonly assumed to be eight or ten degrees (this number arising out of the previous tradition in which there were, for instance, four degrees of coldness and four degrees of hotness, the two perhaps separated by a mean or temperate mid-degree). Within any latitude there are assumed to be a number of "degrees," these degrees being, so to speak, parts of the latitude rather than indivisibles. Swineshead also makes distinctions between the intensities versus the extensions of qualities. In his use of the terminology of latitudes and degrees, Swineshead was by no means an innovator: he was adopting a familiar set of terms. Among others, Roger Swineshead had talked systematically of the relations of degrees and latitudes before him (although Roger had had his idiosyncratic system of "uniform degrees"). In the thoroughness of his discussion of the pros and cons of various conventions for the measurement of intensity and remissness, Richard Swineshead was, however, outstanding.

Treatises II–IV: On Difformly Qualified Subjects; On the Intension of an Element Possessing Two, Unequally Intense, Qualities; On the Intension and Remission of Mixed Subjects. Directly following the determination of the most appropriate "scale of measure" for intension and remission, in general, in treatise I, treatises II–IV form a single, interrelated whole dealing with the intensity and remissness of simple and mixed subjects insofar as the degrees or "overall measures" of these subjects depend upon the degrees had by their various parts.

Thus, treatise II treats the effects of varying intensities of a single quality as these intensities are distributed over a given subject (and hence considers the two dimensions of intensity and exten-

sion) as they bear upon the overall measure of the intensity of the whole, although it only does so for the special cases in which the variation in question is either uniformly difform over the total subject or in which the subject has halves of different, but uniform, intensities. In such cases, Swineshead is in effect asking what measure of intensity is to be assigned the whole. There are, he tells us, two ways (*opiniones* or *positiones*) in which this particular question can be answered: (1) the measure—or as he often calls it, the denomination—of the whole corresponds to the mean degree of the qualified subject (that is, the degree that is equidistant from the initial and final degrees of a uniformly difformly distributed quality or—to take into account the second special case at hand—from the two degrees had by the uniform, but unequally intense, halves of the subject); or (2) the subject should be considered to be just as intense as any of its parts (that is, its overall measure is equivalent to the maximum degree had by the subject [5rb; 6ra]).

Similarly, in treatise III, Swineshead considers how the intensities of two qualities—for example, hotness and dryness—in a given elemental subject (now leaving aside their extension or distribution in this subject) are to be combined in determining the intensity of the whole. We here have to do with three positions: (1) the elemental subject is as intense as the degree equidistant from the degrees of its two qualities, (2) it is as intense as its more remiss quality, or (3) it is as intense as the mean proportional degree between its qualities (9rb).

In treatise IV Swineshead combines the types of variation involved in treatises II and III to consider how both the intensity and the extension of two qualities are to be combined in determining the intensity of a *mixtum* (that is, a compound subject). Four views concerning the measure of such more "complicated" subjects are presented: (1) the intensity of a *mixtum* follows the proportion of the dominant elementary quality to the subdominant elementary quality in it, (2) every *mixtum* is as intense as its dominant elementary quality, (3) every *mixtum* has an intensity in the dominant quality equal to half the difference between its two qualities, (4) the fourth position is presented in two versions: (*a*) The *mixtum* is as intense as the excess of the degree of the dominant quality over the subdominant quality, no account being taken of just what parts of the *mixtum* these qualities are distributed over, or (*b*) it is as intense as the excess between (i) what the dominant quality as extended over such and such a part contributes to the denomination or measure of the whole and (ii) what the subdominant quality as extended over its part of the subject contributes to the denomination of the whole (12va).

However, simply to tabulate the various *positiones* relative to the proper measure of intensity and remissness of the variously qualified simple and mixed subjects that Swineshead presents falls short of representing the substance of treatises II–IV. To begin with, to regard Swineshead's major concern as the unambiguous determination of just which *positio* or theory is the correct one relative to the particular question of measure posed by each treatise is to misrepresent his real interests. At times, Swineshead appears to leave any decision as to the "best theory" an open question. Moreover, even when he does express a preference for a given *positio*, it is seldom without qualifications, and the objections he brings against the opposing, "nonpreferred" *positiones* do not necessarily imply that his primary goal was the "once-and-for-all" rejection of these other *positiones*. His primary concern was rather to show that such and such results follow from this or that *positio*, it being of secondary importance whether these results are, for one reason or another, acceptable or unacceptable (even though they are from time to time so specified); of greater significance was the exhibition of the fact that these results do follow and the explanation of how they follow.

Thus, for example, in treatise III, although Swineshead indicates his preference for the third position (*sustinenda est tertia positio*), it is nonetheless true that the objections or conclusions brought against the second, "less-preferred" position are also relevant to this third position (*sequentur igitur contra istam* [*tertiam*] *positionem inconvenientia sicut contra alias*), with the difference that these same conclusions for the most part are in this instance conceded (11va–12rb). What is more, when we examine Swineshead's procedure in presenting the objections to the presumably rejected positions, there emerges a more accurate picture of his objectives. Hence, for example, from the view that the overall degree of an element corresponds to the degree midway between the degrees of its two constituent qualities, Swineshead states that there follows the conclusion that there would occur continuously operating infinite velocities of action. This result should be rejected because then the agent in question would suddenly corrupt the patient upon which it acts. Inadmissible as this consequent of the conclusion might be, far more interesting to Swineshead (and hence

more deserving of attention) is the fact that this conclusion does indeed follow (*quod tamen ista conclusio sequatur . . .*) from the *positio* under investigation (9va). If all of this is taken into account, one obtains a much better idea of what these treatises of the *Liber calculationum* are all about and is at the same time less puzzled or surprised at Swineshead's lack of emphasis upon the definitive determination of a single, exclusively correct theory or position.

Something more of the general character of this part of the *Liber calculationum* can be derived from a slightly more detailed example drawn from treatise II. The treatise begins by examining the view that the proper measure of the kind of difformly qualified subjects in question corresponds to the mean degree of the subject. Now one of the proofs supporting this view is that, if we take a subject that is, say, either uniformly difformly hot throughout or difformly hot with each half uniformly hot, and remit the more intense half down to the mean degree while equally rapidly intending the more remiss half up to the mean degree, then, since for every part of the subject that is intended there will be a corresponding part remitted equally and no net gain or loss in intensity, it follows that at the beginning the subject contained an intensity equivalent to the mean degree.

However, this proof of the first position or view will not do according to Swineshead, since when combined with the physical assumption that heating rarefies while cooling condenses, the subject will unavoidably be rarefied in one part and condensed in another when the process of equalizing the halves of the subject is carried out; but the moment this equalization commences, the cooler, more remiss, half will, because of the rarefaction caused by heating, become greater than the more intense half, which means that throughout the whole process intension will be occurring over a greater part than is remission; therefore, Swineshead concludes, at the beginning the whole subject must be more remiss than the mean degree. An objection to this procedure is raised, but it is disposed of through a number of replies establishing that the subject must indeed initially have an overall intensity less than the mean degree (5rb–5vb).

All of this would seem to imply that Swineshead definitely rejected the first "mean degree measure" position, especially if we combine this with the fact that in the following paragraphs he appears to regard the second opposing position (that the subjects in question are just as intense as any of their parts) as acceptable (6ra–6va). However, such a judgment would be premature. Swineshead has argued not directly against the first position as such, but rather against a proof given of it. Furthermore, in the remaining (and one should note, larger and more impressive) part of treatise II, Swineshead returns to this first "mean degree" position and allows its application to difformly qualified subjects each half of which is uniform and, more generally, to "stair-step qualities" in which the intensities differ, but are uniform, over certain determinate parts of the qualified subjects. This applicability is grounded upon the fact that in a difform subject with uniform halves, a quality extended through a half "denominates the whole only half as much as it denominates the half through which it is extended." Swineshead then generalizes this "new rule" and states that if a quality is "extended in a proportionally smaller part of the whole, it denominates the whole with a correspondingly more remiss degree than it does the part through which it is extended" (6va), thus opening the possibility of considering "stair-step" distributions.

After giving proofs for the special and general cases of his new "rule of denomination," Swineshead raises an objection against it: "If the first proportional part of something be intense in such and such a degree, and the second [proportional part] were twice as intense, the third three times, and so on *in infinitum*, then the whole would be just as intense as the second proportional part. However, this does not appear to be true. For it is apparent that the quality is infinite and thus, if it exists without a contrary, it will infinitely denominate its subject" (6va).

Swineshead shows that this latter inference to infinite denomination does not follow and that it arises because one has ignored the proper denomination criterion he has just set forth (6vb–7ra). As a preliminary, he devotes considerable space to the important task of establishing that a subject with a quality distribution as specified by the objection is indeed just as intense as its second proportional part, and he presents in detail just how this is so (6va–6vb). The proportional parts in question are to be taken "according to a double proportion" (that is, the succeeding proportional parts of the subject are its half, fourth, eighth, etc.). Now following the arithmetic increase in intensity over the succeeding proportional parts as stipulated by the objection, it follows that the whole will have the intensity of the second proportional part of the subject. Swineshead proves this by taking two subjects—A and B—and dividing them both according

to the required proportional parts. Now take B and "let it be assumed that during the first proportional part of an hour the first [proportional] part of B is intended to its double, and similarly in the second proportional part of the hour the second proportional part of it is intended to its double, and so on *in infinitum* in such a way that at the end [of the hour] B will be uniform in a degree double the degree it now has." Turning then to A, Swineshead asks us to assume that "during the first proportional part of the hour the whole of A except its first proportional part grows more intense by acquiring just as much latitude as the first proportional part of B acquires during that period, while in the second proportional part of the same hour all of A except its first and second proportional parts grows more intense by acquiring just as much latitude as the second proportional part of B then acquires . . . and so on *in infinitum*." Clearly, then, since the whole of A except its first proportional part is equal in extent to its first proportional part, and since the whole of A except its first and second proportional parts is equal to its second proportional part . . . and so on *in infinitum*, it follows that A acquires just as much, and only as much, as B does throughout the hour; therefore, it is overall just as intense as B is at the end of the hour, which is to say that it is doubly intense or has an intensity equivalent to that of its second proportional part [*Q.E.D.*].

In thus determining just how intense A is at the end of its specified intensification, Swineshead has correctly seen that in our terms the infinite geometrical series involved is convergent (if we assume the intensity of the whole of A at the outset to be 1, then $\frac{1}{2} + \frac{2}{4} + \frac{3}{8} + \cdots + \frac{n}{2^n} = 2$). But such an interpretation is misleading. Swineshead gives absolutely no consideration to anything becoming arbitrarily small or tending to zero as we move indefinitely over the specified proportional parts. Swineshead knows where he is going to end up before he even starts; he has merely redistributed what he already knows to be a given finite increase in the intensity of one subject over another subject, something that is found to be true in most instances of the occurrence of "convergent infinite series" in the late Middle Ages. Yet however Swineshead's accomplishment is interpreted, one should note that his major concern was to show that a subject whose quality was distributed in such a manner *in infinitum* over its parts was in fact consistent with his denomination criterion and did not lead to paradox. It is also notable that, in so increasing the intensity of

A, he could have specified that the quality in question was heat, arguing, as he had previously argued against the proof of the first position, that on grounds of the physical assumption that heating causes rarefaction, it followed that A would not be just as intense as its second proportional part. The fact that he did not do so lends further credence to the view that his major interest was in seeing how many "results" could be drawn out of a given position or assumption, the more complicated and surprising the results the better. One such set of results could be derived by applying a physical assumption to the proof of the first position; another, as in the present instance, by ignoring it.

This interest of Swineshead can be even better illustrated if the present example from treatise II is carried yet one step further. Immediately after answering the objection treated above, another objection is put forth claiming that "from this it follows that A is now only finitely intense, yet by means of a merely finite rarefaction will suddenly be made infinitely intense." In Swineshead's reply to the objector's complaint that this is an absurd state of affairs and must be rejected, the important point is again Swineshead's demonstration that this presumably absurd situation can and does obtain (7ra). We can see how this can be so if, Swineshead tells us, we take only every 2^{nth} proportional part of our previously so intensified A and then rarefy the second proportional part of A by any amount howsoever small, while rarefying each of the succeeding proportional parts twice as slowly as the preceding one. Again, in our terms we have to do with a "divergent series," so the conclusion that A is "suddenly made infinitely intense" is a correct one. But to set down the general term of this "series" would be anachronistic and would credit Swineshead with something that was quite outside his thinking. What he should be credited with is ingenious, but much more straightforward. He realized that in selecting only the 2^{nth} proportional parts of A he had chosen parts whose intensities were successively double one another. Therefore, in deliberately specifying that the rarefaction over these parts should be successively "twice as slow," it automatically followed that, considering both the extension and intensity of that amount added to each part by rarefaction, the resulting contribution (no matter how small) to the denomination of the whole would be the same in each instance. And since there were an infinite number of such "added parts," the denomination of the whole immediately became infinite. Once again, in our terms, what Swineshead has done amounts to the adding of a constant amount to each term of an "infinite series." It is more profitable, however, to view Swineshead's concern with the infinite in another, much less modern, way. In the two "objections" that have just been cited, Swineshead has first shown that, astonishing as it might seem, a subject whose quality increases *in infinitum* as distributed over its parts is as a matter of fact only finitely intense overall. One can next take this same finitely intense subject, change it by a finite amount as small as you wish, and it immediately becomes infinitely intense. The switch from infinite to finite and then back to infinite again seems more than incidental. Swineshead was partaking of something that was characteristic of the logical—and by then physical—tradition of solving sophisms. In point of fact, at the end of treatise II he even refers to the conclusions he is dealing with (there are fifteen in all) as *sophismata* (9rb).

The foregoing fairly lengthy discussions of the first four treatises of the *Liber calculationum* should give a good impression of the character of the whole work, not forgetting that the later treatises appear to be slightly more expository in form. The descriptions of some of the special features of the treatises that follow assume the continuation of this same basic character without repeatedly asserting it.

Treatises V–VI: On Rarity and Density; On the Velocity of Augmentation. The fifth and sixth treatises again form a logical unit, this time concerning the quantity or rarity and density of subjects and motions with respect to quantity. The relatively long treatise V (16vb–22rb) has three basic parts. It first addresses directly the question of the proper measures of rarity and density, rejecting the position (1) that rarity depends on the proportion of the quantity of the subject to its matter while density depends on the proportion of matter to quantity, and accepting the position (2) that rarity depends on quantity assuming that the amount of matter remains the same (*raritas attenditur penes quantitatem non simpliciter sed in materia proportionata vel in comparatione ad materiam. Et ponit quod proportionabiliter sicut tota quantitas sit maior manente materia eadem, ita raritas est maior* [17ra]).

It is of interest to the modern historian to realize why Swineshead considered the first position to be significantly different from the second position; it may seem, indeed, to be nothing but an improved and more general version of the second position. The explanation of this point turns out to shed important light on the status of Bradwardine's geometric function relating forces, resistances, and velocities, which had been propounded in his *De proportionibus* in 1328. In fact, for Swineshead, if rarity depended upon the proportion (ratio) of quantity to matter, this would have meant that, for instance, when the proportion of quantity to matter was "doubled" (*dupletur* in his terms, but "squared" in modern terms), then the rarity would be doubled, and the resulting function would have been in modern terms logarithmic or exponential in exactly the same way that Bradwardine's function was logarithmic or exponential. It was their understanding of the meaning of the compounding or "addition" and "subtraction" of proportions (equivalent to multiplying and dividing ratios in the modern sense) that essentially forced fourteenth-century thinkers to this function. Finding it difficult, therefore, to propose the dependence of rarity on the ratio of quantity to matter as this would be understood in the simple modern sense, Swineshead was therefore led to his less elegant second position as a substitute emphasizing quantity and assuming the constancy of matter as a subsidiary consideration in order to avoid the intrusion of a proportion per se.

But having proposed the dependence of rarity on quantity assuming the matter constant, Swineshead enters in the second part of the treatise into a long consideration of how rarity should depend upon quantity. This consideration is subsumed under the question whether both rarity and density are positive entities or whether only one of them is positive, and, if so, which (17ra). Here he can rely in an important way upon his discussion in treatise I of positive and privative entities and their interrelations with regard to intensity and remissness. After an involved discussion, he concludes that density is the positive quality (and rarity privative) and that when a subject is rarefied uniformly for a given period of time it acquires quantity difformly, greater and greater quantities corresponding to equal increments of rarity as the subject becomes more rarefied (*densitas se habet positive et ex uniformi rarefactione alicuius per tempus secundum se totum difformiter acquiritur quantitas et si densius et rarius equalis quantitatis equevelociter rarefierent, rarius maiorem quantitatem acquireret quam densius* [18rb]). Thus, the mathematical characteristics of the measures of rarity become similar to those of the measures of remissness in treatise I, and similar conclusions can be reached. It follows, for instance, that the latitude of rarity between any degree of rarity and zero rarity is infinite (18vb),

just as a similar conclusion had followed for remissness.

The third and last section of treatise V raises and replies to doubts, many of which are parallel to earlier considerations concerning quality. Swineshead concludes that a uniformly difformly dense body or a body with unequal degrees of uniform density in its two halves is as dense as its mean degree (18vb–20vb). Similarly, he says that bodies are as rare as their mean degrees provided that it is understood that the latitudes of rarity and density are really the same (19vb), and he disposes of a whole series of doubts about how density and rarity are to be compared by saying that the situation is the same in this case as it is in the case of intensity and remissness (*ad que omnia possunt consimiliter argui et responderi sicut arguebatur ubi tanguntur illa de intensione et remissione, mutatis illis terminis intensio et remissio in istis terminis raritas et densitas* [20vb]). Finally, he replies to a doubt about whether, if there were an infinite quantity with a part which was infinitely dense, the whole would be infinitely dense (21rb–22rb) by saying that just as in similar cases concerning qualities, so here a density extended through only a finite part of an infinite subject would not contribute anything to the denomination of the whole subject (21vb–22ra).

When to the above description of treatise V is coupled the observation that nowhere in treatise V does Swineshead directly inquire into the physical significance to be properly correlated with the concepts density and rarity, it should be clear that Swineshead's real interest here must have been in the mathematical functions involved in the various positions, and in the consequences, whether more or less startling, that could be shown to be consistent with these functions. And again, as in earlier treatises, he concludes by saying that many more sophisms could be developed concerning this material, all of which can easily be solved if the material he has presented is well understood (22rb).

In treatise VI, Swineshead then turns from rarity and density as such to motions of augmentation, where augmentation is considered to be the same as increase of rarity. Like Roger Swineshead before him, he begins by rejecting the position espoused in Heytesbury's *Regule solvendi sophismata* that motion of augmentation is to be measured by the proportion of the new quantity to the old quantity (22va–24va). Second, he turns to the position on augmentation held by Roger Swineshead, namely that augmentation is to be measured by quantity acquired irrespective of the quantity doing the acquiring (24va–vb), but he also rejects this position because it does not adequately handle cases in which a quantity is lost at the same time as one is added. Swineshead then replaces Roger Swineshead's position with an improved version which he accepts, saying that augmentation and diminution should be measured by the net change of quantity of the subject (24vb). In reply to an objection concerning what happens according to this position to the concept of uniform augmentation, Swineshead admits in effect that the concepts of uniform velocities of alteration and motion will not then have an easy parallel in the case of the motion of augmentation, although one could speak of equal parts of a subject gaining equal qualities.

The most striking thing about treatise VI is perhaps the fact that the largest section of the treatise is devoted to the refutation of Heytesbury's view concerning the proper measure of augmentation. And here there are two points to be noted about the arguments provided. First of all, a significantly large proportion of them involve what are in effect augmentations from zero quantity. Since the first position is obviously not applicable to augmentations from zero (since this would put a zero into the denominator of the proportion of quantities that it proposes as the proper measure of augmentation), one might argue that these supposed refutations of the position are misguided. And secondly, Swineshead himself eventually concedes several of the refuting arguments although he did consider the first position to be refuted. Yet these arguments are left to stand as if they were strikes against the first position. Thus, Swineshead says that the inferences which can be drawn from the first position are amazing and contrary to one's idea of what the proper measure of a motion should be (23va)—some of these conclusions being ones that involve the unfair augmentation from zero quantity—but he then also concedes that some of these conclusions are simply true no matter how the velocity of augmentation is measured (23va). So again one might fairly draw the conclusion that Swineshead's major concern is not really the choice between rival measures, but rather the exhibition of mathematical techniques that one might reasonably use in the discussion of any of the positions.

Treatises VII–VIII: On Reaction; On the Powers of Things. As in the works of the other Oxford calculators where reaction is taken up at a fairly early stage, here too the problem of reaction is really the entire problem of how two qualified bodies act on each other and involves all of the variables dis-

cussed in the preceding treatises. For those who, like Richard Swineshead, held the so-called addition of part to part theory of qualitative change, the problem was particularly acute. There were numerous well-known cases (*experimenta*) in which reaction seemed to occur (25va). Furthermore, under the addition theory it seemed that the parts of a quality present should be able to act and react with the other qualitative parts nearby. Yet the previously accepted Aristotelian and medical theory of qualitative change had assumed that the qualities of a given subject could be represented by the single degrees of hot, cold, wet, or dry of the whole, so that if two bodies were brought close together such that one could act on the other, only that body with the higher degree, say of heat, would act as the agent or force causing change, and only that body with the lower degree would act as patient and be changed. Clearly the calculators were in a position in which they had to improve upon previous theory by taking account of distributions of quality, and yet the theoretical situation was so complex and mathematically difficult that they faced an almost impossible task.

After preliminary arguments, Swineshead takes, as the foundation of his solution to the problem, the position that the power of a subject is determined by the multitude of form (*multitudo forme*) in it, where multitude of form is determined not only by the intensity of the form and the extension, but also by what might be called the density of form (26vb). He takes density as the most important factor and asserts that if a foot length of fire were condensed to half a foot, it would still contain the same multitude of form even if the intensity were the same as before. Swineshead next turns to the question of whether the whole patient resists the agent or only the part acted on. After considering various positions, he concludes that although the whole patient does not necessarily resist the agent, the whole part of the patient directly opposite the agent resists, and that all parts do not resist equally, parts further from the agent resisting less than those closer. Unfortunately, arguments can be raised to show that no simple proportionality obtains between distance from the agent and lesser resistance. Swineshead asserts, however, that it will be more clearly understood when he deals with illuminations how resistance decreases with distance (27rb–28rb).

On the basis of these fundamentals Swineshead concludes that reaction cannot occur between uniform bodies such that the reaction is according to the quality contrary to that of the action (28va–

28vb). (By a uniform body Swineshead means uniform not only according to intensity of quality but also according to the amount of form existing in equal parts of the body.) It is possible for the patient to react according to another quality—so that while the agent heats the patient the patient in turn humidifies the agent. Between difform bodies, on the other hand, there can be action with reaction in the contrary quality in another part. Where such reaction occurs the whole agent and whole patient act and resist according to their power insofar as it is applied in the given situation. Thus, Swineshead appears content in his reply to leave the unspoken and rather improbable implication that in all the observed cases of reaction according to the same quality, the qualities of the two bodies must have been difform.

The rest of treatise VII consists of the solution of three *dubia*. The first, also dealt with by John Dumbleton in his *Summa logicae et philosophiae naturalis*, concerns whether an agent will act more slowly if patients are applied to either side of it than it would if it acted on only one of the patients (29va–30ra). Swineshead is sure that if two actions concur at the same point the action will be faster, but he is not sure of the solution of the doubt if the two patients are far enough apart so that they do not act on each other. In the latter case, he says, the reader may decide for himself whether the patients will assist each other in resisting, since, although some say they do, it is hard to understand how this could be so (30ra). To a second doubt Swineshead concludes that two difform bodies which are similar in those parts nearest each other can nevertheless still act on each other (30ra–30va), and to a third doubt he concludes that bodies having maximum degrees of contraries can act on each other (30va–30vb).

It should be clear that in all of treatise VII one of Swineshead's main questions concerns the additivity or summability of the forces and resistances he is dealing with. Indeed, elsewhere additivity was one of the major concerns of the Oxford calculators in their efforts at quantification. With respect to single dimensions such as that of intensity, the calculators were adamant that the measure of intensity should be an additive measure. Following the addition theory of the intension and remission of forms, they assumed that an intensity was equivalent to the sum of its parts. In dealing with actions and reactions of bodies, however, the basis for such additivity was not so easily found. Here, and again in treatise XI concerning local motion, Swineshead appears to concede, perhaps to his own disappointment, that difficulties appear to ensue if one attempts to treat subjects as the sums of their parts in any simple fashion. The difficulties of considering not only the forces and resistances of the parts, but also the varying distances of the parts from each other and the possible interactions of the parts on each other, made a detailed part-by-part quantitative treatment practically impossible. We may admire Swineshead's ingenuity in the face of such odds while agreeing that it is unfortunate that the slant of Aristotelian physics towards alteration rather than local motion caused Swineshead to concentrate on such a difficult problem.

Treatise VIII again takes up the question dealt with in treatise VII concerning how the powers of things are to be measured, and it appears probable that parts of treatises VII and VIII represent Swineshead's successive reworkings of the same basic problem. Despite nine arguments against the view that power is to be measured by multitude of form, Swineshead reaffirms his earlier conclusion that it is. The only thing that he adds here is the remark that the amount of form induced in a subject will depend upon the amount of matter present (31rb). He concedes the nine arguments or conclusions *de imaginatione*, their supposed difficulty being based on the view that, for a given form, intensity and extension are inversely related, which, he says, is only accidentally so (31rb–31va).

If in the work of Oresme, the concept of the "quantity of quality" was to become fundamental, where quantity of quality was the product of intensity times extension, here we see Swineshead's effort to deal with objections based on a similar concept. Whatever objections there may be to Oresme's concept of "quantity of quality" from a modern point of view, students of medieval science have in recent years become so familiar with the concept that there is a tendency to assume the use of a similar concept in other late medieval authors attempting the quantification of qualities or forms. It deserves emphasizing, therefore, that Richard Swineshead and the other Oxford calculators of 1330–1350 were familiar with concepts like Oresme's quantity of quality, but rejected them in favor of quantifications in terms of intensities alone or in terms of something like Swineshead's multitude of form. This rejection of "quantity of quality" helps explain, among other things, Swineshead's less than total happiness in treatise II with the "mean degree measure" of difform qualities, a measure that he might otherwise have been expected to favor because of its mathematical attractiveness. Swineshead does not always assume, as Oresme's quantity of quality concept implies, that when the extension of a subject is decreased, the form remaining unchanged, the intensity will increase, and he even goes so far as to assert that a form could be condensed to a point without its intensity increasing (31rb).

Treatises IX–X: On the Difficulty of Action; On Maxima and Minima.

The ninth and tenth treatises in a sense carry further Swineshead's treatment of action and the forces causing it. Treatise X has a clear precedent in earlier discussions of maxima and minima, in particular in the discussion found in Heytesbury's *Regule solvendi sophismata*, and treatise IX probably is related, although in a nonobvious way, to Bradwardine's *De proportionibus*. The problem covered in treatise IX (and also in Dumbleton's *Summa*, part VI) seems to have arisen because of the Calculator's acceptance of Bradwardine's function for measuring velocities. For the standard Aristotelian position concerning the relation of forces, resistances, and velocities, there was a simple relationship between forces and the velocities produced with a given resistance, such that each equal part of the force could be interpreted as contributing an equal part of the velocity (and here again arose the question of additivity). For the Bradwardinian position, on the other hand, multiples of a force, with the resistance remaining constant, did not produce equal multiples of the velocity. As a result, one needed some other measure of what a force could do. On this subject, Swineshead first rejects two positions: (1) that the action or difficulty produced depends upon the proportion of greater inequality with which the agent acts, so that an agent acting from a greater proportion produces a greater difficulty (31va); and (2) that the action or difficulty produced depends on a proportion of lesser inequality, because an agent closer in power to the strength of the resistance tires more in acting (31va).

The position that Swineshead adopts is the same as that adopted by Dumbleton, namely that the difficulty produced is proportional to the power acting to its ultimate (31vb). In a given uniform resistance there will be an action of maximum difficulty that cannot be produced in that medium, namely the difficulty equal to the power of the resistance (31vb–32ra). When the power of the agent is doubled, the difficulty it can produce is also doubled. The latitude of difficulty or range of all possible difficulties is infinite (32ra).

The remainder of treatise IX consists of the raising of twelve arguments against Swineshead's preferred position and of his replies to them. In these arguments the connection with Bradwardine's function manifests itself. A common assumption behind the objections is that difficulty (or action) and motion (or velocity) ought to be proportional to each other, so that to move something twice as fast is to produce a double action. As stated above, in the commonly assumed Aristotelian "function," a double force, a double velocity, and presumably a double action or difficulty all seem to be correlated with each other. This is not so in the Bradwardinian function, where a doubling of force does not usually correlate with a doubling of velocity. Swineshead simply asserts here, therefore, that difficulty can be correlated with force or power, and' that velocity and difficulty produced do not necessarily correspond to each other (32vb–33rb). The main effect of treatise IX, therefore, is to clear away objections that might be raised about Bradwardine's function by those still thinking in an Aristotelian framework.

Treatise X concerns maxima and minima only with respect to the traversal of space in local motion, and the ground it covers is quite standard. Having stated some familiar definitions and suppositions concerning maxima and minima of active and passive powers, Swineshead states two rules: (1) that both debilitatable and nondebilitatable powers have a minimum uniform resistance that they cannot traverse (in familiar scholastic terminology, a *minimum quod non*); and (2) that with respect to media there is a maximum power that cannot traverse a given medium, namely the power equal to the resistance of the medium (a *maximum quod non* [34rb]). Thus, for a power, say, equal to 3, there will be a minimum resistance it cannot traverse, that is, the resistance 3, and, conversely, for the resistance equal to 3, the power equal to 3 will be the maximum power that cannot traverse it.

The rest of treatise X consists of rules for assigning maxima and minima under a variety of possible conditions, that is, when the medium is uniform and when it is difform, when there is a time limit and when there is not, when the power is constant and when it weakens in acting, and when the medium is infinite and when it is finite. Although they may take a while to decipher, these conclusions are mostly the simple results of the assumption that the force must be greater than the resistance for motion to occur. Swineshead himself seems to feel that he is traversing familiar ground, and the treatise is therefore quite short.

Treatise XI: On the Place of an Element.

Swineshead's concern in treatise XI is a single problem relating to the motion of a heavy body in the vicinity of its natural place at the center of the universe: whether in free fall, assuming a void or nonresistant medium, the heavy body will ever reach the center of the universe in the sense that the center of the body will eventually coincide with the center of the universe. If we regard the heavy body in question as a thin rod (*simplex columnare*), the variables that Swineshead has to deal with in resolving the problem become evident: as soon as any part of the rod passes the center of the universe, that part may be considered as acting as a resistance against its continued motion. Now one position that can be taken in resolving the problem is that the body acts as the sum of its parts and that therefore the parts of the rod "beyond the center" actually do resist its motion. Assuming this, lengths or segments of the rod will function both as distances traversed as the rod approaches the center and as the forces and resistances involved in determining such a traversal. If we also assume, with Swineshead, Bradwardine's "function" relating velocities with the forces and resistances determining them, then the task to be carried out is to discover a way to apply this "function" to the "distance-determined" forces and resistances acting upon the falling rod in order to calculate the relevant changes in velocity and thus ascertain whether or not the center of the rod ever will reach the center of the universe.

In what is mathematically perhaps the most complicated and sophisticated section of the *Liber calculationum*, Swineshead accomplishes this task and replies that, on the assumption of the rod acting as the sum of its parts, the two centers will never come to coincide. He presents his argument axiomatically, beginning from a number of strictly mathematical *suppositiones* and *regulae* and then moving to their application to the problem at hand. It will be easier to indicate something of the nature of his accomplishment if the order is, at least in part, reversed. Thus, Swineshead clearly realizes and emphasizes the fact that the distance remaining between the center of the rod and the center of the universe will always be equal to half the difference between that (greater) part of the rod which is still on this side of the center of the universe and that (lesser) part which is beyond (37ra) (in terms of Figure 1, $CD = (F_1 - R_1)/2$). This obtains no matter what space intervals we consider in the rod's progressive motion toward the center. When this is added to the fact that, with any given motion of the rod, whatever is subtracted from the segment this side of the center of the universe is added to the segment beyond the center, thus deter-

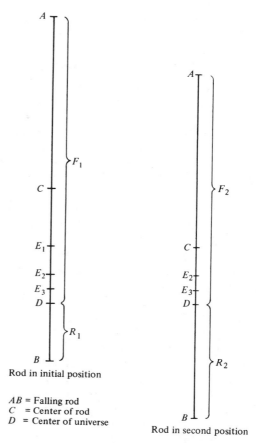

AB = Falling rod
C = Center of rod
D = Center of universe

Rod in initial position

Rod in second position

FIGURE 1

mining the "new" forces and resistances obtaining after that motion, Swineshead then has a way to apply Bradwardine's "function" to the whole problem. Divide, for example, the remaining distance (CD) into proportional parts (according to a double proportion); we know the relation of the distance between the centers to the difference between the relevant forces and resistances: $CD = (F_1 - R_1)/2$, but successively following the particular division specified of the remaining distance it is also true that this same half-difference between F_1 and R_1 is equivalent to the excess of F_1 less one-fourth of $(F_1 - R_1)$ over R_1 plus one-fourth of $(F_1 - R_1)$. But in a strictly mathematical "suppositio" it is stated (and then proved) that the proportion of the thusly decreased F_1 to the thusly increased R_1 will be less than the "sub-double" of the proportion between the original, unaltered F_1 and R_1. (*Si inter aliqua sit proportio maioris inequalitatis, et quarta pars excessus maioris supra minus auferatur a maiori et addatur minori, tunc inter illa in fine erit proportio minor quam subdupla ad proportionem existentem inter ista duo in principio* [35vb].) In modern symbols:

$$\left(F_1 - \frac{F_1 - R_1}{4}\right):\left(R_1 + \frac{F_1 - R_1}{4}\right) < (F_1 : R_1)^{1/2}.$$

At the same time, the decreased F_1 and the increased R_1 have given us the F_2 and R_2 operative after the rod has moved over the first proportional part of the distance between centers, assuming that its speed is uniform throughout this motion, and, moving over the second proportional part, we can similarly derive F_3 and R_3 and relate them to F_2 and R_2 by means of the same "mathematical supposition," and so on, over succeeding proportional parts and F's and R's. However, the ordering of the force-resistance proportions that is the burden of this mathematical supposition is precisely what is at stake in Bradwardine's "function" claiming that increases and (in the particular problem at hand) decreases in velocity correspond to increases and decreases in the proportion between force and resistance. Bradwardine can therefore be directly applied, yielding resultant velocities over succeeding proportional parts each of which is "more remiss" than half the preceding one ($V_1 > 2V_2 > 4V_3 > \cdots$). Since succeeding proportional parts of the distance decrease by exactly half ($CE_1 = 2E_1E_2 = 4E_2E_3 = \cdots$), it follows that the time intervals for each increment of distance must increase *in infinitum*, which means that the center of the rod will never reach the center of the universe (*maius tempus requireretur ad pertransitionem secunde partis proportionalis quam ad pertransitionem prime . . . et sic in infinitum. Ergo in nullo tempore finito transiret C totam illam distantiam* [37rb]).

Swineshead has reached this result by applying a particular, proportional part division to the distance remaining between the centers, but he provides for the generalization of this division by specifying (and proving) his crucial mathematical supposition in a general form (36va); then we may presumably take any succeeding proportional parts whatsoever in determining the fall of the rod. But his own use of this more general supposition occurs in a second, different proof of the conclusion that the rod will never reach the center of the universe. In our terms, the first proof summarized above assumes a constant velocity—and hence constant force-resistance proportions—over the relevant distance intervals, thus employing a discontinuous, step function in resolving the problem. In a more compact, and more difficult, proof Swineshead comes more directly to grip with his variables as exhibiting a continuous function. Less tractable, and hence more difficult to represent adequately in modern terms, than the first proof, its substance is tied to the proportional comparison of decreases or losses with what we would term rates of decrease or loss (for example, *motus velocius proportionabiliter remittetur quam excessus; ergo excessus tardius et tardius proportionabiliter remittetur* [37rb]).

In both proofs Swineshead has in effect assumed that the rod or heavy body in question is a *grave simplex*, a limitation that he addresses himself to by considering, in reply to several objections, the body as a *mixtum* (37va). Far more important, however, is another objection. It claims, in effect, that the assumption behind Swineshead's whole procedure up to that point—namely, that the rod does act as the sum of its parts, must be false because it implies that there would exist natural inclinations that would be totally without purpose and vain (*appetitus . . . omnino otiosus . . . vanus*), an inadmissible consequent (37rb).

Swineshead therefore sets forth a second, alternative position, one in which the heavy body in question acts as a whole, where its parts contribute to the natural inclination or desire (*appetitus*) of the whole in a manner that is not given precise mathematical determination (37vb–38ra). As might be expected, Swineshead spends far less time treating, and seems much less interested in, this second position, in spite of the fact that it is apparently the true one. This brevity fits well with the whole tenor of the *Liber calculationum* and with what has been noted above of the greater interest in deriving results than in just what the results are. The treatment based on the first, "false" *positio* of the whole body as the sum of its parts also fits well with much of the rest of the *Liber calculationum*, where the mathematical and logical determination of the contribution of parts to wholes is so often a central issue.

Treatises XII–XIII: On Light; On the Action of Light. These two treatises are concerned with light, first with respect to the power of the light source and second with respect to the illumination produced.

The power of a light source, Swineshead states, is measured in the same way as the power of other agents, namely by the multitude of form (38ra). Equal light sources, then, will be those that are not only equal in intensity but also equal in multitude of form (38rb). Thus, if sources with equal multitudes of form are intended by equal latitudes of intensity, they will gain equally in power, but if sources with unequal multitudes of form are intended by equal latitudes of intensity, the one with more form will increase more in power than the other.

On the basis of these presuppositions, Swineshead then draws a number of conclusions or rules treating what happens when either the quantity of light source is varied (by adding or subtracting matter so that the multitude of form is changed) or the intensity of these sources is varied. He concludes, for instance, that if there are two light sources of different intensity, which at the outset are either equal or unequal in quantity, but which then diminish equally in quantity, then proportionally as one is more intense than the other it will diminish in power more rapidly (38rb–38va). Swineshead does not believe that changing the quantity (extension) of a light source without adding or subtracting matter will change its power, but he says that his conclusions can be proved even better by those who hold such a view (38vb).

It should be noted that in this treatise Swineshead does assume that there is a correlation between intensity and multitude of form, something which he felt it necessary to state as an explicit hypothesis when he dealt with similar problems in treatise II (for example, 8va) and something which he, in effect, ignored in treatise VIII. Had his interests been in determining the one correct physical theory, it is hard to believe that he would not have brought these contexts together and somewhere stated what he felt to be the true physical situation with regard to the connections between the intensity, extension, and "density" of a form. With his attention falling as entirely on the quantitative side as it does, he lets apparent inconsistencies slide, covered by the remark that the connection between the intensities and extensions of a given form are only accidental (31rb).

Treatise XIII consists of the solution of two major doubts and a long string of conclusions. In reply to the first doubt, Swineshead concludes that every light source produces its entire latitude, from its maximum degree down to zero degree, in every medium in which it suffices to act, but that a source will cast its light to a greater distance in a rarer medium and to a lesser distance in a denser medium (39vb). Light is remitted (is less intense) at more distant points because of the indisposition caused by the medium between the source and the distant point, so since there is no medium between the source and the point next to it there is no remission at that point.

In reply to the second doubt Swineshead concludes that a light source casts a uniformly difform illumination in a uniform medium (40rb–va). Con-

sidering the medium between the source and a distant point as an impediment subtracting from the intensity of illumination, Swineshead comes up with a physically reasonable relation leading to a uniformly difform distribution, avoiding the trap of making the intensity inversely proportional to the distance from the light source. This no doubt is the explanation Swineshead had in mind in treatise VII as being helpful in understanding how distant parts combine their actions and resistances (28rb).

These two replies are then followed by a series of fourteen conclusions (numbered 13–26 in sequence with the conclusions of treatise XII) intended to make clearer what has preceded. They appear quite complex, but we may suppose that he arrived at them by a simple visualization of the situation with few if any mathematical calculations. Thus, Swineshead concludes first that if a light source acts in a uniform medium and if a part of the medium next to the agent is made more dense without changing its quantity (extension), then at every point of the rest of the medium farther from the agent the illumination will be remitted with the same velocity as the illumination at the extreme point of the part made denser is remitted (40vb–41ra). Imagining a graph of the original uniformly

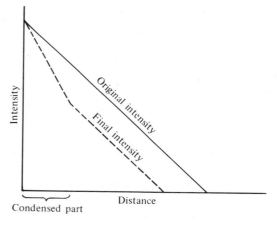

FIGURE 2

difform illumination, we see that this conclusion amounts to saying that when part of the medium is condensed, the slope of decrease of intensity will become steeper in that part, but in the remaining part the slope of decrease will remain the same, being shifted down parallel to itself to connect with the new, more remiss degree at the extreme point of the condensed part (see Figure 2).

Like this first conclusion, Swineshead's other conclusions are easy to understand on the basis of graphs, although he makes no reference to visualizations of the conclusions. In our terms, the variables that he has to work with in the conclusions are that the quantity of the light source determines the rate of decrease of intensity or slope of the distribution of intensities in a given medium, whereas the intensity of the source determines the degree from which that decrease starts. The density of the medium, on the other hand, also determines the slope of the distribution of intensities when the source remains the same. Swineshead can then partially offset changes in the quantity of the light source by changes in the density of the medium, or vice versa, as it suits his purpose (cf. conclusion 19 [41vb]).

It is so natural to us to visualize these conclusions that it is hard to imagine that Swineshead did not do so also. Dumbleton, in the corresponding part of his *Summa*, did make an explicit geometrical analogy, and the tradition of using triangles or cones to represent the dispersal of light in optics would also have prompted mental images of triangles. It is very probable then that the mathematics behind treatise XIII was a simple "visualized geometry."

Treatise XIV: On Local Motion. One of the most exhaustively developed sections of the *Liber calculationum*, treatise XIV begins by stipulating that its contents will be formulated under the assumption "that motion is measured in terms of geometric proportion" (*motum attendi penes proportionem geometricam* [43va]). As immediately becomes obvious, this is Swineshead's elliptical way of informing his readers that he will be accepting Bradwardine's view that variations in velocities correspond directly to variations in the force-resistance proportions determining those velocities (in modern terminology, that arithmetic changes in velocity correspond to geometric changes in the relevant force-resistance ratios). With this as base, what Swineshead accomplishes in setting forth the forty-nine *regulae* that constitute treatise XIV is to give a relatively complete "catalog" of just which *kinds* of changes in velocity correspond to which *kinds* of changes in force and resistance and vice versa.

He does this in strict axiomatic fashion, the first three rules presenting what can be regarded as the basic mathematics of proportion which will serve, together with his assumption of Bradwardine's "function," as the key to all that follows. As indicated above, there is no doubt that the medieval tradition of compounding proportions was at the root of Bradwardine's logarithmic-type function, and it is precisely this that Swineshead makes ex-

plicit in his initial rules. Thus, the first rule tells us that "whenever a force (*potentia*) increases with respect to a constant resistance (*resistentiae non variatae*), then it will acquire as much proportionally relative to that resistance as it will itself be rendered greater" (43va). That is to say, if some force F_1 acting on a constant resistance R increases to F_2, then the proportional increase in F (the proportion $F_2 : F_1$) is equal to the increase of $F_2 : R$ over $F_1 : R$. As Swineshead makes clear in his proof of this rule, this amounts to a compounding of the proportions involved, that is, when $F_2 : F_1$ is "added to" $F_1 : R$ the result is $F_2 : R$. (Note that following the medieval convention proportions are added to one another [just as are numbers or line segments], when we would say they are multiplied.) In the second and third rules Swineshead establishes corresponding relations for the cases of a decrease in force and an increase or decrease in resistance (the force than being held constant [43va]).

That these rules provide the basis of what Swineshead was attempting to do in treatise XIV can be seen as soon as one introduces the motion or velocities that correspond to or "result from" the force-resistance proportions whose "mathematics of change" he has just established. Thus, to return to the first rule as an example, if we assume that a velocity V_1 corresponds to the proportion $F_1 : R$ and a velocity V_2 to the proportion $F_2 : R$, then, because $F_2 : R$ is greater than $F_1 : R$ by the proportion $F_2 : F_1$ (which is what the compounding of these proportions asserts), it follows that the velocity added is precisely the velocity that results from the proportion $F_2 : F_1$ (and which would result from a proportion $F : R$ equal to $F_2 : F_1$ standing alone). Given this, and the corresponding relations when a resistance is allowed to vary while the force is held constant, Swineshead can determine all that he wishes concerning changes in velocity by paying attention only to the relevant force-force or resistance-resistance proportions representing the changes. When, and only when, these proportions are equal will the corresponding positive or negative increments of velocity be equal.

In deducing his succeeding *regulae* on such a basis, Swineshead does not "calculate" velocity increments from given force-force or resistance-resistance proportions, nor velocities from given force-resistance proportions. In this he was strictly medieval. Rather, he always compares (at least) *pairs* of $F : F$ or $R : R$ proportions. Thus, whenever unequal forces increase or decrease with equal swiftness (*equevelociter*)—which means that $F_2 - F_1 = F_4 - F_3$—then the resultant $F_2 : F_1, F_4 : F_3$ proportions will be unequal, whence it follows that the corresponding velocity increments will be unequal. If, on the other hand, the forces increase or decrease proportionally (*eque proportionabiliter*)—which means that $F_2 : F_1 = F_4 : F_3$—then the corresponding velocity increments will be equal. And the same thing holds for increasing or decreasing resistances, the forces being held constant.

Beginning, then, with two rules (4 and 5 [43va]) that apply a change in a *single* force or resistance to, correspondingly, *two* constant resistances or forces (whence the relevant single $F_2 : F_1$ or $R_2 : R_1$ proportions function as pairs since they are applied to pairs of R or F), Swineshead sets forth the implications of his mathematics of force-resistance changes to changes in velocity. In rules 4 and 5, inasmuch as one has a single $F_2 : F_1$ or $R_2 : R_1$ proportion doing double duty, the corresponding velocity increments are naturally the same. (For example, rule 4 reads: "Whenever a force increases or decreases with respect to two equal or unequal, but constant, resistances, it will intend or remit motion with respect to each [of these resistances] with equal swiftness.") Note should be taken of how, throughout treatise XIV, Swineshead handles what we would consider as positive versus negative increments of velocity. Since all determining force and resistance proportions are always of greater inequality (e.g., $F_2 : F_1$ where $F_2 > F_1$ when it is a question of increase in force, $F_1 : F_2$ where $F_1 > F_2$ when decrease is involved), velocity increments are always added, a procedure that follows directly from Swineshead's basic technique of compounding proportions. This means that when it is a question of the remission of motion arising from decreasing forces or increasing resistances, then increments are added to the motion at the end of the change in question, the "sum" of these increments plus the final motion or velocity giving the motion or velocity at the beginning of the change. When the motion is intended, or the velocity increments are positive, the addition is naturally made to the motion obtaining at the beginning of the change.

In rules 6 through 15 (43va–43vb) Swineshead applies the two kinds of force or resistance change, that is, equally swift (*equevelociter*) or equally proportional (*eque proportionabiliter*) increases or decreases, to *pairs* of changing forces or resistances and infers the corresponding changes in velocity. Thus far, the force and resistance changes

can be considered as discrete. However, beginning with rule 19 [43vb] Swineshead faces the case of the uniform and the continuous change of a single force or resistance. Now a single uniformly increasing force acting on a constant resistance, for example, will "generate" pairs of proportions $F_2 : F_1, F_3 : F_2, F_4 : F_3$, etc., where the succeeding proportions have "common terms" because the increase in force is continuous and where $F_2 - F_1 = F_3 - F_2 = F_4 - F_3 = \cdots$ because the increase is uniform. This latter fact entails that $F_2 : F_1 > F_3 : F_2 > F_4 : F_3 > \cdots$, which in turn implies that the increments of velocity will become successively smaller and smaller. Thus, the first half of rule 19 reads: "If a force increases uniformly with respect to a constant resistance, it will intend motion more and more slowly."

It is important, however, to be able to deal with at least certain kinds of nonuniform or difform changes in force and resistance. Hence, in rules 21 and 22 (43vb–44ra), arguing by a *locus a maiori*, Swineshead shows that if (as he has just established) a uniform gain in force or resistance entails a, respectively, slower and slower intension or remission of motion, then a nonuniform, slower and slower gain in force or resistance will necessarily also entail slower and slower intension and remission. Similarly, if a uniform loss in force or resistance entails a, respectively, faster and faster remission or intension of motion, then a nonuniform faster and faster loss in force or resistance also entails faster and faster remission and intension. The difform changes involved in a faster and faster gain, or a slower and slower loss, of force or resistance are not treated, since in such cases no inferences can be made about the resultant $F : F$ and $R : R$ proportions and, hence, about the resultant velocity increments.

However, the types of difform change in force or resistance that Swineshead can and does treat are precisely those needed in much of the remainder of treatise XIV. Up to this point changes in resistance have been independently given. Beginning with rule 23 (44ra) these changes are ascribed to the medium through which a mobile (represented by the force acting upon it) moves. Furthermore, all increase or decrease of resistance has hitherto been considered merely *relative to time* (whether it be *equevelociter* or *eque proportionabiliter*, no matter). But to ascribe variations in resistance to a medium is to speak of increase or decrease *relative to space*. Consequently, the problem facing Swineshead is to connect increments of resistance with respect to space to increments of resistance with respect to time, which is exactly what rule 23 does. Thus, a uniformly difform medium is one in which equal increments of resistance occur over equal spaces or distances. We also know that any body moving through such a medium in the direction of increasing resistance will move continuously more and more slowly (that is, the spaces S_1, S_2, S_3, $\cdots$ traversed in equal times successively decrease). But these two factors imply that, in equal times, the mobile will encounter smaller and smaller increments of resistance. Hence, equal increments of resistance (Swineshead calls them "latitudes of resistance") over space have been connected to decreasing increments of resistance over time. Accordingly, rule 23 reads: "If some force begins to move from the more remiss extreme of a uniformly difform medium and remains constant in strength, then the resistance with respect to it will increase more and more slowly." However, this slower and slower increase in resistance over time is precisely one of those kinds of difform change Swineshead was able to deal with in rules 21 and 22. This allows him to infer in rule 24 (44rb) that the motion of a mobile under a constant force through a uniformly difform medium in the direction of increasing resistance entails that the motion in question will undergo continuously slower and slower remission.

There are media, however, in which the distribution of resistance over equal spaces is difform, but not uniformly difform. What can be said of them? We know what equal changes of velocity are associated with a resistance that changes uniformly proportionally over time (rules 11 and 27 [43va, 44va–44vb]). Thus, if we imagine a medium of uniform resistance which increases in resistance equiproportionally over time as a constant force mobile moves through it, the mobile will remit its motion uniformly, that is, will undergo equal negative increments of velocity in equal times (rule 28 [44vb–45va]). With this rule in hand, Swineshead then imagines another medium with a resistance constant in time but difform with respect to space and having at each point the resistance which was at the corresponding point of the first medium when the mobile was at that point. The mobile will then have the same motion in the second medium as it had in the first, that is, a uniformly difform motion. This means that (rule 29 [45va–45vb]) there can be a medium with resistance distributed difformly over space in such a way as to cause a mobile moving in it under a constant force to remit its motion uniformly (even though Swineshead could not describe this distribution).

Nevertheless, what Swineshead has established in rule 29 is of considerable importance for much of the remainder of treatise XIV. Rules 30–43 [45vb–48rb] all have to do with what will, or will not, occur when other constant or changing forces move through a medium in which (again rule 29) a given constant force uniformly remitted its motion. Thus, in rule 30 [45vb–46rb], Swineshead proves that two unequal constant forces cannot both uniformly remit their motion in the same medium. It is worthy of note that to prove this rule, Swineshead has to determine where the mobile that does remit its motion uniformly is at the middle instant of its motion. To do this he uses the ratio of space traversed in the first half of the time to the space traversed in the second half of the time and to find this ratio he uses the famous "Merton mean speed theorem," which he proves for the occasion (45vb–46ra). Apart from the fact that Swineshead gives four different proofs of the theorem, it here appears as a fairly routine lemma. He does not assign it any special importance, and does not even give it the honor of labeling it as a separate rule or conclusion.

Holding in mind the constant force specified in rule 29 as able to cause the uniform remission of motion in a given medium, Swineshead concludes treatise XIV by considering what will transpire when constant forces greater or lesser than that constant force are brought into play and when greater or lesser forces that are undergoing continuous intensification or remission are involved (rules 31–43). The last of these rules points out that a constant force greater than that specified in rule 29, but acting in the same medium, will give rise to a faster and faster remission of motion, that is, to a difformly difform motion. This leads to the final rules (44–49 [48rb–48vb]) of the treatise, which together function as a kind of appendix stipulating various facts and relations concerning difformly difform motions. As a whole, treatise XIV is an extremely impressive exhibition of just which cases of the different kinds of variation in force, resistance, and velocity that can be drawn out of Bradwardine's "function" are amenable to determination and treatment. As in the case of many of the other treatises of the *Liber calculationum*, there is a substantial increase in complexity from the beginning to the end of treatise XIV. But perhaps one of Swineshead's most signal accomplishments is his success in the latter part of the treatise in connecting variations in resistance over time with variations in resistance over space. For to the medieval supporter of Bradwardine's function (or of "Aristotle's function" as well for relating forces, resistances, and velocities), motion in a medium that was nonuniform was exceedingly problematic. As soon as the resistance in a medium was allowed to vary, one had to face the difficulty that the degree of resistance of the medium determined the velocity of the motion, while at the same time the velocity determined where in the medium the mobile would be and hence the resistance it would encounter. One seemed caught in a situation involving a double dependency of the relevant variables on each other. But Swineshead's "translation" of spatial increments of resistance into temporal ones automatically rendered the resistance of the medium time dependent and thus circumvented the troublesome double dependency.

Treatises XV–XVI: On a Nonresisting Medium or on the Increase of Power and Resistance; On the Induction of the Highest Degree. Treatises XV and XVI are continuations of treatise XIV and add ever more complications. In treatise XV Swineshead again considers the local motions of constant or changing powers in extended media, but this time he allows the resistance of the medium to vary while the mobile is moving through it or (we would say) takes the increase of power as an independent variable. In the key rule 29 of treatise XIV Swineshead had considered the motion of a mobile through a uniform medium with resistance changing over time, but this was a tool to allow him to deal with spatially difform resistances, the distributions of which he could not otherwise describe. Treatise XV, however, begins by dealing with temporally changing resistances in their own right.

The first conclusion of treatise XV is an example of Swineshead's mathematical ingeniousness, not in that he does complex mathematics, but in that he sees how to avoid complex mathematics. The conclusion concerns a nonresisting medium (or, in modern terms, a fixed space or vacuum) in which a resistance begins to be generated. The resistance first appears at one end of the medium and moves progressively across the medium in such a way that the resistance increases uniformly from that end up to the point where the resistance ends. In modern terms, then, we might represent the resistance graphically by a straight line that rotates around the origin, starting in a vertical position, rotating at a decreasing rate (so that any point of the line has a constant horizontal velocity), and increasing in length so that the maximum height of the end point is a constant (see Figure 3). If, Swineshead concludes, a mobile begins to move

from the same extreme of the medium at which the resistance begins to be generated, then it will move with a constant velocity (always keeping pace with the progress of a given degree of resistance), provided that the maximum resistance moves away from the mobile faster than the mobile could move with that resistance (48vb). Swineshead proves this conclusion first by showing that there could not have been any initial period of time during which the mobile increased or decreased its velocity, and second by showing that the mobile could not later begin to move faster or more slowly than its given resistance. In the later proof he argues, for instance, that if the mobile were supposed to increase its velocity, then it would immediately begin to encounter greater resistances, implying a decrease rather than an increase in velocity and thus a contradiction; and if the mobile were supposed to decrease its velocity, then conversely it would immediately begin to encounter lesser resistances implying an increase rather than a decrease in velocity and thus another contradiction. So, therefore, it must continue with a constant velocity. As stated above, from a modern point of view, any position that connects resistance with velocity as Bradwardine's function does would seem to be very problematic when applied to difform resistances, given that position (and therefore resistance) would determine the velocity of the

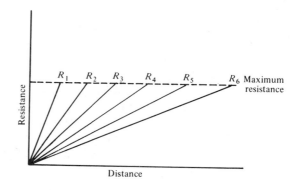

FIGURE 3

mobile, and yet velocity (and initial position) would also determine position, involving a double dependency. We see Swineshead here, however, not only coping with the problems of such a double dependency, but even playing with it and in a sense making sport to come up with ever more intriguing and complicated conclusions. Following the first conclusion, Swineshead proceeds to show that if the motion of the latitude of resistance is accelerated or decelerated the motion of the mobile will accelerate or decelerate also (49ra – 50ra), and he goes on from there to prove nine other conclusions concerned with the generation of a latitude of resistance in a nonresisting medium (50vb – 51rb).

The second main part of treatise XV concerns the motion of powers augmenting from zero degree in uniformly difform resistances. Again, perhaps the first conclusion of this part may serve as an example of the fourteen conclusions proved. If there is a uniformly difform medium terminated at zero degree in which a power begins to move as it augments uniformly from zero degree (always moving according to the proportion of its power to the point of the medium at which it is), then this power will continually move uniformly (51rb – 51va).

The further conclusions of this second part all concern temporally constant uniformly difform resistances, but the powers are allowed to vary in different ways, both uniformly and difformly. These conclusions differ from the conclusions of treatise XIV not only because the resistances involved are uniformly difform rather than difformly difform, but also because the changes of resistance and power are given as the independent variables rather than the velocities, as in treatise XIV.

In this treatise as in the last, the attempt seems to be to give a general description of the possible interrelations of power, resistance, and velocity and their changes. As in the last, too, the main variations of the independent variables considered are uniformly difform variations. This seems to result from the mathematical tractability of such situations rather than from any observational or theoretical context that made such variations likely, as was the case for illumination in treatise XIII, where there was a common belief that the distribution of illumination from a light source was uniformly difform. Within these limitations, Swineshead does, however, manage to build up more and more complex conclusions without doing much explicit mathematics. He rather simply picks those cases, however complex they may appear, about which something can be said on the basis of the general characteristics of the functions involved.

In the third and last main part of treatise XV Swineshead should then have combined his two variables to allow both resistance and power to vary at the same time and to draw conclusions. The treatise simply ends, however, with the words: "It remains to inquire how both [resistance and power] may simultaneously be acquired." (The 1520 edition adds: "and first are posited rules, etc.") Given the complexity of the conclusions that resulted when only resistance or power was allowed to vary, one could hardly blame Swineshead for failing to push on further.

Treatise XVI is broken down into five chapters, each considering a class of problems concerning the induction of the maximum degree. Chapter 1 considers the alterations of larger and smaller uniformly difform subjects altered either uniformly throughout or by a uniformly difform latitude of alteration. Chapter 2 considers cases where a difformly difform latitude of alteration is extended through the part remaining to be brought to maximum degree in the same way as it was extended through the whole at the start.

Chapters 1 and 2 both consider cases where the alteration is extended at the start through the whole subject. Chapter 3, then, considers cases where the alteration does not extend through the whole subject at the start, but rather begins to be generated at the more intense extreme of the subject. Chapter 4 considers how the induction of the maximum degree is to be measured when the subject is rarefied or condensed during the alteration, deciding that such induction should not be measured by the fixed space outside the subject, but rather, with certain qualifications, by the subject itself. Chapter 5 considers how it may occur, through the successive generation of alteration in a subject, that the subject remains or becomes uniformly difform. Treatise XVI may be the most complex of the *Liber calculationum*, but perhaps enough has been said about the previous treatises so that its character can be imagined without the detailed examination of any of its conclusions.

As in the previous treatises, Swineshead in treatise XVI is preoccupied with uniformly difform alterations and the like, probably because they were well defined, whereas with difformly difform alterations the situation becomes overly complex. It might be remembered that, where alterations are concerned, as in this treatise, there was the common view that all qualitative actions, like light, decrease uniformly difformly (that is, linearly) as one moves away from the agent or source. So here again, as in the treatise on illumination, there might be a physical reason for emphasizing uniformly difform distributions. Nevertheless, if there was such a reason, it is well in the background.

Opuscula

Of the three short *opuscula* that may be assigned to Richard Swineshead, two by explicit ascription to a Swineshead as author, and one by its position between the two others, one is a partial commentary on the *De caelo* and the other two are partially repetitive treatments of motion.

In librum de caelo. Apparently part of a commentary, beginning from text 35 of book I of the *De caelo*, this short fragment is in two main parts, the first dealing with Aristotle's proofs that an infinite body cannot move locally, and the second dealing with the relation of substances to their qualities, in connection with the possibility of action and passion between infinite bodies.

In the first main part, Swineshead considers (1) the proofs that an infinite body cannot rotate, drawing paradoxes concerning the intersections of infinite lines during such rotation; (2) the proofs against translational motion of infinites; and (3) Aristotle's arguments that there cannot be an infinite body so that, *a fortiori*, there cannot be any motion of an infinite body.

In the second main part, Swineshead considers (1) Aristotle's discussion of the possible action and passion of infinites, both with relation to simple subjects and with relation to compounds or mixtures; (2) the question of whether substantial forms can vary within some latitude, apparently with the idea that, if elemental forms can be remitted, then a finite action of an infinite subject might be within the range of possibility; (3) a proof that elements can exist without their qualities; (4) a proof that there cannot be mixed bodies of two or more elements of degrees as remiss as desired (in this part, Swineshead mentions Dumbleton by name and refutes some arguments he makes in part IV of his *Summa*); and (5) arguments concerning the possible perpetuation and duration of compounds. The opinions expressed in this work do not seem to be in conflict with the conclusions of the *Liber calculationum*.

De motu. This second short work (following in Cambridge MS Gonville and Caius 499/268 directly after the *De caelo* fragment) is not explicitly ascribed to Swineshead, but its similarity to the last short work of the manuscript, which is ascribed to Swineshead, is so great that there is every reason to ascribe it also to Swineshead. In the Seville manuscript Colombina 7-7-29 the works (the *De motu* and the following *De motu locali*) appear as one, but this seems hardly plausible since there is a great deal of overlap and repetition between them. It is more likely that they are successive drafts of the same work than that they are both sections of a single larger work.

The *De motu* contains an introduction concerning the material, formal, efficient, and final causes

of motion, and two main sections, the first dealing with the measurement of motion with respect to cause and the second with the measurement of motion with respect to effect. Only local motion is considered. The subject matter of both sections is similar to that of treatise XIV of the *Liber calculationum*. Roughly speaking, both the *De motu* and the *De motu locali* seem to occupy an intermediate position between Heytesbury's *Regule* on local motion and the *Calculationes*, a natural supposition being that Swineshead began from Heytesbury's work and went on to develop his ideas from that point.

Concerning the consideration of motion with respect to cause, Swineshead begins by expounding Bradwardine's function relating powers, resistances, and velocities (212ra). This is followed by a number of rules, some of which are the same as, and others similar to, the conclusions of treatise XIV of the *Liber calculationum* (212ra–212va). Swineshead says, for instance, that if a constant power begins to move in the more remiss extreme of a uniformly difform resistance, it will remit its motion more and more slowly (212ra–vb). (Cf. rule 24 of treatise XIV of the *Liber calculationum*.)

In the second section, Swineshead begins with a number of statements concerning the measurement of motion with respect to effect—for instance, that uniform local motion is measured by the line described by the fastest moved point (212vb)—many of which have close analogues in Heytesbury's *Regule*. He states the mean speed rule (213ra) and the rule that in a motion uniformly accelerated from zero or decelerated to zero three times as much is traversed by the more intense half of the motion as by the more remiss half of the motion (213ra), which he derives as a consequence of the mean speed rule.

The second section concludes with five conclusions and a statement concerning the measurement of difform motion. The first three conclusions have to do with the traversal of extended resistances, one of these being the thirtieth rule of treatise XIV of the *Liber calculationum*: if one constant power remits its motion uniformly to zero in a given difform resistance, no other greater or lesser constant power will uniformly intend or remit its motion traversing the same medium (213ra). Concerning velocity in difform motion, Swineshead says that it is not to be measured by the maximum line that is described, but rather by the line that would be described if the velocity were continued for a period of time (213rb).

The *De motu*, then, consists mostly of a series of conclusions along with several stipulations as to how motion is to be measured with respect to cause and with respect to effect. Although the conclusions are so divided, there is little to distinguish them.

De motu locali. This short work receives its title from its explicit, and hence we retain the name despite the fact that this last fragment contains treatments of alteration as well as of local motion. The first two sections of this work correspond to the two main sections of the *De motu,* and many of the rules or conclusions stated are the same.

The work starts with a series of conclusions concerning the effect on velocity of increasing or decreasing the power or resistance in motion (213rb–vb). Many of these conclusions, including eight of the first nine, appear also in the *De motu,* and a similar number, although not always the same ones, appear also in the *Liber calculationum,* treatise XIV. Although these conclusions presuppose Bradwardine's function relating powers, resistances, and velocities, that function is not explicitly stated as it was in the *De motu.*

These rules are followed by a section concerning the measures of resistance, for instance that two resistances of which the most intense degrees are equal must be themselves equal (213vb); and that a motor equal to the maximum degree of a uniformly difform resistance will move in it eternally, never completely traversing it (214ra).

The second section of the *De motu locali* concerns the measures of motion with respect to effect, starting with the stipulation that the velocity of local motion is measured by the line that would be traversed by the fastest moved point (if there is one), provided that it continued its velocity uniformly for a period of time (214rb). Difformly difform motions, Swineshead says, always correspond to some degree within their range of variation *(ibid.),* and uniformly difform motions correspond to their middle degrees (214rb–va). On this basis Swineshead mentions four types of sophisms that can arise from the comparison of accelerations to velocities of which some, he says, are possible, that is, not self-contradictory, and some impossible and to be rejected (214va–vb). A mobile can never begin from an infinite part of a magnitude and traverse some part uniformly (215ra), nor can a motion be remitted uniformly from an infinite degree of velocity *(ibid.).*

If one wants to know how much is traversed by a uniformly difform motion starting and ending at a degree, all one can say in general is that more is traversed than by a mobile moving for the same time with half the maximum degree of the uniform-

ly difform motion (214vb–215ra). All local motions are as fast as any of their parts, and all subjects moved locally are moved as fast as any of their parts, the former being true for all motions but the latter being true only for local motions and not for alterations (215ra).

The third and last section (215ra–215rb) of the *De motu locali* concerns measures of alteration. Like local motion the measure of alteration with respect to cause is the proportion of the power of the altering agent to the power of the altered patient. With respect to effect, the velocity of motion of alteration depends on the maximum latitude of quality that would be acquired by any part of the subject if the velocity were continued for some time period. Irrespective of the measure of velocity of alteration, a subject need not be altered as fast as any of its parts, but often is altered more slowly than a part of it closer to the agent. To determine how fast a subject is altered one has to consider the degree to which it corresponds, calculating the contribution of various degrees to the subject's denomination by the proportion of the subject through which they are extended.

Many sophisms can arise from the comparison of velocities of alteration to the velocities with which subjects are altered. Something may be altered with a faster velocity of alteration and yet be more slowly altered, and hence the two separate measures of alteration must be kept separate. On this basis, it is not contradictory for an agent to alter faster than anything is altered by it. If a uniformly difform alteration is extended throughout a subject, the subject will be altered as the middle degree of that alteration. With brief references to other ways of dealing with alteration the *De motu locali* ends.

Conclusion

As is evident from the discussions of its separate treatises, the *Liber calculationum* places what may seem to be an uncommon emphasis upon the generation of *conclusiones, regulae, objectiones,* and *sophismata.* This unceasing generation of results occurs in other works of the calculatory tradition, but it reaches a high with Richard Swineshead, so much so as to be nearly the defining characteristic of the *Liber calculationum.* Results are drawn to the very limits of manageability. Swineshead's *opuscula, De motu* and *De motu locali,* exhibit the beginnings of this effort to educe results. We, operating with modern mathematics, could generate many more such results, but the subclass that

Swineshead himself generates and treats almost completely exhausts the results he could have dealt with, given the techniques at his disposal. And this excogitation of results occurs whether Swineshead is examining two or more *positiones* or *opiniones* relative to a given topic (when, as said above, only slight attention is paid to deciding definitively between *opiniones*) or only one. The major difference between these two cases appears to be that, in the former, Swineshead is more apt to label as *sophismata* the results he is generating. In any event, he makes it quite clear that *conclusiones* can be elicited, objected to, and resolved on both or all sides when a plurality of *opiniones* is at stake (*multe conclusiones possunt elici ex dictis, ad quarum tamen utramque partem probabiles possunt fieri rationes, que per predicta, si bene intelligantur, satis faciliter solvuntur* [34ra]).

Furthermore, there is almost no discussion in the *Liber calculationum* of the contexts in which one might expect the situations represented by these results to occur, nor, indeed, any time spent investigating whether they can occur. Instead, the work proceeds almost entirely *secundum imaginationem*, as Heytesbury's *Regule solvendi sophismata* had before it. In fact, among all other "Mertonian" works, the *Liber calculationum* is most like Heytesbury's *Regule*. Some of the earlier Oxford calculators, like Walter Burley and Roger Swineshead, had fairly frequently considered natural, as well as *de imaginatione*, situations. Richard Swineshead, by contrast, quite consistently imagines situations that will illustrate and draw results out of various theories rather than taking examples from natural occurrence. The emphasis is upon developing and having a set of techniques as complete as one can make it. If we may trust an inference from the later commentary of Gaetano of Thiene on Heytesbury's *Regule*, one of the reasons for this emphasis was simply the fact that every "calculator" ought to have a system applicable to every conceivable situation (. . . *dicit* [*sc.*, Heytesbury] *quod hoc est tamen impossibile . . . physice loquendo . . . Sed dicit ille magister bene scis hoc, sed quia non implicat contradictionem et est satis imaginabile, ideo calculatores non debent fugere casum* [Venice ed., 1494, 48va]).

The "techniques" that are presented in the *Liber calculationum* may strike the modern reader as basically mathematical. But one must consider such a judgment with care. To begin with, the evidence of the extant manuscripts of the *Liber calculationum* tells us that the medievals themselves did not regard it (or any of the other "calculatory"

works, for that matter) as mathematical in the sense of Euclid, Boethius' *Arithmetica*, or Jordanus de Nemore. When the *Liber calculationum* does not take up an entire codex, it or fragments from it invariably appear with other treatises, questions, or notes on natural philosophy or logic. Nevertheless, there is no doubt that, the evidence of medieval codification aside, mathematical functions and considerations pervade Swineshead's major work. They are applied, however, not in order to understand how some phenomenon normally occurs (as was the case in medieval optics, statics, and astronomy), but in a thoroughly *secundum imaginationem* fashion that is totally different from the Greek-based mathematical tradition inherited by the Middle Ages. A good deal of material from the Greek tradition was, of course, utilized by Swineshead, but he utilized it in a most un-Greek way. Mathematical functions are applied in order to determine all conceivable contributions that parts could make to wholes, to distinguish the discontinuous from the continuous, and to encompass situations or results involving infinite intensities, infinite velocities, and other infinite values. It is for these kinds of problems that the *Liber calculationum* contained the required techniques. To the medieval scholar with the patience and ability needed to comprehend this work, the purpose seems to have been that he should learn to operate with the techniques and rules given by Swineshead—just as one was to learn techniques and rules in the tradition of solving sophisms to which the *Liber calculationum* from time to time refers—so expertly as to be able to handle situations and *casus* in every corner of the fourteenth century realm, be it physical, logical, medical, theological, or whatever.

Dissemination and Influence of the Liber calculationum

Although the work of Swineshead's fellow Mertonians and the English "calculatory" tradition in general is generously represented in later fourteenth-century natural philosophy (very notably so, for example, in the work of Oresme), specific evidence of the *Liber calculationum* during this period is not especially plentiful, although shortly after mid-century the English logician Richard Ferebrich appears to employ parts of treatise XIV in his *Calculationes de motu*. Most of the extant manuscripts of Swineshead's major work are of the fifteenth century, and the records we have of its occurrence in library catalogues for the most part date from 1400 and later. It does appear, however, in at least two "student notebooks" of the later fourteenth century: in one merely in terms of fragmentary traces (MS Bibliothèque Nationale, fonds latin 16621), in the other more substantially (MS Worcester Cathedral, F. 35).

If we ask for evidence of the dissemination and influence not of Mertonian ideas in general or of some particular idea like the so-called Merton mean speed theorem, but rather of parts of the *Liber calculationum* itself, the fifteenth and sixteenth centuries are far richer. The first center of interest is Italy, in the middle and toward the end of the fifteenth century, where Swineshead appears as part of the broader preoccupation with English logic and natural philosophy. He appears, moreover, in terms both *pro* and *contra*. He suffers part of the humanist criticism of the "barbari Britanni" that one finds in the likes of Coluccio Salutati; for Leonardo Bruni he is one of those "quorum etiam nomina perhorresco"; and he even gave his name to the "sophisticas quisquilias et *suisetica* inania" complained about loudly by Ermolao Barbaro and others.

Yet it seems fair to claim that one of the major reasons for these humanist complaints was not Swineshead's works themselves, but rather the fact that they and other English "calculationes" had attracted the attention of a fair number of Italian scholars. Thus, his views are found among those of others treated in works *De reactione* written by Gaietano de Thienis, Giovanni Marliani, Angelus de Fossambruno, Vittore Trincavelli, and Pietro Pomponazzi. He also appears to have been very much in the center of the interest in "calculatory" matters in Padua, and especially Pavia, around the mid-fifteenth century, something that jibes extremely well with the number of times that the *Liber calculationum* was published in these cities. We also know that Nicolletto Vernia, earlier a student of both Paul of Pergola and Gaietano de Thienis, went to Pavia to study the *Calculationes Suisset*, information that fits very well indeed with other things we are able to put together about Vernia's interests. Pomponazzi relates that he engaged in a dispute with Francesco di Nardò armed with *argumentis calculatoriis*; but we have more direct evidence of his concern with Swineshead from the fact that he refers to the "Calculator" in his (unedited) *Questio de anima intellectiva* and from the fact that Vernia owned a copy of the *Liber calculationum* (now Biblioteca Vittorio Emanuele, MS 250).

When one turns to the Italian commentaries or questions on the *Liber calculationum*, the first thing to be noted is that most of this literature is preoccupied only with treatise I: *De intensione et remissione formarum*. It was this part of Swineshead that occupied Pomponazzi in his own treatise of the same title written in 1514, and we have similar sixteenth-century works by Tiberio Baccilieri, Cardinal Domenico Grimani, and Hieronymus Picus. Pomponazzi is critical of Swineshead insofar as the "scale of measure" he proposed in treatise I of the *Liber calculationum* maintains the inverse proportionality of intension and remission and ignores their proper ontological status. Intension and remission should be viewed, Pomponazzi felt, as, respectively, perfection and imperfection; this done, one would not, as Swineshead, "measure" remission by nearness to zero degree, but rather, as an imperfection, in terms of its distance from the maximum degree. Pomponazzi refers to a similar disagreement with Swineshead's "non gradum measure" in his *Super libello de substantia orbis*, where he specifically complains that it runs counter to the *via Aristotelis*. Pomponazzi's criticism can be partially explained by the fact that in his (unedited) lectures on Aristotle's *Physics* he felt that Swineshead and other English "calculators" put too much mathematics (*ille truffe spectant ad mathematicum*) and "geometricalia" into natural philosophy, and (as he complained in his *De intensione et remissione formarum*) constructed a *scientia* that was *media inter physicas et mathematicas*.

Italian *expositiones* or *questiones* on other parts of the *Liber calculationum* are rarer than those on treatise I. Bassanus Politus composed a *Tractatus proportionum* specifically claimed to be *introductorius ad calculationes Suisset*; it sets forth in succinct fashion little more than the standard mathematics of proportion and proportionality drawn from such authors as Euclid and Boethius. More to the content of parts of the *Liber calculationum* is Marliani's *Probatio cuiusdam sententie calculatoris de motu locali*. Its concern is with the views of Swineshead on "mean degree measure" in treatise II and his proofs for the "mean speed theorem" in treatise XIV. The two most complete Italian commentaries on the *Liber calculationum* are unedited and unstudied. One is by Christopher de Recaneto, *doctor in artibus* at Padua in 1454, and covers but treatise I and part of treatise II. The other is more extensive, commenting on treatises I–V and VII–VIII, but we know almost nothing of its author, Philippus Aiuta. All we know is that Marliani wrote a *difficultates* sent to Philippus and (as we learn from the incipit of the present commentary) that he was a doctor in arts and medicine.

The commentary itself, apparently a compilation of Philippus' view made in 1468 by one Magister Bernardinus Antonius de Spanochiis, relates Swineshead to any number of other mathematicians (especially Euclid) and philosophers, both contemporary, earlier medieval, and ancient. But perhaps its most intriguing aspect is the explicit tendency to render Swineshead more comprehensible by the addition of appropriate figures (*quasdam ymagines in marginibus*).

The second major center of interest in Swineshead was Paris at the beginning of the sixteenth century, where a considerable amount of work was done with the *Liber calculationum*, largely by a group of Spanish and Portuguese scholars. The earliest, and certainly most impressive, among them appears to be Alvaro Thomaz. His *Liber de triplici motu*, published in Paris in 1509, contains an extensive, two-part, preliminary treatise expounding all aspects of the mathematics of proportions, and itself treats all parts of the *Liber calculationum* that deal with *motus*. Alvaro also includes much material drawn from Nicole Oresme, not only explaining, but on occasions expanding what he finds in Swineshead and Oresme. One notable instance of such "expansion" is his treatment of the "infinite series" treated by both of these fourteenth-century authors. Following Alvaro by a few years, both John Dullaert of Ghent (in 1512) and Juan de Celaya (in 1517) include comprehensive expositions of "calculatory" material in their *Questiones* on Aristotle's *Physics*. Celaya treats a good number of *conclusiones* drawn from parts (treatises I, II, IV, VI, XIV, XV) of the *Liber calculationum* and appears to have followed Thomaz in at least the structure of much of what he includes. Another Spanish member of this Paris school was Luis Coronel, who does not, like Celaya, include a lengthy connected exposition of Swineshead material in his *Physice perscrutationes* (published in 1511), but who nevertheless does discuss a fair number of issues and passages from scattered treatises (I, II, V, X, XI) of the *Liber calculationum*. At times he seems to lack a proper understanding of what he is discussing from Swineshead and even complains how *prolixissime et tediose* the reasoning is (in this instance referring to treatise XI). The same kind of complaint and lack of comprehension is probably in part behind the remarks of Diego de Astudillo in his *Questiones* on Aristotle's *Physics* when he excuses his omission of "calculatory disputations" since he would "confound the judgments of beginners . . . ignorant of mathematics." Indeed, if it is a proper

appreciation of Swineshead's accomplishments that one has in mind, then none of the "commentators," Italian or Spanish, save Thomaz, qualifies.

Some Renaissance figures continued the fifteenth-century humanist criticism of English "subtilitates" and ridiculed (Luis Vives, for example) Swineshead's work, but others, such as Julius Scaliger and Cardano, praised him as outstandingly acute and ingenious. The most famous later "appreciation" of the Calculator was that of Leibniz. Perhaps initially learning of Swineshead through Scaliger (whom he mentioned in this regard), Leibniz confessed to a certain admiration of Swineshead even before he had had the opportunity to read him. How thoroughly Leibniz finally did read the *Liber calculationum* we do not know; but we do know that he went to the trouble to have the 1520 Venice edition of it transcribed (today Hannover, Niedersächssische Landesbibliothek, MS 615). In Leibniz' eyes, Swineshead's primary accomplishment lay in introducing mathematics into scholastic philosophy, although we should perhaps take "mathematics" to include a certain amount of logic, since at times he coupled Swineshead with Ramon Lull in having accomplished this task. In any event, what Swineshead had done was in his eyes much in harmony with Leibniz' own convictions about the relation of mathematics and "mathematical" logic to philosophy.

Because of the remarks of the likes of Cardano, Scaliger, and Leibniz, Swineshead found his way into eighteenth-century histories of philosophy such as that of Jacob Brucker. After that he was forgotten until Pierre Duhem rediscovered him at the beginning of the twentieth century in his rediscovery of medieval science as a whole.

BIBLIOGRAPHY

I. ORIGINAL WORKS. Manuscripts* of the *Liber calculationum* include Cambridge, Gonville and Caius 499/268, 165r–203v (14c.), tr. I–XI, XV, XII–XIII; *Erfurt, Stadtbibl., Amplon. 0.78, 1r–33r (14c.), contains an abbreviated version of tr. I–II, IV–VIII. Ascribed to one "clymiton" (presumably Killington?) by Schum in his catalogue of the Amplonian MSS, apparently drawing his information from Amplonius Ratinck's fifteenth-century catalogue; *Padua, Bibl. Univ. 924, 51r–70r (15c.), tr. I, VII, VIII, IX; *Paris, Bibl. Nat. lat. 6558, 1r–70v (dated 1375), tr. I–XI, XV, XII–XIII; *Paris, Bibl. Nat. lat. 16621 (14c.), *passim*, fragments (often in altered form); e.g., 52r–v, 212v from tr. XIV; *Pavia, Bibl. Univ., Aldini 314, 1r–83r (15c.), tr. I–XI, XV, XII–XIII, XVI, XIV; Perugia, Bibl. Comm. 1062, 1r–82r (15c.); *Rome, Bibl. Angelica 1963, 1r–106v

(15c.), tr. I–IX, XI–XVI; *Rome, Bibl. Vitt. Emanuele 250, 1r–82r (15c.), contains all tr. except III in the following order: I, II, V, VI, XIV (incomplete), XV, XIV (complete), XVI, XII, XIII, VII, VIII, IX, IV, X, XI; belonged to Nicoletto Vernia; *Vatican, Vat. lat. 3064, 1r–120v (15c.), tr. I–X, XVI, XI, XV, XIV, XII–XIII, III (again); *Vatican, Vat. lat. 3095, 1r–119v (15c.), tr. I–X, XVI, XI, XV, XII–XIV; Vatican, Chigi E. IV. 120, 1r–112v (15c.); Venice, Bibl. Naz. San Marco., lat. VI, 226, 1r–98v (15c.). tr. I–II, IV–XII, III (according to L. Thorndike); *Worcester, Cathedral F. 35, 3r, 27r–65v, 70r–75v (14c.), contains, in following order, fragment (Reg. 1–4) of XIV, I–IV, VI–VII, XII–XIII!, XVI, V; Cesena, Bibl. Malatest., Plut. IX, sin cod VI.

Editions include Padua *ca.* 1477; Pavia 1498; Venice, 1520. A modern edition of treatise XI has been published in the article of Hoskin and Molland cited below.

The *Opuscula* are *In librum de caelo* (Cambridge, Gonville and Caius 499/268, 204r–211v [15c.]; Worcester, Cathedral F. 35, 65v–69v [14c.], incomplete); *De motu* (Cambridge, Gonville and Caius 499/268, 212r–213r [15c.]; Oxford, Bodl., Digby 154, 42r–44v [14c.]; and Seville, Bibl. Colomb. 7-7-29, 28v–30v [15c.]); and *De motu locali* (Cambridge, Gonville and Caius 499/268, 213r–215r [15c.]; Seville, Bibl. Colomb. 7-7-29, 30v–34r [15c.]).

The *De motibus naturalibus* of Roger Swineshead: Erfurt, Stadtbibl., Amplon. F. 135, 25r–47v (14c.); Paris, Bibl. nat., lat. 16621, 39r, 40v–51v, 54v–62r, 66r–84v (14c.), Fragment of part II, all of parts III–VIII; Venice, Bibl. Naz. San Marco lat. VI, 62, 111r (15c.), definitions of part IV. For MSS of the *De obligationibus* and *De insolubilibus* ascribed to Roger, see the article by Weisheipl on Roger cited below.

The *Questiones quatuor super physicas magistri Ricardi* (in MSS Vatican, Vat. lat. 2148, 71r–77v; Vat. 4429, 64r–70r; Venice, San Marco lat. VI, 72, 81r–112r, 168r–169v) that have been tentatively ascribed to Swineshead by Anneliese Maier are in all probability not his, but rather most likely the work of Richard Killington (or Kilvington).

II. SECONDARY LITERATURE. The two basic biographical-bibliographical sources are A. B. Emden, *A Biographical Register of the University of Oxford to A.D. 1500* (Oxford, 1957–1959), 1836–1837, which includes material on Roger and John; and James A. Weisheipl, "Roger Swynesheed, O.S.B., Logician, Natural Philosopher, and Theologian," in *Oxford Studies Presented to Daniel Callus* (Oxford, 1964), 231–252. These both replace G. C. Brodrick, *Memorials of Merton College* (Oxford, 1885), 212–213. Emden has a long list of variant spellings of Swineshead such as Swyneshed, which he prefers, Suicet, Suincet, etc.

*Many of the MSS do not contain all sixteen *tractatus* of the *Liber calculationum*; the incipits and explicits of each *tractatus* have been checked by the authors for those MSS indicated by an asterisk.

On Swineshead and the calculatory tradition in general, see Pierre Duhem, *Études sur Léonard de Vinci,* III, "Les précurseurs parisiens de Galilée" (Paris, 1913), 405–480; most of this material is reprinted with some additions, omissions, and changes in Duhem's *Le système du monde,* VII (Paris, 1956), 601–653. See also Marshall Clagett, *The Science of Mechanics in the Middle Ages* (Madison, Wis., 1959), chs. 4–7; Anneliese Maier, *Die Vorläufer Galileis im 14. Jahrhundert* (=Studien zur Naturphilosophie der Spätscholastik, I), 2nd ed. (Rome, 1966); *Zwei Grundprobleme der scholastischen Naturphilosophie* (=Studien, II), 3rd ed. (Rome, 1968); *An der Grenze von Scholastik und Naturwissenschaft* (=Studien, III), 2nd ed. (Rome, 1952); John Murdoch, "Mathesis in philosophiam scholasticam introducta. The Rise and Development of the Application of Mathematics in Fourteenth Century Philosophy and Theology," in *Arts libéraux et philosophie au moyen âge* (=Acts du quatrième Congrès International de Philosophie Médiévale), (Montreal–Paris, 1969), 215–254; A. G. Molland, "The Geometrical Background to the 'Merton School,'" in *British Journal for the History of Science,* **4** (1968), 108–125; Edith Sylla, *The Oxford Calculators and the Mathematics of Motion, 1320–1350: Physics and Measurement by Latitudes* (unpublished diss., Harvard Univ., 1970); "Medieval Quantifications of Qualities: The 'Merton School,'" in *Archive for History of Exact Sciences,* **8** (1971), 9–39; "Medieval Concepts of the Latitude of Forms: The Oxford Calculators," in *Archives d'histoire doctrinale et littéraire du moyen âge,* **40** (1973), 223–283. More particularly on Swineshead see James A. Weisheipl, "Ockham and Some Mertonians," in *Mediaeval Studies,* **30** (1968), 207–213; Lynn Thorndike, *A History of Magic and Experimental Science,* 8 vols. (New York, 1923–1958), III, 370–385.

See the following on particular treatises of the *Liber calculationum* (although much information is also provided on the individual treatises in some of the more comprehensive literature above): tr. I: Marshall Clagett, "Richard Swineshead and Late Medieval Physics," in *Osiris,* **9** (1950), 131–161; tr. II: John Murdoch, "Philosophy and the Enterprise of Science in the Later Middle Ages," in *The Interaction Between Science and Philosophy,* Y. Elkana, ed. (Atlantic Highlands, N.J., 1974), 67–68; tr. VII: Clagett, *Giovanni Marliani and Late Medieval Physics* (New York, 1941), ch. 2; tr. X: Curtis Wilson, *William Heytesbury: Medieval Logic and the Rise of Mathematical Physics* (Madison, Wis., 1956), ch. 3; tr. XI: M. A. Hoskin and A. G. Molland, "Swineshead on Falling Bodies: An Example of Fourteenth-Century Physics," in *British Journal for the History of Science,* **3** (1966), 150–182; A. G. Molland, "Richard Swineshead on Continuously Varying Quantities," in *Actes du XIIe Congrès International d'Histoire des Sciences,* **4** (Paris, 1968), 127–130; John Murdoch, "Mathesis in philosophiam . . . ," 230–231, 250–254; tr. XIV: John Murdoch, *op. cit.,* 228–230; Marshall Clagett, *The Science of Mechanics . . . ,* 290–304, for Swineshead's proof of the so-called mean speed theorem.

For functions of F, R, and V similar to Roger Swineshead's, one may consult Ernest Moody, "Galileo and Avempace: The Dynamics of the Leaning Tower Experiment," in *Journal of the History of Ideas*, **12** (1951), 163–193, 375–422. For the "addition" theory of qualitative change mentioned in the discussion of treatise VII, see E. Sylla, "Medieval Concepts of the Latitude of Forms. . . ." This article also contains a more complete discussion of the ideas of Roger Swineshead.

The dissemination and influence of the Liber calculationum. To date, the most adequate treatment of the spread of late-medieval natural philosophy in general is Marshall Clagett's chapter on "English and French Physics, 1350–1600," in *The Science of Mechanics in the Middle Ages* (Madison, Wis. 1959). This chapter contains (630–631) a brief account of a segment of Richard Ferebrich's (Feribrigge) *Calculationes de motu*.

The Italian reception of Swineshead. On the humanist criticism of "Suissetica" and other, equally infamous, "English subtleties," the point of departure is Eugenio Garin, "La cultura fiorentina nella seconda metà del trecento e i 'barbari Britanni,'" as in his *L'età nuova. Ricerche di storia della cultura dal XII al XVI secolo* (Naples, 1969), 139–177; the relevant passages from Coluccio Salutati and Leonardo Bruni Aretino, as well as many other similar sources are cited therein. To this one might add the two anonymous letters of Ermolao Barbaro, edited by V. Branca: *Epistolae* (Florence, 1943), II, 22–23 (on which see the article by Dionisotti below). The various works *De reactione* treating Swineshead's opinion are Angelus de Fossambruno, MS Venice, Bibl. Naz. San Marco, VI, 160, ff. 248–252r; Gaietano de Thienis, *Tractatus perutilis de reactione*, Venice ed., 1491; Giovanni Marliani, *Tractatus de reactione* and *In defensionem tractatus de reactione*, both printed in his *Opera omnia*, II (Pavia, 1482) [on which see Clagett, *Giovanni Marliani and Late Medeival Physics*, (New York, 1941), ch. 2]; Victorus Trincavellus, *Questio de reactione iuxta doctrinam Aristotelis et Averrois commentatoris*, printed at the end (69r–74r) of the 1520 Venice ed. of the *Liber calculationum*; Pietro Pomponazzi, *Tractatus acutissimi . . . de reactione* (Venice, 1525).

The case for Pavia as the fifteenth-century center of "calculatory," and especially Swineshead, studies is made by Carlo Dionisotti, "Ermolao Barbaro e la Fortuna di Suiseth," in *Medioevo e Rinascimento: Studi in onore di Bruno Nardi* (Florence, 1955), 219–253. Dionisotti briefly treats the evidence for Nicoletto Vernia's studies in Pavia on the Calculator, but see also Eugenio Garin, "Noterelle sulla filosofia del Rinascimento I: A proposito di N. Vernia," in *Rinascimento*, **2** (1951), 57–62. The reference from Vernia's *De anima intellectiva* (MS Venice, Bibl. Naz. San Marco, VI, 105, ff. 156r–160r) was furnished by Edward Mahoney, who is preparing an edition of the text. The relevant bibliography of the Italian commentaries on treatise I, *De intensione et remissione formarum*, of the *Liber calculationum* is

Tiberio Baccilieri: Bruno Nardi, *Sigieri di Brabante nel pensiero del Rinascimento italiano* (Rome, 1945), 138–139; Pearl Kibre, "Cardinal Domenico Grimani, 'Questio de intensione et remissione qualitatis': A Commentary on the Tractate of that Title by Richard Suiseth (Calculator)," in *Didascaliae: Studies in Honor of Anselm M. Albareda*, Sesto Prete, ed. (New York, 1961), 149–203; Charles Schmitt, "Hieronymus Picus, Renaissance Platonism and the Calculator," to appear in Anneliese Maier Festschrift; Curtis Wilson, "Pomponazzi's Criticism of Calculator," in *Isis*, **44** (1952), 355–363. Other references to Pomponazzi on Swineshead can be found in Pietro Pomponazzi, *Corsi inediti dell'insegnamento padovano*, I: *Super Libello de substantia orbis, expositio et Quaestiones Quattuor* (1507); *Introduzione e testo a cura di Antonino Poppi* (Padua, 1966); and Bruno Nardi, *Saggi sull' Aristotelismo Padovano dal secolo XIV al XVI* (Florence, 1958).

The relevant sources or literature concerning other parts of the *Liber calculationum* are Bassanus Politus, *Tractatus proportionum introductorius ad calculationes Suiset* (Venice, 1505); Giovanni Marliani, *Probatio cuiusdam sentente calculatoris*, in his *Opera omnia*, II (Pavia, 1482), ff. 19r–25r (on which see Clagett, *Giovanni Marliani and Late Medieval Physics* [New York, 1941], ch. 5); Christopher de Recaneto, *Recolecte super calculationes*, MS Venice, Bibl. Naz. San Marco, Lat. VI, 149, ff. 31r–49v. On Recaneto, see Nardi, *Saggi sull'Aristotelismo Padovano dal secolo XIV al XVI* (Florence, 1958), 117–119, 121–122; Philippus Aiuta, "Pro declaratione Suiset calculatoris," MS Bibl. Vaticana, Chigi E. VI, 197, ff. 132r–149r. Finally, mention should be made of a totally unexamined sixteenth-century work on the same part of the *Liber calculationum* by Raggius of Florence, MS Rome, Bibl. Casan. 1431 (B.VI.7).

The Parisian-Spanish reception of Swineshead. The relevant primary sources are [Alvaro Thomaz], *Liber de triplici motu proportionibus annexis magistri Alvari Thome Ulixbonensis philosophicas Suiseth calculationes ex parte declarans* (Paris, 1509); John Dullaert of Ghent, *Questiones super octo libros phisicorum Aristotelis necnon super libros de celo et mundo* (Lyons, 1512); [Juan de Celaya], *Expositio magistri ioannis de Celaya Valentini in octo libros phisicorum Aristotelis: cum questionibus eiusdem secundum triplicem viam beati Thome, realium et nominalium* (Paris, 1517); Ludovicus Coronel, *Physice perscrutationes* (Paris, 1511); Diego de Astudillo, *Quaestiones super octo libros physicorum et super duos libros de generatione Aristotelis, una cum legitima textus expositione eorundem librorum* (Valladolid, 1532). Of the secondary literature on these—and other related—figures, the two basic articles are by William A. Wallace, "The Concept of Motion in the Sixteenth Century," in *Proceedings of the American Catholic Philosophical Association*, **41** (1967), 184–195; "The 'Calculatores' in Early Sixteenth-Century Physics," in *British Journal for the History of Science*, **4** (1969), 221–232. More detailed bio-bibliographical information on the school of Spanish scholars at Paris in the early sixteenth century can be found in H. Elie, "Quelques maîtres de l'université de Paris vers l'an 1500," in *Archives d'histoire doctrinale et littéraire du moyen âge*, **18** (1950–1951), 193–243; and R. Garcia Villoslada, *La universidad de Paris durante los estudios de Francisco de Vitoria, O.P., 1507–1522, Analecta Gregoriana*, XIV (Rome, 1938). On Alvaro Thomaz' treatment of the "infinite series" in Swineshead (and in Nicole Oresme) see Marshall Clagett, *Nicole Oresme and the Medieval Geometry of Qualities and Motions* (Madison, Wis., 1968), 496–499, 514–516; and H. Wieleitner, "Zur Geschichte der unendlichen Reihen im christlichen Mittelalter," in *Bibliotheca mathematica*, **14** (1913–1914), 150–168. Some biographical details on Alvaro can be found in J. Rey Pastor, *Los matemáticos españoles del siglo XVI* (Toledo, 1926), 82–89.

Later sixteenth- and seventeenth-century appreciation of Swineshead. Appropriate references to Cardano's *De subtilitate* and Julius Scaliger's *Exotericarum exercitationum* are given in Jacob Brucker's *Historia critica philosophiae*, III (Leipzig, 1766), 851. This work contains (849–853) numerous quotations from other authors referring (pro and con) to Swineshead as well as a brief example of the *Liber calculationum* itself. Leibniz' references to Swineshead are too numerous (we know of at least eight of them) to cite completely, but some of the most important of them can be found in L. Couturat's *Opuscules et fragments inédits de Leibniz* (Paris, 1903), 177, 199, 330, 340. Indication of the manuscript copy Leibniz had made of Swineshead can be found in Eduard Bodemann, *Die Handschriften der königlichen offentlichen Bibliothek zu Hannover* (Hannover, 1867), 104–105.

JOHN E. MURDOCH
EDITH DUDLEY SYLLA

SYLOW, PETER LUDVIG MEJDELL (*b.* Christiania [now Oslo], Norway, 12 December 1832; *d.* Christiania, 7 September 1918)

Sylow was the son of a cavalry captain, Thomas Edvard Sylow, who later became a minister of the government. After graduation from the Christiania Cathedral School in 1850, he studied at the university, where in 1853 he won a mathematics prize contest. He took the high school teacher examination in 1856, and from 1858 to 1898 he taught in the town of Frederikshald (now Halden). Sylow was awarded a scholarship to travel abroad in 1861, and he visited Berlin and Paris. In 1862–1863 he substituted for Ole-Jacob Broch at Christiania University; but until 1898 his only chance for a university chair came in 1869, and he was not

appointed. Finally, through Sophus Lie, a special chair was created for him at Christiania University in 1898.

From 1873 to 1881 Sylow and Sophus Lie prepared a new edition of the works of N. H. Abel, and for the first four years Sylow was on leave from his school in order to devote himself to the project. In 1902, with Elling Holst, he published Abel's correspondence. He also published a few papers on elliptic functions, particularly on complex multiplication, and on group theory.

Sylow's name is best-known in connection with certain theorems in group theory and certain subgroups of a given group. In 1845 Cauchy had proved that any finite group G has subgroups of any prime order dividing the order of G. In 1872 Sylow published a 10-page paper containing the first extension of Cauchy's result and perhaps the first profound discovery in abstract group theory after Cauchy. Sylow's main theorem read as follows: First, if p^m is the maximal power of p dividing the order of G, then G has subgroups of order p^i for all i with $0 \leq i \leq m$, and in particular subgroups H of order p^m (called p-Sylow groups); and the index j of the normalizer of H is congruent 1 mod p. Second, the p-Sylow groups of G are conjugate with each other. Sylow's theorems were, and still are, a source of discoveries in group theory and are fundamental to most structural research in finite groups.

BIBLIOGRAPHY

I. ORIGINAL WORKS. Sylow's works are listed in H. B. Kragemo, "Bibliographie der Schriften Ludvig Sylows," in *Norsk matematisk forenings skrifter*, 2nd ser., no. 3 (1933), 25–29. They include "Théorèmes sur les groupes de substitutions," in *Mathematische Annalen*, **5** (1872), 584–594; and "Sur la multiplication complexe des fonctions elliptiques," in *Journal de mathématiques pures et appliquées*, 4th ser., **3** (1887), 109–254.

Sylow's MSS are in the Oslo University Library, U.B. MS, fols. 730–808, and U.B. Brevsamling 7–8.

II. SECONDARY LITERATURE. See T. Skolem, "Ludvig Sylow und seine wissenschaftlichen Arbeiten," in *Norsk matematisk forenings skrifter*, 2nd ser., no. 2 (1933), 14–24; and C. Størmer, "Gedächtnisrede auf Professor Dr. P. L. M. Sylow," *ibid.*, no. 1 (1933), 7–13.

HANS FREUDENTHAL

SYLVESTER, JAMES JOSEPH (*b.* London, England, 3 September 1814; *d.* London, 15 March 1897)

Although Sylvester is perhaps most widely remembered for his indefatigable work in the theory of invariants, especially that done in conjunction with Arthur Cayley, he wrote extensively on many other topics in the theory of algebraic forms. He left important theorems in connection with Sturm's functions, canonical forms, and determinants; he especially advanced the theory of equations and the theory of partitions.

James Joseph (Joseph then being his surname) was born into a Jewish family originally from Liverpool. The son of Abraham Joseph, who died while the boy was young, James was the sixth and youngest son of nine children, at least four of whom later assumed the name Sylvester for a reason not now apparent.

Until Sylvester was fifteen, he was educated in London, at first in schools for Jewish boys at Highgate and at Islington, and then for five months at the University of London (later University College), where he met Augustus De Morgan. In 1828 he was expelled "for taking a table knife from the refectory with the intention of sticking it into a fellow student who had incurred his displeasure."[1] In 1829 Sylvester went to the school of the Royal Institution, in Liverpool, where he took the first prize in mathematics by an immense margin and won a prize of $500, offered by the Contractors of Lotteries in the United States, for solving a problem in arrangements. At this school he was persecuted for his faith to a point where he ran away to Dublin. There, in the street, he encountered R. Keatinge, a judge and his mother's cousin, who arranged for his return to school.

Sylvester now read mathematics for a short time with Richard Wilson, at one time a fellow of St. John's College, Cambridge, and in October 1831 he himself entered that college, where he stayed until the end of 1833, when he suffered a serious illness that kept him at home until January 1836. After further bouts of illness, Sylvester took the tripos examination in January 1837, placing second. Since he was not prepared to subscribe to the Thirty-Nine Articles of the Church of England, he was not allowed to take the degree or compete for Smith's mathematical prizes—still less secure a fellowship. He went, therefore, to Trinity College, Dublin, where he took the B.A. and M.A. in 1841. (He finally took the equivalent Cambridge degrees in 1872–1873, the enabling legislation having been passed in 1871.)

In 1838 Sylvester went to what is now University College, London, as De Morgan's colleague. He seems to have found the chair in Natural Philosophy uncongenial. In 1839, at the age of twenty-five, he was elected a fellow of the Royal Society on the strength of his earliest papers, written for *Philosophical Magazine* as soon as he had taken his tripos examination. The first four of these concern the analytical development of Fresnel's theory of the optical properties of crystals, and the motion of fluids and rigid bodies. His attention soon turned to more purely mathematical topics, especially the expression of Sturm's functions in terms of the roots of the equation.

From University College, Sylvester moved in 1841 to a post at the University of Virginia. There are many lurid and conflicting reports of the reasons for his having returned to England in the middle of 1843. He apparently differed from his colleagues as to the way an insubordinate student should be treated. He now left the academic world for a time, and in 1844 was appointed Actuary and Secretary to the Equity and Law Life Assurance Company. He apparently gave private tuition in mathematics, for he had Florence Nightingale as a pupil. In 1846, the same year that Cayley entered Lincoln's Inn, Sylvester entered Inner Temple and was finally called to the bar in November 1850. Cayley and Sylvester soon struck up a friendship. At his Oxford inaugural lecture many years later (1885), Sylvester spoke of Cayley, "who though younger than myself, is my spiritual progenitor—who first opened my eyes and purged them of dross so that they could see and accept the higher mysteries of our common mathematical faith." Both men referred on occasion to theorems they had derived separately through the stimulus of their conversations in the intervals between legal business.

In 1854 Sylvester was an unsuccessful candidate both for the chair of mathematics at the Royal Military Academy, Woolwich, and for the professorship in geometry at Gresham College, London. The successful candidate for the former position soon died, and with the help of Lord Brougham, Sylvester was appointed. He held this post from September 1855 to July 1870. At the same time he became editor, from its first issue in 1855, of the *Quarterly Journal of Pure and Applied Mathematics*, successor to the *Cambridge and Dublin Mathematical Journal*. Assisted as he was by Stokes, Cayley, and Hermite, there was no change in editorship until 1877.

In 1863 Sylvester replaced the geometer Steiner as mathematics correspondent to the French Academy of Sciences. Two years later he delivered a paper on Newton's rule (concerning the number of imaginary roots of an algebraic equation) at King's

College, London. A syllabus to the lecture was the first mathematical paper published by De Morgan's newly founded London Mathematical Society, of which Sylvester was president from 1866 to 1868. In 1869 he presided over the Mathematical and Physical Section of the British Association meeting at Exeter. His address was prompted by T. H. Huxley's charge that mathematics was an almost wholly deductive science, knowing nothing of experiment or causation. This led to a controversy carried on in the pages of *Nature*, relating to Kant's doctrine of space and time; Sylvester, however, was not at his best in this kind of discussion. He reprinted an expanded version of his presidential address, together with the correspondence from *Nature*, as an appendix to *The Laws of Verse* (1870). The thoughts of Matthew Arnold, to whom the book was dedicated, are not known. Sylvester had some slight renown throughout his life, especially among his close friends, for his dirigible flights of poetic fancy; and his book was meant to illustrate the quasi-mathematical "principles of phonetic syzygy." Five original verses introduce a long paper on syzygetic relations, and he used his own verse on several other mathematical occasions.

Sylvester translated verse from several languages. For example, under the nom de plume "Syzygeticus," he translated from the German "The Ballad of Sir John de Courcy";[2] and his *Laws of Verse* includes other examples of his work, which is no worse than that of many a nonmathematician. It could be argued, however, that it was worse in a different way. One of his poems had four hundred lines all rhyming with "Rosalind," while another had two hundred rhyming with "Winn." These were products of his later residence in Baltimore. Sylvester had perhaps a better appreciation of music, and took singing lessons from Gounod.

In 1870 Sylvester resigned his post at Woolwich, and after a bitter struggle that involved correspondence in the *Times*, and even a leading article there (17 August 1871), he secured a not unreasonable pension. It was not until 1876, when he was sixty-one, that he again filled any comparable post. When he did so, it was in response to a letter from the American physicist Joseph Henry. The Johns Hopkins University opened in that year, and Sylvester agreed to accept a chair in mathematics in return for his traveling expenses and an annual stipend of $5,000 "paid in gold." "His first pupil, his first class" was G. B. Halsted. A colleague was C. S. Peirce, with whom, indeed, Sylvester became

embroiled in controversy on a small point of priority. Peirce nevertheless later said of him that he was "perhaps the mind most exuberant in ideas of pure mathematics of any since Gauss." While at Baltimore, Sylvester founded the *American Journal of Mathematics*, to which he contributed thirty papers. His first was a long and uncharacteristic account of the application of the atomic theory to the graphical representation of the concomitants of binary forms (quadratics). He resigned his position at Johns Hopkins in December 1883, when he was appointed to succeed H. J. S. Smith as Savilian professor of geometry at Oxford.

Sylvester was seventy when he delivered his inaugural "On the Method of Reciprocants" (1 December 1885). By virtue of his chair he became a fellow of New College, where he lived as long as he was in Oxford. He collaborated with James Hammond on the theory of reciprocants (functions of differential coefficients the forms of which are invariant under certain linear transformations of the variables) and also contributed several original papers to mathematical journals before his sight and general health began to fail. In 1892 he was allowed to appoint a deputy, William Esson; and in 1894 he retired, living mainly at London and Tunbridge Wells. For a short period in 1896 and 1897 he wrote more on mathematics (for example, on compound partitions and the Goldbach-Euler conjecture). A little more than a fortnight after a paralytic stroke, he died on 15 March 1897 and is buried in the Jewish cemetery at Ball's Pond, Dalston, London.

Sylvester received many honors in his lifetime, including the Royal Medal (1861) and the Copley Medal (1880). It is of interest that in the receipt of such awards he followed rather than preceded Cayley, who was his junior. Sylvester received honorary degrees from Dublin (1865), Edinburgh (1871), Oxford (1880), and Cambridge (1890).

Sylvester never married. He had been anxious to marry a Miss Marston, whom he met in New York in 1842, on his first visit to America. (She was the godmother of William Matthew Flinders Petrie, from whom the story comes.) It seems that although she had formed a strong attachment for him, she refused him on the ground of religious difference, and neither of them subsequently married.

Sylvester's greatest achievements were in algebra. With Cayley he helped to develop the theory of determinants and their application to nonalgebraic subjects. He was instrumental in helping to turn the attention of algebraists from such studies as the theory of equations—in which he nevertheless did important work—to the theory of forms, invariants, and linear associative algebras generally. His part in this movement is often obscured by his flamboyant style. In 1888 P. G. Tait, in a rather strained correspondence with Cayley over the relations between Tait's solution of a quaternionic equation and Sylvester's solution of a linear matrix equation, wrote with some justice: "I found Sylvester's papers hard to assimilate. A considerable part of each paper seems to be devoted to correction of hasty generalizations in the preceding one!"[3]

A number of Sylvester's early writings concern the reality of the roots of numerical equations, Newton's rule for the number of imaginary roots, and Sturm's theorem. His first published researches into these matters date from 1839, and were followed by a steady stream of special results. In due course he found simple expressions for the Sturmian functions (with the square factors removed) in terms of the roots:

$$f_2(x) = \Sigma(a-b)^2 (x-c) (x-d) \cdots$$
$$f_3(x) = \Sigma(a-b)^2 (a-c)^2 (b-c)^2 (x-d) \cdots.$$

Applying Sturm's process of the greatest algebraic common measure to two independent functions $f(x)$ and $\varphi(x)$, rather than to $f(x)$ and $f'(x)$, he found for the resulting functions expressions involving products of differences between the roots of the equations $f(x) = 0$, $\varphi(x) = 0$. Assuming that the real roots of the two equations are arranged in order of magnitude, the functions are of such a character that the roots of the one equation are intercalated among those of the other.

In connection with Newton's rule, the method of Sturm's proof was applied to a quite different problem. Sylvester supposed x to vary continuously, and investigated the increase and decrease in the changes of sign.[4]

Newton's first statement of his incomplete rule for enumerating imaginary roots dates from 1665–1666.[5] Although valid, the rule was not justified before Sylvester's proofs of the complete rule.

Another problem of great importance investigated in two long memoirs of 1853 and 1864 concerns the nature of the roots of a quintic equation. Sylvester took the functions of the coefficients that serve to decide the reality of the roots, and treated them as the coordinates of a point in n-dimensional space. A point is or is not "facultative" according to whether there corresponds, or fails to correspond, an equation with real coefficients. The character of the roots depends on the bounding surface or surfaces of the facultative regions, and on a single surface depending on the discriminant.[6]

Sylvester showed an early interest in the theory of numbers when he published a beautiful theorem on a product formed from numbers less than and prime to a given number.[7] This he described as "a pendant to the elegant discovery announced by the ever-to-be-lamented and commemorated Horner, with his dying voice"; but unfortunately it was later pointed out to him by Ivory that Gauss had given the theorem in his *Disquisitiones arithmeticae* (1801).[8] It is impossible to do justice in a short space to Sylvester's numerous later contributions to the theory of numbers, especially in the partition of numbers. Sylvester applied Cauchy's theory of residues and originated the concept of a denumerant. He also added several results to Euler's treatment of the "problem of the virgins" (the problem of enumerating positive and integral solutions of indeterminate simultaneous linear equations); but his most novel contributions to the subject are to be found in his use of a graphical method. He represented partitions of numbers by nodes placed in order at the points of a rectangular lattice ("graph"). Thus a partition of 9 (5 + 3 + 1) may be represented by the points of the rows in the lattice. The conjugate partition (3 + 2 + 2 + 1 + 1) is then found by considering the lattice of columns, a fact possibly first appreciated by N. M. Ferrers.[9] This

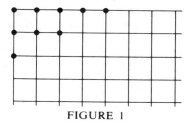

FIGURE 1

representation greatly simplified and showed the way to proofs of many new results in the theory of partitions not only by Sylvester but also by early contributors to his *American Journal of Mathematics*, such as Fabean Franklin.

One of Sylvester's early contributions to the *Journal*, "On Certain Ternary Cubic-Form Equations,"[10] is notable for the geometrical theory of residuation on a cubic curve and the chain rule of rational derivation: From an arbitrary point 1 on the curve it is possible to derive the singly infinite series of points $(1,2,4,5, \cdots 3p \pm 1)$ such that the chord through any two points, m and n, meets the curve again in a point ($m + n$ or $|m - n|$, whichever number is not divisible by 3) of the series. The coordinates of any point m are rational and integral functions of degree m^2 of those of point 1.

Like his friend Cayley, Sylvester was above all an algebraist. As G. Salmon said, the two discussed the algebra of forms for so long that each would often find it hard to say what properly belonged to the other. Sylvester, however, produced the first general theory of contravariants of forms.[11] He was probably the first to recognize that for orthogonal transformations, covariants and contravariants coincide. Moreover, he proved a theorem first given without proof by Cayley, and the truth of which Cayley had begun to doubt. It concerns a certain expression for a number ("Cayley's number") that cannot exceed the number of linearly independent semi-invariants (or invariants) of a certain weight, degree, and extent. Sylvester showed that Cayley's expression for the number of linearly independent ("asyzygetic") semi-invariants of a given type is in fact exact.[12] The result is proved as part of Sylvester's and Cayley's theory of annihilators, which was closely linked to that of generating functions for the tabulation of the partitions of numbers.

Under the influence of Lie's analysis, algebraic invariance was gradually subordinated to a more general theory of invariance under transformation groups. Although Boole had used linear differential operators to generate invariants and covariants, Cayley, Sylvester, and Aronhold were the first to do so systematically. In the calculation of invariants, it may be proved that any invariant I of the binary form (quantic)

$$f = a_0 x^p + p a_1 x^{p-1} y + \cdots + a_p y^p$$

should satisfy the two differential equations

$$\Omega I = 0,$$
$$O I = 0,$$

where Ω and O are linear differential operators:

$$\Omega \equiv a_0 \frac{\partial}{\partial a_1} + 2a_1 \frac{\partial}{\partial a_2} + \cdots + p a_{p-1} \frac{\partial}{\partial a_p},$$

$$O \equiv p a_1 \frac{\partial}{\partial a_0} + (p-1) a_2 \frac{\partial}{\partial a_1} + \cdots + a_p \frac{\partial}{\partial a_{p-1}}.$$

Sylvester called these functions annihilators, built up a rich theory around them, and generalized the method to other forms.[13] With Franklin he exhibited generating functions for all semi-invariants, of any degree, for the forms they studied.[14] Related to these studies is Sylvester's expression, in terms of a linear differential equation, of the condition that a function be an orthogonal covariant or invariant of a binary quantic. Thus the necessary and sufficient

condition that F be a covariant for direct orthogonal transformations is that F have as its annihilator

$$y \frac{\partial}{\partial x} - x \frac{\partial}{\partial y} + O - \Omega.$$

Sylvester played an important part in the creation of the theory of canonical forms. What may be his most widely known theorem states that a general binary form of odd order $(2n - 1)$ is a sum of n $(2n - 1)$-th powers of linear forms. (Thus, for example, a quintic may be reduced to a sum of three fifth powers of linear forms.) Sylvester wrote at length on the canonical reduction of the general $2n$-ic. He showed that even with the ternary quartic, which has fifteen coefficients, the problem was far less simple than it appeared, and that such cannot be simply reduced to a sum of five fourth powers (again with fifteen coefficients). It is here that he introduced the determinant known as the catalecticant, which he showed must vanish if the general $2n$-ic is to be expressed as the sum of n perfect $2n$th powers of linear forms, together with (in general) a term involving the square of the product of these forms.[15]

Early in his study of the effects of linear transformations on real quadratic forms, Sylvester discovered (and named) the law of inertia of quadratic forms.[16] The law was discovered independently by Jacobi.[17] The theorem is that a real quadratic form of rank r may be reduced by means of a real nonsingular linear transformation to the form

$$y_1^2 + \cdots + y_p^2 - y_{p+1}^2 - \cdots - y_r^2,$$

where the index p is uniquely determined. (It follows that two real quadratic forms are equivalent under real and nonsingular transformation if and only if they have the same rank and the same index.)

Another memorable result in the theory of linear transformations and matrices is Sylvester's law of nullity, according to which if r_1 and r_2 are the ranks of two matrices, and if R is the rank of their product,

$$R \leq r_1,$$
$$R \leq r_2,$$
$$R \geq r_1 + r_2 - n,$$

where n is the order of the matrices. For Sylvester the "nullity" of a matrix was the difference between its order and rank, wherefore he wrote his law thus: "The nullity of the product of *two* (and therefore of any number of) matrices cannot be less than the nullity of any factor, nor greater than the sum of the nullities of the *several* factors which make up the product."[18]

Sylvester devised a method (the "dialytic method") for the elimination of one unknown between two equations

$$f(x) \equiv a_0 x^n + a_1 x^{n-1} + \cdots + a_n = 0 \, (a_0 \neq 0),$$
$$\varphi(x) \equiv b_0 x^m + b_1 x^{m-1} + \cdots + b_m = 0 \, (b_0 \neq 0).$$

The method is simpler than Euler's well-known method. Sylvester formed n equations from $f(x)$ by separate and successive multiplication by x^{n-1}, $x^{n-2}, \cdots 1$, and m equations from $\varphi(x)$ by successive multiplication by x^{m-1}, $x^{m-2}, \cdots 1$. From the resulting $m + n$ equations he eliminated the $m + n$ power of x, treating each power as an independent variable. The vanishing of the resulting determinant (E) is a necessary condition for f and φ to have a common root, but the method is deficient to the extent that the condition $E = 0$ is not proved sufficient. This type of approach was superseded in Sylvester's lifetime when Kronecker developed a theory of elimination for systems of polynomials in any number of variables, but elementary texts still quote Sylvester's method alongside Euler's and Bezout's.

Sylvester was inordinately proud of his mathematical vocabulary. He once laid claim to the appellation "Mathematical Adam," asserting that he believed he had "given more names (passed into general circulation) to the creatures of the mathematical reason than all the other mathematicians of the age combined."[19] Much of his vocabulary has been forgotten, although some has survived; but it would be a mistake to suppose that Sylvester bestowed names lightly, or that they were a veneer for inferior mathematics. His "combinants," for example, were an important class of invariants of several q-ary p-ics (q and p constant).[20] His "plagiograph" was less obscure under the title "skew pantograph"; but under either name it was an instrument based on an interesting and unexpected geometrical principle that he was the first to perceive.[21] And in like manner one might run through his works, with their "allotrious" factors, their "zetaic" multiplication, and a luxuriant terminology between.

Sylvester thought his verse to be as important as his mathematics; but he was a poor judge, and the two had little in common beyond an exuberant vocabulary. His mathematics spanned, of course, a far greater range than it is possible to review here. One characteristic of this range is that it was covered without much recourse to the writings of contemporaries. As H. F. Baker has pointed out,

in projective geometry Sylvester seems to have been ignorant of Poncelet's circular points at infinity, and not to have been attracted by Staudt's methods of dispensing with the ordinary notion of length. Sylvester's papers simply ignore most problems in the foundations of geometry. Remarkable as some of his writings in the theory of numbers, elliptic integrals, and theta functions are, he would have benefited from a closer reading of Gauss, Kummer, Cauchy, Abel, Riemann, and Weierstrass. Neither Lie's work on the theory of continuous groups nor the algebraic solution of the fifth-degree equation elicited any attention from him, and it is perhaps surprising that Cayley did not persuade him of their value. An illustration of Sylvester's self-reliance is found at the end of one of the last lengthy papers he composed, "On Buffon's Problem of the Needle," a new approach to this well-known problem in probabilities.[22] The paper was the outcome of conversations with Morgan Crofton, when Sylvester was his senior at Woolwich in the 1860's; yet an extension of Barbier's theorem, now proved by Sylvester, had been published in 1868 by Crofton himself. Sylvester's strength lay in the fact that he could acknowledge this sort of inadvertent duplication without significantly diminishing the enormous mathematical capital he had amassed.

NOTES

1. H. H. Bellot, *University College, London, 1826–1926* (London, 1929), 38.
2. *Gentleman's Magazine*, n.s., **6** (Feb. 1871), 38–48.
3. C. G. Knott, *The Life and Scientific Work of Peter Guthrie Tait* (Cambridge, 1911), 159.
4. For this and the preceding doctrines, see especially "On a Theory of the Syzygetic Functions . . ." (1853), repr. in his *Collected Mathematical Papers* (henceforth abbreviated as *CMP*), I, no. 57, 429–586; and "Algebraical Researches, Containing a Disquisition on Newton's Rule . . .," *ibid.*, II, no. 74 (1864), 376–479. On Newton's rule also see *ibid.*, II, no. 81 (1865), 493–494; no. 84 (1865–1866), 498–513; no. 108 (1871), 704–708; and III, no. 42 (1880), 414–425.
5. See D. T. Whiteside, ed., *The Mathematical Papers of Isaac Newton*, I (Cambridge, 1967), 524.
6. See in particular *CMP*, I, no. 57 (1853), 436.
7. *Ibid.*, no. 5 (1838), 39.
8. *Disquisitiones arithmeticae* (1801), 76.
9. *CMP*, I, no. 59 (1853), 597.
10. *Ibid.*, III, no. 39 (1879–1880), 312–391.
11. *Ibid.*, I, no. 33 (1851), 198–202.
12. *Ibid.*, IV, no. 44 (1886), 515–519; see also no. 42 (1886), 458.
13. See, for example, *ibid.*, III, no. 18 (1878), 117–126; no. 27 (1878), 318–340; IV, no. 41 (1886), 278–302, esp. 288; no. 42 (1886), 305–513, esp. 451.
14. See especially *ibid.*, III, no. 67 (1882), 568–622.
15. See the important memoir in *ibid.*, I, no. 42 (1852), 284–327, with its amusing note to 293: "Meicatalecticizant

would more completely express the meaning of that which, for the sake of brevity, I denote catalecticant."

16. *Ibid.*, no. 47 (1852), 378–381; no. 57 (1853), 511; IV, no. 49 (1887), 532.
17. *Journal für Mathematik*, **53** (1857), 275–281.
18. *CMP*, IV, no. 15 (1884), 134.
19. *Ibid.*, no. 53 (1888), 588.
20. For some further details, see P. Gordan, *Vorlesungen über Invariantentheorie*, II (Leipzig, 1887), 70–78.
21. *CMP*, III, no. 3 (1875), 26–34.
22. *Ibid.*, IV, no. 69 (1890–1891), 663–679.

BIBLIOGRAPHY

I. ORIGINAL WORKS. Sylvester published no lengthy volume of mathematics, although his books on versification and its mathematical principles are numerous, and include *The Law of Continuity as Applied to Versification . . . Illustrated by an English Rendering of "Tyrrhena regnum," Hor. 3, 29 . . .* (London, 1869); *The Laws of Verse, or Principles of Versification Exemplified in Metrical Translations* (London, 1870); *Fliegende Blätter (Rosalind and Other Poems), a Supplement to the Laws of Verse* (London, 1876); *Spring's Debut. A Town Idyll in Two Centuries of Continuous Rhyme* (Baltimore, 1880); *Retrospect. A Verse Composition by the Savilian Professor of Geometry . . . Tr. Into Latin by Undergraduates of New College* (Oxford, 1884); and *Corolla versuum Cantatrici eximiae . . . a professore Saviliano geometriae apud oxonienses* (Oxford, 1895).

Sylvester's mathematical papers are in *The Collected Mathematical Papers of James Joseph Sylvester*, H. F. Baker, ed., 4 vols. (Cambridge, 1904–1912). Thirty of his 87 known letters from American sources are in R. C. Archibald, "Unpublished Letters of James Joseph Sylvester and Other New Information Concerning His Life and Work," in *Osiris*, **1** (1936), 85–154. Archibald gives full bibliographical information on most of the verse writings. Sylvester wrote a sonnet to the Savilian professor of astronomy, Charles Pritchard, on the occasion of his receiving the gold medal of the Royal Astronomical Society, in *Nature*, **33** (1886), 516. One might have imagined that in his literary flamboyance he was imitating Disraeli, had he not also addressed a sonnet to Gladstone (1890).

Thirty-three of Sylvester's lectures were reported by James Hammond in *Lectures Containing an Exposition of the Fundamental Principles of the New Theory of Reciprocants Delivered During . . . 1886 Before the University of Oxford*, repr. from *American Journal of Mathematics* (Oxford–Baltimore, 1888), Lecture 34 is by Hammond. Sylvester contributed well over 300 different mathematical problems to *Educational Times*. These are calendared in *Collected Papers*, IV, 743–747; and several letters concerning the problems are printed in Archibald, *op. cit.*, 124–128.

II. SECONDARY LITERATURE. H. F. Baker included a personal biography of Sylvester in his ed. of the collected papers. R. C. Archibald, *op. cit.*, 91–95, lists 57 publications dealing with Sylvester's life and works. To these may be added R. C. Archibald, "Material Concerning James Joseph Sylvester," in *Studies and Essays Offered to George Sarton* (New York, 1947), 209–217; and R. C. Yates, "Sylvester at the University of Virginia," in *American Mathematical Monthly*, **44** (1937), 194–201.

The most useful discussions of Sylvester's life and work are A. Cayley, "Scientific Worthies XXV: James Joseph Sylvester," in *Nature*, **39** (1889), 217–219, repr. in *The Collected Mathematical Papers of Arthur Cayley*, XIII (Cambridge, 1897), 43–48; F. Franklin, *People and Problems, a Collection of Addresses and Editorials* (New York, 1908), 11–27, first printed in *Bulletin of the American Mathematical Society*, **3** (1897), 299–309; P. A. MacMahon, obituary in *Nature*, **55** (1897), 492–494; and obituary in *Proceedings of the Royal Society*, **63** (1898), ix–xxv; and M. Noether, obituary in *Mathematische Annalen*, **50** (1898), 133–156. Of these, Noether's article is mathematically the most useful. Cayley wrote much invaluable commentary on Sylvester's work, for which see the index to Cayley's collected papers. The *Johns Hopkins University Circulars* are a convenient source of biography, since the editors often reprinted articles on Sylvester that had first been published elsewhere (such as those cited above by Cayley and Franklin, and the first of MacMahon's).

J. D. NORTH

TACQUET, ANDREAS (*b.* Antwerp, Belgium, 23 June 1612; *d.* Antwerp, 22 December 1660)

Tacquet was the son of Pierre Tacquet, a merchant, and Agnes Wandelen of Nuremberg. His father apparently died while the boy was still young but left the family with some means. Tacquet received an excellent education in the Jesuit *collège* of his native town, and a contemporary report describes him as a gifted if somewhat delicate child. In 1629 he entered the Jesuit order as a novice and spent the first two years in Malines and the next four in Louvain, where he studied logic, physics, and mathematics. His mathematics teacher was William Boelmans, a student of and secretary to Gregorius Saint Vincent. After his preliminary training Tacquet taught in various Jesuit *collèges* for five years, notably Greek and poetry at Bruges from 1637 to 1639. From 1640 to 1644 he studied theology in Louvain and in 1644–1645 he taught mathematics there. He took his vows on 1 November 1646 and subsequently taught mathematics in the *collèges* of Louvain (1649–1655) and Antwerp (1645–1649, 1655–1660).

Tacquet's most important mathematical work,

Cylindricorum et annularium, contained a number of original theorems on cylinders and rings. Its main importance, however, lay in its concern with questions of method. Tacquet rejected all notions that solids are composed of planes, planes of lines, and so on, except as heuristic devices for finding solutions. The approach he adopted was that of Luca Valerio and Gregorius, an essentially Archimedean method. The development of his thought can be seen in the fact that in his *Arithmeticae theoria et praxis* he took the value of ax^n ($x < 1$, $n \to \infty$) to be actually zero. Tacquet's most popular work was *Elementa geometriae*, which went through numerous editions during the seventeenth and eighteenth centuries and was edited and revised by Whiston, Musschenbroek, and Bošković. Although little more than a paraphrase of parts of Euclid and Archimedes, the book was distinguished by its clarity and order. Tacquet's *Opera mathematica* was published posthumously and contained, among other previously printed and unprinted works, his *Astronomia*. In the eighth book of this work he rejected the motion of the earth, first, because there was no proof, physical or philosophical, to prove it; second, because his faith required him to believe in its immobility.

Tacquet's importance was mainly pedagogical and his books taught elementary mathematics to many generations of readers, although his influence on Pascal may have been greater. As a creative mathematician he can hardly be deemed more than minor. He was extremely well-read in mathematics, astronomy, and physics, and seemed to have almost total knowledge of the literature. This makes him appear at times as a typical exponent of the irritatingly erudite eclecticism of seventeenth-century scientific Jesuits. However, most of his works were written as textbooks for the Jesuit *collèges* and had no pretensions to originality. His devotion to his church, his order, and his teaching may explain his relative lack of creativity.

BIBLIOGRAPHY

I. ORIGINAL WORKS. The standard bibliography of Tacquet's works is in C. Sommervogel, *Bibliothèque de la Compagnie de Jésus*, VII (Brussels, 1896), cols. 1806–1811. The most important are *Cylindricorum et annularium* (Antwerp, 1651, 1659), also in the *Opera*; *Elementa geometriae* (Antwerp, 1654, 1665, 1672), which was issued in numerous eds. and revs., including translations into English, Italian and Greek, at least until 1805; and *Arithmeticae theoria et praxis* (Louvain, 1656; Antwerp, 1665, 1682). The *Opera mathematica* (Antwerp, 1669, 1707) contains works on astronomy,

spherical trigonometry, practical geometry, and fortification, plus previously published writings on geometry and Aristotle's wheel. Tacquet's correspondence with Huygens is printed in *Oeuvres complètes de Christiaan Huygens, publiées par la Société hollandaise des sciences*, I–III (The Hague, 1888–1890), *passim*.

II. SECONDARY LITERATURE. For biographical information on Tacquet, see H. Bosmans, "Tacquet," in *Biographie nationale*, XXIV (Brussels, 1926–1929), cols. 440–464; and "Le Jésuite mathématicien anversois André Tacquet (1612–1660)," in *Gulden passer*, 3 (1925), 63–87. See also Bosmans' "André Tacquet (S. J.) et son traité d'arithmétique théorique et pratique," in *Isis*, 9 (1927), 66–82. There is no adequate analysis of Tacquet's mathematics and science. For earlier accounts see A. G. Kästner, *Geschichte der Mathematik*, III (Göttingen, 1799), 266–284, 442–449; and J. B. J. Delambre, *Histoire de l'astronomie moderne*, II (Paris, 1821), 531–535. Among modern studies that treat Tacquet is C. R. Wallner, "Über die Entstehung des Grenzbegriffes," in *Bibliotheca mathematica*, 3rd ser., 4 (1903), 246–259.

PER STRØMHOLM

TAIT, PETER GUTHRIE (*b*. Dalkeith, Scotland, 28 April 1831; *d*. Edinburgh, Scotland, 4 July 1901)

Tait was the son of the former Mary Ronaldson and John Tait, who was secretary to the duke of Buccleuch. He was taught first at Dalkeith Grammar School and, after his father's death, at a school in Circus Place and later at the Academy, both in Edinburgh. With his mother and his two sisters Tait lived in Edinburgh with an uncle, John Ronaldson, who introduced the boy to geology, astronomy, and photography. It is interesting to note that the order in the mathematics section of the Edinburgh Academical Club Prize for 1846 was first Tait, then Lewis Campbell, and third J. C. Maxwell. (In the following year Tait was second to Maxwell.) Tait entered Edinburgh University in 1847, and after a session there went in 1848 to Peterhouse, Cambridge, where his tutor was William Hopkins. He graduated as senior wrangler and first Smith's Prizeman in 1852. (Second in the tripos was another student at Peterhouse, W. J. Steele, with whom Tait collaborated on his first book, *Dynamics of a Particle* [1856]. Steele died before completing his portion of the book.)

In 1854 Tait left Cambridge, where he was a fellow of his college, to become professor of mathematics at Queen's College, Belfast. His colleague there was Thomas Andrews, with whom he collaborated in research on the density of ozone and the results of electrical discharge through gases. Other colleagues were Charles Wyville Thomson, who later was scientific leader of the *Challenger* expedition, and James Thomson, brother of William, Lord Kelvin, and discoverer of the effect of pressure on the melting point of ice. Tait's debts to Andrews were undoubtedly great, for the latter introduced him to experimental physics; but he did not, as is occasionally said, introduce Tait to Hamilton's calculus of quaternions, which had occupied Tait while he was at Cambridge.

Tait succeeded J. D. Forbes as professor of natural philosophy at Edinburgh in 1860 and held the chair until shortly before his death. In 1857 he married Margaret Archer Porter, the sister of two Peterhouse friends. One of their four sons, the best amateur golfer of his day, was killed in the Boer War.

At Edinburgh, Tait was confirmed in his recently found liking for experimentation by the duties required of him. In 1862, for example, he wrote a paper jointly with J. A. Wanklyn on electricity developed during evaporation. In 1867, having been greatly taken by Helmholtz's paper on vortex motion, he devised an apparatus for studying vortex smoke rings, thereby giving Kelvin the idea of a vortex atom. His study of vortices was the starting point of a highly important pioneer study of the topology of knots. Tait continued to experiment on thermoelectricity, publishing extensively on the subject and on thermodynamics as a whole. In 1873 he presented a first sketch of his well-known thermoelectric diagram to the Royal Society of Edinburgh. In 1875 he experimented with James Dewar on the behavior of the Crookes radiometer and gave the first satisfactory explanation of it. Between 1876 and 1888, using superb equipment of his own design supplied by the Admiralty, Tait did research on the corrections that it would be necessary to apply to the findings of the *Challenger* expedition regarding deep-sea temperatures. This work led to important experimental studies of compressibility and the behavior of materials under impact. In the same connection Tait wrote a classic paper on the trajectory of a golf ball (1896). The fourth in an important series of papers on the kinetic theory of gases (1886–1892) contained, according to Kelvin, the first proof of the Waterston-Maxwell equipartition theorem.

Tait's life was marked by several controversies, two of which reached a wide public. He felt himself committed to quaternions, having promised Hamilton, only a few days before the latter's death, to publish an elementary treatise on the subject. The work appeared in 1867 and was followed by new editions in 1873 and 1890. Tait disliked intensely the vector methods of J. W. Gibbs and Oliver Heaviside, and in a long exchange of polemics tended to have the worst of the argument. In his controversial *Sketch of the History of Thermodynamics* (1868), a highly prejudiced and pro-British account, the reputations of J. R. Mayer and Clausius suffer, while Kelvin and Joule are often praised at their expense.

BIBLIOGRAPHY

C. G. Knott, *Life and Scientific Work of Peter Guthrie Tait* (Cambridge, 1911), lists 365 papers and 22 books written wholly or partly by Tait. The last two books listed are collected volumes of Tait's *Scientific Papers* (Cambridge, 1898–1900). His best-known work was vol. I of *Treatise on Natural Philosophy* (Oxford, 1867; Cambridge, 1878, 1883), written jointly with Sir William Thomson and widely known as "T and T'." A promised vol. II failed to appear. Tait and Thomson also collaborated on an elementary version.

Knott's biography, which refers to all the important obituaries, is itself the fundamental biographical source, although very uncritical. See also J. H. Hamilton Dickson, in *Dictionary of National Biography*, 2nd supp., III (1912), 471–474; and A. Macfarlane, "P.G.T.," in *Bibliotheca mathematica*, 3rd ser., 4 (1903), 185–200. For the controversy over the history of thermodynamics, see D. S. L. Cardwell, *From Watt to Clausius* (London, 1971), 282–289.

J. D. NORTH

TAKAGI, TEIJI (*b.* Kazuya Village, near Gifu, Japan, 21 April 1875; *d.* Tokyo, Japan [?], 29 February 1960)

Teiji Takagi came from a family of landowners and government officials of a rural part of Gifu prefecture in central Japan. His mother, Tsune Takagi, was married to Mitsuzo Kinomura, of the town of Kitagata, but she returned to her family's home to bear her child and never returned to her husband, allegedly because she was repelled by the leeches on his farm. The boy's uncle, Kansuke Takagi, who was unable to have children of his own, adopted Teiji as his son, a common Japanese practice at the time for propertied families without heirs. The boy was frail and, under the severe discipline of his adoptive father, spent his childhood in study rather than in play with other children. He was an outstanding pupil, advancing through the six-year curriculum of the village school in three years, then graduating five years later, first in his class, from the middle school in Gifu. From 1891 to 1894 he attended the Third National Senior High School in Kyoto.

In 1894 Takagi entered the Imperial University in Tokyo, having already chosen mathematics as his field of study while in Kyoto. After his graduation in 1897, he began graduate study at the same university, but a prestigious government scholarship soon enabled him to go to Germany for three years; he elected to spend the first half of this period in Berlin, the second half in Göttingen.

Takagi read David Hilbert's famous report on the theory of algebraic numbers while he was in Berlin, and he developed an interest in pursuing the subject in the same direction as Hilbert himself—toward Kronecker's *Jugendtraum* ("dream of his youth") theorem on the abelian extensions of imaginary quadratic number fields. Hilbert, however, had shifted to other interests, so his direct influence on Takagi's work during Takagi's year-and-a-half stay in Göttingen was not great. Nonetheless, Takagi believed that his development was profoundly affected by Hilbert, especially by the spirit of mathematical study that Hilbert and Klein generated in turn-of-the-century Göttingen.

Soon after his return home in December 1901, Takagi married Toshi Tani, the sister-in-law of his landlord, in Tokyo on 6 April 1902. The couple had five daughters and three sons. He completed his doctorate at the Imperial University of Tokyo (26 December 1903) on the basis of a paper he had written in Göttingen on a special case of Kronecker's *Jugendtraum* theorem, namely, the case in which the imaginary quadratic field is the one obtained by adjoining i, the square root of -1. This paper and a few brief notes were published in 1902 and 1903, but there was no other published work in the following years prior to World War I. In 1904 he was made full professor at the university.

Class field theory grew out of attempts by Hilbert and Heinrich Weber, among others, to understand and prove the *Jugendtraum* theorem and other works of Leopold Kronecker. Weber gave the original definition of a "class field" (*Klassenkörper*) in terms of a rather complicated construction, the essence of which was to describe the way in which prime ideals of an algebraic number field (called the "ground field") factor in an abelian extension field (that is, a normal extension field whose Galois group over the ground field is an abelian group). Hilbert recast the theory, simplifying it by using a less general definition: Hilbert defined a class field to be what is now called an "absolute" class field, that is, a maximal abelian extension that is "unramified." (An extension is called unramified if the factorization of a prime ideal of the ground field never contains a repeated factor in the extension field.) The existence of class fields in Hilbert's sense was proved by Furtwängler in 1907.

Takagi returned to Weber's original viewpoint, but, instead of considering the way in which primes factor in an abelian extension field, considered the question of determining which ideals of the ground field are relative norms of ideals in the extension field. His main theorems were: (1) For any abelian extension, the ideals of the ground field that are relative norms of ideals of the extension field can be determined by simple multiplicative congruence conditions; (2) conversely, given a set of congruence conditions of the type Takagi describes, there is an abelian extension field in which these congruences determine the ideals that are relative norms of ideals in the extension field; (3) the prime ideals that figure in the muliplicative congruences coincide with the prime divisors of the discriminant of the extension; (4) the Galois group of the extension is isomorphic to the multiplicative group of classes of ideals of the ground field described by the multiplicative congruences; and (5) the way in which a prime ideal factors in the extension field depends only on its image in the Galois group—in particular, the prime ideals that factor into prime ideals of the first degree are precisely the ones that are relative norms (corresponding to the identity of the Galois group).

Takagi, having discovered these sweeping and unexpected theorems in isolation from his German colleagues, doubted they were correct. In fact, by his own account, he was sure they were wrong and spent a great deal of effort looking for an error in his reasoning. By the time the war was over and communication reestablished, however, he had convinced himself and had completed his theory. He set it forth in two long papers (1920, 1922) that constitute, in number of pages, half the volume of his published papers in languages other than Japanese, and contain most of his creative work.

At the International Congress of Mathematicians in Strasbourg in 1920, Takagi gave a brief presentation of his results. Whether because the German mathematicians had been excluded from participation in the congress, or because his presentation was so diffident, the significance of Takagi's work seems not to have been grasped by anyone present. Only in 1922, when C. L. Siegel persuaded Emil Artin to read the first of Takagi's two great papers, did the importance of his work begin to be recognized. A few years later, Helmut Hasse's expository treatises on class field theory made Takagi's theory known to the mathematical world, establishing it in its proper place as a revolutionary advance in algebraic number theory.

Beginning in 1930 Takagi wrote a number of textbooks in Japanese (he had also written one in 1901) dealing with algebra, analysis, the history of mathematics in the nineteenth century, and number theory. These books grew out of his long teaching career at the Imperial University and reportedly had a great effect on the education of later generations of Japanese mathematicians. In addition, he wrote a number of popular works that reached a wide audience and did much to stimulate interest in mathematics in Japan, particularly among young people.

BIBLIOGRAPHY

I. ORIGINAL WORKS. "Über eine Theorie des relativ Abelschen Zahlkörpers," in *Journal of the College of Science, Imperial University of Tokyo*, **41** (1920), 1–133; and "Über das Reciprocitätsgesetz in einem beliebigen algebraischen Zahlkörper," *ibid.*, **44** (1922), 1–50. See also *The Collected Papers of Teiji Takagi*, S. Kuroda, ed. (Tokyo, 1973).

II. SECONDARY LITERATURE. Kin-ya Honda, "Teiji Takagi: A Biography," in *Commentarii mathematici Universitatis Sancti Pauli*, **24**, no. 2 (1975), 141–167.

HAROLD M. EDWARDS

TALBOT, WILLIAM HENRY FOX (*b.* Melbury House, Dorsetshire, England, 11 February 1800; *d.* Lacock Abbey, Wiltshire, England, 17 September 1877)

Talbot was the only child of William Davenport Talbot, an officer of dragoons, and Lady Elisabeth Theresa Fox-Strangways, the eldest daughter of the second earl of Ilchester. Four years after his father's death in July 1800, his mother married Rear Admiral Charles Feilding, who established a warm relationship with his stepson. Talbot grew up with two half sisters in an upper-class family that possessed both social position and culture.

While studying at a boarding school in Rottingdean and later at Harrow, Talbot distinguished himself as a scholar. At age seventeen he entered Trinity College, Cambridge, where he studied classical languages and mathematics, receiving in 1820 the Porson Prize for Greek verse, and graduating

in 1821 as twelfth wrangler and second chancellor's medalist. Soon thereafter he published a half dozen papers on mathematics but spent much of the next decade traveling on the Continent, living the life of a gentleman scholar. He established himself in the late 1820's at the family estate, historic Lacock Abbey, ran successfully as a Liberal from Chippenham for the first reform Parliament (1833–1834), and on 20 December 1832 married Constance Mundy of Markeaton, Derbyshire. Talbot was an active member of numerous scholarly and scientific societies, including the Royal Society, the Royal Astronomical Society, and the British Association for the Advancement of Science.

Talbot's formative years were spent under the influence of the dominant Romantic atmosphere of England and Western Europe. He frequented Romantic operas and concerts and avidly read the works of Goethe, Byron, and Scott, naming two of his daughters after characters in Scott's works. His love of nature manifested itself in his lifelong interest in flowers and in his penchant for travel. His fondness for the past was stimulated not only by Scott's historical novels and by his own historic estate, but also by Young and Champollion's deciphering of the hieroglyphics on the Rosetta Stone in the early 1820's and Rawlinson and Hincks's deciphering of the Assyrian cuneiform in the middle 1840's. These stimuli merged with his flair for languages to initiate a lifelong series of translations from Assyrian and other ancient languages and of historical and philological studies. Beginning with a book of Greek verse, *Legendary Tales* (London, 1830), these translations and studies included four other books and at least sixty-two articles in scholarly journals.

After completing his study at Cambridge, Talbot continued his work in mathematics, systematically studying elliptic integrals. Building upon the earlier achievements of Fagnano dei Toschi, Euler, Legendre, Jacobi, and Abel, he addressed himself to the problem of summing the integrals of any function. His early mathematical work led to his election as a fellow of the Royal Society, while his work on elliptic integrals brought him the Royal Medal of the Society for the year 1838 and an appointment to the Royal Society council.

During the same period Talbot's interests in chemistry and optics quickened, and he gradually adopted a unified, dynamic view of physical phenomena. The early nineteenth century witnessed the adoption and modification of new theoretical frameworks in chemistry and optics. The discovery of many new substances stimulated increasing concern with chemical composition and structure, while the wave theory of light posed problems with dispersion, absorption, photochemical reaction, and other forms of light-matter interaction. Although Talbot counted Wheatstone, Brewster, and Babbage among his scientific friends, he most closely followed the ideas of his friend John Herschel on light. Adopting the wave theory of light and a kinetic interpretation of light, heat, and matter, he pursued the problem of light-matter interaction through the study of optics, crystallography, and spectra. Intrigued by the similar optical characteristics of light and radiant heat as demonstrated by Melloni and Forbes, he sought to show the unity of the chemical rays with visible rays and heat rays. He also sought to use light and optical properties as analytical tools in order to determine the nature and structure of matter and to develop methods of chemical identification. Utilizing the vibratory theory of molecular behavior in gases, he suggested in 1835 a connection between spectral lines and chemical composition. In an 1836 paper he employed the polarizing microscope as a tool to explore "the internal structure of transparent bodies, even in their minutest visible particles" (*London and Edinburgh Philosophical Magazine* [1836], p. 288). This paper brought him the honor of being named the Bakerian lecturer of the Royal Society for the year 1836.

It was with the development of photography that Talbot's love of nature and landscapes merged with his interests in optics and photochemistry. His efforts to sketch Italian scenery had met with repeated frustration. When he realized that he lacked artistic talent, he turned in 1823 to the use of a camera obscura as a drawing aid, but without satisfaction. Again in October of 1833, while honeymooning on the shores of Lake Como, he met with failure when he used Wollaston's recently developed boon to nature lovers and amateur artists, the camera lucida. At that time it occurred to Talbot to imprint the image on chemically sensitized paper. Returning to England in January 1834, he and his assistant, Nicholaas Henneman, conducted many experiments; by 1835 they were able to obtain "negatives" by employing tiny camera obscuras and paper sensitized with excess silver nitrate and fixed with excess common salt. Between 1835 and 1839, Talbot and Henneman continued their experiments, motivated by a desire for an analytic tool for research on radiant heat and light, as well as by a desire for reproducing images from nature. Following Arago's announcement to the Académie des Sciences 7 January 1839 of the existence of Daguerre's photographic process, Talbot became concerned over the priority of his work; he frantically sought to improve his process prior to the disclosure of Daguerre's. Nevertheless, Daguerre's process proved to be vastly superior to Talbot's in the quality of the image. In September 1840 Talbot discovered that gallic acid would develop a latent image on paper, and he called this new process the calotype. He patented and then disclosed the process in a paper presented to the Royal Society in June of 1841.

Although Talbot's photographic efforts did not meet with major commercial success and, because of his efforts to enforce his patents, did not win him popular acclaim, his paper on the calotype did bring him the honor of the Rumford Medal of the Royal Society (1842) for the most outstanding piece of research on light during the previous two years. In the middle 1840's he published two of the earliest books illustrated with photographs. Although twenty-eight of his fifty-nine scientific papers were published after 1840, most of these were minor papers on photography and mathematics. In 1852 he patented and published a method of photoengraving called photoglyphy. From the mid-1850's, with the increasing public clamor over his patent suits, Talbot's interests shifted increasingly to philological and historical studies. Despite the significant contribution he made in these scholarly pursuits. It was his development of the first negative-positive process in photography—that union of his naturalistic and artistic inclinations with his unitary photochemical interests—that brought him his greatest recognition both during his lifetime and after his death.

BIBLIOGRAPHY

I. ORIGINAL WORKS. Talbot's published scientific work appears exclusively in the fifty-nine articles listed in the *Royal Society Catalogue of Scientific Papers*. His two books illustrated with calotypes are *The Pencil of Nature*, parts I–VI (London, 1844–1846), and *Sun Pictures in Scotland* (London, 1845); his own remarks are contained in Appendix A of G. Tissandier, *A History and Handbook of Photography* (London, 1878).

Considerable data are contained in the legal records of the Court of Chancery, Public Record Office, London: Talbot *v* Colls (1852), and Talbot *v* Henderson (1854).

Manuscripts and artifacts are located at: Lacock Abbey, Wiltshire, England; Science Museum, London; Royal Society, London; Kodak Museum, Harrow, England; George Eastman House, Rochester, New York; Stark Library, University of Texas, Austin, Texas; and Soviet Academy of Sciences, Moscow. Some of the manuscript materials held in the U.S.S.R. have been published in T. P. Kravets, ed., *Dokumenti po istorii izobreteniia fotografi* (Moscow, 1949), in English and Russian. See also Wood and Johnston below.

II. SECONDARY LITERATURE. The only biography of Talbot is Arthur H. Booth's *William Henry Fox Talbot . . .* (London, 1965), which is superficial and unreliable. Even the best sources restrict themselves largely to Talbot's photographic work. These include R. Cull, "Biographical Notice of the Late William Henry Fox Talbot," in *Society of Biblical Archaeology. Transactions,* **6** (1878), 543–549; *Dictionary of National Biography;* H. Gernsheim, "Talbot's and Herschel's Photographic Experiments in 1839," in *Image,* **8** (1959), 132–137; H. and A. Gernsheim, *History of Photography . . .* (New York, 1969); A. Jammes, *William H. Fox Talbot, Inventor of the Negative-Positive Process* (New York, 1973); J. D. Johnston, "William Henry Fox Talbot . . .," Part I," and J. D. Johnston and R. C. Smith, "Part II," in *Photographic Journal,* **87A** (1947), 3–13, and **108A** (1968), 361–371; B. Newhall, "William Henry Fox Talbot," in *Image,* **8** (1959), 60–75; E. Ostroff, "Restoration of Photograph . . .," in *Science,* **154** (7 Oct. 1966), 119–123; M. T. Talbot, "The Life and Personality of Fox Talbot," in *Photographic Journal,* **79** (1939), 546–549; D. B. Thomas, *The First Negatives* (London, 1964); and R. D. Wood, "The Involvement of Sir John Herschel in the Photographic Patent Case, Talbot *v* Henderson, 1854," and "J. B. Reade . . .," in *Annals of Science,* **27** (Sept. 1971), 239–264, and **27** (March 1971), 13–83.

REESE V. JENKINS

TANNERY, JULES (*b.* Mantes-sur-Seine, France, 24 March 1848; *d.* Paris, France, 11 November 1910)

Tannery was the youngest of the three children of Delphin Tannery, an engineer with the Compagnie des Chemins de Fer de l'Ouest. The eldest child was a daughter and the second was the engineer and historian of science Paul Tannery. The family moved first to Redon, in Ille-et-Vilaine, where his father supervised the construction of a railroad line, and then to Mondeville near Caen.

At the *lycée* in Caen, he was an excellent student, and he won several prizes in the *concours général.* His brother, who was passionately interested in philosophy and Greek antiquity, gave him a taste for these subjects. In 1866 Tannery was admitted with highest standing to the science section of the École Normale Supérieure and, simultaneously, to the École Polytechnique. He decided to enter the École Normale, and in 1869 placed first in the *agrégation.* He was then assigned to teach mathematics at the *lycée* in Rennes, and in 1871 he was named to a post at the *lycée* in Caen,

where his former classmate Émile Boutroux was also teaching.

During this period Tannery underwent a religious crisis caused by his profound desire to admire without remorse pagan antiquity, the cult of reason, and the ideas of Lucretius.

Tannery returned to Paris in 1872 as *agrégé-préparateur* of mathematics at the École Normale. Encouraged by Hermite, he began work on a thesis inspired by the works of Fuchs ("Propriétés des intégrales des équations différentielles linéaires à coefficients variables"), which he defended in 1874. Two years later he became editor of the *Bulletin des sciences mathématiques,* on which he collaborated with Darboux, Hoüel, and Picard until his death. He wrote a great number of book reviews for the journal—more than 200 for the years 1905–1910 alone. Characterized by rigorous criticism and an excellent style, the reviews are models of their kind in both form and content.

Tannery taught higher mathematics at the Lycée Saint-Louis and substituted for the professor of physical and experimental mechanics at the Sorbonne. In 1881 he was named *maître de conférences* at the École Normale and, shortly afterward, at the École Normale for women located in Sèvres. From 1884 until his death Tannery served as assistant director of scientific studies at the École Normale; in this post he displayed the full measure of his abilities. At the same time, from 1903, he was professor of differential and integral calculus at the Faculty of Sciences of Paris.

A member of several educational commissions and of the Conseil Supérieur de l'Instruction Publique, Tannery played an important role in the pedagogical reforms in France at the beginning of the twentieth century. Through his lectures and supervisory duties at the École Normale this gifted teacher gave valuable guidance to many students and inspired a number of them to seek careers in science (for example, Paul Painlevé, Jules Drach, and Émile Borel). Tannery was elected *membre libre* of the Académie des Sciences on 11 March 1907, replacing Paul Brouardel.

Tannery possessed considerable gifts as a writer. The pure and elegant style of the poems he composed in his free hours clearly bears the stamp of a classic sensibility. His vast culture, nobility of character, and innate sense of a rationally grounded morality are reflected in each of his *Pensées,* a collection of his thoughts on friendship, the arts, and beauty. Often they exhibit a very refined sense of humor.

Among his scientific publications, the *Introduc-*

tion à la théorie des fonctions d'une variable exercised an especially great influence on younger generations of mathematicians. Émile Borel stated that it was a profound, vigorous, and elegant work that taught him how to think. In another book, written with Jules Molk, Tannery presented the results of applying Fuchs's theorems to the linear differential equation that defines the periods of an elliptic function. Tannery also gave a new expansion of the Euler equation. In algebra, following the path opened by Hermite, Tannery studied the similar transformations of the quadratic forms, the invariants of the cubic forms, and the symmetric functions. In geometry, he concentrated his research on the osculating plane of skewed cubic equations and on a fourth degree surface of which the geodesic lines are algebraic. Poincaré highly esteemed Tannery and commented very favorably on his writings. Tannery's work was known abroad, especially in Germany, where a translation of his book *Notions de mathématiques* was published in 1909.

In 1880 Weierstrass published "Zur Funktionenlehre," in which he dealt with the convergence of a series whose terms are rational functions of one variable. Upon reading it, Tannery sent Weierstrass solutions he obtained in a simpler manner, utilizing elementary theorems of function theory. Weierstrass translated Tannery's letter into German and published it in *Monatsberichte der königlich-preussischen Akademie der Wissenschaften zu Berlin* (1881, 228–230).

Tannery reflected a great deal on the role of number in science, and he sought to show how the entire subject of analysis could be built up on the basis merely of the notion of whole number. In his speculations on the notion of infinity, he arrived at the conclusion that it is equivalent to the simple possibility of indefinite addition. Finally, his interest in the history of science—undoubtedly inspired by his brother—led him to publish Galois's unpublished manuscripts and the correspondence between Liouville and Dirichlet.

Galois had entrusted his manuscripts to his friend Auguste Chevalier, who gave them to Liouville. The latter bequeathed his library to one of his sons-in-law, Célestin de Blignières (1823–1905), a former student at the École Polytechnique and a disciple of Auguste Comte. Mme de Blignières, Liouville's daughter, in turn, gave Galois's papers to Tannery, along with her father's correspondence with Dirichlet.

In his *Éloges et discours académiques* (p. 101), Émile Picard drew the following parallel between Jules and Paul Tannery:

They were extremely close all their lives. Of very different natures, the two brothers complement each other. Paul derived a certain tranquillity from his positivist convictions. A philologist and scholar of extraordinary erudition, he sought to follow, in innumerable notes and articles, the historical evolution of science from Greek antiquity until the end of the seventeenth century. Jules's philosophy, on the other hand, did not free him from intellectual anxiety. His outlook was less universal than his brother's, but also more profound. He had both the subtle mind of the metaphysician and the penetrating insight of the disillusioned moralist.

BIBLIOGRAPHY

I. ORIGINAL WORKS. Tannery's books include *Introduction à la théorie des fonctions d'une variable* (Paris, 1886), 2nd ed., 2 vols. (1904–1910); *Eléments de la théorie des fonctions elliptiques*, 4 vols. (Paris, 1893–1902, with Jules Molk); *Leçons d'arithmétique théorique et pratique* (Paris, 1894; 7th ed., 1917); *Introduction à l'étude de la théorie des nombres et de l'algèbre supérieure*, Émile Borel and Jules Drach, eds. (Paris, 1895), taken from Tannery's lectures at the École Normale Superieure; *Notice sur les travaux scientifiques de M Jules Tannery* (Paris, 1901); *Notions de mathématiques* (Paris, 1903), German trans. (Leipzig, 1909), with historical notes by Paul Tannery; *Leçons d'algèbre et d'analyse à l'usage des classes de mathématiques spéciales*, 2 vols. (Paris, 1906), with Paul Tannery; *Liste des travaux de Paul Tannery* (Bordeaux, 1908), prepared by P. Duhem and preceded by obituaries written by Duhem and J. Tannery; and *Science et philosophie* (Paris, 1912), with a brief article by Émile Borel.

Tannery's articles include "Sur l'équation différentielle linéaire qui relie au module la fonction complète de première espèce," in *Comptes rendus hebdomadaires des séances de l'Académie des sciences*, **86** (1878), 811–812; "Sur quelques propriétés des fonctions complètes de première espèce," *ibid.*, 950–953; "Sur les intégrales eulériennes," *ibid.*, **94** (1882), 1698–1701; and "Sur les fonctions symétriques des différences des racines d'une équation," *ibid.*, **98** (1884), 1420–1422; "Les Mathématiques dans l'Enseignement secondaire," in *La revue de Paris*, **4** (1900), 619–641; "Principes fondamentaux de l'arithmétique," with J. Molk, in *Encyclopédie des sciences mathématiques*, pt. 1, I (Paris, 1904), 1–62; "Sur l'aire du parallèlogramme des périodes pour une fonction pu donnée," in *Bulletin des sciences mathématiques*, **28** (1904), 108–117; "Paul Tannery," in *Comptes rendus du IIe Congrès international de philosophie* (Geneva, 1905), 775–797; "Manuscrits et papiers inédits de Galois," in *Bulletin des sciences mathématiques*, **30** (1906), 226–248, 255–263, and **31** (1907), 275–308; "Correspondance entre Liouville et Dirichlet," *ibid.*, **32** (1908), 47–62, 88–95, and **33** (1909), 47–64; "Discours prononcé à Bourg-la-Reine" (at the inauguration of a plaque placed on the house in which Galois was born), *ibid.*, **33** (1909), 158–164; "Pour la science livresque," in *Revue de métaphysique et de morale*, **17** (1909), 161–171; and "Pensées," in *La revue du mois*, **11** (1911), 257–278, 399–435.

II. SECONDARY LITERATURE. The first obituaries of Tannery are the addresses given by P. Painlevé and É. Picard on 13 and 14 November 1910, in *Bulletin des sciences mathématiques*, **34** (1910), 194–197. These were followed by É. Borel, "Jules Tannery, 24 mars 1848–11 novembre 1910," in *La revue du mois*, **11** (1911), 5–16; Émile Hovelaque, "Jules Tannery," in *La revue de Paris*, **1** (1911), 305–322; and A. Châtelet, "Jules Tannery," in *Enseignement mathématique*, **13** (1911), 56–58.

A small book of 140 pages entitled *En souvenir de Jules Tannery MCMXII* was published by subscription by Tannery's friends in 1912; it contains an address by Ernest Lavisse, director of the École Normale, a biographical article by Émile Boutroux, and a selection of Tannery's "Pensées." See also Émile Picard, "La vie et l'oeuvre de Jules Tannery membre de l'Académie," in *Mémoires de l'Académie des sciences de l'Institut de France*, **58** (1926), i–xxxii; the same article, with a few revisions, appeared as "Un géomètre philosophe: Jules Tannery," in *La revue des deux mondes*, **31** (1926), 858–884, and in Picard's *Éloges et discours académiques* (Paris, 1931), 51–104.

See also Poggendorff, III, 1324; IV, 1476; V, 1242; and G. Sarton, "Paul, Jules et Marie Tannery," in *Isis*, **38** (1947–1948), 33–51, which in addition contains a list of Jules Tannery's works on pp. 47–48.

PIERRE SPEZIALI

TANNERY, PAUL (*b.* Mantes-la-Jolie, Yvelines, France, 20 December 1843; *d.* Pantin, Seine–St. Denis, France, 27 November 1904)

An engineer and administrator by profession, Tannery could devote only his leisure hours to scholarship. Despite this limitation, however, he accomplished a vast amount of penetrating and wide-ranging research and became one of the most influential figures in the rapidly developing study of the history of science at the beginning of the twentieth century. Like his younger brother, Jules, who later became a mathematician, Tannery early received a deeply Christian education from his parents, S. Delphin Tannery, an engineer who worked for railroad companies, and the former E. Opportune Perrier. After proving to be a brilliant pupil at a private school in Mantes, Tannery attended the *lycées* of Le Mans and Caen, where he showed great enthusiasm for the classics, although he had

enrolled as a science student. His philosophy teacher, Jules Lachelier, communicated to Tannery a passion for the subject and strengthened his interest in classical antiquity. In 1860 Tannery fulfilled his father's hopes by obtaining one of the highest scores on the competitive entrance examination for the École Polytechnique, where he acquired a solid education in science and technology but devoted much time to other subjects as well. In particular he began to learn Hebrew and developed a strong interest in the teaching of mathematics.

Upon graduating from the École Polytechnique in 1863, Tannery entered the École d'Application des Tabacs as an apprentice engineer. At this time he read Auguste Comte's *Cours de philosophie positive*, an initiation into positivist philosophy that so profoundly influenced him that years later he approached the study of the history of science as a spiritual disciple of Comte.

After working for two years as an assistant engineer at the state tobacco factory in Lille, Tannery was transferred in 1867 to an administrative post at the headquarters of the state tobacco administration in Paris, where he enjoyed a more active intellectual and artistic life. He served in the Franco-Prussian War as an artillery captain and was present during the siege of Paris. An ardent patriot, he was deeply affected by the defeat and never consented to acknowledge the terms of the peace treaty as definitive. Upon demobilization Tannery resumed his former duties. At the same time he eagerly studied philosophy and mathematics, subjects that he discussed with his brother, Jules, who taught at Caen and later at the École Normale Supérieure of Paris, and with such young philosophers as É. Boutroux. In 1872 the tobacco administration sent Tannery to supervise the construction of several buildings in the Périgord region. While there he became seriously ill and was obliged to convalesce for a long period. He used this time to further his knowledge of ancient languages, acquiring a mastery of this field that was evident in his very first publications.

In March 1874 Tannery began to direct an extensive construction project at the state tobacco factory of Bordeaux. This university city had a very active intellectual life, and he soon decided to spend his leisure time investigating various topics in the history of the exact sciences in antiquity, as well as a number of philosophical and philological questions. From 1876 Tannery participated in the work of the Société des Sciences Physiques et Naturelles de Bordeaux and published many studies in its *Mémoires* and in the *Revue philoso-*

phique de la France et de l'étranger, which had recently been founded at Paris. He gradually began to send material to other journals, eventually becoming a fairly regular contributor to about fifteen French and foreign periodicals. He published hundreds of memoirs, articles, notes, and reviews while pursuing a brilliant career in the state tobacco administration. Although many other historians of science have been obliged to conduct their research concurrently with their professional activities, none of them seems to have produced a body of work comparable to Tannery's in scope and importance.

Although his stay at Bordeaux had proved enriching and fruitful, Tannery soon ended it. In 1877, at his own request, he was appointed engineer at the tobacco factory of Le Havre, a city with intellectual resources far inferior to those of Bordeaux but near the region of Caen, where Tannery's parents lived. He continued, however, to take a lively interest in Greek science; and his survey of mathematics at the time of Plato ("L'éducation platonicienne"), published in the *Revue philosophique de la France et de l'étranger*, was enthusiastically received and was translated into English and German. Meanwhile, his professional obligations, already considerable, become still greater in 1880, when he became acting director of the tobacco factory.

In June 1881 Tannery married Marie-Alexandrine Prisset (1856–1945), daughter of a well-to-do notary in Poitiers. Although she had received only a modest education, his young wife encouraged Tannery to pursue his scholarly research. Several trips abroad during this period enabled Tannery to meet leading scholars, notably J. L. Heiberg, H.-G. Zeuthen, G. Eneström, and M. Cantor, with whom he maintained close and fruitful relationships. Since his situation at Le Havre provided little encouragement for his research, however, Tannery soon sought a transfer to Paris.

His request was granted, and in July 1883 he was named appraiser-engineer in a Paris tobacco factory. Once again he was able to devote all his leisure time to scholarship. Although relatively brief, this Paris period was extremely productive. Tannery's principal area of interest was the history of mathematics; he gave a private course on the subject at the Faculty of Sciences in 1884–1885 and published an important series of articles on Greek geometry in the *Bulletin des sciences mathématiques*. He also pursued studies already under way on the origins of Greek science and on various philological questions. In addition he printed previously unpublished Greek texts, as well as original studies on a wide range of topics. Research at the Bibliothèque Nationale and a scholarly visit to Italy enabled him to begin work on two important editorial projects: an edition of the manuscripts of Diophantus, which was entrusted to him in 1883, and one of Fermat's works, for which he received a joint commission with Charles Henry in 1885.

At the end of 1886 Tannery had to leave Paris, in order to direct the tobacco factory at Tonneins (Lot-et-Garonne). Deprived of the resources of the Bibliothèque Nationale, he was limited to editorial work and to perfecting his manuscripts. He revised and completed a series of articles that had been appearing in the *Revue philosophique de la France et de l'étranger* since 1880 and presented them in book form as *Pour l'histoire de la science hellène. De Thalès à Empédocle*, his first separately printed publication. Tannery also regrouped and completed another series of articles, which had been appearing since 1884 in *Bulletin des sciences mathématiques*, into a second, shorter book, *La géométrie grecque, comment son histoire nous est parvenue et ce que nous en savons*, I. *Histoire générale de la géométrie élémentaire* (the only part to be published). In addition, he continued to prepare the edition of Fermat's works.

Promoted to director of the Bordeaux tobacco factory in January 1888, Tannery spent two years in the city in which he had first become aware of his vocation for history. Renewing contact with intellectual circles there, he became friendly with an amateur scholar, Polydore Hochart, who assisted him in collecting material on the Bordeaux correspondents of Mersenne—the first step in a great project that Tannery was not able to complete. He also worked on a study of Greek astronomy, in which he sought, through a very detailed analysis of the *Almagest*, to gain insight into the different theories outlined by Ptolemy. (The study was published in the *Mémoires de la Société des sciences physiques et naturelles de Bordeaux* in 1893.)

At the beginning of 1890 Tannery returned to the Paris headquarters of the state tobacco authority in order to organize the manufacture of matches and to give instruction in the relevant techniques to the apprentice engineers at the École d'Application des Tabacs. In 1893 he was appointed director of the factory at Pantin, near Paris, a post that he held until his death in 1904. Although this appointment entailed heavy administrative and social responsibilities, Tannery did a remarkable amount of research during this final period of his life. He regularly contributed articles, memoirs, notes, and book reviews to about fifteen journals and completed his editions of the works of Diophantus and of Fermat. Tannery also undertook vast new projects, such as collaborating on the *Histoire générale du IVᵉ siècle à nos jours* of Ernest Lavisse and A. N. Rambaud, teaching at the Collège de France for several years, and preparing a new critical edition of the works and correspondence of Descartes. Through his regular correspondence with French and foreign colleagues and through his activities at several congresses, he laid the foundations for international collaboration in the history of science.

A rapid survey of the various aspects of Tannery's work provides some idea of the scope and importance of his accomplishments during these final years. He wrote some 250 articles, notes, and other communications on the most varied issues in the history of the exact sciences, the history of philosophy, and philology, most of them concerning antiquity, Byzantine civilization, and Western civilization from the Middle Ages to the seventeenth century; they occupy five volumes of his collected *Mémoires scientifiques.*

In the years immediately after 1893, however, Tannery concentrated most of his effort on completing his two major editorial projects. The two volumes of Diophantus' *Opera omnia* appeared in 1893 and 1895. (Tannery also began work on a French translation, but he did not complete it.) The three volumes of the *Oeuvres de Fermat,* which Tannery edited with Charles Henry, were published between 1891 and 1896. The first volume contains mathematical works and "Observations sur Diophante"; the second (1894) contains Fermat's correspondence; and the third consists of French translations of the writings and of Latin fragments by Fermat as well as of several texts by J. de Billy and J. Wallis. Tannery, who played the principal role in editing these volumes, also assembled material for a fourth (*Compléments . . .*), which was completed by Henry and published in 1912. A fifth volume, containing further supplementary material, was published by C. de Waard in 1922.

In 1892 Tannery agreed to substitute for Charles Lévêque in the chair of Greek and Latin philosophy at the Collège de France. Without fundamentally altering the character of the chair, Tannery sought to place greater emphasis on the history of ancient scientific thought and to illustrate its influence on the formation of modern sci-

ence. Unfortunately, he did not publish any of his courses, and we have a record only of the main subjects he treated. These included Aristotle's *Physics* and *De caelo,* an interpretation of Plato, ancient theories of matter, the commentaries of Simplicius, and atomistic doctrines, as well as various currents of ancient philosophy and even fragments of Orphic poetry. At the end of the academic year 1896–1897, however, a new project began to occupy almost all Tannery's time: an edition of the works of Descartes. Accordingly, he gave up teaching and thereby renounced the possibility of succeeding Lévêque.

Tannery was interested in Descartes during his first stay in Bordeaux, though only in principle, since all his research during that period pertained to ancient thought. But from 1890 on the preparation of his edition of Fermat's work led him to make a thorough study of Descartes's correspondence and to publish a number of items that had remained in manuscript. The rigor of his editorial work and his deep knowledge of seventeenth-century science brought him, in 1894, the co-editorship (with the historian of modern philosophy Charles Adam) of a new critical edition of the works and correspondence of Descartes that was destined to replace the very dated, eleven-volume edition by Victor Cousin (1824–1826). In the last ten years of Tannery's life this undertaking, the scope and importance of which are obvious, absorbed a growing portion of his leisure. His first—and most difficult—task was the preparation of volumes I–V, devoted to Descartes's correspondence (published 1897–1903). He also participated in editing volumes VI (*Discours de la méthode* and *Essais* [1902]), VII (*Meditationes de prima philosophia* [1904]), and IX (*Méditations* and *Principes* [1904]), and left valuable notes for the other volumes published by Henry. This edition, called the "Adam-Tannery" Descartes, is too well-known to require detailed description here. A major contribution to the history of ideas, and especially to the history of science in the seventeenth century, it sparked a renewal of interest in Cartesian philosophy. By its rigor and precision, and the wealth of its documentation, it far surpassed the earlier editions and marked an important step in the elaboration of modern methods of producing critical editions. Only recently has it been necessary to publish a revised and enlarged edition that takes into account the documentary discoveries made since the beginning of the twentieth century.

Although during the final decade of his career Tannery devoted an ever increasing amount of time to this editorial effort, he still managed to publish a large number of studies, chiefly on ancient science and medieval and Byzantine mathematics. Moreover, his vast erudition enabled him to reply to numerous questions posed in the *Intermédiaire des mathématiciens* and to contribute valuable notes to several fascicles of the *Encyclopédie des sciences mathématiques*. Along with his highly specialized works, he wished to produce a more general account of the history of science, the initial outlines of which he had sketched in his chapters of Lavisse and Rambaud's *Histoire générale*. At the beginning of 1903 it appeared that Tannery would have an especially favorable opportunity to carry out this project. The death of Pierre Laffitte had left vacant the chair of the history of science at the Collège de France, which had been created for him in 1892, and the Assembly of professors at the Collège had voted to maintain the chair. The two consultative bodies, the Assembly and the Académie des Sciences, informed the minister of education that Tannery was their first choice among several candidates. His nomination seemed so certain that he began to write the inaugural lecture of his course. But, for obscure political and philosophical reasons the minister chose the candidate who was second on the list submitted to him: the crystallographer Grégoire Wyrouboff, a positivist philosopher with little competence in the history of science. Strictly speaking the minister was within his rights. Tannery was deeply disappointed by this unjust decision, however, which was vainly opposed by the many French and foreign scholars who considered Tannery one of the leaders in the field. Although the case is not clear, Sarton and Louis have revealed some of Chaumié's motives. First of all it is certain that a militant positivist and freethinker like Wyrouboff fitted more easily into the anticlericalism of Émile Combes's government than a fervid Catholic like Tannery. But it appears also that the minister preferred a course of studies that was oriented toward contemporary science, as Wyrouboff proposed, to the program of general scientific history proposed by Tannery. But there is no doubt that the "scandal of 1903" did great damage to the development of the history of science in France.

Tannery was convinced of the necessity of an international effort to catalog documentary sources and to eliminate the nationalistic interpretations of the history of science that were all too common at that time. The four volumes of his *Mélanges scientifiques* that are devoted to correspondence reveal the extent of his relations with the leading histori-

ans of science in France, Germany, Scandinavia, Italy, and elsewhere. Tannery also was active at the international congresses of historical studies (Paris, 1900; Rome, 1903), philosophy (Paris, 1900; Geneva, 1904), and mathematicians (Heidelberg, 1904). Conscious of the interdisciplinary role of the history of science, Tannery wanted the subject to be recognized as a field in its own right by historians and philosophers, as well as by scientists. He also hoped that students of the field would become aware of the distinctive contribution it could make and that close contacts would be established between historians of science in all countries.

This effort was suddenly interrupted a few weeks after Tannery returned from the Geneva congress of 1904. Suffering from cancer of the pancreas, he died at the end of November in that year. A considerable portion of his work was dispersed in various specialized—and sometimes hard-to-find—journals. His widow soon undertook to collect the publications and regroup them according to major subjects: exact sciences in antiquity, in the Middle Ages, and in the Byzantine world; modern science; history of philosophy; philology; and so on. To these she added the book reviews and the correspondence. A number of distinguished historians of science, including Heiberg, Zeuthen, and Loria, assisted her in this project. Through their devotion and hers, the seventeen volumes of Tannery's *Mémoires scientifiques* now include all his works, except for his three books on ancient science and his editions of Diophantus, Fermat, and Descartes. With the aid of C. de Waard, Marie Tannery also began work on the edition of the *Correspondance du P. Marin Mersenne* that her husband had hoped to undertake.

It would be impossible in an article of this length to convey the importance of a body of work as extensive and varied as Tannery's. Perhaps its most notable characteristic is an unwavering concern for rigor and precision. The detailed studies that constituted the bulk of his output were, in Tannery's view, only a necessary stage in the elaboration of much broader syntheses that would ultimately lead to a comprehensive history of science that he himself could only initiate. While some of the results that he published during thirty years of scholarly activity have been brought into question by documentary discoveries or by new interpretations, a large number of his studies retain their value. Even more important, however, is the fruitful influence that Tannery's work has exerted on historians of science in the twentieth century.

BIBLIOGRAPHY

I. ORIGINAL WORKS. Lists of Tannery's works were published by Marie Tannery in *Mémoires de la Société des sciences physiques et naturelles de Bordeaux*, 6th ser., **4** (1908), 299–382; and by P. Louis in Tannery's *Mémoires scientifiques*, XVII (Toulouse–Paris, 1950), 61–117. G. Eneström presented "Liste des travaux de Paul Tannery sur les mathématiques et la philosophie des mathématiques," in *Bibliotheca mathematica*, 3rd ser., **6** (1905), 292–304. Shorter bibliographies have been offered by G. Sarton in *Osiris*, **4** (1938), 703–705; and by R. Taton in *Revue d'histoire des sciences et de leurs applications*, **7** (1954), 369–371. And on the occasion of his candidacy at the Collège de France in Apr. 1903, Tannery drew up "Titres scientifiques de Paul Tannery," reproduced in *Mémoires*, X, 125–136.

Tannery's published work consists of several books, major editions of scientific writings, and a very large number of articles. The three principal books are devoted to ancient science: *Pour l'histoire de la science hellène. De Thalès à Empédocle* (Paris, 1887); 2nd ed. prepared by A. Diès with a pref. by F. Enriques (Paris, 1930); *La géométrie grecque . . . ,* I, *Histoire générale de la géométrie élémentaire* (Paris, 1887), the only part to be published; and *Recherches sur l'histoire de l'astronomie ancienne* (Paris, 1893). A fourth, briefer publication concerned the preparation of the ed. of Descartes: *La correspondance de Descartes dans les inédits du fonds Libri* (Paris, 1893).

His major eds. of scientific works are *Oeuvres de Fermat*, 3 vols. (Paris, 1891–1896), edited with C. Henry, plus IV (*Compléments*), published by C. Henry (1912), and V (*Suppléments*) (1922), published by C. de Waard; *Diophanti Alexandrini opera omnia*, 2 vols. (Leipzig, 1893–1895); and *Oeuvres de Descartes*, 12 vols. and supp. (Paris, 1897–1913), with C. Adam— Tannery participated in the editing of vols. I–VII and IX. He also began work on eds. that were continued at the urging of Mme Tannery: *Correspondance du P. Marin Mersenne*, C. de Waard, R. Pintard, and B. Rochot, eds. (Paris, 1932–); and Georgius Pachymeres, *Quadrivium*, E. Stéphanou, ed. (Vatican City, 1940).

Most of Tannery's articles, as well as his correspondence, were collected in the *Mémoires scientifiques*, published by Mme Tannery with the aid of several historians of science. The material is grouped as follows: I–III, *Sciences exactes dans l'antiquité* (Toulouse–Paris, 1912–1915); IV, *Sciences exactes chez les Byzantins* (1920); V, *Sciences exactes au Moyen Âge* (1922); VI, *Sciences modernes* (1926); VII, *Philosophie ancienne* (1925); VIII, *Philosophie moderne* (1927); IX, *Philologie* (1929); X, *Supplément au tome VI. Sciences modernes. Généralités historiques* (1930); XI–XII, *Comptes-rendus et analyses* (1931–1933); XIII–XVI, *Correspondance* (1934–1943); and XVII, *Biographie, bibliographie, compléments et tables* (1950). The bibliography given by P. Louis in *Mémoires scientifiques*, XVII, 61–117, which indicates the vol. and first pg. of the works reproduced in this ed., also lists articles not in the *Mémoires*, including the 200 articles Tannery wrote for the *Grand encyclopédie* and his notes to certain chapters of the *Encyclopédie des sciences mathématiques*. Vol. XVII of the *Mémoires* also contains a "Table analytique des mémoires scientifiques," 449–494, which considerably facilitates working with this rich and varied collection of studies, as well as an index of Greek words, 495–506.

II. SECONDARY LITERATURE. See the following, listed chronologically: Charles Adam, "Paul Tannery et l'édition de Descartes," in *Oeuvres de Descartes*, C. Adam and P. Tannery, eds., VIII, v–xviii; H. Bosmans, "Notice sur les travaux de Paul Tannery," in *Revue des questions scientifiques*, 3rd ser., **8** (1905), 544–574; *Discours prononcés aux obsèques de M. Paul Tannery . . .* (Toulouse, 1905); P. Duhem, "Paul Tannery (1843–1904)," in *Revue de philosophie*, 5, no. 1 (1905), 216–230; F. Picavet, "Paul Tannery, historien de la philosophie," in *Archiv für Geschichte der Philosophie*, 3rd ser., **18** (1905), 293–302; J. Tannery, "Notice sur Paul Tannery," in *Rapports et compte-rendus du IIe Congrès international de philosophie* (Geneva, 1905), 775–797, also in *Mémoires de la Société des sciences physiques et naturelles de Bordeaux*, 6th ser., **4** (1908), 269–293; H.-G. Zeuthen, "L'oeuvre de Paul Tannery comme historien des mathématiques," in *Bibliotheca mathematica*, 3rd ser., **6** (1905), 260–292; G. Milhaud, "Paul Tannery," in *Revue des idées*, **3** (1906), 28–39, also in *Nouvelles études sur l'histoire de la pensée scientifique* (Paris, 1911), 1–20; P. Duhem, "Paul Tannery et la Société des sciences physiques et naturelles de Bordeaux," in *Mémoires de la Société des sciences physiques et naturelles de Bordeaux*, 6th ser., **4** (1908), 295–298; and A. Rivaud, "Paul Tannery, historien de la science antique," in *Revue de métaphysique et de morale*, **11** (1913), 177–210.

Later works are G. Loria, "Paul Tannery et son oeuvre d'historien," in *Archeion* (Rome), **11** (1929), lxxx–xcii; J. Nussbaum, *Paul Tannery et l'histoire des physiologues milésiens* (Lausanne, 1929); F. Enriques, "La signification et l'importance de l'histoire de la science et l'oeuvre de Paul Tannery," in Paul Tannery, *Pour l'histoire de la science hellène*, 2nd ed. (Paris, 1930), xi–xxi; Marie Tannery, P. Boutroux, and G. Sarton, "Paul Tannery," "L'oeuvre de Paul Tannery," and "Bibliographie des travaux de Paul Tannery," in *Osiris*, **4** (1938), 633–705; G. Sarton, "Paul, Jules and Marie Tannery," in *Isis*, **38** (1947), 33–51; and P. Louis, "Biographie de Paul Tannery," in Tannery's *Mémoires scientifiques*, XVII, 1–49. The last two articles contain an account of the Wyrouboff affair. See also a group of articles by H. Berr, S. Delorme, J. Itard, R. Lenoble, P.-H. Michel, G. Sarton, P. Sergescu, J. Tannery, and R. Taton in *Revue d'histoire des sciences et de leurs applications*, **7** (1954), 297–368.

There are accounts of the life and work of Marie Tannery by P. Ducassé, in *Osiris*, **4** (1938), 706–709; P.

Louis, in Tannery's *Mémoires scientifiques*, XVII, 51–59; G. Sarton, in *Isis*, **38** (1947), 44–47, 50; and C. de Waard, in *Revue d'histoire des sciences et de leurs applications*, **2** (1948), 90–94.

René Taton

TARSKI, ALFRED (*b.* Warsaw, Poland, 14 January 1901; *d.* Berkeley, California, 27 October 1983)

Trained as both a mathematician and a philosopher, Tarski discovered interconnections between such diverse areas of mathematics as logic, algebra, set theory, and measure theory. He brought clarity and precision to the semantics of mathematical logic, and in so doing he legitimized semantic concepts, such as truth and definability, that had been stigmatized by the logical paradoxes. Tarski was extroverted, quick-witted, strong-willed, energetic, and sharp-tongued. He preferred his research to be collaborative—sometimes working all night with a colleague—and was very fastidious about priority. An inspiring teacher, at Berkeley he supervised the doctoral dissertations of many of the leading mathematical logicians of the next generation. Tarski's influence was especially pervasive in model theory—in forming its concepts, problems, and methodology. Although he did much research in algebra, he remained a logician first and an algebraist second. Collectively, his work can be regarded as an immensely fruitful interplay among algebra, set theory, and logic.

Tarski was the son of Ignacy Tajtelbaum, a successful shopkeeper, and his wife, Rose Prussak Tajtelbaum. (Around 1924 he changed his name from Tajtelbaum to Tarski—to protect his as yet unborn children from anti-Semitism.) He was educated in Warsaw, where he submitted his doctoral dissertation, supervised by Stanislaw Leśniewski, in 1923. His other principal teachers in logic and philosophy were Tadeusz Kotarbiński and Jan Łukasiewicz; in mathematics, Stefan Banach and Wacław Sierpiński. The University of Warsaw granted Tarski a Ph.D. in mathematics in 1924. In 1918, and again in 1920, he served briefly in the Polish army.

From 1922 to 1925 Tarski was an instructor in logic at the Polish Pedagogical Institute in Warsaw. Then he became a *Privatdozent* and an adjunct professor of mathematics and logic at the University of Warsaw. Since this was not a regular university position, in 1925 he also accepted a position as professor at Zeromski's Lycée in Warsaw, teaching there full-time and keeping both positions until 1939.

On 23 June 1929 he married Maria Witkowski; they had a son and a daughter. From January to June 1935 he worked in Vienna, holding a fellowship from Karl Menger's colloquium, where he had lectured by invitation in February 1930. Shortly before the war, Tarski was a candidate for the chair of philosophy at the University of Lvov, but that position went to Leon Chwistek. Tarski's difficulty in obtaining a regular academic appointment, which some have blamed on anti-Semitism, contrasted sharply with his acknowledged role as a leading Warsaw logician. Politically, he was a socialist.

In 1939 Tarski traveled to the United States for a lecture tour. When World War II broke out, he remained there, and was naturalized as an American citizen six years later. With the influx of refugees from Europe, academic positions were scarce. Nevertheless, from 1939 to 1941 Tarski was a research associate in mathematics at Harvard, and in 1940 also served as visiting professor at the City College of New York. During the year 1941–1942 he was a member of the Institute for Advanced Study at Princeton.

Tarski did not obtain a permanent position until 1942, when the University of California at Berkeley hired him as a lecturer. There he remained for the rest of his career, becoming an associate professor in 1945 and full professor a year later. The breadth of his interests is illustrated by his establishment at Berkeley in 1958 of the Group in Logic and the Methodology of Science, bringing together mathematicians and philosophers to study foundational questions. Although Tarski was made emeritus professor in 1968, he continued to teach for five years and to supervise doctoral students and do research until his death. In 1981 he received the Berkeley Citation, the highest award that university gives to its faculty.

Tarski established ties with other academic institutions, serving as Sherman memorial lecturer at University College (London) in 1950 and again in 1966, as lecturer at the Institut Henri Poincaré (Paris) in 1955, and as Flint professor of philosophy at U.C.L.A. in 1967. In addition to his European connections, he had close ties to Latin America. He was visiting professor at the National University of Mexico in 1957, and at the Catholic University of Chile in the year 1974–1975.

Despite his early difficulties in securing a regular position, Tarski received numerous honors. In 1935 he was made a Rockefeller fellow, and a Guggenheim fellow in the year 1941–1942 (and again in the year 1955–1956). From 1958 to 1960 he served as research professor at the Miller Institute for Basic Research in Science. In 1966 he was awarded the Jurzykowski Foundation Prize. The journal *Algebra Universalis* made Tarski honorary editor for his work in universal algebra. He was awarded honorary doctorates by the Catholic University of Chile in 1975 and by the University of Marseilles in 1977.

For many years Tarski was actively involved with mathematical and scientific organizations. From 1935 to 1939 he served as vice president of the Polish Logic Society. In 1940 he was elected to the executive committee of the Association for Symbolic Logic and was the association's president from 1944 to 1946. In 1948 he became a council member of the American Mathematical Society. Tarski served as president of the International Union for the History and Philosophy of Science (1956–1957) and was chairman of the U.S. National Committee on History and Philosophy of Science (1962–1963). In 1965 he was elected to the National Academy of Sciences. In addition, he was a fellow of the American Academy of Arts and Sciences, a foreign member of the Royal Netherlands Academy of Sciences and Letters, and a corresponding fellow of the British Academy.

Tarski was more eclectic than most logicians educated in the 1920's. He drew not only from Bertrand Russell and Alfred North Whitehead's *Principia mathematica* and from David Hilbert, but also from the Peirce-Schröder tradition of algebraic logic and from the Polish logic of Leśniewski and Łukasiewicz. All four traditions repeatedly influenced his work. His dissertation examined the definability of propositional connectives in the theory of types, but his interests were already quite broad. During his career he wrote several hundred articles, as well as monographs, in French, Polish, German, and English. The extreme richness of his work makes it necessary to treat it thematically rather than chronologically.

In 1921 Tarski began publishing in set theory and continued to do so until his death. His first substantial paper (1924), on finite sets, completed several decades of research on this topic by Georg Cantor, Richard Dedekind, Ernst Zermelo, and others. His work often combined foundational concerns with mathematical results, as in the Banach-Tarski paradox (a sphere can be decomposed into a finite number of pieces and reassembled into a sphere of any larger size). Influenced by Sierpiński, Tarski investigated the role of the axiom of choice and showed many propositions (such as the proposition that $M^2 = M$ for every infinite cardinal M) to be equivalent to this axiom. By 1929 he became convinced that cardinal arithmetic divided naturally into those propositions equivalent to this axiom and those independent of it. The latter propositions, he be-

lieved, formed part of a new theory of the equivalence of sets with respect to a given class of one:one mappings, a theory intensively studied by Tarski and Banach. In 1926 Tarski established that the axiom of choice is implied by the generalized continuum hypothesis (that is, for every infinite set A, there is no cardinal between A and its power set). His concern with propositions equivalent to the axiom of choice was lifelong, as was his interest in cardinal arithmetic dispensing with that axiom.

A second theme in Tarski's set-theoretic research was large cardinals. In 1930 he introduced, jointly with Sierpiński, the notion of a strongly inaccessible cardinal, and in 1939 he put forward the axiom of inaccessible sets, a large cardinal axiom that implies the axiom of choice. In 1943, in a joint paper with Paul Erdös, he introduced the seminal notions of strongly compact cardinal and weakly compact cardinal. They observed that every strongly compact cardinal is measurable and that every measurable cardinal is weakly compact. Proofs were not published until 1961, a year after Tarski also established, by using the work of his student William Hanf on infinitary logic, that a measurable cardinal is very large among inaccessible cardinals, thus settling a thirty-year-old problem.

From 1926 to 1928 Tarski conducted a seminar on metamathematics at Warsaw University. There he investigated, in particular, the structure of complete theories in geometry and group theory. He also exploited the technique of quantifier elimination on the theory of discrete order and the theory of real closed fields, thereby establishing the decidability of these theories. The latter work, which yielded the decidability of first-order Euclidean geometry, was not published until 1948. Never published was Tarski's 1949 result that the theory of Boolean algebras is decidable. And his 1939 discovery, with his former student Andrzej Mostowski, that the first-order theory of well-orderings is decidable was published in 1978. The richness of Tarski's discoveries, and the clarity he demanded of their published form, increased the number of his unpublished results and lengthened the time between discovery and publication.

During the 1930's Tarski did much research on the metamathematical notion of deductive system, axiomatizing the notion of consequence with a generality that included all kinds of logic known at the time. He then specialized the notion of consequence to treat specific logics, such as classical propositional logic. Here he was particularly concerned with determining the number of complete extensions of a given mathematical theory. This research was connected with his desire to find purely mathematical (and especially algebraic) equivalents of metamathematical notions.

A recurring theme in Tarski's work was the role of the infinitary in logic. In 1926 he formulated the w-rule (an infinitary version of the principle of mathematical induction), which, by 1933, he considered to be problematical. He showed in 1939 that even in the presence of this rule there are undecidable statements. Around 1957 Tarski investigated first-order logic extended by infinitely long formulas. In 1961 the incompactness of many such languages led to very important results in set theory.

Tarski's famous work on definitions of truth in formalized languages (1933–1935) gave the notion of satisfaction of a sentence in a structure for first-order logic, second-order logic, and so on. This work had a very pronounced influence on philosophers concerned with mathematics, science, and linguistics.

During the mid 1930's Tarski started to do research in algebra, at first as a tool for studying logic and then, in the 1940's, increasingly for its own sake as well. In 1935 he investigated complete and atomic Boolean algebras, notions closely related to logic. His increasing concern in the late 1930's with ideals in Boolean algebras reflected his discovery that such ideals correspond to the metamathematical notion of a mathematical theory. He wrote several joint papers on closure algebras with J. C. C. McKinsey in the 1940's. While Tarski's original motivation for inventing closure algebras was to provide an algebraic analogue for the notion of topological space, he showed that these algebras were intimately related to modal logic and to intuitionistic logic. In 1941 he axiomatized the theory of binary relations and posed the problem of representability: Is every model of this theory isomorphic to an algebra of relations? Although in 1950 Roger Lyndon found the answer to be no, Tarski proved in 1955 that the class of all representable relation algebras is a variety. The following year he determined all complete varieties of rings and of relation algebras. Closely related to this work on varieties was his 1968 paper on equational logic.

Tarski's research on relation algebras led to his most ambitious algebraic creation, cylindrical algebras. During the period 1948–1952 he and his student Fred Thompson formulated the notion of cylindrical algebra as an algebraic analogue of first-order logic. That is, the class of cylindrical algebras was to bear the same relation to first-order logic with identity that the class of Boolean algebras bears to propositional logic. From the 1950's until his death, Tarski investigated cylindrical algebras and

their representability, first with Leon Henkin and then with his former student Donald Monk as well.

Another major area of Tarski's logical research was the undecidability of theories. In 1939 he and Mostowski reduced Gödel's incompleteness theorems to a form that depended only on a finite number of first-order arithmetic axioms, and thereby were able to extend greatly the number of theories known to be undecidable. Their results were published in 1953 in the monograph *Undecidable Theories*, in which Tarski established the undecidability of the first-order theory of groups, of lattices, of abstract projective geometries, and (with Mostowski) of rings.

In his research after World War II, Tarski no longer used the theory of types as his basic logical system; instead, he used first-order logic. At most, he considered certain extensions of first-order logic, such as weak second-order logic and infinitary logics.

Tarski's immense influence cannot be properly judged on the basis of his publications alone. He influenced the many mathematicians with whom he did joint work, and he molded the perspectives of many doctoral students who became leading mathematical logicians. While still at Warsaw, he unofficially supervised Mostowski's dissertation on set theory (1939) as well as M. Presburger's master's thesis on decidability (1930). But it was during his years at Berkeley that Tarski exerted his greatest influence. Those who wrote their dissertations under him included Bjarni Jónsson (1946), Julia Robinson (1948), Robert Vaught (1954), Chen-chung Chang (1955), Solomon Feferman (1957), Robert Montague (1957), Jerome Keisler (1961), Haim Gaifman (1962), William Hanf (1963), and George McNulty (1972). Tarski also molded Dana Scott's approach to logic, although Scott received his Ph.D. at Princeton. Nor was Tarski's influence felt only in mathematics; it was also seen in J. H. Woodger's work on the axiomatic foundations of biology and in Patrick Suppes' research on the axiomatic foundations of physics.

BIBLIOGRAPHY

I. ORIGINAL WORKS. Tarski's *Collected Papers* were published in 4 vols. (1986). His *Nachlass* is in the Bancroft Library, University of California at Berkeley. A complete bibliography is in Steven Givant, "Bibliography of Alfred Tarski," in *Journal of Symbolic Logic*, **51** (1986), 913–941. A list of his Ph.D. students is in the Tarski symposium volume, *Proceedings of Symposia in Pure Mathematics*, **25** (1974), honoring his seventieth birthday and in Hodges (see below).

II. SECONDARY LITERATURE. A series of articles on Tarski's life and work appeared in *Journal of Symbolic Logic*: W. J. Blok and Don Pigozzi, "Alfred Tarski's

Work on General Metamathematics," **53** (1988), 36–50; John Doner and Wilfrid Hodges, "Alfred Tarski and Decidable Theories," *ibid.*, 20–35; John Etchemendy, "Tarski on Truth and Logical Consequence," *ibid.*, 51–79; Wilfrid Hodges, "Alfred Tarski," **51** (1986), 866–868; Bjarni Jónsson, "The Contributions of Alfred Tarski to General Algebra," *ibid.*, 883–889; Azriel Levy, "Alfred Tarski's Work in Set Theory," **53** (1988), 2–6; George F. McNulty, "Alfred Tarski and Undecidable Theories," **51** (1986), 890–898; J. Donald Monk, "The Contributions of Alfred Tarski to Algebraic Logic," *ibid.*, 899–906; Patrick Suppes, "Philosophical Implications of Tarski's Work," **53** (1988), 80–91; L. W. Szczerba, "Tarski and Geometry," **51** (1986), 907–912; Lou van den Dries, "Alfred Tarski's Elimination Theory for Real Closed Fields," **53** (1988), 7–19; and Robert L. Vaught, "Alfred Tarski's Work in Model Theory," **51** (1986), 869–882. On Tarski's contributions to model theory, see C. C. Chang, "Model Theory 1945–1971," in *Proceedings of Symposia in Pure Mathematics*, **25** (1974), 173–186; and R. L. Vaught, "Model Theory Before 1945," *ibid.*, 153–172.

GREGORY H. MOORE

TARTAGLIA (also **Tartalea** or **Tartaia**), **NICCOLÒ** (*b.* Brescia, Italy, 1499 or 1500; *d.* Venice, Italy, 13 December 1557)

The surname Tartaglia, which Niccolò always used, was a nickname given to him in his boyhood because of a speech impediment resulting from a wound in the mouth (*tartagliare* means "to stammer"). According to his will, dated 10 December 1557 and now in the Venice State Archives, he had a brother surnamed Fontana, and some historians have attributed that surname to Niccolò as well.

Tartaglia's father, Michele, a postal courier, died about 1506, leaving his widow and children in poverty. Six years later, during the sack of Brescia, Niccolò, while taking shelter in the cathedral, received five serious head wounds. It was only through the loving care of his mother that he recovered. At the age of about fourteen, he went to a Master Francesco to learn to write the alphabet; but by the time he reached "k," he was no longer able to pay the teacher. "From that day," he later wrote in a moving autobiographical sketch, "I never returned to a tutor, but continued to labor by myself over the works of dead men, accompanied only by the daughter of poverty that is called industry" (*Quesiti*, bk. VI, question 8).

Tartaglia began his mathematical studies at an early age and progressed quickly. He moved to Verona, probably sometime between 1516 and

1518, where he was employed as "teacher of the abacus." Certain documents dating from 1529–1533, preserved in the Verona section of the State Archives, testify that he had a family, that he was in reduced financial circumstances, and that he was in charge of a school in the Palazzo Mazzanti. In 1534 he moved to Venice, where he was "professor of mathematics." Tartaglia also gave public lessons in the Church of San Zanipolo (Santi Giovanni e Paolo). Nearly all his works were printed in Venice, where he remained for the rest of his life except for a return to Brescia for about eighteen months in 1548–1549. During this time he taught at Sant'Afra, San Barnaba, San Lorenzo, and at the academy of the nearby village of Rezzato. He died in Venice, poor and alone, in his dwelling in the Calle del Sturion near the Rialto Bridge.

The most important mathematical subject with which Tartaglia's name is linked is the solution of third-degree equations. The rule for solving them had been obtained by Scipione Ferro in the first or second decade of the sixteenth century but was not published at the time. It was rediscovered by Tartaglia in 1535, on the occasion of a mathematical contest with Antonio Maria Fiore, a pupil of Ferro; but Tartaglia did not publish it either. On 25 March 1539, Tartaglia told Girolamo Cardano about it at the latter's house in Milan. Although Cardano had persistently requested the rule and swore not to divulge it, he included it in his *Ars magna* (1545), crediting Ferro and Tartaglia. This breach of promise angered Tartaglia; and in the *Quesiti* (bk. IX), he presented his own research on third-degree equations and his relations with Cardano, whom he discussed in offensive language.

Lodovico Ferrari, who devised the solution of fourth-degree equations, rose to Cardano's defense and sent a notice (*cartello*) of mathematical challenge to Tartaglia. Between 10 February 1547 and 24 July 1548 they exchanged twelve printed brochures (Ferrari's six *Cartelli* and Tartaglia's six *Risposte*, all usually known as *Cartelli*), which are important for their scientific content and are notable for both polemical liveliness and bibliographical rarity. The exchange was followed by a debate between Tartaglia and Ferrari in the Church of Santa Maria del Giardino, in Milan, on 10 August 1548. The scientific portion of the dispute consisted of the solution of sixty-two problems that the two contestants had posed to each other. Although centering mainly on arithmetic, algebra, and geometry, the questions also dealt with geography, astronomy, architecture, gnomonics, and optics. They offer a vivid picture of the state of the exact sciences in mid-sixteenth-century Italy.

Tartaglia's other mathematical contributions concern fundamentals of arithmetic, numerical calculations, extraction of roots, rationalization of denominators, combinatorial analysis, and various other problems that are now considered quaint and amusing. "Tartaglia's triangle," the triangular array of binomial coefficients also known as "Pascal's triangle," is found in the *General trattato* (pt. II [1556]) but also appears in earlier works by other authors, although in a different configuration.

```
            1
          1   1
        1   2   1
      1   3   3   1
    1   4   6   4   1
 . . . . . . . . . .
```

The *Cartelli* also contain an extreme-value problem proposed by Ferrari that Tartaglia solved without including the relevant demonstration.

In geometry Tartaglia was a pioneer in calculating the volume of a tetrahedron from the lengths of its sides and in inscribing within a triangle three circles tangent to one another (now called Malfatti's problem). In the *Cartelli* Ferrari and Tartaglia contributed to the theory of division of areas and especially to the geometry of the compass with fixed opening—subjects to which Tartaglia returned in the *General trattato*. Of special importance to geometry, as well as to other fields, was Tartaglia's Italian translation, with commentary, of Euclid's *Elements* (1543), the first printed translation of the work into any modern language.

Tartaglia's contribution to the diffusion of the works of the great classical scientists was not confined to this translation, however. One of the first publishers of Archimedes, he produced an edition (1543) of William of Moerbeke's thirteenth-century Latin version of some of Archimedes' works. Tartaglia returned to Archimedes in 1551, publishing an Italian translation, with commentary, of part of Book I of *De insidentibus aquae* that was included in the *Ragionamento primo* on the *Travagliata inventione*. Material left by Tartaglia provided the basis for Curtius Troianus' publication in 1565 of *De insidentibus aquae* (books I and II) and of Jordanus de Nemore's *Opusculum de ponderositate*. The latter work, entitled *Liber Jordani de ratione ponderis* in various thirteenth-century manuscripts, is important in the history of mechanics because it contains the first correct solution of the problem of the equilibrium of a heavy body on an inclined plane. (Tartaglia had also published such a solution in the *Quesiti*.)

Yet, despite these contributions to the dissemination of knowledge, Tartaglia drew criticism—sharp at times—by apparently presenting William of Moerbeke's translation as his own, by not crediting Jordanus with the solution of the inclined-plane problem, and by proposing in the *Travagliata inventione* a procedure mentioned by others for raising submerged ships. Any unbiased judgment must take into consideration that an extremely easygoing attitude then obtained with regard to literary property.

Tartaglia's contributions to the art of warfare aroused widespread and lasting interest, and the broad range of his competence in nonmathematical areas is also demonstrated in the *Quesiti*. In this work Tartaglia dealt with algebraic and geometric material (including the solution of the cubic equation), and such varied subjects as the firing of artillery, cannonballs, gunpowder, the disposition of infantry, topographical surveying, equilibrium in balances, and statics. His various proposals on fortifications were praised by Carlo Promis. In his attempts at a theoretical study of the motion of a projectile—a study in which he was a pioneer—Tartaglia reached the following notable conclusions: the trajectory is a curved line everywhere; and the maximum range, for any given value of the initial speed of the projectile, is obtained with a firing elevation of 45°. The latter result was obtained through an erroneous argument, but the proposition is correct (in a vacuum) and might well be called Tartaglia's theorem. In ballistics Tartaglia also proposed new ideas, methods, and instruments, important among which are "firing tables."

Problems of gunnery led Tartaglia, in *Nova scientia*, to suggest two instruments for determining inaccessible heights and distances. The historian Pietro Riccardi considered them "the first telemeters" and cited their related theories as "the first attempts at modern tachymetry." In the *Quesiti*, Tartaglia showed how to apply the compass to surveying, and in the *General trattato* he presented the first theory of the surveyor's cross. Hence Riccardi also asserted that he was responsible for "the major advances in practical geometry of the first half of the sixteenth century."

Tartaglia's attitude toward military matters is shown in his letter dedicating *Nova scientia* to Francesco Maria della Rovere, duke of Urbino; the letter eloquently demonstrates his discreet reticence and effectively reflects his ethical qualities.

The short work *Travagliata inventione* deals not only with raising sunken ships but also with diving suits, weather forecasting, and specific weights. Tartaglia's experiments on the latter are described in Jordanus de Nemore's *De ponderositate*.

Tartaglia's pupils included the English gentleman Richard Wentworth, who was probably the author of an Italian manuscript now at Oxford (Bodleian Library, MS 584), in which Tartaglia is mentioned several times; Giovanni Antonio Rusconi, author of a book on architecture (Venice, 1540); Maffeo Poveiano, author of a work on arithmetic (Bergamo, 1582); and the mathematician and philosopher Giovanni Battista Benedetti, who in his noted work on the geometry of the compass with fixed opening (Venice, 1553) stated that he began the study of Euclid with Tartaglia.

BIBLIOGRAPHY

I. ORIGINAL WORKS. Tartaglia's works are *Nova scientia* (Venice, 1537); *Euclide Megarense* (Venice, 1543); *Opera Archimedis* (Venice, 1543); *Quesiti et inventioni diverse* (Venice, 1546); *Risposte* to Lodovico Ferrari, 6 pts. (1–4, Venice, 1547; 5–6, Brescia, 1548); *Travagliata inventione* (Venice, 1551), with *Ragionamenti* and *Supplimento*; *General trattato di numeri et misure*, 6 pts. (Venice, 1556–1560); *Archimedis De insidentibus aquae* (Venice, 1565); and *Iordani Opusculum de ponderositate* (Venice, 1565). For further information on the various editions see Pietro Riccardi, *Biblioteca matematica italiana* (Modena, 1870–1928; repr. Milan, 1952), I₂, 496–507, with supplements in the series of *Aggiunte*.

The original copies of the *Cartelli* are very rare, as is the autographed ed. (212 copies) by Enrico Giordani, *I sei cartelli di matematica disfida . . . di Lodovico Ferrari, coi sei contro-cartelli in risposta di Niccolò Tartaglia* (Milan, 1876). Facs. eds. of the *Quesiti* (Brescia, 1959) and the *Cartelli* (Brescia, 1974) have been published with commentaries by Arnaldo Masotti.

Some of Tartaglia's works on the art of warfare were translated during his lifetime into German (1547) and French (1556). Modern eds. include the following:

1. The new. ed. with English trans. and commentary by E. A. Moody, of Jordanus de Nemore's *De ponderositate*, based on thirteenth–fifteenth-century MSS with Tartaglia's ed. as guide, and prepared with the assistance of R. Clements, A. Ditzel, and J. L. Saunders. It is included in E. A. Moody and Marshall Clagett, *The Medieval Science of Weights* (*Scientia de ponderibus*) (Madison, Wis., 1952; 2nd ed., 1960), 167–227, 330–336, 388–413.

2. The new eds. of Thomas Salusbury's seventeenth-century versions of *Travagliata inventione* with *Ragionamenti* and *Supplimento*, and *Archimedis De insidentibus aquae*, in *Mathematical Collections and Translations. In Two Tomes by Thomas Salusbury. London 1661 and 1665* in facs., with analytical and biobibliographical intro. by Stillman Drake (London–Los Angeles, 1967), II, 331–402, 479–516.

3. The English versions, by Stillman Drake, of long excerpts concerning mechanics, from *Nova scientia* and the *Quesiti*, in *Mechanics in Sixteenth-Century Italy*, selections from Tartaglia *et al.*, translated and annotated by S. Drake and I. E. Drabkin (Madison, Wis., 1969), 61–143.

Tartaglia's correspondence (or extracts from it) are in the *Quesiti* and in the *Terzo ragionamento* on the *Travagliata inventione*. Two letters dealing with fortifications were exchanged in 1549 with the military engineer Jacopo Fusto Castriotto; copies, perhaps from the writers' own time, are at the old city archives, at the University of Urbino. They were published by Vincenzo Tonni-Bazza, "Di una lettera inedita di N. Tartaglia," in *Atti dell'Accademia nazionale dei Lincei. Rendiconti*, 5th ser., **10** (1901), 39–42; and "Frammenti di nuove ricerche intorno a N. Tartaglia," in *Atti del Congresso internazionale di scienze storiche, Roma, 1903*, XII (Rome, 1907), 293–307. Facsimiles of the letters are in Masotti, *Studi su N. Tartaglia* (see below), pls. xxiii, xxiv.

II. SECONDARY LITERATURE. Works within each section are listed chronologically.

On Tartaglia's life and works, see Baldassarre Boncompagni, "Intorno ad un testamento inedito di N. Tartaglia," in *In memoriam Dominici Chelini–Collectanea mathematica* (Milan, 1881), 363–412, with full-page facs. of his will; Antonio Favaro, "Intorno al testamento inedito di N. Tartaglia pubblicato da Don B. Boncompagni," in *Rivista periodica dei lavori dell' Accademia di Padova*, **32** (1881–1882), 71–108; Vincenzo Tonni-Bazza, "N. Tartaglia nel quarto centenario natalizio," in *Commentari dell'Ateneo di Brescia* (1900), 160–179; Antonio Favaro, "Per la biografia di N. Tartaglia," in *Archivio storico italiano*, **71** (1913), 335–372; and "Di N. Tartaglia e della stampa di alcune sue opere con particolare riguardo alla 'Travagliata inventione,'" in *Isis*, **1** (1913), 329–340; *Ateneo di Brescia–Scoprendosi il monumento a N. Tartaglia* (Brescia, 1918); *Commentari dell'Ateneo di Brescia* (1918), 77–151; Arnaldo Masotti, "Commemorazione di N. Tartaglia," *ibid.* (1957), 25–48; "Sui 'Cartelli di matematica disfida' scambiati fra L. Ferrari e N. Tartaglia," in *Rendiconti dell'Istituto lombardo di scienze e lettere*, Classe di scienze, sec. A, **94** (1960), 31–41; "Su alcuni possibili autografi di N. Tartaglia," *ibid.*, 42–46; and "N. Tartaglia," in *Storia di Brescia*, II (Brescia, 1963), 597–617, with 4 full-page plates. Masotti's *Studi su N. Tartaglia* (see below) contains many bibliographical details.

On Tartaglia's works, their translations, and certain MSS by Tartaglia or related to him, see "N. Tartaglia e i suoi 'Quesiti'" and "Rarità tartagliane," in *Atti del Convegno di storia delle matematiche, promosso dall'Ateneo* di Brescia nel 1959 in commemorazione del quarto centenario della morte del Tartaglia (Brescia, 1962), 17–56, 119–160, with 37 full-page plates, which are also in A. Masotti, *Studi su N. Tartaglia* (Brescia, 1962).

Tartaglia's algebra is treated in Pietro Cossali, *Origine, trasporto in Italia, primi progressi in essa dell'algebra*, II (Parma, 1799), 96–158; Silvestro Gherardi, "Di alcuni materiali per la storia della Facoltà matematica nell'antica Università di Bologna," in *Nuovi annali delle scienze naturali* (Bologna), 2nd ser., 5 (1846), 161–187, 241–268, 321–356, 401–436, with additions translated into German by Maximilian Curtze in *Archiv der Mathematik und Physik*, 52 (1870–1871), 65–205; Ettore Bortolotti, "I contributi del Tartaglia, del Cardano, del Ferrari, e della scuola matematica bolognese alla teoria algebrica delle equazioni cubiche," in *Studi e memorie per la storia dell'Università di Bologna*, 10 (1926), 55–108; and *The Great Art or The Rules of Algebra, by Girolamo Cardano*, translated and edited by T. Richard Witmer, with foreword by Oystein Ore (Cambridge, Mass., 1968), 8, 9, 52, 96, 239, as well as the foreword and preface, *passim*.

On his contributions to geometry, see Antonio Favaro, "Notizie storico-critiche sulla divisione delle aree," in *Memorie del R. Istituto veneto di scienze, lettere ed arti*, 22 (1883), 151–152; J. S. Mackay, "Solutions of Euclid's Problems, With a Ruler and One Fixed Aperture of the Compasses, by the Italian Geometers of the Sixteenth Century," in *Proceedings of the Edinburgh Mathematical Society*, 5 (1887), 2–22; W. M. Kutta, "Zur Geschichte der Geometrie mit constanter Zirkelöffnung," in *Nova acta Academiae Caesareae Leopoldino Carolinae germanicae naturae curiosorum*, 71 (1896), 80–91; Giovanni Sansone, "Sulle espressioni del volume del tetraedro," in *Periodico di matematiche*, 4th ser., 3 (1923), 26–27; Harald Geppert, "Sulle costruzioni geometriche che si eseguiscono colla riga ed un compasso di apertura fissa," *ibid.*, 9 (1929), 303–309, 313–317; and Giuseppina Biggiogero, "La geometrica del tetraedro," in *Enciclopedia delle matematiche elementari*, II, pt. 1 (Milan, 1936), 220, 245.

Statics and dynamics are discussed in Raffaello Caverni, *Storia del metodo sperimentale in Italia*, 5 vols. (Florence, 1891–1900), I, 53–54; IV, 190–198; Pierre Duhem, *Les origines de la statique*, I (Paris, 1905), 111–112, 119–120, 199; Alexandre Koyré, "La dynamique de N. Tartaglia," in *La science au seizième siècle—Colloque international de Royaumont 1957* (Paris, 1960), 91–116; and S. Drake, "Introduction" to *Mechanics in Sixteenth-Century Italy* (see above), 16–26, which also includes Tartaglia's links with Archimedes and Euclid as well as with Jordanus de Nemore.

Tartaglia's contributions to the military sciences are treated in Max Jähns, *Geschichte der Kriegswissenschaften*, 3 vols. (Munich–Leipzig, 1889–1891; facs. repr. New York, 1965), xix, 507, 596–605, 626, 707–712, 718, 797–802, 850, 985, 1008.

On fortifications, see Carlo Promis, "Della vita e delle opere degl' italiani scrittori di artiglieria, architettura e meccanica militare da Egidio Colonna a Francesco Marchi 1285–1560," in *Francesco di Giorgio Martini, Trattato di architettura civile e militare*, pt. 2 (Turin, 1841), 69–71, 78; H. Wauvermans, "La fortification de N. Tartaglia," in *Revue belge d'art, de sciences et de technologie militaires*, 1, IV (1876), 1–42; and Antonio Cassi Ramelli, *Dalle caverne ai rifugi blindati—Trenta secoli di architettura militare* (Milan, 1964), 320, 326, 346, 354, 360.

Tartaglia's ballistics is discussed in P. Charbonnier, *Essais sur l'histoire de la balistique* (Paris, 1928), 3, 6, 8–38, 41, 54, 66, 75, 87, 266; A. R. Hall, *Ballistics in the Seventeenth Century* (Cambridge, 1952), 33, 36–43, 45–52, 55, 61, 68–70, 81, 83, 95, 105; and E. G. R. Taylor, *The Mathematical Practitioners of Tudor and Stuart England 1485–1714* (Cambridge, 1954,), which mentions Tartaglia especially in connection with William Bourne and Cyprian Lucar, who translated Tartaglia's writings on ballistics into English—see 17, 30–31, 33, 42, 176, 321, 323, 328, 370.

On Tartaglia's topography, see Giovanni Rossi, *Groma e squadro ovvero storia dell'agrimensura italiana dai tempi antichi al secolo XVII°* (Turin, 1877), 7–8, 115–116, 122–138, 140, 142, 156, 157, 161, 166, 169–171, 213; P. Riccardi, "Cenni sulla storia della geodesia in Italia dalle prime epoche fin oltre la metà del secolo XIX," pt. 1, in *Memorie dell'Accademia delle scienze dell'Istituto di Bologna*, 3rd ser., 10 (1879), 474–478; R. T. Gunther, *Early Science in Oxford*, I (Oxford, 1920; repr. London, 1967), 310, 339, 368; and E. G. R. Taylor, "Cartography, Survey and Navigation," in C. Singer et al., *A History of Technology*, III (Oxford, 1957), 539.

Arnaldo Masotti

TAUBER, ALFRED (*b.* Pressburg, Slovakia [now Bratislava, Czechoslovakia], 5 November 1866; *d.* Theresienstadt, Germany [now Terezin, Czechoslovakia], 1942 [?])

Tauber entered the University of Vienna in 1884, concentrating on mathematics, physics, philosophy, and political economy. His doctoral dissertation, "Über einige Sätze der Gruppentheorie" (1888), was written under Gustav von Escherich and was intended for publication, although it never appeared in print. In 1891 Tauber qualified as *Privatdozent* with the *Habilitationsschrift* "Über den Zusammenhang des reellen und imaginären Teiles einer Potenzreihe" and subsequently lectured on the theory of series, trigonometric series, and potential theory. From 1895 he also lectured on the mathematics of insurance, a subject of little interest to him. He was subsequently awarded a monthly salary for this work, and from 1899 he also lectured on the subject at the Technical University of Vienna, where he was appointed *Honorardozent* in 1901. Financial responsibilities obliged Tauber to accept the post of head of the mathematics department of the Phönix insurance company in Vienna (1892–1908). After obtaining an assistant professorship at the university in 1908 he remained adviser to the company until 1912. He had an important role in investigations of mortality tables carried out by a group of insurance companies (1903–1907) and was consultant on insurance to the chamber of commerce and legal adviser to the commerce court of Vienna.

Tauber never assumed the duties of a full professor at the University of Vienna, and the title was not formally conferred upon him until 1919. The reasons for his difficulties are not known, but he was apparently not on good terms with some of the professors there. Almost all of his lectures were given at the Technical University. He retired in 1933 but remained as *Privatdozent* at both universities until 1938. Nothing is known about his last days. The central information office of the Vienna police headquarters contains only one entry, dated 28 June 1942: "Departure to Theresienstadt [concentration camp]."

Tauber's scientific work can be divided into three areas. The first comprises papers on function theory and potential theory; those in the latter area, although overshadowed by the work of Lyapunov, are still important. His most important memoir was "Ein Satz aus der Theorie der unendlichen Reihen" (1897). In 1826 Abel had proved a limit theorem on power series (Abel's limit theorem), the converse of which is true, as Tauber demonstrated, only if an additional condition is stipulated; such conditions are now called Tauberian conditions. These theorems are of fundamental importance in analysis, as was shown especially by G. H. Hardy and J. E. Littlewood, who coined the term "Tauberian theorems," and by N. Wiener. Tauber apparently did not follow subsequent developments of this theorem and, remarkably, did not seem to have considered his memoir of particular importance.

The second group includes papers on linear differential equations and the gamma functions. Although of interest, they did not achieve the importance of his other works.

The third group contains papers and reports on the mathematics of insurance. In "Über die Hypothekenversicherung" (1897) and "Gutachten für die sechste internationale Tagung der Versich-erungswissenschaften" (1909) he formulated his Risiko equation.

BIBLIOGRAPHY

I. ORIGINAL WORKS. A bibliography of Tauber's works may be found in the article by Pinl and Dick (see below). His outstanding work was "Ein Satz aus der Theorie der unendlichen Reihen," in *Monatshefte für Mathematik und Physik*, **8** (1897), 273–277. See also "Über den Zusammenhang des reellen und imaginären Teiles einer Potenzreihe," *ibid.*, **2** (1891), 79–118, his *Habilitationsschrift*; "Über einige Sätze der Potential-theorie," *ibid.*, **9** (1898), 74–88; and "Über die Hypothekenversicherung," in *Österreichische Revue*, **22** (1897), 203–205.

II. SECONDARY LITERATURE. On Tauber and his work, see obituaries by E. Bukovics and J. Rybarz in *Festschrift der technischen Hochschule Wien* (Vienna, 1965–1966), I, 344–346; II, 130–132; and Maximilian Pinl and Auguste Dick, "Kollegen in einer dunkeln Zeit: Schluss," in *Jahresbericht der Deutschen Mathematiker-vereinigung*, **75** (1974), 166–208, especially 202–208, which includes a bibliography.

E. HLAWKA

TAURINUS, FRANZ ADOLPH (*b*. Bad König, Odenwald, Germany, 15 November 1794; *d*. Cologne, Germany, 13 February 1874)

In F. Engel and P. Stäckel's *Die Theorie der Parallellinien von Euklid bis Gauss* two writings of Taurinus are mentioned as contributions to the subject. Since their book is a collection of documents in the prehistory of non-Euclidean geometry, they reproduce the most important passages of the original works, including extracts from those of Taurinus, which in 1895 were available in only a few copies.

According to the information given by Engel and Stäckel, Taurinus was the son of a court official of the counts of Erbach-Schöneberg; his mother was the former Luise Juliane Schweikart. He studied law at Heidelberg, Giessen, and Göttingen, and from 1822 lived in Cologne as a man of independent means; he thus had the leisure to pursue various scientific interests.

Taurinus presented the results of his mathematical investigations in *Die Theorie der Parallellinien* (1825) and *Geometriae prima elementa* (1826). He received the stimulus for these studies from his uncle F. K. Schweikart (1780–1857), who from 1820 was professor of law at the University of Königsberg, and with whom he corresponded concerning his work. Taurinus also communicated several of his results and demonstrations to Gauss, whose replies are printed in Gauss's *Werke* (VII, 186).

According to Engel and Stäckel, Taurinus' investigations on the theory of parallel lines sought to demonstrate that the sole admissible geometry is Euclidean. As the basis for his argumentation Taurinus used the axiom of the straight line, which postulates that through two points there could be exactly one straight line. In this regard, however, he had no choice but to accept the "internal consistency" of the "third system of geometry," in which the sum of the angles of a triangle amounts to less than two right angles.

His remarks in *Geometriae prima elementa* show that by 1826 Taurinus had clearly recognized the lack of contradiction of this "third system," "logarithmic-spherical geometry," as he called it; had even developed the suitable trigonometry; and had successfully applied trigonometry to a series of elementary problems.

Taurinus' works on the problem of parallel lines, like those of his uncle, Schweikart, represent a middle stage in the historical development of this problem between the efforts of Saccheri and Lambert, on the one hand, and those of Gauss, Lobachevsky, and Bolyai, on the other. Although he sought to preserve the hegemony of Euclidean geometry by reference to the infinite number of non-Euclidean geometries; nonetheless, through an idea that was very close to Lambert's, he moved on to non-Euclidean trigonometry as it was later developed by Bolyai and Lobachevsky.

Moreover, Taurinus presented the idea that elliptical geometry can be "realized" on the sphere. This concept was first taken up again by Bernhard Riemann.

BIBLIOGRAPHY

Taurinus' major works are *Die Theorie der Parallellinien* (Cologne, 1825) and *Geometriae prima elementa* (Cologne, 1826).

F. Engel and P. Stäckel, *Die Theorie der Parallellinien von Euklid bis Gauss* (Leipzig, 1895), contains selections from Taurinus' works.

KARLHEINZ HAAS

TAYLOR, BROOK (*b.* Edmonton, Middlesex, England, 18 August 1685; *d.* London, England, 29 December 1731)

Brook Taylor was the son of John Taylor of Bifrons House, Kent, and Olivia, daughter of Sir Nicholas Tempest, Bart. The family was fairly well-to-do, and was connected with the minor nobility. Brook's grandfather, Nathaniel, had supported Oliver Cromwell. John Taylor was a stern parent from whom Brook became estranged in 1721 when he married a woman said to have been of good family but of no fortune. In 1723 Brook returned home after his wife's death in childbirth. He married again in 1725 with his father's approval, but his second wife died in childbirth in 1730. The daughter born at that time survived.

Taylor's home life seems to have influenced his work in several ways. Two of his major scientific contributions deal with the vibrating string and with perspective drawing. His father was interested in music and art, and entertained many musicians in his home. The family archives were said to contain paintings by Brook, and there is an unpublished manuscript entitled *On Musick* among the Taylor materials at St. John's College, Cambridge. This is not the paper said to have been presented to the Royal Society prior to 1713, but a portion of a projected joint work by Taylor, Sir Isaac Newton, and Dr. Pepusch, who apparently was to write on the nonscientific aspects of music.

Taylor was tutored at home before entering St. John's College in 1701, where the chief mathematicians were John Machin and John Keill. Taylor received the LL.B. degree in 1709, was elected to the Royal Society in 1712, and was awarded the LL.D. degree in 1714. He was elected secretary to the Royal Society in January 1714, but he resigned in October 1718 because of ill health and perhaps because of a loss of interest in this rather confining task. He visited France several times both for the sake of his health and for social reasons. Out of these trips grew a scientific correspondence with Pierre Rémond de Montmort dealing with infinite series and Montmort's work in probability. In this Taylor served on some occasions as an intermediary between Montmort and Abraham De Moivre. W. W. Rouse Ball reports that the problem of the knight's tour was first solved by Montmort and De Moivre after it had been suggested by Taylor.[1]

Taylor published his first important paper in the *Philosophical Transactions of the Royal Society* in 1714, but he had actually written it by 1708, according to his correspondence with Keill. The paper dealt with the determination of the center of oscillation of a body, and was typical both of Taylor's work and of the times, in that it dealt with a problem in mechanics, used Newtonian dot notation, and led to a dispute with Johann I Bernoulli.

The period of 1714–1719 was Taylor's most productive, mathematically. The first editions of both his mathematical books, *Methodus incrementorum directa et inversa* and *Linear Perspective*, appeared in 1715. Their second editions appeared in 1717 and 1719 respectively. He also published thirteen articles, some of them letters and reviews, in the *Philosophical Transactions* during the years 1712–1724. These include accounts of experiments with capillarity, magnetism, and the thermometer. In his later years Taylor turned to religious and philosophical writings. His third book, *Comtemplatio philosophica*, was printed posthumously by his grandson in 1793.

Taylor is best known for the theorem or process for expanding functions into infinite series that commonly bears his name. Since it is an important theorem, and since there is disagreement as to the amount of credit that should be given to him for its development, an outline of his derivation of the theorem will be given here. The discussion of Proposition VII, Theorem III of the *Methodus incrementorum* includes the statement:

If z grows to be $z + nz$ then x equals

$$x + \frac{n}{1}\dot{x} + \frac{n}{1}\cdot\frac{n-1}{2}\ddot{x} + \frac{n}{1}\cdot\frac{n-1}{2}\cdot\frac{n-2}{3}\dddot{x}, \text{ etc.}$$

Taylor used dots below the variables to represent increments or finite differences, and dots above to represent Newton's fluxions.

The above statement is a notationally improved version of Newton's interpolation formula as given in Lemma 5 of Book III of his *Principia*. This formula had first appeared in a letter from James Gregory to John Collins in 1670.[2] Taylor had derived this formula inductively from a difference table written in terms of x and its successive differences.

Next, Taylor made the substitutions

$$v = nz, \dot{v} = v - z = (n-1)z, \ddot{v} = \dot{v} - z, \text{ etc.},$$

to derive the statement: "as z growing becomes $z + v$, x likewise growing becomes

$$x + x\frac{v}{1\cdot z} + x\frac{v\dot{v}}{1\cdot 2z^2} + x\frac{v\dot{v}\ddot{v}}{1\cdot 2\cdot 3\cdot z^3} + \cdots \text{ etc.}"$$

The final step in the derivation and Taylor's original statement of the theorem, which in modern notation is

$$f(x+h) = f(x) + \frac{f'(x)}{1!}h + \frac{f''(x)}{2!}h^2 + \frac{f'''(x)}{3!}h^3$$
$$+ \cdots \frac{f^{(n)}(x)}{n!}h^n + \cdots,$$

is finally derived in Corollary II to Theorem III as follows: "for evanescent increments [write] the fluxions which are proportional to them and make all of $\ddot{v}$, $\dot{v}$, v, v, v equal, then as with time flowing uniformly z becomes $z + v$, so will x become

$$x + \dot{x}\frac{v}{1\dot{z}} + \ddot{x}\frac{v^2}{1\cdot 2\dot{z}^2} + \dddot{x}\frac{v^3}{1\cdot 2\cdot 3\dot{z}^3} + \cdots \text{ etc.}"$$

This becomes the modern form of Taylor's series when we realize that with "time flowing uniformly" $\dot{z}$ is a constant, $\frac{\dot{x}}{\dot{z}} = \frac{dx}{dz}$, and v is the increment in the independent variable.

Taylor's first statement of this theorem had been given in a letter of 26 July 1712 to John Machin, which has been reprinted by H. Bateman. In it Taylor remarked that this discovery grew out of a hint from Machin given in a conversation in Child's Coffeehouse about the use of "Sir Isaac Newton's series" to solve Kepler's problem, and "Dr. Halley's method of extracting roots" of polynomial equations, which had been published in the *Transactions* for 1694.

This shows Taylor's fairness, care, and familiarity with the literature. He used his formula to expand functions in series and to solve differential equations, but he seemed to have no foreshadowing of the fundamental role later assigned to it by Lagrange nor to have any qualms about the lack of rigor in its derivation. Colin Maclaurin noted that the special case of Taylor's series now known as Maclaurin's theorem or series was discussed by Taylor on page 27 of the 1717 edition of the *Methodus*. The term "Taylor's series" was probably first used by L'Huillier in 1786, although Condorcet used both the names of Taylor and d'Alembert in 1784.[3]

Although infinite series were in the air at the time, and Taylor himself noted several sources and motivations for his development, it seems that he developed his formula independently and was the first to state it explicitly and in a general form. Peano based his claim for Johann I Bernoulli's priority on an integration in which Bernoulli used an infinite series in 1694.[4] Pringsheim showed that it is possible to derive Taylor's theorem from Bernoulli's formula by some changes of variable. However, there seems to be no indication that

Taylor did this, nor that Bernoulli appreciated the final form or generality of the Taylor theorem. Taylor's Proposition XI, Theorem IV, on the other hand, is directly equivalent to Bernoulli's integration formula. However, Taylor's derivation differs from Bernoulli's in such a way as to entitle him to priority for the process of integration by parts.

Taylor was one of the few English mathematicians who could hold their own in disputes with Continental rivals, although even so he did not always prevail. Bernoulli pointed out that an integration problem issued by Taylor as a challenge to "non-English mathematicians" had already been completed by Leibniz in *Acta eruditorum*. Their debates in the journals occasionally included rather heated phrases and, at one time, a wager of fifty guineas. When Bernoulli suggested in a private letter that they couch their debate in more gentlemanly terms, Taylor replied that he meant to sound sharp and "to show an indignation."

The *Methodus* contained several additional firsts, the importance of which could not have been realized at the time. These include the recognition and determination of a singular solution for a differential equation,[5] a formula involving a change in variables and relating the derivatives of a function to those of its inverse function, the determination of centers of oscillation and percussion, curvature, and the vibrating string problem. The last three problems had been published earlier in the *Philosophical Transactions*, as had been a continued fraction for computing logarithms.

Newton approached curvature by way of the determination of the center of curvature as the limit point of the intersection of two normals. Although this was not published until 1736, Taylor was familiar with Newton's work, since, after applying his own formula, Taylor remarked that the results agreed with those given by Newton for conic sections. Taylor, however, conceived of the radius of curvature as the radius of the limiting circle through three points of a curve, and associated curvature with the problem of the angle of contact dating back to Euclid. He then used curvature and the radius of curvature in giving the first solution for the normal vibrations of the simplest case of the plucked string. In propositions XXII and XXIII he showed that under his conditions each point will vibrate in the manner of a cycloidal pendulum, and he determined the period in terms of the length and weight of the string and a weight supported by the string. There is little doubt that Taylor's work influenced later writers since, for

example, Bernoulli cited Taylor in letters to his son Daniel on this topic.

The *Methodus* qualifies Taylor as one of the founders of the calculus of finite differences, and as one of the first to use it in interpolation and in summation of series.

Taylor contributed to the history of the barometer by explaining a derivation of the variation of atmospheric pressure as a logarithmic function of the altitude, and he also contributed to the study of the refraction of light.

Like all of Taylor's writing, his book on linear perspective was so concise that Bernoulli characterized it as "abstruse to all and unintelligible to artists for whom it was more especially written."[6] Even the second edition, which nearly doubled the forty-two pages of the first, showed little improvement in this matter. Its effect, nevertheless, was very substantial, since it passed through four editions, three translations, and twelve authors who prepared twenty-two editions of extended expositions based on Taylor's concepts. He developed his theory of perspective in a formal and rigorous fashion in a sequence of theorems and proofs. The most outstanding and original of his ideas in this field were his definition and use of vanishing points and vanishing lines for all lines and planes, and his development of a theory and practice for the inverse problem of perspective that later served as a basis for work by Lambert and for the development of photogrammetry. Taylor also made free use of the idea of associating infinitely distant points of intersection with parallel lines, and he sought to devise methods for doing geometric constructions directly in perspective.

A study of Brook Taylor's life and work reveals that his contribution to the development of mathematics was substantially greater than the attachment of his name to one theorem would suggest. His work was concise and hard to follow. The surprising number of major concepts that he touched upon, initially developed, but failed to elaborate further leads one to regret that health, family concerns and sadness, or other unassessable factors, including wealth and parental dominance, restricted the mathematically productive portion of his relatively short life.

NOTES

1. W. W. Rouse Ball, *Mathematical Recreations and Essays* (London, 1912), p. 175.
2. H. W. Turnbull, *James Gregory Tercentenary Memorial Volume* (London, 1939), pp. 119–120.
3. Gino Loria, *Storia delle matematiche*, 2nd ed. (Milan, 1950), p. 649.

4. G. Peano, *Formulario mathematico*, 5th ed. (Turin, 1906–1908), pp. 303–304.

5. E. L. Ince, *Ordinary Differential Equations* (New York, 1944), p. 87.

6. *Contemplatio philosophica*, p. 29, quoted from *Acta eruditorum*.

BIBLIOGRAPHY

I. ORIGINAL WORKS. The major source of biographical data as well as the only publication of his philosophical book is *Contemplatio philosophica: A Posthumous Work of the late Brook Taylor, L.L.D. F.R.S. Some Time Secretary of the Royal Society to Which Is Prefixed a Life of the Author by his Grandson, Sir William Young, Bart., F.R.S. A.S.S. with an appendix containing Sundry Original Papers, Letters from the Count Raymond de Montmort, Lord Bolingbroke, Mercilly de Villette, Bernoulli, & c.* (London, 1793).

This book and the mathematical letters appended to it are reproduced in Heinrich Auchter, *Brook Taylor der Mathematiker und Philosoph* (Würzburg, 1937). Both of these books have a picture of Taylor as secretary of the Royal Society (1714) as a frontispiece. This picture may be derived from a plaque, since it is signed "R. Earlem, Sculp." It is labeled "From an Original Picture in the Possession of Lady Young." A nearly identical picture labeled "J. Dudley, Sculp." is reproduced in *The Mathematics Teacher*, 27 (January 1927), 4. It is also labeled "London, Published March 26, 1811 by J. Taylor, High Holborn."

Charles Richard Wild, in *A History of the Royal Society* (London, 1848), lists a portrait of Taylor painted by Amiconi among the portraits in possession of the Royal Society, but *The Record of the Royal Society*, 3rd ed. (London, 1912), records in its "List of Portraits in Oil in Possession of the Society" "Brook Taylor L.L.D. F.R.S. (1685–1731). Presented by Sir W. Young, Bart., F.R.S. Painter Unknown."

The two editions of Taylor's *Methodus* cited above were both published in London, as were the editions of his *Linear Perspective*. Complete data on the editions and extensions of this book are contained in P. S. Jones, "Brook Taylor and the Mathematical Theory of Linear Perspective," in *The American Mathematical Monthly*, 58 (Nov. 1951), 597–606.

Additional data on Taylor's correspondence is to be found in H. Bateman, "The Correspondence of Brook Taylor," in *Bibliotheca Mathematica*, 3rd ser., 7 (1906–1907), 367–371; Edward M. Langley, "An Interesting Find," in *The Mathematical Gazette*, IV (July 1907), 97–98; Ivo Schneider, "Der Mathematiker Abraham de Moivre," in *Archive for History of Exact Sciences*, 5 (1968/1969), 177–317.

II. SECONDARY LITERATURE. For details of one of Taylor's disputes see Luigi Conte, "Giovanni Bernoulli e le sfida di Brook Taylor," in *Archives de l'histoire des sciences*, 27 (or 1 of new series), 611–622.

The most extensive history of Taylor's theorem is

Alfred Pringsheim, "Zur Geschichte des Taylorschen Lehrsatzes," in *Bibliotheca mathematica*, 3rd ser., I (Leipzig, 1900), 433–479.

PHILLIP S. JONES

TEICHMÜLLER, PAUL JULIUS OSWALD (*b.* Nordhausen im Harz, Germany, 18 June 1913; *d.* Dnieper region, U.S.S.R., September 1943 [?])

Oswald Teichmüller was the only child of Julius Adolf Paul Teichmüller, an independent weaver by trade, and his wife, Gertrud Dinse. He grew up in the provincial Harz region around St. Andreasberg and Nordhausen. In the spring of 1931 he enrolled to study mathematics and physics at Göttingen University. Only a few months later, he joined the Nazi Party and the SA (Storm Troopers). Although he was a brilliant student of mathematics, he supported the expulsion of most of Göttingen's mathematicians by the Nazi regime in 1933.

After Helmut Hasse's call to a vacant chair at Göttingen in the early summer of 1934, Teichmüller engaged in algebraic investigations (nos. 2, 3, 4, and 11 of his collected works) while also preparing a doctoral dissertation on spectral theory in quaternionic Hilbert space (no. 1), finished in 1935. After a short period of postdoctoral work at Göttingen, during which E. Ullrich and R. Nevanlinna introduced him to function theory (nos. 8 and 9), he transferred to the University of Berlin in April 1937, where a group of Nazi mathematicians had gathered around Ludwig Bieberbach and the journal *Deutsche Mathematik*. Teichmüller qualified as university lecturer in March 1938 with a good, though not spectacular, thesis on function theory (no. 13). One of the technical devices used there, quasi-conformal mappings, provided a clue to his main contribution to the theory of Riemann surfaces, the program of which he sketched in 1938 and 1939 while continuing work at Berlin, supported by a modest fellowship (no. 20).

Teichmüller was drafted into the army in the early summer of 1939, just before World War II, but continued his research, first as a soldier in Norway (no. 24), then in Berlin from 1941 to early 1943, working on decoding for the army high command (nos. 29 and 32). In early 1943, however, after the first successes of the Soviet army against the Germans, Teichmüller was sent to the eastern front. He disappeared in September 1943 at the Dnieper and very likely died in the same month, sharing the fate of a great majority of young men in his unit.

Teichmüller's early algebraic investigations dealt with the valuation theory of fields and the structure of algebras. In valuation theory he introduced multiplicative systems of representatives of the residue field of valuation rings (no. 2), which, in a joint effort with E. Witt, led to a characterization of the structure of the whole field in terms of the residue field (no. 11). In the theory of algebras he started to generalize Emmy Noether's concept of crossed products from fields to certain kind of algebras (*Normalringe*, no. 3), gaining new insights, for example, into the structure of p-algebras (algebra of rank p^n over a field of characteristic p; no. 4). Although from 1937 on, his main interests shifted to function theory, Teichmüller did not give up algebra. In a paper published in 1940, he explored further steps toward a Galois theory of algebras, resulting in the introduction of a group that was later recognized as a third Galois cohomology group (no. 22).

After his *Habilitation*, Teichmüller turned energetically to questions in the variation of conformal structures on surfaces, raised earlier by G. F. B. Riemann, H. Poincaré, C. F. Klein, and R. Fricke. His most important innovation was the introduction of quasi-conformal mappings to this field, using ideas first developed by H. Grötzsch and L. Ahlfors in different contexts. That is, considering marked surfaces S of type (g, n), for example (that is, S orientable, closed of genus g with n distinct distinguished points, each S endowed with a homotopy class of sufficiently regular maps $\phi: S_o \rightarrow S$, where S_o is fixed of the same type), he concentrated on sufficiently regular homeomorphisms ϕ such that for z varying in S_o, the dilatation dil $\phi(z)$ (ratio of maximal and minimal diameters of the image of a circle in the tangent plane $T_z S_o$, with respect to conformal metrics on S_o and S) is bounded. Moreover, he analyzed the close relationship between such quasi-conformal ϕ and reciprocal Beltrami differentials q on S_o, ($q = H\dfrac{dz}{dz}$; z is the local parameter, H is the complex-valued function on S_o) as invariants of the conformal metrics pulled back by ϕ.

Teichmüller's main conjecture (I) may be stated as follows: In any homotopy class there is exactly one extremal quasi-conformal mapping ϕ_o—that is, a mapping with dilatation bounded from above by $\inf_\phi \sup_z$ dil (z). That means variation of conformal structure can be realized uniquely by extremal quasi-conformal mappings (no. 20, secs. 46, 52, 122).

Teichmüller established a connection between extremal quasi-conformal mappings and regular quadratic differentials on S_o, using a class of related reciprocal Beltrami differentials. That led him to another conjecture (II) proclaiming the existence of a bicontinuous bijective correspondence Φ between a space T_1 of real parts of certain reciprocal Beltrami differentials and $M_{g,n}$ the moduli space of all conformal structures considered. (T_1 consists of all expressions $c\mathrm{Re}\{''/'\}$, where $''$ is a regular quadratic differential on S_o and $0 < c < 1$.) In fact, he proved existence and injectivity of Φ (theorem A; no. 20, secs. 132–140).

Teichmüller attacked surjectivity along different lines. In his 1939 paper (no. 20) he analyzed infinitesimal deformations of conformal structures on S heuristically, looking upon them as forming the tangent spaces of $M_{g,n}$. After the introduction of an appropriate norm, $M_{g,n}$ was endowed with a Finsler space structure. On that basis he speculated about a possible path to a kind of continuity proof of surjectivity in another central conjecture (III): After appropriate change of norms, T_1 coincides with $T_S M_{g,n}$ and the exponential map of the Finsler metric coincides with Φ of theorem A; thus a Rinow-Hopf type argument can be used to show geodetical completeness of the Finsler space $M_{g,n}$ and the surjectivity of Φ (20, secs. 115–123).

Because his heuristic arguments met with severe criticism, Teichmüller next showed existence of extremal quasi-conformal mappings in the special case of certain simply connected plane regions (pentagons; no. 24). Back in Berlin and working under slightly better conditions, he then gave an existence proof (theorem B) for surfaces of type $(g,0)$ by a classical continuity argument from uniformization theory, avoiding infinitesimal deformations and Finsler metrics (no. 29). But theorem B was also intended as a first step toward a deeper investigation of moduli spaces. In one of his last papers, Teichmüller sketched an idea of how to endow the moduli space $M_{g,o}$ with an analytic structure and how to construct an analytic fiber space of Riemann surfaces parametrized by the points of $M_{g,o}$ (no. 32).

Owing to his being sent to the front and his early death, Teichmüller could not work out most of his ideas. They became seminal, however, for later work.

BIBLIOGRAPHY

I. Original Works. Teichmüller's works are collected in his *Gesammelte Abhandlungen*, Lars V. Alfors and Frederick W. Gehring, eds. (Berlin, Heidelberg, and New York, 1982), with a complete bibliography on 747–749.

II. Secondary Literature. Reference to some of

Teichmüller's algebraic work is made in Saunders MacLane, "Topology and Logic as a Source of Algebra," in *Bulletin of the American Mathematical Society*, **82** (1976), 1–40. On his function theoretical contributions, see L. Bers, "Quasiconformal Mappings with Applications to Differential Equations, Function Theory and Topology," in *Bulletin of the American Mathematical Society*, **83** (1977), 1083–1100. For the broader context, see L. Furtmüller and M. Pinl, "Mathematicians Under Hitler," in *Leo Baeck Yearbook*, XVIII (London, Jerusalem, and New York, 1973), 129–182; H. Mehrtens, "Ludwig Bieberbach and 'Deutsche Mathematik,'" in E. Phillips, ed., *History of Mathematics* (1987); and Norbert Schappacher, "Das Mathematische Institut der Universität Göttingen 1929–1950," in Heinrich Becker, Hans-Joachim Dahms, and Cornelia Wegeler, eds., *Die Universität Göttingen in Nazionalsozialismus* (Munich, 1987), 345–373. See also William Abikoff, "Oswald Teichmüller," in *Mathematical Intelligencer*, **8**, no. 3 (1986), 8–16, 33.

ERHARD SCHOLZ

THĀBIT IBN QURRA, AL-ṢĀBIʾ AL-ḤARRĀNĪ
(*b*. Ḥarrān, Mesopotamia [now Turkey], 836; *d*. Baghdad, 18 February 901)

Life. Thābit ibn Qurra belonged to the Sabian (Mandaean) sect, descended from the Babylonian star worshippers. Because the Sabians' religion was related to the stars they produced many astronomers and mathematicians. During the Hellenistic era they spoke Greek and took Greek names; and after the Arab conquest they spoke Arabic and began to assume Arabic names, although for a long time they remained true to their religion. Thābit, whose native language was Syriac, also knew Greek and Arabic. Most of his scientific works were written in Arabic, but some were in Syriac; he translated many Greek works into Arabic.

In his youth Thābit was a money changer in Ḥarrān. The mathematician Muḥammad ibn Mūsā ibn Shākir, one of three sons of Mūsā ibn Shākir, who was traveling through Ḥarrān, was impressed by his knowledge of languages and invited him to Baghdad; there, under the guidance of the brothers, Thābit became a great scholar in mathematics and astronomy. His mathematical writings, the most studied of his works, played an important role in preparing the way for such important mathematical discoveries as the extension of the concept of number to (positive) real numbers, integral calculus, theorems in spherical trigonometry, analytic geometry, and non-Euclidean geometry. In astronomy Thābit was one of the first reformers of the Ptolemaic system, and in mechanics he was a founder of statics. He was also a distinguished physician and the leader of a Sabian community in Iraq, where he substantially strengthened the sect's influence. During his last years Thābit was in the retinue of the Abbasid Caliph al-Muʿtaḍid (892–902). His son Sinān and his grandsons Ibrāhīm and Thābit were well-known scholars.

Mathematics. Thābit worked in almost all areas of mathematics. He translated many ancient mathematical works from the Greek, particularly all the works of Archimedes that have not been preserved in the original language, including *Lemmata*, *On Touching Circles*, and *On Triangles*, and Apollonius' *Conics*. He also wrote commentaries on Euclid's *Elements* and Ptolemy's *Almagest*.

Thābit's *Kitāb al-Mafrūḍāt* ("Book of Data") was very popular during the Middle Ages and was included by Naṣīr al-Dīn al-Ṭūsī in his edition of the "Intermediate Books" between Euclid's *Elements* and the *Almagest*. It contains thirty-six propositions in elementary geometry and geometrical algebra, including twelve problems in construction and a geometric problem equivalent to solution of a quadratic equation $(a + x)x = b$. *Maqāla fī istikhrāj al-aʿdād al-mutaḥābba bi-suhūlat al-maslak ilā dhālika* ("Book on the Determination of Amicable Numbers") contains ten propositions in number theory, including ones on the constructions of perfect numbers (equal to the sum of their divisors), coinciding with Euclid's *Elements* IX, 36, on the construction of surplus and "defective" numbers (respectively, those greater and less than the sum of their divisors) and the problem, first solved by Thābit, of the construction of "amicable" numbers (pairs of numbers the sum of the divisors of each of which is equal to the other). Thābit's rule is the following: If $p = 3 \cdot 2^n - 1$, $q = 3 \cdot 2^{n-1} - 1$, and $r = 9 \cdot 2^{2n-1} - 1$, are prime numbers, then $M = 2^n \cdot pq$ and $N = 2^n \cdot r$ are amicable numbers.

Kitāb fī Taʾlīf al-nisab ("Book on the Composition of Ratios") is devoted to "composite ratios" (ratios of geometrical quantities), which are presented in the form of products of ratios. The ancient Greeks, who considered only the natural numbers as numbers, avoided applying arithmetical terminology to geometrical quantities, and thus they named the multiplication of ratios by "composition." Composition of ratios is used in the *Elements* (VI, 23), but is not defined in the original text; instead, only particular cases of composite ratios are defined (*Definitions* V, 9–10). An addition by a later commentator (evidently

Theon of Alexandria, in VI, 5) on composite ratios is done in a completely non-Euclidean manner.

Thābit criticizes *Elements* VI, 5, and proposes a definition in the spirit of Euclid: for three quantities A, B, and C, the ratio A/B is composed of the ratios A/C and C/B, and for six quantities A, B, C, D, E, F the ratio A/B is composed of the ratios C/D and E/F, if there are also three quantities L, M, N, such that $A/B = L/M$, $C/D = L/N$, $E/F = N/M$. He later defines the "multiplication of quantities by a quantity" and systematically applies arithmetical terminology to geometrical quantities. He also proves a number of theorems on the composition of ratios and solves certain problems concerning them. This treatise was important in preparing the extension of the concept of number to positive real numbers, produced in a clear form in the eleventh century by al-Bīrūnī (*al-Qānūn al-Masʿūdī*) and al-Khayyāmī (*Sharḥ mā ashkhāla min muṣādarāt Kitāb Uqlīdis*).

In *Risāla fī Shakl al-qiṭāʿ* ("Treatise on the Secant Figure") Thābit gives a new and very elegant proof of Menelaus' theorem of the complete spherical quadrilateral, which Ptolemy had used to solve problems in spherical astronomy; to obtain various forms of this theorem Thābit used his own theory of composite ratios. In *Kitāb fī Misāḥat qaṭʿ al-makhrūṭ alladhī yusammā al-mukāfiʾ* ("Book on the Measurement of the Conic Section Called Parabolic") Thābit computed the area of the segment of a parabola. First he proved several theorems on the summation of a numerical sequence from

$$\sum_{k=1}^{n} (2k-1) = n^2 \text{ to } \sum_{k=1}^{n} (2k-1)^2 + \frac{n}{3}$$

$$= \frac{2}{3} \cdot 2n \sum_{k=1}^{n} (2k-1).$$

He then transferred the last result to segments $a_k = (2k-1)a$, $b_k = 2k \cdot b$ and proved the theorem that for any ratio α/β, however small, there can always be found a natural n for which

$$\frac{n}{2n \cdot \sum_{k=1}^{n} (2k-1)} < \alpha/\beta,$$

which is equivalent to the relation $\lim_{n \to \infty} \frac{1}{n^2} = 0$.

Thābit also applied this result to the segments and divides the diameter of the parabola into segments proportional to odd numbers; through the points of division he then takes chords conjugate with the diameter and inscribes in the segment of the parabola a polygon the apexes of which are the ends of these chords. The area of this polygon is valued by upper and lower limits, on the basis of which it is shown that the area of the segment is equal to 2/3 the product of the base by the height. A. P. Youschkevitch has shown that Thābit's computation is equivalent to that of the integral $\int_0^a \sqrt{x}\, dx$ and not $\int_0^b x^2 dx$, as is done in the computation of the area in Archimedes' *Quadrature of the Parabola*. The computation is based essentially on the application of upper and lower integral sums, and the proof is done by the method of exhaustion; there, for the first time, the segment of integration is divided into unequal parts.

In *Maqāla fī Misāḥat al-mujassamāt al-mukāfiya* ("Book on the Measurement of Parabolic Bodies") Thābit introduces a class of bodies obtained by rotating a segment of a parabola around a diameter: "parabolic cupolas" with smooth, projecting, or squeezed vertex and, around the bases, "parabolic spheres," named cupolas and spheres. As in *Kitāb . . . al-mukāfiʾ* he also proved theorems on the summing of a number sequence; a theorem equivalent to $\lim_{n \to \infty} \alpha^n = 0$ for any α, $0 < \alpha < 1$; and a theorem that the volume of the "parabolic cupola" is equal to half the volume of a cylinder, the base of which is the base of the cupola, and the height is the axis of the cupola: the result is equivalent to the computation of the integral $\int_0^a x dx$.

Kitāb fī Misāḥat al-ashkāl al-musaṭṭaḥa wa'l-mujassama ("Book on the Measurement of Plane and Solid Figures") contains rules for computing the areas of plane figures and the surfaces and volumes of solids. Besides the rules known earlier there is the rule proved by Thābit in "another book," which has not survived, for computing the volumes of solids with "various bases" (truncated pyramids and cones): if S_1 and S_2 are the areas of the bases and h is the height, then the volume is equal to $V = 1/3h\,(S_1 + \sqrt{S_1 S_2} + S_2)$.

Kitāb fi'l-taʾattī li-istikhrāj ʿamal al-masāʾil al-handasiyya ("Book on the Method of Solving Geometrical Problems") examines the succession of operations in three forms of geometrical problems: construction, measurement, and proof (in contrast with Euclid, who examined only problems in construction ["problems"] and in proof ["theorems"]. In *Risāla fi'l-ḥujja al-mansūba ilā Suqrāṭ fi'l-murabbaʿ wa quṭrihi* ("Treatise on the Proof Attributed to Socrates on the Square and Its Diagonals"), Thābit examines the proof, described by Plato in *Meno*, of Pythagoras' theorem for an isosceles right triangle and gives three new proofs for the general case of this theorem. In the first, from a square constructed on the hypotenuse, two triangles congruent to the given triangle and constructed on two adjacent sides of the square are taken out and are added to the two other sides of the square, and the figure obtained thus consists of squares constructed on the legs of the right triangle. The second proof also is based on the division of squares that are constructed on the legs of a right triangle into parts that form the square constructed on the hypotenuse. The third proof is the generalization of Euclid's *Elements* VI, 31. There is also a generalization of the Pythagorean theorem: If in triangle ABC two straight lines are drawn from the vertex B so as to cut off the similar triangles ABE and BCD, then $AB^2 + BC^2 = AC$ ($AE + CD$).

In *Kitāb fī ʿamal shakl mujassam dhī arbaʿ ʿashrat qāʿida tuḥīṭu bihi kura maʿlūma* ("Book on the Construction of a Solid Figure . . .") Thābit constructs a fourteen-sided polyhedron inscribed in a given sphere. He next makes two attempts to prove Euclid's fifth postulate: *Maqāla fī burhān al-muṣādara 'l-mashhūra min Uqlīdis* ("Book of the Proof of the Well-Known Postulate of Euclid") and *Maqāla fī anna 'l-khaṭṭayn idhā ukhrijā ʿalā zawiyatayn aqal min qāʾimatayn iltaqayā* ("Book on the Fact That Two Lines Drawn [From a Transversal] at Angles Less Than Two Right Angles Will Meet"). The first attempt is based on the unclear assumption that if two straight lines intersected by a third move closer together or farther apart on one side of it, then they must, correspondingly, move farther apart or closer together on the other side. The "proof" consists of five propositions, the most important of which is the third, in which Thābit proves the existence of a parallelogram, by means of which Euclid's fifth postulate is proved in the fifth proposition. The second attempt is based on kinematic considerations. In the introduction to the treatise Thābit criticizes the approach of Euclid, who tries to use motion as little as possible in geometry, asserting the necessity of its use. Further on, he postulates that in "one simple motion" (parallel translation) of a body, all its points describe straight lines. The "proof" consists of seven propositions, in the first of which, from the necessity of using motion,

he concludes that equidistant straight lines exist; in the fourth proposition he proves the existence of a rectangle that is used in the seventh proposition to prove Euclid's fifth postulate. These two treatises were an important influence on subsequent attempts to prove the fifth postulate (the latter in particular influenced Ibn al-Haytham's commentaries on Euclid). Similar attempts later led to the creation of non-Euclidean geometry.

Kitāb fī Quṭūʿ al-usṭu wāna wa-basīṭihā ("Book on the Sections of the Cylinder and Its Surface") examines plane sections of an inclined circular cylinder and computes the area of the lateral surfaces of such a cylinder between the two plane sections. The treatise contains thirty-seven propositions. Having shown in the thirteenth that an ellipse is obtained through right-angled compression of the circle, in the next Thābit proves that the area of an ellipse with semiaxes a and b is equal to the area of the circle of radius $\sqrt{ab}$; and in the propositions 15–17 he examines the equiaffine transformation, making the ellipse into a circle equal to it.

Thābit proves that in this case the areas of the segments of the ellipse are equal to the areas of the segments of the circle corresponding to it. In the thirty-seventh proposition he demonstrates that the area of the lateral surface of the cylinder between two plane segments is equal to the product of the length of the periphery of the ellipse that is the least section of the cylinder by the length of the segment of the axis of the cylinder between the sections. This proposition is equivalent to the formula that expresses the elliptical integral of the more general type by means of the simplest type, which gives the length of the periphery of the ellipse.

The algebraic treatise *Qawl fī Taṣḥīḥ masāʾil al-jabr bi 'l-barāhī al-handasiyya* ("Discourse on the Establishment of the Correctness of Algebra Problems . . .") establishes the rules for solving the quadratic equations $x^2 + ax = b$, $x^2 + b = ax$, $x^2 = ax + b$, using *Elements* II, 5–6. (In giving the geometrical proofs of these rules earlier, Al-Khwārizmī did not refer to Euclid.) In *Masʾala fī sʿamal al-mutawassiṭayn waqisma zāwiya maʿlū ma bi-thalāth aqsām mutasāwiya* ("Problem of Constructing Two Means and the Division of a Given Angle Into Three Equal Parts"), Thābit solves classical problems of the trisection of an angle and the construction of two mean proportionals that amount to cubic equations. Here these problems are solved by a method equivalent to Archimedes' method of "insertion" which basically involves finding points of intersection of a hyperbola and a circumference. (In his algebraic treatise al-Khayyāmī later used an analogous method to solve all forms of cubic equations that are not equivalent to linear and quadratic ones and that assume positive roots.)

Thābit studied the uneven apparent motion of the sun according to Ptolemy's eccentricity hypothesis in *Kitāb fī Ibṭāʾ al-ḥaraka fī falak al-burūj wa surʿatihā bi-ḥasab al-mawāḍiʿ allatī yakūnu fīhi min al-falak al-khārij al-markaz* ("Book on the Deceleration and Acceleration of the Motion on the Ecliptic . . ."), which contains points of maximum and minimum velocity of apparent motion and points at which the true velocity of apparent motion is equal to the mean velocity of motion. Actually these points contain the instantaneous velocity of the unequal apparent motion of the sun.

A treatise on the sundial, *Kitāb fī ālāt al-sāʿāt allatī tusammā rukhāmāt*, is very interesting for the history of mathematics. In it the definition of height h of the sun and its azimuth A according to its declination δ, the latitude ϕ of the city and the hour angle t leads to the rules $\sin h = \cos(\phi - \delta) -$ versed $\sin t \cdot \cos \delta \cdot \cos \phi$ and $\sin A = \dfrac{\sin t \cdot \cos \delta}{\cos h}$, which are equivalent to the spherical theorems of cosines and sines for spherical triangles of general forms, the vertexes of which are the sun, the zenith, and the pole of the universe. The rules were formulated by Thābit only for solving concrete problems in spherical astronomy; as a general theorem of spherical trigonometry, the theorem of sines appeared only at the end of the tenth century (Manṣūr ibn ʿIrāq), while the theorem of cosines did not appear until the fifteenth century (Regiomontanus). In the same treatise Thābit examines the transition from the length of the shadow of the gnomon l on the plane of the sundial and the azimuth A of this shadow, which in essence represent the polar coordinates of the point, to "parts of longitude" x and "parts of latitude" y, which represent rectangular coordinates of the same point according to the rule $x = l \sin A$, $y = l \cos A$.

In another treatise on the sundial, *Maqāla fī ṣifat al-ashkāl allatī taḥduthu bi-mamarr ṭaraf ẓill al-miqyās fī saṭḥ al-ufug fī kull yawm wa fī kull balad*, Thābit examines conic sections described by the end of a shadow of the gnomon on the horizontal plane and determines the diameters and centers of these sections for various positions of the sun. In the philosophical treatise *Masāʾil suʾila ʿanhā Thābit ibn Qurra al-Ḥarrānī* ("Questions Posed to Thābit . . ."), he emphasizes the abstract character of number (*ʿadad*), as distinct from the concrete

"counted thing" (*maʿdūd*), and postulates "the existence of things that are actually infinite in contrast with Aristotle, who recognized only potential infinity. Actual infinity is also used by Thābit in *Kitāb fiʾl qarasṭūn* ("Book on Beam Balance").

Astronomy. Thābit wrote many astronomical works. We have already noted his treatise on the investigation of the apparent motion of the sun; his *Kitāb fī Sanat al-shams* ("Book on the Solar Year") is on the same subject. *Qawl fī īḍāḥ al-wajh alladhī dhakara Baṭlamyūs . . .* concerns the apparent motion of the moon, and *Fī ḥisāb ruʾyat al-ahilla*, the visibility of the new moon. In what has been transmitted as *De motu octave spere* and *Risāla ilā Isḥāq ibn Ḥunayn* ("Letter to . . .") Thābit states his kinematic hypothesis, which explains the phenomenon of precession with the aid of the "eighth celestial sphere" (that of the fixed stars); the first seven are those of the sun, moon, and five planets. Thābit explains the "trepidation" of the equinoxes with the help of a ninth sphere. The theory of trepidation first appeared in Islam in connection with Thābit's name.

Mechanics and Physics. Two of Thābit's treatises on weights, *Kitāb fī Ṣifat al-wazn wa-ikhtilāfihi* ("Book on the Properties of Weight and Nonequilibrium") and *Kitāb fiʾl-Qarasṭūn* ("Book on Beam Balance"), are devoted to mechanics. In the first he formulates Aristotle's dynamic principle, as well as the conditions of equilibrium of a beam, hung or supported in the middle and weighted on the ends. In the second treatise, starting from the same principle, Thābit proves the principle of equilibrium of levers and demonstrates that two equal loads, balancing a third, can be replaced by their sum at a midpoint without destroying the equilibrium. After further generalizing the latter proposition for the case in which "as many [equal] loads as desired and even infinitely many" are hung at equal distances, Thābit considers the case of equally distributed continuous loads. Here, through the method of exhaustion and examination of upper and lower integral sums, a calculation equivalent to computation of the integral $\int_a^b x\,ndx$. The result

obtained is used to determine the conditions of equilibrium for a heavy beam.

Thābit's work in natural sciences includes *Qawl fiʾl-Sabab alladhī juʿilat lahu miyāh al-baḥr māliḥa* ("Discourse on the Reason Why Seawater Is Salted"), extant in manuscript, and writings on the reason for the formation of mountains and on the striking of fire from stones. He also wrote two treatises on music.

Medicine. Thābit was one of the best-known physicians of the medieval East. Ibn al-Qiftī, in *Ta'rikh al-hukamā*, tells of Thābit's curing a butcher who was given up for dead. Thābit wrote many works on Galen and medicinal treatises, which are almost completely unstudied. Among these treatises are general guides to medicine—*al-Dhakhīra fī 'ilm al-tibb* ("A Treasury of Medicine"), *Kitāb al-Rawda fi 'l-tibb* ("Book of the Garden of Medicine"), *al-Kunnāsh* ("Collection")—and works on the circulation of the blood, embryology, the cure of various illnesses—*Kitāb fī 'ilm al-'ayn . . .* ("Book on the Science of the Eye . . ."). *Kitāb fi'l-jadarī wa'l-hasbā* ("Book on Smallpox and Measles"), *Risāla fī tawallud al-hasāt* ("Treatise on the Origin of Gallstones"), *Risāla fi'l-bayād alladhī yazharu fi'l-badan* ("Treatise on Whiteness . . . in the Body")—and on medicines. Thābit also wrote on the anatomy of birds and on veterinary medicine (*Kitāb al-baytara*), and commented on *De plantis*, ascribed to Aristotle.

Philosophy and Humanistic Sciences. Thābit's philosophical treatise *Masā'il su'ila 'anhā Thābit ibn Qurra al-Harrānī* comprises his answers to questions posed by his student Abū Mūsā ibn Usayd, a Christian from Iraq. In another extant philosophical treatise, *Maqāla fī talkhīs mā atā bihi Aristūtālīs fī kitābihi fī Mā ba'd al-tābī'a*, Thābit criticizes the views of Plato and Aristotle on the motionlessness of essence, which is undoubtedly related to his opposition to the ancient tradition of not using motion in mathematics. Ibn al-Qiftī (*op. cit.*, 120) says that Thābit commented on Aristotle's *Categories*, *De interpretatione*, and *Analytics*. He also wrote on logic, psychology, ethics, the classification of sciences, the grammar of the Syriac language, politics, and the symbolism in Plato's *Republic*. Ibn al-Qiftī also states that Thābit produced many works in Syriac on religion and the customs of the Sabians.

BIBLIOGRAPHY

I. ORIGINAL WORKS. Thābit's MSS are listed in C. Brockelmann, *Geschichte . . . Literatur*, 2nd ed., I (Leiden, 1943), 241–244, and supp. I (Leiden, 1937), 384–386; Fuat Sezgin, *Geschichte des arabischen Schrifttums*, III (Leiden, 1970), 260–263, and V (Leiden, 1974), 264–272; and H. Suter, *Die Mathematiker und Astronomen der Araber und ihre Werke* (Leipzig, 1900), 34–38, and *Nachträge* (1902), 162–163. Many of his works that are no longer extant are cited by Ibn al-Qiftī in his *Ta'rīkh al-hukamā'*, J. Lippert, ed. (Leipzig, 1903), 115–122.

His published writings include *Kitāb al-Mafrūdāt* ("Book of Data"), in Nasīr al-Dīn al-Tūsī, *Majmū' al-rasā'il*, II (Hyderabad, 1940), pt. 2; *Maqāla fī istikhrāj al-a'dād al-mutahābba bi-suhūlat al-maslak ilā dhālikâ* ("Book on the Determination of Amicable Numbers by an Easy Method"), Russian trans. by G. P. Matvievskaya in *Materialy k istorii . . .*, 90–116; *Kitāb fī ta'līf al-nisab* ("Book on the Composition of Ratios"), Russian trans. by B. A. Rosenfeld and L. M. Karpova in the *Fiziko-matematicheskie Nauki v Stranakh Vostoka* ("Physical-Mathematical Sciences in the Countries of the East"; Moscow, 1966), 9–41; *Risāla fī Shakl al-qitā'* ("Treatise on the Secant Figure"), in Latin trans. by Gerard of Cremona, with notes and German trans.; *Risāla fi'l-hujja al-mansūba ilā Suqrāt fi'l-murabba' wa qutrih* ("Treatise on the Proof Attributed to Socrates on the Square and Its Diagonals"), Arabic text with Turkish trans. in A. Sayili, "Sābit ibn Kurranin Pitagor teoremini temini," and in English in Sayili's "Thābit ibn Qurra's Generalization of the Pythagorean Theorem"; and *Kitāb fī 'amal shakl mujassam dhī arba' 'ashrat qā'ida tuhītu bihi kura ma'lūma* ("Book on the Construction of a Solid Figure With Fourteen Sides About Which a Known Sphere Is Described"), ed. with German trans. in E. Bessel-Hagen and O. Spies, "Tābit b. Qurra's Abhandlung über einen halbregelmässigen Vierzehnflächner."

Additional works are *Maqāla fī burhān al-musādara 'l-mashhūra min Uqlīdis* ("Book of the Proof of the Well-Known Postulate of Euclid"), Russian trans. in B. A. Rosenfeld and A. P. Youschkevitch, *Dokazatelstva pyatogo postulata Evklida . . .*, and English trans. in A. I. Sabra, "Thābit ibn Qurra on Euclid's Parallels Postulate"; *Maqāla fī anna 'l-khattayn idhā ukhrijā 'alā zāwiyatayn aqall min qā'imatayn iltaqayā* ("Book on the Fact That Two Lines Drawn [From a Transversal] at Angles Less Than Two Right Angles Will Meet"), Russian trans. by B. A. Rosenfeld in "Sabit ibn Korra. Kniga o tom, chto dve linii, provedennye pod uglami, shimi dvukh pryamykh, vstretyatsya," *Istoriko-matematicheskie issledovania*, **15** (1962), 363–380, and English trans. in Sabra, *op. cit.*; and *Qawl fī tashīh masā'il al-jabr bi'l-barahīn al-handasiyya* ("Discourse on the Establishment of the Correctness of Algebra Problems With the Aid of Geometrical Proofs"), ed. and German trans. in P. Luckey, "Tābit b. Qurra über die geometrischen Richtigkeitsnachweis der Auflösung der quadratischen Gleichungen."

Further works are *Qawl fī īdāh al-wajh alladhī dhakara Batlamyūs anna bihi istakhraja man taqaddamahu masīrat al-qamar al-dawriyya wa-hiya al-mustawiya* ("Discourse on the Explanation of the Method Noted by Ptolemy That His Predecessors Used for Computation of the Periodic [Mean] Motion of the Moon"), German trans. of the intro. in Hessel-Hagen and Spies, *op. cit.*; *Kitāb fī sanat al-shams* ("Book on the Solar Year"), medieval Latin trans. in F. J. Carmody, *The Astronomi-*

cal *Works of Thabit b. Qurra*, 41–79, and English trans., with commentary, by O. Neugebauer in "Thābit ben Qurra. On the Solar Year and On the Motion of the Eighth Sphere," in *Proceedings of the American Philosophical Society*, **106** (1962), 267–299; medieval Latin trans. of work on the eighth sphere, "De motu octave spere," in Carmody, *op. cit.*, 84–113, and English trans. in Neugebauer, *op. cit.*, 291–299; *Risāla ilā Ishāq ibn Hunayn* ("A Letter to . . ."), included by Ibn Yūnus in his "Great Hakimite *zīj*," Arabic text and French trans. by J. J. Caussin de Parceval, "Le livre de la grande table Hakémite observée par . . . Ebn Younis," 114–118; and *Kitāb fī ālāt al-sāʿāt allatī tusammā rukhāmāt* ("Book on the Timekeeping Instruments Called Sundials"), ed. with German trans. by K. Garbers, ". . . Ein Werk über ebene Sonnenuhren . . .," in *Quellen und Studien zur Geschichte der Mathematik, Astronomie und Physik*, Abt. A, **4** (1936).

Thābit also wrote *Maqāla fī sifat al-ashkāl allatī tahduthu bi-mamarr taraf zill al-miqyās fī sath al-ufuq fī kull yawm wa fī kull balad* ("Book on the Description of Figures Obtained by the Passage of the End of a Shadow of a Gnomon in the Horizontal Plane on Any Day and in Any City"), German trans. in E. Wiedemann and J. Frank, "Über die Konstruktion der Schattenlinien von Thābit ibn Qurra"; *Kitāb fī sifat al-wazn wa-ikhtilāfihi* ("Book on the Properties of Weight and Nonequilibrium"), included by ʿAbd al-Rahman al-Khāzinī in his *Kitāb mīzān al-hikma* ("Book of the Balance of Wisdom"), 33–38; *Kitāb fiʾl-qarastūn* ("Book on Beam Balances"), medieval Latin trans. in F. Buchner, "Die Schrift über der Qarastūn von Thābit b. Qurra," and in E. A. Moody and M. Clagett, *The Medieval Science of Weights*, 77–117 (with English trans.), also German trans. from Arabic MSS in E. Wiedemann, "Die Schrift über den Qarastūn"; and *al-Dhakhīra fī ʿilm al-tibb* ("A Treasury of Medicine"), ed. by G. Subhī (Cairo, 1928).

Recensions of ancient works are Euclid's *Elements*, ed. with additions by Nasīr al-Dīn al-Tūsī, *Tahrīr Uqlīdis fī ʿilm al-handasa* (Teheran, 1881); Archimedes' *Lemmata*, Latin trans. with additions by al-Nasawī, in *Archimedis Opera omnia*, J. L. Heiberg, ed., 2nd ed., II (Leipzig, 1912), 510–525; Archimedes' *On Touching Circles* and *Triangles* in *Rasāʾil ibn Qurra* (Hyderabad, 1940); Apollonius' *Conics*, bks. 5–7, Latin trans. in *Apollonii Pergaei Conicorum libri VII* (Florence, 1661), German trans. in L. Nix, *Das fünfte Buch der Conica des Apollonius von Perga in der arabischen Uebersetzung des Thabit ibn Corrah; De plantis*, ascribed to Aristotle, ed. in A. J. Arberry, "An Early Arabic Translation From the Greek"; and Galen's medical treatises, in F. Sezgin, *Geschichte des arabischen Schrifttums*, III, 68–140.

II. SECONDARY LITERATURE. See A. J. Arberry, "An Early Arabic Translation From the Greek," in *Bulletin of the Faculty of Arts, Cairo*, **1** (1933), 48–76, 219–257, and **2** (1934), 71–105; E. Bessel-Hagen and O. Spies, "Tābit b. Qurra's Abhandlung über einen halbregelmässigen Vierzehnflächner," in *Quellen und Studien*

zur *Geschichte der Mathematik, Astronomie und Physik*, Abt. B, **2** (1933), 186–198; A. Björnbo, "Thābits Werk über den Transversalensatz . . .," in *Abhandlungen zur Geschichte der Naturwissenschaften und der Medizin*, **7** (1924); F. Buchner, "Die Schrift über der Qarastūn von Thābit b. Qurra," in *Sitzungsberichte der Physikalisch-medizinischen Sozietät in Erlangen*, **52–53** (1922), 171–188; F. J. Carmody, *The Astronomical Works of Thabit b. Qurra* (Berkeley–Los Angeles, 1960); J. J. Caussin de Parceval, "Le livre de la grande table Hakémite observée par . . . Ebn Iounis," in *Notices et extraits des manuscrits de la Bibliothèque nationale*, **7**, pt. 1 (1803–1804), 16–240; D. Chvolson, *Die Ssabier und Ssabismus*, I (St. Petersburg, 1856), 546–567; and P. Duhem, *Les origines de la statique*, I (Paris, 1905), 79–92; and *Le système du monde*, II (Paris, 1914), 117–119, 238–246.

Also see Ibn Abi Usaybiʿa, *ʿUyūn al-anbāʾ fī tabaqāt al-atibbāʾ*, A. Müller, ed., I (Königsberg, 1884), 115–122; A. G. Kapp, "Arabische Übersetzer und Kommentatoren Euklids . . .," in *Isis*, **23** (1935), 58–66; L. M. Karpova, "Traktat Sabita ibn Korry o secheniakh tsilindra i ego poverkhnosti" ("Treatise of Thābit ibn Qurra on the Sections of the Cylinder and Its Surface"), in *Trudy XIII Mezhdunarodnogo kongressa po istorii nauki* (Papers of the XIII International Congress on the History of Science), sec. 3–4 (Moscow, 1974), 103–105; E. S. Kennedy, "The Crescent Visibility Theory of Thābit ibn Qurra," in *Proceedings of the Mathematical and Physical Society of the UAR*, **24** (1961), 71–74; ʿAbd al-Rahmān al-Khāzinī, *Kitāb mīzān al-hikma* (Hyderabad, 1940); L. Leclerc, *Histoire de la médecine arabe*, I (Paris, 1876), 168–172; P. Luckey, "Tābit b. Qurra's Buch über die ebenen Sonnenuhren," in *Quellen und Studien zur Geschichte der Mathematik, Astronomie und Physik*, Abt. B, **4** (1938), 95–148; and "Tābit b. Qurra über die geometrischen Richtigkeitsnachweis der Auflösung der quadratischen Gleichungen," in *Berichte de Sächsischen Akademie der Wissenschaften*, Math.-nat. Kl., **13** (1941), 93–114; and G. P. Matvievskaya, *Uchenie o chisle na srednevekovom Blizhnem i Srednem Vostoke* ("Number Theory in the Medieval Near East and Central Asia"; Tashkent, 1967); and "Materialy k istorii ucheniya o chisle na srednevekovom Blizhnem i Srednem Vostoke" ("Materials for a History of Number Theory in the Medieval Near and Middle East"), in *Iz istorii tochnykh nauk na srednevekovom Blizhnem i Srednem Vostoke* ("History of the Exact Sciences in the Medieval Near and Middle East"; Tashkent, 1972), 76–169.

Additional works are M. Meyerhof, "The 'Book of Treasure,' an Early Arabic Treatise on Medicine," in *Isis*, **14** (1930), 55–76; E. A. Moody and M. Clagett, *The Medieval Science of Weights* (Madison, Wis., 1952); L. Nix, *Das fünfte Buch der Conica des Apollonius von Perga in der arabischen Uebersetzung des Thabit ibn Corrah . . .* (Leipzig, 1889); S. Pines, "Thabit b. Qurra's Conception of Number and Theory of the Mathematical Infinite," in *Actes du XIᵉ Congrès inter-*

national d'histoire des sciences, III (Wrocław–Warsaw–Cracow), 160–166; B. A. Rosenfeld and L. M. Karpova, "Traktat Sabita ibn Korry o sostavnykh otnosheniakh" ("Treatise of Thābit ibn Qurra on the Composition of Ratios"), in Fiziko-matematicheskie nauki v strankakh Vostoka ("Physical-Mathematical Sciences in the Countries of the East"), I (Moscow, 1966), 5–8; B. A. Rosenfeld and A. P. Youschkevich, "Dokazatelstva pyatogo postulata Evklida . . ." ("Proofs of Euclid's Fifth Postulate . . ."), in Istoriko-matematicheskie issledovaniia, 14 (1961), 587–592; A. I. Sabra, "Thābit ibn Qurra on Euclid's Parallels Postulate," in Journal of the Warburg and Courtauld Institutes, 31 (1968), 12–32; A. Y. Sansur, Matematicheskie trudy Sabita ibn Korry ("Mathematical Works of Thābit ibn Qurra"; Moscow, 1971); G. Sarton, Introduction to the History of Science, I (Baltimore, 1927), 599–600; A. Sayili, "Sābit ibn Kurranin Pitagor teoremini temini," in Türk Tarih Kurumu. Belleten, 22, no. 88 (1958), 527–549; and "Thabit ibn Qurra's Generalization of the Pythagorean Theorem," in Isis, 51 (1960), 35–37; and O. Schirmer, "Studien zur Astronomie der Araber," in Sitzungsberichte der Physikalisch-medizinischen Sozietät in Erlangen, 58 (1927), 33–88.

See also F. Sezgin, Geschichte des arabischen Schrifttums, III (Leiden, 1970), 260–263; T. D. Stolyarova, "Traktat Sabita ibn Korry 'Kniga o karastune'" ("Thābit ibn Qurra's Treatise 'Book of Qarasṭūn'"), in Iz istorii tochnykh nauk na srednevekovom Blizhnem i Srednem Vostoke ("History of the Exact Sciences in the Medieval Near East and Central Asia"; Tashkent, 1972), 206–210; and Statika v strankakh Blizhnego i Srednego Vostoka v IX–XI vekakh ("Statics in the . . . Near East and Central Asia in the Ninth-Eleventh Centuries"; Moscow, 1973); H. Suter, "Die Mathematiker und Astronomen der Araber und ihre Werke," in Abhandlungen für Geschichte der mathematischen Wissenschaften, 10 (1900); "Über die Ausmessung der Parabel von Thābit ben Kurra al-Harrani," in Sitzungsberichte der Physikalisch-medizinischen Sozietät in Erlangen, 48–49 (1918), 65–86; and "Die Abhandlungen Thābit ben Kurras und Abū Sahl al-Kūhīs über die Ausmessung der Paraboloide," ibid., 186–227; J. Vernet and M. A. Catalá, "Dos tratados de Arquimedes arabe; Tratado de los círculos tangentes y Libro de los triángulos," Publicaciones del Seminario de historia de la ciencia, 2 (1972); E. Wiedemann, "Die Schrift über den Qarasṭūn," in Bibliotheca mathematica, 3rd ser., 12, no. 1 (1912), 21–39; and "Über Thābit, sein Leben und Wirken," in Sitzungsberichte der Physikalisch-medizinischen Sozietät in Erlangen, 52 (1922), 189–219; E. Wiedemann and J. Frank, "Über die Konstruktion der Schattenlinien auf horizontalen Sonnenuhren von Thābit ibn Qurra," in Kongelige Danske Videnskabernes Selskabs Skrifter, Math.-fys. meddel., 4 (1922), 7–30; F. Woepcke, "Notice sur une théorie ajoutée par Thābit ben Korrah à l'arithmétique spéculative des grecs," in Journal asiatique, 4th ser., 20 (1852), 420–429; F. Wüstenfeld, Geschichte der arabischen Ärzte (Leipzig, 1840), 34–36; and A. P. Youschkevitch, "Note sur les déterminations infinitésimales chez Thabit ibn Qurra," in Archives internationales d'histoire des sciences, no. 66 (1964), 37–45; and (as editor), Istoria matematiki s drevneyshikh vremen do nachala XIX stoletiya ("History of Mathematics From Ancient Times to the Beginning of the Nineteenth Century"), I (Moscow, 1970), 221–224, 239–244.

B. A. ROSENFELD
A. T. GRIGORIAN

THALES (b. Miletus, Ionia, 625 B.C. [?]; d. 547 B.C. [?])

Thales is considered by Aristotle to be the "founder" (ἀρχηγός) of Ionian natural philosophy.[1] He was the son of Examyes and Cleobuline, who were, according to some authorities, of Phoenician origin. But the majority opinion considered him a true Milesian by descent (ἰθαγενής Μιλήσιος), and of a distinguished family. This latter view is probably the correct one since his father's name seems to be Carian rather than Semitic, and the Carians had at this time been almost completely assimilated by the Ionians. According to Diogenes Laërtius, Apollodorus put Thales' birth in Olympiad 35.1 (640 B.C.) and his death at the age of 78 in Olympiad 58 (548–545 B.C.). There is a discrepancy in the figures here: probably 35.1 is a mistake for 39.1 (624), since the confusion of $\bar{\epsilon}$ and $\bar{\vartheta}$ is a very common one. Apollodorus would in that case characteristically have made Thales' death correspond with the date of the fall of Sardis, his floruit coincide with the eclipse of the sun dated at 585 B.C.—which he is alleged to have predicted—and assumed his birth to be the conventional forty years before his prime.[2]

Even in antiquity there was considerable doubt concerning Thales' written works. It seems clear that Aristotle did not have access to any book by him, at least none on cosmological matters. Some authorities declare categorically that he left no book behind. Others, however, credit him with the authorship of a work on navigation entitled "The Nautical Star Guide," but in spite of a tradition suggesting that Thales defined the Little Bear and recommended its navigational usefulness to Milesian sailors,[3] it is extremely doubtful that he was the actual author of this work, since Diogenes Laërtius informs us that this book was also attributed to a certain Phokos of Samos. It is most unlikely that a work of Thales would have been ascribed to someone of comparative obscurity, but not the converse.

Much evidence of practical activities associated with Thales has survived, testifying to his versatility as statesman, tycoon, engineer, mathematician, and astronomer. In the century after his death he became an epitome of practical ingenuity.[4] Herodotus records the stories that Thales advised the Ionians to establish a single deliberative chamber at Teos and that he diverted the river Halys so that Croesus' army might be able to cross. (Herodotus is skeptical about the latter explanation.)[5] Aristotle preserves another anecdote that credits Thales with considerable practical knowledge. According to this account, Thales, when reproached for his impracticality, used his skill in astronomy to forecast a glut in the olive crop, went out and cornered the market in the presses, and thereby made a large profit. Aristotle disbelieves the story and comments that this was a common commercial procedure that men attributed to Thales on account of his wisdom.[6] Plato, on the other hand, whose purpose is to show that philosophy is above mere utilitarian considerations, tells the conflicting anecdote that Thales, while stargazing, fell into a well and was mocked by a pretty Thracian servant girl for trying to find out what was going on in the heavens when he could not even see what was at his feet.[7] It is clear that these stories stem from separate traditions — the one seeking to represent the philosopher as an eminently practical man of affairs and the other as an unworldly dreamer.

Thales achieved his fame as a scientist for having predicted an eclipse of the sun. Herodotus, who is our oldest source for this story, tells us that the eclipse (which must have been total or very nearly so) occurred in the sixth year of the war between the Lydians under Alyattes and the Medes under Cyaxares, and that Thales predicted it to the Ionians, fixing as its term the year in which it actually took place.[8] This eclipse is now generally agreed to have occurred on 28 May 585 B.C. (−584 by astronomical reckoning). It has been widely accepted that Thales was able to perform this striking astronomical feat by using the so-called "Babylonian saros," a cycle of 223 lunar months (18 years, 10 days, 8 hours), after which eclipses both of the sun and moon repeat themselves with very little change. Neugebauer, however, has convincingly demonstrated that the "Babylonian saros" was, in fact, the invention of the English astronomer Edmond Halley in rather a weak moment.[9] The Babylonians did not use cycles to predict solar eclipses but computed them from observations of the latitude of the moon made shortly before the expected syzygy. As Neugebauer says,

> . . . there exists no cycle for solar eclipses visible at a given place; all modern cycles concern the earth as a whole. No Babylonian theory for predicting a solar eclipse existed at 600 B.C., as one can see from the very unsatisfactory situation 400 years later, nor did the Babylonians ever develop any theory which took the influence of geographical latitude into account.[10]

Accordingly, it must be assumed that if Thales did predict the eclipse he made an extremely lucky guess and did not do so upon a scientific basis, since he had no conception of geographical latitude and no means of determining whether a solar eclipse would be visible in a particular locality. He could only have said that an eclipse was possible somewhere at some time in the (chronological) year that ended in 585 B.C. But a more likely explanation seems to be simply that Thales happened to be the *savant* around at the time when this striking astronomical phenomenon occurred and the assumption was made that as a savant he *must* have been able to predict it. There is a situation closely parallel to this one in the next century. In 468–467 B.C. a huge meteorite fell at Aegospotami. This event made a considerable impact, and two sources preserve the absurd report that the fall was predicted by Anaxagoras, who was the Ionian *savant* around at that time.[11]

The Greeks themselves claim to have derived their mathematics from Egypt.[12] Eudemus, the author of the history of mathematics written as part of the systematization of knowledge that went on in the Lyceum, is more explicit. He tells us that it was "Thales who, after a visit to Egypt, first brought this study to Greece" and adds "not only did he make numerous discoveries himself, but he laid the foundations for many other discoveries on the part of his successors, attacking some problems with greater generality and others more empirically." Proclus preserves for us some of the discoveries that Eudemus ascribed to Thales, namely, that the circle is bisected by its diameter,[13] that the base angles of an isosceles triangle are equal,[14] and that vertically opposed angles are equal.[15] In addition he informs us that the theorem that two triangles are equal in every respect if they have two angles and one side respectively equal was referred by Eudemus to Thales with the comment that the latter's measuring the distance of ships out at sea necessarily involved the use of this theorem.[16]

From the above it can be seen that Eudemus credited Thales with full knowledge of the theory behind his discoveries. He also held that Thales introduced geometry into Greece from Egypt. Our surviving sources of information about the nature of Egyptian mathematics, however, give us no evidence to suggest that Egyptian geometry had advanced beyond certain rule-of-thumb techniques of practical mensuration. Nowhere do we find any attempt to discover why these techniques worked, nor anything resembling a general and theoretical mathematics. It seems most unlikely, then, that the Greeks derived their mathematics from the Egyptians. But could Thales have been the founder of theoretical mathematics in Greece, as Eudemus claimed? Here again the answer must be negative. The first three discoveries attributed to him by the Peripatetic most probably represent "just the neatest abstract solutions of particular problems associated with Thales."[17] Heath points out that the first of these propositions is not even proved in Euclid.[18] As for the last of them, Thales could very easily have made use of a primitive angle-measurer and solved the problem in one of several ways without necessarily formulating an explicit theory about the principles involved.

Van der Waerden, on the other hand, believes that Thales did develop a logical structure for geometry and introduced into this study the idea of proof.[19] He also seeks to derive Greek mathematics from Babylon. This is a very doubtful standpoint. Although Babylonian mathematics, with its sexagesimal place-value system, had certainly developed beyond the primitive level reached by the Egyptians, here too we find nowhere any attempt at proof. Our evidence suggests that the Greeks were influenced by Babylonian mathematics, but that this influence occurred at a date considerably later than the sixth century B.C. If the Greeks had derived their mathematics from Babylonian sources, one would have expected them to have adopted the much more highly developed place-value system. Moreover, the Greeks themselves, who are extremely generous, indeed overgenerous, in acknowledging their scientific debts to other peoples, give no hint of a Babylonian source for their mathematics.

Our knowledge of Thales' cosmology is virtually dependent on two passages in Aristotle. In the *Metaphysics* (A3, 983b6) Aristotle, who patently has no more information beyond what is given here, is of the opinion that Thales considered water to be the material constituent of things, and in the *De caelo* (B13, 294a28), where Aristotle expressly declares his information to be indirect, we are told that Thales held that the earth floats on water. Seneca provides the additional information (*Naturales quaestiones*, III, 14) that Thales used the idea of a floating earth to explain earthquakes. If we can trust this evidence, which seems to stem ultimately from Theophrastus via a Posidonian source, the implication is that Thales displays an attitude of mind strikingly different from anything that had gone before. Homer and Hesiod had explained that earthquakes were due to the activity of the god Poseidon, who frequently bears the epic epithet "Earth Shaker." Thales, by contrast, instead of invoking any such supernatural agency, employs a simple, natural explanation to account for this phenomenon. Cherniss, however, has claimed that Aristotle's knowledge of Thales' belief that the earth floats on water would have been sufficient to induce him to infer that Thales also held water to be his material substrate.[20] But it is impossible to believe that Aristotle could have been so disingenuous as to make this inference and then make explicit conjectures as to why Thales held water to be his $\dot{\alpha}\rho\chi\dot{\eta}$. Aristotle's conjectured reasons for the importance attached by Thales to water as the ultimate constituent of things are mainly physiological. He suggests that Thales might have been led to this conception by the observation that nutriment and semen are always moist and that the very warmth of life is a damp warmth. Burnet has rejected these conjectures by Aristotle on the ground that in the sixth century interests were meteorological rather than physiological.[21] But, as Baldry has pointed out, an interest in birth and other phenomena connected with sex is a regular feature even of primitive societies long before other aspects of biology are thought of.[22] However this may be, it is noteworthy that, in view of the parallels to be found between Thales' cosmology and certain Near Eastern mythological cosmogonies,[23] there exists the possibility that Thales' emphasis upon water and his theory that the earth floats on water were derived from some such source, and that he conceived of water as a "remote ancestor" rather than as a persistent substrate. But even if Thales was influenced by mythological precedents[24] and failed to approximate to anything like the Aristotelian material cause, our evidence, sparse and controversial though it is, nevertheless seems sufficient to justify the claim that Thales was the first philosopher. This evidence suggests that Thales' thought shared certain basic characteristics with that of his Ionian successors. These Milesian philosophers, abandoning mythopoeic forms of thought, sought to explain the world about them in terms of its visible constituents. Natural explanations were introduced by them, which took the place of supernatural and mystical ones.[25] Like their mythopoeic predecessors, the Milesians firmly believed that there was an orderliness inherent in the world around them. Again like their predecessors, they attempted to explain the world by showing how it had come to be what it is. But, instead of invoking the agency of supernatural powers, they sought for a unifying hypothesis to account for this order and, to a greater or lesser extent, proceeded to deduce their natural explanations of the various phenomena from it. Two elements, then, characterize early Greek philosophy, the search for natural as opposed to supernatural and mystical explanations, and secondly, the search for a unifying hypothesis. Both of these elements proved influential in paving the way for the development of the sciences, and it is in the light of this innovation that Thales' true importance in the history of science must be assessed.

NOTES

1. *Metaphysics*, A3, 983b17 ff. (DK, 11A12).
2. These datings are now approximately in accordance with the figures given by Demetrius of Phalerum, who placed the canonization of the Seven Sages (of whom Thales was universally regarded as a member) in the archonship of Damasias at Athens (582–581 B.C.).
3. Callimachus, *Iambus*, 1, 52 f. 191 Pfeiffer (DK, 11A3a).
4. See Aristophanes, *Birds* 1009; *Clouds* 180.
5. Herodotus, I, 170; I, 75 (DK, 11A4, 11A6).
6. *Politics*, A11, 1259a6 (DK, 11A10).
7. *Theaetetus*, 174A (DK, 11A9). It is odd that Plato should have applied this story to someone as notoriously practical in his interests as Thales. It makes one think that there may be at least a grain of truth in the story. See my review of Moraux's Budé edition of the *De caelo*, in *Classical Review*, n.s., **20** (1970), 174, and M. Landmann and J. O. Fleckenstein, "Tagesbeobachtung von Sternen in Altertum," in *Vierteljahrsschrift der Naturforschenden Gesellschaft in Zürich*, **88** (1943), 98, notwithstanding Dicks' scornful dismissal of their suggestion. Certainly the motive for this story is clear, but it could have been Thales' practice that determined its form. In general Dicks is far too skeptical in his treatment of the stories told of Thales and relegates them to the status of "the famous story of the First World War about the Russians marching through England with 'snow on their boots.'" But on this latter story see Margo Lawrence, *Shadow of Swords* (London, 1971), in which she reveals that soldiers from Russia, wearing Russian uniform, carrying balalaikas, and singing Slavonic songs, did in fact disembark in 1916 at Newcastle upon Tyne. Admittedly the snow on their boots must be left to folklore.
8. I, 74 (DK, 11A5).
9. O. Neugebauer, *The Exact Sciences in Antiquity*, 141.
10. *Ibid.*, 142.
11. See Diogenes Laërtius, II, 10 (DK, 59A1), and Pliny, *Historia naturalis*, II, 149 (DK, 59A11). See also Cicero, *De divinatione*, I.50.112 (DK, 12A5a), and Pliny, *ibid.*, II, 191,

for a sixth-century parallel, where Anaximander is alleged to have predicted an earthquake.
12. See Herodotus, II, 109, who believes that geometry originated from the recurrent need to remeasure land periodically flooded by the Nile; Aristotle, *Metaphysics*, A3, 981b20–25, who believes that mathematics evolved in a highly theoretical way as the invention of a leisured class of Egyptian priests; and Eudemus, who, in spite of being a Peripatetic, sides with Herodotus rather than with Aristotle (see Proclus, *Commentary on Euclid's Elements*, I, 64.16 [Friedlein]).
13. *Commentary on Euclid's Elements*, 157.10 (DK, 11A20).
14. *Ibid.*, 250.20.
15. *Ibid.*, 299.1.
16. *Ibid.*, 352.14.
17. G. S. Kirk, *The Presocratic Philosophers*, 84.
18. T. L. Heath, *Greek Mathematics*, I, 131.
19. B. L. van der Waerden, *Science Awakening*, 89.
20. H. Cherniss, "The Characteristics and Effects of Presocratic Philosophy," in *Journal of the History of Ideas*, **12** (1951), 321.
21. J. Burnet, *Early Greek Philosophy*, 48.
22. H. C. Baldry, "Embryological Analogies in Early Greek Philosophy," in *Classical Quarterly*, **26** (1932), 28.
23. For an excellent account of Egyptian and Mesopotamian cosmogonies, see H. Frankfort, ed., *Before Philosophy* (Penguin Books, London, 1949), pub. orig. as *The Intellectual Adventure of Ancient Man* (Chicago, 1946).
24. Aristotle, it may be noted, cites the parallel in Greek mythology of Oceanus and Tethys, the parents of generation (*Metaphysics*, A3, 983b27ff. [DK,1B10]). But the Greek myth may itself be derived from an oriental source.
25. The gods of whom Thales thought everything was full (see Aristotle, *De anima*, A5, 411a7 [DK, 11A22]) are manifestly different from the personal divinities of traditional mythology.

BIBLIOGRAPHY

For a collection of sources see H. Diels and W. Kranz, *Die Fragmente der Vorsokratiker*, 6th ed., 3 vols. (Berlin, 1951–1952), I, 67–79 (abbreviated as DK above).

See also H. C. Baldry, "Embryological Analogies in Presocratic Cosmogony," in *Classical Quarterly*, **26** (1932), 27–34; J. Burnet, *Greek Philosophy: Part I, Thales to Plato* (London, 1914); and *Early Greek Philosophy*, 4th ed. (London, 1930); H. Cherniss, "The Characteristics and Effects of Presocratic Philosophy," in *Journal of the History of Ideas*, **12** (1951), 319–345; D. R. Dicks, "Thales," in *Classical Quarterly*, n.s. **9** (1959), 294–309; and "Solstices, Equinoxes and the Presocratics," in *Journal of Hellenic Studies*, **86** (1966), 26–40; J. L. E. Dreyer, *A History of the Planetary Systems from Thales to Kepler* (Cambridge, 1906), repr. as *A History of Astronomy from Thales to Kepler* (New York, 1953); W. K. C. Guthrie, *A History of Greek Philosophy*, I (Cambridge, 1962); T. L. Heath, *Aristarchus of Samos* (Oxford, 1913); and *Greek Mathematics*, I (Oxford, 1921); U. Hölscher, "Anaximander und die Anfänge der Philosophie," in *Hermes*, **81** (1953), 257–277, 385–417; repr. in English in Allen and Furley, *Studies in Presocratic Philosophy*, I (New York, 1970), 281–322; C. H. Kahn, "On Early Greek Astronomy," in *Journal of Hellenic Studies*, **90** (1970), 99–116; G. S.

Kirk and J. E. Raven, *The Presocratic Philosophers* (Cambridge, 1957); O. Neugebauer, "The History of Ancient Astronomy, Problems and Methods," in *Journal of Near Eastern Studies*, **4** (1945), 1–38; *The Exact Sciences in Antiquity* (Princeton, 1952; 2nd ed., Providence, R.I., 1957); and "The Survival of Babylonian Methods in the Exact Sciences of Antiquity and Middle Ages," in *Proceedings of the American Philosophical Society*, **107** (1963), 528–535; and B. L. van der Waerden, *Science Awakening*, Arnold Dresden, trans. (Groningen, 1954).

JAMES LONGRIGG

THEAETETUS (*b*. Athens, *ca*. 417 B.C.; *d*. Athens, 369 B.C.)

The son of Euphronius of Sunium, Theaetetus studied under Theodorus of Cyrene and at the Academy with Plato. Although no writing of his has survived, Theaetetus had a major influence in the development of Greek mathematics. His contributions to the theory of irrational quantities and the construction of the regular solids are particularly recorded; and he probably devised a general theory of proportion—applicable to incommensurable and to commensurable magnitudes—before the theory developed by Eudoxus and set out in book V of Euclid's *Elements*.

The *Suda* lexicon has two entries[1] under the name Theaetetus:

"Theaetetus, of Athens, astronomer, philosopher, disciple of Socrates, taught at Heraclea. He was the first to write on (or construct) the so-called five solids. He lived after the Peloponnesian war."

"Theaetetus, of Heraclea in Pontus, philosopher, a pupil of Plato."

Some have supposed that these notices refer to the same person, but it is more probable, as G. J. Allman[2] conjectures, that the second Theaetetus was a son or other relative of the first sent by him while teaching at Heraclea to study at the Academy in his native city.

Plato clearly regarded Theaetetus with a respect and admiration second only to that which he felt for Socrates. He made him a principal character in two dialogues, the eponymous *Theaetetus* and the *Sophist*; and it is from the former dialogue that what we know about the life of Theaetetus is chiefly derived.[3] In the dialogue Euclid of Megara gets a servant boy to read to his friend Terpsion a discussion between Socrates, Theodorus, and Theaetetus that Plato recorded soon after it took place on the day that Socrates faced his accusers, that is,

in 399 B.C. Since Theaetetus is there referred to as a μειράκιον ("a youth"), it is implied that he was an adolescent, say eighteen years old, that is, he was born about 417 B.C.[4] His father, we are told, left a large fortune, which was squandered by trustees; but this did not prevent Theaetetus from being a liberal giver. Although Theaetetus was given the rare Greek compliment of being καλος τε καὶ ἀγαθός ("a thorough gentleman"), it was the beauty of his mind rather than of his body that impressed his compatriots; for, like Socrates, he had a snub nose and protruding eyes. Among the many young men with whom Theodorus had been acquainted, he had never found one so marvelously gifted; the lad's researches were like a stream of oil flowing without sound. Socrates predicted that Theaetetus would become notable if he came to full years. In the preface to the dialogue Euclid relates how he had just seen Theaetetus being carried in a dying condition from the camp at Corinth to Athens; not only had he been wounded in action, after acquitting himself gallantly, but he had contracted dysentery. This would be in the year 369 B.C., for the only other year in that century in which Athens and Corinth were at war, 394 B.C., would hardly allow time for Theaetetus' manifold accomplishments.[5]

The *Theaetetus* is devoted to the problem of knowledge; and the *Sophist*, apart from a method of definition, to the meaning of nonbeing. Although Theaetetus plays a major part in both discussions, there is no reason to think that he was a philosopher in the usual sense of the word. Plato merely used him as a vehicle for thoughts that he wanted expressed. That the two *Suda* passages use the term "philosopher" proves nothing, since the lexicon regularly calls mathematicians philosophers.[6]

In the summary of the early history of Greek geometry given by Proclus, and probably taken from Eudemus, Theaetetus is mentioned along with Leodamas of Thasos and Archytas of Tarentum as having increased theorems and made an advance toward a more scientific grouping,[7] the zeal for which is well shown in the mathematical passage that Plato introduces into the *Theaetetus*.[8] In this passage Theaetetus first relates how Theodorus demonstrated to him and the younger Socrates (a namesake of the philosopher) in each separate case that $\sqrt{3}, \sqrt{5} \cdots \sqrt{17}$ is a surd. He adds: "Since the number of roots[9] seemed to be infinite, it occurred to us to try to gather them together under one name by which we could call all the roots." Accordingly Theaetetus and the younger Socrates divided all numbers into two classes.

A number that could be formed by multiplying equal factors they likened to a square and called "square and equilateral." The other numbers—which could not be formed by multiplying equal factors, but only a greater by a less, or a less by a greater—they likened to an oblong and called "oblong numbers." The lines forming the sides of equilateral numbers they called "lengths," and the lines forming oblong numbers they called "roots." "And similarly," concluded the Theaetetus of the dialogue, "for solids," which can only mean that they attempted a similar classification of cube roots.

The classification may now seem trivial, but the discovery of the irrational was a fairly recent matter[10] and involved a complete recasting of Greek mathematics; and Theaetetus was still only a young man. His more mature work on the subject is recorded in a commentary on the tenth book of Euclid's *Elements*, which has survived only in Arabic and is generally identified with the commentary that Pappus is known to have written. In the introduction to this commentary it is stated:[11]

The aim of Book X of Euclid's treatise on the Elements is to investigate the commensurable and the incommensurable, the rational and irrational continuous quantities. This science had its origin in the school of Pythagoras, but underwent an important development at the hands of the Athenian, Theaetetus, who is justly admired for his natural aptitude in this as in other branches of mathematics. One of the most gifted of men, he patiently pursued the investigation of the truth contained in these branches of science, as Plato bears witness in the book which he called after him, and was in my opinion the chief means of establishing exact distinctions and irrefutable proofs with respect to the above-mentioned quantities. For although later the great Apollonius, whose genius for mathematics was of the highest possible order, added some remarkable species of these after much laborious application, it was nevertheless Theaetetus who distinguished the roots which are commensurable in length from those which are incommensurable, and who divided the more generally known irrational lines according to the different means, assigning the medial line to geometry, the binomial to arithmetic, and the apotome to harmony, as is stated by Eudemus the Peripatetic.

The last sentence gives the key to the achievement of Theaetetus in this field. He laid the foundation of the elaborate classification of irrationals, which is found in Euclid's tenth book; and in particular Theaetetus discovered, and presumably named, the medial, binomial, and apotome. The medial is formed by the product of two magnitudes, the binomial ("of two names") by the sum of two magnitudes, and the apotome (implying that something has been cut off) by the difference of two magnitudes. It is easy to see the correlation between the medial and the geometric mean, for the geometric mean between two irrational magnitudes,[12] a, b, is $\sqrt{ab}$ and is medial. It is also easy to see the correlation between the binomial and the arithmetic mean, for the arithmetic mean between a, b, is $(\frac{1}{2}a + \frac{1}{2}b)$; and this is a binomial. It is not so easy to see the connection between the apotome and the harmonic mean; but a clue is given in the second part of the work, where the commentator returns to the achievement of Theaetetus and observes that if the rectangle contained by two lines is a medial, and one of the sides is a binomial, the other side is an apotome. This in turn recalls Euclid, *Elements* X.112, and amounts to saying that the harmonic mean between a, b, that is, $2ab/(a + b)$, can be expressed as

$$\frac{2ab}{a^2 - b^2} \cdot (a - b).$$

This leads to the question how much of Euclid's tenth book is due to Theaetetus. After a close examination, B. L. van der Waerden concluded that "The entire book is the work of Theaetetus."[13] There are several reasons, however, for preferring to believe that Theaetetus merely identified the medial, binomial, and apotome lines, correlating them with the three means, as the Arabic commentary says, and that the addition of ten other species of irrationals, making thirteen in all, or twenty-five when the binomials and apotomes are further subdivided, is the work of Euclid himself. A scholium to the fundamental proposition X.9 ("the squares on straight lines commensurable in length have to one another the ratio which a square number has to a square number . . .") runs as follows: "This theorem is the discovery of Theaetetus, and Plato recalls it in the *Theaetetus*, but there it is related to particular cases, here treated generally."[14] This would be a pointless remark if Theaetetus were the author of the whole book.

The careful distinction made in the "Eudemian summary" between Euclid's treatment of Eudoxus and Theaetetus is also relevant. Euclid, says the author, "put together the elements, arranging in order many of Eudoxus' theorems, perfecting many of Theaetetus', and bringing to irrefutable demonstration the things which had been only loosely proved by his predecessors."[15] The implication would seem to be that book V is almost entirely the discovery of Eudoxus save in its arrangement, but book X is partly due to Theaetetus and partly to Euclid himself. The strongest argument for believing that Theaetetus had an almost complete knowledge of the Euclidean theory of irrationals is that the correlation of the apotome with the harmonic mean implies a knowledge of book X.112; but it is relevant that the genuine text of Euclid probably stops at book X.111 with the list of the thirteen irrational straight lines.[16]

A related question is the extent to which the influence of Theaetetus can be seen in the arithmetical books of Euclid's *Elements*, VII–IX. Euclid X.9 depends on VIII.11 ("Between two square numbers there is one mean proportional number . . ."), and VIII.11 depends on VII.17 and VII.18 (in modern notation, $ab : ac = b : c$, and $a : b = ac : bc$). H. G. Zeuthen has argued[17] that these propositions are an inseparable part of a whole theory established in book VII and in the early part of book VIII, and that this theory must be due to Theaetetus with the object of laying a sound basis for his treatment of irrationals. It is clear, however, as T. L. Heath has pointed out,[18] that before Theaetetus both Hippocrates and Archytas must have known propositions and definitions corresponding to these in books VII and VIII; and there is no reason to abandon the traditional view that the Pythagoreans had a numerical theory of proportion that was taken over by Euclid in his arithmetical books. Theaetetus merely made use of an existing body of knowledge.

Theaetetus' work on irrationals is closely related to the two other main contributions to mathematics attributed to him. The only use made of book X in the subsequent books of Euclid's *Elements* is to express the sides of the regular solids inscribed in a sphere in terms of the diameter. In the case of the pyramid, the octahedron, and the cube, the length of the side is actually determined; in the case of the icosahedron, it is shown to be a minor; and in the case of the dodecahedron, to be an apotome. It is therefore significant that in the passage from the *Suda* lexicon (cited above) Theaetetus is credited as the first to "write upon" or "construct" the so-called five solids (πρῶτος δὲ τὰ πέντε καλούμενα στερεὰ ἔγραψε). It is also significant that at the end of the mathematical passage in the *Theaetetus* he says that he and his companion proceeded to deal with solids in the same way as with squares and oblongs in the plane. Probably on the authority of Theophrastus, Aëtius[19] attributed the discovery of the five regular solids to the Pythagoreans; and Proclus[20] actually attributes to Pythago-

ras himself the "putting together" (σύστασις) of the "cosmic figures." They are called "cosmic" because of Plato's use of them in the *Timaeus* to build the universe;[21] and no doubt the σύστασις is to be understood as a "putting together" of triangles, squares, and pentagons in order to make solid angles as in that dialogue rather than in the sense of a formal construction. Theaetetus was probably the first to give a theoretical construction for all the five regular solids and to show how to inscribe them in a sphere. A scholium to Euclid, *Elements* XIII, actually attributes to Theaetetus rather than to the Pythagoreans the discovery of the octahedron and icosahedron.[22] On the surface this is puzzling, since the octahedron is a more elementary figure than the dodecahedron, which requires a knowledge of the pentagon; but many objects of dodecahedral form have been found from days much earlier than Pythagoras,[23] and the Pythagorean Hippasus is known to have written on "the construction of the sphere from the twelve pentagons."[24] (It would be in this work, if not earlier, that he would have encountered the irrational, and for his impiety in revealing it, he was drowned at sea.) If the Pythagoreans knew the dodecahedron, almost certainly they knew also the octahedron and probably the icosahedron; and the scholium quoted above may be discounted. The achievement of Theaetetus was to give a complete theoretical construction of all five regular solids such as we find in Euclid, *Elements* XIII; and Theaetetus must be regarded as the main source of the book, although Euclid no doubt arranged the materials in his own impeccable way and put the finishing touches.[25]

The theory of irrationals is also linked with that of proportionals. When the irrational was discovered, it involved a recasting of the Pythagorean theory of proportion, which depended on taking aliquot parts, and which consequently was applicable only to rational numbers, in a more general form applicable also to incommensurable magnitudes. Such a general theory was found by Eudoxus and is embodied in Euclid, *Elements* V. But in 1933[26] Oskar Becker gave a new interpretation of an obscure passage in Aristotle's *Topics*.[27] He suggested that the theory of proportion had already been recast in a highly ingenious form; and if so, the indication is that it was so recast by Eudoxus' older contemporary Theaetetus.

In the passage under discussion Aristotle observes that in mathematics some things are not easily proved for lack of a definition—for example, that a straight line parallel to two of the sides of a parallelogram divides the other two sides and the area in the same ratio; but if the definition is given, it becomes immediately clear, "for the areas have the same ἀνταναίρεσις as the sides, and this is the definition of the same ratio." What does the Greek word mean? The basic meaning is "a taking away," and the older commentators up to Heath

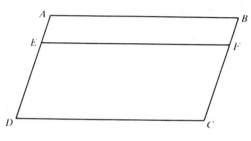

FIGURE 1

and the Oxford translation supposed that it meant "a taking away of the same fraction." In the figure *EF* is the straight line parallel to the sides *AB*, *DC* of the parallelogram *ABCD*, and *AE*, *BF* are the same parts of *AD*, *BC* respectively as the parallelogram *ABFE* is of the parallelogram *ABCD*. This would be in accordance with the Pythagorean theory of proportion, and the passage would contain nothing significant. But Becker drew attention to the comment by Alexander of Aphrodisias on this passage; he uses the word ἀνθυφαίρεσις and observes that this is what Aristotle means by ἀνταναίρεσις. This might not in itself prove very much—the meaning could still be much the same—if it were not, as Becker also noted, that Euclid, although he does not employ the noun ἀνθυφαίρεσις, does in four places[29] use the verb, ἀνθυφαιρεῖν, and—this is the really significant fact—uses it to describe the process of finding the greatest common measure between two magnitudes. In this process the lesser magnitude is subtracted from the greater as many times as possible until a magnitude smaller than itself is left, and then the difference is subtracted as many times as possible from the lesser until a difference smaller than itself is left, and so on continually (ἀνθυφαιρουμένου δὲ ἀεὶ τοῦ ἐλάσσονος ἀπὸ τοῦ μείζονος). In the case of commensurable magnitudes the process comes to an end after a finite number of steps, but in the case of incommensurable magnitudes the process never comes to an end. A mathematician as acute as Theaetetus would realize that this could be made a test of commensurability (as it is in Euclid, *Elements* X.2) and that by adopting a definition of proportion based on this test he could have a the-

ory of proportion applicable to commensurable no less than incommensurable magnitudes.[30]

It is possible that such a general theory was evolved before Eudoxus by some person other than Theaetetus, but in view of Theaetetus' known competence and his interest in irrationals, he is the most likely author. The attribution becomes even more credible if Zeuthen's explanation of how Theodorus proved the square roots of $\sqrt{3}$, $\sqrt{5}$ . . . $\sqrt{17}$ to be irrational is accepted (see the article on Theodorus of Cyrene); for according to his conjecture Theodorus used this method in each particular case, and Theodorus was the teacher of Theaetetus. Although there is no direct evidence that Theaetetus worked out such a pre-Eudoxan theory of proportion, the presumption in favor is strong; and it has convinced all recent commentators.

It is not known whether Theaetetus made any discoveries outside these three fields. In the "Eudemian summary" Proclus says:[31] "Hermotimus of Colophon advanced farther the investigations begun by Eudoxus and Theaetetus; he discovered many propositions in the elements and compiled some portion of the theory of loci." While it is clear that Theaetetus studied mathematics under Theodorus, it is uncertain whether he did so at Cyrene or at Athens. It may be accepted that at some time he taught in Heraclea, and he may have been the teacher of Heraclides Ponticus.[32]

NOTES

1. *Suda Lexicon*, Ada Adler, ed., I, pt. 2 (Leipzig, 1931), Θ 93 and 94, p. 689.6–9.

2. G. J. Allman, "Theaetetus," in *Hermathena*, 6 (1887), 269–278, repr. in *Greek Geometry From Thales to Euclid* (London–Dublin, 1889), 206–215.

3. Plato, *Theaetetus*, *Platonis opera*, J. Burnet, ed., I (Oxford, 1899), 142a–148b; Plato, Loeb Classical Library, H. N. Fowler, ed., VII (London–Cambridge, Mass., 1921; repr. 1967), 6.1–27.24.

4. The birth of Theaetetus has usually been placed in 415 B.C., or even as late as 413, which would make him not more than sixteen years old in 399; but the instances given in H. G. Liddell, R. Scott, and H. Stuart Jones, *A Greek-English Lexicon* (Oxford, 1940), s.vv. μειράκιον and ἔφηβος, show clearly that a μειράκιον would not be younger than eighteen and might be nearly as old as twenty-one. A sentence in the *Chronicle* of Eusebius—preserved in the Armenian and in Jerome's Latin version—*Sancti Hieronymi interpretatio chronicae Eusebii Pamphili*, in *Patrologia Latina*, J.-P. Migne, ed., vol. XXVII = S. Hieronymi, vol. VIII (Paris, 1846), cols. 453–454—which would place the central point of Theaetetus' activity in the third year of the 85th Olympiad (438 B.C.)—must be dismissed as an error. Eusebius' statement is repeated by George Syncellus, *Corpus scriptorum historiae Byzantinae*, B. G. Niebuhr, ed., pt. 7.1; *Georgius Syncellus et Nicephorus*, G. Dindorff, ed., I (Bonn, 1829), p. 471.9.

5. It is one of Eva Sachs's principal achievements in her pioneering inaugural dissertation, *De Theaeteto Atheniensi mathematico* (Berlin, 1914), 16–40, to have established this point irrefutably against E. Zeller and others.

6. But Malcolm S. Brown, in "Theaetetus: Knowledge as Continued Learning," in *Journal of the History of Philosophy*, **7** (1969), 359, maintains that Theaetetus "influenced both the course of mathematics and that of philosophy." Brown quotes Sachs, *op. cit.*, p. 69, in support: "Ille re vera philosophus fuit perfectus"; but it is doubtful if Sachs meant the Latin word to imply that Theaetetus was a metaphysician. Brown seizes on the statement of Theaetetus at the beginning of his conversation with Socrates: "When I make a mistake you will correct me" (*Theaetetus*, 146c.). Brown sees in the mathematical work of Theaetetus a process of successive approximations, which can be construed as "containing errors which are being corrected." He holds also that there is an epistemological analogue, "a well-directed discussion of opinions which, even if unsuccessful in arriving at a final answer, would nevertheless permit of an improvement (even an indefinite improvement) of opinion"; and he believes that in this dialogue at least Plato yielded somewhat to the suggestion of Theaetetus that "knowledge is continued learning" (p. 379).

7. Proclus, *In primum Euclidis*, G. Friedlein, ed. (Leipzig, 1873; repr., Hildesheim, 1967), p. 66.14–18; English trans., Glenn R. Morrow, *Proclus: A Commentary on the First Book of Euclid's Elements* (Princeton, 1970), p. 54.11–14.

8. Plato, *Theaetetus*, *Platonis opera*, J. Burnet, ed., I (Oxford, 1899), 147c–148b; Plato, Loeb Classical Library, H. N. Fowler, ed., VII (London–Cambridge, Mass., 1921; repr., 1967), pp. 24.9–27.24.

9. The Greek word is δυνάμεις, which at a latter date could only mean "squares"; but here its meaning would appear to be "roots," and we can only suppose that at this early stage in Greek mathematics the terminology had not become fixed. It is not necessary with Paul Tannery ("Sur la langue mathématique de Platon," in *Annales de la Faculté des lettres de Bordeaux*, **1** [1884], 96, repr. in *Mémoires scientifiques*, **2** [1912], 92) to alter δύναμις without any MS authority to δυναμένη, the later technical expression for a square root. For a very full discussion of a different interpretation, See Árpád Szabó, *Anfänge der griechischen Mathematik* (Munich–Vienna, 1969), 14–22, 43–57. Szabó holds that δύναμις means *Quadratwert eines Rechtecks* ("square value of a rectangle"), that is, the square equivalent in area to a rectangle. This interpretation has attractions, but the fact that Plato categorically describes δυνάμεις as γραμμαί, "lines," and sets δύναμις in opposition to μῆκος, a rational length, seems fatal to it. But Szabó establishes that δύναμις cannot be power in general.

10. But not so recently as the time of Plato himself. Even if the Athenian stranger in the *Laws* is identified with Plato, it is reading too much into his words αὐτὸς ἀκούσας ὀψέ ποτε τὸ περὶ ταῦτα ἡμῶν πάθος (819d 5–6) to suppose that the irrational was not discovered until the fourth century B.C. Likewise the statement in the "Eudemian summary," in Proclus, *op. cit.*, p. 65.19–21, that Pythagoras "discovered the matter of the irrationals" (τὴν τῶν ἀλόγων πραγματείαν . . . ἀνεῦρεν) must be wrong, and there is almost certainly a textual error–ἀλόγων for ἀναλόγων ("proportionals"). The existence of irrational magnitudes was almost certainly discovered, as Greek tradition asserted, by Hippasus of Metapontum in the middle of the fifth century B.C. The best discussion of the date is Kurt von Fritz, "The Discovery of Incommensurability by Hippasus of Metapontum," in *Studies in Presocratic Philosophy*, David J. Furley and R. E. Allen, eds., I (London–New York, 1970), 382–412. For an attempt to show that the discovery was made in the closing years of the fifth century, see Eric Frank, *Platon und die sogennanten Pythagoreer* (Halle, 1923). Árpád

Szabó, *op. cit.*, pp. 60–69, 111–118, 238, seeks to show that the irrational was discovered in the study of mean proportionals as opposed to the prevailing theory that it arose from the study of diagonals of squares after the discovery of "Pythagoras' theorem."

11. The translation is based in the main on that of William Thomson, in William Thomson and Gustav Junge, *The Commentary of Pappus on Book X of Euclid's Elements* (Cambridge, Mass., 1930; repr., New York, 1968), 63; but his "powers" (that is, the squares), although a faithful rendering of the Arabic, has been modified, since "roots" appears to be the meaning. The ambiguity of the Greek δύναμις, before the terminology became fixed, is reflected in the Arabic.

12. It would be going beyond the evidence to attribute to Theaetetus the Euclidean notion (X, *Definition* 3) that a straight line may be rational but commensurable only in square with a rational straight line; that is, that if r is a rational straight line and m, n integers with m/n in its lowest terms not a square, then $\sqrt{m/n} \cdot r$ is rational. T. L. Heath observes, "It would appear that Euclid's terminology here differed as much from that of his predecessors as it does from ours," and he aptly cites the expression of Plato (following the Pythagoreans), in the *Republic* 546c 4–5: ἄρρητος διάμετρος τοῦ πεμπάδος ("the irrational diameter of five") for the diagonal of a square of side five units; that is, for Plato, and presumably for Theaetetus, as for us, $\sqrt{50}$ is irrational, whereas Euclid would have called it "rational but commensurable in square only." Eva Sachs takes a contrary view, *Die fünf platonischen Körper*, p. 105, but without satisfactory reasons.

13. B. L. van der Waerden, *Science Awakening*, 2nd ed. (Groningen, 1956[?]), p. 172. In full, he writes: "Has the same Theaetetus who studied the medial, the binomial and the apotome, also defined and investigated the ten other irrationalities, or were those introduced later on? It seems to me that all of this is the work of one mathematician. For, the study of the 13 irrationalities is a unit. The same fundamental idea prevails throughout the book, the same methods of proof are applied in all cases. Propositions X.17 and 18 concerning the measurability of the roots of a quadratic equation precede the introduction of binomial and apotome, but these are not used until the higher irrationalities appear on the scene. The theory of the binomial and the apotome is almost inextricably interwoven with that of the 10 higher irrationals. Hence–the entire book is the work of Theaetetus." The conclusion does not follow. The unity may be due to Euclid himself, using some propositions already proved, adding refinements of his own, and welding the whole into one, as Proclus testifies. The division of irrationals into medial, binomial, and apotome can perfectly well be separated from the subdivisions into more complex irrationals. If it were true that X.17 and 18 are not used until after the introduction of the binomial and the apotome, this would prove nothing since they are in their correct logical position; and for that matter, the whole of book X is not used again until book XIII; but, in fact, X.18 is used in X.33, whereas the binomial is not introduced until X.36 and the apotome until X.73.

14. *Euclidis opera omnia*, J. L. Heiberg and H. Menge, eds., V (Leipzig, 1888), Scholium 62 in Elementorum Librum X, p. 450.16–18. There is good reason to believe that the scholiast is Proclus. See H. Knoche, *Untersuchungen über die neu aufgefundenen Scholien des Proklus Diadochus zu Euclids Elementen* (Herford, 1865), p. 24; and J. L. Heiberg, "Paralipomena zu Euclid," in *Hermes*, **38** (1903), p. 341.

15. Proclus, *op. cit.*, p. 68.7–10; Eng. trans. *op. cit.*, p. 56.19–23.

16. J. L. Heiberg gives conclusive reasons for bracketing propositions 112–115, in *Euclidis opera omnia*, J. L. Heiberg

and H. Menge, eds., V, p. lxxxv, and concludes: "non dubito, quin hae quoque propositiones 112–115 e doctrina Apollonii promptae sint; nam antiquae sunt et bonae, hoc saltim constare putaverim, eas ab Euclide scriptas non esse."

17. H. G. Zeuthen, "Sur la constitution des livres arithmétiques des Eléments d'Euclide et leur rapport à la question de l'irrationalité," in *Oversigt over det Kongelige Danske Videnskabernes Selskabs Forhandlinger* (1910), 395–435.

18. Thomas Heath, *A History of Greek Mathematics*, I (Oxford, 1921), 211.

19. Aëtius, *Placita*, II, 6, 5, in H. Diels, *Doxographi Graeci* (Berlin, 1879), p. 334; and *Die Fragmente der Vorsokratiker*, H. Diels and W. Kranz, eds., 6th ed., I (Dublin–Zurich, 1951; repr., 1969), p. 403.8–12.

20. Proclus, *op. cit.*, p. 65.20–21; Eng. trans., *op. cit.*, p. 53.5. Morrow translates the Greek word as "structure."

21. Plato, *Timaeus* 53c–55c; *Platonis opera*, J. Burnet, ed., IV (Oxford, 1915); Loeb Classical Library, *Plato, Timaeus etc.*, R. G. Bury, ed. (London–Cambridge, Mass., 1929; repr., 1966), pp. 126.16–134.4.

22. *Euclidis opera omnia*, J. L. Heiberg and H. Menge, eds., V (Leipzig, 1888), Scholium 1 in Elementorum Librum XIII, p. 654.1–10.

23. One, discovered in 1885 at Monte Loffa in the Colli Euganei near Padua, of Etruscan origin, is dated between 1000 and 500 B.C. (F. Lindemann, "Zur Geschichte der Polyeder und der Zahlzeichen," in *Sitzungsberichte der Bayerischen Akademie der Wissenschaften zu München*, 26 (1897), 725.

24. Iamblichus, *De communi mathematica scientia* 25, N. Festa, ed. (Leipzig, 1891), 77.18–21; *De vita Pythagorica* 18.88, A. Nauck, ed. (Leipzig, 1884; repr., 1965).

25. In the course of a full discussion Eva Sachs, in *Die fünf platonischen Körper* (Berlin, 1917), asserts (p. 105) that the construction of the five solids in Euclid, *Elements*, XIII, 13–17, springs from Theaetetus. She approves H. Vogt, in *Bibliotheca mathematica*, 9, 3rd ser. (1908–1909), p. 47, for controverting Paul Tannery, *La géométrie Grecque* (Paris, 1887), p. 101, who would ascribe the construction of the five solids to the Pythagoreans while leaving to Theaetetus the calculation of the relation of the sides to the radius of the circumscribing sphere: for how, she and Vogt ask, can the exact construction be accomplished without a prior knowledge of this relation? The question how much of Euclid's book XIII is due to Theaetetus is bound up with the difficult question how much, if any, is due to the Aristaeus who is mentioned by Hypsicles in the so-called *Elements*, Book XIV, J. L. Heiberg and H. Menge, eds., vol. V, p. 6.22–23, as the author of a book entitled *Comparison of the Five Figures*, and whether this Aristaeus is to be identified with Aristaeus the Elder, author of a formative book on solid loci, that is, conics. T. L. Heath, in *The Thirteen Books of Euclid's Elements*, III (Cambridge, 1908; 2nd ed., 1925; repr., New York, 1956), p. 439, following C. A. Bretschneider, *Die Geometrie und die Geometer vor Eukleides* (Leipzig, 1870), p. 171, took the view that "as Aristaeus's work was the newest and latest in which, before Euclid's time, this subject was treated, we have in Euclid XIII at least a partial recapitulation of the contents of the treatise of Aristaeus"; but Eva Sachs, *op. cit.*, p. 107, denies this conclusion.

26. Oskar Becker, "Eudoxos Studien I: Eine voreudoxische Proportionenlehre und ihre Spuren bei Aristoteles und Euklid," in *Quellen und Studien zur Geschichte der Mathematik, Astronomie und Physik*, 2B (1933), 311–333. To some extent the theory had already been adumbrated independently by H. G. Zeuthen, "Hvorledes Mathematiken i Tiden fra Platon til Euklid," in *Kongelige Danske Videnskabernes Selskabs Skrifter*, 5 (1915), 108, and E. J. Dijksterhuis, *De Elementen van Euclides*, I (Groningen, 1929), 71, as Becker himself recognizes in *Das mathematischen Denken der Antike* (Göttingen, 1957), p. 103, n. 25. Becker

failed to convince T. L. Heath, *Mathematics in Aristotle* (Oxford, 1949; repr., 1970), 80–83, who in the absence of confirmatory evidence could "only regard Becker's article as a highly interesting speculation" (p. 83). It has also been criticized by K. Reidemeister, *Das exakte Denken der Griechen* (Hamburg, 1949), p. 22, and by Árpád Szabó, "Ein Beleg fur die voreudoxische Proportionlehre?" in *Archiv für Begriffsgeschichte*, 9 (1964), 151–171, and in his *Anfänge der griechischen Mathematik* (Munich–Vienna), 134–135, 180–181. The theory received support, however, from a Leiden dissertation by E. B. Plooij, *Euclid's Conception of Ratio as Criticized by Arabian Commentators* (Rotterdam, 1950). Becker rejected the criticisms in *Archiv für Begriffsgeschichte*, 4 (1959), p. 223, and adhered to his theory in his book *Grundlagen der Mathematik in geschichtlicher Entwicklung* (Bonn, 1954; 2nd ed., 1964). His theory has been wholeheartedly endorsed by B. L. van der Waerden, *Science Awakening*, 2nd ed. (Groningen, 1956 [?]), 175–179; by Kurt von Fritz in "The Discovery of Incommensurability by Hippasus of Metapontum," in *Studies in Presocratic Philosophy*, David J. Furley and R. E. Allen, eds., I (London–New York, 1970), 408–410, esp. note 87; but his statement that Heath "still called the definition 'metaphysical'" is unfair, since Heath said it was "'metaphysical' (as Barrow would say)," and in any case this was in *The Thirteen Books of Euclid's Elements*, II (Cambridge, 1908; 2nd ed., 1925; repr., New York, 1956), p. 121, written before Becker's theory was enunciated; by Malcolm S. Brown, *op. cit.*, pp. 363–364; and by Wilbur Knorr, *The Evolution of the Euclidean Elements* (Dordrecht, 1975).

27. Aristotle, *Topics* VIII.3, 158B 29–159A 1.

28. Alexander of Aphrodisias, *Commentarium in Topica*, Strache and Wallies, eds., in *Commentaria in Aristotelem Graeca*, II (Berlin, 1891), 545.12–17.

29. Euclid, *Elements*, VII.1, VII.2, X.2, and X.3, J. L. Heiberg. ed., II (Leipzig, 1884), 188.13–15, 192.6–7; III (Leipzig, 1886), 12–14, 10.4–5; E. S. Stamatis, ed. (post J. L. Heiberg), II (Leipzig, 1970), 105.8–9, 107.3–4; III (Leipzig, 1972), 3.19–20, 5.8–9.

30. The Arabian commentator al-Māhānī (*fl. ca.* 860), followed by al-Nayrīzī (*fl. ca.* 897), dissatisfied with Euclid's definition, worked out for himself an "anthyphairetic" definition, as was recognized by E. B. Plooij, *op. cit.* For al-Nayrīzī, see *Anaritii in decem libros priores Elementorum Euclidis ex interpretatione Gherardi Cremonensis*, M. Curtze, ed., in *Euclidis opera omnia*, J. L. Heiberg and H. Menge, eds., *Supplementum*, pp. 157–160.

31. Proclus, *op. cit.*, p. 67.20–23; English trans., *op. cit.*, p. 56.9–12.

32. Eva Sachs, *De Theaeteto Atheniensi Mathematico*, p. 64, following Ulrich von Wilamowitz-Moellendorf.

BIBLIOGRAPHY

No original writing by Theaetetus has survived, even in quotation, although his work is undoubtedly embedded in Euclid, *Elements*, X and XIII.

Secondary literature includes G. J. Allman, "Theaetetus," in *Hermathena*, 6 (1887), 269–278, repr. in *Greek Geometry From Thales to Euclid* (London–Dublin, 1889), 206–215; Oskar Becker, "Eudoxos Studien I: Eine voreudoxische Proportionenlehre und ihre Spuren bei Aristoteles und Euklid," in *Quellen und Studien zur Geschichte der Mathematik, Astronomie und Physik*, 2B (1933), 311–333; *ibid.*, 3B (1934), 533–553, repr. in O. Becker, ed., *Zur Geschichte der griechischen Mathematik* (Darmstadt, 1965); in *Archiv für Begriffsgeschich-*

te, **4** (1959), 223; and in *Grundlagen der Mathematik in geschichtlicher Entwicklung* (Bonn, 1954; 2nd ed., 1964), 78–87; Malcolm S. Brown, "Theaetetus: Knowledge as Continued Learning," in *Journal of the History of Philosophy*, **7** (1969), 359–379; Kurt von Fritz, "The Discovery of Incommensurability by Hippasus of Metapontum," in *Annals of Mathematics*, **46** (1945), 242–264; "Platon, Theatet und die antike Mathematik," in *Philologus*, **87** (1932), 40–62, 136–178; and David J. Furley and R. E. Allen, eds., "The Discovery of Incommensurability by Hippasus of Metapontum," in *Studies in Presocratic Philosophy* I (London–New York, 1970), 382–412.

See also Thomas Heath, *A History of Greek Mathematics*, I (Oxford, 1921), 203–204, 209–212; Pauly-Wissowa, *Real-Encyclopädie der classischen Altertumswissenschaft*, 2nd ser., V, cols. 1351–1372; Eva Sachs, *De Theaeteto Atheniensi mathematico* (Inaugural diss., Berlin, 1914): *Die fünf platonischen Körper* (Berlin, 1917), 88–119; Árpád Szabó, "Ein Beleg für die voreudoxische Proportionenlehre?" in *Archiv für Begriffsgeschichte*, **9** (1964), 151–171; "Die Fruhgeschichte der Theorie der Irrationalitaten," in *Anfänge der griechischen Mathematik*, pt. 1 (Munich–Vienna, 1969), 38–130; "Die voreuklidische Proportionlehre," *ibid.*, pt. 2, pp. 131–242; Heinrich Vogt, "Die Entdeckungsgeschichte des Irrationalen nach Plato und anderen Quellen des 4. Jahrhunderts," in *Bibliotheca mathematica*, 3 ser., **10** (1909–1910), 97–155; "Zur Entdeckungsgeschichte des Irrationalen," *ibid.*, **14** (1913–1914), 9–29; B. L. van der Waerden, *Ontwakende Wetenschap* (Groningen, 1950), also in English, Arnold Dresden, trans., *Science Awakening* (Groningen, 1954; 2nd ed., [?], 1956), 165–179; A. Wasserstein, "Theaetetus and the History of the Theory of Numbers," in *Classical Quarterly*, n.s. **8** (1958), 165–179; H. G. Zeuthen, "Notes sur l'histoire des mathématiques VIII; Sur la constitution des livres arithmétiques des Eléments d'Euclide et leur rapport à la question de l'irrationalité," in *Oversigt over det Kongelige Danske Videnskabernes Selskabs Forhandlinger* (1910), 395–435; "Sur les connaissances géométriques des Grecs avant la reforme platonicienne de la géométrie," *ibid.* (1913), 431–473; and "Sur l'origine historique de la connaissance des quantités irrationelles," *ibid.* (1915), 333–362; and Wilbur Knorr, *The Evolution of the Euclidean Elements* (Dordrecht, 1975), chs. 7, 8.

See also the Bibliography of the article on Theodorus of Cyrene.

IVOR BULMER-THOMAS

THEODORUS OF CYRENE (*b*. Cyrene, North Africa, *ca.* 465 B.C.; *d.* Cyrene [?], after 399 B.C.)

Theodorus was the mathematical tutor of Plato and Theaetetus and is known for his contribution to the early development of the theory of irrational quantities. Iamblichus includes him in his catalog of Pythagoreans.[1] According to the account of Eudemus as preserved by Proclus,[2] he was a contemporary of Hippocrates of Chios, and they both came after Anaxagoras and Oenopides of Chios. Diogenes Laërtius[3] states that he was the teacher of Plato; and Plato represents him as an old man in the *Theaetetus*, which is set in 399 B.C. Since Anaxagoras was born *ca.* 500 and Plato in 428 or 427, it is reasonable to suppose that Theodorus was born about 465. This would make him sixty-six years old in the fictive year of the *Theaetetus*. According to the dialogue he had been a disciple of Protagoras but had turned at an early age from abstract speculation to geometry.[4] He was in Athens at the time of the death of Socrates.[5] He is also made a character by Plato in the *Sophist* and the *Politicus*. Plato may have sat at his feet in Athens just before the death of Socrates or at Cyrene during his travels after that event. In the dialogue Theaetetus tells Socrates that he learned geometry, astronomy, harmony, and arithmetic from Theodorus.[6] As with Plato, this could have been at Athens or Cyrene.

In the dialogue[7] Theaetetus is made to relate how Theodorus demonstrated to him and to the younger Socrates, a namesake of the philosopher, that the square roots of 3, 5, and so on up to 17 (excluding 9 and 16, it being understood) are incommensurable with the unit; and Theaetetus goes on to say how he and Socrates tried to find a general formula that would comprehend all square roots. Plato clearly purports to be giving a historical account[8] and to be distinguishing the achievement of Theodorus from that of Theaetetus; and it would appear that Theodorus was the first to demonstrate the irrationality of $\sqrt{3}$, $\sqrt{5}$, $\cdots$, $\sqrt{17}$. Two questions immediately arise. Why did he start at $\sqrt{3}$? Why did he stop at $\sqrt{17}$? The answer to the former question must be that the irrationality of $\sqrt{2}$ was already known. It was, indeed, known to the earlier Pythagoreans; and there is a high probability that it was the discovery of the incommensurability of $\sqrt{2}$ with the unit that revealed to the Greeks the existence of the irrational and made necessary a recasting of Greek mathematical theory.[9] After this discovery it would be natural for Theodorus and others to look for further examples of irrationality.

The answer to the second question depends on how Theodorus proved the irrationality of the numbers under examination, and is not so easy. We may rule out at once the suggestion of F.

Hultsch that Theodorus tried the method of successively closer approximation, because it would never *prove* irrationality.[10] The answer is dependent also on the meaning given to the words $\pi\omega\varsigma$ $\dot{\epsilon}\nu\dot{\epsilon}\sigma\chi\epsilon\tau o$. They usually have been translated "for some reason he stopped."[11] A glance at the uses of $\dot{\epsilon}\nu\dot{\epsilon}\chi\epsilon\iota\nu$ given in the lexicons, however, shows, as R. Hackforth first appreciated, that the Greek must mean "somehow he got into difficulties."[12]

This rules out the possibility that Theodorus stopped at 17 merely because he had to stop somewhere and felt he had proved enough.[13] It also rules out the possibility, despite the contention of A. Wasserstein, that Theodorus merely applied to 3, 5, $\cdots$, 17 the proof of the irrationality of $\sqrt{2}$.[14] This was known to Aristotle and is interpolated in the text of Euclid's *Elements*[15]; it may have been the way in which the irrationality of $\sqrt{2}$ was originally demonstrated. In this proof it is shown that, if the diagonal of a square is commensurable with its side, the same number will be both odd and even.[16] This proof can be generalized for all square roots, and indeed for all roots, in the form "$\sqrt[m]{N}$ is irrational unless N is the m-th power of an integer n."[17] Theodorus would soon have recognized the generality and would have run into no difficulties after 17.

It has been suggested that the Pythagorean devotion to the decad may have led Theodorus to stop where he did.[18] For $\sqrt{3}$ can be represented as $\sqrt{2^2 - 1^2}$, and so on for all the odd numbers up to $\sqrt{17} = \sqrt{9^2 - 8^2}$, at which point all the numerals from 1 to 9 would have been exhausted; Theodorus, however, would not have run into any difficulty in proceeding farther by this method, nor does it afford any proof of irrationality.

The above hypothesis is similar to one propounded by an anonymous commentator on the *Theaetetus*.[19] He first says that Plato made Theaetetus start with $\sqrt{3}$ because he had already shown in the *Meno* that the square on the diagonal of a square is double that on the side. He then proceeded to point out that Theaetetus was both a geometer and a student of musical theory. The tone interval has the ratio 9:8. If we double the two numbers we have 18:16; and between these two numbers the arithmetic mean is 17, dividing the extremes into unequal ratios, "as is shown in the commentaries on the *Timaeus*." The comment of Proclus on Plato, *Timaeus* 35B (*Commentarium in Timaeum*, 195A), is relevant, but we need not pursue it because it is clearly a rather farfetched hypothesis to explain why Theodorus stopped at 17.

An ingenious theory has been put forward by

J. H. Anderhub.[20] If a right-angled isosceles triangle with unit sides is set out as in Figure 1, its

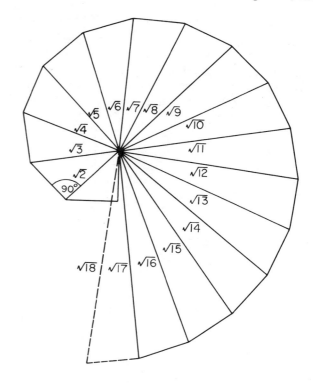

FIGURE 1

hypotenuse is $\sqrt{2}$. If at one extremity of the hypotenuse a perpendicular of unit length is erected, we have a second triangle with hypotenuse = $\sqrt{3}$. The process can be continued with all the hypotenuses $\sqrt{2}$, $\sqrt{3}$ $\cdots$ radiating from a common point, and the angles at the common point can be shown to be 45°, 35°15′, and so on. The total of all the angles up to hypotenuse = $\sqrt{17}$ is approximately 351°10′, and the total up to $\sqrt{18}$ is approximately 364°48′—that is, after $\sqrt{17}$ the circle has been completed and the triangles begin to overlap. But although this would have given Theodorus a reason for stopping, he would have had no difficulty in going on; and the method does not prove the irrationality of any hypotenuse.

There is one theory, put forward by H. G. Zeuthen, that satisfies the requirements that there shall be a separate proof for each number $\sqrt{3}$, $\sqrt{5}$, $\cdots$ as Plato's text suggests, and that after $\sqrt{17}$ the proof will encounter difficulties.[21] Zeuthen's suggestion is that Theodorus used the process of finding the greatest common measure of two magnitudes as set out in Euclid's *Elements*, X.2, and actually made a test of incommensurability by Euclid: "If when the lesser of two unequal magnitudes is continually subtracted from the greater, the remainder never measures the one before it, the magnitudes will be incommensurable."[22] The method may conveniently be illustrated from $\sqrt{17}$ itself. Let ABC be a right-angled triangle in which $AB = 1$, $BC = 4$, so that $CA = \sqrt{17}$. Let CD be cut off from CA equal to CB so that $AD = \sqrt{17} - 4$, and let DE be drawn at right angles to CA. The triangles CDE, CBE are equal and therefore

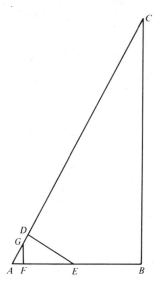

FIGURE 2

$DE = EB$. The triangles ADE, ABC are similar and $DE = 4AD$. We therefore have $DE = 4AD = 4(\sqrt{17} - 4)$. Now from EA let EF be cut off equal to ED and at F let the perpendicular FG be drawn. Then by parity of reasoning

$$AF = AB - BF = AB - 2DE$$
$$= 1 - 8(\sqrt{17} - 4)$$
$$= (\sqrt{17} - 4)(\sqrt{17} + 4)$$
$$- 8(\sqrt{17} - 4)$$
$$= (\sqrt{17} - 4)^2.$$

Obviously, the process can be continued indefinitely, so that ABC, ADE, AFG, $\cdots$ is a diminishing series of triangles such that

$$AB:AD:AF \cdots = 1:(\sqrt{17} - 4):(\sqrt{17} - 4)^2 \cdots$$

and we shall never be left with a magnitude that exactly measures CA, which is accordingly incommensurable.

Theodorus would certainly have used a geometrical proof, but the point can be made as shown be-

low in modern arithmetical notation. The process of finding the greatest common measure of 1 and $\sqrt{17}$ (if any) may be set out as follows:

$$1) \ \sqrt{17} \ (4$$

$$\frac{4}{\sqrt{17}} - 4$$

$$(\sqrt{17} - 4))1(8$$

$$\frac{8(\sqrt{17} - 4)}{1 - 8(\sqrt{17} - 4)}$$
$$= (\sqrt{17} - 4)(\sqrt{17} + 4) - 8(\sqrt{17} - 4)$$
$$= (\sqrt{17} - 4)(\sqrt{17} + 4 - 8)$$
$$= (\sqrt{17} - 4)^2.$$

The next stage in the process would be to divide $(\sqrt{17} - 4)^2$ into $(\sqrt{17} - 4)$, but this is the same as dividing $(\sqrt{17} - 4)$ into 1, which was the previous step. The process is therefore periodic and will never end, so that 1 and $\sqrt{17}$ do not have a greatest common measure. It will be recognized as the same process as that for finding a continued fraction equal to $\sqrt{17}$.

It is a powerful argument in favor of this theory that Plato, in the passage of the *Theaetetus* under discussion, for the first time in Greek literature uses the term οὐ σύμμετρος ("incommensurable") for what had previously been described as ἀρρητος ("inexpressible"). This strongly reinforces the conviction that he was doing something new, and that the novelty consisted in using the test of incommensurability later found in Euclid.

These proofs, geometrical and arithmetical, are simple; and the former would certainly have been within the grasp of Theodorus. So would the earlier proofs for $\sqrt{3}$, $\sqrt{5}$, and so on.[23] The next case, $\sqrt{18}$, would not call for investigation since $\sqrt{18} = 3\sqrt{2}$; but $\sqrt{19}$ presents difficulties at which even a modern mathematician may quail. Recurrence does not take place until after six stages, which, on the basis of the exposition of B. L. van der Waerden, may be set out as follows.[24] We start by subtracting the appropriate multiple of 1 from $\sqrt{19}$ and get a remainder $\sqrt{19} - 4$. We now divide $\sqrt{19} - 4$ into 1. But

$$\frac{1}{\sqrt{19} - 4} = \frac{\sqrt{19} + 4}{3}.$$

We treat $(\sqrt{19} + 4)$ and 3 in exactly the same way, subtracting $2 \cdot 3$ from $\sqrt{19} + 4$ and getting $\sqrt{19} - 2$. Now

$$\frac{3}{\sqrt{19}-2}=\frac{\sqrt{19}+2}{5};$$

and we subtract the 5 from $\sqrt{19}+2$, getting $\sqrt{19}-3$, and divide this into 5. But

$$\frac{5}{\sqrt{19}-3}=\frac{\sqrt{19}+3}{2};$$

and after subtracting $3\cdot 2$ from $\sqrt{19}+3$, we get $\sqrt{19}-3$ again. But

$$\frac{2}{\sqrt{19}-3}=\frac{\sqrt{19}+3}{5},$$

and subtracting 5 from $\sqrt{19}+3$ yields $\sqrt{19}-2$. Now

$$\frac{5}{\sqrt{19}-2}=\frac{\sqrt{19}+2}{3};$$

and by subtracting $2\cdot 3$ from $\sqrt{19}+2$ we obtain $\sqrt{19}-4$. But

$$\frac{3}{\sqrt{19}-4}=\frac{\sqrt{19}+4}{1};$$

subtracting $4\cdot 1$ from $\sqrt{19}+4$ leaves us with $\sqrt{19}$, and dividing 1 into $\sqrt{19}$ brings us back where we started. The process is therefore periodic and will never end, so that $\sqrt{19}$ is incommensurable with 1.

This is formidable enough in modern notation, and impossible to set out in a drawing, particularly a drawing in sand. If this is the method that Theodorus used, it is therefore fully understandable why he stopped at $\sqrt{17}$.

Although this is only a hypothesis, there is no other that fits the facts so well; and if his pupil Theaetetus developed a theory of proportion based on the method of finding the greatest common measure, as is argued in the article devoted to him in this *Dictionary*, it becomes virtually certain that this is the method employed by Theodorus.

Proclus, in analyzing curves in the manner of Geminus, criticizes "Theodorus the mathematician" for speaking of "blending" in lines.[25] He is probably to be identified with Theodorus of Cyrene, since in his only other reference Proclus describes the subject of this article. He may also be identified with the Theodorus whom Xenophon held up as a model of a good mathematician.[26]

NOTES

1. Iamblichus, *De vita Pythagorica*, 267; L. Deubner, ed. (Leipzig, 1937), p. 146.8–9.
2. Proclus, *In primum Euclidis*, G. Friedlein, ed. (Leipzig, 1873; repr. Hildesheim, 1967), 65.21–66.7.

3. Diogenes Laërtius, *Vitae philosophorum*, II.103, III.6; H. S. Long, ed., I (Oxford, 1964), 100.9–13, 123.18.
4. Plato, *Theaetetus* 164E–165A, in *Platonis opera*, J. Burnet, ed., I (Oxford, 1899; frequently repr.).
5. It is not obvious why James Gow, *A Short History of Greek Mathematics* (Cambridge, 1884), 164, should flatly contradict the evidence of Plato's dialogue and say, "He does not seem to have visited Athens."
6. Plato, *Theaetetus*, 145C–D.
7. *Ibid.*, 147D–148B.
8. Jean Itard, *Les livres arithmétiques d'Euclide*, Histoire de la Pensée, X (Paris, 1961), is exceptional in regarding as tenable the view that Theodorus and Theaetetus may not be historical persons but "personnages composites nés dans l'esprit même de Platon."
9. The fullest account of this subject is in Kurt von Fritz, "The Discovery of Incommensurability by Hippasus of Metapontium," in *Studies in Presocratic Philosophy*, David J. Furley and R. E. Allen, eds., I (London–New York, 1970), 382–412. But in his earlier paper with the same title in *Annals of Mathematics*, **46** (1945), 242–264, Fritz exposed himself to some strictures, of which he has not taken notice, from A. Wasserstein, "Theaetetus and the Theory of Numbers," 165, n. 3.
10. F. Hultsch, "Die Näherungswerthe irrationaler Quadratwurzeln bei Archimedes," in *Nachrichten von der königlich Gesellschaft der Wissenschaften zu Göttingen*, **22** (1893), 368–428. Hultsch received some support from T. L. Heath in his early work, *The Works of Archimedes* (Cambridge, 1897), lxxix–lxxx, in which he regarded it as "pretty certain" that Theodorus, like Archimedes after him, represented $\sqrt{3}$ geometrically as the perpendicular from an angular point of an equilateral triangle to the opposite side. He also presumed that Theodorus would start from the identity $3 = 48/16 = (49-1)/16$, so that

$$\sqrt{3}<\sqrt{\frac{48+1}{16}}=\frac{7}{4};$$

but in his later work, *A History of Greek Mathematics*, I (Oxford, 1921), 204, he realized that this "would leave Theodorus as far as ever from *proving* that $\sqrt{3}$ is incommensurable." These approximations may, of course, have played a part in Theodorus' researches until he found a demonstrative proof.
11. "There he stopped" (B. Jowett); "here he somehow came to a pause" (B. J. Kennedy); "il s'était, je ne sais pourquoi, arrêté là" (A. Diès); "there, for some reason, he stopped" (F. M. Cornford); "at that he stopped" (H. N. Fowler); "qui, non so come, si fermò" (M. Timpanaro Cardini). But the latest translator, J. McDowell (Oxford, 1973), has the sense right—"at that point he somehow got tied up."
12. *A Greek-English Lexicon*, H. G. Liddell and R. Scott, eds., new ed. by H. Stuart Jones (Oxford, 1940), see ἐνέχω, II, 565. The general meaning of the passive and middle is "to be held, caught, entangled in"; and a particularly relevant example is given in II.2, [κύρος] ἐνείχετο ἀπορίη͵σι; Herodotus 1.190. *Theatetus* 147D is the only passage quoted for the meaning "come to a standstill" (II.5), and therefore it can hardly determine the meaning of that passage.
R. Hackforth, "Notes on Plato's *Theaetetus*," 128. It is significant that Hackforth's interest is purely literary, and his interpretation is therefore free from any bias in favor of some particular mathematical solution. He is supported by Malcolm S. Brown, "*Theaetetus*: Knowledge as Continued Learning," in *Journal of the History of Philosophy*, **7** (1969), 367.
13. Wasserstein, *op. cit.*, 165, makes this suggestion without necessarily endorsing it. G. H. Hardy and E. M. Wright, *An Introduction to the Theory of Numbers*, 4th ed. (Oxford, 1960), 43, in the light of their views about the difficulty of generalizing the Pythagorean proof for $\sqrt{2}$ (see note 14), regard the suggestion as credible.

14. It is the main burden of Wasserstein's paper (cited above) that this is precisely what Theodorus did. He argues that the difficulties of effecting a valid generalization are such as would have been perceived by Theodorus and that "it was precisely this refusal of the rigorous mathematician to enumerate a general theory based on doubtful foundations that led his pupil Theaetetus to investigate not only the problem of irrationality but also the more fundamental arithmetical questions." Although it may be conceded that Theodorus was an acute mathematician, it is most unlikely that he, or any other ancient mathematician, would have thought about this problem in the manner of G. H. Hardy and E. M. Wright. (See note 16.) Wasserstein's thesis is controverted in detail by Brown, *op cit.*, 366–367, but in part for an irrelevant reason. Brown accepts van der Waerden's view that bk. VII of Euclid's *Elements* was already in "apple-pie order" before the end of the fifth century, whereas Wasserstein, like Zeuthen, regards it as the work of Theaetetus; but Wasserstein's contention that Theodorus applied the traditional proof for $\sqrt{2}$ can be detached from this belief.

15. Aristotle, *Prior Analytics* 1.23.41a23–30; W. D. Ross, ed. (Oxford, 1949, corr. repr. 1965), English trans. by A. J. Jenkinson as *Analytica priora*, in *The Works of Aristotle*, W. D. Ross, ed., I (Oxford, 1928; repr. 1968). Euclid, *Elements*, X, app. 27; *Euclidis opera omnia*, J. L. Heiberg and H. Menge, eds., III (Leipzig, 1886), 408.1–410.16; E. S. Stamatis, ed., in *Euclidis Elementa* post J. L. Heiberg, III (Leipzig, 1972), 231.10–233.13. An alternative proof is also given. In earlier eds. the proof was printed as Euclid, *Elements*, X.117, but it is now recognized as an interpolation.

16. T. L. Heath, *A History of Greek Mathematics*, I (Oxford, 1921), 205, purports to give a fairly easy generalization; but it is logically defective in that he assumes that "if $m^2 = N \cdot n^2$, therefore m^2 is divisible by N, so that m also is a multiple of N," which is true only if N is not itself the multiple of a square number. Wasserstein, *op. cit.*, 168–169, corrects Heath. Hardy and Wright, *op. cit.*, 40, show that the generalization is not so simple as Heath represented it to be and "requires a good deal more than a 'trivial' variation of the Pythagorean proof." This is true; but Hardy and Wright are working to standards of logical rigor far beyond what any mathematician of the fifth century B.C. would have demanded, and Theodorus could fairly easily have found a generalization that would have satisfied his own standards.

17. Hardy and Wright, *op cit.*, 41. The authors discuss Theodorus' work helpfully in the light of modern mathematics on 42–45.

18. See Brown, *op cit.*, 367–368, and his n. 26.

19. *Anonymer Kommentar zu Platons Theaetet*, H. Diels and W. Schubart, eds., Berliner Klassikertexte, II (Berlin, 1905). The passage is reproduced and translated, as is Proclus' commentary on the relevant passage in the *Timaeus*, with illuminating notes, in Wasserstein, *op cit.*, 172–179. The commentator does not appear to accept his own suggestion, saying that Theodorus stopped at 17 because that is the first number after 16, and 16 is the only square in which the number denoting the sum of the sides is equal to the number denoting the area $(4 + 4 + 4 + 4 = 4 \times 4)$.

20. Both B. L. van der Waerden, *Science Awakening*, English trans. by Arnold Dresden of *Ontwakende Wetenschap*, 2nd ed., I (Groningen, n.d.), 143; and Árpád Szabó, *Anfänge der griechischen Mathematik* (Munich–Vienna, 1969), 70, attribute this interesting construction to J. H. Anderhub, *Joco-Seria: Aus den Papieren eines reisenden Kaufmannes*, but I have not been able to obtain a copy.

21. H. G. Zeuthen, "Sur la constitution des livres arithmétiques des Eléments d'Euclide et leur rapport à la question de l'irrationalité," in *Oversigt over det K. Danske Videnskabernes Selskabs Forhandlinger* for 1910 (1910–1911), 422–426. The theory is taken up again in articles in the same periodical in the volumes for 1913 and 1915. Zeu-

then's thesis is supported by O. Toeplitz, 28–29; and by Brown, *op cit.*

22. *Euclidis opera omnia*, J. L. Heiberg and H. Menge, eds., III (Leipzig, 1886), 6.12–8.13; E. C. Stamatis, ed., in *Euclidis Elementa post J. L. Heiberg*, III (Leipzig, 1972), 3.19–4.19.

23. The cases of $\sqrt{5}$ and $\sqrt{10}$ are similar to $\sqrt{17}$. The case of $\sqrt{3}$ is a little more difficult, involving one more step before recurrence takes place. The case of $\sqrt{13}$ is difficult, as may be seen from the process of expressing it as a continued fraction given by G. Chrystal, *Algebra*, II (Edinburgh, 1889), 401–402, where it is shown that recurrence occurs only after five partial quotients:

$$\sqrt{13} = 3 + \frac{1}{1+}\frac{1}{1+}\frac{1}{1+}\frac{1}{1+}\frac{1}{6+}\frac{1}{1+}\cdots,$$

Perhaps it was Theodorus' experience with $\sqrt{13}$ that made him unwilling to embark on $\sqrt{19}$. The same method can be applied to $\sqrt{2}$, although it is probable that $\sqrt{2}$ was originally proved irrational not by this method but by that referred to by Aristotle (see note 15). Zeuthen, *loc. cit.*, and Heath, *loc. cit.*, give the proofs for $\sqrt{5}$ and $\sqrt{3}$; and Heath adds a geometrical proof for $\sqrt{2}$; Hardy and Wright, *op. cit.*, give proofs for $\sqrt{5}$ and $\sqrt{2}$. The method is used by Kurt von Fritz in *Studies in Presocratic Philosophy*, I, 401–406, to prove the incommensurability of the diagonal of a regular pentagon in relation to its side.

24. Van der Waerden, *op. cit.*, 144–146. The method is a simplification of the process of finding the greatest common measure as used in the text for $\sqrt{17}$ by taking new ratios equal to the actual ratios of the process; but van der Waerden's exposition is rather elliptical, and it may more clearly be set out as here.

25. Proclus, *In primum Euclidis*, G. Friedlein, ed., 118.7–9. (The reference in Friedlein's index is incorrect.) In favor of identifying him with Theodorus of Cyrene is the fact that Plato in one place (*Theaetetus* 143B) calls the Cyrenaic "Theodorus the geometer"; and Diogenes Laërtius, *op. cit.*, also calls him "the Cyrenaic geometer" and "the mathematician." Van der Waerden, *op. cit.*, 146, accepts the identification, but it is rejected (by implication) by H. Diels and W. Kranz, eds., *Die Fragmente der Vorsokratiker*, 6th ed. (Dublin–Zurich, 1954; repr. 1969) and most writers; Glenn R. Morrow, *Proclus: A Commentary on the First Book of Euclid's Elements* (Princeton, 1970), 95, n. 70, thinks the reference is to Theodorus of Soli, who is cited by Plutarch on certain mathematical difficulties in the *Timaeus*. Diogenes Laërtius, *loc. cit.*, refers to twenty persons with the name Theodorus, and Pauly-Wissowa lists no fewer than 203. There was even a second Theodorus of Cyrene, a philosopher of some repute, who flourished at the end of the fourth century B.C. In the passage under discussion Proclus is reproducing Geminus' classification of curves; and in treating mixed curves he says the mixing can come about through "composition," "fusing," or "blending." According to Geminus and Proclus, but not Theodorus, planes can be blended but lines cannot.

26. Xenophon, *Memorabilia*, which is *Commentarii* IV.2, 10; *Xenophontis opera omnia*, E. C. Marchant, ed., II (Oxford, 1901; 2nd ed., 1921; repr. 1942), ll. 25–26.

BIBLIOGRAPHY

The works listed in the bibliography of the article on Theaetetus will serve also for Theodorus. In addition, the following, listed chronologically, may be consulted: T. Bonnesen, in *Periodico di mathematiche*, 4th ser., **1** (1921), 16; H. Hasse and H. Scholz, *Die Grundlagen-*

krisis der griechisch Mathematik (Berlin, 1928), 28; K. von Fritz, "Theodorus 31," in Pauly-Wissowa, *Real-Encyclopädie der classischen Altertumswissenschaft*, 2nd ser., V (Stuttgart, 1934), cols. 1811–1825; J. H. Anderhub, *Joco-Seria: Aus den Papieren eines reisenden Kaufmannes* (Wiesbaden, 1941); R. Hackforth, "Notes on Plato's *Theaetetus*," in *Mnemosyne*, 4th ser., **10** (1957), 128; A. Wasserstein, "*Theaetetus* and the History of the Theory of Numbers," in *Classical Quarterly*, n.s. **8** (1958), 165–179; O. Toeplitz, *Kantstudien*, **33**, 28–29; M. Timpanaro Cardini, *Pitagorici, testimonianze e frammenti*, fasc. 2; Bibliotheca di Studi Superiori, **41** (Florence, 1962), 74–81.

IVOR BULMER-THOMAS

THEODOSIUS OF BITHYNIA (*b*. Bithynia, second half of the second century B.C.)

Theodosius was the author of *Sphaerics*, a text-book on the geometry of the sphere, and minor astronomical and astrological works. Strabo, in giving a list of Bithynians worthy of note in various fields, mentions "Hipparchus, Theodosius and his sons, mathematicians."[1] Vitruvius mentions Theodosius as the inventor of a sundial suitable for any region.[2] Strabo's references are usually in chronological order in their respective categories; and since Hipparchus was at the height of his career in 127 B.C., while Strabo and Vitruvius both flourished about the beginning of the Christian era, these statements could refer to the same person and probably do. They harmonize with the fact that Theodosius is quoted by name as the author of the *Sphaerics* by Menelaus (fl. A.D. 100). To allow sufficient time for his sons to be recognized as mathematicians in their own right before Strabo, Theodosius may best be regarded as a younger contemporary of Hipparchus, born in the second half of the second century B.C. and perhaps surviving into the first century; indeed, it is unlikely that such a work as the *Sphaerics* would have been written long after the development of spherical trigonometry by Hipparchus, for this development makes it look old-fashioned.

Confusion has been created, however, by the notice or notices in the notoriously unreliable *Suda Lexicon*. The passage reads:

Theodosius, philosopher, wrote *Sphaerics* in three books, a commentary on the chapter of Theudas, two books *On Days and Nights*, a commentary on the *Method* of Archimedes, *Descriptions of Houses* in three books, *Skeptical Chapters*, astrological works,

On Habitations. Theodosius wrote verses on the spring and other types of works. He was from Tripolis.[3]

It seems probable that the first sentence in this passage confuses the author of the *Sphaerics* with a later skeptical philosopher, for Theudas flourished in the second century of the Christian era;[4] and it also is probable that the second and third sentences should be regarded as a separate notice about a third Theodosius. This would be unimportant if the third sentence had not given rise to the belief that the author of the *Sphaerics* was born at Tripolis in Phoenicia, and in almost all editions until recently he has been described as Theodosius of Tripolis.[5]

Spherics, the geometry of the sphere, was needed for astronomy and was regarded by the ancient Greeks as a branch of astronomy rather than of geometry. Indeed, the Pythagoreans called astronomy "spherics"; and the stereometrical books XII and XIII of Euclid's *Elements*, which lead up to the inscription of the regular solids in a sphere, contain nothing about the geometry of the sphere beyond the proof that the volumes of spheres are in the triplicate ratio of their diameters. Euclid treated this subject in his *Phaenomena*, and just before him Autolycus had dealt with it in his book *On the Moving Sphere*. From a comparison of propositions quoted or assumed by Euclid and Autolycus, it may be inferred that much of Theodosius' *Sphaerics* is derived from some pre-Euclidean textbook, of which some have conjectured that Eudoxus was the author.[6] There is nothing in it that can strictly be called trigonometry, although in III.11 Theodosius proves the equivalent of the formula $\tan a = \sin b \tan A$ for a spherical triangle right-angled at C.

Two of the other works mentioned by the *Suda* have survived. *On Habitations* treats the phenomena caused by the rotation of the earth, particularly what portions of the heavens are visible to the inhabitants of different zones. *On Days and Nights* studies the arc of the ecliptic traversed by the sun each day. Its object is to determine what conditions have to be satisfied in order that the solstice may occur in the meridian at a given place and in order that day and night may really be equal at the equinoxes.

One reason why these three works have survived must be that they were included in the collection that Pappus called "The Little Astronomy"[7]—in contrast with "The Great Astronomy" or *Almagest* of Ptolemy. Pappus also annotated the *Sphaerics* and *On Days and Nights* in some detail.[8] All three works were translated into Arabic toward the end of the ninth century.[9] The translation of the *Sphaerics* up to II.5 is by Qusṭā ibn Lūqā and thereafter by Thābit ibn Qurra. The *Sphaerics* was translated from Arabic into Latin in the twelfth century by Plato of Tivoli and Gerard of Cremona.

There is no reason to doubt that the Theodosius who wrote the *Sphaerics* was also the author of the commentary on the *Method* of Archimedes mentioned by the *Suda*, for the subject matter would be similar. It may be accepted also that he wrote astrological works. It is tempting to think that the Διαγραφαὶ οἰκιῶν, *Descriptions of Houses*, mentioned in the *Suda*, dealt with the "houses of the planets"; but the latter term is always οἶκοι, not οἰκίαι. It must be considered an architectural work, which could, however, be by the author of the *Sphaerics*. The other works mentioned in the *Suda* must be regarded as by another person of the same name. Theodosius' discovery of a sundial suitable for all regions—πρὸς πᾶν κλίμα—may have been recorded in a book, but nothing is known about it.

NOTES

1. Strabo, *Geography* XII.4, 9 c 566, A. Meineke, ed. (Leipzig, 1853), II, 795.13–14.
2. Vitruvius, *De architectura* IX.8,1, F. Krohn, ed. (Leipzig, 1912), p. 218.7.
3. *Suda Lexicon*, under Θεοδόσιος, Ada Adler, ed., II (Leipzig, 1931), Θ 142 and 143, p. 693.
4. Diogenes Laërtius, *Vitae philosophorum* IX.116, H. S. Long, ed. (Oxford, 1964), II, 493.14. He was, according to Diogenes, the fifth skeptical philosopher in succession to Aenesidemus, who flourished at the time of Cicero.
5. Even the definitive ed. by J. L. Heiberg (1927) is entitled "Theodosius Tripolites Sphaerica" but the first entry in the corrigenda (p. xvi) is "Tripolites deleatur ubique."
6. The following propositions in the *Sphaerics* are certainly pre-Euclidean: bk. I, props. 1, 6, 7, 8, 11, 12, 13, 15, 20; bk. II, props. 1, 2, 3, 5, 8, 9, 10, 13, 15, 17, 18, 19, 20; bk. III, prop. 2.
7. Ὁ μικρὸς ἀστρονομούμενος (sc. τόπος). Pappus, *Collection* VI *titulus*, F. Hultsch, ed., *Pappi Alexandrini Collectionis quae supersunt*, II (Berlin, 1877), 475.
8. *Sphaerics, ibid.*, VI.1–33, props. 1–26, F. Hultsch, ed., 475–519; *On Days and Nights, ibid.*, VI.48–68, props. 30–36, F. Hultsch, ed., II, 530–555.
9. H. Wenrich, *De auctorum Graecorum versionibus et commentariis Syriacis Arabicis etc.* (Leipzig, 1842), 206; H. Suter, *Die Mathematiker und Astronomen der Araber und ihre Werke* (Leipzig, 1900), 41.

BIBLIOGRAPHY

I. ORIGINAL WORKS. The three surviving works of Theodosius are in many MSS, of which the most important is Codex Vaticanus Graecus 204 (10th cent.). The *Sphaerics* was first printed in a Latin ed. translated from the Arabic (Venice, 1518), which was followed by Voegelin's Latin ed. (Vienna, 1529), also taken from the Arabic. The *editio princeps* of the Greek text (with Latin trans.) is J. Pena, *Theodosii Tripolitae Sphaericorum libri tres* (Paris, 1558). Subsequent eds. are F. Maurolico (Messina, 1558; Latin trans. only); C. Dasypodius (Strasbourg, 1572; enunciations only in Greek and Latin); C. Clavius (Rome, 1586; Latin trans. only, with works of his own); J. Auria (Rome, 1587); M. Mersenne (Paris, 1644); C. Dechales (Lyons, 1674); I. Barrow (London, 1675); J. Hunt (Oxford, 1707); E. Nizze (Berlin, 1852). The definitive ed. is J. L. Heiberg, "Theodosius Tripolites Sphaerica," in *Abhandlungen der Gesellschaft der Wissenschaften zu Göttingen*, phil.-hist. Kl., n.s. 19, no. 3 (1927), which contains notes on the MSS (i–xv), text with Latin trans. (1–165), and scholia (166–199).

The Greek enunciations of *On Habitations* and *On Days and Nights* were included by Dasypodius in his ed. (Strasbourg, 1572) and Latin translations of the two texts were published by J. Auria (Rome, 1587 and 1591, respectively), but the Greek texts were not printed until the definitive ed. by R. Fecht, "Theodosii *De habitationibus liber De diebus et noctibus libri duo*," in *Abhandlungen der Gesellschaft der Wissenschaften zu Göttingen*, phil.-hist. Kl. n.s. 19, no. 4 (1927), which contains notes (1–12), text and Latin trans. of *On Habitations* (13–43), scholia on *Habitations* (44–52), text and Latin trans. of *On Days and Nights* (53–155), and scholia on *Days and Nights* (156–176). The scholia were first edited by F. Hultsch, "Scholien zur Sphärik des Theodosios," in *Abhandlungen des philosophisch-historische Classe der K. Sächsischen Gesellschaft der Wissenschaften*, 10, no. 5 (1887).

There is a German trans. of the *Sphaerics* by E. Nizze, *Die Sphärik des Theodosios* (Stralsund, 1826). There are French translations by D. Henrion (Paris, 1615); J. B. du Hamel (Paris, 1660); and Paul ver Eecke, *Théodose de Tripoli: Les sphériques* (Paris–Bruges, 1927).

II. SECONDARY LITERATURE. The most useful material on Theodosius is Thomas Heath, *A History of Greek Mathematics* (Oxford, 1921), II, 245–252; the Latin intro. to R. Fecht's ed. (see above), 1–12; and K. Ziegler, "Theodosios 5," in Pauly-Wissowa, *Real-Encyclopädie der classischen Altertumswissenschaft*, n.s. V, cols. 1930–1935. Other sources, listed chronologically, are A. Nokk, *Über die Sphärik des Theodosios* (Karlsruhe, 1847); F. Hultsch, "Die *Sphärik* des Theodosios und einige unedierte Texte," in *Berichte der Sächsischen Gesellschaft der Wissenschaften* (1885); R. Carra de Vaux, "Remaniement des *Sphériques* de Théodose par Jahia ibn Muhammed ibn Abī Schukr al-Maghrabī al Andalusī," in *Journal asiatique*, 17 (1891), 287–295; P. Tannery, *Recherches sur l'histoire de l'astronomie ancienne* (Paris, 1893), 36–37; and A. A. Björnbo, "Studien über Menelaos' *Sphärik*: Beiträge zur Geschichte des Sphärik und Trigonometrie der Griechen," in *Abhandlungen zur Geschichte der mathematischen Wissenschaften*, **14** (1902), 64–65; and "Über zwei mathematische Handschriften," in *Bibliotheca mathematica*, n.s. 3 (1902), 63–75.

IVOR BULMER-THOMAS

THEON OF ALEXANDRIA (*fl.* Alexandria, second half of fourth century)

Theon's scholarly activity is firmly dated by his reports of two eclipses that he observed at Alexandria in 364: the solar eclipse of 16 June and the lunar eclipse of 26 November.[1] Other chronological references in his works all point to the 360's and 370's. The solar eclipse of 364 is used as an example of calculation in both the greater and the lesser commentaries on Ptolemy's *Handy Tables*, the lesser commentary providing examples of calculations that correspond to the dates 15 June 360 and 17 November 377.[2] Also, a list of Roman consuls preserved in one manuscript of Theon's edition of the *Handy Tables* stops with the consuls of the year 372.[3] There is only one ancient biographical notice on Theon, and that very brief.[4] It states that Theon lived under the emperor Theodosius I (reigned 379–395), a date consistent with the above evidence. Theon's daughter, Hypatia, who was famous in her own right as a mathematician (she is credited, among other things, with a revision of book 3 of her father's commentary on the *Almagest*) and as a Neoplatonic philosopher, was torn to pieces by a mob of fanatic Christians at Alexandria in 415. Since there is no mention of Theon in the circumstantial account we have of this event, it is likely that he was already dead. Like his daughter, Theon was certainly a pagan. Whether he, too, favored Neoplatonism cannot be determined.

The ancient biographical notice also informs us that Theon was a member of the "Museum." This was an institution for the support of advanced learning, established at Alexandria about 300 B.C. by Ptolemy I, which had nourished many famous scholars but by Theon's time had declined sadly — if, indeed, it still existed (Theon is the last attested member). Whether he was connected with the Museum or not, Theon was certainly actively engaged in higher education. In the preface to his commentary on the *Almagest*, he says that he has composed the work at the urging of those who attended his lectures on the subject.[5] Indeed, all his extant works are the outcome of his "professorial" activity, being either commentaries on or editions of recognized classics of mathematics and astronomy, intended for the use of students. I will deal with the commentaries in the order in which Theon wrote them, which is established by internal references from one to the other.

Theon's most extensive work is his commentary on Ptolemy's *Almagest*. This was originally in thirteen books, corresponding to the number of books of the *Almagest*; but book 11 is lost, only a fragment of book 5 survives, and there are probably lacunae in other books. The passage in the preface mentioned above suggests that the commentary is a redaction of Theon's lectures, and that is how it reads. It is for the most part a trivial exposition of Ptolemy's text, explaining obvious points at excessive length. Despite Theon's promise to improve over previous commentators on the *Almagest*, "who claim that they will only omit the more obvious points, but in fact prove to have omitted the most difficult,"[6] the commentary is open to precisely this criticism. It is never critical, merely exegetic. To the modern reader it is almost useless for understanding Ptolemy; but it is of value for the occasional information it provides on now-lost mathematical and astronomical works, notably Zenodorus' treatise "On Isoperimetric Figures" in book 1. This passage probably is taken from the earlier commentary on the *Almagest* by Pappus (*fl.* 320), of which only books 5 and 6 survive. Comparison of the two commentaries for book 6 (the only area where they overlap) shows that while Theon borrows much from Pappus, his work is not a mere rewriting of his predecessor's but contains extensive contributions of his own.

Theon also published two commentaries on the *Handy Tables*. The latter, issued by Ptolemy after he had completed the *Almagest*, were meant to provide a convenient means of computing the positions of the heavenly bodies and other astronomical phenomena. In the preface to the larger commentary Theon claims that whereas he had predecessors who commented on the *Almagest*, he is the first to write a commentary on the *Handy Tables*. The earlier of the two commentaries is an extensive one, in five books, addressed to Eulalius and Origenes, whom Theon calls his "companions" (in the Museum ?). In it Theon explains not only how to use the tables but also the reasons for the operations and the basis of the tables' construction, and provides geometrical demonstrations. Thus it frequently covers the same ground as the commentary on the *Almagest*. The second, much smaller, commentary is addressed, like the commentary on the *Almagest*, to Epiphanius, presumably a pupil of

Theon's. In the preface Theon refers to the larger commentary as "the more reasoned (λογικωτέρα) introduction to computation with the *Handy Tables*," and explains that he has written this new work for that majority of his pupils in the subject who are unable to follow geometrical proofs.[7] The smaller commentary, then, merely sets out the rules for computation with the tables, adding occasional worked examples but no reasons. Theon's remark indicating the low mathematical caliber of his students is corroborated by what we should surmise from the nature of his works in general.

All other extant works by Theon are editions of previous authors. "Edition" here does not mean an attempt to establish the authentic text but, rather, a reworking of the original in a form considered more suitable for students. The most notable of Theon's editions is that of Euclid's *Elements*, which was so influential that it consigned the original text to near oblivion. Theon himself attests his work in his commentary on the *Almagest*, book 1, chapter 10, where he says: "That sectors of equal circles are in the ratio of the angles [at the centers] we have proved in our edition of the *Elements* at the end of the sixth book."[8] Indeed, nearly all extant manuscripts of the *Elements* have a proposition to that effect attached to book 6, proposition 33; and many of the manuscripts have titles indicating that they are "from the edition of Theon" or even "from the lectures (συνουσίαι) of Theon."

It was not until the early nineteenth century, however, when Peyrard discovered that the manuscript Vaticanus Graecus 190, which lacks that proposition and is significantly different from the vulgate in other respects, must be an example of the pre-Theonic text, that it became possible to determine the nature of Theon's alterations of Euclid. They are many but mostly trivial, leaving the essential content of the *Elements* almost unchanged. In many places the wording has been altered or expanded to achieve consistency or perspicuity of expression. Of the occasional changes of mathematical substance, a very few are corrections of real mistakes in Euclid's text. More are due to Theon's misunderstanding the original. In some cases he apparently omits what he considers wrong. He makes frequent additions to fill what he considers gaps in Euclid's reasoning, even interpolating whole propositions, as in the above example. On the whole, his edition can hardly be said to improve on the original, although it may well have fulfilled its purpose of being easier for his students to use.

Other works by Euclid of which Theon produced editions are the *Data* (a treatise on what elements of a geometrical figure must be given to determine it) and the *Optics*, both of which exist in Theonic and pre-Theonic versions. The first of these obviously was intended for more advanced students but shows the same general characteristics as the edition of the *Elements*, except that in it Theon is more inclined to abbreviate Euclid's exposition. The Theonic version of the *Optics*, on the other hand, is so different from the original, not only in its language (which is characteristic of the later *koine*) but also in the form of the proofs, that Heiberg conjectured that the text we have consists of Theon's lectures on the subject as taken down by one of his students. This view is supported by the introduction to the Theonic version, which is an exposition of the principles of optics, mostly in indirect speech, occasionally introduced by "he said" or the like. "He" is not identified in the text; but this part clearly has been taken down from a lecture, and it is a plausible guess that "he" is Theon. There is no direct evidence, however, that Theon was responsible for this version, although he is the most likely candidate.

The same may be said of a treatise on catoptrics (theory of visual reflection) that in the manuscripts is attributed to Euclid but must be judged spurious on stylistic grounds alone. Analysis of the contents shows that it is a late compilation containing a mixture of Euclidean and post-Euclidean optical theory. The style and nature of the treatise would be appropriate for Theon, but that does not prove his authorship. Both the *Optics* and the *Catoptrics* are elementary, and are on a far lower scientific level than Ptolemy's *Optics*, which was, however, neglected in later antiquity and has survived only through the Arabic tradition. If, then, it is correct to associate Theon with these "Euclidean" optical works, we have an example in yet another branch of mathematics of his pedagogical activity, directed toward beginning students.

Theon also produced the version in which Ptolemy's *Handy Tables* have come down to us, according to the superscriptions in the manuscripts. The only evidence we have for the original version is Ptolemy's own introduction giving instructions for their use. From this it appears that the changes introduced by Theon were slight, and confined mostly to the arrangement of the tables and updating the chronological list. No one, however, has yet investigated the problem thoroughly.

Among lost works attributed to Theon by the ancient biographical source is a "Treatise on the Small Astrolabe."[9] Arabic bibliographical works also attribute to him a work entitled "On Operation With the Astrolabe."[10] The term "small astrolabe" evidently is used to distinguish this instrument from the "armillary sphere" (which is always the meaning of ἀστρολάβον in the *Almagest*). Thus it must refer to the "astrolabe" in the medieval and modern sense, that is, an instrument used to solve problems in spherical astronomy by means of projection of the celestial sphere onto a plane. This interpretation is confirmed by the Arabic sources, which use *asṭurlāb* only in this sense.

No work on the astrolabe predating the sixth century survives, but we do have the treatise of John Philoponus (*fl.* 520) in Greek, and that of Severus Sebokht (written before 660) in Syriac. The latter draws on a previous treatise, the author of which he calls "the philosopher." The historian al-Yaʿqūbī, writing in Arabic about 875, lists the contents of a treatise on the astrolabe that he ascribes to Ptolemy.[11] Neugebauer has shown that Sebokht's treatise corresponds closely to that described by al-Yaʿqūbī. Since Sebokht distinguishes "the philosopher" from Ptolemy (whose tables he quotes by name), and since al-Yaʿqūbī attributes to Ptolemy works (such as "On the Armillary Sphere") that other Arabic bibliographical sources attribute to Theon,[12] Neugebauer concludes, plausibly, that Theon is the author of the astrolabe treatise described by al-Yaʿqūbī and used by Sebokht. It is most unlikely, however, that Theon invented the astrolabe. The essential mathematical theory (of mapping circles of the celestial sphere onto a plane by stereographic projection) is treated by Ptolemy in his *Planisphaerium*, and the instrument may well predate Ptolemy.

Other lost works attributed to Theon in the Greek biographical source are "On Omens [for weather?] and Examination of Birds and the Cry of Ravens," "On the Rising of the Dog Star," and "On the Rising of the Nile." Nothing is known of these; and some or all should perhaps be attributed to the grammarian Theon of the first century of the Christian era, as should certainly the commentary by "Theon" on Aratus' astronomical poem *Phaenomena*. A slight work on the composition of an astronomical ephemeris found in one manuscript of Theon's commentary on the *Handy Tables* and ascribed to Theon by Delambre[13] certainly belongs to a later period.

Theon was a competent mathematician for his time, but completely unoriginal. He typifies the scholastic of later antiquity who was content to expound recognized classics in his field without ever attempting to go beyond them. The parts of his works that are of most interest for the modern reader, apart from the occasional pieces of historical information, are the worked examples of computations in his commentaries. It is of no small interest to see how the Greeks carried out calculations using their form of the sexagesimal place-value system (Theon provided worked examples of extraction of a square root, as well as multiplication and division). The detailed calculation of the solar eclipse of 364 (which Theon demonstrated both according to the *Almagest* tables and according to the *Handy Tables*) is also most instructive.

For a man of such mediocrity Theon was uncommonly influential. As we have seen, it was his version of Euclid's *Elements* that gained most currency. It was in his edition that the *Handy Tables* passed to Islamic astronomers (among whom it went under his name), and thence (via al-Battānī's work and the Toledan Tables) to Latin Europe in the twelfth century. His commentaries on the *Almagest* and the *Handy Tables* continued to be studied in the Greek-speaking Eastern Empire, and are the basis of at least one Byzantine commentary, that of Stephen of Alexandria on the *Handy Tables*. The work on the astrolabe was probably the main, if not the sole, source of transmission of the theory of that instrument to Islamic astronomy, whence it came to medieval Europe.

One short passage in Theon's shorter commentary on the *Handy Tables* had a remarkable history. He states that "certain ancient astrologers" believed that the tropical and solstitial points had a vibrating back-and-forth motion over eight degrees of the ecliptic. Although not accepting this theory, he explains how to compute the resultant correction to be applied to the positions of the heavenly bodies.[14] According to Theon, the tropical points of "the astrologers" are eight degrees in advance of (to the east of) those of Ptolemy in 158 B.C., and move westward with respect to the latter at a rate of one degree in eighty years. (Thus they would coincide in 483, at which point they would begin to move eastward again.) There is perhaps one other trace of this theory in antiquity, but it was not until Theon's description reached the Islamic astronomers that it bore fruit.

When observational astronomy began to be seriously practiced, under the caliph al-Maʾmūn (early ninth century), it was soon realized that the rate of precession (motion of the tropical points with respect to the fixed stars) as determined by Ptolemy (one degree in one hundred years) was not valid, and that 1.5 degrees in one hundred years was closer to the truth. Rather than impute error to the admired Ptolemy, many preferred to believe that the rate of precession was not a constant, but varied cyclically; the idea undoubtedly came from this passage of Theon's, as is shown by the earliest reference we have, in which the astronomer Ḥabash al-Ḥāsib (*ca.* 850) is said to have introduced into one set of his astronomical tables "the back-and-forth motion of the ecliptic according to the opinion of Theon."[15] Soon afterward Thābit ibn Qurra (*ca.* 870) wrote a treatise expounding the theory and proposing a physical model to account for it. This was translated into Latin in the twelfth century under the title "De motu octave spere," and proved enormously influential in western Europe. The theory, usually known as "trepidation," was adopted by the makers of the Alfonsine Tables, and appears in various forms in the works of Peurbach, Johann Werner, and Copernicus. It was still seriously discussed in the late sixteenth century.

NOTES

1. Both in bk. 6 of his commentary on the *Almagest*, Basel ed., 332 and 319, respectively.
2. *Tables manuelles astronomiques*, N. Halma, ed., I, 77–87; examples are on 31 and 74. In the second passage the "90th" year of Diocletian was corrected by H. Usener in his *Kleine Schriften*, III, 22, n. 20, to "94th" on the basis of MS readings. The correction is confirmed by my computations. This passage, however, is probably an interpolation.
3. "Fasti Theonis Alexandrini," H. Usener, ed., 367–368, 381.
4. *Suda Lexicon*, Ada Adler, ed., II, 702.
5. *Commentaires . . . de Théon . . .*, A. Rome, ed., II, 317.
6. *Ibid.*, 318.
7. *Tables manuelles astronomiques*, I, 27.
8. *Commentaires . . . de Théon . . .*, A. Rome, ed., II, 492.
9. *Suda Lexicon*, loc. cit.
10. For instance, *Fihrist*, G. Flügel, ed., I, 268.
11. Translated by M. Klamroth in *Zeitschrift der Deutschen morgenländischen Gesellschaft*, **42** (1888), 23–25.
12. *Ibid.*, 20–23; compare *Fihrist*, loc. cit.
13. *Histoire de l'astronomie ancienne*, II, 635.
14. *Tables manuelles astronomiques*, I, 53.
15. Ibn al-Qifṭī, J. Lippert, ed., 170.

BIBLIOGRAPHY

I. Original Works. Bks. 1–4 of the commentary on the *Almagest* were edited by A. Rome as *Commentaires de Pappus et de Théon d'Alexandrie sur l'Almageste*, II and III (Vatican City, 1936–1943), the commentary by Pappus being vol. I (1931)—they are Studi e Testi, nos. 72, 106, and 54, respectively. For the remaining books one must still consult the text in the Greek *Almagest*, *Claudii Ptolemaei magnae constructionis . . . lib. xiii. Theonis Alexandrini in eosdem commentariorum lib. xi* (Basel, 1538). On the relationship of Theon's commentary to that by Pappus, see Rome, *op.*

cit., II, lxxxii–lxxxvi; on Hypatia's supposed revision of bk. 3, *ibid.*, III, cxvi–cxxi.

The longer commentary on the *Handy Tables* has never been printed, except for two short passages published by Usener on pp. 360 and 372–373 of his ed. of Theon's list of consuls, "Fasti Theonis Alexandrini," pp. 359–381 in T. Mommsen, ed., *Chronica minora saeculorum IV. V. VI. VII.* (Berlin, 1898), which is *Monumenta Germaniae historica, auctores antiquissimi*, **13**, pt. 3. I have consulted the longer commentary in MS Nuremberg, Stadtbibliothek Cent. Gr. V, 8, fols. 215r–237v. The shorter commentary is printed in the very bad ed. of the *Handy Tables* by N. Halma, *Tables manuelles astronomiques de Ptolémée et de Théon*, I (Paris, 1822), 27–105. Ptolemy's own intro. to the *Handy Tables* is published by J. L. Heiberg in *Claudii Ptolemaei Opera quae exstant omnia*, II, *Opera astronomica minora* (Leipzig, 1907), 159–185.

On Theon's ed. of Euclid's *Elements*, see J. L. Heiberg, *Litterargeschichtliche Studien uber Euklid* (Leipzig, 1882), 174–180; and esp. Heiberg's prolegomena to his critical ed. of the *Elements*, *Euclidis Opera omnia*, V (Leipzig, 1888), li–lxxvi; for the *Data* see H. Menge, *ibid.*, VI (*Euclidis Data cum commentario Marini*), xxxii–xlix; for the *Optics*, Heiberg, *Litterargeschichtliche Studien*, 138–148; for the *Catoptrics, ibid.*, 148–153, and *Euclidis Opera omnia*, VII (*Optica et Catoptrica*), xlix–l.

II. Secondary Literature. A good account is Konrat Ziegler, "Theon 15," in Pauly-Wissowa, *Real-Encyclopädie der classischen Altertumswissenschaft*, 2nd ser., X, cols. 2075–2080. The evidence for Theon's period of activity was collected by H. Usener, "Vergessenes," in his *Kleine Schriften*, III (Leipzig–Berlin, 1914), 21–23. The ancient biographical source is *Suda Lexicon*, Ada Adler, ed., II (Leipzig, 1931), 702, ll. 10–16. On Hypatia, see Socrates Scholasticus, *Historia ecclesiastica*, bk. 7, ch. 15, in J.-P. Migne, ed., *Patrologiae cursus completus*, series Graeca, LXVII, 767–770.

On the sources of the *Catoptrics* see A. Lejeune, "Recherches sur la catoptrique grecque," in *Mémoires de l'Académie royale de Belgique, Classe des lettres*, **52**, no. 2 (1957), 112–151. On Theon and the astrolabe see O. Neugebauer, "The Early History of the Astrolabe," in *Isis*, **40** (1949), 240–256. The treatise of Philoponus was published by H. H. Hase as "Joannis Alexandrini de usu astrolabii . . . libellus," in *Rheinisches Museum für Philologie*, **6** (1839), 127–171; that by Severus Sebokht by F. Nau, "Le traité sur l'astrolabe plan de Sévère Sabokht," in *Journal asiatique*, 9th ser., **13** (1899), 56–101, 238–303.

The passages in al-Yaʿqūbī's work referring to the astrolabe and armillary sphere were translated by M. Klamroth as "Ueber die Auszüge aus griechischen Schriftstellern bei al-Jaʿqûbî IV," in *Zeitschrift der Deutschen morgenländischen Gesellschaft*, **42** (1888), 1–44. What purports to be the Arabic translation of the work on the armillary sphere is extant in the MS Bombay, Mollā Fīrūz 86. See Fuat Sezgin, *Geschichte des* *arabischen Schrifttums,* V (Leiden, 1974), 401. Bibliographical works in Arabic mentioning Theon include Ibn al-Nadīm, *Kitāb al-Fihrist,* G. Flügel, ed., I (Leipzig, 1871), 268; and Ibn al-Qiftī, *Ta'rīkh al-ḥukamā',* J. Lippert, ed. (Leipzig, 1903), 108. Ptolemy's *Planisphaerium,* which exists only in the Arabic tradition, is printed (in the medieval Latin trans. from the Arabic) in his *Opera astronomica minora,* 227–259.

The work on the construction of an ephemeris is in Halma, *op. cit.,* III, 38–42, and described by J.-B. J. Delambre in his *Histoire de l'astronomie ancienne,* II (Paris, 1817), 635–638. Examples of division and extraction of a square root in the sexagesimal system, taken from Theon's commentary on the *Almagest,* are reproduced by T. L. Heath in his *A History of Greek Mathematics,* I (Oxford, 1921), 58–62. On Theon's calculation of the solar eclipse of 364 see A. Rome, "The Calculation of an Eclipse of the Sun According to Theon of Alexandria," in *Proceedings of the International Congress of Mathematicians, Cambridge, Mass., 1950,* I (Providence, R.I., 1952), 209–219. On Stephen of Alexandria's commentary on the *Handy Tables,* see H. Usener, "De Stephano Alexandrino," in his *Kleine Schriften,* III, 247–322.

For a possible use in a fourth-century papyrus of the "trepidation" described by Theon, see J. J. Burckhardt, "Zwei griechische Ephemeriden," in *Osiris,* 13 (1958), 79–92. The reference to Ḥabash's use of trepidation is in Ibn al-Qiftī, *op. cit.,* 170. The Latin text of Thābit's *De motu octave spere* has been printed many times; it is best consulted in J. M. Millás Vallicrosa, *Estudios sobre Azarquiel* (Madrid–Granada, 1943–1950), 496–509, trans. and commentary by O. Neugebauer, "Thabit ben Qurra 'On the Solar Year' and 'On the Motion of the Eighth Sphere,'" in *Proceedings of the American Philosophical Society,* **106** (1962), 264–299. The best discussion of the history of the theory of trepidation in the Latin West is Jerzy Dobrzycki, "Teoria precesji w astronomii średniowiecznej" ("The Theory of Precession in Medieval Astronomy"), with Russian and English summaries, in *Studia i materiały z dziejów nauki polskiej,* ser. C, **11** (1965), 3–47. See also J. L. E. Dreyer, *History of the Planetary Systems From Thales to Kepler* (Cambridge, 1906), index under "Trepidation."

G. J. TOOMER

THEON OF SMYRNA (*fl.* early second century A.D.)

Theon is known chiefly for his handbook, usually called *Expositio rerum mathematicarum ad legendum Platonem utilium.* He may well have been the person called "the old Theon" by Theon of Alexandria in his commentary on the *Almagest.* Ptolemy referred to "Theon the mathematician," who is almost certainly the Theon discussed here,

and ascribed to him observations of the planets Venus and Mercury made in 127, 129, 130, and 132 (*Almagest* 9.9, 10.1, 10.2). The latest writers named by Theon were Thrasyllus, who was active under Tiberius, and Adrastus, the Peripatetic and Aristotelian scholar, who flourished not earlier than A.D. 100. A contemporary bust of Theon from Smyrna has an inscription calling him *Platonikos*: he was thus also known as a philosopher, and his philosophical interests are evident in the *Expositio.*

The treatise is valuable for its wide range of citation from earlier sources. There is little evidence of mathematical originality. Despite the title, the book has little to offer the specialist student of Plato's mathematics. It is, rather, a handbook for philosophy students, written to illustrate how arithmetic, geometry, stereometry, music, and astronomy are interrelated. Geometry and stereometry are cursorily treated, however, perhaps because Theon assumed his readers to be adequately acquainted with them. A promise to provide a lengthy treatment of the harmony of the cosmos (p. 17, l. 24, Hiller edition) is not kept in the extant manuscripts; if that part of the treatise was ever written, it may have been lost early.

The arithmetical section treats the types of numbers in the Pythagorean manner; Theon dealt, for example, with primes, geometrical numbers (such as squares), "side" and "diameter" numbers, and progressions.

Music is divided into three kinds: instrumental, musical intervals expressed numerically (theoretical music), and the harmony of the universe. Theon stated clearly that he is not claiming to have discovered any musical principles himself; his aim is to expand the findings of his predecessors. He therefore quoted amply from his authorities—Thrasyllus, Adrastus, Aristoxenus, Hippasus, Eudoxus, and, of course, Plato. In the account of proportions and ratios the discussion concerns the treatment in Eratosthenes' *Platonikos* of the difference between interval and ratio ($\delta\iota\acute{\alpha}\sigma\tau\eta\mu\alpha$ and $\lambda\acute{o}\gamma o\varsigma$). Eratosthenes is also followed in the exposition of the different kinds of means. Some of the musical part descends into mere number mysticism; it is perhaps the least satisfactory feature of the work. A typical remark (p. 106, Hiller ed.) is that "the decad determines number in all respects. It embraces nature entire within itself, even and odd, moving and unmoved, good and bad."

In contrast, the astronomical section, which also depends much on Adrastus, is of great merit. The earth is a sphere; mountains are minute when compared with the earth, which lies at the center of the universe. The several circles of the heavens are explained, as are the assumed deviations in latitude of the sun, moon, and planets. The various views concerning the order of the heavenly bodies are noted; those of the (neo)Pythagoreans are contrasted with the systems of Eratosthenes and "the mathematicians." Some interesting hexameter verses quoted (pp. 138–140, Hiller ed.) on this topic are said to be by Alexander of Aetolia, but are perhaps by Alexander of Ephesus, a contemporary of Cicero; to the other planets, the earth, the sun, the moon, and the sphere of the fixed stars, Alexander gives a tone, so that all are set in an octave by arrangement of the intervals. Eratosthenes did not count the stationary earth, so in his verses he gave a note each to all seven moving bodies and an eighth to the sphere of the fixed stars. This is as close as Theon came to delivering the promised exposition of the harmony of the cosmos.

Theon explained the progressions, stations, and retrogradations of the planets. He described the eccentric and epicyclic hypotheses, and their equivalence. He seemed to consider Hipparchus as the inventor of the epicyclic hypothesis (p. 188, l. 16, Hiller ed.) that "Hipparchos praised as his own"; but there is a misunderstanding, because Apollonius clearly understood the principle of the epicycle before Hipparchus. Apollonius is not among the authorities cited by Theon.

Estimates of the greatest arcs of Mercury and Venus from the sun are given as 20° and 50° (p. 187, ll. 10–13, Hiller ed.). After an extensive account of the systems of rotating spheres worked out by Eudoxus, Callippus and Aristotle (pp. 178 ff., Hiller ed.), Theon turned to conjunctions, transits, occultations, eclipses, and the axis through the poles and the center of the zodiac.

Historically the most valuable part of the concluding pages is the brief fragment from Eudemus on pre-Socratic astronomy, which is full of problems. For example, the extant archetype manuscript here states that according to Anaximander, the earth is "on high" ($\mu\epsilon\tau\epsilon\omega\rho\sigma$) and "moves" ($\kappa\iota\nu\epsilon\hat{\iota}\tau\alpha\iota$) about the center of the cosmos. Montucla's emendation of $\kappa\iota\nu\epsilon\hat{\iota}\tau\alpha\iota$ to $\kappa\epsilon\hat{\iota}\tau\alpha\iota$ ("rests") (see p. 198, l. 19, Hiller ed.) is attractive but by no means certain, since we do not know what Eudemus wrote, whatever Anaximander's view of the matter may have been. Anaximenes, not Anaxagoras, is here said to have declared that the moon "has her light from the sun."

Other works by Theon are lost. He himself referred to a commentary on Plato's *Republic* (*Expositio* p. 146, l. 4, Hiller ed.). Ibn al-Nadīm's *Fihrist* mentioned a treatise by him on the titles of Plato's writings and the order in which they should be read. He wrote on the ancestry of Plato, but not certainly in a separate treatise; the study may have formed part of the *Republic* commentary (see Hiller ed., p. 146, on Proclus, *On Timaeus*, p. 26A).

BIBLIOGRAPHY

The text of the *Expositio* depends almost entirely on two MSS in Venice: the number theory and the music are in Venet. Marc. 307 (11th–2th cent.), and the astronomy in Venet. Marc. 303 (13th–14th cent.). The first part (pp. 1–119, Hiller ed.) was edited by Ismael Boulliau (Paris, 1644); the other (pp. 120–205, Hiller ed.) by T. H. Martin (Paris, 1849; repr. Groningen, 1971). Both were edited together by E. Hiller in the Teubner version (Leipzig, 1878).

For further discussion, see K. von Fritz, in Pauly-Wissowa, *Real-Encyclopädie der classischen Altertumswissenschaft*, 2nd ser., X (1934), 2067–2075, *s.v.* Theon (14), with bibliography; and T. L. Heath, *A History of Greek Mathematics*, II (Oxford, 1921), 238–244. On the hexameter verses, see E. Hiller, in *Rheinisches Museum für Philologie*, **26** (1871), 586–587; and A. Meineke, *Analecta Alexandrina* (Berlin, 1843; repr. Hildesheim, 1964), 372–374.

G. L. HUXLEY

THEUDIUS OF MAGNESIA (*fl.* fourth century B.C.)

Theudius, an early member of the Academy, is known only from a passage in Proclus' commentary on Euclid's *Elements* (*In primum Euclidis Elementorum librum commentarii*, G. Friedlein, ed. [Leipzig, 1883; repr. 1967], I, pp. 67–68). After mentioning Leo (who made an improved collection of the elements of geometry and invented *diorismi*, means of determining when a problem is soluble and when not) and Eudoxus, Proclus says:

> Amyclas [or, better, Amyntas] of Heraclea, one of Plato's friends, Menaechmus, a pupil of Eudoxus who had also studied with Plato, and Dinostratus his brother, made the whole of geometry still more perfect. Theudius the Magnesian had a reputation for excellence in mathematics and in the rest of philosophy; for he ordered . . . the elements carefully and made many of the limiting [or partial] theorems more general.

Proclus then states that another geometer, Athenaeus of Cyzicus, lived at about the same time.

"These men associated . . . in the Academy and undertook investigations jointly." Next are mentioned Hermotimus of Colophon, who added to the *Elements*, and Philippus of Medma (or Opus), who is said to have revised and published Plato's *Laws*. All these statements by Proclus may well have originated with an excellent authority, the historian of mathematics Eudemus of Rhodes. Theudius may be placed between Eudoxus and Philippus; that is, he was a contemporary of Aristotle. Indeed, T. L. Heath made the reasonable suggestion that the propositions in elementary geometry that are quoted by Aristotle were taken from Theudius' *Elements*. We have, however, no means of knowing which propositions and theorems were his discoveries; nor are we told which Magnesia was his home.

BIBLIOGRAPHY

See K. von Fritz, in Pauly-Wissowa, *Real-Encyclopädie der classischen Altertumswissenschaft*, XI, pt. 2 (1936), 244–246; T. L. Heath, *A History of Greek Mathematics*, I (Oxford, 1921), 319–321; and *The Thirteen Books of Euclid's Elements* (repr. New York, 1956), 116–117; Glenn R. Morrow, *Proclus: A Commentary on the First Book of Euclid's Elements* (Princeton, 1970), 56, n. 45; and F. Wehrli, *Die Schule des Aristoteles*, VII *Eudemos von Rhodos* (Basel, 1955).

G. L. HUXLEY

THIELE, THORVALD NICOLAI (*b.* Copenhagen, Denmark, 24 December 1838; *d.* Copenhagen, 26 September 1910)

Thiele was the son of Just Mathias Thiele, a well-known Danish folklorist and art historian. While studying at the University of Copenhagen, young Thiele was awarded a gold medal for a paper on the geometry of the apparent course of a solar eclipse. In 1866 he took his doctorate, and from 1875 to 1906 he was professor of astronomy at the university and director of the university observatory.

Thiele's scientific work has been characterized by C. Burrau as "a treatment of numerical values derived from observations." If the word "observation" is taken in its widest sense, and if the word "treatment" is taken to mean a penetrating and original mathematical analysis, then this description must be regarded as apt. The topic of Thiele's dissertation was the determination of the orbit of the visual double star γ Virginis. He developed a new method of orbit determination, now known as the Thiele-Innes method (with some of the formulas later arranged for mechanical computation by Robert Innes). Thiele discussed the systematic errors in the observational material for this star and later for other double stars, using in particular the series of observations published in 1878–1879 by Otto W. Struve.

For many years Thiele continued and intensified his studies of the systematic and accidental errors of observation, thus approaching the field of actuarial mathematics. Indeed, for nearly forty years he was the manager of a life insurance company; in this work he satisfied his interest in the practical use of mathematics and numerical computations. In his scientific work, Thiele tried to discover, by means of numerical calculations, the laws for the distribution of the spectral lines of certain elements; and he was an early pioneer in the numerical search for solutions to the three-body problem, developing the Thiele (or Thiele-Burrau) transformation for this purpose.

The mathematical background of his work is given in his books *Theory of Observations* (1903) and *Interpolationsrechnung* (1909). Because of an eye disease, Thiele was unable to do any practical astronomical observation during much of his career, but he took an early part in the development of photography for astronomical purposes.

BIBLIOGRAPHY

I. ORIGINAL WORKS. Thiele's books include *Undersøgelse af Omløbsbevaegelsen i Dobbeltstjernesystemet Gamma Virginis* (Copenhagen, 1866); *Almindelig Iagttagelseslaere: Sandsynlighedsregning og mindste Kvadraters Methode* (Copenhagen, 1889); *Elementaer Iagttagelseslaere* (Copenhagen, 1897); *Theory of Observations* (London, 1903); and *Interpolationsrechnung* (Leipzig, 1909).

His articles include "Castor, calcul du mouvement relatif et critique des observations de cette étoile double," in *Festskrift, Copenhagen University* (1879); review and discussion of Otto W. Struve's measurements of double stars, in *Vierteljahrsschrift der Astronomischen Gesellschaft*, **15** (1880), 314–348; "Note on the Application of Photography to the Micrometric Measurements of Stars," in *Washington Observations for 1885*, appendix I (1889), 58–67; "Om Nutidens Reform af den iagttagende Astronomie," in *Festskrift, Copenhagen University* (1893); "On the Law of Spectral Series," in *Astrophysical Journal*, **6** (1897), 65–76; "Resolution into Series of the Third Band of the Carbon Band Spectrum," *ibid.*, **8** (1898), 1–27; "Tal og Symboler som Bestemmelser mellem Numeraler," in *Festskrift, Copenhagen University* (1901).

Papers are in *Tidsskrift for Matematik* (Copenhagen, 1859–1903); *Royal Danish Academy*, Oversigter and Skrifter (Copenhagen, 1880–1908); and in *Astronomische Nachrichten*, **48–138** (1858–1895). See also Poggendorff, IV, 1488–1489; V, 1250.

II. SECONDARY LITERATURE. Articles on Thiele are in *Dansk Biografisk Leksikon*, XXIII (1942), 503–506; and C. Burrau, in *Vierteljahrsschrift der Astronomischen Gesellschaft*, **46** (1911), 208–210; J. P. Gram, in *Nyt Tidsskrift for Mathematik*, **21B** (1910), 73–78; N. E. Nørlund, in *Fysisk Tidsskrift*, **9** (1910), 1–7; J. P. Gram, "Professor Thiele som Aktuar," in *Dansk Forsikringsaarbog*, **7** (1910), 26–37.

AXEL V. NIELSEN

THOMAZ, ALVARO (also known as **Alvaro Tómas** or **Alvarus Thomas**) (*b.* Lisbon, second half of the fifteenth century; place and date of death unknown)

Biographical data on Thomaz are lacking, save that he was regent of the Collège de Coqueret at Paris on 11 February 1509, as indicated in the colophon of his principal work, and that he is mentioned in the archives of the University of Paris as a master of arts at the same college in 1513. Thomaz is noteworthy for his *Liber de triplici motu proportionibus annexis . . . philosophicas Suiseth calculationes ex parte declarans* ("Book on the Three [Kinds of] Movement, With Ratios Added, Explaining in Part Swineshead's Philosophical [i.e., Physical] Calculations"), printed at Paris in 1509. This work shows Thomaz to be a mathematician and physicist of considerable ability who understood and organized the teachings of fourteenth-century English calculators and Parisian terminists, such as Oresme, making them available to a wide audience of European scholars in the sixteenth century.

Thomaz' work is divided into three parts, the first and second of which are compact expositions of ratios and proportions respectively, while the third is a lengthy application to problems concerning motion. This last part treats, in turn, local motion, augmentation, and alteration. Although designed as a guide to the thought of Richard Swineshead, Thomaz' treatise is not patterned after Swineshead's *Liber calculationum* ("Book of Calculations"), but follows instead an ordering suggested jointly by Thomas Bradwardine's *Tractatus de proportionibus* ("Treatise on Ratios") and by William Heytesbury's *Tractatus de tribus praedicamentis* ("Treatise on the Three Categories").

The first two parts seem to have been inspired by the inferior work of a certain Bassanus Politus, *Tractatus proportionum introductorius ad calculationes Suisset* ("Treatise on Ratios, an Introduction to Swineshead's Calculations"), printed in Venice in 1505, a work that Thomaz effectively castigated as worthless.

Thomaz' citation of authorities was extensive. His mathematics was drawn mainly from Nicomachus, Boethius, Johannes Campanus, and Jordanus de Nemore, while for Euclid he cited "the new translation of Bartholomeus Zambertus." Among the Schoolmen he referred to Thomas Aquinas (and his commentator, Capreolus), Robert Holkot, Duns Scotus, Albert of Saxony, Marsilius of Inghen, Gregory of Rimini, and John Maior. He knew too of the work of Paul of Venice, James of Forli, Cajetan of Thiene, John de Casali, Andrew de Novo Castro, Peter of Mantua, and a writer whom he identified as the Conciliator (Pietro d'Abano). Above all he was conversant with the complex details of Bradwardine's, Heytesbury's, and Swineshead's writings, and also with the little-understood *De proportionibus proportionum* ("On the Ratios of Ratios") of Oresme. Edward Grant states in his edition of the latter work: "Alvarus is the only author known to me who shows an extensive acquaintance with, and understanding of, Oresme's treatise" (p. 71).

Thomaz manifested some originality and considerable independence of judgment, as witness his rejection and reformulation of many of Swineshead's and Oresme's propositions. His treatment of falling bodies was highly imaginative in terms of the types of motive forces and resistive media discussed, but unfortunately was diffuse and inconclusive; contrary to what some scholars have suggested, it contains no explicit adumbration of Galileo's law of uniform acceleration. Thomaz showed facility in the summation of series, generally indicating when they converge and when they do not and, in cases where he cannot determine a precise value, providing limits between which this value must lie.

The influence of Thomaz' work is difficult to assess. Through his colleague at Coqueret, Juan de Celaya, he seems to have assisted in the formation of Celaya's later disciple, Domingo de Soto, who was the first to apply unequivocally the Mertonian "mean-speed theorem" to the case of falling bodies. Thomaz' treatise was cited by many Spaniards, favorably by the Salamancan masters Pedro Margallo and Pedro de Espinosa and by the Dominican Diego de Astudillo, and unfavorably by the Augustinian Alonso de la Veracruz, who blamed Thomaz' "calculatory sophisms" for much wasted time (and midnight oil) on the part of students in arts. At Paris, however, there can be little doubt that Thomaz was the calculator par excellence at the beginning of the sixteenth century, and the principal stimulus for the revival of interest there in the Mertonian approach to mathematical physics.

BIBLIOGRAPHY

I. ORIGINAL WORK. Thomaz' *Liber de triplici motu . . .*, is unavailable in translation; a copy of the original is in the library of the University of Michigan.

II. SECONDARY LITERATURE. For discussions of Thomaz and his work, see Pierre Duhem, *Études sur Léonard de Vinci*, III (Paris, 1913), 531–555, 557, 561; J. Rey Pastor, *Los matemáticos españoles del siglo XVI*, Biblioteca scientia no. 2 (Toledo, 1926), 82–89; Edward Grant, ed. and trans., *Nicole Oresme: De proportionibus proportionum and Ad pauca respicientes* (Madison, 1966), index; and William A. Wallace, "The 'Calculatores' in Early Sixteenth-Century Physics," in *British Journal for the History of Science*, 4 (1969), 221–232.

WILLIAM A. WALLACE, O.P.

THOMPSON, D'ARCY WENTWORTH (*b.* Edinburgh, Scotland, 2 May 1860; *d.* St. Andrews, Scotland, 21 June 1948)

Thompson was the son of D'Arcy Wentworth Thompson, classical master at the Edinburgh Academy and, later, professor of classics at Queen's College, Galway. His mother was Fanny Gamgee, daughter of Joseph Gamgee, a veterinary surgeon. Her brother was Arthur Gamgee, "the first biochemist." Thompson was educated at the Edinburgh Academy and the University of Edinburgh (1877–1880), where he studied anatomy under Turner, chemistry under Crum Brown, and zoology under Wyville Thomson, recently returned from the *Challenger* expedition. He then studied at Trinity College, Cambridge (1880–1883), where he was subsizar and later scholar, and where he read zoology under Francis M. Balfour and physiology under Michael Foster. While there he published his first work, a translation of H. Müller's *Fertilisation of Flowers*, for which Charles Darwin wrote the preface. He gained first-class honors in parts I and II of the natural sciences tripos and for a year taught physiology under Foster. In 1884 Thompson was elected professor of biology at University College, Dundee, and in 1917 was transferred to the chair of natural history at St. Andrews.

Thompson's first marine investigation, that of the fur-seal fisheries, took place in 1896, when he was sent by the British government to the Bering Sea. After representing Great Britain at Washington, D.C., at the Anglo-American commission of inquiry into the Bering Sea seal fishery in 1897, Thompson was made Companion of the Order of the Bath in 1898, in recognition of the success of his mission. A foundation member of the Conseil Permanent International pour l'Exploration de la Mer, he served on the Council from 1902 to 1947, was chairman of the Statistical Committee, and editor of the *Bulletin statistique* (1902–1947).

In 1901 Thompson married Maureen Drury; they had three daughters. In 1916 he was elected fellow of the Royal Society, in 1928 president of the Classical Association (of England and Wales), from 1934–1939 president of the Royal Society of Edinburgh, and in 1936 president of the Scottish Classical Association. He was awarded a knighthood during the coronation honors in 1937.

Thompson did not fit into any particular category; he was equally a scholar, scientist, naturalist, classicist, mathematician, and philosopher. Inheriting a love of the classics from his father and brought up by his scientific grandfather, he straddled two worlds and dominated both.

Thompson's paper "On the Shapes of Eggs and the Causes Which Determine Them," published in *Nature*, 1908, shows the direction in which his thought was taking him. In his 1911 presidential address to section D of the British Association, "Magnalia Naturae; or the Greater Problems of Biology," he discussed, for the first time, what he called "the exploration of the borderline of morphology and physics." This was preparatory to the 1917 *On Growth and Form*, his great contribution to scientific literature. In this work Thompson departed from contemporary zoology, which was occupied with orthodox questions of comparative anatomy and evolution, and treated morphological problems by mathematics. The theme was original, unorthodox, and revolutionary. The chapter "On the Comparison of Related Forms" is a demonstration of the orderly deformation of related organic forms mapped out in accordance with Descartes's method of coordinates. The diagrams of transformation have contributed to other work on problems of growth and have influenced research in embryology, taxonomy, paleontology, and ecology.

Thompson initiated no school of research and was followed by no band of disciples. But the indirect influence of *On Growth and Form* is so wide and so important that it is hard to calculate. Scientists, engineers, architects, painters, and poets have acknowledged their indebtedness to this essay that ranges over a wide field of scientific discovery, thought, and history.

BIBLIOGRAPHY

I. ORIGINAL WORKS. For a list of the published writings of D'Arcy Wentworth Thompson, see *Essays on Growth and Form* (cited below), 386–400.

Major works include H. Müller, *The Fertilisation of Flowers*, Thompson, trans. and ed., with a preface by Charles Darwin (London, 1893); *A Bibliography of Protozoa, Sponges, Coelenterata, and Worms for the Years 1861–1883* (Cambridge, 1885); "John Ray," in *Encyclopaedia Britannica*, 9th ed., XX (1886); *A Glossary of Greek Birds* (Oxford, 1895); "On the Shapes of Eggs, and the Causes Which Determine Them," in *Nature*, **78** (1908), 111–113; Aristotle, *Historia animalium*, Thompson, trans. and ed. (Oxford, 1910); "Magnalia Naturae; or the Greater Problems of Biology," in *Nature*, **87** (1911), 325–328; reprinted in *Smithsonian Institution Annual Report* (1911); *On Aristotle as a Biologist*, with an introduction on Herbert Spencer (Oxford, 1911); "Morphology and Mathematics," in *Transactions of the Royal Society of Edinburgh*, **50** (1915), 857–895; *On Growth and Form* (Cambridge, 1917); "Natural Science: Aristotle," in *The Legacy of Greece*, R. W. Livingstone, ed. (Oxford, 1921); *Science and the Classics* (Oxford, 1940); and *A Glossary of Greek Fishes* (Oxford, 1947).

II. SECONDARY LITERATURE. Important writings on Thompson and his works include Ruth D'Arcy Thompson, *D'Arcy Wentworth Thompson, The Scholar Naturalist, 1860–1948*, with a postscript by P. B. Medawar, "D'Arcy Thompson and Growth and Form" (Oxford, 1958); W. Le Gros Clark and P. B. Medawar, eds., *Essays on Growth and Form* (Oxford, 1945); and Ruth D'Arcy Thompson, *The Remarkable Gamgees* (Edinburgh, 1974).

Brief discussions and obituaries include Clifford Dobell, "D'Arcy Wentworth Thompson," in *Obituary Notices of Fellows of the Royal Society*, **6** (1949), 599–617; W. T. Calman, "Sir D'Arcy Thompson, C.B., LL.D., F.R.S.," in *Royal Society of Edinburgh Year Book* (1946–1948), 44–48; Douglas Young, "Sir D'Arcy Thompson as Classical Scholar," *ibid.*; R. S. Clark, "D'Arcy Wentworth Thompson," in *Journal du Conseil. Conseil permanent international pour l'exploration de la mer*, **16**, no. 1 (1949), 9–13; G. E. Hutchinson, "In Memoriam, D'Arcy Wentworth Thompson," in *American Scientist*, **36** (1948), 577; Lancelot Law Whyte, ed., *Aspects of Form* (London, 1951; 2nd ed., 1968);

S. Brody, *Bioenergetics and Growth* (New York, 1945); J. S. Huxley, *Problems of Relative Growth* (London, 1932); and Jack Burnham, *Beyond Modern Sculpture* (Harmondsworth, Middlesex, 1968).

RUTH D'ARCY THOMPSON

THUE, AXEL (*b.* Tönsberg, Norway, 19 February 1863; *d.* Oslo, Norway, 7 March 1922)

Thue enrolled at Oslo University in 1883 and became a candidate for the doctorate in 1889. From 1891 to 1894 he held a university scholarship in mathematics, and he was a professor of applied mathematics at Oslo from 1903 to 1922.

During 1890–1891 Thue studied at Leipzig under Sophus Lie, but his works do not reveal Lie's influence, probably because of Thue's inability to follow anyone else's line of thought. In 1909 he published his famous article "Über Annäherungswerte algebraischer Zahlen" in Crelle's *Journal*. In 1920 C. L. Siegel found a more precise expression for the approximation of algebraic numbers and K. F. Roth discovered the best possible equation in 1958. Nevertheless, Thue was able to draw a far-reaching conclusion in number theory. He showed that an equation like $y^3 - 2x^3 = 1$ cannot possibly be satisfied by an indefinite number of pairs of numbers x, y, when x and y must be a whole number. Generally formulated, the left side of the equation can be an irreducible homogeneous polynomial in x and y of a degree higher than 2, and the right side can be any whole number. Thue's theorem was characterized by Edmund Landau (1922) as "the most important discovery in elementary number theory that I know."

During 1906–1912 Thue published many articles on series, in one of which he said: "For the development of the logical sciences it will be important to find wide fields for the speculative treatment of difficult problems, without regard to eventual applications." His "Über die gegenseitige Lage gleicher Teile gewisser Zeichenreihen" was characterized as a basic work by G. A. Hedlund (1967).

Thue's most important work in applied mathematics was "De virtuelle hastigheters princip" ("The Principle of Virtual Velocity"), an original statement that has no parallel in the literature. One of the paradoxes Thue liked to state was "The further removed from usefulness or practical application, the more important."

BIBLIOGRAPHY

I. ORIGINAL WORKS. A list of 47 articles (1884–1920) is in *Norsk matematisk tidsskrift*, **4** (1922), 46–49. They include "Über Annäherungswerte algebraischer Zahlen," in *Journal für die reine und angewandte Mathematik*, **135** (1909), 284–305; "Eine Eigenschaft der Zahlen der Fermatschen Gleichung," in *Videnskabsselskabets skrifter* (Oslo) (1911), 1–21; and "De virtuelle hastigheters princip," in *Aars Voss'skoles festskrift* (Oslo, 1913), 194–213. *Selected Mathematical Papers of Axel Thue* (Oslo,   ), with an introduction by Carl Ludwig Siegel, is in press.

II. SECONDARY LITERATURE. There are biographies by C. Størmer, V. Bjerknes, and others in *Norsk matematisk tidsskrift*, **4** (1922), 33–46, with portrait. Viggo Brun and Trygve Nagell published a list of his posthumous works in *Videnskabsselskabets skrifter* (Oslo) (1923), 1–15. Also see G. A. Hedlund, "Remarks on the Work of Axel Thue on Sequences," in *Nordisk matematisk tidsskrift* (1967), 148–150.

VIGGO BRUN

THUNBERG, CARL PETER (*b.* Jönköping, Sweden, 11 November 1743; *d.* Tunaberg, near Uppsala, Sweden, 8 August 1828)

After studying at Jönköping, Thunberg entered Uppsala University in 1761, where he soon came under the influence of Linnaeus. His dissertation for the medical degree, *De ischiade* (1770), was not botanical and Linnaeus did not preside over the disputation; but Thunberg's passion was, nevertheless, natural history and especially botany, and Linnaeus soon considered him a protégé. In order to complete his medical education, Thunberg went to Paris immediately after the disputation, the trip being made possible by a scholarship. Before reaching France he stayed for a while in Holland, where a letter of recommendation from Linnaeus opened the house of Jan and Nikolaus Laurens Burman to him; both were good botanists, and the father was an old friend of Linnaeus.

In Paris, Thunberg received an extraordinary offer: an invitation to follow a Dutch merchant ship to Japan, which was closed to all European nations except Holland. The Burmans had good connections with the rich bourgeoisie of Holland, among whom the enthusiasm for gardening was very great. Thunberg was expected to collect as many Japanese garden plants as possible for his employers. He was, of course, free to make his own purely botanical collections as well, a situation that pleased Linnaeus, with whom Thunberg maintained close correspondence during the voyage. In order to enter Japan, he had to behave in every respect like a good Dutchman. He learned Dutch by stopping off in South Africa, in Cape Colony, where he remained from April 1772 to March 1775, thus fortunately combining language studies with botanical excursions.

There had been very little true botanical investigation of the Cape Colony; during his stay Thunberg made three voyages into the interior, collecting and describing more than three thousand plants, of which about one thousand were new to science. On two trips he was accompanied by the gardener and plant collector Francis Masson, who had been sent to the Cape Colony by Kew Gardens in London. At this time Thunberg began describing species and revising genera from his collections, publishing his papers in the transactions of several Swedish and foreign academies.

In March 1775 Thunberg sailed on a Dutch ship to Batavia. From Java he continued on another Dutch vessel to the island of Deshima in Nagasaki harbor, the only Japanese port open to European trade. For a while Thunberg was able to make short excursions near the town, but bureaucratic difficulties soon curtailed even these few opportunities to collect Japanese plants. A journey to Tokyo with the Dutch ambassador did little to improve the situation. Thunberg nevertheless became the first Western scientist to investigate Japan botanically through the aid of the young Japanese interpreters employed by the traders. Some of them were physicians, eager to learn modern European medicine from Thunberg, who exchanged his knowledge for specimens of Japanese plants. He left the country in December 1776 with a rich collection for further analysis. On his way home he visited Java, Ceylon, and the Cape Colony. Having satisfied his Dutch employers, he went to London, its herbariums and collections being the most important at that time.

Thunberg reached Sweden in 1779 and was appointed botanical demonstrator at Uppsala University. Linnaeus had been succeeded by his son, and it soon became clear that Thunberg and young Linnaeus could not work well together. Although Thunberg was a demonstrator, Linnaeus did not allow him to enter the botanical garden. In 1784 Thunberg succeeded to the professorship of botany (in the Faculty of Medicine), a post he held until his death. He lived quietly on a little estate, Tunaberg, just outside Uppsala, traveling to his daily work in a strange, uncomfortable carriage, well-known among the students as "the rattlesnake." The major event during this long academic period was the transfer of the botanical garden from a low and often flooded region of the town to the much more suitable park of the royal castle, where it is still situated. Most of Thunberg's time as professor was occupied by writing about his extensive collections.

Thunberg's first major work after returning to Sweden was *Flora japonica* (1784), a fundamental account of the floristics and systematics of the vegetation of Japan that describes twenty-one new genera and several hundred new species. His only predecessor of any importance was Engelbert Kaempfer, who traveled in the Far East at the end of the seventeenth century and whose collections Thunberg studied in the British Museum during his visit to London. The vast and important material from the Cape Colony occupied Thunberg for the rest of his life. A preliminary work was *Prodromus plantarum capensium* (1794–1800), a summary of his findings. Much more detailed and important was *Flora capensis* (1807–1823), completed with the help of the German botanist J. A. Schultes. Among his many shorter works are monographs on *Protea, Oxalis, Ixia,* and *Gladiolus.*

Thunberg was exclusively a descriptive botanist who closely followed Linnaeus, using his methods and his already somewhat outmoded sexual system. He modified the latter slightly, reducing its twenty-four classes to twenty by excluding Gynandria, Monoecia, Dioecia, and Polygamia and distributing their members among the other classes. The aim of his reductions, however, seems to have been more practical than theoretical, the plants of the omitted classes often not being constant in their class characters and fitting more smoothly in other parts of the system. Although Linnaeus had been searching for a truly natural system, Thunberg seemed to have no penchant for speculation. His strong points were his keen eye in the field, his indefatigable spirit and eagerness in collecting, and his concise descriptions. Among his contemporaries he was perhaps the one who described the largest number of new plant genera and species. His aims certainly reached no further.

Thunberg's description of his great voyage, published in four parts in Swedish in 1788–1793 and soon translated into English as *Travels in Europe, Africa and Asia* (1793–1795), as well as in French and German, contains material of great ethnographical interest.

BIBLIOGRAPHY

I. ORIGINAL WORKS. T. O. B. N. Krok, *Bibliotheca botanica suecana* (Stockholm–Uppsala, 1925), 705–716, lists all Thunberg's botanical works. Letters from his many correspondents, both Swedish and foreign, are at the University Library, Uppsala, together with other MSS. His published works include *De ischiade* (Uppsala, 1770); *Flora japonica* (Leipzig, 1784); *Travels in Europe, Africa and Asia,* 4 vols. (London, 1793–1795), first published as 4 vols. (Uppsala, 1788–1793); *Prodromus plantarum capensium* (Uppsala, 1794–1800); and *Flora capensis,* 2 vols. (Uppsala, 1807–1823).

II. SECONDARY LITERATURE. See H. O. Juel, *Plantae Thunbergianae* (Uppsala, 1918), in German; and articles about Thunberg by N. Svedelius in *Isis,* **35** (1944–1945), 128–134; in S. Lindroth, ed., *Swedish Men of Science* (Stockholm, 1952), 151–159; and in *Svenska Linnésällskapets årsskrift,* **27** (1944), 29–64.

Thunberg and Cape Colony botany are treated by M. Karsten, in *The Old Company's Garden at the Cape and Its Superintendents* (Cape Town, 1951), 132–134, *passim;* "Carl Peter Thunberg. An Early Investigator of Cape Botany," in *Journal of South African Botany,* **5** (1939), 1–27, 87–155; **12** (1946), 127–190. Thunberg and Japan are treated in C. Gaudon, *Le Japon du XVIIIe siècle vu par Ch. P. Thunberg* (Paris, 1966); and in *Forskningsmaterial rörande C. P. Thunberg* (Tokyo, 1953), in Japanese and Swedish.

See also G. Eriksson, *Botanikens historia i Sverige intill år 1800* (Uppsala, 1969), 258–260, 268–270, 321; and S. Lindroth, *Kungliga Svenska Vetenskapsakademiens historia,* II (Stockholm, 1967), 408–412 and *passim.*

GUNNAR ERIKSSON

THYMARIDAS (*fl.* Paros, first half (?) of fourth century B.C.)

An early Pythagorean of uncertain date, Thymaridas was a number theorist from the Aegean island of Paros. He defined a unit as a "limiting quantity" (see Iamblichus, *In Nicomachi . . . ,* p. 11, 2–3); and he is said to have called a prime number εὐθυγραμμικός ("rectilinear"), because it can only be established one-dimensionally (Iamblichus, *op. cit.,* p. 27, 4–5), since the only measures of a prime number are itself and one. But Thymaridas' chief contribution to number theory was his ἐπάνθημα ("bloom"), which he expressed rather obscurely in generalized form (Iamblichus, *op. cit.,* p. 62, 18 ff.). The rule leads to the solution of a certain set of *n* simultaneous simple equations connecting *n* unknowns. The unknown quantity is called "an undetermined number of units" (that is, *x*); the known quantities are ὡρισμένα ("determined"). The principle of the rule has been explained by Heath as follows:

Let there be n unknown quantities

$$x, x_1, x_2, \cdots x_{n-1}$$

connected by n equations, in such a way that

$$x + x_1 + x_2 + \cdots + x_{n-1} = S$$

$$x + x_1 = a_1,$$

$$x + x_2 = a_2,$$

$$\cdot \cdot \cdot \cdot \cdot \cdot \cdot \cdot \cdot \cdot$$

$$x + x_{n-1} = a_{n-1},$$

the solution is

$$x = \frac{(a_1 + a_2 + \cdots + a_{n-1}) - S}{n - 2}.$$

Iamblichus shows that other equations can be reduced to this form (Iamblichus, *op. cit.*, p. 63, 16 ff.); he gives as an example an indeterminate problem having four unknown quantities in three linear equations. It is not certain that Thymaridas was responsible for the extension of his method.

Of Thymaridas' life we are told only that he fell from prosperity to poverty and that consequently Thestor of Poseidonia sailed to Paros to help him with money specially collected for his benefit (Iamblichus, *De vita pythagorica*, p. 239). "Eumaridas" in a list of Parian Pythagoreans (Iamblichus, *op. cit.*, p. 267) may be a mistake for Thymaridas.

BIBLIOGRAPHY

On Thymaridas and his work, see T. L. Heath, *A History of Greek Mathematics*, I (Oxford, 1921), 69, 72, 94; Iamblichus, in *Nicomachi arithmeticam introductionem*, H. Pistelli, ed. (Leipzig, 1894), 11, 2–3; 27, 4–5; 62, 18 ff.; 63, 16 ff.; and *De vita pythagorica*, L. Deubner, ed. (Leipzig, 1937).

G. HUXLEY

TIETZE, HEINRICH FRANZ FRIEDRICH (*b.* Schleinz, Austria, 31 August 1880; *d.* Munich, Germany, 17 February 1964)

Tietze was the son of Emil Tietze, director of the Geological Institute at the University of Vienna, and of Rosa von Hauer, daughter of the geologist Franz Ritter von Hauer. He was married in 1907 to Leontine Petraschek; they had no children.

Tietze began the study of mathematics at Vienna in 1898. Following the advice of his friend Gustav Herglotz, in 1902 he went for a year to Munich and then returned to Vienna. Gustav von Escherich was his adviser, and for the dissertation "Über Funktionalgleichungen, deren Lösungen keiner algebraischen Differentialgleichung genügen können" Tietze was awarded the Ph.D. in 1904. Through Wilhelm Wirtinger's lectures on algebraic functions and their integrals, Tietze became interested in topological problems, thereafter the focus of his most important mathematical work. In 1908 he qualified as lecturer at Vienna with the *Habilitationsschrift* "Über die topologischen Invarianten mehrdimensionaler Mannigfaltigkeiten." Topology—at this time still in a rudimentary stage—involved studying the properties of geometrical objects, which are invariant with respect to bijective and bicontinous mappings. Today it is one of the most important foundations of mathematics. In his *Habilitationsschrift*, Tietze made essential contributions to combinatory topology, inspired by results of Henri Poincaré. He accepted a position as associate professor of mathematics at the Technical College of Brünn (today Brno) in 1910, and was promoted to full professor in 1913.

Drafted into the Austrian army during World War I, Tietze was forced to interrupt his academic activities. He returned to Brünn after the war, and in 1919 he accepted a full professorship at the University of Erlangen. While at Erlangen he wrote his three-part "Beiträge zur allgemeinen Topologie." Part I is concerned with axioms for different versions of the concept of neighborhood; today one of them bears his name. In 1925 Tietze accepted an offer from the University of Munich, where Constantin Carathéodory and Oskar Perron were colleagues. Most of his some 120 publications were produced during his tenure at Munich. He retired in 1950 but continued his research until a short time before his death in 1964.

As a topologist Tietze did pioneering work. In addition to the papers previously mentioned, his first publication, "Über das Problem der Nachbargebiete im Raum" (1905), should be noted. Whereas in the plane there are at most four domains touching one another along a line, it was already known that in three-dimensional space there exist any number of solids touching one another along a surface. Tietze showed that this can occur even in convex domains. In a further publication, "Einige Bemerkungen über das Problem des Kartenfärbens auf einseitigen Flächen" (1910), he proved that six is the minimum number of colors needed to color any map on the Möbius band or on the projective plane.

In 1914 Tietze stated the important theorem, which

now bears his name, that any function bounded and continous on a closed set can be continously extended to the whole space. With his friend Leopold Vietoris, he published an article in the *Encyklopädie der mathematischen Wissenschaften* ("Beziehungen zwischen den verschiedenen Zweigen der Topologie," 1930), which discusses the relationship between combinatorial topology and set theoretic topology. This work also was crucially important in clarifying the terminology, which was not yet standardized. Tietze's other papers on topology deal with the theory of knots, Jordan curves, and continous mappings of areas, among other subjects.

In addition to topology, Tietze worked in many other fields of mathematics. In 1909 he noticed that the usual criterion for the possibility of constructing a geometrical figure with only compass and ruler as instruments is not sufficient. The arrangement of the constructed points also plays an important role that must be considered. For the theory of continued fractions Tietze developed a decisive criterion of convergence based on geometrical ideas. Further papers involved the theory of convex domains and the fundamental theorem of symmetrical functions, which he proved in a new manner, extending it to the case of an infinite number of variables. In analysis, Tietze gave a new demonstration for J. B. J. Fourier and F. F. D. Budan's rules of signs, generalizing these rules to nonrational holomorphic functions. Tietze's "Über das Schicksal gemischter Populationen nach den Mendelschen Vererbungsgesetzen" (1923) treats a problem belonging to an area of what today is called biomathematics. Between 1940 and 1944 Tietze wrote a series of papers on systems of lattice points and partitions, on the distribution of prime numbers, and on questions of differential geometry.

Tietze's publications mentioned above were addressed to the specialist, but Tietze took great pains to make mathematical problems clear to the general public as well. For this purpose he wrote the two-volume *Gelöste und ungelöste mathematische Probleme aus alter und neuer Zeit* (1949; translated into English and Dutch). It shows his gift for representing even difficult mathematical questions in a very clear and impressive manner for interested people.

In 1929 Tietze was elected a member of the Bavarian Academy of Sciences, and in the years 1934–1942 and 1946–1951 he was secretary of its Mathematical-Natural Sciences Division. He also was a corresponding member of the Austrian Academy of Sciences (elected 1959) and received the Bavarian Verdienstorden (1959).

BIBLIOGRAPHY

I. ORIGINAL WORKS. Complete bibliographies of Tietze's works are with the obituaries by Perron, Seebach and Jacobs, and Vietoris. His works include "Über das Problem der Nachbargebiete im Raum," in *Monatshefte für Mathematik und Physik*, **16** (1905), 211–216; "Über Funktionalgleichungen, deren Lösungen keiner algebraischen Differentialgleichung genügen können," *ibid.*, 329–364, his dissertation; "Über die topologischen Invarianten mehrdimensionaler Mannigfaltigkeiten," *ibid.*, **19** (1908), 1–118; "Einige Bemerkungen über das Problem des Kartenfärbens auf einseitigen Flächen," in *Jahresberichte der Deutschen Mathematiker-Vereinigung*, **19** (1910), 155–159; "Über Funktionen, die auf einer abgeschlossenen Menge stetig sind," in *Journal für die reine und angewandte Mathematik*, **145** (1915), 9–14; "Beiträge zur allgemeine Topologie," pt. 1 in *Mathematische Annalen*, **88** (1923), 290–312, pt. 2, *ibid.*, **91** (1924), 210–224, pt. 3 in *Monatshefte für Mathematik und Physik*, **33** (1923), 15–17; "Über das Schicksal gemischter Populationen nach den Mendelschen Vererbungsgesetzen," in *Zeitschrift für angewandte Mathematik und Mechanik*, **3** (1923); "Beziehungen zwischen den verschiedenen Zweigen der Topologie," in *Encyklopädie der Mathematischen Wissenschaften*, III, 1.2, art. AB 13 (Leipzig, 1930), 141–237, written with Leopold Vietoris; "Systeme von Partitionen und Glitterpunktfiguren I–IX," in *Sitzungsberichte der Bayerischen Akademie der Wissenschaften* (1940), 23–54, 69–166, and (1941), 1–55, 165–191; and *Gelöste und ungelöste mathematische Probleme aus alter und neuer Zeit* (Munich, 1949; 4th ed., 1965).

II. SECONDARY LITERATURE. G. Aumann, "Heinrich Tietze, 31.8.1880–17.2.1964," in *Jahrbuch der Bayerischen Akademie der Wissenschaften (1964)*, 197–201; O. Perron, "Heinrich Tietze, 31.8.1880–17.2.1964," in *Jahresberichte der Deutschen Mathematiker-Vereinigung*, **83** (1981), 182–185; K. Seebach and K. Jacobs, "Verzeichnis der unter H. Tietze angefertigten Dissertationen und Verzeichnis der Veröffentlichungen," *ibid.*, 186–191; and Leopold Vietoris, "Heinrich Tietze," in *Almanach der Österreichischen Akademie der Wissenschaften*, **114** (1964), 360–377.

KARL SEEBACH

TILLY, JOSEPH-MARIE DE (*b.* Ypres, Belgium, 16 August 1837; *d.* Schaerbeek, Belgium, 4 August 1906)

Tilly, one of the most profound Belgian mathematicians, attained the rank of lieutenant general by the time of his retirement. As a second lieutenant in the artillery, he was assigned in 1858 to teach a course in mathematics at the regimental school; and it was there that he studied the principles of geometry. In 1860, in *Recherches sur les éléments de géométrie*, Tilly used Anatole Lamarle's methods to criticize Euclid's fifth postulate and achieved results that Lobachevsky had published but of which he was unaware until about 1866. In *Études de mécanique abstraite* (1870), based on the negation of Euclid's postulate, Tilly worked with a Lobachevskian space. He was the first to study non-Euclidean mechanics, a subject he virtually created. His research brought him into contact with Jules Houël, the only French mathematician then interested in the new geometries. Although they never met, their correspondence (1870–1885) was a valuable stimulus to Tilly, who had been working for nine years without guidance.

In *Essai sur les principes fondamentaux de la géométrie et de la mécanique* (1878), Tilly established the Riemannian, Lobachevskian, and Euclidean geometries on the concept of the distance between two points. In his formulation these geometries were based, respectively, on one, two, and three necessary and sufficient, irreducible axioms.

Tilly also wrote on military science and on the history of mathematics in Belgium, including the centenary report on the mathematical activities of the Belgian Royal Academy from 1772 to 1872. These studies were undertaken in the midst of Tilly's demanding professional duties as director of the arsenal at Antwerp and as commandant and director of studies at the École Militaire for ten years. In *Essai de géométrie analytique générale* (1892), the synthesis and crowning achievement of his work, Tilly stressed the fundamental relationship among the ten distances between any two of a group of five points. In brief, he established that geometry is the mathematical physics of distances.

Tilly's last years were marred by his unjust dismissal as commandant of the École Militaire in December 1899 and his forced early retirement in August 1900. The actions of the minister of war were motivated by complaints that Tilly had unduly emphasized the scientific education of future officers. The inspector of studies at the École Militaire, Gérard-Mathieu Leman (later a general), had forbidden Tilly to use the notions of the infinitely small and of the differential.

In 1870 Tilly was elected corresponding member and, in 1878, full member of the science section of the Belgian Royal Academy, of which he was president in 1887.

BIBLIOGRAPHY

See two articles by P. Mansion, in *Annuaire de l'Académie royale de Belgique*, **80** (1914), 203–285, with portrait and bibliography; and in *Biographie nationale . . .*, XXV (Brussels, 1930–1932), 264–269.

J. PELSENEER

TINSEAU D'AMONDANS, CHARLES DE (*b.* Besançon, France, 19 April 1748; *d.* Montpellier, France, 21 March 1822)

The sixth of the seven children of Marie-Nicolas de Tinseau, *seigneur* of Gennes, and Jeanne Petramand of Velay, Tinseau belonged to the nobility of the Franche-Comté. Admitted to the École Royale du Génie at Mézières in 1769, he graduated as a military engineer at the end of 1771 and until 1791 was an officer in the engineering corps. Gaspard Monge, his professor of mathematics at Mézières, awakened in Tinseau an interest in mathematical research; and in 1772 he presented two memoirs to the Académie des Sciences, one on infinitesimal geometry and the other on astronomy. The following year he was named Bossut's correspondent at the Academy; but after that he seems to have written only one paper, on infinitesimal geometry. Nevertheless, the few items that have survived from his correspondence with Monge before the Revolution attest to a continuing interest in mathematical research.

A participant in the efforts made by the nobility in 1788 to defend the *ancien régime*, Tinseau joined the émigrés gathered at Worms under the leadership of the prince of Condé in 1791. From then on, he lived in various émigré communities, conducting a very active propaganda campaign against the Revolution and later against the Empire. He attempted to organize uprisings in France, and encouraged and aided the Allied powers in their fight against the French armies. Tinseau also fought in several campaigns and, according to his biographer, provided all the coalitions formed until 1813 with strategic plans of the French army. The intransigence of his anti-Revolution convictions is evident in the dozen political pamphlets that he published between 1792 and 1805 at Worms and London.

Devoted to the Bourbons, whom he considered the sole legitimate dynasty, Tinseau refused an offer of amnesty from Napoleon and rejected offers of naturalization extended by the British government. With the rank of brigadier general in the engineering corps, Tinseau acted as aide de camp to the future Charles X and did not return to France until 1816, at which time he immediately went into retirement.

Tinseau married three times. His first marriage took place in France before the Revolution, the other two in England during his exile. His four children from the first marriage all died without issue. From his third marriage he had a son who died in Africa and a daughter who married the engineer and mathematician François Vallès (1805–1887).

Two of the three memoirs that constitute Tinseau's *oeuvre* deal with topics in the theory of surfaces and curves of double curvature: planes tangent to a surface, contact curves of circumscribed cones or cylinders, various surfaces attached to a space curve, the determination of the osculatory plane at a point of a space curve, problems of quadrature and cubature involving ruled surfaces, the study of the properties of certain special ruled surfaces (particularly conoids), and various results in the analytic geometry of space. In these two papers the equation of the tangent plane at a point of a surface was first worked out in detail (the equation had been known since Parent), methods of descriptive geometry were used in determining the perpendicular common to two straight lines in space, and the Pythagorean theorem was generalized to space (the square of a plane area is equal to the sum of the squares of the projections of this area on mutually perpendicular planes).

Although Tinseau published very little, his papers are of great interest as additions to Monge's earliest works. Indeed, Tinseau appears to have been Monge's first disciple.

BIBLIOGRAPHY

I. Original Works. Tinseau's two memoirs on infinitesimal geometry were published as "Solution de quelques problèmes relatifs à la théorie des surfaces courbes et des lignes à double courbure," in *Mémoires de mathématique et de physique présentés . . . sçavans*, **9** (1780), 593–624; and "Sur quelques propriétés des solides renfermés par des surfaces composées des lignes droites," *ibid.*, 625–642. An unpublished memoir dated 1772, "Solution de quelques questions d'astronomie," is in the archives of the Académie des Sciences.

Between 1792 and 1805 Tinseau published many violently anti-Revolution and anti-Napoleonic writings, eleven of which are cited in Michaud (see below).

II. Secondary Literature. The only somewhat detailed article on Tinseau, by Weiss in Michaud's *Biographie universelle*, XLVI (Paris, 1826), 100–102, deals mainly with his political and military careers. Some observations on his mathematical work are in R. Taton, *L'oeuvre scientifique de Gaspard Monge* (Paris, 1951), see index; and C. B. Boyer, *History of Analytic Geome-*

try (New York, 1956), 207. Various documents concerning Tinseau are in his dossiers in the archives of the Académie des Sciences and at the Service Historique de l'Armée.

René Taton

TITCHMARSH, EDWARD CHARLES (*b*. Newbury, England, 1 June 1899; *d*. Oxford, England, 18 January 1963)

Titchmarsh was the son of Edward Harper and Caroline Titchmarsh. In 1925 he married Kathleen Blomfield; they had three children. Titchmarsh received his mathematical training at Oxford; and, like most of his contemporaries, he did not take a doctorate. After teaching at University College, London (1923–1929) and the University of Liverpool (1929–1931), he became Savilian professor of geometry at Oxford. He held this position for the rest of his life.

All of Titchmarsh's extensive research was in various branches of analysis; and in spite of his professorial title, he even lectured exclusively on analysis. He made many significant contributions to Fourier series and integrals; to integral equations (in collaboration with G. H. Hardy); to entire functions of a complex variable; to the Riemann zeta-function; and to eigenfunctions of second-order differential equations, a subject to which he devoted the last twenty-five years of his life.

Titchmarsh wrote a Cambridge tract on the zeta-function (1930), and later expanded it into a much larger book (1951) containing practically everything that was known on the subject. His survey of Fourier integrals (1937) is a definitive account of the classical parts of the theory. His work on eigenfunctions appeared in two parts in 1946 and 1958. His text *The Theory of Functions* (1932) was his best-known book; a generation of mathematicians learned the theory of analytic functions and Lebesgue integration from it, and also learned (by observation) how to write mathematics. He also wrote *Mathematics for the General Reader* (1948).

Titchmarsh made many original contributions to analysis, but his influence was at least as great through his systematization of existing knowledge and his improvements of proofs of known results. He saw physics as a source of interesting mathematical problems; but his interest was exclusively in the mathematics, without any regard for its real applicability. The approach, so often sterile, was successful in his case, for it led him into his study of eigenfunctions, in which the importance of his results was less appreciated in Great Britain than in other countries, especially the Soviet Union.

BIBLIOGRAPHY

Titchmarsh's works are *The Zeta-Function of Riemann* (London, 1930); *The Theory of Functions* (Oxford, 1932); *Introduction to the Theory of Fourier Integrals* (Oxford, 1937); *Eigenfunction Expansions Associated With Second-Order Differential Equations*, pt. 1 (Oxford, 1946), pt. 2 (Oxford, 1958); *Mathematics for the General Reader* (London, 1948); and *The Theory of the Riemann Zeta-Function* (Oxford, 1951).

On Titchmarsh and his work, see the obituary by M. L. Cartwright, in *Journal of the London Mathematical Society*, **39** (1964), 544–565.

R. P. BOAS, JR.

TODHUNTER, ISAAC (*b.* Rye, Sussex, England, 23 November 1820; *d.* Cambridge, England, 1 March 1884)

Todhunter was the second son of George Todhunter, a Congregational minister in Rye, and Mary Hume. Upon the death of his father, the family moved to Hastings, where his mother opened a school for girls and where Todhunter was educated in private schools. Although he is said to have been extremely backward as a child, Todhunter later made good progress under J. B. Austin, with whom he subsequently obtained employment as a schoolmaster. While teaching at schools in Peckham and in Wimbledon, he enrolled as an evening student at University College, London. In 1842 he was awarded the B.A. (obtaining a mathematical scholarship), and in 1884 he received the M.A. (with gold medal). In the same year—acting on the advice of Augustus De Morgan, professor of mathematics at University College—he entered St John's College, Cambridge, where he graduated B.A. (senior wrangler) in 1848 and was given the Smith Prize. Shortly after graduating he was awarded the Burney Prize for an essay in the field of moral science. The following year he was elected to a fellowship, and he remained at St John's College, where for fifteen years he tutored, lectured, wrote, and examined. According to the rules of the college, he resigned his fellowship upon his marriage in 1864 to Louisa Anna Maria Davies. In 1862 Todhunter was elected fellow of the Royal Society of London, and he served on the council of the society from 1871 to 1873. He was also a founding member of the London Mathematical Society.

Throughout his lifetime Todhunter gave much public service as an examiner for the University of Cambridge in moral sciences and also in the mathematical tripos; he also examined for the University of London and for the Indian Civil Service Commission. Most of his time he devoted to writing, and the formidable series of mathematical textbooks he produced established him as one of the most influential figures in mathematical education of the nineteenth century. The textbooks were full and thorough, and were written with meticulous care. Consequently they were extremely popular with schoolmasters and some titles, in particular the *Algebra* (1858) and the *Euclid* (1862), had fifteen or sixteen editions. Many boys went through school and university studying mathematics entirely from Todhunter's textbooks.

Todhunter had little sympathy for the growing spirit of reform and criticism in mathematical education as evidenced in the formation of the Association for the Improvement of Geometrical Teaching (1871). He resisted all attempts to displace Euclid's *Elements* from its central position in mathematics courses. He also defended vigorously the rigors of the examination system as the only sound basis for obtaining and maintaining high standards in mathematics teaching. In *The Conflict of Studies . . .* (1873) he discussed many matters raised by the new reform movements and defended a point of view that, even at that time, was thought conservative. The attack he made on the teaching of experimental science contains the much-quoted statement, "If he [the boy] does not believe the statements of his tutor—probably a clergyman of mature knowledge, recognized ability and blameless character—his suspicion is irrational and manifests a want of the power of appreciating evidence, a want fatal to his success in that branch of science which he is supposed to be cultivating."

Although Todhunter's textbooks continued in use for many years after his death, his reputation rests on the contribution he made to the history of mathematics. The most important works are *A History of the Progress of the Calculus of Variations During the Nineteenth Century* (1861); *A History of the Mathematical Theory of Probability From the Time of Pascal to That of Laplace* (1865); and *A History of the Mathematical Theories of Attraction and the Figure of the Earth From the Time of Newton to That of Laplace* (1873). A further work, *A History of the Theory of Elasticity*, was published posthumously (1886–

1893). In all of these works, Todhunter gave a close and carefully reasoned account of the difficulties involved and the solutions offered by each investigator. His studies and use of source material were thorough and fully documented.

In 1871 Todhunter won the Adams Prize of the Royal Society, for an essay, *Researches in the Calculus of Variations*. The subject arose out of a controversy that had been carried on in the *Philosophical Magazine* some years before, concerning the nature of discontinuity. Todhunter's thesis illuminated some special cases but was obscured by the lack of any adequate definition of continuity.

Todhunter was not an original mathematician. His textbooks were useful in mathematical education but soon became outdated; the histories are still valuable.

BIBLIOGRAPHY

I. ORIGINAL WORKS. None of Todhunter's biographers have found it worthwhile to compile a full list of his elementary textbooks, which ran into a great many editions in his lifetime and, after his death, were revised by others so that they might continue to be useful in schools. The library of St. John's College, Cambridge, contains most of these books and also a collection of journal articles. There is also a small MS collection, which includes the *Arithmetic* on which Todhunter was working immediately prior to his death.

The more important historical works of Todhunter are *A History of the Progress of the Calculus of Variations During the Nineteenth Century* (Cambridge, 1861); *A History of the Mathematical Theory of Probability From the Time of Pascal to That of Laplace* (Cambridge, 1865); *A History of the Mathematical Theories of Attraction and the Figure of the Earth From the Time of Newton to That of Laplace*, 2 vols. (London, 1873); *A History of the Theory of Elasticity and of the Strength of Materials From Galilei to the Present Time*, K. Pearson, ed., 2 vols. (Cambridge, 1886–1893). Essays on education are contained in *The Conflict of Studies and Other Essays* (London, 1873). The Adams Prize essay was printed as *Researches in the Calculus of Variations* (London, 1871). Todhunter also edited George Boole, *Treatise on Differential Equations* (London, 1865) and *William Whewell. An Account of His Writings, With Selections From His Literary and Scientific Correspondence*, 2 vols. (London, 1876).

II. SECONDARY LITERATURE. On Todhunter and his work, see J. E. B. Mayor, "In Memoriam," in *Cambridge Review*, **5** (1884), 228, 245, 260; E. J. Routh, in *Proceedings of the Royal Society*, **37** (1884), xxvii–xxxii; and A. Macfarlane, *Lectures on Ten British Mathematicians of the Nineteenth Century* (New York, 1916), 134–146.

MARGARET E. BARON

TOEPLITZ, OTTO (*b.* Breslau, Germany [now Wrocław, Poland], 1 August 1881; *d.* Jerusalem, 19 February 1940)

Toeplitz' father, Emil Toeplitz, and his grandfather, Julius Toeplitz, were both Gymnasium teachers of mathematics; and they themselves published several mathematical papers. In Breslau, Toeplitz completed the classical Gymnasium and then studied at the university, where he specialized in algebraic geometry and received his Ph.D. in 1905.

The following year Toeplitz moved to Göttingen, where he stayed until he obtained an appointment at the University of Kiel in 1913; he became professor ordinarius in 1920. In 1928 he accepted a chair at the University of Bonn, but soon after Hitler's rise to power in 1933, he was dismissed from the office by the National Socialist regime. For the next few years he was involved in organizational work for the declining Jewish community in Germany. In 1938 he moved to Jerusalem, where he was administrative adviser to the Hebrew University; he also continued to teach in a private seminar, in which he reported the results of his work with G. Köthe.

Toeplitz' chief interest was the theory of infinite linear, bilinear, and quadratic forms, and of the associated infinite matrices, as a framework for concrete problems of analysis. It appears that this interest was sparked by the influence of Hilbert's work on integral equations, which was in the process of publication when Toeplitz arrived in Göttingen; but it was also not unrelated to Toeplitz' earlier work. Thus, following Hilbert, Toeplitz transferred the classical theories on linear, bilinear, and quadratic forms in n-dimensional space as far as possible to the infinite-dimensional cases; and he applied the results to the theory of integral equations and to other areas of analysis, such as Fourier series and complex variable theory.

In 1927 Toeplitz published "Integralgleichungen und Gleichungen mit unendlich vielen Unbekannten," written with E. Hellinger, with whom Toeplitz had closely collaborated. Among the important notions and methods that are given in the article, one of the major concepts was that of a normal bilinear form, which is basic in operator theory.

In the 1930's Toeplitz' mathematical research was based on a more general point of view. With G. Köthe, Toeplitz aimed at the development of a general theory of infinite-dimensional coordinate spaces. By this time S. Banach had published his "Théorie des opérations linéaires," but Toeplitz, having himself contributed much to the emergence of a general theory of linear operators, was critical of the work of Banach and his associates, which he considered too abstract. On the other hand, by deemphasizing the importance of the norm in their theory of coordinate spaces, Toeplitz and Köthe helped to develop the even more general theory of locally convex spaces. As an offshoot of his general interest, Toeplitz established, quite early in his career, the "Toeplitz conditions," which are fundamental in the theory of divergent sequences.

Toeplitz was deeply interested in the history of mathematics and held that only a mathematician of stature is qualified to be a historian of mathematics. In particular, he investigated the relation between Greek mathematics and Greek philosophy. He also wrote "Die Entwicklung der Infinitesimalrechnung" (1949), which was intended as an introduction to the calculus on a historical basis; the work is an example of Toeplitz' concern for the teaching of mathematics at the high school and college level. With H. Rademacher, Toeplitz also wrote *Von Zahlen und Figuren* (1930), one of the most successful attempts to bring higher mathematics before the educated public.

Toeplitz was a typical German-Jewish intellectual, who, while retaining an interest in Jewish matters, felt himself to be a part of his country of birth.

BIBLIOGRAPHY

Toeplitz' major works are *Über Systeme von Formen, deren Funktionaldeterminante identisch verschwindet* (Breslau, 1905); "Über allgemeine lineare Mittelbildungen," in *Prace Matematyczno-fizyczne*, **22** (1911), 113–119; "Integralgleichungen und Gleichungen mit unendlich vielen Unbekannten," in *Encyklopädie der mathematischen Wissenschaften*, **2**, pt. 3 (1927), 1395–1597, written with E. Hellinger; *Von Zahlen und Figuren* (1930), written with H. Rademacher; and "Die Entwicklung der Infinitesimalrechnung," in G. Köthe, ed., *Grundlehren*, LXI (1949). See also Poggendorff, V, 1261–1262; VI, 2672; VIIA, 695.

On Toeplitz and his work, see H. Behnke and G. Köthe, "Otto Toeplitz zum Gedächtnis," in *Jahresbericht der Deutschen Mathematikervereinigung*, **66** (1963), 1–16.

ABRAHAM ROBINSON

TOLMAN, RICHARD CHACE (*b*. West Newton, Massachusetts, 4 March 1881; d. Pasadena, California, 5 September 1948)

Tolman came from a prosperous New England family with close ties to the business and academic world. Following in his father's footsteps, Tolman enrolled at the Massachusetts Institute of Technology after attending the public schools in West Newton. He received a bachelor of science degree in chemical engineering in 1903. He spent the following year in Germany, at the Technische Hochschule at Charlottenburg, and later at Crefeld in an industrial chemical laboratory. Upon his return to M.I.T. in 1904 as a graduate student, Tolman joined Arthur Amos Noyes's Research Laboratory of Physical Chemistry and earned his Ph.D. in 1910. Tolman taught briefly at the University of Michigan and the University of Cincinnati before going to the University of California, Berkeley (1912–1916). He became professor of physical chemistry at the University of Illinois in 1916.

In Washington, D.C., in 1918, while serving as chief of the dispersoid section of the Chemical Warfare Service, Tolman crossed paths again with Noyes, then chairman of the Committee on Nitrate Supply. Noyes was already working hard to persuade the government to continue after the war its research program on the nitrogen products used in explosives and fertilizers. His efforts led to the creation of the Fixed Nitrogen Research Laboratory in 1919, and to Tolman's appointment as associate director (1919–1920) and director (1920–1922). The laboratory flourished under Tolman's direction, and became a mecca for bright young physical chemists. In 1922 Tolman joined the faculty of the California Institute of Technology through Noyes's efforts. As professor of physical chemistry and mathematical physics, Tolman served as dean of the graduate school and was a member of the executive council for many years.

The main thrust of Tolman's work in statistical mechanics, relativistic thermodynamics, and cosmology was mathematical and theoretical. His earliest scientific research (1910) involved measuring the electromotive force produced when a centrifugal force is applied to an electrolytic solution. Tolman based the derivation of an expression for the electromotive force on kinetic arguments, in addition to the customary thermodynamic ones, and showed that both yield the same equation. Turning to metallic conductors next, Tolman, working with T. Dale Stewart at Berkeley, demonstrated the production of an electromotive force by measuring the flow of electric current when a coil of wire rotating about its axis is mechanically accelerated and then brought to a sudden halt. In 1916 they made the first laboratory determination of the mass of the electric carrier in metals.

Tolman also published a number of important papers in the field of chemical kinetics in gaseous systems, that is, the problem of accounting for the rate at which chemical reactions take place. His theoretical treatment of monomolecular thermal and photochemical reaction rates underscored the need to clarify the meaning of the loosely defined concept of the energy of activation. This done, Tolman turned to the experimental work of Farrington Daniels and his co-workers on the decomposition of nitrogen pentoxide, the best example of a first-order unimolecular reaction over a range of concentrations and at a series of temperatures, as a check on the proposed mechanisms of chemical reaction then current. In particular, he showed in 1925 that the simple radiation theory of reaction proposed by Jean Baptiste Perrin and W. C. McC. Lewis did not adequately account for known rates of reaction. The papers not only reveal Tolman's precise reasoning and great physical intuition, but also his consuming interest in the application of statistical mechanics to rates of physical-chemical change.

With Gilbert N. Lewis, Tolman published the first American exposition of the special theory of relativity in 1909. Tolman later wrote *The Theory of the Relativity of Motion* (Berkeley, 1917). This early interest in relativity theory was further stimulated by Hubble's discovery in 1929 that red shifts are proportional to distance, and led to a series of studies on the applications of the general theory to the overall structure and evolution of the universe. In his comprehensive treatise on relativistic thermodynamics, Tolman presented his theory of a universe expanding and contracting rhythmically like a beating heart, arguing that gravity has the effect of counteracting the influence of radiation, thus preventing the complete cessation of motion as predicted by the second law of thermodynamics.

During World War II, Tolman served as vice-chairman of the National Defense Research Committee, as scientific adviser to General Leslie R. Groves on the Manhattan Project, and as United States adviser to the wartime Combined Policy Committee. Afterwards, he became scientific adviser to Bernard Baruch on the United Nations Atomic Energy Commission. Honors received during his lifetime included the Medal for Merit and election to the National Academy of Sciences in 1923.

Tolman married Ruth Sherman, a psychologist, in 1924. They had no children. He willed the bulk of his estate to the California Institute of Technology.

BIBLIOGRAPHY

Tolman published four books and over 100 scientific papers, all of which are chronologically listed in the bibliography appended to the biographical introduction prepared by J. G. Kirkwood, O. R. Wulf, and P. S. Epstein, in *Biographical Memoirs. National Academy of Sciences*, **27** (1952), 139–153. In *Principles of Statistical Mechanics* (Oxford, 1938), a monograph that remains a classic in its field, Tolman refashioned statistical mechanics by using quantum rather than classical mechanics as the starting point for the science. Details about his family and childhood can be gleaned from his brother's autobiographical notes, found in B. F. Ritchie, "Edward Chace Tolman," *ibid.*, **37** (1964), 293–324. Bernard Jaffe, *Outposts of Science* (New York, 1935), 506–516, gives a vivid picture of Tolman's work in cosmology at Caltech in the 1930's. His World War II activities are thoroughly covered in Albert B. Christman's *Sailors, Scientists and Rockets*, I (Washington, D.C., 1971).

Manuscript sources include letters in the papers of Gilbert N. Lewis, now in the office of the Chemistry Department, Berkeley, and several boxes of correspondence and unpublished manuscripts in the archives of the California Institute of Technology.

JUDITH R. GOODSTEIN

TORRICELLI, EVANGELISTA (*b.* Faenza, Italy, 15 October 1608; *d.* Florence, Italy, 25 October 1647)

Eldest of the three children of Gaspare Torricelli and the former Caterina Angetti, Torricelli soon demonstrated unusual talents. His father, a textile artisan in modest circumstances, sent the boy to his uncle, the Camaldolese monk Jacopo (formerly Alessandro), who supervised his humanistic education. In 1625 and 1626 Torricelli attended the mathematics and philosophy courses of the Jesuit school at Faenza, showing such outstanding aptitude that his uncle was persuaded to send him to Rome for further education at the school run by Benedetto Castelli, a member of his order who was a mathematician and hydraulic engineer, and a former pupil of Galileo's. Castelli took a great liking to the youth, realized his exceptional genius, and engaged him as his secretary.

We have direct evidence on the scope and trend

of Torricelli's scientific studies during his stay at Rome in the first letter (11 September 1632) of his surviving correspondence, addressed to Galileo on behalf of Castelli, who was away from Rome. In acknowledging receipt of a letter from Galileo to Castelli, Torricelli seized the opportunity to introduce himself as a mathematician by profession, well versed in the geometry of Apollonius, Archimedes, and Theodosius; he added that he had studied Ptolemy and had seen "nearly everything" by Brahe, Kepler, and Longomontanus. These studies had compelled him to accept the Copernican doctrine and to become "a Galileist by profession and sect"; he had been the first in Rome to make a careful study of Galileo's *Dialogo sopra i due massimi sistemi*, published in February of that year (1632).

After this letter there is a gap in the correspondence until 1640, and it is not known where Torricelli lived or what he did during this period. The most likely hypothesis so far advanced is that from the spring of 1630 to February 1641, he was secretary to Monsignor Giovanni Ciampoli, Galileo's friend and protector, who from 1632 was governor of various cities in the Marches and Umbria (Montalto, Norcia, San Severino, Fabriano). In 1641 Torricelli was again in Rome; he had asked Castelli and other mathematicians for their opinions of a treatise on motion that amplified the doctrine on the motion of projectiles that Galileo had expounded in the third day of the *Discorsi e dimostrazioni matematiche intorno a due nuove scienze* . . . (Leiden, 1638). Castelli considered the work excellent; told Galileo about it; and in April 1641, on his way from Rome to Venice through Pisa and Florence, after appointing Torricelli to give lectures in his absence, submitted the manuscript to Galileo, proposing that the latter should accept Torricelli as assistant in drawing up the two "days" he was thinking of adding to the *Discorsi*. Galileo agreed and invited Torricelli to join him at Arcetri.

But Castelli's delay in returning to Rome and the death of Torricelli's mother, who had moved to Rome with her other children, compelled Torricelli to postpone his arrival at Arcetri until 10 October 1641. He took up residence in Galileo's house, where Vincenzo Viviani was already living, and stayed there in close friendship with Galileo until the latter's death on 8 January 1642. While Torricelli was preparing to return to Rome, Grand Duke Ferdinando II of Tuscany, at Andrea Arrighetti's suggestion, appointed him mathematician and philosopher, the post left vacant by Galileo, with a good salary and lodging in the Medici palace.

Torricelli remained in Florence until his death; these years, the happiest of his life, were filled with the greatest scientific activity. Esteemed for his polished, brilliant, and witty conversation, he soon formed friendships with the outstanding representatives of Florentine culture; the painter Salvatore Rosa, the Hellenist Carlo Dati, and the hydraulic engineer Andrea Arrighetti. In fact, the regular meetings with these friends gave rise to the "Accademia dei Percossi," to whom Torricelli apparently divulged the comedies he was writing, which have not survived but were explicitly mentioned in the memoirs dictated on his deathbed to Lodovico Serenai (*Opere*, IV, 88).

In 1644 Torricelli's only work to be published during his lifetime appeared, the grand duke having assumed all printing costs. The volume, *Opera geometrica*, was divided into three sections: the first dealt with *De sphaera et solidis sphaeralibus libri duo*; the second contained *De motu gravium naturaliter descendentium et proiectorum* (the writing submitted to Galileo for his opinion); and the third section consisted of *De dimensione parabolae*. The work, soon known throughout Italy and Europe, had intrinsic value and, through its clear exposition, diffused the geometry of Cavalieri, whose writings were difficult to read.

The fame that Torricelli acquired as a geometer increased his correspondence with Italian scientists and with a number of French scholars (Carcavi, Mersenne, F. Du Verdus, Roberval), to whom he was introduced by F. Niceron, whom he met while in Rome. The correspondence was the means of communicating Torricelli's greatest scientific discoveries but also the occasion for fierce arguments on priority, which were common during that century. There were particularly serious polemics with Roberval over the priority of discovery of certain properties of the cycloid, including quadrature, center of gravity, and measurement of the solid generated by its rotation round the base. In order to defend his rights, Torricelli formed the intention of publishing all his correspondence with the French mathematicians, and in 1646 he began drafting *Racconto d'alcuni problemi proposti e passati tra gli matematici di Francia et il Torricelli ne i quattro anni prossimamente passati* (*Opere*, III, 1–32). But while he was engaged in this work he died of a violent illness (probably typhoid fever) lasting only a few days. In accordance with his wish he was buried in the Church of San Lorenzo in Florence, but the location of his tomb is unknown.

Mathematical research occupied Torricelli's entire life. During his youth he had studied the classics of Greek geometry, which dealt with infinitesimal questions by the method of progressive elimination. But since the beginning of the seventeenth century the classical method had often been replaced by more intuitive processes; the first examples were given by Kepler, who in determining areas and volumes abandoned Archimedean methods in favor of more expeditious processes differing from problem to problem and hence difficult to imitate. After many years of meditation, Cavalieri, in his geometry of indivisibles (1635), drew attention to an organic process, toward which Roberval, Fermat, and Descartes had been moving almost in the same year; the coincidence shows that the time was ripe for new geometrical approaches.

The new geometry considered every plane figure as being formed by an infinity of chords intercepted within the figure by a system of parallel straight lines; every chord was then considered as a rectangle of infinitesimal thickness—the indivisible, according to the term introduced by Galileo. From the assumed or verified relations between the indivisibles it was possible to deduce the relations between the totalities through Cavalieri's principle, which may be stated as follows: Given two plane figures comprised between parallel straight lines, if all the straight lines parallel thereto determine in the two figures segments having a constant relation, then the areas of the two figures also have the same relation. The principle is easily extended to solid figures. In essence Cavalieri's geometry, the first step toward infinitesimal calculus, replaced the potential mathematical infinity and infinitesimal of the Greek geometricians with the present infinity and infinitesimal.

After overcoming his initial mistrust of the new method, Torricelli used it as a heuristic instrument for the discovery of new propositions, which he then demonstrated by the classical methods. The promiscuous use of the two methods—that of indivisibles for discovery and the Archimedean process for demonstration—is very frequent in the *Opera geometrica*. The first part of *De sphaera et solidis sphaeralibus*, compiled around 1641, studies figures arising through rotation of a regular polygon inscribed in or circumscribed about a circle around one of its axes of symmetry (already mentioned by Archimedes). Torricelli observes that if the regular polygon has equal sides, one of its axes of symmetry joins two opposite vertices or the midpoints of two opposite sides; if, on the other hand, it does not have equal sides, one of its

axes of symmetry joins a vertex with the midpoint of the opposite side. On the basis of this observation he classifies such rotation solids into six kinds, studies their properties, and presents some new propositions and new metrical relations for the round bodies of elementary geometry. The second section of the volume deals with the motion of projectiles, about which more will be said later.

In the third section, apart from giving twenty demonstrations of Archimedes' theorem on squaring the parabola, but without adding anything new of importance, Torricelli shows that the area comprised between the cycloid and its base is equal to three times the area of the generating circle. As an appendix to this part of the work there is a study of the volume generated by a plane area animated by a helicoid motion round an axis of its plane, with the demonstration that it equals the volume generated by the area in a complete rotation round the same axis. Torricelli applies this elegant theorem to various problems and in particular to the surface of a screw with a square thread, which he shows to be equal to a convenient part of a paraboloid with one pitch.

As Torricelli acquired increasing familiarity with the method of indivisibles, he reached the point of surpassing the master—as Cavalieri himself said. In fact he extended the theory by using curved indivisibles, based on the following fundamental concept: In order to allow comparison of two plane figures, the first is cut by a system of curves and the second by a system of parallel straight lines; if each curved indivisible of the first is equal to the corresponding indivisible of the second, the two figures are equal in area. The simplest example is given by comparison of a circle divided into infinitesimal concentric rings with a triangle (having the rectified circumference as base and the radius as height) divided into infinitesimal strips parallel to the base. From the equality of the rings to the corresponding strips it is concluded that the area of the circle is equal to the area of the triangle.

The principle is also extended to solid figures. Torricelli gave the most brilliant application of it in 1641 by proving a new theorem, a gem of the mathematical literature of the time. The theorem, published in *Opera geometrica*, is as follows (*Opere*, I, 191–213): take any point of an equilateral hyperbola (having the equation $xy = 1$) and take the area comprised by the unlimited section of the hyperbola of asymptote x, asymptote x, and the ordinate of the point selected. Although such area is infinite in size, the solid it generates by rotating round the asymptote, although unlimited in extent, nevertheless has a finite volume, calculated by Torricelli as π/a, where a is the abscissa of the point taken on the hyperbola.

Torricelli's proof, greatly admired by Cavalieri and imitated by Fermat, consists in supposing the solid generated by rotation to be composed of an infinite number of cylindrical surfaces of axis x, all having an equal lateral area, all placed in biunivocal correspondence with the sections of a suitable cylinder, and all equal to the surfaces of that cylinder: the principle of curved indivisibles allows the conclusion that the volume of this cylinder is equal to the volume of the solid generated by rotation of the section of the hyperbola considered. In modern terms Torricelli's process is described by saying that an integral in Cartesian coordinates is replaced by an integral in cylindrical coordinates. Still using curved indivisibles, Torricelli found, among other things, the volume of the solid limited by two plane surfaces and by any lateral surface, in particular the volume of barrels. In 1643 the results were communicated to Fermat, Descartes, and Roberval, who found them very elegant and correct.

The example of the hyperbola induced Torricelli to study more general curves, defined today by equations having the form $x^m y^n = c^n$, with m and n positive whole numbers and $m \neq n$. He discovered that their revolution round an asymptote could generate an infinitely long solid with finite volume and that, under particular conditions, the area comprised between the asymptote and the curve could also be finite. Torricelli intended to coordinate all these results, communicated by letter to various mathematicians in 1646 and 1647, in a single work entitled *De infinitis hyperbolis*, but he died before it could be completed. Only after publication of the *Opere* was it possible to reconstruct the paper from scattered notes.

The geometry of indivisibles was also applied by Torricelli to the determination of the center of gravity of figures. In a letter to Michelangelo Ricci dated 7 April 1646, he communicated the "universal theorem," still considered the most general possible even today, which allows determination of the center of gravity of any figure through the relation between two integrals. Among particular cases mention should be made of the determination of the center of gravity of a circular sector, obtained both by the classic procedure and by the method of indivisibles. Torricelli arrived at the same result, perhaps known to him, that Charles de La Faille had reached in 1632.

Torricelli also directed his attention to rectifica-

tion of arcs of a curve, which Descartes in his *Géométrie* of 1637 had declared to be impossible, after having learned from Mersenne that Roberval had demonstrated the equality of length of particular arcs of a parabola and of arcs of an Archimedean spiral. Having conceived the logarithmic spiral, which he termed "geometric," he taught a procedure allowing rectification with ruler and compass of the entire section comprised between any point on the curve and the center, to which the curve tends after an infinite number of revolutions. Torricelli further demonstrated that any Archimedean spiral—or "arithmetic spiral," as he called it—can always be made equal to any particular arc of a suitable parabolic curve.

In addition to these contributions to the integral calculus, Torricelli discovered many relationships of differential calculus. Among the applications he made to the concept of derivative, drawn from the doctrine of motion (see below), mention should be made of his research on maxima and minima. He showed that if the sum $x + y$ is constant, the product $x^m y^n$ is maximum if x and y have the same relation as the exponents. He also determined the point still known as Torricelli's point on the plane of a triangle for which the sum of the distances from the vertices is minimum; the problem had been proposed by Fermat.

Torricelli made other important contributions to mathematics during his studies of mechanics. In *De motu gravium* he continued the study of the parabolic motion of projectiles, begun by Galileo, and observed that if the acceleratory force were to cease at any point of the trajectory, the projectile would move in the direction of the tangent to the trajectory. He made use of this observation, earning Galileo's congratulations, to draw the tangent at a point of the Archimedean spiral, or the cycloid, considering the curves as described by a point endowed with two simultaneous motions. In unpublished notes the question is thoroughly studied in a more general treatment. A point is considered that is endowed with two simultaneous motions, one uniform and the other varying, directed along two straight lines perpendicular to each other. After constructing the curve for distance as a function of time, Torricelli shows that the tangent at any point of the curve forms with the time axis an angle the tangent of which measures the speed of the moving object at that point. In substance this recognizes the inverse character of the operations of integration and differentiation, which form the fundamental theorem of the calculus, published in 1670 by Isaac Barrow, who among his predecessors mentioned Galileo, Cavalieri, and Torricelli. But not even Barrow understood the importance of the theorem, which was first demonstrated by Newton.

Full mastery of the new geometrical methods made Torricelli aware of the inherent dangers, so that his manuscripts contain passages against infinites. His unpublished writings, in fact, include a collection of paradoxes to which the doctrine of indivisibles leads when not applied with the necessary precautions.

In *De motu gravium* Torricelli seeks to demonstrate Galileo's principle regarding equal velocities of free fall of weights along inclined planes of equal height. He bases his demonstration on another principle, now called Torricelli's principle but known to Galileo, according to which a rigid system of a number of bodies can move spontaneously on the earth's surface only if its center of gravity descends. After applying the principle to movement through chords of a circle and parabola, Torricelli turns to the motion of projectiles and, generalizing Galileo's doctrine, considers launching at any oblique angle — whereas Galileo had considered horizontal launching only. He demonstrates in general form Galileo's incidental observation that if at any point of the trajectory a projectile is relaunched in the opposite direction at a speed equal to that which it had at such point, the projectile will follow the same trajectory in the reverse direction. The proposition is equivalent to saying that dynamic phenomena are reversible — that the time of Galileo's mechanics is ordered but without direction. Among the many theorems of external ballistics, Torricelli shows that the parabolas corresponding to a given initial speed and to different inclinations are all tangents to the same parabola (known as the safety parabola or Torricelli's parabola, the first example of an envelope curve of a family of curves).

The treatise concludes with five numerical tables. The first four are trigonometric tables giving the values of sine 2α, sine$^2\alpha$, $\frac{1}{2}$ tan α, and sine α, respectively, for every degree between 0° and 90°; with these tables, when the initial speed and angle of fire are known, all the other elements characteristic of the trajectory can be calculated. The fifth table gives the angle of inclination, when the distance to which the projectile is to be launched and the maximum range of the weapon are known. In the final analysis these are firing tables, the practical value of which is emphasized by the description of their use in Italian, easier than Latin for artillerymen to understand. Italian is also the language used for the concluding description of a new square that made it easier for gunners to calculate elevation of the weapon.

The treatise also refers to the movement of water in a paragraph so important that Ernst Mach proclaimed Torricelli the founder of hydrodynamics. Torricelli's aim was to determine the efflux velocity of a jet of liquid spurting from a small orifice in the bottom of a receptacle. Through experiment he had noted that if the liquid was made to spurt upward, the jet reached a height less than the level of the liquid in the receptacle. He supposed, therefore, that if all the resistances to motion were nil, the jet would reach the level of the liquid. From this hypothesis, equivalent to a conservation principle, he deduced the theorem that bears his name: The velocity of the jet at the point of efflux is equal to that which a single drop of the liquid would have if it could fall freely in a vacuum from the level of the top of the liquid at the orifice of efflux. Torricelli also showed that if the hole is made in a wall of the receptacle, the jet of fluid will be parabolic in form; he then ended the paragraph with interesting observations on the breaking of the fluid stream into drops and on the effects of air resistance. Torricelli's skill in hydraulics was so well known to his contemporaries that he was approached for advice on freeing the Val di Chiana from stagnant waters, and he suggested the method of reclamation by filling.

Torricelli is often credited — although the idea is sometimes attributed to the Grand Duke Ferdinando II — with having converted Galileo's primitive air thermoscope to a liquid thermometer, at first filled with water and later with spirits of wine. On the other hand, there is very good evidence of his technical ability in working telescope lenses, a skill almost certainly acquired during his stay in Florence. By the autumn of 1642 he was already capable of making lenses that were in no way mediocre, although they did not attain the excellence of those made by Francesco Fontana, at that time the most renowned Italian telescope maker. Torricelli had set out to emulate and surpass Fontana. By 1643 he was already able to obtain lenses equal to Fontana's or perhaps even better, but above all he had come to understand that what is really important for the efficiency of a lens is the perfectly spherical machining of the surface, which he carried out with refined techniques. The efficiency of Torricelli's lenses was recognized by the grand duke, who in 1644 presented Torricelli with a gold necklace bearing a medal with the motto "Virtutis praemia."

The fame of Torricelli's excellent lenses quickly became widespread and he received many requests, which he fulfilled at a good profit. He attributed the efficiency of telescopes fitted with his lenses to a machining process that was kept secret at the time but was described in certain papers passed at Torricelli's death to the grand duke, who gave them to Viviani, after which they were lost. An elaborate story has sometimes been woven round this "secret"; but from the surviving documents it seems possible to reconstruct the whole of Torricelli's "secret"—which, apart from the need to enhance the merits of his production in the grand duke's eyes, consisted mainly in very accurate machining of the surfaces, in selecting good-quality glass, and in not fastening the lenses "with pitch, or in any way with fire." But this last precaution—which, according to Torricelli, was known only to God and himself—had been recommended by Hieronymus Sirturi in his *Telescopium* as far back as 1618. In any event, one of Torricelli's telescope lenses, which is now preserved together with other relics at the Museo di Storia della Scienza, Florence, was examined in 1924 by Vasco Ronchi, using the diffraction grating. It was found to be of exquisite workmanship, so much so that one face was seen to have been machined better than the mirror taken as reference surface, and was constructed with the most advanced technique of the period.

The lectures given by Torricelli on various occasions, and collected by Tommaso Bonaventuri in the posthumous volume *Lezioni accademiche*, were by preference on subjects in physics. They include eight lectures to the Accademia della Crusca, of which he was a member (one lecture of thanks for admission to the academy, three on the force of impact, two on lightness, one on wind, and one on fame); one in praise of mathematics, given to the Studio Fiorentino; two on military architecture at the Academy of Drawing, and one of encomium for the "golden century," the fabled epoch of human perfection, delivered to the "Accademia dei Percossi."

From the point of view of physics, the lectures on the force of impact and on wind are of particular interest. In the former he said that he was reporting ideas expressed by Galileo in their informal conversations, and there is no lack of original observations. For example, the assertion that "forces and impetus" (what we call energy) lie in bodies was interpreted by Maxwell in the last paragraph of *A Treatise on Electricity and Magnetism* (1873) as meaning that the propagation of energy is a mediate and not remote action. In the lecture on wind Torricelli refuted the current theory on the formation of wind, which was held to be generated by vaporous exhalations evaporating from the damp earth; on the other hand, he advanced the modern theory that winds are produced by differences of air temperature, and hence of density, between two regions of the earth.

But Torricelli's name is linked above all to the barometric experiment named after him. The argument on vacuum or fullness goes back to the first Greek philosophical schools. In the Middle Ages, Catholic theology replaced Aristotle's doctrine that a vacuum is a contradiction in logic by the concept that nature abhors a vacuum (*horror vacui*). During the Renaissance the argument between supporters of vacuum and those of fullness flared up again. Galileo, joining the rationalist philosophers Telesio and Bruno, opposed Aristotle's arguments against the vacuum and about 1613 experimentally demonstrated the weight of air. But, like the majority of his contemporaries, he believed that an element does not have weight in itself; hence, on the basis of the ascertained weight of air, he was unable to deduce pressures within atmospheric air. To explain the phenomenon that in suction pumps the water does not rise more than eighteen *braccia* (about nine meters), as observed by the Florentine well diggers, Galileo advanced the hypothesis of a force—the "force of vacuum"—that occurred inside the pump and was capable of balancing a column of water eighteen *braccia* high.

In 1630, when Giovanni Battista Baliani asked him why a siphon that was to cross a hill about twenty-one meters high did not work, Galileo replied by reiterating his theory of the force of vacuum. Baliani retorted that in his opinion the failure of the siphon was due to the weight of the air, which by pressing on all sides supported the column of water not under pressure in the top part of the siphon, from which the air had been expelled by the water poured in to fill it. But Galileo did not accept Baliani's ideas, and in the *Discorsi* (1638) he continued to uphold the theory of the force of vacuum. After Galileo's death the discussion continued between his followers in Rome and Florence; and it is probable that the former turned to Torricelli to get his opinion on the working of suction pumps or on a similar experiment that Gasparo Berti is said to have carried out at Rome in 1640 for the purpose of showing that the water in suction pumps rose to more than eighteen *braccia*.

Torricelli, who was perhaps acquainted with

Baliani's concept, proceeded to repeat Berti's or Baliani's experiment, using progressively heavier liquids such as seawater, honey, and mercury, which was mined in Tuscany. The use of mercury also allowed him to simplify the filling process by replacing Baliani's or Berti's siphon with a simple glass tube about one meter long. He planned to fill it to the rim with mercury, to close it with one finger and overturn it, and to immerse the open end in mercury in a bowl. To make such a long tube capable of withstanding the weight of mercury was not an easy task at that time (only in 1646 was Mersenne able to obtain a sufficiently strong tube from the French glassworks); Torricelli asked Viviani to make one, and hence the latter was the first to perform the experiment.

In a letter of 11 June 1644 to Michelangelo Ricci, Torricelli described the experiment and, rejecting the theory of the force of vacuum, interpreted it according to Baliani. But even before carrying out the experiment he was aware of the variations in atmospheric pressure, since in the letter he says that he "wished to make an instrument that would show the changes of air, now heavier and denser, now lighter and thinner." According to a fairly well founded hypothesis, he had acquired a knowledge of the variations in atmospheric pressure through skillful observation of the behavior of hydrostatic toys, perhaps invented by him and later called "Cartesian devils." According to Torricelli the force that supports the mercury column is not internal to the tube but external, produced by the atmosphere that weighs on the mercury in the bowl. If, instead of mercury, the tube had contained water, Torricelli predicted that the height of the column would have been greater by the proportion that the weight of mercury exceeds that of water, a result verified by Pascal in 1647. In confirmation of the hypothesis that the cause of support of the mercury is outside and not inside the tube, Torricelli describes other experiments with tubes blown into a sphere at the top, with which equal heights of the mercury column were obtained, so that the force was not due to the volume of vacuum produced and therefore was not a "force of vacuum."

In his reply to Torricelli's letter Ricci put forward three objections showing how difficult it was for contemporaries to understand the transmission of pressure in air: (1) If the bowl is closed with a lid, the air weighs on the lid and not on the mercury, which should therefore fall in the bowl; (2) The weight of the air acts in a vertical direction from top to bottom, so how can it be transmitted from bottom to top inside the tube? (3) Bodies immersed in a fluid are subject to Archimedes' thrust, so the mercury should be pushed upward by a force equivalent to an equal column of air. Torricelli replied in a letter of 28 June 1644, carefully refuting the objections as follows: (1) If the lid does not change the "degree of condensation" of the air locked between the lid itself and the mercury in the bowl, things remain as before—this is shown by the example of a wood cylinder loaded with a weight and cut crosswise by an iron plate, in which the lower part remains compressed as before; (2) Fluids gravitate downward by nature, but "push and spurt in all directions, even upward"; (3) The mercury in the tube is not immersed in air. In substance Torricelli's two letters elaborate the theory of atmospheric pressure, with a hint at what was to be Pascal's principle.

According to the writings of his contemporaries, Torricelli, after succeeding in the experiment, sought to observe the conditions of life of small animals (fish, flies, butterflies) introduced into the vacuum. The results obtained were almost nil, however, because the creatures were crushed by the weight of the mercury before reaching the top part of the tube; and attempts to ascertain whether sound is propagated in a vacuum also appear to have been unsuccessful. In testimony of his great appreciation Grand Duke Ferdinando II issued a decree praising this experiment of Torricelli's very highly.

Copies of Torricelli's two letters were circulated among Italian scientists and were sent to Mersenne, who, traveling to Italy in October 1644, passed through Florence and obtained a repetition of the experiment from Torricelli himself. On his return to France, he informed his friends of Torricelli's experiment, giving rise to flourishing experimental and theoretical activity. Discovery of the barometer, Vincenzo Antinori wrote, changed the appearance of physics just as the telescope changed that of astronomy; the circulation of the blood, that of medicine; and Volta's pile, that of molecular physics.

BIBLIOGRAPHY

I. ORIGINAL WORKS. The writings and scientific correspondence were published in *Opere di Evangelista Torricelli*, Gino Loria and Giuseppe Vassura, eds., 4 vols. in 5 pts. (I–III, Faenza, 1919; IV, 1944).

Individual works are *Opera geometrica. De sphaera et solidis sphaeralibus libri duo . . . De motu gravium naturaliter descendentium et proiectorum libri duo. De dimensione parabolae* (Florence, 1644), the first sec. repr. with its long title, *De sphaera et solidis sphaeralibus libri duo in quibus Archimedis doctrina de sphaera et cylindro denuo componitur, latius promovetur et in omni specie solidorum, quae vel circa, vel intra sphaeram, ex conversione poligonorum regularium gigni possint, universalius propagatur* (Bologna, 1692); *Lezioni accademiche,* Tommaso Bonaventuri, ed. (Florence, 1715; 2nd ed., Milan, 1813); and "Sopra la bonificazione della Valle di Chiana," in *Raccolta d'autori che trattano del moto delle acque,* IV (Florence, 1768). Other short writings were published in historical works, mentioned below.

The majority of Torricelli's MSS, after complicated vicissitudes and some losses, as recounted in the intro. to the *Opere,* are preserved at the Biblioteca Nazionale Centrale, Florence; Angiolo Procissi, in *Evangelista Torricelli nel terzo centenario della morte* (Florence, 1951), 77–109, gives an accurate catalogue raisonné. The autograph works, except for one, and the souvenirs kept at the Torricelli Museum in Faenza were destroyed in 1944.

There are two oil portraits of Torricelli in the Uffizi Gallery in Florence; another portrait, engraved by Pietro Anichini, is reproduced on the frontispiece of the *Lezioni accademiche.*

II. SECONDARY LITERATURE. All histories of mathematics or physics deal more or less fully with Torricelli's life and work. *Opere,* IV, 341–346, contains a bibliography. Some of the most significant works are Timauro Antiate (pseudonym of Carlo Dati), *Lettera ai Filaleti. Della vera storia della cicloide e della famosissima esperienza dell'argento vivo* (Florence, 1663), the first publication of the correspondence with Ricci on the barometric experiment; [Tommaso Bonaventuri], in *Lezioni accademiche,* preface, v–xlix; Angelo Fabroni, *Vitae Italorum doctrina excellentium qui saeculis XVII et XVIII floruerunt,* I (Pisa, 1778), 340–399, the appendix of which contains *Racconto di alcuni problemi*; and Giovanni Targioni Tozzetti, *Notizie degli aggrandimenti delle scienze fisiche accaduti in Toscana nel corso di anni LX del secolo XVII,* 4 vols. (Florence, 1780).

See also Vincenzo Antinori, *Notizie istoriche relative all'Accademia del Cimento,* in the series Saggi di Naturali esperienze fatte nell'Accademia del Cimento (Florence, 1841), *passim,* esp. 27; Ernst Mach, *Die Mechanik in ihrer Entwickelung historisch-kritisch dargestellt,* 2nd ed. (Leipzig, 1889), 377 ff.; and Raffaello Caverni, *Storia del metodo sperimentale in Italia,* 6 vols. (Florence, 1891–1900; repr. Bologna, 1970)—vols. I, IV, V have unpublished passages from Torricelli.

After publication of the *Opere,* which contained many unpublished writings, the studies on Torricelli received a new impetus. The following works contain many other bibliographical references: Vasco Ronchi, "Sopra una lente di Evangelista Torricelli," in *l'Universo* (Florence), 5, no. 2 (1924); Mario Gliozzi, *Origini e sviluppi dell'esperienza torricelliana* (Turin, 1931), repr. with additions in *Opere,* IV, 231–294; C. de Waard,

L'expérience barométrique, ses antécédents et ses explications (Thouars, 1936); Guido Castelnuovo, *Le origini del calcolo infinitesimale nell'era moderna* (Bologna, 1938; 2nd ed., Milan, 1962), *passim,* esp. 52–53, 58–62; Ettore Bortolotti, "L'opera geometrica di Evangelista Torricelli," in *Monatshefte für Mathematik und Physik,* **48** (1939), repr. in *Opere,* IV, 301–337; Ettore Carruccio, *De infinitis spiralibus,* intro., rearrangement, trans., and notes by Carruccio (Pisa, 1955); Giuseppe Rossini, *Lettere e documenti riguardanti Evangelista Torricelli* (Faenza, 1956); *Convegno di studi torricelliani in occasione del 350° anniversario della nascita di Evangelista Torricelli* (Faenza, 1959); and W. E. Knowles Middleton, *The History of the Barometer* (Baltimore, 1964), ch. 2.

MARIO GLIOZZI

TROPFKE, JOHANNES (*b.* Berlin, Germany, 14 October 1866; *d.* Berlin, 10 November 1939)

Tropfke came from a wealthy family. A bright student, he was encouraged to study a number of different subjects at the Friedrichs Gymnasium, and his wide-ranging interests at the University of Berlin are reflected in the list of subjects Tropfke prepared for the state examination in 1889: mathematics, physics, philosophy, botany, zoology, Latin, and Greek. His dissertation dealt with a topic in the theory of functions. An enthusiastic teacher, he was director of the Kirschner Oberrealschule from 1912 to 1932.

Tropfke's program for changing the secondary school mathematics curriculum, presented in 1899, was published in expanded form as *Geschichte der Elementarmathematik in systematischer Darstellung* (1902–1903). Even in this form, however, it was still based mainly on a study of secondary literature that was largely unchecked by an examination of original sources. Tropfke subsequently produced a second, seven-volume edition (1921–1924) that benefited from the constructive and sympathetic criticism of Heinrich Wieleitner and Gustaf Eneström. This work offered what was, at the time, an excellent overall account of the subject, enriched by a wealth of extremely valuable citations and references. Moreover, it exerted a decisive influence on the reorganization of mathematical education, encouraging teachers to devote greater attention to historical development.

Advances in the study of the history of mathematics led Tropfke to undertake a third, revised and enlarged edition of his work; but it was not completed. He died shortly after the beginning of the war; and the remaining volumes, already in manuscript, were destroyed.

BIBLIOGRAPHY

Tropfke's writings include *Zur Darstellung des ellip-tischen Integrals erster Gattung* (Halle, 1889), his dis-sertation; *Erstmaliges Auftreten der einzelnen Bestand-teile unserer Schulmathematik* (Berlin, 1899); *Geschichte der Elementarmathematik in systematischer Darstel-lung,* 2 vols. (Leipzig, 1902–1903; 2nd ed., 7 vols., Leipzig–Berlin, 1921–1924; 3rd ed., 4 vols., Leipzig–Berlin, 1930–1940); "Archimedes und die Trigonome-trie," in *Archiv für Geschichte der Mathematik, der Naturwissenschaften und der Technik,* n.s. **10** (1928), 432–461; "Zur Geschichte der quadratischen Gleichun-gen über dreieinhalb Jahrtausende," in *Jahresberichte der Deutschen Mathematiker-vereinigung,* **43** (1933), 98–107; and **44** (1934), 26–47, 95–119; and "Die Siebenecksabhandlung des Archimedes," in *Osiris,* **1** (1936), 636–651.

An obituary by J. E. Hofmann, with portrait and bibli-ography, is in *Deutsche Mathematik,* **6** (1941), 114–118.

J. E. HOFMANN

TROUGHTON, EDWARD

TROUGHTON, EDWARD (*b.* Corney, Cumber-land, England, October 1753; *d.* London, England, June 1836)

Troughton was one of the most competent math-ematical instrument makers of the late eighteenth and early nineteenth centuries. In many ways his career was parallel to that of Jesse Ramsden, his earlier counterpart, whom he was to replace as the foremost instrument maker of England.

In 1770 Troughton was apprenticed to his elder brother, John, who specialized in dividing and en-graving instruments for other makers. His shop was on Surrey Street, in the Strand. In 1779 John and Edward Troughton became partners, and in 1782 they bought the business of Benjamin Cole at "The Sign of the Orrery," at 136 Fleet Street. This was a well-established enterprise, having been founded by John Worgan about 1680 and contin-ued, in turn, by John Rowley, Thomas Wright, and the two Benjamin Coles, father and son.

John Troughton died in 1784; and Edward con-ducted the business alone until 1826, when he joined with William Simms, a skilled instrument maker. The firm was renamed Troughton and Simms and, after Troughton's retirement in 1831, continued under that name until 1922 when, through a merger, it became Cooke, Troughton and Simms Ltd.

Troughton's reputation rested on the accuracy and beautiful proportions of his instruments. In 1822 he wrote, "The beauty of the instrument lies not in the flourishes of the engraver, chaser and carver but in the uniformity of figure and just pro-portion alone."

Troughton made many contributions to the de-velopment of instrument making: in 1788 an im-provement of Hadley's quadrant; in 1790 a mer-curial pendulum; and in 1796 a refined version of the Borda, or reflecting circle. He was responsible for substituting spider web filaments for hair or wire in his optical micrometers.

Troughton's most notable achievement was the improvement of the method of dividing a circle. His paper on this in 1809 won him the Copley Medal from the Royal Society of London, which elected him a fellow the following year. In 1822 he was elected a fellow of the Royal Society of Edin-burgh. He was a founding member of the Royal Astronomical Society.

Examples of his instruments are to be found in the Kensington Science Museum, London; the museums of the history of science in Oxford and Florence; the Whipple Museum, Cambridge; the National Maritime Museum, Greenwich; the Pea-body Museum, Salem, Massachusetts; the Conser-vatoire des Arts et Métiers, Paris; and the Smith-sonian Institution, Washington, D.C.

BIBLIOGRAPHY

I. ORIGINAL WORKS. Troughton's works are "An Account of a Method of Dividing Astronomical and Other Instruments by Ocular Inspection, in Which the Usual Tools for Graduating Are Not Employed, etc.," in *Philosophical Transactions of the Royal Society,* **99,** pt. 1 (1809), 105–145; *On the Repeating and Alti-tude-Azimuth Circle* (London, 1812); and "An Account of the Repeating Circle and of the Altitude and Azimuth Instrument, Describing Their Different Constructions, Etc.," in *Memoirs of the Astronomical Society,* **33** (1821), and in *Philosophical Magazine* (1822).

II. SECONDARY LITERATURE. On Troughton's life and work, see the *Dictionary of National Biography,* XIX (London, 1917), 1186–1187. Other works include Mar-ia Luisa Bonelli, *Catalogo degli Strumenti del Museo di Storia della Scienza* (Florence, 1954), pp. 67, 204, 206, 225; Maurice Daumas, *Les instruments scientifiques au XVII et XVIII siècles* (Paris, 1953), 320–321; Nicholas Goodison, *English Barometers, 1680–1860* (New York, 1968), 240; Henry C. King, *The History of the Telescope* (London, 1955), 230–236; J. A. Repsold, *Zur Geschichte der astronomischen Messwerkzeuge, 1450–1830* (Leipzig, 1908), 118–122; E. G. R. Taylor, *The Mathematical Practitioners of Hanoverian England* (London, 1966), 298–299; and E. Wilfred Taylor and J. Simms Wilson, *At the Sign of the Orrery,* pp. 24–30.

RODERICK S. WEBSTER

TSCHIRNHAUS, EHRENFRIED WALTHER (*b.* Kieslingswalde, near Görlitz, Germany, 10 April 1651; *d.* Dresden, Germany, 11 October 1708)

Tschirnhaus was the youngest son of Christoph von Tschirnhaus, a landowner, and Elisabeth Eleonore Freiin Achyll von Stirling, who belonged to a collateral branch of the mathematically gifted Stirling family. His mother died when he was six, but he was brought up by a loving stepmother. After receiving an excellent education from private tutors, Tschirnhaus entered the senior class of the Görlitz Gymnasium in 1666. In the autumn of 1668 he enrolled at the University of Leiden to study philosophy, mathematics, and medicine. He was deeply impressed by the tolerant atmosphere there, as well as by the fiery philosopher Arnold Geulincx, an occasionalist, and the distinguished physician F. de la Boë (Sylvius), who taught Harvey's theory of the circulation of the blood. The most profound influence on him in these years, however, was that of Descartes's philosophy and mathematics, to which he was introduced in private instruction by Pieter van Schooten.

At the beginning of the war between Holland and France in 1672, Tschirnhaus joined the student volunteer corps but did not see action. Following a short visit to Kieslingswalde in 1674, he returned to Leiden and was introduced by his school friend Pieter van Gent to Spinoza, whose teachings he immediately adopted. With a letter of recommendation from Spinoza, he went to London in May 1675 to see Henry Oldenburg. Tschirnhaus had become an excellent algebraist and was able to make a persuasive presentation of his methods for solving equations. He visited John Wallis at Oxford and held discussions with John Collins, to whom he showed examples of his methods. On closer examination, however, they proved to be special cases of a previously known solution.

Bearing recommendations from Oldenburg addressed to Huygens and Leibniz, Tschirnhaus moved to Paris in the fall of 1675. He did not then know French, and when engaged to teach mathematics to one of Colbert's sons, did so in Latin. In an animated exchange with Leibniz, Tschirnhaus reported in general terms on his own methods but only half listened to what Leibniz told him concerning his recent creation of a symbolism for infinitesimal processes. In fact, Tschirnhaus never did grasp the significance of Leibniz' disclosure, and throughout his life he considered the infinitesimal symbolism to be of limited applicability.

Leibniz introduced Tschirnhaus to Clerselier, who had custody of Descartes's papers and allowed them to look through unpublished manuscripts. The two also had an opportunity to examine the posthumous papers of Pascal and Roberval. Tschirnhaus reported on the progress of his studies at Paris in a number of interesting letters to Pieter van Gent, Spinoza, and the latter's friend G. H. Schuller. In the summer of 1676 he corresponded with Oldenburg concerning Descartes's mathematical methods. Tschirnhaus considered them unsurpassable, but Collins had expressed considerable skepticism about them. Consequently, the reports in which Oldenburg and Newton communicated the results obtained by expansions of series were addressed jointly to Leibniz and Tschirnhaus. In his reply of 1 September, Tschirnhaus judged these results somewhat disparagingly; Collins responded with a strong rebuttal, as did Newton in a second letter to Leibniz and Tschirnhaus (3 November 1676).

Also in 1676 Tschirnhaus accompanied Count Nimpsch of Silesia on a trip to southern France and Italy. Everywhere he went, Tschirnhaus sought contact with leading scientists, collected observations, and reported interesting discoveries to Leibniz. Among the matters he communicated to Leibniz was an algorithmic method of reduction that he wrongly believed could be applied to equations of any higher degree. (This method was published in *Acta eruditorum* in 1683.) He also reported on a supposedly new method of quadrature that was in fact merely the result of recasting a procedure devised by Gregory of Saint-Vincent in 1647 in a form better suited for computation. (The improvement had been effected by the use of indivisibles of zero width.) During his return trip in 1679, Tschirnhaus stopped at Paris, at The Hague (where he saw Huygens), and at Hannover (where he visited Leibniz).

While continuing his mathematical research Tschirnhaus constructed effective circular and parabolic mirrors, with which he obtained high temperatures by focusing sunlight. He also made burning glasses, though not without flaws. During a trip to Paris in the summer of 1682, he became a member of the Académie des Sciences. He did not, however, receive the hoped-for royal pension that would have enabled him to pursue his scientific work free from financial concern. After returning from Paris, Tschirnhaus married Elisabeth Eleonore von Lest, who took over most of the details of managing the estate his father had left him, thus permitting him to devote his time entirely to study. Among his achievements was the rediscovery of the process for making hard-paste porcelain. J. F.

Böttger, who is usually given the credit, was a skilled craftsman; but all his work was done under Tschirnhaus' supervision.

Tschirnhaus exhausted his mathematical talents in searching for algorithms. Lacking insight into the more profound relations among mathematical propositions, he was all too ready to assert the existence of general relationships on the basis of particular results that he obtained. Further, he was unwilling to accept suggestions directly from other mathematicians, although he would later adopt them as his own inventions and publish them as such. This tactic led to bitter controversies with Leibniz, Huygens, La Hire, and Jakob I and Johann I Bernoulli; and it ultimately cost him his scientific reputation. Without going into details, we may mention two of these disputes. The first, with Leibniz, concerned the possibility of algebraic quadratures of algebraic curves (1682–1684). The second, with Fatio de Duillier (1687–1689), was provoked by Tschirnhaus' publication of an incorrect method of finding tangents to curves generated by the motion of a drawing pencil within a system of taut threads. The method appeared in a major work of considerable philosophical importance, *Medicina corporis et mentis* (1686–1687), which was influential in the early stages of the Enlightenment. Another work by Tschirnhaus, *Gründliche Anleitung zu den nützlichen Wissenschaften* (1700), was highly praised by Leibniz in 1701. Both books deeply impressed Leibniz' disciple Christian Wolff.

Tschirnhaus was essentially an autodidact. During his university years he lacked the guidance of a kind, experienced, yet strict teacher, who could have restrained his exuberant temperament, moderated his excessive enthusiasm for Descartes's ideas, and instilled in him a greater measure of self-criticism. Even so, Tschirnhaus' achievements—often accomplished with insufficient means—were far more significant than the average contribution made by university teachers of science during his lifetime. Indeed, even his errors proved to be important and fruitful stimuli for other scientists.

BIBLIOGRAPHY

I. ORIGINAL WORKS. The major portion of Tschirnhaus' unpublished papers is in the MS division of the library of the University of Wrocław and among the Leibniz MSS of the Niedersächsische Landesbibliothek, Hannover.

His books are *Medicina corporis et mentis*, 3 pts. in 2 vols. (Amsterdam, 1686–1687; 2nd ed., Leipzig, 1695), also translated into German (Frankfurt, 1688; 2nd ed., Lüneburg, 1705–1708) and recently retranslated into German by J. Haussleiter, in *Acta historica Leopoldina* (Leipzig, 1963), with biography, portrait, and detailed bibliography prepared by R. Zaunick; and *Gründliche Anleitung zu den nützlichen Wissenschaften* (n.p., 1700; 2nd ed., 1708; 3rd ed., 1712).

Tschirnhaus' mathematical papers and reviews appeared in *Journal des sçavans* (Amsterdam), no. 15 (8 June 1682), 210–213; in the following issues of *Acta eruditorum*: (1682), 364–365, 391–393; (1683), 122–124, 204–207, 433–437; (1686), 169–176; (1687), 524–527; (1690), 68–73, 169–172, 481–487, 561–565; (1695), 322–323, 489–493; (1696), 519–524; (1697), 113, 220–223, 409–410; (1698), 259–261; and in *Mémoires de physique et de mathématique de l'Académie royale des sciences* for 1701 (1704), 291–293, and for 1702 (1704), 1–3.

His papers on the burning glass were published in the following issues of *Acta eruditorum*: (1687), 52–54; (1688), 206; (1691), 517–520; (1696), 345–347, 554; (1697), 414–419; (1699), 445–448; and in *Histoire de l'Académie royale des sciences* for 1699 (1702), 90–94, and for 1700 (1703), 131–134.

Some of his correspondence has been published in Huygens, *Oeuvres complètes*, VIII and IX (The Hague, 1899–1900); Spinoza, *Opera*, 3rd ed., III (The Hague, 1914); and in Leibniz, *Briefwechsel mit Mathematikern*, C. I. Gerhardt, ed. (Berlin, 1899; repr. Hildesheim, 1962). The entire Leibniz-Tschirnhaus correspondence will eventually be published in Leibniz, *Sämtliche Schriften und Briefe*, 3rd ser.

II. SECONDARY LITERATURE. See H. Weissenborn, *Lebensbeschreibung des E. W. v. Tschirnhaus . . . und Würdigung seiner Verdienste* (Eisenach, 1866); and the following, more recent, works of J. E. Hofmann: "Das *Opus geometricum* des Gregorius a S. Vincentio und seine Einwirkung auf Leibniz," in *Abhandlungen der Preussischen Akademie der Wissenschaften*, Math.-naturwiss. Kl. (1941), no. 13, 55–69; *Die Entwicklungsgeschichte der Leibnizschen Mathematik während des Aufenthaltes in Paris (1672–1676)* (Munich, 1949), enl. English ed., *Leibniz in Paris, 1672–1676* (London–New York, 1974); *Über Jakob Bernoullis Beiträge zur Infinitesimalmathematik* (Geneva, 1956); "Aus der Frühzeit der Infinitesimalmethoden: Auseinandersetzung um die algebraische Quadratur algebraischer Kurven in der zweiten Hälfte des 17. Jahrhunderts," in *Archive for History of Exact Sciences*, 2, no. 4 (1965), 270–343; and "Drei Sätze von E. W. v. Tschirnhaus über Kreissehnen," in *Studia Leibnitiana*, 3 (1971), 99–115. See also E. Winter, *E. W. von Tschirnhaus und die Frühaufklärung in Mittel- und Osteuropa* (Berlin, 1960).

J. E. HOFMANN

TSU CH'UNG-CHIH (*b.* Fan-yang prefecture [modern Hopeh province], China, *ca.* A.D. 429; *d.* China, *ca.* A.D. 500)

Tsu Ch'ung-chih was in the service of the emperor Hsiao-wu (*r.* 454–464) of the Liu Sung dynasty, first as an officer subordinate to the prefect of Nan-hsü (in modern Kiangsu province), then as an officer on the military staff in the capital city of Chien-k'ang (modern Nanking). During this time he also carried out work in mathematics and astronomy; upon the death of the emperor in 464, he left the imperial service to devote himself entirely to science. His son, Tsu Keng, was also an accomplished mathematician.

Tsu Ch'ung-chih would have known the standard works of Chinese mathematics, the *Chou-pi suan-ching* ("Mathematical Book on the Measurement With the Pole"), the *Hai-tao suan-ching* ("Sea-island Manual"), and especially, the *Chui-chang suan-shu* ("Mathematical Manual in Nine Chapters"), of which Liu Hui had published a new edition, with commentary, in 263. Like his predecessors, Tsu Ch'ung-chih was particularly interested in determining the value of π. This value was given as 3 in the *Chou-pi suan-ching*; as 3.1547 by Liu Hsin (*d.* 23); as $\sqrt{10}$, or $\frac{92}{29}$, by Chang Heng (78–139); and as $\frac{142}{35}$, that is, 3.155, by Wan Fan (219–257). Since the original works of these mathematicians have been lost, it is impossible to determine how these values were obtained, and the earliest extant account of the process is that given by Liu Hui, who reached an approximate value of 3.14. Late in the fourth century, Ho Ch'ēng-tien arrived at an approximate value of $\frac{22}{7}$, or 3.1428.

Tsu Ch'ung-chih's work toward obtaining a more accurate value for π is chronicled in the calendrical chapters (*Lu-li chih*) of the *Sui-shu*, an official history of the Sui dynasty that was compiled in the seventh century by Wei Cheng and others. According to this work,

Tsu Ch'ung-chih further devised a precise method. Taking a circle of diameter 100,000,000, which he considered to be equal to one *chang* [ten *ch'ih*, or Chinese feet, usually slightly greater than English feet], he found the circumference of this circle to be less than 31,415,927 *chang*, but greater than 31,415,926 *chang*. [He deduced from these results] that the accurate value of the circumference must lie between these two values. Therefore the precise value of the ratio of the circumference of a circle to its diameter is as 355 to 113, and the approximate value is as 22 to 7.

The *Sui-shu* historians then mention that Tsu Ch'ung-chih's work was lost, probably because his methods were so advanced as to be beyond the reach of other mathematicians, and for this reason were not studied or preserved. In his *Chun-suan-shih Lung-ts'ung* ("Collected Essays on the History of Chinese Mathematics" [1933]), Li Yen attempted to establish the method by which Tsu Ch'ung-chih determined that the accurate value of

π lay between 3.1415926 and 3.1415927, or $\frac{355}{113}$.

It was his conjecture that

"As $\frac{22}{7} > \pi > 3$, Tsu Ch'ung-chih must have set forth that, by the equality

$$\pi = \frac{22x + 3y}{7x + y} = 3.14159265,$$

one can deduce that

$$x = 15.996y, \text{ that is, that } x = 16y.$$

Therefore

$$\pi = \frac{22 \times 16y + 3y}{7 \times 16y + y} = \frac{22 \times 16 + 3}{7 \times 16 + 1} = \frac{355}{113}.$$"

For the derivation of

$$\pi = \frac{22x + 3y}{7x + y},$$

when *a*, *b*, *c*, and *d* are positive integers, it is easy to confirm that the inequalities

$$\frac{a}{b} \geqslant \frac{a+c}{b+d} \geqslant \frac{c}{d}$$

hold. If these inequalities are taken into consideration, the inequalities

$$\frac{22}{7} \geqslant \frac{22x + 3y}{7x + y} \geqslant \frac{3}{1}$$

may be derived.

Ch'ien Pao-tsung, in *Chung-kuo shu-hsüeh-shih* ("History of Chinese Mathematics" [1964]), assumed that Tsu Ch'ung-chih used the inequality

$$S_{2n} < S < S_{2n} + (S_{2n} - S_n),$$

where S_{2n} is the perimeter of a regular polygon of $2n$ sides inscribed within a circle of circumference S, while S_n is the perimeter of a regular polygon of n sides inscribed within the same circle. Ch'ien Pao-tsung thus found that

$$S_{12288} = 3.14159251$$

and

$$S_{24576} = 3.14159261,$$

resulting in the inequality

$$3.1415926 < \pi < 3.1415927.$$

Of Tsu Ch'ung-chih's astronomical work, the most important was his attempt to reform the calendar. The Chinese calendar had been based upon a cycle of 235 lunations in nineteen years, but in 462 Tsu Ch'ung-chih suggested a new system, the Ta-ming calendar, based upon a cycle of 4,836 lunations in 391 years. His new calendar also incorporated a value of forty-five years and eleven months a *tu* ($365\frac{1}{4}$ *tu* representing 360°) for the precession of the equinoxes. Although Tsu Ch'ung-chih's powerful opponent Tai Fa-hsing strongly denounced the new system, the emperor Hsiao-Wu intended to adopt it in the year 464, but he died before his order was put into effect. Since his successor was strongly influenced by Tai Fa-hsing, the Ta-ming calendar was never put into official use.

BIBLIOGRAPHY

On Tsu Ch'ung-chih and his works see Li Yen, *Chung-suan-shih lun-ts'ung* ("Collected Essays on the History of Chinese Mathematics"), I–III (Shanghai, 1933–1934), IV (Shanghai, 1947), I–V (Peking, 1954–1955); *Chung-kuo shu-hsüeh ta-kang* ("Outline of Chinese Mathematics"; Shanghai 1931, repr. Peking 1958), 45–50; *Chun-kuo suan-hsüeh-shi* ("History of Chinese Mathematics"; Shanghai, 1937, repr. Peking, 1955); "Tsu Ch'ung-chih, Great Mathematician of Ancient China," in *People's China*, **24** (1956), 24; and *Chun-kuo ku-tai shu-hsüeh shi-hua* ("Historical Description of the Ancient Mathematics of China"; Peking, 1961), written with Tu Shih-jan.

See also Ch'ien Pao-tsung, *Chung-kuo shu-hsüeh-shih* ("History of Chinese Mathematics"; Peking, 1964), 83–90; Chou Ch'ing-shu, "Wo-kuo Ku-tai wei-ta ti k'o-hsüeh-chia: Tsu Ch'ung-chih" ("A Great Scientist of Ancient China: Tsu Ch'ung-chih"), in Li Kuang-pi and Ch'ien Chün-hua, *Chung-kuo k'o-hsüeh chi-shu fa-ming ho k'o-hsüeh chi-shu jēn-wu lun-chi* ("Essays on Chinese Discoveries and Inventions in Science and Technology

and the Men Who Made Them"; Peking, 1955), 270–282; Li Ti, *Ta k'o-hsüeh-chia Tsu Ch'ung-chih* ("Tsu Ch'ung-chih the Great Scientist"; Shanghai, 1959); Ulrich Libbrecht, *Chinese Mathematics in the Thirteenth Century* (Cambridge, Mass., 1973), 275–276; Mao I-shēng, "Chung-kuo yüan-chou-lü lüeh-shih" ("Outline History of π in China"), in *K'o-hsüeh*, **3** (1917), 411; Mikami Yashio, *Development of Mathematics in China and Japan* (Leipzig, 1912), 51; Joseph Needham, *Science and Civilization in China*, III (Cambridge, 1959), 102; A. P. Youschkevitch, *Geschichte der Mathematik im Mittelalter* (Leipzig, 1964), 59; and Yen Tun-chieh, "Tsu Keng pieh chuan" ("Special Biography of Tsu Keng") in *K'o-hsüeh*, **25** (1941), 460.

AKIRA KOBORI

TUNSTALL, CUTHBERT (*b*. Hackforth, Yorkshire, England, 1474; *d*. London, England, 18 November 1559)

Tunstall was the natural son of Thomas Tunstall and a daughter of Sir John Conyers, and he was later legitimated (in canon law) by their marriage. He attended Oxford (*ca*. 1491) and Cambridge (*ca*. 1496) but removed to Padua in 1499, where he remained for about six years and became doctor of both canon and civil (Roman) laws. He was appointed bishop of London (1522) and later bishop of Durham (1530, deprived 1552, restored 1553, deprived 1559). Although of strong religious convictions, he was humane and moderate, and was respected even by his opponents in matters of religion. While remaining faithful to Roman Catholic dogma, he was aware that reform was needed. He would protest decisions of Henry VIII (who often kept him away from London when unpopular decisions were to be made), but once they had been made, he would submit. Under Mary he refrained from persecuting Protestants. An outstanding classical scholar, Tunstall was a close friend of Sir Thomas More, to whom his arithmetic was dedicated, and of Erasmus, whom he assisted in the preparation of the second edition of his Greek New Testament.

Tunstall's Latin arithmetic, *De arte supputandi* (1522), was published as a farewell to secular writings just before he was consecrated bishop of London. The work made no claim to originality of material but had been compiled over the years from all available works in Latin or other languages that Tunstall understood. As master of the rolls (1516–1522), and on diplomatic missions to the Continent, he had felt the need to refresh his memory of arithmetic to protect himself in monetary transactions. From the material he had collected he determined to write such a clear treatise that no one who knew Latin would lack an instructor in the art of reckoning. The work seems not to have been popular in England. It has never been translated into English, and all editions but the first were printed on the Continent, where it was greatly admired. For example, Simon Grynaeus dedicated the first Greek text of Euclid's *Elements* (Basel, 1533) to Tunstall, since he had explained the calculating of numbers in so excellent a manner. England had lagged behind the rest of Europe in mathematics. Only a chapter on "Arsemetrike and Whereof It Proceedeth," in Caxton's *The Mirrour of the World* (1481), had preceded Tunstall's *De arte supputandi*; and it was not until 1537 that an arithmetic appeared in English.

BIBLIOGRAPHY

In addition to the London eds. of *De arte supputandi* (1522), there were Paris eds. (1529, 1535, 1538) and Strasbourg eds. (1543, 1544, 1548, 1551). For Tunstall's ecclesiastical writings, see Charles Sturge, *Cuthbert Tunstal* (New York, 1938), which also contains a chapter on the arithmetic. For Erasmian humanism and religious developments in England during Tunstall's lifetime, see L. B. Smith, *Tudor Prelates and Politics, 1536–1558* (Princeton, 1953) and J. K. McConica, *English Humanists and Reformation Politics* (Oxford, 1965).

Joy B. Easton

TURÁN, PAUL (*b.* Budapest, Hungary, 28 August 1910; *d.* Budapest, 26 September 1976)

Turán was the eldest son of Aranha Beck and Béla Turán. He had two brothers and a sister, none of whom survived World War II. While in high school he showed considerable mathematical ability. Turán received his teaching diploma in 1933 and his Ph.D. (under Lipót Féjer) at Pázmány Péter University, Budapest, in 1935. Because of the semifascist conditions in Hungary, Turán, who was Jewish, could not obtain a post even as a high school teacher, and had to support himself by private tutoring. In 1938, when he was an internationally known mathematician, he finally became a teacher in the Budapest rabbinical high school.

After thirty-two months in a Nazi labor camp in Hungary in the years 1941–1944, Turán was liberated. He became a *Privatdozent* at the University of Bu-

dapest. In 1947 he went to Denmark for about six months and then spent six months at the Institute for Advanced Study at Princeton (during this period he completed two papers on polynomials and number theory). In 1948 he was elected corresponding member of the Hungarian Academy of Sciences, and became a full member in 1953. In 1948 and 1952 he received the Kossuth Prize, the highest scientific award in Hungary at that time. He became a full professor at the University of Budapest in 1949 and was the head of the department of algebra and number theory at the university and the head of the department of the theory of functions at the Mathematical Institute of the Hungarian Academy of Sciences.

Turán's first major result, produced when he was twenty-four, was his simple proof of the Hardy-Ramanujan result that the number of prime factors of almost all integers is $(1 + 0(1))\log\log n$. Further developments led to the Turán-Kubilius inequality, one of the starting points of probabilistic number theory.

By 1938 Turán had developed the basic ideas of his most important work, the power-sum method, on which he published some fifty papers, both alone and with collaborators (Stanislav Knapowski, Vera T. Sós [his wife], János Pintz, Gabor Halász, and Istvàn Dancs, among others). Turán worked on the power-sum method until his death (his last paper was a survey of the application of the method in explicit formulas for prime numbers). The method has its most significant applications in analytic number theory, but it also led to many important applications in the theory of differential equations, complex function theory, numerical algebra (approximative solution of algebraic equations), and theory of trigonometric series. Turán devoted three books (with the same title but different—increasingly rich—contents) to this subject. The last and most comprehensive one, *On a New Method in Analysis and Its Applications*, was published in 1984.

The essence of the method is to show that the power sum of n arbitrary complex numbers $z_1, \cdots, z_n$—that is, the sum $g(\nu) = \sum_{j=1}^{n} z_j^\nu$—cannot be small for all ν (compared with the maximal or minimal term, say). In fact, to cite just one (perhaps the most important) result of this theory, choosing ν suitably from any interval of length n, we have

$$\max_{\nu = m+1, \ldots, m+n} \frac{|g(\nu)|}{\max_{1 \le j \le n}|z_i|^\nu} \ge \left(\frac{n}{4e(m+n)}\right)^n.$$

In order to understand this estimate, it should be noted that $g(m + 1) = g(m + 2) = \cdots g(m + n - 1) = 0$ is certainly possible—for instance, the z_j's are nth roots of unity. Similar results can be proved if we consider generalized power sums of the type $\sum_{j=1}^{n} b_j z_j^{\nu}$, supposing very general conditions on the coefficients b_j.

To give an idea of the connection between the theory and its applications, it should be noted that these oscillatory results concerning power sums of complex numbers lead directly to oscillatory results on the solutions of some differential equations; but through a rather sophisticated technique (developed by Turán and Knapowski), via the connection of zeros of Riemann's zeta function and primes, it is also possible to detect irregularities in the distribution of primes using these results. The variety of known applications is so rich that it is difficult to mention any area of classical analysis where the method would have no possible applications.

In 1952 Turán wrote a book in Hungarian and German on the power-sum method. A Chinese translation with some new results of this work appeared in 1954. An English version, *On a New Method of Analysis and Application*, completed by Halász and Pintz, appeared in 1984.

Besides his power-sum method, Turán did work in comparative prime number theory, analytic and quasi-analytic functions, differential equations, and other areas of analysis. In comparative prime number theory inequalities about the distribution of primes in different arithmetic progressions are studied. The subject goes back to Pafnuty Chebyshev and Edmund Landau, but Turán and Knapowski (his student and collaborator, who died young) developed it into a systematic theory.

An elementary power-sum problem posed by Turán in 1938 is the following:

Let $|z_1| = 1$, $|z_i| \leq 1$ $(1 < i < n)$ be n complex numbers.

Let $s_k = \sum_{i=1}^{n} z_i^k$ where $\max_{1<k<n} |s_k| = \mathrm{f}(z_1, \ldots, z_n)$.

Let $\mathrm{f}(n) = \min_{z_1,\ldots,z_n} f(z_1, \cdots, z_n)$.

Turán conjectured first of all that $f(n) > c$ for all n. This was proved by F. V. Atkinson in 1960. Turán further conjectured that $\lim_{n\to\infty} f(n) = 1$. This problem is still open.

Extremal graph theory was begun by Turán while he was in a labor camp. He wrote the first paper on this subject, and several more followed. Finally he gave birth to statistical group theory, in which

he wrote seven fairly substantial papers with the author of this essay.

PAUL ERDÖS

TURING, ALAN MATHISON (*b*. London, England, 23 June 1912; *d*. Wilmslow, England, 7 June 1954)

Turing was the son of Julius Mathias Turing and Ethel Sara Stoney. After attending Sherborne School he entered King's College, Cambridge, in 1931. He was elected a fellow of the college in 1935 for his dissertation "On the Gaussian Error Function," which won a Smith's prize in the following year. From 1936 until 1938 Turing worked at Princeton University with Alonzo Church.

While at Princeton Turing published one of his most important contributions to mathematical logic, his 1937 paper "On Computable Numbers, With an Application to the *Entscheidungsproblem*," which immediately attracted general attention. In it he analyzed the processes that can be carried out in computing a number to arrive at a concept of a theoretical "universal" computing machine (the "Turing machine"), capable of operating upon any "computable" sequence—that is, any sequence of zeros and ones. The paper included Turing's proof that Hilbert's *Entscheidungsproblem* is not solvable by these means. Church had, somewhat earlier, solved Hilbert's problem by employing a λ-definable function as a precise form of the intuitive notion of effectively calculable function, while in 1936, S. C. Kleene had proved the equivalence of λ-definability and the Herbrand-Gödel theory of general recursiveness. In his "Computability and λ-Definability" of 1937, Turing demonstrated that his and Church's ideas were equivalent.

In 1939 Turing published "Systems of Logic Based on Ordinals," in which he examined the question of constructing to any ordinal number α a logic $L\alpha$, such that any problem could be solved within some $L\alpha$. This paper had a far-reaching influence; in 1942 E. L. Post drew upon it for one of his theories for classifying unsolvable problems, while in 1958 G. Kreisel suggested the use of ordinal logics in characterizing informal methods of proof. In the latter year S. Feferman also adapted Turing's ideas to use ordinal logics in predicative mathematics.

In 1939 Turing returned to King's College, where his fellowship was renewed. His research was interrupted by World War II, however, and from the latter part of 1939 until 1948 he was employed in the communications department of the Foreign Office; he was awarded the O.B.E. for his work there. After the war, he declined the offer of a lectureship at Cambridge and, in autumn of 1945, joined the staff of the National Physical Laboratory to work on the design of an automatic computing engine (ACE).

In 1948 Turing became a reader in the University of Manchester and assistant director of the Manchester automatic digital machine (MADAM). He also continued to work in mathematical theory, and improved E. L. Post's demonstration of the existence of a semigroup with unsolvable word problem by exhibiting a semigroup with cancellation for which the word problem is (recursively) unsolvable. He made further contributions to group theory and performed calculations on the Riemann zeta-function in which he incorporated his practical work on computing machines.

In 1950 Turing took up the question of the ability of a machine to think, a subject that had gained general interest with the increasing application of mechanical computing devices to more and more complex tasks. His "Computing Machinery and Intelligence" was addressed to a broad audience and marked by a lively style. *The Programmer's Handbook for the Manchester Electronic Computer*, produced under his direction, was published in the same year.

Throughout his life Turing was also interested in applying mathematical and mechanical theory to the biological problem of life forms. He made a promising approach to this question in his 1952 publication "The Chemical Basis of Morphogenesis." In this work he exploited the mathematical demonstration that small variations in the initial conditions of first-order systems of differential equations may result in appreciable deviations in the asymptotic behavior of their solutions to posit that unknown functions might function biologically as form-producers; he was thus able to account for asymmetry in both mathematical and biological form. He was at work on a general theory when he died of perhaps accidental poisoning.

BIBLIOGRAPHY

I. ORIGINAL WORKS. An edition of Turing's collected works is in preparation by Professor Dr. R. O. Gandy. See especially Turing's "On Computable Numbers, With an Application to the *Entscheidungsproblem*," in *Proceedings of the London Mathematical Society*, **42** (1937), 230–265; "On Computable Numbers, With an Application to the *Entscheidungsproblem*. A Correction," *ibid.*, **43** (1937), 544–547; "Computability and λ-Definability," in *Journal of Symbolic Logic*, **2** (1937), 153–163; "Systems of Logic Based on Ordinals," in *Proceedings of the London Mathematical Society*, **45** (1939), 161–228; "The Word Problem in Semigroups With Cancellation," in *Annals of Mathematics*, **52** (1950), 491–505; "Computing Machinery and Intelligence," in *Mind*, **59** (1950), 433–460, repr. as "Can a Machine Think?" in J. R. Newman, *The World of Mathematics*, IV (New York, 1956), 2099–2133; and "The Chemical Basis of Morphogenesis," in *Philosophical Transactions of the Royal Society*, **237** (1952), 37–72.

II. SECONDARY LITERATURE. S. Turing, *Alan M. Turing* (Cambridge 1959), includes a bibliography of works by and about Turing. See also M. Davis, *Computability and Unsolvability* (New York, 1958); S. Feferman, "Ordinal Logics Re-examined," in *Journal of Symbolic Logic*, **23** (1958), 105; "On the Strength of Ordinal Logics," *ibid.*, 105–106; "Transfinite Recursive Progressions of Axiomatic Theories," *ibid.*, **27** (1962), 259–316; and "Autonomous Transfinite Progressions and the Extent of Predicative Mathematics," in B. van Rootselaar and J. F. Staal, eds., *Logic, Methodology and Philosophy of Science*, III (Amsterdam, 1968), 121–135; S. C. Kleene, *Introduction to Metamathematics* (Amsterdam–Groningen, 1952); and *Mathematical Logic* (New York, 1967); G. Kreisel, "Ordinal Logics and the Characterization of Informal Concepts of Proof," in *Proceedings of the International Congress of Mathematicians, 1958* (Cambridge, 1960), 289–299; and M. H. A. Newman, "Alan Mathison Turing," in *Biographical Memoirs of Fellows of the Royal Society 1955*, I (London, 1955), 253–263, which also has a bibliography.

B. VAN ROOTSELAAR

TURNER, PETER (*b.* London, England, 1586; *d.* London, January 1652)

Turner was the son of Dr. Peter Turner and Pascha Parr, and the grandson of William Turner, the physician and naturalist and dean of Wells. He received his B.A. in 1605 and M.A. in 1612 at Oxford, and became a fellow of Merton College in 1607. Turner was the second Gresham professor of geometry (1620–1630) and second Savilian professor of geometry (1630–1648), in both cases succeeding Henry Briggs. He retained his Merton fellowship, going to London for his Gresham lectures in term time. In 1629 he was appointed to a commission charged with the revision of the Oxford statutes. The final draft was largely the work of Brian Twynne, but it was polished for the press by Turner, who was noted for his Latin style.

He was one of the first scholars to enlist for King Charles in 1641. He was captured at the battle of Edgehill and imprisoned for a time. He was ejected both from his fellowship and his professorship by the Parliamentary Visitors in 1648, and retired to live in straitened circumstances with his widowed sister in Southwark. Both Turner and the Savilian professor of astronomy, John Greaves, were replaced by Cambridge men—Turner by John Wallis, and Greaves by Seth Ward.

It is impossible to judge Turner's abilities in mathematics. He left no mathematical writings, and, indeed, seems to have been noted rather as a Latinist and a linguist, being skilled in Greek, Hebrew, and Arabic. According to Wood he destroyed many of his writings, being of too critical a mind. Further, his effects at Oxford were seized during the Civil War. Some translations from Greek to Latin of the church fathers in the possession of his colleague Mr. Henry Jacobs; Latin poems to the memory of Sir Thomas Bodley (1613); and the preface to the revised Oxford Statutes (1634) are all that are known to have survived.

BIBLIOGRAPHY

Turner's life can be found in John Ward, *Lives of the Professors of Gresham College* (1740; Johnson repr., Sources of Science, no. 71). See also C. E. Mallet, *A History of the University of Oxford*, II (Oxford, 1924–1928; repr., New York, 1968); and the *Calendar of State Papers, Domestic*, during the reign of Charles I.

JOY B. EASTON

AL-ṬŪSĪ, MUḤAMMAD IBN MUḤAMMAD IBN AL-ḤASAN, usually known as **NAṢIR AL-DĪN** (*b.* Ṭūs, Persia, 18 February 1201; *d.* Kadhimain, near Baghdad, 26 June 1274)

Life. Naṣīr al-Dīn, known to his compatriots as Muḥaqqiq-i Ṭūsī, Khwāja-yi Ṭūsī, or Khwāja Naṣīr, is one of the best-known and most influential figures in Islamic intellectual history. He studied the religious sciences and elements of the "intellectual sciences" with his father, a jurisprudent of the Twelve Imām school of Shī'ism at Ṭūs. He also very likely studied logic, natural philosophy, and metaphysics with his maternal uncle in the same city. During this period he also received instruction in algebra and geometry. Afterward he

set out for Nīshāpūr, then still a major center of learning, to complete his formal advanced education; and it was in this city that he gained a reputation as an outstanding scholar. His most famous teachers were Farīd al-Dīn al-Dāmād, who through four intermediaries was linked to Ibn Sīnā and his school and with whom Ṭūsī studied philosophy; Quṭb al-Dīn al-Maṣrī, who was himself the best-known student of Fakhr al-Dīn al-Rāzī (1148–1209), with whom al-Ṭūsī studied medicine, concentrating mostly on the text of Ibn Sīnā's *Canon*; and Kamāl al-Dīn ibn Yūnus (1156–1242), with whom he studied mostly mathematics.

This period was one of the most tumultuous in Islamic history: Mongols were advancing toward Khurasan from Central Asia. Therefore, although already a famous scholar, al-Ṭūsī could not find a suitable position and the tranquillity necessary for a scholarly life. The only islands of peace at this time in Khurasan were the Ismā'īlī forts and mountain strongholds, and he was invited to avail himself of their security by the Ismā'īlī ruler, Naṣir al-Dīn Muḥtashim. Al-Ṭūsī accepted the invitation and went to Quhistan, where he was received with great honor and was held in high esteem at the Ismā'īlī court, although most likely he was not free to leave had he wanted to. The date of his entrance into the service of the Ismā'īlī rulers is not known exactly but was certainly sometime before 1232, for it was during that year that he wrote his famous *Akhlāq-i nāṣirī* for the Ismā'īlī ruler. During his stay at the various Ismā'īlī strongholds, including Alamut, al-Ṭūsī wrote a number of his important ethical, logical, philosophical, and mathematical works, including *Asās al-iqtibās* (on logic) and *Risāla-yi mu'īniyya* (on astronomy). His fame as a scholar reached as far as China.

Hūlāgū ended the rule of the Ismā'īlīs in northern Persia in 1256. His interest in astrology, and therefore his respect for astronomers, combined with al-Ṭūsī's fame in this field, made Hūlāgū especially respectful toward him after he had captured Alamut and "freed" al-Ṭūsī from the fort. Henceforth al-Ṭūsī remained in the service of Hūlāgū as his scientific adviser and was given charge of religious endowments (*awqāf*) and religious affairs. He accompanied Hūlāgū on the expedition that led to the conquest of Baghdad in 1258 and later visited the Shī'ite centers of Iraq, such as Ḥilla.

Having gained the full confidence of Hūlāgū, and benefiting from his interest in astrology, al-Ṭūsī was able to gain his approval to construct a major observatory at Marāgha. Construction began in 1259, and the Īlkhānī astronomical tables were completed in 1272 under Abāqā, after the death of Hūlāgū. In 1274, while at Baghdad, al-Ṭūsī fell ill and died a month later. He was buried near the mausoleum of the seventh Shīʿite imām, Mūsā al-Kāzim, a few miles from Baghdad.

Works. Nearly 150 treatises and letters by Naṣīr al-Dīn al-Ṭūsī are known, of which twenty-five are in Persian and the rest in Arabic. There is even a treatise on geomancy that al-Ṭūsī wrote in Arabic, Persian, and Turkish, demonstrating his mastery of all three languages. It is said that he also knew Greek. His writings concern nearly every branch of the Islamic sciences, from astronomy to philosophy and from the occult sciences to theology. Of the two, Ibn Sīnā was the better physician and al-Ṭūsī the greater mathematician and more competent writer in Persian. But otherwise their breadth of knowledge and influence can be compared very favorably. Moreover, the writings of al-Ṭūsī are distinguished by the fact that so many became authoritative works in the Islamic world.

Al-Ṭūsī composed five works in logic, of which *Asās al-iqtibās* ("Foundations of Inference"), written in Persian, is the most important. In fact, it is one of the most extensive of its kind ever written, surpassed only by the section on logic of Ibn Sīnā's *al-Shifāʾ*. In mathematics al-Ṭūsī composed a series of recensions (*taḥrīr*) upon the works of Autolycus, Aristarchus, Euclid, Apollonius, Archimedes, Hypsicles, Theodosius, Menelaus, and Ptolemy. The texts studied by students of mathematics between Euclid's *Elements* and Ptolemy's *Almagest* were known as the "intermediate works" (*mutawassiṭāt*); and the collection of al-Ṭūsī's works concerning this "intermediate" body of texts became standard in the teaching of mathematics, along with his recensions of Euclid and Ptolemy. He also wrote many original treatises on arithmetic, geometry, and trigonometry, of which the most important are *Jawāmiʿ al-ḥisāb biʾl-takht waʾl turāb* ("The Comprehensive Work on Computation with Board and Dust"), *al-Risāla al-shāfiya* ("The Satisfying Treatise"), and *Kashf al-qināʿ fī asrār shakl al-qiṭāʿ*, known as the *Book of the Principle of Transversal*, which was translated into Latin and influenced Regiomontanus. The best-known of al-Ṭūsī's numerous astronomical works is *Zīj-i īlkhānī* ("The Īlkhānī Tables"), written in Persian and later translated into Arabic and also partially into Latin, by John Greaves, as *Astronomia quaedam ex traditione Shah Cholgii Persae una cum hypothesibus planetarum* (London, 1650). Other major astronomical works are *Tadhkirah* ("Treasury of Astronomy") and his treatises on particular astro-

nomical subjects, such as that on the astrolabe. He also translated the *Ṣuwar al-kawākib* ("Figures of the Fixed Stars") of ʿAbd al-Raḥmān al-Ṣūfī from Arabic into Persian. In the other sciences al-Ṭūsī produced many works, of which *Tanksūkh-nāma* ("The Book of Precious Materials") is particularly noteworthy. He also wrote on astrology.

In philosophy, ethics, and theology al-Ṭūsī composed a commentary on *al-Ishārāt waʾl-tanbīhāt* ("The Book of Directives and Remarks") of Ibn Sīnā; the *Akhlāq-i nāṣirī* (*Nasirean Ethics*), the best-known ethical work in the Persian language, and the *Tajrīd* ("Catharsis"), the main source book of Shiʿite theology, upon which over 400 commentaries and glosses have been composed. Al-Ṭūsī wrote outstanding expositions of Ismāʿīlī doctrine, chief among them the *Taṣawwurāt* ("Notions"), and composed mystical treatises, such as *Awṣāf al-ashrāf* ("Qualifications of the Noble").

Al-Ṭūsī also composed lucid and delicate poetry, mostly in Persian.

Scientific Achievements. In logic al-Ṭūsī followed the teachings of Ibn Sīnā but took a new step in studying the relation between logic and mathematics. He also elucidated the conditional conjunctive (*iqtirānī*) syllogism better than his predecessor. He converted logical terms into mathematical signs and clarified the mathematical signs employed by Abuʾl-Barakāt in his *Kitāb al-muʿtabar* ("The Esteemed Book"). Al-Ṭūsī also distinguished between the meaning of "substance" in the philosophical sense and its use as a scientific term, and clarified the relation of the categories with respect to metaphysics and logic.

In mathematics al-Ṭūsī's contributions were mainly in arithmetic, geometry, and trigonometry. He continued the work of al-Khayyāmī in extending the meaning of number to include irrationals. In his *Shakl al-qiṭāʿ* he showed the commutative property of multiplication between pairs of ratios (which are real numbers) and stated that every ratio is a number. *Jawāmiʿ al-ḥisāb*, which marks an important stage in the development of the Indian numerals, contains a reference to Pascal's triangle and the earliest extant method of extracting fourth and higher roots of numbers. In collaboration with his colleagues at Marāgha, al-Ṭūsī also began to develop computational mathematics, which was pursued later by al-Kāshī and other mathematicians of the Tīmūrid period.

In geometry al-Ṭūsī also followed the work of al-Khayyāmī and in his *al-Risāla al-shāfiya* he examined Euclid's fifth postulate. His attempt to prove it through Euclidean geometry was unsuccessful. He demonstrated that in the quadrilateral *ABCD*, in which *AB* and *DC* are equal and both perpendicular to *BC*, and the angles *A* and *D* are equal, if angles *A* and *D* are acute, the sum of the angles of a triangle will be less than 180°.[1] This is characteristic of the geometry of Lobachevski and shows that al-Ṭūsī, like al-Khayyāmī, had demonstrated some of the properties of the then unknown non-Euclidean geometry. The quadrilateral associated with Saccheri was employed centuries before him by Thābit ibn Qurra, al-Ṭūsī, and al-Khayyāmī.

Probably al-Ṭūsī's most outstanding contribution to mathematics was in trigonometry. In *Shakl al-qitāʿ*, which follows the earlier work of Abu'l-Wafāʾ, Manṣūr ibn ʿIrāq, and al-Bīrūnī, al-Ṭūsī for the first time, as far as modern research has been able to show, developed trigonometry without using Menelaus' theorem or astronomy. This work is really the first in history on trigonometry as an independent branch of pure mathematics and the first in which all six cases for a right-angled spherical triangle are set forth. If *c* = the hypotenuse of a spherical triangle, then:

$$\cos c = \cos a \cos b \qquad \cot A = \tan b \cot c$$
$$\cos c = \cot A \cot B \qquad \sin b = \sin c \sin B$$
$$\cos A = \cos a \sin B \qquad \sin b = \tan a \cot A.$$

He also presents the theorem of sines:

$$\frac{a}{\sin A} = \frac{b}{\sin B} = \frac{c}{\sin C}.$$

It is described clearly for the first time in this book, a landmark in the history of mathematics.

Al-Ṭūsī is best-known as an astronomer. With Hūlāgū's support he gained the necessary financial assistance and supervised the construction of the first observatory in the modern sense. Its financial support, based upon endowment funds; its life-span, which exceeded that of its founder; its use as a center of instruction in science and philosophy; and the collaboration of many scientists in its activities mark this observatory as a major scientific institution in the history of science. The observatory was staffed by Quṭb al-Dīn al-Shīrāzī, Muḥyi ʾl-Dīn al-Maghribī, Fakhr al-Dīn al-Marāghī, Muʾayyad al-Dīn al-ʿUrḍī, ʿAlī ibn ʿUmar al-Qazwīnī, Najm al-Dīn Dabīrān al-Kātibī al-Qazwīnī, Athīr al-Dīn al-Abharī, al-Ṭūsī's sons Aṣīl al-Dīn and Ṣadr al-Dīn, the Chinese scholar Fao Mun-ji, and the librarian Kamāl al-Dīn al-Aykī. It had excellent instruments made by Muʾayyad al-Dīn al-ʿUrḍī in 1261–1262, including a giant mural quadrant, an armillary sphere with five rings and an alidade, a solstitial armill, an azimuth ring with two quadrants, and a parallactic ruler. It was also equipped with a fine library with books on all the sciences. Twelve years of observation and calculation led to the completion of the *Zīj-i īlkhānī* in 1271, to which Muḥyī ʾl-Dīn al-Maghribī later wrote a supplement. The work of the observatory was not confined to astronomy, however; it played a major role in the revival of all the sciences and philosophy.

Al-Ṭūsī's contributions to astronomy, besides the *Zīj* and the recension of the *Almagest*, consist of a criticism of Ptolemaic astronomy in his *Tadhkira*, which is perhaps the most thorough exposition of the shortcomings of Ptolemaic astronomy in medieval times, and the proposal of a new theory of planetary motion. The only new mathematical model to appear in medieval astronomy, this theory influenced not only Quṭb al-Dīn al-Shīrāzī and Ibn al-Shāṭir but also most likely Copernicus, who followed closely the planetary models of Naṣir al-Dīn's students. In chapter 13 of the second treatise of the *Tadhkira*, al-Ṭūsī proves that "if one circle rolls inside the periphery of a stationary circle, the radius of the first being half the second, then any point on the first describes a straight line, a diameter of the second."[2] E. S. Kennedy, who first discovered this late medieval planetary theory issuing from Marāgha, interprets it as "a linkage of two equal length vectors, the second rotating with constant velocity twice that of the first and in a direction opposite the first."[3] He has called this the "Ṭūsī-couple" and has demonstrated (see Figures 1 and 2) its application by al-Ṭūsī, Quṭb al-Dīn, and Ibn al-Shāṭir to planetary motion and its comparison with the Ptolemaic model.[4]

This innovation, which originated with al-Ṭūsī, is without doubt the most important departure from Ptolemaic astronomy before modern times. Except for the heliocentric thesis, the "novelty" of Copernicus' astronomy is already found in the works of al-Ṭūsī and his followers, which probably reached Copernicus through Byzantine intermediaries.

The most important mineralogical work by al-Ṭūsī is *Tanksūkh-nāma*, written in Persian and based on many of the earlier Muslim sources, such as the works of Jābir ibn Ḥayyān, al-Kindī, Muḥammad ibn Zakariyyāʾ, al-Rāzī, ʿUṭārid ibn Muḥammad, and especially al-Bīrūnī, whose *Kitāb al-jamāhir fī maʿrifat al-jawāhir* ("The Book of Multitudes Concerning the Knowledge of Precious Stones") is the main source of al-Ṭūsī's work. In fact the *Tanksūkh-nāma*, which derives its name from the Turco-Mongolian word meaning "some-

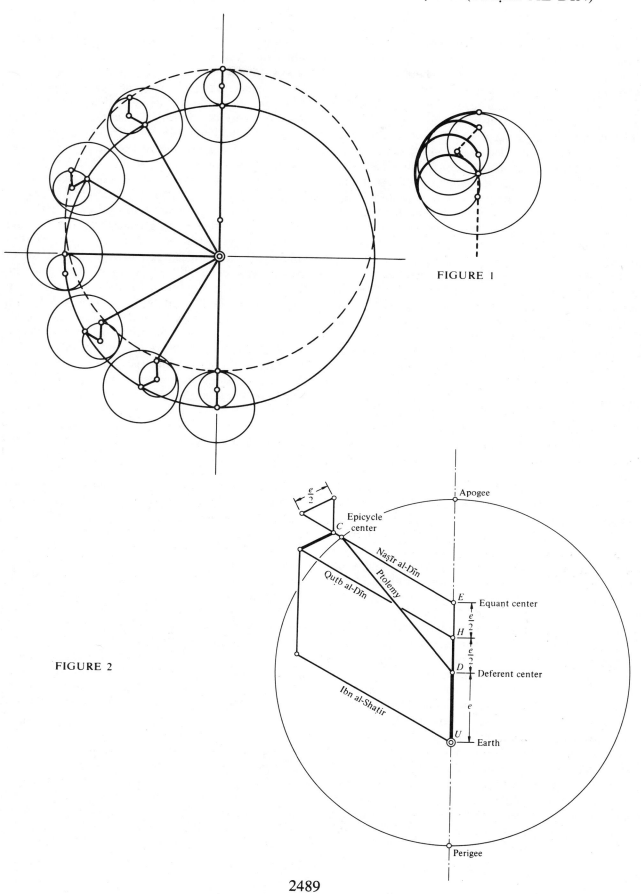

FIGURE 1

FIGURE 2

thing precious," probably is second in importance in the annals of Muslim mineralogy only to al-Bīrūnī's masterpiece.

Al-Ṭūsī's work comprises four chapters. In the first he discusses the nature of compounds; the four elements, their mixture, and the coming into being of a "fifth quality" called temperament (*mizāj*), which can accept the forms of different species; and the role of vapors and the rays of the sun in their formation, in all of this following closely the theories of Ibn Sīnā's *De mineralibus*. An interesting section is devoted to colors, which al-Ṭūsī believes result from the mixture of white and black. In jewels, colors are due to the mixture of earthy and watery elements contained in the substance of the jewel.

The second chapter is devoted exclusively to jewels, their qualities, and their properties. Special attention is paid to rubies, the medical and occult properties of which are discussed extensively. In the third chapter al-Ṭūsī turns to metals and gives an alchemical theory of metallic formation, calling sulfur the father and mercury the mother of metals. He also enumerates the seven traditional metals, including *khārṣīnī*. Like so many Muslim philosopher-scientists, al-Ṭūsī accepts the cosmological and mineralogical theories of alchemy concerning the formation of metals without belonging to the alchemical tradition or even discussing the transmutation of base metal into gold. A section on perfumes ends the book, which is one of the major sources of Muslim mineralogy and is valuable as a source of Persian scientific vocabulary in this field.

Of all the major fields of science, al-Ṭūsī was least interested in medicine, which he nevertheless studied, generally following the teachings of Ibn Sīnā. He also composed a few works on medicine including *Qawānīn al-ṭibb* ("Principles of Medicine") and a commentary on Ibn Sīnā's *Canon*, and exchanged letters with various medical authorities on such subjects as breathing and temperament. He expressed certain differences of opinion with Ibn Sīnā concerning the temperament of each organ of the body but otherwise followed his teachings. Al-Ṭūsī's view of medicine was mainly philosophical; and perhaps his greatest contribution was in psychosomatic medicine, which he discusses, among other places, in his ethical writings, especially *Akhlāq-i nāṣirī* (*Nasirean Ethics*).

Al-Ṭūsī was one of the foremost philosophers of Islam, reviving the Peripatetic (*mashshā'ī*) teachings of Ibn Sīnā after they had been eclipsed for nearly two centuries by *Kalām*. He wrote a masterful commentary on the *Ishārāt wa'l-tanbīhāt* of Ibn Sīnā, which Fakhr al-Dīn al-Rāzī had attacked severely during the previous century. In this work, which is unusual among Muslim philosophical works for its almost mathematical precision, al-Ṭūsī succeeded in rekindling the light of philosophy in Islam. But while claiming in this work to be a mere follower of Ibn Sīnā, in several places questions of God's knowledge of particulars, the nature of space, and the createdness of the physical world clearly shows his debt to Shihāb al-Dīn al-Suhrawardī and some of the Muslim theologians. Al-Ṭūsī in fact marks the first stage in the gradual synthesis of the Peripatetic and Illuminationist (*ishrāqī*) schools, a tendency that became clearer in the writings of his foremost student, Quṭb al-Dīn al-Shīrāzī. He also wrote many philosophical treatises in Persian, so that his prose in this field must be considered, along with the writings of Nāṣir-i Khusraw, Suhrawardī, and Afḍal al-Dīn al-Kāshānī, as the most important in the Persian language.

In ethics al-Ṭūsī composed two major works, both in Persian: the *Akhlāq-i muḥtashimī* ("The Muḥtashimī Ethics") and the much better-known *Nasirean Ethics*, his most famous opus. Based upon the *Tahdhīb al-akhlāq* ("The Refinement of Character") of Muskūya (Miskawayh), the *Nasirean Ethics* expounds a philosophical system combining Islamic teachings with the ethical theories of the Aristotelian and, to a certain extent, the Platonic traditions. The work also contains an elaborate discussion of psychology and psychic healing. For centuries it has been the most popular ethical work among the Muslims of India and Persia.

In Twelve Imām Shiʿism, al-Ṭūsī is considered as much a theologian as a scientist and philosopher because of his *Tajrīd*, which is still central to Shiʿite theological education. A work of great intellectual rigor, the *Tajrīd* represents the first systematic treatment of Shiʿite *Kalām* and is therefore the foundation of systematic theology for the Twelve Imām Shiʿites. In the history of Islam, which is known for its multitalented figures of genius, it is not possible to find another person who was at once an outstanding astronomer and mathematician and the most authoritative theologian of a major branch of Islam.

Influence. Al-Ṭūsī's influence, especially in eastern Islam, was immense. Probably, if we take all fields into account, he was more responsible for the revival of the Islamic sciences than any other individual. His bringing together so many competent scholars and scientists at Marāgha resulted not only in the revival of mathematics and astronomy but also in the renewal of Islamic philosophy and even theology. Al-Ṭūsī's works were for centuries authoritative in many fields of Islamic learning; and his students, such as Quṭb al-Dīn and ʿAllāma Ḥillī, became outstanding scholars and scientists. His astronomical activities influenced the observatories at Samarkand and Istanbul and in the West to a much greater extent than was thought to be the case until recently; and his mathematical studies affected all later Islamic mathematics. In fact, the work of al-Ṭūsī and his collaborators at Marāgha moved eastward to influence Chinese science, which, as a result of the Mongol invasion, had a much closer relationship with Islam. The school of al-Ṭūsī also influenced later Indian science as cultivated under the Moguls and even as late as the eighteenth century, as can be seen in the observatory constructed by Jai Singh II, which indirectly reflects the observatory of Marāgha.

In the West al-Ṭūsī is known almost entirely as an astronomer and mathematician whose significance, at least in these fields, is becoming increasingly evident. In the Muslim East he has always been considered as a foremost example of the "wise man" (ḥakīm), one who, while possessing an acute analytical mind, which he devoted to mathematical, astronomical, and logical studies, extended the horizon of his thought to embrace philosophy and theology and even journeyed beyond the limited horizon of all mental activity to seek ultimate knowledge in the ecstasy provided by gnosis (ʿirfān) and Sufism.

NOTES

1. E. S. Kennedy, "The Exact Sciences in Iran Under the Seljuqs and Mongols," 664.
2. E. S. Kennedy, "Late Medieval Planetary Theory," 369.
3. *Ibid.*
4. *Ibid.*, 369, 367.

BIBLIOGRAPHY

Al-Ṭūsī's major published work is *The Nasirean Ethics*, translated by G. M. Wickens (London, 1964).

Secondary literature includes A. Carathéodory Pasha, *Traité de quadrilatère* (Constantinople, 1891); B. Carra de Vaux, "Les sphères célestes selon Naṣīr-Eddīn Attūsī," in P. Tannery, ed., *Recherches sur l'histoire de l'astronomie ancienne* (Paris, 1893), app. 4, 337–361; A. P. Youschkevitch, and B. A. Rosenfeld, *Die Mathematik der Lander des Ostens in Mittelalter* (Berlin, 1960), 277–288, 304–308; E. S. Kennedy, "Late Medieval Planetary Theory," in *Isis*, 57 (1966), 365–

378; and "The Exact Sciences in Iran Under the Seljuqs and Mongols," in *Cambridge History of Iran*, V (Cambridge, 1968), 659–679; M. Mudarris Raḍawī, *Aḥwal wa āthār-i ustād bashar . . . Khwāja Naṣīr al-Dīn* (Teheran, A.H. 1334, 1955 A.D.); S. H. Nasr, *Three Muslim Sages* (Cambridge, Mass., 1964); and *Science and Civilization in Islam* (Cambridge, Mass., 1968; New York, 1970); G. Sarton, *Introduction to the History of Science*, II, pt. 2 (Baltimore, 1931), 1001–1013; A. Sayili, *The Observatory in Islam* (Ankara, 1960); B. H. Siddiqui, "Naṣīr al-Dīn Ṭūsī," in M. M. Sharif, ed., *A History of Muslim Philosophy*, I (Wiesbaden, 1963), 564–580; A. S. Saidan, "The Comprehensive Work on Computation With Board and Dust by Naṣīr al-Dīn al-Ṭūsī," in *Al-abḥāth*, 20, no. 2 (June 1967), 91–163, and no. 3 (Sept. 1967), 213–293, in Arabic; and *Yādnāmāyi Khwāja Naṣir al-Dīn Ṭūsī*, I (Teheran, A.H. 1336, 1957 A.D.), in Persian.

SEYYED HOSSEIN NASR

AL-ṬŪSĪ, SHARAF AL-DĪN AL-MUZAFFAR IBN MUḤAMMAD IBN AL-MUZAFFAR (*b.* Ṭūs [?], Iran; *d.* Iran, *ca.* 1213/1214)

The name of Sharaf al-Dīn's birthplace, Ṭūs, refers both to a city and to its surrounding region, which with Mashhad and Nīshāpur formed a very prosperous area in the twelfth century.[1] A century earlier, Ṭūs had given Islam one of its most profound thinkers, al-Ghazālī (*d.* 1111); and it was soon to produce a great astronomer and theologian, Naṣir al-Dīn (*d.* 1274). Nothing is known about the first years of al-Ṭūsī's life; but it is reported that, faithful to the tradition of medieval scholars, he went on a long journey to some of the major cities of the time. His itinerary can be reconstructed from undated information preserved in biographies of his contemporaries.

Al-Ṭūsī taught at Damascus, probably about 1165.[2] His most distinguished student there was Abu'l-Faḍl (*b. ca.* 1135), an excellent carpenter who helped make the wood paneling of the Bīmāristān al-Nūrī (1154–1159) before discovering the joys of Euclid and Ptolemy.[3] Al-Ṭūsī most probably then stayed at Aleppo, where one of his pupils was a respected member of the city's Jewish community, Abu'l-Faḍl Binyāmīn (*d.* 1207/1208), whom he instructed in the science of numbers, the use of astronomical tables, and astrology, and, at a less advanced level, in the other rational sciences.[4] From the nature of these courses, it is reasonable to suppose that they lasted about three years.

Al-Ṭūsī's most outstanding pupil, however, was Kamāl al-Dīn Ibn Yūnus (d. 1243) of Mosul, through whom al-Ṭūsī's teachings passed to Naṣīr al-Dīn and Athīr al-Dīn al-Abharī (d. 1263/1265).[5] Al-Ṭūsī was apparently in Mosul in the years preceding 1175,[6] for around this date two physicians from Damascus went there to study with him, but he had already left.[7] One of them then went to the neighboring city of Irbil, where he became a pupil of Ibn al-Dahhān.[8] About this time, however, the latter left Irbil to join Saladin, who had just seized Damascus (1174).[9] Al-Ṭūsī returned to Iran, where he died around 1213, at an advanced age.

Al-Ṭūsī is known for his linear astrolabe (al-Ṭūsī's staff), a simple wooden rod with graduated markings but without sights. It was furnished with a plumb line and a double cord for making angular measurements and bore a perforated pointer. This staff reproduced, in concrete form, the meridian line of the plane astrolabe—that is, the line upon which the engraved markings of that instrument are projected. (These markings are of stars, circles of declination, and heights.) Supplementary scales indicate the right ascensions of the sun at its entry into the signs of the zodiac as well as the hourly shadows. Al-Ṭūsī described the construction and use of the linear astrolabe in several treatises, praising its simplicity and claiming that an amateur could build it in about an hour. His staff made it possible to carry out the observations used to determine the height of the stars, the time, the direction of the Kaʿba, and the ascendants. The instrument, although inexpensive to construct, was less accurate than the ordinary astrolabe. It also was less decorative, and perhaps for this reason it was of little interest to collectors. In any case, not a single linear astrolabe has survived.[10]

Al-Ṭūsī's greatest achievement is recorded in a work that has not yet been analyzed by historians, the manuscript Loth III, 767, in the collection of the India Office, London. This manuscript is actually a reworking of the original by an unknown author who proudly states that he has eliminated

the mathematical tables and shortened some of the long passages. He makes no further claims; and even if he had wished to make more substantial changes, the great difficulty of the work would have discouraged him. The entire contents of the work may, therefore, confidently be attributed to al-Ṭūsī. The treatise, which may have been mentioned by al-Sinjārī,[11] is not the first of its kind by an Arab author. A cross check of citations from Jamshīd al-Kāshī and Ṭāsh Kopru Zādeh reveals that al-Masʿūdī, a disciple of al-Khayyāmī, wrote on the numerical solution of third-degree equations.[12] The existence of an earlier author is not explicitly indicated, but, about 1350, Yaḥyā al-Kāshī noted several similar writings, without specifying dates or names.[13] In the following paragraphs we shall present the most remarkable results in al-Ṭūsī's treatise, but we cannot state the degree of originality for each.

The treatise divides the twenty-five equations of degree $n \leq 3$ into three groups. The first includes twelve equations: those of degree $n \leq 2$ or that reduce to that degree, plus the equation $x^3 = a$. The second contains the eight equations of the third degree that always admit one (positive) solution.[14] The third group is composed of the five equations that can give rise to impossible solutions:[15]

$$x^3 + c = ax^2$$
$$x^3 + c = b^2x$$
$$x^3 + 3ax^2 + c = 3b^2x$$
$$x^3 + b^2x + c = 3ax^2$$
$$x^3 + c = 3ax^2 + 3b^2x$$

We shall not give details of the geometric solutions, since they do not differ from those presented by al-Khayyāmī. (The care that al-Ṭūsī bestows on the study of the problem of the relative position of two conics is, however, worth noting.) On the other hand, the outstanding discussion of the existence of the roots of the group of equations that can give rise to impossible solutions merits the closest ex-

Table I

x_1	4							
N	9	1	7	5	0	0	8	7
N_1	6	4			1	4	4	
	2	7	7	3	5	6	8	7
a						1	2	

Table II

	4	5					
N_1	2	7	7	3	5	6	8	7
		1	2	5			
	2	7	0	0	1	8	0
N_2		6	0	8	8	7
	1	6			1	2
	2	0				

Table III

N_2	6	0	8	8	8	7
						1
	6	0	8	8	8	6
	2	0	2	5	1	2
					4	5

amination. Accordingly, we shall outline, by way of example, al-Ṭūsī's treatment of the fourth equation of this group, which, like the others, is based on the calculation of a maximum. Given that $x^3 < 3ax^2$; therefore $x < 3a$. Then $b^2x < x^2(3a - x)$, so that $b^2 < x(3a - x)$. The maximum of $x(3a - x)$ is $(3a/2)^2$.[16] Therefore $b < 3a/2$. We consider $x^2 + b^2/3 = 2ax$ and take its root $x_1 = a + \sqrt{a^2 - b^2/3}$. A discussion of its existence does not arise, since $b < 3a/2$. We form $f(x_1) = x_1^2(3a - x_1) - b^2x_1$. If $f(x_1) = c$, the equation $x^3 + b^3x + c = 3ax^2$ has a solution $x = x_1$. If $f(x_1) < c$, there is no solution. If $f(x_1) > c$, the equation has two roots separated by x_1. Turning to an evaluation of al-Ṭūsī's treatment in the light of the differential calculus, we set $f(x) = 3ax^2 - x^3 - b^2x$; then $f'(x) = 6ax - 3x^2 - b^2$. Thus $f'(x)$ reduces to zero when $x^2 - 2ax + b^2/3 = 0$. Accordingly, the roots x_0 and x_1 are equal to $a \pm \sqrt{a^2 - b^2/3}$. Finally, $f(x_1) > 0$ implies $b < 3a/2$.

x	0	x_0	x_1	$3a$
$f'(x)$		$-$　0　$+$　0　$-$		
$f(x)$	$0 \searrow f(x_0) \nearrow f(x_1) \searrow -3ab^2$			

The text does not say what led al-Ṭūsī to such profound and beautiful results. The idea of determining the maximum of $x^2(a - x)$, $x(b^2 - x^2)$, $\cdots$ might have been suggested by the solution of $x(a - x) = b^2$. The value of the maximum of $x^2(a - x)$ might have been borrowed from Archimedes, who, unlike al-Ṭūsī, established it geometrically.[17] Yet, even if al-Ṭūsī started from this point, he still had far to go. Pursuing his solution of the equation $x^3 + bx^2 + c = 3ax^2$, he shows that the two solutions are, respectively, $x_1 + X$, where X is the root of $X^3 + 3(x_1 - a)X = f(x_1) - c$, and $x_1 - X$, where X is the root of $X^3 + f(x_1) - c = 3(x_1 - a)X$. This method contains the genesis of a genuine change of variables, and one must admire the author's intention of interrelating the various equations—an approach quite different from traditional Arab thinking on this topic, which emphasized independent solutions of problems (as in the classic solution of the second-degree equations).

We shall conclude with a very schematic presentation of al-Ṭūsī's solution of the equation $x^3 + 3ax = N$, using the example $x^3 + 36x = 91,750,087$.[18] Let x_1 be the number in the hundreds' place of the root; then x_1^3 will represent millions and $3ax_1$ will represent hundreds. Therefore, we place x_1 in the millions' box (the upper line in Table I) and $a = 12$ in the hundreds' box (on the lower line; actually, since a is greater than nine, it is carried over

into that of the thousands). We then calculate the greatest x_1 such that $x_1^3 \leq 91$; this yields $x_1 = 4$. We remove $x_1^3 + 36x_1$ from N, obtaining $N = 27,735,687$. We next place $x_1^2 = 16$ under x_1 in the line containing a and decrease the lower line by one rank and x_1 by two. The result is Table II.

We now calculate the figure in the tens' place. It will be the greatest x_2 such that $3x_2$ multiplied by 16 can be subtracted from 277. Accordingly, $x_2 = 5$, and we place it to the right of 4 in the upper line. In the lower line we put x_1x_2 in the position under $x_1 = 4$. We then subtract from N_1 the total of x_2^3 and the product of $3x_2$ times the lower line—that is, $3x_2(x_1^2 + x_1x_2 + a) = 15(180,012)$. This yields N_2. We add x_1x_2 (that is, 20) to the lower line in the position under $x_1 = 4$ and $x_2^2 = 25$ in the position under $x_2 = 5$. The line becomes 202,512. We decrease it by one rank and decrease the upper line by two. The result is Table III.

Finally, we calculate x_3 such that the product of $3x_3$ times $20 \leq 60$. Thus $x_3 = 1$. We place it to the right of 5. To the lower line we add 45 and subtract from N_2 the total of x_3^3 and the product of $3x_3$ times the lower line (202,962). The remainder is 0. The root of the equation is therefore 451. The method is independent of the system of numeration and permits as close an approximation of the root as desired; it suffices to add a row of three to the last remainder and to continue operating in the same manner. The treatise also gives analogous methods of numerical resolution for the other equations, even for those of the second degree.

NOTES

1. Guy Le Strange, *The Lands of the Eastern Caliphate* (Cambridge, 1909). See the chapter on Khurāsān (with references to the Arab geographers).
2. See Ibn Abī Uṣaybiʿa, *ʿUyūn al-anbāʾ*, II, 190–191.
3. This was a hospital built by Sultan Nūr al-Dīn ibn Zenki, famous for his wars against the Crusaders. See Ibn al-Athīr, *al-Tārīkh al-Bāhir fiʾl dawl ʾl-atābikiyya*, A. A. Ṭulaymāt, ed. (Cairo, 1963), 170; and Shawkat al-Shaṭṭī, *Mūjaz tārīkh al-ṭibb ʿind al-ʿArab* (Damascus, 1959), 22. See also Ibn Abī Uṣaybiʿa, *loc. cit.*
4. Ibn al-Qifṭī, *Tārīkh* (Cairo, 1948), 278.
5. See Ibn Khallikān, *Wafayāt al-aʿyan*, IV, no. 718; and G. Sarton, *Introduction to the History of Science*, II, 600, and II. pt. 2, 1001–1013.
6. In 1193 Ibn Yūnus went to Baghdad to continue his religious studies; see Ibn Khallikān, *loc. cit.* See also Tāsh Kopru Zādeh, *Miftāh al-saʿāda*, II, 214–215.
7. They were Ibn al-Hājib and Muwaffaq al-Dīn. See Ibn Abī Uṣaybiʿa, II, 181–182, 191–192.
8. *Ibid.*
9. See Ibn Khallikān, IV, no. 655.
10. See Henri Michel, *Traité de l'astrolabe*, 22. The same point is also made in L. A. Mayer, *Islamic Astrolabists and Their Works* (Geneva, 1956).

11. Al-Sinjārī. *Irshād al-qāṣid* (Beirut. 1904). 124. Although probably valid, the citation raises some doubt. In fact, the title. *Kitāb al-Muẓaffar al-Ṭūsī*, becomes, in certain editions of Tāsh Kopru Zādeh's *Miftāḥ al-saʿāda* (for instance, I. 327) which, however, derive from al-Sinjārī: *Kitāb al-Ẓafar of al-Ṭūsī* (Naṣīr al-Dīn).

12. Jamshīd al-Kāshī. *Miftāḥ al-ḥisāb*. MS Paris Ar. 5020. fol. 98; and Tāsh Kopru Zādeh. *Miftāḥ al-saʿāda*. I. 327. Sharaf al-Dīn Muḥammad ibn Masʿūd ibn Muḥammad al-Masʿūdī is cited in the article on Muḥammad ibn Aḥmad al-Shurwānī in Ṣafadī. *al-Wāfī*. Ritter. ed. (Istanbul). II. 497. as having taught the *Ishārāt* of Ibn Sīnā to Fakhr al-Dīn al-Rāzī (1164–1238) after having studied under al-Khayyām. He is the author of *al-Kifāya fiʾl-hidāya*; see Ḥājjī Khalīfa. *Kashf al-Ẓunūn*. II. col. 1500. Khalīfa also cites his algebra (I. col. 857).

13. Yaḥya al-Kāshī. *al-Lubāb fiʾl-Ḥisāb*. Aya Sofya MS 2757. See fol. 65r. l. 21; fol. 65v. l. 3; and fol. 67r. l. 25. The MS. written in 1373. bears notes in the author's hand. See the article on al-Kāshī in Sarton. *Introduction to the History of Science*. III. pt. 1. 698.

14. Only $x^3 + ax = bx^2 + c$ can admit up to three positive solutions.

15. *Kitāb fiʾl-jabr waʾl-muqābala*. India Office (London). Loth 767. The equations are found on pp. 101r–112r; 112r–121r; 121r–130r; 130r–142v; and 142v–179r.

16. This is an immediate consequence of Euclid's *Elements*. II. 5.

17. T. L. Heath. *The Works of Archimedes* (New York. 1953). 67–72.

18. In the treatise (fols. 54v–55v) the equation actually solved is $x^3 + 36x = 33,087,717$. the root of which is 321.

BIBLIOGRAPHY

I. ORIGINAL WORKS. Al-Ṭūsī's works include the following:

1. *Kitāb fiʾl jabr waʾl muqābala*. India Office (London). Loth 767.

2. *Risāla fiʾl-asṭurlāb al-khaṭṭī*. British Museum. Or. 5479.

3. *Maʿrifat al-asṭurlāb al-musaṭṭaḥ waʾl-ʿamal bihi*. Leiden 1082. The MS does not bear this title, which was erroneously given to it by some bibliographers, and discusses the linear astrolabe, not the plane astrolabe. The third part, containing demonstrations, is missing from the MS.

4. *Kitāb fī maʿrifat al asṭurlāb al-musaṭṭaḥ waʾl ʿamal bihi*. Seray 3505, 2nd. If Max Krause's identification of this MS with Leiden 1082 is correct, it would be necessary to conclude that we do not have al-Ṭūsī's treatise on the plane astrolabe.

5. *Risāla fiʾl-asṭurlāb al-Khaṭṭī*. Seray 3342, 7.

6. *Risāla fiʾl-asṭurlāb al-Khaṭṭī*. Seray 3464, 1.

7. *Jawāb ʿalā suʾāl liʾamīr al-umarāʾ Shams al-Dīn*. Leiden 1027; Columbia University, Smith, Or. 45, 2. This work concerns the division of a square into three trapezoids and a rectangle, with the relationships preassigned.

8. *Fiʾl-Khaṭṭayn alladhayn yaqrubān wa la yaltaqiyān*. Aya Sofya 2646, 2, 71r–v, deals with the existence of an asymptote to the (equilateral) hyperbola and contains the same demonstration as in *Kitāb fiʾl-jabr waʾl-muqābala*, (1), fols. 38r–40r.

II. SECONDARY LITERATURE. See the following:

9. Ibn Khallikān, *Wafayāt al-aʿyān* (Cairo, 1948).

10. Ibn Abī Uṣaybiʿa, *ʿUyūn al-anbāʾ* (Cairo, 1882).

11. Tāsh Kopru Zādeh, *Miftāḥ al-saʿāda* (Hyderabad, 1910–1911).

12. Ḥājjī Khalīfa, *Kashf al-ẓunūn* (Istanbul, 1941–1943).

13. H. Suter, *Die Mathematiker und Astronomen der Araber* (Leipzig, 1900), 134 (no. 333).

14. Max Krause, "Stambuler Handschriften islamischer Mathematiker," in *Quellen und Studien zur Geschichte der Mathematik, Astronomie und Physik*, Abt. B, Studien, 3 (1936), 437–532, see 490.

15. C. Brockelmann, *Geschichte der arabischen Literatur*, I, 2nd ed. (Leiden, 1943), 472, and supp. I (Leiden, 1937), 858.

16. G. Sarton, *Introduction to the History of Science*, II, pt. 2 (Baltimore, 1950), 622–623.

17. Carlo Nallino, article on the astrolabe (*asṭurlāb*) in *Encyclopaedia of Islam*, 1st ed., I (1913); and by Willy Hartner, *ibid.*, 2nd ed., I, 722–728.

18. Henri Michel, *Traité de l'astrolabe* (Paris, 1947), 115–122; and "L'astrolabe linéaire d'al-Ṭūsī," in *Ciel et terre* (1943), nos. 3–4. A description, sketch, and note on the use of al-Ṭūsī's linear astrolabe can be found on p. 21.

19. R. Carra de Vaux, "L'astrolabe linéaire ou bâton d'al-Tousi," in *Journal asiatique*, 11th ser., 5 (1895), 464–516. This article reproduces the text of al-Ḥasan al Marrākushī with a French translation.

ADEL ANBOUBA

AL-UMAWĪ, ABŪ ʿABDALLĀH YAʿĪSH IBN IBRĀHĪM IBN YŪSUF IBN SIMĀK AL-ANDALUSĪ (*fl.* Damascus, fourteenth century)

Al-Umawī was a Spanish Arab who lived in Damascus, where he taught arithmetic. On the single authority of Ḥājjī Khalīfa, the year of his death is usually given as A.H. 895 (A.D. 1489/1490). But a marginal note on the ninth folio of his arithmetic (MS 1509, 1°, Carullah), written by him to give license to a copyist to teach his work, is dated 17 Dhuʾl-Ḥijja 774 (9 June 1373). The copyist is ʿAbd al-Qādir ibn Muḥammad ibnʿAbd al-Qādir, al-Ḥanbalī, al-Maqdisī. He states that he finished copying the text at Mount Qāsyūn in Damascus on 8 Dhuʾl-Ḥijja 774.

The text referred to is *Marāsim al-intisāb fī ʿilm al-ḥisāb*. A small work in eighteen folios, it is significant in being written by a western Muslim for Easterners, a circumstance that should not discredit the common belief that arithmetic flourished more in eastern than in western Islam. The work represents a trend of Arabic arithmetic in which, as early as the tenth century, the Indian "dust board" calculations had begun to be modified to suit paper and ink; and arithmetic was enriched by concepts from the traditional finger reckoning and the Pythagorean theory of numbers. The trend seems to have started in Damascus; the earliest extant text that shows it is al-Uqlīdisī's *al-Fuṣūl fi'l-ḥisāb al-hindī*, written in A.H. 341 (A.D. 952/3). But there are reasons to believe that the trend had greater influence in the West than in the East.

The forms of the numerals used in the West differed from those in the East, but al-Umawī avoids using numerals except in a table of sequences, in which the western forms appear. The attempts to modify the Indian schemes resulted in several methods, especially of multiplication. Al-Umawī, however, says little about these methods and describes the principal operations briefly, as if his aim is to show what in western arithmetic is unknown, or not widely known, in the East. Thus he insists that the common fraction should be written as $\frac{a}{b}$, whereas the easterners continued to write it as $\overset{a}{\underset{b}{}}$, like the Indians, or as $\overset{0}{\underset{b}{a}}$.

He also insists that the numbers operated upon, say, in multiplication, must be separated from the steps of the operation by placing a straight line under them. Such lines appear in the works of Ibn al-Bannā' of Morocco (*d.* 1321) but not in the East until late in the Middle Ages.

Like the classical Indian authors, in treating addition al-Umawī dispenses with the operation in a few words and moves on to the summation of sequences. Those he discusses are the following:

1. The arithmetical progression in general and the sum of natural numbers, natural odd numbers, and natural even numbers in particular

2. The geometrical progression in general and

2^r and $\sum_{r=0}^{n} 2^r$ in particular

3. The sequences and series of polygonal numbers, namely $\{1 + (r - 1)d\}$ and $Sn = \sum_{r=1}^{n} \{1 + (r - 1)d\}$

4. The sequences and series of pyramidal numbers, namely $\{S_r\}$ and $\sum_{r=1}^{n} \{S_r\}$

5. Summations of r^3, $(2r + 1)^3$, $(2r)^3$ from $r = 1$ to $r = n$

6. Summations of $r(r + 1)$, $(2r + 1)(2r + 3)$, $2r(2r + 2)$ from $r = 1$ to $r = n$.

The sequences of polygonal and pyramidal numbers were transmitted to the Arabs in Thābit ibn Qurra's translation of Nicomachus' *Introduction to Arithmetic*. Also, al-Karajī had given geometrical proofs of Σr^3, $(2r + 1)^3$, $(2r)^3$ in *al-Fakhrī* (see T. Heath, *Manual of Greek Mathematics* [Oxford, 1931], 68).

Without symbolism, al-Umawī often takes the sum of ten terms as an example, a practice started by the Babylonians and adopted by Diophantus and Arabic authors.

In subtraction al-Umawī considers casting out sevens, eights, nines, and elevens. All Hindu-Arabic arithmetic books consider casting out nines; and some add casting out other numbers. Some also treat casting out elevens in the way used today for testing divisibility by 11, which is attributed to Pierre Forcadel (1556). Al-Umawī adds casting out eights and sevens, in a way that leads directly to the following general rule:

Take any integer N in the decimal scale. Clearly $N = a_0 + a_1 \cdot 10 + a_2 \cdot 10^2 + \cdots = \Sigma a_s \cdot 10^s$. It is required to find the remainder after casting out p's from N, where p is any other integer. Let r_s be the remainder of 10^s, that is $10^s \equiv r_s \pmod{p}$; it follows that if $\Sigma a_s \cdot r_s$ is divisible by p so is N. This is a theorem that is attributed to Blaise Pascal (1664); see L. E. Dickson, *Theory of Numbers*, I (New York, 1952), p. 337.

In the text al-Umawī states that the sequence r_s, in the cases he considers, is finite and recurring. Thus for $p = 7$, $r_s = (1, 3, 2, 6, 4, 5)$.

In dealing with square and cube roots, al-Umawī states rules of approximation that are not as well developed as those of the arithmeticians of the East, who had already developed the following rules of approximation.

$$\sqrt{n} = a + \frac{n - a^2}{2a + 1},$$

where a^2 is the greatest integral square in n, and

$$\sqrt[3]{n} = a + \frac{n - a^3}{3a^2 + 3a + 1},$$

where a^3 is the greatest integral cube in n. These rules do not appear in al-Umawī's text. Instead, we find

$$\sqrt{n} = a + \frac{n-a^2}{2a} \text{ or } (a+1) - \frac{(a+1)^2 - n}{2(a+1)}$$

$$\sqrt[3]{n} = a + \frac{n-a^3}{3a^2} \text{ or } (a+1) - \frac{(a+1)^3 - n}{3(a+1)^2}$$

Again, al-Umawī does not consider the method of extracting roots of higher order, which had been known in the East since the eleventh century.

For finding perfect squares and cubes, however, he gives the following rules, most of which have not been found in other texts.

If n is a perfect square:

1. It must end with an even number of zeros, or have 1, 4, 5, 6, or 9 in the units' place.

2. If the units' place is 6, the tens' place must be odd; in all other cases it is even.

3. If the units' place is 1, the hundreds' place and half the tens' place must be both even or both odd.

4. If the units' place is 5, the tens' place is 2.

5. $n \equiv 0, 1, 2, 4 \pmod 7$
   $\equiv 0, 1, 4 \pmod 8$
   $\equiv 0, 1, 4, 7 \pmod 9$

If n is a perfect cube:

1. If it ends with 0, 1, 4, 5, 6, or 9, its cube root ends with 000, 1, 4, 5, 6, or 9, respectively. If it ends with 3, 7, 2, or 8, the root ends with 7, 3, 8, or 2, respectively.

2. $n \equiv 0, 1, 6 \pmod 7$
   $\equiv 0, 1, 3, 5, 7 \pmod 8$
   $\equiv 0, 1, 8 \pmod 9$

Evidently al-Umawī's *Marāsim al-intisāb fī 'ilm al-ḥisāb* is worthy of scholarly interest, especially in connection with the early history of number theory.

Another work by the same author is preserved in MS 5174 h in Alexandria under the name of *Rafᶜ al-ishkāl fī misāḥat al-ashkāl* (removal of doubts concerning the mensuration of figures); it is a small treatise of seventeen folios in which we find nothing on mensuration that the arithmeticians of the East did not know.

BIBLIOGRAPHY

On al-Umawī and his work, see C. Brockelmann, *Geschichte der arabischen Literatur*, supp. 2 (Leiden, 1938), p. 379, and II (Leiden, 1949), p. 344; L. E. Dickson, *History of the Theory of Numbers*, 3 vols. (New York, 1952); Ḥājjī Khalīfa, *Kashf alẓunūn . . .*, 2 vols. (Constantinople, 1941); T. L. Heath, *A History of Greek Mathematics*, 2 vols. (Oxford, 1921); Ibn al-Nadīm, *Al-Fihrist* (Cairo); Nicomachus, *Al-Madkhal ilā ᶜilm al-ᶜadad*, Thābit ibn Qurra, trans., W. Kutch, ed. (Beirut, 1958); and H. Suter, *Die Mathematiker und Astronomen der Araber und ihre Werke* (Leipzig, 1950), no. 453, p. 187.

A. S. SAIDAN

AL-UQLĪDISĪ, ABU'L-ḤASAN AḤMAD IBN IBRĀHĪM (*fl.* Damascus, 952–953)

No source book mentions al-Uqlīdisī. He is known only from a unique copy of his work entitled *Kitāb al-fuṣūl fi'l-ḥisāb al-hindī* (MS 802, Yeni Cami, Istanbul), the front page of which bears the author's name and the statement that the text was written at Damascus in 952–953. The manuscript was copied in A.D. 1157. In the introduction the author states that he has traveled extensively, read all books on Indian arithmetic that he has found, and learned from every noted arithmetician he has met. The epithet al-Uqlīdisī generally was attached to the names of persons who made copies of Euclid's *Elements* for sale, so it is possible that he earned his living in that way. Internal evidence shows that he had experience in teaching Indian arithmetic, for he knows what beginners ask and how to answer their questions.

The book is in four parts. In the first, Hindu numerals are introduced; the place-value concept is explained; and the arithmetical operations, including extraction of square roots, are described, with many examples applied to integers and common fractions in both the decimal and the sexagesimal systems.

In the second part the subject matter is treated at a higher level and includes the method of casting out nines and several variations of the schemes of operations explained in the first part. In the introduction the author states that in this part he has collected the methods used by noted manipulators, expressed in the Indian way. This section contains almost all the schemes of multiplication that appear in later Latin works.

In the third part, justifications of the several concepts and steps suggested in the first two parts are given, generally in answer to questions beginning "Why" or "How is it."

A few words may be necessary for an appreciation of the fourth part. The first few lines of the text state that Indian arithmetic, as transmitted to the Arabs, required the use of the dust abacus.

Later it is said that the operations depended upon shifting the figures and erasing them. For instance, in the example 329×456, the numbers are written as shown below:

$$3\ 2\ 9$$
$$4\ 5\ 6$$

Then 3 is multiplied by 4 and the product is inserted in the top line as 12; 3 is multiplied by 5, which requires putting 5 above, erasing 2, and putting 3 in its place; 3 is multiplied by 6, making it necessary to remove 3 from the top line and write 8 in its place, to erase the 5 before it, and to put 6 in its place. In preparation for the next step, the lower line is shifted one place to the right. The array is now as shown below:

$$1\ 3\ 6\ 8\ 2\ 9$$
$$4\ 5\ 6$$

456 is to be multiplied by 2, which is above the units place of 456; the position of the units digit of the multiplicand in the lower line indicates the multiplier. The remaining steps can now be followed with ease.

Obviously paper and ink cannot be easily used with such schemes. In the fourth part of the text, modifications of the Indian schemes are suggested whereby the abacus can be dispensed with, and ink and paper used instead. We can now judge that al-Uqlīdisī's modification presents a first step in a long chain of attempts that resulted in discarding the abacus completely, first in western Islam and, many centuries later, in the eastern part.

After suggesting a modification of each operation, al-Uqlīdisī proposed that:

1. Greek letters might replace the nine Indian numerals.

2. The Indian numerals with superimposed dots might form a new Arabic alphabet.

3. There might be calculating dice, with one or two numerals on each face, to use instead of the abacus.

4. There might be a calculating board to be used by the blind.

The second idea is cited in other texts, and the third is reminiscent of Boëthius' apexes. It is as likely as not that here al-Uqlīdisī is describing methods used elsewhere rather than making original suggestions. The book ends with a lengthy dis-

cussion of $\Sigma 2^r$ and the method of extracting the cube root.

Al-Uqlīdisī was proud of the following accomplishments in his work:

1. In part 1 he presented the contents of all earlier texts on Indian arithmetic and applied it in the sexagesimal system. We do not have these texts to enable us to judge how far he was correct in this claim. The Latin *Algorismus corpus*, however, indicates that Indian arithmetic as presented by al-Khwārizmī (ninth century) differed basically from that which spread later in the Muslim world. Application of the Indian schemes to the sexagesimal system is found in all later Arabic arithmetic books.

2. In part 2 he gave methods known only to noted arithmeticians, and extended the method of casting out nines to fractions and square roots. On the evidence of later texts, one is inclined to accept this claim of al-Uqlīdisī.

3. In part 4, he showed that Indian arithmetic no longer needed the abacus. This modification was more agreeable to the West than to the East. In support we may note that Ibn al-Bannāʾ (*d.* 1321) of Morocco included as a curiosity in one of his arithmetical works the statement that the ancients had used dust for calculation, whereas Naṣīr al-Dīn al-Ṭūsī (*d.* 1274) of Persia found the dust abacus still important enough to write a book on it.

4. In discussing $\Sigma 2^r$ he distinguished between the nth term and the sum of n terms, which he claimed that some manipulators had confused.

5. He claimed to be the first to have written satisfactorily on the cube root.

There are no documents to decide the last two claims, but we have other reasons to consider al-Uqlīdisī's *Kitāb al-fuṣūl fiʾl-ḥisāb al-hindī* the most important of some one hundred extant Arabic arithmetic texts.

First, it is the earliest known text that contains a direct treatment of decimal fractions. The author suggests a decimal sign, a stroke over the units' place, and insists that it must always be used. In a process of successive division by 2 he obtains the sequence 13, 6.5, 3.25, 1.625, 0.8125. He knows how to regain 13 by successive multiplication by 2 and by ignoring the zeros to the right. In a process of repeatedly increasing 135 by one-tenth, he obtains the array

135	148.5	163.35
13.5	14.85	16.335 and so on.
148.5	163.35	179.685

Again, in finding the approximate roots of numbers, he uses the rules

$$\sqrt{a} = \sqrt{ak^2}/k, \quad \sqrt[3]{a} = \sqrt[3]{ak^3}/k$$

and takes k equal to a multiple of ten.

Although many other arithmeticians used the same rules, all of them rather mechanically transformed the decimal fraction obtained into the sexagesimal system, without showing any sign of comprehension of the decimal idea. Only al-Uqlīdisī gives the root in the decimal scale in several cases. In all operations where powers of ten are involved in the numerator or the denominator, he is well at home.

Second, al-Uqlīdisī's is the first text to tell us clearly that Indian arithmetic depended on the dust abacus. In his introduction, the author compared the Indian system with the then current finger-reckoning and made a correct evaluation of the merits and drawbacks of each. It is now known that Abu'l-Wafā' (940–997/998) and Ibn al-Bannā' made passing statements about the dust abacus in Indian arithmetic, but these references were too terse to catch the attention of the scholars who first studied their works.

BIBLIOGRAPHY

See A. S. Saidan, "The Earliest Extant Arabic Arithmetic," in *Isis*, **57** (1966), 475–490.

A. S. SAIDAN

URYSON, PAVEL SAMUILOVICH (*b.* Odessa, Russia, 3 February 1898; *d.* Batz, France, 17 August 1924)

The son of a distinguished Odessa financier, Uryson attended a private secondary school in Moscow in 1915 and entered the University of Moscow, intending to study physics. The same year he published his first scientific work, on Coolidge tube radiation, prepared under the guidance of P. P. Lazarev. Fascinated by the lectures of D. F. Egorov and N. N. Luzin, Uryson began specializing in mathematics and in 1919, after graduating from the university, he remained there to prepare for a teaching career. Uryson's works were at first concerned with integral equations and with other problems of analysis; but in the summer of 1921, being engaged in solving two problems presented to him by Egorov, he turned to topology. In June

of that year Uryson was appointed assistant professor at the University of Moscow, where, in particular, he lectured on topology and, later, in 1923–1924, on the mathematical theory of relativity. He was also professor at the Second Moscow University (now the Lenin Moscow Pedagogical Institute).

Uryson's publications on topology first appeared in 1922 in the *Comptes rendus* of the Académie des Sciences, as well as in Soviet and Polish journals. His ideas were also presented in lectures, memoirs, and discourses. The reports he delivered at the Mathematical Society of Göttingen in 1923 attracted the attention of Hilbert; and in the summer of 1924, while touring Germany, Holland, and France, he met L. E. J. Brouwer and Felix Hausdorff, who praised his works highly. Uryson drowned off the coast of Brittany at the age of twenty-six while on vacation.

Although his scientific activity lasted for only about five years, he greatly influenced the subsequent development of topology and laid the foundations of the Soviet school of topology, which was then led by his friend P. S. Aleksandrov, with whom he carried out several investigations.

The two cardinal aspects of Uryson's works on topology are topological space (abstract topology) and the theory of dimensionality.

In abstract topology his main results are the introduction and investigation of a class of the so-called normal spaces, metrization theorems, including a theorem on the existence of a topological mapping of any normed space with a countable base into Hilbert space.

The principal tool used in all the most recent investigations of normed spaces is the classical "Uryson's lemma," which proves the existence, for any two disjoint closed sets of a normed space, of a continuous function $f(x)$ which is defined over the given space. It satisfies the inequality $0 \leq f(x) \leq 1$ within that space and assumes on one of the two given sets the value zero, whereas on the other set it assumes the value of unity. Based on this lemma is Uryson's theorem on the metrizability of normed spaces having a countable base, and the theorem on the possibility of extending any continuous function defined on a closed set of a normed space R, to a function continuous over the entire space R. Both theorems are fundamental in general topology.

The theory of dimensionality created by Uryson in 1921–1922 was presented in his memoirs on Cantorian varieties, published posthumously in 1925–1926. In this work Uryson first presented an inductive definition of dimensionality that proved highly fruitful and became classical. Uryson then established that dimensionality, in the sense of the new definition of the n-dimensional Euclidean space R^n, actually equals n. In the process Uryson obtained a number of important results.

For $n = 4$ the equality dim $R^n = n$ was proved only by going beyond the limits of the inductive definition of dimensionality. Uryson's proof of the "theorem of equivalence" appeared to be a turning point in the development of the theory of dimensionality and of a considerable part of topology in general. The second part of this work is devoted to the creation of the theory of one-dimensional continua, in particular, their indexes of branching and continua of condensation.

Concurrently with and independently of Uryson, the Austrian mathematician Karl Menger was engaged in the same field; and the theory of dimensionality is often referred to as the Uryson-Menger theory.

BIBLIOGRAPHY

I. ORIGINAL WORKS. Uryson's collected works on topology and other branches of mathematics were published as *Trudy po topologii i drugim oblastiam matematiki*, 2 vols. (Moscow–Leningrad, 1951). Separately published writings include "Sur l'unicité de la solution des équations linéaires de M. Volterra," in *Bulletin de l'Académie polonaise des sciences*, ser. A (1922), 57–62; "Sur une fonction analytique partout continue," in *Fundamenta mathematica*, **4** (1923), 144–150; "Ein Beitrag zur Theorie der ebenen Gebiete unendlich hohen Zusammenhanges," in *Mathematische Zeitschrift*, **21** (1924), 133–150; "Zur Theorie der topologischen Räume," in *Mathematische Annalen*, **92** (1924), 258–266, written with P. S. Aleksandrov; "Über die Metrisation der kompakten topologischen Räume," *ibid.*, 275–293; and "Mémoire sur les multiplicitées cantoriennes," in *Fundamenta mathematica*, **7** (1925), 30–137; and **8** (1926), 225–356.

II. SECONDARY LITERATURE. For a detailed bibliography of Uryson's works, see *Matematika v SSSR za 40 let* ("Mathematics in the U.S.S.R. for Forty Years"), II (Moscow, 1959), 696–697. On Uryson's life and work, see P. S. Aleksandrov, in *Uspekhi astronomicheskikh nauk*, **5** (1950), 196–202.

A. PAPLAUSCAS

VALERIO (or **VALERI**), **LUCA** (*b.* Naples, Italy, 1552; *d.* Rome, Italy, 17 January 1618)

Valerio was the son of Giovanni Valeri, of Ferrara, and Giovanna Rodomano, of Greek extraction. He was brought up on Corfu and was educated in Rome at the Collegio Romano, where Clavius was one of his teachers. He studied philosophy and theology, although his main interest was mathematics. Most of his life was spent at Rome as a teacher, both private and public. Valerio taught rhetoric and Greek at the Collegio Greco and, from 1600 until his death, mathematics at the Sapienza in Rome. Among his private pupils were the future Pope Clement VIII and the poet Margherita Sarrocchi, with whom he apparently had a love affair. For a time he was also corrector of Greek in the Vatican Library. On 7 June 1612 he was elected a member of the Accademia dei Lincei and was active in its affairs until 1616. Apparently Galileo and Valerio had met about 1590 in Pisa; and around 1610 they were conducting a brisk and friendly correspondence, replete with expressions of mutual admiration. On 24 March 1616, however, Valerio was expelled from the Lincei for reasons that are now obscure. We do know that he objected to its wholehearted support for Galileo's Copernicanism in the controversy of 1616, but all the facts of the case are not available. Valerio spent the last two years of his life in obscurity and disgrace. It is a supreme irony that a few years later Galileo came to a similar end, but for the opposite reason. Galileo, however, rose above their common fate, for in his *Discorsi* of 1638 he called Valerio "greatest geometer, new Archimedes of our time."

Valerio's *De centro gravitatis* consists of the application of Archimedean methods to the determination of the volumes and centers of gravity of the various solids of rotation and their segments. One of the most interesting lemmas of the book says in effect that if lim $x = a$ and lim $y = b$, and if $\frac{x}{y} = c = $ constant, then $\frac{a}{b} = \frac{\lim x}{\lim y} = \lim \frac{x}{y} = c$, which is basically the same as lemma IV of book I of Newton's *Principia* and as Cavalieri's principle. In *Quadratura parabolae* Valerio used the known center of gravity of a hemisphere to find that of a segment of a parabola. He then used this result to determine the area of the segment. Valerio's method was that of Archimedes, although he introduced general lemmas to dispense with the cumbersome *reductio ad absurdum* process. Some of his theorems may be said to make implicit use of a limit approach, but outwardly he was strictly finitist.

Valerio was strongly influenced by Commandino and apparently, in his method for finding centers of gravity, also by Maurolico. Among the mathematicians who studied him and spoke highly of him were Cavalieri, Torricelli, and J. C. de la Faille. He also had a direct influence on Guldin, Gregorius Saint Vincent, and Tacquet.

BIBLIOGRAPHY

I. ORIGINAL WORKS. Valerio published three books: *Subtilium indagationum seu quadratura circuli et aliorum curvilineorum* (Rome, 1582), of which there is an apparently unique copy in the Alexandrine Library in Rome; *De centro gravitatis solidorum* (Rome, 1604; Bologna, 1661 [with *Quadratura*]); and *Quadratura parabolae* (Rome, 1606; Bologna, 1661). The *De piramidis et conis* mentioned in some accounts is probably a bibliographical ghost. Valerio's letters to Galileo, Cesi, and Baldi are printed in the Edizione Nazionale of Galileo's works.

II. SECONDARY LITERATURE. The standard source of information on Valerio is G. Gabrieli, "Luca Valerio Linceo e un episodio memorabile della vecchia Accademia," in *Atti dell'Accademia nazionale dei Lincei. Rendiconti*, Cl. di scienze morali, storiche e filologiche, 6th ser., **9** (1933), 691–728, which has a good bibliography. The first modern historian to draw attention to Valerio as a mathematician was C. R. Wallner, "Über die Entstehung des Grenzbegriffes," in *Bibliotheca mathematica*, 3rd ser., **4** (1903), 246–259. Later accounts include H. Bosmans, "Les démonstrations par l'analyse infinitésimale," in *Annales de la Société scientifique de Bruxelles*, **37** (1913), 211–228; and A. Tosi, "*De centro gravitatis solidorum* di Luca Valerio," in *Periodico di matematiche*, **35** (1957), 189–201. See also H. Wieleitner, "Das Fortleben der Archimedischen Infinitesimalmethoden bis zum Beginn des 17. Jahrh., insbesondere über Schwerpunktbestimmungen," in *Quellen und Studien zur Geschichte der Mathematik, Astronomie und Physik*, Abt. B, Studien, **1** (1931), 201–220.

PER STRØMHOLM

VALLÉE-POUSSIN, CHARLES-JEAN-GUSTAVE-NICOLAS DE LA (*b.* Louvain, Belgium, 14 August 1866; *d.* Louvain, 2 March 1962)

Vallée-Poussin's father was for nearly forty years professor of mineralogy and geology at Louvain. Young Vallée-Poussin entered the Jesuit College at Mons, but he found the teaching in some subjects, notably philosophy, unacceptable. He turned to engineering, although, after obtaining his diploma, he devoted himself to pure mathematics. Since boyhood he had been encouraged in mathematics by Louis-Philippe Gilbert and in 1891 he became Gilbert's assistant at the University of Louvain. Gilbert died in 1892 and, at the age of twenty-six, Vallée-Poussin was elected to his chair. He remained all his life at Louvain.

Vallée-Poussin made a very happy marriage with the gifted daughter of a Belgian family whom he met on holiday in Norway in 1900.

As the outstanding Belgian mathematician of his generation, Vallée-Poussin received many tributes. In accordance with custom, he was honored by celebrations at Louvain in 1928 after thirty-five years in his chair, and again in 1943 after fifty years. On the former occasion, the king of the Belgians conferred on Vallée-Poussin the rank of baron. The Belgian Royal Academy elected him a member in 1909, and he became an associate member of the Paris Académie des Sciences in 1945. He was also a commander of the Legion of Honor and honorary president of the International Mathematical Union.

Vallée-Poussin's earliest investigations were concerned with topics of analysis suggested by his own teaching. He proved in an elegant and general form theorems in the differential and integral calculus. In 1892 his memoir on differential equations was awarded a *couronne* by the Belgian Royal Academy. He quickly showed his analytical power in a spectacular way by his researches into the distribution of primes. After nearly a century of conjectures and proofs of partial results, the prime number theorem—that $\pi(x)$, the number of primes $p \leq x$, is asymptotically $x/\log x$—was proved independently by Hadamard and by Vallée-Poussin in 1896. The two proofs look very different, but each is achieved by difficult arguments of complex function theory applied to the zeta function of Riemann. Vallée-Poussin extended his researches to cover the distribution of primes in arithmetical progressions and primes represented by binary quadratic forms. He also made an advance of the first importance in the original prime number theorem by assigning an upper estimate to the difference between $\pi(x)$ and the logarithmic integral li x, which remained for twenty years the closest known. Apart from his two later papers on the zeta function in 1916, Vallée-Poussin left to others the development of the ideas that he had introduced into the theory of numbers.

Although the proof of the prime number theorem was Vallée-Poussin's highest achievement, his main impact on mathematical thought was his *Cours d'analyse*, a model of style, economy, and lucidity. The sweeping changes that Vallée-Poussin made in successive editions of his work reflected his current interests. The first edition expounded the traditional calculus, differential equations, and differential geometry; it was just too early for the Lebesgue integral. Two sizes of type were used, the larger for a basic course and the smaller for supplementary matter suited to mathematical specialists. In the second edition the part in small type was greatly expanded to take in set theory, measure and the Lebesgue integral, bounded variation, the Jordan curve theorem, and trigonometric series up to the theorems of Parseval des Chênes and Fejér. The third edition of volume I (1914) introduced the Stolz-Fréchet definition of the differentiability of $f(x,y)$. The third edition of volume II was burned when the German army overran Louvain. It would have pursued the discussion of the Lebesgue integral.

Vallée-Poussin, invited to Harvard and to Paris in 1915 and 1916, expanded this work into the Borel tract, *Intégrales de Lebesgue . . .*, which bears the marks of successive refinements of treatment. The second edition of the tract included analytic sets (Lusin, Souslin) and the Stieltjes integral. Vallée-Poussin's *Cours d'analyse* itself reverted after 1919 to a basic course without the small print.

In the decade after 1908 Vallée-Poussin made fundamental advances in the theory of approximation to functions by algebraic and trigonometric polynomials. The fact that any continuous function $f(x)$ can be thus approximated uniformly in a closed interval had been proved in 1885 by Weierstrass by integrating the product of $f(u)$ and a peak function $K(u,x)$, which rises steeply to its maximum at $u = x$. Vallée-Poussin (and Landau independently) applied this singular integral method with $K(u,x)$ of the form

$$\{1-(u-x)^2\}^n \text{ or } \{\cos \tfrac{1}{2}(u-x)\}^{2n}$$

to obtain results about the closeness of approximation to $f(x)$ by polynomials of assigned degree under hypotheses about f and its derivatives.

The Lebesgue integral gave new life to the theory of trigonometric series, and Vallée-Poussin proved a number of results that have become classic, notably his uniqueness theorem, his test for convergence, and a method of summation that is stronger than all the Cesàro methods.

During the first quarter of the twentieth century, Vallée-Poussin's interests were dominated by the Borel-Lebesgue revolution and were centered on the real variable. (His is the one *Cours d'analyse* that contains no complex function theory.) After 1925 he turned again to the complex variable, in particular to potential theory and conformal repre-

sentation. He collected his contributions in a book *Le potentiel logarithmique* (1949), the publication of which was held up by the war. By the time the book appeared some of his ideas had been superseded by those of a younger school of French analysts.

BIBLIOGRAPHY

I. ORIGINAL WORKS. A list of Vallée-Poussin's important papers is in *Journal of the London Mathematical Society*, **39** (1964), 174–175.

Books by Vallée-Poussin are *Cours d'analyse infinitésimale*, 2 vols. (Louvain–Paris, 1903–1906; 2nd ed., 1909–1912; 3rd ed., vol. I only, 1914; 4th ed., 1921–1922)—with changes in each of these editions and fewer changes in succeeding editions (vol. 2 of the 7th ed., 1938; vol. I of the 8th ed., 1938); *Intégrales de Lebesgue fonctions d'ensemble, classes de Baire* (Paris, 1916); *Leçons sur l'approximation des fonctions d'une variable réelle* (Paris, 1919); *Leçons de mécanique analytique* (Paris, 1924); *Les nouvelles méthodes de la théorie du potentiel et le problème généralisé de Dirichlet*. Actualités scientifiques et industrielles (Paris, 1937); *Le potentiel logarithmique, balayage et représentation conforme* (Louvain–Paris, 1949).

II. SECONDARY LITERATURE. Obituary notices are by P. Montel, in *Comptes rendus . . . de l'Académie des sciences*, 2 April 1962; and J. C. Burkill, in *Journal of the London Mathematical Society*, **39** (1964), 165–175.

J. C. BURKILL

VANDERMONDE, ALEXANDRE-THÉOPHILE, also known as **Alexis, Abnit,** and **Charles-Auguste Vandermonde** (*b.* Paris, France, 28 February 1735; *d.* Paris, 1 January 1796)

Vandermonde's father, a physician, directed his sickly son toward a musical career. An acquaintanceship with Fontaine, however, so stimulated Vandermonde that in 1771 he was elected to the Académie des Sciences, to which he presented four mathematical papers (his total mathematical production) in 1771–1772. Later Vandermonde wrote several papers on harmony, and it was said at that time that musicians considered Vandermonde to be a mathematician and that mathematicians viewed him as a musician. This latter view was unfair in that his mathematical work—although small, not generally well known, and a little delayed in publication—was both significant and influential.

Vandermonde's membership in the Academy led to a paper on experiments with cold, made with

Bezout and Lavoisier in 1776, and a paper on the manufacture of steel with Berthollet and Monge in 1786. Vandermonde became an ardent and active revolutionary, being such a close friend of Monge that he was termed "femme de Monge." He was a member of the Commune of Paris and the club of the Jacobins. In 1782 he was director of the Conservatoire des Arts et Métiers and in 1792, chief of the Bureau de l'Habillement des Armées. He joined in the design of a course in political economy for the École Normale and in 1795 was named a member of the Institut National.

Vandermonde is best known for the determinant that is named after him:

$$\begin{vmatrix} 1 & a_1 a_1^2 & \cdots & a_1^{n-1} \\ 1 & a_2 a_2^2 & \cdots & a_2^{n-1} \\ \hline & & \cdots & \\ 1 & a_n a_n^2 & \cdots & a_n^{n-1} \end{vmatrix} = \prod_{i>j} (a_i - a_j).$$

The determinant does not seem to occur in Vandermonde's work, although his third paper dealt with factorials and he did work with products elsewhere. Lebesgue believed that the attribution of this determinant to Vandermonde was due to a misreading of his notation. Muir (see Bibliography) did not mention this particular determinant, which some also attributed to Cauchy, but Muir asserted that Vandermonde's fourth paper was the first to give a connected exposition of determinants because he (1) defined a contemporary symbolism that was more complete, simple, and appropriate than that of Leibniz; (2) defined determinants as functions apart from the solution of linear equations presented by Cramer but also treated by Vandermonde; and (3) gave a number of properties of these functions, such as the number and signs of the terms and the effect of interchanging two consecutive indices (rows or columns), which he used to show that a determinant is zero if two rows or columns are identical. On this basis, Muir said that Vandermonde was "The only one fit to be viewed as the founder of the theory of determinants." Lebesgue, however, felt that this was neither very original, since there had been earlier workers, nor very important, since others were building equivalent theories, but that Vandermonde's real and unrecognized claim to fame was lodged in his first paper, in which he approached the general problem of the solvability of algebraic equations through a study of functions invariant under permutations of the roots of the equations.

Cauchy assigned priority in this to Lagrange and

Vandermonde. Vandermonde read his paper in November 1770, but he did not become a member of the Academy until 1771; and the paper was not published until 1774. During this interval Lagrange published two *mémoires* on the topic. Although Vandermonde's methods were close to those later developed by Abel and Galois for testing the solvability of equations, and although his treatment of the binomial equation $x^m - 1 = 0$ could easily have led to the anticipation of Gauss's results on constructible polygons, Vandermonde himself did not rigorously or completely establish his results nor did he see the implications for geometry. Nevertheless, Kronecker dated the modern movement in algebra to Vandermonde's 1770 paper.

According to Maxwell, Vandermonde's second paper was cited in one of Gauss's notebooks, along with some work of Euler, as being one of two attempts to extend the ideas of Leibniz on the geometry of situation or analysis situs. The paper dealt with the knight's tour and involved the number of interweavings of curves, which Gauss then represented by a double integral and associated with the study of electrical potential.

Unfortunately Vandermonde's spurt of enthusiasm and creativity, which in two years produced four insightful mathematical papers, at least two of which were of substantial importance, was quickly diverted by the exciting politics of the time and, perhaps, by poor health.

BIBLIOGRAPHY

I. ORIGINAL WORKS. Vandermonde's mathematical papers appeared in *Histoire de l'Académie royale des sciences . . .* as follows: "Mémoire sur la résolution des équations" (1771), 365–415; "Remarques sur des problèmes de situation" (1771), 566–574; "Mémoire sur des irrationnelles de différents ordres avec une application au cercle," pt. 1 (1772), 489–498; and "Mémoire sur élimination," pt. 2 (1772), 516–532.

The three algebraic papers were reprinted in C. Itzigsohn, *Abhandlungen aus der reinen Mathematik. In deutscher Sprache herausgegeben* (Berlin, 1888).

II. SECONDARY LITERATURE. The most comprehensive account of Vandermonde's work is Henri Lebesgue, "L'oeuvre mathématique de Vandermonde," in *Thales, recueil des travaux de l'Institut d'histoire des sciences*, IV (1937–1939), 28–42, and in *Enseignement mathématique*, 2nd ser., 1 (1955), 203–223. Also useful are Niels Nielsen, "Vandermonde," in *Géomètres Français sous la revolution* (Copenhagen, 1929), 229–237; Thomas Muir, *The Theory of Determinants in the Historical Order of Their Development*, 2nd ed., I

(London, 1906), repr. (New York, 1960), 17–24; and H. Simon, "Vandermondes Vornamen," in *Zeitschrift für Mathematik und Physik*, **41** (1896), 83–85.

PHILLIP S. JONES

VANDIVER, HARRY SCHULTZ (*b.* Philadelphia, Pennsylvania, 21 October 1882; *d.* Austin, Texas, 9 January 1973)

Harry Schultz Vandiver was the son of John Lyon and Ida Everett Vandiver. At an early age he developed an antagonism to public education that was to last the rest of his life. He dropped out of Central High School and went to work for twelve years as a customshouse broker for his father's firm. He was very much interested in the theory of numbers, and at the age of eighteen began his publishing career in the problem section of the *American Mathematical Monthly*. From 1904 to 1905 he attended some graduate courses in mathematics and made extensive use of the library at the University of Pennsylvania. In 1904 he collaborated with George David Birkhoff on a first-rate paper on the prime factors of $a^n - b^n$ that appeared in the *Annals of Mathematics*.

Vandiver continued to publish three or four papers a year until the end of World War I, during which he served in the U.S. Naval Reserve as a yeoman first class. Then, at the urging of Birkhoff, he turned professional by accepting an instructorship in mathematics at Cornell University in 1919, a position he held until 1924. Vandiver spent his summers at the University of Chicago, working with L. E. Dickson on the latter's monumental *History of the Theory of Numbers* (3 vols., Washington, D.C., 1919–1923) and on the *Report of the Committee on Algebraic Numbers of the National Research Council* (2 vols., Washington, D.C., 1923–1928).

In 1924 Vandiver accepted an associate professorship at the University of Texas at Austin, where he remained until his retirement in 1966. He also continually accepted visiting professorships and lectureships. He was in Princeton in 1934 when he was elected a member of the National Academy of Sciences. More than half of the one hundred papers he wrote thereafter appeared in the *Proceedings* of the academy.

In the summer of 1952 Vandiver visited the National Bureau of Standards Institute at Los Angeles to see what the high-speed computer SWAC could do with Fermat's last theorem. The problem is to show that the equation $x^p + y^p + z^p = 0$ is not solvable in nonzero integers x, y, z, p when p is a prime greater than 2. Vandiver and others had determined various criteria that p has to meet in order for the above equation to hold. He and his students over the years had shown $p > 600$. When the criteria were presented to the SWAC, it eliminated every $p < 2000$ in a couple of hours. (Later the limit of p was set at $p < 4002$ and more recently at $p < 125000$.)

In 1923 Vandiver married Maude Folmsbee. They had one son, Frank Vandiver, who became president of Texas A&M. In accordance with his father's views on public education, Frank was privately tutored for his secondary school and undergraduate college education.

Vandiver was awarded the F. N. Cole Prize in Number Theory by the American Mathematical Society in 1931, and in 1946 the University of Pennsylvania bestowed on him the honorary degree of doctor of science. He was a Guggenheim fellow in the academic year 1927–1928, and his work until 1961 was supported by the National Science Foundation (grants in 1955 and 1957–1961) and the American Philosophical Society (grants in 1934 and 1939).

The Vandivers never owned a home in Austin. For many years they occupied a permanent suite at the Alamo Hotel, where they had a large collection of classical recordings. When he was not doing research or refereeing or reviewing the work of others, Vandiver would relax by listening to Mozart or Beethoven or, on occasion, by attending a campus baseball game. At the age of eighty-four Vandiver gave up research and went into a rest home.

Vandiver's bibliography extends from 1900 to 1963 and contains 173 titles, of which 50 are directly concerned with Fermat's last theorem; the others are mainly on properties of Bernoulli numbers and on cyclotomy and commutative algebra. There are also half a dozen expository papers on Fermat's last theorem and one entitled "On the Desirability of Publishing Classified Bibliographies of the Mathematics Literature" (1960), no doubt inspired by his early work with Dickson's *History*. He also prepared a twenty-two-page bibliography of articles on Bernoulli and Euler numbers for the years 1869–1940, which he never published.

The Fermat problem of showing the nonexistence of integers x, y, z, none zero, such that $x^p + y^p = z^p$ holds for p a prime greater than 2, has long been separated into two cases. Case I is subject to the condition that p fails to divide xyz and is much simpler than case II, in which p may divide xyz. In case I we have Weiferich's criterion that 2^{p-1} is divisible by p^2. This condition is met by $p = 1093$ and $p = 3511$, but for no other prime less than six billion. However, these two primes fail to satisfy the Mirimanoff criterion that p^2 divides 3^{p-1} 1, so that case I is proved for $p < 6 \cdot 10^9$. Many times Vandiver expressed the conviction that case I would be disposed of in the near future.

His approach to case II was along the lines of the early German algebraic number theorist E. E. Kummer, who founded the arithmetic of numbers of the form

$$a_0 + a_1w + a_2w^2 + \ldots + a_{p-1}w^{p-1},$$

where $w^p = 1$, $w \neq 1$, and the a's are ordinary integers.

The Fermat equation can be written

$$x^p = z^p - y^p = (z - y)(z - wy)\ldots(z - w^{p-1}y).$$

Vandiver sought conditions on p alone to make this product a perfect of p. The criteria he derived had to do with the divisibility by p of the Bernoulli numbers $B_2, B_4, B_6, \ldots, B_{p-3}$ and the class number h of the cyclotomic field generated by w. Then there is the problem of combining the criteria to form a condition that should be impossible. Throughout this process one has to try to discover properties of the integers x, y, z, p, which one hopes do not exist after all. This sort of situation was commonplace in the scientific life of H. S. Vandiver.

BIBLIOGRAPHY

I. ORIGINAL WORKS. "On the Integral Divisors of $a^n - b^n$," in *Annals of Mathematics*, 2nd ser., **5** (1904), 173–180, written with G. D. Birkhoff; "Proof of Fermat's Last Theorem for All Prime Exponents Less Than 4002," in *Proceedings of the National Academy of Sciences*, **41** (1955), 970–973, written with C. A. Nicol and J. L. Selfridge; and "On the Desirability of Publishing Classified Bibliographies of the Mathematics Literature," *American Mathematical Monthly*, **67** (1960), 47–50.

II. SECONDARY LITERATURE. An obituary by D. H. Lehmer is in *Bulletin of the American Mathematical Society*, **80** (1974), 817–818. See also D. H. Lehmer, "On Fermat's Quotient, Base Two," in *Mathematics of Computation*, **36** (1981), 289–290; and S. Wagstaff, "The Irregular Primes to 125000," *ibid.*, **32** (1978), 583–591.

D. H. LEHMER

VARIGNON, PIERRE (*b.* Caen, France, 1654; *d.* Paris, France, 23 December 1722)

It is due to Lagrange that Varignon's name gained recognition in the teaching of mechanics in France in the nineteenth century, and until rather recently his name was linked with a theorem on the composition of forces that is now identified with the properties of the vector product. The passage of time diminishes this kind of fame; but historians are discovering in Varignon's work—which, admittedly, is of second rank with regard to substantive results—an importance for the philosophy of science. Expressive of the attempt to reduce the number of basic principles in mechanics in order to improve the organization of the subject, Varignon's accomplishments illustrate the relationship between this effort and progress made in notation and in operational procedures in pure mathematics.

The son and brother of contracting masons, Varignon stated that his entire patrimony consisted of his family's technical knowledge; it proved, however, to be of considerable importance for his later career. He probably studied at the Jesuit *collège* in Caen, which he would have entered at a relatively late age. The only certain information about this period of his life, however, is that relating to his entrance into the religious life: he submitted to the tonsure on 19 December 1676, earned his Master of Arts degree on 15 September 1682, and became a priest in the St.-Ouen parish of Caen on 10 March 1683. An ecclesiastical career enabled him to study at the University of Caen, where he was certainly one of the oldest students.

One of Varignon's fellow students was Charles Castel, Abbé de Saint-Pierre (1658–1743), who later achieved fame for his philanthropy. Saint-Pierre soon offered to share his lodgings and income with Varignon. The two left Caen for Paris in 1686. When Varignon reached Paris, he had already done considerable scientific research; and the contacts he made through Saint-Pierre accomplished the rest. As early as 1687 he had access to Pierre Bayle's periodical, *Nouvelles de la république des lettres*, for the publication of his memoir on tackle blocks for pulleys, and his first published book, *Projet d'une nouvelle méchanique*, was dedicated to the Académie des Sciences.

Although not to be compared with Newton's *Principia*, which appeared in the same year as Varignon's *Projet*, their simultaneous publication perhaps brought the latter work a greater success among French scientists than it would otherwise have had. In any case, the success of the *Projet* brought Varignon nomination as geometer in the Académie des Sciences in 1688, as well as the first appointment to the newly created professorship of mathematics at the Collège Mazarin. Within two years, therefore, Varignon was set in his career. He taught—and resided—at the Collège Mazarin until his death. In 1704 the former secretary of the Academy, Jean-Baptiste du Hamel, resigned in Varignon's favor from the chair of Greek and Latin philosophy at the Collège Royal (now the Collège de France). The title of the chair in no way restricted the scientific topics that could be taught by its holder, who had sole discretion in this regard.

Fully occupied by his teaching duties and his responsibilities as an academician, Varignon had no leisure to prepare works for publication. After a short second work, *Nouvelles conjectures sur la pesanteur* (1690), his literary production consisted of articles for learned journals and a large number of memoirs submitted to the Academy. His correspondence, however, particularly with Leibniz and Johann I Bernoulli, bears witness to his role in the scientific life of his age. From the papers he left at his death, most of which are now lost, his disciples assembled several posthumous works: *Nouvelle mécanique* (announced in the *Projet* of 1687) and *Éclaircissemens sur l'analyse des infiniment petits*, both published in 1725, and *Élémens de mathématiques* (1731), which was based on his courses at the Collège Mazarin.

Varignon's intense pedagogical activity, extending over more than thirty years, constituted his chief contribution to the progress of science and was the source of his fame. By inaugurating a chair devoted specifically to mathematics at the Collège Mazarin, he joined the handful of men who were then teaching advanced mathematics; and it is in this context that his work was of great importance.

Bossut and Montucla, writing the history of mathematics half a century later, were unable to ignore Varignon; but, lacking the necessary historical distance, they were unjustly severe. Bossut, for example, wrote: "Endowed with an excellent memory, Varignon read a great deal, closely examined the writings of the pioneers [*inventeurs*], generalized their methods, and appropriated their ideas; and some students took disguised or enlarged reformulations to be discoveries." But since the essential precondition of a teacher's effectiveness is that he constantly broaden his knowledge and keep it current, Bossut should have praised Varignon for having done just that, instead of condemning him for not sufficiently citing his sources. The latter judgment is, of course, possible; but Varignon's writings offer no incontrovertible support for it. Montucla's evaluation was more penetrating; he criticized Varignon primarily for what may be called a mania for "generalization." Certainly, Varignon had neither a precise nor an ac-

ceptable notion of that process and often confused it with the mere use of algebraic language. Viewed in its historical context, however, this failing is not at all astonishing.

The pejorative assessments of Bossut and Montucla were echoed by Pierre Duhem, who in his *Origines de la statique* (1905–1906) wrote ironically of Varignon's naïve belief in his own originality in mechanics. Yet, like earlier criticisms, Duhem's is not wholly justified. The audacity that average intellects must needs muster in order to fight for progressive ideas always presupposes a certain naïveté on their part. Indeed, the more it becomes evident that Varignon was not a genius, the less the defects of his thought ought to be allowed to weigh against estimates of his real accomplishments.

From this point of view, Lagrange underscored the essential point. In the posthumous edition of the *Nouvelle mécanique* he found the text of a letter from Johann Bernoulli to Varignon (26 January 1717) marking the emergence of the principle of virtual velocities, and he realized that in this matter Varignon deserves credit on two counts: for preparing the way for and eliciting Bernoulli's statement, and for attempting to provide the broadest justification of the principle. Thus the period between the *Projet* of 1687 and the *Nouvelle mécanique* witnessed the development of what appeared a century later to be the very foundation of classical mechanics.

Lagrange was not mistaken, either, about Varignon's active role in the initial development of the principle of the composition of forces. The technique of composing forces by the rule of the parallelogram had undergone more than a century of development when it was published, simultaneously, in 1687 in Newton's *Principia*, Varignon's *Projet*, and the second edition of Bernard Lamy's *Traitez de méchanique*. The enunciation of the principle, which appeared as a consequence of the composition of infinitely small movements and not of finite ones, eliminated a troublesome confusion that had hampered progress in the subject.

The simultaneous publication of the principle makes difficult any judgment regarding priority. Nevertheless, it was Varignon alone who grasped two important points. The first is that the law of the lever does not hold a privileged position in statics, and that the unification of "mechanics" (the science of simple machines) was to be carried out on the basis of the composition of forces. The second concerns the inclined plane: that the real reason for the equilibrium observed is that the resultant of the applied forces is orthogonal to the possible displacement. These two points provide a good indication of Varignon's contribution to the development of the principle of virtual velocities.

It must, of course, be added that his contribution was limited to general statics; but this was the point of departure for d'Alembert's subsequent extension of the principle to dynamics. In the latter field Varignon did not solve any of the important problems of his time—as Bossut correctly observed. Nevertheless, in his memoirs to the Academy, he showed how to apply infinitesimal analysis to the science of motion and how, in specific cases, to use the relationship between force and acceleration. The laborious nature of this work does not detract from its historical importance.

In working with the model of falling bodies, Varignon encountered difficulties in obtaining acceleration as a second derivative. This problem had the advantage, however, of obliging him to reassess the importance of the new differential and integral calculus. His acceptance of the new procedures occurred between 1692 and 1695, and he was among those who gave the most favorable reception to the publication of L'Hospital's *Analyse des infiniment petits* in 1696. The *Éclaircissemens* is composed of critical notes that Varignon, as a professor, considered necessary in presenting L'Hospital's pioneering work to young mathematicians—further evidence of his constructive role in the movement to transform the operations used in mathematics. But Varignon accomplished even more: in 1700–1701 he refuted Rolle's arguments against the new calculus, challenged the cabal that had formed within the Academy, and obliged Leibniz to furnish a more precise account of his ideas. Leibniz, to be sure, did not give him all the aid desired. Nevertheless, he encouraged Varignon to cease debating principles and to start developing mechanical applications of the new mathematics. The questions that Varignon subsequently treated show how faithfully he followed Leibniz' advice.

In his course at the Collège Royal for 1722–1723, Varignon planned to discuss the foundations of infinitesimal calculus but was able to do no more than outline his ideas. Although he died before he could present what was undoubtedly the core of a lifetime's experience, that experience had already borne fruit.

BIBLIOGRAPHY

I. ORIGINAL WORKS. Varignon's books include *Projet d'une nouvelle méchanique* (Paris, 1687); *Nouvelles conjectures sur la pesanteur* (Paris, 1690); *Éclaircisse-mens sur l'analyse des infiniment petits* (Paris, 1725); *Nouvelle mécanique ou statique . . .,* 2 vols. (Paris, 1725); *Traité du mouvement et de la mesure des eaux coulantes et jaillissantes . . .* (Paris, 1725); and *Élémens de mathématiques . . .* (Paris, 1731).

His major published articles are "Démonstration générale de l'usage des poulies à moufle," in *Nouvelles de la république des lettres* (May 1687), 487–498; a sequel to the preceding article containing "une nouvelle démonstration du paradoxe de M. Mariotte," in *Histoire des ouvrages des sçavans,* 1 (Oct. 1687), 172–176; "Règles du mouvement en général," in *Mémoires de mathématiques et de physique tirés des registres de l'Académie . . .* (1692), 190–195; "Des cycloïdes ou roulettes à l'infini," *ibid.* (1693), 43–47; "Règles des mouvemens accélérés suivant toutes les proportions imaginables d'accélérations ordonnées," *ibid.,* 93–96; "Méthode pour trouver des courbes le long desquelles un corps tombant s'approche ou s'eloigne de l'horizon en telle raison des temps qu'on voudra . . .," in *Mémoires de l'Académie royale des sciences* (1699), 1–13.

Later works are "Du mouvement en général par toutes sortes de courbes et des forces centrales tant centrifuges que centripètes, nécessaires aux corps qui les décrivent," *ibid.* (1700), 83–101; "Application au mouvement des planètes," *ibid.,* 218–237; "De la figure ou curvité des fusées des horloges à ressort," *ibid.* (1702), 192–202; "Du mouvement des eaux . . .," *ibid.* (1703), 238–261; "Du mouvement des planètes sur leurs orbes en y comprenant le mouvement de l'apogée on de l'aphélie," *ibid.* (1705), 347–361; "Différentes manières infiniment générales de trouver les rayons osculateurs de toutes sortes de courbes . . .," *ibid.* (1706), 490–507; "Des mouvements faits dans des milieux qui leur résistent en raison quelconque," *ibid.* (1707), 382–476; "Des forces centrales inverses," *ibid.* (1710), 533–544; "Réflexions sur l'usage que la mécanique peut avoir en géométrie," *ibid.* (1714), 77–121; and "Précaution à prendre dans l'usage des suites ou séries infinies . . .," *ibid.* (1715), 203–225.

II. SECONDARY LITERATURE. See Pierre Costabel, "Contribution à l'histoire de la loi de la chute des graves," in *Revue d'histoire des sciences et de leurs applications,* 1 (1947), 193–205; "Le paradoxe de Mariotte," in *Archives internationales d'histoire des sciences,* 2 (1948), 864–886); "Pierre Varignon et la diffusion en France du calcul différentiel et intégral," *Conférences du Palais de la découverte,* ser. D, no. 108 (1965); and "Varignon, Lamy et le parallélogramme des forces," in *Archives internationales d'histoire des sciences,* 19, nos. 74–75 (1966), 103–124; J. O. Fleckenstein, "Pierre Varignon und die mathematischen Wissenschaften in Zeitalter des Cartesianismus," *ibid.,* 2 (1948), 76–138; and Bernard de Fontenelle, "Éloge de M. Varignon," in *Histoire et mémoires de l'Académie des sciences* for 1722, 189–204.

PIERRE COSTABEL

VEBLEN, OSWALD (*b.* Decorah, Iowa, 24 June 1880; *d.* Brooklin, Maine, 10 August 1960)

Veblen's parents were both children of immigrants from Norway. His mother (1851–1908) was born Kirsti Hougen; his father, Andrew Anderson Veblen (1848–1932), was professor of physics at the University of Iowa; and his uncle, Thorstein Veblen (1857–1929), was famous for his book *The Theory of the Leisure Class*. Veblen himself had two B.A. degrees (Iowa, 1898; Harvard, 1900) but was most influenced by his graduate study (Ph.D., 1903) at the University of Chicago under E. H. Moore. He had a happy marriage (1908) to Elizabeth Mary Dixon Richardson. His influential teaching career was at Princeton, both at the University (1905–1932) and at the Institute for Advanced Study (1932–1950).

The axiomatic method, so characteristic of twentieth-century mathematics, had a brilliant start in Hilbert's *Grundlagen der Geometrie* (1899). In this book, precise and subtle analysis corrected the logical inadequacies in Euclid's *Elements*. Veblen's work, starting at this point, was devoted to precise analysis of this and many other branches of geometry, notably topology and differential geometry; his ideas have been extensively developed by many younger American geometers.

The initial step was Veblen's thesis (1903, published 1904), which gave a careful axiomatization for Euclidean geometry, different from that of Hilbert because based on just two primitive notions, "point" and "order" (of points on a line), as initially suggested by Pasch and Peano. With this systematic start on the axiomatic method, Veblen's interests expanded to include the foundations of analysis (where he emphasized the role of the Heine-Borel theorem, that is, of compactness) and finite projective geometries. His work in projective geometry culminated in a magnificent two-volume work, *Projective Geometry* (vol. I, 1910; vol. II, 1918), in collaboration with J. W. Young. This book gives a lucid and leisurely presentation of the whole sweep of these geometries over arbitrary fields and over the real number field, with the properties of conics and projectivities and with the classification of geometries by the Klein-Erlanger program. It includes a masterful exposition of the axiomatic method (independence and categoricity of axioms), which had extensive influence on other workers in algebra and geometry.

Veblen's greatest contribution probably lies in his development of analysis situs. This branch of geometry deals with numerical and algebraic measures of the "connectivity" of geometric figures. It was initiated by Poincaré in a famous but difficult series of memoirs (1895–1904). It came naturally to Veblen's attention through his earlier work on the Jordan curve theorem (that is, how a closed curve separates the plane) and on order and orientation to Euclidean and projective geometry. Veblen's 1916 Colloquium Lectures to the American Mathematical Society led to his 1922 *Analysis Situs*, which for nearly a decade was the only systematic treatment in book form of the pioneering ideas of Poincaré. This book was carefully studied by several generations of mathematicians, who went on to transform and rename the subject (first "combinatorial topology," then "algebraic topology," then "homological algebra") and to found a large American school of topology with wide international influence.

Veblen also did extensive work on differential geometry, especially on the geometry of paths (today treated by affine connections) and on projective relativity (four-component spinors). His more important work in this field would seem to be his part in the transition from purely local differential geometry to global considerations. His expository monograph (1927) on the invariants of quadratic differential forms gave a clear statement of the usual formal local theory; and it led naturally to his later monograph with J. H. C. Whitehead, *The Foundations of Differential Geometry* (1932). This monograph contained the first adequate definition of a global differentiable manifold. Their definition was complicated; for example, they did not assume that the underlying topological space is Hausdorff. Soon afterward H. Whitney, starting from this Veblen-Whitehead definition, developed the simpler definition of a differentiable manifold, which has now become standard (and extended to other cases such as complex analytic manifolds). In this case the Veblen-Whitehead book had influence not through many readers, but essentially through one reformulation, that of Whitney.

Veblen had an extensive mathematical effect upon others; in earlier years through many notable co-workers and students (R. L. Moore, J. W. Alexander, J. H. M. Wedderburn, T. Y. Thomas, Alonzo Church, J. H. C. Whitehead, and many others) and in later years by his activities as a mathematical statesman and as a leader in the development of the School of Mathematics at the Institute for Advanced Study.

BIBLIOGRAPHY

I. ORIGINAL WORKS. Veblen's thesis was published as "A System of Axioms for Geometry," in *Transactions* of the American Mathematical Society, **5** (1904), 343–384. His other works include *Projective Geometry*, I (New York, 1910), written with J. W. Young; II (Boston, 1918); *Analysis Situs*, in *Colloquium Publications. American Mathematical Society*, **5**, pt. 2 (1922); 2nd ed. (1931); "Invariants of Quadratic Differential Forms," in *Cambridge Tracts in Mathematics and Mathematical Physics*, **24** (1927); "The Foundations of Differential Geometry," *ibid.*, **29** (1932), written with J. H. C. Whitehead; and "Projective Relativitätstheorie," in *Ergenbnisse der Mathematik und ihrer Grenzgebiete*, **2**, no. 1 (1933).

II. SECONDARY LITERATURE. On Veblen and his work, see *American Mathematical Society Semicentennial Publications*, **1** (1938), 206–211, with complete list of Veblen's doctoral students; Saunders MacLane, in *Biographical Memoirs. National Academy of Sciences*, **37** (1964), 325–341, with bibliography; Deane Montgomery, in *Bulletin of the American Society*, **69** (1963), 26–36; and *Yearbook. American Philosophical Society* (1962), 187–193.

SAUNDERS MAC LANE

VENN, JOHN (*b.* Hull, England, 4 August 1834; *d.* Cambridge, England, 4 April 1923)

Venn's family was one of a group belonging to the evangelical wing of the Church of England that was noted for its philanthropic work. This group, which included the Macaulays, Thorntons, and Wilberforces, was centered in the London suburb of Clapham and was nicknamed the "Clapham Sect." A pivotal figure was Venn's grandfather, Rev. John Venn, rector of Clapham.

After attending two London schools, at Highgate and Islington, Venn entered Gonville and Caius College, Cambridge, in 1853; took his degree in mathematics in 1857; and was elected a fellow of his college, holding the fellowship until his death. He took holy orders in 1859, but after a short interval of parochial work he returned to Cambridge as college lecturer in moral sciences and played a considerable part in the development of the newly established moral sciences tripos examination. In 1883 Venn resigned his clerical orders, being out of sympathy with orthodox Anglican dogma but remained a devout lay member of the church. He received the Cambridge Sc.D. in 1883 and in that year was elected a fellow of the Royal Society.

Besides his scientific works, Venn conducted much research into historical records and wrote books on the history of his college and on his family. He also undertook the preparation of *Alumni Cantabrigienses*, a tremendous task in which he was assisted by his son, J. A. Venn; two volumes appeared in his lifetime.

Venn's volumes on probability and logic were highly esteemed textbooks in the late nineteenth and early twentieth centuries. The historian H. T. Buckle had discussed the validity of statistical studies of human activities, and De Morgan and Boole had written on the foundations of probability theory; this work stimulated Venn to write his *Logic of Chance*. In this book he disclaimed any attempt to make extensive use of mathematical techniques; he believed that there was a need for a thorough and logical discussion of principles, and his work was an essay in that direction. British predecessors were critically discussed. Venn thought that De Morgan's *Formal Logic* provided a good investigation, but he was not prepared to accept his principles; he was dubious about Boole's *Laws of Thought*, for he was not entirely happy with certain aspects of Boole's algebraic analysis of logic.

Venn attempted to deal with the notorious Petersburg paradox by insisting on the concept of "average gain," which is connected with his revision of the basic definition of probability. The classical definition, given in the early eighteenth century by De Moivre, considers the situation in which there are s successes in m trials and defines the probability of a success as s/m. One weakness of that definition is that if a possible ambiguity is to be evaded by specifying that the m possibilities are all equally likely, we may be led into a circular argument. Venn offered the following definition: If in a large number m of trials there are s successes (and $m - s$ failures), the probability of a success is the limit of s/m as m tends to infinity. This definition avoids the difficulties that arise when the classical definition is applied to, say, a die with bias, but is itself not free from defects. The existence of the limit cannot be proved from the definition; Venn implicitly assumes that a unique limit must exist. In the twentieth century R. von Mises improved Venn's work by adding explicit postulates on the existence of the Venn limit that effectively restrict the nature of the possible trials. The Venn definition also has been criticized on the practical grounds that it alone cannot provide a specific numerical value for the probability and that further hypotheses must be added in order to arrive at such values.

Venn's books on logic were based on a thorough study of earlier works, of which he had a very large collection that is now in the Cambridge University Library. His writings can still be consulted with profit but are chiefly remembered for the use of logical diagrams, although *Symbolic Logic* is largely an attempt to interpret and correct Boole's work. The use of geometric diagrams to represent syllogistic logic has a long history, but Leibniz was the first to use them systematically rather than as casual illustrations. "All A is B" is represented by a circle marked A placed wholly inside another circle marked B; "Some A is B" is represented by two overlapping circles; and the standard syllogisms are depicted by means of three circles. The procedure was further developed by Euler, and in the early nineteenth century many writers offered varieties of diagrammatic representation. In preparing his book Venn had made a careful survey of such writings, and his chapter discussing them is severely critical. Boole's *Laws of Thought* (1854) was the first efficient development of an algebra of logic, but he did not use diagrams.

Venn was strongly influenced by Boole's work, and in his books he clarifies some inconsistencies and ambiguities in Boole's ideas and notations; but his chief contribution to logic was his systematic explanation and development of the method of geometrical representation. He pointed out that diagrams that merely represent the relations between two classes, or two propositions, are not sufficiently general; and he proposed a series of simple closed curves (circles or more elaborate forms) dividing the plane into compartments, such that each successive curve should intersect all the compartments already obtained. For one term, compartments x, $\bar{x}$ (the negation or complement of x) are needed; for two terms, four compartments are needed; for three terms, eight; and so on. By the time five classes are under consideration, the diagram is becoming complicated to the point of uselessness. To illustrate the principles of symbolic logic, Venn deliberately provided a variety of concrete instances, often of the type now found in collections of mathematical puzzles, for he remarked that the subject is sufficiently abstract to present difficulty to the average student, who must be helped by a supply of realizable examples.

Since the null class was not then accepted as a class, Venn also had to discuss whether the diagrams represented compartments or classes—that is, whether compartments could be regarded as unoccupied. A compartment known to be unoccupied could be shown by shading it, and a universal proposition could be represented by a suitable unoccupied compartment: Thus "No A is B" could be represented by shading the area common to the two intersecting circles (or closed curves) representing A and B. Venn's treatment of the "universe of discourse" was somewhat indefinite and was criticized by C. L. Dodgson in his *Symbolic Logic* (published under the pseudonym by which he was better known, Lewis Carroll); Dodgson insisted, in Carollian style, on the use of a closed compartment enclosing the whole diagram to delimit the universe of discourse. Venn diagrams, as they are now generally called, have recently been much used in elementary mathematics to encourage logical thinking at a fairly early stage of a child's education.

BIBLIOGRAPHY

I. Original Works. Venn's books include *The Logic of Chance* (London–Cambridge, 1866); *Symbolic Logic* (London–Cambridge, 1881); and *The Principles of Empirical Logic* (London–Cambridge, 1889).

II. Secondary Literature. A detailed obituary notice of Venn by his son, J. A. Venn, is in *Dictionary of National Biography* for 1922–1930, 869–870. For a critical discussion of definitions of probability, see Harold Jeffreys, *Theory of Probability*, 2nd ed. (Oxford, 1948). A succinct but valuable account of Venn diagrams is M. E. Baron, "A Note on the Historical Development of Logic Diagrams: Leibniz, Euler and Venn," in *Mathematical Gazette*, **53** (May 1969), 113–125.

T. A. A. Broadbent

VER EECKE, PAUL (*b.* Menin, Belgium, 13 February 1867; *d.* Berchem, Belgium, 14 October 1959)

Ver Eecke attended the *collège* in Menin until he was fifteen and completed his secondary education at Bruges. After graduating as a mining engineer from the University of Liège in 1891 and following a short period in private industry, he entered the Administration du Travail in 1894, where he served until his retirement in 1932. His many honors included membership in the Société Mathématique de Belgique, the Académie Internationale d'Histoire des Sciences, and the Comité Belge d'Histoire des Sciences.

While quite young, Ver Eecke became interested in ancient Greek mathematics, especially in the works of Archimedes, and his first publication (1921) was a French translation of the complete works of Archimedes. Nearly all his scholarship concerned the translation of Greek mathematical works into French, the only exceptions being his translations from the Latin into French of the *Liber quadratorum* of Leonardo Fibonacci (written in 1225) and a treatise by Vito Caravelli. He carried out this work not as a philologist but as a scientist, adhering closely to the Greek text. His translations were preceded by surveys of the periods in which the mathematicians lived; and in the footnotes Ver Eecke gave the proofs in modern notation. Ver Eecke thus provided historians of science with a fairly accurate reflection of thought in antiquity and the scientific significance of the works.

In addition to translations Ver Eecke also wrote articles. In "Le théorème dit de Guldin considéré au point de vue historique" he defended the assumption that the law bearing his name was original with Guldin. Ver Eecke's arguments were, however, rejected by R. C. Archibald (*Scripta mathematica*, **1** [1932], 267).

BIBLIOGRAPHY

Ver Eecke's works include *Les oeuvres complètes d'Archimède* (Brussels, 1921); *Les Coniques d'Apollonius de Perge* (Bruges, 1923; repr. Paris, 1963); *Diophante d'Alexandrie. Les six livres arithmétiques et le livre des nombres polygones* (Bruges, 1926); *Les Sphériques de Théodose de Tripoli* (Bruges, 1927); *Serenus d'Antinoë. Le livre "De la section du cylindre" et le livre "De la section du cône"* (Paris–Bruges, 1929); "Note sur le procédé de la démonstration indirecte chez les géomètres d l'antiquité grecque," in *Mathesis*, **44** (1930), 382–384; "Note sur la théorie du plan incliné chez les mathématiciens grecs," *ibid.*, **45** (1931), 352–355; "Le théorème dit de Guldin considéré au point de vue historique," *ibid.*, **46** (1932), 395–397; "La mécanique des Grecs d'après Pappus d'Alexandrie," in *Scientia* (Milan), **54** (1933), 114–122; *Pappus d'Alexandrie. La Collection mathématique* (Paris–Bruges, 1933); "Le traité des hosoèdres de Vito Caravelli (1724–1800)," in *Mathesis*, **49** (1935), 59–82; "Le traité du métrage des divers bois de Didyme d'Alexandrie," in *Annales de la Société scientifique de Bruxelles*, ser. A, **56** (1936), 6–16; "Note sur une démonstration antique d'un théorème de lieu géométrique," in *Mathesis*, **51** (1937), 11–14; *Euclide. L'Optique et la Catoptrique* (Paris–Bruges, 1938); "Note sur une interprétation erronée d'une définition pythagoricienne de la ligne géométrique," in *Antiquité classique*, **7** (1938), 271–273; *Les opuscules mathématiques de Didyme, Diophane et Anthemius, suivis du fragment mathématique de Bobbio* (Paris–Bruges, 1940); *Proclus de Lycie. Les commentaires sur le premier livre des Éléments d'Euclide* (Bruges, 1948); and *Léonard de Pise. Le livre des nombres carrés* (Bruges, 1952).

H. L. L. BUSARD

VERHULST, PIERRE-FRANÇOIS (*b.* Brussels, Belgium, 28 October 1804; *d.* Brussels, 15 February, 1849)

According to Adolphe Quetelet, Verhulst, while on a trip to Rome, "conceived the idea of carrying out a reform in the Papal States and of persuading the Holy Father to give a constitution to his people." The project was, in fact, considered; and Verhulst, ordered to leave Rome, was almost besieged in his apartment.

Verhulst first thought of publishing the complete works of Euler but abandoned this idea in order to study with Quetelet, with whom he eventually collaborated on social statistics. The two did not, however, always share the same views in this field, in which the theoretical foundations were uncertain and observations far from abundant. It was generally assumed, following Malthus, that the tendency of a population to increase follows a geometric progression. Quetelet, however, believed he had grounds for asserting that the sum of the obstacles opposed to the indefinite growth of population increases in proportion to the square of the rate at which the population tends to grow. Verhulst showed in 1846 that these obstacles increase in proportion to the ratio of the excess population to the total population. He was thus led to give the figure of 9,400,000 as the upper limit for the population of Belgium (which, in fact, has grown to 9,581,000 by 1967). Verhulst's research on the law of population growth makes him a precursor of modern students of the subject.

Verhulst was a professor at the Université Libre of Brussels and later at the École Royale Militaire. He was elected to the Académie Royale de Belgique in 1841 and became its president in 1848.

BIBLIOGRAPHY

There are articles on Verhulst by J. Pelseneer, in *Biographie nationale publiée par l'Académie royale de Belgique*, XXVI (Brussels, 1936–1938), cols. 658–663, with bibliography; and A. Quetelet, in *Annuaire de l'Académie r. des sciences, des lettres et des beaux-arts de Belgique*, **16** (1850), 97–124, with a bibliography of Verhulst's works and a portrait.

J. PELSENEER

VERONESE, GIUSEPPE (*b.* Chioggia, Italy, 7 May 1854; *d.* Padua, Italy, 17 July 1917)

Giuseppe Veronese, professor of geometry at the University of Padua from 1881 until his death, was one of the foremost Italian mathematicians of his time. He took part also in political life, first as a member of Parliament for Chioggia (1897–1900), then as a member of the City Council of Padua, and finally as a senator (1904–1917).

Veronese's father was a house painter in Chioggia, then a small fishing town not far from Venice; his mother, Ottavia Duse, was a cousin of the celebrated actress Eleonora Duse. In 1885 Veronese married the Baroness Beatrice Bartolini; they had five children. Veronese was a handsome man, tall and commanding, but in his last years his health was undermined by influenza, which he had contracted in 1912 and which left him with grave cardiovascular disorders.

Because of his parents' poverty, Veronese had to interrupt his studies when he was eighteen and take a minor job in Vienna; but through the generosity of Count Nicolò Papadopoli he was able to resume his studies a year later, first at the Zurich Polytechnic, where he studied engineering and mathematics under Wilhelm Fiedler, and later, following a correspondence with Luigi Cremona, at the University of Rome, from which he graduated in 1877. In the previous year he had become assistant in analytical geometry, an unheard-of distinction for an undergraduate, after demonstrating his exceptional abilities in a paper on Pascal's hexagram, a work he had begun at Zurich. In 1880–1881 Veronese did postgraduate study at Leipzig. Immediately afterward, he won the competition for the professorship of complementary algebra and algebraic geometry at the University of Padua, where he succeeded Giusto Bellavitis. The latter had shown personal liking for Veronese but was fiercely opposed to the new approaches to geometry, which Veronese supported.

Veronese published only about thirty papers; but some of them, also available in German, were extremely important in the history of geometry. In particular he may be considered the main founder of the projective geometry of hyperspaces with n dimensions, which had previously been linear algebra presented geometrically, rather than geometry. Hyperspaces began to assume a more truly geometrical aspect when Veronese used an original recursion method to produce them: a plane can be obtained by projecting the points of a straight line from a point outside it, and a three-dimensional space by projecting the points of a plane from a point outside it, and so on. He is also remembered for "Veronese's surface," a two-dimensional surface of a five-dimensional space, which in its simplest expression can be represented by the parametric equations $x_1 = u^2$, $x_2 = uv$, $x_3 = v^2$, $x_4 = u$, $x_5 = v$, where $x_1, \ldots, x_5$ are the nonhomogeneous coordinates of the space and u and v are two independent parameters. The study of this surface is equivalent, from the point of view of projection, to the study of all the conics of a plane; and one of its projections in ordinary space is Steiner's Roman surface.

Veronese was also one of the first to study non-Archimedean geometry, at first arousing strong opposition, and he demonstrated the independence of Archimedes' postulate—which states that among the multiples of a given magnitude there is always one greater than every fixed magnitude—from the other postulates of geometry. Veronese also wrote useful books for the secondary schools.

Veronese was a member of the Accademia Nazionale dei Lincei and of other Italian academies; and his pupils included Guido Castelnuovo and Tullio Levi-Civita.

When a member of Parliament, Veronese campaigned strenuously for the conservation of the Lagoon of Venice.

BIBLIOGRAPHY

An obituary is C. Segre, "Commemorazione del socio nazionale Giuseppe Veronese," in *Atti dell' Accademia nazionale dei Lincei. Rendiconti*, 5th ser., **26**, pt. 2 (1917), 249–258, with a bibliography of Veronese's publications.

F. G. TRICOMI

VESSIOT, ERNEST (*b.* Marseilles, France, 8 March 1865; *d.* La Bauche, Savoie, France, 17 October 1952)

Vessiot's ancestors were farmers near Langres, in the Haute-Marne. The family rose slowly in the social hierarchy, becoming teachers and, later, school principals. Vessiot's father was a *lycée* teacher and subsequently inspector general of primary schools. Vessiot, the third of six children, became a university professor and member of the Académie des Sciences.

A good record at the *lycée* in Marseilles enabled Vessiot to attend the École Normale Supérieure, which he entered second in his class, after Jacques Hadamard. In 1887 he obtained a teaching post at the *lycée* in Lyons. After receiving the doctorate in 1892, he taught at the universities of Lille, Toulouse, Lyons, and, finally, Paris (1910). Vessiot's first assignment at Paris was to prepare students for the *licence*. Later he taught courses in the theory of functions, in analytical mechanics, and in celestial mechanics. He became director of the École Normale Supérieure (serving in this post until his retirement in 1935) and was elected to the mechanics section of the Académie des Sciences in 1943.

Vessiot's research dealt with the application of the notion of continuous groups, finite or infinite, to the study of differential equations. Extending results obtained by Émile Picard, Vessiot demonstrated in his dissertation (1892) the existence of a group of linear substitutions with constant coefficients operating on a system of n independent solutions of a differential equation. The rigor and depth of his work on groups of linear rational transformations allowed Vessiot to put into more precise form and to develop research begun by Jules Drach (1902) and to extend the results of Élie Cartan on the integration of differential systems (1907). He also completed Volterra's study of Fredholm integrals. The extension of these integrals to partial differential equations led Vessiot to obtain original results concerning perturbations in celestial mechanics, the propagation of waves of discontinuity, and general relativity. During World War I, Vessiot was assigned to work on problems in ballistics, and he corrected certain empirical formulas then in use.

A dedicated teacher, Vessiot wrote useful and well-received textbooks. As director of the École Normale Supérieure he supervised the construction of new laboratories in collaboration with his physicist colleagues Henri Abraham, Léon Bloch, and Georges Bruhat, all of whom fell victim to the Nazis during German occupation.

BIBLIOGRAPHY

Vessiot's writings include "Sur l'interprétation mécanique des transformations de contact infinitésimales," in *Bulletin de la Société mathématique de France*, **34** (1906), 230–269; "Essai sur la propagation des ondes," in *Annales scientifiques de l'École normale supérieure*, 3rd ser., **26** (1909), 404–448; "Sur la réductibilité et l'intégration des systèmes complets," *ibid.*, **29** (1912), 209–278; "Sur la théorie des multiplicités et le calcul des variations," in *Bulletin de la Société mathématique de France*, **40** (1912), 68–139; *Leçons de géométrie supérieure* (Paris, 1919); "Sur une théorie nouvelle des problèmes d'intégration," in *Bulletin de la Société mathématique de France*, **52** (1924), 336–395; "Sur la réductibilité des équations algébriques ou différentielles," in *Annales scientifiques de l'École normale supérieure*, 3rd ser., **57** (1940), 1–60; **58** (1941), 1–36; and **63** (1946), 1–23, also in *Bulletin de la Société mathématique de France*, **75** (1947), 9–26; and *Cours de mathématiques générales*, 3 vols. (Paris, 1921–1952), written with Paul Montel.

For a discussion of Vessiot's work see Élie Cartan, "L'oeuvre scientifique de M. Ernest Vessiot," in *Bulletin de la Société mathématique de France*, **75** (1947), 1–8.

LUCIENNE FÉLIX

VIÈTE, FRANÇOIS (*b*. Fontenay-le-Comte, Poitou [now Vendée], France, 1540; *d*. Paris, France, 23 February 1603)

Viète's father, Étienne, was an attorney in Fontenay and notary at Le Busseau. His mother was Marguerite Dupont, daughter of Françoise Brisson and thus a first cousin of Barnabé Brisson. Viète was married twice: to Barbe Cothereau and, after her death, to Juliette Leclerc. After an education in Fontenay, Viète entered the University of Poitiers to study law. He received a bachelor's degree in law in 1560 but four years later abandoned the profession to enter the service of Antoinette d'Aubeterre, mother of Catherine of Parthenay, supervising the latter's education and remaining her loyal friend and adviser throughout his life. After Antoinette d'Aubeterre was widowed in 1566, Viète followed her to La Rochelle. From 1570 to 1573 he was at Paris, and on 24 October of that year Charles IX appointed him counselor to the *parlement* of Brittany at Rennes. He remained at Rennes for six years, and on 25 March 1580 he became *maître de requêtes* at Paris (an office attached to the *parlement*) and royal privy counselor. From the end of 1584 until April 1589 Viète was banished from the royal court by political enemies and spent some time at Beauvoir-sur-Mer. He was recalled to court by Henry III when the latter was obliged to leave Paris and to move the government to Tours, where Viète became counselor of the *parlement*. During the war against Spain, Viète served Henry IV by decoding intercepted letters written in cipher. A letter from the liaison officer Juan de Moreo to Philip II of Spain, dated 28 October 1589, fell into Henry's hands. The message, in a new cipher that Philip had given Moreo when he departed for France, consisted of the usual alphabet with homophonous substitutions, plus a code list of 413 terms represented by groups of two or three letters or of two numbers, either underlined or dotted. A line above a two-digit group indicated that it could be ignored. It was not until 15 March 1590 that Viète was able to send Henry the completed solution, although he had previously submitted parts of it. He returned to Paris in 1594 and to Fontenay in 1597. He was in Paris in 1599 but was dismissed by Henry IV on 14 December 1602.

Viète had only two periods of leisure (1564–1568 and 1584–1589). His first scientific works were his lectures to Catherine of Parthenay, only one of which has survived in a French translation: *Principes de cosmographie, tirés d'un manuscrit de Viette, et traduits en françois* (Paris, 1637). This tract, containing essays on the sphere, on the elements of geography, and on the elements of astronomy, has little in common with his "Harmonicon coeleste," which was never published but is available in manuscript (an autograph in Florence, Biblioteca Nazionale Centrale, MSS della Biblioteca Magliabechiana, cl. XI, cod. XXXVI, and a copy in cod. XXXVII; a copy by G. Borelli in Rome, Biblioteca Nazionale Centrale Vittorio Emanuele II, fondo San Pantaleone; and the Libri-Carucci copy in Paris, Bibliothèque Nationale, fonds lat. 7274. Part of the treatise is in Paris, Bibliothèque Nationale fonds Nouv. acqu. lat. 1644, fols. 67^r–79^v; and a French index of the part of Bibliothèque Nationale, fonds lat. 7274, is in Bibliothèque Nationale, Nouv. acqu. franç. 3282, fols. 119^r–123^r. The "Harmonicon coeleste," in five books, is Ptolemaic because Viète did not believe that Copernicus' hypothesis was geometrically valid).

All of Viète's mathematical investigations are closely connected with his cosmological and astronomical work. The *Canon mathematicus, seu ad triangula cum appendicibus*, publication of which began in 1571, was intended to form the preparatory, trigonometric part of the "Harmonicon coeleste." The *Canon* is composed of four parts, only the first two of which were published in 1579: "Canon mathematicus," which contains a table of trigonometric lines with some additional tables, and "Universalium inspectionum ad Canonem mathematicum liber singularis," which gives the computational methods used in the construction of the canon and explains the computation of plane and spherical triangles with the aid of the general trigonometric relations existing among the determinant components of such triangles. These relations were brought together in tables that allow the relevant proportion obtaining among three known and one unknown component of the triangle to be read off directly. The two other parts, devoted to astronomy, were not published. Viète certainly knew the work of Rheticus, for he adopted the triangles of three series that the latter had developed.

The *Canon* has six tables, the first of which gives, minute by minute, the values of the six trigonometric lines. For the construction of this table Viète applied the method given by Ptolemy in his *Almagest*, which was improved by the Arabs and introduced into the West through the translation of al-Zarqālī's *Canones sive regulae super tabulas astronomiae* by Gerard of Cremona; John de Lignères's *Canones tabularum primi mobilis* in the fourteenth century; and John of Gmunden's *Tractatus de sinibus, chordis et arcubus*, which inspired Peurbach and Regiomontanus. All these took as their point of departure an arc of 15° called a *kardaga*. The second table, "Canon triangulorum laterum rationalium," was based on the following proposition: "If there is a right-angled triangle having h for the hypotenuse, b for the base, and p for the perpendicular, and the semi-difference $(h-p)/2 = 1$; then $h = (b^2/4) + 1$ and $p = (b^2/4) - 1$. If b is given successive values of an arithmetical progression, the difference will be constant in the table of values of h and p thus formed. The third table, "Ad logisticem per Εξεχονταδας tabella," is a multiplication table in the form of a right triangle that immediately gives, in degrees and minutes, the product $n \cdot n'/60$ for all the numbers n and n' included between 0 and 60. "Fractionum apud mathematicos usitarum, alterius in alterum reductionibus tabella adcommodata," the fourth table, gives the quotients obtaining by dividing the Egyptian year, the day, and the hour, and their principal subdivisions by each other and also by the most commonly used integers. The fifth table, "Mathematici canonis epitome," gives the values of the trigonometric lines from degree to degree and the length of the arc expressed in parts of the radius. The sixth table, "Canon triangulorum ad singulas partes quadranti circuli secundum Εξεχονταδων logisticem," gives the value of the six trigonometric lines from degree to degree, the radius 1 being divided into sixty parts, each part into sixty primes, and each prime into sixty seconds.

After the canon of triangles with rational sides, in the second part of the *Canon*, Viète gave as functions of the radius the values of the sides of inscribed polygons with three, four, six, ten, and fifteen sides and the relations that exist among these trigonometric lines, which permit easy calculation of the tables. In his solution of oblique triangles, Viète solved all the cases (except where three sides are given) by proportionality of sides to the sines of the angles opposite the sides; for the case of three sides, he follows the ancients in subdividing the triangle into right triangles. For spherical triangles he employed the same notation as for plane triangles and established that a spherical right triangle is determined by the total sine and two other elements. In spherical oblique triangles, Viète followed the ancients and Regiomontanus in subdividing the triangle into two right triangles by an arc of a great circle perpendicular to one of the sides and passing through the vertex of the angle opposite. Also in the second part of the *Canon*, Viète wrote decimal fractions with the fractional part printed in smaller type than the integral and separated from the latter by a vertical line.

The most important of Viète's many works on algebra was *In artem analyticem isagoge*, the earliest work on symbolic algebra (Tours, 1591). It also introduced the use of letters both for known quantities, which were denoted by the consonants *B, C, D,* and so on, and for unknown quantities, which were denoted by the vowels. Furthermore, in using *A* to denote the unknown quantity *x*, Viète sometimes employed *A* quadratus, *A* cubus . . . to represent x^2, x^3. . . . This innovation, considered one of the most significant advances in the history of mathematics, prepared the way for the development of algebra.

The two main Greek sources on which Viète drew appear in the opening chapter: book VII of Pappus' *Collection* and Diophantus' *Arithmetica*. The point of departure for Viète's "renovation" was his joining of facts, presented by Pappus only in reference to geometric theorems and problems, to the procedure of Diophantus' *Arithmetica*. On the basis of Pappus' exposition, Viète called this procedure *ars analytice*. In chapter 1 he undertook a new organization of the "analytic" art. To the two kinds of analysis mentioned by Pappus, the "theoretical" and the "problematical" (which he called "zetetic," or "seeking [the truth]," and "poristic," i.e.; "productive [of the proposed theorem]"), he added a third, which he called "rhetic" ("telling" with respect to the numbers), or "exegetic" ("exhibiting" in respect to the geometric magnitudes). He defined the new kind of analysis as the procedure through which the magnitude sought is produced from the equation or proportion set up in canonical form.

In chapter 2 Viète amalgamates some of the "common notions" enumerated in book I of Euclid's *Elements* with some definitions and theorems of book V, of the geometric books II and VI, and of the "arithmetical" books VII and VIII to form his stipulations for equations and proportions. In chapter 3 he gives the fundamental "law of homogeneity," according to which only magnitudes of

"like genus" can be compared with each other, and in the fourth chapter he lays down "the canonical rules of species calculation." These correspond to the rules for addition, subtraction, multiplication, and division used for instruction in ordinary calculation. In this chapter he presents a mode of calculation carried out completely in terms of "species" of numbers and calls it *logistice speciosa*—in contrast with calculation using determinate numbers, which is *logistice numerosa*. Of significance for formation of the concepts of modern mathematics, Viète devotes the *logistice speciosa* to pure algebra, understood as the most comprehensive possible analytic art, applicable indifferently to numbers and to geometric magnitudes. By this process the concept of *eidos*, or species, undergoes a universalizing extension while preserving its link to the realm of numbers. In this general procedure the species represent simply general magnitudes. Viète's *logistice speciosa*, on the other hand, is understood as the procedure analogous to geometric analysis and is directly related to Diophantus' *Arithmetica*.

In chapter 5 Viète presents the *leges zeteticae*, which refer to elementary operations with equations: to antithesis (proposition I), the transfer of one of the parts of one side of the equation to the other; to hypobibasm (proposition II), the reduction of the degree of an equation by the division of all members by the species common to all of them; and to parabolism (proposition III), the removal of the coefficient of the *potestas* (conversion of the equation into the form of a proportion). The sixth chapter, "De theorematum per poristicen examinatione," deals more with synthesis and its relation to analysis than with poristics. It states that the poristic way is to be taken when a problem does not fit immediately into the systematic context.

In chapter 7, on the function of the rhetic art, Viète treats the third kind of analysis (rhetic or exegetic), which is applied to numbers if the search is for a magnitude expressible in a number, as well as to lengths, planes, or solids if the thing itself must be shown, starting from canonically ordered equations.

In chapter 8, the final one, Viète gives some definitions—such as of "equation": An equation is a comparison of an unknown magnitude with a determinate one—some rules, and some outlines of his works *De numerosa potestatum purarum, atque adfectarum ad exegesin resolutione tractatus, Effectionum geometricarum canonica recensio,* and *Supplementum geometriae.* In 1630 the work was translated into French by A. Vasset (very probably Claude Hardy) as *L'algèbre nouvelle de M. Viette* and by J. L. de Vaulezard as *Introduction en l'art analytique, ou nouvelle algèbre de François Viète*. Both also contain a translation of Viète's *Zeteticorum libri quinque*. A modern French translation of the work was published by F. Ritter in *Bullettino di bibliografia. . . ,* 1 (1868), 223–244. An English version by J. W. Smith appeared as an appendix to Jacob Klein's *Greek Mathematical Thought and the Origin of Algebra* (Cambridge, Mass., 1968).

In 1593 Viète published *Zeteticorum libri quinque*, which he very probably had completed in 1591. In it he offered a sample of *logistice speciosa* and contrasted it directly with Diophantus' *Arithmetica*, which, in his opinion, remained too much within the limits of the *logistice numerosa*. In order to stress the parallelism of the two works, Viète ended the fifth book of his *Zetetics* with the same problem that concludes the fifth book of Diophantus' *Arithmetica*. In other parts of the book he also takes series of problems from the Diophantus work. References by Peletier and Peter Ramus, as well as Guilielmus Xylander's translation (1575), must certainly have introduced Viète to the *Arithmetica*, which he undoubtedly also came to know in the original.

Moreover, as K. Reich has proved in her paper "Diophant, Cardano, Bombelli, Viète, ein Vergleich ihrer Aufgaben," he was acquainted with Cardano's *De numerorum proprietatibus, Ars magna*, and *Ars magna arithmeticae* and mentioned his name in problems II,21 and II,22. According to Reich, however, it is not known whether Viète, in preparing his *Zetetics*, considered Bombelli's *Algebra*. The *Zetetics* is composed of five books, the first of which contains ten problems that seek to determine quantities of which the sum, difference, or ratio is known. The problems of the second book give the sum or difference of the squares or cubes of the unknown quantities, their product, and the ratio of this product to the sum or the difference of their squares. In the third book the unknown quantities are proportional, and one is required to find them if the sum or the difference of the extremes or means is given. This book contains the application of these problems to right triangles. The fourth book gives the solutions of second- and third-degree indeterminate problems, such as IV, 2,3, to divide a number, which is the sum of two squares, into two other squares. The fifth book contains problems of the same kind, but generally concerning three numbers: for instance

(V,9), to find a right triangle in such a way that the area augmented with a given number, which is the sum of two squares, is a square.

Viète's notation in his early publications is somewhat different from that in his collected works, edited by F. van Schooten in 1646. For example, the modern $(3\ BD^2 - 3\ BA^2)/4$ is printed in the *Zetetics* as (B in D quadratum $3 - B$ in A quadratum 3)/4, while in 1646 it is reprinted in the form (B in Dq 3 $- B$ in Aq 3)/4. Moreover, the radical sign found in the 1646 edition is a modification introduced by van Schooten. Viète rejected the radical, using instead the letter *l* in the *Zetetics* — for example, $l \cdot 121$ for $\sqrt{121}$. The same holds for Viète's *Effectionum geometricarum canonica recensio*, the outline of which he had given in his *Isagoge*: "With a view to exegetic in geometry, the analytical art selects and enumerates more regular procedures by which equations of 'sides' and 'squares' may be completely interpreted" — that is, it concerns a convenient method for solving geometrical problems by using the coefficients of the equation in question, without solving the corresponding equation. All the solutions he gives in this tract have been carried out by geometric construction with the ruler and compass: for instance, the proof of proposition X, which leads to the equation $x^2 - px = q^2$, and that of proposition XVII, which leads to the equation $x^4 + p^2x^2 = p^2q^2$.

In 1593 at Tours, Jamet Mettayer edited *Francisci Vietae Supplementum geometriae, ex opere restitutae mathematicae analyseos seu algebra nova*. The following statement from proposition XXV — "Enimvero ostensum est in tractatu de aequationum recognitione, aequationes quadratoquadratorum ad aequationes cuborum reduci" — is important because it shows that by 1593 his tract *De aequationum recognitione* had already been completed, long before its publication by Alexander Anderson (1615). The tract begins with the following postulate: A straight line can be drawn from any point across any two lines (or a circle and a straight line) in such a way that the intercept between these two lines (or the line and the circle) will be equal to a given distance, any possible intercept having been predefined. The twenty-five propositions that follow can be divided into four groups:

1. Propositions 1–7 contain the solution of the problem of the mesographicum — to find two mean proportionals between two given straight line segments — and its solution immediately yields the solution of the problem of doubling the cube.

2. Propositions 8–18 contain the solution of the problem of the trisection of an angle and the corre-

sponding cubic equation. The trigonometric solution of the cubic equation occurs twice: in propositions 16 and 17.

3. Propositions 19–24 contain the solution of the problem of finding the side of the regular heptagon that is to be inscribed in a given circle.

4. Proposition 25 explains the importance of the applied method: the construction of two mean proportionals, the trisection of an angle, and all problems that cannot be solved only by means of the ruler and compass but that lead to cubic and biquadratic equations, can be solved with the aid of the ancient *neusis* procedure.

In 1592 Viète began a lively dispute with J. J. Scaliger when the latter published a purported solution of the quadrature of the circle, the trisection of an angle, and the construction of two mean proportionals between two given line segments by means of the ruler and compass only. In that year Viète gave public lectures at Tours and proved that Scaliger's assertions were incorrect, without mentioning the name of the author. For this reason he decided in 1593 to publish book VIII of his *Variorum de rebus mathematicis responsorum Liber VIII, cuius praecipua capita sunt: De duplicatione cubi et quadratione circuli, quae claudit πρόχειρον seu ad usum mathematici canonis methodica*. In chapters 1, 2, and 5 Viète treats the traditional problem of the doubling of the cube, that is, of the construction of two mean proportionals. In the first chapter, on the basis of Plutarch's *Life of Marcellus* (ch. 14), he calls this an irrational problem. In the fifth chapter he treats it synthetically, referring to the "ex Poristicis methodus" that he had presented in the *Supplementum geometriae*. In chapter 3 he is concerned with the trisection of an angle and, in chapter 7, with the construction of the regular heptagon to be inscribed in a given circle, proposed by François de Foix, count of Candale, the most important contemporary editor and reviser of Euclid. Chapters 6 and 14 are related to Archimedes' *On Spirals*, already known in the Latin West through the Moerbeke translation of 1269.

In chapter 8 Viète discusses the quadratrix and, in chapter 11, the lunes that can be squared. He investigates the problem of the corniculate angle in chapter 13 and sides with Peletier, maintaining that the angle of contact is no angle. Viète's proof is new: the circle may be regarded as a plane figure with an infinite number of sides and angles; but a straight line touching a straight line, however short it may be, will coincide with that straight line and will not form an angle. Never before had the meaning of "contact" been stated so plainly. In chapter 16 Viète gives a very interesting construction of the tangent to the Archimedean spiral and, in chapter 18, the earliest explicit expression for π by an infinite number of operations. Considering regular polygons of 4, 8, 16, . . . sides, inscribed in a circle of unit radius, he found that the area of the circle is

$$2 \cdot \frac{1}{\sqrt{\frac{1}{2}} \cdot \sqrt{\frac{1}{2} + \frac{1}{2}\sqrt{\frac{1}{2}}} \cdot \sqrt{\frac{1}{2} + \frac{1}{2}\sqrt{\frac{1}{2} + \frac{1}{2}\sqrt{\frac{1}{2}}} \cdots}}.$$

from which he obtained

$$\frac{\pi}{2} = \frac{1}{\sqrt{\frac{1}{2}} \cdot \sqrt{\frac{1}{2} + \frac{1}{2}\sqrt{\frac{1}{2}} \cdots}}.$$

The trigonometric portion of this treatise begins with chapter 19 and concerns right and oblique plane and spherical triangles. In regard to the polar triangle and Viète's use of it, Braunmühl in his *Vorlesungen* assures the reader that Viète's reciprocal figure is the same as the polar triangle. He arrives at this conclusion because Viète's theorems are arranged in such a manner that each theorem is the dual of the one immediately preceding it.

Since Scaliger could not defend himself against Viète's criticism, he left France for the Netherlands, where soon after his arrival in 1594 he published his *Cyclometrica elementa*, followed some months later by his *Mesolabium*. Viète responded with *Munimen adversus cyclometrica nova* (1594) and *Pseudomesolabium* (1595). In the first, through a nice consideration based on the use of the Archimedean spiral, he gives two interesting approximations of a segment of a circle. In the second he seeks those chords cutting the diameter in such a way that the four parts increase in geometric series. In the appendix Viète refutes Scaliger's assertion that in the inscribed quadrilateral the diameter and both diagonals are in arithmetical proportion.

Viète's mathematical reputation was already considerable when the ambassador from the Netherlands remarked to Henry IV that France did not possess any geometricians capable of solving a problem propounded in 1593 by Adrian Romanus to all mathematicians and that required the solution of a forty-fifth-degree equation. The king thereupon summoned Viète and informed him of the challenge. Viète saw that the equation was satisfied by the chord of a circle (of unit radius) that subtends an angle $2\pi/45$ at the center. In a few minutes he gave the king one solution of the problem written in pencil and, the next day, twenty-two more. He did not find forty-five solutions because the remaining ones involve negative sines, which were unintelligible to him.

Viète published his answer, *Ad problema, quod omnibus mathematicis totius orbis construendum proposuit Adrianus Romanus, responsum*, in 1595. In the introduction he says: "I, who do not profess to be a mathematician, but who, whenever there is leisure, delight in mathematical studies. . . ." Regarding Romanus' equation, Viète had seen at once that since $45 = 3 \cdot 3 \cdot 5$, it was necessary only to divide an angle once into five equal parts, and then twice into three, a division that could be effected by corresponding fifth- and third-degree equations. In the above problem he solved the equation $3x - x^3 = a$: using the roots x he determined y by $3y - y^3 = x$, and by the equation $5z - 5z^3 + z^5 = y$ he found the required roots z.

At the end of his work Viète proposed to Romanus, referring to Apollonius' *Tangencies*, the problem to draw a circle that touches three given circles. Romanus was acquainted with Regiomontanus' statement that he doubted the possibility of a solution by means of the ruler and compass only. He therefore solved the problem by determining the center of the required circle by means of the intersection of two hyperbolas: this solution did not, however, possess the rigor of the ancient geometry. In 1600 Viète presented a solution that had all the rigor desirable in his *Apollonius Gallus, seu exsuscitata Apollonii Pergaei Περὶ ἐπαφῶν geometria ad V. C. A. Romanum*, in which he gave a Euclidean solution using the center of similitude of two circles. Romanus was so impressed that he traveled to Fontenay to meet Viète, beginning an acquaintanceship that soon became warm friendship. Viète himself did not publish the book; very probably it was done by Marino Ghetaldi. A Greek letter dedicated to Viète precedes the text in the original edition. In appendix I, confronted with certain problems that Regiomontanus could solve algebraically but not geometrically, Viète provides their geometric construction and notes, by way of introduction, that these geometric constructions are important. In appendix II he vehemently attacks Copernicus, and there is also a reference to a work intended to correct the errors in the work of Copernicus and the defects in that of Ptolemy. It was to have been entitled *Francelinis* and to have contained a composition, "Epilogistice motuum coelestium Pruteniana," based on hypotheses termed Apollonian, such as the hypothesis of the movable eccentric.

In the 1591 edition of the *Isagoge*, Viète had already given the outline of the *De numerosa potestatum purarum, atque adfectarum ad exegesin resolutione tractatus*. The "numerical resolution of powers" referred to in the title means solving equations that have numerical solutions, such as $x^2 = 2916$ or $x^2 + 7x = 60750$. The work was published in 1600 at Paris, edited by Marino Ghetaldi, with Viète's consent. (All information concerning the edition is taken from a letter written by Ghetaldi to Michel Coignet, dated 15 February 1600, which is printed at the end of the work.) Viète gave some of his manuscripts to Ghetaldi when the latter was in Paris. Ghetaldi took them to Rome and allowed his friends there to make a copy. After Viète's death his heirs gave other manuscripts to his friend Pierre Alleaume, who left them to his son Jacques, a pupil of Viète's. Jacques entrusted Anderson with the treatises *De aequationum recognitione, Notae ad logisticem posteriores*, and *Analytica angularium sectionum*.

In *De numerosa potestatum*, Viète gives a method of approximation to the roots of numerical equations that resembles the one for ordinary root extraction. Taking $f(x) = k$, where k is positive, Viète separates the required root from the rest, then substitutes an approximate value for it and shows that another digit of the root can be obtained by division. A repetition of this process gives the next digit, and so on. Thus, in $x^5 - 5x^3 + 500x = 7,905,504$, he takes $r = 20$, then computes $7,905,504 - r^5 + 5r^3 - 500r$ and divides the result by a value that in modern notation would be $|(f[r + s_1] - f[r])| - s_1{}^n$, where n is the degree of the equation and s_1 is a unit of the denomination of the next digit to be found. Thus, if the required root is 243 and r has been taken to be 200, then s_1 is 10; but if r is taken as 240, then s_1 is 1. In the example above, where $r = 20$, the divisor is 878,295 and the quotient yields the next digit of the root, 4. One obtains $x = 20 + 4 = 24$, the required root.

Viète also had a role in the improvements of the Julian calendar. The yearly determination of the movable feasts had long resulted in great confusion. The rapid progress of astronomy led to the consideration of this subject, and many new calendars were proposed. Pope Gregory XIII convoked a large number of mathematicians, astronomers, and prelates, who decided upon the adoption of the calendar proposed by Clavius. To rectify the errors of the Julian calendar, it was agreed to write 15 October into the new calendar immediately after 4 October 1582. The Gregorian calendar met with great opposition among scientists, including Viète and Tobias Müller. Viète valued the studies involved in a reform of the calendar; and toward the end of his life he allowed himself to be carried away by them and to engage in unjustified polemics against Clavius, the result of which was the publication with Mettayer of *Libellorum supplicum in regia magistri relatio kalendarii vere Gregoriani ad ecclesiasticos doctores exhibita pontifici maximo Clementi VIII anno Christo 1600 iubilaeo* (1600). He gave the work to Cardinal Cinzio Aldobrandini, who transmitted it to Clavius. Since Clavius rejected the proposed corrections, Viète and Pierre Mettayer, the son of Jean, published a libel against Clavius that was as vehement as it was unjust: *Francisci Vietae adversus Christophorum Clavium expostulatio* (1602).

Francisci Vietae fontenaensis de aequationum recognitione et emendatione tractatus duo was published in 1615, under the editorship of Viète's Scottish friend Alexander Anderson. The treatise "De emendatione" contains the subject matter of the work as announced in the *Isagoge* under the title "Ad logisticen speciosam notae posteriores" and sets forth a series of formulas (*notae*) concerning transformations of equations. In particular it presents general methods for solving third- and fourth-degree equations. This work reveals Viète's partial knowledge of the relations between the coefficients and the roots of an equation. Viète demonstrates that if the coefficient of the second term in a second-degree equation is minus the sum of two numbers the product of which is the third term, then the two numbers are roots of the equation. Viète rejected all but positive roots, however, so it was impossible for him to perceive fully the relations in question.

Viète's solution of a cubic equation is as follows: Given $x^3 + 3B^2x = 2Z^3$. To solve this let $y^2 + yx = B^2$. Since from the constitution of such an equation B^2 is understood to be a rectangle of which the lesser of the two sides is y, and the difference between it and the larger side is x, $(B^2 - y^2)/y = x$. Therefore $(B^6 - 3B^4y^2 + 3B^2y^4 - y^6)/y^3 + (3B^4 - 3B^2y^2)/y = 2Z^3$. When all terms have been multiplied by y^3 and properly ordered, one obtains $y^6 + 2Z^3y^3 = B^6$. Since this equation is quadratic with a positive root it also has a cube root. Thus the required reduction is effected. Conclusion: If, therefore, $x^3 + 3B^2x = 2Z^3$, and $\sqrt{B^6 + Z^6} - Z^3 = D^3$, then $(B^2 - D^2)/D$ is x, as required.

In the solution of biquadratics, Viète remains true to his principle of reduction. He first removes the term involving x^3 to obtain the form $x^4 + a^2x^2 + b^3x = c^4$. He then moves the terms involving x^2 and x to the right-hand side of the equation and adds $x^2y^2 + y^4/4$ to each side, so that the equation becomes $(x^2 + y^2/2)^2 = x^2(y^2 - a^2) - b^3x + y^4/4 + c^4$. He then chooses y so that the right-hand side of this equation is a perfect square. Substituting this value of y, he can take the square root of both sides and thus obtain two quadratic equations for x, each of which can be solved.

In theorem 3 of chapter VI, Viète gives a trigonometrical solution of Cardano's irreducible case in cubics. He applies the equation $(2\cos\alpha)^3 - 3(2\cos\alpha) = 2\cos 3\alpha$ to the solution of $x^3 - 3a^2x = a^2b$, when $a > b/2$, by setting $x = 2a\cos\alpha$ and determining 3α from $b = 2a\cos 3\alpha$. In the last chapter Viète resolves into linear factors $x - x_k$ the first member of an algebraic equation $\phi(x) = 0$ from the second up to the fifth degree. Anderson's edition is the only one besides the *Opera* of 1646. There is still a manuscript that contains the text (Paris, Bibliothèque Nationale, Nouv. acqu. lat. 1644, fols. $1^r - 31^r$, "De recognitione aequationum tractatus," and fols. $32^r - 60^v$, "De aequationum emendatione tractatus secundus").

In 1615 Anderson published Viète's treatise on angle sections, *Ad angularium sectionum analyticem theoremata* καθολικώτερα *a Francisco Vieta fontenaensis primum excogitata at absque ulla demonstratione ad nos transmissa, jam tandem demonstrationibus confirmata*. This treatise deals, in part, with general formulas of chords, sines, cosines, and tangents of multiple arcs in terms of the trigonometric lines of the simple arcs. Viète first applies algebraic transformation to trigonometry, particularly to the multisection of angles, but without proofs and calculations, which were added by Anderson. In theorem 6 Viète considers the equations for multiple angles: letting $2\cos a = x$, he expresses $\cos na$ as a function of x for all integers $n < 11$; and at the end he presents a table for determining the coefficients. In theorem 7 he expresses $2x^{n-2}\sin na$ in terms of x and y using $2\sin a = x$ and $2\sin 2a = y$. After theorem 10 Viète states: "Thus the analysis of angular sections involves geometric and arithmetic secrets which hitherto have been penetrated by no one." To the treatises of the *Isagoge* belong "Ad logisticen speciosam notae priores" and "Ad logisticen speciosam notae posteriores," the latter now lost. The first was not published during his life, because Viète believed that the manuscript was not yet suitable for publication. (It was published by Jean de Beaugrand in 1631.) It represents a collection of elementary general algebraic formulas that correspond to the arithmetical propositions of the second and ninth books of Euclid's *Elements*, as well as some interesting propositions that combine algebra with geometry. In propositions 48–51 Viète derives the formulas for sin $2x$; cos $2x$; sin $3x$; cos $3x$; sin $4x$; cos $4x$; sin $5x$ and cos $5x$ expressed in sin x and cos x by applying proposition 46, "From two right-angled triangles construct a third right-angled triangle," to two congruent right triangles; to right triangles with simple and double angles; with simple and triple angles, and with simple and quadruple angles respectively. He remarks, that the coefficients are equal to those in the expansion $(B + D)^n$ (B being the perpendicular and D the base of the original right triangle), that the various terms must be "homogeneous" and that the signs are alternately + and −. (A French translation of this work was published by F. Ritter in *Bullettino di bibliografia* . . ., **1** [1868], 245–276.) Besides Viète's published works there are manuscripts containing works of him or attributed to him. In addition to Nouv. acqu. lat. 1644, Bibliothéque Nationale, fonds lat., nouv. acqu. 1643, contains few new elements. The author was very well acquainted with Viète's work, particularly with his *De numerosa potestatum . . . ad exegesin resolutione . . .*; he betrays the influence of Simon Stevin's *Arithmétique* because his manner of denoting the powers of the unknown depends on the method used by Stevin and he uses the signs for equality and square root. London, British Museum, Sloane 652, fols. 1–9, contains the *Isagoge*, and fols. 10–40 the *Zetetics*.

BIBLIOGRAPHY

I. ORIGINAL WORKS. Note references in text. Additional editions of Viète's works are *Quinque orationes philosophicae* (Paris, 1555); and *Deschiffrement d'une lettre escripte par le Commandeur Moreo au roy d'Espagne son maître* (Tours, 1590). MSS include "Mémoires de la vie de Jean de Parthenay Larchevêque," Bibliothèque Nationale, coll. Dupuy, vol. 743, fols. 189–219; "Généalogie de la maison de Parthenay," Bibliothèque de la Société d'Histoire du Protestantisme, no. 417; "Discours des choses advenues à Lyon, durant que M. de Soubise y commandait," Bibliothèque Nationale, fonds français 20783; and "Manuscrit sur la ligue," Bibliothèque Nationale, fonds français 15499. Viète's collected works were issued as *Opera mathematica* by Frans van Schooten (Leiden, 1646; repr. Hildesheim, 1970).

II. SECONDARY LITERATURE. The best survey of Viète's life and works is in F. Ritter, "François Viète, inventeur de l'algèbre moderne, 1540–1603. Essai sur sa vie et son oeuvre," in *Revue occidentale philosophique, sociale et politique*, 2nd ser., **10** (1895), 234–274, 354–415.

See also the following, listed chronologically: Florian Cajori, *A History of Mathematics* (New York, 1894; repr. New York, 1961), 137–139, 143–144; A. von Braunmühl, *Vorlesungen über Geschichte der Trigonometrie*, I (Leipzig, 1900), 157–183; M. Cantor, *Vorlesungen über Geschichte der Mathematik*, II (Leipzig, 1900; repr. Stuttgart, 1965), 582–591, 629–641; H. G. Zeuthen, *Geschichte der Mathematik im 16. und 17. Jahrhundert* (Leipzig, 1903; repr. Stuttgart, 1966), 95–109; 115–126; M. C. Zeller, *The Development of Trigonometry From Regiomontanus to Pitiscus* (Ann Arbor, Mich., 1944), 73–85; H. Lebesgue, *Commentaires sur l'oeuvre de F. Viète*, Monographies de l'Enseignement Mathématique, No. 4 (Geneva, 1958), 10–17; P. Dedron and J. Itard, *Mathématiques et mathématiciens* (Paris, 1959), 173–185; J. E. Hofmann, "Über Viètes Beiträge zur Geometrie der Einschiebungen," in *Mathematische-physikalische Semesterberichte*, VIII (Göttingen, 1962), 191–214; H. L. L. Busard, "Über einige Papiere aus Viètes Nachlass in der Pariser Bibliothèque Nationale," in *Centaurus*, **10** (1964), 65–126; D. Kahn, *The Codebreakers, the Story of Secret Writing* (New York, 1968), 116–118; J. Klein, *Greek Mathematical Thought and the Origin of Algebra* (Cambridge, 1968), 150–185, 253–285, 315–353; K. Reich, "Diophant, Cardano, Bombelli, Viète, ein Vergleich ihrer Aufgaben," in *Rechenpfennige* (Munich, 1968), 131–150; K. Reich, "Quelques remarques sur Marinus Ghetaldus et François Viète," in *Actes du symposium international "La géométrie et l'algèbre au début du XVIIe siècle"* (Zagreb, 1969), 171–174; J. Grisard, "François Viète mathématicien de la fin du seizième siècle," *Thèse de 3e cycle. École pratique des hautes études*, (Paris, 1968); and K. Reich and H. Gericke, "François Viète, Einführung in die Neue Algebra," in *Historiae scientiarum elementa*, V (Munich, 1973).

H. L. L. BUSARD

VILLALPANDO, JUAN BAUTISTA (*b.* Córdoba, Spain, 1552; *d.* Rome, Italy, 1608)

Little is known about Villalpando's life. After entering the Jesuit order in 1575, he studied under Father Jerome Prado, who was writing a commentary on the book of Ezekiel. Evidently Villalpando's immense erudition was already apparent, and he soon joined Prado in his exegesis. In 1592 the pair moved to Rome to complete their work. Originally commissioned to provide a commentary only on chapters 40, 41, and 42 of Ezekiel, which deal with the architectural description of Solomon's temple, Villalpando suddenly found himself heir to a larger task when Prado died in 1595, having completed only the first twenty-six chapters. Although Villalpando himself died before completing the commentary, he managed to publish three volumes: *Hieronymi Pradi et Ioannis Baptistae*

Villalpandi e Societate Iesu in Ezechielem explanationes et apparatus urbis ac templi Hierosolymitani (Rome, 1596–1604).

Like most Renaissance biblical commentaries, Villalpando's *Ezechiel* is the work of a polymath, containing copious information on subjects ranging from astrology, music, mathematical theories of proportion, and ornate reconstructions of Hebrew, Greek, and Roman systems of weights, measures, and currency to more orthodox etymological and scriptural preoccupations. The widely disparate topics that Villalpando considers in his attempt to re-create the temple would seem to express a Vitruvian vision of the architect. The influence of Vitruvius on Villalpando is crucial, and in this sense his work may be seen as a part of the general Renaissance revival of Vitruvius. Villalpando's great achievement was to have demonstrated in systematic fashion how Solomon's temple, as revealed by God to Ezekiel, was constructed according to Vitruvian principles of harmony and proportion, thus endowing classical architecture with divine approbation. Here, too, Villalpando was continuing an older humanist trend. In showing the celestial locus of classical architecture, he provided further evidence for the preestablished harmony between classical pagan culture and Christian civilization. It is significant that both Philip II of Spain and Pope Clement VIII expressed their approval of Villalpando's *Ezechiel* during the peak of the Counter-Reformation.

The third volume of the exegesis contains the bulk of Villalpando's mathematical and mechanical speculations. While his work on proportion and harmony (II, bk. 1, chs. 1–5) follows earlier Renaissance architectural utilizations of Euclid, his twenty-one propositions on "the center of gravity and the line of direction" (ch. 6) were deemed original enough to be reproduced by Mersenne in his *Synopsis mathematica* (1626). Duhem, who "rediscovered" Villalpando, conjectured that the Jesuit pilfered his propositions and their deductive proofs from a no longer extant manuscript by Leonardo dealing with local motion. Although Taylor has suggested that Villalpando may have had access to Leonardo's manuscripts through his mentor Juan de Herrera, other sources seem more plausible. Given Villalpando's lifelong interest in mathematics, it is highly probable that before his departure for Rome, he may have attended the Academia de Mathemáticas in Madrid, where he may have been introduced to the works of Archimedes. More interesting is the possibility that he knew Christoph Clavius, a fellow Jesuit and friend of Galileo, who was teaching in Rome at the same time. Villalpando relied heavily on Clavius' *Elements of Euclid*, speaking of it in terms of endearment, and it is possible that Clavius introduced him to the work of Commandino and Guido Ubaldo del Monte on the center of gravity. Villalpando, then, can be seen as participating in the sixteenth-century revival of Archimedes and Pappus as reconstructed by Commandino and Guido Ubaldo.

Villalpando's influence has been strongest in the history of architecture. The idea of the Escorial in Spain may have been derived from his earlier designs of the temple, and Inigo Jones certainly utilized his conceptions in introducing Palladian architecture into England. But Villalpando does touch the history of seventeenth-century science in a particularly sensitive area. No less a scientist than Isaac Newton used Villalpando's work in his own attempt to construct Solomon's temple and to determine the dimensions of the biblical cubit.

BIBLIOGRAPHY

I. ORIGINAL WORKS. Aside from the commentary on Ezekiel, Villalpando edited and annotated a medieval exegesis of St. Paul: *S. Remigii Rhemensis episcopi explanationes epistolarum B. Pauli Apostoli* (Rome, 1598). There is also in the Biblioteca Nacional, Madrid, a MS entitled "Relacion de la antigua Jerusalén remitida á Felippe II por el Padre J. B. Villalpando," which establishes Villalpando's connections with the royal court.

II. SECONDARY LITERATURE. The most thorough study of Villalpando's life and architectural accomplishments is René C. Taylor, "El Padre Villalpando (1552–1608) y sus ideas estéticas," in *Academia. Anales y boletín de la Real Academia de San Fernando* (1952), no. 2, 3–65. Taylor revised some of his conclusions, stressing the role of the occult in Villalpando's work, in "Architecture and Magic," in *Essays in the History of Architecture Presented to Rudolph Wittkower* (London, 1967), 81–110, and in "Hermetism and Mystical Architecture in the Society of Jesus," in R. Wittkower and I. B. Jaffe, eds., *Baroque Art: The Jesuit Contribution* (New York, 1972), 63–97, and esp. the documents printed in App. B. The mathematical and aesthetic background of Villalpando's discussion of proportion is discussed in Rudolph Wittkower, *Architectural Principles in the Age of Humanism*, 3rd ed. (London, 1962), 121 ff.

Pierre Duhem's observations on Villalpando's mechanics were first published in *Les origines de la statique*, II (Paris, 1906), 115–126; and were substantially repeated in "Léonard de Vinci et Villalpand," in his *Études sur Léonard de Vinci*, I (Paris, 1906), 53–85.

MICHAEL T. RYAN

VITALI, GIUSEPPE (*b.* Ravenna, Italy, 26 August 1875; *d.* Bologna, Italy, 29 February 1932)

Vitali was unusual, in that for most of his life he worked in relative isolation, although he lived in Genoa and thus was not cut off from intellectual life. Nevertheless, he achieved such valuable results in the theory of functions of a real variable that he is considered one of the greatest predecessors of Lebesgue.

Vitali graduated from the Scuola Normale Superiore at Pisa in 1899 and immediately became assistant to Ulisse Dini, then one of the most authoritative Italian mathematicians, whose recommendation and approval could assure a promising career to a young mathematician. Vitali left this coveted post after two years, however, possibly because of financial need, and taught at various secondary schools, ending at the Liceo C. Colombo in Genoa (1904–1923). He also became involved in politics there, as a Socialist town councillor and municipal magistrate. In 1922, after the rise to power of fascism and the dissolution of the Socialist party, Vitali returned to his studies and made such progress that at the end of 1923 he won the competition for the professorship of infinitesimal analysis at the University of Modena. The following year he moved to Padua and, in 1930, to Bologna.

In 1926 Vitali was struck by a serious circulatory disorder. Weakened in body but not in mind, he returned to research and teaching; about half his published works (of which there are not many) were composed after this illness, even though he could not write.

Vitali was essentially self-taught and accustomed to working alone. This isolation sometimes led him inadvertently to duplicate someone else's discoveries, but he also avoided well-trodden paths. He holds undisputed priority in a number of discoveries: a theorem on set-covering, the notion of an absolutely continuous function, a theorem on the analyticity of the limit of certain successions of equilimited analytical functions, and criteria for closure of systems of orthogonal functions.

In his last years Vitali confined himself to problems of less general interest, such as his new absolute differential calculus and, in collaboration with his friend and colleague A. Tònolo (1885–1962), his "geometry" of Hilbert spaces—neither of which has aroused particular interest.

After Vitali's death Giovanni Sansone published, as coauthors, Vitali's useful *Moderna teoria delle funzioni di variabile reale* (Bologna, 1935; 3rd ed., 1952), the first part of which was written mainly by Vitali.

Vitali was a corresponding fellow of the Academy of Sciences of Turin (1928), of the Accademia dei Lincei (1930), and of the Academy of Bologna (1931).

BIBLIOGRAPHY

See the biographies by S. Pincherle, in *Bollettino dell'Unione matematica italiana*, **11** (1932), 125–126, A. Tònolo, in *Rendiconti del Seminario matematico dell' Università di Padova*, 3 (1932), 67–81, which has a bibliography; and F. G. Tricomi, in *Memorie dell' Accademia delle scienze di Torino*, 4th ser., **4** (1962), 115–116.

F. G. TRICOMI

VIVIANI, VINCENZO (*b.* Florence, Italy, 5 April 1622; *d.* Florence, 22 September 1703)

Viviani was the son of Jacopo di Michelangelo Viviani, a member of the noble Franchi family, and Maria Alamanno del Nente. He studied the humanities with the Jesuits and mathematics with Settimi, a friend of Galileo's. His intelligence and ability led to his presentation in 1638 to Ferdinand II de' Medici, grand duke of Tuscany. Ferdinand introduced him to Galileo, who was so impressed by his talent that he took him into his house at Arcetri as a collaborator in 1639. After Galileo's death, Viviani wrote a historical account of his life and hoped to publish a complete edition of his works. The plan, however, could not be carried out because of opposition by the Church—a serious blow not only to Viviani's reputation but even more to the progress of science in Italy. Since he was unable to pursue the evolution of mathematical ideas that were developing during that period, Viviani turned his talent and inventiveness solely to the study and imitation of the ancients.

Although the Medici court gave him much work, Viviani studied the geometry of the ancients. His accomplishments brought him membership in the Accademia del Cimento, and in 1696 he became a member of the Royal Society of London. In 1699 he was elected one of the eight foreign members of the Académie des Sciences in Paris. He declined offers of high scientific positions from King John II Casimir of Poland and from Louis XIV.

Viviani's first project was an attempted restoration of a work by Aristaeus the Elder, *De locis solidis secunda divinatio geometrica*, which Viviani undertook when he was twenty-four. Aristaeus' work is believed to have been the first methodical exposition of the curves discovered by Menaechmus; but since it has been entirely lost, it is difficult to estimate how close Viviani came to the original work.

Viviani also undertook to reconstruct the fifth book of Apollonius' *Conics*, the first four books of which had been discovered and published. While examining the oriental codices in the grand duke's library in Florence, Borelli discovered a set of papers on which was written "Eight Books of Apollonius' *Conics*." (Actually, the manuscript contained only the first seven books.) Since the manuscript was in Arabic, Borelli obtained the grand duke's permission to take it to Rome, where he turned it over to Abraham Ecchellensis, who was competent to translate it into Latin. The contents of the work were kept secret, however, in order to give Viviani time to complete the publication of his *De maximis et minimis*, which finally appeared at Florence in 1659. Two years later the translation of Apollonius' work was published under Borelli's editorship, and it then became possible to ascertain the substantial similarity between the two works.

Another important work was *Quinto libro degli Elementi di Euclide* (1674). With the rigor and prolixity of the ancients, Viviani devoted an appendix to geometric problems, among which was one on the trisection of an angle, solved by the use of the cylindrical spiral or of a cycloid; another was the problem of duplicating the cube, solved by means of conics or of the cubic $xy^2 = k$.

Viviani also produced the Italian version of Euclid's *Elements* (1690) that was reprinted in 1867 by Betti and Brioschi, in order to raise the level of the teaching of geometry in Italy. Following the example of other learned men of the period, Viviani proposed a problem—known as the "Florentine enigma"—that received wide recognition as soon as the foremost mathematicians began to work on it.[1] The problem was to perforate a hemispheric arch, having four equal windows, in such a way that the residual surface could be squared. Viviani solved the problem by a method that became well known.[2] It is accomplished by the intersection of four right cylinders, the bases of which are tangent to the base of the hemisphere.

There is an Italian translation by Viviani of a work by Archimedes on the rectification of a circumference and the squaring of a circle. He also collected and arranged works by Torricelli after the latter's death.[3]

The search for a point in the plane of a triangle such that the sum of the distances from the vertices shall be the minimum was proposed by Fermat to Torricelli, and by Torricelli to Viviani, who solved the problem (appendix to *De maximis et minimis*, p. 144). This problem was also solved by Torricelli and Cavalieri for triangles with angles less than 120°.[4] It led to a correspondence among Torricelli, Fermat, and Roberval to which Viviani refers (*ibid.*, p. 147).

NOTES

1. During a visit to Italy in 1689, Leibniz met Viviani and solved his problem. It was the first example of the calculation of the area of a curved surface by means of integral calculus (*Acta eruditorum* [1692], 275–279). Jakob I Bernoulli solved the problem (*ibid.*), and that work led to his study of the area of quadrics of revolution (*Acta eruditorum* [Oct. 1696]).

2. Guido Grandi demonstrated the correctness of Viviani's solution by applying the method of indivisibles. There is a reference to this solution in a letter written by Huygens to L'Hospital (*Oeuvres de C. Huygens*, X [The Hague, 1905], 829). In an appendix to this work the publishers inserted a previously unpublished passage by Huygens, in which he demonstrates that the solutions proposed by Leibniz and Viviani are identical.

3. See *Opere di Evangelista Torricelli*, I (Faenza, 1919), pt. 1, 329–407, and pt. 2, 3–43, 49–55.

4. B. Cavalieri, *Exercitationes geometricae sex* (Bologna, 1647), 504–510.

BIBLIOGRAPHY

I. ORIGINAL WORKS. Viviani's writings are *De maximis et minimis geometrica divinatio in quintum Conicorum Apollonii Pergaei, adhuc desideratum* (Florence, 1659); *Quinto libro di Euclide, ovvero scienza universale delle proporzioni, spiegate colla dottrina del Galileo* (Florence, 1674); *Diporto geometrico* (Florence, 1676); *Enodatio problematum universis geometricis praepositorum a D. Claudio Comiers* (Florence, 1677); *Discorso intorno al difendersi dai riempimenti e dalla corrosione dei fiumi* (Florence, 1688); *Elementi piani e solidi di Euclide agl'illustrissimi Sig. dell'Accademia de' Nobili* (Florence, 1690); *Formazione e misura di tutti i cieli* (Florence, 1692); and *De locis solidis secunda divinatio geometrica in quinque libros iniura temporum amissos, Aristaei senioris geometrae* (Florence, 1702).

II. SECONDARY LITERATURE. See L. Conte, "Vincenzo Viviani e l'invenzione di due medie proporzionali," in *Periodico di matematiche*, 25, no. 4 (1952), 185; A. Fabroni, *Vitae italorum doctrina excellentium*, I (Pisa, 1777), 307–344; and Gino Loria, *Curve piane speciali algebriche e trascendenti*, I (Milan, 1930), 373; *Curve sghembe speciali algebriche e trascendenti*, I (Bologna, 1925), 201–233, and II, 63–65; and *Storia delle matematiche*, 2nd ed. (Milan, 1950), see index.

There are biographical articles in L. Berzolari *et al.*, eds., *Enciclopedia delle matematiche elementari*, II, pt. I (Milan, 1937), 61, 172, 193, 523, 524; and II, pt. 2 (Milan, 1938), 48; and Treccani's *Enciclopedia italiana*, XXXV, 529.

A. NATUCCI

VLACQ (VLACK, VLACCUS), ADRIAAN (*b.* Gouda, Netherlands, 1600; *d.* The Hague, Netherlands, late 1666 or early 1667)

A member of a well-to-do family, Vlacq received a good education. Interested in mathematics, he became acquainted with a local surveyor and teacher, Ezechiel De Decker (*ca.* 1595–*ca.* 1657), for whom he translated into Dutch several recent books written in Latin by British authors on the new art of reckoning, notably some by Napier and that by Briggs on logarithms. They decided to publish these and related works in Dutch. *Het eerste deel van de Nieuwe telkonst* appeared in 1626 under the name of De Decker, who in the preface praised Vlacq for his help. It contained Napier's *Rabdologia* in Dutch translation, a paper on business arithmetic by De Decker, and Stevin's *Thiende*. Also that year De Decker published the *Nieuwe telkonst*, a small table of logarithms to base 10 for the numbers from 1 to 10,000, based on Briggs's *Arithmetica logarithmica* (1624). The work promised a full table of logarithms, an accomplishment realized in *Het tweede deel van de Nieuwe telkonst* (1627), again under the name of De Decker with credit to Vlacq. It contained not only the Briggsian logarithms from 1 to 10,000 and from 90,000 to 100,000, already published by Briggs, but also those of all numbers from 1 to 100,000 (to ten decimal places). The latter, the result of Vlacq's computations, did what Briggs had planned to do.

Vlacq took out the privileges on these books and had them published by the Gouda firm of Pieter Rammaseyn, in which he seems to have had a financial interest. Having paid for the publication of tables he himself had computed, Vlacq saw no objection to republishing them under his own name in the *Arithmetica logarithmica* (1628). Although De Decker was not mentioned, there is no indication that he later resented this. Vlacq's fame rests on these tables, which were well received and contain relatively few errors. The *Tweede deel* of 1627, actually the first complete table of decimal logarithms, was long forgotten until a copy was rediscovered in 1920.

To the *Arithmetica logarithmica*, Vlacq added *Canon triangulorum sive tabula artificialium sinuum*, with the decimal logarithms of the trigonometric lines computed from Pitiscus' *Thesaurus mathematicus* (1613). In a letter to John Pell of 25 October 1628, Briggs states that the 1,000 printed copies of this book, with Latin, Dutch, and French prefaces, were almost all sold. The probable reason is that they were used by George Miller for his *Logarithmicall Arithmeticke* (London, 1631), identical with Vlacq's book except for the English preface.

From about 1632 to 1642, Vlacq had a book business in London, which he moved to Paris. After 1648 he was in The Hague, publishing many books and repeatedly involved in business or political quarrels. The books he published include Briggs and Gellibrand's *Trigonometria britannica*, containing the logarithms of the trigonometric lines with angles divided into tenths (Stevin's idea), and his own *Trigonometria artificialis*, using the traditional sexagesimal division of angles. They have log sine, log cosine, log tangent, and log secant for angles increasing by ten seconds. Both books were published by the firm of Rammaseyn (Gouda, 1633).

Since all these tables were large, Vlacq, with his keen business instincts, published the small *Tabulae sinuum, tangentium et secantium et logarithmi sin. tang. et numerorum ab unitate ad 10000* (Gouda, 1636). These tables, carried to seven decimal places, were a great success and were often reprinted and reedited, and were translated into French and German (there is a Leipzig edition of 1821).

From 1652 to 1655 Vlacq waged a pamphlet war, in which he took the English royalist side, thereby provoking an attack by John Milton. In 1654 he is mentioned as successor to Johannes Rammaseyn. Between 1651 and 1662 he was regularly listed as a visitor to the Frankfurt book fair.

BIBLIOGRAPHY

On Vlacq's life and work, see D. Bierens de Haan, "Adriaan Vlack en Ezechiel De Decker," in *Verslagen en mededeelingen der Koninklyke Akademie van wetenschappen*, Afd. Natuurkunde, 2nd ser., 8 (1874), 57–99; and "Adriaan Vlack en zyne logarithmentafels," *ibid.*, 163–199; C. de Waard, "Vlacq (Adriaan)," in *Nieuw nederlandsch biographisch woordenboek*, II (1912), 1503–1506; J. W. L. Glaisher, "Notice Respecting Some New Facts in the Early History of Logarithms," in *Philosophical Magazine*, 4th ser., 44 (1872), 291–

303, and **45** (1873), 376–382; and D. Bierens de Haan, "On Certain Early Logarithmic Tables," *ibid.*, 371–376. The rediscovery of the *Tweede deel* by M. van Haaften is reported in his "Ce n'est pas Vlacq, en 1628, mais De Decker, en 1627, qui a publié une table de logarithmes étendue et complète," in *Nieuw archief voor wiskunde*, **15** (1928), 49–54; he first reported it in *Verzekeringsbode*, **39** (4 Sept. 1920), 383–386. In "Quelques nouvelles données concernant l'histoire des anciennes tables néerlandaises de logarithmes," in *Nieuw archief voor wiskunde*, **21** (1942), 59–64, and in *Nieuw tydschrift voor wiskunde*, **31** (1943–1944), 137–144, van Haaften supplements his account by reference to three documents on the business relationship between De Decker and Vlacq found by P. J. T. Endenburg in the Gouda archives, reported in "De oudste nederlandsche logarithmentafels en hun makers," in *Het Boek*, **25** (1938–1939), 311–320.

D. J. STRUIK

VOLTERRA, VITO (*b.* Ancona, Italy, 3 May 1860; *d.* Rome, Italy, 11 October 1940)

Volterra was the only child of Abramo Volterra, a cloth merchant, and his wife Angelica Almagià. His ancestors had lived in Bologna, whence at the beginning of the fifteenth century one of them had moved to Volterra, a small city in Tuscany—the origin of the family's present name. In 1459 this ancestor's descendants opened a bank in Florence. Volterras are remembered as fifteenth-century writers and travelers and as collectors of books and ancient codices. In the following centuries branches of the family lived in various Italian cities, including Ancona in the 1700's.

Volterra was two years old when his father died. He and his mother, left amost penniless, were taken into the home of her brother, Alfonso Almagià, an employee of the Banca Nazionale. Later they lived in Turin and in Florence. Volterra spent the greater part of his youth in Florence and considered himself almost a native of that city. He attended the Scuola Tecnica Dante Alighieri and the Istituto Tecnico Galileo Galilei, both of which had excellent teachers, including the physicist Antonio Roiti, who played an important part in Volterra's career.

Volterra was a very precocious child. At the age of eleven he began to study Bertrand's *Traité d'arithmétique* and Legendre's *Éléments de géométrie*. He formulated original problems and tried to solve them. At thirteen he worked on ballistic problems and, after reading Jules Verne's novel *From the Earth to the Moon*, tried to determine the trajectory of a gun's projectile in the combined gravitational field of the earth and the moon—a restricted version of the three-body problem. In his solution the time is partitioned into small intervals, for each of which the force is considered as a constant and the trajectory is given as a succession of small parabolic arcs. Almost forty years later, at the age of fifty-two, Volterra demonstrated this solution in a course of lectures given at the Sorbonne. The idea of studying a natural phenomenon by dividing into small intervals the time in which it occurs, and investigating the phenomenon in each such interval by considering the causes that produce it as invariable, was later applied by Volterra to many other kinds of problems, such as differential linear equations, theory of functionals, and linear substitutions.

Although Volterra was greatly interested in science, his family, which had little money, urged him to follow a commercial career. There followed a struggle between his natural inclination and practical necessity. The family appealed to a distant cousin, Edoardo Almagià, a civil engineer with a doctorate in mathematics, hoping that he would persuade the boy to interrupt his studies and devote himself to business. The cousin, however, who later became Volterra's father-in-law, was so impressed by his mathematical ability that he tried to persuade the family to let the boy pursue his scientific studies. Roiti, having learned that his most able student was being urged to become a bank clerk, immediately nominated him as assistant in the physics laboratory at the University of Florence, an unusual occurrence since Volterra had not enrolled at the university.

Volterra completed high school in 1878 and enrolled in the department of natural sciences at the University of Florence. Two years later he won the competition to become a resident student at the Scuola Normale Superiore in Pisa. At the University of Pisa he enrolled in the mathematics and physics courses given by Betti, Dini, and Riccardo Felici. At first he was very interested in Dini's work in analysis. In one of Volterra's early papers, published while he was still a student, he was the first to present examples of derivable functions the derivatives of which are not reconcilable with Riemann's point of view. This observation was used much later as a starting point for Lebesgue's research on this subject. Volterra was fascinated most by Betti's lectures, and under his influence he devoted his research to mechanics and mathematical physics.

In 1882 Volterra graduated with a doctorate in

physics and was immediately appointed Betti's assistant. The following year, at the age of twenty-three, he won the competition for a professorship of mechanics at the University of Pisa. After Betti's death Volterra succeeded him in the chair of mathematical physics. In 1892 Volterra was appointed professor of mechanics at the University of Turin, and in 1900 he succeeded Eugenio Beltrami in the chair of mathematical physics at the University of Rome. In the same year he married Virginia Almagià, who for over forty years was his devoted companion.

In recognition of his scientific achievements, Volterra was made a senator of the kingdom of Italy in 1905. Although he was never attracted by politics, he spoke frequently in the Senate on important issues concerning university organization and problems. He was active in Italian political life during World War I and, later, in the struggle against Fascist oppression.

When World War I broke out, Volterra felt that Italy should join the Allies; and when Italy entered the war, Volterra, although he was fifty-five, enlisted as an officer in the army corps of engineers, joining its air branch. He perfected a new type of airship, studied the possibility of mounting guns in it, and was the first to fire a gun from an airship. He also experimented with airplanes. For these accomplishments he was mentioned in dispatches and decorated with the War Cross.

At the beginning of 1917 Volterra established the Italian Office of War Inventions and became its chairman. He made frequent trips to France and to Great Britain in the process of wartime scientific and technical collaboration among the Allies. He was the first to propose the use of helium as a substitute for hydrogen in airships.

In October 1922 Fascism came to power in Italy. Volterra was one of the few to understand, from the beginning, its threat to the country's democratic institutions. He was one of the principal signatories of the "Intellectuals' Declaration" against Fascism, an action he took while president of the Accademia dei Lincei. When the proposed "laws of national security" were discussed by the Italian Senate, a small group of opposition senators, headed by Volterra and Benedetto Croce, appeared—at great personal risk—at all the Senate's meetings and always voted against Mussolini. By 1930 the parliamentary government created by Cavour in the nineteenth century was abolished, and Volterra never again attended sessions of the Italian Senate.

In 1931, having refused to sign the oath of allegiance imposed upon professors by the Fascist government, Volterra was dismissed from the University of Rome; and in 1932, for the same reason, he was deprived of all his memberships in Italian scientific academies. In 1936, however, on the nomination of Pope Pius XI he was elected to the Pontifical Academy of Sciences.

After 1931 Volterra lectured in Paris at the Sorbonne, in Rumania, in Spain, in Belgium, in Czechoslovakia, and in Switzerland. He spent only short periods in Italy, mainly at his country house at Ariccia, in the Alban Hills south of Rome. From December 1938 he was afflicted by phlebitis, but his mind remained clear and he continued his passionate pursuit of science until his death.

Volterra's scientific work covers the period from 1881, when he published his first papers, to 1940 when his last paper was published in the *Acta* of the Pontifical Academy of Sciences. His most important contributions were in higher analysis, mathematical physics, celestial mechanics, the mathematical theory of elasticity, and mathematical biometrics. His major works in these fields included the foundation of the theory of functionals and the solution of the type of integral equations with variable limits that now bear his name, methods of integrating hyperbolic partial differential equations, the study of hereditary phenomena, optics of birefringent media, the motion of the earth's poles and elastic dislocations of multiconnected bodies, and, in his last years, placing the laws of biological fluctuations on mathematical bases and establishing principles of a demographic dynamics that present analogies to the dynamics of material systems.

Volterra received numerous honors, was a member of almost every major scientific academy and was awarded honorary doctorates by many universities. In 1921 he received an honorary knighthood from George V of England.

Scientific research did not, however, occupy all of Volterra's activity. He was an intimate friend of many well-known scientific, political, literary, and artistic men of his time. He has been compared to a typical man of the Italian Renaissance for the variety of his interests and knowledge, his great scientific curiosity, and his sensitivity to art, literature, and music.

BIBLIOGRAPHY

I. ORIGINAL WORKS. Volterra's works were collected as *Opere matematiche. Memorie e note*, 5 vols. (Rome, 1954–1962).

His writings include *Trois leçons sur quelques progrès récents de la physique mathématique* (Worcester, Mass., 1912), also in *Lectures Delivered . . . by V. Volterra, E. Rutherford, R. W. Wood, C. Barus* (Worcester, Mass., 1912), and translated into German (Leipzig, 1914); *Leçons sur les équations intégrales et les équations intégro-différentielles*, M. Tomassetti and F. S. Zarlatti, eds. (Paris, 1913); *Leçons sur les fonctions de lignes*, collected and edited by Joseph Pérès (Paris, 1913); "Henri Poincaré: L'oeuvre mathématique," in *Revue du mois*, **15** (1913), 129–154; *Saggi scientifici* (Bologna, 1920); and *Leçons sur la composition et les fonctions permutables* (Paris, 1924), written with J. Pérès.

Additional works are *Theory of Functionals and of Integral and Integro-Differential Equations*, Luigi Fantapié, ed., M. Long, trans. (London–Glasgow, 1930), repr. with a preface by Griffith C. Evans and an almost complete bibliography of Volterra's works and a biography by Sir Edmund Whittaker (New York, 1959); *Leçons sur la théorie mathématique de la lutte pour la vie*, Marcel Brelot, ed. (Paris, 1931); *Les associations biologiques au point de vue mathématique* (Paris, 1935), written with U. D'Ancona; *Théorie générale des fonctionnelles* (Paris, 1936), written with J. Pérès; and *Sur les distorsions des corps élastiques (théorie et applications)* (Paris, 1960), written with E. Volterra, preface by J. Pérès.

II. SECONDARY LITERATURE. Biographies of Volterra and descriptions of his scientific work were published immediately after his death in 1940. A year later Sir Edmund Whittaker published a biography in *Obituary Notices of Fellows of the Royal Society of London*, **3** (1941), 691–729, with a bibliography; an abridged version appeared in *Journal of the London Mathematical Society*, **16** (1941), 131–139.

Other biographies and commemorations of Volterra, listed chronologically, include *Enciclopedia italiana di scienze, lettere ed arti*, XXXV (Rome, 1938), 582–583; Émile Picard, in *Comptes rendus . . . de l'Académie des sciences*, **211** (1940), 309–312; S. Mandelbrojt, in *Yearbook. American Philosophical Society* (1940), 448–451; D'Arcy W. Thompson and Sir Sydney Chapman, in *Nature*, **147** (22 Mar. 1941), 349–350; C. Somigliana, in *Acta Pontificiae Accademiae scientiarum*, **6** (1942), 57–86; C. Somigliana, in *Rendiconti del Seminario matematico e fisico di Milano*, **17** (1946), 3–61, with bibliography; Guido Castelnuovo and Carlo Somigliana, "Vito Volterra e la sua opera scientifica," in *Atti dell' Accademia nazionale dei Lincei* (1947), session of 17 Oct.; and J. Pérès, in *Ricerca scientifica*, **18** (1948), 1–9.

See also *Enciclopedia italiana di scienze, lettere ed arti, seconda appendice 1938–1948* (Rome, 1949); and G. Armellini, *Discorso pronunciato . . . per le onoranze a V. Volterra . . .* (Ancona, 1951); Guido Corbellini, *Vito Volterra nel centenario della sua nascita* (Rome, 1960); Accademia Nazionale dei Lincei, *Vito Volterra nel I centenario della nascita* (Rome, 1961); and Fran-

cesco G. Tricomi, "Matematici italiani del primo secolo dello stato unitario," *Memorie dell'Accademia delle scienze di Torino*, Cl. di scienze fisiche, matematiche e naturali, 4th ser., no. 1 (1962), 118.

E. VOLTERRA

VON NEUMANN, JOHANN (or JOHN) (*b.* Budapest, Hungary, 28 December 1903; *d.* Washington, D.C., 8 February 1957)

Von Neumann, the eldest of three sons of Max von Neumann, a well-to-do Jewish banker, was privately educated until he entered the Gymnasium in 1914. His unusual mathematical abilities soon came to the attention of his teachers, who pointed out to his father that teaching him conventional school mathematics would be a waste of time; he was therefore tutored in mathematics under the guidance of university professors, and by the age of nineteen he was already recognized as a professional mathematician and had published his first paper. Von Neumann was *Privatdozent* at Berlin from 1927 to 1929 and at Hamburg in 1929–1930, then went to Princeton University for three years; in 1933 he was invited to join the newly opened Institute for Advanced Study, of which he was the youngest permanent member at that time. At the outbreak of World War II, von Neumann was called upon to participate in various scientific projects related to the war effort; in particular, from 1943 he was a consultant on the construction of the atomic bomb at Los Alamos. After the war he retained his membership in numerous government boards and committees, and in 1954 he became a member of the Atomic Energy Commission. His health began to fail in 1955, and he died of cancer two years later.

Von Neumann may have been the last representative of a once-flourishing and numerous group, the great mathematicians who were equally at home in pure and applied mathematics and who throughout their careers maintained a steady production in both directions. Pure and applied mathematics have now become so vast and complex that mastering both seems beyond human capabilities. In von Neumann's generation his ability to absorb and digest an enormous amount of extremely diverse material in a short time was exceptional; and in a profession where quick minds are somewhat commonplace, his amazing rapidity was proverbial. There is hardly a single important part of the mathematics of the 1930's with which he had not at least a passing acquaintance, and the same is probably true of theoretical physics.

Despite his encyclopedic background, von Neumann's work in pure mathematics had a definitely smaller range than that of Poincaré or Hilbert, or even of H. Weyl. His genius lay in analysis and combinatorics, the latter being understood in a very wide sense, including an uncommon ability to organize and axiomatize complex situations that a priori do not seem amenable to mathematical treatment, as in quantum mechanics and the theory of games. As an analyst von Neumann does not belong to the classical school represented by the French and English mathematicians of the early 1900's but, rather, to the tradition of Hilbert, Weyl, and F. Riesz, in which analysis, while being as "hard" as any classical theory, is based on extensive foundations of linear algebra and general topology; however, he never did significant work in number theory, algebraic topology, algebraic geometry, or differential geometry. It is only in comparison with the greatest mathematical geniuses of history that von Neumann's scope in pure mathematics may appear somewhat restricted; it was far beyond the range of most of his contemporaries, and his extraordinary work in applied mathematics, in which he certainly equals Gauss, Cauchy, or Poincaré, more than compensates for its limitations.

Pure Mathematics. Von Neumann's work in pure mathematics was accomplished between 1925 and 1940, which might be called his *Sturm und Drang* period, when he seemed to be advancing at a breathless speed on all fronts of logic and analysis at once, not to speak of mathematical physics. This work, omitting a few minor papers, can be classified under five main topics.

Logic and Set Theory. Von Neumann's interest in set theory arose very early: in his second paper (1923) he gave an elegant new definition of ordinal numbers, and in the third (1925) he introduced an axiomatic system for set theory quite different from the one proposed by Zermelo and Fraenkel (it was later adopted by Gödel in his research on the continuum hypothesis). In the late 1920's von Neumann also participated in the Hilbert program of metamathematics and published a few papers on proofs of noncontradiction for parts of arithmetic, before Gödel shattered the hopes for a better result.

Measure Theory. Although it was not in the center of von Neumann's preoccupation, he made several valuable contributions to measure theory. His knowledge of group theory enabled him to "explain" the Hausdorff-Banach-Tarski "paradox," in which two balls of different radii in $\mathbf{R}^n$ ($n \geqslant 3$) are decomposed into a finite number of (nonmeasurable) subsets that are pairwise congruent (such decompositions cannot exist for $n = 1$ or $n = 2$); he showed that $n = 1$ or $n = 2$ is impossible because the orthogonal group in three or more variables contains free non-Abelian groups, whereas it does not for $n \leqslant 2$.

Another highly ingenious paper established the existence of an algebra of bounded measurable functions on the real line that forms a complete system of representatives of the classes of almost-everywhere-equal measurable bounded functions (each class contains one, and only one, function of the algebra). This theorem, later generalized to arbitrary measure spaces by Dorothy Maharam, holds the key to the "disintegration" process of measures (corresponding to the classical notion of "conditional probability"). It is a curious coincidence that in "Operator Methods in Classical Mechanics" von Neumann was the first to prove, by a completely different method, the existence of such disintegrations for fairly general types of measures.

On the borderline between this group of papers and the next lies von Neumann's basic work on Haar's measure, which he proved to be unique up to a constant factor; the first proof was valid only for compact groups and used his direct definition of the "mean" of a continuous function over such a group. The extension of that idea to more general groups was the starting point of his subsequent papers, some written in collaboration with Solomon Bochner, on almost-periodic functions on groups.

Lie Groups. One of the highlights of von Neumann's career was his 1933 paper solving Hilbert's "fifth problem" for compact groups, proving that such a group admits a Lie group structure once it is locally homeomorphic with Euclidean space. He had discovered the basic idea behind that paper six years earlier: the fact that closed subgroups of the general linear group are in fact Lie groups. The method of proof of that result was shown a little later by E. Cartan to apply as well to closed subgroups of arbitrary Lie groups.

Spectral Theory of Operators in Hilbert Space. This topic is by far the dominant theme in von Neumann's work. For twenty years he was the undisputed master in this area, which contains what is now considered his most profound and most original creation, the theory of rings of operators. The first papers (1927) in which Hilbert space theory appears are those on the foundations of quantum mechanics (see below). These investigations later led von Neumann to a systematic study of unbounded hermitian operators, which previously had been considered only in a few special cases by Weyl and T. Carleman. His papers on unbounded hermitian operators have not been improved upon since their publication, yet within a few years he realized that the traditional idea of representing an operator by an infinite matrix was totally inadequate, and discovered the topological devices that were to replace it: the use of the graph of an unbounded operator and the extension to such an operator of the classical "Cayley transform," which reduced the structure of a self-adjoint operator to that of a unitary operator (known since Hilbert). At the same time this work led him to discover the defects of a general, densely defined hermitian operator, which later were seen to correspond to the "boundary conditions" for operators stemming from differential and partial differential equations.

The same group of papers includes another famous result from von Neumann's early years, his proof in 1932 of the ergodic theorem in its "L^2 formulation" given by B. O. Koopman a few months earlier. With G. D. Birkhoff's almost simultaneous proof of the sharper "almost everywhere" formulation of the theorem, von Neumann's results were to form the starting point of all subsequent developments in ergodic theory.

Rings of Operators. Most of von Neumann's results on unbounded operators in Hilbert space were independently discovered a little later by M. H. Stone. But von Neumann's ideas on rings of operators broke entirely new ground. He was well acquainted with the noncommutative algebra beautifully developed by Emmy Noether and E. Artin in the 1920's, and he realized how these concepts simplified and illuminated the theory of matrices. This probably provided the motivation for extending such concepts to algebras consisting of (bounded) operators in a given separable Hilbert space, to which he gave the vague name "rings of operators" and which are now known as "von Neumann algebras." He introduced their theory in the same year as his first paper on unbounded operators, and from the beginning he had the insight to select the two essential features that would allow him further progress: the algebra must be self-adjoint (that is, for any operator in the algebra, its adjoint must also belong to the algebra) and closed under the strong topology of operators and not merely in the finer topology of the norm.

Von Neumann's first result was the "double commutant theorem," which states that the von Neumann algebra generated by a self-adjoint family $\mathscr{F}$ of operators is the commutant of the commutant of $\mathscr{F}$, a generalization of a similar result obtained by I. Schur for semisimple algebras of finite dimension that was to become one of the main tools in his later work. After elucidating the relatively easy study of commutative algebras, von Neumann embarked in 1936, with the partial collaboration of F. J. Murray, on the general study of the noncommutative case. The six major papers in which they developed that theory between 1936 and 1940 certainly rank among the masterpieces of analysis in the twentieth century. They immediately realized that among the von Neumann algebras, the "factors" (those with the center reduced to the scalars) held the key to the structure of the general von Neumann algebras; indeed, in his last major paper on the subject (published in 1949 but dating from around 1940), von Neumann showed how a process of "direct integration" (the analogue of the "direct sum" of the finite dimensional theory) explicitly gave all von Neumann algebras from factors as "building blocks."

The evidence from classical study of noncommutative algebras seemed to lead to the conjecture that all factors would be isomorphic to the algebra $\mathscr{B}(H)$ of all bounded operators in a Hilbert space H (of finite or separable dimension). Murray and von Neumann therefore startled the mathematical world when they showed that the situation was far more complicated. As in the classical theory, their main tool consisted of the self-adjoint idempotents in the algebra, which are simply orthogonal projections on closed subspaces of the Hilbert space; the novelty was that, in contrast with the classical case (or the case of $\mathscr{B}[H]$), minimal idempotents may fail to exist in the algebra, which implies that all idempotents are orthogonal projections on infinite-dimensional subspaces. Nevertheless, they may be *compared*, the projection on a subspace E being considered as "smaller" than one on a subspace F when the algebra contains a partial isometry V sending E onto a subspace of F. This is only a "preorder"; but when one considers the corresponding order relation (between equivalence classes), it turns out that in a factor this is a total order relation that may be described by a "dimension function" that attaches to each equivalence class of projections a real number ≥ 0 or $+\infty$. Murray and von Neumann showed that after proper normalization the range of the dimension could be one of five possibilities: $\{1, 2, \cdots, n\}$ (type I_n, the classical algebras of matrices), $\{1, 2, \cdots, +\infty\}$ (type I_∞, corresponding to the algebras $\mathscr{B}[H]$), the whole interval $[0, 1]$ in the real line (type II_1), the whole interval $[0, +\infty]$ in the extended real line (type II_∞), and the two-element set $\{0, +\infty\}$ (type III).

It may be said that the algebraic structure of a factor imposes on the set of corresponding subspaces of H (images of H by the projections belonging to the factor) an order structure similar to that of the subspaces of a usual projective space, but with completely new possibilities regarding the "dimension" attached to these subspaces. Intrigued by this geometric interpretation of his results, von Neumann developed it in a series of papers on "continuous geometries" and their algebraic satellites, the "regular rings" (which are to continuous geometries as rings of matrices are to vector spaces). This classification, which required great technical skill in the handling of the spectral theory of operators, immediately led to the question of existence for the new "factors." Murray and von Neumann devoted many of their papers to this question; and they were able to exhibit factors of types II_1, II_∞, and III by using ingenious constructions from ergodic theory (at a time when the subject of actions of groups on measure spaces was still in its infancy) and algebras generated by convolution operators. They went even further and initiated the study of isomorphisms between factors, succeeding, in particular, in obtaining two nonisomorphic factors of type II_1; only very recently has it been proved that there are uncountably many isomorphism classes for factors of types II_1 and III.

Applied Mathematics. *Mathematical Physics.* Von Neumann's most famous work in theoretical physics is his axiomatization of quantum mechanics. When he began work in that field in 1927, the methods used by its founders were hard to formulate in precise mathematical terms: "operators" on "functions" were handled without much consideration of their domain of definition or their topological properties; and it was blithely assumed that such "operators," when self-adjoint, could always be "diagonalized" (as in the finite dimensional case), at the expense of introducing "Dirac functions" as "eigenvectors." Von Neumann showed that mathematical rigor could be restored by taking as basic axioms the assumptions that the states of a physical system were points of a Hilbert space and that the measurable quantities were Hermitian (generally unbounded) operators densely defined in that space. This formalism, the practical use of which became available after von Neumann had developed the spectral theory of unbounded Hermitian operators (1929), has survived subsequent developments of quantum mechanics and is still the basis of nonrelativistic quantum theory; with the introduction of the theory of distributions, it has even become possible to interpret its results in a way similar to Dirac's original intuition.

After 1927 von Neumann also devoted much effort to more specific problems of quantum mechanics, such as the problem of measurement and the foundation of quantum statistics and quantum thermodynamics, proving in particular an ergodic theorem for quantum systems. All this work was developed and expanded in *Mathematische Grundlagen der Quantenmechanik* (1932), in which he also discussed the much-debated question of "causality" versus "indeterminacy" and concluded that no introduction of "hidden parameters" could keep the basic structure of quantum theory and restore "causality."

Quantum mechanics was not the only area of theoretical physics in which von Neumann was active. With Subrahmanyan Chandrasekhar he published two papers on the statistics of the fluctuating gravitational field generated by randomly distributed stars. After he started work on the Manhattan project, leading to atomic weapons, he became interested in the theory of shock waves and wrote many reports on their theoretical and computational aspects.

Numerical Analysis and Computers. Von Neumann's uncommon grasp of applied mathematics, treated as a whole without divorcing theory from experimental realization, was nowhere more apparent than in his work on computers. He became interested in numerical computations in connection with the need for quick estimates and approximate results that developed with the technology used for the war effort—particularly the complex problems of hydrodynamics—and the completely new problems presented by the harnessing of nuclear energy, for which no ready-made theoretical solutions were available. Dissatisfied with the computing machines available immediately after the war, he was led to examine from its foundations the optimal method that such machines should follow, and he introduced new procedures in their logical organization, the "codes" by which a fixed system of wiring could solve a great variety of problems. Von Neumann devised various methods of programming a computer, particularly for finding eigenvalues and inverses of matrices, extrema of functions of several variables, and production of random numbers. Although he never lost sight of the theoretical questions involved (as can be seen in his remarkably original papers with Herman Goldstine, on the limitation of the errors in the numerical inversion of a matrix of large order), he also wanted to have a direct acquaintance with the engineering problems that had to be faced, and supervised the construction of a computer at the Institute for Advanced Study; many fundamental devices in the present machines bear the imprint of his ideas.

In the last years of his life, von Neumann broadened his views to the general theory of automata, in a kind of synthesis of his early interest in logic and his later work on computers. With his characteristic boldness and scope of vision, he did not hesitate to attack two of the most complex questions in the field: how to design reliable machines using unreliable components, and the construction of self-reproducing machines. As usual he brought remarkably new ideas in the approach to solutions of these problems and must be considered one of the founders of a flourishing new mathematical discipline.

Theory of Games. The role as founder is even more obvious for the theory of games, which von Neumann, in a 1926 paper, conjured—so to speak—out of nowhere. To give a quantitative mathematical model for games of chance such as poker or bridge might have seemed a priori impossible, since such games involve free choices by the players at each move, constantly reacting on each other. Yet von Neumann did precisely that, by introducing the general concept of "strategy" (qualitatively considered a few years earlier by E. Borel) and by constructing a model that made this concept amenable to mathematical analysis. That this model was well adapted to the problem was shown conclusively by von Neumann in the same paper, with the proof of the famous minimax theorem: for a game with two players in a normalized form, it asserts the existence of a unique numerical value, representing a gain for one player and a loss for the other, such that each can achieve at least this favorable expectation from his own point of view by using a "strategy" of his own choosing: such strategies for the two players are termed optimal strategies, and the unique numerical value, the minimax value of the game.

This was the starting point for far-reaching generalizations, including applications to economics, a topic in which von Neumann became interested as early as 1937 and that he developed in his major treatise written with O. Morgenstern, *Theory of Games and Economic Behavior* (1944). These the-

ories have developed into a full-fledged mathematical discipline, attracting many researchers and branching into several types of applications to the social sciences.

BIBLIOGRAPHY

Von Neumann's works were brought together as *Collected Works of John Von Neumann*, A. H. Taub, ed., 6 vols. (New York, 1961). His books include *Mathematische Grundlagen der Quantenmechanik* (Berlin, 1932); and *Theory of Games and Economic Behavior* (Princeton, 1944), written with O. Morgenstern. A memorial volume is "John von Neumann, 1903–1957," which is *Bulletin of the American Mathematical Society*, **64**, no. 654 (May 1958).

J. Dieudonné

VORONOY, GEORGY FEDOSEEVICH (*b.* Zhuravka, Poltava guberniya, Russia, 28 April 1868; *d.* Warsaw, Poland, 20 November 1908)

Voronoy's father was superintendent of Gymnasiums in Kishinev and in other towns in the southern Ukraine. After graduating from the Gymnasium in Priluki in 1885, Voronoy enrolled in the mathematics section of the Faculty of Physics and Mathematics of the University of St. Petersburg. He graduated in 1889 and was retained to prepare for a teaching career. In 1894 he defended his master's dissertation, on algebraic integers associated with the roots of an irreducible third-degree equation. He then became professor in the Department of Pure Mathematics at the University of Warsaw. He defended his doctoral dissertation, on a generalization of the algorithm of continued fractions, at St. Petersburg in 1897; both dissertations were awarded the Bunyakovsky Prize of the St. Petersburg Academy of Sciences.

Voronoy subsequently elaborated his own ideas on the geometry of numbers and conducted investigations on the analytic theory of numbers. In 1904 he participated in the Third International Congress of Mathematicians in Heidelberg, where he met Minkowski, who was then working on topics closely related to those in which Voronoy was interested.

Voronoy's work, all of which concerns the theory of numbers, can be divided into three groups: algebraic theory of numbers, geometry of numbers, and analytic theory of numbers.

In his doctoral dissertation Voronoy gave the best algorithm known at the time for calculating fundamental units of a general cubic field, for both a positive and negative discriminant.

Voronoy completed two of a planned series of memoirs in which he intended to apply the principle of continuous Hermite parameters to problems of the arithmetical theory of definite and indefinite quadratic forms. In the first of these works, which dealt with certain characteristics of complete quadratic forms, he solved the question posed by Hermite concerning the precise upper limit of the minima of the positive quadratic forms of a given discriminant of n variables. E. I. Zolotarev and A. N. Korkin had given solutions for $n = 4$ and $n = 5$; with the aid of the methods of the geometrical theory of numbers Voronoy gave a full algorithmic solution for any n. In the second paper, which concerned simple parallelepipeds, Voronoy dealt with the determination of all possible methods of filling an n-dimensional Euclidean space with identical convex nonintersecting polyhedra having completely contiguous boundaries (parallelepipeds). A solution of this problem for three-dimensional space had been given by the crystallographer E. S. Fedorov, but his proofs were incomplete. In 1896 Minkowski demonstrated that the parallelepipeds must have centers of symmetry and that the number of their boundaries did not exceed $2(2^n - 1)$. Voronoy imposed the further requirement that $n + 1$ parallelepipeds converge at each summit and completely solved the problem for these conditions.

In a memoir concerning a problem from the theories of asymptotic functions Voronoy solved Dirichlet's problem concerning the determination of the number of whole points under the hyperbola $xy = n$. Dirichlet had found that the number of such points lying in the area $x > 0$, $y > 0$, $xy \leq n$ was expressed by the formula $F(n) = n(\log n + 2C - 1) + R(n)$, where $R(n) = O(\sqrt{n})$. By introducing series similar to a Farey series and by dividing the area of summation into the subsets associated with these series, Voronoy substantially improved the evaluation, obtaining $R(n) = O(\sqrt[3]{n} \cdot \log n)$. His paper served as the starting point for the work of I. M. Vinogradov, and the Farey series that he introduced was employed in the investigation of problems in the additive theory of numbers by Vinogradov, G. H. Hardy, and J. E. Littlewood.

BIBLIOGRAPHY

Voronoy's collected works were published as *Sobranie sochineny*, 3 vols. (Kiev, 1952–1953). Papers mentioned in the article are "Sur un problème du calcul des fonctions asymptotiques," in *Journal für die reine und angewandte Mathematik*, **126** (1903), 241–282; "Sur quelques propriétés des formes quadratiques positives parfaites," *ibid.*, **133** (1908), 97–178; and "Recherches sur les paralleloèdres primitifs," *ibid.*, **136** (1909), 67–179. These papers are reprinted in *Sobranie sochineny*, II, 5–50, 171–238, 239–368. On his work, see B. N. Delone, *Peterburgskaya shkola teorii chisel* ("The St. Petersburg School of the Theory of Numbers"; Moscow–Leningrad, 1947).

I. G. BASHMAKOVA

WALD, ABRAHAM (*b.* Cluj, Rumania, 31 October 1902; *d.* India, 13 December 1950)

Wald was born into a family which had considerable intellectual interests but had to earn its livelihood in petty trade because of anti-Jewish restrictions. These restrictions made his education at the University of Cluj, and later at the University of Vienna, very difficult. After Hitler occupied Austria in 1938, Wald moved to the United States, which saved him from death in a German concentration camp—the fate of all but one other member of his numerous family. He later married Lucille Lang, an American, who died with him in an airplane crash.

At Vienna, Wald was a student and a protégé, and later a friend, of Karl Menger. His work in pure mathematics was largely, although not wholly, in geometry. Menger later directed Wald toward mathematical statistics and mathematical economics, so that he was able to find employment with the distinguished economist Oskar Morgenstern.

It seems reasonable to say that Wald's most important work was in statistics, both because of his relative importance in the field and because of the current assessment of the field's importance. One of his great contributions to statistics was to bring to it mathematical precision in the formulation of problems and mathematical rigor in argument. These qualities, which were often lacking when he began his statistical career in 1938, have transformed the subject—although not necessarily to the satisfaction of everyone. It should be emphasized, however, that these accomplishments were a by-product and consequence of his extraordinary ability and the breadth of his statistical interests. Wald wrote lucidly and unambiguously on many statistical subjects, and there is scarcely a branch of modern statistics to which he did not contribute. His writings and lectures were so lucid and so unambiguous because of this precision, and he achieved so much in the way of results, that the superiority of mathematical precision became apparent to all. It is impossible to discuss Wald's statistical results in detail; rather, we shall single out the two most important fields of his work, which he founded and in which his results still dominate: sequential analysis and the theory of decision functions.

In sequential analysis one takes observations seriatim until the evidence is sufficiently strong, bearing in mind certain previously imposed bounds on the probabilities of error. When there are only two possible hypotheses, the "Wald sequential probability ratio test" has the property that it requires the smallest average number of observations under either hypothesis. This famous "optimum property of the sequential probability ratio test" was brilliantly conjectured by Wald in 1943 and proved jointly by him and a colleague in 1948. Wald proved many theorems on the distribution of the required number of observations and obtained many approximations on probabilities of error and average required numbers of observations, that are still used in applications. Most, although not all, of his results were summed up in *Sequential Analysis* (1947). With minor exceptions, the entire contents of this book were obtained by him. Such a phenomenon is rare in mathematical books and indicates the extent to which he founded and dominated the field of sequential analysis.

When Wald began his work in statistics, a large part of the field was concerned with the theory of testing hypotheses. He regarded this theory as, at best (when properly interpreted), one of deciding between exactly two courses of action. Consequently very many statistical problems actually fall outside the scope of this theory. There was no consistent theory for deciding among more than two courses of action, and attempts to force such problems into the framework of the theory of testing hypotheses had yielded very unsatisfactory results. It is interesting that these objections were clearly realized by a theoretician like Wald and not by the practical statisticians in industrial and agricultural laboratories who applied the theory. (For a recent criticism of the theory see Wolfowitz, "Remarks on the Theory of Testing Hypotheses.") Wald's theory of statistical decision functions considers the problem of deciding among any number of (possibly infinitely many) courses of action, both sequentially and nonsequentially. The statistician introduces a loss function that measures the consequences of various actions under different situations. With each statistical procedure (decision function) there is associated a vector, or function, of average loss under the various possible situations (the risk function). The statistical procedures of which the risk functions are not inferior to those of any other form a "complete" class, and the statistician can properly ignore the procedures not in the complete class.

At Wald's death the theory of statistical decision functions was far from the point of application to everyday, practical statistical problems; and little progress has been made in this direction since then. The theory is still of great conceptual and theoretical importance, and provides a logical basis for the formulation of many research problems. Recent research in the theory itself has, however, been chiefly in the direction of very technical mathematical refinements and has not achieved any essential breakthroughs.

Some of Wald's work in statistics originated in economic problems and properly belongs to both subjects. One such example is his work on the identification of economic relations—roughly speaking, the problem whether the distributions, which result from a model of the observed chance variables, uniquely determine all or certain specified parameters of the model. Also included in this category is his work on stochastic difference equations—models involving sequences of chance variables connected by difference equations with "error" chance variables. Wald also proved theorems on the existence of unique solutions for systems of equations for several types of economic systems and studied cost-of-living index numbers, the empirical determination of indifference surfaces, and the elimination of seasonal variation in time series. In all these his methods were ingenious and his contributions very important.

In pure mathematics, Wald's first three published papers and "Zur Axiomatik des Zwischenbegriffes" dealt with the characterization of "betweenness" in metric spaces. He also extended Steinitz's theorem to vectors with infinitely many elements; the theorem states that a divergent series, the elements of which are finite vectors, can, by a permutation of its terms, be made to converge to any element of a linear manifold. Perhaps his best result was the development of a differential geometry that starts from the assumption of a convex, compact metric space that at every point admits what should be called a Wald curvature. From this he was able to derive properties of differential geometry that are postulated in other systems.

Relatively uninterested in mathematical elegance, Wald spent little time in polishing a paper after a problem was solved to his satisfaction. In his masterly hands simple methods sometimes yielded the most amazing results. Although he was readily accessible, he had very few students. With one of these, J. Wolfowitz, who became his friend and colleague, he wrote fifteen joint papers. His American, and largely statistical, period was relatively brief (1938–1950) and extraordinarily productive. During this time he learned mathematical statistics, contributed deeply to it, changed it essentially, and dominated the subject. It has borne his impress since, and the paths he opened are still being pursued.

BIBLIOGRAPHY

I. ORIGINAL WORKS. A comprehensive bibliography of Wald's writings follows Tintner's memoir (see below). His works include "Zur Axiomatik des Zwischenbegriffes," in *Ergebnisse eines mathematischen Kolloquiums*, **4** (1933), 23–24; *Sequential Analysis* (New York–London, 1947); and "Optimum Character of the Sequential Probability Ratio Test," in *Annals of Mathematical Statistics*, **19** (1948), 326–339, written with J. Wolfowitz.

II. SECONDARY LITERATURE. On Wald and his work, see J. Wolfowitz, "Abraham Wald, 1902–1950," in *Annals of Mathematical Statistics*, **23** (1952), 1–13; Karl Menger, "The Formative Years of Abraham Wald and His Work in Geometry," *ibid.*, 14–20; G. Tintner, "Abraham Wald's Contributions to Econometrics," *ibid.*, 21–28; and "The Publications of Abraham Wald," *ibid.*, 29–33, which lists 103 works (1931–1952).

See also J. Wolfowitz, "Remarks on the Theory of Testing Hypotheses," in *New York Statistician*, **18**, no. 7 (Mar. 1967), 1–3.

J. WOLFOWITZ

WALLACE, WILLIAM (*b.* Dysart, Scotland, 23 September 1768; *d.* Edinburgh, Scotland, 28 April 1843)

Wallace had no schooling after the age of eleven, when he was apprenticed to a bookbinder; he subsequently taught himself mathematics and became a teacher at Perth. In 1803 he was appointed to the Royal Military College at Great Marlow and in 1819 became professor of mathematics at the University of Edinburgh, where he remained until his retirement in 1838. Wallace wrote many articles for encyclopedias and numerous papers in *Proceedings of the Royal Society of Edinburgh*, including some on mechanical devices. He also played a large part in the establishment of the observatory on Calton Hill, Edinburgh.

The feet of the perpendiculars to the sides of a triangle from a point P on its circumcircle are collinear. This line is sometimes called the pedal line but more often, incorrectly, the Simson line of the triangle relative to P. It was stated by J. S. Mackay that no such theorem is in Simson's published works. The result appears in an article by Wallace in Thomas Leybourn's *Mathematical Repository* (**2** [1799–1800], 111), and Mackay could find no earlier publication. In the preceding volume Wallace had proved that if the sides of a triangle touch a parabola, the circumcircle of the triangle passes through the focus of the parabola, a result already obtained by Lambert. To demonstrate this, Wallace showed that the feet of the perpendiculars from the focus to the sides of the triangle lie on the tangent at the vertex of the parabola, which is equivalent to saying that the pedal line of the triangle is the tangent at the vertex. The close connection of this theorem with the pedal line suggests that Wallace was led to the property of the pedal line from the parabolic property.

In 1804 the following result was proposed for proof in *Mathematical Repository* (n.s. **1**, 22): If four straight lines intersect each other to form four triangles by omitting one line in turn, the circumcircles of these triangles have a point in common. The proposer was "Scoticus," which Leybourn later said was a pseudonym for Wallace. Two solutions were given in the same volume (170). Miquel later proved that five lines determine five sets of four lines, by omitting each in turn; and the five points, one arising from each such set, lie on a circle. Clifford proved that the theorems of Wallace and Miquel are parts of an endless chain of theorems: $2n$ lines determine a point as the intersection of $2n$ circles; taking one more line, $2n + 1$ lines determine $2n + 1$ sets of $2n$ lines, each such set determines a point, and these $2n + 1$ points lie on a circle.

BIBLIOGRAPHY

Two articles by J. S. Mackay in *Proceedings of the Edinburgh Mathematical Society*—**9** (1891), 83–91, and **23** (1905), 80–85—give the bibliography of Wallace's two theorems and later extensions and generalizations with scholarly thoroughness.

For a full account of Wallace's life, see the unsigned but evidently authoritative obituary in *Monthly Notices of the Royal Astronomical Society*, **6** (1845), 31–36.

T. A. A. BROADBENT

WALLIS, JOHN (*b*. Ashford, Kent, England, 3 December 1616; *d*. Oxford, England, 8 November 1703)

Wallis was the third child of John Wallis and his second wife, Joanna Chapman. His father studied at Trinity College, Cambridge, and after having taken holy orders became minister at Ashford, about 1603. Standing in great esteem and reputation in his town and parish, he died when John was barely six.

Young John grew up, together with his two older sisters and two younger brothers, in the care of his mother. After he had received his first education, he was sent in 1625 to a grammar school at Tenterden, Kent, where, according to his autobiography,[1] he enjoyed a thorough training in Latin. In 1631–1632 Wallis attended the famous school of Martin Holbeach at Felsted, Essex. Besides more Latin and Greek he also learned some Hebrew and was introduced to the elements of logic. As mathematics was not part of the grammar school curriculum, he obtained his first insight into this field during a vacation; he studied what a brother of his had learned in approximately three months as preparation for a trade.

Wallis entered Emanuel College, Cambridge, the "Puritan College," about Christmas 1632 as a pensioner. He not only took the traditional undergraduate courses (obtaining his bachelor of arts degree early in 1637), followed by studies in theology, but he also studied physic, anatomy, astronomy, geography, and other parts of natural philosophy and what was then called mathematics—although the latter "were scarce looked upon, with us, as Academical Studies then in fashion." He was the first student of Francis Glisson to defend the doctrine of the circulation of the blood in a public disputation.

In 1640 Wallis received the degree of master of arts and was ordained by the bishop of Winchester. For some years he earned his living as private chaplain and as minister in London. From 1644, after the outbreak of the Civil War, he also acted as secretary to the Assembly of Divines at Westminster, which was charged with proposing a new form of church government. For about a year he also held a fellowship at Queens' College, Cambridge, in consequence of a Parliamentary ordinance. He gave up this position when he married Susanna Glyde of Northiam, Sussex, on 14 March 1645.

Wallis' appointment as Savilian professor of geometry at Oxford on 14 June 1649 must have come as a surprise to many; his accomplishments thus far, with one exception, had had little to do with mathematics. His predecessor, Peter Turner, was a Royalist who had been dismissed by an order of Parliament; Wallis had rendered valuable services not only as a secretary to the Assembly of Divines but also by his skill in deciphering captured coded letters for the Parliamentarians. Few people in 1649 could have foreseen that within a few years the thirty-two-year-old theologian would become one of the leading mathematicians of his time.

This appointment determined Wallis' career; he held the chair until his death more than half a century later. In addition, in 1657–1658 he was elected—by a somewhat doubtful procedure—custos arch.varum (keeper of the archives) to the university, an office he also held for life. In 1654 he had been admitted doctor of divinity. At the Restoration Wallis was confirmed in his offices for having possessed the courage to sign the remonstrance against the execution of King Charles I; he also received the title of royal chaplain to Charles II. When in 1692 Queen Mary II offered Wallis the deanery of Hereford, he declined, hinting that favors for his son and his son-in-law Blencowe would be more welcome signs of recognition of his services to his country.

These achievements include the mathematical works, helping found the Royal Society; his work in the decipherment of code letters for the government; logic; teaching deaf mutes to speak and the related grammatical and phonetical writings; archival studies and his assistance to the university in legal affairs; theological activities as a preacher and author of treatises and books; and the editions (many of them first editions) of mathematical and musical manuscripts of ancient Greek authors.

The first two decades of the Savilian professorship were the most creative period in Wallis' life. He later increasingly turned to editing works of other scientists (J. Horrox, W. Oughtred, and Greek authors) and his own earlier works, and to the preparation of historical and theological discourses. His *Opera mathematica* appeared between 1693 and 1699, financed by and printed at the university.

Wallis enjoyed vigorous health throughout his life. His powers of intellect were remarkable, and he was renowned for his skill in public disputations. But he also possessed a highly contentious disposition and became involved in many violent controversies—the more so since modesty does not seem to have been one of his virtues. Nevertheless he had many devoted friends. It was for

Thomas Smith, vice-president of Magdalen College, Oxford, and librarian at the Cottonian Library, London, that Wallis wrote his autobiography in 1697; and Samuel Pepys commissioned Sir Godfrey Kneller to paint a full-length portrait of "that great man and my most honoured friend, Dr. Wallis, to be lodged as an humble present of mine (though a Cambridge-man) to my dear Aunt the University of Oxford."[2] Wallis was interred in St. Mary's, the university church, and an epitaph by his son was placed in the wall near his burial place: "Joannes Wallis, S.T.P., Geometriae Professor Savilianus, et Custos Archivarum Oxon. Hic dormit. Opera reliquit immortalia . . ." ("Here sleeps John Wallis, Doctor of Theology, Savilian Professor of Geometry, and Keeper of the Oxford Archives. He left immortal works. . . ."[3])

Mathematics. Wallis reports in his *Algebra*[4] that his interest in mathematics (beyond the little that he may have learned at Cambridge) was first aroused in 1647 or 1648, when he chanced upon a copy of William Oughtred's *Clavis mathematicae*. After having mastered it in a few weeks, he rediscovered Cardano's solution of the cubic equation (not given by Oughtred) and, continuing where Oughtred had left off, composed in 1648 a *Treatise of Angular Sections*, which remained unpublished until 1685. In the same year, at the request of Cambridge professor of mathematics John Smith, the Platonist (1618–1652), he gave an explanation of Descartes's treatment of the fourth-degree equation. The basic idea, to write the equation as a product of two quadratic factors, could be derived from Harriot's *Artis analyticae praxis* (published posthumously in 1631); yet Wallis repeatedly claimed not to have known this book in 1648. Such was the total evidence of his mathematical talents that Wallis presented when he was made Savilian professor of geometry in 1649.

With a rare energy and perseverance, he now took up the systematic study of all the major mathematical literature available to him in the Savilian and the Bodleian libraries in Oxford. According to the statutes of his chair, Wallis had to give public lectures on the thirteen books of Euclid, on the *Conics* of Apollonius, and on all of Archimedes' work. He was also to offer introductory courses in practical and theoretical arithmetic—with a free choice of textbooks therein. Lectures on other subjects such as cosmography, plane and spherical trigonometry, applied geometry, mechanics, and the theory of music were suggested but not obligatory according to the statutes.

An outcome of his elementary lectures was the *Mathesis universalis, seu opus arithmeticum* (1657). Its treatment of notation, including a historical survey, stressed the great advantages of a suggestive and unified symbolism; yet the influence of Oughtred (who had developed a rather special notation) sometimes makes itself felt—to no great advantage. On the whole, this work reflects the rather weak state of mathematical learning in the universities at the time.

In the treatise *De sectionibus conicis* (1655) Wallis dealt with a classical subject in a new way.[5] He considered the conic sections merely as plane curves, once he had obtained them by sections of a cone, and subjected them to the analytical treatment introduced by Descartes rather than to the traditional synthetic approach. In addition, he employed infinitesimals in the sense of Cavalieri and Torricelli. Here he also first introduced the sign for infinity and used $1/\infty$ to represent, for example, the height of an infinitely small triangle. Although Mydorge in adherence to the ancient methods had obtained a certain simplification of the treatment in 1631, Wallis was rather proud of his achievement; he may not have known Mydorge's *De sectionibus conicis* at the time of writing. Shortly afterward, in 1659, Jan de Witt's valuable treatise *Elementa curvarum linearum*, also employing the analytic symbolism, appeared in Amsterdam. Yet, on the whole, the new viewpoint was accepted only slowly by mathematicians.

Together with his conic sections Wallis published the book on which his fame as a mathematician is grounded, *Arithmetica infinitorum*; the title page is dated 1656, but printing had been completed in the summer of 1655. It resulted mainly from his study of Torricelli's *Opera geometrica* (1644), for Cavalieri's basic work on the methods of indivisibles was unavailable. At first Wallis' attempts to apply these methods to the quadrature of the circle met with failure; and not even a study of the voluminous *Opus geometricum* (1647) of Gregory of St. Vincent, which was devoted to this subject, would help. But then, by an ingenious and daring sequence of interpolations, he produced his famous result[6]

$$\frac{4}{\pi} = \frac{3}{2} \cdot \frac{3}{4} \cdot \frac{5}{4} \cdot \frac{5}{6} \cdot \frac{7}{6} \cdots .$$

Although the method was mistrusted by such eminent mathematicians as Fermat and Huygens, the result was ascertained by numerical computation. Wallis' main interest lay not with the demonstration, but with the investigation. Actually searching for the value of

$$\int_0^1 (1 - x^2)^{\frac{1}{2}}\, dx = \frac{\pi}{4},$$

he considered the generalized integral

$$I(k, n) = \int_0^1 (1 - x^{1/k})^n\, dx.$$

Its reciprocal $1 : I(k, n)$ he tabulated first for integral values of k and n (receiving the symmetric array of the binomical coefficients or figurated numbers), then for the fractions $k = \frac{1}{2}, \frac{3}{2}, \frac{5}{2}, \cdots$; for, with $k = n = 1/2$, this should yield $1 : I\left(\frac{1}{2}, \frac{1}{2}\right) = \frac{4}{\pi}$, for which he wrote the symbol $\square$. Then each second value of the row and column which met at $\square$ was a certain (fractional) multiple of $\square$. Assuming that all rows and columns in his table would continually increase, Wallis was able to derive two sequences of upper and lower bounds for $\square$, respectively. When these sequences are continued indefinitely, they yield his famous infinite product. William Brouncker soon transformed it into a regular continued fraction, which Wallis included in his book.

Wallis' method of interpolation—he himself gave it this name, which has become a *terminus technicus*—is based on the assumption of continuity, and, incidentally, seems closely related to the procedure he had to apply when he deciphered coded letters. To preserve this continuity and thereby the underlying mathematical law in his table, Wallis went to the utmost limit. He admitted fractional multiples of the type $A \cdot \frac{0}{1} \cdot \frac{2}{3} \cdot \frac{4}{5} \cdot \frac{6}{7} \cdots$, claiming that A here should be infinite so that the value of the product was a finite number. One must emphasize the kind of "functional thinking" revealed here—not on the basis of geometric curves but of sequences of numerical expressions, that is, tabulated functions.

There are many more remarkable results of a related nature in the *Arithmetica infinitorum*, in the tracts on the cycloid and the cissoid, and in the *Mechanica*.[7] The integral $I(k, n)$ may in fact, by the substitution $x \rightarrow y^k$, be transformed into the normal form of the beta integral. He soon derived analytically the integral for the arc length of an ellipse and reduced other integrals to the elliptic one. But more important than the individual problems that Wallis mastered was the novelty of his approach—his analytic viewpoint, in contrast to the traditional geometric one—at a time when the symbolism of analysis had not yet been properly developed. The best documentation of his new "functional thinking" is provided in the *Arithmetica infinitorum*; he finally plots the graphs of the family of functions the values of which he had so far evaluated only for a sequence of distinct points. There he considers not so much the single curves as the sequence of them, since the parameter changes from one integral value to the next. The answer to his question of what the equations of these curves would be for fractional values of the parameter—another type of interpolation and example of "continuous thinking"—was given by Euler by means of the gamma function, the generalized factorial.

The *Arithmetica infinitorum* exerted a singularly important effect on Newton when he studied it in the winter of 1664–1665.[8] Newton generalized even more than Wallis by keeping the upper limit of the integrals $I(k, n)$ variable. He thus arrived at the binomial theorem by way of Wallisian interpolation procedures. In a few cases the binomial expansion could be checked by algebraic division and root extraction; but, just as in the case of Wallis' product, a rigorous justification had to wait until mathematical techniques had been much refined.

The publication of the *Arithmetica infinitorum* immediately provoked a mathematical challenge from Fermat. He directed "to Wallis and the other English mathematicians," some numerical questions: To find a cube, which added to all its aliquot parts will make a square (such as $7^3 + 7^2 + 7 + 1 = 20^2$), and to find a square number, which added to all its aliquot parts, will make a cube.[9] Fermat, lawyer and councillor of the *parlement* in Toulouse, had added: "We await these solutions, which, if England or Belgic or Celtic Gaul do not produce, Narbonese Gaul will." Besides Wallis, Brouncker, later the first president of the Royal Society, participated in the contest on the side of the English. On the Continent, Frenicle de Bessy applied his great skill in handling large numbers. Wallis at first highly underestimated the difficulty as well as the theoretical foundation of Fermat's questions; and Fermat added further problems in 1657–1658. Wallis maintained the number 1 to be a valid solution, and in return drew up some superficially similar questions. His method of solution was more or less that of trial and error, based on intelligent guessing, and in some ways was not unrelated to the procedures employed in his *Arithmetica infinitorum*. Until the end of his life Wallis had no idea of the number-theoretical insights that Fermat had obtained—nor could he, since his challenger did not reveal them. Afraid that the French mathematicians might reap all the glory from this contest, Wallis obtained permission to publish the letters: the *Commercium epistolicum* appeared in 1658. The last chapter of his *Discourse of Combinations, Alternations, and Aliquot Parts* (1685) deals with "Monsieur Fermat's Problems Concerning Divisors and Aliquot Parts." Finally, among his manuscripts there are also a number of attempts to solve some of Fermat's problems, including the "Theorema Fermatianum Negativum" that $a^3 + b^3 = c^3$ is not possible in integral or rational numbers and another negative theorem that there does not exist a right triangle with square area.[10]

But number theory had no special appeal to Wallis—nor to any other mathematician of the time, Frenicle excepted. This was so partly because it was hardly applicable, as Wallis himself emphasized and partly because it did not suit the taste of seventeenth- and eighteenth-century mathematicians, Euler being a notable exception. Fermat, who had glimpsed the treasures of number theory and had recognized its intrinsic mathematical value, did little to introduce his fellow mathematicians to the subject. Thus the general judgment about the contest had to be based on Wallis' *Commercium epistolicum*, and the editor did not hesitate to underline the achievements he and Brouncker had made. No wonder that his fame was now firmly established throughout Europe.

Wallis also participated in the competition in which Pascal in the summer of 1658 asked for quadratures, cubatures, and centers of gravity of certain figures limited by cycloidal arcs.[11] Neither Wallis nor Lalouvère, who also competed for the prize, satisfied Pascal, and no prize was awarded. This was not quite fair, and in 1659 Wallis replied with *Tractatus duo . . . de cycloide et . . . de cissoide*. Here, as well as in the second part of his voluminous *Mechanica, sive de motu tractatus geometricus* (1669–1671), he again relied on his analytic methods. This second part, on the calculation of centers of gravity, is the major part of the *Mechanica*, and in it Wallis carried on the analytical investigations of the 1650's.

The first part deals with various forms of motion in a strictly "geometrical," that is, Euclidean, manner, starting with definitions followed by propositions. The motion of bodies under the action of gravity is covered in particular. The final chapter of the first part is devoted to a treatment of the balance and introduces the idea of moment, which is essential for the inquiries into the centers of gravity. In the third part, Wallis returns not only to

the elementary machines, according to ancient tradition, but above all to a thorough treatment of the problems on percussion. In 1668 percussion and impact were a major topic of discussion at the Royal Society, and Wallis, Wren, and Huygens submitted papers.[12] In the *Mechanica*, Wallis extended his investigations, studying the behavior of both elastic and inelastic bodies. Although in style and subject matter it is not a uniform book, at the time it certainly was one of the most important and comprehensive in its field. It represents a major advance in the mathematization of mechanics, but it was superseded in 1687 by a much greater one—Newton's *Principia*.

Wallis' last great mathematical book was *Treatise of Algebra, Both Historical and Practical* (1685), the fruit of many years' labor.[13] As its title suggests, it was to combine a full exposition of algebra with its history, a feat never previously attempted by any author. The book was Wallis' only major mathematical work to be published in the vernacular. (In 1693 an augmented Latin translation was issued as vol. II of his *Opera mathematica*.)

Of the 100 chapters, the first fourteen trace the history of the subject up to the time of Viète, with emphasis on the development of mathematical notation. The subsequent practical introduction to algebra (chapters 15–63) was based almost entirely on Oughtred's *Clavis mathematicae*, Harriot's *Artis analyticae praxis*, and *An Introduction to Algebra* (1668), Thomas Brancker's translation of J. H. Rahn's *Teutsche Algebra* (1659), with numerous additions by John Pell, Rahn's former teacher. This fact alone signals the great bias Wallis had developed in favor of his countrymen. It becomes even more obvious in the passages where the author claimed that Descartes had obtained his algebraical knowledge from Harriot. Criticisms of Wallis' one-sided account were raised immediately and have continued since. After an insertion concerning the application of algebra to geometry and geometrical interpretations of algebraic facts (chapters 64–72, including an attempt to give a representation of imaginary numbers),[14] Wallis devoted the final twenty-eight chapters to a subject that one would hardly look for in a book on algebra today: a discussion of the methods of exhaustion and of indivisibles, again with reference to the *Arithmetica infinitorum*. Thus the new methods were still considered as an extension of an old subject rather than as a wholly new field of mathematics.

The *Algebra* also includes an exposition of the method of infinite series and the first printed account, much augmented in the second edition, of some of Newton's pioneering results. Wallis had long been afraid that foreigners might claim the glory of Newton's achievements by publishing some of his ideas as their own before Newton himself had done so. He therefore repeatedly warned his younger colleague at Cambridge not to delay but to leave perfection of his methods to later editions.[15] (Volume III of the *Opera* [1699] contains an *Epistolarum collectio*, of which the most important part is the correspondence between Newton and Leibniz, in particular Newton's famous "Epistola prior" and "Epistola posterior" of 1676.)

Apart from some editions of Greek mathematical classics, the *Algebra* with its several supplementary treatises—*Cono-Cuneus* (a study in analytic three-dimensional geometry), *Angular Sections*,[16] *Angle of Contact*, and *Combinations, Alternations, and Aliquot Parts*—marked the end of the stream of mathematical works. Even without the polemics against Hobbes and some minor pieces, they fill three large volumes.

Wallis helped shape over half a century of mathematics in England. He bore the greatest share of all the efforts made during this time to raise mathematics to the eminence it enjoyed on the Continent. The center of mathematical research and of the "new science" in Galileo's time lay in Italy. It then shifted northward, especially to France and the Netherlands. Because of Wallis' preparative work and Newton's genius, it rested in Britain for a while, until through the influence of Leibniz, the Bernoullis, and Euler it moved back to the Continent.

Nonmathematical Work. Wallis first exhibited his mental powers early in the Civil War (1642 or 1643), when by chance he was shown a letter written in cipher and succeeded in decoding it within a few hours.[17] Because more letters were given to him by the Parliamentarians, rumors were later spread that he had deciphered important royal letters that had fallen into their hands. Wallis strenuously denied the accusation, and it is very unlikely that he revealed anything harmful to the royal family or the public safety—if indeed he came across such information. On the contrary, the confirmation of his offices at the Restoration may well have been a sign of gratitude to him by Charles II. For many years Wallis continued to decipher intercepted letters for the government, especially after the Revolution. In old age he taught the art to his grandson William Blencowe but refused to disclose it when Leibniz on behalf of his government requested information on it.

In his autobiography, written in January 1697, when he was over eighty, Wallis referred to one of his first successes more than half a century earlier:

> Being encouraged by this success, beyond expectation; I afterwards ventured on many others (some of more, some of less difficulty) and scarce missed of any that I undertook, for many years, during our civil Wars, and afterwards. But of late years, *the French Methods of Cipher* are grown so intricate beyond what it was wont to be, that I have failed of many; tho' I did have master'd divers of them.[18]

Of great importance for much of his later scientific work was his introduction, while living in London, to a group interested in the "new" natural and experimental sciences—the circle from which the Royal Society emerged soon after the Restoration.[19] To Wallis we owe one of the few reports on those early meetings that give direct evidence.

> About the year 1645, while I lived in *London* (at a time, when, by our Civil Wars, Academical Studies were much interrupted in both our Universities:) beside the Conversation of divers eminent Divines, as to matters Theological; I had the opportunity of being acquainted with divers worthy Persons, inquisitive into Natural Philosophy, and other parts of Humane Learning; and Particularly of what hath been called the *New Philosophy* or *Experimental Philosophy*.
>
> We did by agreement, divers of us, meet weekly in *London* on a certain day, to treat and discours of such affairs. . . .
>
> These meetings we held sometimes at *Dr. Goddards* lodgings in *Woodstreet* (or some convenient place near) on occasion of his keeping an Operator in his house, for grinding Glasses for Telescopes and Microscopes; and sometime at a convenient place in *Cheap-side*; sometime at *Gresham College* or some place near adjoyning.
>
> Our business was (precluding matters of Theology and State Affairs) to discours and consider of *Philosophical Enquiries*, and such as related thereunto; as *Physick, Anatomy, Geometry, Astronomy, Navigation, Staticks, Magneticks, Chymicks, Mechanicks,* and *Natural Experiments*; with the State of these Studies, as then cultivated, at home and abroad. We there discoursed of the *Circulation of the Blood, the Valves in the Veins, the Venae Lacteae, the Lymphatick vessels, the Copernican Hypothesis, the Nature of Comets, and New Stars, the Satellites of Jupiter, the Oval Shape* (as it then appeared) *of Saturn, the spots in the Sun, and its Turning on its own Axis, the Inequalities and Selenography of the Moon, the several Phases of Venus and Mercury, the Improvement of Telescopes, and grinding of Glasses for that purpose, the Weight of Air, the Possibility or Impossibility of Vacuities, and Natures Abhorrence*

thereof; the Torricellian Experiment in Quicksilver, the Descent of heavy Bodies, and the degrees of Acceleration therein; and divers other things of like nature. Some of which were then but New Discoveries, and others not so generally known and imbraced, as now they are; With other things appertaining to what hath been called *The New Philosophy;* which from the times of *Galileo* at *Florence,* and *Sr Francis Bacon (Lord Verulam)* in *England,* hath been much cultivated in *Italy, France, Germany,* and other Parts abroad, as well as with us in *England.*

About the year 1648, 1649, some of our company being removed to *Oxford* (first Dr *Wilkins,* then I, and soon after Dr *Goddard*) our company divided. Those in *London* continued to meet there as before (and we with them, when we had occasion to be there;) and those of us at *Oxford* . . . continued such meetings in *Oxford;* and brought those Studies into fashion there. . . .

Those meetings in *London* continued, and (after the Kings Return in 1660) were increased with the accession of divers worthy and Honorable Persons; and were afterwards incorporated by the name of *the Royal Society,* etc. and so continue to this day.

While the Royal Society of London did indeed grow and continue, the Oxford offspring suffered a less happy fate. After a period of decline and interruption it seems to have flourished again in the 1680's when Wallis was elected its president and tried to establish closer contacts with the mother society and similar groups in Scotland. But Oldenburg, secretary of the London society, initiated publication of the *Philosophical Transactions* and thereby provided a more permanent means of scientific exchange than personal intercourse and weekly discussions.[20] Wallis made ample use of the *Transactions;* and between 1666 and 1702 he published more than sixty papers and book reviews. The reviews concerned mathematical books, but the papers were more wide-ranging.[21] One of the leading scientists among the early fellows of the Royal Society, he was also one of the most energetic in promoting it and helping it to achieve its goals, at a time when not a few of these virtuosi were men without a real understanding of the scientific experiments conducted and of the complex theories behind them.

Wallis' most successful work was his *Grammatica linguae anglicanae,* with a *Praxis grammatica* and a treatise, *De loquela,* on the production of the sounds of speech. First published in 1652, the sixth, and last, edition in England appeared in 1765; it was also published on the Continent.

In his *History of Modern Colloquial English,* H. C. Wyld emphasized that Wallis "has consider-able merits as an observer of sounds, he has good powers of discrimination, nor is he led astray by the spelling like all the sixteenth-century grammarians, and Bullokar, Gill, and Butler in the seventeenth."[22] He then continued to discuss some of Wallis' more noteworthy observations. A much more detailed account is given in M. Lehnert's monograph.[23]

Wallis' *Treatise of Speech* formed a useful theoretical foundation for his pioneering attempts to teach deaf-mutes how to speak. In 1661 and 1662 Wallis instructed two young men, Daniel Whaley and Alexander Popham; the latter had previously been taught by Dr. William Holder. Wallis presented Whaley to the Royal Society on 21 May 1662 and in 1670 reported on his instruction of Popham in the *Philosophical Transactions*—failing to mention Holder's teaching.[24] This unfair act eventually (1678) led to a bitter attack by Holder, to which Wallis replied in no less hostile words.[25]

This was one of the many violent quarrels in which Wallis became involved. Although readily inclined to boast of his achievements and to appropriate the ideas of others for further development, he did not always acknowledge his debt to his predecessors. Furthermore he was often carried away by his temper and would reply without restraint to criticism. He thus quarreled with Holder, Henry Stubbe, Lewis Maydwell, and Fermat; and his longest and most bittered dispute, with Thomas Hobbes, dragged on for over a quarter of a century.[26] Despite, or rather because of, his limited mathematical knowledge, Hobbes claimed in 1655 to possess an absolute quadrature of the circle. Somewhat later he also purported to have solved another of the great mathematical problems—the duplication of the cube. Hobbes's chief transgression, however, was in having dared to criticize Wallis' *Arithmetica infinitorum.* The controversy soon degenerated into the most virulent hostility, which gave rise to wild accusations and abusive language. The quarrel ended only with Hobbes's death in 1679. J. F. Scott has suggested that Wallis' relentless attacks may have been partly motivated by Hobbes's increasing influence, especially as author of the *Leviathan,* and by Wallis' fear that Hobbes's teachings would undermine respect for the Christian religion.

As keeper of the archives, Wallis rendered considerable services to his university. In his brief account of Wallis' life, David Gregory said, "He put the records, and other papers belonging to the University that were under his care into such exact order, and managed its lawsuits with such dexterity and success that he quickly convinced all, even those who made the greatest noise against this election, how fitt he was for the post."[27] A successor as keeper, Reginald L. Poole, also praised Wallis' work: "He left his mark on the Archives in numerous transcripts, but above all by the Repertory of the entire collection which he made on the basis of Mr. Twyne's list in 1664 and which continues to this day the standard catalogue."[28] Wallis' catalogue was not replaced until even later in the twentieth century. Although not a practicing musician, Wallis composed some papers on musical theory that were published in the *Philosophical Transactions*,[29] and he edited works on harmony by Ptolemy, Porphyrius, and Bryennius. One of his papers reports his observation of the "trembling" of consonant strings, while others contain a mathematical discussion of the intervals of the musical scale and the resulting need for temperament in tuning an organ or other keyboard instrument. In an appendix to Ptolemy's *Harmonics*, Wallis attempted to explain the surprising effects attributed to ancient music (which he rendered in modern notation); and he also dealt with these effects in a separate paper. Finally he contributed extended remarks on Thomas Salmon's *Proposal to Perform Musick, in Perfect and Mathematical Proportions* (London, 1688), the forerunner of which, *An Essay to the Advancement of Musick* (London, 1672), had aroused great interest as well as conflicting views.

Theology. From 1690 to 1692 Wallis published a series of eight letters and three sermons on the doctrine of the Holy Trinity, directed against the Unitarians. In order to explain this doctrine he introduced an analogous example from mathematics: a cubical body with three dimensions, length, breadth, and height; and compared the mystery of the Trinity with the cube:

> This *longum, latum, profundum,* (Long, Broad, and Tall), is but *One* Cube; of *Three Dimensions,* and yet but *One Body.* And this *Father, Son,* and *Holy-Ghost:* Three Persons, and yet but One God.[30]

Wallis' discourses on the Trinity met with marked approval from various theological quarters. It was even used in Pierre Bayle's famous *Dictionnaire historique et critique* in a note to the article on Abailard. Bayle wished to vindicate Abailard of the charge of Tritheism,[31] which had been raised against him for having used an analogy between the Trinity and the syllogism that consists of proposition, assumption, and conclusion. Just as no-body doubts the orthodoxy of Wallis on the basis of his geometrical example, Bayle argued, there was no reason to attack Abailard for his analogy of the syllogism.

Wallis' sermons and other theological works, often praised for their simple and straightforward language, testify that his religious principles were Calvinist, according to the literal sense of the Church of England. He never denied the Puritanism in which he had grown up, although he remained a loyal member of the official church.

From his student days, Wallis sided with the Parliamentarians, and Cromwell is said to have had a great respect for him. As secretary to the Assembly of Divines at Westminster during the Civil War, Wallis became thoroughly familiar with the controversial issues within the Episcopal Church and between the Church and Parliament. Included in his autobiography is a rather long intercalation about this assembly, which was convened to suggest a new form of church government in place of the episcopacy.[32] His interpretation of proceedings carried on half a century earlier might have been somewhat colored by the actual events that followed. The episcopacy was, after all, not abolished; and Wallis had tried to stay on good terms with the bishops and archbishops. Toward the end of the century he strongly opposed the introduction of the Gregorian calendar in England, considering it a kind of submission to Rome. The new calendar was not in fact adopted in Britain until 1752. Some of Wallis' friends and colleagues in the Royal Society exchanged their university posts for careers in the church, but Wallis himself was never given the opportunity. Obviously his trimming politics had made him not totally acceptable to the monarchy, although he did enjoy signs of royal favor. As he himself expressed it, he was "willing whatever side was upmost, to promote (as I was able) any good design for the true Interest of Religion, of Learning, and the publick good."[33]

NOTES

1. C. J. Scriba, "The Autobiography . . .," 24.
2. J. R. Tanner, ed., *Private Correspondence and Miscellaneous Papers of Samuel Pepys, 1679–1703,* II (London, 1926), 257.
3. "S.T.P." is the usual abbreviation for Doctors of Divinity in inscriptions; Wallis was never created professor of theology.
4. J. Wallis, *Algebra,* ch. 46.
5. See H. Wieleitner, "Die Verdienste."
6. For a more detailed description, see Sir T. P. Nunn, "The Arithmetic"; J. F. Scott, *The Mathematical Work,* ch. 4; and D. T. Whiteside, "Patterns of Mathematical Thought in the Later Seventeenth Century," in *Archives for History of Exact Sciences,* 1 (1961), 179–388, esp. 236–243.

7. See W. Kutta, "Elliptische," and A. Prag, "John Wallis," esp. 391–395.

8. D. T. Whiteside, "Newton's Discovery of the General Binomial Theorem," in *Mathematical Gazette*, **45** (1961), 175–180; and *The Mathematical Papers of Isaac Newton*, D. T. Whiteside, ed., I (Cambridge, 1967), 96–111.

9. See G. Wertheim, "P. Fermats Streit . . . .," and J. E. Hofmann, "Neues über Fermats. . . ."

10. See C. J. Scriba, *Studien . . .*, chs. 2–3.

11. See K. Hara, "Pascal et Wallis . . . ," and J. Hofmann and J. E. Hofmann, "Erste Quadratur der Kissoide," in *Deutsche Mathematik*, **5** (1941), 571–584.

12. See A. R. Hall, "Mechanics and the Royal Society, 1668–1670," in *British Journal for the History of Science*, **3** (1966–1967), 24–38.

13. See J. F. Scott, "John Wallis."

14. See G. Eneström, "Die geometrische Darstellung."

15. See C. J. Scriba, "Neue Dokumente zur Entstehungsgeschichte des Prioritätsstreites zwischen Leibniz und Newton um die Erfindung der Infinitesimalrechnung," in *Akten des Internationalen Leibniz-Kongresses Hannover, 14.–19. November 1966*, II. *Mathematik-Naturwissenschaften* (Wiesbaden, 1969), 69–78.

16. See C. J. Scriba, *Studien*, ch. 1.

17. See D. E. Smith, "John Wallis," and D. Kahn, *The Codebreakers* (New York, 1967), 166–169.

18. See C. J. Scriba, "The Autobiography," 38.

19. Different opinions have been expressed as to whether the Royal Society emerged from the London group described by Wallis or from an independent Oxford group in existence before Wallis came to Oxford in 1649. For a champion of the latter view, see M. Purver, *The Royal Society: Concept and Creation* (London, 1967). A brief review of this is C. J. Scriba, "Zur Entstehung der Royal Society," in *Sudhoffs Archiv für Geschichte der Medizin und der Naturwissenschaften*, **52** (1968), 269–271. There is an extended debate, in three articles by P. M. Rattansi, C. Hill, and A. R. Hall and M. B. Hall, in *Notes and Records. Royal Society of London*, **23** (1968), 129–168, where further references are given. It seems to be without doubt that the London group cannot be ignored. Wallis' report is taken from "The Autobiography," 39–40.

20. Wallis' correspondence with Oldenburg is printed in *The Correspondence of Henry Oldenburg*, A. R. Hall and M. Boas Hall, eds. (Madison, Wis., 1965–).

21 For a not quite complete list of Wallis' publications in the *Philosophical Transactions of the Royal Society*, see J. F. Scott, *The Mathematical Work*, 231–233; paper no. 62 is not by Wallis.

22. H. C. Wyld, *A History of Modern Colloquial English*, 3rd ed. (Oxford, 1936; repr. 1953), 170.

23. M. Lehnert, in *Die Grammatik*, criticizes the older work by L. Morel, *De Johannis Wallisii*, as insufficient. See also A. B. Melchior, "Sir Thomas Smith and John Wallis," in *English Studies*, **53** (1972), and his review of John Wallis, "Grammar of the English Language," in *English Studies*, **55** (1974), 83–85.

24. *Philosophical Transactions of the Royal Society*, **5**, no. 61 (18 July 1670), 1087–1097 (pagination repeated).

25. W. Holder, *A Supplement*; J. Wallis, *A Defense*.

26. See J. F. Scott, *The Mathematical Work*, ch. 10.

27. Bodleian Library Oxford, MS Smith 31, p. 58; J. Collier, *A Supplement*.

28. R. L. Poole, *A Lecture on the History of the University Archives* (Oxford, 1912), 25.

29. *Philosophical Transactions of the Royal Society*, **12**, no. 134 (23 Apr. 1677), 839–842; **20**, no. 238 (Mar. 1698), 80–84; **20**, no. 242 (July 1698), 249–256; **20**, no. 243 (Aug. 1698), 297–303. See L. S. Lloyd, "Musical Theory in the Early *Philosophical Transactions*," in *Notes and Records. Royal Society of London*, **3** (1940–1941), 149–157.

30. Quoted from R. C. Archibald, "Wallis on the Trinity," 36.

31. See the query by E. H. Neville, "Wallis on the Trinity," 197, who quotes the 5th ed., I (Amsterdam, 1734), 30. In the new ed. (Paris, 1820), it is I, 59–60, note M.

32. See Scriba, "The Autobiography," 31–37.

33. *Ibid.*, 43.

BIBLIOGRAPHY

I. ORIGINAL WORKS. Most of Wallis' publications (including pamphlets and sermons) are listed in the British Museum catalog, but a complete bibliography is still a desideratum. Wallis collected his more important books and some articles in his *Opera mathematica*, 3 vols. (Oxford, 1693–1699), repr. with intro. by C. J. Scriba (Hildesheim–New York, 1972). The table of contents in vol. I contains a list of books that were originally not planned for inclusion in the *Opera mathematica*, which was to consist of two volumes only. A selection of mathematical and nonmathematical works taken from this list and augmented by additional material is included in vol. III.

The *Opera mathematica* should not be confused with the *Operum mathematicorum pars prima* and *pars secunda*, published in 1657 and 1656 [sic], respectively. Vol. I contains *Oratio inauguralis*; *Mathesis universalis, sive arithmeticum opus integrum*; *Adversus Meibomii De proportionibus dialogus, tractatus elenctibus*; and *M. Mersenni locus notatur*. Vol. II contains *De angulo contactus et semicirculo disquisitio geometrica*; *De sectionibus conicis, nova methodo expositis, tractatus*; *Arithmetica infinitorum* (already printed and in some copies distributed in 1655), and the brief *Eclipsis solaris observatio*.

Works cited in the text and in the notes include the reply to W. Holder, *A Supplement to the Philosophical Transactions of July 1670, With Some Reflexions on Dr. John Wallis, His Letter There Inserted* (London, 1678), which Wallis issued under the title *A Defence of the Royal Society, and the Philosophical Transactions, Particularly Those of July 1670, in Answer to the Cavils of Dr. William Holder* (London, 1678); and the voluminous *Treatise of Algebra, Both Historical and Practical, Showing the Original, Progress, and Advancement Thereof, From Time to Time; and by What Steps It Hath Attained to the Height at Which Now It Is* (London, 1685; enl. Latin version in vol. II of the *Opera mathematica*). There is a facs. ed. of the *Grammatica linguae anglicanae* of 1653 (Menston, 1969), and a new ed. with translation and commentary by J. A. Kemp, *Grammar of the English Language* (London, 1972).

Wallis' autobiography was reprinted in C. J. Scriba, "The Autobiography of John Wallis, F.R.S.," in *Notes and Records. Royal Society of London*, **25** (1970), 17–46; this includes a survey of other early biographies of Wallis, including that by David Gregory, which is printed in J. Collier, *A Supplement to the Great Historical, Geographical, Genealogical and Poetical Dictionary . . . Together With a Continuation From the Year*

1688, to 1705, by Another Hand (London, 1705; 2nd ed., 1727).

II. SECONDARY LITERATURE. The book-length monographs on Wallis the mathematician are J. F. Scott, *The Mathematical Work of John Wallis, D.D., F.R.S. (1616–1703)* (London, 1938); and C. J. Scriba, *Studien zur Mathematik des John Wallis (1616–1703). Winkelteilungen, Kombinationslehre und zahlentheoretische Probleme* (Wiesbaden, 1966). Scott surveys Wallis' life and his main published mathematical works; Scriba concentrates on the topics stated in his title, making use also of unpublished MSS, and includes a list of books owned by Wallis, which are now in the Bodleian, as well as a brief survey of the MS material. An index to the correspondence is C. J. Scriba, "A Tentative Index of the Correspondence of John Wallis, F.R.S.," in *Notes and Records. Royal Society of London*, 22 (1967), 58–93.

Wallis the grammarian and phonetician is the subject of L. Morel, *De Johannis Wallisii grammatica linguae anglicanae et tractatu de loquela thesis* (Paris, 1895), which is superseded by M. Lehnert, *Die Grammatik des englischen Sprachmeisters John Wallis (1616–1703)* (Wrocław, 1936). The following articles deal with Wallis or his work: R. C. Archibald, "Wallis on the Trinity," in *American Mathematical Monthly*, 43 (1936), 35–37, and in *Scripta mathematica*, 4 (1936), 202; L. I. Cherkalova, "Sostavnye otnoshenia u Vallisa," in *Doklady na nauchnykh konferentsiakh*, 2, no. 3 (1964), 153–160; G. Eneström, "Die geometrische Darstellung imaginärer Grössen bei Wallis," in *Bibliotheca mathematica*, 3rd ser., 7 (1906–1907), 263–269; K. Hara, "Pascal et Wallis au sujet de la cycloïde," in *Annals of the Japanese Association of the Philosophy of Science*, 3 (1969), 166–187; J. E. Hofmann, "Neues über Fermats zahlentheoretische Herausforderungen von 1657," in *Abhandlungen der Preussischen Akademie der Wissenschaften*, Math. naturwiss. Kl. (1943), no. 9 (Berlin, 1944); M. Koppe, "Die Bestimmung sämtlicher Näherungsbrüche einer Zahlengrösse bei John Wallis (1672)," in *Sitzungsberichte der Berliner mathematischen Gesellschaft*, 2 (1903), 56–60; F. D. Kramar, "Integratsionnye metody Dzhona Vallisa," in *Istoriko-matematicheskie issledovaniya*, 14 (1961), 11–100; W. Kutta, "Elliptische und andere Integrale bei Wallis," in *Bibliotheca mathematica*, 3rd ser., 2 (1901), 230–234; E. H. Neville, "Wallis on the Trinity," in *Scripta mathematica*, 2 (1934), 197; T. F. Nikonova, "Pervy opyt postroeni istorii algebry anglyskim matematikom Dzhonom Vallisom," in *Uchenye zapiski. Moskovskoi oblastnoi pedagogicheskii institut*, 202 (1968), 379–392; T. P. Nunn, "The Arithmetic of Infinites," in *Mathematical Gazette*, 5 (1910–1911), 345–357, 378–386; H. C. Plummer, "Jeremiah Horrocks and his *Opera posthuma*," in *Notes and Records. Royal Society of London*, 3 (1940–1941), 39–52. Wallis was instrumental in selecting the material for the posthumous ed. of Horrocks' astronomical work.

See also A. Prag, "John Wallis. 1616–1703. Zur Ideengeschichte der Mathematik im 17. Jahrhundert," in

Quellen und Studien zur Geschichte der Mathematik, Astronomie und Physik, Abt. B, 1 (1931), 381–412, mainly devoted to the *Arithmetica infinitorum* and the *Algebra*, but with many astute remarks on the general state of seventeenth-century mathematics; J. F. Scott, "John Wallis as a Historian of Mathematics," in *Annals of Science*, 1 (1936), 335–357; and "The Reverend John Wallis, F.R.S. (1616–1703)," in *Notes and Records. Royal Society of London*, 15 (1960), 57–67, with selected bibliography by D. T. Whiteside, 66–67; C. J. Scriba, "Wallis and Harriot," in *Centaurus*, 10 (1964), 248–257; "John Wallis' *Treatise of Angular Sections* and Thâbit ibn Qurra's Generalization of the Pythagorean Theorem," in *Isis*, 57 (1966), 56–66; "Das Problem des Prinzen Ruprecht von der Pfalz," in *Praxis der Mathematik*, 10 (1968), 241–246; "Wie läuft Wasser aus einem Gefäss? Eine mathematisch-physikalische Aufzeichnung von John Wallis aus dem Jahr 1667," in *Sudhoffs Archiv*, 52 (1968), 193–210; and "Eine mathematische Festvorlesung vor 300 Jahren," in *Janus*, 56 (1969), 182–190; D. E. Smith, "John Wallis as a Cryptographer," in *Bulletin of the American Mathematical Society*, 24 (1917), 82–96; L. Tenca, "Giovanni Wallis e gli italiani," in *Bollettino dell' Unione matematica italiana*, 3rd ser., 10 (1955), 412–418; G. Wertheim, "P. Fermats Streit mit J. Wallis," in *Abhandlungen zur Geschichte der Mathematik*, 9 (1899), 555–576; H. Wieleitner, "Die Verdienste von John Wallis um die analytische Geometrie," in *Weltall*, 29 (1929–1930), 56–60; and G. U. Yule, "John Wallis, D.D., F.R.S. 1616–1703," in *Notes and Records. Royal Society of London*, 2 (1939), 74–82.

CHRISTOPH J. SCRIBA

WANG, HSIEN CHUNG (*b.* Peking [Beijing], China, 18 April 1918; *d.* New York City, 25 June 1978)

H. C. Wang was a distinguished and versatile mathematician who made important contributions to algebraic topology, Lie groups and their homogeneous spaces, and discrete subgroups of Lie groups. Wang came from a family with an impressive intellectual and scholarly tradition. His great-grandfather, Wang I Rong (1845–1900), was a famous archaeologist and president of the Imperial Academy who, with his wife, committed a glorious suicide, that is, suicide as a protest, when foreign troops entered Peking during the Boxer Rebellion. His eldest brother, Wang Xian Jun, became a professor of philosophy and logic at Peking University. Another elder brother, Wang Xian Zhao, is a well-known meteorologist, and his elder sister, Wang Xian Tian, is a professor at the Institute of Psychology of the Academia Sinica (PRC).

Upon graduation from Nankai High School in Tientsin, Wang entered Tsing Hua University in Peking in 1936 as a student of physics. After the Japanese invasion in July 1937 the university fled to Kunming in southwest China and merged with Nankai and Peking universities. After a difficult journey of almost a year, Wang rejoined the university and resumed his studies, changing his field to mathematics. He graduated in 1941 and began graduate work under Shiing Shen Chern, one of the leading differential geometers of the twentieth century. By 1944 he had obtained an M.A. degree and written his first research paper. After a year of high school teaching he won a British Council scholarship and set sail for England, where he studied first at Sheffield, and then at Manchester under M. H. A. Newman. By this time Wang was a productive research mathematician and had written about a dozen papers, including two of his most important ones. In the first of these he discovered an important exact sequence (the Wang sequence) involving the homology groups associated with fiber bundles over spheres. It was used in Leray's work on spectral sequences. In the second he gave an essentially complete solution to a problem arising from the work of Hopf and Samelson: determine the closed subgroups of maximum rank of a compact Lie group G.

After receiving a Ph.D. from Manchester in 1948, Wang returned to China as a research fellow of the Institute of Mathematics of the Academia Sinica (Chinese National Academy of Science), and followed the institute to Taiwan shortly thereafter. In the fall of 1949 he became a lecturer at Louisiana State University and began a long, fruitful career in the United States.

During his two years at Baton Rouge he wrote several more papers, among them his beautiful paper on two-point homogeneous spaces. In this paper he showed that a connected, compact metric space E, whose group of isometries carries a pair of points (p, q) to any pair (p', q') the same distance apart, is, in fact, a homogeneous space of a compact Lie group. Using this information he was able to enumerate all such spaces. Even in the noncompact case he obtained some results, later completed by J. Tits.

In the fall of 1951 he was invited for his first one-year appointment to the Institute for Advanced Study in Princeton, New Jersey, after which he was appointed for two years at Alabama Polytechnic Institute, followed again by a year (1954–1955) at the Institute for Advanced Study. It was during this period that he wrote a basic and important paper characterizing and classifying homogeneous complex manifolds, one of his works most often cited.

This was a very difficult time to secure employment in mathematics, especially for immigrants. Although this changed drastically by the late 1950's, it was still several years before Wang obtained a permanent position. The years from 1955 to 1957 were spent at the University of Washington in Seattle and then at Columbia University in New York. In 1956 he married Lung Hsien (Lucy) Kuan. His first tenured position, at Northwestern University, came in 1957; he was made a full professor there the following year.

In 1958, in recognition of the importance of his work, Wang was invited to address the quadrennial International Mathematical Congress at Edinburgh, and in 1960 he was awarded a Guggenheim Fellowship to spend another year at the Institute for Advanced Study. At about this time he broke new ground in his research with an important study of transformation groups of $n-$ spheres with an orbit of dimension $n - 1$. This paper involves some clever and original ideas, as well as some formidable computations, and is a major departure from his earlier work.

As early as 1955 Wang had become interested in discrete subgroups of Lie groups, and in 1956 he published his first paper on this subject. This now became his major research area until the end of his career, resulting in several further important articles.

In 1965 and 1966 Wang spent a fourth year at the Institute for Advanced Study and then accepted a position at Cornell University, which he held until his death. During his tenure there, as a result of the rapprochement between the United States and the People's Republic of China, he was at last able to visit his family and friends. He went to China again in 1973 after a sabbatical year in England at the University of Warwick, this time with his wife and three daughters, and he returned for a third time in 1977. A fourth visit was being planned at the time of his death.

Wang's last paper was published in 1973, after which his research was much curtailed because of his anxiety for his wife, who had developed cancer. His teaching and other mathematical and administrative activities continued unabated, however, and he played an important role in the department at Cornell. He was very much liked there, as everywhere, for his modesty, generosity, kindness, and courtesy. He was a fine teacher and lecturer, and he guided several students to Ph.D.s and subsequent productive careers. He enjoyed excellent health until he was suddenly stricken with leukemia in June 1978. He succumbed within weeks, to be survived for only a few months by his wife.

BIBLIOGRAPHY

I. ORIGINAL WORKS. "The Homology Groups of the Fibre Bundles over a Sphere," in *Duke Mathematical Journal*, **16** (1949), 33–38; "Homogeneous Space with Non-vanishing Euler Characteristics," in *Annals of Mathematics*, **50** (1949), 925–953; "Two-point Homogeneous Spaces," *ibid.*, **55** (1952), 177–191; "Closed Manifolds with Homogeneous Complex Structure," in *American Journal of Mathematics*, **76** (1954), 1–32; "Compact Transformation Groups of S^n with an $(n - 1)$-Dimensional Orbit," *ibid.*, **82** (1960), 698–748; "Topics on Totally Discontinuous Groups," in W. M. Boothby and G. Weiss, eds., *Symmetric Spaces* (New York, 1972), 459–487.

II. SECONDARY LITERATURE. A memorial volume of the *Bulletin of the Institute of Mathematics, Academia Sinica*, **8** (1980), contains a discussion of Wang's life by S. T. Hu and of his work by W. M. Boothby, S. S. Chern, and S. P. Wang.

WILLIAM M. BOOTHBY

WANGERIN, ALBERT (*b.* Greiffenberg, Pomerania, Germany, 18 November 1844; *d.* Halle, Germany, 25 October 1933)

Wangerin studied mathematics and physics from 1862 to 1866 at the universities of Halle and Königsberg, receiving the Ph.D. from the latter in 1866. Until 1876 he taught in high schools in Posen (now Poznan, Poland) and Berlin. He began to teach on the university level at Easter 1876, when he assumed the post of extraordinary professor at the University of Berlin. In 1882 he was named full professor at the University of Halle, where he remained until his retirement in 1919.

At Königsberg, Wangerin studied under Richelot, a supporter of the Jacobian tradition, and under Franz Neumann. It was Neumann who suggested the subject of his dissertation, and Wangerin later wrote a book (1907) and a highly appreciative article on his former teacher. Wangerin's admiration for Neumann remained an important influence on his choice of research problems. He became an expert on potential theory, spherical functions, and the fields of mathematical physics related to these subjects. For example, in one of his papers he calculated the potential of certain ovaloids and surfaces of revolution. Wangerin also worked, although less intensely, in differential geometry. In 1894 he wrote an article showing how to determine many bending surfaces of a given surface of revolution of constant curvature without knowing its geodetic lines.

Wangerin's importance, however, does not lie in the authorship of enduring scientific works but, rather, in his astonishingly varied activities as university teacher, textbook author, contributor to encyclopedias and journals, editor of historical writings, and president of a scientific academy. While at Berlin he directed his lectures to a fairly broad audience, and even at Halle he continued to be greatly interested in the training of high school teachers. He also wrote a two-volume work on potential theory and spherical functions for the series Sammlung Schubert.

Wangerin wrote two articles for *Encyklopädie der mathematischen Wissenschaften*. The first (1904) deals with the theory of spherical and related functions, especially Lamé and Bessel functions. The second, "Optik; ältere Theorien" (1907), appeared in the physics volume of the *Encyklopädie*. In it Wangerin displays a familiarity with the history of physical theory that is unusual for a mathematician. His sensitivity to historical questions evokes his study, four decades earlier, under Neumann. Wangerin's historical interests are also evident in his editing of works by Gauss, Euler, Lambert, and Lagrange for *Ostwalds Klassiker der exakten Wissenschaften*.

From 1869 to 1924 Wangerin was a coeditor of *Fortschritte der Mathematik*, then the only periodical devoted to reviewing mathematical literature. In this capacity he reviewed almost all the works in his special field published during this period. For 1906 to 1921 Wangerin was president of the Deutsche Akademie der Naturforscher Leopoldina in Halle.

BIBLIOGRAPHY

Wangerin's writings include "Über die Abwicklung von Flächen konstanten Krümmungsmasses sowie einiger anderer Flächen aufeinander," in *Festschrift zur 200-jährigen Jubelfeier der Universität Halle* (Halle, 1894), 1–21; "Theorie der Kugelfunktionen und der verwandten Funktionen, insbesondere der Laméschen und Besselschen (Theorie spezieller, durch lineare Differentialgleichungen definierter, Funktionen)," in *Encyklopädie der mathematischen Wissenschaften*, II, pt. 1 (Leipzig, 1904), 699–759; *Franz Neumann und sein Wirken als Forscher und Lehrer* (Brunswick, 1907);

"Optik, ältere Theorien," in *Encyklopädie der mathematischen Wissenschaften*, V, pt. 3 (Leipzig, 1907), 1–93; *Theorie des Potentials und der Kugelfunktionen*, 2 vols., nos. 58 and 59 in Sammlung Schubert (Leipzig, 1908–1921); "Franz Neumann als Mathematiker," in *Physikalische Zeitschrift*, **11** (1910), 1066–1072; and "Über das Potential gewisser Ovaloide," in *Nova acta Leopoldina*, **6**, no. 1 (1915), 1–80.

Secondary literature includes W. Lorey, "Zum 70. Geburtstag des Mathematikers A. Wangerin," in *Zeitschrift für mathematischen und naturwissenschaftlichen Unterricht*, **46** (1915), 53–57; and "Bericht über die Feier der 80. Wiederkehr des Geburtstages des Herrn Geh. Rats Prof. Dr. Wangerin," in *Jahresberichte der Deutschen Mathematiker-vereinigung*, **34** (1926), 108–111.

WERNER BURAU

WARING, EDWARD (*b*. Shrewsbury, England, *ca.* 1736; *d*. Plealey, near Shrewsbury, 15 August 1798)

Little is known of Waring's early life. In 1753 he was admitted to Magdalene College, Cambridge, as a sizar, and his mathematical talent immediately attracted attention. He graduated B.A. as senior wrangler in 1757, was elected a fellow of the college, and in 1760 received the M.A. and resigned his fellowship to accept appointment, on the death of John Colson, as sixth Lucasian professor of mathematics. Although his Lucasian professorship was opposed in some quarters because of his age—he was still in his twenties—Waring soon effectively silenced his critics by publishing, in 1762, his *Miscellanea analytica de aequationibus algebraicis et curvarum proprietatibus*, which gave indisputable proof of his ability and at once established him as a mathematician of the first rank. He was elected a fellow of the Royal Society the following year.

The *Miscellanea* was described by Charles Hutton (in *Mathematical and Philosophical Dictionary*, II [1795], 584) as "one of the most abstruse books written in the abstrusest parts of Algebra." It deals largely with the theory of numbers (some of its chapters are "De fluxionibus fluentium inveniendis," "De methodo incrementorum," and "De infinitis seriebus"), a branch of mathematics for which Waring had a special gift. It contains, without proof, the theorem that every integer is the sum of four squares, nine cubes, nineteen biquadrates, "and so on." In 1770 Waring published *Meditationes algebraicae*, a work that was highly praised by Lagrange; in 1772 he brought out *Proprietates algebraicarum curvarum*; and 1776 saw

the publication of *Meditationes analyticae*. In addition to these important treatises, he also, during this period, published a number of learned papers in the *Philosophical Transactions of the Royal Society*. His last major work, *Essay on the Principles of Human Knowledge*, published in 1794, is notable for his application of abstract science to philosophy.

As a mathematician, Waring was unfortunate in working at a time in which English mathematics were in a state of decline. This was in part due to the clumsy notation in which Newton had expounded his calculus and to the geometrical exposition that gave the *Principia* a somewhat archaic appearance and persuaded English readers that the great new mathematical tool forged by Newton and Leibniz (which was then being employed with great vigor and skill on the Continent, particularly by the Bernoullis) was, in fact, not really necessary. This melancholy state of affairs persisted for more than a century, despite the efforts of such distinguished mathematicians as Brook Taylor, Colin Maclaurin, and John Wallis, and led Lalande to observe in a "Notice sur la vie de Condorcet" (*Mercure de France*, 20 Jan. 1796, p. 143) that there was not a single first-rate analyst in all England. (Waring, however, stoutly maintained that his *Miscellanea Analytica* disproved Lalande's charge, and cited its commendation by d'Alembert, Lagrange, and Euler.)

Despite the spectacular improvements in notation by which fundamental mathematical operations were expressed on the Continent, Waring, in his own works, used both the *de*ism of Leibniz and the *do*tage of Newton—the two great rival systems—indifferently, and made no notable contribution to the establishment of a permanent notation in any branch of mathematics. His method of writing exponents (as, for example, on page 8 of the 1785 edition of his *Meditationes analyticae*) was clumsy in the extreme, and in general his presentation is unattractive and his books difficult to follow. He suffered from an apparent lack of intellectual order that rendered his mathematical compositions so confused that they are almost impossible to follow in manuscript, while his published works, perhaps because of his extreme myopia, are riddled with typographical errors. His language, at best, was obscure.

Waring received the Copley Medal of the Royal Society in 1784. He was also elected a member of a number of European scientific societies, notably those of Göttingen and Bologna. He served as Lucasian professor until his death; he was also a commissioner of the important Board of Longitude. Nor were his activities exclusively mathematical; simultaneously with his composition of his books he turned to medicine, and received the M.D. from Cambridge in 1770. He does not appear ever to have practiced medicine, but it is believed that he carried out dissections in the privacy of his Cambridge rooms.

BIBLIOGRAPHY

I. ORIGINAL WORKS. Waring's books include *Miscellanea analytica de aequationibus algebraicis et curvarum proprietatibus . . .* (Cambridge, 1762), his best-known work; *Meditationes algebraicae* (Cambridge, 1770; 3rd ed., 1782); *Proprietates algebraicarum curvarum* (Cambridge, 1772); *Meditationes analyticae* (Cambridge, 1776; 2nd ed., enl., 1785); *On the Principles of Translating Algebraic Quantities Into Probable Relations and Annuities* (Cambridge, 1792); and *Essay on the Principles of Human Knowledge* (Cambridge, 1794).

His papers in the *Philosophical Transactions of the Royal Society* are "Problems," **53** (1763), 294–298; "Some New Properties in Conic Sections," **54** (1764), 193–197; "Two Theorems," **55** (1765), 143–145; "Problems Concerning Interpolations," **69** (1779), 59–67; and "On the General Resolution of Algebraical Equations," *ibid.*, 86–104.

II. SECONDARY LITERATURE. British historians of mathematics have hardly done justice to Waring. *Gentleman's Magazine*, **68**, pt. 2 (1798), 730, 807, contains a brief biography and a list of his principal contributions to mathematics; as does J. A. Venn, *Alumni Cantabrigienses*, pt. 2, IV (Cambridge, 1954), 352. The most exhaustive account of his work is Moritz Cantor, *Vorlesungen über Geschichte der Mathematik*, IV (Leipzig, 1908), 92–95. See also Florian Cajori, *History of Mathematical Notations*, 2 vols. (Chicago, 1928–1929), see indexes and I, 244, which reproduces p. 8 of the 1785 ed. of Waring's *Meditationes analyticae*; and R. T. Gunther, *Early Science in Cambridge* (Oxford, 1937), 60.

J. F. SCOTT

WATSON, GEORGE NEVILLE (*b*. Westward Ho!, Devon, England, 31 January 1886; *d*. Leamington Spa, England, 2 February 1965)

Watson went up to Cambridge University in 1904 as a major scholar of Trinity College, to which he was intensely devoted throughout his life, and held a fellowship there from 1910 to 1916. After a brief period at University College, London, he went to Birmingham in 1918 as professor of mathematics and remained in this post until his retirement in 1951.

Almost all Watson's work was done in complex variable theory. Within this field he was no narrow specialist, his interests ranging widely over problems arising in the theories of difference and differential equations, number theory, special functions, and asymptotic expansions. As a classical analyst Watson showed great power and an outstanding ability to find rigorous and manageable approximations to complicated mathematical expressions; unlike many pure mathematicians, he was not averse to numerical computation, which he performed on his own Brunsviga machine and in which he found relaxation.

Watson wrote over 150 mathematical papers and three books. The first of these books, a Cambridge tract on complex integration, is now rarely consulted; but the remaining two had, and still have, a wide influence, particularly among applied mathematicians and theoretical physicists. The second, *A Course of Modern Analysis*, was written in collaboration with E. T. Whittaker, who had been one of the younger fellows of Trinity when Watson was an undergraduate. The first edition had appeared in 1902 under Whittaker's sole authorship and Watson offered to share the work of preparing the second, which appeared in 1915 and was a considerably expanded version of the original work. The first part of the book develops the basic principles and techniques of analysis and these are applied in the second part to obtain the properties of the many special functions that occur in applications. "Whittaker and Watson" has appeared in several editions and numerous reprints; Watson never lost his interest in it and, in his retirement, embarked upon a much enlarged version, which was never published.

The first fifty of Watson's mathematical papers are concerned mainly with properties and expansions of special mathematical functions. These investigations culminated in the publication of his monumental and definitive *Treatise on the Theory of Bessel Functions* (1922). A second edition, containing only minimal alterations, appeared in 1944; for by then Watson had lost interest in the subject and, unfortunately for the mathematical public, was not prepared to undertake the continuous revision and expansion that would have kept the book up to date. By 1929, also, he had already embarked on his "Ramanujan period"; and during the next ten years a succession of papers appeared in which he proved and extended numerous results that had been stated in the notebooks of the Indian mathematical genius Srinivasa Ramanujan, who had died in 1920. Watson and B. M. Wilson of Liverpool were invited by the University of Madras to become joint editors of a projected work, of an estimated 600 pages, which would contain proofs of Ramanujan's results.

Both editors made considerable progress, and much of their work was published as original papers. The mass of Ramanujan material was so extensive, however, that the fruit of their combined labors never reached the stage of publication in book form. Wilson died in 1935; and by 1939 Watson's impetus had diminished, possibly because of his increased administrative and teaching commitments following the outbreak of World War II. His work not only had provided proofs of formulas and congruences stated by Ramanujan, but also had considerably extended Ramanujan's work on singular moduli and set his work on mock theta functions on a proper foundation. These investigations were admirably suited to Watson's analytical abilities, since they demanded not only great ingenuity but also enormous industry. Much of this work would now be regarded as being outside the main stream of mathematics; but fashions change! His efforts during this period were not devoted solely to problems arising from Ramanujan's notebooks; his important work on what are now called Watson transforms also dates from this time.

With the exception of his investigations on periodic sigma functions, Watson's papers during the last twenty years of his life are of lesser interest.

BIBLIOGRAPHY

A complete list of Watson's mathematical writings is in the obituary notice by R. A. Rankin that appeared in *Journal of the London Mathematical Society*, **41** (1966), 551–565, where a more detailed discussion of some of his work is given. See also the obituary notice by J. M. Whittaker in *Biographical Memoirs of Fellows of the Royal Society*, **12** (1966), 521–530, which supplements the latter and includes a photograph.

Watson's unpublished work on the Ramanujan notebooks is in a collection of MSS deposited in the library of Trinity College, Cambridge.

R. A. RANKIN

WEBER, HEINRICH (*b.* Heidelberg, Germany, 5 May 1842; *d.* Strasbourg, Germany [now France], 17 May 1913)

Weber, son of the the historian G. Weber, began the study of mathematics and physics in 1860 at the University of Heidelberg. He then went to Leipzig for a year but subsequently returned to Heidelberg, where he obtained the Ph.D. in 1863. After working at Königsberg under Franz Neumann and F. J. Richelot, he qualified as *Privatdozent* in 1866 at Heidelberg and obtained a post as extraordinary professor there in 1869. He subsequently taught at the Eidgenössische Polytechnikum in Zurich, the University of Königsberg, the Technische Hochschule in Charlottenburg, the universities of Marburg and Göttingen, and, from 1895, at Strasbourg.

Weber was rector of the universities of Königsberg, Marburg, and Strasbourg; member of many German and foreign academies; and recipient of an honorary doctorate from the University of Christiania (now Oslo). He was a cofounder of the Deutsche Mathematiker-Vereinigung and member of the editorial board of *Mathematische Annalen*.

In 1870 Weber married Emilie Dittenberger, daughter of a Weimar court chaplain. Their daughter translated the philosophical writings of Henri Poincaré into German, and their son Rudolf Heinrich became professor of theoretical physics at Rostock. Weber's closest friend was Richard Dedekind, with whom he often collaborated and with whom he edited Riemann's works (1876). Weber's students included Hermann Minkowski and David Hilbert.

An immensely versatile mathematician, Weber focused his research mainly on analysis and its application to mathematical physics and number theory. The direction of his work was decisively influenced by his stay at Königsberg, where Jacobian mathematics still flourished. There he was encouraged by Neumann to investigate physical problems and by Richelot to study algebraic functions. Weber began his research with an examination of the theory of differential equations, which he conducted in Jacobi's manner. Then, building on Carl Neumann's book on Riemann's theory of algebraic functions and on the work of Alfred Clebsch and Paul Gordan on Abelian functions, Weber demonstrated Abel's theorem in its most general form. He also worked on the mathematical treatment of physical problems concerning heat, static and current electricity, the motion of rigid bodies in liquids, and electrolytic displacement. He brought together a portion of this research in *Die partiellen Differentialgleichungen der mathematischen Physik* (1900–1901), a complete reworking and development of a similarly titled book prepared by Karl Hattendorff from Riemann's lectures that had gone through three editions.

Weber investigated important contemporary problems in algebra and number theory, the fields in which he did his most penetrating work. With Dedekind he wrote a fundamental work on algebraic functions that contained a purely arithmetical theory of these functions. One of Weber's outstanding accomplishments was the proof of Kronecker's theorem, which states that the absolute Abelian fields are cyclotomic—that is, they are obtained from the rational numbers through adjunction of roots of unity. In 1891 Weber gave a complete account of the problems of complex multiplication, a topic in which analysis and number theory are inseparably linked. His studies culminated in the two-volume *Lehrbuch der Algebra* (1895–1896), which for decades was indispensable in teaching and research.

Weber was an enthusiastic and inspiring teacher who took great interest in educational questions. In collaboration with Joseph Wellstein and with the assistance of other mathematicians, he edited the *Enzyklopädie der Elementar-Mathematik*, a three-volume work designed for both teachers and students.

BIBLIOGRAPHY

Weber's works include "Ueber singuläre Auflösungen partieller Differentialgleichungen erster Ordnung," in *Journal für die reine und angewandte Mathematik*, **66** (1866), 193–236; "Neuer Beweis des Abelschen Theorems," in *Mathematische Annalen*, **8** (1874), 49–53; "Theorie der algebraischen Funktionen einer Veränderlichen," in *Journal für die reine und angewandte Mathematik*, **92** (1882), 181–290, written with R. Dedekind; *Elliptische Funktionen und algebraische Zahlen* (Brunswick, 1891; 2nd ed., 1908, as vol. III of *Lehrbuch der Algebra*); *Lehrbuch der Algebra*, 2 vols. (Brunswick, 1895–1896; 2nd ed., 1898–1899); *Die partiellen Differentialgleichungen der mathematischen Physik*, 2 vols. (Brunswick, 4th ed., 1900–1901; 5th ed., 1910–1912); and *Enzyklopädie der Elementar-Mathematik*, 3 vols. (Leipzig, 1903–1907), written with Joseph Wellstein *et al.*

There is an obituary by A. Voss in *Jahresberichte der Deutschen Mathematiker-Vereinigung*, **23** (1914), 431–444, with portrait.

BRUNO SCHOENEBERG

WEDDERBURN, JOSEPH HENRY MACLAGAN (*b.* Forfar, Scotland, 26 February 1882; *d.* Princeton, New Jersey, 9 October 1948)

Wedderburn was the tenth of fourteen children. His father, Alexander Wedderburn, was a physician in a family of ministers (on his father's side) and lawyers (on his mother's side). In 1898 Wedderburn matriculated at the University of Edinburgh; in 1903 he received an M.A. degree with first-class honors in mathematics. No doubt influenced by the work of Frobenius and Schur, he went to Leipzig and Berlin in 1904. During the same year he proceeded to the United States as a Carnegie fellow at the University of Chicago (E. H. Moore and L. E. Dickson were there). From 1905 to 1909 he was lecturer at the University of Edinburgh and assistant to Chrystal. During this time Wedderburn edited the *Proceedings of the Edinburgh Mathematical Society*, and in 1908 was awarded the doctorate of science.

In 1909 Wedderburn became one of the "preceptors" appointed under Woodrow Wilson at Princeton University. At the outbreak of World War I he enlisted in the British Army and fought in France. After the war he returned to Princeton, where he continued to teach until his retirement in 1945. When the mathematics department at Princeton assumed responsibility for publishing the *Annals of Mathematics*, Wedderburn was its editor from 1912 to 1928. Toward the close of the 1920's, he suffered what appears to have been a nervous breakdown. He led an increasingly solitary life and retired from his university post some years before the normal time. Wedderburn published thirty-eight papers and a textbook, *Lectures on Matrices* (1934), which in the last chapter contains an excellent account of his theorems and their background as well as some original contributions to the subject.

Wedderburn's mathematical work includes two famous theorems, which bear his name; both were established in the years 1905–1908. Before Wedderburn began his investigations, the classification of the semisimple algebras was done only if the ground field was the field of real or complex numbers. This did not lead to deeper insight into hypercomplex numbers (linear associative algebra). Wedderburn attacked the problem in a completely general way and introduced new methods and arrived at a complete understanding of the structure of semisimple algebras over any field. He showed that they are a direct sum of simple algebras and finally—in a celebrated paper ("On Hyper-complex Numbers") that was to be the beginning of a new era in the theory—proved that a simple algebra consists of all matrices of a given degree with elements taken from a division algebra.

Wedderburn's second important contribution concerns the investigation of skew fields with a finite number of elements. The commutative case had been investigated before Moore in 1903, and had led to a complete classification of all commutative fields with a given number of fields. Moore showed that for a given number p^r of elements there exists (apart from isomorphisms) only one field, namely the Galois field of degree r and characteristic k. Since a noncommutative finite field had never been found, one could suspect that it did not exist. In 1905 Wedderburn showed that every field with a finite number of elements is indeed commutative (under multiplication) and therefore a Galois field. This second theorem ("A Theorem on Finite Algebras") gives at once the complete classification of all semisimple algebras with a finite number of elements. But the theorem also had many other applications in number theory and projective geometry. It gave at once the complete structure of all projective geometries with a finite number of points, and it showed that in all these geometries Pascal's theorem was a consequence of Desargues's theorem. The structure of semisimple groups was now reduced to that of noncommutative fields. Wedderburn's theorem had been the special case of a more general Diophantine property of fields and thus opened an entirely new line of research.

BIBLIOGRAPHY

I. Original Works. Wedderburn's works are "A Theorem on Finite Algebras," in *Transactions of the American Mathematical Society*, **6** (1905), 349–352; "Non-Desarguesian and Non-Pascalian Geometries," *ibid.*, **8** (1907), 379–388, written with O. Veblen; "On Hypercomplex Numbers," in *Proceedings of the London Mathematical Society*, **6**, 2nd ser. (1907–1908), 77–118; "The Automorphic Transformation of a Bilinear Form," in *Annals of Mathematics*, **23**, 2nd ser. (1921–1923), 122–134; "Algebraic Fields," *ibid.*, **24**, 2nd ser. (1922–1923), 237–264; "Algebras Which Do Not Possess a Finite Basis," in *Transactions of the American Mathematical Society*, **26** (1924), 395–426; "A Theorem on Simple Algebras," in *Bulletin of the American Mathematical Society*, **31** (1925), 11–13; "Non-commutative Domains of Integrity," in *Journal für die reine und angewandte Mathematik*, **167** (1931), 129–141; *Lectures on Matrices* (New York, 1934); "Boolean Linear Associative Algebra," in *Annals of Mathematics*, **35**, 2nd ser. (1934), 185–194; and "The Canonical Form of a Matrix," *ibid.*, **39**, 2nd ser. (1938), 178–180.

II. Secondary Literature. See E. Artin, "The Influence of J. H. M. Wedderburn on the Development of Modern Algebra," in *Bulletin of the American Mathematical Society*, **56** (1950), 65–72.

HENRY NATHAN

WEIERSTRASS, KARL THEODOR WILHELM

(*b*. Ostenfelde, Westphalia, Germany, 31 October 1815; *d*. Berlin, Germany, 19 February 1897)

Weierstrass was the first child of Wilhelm Weierstrass, secretary to the mayor of Ostenfelde, and Theodora Vonderforst, who were married five months before his birth. The family name first appeared in Mettmann, a small town between Düsseldorf and Elberfeld; since the sixteenth century they had been artisans and small merchants. Weierstrass' father, an intelligent, educated man with knowledge of the arts and sciences, could have held higher posts than he actually did; little is known about his mother's family. Weierstrass had a brother and two sisters, none of whom ever married. When Weierstrass was eight his father entered the Prussian taxation service; and as a result of his frequent transfers, young Karl attended several primary schools. In 1829, at the age of fourteen, he was accepted at the Catholic Gymnasium in Paderborn, where his father was assistant and subsequently treasurer at the main customs office.

A distinguished student at the Gymnasium, Weierstrass received several prizes before graduating. Unlike many mathematicians, he had no musical talent; nor did he ever acquire an interest in the theater, painting, or sculpture. He did, however, value lyric poetry and occasionally wrote verses himself. In 1828, a year after his mother's death, Weierstrass' father remarried. At the age of fifteen Weierstrass reportedly worked as a bookkeeper for a merchant's wife—both to utilize his abilities and to ease the strain of his family's financial situation. A reader of Crelle's *Journal für die reine und angewandte Mathematik* while in his teens, he also gave his brother Peter mathematical coaching that does not seem to have proved helpful: Weierstrass' proofs were generally "knocking," his brother later admitted.

After leaving the Gymnasium in 1834, Weierstrass complied with his father's wish that he study public finance and administration, and entered the University of Bonn. The course of studies that he pursued was planned to permit him to obtain a background in law, administration, and economics—the requisites for those seeking higher administrative posts in Prussia. The study of mathematics or related areas was his first choice, however; and the conflict between duty and inclination led to physical and mental strain. He tried, in vain, to overcome his problems by participating in carefree student life, but he soon came to shun lectures and to restrict himself to studying mathematics on his own, beginning with the *Mécanique céleste* of Laplace. Weierstrass was fortunate in having an understanding adviser in astronomy, mathematics, and physics, Dietrich von Münchow. However, Münchow was of the old school and, because he gave only elementary lectures, was remote from the advances of modern mathematics.

Around this time Weierstrass read Jacobi's *Fundamenta nova theoriae functionum ellipticarum* (1829); the work proved difficult for him, based, as it was, on prior knowledge of Legendre's *Traité des fonctions elliptiques*, published shortly beforehand. A transcript of Christof Gudermann's lecture on modular functions rendered the theory of elliptic variables understandable to him and inspired him to initiate his own research. In a letter to Sophus Lie of 10 April 1882, Weierstrass explained his definitive decision to study mathematics:

> For me this letter [from Abel to Legendre], when I became aware of it in Crelle's *Journal* [6 (1830), 73–80] during my student years, was of the utmost importance. The immediate derivation of the form of representation of the function given by Abel and designated by him by $\lambda(x)$, from the differential equation defining this function, was the first mathematical task I set myself; and its fortunate solution made me determined to devote myself wholly to mathematics; I made this decision in my seventh semester [winter semester 1837–1838], although originally I undertook the study of public finance and administration [*N. H. Abel, Mémorial* (1902), 108].

After eight semesters Weierstrass left the university without taking the examination. Although his father was greatly disappointed, a family friend, president of the court of justice of Paderborn, persuaded him to send Weierstrass to the Theological and Philosophical Academy at Münster, where he would be able to take the teacher's examination after a short time. Weierstrass enrolled on 22 May 1839. Helped and encouraged by Gudermann— Weierstrass was the only university student at his lectures on elliptic functions, he left Münster that autumn to prepare for the state examination.

In January 1840 Weierstrass' father assumed the more remunerative post of director of the saltworks and the family moved to Westernkotten, near Lippstadt. Two months later Weierstrass registered for the examination, and at the beginning of May he received the philological, pedagogical, and mathematical problems for the written examination. The first mathematical problem was one that Weierstrass himself had requested, the representation of elliptic functions. Following Abel, for whose work he had always had the highest regard, Weierstrass presented in his examination an important advance in the new theory of elliptic functions, and this work contains important starting points for his subsequent investigations. Gudermann recognized the significance of his accomplishment and wrote in his evaluation that Weierstrass was "of equal rank with the discoverers who were crowned with glory." The school superintendent was somewhat more restrained. When Weierstrass later read Gudermann's complete critique, he admitted that had he learned of it earlier, he would have published the work immediately and most certainly would have obtained a university chair sooner. He considered it especially fine of Gudermann to have praised him so highly, even though his work contained sharp criticism of Gudermann's method. It is of interest that one of the other mathematical problems that Weierstrass was assigned, on elementary geometry, gave him much difficulty, at least according to his brother's account.

After having passed the oral examinations in April 1841, Weierstrass taught for a one-year probationary period at the Gymnasium in Münster, before transferring to the Catholic secondary school in Deutsch-Krone, West Prussia (1842–1848), and then to the Catholic Gymnasium in Braunsberg, East Prussia (1848–1855). In addition to mathematics and physics, he taught German, botany, geography, history, gymnastics, and even calligraphy. (Reminiscent of this is his peculiar $\mathscr{P}$ of the Weierstrassian p-function.) In recalling the misery of these years, Weierstrass remarked that he had neither a colleague for mathematical discussions nor access to a mathematical library, and that the exchange of scientific letters was a luxury that he could not afford. The "unending dreariness and boredom" would have been unbearable for him without hard work, and his every free minute was devoted to mathematics.

Fortunately he found an understanding senior colleague in Ferdinand Schultz, director of the Braunsberg Institute. Weierstrass was in Deutsch-Krone during the Revolution of 1848. Dirichlet had stated that a mathematician could only be a democrat, and Weierstrass' beliefs were not contrary to this belief. Commissioned to oversee the belletristic section of the local newspaper, he approved reprinting the freedom songs of Georg Herwegh—under the eyes of the censor.

Although not involved in nationalistic struggles, Weierstrass was no stranger to national feelings. He aspired to neither title nor decorations and was reluctant to exchange the simple title of professor for the more pretentious one of privy councillor. His religious views were moderate and tolerant, and he eschewed political as well as religious bigots. Reared a Catholic, he paid homage in a public speech as rector to the cultural significance of the Reformation. In his philosophical outlook he was a frank adherent of Kant and an opponent of Fichte and Schelling.

Weierstrass' first publications on Abelian functions, which appeared in the Braunsberg school prospectus (1848–1849), went unnoticed; but the following work, "Zur Theorie der Abelschen Functionen" (Crelle's *Journal*, **47** [1854], 289–306), elicited enormous interest and marked a decisive turning point in his life. In this memoir he demonstrated the solution to the problem of inversion of the hyperelliptic integrals, which he accomplished by representing Abelian functions as the quotients of constantly converging power series. Many of his results were only hinted at in this work, for since 1850 he had suffered painful attacks of vertigo, which lasted up to an hour and subsided only after a tormenting attack of vomiting. These attacks, which contemporaries called brain spasms, recurred for about twelve years and made it impossible for him to work. Although the 1854 paper was merely a preliminary statement, Liouville called it "one of those works that marks an epoch in science." On 31 March 1854 the University of Königsberg awarded Weierstrass an honorary doctorate. He was promoted to senior lecturer at Braunsberg and in the fall of 1855 was granted a year's leave to continue his studies. Firmly determined not to return to the school, he applied in August 1855 for the post of Kummer's successor at the University of Breslau—an unusual mode of procedure. (Kummer had been called to Berlin to succeed Dirichlet, who had assumed Gauss's chair at Göttingen.) Weierstrass did not receive the appointment at Breslau.

In the famous "Theorie der Abelschen Functionen" (Crelle's *Journal*, **52** [1856], 285–380), which contains an excerpt from the previously mentioned examination work, Weierstrass proved what previously he had only hinted. According to Hilbert, he had realized one of the greatest achievements of analysis, the solution of the Jacobian inversion problem for hyperelliptic integrals. There was talk of appointment to a post in Austria, but before formal discussions could take place Weierstrass accepted on 14 June 1856 an appointment as professor at the Industry Institute in Berlin, a forerunner of the Technische Hochschule. While he did not have to return to the Gymnasium in Braunsberg, his hopes for appointment to the University of Berlin had not been realized. In September 1856, while attending a conference of natural scientists in Vienna, Weierstrass was offered a special professorship at any Austrian university of his choice. He was still undecided a month later, when he was invited to the University of Berlin as associate professor. He accepted. On 19 November 1856 he became a member of the Berlin Academy. It was not until July 1864 that he was able to leave the Industry Institute and assume a chair at the university.

Having spent the most productive years of his life teaching elementary classes, far from the centers of scientific activity, Weierstrass had found time for his own research only at the expense of his health. Heavy demands were again made on him at Berlin, and on 16 December 1861 he suffered a complete collapse; he did not return to scientific work until the winter semester of 1862–1863. Henceforth he always lectured while seated, consigning the related work at the blackboard to an advanced student. The "brain spasms" were replaced by recurrent attacks of bronchitis and phlebitis, which afflicted him until his death at the age of eighty-one. Nevertheless, he became a recognized master, primarily through his lectures. He delayed publication of his results not—as has often been charged—because of a "basic aversion to printer's ink" but, rather, because his critical sense invariably compelled him to base any analysis on a firm foundation, starting from a fresh approach and continually revising and expanding.

It was only gradually that Weierstrass acquired the masterly skill in lecturing extolled by his later students. Initially his lectures were seldom clear, orderly, or understandable. His ideas simply streamed forth. Yet his reputation for lecturing on new theories attracted students from around the world, and eventually some 250 students attended his classes. Since no one else offered the same subject matter, graduate students as well as university lecturers were attracted to Berlin. Moreover, he was generous in suggesting topics for dissertations and continuing investigations.

One of Weierstrass' first lectures at Berlin was on the application of Fourier series and integrals to problems of mathematical physics. But the lack of rigor that he detected in all available works on the subject, as well as the fruitlessness of his own efforts to surmount this deficiency, frustrated him to the degree that he decided not to present this course again. It was not until 1885 that he took up the representation of single-valued functions of a real variable by means of trigonometric series, stressing that "he had considered the needs of mathematical physics." Here again are manifest his proverbial striving for the characteristic "Weierstrassian rigor" that virtually compelled him to carry his investigations to an ever higher degree of maturity and completion. His position concerning the applications of his research was clarified in his inaugural speech at the Berlin Academy on 9 July 1857, in which he stated that mathematics occupies an especially high place because only through its aid can a truly satisfying understanding of natural phenomena be obtained. To some degree his outlook approached that of Gauss, who believed that mathematics should be the friend of practice, but never its slave.

Over the years Weierstrass developed a great lecture cycle: "Introduction to the Theory of Analytic Functions"; "Theory of Elliptic Functions," sometimes beginning with the differential calculus, at other times starting with the theory of functions, the point of departure being the algebraic addition theorem; "Application of Elliptic Functions to Problems in Geometry and Mechanics"; "Theory of Abelian Functions"; "Application of Abelian Functions to the Solution of Selected Geometric Problems"; and "Calculus of Variations." Within this cycle Weierstrass erected the entire structure of his mathematics, using as building blocks only that which he himself had proven.

During seven semesters (1864–1873) Weierstrass also lectured on synthetic geometry, thereby honoring his promise to Jakob Steiner before the latter's death in 1863. Steiner's discussions, which Weierstrass had read in Crelle's *Journal* as a student, had especially stimulated his interest; and he was one of the few people in Berlin with whom the old crank had remained on good terms. These lectures were given only out of a sense of obligation, however—not from any interest in the subject; for Weierstrass considered geometric demonstrations to be in very poor taste. If, as has been alleged, he sometimes permitted himself to clarify a point by using a diagram, it was carefully erased.

In addition to lecturing, Weierstrass introduced the first seminar devoted exclusively to mathematics in Germany, a joint undertaking with Kummer

at the University of Berlin in 1861. Here again he developed many fruitful concepts that were frequently used by his students as subjects for papers. In his inaugural lecture as rector of the University of Berlin, Weierstrass called for lecturers to "designate the boundaries that had not yet been crossed by science . . . from which positions further advances would then be made possible." The lecturer should neither deny his students "a deeper insight into the progress of his own investigations, nor should he remain silent about his own errors and disappointments."

Weierstrass' students included Heinrich Bruns, Georg Frobenius, Georg Hettner, Ludwig Kiepert, Wilhelm Killing, Johannes Knoblauch, Ernst Kötter, Reinhold von Lilienthal, Hans von Mangoldt, Felix Müller, Eugen Netto, Friedrich Schottky, Ludwig Stickelberger, and Wilhelm Ludwig Thomé. Auditors or participants in the seminar included Paul Bachmann, Oskar Bolza, Friedrich Engel, Leopold Gegenbauer, August Gutzmer, Lothar Heffter, Kurt Hensel, Otto Hölder, Adolf Hurwitz, Felix Klein, Adolf Kneser, Leo Koenigsberger, Fritz Kötter, Mathias Lerch, Sophus Lie, Jacob Lüroth, Franz Mertens, Hermann Minkowski, Gösta Mittag-Leffler, Hermann Amandus Schwarz, and Otto Stolz. The philosopher Edmund Husserl—insofar as he was a mathematician—was also a student of Weierstrass.

Weierstrass was not without his detractors: Felix Klein, for instance, remarked that he and Lie had merely fought for their own points of view in the seminars. Most of Weierstrass' students, however, accepted his theories as an unassailable standard. Doubts were not permitted to arise, and checking was hardly possible since Weierstrass cited very few other sources and arranged his methodical structure so that he was obliged to refer only to himself. Independent opinions, such as Klein's, were the exception.

Weierstrass' criticism of Riemann's basic concept of the theory of functions, namely the application and use of the principle of Dirichlet, resulted in the fact that until the twentieth century his approach to the theory of functions, starting with the power series, was preferred to Riemann's, which originated with complex differentiation. Weierstrass formulated his credo in a letter to his student H. A. Schwarz (3 October 1875):

> The more I ponder the principles of function theory—and I do so incessantly—the more I am convinced that it must be founded on simple algebraic truths and that one is therefore on the wrong path if,

instead of building on simple and fundamental algebraic propositions, one has recourse to the "transcendental" (to put it briefly), no matter how impressive at first glance, for example, seem the reflections by means of which Riemann discovered so many of the most important properties of algebraic functions. It is self-evident that any and all paths must be open to a researcher during the actual course of his investigations; what is at issue here is merely the question of a systematic theoretical foundation.

Although Weierstrass enjoyed considerable authority at Berlin, he occasionally encountered substantial resistance from his colleagues; and such criticism hurt him deeply. In the late 1870's his relations with his close friend Leopold Kronecker cooled considerably when Kronecker imparted to Weierstrass his antipathy for the work of Georg Cantor. Weierstrass had been one of the first to recognize the value of Cantor's accomplishments and had in fact stimulated his work on the concept of countability. Kronecker, by contrast, proclaimed that he had set himself the task "of investigating the error of every conclusion used in the so-called present method of analysis." Weierstrass' reaction to Kronecker's attack may well have been excessive; but in 1885 he decided to leave Germany and go to Switzerland, believing that everything for which he had worked was near collapse. Determined to prevent such a catastrophe, he resolved to remain in Berlin after all. The choice of his successor and publication of his works were problems still to be resolved—and his successor would have to be endorsed by Kronecker. Kronecker's death in 1891 cleared the path for the appointment of Hermann Amandus Schwarz.

But the publication of Weierstrass' writings was another matter. He was satisfied with neither the circulating transcripts of his lectures nor with the textbooks that followed his concepts and that he had, to some degree, authorized; and his major ideas and methodology remained unpublished. In 1887, having already edited the works of Steiner and Jacobi, Weierstrass decided to publish his own mathematical lifework, assured of the help of the younger mathematicians of his school. He lived to see only the first two volumes appear in print (1894, 1895). According to his wishes, volume IV was given preferential treatment, and it appeared in 1902. The altered title, "Lectures on the Theory of Abelian Transcendentals"—they had always been called the theory of Abelian functions—more accurately reflects the scope of his lectures. Volume III was published the following year. Twelve

years elapsed before the appearance of volume V ("Lectures on Elliptic Functions") and volume VI ("Selected Problems of Geometry and Mechanics to be Solved With the Aid of the Theory of Elliptic Functions"), and another dozen years before volume VII ("Lectures on the Calculus of Variations"). All of Weierstrass' efforts to ensure the publication soon after his death of a complete edition of his works were fruitless: volumes VIII–X, intended to contain works on hyperelliptic functions, a second edition of his lectures on elliptic functions, and the theory of functions, remain unpublished.

In 1870, at the age of fifty-five, Weierstrass met the twenty-year-old Russian Sonya Kovalevsky, who had come to Berlin from Heidelberg, where she had taken her first semester under Leo Koenigsberger. Unable to secure her admission to the university, Weierstrass taught her privately; and his role in both her scientific and personal affairs far transcended the usual teacher-student relationship. In her he found a "refreshingly enthusiastic participant" in all his thoughts, and much that he had suspected or fumbled for became clear in his conversations with her. In a letter to her of 20 August 1873, Weierstrass wrote of their having "dreamed and been enraptured of so many riddles that remain for us to solve, on finite and infinite spaces, on the stability of the world system, and on all the other major problems of the mathematics and the physics of the future." It seemed to him as though she had "been close . . . throughout [his] entire life . . . and never have I found anyone who could bring me such understanding of the highest aims of science and such joyful accord with my intentions and basic principles as you!" Through his intercession she received the doctorate *in absentia* at Göttingen in 1874.

Yet their friendship did not remain untroubled. Her links with socialist circles, her literary career as author of novels, and her advocacy of the emancipation of women strongly biased the judgment of her contemporaries, and resulted in defamation of the friendship. On the other hand, many of his letters to her were unanswered. At one juncture she remained silent for three years. He was instrumental in her obtaining an appointment as lecturer in mathematics at Stockholm in 1883 and a life professorship in mathematics in 1889. The misinterpretation of their relationship and her early death in 1891 brought him additional physical suffering. During his last three years he was confined to a wheelchair, immobile and dependent. He died of pneumonia.

In his inaugural speech to the Berlin Academy, Weierstrass characterized his scientific activity as having centered on the search for "those values of a wholly new type of which analysis had not yet had an example, their actual representation, and the elucidation of their properties." One of his earliest attempts at solving this problem was a treatise (1841) on the representation of an analytic function exhibiting an absolute value that lies between two given boundaries. It contained the Cauchy integral proposition and the Laurent proposition. It was published only fifty-three years later, however, when it became clear that Weierstrass at the age of twenty-six had already had at his disposal the principles of his theory of functions, to the development of which he subsequently devoted his lifework. Yet his contribution to reestablishing the theory of analytic functions ultimately served only to achieve his final aim: the erection of a general theory of Abelian integrals (all integrals over algebraic functions) and the consideration of their converse functions, the Abelian functions.

What Weierstrass considered to be his main scientific task is now held to be less important than his accomplishments in the foundation of his theory. The special functions which he investigated, and the theory of which he lucidly elaborated or transformed, now elicit less interest than his criticism, rigor, generally valid concepts, and the procedures and propositions of the theory of functions. Weierstrass' name remains linked to his preliminary proposition, approximation propositions, double series proposition, proposition of products, and fundamental proposition—as well as the Casorati-Weierstrass proposition. Hundreds of mathematicians were influenced by his uncompromising development of a systematic foundation and his pursuit of a fixed plan after appropriate preparation of detail; and they in turn instilled in their students Weierstrass' concepts of the necessity of clarity and truth, and his belief that the highest aim of science is to achieve general results. Admired by Poincaré for his "unity of thought," Weierstrass was the most important nineteenth-century German mathematician after Gauss and Riemann.

BIBLIOGRAPHY

I. ORIGINAL WORKS. Weierstrass' writings were published as *Mathematische Werke*, 7 vols. (Berlin, 1894–1927). His papers are listed in Poggendorff, II, 1282; III, 1424; IV, 1610; V, 1345; and VI, 2831.

The following letters have been published: to Paul du Bois-Reymond, G. Mittag-Leffler, ed., in *Acta mathematica*, 39 (1923), 199–225; to Leo Koenigsberger, G. Mittag-Leffler, ed., ibid., 226–239; to Lazarus Fuchs, M. Wentscher and L. Schlesinger, ed., ibid., 246–256. Excerpts of Weierstrass' correspondence with Sonya Kovalevsky were included by Mittag-Leffler in his discussion, "Une page de la vie de Weierstrass," in *Compte rendu du deuxième Congrès international des mathématiciens* (Paris, 1902), 131–153; and in "Zur Biographie von Weierstrass," in *Acta mathematica*, 35 (1912), 29–65, which also includes Weierstrass' letters to Mittag-Leffler. His letters to Kovalevsky were also used by Mittag-Leffler in "Weierstrass et Sonja Kowalewsky," ibid., 39 (1923), 133–198; by P. Y. Polubarinova-Kochina, in "K biografii S. V. Kovalevskoy" ("Toward a Biography . . ."), in *Istoriko-matematicheskie issledovaniya*, 7 (1954), 666–712; and by K.-R. Biermann, "Karl Weierstrass," in *Journal für die reine und angewandte Mathematik*, 223 (1966), 191–220, which presents a survey of the known archives and their places of deposition. The Weierstrass letters to Kovalevsky have been published completely in P. Y. Polubarinova-Kochina, *Pisma Karla Weierstrassa K Sof'e Kovalevskoj 1871–1891* (Moscow, 1973).

Propositions for academic elections of Weierstrass are in K.-R. Biermann, "Vorschläge zur Wahl von Mathematikern in die Berliner Akademie," in *Abhandlungen der Deutschen Akademie der Wissenschaften zu Berlin*, Kl. für Mathematik, Physik und Technik (1960), no. 3, 25–34, passim. Weierstrass' analysis is discussed in Pierre Duac, "Éléments d'analyse de Karl Weierstrass," in *Archive for History of Exact Sciences*, nos. 1–2, 10 (1973), 41–176.

II. SECONDARY LITERATURE. See Henri Poincaré, "L'oeuvre mathématique de Weierstrass," in *Acta mathematica*, 22 (1899), 1–18; and G. Mittag-Leffler, "Die ersten 40 Jahre des Lebens von Weierstrass," ibid., 39 (1923), 1–57. A number of Weierstrass' students and auditors have published reminiscences of him; see the bibliography to Biermann's memoir (cited above), in *Journal für die reine und angewandte Mathematik*, 223 (1966), 219–220. See also *Festschrift zur Gedächtnisfeier für Karl Weierstrass*, H. Behnke and K. Kopfermann, eds. (Cologne–Opladen, 1966); and especially Heinrich Behnke, "Karl Weierstrass und seine Schule," 13–40; as well as K.-R. Biermann, "Die Berufung von Weierstrass nach Berlin," 41–52. See also the following articles by Biermann: "Dirichlet über Weierstrass," in *Praxis der Mathematik*, 7 (1965), 309–312; "K. Weierstrass und A. v. Humboldt," in *Monatsberichte der Deutschen Akademie der Wissenschaften zu Berlin*, 8 (1966), 33–37; "Karl Weierstrass in seinen wissenschaftlichen Grundsätzen," in *Sudhoffs Archiv*, 50 (1966), 305–309; and the book by Biermann, *Die mathematik und ihre Dozenten an der Berliner Universität 1810–1920* (Berlin, 1973).

KURT-R. BIERMANN

WEINGARTEN, JULIUS (*b.* Berlin, Germany, 2 March 1836; *d.* Freiburg im Breisgau, Germany, 16 June 1910)

The son of a weaver who had emigrated from Poland, Weingarten graduated from the Berlin municipal trade school in 1852 and then studied mathematics and physics at the University of Berlin and chemistry at the Berlin Gewerbeinstitut. Between 1858 and 1864 he was an assistant teacher at various schools in Berlin. After receiving the Ph.D. from the University of Halle in 1864, Weingarten taught at the Bauakademie in Berlin, where he was promoted to the rank of professor in 1871. His next position was at the newly founded Technische Hochschule in Berlin. In 1902, for reasons of health, he moved to Freiburg im Breisgau, where he taught as honorary professor until 1908.

Weingarten was inspired by Dirichlet's lectures to study potential theory and later in his career he occasionally published papers on theoretical physics. It was, however, in pure mathematics, particularly in differential geometry, that he made his greatest contribution. Lack of money obliged Weingarten to accept unsatisfactory teaching positions for many years. It was not until he came to Freiburg that, at an advanced age, he found a suitable academic post.

In 1857 the University of Berlin awarded Weingarten a prize for a work on the lines of curvature of a surface, and in 1864 he received the doctorate for the same work. In the meantime he had written other major papers on the theory of surfaces (1861, 1863). This was the most important subject in differential geometry in the nineteenth century, and one of its main problems was that of stating all the surfaces isometric to a given surface. The only class of such surfaces known before Weingarten consisted of the developable surfaces isometric to the plane. These included the cones.

Weingarten was the first to go beyond this stage. For example, he gave the class of surfaces isometric to a given surface of revolution. He had the important insight of introducing those surfaces for which there exists a definite functional relationship between their principal curvatures (1863). These are now called W-surfaces in his honor. Weingarten showed that the one nappe of the central surface of a W-surface is isometric to a surface of revolution and, conversely, that all surfaces isometric to surfaces of revolution can also be obtained in this manner. The W-surfaces are best conceived by considering their spherical image and, operating from this point of view, Weingarten also described various classes of surfaces that are isomorphic to each other. Later he cited classes of this kind in which there are no surfaces of revolution (1884).

In 1886 and 1887 Weingarten studied the infinitesimal deformation of surfaces. Jean-Gaston Darboux, the leading differential geometer of the nineteenth century and author of the four-volume *Leçons sur la théorie générale des surfaces . . .*, stated that Weingarten's achievements were worthy of Gauss. Darboux's work inspired Weingarten to undertake further research, which appeared in a long paper that was awarded a prize by the Paris Academy of Sciences in 1894 and was published in *Acta mathematica* in 1897. In this paper Weingarten reduced the problem of determining all the surfaces isometric to a given surface F to that of determining all solutions of a certain partial differential equation of the Monge-Ampère type.

BIBLIOGRAPHY

Weingarten's writings include "Über die Oberflächen, für welche einer der beiden Hauptkrümmungsmesser eine Funktion des anderen ist," in *Journal für die reine und angewandte Mathematik*, **62** (1863), 160–173; "Über die Theorie der aufeinander abwickelbaren Oberflächen," in *Festschrift der Königlichen Technischen Hochschule zu Berlin* (Berlin, 1884), 1–43; "Über die Deformation einer biegsamen unausdehnbaren Fläche," in *Journal für die reine und angewandte Mathematik*, **100** (1887), 296–310; "Sur la déformation des surfaces," in *Acta mathematica*, **20** (1897), 159–200; and "Mémoire sur la déformation des surfaces," in *Mémoires présentés par divers savants*, 2nd ser., **32** (1902), 1–46.

An obituary is Stanislaus Jolles, "Julius Weingarten," in *Sitzungsberichte der Berliner mathematischen Gesellschaft*, **10** (1911), 8–11.

WERNER BURAU

WERNER, JOHANN(ES) (*b.* Nuremberg, Germany, 14 February 1468; *d.* Nuremberg, May [?] 1522)

While still a student in Nuremberg, Werner was drawn to the exact sciences and later said that he was intended for the study of mathematics from his early childhood. He enrolled at the University of Ingolstadt on 21 September 1484; and in 1490 he was appointed chaplain in Herzogenaurach. While studying in Rome (1493–1497) Werner was ordained a priest and met Italian scholars. By then his knowledge of mathematics, astronomy, and geography had increased; and he was allowed to inspect scientific manuscripts. He owned a Menelaus manuscript and was acquainted with unpublished works by Jābir ibn Aflaḥ (Geber) and Theodosius. Werner probably acquired his excellent knowledge of Greek in Italy. After his return to Nuremberg he celebrated his first mass in the church of St. Sebald on 29 April 1498. Probably in response to the requests of Empress Bianca Maria, in 1503 he was appointed priest at Wöhrd, just outside Nuremberg. In 1508 he was serving at St. Johannis Church in Nuremberg, where he remained until his death (between 12 March and 11 June 1522).

Werner was reputed to have been "very diligent" in carrying out all official responsibilities. Since his pastoral duties were rather limited, he devoted much of his time to scientific study. His works brought him recognition from such Nuremberg scholars as Willibald Pirkheimer (1470–1530), Sebald Schreyer (1446–1520), and Cardinal Matthäus Lang (1468–1540). He was friendly with Bernhard Walther (*ca.* 1430–1504) and the choirmaster Lorenz Beheim (1457[?]–1521) from Bamberg, as well as Albrecht Dürer, who occasionally asked his advice on mathematical problems. Werner enjoyed an excellent reputation even among scholars from Vienna: in 1514 the mathematician and imperial historiographer Johannes Stabius arranged the publication of a collection of writings on geography that included works by Werner. The humanist Konrad Celtis, whom Werner regarded as his "most beloved teacher," tried in 1503 to have Werner transferred to Vienna. Emperor Maximilian I appointed him chaplain at his court.

Not all of Werner's numerous works were published during his lifetime. Some remain unprinted, and others have been lost. Besides the 1514 collection containing Werner's and other authors' writings on geography, a collection of mathematical and astronomical works was published at Nuremberg in 1522. A handwritten remark in the Munich copy of the latter work leads us to believe that Werner died while the work was being printed. His meteorological treatise appeared after his death, and his works on spherical trigonometry and meteoroscopes were not published until 1907 and 1913, respectively.

Astronomy. In a sense Werner can be regarded as a student of Regiomontanus, for he had access to the latter's writings. Although a skilled maker of astronomical instruments, he showed less talent in theoretical work. The Germanisches Nationalmuseum in Nuremberg possesses a gold-plated brass astrolabe from 1516, probably made by Werner

(see Zinner, pl. 25, 4). The clock on the south side of the parish church in Herzogenaurach and the two sundials in the choir of the church at Rosstal may be by Werner. He improved the Jacob's staff that had been used by Regiomontanus to measure interstellar distances, and he described it in the 1514 collection ("In eundem primum librum . . . Ptholomaei . . .," ch. 4, annotations 3–5).

Werner also invented an instrument that he called a "meteoroscope" to solve problems in spherical astronomy. It consists of a metal disk divided into quadrants with a pointer attached. Like the saphea, the first and fourth quadrants contain a stereographic projection of the circles of latitude and longitude, while the second and third quadrants have two different types of sine divisions. The device, which is only known from the description in "De meteoroscopiis," was built not for observational purposes but to replace as many mathematical tables as possible. Even here Werner proved to be a student of Regiomontanus, although his meteoroscope had nothing in common with the device of the same name built by his famous predecessor: Regiomontanus' instrument, the directions for use of which were published by Werner, is an armillary sphere. Werner's treatises on sundials and on astronomical and geographical problems that can be solved by methods of spherical trigonometry have been lost.

A manuscript dated 1521 concerning the making of a device designed to determine the latitudes of planets and one containing tables for the five planets are among Werner's unpublished works, as is a letter to Sebald Schreyer about the comet of 1500. Several horoscopes give evidence of Werner's work in astrology. They were cast for Ursula Gundelfinger, Erasmus Topler, Willibald Pirkheimer, Christoph Scheurl, and Sebald Schreyer.

Werner had less success with his treatises on the movement of the eighth sphere, which constitute the last section of the collection of works published in 1522. He maintains that the so-called precession of the stars would be an irregular movement, thus showing that he was a disciple of the Arab trepidation theory. In a letter to the canon of Cracow cathedral, Bernhard Wapowski, Copernicus attacked the treatise vigorously; and Tycho Brahe criticized it by accusing Werner of having failed to observe accurately enough the three stars that Werner took as the basis of the movement of the eighth sphere.

Mathematics. Werner's mathematical works are in spherical trigonometry and the theory of conic sections. His principal work on spherical triangles was printed in 1907 from the copy in Codex Vaticanus Reginensis Latinus 1259 (fols. 1r–184r). A second copy of the autograph that contains figures was later discovered by Ernst Zinner (Landesbibliothek Weimar, no. f 324, fols. 1–103). Rheticus intended to publish the two writings, but only the letter of dedication to Ferdinand I of Bohemia and Hungary appeared (Cracow, 1557). The work, in four parts, which was written between 1505 and 1513, was not revised for publication by Werner. A fifth part for which he collected material has been lost. Although the treatise is incomplete, Werner's work was the best of its kind at the time, and its presentation surpassed that in Regiomontanus' books on triangles. In comparison with Regiomontanus' treatise, Werner's work is notable for its methodical presentation and practical applicability.

The various types of triangles are systematically described in part I. The following parts, which probably were written earlier, contain a theory of triangular calculation suitable for practical purposes. The basic formulas of spherical trigonometry and instructions for the solution of right spherical triangles are given in part II, and parts III and IV concern the calculation of oblique-angled triangles. In part IV Werner uses formulas that correspond to the cosine formula. Thus in proposition 5 he does not use the cosine formula as it is known today,

$$\cos b = \cos a \cos c + \sin a \sin c \cos B$$

(angle B is sought; a, b, c are the sides), but writes

$$\frac{\frac{1}{2}(\sin[90° - a + c] - \sin[90° - c - a])}{\sin(90° - b) - \sin(90° - c - a)} = \frac{r}{\sin \text{vers}(180° - B)}.$$

This means that Werner implicitly used the formula

$$2 \sin a \sin c = \cos(a - c) - \cos(a + c),$$

whereby he could replace multiplication and division with addition and subtraction. This method, which later became known as prosthaphaeresis, was first used by Werner, but mathematicians soon realized that it simplified calculation. Perhaps through Rheticus, Tycho Brahe learned of this procedure, which was used until the introduction of logarithms.

The treatise containing twenty-two theorems on conic sections was intended as an introduction to his work on duplication of the cube. For that reason Werner dealt only with the parabola and hyperbola but not with the ellipse. In a manner similar to the methods of Apollonius, Werner produced a cone by passing through the points of the circumference straight lines that also pass through a point not in the plane of the circle. In contrast to the ancients he did not consider the parabola and the hyperbola to be defined as plane curves but regarded them in connection with the cone by which they were formed. He proved the theorems on conic sections through geometrical observations on the cone.

Werner's report on duplication of the cube contained nothing new, being only a revision of the eleven solutions to this problem found in classical antiquity; they were known to Werner from the translation of the commentary by Eutocius on Archimedes prepared by Giorgio Valla. Werner added twelve supplementary notes to his treatise. The first ten dealt with the transformation of parallelepipeds and cylinders. In the eleventh note Werner proved that the sun's rays fall on the earth in parallel, and in the twelfth he showed that the rays are gathered in one point on a parabolic mirror.

The third writing in the collection of works dated 1522 also contained an Archimedean problem already treated by Eutocius, in which a sphere is to be cut by a plane so that the volumes of the two spherical sections are in a given proportion to each other (*De sphaera et cylindro* II, 4). Werner added his own solution, in which a parabola and hyperbola intersect each other, to those of Dionysodorus and Diocles.

Some mathematical works by Werner have been lost, including one on arithmetic, a work that apparently was influenced by Euclid's *Data*, and a translation of Euclid's *Elements* into German that Werner completed at the request of Pirkheimer and Sebald Beheim for the sum of 100 taler.

Geography and Meteorology. The collection dated 1514 contains Werner's works on mathematical geography. In the commentary on the first book of Ptolemy's *Geography*, Werner explains the basic concepts of spherical geography and then turns to the measurement of degrees on the sphere. When determining the declination of the sun, he refers to the tables compiled by Georg von Peuerbach and Domenico Maria. Werner's method is interesting in that it determines simultaneously the longitude and the latitude of a place (ch. 3, annotation 8): For the first time it was possible for two sites the locations of which are being sought to be found by a combined series of observations. Since for the determination of latitude it is necessary merely to observe the upper and lower culmination of a circumpolar star, but not the position of the sun, quite a few sources of errors were removed. The fourth chapter deals with the determination of the difference in longitude of two places, which can be obtained by simultaneous observation of a lunar eclipse. Another method is based on the determination of the distance of a zodiac star from the moon as seen from two places (ch. 4, annotation 8). This method of calculating the distances to the moon requires only the determination of the angular distances, which can be carried out by means of the Jacob's staff, and the precise knowledge of the true and mean motions of the moon. This method soon replaced the older ones and was then used as the principal method for determining longitude in nautical astronomy.

The methods used by Werner enabled him to improve or to explain certain details of the ancient geographers, especially those of Marinus. Werner's remarks in chapters 7–10 refer to Marinus' determination of places, which he proves to be often incorrect, or to the sea voyages mentioned and explained by Marinus. Werner demonstrated a knowledge of the existence and direction of the trade winds and explained their origin. In addition, he tried to present a theoretical proof of approximate formulas for the determination of distances that were used in navigation.

Werner's contributions to cartography are based on his criticism of Marinus; they can be found at the end of the commentary on Ptolemy and in the "Libellus quatuor terrarum orbis . . . ." The remarks on chapter 24 of the *Geography* lead us to believe that Werner understood the two projections used by Ptolemy (simple conic projection and modified spherical projection) and developed them. The treatise on four other projections of the terrestrial globe, which is dedicated to Pirkheimer, contains more new ideas. In it Werner outlines the principles of stereographic projection and emphasizes that any point on the surface of the sphere can be chosen as the center of projection. In addition, Werner develops three cordiform map projections that resemble one another; the second gives an equal-area projection of the sphere. The idea of an equivalent projection occurred earlier in the works of Bernard Sylvanus, but Werner and Johannes Stabius were the first to work it out mathematically. Later, Oronce Fine, Peter Apian, and Gerardus Mercator adopted the cordiform projection. It is not known whether Werner designed a map of the world.

Werner's work in geography gained widespread recognition. Peter Apian, in particular, was a student of Werner's in theoretical cartography. The treatises contained in the collection dated 1514 were included almost unchanged in Apian's *Introductio geographica* (1533); Apian even used the proof sheets from the beginning of "In eundem primum librum . . . argumenta" to the end of "Joannis de Regiomonte epistola . . . de compositione et usu cuiusdam meteoroscopii," and admits in several places in his writings how much he had learned from Werner.

In meteorology Werner paved the way for a scientific interpretation. Meteorology and astrology were connected, but he nevertheless attempted to explain this science rationally. A short text on weather forecasting is still available in the manuscript "Regula aurea . . . ." The "guidelines that explain the principles and observations of the changes in the atmosphere," published in 1546 by Johann Schöner, contain meteorological notes for 1513–1520. The weather observations are based mainly on stellar constellations, and hence the course of the moon is of less importance. Although Werner did not collect the data systematically, as Tycho Brahe did, he attempted to incorporate meteorology into physics and to take into consideration the geographical situation of the observational site. Thus he can be regarded as a pioneer of modern meteorology and weather forecasting.

Other Works. The manuscript Codex Guelf. 17.6 Aug. 4° (Herzog-August Bibliothek, Wolfenbüttel) is an autograph in which words occasionally are crossed out and numerous addenda appear in the margin. The treatise gives an annal-like presentation of important events that occurred in Nuremberg between 1506 and 1521, most of which were political. On folios 41v and 70v two astronomical drawings that refer to Nuremberg are incorporated into the text.

BIBLIOGRAPHY

I. ORIGINAL WORKS. Writings published during Werner's lifetime were a collection on geography, *In hoc opere haec continentur . . . .* (Nuremberg, 1514), opusculum," "In idem Georgii Amirucii opusculum appendices," and "Ioannis de Regiomonte epistola ad reverendissimum patrem et dominum Bessarionem de which contained as well as "Nova translatio primi libri geographiae Cl. Ptolomaei," "In eundem primum librum geographiae Cl. Ptolomaei argumenta, paraphrases, quibus idem liber per sententias ac summatim explicatur, et annotationes," "Libellus de quatuor terrarum orbis in plano figurationibus ab eodem I.V. novissime compertis et enarratis," "Ex fine septimi libri eiusdem geographiae Cl. Ptolomaei super plana terrarum orbis descriptione a priscis instituta geographis," "De his quae geographiae debent adesse Georgii Amirucii Constantinopolitani compositione et usu cuiusdam meteoroscopii"—all re-edited by Peter Apian in his *Introductio geographica in doctissimas in Verneri annotationes* (Ingolstadt, 1533); and works on mathematics and astronomy, *In hoc opere haec continentur . . .* (Nuremberg, 1522), which contains "Libellus super vigintiduobus elementis conicis," "Commentarius seu paraphrastica enarratio in undecim modos conficiendi eius problematis quod cubi duplicatio dicitur," "Commentatio in Dionysodori problema, quo data sphaera plano sub data secatur ratione," "Alius modus idem problema conficiendi ab eodem I.V. novissime compertus demonstratusque," "De motu octavae sphaerae tractatus duo," and "Summaria enarratio theoricae motus octavae sphaerae."

Published after Werner's death were *Canones sicut brevissimi, ita etiam doctissimi, complectentes praecepta et observationes de mutatione aurae clarissimi mathematici Ioannis Verneri,* J. Schöner, ed. (Nuremberg, 1546); *Ioannis Verneri de triangulis sphaericis libri quatuor,* A. A. Björnbo, ed., XXIV. pt. 1, of the series Abhandlungen zur Geschichte der Mathematischen Wissenschaften mit Einschluss Ihrer Anwendungen (Leipzig, 1907); and *Ioannis Verneri de meteoroscopiis libri sex,* Joseph Würschmidt, ed., XXIV, pt. 2, of the same series (Leipzig, 1913). Some of Werner's letters are published in H. Rupprich, ed., *Der Briefwechsel des Konrad Celtis* (Munich, 1934).

The following writings remain in MS: "Tabulae latitudinum Saturni, Jovis, Martis, Veneris et Mercurii" (1521), Codex Oxoniensis Digby 132, fols. 1r–28v; "Compositiones et usus organorum latitudinum lunae et quinque planetarum" (1521), *ibid.,* fols. 29r–64r; "Judicium de cometa anni 1500 ad Sebaldum Clamosum alias Schreyer civem Nurembergensem" (1500), Vienna, Codex Vind. lat. 4756, fols. 143r–146v; two horoscopes, *ibid.,* 5002, fols. 104r–111v; "Regula aurea de aeris dispositione diiudicanda singulis diebus," *ibid.,* 5212, fols. 5v–6v; astrological writings, *ibid.,* 10534, fols. 248v, 260r; horoscopes (1498), *ibid.,* 10650, fols. 42r–87r; horoscope (1513), Munich, Clm 27083, fols. 1r–8v; horoscope, Paris, BN Reg. 7417; and "Historicus diarius inde ab anno 1506–1521 Johannis Verneri presbiteri Bambergensis diocesis et vicarii seu rectoris cappelle beatorum Johannis baptiste et Johannis evangeliste Norinbergensis," Wolfenbüttel, Codex Guelf. 17.6 Aug. 4°.

Lost works written before 1514 are "Liber de multimodis tam in astronomia quam in geographia problematis, quae ope arteque horum quinque librorum (Libri quinque de triangulis) absolvuntur"; "Opusculum de nonnullis scioteris, quibus linea meridiana, sublimitas axis mundani et hora diei sub omni climate per umbram solis simul examinantur"; "Tractatus resolutorius, qui prope pedissequus existit libris *Datorum* Euclidis"; and "Libellus arithmeticus, qui complectitur quaedam commenta numeralia." Also lost is a translation of Euclid's *Elements* into German.

II. SECONDARY LITERATURE. On Werner's life, see Johann Gabriel Doppelmayr, *Historische Nachricht von den Nürnbergischen Mathematicis und Künstlern* (Nuremberg, 1730), 31–35; Siegmund Günther, in *Allgemeine deutsche Biographie,* XLII (Leipzig, 1897), 56–58; Abraham Gotthilf Kästner, *Geschichte der Mathematik seit der Wiederherstellung der Wissenschaften bis ans Ende des 18. Jahrhunderts,* II (Göttingen, 1797; repr. Hildesheim–New York, 1970), 52–64; Hans Kressel, "Hans Werner. Der gelehrte Pfarrherr von St. Johannis. Der Freund und wissenschaftliche Lehrmeister Albrecht Dürers," in *Mitteilungen des Vereins für Geschichte der Stadt Nürnberg,* **52** (1963–1964), 287–304; Karl Schottenloher, "Der Mathematiker und Astronom Johann Werner aus Nürnberg. 1466 [*sic*]–1522," in *Festgabe an Hermann Grauert* (Freiburg im Breisgau, 1910), 147–155; and Ernst Zinner, "Die fränkische Sternkunde im 11, bis 16. Jahrhundert," in *Bericht der Naturforschenden Gesellschaft in Bamberg,* **27** (1934), 111–113. A biography of Werner is being prepared by Kurt Pilz as part of his work *600 Jahre Astronomie in Nürnberg.*

Werner's achievements in astronomy are discussed in Ernst Zinner, *Verzeichnis der astronomischen Handschriften des deutschen Kulturgebietes* (Munich, 1925), nos. 11641–11650; and *Deutsche und niederländische astronomische Instrumente des 11.–18. Jahrhunderts* (2nd ed., Munich, 1967), 148, 151 f., 208 f., 584.

Copernicus' criticism of Werner is presented in Maximilian Curtze, "Der Brief des Coppernicus an den Domherrn Wapowski zu Krakau über das Buch des Johannes Werner *De motu octavae sphaerae,*" in *Mittheilungen des Coppernicus-Vereins für Wissenschaft und Kunst, Thorn,* no. 1 (1878), 18–33; Siegmund Günther, "Der Wapowski-Brief des Coppernicus und Werners Tractat über die Praecession," *ibid.,* no. 2 (1880), 1–11; and *Three Copernican Treatises,* translated with intro. and notes by Edward Rosen (2nd ed., New York, 1959), 7–9, 91–106.

Brahe's criticism of Werner appears in *Tychonis Brahe opera omnia,* J. L. E. Dreyer, ed., VII (Copenhagen, 1924), 295, ll. 23–42.

Werner's achievements in mathematics are treated in Moritz Cantor, *Vorlesungen über Geschichte der Mathematik,* II, *Vom Jahre 1200 bis zum Jahre 1668* (2nd ed., Leipzig, 1900; repr. New York–Stuttgart, 1965), 452–459; C. J. Gerhardt, *Geschichte der Mathematik in Deutschland,* which is vol. XVII of Geschichte der Wissenschaften in Deutschland (Munich, 1877; repr. New York–London, 1965), 23–25; and Johannes Tropfke, *Geschichte der Elementar-Mathematik in systematischer Darstellung,* 2nd ed., V (Berlin–Leipzig, 1923), 62, 107–110.

On the history of the text of Werner's trigonometry, see A. A. Björnbo, *Ioannis Verneri,* 140–175; E. Zinner, *Deutsche . . . Instrumente . . .,* 358; and Karl Heinz Burmeister, *Georg Joachim Rhetikus 1514–1574. Eine Bio-Bibliographie* (Wiesbaden, 1967), I, 78, 134, 159 f., 181 f., and II, 78.

Werner's achievements in geography and meteorology are discussed in Siegmund Günther, *Studien zur Geschichte der mathematischen und physikalischen Geographie* (Halle, 1878), 273–332.

MENSO FOLKERTS

WESSEL, CASPAR (*b.* Vestby, near Dröbak, Norway, 8 June 1745; *d.* Copenhagen, Denmark, 25 March 1818)

Although he was born when Norway was part of Denmark and spent most of his life in Denmark, Wessel is regarded as a Norwegian. (Niels Nielsen, in his *Matematiken i Danmark, 1528–1800* [Copenhagen–Christiania, 1912], gives his birthplace as Jonsrud in Akershus.) His father, Jonas Wessel, was a vicar in the parish of which his grandfather was the pastor; his mother was Maria Schumacher.

After attending the Christiania Cathedral School in Oslo from 1757 to 1763, Wessel spent a year at the University of Copenhagen. In 1764 he began work on the cartography of Denmark, as an assistant with the Danish Survey Commission operating under the Royal Danish Academy of Sciences. He passed the university examination in Roman law in 1778 and became survey superintendent in 1798. He continued as a surveyor and cartographer even after his retirement in 1805, working on special projects until rheumatism forced him to stop in 1812. He was frequently in financial difficulty; but since he would accept no remuneration for special maps of Schleswig and Holstein requested by the French government, the Royal Danish Academy awarded him a silver medal and a set of its *Mémoires* and maps. He was made a knight of Danebrog in 1815.

Wessel's fame as a mathematician is based entirely on one paper, written in Danish and published in the *Mémoires* of the Royal Danish Academy, that established his priority in publication of the geometric representation of complex numbers. John Wallis had given a geometric representation of the complex roots of quadratic equations in 1685; Gauss had had the idea as early as 1799 but did not explicitly publish it until 1831. Robert Argand's independent publication in 1806 must be credited as the source of this concept in modern mathematics because Wessel's work remained essentially unknown until 1895, when its significance was pointed out by Christian Juel. Despite its lack of influence upon the development of mathematics, Wessel's publication was remarkable in many ways: he was not a professional mathematician; Norway and Denmark were not mathematically productive or stimulating at that time; he was not a member of the Royal Danish Academy (he had been helped and encouraged by J. N. Tetens, councillor of state and president of the science section of the Academy); and yet his exposition was, in some respects, superior to and more modern in spirit than Argand's.

The title of Wessel's treatise calls it an "attempt" to give an analytic representation of both distance and direction that could be used to solve plane and spherical polygons. The connection of this goal with Wessel's work as a surveyor and cartographer is obvious. The statement of the problem also suggests that Wessel should be credited with an early formulation of vector addition. In fact, Michael J. Crowe, in *A History of Vector Analysis* (University of Notre Dame Press, 1967), defines the first period in that history as that of a search for hypercomplex numbers to be used in space analysis and dates it from the time of Wessel, whom he calls the first to add vectors in three-dimensional space. Wessel's first step was to note that two segments of the same line, whether of the same or opposite sense, are added by placing the initial point of one at the terminus of the other and defining the sum to be the segment extending from the initial point of the first to the terminal point of the second. He immediately defined the sum of two nonparallel segments in the same way and extended this definition to apply to any number of segments.

For multiplication of line segments, Wessel drew his motivation from the fact that, in arithmetic, a product of two factors has the same ratio to one factor as the other factor has to 1. Assuming that the product and the two factors are in the same plane and have the same initial point as the unit segment, he reasoned that the product vector should differ in direction from one factor by the same amount by which the other factor differed from unity. Wessel then designated two oppositely directed unit segments having the same origin by $+1$ and -1, and assigned to them the direction angles $0°$ and $180°$. To unit segments perpendicular to these he assigned the symbols $+\epsilon$ and $-\epsilon$ and the angles $90°$ and either $270°$ or $-90°$. Wessel immediately pointed out that multiplication of these numbers corresponded to addition of their angles and gave a table in which $(+\epsilon) \cdot (+\epsilon) = -1$. He then noted that this means that $\epsilon = \sqrt{-1}$, and that these operations do not contradict the ordinary rules of algebra. From this and his definition of addition of vectors, Wessel next wrote cos $v + \epsilon$ sin v as the algebraic formula for a unit segment and then derived the algebraic formula $(a + \epsilon b) \cdot (c + \epsilon d) = ac - bd + \epsilon(ad + bc)$ for the product of any two segments from the formula for the product of two unit segments derived from the equation $(\cos v + \epsilon \sin v)$ $(\cos u + \epsilon \sin u) = \cos(u + v) + \epsilon \sin (u + v)$, using trigonometric identities.

Thus Wessel's development proceeded rather directly from a geometric problem, through geometric-intuitive reasoning, to an algebraic formula. Argand began with algebraic quantities and sought a geometric representation for them.

Wessel was more modern than Argand in his recognition of the arbitrary nature of the definitions of operations that Argand initially attempted to justify by intuitive arguments. Wessel also sought to extend his definition of multiplication to lines in space. T. N. Thiele's view that Wessel should be credited with anticipating Hamilton's formulation of quaternion multiplication, however, seems to exaggerate the extent of his work, which Wessel himself recognized as incomplete.

Wessel used in his development trigonometric identities that Argand derived by means of his definitions of operations on complex numbers. Argand presented a greater variety of applications of his work, including a proof of the fundamental theorem of algebra and of Ptolemy's theorem. Wessel worked at his original problem of applying algebra to the solution of plane and spherical polygons, after expanding his discussion to include formulas for division, powers, and roots of complex numbers.

Wessel's initial formulation was remarkably clear, direct, concise, and modern. It is regrettable that it was not appreciated for nearly a century and hence did not have the influence it merited.

BIBLIOGRAPHY

I. Original Works. Wessel's paper "Om directionens analytiske betegning, et forsøg, anvendt fornemmelig til plane og sphaeriske polygoners opløsning," read to the Royal Danish Academy of Sciences on 10 Mar. 1797, was printed in 1798 by J. R. Thiele and was incorporated in *Nye samling af det Kongelige Danske Videnskabernes Selskabs Skrifter*, 2nd ser., **5** (1799), 496–518. Almost a century later the Academy published a French trans., *Essai sur la représentation analytique de la direction, par Caspar Wessel* (Copenhagen, 1897), with prefaces by H. Valentiner and T. N. Thiele.

In the meantime, Sophus Lie published a reproduction in *Archiv for mathematik og naturvidenskab*, **18** (1896).

The English trans. by Martin A. Nordgaard of portions of the original paper first appeared in D. E. Smith, ed., *A Source Book in Mathematics* (New York, 1929), 55–66, repr. in H. O. Midonick, ed., *The Treasury of Mathematics* (New York, 1965), 805–814.

II. Secondary Literature. The most complete discussions are Viggo Brun, *Regnekunsten i det gamle Norge* (Oslo, 1962), 92–111, with English summary on 120–122; and "Caspar Wessel et l'introduction géométrique des nombres complexes," in *Revue d'histoire des sciences et de leurs applications*, **12** (Jan.-Mar. 1959), 19–24; and Webster Woodruff Beman, "A Chapter in the History of Mathematics," in *Proceedings of the American Association for the Advancement of Science*, **46** (1897), 33–50, which includes a survey of the development of the concept of a complex number with especial emphasis on graphical representation, particularly the work of Wessel—French trans. in *Enseignement mathématique*, **1** (1899), 162–184.

Much information on Wessel's cartographic and surveying activity is in Otto Harms, "Die amtliche Topographie in Oldenburg und ihre kartographischen Ergebnisse," in *Oldenburger Jahrbuch*, **60**, pt. 1 (1961), 1–38.

PHILLIP S. JONES

WEYL, HERMANN (*b.* Elmshorn, near Hamburg, Germany, 9 November 1885; *d.* Zurich, Switzerland, 8 December 1955)

Weyl attended the Gymnasium at Altona and, on the recommendation of the headmaster of his Gymnasium, who was a cousin of Hilbert, decided at the age of eighteen to enter the University of Göttingen. Except for one year at Munich he remained at Göttingen, as a student and later as *Privatdozent*, until 1913, when he became professor at the University of Zurich. After Klein's retirement in 1913, Weyl declined an offer to be his successor at Göttingen but accepted a second offer in 1930, after Hilbert had retired. In 1933 he decided he could no longer remain in Nazi Germany and accepted a position at the Institute for Advanced Study at Princeton, where he worked until his retirement in 1951. In the last years of his life he divided his time between Zurich and Princeton.

Weyl undoubtedly was the most gifted of Hilbert's students. Hilbert's thought dominated the first part of his mathematical career; and although later he sharply diverged from his master, particularly on questions related to foundations of mathematics, Weyl always shared his convictions that the value of abstract theories lies in their success in solving classical problems and that the proper way to approach a question is through a deep analysis of the concepts it involves rather than by blind computations.

Weyl arrived at Göttingen during the period when Hilbert was creating the spectral theory of self-adjoint operators, and spectral theory and harmonic analysis were central in his mathematical research throughout his life. Very soon, however, he considerably broadened the range of his interests, including areas of mathematics into which Hilbert had never penetrated, such as the theory of Lie groups and the analytic theory of numbers, thereby becoming one of the most universal mathematicians of his generation. He also had an important role in the development of mathematical physics, the field to which his most famous books, *Raum, Zeit und Materie* (1918), on the theory of relativity, and *Gruppentheorie und Quantenmechanik* (1928), are devoted.

Weyl's first important work in spectral theory was his *Habilitationsschrift* (1910), on singular boundary conditions for second-order linear differential equations. The classical Sturm-Liouville problem consists in determining solutions of a self-adjoint differential equation

$$(1) \qquad (py')' - (q - \lambda)y = 0$$

in a compact interval $0 \leq x \leq l$, with $p(x) > 0$ and q real in that interval, the solutions being subject to boundary conditions

$$(2) \qquad y'(0) - wy(0) = 0$$

$$(3) \qquad y'(l) - hy(l) = 0$$

with real numbers w, h; it is known that nontrivial solutions exist only when λ takes one of an increasing sequence (λ_n) of real numbers ≥ 0 and tending to $+\infty$ (the spectrum of the equation). Weyl investigated the case in which $l = +\infty$; his idea was to give arbitrary complex values to λ. Then, for given real h, there is a unique solution satisfying (2) and (3), provided w is taken as a complex number $w(\lambda, h)$. When h takes all real values, the points $w(\lambda, h)$ are on a circle $C_l(\lambda)$ in the complex plane. Weyl also showed that when l tends to $+\infty$, the circles $C_l(\lambda)$ (for fixed λ) form a nested family that has a circle or a point as a limit. The distinction between the two cases is independent of the choice of λ, for in the "limit circle" case all solutions of (1) are square-integrable on $[0, +\infty]$, whereas in the "limit point" case only one solution (up to a constant factor) has that property. This was actually the first example of the general theory of defects of an unbounded Hermitian oper-

ator, which was created later by von Neumann. Weyl also showed how the classical Fourier series development of a function in a series of multiples of the eigenfunctions of the Sturm-Liouville problem was replaced, when $l - +\infty$, by an expression similar to the Fourier integral (the spectrum then being generally a nondiscrete subset of **R**); he thus anticipated the later developments of the Carleman integral operators and their applications to differential linear equations of arbitrary order and to elliptic linear partial differential equations.

In 1911 Weyl inaugurated another important chapter of spectral theory, the asymptotic study of the eigenvalues of a self-adjoint compact operator U in Hilbert space H, with special attention to applications to the theory of elasticity. For this purpose he introduced the "maximinimal" method for the direct computation of the nth eigenvalue λ_n of U (former methods gave the value of λ_n only after those of $\lambda_1, \lambda_2, \cdots, \lambda_{n-1}$ had been determined). One considers an arbitrary linear subspace F of codimension $n - 1$ in H and the largest value of the scalar product $(U \cdot x \mid x)$ when x takes all values on the intersection of F and the unit sphere $\|x\| = 1$ of H; λ_n is the smallest of these largest values when F is allowed to run through all subspaces of codimension 1. This method has a very intuitive geometric interpretation in the theory of quadrics when H is finite-dimensional; it was used with great efficiency in many problems of functional analysis by Weyl himself and later by Richard Courant, who did much to popularize it and greatly extend its range of applications.

Weyl published the famous paper on equidistribution modulo 1, one of the highlights of his career, in 1916. A sequence (x_n) of real numbers is equidistributed modulo 1 if for any interval $[\alpha, \beta]$ contained in $[0,1]$, the number $\nu(\alpha, \beta; n)$ of elements x_k such that $k \leq n$ and $x_k = N_k + y_k$, with $\alpha \leq y_k \leq \beta$ and N_k a (positive or negative) integer, is such that $\nu(\alpha, \beta; n)/n$ tends to the length $\beta - \alpha$ of the interval when n tends to $+\infty$. Led to such questions by his previous work on the Gibbs phenomenon for series of spherical harmonics, Weyl approached the problem by a completely new — and amazingly simple — method. For any sequence (y_n) of real numbers, write $M((y_n))$ the limit (when it exists) of the arithmetic mean $(y_1 + \cdots + y_n)/n$ when n tends to $+\infty$; then to say that (x_n) is equidistributed means that $M((f(x_n))) = \int_0^1 f(t)dt$ for any function of period 1 coinciding on $[0,1]$ with the characteristic function of any interval $[\alpha, \beta]$. Weyl's familiarity with harmonic analysis enabled him to conclude (1) that this property was equivalent to the existence of $M((f(x_n)))$ for all Riemann integrable functions of period 1 and (2) that it was enough to check the existence of that limit for the particular functions $\exp(2\pi ikx)$ for any integer $k \in Z$. This simple criterion immediately yields the equidistribution of the sequence $(n\alpha)$ for irrational α (proved independently a little earlier by Weyl, Bohl, and Wacław Sierpiński by purely arithmetic methods), as well as a quantitative form of the Kronecker theorems on simultaneous Diophantine approximations.

Weyl's most profound result was the proof of the equidistribution of the sequence $(P(n))$, where P is a polynomial of arbitrary degree, the leading coefficient of which is irrational; this amounts to showing that

$$s_N = \sum_{n=0}^{N} \exp(2\pi i P(n)) = o(N)$$

for N tending to $+\infty$. To give an idea of Weyl's ingenious proof, consider the case when $P(n) = \alpha n^2 + \beta n$ with irrational α. One writes

$$|s_N|^2 = s_N \bar{s}_N = \sum_{m,n=0}^{N} \exp(2\pi i(\alpha(m^2 - n^2) + \beta(m - n)))$$

$$= \sum_{r=-N}^{N} \sigma_r \cdot \exp(2\pi i(\alpha r^2 + \beta r)),$$

where $\sigma_r = \sum_{n \epsilon I_r} \exp(2\pi i \alpha rn)$, I_r being the interval intersection of $[0,N]$ and $[-r, N - r]$ in $\mathbf{Z}$. This yields $|s_N|^2 \leq \sum_{r=-N}^{N} |\sigma_r|$. One has two majorations, $|\sigma_r| \leq N + 1$ and $|\sigma_r| \leq 1/\sin(2\pi\alpha r)$. For a given $\epsilon \in [0,\frac{1}{2}]$, the number of integers $r \in [-N,N]$ such that $2\alpha r$ is congruent to a number in the interval $[-\epsilon,\epsilon]$ has the form $4\pi\epsilon N + o(N)$ by equidistribution; hence it is $\leq 5\epsilon N$ for large N. Applying to these integers r the first majoration, and the second to the others, one obtains

$$|s_N|^2 \leq 5\epsilon N(N + 1) + (2N + 1) / \sin(\pi\epsilon) \leq 6\epsilon N^2$$

for large N, thus proving the theorem. The extension of that idea to polynomials of higher degree d is not done by induction on d, but by a more elaborate device using the equidistribution of a multilinear function of d variables. Weyl's results, through the improvements made later by I. M. Vinogradov and his school, have remained fundamental tools in the application of the Hardy-Littlewood method in the additive theory of numbers.

Weyl's versatility is illustrated in a particularly striking way by the fact that immediately after these original advances in number theory (which he obtained in 1914), he spent more than ten years as a geometer—a geometer in the most modern sense of the word, uniting in his methods topology, algebra, analysis, and geometry in a display of dazzling virtuosity and uncommon depth reminiscent of Riemann. His familiarity with geometry and topology had been acquired a few years earlier when, as a young *Privatdozent* at Göttingen, he had given a course on Riemann's theory of functions; but instead of following his predecessors in their constant appeal to "intuition" for the definition and properties of Riemann surfaces, he set out to give to their theory the same kind of axiomatic and rigorous treatment that Hilbert had given to Euclidean geometry. Using Hilbert's idea of defining neighborhoods by a system of axioms, and influenced by Brouwer's clever application of Poincaré's simplicial methods (which had just been published), he gave the first rigorous definition of a complex manifold of dimension 1 and a thorough treatment (without any appeal to intuition) of all questions regarding orientation, homology, and fundamental groups of these manifolds. *Die Idee der Riemannschen Fläche* (1913) immediately became a classic and inspired all later developments of the theory of differential and complex manifolds.

The first geometric problem that Weyl attempted to solve (1915) was directly inspired by Hilbert's previous work on the rigidity of convex surfaces. Hilbert had shown how the "mixed volumes" considered by Minkowski could be expressed in terms of a second-order elliptic differential linear operator L_H attached to the "Stützfunktion" H of a given convex body; Blaschke had observed that this operator was the one that intervened in the theory of infinitesimal deformation of surfaces, and this knowledge had enabled Hilbert to deduce from his results that such infinitesimal deformations for a convex body could only be Euclidean isometries. Weyl attempted to prove that not only infinitesimal deformations, but finite deformations of a convex surface as well, were necessarily Euclidean isometries. His very original idea, directly inspired by his work on two-dimensional "abstract" Riemannian manifolds, was to prove simultaneously this uniqueness property and an existence statement, namely that any two-dimensional Riemannian compact manifold with everywhere positive curvature was uniquely (up to isometries) imbeddable in Euclidean three-dimensional space. The bold method he proposed for the proof was to proceed by continuity, starting from the fact that (by another result of Hilbert's) the problem of existence and uniqueness was already solved for the ds^2 of the sphere, and using a family of ds^2 depending continuously on a real parameter linking the given ds^2 to that of the sphere and having all positive curvature. This led him to a "functional differential equation" that he did not completely solve, but later work by L. Nirenberg showed that a complete proof of the theorem could be obtained along these lines.

Interrupted in this work by mobilization into the German army, Weyl did not resume it when he was allowed to return to civilian life in 1916. At Zurich he had worked with Einstein for one year, and he became keenly interested in the general theory of relativity, which had just been published; with his characteristic enthusiasm he devoted most of the next five years to exploring the mathematical framework of the theory. In these investigations Weyl introduced the concept of what is now called a linear connection, linked not to the Lorentz group of orthogonal transformations of a quadratic form of signature (1, 3) but to the enlarged group of similitudes (reproducing the quadratic form only up to a factor); he even thought for a time that this would give him a "unitary theory" encompassing both gravitation and electromagnetism. Although these hopes did not materialize, Weyl's ideas undoubtedly were the source from which E. Cartan, a few years later, developed his general theory of connections (under the name of "generalized spaces").

Weyl's use of tensor calculus in his work on relativity led him to reexamine the basic methods of that calculus and, more generally, of classical invariant theory that had been its forerunner but had fallen into near oblivion after Hilbert's work of 1890. On the other hand, his semiphilosophical, semimathematical ideas on the general concept of "space" in connection with Einstein's theory had directed his investigations to generalizations of Helmholtz's problem of characterizing Euclidean geometry by properties of "free mobility." From these two directions Weyl was brought into contact with the theory of linear representations of Lie groups; his papers on the subject (1925–1927) certainly represent his masterpiece and must be counted among the most influential ones in twentieth-century mathematics.

In the early 1900's Frobenius, I. Schur, and A. Young had completely determined the irreducible rational linear representations of the general linear group $GL(n,C)$ of complex matrices of order n; it was easy to deduce from Schur's results that all

rational linear representations of the special linear group $SL(n,C)$ (matrices of determinant 1) were completely reducible—that is, direct sums of irreducible representations. Independently, E. Cartan in 1913 had described all irreducible linear representations of the simple complex Lie algebras without paying much attention to the exact relation between these representations and the corresponding ones for the simple groups, beyond exhibiting examples of group representations for each type of Lie algebra representations. Furthermore, Cartan apparently had assumed without proof that any (finite-dimensional) linear representation of a semisimple Lie algebra is completely reducible.

Weyl inaugurated a new approach by deliberately focusing his attention on global groups, the Lie algebras being reduced to the status of technical devices. In 1897 Hurwitz had shown how one may form invariants for the orthogonal or unitary group by substituting, for the usual averaging process on finite groups, integration on the (compact) group with respect to an invariant measure. He also had observed that this yields invariants not only of the special unitary group $SU(n)$ but also of the special linear group $SL(n,C)$ (the first example of what Weyl later called the "unitarian trick"). Using Hurwitz's method, I. Schur in 1924 had proved the complete reducibility of all continuous linear representations of $SU(n)$ by showing the existence, on any representation space of that group, of a Hermitian scalar product invariant under the action of $SU(n)$; by using the "unitarian trick" he also was able to prove the complete reducibility of the continuous linear representations of $SL(n,C)$ and to obtain orthogonality relations for the characters of $SU(n)$, generalizing the well-known Frobenius relations for the characters of a finite group. These relations led to the explicit determination of the characters of $SL(n,C)$, which Schur had obtained in 1905 by purely algebraic methods.

Starting from these results, Weyl first made the connection between the methods of Schur and those of E. Cartan for the representations of the Lie algebra of $SL(n,C)$ by pointing out for the first time that the one-to-one correspondence between both types of representations was due to the fact that $SU(n)$ is simply connected. He next extended the same method to the orthogonal and symplectic complex groups, observing, apparently for the first time, the existence of the two-sheeted covering group of the orthogonal group (the "spin" group, for which Cartan had only obtained the linear representations by spinors). Finally, Weyl turned to the global theory of all semisimple complex groups. First he showed that the "unitarian trick" had a validity that was not limited to the classical groups by proving that every semisimple complex Lie algebra $\mathfrak{g}$ could be considered as obtained by complexification from a well-determined real Lie algebra $\mathfrak{g}_u$, which was the Lie algebra of a compact group G_u; E. Cartan had obtained that result through a case-by-case examination of all simple complex Lie groups, whereas Weyl obtained a general proof by using the properties of the roots of the semisimple algebra. This established a one-to-one correspondence between linear representations of $\mathfrak{g}$ and linear representations of $\mathfrak{g}_u$; but to apply Hurwitz's method, one had to have a compact Lie group having $\mathfrak{g}_u$ as Lie algebra and being simply connected. This is not necessarily the case for the group G_u, and to surmount that difficulty, one had to prove that the universal covering group G_u^* of G_u is also compact; the a priori proof that such is the case is one of the deepest and most original parts of Weyl's paper. It is linked to a remarkable geometric interpretation of the roots of the Lie algebra $\mathfrak{g}_u$ relative to a maximal commutative subalgebra $\mathfrak{t}$, which is the Lie algebra of a maximal torus T of G_u. Each root vanishes on a hyperplane of $\mathfrak{t}$, and the connected components of the complement of the union of these hyperplanes in the vector space $\mathfrak{t}$ are polyhedrons that are now called Weyl chambers; each of these chambers has as boundary a number of "walls" equal to the dimension of $\mathfrak{t}$.

Using this description (and some intuitive considerations of topological dimension that he did not bother to make rigorous), Weyl showed simultaneously that the fundamental group of G_u was finite (hence G_u^* was compact) and that for G_u the maximal torus T played a role similar to that of the group of diagonal matrices in $\mathrm{SU}(n)$: every element of G_u is a conjugate of an element of T. Furthermore, he proved that the Weyl chambers are permuted in a simply transitive way by the finite group generated by the reflections with respect to their walls (now called the Weyl group of $\mathfrak{g}$ or of G_u); this proof gave him not only a new method of recovering Cartan's "dominant weights" but also the explicit determination of the character of a representation as a function of its dominant weight.

In this determination Weyl had to use the orthogonality relations of the characters of G_u (obtained through an extension of Schur's method) and a property that would replace Frobenius' fundamental theorem in the theory of linear representations of finite groups: that all irreducible representations are obtained by "decomposing" the regular representation. Weyl conceived the extraordinarily bold idea (for the time) of obtaining all irreducible representations of a semisimple group by "decomposing" an infinite-dimensional linear representation of G_u. To replace the group algebra introduced by Frobenius, he considered the continuous complex-valued functions on G_u and took as "product" of two such functions f,g what we now call the convolution $f*g$, defined by $(f*g)(t) = \int f(st^{-1})g(t)dt$, integration being relative to an invariant measure. To each continuous function f the operator $R(f)$: $g \rightarrow f*g$ is then associated; the "decomposition" is obtained by considering the space of continuous functions on G_u as a pre-Hilbert space and by showing that for suitable f (those of the form $h*h$, where $\bar{h}(t) = \overline{h(t^{-1})}$), $R(f)$ is Hermitian and compact, so that the classical Schmidt-Riesz theory of compact operators can be applied. It should be noted that in this substitute for the group algebra formed by the continuous functions on G_u, there is no unit element if G_u is not trivial (in contrast with what happens for finite groups); again it was Weyl who saw the way out of this difficulty by using the "regularizing" property of the convolution to introduce "approximate units"—that is, sequences (u_n) of functions that are such that the convolutions u_n*f tend to f for every continuous function f.

Very few of Weyl's 150 published books and papers—even those chiefly of an expository character—lack an original idea or a fresh viewpoint. The influence of his works and of his teaching was considerable: he proved by his example that an "abstract" approach to mathematics is perfectly compatible with "hard" analysis and, in fact, can be one of the most powerful tools when properly applied.

Weyl had a lifelong interest in philosophy and metaphysics, and his mathematical activity was seldom free from philosophical undertones or afterthoughts. At the height of the controversy over the foundations of mathematics, between the formalist school of Hilbert and the intuitionist school of Brouwer, he actively fought on Brouwer's side; and if he never observed too scrupulously the taboos of the intuitionists, he was careful in his papers never to use the axiom of choice. Fortunately, he dealt with theories in which he could do so with impunity.

BIBLIOGRAPHY

Weyl's writings were brought together in his *Gesammelte Abhandlungen*, K. Chandrasekharan, ed., 4 vols.

(Berlin – Heidelberg – New York, 1968). See also *Selecta Hermann Weyl* (Basel – Stuttgart, 1956).

J. DIEUDONNÉ

WHISTON, WILLIAM (*b.* Norton, Leicester, England, 9 December 1667; *d.* Lyndon, Rutland, England, 22 August 1752)

Whiston's father, Josiah Whiston, who was also his first teacher, was a pastor. Whiston studied mathematics at Cambridge, where he earned the master's degree in 1693. He was then, successively, tutor to the nephew of John Tillotson; chaplain of the bishop of Norwich; and rector of Lowestoft and Kessingland, Suffolk. Isaac Newton, who liked and admired Whiston, engaged him as his assistant lecturer in mathematics at Cambridge and in 1701 arranged for Whiston to succeed him as Lucasian professor. But the two men became estranged because of a difference of opinion concerning the interpretation of Biblical chronology. Whiston published several theological works in which he defended heterodox opinions and supported Arianism against the dogma of the Trinity. In 1710 he was deprived of his chair and driven from the university. Newton did nothing at all to help him, even though he himself was secretly anti-Trinitarian.

Whiston moved to London, where he led a bohemian life, while continuing to occupy himself with literature and theology. He often had no money, but he nevertheless frequented the court and high society. He wrote many theological and scientific works in this period, and fell into mystic and prophetic trances. At the age of eighty he became an Anabaptist. He retired to the home of his daughter in Lyndon, where he died in 1752.

Whiston's scientific writings include several mathematical treatises, notably a Latin edition of Euclid (Cambridge, 1703), and *Praelectiones astronomicae* (1707). His most important work is *A New Theory of the Earth, From Its Original to the Consummation of All Things. Wherein the Creation of the World in Six Days, the Universal Deluge, and the General Conflagration, as Laid Down in the Holy Scriptures, Are Shewn to be Perfectly Agreeable to Reason and Philosophy* (London, 1696), which went through six editions, an indication of considerable success. It was dedicated to Newton, and its goal was to redo, with the aid of Newtonian cosmology, what Burnet had done with the aid of Descartes in *Telluris theoria sacra* (London, 1681). Whiston prefaced his book by a long dissertation entitled "A Discourse Concerning the Nature, Stile, and Extent of the Mosaick History of the Creation." In its ninety-four separately numbered pages he set forth the principles of a very free interpretation of *Genesis*. In particular, like Burnet, he contended that the Mosaic account (except for the general introduction consisting of the first verse: "In the beginning God created the heaven and the earth") concerns only the earth, and not even the entire solar system. Again like Burnet, Whiston thought that Moses, whose audience consisted of illiterate Jews, was not able to give a scientific account of the formation of the earth.

Seeking to give his arguments a geometric rigor, Whiston presented the theory itself in four books entitled *Lemmata, Hypotheses, Phaenomena,* and *Solutions*. According to the theory, the earth was originally a comet, revolving around the sun in a very eccentric orbit. This is the situation commonly described by the term "chaos." Then one day God decided to make the earth a planet, and the chaos vanished; this is the transformation recounted in Genesis. From this time and until the Flood, the earth revolved around the sun in a perfectly circular orbit; the axis of its poles was perpendicular to the plane of the ecliptic, and there were no seasons and no daily rotation. The Flood, which put an end to this state of affairs, was produced by a comet guided by God. The head of the comet, by its attraction or by its impact, broke the surface layer of the earth, causing the waters of the "great abyss" to overflow; the vapors of the tail of the comet condensed to form torrential rains. The oblique impact of the comet displaced the axis of the poles, transformed the circular orbit into an ellipse, and imparted to the earth its rotational movement. Like Woodward, Whiston thought that the layers of sedimentary rocks and the marine fossils discovered on the continents resulted from this flood. Whiston's exposition of his system lacks clarity, and he sometimes contradicted himself.

Like Newton, but less cautiously, Whiston pictured God as intervening in nature, not only to create matter and endow it with gravitation, but also to direct the course of the history of the earth. Whiston's view was that God intervenes both directly (for example, in the creation of man) and through the intermediary of physical agents (such as a comet). Whiston explicitly stated that these two modes ultimately amount to the same thing. The ideas expressed on this point in *A New Theory of the Earth* were taken up again and made more precise in *Astronomical Principles of Reli-*

gion Natural and Reveal'd, which Whiston published in London in 1717. His thinking was similar to that of Richard Bentley and Samuel Clarke but displayed less precision and clarity. Whiston also attempted to justify his hypotheses by an interesting theory of scientific knowledge, derived from Newton but also showing the deep influence of Burnet and Cartesianism.

Whiston was more than simply a representative of an age and of a group of scientists who sought to reconcile science and Revelation. As in the case of Burnet, from whom he took a great deal, his writings were much disputed but also widely read, throughout the entire eighteenth century, and not just in England. For example, Buffon, who summarized Whiston's theory in order to ridicule it, borrowed more from him than he was willing to admit and thus unconsciously promoted the spread of his ideas. It may be said that all the cosmogonies based on the impact of celestial bodies, including that of Jeans, owed something, directly or indirectly, to Whiston's inventions.

BIBLIOGRAPHY

On Whiston and his work, see Paolo Casini, *L'universo-macchina. Origini della filosofia newtoniana* (Bari, 1969); Hélène Metzger, *Attraction universelle et religion naturelle chez quelques commentateurs anglais de Newton* (Paris, 1938); and Victor Monod, *Dieu dans l'univers* (Paris, 1933).

JACQUES ROGER

WHITEHEAD, ALFRED NORTH (*b*. Ramsgate, Kent, England, 15 February 1861; *d*. Cambridge, Massachusetts, 30 December 1947)

Education, religion, and local government were the traditional interests of the family into which Whitehead was born, the son of a southern English schoolteacher turned Anglican clergyman. As a child Whitehead developed a strong sense of the enduring presence of the past, surrounded as he was by relics of England's history. The school to which he was sent in 1875, Sherborne in Dorset, traced its origin to the eighth century. At Sherborne, Whitehead excelled in mathematics, grew to love the poetry of Wordsworth and Shelley, and in his last year acted as head of the school and captain of games. In the autumn of 1880 he entered Trinity College, Cambridge. Although during his

whole undergraduate study all his courses were on pure or applied mathematics, he nevertheless developed a considerable knowledge of history, literature, and philosophy. His residence at Cambridge, first as scholar, then as fellow, and finally as senior lecturer in mathematics, lasted from 1880 to 1910. During the latter part of this period he used to give political speeches in the locality; these favored the Liberal party and often entailed his being struck by rotten eggs and oranges. In 1890 he married Evelyn Willoughby Wade, whose sense of beauty and adventure fundamentally influenced Whitehead's philosophical thought. Three children were born to them between 1891 and 1898: Thomas North, Jessie Marie, and Eric Alfred, who was killed in action with the Royal Flying Corps in 1918.

In 1910 Whitehead moved to London, where he held a variety of posts at University College and was professor at the Imperial College of Science and Technology. During this period, while active in assisting to frame new educational programs, he turned his reflective efforts toward formulating a philosophy of science to replace the prevailing materialistic mechanism, which in his view was unable to account for the revolutionary developments taking place in science.

In 1924, at the age of sixty-three, Whitehead became a professor of philosophy at Harvard University. There his previous years of reflection issued in a rapid succession of philosophical works of first importance, principally *Process and Reality: An Essay in Cosmology* (1929). He retired from active teaching only in June 1937, at the age of seventy-six. Whitehead died in his second Cambridge ten years later, still a British subject, but with a great affection for America. He had enjoyed the rare distinction of election to fellowships both in the Royal Society and in the British Academy. In 1945 he was also awarded the British Order of Merit.

Whitehead's life and work thus fall naturally into three periods which, although distinct, manifest a unity of development in his thought. At Cambridge University his writings dealt with mathematics and logic, although his thought already displayed those more general interests that would lead him to philosophy. In his second, or London, period, Whitehead devoted himself to rethinking the conceptual and experiential foundations of the physical sciences. He was stimulated in this work by participating in the discussions of the London Aristotelian Society. The writings of his third, or Harvard, period were distinctly philosophical, commencing with *Science and the Modern World* (1925), and culminating in *Process and Reality* (1929) and *Adventures of Ideas* (1933). These three works contain the essentials of his metaphysical thinking. Noteworthy among his several other books are *The Aims of Education* (1929) and *Religion in the Making* (1926), in which he combines a sensitivity to religious experience with a criticism of traditional religious concepts.

Although Whitehead's intellectual importance lies mainly in philosophy itself, he did significant work in mathematics, mathematical logic, theoretical physics, and philosophy of science.

Mathematics and Mathematical Logic. Whitehead's mathematical work falls into three general areas, the first two of which belong to his residence at Cambridge University, the third to his London period. The first area, algebra and geometry, contains his writings in pure mathematics, chief among which is his first book, *A Treatise on Universal Algebra* (1898). Other examples are papers on "The Geodesic Geometry of Surfaces in Non-Euclidean Space" (1898) and "Sets of Operations in Relation to Groups of Finite Order" (1899). The second area consists in work that would today be termed logic and foundations. It includes work on axiomatics (projective and descriptive geometry), cardinal numbers, and algebra of symbolic logic; it culminates in the three-volume *Principia Mathematica*, written with Bertrand Russell. The third area—less relevant from a mathematical point of view—contains the mathematical work that overlaps other fields of Whitehead's scientific activity, mainly his physics and his philosophy of mathematics. His paper "On Mathematical Concepts of the Material World" (1906) is typical of the former; his *Introduction to Mathematics* (1911) lies in the border area between mathematics and the philosophy of mathematics.

Algebra and Geometry. Whitehead's first book, *A Treatise on Universal Algebra*, seems at first glance entirely mathematical. Only in view of his subsequent development are several of his introductory remarks seen to have a philosophical import. This lengthy book, begun in 1891 and published in 1898, formed part of that nineteenth-century pioneering development sometimes referred to as the "liberation of algebra" (from restriction to quantities). Although the movement was not exclusively British, there was more than half a century of British tradition on the subject (George Peacock, Augustus De Morgan, and William Rowan Hamilton), to which Whitehead's mathematical work belonged.

Whitehead acknowledged that the ideas in the *Universal Algebra* were largely based on the work of Hermann Grassmann, Hamilton, and Boole. He even stated that his whole subsequent work on mathematical logic was derived from these sources, all of which are classical examples of structures that do not involve quantities.

After an initial discussion of general principles and of Boolean algebra, the *Universal Algebra* is devoted to applications of Grassmann's calculus of extension, which can be regarded as a generalization of Hamilton's quaternions and an extension of arithmetic. Major parts of the modern theory of matrices and determinants, of vector and tensor calculus, and of geometrical algebra are implied in the calculus of extension. Whitehead's elaboration of Grassmann's work consists mainly in applications to Euclidean and non-Euclidean geometry.

Although the *Universal Algebra* displayed great mathematical skill and erudition, it does not seem to have challenged mathematicians or to have contributed in a direct way to further development of the topics involved. It was never reprinted during Whitehead's lifetime. It is plausible to think that, by the time the mathematical world became aware of the many valuable items of the work, these had been incorporated elsewhere in more accessible contexts and more modern frameworks.

Logic and Foundations. Confining itself to the algebras of Boole and Grassmann, the *Universal Algebra* never became what it was intended to be, a comparative study of algebras as symbolic structures. Whitehead planned to make such a comparison in a second volume along with studies of quaternions, matrices, and the general theory of linear algebras. Between 1898 and 1903 he worked on this second volume. It never appeared, and neither did the second volume of Bertrand Russell's *Principles of Mathematics* (1903). The two authors discovered that their projected second volumes "were practically on identical topics," and decided to cooperate in a joint work. In doing so their vision expanded, and it was eight or nine years before their monumental *Principia Mathematica* appeared.

The *Principia Mathematica* consists of three volumes which appeared successively in 1910, 1912, and 1913. A fourth volume, on the logical foundations of geometry, was to have been written by Whitehead alone but was never completed. The *Principia* was mainly inspired by the writings of Gottlob Frege, Georg Cantor, and Giuseppe Peano. At the heart of the treatment of mathematical logic in the *Principia* lies an exposition of sentential logic so well done that it has hardly been improved upon since. Only one axiom (Axiom 5, the "associative principle") was later (1926) proved redundant by Paul Bernays. The development of predicate logic uses Russell's theory of types, as expounded in an introductory chapter in the first volume. The link with set theory is made by considering as a set all the objects satisfying some propositional function. Different types, or levels, of propositional functions yield different types, or levels, of sets, so that the paradoxes in the construction of a set theory are avoided. Subsequently several parts of classical mathematics are reconstructed within the system.

Although the thesis about the reduction of mathematics to logic is Russell's, as is the theory of types, Russell himself stressed that the book was truly a collaboration and that neither he nor Whitehead could have written it alone.[1] The second edition (1925), however, was entirely under Russell's supervision, and the new introduction and appendices were his, albeit with Whitehead's tacit approval.

Taken as a whole, the *Principia* fills a double role. First, it constitutes a formidable effort to prove, or at least make plausible, the philosophical thesis best described by Russell in his preface to *The Principles of Mathematics*: "That all pure mathematics deals exclusively with concepts definable in terms of a very small number of fundamental logical concepts, and that all its propositions are deducible from a very small number of fundamental logical principles." This thesis is commonly expressed by the assertion that logic furnishes a basis for all mathematics. Some time later this assertion induced the so-called logicist thesis, or logicism, developed by Wittgenstein—the belief that both logic and mathematics consist entirely of tautologies. There is no evidence that Whitehead ever agreed with this; on the contrary, his later philosophical work indicates a belief in ontological referents for mathematical expressions. The thesis that logic furnishes a basis for all mathematics was first maintained by Frege but later (1931) refuted by Kurt Gödel, who showed that any system containing arithmetic, including that of the *Principia*, is essentially incomplete.

The second role of the *Principia* is the enrichment of mathematics with an impressive system, based on a thoroughly developed mathematical logic and a set theory free of paradoxes, by which a substantial part of the body of mathematical knowledge becomes organized. The *Principia* is considered to be not only a historical masterpiece of mathematical architecture, but also of contem-

porary value insofar as it contains subtheories that are still very useful.

Other Mathematical Work. At about the time Whitehead was occupied with the axiomatization of geometric systems, he turned his attention to the mathematical investigation of various possible ways of conceiving the nature of the material world. His paper "On Mathematical Concepts of the Material World" (1906) is just such an effort to create a mathematical although qualitative model of the material world. This effort differs from applied mathematics insofar as it does not apply known mathematics to situations and processes outside mathematics but creates the mathematics *ad hoc* to suit the purpose; yet it resembles applied mathematics insofar as it applies logical-mathematical tools already available. The paper conceives the material world in terms of a set of relations, and of entities that form the "fields" of these relations. The axiomatic mathematical system is not meant to serve as a cosmology but solely to exhibit concepts not inconsistent with some, if not all, of the limited number of propositions believed to be true concerning sense perceptions. Yet the system does have a cosmological character insofar as it tries to comprehend the entire material world. Unlike theoretical physics the paper is entirely devoid of quantitative references. It is thus an interesting attempt to apply logical-mathematical concepts to ontological ones, and is an early indication of Whitehead's dissatisfaction with the Newtonian conception of space and time. In a qualitative way the paper deals with field theory and can be regarded as a forerunner of later work in physics.

The delightful little book *An Introduction to Mathematics* (1911) is another early example of Whitehead's drifting away from the fields of pure mathematics and logic, this time more in the direction of philosophy of mathematics. The book contains a fair amount of solid although mainly fundamental and elementary mathematics, lucidly set out and explained. The object of the book, however, "is not to teach mathematics, but to enable students from the very beginning of their course to know what the science is about, and why it is necessarily the foundation of exact thought as applied to natural phenomena" (p. 2). In it Whitehead stresses the three notions of variable, form, and generality.

Theoretical Physics. Whitehead's contributions to relativity, gravitation, and "unified field" theory grew out of his preoccupations with the principles underlying our knowledge of nature. These philosophical considerations are presented chiefly in *An Enquiry Concerning the Principles of Natural Knowledge* (1919), *The Concept of Nature* (1920), and *The Principle of Relativity* (1922). A. S. Eddington, in his own book *The Nature of the Physical World* (Cambridge, 1929), comments: "Although this book may in most respects seem diametrically opposed to Dr. Whitehead's widely read philosophy of Nature, I think it would be truer to regard him as an ally who from the opposite side of the mountain is tunnelling to meet his less philosophically minded colleagues" (pp. 249–250).

In a chapter on motion in the *Principles of Natural Knowledge*, Whitehead derives the Lorentz transformation equations, now so familiar in Einstein's special theory of relativity. Whitehead's derivation, however, was based on his principle of kinematic symmetry,[2] and was carried through without reference to the concept of light signals. Consequently the velocity c in the equations is not necessarily that of light, although it so happens that in our "cosmic epoch," c is most clearly realized in nature as the velocity of light. There are three types of kinematics, which Whitehead termed "hyperbolic," "elliptic," or "parabolic," according to whether c^2 is positive, negative, or infinite. Whitehead pointed out that the hyperbolic type of kinematics corresponds to the Larmor-Lorentz-Einstein theory of electromagnetic relativity and that the parabolic type reduces to the ordinary Newtonian relativity (Galilean transformation). He rejected the elliptic type as inapplicable to nature.

In *The Principle of Relativity* Whitehead challenged the conceptual foundations of both the special and general theories of Einstein by offering "an alternative rendering of the theory of relativity" (page v). One of Whitehead's fundamental hypotheses was that space-time must possess a uniform structure everywhere and at all times—a conclusion that Whitehead drew from a consideration of the character of our knowledge in general and of our knowledge of nature in particular. He argued that Einstein's view that space-time may exhibit a local curvature fails to provide an adequate theory of measurement:

> Einstein, in my opinion, leaves the whole antecedent theory of measurement in confusion when it is confronted with the actual conditions of our perceptual knowledge. . . . Measurement on his theory lacks systematic uniformity and requires a knowledge of the actual contingent field before it is possible.[3]

Whitehead proposed an action-at-a-distance theory rather than a field theory. He relieved the physicist of the task of having to solve a set of nonlinear partial differential equations. J. L. Synge, who ignored any consideration of the philosophical foundations of the theory, has clearly presented the mathematical formulas of Whitehead's gravitational theory in modern notation.[4]

Using Synge's notation, the world lines of test particles and light rays in Whitehead's theory may be conveniently discussed by the Euler-Lagrange equations:

$$\frac{d}{d\lambda}\frac{\partial L}{\partial \dot{x}_p} - \frac{\partial L}{\partial x_p} = 0, \qquad (1)$$

where $2L = -1$ for test particles; $2L = 0$ for light rays; and $\dot{x}_p = \dfrac{dx_p}{d\lambda}$. The Lagrangian L is defined:

$$L = \frac{1}{2}g_{mn}\dot{x}_m\dot{x}_n, \qquad (2)$$

where g_{mn} is a symmetrical tensor defined by

$$g_{mn} = \delta_{mn} + \frac{2mG}{c^2 w^3}y_m y_n. \qquad (3)$$

In equation (3) δ_{mn} is the Kronecker delta; G is the gravitational constant; c is a fundamental velocity; and m is the mass of a particle with a world line given by $x'_n = x'_n(s')$, where s' is the Minkowskian arc length such that $ds'^2 = -dx'_n dx'_n$; $y_m = x_m - x'_m$; and $w = -y_n\dfrac{dx'_n}{ds'}$. The parameter λ in equation (1) is such that $d\lambda = (-g_{mn}dx_m dx_n)^{\frac{1}{2}}$. Latin suffixes have the range 1, 2, 3, 4. Thus Whitehead's theory of gravitation is described in terms of Minkowskian space-time with $x_4 = ict$ (where $i = \sqrt{-1}$ and c is the speed of light in a vacuum).[5] The basic physical laws of the Whitehead theory are invariant with respect to Lorentz transformations but not necessarily with respect to general coordinate transformations. Whitehead invoked neither the principle of equivalence nor the principle of covariance.

Clifford M. Will has challenged the viability of Whitehead's theory by arguing that it predicts "an anisotropy in the Newtonian gravitational constant G, as measured locally by means of Cavendish experiments."[6] Using Synge's notation, Will calculated Whitehead's prediction of twelve-hour sidereal-time earth tides, which are produced by the galaxy, and found Whitehead's prediction in disagreement with the experimentally measured value of these geotidal effects. In Whitehead's theory the anisotropy in G is a result of the uniform structure of space-time demanded by the theory.

In order to understand the relation of the anisotropy to uniformity we must recognize that in Whitehead's theory gravitational forces are propagated along the geodesics of the uniform structure of space-time, while electromagnetic waves are deflected by the contingencies of the universe.[7] This restriction in the propagation of gravity produces the variation in the gravitational constant. While Whitehead's mathematical formulas imply this restriction, it is not demanded by his philosophy of nature. For Whitehead, gravitational forces share in the contingency of nature, and may therefore be affected, as electromagnetic waves are, by the contingencies of the universe.

In addition to the consideration of gravitation, in chapter 5 of *The Principle of Relativity* Whitehead extends his equations of motion to describe the motion of a particle in a combined gravitational and electromagnetic field. As Rayner points out,[8] this is not a "true" unified field theory since it does not interpret gravitational and electromagnetic phenomena in terms of a single primitive origin.

It is possible to demonstrate, as did Eddington[9] and Synge,[10] that the predictions of Whitehead's theory and those of Einstein's general theory of relativity are equivalent with respect to the four tests of relativity: the deflection of a light ray, the red shift, the advance in the perihelion of a satellite, and radar time delay. The equivalence of the two theories with respect to these tests rests in the remarkable fact that both theories, when solved for a static, spherically symmetrical gravitational field, produce the Schwarzschild solution of the field equations.

In accordance with his usual practice, Whitehead assembled *Relativity* from lectures that he delivered at the Imperial College, the Royal Society of Edinburgh, and Bryn Mawr College. He did not publish in the journals of physical science nor enter into active discourse with members of the scientific community. His gravitational theory is not referred to in the formal treatments of relativity given by such authors as Bergmann, Einstein, and Pauli. The mathematical physicists who studied and extended Whitehead's physical theories in the 1950's had difficulty understanding his esoteric language and his philosophical ideas. While the two ends of Eddington's tunnel have not yet been joined under the mountain, considerable progress has been made by the careful exposition of Whitehead's philosophy of science by Robert M. Palter.[11]

In 1961 C. Brans and R. H. Dicke developed a modified relativistic theory of gravitation apparently compatible with Mach's principle.[12] It is significant that the Einstein, Whitehead, and Brans-Dicke theories represent distinct conceptual formulations, the predictions of which with regard to observational tests are all so close that it is not yet possible on this basis to make a choice among them. New experiments of high precision on the possible Machian time variation of G and on the precession of the spin axis of a gyroscope,[13] as well as theoretical considerations such as the "parametrized post-Newtonian" (PPN) formalism,[14] may be decisive. At present the Einstein theory is regarded as the most influential and elegant; the Brans-Dicke theory has perhaps the most attractive cosmological consequences;[15] and the Whitehead theory, although clearly the simplest, suffers from its obscurity.

Philosophy of Science. Whitehead once remarked that what worried him was "the muddle geometry had got into" in relation to the physical world.[16] Particularly in view of Einstein's theory of relativity, it was unclear what relation geometrical space had to experience. It was therefore necessary to find a basis in physical experience for the scientific concepts of space and time. These are, Whitehead thought, "the first outcome of the simplest generalisations from experience, and . . . not to be looked for at the tail end of a welter of differential equations."[17] The supposed divorce of abstract scientific concepts from actual experience had resulted in a "bifurcation of nature," a splitting into two disparate natures, of which one was a merely apparent world of sense experience, the other a conjectured, causal world perpetually behind a veil. Aside from extrinsic quantitative relations, the elements of this latter world were presumed to be intrinsically self-contained and unrelated to one another. Somehow this conjectured, monadically disjunctive nature, although itself beyond experience, was supposed to account causally for the unified nature of experience. Whitehead rejected this view as incoherent and as an unsatisfactory foundation for the sciences. According to Whitehead, "we must reject the distinction between nature as it really is and experiences of it which are purely psychological. Our experiences of the apparent world are nature itself."[18]

In his middle writings Whitehead examined how space and time are rooted in experience, and in general laid the foundations of a natural philosophy that would be the necessary presupposition of a reorganized speculative physics. He investigated the coherence of "Nature," understood as the object of perceptual knowledge; and he deliberately, although perhaps unsuccessfully, distinguished nature as thus known from the synthesis of knower and known, which falls within the ambit of metaphysical analysis.

Two special characteristics of Whitehead's analysis are of particular importance: his identification of noninstantaneous events as the basic elements of perceived nature, and the intrinsically relational constitution of these events (as displayed in his doctrine of "significance"). Space and time (or space-time) are then shown to be derivative from the fundamental process by which events are interrelated, rather than a matrix within which events are independently situated. This view contrasts sharply with the prevalent notion that nature consists in an instantaneous collection of independent bodies situated in space-time. Such a view, Whitehead thought, cannot account for the perception of the continuity of existence, nor can it represent the ultimate scientific fact, since change inevitably imports the past and the future into the immediate fact falsely supposed to be embodied in a durationless present instant.

Whitehead's philosophy of nature attempts to balance the view of nature-in-process with a theory of elements ingredient within nature ("objects"), which do not themselves share in nature's passage. Whitehead's boyhood sense of permanences in nature thus emerged both in his mathematical realism and in his philosophic recognition of unchanging characters perpetually being interwoven within the process of nature.

Method of Extensive Abstraction. "Extensive abstraction" is the term Whitehead gave to his method for tracing the roots within experience of the abstract notions of space and time, and of their elements.

In this theory it is experienced events, not physical bodies, that are related; their fundamental relation lies in their overlapping, or "extending over," one another. Later Whitehead recognized that this relation is itself derivative from something more fundamental.[19] The notions of "part," "whole," and "continuity" arise naturally from this relation of extending-over. These properties lead to defining an "abstractive set" as "any set of events that possesses the two properties, (i) of any two members of the set one contains the other as a part, and (ii) there is no event which is a common part of every member of the set."[20] Such a set of events must be infinite toward the small end, so that there is no least event in the set. Corresponding to the abstractive set of events there is an ab-

stractive set of the intrinsic characters of the events. The latter set converges to an exactly defined locational character. For instance, the locational character of an abstractive set of concentric circles or squares converges to a nondimensional but located point. In analogous fashion, an abstractive set of rectangles, all of which have a common length but variable widths, defines a line segment. With the full development of this technique Whitehead was able to define serial times, and, in terms of them, space. He concluded that all order in space is merely the expression of order in time. "Position in space is merely the expression of diversity of relations to alternative time-systems."[21]

In general Whitehead held that there are two basic aspects in nature. One is its passage or creative advance; the other its character as extended—that is, that its events extend over one another, thus giving nature its continuity. These two facts are the qualities from which time and space originate as abstractions.

The purpose of the method of extensive abstraction is to show the connection of the abstract with the concrete. Whitehead showed, for instance, how the abstract notion of a point of instantaneous space is naturally related to the experience of events in nature, which have the immediately given property of extension. Whitehead's procedure, however, is easily subject to misunderstanding. Most Whitehead scholars agree that Whitehead was trying neither to deduce a geometry from sense experience, nor to give a psychological description of the genesis of geometric concepts. Rather, he was using a mathematical model to clarify relations appearing in perception. Another misinterpretation would be to assume that Whitehead took as the immediate data for sense awareness some kind of Humean sensa instead of events themselves.

In his notes to the second edition of the *Principles of Natural Knowledge* Whitehead suggested certain improvements in his procedure. The final outcome of extensive abstraction is found in part 4 of *Process and Reality*, "The Theory of Extension," in which Whitehead defines points, lines, volumes, and surfaces without presupposing any particular theory of parallelism, and defines a straight line without any reference to measurement.

Uniformity of Spatiotemporal Relations. In the Preface to *The Principle of Relativity* Whitehead states:

> As the result of a consideration of the character of our knowledge in general, and of our knowledge of nature in particular, . . . I deduce that our experi-

ence requires and exhibits a basis of uniformity, and that in the case of nature this basis exhibits itself as the uniformity of spatio-temporal relations. This conclusion entirely cuts away the casual heterogeneity of these relations which is the essential of Einstein's later theory.

The mathematical consequences of this conclusion for Whitehead's theory of relativity have already been noted. It remains to indicate summarily the reasons that persuaded Whitehead to adopt this view.

Consonance with the general character of direct experience was one of the gauges by which Whitehead judged any physical theory, for he was intent on discovering the underlying structures of nature as observed. Further, he maintained the traditional division between geometry and physics: it is the role of geometry to reflect the relatedness of events; that of physics to describe the contingency of appearance. He also claimed that it is events, not material bodies, that are the terms of the concrete relations of nature. But since for Whitehead these relations were essentially constitutive of events, it might seem that no event can be known apart from knowledge of all those other events to which it is related. Thus, nothing can be known until everything is known—an impossible requirement for knowledge.

Whitehead met this objection by distinguishing between essential and contingent relations of events. One can know that an event or factor is related to others without knowing their precise character. But since in our knowledge no event discloses the particular individuals constituting the aggregate of events to which it is related, even contingently, this relatedness must embody an intrinsic uniformity apart from particular relationships to particular individuals. This intrinsic and necessary uniformity of the relatedness of events is precisely the uniformity of their spatiotemporal structure.

Whitehead provided an illustration of this in a discussion of equality.[22] Equality presupposes measurement, and measurement presupposes matching (not vice versa). It must follow that "measurement presupposes a structure yielding definite stretches which, in some sense inherent in the structure, match each other."[23] This inherent matching is spatiotemporal uniformity.

It is well known that in his later philosophy Whitehead came to hold—contrary to his earlier belief—that nature is not continuous in fact, but "incurably atomic." Continuity was recognized to belong to potentiality, not to actuality.[24] It has

even been claimed that this later revision removes the basic difference between Einstein and Whitehead, so that the Whitehead of *Process and Reality* offers only an alternative interpretation of Einstein's theory of relativity, not an alternative theory.[25] This claim, however, has not found wide support.

Despite some recent interest in it, Whitehead's theory of relativity has been mainly ignored and otherwise not well understood. *The Principle of Relativity* has long been out of print, and it is impossible now to say whether it has a scientific future.

NOTES

1. Bertrand Russell, "Whitehead and Principia Mathematica," *Mind*, n.s. **57** (1948), 137–138.
2. For a discussion and derivation, see C. B. Rayner, "Foundations and Applications of Whitehead's Theory of Relativity," University of London thesis, 1953; "The Application of the Whitehead Theory of Relativity to Non-static, Spherically Symmetrical Systems," in *Proceedings of the Royal Society of London*, **222A** (1954), 509–526.
3. *The Principle of Relativity*, p. 83.
4. J. L. Synge, in *Proceedings of the Royal Society of London*, **211A** (1952), 303–319.
5. Whitehead's requirement that space-time be homogeneous is not violated by a space-time of constant curvature. This extension of Whitehead's theory has been carried out by G. Temple, "A Generalisation of Professor Whitehead's Theory of Relativity," in *Proceedings of the Physical Society of London*, **36** (1923), 176–193; and by C. B. Rayner, "Whitehead's Law of Gravitation in a Space-Time of Constant Curvature," in *Proceedings of the Physical Society of London*, **68B** (1955), 944–950.
6. Clifford M. Will, "Relativistic Gravity in the Solar System . . .," p. 141.
7. Misner, Thorne, and Wheeler, *Gravitation*, p. 430. Whitehead's theory is termed a "two metric" theory of gravitation. The first metric defines the uniform structure of space-time; the second, the physically contingent universe.
8. Rayner, "Foundations and Applications . . .," p. 23.
9. Sir A. S. Eddington, "A Comparison of Whitehead's and Einstein's Formulae," p. 192.
10. J. L. Synge, *The Relativity Theory of A. N. Whitehead* (1951). In ch. 13 of *The Principle of Relativity* Whitehead obtains a red shift that disagrees with Einstein's by a factor of 7/6. This is in disagreement with the terrestrial Mössbauer experiments (see R. V. Pound and G. A. Rebka, Jr., "Apparent Weight of Photons," *Physical Review Letters*, **4** [1960], 337–341). Synge observes, however, that the discrepancy lies in Whitehead's use of a classical rather than a quantum mechanical model of an atom and is not due to Whitehead's gravitational theory. See also C. B. Rayner, "The Effects of Rotation of the Central Body on Its Planetary Orbits, After the Whitehead Theory of Gravitation," in *Proceedings of the Royal Society of London*, **232A** (1955), 135–148.
11. Robert M. Palter, *Whitehead's Philosophy of Science.*
12. C. Brans and R. H. Dicke, in *Physical Review*, **124** (1961), 925–935.
13. L. I. Schiff, "Experimental Tests of Theories of Relativity," in *Physics Today*, **14**, no. 11 (November 1961), 42–48.
14. C. M. Will, *op. cit.*

15. R. H. Dicke, "Implications for Cosmology of Stellar and Galactic Evolution Rates," in *Review of Modern Physics*, **34** (1962), 110–122.
16. Lowe, *Understanding Whitehead*, p. 193.
17. *Principles of Natural Knowledge*, p. vi.
18. *The Principle of Relativity*, p. 62.
19. *Principles of Natural Knowledge*, p. 202.
20. *The Concept of Nature*, p. 79; *Principles of Natural Knowledge*, p. 104.
21. *The Principle of Relativity*, p. 8.
22. *Ibid.*, ch. 3.
23. *Ibid.*, p. 59.
24. Leclerc, "Whitehead and the Problem of Extension."
25. Seaman, "Whitehead and Relativity."

BIBLIOGRAPHY

I. Original Works. A chronological list of all Whitehead's writings may be found in P. A. Schilpp (see below). The following works are of most scientific importance: *A Treatise on Universal Algebra, With Applications* (Cambridge, 1898); "On Mathematical Concepts of the Material World," in *Philosophical Transactions of the Royal Society of London*, **205A** (1906), 465–525, also available in the Northrop and Gross anthology (see below); *Principia Mathematica*, 3 vols. (Cambridge, 1910–1913), written with Bertrand Russell; *An Introduction to Mathematics* (London, 1911); "Space, Time, and Relativity," in *Proceedings of the Aristotelian Society*, n.s. **16** (1915–1916), 104–129, also available in the Johnson anthology (see below); *An Enquiry Concerning the Principles of Natural Knowledge* (Cambridge, 1919); *The Concept of Nature* (Cambridge, 1920); *The Principle of Relativity, With Applications to Physical Science* (Cambridge, 1922), which is out-of-print but may be obtained from University Microfilms, Ann Arbor, Mich.; also, pt. 1, "General Principles," is reprinted in the Northrop and Gross anthology; *Science and the Modern World* (New York, 1925); *Process and Reality: An Essay in Cosmology* (New York; 1929), which is of scientific interest chiefly insofar as it gives Whitehead's final version of his theory of extensive abstraction; and *Essays in Science and Philosophy* (New York, 1947), a collection of earlier essays.

Two useful anthologies of Whitehead's writings are F. S. C. Northrop and Mason W. Gross, eds., *Alfred North Whitehead: An Anthology* (New York, 1961); and A. H. Johnson, ed., *Alfred North Whitehead: The Interpretation of Science, Selected Essays* (Indianapolis, 1961).

II. Secondary Literature. Paul Arthur Schilpp, ed., *The Philosophy of Alfred North Whitehead*, Library of Living Philosophers Series (New York, 1951), contains Whitehead's "Autobiographical Notes," a complete chronological list of Whitehead's writings, and essays pertinent to Whitehead's science by Lowe, Quine, and Northrop. Victor Lowe, *Understanding Whitehead* (Baltimore, 1962), is a valuable tool, especially pt. 2, "The Development of Whitehead's Philosophy," which is an enlargement of Lowe's essay in the Schilpp volume. Robert M. Palter, *Whitehead's Philosophy of Science* (Chicago, 1960), is a perceptive mathematical exposition of Whitehead's views on extension and on relativity. In 1971 appeared *Process Studies* (published at the School of Theology at Claremont, California), a journal devoting itself to exploring the thought of Whitehead and his intellectual associates. The fourth issue of vol. 1 (Winter 1971) contains a bibliography of secondary literature on Whitehead, to be periodically updated.

The following are cited as examples of the influence of Whitehead's thought on scientists or philosophers of science. In *Experience and Conceptual Activity* (Cambridge, Mass., 1965), J. M. Burgers, a physicist of some distinction, presents for scientists a case for a Whiteheadian rather than a physicalistic world view. Also, a strong Whiteheadian perspective dominates Milič Čapek, *The Philosophical Impact of Contemporary Physics* (New York, 1961).

Whitehead's later metaphysics, although consistent with and developed out of his reflections on science, forms another story altogether. For a more general introduction to his thought and to the literature, see the article on Whitehead in Paul Edwards, ed., *The Encyclopedia of Philosophy*, VIII (New York–London, 1967), 290–296.

On Whitehead's mathematics and logic, see Granville C. Henry, Jr., "Whitehead's Philosophical Response to the New Mathematics," in *Southern Journal of Philosophy*, **7** (1969–1970), 341–349; George L. Kline, ed., *Alfred North Whitehead: Essays on His Philosophy*, pt. 2 (Englewood Cliffs, N.J., 1963); J. J. C. Smart, "Whitehead and Russell's Theory of Types," in *Analysis*, **10** (1949–1950), 93–96, which is critical of the theory of types; Martin Shearn, "Whitehead and Russell's Theory of Types: A Reply," *ibid.*, **11** (1950–1951), 45–48.

On Whitehead's theoretical physics, see Sir A. S. Eddington, "A Comparison of Whitehead's and Einstein's Formulae," in *Nature*, **113** (1924), 192; Charles W. Misner, Kip S. Thorne, John Archibald Wheeler, *Gravitation* (San Francisco, 1973); C. B. Rayner, "Foundations and Applications of Whitehead's Theory of Relativity" (Ph.D. thesis, University of London, 1953); A. Schild, "Gravitational Theories of the Whitehead Type and the Principle of Equivalence," in *Proceedings of the International School of Physics*, "Enrico Fermi," course 20 (Italian Physical Society and Academic Press, 1963), 69–115; Francis Seaman, "Discussion: In Defense of Duhem," in *Philosophy of Science*, **32** (1965), 287–294, which argues that Whitehead's physical theory in *Process and Reality* illustrates the assumption of geometric, without physical, continuity; J. L. Synge, *The Relativity Theory of Alfred North Whitehead* (College Park, Md., 1951); Clifford M. Will, "Relativistic Gravity in the Solar System, II: Anisotropy in the Newtonian Gravitational Constant," in *Astrophysical Journal*, **169** (1971), 141–155; and "Gravitation Theory," in *Scientific American*, **231**, no. 5 (1974), 24–33, which compares competing theories.

On Whitehead's philosophy of science, see Ann P. Lowry, "Whitehead and the Nature of Mathematical Truth," in *Process Studies*, 1 (1971), 114–123; Thomas N. Hart, S. J., "Whitehead's Critique of Scientific Materialism," in *New Scholasticism*, 43 (1969), 229–251; Nathaniel Lawrence, "Whitehead's Method of Extensive Abstraction," in *Philosophy of Science*, 17 (1950), 142–163; Adolf Grünbaum, "Whitehead's Method of Extensive Abstraction," in *British Journal for the Philosophy of Science*, 4 (1953), 215–226, which attacks the validity of Whitehead's method (see Lowe's reply in *Understanding Whitehead*, pp. 79–80); Caroline Whitbeck, "Simultaneity and Distance," in *Journal of Philosophy*, 66 (1969), 329–340; Wolfe Mays, "Whitehead and the Philosophy of Time," in *Studium generale*, 23 (1970), 509–524; Robert R. Llewellyn, "Whitehead and Newton on Space and Time Structure," in *Process Studies*, 3 (1973), 239–258; Ivor Leclerc, "Whitehead and the Problem of Extension," in *Journal of Philosophy*, 58 (1961), 559–565; Robert M. Palter, "Philosophic Principles and Scientific Theory," in *Philosophy of Science*, 23 (1956), 111–135, compares the theories of Einstein and Whitehead.

See also Francis Seaman, "Whitehead and Relativity," in *Philosophy of Science*, 22 (1955), 222–226; A. P. Ushenco, "A Note on Whitehead and Relativity," in *Journal of Philosophy*, 47 (1950), 100–102; Dean R. Fowler, "Whitehead's Theory of Relativity," in *Process Studies*, 5 (1975), which treats the philosophical foundations of Whitehead's theory of relativity; and Richard J. Blackwell, "Whitehead and the Problem of Simultaneity," in *Modern Schoolman*, 41 (1963–1964), 62–72. The extent to which applications of Whitehead's philosophical scheme agree with modern quantum theory has been discussed by Abner Shimony, "Quantum Physics and the Philosophy of Whitehead," in *Boston Studies in the Philosophy of Science*, II (New York, 1965), 307–330; and by J. M. Burgers, "Comments on Shimony's Paper," *ibid.*, pp. 331–342. Henry J. Foise, Jr., "The Copenhagen Interpretation of Quantum Theory and Whitehead's Philosophy of Organism," in *Tulane Studies in Philosophy*, 23 (1974), 32–47, challenges Shimony's conclusions.

WILLIAM A. BARKER
KAREL L. DE BOUVÈRE, S.C.J.
JAMES W. FELT, S.J.
DEAN R. FOWLER

WHITEHEAD, JOHN HENRY CONSTANTINE (*b.* Madras, India, 11 November 1904; *d.* Princeton, New Jersey, 8 May 1960)

Whitehead is perhaps best remembered for his idea of developing the theory of homotopy equivalence by the strictly combinatorial method of allowed transformations. He built up an important school of topology at Oxford.

Whitehead was the son of the Right Reverend Henry Whitehead, from 1899 to 1922 bishop of Madras, and of Isobel Duncan of Calne, Wiltshire. She had been one of the first undergraduates to study mathematics at Lady Margaret Hall, Oxford. Bishop Whitehead was the brother of the mathematician Alfred North Whitehead.

Sent to England before he was two, Whitehead saw little of his parents until his father's retirement to England in 1922. He was educated at Eton and Balliol College, Oxford. His Balliol tutor was J. W. Nicholson, who had studied under A. N. Whitehead. Whitehead boxed for the university, was a good cricketer, and an even better poker player. After graduating in mathematics he joined a firm of stockbrokers, but in 1928 he returned to Oxford to do further mathematical work. There he met Oswald Veblen, on leave from Princeton University, and it was arranged that Whitehead should visit Princeton on a Commonwealth fellowship. He was there from 1929 to 1932, when, having taken a Ph.D., he returned to Oxford and a fellowship at Balliol. In 1934 Whitehead married Barbara Shiela Carew Smyth, a concert pianist. They had two sons.

From 1941 to 1945 Whitehead worked at the Admiralty and Foreign Office. He was elected a fellow of the Royal Society in 1944, and Waynflete professor of pure mathematics and fellow of Magdalen College, Oxford, in 1947. He was president of the London Mathematical Society from 1953 to 1955. He died of a heart attack during a visit to Princeton.

On Whitehead's first visit to Princeton he took up the studies that were to occupy the remainder of his life. There he collaborated with S. Lefschetz on a proof that all analytic manifolds can be triangulated (*Mathematical Works*, II, no. 15 [1933]; see bibliography for details of the edition). He offered a proof (*ibid.*, no. 16 [1934]; corrected in no. 18 [1935]) of the Poincaré hypothesis that a simply connected 3-manifold, compact and without boundary, is a topological 3-sphere. Although Whitehead soon found his proof to have been erroneous, work on it committed him to topology. One memorable early discovery was of a counterexample for open 3-manifolds (*ibid.*, no. 20 [1935]). Before turning to topology, Whitehead had made an important study of the geometry of paths. A monograph on the foundations of differential geometry, written with Veblen, contains the first precise definition, through axioms, of a differential manifold (*Mathematical Works*, I, no. 7 [1932]). This definition was much more precise than the concept of a global differential manifold offered, for example, by Robert König (1919) and E. Cartan (1928). In another work written with Veblen (*ibid.*, no. 6 [1931]) the independence of the axioms is proved.

Under the influence of Marston Morse, Whitehead studied differential geometry in the large, and his paper "On the Covering of a Complete Space by the Geodesics Through a Point" (*Mathematical Works*, I, no. 17 [1935]) marks a turning point in this subject. Assuming an analytic manifold with a Finsler metric, he discussed the relationship between different concepts of completeness in the manifold. He also made a detailed investigation of the properties of the locus of characteristic points of a given point. Other notable work in differential geometry includes his new and elegant proof of a theorem first stated by E. E. Levi and of an important analogue (*ibid.*, no. 22 [1936], and no. 36 [1941]).

After 1941 Whitehead was mainly concerned with topology. He had never lost his early interest in the subject, and J. W. Milnor describes his "Simplicial Spaces, Nuclei and *M*-Groups" (*Mathematical Works*, II, no. 28 [1939]) as the paper that will probably be remembered as his most significant work. Milnor discusses this and related work at length (*Mathematical Works*, I, xxv–xxxiii). The 1939 paper was a brilliant extension of the strictly combinatorial type of topology developed by J. W. Alexander and M. H. A. Newman between 1925 and 1932. (Whitehead had met Newman on his first visit to Princeton.) The contents of the paper were characterized by Whitehead's idea of using the strictly combinatorial method of allowed transformations to solve problems in the theory of homotopy equivalence.

Whitehead's interests gradually shifted toward algebraic topology as a result of his search for invariants to characterize the homotopy type of complexes, and for methods of computing their homotopy groups. Newman explains how Whitehead's discovery of certain mistakes he had made in a paper written in 1941 persuaded him to avoid a free "geometrical" style of composition. Whitehead therefore undertook a complete restatement of his earlier work on homotopy, in a way expertly outlined by Newman. In the last three years of Whitehead's life there was a revival of geometrical topology, which led him to offer, jointly with A. Shapiro, a proof of Dehn's lemma much simpler than the one given in 1957 by C. D. Papakyriako-poulos (*Mathematical Works*, IV, no. 84 [1958]). Here, and in his elaboration of methods laid down by B. Mazur (1958) and Morton Brown (1960),

there is ample evidence that Whitehead died at the height of his mathematical powers.

BIBLIOGRAPHY

I. ORIGINAL WORKS. Ninety papers, some of them lengthy memoirs, are collected in *Mathematical Works of J. H. C. Whitehead*, I. M. James, ed., 4 vols. (Oxford, 1962). References in text are to this collection, the numbers corresponding to the list of Whitehead's publications in I, ix–xiii, and the original year of publication being added in brackets. The papers are classified as follows: vol. I, differential geometry; vol. II, complexes and manifolds; vol. III, homotopy theory; vol. IV, algebraic and classical topology. Whitehead collaborated with Oswald Veblen on *The Foundations of Differential Geometry* (Cambridge, 1932), included in *Mathematical Works*, I. His Oxford lectures on Riemannian geometry and linear algebras, which were separately duplicated and circulated by the Mathematical Institute, Oxford, in 1959, are not included in the collected edition.

II. SECONDARY LITERATURE. Vol. I of the *Mathematical Works* is prefaced by a biographical note by M. H. A. Newman and Barbara Whitehead, and by a mathematical appreciation by John W. Milnor. Two other valuable surveys of Whitehead's work are M. H. A. Newman's obituary notice in *Biographical Memoirs of Fellows of the Royal Society*, 7 (1961), 349–363; and P. J. Hilton, "Memorial Tribute to J. H. C. Whitehead," in *L'enseignement mathématique*, 2nd ser., 7 (1961), 107–124.

J. D. NORTH

WHITTAKER, EDMUND TAYLOR (*b.* Birkdale, Lancashire, England, 24 October 1873; *d.* Edinburgh, Scotland, 24 March 1956)

Whittaker was educated at Manchester Grammar School and Trinity College, Cambridge. He was bracketed second wrangler in the mathematical tripos of 1895, was elected a fellow of Trinity College the following year, and was first Smith's prizeman in 1897. In 1905 he was elected a fellow of the Royal Society, and was awarded the Sylvester and Copley medals of the society in 1931 and 1954 respectively. In 1906 he became astronomer royal for Ireland and from 1912 until his retirement in 1946 was professor of mathematics at the University of Edinburgh. From 1939 to 1944 Whittaker was president of the Royal Society of Edinburgh, and was an honorary member of several learned societies. In 1935 Pope Pius XI conferred on him the cross *pro ecclesia et pontifice* and a year later appointed him to the Pontifical Academy of Sciences. In 1945 Whittaker was knighted and in 1949 became an honorary fellow of Trinity College, Cambridge.

In 1901 Whittaker married Mary Boyd, daughter of the Reverend Thomas Boyd of Cambridge; they had three sons and two daughters. The second son, J. M. Whittaker, became a mathematician and was vice-chancellor of the University of Sheffield. Whittaker's elder daughter married the mathematician E. T. Copson.

Whittaker's deepest interest was in fundamental mathematical physics, and consequently much of his earlier work was concerned with the theory of differential equations. Perhaps his most significant paper in this field was the one published in 1902 in which he obtained the most general solution of Laplace's equation in three dimensions, which is analytic about the origin, in the form

$$\int_0^{2\pi} f(x \cos \alpha + y \sin \alpha + iz, \alpha)\, d\alpha$$

and the corresponding solution of the wave equation in the form

$$\int_0^{\pi}\int_0^{2\pi} f(x \sin \alpha \cos \beta + y \sin \alpha \sin \beta + z \cos \alpha + ct,$$
$$\alpha, \beta)\, d\alpha\, d\beta.$$

The discovery of the general integral representation of any harmonic function brought a new unity into potential theory; the integral representations of Legendre and Bessel functions, for example, were immediate consequences. Moreover, entirely new fields of research in the theory of Mathieu and Lamé functions were opened up. Whittaker also made a detailed study of the differential equation obtained from the hypergeometric equation by a confluence of two singularities, and he introduced the functions $W_{k,m}(z)$, which now bear his name. Another lifelong interest of Whittaker's was the theory of automorphic functions and the standard English book on the subject by L. R. Ford owes much to Whittaker. He also wrote a few papers on special problems in algebra and on numerical analysis.

Whittaker had an intense interest in the theory of relativity and from 1921 onward wrote ten papers on the subject. In one of the papers he gave a definition of spatial distance in curved space-time, which is both mathematically elegant and practical. In other papers he extended well-known formulas in electromagnetism to general relativity, gave a relativistic formulation of Gauss's theorem, and

dealt with the relation between tensor calculus and spinor calculus.

Whittaker will long be read, since his textbooks on several diverse branches of mathematics have become classics. *Modern Analysis* (1902) was the first book in English to present the theory of functions of a complex variable at a level suitable for undergraduate and beginning graduate students. Forsyth's *Theory of Functions* had appeared in 1893, but its contents had not penetrated to the general body of mathematicians. *Modern Analysis* was extensively revised and enlarged in 1915 in collaboration with G. N. Watson, whose name was then added to the title page. Whittaker's *Analytical Dynamics*, which was published in 1904, was the first book to give a systematic account in English of the superbly beautiful theory that springs from Hamilton's equations; and it was of fundamental importance in the development of the quantum theory. Then, in 1910 there appeared *The History of the Theories of Aether and Electricity*. In 1951 a revised version of the book was published and constituted the first volume of a new treatise with the same title; it deals with the history up to the end of the nineteenth century. The second volume, which appeared in 1953, describes the developments made between 1900 and 1926 and is concerned mainly with relativity and quantum theory. The two volumes together form Whittaker's *magnum opus*. A contemplated third volume dealing with later theories was never completed.

Notwithstanding the excellence of *Aether and Electricity*, the chapter in the second volume dealing with the special theory of relativity has been criticized for the emphasis it places on the work of Lorentz and Poincaré, and for the consequent impression it gives that the work of Einstein was of minor importance. The consensus is that Whittaker made an error of judgment. As early as 1899 Poincaré had thought it possible that there might not be such a thing as absolute space, and in 1904 he had discussed without mathematics the possibility of a new mechanics in which mass would depend on velocity and in which the velocity of light would be an upper limit to all physically possible velocities. Also, Lorentz had derived the transformation that now bears his name before Einstein published his paper in 1905, but Lorentz interpreted it in terms of absolute space and time, concepts that, according to Born, he was still clinging to a few years before his death in 1928. Likewise, Poincaré seemed to regard the Lorentz transformation (which he discussed in a mathematically impressive paper in 1906) as physically important only because Maxwell's equations are invariant under it. It was Einstein (who had doubts about the ultimate validity of Maxwell's equations) who derived the transformation law from more fundamental physical principles.

Soon after his arrival at the University of Edinburgh, Whittaker instituted a mathematical laboratory and lectured on numerical analysis. His book *The Calculus of Observations*, written with G. Robinson, grew out of these lectures and was published in 1924. At that time very little of its content was to be found in any other book in English.

Although Whittaker expended a tremendous effort on advanced study and research, he regarded his undergraduate teaching as of paramount importance and, in addition to lecturing to the honors classes, he lectured once a week to the first-year class on the history and development of mathematics. He was an outstanding lecturer and by his dignified bearing, his great command of language, his eloquent delivery, and his obvious mastery of his subject, he made a tremendous impression upon young students. They knew at once that they were in the presence of a scholar and teacher of the first rank and in all his prelections they saw at work a mind of astonishing accuracy and force, ranging at will over the whole field of ancient and modern mathematics and presenting with insight and great persuasive power the profundities there disclosed.

Whittaker was a deeply religious man all through his life and, after having belonged to several branches of the Protestant faith—including the Church of Scotland, of which he was an elder—he was received into the Roman Catholic Church in 1930. After retiring from his chair at Edinburgh, Whittaker spent much of his time studying the philosophical aspects of modern physics and the repercussions that recent developments might have on theology. He expounded his views in *The Beginning and End of the World* (1942), *Space and Spirit* (1947), *From Euclid to Eddington* (1949), and in a large number of papers. He wrote from an orthodox Roman Catholic point of view with great emphasis on natural theology and the work of Thomas Aquinas. He deplored that in modern life "the sense of creatureliness and dependence has passed away, and God is left out of account." He was undoubtedly one of the few men of his time who could speak with authority on both physics and theology.

BIBLIOGRAPHY

An extensive account of Whittaker's life and work is in the Whittaker Memorial Number of *Proceedings of the Edinburgh Mathematical Society*, **11**, pt. 1 (1958), 1–70, which includes a general biographical notice and articles by five contributors on different aspects of Whittaker's work. See also biographical notices by G. F. J. Temple, in *Biographical Memoirs of Fellows of the Royal Society*, **2** (1956), 299–325; and by W. H. McCrea, in *Journal of the London Mathematical Society*, **32** (1957), 234–256.

The question concerning the origin of the special theory of relativity is discussed by G. Holton, in *American Journal of Physics*, **28** (1960), 627–636; and M. Born, *The Born-Einstein Letters* (New York, 1971), 197–199.

DANIEL MARTIN

WIDMAN (or **WEIDEMAN** or **WIDEMAN**), **JOHANNES** (*b.* Eger, Bohemia [now Czechoslovakia], *ca.* 1462; *d.* Leipzig, Germany, after 1498)

The little known about Widman's life is based on the records of the University of Leipzig. He was entered in the matriculation register in 1480 as "Iohannes Weideman de Egra."[1] He received the bachelor's degree in 1482 and the master's degree in 1485.[2] He then lectured on the fundamentals of arithmetic, on computation on lines, and on algebra, as can be seen from the announcements for and invitations to his courses.[3] Widman's algebra lecture of 1486, the first given in Germany, is preserved in a student's notebook.[4] In this lecture he discussed the twenty-four types of equations generally treated by the Cossists and illustrated them with many problems. He employed the Cossist signs for the powers of the unknowns, as well as symbols for plus, minus, and the root.[5] As Widman explicitly stated elsewhere,[6] he considered computation with irrational numbers and polynomials (*De additis et diminutis*) to be part of the subject matter of algebra. He also treated fractions and proportions in order to prepare his students for the study of algebra.

The work for which Widman is best known, *Behend und hüpsch Rechnung uff allen Kauffmanschafften*, appeared in 1489. After the Trent *Algorismus* (1475) and the Bamberg arithmetic books (1482, 1483), it was the first printed arithmetic book in German; and it far surpassed its predecessors in the scope and number of its examples.[7] It also was notable for containing the first appearance in print of the plus and minus signs. Widman dedicated the book to Sigismund Altmann of Schmidtmühlen, who also enrolled at Leipzig in 1480.[8] There are no direct reports of Widman's activities after 1489; his brief mathematical works that were printed later appeared anonymously and without date of publication. Yet, according to Conrad Wimpina, Widman was still working on mathematical topics in 1498.

Widman's knowledge of arithmetic was based on the *Algorismus Ratisbonensis* and the Bamberg arithmetic book of 1483, as can be seen by comparing the problems treated in these works with those in his own. His arithmetic book of 1489 went through several editions until 1526,[9] when it was superseded by those of Köbel, Adam Ries, and others.

Widman learned algebra primarily from a volume of manuscripts he owned (now known as Codex Dresdensis C 80)[10] that later came into the possession of Georg Sturtz of Erfurt, who about 1523 placed it at the disposition of Ries. A compilation of all that was then known about arithmetic and algebra, the volume contained, in particular, a German algebra of 1471 and one in Latin.[11] The Latin algebra, in the margins of which Widman entered further examples of the twenty-four types of equations, was the basis of his algebra lecture of 1486.[12] The lecture also is partially preserved in another Dresden manuscript (C 80^m) and in manuscripts from Munich and Vienna.[13] This manuscript (C 80) was also the source of Widman's writings that were printed at Leipzig about 1495.[14] Ries borrowed problems for his *Coss* from Widman's algebra, but he was not aware of the author's identity.[15] Following the appearance of printed works on algebra by Grammateus, Rudolff, and Stifel at the beginning of the sixteenth century, Widman's writings fell into neglect.

NOTES

1. See G. Erler, *Die Matrikel der Universität Leipzig*, I, 323. Widman was a member of the Natio Bavarorum.
2. *Ibid.*, II, 228, 289. Master Widman was allowed to live outside the dormitory (*petivit dimissionem burse et obtinuit*).
3. See W. Kaunzner, "Über Johannes Widmann von Eger." 1 f., 45; and E. Wappler, "Zur Geschichte der deutschen Algebra im 15. Jahrhundert," 9 f.; and "Beitrag zur Geschichte der Mathematik," 149, 167.
4. The fee for the lecture was 42 groschen (2 florins). See Kaunzner, *op. cit.*, 45.
5. On the root symbol see Wappler, "Zur Geschichte der deutschen Algebra im 15. Jahrhundert," 13. On the earliest use of the minus sign see Kaunzner, "Deutsche Mathematiker des 15. und 16. Jahrhunderts und ihre Symbolik," 22 f.
6. In Codex Lipsiensis 1470, fol. 432. On this point see Kaunzner, "Über Johannes Widmann von Eger," 41, 92 f.
7. Widman did not use line reckoning; he did, however, present a thorough treatment of proportions using the traditional terminology.
8. He was *Dr. utriusque juris* and rector in 1504.
9. See D. E. Smith, *Rara arithmetica*, 36 f.

10. Widman knew the Regensburg algebra of 1461, and he took certain problems from it (*Regula dele cose super quartum capitulum*). On this point see M. Curtze, in *Abhandlungen zur Geschichte der Mathematik*, 7 (1895), 72; and Wappler, "Zur Geschichte der deutschen Algebra," 540.
11. A description of Codex Dresdensis C 80 is in Kaunzner, "Über Johannes Widmann von Eger," 27–39.
12. See Codex Lipsiensis 1470, fols. 479–493. On this point see Kaunzner, "Über . . . Widmann . . .," 45.
13. See Kaunzner, "Deutsche Mathematiker des 15. und 16. Jahrhunderts und ihre Symbolik," 21.
14. Wappler, "Beitrag zur Geschichte der Mathematik," 167, proposes 1490 as the year of publication. All six treatises have the same format, the same type, and the same size pages and length of lines. They all appeared anonymously, without date and, with one exception (Leipzig), without city. Wimpina (*b.* 1460; enrolled at Leipzig in 1479) enumerated all these works except *Regula falsi*; at the time he made his list the works were commercially available.
15. They are problems that Widman had entered in the margins of Codex Dresdensis C 80. See Wappler, "Zur Geschichte der deutschen Algebra," 541 ff.

BIBLIOGRAPHY

I. ORIGINAL WORKS. Widman's *Behend und hüpsch Rechnung uff allen Kauffmanschafften* appeared at Leipzig in 1489. The rest of his works, published anonymously and without city or date, are *Algorithmus integrorum cum probis annexis; Algorithmus linealis; Algorithmus minutiarum phisicarum; Algorithmus minutiarum vulgarium; Regula falsi apud philozophantes augmenti et decrementi appellata;* and *Tractatus proportionum plusquam aureus*. On these latter works, see Klebs (below), 35, 36, 281, 324; Wimpina (below), 50; and Wappler, "Beitrag zur Geschichte der Mathematik" (below).

II. SECONDARY LITERATURE. See M. Cantor, *Vorlesungen zur Geschichte der Mathematik*, 2nd ed., II (Leipzig; 1913), 228 ff.; M. W. Drobisch, *De Ioanni Widmanni Egeriani compendio arithmeticae mercatorum* (Leipzig; 1840); G. Erler, *Die Matrikel der Universität Leipzig*, 3 vols. (Leipzig, 1895–1902), I, 323; II, 228, 289; W. Kaunzner, "Über Johannes Widmann von Eger. Ein Beitrag zur Geschichte der Rechenkunst im ausgehenden Mittelalter," *Veröffentlichungen des Forschungsinstituts des Deutschen Museums für die Geschichte der Naturwissenschaften und der Technik*, ser. C., no. 4 (1968); and "Deutsche Mathematiker des 15. und 16. Jahrhunderts und ihre Symbolik," *ibid.*, ser. A, no. 90 (1971); A. C. Klebs, "Incunabula scientifica et medica," in *Osiris*, 4 (1938), 1–359; D. E. Smith, *Rara arithmetica* (Boston–London, 1908), 36, 40, 44; E. Wappler, "Zur Geschichte der deutschen Algebra im 15. Jahrhundert," in *Programm Gymnasium Zwickau* (1887), 1–32; "Beitrag zur Geschichte der Mathematik," in *Abhandlungen zur Geschichte der Mathematik*, 5 (1890), 147–169; and "Zur Geschichte der deutschen Algebra," *ibid.*, 9 (1899), 537–554; and C. Wimpina, *Scriptorum insignium, qui in celeberrimis praesertim Lipsiensi, Wittenbergensi, Francofurdiana ad Viadrum academiis, a fundatione ipsarum usque ad annum Christi MDXV floruerunt centuria, quondam ab J. J. Madero Hanno-verano edita, ex mspto autographo emendata, completa, annotationibusque brevibus ornata,* J. F. T. Merzdorf, ed. (Leipzig, 1839), 50 f.

KURT VOGEL

WIELEITNER, HEINRICH (*b.* Wasserburg am Inn, Germany, 31 October 1874: *d.* Munich, Germany, 27 December 1931)

Wieleitner received his higher education at the Catholic seminaries at Scheyern and Freising but subsequently decided to study mathematics (rather than classical languages and theology) at the University of Munich. Since his parents lived in simple circumstances, C. L. F. Lindemann proposed that Wieleitner be allotted the Lamont stipend for Catholic students of mathematics in 1895. This enabled the gifted young man to complete his studies in 1897 with excellent marks. Three years later he obtained the doctorate with a dissertation on third-order surfaces with oval points, a subject suggested to him by Lindemann.

Meanwhile, Wieleitner had become a high school teacher, his first appointment being at the Gymnasium at Speyer. In 1909 he was made *Gymnasialprofessor* at Pirmasens: in 1915 he returned to Speyer as headmaster of the *Realschule*: in 1920 he moved to Augsburg, and in 1926 he was promoted to *Oberstudiendirektor* at the Neue Realgymnasium in Munich, a post he held until his death. Parallel to his career as an educator, Wieleitner established a reputation as a geometer and—increasingly so—as a historian of mathematics. Probably during the International Congresses of Mathematicians at Heidelberg (1904) and Rome (1908), he met Italian geometers. He translated an article by Gino Loria and, with E. Ciani, contributed to the revised German edition of *Pascals Repertorium der höheren Mathematik.*[1] In 1905 his *Theorie der ebenen algebraischen Kurven höherer Ordnung* had been published, and in 1908 it was supplemented by *Spezielle ebene Kurven.* In 1914 and 1918 the two volumes of Wieleitner's *Algebraische Kurven* followed. Wieleitner's books were noted for their simple, straightforward presentation and the author's great didactic skill, which made ample use of geometric intuition and insight.

Although always interested in the history of mathematics, Wieleitner would most probably not have become involved in the field had Anton von Braunmühl not died in 1908. With Siegmund Günther, Braunmühl had undertaken to write a

Geschichte der Mathematik in two volumes. Günther's volume (antiquity to Descartes)[2] appeared in 1908, but his partner left an unfinished manuscript. Wieleitner was persuaded to step in. Thoroughly going through G. Eneström's many critical remarks about Cantor's *Vorlesungen über Geschichte der Mathematik,*[3] he revised and completed part I of Braunmühl's work (arithmetic, algebra, analysis), which was published in 1911: part II (geometry, trigonometry) appeared in 1921. Apart from being based on a detailed study of primary sources, Wieleitner's presentation always stressed the notion of development and progress of mathematics. Giving only minor attention to individual biographies, the author brought the leading ideas to the fore, and wrote a history of mathematical ideas. He followed the same general concept in his *Geschichte der Mathematik,* published in two small volumes in the Sammlung Göschen in 1922–1923.

Shortly after moving to Munich in 1928, Wieleitner, at Sommerfeld's suggestion, was made *Privatdozent,* and in 1930 honorary professor, at the university. Since 1919 he had been corresponding member of the Deutsche Akademie der Naturforscher Leopoldina, and in 1929 he was elected member of the Académie Internationale d'Histoire des Sciences.

Wieleitner published about 150 books and articles and more than 2,500 book reviews. Many of his papers and books—in geometry and the history of mathematics—were addressed to teachers and students of mathematics. In inexpensive source booklets he presented carefully chosen excerpts from mathematical classics for classroom use. His work in the history of mathematics was continued in the same spirit and with the same close connection to mathematical education by Kurt Vogel and J. E. Hofmann.

NOTES

1. *Pascals Repertorium der höheren Mathematik,* 2nd, completely rev. German ed., E. Salkowski and H. E. Timerding, eds., II, pt. 1, *Grundlagen und ebene Geometrie* (Leipzig – Berlin, 1910).
2. Siegmund Günther, *Geschichte der Mathematik,* I, *Von den ältesten Zeiten bis Cartesius* (Leipzig, 1908).
3. Moritz Cantor, *Vorlesungen über Geschichte der Mathematik,* 4 vols. (I: Leipzig, 1880; 2nd ed., 1894; 3rd ed., 1907: II: 1892; 2nd ed., 1899–1900: III: 1894–1898; 2nd ed., 1900–1901: IV: 1908).

BIBLIOGRAPHY

I. ORIGINAL WORKS. Wieleitner's most important books are *Theorie der ebenen algebraischen Kurven höherer Ordnung* (Leipzig, 1905), Sammlung Schubert no. 43; *Spezielle ebene Kurven* (Leipzig, 1908), Sammlung Schubert no. 56; *Geschichte der Mathematik, II, Von Cartesius bis zur Wende des 18. Jahrhunderts*, 2 vols. (Leipzig, 1911–1921), Sammlung Schubert nos. 63, 64; *Algebraische Kurven*, 2 vols. (Berlin–Leipzig, 1914–1918; I: 2nd ed., 1919; 3rd ed., 1930; II: 2nd ed., 1919), Sammlung Göschen nos. 435, 436; *Geschichte der Mathematik*, 2 vols. (Berlin–Leipzig, 1922–1923), Sammlung Göschen nos. 226, 875; *Die Geburt der modernen Mathematik*, 2 vols. (Karlsruhe, 1924–1925); and *Mathematische Quellenbücher*, 4 vols. (Berlin, 1927–1929). A combined Russian trans. of the 2 vols. of *Geschichte der Mathematik*, II (Sammlung Schubert nos. 63, 64) and of *Geschichte der Mathematik*, II (Sammlung Göschen no. 875), 53–147, was edited under the title *Istoria matematiki ot Dekarta do serednii XIX stoletia* by A. P. Youschkevitch (Moscow, 1966).

II. SECONDARY LITERATURE. The most extensive obituaries (including bibliographies and a portrait) are J. E. Hofmann, in *Jahresbericht der Deutschen Mathematiker-vereinigung*, **42** (1933), 199–223, with portrait; and J. Ruska, in *Isis*, **18** (1932), 150–165.

CHRISTOPH J. SCRIBA

WIENER, LUDWIG CHRISTIAN (*b*. Darmstadt, Germany, 7 December 1826; *d*. Karlsruhe, Germany, 31 July 1896)

In mathematics Christian Wiener did important work in descriptive geometry and the construction of mathematical models. As a physicist he studied chiefly molecular phenomena and atmospheric radiation. In his philosophical writings he advocated a point of view based on the methodology of natural science.

The son of a judge, Wiener attended the gymnasium in Darmstadt and from 1843 to 1847 studied engineering and architecture at the University of Giessen, where he passed the state architecture examination. In 1848 he obtained a post as teacher of physics, mechanics, hydraulics, and descriptive geometry at the Höhere Gewerbeschule (later the Technische Hochschule) of Darmstadt. Two years later he earned the Ph.D. and qualified as a *Privatdozent* in mathematics at the University of Giessen. To further his education he attended the Technical University in Karlsruhe, working for about a year under Ferdinand Redtenbacher, the professor of mechanical engineering. He returned to Giessen in the autumn of 1851; but the following year he accepted a professorship of descriptive geometry at the Technische Hochschule in Karlsruhe, retaining the position until 1896.

An able and respected teacher, Wiener trained a great number of students while conducting important research. Elected rector of the Technische Hochschule three times, he was also a member of the Gewerbeschulrat and the Oberschulrat of the state of Baden. Wiener was liked and esteemed for his upright character, his sense of justice, and his kindliness.

In his mathematical works Wiener frequently used direct intuition as an aid in carrying out proofs. This led him into the realm of aesthetics, as can be seen from his philosophical essay "Über die Schönheit der Linien" (1896), which contains an appendix on the relationship between mathematical continuity and the regularity of forms.

Wiener's chief work was the two-volume *Lehrbuch der darstellenden Geometrie* (1884–1887), based on his teaching experience and numerous publications on descriptive geometry. In the introduction to the *Lehrbuch* he presented a valuable historical survey, based on a firsthand study of the sources, that constituted an important supplement to Chasles's *Aperçu historique sur l'origine et le développement des méthodes en géométrie* (1837). Wiener treated the basic problems of descriptive geometry by a single method: a varied use of the principal lines of a plane. He also sought to simplify individual problems as much as possible and to find the easiest graphical solutions for them. He was not, however, concerned merely with graphical methods, of which he was a master. He was also interested in the problems and their solutions (such as shadow construction and brightness distribution), as well as in the development of the necessary geometric aids. For example, he used imaginary projection and developed a grid method that can be derived from the theory of cyclically projected point series.

Wiener also became known for his mathematical models. In 1869, at the suggestion of R. F. A. Clebsch, he constructed a plaster-of-Paris model of the third-order surface. He displayed his models at expositions of mathematical teaching aids in London (1876), Munich (1893), and Chicago (1893). In analysis he discussed and drew the Weierstrass function, which is everywhere continuous and yet at no point has a derivative.

Extending his works on descriptive geometry into physics, Wiener investigated the illumination conditions for various bodies. Thus, he calculated the amounts of solar radiation received at different latitudes and during the varying lengths of days in the course of the year. His numerical values are still fundamental for the study of atmospheric optics and of the effect of radiation on the earth's climate. In a posthumously published article Wiener examined the total radiation received by the atmosphere and considered problems related to color theory and strengths of perceptions.

In his studies on molecular physics, Wiener demonstrated by extremely careful observations that Brownian movement is an "internal motion peculiar to the liquid state." He developed an atomistic cosmology, which he set forth in *Atomlehre* (1869), the first volume of his chief philosophical work, *Die Grundzüge der Weltordnung*. He presupposed the causality of all natural phenomena and the existence of a real external world but, in accordance with a view widely held at the time, he still accepted the existence of an ether. In his treatment of crystalline forms Wiener developed the concept of the regular point system, which became important in crystallography.

Among the topics Wiener discussed in his writings on moral philosophy were will and morality. He defined free will as independence from external, determining circumstances only, thus precluding full independence—that is, absolute freedom. He opposed the view of some of his contemporaries that scientific research, with its analytic methods, could become a danger to man's sense of morality and beauty. Unlike his other publications, Wiener's philosophical works found only a limited audience.

BIBLIOGRAPHY

I. ORIGINAL WORKS. Bibliographies of Wiener's approximately 100 scientific books and papers are in Poggendorff, II, 1322, and III, 1442; and in the unsigned *Zur Erinnerung an Dr. Christian Wiener* (see below). Mathematical works include *Über Vielecke und Vielflache* (Leipzig, 1864); *Stereoskopische Photographie des Modells einer Fläche dritter Ordnung mit 27 reellen Geraden* (Leipzig, 1869); "Direkte Lösung der Aufgabe: Einen durch fünf Punkte oder durch fünf Tangenten gegebenen Kegelschnitt auf einen Umdrehungskegel zu legen," in *Zeitschrift für Mathematik und Physik*, **20** (1875), 317–325; "Geometrische und analytische Untersuchung der Weierstrass'schen Funktion," in *Journal für die reine und angewandte Mathematik*, **90** (1880), 221–252; and *Lehrbuch der darstellenden Geometrie*, 2 vols. (Leipzig, 1884–1887).

Writings in physics are "Erklärung des atomistischen Wesens des tropfbar-flüssigen Körperzustandes und Bestätigung desselben durch die sogenannten Molekularbewegungen," in *Annalen der Physik und Chemie*, **118** (1863), 79–94; "Über die Stärke der Bestrahlung der Erde durch die Sonne in ihren verschiedenen Breiten und Jahreszeiten," in *Zeitschrift für Mathematik und Physik*, **22** (1877), 341–368, also abridged in *Osterreichische Zeitschrift für Meteorologie*, **14** (1879), 113–129; and "Die Helligkeit des klaren Himmels und die Beleuchtung durch Sonne, Himmel und Rückstrahlung," H. Wiener, O. Wiener, and W. Möbius, eds., 2 pts., *Nova acta Leopoldina*, **73**, no. 1 (1900), and **91**, no. 2 (1909).

On philosophy, see *Die Grundzüge der Weltordnung* (Leipzig–Heidelberg, 1863), 2nd ed., 2 vols.: I, *Atomlehre* (1869), II, *Die geistige Welt und der Ursprung der Dinge* (1869); and "Über die Schönheit der Linien," in *Abhandlungen des Naturwissenschaftlichen Vereins in Karlsruhe*, **11** (1896), 47–73.

II. SECONDARY LITERATURE. See the unsigned *Zur Erinnerung an Dr. Christian Wiener* (Karlsruhe, 1896); A. Brill and L. Sohnke, "Christian Wiener," in *Jahresberichte der Deutschen Mathematiker-Vereinigung*, **6** (1897), 46–69; and H. Wiener, "Wiener, Christian," in *Allgemeine deutsche Biographie*, XLII (1897), 790–792.

HANS-GÜNTHER KÖRBER

WIENER, NORBERT (*b*. Columbia, Missouri, 26 November 1894; *d*. Stockholm, Sweden, 18 March 1964)

Wiener was the son of Leo Wiener, who was born in Byelostok, Russia, and Bertha Kahn. Although a child prodigy, he matured into a renowned mathematician rather slowly. At first he was taught by his father. He entered high school at the age of nine and graduated two years later. After four years in college, he enrolled at the Harvard Graduate School at the age of fifteen in order to study zoology. That soon turned out to be a wrong choice. He next tried philosophy at Cornell. "A philosopher in spite of himself," Wiener took a Ph.D. at Harvard in 1913 with a dissertation on the boundary between philosophy and mathematics. A Harvard traveling fellowship paid his way to Europe. Bertrand Russell was his chief mentor at Cambridge and advised him to learn more mathematics. Neither the examples of Hardy and Littlewood at Cambridge, however, nor those of Hilbert and Landau at Göttingen, converted him to mathematics. Back in the United States in 1915, Wiener tried various jobs teaching philosophy, mathematics, and engineering. In the spring of 1919 he got a position in the mathematics department of the Massachusetts Institute of Technology, not then particularly distinguished in that discipline. An assistant professor in 1924, associate in 1929, and full professor in 1932, he remained at MIT until his retirement. Although his genius contributed to establishing the institute's present reputation, he could never comfort himself over the failure of other American universities, and particularly of Harvard, to show much interest in him. He traveled a great deal, to Europe and to Asia, and his visits to Germany in the interwar years left their traces in many anecdotes told in Continental circles. His *Cybernetics* made him a public figure. President Lyndon Johnson awarded him the National Medal of Science two months before his death. He died during a trip to Sweden and left two daughters. His wife was the former Margaret Engemann.

In appearance and behavior, Norbert Wiener was a baroque figure, short, rotund, and myopic, combining these and many qualities in extreme degree. His conversation was a curious mixture of pomposity and wantonness. He was a poor listener. His self-praise was playful, convincing, and never offensive. He spoke many languages but was not easy to understand in any of them. He was a famously bad lecturer.

Wiener was a great mathematician who opened new perspectives onto fields in which the activity became intense, as it still is. Although most of his ideas have become standard knowledge, his original papers, and especially his books, remain difficult to read. His style was often chaotic. After proving at length a fact that would be too easy if set as an exercise for an intelligent sophomore, he would assume without proof a profound theorem that was seemingly unrelated to the preceding text, then continue with a proof containing puzzling but irrelevant terms, next interrupt it with a totally unrelated historical exposition, meanwhile quote something from the "last chapter" of the book that had actually been in the first, and so on. He would often treat unrelated questions consecutively, and although the discussion of any one of them might be lucid, rigorous, and beautiful, the reader is left puzzled by the lack of continuity. All too often Wiener could not resist the temptation to tell everything that cropped up in his comprehensive mind, and he often had difficulty in separating the relevant mathematics neatly from its scientific and social implications and even from his personal experiences. The reader to whom he appears to be addressing himself seems to alternate in a random order between the layman, the undergraduate student of mathematics, the average mathematician, and Wiener himself.

Wiener wrote a most unusual autobiography. Although it conveys an extremely egocentric view of the world, I find it an agreeable story and not offensive, because it is naturally frank and there is no pose, least of all that of false modesty. All in all

it is abundantly clear that he never had the slightest idea of how he appeared in the eyes of others. His account of the ill-starred trip to Europe in 1926–1927 is a particularly good example. Although he says almost nothing about the work of the mathematicians whom he met, he recalled after twenty-five years meeting J. B. S. Haldane and setting him straight over an error in his book *The Gold-Makers*: Haldane had used a Danish name for a character supposed to be an Icelander (*I Am a Mathematician*, 160). In his autobiography Wiener comes through as a fundamentally good-natured person, realistic about his human responsibilities and serious enough to be a good friend, a good citizen, and a good cosmopolite. Despite his broad erudition, the philosophical interludes are no more than common sense, if not downright flat. Unlike many autobiographers, he never usurps the role of a prophet who long ago predicted the course that things have taken. A good biography ought to be written of him, one that would counterbalance his autobiography and do him more justice than anyone can do in a book about himself.

According to his own account, Wiener's understanding of modern mathematics began in 1918, when he came across works on integration, functionals, and differential equations among the books of a young Harvard student who had died. At that time he met I. A. Barnett, who by suggesting that he work on integration in function spaces, put Wiener on the track that would lead him to his greatest achievements, the first of which was differential space. It was already characteristic of Wiener's openness of mind that, rather than being satisfied with a general integration theory, he looked for physical embodiments to test the theory. The first he tried, turbulence, was a failure; but the next, Brownian motion (1921), studied earlier by Einstein, was a success. Wiener conceived a measure in the space of one-dimensional paths that leads to the application of probability concepts in that space (see *Selected Papers*, no. 2). The construction is surprisingly simple. Take the set of continuous functions $x(t)$ of $t \geqq 0$ with $x(0) = 0$ and require that the probability of x passing for t_i between α_i and β_i ($i = 1, \ldots, k$) is provided by the Einstein-Smoluchowski formula that gives for the probability density of a point at x staying at y after a lapse of time t the expression

$$(2 \pi t)^{\frac{1}{2}} \exp (-[y - x]^2/2t).$$

In later work Wiener made this measure more explicit by a measure-preserving mapping of the real number line on function space. He also proved that almost all paths are nondifferentiable and that almost all of them satisfy a Lipschitz condition of any degree $<1/2$, although almost none does so with such a condition of degree $>1/2$. "Differential space" is a strange term for this function space with a measure, promising a measure defined not by finite but by differential methods. Although vaguely operative on the background, this idea was never made explicit by Wiener when he resumed use of the term "differential space" in later work.

In 1923–1925 Wiener published papers that greatly influenced potential theory: Dirichlet's problem, in its full generality (see *Selected Papers*, no. 3). The exterior problem of a compact set K in 3-space led him to the capacitory potential of a measure with support K as a basic tool.

From Brownian motion Wiener turned to the study of more general stochastic processes, and the mathematical needs of MIT's engineering department set him on the new track of harmonic analysis. His work during the next five years culminated in a long paper (1930) on generalized harmonic analysis (see *Selected Papers*, no. 4), which as a result of J. D. Tamarkin's collaboration is very well written. Rather than on the class L^2, Wiener focused on that of measurable functions f with

$$\Phi(x) = \lim_{T \to \infty} \frac{1}{2T} \int_{-T}^{T} f(x+t) \bar{f}(t) dt$$

existing for all x, which is even broader than that of almost periodic functions. He borrowed the function Φ from physics as a key to harmonic analysis and connected it later to communication theory. Writing Φ as a Fourier transform,

$$\Phi(t) = (2\pi)^{-\frac{1}{2}} \int_{-\infty}^{\infty} e^{-itu} dS(u),$$

he obtained what is now called the spectral distribution S. The most difficult step was to connect S to the integrated Fourier transform g of f by an analogue of the classical formula $S(t) = \int_{-\infty}^{t} |g(\lambda)|^2 d\lambda$. A brilliant example is: If $f(x) = \pm 1$ for $x_n \leq x < x_{n+1}$, where the signs are fixed by spinning a coin, then the spectral distribution of f is almost certainly continuous.

A key formula in this field was placed by Wiener on the cover of the second part of his autobiography:

$$\lim_{\epsilon \to 0} \frac{1}{2\epsilon} \int_{-\infty}^{\infty} (g(\omega+\epsilon) - g(\omega-\epsilon))^2 d\omega$$

$$= \frac{2}{\pi} \lim_{A \to \infty} \frac{1}{2A} \int_{-A}^{A} |f(t)|^2 dt.$$

When Wiener attempted to prove this, A. E. Ingham led him to what Hardy and Littlewood had called Tauberian theorems; but Wiener did more than adapt their results to his own needs. He gave a marvelous example of the unifying force of mathematical abstraction by recasting the Tauberian question as follows (see *Selected Papers*, no. 5): To prove the validity of

$$\lim_{x \to \infty} \int_{-\infty}^{\infty} K(x-y) f(y) dy = A \int_{-\infty}^{\infty} K(x) dx,$$

by which kind of more tractable kernel K_1, K may be replaced. The answer is (for K and $K_1 \in L_1$): If the Fourier transform of K_1 vanishes nowhere, the validity with K_1 implies that with K. Tauberian theorems have lost much of their interest today, but the argument by which Wiener proved his theorem is still vigorous. Wiener showed that in L_1 the linear span of the translates of a function is dense if its Fourier transform vanishes nowhere. This, again, rests on the remark that the Fourier transform class L_1 is closed with respect to division (as far as possible). Wiener's work in this area became the historical source of the theory of Banach algebras. The "Wiener problem," that is, the problem of deciding whether it is true that in L_1 a function f_1 belongs to the closure of the span of the translates of f_2 if and only if the Fourier transform of f_1 always vanishes together with that of f_2, greatly influenced modern harmonic analysis; it was proved to be wrong by Paul Malliavin in 1959.

Fourier transforms and Tauberian theorems were also the subject of Wiener and R. E. A. C. Paley's collaboration, which led to *Fourier Transforms* (1934). Another cooperative achievement was the study of the Wiener-Hopf equation (see *Selected Papers*, no. 6),

$$f(x) = \int_{0}^{\infty} K(x-y) f(y) dy,$$

generalizing Eberhard Hopf's investigation on radiation equilibrium. In *I Am a Mathematician* (p. 177), Wiener remarked that although originally accounting for the discontinuity of two physical media at $x = 0$, it can even better serve to embody the discontinuity of knowledge at the boundary of future and past. The previous work on the Wiener-Hopf equation became influential in Wiener's prediction theory.

Until the late 1930's stochastic processes, as exemplified by Brownian motion, and harmonic analysis were loose ends in the fabric of Wiener's thought. To be sure, they were not isolated from each other: the spectrally analyzed function f was thought of as a single stochastic happening, and the earlier cited example shows that such a happening could even be conceived as embedded in a stochastic process. Work of others in the 1930's shows the dawning of the idea of spectral treatment of stationary stochastic processes; at the end of the decade it became clear that the "Hilbert space trick" of ergodic theory could serve this aim also. Initially Wiener had neglected ergodic theory; in 1938–1939 he fully caught up (see *Selected Papers*, nos. 7–8), although in later work he did not avail himself of these methods as much as he might have done.

Communication theory, which for a long time had been Wiener's background thought, became more prominent in his achievements after 1940. From antiaircraft fire control and noise filtration in radar to control and communication in biological settings, it was technical problems that stimulated his research. Although linear prediction was investigated independently by A. N. Kolmogorov, Wiener's approach had the merit of dealing with prediction and filtering under one heading. If on the strength of ergodicity of the stationary stochastic process $f(f_t \in L_2)$, the covariances $\varphi(t) = (f_t, f_0)$ are supposed to be provided by the data of the past, linear predicting means estimating the future of f by its projection on the linear span of the past f_t. On the other hand, linear filtering means separating the summands "message" and "noise" in $f_t = f_t^1 + f_t^2$, where again the autocovariances and cross covariances $\Phi(t) = (f_t, f_0)$ and $\Phi_1(t) = (f_t^1, f_0)$ are supposed to be known and the message is estimated by its projection on the linear span of the past signals f_t. Both tasks lead to Wiener-Hopf equations for a weighting distribution w,

$$\varphi(t+h) = \int_0^\infty \varphi(t-\tau)\,dw(\tau) \qquad (t \geqq 0),$$

$$\varphi_1(t+h) = \int_0^\infty \varphi(t-\tau)\,dw(\tau) \qquad (t \geqq 0),$$

respectively.

The implications of these fundamental concepts were elaborated in a wartime report that was belatedly published in 1949; it is still difficult to read, although its contents have become basic knowledge in communication theory. Nonlinear filtering was the subject of Wiener's unpublished memorandum (1949) that led to combined research at MIT, as reported by his close collaborator Y. W. Lee

(see *Selected Papers*, pp. 17–33). A series of lectures on this subject was published in 1958. One of its main subjects is the use of an orthogonal development of nonlinear (polynomial) Volterra functionals by R. H. Cameron and W. T. Martin (1947) in a spectral theory and in the analysis and synthesis of nonlinear filters, which, rather than with trigonometric inputs, are probed with white Gaussian inputs.

After this brief exposition of Wiener's mathematics of communication, it remains to inspect the broad field that Wiener himself vaguely indicated as cybernetics; he tells how he coined this term, although it had not been unusual in the nineteenth century to indicate government theory. While studying antiaircraft fire control, Wiener may have conceived the idea of considering the operator as part of the steering mechanism and of applying to him such notions as feedback and stability, which had been devised for mechanical systems and electrical circuits. No doubt this kind of analogy had been operative in Wiener's mathematical work from the beginning and sometimes had even been productive. As time passed, such flashes of insight were more consciously put to use in a sort of biological research for which Wiener consulted all kinds of people, except mathematicians, whether or not they had anything to do with it. *Cybernetics, or the Control and Communication in the Animal and the Machine* (1948) is a rather eloquent report of these abortive attempts, in the sense that it shows there is not much to be reported. The value and influence of *Cybernetics*, and other publications of this kind, should not, however, be belittled. It has contributed to popularizing a way of thinking in communication theory terms, such as feedback, information, control, input, output, stability, homeostasis, prediction, and filtering. On the other hand, it also has contributed to spreading mistaken ideas of what mathematics really means. *Cybernetics* suggests that it means embellishing a nonmathematical text with terms and formulas from highbrow mathematics. This is a style that is too often imitated by those who have no idea of the meaning of the mathematical words they use. Almost all so-called applications of information theory are of this kind.

Even measured by Wiener's standards, *Cybernetics* is a badly organized work—a collection of misprints, wrong mathematical statements, mistaken formulas, splendid but unrelated ideas, and logical absurdities. It is sad that this work earned Wiener the greater part of his public renown, but this is an afterthought. At that time mathematical readers were more fascinated by the richness of its ideas than by its shortcomings. Few, if any, reviewers voiced serious criticism.

Wiener published more writings of this kind. The last was a booklet entitled *God and Golem, Inc.* It would have been more appropriate as the swan song of a lesser mathematician than Wiener.

BIBLIOGRAPHY

I. ORIGINAL WORKS. Many of Wiener's writings were brought together in his *Selected Papers* (Cambridge, Mass., 1964), which includes contributions by Y. W. Lee, N. Levinson, and W. T. Martin. Among his works are *Fourier Transforms in the Complex Domain* (New York, 1934), written with Raymond E. A. C. Paley; *Cybernetics, or the Control and Communication in the Animal and the Machine* (Paris–Cambridge, Mass., 1948); *Extrapolation, Interpolation and Smoothing of Stationary Time Series, With Engineering Applications* (Cambridge, Mass.–New York–London, 1949); *Ex-Prodigy–My Childhood and Youth* (New York, 1953; Cambridge, Mass., 1955); *I Am a Mathematician–the Later Life of a Prodigy* (Garden City, N.Y., 1956; repr. Cambridge, Mass., 1964); *Nonlinear Problems in Random Theory* (Cambridge, Mass.–New York–London, 1958); *God and Golem, Inc.* (Cambridge, Mass., 1964); and *Differential Space, Quantum Systems, and Prediction* (Cambridge, Mass., 1966), written with Armand Siegel, Bayard Rankin, and William Ted Martin.

II. SECONDARY LITERATURE. See "Norbert Wiener," *Bulletin of the American Mathematical Society*, spec. iss., **72**, no. 1, pt. 2 (1966), with contributions by N. Levinson, W. Rosenblith and J. Wiesner, M. Brelot, J. P. Kahane, S. Mandelbrojt, M. Kac, J. L. Doob, P. Masani, and W. L. Root, with bibliography of 214 items (not including posthumous works). See also Constance Reid, *Hilbert* (Berlin, 1970), esp. 169–170.

HANS FREUDENTHAL

WILCZYNSKI, ERNEST JULIUS (*b*. Hamburg, Germany, 13 November 1876; *d*. Denver, Colorado, 14 September 1932)

Wilczynski was a son of Max Wilczynski and Friederike Hurwitz, who settled in Chicago when he was young. He returned to Germany for advanced study, receiving the Ph.D. from the University of Berlin in 1897 with a dissertation entitled "Hydrodynamische Untersuchungen mit Anwendung auf die Theorie der Sonnenrotation." Upon returning to the United States, he spent a year as a computer in the Office of the Nautical Almanac in Washington. In 1898 Wilczynski went to the University of California as an instructor; he rose to the rank of associate professor and served there until 1907. From 1903 to 1905 he was in Europe as assistant and associate of the Carnegie Institution of Washington, which provided the financial support that enabled him to write *Projective Differential Geometry of Curves and Ruled Surfaces* (1906). In 1906 he married Countess Ines Masola, of Verona. He was associate professor at the University of Illinois from 1907 to 1910 and at the University of Chicago from 1910 to 1914, achieving full professorship in the latter year.

Wilczynski's main work was in projective differential geometry, a subject of which he is generally considered the creator. A prolific worker, he published seventy-seven books and papers. He was also active in scientific organizations, serving as vice-president of the American Mathematical Society, as a member of the council of the Mathematical Association of America, and as an associate editor of the *Transactions of the American Mathematical Society*. Wilczynski won a prize (and was named laureate) of the Royal Belgian Academy in 1909, and in 1919 he was elected a member of the National Academy of Sciences.

What is now called classical differential geometry studied the local metric properties of geometrical configurations; projective differential geometry proposed similarly to study the local properties invariant under projective transformations. When Wilczynski started his work, about 1900, Halphen's projective differential geometry of curves already existed; but Wilczynski devised new methods, deepened the theory for curves, extended it to surfaces, and brought it to its present form.

In 1900, classical differential geometry was already a century old. Although it could still provide much interesting detail, it had lost its vitality; and by 1920 it had been declared dead. E. T. Bell has suggested that classical differential geometry lacked method and aim. Projective differential geometry, although it contained new points of view, was only a part of that larger subject and, therefore, shared its fate, although classical metric differential geometry is still a staple university course.

BIBLIOGRAPHY

See E. T. Bell, *Development of Mathematics* (New York, 1940), 332; and E. P. Lane, "Ernest Julius Wilczynski," in *American Mathematical Monthly*, **39** (1932),

567–569, see also 500; and "Ernest Julius Wilczynski – In Memoriam," in *Bulletin of the American Mathematical Society*, **39** (1933), 7–14, with bibliography of 77 works published by Wilczynski from 1895 to 1923.

A. SEIDENBERG

WILKS, SAMUEL STANLEY (*b.* Little Elm, Texas, 17 June 1906; *d.* Princeton, New Jersey, 7 March 1964)

Wilks was the eldest of the three children of Chance C. and Bertha May Gammon Wilks. His father trained for a career in banking but after a few years chose to operate a 250-acre farm near Little Elm. His mother had a talent for music and art and instilled her own lively curiosity in her three sons.[1] Wilks obtained his grade-school education in a one-room schoolhouse and attended high school in Denton, where during his final year he skipped study hall regularly in order to take a mathematics course at North Texas State Teachers College, where he received an A.B. in architecture in 1926.

Believing his eyesight inadequate for architecture, Wilks embarked on a career in mathematics. During the school year 1926–1927, he taught mathematics and manual training in a public school in Austin, Texas, and began graduate study of mathematics at the University of Texas. He continued his studies as a part-time instructor in 1927–1928, received an M.A. in mathematics in 1928, and remained as an instructor during the academic year 1928–1929.

Granted a two-year fellowship by the University of Iowa, in the summer of 1929 Wilks began a program of study and research leading to receipt, in June 1931, of a Ph.D. in mathematics. National research fellowships enabled him to continue research and training in mathematical statistics at Columbia University (1931–1932), University College, London (1932), and Cambridge University (1933). Wilks's scientific career was subsequently centered at Princeton, where he rose from instructor in mathematics (1933) to professor of mathematical statistics (1944).

Wilks married Gena Orr, of Denton, in September 1931; they had one son, Stanley Neal Wilks. He was a member of the American Philosophical Society, the International Statistical Institute, and the American Academy of Arts and Sciences, and a fellow of the American Association for the Advancement of Science. He also belonged to most major societies in his field.

Wilks's education was extraordinary for the number of prominent people involved in it. At the University of Texas, his first course in advanced mathematics was set theory, taught by R. L. Moore, noted for his researches in topology, his unusual methods of teaching, and his contempt for applied mathematics. Having a strong practical bent, however, Wilks was more interested in probability and statistics, taught by Edward L. Dodd; known for his researches on mathematical and statistical properties of various types of means, Dodd encouraged Wilks to pursue further study of these subjects at the University of Iowa (now the State University of Iowa).

At Iowa, Wilks was introduced by Henry L. Rietz to "the theory of small samples" pioneered by "Student" (W. S. Gossett) and fully developed by R. A. Fisher, and to statistical methods employed in experimental psychology and educational testing by E. F. Lindquist.

Wilks chose Columbia University for his first year of postdoctoral study and research because Harold Hotelling, a pioneer in multivariate analysis and the person in the United States most versed in the "Student"-Fisher theory of small samples, had just been appointed professor there in the economics department. At Columbia, Wilks attended the lectures at Teachers College of Charles E. Spearman, considered the father of factor analysis, and became acquainted with the work at Bell Telephone Laboratories of Walter A. Shewhart, originator of statistical quality control of manufacturing processes.

Wilks spent the first part of his second year writing a joint paper with Egon S. Pearson in the department of Karl Pearson at University College, London. At Cambridge University he worked with John Wishart who had been a research assistant to both Karl Pearson and Fisher, and whose work in multivariate analysis was close to Wilks's main interest.

Wilks's first ten published papers were contributions to the branch of statistical theory and methodology known as multivariate analysis, and it was to this area that he made his greatest contributions. His doctoral dissertation, written under Henry L. Rietz, provided the small-sample theory for answering a number of questions arising in use of the technique of "matched" groups in experimental work in educational psychology. It was preceded by a short note, "The Standard Error of the Means of 'Matched' Samples" (1931). This note and dissertation are the first in a long series of papers on topics in multivariate analysis suggested to Wilks by problems in experimental psychology and educational testing.

It was, however, his paper, "Certain Generalizations in the Analysis of Variance," that immediately established Wilks's stature. In this paper he defined the "generalized variance" of a sample of n individuals from a multivariate population, constructed multivariate generalizations of the correlation ratio and coefficient of multiple correlation, deduced the moments of the sampling distributions of these and other related functions in random samples from a normal multivariate population from Wishart's generalized product moment distribution (1928), constructed the likelihood ratio criterion for testing the null hypothesis that k multivariate samples of sizes $n_1, n_2, \cdots, n_k$ are random samples from a common multivariate normal population (now called Wilks's Λ criterion) and derived its sampling distribution under the null hypothesis, and similarly explored various other multivariate likelihood ratio criteria.

Three other papers written in 1931–1932 concerned derivation of the sampling distributions of estimates of the parameters of a bivariate normal distribution from "fragmentary samples"—that is, when some of the individuals in a sample yield observations on both variables, x and y, and some only on x, or on y, alone; derivation of the distribution of the multiple correlation coefficient in samples from a normal population with a nonzero multiple correlation coefficient directly from Wishart's generalized product moment distribution (1928) without using the geometrical notions and an invariance property utilized by Fisher in his derivation (1928); and derivation of an exact expression for the standard error of an observed "tetrad difference," an outgrowth of attending Spearman's lectures.

"Methods of Statistical Analysis . . . for k Samples of Two Variables" (1933), written with E. S. Pearson, and "Moment-Generating Operators for Determinants of Product Moments . . ." (1934) are the products of Wilks's year in England. The first consists of elaboration in greater detail for the bivariate normal case of the techniques developed for the multivariate normal in his "Certain Generalizations . . .," and reflects his and Pearson's growing interest in industrial applications by including a worked example based on data from W. A. Shewhart (1931). The second may be regarded as an extension of the work of J. Wishart and M. S. Bartlett, who had just completed an "independent" derivation of Wishart's product moment distribution "by purely algebraic methods" when

Wilks arrived in Cambridge. His next important contribution to multivariate analysis, "On the Independence of k Sets of Normally Distributed . . . Variables" (1935), appears to have been written to meet a need encountered in his work with the College Entrance Examination Board, as do many of his later contributions to multivariate analysis.

In addition to his extensive and penetrating studies of likelihood ratio tests for various hypotheses relating to multivariate normal distributions, Wilks made similar investigations (1935) relating to multinomial distributions and to independence in two-, three-, and higher-dimensional contingency tables. He also provided (1938) a compact proof of the basic theorem on the large-sample distribution of the likelihood ratio criterion for testing "composite" statistical hypotheses—that is, when the "null hypothesis" tested specifies the values of, say, only m out of the h parameters of the probability distribution concerned. Jerzy Neyman's basic paper on the theory confidence-interval estimation appeared in 1937. The following year Wilks showed that under fairly general conditions confidence intervals for a parameter of a probability distribution based upon its maximum-likelihood estimator are, on the average, the shortest obtainable in large samples.

In response to a need expressed by Shewhart, Wilks in 1941 laid the foundations of the theory of statistical "tolerance limits," which actually are confidence limits, in the sense of Neyman's theory—not, however, for the value of some parameter of the distribution sampled, as in Neyman's development but, rather, for the location of a specified fraction of the distribution sampled. He showed that a suitably selected pair of ordered observations ("order statistics") in a sample of sufficient size from an arbitrary continuous distribution provides a pair of limits (statistical "tolerance limits") to which there corresponds a stated chance that at least a specified fraction of the underlying distribution is contained between these limits, thus providing the "distribution-free" solution needed when the assumption of an underlying normal distribution of industrial production is unwarranted. Wilks also derived the corresponding parametric solution of maximum efficiency in the case of sampling from a normal distribution (based on the sample mean and standard deviation) and an expression for the relative efficiency of the distribution-free solution in this case.

In 1942 Wilks developed formulas for the probabilities that at least a fraction N_0/N of a second random sample of N observations from an arbitrary continuous distribution (a) would lie above the rth "order statistic" (rth observation in increasing order of size), $1 \leq r \leq n$, in a first random sample of size n from the same distribution, or (b) would be included between the rth and sth order statistics, $1 \leq r < s \leq n$, of the first sample; and illustrated the application of these results to the setting of one- and two-sided statistical tolerance limits. This work was Wilks's earliest contribution to "nonparametric" or "distribution-free" methods of statistical inference, an area of research of which he provided an extensive review in depth in "Order Statistics" (1948).

Wilks was a founder of the Institute of Mathematical Statistics (1935) and remained an active member. The Institute took full responsibility for the *Annals of Mathematical Statistics*, and Wilks became editor, with the June 1938 issue.[2] He served through the December 1949 issue, guiding the development of the *Annals* from a marginal journal, with a small subscription list, to the foremost publication in its field.

Although Wilks became an instructor in the department of mathematics at Princeton University at the beginning of the academic year 1933–1934, he did not give a formal course in statistics at Princeton until 1936, owing to a prior commitment that the university had made with an instructor in the department of economics and social institutions who had been sent off at university expense to develop a course on "modern statistical theory" two years before; and owing to the need for resolution by the university's administration of an equitable division of responsibility for the teaching of statistics between that department (which theretofore had been solely responsible for all teaching of statistics) and the department of mathematics.[3] Wilks was promoted to assistant professor in 1936. In the fall term he taught a graduate course, the substance of which he published as his *Lectures . . . on . . . Statistical Inference, 1936–37 . . .*; and in the spring of 1937 he gave an undergraduate course, quite possibly the first carefully formulated college undergraduate course in mathematical statistics based on one term of calculus.

Wilks's service to the federal government began with his appointment in 1936 as a collaborator in the Soil Conservation Program of the U.S. Department of Agriculture. He continued to serve the government as a member of the Applied Mathematics Panel, National Defense Research Committee, Office of Scientific Research and Development; chairman of the mathematics panel, Research and Development Board, Defense Department; adviser to the Selective Service System and the Bureau of the Budget; a member of various committees of the National Science Foundation, the National Academy of Sciences, and NASA; and an academic member of the Army Mathematics Advisory Panel. In 1947 he was awarded the Presidential Certificate of Merit for his contributions to antisubmarine warfare and the solution of convoy problems.

Wilks was deeply interested in the whole spectrum of mathematical education. In "Personnel and Training Problems in Statistics" (1947) he outlined the growing use of statistical methods, the demand for personnel, and problems of training, and made recommendations that served as a guide in the rapid growth of university centers of training in statistics after World War II. Drawing on his experience at Princeton, he urged, in "Teaching Statistical Inference in Elementary Mathematics Courses" (1958), teaching the principles of statistical inference to freshmen and sophomores, and further proposed revamping high school curricula in mathematics and the sciences to provide instruction in probability, statistics, logic, and other modern mathematical subjects. During his last few years he worked with an experimental program in a school at Princeton that introduced mathematics at the elementary level, down to kindergarten.

NOTES

1. An unfortunate consequence of the father's predilection for alliteration in naming his sons is that publications of Samuel Stanley and Syrrel Singleton Wilks (a physiologist and expert in aerospace medicine) are sometimes lumped together under "S. S. Wilks" in bibliographic works, such as *Science Citation Index.*

2. For a fuller account of the founding and early years of the *Annals of Mathematical Statistics*, see the letter from Harry C. Carver, dated 14 Apr. 1972, to professor [W. J.] Hall, reproduced in *Bulletin of the Institute of Mathematical Statistics*, **2**, no. 1 (Jan. 1973), 11–14; and Allen T. Craig, "Our Silver Anniversary," in *Annals of Mathematical Statistics*, **31**, no. 4 (Dec. 1960), 835–837.

3. The background of this delay and its ultimate resolution are discussed in detail by Churchill Eisenhart, in "Samuel S. Wilks and the Army Experiment Design Conference Series," an address at the twentieth Conference on the Design of Experiments in Army Research, Development and Testing, held at Fort Belvoir, Va., 23–25 Oct. 1974, published in the *Proceedings* of this conference (U.S. Army Research Office Report 75–2 June 1975), 1–47. This account also contains material unavailable elsewhere on Wilks's family and early career, together with extensive notes on the American institutions and personages that played important roles in it.

BIBLIOGRAPHY

I. ORIGINAL WORKS. "The Publications of S. S. Wilks," prepared by T. W. Anderson, in *Annals of Mathematical Statistics*, **36**, no. 1 (Feb. 1965), 24–27, which gives bibliographic details for five books, forty-eight articles, and twelve "other writings," appears to be complete with respect to the first two categories but not to the last. All forty-eight articles are repr. in T. W. Anderson, *S. S. Wilks: Collected Papers — Contributions to Mathematical Statistics* (New York, 1967), as are Anderson's lists of Wilks's publications, in rearranged form (xxvii–xxxiii). Particulars on thirty-one additional "other writings" are given by Churchill Eisenhart, "A Supplementary List of Publications of S. S. Wilks," in *American Statistician*, **29**, no. 1 (Feb. 1975), 25–27.

Among the more important of Wilks's publications are three holograph books: *Lectures by S. S. Wilks on the Theory of Statistical Inference 1936–1937, Princeton University* (Ann Arbor, Mich., 1937); *Elementary Statistical Analysis* (Princeton, 1948), quite conceivably the first carefully developed undergraduate course in mathematical statistics based on one term of calculus; and *Mathematical Statistics* (New York, 1962), a far more advanced, comprehensive treatment — *Mathematical Statistics* (Princeton, 1943) was an early version of some of the same material, prepared partly with the help of his students. He also wrote *Introductory Probability and Statistical Inference: An Experimental Course* (New York, 1957; rev. ed., Princeton, 1959; Spanish trans., Rosario, Argentina, 1961), with E. C. Douglas, F. Mosteller, R. S. Pieters, D. E. Richmond, R. E. K. Rourke, and G. B. Thomas; and *Introductory Engineering Statistics* (New York, 1965; 2nd ed., 1971), with Irwin Guttman (2nd ed. with Guttman and J. S. Hunter).

Of his research papers, the most notable are "The Standard Error of the Means of 'Matched' Samples," in *Journal of Educational Psychology*, **22**, no. 3 (Mar. 1931), 205–208, repr. as paper 1 in *Collected Papers*; "On the Distributions of Statistics in Samples From a Normal Population of Two Variables With Matched Sampling of One Variable," in *Metron*, **9**, nos. 3–4 (Mar. 1932), 87–126, repr. as paper 2 in *Collected Papers*, his doctoral dissertation; "Certain Generalizations in the Analysis of Variance," in *Biometrika*, **24**, pts. 3–4 (Nov. 1932), 471–494, repr. as paper 6 in *Collected Papers*; "Methods of Statistical Analysis Appropriate for *k* Samples of Two Variables," *ibid.*, **25**, pts. 3–4 (Dec. 1933), 353–378, repr. as paper 7 in *Collected Papers*, written with E. S. Pearson; "Moment-Generating Operators for Determinants of Product Moments in Samples From a Normal System," in *Annals of Mathematics*, 2nd ser., **35**, no. 2 (Apr. 1934), 312–340, repr. as paper 8 in *Collected Papers*; "On the Independence of *k* Sets of Normally Distributed Statistical Variables," in *Econometrica*, **3**, no. 3 (July 1935), 309–326, repr. as paper 9 in *Collected Papers*; "The Likelihood Test of Independence in Contingency Tables," in *Annals of Mathematical Statistics*, **6**, no. 4 (Dec. 1935), 190–196,

repr. as paper 11 in *Collected Papers*; "The Large-Sample Distribution of the Likelihood Ratio for Testing Composite Hypotheses," *ibid.*, **9**, no. 1 (Mar. 1938), 60–62, repr. as paper 14 in *Collected Papers*; and "Weighting Systems for Linear Functions of Correlated Variables When There Is No Dependent Variable," in *Psychometrika*, **3**, no. 1 (Mar. 1938), 23–40, repr. as paper 16 in *Collected Papers*.

See also "Shortest Average Confidence Intervals From Large Samples," in *Annals of Mathematical Statistics*, **9**, no. 3 (Sept. 1938), 166–175, repr. as paper 17 in *Collected Papers*; "An Optimum Property of Confidence Regions Associated With the Likelihood Function," *ibid.*, **10**, no. 4 (Dec. 1939), 225–235, repr. as paper 20 in *Collected Papers*, written with J. F. Daly; "Determination of Sample Sizes for Setting Tolerance Limits," *ibid.*, **12**, no. 1 (Mar. 1941), 91–96, repr. as paper 23 in *Collected Papers*; "Statistical Prediction With Special Reference to the Problem of Tolerance Limits," *ibid.*, **13**, no. 4 (Dec. 1942), 400–409, repr. as paper 26 in *Collected Papers*; "Sample Criteria for Testing Equality of Means, Equality of Variances, and Equality of Covariances in a Normal Multivariate Population," *ibid.*, **17**, no. 3 (Sept. 1946), 257–281, repr. as paper 28 in *Collected Papers*; "Order Statistics," in *Bulletin of the American Mathematical Society*, **54**, no. 1 (Jan. 1948), 6–50, repr. as paper 32 in *Collected Papers*; and "Multivariate Statistical Outliers," in *Sankhya*, **25A**, pt. 4 (Dec. 1963), 407–426, repr. as paper 48 in *Collected Papers*.

Two important papers on teaching and training in statistics are "Personnel and Training Problems in Statistics," in *American Mathematical Monthly*, **54**, no. 9 (Nov. 1947), 525–528; and "Teaching Statistical Inference in Elementary Mathematics Courses," *ibid.*, **65**, no. 3 (Mar. 1958), 143–152.

Following Wilks's death, his "working papers on subjects requiring statistical analysis; letters, reports and papers relating to professional organizations," were donated by his widow and Princeton University to the American Philosophical Society; for further details see *Guide to the Archives and Manuscript Collections of the American Philosophical Society* (Philadelphia, 1966), 146. Another dozen items of correspondence (1946, 1961–1962) are preserved in the Leonard J. Savage Papers (MS group 695), Sterling Memorial Library, Yale University. Wilks's professional books and journals have been placed in the S. S. Wilks Room in New Fine Hall, Princeton University.

II. SECONDARY LITERATURE. The biography of Wilks by Frederick Mosteller in *International Encyclopedia of the Social Sciences*, XVI (New York, 1968), 550–553, provides an informative summary of the highlights of Wilks's life, work, and impact in diverse professional roles. Wilks's research contributions and other writings are reviewed in the comprehensive obituary by T. W. Anderson in *Annals of Mathematical Statistics*, **36**, no. 1 (Feb. 1965), 1–23 (repr. in *S. S. Wilks: Collected Papers*), which is preceded by a photograph — not in *Col-*

lected Papers – of Wilks at his desk. A less technical but equally full account of Wilks's life and work is Frederick Mosteller, "Samuel S. Wilks: Statesman of Statistics," in *American Statistician*, **18**, no. 2 (Apr. 1964), 11–17; there is some additional illuminating information in the obituaries by W. G. Cochran, in *Review of the International Statistical Institute*, **32**, nos. 1–2 (June 1964), 189–191; and John W. Tukey, in *Yearbook, American Philosophical Society* for 1964 (1965), 147–154. The obituary in *Estadística* (Washington, D.C.), **22**, no. 83 (June 1964), 338–340, tells of his activities in connection with the Inter-American Statistical Institute.

The eight articles that constitute "Memorial to Samuel S. Wilks" in *Journal of the American Statistical Association*, **60**, no. 312 (Dec. 1965), 938–966, are rich sources of further information, insight, and perspective: Frederick F. Stephan and John W. Tukey, "Sam Wilks in Princeton," 939–944; Frederick Mosteller, "His Writings in Applied Statistics," 944–953; Alex M. Mood, "His Philosophy About His Work," 953–955; Morris H. Hansen, "His Contributions to Government," 955–957; Leslie E. Simon, "His Stimulus to Army Statistics," 957–962; Morris H. Hansen, "His Contributions to the American Statistical Association," 962–964; W. J. Dixon, "His Editorship of the *Annals of Mathematical Statistics*," 964–965; and the unsigned "The Wilks Award," 965–966.

Other publications cited or mentioned in the text are: R. A. Fisher, "On the Mathematical Foundations of Theoretical Statistics," in *Philosophical Transactions of the Royal Society*, **222A**, no. 602 (19 Apr. 1922), 309–368; and "The General Sampling Distribution of the Multiple Correlation Coefficient," in *Proceedings of the Royal Society*, **121A**, no. A788 (1 Dec. 1928), 654–673; E. F. Lindquist, "The Significance of a Difference Between 'Matched' Groups," in *Journal of Educational Psychology*, **22** (Mar. 1931), 197–204; J. Neyman, "Outline of a Theory of Statistical Estimation Based on the Classical Theory of Probability," in *Philosophical Transactions of the Royal Society*, **236A**, no. 767 (30 Aug. 1937), 333–380, repr. as paper no. 20 in *A Selection of Early Statistical Papers of J. Neyman* (Cambridge – Berkeley – Los Angeles, 1967); J. Neyman and E. S. Pearson, "On the Use and Interpretation of Certain Test Criteria. Part I," in *Biometrika*, **20A**, pts. 1–2 (July 1928), 175–240, repr. as paper no. 1 in *Joint Statistical Papers of J. Neyman and E. S. Pearson* (Cambridge – Berkeley – Los Angeles, 1967); "On the Use and Interpretation of Certain Test Criteria. Part II," *ibid.*, pts. 3–4 (Dec. 1928), 263–294, repr. as paper no. 2 in *Joint . . . Papers*; and "On the Problem of k Samples," in *Bulletin international de l'Académie polonaise des sciences et des lettres*, no. 6A (June 1931), 460–481, repr. as paper no. 4 in *Joint . . . Papers*; Walter A. Shewhart, *Economic Control of Quality of Manufactured Product* (New York, 1931), 42; J. Wishart, "The Generalized Product Moment Distribution in Samples From a Normal Multivariate Population," in *Biometrika*, **20A**, pts. 1–2 (July 1928), 32–52; and

J. Wishart and M. S. Bartlett, "The Generalized Product Moment Distribution in a Normal System," in *Proceedings of the Cambridge Philosophical Society. Mathematical and Physical Sciences*, **29**, pt. 2 (10 May 1933), 260–270.

CHURCHILL EISENHART

WILSON, EDWIN BIDWELL (*b.* Hartford, Connecticut, 25 April 1879; *d.* Brookline, Massachusetts, 28 December 1964)

The son of a schoolteacher, Wilson graduated B.A. from Harvard in 1899 and Ph.D. from Yale two years later. He studied for a while in Paris, taught mathematics at Yale, and then moved to the Massachusetts Institute of Technology, becoming head of the department of physics there in 1917. Five years later he was appointed professor of vital statistics at the Harvard School of Public Health. Wilson's work in that capacity earned him two presidencies in 1929: of the American Statistical Association and the Social Sciences Research Council, New York. Following his retirement in 1945 he acted as consultant to the Office of Naval Research. Throughout his long and varied career (among other things he was managing editor of the *Proceedings of the National Academy of Sciences*, Washington, for half a century) Wilson combined a quiet if somewhat crotchety Yankee charm with a firm sense of high standards in research and exposition.

In each of his fields Wilson made characteristic contributions. As a student of Willard Gibbs at Yale, he codified the great physicist's lectures on vector analysis into a textbook. This beautiful work, published when Wilson was only twenty-two years old, had a profound and lasting influence on the notation for and use of vector analysis. Meantime, Wilson's mind and pen began to range over many other areas of mathematics, including the foundations of projective and differential geometry; and in 1903 he criticized, with bold sharpness, Hilbert's "so-called foundations" of geometry. In 1912 Wilson published a comprehensive text on advanced calculus that was the first really modern book of its kind in the United States. Immediately successful, it had no rival for many years. Wilson's interest in theoretical physics, inspired by Gibbs, resulted in papers on mechanics and relativity. World War I led him to study aerodynamics, in which he gave a course; and he did research on the theory of the effects of gusts on airplane flight. Outcomes of this work were the publication of a book on aeronautics in 1920 and the stimulation of a group of students who were to make a mark in that field.

Early in the 1920's Wilson began to think carefully about probability and statistics. Because of his Harvard professorship he naturally focused on vital statistics, but he also pondered the theory of errors and its relation to quantitative biology and astronomy. In this field he was both innovative and evangelical—constantly drawing attention to the role of statistics in biology and urging the recruitment of full-time statisticians.

A major contribution to inferential statistics was Wilson's restructuring of interval estimation. For long before his time it had been vaguely implicit that the attachment of a standard error to a point estimate was a crude interval estimate. Thus, noting, say, that a series of observations yielded 129 ± 22 mm. as the mean length of a sample of Armadillidiidae, the researcher could add that the true (parametric) value lay, with a probability of about 2/3, in the interval 107–151. In an admirably concise note published in 1927, Wilson pointed out that, logically, a true value cannot have a probable location. He also showed how a rigorous and unelliptic statement could be made about the probability that an estimated interval will embrace the (fixed) parameter. This interval was essentially what became known as a confidence interval, as rediscovered and developed by Jerzy Neyman and his school. The priority must, however, be given to Wilson.

In studying cumulative population growth, and in handling quantal-response bioassay (which involves "all-or-none" reactions of members of a biological population to an agent), Wilson was an early and effective advocate of the logistic function, $P = (1 + \exp[-(\alpha + \beta X)])^{-1}$, where P is the probability of response to the amount X of the agent, and α and β are parameters. He published methods of handling data that fitted this function, and thus of estimating the potency of the agent.

Wilson exhibited a constructively critical mind, quick to expose flaws and errors. Each of his books was an effective and timely exposition of a major subject, and his best papers made lasting impressions. He contributed to many disciplines other than his specialties, including epidemiology, sociology, and economics. His greatest originality may have been reached in his papers on statistics—which, interestingly, was a subject he did not explore deeply until middle age.

BIBLIOGRAPHY

Wilson's three important books are *Vector Analysis* (New York, 1901); *Advanced Calculus* (Boston, 1912); and *Aeronautics* (New York, 1920). Some noteworthy papers are "The So-Called Foundations of Geometry," in *Archiv der Mathematik und Physik*, **6** (1903), 104–122; "The Space-Time Manifold of Relativity; the non-Euclidean Geometry of Mechanics and Electromagnetics," in *Proceedings of the American Academy of Arts and Sciences*, **48** (1912), 389–507, written with G. N. Lewis; "Differential Geometry of Two-Dimensional Surfaces in Hyperspace," *ibid.*, **52** (1916), 270–386, written with C. L. E. Moore; "Probable Inference, the Law of Succession, and Statistical Inference," in *Journal of the American Statistical Association*, **22** (1927), 209–212; "Periodogram of American Business Activity," in *Quarterly Journal of Economics*, **48** (1934), 375–417; and "The Determination of LD-50 and Its Sampling Error in Bioassay," in *Proceedings of the National Academy of Sciences of the United States of America*, **29** (1943), 79–85, 114–120, 257–262, written with Jane Worcester.

A full account of Wilson's life and work, by Jerome Hunsaker and Saunders Mac Lane, is in *Biographical Memoirs. National Academy of Sciences*, **43** (1973), 285–320, with bibliography.

NORMAN T. GRIDGEMAN
SAUNDERS MAC LANE

WILSON, JOHN (*b.* Applethwaite, Westmorland, England, 6 August 1741; *d.* Kendal, Westmorland, 18 October 1793)

Wilson was educated at Kendal and at Peterhouse, Cambridge, where in the mathematical tripos of 1761 he was senior wrangler. He was elected a fellow of Peterhouse in 1764 and a fellow of the Royal Society in 1782. As an undergraduate he attracted notice in the university by his defense of Waring, then Lucasian professor of mathematics, against adverse criticism of the latter's *Miscellanea analytica* (1762).

As a private tutor at Cambridge, Wilson had a high reputation; but after a short period of teaching, he was called to the bar in 1766 and acquired a considerable practice on the northern circuit. In 1786 he was raised to the bench of the Court of Common Pleas; later he served for a short time as one of the commissioners for the great seal, between the retirement of Lord Edward Thurlow from the office of lord chancellor and the appointment of Lord Loughborough.

Wilson's name is given to the theorem that if p is a prime number, then $1 + (p-1)!$ is divisible by p.

The first published statement of the theorem was by Waring in his *Meditationes algebraicae* (1770), although manuscripts in the Hannover Library show that the result had been found by Leibniz. Waring ascribed the theorem to Wilson but did not prove it; the first published proof was given by Lagrange (1773), who provided a direct proof from which Fermat's theorem (1640), first proved by Euler in 1736, can be deduced: If p is a prime and a is not divisible by p, then $a^{p-1} - 1$ is divisible by p. Lagrange also showed that Wilson's theorem can be deduced from Fermat's theorem, and that the converse of Wilson's theorem is true: if n divides $1 + (n - 1)!$, then n is a prime.

In a series of letters exchanged between Sir Frederick Pollock and Augustus De Morgan, published by W. W. Rouse Ball, Pollock described the mathematical work done at Cambridge in the first decade of the nineteenth century, and asserted that Wilson's theorem was a guess that neither he nor Waring could prove.

Wilson's result has been generalized to provide a series of theorems relating to the symmetric functions of the integers $1, 2, \cdots, p - 1$, and in other ways. The history of the theorem and its generalizations is given in detail by L. E. Dickson.

BIBLIOGRAPHY

For Wilson's life, see *Dictionary of National Biography*, XXI, p. 578; and Atkinson, *Worthies of Westmorland*, II (London, 1850); for personal details, Augustus De Morgan, *Budget of Paradoxes*, 2nd ed. (Chicago–London, 1915); W. W. Rouse Ball, *A History of the Study of Mathematics at Cambridge* (Cambridge, 1889).

For Wilson's theorem, see the following, listed chronologically: E. Waring, *Meditationes algebraicae* (Cambridge, 1770); J. L. Lagrange, in *Nouveaux mémoires de l'Académie de Berlin* (1773); and L. E. Dickson, *History of the Theory of Numbers*, I (repr. New York, 1934), ch. 3.

T. A. A. BROADBENT

WINLOCK, JOSEPH (*b.* Shelby County, Kentucky, 6 February 1826; *d.* Cambridge, Massachusetts, 11 June 1875)

Immediately upon graduation from Shelby College in 1845, Winlock was appointed professor of mathematics and astronomy in that school. At the meeting in 1851 of the American Association for the Advancement of Science, Winlock met Benjamin Peirce; thenceforth he was esteemed and promoted by the scientific lazzaroni. In 1852 he moved to Cambridge, as a computer for the *American Ephemeris and Nautical Almanac*. Using the refracting telescope from Shelby set up in the Cloverden Observatory in Cambridge, Winlock and B. A. Gould made astronomical observations. In 1857 Winlock was appointed professor of mathematics at the U.S. Naval Observatory. The following year he was promoted to superintendent of the Nautical Almanac office, which position he resigned in 1859 to take charge of the mathematics department of the U.S. Naval Academy. Following the outbreak of the Civil War, Winlock again took superintendence of the Nautical Almanac. In 1863 he was made an original member of the National Academy of Sciences. In 1866, backed by the "Coast Survey Clique," he was appointed Phillips professor of astronomy and director of the Harvard College Observatory. In 1871 the professorship of geodesy in the Lawrence Scientific School was added to his duties.

While at Harvard, Winlock's primary concern was to develop and obtain more accurate and efficient instruments. In this he was quite successful. Had he lived longer he would probably have used them to even better advantage than he did. Troughton & Simms, after extensive collaboration with Winlock, supplied a large and improved meridian circle. With this the Harvard zone of stars for the Astronomische Gesellschaft was determined; after Winlock's death the observations were continued by William A. Rogers, and the computations by Winlock's oldest daughter, Anna.

Among Winlock's several contributions to solar photography was the development of fixed-horizontal long-focus refracting telescopes. One of these instruments, installed at Harvard in 1870, took daily pictures of the sun. Similar telescopes were used by the eight U.S. government-sponsored expeditions to record the 1874 transit of Venus. Also worthy of mention are Winlock's particularly detailed photographs of the solar corona during the eclipse of 1869. Celestial spectroscopy also received Winlock's attention, and he obtained several fine spectroscopes for the observatory. To take the fullest possible advantage offered by the 1870 solar eclipse, Winlock devised a mechanical method of recording the positions of spectral lines. Throughout his tenure at Harvard he collaborated with the Coast Survey on both astronomical and geographical projects.

BIBLIOGRAPHY

The Royal Society of London, *Catalogue of Scientific Papers,* Poggendorff, and the *Bibliographie Générale de l'Astronomie* list about two dozen Winlock papers. Winlock's influence as an astronomer, both his own work and the work he inspired in others, is best seen in the *Annals* of the Harvard College Observatory. Vols. **5, 6, 7**, published by Winlock, contain work done by his predecessors, W. C. Bond and G. P. Bond. Published after Winlock's death, vol. **8**, pt. 1, "Historical Account of the Astronomical Observatory of Harvard College," details the instrumental additions and improvements engineered by Winlock; pt. 2 contains "Astronomical Engravings of the Moon, Planets, etc.; Prepared [by L. Trouvelot] at the Astronomical Observatory of Harvard College Under the Direction of the Late Joseph Winlock, A.M." Vol. **9** contains C. S. Peirce's photometrical researches, also supported by Winlock. Vols. **10, 12, 14, 16, 25, 35,** and **36** contain astrometric catalogs prepared by William A. Rogers under the direction of Winlock and his successor, E. C. Pickering (in many cases these observations had been begun by Winlock). Vol. **13** contains micrometric observations from 1866 to 1881, made under, and in some cases by, Winlock and Pickering.

The most extensive obituary is in *Proceedings of the American Academy of Arts and Sciences,* **11** (1875–1876), 339–350, republished verbatim in *Biographical Memoirs of the National Academy of Sciences,* **1** (Washington, D.C., 1875). See also *Nature,* **12** (1875), 191–192; *American Journal of Science,* **10** (1875), 159–160 (quoted in *Scientific American*); *Dictionary of American Biography,* XX (New York, 1936); and the various published histories of the Harvard College Observatory.

DEBORAH JEAN WARNER

WINTHROP, JOHN (*b.* Boston, Massachusetts, 19 December 1714; *d.* Cambridge, Massachusetts, 3 May 1779)

One of sixteen children of Adam Winthrop and Anne Wainwright, John Winthrop was born into a New England family that was already famous both politically and scientifically. His great-granduncle and namesake, the son of Winthrop the elder, who immigrated to Massachusetts in 1630, was a founding member of the Royal Society of London, and governor of Connecticut from 1660 until his death in 1676. He was a notable administrator of the new settlements and a practical student of chemistry. It is interesting to note that one of his communications to the Royal Society concerned a fifth satellite of Jupiter. Here he anticipated his descendant's far more extensive astronomical studies.

Winthrop attended the Boston Latin School and Harvard College, from which he graduated in 1732. For the next six years he lived at home and studied privately to such effect that in 1738, at the age of twenty-four, he was appointed the second Hollis professor of mathematics and natural philosophy at Harvard, succeeding Isaac Greenwood. His duties included giving illustrated public lectures and taking charge of the considerable collection of philosophical instruments in Harvard Hall, used for demonstrations.

During his long tenure of the Hollis chair, which ceased only with his death, Winthrop established the first experimental physics laboratory in America; taught the laws of mechanics, optics, and astronomy according to Newton's principles; and introduced into the mathematics curriculum the study of the calculus. Perhaps his most important work for Harvard followed the disastrous fire that destroyed Harvard Hall on the night of 24 January 1764. The fire gutted the last of Harvard's original buildings and wiped out the valuable collection of scientific instruments. It fell to Winthrop to arrange for the replacement of the collection, which he was well equipped to do, both because of his scientific knowledge and because of his family connections and many friends on both sides of the Atlantic. The most active and influential of these friends was Franklin, who knew many of the finest instrument makers in London. The first orders for new apparatus went to London in June 1764, and over the next few years, instruments bearing such names as John Ellicott, Jeremiah Sisson, James Short, Peter Dollond, Benjamin Martin, Edward Nairne, and George Adams were dispatched to Harvard. The two major shipments were valued together at about £540. Among the instruments were two telescopes produced by Short. Winthrop himself owned a telescope by Short (made *ca.* 1755), which appears in the portrait of him painted by John Singleton Copley about 1773.

After 1739 Winthrop carried out many astronomical observations, the majority of which were reported in the *Philosophical Transactions of the Royal Society.* He observed the transits of Mercury in 1740, 1743, and again in 1769; and he used his observations to help determine the difference in longitude between Cambridge, Massachusetts, and Greenwich, England. In April 1759 he delivered lectures on the return of Halley's comet of 1682. Perhaps his most important astronomical work was concerned with the two transits of Venus in 1761 and 1769, which engaged astronomers all over the world. For the 1761 transit Winthrop organized an expedition from Harvard to St. John's, Newfoundland, which provided the material for one of his most important papers. In 1769 he published the results of further work in *Two Lectures on the Parallax and Distance of the Sun, as Deducible From the Transit of Venus*. Winthrop was also interested in magnetism and meteorology, and carried out systematic observations over a period of twenty years, reporting in 1756 on the effects of the severe earthquake in New England.

A number of honors were awarded to Winthrop in his later years. On 27 June 1765 he was proposed as a fellow of the Royal Society at the instigation of Franklin; Short was another of his supporters. Winthrop must have been closely associated with both men at this time, over replacement instruments for his college, and in work on the transits of Venus. Not only did Short make telescopes for observatories throughout the world, but he was also closely concerned with the Royal Society's plans for observing the phenomena. Winthrop's election was delayed until February 1766, when the ballot finally took place. Franklin signed a bond for his contributions, and the Harvard records show that his fees, not exceeding fifty-two shillings, were paid out of the treasury of the society in return for his placing a volume of the *Philosophical Transactions* annually in the library. In 1769 Winthrop became a member of the American Philosophical Society. He received the honorary degrees of LL.D. from the University of Edinburgh and from Harvard in 1771 and 1773, respectively.

Winthrop's first wife, whom he married in 1746, was Rebecca Townsend; and three years after her death in 1756, he married Hannah Fayerweather, a widow, who survived him. Winthrop was an ardent patriot, and a friend and adviser of George Washington. His career maintained the family tradition of public service allied with learning.

BIBLIOGRAPHY

I. ORIGINAL WORKS. Winthrop's works include "Concerning the Transit of Mercury Over the Sun, April 21, 1740 and of an Eclipse of the Moon, Dec. 21, 1740," in *Philosophical Transactions of the Royal Society*, **42** (1742–1743), 572–578; "An Account of the Earthquake Felt in New England, and the Neighbouring Parts of America, on the 18th of November 1755," *ibid.*, **50** (1757–1758), 1–18; "An Account of a Meteor Seen in New England, and of a Whirlwind Felt in That Country," *ibid.*, **52** (1761–1762), 6–16; "An Account of Several Fiery Meteors Seen in North America," *ibid.*, **54** (1764), 185–188; "Extract of a Letter . . . to James Short," *ibid.*, 277–278, on longitude and the equation of time; "Observations on the Transit of Venus, June 6, 1761, at St. John's, Newfoundland." *ibid.*, 279–283; "Cogitata de Cometis," *ibid.*, **57** (1767), 132–154; "Observations of the Transit of Venus Over the Sun, June 3, 1769," *ibid.*, **59** (1769), 351–358; "Observations of the Transit of Mercury Over the Sun, October 25, 1743," *ibid.*, 505–506; "Extract of a Letter . . . to B. Franklin," *ibid.*, **60** (1770), 358–362, on the transit of Venus and the aberration of light; "Observations of the Transit of Mercury Over the Sun, November 9th, 1769," *ibid.*, **61** (1771), 51–52; and "Remarks Upon a Passage in Castillione's Life of Sir Isaac Newton," *ibid.*, **64** (1774), 153–157.

Some of the material in the above papers was published separately including *Relation of a Voyage From Boston to Newfoundland for the Observation of the Transit of Venus, June 6, 1761* (Boston, 1761); and *Two Lectures on the Parallax and Distance of the Sun, as Deducible From the Transit of Venus. Read in Holden-Chapel at Harvard-College in Cambridge, New England, in March 1769* (Boston, 1769).

II. SECONDARY LITERATURE. On Winthrop and his work, see I. Bernard Cohen, *Some Early Tools of American Science. An Account of the Early Scientific Instruments and Mineralogical and Biological Collections in Harvard University* (Cambridge, Mass., 1950), *passim* (225 ff.); Raymond Phineas Stearns, "Colonial Fellows of the Royal Society of London, 1661–1788," in *Notes and Records of the Royal Society of London*, **8** (1951), 178–246; Raymond Phineas Stearns, *Science in the British Colonies of America* (Urbana, Ill., 1970), esp. 642–670; G. L'E. Turner, "The Apparatus of Science," in *History of Science*, **9** (1970), 129–138, an essay review of David P. Wheatland, *The Apparatus of Science at Harvard 1766–1800. Collection of Historical Scientific Instruments, Harvard University* (Cambridge, Mass., 1968), written with Barbara Carson; and *Dictionary of American Biography*, X, pp. 414–416.

G. L'E. TURNER

WINTNER, AUREL (*b.* Budapest, Hungary, 8 April 1903; *d.* Baltimore, Maryland, 15 January 1958)

Wintner studied mathematics at the University of Leipzig from 1927 to 1929. During that period he was an editorial assistant for *Mathematische Zeitschrift* and *Jahrbuch über die Fortschritte der Mathematik*, serving under the direction of Leon Lichtenstein, who for many years was editor of those journals. This period of apprenticeship had a profound influence on Wintner, and he often expressed his gratitude for his training under Lichtenstein.

Wintner's mathematical reputation was established by a series of papers on the Hill lunar theory that gave the first mathematically rigorous proof of the convergence of George Hill's method involving infinitely many unknowns. He received the Ph.D. at Leipzig in 1929, then spent a semester in Rome as a Rockefeller fellow and another in Copenhagen, where he worked with Elis Stromgren. As a result of that collaboration, Wintner was able to provide a theoretical basis for Stromgren's "natural termination principle" for orbit periods, which was an empirical analysis of the degeneration of periodic orbits.

In 1929 Wintner published *Spektraltheorie der unendlichen Matrizen*, which contains the first proofs of the basic facts in Hilbert space—the fundamental mathematical construct in the then-developing physical theory of quantum mechanics. Unfortunately, Wintner's fundamental contributions to this subject were (and are) not adequately appreciated because he formulated his results in the language of matrices rather than in the more abstract language of operators, made popular by von Neumann. This lack of recognition embittered Wintner and made him suspicious of the (genuine) merits of the more abstract developments in recent mathematics.

In 1930 Wintner married the daughter of Otto Hölder, one of his teachers at Leipzig. In the same year he joined the faculty of the Johns Hopkins University, where he remained until his death. In 1944 he became an editor of *American Journal of Mathematics*, to which he devoted most of his energy, both through his scientific contributions (a substantial part of his most valuable work after he came to America was published there) and through his editorial work.

Wintner's work in America covered the entire range of classical analysis, from probability and analytic number theory to differential equations and basic questions in local differential geometry. Much of his work from 1936 to 1958 was done in collaboration with his student and colleague Philip Hartman. He published several papers with Norbert Wiener in a branch of probability theory that is now coming back into fashion. He also produced works with several other mathematicians. In 1941 Wintner published *Analytical Foundations of Celestial Mechanics*, which combines great astronomical and mathematical scholarship with deep and meticulous analysis. He is best known for this work.

Wintner, a man of high moral principles, opposed direct government support of scholarly research, for fear of interference. He not only accepted considerable financial hardship by personally refusing such support but also was willing to

forgo fruitful scientific collaboration in order to maintain his ideals.

Shlomo Sternberg

WITT, JAN DE (*b.* Dordrecht, Netherlands, 24 September 1625; *d.* The Hague, Netherlands, 20 August 1672)

De Witt was the son of Jacob de Witt, burgomeister of Dordrecht, and Anna van de Corput. Both families were prominent members of the regent class which governed the towns and provinces of the Netherlands. He entered Dordrecht Latin school in 1636, and went to the University of Leiden in 1641. There he studied law, leaving for France in 1645 to take his degree at Angers. At Leiden he studied mathematics privately with Frans van Schooten the Younger, and received from him an excellent training in Cartesian mathematics. De Witt was a talented mathematician who had little time to devote to mathematics. He became pensionary of Dordrecht in 1650, and grand pensionary of Holland in 1653, making him the leader of the States Party, and, in effect, the prime minister of the Netherlands. He was a statesman of unusual ability and strength of character who guided the affairs of the United Provinces during the twenty-year interregnum in the Stadtholdership during the minority of William of Orange. This was one of the most critical periods in Dutch history, with the three Anglo-Dutch wars; the hostility of the Orange faction culminated in the murder of de Witt and his brother Cornelis by a mob in 1672.

De Witt's most important mathematical work was his *Elementa curvarum linearum*, written before 1650 and printed in Van Schooten's second Latin edition of Descartes's *Géométrie* (1659–1661). It is in two books: the first, a synthetic treatment of the geometric theory found in the early books of Apollonius' *Conics*; and the second, one of the first systematic developments of the analytic geometry of the straight line and conic. In the first book the *symptomae* (expressed as proportions) of the parabola, ellipse, and hyperbola are derived as plane loci, rather than as sections of the cone. His locus definitions of the ellipse are familiar to us today: the eccentric angle construction (a point fixed with respect to a rotating segment); the trammel construction (a fixed point on a given segment moving on two intersecting lines); and the "string" construction, based on the two-focus definition. For the hyperbola and parabola the locus is constructed as the intersection of corresponding members of two pencils of lines, one parallel and one concurrent. In modern terms these are interesting unintentional examples of the Steiner-Chasles projective definition of the conics, where the vertex of one pencil is at infinity.

De Witt is credited with introducing the term "directrix" for the parabola, but it is clear from his derivation that he does not use the term for the fixed line of our focus-directrix definition. Given fixed lines *DB* and *EF* intersecting at *D*, with *B* the pole and *EF* the directrix: for any point *H* on *EF*, if ∠*HBL* is constructed equal to ∠*FDB*, a line through *H* parallel to *BD* cuts *BL* in *G*, a point on the locus. *AC* is drawn through *B* with ∠*DBC* = ∠*BDF*, cutting *HG* in *I*, and *GK* is drawn parallel to *AC*. Since triangles *BDH* and *GKB* are similar, $(BI)^2 = (BD)(BK)$ or $y^2 = px$, a parabola with vertex at *B*, abscissa *BK* = *x*, and ordinate *KG* = *y*. If *EF* is perpendicular to *DB*, a rectangular coordinate system results, but *EF* is not our directrix.

In the first book of the *Elementa* de Witt not only freed the conics from the cone with his kinematic constructions, but satisfied the Cartesian criteria of constructibility. This book was written, as he reported to van Schooten, to give a background for the new analytic development of the second book. He began the analytic treatment by showing that equations of the first degree represent straight lines. As was usual at the time he did not use negative coordinates, graphing only segments or rays in the first quadrant. He carefully explained the actual construction of the lines for arbitrary coeffi-

cients since they would be needed in his transformations reducing general quadratic equations to type conics. For each conic de Witt began with simplified equations equivalent to his standard forms in book I, and then used translations and rotations to reduce more complicated equations to the canonical forms. For example, in the hyperbola

$$yy + \frac{2bxy}{a} + 2cy = \frac{fxx}{a} + ex + dd$$

he lets

$$z = y + \frac{b}{a}x + c$$

and then

$$v = x + h$$

where *h* is the coefficient of the linear term in *x* after the first substitution, giving

$$\frac{aazz}{fa + bb} = vv - hh + \frac{aadd + aacc}{fa + bb},$$

a standard hyperbola which cuts the new *v* or *z* axes according as *hh* is greater than or less than $\frac{aadd + aacc}{fa + bb}$. Although de Witt seems to be aware of the characteristic of the general quadratic equation in choosing his examples, he does not explicitly mention its use to determine the type of conic except in the case of the parabola. There he states that, if the terms of the second degree are a perfect square, the equation represents a parabola.

The last chapter is a summing up of the various transformations showing how to construct the graphs of all equations of second degree. Each case of positive and negative coefficients must be handled separately in a drawing, but the discussion for each curve is completely general, and both original and transformed axes are drawn.

In addition to the algebraic simplifications of the curves to normal form, book II contains the usual focus-directrix property of the parabola, and the analytic derivations of the ellipse and hyperbola as the locus of points the sum or difference of whose distances from two fixed points is a constant. These are done in the modern manner, squaring twice, with the explicit use of the Pythagorean theorem in place of the more recent distance formula.

De Witt's *Elementa* and John Wallis' *Tractatus de sectionibus conicis* (1655) are considered the first textbooks in analytic geometry. Although Wallis raised the question of priority, their ap-

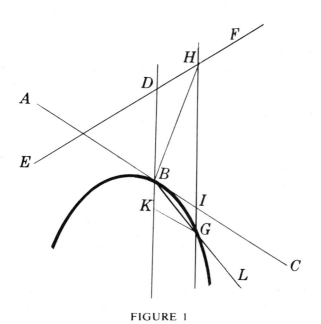

FIGURE 1

proaches were different and completely independent. Wallis first defined the conics as second-degree equations and deduced the properties of the curves from the equations, while de Witt defined them geometrically in the plane, and then showed that quadratic equations could be reduced to his normal forms.

Christiaan Huygens once wrote John Wallis of de Witt: "Could he have spared all his strength for mathematical works, he would have surpassed us all." His geometry was his only contribution to pure mathematics, but he turned his mathematical interests to the financial problems of the province of Holland throughout his long tenure as grand pensionary. The chief means of raising money for the States was by life or fixed annuities. In 1665 de Witt succeeded in reducing the interest rate from 5 to 4 percent and established a sinking fund with the interest saved by the conversion accumulated at compound interest to be applied to the debt of Holland, which could thus be paid in forty-one years. The second Anglo-Dutch War (1665–1667), however, defeated this scheme. The English wars were a perpetual financial drain, and more than half of the expenditure of the province of Holland (which had to defray the costs of the war almost alone) was swallowed up in interest payments.

In April 1671 it was resolved to negotiate funds by life annuities, thereby limiting the debt to one generation. De Witt prepared a treatise for the States of Holland demonstrating mathematically that life annuities were being offered at too high a rate of interest in comparison with fixed annuities. For many years the rule-of-thumb rates for life annuities had been twice the standard rate of interest. Holland had recently reduced the rate of interest to twenty-five years' purchase (4 percent) and was selling life annuities at fourteen years' purchase (7¹/₇ percent). De Witt wanted to raise the price to sixteen years' purchase (6¼ percent). His *Waerdye van Lyf-renten naer proportie van Losrenten* (July, 1671) is certainly among the first attempts to apply the theory of probability to economic problems. It was written as a political paper, and remained buried in the archives for almost two hundred years. Since its discovery and publication by Frederick Hendriks in 1852 there have been many articles (some of which are listed in the bibliography) explaining or criticizing it on the basis of modern actuarial science. It is actually a very simple and ingenious dissertation based only on the use of the principle of mathematical expectation to form equal contracts.

De Witt listed the present values at 4 percent of annuity payments of 10,000,000 stuyvers (to avoid decimals) per half year, and summed the mathematical expectations using hypothetical mortality rates for different ages. He first presupposed that a man is equally likely to die in the first or last half of any year, and then, since annuities were generally purchased on young lives, extended this to any half year of the "years of full vigor" from age three to fifty-three. For simplicity he considered the first hundred half years equally destructive or mortal, although he stated that the likelihood of decease is actually smaller in the first years. So too, he stopped at age eighty, although many live beyond that age. In the next ten years, fifty-three to sixty-three, the chance of dying does not exceed more than in the proportion of 3 to 2 the chance of dying in the first period; from sixty-three to seventy-three, the chance of dying is not more than 2 to 1; and from seventy-three to eighty, not more than 3 to 1.

De Witt gives many examples to explain the use of the concept of mathematical expectation. The following one is basic to his later calculations, and has been overlooked by many commentators. Consider a man of forty and a man of fifty-eight. According to his presuppositions the chances of the older man dying compared with the younger man are as 3 to 2. An equal contract could be devised: if the person of fifty-eight dies in six months, the younger man inherits 2,000 florins, but if the man of forty dies in six months, the elder inherits 3,000 florins. That is, the chance of the man of fifty-eight gaining 3,000 florins. is as 2 to 3, or, in terms of de Witt's annuity calculations, the chance of receiving a particular annuity payment in the second period is two-thirds that in the first period.

From this reasoning de Witt's calculations are straightforward: He sums the present values for the first hundred half years; two-thirds the present values for the next twenty half years; for the next twenty, one-half the present values; and one-third for the last fourteen. All these are summed and the average taken, giving a little more than sixteen florins as the present value of one florin of annuity on a young and healthy life. If the method had been applied to actual mortality tables, the labor would have been formidable. Later in 1671 de Witt and Jan Hudde corresponded on the problem of survivorship annuities on more than one life, and here both used actual mortality figures taken from the annuity records of Holland. Working with several groups of at least a hundred persons of a given age de Witt developed appropriate rates for annuities on two lives. These were extended a posteriori to any number of lives by a Pascal triangle, with a promise to Hudde to establish the results a priori. This was the culmination of de Witt's work with annuities, but for political reasons he suggested to Hudde that the public not be informed of the results of their study, since they were willing to buy annuities on more than one life at the current rate, which was favorable to the government.

BIBLIOGRAPHY

I. ORIGINAL WORKS. *Elementa curvarum linearum,* in Frans van Schooten's Latin ed. of Descartes's *Géométrie, Geometria a Renato Descartes* (Amsterdam, 1659–1661). *Waerdye van Lyf-renten naer proportie van Los-renten* (The Hague, 1671; facs. ed. Haarlem, 1879). Six volumes of letters in *Werken van het Historisch Genootschap te Utrecht,* 3d ser., XVIII, XXV, XXXI, XXXIII, XLII, XLIV (1906–1922). Volume XXXIII contains letters to and from mathematicians including the letters to Jan Hudde on annuities on more than one life.

II. SECONDARY LITERATURE. Of the many biographies of de Witt, Nicolaas Japikse, *Johan de Witt* (Amsterdam, 1915), is indispensable. Still valuable is G. A. Lefèvre-Pontalis, *Jean de Witt, Grand Pensionnaire de Hollande,* 2 vols. (Paris, 1884); English trans., S. F. Stephenson and A. Stephenson (London, 1885). For a reliable discussion of the period, and the relations between de Witt and William III, see Pieter Geyl, *The Netherlands in the Seventeenth Century, Part Two 1648–1715* (London, 1964), and his *Oranje en Stuart* (Utrecht, 1939), English trans., Arnold Pomerans (London, 1969). For the geometry see P. van Geer, "Johan de Witt als Wiskundige," in *Nieuw Archief voor Wiskundige,* 2nd ser., 11 (1915), 98–126; and C. B. Boyer, *History of Analytic Geometry* (New York, 1956).

An English translation of the work on life annuities can be found in Frederick Hendriks, "Contributions to the History of Insurance . . . a Restoration of the Grand Pensionary De Witt's Treatise on Life Annuities," in *The Assurance Magazine* (now *Journal of the Institute of Actuaries*), 2 (1852), 230–258. Vols. 3 (1901), 10 (1908), and 11 (1909) of the *Archief voor Verzekeringe Wetenschap* contain articles offering varying criticisms and explanations of de Witt's writings on annuities.

JOY B. EASTON

WITTICH (or **WITTICHIUS**), **PAUL** (*b.* Breslau, Silesia [now Wrocław, Poland], 1555 [?]; *d.* Breslau, 9 January 1587)

Little is known about Wittich's life. In the summer of 1580, with a letter of introduction from Hagecius, he went for a short time to Uraniborg to work with Tycho Brahe.[1] He soon showed himself to be a skillful mathematician, for with Tycho he discovered—or, more precisely, rediscovered—the method of prostaphaeresis, by which the products and quotients of trigonometric functions appearing in trigonometric formulas can be replaced by simpler sums and differences.[2] The two formulas involved in this method are $\sin a \cdot \sin b = \frac{1}{2}(\cos [a - b] - \cos [a + b])$ and $\cos a \cdot \cos b = \frac{1}{2}(\cos [a - b] + \cos [a + b])$.

The individual contributions of Tycho Brahe and Wittich cannot be established with certainty, but that of Wittich, who was the better mathematician, was probably the greater.[3] A letter is extant in which Tycho reported on this period of collaboration, during which each freely and fully shared his results with the other.[4] It is therefore understandable that he was very angry with Wittich when he learned that the method of prostaphaeresis had become known in Kassel, which Wittich had visited in 1584, and that Nicolai Reymers Bär (Ursus) had published it as his own discovery in 1588.[5]

Actually, Ursus also had been at Uraniborg in 1584 and had secretly noted down the method, although he did not discover the proof, which Brahe kept more carefully concealed. Wittich, who taught mathematics in Breslau from 1582 to 1584, was in Kassel in 1584.[6] There he described to Joost Bürgi, the clockmaker for Landgrave Wilhelm IV, the instruments used by Tycho in his observatory,[7] which Bürgi reproduced and improved. Wittich also showed him the proof of prostaphaeresis; and it was from Bürgi that Ursus learned the *mysteria triangulorum.* Wittich left Kassel before 1586 and died in Breslau at the beginning of 1587. On learning of Wittich's death, Tycho regretted that he had doubted his honesty.[8]

The method of prostaphaeresis originated with Johann Werner, who developed it in conjunction with the law of cosines for sides of a spherical triangle. In Regiomontanus' formulation the law reads: sinvers A: sinvers a − sinvers $[b - c] = r^2$: $(\sin b \cdot \sin c)$.[9] If one eliminates the *sinus versus* and takes $r = sinus totus = 1$, the result is

$$\frac{1}{\cos A} = \frac{\sin b \cdot \sin c}{\cos a - \cos b \cdot \cos c}.$$

Here Werner, who preserved the *sinus versus,* used the first formula of prostaphaeresis in handling the term $\sin b \cdot \sin c$; whereas Tycho and Wittich also knew the cosine law with the term $\cos b \cdot \cos c$.[10] They also used prostaphaeresis for problems that Werner solved without this method.[11]

It is unlikely that Tycho and Wittich ever saw Werner's *De triangulis sphaericis libri quatuor*. Its manuscript, which Rheticus wanted to publish at Cracow in 1557, was not printed until 1907.[12] On the other hand, Tycho knew that such a work existed and sought, unsuccessfully, to obtain a copy of it.[13] He and Wittich might, therefore, have been encouraged by this knowledge to work out the details of such a method, which Ursus stole and published in 1588.[14]

In 1580 Tycho and Wittich probably had not seen Viète's *Canon mathematicus* of 1579. Further evidence on this point is provided by Longomontanus, who was Tycho's assistant at Uraniborg from 1589 to 1597.[15] The method of converting products to sums or differences was further developed by Bürgi, Clavius, and Jöstel, among others. Specifically, Bürgi took as his starting point the relationship between arithmetic and geometric series and introduced logarithms.[16] He thereby definitively replaced the older method with an improved one that Pitiscus called *modus Byrgii*.[17] Kepler, who was thoroughly acquainted with Tycho's computations, mentions the *negotium prostaphaereticum Wittichianum* in his book on optics (1604).[18]

NOTES

1. Wittich, who left Uraniborg because of a matter concerning an inheritance, carried with him a letter from Brahe to Hagecius dated 4 Nov. 1580. Since Brahe received no answer, Wittich was suspected of not having delivered it. Hagecius later cleared up the matter (23 Sept. 1582). On this point see Brahe, *Opera*, VII, 72.
2. In the letter of 4 Nov. 1580 Brahe speaks of their efforts to develop this method, "quae per προσταφαίρεσιν procedit absque taediosa multiplicacione et divisione." *Ibid.*, 58.
3. See R. Wolf, *Handbuch der Astronomie*, 227 f.
4. See Brahe's letter to Hagecius of 14 Mar. 1592. Brahe, *Opera*, VII, 323.
5. See Brahe's letter to Hagecius of 1 July 1586, in which he writes that Wittich "agit sane minus sincere mecum." *Ibid.*, 108.
6. See J. L. E. Dreyer, *Tycho Brahe*, 121, n. 4.
7. Among these were the mural quadrant with transverse calibration. On this see C. D. Hellman, "Brahe," 405.
8. See his letter of 14 Jan. 1595: "nec vivum nec defunctum suis privavi honoribus." *Opera*, VI, 327.
9. See A. von Braunmühl, *Vorlesungen über Geschichte der Trigonometrie*, 131; and J. Tropfke, *Geschichte der Elementar-Mathematik*, 139 ff.
10. In the process *cos* is replaced by the *sin* of the complement. See A. A. Björnbo, "Ioannis Verneri . . . ." 169; and M. Cantor, *Vorlesungen über Geschichte der Mathematik*, 642f. Ibn Yūnus also knew prostaphaeresis for the operation involving cos *a* · cos *b*. See G. Sarton, *Introduction to the History of Science*, 716 ff. Traces of the law can be found in a special case in Indian mathematics (see Braunmühl, 41), and in a more complete form in the work of al-Battānī (see

Sarton, *op. cit.*, 603; and Braunmühl, *op. cit.*, 53). Peuerbach also knew this law and derived it independently in *Compositio tabule altitudinis solis ad omnes horas* (in Codex Vindobonensis 5203, fols. 54r–55r).
11. See Björnbo, *op. cit.*, 169.
12. It was published by Björnbo with the preface by Rheticus that was printed in 1557.
13. See Tycho's letter to Hagecius of 25 Aug. 1585. *Opera*, VII, 95.
14. See Björnbo, *op. cit.*, 171.
15. See Dreyer, *op. cit.*, 361, n. 3, and 383.
16. Even before Stifel's *Arithmetica integra* (1544) others, including Chuquet and Heinrich Grammateus, compared the two types of series. On this point see L. Nový, "Bürgi," 602.
17. See Bartholomeo Pitiscus, *Trigonometriae sive de dimensione triangulorum libri quinque*, 3rd ed. (Frankfurt, 1612), 177.
18. Kepler, *Gesammelte Werke*, II (Munich, 1939), 336.

BIBLIOGRAPHY

See A. A. Björnbo, "Ioannis Verneri De triangulis sphaericis libri quatuor, de meteoroscopiis libri sex cum prooemio Georgii Ioachimi Rhetici. I. De triangulis sphaericis," in *Abhandlungen zur Geschichte der mathematischen Wissenschaften*, 24 (1907), 150–175; A. von Braunmühl, *Vorlesungen über Geschichte der Trigonometrie*, I (Leipzig, 1900), 256; 260; and "Zur Geschichte der prosthaphaeretischen Methode in der Trigonometrie," in *Abhandlungen zur Geschichte der Mathematik*, 9 (1899), 15–29; M. Cantor, *Vorlesungen über Geschichte der Mathematik*, 2nd ed., II (Leipzig, 1913), 937; J. L. E. Dreyer, *Tycho Brahe, a Picture of Scientific Life and Work in the Sixteenth Century* (Edinburgh, 1890; New York, 1963), 405; and *Tychonis Brahe Opera omnia*, XV (Copenhagen, 1913; 1929), 50; C. D. Hellman, "Brahe," in *Dictionary of Scientific Biography*, II, 401–416; L. Nový, "Bürgi," *ibid.*, 602–603; G. Sarton, *Introduction to the History of Science*, I (Baltimore, 1927); J. Tropfke, *Geschichte der Elementar-Mathematik*, 2nd ed., V (Berlin–Leipzig, 1923), 108 ff; and R. Wolf, *Handbuch der Astronomie, ihrer Geschichte und Litteratur*, I (Zurich, 1890).

KURT VOGEL

WOEPCKE, FRANZ (*b.* Dessau, Germany, 6 May 1826; *d.* Paris, France, 25 March 1864)

Woepcke was the son of Ernst Woepcke, the Wittenberg postmaster, and Karolina Chapon. He studied mathematics and physics at Berlin from 1843 to 1847, receiving the Ph.D. *magna cum laude* in the latter year for a work on sundials in antiquity. In addition to pure mathematics, he was particularly interested in its history, a subject that Humboldt encouraged him to pursue.[1] In the mid-nineteenth century very little was known of the Arab contribution to the development of mathematics. Many Latin translations from the Arabic had existed since the twelfth century; but the texts themselves were not accessible, and further research was thus effectively blocked.[2] Woepcke therefore went to Bonn in 1848 to learn Arabic.[3] After qualifying as *Privatdozent* in the spring of 1850, he went to Leiden, where there were many Arabic manuscripts, and in May of the same year, to Paris, then the center of Oriental studies in Europe.[4] In Paris he studied Persian (under Julius von Mohl) and Sanskrit (under P. O. Foucaux), as well as mathematics (under J. Liouville).

Woepcke interrupted his stay in Paris only from 1856 to 1858, when he taught mathematics and physics at the French Gymnasium in Berlin. He resigned his post because it left him no time for research. His tireless work on Arabic and Persian manuscripts enabled Woepcke to publish some thirty texts.[5] His edition of al-Khayyāmī's *Algebra*, which appeared in 1851, was followed in 1853 by a selection from al-Karajī's *Algebra*. In 1861 and 1863 Woepcke worked on manuscripts in Oxford and in London. He was obliged to return to Paris in December 1863 because his health, always weak, was failing rapidly. He died at the age of thirty-seven and was buried in Père Lachaise cemetery.

Woepcke's contemporaries praised him as modest but confident in his own judgment and as an enemy of all superficiality.[6] He valued only facts and left the working out of unproved conclusions to others.

A member of many learned societies, Woepcke made an outstanding contribution to the knowledge of Eastern contributions in the history of mathematics. Although he investigated many specific problems in various fields, his studies centered on the algebra of the Arabs (its symbolism and the determination of its Greek and Indian components) and on the Indian and Arab influence on the West (the spread of Hindu numerals and methods and the sources of the work of Leonardo Fibonacci).[7] He also attempted to reconstruct lost texts of Apollonius and Euclid on the basis of Arab manuscripts.[8]

Woepcke's own mathematical research dealt mainly with curves and surfaces, equations of the *n*th degree, and function theory. He also translated into French works by J. Steiner (central curves) and by Weierstrass (theory of Abelian functions). Because of Woepcke's early death, many of his editorial projects—for which he had already copied or translated the Arabic texts—were left unfinished or were continued by others.[9] Among the material that came into the possession of Boncompagni were 174 letters and a codex with twenty-five unpublished works, including selections from texts, translations, and notes.[10]

NOTES

1. In 1851 Woepcke translated Humboldt's *Über die bei verschiedenen Völkern üblichen Systeme von Zahlzeichen* (1829) into French.
2. Exceptions were the *Algebra* of al-Khwārizmī, edited by Frederic Rosen (London, 1831), and the *Jawāmi'* of al-Farghānī edited by Jacob Golius (Amsterdam, 1669).
3. He studied Arabic under G. W. F. Freytag and J. Gildemeister, as well as astronomy under F. W. A. Argelander.
4. Among the scholars who had worked there were Silvestre de Sacy, J. J. Sédillot, and L. A. Sédillot. See G. Sarton, *Introduction to the History of Science*, I, 665, 667, 717; II, 622.
5. See E. Narducci, "Intorno alla vita ed agli scritti di Francesco Woepcke," 123.
6. *Ibid.*, 123 ff.
7. His investigations include Leonardo Fibonacci's solution of the third-degree equation, two Arab approximation methods for determining sine 1°, Indian methods for calculating the sine, ancient methods of multiplication, and astrolabes. On Woepcke's works see Sarton, *op. cit.*, I, 600 (Thābit ibn Qurra), 663 (number symbols in a MS of 970), 667 (Abu'l-Wafā'), 718 (Abū Ja'far ibn al-Ḥusain), 719 (al-Karkhī); II, 401 (Muḥammad ibn al-Ḥusain); III, 1765 (al-Qalasādī), 1766 (spread of Hindu numerals and algebraic symbolism).
8. *Ibid.*, I, 154, 174; also R. C. Archibald, *Euclid's Book on Divisions of Figures With a Restoration Based on Woepcke's Text and on the Practica Geometriae of Leonardo Pisano* (Cambridge, 1915), 9–13.
9. Baron de Slane (see Sarton, I, 665; II, 401) edited works on al-Qūhī, al-Sijzī, and Muḥammad ibn al-Ḥusain (dealing with universal compasses for all conic sections); and Aristide Marre (see Sarton, II, 1000) edited the *Talkhīṣ* of Ibn al-Bannā'—for Woepcke's preliminary work on this text see Narducci, *op. cit.*, 129, 151.
10. See Narducci, *op. cit.*, 151 f.

BIBLIOGRAPHY

I. ORIGINAL WORKS. There are complete bibliographies in Narducci (see below), 133–152; and in Poggendorff, II, 1353–1354, and III, 1458. His writings include *Disquisitiones archaeologico-mathematicae circa solaria veterum* (Berlin, 1847), his doctoral dissertation; *L'Algèbre d'Omar Alkhayyāmī* (Paris, 1851); *Extrait du Fakhrī, Traité d'algèbre par Aboū Bekr Mohammed ben Alhaçan Alkarkhī* (Paris, 1853); *Sur l'introduction de l'arithmétique indienne en Occident*, (Rome, 1859); and "Recherches sur plusieurs ouvrages de Léonard de Pise . . . et sur les rapports qui existent entre ces ouvrages et les travaux mathématiques des arabes," in *Atti dell'Accademia pontificia dei Nuovi Lincei*, **10** (1856–1857), 236–248; **12** (1858–1859), 399–438; and **14** (1860–1861), 211–227, 241–269, 301–356.

II. SECONDARY LITERATURE. See J. Fück, *Die arabischen Studien in Europa* (Leipzig, 1955), 204; E. Narducci, "Intorno alla vita ed agli scritti di Francesco Woepcke," in *Bullettino di bibliografia e di storia delle scienze matematiche e fisiche*, **2** (1869), 119–152; and G. Sarton, *Introduction to the History of Science*, 3 vols. (Baltimore, 1927–1948).

KURT VOGEL

WOLFOWITZ, JACOB (*b*. Warsaw, Russian Poland, 19 March 1910; *d*. Tampa, Florida, 16 July 1981)

Jacob Wolfowitz was born into a Jewish family, the son of Samuel and Chaya Wolfowitz. Samuel emigrated to the United States shortly before the outbreak of World War I, planning to have his family join him after a brief period. The outbreak of the war prevented this, and the family was not able to join Samuel in New York City until 1920. The war years were particularly difficult times for the family. Jacob Wolfowitz was educated in the public schools of Brooklyn, New York, and graduated from the College of the City of New York with the degree of bachelor of science in 1931. This was during the Great Depression, and Wolfowitz secured whatever employment he could, including high-school teaching, while continuing his education part-time. He obtained the M.A. degree from Columbia University in 1933, and the Ph.D. in mathematics from New York University in 1942. In 1934 he married Lillian Dundes. Their children, Laura Mary and Paul Dundes, were born in 1941 and 1943, respectively.

In 1942 Wolfowitz joined the Statistical Research Group of Columbia University, doing war-related research. In 1945 he became associate professor of statistics at the University of North Carolina. In 1946 he joined the newly formed Department of Mathematical Statistics at Columbia University. In 1951 he became professor of mathematics at Cornell University, and in 1970 he joined the Department of Mathematics at the University of Illinois. After retiring from Illinois in 1978, he became distinguished professor of mathematics at the University of South Florida, a position he held until his death. He also held visiting professorships at the universities of Paris, Heidelberg, and California at Los Angeles, and the Technion (Israel Institute of Technology).

His research accomplishments were recognized by a long list of honors, including an honorary doctorate from the Technion; election to the U.S. National Academy of Sciences and to the American Academy of Arts and Sciences; election as fellow of the International Statistics Institute, the Econometric Society, the American Statistical Association, and the Institute of Mathematical Statistics; a term as president of the Institute of Mathematical Statistics; and selection as Shannon Lecturer of the Institute of Electrical and Electronic Engineers and as the Wald and the Rietz lecturer of the Institute of Mathematical Statistics. He was an excellent lecturer, with a remarkable ability to clarify some very complicated mathematics. Wolfowitz was a physically vigorous man who played handball while he lived in New York City and took long, brisk walks when he moved away from the city. He was an omnivorous reader, with a remarkable knowledge of political, social, and economic conditions in all of the large countries and many of the small countries of the world. He was a lifelong and committed Zionist and was active in organizing protests against Soviet repression of dissidents, intellectuals, and minorities.

Wolfowitz met Abraham Wald soon after Wald arrived in New York City in the autumn of 1938. Wald was well known for his research on geometry and econometrics in Vienna, and the two men quickly became close friends and collaborators. Their earliest joint work was in the area of nonparametric statistical inference, their first paper appearing in 1939. Nonparametric statistical inference is necessary when the statistician is unable to assume that he is sampling from a population whose form is known, and that the only unknowns are a finite number of parameters. The first appearance of the word "nonparametric" was in a 1942 paper by Wolfowitz. Wald and Wolfowitz constructed confidence bands for a completely unknown distribution function and constructed a test to determine whether two samples come from the same population, without making any assumptions about the form of the populations.

Another important subject on which Wald and Wolfowitz collaborated was sequential analysis. While working with the Columbia University Statistical Research Group, Wald had developed what he called the "sequential probability ratio test." This test decides which of two populations is being sampled by taking observations one at a time and determining after each observation whether another observation should be taken or whether sampling should be terminated and a final choice made. The conventional technique was to take a predetermined number of observations. Wald conjectured that the sequential probability ratio test minimizes the average number of observations required, but no rigorous proof existed until Wald and Wolfowitz published one in 1948. This 1948 paper may have been the paper of which Wolfowitz was proudest. Wolfowitz published many other papers on sequential methods, including several that constructed estimators of unknown parameters using sequential sampling.

Wald died in 1950, and his death removed the strongest tie binding Wolfowitz to Columbia University. He moved to Cornell University in 1951. Jack Kiefer, who was just completing his doctorate at Columbia, moved to Cornell at the same time, and Wolfowitz and Kiefer started a long and fruitful collaboration. One important area they explored was the optimal design of experiments, which is the theory specifying where to take observations in order to estimate unknown parameters with the smallest possible error. Kiefer and Wolfowitz also made important contributions to the mathematical theory describing the properties of queues. In collaboration with A. Dvoretzky they published fundamental research on the inventory problem, which is the problem of deciding how much inventory to hold in each of a sequence of intervals when there are penalties for holding too much or too little inventory and demand is random. This research was an early example of what came to be known as dynamic programming.

Starting in 1957 Wolfowitz devoted an increasing proportion of his research to information theory. Information theory describes how rapidly information can be sent over a channel when random errors occur in the transmission and the probability of correct decipherment must be at least equal to a preassigned value. Wolfowitz gave various limits on the rate at which information can be sent for various types of channels. His monograph *Coding Theorems of Information Theory* contains most of these results.

BIBLIOGRAPHY

Wolfowitz's research covered all of the major areas in mathematical statistics. *Jacob Wolfowitz: Selected Papers* (New York, 1980) contains a complete list of his 120 publications, the complete text of 49 papers he chose as among his most important, a brief biography, and a detailed discussion of his research. See also *Coding Theorems of Information Theory*, 3rd ed. (New York, 1978). An obituary by Rudolph Ahlswede, with bibliography, appeared in *IEEE Transactions on Information Theory*, **28** (1982), 687–690.

LIONEL WEISS

WOODHOUSE, ROBERT (*b.* Norwich, England, 28 April 1773; *d.* Cambridge, England, 28 [23?] December 1827)

Woodhouse was a critic and reformer. The son of Robert Woodhouse, a linen draper, and of the daughter of J. Alderson, a nonconformist minister, Woodhouse attended the grammar school at North Walsham. In 1790 he was admitted to Caius College, Cambridge, and four years later graduated with the B.A., as senior wrangler and first Smith's prizeman. In 1798 he received the M.A. from the university, and was successively fellow (1798–1823), Lucasian professor of mathematics (1820–1822), and Plumian professor of astronomy and experimental philosophy (1822–1827). Woodhouse also served as the first superintendent of the astronomical observatory at Cambridge. In 1802 he was elected a fellow of the Royal Society. He married Harriet Wilkens in 1823; they had one son, Robert.

Woodhouse was primarily interested in what was then called the metaphysics of mathematics; that is, he was concerned with questions such as the proper theoretical foundations of the calculus, the role of geometric and analytic methods, the importance of notation, and the nature of imaginary numbers. Many of these questions are discussed in his *Principles of Analytical Calculation* (1803), a polemic aimed primarily at the fellows and professors at Cambridge. In this work Woodhouse defended analytic methods, the differential notation, and a theory of calculus based, like that of Lagrange, on series expansions. It does not appear to have had much influence in the introduction of continental methods at Cambridge. His elementary text on trigonometry (1809), however, was widely used. George Peacock, who himself played a decisive role in the reform of mathematical studies at Cambridge, considered this work to be of major importance in achieving this goal. It was not polemical, but used analytic methods and the differential notation throughout.

Woodhouse's other writings include a history of the calculus of variations (1810), a treatise on astronomy (1812), and a work on the theory of gravitation, somewhat misnamed *Physical Astronomy* (1818). In all these works Woodhouse presented the results of continental research from the time of Newton up to his own time.

BIBLIOGRAPHY

I. ORIGINAL WORKS. Woodhouse's papers include "On the Necessary Truth of Certain Conclusions Obtained by Means of Imaginary Quantities," in *Philosophical Transactions of the Royal Society*, **91** (1801), 89–119; and "On the Independence of the Analytical and Geometrical Methods of Investigation; and on the Advantages To Be Derived From Their Separation," *ibid.*, **92** (1809), 85–125. His books are *Principles of Analytical Calculation* (Cambridge, 1803); *A Treatise on Plane and Spherical Trigonometry* (Cambridge, 1809; 5th rev. ed., 1827); *A Treatise on Isoperimetrical Problems and the Calculus of Variations* (Cambridge, 1810), reprinted as *A History of the Calculus of Variations in the Eighteenth Century* (New York, n.d.); *Treatise on Astronomy* (Cambridge, 1812); and *Physical Astronomy* (Cambridge, 1818).

II. SECONDARY LITERATURE. The fullest account of Woodhouse's life and work is in Augustus DeMorgan, "Robert Woodhouse," in *Penny Cyclopaedia*, XXVII (London, 1843), 526–527. Woodhouse's influence is considered in Elaine Koppelman, *Calculus of Operations: French Influence in British Mathematics in the First Half of the Nineteenth Century* (Ph.D. diss., Johns Hopkins University, 1969).

ELAINE KOPPELMAN

WOODWARD, ROBERT SIMPSON (*b.* Rochester, Michigan, 21 July 1849; *d.* Washington, D.C., 29 June 1924)

Woodward was part of the tradition of mathematical physics that saw the earth as the great object of study. In 1904 he asserted, "The earth is thus at once the grandest of laboratories and the grandest of museums available to man." To this laboratory and museum Woodward brought a great skill in mathematics and an insistence on obtaining data of the highest precision in a form suitable for computation. The last point greatly influenced the young John Hayford, who worked with Woodward at the Coast and Geodetic Survey.

After receiving a degree in civil engineering in 1872 from the University of Michigan, Woodward worked for ten years with the Lake Survey of the U.S. Corps of Engineers. From 1882 to 1884 he was an astronomer with the U.S. Transit of Venus Commission. Woodward next served for six years with the U.S. Geological Survey, successively occupying the posts of astronomer, geographer, and chief geographer.

His most notable scientific contributions occurred during this period. For G. K. Gilbert he calculated the effects on shore lines of the removal of superficial masses by means of potential theory. In this work and his passing consideration of isostasy, Woodward considered thermal effects, clearly related to the concern with how heat influenced base bars and other instruments of precision. In a series of papers in 1887–1888, Woodward explored the cooling of homogeneous spheres and the diffusion of heat in rectangular masses. The find-

ings were applied to Kelvin's work on the age of the earth. By 1889 Woodward criticized Kelvin for the "unverified assumption of an initial uniform temperature and a constant diffusivity." As the data for Kelvin's calculations were derived from observations of continental areas, Woodward felt the probabilities were against obtaining satisfactory numerical results for the entire earth. His position strengthened the opposition of many geologists, at least in America, to Kelvin's constriction of geological time.

From 1890 to 1893 Woodward was with the U.S. Coast and Geodetic Survey. In 1893 he became professor of mechanics and mathematical physics at Columbia University; and in 1895 he was named dean of the College of Pure Science. From 1904 through 1920 Woodward was president of the Carnegie Institution of Washington, succeeding D. C. Gilman. As chairman of two advisory committees, he had previously played a role in the development of the policies of the Institution. He was a strong administrator and largely responsible for the direction taken by the Carnegie Institution.

BIBLIOGRAPHY

F. E. Wright's memoir in *Biographical Memoirs. National Academy of Sciences*, **19** (1938), 1–24, has a good bibliography. The archives of the Carnegie Institution of Washington and the papers of many of his contemporaries contain manuscripts by or about Woodward. The correspondence of J. McK. Cattell in the Library of Congress and T. W. Richards in the Harvard University Archives are valuable for his views on the policies of the Carnegie Institution. The correspondence of Presidents Low and Butler in the Office of the Secretary, Columbia University, contains a small number of interesting items.

NATHAN REINGOLD

WREN, CHRISTOPHER (*b.* East Knoyle, Wiltshire, England, 20 October 1632; *d.* London, England, 25 February 1723)

Wren came from a family with strong ecclesiastical traditions. His father, for whom he was named, was rector of East Knoyle, chaplain to Charles I, and later (1634) dean of Windsor. His uncle, Matthew Wren, was successively bishop of Hereford, Norwich, and Ely. Wren was frail as a child, yet even in his earliest years he manifested an interest in the construction of mechanical instruments that included a rain gauge and a "pneumatic engine." He was educated at Westminster School, whence he proceeded in 1649 to Wadham College, Oxford. There he became closely associated with John Wilkins, who was later bishop of Chester and a member of that distinguished group whose activities led to the formation of the Royal Society. At Wadham College, Wren's talent for mathematical and scientific pursuits soon attracted attention. He graduated B.A. in 1651, and three years later received the M.A. He was elected a fellow of All Souls College, Oxford, in 1653 and remained in residence there until 1657.

Wren's interest in astronomy appears to have manifested itself about that time, and it led to his appointment, as professor of astronomy at Gresham College in 1657. In his inaugural lecture, after mentioning the relation of astronomy to mathematics, to theology in the interpretation of the Scriptures, to medicine, and above all to navigation, he praised the new liberty in the study and observation of nature, and the rejection of the tyranny of ancient opinions. He retained this professorship until 1661, when he was appointed Savilian professor of astronomy at Oxford, a post he occupied until 1673.

Wren is best remembered as an architect. His fame as the most distinguished architect England has produced probably has obscured his accomplishments in other branches of science. He was perhaps the most accomplished man of his day. While at Oxford he ranked high in his knowledge of anatomy; and his abilities as a demonstrator in that subject were acknowledged with praise by Thomas Willis in his *Cerebri anatome*, for which Wren made all the drawings. Wren also is said to have been the pioneer in the physiological experiments of injecting various liquids into the veins of living animals (Weld, *History*, I, 273).

Wren made important contributions to mathematics; and Newton, in the second edition of his *Principia* (1713), classed him with John Wallis and Christiaan Huygens as the leading geometers of the day ("Christopherus Wrennus, eques auratus, geometrarum facile principes," p. 19). Chief among his contributions was his rectification of the cycloid. This curve, because of its singularly beautiful properties, had long been a favorite of geometers since its discovery early in the sixteenth century. Many of its properties had been discovered by Pascal; its rectification, the finding of a straight line equal to an arc of the curve, was effected by Wren in 1658 and also by Fermat.

In 1668 Oldenburg asked Wren, along with Wallis and Huygens, to inform the Royal Society of his research into the laws of impact. In a terse paper read on 17 December 1668 and published on 11 January 1669 in the *Philosophical Transactions*, Wren offered a theoretical solution based on the model of a balance beam on which the impacting bodies are suspended at distances from the point of impact proportional to their initial speeds. Equilibrium in the model corresponds to an impact situation in which bodies approach one another at speeds inversely proportional to their sizes and, Wren postulated as a "Law of Nature," rebound at their initial speeds, which Wren termed their "proper speeds." In cases in which the center of motion does not coincide with the center of gravity of the system, Wren postulated that impact shifts the center of motion to a point equidistant from the center of gravity on the opposite side. Employing the further postulate that the speed of approach equals the speed of separation, Wren set forth rules of calculation that yield the center of gravity from the known sizes and initial speeds of the bodies, and then use the speeds and the center of gravity to compute the final speeds. The close fit of these results with experiment seems to have been the basic source of Wren's confidence in his solution. Wren also made a number of pendulum experiments, and Wilkins declared that he was the first to suggest the determination of standard measure of length by means of the oscillation of the pendulum (Weld, *History*, I, 196).

Even as a boy Wren had shown that he had the capacity to become a draftsman of exceptional ability. He probably applied himself to the serious study of the subject when he was commissioned to submit plans for the building of the chapel of Pembroke College, Cambridge, which was completed in 1663. His next major achievement was the building of the Sheldonian Theatre, Oxford, a model of which was exhibited before the newly formed Royal Society in April 1663. It was completed in 1669, and in that year Charles II appointed Wren surveyor of the royal works, a post he retained for half a century.

Meanwhile, the Great Fire had given Wren a unique opportunity to display his skill as an architect. Much of the City of London had been destroyed in the conflagration, including the old St. Paul's. This building, ancient and ruinous, had long been in urgent need of repairs; and just before the fire Wren had been invited by the dean to prepare plans for the building of a new cathedral. Wren's original plans were not approved, so he prepared a second scheme, having meanwhile obtained the concession that he might make such alterations as he deemed advisable. This second scheme was accepted, and a warrant for the building of the cathedral was issued in 1675. The first stone was laid on 21 June 1675, and after many delays the cathedral was finished in 1710.

Much of the City having been destroyed, Wren was invited to submit plans for the rebuilding of some fifty churches consumed in the flames. (These are described in *Parentalia*, 309–318.) At Oxford he built, in addition to the Sheldonian Theatre, the Tom Tower of Christ Church and Queen's College Chapel. At Cambridge, besides the chapel at Pembroke College, he built the library of Trinity College.

Wren received many honors. The University of Oxford conferred upon him the degree of doctor of Civil Laws; Cambridge awarded him the LL.D. In 1673 he was knighted. Wren also represented many constituencies in Parliament at different periods. In 1669 he married Faith Coghill, of Blechingdon, Oxford, by whom he had two sons, one of whom survived him. On the death of Lady Wren he married Jane Fitzwilliam, by whom he had a son and a daughter.

Wren played a prominent part in the formation of the Royal Society of London, which arose out of the informal gatherings of the votaries of experimental science that took place about the middle of the seventeenth century. These gatherings doubtless were inspired by the growing desire for learning that had been stimulated by the writings of Francis Bacon, notably the *Novum Organum*; but they also owed much to the institution founded under the will of Sir Thomas Gresham, according to which seven professors were employed to lecture on successive days of the week on divinity, astronomy, geometry, physic, law, rhetoric, and music. Of those whose enthusiasm prompted them to associate themselves with the new venture, the best-known, besides Wren, were Robert Boyle, John Wilkins, John Wallis, John Evelyn, Robert Hooke, and William Petty. The meetings, held at Gresham College, were suspended during the troubled times that followed the Civil War. On the return of Charles II in May 1660, they were revived and the need for a more formal organization was at once recognized. Accordingly, on 28 November 1660 the following memorandum was drawn up: "These persons following . . . mett together at Gresham Colledge to heare Mr. Wren's lecture." At the end of Wren's lecture it was proposed that the meetings should continue weekly. A list was drawn up of those interested; and at a meeting held on 19 December 1660, it was ordered that subsequent meetings should be held at Gresham College.

The charter of incorporation passed the great seal on 15 July 1662 (which thus is the date of the formation of the Royal Society); Wren is said to have prepared its preamble. A Council was formed, with Wren as one of the members. He was the Society's third president, serving from 30 November 1680 to 30 November 1682. *The Record Book of the Royal Society of London* (1940, 18) pays tribute to Wren's zeal and encouragement despite the difficulties facing the young organization: "To him the Royal Society owes a deep debt of gratitude for the constant and loyal service which he rendered to it in its early days."

Wren also studied meteorology long before it had become an exact science through the work of Mariotte, Boyle, and Hooke. He was one of the earliest naturalists to investigate, by means of the microscope, the structure of insects; and his remarkable skill as a draftsman enabled him to make accurate drawings of what he saw.

Wren was largely instrumental in arranging for the (unauthorized) publication of Flamsteed's *Historia coelestis Britannica* (1712), which had been financed by Prince George, Queen Anne's consort, but had ceased with his death in 1708. When at length printing was resumed, many obstacles were placed in Flamsteed's way. Wren had been appointed a member of the committee to oversee the printing of the work; and despite much opposition, he gave Flamsteed great encouragement. Nevertheless, Flamsteed's wishes met with little response; and after the work eventually appeared under Halley's editorship, Flamsteed managed to secure three hundred of the four hundred copies printed and at once consigned them to the flames.

In 1718 Wren was superseded as surveyor of the royal works, after more than fifty years of active and laborious service to the crown and the public. He then retired to Hampton Court, where he spent the last five years of his life. He is buried in St. Paul's Cathedral, where a tablet to his memory has been erected.

BIBLIOGRAPHY

I. ORIGINAL WORKS. Among Wren's papers that appeared in *Philosophical Transactions of the Royal Society* are "Lex collisionis corporum" (Mar. 1669); "Description of an Instrument Invented Divers Years Ago for Drawing the Out-line of Any Objective in Perspective" (1669); "The Generation of an Hyperbolical Cylindroid Demonstrated, and the Application Thereof to the Grinding of Hyperbolical Glasses" (June 1669); "A Description of Dr. Christopher Wren's Engin Designed for Grinding Hyperbolical Glasses" (Nov. 1669); and "On Finding a Straight Line Equal to That of a Cycloid and to the Parts Thereof" (Nov. 1673).

II. SECONDARY LITERATURE. See Sir Harold Hartley, ed., *The Royal Society: Its Origins and Founders* (London, 1960); *Parentalia, or Memoirs of the Family of Wrens* (London, 1750), compiled by his son Christopher and published by his grandson Stephen; *Record Book of the Royal Society of London* (1940); and C. R. Weld, *History of the Royal Society*, 2 vols. (London, 1848).

For Wren's work on impact, see A. R. Hall and M. B. Hall, eds., *The Correspondence of Henry Oldenburg*, V (Madison, Wis., 1968), 117–118, 125, 134–135, 193, 263, 265, and in particular 319–320 (Wren's paper in the original Latin) and 320–321 (an English translation).

J. F. SCOTT

WRIGHT, EDWARD (*b.* Garveston, Norfolk, England, October 1561; *d.* London, England, November 1615)

Details of Wright's life are unusually scanty and must be supplemented from facts about his relatives and friends. His father, Henry, was described as "mediocris fortunae, deceased" when an elder brother, Thomas, entered Gonville and Caius College, Cambridge, as a pensioner in 1574. Probably both boys were taught by John Hayward at a neighboring school in Hardingham. Edward joined his brother at Caius College, Cambridge, in December 1576; but Thomas' support for him was short-lived, since he died early in 1579. Wright's academic career closely paralleled that of John Fletcher: both graduated B.A. in 1581 and M.A. in 1584, and obtained their fellowships on Lady Day 1587. Fletcher had returned for his fellowship after teaching for a few years at Dronfield Grammar School, Derbyshire, so it is possible that Wright was also away from Cambridge in 1581–1584. Fletcher had a reputation as a medical writer, collaborator with Sir Christopher Heydon on his *Defence of Judiciall Astrologie* (1603), and as mathematics teacher to Henry Briggs. Contemporary with Briggs at St. John's College was Thomas Bernhere, later Wright's brother-in-law; both graduated M.A. in 1585, became fellows of their college, and were closely associated with Henry Alvey, one of the leaders of Cambridge Puritanism.[1]

In 1589 Wright received royal permission to absent himself from Cambridge in order to accompany George, earl of Cumberland, on an expedition to the Azores that was intended to acquire booty from Spanish ships. In 1599 Wright wrote that "the time of my first employment at sea" was "more than tenne yeares since." This suggests that he may have been to sea previously, possibly in 1581–1584. There seems little doubt that he had already acquired a reputation in mathematical navigation, and none at all that his 1589 voyage contributed greatly to his main achievements (described below). Wright returned to Cambridge at the end of 1589 and prepared a draft of his most important book, *Certaine Errors in Navigation*, in the next year or so. The 1599 printed version incorporates results obtained from observations made at London in the period May 1594–November 1597. It would seem that Wright had moved from Cambridge before the expiration of his fellowship in 1596, and that he had married the sister of Thomas Bernhere in 1595. Their only son, Samuel, entered his father's college after schooling in London but died before graduation, "a youth of much promise."

The succession of London mathematical lecturers is confused, but it is probable that Wright had some such employment after leaving Cambridge. These lecturers had been supported by Sir Thomas Smith and Sir John Wolstenholme, two rich city merchants closely connected with several trading companies. Thomas Hood was an early lecturer, and it has been suggested that Wright succeeded him. The position was complicated by the starting of Gresham College, where Henry Briggs was first professor of geometry.

There was, however, still a need for lecturers in navigation; Wright was serving in this capacity in 1614 when the East India Company took over the patronage and paid him an annual salary of £50. He may have held this post from 1612, the year of the death of Prince Henry, whom he had tutored in mathematics and whose librarianship he had been expecting. About the same time Wright was surveyor for the New River project, under Sir Hugh Myddleton, for bringing water to London.[2] During this London period he also wrote and published a number of mathematical tracts.

The publishing history of Wright's main work, *Certaine Errors in Navigation*, is complex. Wright himself outlined the impetus for the chief feature of this work, the justification of the so-called Mercator map projection, described as "the greatest advance ever made in marine cartography."[3] He criticized the usual sea charts as "like an inextricable labyrinth of error," offering as an instance his own experience in 1589: land was sighted "when by account of the ordinary chart we should have beene 50 leagues short of it." He admitted that his development had been prompted by Mercator's 1569 map of the world, but stated that neither Mercator nor anybody else had shown him how to do it. Wright's principle was very simple: to increase the distance apart of the parallels of latitude to match the exaggeration arising from the assumption that they were equally long. Since the lengths of the parallels varied according to a factor cos λ, the correction factor was sec λ at any point. In order to plot the parallels on the new charts, Wright had effectively to perform the integration $\int_0^\lambda \sec \lambda d\lambda$. This was done numerically—in his own words, "by perpetual addition of the Secantes answerable to the latitudes of each point or parallel into the summe compounded of all the former secantes. . . ."

Wright's development of the Mercator projection was first published by others. *Thomas Blundevile His Exercises Containing Six Treatises* (1594) was an important navigation compilation, the first to describe the use of the sine, tangent, and secant trigonometric functions. The author was at a loss to explain the new (Mercator) arrangement, which had been constructed "by what rule I knowe not, unless it be by such a table, as my friende M. Wright of Caius College in Cambridge at my request sent me (I thanke him) not long since for that purpose, which table with his consent, I have here plainlie set down together with the use thereof as followeth." The table of meridional parts was given at degree intervals.[4]

Two years later, following his publication of a Dutch version of Emery Molyneux's globe, Jodocus Hondius published at Amsterdam the well-known "Christian-Knight" maps of the world and of the four continents. These were based on Wright's theory of Mercator's projection, but were issued without acknowledgment. It seems that when he was in England, Hondius had been allowed to see the manuscript of Wright's *Certaine Errors*. In 1598–1600 Richard Hakluyt published his *Principal Navigations*, which contains two world charts on the new projection, that of 1600 a revision of the first. Although there is no attribution, it is clear that Wright was a major collaborator; further revisions in Hakluyt's work were made for versions in the 1610 and 1657 editions of his *Certaine Errors*.

Before the Hakluyt maps, William Barlow had included in his *The Navigator's Supply* (1597) a demonstration of Wright's projection "obtained of a friend of mine of like profession unto myself." This evidence of interest in his work was brought home to Wright when the earl of Cumberland showed him a manuscript that had been found among the possessions of Abraham Kendall and was being prepared for the press. Wright was surprised to find it was a copy of his own *Certaine Errors*, an experience that convinced him it was time to publish the work himself.

Ultimately Wright included his "The Voyage of the Earl of Cumberland to the Azores," which had been printed in Hakluyt's second volume. With it was a chart of the Azores on the new projection, showing Cumberland's route; this has been judged to be more significant than the world charts, since it was large enough to be used. *Certaine Errors* discussed other navigation problems, and was considerably extended in the second edition (1610), dedicated to Prince Henry. Wright also contributed to two seminal works. In 1600 he helped, particularly with a preface, to produce William Gilbert's *De magnete*. His translation of John Napier's *Mirifici logarithmorum canonis descriptio, A Description of the Admirable Table of Logarithmes*, appeared posthumously. It was approved by Napier and brought out by his friend Henry Briggs after the death of Wright's son Samuel, who contributed the dedication to the East Indies Company. The book marks the lifelong collaboration between Briggs and Wright, and the latter's efforts to spread a better understanding of navigation.[5] Nobody had done more to "set the seal on the supremacy of the English in the theory and practice of the art of navigation at this time."

NOTES

1. The baptism at Garveston took place on 8 October 1561: the father's will, dated 17 January 1573, left his house to his wife, Margaret, and then to Edward. (This information was provided by the Norfolk and Norwich Record Office.) J. Venn, *Biographical History of Gonville and Caius College*, 1 (Cambridge, 1897), 88–89; "From the Library," in *Midland Medical Review*, 1 (1961), 185–187; H. C. Porter, *Reformation and Reaction in Tudor Cambridge* (Cambridge, 1958).

2. See J. E. C. Hill, *Intellectual Origins of the English Revolution*, 39–40; D. W. Waters, *The Art of Navigation . . .*, 239, 278. It is possible that Wright lectured at Trinity House, Deptford, since he dedicated his 1599 translation to its master, Richard Polter.

3. Waters, *op. cit.*, 121.

4. R. C. Archibald, in *Mathematical Tables and Other Aids to Computation*, 3 (1948), 223–225, ignores these earlier eds. of the table, as well as the (independent) MS calculations by Thomas Harriot, discussed by Waters.

5. The final quotation is from Waters (p. 219), who also mentions several mathematical instruments that Wright helped to develop.

BIBLIOGRAPHY

I. ORIGINAL WORKS. Wright's main work, *Certaine Errors in Navigation, Arising Either of the Ordinarie Erroneous Making or Using of the Sea Chart, Compasse, Crosse Staffe, and Tables of Declinations of the Sunne, and Fixed Starres Detected and Corrected* (London, 1599; 2nd ed., enl., 1610; 3rd ed., Joseph Moxon, ed., 1657), includes, at the end, "The Voyage of the . . . Earle of Cumberland to the Azores," also printed by Hakluyt (1599) and at Lisbon (1911). Other writings are *The Haven-Finding Art*, translated from the Dutch of Simon Stevin (London, 1599), repr. in *Certaine Errors* (1657) and, in part, by H. D. Harradon in *Territorial Magazine*, **50** (Mar. 1945); *Description and Use of the Sphaere* (London, 1614; 1627); *A Short Treatise of Dialling: Shewing the Making of All Sorts of Sun-Dials* (London, 1614); and *A Description of the Admirable Tables of Logarithmes*, translated from the Latin of John Napier (London, 1616; 1618).

The MSS at Dublin are briefly listed by T. K. Abbott, *Catalogue of the Manuscripts in the Library of Trinity College* (Dublin, 1900).

II. SECONDARY LITERATURE. See W. W. R. Ball, *A History of the Study of Mathematics at Cambridge* (Cambridge, 1889), 25–27; F. Cajori, "On an Integration Ante-dating the Integral Calculus," in *Bibliotheca mathematica*, 3rd ser., **14** (1914), 312–319; and "Algebra in Napier's Day and Alleged Prior Inventions," in C. G. Knott, ed., *Napier Tercentenary Memorial Volume* (Edinburgh, 1915), 93–109; J. E. C. Hill, *Intellectual Origins of the English Revolution* (Oxford, 1965); C. Hutton, *A Philosophical and Mathematical Dictionary*, new ed., II (London, 1815), 619–620; J. K. Laughton, *Dictionary of National Biography*, LXIII; E. J. S. Parsons and W. F. Morris, "Edward Wright and His Work," in *Imago mundi*, **3** (1939), 61–71; Helen M. Wallis, "The First English Globe: A Recent Discovery," in *Geographical Journal*, **108** (1951), 275–290; "Further Light on the Molyneux Globes," *ibid.*, **121** (1955), 304–311; and "World Map in Principal Navigations, 1599: Evidence to Suggest That Edward Wright was the Main Author," an unpublished note (1972); and D. W. Waters, *The Art of Navigation in England in Elizabethan and Early Stuart Times* (London, 1958).

P. J. WALLIS

XENOCRATES OF CHALCEDON (*b.* Chalcedon [now Kadiköy], Bithynia [now Turkey], 396/395 B.C.; *d.* Athens, 314/313 B.C.)

Xenocrates was a student of Plato and, as head of the Academy from 339 B.C. to 314/313 B.C., was one of the founders of the ancient Academic tradition. He entered the Academy (in 378 B.C. at the earliest or 373 B.C. at the latest) and about ten years later accompanied Plato to Syracuse, the latter's second or third voyage to that city.

After Plato's death, Xenocrates and Aristotle were invited to Assos, where they remained until the overthrow of Hermias of Atarneus, in 342 B.C. Plato's successor, his nephew Speusippus, headed the Academy until his death in 340/339 B.C. He sent for Xenocrates, who was not in Athens at this time, and designated him his successor. Nevertheless, an election was held, which Xenocrates won by only a few votes. The opposing candidates, Heraclitus Ponticus and Menedemus of Pyrrha, thereupon left the Academy. (Aristotle was not a candidate.)

In 322 B.C. Xenocrates was appointed to an Athenian legation sent to negotiate with Antipatrus of Macedonia, but it was compelled, instead, to acknowledge Athens' submission. Since Xenocrates was not a citizen of Athens, Antipatrus did not recognize his status as a legitimate ambassador. Both before and after this incident, Xenocrates refused to seek Athenian citizenship, since he disapproved of the city's close relations with Macedonia. On this point he was at odds with the political views of his predecessor Speusippus, who had supported Athens' pro-Macedonian policies. After Xenocrates' death, the leadership of the Academy passed to Polemo.

According to a number of less substantiated anecdotes about Xenocrates, he is depicted as good-natured, gentle, and considerate—but it is also quite clear that he lacked the *charis* ("graciousness") of his teacher Plato. Along with these traits, Xenocrates is reported to have displayed singular diligence. The list of his writings, which is entirely preserved in Diogenes Laërtius (IV, 11–14), contains about seventy titles. The biographical anecdotes state that he never left the Academy (where all his work was done) more than once a year.

None of Xenocrates' writings has survived. They presumably were never published—that is, copied; rather, the single copies in his own hand were deposited at the Academy. When Athens was stormed by Sulla's troops in March 86 B.C., the Academy, located in front of the western gate, was destroyed together with its priceless library.[1]

Unlike Aristotle, Xenocrates did not wish to develop philosophy in new ways but considered it his task to maintain Plato's theory as he had received and understood it. This motivation underlay his extensive literary activity, in which enterprise Xenocrates relied primarily upon his memory—

recalling, in some instances, what he had learned as much as twenty-five years earlier. Curiously, Xenocrates did not respect an important request made by Plato, who considered language unreliable and conducive to misunderstanding. Plato apparently insisted that the contents of philosophical doctrines be communicated only to those who would strictly observe definite precautions, and consequently he often veiled his meaning through the use of metaphors and myths. Xenocrates, seeking to render Plato's theories teachable without recourse to such means, established a system of doctrinal propositions. Xenocrates' lifework consisted in producing a kind of codification—and thus, of necessity, a transformation—of Plato's philosophy. But it immediately became apparent that others, especially Aristotle, understood Plato in a wholly different way with respect to certain key questions. Crantor of Soli, for example—himself the pupil of Xenocrates—was to some extent justified in reproaching him for having taught things that differed from elements of Plato's surviving written works. Although Xenocrates did not attribute to Plato anything that he had not actually taught, he did choose single aspects—often overly narrow ones—from among the many possible ways of presenting Plato's conceptions and raised them to the status of official doctrine.

Xenocrates probably found himself confronted with a difficult situation. After it had been decided to preserve Plato's teachings, everything that could not be encompassed in words—that is, everything that Plato had not wished to set forth in words—had to be abandoned in the interest of a clear and systematic presentation. In the process of achieving this sort of systematization, Xenocrates sacrificed Plato's dialectical approach.

Xenocrates was no more a dualist than Plato. Rather, he belongs to the long line of those who have attempted to overcome a type of dualism within the philosophical tradition. In particular, in his comprehensive outline, Xenocrates provided for a gradation of all the elements that make up ontology, physics, ethics, and epistemology. This scheme assumed major importance in the development of Neoplatonism. Xenocrates' real legacy lies in the conception he sketched of a hierarchy of all existing things that culminates in a single, highest point, the One.

NOTES

1. Reports of Xenocrates' teaching have survived only in the works of Aristotle and in Cicero and other Roman authors. The so-called fragments have been collected by Richard

Heinze (see below). All knowledge of Xenocrates was probably based on an indirect tradition. Reports of his teaching are only rarely supported by mention of the title of one of his works (cf. Heinze, 157, 158). The only quotation that seems to bear the stamp of authenticity is in Themistius' (A.D. 317[?]–ca. 388) commentary on Aristotle's *De anima*; see *Commentaria in Aristotelem Graeca*, V, pt. 3, R. Heinze, ed. (Berlin, 1899); and Heinze, *Xenocrates*, frag. 61. In Themistius' reference to the fifth book of περὶ φύσεως, it is possible to glean an indication that Xenocrates may have introduced the definition of soul as number. In this instance it cannot be ruled out that περὶ φύσεως had been published either in whole or in part. But such a quotation may also have originated in Crantor's interpretation of the *Timaeus*, where he suddenly attacks Xenocrates' theory of the soul as number. On this point, see H. F. Cherniss, *Aristotle's Criticism of Plato and the Academy*, I (Baltimore, 1944; repr. New York, 1962), p. 399, n. 325.

BIBLIOGRAPHY

See H. F. Cherniss, *The Riddle of the Early Academy* (Berkeley, Calif., 1945; repr. New York, 1962), esp. 31–59; H. Dörrie, "Xenokrates," in Pauly-Wissowa, *Real Encyclopädie der classischen Altertumswissenschaft*, 2nd ser., IX, 1512–1528; R. Heinze, *Xenocrates. Darstellung der Lehre und Sammlung der Fragmente* (Leipzig, 1892; repr., Hildesheim, 1965); S. Mekler, ed., *Academicorum philosophorum index Herculanensis* (Berlin, 1902), esp. 38–39; Diogenes Laërtius, *De vitis philosophorum*, IV, ch. 2—also in English, R. D. Hicks, trans., *Lives of Eminent Philosophers*, I (Cambridge, Mass.–London, 1966), 380–393; and U. von Wilamowitz-Moellendorff, *Platon, sein Leben und seine Werke*, 4th ed., I (Berlin, 1948), 579–581.

H. DÖRRIE

YANG HUI (*fl.* China, *ca.* 1261–1275)

The thirteenth century was perhaps the most significant period in the history of Chinese mathematics. It began with the appearance of Ch'in Chiu-shao's *Shu-shu chiu-chang* in 1247, and the following year Li Chih issued an equally important work, the *Ts'e-yüan hai-ching*. These two great algebraists were later joined by Yang Hui (literary name, Yang Ch'ien-kuang), whose publications far surpassed those of his predecessors, and of whom we have absolutely no knowledge. The golden age of Chinese mathematics came to an end after the appearance of Chu Shih-chieh's *Ssu-yüan yü-chien* in 1303. Of the works of these four great Chinese mathematicians, those by Yang Hui have, until very recently, been the least studied and analyzed.

Nothing is known about the life of Yang Hui, except that he produced mathematical writings. From the prefaces to his works we learn that he was a native of Ch'ien-t'ang (now Hangchow). He seems to have been a civil servant, having served in T'ai-chou, and he had probably visited Su-chou (modern Soochow). His friends and acquaintances included Ch'en Chi-hsien, Liu Pi-chien, Ch'iu Hsü-chü, and Shih Chung-yung, the last having collaborated with him on one of his works; but we know nothing else about their personal history. Yang Hui also names as his teacher another mathematician, Liu I, a native of Chung-shan, of whom nothing is known.

In 1261 Yang Hui wrote *Hsiang-chieh chiu-chang suan-fa* ("Detailed Analysis of the Mathematical Rules in the Nine Chapters"), a commentary on the old Chinese mathematical classic *Chiu-chang suan-shu*, by Liu Hui. The present version of the *Hsiang-chieh chiu-chang suan-fa*, which is based on the edition in the *I-chia-t'ang ts'ung-shu* (1842) collection, is incomplete and consists of only five chapters; two additional chapters have been restored from the *Yung-lo ta-tien* encyclopedia. Besides the original nine chapters of the *Chiu-chang suan-shu*, Yang Hui's *Hsiang-chieh chiu-chang suan-fa* included three additional chapters, making a total of twelve. According to the preface written by Yang Hui, he had selected 80 of the 246 problems in the *Chiu-chang suan-shu* for detailed discussion. The now-lost introductory chapter of the *Hsiang-chieh chiu-chang suan-fa*, as we learn from the *shao-kuang* ("Diminishing Breadth") chapter of the text and from a quotation in another of Yang Hui's works, *Suan-fa t'ung-pien pen-mo*, contained diagrams and illustrations.

Chapter 1, according to what Yang Hui describes in *Suan-fa t'ung-pien pen-mo* and *Ch'eng-ch'u t'ung-pien suan-pao*, dealt with the ordinary methods of multiplication and division. This chapter is also lost, but two of its problems have been restored from the *Yung-lo ta-tien* encyclopedia by Li Yen; it was entitled *Chu-chia suan-fa*. Chapter 2, *Fang-t'ien* ("Surveying of Land"), is now lost. Chapter 3, *Su-mi* ("Millet and Rice") is also lost, but three problems have been restored from the *Yung-lo ta-tien* encyclopedia. Chapter 4, *Ts'ui-fen* ("Distribution by Progression"), is no longer extant; but eleven of its problems have been restored from the *Yung-lo ta-tien* encyclopedia. Chapter 5, *Shao-kuang* ("Diminishing Breadth"), also has been partially restored from the *Yung-lo ta-tien* encyclopedia. As for Chapter 6, *Shang-kung* ("Consultations on Engineering Works"), the *I-chia-t'ang ts'ung-shu* collection contains thirteen problems (fifteen problems are missing). Chapter 7, *Chün-shu* ("Impartial Taxation"); chapter 8, *Ying-pu-tsu* ("Excess and Deficiency"); chapter 9,

Fang-ch'eng ("Calculation by Tabulation"); chapter 10, *Kou-ku* ("Right Angles"); and chapter 11, *Tsuan-lei* ("Reclassifications") remain more or less intact in the *I-chia-t'ang ts'ung-shu* collection, except for one missing problem in chapter 7 and four in chapter 9.

In 1450 the Ming mathematician Wu Ching wrote the *Chiu-chang hsiang-chu pi-lei suan-fa* ("Comparative Detailed Analysis of the Mathematical Rules in the Nine Chapters"), in which the "old questions" (*ku-wen*) are referred to. Yen Tun-chieh has shown that Wu Ching's "old questions" were based on Yang Hui's *Hsiang-chieh chiu-chang suan-fa*, and he has been engaged in restoring this text. A substantial part of the *I-chia-t'ang ts'ung-shu* edition of the text has been rendered into English by Lam Lay Yong of the University of Singapore.

Yang Hui published his second mathematical work, the two-volume *Jih-yung suan-fa* ("Mathematical Rules in Common Use"), in 1262. This book is no longer extant. Some sections have, however, been restored by Li Yen from the *Chu-chia suan-fa* in the *Yung-lo ta-tien* encyclopedia. The book seems to be quite elementary.

In 1274 Yang Hui produced the *Ch'eng-ch'u t'ung-pien pen-mo* ("Fundamental Mutual Changes in Multiplications and Divisions") in three volumes. The first volume was originally known as the *Suan-fa t'ung-pien pen-mo* ("Fundamental Mutual Changes in Calculations"); the second as *Ch'eng-ch'u t'ung-pien suan-pao* ("Treasure of Mathematical Arts on the Mutual Changes in Multiplications and Divisions"); and the last volume, written in collaboration with Shih Chung-yung, was originally called *Fa-suan ch'ü-yung pen-mo* ("Fundamentals of the Applications of Mathematics"). The next year Yang Hui wrote the *T'ien-mou pi-lei ch'eng-ch'u chieh-fa* ("Practical Rules of Mathematics for Surveying") in two volumes. This was followed in the same year by the *Hsü-ku chai-ch'i suan-fa* ("Continuation of Ancient Mathematical Methods for Elucidating the Strange Properties of Numbers"), written after Yang Hui had been shown old mathematical documents by his friends Liu Pi-chien and Ch'iu Hsü-chü. Subsequently all seven volumes that Yang Hui wrote in 1274–1275 came to be known under a single title, *Yang Hui suan-fa* ("The Mathematical Arts of Yang Hui"). The work was first printed in 1378 by the Ch'in-te shu-t'ang Press and was reprinted in Korea in 1433. A handwritten copy of the Korean reprint was made by the seventeenth-century Japanese mathematician Seki Takakazu. (A copy of the Korean reprint is in the Peking National Library.) Li Yen had Seki Takakazu's handwritten copy of the *Yang Hui suan-fa* dated 1661; it became the property of the Academia Sinica after his death in 1963. At the beginning of the seventeenth century Mao Chin (1598–1652) made a handwritten copy of the fourteenth-century edition of the *Yang Hui suan-fa.*

All of Yang Hui's writings, including the *Yang Hui suan-fa,* seem to have been forgotten during the eighteenth century. Efforts were made in 1810 to reconstruct the text from the *Yung-lo ta-tien* encyclopedia by Juan Yuan (1764–1849), but they were confined to a portion of the *Hsü-ku chai-ch'i suan-fa.* In 1776 Pao T'ing-po included a portion of the *Hsü-ku chai-ch'i suan-fa* in his *Chih-pu-tsu ts'ung-shu* collection that may have come from the restoration by Juan Yuan. In 1814 Huang P'ei-lieh discovered an incomplete and disarranged copy of the *Yang Hui suan-fa.* He and the mathematician Li Jui put the text in order. Lo Shih-lin had a handwritten copy made of this corrected text. This version of the *Yang Hui suan-fa,* consisting of only six volumes, was incorporated into the *I-chia-t'ang ts'ung-shu* collection by Yu Sung-nien (1842). Later reproduction of the text in the *Ts'ung-shu chi-ch'eng* collection (1936) is based on the version in the *I-chia-t'ang ts'ung-shu* collection. Some of the textual errors in the book have been corrected by Sung Ching-ch'ang in his *Yang Hui suan-fa cha-chi.* A full English translation and commentary of the *Yang Hui suan-fa* was made by Lam Lay Yong in 1966 for her doctoral dissertation at the University of Singapore.

The *Hsiang-chieh chiu-chang suan-fa* is perhaps the best-known, but certainly not the most interesting, of Yang Hui's writings. In it he explains the questions and problems in the *Chiu-chang suan-shu,* sometimes illustrating them with diagrams, and gives the detailed solutions. Problems of the same nature also are compared with each other. In the last chapter, the *Tsuan lei,* Yang Hui reclassifies all the 246 problems in the *Chiu-chang suan-shu* in order of progressive difficulty, for the benefit of students of mathematics. Some examples of algebraic series given by Yang Hui in this book are

$$m^2 + (m+1)^2 + \cdots + (m+n)^2 = \frac{m+1}{3}$$

$$\left\{ m^2 + (m+n)^2 + m(m+n) + \frac{1}{2}\left[(m+n) - m \right] \right\}$$

$$1 + 3 + 6 + \cdots + \frac{n(n+1)}{2} = \frac{1}{6}n(n+1)(n+2)$$

$$1^2 + 2^2 + 3^2 + \cdots + n^2 = \frac{1}{3}n\left(n+\frac{1}{2}\right)(n+1)$$

$$1^2 + (a+1)^2 + \cdots + (c-1)^2 + c^2$$
$$= \frac{1}{3}(c-a)\left(c^2 + a^2 + ca + \frac{c-a}{2}\right).$$

The portions restored from the *Yung-lo ta-tien* encyclopedia contain the earliest illustration of the "Pascal triangle." Yang Hui states that this diagram was derived from an earlier mathematical text, the *Shih-so suan-shu* of Chia Hsien (*fl. ca.* 1050). This diagram shows the coefficients of the expansion of $(x + a)^n$ up to the sixth power. Another diagram showing coefficients up to the eighth power was later found in the early fourteenth-century work *Ssu-yüan yü-chien* of Chu Shih-chieh. Other Chinese mathematicians using the Pascal triangle before Blaise Pascal were Wu Ching (1450), Chou Shu-hsüeh (1588), and Ch'eng Ta-wei (1592).

The *Tsuan-lei* also quotes a method of solving numerical equations higher than the second degree taken from Chia Hsien's *Shih-so suan-shu.* The method is similar to that rediscovered independently in the early nineteenth century, by Ruffini and Horner, for solving numerical equations of all orders by continuous approximation. A method called the *tseng-ch'eng k'ai-li-fang fa* for solving a cubic equation $x^3 - 1860867 = 0$ is given in detail below.

The number 1860867 is set up in the second row of a counting board in which five rows are used—the top row (*shang*) is for the root to be obtained, the second row (*shih*) is for the constant, the third row (*fang*) is for the coefficient of x, the fourth row (*lien*) is for the coefficient of x^2, and the last row (*hsia-fa*) is for the coefficient of x^3. Thus 1 is placed in the last row, and this coefficient is shifted to the left, moving two place values at a time until it comes in line with the number 1860867, at the extreme left in this case, as shown in Figure 1a.

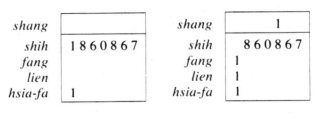

shang			*shang*	1
shih	1 860 867		*shih*	860 867
fang			*fang*	1
lien			*lien*	1
hsia-fa	1		*hsia-fa*	1

FIGURE 1a   FIGURE 1b

Since x lies between 100 and 200, 1 is placed at the hundreds' place of the first row. Multiplying this number by the number in the last row yields 1, which is entered on the fourth row as the *lien*. Again, multiplying the number 1 on the top row by the *lien* gives 1, which is entered in the third row as the *fang*. The number in the *fang* row is subtracted from the number in the same column in the *shih* row. The result is shown in Figure 1b. The number on the last row is multiplied a second time by the number in the top row and the product is added to the *lien*. The number in the *lien* is multiplied by the number on the top row and added to the *fang*. The number on the last row is multiplied a third time by the number on the top row, and the product is added to the number in the fourth row. The result is shown in Figure 1c.

shang	1
shih	860867
fang	3
lien	3
hsia-fa	1

FIGURE 1c

shang	1
shih	860867
fang	3
lien	3
hsia-fa	1

FIGURE 1d

The number in the third row (*fang*) is moved to the right by one place, that in the fourth row (*lien*) is moved to the right by two places, and that in the fifth row (*hsia-fa*) is moved to the right by three places, as in Figure 1d.

For the next approximation, x is found to lie between 120 and 130. Hence 2 is placed in the upper row in the tens' place. The same process is repeated, using 2 as the multiplier. We have $2 \times 1 = 2$, which is then added to the *lien*, giving a sum 32; and $2 \times 32 = 64$, which, when added to the *fang*, gives 364. Then 364 is multiplied by 2, giving 728, which is subtracted from 860867 to give 132867, as shown in Figure 1e.

shang	1 2
shih	132867
fang	364
lien	32
hsia-fa	1

FIGURE 1e

shang	1 2
shih	132867
fang	364
lien	36
hsia-fa	1

FIGURE 1f

Then the *hsia-fa* is multiplied a second time by 2 and added to the *lien*, giving a sum of 34, which again is multiplied by 2 and added to the *fang*, giv-

ing 432. The *hsia-fa* is multiplied a third time by 2 and added to the number 34 in the *lien* row to give 36, as shown in Figure 1f. The number in the *fang* row is now shifted one place, that in the *lien* row two places, and that in the *hsia-fa* row three places to the right, as shown in Figure 1g.

shang	1 2
shih	132867
fang	432
lien	36
hsia-fa	1

FIGURE 1g

shang	1 2 3
shih	0
fang	44289
lien	363
hsia-fa	1

FIGURE 1h

The last digit of x is found to be 3. This is placed on the top row in the units' column. Three times the *hsia-fa* gives 3, which, when added to the *lien*, gives 363. $3 \times 363 = 1089$, which, when added to the *fang*, gives 44289. Then $3 \times 44289 = 132867$, which, when subtracted from the *shih* row, leaves no remainder, as shown in Figure 1h. The root is therefore 123.

The *Hsiang-chieh chiu-chang suan-fa* also contains a method for solving quartic equations called the *tseng san-ch'eng k'ai-fang fa*. This involves the equation $x^4 - 1{,}336{,}336 = 0$. The method used is similar to that employed above for cubic equations. The solution is presented below in a slightly modified form, in order to show the resemblance to Horner's method.

$$x^4 - 1336336 = 0, \quad x = 34$$

$$
\begin{array}{l}
1(10)^4 + \quad 0 \times (10)^3 + \quad\quad 0 \times (10)^2 + \quad\quad 0 \times (10) - 1336336 \quad\quad \underline{30} \\
\quad\quad + \; 30 \times (10)^3 + \; 900 \times (10)^2 + \; 27000 \times (10) + \; 810000 \\
\hline
1(10)^4 + \; 30 \times (10)^3 + \; 900 \times (10)^2 + \; 27000 \times (10) - \; 526336 \\
\quad\quad + \; 30 \times (10)^3 + 1800 \times (10)^2 + \; 81000 \times (10) \\
\hline
1(10)^4 + \; 60 \times (10)^3 + 2700 \times (10)^2 + 108000 \times (10) \\
\quad\quad + \; 30 \times (10)^3 + 2700 \times (10)^2 \\
\hline
1(10)^4 + \; 90 \times (10)^3 + 5400 \times (10)^2 \\
\quad\quad + \; 30 \times (10)^3 \\
\hline
1(10)^4 + 120 \times (10)^3 \\
1(10)^4 + 120 \times (10)^3 + 5400 \times (10)^2 + 108000 \times (10) - 526336 \quad\quad \underline{4} \\
\quad\quad\quad + \; 4 \times (10)^3 + \; 496 \times (10)^2 + \; 23584 \times (10) + 526336 \\
\hline
1(10)^4 + 124 \times (10)^3 + 5896 \times (10)^2 + 131584 \times (10) + \quad\quad 0
\end{array}
$$

Both the few remaining problems of the *Jih-yung suan-fa* restored from the *Yung-lo ta-tien* encyclopedia and its title *Jih-yung*, meaning "daily or common use," suggest that the book must be of an elementary and practical nature, although we no longer have access to its entire text. Two examples follow:

a. A certain article actually weighs 112 pounds.

How much does it weigh on the provincial steelyard? Answer: 140 pounds. (Note that on the provincial steelyard 100 pounds would read 125 pounds.)

b. The weight of a certain article reads 391 pounds, 4 ounces, on a provincial steelyard. What is its actual weight? Answer: 313 pounds.

The first volume of the *Ch'eng-ch'u t'ung-pien pen-mo* (the *Suan-fa t'ung-pien pen-mo*) gives a syllabus or program of study for the beginner that is followed by a detailed explanation of variations in the methods of multiplication. In it Yang Hui shows how division can be conveniently replaced by multiplication by using the reciprocal of the divisor as the multiplier. For example, $2746 \div 25 = 27.46 \times 4$; $2746 \div 14.285 = 27.46 \times 7$; and $2746 \div 12.5 = 27.46 \times 8$. Sometimes he multiplies successively by the factors of the multiplier—for example, $274 \times 48 = 274 \times 6 \times 8$—and at other times he shows that the multiplier can be multiplied by the multiplicand—for example, $247 \times 7360 = 7360 \times 247$. Of special interest are the "additive" and "subtractive" methods that are applied to multiplication. These methods are quite conveniently used on the counting board, or even on an abacus, where the numbers are set up rather than written on a piece of paper. If the multiplier is 21, 31, 41, 51, 61, 71, 81, or 91, multiplication can be performed by multiplying only with the tens' digit and the result, shifted one decimal place to the left, is added to the multiplicand. Yang Hui gives a number of examples to illustrate this method, such as $232 \times 31 = 232 \times 30 + 232$; $234 \times 410 = 234 \times 400 + 2340$. In the "subtractive" method of multiplication, if the multiplier x is a number of n digits, the multiplicand p is first multiplied by 10^n, and from the result the product of the multiplicand and the difference between 10^n and the multiplier x is subtracted, that is, $xp = 10^n p - (10^n - x)p$. Yang Hui gives the example $26410 \times 7 = 264100 - (2641 \times 3) = 1848700$. The book ends with an account of how division can be performed.

In the second volume of the *Ch'eng-ch'u t'ung-pien pen-mo* (the *Ch'eng-ch'u t'ung-pien suan-pao*), Yang Hui proceeds further in showing how division can be avoided by multiplying with the reciprocal of the divisor. He also elaborates on the "additive" and "subtractive" methods for multiplication. He states the rule that in division, the result remains unchanged if both the dividend and the divisor are multiplied or divided by the same quantity. The examples he gives include the following:

$$
\begin{aligned}
(a)\ 274 \div 6.25 &= (274 \times 16) \div (6.25 \times 16) \\
&= 2.74 \times 16 \\
&= 27.4 + (2.74 \times 6) \\
(b)\ 342 \times 56 &= \frac{342}{2} \times 112 \\
&= \tfrac{1}{2}[34200 + 3420 + (342 \times 2)] \\
(c)\ 247 \times 1.95 &= 247 \times 1.3 \times 1.5 \\
&= [247 + (247 \times 0.3)] \times 1.5 \\
&= [247 + (247 \times 0.3)] \\
&\quad + [247 + (247 \times 0.3)] \times 0.5 \\
(d)\ 107 \times 10600 &= 1070000 + (107 \times 600) \\
(e)\ 19152 \div 56 &= \frac{19152}{4} \div \frac{56}{4} \\
&= 4788 \div 14 \\
(f)\ 9731 \div 37 &= (9731 \times 3) \div (37 \times 3) \\
&= 29193 \div 111
\end{aligned}
$$

The "subtractive" method for division is applied to cases (e) and (f). The steps for solving (e) are shown below:

```
              3 | 4 | 2
       14 | 4  7   8   8
            3 0
            1 7   8   8
            1 2
              5   8   8
              4   0
              1   8   8
              1   6
                  2   8
                  2   0
                      8
                      8
```

Yang Hui also states the rule that in multiplication, the result remains unchanged if the multiplicand is multiplied by a number and the multiplier by the reciprocal of the same number. Then he shows how to apply the rule to make the methods of "additive" and "subtractive" multiplication applicable. For example, $237 \times 56 = \frac{237}{2} \times (56 \times 2) = 118.5 \times 112 = 11850 + 1185 + (118.5 \times 2)$. The last part of the volume contains the division tables, the first instance of such tables in Chinese mathematical texts. They were later used by the Chinese in division operations involving the abacus.

The last volume of the *Ch'eng-ch'u t'ung-pien pen-mo* (the *Fa-suan ch'ü-yung pen-mo*) gives various rapid methods for multiplication and division for multipliers and divisors from 2 to 300 that are based on the rules described in the first two volumes. For example, when the multiplier is 228, Yang Hui and his collaborator Shih Chung-yung recommend the use of the factors 12 and 19 and the successive application of the "additive" method of multiplication; and when the multiplier is 125, they recommend shifting the multiplicand three places to the left and then halving it three times successively.

The *T'ien-mou pi-lei ch'eng-ch'u chieh-fa*, interesting mainly for its theory of equations, consists of two chapters. The first begins with a method for finding the area of a rectangular farm that is extended to problems involving other measures—weights, lengths, volumes, and money. These problems indicate that the length measurements for the sides of a rectangle can be employed as "dummy variables." Yang Hui was hence on the path leading to algebra, although neither he nor his Chinese contemporaries made extensive use of symbols. The text shows that Yang Hui had a highly developed conception of decimal places, simplified certain divisions by multiplication with reciprocals, and avoided the use of common fractions and showed his preference for decimal fractions. The words *chieh-fa* (literally, "shorter method") in the title must have referred to these and other simplified methods that he introduced. Three different values for the ratio of the circumference to the diameter of a circle are used: 3, 22/7, and 3.14. The rest of the first chapter deals with the area of the annulus, the isosceles triangle, and the trapezium; series; and arithmetic progressions exemplified by problems involving bundles of arrows with either square or circular cross sections.

The second chapter of the *T'ien-mou pi-lei ch'eng-ch'u chieh-fa* contains the earliest explanations of the Chinese methods for solving quadratic equations. For equations of the type $x^2 + 12x = 864$, Yang Hui recommends the *tai tsung k'ai fang* method, literally the method of extracting the root by attaching a side rectangle (*tsung*). The constant 864 is called *chi* ("total area"). If $x = 10x_1 + x_2$, $10x_1$ is called the *ch'u shang* ("first deliberation") and x_2 the *tz'u shang* ("second deliberation"), then $(10x_1)^2$ is the *fang fa*, x_2^2 the *yü*, and $10x_1x_2$ the *lien*. Also, $12x = 12(10x_1 + x_2)$, with 12 $(10x_1)$ being called *tsung fang* and $12x_2$ the *tsung*. Five rows on the counting board are used: *shang, chih, fang-fa, tsung-fang,* and *yü* or *yü suan*, in descending order. The constant 864 is first placed in the second row (*chih*), then the coefficient of x on the fourth row (*tsung-fang*), and the coefficient for x^2

on the last row (*yü suan*). The coefficient of x is moved one place to the left and that of x^2 two places to the left, as shown in Figure 2a. The value of x lies between 20 and 30. The number 20, called the *ch'u shang*, is placed on the top row. Taking the number 2 of the *ch'u shang* as the multiplier, the product with the *yü suan* is 20. This is entered in the third row (*fang-fa*), as shown in Figure 2b. The number 2 of the *ch'u shang* is again used as the multiplier to find the products of the *fang-fa* and the *tsung-fang*. The sum of these two products (640) is subtracted from the *chih*, giving a remainder 224. The third row, now known as *lien*, and the fourth row, now known as *tsung*, are moved one place to the right, while the *yü suan* is moved by two places, as shown in Figure 2c.

shang			
chih	8	6	4
tsung-fang	1	2	
yü suan	1	0	

FIGURE 2a

shang	2		
chih	8	6	4
fang-fa	2	0	
tsung-fang	1	2	
yü suan	1	0	

FIGURE 2b

shang	2		
chih	2	2	4
lien		4	0
tsung		1	2
yü suan			1

FIGURE 2c

shang	2	4	
chih	2	2	4
lien yü		4	4
tsung		1	2
yü suan			1

FIGURE 2d

The "second deliberation" (*tz'u shang*) is found to be 4. This is placed in the first row after the number 2. The product of the "second deliberation" and the *yü suan*, called *yü*, is added to the third row, which then becomes known as the *lien yü* (44 in this case). See Figure 2d. The sum of the products of the "second deliberation" and each of the *lien yü* and the *tsung* (224), when subtracted from the *chih*, leaves no remainder. Hence $x = 24$.

The solution is also illustrated by Yang Hui in a diagram as shown in Figure 3. If $x = (10x_1 + x_2)$, where $x_1 = 2$ and $x_2 = 4$, then from the equation $(10x_1 + x_2)^2 + 12(10x_1 + x_2) = 864$ we obtain $100x_1^2 + 20x_1x_2 + x_2^2 + 120x_1 + 12x_2 = 864$. Here the *fang-fa* is given by $100x_1^2$, the two *lien* by $20x_1x_2$, *yü* by x_2^2, *tsung-fang* by $120x_1$, *tsung* by $12x_2$, and the total *chih* by 864.

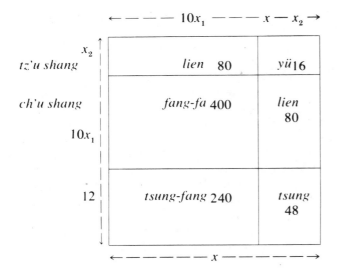

FIGURE 3

For equations of the type $x^2 - 12x = 864$, Yang Hui gives two different methods: the *i chi k'ai fang* (extracting the root by increasing the area) and the *chien ts'ung k'ai fang* (extracting the root by detaching a side rectangle, or *ts'ung*). For finding the smaller root of an equation of the type $-x^2 + 60x = 84$, Yang Hui recommends either of the two methods of *i yu* ("adding a corner square") and *chien ts'ung* ("detaching a side rectangle"). Finally, for finding the larger root of the same equation, he gives the *fan chi* ("inverted area") method. The geometrical illustrations of these methods suggest that means for solving quadratic equations may have been first derived geometrically by Yang Hui. Negative roots are also discussed, and the general solutions given are similar to Horner's method.

In the second chapter of his *T'ien-mou pi-lei ch'eng-ch'u chieh-fa*, Yang Hui also describes a method of solving equations of the type $x^4 = c$ as given by Liu I and Chia Hsien. There are also quadratic equations in which either the product and the difference of the two roots, or the product and the sum of the two roots, are given, such as an equation in the form

$$(x + y)^2 = (x - y)^2 + 4xy.$$

In addition he gives a general formula for the positive roots in the form

$$x = \frac{-b \pm \sqrt{(b^2 - 4ac)}}{2a}.$$

The methods used by Yang Hui for solving quadratic equations appear to be more flexible than those used in the West. He also demonstrated how to solve a biquadratic equation of the form

$$-5x^4 + 52x^3 + 128x^2 = 4096$$

by means of the *san-ch'eng-fang* ("quartic root") method, which is very similar to the method rediscovered in the early nineteenth century by Horner and Ruffini. The rest of the chapter deals with dissection of areas: a rectangle cut off from a larger isosceles triangle, a trapezium cut away from a larger trapezium, and an annulus cut off from a larger annulus.

The *Hsü-ku chai-ch'i suan-fa* consists of two chapters. The first has recently aroused considerable interest because of its magic squares. It is found only in the rare Sung edition and is missing from the *I-chia-t'ang ts'ung-shu* version, which is more commonly available. The *Hsü-ku chai-ch'i suan-fa* is the earliest Chinese text extant that gives magic squares higher than the third order and magic circles as well. In the preface Yang Hui disclaims originality in regard to its contents, saying that the material was among the old manuscripts and mathematical texts brought to him by his friends Liu Pi-chien and Ch'iu Hsü-chü. After Yang Hui, magic squares were discussed by Ch'eng Ta-wei in his *Suan-fa t'ung-tsung* (1593), by Fang Chung-t'ung in his *Shu-tu yen* (1661), by Chang Ch'ao in his *Hsin-chai tsa tsu* (ca. 1670), and by Pao Ch'i-shou in his *Pi-nai-shan-fang chi* (ca. 1880). In 1935 Li Yen published a paper on Chinese magic squares and reproduced the entire section on magic squares in Yang Hui's book, but with some misprints. In 1959 a subsection on magic squares was included in volume III of Joseph Needham's *Science and Civilisation in China*. Through the courtesy of Li Yen, a microfilm of his personal copy of the Sung edition of *Yang Hui suan-fa*, containing the full chapter on magic squares, was obtained for the preparation of Lam Lay Yong's doctoral dissertation. Some of Yang Hui's magic squares are shown in Figure 4a–4h.

④　　⑨　　②

③　　⑤　　⑦

⑧　　①　　⑥

2	16	13	3
11	5	8	10
7	9	12	6
14	4	1	15

FIGURE 4a. The *lo-shu*, magic square of order 3.

FIGURE 4b. One of the two magic squares of order 4.

12	27	33	23	10
28	18	13	26	20
11	25	21	17	31
22	16	29	24	14
32	19	9	15	30

FIGURE 4c. One of the two magic squares of order 5.

13	22	18	27	11	20
31	4	36	9	29	2
12	21	14	23	16	25
30	3	5	32	34	7
17	26	10	19	15	24
8	35	28	1	6	33

FIGURE 4d. One of the two magic squares of order 6.

46	8	16	20	29	7	49
3	40	35	36	18	41	2
44	12	33	23	19	38	6
28	26	11	25	39	24	22
5	7	31	27	17	13	45
48	9	15	14	32	10	47
1	43	34	30	21	42	4

FIGURE 4e. One of the two magic squares of order 7.

61	3	2	64	57	7	6	60
12	54	55	9	16	50	51	13
20	46	47	17	24	42	43	21
37	27	26	40	33	31	30	36
29	35	34	32	25	39	38	28
44	22	23	41	48	18	19	45
52	14	15	49	56	10	11	53
5	59	58	8	1	63	62	4

FIGURE 4f. One of the two magic squares of order 8.

31	76	13	36	81	18	29	74	11
22	40	58	27	45	63	20	38	56
67	4	49	72	9	54	65	2	47
30	75	12	32	77	14	34	79	16
21	39	57	23	41	59	25	43	61
66	3	48	68	5	50	70	7	52
35	80	17	28	73	10	33	78	15
26	44	62	19	37	55	24	42	60
71	8	53	64	1	46	69	6	51

FIGURE 4g. Magic square of order 9 (the number 43 is incorrectly written in Seki Takakazu's copy as 42).

1	20	21	40	41	60	61	80	81	100
99	82	79	62	59	42	39	22	19	2
3	18	23	38	43	58	63	78	83	98
97	84	77	64	57	44	37	24	17	4
5	16	25	36	45	56	65	76	85	96
95	86	75	66	55	46	35	26	15	6
14	7	34	27	54	47	74	67	94	87
88	93	68	73	48	53	28	33	8	13
12	9	32	29	52	49	72	69	92	89
91	90	71	70	51	50	31	30	11	10

FIGURE 4h. Magic square of order 10.

Besides magic squares and magic circles, the first chapter deals with problems on indeterminate analysis, calendar computation, geometrical progressions, and volumes and areas of objects of various regular shapes. For indeterminate analysis Yang Hui also gives the common names used in his time, such as *Ch'in Wang an tien ping* ("the Prince of Ch'in's secret method of counting soldiers"), *chien kuan shu* ("method of cutting lengths of tube"), and *fu shê chih shu* ("method of repeating trials"). (For further details on the Chinese method of indeterminate analysis, see "Ch'in Chiushao.")

The first problem of the second chapter reads: "A number of pheasants and rabbits are placed together in the same cage. Thirty-five heads and ninety-four feet are counted. Find the number of each." Besides simultaneous linear equations of two unknowns, this chapter deals with three unknowns. The chapter then considers miscellaneous examples taken from several mathematical texts, including Liu Hui's *Chiu-chang suan-shu* and *Hai-tao suan-ching*, the *Sun-tzu suan-ching*, the *Chang Ch'iu-chien suan-ching*, the *Ying-yung suan-fa*, the *Chih-nan suan-fa*, and the *Pien-ku t'ung-yuan*. The last three mathematical texts were printed during the eleventh and twelfth centuries in China, but are now lost. It is only through the works of Yang Hui that fragments of them and some of the other texts printed in the same era are extant. In the last problem of the chapter, Yang Hui gives a detailed analysis of the method employed by Liu Hui in his *Hai-tao suan-ching*. It is interesting that Yang Hui's first publication, the *Hsiang-chieh chiu-chang suan-fa*, is a study of Liu Hui's *Chiu-chang suan-shu*, which had been authoritative in China for about 1,000 years. Thus, with the last problem in his last publication, Yang Hui had completed a total analysis of Liu Hui's writings.

BIBLIOGRAPHY

See Schuyler Cammann, "The Evolution of Magic Squares in China," in *Journal of the American Oriental Society*, **80**, no. 2 (1960), 116; and "Old Chinese Magic Squares," in *Sinologica*, **7**, no. 1 (1962), 14; Ch'ien Pao-tsung, *Chung-kuo Shu-hsüeh-shih* (Peking, 1964); Ch'ien Pao-tsung *et al.*, *Sung Yuan shu-hsüeh-shih lun-wen-chi* (Peking, 1966); Hsü Shun-fang, *Chung-suan-chia ti tai-shu-hsüeh yen chiu* (Peking, 1952); Lam Lay Yong, *The Yang Hui Suan Fa, a Thirteenth-Century Chinese Mathematical Treatise* (Singapore); Li Yen, "Chung-suan-shih lun-ts'ung," in *Gesammelte Abhandlungen über die Geschichte der Chinesischen Mathematik*, II and III (Shanghai, 1935); and *Chung-kuo suan-hsüeh-shih* (Shanghai, 1937; rev. ed., 1955); Li Yen and Tu Shih-jan, *Chung-kuo ku-tai shu-hsüeh chien-shih*, II (Peking, 1964); Yoshio Mikami, *Mathematics in China and Japan* (1913; repr. New York, 1961); and Joseph Needham, *Science and Civilisation in China*, III (Cambridge, 1959).

HO PENG-YOKE

YATIVṚṢABHA (*fl.* India, sixth century)

Yativṛṣabha (in Prākrit, Jadivasaha) was a Jain author who studied under Ārya Maṅkṣu and Nāgahastin, and compiled several works in Prākrit expounding Jain traditions. One of these, the *Tiloyapaṇṇattī*, a description of the universe and its parts, is of some importance to historians of Indian science because it incorporates formulas representative of developments in Jain mathematics between the older canonical works and the later texts of the ninth and following centuries. Unfortunately, almost nothing is known of Yativṛṣabha himself; his lifetime is fixed by the general character of his work, as well as by his references to the *Loyavibhāga* (probably that written by Sarvanandin in 458) and by the reference to him by Jinabhadra Kṣamāśramaṇa (*fl.* 609). Yativṛṣabha's statement that the end of the Gupta dynasty occurred after 231 years of rule must refer to a contemporary event in Gupta Era 231 (A.D. 551).

BIBLIOGRAPHY

The *Tiloyapaṇṇattī* was edited by Ādinātha Upādhyāya and Hīrālāla Jaina with a Hindi paraphrase by Balchandra, 2 vols. (Śolāpura, 1943–1951; I, 2nd ed., 1956). There is a study in Hindi of the mathematics of Yativṛṣabha by Lakṣmīcandra Jaina, *Tiloyapaṇṇattī kā gaṇita* (Śolāpura, 1958).

DAVID PINGREE

YOUDEN, WILLIAM JOHN (*b.* Townsville, Australia, 12 April 1900; *d.* Washington, D.C., 31 March 1971)

Youden was the eldest child of William John Youden, an English engineer, and Margaret Hamilton of Carluke, Scotland. In 1902 the family returned to the father's birthplace—Dover, England—and resided there until 1907, when they left for America. They lived for a while in Connecticut and at Niagara Falls, New York, where Youden attended public school, before moving to Rochester, New York, in 1916. Youden attended the University of Rochester from 1917 to 1921, except for three months in the U.S. Army in 1918, receiving a B.S. in chemical engineering in 1921. He began graduate work in September 1922 at Columbia University, earning an M.A. in chemistry in 1923 and a Ph.D. the following year.

Immediately after receiving his doctorate, Youden joined the Boyce Thompson Institute for Plant Research in Yonkers, New York, as a physical chemist. He held this post until May 1948, when he joined the National Bureau of Standards as assistant chief of the Statistical Engineering Laboratory, Applied Mathematics Division. Three years later he became a consultant on statistical design and analysis of experiments to the chief of this division, a position he retained until his retirement in 1965.

He was an honorary fellow of the Royal Statistical Society (1965), and was awarded the Medal of Freedom in 1964, the 1969 Samuel S. Wilks Memorial Medal of the American Statistical Association, and the 1969 Shewhart Medal of the American Society for Quality Control.

In 1922 Youden married Gladys Baxter of Rochester, New York; they had two sons, William Wallace (1925–1968) and Robert Hamilton, both of whom chose careers in the computer field. In 1938 he married Grethe Hartmann of Copenhagen, Denmark; they had one son, Julius Hartmann, now a teacher in Copenhagen. In 1957 Youden married Didi Stockfleth of the Norwegian Embassy staff in Washington, D.C. Survivors of his immediate family include his widow, Didi; two sons; and eight grandchildren. Youden is buried in the National Cemetery, Gettysburg National Military Park, Gettysburg, Pennsylvania, in deference to his expressed wishes to remain in his adopted country.

Youden began his professional career as a physical chemist. His first paper to exhibit any knowledge of statistical methods, "A Nomogram for Use in Connection With Gutzeit Arsenic Determinations on Apples" (September 1931), was expository in nature: he noted that the differences between repeated determinations of a physicochemical property of a particular biological material reflect not only the "probable error" of the method of chemical analysis but also the "probable error" of the technique of sampling the material under investigation, and then, with guidance from a 1926 paper of W. A. Shewhart, outlined the requisite theory, illustrated its application, furnished a nomogram to facilitate correct evaluation of the precision of a particular procedure, and pointed out statistical errors that marred a number of earlier publications on sampling of apples for determination of arsenical sprayed residue. This paper marks the beginning of Youden's "missionary" efforts to acquaint research workers with statistical methods of value in their work.

About 1928 Youden "obtained one of the 1050 copies . . . of the first edition" of R. A. Fisher's *Statistical Methods . . .* (1925). At that time he was "so discouraged by what was called 'measurement' in biology that [he] was on the point of resigning" his post at Boyce Thompson. "Fisher's book opened a ray of hope," however, and Youden soon realized that at Boyce Thompson "he had the opportunity to perform agricultural experiments, both in the field and in the greenhouse, and to try out the early experiment designs" and Fisher's new small-sample methods of data analysis. The publicity for the visit of Fisher to Iowa State College in 1931 came to Youden's attention and aroused his curiosity, but he was unable to attend. When Fisher visited Cornell on his way home from Iowa, Youden "drove there . . . to show him an experimental arrangement."[1] During the academic year 1931–1932, he commuted to Columbia University to attend Harold Hotelling's lectures on statistical inference.[2] During the next few years he published a number of mathematical-statistical papers describing the application of statistical techniques to problems arising in studies of seeds, soils, apples, leaves, and trees.

During this period Youden devoted increasing attention to statistical design of experiments, in order to cope with the enormous variability of biological material; he found many of the standard experiment designs developed for agricultural field trials to be directly applicable in greenhouse work, a situation that led to vastly improved precision. Recognizing that the limited number of leaves per plant thwarted the use of Latin square designs to effect precise within-plant comparisons of a large number of proposed treatments for plant ailments, Youden devised new symmetrically balanced, incomplete block designs that had the characteristic "double control" of Latin square designs but not the restriction that each "treatment" (or "variety") must occur once, and only once, in each row and column. He brought these new designs to R. A. Fisher's attention in 1936 and subsequently completed "Use of Incomplete Block Replications in Estimating Tobacco Mosaic Virus" (1937), in which he presented and illustrated the application of four of the new rectangular experimental arrangements. In a subsequent paper (1940) he gave eight additional designs and, for six of these, the complementary designs. Youden's new rectangular experiment designs, called "Youden squares" by R. A. Fisher and F. Yates in the introduction to their *Statistical Tables . . .* (1938, p. 18), were immediately found to be of broad utility in biological and medical research generally; to be applicable but of less value in agricultural field trials; and, with the advent of World War II, to be of great value in the scientific and engineering experimentation connected with research and development. To gain further knowledge of statistical theory and methodology, Youden audited the courses on mathematical statistics and design of experiments, by Harold Hotelling and Gertrude M. Cox respectively, and took part in a number of statistical seminars at North Carolina State College in 1941.

Youden served as an operations analyst with the U.S. Army Air Force (1942–1945), first in Britain, where he directed a group of civilian scientists seeking to determine the controlling factor in bombing accuracy; in the latter part of the war, he conducted similar studies in India, China, and the Marianas, preparatory to the assault on Japan. He displayed exceptional skill in the invention of novel, and adaptation of standard, statistical tools of experiment design and analysis to cope with problems arising in the study of bombing accuracy.

In a lecture delivered at the National Bureau of Standards in 1947 Youden exposed the fallaciousness of the all-too-common belief that statistical methods—and a statistician—can be of no help unless one has a vast amount of data; demonstrated that one can obtain valuable information on the precision—and even on the accuracy—of a measurement process without making a large number of measurements on any single quantity; and showed how in routine work one can often obtain useful auxiliary information on personnel or equipment at little or no additional cost through skillful preliminary planning of the measurements to be taken.

On joining the National Bureau of Standards in 1948, Youden revealed the advantages of applying carefully selected statistical principles and techniques in the planning stages of the Bureau's experiments or tests. In the course of these demonstrations he noticed, and was one of the first to capitalize on, important differences between experimentation in the biological and agricultural sciences and in the physical and chemical sciences.[3]

Youden began to devise new forms of experimental arrangements, the first of which were his "linked blocks" (1951) and "chain blocks" (1953), developed to take advantage of special circumstances of spectrographic determinations of chemical elements carried out by comparing spectrum lines recorded on photographic plates.[4] In 1952 Youden and W. S. Connor began to exploit a special class of experiment designs having block size 2 in the thermometer, meter-bar and radium-standards calibration programs of the Bureau. The thermometer calibration application involved observation of the reading of each of the two thermometers forming a "block"; the meter-bar application involved observation of only the difference of the lengths of the two meter bars making up a block, and marked the start of the development of a system of "calibration designs" that Youden did not develop further and exploit as a special subclass until 1962; and the radium-standards application, observation of only ratios of pairs of standards. Meanwhile, Youden and J. S. Hunter had originated a class of designs that they termed "partially replicated Latin squares" (1955), to provide a means of checking whether the assumption of additivity of row, column, and treatment effects is valid. In an epochal 1956 address, "Randomization and Experimentation," Youden introduced a technique for constrained randomization that obviates "the difficult position of the statistician who rules against . . . a systematic sequence when advanced on the grounds of convenience and insists on it when it pops out of the hat" (p. 16).

In the early 1960's Youden exploited a class of selected experiment designs with the specific purpose of identifying and estimating the effects of sources of systematic error. "Systematic Errors in Physical Constants" (1961) contains his first "ruggedness test" based on the observation that some of the fractional factorial designs, developed a decade earlier for optimum multifactor experiments, were ready-made for testing the "ruggedness" (insensitivity) of a method of measurement with respect to recognized sources of systematic error and changes of conditions likely to be encountered in practice.

Youden also originated at least three new statistical techniques: an index for rating diagnostic tests (1950), the two-sample chart for graphical diagnosis of interlaboratory test results (1959), and an extreme rank sum test for outliers (1963), devised to test the statistical significance of outlier laboratories in interlaboratory collaborative tests. The two-sample chart has the same advantage as Shewhart's control chart: simplicity of construction, visual pinpointing of trouble spots, and comparative ease of more refined analysis.[5] Although developed in the setting of test methods for properties of materials, it has become a standard tool of the National Conference of Standard Laboratories in its nationwide program of searching for and rectifying systematic differences in the most accurate programs for instrument calibration.[6] This technique is now used in all measurement fields where interlaboratory agreement is important, and the term "Youden plot" specifies not only the plotting technique but also the experimental procedure for sampling the performance of each laboratory through the results obtained on paired test items.[7] In the case of the extreme rank sum test, Youden's ideas had been anticipated by R. Doornbos and H. J. Prins (1958), but it was characteristic of Youden that he had independently conceived his test primarily as a device to dramatize and clarify the messages contained in experimental results, rather than as a contribution to distribution-free statistical methods.

By his publications and by his example, Youden contributed substantially to the achievement of objectivity in experimentation and to the establishment of more exact standards for drawing scientific conclusions. "Enduring Values," his address as retiring president of the Philosophical Society of Washington, is an exposition of schemes for incorporating investigations of systematic errors into experimental determinations of fundamental physical constants and a plea for efforts by scientists to accumulate objective evidence for the description of the precision and accuracy of their work. Shortly before his death Youden completed the manuscript of another "missionary" effort, *Risk, Choice and Prediction* (1974), formally intended to familiarize students in the seventh grade and above with basic statistical concepts but actually meant "for anyone . . . who wants to learn in a relatively painless way how the concept and techniques of statistics can help us better understand today's complex world" (p. vii).

NOTES

1. The first and last quotations are from W. J. Youden, "Memorial to Sir Ronald Aylmer Fisher," in *Journal of the American Statistical Association*, **57**, no. 300 (Dec. 1962), 727; the others, from Youden's "The Evolution of Designed Experiments," 59.

2. At this time Hotelling was the person in the United States most versed in the Student-Fisher theory of small samples.

3. Of paramount importance, he noted, is the difference in the magnitude of the errors of measurement: in agricultural and biological experimentation unavoidable variation is likely to be large, so the early experiment designs developed for application in these fields compensate by incorporating many determinations of the quantities of principal interest; physical measurements, in contrast, can often be made with high precision and the experimental material usually is comparatively homogeneous, so that the quantities of interest often can be determined with acceptably small standard errors from as few as two or three, or even from a single, indirect determination. Also, in many experimental situations in the physical sciences and engineering, a "block" and the "plots" within a block are sharply and naturally defined, and often are quite distinct; this is in marked contrast with the arbitrary division of a given land area into "blocks" in agricultural field trials, and the subdivision of a block into contiguous "plots." Consequently, various "interactions" commonly present in agricultural field trials are often absent or negligible in physical-science experimentation.

4. "Linked block" designs are incomplete block designs for which every pair of blocks has the same number of treatments in common; they were subsequently shown to be special cases of partially balanced incomplete block designs with two associate classes of triangular type. "Chain block" designs were developed for situations in which the number of treatments considerably exceeds the block size while, within blocks, comparisons are of such high precision that at most two replications are needed, some treatments occurring only once. Chain block designs with two-way elimination of heterogeneity were subsequently devised by Mandel (1954).

5. See, for example, Acheson J. Duncan, *Quality Control and Industrial Statistics*, 3rd ed. (Homewood, Ill., 1965), pt. 4.

6. See *Proceedings of the 1966 Standards Laboratory Conference*, National Bureau of Standards Miscellaneous Publication 291 (Washington, D.C., 1967), 19, 20, 27–29, 42, 45, 48, 51, 61, 62.

7. "Graphical Diagnosis of Interlaboratory Test Results" (May 1959) is the basic reference on the "Youden plot." A condensed version appeared in *Technical News Bulletin. National Bureau of Standards*, **43**, no. 1 (Jan. 1959), 16–18; and its evolution can be followed in four columns in *Industrial and Engineering Chemistry*: "Presentation for Action," **50**, no. 8 (Aug. 1958), 83A–84A; "Product Specifications and Test Procedures," *ibid.*, no. 10 (Oct. 1958), 91A–92A; "Circumstances Alter Cases," *ibid.*, no. 12 (Dec. 1958), 77A–78A; and "What Is Measurement?" **51**, no. 2 (Feb. 1959), 81A–82A.

BIBLIOGRAPHY

I. ORIGINAL WORKS. Brian L. Joiner and Roy H. Wampler, "Bibliography of W. J. Youden," in *Journal of Quality Technology (JQT)*, **4**, no. 1 (Jan. 1972), 62–66, lists 5 books and 110 papers (including book chapters, encyclopedia articles, editorials, and military documents, but excluding the 36 columns "Statistical Design" [see below], 9 book reviews, and a foreword to a book by another author). It appears to be complete and correct, except for omission of the 1969 and 1970 papers noted below, a premature date for his posthumous book, and the unfortunate substitution of "Quality" for the third word in the title "Simplified Statistical Quantity Control" (1963). Dedicated to Youden, this issue of *JQT* also contains a portrait; a biographical essay by Churchill Eisenhart; "Summary and Index for 'Statistical Design,'" prepared by Mary G. Natrella, which covers his column "Statistical Design," in *Industrial and Engineering Chemistry* (1954–1959); and reproductions of several papers and other materials.

Youden's doctoral dissertation, *A New Method for the Gravimetric Determination of Zirconium*, was privately printed (New York, 1924). As a member of the staff of the Boyce Thompson Institute, he published 15 research papers on chemical and biological studies and instrumentation pertinent to the work of the Institute in *Contributions From Boyce Thompson Institute*. The items below that are marked "repr. in *JQT*" were reprinted in *Journal of Quality Technology*, **4**, no. 1; and those marked "repr. in *SP 300-1*," in Harry H. Ku, ed., *Precision Measurement and Calibration: Selected Papers on Statistical Concepts and Procedures*, National Bureau of Standards Special Publication 300, vol. 1 (Washington, D.C., 1969).

Youden's earlier works include "A Nomogram for Use in Connection With Gutzeit Arsenic Determinations on Apples," in *Contributions From Boyce Thompson Institute*, **3**, no. 3 (Sept. 1931), 363–373; "Statistical Analysis of Seed Germination Data Through the Use of the Chi-Square Test," *ibid.*, **4**, no. 2 (June 1932), 219–232; "A Statistical Study of the Local Lesion Method for Estimating Tobacco Mosaic Virus," *ibid.*, **6**, no. 3 (July–Sept. 1934), 437–454, written with Helen P. Beale; "Relation of Virus Concentration to the Number of Lesions Produced," *ibid.*, **7**, no. 1 (Jan.–Mar. 1935), 37–53, written with H. P. Beale and J. D. Guthrie; "Field Trials With Fibre Pots," *ibid.*, **8**, no. 4 (Oct.–Dec. 1936), 317–331, written with P. W. Zimmerman; "Use of Incomplete Block Replications in Estimating Tobacco Mosaic Virus," *ibid.*, **9**, no. 1 (Nov. 1937), 41–48 (repr. in *JQT*), the paper in which the first four members of a new class of rectangular experimental arrangements, now called "Youden squares," appeared—the paper that catapulted him to fame; "Selection of Efficient Methods for Soil Sampling," *ibid.*, 59–70; "Experimental Designs to Increase the Accuracy of Greenhouse Studies," *ibid.*, **11**, no. 3 (Apr.–June 1940), 219–228; "Burette Experiment," part of the lecture "A Statistical Technique for Analytical Data," delivered at the National Bureau of Standards, 29 Apr. 1947, repr. in *JQT* from pp. 344–346, 350, of Churchill Eisenhart, "Some Canons of Sound Experimentation," in *Bulletin de l'Institut international de statistique*, **37**, no. 3 (1960), 339–350; and "Technique for Testing the Accuracy of Analytical Data," in *Analytical Chemistry*, **19**, no. 12 (Dec. 1947), 946–950.

Later works are "Index for Rating Diagnostic Tests," in *Cancer*, **3**, no. 1 (Jan. 1950), 32–35; "Linked Blocks: A New Class of Incomplete Block Designs" (abstract only), in *Biometrics*, **7**, no. 1 (Mar. 1951), 124; *Statistical Methods for Chemists* (New York, 1951); also in Italian (Genoa, 1964), his first book; "Statistical Aspects of Analytical Determinations," in *Analyst* (London), **77**, no. 921 (Dec. 1952), 874–878 (repr. in *JQT*); "The Chain Block Design," in *Biometrics*, **9**, no. 2 (June 1953), 127–140, written with W. S. Connor; "Sets of Three Measurements," in *Scientific Monthly*, **77**, no. 3 (Sept. 1953), 143–147 (repr. in *JQT*); "Making One Measurement Do the Work of Two," in *Chemical Engineering Progress*, **49**, no. 10 (Oct. 1953), 549–552 (repr. in *JQT*), written with W. S. Connor; "New Experimental Designs for Paired Observations," in *Journal of Research of the National Bureau of Standards*, **53**, no. 3 (Sept. 1954), 191–196 (repr. in *SP 300-1*), written with W. S. Connor; "Instrumental Drift," in *Science*, **120**, no. 3121 (22 Oct. 1954), 627–631 (repr. in *SP 300-1*); "Comparison of Four National Radium Standards: Part 2. Statistical Procedures and Survey," in *Journal of Research of the National Bureau of Standards*, **53**, no. 5 (Nov. 1954), 273–275 (repr. in *SP 300-1*), written with W. S. Connor; "Partially Replicated Latin Squares," in *Biometrics*, **11**, no. 4 (Dec. 1955), 399–405, written with J. S. Hunter; "Graphical Diagnosis of Interlaboratory Test Results," in *Industrial Quality Control*, **15**, no. 11 (May 1959), 24–28 (repr. in *JQT* and *SP 300-1*), the basic reference on Youden's two-sample procedure and diagram, collectively known as the "Youden Plot"; and "Measurements Made by Matching With Known Standards," in *Technometrics*, **1**, no. 2 (May 1959), 101–109, written with W. S. Connor and N. C. Severo.

See also *Statistical Design* (Washington, D.C., 1960), a collection of 36 articles published in a column with this title in *Industrial and Engineering Chemistry*, **46**, no. 2 (Feb. 1954)–**51**, no. 12 (Dec. 1959); "Physical Measurements and Experiment Design," in *Colloques internationaux du Centre national de la recherche scientifique* (Paris, 1961), no. 110, le Plan d'Expériences, 115–128 (repr. in *SP-300-1*); "Systematic Errors in Physical Constants," in *Physics Today*, **14**, no. 9 (Sept. 1961), 32–42, repr. in *Technometrics*, **4**, no. 1 [Feb. 1962], 111–123, and in *SP-300-1*; "Experimental Design and ASTM Committees," in *Materials Research and Standards*, **1**, no. 11 (Nov. 1961), 862–867 (repr. in *SP-300-1*); *Experimentation and Measurement* (New York, 1962); "Uncertainties in Calibration," in *I.R.E. Transactions on Instrumentation*, I-11, nos. 3–4 (Dec. 1962), 133–138 (repr. in *JQT* and *SP-300-1*); "Ranking Laboratories by Round-Robin Tests," in *Materials Research and Standards*, **3**, no. 1 (Jan. 1963), 9–13 (repr. in *SP-300-1*); "Measurement Agreement Comparisons," in *Proceedings of the 1962 Standards Laboratory Con-*

ference, National Bureau of Standards Miscellaneous Publication 248 (Washington, D.C., 1963), 147–151 (repr. in *SP-300-1*), the paper that inspired the work of Bose and Cameron (1965, 1967) and Eicke and Cameron (1967) on "calibration designs." "The Collaborative Test," in *Journal of the Association of Official Agricultural Chemists*, **46**, no. 1 (Feb. 1963), 55–62 (repr. in *SP-300-1*); and "The Evolution of Designed Experiments," in *Proceedings of the [1963] IBM Scientific Computing Symposium on Statistics* (White Plains, N.Y., 1965), 59–67 (repr. in *JQT*).

Additional works are *Statistical Techniques for Collaborative Tests* (Washington, D.C., 1967); "How Mathematics Appraises Risks and Gambles," in T. L. Saaty and F. J. Weyl, eds., *The Spirit and Uses of Mathematics* (New York, 1969), 167–187; "A Revised Scheme for the Comparison of Quantitative Methods," in *American Journal of Clinical Pathology*, **54**, no. 3 (Sept. 1970), 454–462, written with R. N. Barnett; "Enduring Values," in *Technometrics*, **14**, no. 1 (Feb. 1972), 1–11; "Randomization and Experimentation," *ibid.*, 13–22; and *Risk, Choice and Prediction: An Introduction to Experimentation* (North Scituate, Mass., 1974).

Copies of all of Youden's journal articles and book reviews, and many of his book chapters, published in 1924–1965, are bound together, generally in chronological order, along with copies of his Air Force manuals, his patents, and his paperbound books *Statistical Design* and *Experimentation and Measurement*, in "W. J. Youden Publications," 2 vols., in the Historical Collection of the Library of the National Bureau of Standards at Gaithersburg, Md. His publications of 1966–1972 have been assembled for a 3rd vol. There is also a vol. containing abstracts of his talks given during 1949–1965. In addition, among the records of the Bureau's Applied Mathematics Division are eight boxes of "Youdeniana" covering 1920–1971: personal records given by his widow in 1973, professional correspondence, reports, commendations, certificates of awards, photographs, handwritten notes and computations, and a considerable number of Youden's papers, lectures, and speeches.

II. SECONDARY LITERATURE. Youden's career and contributions to statistical theory and practice are summarized briefly in an unsigned obituary in *American Statistician*, **25**, no. 3 (June 1971), 51; and more fully by Churchill Eisenhart, in *Journal of Quality Technology*, **4**, no. 1 (Jan. 1972), 1–6. His contributions to the theory of statistical design and analysis of experiments are given special attention by Churchill Eisenhart and Joan R. Rosenblatt, in *Annals of Mathematical Statistics*, **43**, no. 4 (Aug. 1972), 1035–1040. A biography of Youden, with portrait, is scheduled for publication in *National Cyclopedia of American Biography*, LVI (1975), 99–100. A biographical essay on Youden's contributions to statistical theory, methodology, by Harry H. Ku is to appear in a volume tentatively titled *Statistics: Articles From the International Encyclopedia of the Social Sciences* (New York, 1976 or 1977).

Other publications are R. N. Barnett, "A Scheme for

the Comparison of Quantitative Methods," in *American Journal of Clinical Pathology*, **43**, no. 6 (June 1965), 562–569; R. C. Bose and J. M. Cameron, "The Bridge Tournament Problem and Calibration Designs for Comparing Pairs of Objects," in *Journal of Research of the National Bureau of Standards*, **69B**, no. 4 (Oct.–Dec. 1965), 323–332; "Calibration Designs Based on Solutions to the Tournament Problem," *ibid.*, **71B**, no. 4 (Oct.–Dec. 1967), 149–160; Willard H. Clatworthy, *Tables of Two-Associate-Class Partially Balanced Designs*, National Bureau of Standards Applied Mathematics Series, no. 63 (Washington, D.C., 1973); W. G. Eicke and J. M. Cameron, *Designs for Surveillance of the Volt Maintained by a Small Group of Saturated Standard Cells*, National Bureau of Standards Technical Note 430 (Washington, D.C., 1967); R. A. Fisher, *Statistical Methods for Research Workers* (Edinburgh–London, 1925; 14th ed., Edinburgh–London–Darien, Conn., 1970); R. A. Fisher and F. Yates, *Statistical Tables for Biological, Agricultural, and Medical Research* (Edinburgh–London, 1938; 6th ed., London–New York, 1963); H. O. Halvorson and N. R. Ziegler, "Application of Statistics to Problems in Bacteriology. I. A Means of Determining Bacterial Population by the Dilution Method," in *Journal of Bacteriology*, **25**, no. 2 (Feb. 1933), 101–121; J. Mandel, "Chain Block Designs With Two-Way Elimination of Homogeneity," in *Biometrics* **10**, no. 2 (June 1954), 251–272; Benjamin L. Page, "Calibration of Meter Line Standards of Length at the National Bureau of Standards," in *Journal of Research of the National Bureau of Standards*, **54**, no. 1 (Jan. 1955), 1–14; Gary J. Sutter, George Zyskind, and Oscar Kempthorne, "Some Aspects of Constrained Randomization," Aeronautical Research Laboratories Report 63-18 (Wright-Patterson Air Force Base, Ohio, 1963); and Walter A. Shewhart, "Correction of Data for Errors of Measurement," in *Bell System Technical Journal*, **5**, no. 1 (Jan. 1926), 11–26.

CHURCHILL EISENHART

YOUNG, JOHN WESLEY (*b.* Columbus, Ohio, 17 November 1879; *d.* Hanover, New Hampshire, 17 February 1932)

Young's father, William Henry Young, a lieutenant colonel during the Civil War and professor of ancient languages at Ohio University, served as United States consul in Karlsruhe, Germany, from 1869 to 1876. His mother was Marie Widdenhorn.

After graduating from the Gymnasium in Baden-Baden, Young entered Ohio State University and earned a Ph.B. there in 1899. He received the A.M. (1901) and the Ph.D. (1904) from Cornell University. In 1907 he married Mary Louise Aston of Columbus. After teaching at Northwestern University (1903–1905), Princeton (preceptor, 1905–1908), the University of Illinois (1908–1910), the University of Kansas (head of the mathematics department, 1910–1911), and the University of Chicago (summer of 1911), he settled for the rest of his life at Dartmouth College, where he modernized and humanized the mathematics curriculum.

Young was influential in many learned societies, both in the United States and in Europe. He served as an editor of *Mathematics Teacher; Bulletin* and *Colloquium Publications, American Mathematical Society*; and *Carus Mathematical Monographs*. His active participation in the American Mathematical Society included membership on its Council (1907–1925) and vice-presidency (1928–1930). He was also instrumental in the founding of the Mathematical Association of America, of which he was vice-president in 1918 and president in 1929–1931. As chairman of its Committee on Mathematical Requirements (1916–1924), he edited a 652-page report, *The Reorganization of Mathematics in Secondary Education* (1923), which circulated widely and profoundly influenced educational thought and practice.

Throughout his professional career three themes dominated Young's publications: the concept of generalization, the presentation of advanced mathematics from an elementary viewpoint, and, in conjunction with these, the "popularization" of mathematics. His *Lectures on the Fundamental Concepts of Algebra and Geometry* (1911) is excellently written and is still highly regarded. At Dartmouth his synoptic course gave the nonspecialist an understanding of topics in advanced mathematics.

In 1908, Young, with Oswald Veblen, created a set of postulates for projective geometry that embodied the first fully independent set of assumptions for that branch of geometry. This formulation served as the basis for the first volume of the classic *Projective Geometry* (1910), written with Veblen.

BIBLIOGRAPHY

I. ORIGINAL WORKS. Young's A.M. thesis, "On the Homomorphisms of a Group," in *Transactions of the American Mathematical Society*, **3** (1902), 186–191; and "On a Certain Group of Isomorphisms," in *American Journal of Mathematics*, **25** (1903), 206–212, were written under the direction of G. A. Miller. His Ph.D. dissertation, "On the Group of Sign $(0, 3; 2,4,\infty)$ and the Functions Belonging to It," in *Transactions of the American Mathematical Society*, **5** (1904), 81–104, used methods developed by Klein in treating the elliptic modular group. Other papers are "The Use of Hypercomplex Numbers in Certain Problems of the Modular Group," in *Bulletin of the American Mathematical Society*, **11** (1905), 363–367; "A Class of Discontinuous ζ-Groups Defined by the Normal Curves of the Fourth Order in a Space of Four Dimensions," in *Rendiconti del Circulo matematico di Palermo*, **23** (1907), 97–106; "A Fundamental Invariant of the Discontinuous ζ-Groups Defined by the Normal Curves of Order *n* in a Space of *n* Dimensions," in *Bulletin of the American Mathematical Society*, **14** (1908), 363–367; "A Set of Assumptions for Projective Geometry," in *American Journal of Mathematics*, **30** (1908), 347–380, written with O. Veblen; "The Discontinuous ζ-Groups Defined by Rational Normal Curves in a Space of *n* Dimensions," in *Bulletin of the American Mathematical Society*, **16** (1910), 363–368; "The Geometries Associated With a Certain System of Cremona Groups," in *Transactions of the American Mathematical Society*, **17** (1916), 233–244, written with F. M. Morgan; and "A New Formulation for General Algebra," in *Annals of Mathematics*, 2nd ser., **29** (1921), 47–60.

Lectures on the Fundamental Concepts of Algebra and Geometry (New York, 1911) was translated into Italian by L. Pierro (Naples, 1919). *Projective Geometry* (Boston, 1910) consisted of 2 vols.: vol. I written with O. Veblen and vol. II, published under the names of Veblen and Young, but written by Veblen alone. *Projective Geometry* was Carus Mathematical Monograph no. 4 (Chicago, 1930). Young wrote a number of elementary mathematical textbooks, of which *Elementary Mathematical Analysis* (New York, 1918), written with F. M. Morgan, a pioneer text in the reorganization of freshman college courses, is structured around the unifying concept of function.

Other works are *The Reorganization of Mathematics in Secondary Education* (Oberlin, Ohio, 1923); "The Organization of College Courses in Mathematics for Freshmen," in *American Mathematical Monthly*, **30** (1923), 6–14; "Geometry," (in part) in *Encyclopaedia Britannica*, 14th ed. (1929), X, 174–178; and "The Adjustment Between Secondary School and College Work," in *Journal of Engineering Education*, **22** (1932), 586–595, his last paper, which is typical of a number of papers on collegiate mathematical teaching. Young's retiring presidential address, "Functions of the Mathematical Association of America," in *American Mathematical Monthly*, **39** (1932), 6–15, is an excellent example of the range of his interests and involvement in mathematics.

II. SECONDARY LITERATURE. K. D. Beetle and C. E. Wilder, "John Wesley Young: In Memoriam," in *Bulletin of the American Mathematical Society*, **38** (1932), 603–610, is a good biography complete with bibliography. Another, by E. M. Hopkins, L. L. Silverman, and H. E. Slaught, is in *American Mathematical Monthly*, **39** (1932), 309–314. For additional material on Young's role in American mathematics and the work and impact of the National Committee on Mathematical Requirements, see K. O. May, ed., *The Mathematical Association of America: Its First Fifty Years* (1972), 26–30, 39–40, 44; and

the *American Mathematical Monthly*, **23** (1916), 226, 283; **24** (1917), 463–464; **25** (1918), 56–59; **26** (1919), 223–234, 279–280, 439–440, 462–463; **27** (1920), 101–104, 145–146, 194, 341–342, 441–442; **28** (1921), 357–358; **29** (1922), 46; and **32** (1925), 157.

HENRY S. TROPP

YOUNG, WILLIAM HENRY (*b.* London, England, 20 October 1863; *d.* Lausanne, Switzerland, 7 July 1942)

Young was the eldest son of Henry Young and Hephzibah Jeal. The Young family had been bankers in the City for some generations. Young went to the City of London School, of which the headmaster, Edwin A. Abbott, author of the mathematical fantasy *Flatland*, recognized his flair for mathematics. Young entered Peterhouse, Cambridge, in 1881. In the mathematical tripos of 1884 he was expected to be senior wrangler but was placed fourth. In later years he related that he refused to restrict his interests (intellectual and athletic) to the intensive training in mathematics necessary for the highest place in the order of merit. The first books he borrowed from the College library were the works of Molière. Instead of writing a mathematical essay for a Smith's prize, he competed for and won a prize in theology. He was of Baptist stock and, at Cambridge, was baptized into the Church of England.

Young was a fellow of Peterhouse from 1886 to 1892, but he held no official position in the college or the university. It is surprising that between the ages of twenty-five and thirty-five he did not turn to research, but deliberately set himself to earn a large income and accumulate savings by private teaching of undergraduates from early morning until late at night.

In 1896 Young married Grace Emily, daughter of Henry W. Chisholm. She had taken the mathematical tripos and was ranked equal to a wrangler; as Grace Chisholm Young, she became a mathematician of international reputation. At the end of their first year together, she said, " . . . he proposed, and I eagerly agreed, to throw up lucre, go abroad, and devote ourselves to research." They lived mainly in Göttingen until 1908 and then in Switzerland, first in Geneva and later in Lausanne.

In striking contrast with most mathematicians, Young did hardly any research until he was over thirty-five, but between 1900 and 1924 he wrote more than two hundred papers. At the turn of the century, the theory of real functions was subject to artificial and unaesthetic restrictions. For instance, the standard process (Riemann's) of reconstructing an integral from its derivative required the continuity of the derivative. In the late 1890's the Paris school, led by Baire and Borel, laid the foundations of an essentially more powerful theory, based on the concept of the measure of a set of points. Lebesgue's famous thesis, "Intégrale, longueur, aire," appeared in 1902. Young, working independently, arrived at a definition of integration, different in form from, but essentially equivalent to, Lebesgue's. He was anticipated by about two years, and it must have been a heavy blow to one who had become conscious of his power to make fundamental discoveries; but he bore the disappointment magnanimously, and himself called the integral that of Lebesgue. Many aspects of the later development are Young's own, notably his method of monotone sequences as used in the Stieltjes integral.

Young showed supreme power in two other fields of analysis. The first is the theory of Fourier series. In 1912 he established the connection between the sum of the qth powers of the Fourier constants of a function f and the integral of f^p, where p and q are conjugate indices and q is an even integer. The completion for unrestricted q was achieved after eleven years by Hausdorff. Young proved many other theorems, some of striking simplicity and beauty, about Fourier series and more general orthogonal series. The second field—in which lay what was probably Young's most far-reaching work—was the basic differential calculus of functions of more than one variable. The best tribute to it is that, since 1910, every author of an advanced calculus textbook has adopted Young's approach.

Every word and every movement of Young gave evidence of restless vitality. His appearance was striking; after his marriage he grew a beard—red in contrast with his dark hair—and wore it very long in later years. Of his three sons and three daughters, Professor Laurence Chisholm Young and Dr. Rosalind Cecily Tanner continued their parents' work in pure mathematics. The eldest son was killed flying in France in 1917.

Young held part-time chairs at Calcutta (1913–1916) and Liverpool (1913–1919), and he was professor at Aberystwyth from 1919 to 1923. More than once electors to a chair passed him over in favor of men less powerful as mathematicians but less exacting as colleagues. He was an honorary doctor of the universities of Calcutta, Geneva, and Strasbourg; and his honors included the Sylvester Medal of the Royal Society (1928). He was president of the International Union of Mathematicians in 1929–1936.

When France fell in 1940 he was at Lausanne, cut off from his family, and he had to remain there, unhappy and restive, for the last two years of his life.

BIBLIOGRAPHY

I. ORIGINAL WORKS. Young wrote more than 200 papers; for a list of the most important of them see the obituary notices below. His books are *The First Book of Geometry* (London, 1905), written with Grace Chisholm Young, an excellent and original book doubtless composed for the education of their children; *The Theory of Sets of Points* (Cambridge, 1906), written with Grace Chisholm Young; and *The Fundamental Theorems of the Differential Calculus* (Cambridge, 1910).

II. SECONDARY LITERATURE. See *Obituary Notices of Fellows of the Royal Society of London*, **3** (1943), 307–323, with portrait; *Journal of the London Mathematical Society*, **17** (1942), 218–237; and *Dictionary of National Biography, 1941–1950* (1959), 984–985.

J. C. BURKILL

YULE, GEORGE UDNY (*b.* Morham, near Haddington, Scotland, 18 February 1871; *d.* Cambridge, England, 26 June 1951)

Yule was the son of Sir George Udny Yule and his wife, Henrietta Peach. Sir George was an administrator in the Indian Civil Service and a member of an old Scottish farming family with a history of some government, military, and literary distinction. In 1875 Sir George moved his family to London; and Yule was sent first to a day school there, and then to a preparatory school near Rugby. He was subsequently educated at Winchester College and University College, London, where, between 1887 and 1890, he read civil engineering but did not take a degree, there being none in the subject at the time. After two years' training in a small engineering works, however, Yule decided against engineering as a career and spent a year under Heinrich Hertz at Bonn, investigating the passage of electric waves through dielectrics. This was the subject of his first published paper.

Yule returned to London in 1893, at the invitation of Karl Pearson, to become demonstrator (lecturer) at University College. In 1896 he was promoted to assistant professor of applied mathematics. Three years later he married May Winifred Cummings, but the marriage was annulled in 1912.

One consequence of his marriage was that Yule felt obliged to earn a higher salary, and he accepted a dreary administrative post at the City and Guilds of London Institute. Between 1902 and 1909 he held concurrently a lectureship in statistics at University College, delivering evening lectures that were the basis of his first book, *An Introduction to the Theory of Statistics* (1911). This was for long the only comprehensive textbook on the subject (the fourteenth edition, revised by M. G. Kendall, appeared in 1958). The *Introduction*, and his reputation as a lecturer, led to his being offered the newly created lectureship in statistics at Cambridge in 1912.

Yule soon had a range of practical statistical experience. He was statistician to the School of Agriculture at Cambridge while he was university lecturer; and during World War I he was statistician first to the director of army contracts, and later to the Ministry of Food. In 1922 Yule became a fellow of both St. John's College, Cambridge, and the Royal Society. He resigned his university position in 1931. The following year he obtained a pilot's license; but a serious heart ailment obliged him to spend most of his retirement in a quieter pursuit, a study of the statistical aspects of literary style.

Yule's principal achievements in statistical theory concern regression and correlation, association, time series, Mendelian inheritance, and epidemiology. His early memoirs on correlation (1897, 1907) and association (1900) have proved to be fundamental. In the first of these he introduced the concept of partial ("net") correlation, and in 1907 he demonstrated that the sampling distributions for partial correlation coefficients are of the same form as those for total correlation coefficients. In the paper of 1900, Yule presented the coefficient of association for the measurement of the degree of association in 2×2 contingency tables. His introduction of this coefficient led to a long controversy with his former mentor and friend Karl Pearson, who joined forces with David Heron in a protest that M. G. Kendall said was "remarkable for having missed the point over more pages (173) than perhaps any other memoir in statistical history" (*The Advanced Theory of Statistics*, I [1943], 322).

From 1912 Yule and Major M. Greenwood laid the foundations of the theory of accident distributions. In 1921 he wrote on time correlation and began work leading to a well-known paper on sunspots (1927) that marked the beginning of the modern theory of oscillatory time series.

Yule introduced many new ideas into statistical theory and corrected many errors, especially in biometrics. He made important studies of the mathematics of biological evolution and of the statistics of agricultural field trials. He was perhaps the first to consider (1902) whether the observed correlations between parents and offspring could be accounted for by multifactorial Mendelian inheritance, a problem taken up later by R. A. Fisher.

BIBLIOGRAPHY

Yule wrote two books: *An Introduction to the Theory of Statistics* (London, 1911) and *The Statistical Study of Literary Vocabulary* (Cambridge, 1944). A bibliography of 71 scientific papers, plus 12 on other subjects, is in the notice by F. Yates, in *Obituary Notices of Fellows of the Royal Society of London*, **8** (1952), 309–323, with portrait.

J. D. NORTH

IBN YŪNUS, ABUʾL-ḤASAN ʿALĪ IBN ʿABD AL-RAḤMĀN IBN AḤMAD IBN YŪNUS AL-ṢADAFĪ (*d.* Fusṭāṭ, Egypt, 1009)

Ibn Yūnus was one of the greatest astronomers of medieval Islam. He came from a respected family, his great-grandfather Yūnus having been a companion of the famous legal scholar al-Shāfiʿī and his father, ʿAbd al-Raḥmān, being a distinguished historian and scholar of *ḥadīth* (the sayings of Muḥammad). Besides being famous as an astronomer and astrologer, Ibn Yūnus was widely acclaimed as a poet, and some of his poems have been preserved. Unfortunately nothing of consequence is known about his early life or education.

We know that as a young man Ibn Yūnus witnessed the Fatimid conquest of Egypt and the foundation of Cairo in 969. In the period from 977 to 996, which corresponds roughly to the reign of Caliph al-ʿAzīz, he made astronomical observations that were renewed by order of Caliph al-Ḥākim, who succeeded al-ʿAzīz in 996 at the age of eleven and was much interested in astrology. Ibn Yūnus' recorded observations continued until 1003.

Ibn Yūnus' major work was *al-Zīj al-Ḥākimī al-kabīr*, *zīj* meaning an astronomical handbook with tables. It is a particularly fine representative of a class of astronomical handbooks, numbering perhaps 200, compiled in medieval Islam. The *Zīj* of Ibn Yūnus was dedicated to Caliph al-Ḥākim and was aptly named *al-kabīr* ("large"). The text of the first forty-four of the eighty-one chapters of the original work is twice the length of the text of the

Zīj by al-Battānī and contains more than twice as many tables as the earlier work. The only extant chapters of the *Ḥākimī zīj* are in two unpublished manuscripts at Leiden and Oxford, comprising about three hundred folios. A manuscript in Paris contains an anonymous abridgment of part of the *Zīj* and is a source for some additional chapters up to chapter 57, and chapters 77–81.

The importance of Ibn Yūnus was realized in the West when the Leiden manuscript was first seriously studied. In 1804, Armand-Pierre Caussin de Perceval published the text of Ibn Yūnus' observational reports with a French translation. He also included the introduction to the *Zīj*, which contains the titles of the eighty-one chapters. J.-J. Sédillot's translation (now lost) of the Leiden and Paris manuscripts was summarized by Delambre in 1819. The German scholar Carl Schoy published several articles containing translations and analyses of individual chapters of the *Zīj* relating to spherical astronomy and sundial theory.

The *Ḥākimī zīj* deals with the standard topics of Islamic astronomy but is distinguished from all other extant *zījes* by beginning with a list of observations made by Ibn Yūnus and of observations made by some of his predecessors, quoted from their works. Despite the critical attitude of Ibn Yūnus toward these earlier scholars and his careful recording of their observations and some of his own, he completely neglects to describe the observations that he used in establishing his own planetary parameters—nor does he indicate whether he used any instruments for these observations. Indeed, the *Ḥākimī zīj* is a poor source of information about the instruments used by Ibn Yūnus. In his account of measurements of the latitude of Fusṭāṭ and of the obliquity of the ecliptic from solar meridian altitudes at the solstices, Ibn Yūnus states that he used an instrument provided by Caliph al-ʿAzīz and Caliph al-Ḥākim. Although he describes it only by mentioning that the divisions for each minute of arc were clearly visible on its scale, the instrument was probably a large meridian ring. His only other references to instruments used for simple observations are to an astrolabe and a gnomon.

In view of the paucity of this information, it is remarkable that the statement that Ibn Yūnus worked in a "well-equipped observatory" is often found in popular accounts of Islamic astronomy. A. Sayili, *The Observatory in Islam*, has shown how this notion gained acceptance in Western literature.

There are two sources, however, that might cast a little more light on the situation if their reliability could be established. First, the historian Ibn Ḥammād (*fl. ca.* 1200) mentions a copper instrument, resembling an astrolabe three cubits in diameter, that a contemporary of his had seen and associated with the Ḥākimī observations. Likewise the Yemenite Sultan al-Ashraf (*fl. ca.* 1290), who was an astronomer, records that al-Ḥākim had an armillary sphere consisting of nine rings, each of which weighed 2,000 pounds and was large enough for a man to ride through on horseback. The possibility that this large instrument was that known to have been constructed in Cairo about 1125—over a century after the death of Ibn Yūnus—cannot yet be discounted.

There is evidence that al-Ḥākim had a house on the Muqaṭṭam hills overlooking Cairo, which may have contained astronomical instruments: Ibn Yūnus is known to have visited this house on one occasion to make observations of Venus. Nevertheless, al-Ḥākim's unsuccessful attempt to build an observatory in Cairo took place after Ibn Yūnus' death; and the only locations mentioned by Ibn Yūnus in his own accounts of his observations are the Mosque of Ibn Naṣr al-Maghribī at al-Qarāfa, and the house of his great-grandfather Yūnus, in nearby Fusṭāṭ. A note written in the fifteenth century on the title folio of the Leiden manuscript of the *Ḥākimī zīj* states that Ibn Yūnus' observations were made in the area of Birkat al-Ḥabash in Fusṭāṭ.

Ibn Yūnus explains in the introduction to his *Zīj* that the work is intended to replace the *Mumtaḥan zīj* of Yaḥyā ibn Abī Manṣūr, prepared for the Abbasid Caliph al-Maʾmūn in Baghdad almost 200 years earlier. Ibn Yūnus reports the observations of some astronomers before his own time, in which what was observed was at variance with what was calculated with the tables of the *Mumtaḥan zīj*. When reporting his own observations, Ibn Yūnus often compares what he observed with what he had computed with the *Mumtaḥan* tables.

From the introduction and chapters 4, 5, and 6 of the *Ḥākimī zīj*, which contain the observation accounts, it is clear that Ibn Yūnus was familiar with the *zījes* of Ḥabash al-Ḥāsib, al-Battānī, and al-Nayrīzī, as well as the *Mumtaḥan zīj*. The observations made by Ḥabash that Ibn Yūnus quotes are not in the two extant versions of Ḥabash's *Zīj*. Ibn Yūnus also records observations made by al-Māhānī, whose works are not extant. He lists the planetary parameters of the *Mumtaḥan zīj*, and this has enabled the positive identification of at least the planetary tables in the only extant manuscript of this early work, which contains considerable spurious material. Ibn Yūnus also quotes observations made by the Banū Amājūr family in Baghdad; their five *zījes* are not extant. Other works quoted by Ibn Yūnus, although not necessarily directly, are the *zījes* of al-Nihāwandī, Ibn al-Adamī, the Banū Mūsā, Abū Maʿshar, Ibn al-Aʿlam, al-Ṣūfī, and Muḥammad al-Samarqandī; none of these works is extant, and Ibn Yūnus' references provide valuable information about them.

The observations described by Ibn Yūnus are of conjunctions of planets with each other and with Regulus, solar and lunar eclipses, and equinoxes; he also records measurements of the obliquity of the ecliptic (chapter 11) and of the maximum lunar latitude (chapter 38). All of these accounts are notable for their lack of information on observational procedures. The following passage is a translation of one of Ibn Yūnus' accounts of a planetary conjunction that he had observed:

A conjunction of Venus and Mercury in Gemini, observed in the western sky: The two planets were in conjunction after sunset on the night whose morning was Monday, the thirteenth day of Jumādā II 390 Hegira era. The time was approximately eight equinoctial hours after midday on Sunday, which was the fifth day of Khardādh, 369 Yazdigird era. Mercury was north of Venus and their latitude difference was a third of a degree. According to the *Mumtaḥan Zīj* their longitude difference was four and a half degrees [A. P. Caussin de Perceval, "Le livre de la grande table Hakémite," in *Notices et extraits des manuscrits de la Bibliothèque nationale*, 7 (1804), p. 217].

The Sunday mentioned was 19 May 1000, and computation with modern tables confirms that there was a conjunction in longitude that evening and that Mercury was indeed one-third degree north of Venus. About forty such planetary conjunctions observed by Ibn Yūnus are described in the *Zīj*.

The following passage is a translation of Ibn Yūnus' account of the lunar eclipse that occurred on 22 April 981 (Oppolzer no. 3379):

This lunar eclipse was in the month of Shawwāl, 370 Hegira era, on the night whose morning was Friday, the third day of Urdibihisht, 350 Yazdigird era. We gathered to observe this eclipse at al-Qarāfa, in the Mosque of Ibn Naṣr al-Maghribī. We perceived first contact when the altitude of the moon was approximately 21°. About a quarter of the lunar diameter was eclipsed, and reemergence occurred about a quarter of an hour before sunrise [A. P. Caussin de Perceval, p. 187].

Some of the thirty eclipses reported by Ibn Yūnus were used by Simon Newcomb in his determination of the secular acceleration of the moon. More recently, other observations recorded in the *Ḥākimī zīj* have been used by R. Newton.

The first chapter of the *Zīj* is the longest of the extant chapters and deals with the Muslim, Coptic, Syrian, and Persian calendars. There are detailed instructions for converting a date in one calendar to any of the other calendars, and extensive tables for that purpose. There are also tables for determining the dates of Lent and Easter in both the Syrian and the Coptic calendars. Such tables are found in several Islamic *zījes*.

Chapters 7 and 9, on planetary longitudes, contain instructions for determining true longitudes from the tables of mean motion and equations. No theory is described, but the theory underlying the instructions and tables is entirely Ptolemaic. The mean motions differ from those used by Ibn Yūnus' predecessors, and his values for the sun and moon were deemed sufficiently reliable by al-Ṭūsī to be used in the *Īlkhānī zīj* 250 years later. Ibn Yūnus' planetary tables are computed for both the Muslim and Persian calendars, and define the mean positions of the sun, moon, and planets, as well as the astrologically significant "comet" *al-kayd*, for over 2,700 Muslim and 1,800 Persian years from the respective epochs 622 and 632.

For the year 1003, Ibn Yūnus gives the solar apogee as Gemini 26;10° and the maximum solar equation as 2;0,30°, corresponding to a double eccentricity of 2;6,10° (where the solar deferent radius is 60). No solar observations made by Ibn Yūnus are recorded in the *Zīj*. He changes the values of the lunar epicyclic radius and the eccentricity from Ptolemy's 5;15° and 10;19°, also used in the *Mumtaḥan zīj*, to 5;1,14° and 11;7°, respectively (the latter is not used consistently), again without explanation. His planetary equation tables are identical with those of Ptolemy's *Handy Tables* and the *Mumtaḥan zīj* for Saturn, Jupiter, and Mars. For Venus, Ibn Yūnus assumes an eccentricity exactly half that of the sun and uses an epicyclic radius of 43;42 rather than Ptolemy's 43;10. For Mercury he adopts a maximum equation of 4;2°, an Indian parameter previously used in the *Zīj* of al-Khwārizmī, rather than Ptolemy's 3;2°. Ibn Yūnus' tables of equations for the moon, Venus, and Mercury contain the same inconsistencies as al-Battānī's tables for Venus, in that some of the columns are not adjusted for the new parameters; this is a fairly common feature in Islamic *zījes*. There is evidence that Ibn Yūnus was not altogether satisfied with his determination of the planetary apogees: the *Ḥākimī zīj* contains three different sets of values (chapters 6, 8, and 9).

In his discussion of solar and lunar distances (chapters 55, 56), Ibn Yūnus assumes a maximum solar parallax of 0;1,57°, instead of Ptolemy's value of 0;2,51°. Chapters 59–75, on parallax and eclipse theory and the associated tables, are not in the known manuscripts; and their recovery in other sources would be extremely valuable for the study of Islamic astronomy.

In chapter 38, on lunar and planetary latitudes, Ibn Yūnus states that he found the maximum lunar latitude to be 5;3°. Although he says that he measured it many times and repeatedly found this value, he does not say how the measurements were made. He did not pursue the suggestion of the Banū Amājūr that he quotes: that the maximum lunar latitude was not constant. His planetary latitude tables are derived from those in the *Almagest*, except in the case of Venus, for which he used values originally taken from the *Handy Tables*.

Ibn Yūnus measured the position of Regulus as Leo 15;55° in 1003. His value for the motion of the fixed stars is 1° in 70 1/4 Persian years (of 365 days) and apparently was computed by using his own observation of Regulus and that made by Hipparchus; it is the most accurate of all known Islamic values. He had information at his disposal from which he might have deduced that the motion of the planetary apogees was different from the motion of the fixed stars, but he chose to conclude that the apogees moved at the same rate as the stars (chapter 8).

The trigonometric functions used by Ibn Yūnus are functions of arcs rather than angles, and are computed for radius 60, as was standard in Islamic works. Chapter 10 of the *Zīj* contains a table of sines for each 0;10° of arc, computed to four significant sexagesimal digits. The values are seldom in error by more than ±2 in the fourth digit. Ibn Yūnus determined the sine of 1° to be 1;2,49,43,28 (to base 60), using a method equivalent to interpolating linearly between the values of sin x/x for $x =$ 15/16° and 9/8°. He then improved this value by a rather dubious technique to obtain 1;2,49,43,4. The accurate value to this degree of precision is 1;2,49,43,11. Ibn Yūnus' younger contemporary al-Bīrūnī was able to calculate the chord of a unit circle subtended by an angle of 1° correctly to five significant sexagesimal digits. Although in chapter 11 of the *Zīj* Ibn Yūnus tabulates the cotangent function to three sexagesimal digits for each ten minutes of arc, he does not take full advantage of

it. Many of the methods he suggests throughout the *Zīj* require divisions of sines by cosines; and he uses the cotangent function, which he calls the shadow, only when the argument is an altitude arc.

In spherical astronomy (chapters 12–54) Ibn Yūnus reached a very high level of sophistication. Although none of his formulas is explained, it seems probable that most of them were derived by means of orthogonal projections and analemma constructions, rather than by the application of the rules of spherical trigonometry that were being developed by Muslim scholars in Iraq and Persia. Altogether, there are several hundred formulas outlined in the *Zīj*, many of which are trivially equivalent. These are stated in words and without recourse to any symbols. For each method outlined, Ibn Yūnus generally gives at least one numerical example. The problems of spherical astronomy discussed in the *Ḥākimī zīj* are more varied than those in most major Islamic *zījes*, and the following examples are intended to illustrate the scope of the treatment.

Ibn Yūnus describes several methods for computing right and oblique ascensions (chapters 13, 14). He also computes both, the latter for each degree of the ecliptic and for each degree of terrestrial latitude from 1° to 48° (beyond which limit, according to Manṣūr ibn 'Irāq, "there is no one who studies this sort of thing or even thinks about it"). Ibn Yūnus discusses in great detail the determination of time and solar azimuth from solar altitude, and it will be clear from the tables mentioned below that he devoted much effort to these problems. Certain functions that he discusses in the text are also tabulated, such as the solar altitude in the prime vertical and the rising amplitude of the sun (that is, the distance of the rising sun from the east point). The problem of finding solar altitude from solar azimuth (chapter 24) is not so simple as the inverse problem; but Ibn Yūnus solves it in several ways, including the use of an algebraic method. He also tabulates the solar altitude for certain azimuths, such as that of the *qibla*, the direction of Mecca (chapter 28), and ten different azimuths (chapter 24), to be used for finding the meridian. Several geometric solutions to the problem of determining the *qibla*, a favorite of the Islamic astronomers, are also outlined. One of Ibn Yūnus' solutions is equivalent to successive applications of the cosine rule and sine rule for spherical triangles, but is derived by a projection method that was also used by the contemporary Egyptian scholar Ibn al-Haytham.

Particularly elegant solutions are presented for

finding the meridian from three solar observations on the same day (chapter 23) and for finding the time between two solar observations on the same day (chapter 33). The latter problem is solved by a direct application of the cosine rule for plane triangles, the earliest attested use of this rule. Ibn Yūnus transforms ecliptic to equatorial coordinates (chapter 39) by a method equivalent to the cosine rule for spherical triangles but probably derived by means of an analemma construction. His sundial theory (chapters 26, 27, 35) is also of considerable sophistication. It deals with horizontal and vertical sundials, the latter oriented in the meridian, the prime vertical, or a general direction inclined to both. He proves geometrically that for a horizontal sundial the gnomon shadow measures the altitude of the upper rim of the solar disk, and stresses the precautions to be taken when setting the gnomon on a marble slab to ensure that it is aligned correctly.

The chapters of the Zīj dealing with astrological calculations (77–81), although partially extant in the anonymous abridgment of the work, have never been studied. Ibn Yūnus was famous as an astrologer and, according to his biographers, devoted much time to making astrological predictions. His Kitāb bulūgh al-umniyya ("On the Attainment of Desire") consists of twelve chapters devoted to the significance of the heliacal risings of Sirius when the moon is in any of the twelve zodiacal signs, and to predictions based on the day of the week on which the first day of the Coptic year falls.

In chapter 10 of the Ḥākimī zīj Ibn Yūnus states that he had prepared a shorter version of his major work; this, unfortunately, is no longer extant. There are, however, numerous later zījes compiled in Egypt, Persia, and Yemen that are extant and contain material ultimately due to Ibn Yūnus. For example, the thirteenth-century Egyptian Muṣṭalaḥ zīj, as well the Īlkhānī zīj of al-Ṭūsī and the Zīj of Muhyi'l-Dīn al-Maghribī, both compiled at the observatory in Maragha, Persia, in the thirteenth century, relied on the Ḥākimī zīj. Likewise, the Mukhtār zīj by the thirteenth-century Yemenite astronomer Abu'l-ʿUqūl is based mainly on a zīj by Ibn Yūnus other than the Ḥākimī; and an anonymous fourteenth-century Yemenite zīj is adapted from the Ḥākimī zīj.

There are other sets of tables preserved in the manuscript sources and attributed to Ibn Yūnus that are distinct from those in the Ḥākimī zīj but based on them. First, Ibn Yūnus appears to be the author of tables of the sine and tangent functions for each minute of arc, as well as tables of solar declination for each minute of solar longitude. These sine tables display values of the sine function to five sexagesimal digits, which is roughly equivalent to nine decimal digits. The values are often in error in the fourth sexagesimal digit, however, so that it was a premature undertaking. Indeed, over four centuries passed before the compilation of the trigonometric tables in the Zīj of Ulugh Beg in Samarkand, in which values are also given to five sexagesimal digits for each minute of arc — but are generally correct. Second, it appears that Ibn Yūnus was the author of an extensive set of tables, called al-Taʿdīl al-muḥkam, that display the equations of the sun and moon; the latter are of particular interest. They are based on those in the Ḥākimī zīj but are arranged so as to facilitate computation of the lunar position: the equation is tabulated as a function of the double elongation and mean anomaly, both of which can be taken from the mean motion tables; thus there is no need to find the true anomaly. The table, which accurately defines the Ptolemaic lunar equation for Ibn Yūnus' parameters, contains over 34,000 entries.

Ibn Yūnus' second major work was part of the corpus of spherical astronomical tables for timekeeping used in Cairo until the nineteenth century. It is difficult to ascertain precisely how many tables in this corpus, which later became known as the Kitāb ghayat al-intifaʿ ("Very Useful Tables"), were actually computed by Ibn Yūnus. Some appear to have been compiled by the late thirteenth-century astronomer al-Maqsī. The corpus exists in numerous manuscript sources, each containing different arrangements of the tables or only selected sets of tables; and in its entirety the corpus consists of about 200 pages of tables, most of which contain 180 entries. The tables are generally rather accurately computed and are all based on Ibn Yūnus' values of 30;0° for the latitude of Cairo and 23;35° for the obliquity of the ecliptic.

The main tables in the corpus display the time since sunrise, the time remaining to midday, and the solar azimuth as functions of the solar altitude and solar longitude. Entries are tabulated for each degree of solar altitude and longitude, and each of the three sets contains over ten thousand entries. The remaining tables in the corpus are of spherical astronomical functions, some of which relate to the determination of the five daily prayers of Islam.

The times of Muslim prayer are defined with reference to the apparent daily motion of the sun across the sky and vary throughout the year. The prayers must be performed within certain intervals of time, which are variously defined. The following general definitions underlie the tables in the corpus. The day is considered to begin at sunset, and the evening prayer is performed between sunset and nightfall. The permitted interval for the night prayer begins at nightfall. The interval for the morning prayer begins at daybreak and the prayer must be completed by sunrise. The period for the noon prayer begins when the sun is on the meridian, and that for the afternoon prayer begins when the shadow of any object is equal to its midday shadow plus the length of the object.

Examples of functions relating to the prayer times, which are tabulated in the corpus for each degree of solar longitude, include the following:

1. The length of morning and evening twilights, defining the permitted times for the morning and evening prayers, based on the assumption that twilight appears or disappears when the sun reaches a particular angle of depression below the horizon. (The angles suggested by Ibn Yūnus in the *Ḥākimī zīj* are 18° for both phenomena, but in a later work he suggests 20° and 16° for morning and evening, respectively. The main twilight tables in the corpus are based on 19° and 17°.)

2. The time from nightfall to daybreak, defining the permitted interval for the night prayer.

3. The time from sunrise to midday.

4. The time from midday to the beginning of the time for the afternoon prayer, defining the interval for the noon prayer; and the time from the beginning of the afternoon prayer to sunset, defining the interval for the afternoon prayer.

5. Corrections to the semidiurnal arc for the effect of refraction at the horizon, apparently based on the assumption that the true horizon is about 2/3° below the visible horizon. (These corrections, which are specifically attributed to Ibn Yūnus, represent the earliest attested quantitative estimate of the effect of refraction on horizon phenomena.)

6. The solar altitude in the azimuth of Mecca, and the time when the sun has this azimuth. (Such tables were used to establish the direction of prayer and the orientation of *miḥrābs* in mosques.)

Virtually all later Egyptian prayer tables until the nineteenth century were based on those in this main corpus. In certain cases the original tables were well-disguised, the entries being written out in words for each day of the Coptic year or a given Muslim year. The impressive developments in astronomical timekeeping in thirteenth-century Yemen and fourteenth-century Syria, particularly the tables of Abu'l-ʿUqūl for Taʿizz and of al-

Khalīlī for Damascus, also owe their inspiration to the main Cairo corpus.

It is clear from the biography of Ibn Yūnus by his contemporary al-Musabbiḥī, preserved in the writings of later authors, that Ibn Yūnus was an eccentric. Al-Musabbiḥī describes him as a careless and absent-minded man who dressed shabbily and had a comic appearance. One day, when he was in good health, he predicted his own death in seven days. He attended to his personal business, locked himself in his house, and washed the ink off his manuscripts. He then recited the Koran until he died—on the day he had predicted. According to his biographer, Ibn Yūnus' son was so stupid that he sold his father's papers by the pound in the soap market.

BIBLIOGRAPHY

I. ORIGINAL WORKS. Ibn Yūnus' works are the following:

1. *al-Zīj al-Ḥākimī al-kabīr*: MS Leiden Cod. Or. 143 contains chs. 1–22; MS Oxford Hunt. 331 contains chs. 21–44; MS Paris B.N. ar. 2496 is an anonymous abridgment containing some additional chs. up to 57 and chs. 77–81; MS Leiden Cod. Or. 2813 contains part of ch. 1. Extracts from Ibn Yūnus' mean motion tables are in numerous later sources, such as MS Princeton Yahuda 3475, fols. 16r–21r; and MS Cairo Dār al-Kutub, *mīqāt* 116M.

2. Other *zījes* are not extant. A treatise on the compilation of solar, lunar, and planetary ephemerides, which appears to be taken from a *zīj* by Ibn Yūnus other than the *Ḥākimī*, survives in MS Cairo Dār al-Kutub, *mīqāt* 116M, fols. 8v–9r; and probably in MS Berlin Ahlwardt no. 5742, pt. 2. A fragment of an Egyptian *zīj* containing tables due to Ibn Yūnus is MS Berlin Ahlwardt 5733. The late thirteenth-century Yemenite *Mukhtār zīj*, extant in MS British Museum 768 (Or. 3624), appears to be based on a *zīj* by Ibn Yūnus compiled prior to the *Ḥākimī zīj*.

The following *zījes* are incorrectly attributed to Ibn Yūnus on their title folios: MS Aleppo Awqāf 947; MS Cairo Ṭalʿat, *mīqāt* 138; MSS Paris B.N. ar. 2520 and 2513. The first two are quite unrelated to the Egyptian astronomer. The two Paris MSS are copies of the thirteenth-century Egyptian *Muṣṭalaḥ zīj* and a later recension: they both contain material due to Ibn Yūnus. Two treatises purporting to be commentaries on a *zīj* by Ibn Yūnus—MS Gotha Forschungsbibliothek A1401 and MS Cairo Dār al-Kutub, *mīqāt* 1106—are based on the *Muṣṭalaḥ zīj*.

Short notices on topics in spherical astronomy attributed to Ibn Yūnus are in MS Milan Ambrosiana 281e (C49) and MS Paris B.N. ar. 2506.

3. *Kitāb ghāyat al-intifāʿ* ("Very Useful Tables," a later title given to the corpus). The following sources

contain most of the tables: MS Dublin Chester Beatty 3673 and MS Cairo Dār al-Kutub, *mīqāt* 108.

Ibn Yūnus' original solar azimuth tables, entitled *Kitāb al-samt*, are extant in MS Dublin Chester Beatty no. 3673, pt. 1; MS Gotha Forschungsbibliothek no. A1410, pt. 1; MS Cairo Dār al-Kutub, *mīqāt* 137M; and MS Cairo Azhar, *falak* no. 4382, pt. 2.

The tables of time since sunrise, entitled *Kitāb al-dāʾir* and associated with al-Maqsī (*fl.* 1275), are in MS Gotha Forschungsbibliothek A1402. The hour-angle tables and numerous prayer tables in the version by Ibn al-Kattānī (*fl.* 1360) are preserved in MS Istanbul Kiliç Ali Paša 684. The hour-angle tables, entitled *Kitāb fadl al-dāʾir*, are copied separately in MS Cairo Taymūriyya, *riyāḍiyyāt* 191; and MS Cairo Azhar, *falak* no. 4382, pt. 1; they are copied together with the tables of time since sunrise in MS Dublin Chester Beatty no. 3673, pt. 2; and MS Dublin Chester Beatty 4078. The edition of the corpus by al-Bakhāniqī (*fl.* 1350) is extant in MS Cairo Dār al-Kutub, *mīqāt* 53 and 108.

There are literally dozens of MSS that contain extracts from the corpus in varying degrees of confusion.

MSS Cairo Taymūriyya, *riyāḍiyyāt* 354; and Dār al-Kutub, *mīqāt* 1207, together constitute a corpus of tables for timekeeping computed for the latitude of Alexandria. In the first the tables are falsely attributed to Ibn Yūnus.

4. *Kitāb al-jayb* (sine tables) are extant in MS Berlin Ahlwardt no. 5752, pt. 1; and MS Damascus Ẓāhiriyya 3109.

5. *Kitāb al-ẓill* (cotangent tables) apparently are not extant. The tangent tables in MS Berlin Ahlwardt no. 5767, pt. 3, attributed to Ibn Yūnus are not based on the cotangent tables in the *Ḥākimī zīj*.

6. *Kitāb al-mayl* (solar declination tables) are MS Berlin Ahlwardt 5752,2.

7. *Kitāb al-taʿdīl al-muḥkam* (solar and lunar equation tables) are extant in MS Cairo Dār al-Kutub, *mīqāt* 29, which contains the complete set of lunar tables; MS Gotha Forschungsbibliothek no. A1410, pt. 2, which contains an incomplete set; and MS British Museum Or. 3624, fols. 111v–129r, 113v–151r, which contains the solar tables and a related set of lunar tables.

8. A short treatise on a candle clock is in MS Beirut St. Joseph, Arabe 223/12. This is attributed to Ibn Yūnus al Miṣrī (the Egyptian) in the introduction but is attributed by the Syrian engineer al-Jazarī (*fl. ca.* 1200) to Yūnus al-Aṣṭurlābī (the astrolabe maker), who may not be identical with the celebrated Egyptian astronomer. On the clock itself, see E. S. Kennedy and W. Ukashah, "The Chandelier Clock of Ibn Yūnis," in *Isis*, **60** (1969), 543–545.

9. *Kitāb bulūgh al-umniyya fī mā yataʿallaq biṭulūʿ al-Shiʿrā l-yamāniyya* (astrological treatise) is in MS Manchester Mingana 927 (916); MS Gotha Forschungsbibliothek A1459; and MS Cairo Dār al-Kutub, *majāmīʿ* 289.

10. The poem on the times of prayer attributed to Ibn Yūnus in MS Cairo Dār al-Kutub, *mīqāt* 181M, fols. 46v–48r, also occurs in two corrupt versions attributed to the Imām al-Shāfiʿī in MSS Berlin Ahlwardt 5700, fol. 11r, and 5820, fol. 65r. Poems by Ibn Yūnus are found in several medieval Arabic anthologies.

II. SECONDARY LITERATURE. Early studies of the *Ḥākimī zīj* are A. P. Caussin de Perceval, "Le livre de la grande table Hakémite," in *Notices et extraits des manuscrits de la Bibliothèque nationale*, **7** (1804), 16–240, on the observation accounts; and J.-B. Delambre, *Histoire de l'astronomie du moyen âge* (Paris, 1819, repr. New York–London, 1965), containing a summary of the contents of the *Zīj*. The major studies by Carl Schoy on Ibn Yūnus are his "Beiträge zur arabischen Trigonometrie," in *Isis*, **5** (1923), 364–399; *Gnomonik der Araber*, which is I, pt. 6, of E. von Bassermann-Jordan, ed., *Die Geschichte der Zeitmessung und der Uhren* (Berlin–Leipzig, 1923); and *Über den Gnomonschatten und die Schattentafeln der arabischen Astronomie* (Hannover, 1923). Articles by Schoy on individual chapters of the *Ḥākimī zīj* were published in *Annalen der Hydrographie und maritimen Meteorologie*, **48** (1920), 97–111; **49** (1921), 124–133; and **50** (1922), 3–20, 265–271. A more recent study of the spherical astronomy in the *Ḥākimī zīj* is D. A. King, "The Astronomical Works of Ibn Yūnus" (Ph.D. diss., Yale University, 1972). The tables entitled *Kitāb al-taʿdīl al-muḥkam* are discussed in D. A. King, "A Double-Argument Table for the Lunar Equation Attributed to Ibn Yūnus," in *Centaurus*, **18** (1974), 129–146.

On the observatories in medieval Cairo, see A. Sayili, *The Observatory in Islam* (Ankara, 1960), 130–156, 167–175.

For modern studies relying on data from Ibn Yūnus' observational accounts, see S. Newcomb, "Researches on the Motion of the Moon. Part I . . .," in *Washington Observations for 1875* (1878), app. 2; and R. Newton, *Ancient Astronomical Observations and the Acceleration of the Earth and Moon* (Baltimore, 1970).

On the corpus of spherical astronomical tables for Cairo attributed to Ibn Yūnus, see D. A. King, "Ibn Yūnus' *Very Useful Tables* for Reckoning Time by the Sun," in *Archive for History of Exact Sciences*, **10** (1973), 342–394. The problems of their attribution, and all other known medieval tables for regulating the times of prayer, are discussed in D. A. King, *Studies on Astronomical Timekeeping in Medieval Islam*, which is in preparation.

DAVID A. KING

ZANOTTI, EUSTACHIO (*b.* Bologna, Italy, 27 November 1709; *d.* Bologna, 15 May 1782)

Like the astronomer Eustachio Manfredi, his godfather, Zanotti belonged to a prominent family distinguished in the arts, letters, and sciences. The son of Gian Pietro Zanotti and Costanza

Gambari, he was educated by the Jesuits and entered the University of Bologna, becoming Manfredi's assistant at the Institute of Sciences in 1729. He graduated in philosophy in 1730 and obtained his first university post, as reader in mechanics at Bologna, in 1738, after presenting his trial lecture on the Newtonian theory of light. The following year he succeeded Manfredi as director of the Institute observatory, a post to which he dedicated himself almost exclusively for the next forty years, never marrying and declining all offers from other universities. He began teaching hydraulics at the university in 1760, having been requested by the government to supervise works on rivers and waterways. His publications in this field include a work on the characteristics of riverbeds near the sea (1760) that remained in print for almost a century. Zanotti wrote the last part of Manfredi's *Elementi della geometria*, "according to the method of indivisibles"; and his lucid and informative *Trattato teorico-pratico di prospettiva* (1766) was intended for painters as well as mathematicians.

Zanotti established a reputation as an astronomer even before Manfredi's death, through the discovery of two comets, to the second of which (1739) he attributed a parabolic orbit. In 1741, under his direction, the new instruments that Manfredi had ordered from Sisson's were installed at the Bologna observatory: a mural quadrant 1.2 meters in radius and a transit instrument with a focal length of about one meter. In 1780 he added a movable equatorial telescope made by Dollond's.

With the acquisition of Sisson's instruments, Zanotti's observatory became one of the finest in Europe. In 1748 and 1749, with his assistants G. Brunelli and Petronio Matteucci, he carried out repeated observations of the sun and planets, and compiled a catalog of 447 stars, all but thirty-three of them within the zodiac. The work was published with additions in 1750 as an appendix to the new edition of Manfredi's introductory volume to his ephemerides. Zanotti continued to publish the ephemerides with scrupulous care: three volumes covered the period 1751–1774, and a fourth was published posthumously by Matteucci in 1786.

Zanotti's principal observations and descriptions, including some on occultations of stars by the moon, concern six comets (1737, 1739, 1742, 1743–1744, Halley's comet of 1758, and 1769), four lunar eclipses (December 1739, January 1740, November 1745, June 1750), three solar eclipses (August 1738, July 1748, January 1750), the aurora borealis (December 1737, March 1739), and

transits of Mercury (1743, 1753) and of Venus (1751) on the sun.

In 1750 Zanotti was invited by the Paris Academy of Sciences to participate in a major international research project, the main purpose of which was to measure the lunar parallax. His observations provided the program with some of its most accurate results.

Zanotti's accomplishments also included the restoration in 1776 of Gian Domenico Cassini's sundial in the church of San Petronio. The displaced perforated roofing slab forming the gnomon was raised slightly, restoring the instrument to its original height. The old deformed iron ship representing the meridian was removed and a solid foundation was laid as a base for new level marble slabs with the new brass meridian strip. Accurate geodetic and topographic measurements made in 1904 and 1925 have verified that the instrument has remained as Zanotti left it, that is, in the position that perfectly reproduces Cassini's original conditions of construction.

According to L. Palcani-Caccianemici, his collaborator and principal biographer, Zanotti was also a pioneer in the study of variable stars, a little-understood phenomenon that was then considered to represent an error of vision or an effect caused by the intervening atmosphere. Zanotti, however, maintained that changes of light occur even when the possibility of such causes is entirely ruled out. "If you observe with a telescope two stars extremely near to each other," he said, "you will see that one remains exactly the same and that the other, altered in intensity, no longer appears as before."

Unfortunately, no trace of these observations appears in Zanotti's published writings, possibly because he did not wish to seem to be questioning the incorruptibility and constancy of the heavens—a subject about which the Aristotelians who controlled the University of Bologna were particularly sensitive and uncompromising.

BIBLIOGRAPHY

I. ORIGINAL WORKS. Most of Zanotti's astronomical memoirs appeared in the *Commentarii* of the Istituto e Accademia delle scienze di Bologna, beginning with **2**, pt. 1 (1745); the last one appeared in **7** (1791)—see index. There are also three papers, in English, in *Philosophical Transactions of the Royal Society*: on the aurora borealis, **41** (1741), 593–601; on the comet of 1739, *ibid.*, 809; and on the 1761 transit of Venus, **52** (1761), 399–414.

His most important separately published works are

Ephemerides motuum coelestium ex anno 1751 ad annum 1786, 3 vols. (Bologna, 1750–1774); *Trattato teorico-pratico di prospettiva* (Bologna, 1766); and *La meridiana del tempio di San Petronio rinnovata l'anno 1776* (Bologna, 1779).

II. SECONDARY LITERATURE. See the following, listed chronologically: L. Palcani-Caccianemici, *De vita Eustachii Zanotti commentarius* (Bologna, 1782), translated into Italian by G. A. Maggi as "Elogio di Eustachio Zanotti" and prefixed, with a bibliography, to the new ed. of Zanotti's *Trattato teorico-pratico di prospettiva* (Milan, 1825); *Vita di Eustachio Zanotti* (n.p., n.d.), an extract from *Giornale dei letterati* (Pisa), **58** (1785), 175–197; G. Fantuzzi, *Notizie degli scrittori bolognesi*, VIII (Bologna, 1790; repr. 1965), 265–270; Noël Poudra, *Histoire de la perspective* (Paris, 1864), 529–533; and P. Riccardi, *Biblioteca matematica italiana*, II (Modena, 1873–1876; repr. Milan, 1952), 651–657.

More recent works include M. Rajna, "L'astronomia in Bologna," in *Memorie della Società degli spettroscopisti italiani*, **32** (1903), 241–250, esp. 245; Federigo Guarducci, *La meridiana di Gian Domenico Cassini nel tempio di San Petronio di Bologna riveduta nel 1904 e nel 1925* (Bologna, 1925); E. Bortolotti, *La storia della matematica nella Università di Bologna* (Bologna, 1947), 177–178; G. Horn d'Arturo, *Piccola enciclopedia astronomica*, II (Bologna, 1960), 364; and Anna Maria Matteucci, *Carlo Francesco Dotti e l'architettura bolognese del settecento*, 2nd ed. (Bologna, 1969), 44–49, *passim*.

GIORGIO TABARRONI

ZARANKIEWICZ, KAZIMIERZ (*b.* Czestochowa, Poland, 2 May 1902; *d.* London, England, 5 September 1959)

Zarankiewicz's contributions to mathematics were in topology, the theory of graphs, the theory of complex functions, number theory, and mathematical education. In addition, he founded and for several years headed the Polish Astronautical Society.

Zarankiewicz was born and raised in a moderately well-to-do family. After obtaining his baccalaureate degree in 1919 in Bedzin, near Czestochowa, he studied mathematics at the University of Warsaw. He was awarded a Ph.D. there in 1923 for a dissertation (published in 1927) on the cut points in connected sets, and in 1924 he was made assistant to the professor of mathematics at the Warsaw Polytechnic. In 1929, following publication of his habilitation essay on a topological property of the plane (concerning the mutual cuttings of three regions and three continua), Zarankiewicz became *Dozent* in mathematics. He spent the aca-

demic year 1930–1931 working with Karl Menger at Vienna and with Richard von Mises at Berlin, where he collaborated with Stefan Bergman and other mathematicians. Upon returning to Warsaw, Zarankiewicz was assigned to teach a course in rational mechanics at the Polytechnic and courses in mathematics and statistics at the High Agricultural College. In 1936 he was invited to the University of Tomsk to lecture for a semester on conformal mappings, particularly on several problems that he had solved. He was named substitute for the professor at the Warsaw Polytechnic in 1937; but his nomination to the professorship (1939) was not confirmed until after the war.

During the German occupation of Poland, Zarankiewicz taught mathematics, clandestinely, to underground groups of high school and college students. In 1944 he was deported to a forced labor camp in Germany. Returning to the ruins of Warsaw in 1945, he resumed his courses at the Polytechnic and continued them for the rest of his life.

Zarankiewicz was appointed full professor in 1948 and spent several months of that year working at Harvard and at several other American universities. From 1949 to 1957 he supervised in Poland the Mathematical Olympics for high school students, remaining a member of its central board thereafter. At the same time he was a member of the editorial committees of *Applied Mechanics Reviews* and *Matematyka*, a Polish journal written primarily for secondary-school teachers. From 1948 to 1951 Zarankiewicz headed the Warsaw section of the Polish Mathematical Society. He maintained a long-standing active interest in astronautics and in the organization in Poland of a society founded in 1956 devoted to this field. Zarankiewicz died in London while presiding over a plenary session of the Tenth Congress of the International Astronautical Federation, of which he was vice-president. His funeral was held in Warsaw, and one of the city's streets is named for him. Zarankiewicz's topological writings deal mainly with cut points, that is, those points which disconnect (and locally disconnect) the continua, and with the continua that disconnect the spaces. In 1926 he showed, among other things, that if C is a locally connected continuum (a continuous image of an interval), then the set $\tau(C)$ of all the cut points of C possesses a special structure, which he characterized. In particular, the closures of the constituents of $\tau(C)$ are dendrites, that is, one-dimensional, acyclic, locally connected continua. In his doctoral dissertation Zarankiewicz introduced and investigated the important notion of the continua of convergence. He characterized the locally connected continua by the equivalence, for their closed subsets F, of the connectedness and of the semicontinuity of the set $C \setminus F$ between all the pairs of its points. He also characterized the dendrites C by the structure of the set $C \setminus \tau(C)$ and—independently of Pavel Urysohn—the hereditarily locally connected continua by the absence, among their subsets, of continua of convergence (1927). In 1932 and in 1951 Zarankiewicz resumed and extended the study of the set $\tau(C)$ by a series of remarkable theorems. In particular, he gave a new definition of the cyclic element in G. T. Whyburn's sense, for the locally connected continua.

Zarankiewicz's studies of the cutting of spaces by continua were concerned especially with local cuttings of the plane or, which is topologically equivalent, of the sphere. In publications of 1927, 1929, and 1932, he established interesting topological characterizations of the circumference, of the straight line, and of several other lines with the aid of the number of their connectedness points, another notion that he originated. These theorems, which are more quantitative than qualitative, reflect Zarankiewicz's tendency to seek numerical solutions in every field of mathematics in which he worked, For example, generalizing R. L. Moore's theorem concerning triods in the plane, he showed that in Euclidean spaces of more than two dimensions, every family of disjoint continua each of which locally cuts the space at a point that cuts locally itself (*doppelt zerlegender Punkt*) is, at most, countable (1934).

Zarankiewicz's last publication in topology (1952), written with C. Kuratowski, deals with a problem that is still unsolved: Given n disjoint regions in the plane (or on the sphere) with connected boundaries $R_1, R_2, \cdots, R_n$ and k continua $C_1, C_2, \cdots, C_k$, each of which meets each of these regions, what is the minimum number $s_{k,n}$ of couples i,j such that C_i cuts R_j (where $i = 1, 2, \cdots, k$ and $j = 1, 2, \cdots, n$)? Zarankiewicz's conjecture is that $s_{k,n} = (k - 2)(n - 2)$ for all integers $k \geq 2$ and $n \geq 2$. In 1928 he showed that $s_{3,3} = 1$ and, in the joint work of 1952, that the presumed formula holds for all $k \geq 4$ and $n \leq 4$.

In theory of graphs Zarankiewicz developed, among other topics, a criterion for the existence of a complete subgraph of highest possible order in every graph of a given order in which the minimum number of edges arising from a vertex is sufficiently high (1947). Later, Pál Turán improved this criterion and devoted an interesting study to it. Zar-

ankiewicz, in publications of 1953 and 1954, solved, independently of K. Urbanik, a problem posed by Turán by showing that if A and B are finite sets of the plane, composed of a and b points, respectively, and if each point of A is joined by a simple arc to all the points of B in such a way that outside of A and B every point of intersection belongs to two arcs, then the number of these points of intersection is at least equal to

$$\mathrm{E}(\tfrac{1}{2}a) \cdot \mathrm{E}(\tfrac{1}{2}a - 1) \cdot \mathrm{E}(\tfrac{1}{2}b) \cdot \mathrm{E}(\tfrac{1}{2}b - 1),$$

and that this minimum is attained. In 1951 Zarankiewicz posed the problem of finding the least number $k_j(n)$ such that every set of $k_j(n)$ points of a plane net of n^2 points (where $n > 3$) contains j^2 points on j lines and on j columns. Several other authors have subsequently treated this problem.

Zarankiewicz's works on complex functions (1934, 1938, 1956) deal principally with the kernel (*Kernfunktion*) and its applications. Given a complete system $\{\phi_\nu(z)\}$, where $\nu = 1, 2, \cdots$, of orthonormal analytic functions in a domain D of the complex plane of $z = x + iy$, the function $K_D(z,\zeta) = \sum_{\nu=1}^{\infty} \phi_\nu(z) \overline{\phi_\nu(\zeta)}$ is called the kernel of the domain D. It is known that it exists for all z and ζ of D and depends only on D; that if D is simply connected— that is, if the boundary of D is connected—the function $W(z) = \int_0^z K_D(z,\zeta)dz$ transforms D onto the interior of the circle $|W| < c$, where c is a constant; that the function K_D is a relative invariant—that is,

$$K_D(z,\bar{z}) = K_{D^*}(z^*[z], \overline{z^*[z]}) \cdot |dz^*(z)/dz|^2$$

for every analytic function z^*z mapping the domain D of the complex z-plane onto the domain D^* of the complex z^*-plane—and, consequently, that the formula

$$ds_D^2(z) = K_D(z,\bar{z}) \cdot |dz|^2 =$$
$$K_{D^*}(z^*,\overline{z^*}) \cdot |dz^*|^2 = ds_{D^*}^2(z^*)$$

represents the square of the length of the line or element of an invariant metric; that the curvature of the metric

$$J_D(z,\bar{z}) = -\frac{2}{K_D(z,\bar{z})} \cdot \frac{d^2 \log K_D(z,\bar{z})}{dz d\bar{z}}$$

is an absolute invariant of the conformal mappings; and that if the boundary of D is connected, $J_D(z,\bar{z})$ is a constant.

Zarankiewicz showed that when the boundary of D is doubly connected—that is, has exactly two components—the function $J_D(z,\bar{z})$ is no longer constant; in this case he represented it by doubly periodic functions. He established a criterion for recognizing, with the aid of this representation, when it is that a boundary domain with two components can be transformed conformally into another domain of this type. (P. P. Kufarev determined the minimum domain, that is, into which every domain of which the boundary consists of two components is transformable by the function $W[z]$.) This Zarankiewicz result played an important role in the development of the theory of the kernel and its generalizations to several variables, notably to pseudo-conformal transformations in space of more than three dimensions.

In number theory Zarankiewicz devoted particular attention to what are called triangular numbers—that is, triplets of integers equal to the lengths of the sides of right triangles (1949). His ideas inspired a work by Sierpiński (1954), at the end of which the author reproduces an ingenious example, inspired by Zarankiewicz, of a decomposition of the set of natural numbers into two disjoint classes, neither of which contains a triplet of consecutive numbers or an infinite arithmetic progression.

BIBLIOGRAPHY

I. ORIGINAL WORKS. A list of Zarankiewicz's 45 publications is in *Colloquium mathematicum*, **12** (1964), 285–288. The most important are "Sur les points de division dans les ensembles connexes," in *Fundamenta mathematicae*, **9** (1927), 124–171; "Über eine topologische Eigenschaft der Ebene," *ibid.*, **11** (1928), 19–26; "Uber die lokale Zerschneidung der Ebene," in *Monatshefte für Mathematik und Physik*, **39** (1932), 43–45; "Sur la représentation conforme d'un domaine doublement connexe sur un anneau circulaire," in *Comptes rendus . . . de l'Académie des sciences*, **198** (1934), 1347–1349; "Über doppeltzerlegende Punkte," in *Fundamenta mathematicae*, **23** (1934), 166–171; "O liczbach trójkątowych" ("On Triangular Numbers"), in *Matematyka*, **2** (1949), nos. 4–5; "Sur un problème concernant les coupures des régions par des continus," in *Fundamenta mathematicae*, **39** (1952), 15–24, written with C. Kuratowski; and "On a Problem of P. Turán Concerning Graphs," *ibid.*, **41** (1954), 137–145.

II. SECONDARY LITERATURE. See S. Bergman, R. Duda, B. Knaster, Jan Mycielski, and A. Schinzel, "Kazimierz Zarankiewicz," in *Wiadomości matematyczne*, 2nd ser., **9** (1966), 175–184 (in Polish), also in *Colloquium mathematicum*, **12** (1964), 277–288 (in French), which contains a list of Zarankiewicz's works.

BRONISLAW KNASTER

ZENODORUS (*b.* Athens [?]; *fl.* early second century B.C.)

Zenodorus is known to have been the author of a treatise on isoperimetric figures—plane figures of equal perimeter but differing areas, and solid figures of equal surface but differing volumes.[1] This has not survived as such, but it is epitomized in Pappus' *Collection*, in the commentary by Theon of Alexandria on Ptolemy's *Almagest*, and in the anonymous *Introduction to the Almagest*.

Older writers placed the date of Zenodorus in the fifth century B.C., but this was through a mistaken identification with a Zenodorus who is said by Proclus to have belonged "to the succession of Oenopides."[2] From several references by Zenodorus to Archimedes, Nokk rightly concluded that he must have flourished after, say, 200 B.C.[3] Because Quintilian showed awareness of isoperimetry, F. Hultsch and M. Cantor conjectured a lower limit of A.D. 90 for his life; but Zenodorus made no claim to have been the only, or even the first, person to have written on the subject and the deduction is erroneous.[4] Until recently all that could be said with certainty was that he lived after Archimedes and before Pappus, say 200 B.C.–A.D. 300; but it is now established that he must have flourished in the early part of the second century B.C. A fragment from a biography of the Epicurean philosopher Philonides, found in the Herculaneum papyrus roll no. 1044, mentions among his acquaintances a Zenodorus at least once and perhaps twice. In publishing the fragment, W. Crönert identified him with the mathematician.[5] G. J. Toomer, in an elaborate study of occurrences of the name, concluded that unless Zenodorus was a Hellenized Semite (which is not impossible), the comparative rarity of the name confirms Crönert's identification.[6] This is made certain by the fact that in the Arabic translation of Diocles' treatise *On Burning Mirrors*, which has been discovered and edited by Toomer, Zenodorus is mentioned as having posed a problem to Diocles. Toomer's literal translation reads:

> The book of Diocles on burning mirrors. He said: Pythion the geometer, who was of the people of Thasos, wrote a letter to Conon in which he asked him how to find a mirror surface such that when it is placed facing the sun the rays reflected from it meet the circumference of a circle. And when Zenodorus the astronomer came down to Arcadia and was introduced [?] to us, he asked us how to find a mirror surface such that when it is placed facing the sun the rays reflected from it meet a point and thus cause burning. So we want to explain the answer to the

problem posed by Pythion and to that posed by Zenodorus; in the course of this we shall make use of the premises established by our predecessors.[7]

It is no bar to the identification of this Zenodorus with the author of the isoperimetric propositions that he is here called an astronomer. There was considerable overlap between mathematics and astronomy—Euclid, Archimedes, and Apollonius are notable examples—and Zenodorus may well have written astronomical works of which we have no knowledge. A Vatican manuscript gives a catalog of astronomers—οἱ περὶ τοῦ πόλου συντάξαντες—which includes the name Zenodorus.[8] In accordance with the principle of not multiplying entities unnecessarily, it would seem that he, too, should be identified with the mathematician.

The Herculaneum fragments mention two visits by Zenodorus to Athens. On the onomastic evidence he could be from Cyrene, or Ptolemaic Egypt, or possibly from Chios or Erythrae. But the name is attested eight or nine times in Athens; and on the assumption that he was an Athenian, Toomer has plausibly identified him with a member of the Lamptrai family mentioned in an inscription that lists contributions for some unknown purpose during the archonship of Hermogenes (183–182 B.C.).[9]

It is only in Theon's commentary that the isoperimetric propositions are specifically attributed to Zenodorus, but the passages in Pappus' *Collection* and the *Introduction* are so similar that they also must be derived from him. They are not, however, simply lifted from Zenodorus: there are considerable differences in the order and wording of the propositions in the three sources, and the question which is nearest to the original has given rise to some discussion. In all probability Pappus, like Theon, reproduced the propositions of Zenodorus at the relevant point in his commentary on the first book of the *Almagest*, where Ptolemy says, "Among different figures having an equal perimeter, since that which has the more angles is greater, of plane figures the circle is the greatest and of solid figures the sphere."[10] If so, this may have been the most exact reproduction of Zenodorus' text, ascribed to him by name, as in Theon; when he came to compile his *Collection*, Pappus varied the presentation, added the proposition "Of all segments of a circle having equal circumferences, the semicircle is the greatest in area," and proceeded to a disquisition on the semiregular solids of Archimedes.[11] Theon would have drawn upon Pappus, and the anonymous author of the *Introduction* upon both.

It would appear that Zenodorus' treatise contained fourteen propositions. There is agreement in the three versions that the first was "Of regular polygons having the same perimeter, the greater is that which has the more angles." The final proposition, stated but not actually proved, was almost certainly "If a sphere and a regular polyhedron have the same surface [area], the sphere is the greater." In between came such propositions as the following:

"If a circle and a regular polygon have the same perimeter, the circle is the greater."

"If on the base of an isosceles triangle there be set up a non-isosceles triangle having the same perimeter, the isosceles triangle is the greater."

"Given two similar right-angled triangles, the square on the sum of the hypotenuses is equal to the sum of the squares on the corresponding sides taken together."

"If on unequal bases there be set up two similar isosceles triangles, and on the same bases there be set up two dissimilar isosceles triangles having together the same perimeter as the two similar triangles, the sum of the similar triangles is greater than the sum of the dissimilar triangles."

"Among polygons with an equal perimeter and an equal number of sides, the regular polygon is the greatest."

"If a regular polygon [with an even number of sides] revolves about one of the longest diagonals, there is generated a solid bounded by conical surfaces that is less than the sphere having the same surface."

"Each of the five regular solids is less than the sphere with equal surface."

There is no little subtlety in the reasoning; indeed, rigorous proofs of the isoperimetric properties of the circle and sphere had to wait until H. A. Schwarz provided them in 1884.[12]

NOTES

1. The Greek title is given by Theon, *Commentaires de Pappus et de Théon d'Alexandrie sur l'Almageste*, A. Rome, ed. II, 355.4, as Περὶ ἰσοπεριμέτρων σχημάτων. The earlier editors had read ἰσομέτρων, but Rome showed that this was a variant reading in some MSS. "Isoperimetric" makes better sense than "isometric" and is confirmed by the comment of Simplicius in his *Commentarium in Aristotelis de caelo*, J. L. Heiberg, ed., in *Commentaria in Aristotelem Graeca*, VII (Berlin, 1894), 412; δέδεικται . . . παρὰ Ἀρχιμήδους καὶ παρὰ Ζηνοδώρου πλατύτερον, ὅτι τῶν ἰσοπεριμέτρων σχημάτων πολυχωρητότερός ἐστιν ἐν μὲν τοῖς ἐπιπέδοις ὁ κύκλος, ἐν δὲ τοῖς στερεοῖσιν ἡ σφαῖρα.
2. Proclus, *In primum Euclidis*, G. Friedlein, ed. (Leipzig, 1873; repr. Hildesheim, 1967), 80.15–16; English trans. by

Glenn R. Morrow, *Proclus: A Commentary on the First Book of Euclid's Elements* (Princeton, 1970), 66. There is one genuine reference to Zenodorus in Proclus, Friedlein ed., 165.24, where it is asserted that there are four-sided triangles, called "barblike" by some but "hollow-angled" (κοιλογώνια) by Zenodorus. The reference is to a quadrilateral with one angle greater than two right angles, called a reentrant angle. It was formerly believed that this word occurred in Theon's version, and Nokk (see note 3) used this as an argument for believing Theon's text to be the nearest the original; but Rome, *op. cit.*, 371, has shown that the word is interpolated and may, indeed, have been interpolated before Proclus read Theon. It remains in the *Introduction to the Almagest: Pappi Alexandrini Collectionis quae supersunt . . .*, F. Hultsch, ed., III, 1194.12, 13, 16.

3. Nokk, *Zenodorus' Abhandlung über die isoperimetrischen Figuren*, 27–29.
4. Quintilian, *De institutione oratoria* (I.10, 39–45), L. Radermacher, ed. (Leipzig, 1907; 6th ed., enl. and corr. by V. Buchheit, 1971), I, 63.12–64.12; also M. Winterbottom, ed. (Oxford, 1970), I, 65.28–66.31. But B. L. van der Waerden, *Science Awakening*, 2nd English ed., 268, is in error in saying that Quintilian "mentions" Zenodorus. Also see F. Hultsch, *op. cit.*, III, 1190; and M. Cantor, *Vorlesungen über Geschichte der Mathematik*, 3rd ed., I (Leipzig, 1907), 549.
5. W. Crönert, "Der Epikureer Philonides." The name occurs in fr. 31, ll. 4–5 (Crönert, 953–954) and probably in fr. 34, l. 1 (Crönert, 954).
6. G. J. Toomer, "The Mathematician Zenodorus," 186.
7. *Ibid.*, 190–191. In both cases where the name occurs, Zenodorus is an emendation, but Toomer regards it as certain.
8. Vaticanus Graecus 381, published by Ernst Maass in *Hermes*, **16** (1881), 388, and more definitively in his *Aratea* (Berlin, 1892), 123. Maass himself identified the Zenodorus of the catalog with the mathematician.
9. Toomer, *op. cit.*, 187–190.
10. Ptolemy, *Syntaxis mathematica (Almagest)*, I.3: *Claudii Ptolemaei Opera quae exstant omnia*, J. L. Heiberg, ed., I (Leipzig, 1898), 13.16–19.
11. If Pappus in his commentary gave credit to Zenodorus, as Theon did, this would help to explain why Zenodorus is not mentioned in the *Collection*; there is no question of Pappus' trying to appropriate another's work as his own.
12. H. A. Schwarz, "Beweis des Satzes, dass die Kugel kleinere Oberfläche besitzt, als jeder andere Körper gleichen Volumens," in *Nachrichten von der Gesellschaft der Wissenschaften zu Göttingen* (1884), 1–13, repr. in Schwarz's *Gesammelte mathematische Abhandlungen*, II (Berlin, 1890), 327–340.

BIBLIOGRAPHY

I. ORIGINAL WORKS. Zenodorus' one known work was entitled Περὶ ἰσοπεριμέτρων. It has not survived as such but is epitomized in three other works: Pappus, *Collection*, V. 3–19: *Pappi Alexandrini Collectionis quae supersunt*, F. Hultsch, ed., I (Berlin, 1876), 308.2–334.21; Theon of Alexandria, *Commentary on the Almagest* I.3: *Commentaires de Pappus et de Théon d'Alexandrie sur l'Almageste*, A. Rome, ed., II, *Théon d'Alexandrie* (Vatican City, 1936), 354.19–379.15, which was translated into Latin and collated with the passages in Pappus in Hultsch, *op. cit.*, III (Berlin, 1878), 1189–1211; and an anonymous work usually known as the *Introduction to the Almagest* and published in F. Hultsch,

op. cit., III, as "Anonymi commentarius de figuris planis isoperimetris," 1138–1165.

II. SECONDARY LITERATURE. See the following, listed chronologically: Nokk, *Zenodorus' Abhandlung über die isoperimetrischen Figuren nach den Auszügen welche uns die Alexandriner Theon und Pappus aus derselben überliefert haben* (Freiburg im Breisgau, 1860); James Gow, *A Short History of Greek Mathematics* (Cambridge, 1884), 271–272; W. Crönert, "Der Epikureer Philonides," in *Sitzungsberichte der Preussischen Akademie der Wissenschaften zu Berlin* (1900), 942–959; W. Schmidt, "Zur Geschichte der Isoperimetrie im Altertum," in *Bibliotheca mathematica*, 3rd ser., **2** (1901), 5–8; T. L. Heath, *A History of Greek Mathematics*, II (Oxford, 1921), 207–213; W. Müller, "Das isoperimetrische Problem im Altertum," in *Sudhoffs Archiv*, **37** (1953), 39–71, with a German trans. of Theon's epitome; B. L. van der Waerden, *Science Awakening*, English trans. of *Ontwakende Wetenschap* with author's additions, 2nd ed. (Groningen, n.d.), 268–269; and G. J. Toomer, "The Mathematician Zenodorus," in *Greek, Roman and Byzantine Studies*, **13** (1972), 177–192.

IVOR BULMER-THOMAS

ZENO OF ELEA (*b.* Elea, Lucania, *ca.* 490 B.C.; *d.* Elea, *ca.* 425 B.C.)

Zeno became a friend and disciple of Parmenides, with whom, according to Plato's dialogue *Parmenides*, he visited Athens in the middle of the fifth century B.C. Some later Greek authors, however, considered this visit an invention of Plato's. According to a widespread legend with many greatly differing versions, Zeno was tortured and killed by a tyrant of Elea or of Syracuse, against whom he had conspired.

Zeno's fame and importance both for philosophy and for the mathematical theory of the continuum rest on his famous paradoxes. There is, however, a tradition, preserved by Diogenes Laërtius (IX,5,29), that he also developed a cosmology, according to which there existed several "worlds" (κόσμοι), composed of "warm" and "cold," "dry" and "wet," but no empty space. Since it is difficult to find any direct connection between this cosmology and Zeno's paradoxes, that tradition has been questioned in recent times. The cosmology has some affinity, however, to certain medical doctrines of the fifth century B.C. There is at least the possibility that it was part of a theory of the phenomenal world analogous to Parmenides' theory of the world of belief (δόξα); and there is no other known Greek philosopher who held exactly these beliefs. Thus there is no compelling reason to reject the tradition.

According to Plato (*Parmenides*, 127 ff.), as a young man Zeno elaborated his paradoxes in defense of the philosophy of Parmenides but did not, like Parmenides, try to prove positively that there is nothing but the One and that plurality, change, and motion are mere illusions. He simply tried to show that if one assumes the existence of plurality and motion, no less strange consequences follow than if one denies their existence. In his commentary on Plato's *Parmenides* (127D), Proclus affirms that Zeno elaborated forty different paradoxes following from the assumption of plurality and motion, all of them apparently based on the difficulties deriving from an analysis of the continuum.

The best-known of the paradoxes is that of Achilles and the tortoise, according to which Achilles cannot overtake the tortoise. Though he always runs a hundred times faster than the tortoise, the latter will, before Achilles has reached the tortoise's starting point, have moved 1/100 of the original distance; and while Achilles traverses this second distance, the tortoise will have traversed 1/100 of the latter; and so on ad infinitum—so that Achilles can never catch the tortoise. Aristotle tried to refute this argument by pointing out that not only space but also time is infinitely divisible, so that the time particles, the sum of which is finite, correspond to the particles to be traversed and no difficulty arises for Achilles. At first sight this argument appears all the more convincing because in what seems to be the original formulation of the paradox, Achilles apparently finds it easy to traverse the distance between his starting point and that of the tortoise and experiences difficulty only after the distance between him and the tortoise has become smaller. There is, however, a much more subtle form of the argument, according to which Achilles cannot even begin: Before he can traverse the distance between his starting point and that of the tortoise, he has first to traverse half of that distance, and before that one-quarter, before that one-eighth, and so on ad infinitum. Thus he never gets going.

That this difficulty cannot be overcome quite so easily by referring to the infinite divisibility of time is shown by the second famous paradox of Zeno, that of the flying arrow that cannot move. In its simplest form this paradox says that the arrow can move neither in the place where it is nor in a place where it is not. In a more elaborate form it says that at any given instant, the arrow occupies a space equal to its size. It can neither occupy a larg-er space nor be in two different places at the same time. Since there is nothing between one instant and the next, and since the arrow cannot move in an instant, it cannot move at all. Aristotle tried to refute this argument by pointing out that the "now" ($\nu\hat{\nu}\nu$), although it divides time into past and future, is not a part of time, since time is extensive and since any part of that which has extension must in its turn have extension. In other words, time is not composed of "nows" or instants.

In recent times interest in the problem has been so great that hardly a year has passed without the publication of one or more attempts at its solution. G. Vlastos very cleverly pointed out that if we use the mathematical formula for velocity $v = s/t$ and apply it to the instant, which is supposed to be extensionless, we obtain the value $v = 0/0$, which is no fixed value at all and certainly not the fixed value of 0, thus indicating that the arrow has no velocity but remains at rest. In order to obtain the result 0, t must have a positive value: $v = 0/t = 0$. This is quite true. But Vlastos' further observation that the problem is similar to the problem of how a circle can be curved although it is supposed to be composed of points—and points are not curved—shows that what the mathematical formula reveals so clearly is still not quite realizable by human imagination.

The most thorough study of the problem from this latter point of view has been made by A. Grünbaum. He begins by distinguishing between two different concepts of time, one "mind-dependent" and one "mind-independent." The former is characterized by the experience of the fleeting "now," which—as in Aristotle's theory of time—divides time into a constantly approaching future and into a constantly receding past into which what until "now" had been future sinks back, and in virtue of which things come into being and pass away. This kind of time, according to Grünbaum, can exist only in a mind consciously experiencing time. From it he distinguishes what he calls the "mind-independent" time of the physicist, within which one can clearly distinguish between an "earlier" and a "later" but within which, strictly speaking, there is no future, present, or past. In analogy to mind-dependent time, however, mind-independent time can be divided by "points of simultaneity," which can be assumed in any point of the time coordinate. These points of simultaneity can more strictly be considered as (extensionless) mathematical points than can the "now points" of mind-dependent time, which permits a kind of quasi-instantaneous awareness of succession—as, for instance, in the perception of the unity of a melody consisting of a succession of sounds.

By this distinction between two sorts of time, Grünbaum tries to eliminate from the discussion the result of observations made by William James and A. N. Whitehead, who tried to show that time cannot strictly be considered a continuum in the sense of Georg Cantor's theory of aggregates, since, as careful self-observation shows, human time-consciousness is not continuous, but discrete ("pulsating," not "punctual"). This, according to Grünbaum, is true of mind-dependent, but not of mind-independent, time. The latter is strictly a continuum with an absolute density of mathematical points. Within the context of this theory an attempt is then made to solve the Zenonian problem on the basis of the assumption that any extended magnitude or interval contains (in the sense of Cantor's theory of aggregates) an indenumerable or superdenumerable infinity of extensionless (or, as Grünbaum expresses it, degenerative) elements, which has extension although its elements do not. In other words, the theory, in contrast with that of Aristotle, who admitted only the "potential infinity" of unending division, postulates that any line or curve actually represents (or is composed of) a nondenumerable infinity of nonextended points that nevertheless has extension.

In a way, then, the paradox that the arrow cannot move in any given instant, but appears to move in a succession of instants, is "solved" by replacing it with the paradox that an infinite aggregate of nonextended points nevertheless has extension; that is, the paradox becomes connected with the intricacies of the modern theory of the continuum, which is still hotly debated. Grünbaum unquestionably, however, drew attention to the psychological aspects of the problem—or, rather, to those aspects where it touches upon the theory of knowledge. As H. Fränkel pointed out, the paradoxes discussed really derive from the fact that

> The human mind, when trying to give itself an accurate account of motion, finds itself confronted with two aspects of the phenomenon. Both are inevitable but at the same time they are mutually exclusive. Either we look at the continuous flow of motion; then it will be impossible for us to think of the object in any particular position. Or we think of the object as occupying any of the positions through which its course is leading it; and while fixing our thought on that particular position we cannot help fixing the object itself and putting it at rest for one short instant ["Zeno of Elea's Attacks on Plurality," pp. 8–9].

The two main arguments against motion discussed so far have not survived in their original wording but appear in the ancient tradition in more or less refined formulations. Zeno's arguments against plurality, however, are—at least in part—quoted literally by Simplicius. These quotations are much less clearly and precisely formulated than the paradoxes of Achilles and the tortoise and the flying arrow. They show with what difficulties Zeno had to struggle when trying to express his thoughts, and they therefore require a good deal more interpretation. The difficulty is increased by the fact that Simplicius quotes only the second part of the argument literally and summarizes the first part. In his introduction he says that Zeno had first tried to prove that that which has no "magnitude" (extension [?]; $\mu\acute{\epsilon}\gamma\epsilon\vartheta o\varsigma$) nor thickness ($\pi\acute{\alpha}\chi o\varsigma$) nor body ($\ddot{o}\gamma\kappa o\varsigma$) cannot exist. "For if it is added to something else, it will not make it bigger, and if it is subtracted, it will not make it smaller. But if it does not make a thing bigger when added to it nor smaller when subtracted from it, then it appears obvious that what was added or subtracted was nothing." The literal quotation then continues:

> If this is [so?], then it is necessary that the one must have a certain distance ($\dot{\alpha}\pi\acute{\epsilon}\chi\epsilon\iota\nu$) from the other, and this is also so with that which protrudes ($\pi\epsilon\rho\grave{\iota}\ \tau o\bar{\upsilon}\ \pi\rho o\acute{\epsilon}\chi o\nu\tau o\varsigma$). For this also will have "magnitude" [extension] and something of it will protrude. And to say this once and to say it again and again is the same thing. For nothing of it in this way will be the outermost ($\tau\grave{o}\ \breve{\epsilon}\sigma\chi\alpha\tau o\nu$) and never will any of them be without proportion to the others. Therefore, if there are many things it is necessary that they are small and big: small to the extent of having no size [extension] at all and big to the extent of infinite extension [H. Diels and W. Kranz, *Die Fragmente der Vorsokratiker*, 7th ed., I, no. 29, p. 266].

The use of the word $\dot{\alpha}\pi\acute{\epsilon}\chi\epsilon\iota\nu$, which usually means "to be away from" or "to be at a distance from," has induced some commentators to interpret Zeno's argument in the following way: If there are many things, they must be distinguished from one another. If they are distinguished, they must be separate. If they are separate, there must be something between them. Since Zeno (according to his cosmology) denied the existence of empty space, what separates things must itself be a thing, which in its turn must be separated by another thing that separates it from the things that it separates from one another, and so on ad infinitum. But this interpretation is hardly reconcilable with what precedes and what follows in Simplicius' account.

The argument as a whole is understandable only on the assumption that ἀπέχειν is used as a synonym of προέχειν, the term that is used in the remainder of the argument. The gist of the argument then appears to have been: What has size is divisible. What is divisible is not a real One, since it has parts. But any part that "lies beyond" or protrudes from a given part of something that has size, has size in its turn; hence it has parts, and so on ad infinitum, so that it becomes both small and big beyond all measure. If this is the meaning of the argument, we are back with the problem of the continuum.

Vlastos has claimed that in the last sentence of the fragment quoted, Zeno committed "a logical gaffe" by assuming that through infinitely continued division, one finally ends with particles "of no size!" But on closer inspection it seems clear that Zeno, at least in the first half of his last argument, committed no such logical error. Far from assuming that by infinitely continued division one finally comes to particles "of no size," his argument is based on the very opposite assumption: however far the division may have proceeded, what remains still always has size, hence is further divisible, hence has parts, hence is not really One. Therefore, in order to be really One (indivisible)—and this conclusion, if one starts from Zeno's assumption, is perfectly sound—it must be without size. But—and here the preliminary argument reported by Simplicius is brought in—what has no size does not make a thing to which it is added bigger, nor a thing from which it is subtracted smaller, and hence appears to be nothing.

This interpretation and analysis of the argument is also in perfect agreement with a statement elsewhere attributed to Zeno, to the effect that if someone could really explain to him what the One is, then he would also be in a position to explain plurality. At the same time it shows that Plato was right when he reported that Zeno did not try to give direct support to Parmenides' doctrine that only the One exists, but merely tried to show that from the assumption of a plurality of things, no less strange conclusions could be drawn than from the assumption that there is nothing but the One.

Granting this, one may still contend that Zeno committed a "logical gaffe" in the second part of his last argument, where he speaks of an infinite number of parts that would make the size of the object composed of them grow beyond all measure; this statement appears to be at variance with one of the most elementary applications of the theory of convergent series: that the sum of the infinite series $1/2 + 1/4 + 1/8 + 1/16 + \cdots = 1$. But this mathematical formula is a convenient symbol for the fact that infinitely continued bisection of a unit cannot exceed the unit, a fact of which Zeno, as other fragments clearly show, was perfectly aware. What he obviously did try to point out is that it is not possible for the human mind to build up the sum of such an infinite series starting, so to speak, from the other end, the end with the "degenerative elements," as Grünbaum calls them. When building up a sum, one has always to start with elements that have size. The difficulty is essentially that which H. Fränkel so lucidly described in regard to motion.

The other paradoxes of Zeno that have been preserved by ancient tradition are not so profound and can be resolved completely. One of them is that of the falling millet: If a falling bushel of millet makes a noise, so must an individual grain; if the latter makes no noise, neither can the bushel of grain, for the size of the grain has a definite ratio to that of the heap. The same must then be true of the noises. The resolution here lies in the limitation of perception, which also plays a role in the modern discussion of the perception of time. Interestingly, Zeno argues on the basis of the mathematical argument that there must be a definite proportion.

Another is the paradox of the moving blocks: If four blocks *BBBB* of equal size move along four blocks *AAAA* of the same size which are at rest, and at the same time four blocks *CCCC*, again of the same size and the first two of which have arrived below the last two of the row *AAAA*, move with the same speed as *BBBB* in the opposite direction from *BBBB*, then *BBBB* will pass two blocks of *AAAA* in the same time in which they pass four blocks of *CCCC*. But since their speed remains the same, and yet time is measured by the distance traveled at the same time, half the time is equal to the double time.

Alexander of Aphrodisias made the following diagram to illustrate Zeno's moving blocks argument:

$$AAAA$$
$$BBBB \rightarrow$$
$$\leftarrow CCCC$$

It is interesting that this argument contains the first glimpse in ancient literature of an awareness of the relativity of motion. It is the only Zenonian paradox preserved that has nothing to do with the problem of the continuum, although there have been some attempts in modern times by Paul Tannery and R. E. Siegel to show that there is a connection.

Concerning Zeno's importance for the development of ancient Greek mathematics, the most various views have been held and are still held by modern historians of science. Tannery was the first to suggest that Zeno's relation to the philosophy of Parmenides may have been less close than ancient tradition affirms and that Zeno was much more deeply influenced by problems arising from the discovery of incommensurability by the Pythagoreans. On the basis of the same assumption, H. Hasse and H. Scholz tried to show that Zeno was the "man of destiny" of ancient mathematics. They attempted to prove that the Pythagoreans, after having discovered the incommensurability of the diameter of a square with its side, had tried to overcome the resultant difficulties by assuming the existence of infinitely small elementary lines (*lineae indivisibiles*). It was against this inaccurate handling of the infinitesimal that Zeno protested, thus forcing the next generation of Pythagorean mathematicians to give the theory a better and more accurate foundation.

Other scholars (W. Burkert, A. Szabó, J. A. Philip) contend that since, according to ancient tradition, the Pythagoreans engaged in a rather abstruse number mysticism such a profound mathematical discovery as that of incommensurability cannot have been made by them, but must have been made by "practical mathematicians" influenced by Zeno's paradoxes. But there is no direct road leading from Zeno's paradoxes to the proof of incommensurability in specific cases, whereas some of the speculations supporting the Pythagoreans (when carried through with the consistency characteristic of the philosophers of the first century) must almost inevitably have led to the discovery, although we do not know exactly how it was first made; and there is no tradition concerning an effect of Zeno's speculations on the development of mathematics in the second half of the fifth century B.C. B. L. van der Waerden has shown that what we know of mathematical theories of the second half of the fifth century B.C.—when the discovery of incommensurability undoubtedly was made—is rather at variance with the assumption that Zeno had any considerable influence on the development of mathematics at that time.

This, however, does not necessarily mean that Zeno's name has to be stricken from the history of ancient Greek mathematics. In all likelihood he received the first impulse toward the invention of his paradoxes not from mathematics but, as attested by Plato, from the speculations of Parmenides, and did not immediately have a strong influence on

the development of Greek mathematics. But it is hardly by chance that Plato wrote his dialogue *Parmenides*, in which he refers to Zeno's paradoxes, around the time that Eudoxus of Cnidus, who revised the theory of proportions in such a way as to enable him to handle the infinitesimal with an accuracy that has remained unsurpassed, spent some years at Athens and was a member of Plato's academy. Zeno's paradoxes can hardly have failed to have been thoroughly discussed then, and so Zeno may still have had some influence on Greek mathematics at that decisive point in its development.

BIBLIOGRAPHY

I. ORIGINAL WORKS. An extensive bibliography is in W. Totok, *Handbuch der Geschichte der Philosophie*, I, *Altertum* (Frankfurt, 1964), 123–124. The text ed. most convenient for English-speaking readers is H. D. P. Lee, *Zeno of Elea. A Text With Translation and Commentary* (Cambridge, 1936). In the secondary literature, however, the fragments are usually quoted according to H. Diels and W. Kranz, *Die Fragmente der Vorsokratiker*, 7th ed., I, no. 29, 247–258.

II. SECONDARY LITERATURE. See Guido Calogero, *Studi sull'Eleatismo* (Rome, 1932); and *Storia della logica antica*, I (Bari, 1967), 171–208; H. Fränkel, "Zeno of Elea's Attacks on Plurality," in *American Journal of Philology*, 63 (1942), 1–25, 193–206; Adolf Grünbaum, "A Consistent Conception of the Extended Linear Continuum as an Aggregate of Unextended Elements," in *Philosophy of Science*, 19 (1952), 288–305; "The Nature of Time," in *Frontiers of Science and Philosophy*, 1 (1962), 149–184; and *Modern Science and Zeno's Paradoxes* (Middletown, Conn., 1967); H. Hasse and H. Scholz, *Die Grundlagenkrisis der griechischen Mathematik* (Berlin–Charlottenburg, 1928); J. A. Philip, *Pythagoras and Early Pythagoreanism* (Toronto, 1966), 206–207; R. E. Siegel, "The Paradoxes of Zeno," in *Janus*, 48 (1959), 42 ff.; A. Szabó, *Anfänge der griechischen Mathematik* (Munich–Vienna, 1939), 333 ff.; P. Tannery, "Le concept scientifique du continu. Zénon d'Élée et Georg Cantor," in *Revue philosophique de la France et de l'étranger*, 20 (1885), 385–410, esp. 393–394; and *Pour l'histoire de la science hellène*, 2nd ed. (Paris, 1930), 248 ff.; B. L. van der Waerden, "Zenon und die Grundlagenkrise der griechischen Mathematik," in *Mathematische Annalen*, 117, no. 2 (1940), 141–161, esp. 151 ff.; and G. Vlastos, "A Note on Zeno's Arrow," in *Phronesis*, 11 (1966), 3–18; and "Zeno's Race Course," in *Journal of the History of Philosophy*, 4 (1966), 95–108.

Concerning the influence of Zeno and of the methods developed by Eudoxus on the nineteenth-century attempts to give the calculus a more exact foundation, see M. Black, "Achilles and the Tortoise," in *Analysis*, 11

(1951), 91–101; J. M. Hinton and C. B. Martin, "Achilles and the Tortoise," *ibid.*, **14** (1953), 56–68; G. E. L. Owen, "Zeno and the Mathematicians," in *Proceedings of the Aristotelian Society*, n.s. **58** (1957–1958), 199–222; L. E. Thomas, "Achilles and the Tortoise," in *Analysis*, **12** (1952), 92–94; R. Taylor, "Mr. Black on Temporal Paradoxes," *ibid.*, 38–44; and J. O. Wisdom, "Achilles on a Physical Racecourse," *ibid.*, 67–72. There is also an especially instructive earlier paper by M. Dehn, "Raum, Zeit, Zahl bei Aristoteles vom mathematischen Standpunkt aus," in *Scientia*, **40** (1936), 12–21, 69–74, which deals with Aristotle's criticism of Zeno's paradoxes and its importance for modern mathematics.

Concerning the general problems underlying Zeno's paradoxes, see also P. Beisswanger, *Die Anfechtbarkeit der klassischen Mathematik* (Stuttgart, 1965); P. Bennacerraf, "What Numbers Could Not Be," in *Philosophical Review*, **74** (1965), 47–73; and Hermann Weyl, "Über die neue Grundlagenkrise der Mathematik," in *Mathematische Zeitschrift*, **10** (1921), 39–79.

KURT VON FRITZ

ZENO OF SIDON (*b.* Sidon, *ca.* 150 B.C.; *d.* Athens, *ca.* 70 B.C.)

According to ancient tradition, Zeno of Sidon was a very prolific writer who discussed theory of knowledge, logic, various aspects of ancient atomic theory, the fundamental differences of the sexes (from which it follows that they have different diseases), problems of Epicurean ethics, literary criticism, style, oratory, poetry, and mathematics. Very little is known of the contents of these writings except those on mathematics and logic, which are of great interest.

Epicurus had been a very severe critic of mathematics as a science; but what he said about it is very superficial and shows that he did not understand what mathematics is. This is not at all the case with Zeno's criticism of Euclid's axiomatics. In his commentary on Euclid, Proclus says that Zeno attacked the first theorem of the *Elements* (the construction of an equilateral triangle) on the ground that it is valid only if one assumes that two straight lines cannot have more than one point in common, and that Euclid has not set this down as an axiom. On the same ground he attacked Euclid's fourth postulate, which asserts the equality of all right angles, observing that it presupposes the construction of a right angle, which is not given until I, 11. In addition, Proclus and Sextus Empiricus mention several criticisms of Euclid that they attribute to an unnamed Epicurean and that are

similar to Zeno's criticisms: for instance, that there is no axiom establishing the infinite divisibility of curves, which is connected with a discussion of various consequences following from the assumption that curves are not infinitely divisible but, rather, are composed of the smallest units of indivisible lines. There is also a criticism anticipating Schopenhauer's of Euclid's method of superimposition, by which he proves the first theorem of congruence and a few other theorems: namely, that only matter can be moved in space.

On the basis of these criticisms of Euclid's axiomatics, E. M. Bruins has claimed that Zeno of Sidon was the first to discover the possibility of non-Euclidean geometry. This claim appears exaggerated, since there is not the slightest tradition indicating that Zeno elaborated his criticism in such a way as to show positively how a non-Euclidean geometrical system could be built up. Zeno's criticisms of Euclid are pertinent, however, and if any of the ancient philosophers and mathematicians who tried to refute them had been able to grasp their full implications, the development of mathematics might have taken a different turn.

Lengthy fragments of a treatise by the Epicurean philosopher Philodemus of Gadara have been found on a papyrus from Herculaneum (no. 1065), and most of those preserved contain a report on a controversy between Zeno and contemporary Stoics over the foundations of knowledge. In this dispute Zeno defended the old Epicurean doctrine that all human knowledge is derived exclusively from experience. What makes it interesting, however, is that he bases his defense on a theory that he calls "transition according to similarity" ($\mu\epsilon\tau\acute{\alpha}\beta\alpha\sigma\iota\varsigma$ $\kappa\alpha\vartheta$' $\acute{o}\mu o\iota\acute{o}\tau\eta\tau\alpha$) or "transition from the apparent to the not apparent" ($\mu\epsilon\tau\acute{\alpha}\beta\alpha\sigma\iota\varsigma$ $\acute{\alpha}\pi\grave{o}$ $\tau\tilde{\omega}\nu$ $\phi\alpha\iota\nu o\mu\acute{\epsilon}\nu\omega\nu$ $\acute{\epsilon}\varsigma$ $\tau\grave{\alpha}$ $\acute{\alpha}\phi\alpha\nu\tilde{\eta}$), but that is essentially an anticipation of John Stuart Mill's theory of induction.

In contrast to Aristotle's theory of induction, according to which the most certain kind of induction is that in which one case is sufficient to make it evident that the same must be true in all similar cases, and in opposition to the Stoic doctrine that no number of cases ever permits the conclusion that the same must be true in all cases, Zeno insisted that all knowledge is fundamentally derived by inference to all cases from a great many cases without observed counter-instance. He carried this principle to the extreme by asserting that the knowledge that the square with a side of length 4 is the only square in which the sum of the length of the sides (16) is equal to the contents ($4 \times 4 = 16$)

was derived from measuring innumerable squares, although here it is evident that the result—insofar as it is correct, one-dimensional measures being equated with two-dimensional measures—can be derived from a simple deduction and that nobody will be so foolish as to "verify" it in innumerable squares. The recent proof by computers that the principle is not altogether applicable to mathematics and number theory shows that certain theorems of Pólya's that had been considered universally valid because they had been proved up to very high numbers were not valid beyond higher numbers unreachable by human calculation.

The details of the controversy between Zeno and the Stoics is extremely interesting because sometimes the positions become curiously reversed, and because it provides a kind of phenomenology of induction going beyond most modern works.

BIBLIOGRAPHY

I. ORIGINAL WORKS. Extracts of Zeno's lectures are in T. Gomperz, *Herkulanische Studien*, I (Leipzig, 1865), 24–27; and P. H. and E. A. de Lacy, eds., *Philodemos: On Methods of Inference*, which is Philological Monographs of the American Philological Association, no. 10 (Philadelphia, 1941)—see index. (Pp. 22–66, columns Ia, 1–XIX, 4, are mostly extracts from Zeno's lectures, but it is not certain how far they are literal.)

II. SECONDARY LITERATURE. See Ludger Adam. "Das Wahrheits- und Hypothesenproblem bei Demokrit, Epikur und Zeno, dem Epikureer" (Ph.D. diss., Göttingen, 1947); E. M. Bruins, *La géométrie non-euclidienne dans l'antiquité*, Publications de l'Université de Paris, D121 (Paris, 1967); and G. Vlastos, "Zeno of Sidon as a Critic of Euclid," in *The Classical Tradition: Literary and Historical Studies in Honor of Harry Caplan* (New York, 1966), 148–159.

On problems arising in connection with Zeno's theory of induction, see C. B. Haselgrove, "A Disproof of a Conjecture of Pólya," in *Mathematica*, 5 (1958), 141; K. von Fritz, "Die ἐπαγωγή bei Aristoteles," in *Sitzungsberichte der Bayerischen Akademie der Wissenschaften zu München*, Phil.-hist. Kl. (1964), no. 3, 40 ff., 62 ff.; and R. Queneau, "Conjectures fausses en théorie des nombres," in *Mélanges Koyré*, I (Paris, 1964), 475 ff.

KURT VON FRITZ

ZERMELO, ERNST FRIEDRICH FERDINAND (*b.* Berlin, Germany, 27 July 1871; *d.* Freiburg im Breisgau, Germany, 21 May 1953)

The son of Ferdinand Rudolf Theodor Zermelo, a college professor, and Maria Augusta Elisabeth Zieger, Zermelo received his secondary education at the Luisenstädtisches Gymnasium in Berlin, where he passed his final examination in 1889. He subsequently studied mathematics, physics, and philosophy at Berlin, Halle, and Freiburg, taking courses taught by Frobenius, Lazarus Fuchs, Planck, Erhard Schmidt, H. A. Schwarz, and Edmund Husserl. In 1894 he received the doctorate at Berlin with the dissertation *Untersuchungen zur Variationsrechnung*. Zermelo went to Göttingen and in 1899 was appointed *Privatdozent* after having submitted the *Habilitationsschrift* "Hydrodynamische Untersuchungen über die Wirbelbewegungen in einer Kugelfläche." In December 1905, shortly after his sensational proof of the well-ordering theorem (1904), Zermelo was named titular professor at Göttingen. In 1910 he accepted a professorship at Zurich, which poor health forced him to resign in 1916. A year after he had left Göttingen, 5000 marks from the interest of the Wolfskehl Fund was awarded him on the initiative of David Hilbert in recognition of his results in set theory (and to enable him to recover his health). After resigning his post at Zurich, Zermelo lived in the Black Forest until 1926, when he was appointed honorary professor at the University of Freiburg im Breisgau. He renounced connection with the university in 1935 because of his disapproval of the Hitler regime. After the war he requested reinstatement, which was granted him in 1946.

Zermelo had a lively interest in physics and a keen sense for the application of mathematics to practical problems. He prepared German editions of Glazebrook's *Light* and Gibbs's *Elementary Principles in Statistical Mechanics*; and after having shown in "Ueber einen Satz der Dynamik" how application of Poincaré's recurrence theorem leads to the nonexistence of irreversible processes in the kinetic theory of gases, he had a penetrating discussion with Boltzmann on the explanation of irreversible processes.

In Zermelo's dissertation, which dealt with the calculus of variations, he extended Weierstrass' method for the extrema of integrals over a class of curves to the case of integrands depending on derivatives of arbitrarily high order, at the same time giving a careful definition of the notion of neighborhood in the space of curves. Throughout his life he was faithful to the calculus of variations, on which he often lectured and to which he contributed a report on its progress written with H. Hahn for the *Encyklopädie der mathematischen Wissen-*

schaften (1904) and the paper "Über die Navigation . . ." (1929).

Further examples of his original contributions to practical questions are his method for estimating the strength of participants in tournaments ("Die Berechnung der Turnier-Ergebnisse," 1929), which has been used in chess tournaments, and his investigation of the fracture of a cube of sugar ("Über die Bruchlinien zentrierter Ovale," 1933).

As an assistant at Göttingen, Zermelo lectured during the winter semester of 1900–1901 on set theory, to the development of which he was to contribute decisively. He had studied Cantor's work thoroughly, and his conversations with Erhard Schmidt led to his ingenious proof of the well-ordering theorem, which states that every set can be well-ordered; that is, in every set a relation $a \prec b$, to be read as "*a* comes before *b*," can be introduced, such that (1) for any two elements *a* and *b*, either $a = b$ or $a \prec b$ or $b \prec a$; (2) if for three elements *a*, *b*, *c* we have $a \prec b$ and $b \prec c$, then $a \prec c$; (3) any nonvoid subset has a first element. In a commentary to his own proof, Zermelo pointed out the underlying hypothesis that for any infinite system of sets there always are relations under which every set corresponds to one of its elements. The proof stirred the mathematical world and produced a great deal of criticism—most of it unjustified—which Zermelo answered elegantly in "Neuer Beweis" (1908), where he also gave a second proof of the theorem. His answer to Poincaré's accusation of impredicativity is of some historical interest because he points out certain consequences and peculiarities of the predicative position that have played a role in the development of predicative mathematics.

Also in 1908 Zermelo set up an axiom system for Cantor's set theory that has proved of tremendous importance for the development of mathematics. It consists of seven axioms and uses only two technical terms: set and $\in$, the symbol for the "element of" relation. Zermelo emphasized the descriptive nature of the axioms, starting with a domain *B* of objects and then specifying under what conditions (the axioms) an object is to be called a set. With the exception of the null set introduced in axiom 2, every set *a* is an object of *B* for which there is another object *b* of *B* such that $a \in b$.

Axiom 1 (extensionality): $m = n$ if and only if $a \in m$ is equivalent to $a \in n$.

Axiom 2 (elementary sets): There is a null set, having no element at all. Every object *a* of *B* determines a set $\{a\}$ with *a* as its only element. Any two objects *a*, *b* of *B* determine a set $\{a,b\}$ with precisely *a* and *b* as elements.

Axiom 3 (separation): If a property *E* is definite for the elements of a set *m*, then there is a subset m_E of *m* consisting of exactly those elements of *m* for which *E* holds.

Axiom 4 (power set): To any set *m* there is a set $P(m)$ that has the subsets of *m* for its elements.

Axiom 5 (union): To any set *m* there is a set $\cup m$, the union of *m*, consisting of the elements of the elements of *m*.

Axiom 6 (axiom of choice): If *m* is a set of disjoint nonvoid sets, then $\cup m$ contains a subset *n* that contains exactly one element from every set of *m*.

Axiom 7 (infinity): There is a set *z* that has the null set as an element and has the property that if *a* is an element of *z*, then $\{a\}$ is also an element of *z*.

In order to avoid the paradoxes, particularly Russell's paradox, which would render the system useless, Zermelo restricted set formation by the condition of definiteness of the defining property of a subset. A property *E* definite for set *m* is explained as one for which the basic relations of *B* permit one to decide whether or not *E* holds for any element of *m*. Although this condition seemed to preclude contradictions in the system, Zermelo explicitly left aside the difficult questions of independence and consistency. This was a wise decision, as one may realize after having seen the solutions of the questions of relative consistency and independence of axiom 6 by Kurt Gödel (1938) and P. J. Cohen (1963), respectively.

Because of its generality the notion of definite property is very elegant. It is rather difficult to apply, however, because it does not yield a general method for proving a proposed property to be definite.

Although nonaxiomatic Cantorian set theory was then flourishing, particularly the branch that developed into point-set topology, there was no progress in axiomatic set theory until 1921, when A. Fraenkel, in his attempts to prove the independence of the axiom of choice, pointed out some defects in Zermelo's system. Fraenkel's objections were threefold. First, the axiom of infinity is too weak; second, the system is by no means categorical; and third, the notion of definite property is too vague to handle in proofs of independence and consistency. These remarks led Fraenkel to add the powerful axiom of replacement, which adds to any set *s* its image under some function *F*, while the notion of function is introduced by definition. Another way of obtaining a similar result was achieved by T. Skolem, who specified a definite property as one expressible in first-order logic.

After having realized the importance of Fraenkel's and Skolem's remarks, Zermelo set out in "Über den Begriff der Definitheit in der Axiomatik" (1929) to axiomatize this notion by describing the set of definite properties as the smallest set containing the basic relations of the domain *B* and satisfying certain closure conditions. He admitted that the reason for doing so was methodological: to keep to the "pure axiomatic" method, in avoidance of the genetic method and the use of the notion of finite number. Since there is no categoricity, an investigation of the structure of the possible domains *b*—models for axiomatic set theory—makes sense. In "Über Grenzzahlen und Mengenbereiche" (1930) Zermelo investigated the structure of models of an axiom system consisting of his earlier axioms 1, 4, 5, the last part of 2, the unrestricted form of 3, a liberal axiom of replacement, and an axiom of well-foundedness (with respect to ∈) stating that every subdomain *T* of domain *B* contains at least one element t_0 that has no element *t* in *T*.

Zermelo's fragmentary attempt, in "Grundlagen einer allgemeinen Theorie der mathematischen Satzsysteme" (1935), to abolish the limitations of proof theory has not been of great consequence because his conception of a proof as a system of theorems, well-founded with respect to the relation of consequence, seems too general to lead to results of sufficient interest.

BIBLIOGRAPHY

I. ORIGINAL WORKS. Zermelo's writings include *Untersuchungen zur Variationsrechnung* (Berlin, 1894), his dissertation; "Ueber einen Satz der Dynamik und die mechanische Wärmetheorie," in *Annalen der Physik und Chemie*, n.s. 57 (1896), 485–494; "Ueber mechanische Erklärungen irreversibler Vorgänge. Eine Antwort auf Hrn. Boltzmann's 'Entgegnung,'" *ibid.*, 59 (1896), 793–801; *Das Licht. Grundriss der Optik für Studierende und Schüler*, his trans. of R. T. Glazebrook's *Light* (Berlin, 1897); "Ueber die Bewegung eines Punktsystemes bei Bedingungsungleichungen," in *Nachrichten von der K. Gesellschaft der Wissenschaften zu Göttingen*, math.-phys. Kl. (1899), 306–310; "Über die Anwendung der Wahrscheinlichkeitsrechnung auf dynamische Systeme," in *Physikalische Zeitschrift*, 1 (1899–1900), 317–320; "Ueber die Addition transfiniter Cardinalzahlen," in *Nachrichten von der K. Gesellschaft der Wissenschaften zu Göttingen*, math.-phys. Kl. (1901), 34–38; "Hydrodynamische Untersuchungen über die Wirbelbewegungen in einer Kugelfläche," in *Zeitschrift für Mathematik und Physik*, 47 (1902), 201–237, his *Habilitationsschrift*; and "Zur Theorie der kürzesten Linien," in *Jahresberichte der Deutschen Mathematikervereinigung*, 11 (1902), 184–187.

Further works are "Über die Herleitung der Differentialgleichung bei Variationsproblemen," in *Mathematische Annalen*, 58 (1904), 558–564; "Beweis, dass jede Menge wohlgeordnet werden kann," *ibid.*, 59 (1904), 514–516; "Weiterentwickelung der Variationsrechnung in den letzten Jahren," in *Encyklopädie der mathematischen Wissenschaften*, II, pt. 1 (Leipzig, 1904), 626–641, written with H. Hahn; *Elementare Grundlagen der statistischen Mechanik*, his trans. of Gibbs's work (Leipzig, 1905); "Neuer Beweis für die Möglichkeit einer Wohlordnung," in *Mathematische Annalen*, 65 (1908), 107–128; "Untersuchungen über die Grundlagen der Mengenlehre I," *ibid.*, 261–281; "Sur les ensembles finis et le principe de l'induction complète," in *Acta mathematica*, 32 (1909), 185–193; "Die Einstellung der Grenzkonzentrationen an der Trennungsfläche zweier Lösungsmittel," in *Physikalische Zeitschrift*, 10 (1909), 958–961, written with E. H. Riesenfeld; and "Ueber die Grundlagen der Arithmetik," in *Atti del IV Congresso internazionale dei matematici*, II (Rome, 1909), 8–11.

See also "Über eine Anwendung der Mengenlehre auf die Theorie des Schachspiels," in *Proceedings of the Fifth International Congress of Mathematicians*, II (Cambridge, 1913), 501–504; "Über ganze transzendente Zahlen," in *Mathematische Annalen*, 75 (1914), 434–442; "Ueber das Masz und die Diskrepanz von Punktmengen," in *Journal für die reine und angewandte Mathematik*, 158 (1927), 154–167; "Über den Begriff der Definitheit in der Axiomatik," in *Fundamenta mathematicae*, 14 (1929), 339–344; "Die Berechnung der Turnier-Ergebnisse als ein Maximumproblem der Wahrscheinlichkeitsrechnung," in *Mathematische Zeitschrift*, 29 (1929), 436–460; and "Über die Navigation in der Luft als Problem der Variationsrechnung," in *Jahresberichte der Deutschen Mathematikervereinigung*, 39 (1929), 44–48.

Additional works are "Über Grenzzahlen und Mengenbereiche. Neue Untersuchungen über die Grundlagen der Mengenlehre," in *Fundamenta mathematicae*, 16 (1930), 29–47; "Über die logische Form der mathematischen Theorien," in *Annales de la Société polonaise de mathématique*, 9 (1930), 187; "Über das Navigationsproblem bei ruhender oder veränderlicher Windverteilung," in *Zeitschrift für angewandte Mathematik und Mechanik*, 11 (1931), 114–124; "Über mathematische Systeme und die Logik des Unendlichen," in *Forschungen und Fortschritte*, 8 (1932), 6–7; "Über Stufen der Quantifikation und die Logik des Unendlichen," in *Jahresberichte der Deutschen Mathematikervereinigung*, 41 (1932), 85–88; "Über die Bruchlinien zentrierter Ovale. (Wie zerbricht ein Stück Zucker?)," in *Zeitschrift für angewandte Mathematik und Mechanik*, 13 (1933), 168–170; "Elementare Betrachtungen zur Theorie der

Primzahlen," in *Nachrichten von der Gesellschaft der Wissenschaften zu Göttingen*, Fachgruppe 1, **1** (1934), 43–46; and "Grundlagen einer allgemeinen Theorie der mathematischen Satzsysteme. (Erste Mitteilung)," in *Fundamenta mathematicae*, **25** (1935), 136–146.

A collection of papers left by Zermelo is in the library of the University of Freiburg im Breisgau. A short description, furnished by H. Gericke, is as follows: a set of copies of articles by Zermelo and other mathematicians, a collection of letters and MSS and sketches of published papers, lecture notes in shorthand, parts of a translation of Homer in German verse, the second part of his *Habilitationsschrift*, and a sketch of a patent application "Kreisel zur Stabilisierung von Fahr- und Motorrädern" (gyroscope for stabilizing bicycles and motorcycles).

II. SECONDARY LITERATURE. Quite a number of relevant papers on set theory, including three memoirs by Zermelo, are reprinted in J. van Heijenoort, *From Frege to Gödel* (Cambridge, Mass., 1967), which also contains references to the literature up to 1966. See also P. J. Cohen, *Set Theory and the Continuum Hypothesis* (New York, 1966); S. Fefermann, "Systems of Predicative Analysis," in *Journal of Symbolic Logic*, **29** (1964), 1–30; A. Fraenkel, "Über die Zermelosche Begründung der Mengenlehre," in *Jahresberichte der Deutschen Mathematikervereinigung*, **30** (1921), 97–98; "Zu den Grundlagen der Cantor-Zermeloschen Mengenlehre," in *Mathematische Annalen*, **86** (1922), 230–237; "Der Begriff 'definit' und die Unabhängigkeit des Auswahlsaxioms," in *Sitzungsberichte der Preussischen Akademie der Wissenschaften zu Berlin* (1922), 253–257; and *Foundations of Set Theory* (Amsterdam, 1958), written with Y. Bar-Hillel; H. Gericke, *Beiträge zur Freiburger Wissenschafts- und universitätsgeschichte*, VII, *Zur Geschichte der Mathematik an der Universität Freiburg i.Br.*, J. Vincke, ed. (Freiburg im Breisgau, 1955), 72–73; K. Gödel, *The Consistency of the Continuum Hypothesis* (Princeton, N.J., 1940); G. Kreisel and J. L. Krivine, *Elements of Mathematical Logic* (Amsterdam, 1967); M. Pinl, "Kollegen in einer dunklen Zeit," in *Jahresberichte der Deutsche Mathematikervereinigung*, **71** (1969), 167–228, esp. 221–222; C. Reid, *Hilbert* (Berlin, 1970); and J. Barkeley Rosser, *Simplified Independence Proofs* (New York, 1969).

Also see T. Skolem, "Logisch-kombinatorische Untersuchungen über die Erfüllbarkeit oder Beweisbarkeit mathematischer Sätze nebst einem Theoreme über dichte Mengen," in *Skrifter utgitt av Videnskapsselskapet i Kristiania*, I. Mat.-naturvid. kl. (1920), no. 4; "Einige Bemerkungen zur axiomatischen Begründung der Mengenlehre," in *Matematiker kongressen i Helsinfors den 4–7 Juli 1922* (Helsinki, 1923), 217–232; "Über einige Grundlagenfragen der Mathematik," in *Skrifter utgitt av det Norske videnskaps-akademi i Oslo*, I. Mat.-naturvid. kl. (1929), no. 4; and "Einige Bemerkungen zu der Abhandlung von E. Zermelo: 'Über die Definitheit in der Axiomatik,'" in *Fundamenta mathematicae*, **15** (1930), 337–341; and L. Zoretti and A. Rosenthal, "Die

Punktmengen," in *Encyklopädie der mathematischen Wissenschaften*, II, pt. 3 (Leipzig, 1923), 855–1030.

B. VAN ROOTSELAAR

ZEUTHEN, HIERONYMUS GEORG (*b.* Grimstrup, West Jutland, Denmark, 15 February 1839; *d.* Copenhagen, Denmark, 6 January 1920)

The son of a minister, Zeuthen received his earliest education in Grimstrup and at the age of ten entered the secondary school in Sorø, where his father had been transferred. From 1857 to 1862 he studied pure and applied mathematics at the University of Copenhagen. After passing the examination for a master's degree, he received a stipend in 1863 to travel to Paris for further study with Chasles. Having become familiar with his writings, Zeuthen followed Chasles's lead in his own work on enumerative methods in geometry and also in undertaking research on the history of mathematics.

Zeuthen found in enumerative methods in geometry ("number geometry") a fertile area for research. His first work on this subject was his doctoral dissertation at the University of Copenhagen, *Nyt Bidrag til Laeren on Systemer af Keglesnit* (1865), which was also published in French in *Nouvelles annales de mathématiques* (2nd ser., **5** [1866]) as "Nouvelle méthode pour déterminer les caractéristiques des systèmes de coniques." In this work Zeuthen adhered closely to Chasles's theory of the characteristics of conic systems but also presented new points of view: for the elementary systems under consideration, he first ascertained the numbers for point or line conics in order to employ them to determine the characteristics. Arthur Cayley presented a thorough discussion of the relationships and an exposition of the entire theory in "On the Curves Which Satisfy Given Conditions" (*Philosophical Transactions of the Royal Society*, **158** [1868], 75–143).

The first decade of Zeuthen's scientific activity was devoted entirely to enumerative methods in geometry, and his works were published in *Tidsskrift for Mathematik*, of which he was editor from 1871 to 1889; he was also a contributor to *Mathematische Annalen* and other European scientific journals. A summary of this work was presented in *Lehrbuch der abzählenden Methoden der Geometrie* (1914); and as a leading expert in the field, he was chosen to write "Encyklopädiebericht über abzählende Methoden" for the *Encyklopädie der mathematischen Wissenschaften* (III, pt. 2 [1905], 257–312).

In 1871 Zeuthen became assistant professor and in 1886 full professor at the University of Copenhagen, where he remained until his death, serving as rector in 1896. While at the university he also taught at the nearby Polytechnic Academy and for many years was secretary of the Royal Danish Academy of Sciences.

After 1875, in addition to teaching, Zeuthen wrote on mechanics, geometry, and the history of mathematics. In his first major work on this subject, "Kegelsnitlaeren in Oltiden" (1885), he presented an exposition of Apollonius of Perga's theory of conic sections, in which he showed that Apollonius had employed oblique coordinates in deriving the properties of conics. Zeuthen also found in his work the projective production of the conics from two pencils of lines.

In a second, larger work (1896), Zeuthen traced the development of mathematics to the Middle Ages, presenting the influences of the Greek tradition that were transmitted to medieval mathematics through the Arabs and the rediscovery of the original works. He continued his historical studies in *Geschichte der Mathematik im 16. und 17. Jahrhundert* (1903), a large portion of which is devoted to Descartes and Viète, with regard not only to algebra and analytic geometry but also to the history of analysis, the development of which Zeuthen traced from its beginnings to Newton and Leibniz. Zeuthen also emphasized the importance of Barrow's works in the emergence of this discipline.

Although in these works Zeuthen naturally drew on the findings and references of other authors, his results were based essentially on careful study of original texts. Moreover, he strove to attune his thinking to the ancient forms of mathematics, in order to appraise the value of the resources and methods available in earlier periods. Although he was criticized for not providing full details concerning his sources, it is widely conceded that Zeuthen was the foremost historian of mathematics of his time, perhaps superior to Moritz Cantor and Siegmund Günther.

Zeuthen saw things intuitively: he constantly strove to attain an overall conception that would embrace the details of the subject under investigation and afford a way of seizing their significance. This approach characterized his historical research equally with his work on enumerative methods in geometry.

A *Festschrift* was dedicated to Zeuthen on his seventieth birthday, and in honor of his eightieth birthday a medal with his likeness was struck.

BIBLIOGRAPHY

I. ORIGINAL WORKS. A list of Zeuthen's 161 published writings is in M. Noether, "Hieronymus Georg Zeuthen" (see below), 15–23. Among his most important monographs are *Grundriss einer elementargeometrischen Kegelschnittslehre* (Leipzig, 1882); "Kegelsnitlaeren in Oltiden," which is *Kongelige Danske Videnskabernes Selskabs Skrifter*, 6th ser., **3**, no. 1 (1885), 1–319, 2nd ed. by O. Neugebauer (Copenhagen, 1949); German trans. by R. Fischer-Benzon as *Die Lehre von den Kegelschnitten im Altertum* (Copenhagen, 1886), 2nd ed. by J. E. Hofmann (Hildesheim, 1966); *Forelaesning over Mathematikens Historie: Oldtig i Middelalder* (Copenhagen, 1893), German trans. as *Geschichte der Mathematik im Altertum und Mittelalter* (Copenhagen, 1896), French trans. by J. Mascart (Paris, 1902); *Geschichte der Mathematik im 16. und 17. Jahrhundert* (Copenhagen, 1903), also in German (Leipzig, 1903) and Russian (Moscow–Leningrad, 1933); and *Lehrbuch der abzählenden Methoden der Geometrie* (Leipzig–Berlin, 1914).

II. SECONDARY LITERATURE. See Johannes Hjelmslev, "Hieronymus Georg Zeuthen," in *Matematisk Tidsskrift*, ser. A (1939), 1–10; and Max Noether, "Hieronymus Georg Zeuthen," in *Mathematische Annalen*, **83** (1921), 1–23. Luigi Berzolari, "Bericht über die allgemeine Theorie der höheren ebenen algebraischen Kurven," in *Encyklopädie mathematischen Wissenschaften*, III, pt. 2 (Leipzig, 1906), 313–455, contains many references to Zeuthen's work and results.

KARLHEINZ HAAS

ZHUKOVSKY, NIKOLAY EGOROVICH (*b.* Orekhovo, Vladimir province, Russia, 17 January 1847; *d.* Moscow, U.S.S.R., 17 March 1921)

The son of a communications engineer, Zhukovsky completed his secondary education at the Fourth Gymnasium for Men in Moscow in 1864 and graduated in 1868 from the Faculty of Physics and Mathematics of the University of Moscow, having specialized in applied mathematics. In 1870 he began teaching at the Second Gymnasium for Women in Moscow, and at the beginning of 1872 he was invited to teach mathematics at the Moscow Technical School, at which he also lectured on theoretical mechanics from 1874. Two years later he defended a dissertation at the Technical School on the kinematics of a liquid and was awarded the degree of master of applied mathematics; a separate chair of mechanics was subsequently established for him at the school. In 1882 he defended his doctoral dissertation, on the stability of motion, at Moscow University and four years later became head of the department of mechanics there. In 1894 he was elected corresponding member of the St. Petersburg Academy of Sciences, and in 1900 he was promoted to member. Unwilling to leave his teaching posts in Moscow and undertake the requisite move to St. Petersburg, however, Zhukovsky withdrew his candidacy. A member of the Moscow Mathematical Society, he also served as vice-president from 1903 to 1905, and as president from 1905 until his death he proved to be an outstanding administrator.

Zhukovsky's approximately 200 publications in mechanics and its applications to technology reveal the wide range of his interests. Several works are devoted to the motion of a solid around a fixed point, in particular, to the case of Sonya Kovalevsky, for which he gave an elegant geometrical interpretation. He also wrote on the theory of ships, on the resistance of materials, and on practical mechanics. From the beginning of the twentieth century his interest focused primarily on aerodynamics and aviation, to which he devoted himself exclusively in his later years.

In his clear and well-organized lectures Zhukovsky made extensive use of geometric methods, which he valued highly. His lectures on hydrodynamics were standard works for many years, and his course on the theory of regulation of mechanical action (1908–1909) was the first rigorous presentation in Russian of the fundamentals of that subject. His lectures at the Moscow Technical School on the theoretical basis of aeronautics (1911–1912) were the world's first systematic course in aviation theory and were based largely on his own theoretical research and on experiments conducted in laboratories that he had established. During World War I Zhukovsky and his students taught special courses for pilots at the Technical School.

Instrumental in the development of Soviet aviation, Zhukovsky was named head of the Central Aerohydrodynamics Institute, established in 1918. The school of aviation that subsequently developed from it was based on his teaching and became the N. E. Zhukovsky Academy of Military and Aeronautical Engineering in 1922.

Zhukovsky is considered the founder of Russian hydromechanics and aeromechanics. In his master's thesis (1876) he made extensive use of geometric, as well as analytic, methods to establish the kinematic laws of particles in a current. In 1885 he was awarded the N. D. Brashman Prize for a major theoretical work on the motion of a solid containing a homogeneous liquid. The methods that he

developed in this memoir made it possible to solve certain problems of astronomy, concerning the laws of planetary rotation, and of ballistics, on the theory of projectiles having liquid cores. In a work dealing with a modification of the Kirchhoff method for determining the motion of a liquid in two dimensions with constant velocity and an unknown line of flow (1890), Zhukovsky used the theory of functions of a complex variable to elaborate a method for determining the resistance of a profile having any number of critical points. In addition to solving the problems studied by Kirchhoff, he resolved others, the solution of which had been extremely complicated with the use of existing methods. A memoir written with S. A. Chaplygin (1906) gave a precise solution to the problem of the motion of a lubricant between pin and bearings, and stimulated a number of other investigations.

In hydraulics, Zhukovsky in 1888 undertook theoretical research on the movement of subsurface water and studied the influence of pressure on water-permeated sand, establishing the relation between changes in the water level and changes in barometric pressure. Showing that the variation in the water level depends on the thickness of the water-bearing layer, he introduced formulas to determine the undergound water supply, using experimental data extensively. This research was summarized in a work on hydraulic shock in water pipes (1898), in which Zhukovsky established that the reason for damage to water mains was the sudden increase in pressure that followed the rapid closing of the valves. Extensive experiments enabled him to present the physical nature of hydraulic shock, to give a formula for determining the time needed for safe closing of the mains, and to elaborate a method for preserving them from damage effected by hydraulic shock. Zhukovsky acquired an international reputation for this theory, which has remained fundamental to problems of hydraulic shock.

Zhukovsky's other works in hydrodynamics concern the formation of riverbeds (1914) and the selection of a river site for constructing dams and for withdrawing water used to cool machines at large power stations (1915).

Known as "the father of Russian aviation," Zhukovsky became interested in the late 1880's in flight in heavier-than-air machines, a basic problem of which was lift. The experimental data that had been obtained proved useful only in particular cases; attempts to determine lift on the basis of theoretical premises—especially existing theories of jet stream—yielded results that differed considerably from experimental findings.

Considering it necessary to first establish a physical picture of lift, Zhukovsky in 1890 considered the possibility that it can result from certain vortical motions caused by the viscosity of the surrounding medium. His subsequent experiments with disks rotating in an air current (1890–1891) anticipated his concept of bound vortices, the basis of his theory of lift. In 1891 Zhukovsky began studying the dynamics of flight in heavier-than-air machines, theoretically substantiating the possibility of complex motion of an airborne craft, in particular the existence of loops. In 1890–1891 Zhukovsky undertook experiments designed to study the changing position of the center of pressure of a wing with the simplest profile, a flat disk. By that time he had already turned his attention to the question of stability and was conducting tests of gliders and kites. In studying propeller thrust, Zhukovsky considered heavier-than-air craft powered by flapping wings, multipropellered helicopters, and screw propellors. In 1897 he presented a method of computing the most efficient angle of attack of a wing.

Zhukovsky's works on the motion of a substance in a liquid, published in the 1880's and 1890's, included a memoir on the paradox of Du Buat (1734–1809), for which he gave a physical explanation. In 1779 Du Buat had shown experimentally that the resistance of an immobile disk in a moving liquid is greater than the resistance of a disk moving at the same speed in a stationary liquid—a phenomenon that seemed to contradict the general laws of mechanics. Zhukovsky explained the discrepancy by the fact that, in practice, turbulence always occurs on the walls and the free surface of a liquid. To support his explanation he constructed a small device by means of which he showed that when there is no turbulence the pressure remains the same in both cases.

Zhukovsky established that lift results from the flow in an airstream of an immobile bound vortex (or system of vortices) by which the object can be replaced. From this starting point, he derived a formula for lift, equal to the product of the density of air, the circulation velocity of the surrounding airstream, and the velocity of the body. The theorem was confirmed in experiments with rotating oblong disks, conducted in 1905–1906 at the Aerodynamics Institute at Kuchino, near Moscow.

The formulation in 1910 of the Zhukovsky-Chaplygin postulate, concerning the determination of the rate of circulation around a wing, made it possible to solve the problem of lift, to determine its moment, and to develop a profile for airplane wings. Zhukovsky also investigated the profile of resistance of a wing and established the existence of resistance caused by the flow of turbulence from the wing's sharp leading edge.

In high-speed aerodynamics, Zhukovsky in 1919 presented a theory of the distribution of high-velocity plane and spherical waves, and demonstrated its possible application to determine the resistance of projectiles. His work in airplane stability included a major monograph (1918) in which he considered the construction of airplanes on the assumption that the longerons bear uniform loads arising from the weight of the wings and from the air pressure.

Zhukovsky initiated the study in Russia of the theory of bombing from airplanes. In 1915 he offered a method of determining the trajectory and bomb velocity when the air resistance is proportional to the square of the velocity; he provided a method of calculating the change of air density from a given altitude; and he examined various practical methods for using bombing and sighting apparatus.

S. A. Chaplygin was the most distinguished member of Zhukovsky's school, which included A. I. Nekrasov, L. S. Leybenzon, V. P. Vetchinkin, B. N. Yuriev, and A. N. Tupolev.

BIBLIOGRAPHY

I. ORIGINAL WORKS. Zhukovsky's complete collected works were published as *Polnoe sobranie sochineny*, 9 vols. (Moscow–Leningrad, 1935–1937). Other collections are *Izbrannye sochinenia* ("Selected Works"), 2 vols. (Moscow–Leningrad, 1948); and *Sobranie sochineny* ("Collected Works"), 7 vols. (Moscow–Leningrad, 1948–1950).

II. SECONDARY LITERATURE. On Zhukovsky and his work, see V. A. Dombrovskaya, *Nikolay Egorovich Zhukovsky* (Moscow–Leningrad, 1939), with bibliography of his writings; V. V. Golubev, *Nikolay Egorovich Zhukovsky* (Moscow, 1947); A. T. Grigorian, *Ocherki istorii mekhaniki v Rossii* ("Sketches of the History of Mechanics in Russia"; Moscow, 1961); "Vklad N. E. Zhukovskogo i S. A. Chaplygina v gidro-dinamiky i aerodinamiku" ("The Contribution of Zhukovsky and Chaplygin to Hydrodynamics and Aerodynamics"), in *Evolyutsia mekhaniki v Rossii* ("Evolution of Mechanics in Russia"; Moscow, 1967); and *Mekhanika ot antichnosti do nashikh dney* ("Mechanics From Antiquity to Our Time"; Moscow, 1971); A. A. Kosmodemyansky, "Nikolay Egorovich Zhukovsky," in *Lyudi russkoy nauki*

("Men of Russian Science"; Moscow, 1961), 169–177; and L. S. Leybenzon, *Nikolay Egorovich Zhukovsky* (Moscow–Leningrad, 1947).

A. T. GRIGORIAN

ZOLOTAREV, EGOR IVANOVICH (*b.* St. Petersburg, Russia [now Leningrad, U.S.S.R.], 12 April 1847; *d.* St. Petersburg, 19 July 1878)

Zolotarev was the son of a watchmaker. After graduating in 1863 with a silver medal from the Gymnasium, he enrolled at the Faculty of Physics and Mathematics of St. Petersburg, where he attended the lectures of Chebyshev and his student A. N. Korkin. He graduated with the candidate's degree in 1867 and the following year became assistant professor there. In 1869 he defended his master's dissertation, on an indeterminate third-degree equation; his doctoral dissertation (1874) was devoted to the theory of algebraic integers. In 1876 he was appointed professor of mathematics at St. Petersburg and junior assistant of applied mathematics at the St. Petersburg Academy of Sciences.

On two trips abroad Zolotarev attended the lectures of Kummer and Weierstrass, and met with Hermite. He shared his impressions of noted scholars and discussed mathematical problems with Korkin, whose collaborator he subsequently became. Zolotarev died at the age of thirty-one, of blood poisoning, after having fallen under a train.

The most gifted member of the St. Petersburg school of mathematics, Zolotarev produced fundamental works on mathematical analysis and the theory of numbers during his eleven-year career. Independent of Dedekind and Kronecker, he constructed a theory of divisibility for the whole numbers of any field of algebraic numbers, working along the lines developed by Kummer and elaborating the ideas and methods that now comprise the core of local algebra. He operated with the numbers of the local ring Z_p and its full closure in the field $Q(\theta)$ and, in essence, brought under examination the semilocal ring O_p. In modern terminology Zolotarev's results consisted in proving that (1) the ring O_p is a finite type of Z_p-modulus and (2) O_p is a ring of principal ideals. In his local approach to the concept of a number of the field $Q(\theta)$ Zolotarev demonstrated that the ring O of the whole numbers in $Q(\theta)$ is the intersection of all semilocal rings O_p. Zolotarev defined ideal numbers in O as essentially valuations and found the simple elements of O_p with the aid of a lemma that is the analog of the theory of expansion into Puiseux series.

Zolotarev employed a theory that he had constructed for determining, with a finite number of operations, the possibility of selecting a number, A, such that the second-order elliptical differential $(x + A) \, dx \, / \sqrt{R(x)}$, where $R(x)$ is a fourth-degree polynomial with real coefficients, can be integrated in logarithms. Abel demonstrated that for an affirmative solution it is necessary and sufficient that $\sqrt{R(x)}$ be expandable into a periodic continuous fraction; but because he did not give an evaluation of the length of the period, his solution was ineffective. Zolotarev provided the required evaluation, applying the equation of the division of elliptic functions.

With Korkin, Zolotarev worked on the problem posed by Hermite of determining the minima of positive quadratic forms of n variables having real coefficients; they gave exhaustive solutions for the cases $n = 4$ and $n = 5$.

Among Zolotarev's other works are an original proof of the law of quadratic reciprocity, based on the group-theoretic lemma that Frobenius had called "the most interesting," as well as solutions of difficult individual questions in the theory of the optimal approximation of functions. Thus, Zolotarev found the nth-degree polynomial, the first coefficient of which is equal to unity and the second coefficient of which is fixed, that deviates least from zero.

BIBLIOGRAPHY

I. ORIGINAL WORKS. Zolotarev's complete writings were published by the V. A. Steklov Institute of Physics and Mathematics as *Polnoe sobranie sochineny*, 2 vols. (Leningrad, 1931–1932); see esp. II, 72–129; and "Sur la théorie des nombres complexes," in *Journal de mathématiques pures et appliquées*, 3rd ser., **6** (1880), 51–84, 129–166.

II. SECONDARY LITERATURE. On Zolotarev's life and work, see I. G. Bashmakova, "Obosnovanie teorii delimosti v trudakh E. I. Zolotareva" ("Foundation of the Theory of Divisibility in Zolotarev's Works"), in *Istoriko-matematicheskie issledovaniya*, **2** (1949), 231–351; N. G. Chebotarev, "Ob osnovanii teorii idealov po Zolotarevu" ("On the Foundation of the Theory of Ideals According to Zolotarev"), in *Uspekhi matematicheskikh nauk*, **2**, no. 6 (1947), 52–67; B. N. Delone, *Peterburgskaya shkola teorii chisel* ("The St. Petersburg School of the Theory of Numbers"; Moscow–Leningrad, 1947); R. O. Kuzmin, "Zhizn i nauchnaya deyatelnost Egora Ivanovicha Zolotareva" ("Zolotarev's Life and Scientific Activity"), in *Uspekhi matematicheskikh nauk*, **2**, no. 6 (1947), 21–51; and E. P. Ozhigova, *Egor Ivanovich Zolotarev* (Moscow–Leningrad, 1966).

I. G. BASHMAKOVA

ZUCCHI, NICCOLÒ (*b.* Parma, Italy, 6 December 1586; *d.* Rome, Italy, 21 May 1670)

Zucchi taught rhetoric, and later theology and mathematics, at the Jesuits' Roman College, of which he was also rector and from which he moved to the one in Ravenna. Returning to Rome, he held the office of preacher in the Apostolic Palace for at least seven years and was in charge of his religious order's mother house. Because of the esteem in which he was held, he was a member of the retinue of the papal legate sent to the court of the Emperor Ferdinand II, where he met Kepler; Zucchi considered this event one of the most important in his life.

Zucchi is remembered today for his research, "partly the fruit of experiment and partly of reasoning," in optics. In 1616 (or perhaps 1608) he had constructed an apparatus in which an ocular lens was used to observe the image produced by reflection from a concave metal mirror. This was one of the earliest reflecting telescopes, in which the enlargement is obtained by the interaction of mirrors and lenses.

Later, in *Optica philosophia* . . ., Zucchi described the apparatus, from which, wittingly or not, the most improved models of a slightly later date were derived (those of Gregory and Newton, for instance).

This apparatus enabled Zucchi to make a more thorough examination of the spots on Mars (1640), observed four years earlier by F. Fontana, and thus to supply material for Cassini's discovery of the rotation of that planet (1666).

Zucchi worked in a period of contradictory thought and scientific investigation. Alongside the clarity of Galileo's ideas were beliefs at once highly ingenuous and abstruse, as well as extravagant errors.

Hence, Zucchi accepted strange astronomical theories, which he expounded with the utmost certainty in his sermons. In the cathedral of Pisa (Galileo's native city) he asserted in 1638 that the sun is further from the earth during the summer than in winter and that this is proved by the need to alter the length of the telescope in those seasons in order to be able to observe sunspots. But this was not enough: he stated that Venus is nearer the sun than Mercury is, because the former represents beauty and the latter skill. Such statements elicited laughter in some circles but were simultaneously accepted in others as a sign of profound doctrine.

BIBLIOGRAPHY

Zucchi's main work is *Optica philosophia experimentalis et ratione a fundamentis constituta* . . ., 2 vols. (Leiden, 1652–1656). He was also author of *Nova de machinis philosophia* (Rome, 1649).

LUIGI CAMPEDELLI

Mathematicians by Field

ALGEBRA

Abel
Abraham Bar Hiyya
Abū Kāmil
Agnesi
Albert
Argand
Aronhold
Artin
Ibn Al-Bannā'

Bartholin
Bertrand
Betti
Bezout
Blichfeldt
Bombelli
Boole
Borchardt
Bourbaki
Brauer
Bring
Brioschi
Bromwich
Brożek
Budan de Boislaurent
Bugaev
Burnside

Cardano
Cartan
Cauchy
Cayley
Chebotaryov
Chu Shih-Chieh
Chuquet
Clebsch
Clifford
Cole

Dantzig
Dedekind

De Morgan
Dickson
Diophantus of Alexandria
Dyck

Eisenstein
Euler

Fagnano dei Toschi, G. C.
Fermat
Ferrari
Ferro
Fibonacci
Frobenius

Galois
Gauss
Gordan
Gräffe
Grave

Hamilton, W. R.
Harish-Chandra
Harriot
Herbrand
Hilbert
Hindenberg
Hoëné-Wroński
Horner
Hudde

Jerrard
Jordan

Al-Karajī
Al-Khayyāmī
Al-Khwārizmī
Kirkman
Klein

Koenig, J.
Kramp
Kronecker
Krull

Lagrange
Leibniz
Li Chih
Lie
Liouville
Lipschitz
Liu Hui

MacMahon
Malfatti
Maltsev
Mathieu
Meyer
Miller, G. A.
Minkowski
Molin
Moore, E. H.

Naimark
Nārāyaṇa
Netto
Noether, A. E.

Oughtred

Peacock
Peirce, B.
Peirce, C. S.
Peletier
Pell
Poincaré

Al-Qaladṣādī

Ries
Robinson
Rolle
Rudolff
Ruffini

Al-Samaw'al
Schläfli
Schur
Segner
Seki
Servois
Skolem
Sluse
Stampioen
Steinitz
Stevin
Stifel
Sylow
Sylvester

Tartaglia
Tschirnhaus
Al-Ṭūsī (Nasir al-Dīn)

Vandermonde
Viète
Von Neumann

Wallis
Weber
Wedderburn
Weyl

Yang Hui

ANALYSIS, DIFFERENTIAL EQUATIONS

Agnesi
Akhieyer
Arbogast

Baire
Banach
Bergman
Bernoulli, Jakob I
Bernoulli, Johann I
Bernstein, S.
Besicovitch
Birkhoff
Bliss
Bôcher
Bochner
Bohl
Bohr

Bolza
Bolzano
Borel
Bougainville
Bouquet
Boutroux
Briot
Brisson
Bunyakovsky

Carathéodory
Carnot
Cauchy
Chebyshev
Cheyne
Christoffel

Cotes
Craig

Davidov
Delsarte
Denjoy
Dini
Dirichlet
Douglas
Drach
Du Bois-Reymond
Dyck

Egorov
Engel
Erdélyi

Euler
Evans

Fatou
Fejér
Fontaine
Forsyth
Fourier
Français, F. J.
Fréchet
Fredholm
Fubini
Fuchs
Fuss

Gauss

Gelfond
Göpel
Goursat
Grave
Gregory, D. F.
Gudermann

Haar
Halphen
Hamilton, W. R.
Hardy, G. H.
Heine
Hellinger
Helly
Hermann, J.
Hermite
Hilbert
Hobson
Hölder
Hoüel
Humbert
Hurwitz

Jensen

Kneser
Knopp
Koch
Koebe
Königsberger
Kovalevsky
Kronecker
Krylov, N. M.
Kummer

Lacroix
Lagrange

Laguerre
Landau
Landen
Landsberg
Laplace
Laurent, P. A.
Lebesgue
Legendre
Leibniz
Lerch
Levi-Civita
Levinson
Lexell
L'Hospital
Lie
Lindelöf
Liouville
Lipschitz
Littlewood
Loewner
Luzin
Lyapunov

Maclaurin
Markov
Mayer
Méray
Mineur
Mittag-Leffler
Monge
Montel
Moore, E. H.

Naimark
Nevanlinna
Newton, I.
Nielsen
Nieuwentijt

Osgood
Ostrogradsky

Painlevé
Parseval des Chênes
Peano
Pérès
Petrovsky
Pfaff
Picard
Pincherle
Plana
Poincaré
Pringsheim
Privolov
Puiseux

Radó
Radon
Ramanujan
Razmadze
Ricatti, J. F.
Ricatti, V.
Ricci-Curbastro
Riemann
Riesz, F.
Riesz, M.
Ritt
Rosenhain
Runge

Saks
Salem
Schläfli
Schmidt
Schottky
Schouten
Schwarz

Serret
Servois
Shnirelman
Siegel
Simpson
Sokhotsky
Sonin
Steklov
Stepanov
Stieltjes
Sturm, C.-F.

Talbot
Tannery, J.
Tauber
Taylor
Titchmarsh
Toeplitz

Vallée-Poussin
Vessiot
Vitali
Volterra
Von Neumann

Watson
Weber
Weierstrass
Weyl
Wiener, N.
Wilson, E. B.
Wintner

Young, J. H.

Zolotarev

ARITHMETIC, COMPUTING, NUMBER THEORY

Abū'l-Wafā

Babbage
Bachet de Méziriac
Bachmann
Al-Baghdādī
Bell
Berwick
Billy
Boethius
Briggs
Brouncker
Bugaev
Bunyakovsky
Bügi

Caramuel y Lobkowitz
Cataldi
Ceulen
Chebyshev
Ch'in Chiu-Shao
Chu Shih-Chieh
Chuquet

Davenport
Dedekind
Delamain
Dickson
Diophantus of Alexandria

Dirichlet
Domninus of Larissa

Eisenstein
Eratosthenes
Euler
Ibn Ezra

Fermat
Fibonacci
Fueter

Galois
Gauss
Gelfond
Germain
Goldbach
Grave

Hadamard
Hardy, G. H.
Hartree
Hasse
Hecke
Heilbronn
Hensel
Hermite
Hilbert

Hill, L. S.
Humbert
Hurwitz

Jacobi
John of Murs
Jordanus de Nemore

Al-Kāshī
Al-Khayyāmī
Klein
Kronecker
Kummer
Kürschák
Kushyār

Lagny
Lagrange
Lambert
Landau, E.
La Roche
Legendre
Li Chih
Lindemann
Linnick
Liouville
Liu Hui
Littlewood
Lucas

Markov
Mathews
Mersenne
Minkowski
Mordell

Napier
Nārāyaṇa
Al-Nasawī
Nicomachus of Gerasa

Ortega
Oughtred

Pascal, B.
Pell
Poincaré
Pythagoras of Samos

Al-Qaladṣādī

Rademacher
Ramanujan
Ramsden
Riemann
Ries
Runge

Seidel	Takagi	Al-Uqlīdīsī	Waring
Seki	Thue		Weber
Shanks	Thymaridas		Wessel
Shnirelman	Tsu Ch'ung-Chih	Vallée-Poussin	Weyl
Siegel	Tunstall	Vandiver	Wilson, J.
Sierpiński	Turán	Vlacq	
Skolem	Turing	Von Neumann	
Smith	Al-Ṭūsī (Nasir al-Dīn)	Voronov	Yang Hui
Śrīdhara			
Stifel			
Stirling	Al-Umawī	Wallis	Zolotarev

ASTRONOMY, GEODESY, TRIGONOMETRY

Abū'l-Wafā	Eratosthenes	La Condamine	Qāḍī Zāda
Adams	Esclangon	Lagrange	
Andoyer	Eudoxus of Cnidus	Lambert	
Aristarchus of Samos	Euler	Lansberge	
Āryabhaṭa I	Ibn Ezra	Laplace	Regiomontanus
Āryabhaṭa II		Lavanha	Rheticus
Autolycus of Pitane		Levi ben Gerson	Richard of Wallingford
Auzout	Fine, O.	Loomis	Roomen
Azara			Rumovsky
	Gauss		
Balbus	Gemma Frisius	Macmillan	
Banū Mūsā	Glaisher	Magini	Sacrobosco
Barbier	Gregory, D.	Manṣūr	Schickard
Al-Battānī	Gregory, J.	Menelaus of Alexandria	Seidel
Bernoulli, Johann III	Gunter	Mercator	Shen Kua
Bessel		Mineur	Sigüenza y Góngora
Bhāskara II		Möbius	Al-Sijzī
Al-Bīrūnī	Ḥabash al-Ḥāsib	Moiseev	Sinān
Borelli	Halley	Mollweide	Snel
Boulliau	Hartmann, G.	Moulton	Śrīpati
Bredon	Hartmann, J.	Mouton	Subbotin
Brinkley	Ibn al-Haytham	Muḥyi 'l-Dīn	
Buot	Heraclides Ponticus	Munīśvara Viśvarūpa	
Bürgi	Hill, G. W.		Thābit ibn Qurra
	Hipparchus		Theodosius of Bithynia
	Huygens	Al-Nayrīzī	Thiele
Calandrelli	Hysicles of Alexandria	Newcomb	Tsu Ch'ung-Chih
Callippus		Newton, H. A.	Al-Ṭūsī (Nasir al-Dīn)
Campanus of Novara	Ibrāhīm ibn Sinān	Newton, I.	Al-Ṭūsī (Sharaf al-Dīn)
Castillon		Norwood	
Ch'in Chiu-Shao		Nuñez Salaciense	
Christmann	Jābir ibn Aflah		Volterra
Clausen	Al-Jawharī		
Clavius	Al-Jayyānī	Oenopides of Chios	
Conon of Samos	John of Gmunden	Oughtred	Werner
Cosserat	John of Lignères		Winlock
	John of Murs		Winthrop
		Peirce, B.	Wintner
Danti		Peirce, C. S.	Wittich
Darwin, G. H.	Al-Kāshī	Peter Philomena of Dacia	Wright
Dasypodius	Al-Khalīlī	Peurbach	
Dee	Al-Khayyāmī	Pitiscus	
Digges, L.	Al-Khāzin	Plana	
Digges, T.	Al-Khujandī	Poincaré	Ibn Yūnus
Dionis du Séjour	Al-Khwārizmī	Poisson	
Dositheus	Krasovsky	Pratt, J. H.	
Dudith	Kushyār	Ptolemy	Zucchi

FOUNDATIONS, LOGIC, SET THEORY

Aristotle	Bolzano	Cantor, G.	Fraenkel
	Boole	Couturat	Frege
	Bourbaki		
	Bradwardine		
Bernays	Brouwer	De Morgan	Gentzen
Bernstein, F.	Burali-Forti	Dodgson	Gödel

Hamilton, W.	Löwenheim	Ramsey	Tarski
Herbrand	Lukasiewicz	Richard, J. A.	Turing
Heytesbury		Robinson	Al-Ṭūsī (Nasir al-Dīn)
Heyting	McColl	Russell	
Hilbert	Maltsev		
Huntington	Mostowski		Venn
			Von Neumann
Jevons			
Johnson	Novikov	Saccheri	
		Al-Samarquandī	
		Schoenflies	Weyl
Kalmár	Padoa	Schröder	Whitehead, A. N.
Kronecker	Peano	Segner	
	Peirce, C. S.	Shatunovsky	
	Poretsky	Sierpiński	
Leibniz	Post	Skolem	Zeno of Elea
Leśniewski		Swineshead	Zermelo

GEOMETRY, TOPOLOGY

Abraham Bar Hivya	Ceva, T.	Grandi	Lacroix
Abū Kāmil	Chasles	Grassmann	Laguerre
Aida Yasuaki	Clebsch	Gregory, J.	La Hire
Ajima Naonobu	Clifford	Grossmann	Lalouvere
Alexsandrov	Codazzi	Gua de Malves	Lambert
Antiphon	Coolidge	Guccia	Lamé
Apollonius of Perga	Cramer	Guldin	Lancret
Archimedes	Cremona		Lefschetz
Archytas of Tarentum			Legendre
Argand		Hachette	Leibniz
Aristaeus	Dandelin	Halphen	Lemoine
Arnauld	Darboux	Halsted	Leo
	DeGroot	Hausdorff	Leodamas of Thasos
	Dehn	Ibn al-Haytham	Leonardo da Vinci
Ibn Al-Bannā'	Desargues	Hero of Alexandria	Le Paige
Banū Mūsā	Descartes	Hesse	Le Poivre
Barbier	Dini	Heuraet	Le Tenneur
Barrow	Dinostratus	Hilbert	Levi-Civita
Bellavitis	Diocles	Hippias of Elis	Lexell
Beltrami	Dionysodorus	Hippocrates of Chios	Lie
Bernstein, S.	Douglas	Hobbes	Lindemann
Bertini	Dupin	Hodge	Lipschitz
Bertrand	Dürer	Hölder	Liu Hui
Betti		Hopf	Lobachevsky
Bezout		Huygens	Loria
Bhāskara II	Egorov	Hysicles of Alexandria	Lueroth
Bianchi	Ehresmann		
Blaschke	Eisenhart		
Bobilier	Enriques	Ibrahīm ibn Sinān	Macaulay
Bolyai, F.	Euclid		Maclaurin
Bolyai, J.	Eudoxus of Cnidus		Al-Māhānī
Bonnet	Euler	Janiszewski	Malfatti
Borelli		Al-Jawharī	Mannheim
Bosse		Al-Jayyānī	Mascheroni
Bour	Fabri	Joachimsthal	Mazurkiewicz
Bouvelles	Fagnano dei Toschi, G. F.	Jonquières	Menaechmus
Braikenridge	Fagnano dei Toschi, G. C.	Jordan	Menelaus of Alexandria
Bret	Fano	Jordanus de Nemore	Mengoli
Brianchon	Fermat	Juel	Meusnier de la Place
Brill	Feuerbach		Meyer
Brocard	Francesca		Minding
Brouwer	Frenet	Kagan	Minkowski
Bryson of Heraclea	Frenicle de Bessy	Kamāl al-Dīn	Möbius
Burali-Forti	Fubini	Keckermann	Mohr
Buteo	Fuss	Keill	Monge
	Fyodorov	Kerékjártó	Moore, E. H.
		Al-Khayyāmī	Moore, R. L.
Carnot		Al-Khujandī	Moufang
Cartan	Galerkin	Klein	Moutard
Castelnuovo	Gauss	Klügel	Mydorge
Cavalieri	Geiser	Koenigs	
Cayley	Gerard of Brussels	Kotelnikov	
Čech	Gergonne	Kummer	Al-Nasawī
Cesàro	Ghetaldi	Kuratowski	Al-Nayrīzī
Ceva, G.	Göpel		Neuberg

Newton, I.
Nicomedes
Noether, M.

Oenopides of Chios
Oresme

Pacioli
Pappus of Alexandria
Pascal, B.
Pascal, E.
Pasch
Patrizi
Peano
Perseus
Petersen
Peterson
Petrovsky
Pieri
Playfair
Plücker
Poincaré
Poncelet
Pythagoras of Samos

Al-Qūhī

Réumur
Reidemeister
Reye
Ribaucour
Ricci, Michelangelo
Ricci-Curbastro
Riemann
Roberval
Rohn
Rosanes
Rudio

Saccheri
Saint-Vincent
Salmon
Scheffers
Scheuchzer
Schläfli
Schoenflies
Schooten
Schoute
Schouten
Schroeter
Schubert
Schwarz
Schweikart
Segre
Serenus
Serret

Servois
Severi
Sierpiński
Al-Sijzī
Sinān
Sluse
Sommerville
Sporus of Nicaea
Stäckel
Staudt
Steiner
Stewart
Stolz
Study
Sturm, F. O. R.

Tacquet
Taurinus
Taylor
Teichmüller
Thales
Theaetetus
Theodorus of Cyrene
Theudius of Magnesia
Tietze
Tilly
Tinseau d'Amondans
Torricelli

Tschirnhaus
Al-Ṭūsī (Nasir al-Dīn)

Uryson

Valerio
Varignon
Veblen
Veronese

Wallace
Wallis
Wang
Weingarten
Weyl
Whitehead, J. H. C.
Wilczynski
Witt
Wren

Young, J. W.

Zarankiewicz
Zenodorus
Zeuthen

HISTORY, PHILOSOPHY, DISSEMINATION OF KNOWLEDGE

Adelard of Bath
Aḥmad Ibn Yūsuf
Albert of Saxony
Alberti
Albertus Magnus
Alzate y Ramírez
Anatolius of Alexandria
Anderson
Aristotle

Bacon
Barocius
Bernoulli, Nikolaus II
Bortolotti
Boutroux
Bradwardine
Braunmühl

Campanus of Novara
Cantor, M. B.
Clarke
Carcavi
Chrystal
Ciruelo
Clifford
Collins
Cotes
Commandino
Comte
Condorcet
Coolidge
Crelle
Crousaz
Cunha
Curtze
Cusa

Debeaune
Dechales
Democritus

Descartes
Dickstein
Dominicus de Clavasio
Doppelmayr

Engel
Enriques
Eutocius of Ascalon

Farrar
Faulhaber
Feigl
Fibonacci
Fields
Fine, H. B.
Fink
Fontenelle
Forsyth
Français, J. F.
Frank
Fries

Geminus
Gerbert
Gergonne
Ghetaldi
Girard
Glaisher
Goldbach
Grandi
'sGravesande
Guccia
Guenther

Halley
Halsted
Hankel
Hardy, C.
Heath

Henrion
Hérigone
Hermann the Lame
Holmboe
Hugh of St. Victor
Hypatia

Isidorus of Miletus

Jagannātha
Jevons
Jones
Jungius

Kaestner
Klein
Köbel
Korteweg
Kraft
Krylov, A. N.

Lacroix
Lambert
Laplace
Laurent, M. P. H.
Lax
Leibniz
Leo the Mathematician
Le Roy
Leurechon
L'Hospital
Loria
Lull

Magnitsky
Mahāvīra
Maior
Malebranche

Mansion
Martianus Capella
Maseres
Maupertuis
Maurolico
Mello
Mersenne
Milhaud
Mittag-Leffler
Moerbeke
Montucla
Mylon

Neander
Nicomachus of Gerasa

Oresme
Ozanam

Pacioli
Pappus of Alexandria
Pecham
Peletier
Pemberton
Planudes
Plato
Plato of Tivoli
Poincaré
Poleni
Porta
Prévost
Privat de Molières
Proclus
Pythagoras of Samos

Ramus
Recorde
Reichenbach
Ricci, Matteo

Mathematicians by Field

Ricci, O.
Ricard, L. P. E.
Risner
Rowning
Rudio
Russell

Saurin
Schooten
Schott
Shen Kua
Shirakatski
Simson

Somerville
Stäckel
Stephanus of Alexandria
Stepling
Suter
Swineshead

Tannery, P.
Tartaglia
Thābit ibn Qurra
Theon of Alexandria
Theon of Smyrna
Thomaz

Todhunter
Tropfke
Al-Ṭūsī (Nasir al-Dīn)

Ver Eecke
Viviani

Weyl
Whiston
Whitehead, A. N.
Widman
Wieleitner

Woepcke
Woodhouse

Xenocrates of Chalcedon

Yativṛṣabha

Zeno of Sidon
Zeuthen

MECHANICS, PHYSICS, TECHNOLOGY

Aepinus
Ampère
Amsler
Alembert
Aguilon
Angeli
Anthemius of Tralles
Appell
Archimedes
Archytas of Tarentum
Aristoxenus
Atwood

Balmer
Barlow
Bateman
Beaugrand
Benedetti
Bernoulli, D.
Bernoulli, Jakob I
Bernoulli, Jakob II
Bernoulli, Johann I
Bernoulli, Johann II
Bessel
Betti
Birkhoff
Bjerknes
Blasius of Parma
Bobilier
Borda
Borelli
Bošković
Bossut
Bour
Boussinesq
Bowen
Bramer
Brashman
Brillouin
Bunyakovsky
Burrau

Cabeo
Camus
Carnot
Castel
Cauchy
Ceva, G.
Chaplygin
Clairaut
Cosserat
Crelle
Culmann

D'Arcy
Darwin, C. G.
Davidov

De Groot
Descartes
Dirichlet
Doppler
Duhamel
Dupré

Euler

Ferrel
Fourier
Frank
Friedmann
Frisi
Fuss
Fyodorov

Gauss
Gellibrand
Germain
Giorgi
Green
Gregory, D.
Gregory, O. G.

Hachette
Hadamard
Halley
Hamilton, W. R.
Hartree
Ibn al-Haytham
Hecht
Hermann, J.
Hero of Alexandria
Hilbert
Hodgkinson
Hopkins, W.
Hutton, C.
Huygens

Ivory

Jacobi
Joachimsthal
Jordanus de Nemore

Kaluza
Kamāl al-Dīn
Klein
Kochin
Koenig, J. S.
Koenigs
Kolosov

Korteweg
Kotelnikov
Kovalevsky
Krylov, A. N.

La Faille
Lagrange
La Hire
Lamb
Lambert
Lamé
Lamy
Laplace
Leonardo da Vinci
Le Tenneur
Lévy
Liouville
Loewner
Love
Lyapunov

Maclaurin
Macmillan
Marci of Kronland
Mathieu
Mayer
Menabrea
Meshchersky
Metius, A.
Metius, A. A.
Metius, J.
Miller, W. H.
Minkowski
Mises
Möbius
Monge
Monte
Morland

Nairne
Navier
Nekrasov
Neumann, C. G.
Neumann, F. E.
Newton, I.
Nicholson, J. W.
Noether, A. E.

Ocagne
Oresme
Ostrogradsky

Peirce, B.
Peirce, B. O. II
Pérès

Poincaré
Poinsot
Poisson
Poncelet
Ptolemy
Puiseux

Reyneau
Rey Pastor
Rheticus
Ricatti, J. F.
Ricatti, V.
Riemann
Robins
Runge
Rydberg

Saint-Venant
Schoenflies
Schuster
Sezawa
Siegel
Somov
Stäckel
Steklov
Stevin
Stokes
Stoney
Størmer
Sturm, C.-F.

Tait
Tartaglia
Thābit ibn Qurra
Thompson
Tilly
Tolman
Torricelli
Troughton
Turner

Varignon
Villalpando
Volterra
Von Neumann

Wangerin
Weyl
Whittaker
Wiener, L. C.
Wiener, N.
Woodward

Zanotti
Zhukovsky

PROBABILITY, STATISTICS

Adrain
Arbuthnot

Bachelier
Bayes
Bernoulli, D.
Bernoulli, Jakob I
Bernoulli, Nikolaus I
Bernstein, F.
Bertrand
Bienayme
Bortkiewicz

Cardano
Chebyshev
Cochran
Condorcet
Cournot
Cramer

Deparcieux

Feller
Fermat
Fisher

Galton
Gauss
Gompertz
Gosset
Graunt

Keynes
Khinchin

Laplace
Legendre
L'Huillier

Linnick
Lotka
Lyapunov

Markov
Mazurkiewicz
Mises
Moivre
Montmort

Neyman

Pascal, B.
Pearson
Petrovsky
Poisson

Quetelet

Rényi

Salem
Savage
Scheffé
Semyonov-Tyan-Shansky
Shewhart
Slutsky

Verhuslt

Wald
Wilks
Wilson, E. B.
Wolfowitz

Youden
Yule

CHRONOLOGY

2700 B.C.	Introduction of Egyptian calendar
2100	Sumerian cuneiform texts utilize base 60 positional system
1950	Old Babylonian tablets solving problems of arithmetical-algebraic character
1850	Moscow Papyrus
1650	Rhind Papyrus
585	Thales of Miletus: origins of deductive geometry
520	Pythagoras founds cult based on number worship
500	Indian *Súlvasútras*
450	Pythagorean discovery of incommensurable magnitudes
430	Democritus and Greek atomism Hippocrates of Chios: quadrature of lunes
360	Eudoxus of Cnidus: proportion theory; method of exhaustion
330	Autolycus: *On the Moving Sphere*
323	Death of Alexander the Great; Alexandria emerges as center of learning for Hellenistic world
300	Euclid's *Elements*
280	Aristarchus of Samos: heliocentric hypothesis
250	Eratosthenes calculates the circumference of the earth and the obliquity of the ecliptic
225	Apollonius' *Conics*
150	Astronomical work of Hipparchus of Nicaea
A.D. 75	*Metrica* of Heron of Alexander
100	Nicomachus: *Arithmetica* Menelaus: *Sphaerica*
150	Ptolemy's *Almagest*
250	Diophantus: *Arithmetica*
263	Liu Hui's commentary on the *Nine Chapters*
320	Pappus's *Synagoge* (*Mathematical Collection*)
390	Theon of Alexandria's edition of Euclid's *Elements*
415	Death of Hypatia of Alexandria
470	Computations of π by Tsu Ch'ung Chih
500	Āryabhata I's work on indeterminate equations
560	Eutocius' commentary on works of Archimedes
625	Brahmagupta of Ujjain
650	Hindu numeral system
773	Al-Fazārī's translation of the *Siddhāntās* into Arabic
820	Al-Ma'-mūn establishes "House of Wisdom" (*Bait al-hikma*) in Baghdad
825	Al-Khwarizmi's treatise on algebra, *Ḥisāb al-jabr wal-muqābala*
1000	Al-Battānī's work on astronomy and trigonometry Ibn al-Haytham's *Optics*
1079	Omar Khayyam reforms the Persian calendar
1150	Bhāskara's *Lilāvati* advances theory of Diophantine equations
1202	Leonardo of Pisa's *Liber abaci*
1247	Ch'in Chiu-Shao publishes work on indeterminate equations
1260	Naṣir al-Dīn leads new Mongol center at Maragha
1261	Yang Hui's arithmetical computations using decimal system
1270	William of Moerbeke's translation of works of Archimedes
1303	Yang Hui's introduction of "Pascal's triangle" published by Chu-Shih-Chieh
1328	Bradwardine's *Liber de proportionibus*
1360	Oresme's theory of forms
1400	Al-Kāshī applies Horner's method to solve algebraic equations
1464	Regiomontanus: *De triangulabis omnimodus libri quinque*
1482	Publication of first printed edition of Euclid's *Elements*
1494	Luca Pacioli: *Summa de Arithmetica*
1543	Copernicus's *De revolutionibus orbium coelestium* Tartaglia's Italian translation of Euclid's *Elements* Tartaglia's edition of William of Moerbeke's *Archimedes*
1545	Cardano's *Ars Magna*
1550	Adam Ries's *Rechenung nach der lenge, auff den Linihen und Feder*

Chronology

First volume of Plücker's *Analytisch-geometrische Entwickelungen*

1829 Abel's death at age 27

Jacobi's *Fundamenta nova theoriae functionum ellipticarum*

1830 Lobachevsky publishes work on non-Euclidean geometry

1832 Galois, age 20, mortally wounded in a duel

Janos Bolyai publishes an appendix on non-Euclidean geometry to a book published by his father, Wolfgang

1834 Poinsot: *Theorie nouvelle de la rotation des corps*

1835 Hamilton: *General Method in Dynamics*

1836 Founding of Liouville's *Journal des mathématiques pures et appliquées*

1837 Founding of *Cambridge and Dublin Mathematical Journal*

1843 Hamilton introduces quaternions

1844 First edition of Grassmann's *Ausdehnungslehre*

Liouville gives first rigorous proof of the existence of transcendental numbers

1846 Kummer introduces "ideal numbers" to formulate his reciprocity law for algebraic number fields

Liouville publishes some of Galois's posthumous manuscripts

1847 Staudt's *Geometrie der Lage*

1848 First of Salmon's texts on modern geometry

1851 Riemann's doctoral thesis on complex variable theory introduces Riemann surfaces

1854 Riemann delivers his *Habilitationsvortrag* at Göttingen

Boole's *Investigation in the Laws of Thought*

First of Cayley's nine *Memoirs on Quantics*

1856 Weierstrass begins his teaching career at the University of Berlin

1858 Brioschi founds *Annali de matematica pura et applicata*

1859 Riemann studies the zeta function and introduces the Riemann hypothesis in *"Ueber die Anzahl der Primzahlen unter einer gegebenen Grösse"*

Cayley's *Sixth Memoir on Quantics* introduces a metric for projective geometry in relation to a conic section

1863 Dedekind's first edition of Dirichlet's *Vorlesungen über Zahlentheorie*

Cremona introduces "Cremona transformations"

1868 Volume I of Plücker's *Neue Geometrie des Raumes*

1869 Clebsch and C. Neumann found *Mathematische Annalen*

1870 Jordan: *Traité des substitutions et des équations algébriques*

Benjamin Peirce's *Linear Associative Algebra*

1872 Klein's *Erlanger Programm*

Dedekind's *Stetigkeit und irrationale Zahlen*

1879 Schubert's *Kalkül der abzählenden Geometrie*

1881 Poincaré's first publications on automorphic functions

1882 Lindemann proves that π is a transcendental number, thereby showing that the quadrature of the circle is impossible by means of constructions using straightedge and compass alone

Dedekind's *Was sind und was sollen die Zahlen?*

First volume of Jordan's *Cours d'analyse*

1883 Cantor's *Grundlagen einer allgemeinen Manigfaltigkeitslehre*

1884 Frege's *Die Grundlagen der Arithmetik*

Klein's *Vorlesungen über das Ikosaeder*

1887 First volume of Darboux's *Leçons sur la théorie générale des surfaces*

1888 Founding of the New York Mathematical Society, later renamed the American Mathematical Society

First volume of Lie's *Theorie der Transformationsgruppen*

1890 Founding of the *Deutsche Mathematiker-Vereinigung*

1891 First volume of Picard's *Cours d'analyse*

1892 First volume of Poincaré's *Les méthodes nouvelles de la méchanique céleste*

1895 First volume of Poincaré's *Leçons de méchanique céleste*

Poincaré's *Analysis Situs*: origin of combinatorial topology

1896 First International Congress of Mathematicians held in Zürich

Hadamard and De la Vallée-Poussin prove the prime number theorem

1898 Recovery of Gauss's scientific diary

1899 Hilbert's *Grundlagen der Geometrie*

1900 Hilbert's speech, *"Mathematische Probleme,"* delivered at the Second International Congress of Mathematicians in Paris

1902 First volume of Bianchi's *Lezioni di goemtria differenziale*

Chronology

BIOGRAPHICAL DICTIONARY
OF MATHEMATICIANS

INDEX

F

J

K

Logica moderna, 1047a
Logical piano, 1161b
logicism, 901b
Logicomathematical techniques, 2370a–2388b
Logistice numerosa, 2514b, 2515a
Logistice speciosa, 2514b, 2515a
Lomonosov, M.V., 21a
Longitude, 879b–880a
Loomis, Elias (1811–1889), 1620–1621
Lorentz, Hendrik Antoon
    Lorentz transformations, 827b, 2577b–2578a
Loria, Gino (1862–1954), 1621–1622
Lotka, Alfred James (1880–1949), 1622–1623
Love, Augustus Edward Hough (1863–1940), 1623–1624
    Löwenheim-Skolem paradox, 1057a, 1617b, 1762b–1736a
    Löwenheim-Skolem-Tarski theorem, 1762b
Loxodromes, 2301b
Lucas, François-Edouard-Anatole (1842–1891), 1624
Lueroth (or Lüroth), Jakob (1844–1910), 1624–1625
Łukasiewicz, Jan (1878–1956), 1625–1626
Lull, Ramón (*ca.* 1232–1316), 1626–1630
Lunes
    quadrature of, 1010b–1011a, 1084b–1087b
Luzin, Nikolai Nikolaievich (1883–1950), 1630–1632, 39b, 2049a,b
Lyapunov, Aleksandr Mikhailovich (1857–1918), 1632–1636

M

Macaulay, Francis Sowerby (1862–1937), 1636
McColl, Hugh (1837–1909), 1637
MacCullagh, James, 974b
Mach, Ernst, 94b
Maclaurin, Colin (1698–1746), 1637–1640, 547b–548a
    Braikenridge-Maclaurin theorem, 356a
    ellipsoid, 1634b–1635a
    Maclaurin's series, 2424b
    theorem of, 312a
MacMahon, Percy Alexander (1854–1929), 1640–1641
MacMillan, William Duncan (1871–1948), 1641
Magalotti, Lorenzo, 321b
Magazin for Naturvidenskaben, 2a
Magic, natural, 164a
Magic circles, 2616b
Magic squares, 838a–b, 2616b–2617b
Magini, Giovanni Antonio (1555–1617), 1641–1642
Magistros, Gregory, 717a
Magni, Domenico, 322
Magnitsky, Leonty Filippovich (1669–1739), 1642–1643
Magnitudes
    in geometry, 1157b

homogeneous, 1484b
infinitely great and small, 334a
irrational, 696b
qua, 289b
ration to one another, 87b
theory of, 684a–b
al-Māhānī, Abū ᶜAbd Allāh Muḥammad ibn ᶜĪsā (*fl. ca.* 860–880), 1643–1644, 713b, 716a
Maine de Biran, Marie-Françoise-Pierre, 52b
Maior (or Maioris), John (or Jean Mair) (1469–1550), 1644–1645
Malebranche, Nicolas (1638–1715), 1645–1651
Malfatti, Gian Francesco (1731–1807), 1651–1652, 27b
    Malfatti problem, 27b, 1652a, 2419a
Maltsev (or Malcev), Anatoly Ivanovich (1909–1967), 1652–1653
Malvasia, Cornelio
    micrometer, 154b
Manetti, Gianozzo, 138a
Manifolds, 670a
    absolute neighborhood retract, 326b
    algebraic, 1102a,b
    analytic, 2575b–2576a
    compact complex, 283b
    compact orientable, 1474b
    complex, 669a–b, 1100a, 1103a–b
    differentiable, 421b, 668b, 669a, 2507b, 2575b–2576a
    five-dimensional, 1200b–1201a
    Grassmann, 920b
    H manifolds, 1110b
    homogeneous, 668b
    mappings of, 1110a
    n-dimensional, 2146b
    Riemannian, 668b, 1102b–1103a, 1601a
    topological, 583b–584a
Mannheim, Victor Mayer Amédée (1831–1906), 1653–1654
Mans, Jacques Peletier du, 724a
Mansion, Paul (1844–1919), 1654
Manṣūr ibn ᶜAlī ibn ᶜIrāq, Abū Naṣr (d. *ca.* A.D. 1036), 1655–1657
Mappings
    bounded families, 174a
    conformal, 27b, 184b–185a, 771a, 1266b, 1967b, 2016a, 2141a, 2233a
    continuous, 42a, 174a, 292b, 379b
    equicontinuous, 1225b
    kinematic, 272a
    n dimensional, 1110a
    pseudo-conformal, 206a
    quasi-conformal, 2427a–b
    Riemann's theorem, 2143b
    of sets, 402a,b
    square onto a line segment, 402b
    topological, 379b
Marchenko, V. A., 28b
Marci of Kronland, Johannes Marcus (1599–1667), 1657–1658
Marcolongo, Roberto, 388a,b
Maricourt, Pierre de
    see Peter Peregrinus
Marinus of Naples, 700b, 705a
Mariotte, Edme, 54b
Markov, Andrei Andreevich (1856–1922),

1658–1664
    Markov chains, 348b, 1662b–1663b
    Markov partition, 348b
    Markov processes, 772a, 1663a,b
    stochastic methods, 158b
Marre, Aristide, 501a
Martianus Capella (*fl. ca.* A.D. 365–440), 1664–1665
Mascheroni, Lorenzo (1750–1800), 1665–1667
Maseres, Francis (1731–1824), 1667–1669
Mathematica, 1117a
Mathematics
    as abstract science, 36b–37a
    d'Alembert on, 45a, 48a
    applied, 2178b
    Arabic, 176a
    Aristotle's model, 115a–116a
    arithmetization of, 2022b–2023a
    axiomatic approach, 343a, 379a, 380a
    Babylonia, 2436a
    Bacon, 164b–165b
    Bourbaki, 343b
    Chinese, 2239b, 2257a–2258a, 2610b–2618a
    classical, 901b
    combinatorial, 1061b–1062a
    computational, 1300b–1301a
    Egyptian, 2436a
    and experience, 162b
    formalism, 1056b–1057a
    foundations of, 1056b, 1108a–b, 1120a, 2022b–2023a, 2251a
    Greek, 181b, 1019a–b, 2435b–2436a
    in hierarchy of sciences, 1966b
    history of, 345b–346a, 363b, 407a, 425a, 426b, 593a, 618b, 1152a, 1621a, 1716a, 1753b–1754a, 2467b–2468a, 2580a–b
    ideal and factual, 1868b–1869a
    intuitionistic, 379b, 380a,b
    logic and, 165a, 2569a
    metaphysics of, 2603b
    methodology of 368b
    an nonmathematical sciences, 142b–143a
    and philosophy, 354a, 558b–559a
    philosophy of, 900a–b
    and physics, 120a–121b, 644a
    rigorous proofs in, 300b
    and science, 115a, 164b–165a
    social, 532a–533b
    teaching of, 156a
    see also Algebra; Analysis; Arithmetic; Calculation; Geometry; Number(s); Number theory; Trigonometry
Mathews, George Ballard (1861–1922), 1669
Mathieu, Émile Léonard (1835–1980), 1669–1671
Matrices
    Riemann, 29b–30a
    theory of, 453b–454a
Matsunaga, Yoshisuke, 26b, 27a
Maupertuis, Pierre Louis Moreau de (1698–1759), 1671–1674
    and Koenig, 1267b
    least action principle, 740a–b
Maurolico, Francesco (1494–1575), 1674–1678, 101b

O

P

Population (cont.)
  Laplace studies, 1370b–1371b
  statistics, 216a
Poretsky, Platon Sergeevich (1864–1907), 2042
Porisms, 632b, 710a–b
Porta, Giambattista della (1535–1615), 2042–2045
Positivism, 524a–b, 851a, 2157a
Possibility, physical, 540b
Post, Emil Leon (1897–1954), 2045–2047
Potential
  coining of term, 927b
  equation, 184b, 687a
  logarithmic, 344b, 1785b
  spherical, 344b
  theory, 205b, 506a, 1107a, 1670a, 1785b
Powers
  boundaries of, 1048a–b
  laws, 411b
  for natural numbers, 766b
  of the unknown, 628a–b
  see also Exponents
Power-sum method, 2483b–2484a
Pragmaticism, 1969b
Pratt, John Henry (1809–1871), 2047
Predicate
  quantification of, 969b, 970a
Prestet, Jean, 1646a, 1647b–1648a
Prévost, Isaac-Bénédict (1755–1819), 2047–2048
Price, Richard, 195a
Price index-numbers, 1160b–1161a
Prime number theorem, 1020b, 1327a, 1332a, 2500b
Prime spots, 1054b
Primeness, 780b
Primes
  and almost primes, 2118b
  in arithmetic progressions, 646b
  distribution of, 2500b
Princeton University, 801b
Pringsheim, Alfred (1850–1941), 2048–2049
Privalov, Ivan Ivanovich (1891–1941), 2049–2050
Privat de Molières, Joseph (1677–1742), 2050–2051
Probabilism, 541b–542a
Probability, 51b, 772a
  Bayes's theorem, 1343a–b
  binomial, 1737a–b
  calculus of, 178b, 531b–532a, 540b–541a, 1918b–1919a
  chance, 1737a
  continuity in, 158b
  control chart techniques, 2277b–2278a
  denumerable, 316b
  error theory, 1425b–1429a
  of events, 1341b–1348a
  fiducial theory, 911b
  gambling, 2208b
  Laplace, 1365b–1368a, 1370b, 1429a–1438b
  and likelihood, 807b–808a
  number theory, 2118a
  objective, 540b–541a
  population statistics, 216a
  quantum mechanics, 639b
  sequential ratio test, 2602b

small events, 2033b–2034a
subjective, 540b–541a
Venn, 2508b
theory of, 48b–49a, 84a–b, 194a–195a, 223b–224a, 230b, 234a, 310a, 313a, 328a–b, 411b, 472a, 478a, 771b, 781b, 1162a–b, 1181b, 1182a
  De Moivre's theorem, 1737b–1738a
  frequency theory, 1723b–1724a, 2115a–b
  Huygens, 1125b, 1126a–b
  Keynes, 1226b–1277a
  Khinchin, 1243a
  Linnik, 1593b
  Markov, 1661a–1663b
  Von Mises, 1723b–1724a
Problem, correctly posed, 962a–b
Problems
  solving methods, 630b–633a, 793a–794b, 795a–b
Probus (Probha), 138b
Proclus (*ca.* 410–485), 2051–2053
  on Euclid, 179b–180a, 689a, 690b, 694a, 698a–b, 699a, 700b–701b, 703b–705a, 712a
  on Eudoxus, 735a
  quadratrix, 621b
  translations of, 1731a, 1732a
Progressions
  broken, 2196a
  natural, 2196a
Projection
  and perspective, 596a
  stereographic, 24a, 562b, 985a–b
  theory of, 1801a
Proof
  method of, 796a
  theory of, 115a, 208b, 2045b, 2046a
Proportion
  definitions of, 24b–25a
  Dürer, 664a–b, 665a, 666a
  equal, 1120b
  Eudoxus, 734b–735a
  metric, 279b
  theory of, 694a–b, 696a, 2440b–2441b
Proportionals, mean, 177a, 1865a–1866a, 2430b, 2516a
Propositions
  conversion of, 1683a
  logical calculus of, 1637a
  problems and theorems, 1683a
Prosthaphaeresis, 389b, 489a, 514a–b, 1776a, 2557a, 2599b–2600a
Protagoras, 65b
Protophysics
  Leibniz, 1489a–b
Protothetic theory, 1567a
Psuedo-Hippocrates
  translations, 1731b, 1732a
Pseudosphere, 198b, 200a
Pseudo-versiera, 22b–23a
Ptolemy (or Claudius Ptolemaeus) (*ca.* 100–ca. 170), 2053–2073, 79a
  Almagest, 25a, 395b
    commentaries, 364b, 1907a–b, 2451b
    editions, 522b, 1986b–1987b
    translations, 15b, 17b, 1145b, 1731b
    and al-Battānī, 189a–b
  Handy Tables, 2451b, 2452b, 2453b

heliocentrism, 111b
music ratios, 146b
Puiseux, Victor (1820–1883), 2073–2074
Pulley, compound, 85b
Putnam, D. C., 237b
Pythagoras of Samos (*ca.* 560–*ca.* 480 B.C.), 2074–2080
  heliocentrism, 110b
  music theory, 146a
  Pythagorean theorem, 693a, 694a, 696a, 699a, 767b, 795a, 1607b, 1903a, 2077a, 2430a
  Pythagorean triplets, 797b
Pythagoreanism, 587b, 696a–b, 699a, 2440a–b, 2642a

Q

Q numbers, 638a–b
Q quotient, 328b
Ibn al-Qāḍī, 174b
Qāḍī Zāda al-Rūmī (Salah al-Dīn Mūsā Pasha) (*ca.* 1364–*ca.* 1436), 2080–2083
al-Qalaṣādī (al-Qalṣādī), Abu'l-Ḥasan ᶜAlī ibn Muḥammad ibn ᶜAlī (1412–1486), 2083–2084
Quadrant, 397a, 1033a,b, 1167b, 1979a–b
  plane of the, 333a
  trigonometric uses of, 804a
Quadratics, 8a, 633a, 2132b, 2133b, 2299b, 2518a–b
Quadratrix, 621b–622b, 1080a–1081a
Quadrature
  of circle, 65a–b, 347a–b, 382b, 383a, 391b, 409a, 489a, 560b, 621b–622a, 779b, 1011a, 1081a, 1085b–1087b, 1126a, 1180b, 1320b, 1499a, 1500a, 1501b, 1554b–1555b, 1903b, 2108a–b, 2311a, 2535b
  of crescent-shaped figures, 1010b
  of curvilinear figures, 545a–b
  Grandi, 914b
  of hyperbola, 378a, 1126a,b
  of lunes, 1010b–1011a, 1084b, 1087b
  mechanical, 771a
  methods of, 182a, 778a–780a, 935a,b, 1799a–1800a, 2198a
  of parabola, 1126a, 1141b–1142a
Quadrics, 1046a
Quadrilaterials, 894b, 2192b
Quadrivium, 285a–b, 287a, 289b, 1664b
Quantal-response bioassay, 2592a
Quantification theory, 1031b
Quantities
  extensive, 919a–920a
  negative, 418b–419a
  theory of
    see Numbers, real
Quasianalyticity, 959b
Quaternions, 310b, 978a
  discovery of, 976a, 977a–b, 978a–b
  integrity in, 1122a
  theory of, 198a,b, 919a, 920a, 921a
Quetelet, Lambert-Adolphe-Jacques (1796–1874), 2084–2086
Queues, 2603a

Riesz, Frigyes (Fréderic) (cont.)
Riesz-Fejér theorem, 721a
Riesz-Fischer theorem, 2150b–2151a
Riesz, Marcel (1886–1969), 2152–2153
Rings
Artin, 150a
associative, 150
concept of, 580b
and ideals, 1870b
Krull rings, 1283a
Noetherian, 1282b–1283a
noncummutative, 1871a
theory of, 1283a, 2527b, 2528a–2529a
Zolotarev, 2651a
Risner, Friedrich (d. ca. 1580), 2153–2154
Rithmomachia, 1033b
Ritt, Joseph Fels (1893–1951), 2154
Ritz, Walter
convergence method, 1285b
Rivault, David, 102a
Robert of Chester, 798b
Roberval, Gilles Personne (or Personier) de
(1602–1675), 2154–2159, 181b, 196a,
409b
Robins, Benjamin (1707–1751), 2159
Robinson, Abraham (1918–1974), 2159–
2163
Robinson forcing, 2161b
Rodonea, 914a–b
Rohn, Karl (1855–1920), 2163
Rolle, Michel (1652–1719), 2163–2165
theorem of, 2164b
Romain, Adrien, 307b
Romanus, Adrian
see Rooman, Adriaan van
Rømer, Ole, 183b
Roomen, Adriaan van (1561–1615), 2165–
2167
Roots
approximation rules, 2495b–2496a
cube, 99b, 894b, 1556a–b, 1605a–b
extraction of, 1232b–1233a, 1794b–1795b
geometrical construction of, 1236a
imaginary, 986a, 1309a, 2399a
of integers, 1216a
of large numbers, 94a
Leonardo da Vinci, 1552b
of numerical equations, 2399a
square, 3b, 426b–427a, 428b, 861a,
1605a–b, 1889a, 2204a, 2344a
tenth, 27b
Rosanes, Jakob (1842–1922), 2167
Rosenhain, Johann Georg (1816–1887),
2167–2168
Rosser, Barkley, 890a
Rossi, Roberto de, 138a
Rotation
areas in, 885b
axes of, 2235a
geometrical figures in, 885b
Rotundum, 805b
Rowning, John (ca. 1701–1771), 2168–2169
Rudio, Ferdinand (1856–1929), 2169
Rudolf of Bruges, 7a
Rudolff (or Rudolf), Christoff (fl. end of
fifteenth century–first half of six-
teenth century), 2169–2172
Coss, 2343a,b
Ruelle, David, 348b–349a

Ruffini, Paolo (1765–1822), 2172–2174
Abel-Ruffini theorem, 3b, 2172a–b
and Bortolotti, 329b
Ruffini-Horner method, 1216a
Ruffini's rule, 2172b
Rule of the drinkers problem, 799a
Rumovsky, Stepan Yakovlevich (1734–
1812), 2174–2175
Runge, Carol David Tolmé (1856–1927),
2175–2180
Lagrange interpolation, 771a
Runge-Kutta procedure, 2178b
Ibn Rushd, Abu'l Walīd Muḥammad ibn
Aḥmad ibn Muḥammad, 716b
Russell, Bertrand Arthur William (1872–
1970), 2180–2188
and Frege, 833a
and Gödel, 904b
on Keynes, 1226b
logic, 901b
and Whitehead, 2568a–b–2569a
Rydberg, Johannes (Janne) Robert (1854–
1919), 2188–2191
Rydberg's constant, 2189b
Rydberg's formula, 2189b
Rydberg-Schuster law, 2189b
Rythmomachia, 180a

S

S method of simultaneous confidence inter-
vals, 2211b
Saccheri, (Giovanni) Girolamo (1667–
1733), 2191–2193, 200a, 692a–b,
726a
Saccheri's quadrangle, 1327b
Sacrobosco, Johannes de (or John of Holy-
wood) (d. ca. 1256), 2193–2196,
180a, 802a
Šafarevič, I. R., 149b
Ibn al-Ṣaffar, 2007a,b
Saigey, Frédéric, 4a
Saijyo school, 26a
Saint Petersburg mathematical school,
473a–474b
Saint-Venant, Adhémar Jean Claude Barré
de (1797–1886), 2196–2197, 917a
Saint Vincent, Gregorius (1584–1667),
2197–2198
Sakabe, Hiroyasu, 26b
Saks, Stanisław (1897–1942), 2199
Salaciense, Pedro Nunez, 803b
Saladini, Girolamo, 2126b–2127a,b
Salem, Raphaël (1898–1963), 2199–2201
Salmon, George (1819–1904), 2201–2202
al-Samarqandī, Shams al-Dīn Muḥammad
ibn Ashraf al-Ḥusaynī (fl. 1276),
2202
al-Samawʾal, ibn Yaḥyā al-Maghribī
(d. ca. 1180), 2202–2206, 1209b,
1210a,b, 1211a
Sampling, statistical, 923a
distribution, 911a–b, 1938a–1947b,
2588a–2589a
errors, 1944b–1946a
large samples, 911a
methods, 60b

random, 2588a, 2589a
sequential probability ratio test, 2602b
small, 806b, 808b, 1856b–1857a
Sangaku tablets, 25b
Santone, Elia Vineto, 725b–726a
Saphea, 1173a
Ibn al-Sarī, 717a
Sarzosa, Francisco, 802a
Saturn's rings
mathematical theory of, 1963b
Saurin, Joseph (1659–1737), 2206–2208
Savage, Leonard Jimmie (1917–1971),
2208–2209
Savart, Félix
Biot-Savart law, 57a,b
Savasorda
see Abraham bar Ḥiyya ha-Nasi
Savile, Henry, 726a
Scaliger, Joseph Justus, 2516a,b
Schauder, Juliusz Pawel (1899–1934), 2209–
2211, 379b
Scheffé, Henry (1907–1977), 2211–2212
Scheffers, Georg (1866–1945), 2212–2213,
1589a
Scheubel, Johann, 724b
Scheuchzer, Johann Jakob (1672–1733),
2213
Scheutz, Georg, 157b
Schiaparelli, G. V., 1977b
Schickard, Wilhelm (1592–1635), 2213–
2214
Schiffer, M., 206b
Schiipp, Paul, 904b–905a
Schläfli, Ludwig (1814–1895), 2214–2217
Schmidt, Erhard (1876–1959), 2217–2220,
205b
Schoenflies, Arthur Moritz (1853–1928),
2220–2221, 850a
Scholasticism, 32b, 162b
Scholz, Heinrich, 1050b
Schooten, Frans van (ca. 1615–1660), 2221–
2223, 183b, 1045b–1046a
Schott, Gaspar (1608–1666), 2223–2224
Schottky, Friedrich Hermann (1851–1935),
2224–2225
Schottky's functions, 27b
Schoute, Pieter Hendrik (1846–1923), 2225
Schouten, Jan Arnoldus (1883–1971),
2225–2226
Schreier, Otto, 150a
Schröder, Friedrich Wilhelm Karl Ernst
(1841–1902), 2226–2227, 312a,b
Schrödinger, Erwin
Schrödinger equation, 638b–639a
Schroeter, Heinrich Eduard (1829–1892),
2227–2228
Schubert, Hermann Cäsar Hannibal (1848–
1911), 2228–2230
calculus, 1058a
Schur, Issai (1875–1941), 2230–2231,
359a–b, 360a–b, 2564b
Schur index, 360a, 2230b
Schur's lemma, 2230b
splitting fields theory, 359b–360a, 362a,b
Schuster, Arthur (1851–1934), 2231–2232,
172a
Schwarz, Hermann Amandus (1843–1921),
2232–2234, 386a
Riemann's mapping theorem, 2143b

T

Y

Z